MW00806637

TIMELESS TRUTHS BIBLE

PRESENTED TO

BY

ON

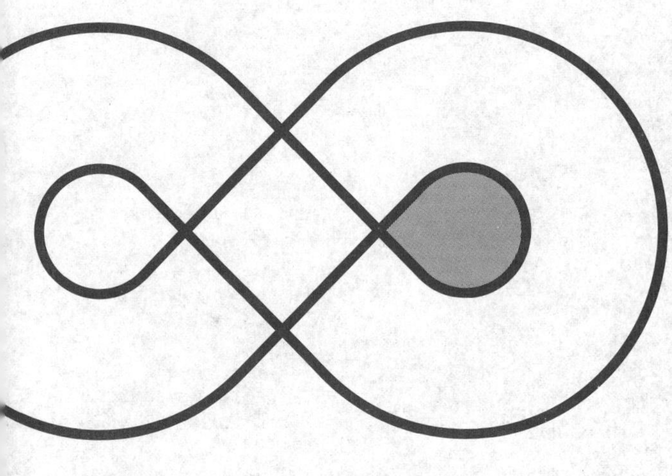

TIMELESS TRUTHS BIBLE

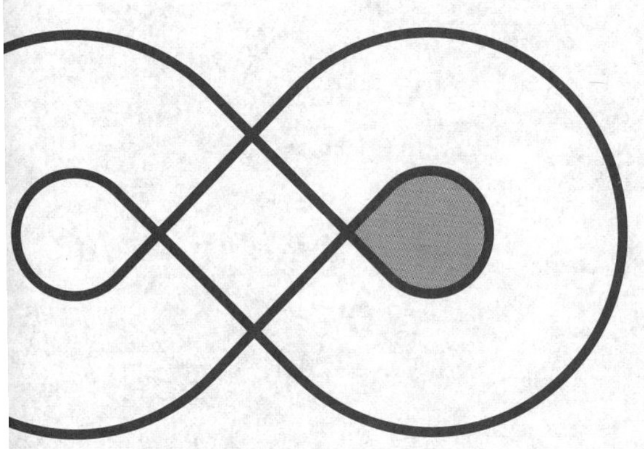

TIMELESS TRUTHS BIBLE

ONE FAITH.
HANDED DOWN.
FOR ALL THE SAINTS.

MATTHEW Z. CAPPS, GENERAL EDITOR

THOMAS NELSON
Since 1798

www.ThomasNelson.com

ess Truths Bible, NET

shed in Nashville, TN, by Thomas Nelson. Thomas Nelson is a registered trademark of
erCollins Christian Publishing, Inc.

ry of Congress Control Number: 2023932144

Printed in India

'3 22 ~ 20 19 18 17 16 15 14 / BPI / 10 9 8 7 6 5 4 3 2 1

CONTENTS

LIST OF ABBREVIATIONS

Alphabetical list of Bible books and abbreviations:

Acts.......... Acts
Amos .... Amos
1 Chr .... 1 Chronicles
2 Chr......... 2 Chronicles
Col........... Colossians
1 Cor .... 1 Corinthians
2 Cor......... 2 Corinthians
Dan.......... Daniel
Deut......... Deuteronomy
Eccl.......... Ecclesiastes
Eph .... Ephesians
Esth.......... Esther
Exod......... Exodus
Ezek .... Ezekiel
Ezra.......... Ezra
Gal........... Galatians
Gen .... Genesis
Hab.......... Habakkuk
Hag .... Haggai
Heb.......... Hebrews
Hos.......... Hosea
Isa .... Isaiah
Jas .... James
Jer .... Jeremiah
Job........... Job
Joel .... Joel
John .... John
1 John........ 1 John
2 John........ 2 John
3 John........ 3 John
Jonah .... Jonah
Josh.......... Joshua
Jude.......... Jude
Judg.......... Judges
1 Kgs .... 1 Kings
2 Kgs......... 2 Kings
Lam.......... Lamentations
Lev........... Leviticus
Luke .... Luke
Mal .... Malachi
Mark .... Mark
Matt......... Matthew
Mic .... Micah
Nah.......... Nahum
Neh.......... Nehemiah
Num......... Numbers
Obad......... Obadiah
1 Pet .... 1 Peter
2 Pet .... 2 Peter
Phlm......... Philemon
Phil .... Philippians
Prov .... Proverbs
Ps(s) .... Psalms
Rev .... Revelation
Rom .... Romans
Ruth .... Ruth
1 Sam .... 1 Samuel
2 Sam......... 2 Samuel
Song......... Song of Songs
1 Thess....... 1 Thessalonians
2 Thess ...... 2 Thessalonians
1 Tim......... 1 Timothy
2 Tim .... 2 Timothy
Titus......... Titus
Zech .... Zechariah
Zeph......... Zephaniah

Additional abbreviations used in the notes:

LXX......... Septuagint (the Greek Old Testament, translated between 250 and 100 BC)
MT.......... Masoretic Text (the traditional rabbinical text of the Hebrew Bible, dating from the medieval period)

TO THE READER

AN INTRODUCTION TO THE NEW ENGLISH TRANSLATION

You have been born anew . . . through the living and enduring word of God.
1 PETER 1:23

The New English Translation (NET) is the newest complete translation of the original biblical languages into English. In 1995 a multidenominational team of more than twenty-five of the world's foremost biblical scholars gathered around the shared vision of creating an English Bible translation that could overcome old challenges and boldly open the door for new possibilities. The translators completed the first edition in 2001 and incorporated revisions based on scholarly and user feedback in 2003 and 2005. In 2019 a major update reached its final stages. The NET's unique translation process has yielded a beautiful, faithful English Bible for the worldwide church today.

What sets the NET Bible apart from other translations? We encourage you to read the full story of the NET's development and additional details about its translation philosophy at netbible.com/net-bible-preface. But we would like to draw your attention to a few features that commend the NET to all readers of the Word.

TRANSPARENT AND ACCOUNTABLE

Have you ever wished you could look over a Bible translator's shoulder as he or she worked?

Bible translation usually happens behind closed doors—few outside the translation committee see the complex decisions underlying the words that appear in their English Bibles. Fewer still have the opportunity to review and speak into the translators' decisions.

Throughout the NET's translation process, every working draft was made publicly available on the Internet. Bible scholars, ministers, and laypersons from around the world logged millions of review sessions. No other translation is so openly accountable to the worldwide church or has been so thoroughly vetted.

And yet the ultimate accountability was to the biblical text itself. The NET Bible is neither crowdsourced nor a "translation by consensus." Rather, the NET translators filtered every question and suggestion through the very best insights from biblical linguistics, textual criticism, and their unswerving commitment to following the text wherever it leads. Thus, the NET remains supremely accurate and trustworthy while also benefiting from extensive review by those who would be reading, studying, and teaching from its pages.

BEYOND THE "READABLE VS. ACCURATE" DIVIDE

The uniquely transparent and accountable translation process of the NET has been crystallized in the most extensive set of Bible translators' notes ever created. More than 60,000 notes highlight every major decision, outline alternative views, and explain difficult or nontraditional renderings. Freely available at netbible.org and in print in the *NET Bible, Full Notes Edition*, these notes help the NET overcome one of the biggest challenges facing any Bible translation: the tension between *accuracy* and *readability*.

If you have spent more than a few minutes researching the English version of the Bible, you have probably encountered a "translation spectrum"—a simple chart with the most wooden-but-precise translations and paraphrases on the far left (representing a "word-for-word" translation approach) and the loosest-but-easiest-to-read translations and paraphrases on the far right (representing a "thought-for-thought" philosophy of translation). Some translations intentionally lean toward one end of the spectrum or the other, embracing the strengths and weaknesses of their chosen approach. Most try to strike a balance between the extremes, weighing accuracy against readability—striving to reflect the grammar of the underlying biblical languages while still achieving acceptable English style.

But the NET moves beyond that old dichotomy. Because of the extensive translators' notes, the NET never has to compromise. Whenever faced with a difficult translation choice, the translators were free to put the strongest option in the main text while documenting the challenge, their thought process, and the solution in the notes.

The benefit to you, the reader? You can be sure that the NET is a translation you can trust—nothing has been lost in translation or obscured by a translator's dilemma. Instead, you are invited to see for yourself and gain the kind of transparent access to the biblical languages previously available only to scholars.

MINISTRY FIRST

One more reason to love the NET: Modern Bible translations are typically copyrighted, posing a challenge for ministries hoping to quote more than a few passages in their Bible study resources, curriculum, or other programming. But the NET is for everyone, with "ministry first" copyright innovations that encourage ministries to quote and share the life-changing message of Scripture as freely as possible. In fact, one of the major motivations behind the creation of the NET was the desire to ensure that ministries had unfettered access to a top-quality modern Bible translation without needing to embark on a complicated process of securing permissions.

Visit netbible.com/net-bible-copyright to learn more.

TAKE UP AND READ

With its balanced, easy-to-understand English text and a transparent translation process that invites you to see for yourself the richness of the biblical languages, the NET is a Bible you can embrace as your own. Clear, readable, elegant, and accurate, the NET presents Scripture as meaningfully and powerfully today as when these words were first communicated to the people of God.

Our prayer is that the NET will be a fresh and exciting invitation to you—and Bible readers everywhere—to "let the word of Christ dwell in you richly" (Col 3:16).

The Publishers

HOW TO USE THIS BIBLE

The *Timeless Truths Bible* is designed to give explanations of the scriptures from people throughout the history of the church. In this Bible edition using the New English Translation, you'll encounter various features that clarify the meaning of the text so that you will better understand God's revelation about himself, us, and the world.

COMMENTARY: Each chapter of the Bible will contain commentary from a person in church history. Doctrinal insights about a portion or the whole chapter are placed in the outer margins. As you read the Bible, these notes will illustrate the doctrinal unity of the church throughout the ages. Each note includes the name of the person who stated or wrote the piece of commentary. We adapted the quotations in this collection for our use: we removed extraneous punctuation, updated archaic language, lowercased deity pronouns to match the NET, and changed Bible quotations to match the NET. In the back matter of this edition, you will find a master index of all the sources cited in these notes.

BOOK INTRODUCTIONS: Before each book of the Bible, you can read an introduction about the history, author, and context for that book. This background information gives special attention to the book's significance in church history and continued applicability today.

BIOGRAPHIES: Dozens of full-page articles share the inspiring life stories of men and women who were transformed by the gospel. Their stories of serving Christ with courage and creativity will inspire your life of faith.

SACRED ART: Scattered throughout the edition you will discover selected works of art on full-color pages. The art comes from various time periods of church history and from artists representing differing cultures. The artwork gives a visual representation of the Bible's timeline; it also displays the place that beauty and creativity have had throughout the history of the church. Use it as a means to reflect upon the Bible story to which each piece is connected.

CREEDS AND CONFESSIONS: A collection of creeds, confessions, catechisms, and covenants used during the church's history are included throughout this edition. As you read them, you have the opportunity to consider how the church has always valued the Word of God. These documents used by the church, denominations, and various networks remind us that God has been at work in his people throughout all human history.

As you read this edition of God's Word, the notes will give you a fresh experience of God's majesty, his faithfulness, and his redemptive plan for everyone. Enjoy the journey as you explore these timeless truths.

> To search the Scriptures is a work most fair and most profitable for souls . . . For through the Holy Scriptures we are trained to action that is pleasing to God and untroubled contemplation. For in these we find both exhortation to every virtue and dissuasion from every vice . . . Therefore let us knock at that very fair garden of the Scriptures, so fragrant and sweet and blooming.
>
> JOHN OF DAMASCUS, *ORTHODOX FAITH*

The book you hold in your hands is God's perfect treasure, a revelation of himself to humankind. In fact, Christianity is dependent upon the belief that God has graciously, intentionally, and lovingly chosen to reveal himself and his will to humanity. If God has revealed himself to us, our desire should be that as we study God's Word, we do so in a way that seeks to understand every passage accurately in light of his divine self-disclosure.

There are times when the historical distance between the modern reader and ancient text makes it difficult to understand certain parts of scripture. Even so, the good news is that when you read the Bible you are not alone. Because the Bible is one of the most printed books in human history, it also has one of the deepest wells of insightful commentary that we as modern readers can draw from.

In a modern world that too often sprints along in what C. S. Lewis called in *Surprised by Joy* "chronological snobbery," that is, believing that ancient resources are obstacles to our progress, retrieving the past can help clarify our historical shortsightedness and cultural biases. In short, we cannot underestimate the contributions of the past or exaggerate the wisdom of the present. We must approach the Bible with the humble belief that every generation in the church has unique contributions to offer. The wisest of Christians in history have always drawn from the past to understand how to live in the present.

As you study the *Timeless Truths Bible*, we welcome you into an ancient conversation, an interpretive community that stretches across time and knows no geographical boundaries. It is a community that includes people from the very earliest disciples of Jesus living in Jerusalem, the second-century converts in Roman-ruled Africa and Europe, medieval monastics, the Reformers, English Puritans, American revivalists, and many more. This rich history affords us the opportunity to cultivate theological instincts and values from trusted guides. Historically, Christians have held the belief that biblical interpretation is an activity to be practiced in the church and for the church. And while the church has differed on certain issues, by and large she has been held together by the book you're holding in your hands—the living Word of God.

WHY WE SHOULD LISTEN TO VOICES FROM CHURCH HISTORY

The *Timeless Truths Bible* is designed with this history in mind. It will remind you that, as you read the Word of God, you're a part of a sacred communion made up of believers past and present. Not only is this particular Bible beautifully designed, it has also been carefully crafted with selected features to help you in your journey through the text.

Regardless of your spiritual journey, if you are new to the Bible or a seasoned saint, hearing from voices of the past will deeply enrich your understanding of God's Word. The church in every generation has gathered around the Bible to read, study, ponder, debate, and meditate on the scriptures. Through personal study and communal discussion on the Bible, God has shaped his people, setting them apart to love him and each other, to worship, and to work toward advancing his good news to the whole world.

My prayer is that the *Timeless Truths Bible* will encourage and strengthen you, and that your own study of this incomparable book will be enriched by the reflections and insights of faithful saints from across the centuries who, just like you, came to scripture to learn from the Author of life. As you read, do so with an open mind and heart. There is a sense in which we do not simply read the Bible, the Bible also reads us. As Charles Spurgeon once said, "Nobody ever outgrows Scripture! The Book widens and deepens with our years! It is true, it cannot really grow, for it is perfect, but it does so to our apprehension. The deeper you dig into Scripture, the more you find that it is a great abyss of truth."

MATTHEW Z. CAPPS, GENERAL EDITOR

*__1 Samuel 13:1__ MT *a son of a year*; a few Greek manuscripts read *thirty.*

†**1 Samuel 13:1** MT *two years*; Acts 13:21 has *forty*; some English translations add these two, resulting in *forty-two.*

‡**Ezra 4:7** Since it makes no sense to say the letter was first written in Aramaic and then translated into Aramaic, the second mention of Aramaic is probably a scribal notation that what follows is in Aramaic.

§**Matthew 17:20** Many significant manuscripts omit **17:21** *But this kind does not go out except by prayer and fasting.*

||**Matthew 18:10** The most significant manuscripts do not include **18:11** *For the Son of Man came to seek the lost.*

¶**Matthew 23:13** The most important manuscripts omit **23:14** *Woe to you experts in the law and you Pharisees, hypocrites! You devour widows' houses and for show you pray long prayers! Therefore you will receive the greater condemnation.*

*__Mark 7:15__ The best manuscripts omit **7:16** *Let anyone with ears to hear, listen.*

†**Mark 9:43** The best manuscripts omit **9:44** *where their worm never dies and the fire is never quenched.* (identical to v. 48)

‡**Mark 9:45** The best manuscripts omit **9:46** *where their worm never dies and the fire is never quenched.* (identical to v. 48)

§**Mark 11:25** The best manuscripts omit **11:26** *But if you do not forgive, neither will your Father in heaven forgive your sins.*

||**Mark 15:27** The best manuscripts omit **15:28** *And the scripture was fulfilled that says, "He was counted with the lawless ones."*

¶**Mark 16:8** Mark ends at this point in some manuscripts, including two of the most respected ones. Other manuscripts supply a shorter ending: "They reported briefly to those around Peter all that they had been commanded. After these things Jesus himself sent out through them, from the east to the west, the holy and imperishable preaching of eternal salvation. Amen." Some manuscripts supply both endings. Because of questions about the authenticity of these alternative endings, 16:8 is usually regarded as the last verse of the Gospel of Mark.

*__Luke 17:35__ The best manuscripts do not include **17:36** *There will be two in the field; one will be taken and other left.*

EXPLANATORY NOTES

†**Luke 22:44** Some important manuscripts lack **22:43–44**.

‡**Luke 23:16** Many of the best manuscripts do not include **23:17** *(Now he was obligated to release one individual for them at the feast.)*

§**Luke 23:34** Many significant manuscripts omit v. 34a; because of uncertainty of its authenticity it has been placed in brackets in the translation.

||**John 5:3** Some manuscripts add *waiting for the moving of the water.* **5:4** *For an angel of the Lord went down and stirred up the water at certain times. Whoever first stepped in after the stirring of the water was healed from whatever disease which he suffered.*

¶John 7:53–8:11 is not contained in the earliest and best manuscripts and was almost certainly not an original part of the Gospel of John; one group of manuscripts places it after Luke 21:38.

***John 9:39** Some significant manuscripts lack v. 38 and the first part of v. 39; because of uncertainty over the authenticity of this material it has been placed in brackets in the translation.

†**Acts 8:36** A few later manuscripts add **8:37** *He said to him, "If you believe with your whole heart, you may." He replied, "I believe that Jesus Christ is the Son of God."*

‡**Acts 15:33** A few later manuscripts add **15:34** *But Silas decided to stay there.*

§**Acts 24:6** Some later manuscripts include 24:7 and parts of vv. 6 and 8: *and we wanted to judge him according to our law.* **24:7** *But Lysias the commanding officer came and took him out of our hands with a great deal of violence,* **24:8** *ordering those who accused him to come before you.*

||**Acts 28:28** Some later manuscripts include **28:29** *When he had said these things, the Jews departed, having a great dispute among themselves.*

¶**Romans 16:23** Some later manuscripts add **16:24** *The grace of our Lord Jesus Christ be with all of you. Amen.*

***Ephesians 1:1** The earliest and most significant manuscripts omit *in Ephesus* (for further discussion of this complex problem see the note in the full-notes edition of the NET or online at netbible.org).

THE OLD TESTAMENT

AUTHOR	AUDIENCE	DATE	PURPOSE	THEMES
Moses	God's chosen people, the Israelites	Between 1446 and 1406 BC	Moses wrote this historical account to chronicle the beginning of the story of God's people, from creation to covenant.	God the Creator; creation; humanity; the fall; covenant; and God's people

For generations the communion of saints has looked to the first book of Moses called Genesis in an attempt to understand the nature of God and the world that he made. John Calvin encapsulated the purpose and themes of this book well in the introduction to his commentary on Genesis:

> This one consideration stamps an inestimable value on the book—that it alone reveals those things which are of primary necessity to be known; namely, in what manner God, after the destructive fall of man, adopted to himself a church; what constituted the true worship of himself, and in what offices of piety the holy fathers exercised themselves; in which way pure religion, having for a time declined through the indolence of men, was restored to its integrity. We also learn when God deposited with a special people his gratuitous covenant of eternal salvation; in what manner a small progeny gradually proceeding from one man, who was both barren and withering, almost half-dead, and (as Isaiah calls him) solitary, yet suddenly grew to an immense multitude; by what unexpected means God both exalted and defended a family chosen by himself although poor, destitute of protection, exposed to every storm, and surrounded on all sides by innumerable hosts of enemies.

Genesis opens with two creation narratives that explore the nature of God's creative work. There is largely unity among the patristics, medievalists, and Reformers who read these creation accounts as theologically foundational, recounting the origins of the universe from "God the Father, creator of heaven and earth" as the Nicene Creed begins. In part the early church fathers connected the doctrine of creation to the doctrine of the incarnation. Consider Athanasius's words: "But as we proceed in our exposition of this [the incarnation of the Word], we must first speak about the creation of the universe and its Creator, God, so that in this way we may consider as fitting that its renewal was effected by the Word who created it in the beginning." While modern approaches have attempted to read Enlightenment science into the early chapters of Genesis, a more theological understanding is more common to the communion of saints down through the centuries.

Similarly, there is unity concerning the doctrine of the Trinity in Genesis, with many theologians homing in on the plural language of Genesis 1:26: "Let us make humankind in our image, after our likeness." The early church fathers generally regarded this divine "image" and "likeness" language of the so-called *Imago Dei* (Image of God) as

GENESIS

relating to human reason. Medieval exegesis generally distinguished the two terms as representing two parts of the human: faculty of reason (image) and moral nature (likeness), where the former was damaged by sin and the latter was obliterated. Given the Reformers' emphasis on recapturing the original meaning of scripture, and armed with a reclaimed knowledge of Hebrew, they could not separate the two terms, understanding the use of "image" and "likeness" as Hebrew parallelism, a view that is still dominant among theologians today.

Genesis 3 explains how God's good creation was torn apart through human rebellion. The fall of Adam was understood by the early church in parallel with Christ, who was the Second Adam come to redeem fallen humanity, announced in what is known as the *protoevangelion*, an early proclamation of the gospel found in Genesis 3:15. The woman's offspring is promised to redeem humanity. From Augustine to Luther, this Offspring was understood to refer to Christ.

Chapters 4–11 chronicle cascading episodes of sin and wickedness, which culminate in the destruction of the earth with a flood and the renewal of creation. This account is followed by the dispersion of humanity at Babel and the calling of Abram. God established a covenant with Abram, later called Abraham, and his descendants and promised to bless them—and the world through them. The remainder of the book, chapters 12–50, tells the story of the patriarchs of Israel, the generations from Abraham to the sons of Jacob. Early Christian interpretation of these narratives mostly relied on the Jewish scholar Philo, who integrated the allegorical methods of Greek thought into his understanding of the Hebrew scriptures. From Origen to Ambrose and Chrysostom to Augustine, these early saints taught doctrinal and moral lessons from the lives of Abraham, Isaac, Jacob, and Joseph. They also used these stories to illustrate important truths about the sovereignty of God and the promises of Christ to the church. This practice, in some form, continued down through church history. For example, the Venerable Bede, in the eighth century, applied the blessings of Genesis 12:1–3 to the church in a spiritual sense, and the Reformer John Calvin used the story of Joseph to illustrate the providence of God.

Genesis is part of a larger collection of books called the Pentateuch, and it should be read in that light. When read together, these first five books of the Bible tell of God's faithfulness to his people in the early years. Genesis sets the stage by revealing God as creator and sustainer but also as a friend to Abraham, Isaac, Jacob, and his children.

THE CREATION OF THE WORLD

1 In the beginning God created the heavens and the earth.
2 Now the earth was without shape and empty, and darkness
was over the surface of the watery deep, but the Spirit of God
was moving over the surface of the water. 3 God said, "Let there
be light." And there was light! 4 God saw that the light was good,
so God separated the light from the darkness. 5 God called the
light "day" and the darkness "night." There was evening, and
there was morning, marking the first day.
6 God said, "Let there be an expanse in the midst of the waters and let it separate water from water." 7 So God made the
expanse and separated the water under the expanse from the
water above it. It was so. 8 God called the expanse "sky." There
was evening, and there was morning, a second day.
9 God said, "Let the water under the sky be gathered to one
place and let dry ground appear." It was so. 10 God called the dry
ground "land" and the gathered waters he called "seas." God
saw that it was good.
11 God said, "Let the land produce vegetation: plants yielding
seeds and trees on the land bearing fruit with seed in it, according to their kinds." It was so. 12 The land produced vegetation—
plants yielding seeds according to their kinds, and trees bearing
fruit with seed in it according to their kinds. God saw that it was
good. 13 There was evening, and there was morning, a third day.
14 God said, "Let there be lights in the expanse of the sky
to separate the day from the night, and let them be signs to
indicate seasons and days and years, 15 and let them serve as
lights in the expanse of the sky to give light on the earth." It
was so. 16 God made two great lights—the greater light to rule
over the day and the lesser light to rule over the night. He made
the stars also. 17 God placed the lights in the expanse of the sky
to shine on the earth, 18 to preside over the day and the night,
and to separate the light from the darkness. God saw that it was
good. 19 There was evening, and there was morning, a fourth day.
20 God said, "Let the water swarm with swarms of living creatures and let birds fly above the earth across the expanse of
the sky." 21 God created the great sea creatures and every living
and moving thing with which the water swarmed, according to
their kinds, and every winged bird according to its kind. God
saw that it was good. 22 God blessed them and said, "Be fruitful
and multiply and fill the water in the seas, and let the birds
multiply on the earth." 23 There was evening, and there was
morning, a fifth day.
24 God said, "Let the land produce living creatures according
to their kinds: cattle, creeping things, and wild animals, each
according to its kind." It was so. 25 God made the wild animals
according to their kinds, the cattle according to their kinds,
and all the creatures that creep along the ground according to
their kinds. God saw that it was good.
26 Then God said, "Let us make humankind in our image, after
our likeness, so they may rule over the fish of the sea and the
birds of the air, over the cattle, and over all the earth, and over
all the creatures that move on the earth."

27 God created humankind in his own image,
in the image of God he created them,
male and female he created them.

28 God blessed them and said to them, "Be fruitful and multiply! Fill the earth and subdue it! Rule over the fish of the sea

1:26–30 When he wished to create humankind, God employed much deliberation and great counsel. Indeed, he did not merely say, "Let the water under the sky be gathered to one place and let dry ground appear" as with the earlier things, but descending into himself from on high, he fortified his speech with weighty words, saying "Let us make!" We are thus to learn of our nobility and dignity. For even if man was made from earth, God nonetheless made him with his own hand so that we might see how highly God regarded humans.

ULRICH ZWINGLI (1484–1531)
ANNOTATIONS ON GENESIS

and the birds of the air and every creature that moves on the
ground." 29 Then God said, "I now give you every seed-bearing
plant on the face of the entire earth and every tree that has
fruit with seed in it. They will be yours for food. 30 And to all
the animals of the earth, and to every bird of the air, and to
all the creatures that move on the ground—everything that
has living breath in it—I give every green plant for food."
It was so.
31 God saw all that he had made—and it was very good! There
was evening, and there was morning, the sixth day.

2 The heavens and the earth were completed with everything
that was in them. 2 By the seventh day God finished the work
that he had been doing, and he ceased on the seventh day all
the work that he had been doing. 3 God blessed the seventh day
and made it holy because on it he ceased all the work that he
had been doing in creation.

THE CREATION OF MAN AND WOMAN

4 This is the account of the heavens and the earth when
they were created—when the LORD God made the earth and
heavens.
5 Now no shrub of the field had yet grown on the earth, and
no plant of the field had yet sprouted, for the LORD God had not
caused it to rain on the earth, and there was no man to cultivate
the ground. 6 Springs would well up from the earth and water
the whole surface of the ground. 7 The LORD God formed the
man from the soil of the ground and breathed into his nostrils
the breath of life, and the man became a living being.
8 The LORD God planted an orchard in the east, in Eden; and
there he placed the man he had formed. 9 The LORD God made
all kinds of trees grow from the soil, every tree that was pleasing to look at and good for food. (Now the tree of life and the
tree of the knowledge of good and evil were in the middle of
the orchard.)
10 Now a river flows from Eden to water the orchard, and
from there it divides into four headstreams. 11 The name of
the first is Pishon; it runs through the entire land of Havilah,
where there is gold. 12 (The gold of that land is pure; pearls and
lapis lazuli are also there.) 13 The name of the second river is
Gihon; it runs through the entire land of Cush. 14 The name of
the third river is Tigris; it runs along the east side of Assyria.
The fourth river is the Euphrates.
15 The LORD God took the man and placed him in the orchard
in Eden to care for it and to maintain it. 16 Then the LORD God
commanded the man, "You may freely eat fruit from every tree
of the orchard, 17 but you must not eat from the tree of the
knowledge of good and evil, for when you eat from it you will
surely die."
18 The LORD God said, "It is not good for the man to be alone. I
will make a companion for him who corresponds to him." 19 The
LORD God formed out of the ground every living animal of the
field and every bird of the air. He brought them to the man to
see what he would name them, and whatever the man called
each living creature, that was its name. 20 So the man named
all the animals, the birds of the air, and the living creatures of
the field, but for Adam no companion who corresponded to
him was found. 21 So the LORD God caused the man to fall into
a deep sleep, and while he was asleep, he took part of the man's
side and closed up the place with flesh. 22 Then the LORD God

2:1–7 In this manner and order was the stately fabric of the world produced and erected, but as yet it remained as a fair and well-furnished house without an inhabitant. God had employed infinite wisdom and power about it and engraved his name upon the meanest creature in it, but there was no creature yet made to read the name and celebrate the praises of the almighty Creator. He therefore thought the world imperfect till there was a creature made that could contemplate, praise, and worship the Maker of it: For this very use and purpose were human beings created, that they might not only see but also consider the things they saw and both praise and love the Maker for and in them all.

JOHN FLAVEL (1627–1691)
THE WORKS

made a woman from the part he had taken out of the man, and
he brought her to the man. 23 Then the man said,

"This one at last is bone of my bones
and flesh of my flesh;
this one will be called 'woman,'
for she was taken out of man."

24 That is why a man leaves his father and mother and unites
with his wife, and they become one family. 25 The man and his
wife were both naked, but they were not ashamed.

THE TEMPTATION AND THE FALL

3 Now the serpent was shrewder than any of the wild animals
that the LORD God had made. He said to the woman, "Is it
really true that God said, 'You must not eat from any tree of the
orchard'?" 2 The woman said to the serpent, "We may eat of the
fruit from the trees of the orchard; 3 but concerning the fruit
of the tree that is in the middle of the orchard God said, 'You
must not eat from it, and you must not touch it, or else you will
die.'" 4 The serpent said to the woman, "Surely you will not die,
5 for God knows that when you eat from it your eyes will open
and you will be like God, knowing good and evil."
6 When the woman saw that the tree produced fruit that
was good for food, was attractive to the eye, and was desirable
for making one wise, she took some of its fruit and ate it. She
also gave some of it to her husband who was with her, and he
ate it. 7 Then the eyes of both of them opened, and they knew
they were naked; so they sewed fig leaves together and made
coverings for themselves.

THE JUDGMENT ORACLES OF GOD AT THE FALL

8 Then the man and his wife heard the sound of the LORD God
moving about in the orchard at the breezy time of the day, and
they hid from the LORD God among the trees of the orchard. 9 But
the LORD God called to the man and said to him, "Where are you?"
10 The man replied, "I heard you moving about in the orchard, and I
was afraid because I was naked, so I hid." 11 And the LORD God said,
"Who told you that you were naked? Did you eat from the tree that
I commanded you not to eat from?" 12 The man said, "The woman
whom you gave me, she gave me some fruit from the tree and I ate
it." 13 So the LORD God said to the woman, "What is this you have
done?" And the woman replied, "The serpent tricked me, and I ate."
14 The LORD God said to the serpent,

"Because you have done this,
cursed are you above all the cattle
and all the living creatures of the field!
On your belly you will crawl
and dust you will eat all the days of your life.
15 And I will put hostility between you and the woman
and between your offspring and her offspring;
he will strike your head,
and you will strike his heel."

16 To the woman he said,

"I will greatly increase your labor pains;
with pain you will give birth to children.
You will want to control your husband,
but he will dominate you."

3:1–6 Satan had indeed been already accustomed to lie against God for the purpose of leading men astray. In the garden of God he disputed about God as if God were not there, for he was ignorant of the greatness of God. And then, in the next place, after he had learned from the woman that God had said that they should die if they tasted the aforesaid tree, opening his mouth he uttered falsehood, "Surely you will not die." But that God was true and the serpent a liar was proved by the result, death having passed upon them who had eaten. For along with the fruit they did also fall under the power of death because they did eat in disobedience, and disobedience to God entails death. Therefore, as they became forfeit to death, from that moment they were handed over to it.

IRENAEUS (C. 130–C. 202)
AGAINST HERESIES

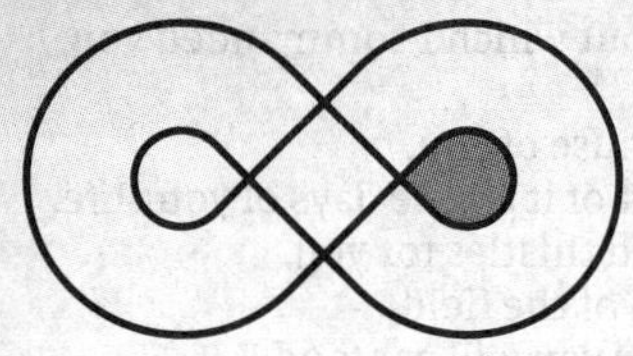

THE APOSTLES' CREED (c. 140)

THE APOSTLES' CREED was written in the second century, the earliest creed in church history. Its name is derived from the belief that it preserves the "rule of faith" (Augustine, *A Sermon to Catechumens on the Creed*) handed down from the apostles, an outline of the main tenets of the doctrine from the New Testament. This creed has been used so widely and by so many church traditions that it is one of the rare documents that unites all Christians in common belief.

I BELIEVE in God, the Father Almighty,
Creator of heaven and earth.

I BELIEVE in Jesus Christ, God's only Son, our Lord,
who was conceived by the Holy Spirit,
born of the Virgin Mary,
suffered under Pontius Pilate,
was crucified, died, and was buried;
he descended to the dead.
On the third day he rose again;
he ascended into heaven,
he is seated at the right hand of the Father,
and he will come to judge the living and the dead.

I BELIEVE in the Holy Spirit,
the holy catholic church,
the communion of saints,
the forgiveness of sins,
the resurrection of the body,
and the life everlasting. Amen.

17 But to Adam he said,
"Because you obeyed your wife
and ate from the tree about which I commanded you,
'You must not eat from it,'
the ground is cursed because of you;
in painful toil you will eat of it all the days of your life.
18 It will produce thorns and thistles for you,
but you will eat the grain of the field.
19 By the sweat of your brow you will eat food
until you return to the ground,
for out of it you were taken;
for you are dust, and to dust you will return."

20 The man named his wife Eve, because she was the mother
of all the living. 21 The LORD God made garments from skin for
Adam and his wife, and clothed them. 22 And the LORD God said,
"Now that the man has become like one of us, knowing good
and evil, he must not be allowed to stretch out his hand and
take also from the tree of life and eat, and live forever." 23 So the
LORD God expelled him from the orchard in Eden to cultivate
the ground from which he had been taken. 24 When he drove
the man out, he placed on the eastern side of the orchard in
Eden angelic sentries who used the flame of a whirling sword
to guard the way to the tree of life.

THE STORY OF CAIN AND ABEL

4 Now the man was intimate with his wife Eve, and she became
pregnant and gave birth to Cain. Then she said, "I have created a man just as the LORD did!" 2 Then she gave birth to his
brother Abel. Abel took care of the flocks, while Cain cultivated
the ground.
3 At the designated time Cain brought some of the fruit of
the ground for an offering to the LORD. 4 But Abel brought some
of the firstborn of his flock—even the fattest of them. And the
LORD was pleased with Abel and his offering, 5 but with Cain
and his offering he was not pleased. So Cain became very angry,
and his expression was downcast.
6 Then the LORD said to Cain, "Why are you angry, and why is
your expression downcast? 7 Is it not true that if you do what is
right, you will be fine? But if you do not do what is right, sin
is crouching at the door. It desires to dominate you, but you
must subdue it."
8 Cain said to his brother Abel, "Let's go out to the field."
While they were in the field, Cain attacked his brother Abel
and killed him.
9 Then the LORD said to Cain, "Where is your brother Abel?"
And he replied, "I don't know! Am I my brother's guardian?"
10 But the LORD said, "What have you done? The voice of your
brother's blood is crying out to me from the ground! 11 So now
you are banished from the ground, which has opened its mouth
to receive your brother's blood from your hand. 12 When you try
to cultivate the ground it will no longer yield its best for you.
You will be a homeless wanderer on the earth."
13 Then Cain said to the LORD, "My punishment is too great
to endure! 14 Look, you are driving me off the land today, and I
must hide from your presence. I will be a homeless wanderer
on the earth; whoever finds me will kill me!" 15 But the LORD
said to him, "All right then, if anyone kills Cain, Cain will be
avenged seven times as much." Then the LORD put a special

4:1–8 What was it that made Abel more beloved by God than his brother, Cain? Without a doubt faith, by which he wholly depended on God. Cain, however, was more or less distrustful and, not content with those things that the soil freely sent forth for food as an innocent means of livelihood, he plowed up the ground. They both offered God sacrifices from their means, but the sacrifice of Abel alone was accepted by God because with a pure heart the innocent man trusted in God's goodness and was not intent on the goods of this world but waited for his piety's reward in heaven. Therefore through his faith did he deserve that God, embracing his offerings, should testify that he was righteous with fire sent down from heaven.

ERASMUS (1466–1536)
PARAPHRASE ON THE EPISTLES

mark on Cain so that no one who found him would strike him
down. 16So Cain went out from the presence of the LORD and
lived in the land of Nod, east of Eden.

THE BEGINNING OF CIVILIZATION

17Cain was intimate with his wife, and she became pregnant and
gave birth to Enoch. Cain was building a city, and he named the
city after his son Enoch. 18To Enoch was born Irad, and Irad was
the father of Mehujael. Mehujael was the father of Methushael,
and Methushael was the father of Lamech.
19Lamech took two wives for himself; the name of the first
was Adah, and the name of the second was Zillah. 20Adah gave
birth to Jabal; he was the first of those who live in tents and
keep livestock. 21The name of his brother was Jubal; he was
the first of all who play the harp and the flute. 22Now Zillah
also gave birth to Tubal-Cain, who heated metal and shaped
all kinds of tools made of bronze and iron. The sister of Tubal-
Cain was Naamah.
23Lamech said to his wives,
"Adah and Zillah, listen to me!
You wives of Lamech, hear my words!
I have killed a man for wounding me,
a young man for hurting me.
24 If Cain is to be avenged seven times as much,
then Lamech seventy-seven times!"

25And Adam was intimate with his wife again, and she gave
birth to a son. She named him Seth, saying, "God has given me
another child in place of Abel because Cain killed him." 26And
a son was also born to Seth, whom he named Enosh. At that
time people began to worship the LORD.

FROM ADAM TO NOAH

5 This is the record of the family line of Adam.
When God created humankind, he made them in the likeness of God. 2He created them male and female; when they
were created, he blessed them and named them "humankind."
3When Adam had lived 130 years he fathered a son in his
own likeness, according to his image, and he named him Seth.
4The length of time Adam lived after he became the father of
Seth was 800 years; during this time he had other sons and
daughters. 5The entire lifetime of Adam was 930 years, and
then he died.
6When Seth had lived 105 years, he became the father of
Enosh. 7Seth lived 807 years after he became the father of
Enosh, and he had other sons and daughters. 8The entire lifetime of Seth was 912 years, and then he died.
9When Enosh had lived 90 years, he became the father of
Kenan. 10Enosh lived 815 years after he became the father of
Kenan, and he had other sons and daughters. 11The entire lifetime of Enosh was 905 years, and then he died.
12When Kenan had lived 70 years, he became the father of
Mahalalel. 13Kenan lived 840 years after he became the father
of Mahalalel, and he had other sons and daughters. 14The entire
lifetime of Kenan was 910 years, and then he died.
15When Mahalalel had lived 65 years, he became the father
of Jared. 16Mahalalel lived 830 years after he became the father
of Jared, and he had other sons and daughters. 17The entire
lifetime of Mahalalel was 895 years, and then he died.

5:1–32 Adam was created after the image and similitude of God, or the image was created by God and not begotten, for Adam did not have parents. He did not remain in this image but fell away from it through sin. And so Seth, who was born later on, was not born after the image of God but after that of his father, Adam. That is, he was like Adam; he was the image of his father, Adam, not only in the shape of his face but also in likeness. This image includes original sin and the punishment of eternal death that were inflicted on Adam on account of his sin. But just as Adam recovered the lost image in the future Seed, so Seth did also after he had grown up, for through his word God stamped his likeness upon him.

MARTIN LUTHER (1483–1546)
LECTURES ON GENESIS

[18]When Jared had lived 162 years, he became the father of Enoch. [19]Jared lived 800 years after he became the father of Enoch, and he had other sons and daughters. [20]The entire lifetime of Jared was 962 years, and then he died.

[21]When Enoch had lived 65 years, he became the father of Methuselah. [22]After he became the father of Methuselah, Enoch walked with God for 300 years, and he had other sons and daughters. [23]The entire lifetime of Enoch was 365 years. [24]Enoch walked with God, and then he disappeared because God took him away.

[25]When Methuselah had lived 187 years, he became the father of Lamech. [26]Methuselah lived 782 years after he became the father of Lamech, and he had other sons and daughters. [27]The entire lifetime of Methuselah was 969 years, and then he died.

[28]When Lamech had lived 182 years, he had a son. [29]He named him Noah, saying, "This one will bring us comfort from our labor and from the painful toil of our hands because of the ground that the LORD has cursed." [30]Lamech lived 595 years after he became the father of Noah, and he had other sons and daughters. [31]The entire lifetime of Lamech was 777 years, and then he died.

[32]After Noah was 500 years old, he became the father of Shem, Ham, and Japheth.

GOD'S GRIEF OVER HUMANKIND'S WICKEDNESS

6 When humankind began to multiply on the face of the earth, and daughters were born to them, [2]the sons of God saw that the daughters of humankind were beautiful. Thus they took wives for themselves from any they chose. [3]So the LORD said, "My Spirit will not remain in humankind indefinitely, since they are mortal. They will remain for 120 more years."

[4]The Nephilim were on the earth in those days (and also after this) when the sons of God would sleep with the daughters of humankind, who gave birth to their children. They were the mighty heroes of old, the famous men.

[5]But the LORD saw that the wickedness of humankind had become great on the earth. Every inclination of the thoughts of their minds was only evil all the time. [6]The LORD regretted that he had made humankind on the earth, and he was highly offended. [7]So the LORD said, "I will wipe humankind, whom I have created, from the face of the earth—everything from humankind to animals, including creatures that move on the ground and birds of the air, for I regret that I have made them."

[8]But Noah found favor in the sight of the LORD.

THE JUDGMENT OF THE FLOOD

[9]This is the account of Noah.

Noah was a godly man; he was blameless among his contemporaries. He walked with God. [10]Noah had three sons: Shem, Ham, and Japheth.

[11]The earth was ruined in the sight of God; the earth was filled with violence. [12]God saw the earth, and indeed it was ruined, for all living creatures on the earth were sinful. [13]So God said to Noah, "I have decided that all living creatures must die, for the earth is filled with violence because of them. Now I am about to destroy them and the earth. [14]Make for yourself an ark of cypress wood. Make rooms in the ark, and cover it with pitch inside and out. [15]This is how you should make it: The ark is to be 450 feet long, 75 feet wide, and 45 feet high. [16]Make a roof for

6:13–22 Both the providence and the grace of God own and crown the obedient and diligent. God gave Noah particular orders how to make the ark that could not therefore but be well fitted for the purpose. God promised Noah that he and his family should be kept alive in the ark. What we do in obedience to God, we and our families are likely to have the benefit of. The piety of parents gets their children good in this life and furthers them in the way to eternal life if they improve it.

MATTHEW HENRY (1662–1714)
COMMENTARY ON THE WHOLE BIBLE

the ark and finish it, leaving 18 inches from the top. Put a door
in the side of the ark, and make lower, middle, and upper decks.
17I am about to bring floodwaters on the earth to destroy from
under the sky all the living creatures that have the breath of
life in them. Everything that is on the earth will die, 18but I will
confirm my covenant with you. You will enter the ark—you, your
sons, your wife, and your sons' wives with you. 19You must bring
into the ark two of every kind of living creature from all flesh,
male and female, to keep them alive with you. 20Of the birds
after their kinds, and of the cattle after their kinds, and of every
creeping thing of the ground after its kind, two of every kind
will come to you so you can keep them alive. 21And you must
take for yourself every kind of food that is eaten, and gather it
together. It will be food for you and for them."
22And Noah did all that God commanded him—he did indeed.
7 The LORD said to Noah, "Come into the ark, you and all your
household, for I consider you godly among this generation.
2You must take with you seven pairs of every kind of clean animal, the male and its mate, two of every kind of unclean animal,
the male and its mate, 3and also seven pairs of every kind of
bird in the sky, male and female, to preserve their offspring on
the face of the entire earth. 4For in seven days I will cause it
to rain on the earth for 40 days and 40 nights, and I will wipe
from the face of the ground every living thing that I have made."
5And Noah did all that the LORD commanded him.
6Noah was 600 years old when the floodwaters engulfed
the earth. 7Noah entered the ark along with his sons, his wife,
and his sons' wives because of the floodwaters. 8Pairs of clean
animals, of unclean animals, of birds, and of everything that
creeps along the ground, 9male and female, came into the ark
to Noah, just as God had commanded him. 10And after seven
days the floodwaters engulfed the earth.
11In the six hundredth year of Noah's life, in the second
month, on the seventeenth day of the month—on that day all
the fountains of the great deep burst open and the floodgates
of the heavens were opened. 12And the rain fell on the earth
40 days and 40 nights.
13On that very day Noah entered the ark, accompanied by his
sons Shem, Ham, and Japheth, along with his wife and his sons'
three wives. 14They entered, along with every living creature after
its kind, every animal after its kind, every creeping thing that
creeps on the earth after its kind, and every bird after its kind, everything with wings. 15Pairs of all creatures that have the breath of
life came into the ark to Noah. 16Those that entered were male and
female, just as God commanded him. Then the LORD shut him in.
17The flood engulfed the earth for 40 days. As the waters
increased, they lifted the ark and raised it above the earth.
18The waters completely overwhelmed the earth, and the ark
floated on the surface of the waters. 19The waters completely
inundated the earth so that even all the high mountains under
the entire sky were covered. 20The waters rose more than 20
feet above the mountains. 21And all living things that moved
on the earth died, including the birds, domestic animals, wild
animals, all the creatures that swarm over the earth, and all
humankind. 22Everything on dry land that had the breath of
life in its nostrils died. 23So the LORD destroyed every living
thing that was on the surface of the ground, including people,
animals, creatures that creep along the ground, and birds of
the sky. They were wiped off the earth. Only Noah and those

7:7–15 Christ was represented in Noah and the world in that ark. For why were all living creatures shut up in that ark except to signify all the nations? For God did not lack the capability of creating anew every species of living things. For when no creatures were in existence, did he not say, "Let the land produce" and the land produced? So from the same source as he made them then, he could remake them. God made them by a word, so God could remake them by a word.

AUGUSTINE **(354–430)**
TRACTATES ON THE GOSPEL OF JOHN

who were with him in the ark survived. [24]The waters prevailed over the earth for 150 days.

8 But God remembered Noah and all the wild animals and domestic animals that were with him in the ark. God caused a wind to blow over the earth and the waters receded. [2]The fountains of the deep and the floodgates of heaven were closed, and the rain stopped falling from the sky. [3]The waters kept receding steadily from the earth, so that they had gone down by the end of the 150 days. [4]On the seventeenth day of the seventh month, the ark came to rest on one of the mountains of Ararat. [5]The waters kept on receding until the tenth month. On the first day of the tenth month, the tops of the mountains became visible.

[6]At the end of 40 days, Noah opened the window he had made in the ark [7]and sent out a raven; it kept flying back and forth until the waters had dried up on the earth.

[8]Then Noah sent out a dove to see if the waters had receded from the surface of the ground. [9]The dove could not find a resting place for its feet because water still covered the surface of the entire earth, and so it returned to Noah in the ark. He stretched out his hand, took the dove, and brought it back into the ark. [10]He waited seven more days and then sent out the dove again from the ark. [11]When the dove returned to him in the evening, there was a freshly plucked olive leaf in its beak! Noah knew that the waters had receded from the earth. [12]He waited another seven days and sent the dove out again, but it did not return to him this time.

[13]In Noah's six hundred and first year, in the first day of the first month, the waters had dried up from the earth, and Noah removed the covering from the ark and saw that the surface of the ground was dry. [14]And by the twenty-seventh day of the second month the earth was dry.

[15]Then God spoke to Noah and said, [16]"Come out of the ark, you, your wife, your sons, and your sons' wives with you. [17]Bring out with you all the living creatures that are with you. Bring out every living thing, including the birds, animals, and every creeping thing that creeps on the earth. Let them increase and be fruitful and multiply on the earth!"

[18]Noah went out along with his sons, his wife, and his sons' wives. [19]Every living creature, every creeping thing, every bird, and everything that moves on the earth went out of the ark in their groups.

[20]Noah built an altar to the LORD. He then took some of every kind of clean animal and clean bird and offered burnt offerings on the altar. [21]And the LORD smelled the soothing aroma and said to himself, "I will never again curse the ground because of humankind, even though the inclination of their minds is evil from childhood on. I will never again destroy everything that lives, as I have just done.

[22]"While the earth continues to exist,
planting time and harvest,
cold and heat,
summer and winter,
and day and night will not cease."

GOD'S COVENANT WITH HUMANKIND THROUGH NOAH

9 Then God blessed Noah and his sons and said to them, "Be fruitful and multiply and fill the earth. [2]Every living creature of the earth and every bird of the sky will be terrified of

8:1–19 It is not idle chatter when the Holy Spirit says that God remembered Noah. It indicates that from the day when Noah entered the ark nothing was said to him, nothing was revealed to him, and he saw no ray of grace shining; but he clung only to the promise he had received although meanwhile the waters and the waves were raging as though God had surely forgotten him. His children, the cattle, and the other animals of every kind experienced the same peril throughout the entire 150 days in the ark. Even through a rich measure of the Spirit, it did not overcome them without great affliction of the flesh, without tears and great fear, which I think the dumb animals experienced too.

MARTIN LUTHER (1483–1546)
LECTURES ON GENESIS

you. Everything that creeps on the ground and all the fish of
the sea are under your authority. 3You may eat any moving
thing that lives. As I gave you the green plants, I now give
you everything.
4"But you must not eat meat with its life (that is, its blood)
in it. 5For your lifeblood I will surely exact punishment, from
every living creature I will exact punishment. From each person
I will exact punishment for the life of the individual since the
man was his relative.

6 "Whoever sheds human blood,
by other humans
must his blood be shed;
for in God's image
God has made humankind.

7"But as for you, be fruitful and multiply; increase abundantly
on the earth and multiply on it."
8God said to Noah and his sons, 9"Look. I now confirm my
covenant with you and your descendants after you 10and with
every living creature that is with you, including the birds, the
domestic animals, and every living creature of the earth with
you, all those that came out of the ark with you—every living
creature of the earth. 11I confirm my covenant with you: Never
again will all living things be wiped out by the waters of a flood;
never again will a flood destroy the earth."
12And God said, "This is the guarantee of the covenant I
am making with you and every living creature with you, a
covenant for all subsequent generations: 13I will place my
rainbow in the clouds, and it will become a guarantee of the
covenant between me and the earth. 14Whenever I bring
clouds over the earth and the rainbow appears in the clouds,
15then I will remember my covenant with you and with all living creatures of all kinds. Never again will the waters become
a flood and destroy all living things. 16When the rainbow is
in the clouds, I will notice it and remember the perpetual
covenant between God and all living creatures of all kinds
that are on the earth."
17So God said to Noah, "This is the guarantee of the covenant
that I am confirming between me and all living things that are
on the earth."

THE CURSE ON CANAAN

18The sons of Noah who came out of the ark were Shem, Ham,
and Japheth. (Now Ham was the father of Canaan.) 19These
were the three sons of Noah, and from them the whole earth
was populated.
20Noah, a man of the soil, began to plant a vineyard. 21When
he drank some of the wine, he got drunk and uncovered himself
inside his tent. 22Ham, the father of Canaan, saw his father's
nakedness and told his two brothers who were outside. 23Shem
and Japheth took the garment and placed it on their shoulders.
Then they walked in backwards and covered up their father's
nakedness. Their faces were turned the other way so they did
not see their father's nakedness.
24When Noah awoke from his drunken stupor he learned
what his youngest son had done to him. 25So he said,

"Cursed be Canaan!
The lowest of slaves
he will be to his brothers."

9:8–17 Mark the form of the promise. God does not say, *And when you shall look upon the rainbow and you shall remember my covenant, then I will not destroy the earth,* but it is gloriously put not upon our memory, which is fickle and frail, but upon God's memory, which is infinite and immutable. Oh! It is not my remembering God—it is God's remembering me that is the ground of my safety; it is not my laying hold of his covenant, but his covenant's laying hold of me. Glory be to God!

CHARLES SPURGEON
(1834–1892)
MORNING AND EVENING

26 He also said,
"Worthy of praise is the LORD, the God of Shem!
May Canaan be the slave of Shem!
27 May God enlarge Japheth's territory and numbers!
May he live in the tents of Shem
and may Canaan be the slave of Japheth!"

28 After the flood Noah lived 350 years. 29 The entire lifetime
of Noah was 950 years, and then he died.

THE TABLE OF NATIONS

10 This is the account of Noah's sons: Shem, Ham, and
Japheth. Sons were born to them after the flood.
2 The sons of Japheth were Gomer, Magog, Madai, Javan, Tubal, Meshech, and Tiras. 3 The sons of Gomer were Ashkenaz,
Riphath, and Togarmah. 4 The sons of Javan were Elishah, Tarshish, the Kittim, and the Dodanim. 5 From these the coastlands
of the nations were separated into their lands, every one according to its language, according to their families, by their nations.
6 The sons of Ham were Cush, Mizraim, Put, and Canaan. 7 The
sons of Cush were Seba, Havilah, Sabtah, Raamah, and Sabteca.
The sons of Raamah were Sheba and Dedan.
8 Cush was the father of Nimrod; he began to be a valiant
warrior on the earth. 9 He was a mighty hunter before the LORD.
(That is why it is said, "Like Nimrod, a mighty hunter before
the LORD.") 10 The primary regions of his kingdom were Babel,
Erech, Akkad, and Calneh in the land of Shinar. 11 From that land
he went to Assyria, where he built Nineveh, Rehoboth Ir, Calah,
12 and Resen, which is between Nineveh and the great city Calah.
13 Mizraim was the father of the Ludites, Anamites, Leha-
bites, Naphtuhites, 14 Pathrusites, Casluhites (from whom the
Philistines came), and Caphtorites.
15 Canaan was the father of Sidon his firstborn, Heth, 16 the
Jebusites, Amorites, Girgashites, 17 Hivites, Arkites, Sinites, 18 Arvadites, Zemarites, and Hamathites. Eventually the families
of the Canaanites were scattered 19 and the borders of Canaan
extended from Sidon all the way to Gerar as far as Gaza, and
all the way to Sodom, Gomorrah, Admah, and Zeboyim, as far
as Lasha. 20 These are the sons of Ham, according to their families, according to their languages, by their lands, and by their
nations.
21 And sons were also born to Shem (the older brother of
Japheth), the father of all the sons of Eber.
22 The sons of Shem were Elam, Asshur, Arphaxad, Lud, and
Aram. 23 The sons of Aram were Uz, Hul, Gether, and Mash. 24 Arphaxad was the father of Shelah, and Shelah was the father
of Eber. 25 Two sons were born to Eber: One was named Peleg
because in his days the earth was divided, and his brother's
name was Joktan. 26 Joktan was the father of Almodad, Sheleph,
Hazarmaveth, Jerah, 27 Hadoram, Uzal, Diklah, 28 Obal, Abimael,
Sheba, 29 Ophir, Havilah, and Jobab. All these were sons of Joktan.
30 Their dwelling place was from Mesha all the way to Sephar
in the eastern hills. 31 These are the sons of Shem according to
their families, according to their languages, by their lands, and
according to their nations.
32 These are the families of the sons of Noah, according to
their genealogies, by their nations, and from these the nations
spread over the earth after the flood.

10:1—11:1 When the generations of the sons of Noah are recounted, it is said, "These are the sons of Ham, according to their families, according to their languages, by their lands, and by their nations." The addition of this sentence, "The whole earth had a common language and a common vocabulary," seems to indicate that at the time when the nations were scattered over the earth they had all one language in common; but this is evidently inconsistent with the previous words, "according to their families, according to their languages." For each family or nation could not be said to have its own language if all had one language in common. And so it is by way of recapitulation it is added, "The whole earth had a common language and a common vocabulary," the narrative here going back without indicating the change to tell how it was that from having one language in common, the nations were divided into a multitude of tongues.

AUGUSTINE **(354–430)**
ON CHRISTIAN DOCTRINE

THE DISPERSION OF THE NATIONS AT BABEL

11 The whole earth had a common language and a common vocabulary. 2 When the people moved eastward, they found a plain in Shinar and settled there. 3 Then they said to one another, "Come, let's make bricks and bake them thoroughly." (They had brick instead of stone and tar instead of mortar.) 4 Then they said, "Come, let's build ourselves a city and a tower with its top in the heavens so that we may make a name for ourselves. Otherwise we will be scattered across the face of the entire earth."

5 But the LORD came down to see the city and the tower that the people had started building. 6 And the LORD said, "If as one people all sharing a common language they have begun to do this, then nothing they plan to do will be beyond them. 7 Come, let's go down and confuse their language so they won't be able to understand each other."

8 So the LORD scattered them from there across the face of the entire earth, and they stopped building the city. 9 That is why its name was called Babel—because there the LORD confused the language of the entire world, and from there the LORD scattered them across the face of the entire earth.

THE GENEALOGY OF SHEM

10 This is the account of Shem.

Shem was 100 years old when he became the father of Arphaxad, two years after the flood. 11 And after becoming the father of Arphaxad, Shem lived 500 years and had other sons and daughters.

12 When Arphaxad had lived 35 years, he became the father of Shelah. 13 And after he became the father of Shelah, Arphaxad lived 403 years and had other sons and daughters.

14 When Shelah had lived 30 years, he became the father of Eber. 15 And after he became the father of Eber, Shelah lived 403 years and had other sons and daughters.

16 When Eber had lived 34 years, he became the father of Peleg. 17 And after he became the father of Peleg, Eber lived 430 years and had other sons and daughters.

18 When Peleg had lived 30 years, he became the father of Reu. 19 And after he became the father of Reu, Peleg lived 209 years and had other sons and daughters.

20 When Reu had lived 32 years, he became the father of Serug. 21 And after he became the father of Serug, Reu lived 207 years and had other sons and daughters.

22 When Serug had lived 30 years, he became the father of Nahor. 23 And after he became the father of Nahor, Serug lived 200 years and had other sons and daughters.

24 When Nahor had lived 29 years, he became the father of Terah. 25 And after he became the father of Terah, Nahor lived 119 years and had other sons and daughters.

26 When Terah had lived 70 years, he became the father of Abram, Nahor, and Haran.

THE RECORD OF TERAH

27 This is the account of Terah.

Terah became the father of Abram, Nahor, and Haran. And Haran became the father of Lot. 28 Haran died in the land of his birth, in Ur of the Chaldeans, while his father Terah was still alive. 29 And Abram and Nahor took wives for themselves. The name of Abram's wife was Sarai. And the name of Nahor's wife was Milcah; she was the daughter of Haran, who was the father of both Milcah and Iscah. 30 But Sarai was barren; she had no children.

31 Terah took his son Abram, his grandson Lot (the son of
Haran), and his daughter-in-law Sarai, his son Abram's wife, and
with them he set out from Ur of the Chaldeans to go to Canaan.
When they came to Haran, they settled there. 32 The lifetime
of Terah was 205 years, and he died in Haran.

THE OBEDIENCE OF ABRAM

12 Now the LORD said to Abram,
"Go out from your country, your relatives, and your
father's household
to the land that I will show you.
2 Then I will make you into a great nation, and I will bless
you,
and I will make your name great,
so that you will exemplify divine blessing.
3 I will bless those who bless you,
but the one who treats you lightly I must curse,
so that all the families of the earth may receive blessing
through you."

4 So Abram left, just as the LORD had told him to do, and Lot
went with him. (Now Abram was 75 years old when he departed
from Haran.) 5 And Abram took his wife Sarai, his nephew Lot,
and all the possessions they had accumulated and the people
they had acquired in Haran, and they left for the land of Canaan.
They entered the land of Canaan.
6 Abram traveled through the land as far as the oak tree of
Moreh at Shechem. (At that time the Canaanites were in the
land.) 7 The LORD appeared to Abram and said, "To your descendants I will give this land." So Abram built an altar there to the
LORD, who had appeared to him.
8 Then he moved from there to the hill country east of Bethel
and pitched his tent, with Bethel on the west and Ai on the east.
There he built an altar to the LORD and worshiped the LORD.
9 Abram continually journeyed by stages down to the Negev.

12:1–9 That our faith was also prefigured in Abraham, and that he was the patriarch of our faith and the prophet of it, the apostle has very fully taught: "Just as Abraham believed God, and it was credited to him as righteousness, so then, understand that those who believe are the sons of Abraham" (Gal 3:6–7). For which reasons the apostle declared that this man was not only the prophet of faith, but also the father of those who from among the Gentiles believe in Jesus Christ because he believed in things future as if they were already accomplished because of the promise of God; and in like manner do we also, because of the promise of God, behold through faith that inheritance is laid up for us in the future kingdom.

IRENAEUS (C. 130–C. 202)
AGAINST HERESIES

THE PROMISED BLESSING JEOPARDIZED

10 There was a famine in the land, so Abram went down to
Egypt to stay for a while because the famine was severe. 11 As
he approached Egypt, he said to his wife Sarai, "Look, I know
that you are a beautiful woman. 12 When the Egyptians see
you they will say, 'This is his wife.' Then they will kill me but
will keep you alive. 13 So tell them you are my sister so that it
may go well for me because of you and my life will be spared
on account of you."
14 When Abram entered Egypt, the Egyptians saw that the
woman was very beautiful. 15 When Pharaoh's officials saw her,
they praised her to Pharaoh. So Abram's wife was taken into
the household of Pharaoh, 16 and he did treat Abram well on
account of her. Abram received sheep and cattle, male donkeys,
male servants, female servants, female donkeys, and camels.
17 But the LORD struck Pharaoh and his household with
severe diseases because of Sarai, Abram's wife. 18 So Pharaoh
summoned Abram and said, "What is this you have done to
me? Why didn't you tell me that she was your wife? 19 Why did
you say, 'She is my sister,' so that I took her to be my wife? Now,
here is your wife. Take her and go!" 20 Pharaoh gave his men
orders about Abram, and so they expelled him, along with his
wife and all his possessions.

ABRAM'S SOLUTION TO THE STRIFE

13 So Abram went up from Egypt into the Negev. He took
his wife and all his possessions with him, as well as Lot.
2(Now Abram was very wealthy in livestock, silver, and gold.)
3And he journeyed from place to place from the Negev as
far as Bethel. He returned to the place where he had pitched
his tent at the beginning, between Bethel and Ai. 4This was
the place where he had first built the altar, and there Abram
worshiped the LORD.
5Now Lot, who was traveling with Abram, also had flocks, herds,
and tents. 6But the land could not support them while they were
living side by side. Because their possessions were so great, they
were not able to live alongside one another. 7So there were quarrels between Abram's herdsmen and Lot's herdsmen. (Now the
Canaanites and the Perizzites were living in the land at that time.)
8Abram said to Lot, "Let there be no quarreling between me
and you, and between my herdsmen and your herdsmen, for we
are close relatives. 9Is not the whole land before you? Separate
yourself now from me. If you go to the left, then I'll go to the
right, but if you go to the right, then I'll go to the left."
10Lot looked up and saw the whole region of the Jordan. He
noticed that all of it was well watered (this was before the LORD
obliterated Sodom and Gomorrah) like the garden of the LORD,
like the land of Egypt, all the way to Zoar. 11Lot chose for himself
the whole region of the Jordan and traveled toward the east.
So the relatives separated from each other. 12Abram settled in
the land of Canaan, but Lot settled among the cities of the Jordan
plain and pitched his tents next to Sodom. 13(Now the people of
Sodom were extremely wicked rebels against the LORD.)
14After Lot had departed, the LORD said to Abram, "Look
from the place where you stand to the north, south, east, and
west. 15I will give all the land that you see to you and your descendants forever. 16And I will make your descendants like the
dust of the earth, so that if anyone is able to count the dust of
the earth, then your descendants also can be counted. 17Get up
and walk throughout the land, for I will give it to you."
18So Abram moved his tents and went to live by the oaks
of Mamre in Hebron, and he built an altar to the LORD there.

THE BLESSING OF VICTORY FOR GOD'S PEOPLE

14 At that time Amraphel king of Shinar, Arioch king of Ellasar, Kedorlaomer king of Elam, and Tidal king of nations
2went to war against Bera king of Sodom, Birsha king of Gomorrah, Shinab king of Admah, Shemeber king of Zeboyim,
and the king of Bela (that is, Zoar). 3These last five kings joined
forces in the Valley of Siddim (that is, the Salt Sea). 4For twelve
years they had served Kedorlaomer, but in the thirteenth year
they rebelled. 5In the fourteenth year, Kedorlaomer and the
kings who were his allies came and defeated the Rephaites in
Ashteroth Karnaim, the Zuzites in Ham, the Emites in Shaveh
Kiriathaim, 6and the Horites in their hill country of Seir, as far
as El Paran, which is near the desert. 7Then they attacked En
Mishpat (that is, Kadesh) again, and they conquered all the
territory of the Amalekites, as well as the Amorites who were
living in Hazezon Tamar.
8Then the king of Sodom, the king of Gomorrah, the king
of Admah, the king of Zeboyim, and the king of Bela (that is,
Zoar) went out and prepared for battle. In the Valley of Siddim
they met 9Kedorlaomer king of Elam, Tidal king of nations,

13:1–18 Moses commemorates the goodness of God in protecting Abram: He not only returned in safety but took with him great wealth. Moses next shows that riches proved no sufficient obstacle to prevent Abram from having respect continually to his proposed end and from moving toward it with unremitting pace. We know how greatly even a moderate share of wealth hinders many from raising their heads toward heaven. Therefore Moses places the virtue of Abram in contrast with the common vice of others when he relates that he was not to be prevented by any impediments from seeking again the land of Canaan. He did not forget what had been divinely commanded him and therefore, as one unfettered, he hastened to the place whither he was called.

JOHN CALVIN **(1509–1564)**
COMPLETE COMMENTARY ON THE BIBLE

Amraphel king of Shinar, and Arioch king of Ellasar. Four kings
fought against five. 10 Now the Valley of Siddim was full of tar
pits. When the kings of Sodom and Gomorrah fled, they fell
into them, but some survivors fled to the hills. 11 The four victorious kings took all the possessions and food of Sodom and
Gomorrah and left. 12 They also took Abram's nephew Lot and
his possessions when they left, for Lot was living in Sodom.
13 A fugitive came and told Abram the Hebrew. Now Abram
was living by the oaks of Mamre the Amorite, the brother of
Eshcol and Aner. (All these were allied by treaty with Abram.)
14 When Abram heard that his nephew had been taken captive,
he mobilized his 318 trained men who had been born in his
household, and he pursued the invaders as far as Dan. 15 Then,
during the night, Abram divided his forces against them and
defeated them. He chased them as far as Hobah, which is north
of Damascus. 16 He retrieved all the stolen property. He also
brought back his nephew Lot and his possessions, as well as
the women and the rest of the people.
17 After Abram returned from defeating Kedorlaomer and
the kings who were with him, the king of Sodom went out to
meet Abram in the Valley of Shaveh (known as the King's Valley). 18 Melchizedek king of Salem brought out bread and wine.
(Now he was the priest of the Most High God.) 19 He blessed
Abram, saying,

"Blessed be Abram by the Most High God,
Creator of heaven and earth.
20 Worthy of praise is the Most High God,
who delivered your enemies into your hand."

Abram gave Melchizedek a tenth of everything.
21 Then the king of Sodom said to Abram, "Give me the people
and take the possessions for yourself." 22 But Abram replied
to the king of Sodom, "I raise my hand to the LORD, the Most
High God, Creator of heaven and earth, and vow 23 that I will
take nothing belonging to you, not even a thread or the strap
of a sandal. That way you can never say, 'It is I who made Abram
rich.' 24 I will take nothing except compensation for what the
young men have eaten. As for the share of the men who went
with me—Aner, Eshcol, and Mamre—let them take their share."

THE CUTTING OF THE COVENANT

15 After these things the LORD's message came to Abram in
a vision: "Fear not, Abram! I am your shield and the one
who will reward you in great abundance."
2 But Abram said, "O Sovereign LORD, what will you give me
since I continue to be childless, and my heir is Eliezer of Damascus?" 3 Abram added, "Since you have not given me a descendant,
then look, one born in my house will be my heir!"
4 But look, the LORD's message came to him: "This man will
not be your heir, but instead a son who comes from your own
body will be your heir." 5 The LORD took him outside and said,
"Gaze into the sky and count the stars—if you are able to count
them!" Then he said to him, "So will your descendants be."
6 Abram believed the LORD, and the LORD credited it as righteousness to him.
7 The LORD said to him, "I am the LORD who brought you
out from Ur of the Chaldeans to give you this land to possess."
8 But Abram said, "O Sovereign LORD, by what can I know that
I am to possess it?"

14:18–24 The sacrifice of the Lord prefigured according to what the divine scripture testifies and says, "Melchizedek king of Salem brought out bread and wine. (Now he was the priest of the Most High God.) He blessed Abram." But that Melchizedek portrayed a type of Christ the Holy Spirit declares in the Psalms, saying in the person of the Father to the Son: "You are an eternal priest after the pattern of Melchizedek" (Ps 110:4). The order proceeds first from the sacrifice and then descends to Melchizedek, a priest of the Most High God, because he offered bread and because he blessed Abraham. For who is more a priest of the Most High God than our Lord Jesus Christ, who offered sacrifice to God the Father and offered the very same thing that Melchizedek had offered, bread and wine, that were actually his body and blood?

CYPRIAN OF CARTHAGE
(C. 210–258)
LETTERS

15:1–6 It is patience that is both subsequent and antecedent to faith. In short, Abraham believed God and was accredited by him with righteousness; but it was patience that proved his faith when he was bidden to sacrifice his son with a view to the typical attestation of his faith. But God knew whom he had accredited with righteousness. The trial was necessary not to prove his faith to God, who knows all whom he accounts righteous. Deservedly then was he blessed because he was faithful, deservedly faithful because patient (see Heb 6:15). So faith illumined by patience, when it was becoming propagated among the nations through Abraham's seed, "who is Christ" (Gal 3:16) and was superinducing grace over the law, made patience her preeminent assistant for amplifying and fulfilling the law because that alone had been lacking unto the doctrine of righteousness.

TERTULLIAN (155–C. 220)
ON PATIENCE

9 The LORD said to him, "Take for me a heifer, a goat, and a
ram, each three years old, along with a dove and a young pigeon."
10 So Abram took all these for him and then cut them in two
and placed each half opposite the other, but he did not cut the
birds in half. 11 When birds of prey came down on the carcasses,
Abram drove them away.
12 When the sun went down, Abram fell sound asleep, and
great terror overwhelmed him. 13 Then the LORD said to Abram,
"Know for certain that your descendants will be strangers in a
foreign country. They will be enslaved and oppressed for 400
years. 14 But I will execute judgment on the nation that they
will serve. Afterward they will come out with many possessions.
15 But as for you, you will go to your ancestors in peace and
be buried at a good old age. 16 In the fourth generation your
descendants will return here, for the sin of the Amorites has
not yet reached its limit."
17 When the sun had gone down and it was dark, a smoking
firepot with a flaming torch passed between the animal parts.
18 That day the LORD made a covenant with Abram: "To your
descendants I give this land, from the river of Egypt to the great
river, the Euphrates River—19 the land of the Kenites, Kenizzites,
Kadmonites, 20 Hittites, Perizzites, Rephaites, 21 Amorites, Canaanites, Girgashites, and Jebusites."

THE BIRTH OF ISHMAEL

16 Now Sarai, Abram's wife, had not given birth to any children, but she had an Egyptian servant named Hagar. 2 So
Sarai said to Abram, "Since the LORD has prevented me from
having children, please sleep with my servant. Perhaps I can
have a family by her." Abram did what Sarai told him.
3 So after Abram had lived in Canaan for ten years, Sarai,
Abram's wife, gave Hagar, her Egyptian servant, to her husband
to be his wife. 4 He slept with Hagar, and she became pregnant.
Once Hagar realized she was pregnant, she despised Sarai.
5 Then Sarai said to Abram, "You have brought this wrong on
me! I gave my servant into your embrace, but when she realized
that she was pregnant, she despised me. May the LORD judge
between you and me!"
6 Abram said to Sarai, "Since your servant is under your authority, do to her whatever you think best." Then Sarai treated
Hagar harshly, so she ran away from Sarai.
7 The angel of the LORD found Hagar near a spring of water
in the wilderness—the spring that is along the road to Shur.
8 He said, "Hagar, servant of Sarai, where have you come from,
and where are you going?" She replied, "I'm running away from
my mistress, Sarai."
9 Then the angel of the LORD said to her, "Return to your
mistress and submit to her authority. 10 I will greatly multiply
your descendants," the angel of the LORD added, "so that they
will be too numerous to count." 11 Then the angel of the LORD
said to her,

"You are now pregnant
and are about to give birth to a son.
You are to name him Ishmael,
for the LORD has heard your painful groans.
12 He will be a wild donkey of a man.
He will be hostile to everyone,
and everyone will be hostile to him.
He will live away from his brothers."

16:1–5 We have here the ill consequences of Abram's marriage to Hagar. Hagar no sooner perceived herself with child but she looked scornfully upon her mistress, upbraided her perhaps with her barrenness, and insulted her. Sarai fell upon Abram and very unjustly charged him with the injury, suspecting that he had countenanced Hagar's insolence. And as one not willing to hear what Abram had to say, she rashly appealed to God—"May the LORD judge between you and me!"—as if Abram had refused to right her. When passion is upon the throne, reason is out of doors and is neither heard nor spoken. Those are not always in the right who are most forward in appealing to God. Rash and bold imprecations are commonly evidences of guilt and a bad cause.

JOHN WESLEY (1703–1791)
EXPLANATORY NOTES ON THE BIBLE

[13]So Hagar named the LORD who spoke to her, "You are the
God who sees me," for she said, "Here I have seen one who sees
me!" [14]That is why the well was called Beer Lahai Roi. (It is
located between Kadesh and Bered.)
[15]So Hagar gave birth to Abram's son, whom Abram named
Ishmael. [16](Now Abram was eighty-six years old when Hagar
gave birth to Ishmael.)

THE SIGN OF THE COVENANT

17 When Abram was ninety-nine years old, the LORD appeared to him and said, "I am the Sovereign God. Walk
before me and be blameless. [2]Then I will confirm my covenant between me and you, and I will give you a multitude of
descendants."
[3]Abram bowed down with his face to the ground, and God
said to him, [4]"As for me, this is my covenant with you: You will
be the father of a multitude of nations. [5]No longer will your
name be Abram. Instead, your name will be Abraham because
I will make you the father of a multitude of nations. [6]I will
make you extremely fruitful. I will make nations of you, and
kings will descend from you. [7]I will confirm my covenant as a
perpetual covenant between me and you. It will extend to your
descendants after you throughout their generations. I will be
your God and the God of your descendants after you. [8]I will
give the whole land of Canaan—the land where you are now
residing—to you and your descendants after you as a permanent
possession. I will be their God."
[9]Then God said to Abraham, "As for you, you must keep the
covenantal requirement I am imposing on you and your descendants after you throughout their generations. [10]This is
my requirement that you and your descendants after you must
keep: Every male among you must be circumcised. [11]You must
circumcise the flesh of your foreskins. This will be a reminder
of the covenant between me and you. [12]Throughout your generations every male among you who is eight days old must be
circumcised, whether born in your house or bought with money
from any foreigner who is not one of your descendants. [13]They
must indeed be circumcised, whether born in your house or
bought with money. The sign of my covenant will be visible
in your flesh as a permanent reminder. [14]Any uncircumcised
male who has not been circumcised in the flesh of his foreskin
will be cut off from his people—he has failed to carry out my
requirement."
[15]Then God said to Abraham, "As for your wife, you must
no longer call her Sarai; Sarah will be her name. [16]I will bless
her and will give you a son through her. I will bless her and
she will become a mother of nations. Kings of countries will
come from her!"
[17]Then Abraham bowed down with his face to the ground
and laughed as he said to himself, "Can a son be born to a man
who is a hundred years old? Can Sarah bear a child at the age
of ninety?" [18]Abraham said to God, "O that Ishmael might live
before you!"
[19]God said, "No, Sarah your wife is going to bear you a son,
and you will name him Isaac. I will confirm my covenant with
him as a perpetual covenant for his descendants after him. [20]As
for Ishmael, I have heard you. I will indeed bless him, make
him fruitful, and give him a multitude of descendants. He will
become the father of twelve princes; I will make him into a great

17:15–27 The fact that Abraham laughed when he had been promised a son through Sarah was an expression of joy. Indeed, he "bowed down with his face to the ground"—in worship. He was not incredulous, nor was he greedy. *I have no doubt that you will come through, granting a son to an old man of a hundred years and that, as the author of nature, you will effectively stretch its limits. Blessed indeed is the one on whom this gift is bestowed; but I will be doubly favored if even Ishmael should live in your presence.* And so the Lord approved Abraham's sentiments, did not deny his request, and confirmed his own promises.

AMBROSE **(C. 339–C. 397)**
ON ABRAHAM

nation. 21 But I will establish my covenant with Isaac, whom
Sarah will bear to you at this set time next year." 22 When he
finished speaking with Abraham, God went up from him.
23 Abraham took his son Ishmael and every male in his household (whether born in his house or bought with money) and
circumcised them on that very same day, just as God had told
him to do. 24 Now Abraham was ninety-nine years old when he
was circumcised; 25 his son Ishmael was thirteen years old when
he was circumcised. 26 Abraham and his son Ishmael were circumcised on the very same day. 27 All the men of his household,
whether born in his household or bought with money from a
foreigner, were circumcised with him.

THREE SPECIAL VISITORS

18 The LORD appeared to Abraham by the oaks of Mamre
while he was sitting at the entrance to his tent during the
hottest time of the day. 2 Abraham looked up and saw three men
standing across from him. When he saw them he ran from the
entrance of the tent to meet them and bowed low to the ground.
3 He said, "My lord, if I have found favor in your sight, do not
pass by and leave your servant. 4 Let a little water be brought
so that you may all wash your feet and rest under the tree.
5 And let me get a bit of food so that you may refresh yourselves since you have passed by your servant's home. After
that you may be on your way." "All right," they replied, "you
may do as you say."
6 So Abraham hurried into the tent and said to Sarah, "Quick!
Take three measures of fine flour, knead it, and make bread."
7 Then Abraham ran to the herd and chose a fine, tender calf,
and gave it to a servant, who quickly prepared it. 8 Abraham then
took some curds and milk, along with the calf that had been
prepared, and placed the food before them. They ate while he
was standing near them under a tree.
9 Then they asked him, "Where is Sarah your wife?" He replied, "There, in the tent." 10 One of them said, "I will surely
return to you when the season comes round again, and your
wife Sarah will have a son!" (Now Sarah was listening at the
entrance to the tent, not far behind him. 11 Abraham and Sarah
were old and advancing in years; Sarah had long since passed
menopause.) 12 So Sarah laughed to herself, thinking, "After I
am worn out will I have pleasure, especially when my husband
is old too?"
13 The LORD said to Abraham, "Why did Sarah laugh and
say, 'Will I really have a child when I am old?' 14 Is anything
impossible for the LORD? I will return to you when the season
comes round again and Sarah will have a son." 15 Then Sarah
lied, saying, "I did not laugh," because she was afraid. But the
LORD said, "No! You did laugh."

ABRAHAM PLEADS FOR SODOM

16 When the men got up to leave, they looked out over Sodom.
(Now Abraham was walking with them to see them on their
way.) 17 Then the LORD said, "Should I hide from Abraham what
I am about to do? 18 After all, Abraham will surely become a
great and powerful nation, and all the nations on the earth may
receive blessing through him. 19 I have chosen him so that he
may command his children and his household after him to keep
the way of the LORD by doing what is right and just. Then the
LORD will give to Abraham what he promised him."

18:1–15 A sign would have been given Sarah if she had asked to hear or to see and then believe: first, because she was a woman, old and barren; and second, because nothing like this had ever been done before. God then gave a sign specifically to her who had not asked for a sign and said, "Why did Sarah laugh and say, 'Will I really have a child when I am old?'" But Sarah, instead of accepting the sign that was given to her, persisted by this falsehood in denying the true sign that had been given to her. Even though she had denied it because she was afraid, nevertheless in order to make her know that a false excuse did not convince him, God said to her, *But you did laugh in your heart; even your heart is denying the foolishness of your tongue*.

EPHREM THE SYRIAN
(C. 306–373)
COMMENTARY ON GENESIS

[20]So the LORD said, "The outcry against Sodom and Gomorrah is so great and their sin so blatant [21]that I must go down and see if they are as wicked as the outcry suggests. If not, I want to know."

[22]The two men turned and headed toward Sodom, but Abraham was still standing before the LORD. [23]Abraham approached and said, "Will you really sweep away the godly along with the wicked? [24]What if there are 50 godly people in the city? Will you really wipe it out and not spare the place for the sake of the 50 godly people who are in it? [25]Far be it from you to do such a thing—to kill the godly with the wicked, treating the godly and the wicked alike! Far be it from you! Will not the judge of the whole earth do what is right?"

[26]So the LORD replied, "If I find in the city of Sodom 50 godly people, I will spare the whole place for their sake."

[27]Then Abraham asked, "Since I have undertaken to speak to the Lord (although I am but dust and ashes), [28]what if there are five less than the 50 godly people? Will you destroy the whole city because five are lacking?" He replied, "I will not destroy it if I find 45 there."

[29]Abraham spoke to him again, "What if 40 are found there?" He replied, "I will not do it for the sake of the 40."

[30]Then Abraham said, "May the Lord not be angry so that I may speak! What if 30 are found there?" He replied, "I will not do it if I find 30 there."

[31]Abraham said, "Since I have undertaken to speak to the Lord, what if only 20 are found there?" He replied, "I will not destroy it for the sake of the 20."

[32]Finally Abraham said, "May the Lord not be angry so that I may speak just once more. What if 10 are found there?" He replied, "I will not destroy it for the sake of the 10."

[33]The LORD went on his way when he had finished speaking to Abraham. Then Abraham returned home.

THE DESTRUCTION OF SODOM AND GOMORRAH

19 The two angels came to Sodom in the evening while Lot was sitting in the city's gateway. When Lot saw them, he got up to meet them and bowed down with his face toward the ground.

[2]He said, "Here, my lords, please turn aside to your servant's house. Stay the night and wash your feet. Then you can be on your way early in the morning." "No," they replied, "we'll spend the night in the town square."

[3]But he urged them persistently, so they turned aside with him and entered his house. He prepared a feast for them, including bread baked without yeast, and they ate. [4]Before they could lie down to sleep, all the men—both young and old, from every part of the city of Sodom—surrounded the house. [5]They shouted to Lot, "Where are the men who came to you tonight? Bring them out to us so we can take carnal knowledge of them!"

[6]Lot went outside to them, shutting the door behind him. [7]He said, "No, my brothers! Don't act so wickedly! [8]Look, I have two daughters who have never been intimate with a man. Let me bring them out to you, and you can do to them whatever you please. Only don't do anything to these men, for they have come under the protection of my roof."

[9]"Out of our way!" they cried, "This man came to live here as a foreigner, and now he dares to judge us! We'll do more harm

19:1–38 As we would not be partakers of Sodom's curse and would not be destroyed, we should flee out of it and not look behind us. There is nothing in Sodom worth looking back upon. All the enjoyments of Sodom will soon perish in the common destruction; all will be burned up. Therefore it is foolish for any who are fleeing out of Sodom to hanker anymore after them. Remember Lot's wife, for she looked back, as being loathe utterly and forever to leave the ease, the pleasure, and plenty that she enjoyed in Sodom, and as having a mind to return to them again: Remember what became of her.

JONATHAN EDWARDS
(1703–1758)
SELECTIONS FROM THE UNPUBLISHED WRITINGS

to you than to them!" They kept pressing in on Lot until they
were close enough to break down the door.
10So the men inside reached out and pulled Lot back into the
house as they shut the door. 11Then they struck the men who
were at the door of the house, from the youngest to the oldest,
with blindness. The men outside wore themselves out trying to
find the door. 12Then the two visitors said to Lot, "Who else do
you have here? Do you have any sons-in-law, sons, daughters, or
other relatives in the city? Get them out of this place 13because
we are about to destroy it. The outcry against this place is so
great before the LORD that he has sent us to destroy it."
14Then Lot went out and spoke to his sons-in-law who were
going to marry his daughters. He said, "Quick, get out of this
place because the LORD is about to destroy the city!" But his
sons-in-law thought he was ridiculing them.
15At dawn the angels hurried Lot along, saying, "Get going!
Take your wife and your two daughters who are here, or else
you will be destroyed when the city is judged!" 16When Lot
hesitated, the men grabbed his hand and the hands of his wife
and two daughters because the LORD had compassion on them.
They led them away and placed them outside the city. 17When
they had brought them outside, they said, "Run for your lives!
Don't look behind you or stop anywhere in the valley! Escape
to the mountains or you will be destroyed!"
18But Lot said to them, "No, please, Lord! 19Your servant has
found favor with you, and you have shown me great kindness by
sparing my life. But I am not able to escape to the mountains because this disaster will overtake me and I'll die. 20Look, this town
over here is close enough to escape to, and it's just a little one.
Let me go there. It's just a little place, isn't it? Then I'll survive."
21"Very well," he replied, "I will grant this request too and will
not overthrow the town you mentioned. 22Run there quickly,
for I cannot do anything until you arrive there." (This incident
explains why the town was called Zoar.)
23The sun had just risen over the land as Lot reached Zoar.
24Then the LORD rained down sulfur and fire on Sodom and
Gomorrah. It was sent down from the sky by the LORD. 25So
he overthrew those cities and all that region, including all the
inhabitants of the cities and the vegetation that grew from the
ground. 26But Lot's wife looked back longingly and was turned
into a pillar of salt.
27Abraham got up early in the morning and went to the place
where he had stood before the LORD. 28He looked out toward
Sodom and Gomorrah and all the land of that region. As he
did so, he saw the smoke rising up from the land like smoke
from a furnace.
29So when God destroyed the cities of the region, God honored Abraham's request. He removed Lot from the midst of
the destruction when he destroyed the cities Lot had lived in.
30Lot went up from Zoar with his two daughters and settled
in the mountains because he was afraid to live in Zoar. So he
lived in a cave with his two daughters. 31Later the older daughter said to the younger, "Our father is old, and there is no man
in the country to sleep with us, the way everyone does. 32Come,
let's make our father drunk with wine so we can go to bed with
him and preserve our family line through our father."
33So that night they made their father drunk with wine, and
the older daughter came in and went to bed with her father.
But he was not aware of when she lay down with him or when

she got up. [34]So in the morning the older daughter said to the
younger, "Since I went to bed with my father last night, let's
make him drunk again tonight. Then you go in and go to bed
with him so we can preserve our family line through our father."
[35]So they made their father drunk that night as well, and the
younger one came and went to bed with him. But he was not
aware of when she lay down with him or when she got up.
[36]In this way both of Lot's daughters became pregnant by
their father. [37]The older daughter gave birth to a son and named
him Moab. He is the ancestor of the Moabites of today. [38]The
younger daughter also gave birth to a son and named him Ben
Ammi. He is the ancestor of the Ammonites of today.

20:1–18 Let the chaste learn not to dread calumny. For she who preferred chastity to life did not suffer the loss of life and retained the glory of chastity. So too Abraham, once bidden to go to foreign lands and not being held back either by the danger to his wife's modesty or by the fear of death before him, preserved both his own life and his wife's chastity. So no one has ever repented of trusting God, and chastity increased devotion in Sarah, and devotion chastity.

AMBROSE (C. 339–C. 397)
DOGMATIC TREATISES

ABRAHAM AND ABIMELECH

20 Abraham journeyed from there to the Negev region and
settled between Kadesh and Shur. While he lived as a
temporary resident in Gerar, [2]Abraham said about his wife
Sarah, "She is my sister." So Abimelech, king of Gerar, sent for
Sarah and took her.
[3]But God appeared to Abimelech in a dream at night and
said to him, "You are as good as dead because of the woman
you have taken, for she is someone else's wife."
[4]Now Abimelech had not gone near her. He said, "Lord, would
you really slaughter an innocent nation? [5]Did Abraham not say
to me, 'She is my sister'? And she herself said, 'He is my brother.' I
have done this with a clear conscience and with innocent hands!"
[6]Then in the dream God replied to him, "Yes, I know that
you have done this with a clear conscience. That is why I have
kept you from sinning against me and why I did not allow you
to touch her. [7]But now give back the man's wife. Indeed he is a
prophet and he will pray for you; thus you will live. But if you
don't give her back, know that you will surely die along with
all who belong to you."
[8]Early in the morning Abimelech summoned all his servants.
When he told them about all these things, they were terrified.
[9]Abimelech summoned Abraham and said to him, "What have
you done to us? What sin did I commit against you that would
cause you to bring such great guilt on me and my kingdom? You
have done things to me that should not be done!" [10]Then Abimelech asked Abraham, "What prompted you to do this thing?"
[11]Abraham replied, "Because I thought, 'Surely no one fears
God in this place. They will kill me because of my wife.' [12]What's
more, she is indeed my sister, my father's daughter, but not my
mother's daughter. She became my wife. [13]When God made me
wander from my father's house, I told her, 'This is what you can
do to show your loyalty to me: Every place we go, say about me,
"He is my brother."'"
[14]So Abimelech gave sheep, cattle, and male and female
servants to Abraham. He also gave his wife Sarah back to him.
[15]Then Abimelech said, "Look, my land is before you; live wherever you please."
[16]To Sarah he said, "Look, I have given 1,000 pieces of silver
to your 'brother.' This is compensation for you so that you will
stand vindicated before all who are with you."
[17]Abraham prayed to God, and God healed Abimelech, as
well as his wife and female slaves so that they were able to
have children. [18]For the LORD had caused infertility to strike
every woman in the household of Abimelech because he took
Sarah, Abraham's wife.

IGNATIUS OF ANTIOCH:

CHAMPION OF THE CATHOLIC CHURCH

c. 35–c. 115

After the death of the last apostle, John the Beloved, the early church lost a vital link to Jesus' ministry and teachings. Men known as *apostolic fathers* bridged that gap. These apostolic fathers were closely associated with those who had firsthand experience with Jesus. Along with Clement of Rome and Polycarp of Smyrna, Ignatius of Antioch was one of those influential links.

Born in AD 35 in the Roman province of Syria, Ignatius found Christ at an early age and is reported to have been a disciple of John the apostle. He eventually became the third bishop over the church of Antioch, having been appointed by the apostle Peter himself according to the tradition of the Eastern Orthodox Church. He is significant in part because of survival of the seven letters he wrote while traveling to Rome under arrest for his refusal to worship the Roman gods. One of the letters was addressed to Polycarp; the remaining six were addressed to six city churches: Ephesus, Magnesia, Tralles, Rome, Philadelphia, and Smyrna.

These letters addressed major themes similar to those covered by other early leaders like Clement and Polycarp: false teaching, disunity, and church leadership. But Ignatius stands out as being the first to refer explicitly to the Christian church as *katholikos*, or universal: "Wherever the bishop shall appear, there let the multitude [of the people] also be; even as, wherever Jesus Christ is, there is the *catholic* church."

Reflecting his concern for the unity of believers and the unity of the faith, Ignatius's letter to the church of Smyrna appealed to the idea of the catholic, universal church made up of local communities of faith. Although this was the first time a Christian leader had referred to the church in this way, it reflected an early understanding that the church should be single-minded in its beliefs and in its fellowship across all times and places.

In an effort to foster such unity, Ignatius urged believers to submit themselves to the church leadership established by God. In his letter to the church of Magnesia, he encouraged believers "to do all things with a divine harmony," united under the leadership of the bishop, presbyters, and deacons who are all "entrusted with the ministry of Jesus Christ."

In the end, this champion of the catholic church was martyred around AD 115 in the Colosseum of Rome, most likely in the infamous wild animal games. As Ignatius awaited his death, he set a courageous example for future martyrs by connecting his death with Christ's own obedience unto death on the cross. Drawing on the imagery of the Last Supper, he described his body as "the wheat of God" which was soon to be "ground by the teeth of the wild beasts, that I may be found the pure bread of Christ."

IMPORTANT WORKS

EPISTLE TO THE EPHESIANS

EPISTLE TO THE MAGNESIANS

EPISTLE TO THE ROMANS

EPISTLE TO POLYCARP

21:1–7 It was far above the power of nature and even contrary to its laws that the aged Sarah should be honored with a son; and even so it is beyond all ordinary rules that I, a poor, helpless, undone sinner should find grace to bear about in my soul the indwelling Spirit of the Lord Jesus. Even I have been made to bring forth fruit unto holiness. Well may my mouth be filled with joyous laughter because of the singular, surprising grace I have received of the Lord. Sarah looked on her Isaac and laughed with excess of rapture, and all her friends laughed with her; and you, my soul, look on your Jesus, and bid heaven and earth unite in your joy unspeakable.

CHARLES SPURGEON
(1834–1892)
MORNING AND EVENING

THE BIRTH OF ISAAC

21 The LORD visited Sarah just as he had said he would and
did for Sarah what he had promised. 2 So Sarah became
pregnant and bore Abraham a son in his old age at the appointed
time that God had told him. 3 Abraham named his son—whom
Sarah bore to him—Isaac. 4 When his son Isaac was eight days
old, Abraham circumcised him just as God had commanded
him to do. 5 (Now Abraham was one hundred years old when
his son Isaac was born to him.)
6 Sarah said, "God has made me laugh. Everyone who hears
about this will laugh with me." 7 She went on to say, "Who would
have said to Abraham that Sarah would nurse children? Yet I
have given birth to a son for him in his old age!"
8 The child grew and was weaned. Abraham prepared a great
feast on the day that Isaac was weaned. 9 But Sarah noticed the
son of Hagar the Egyptian—the son whom Hagar had borne to
Abraham—mocking. 10 So she said to Abraham, "Banish that
slave woman and her son, for the son of that slave woman will
not be an heir along with my son Isaac!"
11 Sarah's demand displeased Abraham greatly because Ishmael was his son. 12 But God said to Abraham, "Do not be upset
about the boy or your slave wife. Do all that Sarah is telling you
because through Isaac your descendants will be counted. 13 But
I will also make the son of the slave wife into a great nation, for
he is your descendant too."
14 Early in the morning Abraham took some food and a skin
of water and gave them to Hagar. He put them on her shoulders,
gave her the child, and sent her away. So she went wandering
aimlessly through the wilderness of Beer Sheba. 15 When the
water in the skin was gone, she shoved the child under one of
the shrubs. 16 Then she went and sat down by herself across
from him at quite a distance, about a bowshot, away; for she
thought, "I refuse to watch the child die." So she sat across from
him and wept uncontrollably.
17 But God heard the boy's voice. The angel of God called to
Hagar from heaven and asked her, "What is the matter, Hagar?
Don't be afraid, for God has heard the boy's voice right where he
is crying. 18 Get up! Help the boy up and hold him by the hand,
for I will make him into a great nation." 19 Then God enabled
Hagar to see a well of water. She went over and filled the skin
with water, and then gave the boy a drink.
20 God was with the boy as he grew. He lived in the wilderness
and became an archer. 21 He lived in the wilderness of Paran. His
mother found a wife for him from the land of Egypt.
22 At that time Abimelech and Phicol, the commander of his
army, said to Abraham, "God is with you in all that you do. 23 Now
swear to me right here in God's name that you will not deceive
me, my children, or my descendants. Show me, and the land
where you are staying, the same loyalty that I have shown you."
24 Abraham said, "I swear to do this." 25 But Abraham lodged
a complaint against Abimelech concerning a well that Abimelech's servants had seized. 26 "I do not know who has done this
thing," Abimelech replied. "Moreover, you did not tell me. I did
not hear about it until today."
27 Abraham took some sheep and cattle and gave them to
Abimelech. The two of them made a treaty. 28 Then Abraham set
seven ewe lambs apart from the flock by themselves. 29 Abimelech asked Abraham, "What is the meaning of these seven
ewe lambs that you have set apart?" 30 He replied, "You must

take these seven ewe lambs from my hand as legal proof that I dug this well." 31That is why he named that place Beer Sheba, because the two of them swore an oath there.

32So they made a treaty at Beer Sheba; then Abimelech and Phicol, the commander of his army, returned to the land of the Philistines. 33Abraham planted a tamarisk tree in Beer Sheba. There he worshiped the LORD, the eternal God. 34So Abraham stayed in the land of the Philistines for quite some time.

THE SACRIFICE OF ISAAC

22 Some time after these things God tested Abraham. He said to him, "Abraham!" "Here I am!" Abraham replied. 2God said, "Take your son—your only son, whom you love, Isaac—and go to the land of Moriah! Offer him up there as a burnt offering on one of the mountains which I will indicate to you."

3Early in the morning Abraham got up and saddled his donkey. He took two of his young servants with him, along with his son Isaac. When he had cut the wood for the burnt offering, he started out for the place God had spoken to him about.

4On the third day Abraham caught sight of the place in the distance. 5So he said to his servants, "You two stay here with the donkey while the boy and I go up there. We will worship and then return to you."

6Abraham took the wood for the burnt offering and put it on his son Isaac. Then he took the fire and the knife in his hand, and the two of them walked on together. 7Isaac said to his father Abraham, "My father?" "What is it, my son?" he replied. "Here is the fire and the wood," Isaac said, "but where is the lamb for the burnt offering?" 8"God will provide for himself the lamb for the burnt offering, my son," Abraham replied. The two of them continued on together.

9When they came to the place God had told him about, Abraham built the altar there and arranged the wood on it. Next he tied up his son Isaac and placed him on the altar on top of the wood. 10Then Abraham reached out his hand, took the knife, and prepared to slaughter his son. 11But the angel of the LORD called to him from heaven, "Abraham! Abraham!" "Here I am!" he answered. 12"Do not harm the boy!" the angel said. "Do not do anything to him, for now I know that you fear God because you did not withhold your son, your only son, from me."

13Abraham looked up and saw behind him a ram caught in the bushes by its horns. So he went over and got the ram and offered it up as a burnt offering instead of his son. 14And Abraham called the name of that place "The LORD provides." It is said to this day, "In the mountain of the LORD provision will be made."

15The angel of the LORD called to Abraham a second time from heaven 16and said, "I solemnly swear by my own name, decrees the LORD, that because you have done this and have not withheld your son, your only son, 17I will indeed bless you, and I will greatly multiply your descendants so that they will be as countless as the stars in the sky or the grains of sand on the seashore. Your descendants will take possession of the strongholds of their enemies. 18Because you have obeyed me, all the nations of the earth will pronounce blessings on one another using the name of your descendants."

19Then Abraham returned to his servants, and they set out together for Beer Sheba where Abraham stayed.

20After these things Abraham was told, "Milcah also has borne children to your brother Nahor—21Uz the firstborn, his brother

22:11–19 By an oath God gave and confirmed the promise to Abraham that "all the nations of the earth will pronounce blessings on one another using the name of your descendants." With what comfort may we suppose the good old man and his son went down from the mount and returned unto the young men! With what joy may we imagine he went home and related all that had passed to Sarah! And above all, with what triumph is he now exulting in the paradise of God and adoring rich, free, distinguishing, electing, everlasting love, which alone made him differ from the rest of humankind and rendered him worthy of that title he will have so long as the sun and the moon endure, the "father of the faithful"!

GEORGE WHITEFIELD
(1714–1770)
THE WORKS

Buz, Kemuel (the father of Aram), [22]Kesed, Hazo, Pildash, Jidlaph,
and Bethuel." [23](Now Bethuel became the father of Rebekah.)
These were the eight sons Milcah bore to Abraham's brother
Nahor. [24]His concubine, whose name was Reumah, also bore
him children—Tebah, Gaham, Tahash, and Maacah.

THE DEATH OF SARAH

23 Sarah lived 127 years. [2]Then she died in Kiriath Arba (that
is, Hebron) in the land of Canaan. Abraham went to mourn
for Sarah and to weep for her.
[3]Then Abraham got up from mourning his dead wife and
said to the sons of Heth, [4]"I am a foreign resident, a temporary
settler, among you. Grant me ownership of a burial site among
you so that I may bury my dead."
[5]The sons of Heth answered Abraham, [6]"Listen, sir, you are a
mighty prince among us! You may bury your dead in the choicest of our tombs. None of us will refuse you his tomb to prevent
you from burying your dead."
[7]Abraham got up and bowed down to the local people, the
sons of Heth. [8]Then he said to them, "If you agree that I may
bury my dead, then hear me out. Ask Ephron the son of Zohar
[9]if he will sell me the cave of Machpelah that belongs to him;
it is at the end of his field. Let him sell it to me publicly for the
full price, so that I may own it as a burial site."
[10](Now Ephron was sitting among the sons of Heth.) Ephron
the Hittite replied to Abraham in the hearing of the sons of
Heth—before all who entered the gate of his city—[11]"No, my lord!
Hear me out. I sell you both the field and the cave that is in it.
In the presence of my people I sell it to you. Bury your dead."
[12]Abraham bowed before the local people [13]and said to Ephron
in their hearing, "Hear me, if you will. I pay to you the price of
the field. Take it from me so that I may bury my dead there."
[14]Ephron answered Abraham, saying to him, [15]"Hear me,
my lord. The land is worth 400 pieces of silver, but what is that
between me and you? So bury your dead."
[16]So Abraham agreed to Ephron's price and weighed out for
him the price that Ephron had quoted in the hearing of the
sons of Heth—400 pieces of silver, according to the standard
measurement at the time.
[17]So Abraham secured Ephron's field in Machpelah, next to
Mamre, including the field, the cave that was in it, and all the
trees that were in the field and all around its border, [18]as his
property in the presence of the sons of Heth before all who
entered the gate of Ephron's city.
[19]After this Abraham buried his wife Sarah in the cave in
the field of Machpelah next to Mamre (that is, Hebron) in the
land of Canaan. [20]So Abraham secured the field and the cave
that was in it as a burial site from the sons of Heth.

23:1–19 Abraham was a sojourner who did not possess even so much land as to set his foot on, and when he needed a tomb, bought one for money. The Word teaches us that as long as he lives in the flesh he is a sojourner, and when he removes from this life, rests in his own home. And truly blessed is it not to rot with things of earth as though they were one's own, nor cling to all that is about us here as though here were our natural fatherland. Hard it is to find people who will not heed present things as though they were their own; who knows that he has the use of wealth but for a season, who reckons on the brief duration of his health, who remembers that the bloom of human glory fades away.

BASIL THE GREAT **(330–379)**
PROLEGOMENA

THE WIFE FOR ISAAC

24 Now Abraham was old, well advanced in years, and the
LORD had blessed him in everything. [2]Abraham said to his
servant, the senior one in his household who was in charge of
everything he had, "Put your hand under my thigh [3]so that I may
make you solemnly promise by the LORD, the God of heaven
and the God of the earth: You must not acquire a wife for my
son from the daughters of the Canaanites, among whom I am
living. [4]You must go instead to my country and to my relatives
to find a wife for my son Isaac."

5The servant asked him, "What if the woman is not willing
to come back with me to this land? Must I then take your son
back to the land from which you came?"
6"Be careful never to take my son back there!" Abraham told
him. 7"The LORD, the God of heaven, who took me from my
father's house and the land of my relatives, promised me with
a solemn oath, 'To your descendants I will give this land.' He
will send his angel before you so that you may find a wife for my
son from there. 8But if the woman is not willing to come back
with you, you will be free from this oath of mine. But you must
not take my son back there!" 9So the servant placed his hand
under the thigh of his master Abraham and gave his solemn
promise he would carry out his wishes.
10Then the servant took ten of his master's camels and departed with all kinds of gifts from his master at his disposal.
He journeyed to the region of Aram Naharaim and the city of
Nahor. 11He made the camels kneel down by the well outside
the city. It was evening, the time when the women would go out
to draw water. 12He prayed, "O LORD, God of my master Abraham, guide me today. Be faithful to my master Abraham. 13Here
I am, standing by the spring, and the daughters of the people
who live in the town are coming out to draw water. 14I will say
to a young woman, 'Please lower your jar so I may drink.' May
the one you have chosen for your servant Isaac reply, 'Drink,
and I'll give your camels water too.' In this way I will know that
you have been faithful to my master."
15Before he had finished praying, there came Rebekah with
her water jug on her shoulder. She was the daughter of Bethuel
son of Milcah (Milcah was the wife of Abraham's brother Nahor).
16Now the young woman was very beautiful. She was a virgin;
no man had ever been physically intimate with her. She went
down to the spring, filled her jug, and came back up. 17Abraham's
servant ran to meet her and said, "Please give me a sip of water
from your jug." 18"Drink, my lord," she replied, and quickly lowering her jug to her hands, she gave him a drink. 19When she
had done so, she said, "I'll draw water for your camels too, until
they have drunk as much as they want." 20She quickly emptied
her jug into the watering trough and ran back to the well to
draw more water until she had drawn enough for all his camels.
21Silently the man watched her with interest to determine if
the LORD had made his journey successful or not.
22After the camels had finished drinking, the man took out
a gold nose ring weighing a beka and two gold wrist bracelets
weighing ten shekels and gave them to her. 23"Whose daughter
are you?" he asked. "Tell me, is there room in your father's house
for us to spend the night?"
24She said to him, "I am the daughter of Bethuel the son of
Milcah, whom Milcah bore to Nahor. 25We have plenty of straw
and feed," she added, "and room for you to spend the night."
26The man bowed his head and worshiped the LORD, 27saying,
"Praised be the LORD, the God of my master Abraham, who has
not abandoned his faithful love for my master! The LORD has
led me to the house of my master's relatives!"
28The young woman ran and told her mother's household
all about these things. 29(Now Rebekah had a brother named
Laban.) Laban rushed out to meet the man at the spring. 30When
he saw the bracelets on his sister's wrists and the nose ring and
heard his sister Rebekah say, "This is what the man said to me,"
he went out to meet the man. There he was, standing by the

24:26–28 When the servant of Abraham heard that he had alighted upon the daughter of Bethuel, he was elated with hope. He gave thanks to God regarding it as the result of providence that he had been thus opportunely led straight to the place he had wished. He did not therefore boast of his good fortune; he declared that God had dealt kindly and faithfully with Abraham and that God had been faithful in fulfilling his promises. God gratuitously confers favors upon humankind and is specially inclined to beneficence; and by never frustrating their hope, he proves himself to be faithful and true. This thanksgiving therefore teaches us always to have the providence of God before our eyes in order that we may ascribe to him whatever happens prosperously to us.

JOHN CALVIN **(1509–1564)**
COMPLETE COMMENTARY ON THE BIBLE

camels near the spring. 31 Laban said to him, "Come, you who
are blessed by the LORD! Why are you standing out here when
I have prepared the house and a place for the camels?"
32 So Abraham's servant went to the house and unloaded the
camels. Straw and feed were given to the camels, and water was
provided so that he and the men who were with him could wash
their feet. 33 When food was served, he said, "I will not eat until
I have said what I want to say." "Tell us," Laban said.
34 "I am the servant of Abraham," he began. 35 "The LORD has
richly blessed my master and he has become very wealthy. The
LORD has given him sheep and cattle, silver and gold, male and
female servants, and camels and donkeys. 36 My master's wife
Sarah bore a son to him when she was old, and my master has
given him everything he owns. 37 My master made me swear an
oath. He said, 'You must not acquire a wife for my son from the
daughters of the Canaanites, among whom I am living, 38 but you
must go to the family of my father and to my relatives to find a
wife for my son.' 39 But I said to my master, 'What if the woman
does not want to go with me?' 40 He answered, 'The LORD, before
whom I have walked, will send his angel with you. He will make
your journey a success and you will find a wife for my son from
among my relatives, from my father's family. 41 You will be free
from your oath if you go to my relatives and they will not give her
to you. Then you will be free from your oath.' 42 When I came to
the spring today, I prayed, 'O LORD, God of my master Abraham,
if you have decided to make my journey successful, may events
unfold as follows: 43 Here I am, standing by the spring. When the
young woman goes out to draw water, I'll say, "Please give me a
little water to drink from your jug." 44 Then she will reply to me,
"Drink, and I'll draw water for your camels too." May that woman
be the one whom the LORD has chosen for my master's son.'
45 "Before I finished praying in my heart, along came Rebekah
with her water jug on her shoulder! She went down to the spring
and drew water. So I said to her, 'Please give me a drink.' 46 She
quickly lowered her jug from her shoulder and said, 'Drink, and
I'll give your camels water too.' So I drank, and she also gave the
camels water. 47 Then I asked her, 'Whose daughter are you?' She
replied, 'The daughter of Bethuel the son of Nahor, whom Milcah
bore to Nahor.' I put the ring in her nose and the bracelets on her
wrists. 48 Then I bowed down and worshiped the LORD. I praised
the LORD, the God of my master Abraham, who had led me on
the right path to find the granddaughter of my master's brother
for his son. 49 Now, if you will show faithful love to my master,
tell me. But if not, tell me as well, so that I may go on my way."
50 Then Laban and Bethuel replied, "This is the LORD's doing.
Our wishes are of no concern. 51 Rebekah stands here before
you. Take her and go so that she may become the wife of your
master's son, just as the LORD has decided."
52 When Abraham's servant heard their words, he bowed
down to the ground before the LORD. 53 Then he brought out
gold, silver jewelry, and clothing and gave them to Rebekah.
He also gave valuable gifts to her brother and to her mother.
54 After this, he and the men who were with him ate a meal and
stayed there overnight.
When they got up in the morning, he said, "Let me leave
now so I can return to my master." 55 But Rebekah's brother and
her mother replied, "Let the girl stay with us a few more days,
perhaps ten. Then she can go." 56 But he said to them, "Don't
detain me—the LORD has granted me success on my journey.

Let me leave now so I may return to my master." [57]Then they
said, "We'll call the girl and find out what she wants to do." [58]So
they called Rebekah and asked her, "Do you want to go with this
man?" She replied, "I want to go."
[59]So they sent their sister Rebekah on her way, accompanied
by her female attendant, with Abraham's servant and his men.
[60]They blessed Rebekah with these words:
"Our sister, may you become the mother of thousands
of ten thousands!
May your descendants possess the strongholds of their
enemies."

[61]Then Rebekah and her female servants mounted the camels and rode away with the man. So Abraham's servant took
Rebekah and left.
[62]Now Isaac came from Beer Lahai Roi, for he was living in the
Negev. [63]He went out to relax in the field in the early evening.
Then he looked up and saw that there were camels approaching. [64]Rebekah looked up and saw Isaac. She got down from
her camel [65]and asked Abraham's servant, "Who is that man
walking in the field toward us?" "That is my master," the servant
replied. So she took her veil and covered herself.
[66]The servant told Isaac everything that had happened.
[67]Then Isaac brought Rebekah into his mother Sarah's tent.
He took her as his wife and loved her. So Isaac was comforted
after his mother's death.

THE DEATH OF ABRAHAM

25 Abraham had taken another wife, named Keturah. [2]She
bore him Zimran, Jokshan, Medan, Midian, Ishbak, and
Shuah. [3]Jokshan became the father of Sheba and Dedan. The
descendants of Dedan were the Asshurites, Letushites, and
Leummites. [4]The sons of Midian were Ephah, Epher, Hanoch,
Abida, and Eldaah. All these were descendants of Keturah.
[5]Everything he owned Abraham left to his son Isaac. [6]But
while he was still alive, Abraham gave gifts to the sons of his concubines and sent them off to the east, away from his son Isaac.
[7]Abraham lived a total of 175 years. [8]Then Abraham breathed
his last and died at a good old age, an old man who had lived a
full life. He joined his ancestors. [9]His sons Isaac and Ishmael
buried him in the cave of Machpelah near Mamre, in the field
of Ephron the son of Zohar, the Hittite. [10]This was the field
Abraham had purchased from the sons of Heth. There Abraham
was buried with his wife Sarah. [11]After Abraham's death, God
blessed his son Isaac. Isaac lived near Beer Lahai Roi.

THE SONS OF ISHMAEL

[12]This is the account of Abraham's son Ishmael, whom Hagar
the Egyptian, Sarah's servant, bore to Abraham.
[13]These are the names of Ishmael's sons, by their names according to their records: Nebaioth (Ishmael's firstborn), Kedar,
Adbeel, Mibsam, [14]Mishma, Dumah, Massa, [15]Hadad, Tema,
Jetur, Naphish, and Kedemah. [16]These are the sons of Ishmael, and these are their names by their settlements and their
camps—twelve princes according to their clans.
[17]Ishmael lived a total of 137 years. He breathed his last and
died; then he joined his ancestors. [18]His descendants settled
from Havilah to Shur, which runs next to Egypt all the way to
Asshur. They settled away from all their relatives.

25:12–34 Although we must be of Jacob's judgment in seeking the birthright, we ought carefully to avoid all guile in seeking to obtain even the greatest advantages. Jacob's pottage pleased Esau's eye. "Feed me some of the red stuff"; for this he was called Edom, or Red. Gratifying the sensual appetite ruins thousands of precious souls. Esau ate and drank, pleased his palate, satisfied his appetite, and then carelessly rose up and went his way without any serious thought or any regret about the bad bargain he had made. People are ruined, not so much by doing what is amiss, as by doing it and not repenting of it.

MATTHEW HENRY (1662–1714)
COMMENTARY ON THE WHOLE BIBLE

JACOB AND ESAU

[19]This is the account of Isaac, the son of Abraham.

Abraham became the father of Isaac. [20]When Isaac was forty years old, he married Rebekah, the daughter of Bethuel the Aramean from Paddan Aram and sister of Laban the Aramean.

[21]Isaac prayed to the LORD on behalf of his wife because she was childless. The LORD answered his prayer, and his wife Rebekah became pregnant. [22]But the children struggled inside her, and she said, "Why is this happening to me?" So she asked the LORD, [23]and the LORD said to her,

"Two nations are in your womb,
and two peoples will be separated from within you.
One people will be stronger than the other,
and the older will serve the younger."

[24]When the time came for Rebekah to give birth, there were twins in her womb. [25]The first came out reddish all over, like a hairy garment, so they named him Esau. [26]When his brother came out with his hand clutching Esau's heel, they named him Jacob. Isaac was sixty years old when they were born.

[27]When the boys grew up, Esau became a skilled hunter, a man of the open fields, but Jacob was an even-tempered man, living in tents. [28]Isaac loved Esau because he had a taste for fresh game, but Rebekah loved Jacob.

[29]Now Jacob cooked some stew, and when Esau came in from the open fields, he was famished. [30]So Esau said to Jacob, "Feed me some of the red stuff—yes, this red stuff—because I'm starving!" (That is why he was also called Edom.)

[31]But Jacob replied, "First sell me your birthright." [32]"Look," said Esau, "I'm about to die! What use is the birthright to me?" [33]But Jacob said, "Swear an oath to me now." So Esau swore an oath to him and sold his birthright to Jacob.

[34]Then Jacob gave Esau some bread and lentil stew; Esau ate and drank, then got up and went out. So Esau despised his birthright.

ISAAC AND ABIMELECH

26:1–11 God promised Abraham a religious and righteous nation of similar faith and a delight to the Father. Notice how he makes the same promises to Isaac and Jacob. To Isaac: "All the nations of the earth will pronounce blessings on one another using the name of your descendants." To Jacob: "And so all the families of the earth may receive blessings through you and through your descendants" (Gen 28:14). But God does not address this blessing to Esau but only to them from whom Christ was to come through the Virgin Mary. For the seed is divided after Jacob and comes down through Judah and Perez and Jesse and David. This was a sign that some Jews would be certainly children of Abraham and at the same time would share in the lot of Christ.

JUSTIN MARTYR (C. 100–C. 165)
DIALOGUE WITH TRYPHO

26 There was a famine in the land, subsequent to the earlier famine that occurred in the days of Abraham. Isaac went to Abimelech king of the Philistines at Gerar. [2]The LORD appeared to Isaac and said, "Do not go down to Egypt; settle down in the land that I will point out to you. [3]Stay in this land. Then I will be with you and will bless you, for I will give all these lands to you and to your descendants, and I will fulfill the solemn promise I made to your father Abraham. [4]I will multiply your descendants so they will be as numerous as the stars in the sky, and I will give them all these lands. All the nations of the earth will pronounce blessings on one another using the name of your descendants. [5]All this will come to pass because Abraham obeyed me and kept my charge, my commandments, my statutes, and my laws." [6]So Isaac settled in Gerar.

[7]When the men of that place asked him about his wife, he replied, "She is my sister." He was afraid to say, "She is my wife," for he thought to himself, "The men of this place will kill me to get Rebekah because she is very beautiful."

[8]After Isaac had been there a long time, Abimelech king of the Philistines happened to look out a window and observed Isaac caressing his wife Rebekah. [9]So Abimelech summoned

Isaac and said, "She is really your wife! Why did you say, 'She is
my sister'?" Isaac replied, "Because I thought someone might
kill me to get her."
10Then Abimelech exclaimed, "What in the world have you
done to us? One of the men nearly took your wife to bed, and
you would have brought guilt on us!" 11So Abimelech commanded all the people, "Whoever touches this man or his wife will
surely be put to death."
12When Isaac planted in that land, he reaped in the same
year a hundred times what he had sown, because the LORD
blessed him. 13The man became wealthy. His influence continued to grow until he became very prominent. 14He had so
many sheep and cattle and such a great household of servants
that the Philistines became jealous of him. 15So the Philistines
took dirt and filled up all the wells that his father's servants
had dug back in the days of his father Abraham.
16Then Abimelech said to Isaac, "Leave us and go elsewhere,
for you have become much more powerful than we are." 17So
Isaac left there and settled in the Gerar Valley. 18Isaac reopened
the wells that had been dug back in the days of his father Abraham, for the Philistines had stopped them up after Abraham
died. Isaac gave these wells the same names his father had
given them.
19When Isaac's servants dug in the valley and discovered a
well with fresh flowing water there, 20the herdsmen of Gerar
quarreled with Isaac's herdsmen, saying, "The water belongs to
us!" So Isaac named the well Esek because they argued with him
about it. 21His servants dug another well, but they quarreled
over it too, so Isaac named it Sitnah. 22Then he moved away
from there and dug another well. They did not quarrel over
it, so Isaac named it Rehoboth, saying, "For now the LORD has
made room for us, and we will prosper in the land."
23From there Isaac went up to Beer Sheba. 24The LORD appeared to him that night and said, "I am the God of your father
Abraham. Do not be afraid, for I am with you. I will bless you and
multiply your descendants for the sake of my servant Abraham."
25Then Isaac built an altar there and worshiped the LORD. He
pitched his tent there, and his servants dug a well.
26Now Abimelech had come to him from Gerar along with
Ahuzzah his friend and Phicol the commander of his army.
27Isaac asked them, "Why have you come to me? You hate
me and sent me away from you." 28They replied, "We could
plainly see that the LORD is with you. So we decided there
should be a pact between us—between us and you. Allow us to
make a treaty with you 29so that you will not do us any harm,
just as we have not harmed you, but have always treated you
well before sending you away in peace. Now you are blessed
by the LORD."
30So Isaac held a feast for them and they celebrated. 31Early
in the morning the men made a treaty with each other. Isaac
sent them off; they separated on good terms.
32That day Isaac's servants came and told him about the
well they had dug. "We've found water," they reported. 33So
he named it Shibah; that is why the name of the city has been
Beer Sheba to this day.
34When Esau was forty years old, he married Judith the
daughter of Beeri the Hittite, as well as Basemath the daughter of Elon the Hittite. 35They caused Isaac and Rebekah great
anxiety.

27:1–17 One son considered himself to hold pride of place by birthright and by his father's preference for him, and yet he was suddenly found to be bereft of all this. The other son, being endowed with homely virtues and enjoying the help of favor from above, won his father's blessing against his will. Nothing is more powerful than the person helped by that mighty right hand. In any case, look carefully at all this so as to learn the extraordinary nature of God's designs: One man enjoyed favor from that source and was accorded great cooperation in everything so that the father's blessing was transferred to him. The other lost everything, forfeiting what was his because of the evil of his ways.

CHRYSOSTOM (C. 347–407)
HOMILIES ON GENESIS

JACOB CHEATS ESAU OUT OF THE BLESSING

27 When Isaac was old and his eyes were so weak that he was almost blind, he called his older son Esau and said to him, "My son!" "Here I am!" Esau replied. [2]Isaac said, "Since I am so old, I could die at any time. [3]Therefore, take your weapons—your quiver and your bow—and go out into the open fields and hunt down some wild game for me. [4]Then prepare for me some tasty food, the kind I love, and bring it to me. Then I will eat it so that I may bless you before I die."

[5]Now Rebekah had been listening while Isaac spoke to his son Esau. When Esau went out to the open fields to hunt down some wild game and bring it back, [6]Rebekah said to her son Jacob, "Look, I overheard your father tell your brother Esau, [7]'Bring me some wild game and prepare for me some tasty food. Then I will eat it and bless you in the presence of the LORD before I die.' [8]Now then, my son, do exactly what I tell you! [9]Go to the flock and get me two of the best young goats. I'll prepare them in a tasty way for your father, just the way he loves them. [10]Then you will take it to your father. Thus he will eat it and bless you before he dies."

[11]"But Esau my brother is a hairy man," Jacob protested to his mother Rebekah, "and I have smooth skin! [12]My father may touch me! Then he'll think I'm mocking him and I'll bring a curse on myself instead of a blessing." [13]So his mother told him, "Any curse against you will fall on me, my son! Just obey me! Go and get them for me!"

[14]So he went and got the goats and brought them to his mother. She prepared some tasty food, just the way his father loved it. [15]Then Rebekah took her older son Esau's best clothes, which she had with her in the house, and put them on her younger son Jacob. [16]She put the skins of the young goats on his hands and the smooth part of his neck. [17]Then she handed the tasty food and the bread she had made to her son Jacob.

[18]He went to his father and said, "My father!" Isaac replied, "Here I am. Which are you, my son?" [19]Jacob said to his father, "I am Esau, your firstborn. I've done as you told me. Now sit up and eat some of my wild game so that you can bless me." [20]But Isaac asked his son, "How in the world did you find it so quickly, my son?" "Because the LORD your God brought it to me," he replied. [21]Then Isaac said to Jacob, "Come closer so I can touch you, my son, and know for certain if you really are my son Esau." [22]So Jacob went over to his father Isaac, who felt him and said, "The voice is Jacob's, but the hands are Esau's." [23]He did not recognize him because his hands were hairy, like his brother Esau's hands. So Isaac blessed Jacob. [24]Then he asked, "Are you really my son Esau?" "I am," Jacob replied. [25]Isaac said, "Bring some of the wild game for me to eat, my son. Then I will bless you." So Jacob brought it to him, and he ate it. He also brought him wine, and Isaac drank. [26]Then his father Isaac said to him, "Come here and kiss me, my son." [27]So Jacob went over and kissed him. When Isaac caught the scent of his clothing, he blessed him, saying,

"Yes, my son smells
like the scent of an open field
which the LORD has blessed.
[28] May God give you
the dew of the sky
and the richness of the earth,
and plenty of grain and new wine.

29 May peoples serve you
and nations bow down to you.
You will be lord over your brothers,
and the sons of your mother will bow down to you.
May those who curse you be cursed,
and those who bless you be blessed."

30Isaac had just finished blessing Jacob, and Jacob had scarcely left his father's presence, when his brother Esau returned
from the hunt. 31 He also prepared some tasty food and brought
it to his father. Esau said to him, "My father, get up and eat some
of your son's wild game. Then you can bless me." 32His father
Isaac asked, "Who are you?" "I am your firstborn son," he replied,
"Esau!" 33Isaac began to shake violently and asked, "Then who
else hunted game and brought it to me? I ate all of it just before you arrived, and I blessed him. He will indeed be blessed!"
34When Esau heard his father's words, he wailed loudly and
bitterly. He said to his father, "Bless me too, my father!" 35But
Isaac replied, "Your brother came in here deceitfully and took
away your blessing." 36Esau exclaimed, "Jacob is the right name
for him! He has tripped me up two times! He took away my
birthright, and now, look, he has taken away my blessing!" Then
he asked, "Have you not kept back a blessing for me?"
37Isaac replied to Esau, "Look! I have made him lord over you.
I have made all his relatives his servants and provided him with
grain and new wine. What is left that I can do for you, my son?"
38Esau said to his father, "Do you have only that one blessing,
my father? Bless me too!" Then Esau wept loudly.
39So his father Isaac said to him,
"See here, your home will be by the richness of the
earth,
and by the dew of the sky above.
40 You will live by your sword
but you will serve your brother.
When you grow restless,
you will tear off his yoke
from your neck."

41So Esau hated Jacob because of the blessing his father had
given to his brother. Esau said privately, "The time of mourning
for my father is near; then I will kill my brother Jacob!"
42When Rebekah heard what her older son Esau had said,
she quickly summoned her younger son Jacob and told him,
"Look, your brother Esau is planning to get revenge by killing
you. 43Now then, my son, do what I say. Run away immediately
to my brother Laban in Haran. 44Live with him for a little while
until your brother's rage subsides. 45Stay there until your brother's anger against you subsides and he forgets what you did to
him. Then I'll send someone to bring you back from there. Why
should I lose both of you in one day?"
46Then Rebekah said to Isaac, "I am deeply depressed because
of the daughters of Heth. If Jacob were to marry one of these
daughters of Heth who live in this land, I would want to die!"

28 So Isaac called for Jacob and blessed him. Then he commanded him, "You must not marry a Canaanite woman! 2Leave immediately for Paddan Aram! Go to the house of
Bethuel, your mother's father, and find yourself a wife there,
among the daughters of Laban, your mother's brother. 3May
the Sovereign God bless you! May he make you fruitful and give

28:1–9 Two great promises Abraham was blessed with, and Isaac here entails them both upon Jacob. First, there is the promise of heirs: "May he make you fruitful and give you a multitude of descendants!" Through his loins should descend from Abraham that person in whom all the families of the earth should be blessed. Second, there is the promise of an inheritance for those heirs: "That you may possess the land God gave to Abraham." Canaan was hereby entailed upon the seed of Jacob exclusive of the seed of Esau. Isaac was now sending Jacob away into a distant country to settle there for some time; and lest this should look like disinheriting him, he here confirms the settlement of it upon him. This promise looks as high as heaven, of which Canaan was a type.

JOHN WESLEY **(1703–1791)**
EXPLANATORY NOTES ON THE BIBLE

you a multitude of descendants! Then you will become a large
nation. 4May he give you and your descendants the blessing he
gave to Abraham so that you may possess the land God gave to
Abraham, the land where you have been living as a temporary
resident." 5So Isaac sent Jacob on his way, and he went to Paddan
Aram, to Laban son of Bethuel the Aramean and brother of
Rebekah, the mother of Jacob and Esau.

6Esau saw that Isaac had blessed Jacob and sent him off to
Paddan Aram to find a wife there. As he blessed him, Isaac
commanded him, "You must not marry a Canaanite woman."
7Jacob obeyed his father and mother and left for Paddan Aram.
8Then Esau realized that the Canaanite women were displeasing to his father Isaac. 9So Esau went to Ishmael and married
Mahalath, the sister of Nebaioth and daughter of Abraham's
son Ishmael, along with the wives he already had.

JACOB'S DREAM AT BETHEL

10Meanwhile Jacob left Beer Sheba and set out for Haran. 11He
reached a certain place where he decided to camp because the
sun had gone down. He took one of the stones and placed it near
his head. Then he fell asleep in that place 12and had a dream. He
saw a stairway erected on the earth with its top reaching to the
heavens. The angels of God were going up and coming down it
13and the LORD stood at its top. He said, "I am the LORD, the God
of your grandfather Abraham and the God of your father Isaac.
I will give you and your descendants the ground you are lying
on. 14Your descendants will be like the dust of the earth, and
you will spread out to the west, east, north, and south. And so
all the families of the earth may receive blessings through you
and through your descendants. 15I am with you! I will protect
you wherever you go and will bring you back to this land. I will
not leave you until I have done what I promised you!"

16Then Jacob woke up and thought, "Surely the LORD is in
this place, but I did not realize it!" 17He was afraid and said,
"What an awesome place this is! This is nothing else than the
house of God! This is the gate of heaven!"

18Early in the morning Jacob took the stone he had placed
near his head and set it up as a sacred stone. Then he poured oil
on top of it. 19He called that place Bethel, although the former
name of the town was Luz. 20Then Jacob made a vow, saying,
"If God is with me and protects me on this journey I am taking
and gives me food to eat and clothing to wear, 21and I return
safely to my father's home, then the LORD will become my God.
22Then this stone that I have set up as a sacred stone will be
the house of God, and I will surely give you back a tenth of
everything you give me."

THE MARRIAGES OF JACOB

29 So Jacob moved on and came to the land of the eastern
people. 2He saw in the field a well with three flocks of
sheep lying beside it, because the flocks were watered from that
well. Now a large stone covered the mouth of the well. 3When
all the flocks were gathered there, the shepherds would roll the
stone off the mouth of the well and water the sheep. Then they
would put the stone back in its place over the well's mouth.

4Jacob asked them, "My brothers, where are you from?" They
replied, "We're from Haran." 5So he said to them, "Do you know
Laban, the grandson of Nahor?" "We know him," they said. 6"Is
he well?" Jacob asked. They replied, "He is well. Now look, here

29:1–30 There are some things that must be taken in order. For instance, many men desire the beautiful and well-favored Rachel of joy and peace in believing, but they must first be wedded to the tender-eyed Leah of repentance. What say you, are you so vain as to hope to break through the heavenly rule? Do you hope for reward without labor or honor without toil? Dismiss the idle expectation, and be content to take the ill-favored things for the sake of the sweet love of Jesus, which will recompense you for all. In such a spirit, laboring and suffering, you will find bitters grow sweet and hard things easy. As with Jacob, your years of service will seem to you but a few days for the love you have for Jesus.

CHARLES SPURGEON
(1834–1892)
MORNING AND EVENING

comes his daughter Rachel with the sheep." 7Then Jacob said,
"Since it is still the middle of the day, it is not time for the flocks
to be gathered. You should water the sheep and then go and
let them graze some more." 8"We can't," they said, "until all the
flocks are gathered and the stone is rolled off the mouth of the
well. Then we water the sheep."
9While he was still speaking with them, Rachel arrived with
her father's sheep, for she was tending them. 10When Jacob
saw Rachel, the daughter of his uncle Laban, and the sheep
of his uncle Laban, he went over and rolled the stone off the
mouth of the well and watered the sheep of his uncle Laban.
11Then Jacob kissed Rachel and began to weep loudly. 12When
Jacob explained to Rachel that he was a relative of her father
and the son of Rebekah, she ran and told her father. 13When
Laban heard this news about Jacob, his sister's son, he rushed
out to meet him. He embraced him and kissed him and brought
him to his house. Jacob told Laban how he was related to him.
14Then Laban said to him, "You are indeed my own flesh and
blood." So Jacob stayed with him for a month.
15Then Laban said to Jacob, "Should you work for me for
nothing because you are my relative? Tell me what your wages
should be." 16(Now Laban had two daughters; the older one was
named Leah, and the younger one Rachel. 17Leah's eyes were
tender, but Rachel had a lovely figure and beautiful appearance.)
18Since Jacob had fallen in love with Rachel, he said, "I'll serve
you seven years in exchange for your younger daughter Rachel."
19Laban replied, "I'd rather give her to you than to another man.
Stay with me." 20So Jacob worked for seven years to acquire
Rachel. But they seemed like only a few days to him because
his love for her was so great.
21Finally Jacob said to Laban, "Give me my wife, for my time
of service is up. And I want to sleep with her." 22So Laban invited
all the people of that place and prepared a feast. 23In the evening
he brought his daughter Leah to Jacob, and he slept with her.
24(Laban gave his female servant Zilpah to his daughter Leah
to be her servant.)
25In the morning Jacob discovered it was Leah! So Jacob said
to Laban, "What in the world have you done to me? Didn't I work
for you in exchange for Rachel? Why have you tricked me?" 26"It
is not our custom here," Laban replied, "to give the younger
daughter in marriage before the firstborn. 27Complete my older
daughter's bridal week. Then we will give you the younger one
too, in exchange for seven more years of work."
28Jacob did as Laban said. When Jacob completed Leah's bridal week, Laban gave him his daughter Rachel to be his wife.
29(Laban gave his female servant Bilhah to his daughter Rachel
to be her servant.) 30Jacob slept with Rachel as well. He also
loved Rachel more than Leah. Then he worked for Laban for
seven more years.

THE FAMILY OF JACOB

31When the LORD saw that Leah was unloved, he enabled her
to become pregnant while Rachel remained childless. 32So
Leah became pregnant and gave birth to a son. She named
him Reuben, for she said, "The LORD has looked with pity on
my oppressed condition. Surely my husband will love me now."
33She became pregnant again and had another son. She said,
"Because the LORD heard that I was unloved, he gave me this
one too." So she named him Simeon.

34 She became pregnant again and had another son. She said,
"Now this time my husband will show me affection, because
I have given birth to three sons for him." That is why he was
named Levi.
35 She became pregnant again and had another son. She said,
"This time I will praise the LORD." That is why she named him
Judah. Then she stopped having children.

30 When Rachel saw that she could not give Jacob children,
she became jealous of her sister. She said to Jacob, "Give
me children or I'll die!" 2 Jacob became furious with Rachel and
exclaimed, "Am I in the place of God, who has kept you from
having children?" 3 She replied, "Here is my servant Bilhah!
Sleep with her so that she can bear children for me and I can
have a family through her."
4 So Rachel gave him her servant Bilhah as a wife, and Jacob
slept with her. 5 Bilhah became pregnant and gave Jacob a son.
6 Then Rachel said, "God has vindicated me. He has responded to
my prayer and given me a son." That is why she named him Dan.
7 Bilhah, Rachel's servant, became pregnant again and gave
Jacob another son. 8 Then Rachel said, "I have fought a desperate struggle with my sister, but I have won." So she named him
Naphtali.
9 When Leah saw that she had stopped having children, she
gave her servant Zilpah to Jacob as a wife. 10 Soon Leah's servant
Zilpah gave Jacob a son. 11 Leah said, "How fortunate!" So she
named him Gad.
12 Then Leah's servant Zilpah gave Jacob another son. 13 Leah
said, "How happy I am, for women will call me happy!" So she
named him Asher.
14 At the time of the wheat harvest Reuben went out and
found some mandrake plants in a field and brought them to
his mother Leah. Rachel said to Leah, "Give me some of your
son's mandrakes." 15 But Leah replied, "Wasn't it enough that
you've taken away my husband? Would you take away my son's
mandrakes too?" "All right," Rachel said, "he may go to bed with
you tonight in exchange for your son's mandrakes." 16 When
Jacob came in from the fields that evening, Leah went out to
meet him and said, "You must sleep with me because I have paid
for your services with my son's mandrakes." So he went to bed
with her that night. 17 God paid attention to Leah; she became
pregnant and gave Jacob a son for the fifth time. 18 Then Leah
said, "God has granted me a reward because I gave my servant
to my husband as a wife." So she named him Issachar.
19 Leah became pregnant again and gave Jacob a son for the
sixth time. 20 Then Leah said, "God has given me a good gift.
Now my husband will honor me because I have given him six
sons." So she named him Zebulun.
21 After that she gave birth to a daughter and named her
Dinah.
22 Then God took note of Rachel. He paid attention to her
and enabled her to become pregnant. 23 She became pregnant
and gave birth to a son. Then she said, "God has taken away my
shame." 24 She named him Joseph, saying, "May the LORD give
me yet another son."

THE FLOCKS OF JACOB

25 After Rachel had given birth to Joseph, Jacob said to Laban,
"Send me on my way so that I can go home to my own country.
26 Let me take my wives and my children whom I have acquired

30:1 The foundation of this impatient and unbecoming behavior in Rachel was envy and jealousy of her sister. Therefore, though sterility was counted a very great evil among the Hebrew women, and that principally from their hope of being respectively the mother of the blessed Seed, yet it is not evident that Rachel was now actuated by this hope but solely by envy of her sister, as appears further from the names she gave her handmaid's children. That, in her cooler and more serious hours, she was affected by the reproach of barrenness there is no doubt (see Gen 30:23), as well as anxious to bear that she might be the mother of that Seed of Abraham in whom all nations should be blessed.

THOMAS COKE **(1747–1814)**
COMMENTARY ON THE HOLY BIBLE

by working for you. Then I'll depart, because you know how hard I've worked for you."

27But Laban said to him, "If I have found favor in your sight, please stay here, for I have learned by divination that the LORD has blessed me on account of you." 28He added, "Just name your wages—I'll pay whatever you want."

29"You know how I have worked for you," Jacob replied, "and how well your livestock have fared under my care. 30Indeed, you had little before I arrived, but now your possessions have increased many times over. The LORD has blessed you wherever I worked. But now, how long must it be before I do something for my own family too?"

31So Laban asked, "What should I give you?" "You don't need to give me a thing," Jacob replied, "but if you agree to this one condition, I will continue to care for your flocks and protect them: 32Let me walk among all your flocks today and remove from them every speckled or spotted sheep, every dark-colored lamb, and the spotted or speckled goats. These animals will be my wages. 33My integrity will testify for me later on. When you come to verify that I've taken only the wages we agreed on, if I have in my possession any goat that is not speckled or spotted or any sheep that is not dark-colored, it will be considered stolen."

34"Agreed!" said Laban, "It will be as you say."

35So that day Laban removed the male goats that were streaked or spotted, all the female goats that were speckled or spotted (all that had any white on them), and all the dark-colored lambs, and put them in the care of his sons. 36Then he separated them from Jacob by a three-day journey, while Jacob was taking care of the rest of Laban's flocks.

37But Jacob took fresh-cut branches from poplar, almond, and plane trees. He made white streaks by peeling them, making the white inner wood in the branches visible. 38Then he set up the peeled branches in all the watering troughs where the flocks came to drink. He set up the branches in front of the flocks when they were in heat and came to drink. 39When the sheep mated in front of the branches, they gave birth to young that were streaked or speckled or spotted. 40Jacob removed these lambs, but he made the rest of the flock face the streaked and completely dark-colored animals in Laban's flock. So he made separate flocks for himself and did not mix them with Laban's flocks. 41When the stronger females were in heat, Jacob would set up the branches in the troughs in front of the flock, so they would mate near the branches. 42But if the animals were weaker, he did not set the branches there. So the weaker animals ended up belonging to Laban and the stronger animals to Jacob. 43In this way Jacob became extremely prosperous. He owned large flocks, male and female servants, camels, and donkeys.

JACOB'S FLIGHT FROM LABAN

31 Jacob heard that Laban's sons were complaining, "Jacob has taken everything that belonged to our father! He has gotten rich at our father's expense!" 2When Jacob saw the look on Laban's face, he could tell his attitude toward him had changed.

3The LORD said to Jacob, "Return to the land of your fathers and to your relatives. I will be with you." 4So Jacob sent a message for Rachel and Leah to come to the field where his flocks were. 5There he said to them, "I can tell that your father's attitude toward me has changed, but the God of my father has been

31:1–21 Do you see the good man's great meekness on the one hand, and Laban's sons' ingratitude on the other, and how they could not bear to hold their envy in check but even affected their father's attitude? See now God's ineffable care and the degree of considerateness he employs when he sees us doing our best. When he saw the good man, the object of their envy, he said to Jacob, "Return to the land of your fathers and to your relatives. I will be with you." We learn from this passage that whenever we bear people's wrongdoing meekly and mildly, we enjoy help from on high in a richer and more abundant measure. Accordingly, far from resisting those bent on abusing us, let us bear it nobly in the knowledge that the Lord of all will not forget us. Hence Jacob also said, "God has not permitted him to do me any harm."

CHRYSOSTOM **(C. 347–407)**
HOMILIES ON GENESIS

with me. [6]You know that I've worked for your father as hard as
I could, [7]but your father has humiliated me and changed my
wages ten times. But God has not permitted him to do me any
harm. [8]If he said, 'The speckled animals will be your wage,' then
the entire flock gave birth to speckled offspring. But if he said,
'The streaked animals will be your wage,' then the entire flock
gave birth to streaked offspring. [9]In this way God has snatched
away your father's livestock and given them to me.
[10]"Once during breeding season I saw in a dream that the
male goats mating with the flock were streaked, speckled, and
spotted. [11]In the dream the angel of God said to me, 'Jacob!'
'Here I am!' I replied. [12]Then he said, 'Observe that all the male
goats mating with the flock are streaked, speckled, or spotted,
for I have observed all that Laban has done to you. [13]I am the
God of Bethel, where you anointed the sacred stone and made
a vow to me. Now leave this land immediately and return to
your native land.'"
[14]Then Rachel and Leah replied to him, "Do we still have
any portion or inheritance in our father's house? [15]Hasn't he
treated us like foreigners? He not only sold us, but completely
wasted the money paid for us! [16]Surely all the wealth that God
snatched away from our father belongs to us and to our children.
So now do everything God has told you."
[17]So Jacob immediately put his children and his wives on
the camels. [18]He took away all the livestock he had acquired
in Paddan Aram and all his moveable property that he had
accumulated. Then he set out toward the land of Canaan to
return to his father Isaac.
[19]While Laban had gone to shear his sheep, Rachel stole
the household idols that belonged to her father. [20]Jacob also
deceived Laban the Aramean by not telling him that he was
leaving. [21]He left with all he owned. He quickly crossed the
Euphrates River and headed for the hill country of Gilead.
[22]Three days later Laban discovered Jacob had left. [23]So he
took his relatives with him and pursued Jacob for seven days.
He caught up with him in the hill country of Gilead. [24]But God
came to Laban the Aramean in a dream at night and warned
him, "Be careful that you neither bless nor curse Jacob."
[25]Laban overtook Jacob, and when Jacob pitched his tent
in the hill country of Gilead, Laban and his relatives set up
camp there too. [26]"What have you done?" Laban demanded of
Jacob. "You've deceived me and carried away my daughters as
if they were captives of war! [27]Why did you run away secretly
and deceive me? Why didn't you tell me so I could send you off
with a celebration complete with singing, tambourines, and
harps? [28]You didn't even allow me to kiss my daughters and my
grandchildren goodbye. You have acted foolishly! [29]I have the
power to do you harm, but the God of your father told me last
night, 'Be careful that you neither bless nor curse Jacob.' [30]Now
I understand that you have gone away because you longed desperately for your father's house. Yet why did you steal my gods?"
[31]"I left secretly because I was afraid!" Jacob replied to Laban.
"I thought you might take your daughters away from me by
force. [32]Whoever has taken your gods will be put to death! In
the presence of our relatives identify whatever is yours and
take it." (Now Jacob did not know that Rachel had stolen them.)
[33]So Laban entered Jacob's tent, and Leah's tent, and the tent
of the two female servants, but he did not find the idols. Then he
left Leah's tent and entered Rachel's. [34](Now Rachel had taken

the idols and put them inside her camel's saddle and sat on
them.) Laban searched the whole tent, but did not find them.
[35]Rachel said to her father, "Don't be angry, my lord. I cannot
stand up in your presence because I am having my period." So
he searched thoroughly, but did not find the idols.
[36]Jacob became angry and argued with Laban. "What did I do
wrong?" he demanded of Laban. "What sin of mine prompted
you to chase after me in hot pursuit? [37]When you searched
through all my goods, did you find anything that belonged to
you? Set it here before my relatives and yours, and let them
settle the dispute between the two of us!
[38]"I have been with you for the past 20 years. Your ewes and
female goats have not miscarried, nor have I eaten rams from
your flocks. [39]Animals torn by wild beasts I never brought to
you; I always absorbed the loss myself. You always made me
pay for every missing animal, whether it was taken by day or at
night. [40]I was consumed by scorching heat during the day and by
piercing cold at night, and I went without sleep. [41]This was my
lot for 20 years in your house: I worked like a slave for you—14
years for your two daughters and 6 years for your flocks—but
you changed my wages 10 times! [42]If the God of my father—the
God of Abraham, the one whom Isaac fears—had not been with
me, you would certainly have sent me away empty-handed! But
God saw how I was oppressed and how hard I worked, and he
rebuked you last night."
[43]Laban replied to Jacob, "These women are my daughters,
these children are my grandchildren, and these flocks are my
flocks. All that you see belongs to me. But how can I harm these
daughters of mine today or the children to whom they have
given birth? [44]So now, come, let's make a formal agreement, you
and I, and it will be proof that we have made peace."
[45]So Jacob took a stone and set it up as a memorial pillar.
[46]Then he said to his relatives, "Gather stones." So they brought
stones and put them in a pile. They ate there by the pile of stones.
[47]Laban called it Jegar Sahadutha, but Jacob called it Galeed.
[48]Laban said, "This pile of stones is a witness of our agreement today." That is why it was called Galeed. [49]It was also called
Mizpah because he said, "May the LORD watch between us when
we are out of sight of one another. [50]If you mistreat my daughters or if you take wives besides my daughters, although no
one else is with us, realize that God is witness to your actions."
[51]"Here is this pile of stones and this pillar I have set up between me and you," Laban said to Jacob. [52]"This pile of stones
and the pillar are reminders that I will not pass beyond this
pile to come to harm you and that you will not pass beyond
this pile and this pillar to come to harm me. [53]May the God of
Abraham and the god of Nahor, the gods of their father, judge
between us." Jacob took an oath by the God whom his father
Isaac feared. [54]Then Jacob offered a sacrifice on the mountain
and invited his relatives to eat the meal. They ate the meal and
spent the night on the mountain.
[55]Early in the morning Laban kissed his grandchildren and
his daughters goodbye and blessed them. Then Laban left and
returned home.

JACOB WRESTLES AT PENIEL

32 So Jacob went on his way and the angels of God met him.
[2]When Jacob saw them, he exclaimed, "This is the camp
of God!" So he named that place Mahanaim.

3 Jacob sent messengers on ahead to his brother Esau in the
land of Seir, the region of Edom. 4 He commanded them, "This
is what you must say to my lord Esau: 'This is what your servant
Jacob says: I have been staying with Laban until now. 5 I have oxen,
donkeys, sheep, and male and female servants. I have sent this
message to inform my lord, so that I may find favor in your sight.'"
6 The messengers returned to Jacob and said, "We went to
your brother Esau. He is coming to meet you and has 400 men
with him." 7 Jacob was very afraid and upset. So he divided the
people who were with him into two camps, as well as the flocks,
herds, and camels. 8 "If Esau attacks one camp," he thought, "then
the other camp will be able to escape."
9 Then Jacob prayed, "O God of my father Abraham, God of my
father Isaac, O LORD, you said to me, 'Return to your land and
to your relatives and I will make you prosper.' 10 I am not worthy
of all the faithful love you have shown your servant. With only
my walking stick I crossed the Jordan, but now I have become
two camps. 11 Rescue me, I pray, from the hand of my brother
Esau, for I am afraid he will come and attack me, as well as the
mothers with their children. 12 But you said, 'I will certainly
make you prosper and will make your descendants like the
sand on the seashore, too numerous to count.'"
13 Jacob stayed there that night. Then he sent as a gift to his
brother Esau 14 200 female goats and 20 male goats, 200 ewes
and 20 rams, 15 30 female camels with their young, 40 cows and
10 bulls, and 20 female donkeys and 10 male donkeys. 16 He entrusted them to his servants, who divided them into herds. He
told his servants, "Pass over before me, and keep some distance
between one herd and the next." 17 He instructed the servant
leading the first herd, "When my brother Esau meets you and
asks, 'To whom do you belong? Where are you going? Whose
herds are you driving?' 18 then you must say, 'They belong to
your servant Jacob. They have been sent as a gift to my lord
Esau. In fact Jacob himself is behind us.'"
19 He also gave these instructions to the second and third
servants, as well as all those who were following the herds,
saying, "You must say the same thing to Esau when you meet
him. 20 You must also say, 'In fact your servant Jacob is behind
us.'" Jacob thought, "I will first appease him by sending a gift
ahead of me. After that I will meet him. Perhaps he will accept
me." 21 So the gifts were sent on ahead of him while he spent
that night in the camp.
22 During the night Jacob quickly took his two wives, his two
female servants, and his eleven sons and crossed the ford of the
Jabbok. 23 He took them and sent them across the stream along
with all his possessions. 24 So Jacob was left alone. Then a man
wrestled with him until daybreak. 25 When the man saw that
he could not defeat Jacob, he struck the socket of his hip so the
socket of Jacob's hip was dislocated while he wrestled with him.
26 Then the man said, "Let me go, for the dawn is breaking." "I
will not let you go," Jacob replied, "unless you bless me." 27 The
man asked him, "What is your name?" He answered, "Jacob."
28 "No longer will your name be Jacob," the man told him, "but
Israel, because you have fought with God and with men and
have prevailed."
29 Then Jacob asked, "Please tell me your name." "Why do you
ask my name?" the man replied. Then he blessed Jacob there.
30 So Jacob named the place Peniel, explaining, "Certainly I have
seen God face to face and have survived."

32:22–32 A great while before day, Jacob, being alone, more fully spread his fears before God in prayer. While thus employed, one in the likeness of a man wrestled with him. When the Spirit helps our infirmities, and our earnest and vast desires can scarcely find words to utter them, then prayer is indeed wrestling with God. However tried or discouraged, we shall prevail. Jacob kept his ground; though the struggle continued long, this did not shake his faith or silence his prayer. He will have a blessing—and had rather have his bone put out of joint than go away without one. Those who would have the blessing of Christ must resolve to take no denial. The fervent prayer is the effectual prayer.

MATTHEW HENRY **(1662–1714)**
COMMENTARY ON THE WHOLE BIBLE

31 The sun rose over him as he crossed over Penuel, but he was limping because of his hip. 32 That is why to this day the Israelites do not eat the sinew which is attached to the socket of the hip, because he struck the socket of Jacob's hip near the attached sinew.

JACOB MEETS ESAU

33 Jacob looked up and saw that Esau was coming along with 400 men. So he divided the children among Leah, Rachel, and the two female servants. 2 He put the servants and their children in front, with Leah and her children behind them, and Rachel and Joseph behind them. 3 But Jacob himself went on ahead of them, and he bowed toward the ground seven times as he approached his brother. 4 But Esau ran to meet him, embraced him, hugged his neck, and kissed him. Then they both wept. 5 When Esau looked up and saw the women and the children, he asked, "Who are these people with you?" Jacob replied, "The children whom God has graciously given your servant." 6 The female servants came forward with their children and bowed down. 7 Then Leah came forward with her children and they bowed down. Finally Joseph and Rachel came forward and bowed down.

8 Esau then asked, "What did you intend by sending all these herds to meet me?" Jacob replied, "To find favor in your sight, my lord." 9 But Esau said, "I have plenty, my brother. Keep what belongs to you." 10 "No, please take them," Jacob said. "If I have found favor in your sight, accept my gift from my hand. Now that I have seen your face and you have accepted me, it is as if I have seen the face of God. 11 Please take my present that was brought to you, for God has been generous to me and I have all I need." When Jacob urged him, he took it.

12 Then Esau said, "Let's be on our way! I will go in front of you." 13 But Jacob said to him, "My lord knows that the children are young, and that I have to look after the sheep and cattle that are nursing their young. If they are driven too hard for even a single day, all the animals will die. 14 Let my lord go on ahead of his servant. I will travel more slowly, at the pace of the herds and the children, until I come to my lord at Seir."

15 So Esau said, "Let me leave some of my men with you." "Why do that?" Jacob replied. "My lord has already been kind enough to me."

16 So that same day Esau made his way back to Seir. 17 But Jacob traveled to Sukkoth where he built himself a house and made shelters for his livestock. That is why the place was called Sukkoth.

18 After he left Paddan Aram, Jacob came safely to the city of Shechem in the land of Canaan, and he camped near the city. 19 Then he purchased the portion of the field where he had pitched his tent; he bought it from the sons of Hamor, Shechem's father, for 100 pieces of money. 20 There he set up an altar and called it "The God of Israel is God."

DINAH AND THE SHECHEMITES

34 Now Dinah, Leah's daughter whom she bore to Jacob, went to meet the young women of the land. 2 When Shechem son of Hamor the Hivite, who ruled that area, saw her, he grabbed her, forced himself on her, and sexually assaulted her. 3 Then he became very attached to Dinah, Jacob's daughter. He fell in love with the young woman and spoke romantically to

33:1–20 That Esau met his brother with unexpected benevolence and kindness is the effect of the special favor of God. By this method God proved that he has the hearts of human beings in his hand to soften their hardness and to mitigate their cruelty as often as he pleases. He can easily render them tolerant toward us, and we here see that Esau became so toward his brother Jacob. For even in the reprobate, God's established order of nature prevails.

JOHN CALVIN (1509–1564)
COMPLETE COMMENTARY ON THE BIBLE

34:1–31 The pastures at Succoth and Shechem were attractive, Jacob's possessions had so largely increased that movement was difficult, and circumstances were perhaps conceived of as having changed, making the realization of the vow almost impracticable. And so Jacob settled down to ordinary life, having either put off or else put aside the fulfillment of his promise. Not only did Jacob's worldliness lead to danger and disaster to himself and his household, but it also necessarily hindered him at the same time from bearing witness to God. "The Canaanites were in the land" (Gen 12:6) and, as with Lot before him, there was no real testimony because there was no real difference between him and them. Worldliness lowers tone and prevents testimony.

W. H. GRIFFITH THOMAS (1861–1924)
GENESIS: A DEVOTIONAL COMMENTARY

her. [4]Shechem said to his father Hamor, "Acquire this young girl as my wife." [5]When Jacob heard that Shechem had violated his daughter Dinah, his sons were with the livestock in the field. So Jacob remained silent until they came in.

[6]Then Shechem's father Hamor went to speak with Jacob about Dinah. [7]Now Jacob's sons had come in from the field when they heard the news. They were offended and very angry because Shechem had disgraced Israel by sexually assaulting Jacob's daughter, a crime that should not be committed.

[8]But Hamor made this appeal to them: "My son Shechem is in love with your daughter. Please give her to him as his wife. [9]Intermarry with us. Let us marry your daughters, and take our daughters as wives for yourselves. [10]You may live among us, and the land will be open to you. Live in it, travel freely in it, and acquire property in it."

[11]Then Shechem said to Dinah's father and brothers, "Let me find favor in your sight, and whatever you require of me I'll give. [12]You can make the bride price and the gift I must bring very expensive, and I'll give whatever you ask of me. Just give me the young woman as my wife!"

[13]Jacob's sons answered Shechem and his father Hamor deceitfully when they spoke because Shechem had violated their sister Dinah. [14]They said to them, "We cannot give our sister to a man who is not circumcised, for it would be a disgrace to us. [15]We will give you our consent on this one condition: You must become like us by circumcising all your males. [16]Then we will give you our daughters to marry, and we will take your daughters as wives for ourselves, and we will live among you and become one people. [17]But if you do not agree to our terms by being circumcised, then we will take our sister and depart."

[18]Their offer pleased Hamor and his son Shechem. [19]The young man did not delay in doing what they asked because he wanted Jacob's daughter Dinah badly. (Now he was more important than anyone in his father's household.) [20]So Hamor and his son Shechem went to the gate of their city and spoke to the men of their city, [21]"These men are at peace with us. So let them live in the land and travel freely in it, for the land is wide enough for them. We will take their daughters for wives, and we will give them our daughters to marry. [22]Only on this one condition will these men consent to live with us and become one people: They demand that every male among us be circumcised just as they are circumcised. [23]If we do so, won't their livestock, their property, and all their animals become ours? So let's consent to their demand, so they will live among us."

[24]All the men who assembled at the city gate agreed with Hamor and his son Shechem. Every male who assembled at the city gate was circumcised. [25]In three days, when they were still in pain, two of Jacob's sons, Simeon and Levi, Dinah's brothers, each took his sword and went to the unsuspecting city and slaughtered every male. [26]They killed Hamor and his son Shechem with the sword, took Dinah from Shechem's house, and left. [27]Jacob's sons killed them and looted the city because their sister had been violated. [28]They took their flocks, herds, and donkeys, as well as everything in the city and in the surrounding fields. [29]They captured as plunder all their wealth, all their little ones, and their wives, including everything in the houses.

[30]Then Jacob said to Simeon and Levi, "You have brought ruin on me by making me a foul odor among the inhabitants

of the land—among the Canaanites and the Perizzites. I am few
in number; they will join forces against me and attack me, and
both I and my family will be destroyed!" 31But Simeon and Levi
replied, "Should he treat our sister like a common prostitute?"

THE RETURN TO BETHEL

35 Then God said to Jacob, "Go up at once to Bethel and
live there. Make an altar there to God, who appeared to
you when you fled from your brother Esau." 2So Jacob told his
household and all who were with him, "Get rid of the foreign
gods you have among you. Purify yourselves and change your
clothes. 3Let us go up at once to Bethel. Then I will make an
altar there to God, who responded to me in my time of distress
and has been with me wherever I went."
4So they gave Jacob all the foreign gods that were in their
possession and the rings that were in their ears. Jacob buried
them under the oak near Shechem 5and they started on their
journey. The surrounding cities were afraid of God, and they
did not pursue the sons of Jacob.
6Jacob and all those who were with him arrived at Luz (that
is, Bethel) in the land of Canaan. 7He built an altar there and
named the place El Bethel because there God had revealed
himself to him when he was fleeing from his brother. 8(Deborah,
Rebekah's nurse, died and was buried under the oak below
Bethel; thus it was named Oak of Weeping.)
9God appeared to Jacob again after he returned from Paddan
Aram and blessed him. 10God said to him, "Your name is Jacob,
but your name will no longer be called Jacob; Israel will be your
name." So God named him Israel. 11Then God said to him, "I
am the Sovereign God. Be fruitful and multiply! A nation—even
a company of nations—will descend from you; kings will be
among your descendants! 12The land I gave to Abraham and
Isaac I will give to you. To your descendants I will also give this
land." 13Then God went up from the place where he spoke with
him. 14So Jacob set up a sacred stone pillar in the place where
God spoke with him. He poured out a drink offering on it, and
then he poured oil on it. 15Jacob named the place where God
spoke with him Bethel.
16They traveled on from Bethel, and when Ephrath was still
some distance away, Rachel went into labor—and her labor was
hard. 17When her labor was at its hardest, the midwife said to
her, "Don't be afraid, for you are having another son." 18With
her dying breath, she named him Ben Oni. But his father called
him Benjamin instead. 19So Rachel died and was buried on the
way to Ephrath (that is, Bethlehem). 20Jacob set up a marker
over her grave; it is the Marker of Rachel's Grave to this day.
21Then Israel traveled on and pitched his tent beyond Migdal
Eder. 22While Israel was living in that land, Reuben went to bed
with Bilhah, his father's concubine, and Israel heard about it.
Jacob had twelve sons:

23 The sons of Leah were Reuben, Jacob's firstborn, as well as Simeon, Levi, Judah, Issachar, and Zebulun.
24 The sons of Rachel were Joseph and Benjamin.
25 The sons of Bilhah, Rachel's servant, were Dan and Naphtali.
26 The sons of Zilpah, Leah's servant, were Gad and Asher.

These were the sons of Jacob who were born to him in Paddan Aram.

35:1–15 After he was called by God, Jacob ascended to Bethel, that is, to the house of God, offered sacrifices to God, and was declared chief and master of the holy rites. He taught his successors and descendants how to enter the house of God. He ordered the foreign gods to be rejected and to change the garments. It is fitting for us to do likewise when we are called before God or enter the divine temple. We also must change completely our garment by stripping off "the old man who is being corrupted in accordance with deceitful desires" (Eph 4:22) and by clothing ourselves with "the new man that is being renewed in knowledge according to the image of the one who created it" (Col 3:10).

CYRIL OF ALEXANDRIA
(C. 376–444)
GLAPHYRA ON GENESIS

27 So Jacob came back to his father Isaac in Mamre, to Kiriath Arba (that is, Hebron), where Abraham and Isaac had stayed. 28 Isaac lived to be 180 years old. 29 Then Isaac breathed his last and joined his ancestors. He died an old man who had lived a full life. His sons Esau and Jacob buried him.

THE DESCENDANTS OF ESAU

36 What follows is the account of Esau (also known as Edom). 2 Esau took his wives from the Canaanites: Adah the daughter of Elon the Hittite, and Oholibamah the daughter of Anah and granddaughter of Zibeon the Hivite, 3 in addition to Basemath the daughter of Ishmael and sister of Nebaioth.

4 Adah bore Eliphaz to Esau, Basemath bore Reuel, 5 and Oholibamah bore Jeush, Jalam, and Korah. These were the sons of Esau who were born to him in the land of Canaan.

6 Esau took his wives, his sons, his daughters, all the people in his household, his livestock, his animals, and all his possessions that he had acquired in the land of Canaan, and he went to a land some distance away from Jacob his brother 7 because they had too many possessions to be able to stay together, and the land where they had settled was not able to support them because of their livestock. 8 So Esau (also known as Edom) lived in the hill country of Seir.

9 This is the account of Esau, the father of the Edomites, in the hill country of Seir.

10 These were the names of Esau's sons: Eliphaz, the son of Esau's wife Adah, and Reuel, the son of Esau's wife Basemath.

11 These were the sons of Eliphaz: Teman, Omar, Zepho, Gatam, and Kenaz.

12 Timna, a concubine of Esau's son Eliphaz, bore Amalek to Eliphaz. These were the sons of Esau's wife Adah.

13 These were the sons of Reuel: Nahath, Zerah, Shammah, and Mizzah. These were the sons of Esau's wife Basemath.

14 These were the sons of Esau's wife Oholibamah the daughter of Anah and granddaughter of Zibeon: She bore Jeush, Jalam, and Korah to Esau.

15 These were the chiefs among the descendants of Esau, the sons of Eliphaz, Esau's firstborn: chief Teman, chief Omar, chief Zepho, chief Kenaz, 16 chief Korah, chief Gatam, chief Amalek. These were the chiefs descended from Eliphaz in the land of Edom; these were the sons of Adah.

17 These were the sons of Esau's son Reuel: chief Nahath, chief Zerah, chief Shammah, chief Mizzah. These were the chiefs descended from Reuel in the land of Edom; these were the sons of Esau's wife Basemath.

18 These were the sons of Esau's wife Oholibamah: chief Jeush, chief Jalam, chief Korah. These were the chiefs descended from Esau's wife Oholibamah, the daughter of Anah.

19 These were the sons of Esau (also known as Edom), and these were their chiefs.

20 These were the sons of Seir the Horite, who were living in the land: Lotan, Shobal, Zibeon, Anah, 21 Dishon, Ezer, and Dishan. These were the chiefs of the Horites, the descendants of Seir in the land of Edom.

22 The sons of Lotan were Hori and Homam; Lotan's sister was Timna.

23 These were the sons of Shobal: Alvan, Manahath, Ebal, Shepho, and Onam.

36:1–43 To the two sons of Isaac had been promised the honor that kings should spring from them. The Edomites first began to reign, and thus the condition of Israel seemed to be inferior. But at length, lapse of time taught how much better it is, by creeping on the ground, to strike the roots deep than to acquire an extravagant preeminence for a moment that speedily vanishes away. There is therefore no reason why the faithful who slowly pursue their way should envy the quick children of this world their rapid succession of delights, since the felicity the Lord promises them is far more stable.

JOHN CALVIN **(1509–1564)**
COMPLETE COMMENTARY ON THE BIBLE

24These were the sons of Zibeon: Aiah and Anah (who discovered the hot springs in the wilderness as he pastured the
donkeys of his father Zibeon).
25These were the children of Anah: Dishon and Oholibamah,
the daughter of Anah.
26These were the sons of Dishon: Hemdan, Eshban, Ithran,
and Keran.
27These were the sons of Ezer: Bilhan, Zaavan, and Akan.
28These were the sons of Dishan: Uz and Aran.
29These were the chiefs of the Horites: chief Lotan, chief
Shobal, chief Zibeon, chief Anah, 30chief Dishon, chief Ezer,
chief Dishan. These were the chiefs of the Horites, according
to their chief lists in the land of Seir.
31These were the kings who reigned in the land of Edom
before any king ruled over the Israelites:
32Bela the son of Beor reigned in Edom; the name of his city
was Dinhabah.
33When Bela died, Jobab the son of Zerah from Bozrah
reigned in his place.
34When Jobab died, Husham from the land of the Temanites
reigned in his place.
35When Husham died, Hadad the son of Bedad, who defeated
the Midianites in the land of Moab, reigned in his place; the
name of his city was Avith.
36When Hadad died, Samlah from Masrekah reigned in his
place.
37When Samlah died, Shaul from Rehoboth on the River
reigned in his place.
38When Shaul died, Baal Hanan the son of Achbor reigned
in his place.
39When Baal Hanan the son of Achbor died, Hadad reigned
in his place; the name of his city was Pau. His wife's name was
Mehetabel, the daughter of Matred, the daughter of Me-Zahab.
40These were the names of the chiefs of Esau, according to
their families, according to their places, by their names: chief
Timna, chief Alvah, chief Jetheth, 41chief Oholibamah, chief
Elah, chief Pinon, 42chief Kenaz, chief Teman, chief Mibzar,
43chief Magdiel, chief Iram. These were the chiefs of Edom,
according to their settlements in the land they possessed. This
was Esau, the father of the Edomites.

JOSEPH'S DREAMS

37 But Jacob lived in the land where his father had stayed,
in the land of Canaan.
2This is the account of Jacob.
Joseph, his seventeen-year-old son, was taking care of the
flocks with his brothers. Now he was a youngster working with
the sons of Bilhah and Zilpah, his father's wives. Joseph brought
back a bad report about them to their father.
3Now Israel loved Joseph more than all his sons because he
was a son born to him late in life, and he made a special tunic
for him. 4When Joseph's brothers saw that their father loved
him more than any of them, they hated Joseph and were not
able to speak to him kindly.
5Joseph had a dream, and when he told his brothers about
it they hated him even more. 6He said to them, "Listen to this
dream I had: 7There we were, binding sheaves of grain in the
middle of the field. Suddenly my sheaf rose up and stood upright and your sheaves surrounded my sheaf and bowed down

37:1–5 No submission on the part of their harmless brother could soften the envy of the eleven patriarchs so that scripture relates of them: "When Joseph's brothers saw that their father loved him more than any of them, they hated Joseph and were not able to speak to him kindly" until their jealousy, which would not listen to any entreaties on the part of their obedient and submissive brother, desired his death and would scarcely be satisfied with the sin of selling a brother. It is plain then that envy is worse than all faults and harder to get rid of as it is inflamed by those remedies by which the others are destroyed.

JOHN CASSIAN
(C. 360–C. 435)
THE CONFERENCES

to it!" [8]Then his brothers asked him, "Do you really think you
will rule over us or have dominion over us?" They hated him
even more because of his dream and because of what he said.
[9]Then he had another dream, and told it to his brothers.
"Look," he said. "I had another dream. The sun, the moon, and
eleven stars were bowing down to me." [10]When he told his father
and his brothers, his father rebuked him, saying, "What is this
dream that you had? Will I, your mother, and your brothers
really come and bow down to you?" [11]His brothers were jealous
of him, but his father kept in mind what Joseph said.
[12]When his brothers had gone to graze their father's flocks
near Shechem, [13]Israel said to Joseph, "Your brothers are grazing the flocks near Shechem. Come, I will send you to them."
"I'm ready," Joseph replied. [14]So Jacob said to him, "Go now and
check on the welfare of your brothers and of the flocks, and
bring me word." So Jacob sent him from the valley of Hebron.

[15]When Joseph reached Shechem, a man found him wandering in the field, so the man asked him, "What are you looking
for?" [16]He replied, "I'm looking for my brothers. Please tell me
where they are grazing their flocks." [17]The man said, "They left
this area, for I heard them say, 'Let's go to Dothan.'" So Joseph
went after his brothers and found them at Dothan.
[18]Now Joseph's brothers saw him from a distance, and before
he reached them, they plotted to kill him. [19]They said to one
another, "Here comes this master of dreams! [20]Come now, let's
kill him, throw him into one of the cisterns, and then say that a
wild animal ate him. Then we'll see how his dreams turn out!"

[21]When Reuben heard this, he rescued Joseph from their
hands, saying, "Let's not take his life!" [22]Reuben continued,
"Don't shed blood! Throw him into this cistern that is here
in the wilderness, but don't lay a hand on him." (Reuben said
this so he could rescue Joseph from them and take him back
to his father.)
[23]When Joseph reached his brothers, they stripped him of
his tunic, the special tunic that he wore. [24]Then they took him
and threw him into the cistern. (Now the cistern was empty;
there was no water in it.)
[25]When they sat down to eat their food, they looked up and
saw a caravan of Ishmaelites coming from Gilead. Their camels
were carrying spices, balm, and myrrh down to Egypt. [26]Then
Judah said to his brothers, "What profit is there if we kill our
brother and cover up his blood? [27]Come, let's sell him to the
Ishmaelites, but let's not lay a hand on him, for after all, he is
our brother, our own flesh." His brothers agreed. [28]So when the
Midianite merchants passed by, Joseph's brothers pulled him
out of the cistern and sold him to the Ishmaelites for 20 pieces
of silver. The Ishmaelites then took Joseph to Egypt.
[29]Later Reuben returned to the cistern to find that Joseph
was not in it! He tore his clothes, [30]returned to his brothers,
and said, "The boy isn't there! And I, where can I go?" [31]So they
took Joseph's tunic, killed a young goat, and dipped the tunic
in the blood. [32]Then they brought the special tunic to their
father and said, "We found this. Determine now whether it is
your son's tunic or not."
[33]He recognized it and exclaimed, "It is my son's tunic! A wild
animal has eaten him! Joseph has surely been torn to pieces!"
[34]Then Jacob tore his clothes, put on sackcloth, and mourned
for his son many days. [35]All his sons and daughters stood by
him to console him, but he refused to be consoled. "No," he

said, "I will go to the grave mourning my son." So Joseph's father wept for him.

36 Now in Egypt the Midianites sold Joseph to Potiphar, one of Pharaoh's officials, the captain of the guard.

JUDAH AND TAMAR

38 At that time Judah left his brothers and stayed with an Adullamite man named Hirah. 2 There Judah saw the daughter of a Canaanite man named Shua. Judah acquired her as a wife and slept with her. 3 She became pregnant and had a son. Judah named him Er. 4 She became pregnant again and had another son, whom she named Onan. 5 Then she had yet another son, whom she named Shelah. She gave birth to him in Kezib.

6 Judah acquired a wife for Er his firstborn; her name was Tamar. 7 But Er, Judah's firstborn, was evil in the LORD's sight, so the LORD killed him.

8 Then Judah said to Onan, "Sleep with your brother's wife and fulfill the duty of a brother-in-law to her so that you may raise up a descendant for your brother." 9 But Onan knew that the child would not be considered his. So whenever he slept with his brother's wife, he wasted his emission on the ground so as not to give his brother a descendant. 10 What he did was evil in the LORD's sight, so the LORD killed him too.

11 Then Judah said to his daughter-in-law Tamar, "Live as a widow in your father's house until Shelah my son grows up." For he thought, "I don't want him to die like his brothers." So Tamar went and lived in her father's house.

12 After some time Judah's wife, the daughter of Shua, died. After Judah was consoled, he left for Timnah to visit his sheepshearers, along with his friend Hirah the Adullamite. 13 Tamar was told, "Look, your father-in-law is going up to Timnah to shear his sheep." 14 So she removed her widow's clothes and covered herself with a veil. She wrapped herself and sat at the entrance to Enaim which is on the way to Timnah. (She did this because she saw that she had not been given to Shelah as a wife, even though he had now grown up.)

15 When Judah saw her, he thought she was a prostitute because she had covered her face. 16 He turned aside to her along the road and said, "Come, please, I want to sleep with you." (He did not realize it was his daughter-in-law.) She asked, "What will you give me so that you may sleep with me?" 17 He replied, "I'll send you a young goat from the flock." She asked, "Will you give me a pledge until you send it?" 18 He said, "What pledge should I give you?" She replied, "Your seal, your cord, and the staff that's in your hand." So he gave them to her, then slept with her, and she became pregnant by him. 19 She left immediately, removed her veil, and put on her widow's clothes.

20 Then Judah had his friend Hirah the Adullamite take a young goat to get back from the woman the items he had given in pledge, but Hirah could not find her. 21 He asked the men who were there, "Where is the cult prostitute who was at Enaim by the road?" But they replied, "There has been no cult prostitute here." 22 So he returned to Judah and said, "I couldn't find her. Moreover, the men of the place said, 'There has been no cult prostitute here.'" 23 Judah said, "Let her keep the things for herself. Otherwise we will appear to be dishonest. I did indeed send this young goat, but you couldn't find her."

24 After three months Judah was told, "Your daughter-in-law Tamar has turned to prostitution, and as a result she has

38:1–29 If we were to form a character of Judah by this story, we should not say, "Judah, your brothers will praise you" (Gen 49:8). But God will show that his choice is of grace and not of merit, and that Christ came into the world to save sinners, even the chief, and is not ashamed upon their repentance to be allied to them; also that the worth and worthiness of Jesus Christ are personal of himself and not derived from his ancestors. Humbling himself to be made "in the likeness of sinful flesh" (Rom 8:3), he was pleased to descend from some that were infamous. How little reason had the Jews, who were so called from this Judah, to boast as they did that they were not born of fornication!

MATTHEW HENRY **(1662–1714)**
COMMENTARY ON THE WHOLE BIBLE

become pregnant." Judah said, "Bring her out and let her be burned!" [25]While they were bringing her out, she sent word to her father-in-law: "I am pregnant by the man to whom these belong." Then she said, "Identify the one to whom the seal, cord, and staff belong." [26]Judah recognized them and said, "She is more upright than I am, because I wouldn't give her to Shelah my son." He was not physically intimate with her again.

[27]When it was time for her to give birth, there were twins in her womb. [28]While she was giving birth, one child put out his hand, and the midwife took a scarlet thread and tied it on his hand, saying, "This one came out first." [29]But then he drew back his hand, and his brother came out before him. She said, "How you have broken out of the womb!" So he was named Perez. [30]Afterward his brother came out—the one who had the scarlet thread on his hand—and he was named Zerah.

JOSEPH AND POTIPHAR'S WIFE

39 Now Joseph had been brought down to Egypt. An Egyptian named Potiphar, an official of Pharaoh and the captain of the guard, purchased him from the Ishmaelites who had brought him there. [2]The LORD was with Joseph. He was successful and lived in the household of his Egyptian master. [3]His master observed that the LORD was with him and that the LORD made everything he was doing successful. [4]So Joseph found favor in his sight and became his personal attendant. Potiphar appointed Joseph overseer of his household and put him in charge of everything he owned. [5]From the time Potiphar appointed him over his household and over all that he owned, the LORD blessed the Egyptian's household for Joseph's sake. The blessing of the LORD was on everything that he had, both in his house and in his fields. [6]So Potiphar left everything he had in Joseph's care; he gave no thought to anything except the food he ate.

Now Joseph was well built and good-looking. [7]Soon after these things, his master's wife took notice of Joseph and said, "Come to bed with me." [8]But he refused, saying to his master's wife, "Look, my master does not give any thought to his household with me here, and everything that he owns he has put into my care. [9]There is no one greater in this household than I am. He has withheld nothing from me except you because you are his wife. So how could I do such a great evil and sin against God?" [10]Even though she continued to speak to Joseph day after day, he did not respond to her invitation to go to bed with her.

[11]One day he went into the house to do his work when none of the household servants were there in the house. [12]She grabbed him by his outer garment, saying, "Come to bed with me!" But he left his outer garment in her hand and ran outside. [13]When she saw that he had left his outer garment in her hand and had run outside, [14]she called for her household servants and said to them, "See, my husband brought in a Hebrew man to us to humiliate us. He tried to go to bed with me, but I screamed loudly. [15]When he heard me raise my voice and scream, he left his outer garment beside me and ran outside."

[16]So she laid his outer garment beside her until his master came home. [17]This is what she said to him: "That Hebrew slave you brought to us tried to humiliate me, [18]but when I raised my voice and screamed, he left his outer garment and ran outside."

[19]When his master heard his wife say, "This is the way your slave treated me," he became furious. [20]Joseph's master took

39:1–23 What is the meaning of "the LORD was with Joseph"? Grace from on high stood by him, it is saying, and smoothed over all his difficulties. It arranged all his affairs so that he should advance gradually and, by proceeding through those trials, manage to reach the throne of the kingdom. But you, hearing that Joseph endured slavery at the hands of the traders and then experienced the slavery of the chief steward, consider how he was not alarmed and did not give up hope. On the contrary he bore everything meekly and nobly. "The LORD was with Joseph" after all, "the LORD made everything he was doing successful."

CHRYSOSTOM (C. 347–407)
HOMILIES ON GENESIS

him and threw him into the prison, the place where the king's
prisoners were confined. So he was there in the prison.
21 But the LORD was with Joseph and showed him kindness.
He granted him favor in the sight of the prison warden. 22 The
warden put all the prisoners under Joseph's care. He was in
charge of whatever they were doing. 23 The warden did not concern himself with anything that was in Joseph's care because
the LORD was with him and whatever he was doing the LORD
was making successful.

THE CUPBEARER AND THE BAKER

40 After these things happened, the cupbearer to the king
of Egypt and the royal baker offended their master, the
king of Egypt. 2 Pharaoh was enraged with his two officials, the
cupbearer and the baker, 3 so he imprisoned them in the house
of the captain of the guard in the same facility where Joseph
was confined. 4 The captain of the guard appointed Joseph to
be their attendant, and he served them.
They spent some time in custody. 5 Both of them, the cupbearer and the baker of the king of Egypt, who were confined in the
prison, had a dream the same night. Each man's dream had its
own meaning. 6 When Joseph came to them in the morning, he
saw that they were looking depressed. 7 So he asked Pharaoh's
officials, who were with him in custody in his master's house,
"Why do you look so sad today?" 8 They told him, "We both had
dreams, but there is no one to interpret them." Joseph responded, "Don't interpretations belong to God? Tell them to me."
9 So the chief cupbearer told his dream to Joseph: "In my
dream, there was a vine in front of me. 10 On the vine there
were three branches. As it budded, its blossoms opened and
its clusters ripened into grapes. 11 Now Pharaoh's cup was in
my hand, so I took the grapes, squeezed them into his cup, and
put the cup in Pharaoh's hand."
12 "This is its meaning," Joseph said to him. "The three branches represent three days. 13 In three more days Pharaoh will rein-
state you and restore you to your office. You will put Pharaoh's
cup in his hand, just as you did before when you were cupbearer.
14 But remember me when it goes well for you, and show me
kindness. Make mention of me to Pharaoh and bring me out
of this prison, 15 for I really was kidnapped from the land of the
Hebrews and I have done nothing wrong here for which they
should put me in a dungeon."
16 When the chief baker saw that the interpretation of the
first dream was favorable, he said to Joseph, "I also appeared in
my dream and there were three baskets of white bread on my
head. 17 In the top basket there were baked goods of every kind
for Pharaoh, but the birds were eating them from the basket
that was on my head."
18 Joseph replied, "This is its meaning: The three baskets
represent three days. 19 In three more days Pharaoh will de-
capitate you and impale you on a pole. Then the birds will eat
your flesh from you."
20 On the third day it was Pharaoh's birthday, so he gave a
feast for all his servants. He "lifted up" the head of the chief
cupbearer and the head of the chief baker in the midst of his
servants. 21 He restored the chief cupbearer to his former position so that he placed the cup in Pharaoh's hand, 22 but the chief
baker he impaled, just as Joseph had predicted. 23 But the chief
cupbearer did not remember Joseph—he forgot him.

40:1–23 The venerable Joseph addressed us in these words: "Why do you look so sad today?" to which we answered: *We have passed a sleepless night and there is no one to lighten the weight of our troubles unless the Lord may remove them by your wisdom.* Then he who recalled the excellence of the patriarch both by his merits and name said: *Does not the cure of man's perplexities come from the Lord? Let them be brought forward: For the divine compassion is able to give a remedy for them by means of our advice according to your faith.*

JOHN CASSIAN
(C. 360–C. 435)
THE CONFERENCES

IRENAEUS OF LYON:

DEFENDER AGAINST HERESIES

c. 120–202

The first few generations of Christians frequently suffered from punishment and persecution for their commitment to the way of Christ. But they also suffered from a number of confusing alternative teachings that warred against the true faith. Those who attempted to protect the faith and fight against heresies were *apologists*, people who explained and defended the Christian worldview. One such person was Irenaeus.

Born around AD 120 and raised in a Christian home near Smyrna in Asia Minor, Irenaeus was discipled in the faith by the bishop of his hometown, the great Polycarp. Eventually Irenaeus moved to Lyons in modern-day France, where he served as a pastor to Christian immigrants from the eastern part of the Roman Empire. After surviving deadly anti-Christian persecution launched by the Roman emperor Marcus Aurelius in AD 177, he became bishop of Lyons and devoted himself to defending against heresies rising up within the church.

Irenaeus was particularly passionate about defending the faith against Gnosticism (from the Greek word for "knowledge")—a collection of alternative spiritual worldviews and teachings opposed to orthodox Christianity. The Gnostics claimed a certain kind of salvation through secret knowledge transmitted by Jesus himself mixed with philosophy and ritual magic that emphasized spiritual escape rather than redemption and restoration. In his famous work *Against Heresies*, Irenaeus contended for the faith by holding to a high view of scripture and meticulously expositing its truth. He was the first theologian to refer to the two parts of the biblical canon as the Old and New Testaments, reflecting the unity of the one message of God's redemption through Christ. He also referenced the four Gospels—Matthew, Mark, Luke, and John—as being the true testimony of Jesus' life and teaching, death and resurrection.

One of Irenaeus's more enduring contributions also proved controversial: he is the first known Christian theologian to have defended the primacy of the church in Rome, indicating that it had authority over other churches. Because it had been founded by both Peter and Paul, and their teachings were passed down through a succession of bishops, Irenaeus argued, "It is a matter of necessity that every church should agree with this Church [of Rome] on account of its preeminent authority, that is, the faithful everywhere, inasmuch as the apostolical tradition has been preserved continuously."

Irenaeus's passion for defending the Christian faith against heresies led him to elevate the church in Rome, based on its vital role in preserving apostolic tradition. By the time of Irenaeus's death in 202, the bishop of Rome had risen in status within the broader ecclesial world, in part through Irenaeus's faithful defense of the church against heresies.

IMPORTANT WORKS

AGAINST HERESIES

PROOF OF THE APOSTOLIC PREACHING

JOSEPH'S RISE TO POWER

41 At the end of two full years Pharaoh had a dream. As he
was standing by the Nile, [2]seven fine-looking, fat cows
were coming up out of the Nile, and they grazed in the reeds.
[3]Then seven bad-looking, thin cows were coming up after them
from the Nile, and they stood beside the other cows at the
edge of the river. [4]The bad-looking, thin cows ate the seven
fine-looking, fat cows. Then Pharaoh woke up.
[5]Then he fell asleep again and had a second dream: There
were seven heads of grain growing on one stalk, healthy and
good. [6]Then seven heads of grain, thin and burned by the east
wind, were sprouting up after them. [7]The thin heads swallowed
up the seven healthy and full heads. Then Pharaoh woke up and
realized it was a dream.
[8]In the morning he was troubled, so he called for all the
diviner-priests of Egypt and all its wise men. Pharaoh told
them his dreams, but no one could interpret them for him.
[9]Then the chief cupbearer said to Pharaoh, "Today I recall my
failures. [10]Pharaoh was enraged with his servants, and he put
me in prison in the house of the captain of the guards—me
and the chief baker. [11]We each had a dream one night; each
of us had a dream with its own meaning. [12]Now a young man,
a Hebrew, a servant of the captain of the guards, was with us
there. We told him our dreams, and he interpreted the meaning
of each of our respective dreams for us. [13]It happened just as
he had said to us—Pharaoh restored me to my office, but he
impaled the baker."
[14]Then Pharaoh summoned Joseph. So they brought him
quickly out of the dungeon; he shaved himself, changed his
clothes, and came before Pharaoh. [15]Pharaoh said to Joseph,
"I had a dream, and there is no one who can interpret it. But I
have heard about you, that you can interpret dreams." [16]Joseph
replied to Pharaoh, "It is not within my power, but God will
speak concerning the welfare of Pharaoh."
[17]Then Pharaoh said to Joseph, "In my dream I was standing
by the edge of the Nile. [18]Then seven fat and fine-looking cows
were coming up out of the Nile, and they grazed in the reeds.
[19]Then seven other cows came up after them; they were scrawny,
very bad looking, and lean. I had never seen such bad-looking
cows as these in all the land of Egypt! [20]The lean, bad-looking
cows ate up the seven fat cows. [21]When they had eaten them,
no one would have known that they had done so, for they were
just as bad looking as before. Then I woke up. [22]I also saw in my
dream seven heads of grain growing on one stalk, full and good.
[23]Then seven heads of grain, withered and thin and burned
with the east wind, were sprouting up after them. [24]The thin
heads of grain swallowed up the seven good heads of grain. So
I told all this to the diviner-priests, but no one could tell me
its meaning."
[25]Then Joseph said to Pharaoh, "Both dreams of Pharaoh
have the same meaning. God has revealed to Pharaoh what he
is about to do. [26]The seven good cows represent seven years,
and the seven good heads of grain represent seven years. Both
dreams have the same meaning. [27]The seven lean, bad-looking
cows that came up after them represent seven years, as do the
seven empty heads of grain burned with the east wind. They
represent seven years of famine. [28]This is just what I told Pharaoh: God has shown Pharaoh what he is about to do. [29]Seven
years of great abundance are coming throughout the whole land

41:1–57 When Joseph was in honor, then was he in danger; when he was in dishonor, then was he in safety. The eunuch did not remember him, and right well it was that he did not that the occasion of his deliverance might be more glorious: that the whole might be ascribed not to humans' favor but to God's providence. Therefore it is that the eunuch forgets him, that Egypt might not forget him, that the king might not be ignorant of him. Had he been delivered at that time, it is likely he would have desired to depart to his own country. Therefore he is kept back by numberless constraints, first by subjection to a master, second by being in prison, and third by being over the kingdom, to the end that all this might be brought about by the providence of God.

CHRYSOSTOM (C. 347–407)
HOMILIES ON GENESIS

of Egypt. 30 But seven years of famine will occur after them, and
all the abundance will be forgotten in the land of Egypt. The
famine will devastate the land. 31 The previous abundance of
the land will not be remembered because of the famine that
follows, for the famine will be very severe. 32 The dream was
repeated to Pharaoh because the matter has been decreed by
God, and God will make it happen soon.

33 "So now Pharaoh should look for a wise and discerning man
and give him authority over all the land of Egypt. 34 Pharaoh
should do this—he should appoint officials throughout the
land to collect one-fifth of the produce of the land of Egypt
during the seven years of abundance. 35 They should gather all
the excess food during these good years that are coming. By
Pharaoh's authority they should store up grain so the cities will
have food, and they should preserve it. 36 This food should be
held in storage for the land in preparation for the seven years
of famine that will occur throughout the land of Egypt. In this
way the land will survive the famine."

37 This advice made sense to Pharaoh and all his officials. 38 So
Pharaoh asked his officials, "Can we find a man like Joseph, one
in whom the Spirit of God is present?" 39 So Pharaoh said to
Joseph, "Because God has enabled you to know all this, there is
no one as wise and discerning as you are! 40 You will oversee my
household, and all my people will submit to your commands.
Only I, the king, will be greater than you.

41 "See here," Pharaoh said to Joseph, "I place you in authority over all the land of Egypt." 42 Then Pharaoh took his signet
ring from his own hand and put it on Joseph's. He clothed him
with fine linen clothes and put a gold chain around his neck.
43 Pharaoh had him ride in the chariot used by his second-in-
command, and they cried out before him, "Kneel down!" So he
placed him over all the land of Egypt. 44 Pharaoh also said to
Joseph, "I am Pharaoh, but without your permission no one will
move his hand or his foot in all the land of Egypt." 45 Pharaoh
gave Joseph the name Zaphenath-Paneah. He also gave him
Asenath daughter of Potiphera, priest of On, to be his wife. So
Joseph took charge of all the land of Egypt.

46 Now Joseph was 30 years old when he began serving Pharaoh king of Egypt. Joseph was commissioned by Pharaoh and
was in charge of all the land of Egypt. 47 During the seven years
of abundance the land produced large, bountiful harvests. 48 Joseph collected all the excess food in the land of Egypt during
the seven years and stored it in the cities. In every city he put
the food gathered from the fields around it. 49 Joseph stored up
a vast amount of grain, like the sand of the sea, until he stopped
measuring it because it was impossible to measure.

50 Two sons were born to Joseph before the famine came.
Asenath daughter of Potiphera, priest of On, was their mother.
51 Joseph named the firstborn Manasseh, saying, "Certainly God
has made me forget all my trouble and all my father's house."
52 He named the second child Ephraim, saying, "Certainly God
has made me fruitful in the land of my suffering."

53 The seven years of abundance in the land of Egypt came to
an end. 54 Then the seven years of famine began, just as Joseph
had predicted. There was famine in all the other lands, but
throughout the land of Egypt there was food. 55 When all the
land of Egypt experienced the famine, the people cried out to
Pharaoh for food. Pharaoh said to all the people of Egypt, "Go
to Joseph and do whatever he tells you."

56While the famine was over all the earth, Joseph opened
the storehouses and sold grain to the Egyptians. The famine
was severe throughout the land of Egypt. 57People from every
country came to Joseph in Egypt to buy grain because the famine was severe throughout the earth.

JOSEPH'S BROTHERS IN EGYPT

42 When Jacob heard there was grain in Egypt, he said to his
sons, "Why are you looking at each other?" 2He then said,
"Look, I hear that there is grain in Egypt. Go down there and
buy grain for us so that we may live and not die."
3So ten of Joseph's brothers went down to buy grain from
Egypt. 4But Jacob did not send Joseph's brother Benjamin with
his brothers, for he said, "What if some accident happens to
him?" 5So Israel's sons came to buy grain among the other travelers, for the famine was severe in the land of Canaan.
6Now Joseph was the ruler of the country, the one who sold
grain to all the people of the country. Joseph's brothers came
and bowed down before him with their faces to the ground.
7When Joseph saw his brothers, he recognized them, but he
pretended to be a stranger to them and spoke to them harshly.
He asked, "Where do you come from?" They answered, "From
the land of Canaan, to buy grain for food."
8Joseph recognized his brothers, but they did not recognize
him. 9Then Joseph remembered the dreams he had dreamed
about them, and he said to them, "You are spies; you have come
to see if our land is vulnerable!"
10But they exclaimed, "No, my lord! Your servants have come
to buy grain for food! 11We are all the sons of one man; we are
honest men! Your servants are not spies."
12"No," he insisted, "but you have come to see if our land is
vulnerable." 13They replied, "Your servants are from a family
of twelve brothers. We are the sons of one man in the land of
Canaan. The youngest is with our father at this time, and one
is no longer alive."
14But Joseph told them, "It is just as I said to you: You are
spies! 15You will be tested in this way: As surely as Pharaoh lives,
you will not depart from this place unless your youngest brother
comes here. 16One of you must go and get your brother, while
the rest of you remain in prison. In this way your words may be
tested to see if you are telling the truth. If not, then, as surely
as Pharaoh lives, you are spies!" 17He imprisoned them all for
three days. 18On the third day Joseph said to them, "Do as I say
and you will live, for I fear God. 19If you are honest men, leave
one of your brothers confined here in prison while the rest of
you go and take grain back for your hungry families. 20But you
must bring your youngest brother to me. Then your words will
be verified and you will not die." They did as he said.
21They said to one another, "Surely we're being punished
because of our brother, because we saw how distressed he was
when he cried to us for mercy, but we refused to listen. That
is why this distress has come on us!" 22Reuben said to them,
"Didn't I say to you, 'Don't sin against the boy,' but you wouldn't
listen? So now we must pay for shedding his blood!" 23(Now
they did not know that Joseph could understand them, for he
was speaking through an interpreter.) 24He turned away from
them and wept. When he turned around and spoke to them
again, he had Simeon taken from them and tied up before
their eyes.

42:1–24 Famine pinched all the nations, and it seemed inevitable that Jacob and his family should suffer great want; but the God of providence, who never forgets the objects of electing love, had stored a granary for his people by giving the Egyptians warning of the scarcity and leading them to treasure up the grain of the years of plenty. Believer, though all things are apparently against you, rest assured that God has made a reservation on your behalf; in the roll of your griefs there is a saving clause. Somehow he will deliver you, and somewhere he will provide for you. The quarter from which your rescue shall arise may be a very unexpected one, but help will assuredly come in your extremity, and you shall magnify the name of the Lord.

CHARLES SPURGEON
(1834–1892)
MORNING AND EVENING

25Then Joseph gave orders to fill their bags with grain, to return each man's money to his sack, and to give them provisions for the journey. His orders were carried out. 26So they loaded their grain on their donkeys and left.

27When one of them opened his sack to get feed for his donkey at their resting place, he saw his money in the mouth of his sack. 28He said to his brothers, "My money was returned! Here it is in my sack!" They were dismayed; they turned trembling to one another and said, "What in the world has God done to us?"

29They returned to their father Jacob in the land of Canaan and told him all the things that had happened to them, saying, 30"The man, the lord of the land, spoke harshly to us and treated us as if we were spying on the land. 31But we said to him, 'We are honest men; we are not spies! 32We are from a family of twelve brothers; we are the sons of one father. One is no longer alive, and the youngest is with our father at this time in the land of Canaan.'

33"Then the man, the lord of the land, said to us, 'This is how I will find out if you are honest men. Leave one of your brothers with me, and take grain for your hungry households and go. 34But bring your youngest brother back to me so I will know that you are honest men and not spies. Then I will give your brother back to you and you may move about freely in the land.'"

35When they were emptying their sacks, there was each man's bag of money in his sack! When they and their father saw the bags of money, they were afraid. 36Their father Jacob said to them, "You are making me childless! Joseph is gone. Simeon is gone. And now you want to take Benjamin! Everything is against me."

37Then Reuben said to his father, "You may put my two sons to death if I do not bring him back to you. Put him in my care and I will bring him back to you." 38But Jacob replied, "My son will not go down there with you, for his brother is dead and he alone is left. If an accident happens to him on the journey you have to make, then you will bring down my gray hair in sorrow to the grave."

THE SECOND JOURNEY TO EGYPT

43 Now the famine was severe in the land. 2When they finished eating the grain they had brought from Egypt, their father said to them, "Return, buy us a little more food."

3But Judah said to him, "The man solemnly warned us, 'You will not see my face unless your brother is with you.' 4If you send our brother with us, we'll go down and buy food for you. 5But if you will not send him, we won't go down there because the man said to us, 'You will not see my face unless your brother is with you.'"

6Israel said, "Why did you bring this trouble on me by telling the man you had one more brother?"

7They replied, "The man questioned us thoroughly about ourselves and our family, saying, 'Is your father still alive? Do you have another brother?' So we answered him in this way. How could we possibly know that he would say, 'Bring your brother down'?"

8Then Judah said to his father Israel, "Send the boy with me and we will go immediately. Then we will live and not die—we and you and our little ones. 9I myself pledge security for him; you may hold me liable. If I do not bring him back to you and place him here before you, I will bear the blame before you

all my life. [10]But if we had not delayed, we could have traveled
there and back twice by now!"
[11]Then their father Israel said to them, "If it must be so,
then do this: Take some of the best products of the land in
your bags, and take a gift down to the man—a little balm and a
little honey, spices and myrrh, pistachios and almonds. [12]Take
double the money with you; you must take back the money
that was returned in the mouths of your sacks—perhaps it was
an oversight. [13]Take your brother too, and go right away to the
man. [14]May the Sovereign God grant you mercy before the man
so that he may release your other brother and Benjamin! As
for me, if I lose my children I lose them."
[15]So the men took these gifts, and they took double the money with them, along with Benjamin. Then they hurried down to
Egypt and stood before Joseph. [16]When Joseph saw Benjamin
with them, he said to the servant who was over his household,
"Bring the men to the house. Slaughter an animal and prepare
it, for the men will eat with me at noon." [17]The man did just as
Joseph said; he brought the men into Joseph's house.
[18]But the men were afraid when they were brought to Joseph's house. They said, "We are being brought in because of
the money that was returned in our sacks last time. He wants
to capture us, make us slaves, and take our donkeys!" [19]So they
approached the man who was in charge of Joseph's household
and spoke to him at the entrance to the house. [20]They said,
"My lord, we did indeed come down the first time to buy food.
[21]But when we came to the place where we spent the night,
we opened our sacks and each of us found his money—the full
amount—in the mouth of his sack. So we have returned it. [22]We
have brought additional money with us to buy food. We do not
know who put the money in our sacks!"
[23]"Everything is fine," the man in charge of Joseph's household told them. "Don't be afraid. Your God and the God of your
father has given you treasure in your sacks. I had your money."
Then he brought Simeon out to them.
[24]The servant in charge brought the men into Joseph's house.
He gave them water, and they washed their feet. Then he gave
food to their donkeys. [25]They got their gifts ready for Joseph's
arrival at noon, for they had heard that they were to have a
meal there.
[26]When Joseph came home, they presented him with the gifts
they had brought inside, and they bowed down to the ground
before him. [27]He asked them how they were doing. Then he
said, "Is your aging father well, the one you spoke about? Is he
still alive?" [28]"Your servant our father is well," they replied. "He
is still alive." They bowed down in humility.
[29]When Joseph looked up and saw his brother Benjamin, his
mother's son, he said, "Is this your youngest brother, whom you
told me about?" Then he said, "May God be gracious to you, my
son." [30]Joseph hurried out, for he was overcome by affection
for his brother and was at the point of tears. So he went to his
room and wept there.
[31]Then he washed his face and came out. With composure
he said, "Set out the food." [32]They set a place for him, a separate
place for his brothers, and another for the Egyptians who were
eating with him. (The Egyptians are not able to eat with Hebrews, for the Egyptians think it is disgusting to do so.) [33]They
sat before him, arranged by order of birth, beginning with the
firstborn and ending with the youngest. The men looked at each

43:18–34 Observe the great respect Joseph's brethren paid to him. Thus were Joseph's dreams more and more fulfilled. Joseph showed great kindness to them. He treated them nobly. In a day of famine it is enough to be fed, but they were feasted. Their cares and fears were now over, and they ate their bread with joy, reckoning they were upon good terms with the lord of the land. Joseph showed special regard for Benjamin that he might test whether his brethren would envy him. It must be our rule to be content with what we have and not to grieve at what others have.

MATTHEW HENRY (1662–1714)
COMMENTARY ON THE WHOLE BIBLE

other in astonishment. [34]He gave them portions of the food set before him, but the portion for Benjamin was five times greater than the portions for any of the others. They drank with Joseph until they all became drunk.

THE FINAL TEST

44 He instructed the servant who was over his household, "Fill the sacks of the men with as much food as they can carry and put each man's money in the mouth of his sack. [2]Then put my cup—the silver cup—in the mouth of the youngest one's sack, along with the money for his grain." He did as Joseph instructed.

[3]When morning came, the men and their donkeys were sent off. [4]They had not gone very far from the city when Joseph said to the servant who was over his household, "Pursue the men at once! When you overtake them, say to them, 'Why have you repaid good with evil? [5]Doesn't my master drink from this cup and use it for divination? You have done wrong!'"

[6]When the man overtook them, he spoke these words to them. [7]They answered him, "Why does my lord say such things? Far be it from your servants to do such a thing! [8]Look, the money that we found in the mouths of our sacks we brought back to you from the land of Canaan. Why then would we steal silver or gold from your master's house? [9]If one of us has it, he will die, and the rest of us will become my lord's slaves!"

[10]He replied, "You have suggested your own punishment! The one who has it will become my slave, but the rest of you will go free." [11]So each man quickly lowered his sack to the ground and opened it. [12]Then the man searched. He began with the oldest and finished with the youngest. The cup was found in Benjamin's sack! [13]They all tore their clothes! Then each man loaded his donkey, and they returned to the city.

[14]So Judah and his brothers came back to Joseph's house. He was still there, and they threw themselves to the ground before him. [15]Joseph said to them, "What did you think you were doing? Don't you know that a man like me can find out things like this by divination?"

[16]Judah replied, "What can we say to my lord? What can we speak? How can we clear ourselves? God has exposed the sin of your servants! We are now my lord's slaves, we and the one in whose possession the cup was found."

[17]But Joseph said, "Far be it from me to do this! The man in whose hand the cup was found will become my slave, but the rest of you may go back to your father in peace."

[18]Then Judah approached him and said, "My lord, please allow your servant to speak a word with you. Please do not get angry with your servant, for you are just like Pharaoh. [19]My lord asked his servants, 'Do you have a father or a brother?' [20]We said to my lord, 'We have an aged father, and there is a young boy who was born when our father was old. The boy's brother is dead. He is the only one of his mother's sons left, and his father loves him.'

[21]"Then you told your servants, 'Bring him down to me so I can see him.' [22]We said to my lord, 'The boy cannot leave his father. If he leaves his father, his father will die.' [23]But you said to your servants, 'If your youngest brother does not come down with you, you will not see my face again.' [24]When we returned to your servant my father, we told him the words of my lord.

[25]"Then our father said, 'Go back and buy us a little food.' [26]But we replied, 'We cannot go down there. If our youngest

44:16 What shall we admire first? Joseph's powers of mind, with which he descended to the very resting place of truth? Or his counsel, whereby he foresaw so great and lasting a need? And what am I to say of his greatness of mind? For though sold by his brothers into slavery, he took no revenge for this wrong but put an end to their want. What of his gentleness, whereby by a pious fraud he sought to gain the presence of his beloved brother who, under pretense of a well-planned theft, he declared to have stolen his property, that he might hold him as a hostage of his love?

AMBROSE **(C. 339–C. 397)**
ON THE DUTIES OF THE CLERGY

brother is with us, then we will go, for we won't be permitted
to see the man's face if our youngest brother is not with us.'
27"Then your servant my father said to us, 'You know that my
wife gave me two sons. 28The first disappeared and I said, "He
has surely been torn to pieces." I have not seen him since. 29If
you take this one from me too and an accident happens to him,
then you will bring down my gray hair in tragedy to the grave.'
30"So now, when I return to your servant my father, and the
boy is not with us—his very life is bound up in his son's life.
31When he sees the boy is not with us, he will die, and your
servants will bring down the gray hair of your servant our father
in sorrow to the grave. 32Indeed, your servant pledged security
for the boy with my father, saying, 'If I do not bring him back
to you, then I will bear the blame before my father all my life.'
33"So now, please let your servant remain as my lord's slave
instead of the boy. As for the boy, let him go back with his brothers. 34For how can I go back to my father if the boy is not with
me? I couldn't bear to see my father's pain."

THE RECONCILIATION OF THE BROTHERS

45 Joseph was no longer able to control himself before all his
attendants, so he cried out, "Make everyone go out from
my presence!" No one remained with Joseph when he made
himself known to his brothers. 2He wept loudly; the Egyptians
heard it and Pharaoh's household heard about it.
3Joseph said to his brothers, "I am Joseph! Is my father still
alive?" His brothers could not answer him because they were
dumbfounded before him. 4Joseph said to his brothers, "Come
closer to me," so they came near. Then he said, "I am Joseph
your brother, whom you sold into Egypt. 5Now, do not be upset
and do not be angry with yourselves because you sold me here,
for God sent me ahead of you to preserve life! 6For these past
two years there has been famine in the land and for five more
years there will be neither plowing nor harvesting. 7God sent
me ahead of you to preserve you on the earth and to save your
lives by a great deliverance. 8So now, it is not you who sent me
here, but God. He has made me an adviser to Pharaoh, lord over
all his household, and ruler over all the land of Egypt. 9Now
go up to my father quickly and tell him, 'This is what your son
Joseph says: "God has made me lord of all Egypt. Come down to
me; do not delay! 10You will live in the land of Goshen, and you
will be near me—you, your children, your grandchildren, your
flocks, your herds, and everything you have. 11I will provide you
with food there because there will be five more years of famine.
Otherwise you would become poor—you, your household, and
everyone who belongs to you."' 12You and my brother Benjamin
can certainly see with your own eyes that I really am the one
who speaks to you. 13So tell my father about all my honor in
Egypt and about everything you have seen. But bring my father
down here quickly!"
14Then he threw himself on the neck of his brother Benjamin
and wept, and Benjamin wept on his neck. 15He kissed all his
brothers and wept over them. After this his brothers talked
with him.
16Now it was reported in the household of Pharaoh, "Joseph's
brothers have arrived." It pleased Pharaoh and his servants.
17Pharaoh said to Joseph, "Say to your brothers, 'Do this: Load
your animals and go to the land of Canaan! 18Get your father and
your households and come to me! Then I will give you the best

45:1–15 If a person is angry with his brother or sister, how will he appease his Father since all anger is forbidden? For even Joseph, when dismissing his brethren for the purpose of fetching their father, said, *"Do not be angry."* He warned us, to be sure, to go not to the Father with anger. Not even by an evil word does he permit it to be vented. But how rash is it either to pass a day without prayer, while you refuse to make satisfaction to your brother or sister, or else by perseverance in anger to lose your prayer?

TERTULLIAN **(155–C. 220)**
ON PRAYER

land in Egypt and you will eat the best of the land.’ 19You are also commanded to say, ‘Do this: Take for yourselves wagons from the land of Egypt for your little ones and for your wives. Bring your father and come. 20Don’t worry about your belongings, for the best of all the land of Egypt will be yours.’”

21So the sons of Israel did as he said. Joseph gave them wagons as Pharaoh had instructed, and he gave them provisions for the journey. 22He gave sets of clothes to each one of them, but to Benjamin he gave 300 pieces of silver and five sets of clothes. 23To his father he sent the following: ten donkeys loaded with the best products of Egypt and ten female donkeys loaded with grain, food, and provisions for his father’s journey. 24Then he sent his brothers on their way and they left. He said to them, “As you travel don’t be overcome with fear.”

25So they went up from Egypt and came to their father Jacob in the land of Canaan. 26They told him, “Joseph is still alive and he is ruler over all the land of Egypt!” Jacob was stunned, for he did not believe them. 27But when they related to him everything Joseph had said to them, and when he saw the wagons that Joseph had sent to transport him, their father Jacob’s spirit revived. 28Then Israel said, “Enough! My son Joseph is still alive! I will go and see him before I die.”

THE FAMILY OF JACOB GOES TO EGYPT

46 So Israel began his journey, taking with him all that he had. When he came to Beer Sheba he offered sacrifices to the God of his father Isaac. 2God spoke to Israel in a vision during the night and said, “Jacob, Jacob!” He replied, “Here I am!” 3He said, “I am God, the God of your father. Do not be afraid to go down to Egypt, for I will make you into a great nation there. 4I will go down with you to Egypt and I myself will certainly bring you back from there. Joseph will close your eyes.”

5Then Jacob started out from Beer Sheba, and the sons of Israel carried their father Jacob, their little children, and their wives in the wagons that Pharaoh had sent along to transport him. 6Jacob and all his descendants took their livestock and the possessions they had acquired in the land of Canaan, and they went to Egypt. 7He brought with him to Egypt his sons and grandsons, his daughters and granddaughters—all his descendants.

8These are the names of the sons of Israel who went to Egypt—Jacob and his sons: Reuben, the firstborn of Jacob.

9 The sons of Reuben: Hanoch, Pallu, Hezron, and Carmi.
10 The sons of Simeon: Jemuel, Jamin, Ohad, Jakin, Zohar, and Shaul (the son of a Canaanite woman).
11 The sons of Levi: Gershon, Kohath, and Merari.
12 The sons of Judah: Er, Onan, Shelah, Perez, and Zerah (but Er and Onan died in the land of Canaan).
The sons of Perez were Hezron and Hamul.
13 The sons of Issachar: Tola, Puah, Jashub, and Shimron.
14 The sons of Zebulun: Sered, Elon, and Jahleel.
15 These were the sons of Leah, whom she bore to Jacob in Paddan Aram, along with Dinah his daughter. His sons and daughters numbered thirty-three in all.
16 The sons of Gad: Zephon, Haggi, Shuni, Ezbon, Eri, Arodi, and Areli.
17 The sons of Asher: Imnah, Ishvah, Ishvi, Beriah, and Serah their sister.
The sons of Beriah were Heber and Malkiel.

46:1–26 In his generosity God exceeds our requests out of fidelity to his characteristic love. “Do not be afraid to go down to Egypt,” he said. Because Jacob dreaded the length of the journey, accordingly he said, *I will accompany you and make everything easy for you.* Notice the considerateness of the expression: “I will go down with you to Egypt.” What could be more blessed than to have God as traveling companion? Then he spoke the consoling thought that the old man had particular need of: *That dearly beloved son of yours will personally prepare your body for burial, and his hands will close your eyes in death.* So, quite happy and free from all concern, Jacob took to the road. Consider at this point, I ask you, with what cheerfulness the good man made the journey, being so reassured by God’s promise.

CHRYSOSTOM **(C. 347–407)**
HOMILIES ON GENESIS

18 These were the sons of Zilpah, whom Laban gave to Leah
his daughter. She bore these to Jacob, sixteen in all.
19 The sons of Rachel the wife of Jacob: Joseph and
Benjamin.
20 Manasseh and Ephraim were born to Joseph in the land
of Egypt. Asenath daughter of Potiphera, priest of
On, bore them to him.
21 The sons of Benjamin: Bela, Beker, Ashbel, Gera,
Naaman, Ehi, Rosh, Muppim, Huppim and Ard.
22 These were the sons of Rachel who were born to Jacob,
fourteen in all.
23 The son of Dan: Hushim.
24 The sons of Naphtali: Jahziel, Guni, Jezer, and Shillem.
25 These were the sons of Bilhah, whom Laban gave to Rachel
his daughter. She bore these to Jacob, seven in all.

26 All the direct descendants of Jacob who went to Egypt with
him were sixty-six in number. (This number does not include
the wives of Jacob's sons.) 27 Counting the two sons of Joseph
who were born to him in Egypt, all the people of the household
of Jacob who were in Egypt numbered seventy.
28 Jacob sent Judah before him to Joseph to accompany him to
Goshen. So they came to the land of Goshen. 29 Joseph harnessed
his chariot and went up to meet his father Israel in Goshen.
When he met him, he hugged his neck and wept on his neck
for quite some time.
30 Israel said to Joseph, "Now let me die since I have seen your
face and know that you are still alive." 31 Then Joseph said to
his brothers and his father's household, "I will go up and tell
Pharaoh, 'My brothers and my father's household who were in
the land of Canaan have come to me. 32 The men are shepherds;
they take care of livestock. They have brought their flocks and
their herds and all that they have.' 33 Pharaoh will summon you
and say, 'What is your occupation?' 34 Tell him, 'Your servants
have taken care of cattle from our youth until now, both we
and our fathers,' so that you may live in the land of Goshen, for
everyone who takes care of sheep is disgusting to the Egyptians."

JOSEPH'S WISE ADMINISTRATION

47 Joseph went and told Pharaoh, "My father, my brothers,
their flocks and herds, and all that they own have arrived
from the land of Canaan. They are now in the land of Goshen."
2 He took five of his brothers and introduced them to Pharaoh.
3 Pharaoh said to Joseph's brothers, "What is your occupation?" They said to Pharaoh, "Your servants take care of flocks,
just as our ancestors did." 4 Then they said to Pharaoh, "We have
come to live as temporary residents in the land. There is no
pasture for your servants' flocks because the famine is severe
in the land of Canaan. So now, please let your servants live in
the land of Goshen."
5 Pharaoh said to Joseph, "Your father and your brothers have
come to you. 6 The land of Egypt is before you; settle your father
and your brothers in the best region of the land. They may live
in the land of Goshen. If you know of any highly capable men
among them, put them in charge of my livestock."
7 Then Joseph brought in his father Jacob and presented him before Pharaoh. Jacob blessed Pharaoh. 8 Pharaoh said to Jacob, "How
long have you lived?" 9 Jacob said to Pharaoh, "All the years of my
travels are 130. All the years of my life have been few and painful;

47:9 Jacob may here seem to complain. Why did he not rather recount the great and manifold favors of God that formed an abundant compensation for every kind of evil? Besides, his complaint respecting the shortness of life seems unworthy of him: Why did he not deem a whole century and a third part of another sufficient for him? But if anyone will rightly weigh his words, he rather expressed his own gratitude in celebrating the goodness of God toward his fathers. For he did not so much deplore his own decrepitude as he extolled the vigor divinely afforded to his fathers. This comparison was only intended to ascribe glory to God, whose blessing toward Abraham and Isaac had been greater than to himself.

JOHN CALVIN **(1509–1564)**
COMPLETE COMMENTARY ON THE BIBLE

the years of my travels are not as long as those of my ancestors."
10Then Jacob blessed Pharaoh and went out from his presence.
11So Joseph settled his father and his brothers. He gave them
territory in the land of Egypt, in the best region of the land, the
land of Rameses, just as Pharaoh had commanded. 12Joseph also
provided food for his father, his brothers, and all his father's
household, according to the number of their little children.
13But there was no food in all the land because the famine was very severe; the land of Egypt and the land of Canaan
wasted away because of the famine. 14Joseph collected all the
money that could be found in the land of Egypt and in the land
of Canaan as payment for the grain they were buying. Then
Joseph brought the money into Pharaoh's palace. 15When the
money from the lands of Egypt and Canaan was used up, all the
Egyptians came to Joseph and said, "Give us food! Why should
we die before your very eyes because our money has run out?"
16Then Joseph said, "If your money is gone, bring your livestock, and I will give you food in exchange for your livestock."
17So they brought their livestock to Joseph, and Joseph gave
them food in exchange for their horses, the livestock of their
flocks and herds, and their donkeys. He got them through that
year by giving them food in exchange for all their livestock.
18When that year was over, they came to him the next year
and said to him, "We cannot hide from our lord that the money
is used up and the livestock and the animals belong to our lord.
Nothing remains before our lord except our bodies and our
land. 19Why should we die before your very eyes, both we and
our land? Buy us and our land in exchange for food, and we, with
our land, will become Pharaoh's slaves. Give us seed that we
may live and not die. Then the land will not become desolate."
20So Joseph bought all the land of Egypt for Pharaoh. Each of
the Egyptians sold his field, for the famine was severe. So the
land became Pharaoh's. 21Joseph made all the people slaves
from one end of Egypt's border to the other end of it. 22But he
did not purchase the land of the priests because the priests had
an allotment from Pharaoh and they ate from their allotment
that Pharaoh gave them. That is why they did not sell their land.
23Joseph said to the people, "Since I have bought you and
your land today for Pharaoh, here is seed for you. Cultivate the
land. 24When the crop comes in, give one-fifth of it to Pharaoh.
The remaining four-fifths will be yours for seed for the fields
and for you to eat, including those in your households and your
little children." 25They replied, "You have saved our lives! You
are showing us favor, and we will be Pharaoh's slaves."
26So Joseph made it a statute, which is in effect to this day
throughout the land of Egypt: One-fifth belongs to Pharaoh.
Only the land of the priests did not become Pharaoh's.
27Israel settled in the land of Egypt, in the land of Goshen,
and they owned land there. They were fruitful and increased
rapidly in number.
28Jacob lived in the land of Egypt 17 years; the years of Jacob's
life were 147 in all. 29The time for Israel to die approached,
so he called for his son Joseph and said to him, "If now I have
found favor in your sight, put your hand under my thigh and
show me kindness and faithfulness. Do not bury me in Egypt,
30but when I rest with my fathers, carry me out of Egypt and
bury me in their burial place." Joseph said, "I will do as you say."
31Jacob said, "Swear to me that you will do so." So Joseph gave
him his word. Then Israel bowed down at the head of his bed.

MANASSEH AND EPHRAIM

48 After these things Joseph was told, "Your father is weaken-
ing." So he took his two sons Manasseh and Ephraim with
him. [2]When Jacob was told, "Your son Joseph has just come to you,"
Israel regained strength and sat up on his bed. [3]Jacob said to Joseph,
"The Sovereign God appeared to me at Luz in the land of Canaan
and blessed me. [4]He said to me, 'I am going to make you fruitful
and will multiply you. I will make you into a group of nations, and I
will give this land to your descendants as an everlasting possession.'
[5]"Now, as for your two sons, who were born to you in the
land of Egypt before I came to you in Egypt, they will be mine.
Ephraim and Manasseh will be mine just as Reuben and Simeon are. [6]Any children that you father after them will be yours;
they will be listed under the names of their brothers in their
inheritance. [7]But as for me, when I was returning from Paddan,
Rachel died—to my sorrow—in the land of Canaan. It happened
along the way, some distance from Ephrath. So I buried her
there on the way to Ephrath" (that is, Bethlehem).
[8]When Israel saw Joseph's sons, he asked, "Who are these?"
[9]Joseph said to his father, "They are the sons God has given
me in this place." His father said, "Bring them to me so I may
bless them." [10]Now Israel's eyes were failing because of his age;
he was not able to see well. So Joseph brought his sons near to
him, and his father kissed them and embraced them. [11]Israel
said to Joseph, "I never expected to see you again, but now God
has allowed me to see your children too."
[12]So Joseph moved them from Israel's knees and bowed down
with his face to the ground. [13]Joseph positioned them; he put
Ephraim on his right hand across from Israel's left hand, and
Manasseh on his left hand across from Israel's right hand. Then
Joseph brought them closer to his father. [14]Israel stretched
out his right hand and placed it on Ephraim's head, although
he was the younger. Crossing his hands, he put his left hand on
Manasseh's head, for Manasseh was the firstborn.
[15]Then he blessed Joseph and said,

"May the God before whom my fathers
Abraham and Isaac walked—
the God who has been my shepherd
all my life long to this day,
16 the angel who has protected me
from all harm—
bless these boys.
May my name be named in them,
and the name of my fathers Abraham and Isaac.
May they grow into a multitude on the earth."

[17]When Joseph saw that his father placed his right hand on
Ephraim's head, it displeased him. So he took his father's hand
to move it from Ephraim's head to Manasseh's head. [18]Joseph
said to his father, "Not so, my father, for this is the firstborn.
Put your right hand on his head."
[19]But his father refused and said, "I know, my son, I know.
He too will become a nation and he too will become great. In
spite of this, his younger brother will be even greater and his descendants will become a multitude of nations." [20]So he blessed
them that day, saying,

"By you will Israel bless, saying,
'May God make you like Ephraim and Manasseh.'"
Thus he put Ephraim before Manasseh.

48:1–22 The patriarch gives this his dying testimony of the faithfulness of God and declares that he has been delivered from all evil. The good was present to him. And so, leaving life, he left it according to his own word, "overflowing with favor, and full of the LORD's blessing" (Deut 33:23). So we in our turns may at the last hope that what we know not now will largely be explained, and we may seek to anticipate our dying verdict by a living confidence, in the midst of our toils and our sorrows, that "all things work together for good for those who love God" (Rom 8:28).

ALEXANDER MACLAREN
(1826–1910)
EXPOSITIONS OF THE HOLY SCRIPTURES

21 Then Israel said to Joseph, "I am about to die, but God will be
with you and will bring you back to the land of your fathers. 22 As
one who is above your brothers, I give to you the mountain slope,
which I took from the Amorites with my sword and my bow."

THE BLESSING OF JACOB

49 Jacob called for his sons and said, "Gather together so I
can tell you what will happen to you in future days.

2 "Assemble and listen, you sons of Jacob;
listen to Israel, your father.
3 Reuben, you are my firstborn,
my might and the beginning of my strength,
outstanding in dignity, outstanding in power.
4 You are destructive like water and will not excel,
for you got on your father's bed,
then you defiled it—he got on my couch!
5 Simeon and Levi are brothers,
weapons of violence are their knives!
6 O my soul, do not come into their council,
do not be united to their assembly, my heart,
for in their anger they have killed men,
and for pleasure they have hamstrung oxen.
7 Cursed be their anger, for it was fierce,
and their fury, for it was cruel.
I will divide them in Jacob,
and scatter them in Israel!
8 Judah, your brothers will praise you.
Your hand will be on the neck of your enemies,
your father's sons will bow down before you.
9 You are a lion's cub, Judah,
from the prey, my son, you have gone up.
He crouches and lies down like a lion;
like a lioness—who will rouse him?
10 The scepter will not depart from Judah,
nor the ruler's staff from between his feet,
until he comes to whom it belongs;
the nations will obey him.
11 Binding his foal to the vine,
and his colt to the choicest vine,
he will wash his garments in wine,
his robes in the blood of grapes.
12 His eyes will be red from wine,
and his teeth white from milk.
13 Zebulun will live by the haven of the sea
and become a haven for ships;
his border will extend to Sidon.
14 Issachar is a strong-boned donkey
lying down between two saddlebags.
15 When he sees a good resting place,
and the pleasant land,
he will bend his shoulder to the burden
and become a slave laborer.
16 Dan will judge his people
as one of the tribes of Israel.
17 May Dan be a snake beside the road,
a viper by the path,
that bites the heels of the horse
so that its rider falls backward.
18 I wait for your deliverance, O LORD.

19 Gad will be raided by marauding bands,
but he will attack them at their heels.
20 Asher's food will be rich,
and he will provide delicacies to royalty.
21 Naphtali is a free running doe,
he speaks delightful words.
22 Joseph is a fruitful bough,
a fruitful bough near a spring
whose branches climb over the wall.
23 The archers will attack him,
they will shoot at him and oppose him.
24 But his bow will remain steady,
and his hands will be skillful;
because of the hands of the Powerful One of Jacob,
because of the Shepherd, the Rock of Israel,
25 because of the God of your father,
who will help you,
because of the Sovereign God,
who will bless you
with blessings from the sky above,
blessings from the deep that lies below,
and blessings of the breasts and womb.
26 The blessings of your father are greater
than the blessings of the eternal mountains
or the desirable things of the age-old hills.
They will be on the head of Joseph
and on the brow of the prince of his brothers.
27 Benjamin is a ravenous wolf;
in the morning devouring the prey,
and in the evening dividing the plunder."

28These are the twelve tribes of Israel. This is what their
father said to them when he blessed them. He gave each of
them an appropriate blessing.
29Then he instructed them, "I am about to go to my people.
Bury me with my fathers in the cave in the field of Ephron the
Hittite. 30It is the cave in the field of Machpelah, near Mamre
in the land of Canaan, which Abraham bought for a burial plot
from Ephron the Hittite. 31There they buried Abraham and his
wife Sarah; there they buried Isaac and his wife Rebekah; and
there I buried Leah. 32The field and the cave in it were acquired
from the sons of Heth."
33When Jacob finished giving these instructions to his sons,
he pulled his feet up onto the bed, breathed his last breath, and
went to his people.

49:22–28 That strength God gives to his Josephs is true divine strength. Why does Joseph stand against temptation? Because God gives him aid. There is nothing we can do without the power of God. Notice in what a blessedly familiar way God gives this strength to Joseph—"His hands will be skillful; because of the hands of the Powerful One of Jacob." Thus God is represented as putting his hands on Joseph's hands, placing his arms on Joseph's arms. Marvelous condescension! God almighty, eternal, omnipotent stoops from his throne and lays his hand upon the child's hand, stretching his arm upon the arm of Joseph that he may be made strong!

CHARLES SPURGEON
(1834–1892)
MORNING AND EVENING

THE BURIALS OF JACOB AND JOSEPH

50 Then Joseph hugged his father's face. He wept over him
and kissed him. 2Joseph instructed the physicians in his
service to embalm his father, so the physicians embalmed Israel. 3They took 40 days, for that is the full time needed for
embalming. The Egyptians mourned for him 70 days.
4When the days of mourning had passed, Joseph said to Pharaoh's royal court, "If I have found favor in your sight, please say
to Pharaoh, 5'My father made me swear an oath. He said, "I am
about to die. Bury me in my tomb that I dug for myself there
in the land of Canaan." Now let me go and bury my father; then
I will return.'" 6So Pharaoh said, "Go and bury your father, just
as he made you swear to do."

50:1–25 From these things we may not only argue that the patriarchs continued to be and did enjoy something after they were dead, but also that they lived to see and enjoy the fulfillment of those promises that were made to them. God calls himself their God, both before and after their death, and their happiness in great part consisted in seeing the fulfillment of those promises in the course of his providence to their seed.

JONATHAN EDWARDS
(1703–1758)
SELECTIONS FROM THE UNPUBLISHED WRITINGS

[7]So Joseph went up to bury his father; all Pharaoh's officials went with him—the senior courtiers of his household, all the senior officials of the land of Egypt, [8]all Joseph's household, his brothers, and his father's household. But they left their little children and their flocks and herds in the land of Goshen. [9]Chariots and horsemen also went up with him, so it was a very large entourage.

[10]When they came to the threshing floor of Atad on the other side of the Jordan, they mourned there with very great and bitter sorrow. There Joseph observed a seven-day period of mourning for his father. [11]When the Canaanites who lived in the land saw them mourning at the threshing floor of Atad, they said, "This is a very sad occasion for the Egyptians." That is why its name was called Abel Mizraim, which is beyond the Jordan.

[12]So the sons of Jacob did for him just as he had instructed them. [13]His sons carried him to the land of Canaan and buried him in the cave of the field of Machpelah, near Mamre. This is the field Abraham purchased as a burial plot from Ephron the Hittite. [14]After he buried his father, Joseph returned to Egypt, along with his brothers and all who had accompanied him to bury his father.

[15]When Joseph's brothers saw that their father was dead, they said, "What if Joseph bears a grudge and wants to repay us in full for all the harm we did to him?" [16]So they sent word to Joseph, saying, "Your father gave these instructions before he died: [17]'Tell Joseph this: Please forgive the sin of your brothers and the wrong they did when they treated you so badly.' Now please forgive the sin of the servants of the God of your father." When this message was reported to him, Joseph wept. [18]Then his brothers also came and threw themselves down before him; they said, "Here we are; we are your slaves." [19]But Joseph answered them, "Don't be afraid. Am I in the place of God? [20]As for you, you meant to harm me, but God intended it for a good purpose, so he could preserve the lives of many people, as you can see this day. [21]So now, don't be afraid. I will provide for you and your little children." Then he consoled them and spoke kindly to them.

[22]Joseph lived in Egypt, along with his father's family. Joseph lived 110 years. [23]Joseph saw the descendants of Ephraim to the third generation. He also saw the children of Makir the son of Manasseh; they were given special inheritance rights by Joseph.

[24]Then Joseph said to his brothers, "I am about to die. But God will surely come to you and lead you up from this land to the land he swore on oath to give to Abraham, Isaac, and Jacob." [25]Joseph made the sons of Israel swear an oath. He said, "God will surely come to you. Then you must carry my bones up from this place." [26]So Joseph died at the age of 110. After they embalmed him, his body was placed in a coffin in Egypt.

AUTHOR	AUDIENCE	DATE	PURPOSE	THEMES
Moses	God's chosen people, the Israelites	Between 1446 and 1406 BC	Moses wrote this historical account of Israel's exodus out of Egypt to reveal Yahweh and show how Israel came to be a nation set apart by God.	The nature and character of God; redemption and salvation; and the covenant relationship and its requirements

The second book of Moses called Exodus contains a rich portrait of redemption, for it is God who redeems his people in a most spectacular way. After hearing the cries of oppression from his people, God acted on their behalf to rescue and claim them as his own in a covenant relationship. John Wesley explained the nature of Exodus by comparing and contrasting it with Genesis: "The beginning of the former book shows us how God formed the world for himself, the beginning of this shows us how he formed Israel for himself. There we have the creation of the world in history, here the redemption of the world in type." Moses wrote this historical account of Israel's exodus out of Egypt to reveal Yahweh, the God of Israel, and to show how Israel came to be a special nation set apart by God.

Who is the God of Israel? "The Lord—the God of your fathers, the God of Abraham, the God of Isaac, and the God of Jacob" (3:15). He is the same God who gave promises and blessings to Abraham and his descendants in Genesis 12. After Moses encountered God in the burning bush, more of the Lord's character was revealed: "I have surely seen the affliction of my people . . . have heard their cry . . . I know their sorrows" (3:7). John Calvin commented on God's character, saying: "It ought to afford no common consolation in the troubles of us all when we are groaning under any unjust burden, for God, whose sight was then so clear, is not now so blind as not to see all injustice and to pity those who call upon him."

Perhaps the culminating revelation of God's character in the book of Exodus is found in 34:6–7, where the Lord proclaims himself the "compassionate and gracious God, slow to anger, and abounding in loyal love and faithfulness, keeping loyal love for thousands, forgiving iniquity and transgression and sin." This is who the Lord is in all of his fullness!

What's more is that God has come down "to deliver" the Israelites as their *go'el*, their Redeemer, in order to "bring them up . . . to a land flowing with milk and honey" (3:8). Exodus offers us a clear picture of redemption in which the Lord goes to great lengths to rescue his people from calamity and carry them into renewal and blessing. The climax of this redemption came through the blood of the lamb applied to the doorposts of Israel's homes. The church has always understood this as foreshadowing the blood

of the Lamb, Jesus Christ. John Wesley, seeing embedded in Exodus rich imagery related to the person and work of Christ, said: "There are more types of Christ in this book than perhaps in any other book of the Old Testament. The way of man's reconciliation to God and coming into covenant and communion with him by a mediator is here variously represented, and it is of great use to us for the illustration of the New Testament."

As the climax of Exodus, God established a covenant with his people on Mount Sinai. There he took Israel as his people and established a covenant relationship with them, just as he had promised Abraham. They became a "special possession out of all the nations . . . a kingdom of priests and a holy nation" (19:5–6). The Venerable Bede rightly saw in this designation the same call of the church: "The apostle Peter rightly gives to the Gentiles this attestation of praise that formerly was given by Moses to the ancient people of God because they believed in Christ, who like a cornerstone brought the Gentiles into that salvation which Israel had had for itself."

As part of their covenant with Yahweh, the Israelites had obligations to keep. Those requirements were known as the Decalogue, the Ten Words or Ten Commandments. Caesarius of Arles applied these words to the church, saying: "We should also know that the Ten Commandments of the law are also fulfilled by the two gospel precepts, love of God and love of neighbor. For the three commandments which were written on the first tablet pertain to the love of God, while on the second tablet seven commandments were inscribed . . . doubtless all of the latter are recognized as pertaining to love of neighbor." Further regulations were given that detailed instructions for worship and for creating God's dwelling place among them, the tabernacle.

Though the Israelites would violate these regulations in short order, erecting a golden calf idol, the book of Exodus reveals God's commitment to his people and to his promises. It is a book relevant to our own relationship with God, for it reveals his character, recalls the lengths to which God will go to redeem us, and reminds us of the necessity to love the Lord and love our neighbor.

1:1–22 We were led out of Egypt where we were serving the devil as a pharaoh, where we were doing works of clay amid earthly desires, and we were laboring much in them. For Christ cried out to us, as if we were making bricks, "Come to me, all you who are weary and burdened" (Matt 11:28). Led out of there, we were led over through baptism as through the Red Sea—red because consecrated by the blood of Christ—when all our enemies who were assailing us were dead, that is, when our sins were wiped out.

AUGUSTINE **(354–430)**
TRACTATES ON THE GOSPEL OF JOHN

BLESSING DURING BONDAGE IN EGYPT

1 These are the names of the sons of Israel who entered Egypt—
each man with his household entered with Jacob: [2]Reuben,
Simeon, Levi, and Judah, [3]Issachar, Zebulun, and Benjamin,
[4]Dan and Naphtali, Gad and Asher. [5]All the people who were
directly descended from Jacob numbered 70. But Joseph was
already in Egypt, [6]and in time Joseph and his brothers and all
that generation died. [7]The Israelites, however, were fruitful,
increased greatly, multiplied, and became extremely strong,
so that the land was filled with them.
[8]Then a new king, who did not know about Joseph, came to
power over Egypt. [9]He said to his people, "Look at the Israelite
people, more numerous and stronger than we are! [10]Come, let's
deal wisely with them. Otherwise they will continue to multiply, and if a war breaks out, they will ally themselves with our
enemies and fight against us and leave the country."
[11]So they put foremen over the Israelites to oppress them
with hard labor. As a result they built Pithom and Rameses as
store cities for Pharaoh. [12]But the more the Egyptians oppressed
them, the more they multiplied and spread. As a result the Egyptians loathed the Israelites, [13]and they made the Israelites serve
rigorously. [14]They made their lives bitter by hard service with
mortar and bricks and by all kinds of service in the fields. Every
kind of service the Israelites were required to give was rigorous.
[15]The king of Egypt said to the Hebrew midwives, one of
whom was named Shiphrah and the other Puah, [16]"When you
assist the Hebrew women in childbirth, observe at the delivery:
If it is a son, kill him, but if it is a daughter, she may live." [17]But
the midwives feared God and did not do what the king of Egypt
had told them; they let the boys live.
[18]Then the king of Egypt summoned the midwives and said
to them, "Why have you done this and let the boys live?" [19]The
midwives said to Pharaoh, "Because the Hebrew women are
not like the Egyptian women—for the Hebrew women are vigorous; they give birth before the midwife gets to them!" [20]So
God treated the midwives well, and the people multiplied and
became very strong. [21]And because the midwives feared God,
he made households for them.
[22]Then Pharaoh commanded all his people, "All sons that
are born you must throw into the river, but all daughters you
may let live."

2:1–10 Let us come now again to that word of Moses in which he says: "The Lord your God will raise up for you a prophet like me from among your brothers" (Acts 3:22). For there Moses after his birth was placed by his mother in an ark and exposed beside the banks of the river; here our Lord Jesus Christ, after his birth by Mary his mother, was sent off in flight into Egypt through the instrumentality of an angel. There Moses led forth his people from the midst of the Egyptians and saved them; and here Jesus, leading forth his people from the midst of the Pharisees, transferred them to an eternal salvation.

ARCHELAUS, BISHOP OF CARRHAE **(C. 278)**
THE ACTS OF THE DISPUTATION WITH THE HERESIARCH MANES

THE BIRTH OF THE DELIVERER

2 A man from the household of Levi married a woman who was
a descendant of Levi. [2]The woman became pregnant and gave
birth to a son. When she saw that he was a healthy child, she
hid him for three months. [3]But when she was no longer able to
hide him, she took a papyrus basket for him and sealed it with
bitumen and pitch. She put the child in it and set it among the
reeds along the edge of the Nile. [4]His sister stationed herself
at a distance to find out what would happen to him.
[5]Then the daughter of Pharaoh came down to wash herself
by the Nile, while her attendants were walking alongside the
river, and she saw the basket among the reeds. She sent one of
her attendants, took it, [6]opened it, and saw the child—a boy,
crying!—and she felt compassion for him and said, "This is one
of the Hebrews' children."
[7]Then his sister said to Pharaoh's daughter, "Shall I go and
get a nursing woman for you from the Hebrews, so that she

may nurse the child for you?" 8Pharaoh's daughter said to her,
"Yes, do so." So the young girl went and got the child's mother.
9Pharaoh's daughter said to her, "Take this child and nurse him
for me, and I will pay your wages." So the woman took the child
and nursed him.
10When the child grew older she brought him to Pharaoh's
daughter, and he became her son. She named him Moses, saying,
"Because I drew him from the water."

THE PRESUMPTION OF THE DELIVERER

11In those days, when Moses had grown up, he went out to his
people and observed their hard labor, and he saw an Egyptian
man attacking a Hebrew man, one of his own people. 12He
looked this way and that and saw that no one was there, and
then he attacked the Egyptian and concealed the body in the
sand. 13When he went out the next day, there were two Hebrew
men fighting. So he said to the one who was in the wrong, "Why
are you attacking your fellow Hebrew?"
14The man replied, "Who made you a ruler and a judge over
us? Are you planning to kill me like you killed that Egyptian?"
Then Moses was afraid, thinking, "Surely what I did has become
known." 15When Pharaoh heard about this event, he sought to
kill Moses. So Moses fled from Pharaoh and settled in the land
of Midian, and he settled by a certain well.
16Now a priest of Midian had seven daughters, and they
came and began to draw water and fill the troughs in order to
water their father's flock. 17When some shepherds came and
drove them away, Moses came up and defended them and then
watered their flock. 18So when they came home to their father
Reuel, he asked, "Why have you come home so early today?"
19They said, "An Egyptian man rescued us from the shepherds,
and he actually drew water for us and watered the flock!" 20He
said to his daughters, "So where is he? Why in the world did
you leave the man? Call him, so that he may eat a meal with us."
21Moses agreed to stay with the man, and he gave his daughter Zipporah to Moses in marriage. 22When she bore a son, Moses named him Gershom, for he said, "I have become a resident
foreigner in a foreign land."

THE CALL OF THE DELIVERER

23During that long period of time the king of Egypt died, and
the Israelites groaned because of the slave labor. They cried
out, and their desperate cry because of their slave labor went
up to God. 24God heard their groaning; God remembered his
covenant with Abraham, with Isaac, and with Jacob. 25God saw
the Israelites, and God understood.

3 Now Moses was shepherding the flock of his father-in-law
Jethro, the priest of Midian, and he led the flock to the far
side of the desert and came to the mountain of God, to Horeb.
2The angel of the LORD appeared to him in a flame of fire from
within a bush. He looked, and the bush was ablaze with fire,
but it was not being consumed! 3So Moses thought, "I will turn
aside to see this amazing sight. Why does the bush not burn
up?" 4When the LORD saw that he had turned aside to look, God
called to him from within the bush and said, "Moses, Moses!"
And Moses said, "Here I am." 5God said, "Do not approach any
closer! Take your sandals off your feet, for the place where you
are standing is holy ground." 6He added, "I am the God of your
father, the God of Abraham, the God of Isaac, and the God of

3:1–5 We have then learned that we must do penance, and this at a time when the heat of luxury and sin is giving way; and that we, when under the dominion of sin, must show ourselves God-fearing by refraining rather than allowing ourselves in evil practices. For if it is said to Moses when he was desiring to draw nearer, "Take your sandals off your feet," how much more must we free the feet of our soul from the bonds of the body and clear our steps from all connection with this world.

AMBROSE (C. 339–C. 397)
CONCERNING REPENTANCE

Jacob." Then Moses hid his face, because he was afraid to look
at God.
7The LORD said, "I have surely seen the affliction of my people
who are in Egypt. I have heard their cry because of their taskmas-
ters, for I know their sorrows. 8I have come down to deliver them
from the hand of the Egyptians and to bring them up from that
land to a land that is both good and spacious, to a land flowing
with milk and honey, to the region of the Canaanites, Hittites,
Amorites, Perizzites, Hivites, and Jebusites. 9And now indeed the
cry of the Israelites has come to me, and I have also seen how
severely the Egyptians oppress them. 10So now go, and I will send
you to Pharaoh to bring my people, the Israelites, out of Egypt."
11Moses said to God, "Who am I that I should go to Pharaoh,
or that I should bring the Israelites out of Egypt?" 12He replied,
"Surely I will be with you, and this will be the sign to you that
I have sent you: When you bring the people out of Egypt, you
and they will serve God at this mountain."
13Moses said to God, "If I go to the Israelites and tell them,
'The God of your fathers has sent me to you,' and they ask me,
'What is his name?'—what should I say to them?"
14God said to Moses, "I AM that I AM." And he said, "You must
say this to the Israelites, 'I AM has sent me to you.'" 15God also
said to Moses, "You must say this to the Israelites, 'The LORD—
the God of your fathers, the God of Abraham, the God of Isaac,
and the God of Jacob—has sent me to you. This is my name
forever, and this is my memorial from generation to generation.'
16"Go and bring together the elders of Israel and tell them,
'The LORD, the God of your fathers, appeared to me—the God
of Abraham, Isaac, and Jacob—saying, "I have attended carefully
to you and to what has been done to you in Egypt, 17and I have
promised that I will bring you up out of the affliction of Egypt
to the land of the Canaanites, Hittites, Amorites, Perizzites,
Hivites, and Jebusites, to a land flowing with milk and honey."'
18"The elders will listen to you, and then you and the elders
of Israel must go to the king of Egypt and tell him, 'The LORD,
the God of the Hebrews, has met with us. So now, let us go three
days' journey into the wilderness, so that we may sacrifice to
the LORD our God.' 19But I know that the king of Egypt will not
let you go, not even under force. 20So I will extend my hand and
strike Egypt with all my wonders that I will do among them,
and after that he will release you.
21"I will grant this people favor with the Egyptians, so that
when you depart you will not leave empty-handed. 22Every
woman will ask her neighbor and the one who happens to be
staying in her house for items of silver and gold and for clothing.
You will put these articles on your sons and daughters—thus
you will plunder Egypt!"

THE SOURCE OF SUFFICIENCY

4 Moses answered again, "And if they do not believe me or
pay attention to me, but say, 'The LORD has not appeared to
you'?" 2The LORD said to him, "What is that in your hand?" He
said, "A staff." 3The LORD said, "Throw it to the ground." So he
threw it to the ground, and it became a snake, and Moses ran
from it. 4But the LORD said to Moses, "Put out your hand and
grab it by the tail"—so he put out his hand and caught it, and
it became a staff in his hand—5"that they may believe that the
LORD, the God of their fathers, the God of Abraham, the God
of Isaac, and the God of Jacob, has appeared to you."

6 The LORD also said to him, "Put your hand into your robe." So he put his hand into his robe, and when he brought it out—there was his hand, leprous like snow! 7 He said, "Put your hand back into your robe." So he put his hand back into his robe, and when he brought it out from his robe—there it was, restored like the rest of his skin! 8 "If they do not believe you or pay attention to the former sign, then they may believe the latter sign. 9 And if they do not believe even these two signs or listen to you, then take some water from the Nile and pour it out on the dry ground. The water you take out of the Nile will become blood on the dry ground."

10 Then Moses said to the LORD, "O my Lord, I am not an eloquent man, neither in the past nor since you have spoken to your servant, for I am slow of speech and slow of tongue."

11 The LORD said to him, "Who gave a mouth to man, or who makes a person mute or deaf or seeing or blind? Is it not I, the LORD? 12 So now go, and I will be with your mouth and will teach you what you must say."

13 But Moses said, "O my Lord, please send anyone else whom you wish to send!"

14 Then the LORD became angry with Moses, and he said, "What about your brother Aaron the Levite? I know that he can speak very well. Moreover, he is coming to meet you, and when he sees you he will be glad in his heart.

15 "So you are to speak to him and put the words in his mouth. And as for me, I will be with your mouth and with his mouth, and I will teach you both what you must do. 16 He will speak for you to the people, and it will be as if he were your mouth and as if you were his God. 17 You will also take in your hand this staff, with which you will do the signs."

THE RETURN OF MOSES

18 So Moses went back to his father-in-law Jethro and said to him, "Let me go, so that I may return to my relatives in Egypt and see if they are still alive." Jethro said to Moses, "Go in peace." 19 The LORD said to Moses in Midian, "Go back to Egypt, because all the men who were seeking your life are dead." 20 Then Moses took his wife and sons and put them on a donkey and headed back to the land of Egypt, and Moses took the staff of God in his hand. 21 The LORD said to Moses, "When you go back to Egypt, see that you do before Pharaoh all the wonders I have put under your control. But I will harden his heart and he will not let the people go. 22 You must say to Pharaoh, 'This is what the LORD has said, "Israel is my son, my firstborn, 23 and I said to you, 'Let my son go that he may serve me,' but since you have refused to let him go, I will surely kill your son, your firstborn!"'"

24 Now on the way, at a place where they stopped for the night, the LORD met Moses and sought to kill him. 25 But Zipporah took a flint knife, cut off the foreskin of her son and touched it to Moses' feet, and said, "Surely you are a bridegroom of blood to me." 26 So the LORD let him alone. (At that time she said, "A bridegroom of blood," referring to the circumcision.)

27 The LORD said to Aaron, "Go to the wilderness to meet Moses. So he went and met him at the mountain of God and greeted him with a kiss. 28 Moses told Aaron all the words of the LORD who had sent him and all the signs that he had commanded him. 29 Then Moses and Aaron went and brought together all the Israelite elders. 30 Aaron spoke all the words that the LORD had spoken to Moses and did the signs in the sight of the people,

4:10–17 In Exodus God spoke to Moses when he delayed and feared to go to the people, saying, "Who gave a mouth to man, or who makes a person mute or deaf or seeing or blind? Is it not I, the LORD? So now go, and I will be with your mouth and will teach you what you must say." It is not difficult for God to open the mouth of a person devoted to him and to inspire constancy and confidence in speaking in one who confesses him. Therefore let no one consider in persecutions what danger the devil brings, but rather let him bear in mind what assistance God affords. Let not the disturbances of human beings weaken the mind, but let divine protection strengthen the faith.

CYPRIAN OF CARTHAGE
(C. 210–258)
EXHORTATION TO MARTYRDOM

31 and the people believed. When they heard that the LORD had attended to the Israelites and that he had seen their affliction, they bowed down close to the ground.

OPPOSITION TO THE PLAN OF GOD

5 Afterward Moses and Aaron went to Pharaoh and said, "This is what the LORD, the God of Israel, has said, 'Release my people so that they may hold a pilgrim feast to me in the wilderness.'" 2 But Pharaoh said, "Who is the LORD that I should obey him by releasing Israel? I do not know the LORD, and I will not release Israel!" 3 And they said, "The God of the Hebrews has met with us. Let us go a three-day journey into the wilderness so that we may sacrifice to the LORD our God, so that he does not strike us with plague or the sword." 4 The king of Egypt said to them, "Moses and Aaron, why do you cause the people to refrain from their work? Return to your labor!" 5 Pharaoh was thinking, "The people of the land are now many, and you are giving them rest from their labor."

6 That same day Pharaoh commanded the slave masters and foremen who were over the people: 7 "You must no longer give straw to the people for making bricks as before. Let them go and collect straw for themselves. 8 But you must require of them the same quota of bricks that they were making before. Do not reduce it, for they are slackers. That is why they are crying, 'Let us go sacrifice to our God.' 9 Make the work harder for the men so they will keep at it and pay no attention to lying words!"

10 So the slave masters of the people and their foremen went to the Israelites and said, "Thus says Pharaoh: 'I am not giving you straw. 11 You go get straw for yourselves wherever you can find it, because there will be no reduction at all in your workload.'" 12 So the people spread out through all the land of Egypt to collect stubble for straw. 13 The slave masters were pressuring them, saying, "Complete your work for each day, just like when there was straw!" 14 The Israelite foremen whom Pharaoh's slave masters had set over them were beaten and were asked, "Why did you not complete your requirement for brickmaking as in the past—both yesterday and today?"

15 The Israelite foremen went and cried out to Pharaoh, "Why are you treating your servants this way? 16 No straw is given to your servants, but we are told, 'Make bricks!' Your servants are even being beaten, but the fault is with your people."

17 But Pharaoh replied, "You are slackers! Slackers! That is why you are saying, 'Let us go sacrifice to the LORD.' 18 So now, get back to work! You will not be given straw, but you must still produce your quota of bricks!" 19 The Israelite foremen saw that they were in trouble when they were told, "You must not reduce the daily quota of your bricks."

20 When they went out from Pharaoh, they encountered Moses and Aaron standing there to meet them, 21 and they said to them, "May the LORD look on you and judge, because you have made us stink in the opinion of Pharaoh and his servants, so that you have given them an excuse to kill us!"

THE ASSURANCE OF DELIVERANCE

22 Moses returned to the LORD, and said, "Lord, why have you caused trouble for this people? Why did you ever send me? 23 From the time I went to speak to Pharaoh in your name, he has caused trouble for this people, and you have certainly not rescued them!"

5:1–21 The more God exerts his power, the more is Satan's rage excited on the other side, and the wicked become more fiercely cruel. This offense would greatly shake us unless we knew, from the admonition of this example, that the inestimable grace that is offered us in Christ ought to be so valued by us that in comparison with it, riches, honors, and all that people seek after should be accounted nothing; and that we should find no difficulty in despising inconveniences of whatever kind.

JOHN CALVIN (1509–1564)
COMPLETE COMMENTARY ON THE BIBLE

6 Then the LORD said to Moses, "Now you will see what I will
do to Pharaoh, for compelled by my strong hand he will release them, and by my strong hand he will drive them out of
his land."
2 God spoke to Moses and said to him, "I am the LORD. 3 I
appeared to Abraham, to Isaac, and to Jacob as God Almighty,
but by my name 'the LORD' I was not known to them. 4 I also
established my covenant with them to give them the land of
Canaan, where they were living as resident foreigners. 5 I have
also heard the groaning of the Israelites, whom the Egyptians
are enslaving, and I have remembered my covenant. 6 Therefore,
tell the Israelites, 'I am the LORD. I will bring you out from your
enslavement to the Egyptians, I will rescue you from the hard
labor they impose, and I will redeem you with an outstretched
arm and with great judgments. 7 I will take you to myself for a
people, and I will be your God. Then you will know that I am the
LORD your God, who brought you out from your enslavement
to the Egyptians. 8 I will bring you to the land I swore to give
to Abraham, to Isaac, and to Jacob—and I will give it to you as
a possession. I am the LORD.'"
9 Moses told this to the Israelites, but they did not listen to
him because of their discouragement and hard labor. 10 Then
the LORD said to Moses, 11 "Go, tell Pharaoh king of Egypt that
he must release the Israelites from his land." 12 But Moses replied to the LORD, "If the Israelites did not listen to me, then
how will Pharaoh listen to me, since I speak with difficulty?"
13 The LORD spoke to Moses and Aaron and gave them a
charge for the Israelites and Pharaoh king of Egypt to bring
the Israelites out of the land of Egypt.

THE ANCESTRY OF MOSES AND AARON

14 These were the heads of their fathers' households:
The sons of Reuben, the firstborn son of Israel, were Hanoch
and Pallu, Hezron and Carmi. These were the clans of Reuben.
15 The sons of Simeon were Jemuel, Jamin, Ohad, Jakin, Zohar, and Shaul, the son of a Canaanite woman. These were the
clans of Simeon.
16 Now these were the names of the sons of Levi, according
to their records: Gershon, Kohath, and Merari. (The length of
Levi's life was 137 years.)
17 The sons of Gershon, by their families, were Libni and
Shimei.
18 The sons of Kohath were Amram, Izhar, Hebron, and Uzziel.
(The length of Kohath's life was 133 years.)
19 The sons of Merari were Mahli and Mushi. These were the
clans of Levi, according to their records.
20 Amram married his father's sister Jochebed, and she bore
him Aaron and Moses. (The length of Amram's life was 137 years.)
21 The sons of Izhar were Korah, Nepheg, and Zikri.
22 The sons of Uzziel were Mishael, Elzaphan, and Sithri.
23 Aaron married Elisheba, the daughter of Amminadab and
sister of Nahshon, and she bore him Nadab and Abihu, Eleazar
and Ithamar.
24 The sons of Korah were Assir, Elkanah, and Abiasaph. These
were the Korahite clans.
25 Now Eleazar son of Aaron married one of the daughters
of Putiel and she bore him Phinehas.
These were the heads of the fathers' households of Levi according to their clans.

6:26—7:13 God said, "I will harden Pharaoh's heart, and . . . I will multiply my signs and wonders in the land of Egypt." God makes good use of bad hearts for what he wishes. That Pharaoh had such a heart that was not moved by God's patience to piety but rather to impiety was the result of his own vice. But that those things happened by which his heart, so evil by its own vice, resisted God's command—it is called "hardened" because it did not bend and agree but resisted unbendingly—was of divine dispensation. We should consider whether the phrase can be understood in this way: "I will harden" as if he were saying, *I shall show how hard his heart is.*

AUGUSTINE **(354–430)**
QUESTIONS ON EXODUS

26It was the same Aaron and Moses to whom the LORD said,
"Bring the Israelites out of the land of Egypt by their regiments."
27They were the men who were speaking to Pharaoh king of
Egypt, in order to bring the Israelites out of Egypt. It was the
same Moses and Aaron.

THE AUTHENTICATION OF THE WORD

28When the LORD spoke to Moses in the land of Egypt, 29he said
to him, "I am the LORD. Tell Pharaoh king of Egypt all that I am
telling you." 30But Moses said before the LORD, "Since I speak
with difficulty, why should Pharaoh listen to me?"

7 So the LORD said to Moses, "See, I have made you like God
to Pharaoh, and your brother Aaron will be your prophet.
2You are to speak everything I command you, and your brother
Aaron is to tell Pharaoh that he must release the Israelites
from his land. 3But I will harden Pharaoh's heart, and although
I will multiply my signs and my wonders in the land of Egypt,
4Pharaoh will not listen to you. I will reach into Egypt and bring
out my regiments, my people the Israelites, from the land of
Egypt with great acts of judgment. 5Then the Egyptians will
know that I am the LORD when I extend my hand over Egypt
and bring the Israelites out from among them."

6And Moses and Aaron did so; they did just as the LORD
commanded them. 7Now Moses was eighty years old and Aaron
was eighty-three years old when they spoke to Pharaoh.

8The LORD said to Moses and Aaron, 9"When Pharaoh says
to you, 'Do a miracle,' and you say to Aaron, 'Take your staff and
throw it down before Pharaoh,' it will become a snake." 10When
Moses and Aaron went to Pharaoh, they did so, just as the LORD
had commanded them—Aaron threw down his staff before
Pharaoh and his servants, and it became a snake. 11Then Pharaoh
also summoned wise men and sorcerers, and the magicians of
Egypt by their secret arts did the same thing. 12Each man threw
down his staff, and the staffs became snakes. But Aaron's staff
swallowed up their staffs. 13Yet Pharaoh's heart became hard,
and he did not listen to them, just as the LORD had predicted.

PLAGUE ONE: WATER TO BLOOD

14The LORD said to Moses, "Pharaoh's heart is hard; he refuses
to release the people. 15Go to Pharaoh in the morning when he
goes out to the water. Position yourself to meet him by the edge
of the Nile, and take in your hand the staff that was turned into
a snake. 16Tell him, 'The LORD, the God of the Hebrews, has sent
me to you to say, "Release my people, that they may serve me
in the wilderness!" But until now you have not listened. 17This
is what the LORD has said: "By this you will know that I am the
LORD: I am going to strike the water of the Nile with the staff
that is in my hand, and it will be turned into blood. 18Fish in
the Nile will die, the Nile will stink, and the Egyptians will be
unable to drink water from the Nile."'" 19Then the LORD said to
Moses, "Tell Aaron, 'Take your staff and stretch out your hand
over Egypt's waters—over their rivers, over their canals, over
their ponds, and over all their reservoirs—so that it becomes
blood.' There will be blood everywhere in the land of Egypt,
even in wooden and stone containers." 20Moses and Aaron did
so, just as the LORD had commanded. He raised the staff and
struck the water that was in the Nile right before the eyes of
Pharaoh and his servants, and all the water that was in the
Nile was turned to blood. 21When the fish that were in the Nile

died, the Nile began to stink, so that the Egyptians could not
drink water from the Nile. There was blood everywhere in the
land of Egypt! 22But the magicians of Egypt did the same by
their secret arts, and so Pharaoh's heart remained hard, and
he refused to listen to Moses and Aaron—just as the LORD had
predicted. 23And Pharaoh turned and went into his house. He
did not pay any attention to this. 24All the Egyptians dug around
the Nile for water to drink, because they could not drink the
water of the Nile.

PLAGUE TWO: FROGS

25Seven full days passed after the LORD struck the Nile.
8 1Then the LORD said to Moses, "Go to Pharaoh and tell him,
'This is what the LORD has said: "Release my people in order
that they may serve me! 2But if you refuse to release them,
then I am going to plague all your territory with frogs. 3The
Nile will swarm with frogs, and they will come up and go into
your house, in your bedroom, and on your bed, and into the
houses of your servants and your people, and into your ovens
and your kneading troughs. 4Frogs will come up against you,
your people, and all your servants."'"
5The LORD spoke to Moses, "Tell Aaron, 'Extend your hand
with your staff over the rivers, over the canals, and over the
ponds, and bring the frogs up over the land of Egypt.'" 6So Aaron
extended his hand over the waters of Egypt, and frogs came up
and covered the land of Egypt.
7The magicians did the same with their secret arts and
brought up frogs on the land of Egypt too.
8Then Pharaoh summoned Moses and Aaron and said, "Pray
to the LORD that he may take the frogs away from me and my
people, and I will release the people that they may sacrifice to
the LORD." 9Moses said to Pharaoh, "You may have the honor
over me—when shall I pray for you, your servants, and your
people, for the frogs to be removed from you and your houses,
so that they will be left only in the Nile?" 10He said, "Tomorrow."
And Moses said, "It will be as you say, so that you may know that
there is no one like the LORD our God. 11The frogs will depart
from you, your houses, your servants, and your people; they
will be left only in the Nile."
12Then Moses and Aaron went out from Pharaoh, and Moses
cried to the LORD because of the frogs that he had brought on
Pharaoh. 13The LORD did as Moses asked—the frogs died in the
houses, the villages, and the fields. 14The Egyptians piled them
in countless heaps, and the land stank. 15But when Pharaoh saw
that there was relief, he hardened his heart and did not listen
to them, just as the LORD had predicted.

PLAGUE THREE: GNATS

16The LORD said to Moses, "Tell Aaron, 'Extend your staff and
strike the dust of the ground, and it will become gnats throughout all the land of Egypt.'" 17They did so; Aaron extended his
hand with his staff, he struck the dust of the ground, and it became gnats on people and on animals. All the dust of the ground
became gnats throughout all the land of Egypt. 18When the
magicians attempted to bring forth gnats by their secret arts,
they could not. So there were gnats on people and on animals.
19The magicians said to Pharaoh, "It is the finger of God!" But
Pharaoh's heart remained hard, and he did not listen to them,
just as the LORD had predicted.

8:1–15 Take the example of Pharaoh, a man given to vain, empty thoughts. His land of Egypt was afflicted with a plague of frogs. They gave forth a surfeit of sound, meaningless and senseless. Moses said to Pharaoh, "You may have the honor over me—when shall I pray for you, your servants, and your people, for the frogs to be removed from you and your houses?" Pharaoh, who because of his plight should have besought him to offer prayer, replied, "Tomorrow," thus showing himself indifferent to the punishment that the delay would bring, although he was still intent on saving Egypt from the plague. And so, when his prayer was finally granted, he was unmindful of gratitude. Being puffed up in heart, he forgot God.

AMBROSE (C. 339–C. 397)
CAIN AND ABEL

PLAGUE FOUR: FLIES

[20]The LORD said to Moses, "Get up early in the morning and position yourself before Pharaoh as he goes out to the water, and tell him, 'This is what the LORD has said, "Release my people that they may serve me! [21]If you do not release my people, then I am going to send swarms of flies on you and on your servants and on your people and in your houses. The houses of the Egyptians will be full of flies, and even the ground they stand on. [22]But on that day I will mark off the land of Goshen, where my people are staying, so that no swarms of flies will be there, that you may know that I am the LORD in the midst of this land. [23]I will put a division between my people and your people. This sign will take place tomorrow."'" [24]The LORD did so; a thick swarm of flies came into Pharaoh's house and into the houses of his servants, and throughout the whole land of Egypt the land was ruined because of the swarms of flies.

[25]Then Pharaoh summoned Moses and Aaron and said, "Go, sacrifice to your God within the land." [26]But Moses said, "That would not be the right thing to do, for the sacrifices we make to the LORD our God would be an abomination to the Egyptians. If we make sacrifices that are an abomination to the Egyptians right before their eyes, will they not stone us? [27]We must go on a three-day journey into the wilderness and sacrifice to the LORD our God, just as he is telling us."

[28]Pharaoh said, "I will release you so that you may sacrifice to the LORD your God in the wilderness. Only you must not go very far. Do pray for me."

[29]Moses said, "I am going to go out from you and pray to the LORD, and the swarms of flies will go away from Pharaoh, from his servants, and from his people tomorrow. Only do not let Pharaoh deal falsely again by not releasing the people to sacrifice to the LORD." [30]So Moses went out from Pharaoh and prayed to the LORD, [31]and the LORD did as Moses asked—he removed the swarms of flies from Pharaoh, from his servants, and from his people. Not one remained! [32]But Pharaoh hardened his heart this time also and did not release the people.

PLAGUE FIVE: DISEASE

9 Then the LORD said to Moses, "Go to Pharaoh and tell him, 'This is what the LORD, the God of the Hebrews, has said, "Release my people that they may serve me! [2]For if you refuse to release them and continue holding them, [3]then the hand of the LORD will surely bring a very terrible plague on your livestock in the field, on the horses, the donkeys, the camels, the herds, and the flocks. [4]But the LORD will distinguish between the livestock of Israel and the livestock of Egypt, and nothing will die of all that the Israelites have."'"

[5]The LORD set an appointed time, saying, "Tomorrow the LORD will do this in the land." [6]And the LORD did this on the next day; all the livestock of the Egyptians died, but of the Israelites' livestock not one died. [7]Pharaoh sent representatives to investigate, and indeed, not even one of the livestock of Israel had died. But Pharaoh's heart remained hard, and he did not release the people.

PLAGUE SIX: BOILS

[8]Then the LORD said to Moses and Aaron, "Take handfuls of soot from a furnace, and have Moses throw it into the air while Pharaoh is watching. [9]It will become fine dust over the whole

9:1–12 In the fifth plague Egypt was struck with the slaughter of animals or cattle. Frenzy is demonstrated here, and the stupidity of people who, like irrational animals, gave worship and the name of "god" to figures carved in wood or stone—figures not only of human beings but of animals too. They believed that the divine splendor was present in these forms and offered pathetic acts of worship to them. After these plagues came rotten and swollen cysts, along with fever, as the sixth plague. In the ulcers the troubled and purulent evil of this age is signified, in the cysts swollen and inflated pride, and in the fevers anger and the madness of rage. Up to this point such punishments as were inflicted on the world were tempered, insofar as its errors were represented by signs.

ISIDORE OF SEVILLE
(C. 560–636)
QUESTIONS ON THE OLD TESTAMENT

land of Egypt and will cause boils to break out and fester on both people and animals in all the land of Egypt." [10]So they took soot from a furnace and stood before Pharaoh, Moses threw it into the air, and it caused festering boils to break out on both people and animals.

[11]The magicians could not stand before Moses because of the boils, for boils were on the magicians and on all the Egyptians. [12]But the LORD hardened Pharaoh's heart, and he did not listen to them, just as the LORD had predicted to Moses.

PLAGUE SEVEN: HAIL

[13]The LORD said to Moses, "Get up early in the morning, stand before Pharaoh, and tell him, 'This is what the LORD, the God of the Hebrews, has said: "Release my people so that they may serve me! [14]For this time I will send all my plagues on your very self and on your servants and your people, so that you may know that there is no one like me in all the earth. [15]For by now I could have stretched out my hand and struck you and your people with plague, and you would have been destroyed from the earth. [16]But for this purpose I have caused you to stand: to show you my strength, and so that my name may be declared in all the earth. [17]You are still exalting yourself against my people by not releasing them. [18]I am going to cause very severe hail to rain down about this time tomorrow, such hail as has never occurred in Egypt from the day it was founded until now. [19]So now, send instructions to gather your livestock and all your possessions in the fields to a safe place. Every person or animal caught in the field and not brought into the house—the hail will come down on them, and they will die!"'"

[20]Those of Pharaoh's servants who feared the LORD's message hurried to bring their servants and livestock into the houses, [21]but those who did not take the LORD's message seriously left their servants and their cattle in the field.

[22]Then the LORD said to Moses, "Extend your hand toward the sky that there may be hail in all the land of Egypt, on people and on animals, and on everything that grows in the field in the land of Egypt." [23]When Moses extended his staff toward the sky, the LORD sent thunder and hail, and fire fell to the earth; so the LORD caused hail to rain down on the land of Egypt. [24]Hail fell and fire mingled with the hail; the hail was so severe that there had not been any like it in all the land of Egypt since it had become a nation. [25]The hail struck everything in the open fields, both people and animals, throughout all the land of Egypt. The hail struck everything that grows in the field, and it broke all the trees of the field to pieces. [26]Only in the land of Goshen, where the Israelites lived, was there no hail.

[27]So Pharaoh sent and summoned Moses and Aaron and said to them, "I have sinned this time! The LORD is righteous, and I and my people are guilty. [28]Pray to the LORD, for the mighty thunderings and hail are too much! I will release you and you will stay no longer."

[29]Moses said to him, "When I leave the city I will spread my hands to the LORD, the thunder will cease, and there will be no more hail, so that you may know that the earth belongs to the LORD. [30]But as for you and your servants, I know that you do not yet fear the LORD God."

[31](Now the flax and the barley were struck by the hail, for the barley had ripened and the flax was in bud. [32]But the wheat and the spelt were not struck, for they are later crops.)

33So Moses left Pharaoh, went out of the city, and spread out
his hands to the LORD, and the thunder and the hail ceased,
and the rain stopped pouring on the earth. 34When Pharaoh
saw that the rain and hail and thunder ceased, he sinned again:
both he and his servants hardened their hearts. 35So Pharaoh's
heart remained hard, and he did not release the Israelites, as
the LORD had predicted through Moses.

PLAGUE EIGHT: LOCUSTS

10 The LORD said to Moses, "Go to Pharaoh, for I have hardened his heart and the heart of his servants, in order to
display these signs of mine before him, 2and in order that in
the hearing of your son and your grandson you may tell how I
made fools of the Egyptians and about my signs that I displayed
among them, so that you may know that I am the LORD."
3So Moses and Aaron came to Pharaoh and told him, "This is
what the LORD, the God of the Hebrews, has said: 'How long do
you refuse to humble yourself before me? Release my people so
that they may serve me! 4But if you refuse to release my people,
I am going to bring locusts into your territory tomorrow. 5They
will cover the surface of the earth, so that you will be unable to
see the ground. They will eat the remainder of what escaped—
what is left over for you—from the hail, and they will eat every
tree that grows for you from the field. 6They will fill your houses,
the houses of your servants, and all the houses of Egypt, such
as neither your fathers nor your grandfathers have seen since
they have been in the land until this day!'" Then Moses turned
and went out from Pharaoh.
7Pharaoh's servants said to him, "How long will this man be
a menace to us? Release the people so that they may serve the
LORD their God. Do you not know that Egypt is destroyed?"
8So Moses and Aaron were brought back to Pharaoh, and
he said to them, "Go, serve the LORD your God. Exactly who is
going with you?" 9Moses said, "We will go with our young and
our old, with our sons and our daughters, and with our sheep
and our cattle we will go, because we are to hold a pilgrim feast
for the LORD."
10He said to them, "The LORD will need to be with you if I
release you and your dependents! Watch out! Trouble is right
in front of you. 11No! Go, you men only, and serve the LORD, for
that is what you want." Then Moses and Aaron were driven out
of Pharaoh's presence.
12The LORD said to Moses, "Extend your hand over the land
of Egypt for the locusts, that they may come up over the land of
Egypt and eat everything that grows in the ground, everything
that the hail has left." 13So Moses extended his staff over the land
of Egypt, and then the LORD brought an east wind on the land all
that day and all night. The morning came, and the east wind had
brought up the locusts! 14The locusts went up over all the land of
Egypt and settled down in all the territory of Egypt. It was very
severe; there had been no locusts like them before, nor will there
be such ever again. 15They covered the surface of all the ground
so that the ground became dark with them, and they ate all the
vegetation of the ground and all the fruit of the trees that the hail
had left. Nothing green remained on the trees or on anything that
grew in the fields throughout the whole land of Egypt.
16Then Pharaoh quickly summoned Moses and Aaron and
said, "I have sinned against the LORD your God and against
you! 17So now, forgive my sin this time only, and pray to the

10:12–20 See how Pharaoh is obliged to come to his knees at length. He will be up again soon, for his heart is not humbled though he is eating his own words. An unhumbled heart is not subdued by judgments; it is so apparently, but really it is still a heart of stone. God kept his grace back from him so that he relapsed into his natural state of hard-heartedness. Pharaoh is the great mirror of pride and obstinacy.

CHARLES SPURGEON
(1834–1892)
METROPOLITAN TABERNACLE SERMONS

JUSTIN MARTYR:

PASSIONATE DEFENDER OF THE FAITH

c. 100–c. 165

Whether from Jewish religious leaders, pagan Greek philosophers, or the Roman imperial court, early Christians were on the defensive from the very start. Certain men known as *apologists* took up the challenge of defending the faith. Chief among them was Justin Martyr.

Born to Christian parents in Judea in AD 100, Justin displayed curiosity about life from an early age. Such curiosity led him to seek answers to life's big questions in the most influential philosophies of the day. After happening upon an older man in an obscure seaside town, Justin heard the good news, which led to his conversion. As he described it: "Straightway a flame was kindled in my soul; and a love of the prophets, and of those men who are friends of Christ, possessed me; and whilst revolving his words in my mind, I found this philosophy alone to be safe and profitable."

Not long after, Justin devoted his life to sharing the gospel and defending the faith. One of his most important works is *Dialogues with Trypho*, an extended discourse between a Christian and a Jew named Trypho, modeled after Plato's dialogues. Through the course of the interaction, the reader is treated to an expertly crafted argument demonstrating how Christianity fulfills the Old Testament. Justin's skills at interpreting the Hebrew scriptures were useful later when he defended against the heresy of Marcionism, a false teaching that rejected all things Jewish and taught that the God of the Hebrews was a different, lower god than the God of the New Testament.

This passion for defending the Christian faith extended into two more apologies. The *First Apology*, addressed to Emperor Antonius Pius, argued against the indiscriminate punishment of Christians, explained the essentials of Christianity, outlined Christian ethics, and declared the supremacy of the Christian religion.

Justin's *Second Apology* was written to the Roman Senate. In this work, Justin's anger boiled over the continued unjust punishment and persecution of Christians. He addressed a particular situation in which a pastor had been arrested, thrown into prison, and eventually martyred for his faith.

Justin himself said he "expected to be plotted against and fixed to the stake." He was right. After an antagonistic philosopher, Crescens, entrapped Justin and six other believers, he was beheaded around AD 165—earning his "martyr" moniker and going down in history as one of the most passionate defenders of the faith.

IMPORTANT WORKS

DIALOGUE WITH TRYPHO THE JEW

FIRST APOLOGY

SECOND APOLOGY

THE DISCOURSE TO THE GREEKS

LORD your God that he would only take this death away from me." [18]Moses went out from Pharaoh and prayed to the LORD, [19]and the LORD turned a very strong west wind, and it picked up the locusts and blew them into the Red Sea. Not one locust remained in all the territory of Egypt. [20]But the LORD hardened Pharaoh's heart, and he did not release the Israelites.

PLAGUE NINE: DARKNESS

[21]The LORD said to Moses, "Extend your hand toward heaven so that there may be darkness over the land of Egypt, a darkness so thick it can be felt."

[22]So Moses extended his hand toward heaven, and there was absolute darkness throughout the land of Egypt for three days. [23]No one could see another person, and no one could rise from his place for three days. But the Israelites had light in the places where they lived.

[24]Then Pharaoh summoned Moses and said, "Go, serve the LORD—only your flocks and herds will be detained. Even your families may go with you."

[25]But Moses said, "Will you also provide us with sacrifices and burnt offerings that we may present them to the LORD our God? [26]Our livestock must also go with us! Not a hoof is to be left behind! For we must take these animals to serve the LORD our God. Until we arrive there, we do not know what we must use to serve the LORD."

[27]But the LORD hardened Pharaoh's heart, and he was not willing to release them. [28]Pharaoh said to him, "Go from me! Watch out for yourself! Do not appear before me again, for when you see my face you will die!" [29]Moses said, "As you wish! I will not see your face again."

PLAGUE TEN: DEATH

11 The LORD said to Moses, "I will bring one more plague on Pharaoh and on Egypt; after that he will release you from this place. When he releases you, he will drive you out completely from this place. [2]Instruct the people that each man and each woman is to request from his or her neighbor items of silver and gold."

[3](Now the LORD granted the people favor with the Egyptians. Moreover, the man Moses was very great in the land of Egypt, respected by Pharaoh's servants and by the Egyptian people.)

[4]Moses said, "This is what the LORD has said: 'About midnight I will go throughout Egypt, [5]and all the firstborn in the land of Egypt will die, from the firstborn son of Pharaoh who sits on his throne, to the firstborn son of the slave girl who is at her hand mill, and all the firstborn of the cattle. [6]There will be a great cry throughout the whole land of Egypt, such as there has never been, nor ever will be again. [7]But against any of the Israelites not even a dog will bark against either people or animals, so that you may know that the LORD distinguishes between Egypt and Israel.' [8]All these your servants will come down to me and bow down to me, saying, 'Go, you and all the people who follow you,' and after that I will go out." Then Moses went out from Pharaoh in great anger.

[9]The LORD said to Moses, "Pharaoh will not listen to you, so that my wonders may be multiplied in the land of Egypt." [10]So Moses and Aaron did all these wonders before Pharaoh, but the LORD hardened Pharaoh's heart, and he did not release the Israelites from his land.

11:7 A principal intent of God in the various dispensations of his providence is to make himself known to the world. By some of his works he makes known his natural perfections of wisdom and power; by others his moral perfections of goodness and truth. In his dealings with Pharaoh in particular, we are expressly told that he had this end in view. The exercise of his sovereignty was in that instance intended to be displayed as also in "the LORD distinguishes between Egypt and Israel." But if we consider these two nations as types or representatives of the friends and enemies of God, we shall be rather led to contemplate the equity of all his dispensations toward them.

CHARLES SIMEON
(1759–1836)
HORAE HOMILETICAE

THE INSTITUTION OF THE PASSOVER

12 The LORD said to Moses and Aaron in the land of Egypt,
2"This month is to be your beginning of months; it will
be your first month of the year. 3Tell the whole community
of Israel, 'On the tenth day of this month they each must take
a lamb for themselves according to their families—a lamb for
each household. 4If any household is too small for a lamb, the
man and his next-door neighbor are to take a lamb according to
the number of people—you will make your count for the lamb
according to how much each one can eat. 5Your lamb must be
perfect, a male, one year old; you may take it from the sheep or
from the goats. 6You must care for it until the fourteenth day of
this month, and then the whole community of Israel will kill it
around sundown. 7They will take some of the blood and put it
on the two side posts and top of the doorframe of the houses
where they will eat it. 8They will eat the meat the same night;
they will eat it roasted over the fire with bread made without
yeast and with bitter herbs. 9Do not eat it raw or boiled in water,
but roast it over the fire with its head, its legs, and its entrails.
10You must leave nothing until morning, but you must burn
with fire whatever remains of it until morning. 11This is how
you are to eat it—dressed to travel, your sandals on your feet,
and your staff in your hand. You are to eat it in haste. It is the
LORD's Passover.
12"'I will pass through the land of Egypt in the same night,
and I will attack all the firstborn in the land of Egypt, both
of humans and of animals, and on all the gods of Egypt I will
execute judgment. I am the LORD. 13The blood will be a sign
for you on the houses where you are, so that when I see the
blood I will pass over you, and this plague will not fall on you
to destroy you when I attack the land of Egypt.
14"'This day will become a memorial for you, and you will
celebrate it as a festival to the LORD—you will celebrate it perpetually as a lasting ordinance. 15For seven days you must eat
bread made without yeast. Surely on the first day you must put
away yeast from your houses because anyone who eats bread
made with yeast from the first day to the seventh day will be
cut off from Israel.
16"'On the first day there will be a holy convocation, and
on the seventh day there will be a holy convocation for you.
You must do no work of any kind on them, only what every
person will eat—that alone may be prepared for you. 17So you
will keep the Feast of Unleavened Bread, because on this very
day I brought your regiments out from the land of Egypt, and
so you must keep this day perpetually as a lasting ordinance.
18In the first month, from the fourteenth day of the month, in
the evening, you will eat bread made without yeast until the
twenty-first day of the month in the evening. 19For seven days
yeast must not be found in your houses, for whoever eats what
is made with yeast—that person will be cut off from the community of Israel, whether a resident foreigner or one born in
the land. 20You will not eat anything made with yeast; in all the
places where you live you must eat bread made without yeast.'"
21Then Moses summoned all the elders of Israel, and told
them, "Go and select for yourselves a lamb or young goat for
your families, and kill the Passover animals. 22Take a branch
of hyssop, dip it in the blood that is in the basin, and apply to
the top of the doorframe and the two side posts some of the
blood that is in the basin. Not one of you is to go out the door

12:1–20 It was declared by God that in the first month of the year on the fourteenth day of the month, a year-old lamb without blemish should be sacrificed. With its blood they were to make signs upon the doorposts of their houses, lest they be frightened by the angel of destruction. And on that very night when the lamb was eaten in their homes, which was the celebration of the Passover, they should receive liberation through the figure of slavery. It is not difficult to interpret the spotless Lamb of Christ and his sacrifice made to free the slavery of our death. For, marked by the sign of his cross as by the sprinkling of blood, we shall be saved from the angels of destruction even to the consummation of the world.

MARTIN OF BRAGA
(520–580)
ON THE PASCHA

of his house until morning. [23]For the LORD will pass through to strike Egypt, and when he sees the blood on the top of the doorframe and the two side posts, then the LORD will pass over the door, and he will not permit the destroyer to enter your houses to strike you. [24]You must observe this event as an ordinance for you and for your children forever. [25]When you enter the land that the LORD will give to you, just as he said, you must observe this ceremony. [26]When your children ask you, 'What does this ceremony mean to you?'—[27]then you will say, 'It is the sacrifice of the LORD's Passover, when he passed over the houses of the Israelites in Egypt, when he struck Egypt and delivered our households.'" The people bowed down low to the ground, [28]and the Israelites went away and did exactly as the LORD had commanded Moses and Aaron.

THE DELIVERANCE FROM EGYPT

[29]It happened at midnight—the LORD attacked all the firstborn in the land of Egypt, from the firstborn of Pharaoh who sat on his throne to the firstborn of the captive who was in the prison, and all the firstborn of the cattle. [30]Pharaoh got up in the night, along with all his servants and all Egypt, and there was a great cry in Egypt, for there was no house in which there was not someone dead. [31]Pharaoh summoned Moses and Aaron in the night and said, "Get up, get out from among my people, both you and the Israelites! Go, serve the LORD as you have requested! [32]Also, take your flocks and your herds, just as you have requested, and leave. But bless me also."

[33]The Egyptians were urging the people on, in order to send them out of the land quickly, for they were saying, "We are all dead!" [34]So the people took their dough before the yeast was added, with their kneading troughs bound up in their clothing on their shoulders. [35]Now the Israelites had done as Moses told them—they had requested from the Egyptians silver and gold items and clothing. [36]The LORD gave the people favor in the sight of the Egyptians, and they gave them whatever they wanted, and so they plundered Egypt.

[37]The Israelites journeyed from Rameses to Sukkoth. There were about 600,000 men on foot, plus their dependents. [38]A mixed multitude also went up with them, and flocks and herds—a very large number of cattle. [39]They baked cakes of bread without yeast using the dough they had brought from Egypt, for it was made without yeast. Because they were thrust out of Egypt and were not able to delay, they could not prepare food for themselves either.

[40]Now the length of time the Israelites lived in Egypt was 430 years. [41]At the end of the 430 years, on the very day, all the regiments of the LORD went out of the land of Egypt. [42]It was a night of vigil for the LORD to bring them out from the land of Egypt, and so on this night all Israel is to keep the vigil to the LORD for generations to come.

PARTICIPATION IN THE PASSOVER

[43]The LORD said to Moses and Aaron, "This is the ordinance of the Passover. No foreigner may share in eating it. [44]But everyone's servant who is bought for money, after you have circumcised him, may eat it. [45]A foreigner and a hired worker must not eat it. [46]It must be eaten in one house; you must not bring any of the meat outside the house, and you must not break a bone of it. [47]The whole community of Israel must observe it.

48“When a resident foreigner lives with you and wants to
observe the Passover to the LORD, all his males must be circumcised, and then he may approach and observe it, and he will be
like one who is born in the land—but no uncircumcised person
may eat of it. 49The same law will apply to the person who is
native-born and to the resident foreigner who lives among you.”
50So all the Israelites did exactly as the LORD commanded
Moses and Aaron. 51And on this very day the LORD brought the
Israelites out of the land of Egypt by their regiments.

THE LAW OF THE FIRSTBORN

13 The LORD spoke to Moses, 2“Set apart to me every firstborn male—the first offspring of every womb among the
Israelites, whether human or animal; it is mine.”
3Moses said to the people, “Remember this day on which you
came out from Egypt, from the place where you were enslaved,
for the LORD brought you out of there with a mighty hand—and
no bread made with yeast may be eaten. 4On this day, in the
month of Abib, you are going out.
5“When the LORD brings you to the land of the Canaanites,
Hittites, Amorites, Hivites, and Jebusites, which he swore to
your fathers to give you, a land flowing with milk and honey,
then you will keep this ceremony in this month. 6For seven days
you must eat bread made without yeast, and on the seventh
day there is to be a festival to the LORD. 7Bread made without
yeast must be eaten for seven days; no bread made with yeast
shall be seen among you, and you must have no yeast among
you within any of your borders.
8“You are to tell your son on that day, ‘It is because of what
the LORD did for me when I came out of Egypt.’ 9It will be a sign
for you on your hand and a memorial on your forehead, so that
the law of the LORD may be in your mouth, for with a mighty
hand the LORD brought you out of Egypt. 10So you must keep
this ordinance at its appointed time from year to year.
11“When the LORD brings you into the land of the Canaanites,
as he swore to you and to your fathers, and gives it to you, 12then
you must give over to the LORD the first offspring of every
womb. Every firstling of a beast that you have—the males will
be the LORD’s. 13Every firstling of a donkey you must redeem
with a lamb, and if you do not redeem it, then you must break
its neck. Every firstborn of your sons you must redeem.
14“In the future, when your son asks you ‘What is this?’ you
are to tell him, ‘With a mighty hand the LORD brought us out
from Egypt, from the land of slavery. 15When Pharaoh stubbornly refused to release us, the LORD killed all the firstborn
in the land of Egypt, from the firstborn of people to the firstborn of animals. That is why I am sacrificing to the LORD the
first male offspring of every womb, but all my firstborn sons I
redeem.’ 16It will be for a sign on your hand and for frontlets
on your forehead, for with a mighty hand the LORD brought
us out of Egypt.”

THE LEADING OF GOD

17When Pharaoh released the people, God did not lead them by
the way to the land of the Philistines, although that was nearby,
for God said, “Lest the people change their minds and return to
Egypt when they experience war.” 18So God brought the people
around by the way of the wilderness to the Red Sea, and the
Israelites went up from the land of Egypt prepared for battle.

13:1–16 In remembrance of the destruction of the firstborn of Egypt, both of man and of beast, and the deliverance of the Israelites out of bondage, the firstborn males of the Israelites were set apart to the Lord. By this was set before them that their lives were preserved through the ransom of the atonement, which in due time was to be made for sin. They were also to consider their lives, thus ransomed from death, as now to be consecrated to the service of God. The parents were not to look upon themselves as having any right in their firstborn till they solemnly presented them to God and allowed his title to them. The remembrance of their coming out of Egypt must be kept up every year.

MATTHEW HENRY (1662–1714)
COMMENTARY ON THE WHOLE BIBLE

19 Moses took the bones of Joseph with him, for Joseph had
made the Israelites solemnly swear, "God will surely attend to
you, and you will carry my bones up from this place with you."
20 They journeyed from Sukkoth and camped in Etham, on
the edge of the desert. 21 Now the LORD was going before them
by day in a pillar of cloud to lead them in the way, and by night
in a pillar of fire to give them light, so that they could travel
day or night. 22 He did not remove the pillar of cloud by day nor
the pillar of fire by night from before the people.

THE VICTORY AT THE RED SEA

14 The LORD spoke to Moses, 2 "Tell the Israelites that they
must turn and camp before Pi Hahiroth, between Migdol
and the sea; you are to camp by the sea before Baal Zephon
opposite it. 3 Pharaoh will think regarding the Israelites, 'They
are wandering around confused in the land—the desert has
closed in on them.' 4 I will harden Pharaoh's heart, and he will
chase after them. I will gain honor because of Pharaoh and
because of all his army, and the Egyptians will know that I am
the LORD." So this is what they did.
5 When it was reported to the king of Egypt that the people
had fled, the heart of Pharaoh and his servants was turned
against the people, and the king and his servants said, "What
in the world have we done? For we have released the people
of Israel from serving us!" 6 Then he prepared his chariots and
took his army with him. 7 He took 600 select chariots, and all
the rest of the chariots of Egypt, and officers on all of them.
8 But the LORD hardened the heart of Pharaoh king of Egypt,
and he chased after the Israelites. Now the Israelites were going out defiantly. 9 The Egyptians chased after them, and all
the horses and chariots of Pharaoh and his horsemen and his
army overtook them camping by the sea, beside Pi Hahiroth,
before Baal Zephon. 10 When Pharaoh got closer, the Israelites
looked up, and there were the Egyptians marching after them,
and they were terrified. The Israelites cried out to the LORD,
11 and they said to Moses, "Is it because there are no graves in
Egypt that you have taken us away to die in the desert? What
in the world have you done to us by bringing us out of Egypt?
12 Isn't this what we told you in Egypt, 'Leave us alone so that
we can serve the Egyptians, because it is better for us to serve
the Egyptians than to die in the desert!'"
13 Moses said to the people, "Do not fear! Stand firm and see
the salvation of the LORD that he will provide for you today; for
the Egyptians that you see today you will never, ever see again.
14 The LORD will fight for you, and you can be still."
15 The LORD said to Moses, "Why do you cry out to me? Tell
the Israelites to move on. 16 And as for you, lift up your staff
and extend your hand toward the sea and divide it, so that
the Israelites may go through the middle of the sea on dry
ground. 17 And as for me, I am going to harden the hearts of
the Egyptians so that they will come after them, that I may
be honored because of Pharaoh and his army and his chariots
and his horsemen. 18 And the Egyptians will know that I am
the LORD when I have gained my honor because of Pharaoh,
his chariots, and his horsemen."
19 The angel of God, who was going before the camp of Israel,
moved and went behind them, and the pillar of cloud moved
from before them and stood behind them. 20 It came between
the Egyptian camp and the Israelite camp; it was a dark cloud

14:15–31 For it is better that people should acknowledge their transgressions than that they should harden their hearts as the hearts of those who stirred up sedition against Moses the servant of God, and whose condemnation was made manifest to all. For they went down alive into Hades, and death swallowed them up. Pharaoh with his army and all the princes of Egypt, and the chariots with their riders, were sunk in the depths of the Red Sea and perished for no other reason than that their foolish hearts were hardened after so many signs and wonders had been wrought in the land of Egypt by Moses the servant of God.

CLEMENT OF ROME (D. 99)
FIRST CLEMENT

and it lit up the night so that one camp did not come near the
other the whole night. 21 Moses stretched out his hand toward
the sea, and the LORD drove the sea apart by a strong east wind
all that night, and he made the sea into dry land, and the water
was divided. 22 So the Israelites went through the middle of the
sea on dry ground, the water forming a wall for them on their
right and on their left.
23 The Egyptians chased them and followed them into the
middle of the sea—all the horses of Pharaoh, his chariots, and
his horsemen. 24 In the morning watch the LORD looked down
on the Egyptian army through the pillar of fire and cloud, and
he threw the Egyptian army into a panic. 25 He jammed the
wheels of their chariots so that they had difficulty driving, and
the Egyptians said, "Let's flee from Israel, for the LORD fights
for them against Egypt!"
26 The LORD said to Moses, "Extend your hand toward the
sea, so that the waters may flow back on the Egyptians, on
their chariots, and on their horsemen!" 27 So Moses extended
his hand toward the sea, and the sea returned to its normal
state when the sun began to rise. Now the Egyptians were
fleeing before it, but the LORD overthrew the Egyptians in the
middle of the sea. 28 The water returned and covered the chariots and the horsemen and all the army of Pharaoh that was
coming after the Israelites into the sea—not so much as one
of them survived! 29 But the Israelites walked on dry ground
in the middle of the sea, the water forming a wall for them
on their right and on their left. 30 So the LORD saved Israel on
that day from the power of the Egyptians, and Israel saw the
Egyptians dead on the shore of the sea. 31 When Israel saw the
great power that the LORD had exercised over the Egyptians,
they feared the LORD, and they believed in the LORD and in
his servant Moses.

THE SONG OF TRIUMPH

15 Then Moses and the Israelites sang this song to the LORD.
They said,

"I will sing to the LORD, for he has triumphed gloriously,
the horse and its rider he has thrown into the sea.
2 The LORD is my strength and my song,
and he has become my salvation.
This is my God, and I will praise him,
my father's God, and I will exalt him.
3 The LORD is a warrior—
the LORD is his name.
4 The chariots of Pharaoh and his army he has thrown
into the sea,
and his chosen officers were drowned in the Red Sea.
5 The depths have covered them;
they went down to the bottom like a stone.
6 Your right hand, O LORD, was majestic in power;
your right hand, O LORD, shattered the enemy.
7 In the abundance of your majesty you have overthrown
those who rise up against you.
You sent forth your wrath;
it consumed them like stubble.
8 By the blast of your nostrils the waters were piled up,
the flowing water stood upright like a heap,
and the deep waters were solidified in the heart of the
sea.

15:1–11 The bridge over the river being broken, the passageway settled down, and immediately the chariots with the men disappeared in the depths, and that most impious one himself first of all, then the shield bearers who were with him, as the divine oracles foretold, "sank like lead in the mighty waters"; so that those who obtained the victory from God, if not in words at least in deeds, like Moses, the great servant of God, and those who were with him, fittingly sang as they had sung against the impious tyrant of old, saying, "I will sing to the LORD, for he has triumphed gloriously, the horse and its rider he has thrown into the sea. The LORD is my strength and my song, and he has become my salvation." And "Who is like you, O LORD, among the gods? Who is like you—majestic in holiness, fearful in praises, working wonders?"

EUSEBIUS OF CAESAREA
(C. 260–339)
ECCLESIASTICAL HISTORY

9 The enemy said, 'I will chase, I will overtake,
I will divide the spoil;
my desire will be satisfied on them.
I will draw my sword, my hand will destroy them.'
10 But you blew with your breath, and the sea covered them.
They sank like lead in the mighty waters.
11 Who is like you, O LORD, among the gods?
Who is like you—majestic in holiness, fearful in praises,
working wonders?
12 You stretched out your right hand,
the earth swallowed them.
13 By your loyal love you will lead the people whom you
have redeemed;
you will guide them by your strength to your holy
dwelling place.
14 The nations will hear and tremble;
anguish will seize the inhabitants of Philistia.
15 Then the chiefs of Edom will be terrified,
trembling will seize the leaders of Moab,
and the inhabitants of Canaan will shake.
16 Fear and dread will fall on them;
by the greatness of your arm they will be as still as stone
until your people pass by, O LORD,
until the people whom you have bought pass by.
17 You will bring them in and plant them in the mountain
of your inheritance,
in the place you made for your residence, O LORD,
the sanctuary, O Lord, that your hands have established.
18 The LORD will reign forever and ever!
19 For the horses of Pharaoh came with his chariots and
his footmen into the sea,
and the LORD brought back the waters of the sea on them,
but the Israelites walked on dry land in the middle of
the sea."

20 Miriam the prophetess, the sister of Aaron, took a hand
drum in her hand, and all the women went out after her with
hand drums and with dances. 21 Miriam sang in response to them,
"Sing to the LORD, for he has triumphed gloriously;
the horse and its rider he has thrown into the sea."

THE BITTER WATER

22 Then Moses led Israel to journey away from the Red Sea. They
went out to the wilderness of Shur, walked for three days into
the wilderness, and found no water. 23 Then they came to Marah,
but they were not able to drink the waters of Marah, because
they were bitter. (That is why its name was Marah.)

24 So the people murmured against Moses, saying, "What can
we drink?" 25 He cried out to the LORD, and the LORD showed
him a tree. When Moses threw it into the water, the water became safe to drink. There the LORD made for them a binding
ordinance, and there he tested them. 26 He said, "If you will
diligently obey the LORD your God, and do what is right in his
sight, and pay attention to his commandments, and keep all his
statutes, then all the diseases that I brought on the Egyptians I
will not bring on you, for I, the LORD, am your healer."

27 Then they came to Elim, where there were twelve wells
of water and seventy palm trees, and they camped there by
the water.

THE PROVISION OF MANNA

16 When they journeyed from Elim, the entire company of
Israelites came to the wilderness of Sin, which is between
Elim and Sinai, on the fifteenth day of the second month after
their exodus from the land of Egypt. 2The entire company of Israelites murmured against Moses and Aaron in the wilderness.
3The Israelites said to them, "If only we had died by the hand
of the LORD in the land of Egypt, when we sat by the pots of
meat, when we ate bread to the full, for you have brought us out
into this wilderness to kill this whole assembly with hunger!"
4Then the LORD said to Moses, "I am going to rain bread
from heaven for you, and the people will go out and gather the
amount for each day, so that I may test them. Will they walk
in my law or not? 5On the sixth day they will prepare what
they bring in, and it will be twice as much as they gather every
other day."
6Moses and Aaron said to all the Israelites, "In the evening
you will know that the LORD has brought you out of the land of
Egypt, 7and in the morning you will see the glory of the LORD,
because he has heard your murmurings against the LORD. As
for us, what are we, that you should murmur against us?"
8Moses said, "You will know this when the LORD gives you
meat to eat in the evening and bread in the morning to satisfy
you, because the LORD has heard your murmurings that you
are murmuring against him. As for us, what are we? Your murmurings are not against us, but against the LORD."
9Then Moses said to Aaron, "Tell the whole community of
the Israelites, 'Come before the LORD, because he has heard
your murmurings.'"
10As Aaron spoke to the whole community of the Israelites
and they looked toward the wilderness, there the glory of the
LORD appeared in the cloud, 11and the LORD spoke to Moses,
12"I have heard the murmurings of the Israelites. Tell them,
'During the evening you will eat meat, and in the morning you
will be satisfied with bread, so that you may know that I am
the LORD your God.'"
13In the evening the quail came up and covered the camp,
and in the morning a layer of dew was all around the camp.
14When the layer of dew had evaporated, there on the surface
of the wilderness was a thin flaky substance, thin like frost on
the earth. 15When the Israelites saw it, they said to one another,
"What is it?" because they did not know what it was. Moses said
to them, "It is the bread that the LORD has given you for food.
16"This is what the LORD has commanded: 'Each person is
to gather from it what he can eat, an omer per person according to the number of your people; each one will pick it up for
whoever lives in his tent.'" 17The Israelites did so, and they
gathered—some more, some less. 18When they measured with
an omer, the one who gathered much had nothing left over,
and the one who gathered little lacked nothing; each one had
gathered what he could eat.
19Moses said to them, "No one is to keep any of it until morning." 20But they did not listen to Moses; some kept part of it until
morning, and it was full of worms and began to stink, and Moses
was angry with them. 21So they gathered it each morning, each
person according to what he could eat, and when the sun got
hot, it would melt. 22And on the sixth day they gathered twice
as much food, two omers per person; and all the leaders of the
community came and told Moses. 23He said to them, "This is

16:22–31 All, both poor and rich, they gathered manna. Christ is a common food for king and subject; all take part of Christ. Neither Jew nor Gentile is exempt, but all may come and buy freely without money. Of this manna they who had least had enough. So here, they that have the least of Christ, though they take him with trembling hands, yet they shall have enough, for Christ is theirs. Whosoever has the least grace, if it be true and sound, has grace enough to bring him or her to eternal life.

RICHARD SIBBES (1577–1635)
BETWEEN CHRIST AND HIS CHURCH

what the LORD has said: 'Tomorrow is a time of cessation from work, a holy Sabbath to the LORD. Whatever you want to bake, bake today; whatever you want to boil, boil today; whatever is left put aside for yourselves to be kept until morning.'"

24 So they put it aside until the morning, just as Moses had commanded, and it did not stink, nor were there any worms in it. 25 Moses said, "Eat it today, for today is a Sabbath to the LORD; today you will not find it in the area. 26 Six days you will gather it, but on the seventh day, the Sabbath, there will not be any."

27 On the seventh day some of the people went out to gather it, but they found nothing. 28 So the LORD said to Moses, "How long do you refuse to obey my commandments and my instructions? 29 See, because the LORD has given you the Sabbath, that is why he is giving you food for two days on the sixth day. Each of you stay where you are; let no one go out of his place on the seventh day." 30 So the people rested on the seventh day.

31 The house of Israel called its name "manna." It was like coriander seed and was white, and it tasted like wafers with honey.

32 Moses said, "This is what the LORD has commanded: 'Fill an omer with it to be kept for generations to come, so that they may see the food I fed you in the wilderness when I brought you out from the land of Egypt.'" 33 Moses said to Aaron, "Take a jar and put in it an omer full of manna, and place it before the LORD to be kept for generations to come." 34 Just as the LORD commanded Moses, so Aaron placed it before the ark of the testimony for safekeeping.

35 Now the Israelites ate manna 40 years, until they came to a land that was inhabited; they ate manna until they came to the border of the land of Canaan. 36 (Now an omer is one-tenth of an ephah.)

WATER AT MASSAH AND MERIBAH

17 The whole community of the Israelites traveled on their journey from the wilderness of Sin according to the LORD's instruction, and they pitched camp in Rephidim. Now there was no water for the people to drink. 2 So the people contended with Moses, and they said, "Give us water to drink!" Moses said to them, "Why do you contend with me? Why do you test the LORD?" 3 But the people were very thirsty there for water, and they murmured against Moses and said, "Why in the world did you bring us up from Egypt—to kill us and our children and our cattle with thirst?"

4 Then Moses cried out to the LORD, "What will I do with this people?—a little more and they will stone me!" 5 The LORD said to Moses, "Go over before the people; take with you some of the elders of Israel and take in your hand your staff with which you struck the Nile and go. 6 I will be standing before you there on the rock in Horeb, and you will strike the rock, and water will come out of it so that the people may drink." And Moses did so in plain view of the elders of Israel.

7 He called the name of the place Massah and Meribah, because of the contending of the Israelites and because of their testing the LORD, saying, "Is the LORD among us or not?"

17:1–7 Though they spoke of stoning Moses, he must take his rod with him, not to summon some plague to chastise them but to fetch water for their supply. O the wonderful patience and forbearance of God toward provoking sinners! He maintains those who are at war with him and reaches out the hand of his bounty to those who lift up the heel against him. If God had only showed Moses a fountain of water in the wilderness, that had been a great favor; but that he might show his power as well as his pity and make it a miracle of mercy, he gave them water out of a rock. Let this direct us to live in a dependence upon God's providence even in the greatest straits and difficulties, and upon Christ's grace; that rock was Christ.

JOHN WESLEY (1703–1791)
EXPLANATORY NOTES ON THE BIBLE

VICTORY OVER THE AMALEKITES

8 Amalek came and attacked Israel in Rephidim. 9 So Moses said to Joshua, "Choose some of our men and go out, fight against Amalek. Tomorrow I will stand on top of the hill with the staff of God in my hand."

[10]So Joshua fought against Amalek just as Moses had instructed him, and Moses and Aaron and Hur went up to the
top of the hill. [11]Whenever Moses would raise his hands, then
Israel prevailed, but whenever he would rest his hands, then
Amalek prevailed. [12]When the hands of Moses became heavy,
they took a stone and put it under him, and Aaron and Hur
held up his hands, one on one side and one on the other, and
so his hands were steady until the sun went down. [13]So Joshua
destroyed Amalek and his army with the sword.
[14]The LORD said to Moses, "Write this as a memorial in the
book, and rehearse it in Joshua's hearing; for I will surely wipe
out the remembrance of Amalek from under heaven." [15]Moses
built an altar, and he called it "The LORD is my Banner," [16]for
he said, "For a hand was lifted up to the throne of the LORD—
that the LORD will have war with Amalek from generation to
generation."

THE ADVICE OF JETHRO

18 Jethro, the priest of Midian, Moses' father-in-law, heard
about all that God had done for Moses and for his people
Israel, that the LORD had brought Israel out of Egypt.
[2]Jethro, Moses' father-in-law, took Moses' wife Zipporah after he had sent her back, [3]and her two sons, one of whom was
named Gershom (for Moses had said, "I have been a foreigner
in a foreign land") [4]and the other Eliezer (for Moses had said,
"The God of my father has been my help and delivered me from
the sword of Pharaoh").
[5]Jethro, Moses' father-in-law, together with Moses' sons and
his wife, came to Moses in the wilderness where he was camping
by the mountain of God. [6]He said to Moses, "I, your father-in-
law Jethro, am coming to you, along with your wife and her
two sons with her." [7]Moses went out to meet his father-in-law
and bowed down and kissed him; they each asked about the
other's welfare, and then they went into the tent. [8]Moses told
his father-in-law all that the LORD had done to Pharaoh and
to Egypt for Israel's sake, and all the hardship that had come
on them along the way, and how the LORD had delivered them.
[9]Jethro rejoiced because of all the good that the LORD had
done for Israel, whom he had delivered from the hand of Egypt.
[10]Jethro said, "Blessed be the LORD who has delivered you from
the hand of Egypt, and from the hand of Pharaoh, who has delivered the people from the Egyptians' control! [11]Now I know
that the LORD is greater than all the gods, for in the thing in
which they dealt proudly against them he has destroyed them."
[12]Then Jethro, Moses' father-in-law, brought a burnt offering
and sacrifices for God, and Aaron and all the elders of Israel
came to eat food with the father-in-law of Moses before God.
[13]On the next day Moses sat to judge the people, and the people stood around Moses from morning until evening. [14]When
Moses' father-in-law saw all that he was doing for the people,
he said, "What is this that you are doing for the people? Why
are you sitting by yourself, and all the people stand around you
from morning until evening?"
[15]Moses said to his father-in-law, "Because the people come
to me to inquire of God. [16]When they have a dispute, it comes
to me and I decide between a man and his neighbor, and I make
known the decrees of God and his laws."
[17]Moses' father-in-law said to him, "What you are doing is not
good! [18]You will surely wear out, both you and these people who

18:1–27 Moses, who spoke with God, was judged by the reproof of Jethro, who was of alien race, because with ill-advised labor he devoted himself to the people's earthly affairs. And counsel too was presently given him that he should appoint others in his stead for settling earthly conflicts, and he himself should be freer to learn spiritual secrets for the instruction of the people.

GREGORY THE GREAT
(C. 540–604)
PASTORAL CARE

are with you, for this is too heavy a burden for you; you are not
able to do it by yourself. [19]Now listen to me, I will give you advice,
and may God be with you. You be a representative for the people
to God, and you bring their disputes to God; [20]warn them of the
statutes and the laws, and make known to them the way in which
they must walk and the work they must do. [21]But you choose
from the people capable men, God-fearing men, men of truth,
those who hate bribes, and put them over the people as rulers
of thousands, rulers of hundreds, rulers of fifties, and rulers of
tens. [22]They will judge the people under normal circumstances,
and every difficult case they will bring to you, but every small
case they themselves will judge, so that you may make it easier
for yourself, and they will bear the burden with you. [23]If you do
this thing, and God so commands you, then you will be able to
endure, and all these people will be able to go home satisfied."
[24]Moses listened to his father-in-law and did everything he
had said. [25]Moses chose capable men from all Israel, and he made
them heads over the people, rulers of thousands, rulers of hundreds, rulers of fifties, and rulers of tens. [26]They judged the people
under normal circumstances; the difficult cases they would bring
to Moses, but every small case they would judge themselves.
[27]Then Moses sent his father-in-law on his way, and so Jethro
went to his own land.

ISRAEL AT SINAI

19 In the third month after the Israelites went out from the
land of Egypt, on the very day, they came to the desert of
Sinai. [2]After they journeyed from Rephidim, they came to the
desert of Sinai, and they camped in the desert; Israel camped
there in front of the mountain.
[3]Moses went up to God, and the LORD called to him from the
mountain, "Thus you will tell the house of Jacob, and declare
to the people of Israel: [4]'You yourselves have seen what I did to
Egypt and how I lifted you on eagles' wings and brought you to
myself. [5]And now, if you will diligently listen to me and keep
my covenant, then you will be my special possession out of all
the nations, for all the earth is mine, [6]and you will be to me a
kingdom of priests and a holy nation.' These are the words that
you will speak to the Israelites."
[7]So Moses came and summoned the elders of Israel. He set
before them all these words that the LORD had commanded
him, [8]and all the people answered together, "All that the LORD
has commanded we will do!" So Moses brought the words of
the people back to the LORD.
[9]The LORD said to Moses, "I am going to come to you in a
dense cloud, so that the people may hear when I speak with you
and so that they will always believe in you." And Moses told the
words of the people to the LORD.
[10]The LORD said to Moses, "Go to the people and sanctify
them today and tomorrow, and make them wash their clothes
[11]and be ready for the third day, for on the third day the LORD
will come down on Mount Sinai in the sight of all the people.
[12]You must set boundaries for the people all around, saying,
'Take heed to yourselves not to go up on the mountain nor
touch its edge. Whoever touches the mountain will surely be
put to death! [13]No hand will touch him—but he will surely be
stoned or shot through, whether a beast or a human being; he
must not live.' When the ram's horn sounds a long blast they
may go up on the mountain."

19:1–25 "For the commandments . . . are summed up in this, 'Love your neighbor as yourself.' Love does no wrong to a neighbor. Therefore love is the fulfillment of the law" (Rom 13:9–10). Now this was not written on the tablets of stone but "has been poured out in our hearts through the Holy Spirit who was given to us" (Rom 5:5). God's law, therefore, is love. "The outlook of the flesh is hostile to God, for it does not submit to the law of God, nor is it able to do so" (Rom 8:7). But when the works of love are written on tablets to alarm the carnal mind, there arises the law of works and "the letter kills" the transgressor (2 Cor 3:6); but when love itself is shed abroad in the hearts of believers, then we have the law of faith, and the Spirit who gives life to those who love.

AUGUSTINE **(354–430)**
ANTI-PELAGIAN WRITINGS

[14]Then Moses went down from the mountain to the people
and sanctified the people, and they washed their clothes. [15]He
said to the people, "Be ready for the third day. Do not approach
your wives for marital relations."
[16]On the third day in the morning there was thunder and
lightning and a dense cloud on the mountain, and the sound
of a very loud horn; all the people who were in the camp trembled. [17]Moses brought the people out of the camp to meet God,
and they took their place at the foot of the mountain. [18]Now
Mount Sinai was completely covered with smoke because the
LORD had descended on it in fire, and its smoke went up like
the smoke of a great furnace, and the whole mountain shook
violently. [19]When the sound of the horn grew louder and louder,
Moses was speaking and God was answering him with a voice.
[20]The LORD came down on Mount Sinai, on the top of the
mountain, and the LORD summoned Moses to the top of the
mountain, and Moses went up. [21]The LORD said to Moses, "Go
down and solemnly warn the people, lest they force their way
through to the LORD to look, and many of them perish. [22]Let
the priests also, who approach the LORD, sanctify themselves,
lest the LORD break through against them."
[23]Moses said to the LORD, "The people are not able to come
up to Mount Sinai, because you solemnly warned us, 'Set boundaries for the mountain and set it apart.'" [24]The LORD said to
him, "Go, get down, and then come up, and Aaron with you, but
do not let the priests and the people force their way through to
come up to the LORD, lest he break through against them." [25]So
Moses went down to the people and spoke to them.

THE DECALOGUE

20 God spoke all these words:
[2]"I, the LORD, am your God, who brought you from the
land of Egypt, from the house of slavery.
[3]"You shall have no other gods before me.
[4]"You shall not make for yourself a carved image or any likeness of anything that is in heaven above or that is on the earth
beneath or that is in the water below. [5]You shall not bow down
to them or serve them, for I, the LORD, your God, am a jealous
God, responding to the transgression of fathers by dealing with
children to the third and fourth generations of those who reject
me, [6]and showing covenant faithfulness to a thousand generations of those who love me and keep my commandments.
[7]"You shall not take the name of the LORD your God in vain,
for the LORD will not hold guiltless anyone who takes his name
in vain.
[8]"Remember the Sabbath day to set it apart as holy. [9]For six
days you may labor and do all your work, [10]but the seventh day
is a Sabbath to the LORD your God; on it you shall not do any
work, you, or your son, or your daughter, or your male servant,
or your female servant, or your cattle, or the resident foreigner who is in your gates. [11]For in six days the LORD made the
heavens and the earth and the sea and all that is in them, and
he rested on the seventh day; therefore the LORD blessed the
Sabbath day and set it apart as holy.
[12]"Honor your father and your mother, that you may live a
long time in the land the LORD your God is giving to you.
[13]"You shall not murder.
[14]"You shall not commit adultery.
[15]"You shall not steal.

16 “You shall not give false testimony against your neighbor. 17 “You shall not covet your neighbor’s house. You shall not covet your neighbor’s wife, nor his male servant, nor his female servant, nor his ox, nor his donkey, nor anything that belongs to your neighbor.”

18 All the people were seeing the thundering and the lightning, and heard the sound of the horn, and saw the mountain smoking—and when the people saw it they trembled with fear and kept their distance. 19 They said to Moses, “You speak to us and we will listen, but do not let God speak with us, lest we die.” 20 Moses said to the people, “Do not fear, for God has come to test you, that the fear of him may be before you so that you do not sin.” 21 The people kept their distance, but Moses drew near the thick darkness where God was.

20:18–21 Think not that this thunder and fire are designed to consume you. No; it was intended (1) To prove them, to try how they could like dealing with God immediately, without a mediator, and so to convince them how admirably well God had chosen for them in putting Moses into that office. Ever since Adam fled upon hearing God’s voice in the garden, sinful humanity could not bear either to speak to God or hear from him immediately. (2) To keep them to their duty and prevent their sinning against God. We must not fear with amazement, but we must always have in our minds a reverence of God’s majesty, a dread of his displeasure, and an obedient regard to his sovereign authority.

JOHN WESLEY (1703–1791)
EXPLANATORY NOTES ON THE BIBLE

THE ALTAR

22 The LORD said to Moses, “Thus you will tell the Israelites: ‘You yourselves have seen that I have spoken with you from heaven. 23 You must not make gods of silver alongside me, nor make gods of gold for yourselves.

24 “‘You must make for me an altar made of earth, and you will sacrifice on it your burnt offerings and your peace offerings, your sheep and your cattle. In every place where I cause my name to be honored I will come to you and I will bless you. 25 If you make me an altar of stone, you must not build it of stones shaped with tools, for if you use your tool on it you have defiled it. 26 And you must not go up by steps to my altar, so that your nakedness is not exposed.’

THE ORDINANCES

21 “These are the ordinances that you will set before them:

HEBREW SERVANTS

2 “If you buy a Hebrew servant, he is to serve you for six years, but in the seventh year he will go out free without paying anything. 3 If he came in by himself he will go out by himself; if he had a wife when he came in, then his wife will go out with him. 4 If his master gave him a wife, and she bore sons or daughters, the wife and the children will belong to her master, and he will go out by himself. 5 But if the servant should declare, ‘I love my master, my wife, and my children; I will not go out free,’ 6 then his master must bring him to the judges, and he will bring him to the door or the doorpost, and his master will pierce his ear with an awl, and he shall serve him forever.

7 “If a man sells his daughter as a female servant, she will not go out as the male servants do. 8 If she does not please her master, who has designated her for himself, then he must let her be redeemed. He has no right to sell her to a foreign nation, because he has dealt deceitfully with her. 9 If he designated her for his son, then he will deal with her according to the customary rights of daughters. 10 If he takes another wife, he must not diminish the first one’s food, her clothing, or her marital rights. 11 If he does not provide her with these three things, then she will go out free, without paying money.

21:12–27 But what parts of the law can I defend as good with a greater confidence than those that heresy has shown such a longing for—[such as] the statute of retaliation (vv. 23–25)? Now there is not here any smack of permission to mutual injury. There is rather, on the whole, a provision for restraining violence. To a people who were very hard-hearted and wanting in faith toward God, the commission of wrong was to be checked by the fear of retribution immediately to happen. So the permission of this retribution was to be the prohibition of provocation. In this way a stop might thus be put to all hot-blooded injury. By the permission of the second, the first is prevented by fear. By this deterring of the first, the second act of wrong fails to be committed.

TERTULLIAN (155–C. 220)
AGAINST MARCION

PERSONAL INJURIES

12 “Whoever strikes someone so that he dies must surely be put to death. 13 But if he does not do it with premeditation, but it happens by accident, then I will appoint for you a place where

he may flee. 14But if a man willfully attacks his neighbor to kill him cunningly, you will take him even from my altar that he may die.

15"Whoever strikes his father or his mother must surely be put to death.

16"Whoever kidnaps someone and sells him, or is caught still holding him, must surely be put to death.

17"Whoever treats his father or his mother disgracefully must surely be put to death.

18"If men fight, and one strikes his neighbor with a stone or with his fist and he does not die, but must remain in bed, 19and then if he gets up and walks about outside on his staff, then the one who struck him is innocent, except he must pay for the injured person's loss of time and see to it that he is fully healed.

20"If a man strikes his male servant or his female servant with a staff so that he or she dies as a result of the blow, he will surely be punished. 21However, if the injured servant survives one or two days, the owner will not be punished, for he has suffered the loss.

22"If men fight and hit a pregnant woman and her child is born prematurely, but there is no serious injury, the one who hit her will surely be punished in accordance with what the woman's husband demands of him, and he will pay what the court decides. 23But if there is serious injury, then you will give a life for a life, 24eye for eye, tooth for tooth, hand for hand, foot for foot, 25burn for burn, wound for wound, bruise for bruise.

26"If a man strikes the eye of his male servant or his female servant so that he destroys it, he will let the servant go free as compensation for the eye. 27If he knocks out the tooth of his male servant or his female servant, he will let the servant go free as compensation for the tooth.

LAWS ABOUT ANIMALS

28"If an ox gores a man or a woman so that either dies, then the ox must surely be stoned and its flesh must not be eaten, but the owner of the ox will be acquitted. 29But if the ox had the habit of goring, and its owner was warned but he did not take the necessary precautions, and then it killed a man or a woman, the ox must be stoned and the man must be put to death. 30If a ransom is set for him, then he must pay the redemption for his life according to whatever amount was set for him. 31If the ox gores a son or a daughter, the owner will be dealt with according to this rule. 32If the ox gores a male servant or a female servant, the owner must pay thirty shekels of silver, and the ox must be stoned.

33"If a man opens a pit or if a man digs a pit and does not cover it and an ox or a donkey falls into it, 34the owner of the pit must repay the loss. He must give money to its owner, and the dead animal will become his. 35If the ox of one man injures the ox of his neighbor so that it dies, then they will sell the live ox and divide its proceeds, and they will also divide the dead ox. 36Or if it is known that the ox had the habit of goring, and its owner did not take the necessary precautions, he must surely pay ox for ox, and the dead animal will become his.

LAWS ABOUT PROPERTY

22 "If a man steals an ox or a sheep and kills it or sells it, he must pay back five head of cattle for the ox, and four sheep for the one sheep.

22:1–15 To burn the food of a person is bad enough, but how much worse to destroy the soul! It may be useful to us to reflect how far we may have been guilty in the past and to inquire whether, even in the present, there may not be evil in us that has a tendency to bring damage to the souls of our relatives, friends, or neighbors. O Lord and giver of peace, make us peacemakers, and never let us aid and abet the people of strife or even unintentionally cause the least division among your people.

CHARLES SPURGEON
(1834–1892)
MORNING AND EVENING

2“If a thief is caught breaking in and is struck so that he dies, there will be no blood guilt for him. 3If the sun has risen on him, then there is blood guilt for him. A thief must surely make full restitution; if he has nothing, then he will be sold for his theft. 4If the stolen item should in fact be found alive in his possession, whether it be an ox or a donkey or a sheep, he must pay back double.

5“If a man grazes his livestock in a field or a vineyard and he lets the livestock loose and they graze in the field of another man, he must make restitution from the best of his own field and the best of his own vineyard.

6“If a fire breaks out and spreads to thorn bushes, so that stacked grain or standing grain or the whole field is consumed, the one who started the fire must surely make restitution.

7“If a man gives his neighbor money or articles for safekeeping and it is stolen from the man’s house, if the thief is caught, he must repay double. 8If the thief is not caught, then the owner of the house will be brought before the judges to see whether he has laid his hand on his neighbor’s goods. 9In all cases of illegal possessions, whether for an ox, a donkey, a sheep, a garment, or any kind of lost item, about which someone says ‘This belongs to me,’ the matter of the two of them will come before the judges, and the one whom the judges declare guilty must repay double to his neighbor. 10If a man gives his neighbor a donkey or an ox or a sheep or any beast to keep, and it dies or is injured or is carried away without anyone seeing it, 11then there will be an oath to the Lord between the two of them, that he has not laid his hand on his neighbor’s goods, and its owner will accept this, and he will not have to pay. 12But if it was stolen from him, he will pay its owner. 13If it is torn in pieces, then he will bring it for evidence, and he will not have to pay for what was torn.

14“If a man borrows an animal from his neighbor and it is hurt or dies when its owner was not with it, the man who borrowed it will surely pay. 15If its owner was with it, he will not have to pay; if it was hired, what was paid for the hire covers it.

MORAL AND CEREMONIAL LAWS

16“If a man seduces a virgin who is not engaged and goes to bed with her, he must surely pay the marriage price for her to be his wife. 17If her father refuses to give her to him, he must pay money for the bride price of virgins.

18“You must not allow a sorceress to live.

19“Whoever has sexual relations with a beast must surely be put to death.

20“Whoever sacrifices to a god other than the Lord alone must be utterly destroyed.

21“You must not wrong a resident foreigner nor oppress him, for you were foreigners in the land of Egypt.

22“You must not afflict any widow or orphan. 23If you afflict them in any way and they cry to me, I will surely hear their cry, 24and my anger will burn and I will kill you with the sword, and your wives will be widows and your children will be fatherless.

25“If you lend money to any of my people who are needy among you, do not be like a moneylender to him; do not charge him interest. 26If you do take the garment of your neighbor in pledge, you must return it to him by the time the sun goes down, 27for it is his only covering—it is his garment for his body. What else can he sleep in? And when he cries out to me, I will hear, for I am gracious.

28“You must not blaspheme God or curse the ruler of your
people.
29“Do not hold back offerings from your granaries or your
vats. You must give me the firstborn of your sons. 30You must
also do this for your oxen and for your sheep; seven days they
may remain with their mothers, but give them to me on the
eighth day.
31“You will be holy people to me; you must not eat any meat
torn by animals in the field. You must throw it to the dogs.

JUSTICE

23 “You must not give a false report. Do not make common
cause with the wicked to be a malicious witness.
2“You must not follow a crowd in doing evil things; in a lawsuit you must not offer testimony that agrees with a crowd so
as to pervert justice, 3and you must not show partiality to a
poor man in his lawsuit.
4“If you encounter your enemy’s ox or donkey wandering off,
you must by all means return it to him. 5If you see the donkey
of someone who hates you fallen under its load, you must not
ignore him, but be sure to help him with it.
6“You must not turn away justice for your poor people in their
lawsuits. 7Keep your distance from a false charge—do not kill
the innocent and the righteous, for I will not justify the wicked.
8“You must not accept a bribe, for a bribe blinds those who
see and subverts the words of the righteous.
9“You must not oppress a resident foreigner, since you know
the life of a foreigner, for you were foreigners in the land of
Egypt.

SABBATHS AND FEASTS

10“For six years you are to sow your land and gather in its produce. 11But in the seventh year you must let it lie fallow and
leave it alone so that the poor of your people may eat, and what
they leave any animal in the field may eat; you must do likewise
with your vineyard and your olive grove. 12For six days you are
to do your work, but on the seventh day you must cease, in
order that your ox and your donkey may rest and that your
female servant’s son and the resident foreigner may refresh
themselves.
13“Pay attention to do everything I have told you, and do
not even mention the names of other gods—do not let them
be heard on your lips.
14“Three times in the year you must make a pilgrim feast to
me. 15You are to observe the Feast of Unleavened Bread; seven
days you must eat bread made without yeast, as I commanded
you, at the appointed time of the month of Abib, for at that
time you came out of Egypt. No one may appear before me
empty-handed.
16“You are also to observe the Feast of Harvest, the firstfruits
of your labors that you have sown in the field, and the Feast
of Ingathering at the end of the year when you have gathered
in your harvest out of the field. 17At three times in the year all
your males will appear before the Sovereign LORD.
18“You must not offer the blood of my sacrifice with bread
containing yeast; the fat of my festal sacrifice must not remain
until morning. 19The first of the firstfruits of your soil you must
bring to the house of the LORD your God.
“You must not cook a young goat in its mother’s milk.

23:10–19 Every seventh year the land was to rest. They must not plow or sow it; what the earth produced of itself should be eaten and not laid up. This law seems to have been intended to teach dependence on providence and God’s faithfulness in sending the larger increase while they kept his appointments. It was also typical of the heavenly rest, when all earthly labors, cares, and interests shall cease forever. What a good Master do we serve, who has made it our duty to rejoice before him! Let us devote with pleasure to the service of God that portion of our time that he requires and count his sabbaths and ordinances to be a feast unto our souls. They were not to come empty-handed, so now we must not come to worship God empty-hearted; our souls must be filled with holy desires toward him and dedications of ourselves to him, for with such sacrifices God is well pleased.

MATTHEW HENRY (1662–1714)
COMMENTARY ON THE WHOLE BIBLE

THE ANGEL OF THE PRESENCE

[20]"I am going to send an angel before you to protect you as you
journey and to bring you into the place that I have prepared.
[21]Take heed because of him, and obey his voice; do not rebel
against him, for he will not pardon your transgressions, for
my Name is in him. [22]But if you diligently obey him and do all
that I command, then I will be an enemy to your enemies, and
I will be an adversary to your adversaries. [23]For my angel will
go before you and bring you to the Amorites, the Hittites, the
Perizzites, the Canaanites, the Hivites, and the Jebusites, and
I will destroy them completely.

[24]"You must not bow down to their gods; you must not serve
them or do according to their practices. Instead you must completely overthrow them and smash their standing stones to
pieces. [25]You must serve the LORD your God, and he will bless
your bread and your water, and I will remove sickness from
your midst. [26]No woman will miscarry her young or be barren
in your land. I will fulfill the number of your days.

[27]"I will send my terror before you, and I will alarm all the
people whom you encounter; I will make all your enemies turn
their backs to you. [28]I will send hornets before you that will
drive out the Hivite, the Canaanite, and the Hittite before you.
[29]I will not drive them out before you in one year, lest the land
become desolate and the wild animals multiply against you.
[30]Little by little I will drive them out before you, until you become fruitful and inherit the land. [31]I will set your boundaries
from the Red Sea to the Sea of the Philistines, and from the
desert to the River, for I will deliver the inhabitants of the land
into your hand, and you will drive them out before you.

[32]"You must make no covenant with them or with their gods.
[33]They must not live in your land, lest they make you sin against
me, for if you serve their gods, it will surely be a snare to you."

THE LORD RATIFIES THE COVENANT

24 But to Moses the LORD said, "Come up to the LORD, you
and Aaron, Nadab and Abihu, and seventy of the elders
of Israel, and worship from a distance. [2]Moses alone may come
near the LORD, but the others must not come near, nor may
the people go up with him."

[3]Moses came and told the people all the LORD's words and
all the decisions. All the people answered together, "We are
willing to do all the words that the LORD has said," [4]and Moses
wrote down all the words of the LORD. Early in the morning he
built an altar at the foot of the mountain and arranged twelve
standing stones—according to the twelve tribes of Israel. [5]He
sent young Israelite men, and they offered burnt offerings and
sacrificed young bulls for peace offerings to the LORD. [6]Moses
took half of the blood and put it in bowls, and half of the blood
he splashed on the altar. [7]He took the Book of the Covenant
and read it aloud to the people, and they said, "We are willing
to do and obey all that the LORD has spoken." [8]So Moses took
the blood and splashed it on the people and said, "This is the
blood of the covenant that the LORD has made with you in
accordance with all these words."

[9]Moses and Aaron, Nadab and Abihu, and the seventy elders
of Israel went up, [10]and they saw the God of Israel. Under his feet
there was something like a pavement made of sapphire, clear
like the sky itself. [11]But he did not lay a hand on the leaders of
the Israelites, so they saw God, and they ate and they drank.

24:1–18 Moses, of course, might be thought to have seen God with bodily eyes, if not only the Wisdom of God that is Christ but even the wisdom itself, which can be seen with the eyes of the flesh, or because it is written of the elders of Israel that "they saw the God of Israel" and "under his feet there was something like a pavement made of sapphire, clear like the sky itself" (Exod 24:10). We might therefore be led to imagine that the Word and the Wisdom of God, who extends from end to end mightily and orders all things sweetly, stood in his own substance within the space of an earthly place. As we have often declared, all these visible and tangible signs were displayed through a creature that has been made subject in order to signify the invisible and intelligible God, not only the Father but also the Son and the Holy Spirit, from whom are all things, through whom are all things, and in whom are all things.

AUGUSTINE (354–430)
ON THE TRINITY

12The LORD said to Moses, "Come up to me on the mountain and remain there, and I will give you the stone tablets with the law and the commandments that I have written, so that you may teach them." 13So Moses set out with Joshua his attendant, and Moses went up the mountain of God. 14He told the elders, "Wait for us in this place until we return to you. Here are Aaron and Hur with you. Whoever has any matters of dispute can approach them."

15Moses went up the mountain, and the cloud covered the mountain. 16The glory of the LORD resided on Mount Sinai, and the cloud covered it for six days. On the seventh day he called to Moses from within the cloud. 17Now the appearance of the glory of the LORD was like a devouring fire on the top of the mountain in plain view of the people. 18Moses went into the cloud when he went up the mountain, and Moses was on the mountain 40 days and 40 nights.

THE MATERIALS FOR THE TABERNACLE

25 The LORD spoke to Moses, 2"Tell the Israelites to take an offering for me; from every person motivated by a willing heart you are to receive my offering. 3This is the offering you are to accept from them: gold, silver, bronze, 4blue, purple, scarlet, fine linen, goats' hair, 5ram skins dyed red, fine leather, acacia wood, 6oil for the light, spices for the anointing oil and for fragrant incense, 7onyx stones, and other gems to be set in the ephod and in the breastpiece. 8Let them make for me a sanctuary, so that I may live among them. 9According to all that I am showing you—the pattern of the tabernacle and the pattern of all its furnishings—you must make it exactly so.

THE ARK OF THE TESTIMONY

10"They are to make an ark of acacia wood—its length is to be 45 inches, its width 27 inches, and its height 27 inches. 11You are to overlay it with pure gold—both inside and outside you must overlay it, and you are to make a surrounding border of gold over it. 12You are to cast four gold rings for it and put them on its four feet, with two rings on one side and two rings on the other side. 13You are to make poles of acacia wood, overlay them with gold, 14and put the poles into the rings at the sides of the ark in order to carry the ark with them. 15The poles must remain in the rings of the ark; they must not be removed from it. 16You are to put into the ark the testimony that I will give to you.

17"You are to make an atonement lid of pure gold; its length is to be 45 inches, and its width is to be 27 inches. 18You are to make two cherubim of gold; you are to make them of hammered metal on the two ends of the atonement lid. 19Make one cherub on one end and one cherub on the other end; from the atonement lid you are to make the cherubim on the two ends. 20The cherubim are to be spreading their wings upward, overshadowing the atonement lid with their wings, and the cherubim are to face each other, looking toward the atonement lid. 21You are to put the atonement lid on top of the ark, and in the ark you are to put the testimony I am giving you. 22I will meet with you there, and from above the atonement lid, from between the two cherubim that are over the ark of the testimony, I will speak with you about all that I will command you for the Israelites.

THE TABLE FOR THE BREAD OF THE PRESENCE

23"You are to make a table of acacia wood; its length is to be 36 inches, its width 18 inches, and its height 27 inches.

25:10–22 The ark was united to the Godhead; it had the cloud of glory over it and upon it, which was the symbol of God's immediate presence. The ark was the throne of God and where he was present in a higher manner than he was in any other place. The ark contained the precious treasure of the law of God and the pot of manna, the one signifying divine holiness, of which the law of God is an emanation and expression, and the other signifying divine happiness, for manna was spiritual and heavenly bread or food. But food is the common figure in scripture to represent happiness, delight, and satisfaction; or in one word, those two things that were contained in this cabinet signified the Holy Spirit, which is the same with the divine good or fullness of God, his infinite holiness and joy.

JONATHAN EDWARDS
(1703–1758)
THE COMPLETE WORKS

24You are to overlay it with pure gold, and you are to make
a surrounding border of gold for it. 25You are to make a surrounding frame for it about three inches broad, and you are to
make a surrounding border of gold for its frame. 26You are to
make four rings of gold for it and attach the rings at the four
corners where its four legs are. 27The rings are to be close to
the frame to provide places for the poles to carry the table.
28You are to make the poles of acacia wood and overlay them
with gold, so that the table may be carried with them. 29You
are to make its plates, its ladles, its pitchers, and its bowls,
to be used in pouring out offerings; you are to make them of
pure gold. 30You are to set the Bread of the Presence on the
table before me continually.

THE LAMPSTAND

31"You are to make a lampstand of pure gold. The lampstand
is to be made of hammered metal; its base and its shaft, its
cups, its buds, and its blossoms are to be from the same piece.
32Six branches are to extend from the sides of the lampstand,
three branches of the lampstand from one side of it and three
branches of the lampstand from the other side of it. 33Three
cups shaped like almond flowers with buds and blossoms are to
be on one branch, and three cups shaped like almond flowers
with buds and blossoms are to be on the next branch, and the
same for the six branches extending from the lampstand. 34On
the lampstand there are to be four cups shaped like almond
flowers with buds and blossoms, 35with a bud under the first
two branches from it, and a bud under the next two branches
from it, and a bud under the third two branches from it, according to the six branches that extend from the lampstand.
36Their buds and their branches will be one piece, all of it one
hammered piece of pure gold.

37"You are to make its seven lamps and then set its lamps
up on it, so that it will give light to the area in front of it. 38Its
trimmers and its trays are to be of pure gold. 39About 75 pounds
of pure gold is to be used for it and for all these utensils. 40Now
be sure to make them according to the pattern you were shown
on the mountain.

THE TABERNACLE

26 "The tabernacle itself you are to make with ten curtains
of fine twisted linen and blue and purple and scarlet; you
are to make them with cherubim that are the work of an artistic
designer. 2The length of each curtain is to be 42 feet, and the
width of each curtain is to be 6 feet—the same size for each of
the curtains. 3Five curtains are to be joined, one to another,
and the other five curtains are to be joined, one to another.
4You are to make loops of blue material along the edge of the
end curtain in one set, and in the same way you are to make
loops in the outer edge of the end curtain in the second set.
5You are to make 50 loops on the one curtain, and you are to
make 50 loops on the end curtain which is on the second set,
so that the loops are opposite one to another. 6You are to make
50 gold clasps and join the curtains together with the clasps,
so that the tabernacle is a unit.

7"You are to make curtains of goats' hair for a tent over the
tabernacle; you are to make eleven curtains. 8The length of
each curtain is to be 45 feet, and the width of each curtain is
to be 6 feet—the same size for the eleven curtains. 9You are to

26:1–37 The veils are here ordered to be made, one for a partition between the Holy Place and the Most Holy Place, which not only forbade any to enter but so much as to look into the holiest of all. Under that dispensation divine grace was veiled, but now we behold it with open face. The apostle tells us this veil intimated that the ceremonial law could not make the comers thereunto perfect. The way into the holiest was not made manifest while the first tabernacle was standing; life and immortality lay concealed till they were brought to light by the gospel, which was therefore signified by the rending of this veil at the death of Christ. We have now boldness to enter into the holiest in all acts of devotion by the blood of Jesus, yet such as obliges us to a holy reverence and a humble sense of our distance.

JOHN WESLEY (1703–1791)
EXPLANATORY NOTES ON THE BIBLE

join five curtains by themselves and six curtains by themselves. You are to double over the sixth curtain at the front of the tent. [10]You are to make 50 loops along the edge of the end curtain in one set and 50 loops along the edge of the curtain that joins the second set. [11]You are to make 50 bronze clasps and put the clasps into the loops and join the tent together so that it is a unit. [12]Now the part that remains of the curtains of the tent—the half curtain that remains will hang over at the back of the tabernacle. [13]The foot and a half on the one side and the foot and a half on the other side of what remains in the length of the curtains of the tent will hang over the sides of the tabernacle, on one side and the other side, to cover it.

[14]"You are to make a covering for the tent out of ram skins dyed red and over that a covering of fine leather.

[15]"You are to make the frames for the tabernacle out of acacia wood as uprights. [16]Each frame is to be 15 feet long, and each frame is to be 27 inches wide, [17]with two projections per frame parallel one to another. You are to make all the frames of the tabernacle in this way. [18]So you are to make the frames for the tabernacle: 20 frames for the south side, [19]and you are to make 40 silver bases to go under the 20 frames—two bases under the first frame for its two projections, and likewise two bases under the next frame for its two projections; [20]and for the second side of the tabernacle, the north side, 20 frames, [21]and their 40 silver bases, two bases under the first frame, and two bases under the next frame. [22]And for the back of the tabernacle on the west you will make six frames. [23]You are to make two frames for the corners of the tabernacle on the back. [24]At the two corners they must be doubled at the lower end and finished together at the top in one ring. So it will be for both. [25]So there are to be eight frames and their silver bases, sixteen bases, two bases under the first frame, and two bases under the next frame.

[26]"You are to make bars of acacia wood, five for the frames on one side of the tabernacle, [27]and five bars for the frames on the second side of the tabernacle, and five bars for the frames on the back of the tabernacle on the west. [28]The middle bar in the center of the frames will reach from end to end. [29]You are to overlay the frames with gold and make their rings of gold to provide places for the bars, and you are to overlay the bars with gold. [30]You are to set up the tabernacle according to the plan that you were shown on the mountain.

[31]"You are to make a special curtain of blue, purple, and scarlet yarn and fine twisted linen; it is to be made with cherubim, the work of an artistic designer. [32]You are to hang it with gold hooks on four posts of acacia wood overlaid with gold, set in four silver bases. [33]You are to hang this curtain under the clasps and bring the ark of the testimony in there behind the curtain. The curtain will make a division for you between the Holy Place and the Most Holy Place. [34]You are to put the atonement lid on the ark of the testimony in the Most Holy Place. [35]You are to put the table outside the curtain and the lampstand on the south side of the tabernacle, opposite the table, and you are to place the table on the north side.

[36]"You are to make a hanging for the entrance of the tent of blue, purple, and scarlet yarn and fine twisted linen, the work of an embroiderer. [37]You are to make for the hanging five posts of acacia wood and overlay them with gold, and their hooks will be gold, and you are to cast five bronze bases for them.

27:1–8 There were two altars in the temple that expressed the two covenants in the church. The first, the altar of burnt offerings, which was plated with bronze and was situated in front of the doors of the temple, was for the offering up of victims and sacrifices. It signified the fleshly minded worshipers of the old covenant. And then there was the altar of incense, which was covered with gold and set near the entrance of the Most Holy Place and was to burn fragrant gums on. This prefigured the interior and more perfect grace of the new covenant and its worshipers.

VENERABLE BEDE
(C. 672–735)
HOMILIES ON THE GOSPELS

THE ALTAR

27 "You are to make the altar of acacia wood, 7½ feet long, and
7½ feet wide; the altar is to be square, and its height is to
be 4½ feet. 2You are to make its four horns on its four corners;
its horns will be part of it, and you are to overlay it with bronze.
3You are to make its pots for the ashes, its shovels, its tossing
bowls, its meat hooks, and its fire pans—you are to make all its
utensils of bronze. 4You are to make a grating for it, a network
of bronze, and you are to make on the network four bronze
rings on its four corners. 5You are to put it under the ledge of
the altar below, so that the network will come halfway up the
altar. 6You are to make poles for the altar, poles of acacia wood,
and you are to overlay them with bronze. 7The poles are to be
put into the rings so that the poles will be on two sides of the
altar when carrying it. 8You are to make the altar hollow, out
of boards. Just as it was shown you on the mountain, so they
must make it.

THE COURTYARD

9"You are to make the courtyard of the tabernacle. For the south
side there are to be hangings for the courtyard of fine twisted
linen, 150 feet long for one side, 10with 20 posts and their 20
bronze bases, with the hooks of the posts and their bands of
silver. 11Likewise for its length on the north side, there are to
be hangings for 150 feet, with 20 posts and their 20 bronze
bases, with silver hooks and bands on the posts. 12The width of
the court on the west side is to be 75 feet with hangings, with
their 10 posts and their 10 bases. 13The width of the court on
the east side, toward the sunrise, is to be 75 feet. 14The hangings on one side of the gate are to be 22½ feet long, with their
three posts and their three bases. 15On the second side there
are to be hangings 22½ feet long, with their three posts and
their three bases. 16For the gate of the courtyard there is to be
a curtain of 30 feet, of blue, purple, and scarlet yarn and fine
twisted linen, the work of an embroiderer, with four posts and
their four bases. 17All the posts around the courtyard are to
have silver bands; their hooks are to be silver, and their bases
bronze. 18The length of the courtyard is to be 150 feet and the
width 75 feet, and the height of the fine twisted linen hangings
is to be 7½ feet, with their bronze bases. 19All the utensils of
the tabernacle used in all its service, all its tent pegs, and all the
tent pegs of the courtyard are to be made of bronze.

OFFERING THE OIL

20"You are to command the Israelites that they bring to you
pure oil of pressed olives for the light, so that the lamps will
burn regularly. 21In the tent of meeting outside the curtain
that is before the testimony, Aaron and his sons are to arrange
it from evening to morning before the LORD. This is to be a
lasting ordinance among the Israelites for generations to come.

THE CLOTHING OF THE PRIESTS

28 "And you, bring near to you your brother Aaron and his
sons with him from among the Israelites, so that they may
minister as my priests—Aaron, Nadab and Abihu, Eleazar and
Ithamar, Aaron's sons. 2You must make holy garments for your
brother Aaron, for glory and for beauty. 3You are to speak to all
who are specially skilled, whom I have filled with the spirit of
wisdom, so that they may make Aaron's garments to set him

apart to minister as my priest. 4Now these are the garments
that they are to make: a breastpiece, an ephod, a robe, a fitted
tunic, a turban, and a sash. They are to make holy garments for
your brother Aaron and for his sons, that they may minister
as my priests. 5The artisans are to use the gold, blue, purple,
scarlet, and fine linen.
6"They are to make the ephod of gold, blue, purple, scarlet,
and fine twisted linen, the work of an artistic designer. 7It is to
have two shoulder pieces attached to two of its corners, so it
can be joined together. 8The artistically woven waistband of the
ephod that is on it is to be like it, of one piece with the ephod,
of gold, blue, purple, scarlet, and fine twisted linen.
9"You are to take two onyx stones and engrave on them the
names of the sons of Israel, 10six of their names on one stone,
and the six remaining names on the second stone, according
to the order of their birth. 11You are to engrave the two stones
with the names of the sons of Israel with the work of an engrav-
er in stone, like the engravings of a seal; you are to have them
set in gold filigree settings. 12You are to put the two stones on
the shoulders of the ephod, stones of memorial for the sons
of Israel, and Aaron will bear their names before the LORD on
his two shoulders for a memorial. 13You are to make filigree
settings of gold 14and two braided chains of pure gold, like a
cord, and attach the chains to the settings.
15"You are to make a breastpiece for use in making decisions, the work of an artistic designer; you are to make it in
the same fashion as the ephod; you are to make it of gold, blue,
purple, scarlet, and fine twisted linen. 16It is to be square when
doubled, nine inches long and nine inches wide. 17You are to
set in it a setting for stones, four rows of stones, a row with a
ruby, a topaz, and a beryl—the first row; 18and the second row,
a turquoise, a sapphire, and an emerald; 19and the third row,
a jacinth, an agate, and an amethyst; 20and the fourth row, a
chrysolite, an onyx, and a jasper. They are to be enclosed in gold
in their filigree settings. 21The stones are to be for the names
of the sons of Israel, twelve, according to the number of their
names. Each name according to the twelve tribes is to be like
the engravings of a seal.
22"You are to make for the breastpiece braided chains like
cords of pure gold, 23and you are to make for the breastpiece
two gold rings and attach the two rings to the upper two ends
of the breastpiece. 24You are to attach the two gold chains to
the two rings at the ends of the breastpiece; 25the other two
ends of the two chains you will attach to the two settings and
then attach them to the shoulder pieces of the ephod at the
front of it. 26You are to make two rings of gold and put them
on the other two ends of the breastpiece, on its edge that is
on the inner side of the ephod. 27You are to make two more
gold rings and attach them to the bottom of the two shoulder
pieces on the front of the ephod, close to the juncture above the
waistband of the ephod. 28They are to tie the breastpiece by its
rings to the rings of the ephod by blue cord, so that it may be
above the waistband of the ephod, and so that the breastpiece
will not be loose from the ephod. 29Aaron will bear the names
of the sons of Israel in the breastpiece of decision over his heart
when he goes into the Holy Place, for a memorial before the
LORD continually.
30"You are to put the Urim and the Thummim into the breastpiece of decision; and they are to be over Aaron's heart when he

28:1–30 It is rightly enjoined that the humeral veil be made of gold, hyacinth, purple, scarlet twice dyed, and fine-twisted linen so that it may be evident with what variety of virtues the priest should be conspicuous. Thus in the vesture of the priest the gold is resplendent beyond all else; so should he especially shine beyond all others in the understanding of wisdom. Now to gold, blue, and purple is added twice-dyed scarlet to signify that in the eyes of the Judge of the heart all that is good in virtues must be adorned with charity. Moreover, because this charity embraces both God and neighbor, its radiance is of a double hue. He therefore who sighs for the beauty of his Maker but neglects the care of his neighbor, or who so compasses the care of the neighbor as to grow listless in divine love, in neglecting either of these does not know what it means to have twice-dyed scarlet in the adornment of the humeral.

GREGORY THE GREAT
(C. 540–604)
PASTORAL CARE

goes in before the LORD. Aaron is to bear the decisions of the
Israelites over his heart before the LORD continually.
31“You are to make the robe of the ephod completely blue.
32There is to be an opening in its top in the center of it, with
an edge all around the opening, the work of a weaver, like the
opening of a collar, so that it cannot be torn. 33You are to make
pomegranates of blue, purple, and scarlet all around its hem
and bells of gold between them all around. 34The pattern is to
be a gold bell and a pomegranate, a gold bell and a pomegranate,
all around the hem of the robe. 35The robe is to be on Aaron
as he ministers, and his sound will be heard when he enters
the Holy Place before the LORD and when he leaves, so that
he does not die.
36“You are to make a plate of pure gold and engrave on it
the way a seal is engraved: ‘Holiness to the LORD.’ 37You are to
attach to it a blue cord so that it will be on the turban; it is to
be on the front of the turban. 38It will be on Aaron’s forehead,
and Aaron will bear the iniquity of the holy things, which the
Israelites are to sanctify by all their holy gifts; it will always be
on his forehead, for their acceptance before the LORD. 39You
are to weave the tunic of fine linen and make the turban of fine
linen, and make the sash the work of an embroiderer.
40“For Aaron’s sons you are to make tunics, sashes, and headbands for glory and for beauty.
41“You are to clothe them—your brother Aaron and his sons
with him—and anoint them and ordain them and set them apart
as holy, so that they may minister as my priests. 42Make for them
linen undergarments to cover their naked bodies; they must
cover from the waist to the thighs. 43These must be on Aaron
and his sons when they enter the tent of meeting, or when they
approach the altar to minister in the Holy Place, so that they
bear no iniquity and die. It is to be a perpetual ordinance for
him and for his descendants after him.

THE CONSECRATION OF AARON AND HIS SONS

29 “Now this is what you are to do for them to consecrate
them so that they may minister as my priests. Take a
young bull and two rams without blemish; 2and bread made
without yeast, and perforated cakes without yeast mixed with
oil, and wafers without yeast spread with oil—you are to make
them using fine wheat flour. 3You are to put them in one basket
and present them in the basket, along with the bull and the
two rams.
4“You are to present Aaron and his sons at the entrance of
the tent of meeting. You are to wash them with water 5and take
the garments and clothe Aaron with the tunic, the robe of the
ephod, the ephod, and the breastpiece; you are to fasten the
ephod on him by using the skillfully woven waistband. 6You
are to put the turban on his head and put the holy diadem
on the turban. 7You are to take the anointing oil and pour it
on his head and anoint him. 8You are to present his sons and
clothe them with tunics 9and wrap the sashes around Aaron
and his sons and put headbands on them, and so the ministry
of priesthood will belong to them by a perpetual ordinance.
Thus you are to consecrate Aaron and his sons.
10“You are to present the bull at the front of the tent of meeting, and Aaron and his sons are to put their hands on the head
of the bull. 11You are to kill the bull before the LORD at the
entrance to the tent of meeting 12and take some of the blood

29:1–46 Aaron and his sons were to be set apart for the priest’s office with ceremony and solemnity. All believers are spiritual priests to offer spiritual sacrifices (1 Pet 2:5), washed in the blood of Christ, and so made to our God priests (Rev 1:5–6). They also are clothed with the beauty of holiness and have received the anointing (1 John 2:27). The Spirit of God is called the finger of God (Luke 11:20), and by him the merit of Christ is applied to our souls. This consecration signifies the admission of a sinner into the spiritual priesthood to offer spiritual sacrifices acceptable to God through Jesus Christ.

MATTHEW HENRY (1662–1714)
COMMENTARY ON THE WHOLE BIBLE

of the bull and put it on the horns of the altar with your finger;
all the rest of the blood you are to pour out at the base of the
altar. 13You are to take all the fat that covers the entrails, and
the lobe that is above the liver, and the two kidneys and the fat
that is on them, and burn them on the altar. 14But the meat of
the bull, its skin, and its dung you are to burn up outside the
camp. It is the purification offering.
15"You are to take one ram, and Aaron and his sons are to
lay their hands on the ram's head, 16and you are to kill the ram
and take its blood and splash it all around on the altar. 17Then
you are to cut the ram into pieces and wash the entrails and
its legs and put them on its pieces and on its head 18and burn
the whole ram on the altar. It is a burnt offering to the LORD,
a soothing aroma; it is an offering made by fire to the LORD.
19"You are to take the second ram, and Aaron and his sons
are to lay their hands on the ram's head, 20and you are to kill
the ram and take some of its blood and put it on the tip of the
right ear of Aaron, on the tip of the right ear of his sons, on
the thumb of their right hand, and on the big toe of their right
foot, and then splash the blood all around on the altar. 21You
are to take some of the blood that is on the altar and some of
the anointing oil and sprinkle it on Aaron, on his garments,
on his sons, and on his sons' garments with him, so that he
may be holy, he and his garments along with his sons and his
sons' garments.
22"You are to take from the ram the fat, the fat tail, the fat
that covers the entrails, the lobe of the liver, the two kidneys
and the fat that is on them, and the right thigh—for it is the
ram for consecration—23and one round flat cake of bread, one
perforated cake of oiled bread, and one wafer from the basket
of bread made without yeast that is before the LORD. 24You
are to put all these in Aaron's hands and in his sons' hands,
and you are to wave them as a wave offering before the LORD.
25Then you are to take them from their hands and burn them
on the altar for a burnt offering, for a soothing aroma before
the LORD. It is an offering made by fire to the LORD. 26You are
to take the breast of the ram of Aaron's consecration; you are
to wave it as a wave offering before the LORD, and it is to be
your share. 27You are to sanctify the breast of the wave offering
and the thigh of the contribution, which were waved and lifted
up as a contribution from the ram of consecration, from what
belongs to Aaron and to his sons. 28It is to belong to Aaron and
to his sons from the Israelites, by a perpetual ordinance, for it
is a contribution. It is to be a contribution from the Israelites
from their peace offerings, their contribution to the LORD.
29"The holy garments that belong to Aaron are to belong to
his sons after him, so that they may be anointed in them and
consecrated in them. 30The priest who succeeds him from his
sons, when he first comes to the tent of meeting to minister
in the Holy Place, is to wear them for seven days.
31"You are to take the ram of the consecration and cook its
meat in a holy place. 32Aaron and his sons are to eat the meat
of the ram and the bread that was in the basket at the entrance
of the tent of meeting. 33They are to eat those things by which
atonement was made to consecrate and to set them apart, but
no one else may eat them, for they are holy. 34If any of the meat
from the consecration offerings or any of the bread is left over
until morning, then you are to burn up what is left over. It must
not be eaten, because it is holy.

35"Thus you are to do for Aaron and for his sons according to all that I have commanded you; you are to consecrate them for seven days. 36Every day you are to prepare a bull for a purification offering for atonement. You are to purify the altar by making atonement for it, and you are to anoint it to set it apart as holy. 37For seven days you are to make atonement for the altar and set it apart as holy. Then the altar will be most holy. Anything that touches the altar will be holy.

38"Now this is what you are to prepare on the altar every day continually: two lambs a year old. 39The first lamb you are to prepare in the morning, and the second lamb you are to prepare around sundown. 40With the first lamb offer a tenth of an ephah of fine flour mixed with a fourth of a hin of oil from pressed olives, and a fourth of a hin of wine as a drink offering. 41The second lamb you are to offer around sundown; you are to prepare for it the same meal offering as for the morning and the same drink offering, for a soothing aroma, an offering made by fire to the LORD.

42"This will be a regular burnt offering throughout your generations at the entrance of the tent of meeting before the LORD, where I will meet with you to speak to you there. 43There I will meet with the Israelites, and it will be set apart as holy by my glory.

44"So I will set apart as holy the tent of meeting and the altar, and I will set apart as holy Aaron and his sons that they may minister as priests to me. 45I will reside among the Israelites, and I will be their God, 46and they will know that I am the LORD their God, who brought them out from the land of Egypt, so that I may reside among them. I am the LORD their God.

THE ALTAR OF INCENSE

30 "You are to make an altar for burning incense; you are to make it of acacia wood. 2Its length is to be 18 inches and its width 18 inches; it will be square. Its height is to be 36 inches, with its horns of one piece with it. 3You are to overlay it with pure gold—its top, its four walls, and its horns—and make a surrounding border of gold for it. 4You are to make two gold rings for it under its border, on its two flanks; you are to make them on its two sides. The rings will be places for poles to carry it with. 5You are to make the poles of acacia wood and overlay them with gold.

6"You are to put it in front of the curtain that is before the ark of the testimony (before the atonement lid that is over the testimony), where I will meet you. 7Aaron is to burn sweet incense on it morning by morning; when he attends to the lamps he is to burn incense. 8When Aaron sets up the lamps around sundown he is to burn incense on it; it is to be a regular incense offering before the LORD throughout your generations. 9You must not offer strange incense on it, nor burnt offering, nor meal offering, and you must not pour out a drink offering on it. 10Aaron is to make atonement on its horns once in the year with some of the blood of the sin offering for atonement; once in the year he is to make atonement on it throughout your generations. It is most holy to the LORD."

30:1–10 If I should consider how the true high priest, my Lord Jesus Christ, having indeed been placed in the flesh was with the people all year, that year about which he himself said, "He has anointed me to proclaim good news to the poor . . . to proclaim the year of the Lord's favor" (Luke 4:18–19), I perceive how "once" in this "year" on the Day of Atonement he enters into the Most Holy Place, that is, when with his dispensation fulfilled he penetrates the heavens and goes to the Father to make atonement for the human race and prays for all those who believe in him. Therefore the Day of Atonement remains for us until the sun sets, that is, until the world comes to an end.

ORIGEN (C. 185–C. 253)
HOMILIES ON LEVITICUS

THE RANSOM MONEY

11The LORD spoke to Moses, 12"When you take a census of the Israelites according to their number, then each man is to pay a ransom for his life to the LORD when you number them, so that there will be no plague among them when you number them. 13Everyone who crosses over to those who are numbered is to pay this: a half shekel according to the shekel of the sanctuary (a shekel weighs 20 gerahs). The half shekel is to be an offering to the LORD. 14 Everyone who crosses over to those numbered, from twenty years old and up, is to pay an offering to the LORD. 15 The rich are not to pay more and the poor are not to pay less than the half shekel when giving the offering of the LORD, to make atonement for your lives. 16 You are to receive the atonement money from the Israelites and give it for the service of the tent of meeting. It will be a memorial for the Israelites before the LORD, to make atonement for your lives."

THE BRONZE LAVER

17 The LORD spoke to Moses, 18 "You are also to make a large bronze basin with a bronze stand for washing. You are to put it between the tent of meeting and the altar and put water in it, 19 and Aaron and his sons must wash their hands and their feet from it. 20 When they enter the tent of meeting, they must wash with water so that they do not die. Also, when they approach the altar to minister by burning incense as an offering made by fire to the LORD, 21 they must wash their hands and their feet so that they do not die. And this will be a perpetual ordinance for them and for their descendants throughout their generations."

OIL AND INCENSE

22 The LORD spoke to Moses, 23 "Take choice spices: 12½ pounds of free-flowing myrrh, half that—about 6¼ pounds—of sweet-smelling cinnamon, 6¼ pounds of sweet-smelling cane, 24 and 12½ pounds of cassia, all weighed according to the sanctuary shekel, and four quarts of olive oil. 25 You are to make this into a sacred anointing oil, a perfumed compound, the work of a perfumer. It will be sacred anointing oil.

26 "With it you are to anoint the tent of meeting, the ark of the testimony, 27 the table and all its utensils, the lampstand and its utensils, the altar of incense, 28 the altar for the burnt offering and all its utensils, and the laver and its base. 29 So you are to sanctify them, and they will be most holy; anything that touches them will be holy.

30 "You are to anoint Aaron and his sons and sanctify them so that they may minister as my priests. 31 And you are to tell the Israelites: 'This is to be my sacred anointing oil throughout your generations. 32 It must not be applied to people's bodies, and you must not make any like it with the same recipe. It is holy, and it must be holy to you. 33 Whoever makes perfume like it and whoever puts any of it on someone not a priest will be cut off from his people.'"

34 The LORD said to Moses, "Take spices, gum resin, onycha, galbanum, and pure frankincense of equal amounts 35 and make it into an incense, a perfume, the work of a perfumer. It is to be finely ground, and pure and sacred. 36 You are to beat some of it very fine and put some of it before the ark of the testimony in the tent of meeting where I will meet with you; it is to be most holy to you. 37 And the incense that you are to make, you must not make for yourselves using the same recipe; it is to be most holy to you, belonging to the LORD. 38 Whoever makes anything like it, to use as perfume, will be cut off from his people."

WILLING ARTISANS

31 The LORD spoke to Moses, 2 "See, I have chosen Bezalel son of Uri, the son of Hur, of the tribe of Judah, 3 and I have filled him with the Spirit of God in skill, in understanding,

31:1–11 To be chosen is equivalent to rendering eminent so that Moses signifies that Bezalel should be something extraordinary as being endowed with a peculiar gift. Still, although the call of Bezalel was special because God entrusted to him an unusual and by no means ordinary work, we gather that no one excels even in the most despised and humble handicraft except insofar as God's Spirit works in him. For although "there are different gifts" (1 Cor 12:4), still it is the same Spirit from whom they all flow and also as God has seen fit to distribute and measure them out to every person.

JOHN CALVIN (1509–1564)
COMPLETE COMMENTARY ON THE BIBLE

in knowledge, and in all kinds of craftsmanship, [4]to make artistic designs for work with gold, with silver, and with bronze, [5]and with cutting and setting stone, and with cutting wood, to work in all kinds of craftsmanship. [6]Moreover, I have also given him Oholiab son of Ahisamach, of the tribe of Dan, and I have given ability to all the specially skilled, that they may make everything I have commanded you: [7]the tent of meeting, the ark of the testimony, the atonement lid that is on it, all the furnishings of the tent, [8]the table with its utensils, the pure lampstand with all its utensils, the altar of incense, [9]the altar for the burnt offering with all its utensils, the large basin with its base, [10]the woven garments, the holy garments for Aaron the priest and the garments for his sons, to minister as priests, [11]the anointing oil, and sweet incense for the Holy Place. They will make all these things just as I have commanded you."

SABBATH OBSERVANCE

[12]The LORD said to Moses, [13]"Tell the Israelites, 'Surely you must keep my Sabbaths, for it is a sign between me and you throughout your generations, that you may know that I am the LORD who sanctifies you. [14]So you must keep the Sabbath, for it is holy for you. Everyone who defiles it must surely be put to death; indeed, if anyone does any work on it, then that person will be cut off from among his people. [15]Six days work may be done, but on the seventh day is a Sabbath of complete rest, holy to the LORD; anyone who does work on the Sabbath day must surely be put to death. [16]The Israelites must keep the Sabbath by observing the Sabbath throughout their generations as a perpetual covenant. [17]It is a sign between me and the Israelites forever; for in six days the LORD made the heavens and the earth, and on the seventh day he rested and was refreshed.'"

[18]He gave Moses two tablets of testimony when he had finished speaking with him on Mount Sinai, tablets of stone written by the finger of God.

32:1–35 When Moses went up into the mount and abode there, with fasting and humiliation, 40 days and 40 nights, the Lord said unto him, *Moses, Moses, get down quickly, for your people whom you brought out of the land of Egypt have committed iniquity.* And the Lord said unto him, *I have seen this people, and behold, it is a stiff-necked people. Let me destroy them and blot out their name from under heaven.* But Moses said, *Far be it from you, Lord! Pardon the sin of this people; else blot me also out of the book of the living.* O marvelous love! O insuperable perfection! The servant speaks freely to his Lord and asks forgiveness for the people or begs that he himself might perish along with them.

CLEMENT OF ROME **(D. 99)**
FIRST CLEMENT

THE SIN OF THE GOLDEN CALF

32 When the people saw that Moses delayed in coming down from the mountain, they gathered around Aaron and said to him, "Get up, make us gods that will go before us. As for this fellow Moses, the man who brought us up from the land of Egypt, we do not know what has become of him!"

[2]So Aaron said to them, "Break off the gold earrings that are on the ears of your wives, your sons, and your daughters, and bring them to me." [3]So all the people broke off the gold earrings that were on their ears and brought them to Aaron. [4]He accepted the gold from them, fashioned it with an engraving tool, and made a molten calf. Then they said, "These are your gods, O Israel, who brought you up out of Egypt."

[5]When Aaron saw this, he built an altar before it, and Aaron made a proclamation and said, "Tomorrow will be a feast to the LORD." [6]So they got up early on the next day and offered up burnt offerings and brought peace offerings, and the people sat down to eat and drink, and they rose up to play.

[7]The LORD spoke to Moses, "Go quickly, descend, because your people, whom you brought up from the land of Egypt, have acted corruptly. [8]They have quickly turned aside from the way that I commanded them—they have made for themselves a molten calf and have bowed down to it and sacrificed to it

and said, 'These are your gods, O Israel, which brought you up
from the land of Egypt.'"
9Then the LORD said to Moses, "I have seen this people. Look
what a stiff-necked people they are! 10So now, leave me alone so
that my anger can burn against them and I can destroy them,
and I will make from you a great nation."
11But Moses sought the favor of the LORD his God and said,
"O LORD, why does your anger burn against your people, whom
you have brought out from the land of Egypt with great power and
with a mighty hand? 12Why should the Egyptians say, 'For evil he
led them out to kill them in the mountains and to destroy them
from the face of the earth'? Turn from your burning anger, and
relent of this evil against your people. 13Remember Abraham,
Isaac, and Israel your servants, to whom you swore by yourself
and told them, 'I will multiply your descendants like the stars of
heaven, and all this land that I have spoken about I will give to your
descendants, and they will inherit it forever.'" 14Then the LORD
relented over the evil that he had said he would do to his people.
15Moses turned and went down from the mountain with
the two tablets of the testimony in his hands. The tablets were
written on both sides—they were written on the front and on
the back. 16Now the tablets were the work of God, and the writing was the writing of God, engraved on the tablets. 17When
Joshua heard the noise of the people as they shouted, he said
to Moses, "It is the sound of war in the camp!" 18Moses said,
"It is not the sound of those who shout for victory, nor is it the
sound of those who cry because they are overcome, but the
sound of singing I hear."
19When he approached the camp and saw the calf and the
dancing, Moses became extremely angry. He threw the tablets
from his hands and broke them to pieces at the bottom of the
mountain. 20He took the calf they had made and burned it in
the fire, ground it to powder, poured it out on the water, and
made the Israelites drink it.
21Moses said to Aaron, "What did this people do to you, that
you have brought on them so great a sin?" 22Aaron said, "Do
not let your anger burn hot, my lord; you know these people,
that they tend to evil. 23They said to me, 'Make us gods that
will go before us, for as for this fellow Moses, the man who
brought us up out of the land of Egypt, we do not know what
has happened to him.' 24So I said to them, 'Whoever has gold,
break it off.' So they gave it to me, and I threw it into the fire,
and this calf came out."
25Moses saw that the people were running wild, for Aaron
had let them get completely out of control, causing derision
from their enemies. 26So Moses stood at the entrance of the
camp and said, "Whoever is for the LORD, come to me." All the
Levites gathered around him, 27and he said to them, "This is
what the LORD, the God of Israel, has said 'Each man fasten
his sword on his side, and go back and forth from entrance to
entrance throughout the camp, and each one kill his brother,
his friend, and his neighbor.'"
28The Levites did what Moses ordered, and that day about
3,000 men of the people died. 29Moses said, "You have been consecrated today for the LORD, for each of you was against his son
or against his brother, so he has given a blessing to you today."
30The next day Moses said to the people, "You have committed a very serious sin, but now I will go up to the LORD—perhaps
I can make atonement on behalf of your sin."

31 So Moses returned to the LORD and said, "Alas, this people has committed a very serious sin, and they have made for themselves gods of gold. 32 But now, if you will forgive their sin..., but if not, wipe me out from your book that you have written."
33 The LORD said to Moses, "Whoever has sinned against me—that person I will wipe out of my book. 34 So now go, lead the people to the place I have spoken to you about. See, my angel will go before you. But on the day that I punish, I will indeed punish them for their sin."
35 And the LORD sent a plague on the people because they had made the calf—the one Aaron made.

33 The LORD said to Moses, "Go up from here, you and the people whom you brought up out of the land of Egypt, to the land I promised on oath to Abraham, to Isaac, and to Jacob, saying, 'I will give it to your descendants.' 2 I will send an angel before you, and I will drive out the Canaanite, the Amorite, the Hittite, the Perizzite, the Hivite, and the Jebusite. 3 Go up to a land flowing with milk and honey. But I will not go up among you, for you are a stiff-necked people, and I might destroy you on the way."
4 When the people heard this troubling word they mourned; no one put on his ornaments. 5 For the LORD had said to Moses, "Tell the Israelites, 'You are a stiff-necked people. If I went up among you for a moment, I might destroy you. Now take off your ornaments that I may know what I should do to you.'" 6 So the Israelites stripped off their ornaments by Mount Horeb.

THE PRESENCE OF THE LORD

7 Moses took the tent and pitched it outside the camp, at a good distance from the camp, and he called it the tent of meeting. Anyone seeking the LORD would go out to the tent of meeting that was outside the camp.
8 And when Moses went out to the tent, all the people would get up and stand at the entrance to their tents and watch Moses until he entered the tent. 9 And whenever Moses entered the tent, the pillar of cloud would descend and stand at the entrance of the tent, and the LORD would speak with Moses. 10 When all the people would see the pillar of cloud standing at the entrance of the tent, all the people, each one at the entrance of his own tent, would rise and worship. 11 The LORD would speak to Moses face to face, the way a person speaks to a friend. Then Moses would return to the camp, but his servant, Joshua son of Nun, a young man, did not leave the tent.
12 Moses said to the LORD, "See, you have been saying to me, 'Bring this people up,' but you have not let me know whom you will send with me. But you said, 'I know you by name, and also you have found favor in my sight.' 13 Now if I have found favor in your sight, show me your way, that I may know you, that I may continue to find favor in your sight. And see that this nation is your people."
14 And the LORD said, "My presence will go with you, and I will give you rest."
15 And Moses said to him, "If your presence does not go with us, do not take us up from here. 16 For how will it be known then that I have found favor in your sight, I and your people? Is it not by your going with us, so that we will be distinguished, I and your people, from all the people who are on the face of the earth?"
17 The LORD said to Moses, "I will do this thing also that you have requested, for you have found favor in my sight, and I know you by name."

33:12–23 Moses says to him, *Show me yourself.* You see that then also the prophets saw Christ in the measure each was able. *Show me yourself, that I may see you clearly.* But he said, *No one sees me and still lives.* How could anyone gaze upon the majesty of the Godhead? *It is a great thing that you desire, O Moses,* the Lord says, *and I approve your insatiable longing and I will do this thing for you, but according to your capacity. You will station yourself on a rock, for as you are small, you will lodge in a small place.*

CYRIL OF JERUSALEM
(C. 313–386)
CATECHETICAL LECTURES

18And Moses said, "Show me your glory."
19And the LORD said, "I will make all my goodness pass before your face, and I will proclaim the LORD by name before
you; I will be gracious to whom I will be gracious; I will show
mercy to whom I will show mercy." 20But he added, "You cannot see my face, for no one can see me and live." 21The LORD
said, "Here is a place by me; you will station yourself on a rock.
22When my glory passes by, I will put you in a cleft in the rock
and will cover you with my hand while I pass by. 23Then I will
take away my hand, and you will see my back, but my face
must not be seen."

THE NEW TABLETS OF THE COVENANT

34 The LORD said to Moses, "Cut out two tablets of stone like
the first, and I will write on the tablets the words that
were on the first tablets, which you smashed. 2Be prepared in
the morning, and go up in the morning to Mount Sinai, and
station yourself for me there on the top of the mountain. 3No
one is to come up with you; do not let anyone be seen anywhere
on the mountain; not even the flocks or the herds may graze in
front of that mountain." 4So Moses cut out two tablets of stone
like the first; early in the morning he went up to Mount Sinai,
just as the LORD had commanded him, and he took in his hand
the two tablets of stone.
5The LORD descended in the cloud and stood with him there
and proclaimed the LORD by name. 6The LORD passed by before
him and proclaimed: "The LORD, the LORD, the compassionate
and gracious God, slow to anger, and abounding in loyal love
and faithfulness, 7keeping loyal love for thousands, forgiving
iniquity and transgression and sin. But he by no means leaves
the guilty unpunished, responding to the transgression of fathers by dealing with children and children's children, to the
third and fourth generation."
8Moses quickly bowed to the ground and worshiped 9and
said, "If now I have found favor in your sight, O Lord, let my
Lord go among us, for we are a stiff-necked people; pardon our
iniquity and our sin, and take us for your inheritance."
10He said, "See, I am going to make a covenant before all
your people. I will do wonders such as have not been done in
all the earth, nor in any nation. All the people among whom
you live will see the work of the LORD, for it is a fearful thing
that I am doing with you.
11"Obey what I am commanding you this day. I am going to
drive out before you the Amorite, the Canaanite, the Hittite,
the Perizzite, the Hivite, and the Jebusite. 12Be careful not to
make a covenant with the inhabitants of the land where you
are going, lest it become a snare among you. 13Rather you must
destroy their altars, smash their images, and cut down their
Asherah poles. 14For you must not worship any other god, for
the LORD, whose name is Jealous, is a jealous God. 15Be careful
not to make a covenant with the inhabitants of the land, for
when they prostitute themselves to their gods and sacrifice
to their gods, and someone invites you, you will eat from his
sacrifice; 16and you then take his daughters for your sons, and
when his daughters prostitute themselves to their gods, they
will make your sons prostitute themselves to their gods as well.
17You must not make yourselves molten gods.
18"You must keep the Feast of Unleavened Bread. For seven
days you must eat bread made without yeast, as I commanded

34:19–20 God will take away the spiritual veil that covers the souls of his people that is between them and divine truths. It has allusion to Moses when he came from the mount; he had a veil, for the people could not behold him. He had a glory put upon his face that they could not look upon him with a direct eye. To this day, says he, when Moses is read, there is a veil put upon their hearts. Nevertheless, when they shall turn to the Lord, the veil shall be taken away.

RICHARD SIBBES (1577–1635)
THE GLORIOUS FEAST OF THE GOSPEL

you; do this at the appointed time of the month Abib, for in the month Abib you came out of Egypt.

19“Every firstborn of the womb belongs to me, even every firstborn of your cattle that is a male, whether ox or sheep. 20Now the firstling of a donkey you may redeem with a lamb, but if you do not redeem it, then break its neck. You must redeem all the firstborn of your sons.

“No one will appear before me empty-handed.

21“On six days you may labor, but on the seventh day you must rest; even at the time of plowing and of harvest you are to rest.

22“You must observe the Feast of Weeks—the firstfruits of the harvest of wheat—and the Feast of Ingathering at the end of the year. 23At three times in the year all your men must appear before the Sovereign LORD, the God of Israel. 24For I will drive out the nations before you and enlarge your borders; no one will covet your land when you go up to appear before the LORD your God three times in the year.

25“You must not offer the blood of my sacrifice with yeast; the sacrifice from the Feast of Passover must not remain until the following morning.

26“The first of the firstfruits of your soil you must bring to the house of the LORD your God.

“You must not cook a young goat in its mother's milk.”

27The LORD said to Moses, “Write down these words, for in accordance with these words I have made a covenant with you and with Israel.” 28So he was there with the LORD 40 days and 40 nights; he did not eat bread, and he did not drink water. He wrote on the tablets the words of the covenant, the Ten Commandments.

THE RADIANT FACE OF MOSES

29Now when Moses came down from Mount Sinai with the two tablets of the testimony in his hand—when he came down from the mountain, Moses did not know that the skin of his face shone while he talked with him. 30When Aaron and all the Israelites saw Moses, the skin of his face shone, and they were afraid to approach him. 31But Moses called to them, so Aaron and all the leaders of the community came back to him, and Moses spoke to them. 32After this all the Israelites approached, and he commanded them all that the LORD had spoken to him on Mount Sinai. 33When Moses finished speaking with them, he would put a veil on his face. 34But when Moses went in before the LORD to speak with him, he would remove the veil until he came out. Then he would come out and tell the Israelites what he had been commanded. 35When the Israelites would see the face of Moses, that the skin of Moses' face shone, Moses would put the veil on his face again, until he went in to speak with the LORD.

SABBATH REGULATIONS

35 Moses assembled the whole community of the Israelites and said to them, “These are the things that the LORD has commanded you to do. 2In six days work may be done, but on the seventh day there must be a holy day for you, a Sabbath of complete rest to the LORD. Anyone who does work on it will be put to death. 3You must not kindle a fire in any of your homes on the Sabbath day.”

WILLING WORKERS

4Moses spoke to the whole community of the Israelites, “This is the word that the LORD has commanded: 5‘Take an offering for

the LORD. Let everyone who has a willing heart bring an offering
to the LORD: gold, silver, bronze; [6]blue, purple, and scarlet yarn;
fine linen; goats' hair; [7]ram skins dyed red; fine leather; acacia
wood; [8]olive oil for the light; spices for the anointing oil and for
the fragrant incense; [9]onyx stones, and other gems for mounting on the ephod and the breastpiece. [10]Every skilled person
among you is to come and make all that the LORD has commanded: [11]the tabernacle with its tent, its covering, its clasps,
its frames, its crossbars, its posts, and its bases; [12]the ark, with its
poles, the atonement lid, and the special curtain that conceals
it; [13]the table with its poles and all its vessels, and the Bread of
the Presence; [14]the lampstand for the light and its accessories,
its lamps, and oil for the light; [15]and the altar of incense with its
poles, the anointing oil, and the fragrant incense; the hanging
for the door at the entrance of the tabernacle; [16]the altar for the
burnt offering with its bronze grating that is on it, its poles, and
all its utensils; the large basin and its pedestal; [17]the hangings
of the courtyard, its posts and its bases, and the curtain for the
gateway to the courtyard; [18]tent pegs for the tabernacle and tent
pegs for the courtyard and their ropes; [19]the woven garments
for serving in the Holy Place, the holy garments for Aaron the
priest, and the garments for his sons to minister as priests.'"

[20]So the whole community of the Israelites went out from
the presence of Moses. [21]Everyone whose heart stirred him
to action and everyone whose spirit was willing came and
brought the offering for the LORD for the work of the tent of
meeting, for all its service, and for the holy garments. [22]They
came, men and women alike, all who had willing hearts. They
brought brooches, earrings, rings and ornaments, all kinds of
gold jewelry, and everyone came who waved a wave offering
of gold to the LORD.

[23]Everyone who had blue, purple, or scarlet yarn, fine linen,
goats' hair, ram skins dyed red, or fine leather brought them.
[24]Everyone making an offering of silver or bronze brought it
as an offering to the LORD, and everyone who had acacia wood
for any work of the service brought it. [25]Every woman who was
skilled spun with her hands and brought what she had spun,
blue, purple, or scarlet yarn, or fine linen, [26]and all the women
whose heart stirred them to action and who were skilled spun
goats' hair.

[27]The leaders brought onyx stones and other gems to be
mounted for the ephod and the breastpiece, [28]and spices and
olive oil for the light, for the anointing oil, and for the fragrant
incense.

[29]The Israelites brought a freewill offering to the LORD, every
man and woman whose heart was willing to bring materials for
all the work that the LORD through Moses had commanded
them to do.

[30]Moses said to the Israelites, "See, the LORD has chosen
Bezalel son of Uri, the son of Hur, of the tribe of Judah. [31]He
has filled him with the Spirit of God—with skill, with understanding, with knowledge, and in all kinds of work—[32]to design
artistic designs, to work in gold, in silver, and in bronze, [33]and in
cutting stones for their setting, and in cutting wood, to do work
in every artistic craft. [34]And he has put it in his heart to teach,
he and Oholiab son of Ahisamach, of the tribe of Dan. [35]He
has filled them with skill to do all kinds of work as craftsmen,
as designers, as embroiderers in blue, purple, and scarlet yarn
and in fine linen, and as weavers. They are craftsmen in all the

35:20–29 What they did they did cheerfully. They were willing, and it was not any external inducement that made them so, but their spirits. It was from a principle of love to God and his service, a desire of his presence with them by his ordinances, gratitude for the great things he had done for them, and faith in his promises of what he would do further.

JOHN WESLEY (1703–1791)
EXPLANATORY NOTES ON THE BIBLE

36:1–38 The readiness and zeal with which these builders set about their work, the exactness with which they performed it, and the faithfulness with which they objected to receive more contributions are worthy of our imitation. Thus should we serve God and our superiors also in all things lawful. Where have we the representation of God's love toward us, that we by love dwell in him and he in us, save in Emmanuel? (Matt 1:23). This was the design of the "tent of the testimony," a visible testimony of the love of God to the race of human beings, as shown by Christ's taking up his abode on earth wherein, as the original expresses it, he did tabernacle among us.

MATTHEW HENRY (1662–1714)
COMMENTARY ON THE WHOLE BIBLE

36 work and artistic designers. 1 So Bezalel and Oholiab and
every skilled person in whom the LORD has put skill and
ability to know how to do all the work for the service of the
sanctuary are to do the work according to all that the LORD
has commanded."
2 Moses summoned Bezalel and Oholiab and every skilled
person in whom the LORD had put skill—everyone whose heart
stirred him to volunteer to do the work. 3 They received from
Moses all the offerings the Israelites had brought to do the
work for the service of the sanctuary, and they still continued
to bring him a freewill offering each morning. 4 So all the skilled
people who were doing all the work on the sanctuary came
from the work they were doing 5 and told Moses, "The people
are bringing much more than is needed for the completion of
the work which the LORD commanded us to do!"
6 Moses instructed them to take his message throughout
the camp, saying, "Let no man or woman do anymore work for
the offering for the sanctuary." So the people were restrained
from bringing any more. 7 Now the materials were more than
enough for them to do all the work.

THE BUILDING OF THE TABERNACLE

8 All the skilled among those who were doing the work made
the tabernacle with ten curtains of fine twisted linen and blue
and purple and scarlet yarn; they were made with cherubim
that were the work of an artistic designer. 9 The length of one
curtain was 42 feet, and the width of one curtain was 6 feet—
the same size for each of the curtains. 10 He joined five of the
curtains to one another, and the other five curtains he joined
to one another. 11 He made loops of blue material along the edge
of the end curtain in the first set; he did the same along the
edge of the end curtain in the second set. 12 He made 50 loops
on the first curtain, and he made 50 loops on the end curtain
that was in the second set, with the loops opposite one another.
13 He made 50 gold clasps and joined the curtains together to
one another with the clasps, so that the tabernacle was a unit.
14 He made curtains of goats' hair for a tent over the tabernacle; he made eleven curtains. 15 The length of one curtain
was 45 feet, and the width of one curtain was 6 feet—one size
for all eleven curtains. 16 He joined five curtains by themselves
and six curtains by themselves. 17 He made 50 loops along the
edge of the end curtain in the first set and 50 loops along the
edge of the curtain that joined the second set. 18 He made 50
bronze clasps to join the tent together so that it might be a
unit. 19 He made a covering for the tent out of ram skins dyed
red and over that a covering of fine leather.
20 He made the frames for the tabernacle of acacia wood as uprights. 21 The length of each frame was 15 feet, the width of each
frame was 2¼ feet, 22 with two projections per frame parallel
one to another. He made all the frames of the tabernacle in this
way. 23 So he made frames for the tabernacle: 20 frames for the
south side. 24 He made 40 silver bases under the 20 frames—two
bases under the first frame for its two projections, and likewise
two bases under the next frame for its two projections, 25 and
for the second side of the tabernacle, the north side, he made
20 frames 26 and their 40 silver bases, two bases under the first
frame and two bases under the next frame. 27 And for the back of
the tabernacle on the west he made six frames. 28 He made two
frames for the corners of the tabernacle on the back. 29 At the

two corners they were doubled at the lower end and finished
together at the top in one ring. So he did for both. 30So there
were eight frames and their silver bases, 16 bases, two bases
under each frame.
31He made bars of acacia wood, five for the frames on one
side of the tabernacle 32and five bars for the frames on the
second side of the tabernacle, and five bars for the frames of the
tabernacle for the back side on the west. 33He made the middle
bar to reach from end to end in the center of the frames. 34He
overlaid the frames with gold and made their rings of gold to
provide places for the bars, and he overlaid the bars with gold.
35He made the special curtain of blue, purple, and scarlet
yarn and fine twisted linen; he made it with cherubim, the work
of an artistic designer. 36He made for it four posts of acacia wood
and overlaid them with gold, with gold hooks, and he cast for
them four silver bases.
37He made a hanging for the entrance of the tent of blue, purple, and scarlet yarn and fine twisted linen, the work of an embroiderer, 38and its five posts and their hooks. He overlaid their
tops and their bands with gold, but their five bases were bronze.

THE MAKING OF THE ARK

37 Bezalel made the ark of acacia wood; its length was 45
inches, its width 27 inches, and its height 27 inches. 2He
overlaid it with pure gold, inside and out, and he made a surrounding border of gold for it. 3He cast four gold rings for it
that he put on its four feet, with two rings on one side and two
rings on the other side. 4He made poles of acacia wood, overlaid
them with gold, 5and put the poles into the rings on the sides
of the ark in order to carry the ark.
6He made an atonement lid of pure gold; its length was 45
inches, and its width was 27 inches. 7He made two cherubim
of gold; he made them of hammered metal on the two ends of
the atonement lid, 8one cherub on one end and one cherub
on the other end. He made the cherubim from the atonement
lid on its two ends. 9The cherubim were spreading their wings
upward, overshadowing the atonement lid with their wings. The
cherubim faced each other, looking toward the atonement lid.

THE MAKING OF THE TABLE

10Bezalel made the table of acacia wood; its length was 36 inches,
its width 18 inches, and its height 27 inches. 11He overlaid it with
pure gold, and he made a surrounding border of gold for it. 12He
made a surrounding frame for it about three inches wide, and
he made a surrounding border of gold for its frame. 13He cast
four gold rings for it and attached the rings at the four corners
where its four legs were. 14The rings were close to the frame
to provide places for the poles to carry the table. 15He made
the poles of acacia wood and overlaid them with gold, to carry
the table. 16He made the vessels which were on the table out
of pure gold, its plates, its ladles, its pitchers, and its bowls, to
be used in pouring out offerings.

THE MAKING OF THE LAMPSTAND

17Bezalel made the lampstand of pure gold. He made the lampstand of hammered metal; its base and its shaft, its cups, its
buds, and its blossoms were from the same piece. 18Six branches
were extending from its sides, three branches of the lampstand
from one side of it, and three branches of the lampstand from

37:1–29 The reason why so minute and elaborate details are given in these chapters seems to be to show to us that Moses carried out exactly, rigidly, and minutely every order that he received, not determining in his own mind, *This is not important, and therefore I may omit it*, and *That is important, and therefore I must do it*; but acting rigidly and strictly according to the pattern that was showed him on the mount and the prescriptions set forth by God. This chapter, like those that succeed it, records the fact that Moses did so.

JOHN CUMMING **(1807-1881)**
SABBATH MORNING READINGS ON THE OLD TESTAMENT

the other side of it. [19]Three cups shaped like almond flowers with buds and blossoms were on the first branch, and three cups shaped like almond flowers with buds and blossoms were on the next branch, and the same for the six branches that were extending from the lampstand. [20]On the lampstand there were four cups shaped like almond flowers with buds and blossoms, [21]with a bud under the first two branches from it, and a bud under the next two branches from it, and a bud under the third two branches from it; according to the six branches that extended from it. [22]Their buds and their branches were of one piece; all of it was one hammered piece of pure gold. [23]He made its seven lamps, its trimmers, and its trays of pure gold. [24]He made the lampstand and all its accessories with seventy-five pounds of pure gold.

THE MAKING OF THE ALTAR OF INCENSE

[25]Bezalel made the incense altar of acacia wood. Its length was 18 inches and its width 18 inches—a square—and its height was 36 inches. Its horns were of one piece with it. [26]He overlaid it with pure gold—its top, its four walls, and its horns—and he made a surrounding border of gold for it. [27]He also made two gold rings for it under its border, on its two sides, on opposite sides, as places for poles to carry it with. [28]He made the poles of acacia wood and overlaid them with gold.

[29]He made the sacred anointing oil and the pure fragrant incense, the work of a perfumer.

THE MAKING OF THE ALTAR FOR THE BURNT OFFERING

38 Bezalel made the altar for the burnt offering of acacia wood 7½ feet long and 7½ feet wide—it was square—and its height was 4½ feet. [2]He made its horns on its four corners; its horns were part of it, and he overlaid it with bronze. [3]He made all the utensils of the altar—the pots, the shovels, the tossing bowls, the meat hooks, and the fire pans—he made all its utensils of bronze. [4]He made a grating for the altar, a network of bronze under its ledge, halfway up from the bottom. [5]He cast four rings for the four corners of the bronze grating, to provide places for the poles. [6]He made the poles of acacia wood and overlaid them with bronze. [7]He put the poles into the rings on the sides of the altar, with which to carry it. He made the altar hollow, out of boards.

[8]He made the large basin of bronze and its pedestal of bronze from the mirrors of the women who served at the entrance of the tent of meeting.

THE CONSTRUCTION OF THE COURTYARD

[9]Bezalel made the courtyard. For the south side the hangings of the courtyard were of fine twisted linen, 150 feet long, [10]with their 20 posts and their 20 bronze bases, with the hooks of the posts and their bands of silver. [11]For the north side the hangings were 150 feet, with their 20 posts and their 20 bronze bases, with the hooks of the posts and their bands of silver. [12]For the west side there were hangings 75 feet long, with their 10 posts and their 10 bases, with the hooks of the posts and their bands of silver. [13]For the east side, toward the sunrise, it was 75 feet wide, [14]with hangings on one side of the gate that were 22½ feet long, with their three posts and their three bases, [15]and for the second side of the gate of the courtyard, just like the

38:1–8 On this altar of burnt offering, all their sacrifices were offered. Christ was himself the altar to his own sacrifice of atonement, and so he is to all our sacrifices of acknowledgment. We must have an eye to him in offering them as God has in accepting them. This basin of bronze signified the provision that is made in the gospel for cleansing our souls from the pollution of sin by the merit of Christ, that we may be fit to serve the holy God in holy duties.

JOHN WESLEY (1703–1791)
EXPLANATORY NOTES ON THE BIBLE

other, the hangings were 22½ feet long, with their three posts
and their three bases. [16]All the hangings around the courtyard
were of fine twisted linen. [17]The bases for the posts were bronze.
The hooks of the posts and their bands were silver, their tops
were overlaid with silver, and all the posts of the courtyard had
silver bands. [18]The curtain for the gate of the courtyard was of
blue, purple, and scarlet yarn and fine twisted linen, the work
of an embroiderer. It was 30 feet long and, like the hangings in
the courtyard, it was 7½ feet high, [19]with four posts and their
four bronze bases. Their hooks and their bands were silver,
and their tops were overlaid with silver. [20]All the tent pegs of
the tabernacle and of the courtyard all around were bronze.

THE MATERIALS OF THE CONSTRUCTION

[21]This is the inventory of the tabernacle, the tabernacle of the
testimony, which was counted by the order of Moses, being
the work of the Levites under the direction of Ithamar, son of
Aaron the priest. [22]Now Bezalel son of Uri, the son of Hur, of the
tribe of Judah, made everything that the LORD had commanded
Moses; [23]and with him was Oholiab son of Ahisamach, of the
tribe of Dan, an artisan, a designer, and an embroiderer in blue,
purple, and scarlet yarn and fine linen.

[24]All the gold that was used for the work, in all the work
of the sanctuary (namely, the gold of the wave offering) was
29 talents and 730 shekels, according to the sanctuary shekel.

[25]The silver of those who were numbered of the community
was 100 talents and 1,775 shekels, according to the sanctuary
shekel, [26]one beka per person, that is, a half shekel, according to the sanctuary shekel, for everyone who crossed over to
those numbered, from twenty years old or older, 603,550 in all.
[27]The 100 talents of silver were used for casting the bases of
the sanctuary and the bases of the special curtain—100 bases
for 100 talents, one talent per base. [28]From the remaining 1,775
shekels he made hooks for the posts, overlaid their tops, and
made bands for them.

[29]The bronze of the wave offering was seventy talents and
2,400 shekels. [30]With it he made the bases for the door of the
tent of meeting, the bronze altar, the bronze grating for it, and
all the utensils of the altar, [31]the bases for the courtyard all
around, the bases for the gate of the courtyard, all the tent
pegs of the tabernacle, and all the tent pegs of the courtyard
all around.

THE MAKING OF THE PRIESTLY GARMENTS

39 From the blue, purple, and scarlet yarn they made woven
garments for serving in the sanctuary; they made holy
garments that were for Aaron, just as the LORD had commanded
Moses.

THE EPHOD

[2]He made the ephod of gold, blue, purple, scarlet yarn, and fine
twisted linen. [3]They hammered the gold into thin sheets and
cut it into narrow strips to weave them into the blue, purple,
and scarlet yarn, and into the fine linen, the work of an artistic
designer. [4]They made shoulder pieces for it, attached to two
of its corners, so it could be joined together. [5]The artistically
woven waistband of the ephod that was on it was like it, of one
piece with it, of gold, blue, purple, and scarlet yarn and fine
twisted linen, just as the LORD had commanded Moses.

39:1–43 We have seen how great mysteries were contained in the turban, which was "Holiness to the LORD," and in the ephod, in which shone forth the light of truth and integrity of life, and in which were the symbols of the ten tribes, so that the priest bore the people itself upon his shoulders and before his breast in such a manner that in the person of one all might be presented familiarly before God. For this reason he repeats many times the clause "as the LORD had commanded Moses," which certainly has the effect of awakening attention.

JOHN CALVIN (1509–1564)
COMPLETE COMMENTARY ON THE BIBLE

6They set the onyx stones in gold filigree settings, engraved as with the engravings of a seal with the names of the sons of Israel. 7He put them on the shoulder pieces of the ephod as stones of memorial for the Israelites, just as the LORD had commanded Moses.

THE BREASTPIECE OF DECISION

8He made the breastpiece, the work of an artistic designer, in the same fashion as the ephod, of gold, blue, purple, and scarlet yarn, and fine twisted linen. 9It was square—they made the breastpiece doubled, nine inches long and nine inches wide when doubled. 10They set on it four rows of stones: a row with a ruby, a topaz, and a beryl—the first row; 11and the second row, a turquoise, a sapphire, and an emerald; 12and the third row, a jacinth, an agate, and an amethyst; 13and the fourth row, a chrysolite, an onyx, and a jasper. They were enclosed in gold filigree settings. 14The stones were for the names of the sons of Israel, twelve, corresponding to the number of their names. Each name corresponding to one of the twelve tribes was like the engravings of a seal.

15They made for the breastpiece braided chains like cords of pure gold, 16and they made two gold filigree settings and two gold rings, and they attached the two rings to the upper two ends of the breastpiece. 17They attached the two gold chains to the two rings at the ends of the breastpiece; 18the other two ends of the two chains they attached to the two settings, and they attached them to the shoulder pieces of the ephod at the front of it. 19They made two rings of gold and put them on the other two ends of the breastpiece on its edge, which is on the inner side of the ephod. 20They made two more gold rings and attached them to the bottom of the two shoulder pieces on the front of the ephod, close to the juncture above the waistband of the ephod. 21They tied the breastpiece by its rings to the rings of the ephod by blue cord, so that it was above the waistband of the ephod, so that the breastpiece would not be loose from the ephod, just as the LORD had commanded Moses.

THE OTHER GARMENTS

22He made the robe of the ephod completely blue, the work of a weaver. 23There was an opening in the center of the robe, like the opening of a collar, with an edge all around the opening so that it could not be torn. 24They made pomegranates of blue, purple, and scarlet yarn and twisted linen around the hem of the robe. 25They made bells of pure gold and attached the bells between the pomegranates around the hem of the robe between the pomegranates. 26There was a bell and a pomegranate, a bell and a pomegranate, all around the hem of the robe, to be used in ministering, just as the LORD had commanded Moses.

27They made tunics of fine linen—the work of a weaver, for Aaron and for his sons—28and the turban of fine linen, the headbands of fine linen, and the undergarments of fine twisted linen. 29The sash was of fine twisted linen and blue, purple, and scarlet yarn, the work of an embroiderer, just as the LORD had commanded Moses. 30They made a plate, the holy diadem, of pure gold and wrote on it an inscription, as on the engravings of a seal, "Holiness to the LORD." 31They attached to it a blue cord to attach it to the turban above, just as the LORD had commanded Moses.

MOSES INSPECTS THE TABERNACLE

32So all the work of the tabernacle, the tent of meeting, was
completed, and the Israelites did according to all that the LORD
had commanded Moses—they did it exactly so. 33They brought
the tabernacle to Moses, the tent and all its furnishings, clasps,
frames, bars, posts, and bases; 34and the coverings of ram skins
dyed red, the covering of fine leather, and the protecting curtain; 35the ark of the testimony and its poles, and the atonement
lid; 36the table, all its utensils, and the Bread of the Presence;
37the pure lampstand, its lamps, with the lamps set in order,
and all its accessories, and oil for the light; 38and the gold altar,
and the anointing oil, and the fragrant incense; and the curtain
for the entrance to the tent; 39the bronze altar and its bronze
grating, its poles, and all its utensils; the large basin with its
pedestal; 40the hangings of the courtyard, its posts and its bases, and the curtain for the gateway of the courtyard, its ropes
and its tent pegs, and all the furnishings for the service of the
tabernacle, for the tent of meeting; 41the woven garments for
serving in the sanctuary, the holy garments for Aaron the priest,
and the garments for his sons to minister as priests.

42The Israelites did all the work according to all that the
LORD had commanded Moses. 43Moses inspected all the work,
and they had done it just as the LORD had commanded—they
had done it exactly—and Moses blessed them.

SETTING UP THE SANCTUARY

40 Then the LORD spoke to Moses: 2"On the first day of the
first month you are to set up the tabernacle, the tent of
meeting. 3You are to place the ark of the testimony in it and
shield the ark with the special curtain. 4You are to bring in the
table and set out the things that belong on it; then you are to
bring in the lampstand and set up its lamps. 5You are to put the
gold altar for incense in front of the ark of the testimony and
put the curtain at the entrance to the tabernacle. 6You are to
put the altar for the burnt offering in front of the entrance to
the tabernacle, the tent of meeting. 7You are to put the large
basin between the tent of meeting and the altar and put water
in it. 8You are to set up the courtyard around it and put the
curtain at the gate of the courtyard. 9And take the anointing
oil, and anoint the tabernacle and all that is in it, and sanctify
it and all its furnishings, and it will be holy. 10Then you are to
anoint the altar for the burnt offering with all its utensils; you
are to sanctify the altar, and it will be the most holy altar. 11You
must also anoint the large basin and its pedestal, and you are
to sanctify it.

12"You are to bring Aaron and his sons to the entrance of the
tent of meeting and wash them with water. 13Then you are to
clothe Aaron with the holy garments and anoint him and sanctify him so that he may minister as my priest. 14You are to bring
his sons and clothe them with tunics 15and anoint them just
as you anointed their father, so that they may minister as my
priests; their anointing will make them a priesthood that will
continue throughout their generations." 16This is what Moses
did, according to all the LORD had commanded him—so he did.

17So the tabernacle was set up on the first day of the first
month, in the second year. 18When Moses set up the tabernacle
and put its bases in place, he set up its frames, attached its bars,
and set up its posts. 19Then he spread the tent over the tabernacle and put the covering of the tent over it, as the LORD had

40:1–38 Why did God command Moses to erect the tabernacle on the first day of the first month? Because at that time he created the world. So too in this very season God set Israel free from slavery under the Egyptians, and the archangel Gabriel brought the holy Virgin the good news of her mysterious childbearing. In this same season the Lord Christ underwent his saving Passion.

THEODORET OF CYR
(C. 393–C. 458)
QUESTIONS ON EXODUS

TERTULLIAN:

A FOUNDER OF WESTERN THEOLOGY

c. 160–c. 212

"What has Athens to do with Jerusalem?" Another way of framing this question: "What does the culture of the day have to do with Christianity?" So wondered Tertullian, one of the early influential Latin theologians from Northern Africa. He was skeptical about his contemporaries' efforts to bring Greek philosophy into conversation with the truth of Christianity—and the underlying issues in that debate remain even today.

Born around AD 160 and raised as a pagan in Carthage, Tertullian was already a skilled lawyer and orator when he became a Christian in the 190s. He put those skills to good use for the sake of the church. Tertullian's conversion represents a fascinating development in the church's growth at that time: Roman intellectuals and average citizens were paying closer attention to Christianity and embracing the faith. "The outcry is that the State is filled with Christians," he wrote, "that they are in the fields, in the citadels, in the islands . . . both sexes, every age and condition, even high rank, are passing over to the profession of the Christian faith." He joined other Christian intellectuals to make the case to the broader culture that Christianity was not only respectable, but intellectually sound.

While many Christian thinkers of the time had an optimistic view of the human ability to discover truth and its connection with the Christian faith (frequently declaring that "All truth is God's truth"), Tertullian said differently. He was skeptical and pessimistic about the human mind's ability to grasp truth without the help of God's divine revelation. Hence, he questioned what the Greek philosophy of Athens had to do with the revealed faith of Jerusalem.

Like Irenaeus before him, Tertullian prioritized apostolic succession, insisting that only those churches founded by apostles or led by their successors were capable of preserving and teaching Christian truth. "All doctrine," he said, "must be prejudged as false that savors of contradiction to the truth of the churches and apostles of Christ and God." Consequently, given that the Church of Rome was founded by the great apostles Peter and Paul, Tertullian believed it had a special place within Christianity to preserve right teaching and belief.

Additionally, Tertullian was an influential voice in the early development of the terminology used to describe the triune God. The first writer known to have used the Latin term *trinitas*, Tertullian declared that the Trinity was "three persons, one substance," thus helping to establish a thread of thought that culminated with the declarations at Nicea (325) and Constantinople (381).

Though Tertullian was never officially sainted, his legacy remains as a champion of the primacy of divine revelation and as an important theologian of the Western church.

IMPORTANT WORKS

APOLOGY

AGAINST MARCION

AGAINST PRAXEAS

commanded him. 20He took the testimony and put it in the ark,
attached the poles to the ark, and then put the atonement lid
on the ark. 21And he brought the ark into the tabernacle, hung
the protecting curtain, and shielded the ark of the testimony
from view, just as the LORD had commanded him.
22And Moses put the table in the tent of meeting, on the
north side of the tabernacle, outside the curtain. 23And he set
the bread in order on it before the LORD, just as the LORD had
commanded him.
24And he put the lampstand in the tent of meeting opposite
the table, on the south side of the tabernacle. 25Then he set up
the lamps before the LORD, just as the LORD had commanded
him.
26And he put the gold altar in the tent of meeting in front
of the curtain, 27and he burned fragrant incense on it, just as
the LORD had commanded him.
28Then Moses put the curtain at the entrance to the tabernacle. 29He also put the altar for the burnt offering by the
entrance to the tabernacle, the tent of meeting, and offered
on it the burnt offering and the meal offering, just as the LORD
had commanded him.
30Then he put the large basin between the tent of meeting
and the altar and put water in it for washing. 31Moses and Aaron and his sons would wash their hands and their feet from it.
32Whenever they entered the tent of meeting, and whenever
they approached the altar, they would wash, just as the LORD
had commanded Moses.
33And he set up the courtyard around the tabernacle and
the altar, and put the curtain at the gate of the courtyard. So
Moses finished the work.
34Then the cloud covered the tent of meeting, and the glory
of the LORD filled the tabernacle. 35Moses was not able to enter
the tent of meeting because the cloud settled on it and the
glory of the LORD filled the tabernacle. 36But when the cloud
was lifted up from the tabernacle, the Israelites would set out
on all their journeys; 37but if the cloud was not lifted up, then
they would not journey farther until the day it was lifted up.
38For the cloud of the LORD was on the tabernacle by day, but
fire would be on it at night, in plain view of all the house of
Israel throughout all their journeys.

AUTHOR	AUDIENCE	DATE	PURPOSE	THEMES
Moses	God's chosen people, the Israelites	Between 1446 and 1406 BC	Moses wrote this book of ceremony and law to detail the sacrifices that atoned for sin and so that the children of Israel might be holy.	Sacrifice and offerings; trespasses and sins; and holiness and obedience

The contents of Leviticus often seem foreign and inapplicable to us with all the rituals and blood sacrifices, ceremonial laws, and prohibitions. Yet there is something deep and abiding here. Reformed pastor and Bible scholar Matthew Henry explained the relevance of Leviticus for us today:

> God ordained diverse kinds of oblations and sacrifices to assure his people of the forgiveness of their offenses, if they offered them in true faith and obedience. Also he appointed the priests and Levites, their apparel, offices, conduct, and portion. He showed what feasts they should observe and at what times. He declared by these sacrifices and ceremonies that the reward of sin is death, and that without the blood of Christ, the innocent Lamb of God, there can be no forgiveness of sins.

These sacrifices for sins and religious ceremonies were meant to set God's people apart as holy.

From the beginning, the reader of Leviticus is confronted with a list of offerings and sacrifices: the burnt, grain, fellowship, sin, guilt, and fellowship offerings. In the ancient Near East, people would often offer animals or baked goods to placate or curry favor with the gods. The sacrifices of the Israelites served different purposes however: They were offered as signs of commitment on the one hand and the means of relationship on the other. In the early church, these passages pertaining to Israel's offerings were often interpreted allegorically. Here is how Paterius explained the burnt offering:

> We strip off the skin of a victim when we remove the illusion of virtue from the eyes of our mind. We cut its limbs into pieces when we carefully distinguish the content of a virtue and ponder it step by step . . . Hence the priest of the law is bidden to burn in fire part of the victim that has been cut into pieces, namely, the head and the parts around the liver; but the feet and the intestines of the victim he must first wash in water. We burn the head and what is near the liver when, in the senses that rule the whole body and in our hidden desires, we burn with the flame of divine love.

LEVITICUS

Such sacrifices were meant primarily to deal with the trespasses the Israelites committed against God, but they also dealt with issues of ritual purity. Trespasses were those overt acts that were deliberate sins against the Lord or a neighbor. Included among these were the so-called sins of omission, where an individual trespassed without knowing it but still violated God's laws.

Because God is holy, his people needed to be holy; the laws set forth in Leviticus were given so that the people of God could draw near their Maker: "For I am the Lord your God and you are to sanctify yourselves and be holy because I am holy . . . for I am the Lord who brought you up from the land of Egypt to be your God, and you are to be holy because I am holy" (11:44–45). This call to holiness is directly linked to the covenantal relationship God created with his people when he brought them out of Egypt. They were not to do that which was done in the land of Egypt or in the land of Canaan. Instead: "You must observe my regulations and you must be sure to walk in my statutes. I am the Lord your God" (18:4). Although Christians "have been made holy through the offering of the body of Jesus Christ once for all," and "where there is forgiveness of these, there is no longer any offering for sin" (Heb 10:10, 18), the command to choose the Lord every day and do what pleases him stands.

John Wesley commented on the ongoing relevance of Leviticus for the communion of saints: "The records of even these abrogated laws are of use to us for the strengthening of our faith . . . and for the increase of our thankfulness to God, for freeing us from that heavy yoke."

1:1–17 Our Lord's being made "sin for us" (2 Cor 5:21) is set forth here by the very significant transfer of sin to the bull, which was made by the elders of the people. The laying of the hand was not a mere touch of contact. Surely this is the very essence and nature of faith, which not only brings us into contact with the great Substitute but teaches us to lean upon him with all the burden of our guilt. Jehovah made to meet upon the head of the Substitute all the offenses of his covenant people, but each one of the chosen is brought personally to ratify this solemn covenant act when by grace he or she is enabled by faith to lay a hand upon the head of the "Lamb slain from the foundation of the world" (Rev 13:8 KJV).

CHARLES SPURGEON
(1834–1892)
MORNING AND EVENING

INTRODUCTION TO THE SACRIFICIAL REGULATIONS

1 Then the LORD called to Moses and spoke to him from the
Meeting Tent: 2"Speak to the Israelites and tell them, 'When
someone among you presents an offering to the LORD, you must
present your offering from the domesticated animals, either
from the herd or from the flock.

BURNT-OFFERING REGULATIONS: ANIMAL FROM THE HERD

3"'If his offering is a burnt offering from the herd, he must present it as a flawless male; he must present it at the entrance of
the Meeting Tent for its acceptance before the LORD. 4He must
lay his hand on the head of the burnt offering, and it will be
accepted for him to make atonement on his behalf. 5Then the
one presenting the offering must slaughter the bull before the
LORD, and the sons of Aaron, the priests, must present the blood
and splash the blood against the sides of the altar, which is at
the entrance of the Meeting Tent. 6Next, the one presenting the
offering must skin the burnt offering and cut it into parts, 7and
the sons of Aaron, the priests, must put fire on the altar and
arrange wood on the fire. 8Then the sons of Aaron, the priests,
must arrange the parts with the head and the suet on the wood
that is in the fire on the altar. 9Finally, the one presenting the
offering must wash its entrails and its legs in water, and the
priest must offer all of it up in smoke on the altar—it is a burnt
offering, a gift of a soothing aroma to the LORD.

ANIMAL FROM THE FLOCK

10"'If his offering is from the flock for a burnt offering—from
the sheep or the goats—he must present a flawless male, 11and
must slaughter it on the north side of the altar before the LORD,
and the sons of Aaron, the priests, will splash its blood against
the altar's sides. 12Next, the one presenting the offering must
cut it into parts, with its head and its suet, and the priest must
arrange them on the wood that is in the fire on the altar. 13Then
the one presenting the offering must wash the entrails and the
legs in water, and the priest must present all of it and offer it up
in smoke on the altar—it is a burnt offering, a gift of a soothing
aroma to the LORD.

OFFERING OF BIRDS

14"'If his offering to the LORD is a burnt offering of birds, he
must present his offering from the turtledoves or from the
young pigeons. 15The priest must present it at the altar, pinch
off its head and offer the head up in smoke on the altar, and its
blood must be drained out against the side of the altar. 16Then
the priest must remove its entrails by cutting off its tail feathers, and throw them to the east side of the altar into the place
of fatty ashes, 17and tear it open by its wings without dividing
it into two parts. Finally, the priest must offer it up in smoke on
the altar on the wood which is in the fire—it is a burnt offering,
a gift of a soothing aroma to the LORD.

GRAIN-OFFERING REGULATIONS: OFFERING OF RAW FLOUR

2 "'When a person presents a grain offering to the LORD, his
offering must consist of choice wheat flour, and he must pour
olive oil on it and put frankincense on it. 2Then he must bring

it to the sons of Aaron, the priests, and the priest must scoop
out from there a handful of its choice wheat flour and some of
its olive oil in addition to all of its frankincense, and the priest
must offer its memorial portion up in smoke on the altar—it is
a gift of a soothing aroma to the LORD. 3The remainder of the
grain offering belongs to Aaron and to his sons—it is most holy
from the gifts of the LORD.

PROCESSED GRAIN OFFERINGS

4"'When you present an offering of grain baked in an oven, it
must be made of choice wheat flour baked into unleavened
loaves mixed with olive oil or unleavened wafers smeared with
olive oil. 5If your offering is a grain offering made on the griddle,
it must be choice wheat flour mixed with olive oil, unleavened.
6Crumble it in pieces and pour olive oil on it—it is a grain offering. 7If your offering is a grain offering made in a pan, it must
be made of choice wheat flour deep fried in olive oil.
8"'You must bring the grain offering that must be made from
these to the LORD. Present it to the priest, and he will bring it to
the altar. 9Then the priest must take up from the grain offering
its memorial portion and offer it up in smoke on the altar—it
is a gift of a soothing aroma to the LORD. 10The remainder of
the grain offering belongs to Aaron and to his sons—it is most
holy from the gifts of the LORD.

ADDITIONAL GRAIN-OFFERING REGULATIONS

11"'No grain offering which you present to the LORD can be
made with yeast, for you must not offer up in smoke any yeast
or honey as a gift to the LORD. 12You can present them to the
LORD as an offering of firstfruit, but they must not go up to
the altar for a soothing aroma. 13Moreover, you must season
every one of your grain offerings with salt; you must not allow
the salt of the covenant of your God to be missing from your
grain offering—on every one of your grain offerings you must
present salt.
14"'If you present a grain offering of first ripe grain to the
LORD, you must present your grain offering of first ripe grain as
soft kernels roasted in fire—crushed bits of fresh grain. 15And
you must put olive oil on it and set frankincense on it—it is a
grain offering. 16Then the priest must offer its memorial portion up in smoke—some of its crushed bits, some of its olive
oil, in addition to all of its frankincense—it is a gift to the LORD.

PEACE-OFFERING REGULATIONS: ANIMAL FROM THE HERD

3 "'Now if his offering is a peace-offering sacrifice, if he presents
an offering from the herd, he must present before the LORD
a flawless male or a female. 2He must lay his hand on the head
of his offering and slaughter it at the entrance of the Meeting
Tent, and the sons of Aaron, the priests, must splash the blood
against the altar's sides. 3Then the one presenting the offering must present a gift to the LORD from the peace-offering
sacrifice: He must remove the fat that covers the entrails and
all the fat that surrounds the entrails, 4the two kidneys with
the fat on their sinews, and the protruding lobe on the liver
(which he is to remove along with the kidneys). 5Then the sons
of Aaron must offer it up in smoke on the altar atop the burnt
offering that is on the wood in the fire as a gift of a soothing
aroma to the LORD.

2:3–10 The grain offering is most holy, and it is taken from the fire offerings of the Lord, expressing complete appropriation by the Lord of the things offered to him. We may not say, "I give myself to the Lord" and then do as we please. The Lord takes us at our word. We are no more our own, nor is our body ours, nor our members, nor our money, nor our health, nor our talents, nor our reputation, nor our affections, nor our relations, nor our very life itself. All is the Lord's–in his treasury–of the offerings of the Lord made by fire that ascend up to heaven in the smoke of the altar.

ANDREW BONAR (1810–1892)
A COMMENTARY ON LEVITICUS

3:1–17 The peace offerings had regard to God as the giver of all good things. These were divided between the altar, the priest, and the owner. They were called *peace offerings* because in them God and his people did, as it were, feast together in token of friendship. The peace offerings were offered by way of supplication. If a person were in pursuit of any mercy, he or she would add a peace offering to prayer for it. Christ is our peace, our peace offering; for through him alone it is that we can obtain an answer of peace to our prayers. Or the peace offering was offered by way of thanksgiving for some mercy received. We must offer to God the sacrifice of praise continually, by Christ our peace, and then this shall please the Lord better than an ox or bullock.

MATTHEW HENRY (1662–1714)
COMMENTARY ON THE WHOLE BIBLE

ANIMAL FROM THE FLOCK

[6]"'If his offering for a peace-offering sacrifice to the LORD is from the flock, he must present a flawless male or female. [7]If he presents a sheep as his offering, he must present it before the LORD. [8]He must lay his hand on the head of his offering and slaughter it before the Meeting Tent, and the sons of Aaron must splash its blood against the altar's sides. [9]Then he must present a gift to the LORD from the peace-offering sacrifice: He must remove all the fatty tail up to the end of the spine, the fat covering the entrails, and all the fat on the entrails, [10]the two kidneys with the fat on their sinews, and the protruding lobe on the liver (which he is to remove along with the kidneys). [11]Then the priest must offer it up in smoke on the altar as a food gift to the LORD.

[12]"'If his offering is a goat, he must present it before the LORD, [13]lay his hand on its head, and slaughter it before the Meeting Tent, and the sons of Aaron must splash its blood against the altar's sides. [14]Then he must present from it his offering as a gift to the LORD: the fat which covers the entrails and all the fat on the entrails, [15]the two kidneys with the fat on their sinews, and the protruding lobe on the liver (which he is to remove along with the kidneys). [16]Then the priest must offer them up in smoke on the altar as a food gift for a soothing aroma—all the fat belongs to the LORD. [17]This is a perpetual statute throughout your generations in all the places where you live: You must never eat any fat or any blood.'"

SIN-OFFERING REGULATIONS

4 Then the LORD spoke to Moses: [2]"Tell the Israelites, 'When a person sins by straying unintentionally from any of the LORD's commandments which must not be violated, and violates any one of them—

FOR THE PRIEST

[3]"'If the high priest sins so that the people are guilty on account of the sin he has committed, he must present a flawless young bull to the LORD for a sin offering. [4]He must bring the bull to the entrance of the Meeting Tent before the LORD, lay his hand on the head of the bull, and slaughter the bull before the LORD. [5]Then that high priest must take some of the blood of the bull and bring it to the Meeting Tent. [6]The priest must dip his finger in the blood and sprinkle some of it seven times before the LORD toward the front of the special curtain of the sanctuary. [7]The priest must put some of the blood on the horns of the altar of fragrant incense that is before the LORD in the Meeting Tent, and all the rest of the bull's blood he must pour out at the base of the altar of burnt offering that is at the entrance of the Meeting Tent.

[8]"'Then he must take up all the fat from the sin-offering bull: the fat covering the entrails and all the fat surrounding the entrails, [9]the two kidneys with the fat on their sinews, and the protruding lobe on the liver (which he is to remove along with the kidneys) [10]—just as it is taken from the ox of the peace-offering sacrifice—and the priest must offer them up in smoke on the altar of burnt offering. [11]But the hide of the bull, all its flesh along with its head and its legs, its entrails, and its dung—[12]all the rest of the bull—he must bring outside the camp to a ceremonially clean place, to the fatty-ash pile, and he must burn it on a wood fire; it must be burned on the fatty-ash pile.

4:1–12 God accused the Israelites more vehemently and showed that they were worthy of greater chastisement because they sinned after so many honors had come to them from him. And before the times of the prophets, wishing to show that sins receive sorer punishment by far when they occur in the case of the priest than in the case of the laity, he enjoins as great a sacrifice to be offered for the priest as for the whole people, and this amounts to a proof on his part that the wounds of the priesthood need more assistance.

CHRYSOSTOM (C. 347–407)
ON THE PRIESTHOOD

FOR THE WHOLE CONGREGATION

[13]“‘If the whole congregation of Israel strays unintentionally and the matter is not noticed by the assembly, and they violate one of the LORD’s commandments, which must not be violated, so they become guilty, [14]the assembly must present a young bull for a sin offering when the sin they have committed becomes known. They must bring it before the Meeting Tent, [15]the elders of the congregation must lay their hands on the head of the bull before the LORD, and someone must slaughter the bull before the LORD. [16]Then the high priest must bring some of the blood of the bull to the Meeting Tent, [17]and that priest must dip his finger in the blood and sprinkle some of the blood seven times before the LORD toward the front of the curtain. [18]He must put some of the blood on the horns of the altar which is before the LORD in the Meeting Tent, and all the rest of the blood he must pour out at the base of the altar of burnt offering that is at the entrance of the Meeting Tent.

[19]“‘Then the priest must take all its fat and offer the fat up in smoke on the altar. [20]He must do with the rest of the bull just as he did with the bull of the sin offering; this is what he must do with it. So the priest will make atonement on their behalf, and they will be forgiven. [21]He must bring the rest of the bull outside the camp and burn it just as he burned the first bull—it is the sin offering of the assembly.

FOR THE LEADER

[22]“‘Whenever a leader, by straying unintentionally, sins and violates one of the commandments of the LORD his God which must not be violated, and he pleads guilty, [23]or his sin that he committed is made known to him, he must bring a flawless male goat as his offering. [24]He must lay his hand on the head of the male goat and slaughter it in the place where the burnt offering is slaughtered before the LORD—it is a sin offering. [25]Then the priest must take some of the blood of the sin offering with his finger and put it on the horns of the altar of burnt offering, and he must pour out the rest of its blood at the base of the altar of burnt offering. [26]Then the priest must offer all of its fat up in smoke on the altar like the fat of the peace-offering sacrifice. So the priest will make atonement on his behalf for his sin, and he will be forgiven.

FOR THE COMMON PERSON

[27]“‘If an ordinary individual sins by straying unintentionally when he violates one of the LORD’s commandments which must not be violated, and he pleads guilty, [28]or his sin that he committed is made known to him, he must bring a flawless female goat as his offering for the sin that he committed. [29]He must lay his hand on the head of the sin offering and slaughter the sin offering in the place where the burnt offering is slaughtered. [30]Then the priest must take some of its blood with his finger and put it on the horns of the altar of burnt offering, and he must pour out all the rest of its blood at the base of the altar. [31]Then he must remove all of its fat (just as fat was removed from the peace-offering sacrifice), and the priest must offer it up in smoke on the altar for a soothing aroma to the LORD. So the priest will make atonement on his behalf, and he will be forgiven.

[32]“‘But if he brings a sheep as his offering, for a sin offering, he must bring a flawless female. [33]He must lay his hand on the

head of the sin offering and slaughter it for a sin offering in the place where the burnt offering is slaughtered. [34]Then the priest must take some of the blood of the sin offering with his finger and put it on the horns of the altar of burnt offering, and he must pour out all the rest of its blood at the base of the altar. [35]Then the one who brought the offering must remove all its fat (just as the fat of the sheep is removed from the peace-offering sacrifice), and the priest must offer them up in smoke on the altar on top of the other gifts for the LORD. So the priest will make atonement on his behalf for his sin that he has committed, and he will be forgiven.

ADDITIONAL SIN-OFFERING REGULATIONS

5 "'When a person sins in that he hears a public curse against one who fails to testify and he is a witness (he either saw or knew what had happened) and he does not make it known, then he will bear his punishment for iniquity. [2]Or when there is a person who touches anything ceremonially unclean, whether the carcass of an unclean wild animal, or the carcass of an unclean domesticated animal, or the carcass of an unclean creeping thing, even if he did not realize it, he has become unclean and is guilty; [3]or when he touches human uncleanness with regard to anything by which he can become unclean, even if he did not realize it, but he has later come to know it and is guilty; [4]or when a person swears an oath, speaking thoughtlessly with his lips, whether to do evil or to do good, with regard to anything which the individual might speak thoughtlessly in an oath, even if he did not realize it, but he has later come to know it and is guilty with regard to one of these oaths—[5]when an individual becomes guilty with regard to one of these things he must confess how he has sinned, [6]and he must bring his penalty for guilt to the LORD for his sin that he has committed—a female from the flock, whether a female sheep or a female goat, for a sin offering. So the priest will make atonement on his behalf for his sin.

[7]"'If he cannot afford an animal from the flock, he must bring his penalty for guilt for his sin that he has committed, two turtledoves or two young pigeons, to the LORD, one for a sin offering and one for a burnt offering. [8]He must bring them to the priest and present first the one that is for a sin offering. The priest must pinch its head at the nape of its neck, but must not sever the head from the body. [9]Then he must sprinkle some of the blood of the sin offering on the wall of the altar, and the remainder of the blood must be squeezed out at the base of the altar—it is a sin offering. [10]The second bird he must make a burnt offering according to the standard regulation. So the priest will make atonement on behalf of this person for his sin which he has committed, and he will be forgiven.

[11]"'If he cannot afford two turtledoves or two young pigeons, he must bring as his offering for his sin which he has committed a tenth of an ephah of choice wheat flour for a sin offering. He must not place olive oil on it, and he must not put frankincense on it, because it is a sin offering. [12]He must bring it to the priest, and the priest must scoop out from it a handful as its memorial portion and offer it up in smoke on the altar on top of the other gifts of the LORD—it is a sin offering. [13]So the priest will make atonement on his behalf for his sin which he has committed by doing one of these things, and he will be forgiven. The remainder of the offering will belong to the priest like the grain offering.'"

5:1–13 "When a person sins in that he hears a public curse against one who fails to testify and he is a witness (he either saw or knew what had happened) and he does not make it known, then he will bear his punishment for iniquity." That is, if he does not make it known, he will incur sin. This seems to say that a man sins when someone swears falsely in his hearing, and he knows that that man is swearing falsely and remains silent. But between fear of this sin and fear of the treachery of men, there often arises no small temptation.

AUGUSTINE (354–430)
QUESTIONS ON LEVITICUS

GUILT-OFFERING REGULATIONS: KNOWN TRESPASS

[14]Then the LORD spoke to Moses: [15]"When a person commits a trespass and sins by straying unintentionally from the regulations about the LORD's holy things, then he must bring his penalty for guilt to the LORD, a flawless ram from the flock, convertible into silver shekels according to the standard of the sanctuary shekel, for a guilt offering. [16]And whatever holy thing he violated he must restore and must add one-fifth to it and give it to the priest. So the priest will make atonement on his behalf with the guilt-offering ram, and he will be forgiven.

UNKNOWN TRESPASS

[17]"If a person sins and violates any of the LORD's commandments that must not be violated (although he did not know it at the time, but later realizes he is guilty), then he will bear his punishment for iniquity [18]and must bring a flawless ram from the flock, convertible into silver shekels, for a guilt offering to the priest. So the priest will make atonement on his behalf for his error that he committed (although he himself had not known it), and he will be forgiven. [19]It is a guilt offering; he was surely guilty before the LORD."

TRESPASS BY DECEPTION AND FALSE OATH

6 Then the LORD spoke to Moses: [2]"When a person sins and commits a trespass against the LORD by deceiving his fellow citizen in regard to something held in trust, or a pledge, or something stolen, or by extorting something from his fellow citizen, [3]or has found something lost and denies it and swears falsely concerning any one of the things that someone might do to sin—[4]when it happens that he sins and he is found guilty, then he must return whatever he had stolen, or whatever he had extorted, or the thing that he had held in trust, or the lost thing that he had found, [5]or anything about which he swears falsely. He must restore it in full and add one-fifth to it; he must give it to its owner when he is found guilty. [6]Then he must bring his guilt offering to the LORD, a flawless ram from the flock, convertible into silver shekels, for a guilt offering to the priest. [7]So the priest will make atonement on his behalf before the LORD and he will be forgiven for whatever he has done to become guilty."

SACRIFICIAL INSTRUCTIONS FOR THE PRIESTS: THE BURNT OFFERING

[8]Then the LORD spoke to Moses: [9]"Command Aaron and his sons, 'This is the law of the burnt offering. The burnt offering is to remain on the hearth on the altar all night until morning, and the fire of the altar must be kept burning on it. [10]Then the priest must put on his linen robe and must put linen leggings over his bare flesh, and he must take up the fatty ashes of the burnt offering that the fire consumed on the altar, and he must place them beside the altar. [11]Then he must take off his clothes and put on other clothes, and he must bring the fatty ashes outside the camp to a ceremonially clean place, [12]but the fire which is on the altar must be kept burning on it. It must not be extinguished. So the priest must kindle wood on it morning by morning, and he must arrange the burnt offering on it and offer the fat of the peace offering up in smoke on it. [13]A continual fire must be kept burning on the altar. It must not be extinguished.

6:8–13 Keep the altar of private prayer burning. This is the very life of all piety. The sanctuary and family altars borrow their fires here, therefore let this burn well. Secret devotion is the very essence, evidence, and barometer of vital and experimental religion. Burn here the fat of your sacrifices. Let your closet seasons be, if possible, regular, frequent, and undisturbed. Let us use texts of scripture as fuel for our heart's fire, they are live coals; let us attend sermons, but above all, let us be much alone with Jesus.

CHARLES SPURGEON **(1834–1892)**
MORNING AND EVENING

THE GRAIN OFFERING OF THE COMMON PERSON

[14]"'This is the law of the grain offering. The sons of Aaron are to present it before the LORD in front of the altar, [15]and the priest must take up with his hand some of the choice wheat flour of the grain offering and some of its olive oil, and all of the frankincense that is on the grain offering, and he must offer its memorial portion up in smoke on the altar as a soothing aroma to the LORD. [16]Aaron and his sons are to eat what is left over from it. It must be eaten unleavened in a holy place; they are to eat it in the courtyard of the Meeting Tent. [17]It must not be baked with yeast. I have given it as their portion from my gifts. It is most holy, like the sin offering and the guilt offering. [18]Every male among the sons of Aaron may eat it. It is a perpetual allotted portion throughout your generations from the gifts of the LORD. Anyone who touches these gifts must be holy.'"

THE GRAIN OFFERING OF THE PRIESTS

[19]Then the LORD spoke to Moses: [20]"This is the offering of Aaron and his sons which they must present to the LORD on the day when he is anointed: a tenth of an ephah of choice wheat flour as a continual grain offering, half of it in the morning and half of it in the evening. [21]It must be made with olive oil on a griddle, and you must bring it well soaked, so you must present a grain offering of broken pieces as a soothing aroma to the LORD. [22]The high priest who succeeds him from among his sons must do it. It is a perpetual statute; it must be offered up in smoke as a whole offering to the LORD. [23]Every grain offering of a priest must be a whole offering; it must not be eaten."

THE SIN OFFERING

[24]Then the LORD spoke to Moses: [25]"Tell Aaron and his sons, 'This is the law of the sin offering. In the place where the burnt offering is slaughtered the sin offering must be slaughtered before the LORD. It is most holy. [26]The priest who offers it for sin is to eat it. It must be eaten in a holy place, in the courtyard of the Meeting Tent. [27]Anyone who touches its meat must be holy, and whoever spatters some of its blood on a garment must wash whatever he spatters it on in a holy place. [28]Any clay vessel it is boiled in must be broken, and if it was boiled in a bronze vessel, then that vessel must be rubbed out and rinsed in water. [29]Any male among the priests may eat it. It is most holy. [30]But any sin offering from which some of its blood is brought into the Meeting Tent to make atonement in the sanctuary must not be eaten. It must be burned up in the fire.

THE GUILT OFFERING

7 "'This is the law of the guilt offering. It is most holy. [2]In the place where they slaughter the burnt offering they must slaughter the guilt offering, and the officiating priest must splash the blood against the altar's sides. [3]Then the one making the offering must present all its fat: the fatty tail, the fat covering the entrails, [4]the two kidneys and the fat on their sinews, and the protruding lobe on the liver (which he must remove along with the kidneys). [5]Then the priest must offer them up in smoke on the altar as a gift to the LORD. It is a guilt offering. [6]Any male among the priests may eat it. It must be eaten in a holy place. It is most holy. [7]The law is the same for the sin offering and the guilt offering; it belongs to the priest who makes atonement with it.

PRIESTLY PORTIONS OF BURNT AND GRAIN OFFERINGS

8"'As for the priest who presents someone's burnt offering, the
hide of that burnt offering which he presented belongs to him.
9Every grain offering which is baked in the oven or made in
the pan or on the griddle belongs to the priest who presented
it. 10Every grain offering, whether mixed with olive oil or dry,
belongs to all the sons of Aaron, each one alike.

THE PEACE OFFERING

11"'This is the law of the peace-offering sacrifice which he is to
present to the LORD. 12If he presents it on account of thanksgiving, along with the thank-offering sacrifice he must present
unleavened loaves mixed with olive oil, unleavened wafers
smeared with olive oil, and well-soaked, ring-shaped loaves made
of choice wheat flour mixed with olive oil. 13He must present
this grain offering in addition to ring-shaped loaves of leavened
bread which regularly accompany the sacrifice of his thanksgiving peace offering. 14He must present one of each kind of grain
offering as a contribution offering to the LORD; it belongs to
the priest who splashes the blood of the peace offering. 15The
meat of his thanksgiving peace offering must be eaten on the
day of his offering; he must not set any of it aside until morning.
16"'If his offering is a votive or freewill sacrifice, it may be
eaten on the day he presents his sacrifice, and also the leftovers
from it may be eaten on the next day, 17but the leftovers from
the meat of the sacrifice must be burned up in the fire on the
third day. 18If some of the meat of his peace-offering sacrifice
is ever eaten on the third day, it will not be accepted; it will not
be accounted to the one who presented it since it is spoiled,
and the person who eats from it will bear his punishment for
iniquity. 19The meat which touches anything ceremonially unclean must not be eaten; it must be burned up in the fire. As for
ceremonially clean meat, everyone who is ceremonially clean
may eat the meat. 20The person who eats meat from the peace-
offering sacrifice which belongs to the LORD while that person's
uncleanness persists will be cut off from his people. 21When a
person touches anything unclean (whether human uncleanness,
or an unclean animal, or an unclean detestable creature) and
eats some of the meat of the peace-offering sacrifice which belongs to the LORD, that person will be cut off from his people.'"

SACRIFICIAL INSTRUCTIONS FOR THE COMMON PEOPLE: FAT AND BLOOD

22Then the LORD spoke to Moses: 23"Tell the Israelites, 'You
must not eat any fat of an ox, sheep, or goat. 24Moreover, the
fat of an animal that has died of natural causes and the fat of an
animal torn by beasts may be used for any other purpose, but
you must certainly never eat it. 25If anyone eats fat from the
animal from which he presents a gift to the LORD, that person
will be cut off from his people. 26And you must not eat any blood
of the birds or of the domesticated land animals in any of the
places where you live. 27Any person who eats any blood—that
person will be cut off from his people.'"

PRIESTLY PORTIONS OF PEACE OFFERINGS

28Then the LORD spoke to Moses: 29"Tell the Israelites, 'The
one who presents his peace-offering sacrifice to the LORD must
bring part of his offering to the LORD as his sacrifice. 30With

7:11–13 The Jews say that the peace offerings for thanksgiving were brought on such occasions of deliverance from danger in traveling the desert, voyaging the sea, captivity, or sickness. Peace offerings brought on occasion of a vow were probably very similar, but with this difference, that in the time of danger—e.g., a storm at sea or violent wind in the desert—they were promised or vowed to the Lord. Such vowed peace offerings go under the name of "sacrifices of thanksgiving." Those called "freewill" were probably brought just because the soul of the worshiper was, at the time, overflowing with gratitude.

ANDREW BONAR (1810–1892)
A COMMENTARY ON LEVITICUS

his own hands he must bring the LORD's gifts. He must bring the fat with the breast to wave the breast as a wave offering before the LORD, 31and the priest must offer the fat up in smoke on the altar, but the breast will belong to Aaron and his sons. 32The right thigh you must give as a contribution offering to the priest from your peace-offering sacrifice. 33The one from Aaron's sons who presents the blood of the peace offering and fat will have the right thigh as his share, 34for the breast of the wave offering and the thigh of the contribution offering I have taken from the Israelites out of their peace-offering sacrifices and have given them to Aaron the priest and to his sons from the people of Israel as a perpetual allotted portion.'"

35This is the allotment of Aaron and the allotment of his sons from the LORD's gifts on the day Moses presented them to serve as priests to the LORD. 36This is what the LORD commanded to give to them from the Israelites on the day Moses anointed them—a perpetual allotted portion throughout their generations.

SUMMARY OF SACRIFICIAL REGULATIONS IN LEVITICUS 6:8–7:36

37This is the law for the burnt offering, the grain offering, the sin offering, the guilt offering, the ordination offering, and the peace-offering sacrifice, 38which the LORD commanded Moses on Mount Sinai on the day he commanded the Israelites to present their offerings to the LORD in the desert of Sinai.

ORDINATION OF THE PRIESTS

8 Then the LORD spoke to Moses: 2"Take Aaron and his sons with him, and the garments, the anointing oil, the sin-offering bull, the two rams, and the basket of unleavened bread, 3and assemble the whole congregation at the entrance of the Meeting Tent." 4So Moses did just as the LORD commanded him, and the congregation assembled at the entrance of the Meeting Tent. 5Then Moses said to the congregation: "This is what the LORD has commanded to be done."

> 8:1–9 Well is the church named *ecclesia* ("assembly" or "gathering") because it calls forth and assembles all people, as the Lord says in Leviticus: "Assemble the whole congregation at the entrance of the Meeting Tent." It is worthy of note that this word "assemble" is used in the scriptures for the first time in the passage when the Lord established Aaron in the high priesthood. In Deuteronomy God said to Moses, "Assemble the people before me so that I can tell them my commands. Then they will learn to revere me" (Deut 4:10).
>
> CYRIL OF JERUSALEM
> (C. 313–386)
> *CATECHETICAL LECTURES*

CLOTHING AARON

6So Moses brought Aaron and his sons forward and washed them with water. 7Then he put the tunic on Aaron, wrapped the sash around him, and clothed him with the robe. Next he put the ephod on him and placed on him the decorated band of the ephod, and fastened the ephod closely to him with the band. 8He then set the breastpiece on him and put the Urim and Thummim into the breastpiece. 9Finally, he set the turban on his head and attached the gold plate, the holy diadem, to the front of the turban just as the LORD had commanded Moses.

ANOINTING THE TABERNACLE AND AARON, AND CLOTHING AARON'S SONS

10Then Moses took the anointing oil and anointed the tabernacle and everything in it, and so consecrated them. 11Next he sprinkled some of it on the altar seven times and so anointed the altar, all its vessels, and the washbasin and its stand to consecrate them. 12He then poured some of the anointing oil on the head of Aaron and anointed him to consecrate him. 13Moses also brought forward Aaron's sons, clothed them with tunics, wrapped sashes around them, and wrapped headbands on them just as the LORD had commanded Moses.

CONSECRATION OFFERINGS

[14]Then he brought near the sin-offering bull, and Aaron and his sons laid their hands on the head of the sin-offering bull, [15]and he slaughtered it. Moses then took the blood and put it all around on the horns of the altar with his finger and purified the altar, and he poured out the rest of the blood at the base of the altar and so consecrated it to make atonement on it. [16]Then he took all the fat on the entrails, the protruding lobe of the liver, and the two kidneys and their fat, and Moses offered it all up in smoke on the altar, [17]but the rest of the bull—its hide, its flesh, and its dung—he completely burned up outside the camp just as the LORD had commanded Moses.

[18]Then he presented the burnt-offering ram, and Aaron and his sons laid their hands on the head of the ram, [19]and he slaughtered it. Moses then splashed the blood against the altar's sides. [20]Then he cut the ram into parts, and Moses offered the head, the parts, and the suet up in smoke, [21]but the entrails and the legs he washed with water, and Moses offered the whole ram up in smoke on the altar—it was a burnt offering for a soothing aroma, a gift to the LORD, just as the LORD had commanded Moses.

[22]Then he presented the second ram, the ram of ordination, and Aaron and his sons laid their hands on the head of the ram, [23]and he slaughtered it. Moses then took some of its blood and put it on Aaron's right earlobe, on the thumb of his right hand, and on the big toe of his right foot. [24]Next he brought Aaron's sons forward, and Moses put some of the blood on their right earlobes, on their right thumbs, and on the big toes of their right feet, and Moses splashed the rest of the blood against the altar's sides.

[25]Then he took the fat (the fatty tail, all the fat on the entrails, the protruding lobe of the liver, and the two kidneys and their fat) and the right thigh, [26]and from the basket of unleavened bread that was before the LORD he took one unleavened loaf, one loaf of bread mixed with olive oil, and one wafer, and placed them on the fat parts and on the right thigh. [27]He then put all of them on the palms of Aaron and his sons, who waved them as a wave offering before the LORD. [28]Moses then took them from their palms and offered them up in smoke on the altar on top of the burnt offering—they were an ordination offering for a soothing aroma; it was a gift to the LORD. [29]Finally, Moses took the breast and waved it as a wave offering before the LORD from the ram of ordination. It was Moses' share just as the LORD had commanded Moses.

ANOINTING AARON, HIS SONS, AND THEIR GARMENTS

[30]Then Moses took some of the anointing oil and some of the blood which was on the altar and sprinkled it on Aaron and his garments, and on his sons and his sons' garments. So he consecrated Aaron, his garments, and his sons and his sons' garments. [31]Then Moses said to Aaron and his sons, "Boil the meat at the entrance of the Meeting Tent, and there you are to eat it and the bread which is in the ordination-offering basket, just as I have commanded, saying, 'Aaron and his sons are to eat it,' [32]but the remainder of the meat and the bread you must burn with fire. [33]And you must not go out from the entrance of the Meeting Tent for seven days, until the day when your days of ordination are completed, because you must be ordained

over a seven-day period. [34]What has been done on this day the
LORD has commanded to be done to make atonement for you.
[35]You must reside at the entrance of the Meeting Tent day and
night for seven days and keep the charge of the LORD so that
you will not die, for this is what I have been commanded." [36]So
Aaron and his sons did all the things the LORD had commanded
through Moses.

9:1–24 Aaron and his sons began to execute their office. It was necessary that he should be his brother's disciple in order to follow the pattern laid down by God. Sacrifices were approved by a divine miracle in ratification of the priesthood that God had instituted. Aaron sacrificed according to God's command and the legal ritual. He lifted up his hand toward the people. When by the lifting up of their hands the priests testified of God's paternal favor to the people, their commission was ratified and efficacious.

JOHN CALVIN (1509–1564)
COMPLETE COMMENTARY ON THE BIBLE

INAUGURATION OF TABERNACLE WORSHIP

9 On the eighth day Moses summoned Aaron and his sons
and the elders of Israel, [2]and said to Aaron, "Take for yourself a bull calf for a sin offering and a ram for a burnt offering,
both flawless, and present them before the LORD. [3]Then tell
the Israelites: 'Take a male goat for a sin offering and a calf
and a lamb, both a year old and flawless, for a burnt offering,
[4]and an ox and a ram for peace offerings to sacrifice before the
LORD, and a grain offering mixed with olive oil, for today the
LORD is going to appear to you.'" [5]So they took what Moses had
commanded to the front of the Meeting Tent, and the whole
congregation presented them and stood before the LORD. [6]Then
Moses said, "This is what the LORD has commanded you to do
so that the glory of the LORD may appear to you." [7]Moses then
said to Aaron, "Approach the altar and make your sin offering
and your burnt offering, and make atonement on behalf of
yourself and on behalf of the people; and also make the people's
offering and make atonement on behalf of them just as the
LORD has commanded."

THE SIN OFFERING FOR THE PRIESTS

[8]So Aaron approached the altar and slaughtered the sin-offering
calf which was for himself. [9]Then Aaron's sons presented the
blood to him, and he dipped his finger in the blood and put it
on the horns of the altar, and the rest of the blood he poured
out at the base of the altar. [10]The fat and the kidneys and the
protruding lobe of the liver from the sin offering he offered
up in smoke on the altar just as the LORD had commanded
Moses, [11]but the flesh and the hide he completely burned up
outside the camp.

THE BURNT OFFERING FOR THE PRIESTS

[12]He then slaughtered the burnt offering, and his sons handed
the blood to him, and he splashed it against the altar's sides.
[13]The burnt offering itself they handed to him by its parts, including the head, and he offered them up in smoke on the altar,
[14]and he washed the entrails and the legs and offered them up
in smoke on top of the burnt offering on the altar.

THE OFFERINGS FOR THE PEOPLE

[15]Then he presented the people's offering. He took the sin-
offering male goat which was for the people, slaughtered it,
and performed a purification rite with it like the first one. [16]He
then presented the burnt offering, and did it according to the
standard regulation. [17]Next he presented the grain offering,
filled his hand with some of it, and offered it up in smoke on
the altar in addition to the morning burnt offering. [18]Then he
slaughtered the ox and the ram—the peace-offering sacrifices
which were for the people—and Aaron's sons handed the blood
to him, and he splashed it against the altar's sides. [19]As for the
fat parts from the ox and from the ram (the fatty tail, the fat

covering the entrails, the kidneys, and the protruding lobe of the liver), 20they set those on the breasts, and he offered the fat parts up in smoke on the altar. 21Finally Aaron waved the breasts and the right thigh as a wave offering before the LORD just as Moses had commanded.

22Then Aaron lifted up his hands toward the people and blessed them and descended from making the sin offering, the burnt offering, and the peace offering. 23Moses and Aaron then entered into the Meeting Tent. When they came out, they blessed the people, and the glory of the LORD appeared to all the people. 24Then fire went out from the presence of the LORD and consumed the burnt offering and the fat parts on the altar, and all the people saw it, so they shouted loudly and fell down with their faces to the ground.

NADAB AND ABIHU

10 Then Aaron's sons, Nadab and Abihu, each took his fire pan and put fire in it, set incense on it, and presented strange fire before the LORD, which he had not commanded them to do. 2So fire went out from the presence of the LORD and consumed them so that they died before the LORD. 3Moses then said to Aaron, "This is what the LORD spoke: 'Among the ones close to me I will show myself holy, and in the presence of all the people I will be honored.'" So Aaron kept silent. 4Moses then called to Mishael and Elzaphan, the sons of Uzziel, Aaron's uncle, and said to them, "Come near, carry your brothers from the front of the sanctuary to a place outside the camp." 5So they came near and carried them away in their tunics to a place outside the camp just as Moses had spoken. 6Then Moses said to Aaron and to Eleazar and Ithamar his other two sons, "Do not dishevel the hair of your heads and do not tear your garments, so that you do not die and so that wrath does not come on the whole congregation. Your brothers, all the house of Israel, are to mourn the burning that the LORD has caused, 7but you must not go out from the entrance of the Meeting Tent lest you die, for the LORD's anointing oil is on you." So they acted according to the word of Moses.

10:1–7 The sons of Aaron also, who set upon the altar a strange fire not commanded by the Lord, were at once blotted out in the sight of the avenging Lord. These examples, you will see, are being followed wherever the tradition that comes from God is despised by lovers of strange doctrine and replaced by teaching of merely human authority.

CYPRIAN OF CARTHAGE
(C. 210–258)
THE UNITY OF THE CATHOLIC CHURCH

PERPETUAL STATUTES THE LORD SPOKE TO AARON

8Then the LORD spoke to Aaron, 9"Do not drink wine or strong drink, you and your sons with you, when you enter into the Meeting Tent, so that you do not die. This is a perpetual statute throughout your generations, 10as well as to distinguish between the holy and the common, and between the unclean and the clean, 11and to teach the Israelites all the statutes that the LORD has spoken to them through Moses."

PERPETUAL STATUTES MOSES SPOKE TO AARON

12Then Moses spoke to Aaron and to Eleazar and Ithamar, his remaining sons, "Take the grain offering which remains from the gifts of the LORD and eat it unleavened beside the altar, for it is most holy. 13You must eat it in a holy place because it is your allotted portion and the allotted portion of your sons from the gifts of the LORD, for this is what I have been commanded. 14Also, the breast of the wave offering and the thigh of the contribution offering you must eat in a ceremonially clean place, you and your sons and daughters with you, for the foods have been given as your allotted portion and the allotted portion of

your sons from the peace-offering sacrifices of the Israelites.
[15]The thigh of the contribution offering and the breast of the
wave offering they must bring in addition to the gifts of the fat
parts to wave them as a wave offering before the LORD, and it
will belong to you and your sons with you for a perpetual statute
just as the LORD has commanded."

THE PROBLEM WITH THE INAUGURAL SIN OFFERING

[16]Later Moses sought diligently for the sin-offering male goat,
but it had actually been burnt. So he became angry at Eleazar
and Ithamar, Aaron's remaining sons, saying, [17]"Why did you
not eat the sin offering in the sanctuary? For it is most holy,
and he gave it to you to bear the iniquity of the congregation, to
make atonement on their behalf before the LORD. [18]See here! Its
blood was not brought into the Holy Place within! You should
certainly have eaten it in the sanctuary just as I commanded!"
[19]But Aaron spoke to Moses, "See here! Just today they presented their sin offering and their burnt offering before the LORD,
and such things as these have happened to me! If I had eaten a
sin offering today, would the LORD have been pleased?" [20]When
Moses heard this explanation, he was satisfied.

CLEAN AND UNCLEAN LAND CREATURES

11 The LORD spoke to Moses and Aaron, saying to them, [2]"Tell
the Israelites: 'This is the kind of creature you may eat
from among all the animals that are on the land. [3]You may eat
any among the animals that has a divided hoof (the hooves are
completely split in two) and that also chews the cud. [4]However,
you must not eat these from among those that chew the cud
and have divided hooves: The camel is unclean to you because
it chews the cud even though its hoof is not divided. [5]The rock
badger is unclean to you because it chews the cud even though
its hoof is not divided. [6]The hare is unclean to you because it
chews the cud even though its hoof is not divided. [7]The pig is
unclean to you because its hoof is divided (the hoof is completely split in two), even though it does not chew the cud. [8]You
must not eat from their meat, and you must not touch their
carcasses; they are unclean to you.

CLEAN AND UNCLEAN WATER CREATURES

[9]"'These you can eat from all creatures that are in the water: Any
creatures in the water that have both fins and scales, whether in
the seas or in the streams, you may eat. [10]But any creatures that
do not have both fins and scales, whether in the seas or in the
streams, from all the swarming things of the water and from all
the living creatures that are in the water, are detestable to you.
[11]Since they are detestable to you, you must not eat their meat,
and their carcass you must detest. [12]Any creature in the water
that does not have both fins and scales is detestable to you.

CLEAN AND UNCLEAN BIRDS

[13]"'These you are to detest from among the birds—they must
not be eaten, because they are detestable: the griffon vulture,
the bearded vulture, the black vulture, [14]the kite, the buzzard of
any kind, [15]every kind of crow, [16]the eagle owl, the short-eared
owl, the long-eared owl, the hawk of any kind, [17]the little owl, the
cormorant, the screech owl, [18]the white owl, the scops owl, the
osprey, [19]the stork, the heron of any kind, the hoopoe, and the bat.

CLEAN AND UNCLEAN INSECTS

[20]"'Every winged swarming thing that walks on all fours is detestable to you. [21]However, this you may eat from all the winged swarming things that walk on all fours, which have jointed legs to hop with on the land. [22]These you may eat from them: the locust of any kind, the bald locust of any kind, the cricket of any kind, the grasshopper of any kind. [23]But any other winged swarming thing that has four legs is detestable to you.

CARCASS UNCLEANNESS

[24]"'By these you defile yourselves—anyone who touches their carcass will be unclean until the evening, [25]and anyone who carries their carcass must wash his clothes and will be unclean until the evening.

INEDIBLE LAND QUADRUPEDS

[26]"'All animals that divide the hoof, but it is not completely split in two, and do not chew the cud are unclean to you; anyone who touches them becomes unclean. [27]All that walk on their paws among all the creatures that walk on all fours are unclean to you. Anyone who touches their carcass will be unclean until the evening, [28]and the one who carries their carcass must wash his clothes and be unclean until the evening; they are unclean to you.

CREATURES THAT SWARM ON THE LAND

[29]"'Now this is what is unclean to you among the swarming things that swarm on the land: the rat, the mouse, the large lizard of any kind, [30]the Mediterranean gecko, the spotted lizard, the wall gecko, the skink, and the chameleon. [31]These are the ones that are unclean to you among all the swarming things. Anyone who touches these creatures when they die will be unclean until evening. [32]Also, anything they fall on when they die will become unclean—any wood vessel or garment or article of leather or sackcloth. Any such vessel with which work is done must be immersed in water and will be unclean until the evening. Then it will become clean. [33]As for any clay vessel they fall into, everything in it will become unclean, and you must break it. [34]Any food that may be eaten which becomes soaked with water will become unclean. Anything drinkable in any such vessel will become unclean. [35]Anything their carcass may fall on will become unclean. An oven or small stove must be smashed to pieces; they are unclean, and they will stay unclean to you. [36]However, a spring or a cistern which collects water will be clean, but one who touches the creature's carcass will be unclean. [37]Now, if such a carcass falls on any sowing seed which is to be sown, it is clean, [38]but if water is put on the seed and such a carcass falls on it, it is unclean to you.

EDIBLE LAND ANIMALS

[39]"'Now if an animal that you may eat dies, whoever touches its carcass will be unclean until the evening. [40]One who eats from its carcass must wash his clothes and be unclean until the evening, and whoever carries its carcass must wash his clothes and be unclean until the evening. [41]Every swarming thing that swarms on the land is detestable; it must not be eaten. [42]You must not eat anything that crawls on its belly or anything that walks on all fours or on any number of legs of all the swarming things that swarm on the land, because they are detestable. [43]Do not make yourselves detestable by any of the swarming

11:24–47 He himself says, "Be holy because I am holy," that is to say, *Choose me and keep away from what displeases me. Do what I love; love what I do. If what I order seems difficult, come back to me who ordered it so that from where the command was given help might be offered. I who furnished the desire will not refuse support. Fast from contradiction, abstain from opposition. Let me be your food and drink. None desire in vain what is mine, for those who stretch out toward me seek me because I first sought them.*

LEO THE GREAT (C. 400–461)
SERMONS

things. You must not defile yourselves by them and become unclean by them, [44]for I am the LORD your God, and you are to sanctify yourselves and be holy because I am holy. You must not defile yourselves by any of the swarming things that creep on the ground, [45]for I am the LORD who brought you up from the land of Egypt to be your God, and you are to be holy because I am holy. [46]This is the law of the land animals, the birds, all the living creatures that move in the water, and all the creatures that swarm on the land, [47]to distinguish between the unclean and the clean, between the living creatures that may be eaten and the living creatures that must not be eaten.'"

PURIFICATION OF A WOMAN AFTER CHILDBIRTH

12 The LORD spoke to Moses: [2]"Tell the Israelites, 'When a woman produces offspring and bears a male child, she will be unclean seven days, as she is unclean during the days of her menstruation. [3]On the eighth day the flesh of his foreskin must be circumcised. [4]Then she will remain thirty-three days in blood purity. She must not touch anything holy, and she must not enter the sanctuary until the days of her purification are fulfilled. [5]If she bears a female child, she will be impure fourteen days as during her menstrual flow, and she will remain sixty-six days in blood purity.

[6]"'When the days of her purification are completed for a son or for a daughter, she must bring a one-year-old lamb for a burnt offering and a young pigeon or turtledove for a sin offering to the entrance of the Meeting Tent, to the priest. [7]The priest is to present it before the LORD and make atonement on her behalf, and she will be clean from her flow of blood. This is the law of the one who bears a child, for the male or the female child. [8]If she cannot afford a sheep, then she must take two turtledoves or two young pigeons, one for a burnt offering and one for a sin offering, and the priest is to make atonement on her behalf, and she will be clean.'"

12:1–8 It was certainly not for nothing that the commandment was given for the child to be circumcised on the eighth day; it can only have been because the rock, the stone with which we are circumcised, was Christ. It was with knives of rock or stone that the people were circumcised; "the rock was Christ" (1 Cor 10:4). So why on the eighth day? Because in seven-day weeks the first is the same as the eighth; once you've completed the seven days, you are back at the first. The seventh is finished, the Lord is buried; we are back at the first, the Lord is raised up.

AUGUSTINE (354–430)
SERMONS

INFECTIONS ON THE SKIN

13 The LORD spoke to Moses and Aaron: [2]"When someone has a swelling or a scab or a bright spot on the skin of his body that may become a diseased infection, he must be brought to Aaron the priest or one of his sons, the priests. [3]The priest must then examine the infection on the skin of the body, and if the hair in the infection has turned white and the infection appears to be deeper than the skin of the body, then it is a diseased infection, so when the priest examines it, he must pronounce the person unclean.

A BRIGHT SPOT ON THE SKIN

[4]"If it is a white bright spot on the skin of his body, but it does not appear to be deeper than the skin, and the hair has not turned white, then the priest is to quarantine the person with the infection for seven days. [5]The priest must then examine it on the seventh day, and if, as far as he can see, the infection has stayed the same and has not spread on the skin, then the priest is to quarantine the person for another seven days. [6]The priest must then examine it again on the seventh day, and if the infection has faded and has not spread on the skin, then the priest is to pronounce the person clean. It is a scab, so he must wash his clothes and be clean. [7]If, however, the scab is spreading further on the skin after he has shown himself to the

13:1–17 When people see themselves to be altogether lost and ruined, when they disclaim all righteousness of their own and plead guilty before the Lord, then they are clean through the blood of Jesus and the grace of God. Hidden, unfelt, unconfessed iniquity is the true leprosy, but when sin is seen and felt, it has received its deathblow, and the Lord looks with eyes of mercy upon the soul afflicted with it. Nothing is more deadly than self-righteousness or more hopeful than contrition.

CHARLES SPURGEON (1834–1892)
MORNING AND EVENING

ORIGEN:

PROLIFIC THINKER WITH A MIXED LEGACY

c. 185–c. 254

One of the most controversial Christian thinkers of the third century was also one of the most influential. Some have said that his influence on Christian theology during his era was surpassed only by the apostle Paul himself.

Born in Alexandria, Egypt, to Christian parents around AD 185, Origen had a hunger for truth at an early age, desiring to know and understand scripture more deeply. As a young student at the Alexandria Christian school, he was mentored by Clement of Alexandria, who sharpened his understanding of Greek philosophy and deepened his love for the faith.

When Origen was seventeen, his father was martyred. Though he fully expected to follow in his father's footsteps and become a martyr himself, Origen became a teacher instead at the school at Alexandria after persecutions resulted in the martyrdom or departure of several teachers. Although he taught the range of secular subjects, such as grammar and rhetoric, he was more keen to teach religious subjects, eventually taking over for Clement as head of the school and continuing Clement's work of raising the next generation of Christian thinkers.

During this time, Origen adopted an ascetic lifestyle, giving up worldly pleasures in the interest of his spiritual life. He slept on the floor, gave up alcohol and limited his food, owned only one cloak and no shoes, and thoroughly immersed himself in the scriptures. Remarkably—and controversially—he was so committed to dying to this world and living for Christ that he physically castrated himself, an act that brought him fame throughout the region.

As one of the most prolific of early Christian thinkers, Origen carries a mixed legacy. He was mostly consistent with the apostolic tradition handed down from early church fathers, writing: "Nothing which is at variance with the tradition of apostles and of the church is to be accepted as true." He was also one of the fiercest defenders of the faith, going toe-to-toe with the Roman pagan philosopher Celsus. In *Against Celsus,* Origen responded to attacks against Christianity and showed the superiority of scripture to Greek philosophy. He also provided a system of Christian philosophy in *On First Principles*, where he commented on topics ranging from the nature of God to creation to salvation. Origen should be credited for articulating the vital Christological doctrine of "eternal generation of the Son"—which basically says that Jesus Christ is eternally the fully divine Son of God, not a lesser, subdivine being. And he offered an enduring contribution to textual criticism, particularly for the Old Testament.

Origen remains one of the faith's most influential thinkers, with his writings guiding the development of Christian theology well into the Middle Ages and beyond. He was martyred for his faith in 254.

IMPORTANT WORKS

AGAINST CELSUS

ON FIRST PRINCIPLES

priest for his purification, then he must show himself to the
priest a second time. 8The priest must then examine it, and if
the scab has spread on the skin, then the priest is to pronounce
the person unclean. It is a disease.

A SWELLING ON THE SKIN

9"When someone has a diseased infection, he must be brought to
the priest. 10The priest will then examine it, and if a white swelling is on the skin, it has turned the hair white, and there is raw
flesh in the swelling, 11it is a chronic disease on the skin of his
body, so the priest is to pronounce him unclean. The priest must
not merely quarantine him, for he is unclean. 12If, however, the
disease breaks out on the skin so that the disease covers all the
skin of the person with the infection from his head to his feet,
as far as the priest can see, 13the priest must then examine it,
and if the disease covers his whole body, he is to pronounce the
person with the infection clean. He has turned all white, so he is
clean. 14But whenever raw flesh appears in it, he will be unclean,
15so the priest is to examine the raw flesh and pronounce him
unclean—it is diseased. 16If, however, the raw flesh once again
turns white, then he must come to the priest. 17The priest will
then examine it, and if the infection has turned white, the priest
is to pronounce the person with the infection clean—he is clean.

A BOIL ON THE SKIN

18"When someone's body has a boil on its skin and it heals, 19and
in the place of the boil there is a white swelling or a reddish
white bright spot, he must show himself to the priest. 20The
priest will then examine it, and if it appears to be deeper than
the skin and its hair has turned white, then the priest is to
pronounce the person unclean. It is a diseased infection that
has broken out in the boil. 21If, however, the priest examines it,
and there is no white hair in it, it is not deeper than the skin,
and it has faded, then the priest is to quarantine him for seven
days. 22If it is spreading farther on the skin, then the priest is
to pronounce him unclean. It is an infection. 23But if the bright
spot stays in its place and has not spread, it is the scar of the
boil, so the priest is to pronounce him clean.

A BURN ON THE SKIN

24"When a body has a burn on its skin and the raw area of the
burn becomes a reddish white or white bright spot, 25the priest
must examine it, and if the hair has turned white in the bright
spot and it appears to be deeper than the skin, it is a disease
that has broken out in the burn. The priest is to pronounce the
person unclean. It is a diseased infection. 26If, however, the priest
examines it and there is no white hair in the bright spot, it is
not deeper than the skin, and it has faded, then the priest is to
quarantine him for seven days. 27The priest must then examine it
on the seventh day, and if it is spreading further on the skin, then
the priest is to pronounce him unclean. It is a diseased infection.
28But if the bright spot stays in its place, has not spread on the
skin, and it has faded, then it is the swelling of the burn, so the
priest is to pronounce him clean, because it is the scar of the burn.

SCALL ON THE HEAD OR IN THE BEARD

29"When a man or a woman has an infection on the head or in the
beard, 30the priest is to examine the infection, and if it appears
to be deeper than the skin and the hair in it is reddish yellow

and thin, then the priest is to pronounce the person unclean.
It is scall, a disease of the head or the beard. 31 But if the priest
examines the scall infection and it does not appear to be deeper
than the skin, and there is no black hair in it, then the priest is
to quarantine the person with the scall infection for seven days.
32 The priest must then examine the infection on the seventh
day, and if the scall has not spread, there is no reddish yellow hair
in it, and the scall does not appear to be deeper than the skin,
33 then the individual is to shave himself, but he must not shave
the area affected by the scall, and the priest is to quarantine the
person with the scall for another seven days. 34 The priest must
then examine the scall on the seventh day, and if the scall has not
spread on the skin and it does not appear to be deeper than the
skin, then the priest is to pronounce him clean. So he is to wash
his clothes and be clean. 35 If, however, the scall spreads further on
the skin after his purification, 36 then the priest is to examine it,
and if the scall has spread on the skin, the priest is not to search
further for reddish yellow hair. The person is unclean. 37 If, as far
as the priest can see, the scall has stayed the same and black hair
has sprouted in it, the scall has been healed; the person is clean.
So the priest is to pronounce him clean.

BRIGHT WHITE SPOTS ON THE SKIN

38 "When a man or a woman has bright spots—white bright
spots—on the skin of their body, 39 the priest is to examine
them, and if the bright spots on the skin of their body are faded white, it is a harmless rash that has broken out on the skin.
The person is clean.

BALDNESS ON THE HEAD

40 "When a man's head is bare so that he is balding in back, he is
clean. 41 If his head is bare on the forehead so that he is balding
in front, he is clean. 42 But if there is a reddish white infection
in the back or front bald area, it is a disease breaking out in his
back or front bald area. 43 The priest is to examine it, and if the
swelling of the infection is reddish white in the back or the front
bald area like the appearance of a disease on the skin of the body,
44 he is a diseased man. He is unclean. The priest must surely
pronounce him unclean because of his infection on his head.

THE LIFE OF THE PERSON WITH SKIN DISEASE

45 "As for the diseased person who has the infection, his clothes
must be torn, the hair of his head must be unbound, he must
cover his mustache, and he must call out 'Unclean! Unclean!'
46 The whole time he has the infection he will be continually
unclean. He must live in isolation, and his place of residence
must be outside the camp.

INFECTIONS IN GARMENTS, CLOTH, OR LEATHER

47 "When a garment has a diseased infection in it, whether a wool
or linen garment, 48 or in the warp or woof of the linen or the
wool, or in leather or anything made of leather, 49 if the infection in the garment or leather or warp or woof or any article of
leather is yellowish green or reddish, it is a diseased infection,
and it must be shown to the priest. 50 The priest is to examine
and then quarantine the article with the infection for seven
days. 51 He must then examine the infection on the seventh
day. If the infection has spread in the garment, or in the warp,
or in the woof, or in the leather—whatever the article into which

the leather was made—the infection is a malignant disease. It is unclean. [52]He must burn the garment or the warp or the woof, whether wool or linen, or any article of leather which has the infection in it. Because it is a malignant disease it must be burned up in the fire. [53]But if the priest examines it and the infection has not spread in the garment or in the warp or in the woof or in any article of leather, [54]the priest is to command that they wash whatever has the infection and quarantine it for another seven days. [55]The priest must then examine it after the infection has been washed out, and if the infection has not changed its appearance even though the infection has not spread, it is unclean. You must burn it up in the fire. It is a fungus, whether on the back side or front side of the article. [56]But if the priest has examined it and the infection has faded after it has been washed, he is to tear it out of the garment or the leather or the warp or the woof. [57]Then if it still appears again in the garment or the warp or the woof, or in any article of leather, it is an outbreak. Whatever has the infection in it you must burn up in the fire. [58]But the garment or the warp or the woof or any article of leather which you wash and infection disappears from it is to be washed a second time, and it will be clean."

SUMMARY OF INFECTION REGULATIONS

[59]This is the law of the diseased infection in the garment of wool or linen, or the warp or woof, or any article of leather, for pronouncing it clean or unclean.

PURIFICATION OF DISEASED SKIN INFECTIONS

14 The LORD spoke to Moses: [2]"This is the law of the diseased person on the day of his purification, when he is brought to the priest. [3]The priest is to go outside the camp and examine the infection. If the infection of the diseased person has been healed, [4]then the priest will command that two live clean birds, a piece of cedar wood, a scrap of crimson fabric, and some twigs of hyssop be taken up for the one being cleansed. [5]The priest will then command that one bird be slaughtered into a clay vessel over fresh water. [6]Then he is to take the live bird along with the piece of cedar wood, the scrap of crimson fabric, and the twigs of hyssop, and he is to dip them and the live bird in the blood of the bird slaughtered over the fresh water, [7]and sprinkle it seven times on the one being cleansed from the disease, pronounce him clean, and send the live bird away over the open countryside.

THE SEVEN DAYS OF PURIFICATION

[8]"The one being cleansed must then wash his clothes, shave off all his hair, and bathe in water, and so be clean. Then afterward he may enter the camp, but he must live outside his tent seven days. [9]When the seventh day comes, he must shave all his hair—his head, his beard, his eyebrows, all his hair—and he must wash his clothes, bathe his body in water, and so be clean.

THE EIGHTH-DAY ATONEMENT RITUALS

[10]"On the eighth day he must take two flawless male lambs, one flawless yearling female lamb, three-tenths of an ephah of choice wheat flour as a grain offering mixed with olive oil, and one log of olive oil, [11]and the priest who pronounces him clean will have the man who is being cleansed stand along with these offerings before the LORD at the entrance of the Meeting Tent.

14:10–32 The offering of flour, which was ordered to be presented for those cleansed from leprosy, was a prototype of the eucharistic bread that our Lord Jesus Christ commanded us to offer in remembrance of the Passion he endured for all those souls who are cleansed from sin. And at the same time we should thank God for having created the world and everything in it for the sake of humankind, for having saved us from the sin in which we were born, and for the total destruction of the powers and principalities of evil through him who suffered in accordance with his will.

JUSTIN MARTYR (C. 100–C. 165)
DIALOGUE WITH TRYPHO

12“The priest is to take one male lamb and present it for a
guilt offering along with the log of olive oil and present them
as a wave offering before the LORD. 13He must then slaughter the male lamb in the place where the sin offering and the
burnt offering are slaughtered, in the sanctuary, because, like
the sin offering, the guilt offering belongs to the priest; it is
most holy. 14Then the priest is to take some of the blood of the
guilt offering and put it on the right earlobe of the one being
cleansed, on the thumb of his right hand, and on the big toe
of his right foot. 15The priest will then take some of the log of
olive oil and pour it into his own left hand. 16Then the priest
is to dip his right forefinger into the olive oil that is in his left
hand, and sprinkle some of the olive oil with his finger seven
times before the LORD. 17The priest will then put some of the
rest of the olive oil that is in his hand on the right earlobe of
the one being cleansed, on the thumb of his right hand, and on
the big toe of his right foot, on the blood of the guilt offering,
18and the remainder of the olive oil that is in his hand the priest
is to put on the head of the one being cleansed. So the priest is
to make atonement for him before the LORD.
19“The priest must then perform the sin offering and make
atonement for the one being cleansed from his impurity. After
that he is to slaughter the burnt offering, 20and the priest is to
offer the burnt offering and the grain offering on the altar. So
the priest is to make atonement for him and he will be clean.

THE EIGHTH-DAY ATONEMENT RITUALS FOR THE POOR PERSON

21“If the person is poor and does not have sufficient means,
he must take one male lamb as a guilt offering for a wave offering to make atonement for himself, one-tenth of an ephah
of choice wheat flour mixed with olive oil for a grain offering,
a log of olive oil, 22and two turtledoves or two young pigeons,
which are within his means. One will be a sin offering and the
other a burnt offering.
23“On the eighth day he must bring them for his purification
to the priest at the entrance of the Meeting Tent before the
LORD, 24and the priest is to take the male lamb of the guilt offering and the log of olive oil and wave them as a wave offering
before the LORD. 25Then he is to slaughter the male lamb of the
guilt offering, and the priest is to take some of the blood of the
guilt offering and put it on the right earlobe of the one being
cleansed, on the thumb of his right hand, and on the big toe of
his right foot. 26The priest will then pour some of the olive oil
into his own left hand, 27and sprinkle some of the olive oil that
is in his left hand with his right forefinger seven times before
the LORD. 28Then the priest is to put some of the olive oil that
is in his hand on the right earlobe of the one being cleansed,
on the thumb of his right hand, and on the big toe of his right
foot, on the place of the blood of the guilt offering, 29and the
remainder of the olive oil that is in the hand of the priest he is
to put on the head of the one being cleansed to make atonement
for him before the LORD.
30“He will then make one of the turtledoves or young pigeons,
which are within his means, 31a sin offering and the other a
burnt offering along with the grain offering. So the priest is to
make atonement for the one being cleansed before the LORD.
32This is the law of the one in whom there is a diseased infection, who does not have sufficient means for his purification.”

PURIFICATION OF DISEASE-INFECTED HOUSES

33 The Lord spoke to Moses and Aaron: 34 "When you enter the land of Canaan which I am about to give to you for a possession, and I put a diseased infection in a house in the land you are to possess, 35 then whoever owns the house must come and declare to the priest, 'Something like an infection is visible to me in the house.' 36 Then the priest will command that the house be cleared before the priest enters to examine the infection so that everything in the house does not become unclean, and afterward the priest will enter to examine the house. 37 He is to examine the infection, and if the infection in the walls of the house consists of yellowish green or reddish eruptions, and it appears to be deeper than the surface of the wall, 38 then the priest is to go out of the house to the doorway of the house and quarantine the house for seven days. 39 The priest must return on the seventh day and examine it, and if the infection has spread in the walls of the house, 40 then the priest is to command that the stones that had the infection in them be pulled and thrown outside the city into an unclean place. 41 Then they shall scrape the house all around on the inside, and the plaster which they have scraped off must be dumped outside the city into an unclean place. 42 They are then to take other stones and replace those stones, and he is to take other plaster and replaster the house.

43 "If the infection returns and breaks out in the house after he has pulled out the stones, scraped the house, and it is replastered, 44 the priest is to come and examine it, and if the infection has spread in the house, it is a malignant disease in the house. It is unclean. 45 He must tear down the house, its stones, its wood, and all the plaster of the house, and bring all of it outside the city to an unclean place. 46 Anyone who enters the house all the days the priest has quarantined it will be unclean until evening. 47 Anyone who lies down in the house must wash his clothes. Anyone who eats in the house must wash his clothes.

48 "If, however, the priest enters and examines it, and the infection has not spread in the house after the house has been replastered, then the priest is to pronounce the house clean because the infection has been healed. 49 Then he is to take two birds, a piece of cedar wood, a scrap of crimson fabric, and some twigs of hyssop to purify the house, 50 and he is to slaughter one bird into a clay vessel over fresh water. 51 He must then take the piece of cedar wood, the twigs of hyssop, the scrap of crimson fabric, and the live bird, and dip them in the blood of the slaughtered bird and in the fresh water, and sprinkle the house seven times. 52 So he is to purify the house with the blood of the bird, the fresh water, the live bird, the piece of cedar wood, the twigs of hyssop, and the scrap of crimson fabric, 53 and he is to send the live bird away outside the city into the open countryside. So he is to make atonement for the house, and it will be clean.

SUMMARY OF PURIFICATION REGULATIONS FOR INFECTIONS

54 "This is the law for all diseased infections, for scall, 55 for the diseased garment, for the house, 56 for the swelling, for the scab, and for the bright spot, 57 to teach when something is unclean and when it is clean. This is the law for dealing with infectious disease."

MALE BODILY DISCHARGES

15 The LORD spoke to Moses and Aaron: 2"Speak to the Israelites and tell them, 'When any man has a discharge from his body, his discharge is unclean. 3Now this is his uncleanness in regard to his discharge—whether his body secretes his discharge or blocks his discharge, he is unclean. All the days that his body has a discharge or his body blocks his discharge, this is his uncleanness.

4"'Any bed the man with a discharge lies on will be unclean, and any furniture he sits on will be unclean. 5Anyone who touches his bed must wash his clothes, bathe in water, and be unclean until evening. 6The one who sits on the furniture the man with a discharge sits on must wash his clothes, bathe in water, and be unclean until evening. 7The one who touches the body of the man with a discharge must wash his clothes, bathe in water, and be unclean until evening. 8If the man with a discharge spits on a person who is ceremonially clean, that person must wash his clothes, bathe in water, and be unclean until evening. 9Any means of riding that the man with a discharge rides on will be unclean. 10Anyone who touches anything that was under him will be unclean until evening, and the one who carries those items must wash his clothes, bathe in water, and be unclean until evening. 11Anyone whom the man with the discharge touches without having rinsed his hands in water must wash his clothes, bathe in water, and be unclean until evening. 12A clay vessel which the man with the discharge touches must be broken, and any wooden utensil must be rinsed in water.

PURITY REGULATIONS FOR MALE BODILY DISCHARGES

13"'When the man with the discharge becomes clean from his discharge, he is to count off for himself seven days for his purification, and he must wash his clothes, bathe in fresh water, and be clean. 14Then on the eighth day he is to take for himself two turtledoves or two young pigeons, and he is to present himself before the LORD at the entrance of the Meeting Tent and give them to the priest, 15and the priest is to make one of them a sin offering and the other a burnt offering. So the priest is to make atonement for him before the LORD for his discharge.

16"'When a man has a seminal emission, he must bathe his whole body in water and be unclean until evening, 17and he must wash in water any clothing or leather that has semen on it, and it will be unclean until evening. 18As for a woman whom a man goes to bed with, then has a seminal emission, they must bathe in water and be unclean until evening.

FEMALE BODILY DISCHARGES

19"'When a woman has a discharge and her discharge is blood from her body, she is to be in her menstruation seven days, and anyone who touches her will be unclean until evening. 20Anything she lies on during her menstruation will be unclean, and anything she sits on will be unclean. 21Anyone who touches her bed must wash his clothes, bathe in water, and be unclean until evening. 22Anyone who touches any furniture she sits on must wash his clothes, bathe in water, and be unclean until evening. 23If there is something on the bed or on the furniture she sits on, when he touches it, he will be unclean until evening, 24and if a man actually goes to bed with her so that her menstrual impurity touches him, then he will be unclean seven days, and any bed he lies on will be unclean.

15:1–12 **For from the beginning the Spirit of God moved upon the face of the waters, and anew the scripture witnesses that water has the power of purification. In the time of Noah God washed away the sin of the world by water. By water every impure person is purified, according to the law, even the very garments being washed with water.**

JOHN OF DAMASCUS
(C. 675–749)
AN EXACT EXPOSITION OF THE ORTHODOX FAITH

25“‘When a woman’s discharge of blood flows many days not at the time of her menstruation, or if it flows beyond the time of her menstruation, all the days of her discharge of impurity will be like the days of her menstruation—she is unclean. 26Any bed she lies on all the days of her discharge will be to her like the bed of her menstruation, any furniture she sits on will be unclean like the impurity of her menstruation, 27and anyone who touches them will be unclean, and he must wash his clothes, bathe in water, and be unclean until evening.

PURITY REGULATIONS FOR FEMALE BODILY DISCHARGES

28“‘If she becomes clean from her discharge, then she is to count off for herself seven days, and afterward she will be clean. 29Then on the eighth day she must take for herself two turtledoves or two young pigeons, and she must bring them to the priest at the entrance of the Meeting Tent, 30and the priest is to make one a sin offering and the other a burnt offering. So the priest is to make atonement for her before the LORD from her discharge of impurity.

SUMMARY OF PURIFICATION REGULATIONS FOR BODILY DISCHARGES

31“‘Thus you are to set the Israelites apart from their impurity so that they do not die in their impurity by defiling my tabernacle which is in their midst. 32This is the law for the one with a discharge: for the one who has a seminal emission and becomes unclean by it, 33for the one who is sick in her menstruation, for the one with a discharge, whether male or female, and for a man who goes to bed with an unclean woman.’”

THE DAY OF ATONEMENT

16 The LORD spoke to Moses after the death of Aaron’s two sons when they approached the presence of the LORD and died, 2and the LORD said to Moses: “Tell Aaron your brother that he must not enter at any time into the Holy Place inside the special curtain in front of the atonement lid that is on the ark so that he may not die, for I will appear in the cloud over the atonement lid.

16:1–14 May I offer an interpretation of the two goats that were presented on the great Day of Atonement? Do they not also prefigure the two natures of Christ? One of these goats was bound with scarlet and driven by the people out of the camp into the wilderness amid cursing and spitting, being thus marked with all the signs of the Lord’s own Passion. The other, by being offered up for sins and given to the priests of the temple for meat, afforded proofs of his second appearance when (after all sins have been expiated) the priests of the spiritual temple, that is, the church, are to enjoy the flesh of the Lord’s own grace.

TERTULLIAN (155–C. 220)
AGAINST MARCION

DAY OF ATONEMENT OFFERINGS

3“In this way Aaron is to enter into the sanctuary—with a young bull for a sin offering and a ram for a burnt offering. 4He must put on a holy linen tunic, linen leggings are to cover his body, and he is to wrap himself with a linen sash and wrap his head with a linen turban. They are holy garments, so he must bathe his body in water and put them on. 5He must also take two male goats from the congregation of the Israelites for a sin offering and one ram for a burnt offering. 6Then Aaron is to present the sin-offering bull which is for himself and is to make atonement on behalf of himself and his household. 7Next he must take the two goats and stand them before the LORD at the entrance of the Meeting Tent, 8and Aaron is to cast lots over the two goats, one lot for the LORD and one lot for Azazel. 9Aaron must then present the goat which has been designated by lot for the LORD, and he is to make it a sin offering, 10but the goat which has been designated by lot for Azazel is to be stood alive before the LORD to make atonement on it by sending it away into the desert to Azazel.

THE SIN-OFFERING SACRIFICIAL PROCEDURES

[11]"Aaron is to present the sin-offering bull which is for himself, and he is to make atonement on behalf of himself and his
household. He is to slaughter the sin-offering bull which is for
himself, [12]and take a censer full of coals of fire from the altar
before the LORD and a full double handful of finely ground
fragrant incense, and bring them inside the curtain. [13]He must
then put the incense on the fire before the LORD, and the cloud
of incense will cover the atonement lid which is above the ark
of the testimony, so that he will not die. [14]Then he is to take
some of the blood of the bull and sprinkle it with his finger
on the eastern face of the atonement lid, and in front of the
atonement lid he is to sprinkle some of the blood seven times
with his finger.

[15]"Aaron must then slaughter the sin-offering goat which
is for the people. He is to bring its blood inside the curtain,
and he is to do with its blood just as he did to the blood of
the bull: He is to sprinkle it on the atonement lid and in front
of the atonement lid. [16]So he is to make atonement for the
Holy Place from the impurities of the Israelites and from their
transgressions with regard to all their sins, and thus he is to do
for the Meeting Tent which resides with them in the midst of
their impurities. [17]Nobody is to be in the Meeting Tent when
he enters to make atonement in the Holy Place until he goes
out, and he has made atonement on his behalf, on behalf of
his household, and on behalf of the whole assembly of Israel.

[18]"Then Aaron is to go out to the altar which is before the
LORD and make atonement for it. He is to take some of the
blood of the bull and some of the blood of the goat, and put it
all around on the horns of the altar. [19]Then he is to sprinkle on
it some of the blood with his finger seven times, and cleanse
and consecrate it from the impurities of the Israelites.

THE LIVE GOAT RITUAL PROCEDURES

[20]"When Aaron has finished purifying the Holy Place, the Meeting
Tent, and the altar, he is to present the live goat. [21]Aaron is to lay
his two hands on the head of the live goat and confess over it all
the iniquities of the Israelites and all their transgressions in regard
to all their sins, and thus he is to put them on the head of the goat
and send it away into the desert by the hand of a man standing
ready. [22]The goat is to bear on itself all their iniquities into an
inaccessible land, so he is to send the goat away into the desert.

THE CONCLUDING RITUALS

[23]"Aaron must then enter the Meeting Tent and take off the
linen garments which he had put on when he entered the sanctuary, and leave them there. [24]Then he must bathe his body in
water in the Holy Place, put on his clothes, and go out and make
his burnt offering and the people's burnt offering. So he is to
make atonement on behalf of himself and the people.

[25]"Then he is to offer up the fat of the sin offering in smoke on
the altar, [26]and the one who sent the goat away to Azazel must
wash his clothes, bathe his body in water, and afterward he may
reenter the camp. [27]The bull of the sin offering and the goat of
the sin offering, whose blood was brought to make atonement
in the Holy Place, must be brought outside the camp and their
hide, their flesh, and their dung must be burned up, [28]and the
one who burns them must wash his clothes and bathe his body
in water, and afterward he may reenter the camp.

REVIEW OF THE DAY OF ATONEMENT

29“This is to be a perpetual statute for you. In the seventh month, on the tenth day of the month, you must humble yourselves and do no work of any kind, both the native citizen and the resident foreigner who lives in your midst, 30for on this day atonement is to be made for you to cleanse you from all your sins; you must be clean before the LORD. 31It is to be a Sabbath of complete rest for you, and you must humble yourselves. It is a perpetual statute.

32“The priest who is anointed and ordained to act as high priest in place of his father is to make atonement. He is to put on the linen garments, the holy garments, 33and he is to purify the Most Holy Place, he is to purify the Meeting Tent and the altar, and he is to make atonement for the priests and for all the people of the assembly. 34This is to be a perpetual statute for you to make atonement for the Israelites for all their sins once a year.” So he did just as the LORD had commanded Moses.

THE SLAUGHTER OF ANIMALS

17 The LORD spoke to Moses, 2“Speak to Aaron, his sons, and all the Israelites, and tell them, ‘This is the word that the LORD has commanded, 3“Blood guilt will be accounted to any man from the house of Israel who slaughters an ox or a lamb or a goat inside the camp or outside the camp, 4but has not brought it to the entrance of the Meeting Tent to present it as an offering to the LORD before the tabernacle of the LORD. He has shed blood, so that man will be cut off from the midst of his people. 5This is so that the Israelites will bring their sacrifices that they are sacrificing in the open field to the LORD at the entrance of the Meeting Tent—to the priest—and sacrifice them there as peace-offering sacrifices to the LORD. 6The priest is to splash the blood on the altar of the LORD at the entrance of the Meeting Tent, and offer the fat up in smoke for a soothing aroma to the LORD. 7So the people must no longer offer their sacrifices to the goat demons, acting like prostitutes by going after them. This is to be a perpetual statute for them throughout their generations.”’

8“You are to say to them: ‘Any man from the house of Israel or from the resident foreigners who live in their midst, who offers a burnt offering or a sacrifice 9but does not bring it to the entrance of the Meeting Tent to offer it to the LORD—that person will be cut off from his people.

17:1–16 In the case of the human person, first its body is created from the dust, and afterward the power of life is given to it, and this is the being of the soul. Accordingly Moses said about the beasts, “The life of every living thing is in the blood.” But in the case of the human person, its being is incorporeal and immortal and has a great superiority over the body, to the same extent as incorporeal form surpasses the corporeal.

CHRYSOSTOM (C. 347–407)
HOMILIES ON GENESIS

PROHIBITION AGAINST EATING BLOOD

10“‘Any man from the house of Israel or from the resident foreigners who live in their midst who eats any blood, I will set my face against that person who eats the blood, and I will cut him off from the midst of his people, 11for the life of every living thing is in the blood. So I myself have assigned it to you on the altar to make atonement for your lives, for the blood makes atonement by means of the life. 12Therefore, I have said to the Israelites: No person among you is to eat blood, and no resident foreigner who lives among you is to eat blood.

13“‘Any man from the Israelites or from the resident foreigners who live in their midst who hunts a wild animal or a bird that may be eaten must pour out its blood and cover it with soil, 14for the life of all flesh is its blood. So I have said to the Israelites: You must not eat the blood of any living thing because the life of every living thing is its blood—all who eat it will be cut off.

REGULATIONS FOR EATING CARCASSES

15“‘Any person who eats an animal that has died of natural causes or an animal torn by beasts, whether a native citizen or a resident foreigner, must wash his clothes, bathe in water, and be unclean until evening; then he will be clean. 16But if he does not wash his clothes and does not bathe his body, he will bear his punishment for his iniquity.’”

EXHORTATION TO OBEDIENCE AND LIFE

18 The LORD spoke to Moses: 2“Speak to the Israelites and tell them, ‘I am the LORD your God! 3You must not do as they do in the land of Egypt where you have been living, and you must not do as they do in the land of Canaan into which I am about to bring you; you must not walk in their statutes. 4You must observe my regulations, and you must be sure to walk in my statutes. I am the LORD your God. 5So you must keep my statutes and my regulations; anyone who does so will live by keeping them. I am the LORD.

LAWS OF SEXUAL RELATIONS

6“‘No man is to approach any close relative to have sexual relations with her. I am the LORD. 7You must not expose your father’s nakedness by having sexual relations with your mother. She is your mother; you must not have sexual relations with her. 8You must not have sexual relations with your father’s wife; she is your father’s nakedness. 9You must not have sexual relations with your sister, whether she is your father’s daughter or your mother’s daughter, whether she is born in the same household or born outside it; you must not have sexual relations with either of them. 10You must not expose the nakedness of your son’s daughter or your daughter’s daughter by having sexual relations with them, because they are your own nakedness. 11You must not have sexual relations with the daughter of your father’s wife born of your father; she is your sister. You must not have sexual relations with her. 12You must not have sexual relations with your father’s sister; she is your father’s flesh. 13You must not have sexual relations with your mother’s sister, because she is your mother’s flesh. 14You must not expose the nakedness of your father’s brother; you must not approach his wife to have marital relations with her. She is your aunt. 15You must not have sexual relations with your daughter-in-law; she is your son’s wife. You must not have sexual relations with her. 16You must not have sexual relations with your brother’s wife; she is your brother’s nakedness. 17You must not have sexual relations with both a woman and her daughter; you must not take as wife either her son’s daughter or her daughter’s daughter to have sexual relations with them. They are closely related to her—it is lewdness. 18You must not take a woman in marriage and then marry her sister as a rival wife while she is still alive, to have sexual relations with her.

19“‘You must not approach a woman in her menstrual impurity to have sexual relations with her. 20You must not have sexual relations with the wife of your fellow citizen to become unclean with her. 21You must not give any of your children as an offering to Molech, so that you do not profane the name of your God. I am the LORD! 22You must not have sexual relations with a male as one has sexual relations with a woman; it is a detestable act. 23You must not have sexual relations with any animal to become defiled with it, and a woman must not stand before an animal to have sexual relations with it; it is a perversion.

18:1–30 The sin of Sodom is contrary to nature as is also that with brute beasts. But adultery and fornication are against the law; the one whereof is impiety, the other injustice and in a word, no other than a great sin. But neither sort of them is without its punishment in its own proper nature. For the practicers of one sort attempt the dissolution of the world and endeavor to make the natural course of things to change for one that is unnatural, but those of the second sort—the adulterers—are unjust by corrupting others’ marriages.

CONSTITUTIONS OF THE HOLY APOSTLES (C. 375–390)

WARNING AGAINST THE ABOMINATIONS OF THE NATIONS

[24]"'Do not defile yourselves with any of these things, for the
nations that I am about to drive out before you have been defiled with all these things. [25]Therefore the land has become
unclean, and I have brought the punishment for its iniquity
upon it, so that the land has vomited out its inhabitants. [26]You
yourselves must obey my statutes and my regulations and must
not do any of these abominations, both the native citizen and
the resident foreigner in your midst, [27]for the people who were
in the land before you have done all these abominations, and
the land has become unclean. [28]So do not make the land vomit
you out because you defile it just as it has vomited out the
nations that were before you. [29]For if anyone does any of these
abominations, that person who does them will be cut off from
the midst of the people. [30]You must obey my charge not to
practice any of the abominable statutes that have been done
before you, so that you do not defile yourselves by them. I am
the LORD your God.'"

RELIGIOUS AND SOCIAL REGULATIONS

19 The LORD spoke to Moses: [2]"Speak to the whole congregation of the Israelites and tell them, 'You must be holy because I, the LORD your God, am holy. [3]Each of you must respect
his mother and his father, and you must keep my Sabbaths. I
am the LORD your God. [4]Do not turn to idols, and you must not
make for yourselves gods of cast metal. I am the LORD your God.

EATING THE PEACE OFFERING

[5]"'When you sacrifice a peace-offering sacrifice to the LORD, you
must sacrifice it so that it is accepted for you. [6]It must be eaten
on the day of your sacrifice and on the following day, but what
is left over until the third day must be burned up. [7]If, however,
it is eaten on the third day, it is spoiled; it will not be accepted,
[8]and the one who eats it will bear his punishment for iniquity
because he has profaned what is holy to the LORD. That person
will be cut off from his people.

LEAVING THE GLEANINGS

[9]"'When you gather in the harvest of your land, you must not
completely harvest the corner of your field, and you must not
gather up the gleanings of your harvest. [10]You must not pick
your vineyard bare, and you must not gather up the fallen grapes
of your vineyard. You must leave them for the poor and the
resident foreigner. I am the LORD your God.

DEALING HONESTLY

[11]"'You must not steal, you must not tell lies, and you must
not deal falsely with your fellow citizen. [12]You must not swear
falsely in my name, so that you do not profane the name of your
God. I am the LORD. [13]You must not oppress your neighbor or
commit robbery against your neighbor. You must not withhold
the wages of the hired laborer overnight until morning. [14]You
must not curse a deaf person or put a stumbling block in front
of a blind person. You must fear your God; I am the LORD.

JUSTICE, LOVE, AND PROPRIETY

[15]"'You must not deal unjustly in judgment: You must neither
show partiality to the poor nor honor the rich. You must judge

19:9–10 In the harvest the owners are prohibited from appropriating what falls from the handfuls as also in reaping the law enjoins a part to be left unreaped, signally thereby training those who possess to sharing and to large-heartedness by foregoing of their own to those who are in want and thus providing means of subsistence for the poor. You see how the law proclaims at once the righteousness and goodness of God, who dispenses food to all ungrudgingly. Blessing is on the head of him who bestows; and he who pities the poor shall be blessed.

CLEMENT OF ALEXANDRIA (C. 150–C. 215)
STROMATEIS

your fellow citizen fairly. 16You must not go about as a slanderer among your people. You must not stand idly by when your neighbor's life is at stake. I am the LORD. 17You must not hate your brother in your heart. You must surely reprove your fellow citizen so that you do not incur sin on account of him. 18You must not take vengeance or bear a grudge against any of your people, but you must love your neighbor as yourself. I am the LORD. 19You must keep my statutes. You must not allow two different kinds of your animals to breed together, you must not sow your field with two different kinds of seed, and you must not wear a garment made of two different kinds of material.

LYING WITH A SLAVE WOMAN

20"'When a man goes to bed with a woman for intercourse, although she is a slave woman designated for another man and she has not yet been ransomed, or freedom has not been granted to her, there will be an obligation to pay compensation. They must not be put to death, because she was not free. 21He must bring his guilt offering to the LORD at the entrance of the Meeting Tent, a guilt-offering ram, 22and the priest is to make atonement for him with the ram of the guilt offering before the LORD for his sin that he has committed, and he will be forgiven of his sin that he has committed.

THE PRODUCE OF FRUIT TREES

23"'When you enter the land and plant any fruit tree, you must consider its fruit to be forbidden. Three years it will be forbidden to you; it must not be eaten. 24In the fourth year all its fruit will be holy, praise offerings to the LORD. 25Then in the fifth year you may eat its fruit to add its produce to your harvest. I am the LORD your God.

BLOOD, HAIR, BODY, AND PROSTITUTION

26"'You must not eat anything with the blood still in it. You must not practice either divination or soothsaying. 27You must not round off the corners of the hair on your head or ruin the corners of your beard. 28You must not slash your body for a dead person or incise a tattoo on yourself. I am the LORD. 29Do not profane your daughter by making her a prostitute, so that the land does not practice prostitution and become full of lewdness.

SABBATHS, PURITY, HONOR, RESPECT, AND HONESTY

30"'You must keep my Sabbaths and fear my sanctuary. I am the LORD. 31Do not turn to the spirits of the dead and do not seek familiar spirits to become unclean by them. I am the LORD your God. 32You must stand up in the presence of the aged, honor the presence of an elder, and fear your God. I am the LORD. 33When a resident foreigner lives with you in your land, you must not oppress him. 34The resident foreigner who lives with you must be to you as a native citizen among you; so you must love the foreigner as yourself, because you were foreigners in the land of Egypt. I am the LORD your God. 35You must not do injustice in the regulation of measures, whether of length, weight, or volume. 36You must have honest balances, honest weights, an honest ephah, and an honest hin. I am the LORD your God who brought you out from the land of Egypt. 37You must be sure to obey all my statutes and regulations. I am the LORD.'"

20:1–27 Renounce we things carnal, that we may at length bear fruits spiritual. If he is making prayer to the Lord, he is near heaven. If he is bending over the scriptures, he is wholly in them. If he is singing a psalm, he satisfies himself. For there is a prophetic utterance of the Old Testament: "You must sanctify yourselves and be holy, because I am the LORD your God." For it is our duty so to walk in the Lord's discipline as is "worthy," not according to the filthy desires of the flesh.

TERTULLIAN (155–C. 220)
EXHORTATION TO CHASTITY AND TO HIS WIFE

PROHIBITIONS AGAINST ILLEGITIMATE FAMILY WORSHIP

20 The LORD spoke to Moses: 2"You are to say to the Israelites, 'Any man from the Israelites (or any of the resident
foreigners who live in Israel) who gives any of his children to
Molech must be put to death; the people of the land must pelt
him with stones. 3I myself will set my face against that man
and cut him off from the midst of his people, because he has
given some of his children to Molech and thereby defiled my
sanctuary and profaned my holy name. 4If, however, the people
of the land shut their eyes to that man when he gives some of
his children to Molech so that they do not put him to death, 5I
myself will set my face against that man and his clan. I will cut
off from the midst of the people both him and all who follow
after him in spiritual prostitution, committing prostitution
by worshiping Molech.

PROHIBITION AGAINST SPIRITISTS AND MEDIUMS

6"'The person who turns to the spirits of the dead and familiar
spirits to commit prostitution by going after them, I will set
my face against that person and cut him off from the midst of
his people.

EXHORTATION TO HOLINESS AND OBEDIENCE

7"'You must sanctify yourselves and be holy, because I am the
LORD your God. 8You must be sure to obey my statutes. I am
the LORD who sanctifies you.

FAMILY LIFE AND SEXUAL PROHIBITIONS

9"'If anyone curses his father or mother, he must be put to
death. He has cursed his father or mother; his blood guilt is on
himself. 10If a man commits adultery with his neighbor's wife,
both the adulterer and the adulteress must be put to death.
11If a man goes to bed with his father's wife, he has exposed his
father's nakedness. Both of them must be put to death; their
blood guilt is on themselves. 12If a man goes to bed with his
daughter-in-law, both of them must be put to death. They have
committed perversion; their blood guilt is on themselves. 13If a
man goes to bed with a male as one goes to bed with a woman,
the two of them have committed an abomination. They must
be put to death; their blood guilt is on themselves. 14If a man
has marital relations with both a woman and her mother, it is
lewdness. Both he and they must be burned to death, so there
is no lewdness in your midst. 15If a man has sexual relations
with any animal, he must be put to death, and you must kill
the animal. 16If a woman approaches any animal to copulate
with it, you must kill the woman, and the animal must be put
to death; their blood guilt is on themselves.

17"'If a man has marital relations with his sister, whether
the daughter of his father or of his mother, so that he sees her
nakedness and she sees his nakedness, it is a disgrace. They
must be cut off in the sight of the children of their people. He
has exposed his sister's nakedness; he will bear his punishment
for iniquity. 18If a man goes to bed with a menstruating woman and uncovers her nakedness, he has laid bare her fountain
of blood, and she has exposed the fountain of her blood, so
both of them must be cut off from the midst of their people.
19You must not expose the nakedness of your mother's sister
or your father's sister, for such a person has exposed his own

close relative. They must bear their punishment for iniquity.
20If a man goes to bed with his aunt, he has exposed his uncle's
nakedness; they must bear responsibility for their sin, they will
die childless. 21If a man has marital relations with his brother's
wife, it is indecency. He has exposed his brother's nakedness;
they will be childless.

EXHORTATION TO HOLINESS AND OBEDIENCE

22"'You must be sure to obey all my statutes and regulations,
so that the land to which I am about to bring you to take up
residence does not vomit you out. 23You must not walk in the
statutes of the nations which I am about to drive out before
you, because they have done all these things and I am filled
with disgust against them. 24So I have said to you: You yourselves will possess their land and I myself will give it to you
for a possession, a land flowing with milk and honey. I am the
LORD your God who has set you apart from the other peoples.
25Therefore you must distinguish between the clean animal
and the unclean, and between the unclean bird and the clean,
and you must not make yourselves detestable by means of an
animal or bird or anything that creeps on the ground—creatures
I have distinguished for you as unclean. 26You must be holy to
me because I, the LORD, am holy, and I have set you apart from
the other peoples to be mine.

PROHIBITION AGAINST SPIRITISTS AND MEDIUMS

27"'A man or woman who has in them a spirit of the dead or a
familiar spirit must be put to death. They must pelt them with
stones; their blood guilt is on themselves.'"

RULES FOR THE PRIESTS

21 The LORD said to Moses, "Say to the priests, the sons of
Aaron—say to them: 'For a dead person no priest is to
defile himself among his people, 2except for his close relative
who is near to him—his mother, his father, his son, his daughter,
his brother, 3and his virgin sister who is near to him, who has
no husband—he may defile himself for her. 4He must not defile
himself as a husband among his people so as to profane himself.
5Priests must not have a bald spot shaved on their head, they
must not shave the corner of their beard, and they must not
cut slashes in their body.

6"'They must be holy to their God, and they must not profane
the name of their God, because they are the ones who present
the LORD's gifts, the food of their God. Therefore they must be
holy. 7They must not take a wife defiled by prostitution, nor are
they to take a wife divorced from her husband, for the priest is
holy to his God. 8You must sanctify him because he presents
the food of your God. He must be holy to you because I, the
LORD who sanctifies you all, am holy. 9If a daughter of a priest
profanes herself by engaging in prostitution, she is profaning
her father. She must be burned to death.

RULES FOR THE HIGH PRIEST

10"'The high priest—who is greater than his brothers, and on
whose head the anointing oil is poured, and who has been ordained to wear the priestly garments—must neither dishevel
the hair of his head nor tear his garments. 11He must not go
where there is any dead person; he must not defile himself
even for his father or for his mother. 12He must not go out from

21:1–24 None of the priests shall pollute themselves in such a way that they would be excluded from conversing with men, to whom by their function they were to be serviceable upon all occasions, and from the handling of holy things. And God would hereby teach them, and in them all successive ministers, that they ought entirely to give themselves to the service of God. Yes, to renounce all expressions of natural affection and all worldly employments as far as they are impediments to the discharge of their holy services. By being "holy to their God," they are to be devoted to God's service and always prepared for it and therefore shall keep themselves from all defilements.

JOHN WESLEY (1703–1791)
EXPLANATORY NOTES ON THE OLD TESTAMENT

the sanctuary and must not profane the sanctuary of his God, because the dedication of the anointing oil of his God is on him. I am the LORD. [13]He must take a wife who is a virgin. [14]He must not marry a widow, a divorced woman, or one profaned by prostitution; he may only take a virgin from his people as a wife, [15]so that he does not profane his children among his people, for I am the LORD who sanctifies him.'"

RULES FOR THE PRIESTHOOD

[16]The LORD spoke to Moses: [17]"Tell Aaron, 'No man from your descendants throughout their generations who has a physical flaw is to approach to present the food of his God. [18]Certainly no man who has a physical flaw is to approach: a blind man, or one who is lame, or one with a slit nose, or who has a limb too long, [19]or a man who has had a broken leg or arm, [20]or a hunchback, or a dwarf, or one with a spot in his eye, or a festering eruption, or a feverish rash, or a crushed testicle. [21]No man from the descendants of Aaron the priest who has a physical flaw may step forward to present the LORD's gifts; he has a physical flaw, so he must not step forward to present the food of his God. [22]He may eat both the most holy and the holy food of his God, [23]but he must not go near the special curtain or step forward to the altar because he has a physical flaw. Thus he must not profane my holy places, for I am the LORD who sanctifies them.'"

[24]So Moses spoke these things to Aaron, his sons, and all the Israelites.

REGULATIONS FOR THE EATING OF PRIESTLY STIPENDS

22:1–33 It was not lawful for everyone to touch the priestly vesture or any of the holy vessels; nor might the sacrifices themselves be consumed except by the proper persons and at the proper time and place; nor might the anointing oil or the compounded incense be imitated; nor might anyone enter the temple who was not in the most minute particular pure in both soul and body; so far was the Most Holy Place removed from presumptuous access that it might be entered by one man only once a year. No one is worthy of the mightiness of God.

GREGORY OF NAZIANZUS
(C. 329–390)
IN DEFENSE OF HIS FLIGHT TO PONTUS

22 The LORD spoke to Moses: [2]"Tell Aaron and his sons that they must deal respectfully with the holy offerings of the Israelites, which they consecrate to me, so that they do not profane my holy name. I am the LORD. [3]Say to them, 'Throughout your generations, if any man from all your descendants approaches the holy offerings, which the Israelites consecrate to the LORD, while he is impure, that person must be cut off from before me. I am the LORD. [4]No man from the descendants of Aaron who is diseased or has a discharge may eat the holy offerings until he becomes clean. The one who touches anything made unclean by contact with a dead person, or with a man who has a seminal emission, [5]or with a man who touches a swarming thing by which he becomes unclean, or who touches a person by which he becomes unclean, whatever that person's impurity–[6]the person who touches any of these will be unclean until evening and must not eat from the holy offerings unless he has bathed his body in water. [7]When the sun goes down he will be clean, and afterward he may eat from the holy offerings, because they are his food. [8]He must not eat an animal that has died of natural causes or an animal torn by beasts and thus become unclean by it. I am the LORD. [9]They must keep my charge so that they do not incur sin on account of it and therefore die because they profane it. I am the LORD who sanctifies them.

[10]"'No lay person may eat anything holy. Neither a priest's lodger nor a hired laborer may eat anything holy, [11]but if a priest buys a person with his own money, that person may eat the holy offerings, and those born in the priest's own house may eat his food. [12]If a priest's daughter marries a lay person, she may not eat the holy contribution offerings, [13]but if a priest's

daughter is a widow or divorced, and she has no children so
that she returns to live in her father's house as in her youth,
she may eat from her father's food, but no lay person may eat it.
14"'If a man eats a holy offering by mistake, he must add
one-fifth to it and give the holy offering to the priest. 15They
must not profane the holy offerings which the Israelites contribute to the LORD, 16and so cause them to incur a penalty
for guilt when they eat their holy offerings, for I am the LORD
who sanctifies them.'"

REGULATIONS FOR OFFERING VOTIVE AND FREEWILL OFFERINGS

17The LORD spoke to Moses: 18"Speak to Aaron, his sons, and
all the Israelites and tell them, 'When any man from the house
of Israel or from the resident foreigners in Israel presents his
offering for any of the votive or freewill offerings, which they
present to the LORD as a burnt offering, 19if it is to be acceptable for your benefit, it must be a flawless male from the cattle,
sheep, or goats. 20You must not present anything that has a flaw,
because it will not be acceptable for your benefit. 21If a man
presents a peace-offering sacrifice to the LORD for a special
votive offering or for a freewill offering from the herd or the
flock, it must be flawless to be acceptable; it must have no flaw.
22"'You must not present to the LORD something blind, or
with a broken bone, or mutilated, or with a running sore, or
with a festering eruption, or with a feverish rash. You must not
give any of these as a gift on the altar to the LORD. 23As for an
ox or a sheep with a limb too long or stunted, you may present
it as a freewill offering, but it will not be acceptable for a votive
offering. 24You must not present to the LORD something with
testicles that are bruised, crushed, torn, or cut off; you must
not do this in your land. 25Even from a foreigner you must not
present the food of your God from such animals as these, for
they are ruined and flawed; they will not be acceptable for your
benefit.'"
26The LORD spoke to Moses: 27"When an ox, lamb, or goat is
born, it must be under the care of its mother seven days, but
from the eighth day onward it will be acceptable as an offering
gift to the LORD. 28You must not slaughter an ox or a sheep and
its young on the same day. 29When you sacrifice a thanksgiving
offering to the LORD, you must sacrifice it so that it is acceptable for your benefit. 30On that very day it must be eaten; you
must not leave any part of it over until morning. I am the LORD.
31"You must be sure to do my commandments. I am the LORD.
32You must not profane my holy name, and I will be sanctified
in the midst of the Israelites. I am the LORD who sanctifies
you, 33the one who brought you out from the land of Egypt to
be your God. I am the LORD."

REGULATIONS FOR ISRAEL'S APPOINTED TIMES

23 The LORD spoke to Moses: 2"Speak to the Israelites and
tell them, 'These are the LORD's appointed times which
you must proclaim as holy assemblies—my appointed times.

THE WEEKLY SABBATH

3"'Six days work may be done, but on the seventh day there
must be a Sabbath of complete rest, a holy assembly. You must
not do any work; it is a Sabbath to the LORD in all the places
where you live.

THE PASSOVER AND FEAST OF UNLEAVENED BREAD

4"'These are the LORD's appointed times, holy assemblies, which
you must proclaim at their appointed time. 5In the first month,
on the fourteenth day of the month, at twilight, is a Passover
offering to the LORD. 6Then on the fifteenth day of the same
month will be the Feast of Unleavened Bread to the LORD; seven
days you must eat unleavened bread. 7On the first day there will
be a holy assembly for you; you must not do any regular work.
8You must present a gift to the LORD for seven days, and the seventh day is a holy assembly; you must not do any regular work.'"

THE PRESENTATION OF FIRSTFRUITS

9The LORD spoke to Moses: 10"Speak to the Israelites and tell
them, 'When you enter the land that I am about to give to you
and you gather in its harvest, then you must bring the sheaf of
the first portion of your harvest to the priest, 11and he must
wave the sheaf before the LORD to be accepted for your benefit—
on the day after the Sabbath the priest is to wave it. 12On the
day you wave the sheaf you must also offer a flawless yearling
lamb for a burnt offering to the LORD, 13along with its grain
offering, two-tenths of an ephah of choice wheat flour mixed
with olive oil, as a gift to the LORD, a soothing aroma, and its
drink offering, one-fourth of a hin of wine. 14You must not eat
bread, roasted grain, or fresh grain until this very day, until
you bring the offering to your God. This is a perpetual statute
throughout your generations in all the places where you live.

THE FEAST OF WEEKS

15"'You must count for yourselves seven weeks from the day
after the Sabbath, from the day you bring the wave-offering
sheaf; they must be complete weeks. 16You must count 50 days—
until the day after the seventh Sabbath—and then you must
present a new grain offering to the LORD. 17From the places
where you live you must bring two loaves of bread for a wave
offering; they must be made from two-tenths of an ephah of
fine wheat flour, baked with yeast, as firstfruits to the LORD.
18Along with the loaves of bread, you must also present seven
flawless yearling lambs, one young bull, and two rams. They
are to be a burnt offering to the LORD along with their grain
offering and drink offerings, a gift of a soothing aroma to the
LORD. 19You must also offer one male goat for a sin offering
and two yearling lambs for a peace-offering sacrifice, 20and the
priest is to wave them—the two lambs—along with the bread
of the firstfruits, as a wave offering before the LORD; they will
be holy to the LORD for the priest.

21"'On this very day you must proclaim an assembly; it is to be
a holy assembly for you. You must not do any regular work. This
is a perpetual statute in all the places where you live throughout
your generations. 22When you gather in the harvest of your
land, you must not completely harvest the corner of your field,
and you must not gather up the gleanings of your harvest. You
must leave them for the poor and the resident foreigner. I am
the LORD your God.'"

THE FEAST OF HORN BLASTS

23The LORD spoke to Moses: 24"Tell the Israelites, 'In the seventh month, on the first day of the month, you must have a
complete rest, a memorial announced by loud horn blasts, a

23:15–44 The Feast of Weeks was held in remembrance of the giving of the law 50 days after the departure from Egypt and looked forward to the outpouring of the Holy Ghost 50 days after Christ our Passover was sacrificed for us. In the Feast of Shelters there was a remembrance of their dwelling in tents in the wilderness as well as their fathers' dwelling in tents in Canaan to remind them of their origin and their deliverance. Christ's tabernacling on earth in human nature might also be prefigured. God appointed these feasts "besides the Sabbaths of the LORD and all your gifts, votive offerings, and freewill offerings." Calls to extraordinary services will not excuse from constant and stated ones.

MATTHEW HENRY **(1662–1714)**
COMMENTARY ON THE WHOLE BIBLE

holy assembly. [25]You must not do any regular work, but you must present a gift to the LORD.'"

THE DAY OF ATONEMENT

[26]The LORD spoke to Moses: [27]"The tenth day of this seventh month is the Day of Atonement. It is to be a holy assembly for you, and you must humble yourselves and present a gift to the LORD. [28]You must not do any work on this particular day, because it is a day of atonement to make atonement for yourselves before the LORD your God. [29]Indeed, any person who does not behave with humility on this particular day will be cut off from his people. [30]As for any person who does any work on this particular day, I will exterminate that person from the midst of his people—[31]you must not do any work! This is a perpetual statute throughout your generations in all the places where you live. [32]It is a Sabbath of complete rest for you, and you must humble yourselves on the ninth day of the month in the evening, from evening until evening you must observe your Sabbath."

THE FEAST OF TEMPORARY SHELTERS

[33]The LORD spoke to Moses: [34]"Tell the Israelites, 'On the fifteenth day of this seventh month is the Feast of Shelters for seven days to the LORD. [35]On the first day is a holy assembly; you must do no regular work. [36]For seven days you must present a gift to the LORD. On the eighth day there is to be a holy assembly for you, and you must present a gift to the LORD. It is a solemn assembly day; you must not do any regular work.

[37]"'These are the appointed times of the LORD that you must proclaim as holy assemblies to present a gift to the LORD—burnt offering, grain offering, sacrifice, and drink offerings, each day according to its regulation, [38]besides the Sabbaths of the LORD and all your gifts, votive offerings, and freewill offerings which you must give to the LORD.

[39]"'On the fifteenth day of the seventh month, when you gather in the produce of the land, you must celebrate a pilgrim festival of the LORD for seven days. On the first day is a complete rest and on the eighth day is complete rest. [40]On the first day you must take for yourselves branches from majestic trees—palm branches, branches of leafy trees, and willows of the brook—and you must rejoice before the LORD your God for seven days. [41]You must celebrate it as a pilgrim festival to the LORD for seven days in the year. This is a perpetual statute throughout your generations; you must celebrate it in the seventh month. [42]You must live in temporary shelters for seven days; every native citizen in Israel must live in shelters, [43]so that your future generations may know that I made the Israelites live in shelters when I brought them out from the land of Egypt. I am the LORD your God.'"

[44]So Moses spoke to the Israelites about the appointed times of the LORD.

REGULATIONS FOR THE LAMPSTAND AND THE TABLE OF BREAD

24 The LORD spoke to Moses: [2]"Command the Israelites to bring to you pure oil of beaten olives for the light, to make a lamp burn continually. [3]Outside the special curtain of the congregation in the Meeting Tent, Aaron must arrange it from evening until morning before the LORD continually. This is a perpetual statute throughout your generations. [4]On

the ceremonially pure lampstand he must arrange the lamps before the LORD continually.

5“You must take choice wheat flour and bake twelve loaves; there must be two-tenths of an ephah of flour in each loaf, 6and you must set them in two rows, six in a row, on the ceremonially pure table before the LORD. 7You must put pure frankincense on each row, and it will become a memorial portion for the bread, a gift to the LORD. 8Each Sabbath day Aaron must arrange it before the LORD continually; this portion is from the Israelites as a perpetual covenant. 9It will belong to Aaron and his sons, and they must eat it in a holy place because it is most holy to him, a perpetually-allotted portion from the gifts of the LORD.”

A CASE OF BLASPHEMING THE NAME

10Now an Israelite woman’s son whose father was an Egyptian went out among the Israelites, and the Israelite woman’s son and an Israelite man had a fight in the camp. 11The Israelite woman’s son misused the Name and cursed, so they brought him to Moses. (Now his mother’s name was Shelomith, daughter of Dibri, of the tribe of Dan.) 12So they placed him in custody until they were able to make a clear legal decision for themselves based on words from the mouth of the LORD.

13Then the LORD spoke to Moses: 14“Bring the one who cursed outside the camp, and all who heard him are to lay their hands on his head, and the whole congregation is to stone him to death. 15Moreover, you are to tell the Israelites, ‘If any man curses his God, he will bear responsibility for his sin, 16and one who misuses the name of the LORD must surely be put to death. The whole congregation must surely stone him, whether he is a resident foreigner or a native citizen; when he misuses the Name he must be put to death.

17“‘If a man beats any person to death, he must be put to death. 18One who beats an animal to death must make restitution for it, life for life. 19If a man inflicts an injury on his fellow citizen, just as he has done it must be done to him—20fracture for fracture, eye for eye, tooth for tooth—just as he inflicts an injury on another person that same injury must be inflicted on him. 21One who beats an animal to death must make restitution for it, but one who beats a person to death must be put to death. 22There will be one regulation for you, whether a resident foreigner or a native citizen, for I am the LORD your God.’”

23Then Moses spoke to the Israelites and they brought the one who cursed outside the camp and stoned him with stones. So the Israelites did just as the LORD had commanded Moses.

REGULATIONS FOR THE SABBATICAL YEAR

25 The LORD spoke to Moses at Mount Sinai: 2“Speak to the Israelites and tell them, ‘When you enter the land that I am giving you, the land must observe a Sabbath to the LORD. 3Six years you may sow your field, and six years you may prune your vineyard and gather the produce, 4but in the seventh year the land must have a Sabbath of complete rest—a Sabbath to the LORD. You must not sow your field or prune your vineyard. 5You must not gather in the aftergrowth of your harvest, and you must not pick the grapes of your unpruned vines; the land must have a year of complete rest. 6You may have the Sabbath produce of the land to eat—you, your male servant, your female servant, your hired worker, the resident foreigner who stays with you, 7your cattle, and the wild animals that are in your land—all its produce will be for you to eat.

24:5–9 The 12 loaves on the table of the tabernacle then are the 12 apostles and all those in the church who follow their teaching. Since until the end of time they do not cease to renew the people of God with the nourishment of the Word, they are the 12 loaves of proposition that never depart from the table of the Lord. Those same loaves are also properly commanded to be set on the table in two rows of six for the sake of concord (that is to say, charity and fellowship), for the Lord is also said to have sent his disciples out to preach two by two. This suggests figuratively that the holy teachers never disagree with one another in either their defense of truth or their ardor for love.

VENERABLE BEDE
(C. 672–735)
ON THE TABERNACLE

REGULATIONS FOR THE JUBILEE YEAR OF RELEASE

8 "'You must count off seven weeks of years, seven times seven
years, and the days of the seven weeks of years will amount to 49
years. 9 You must sound loud horn blasts—in the seventh month,
on the tenth day of the month, on the Day of Atonement—you
must sound the horn in your entire land. 10 So you must consecrate the fiftieth year, and you must proclaim a release in the
land for all its inhabitants. That year will be your Jubilee; each
one of you must return to his property, and each one of you
must return to his clan. 11 That fiftieth year will be your Jubilee;
you must not sow the land, harvest its aftergrowth, or pick the
grapes of its unpruned vines. 12 Because that year is a Jubilee,
it will be holy to you—you may eat its produce from the field.

RELEASE OF LANDED PROPERTY

13 "'In this Year of Jubilee you must each return to your property. 14 If you make a sale to your fellow citizen or buy from your
fellow citizen, no one is to wrong his brother. 15 You may buy it
from your fellow citizen according to the number of years since
the last Jubilee; he may sell it to you according to the years of
produce that are left. 16 The more years there are, the more
you may make its purchase price, and the fewer years there
are, the less you must make its purchase price, because he is
only selling to you a number of years of produce. 17 No one is to
oppress his fellow citizen, but you must fear your God, because
I am the LORD your God. 18 You must obey my statutes and my
regulations; you must be sure to keep them so that you may
live securely in the land.

19 "'The land will give its fruit, and you may eat until you are
satisfied, and you may live securely in the land. 20 If you say,
"What will we eat in the seventh year if we do not sow and gather
our produce?" 21 I will command my blessing for you in the sixth
year so that it may yield the produce for three years, 22 and you
may sow the eighth year and eat from that sixth year's produce—
old produce. Until you bring in the ninth year's produce, you may
eat old produce. 23 The land must not be sold without reclaim
because the land belongs to me, for you are foreign residents,
temporary settlers, with me. 24 In all your landed property you
must provide for the right of redemption of the land.

25 "'If your brother becomes impoverished and sells some of his
property, his near redeemer is to come to you and redeem what
his brother sold. 26 If a man has no redeemer, but he prospers and
gains enough for its redemption, 27 he is to calculate the value of
the years it was sold, refund the balance to the man to whom he
had sold it, and return to his property. 28 If he has not prospered
enough to refund a balance to him, then what he sold will belong
to the one who bought it until the Jubilee year, but it must revert
in the Jubilee and the original owner may return to his property.

RELEASE OF HOUSES

29 "'If a man sells a residential house in a walled city, its right
of redemption must extend until one full year from its sale; its
right of redemption must extend to a full calendar year. 30 If
it is not redeemed before the full calendar year is ended, the
house in the walled city will belong without reclaim to the one
who bought it throughout his generations; it will not revert in
the Jubilee. 31 The houses of villages, however, which have no
wall surrounding them must be considered as the field of the
land; they will have the right of redemption and must revert in

the Jubilee. 32As for the cities of the Levites, the houses in the
cities which they possess, the Levites must have a perpetual
right of redemption. 33Whatever someone among the Levites
might redeem—the sale of a house which is his property in a
city—must revert in the Jubilee, because the houses of the cities
of the Levites are their property in the midst of the Israelites.
34Moreover, the open field areas of their cities must not be
sold, because that is their perpetual possession.

DEBT AND SLAVE REGULATIONS

35"'If your brother becomes impoverished and is indebted to
you, you must support him; he must live with you like a foreign resident. 36Do not take interest or profit from him, but
you must fear your God, and your brother must live with you.
37You must not lend him your money at interest, and you must
not sell him food for profit. 38I am the LORD your God who
brought you out from the land of Egypt to give you the land of
Canaan—to be your God.

39"'If your brother becomes impoverished with regard to
you so that he sells himself to you, you must not subject him to
slave service. 40He must be with you as a hired worker, as a resident foreigner; he must serve with you until the Year of Jubilee,
41but then he may go free, he and his children with him, and
may return to his family and to the property of his ancestors.
42Since the Israelites are my servants whom I brought out from
the land of Egypt, they must not be sold in a slave sale. 43You
must not rule over them harshly, but you must fear your God.

44"'As for your male and female slaves who may belong to
you—you may buy male and female slaves from the nations all
around you. 45Also, you may buy slaves from the children of the
foreigners who reside with you and from their families that
are with you, whom they have fathered in your land; they may
become your property. 46You may give them as an inheritance to
your children after you to possess as property. You may enslave
them perpetually. However, as for your brothers the Israelites,
no man may rule over his brother harshly.

47"'If a resident foreigner who is with you prospers and your
brother becomes impoverished with regard to him so that he
sells himself to a resident foreigner who is with you or to a
member of a foreigner's family, 48after he has sold himself he
retains a right of redemption. One of his brothers may redeem
him, 49or his uncle or his cousin may redeem him, or any one of
the rest of his blood relatives—his family—may redeem him, or
if he prospers, he may redeem himself. 50He must calculate with
the one who bought him the number of years from the year he
sold himself to him until the Jubilee year, and the cost of his
sale must correspond to the number of years, according to the
rate of wages a hired worker would have earned while with him.
51If there are still many years, in keeping with them, he must
refund most of the cost of his purchase for his redemption, 52but
if only a few years remain until the Jubilee, he must calculate
for himself in keeping with the remaining years and refund
it for his redemption. 53He must be with the one who bought
him like a yearly hired worker. The one who bought him must
not rule over him harshly in your sight. 54If, however, he is not
redeemed in these ways, he must go free in the Jubilee year,
he and his children with him, 55because the Israelites are my
own servants; they are my servants whom I brought out from
the land of Egypt. I am the LORD your God.

25:35–36 Don't you see how great a punishment is appointed for the deed? Don't you hear that even in the old law this is forbidden? But what is the plea of the many? "When I have received the interest, I give to the poor," one tells me. Speak reverently, O man; God desires not such sacrifices. Deal not subtly with the law. Better not give to a poor man than give from that source, for the money that has been collected by honest labors you often make to become unlawful because of that wicked increase, as if one should compel a fair womb to give birth to scorpions.

CHRYSOSTOM **(C. 347–407)**
HOMILIES ON THE GOSPEL OF MATTHEW

EXHORTATION TO OBEDIENCE

26 "'You must not make for yourselves idols, so you must not set up for yourselves a carved image or a pillar, and you must not place a sculpted stone in your land to bow down before it, for I am the LORD your God. 2You must keep my Sabbaths and reverence my sanctuary. I am the LORD.

THE BENEFITS OF OBEDIENCE

3"'If you walk in my statutes and are sure to obey my commandments, 4I will give you your rains in their time so that the land will give its yield and the trees of the field will produce their fruit. 5Threshing season will extend for you until the season for harvesting grapes, and the season for harvesting grapes will extend until sowing season, so you will eat your bread until you are satisfied, and you will live securely in your land. 6I will grant peace in the land so that you will lie down to sleep without anyone terrifying you. I will remove harmful animals from the land, and no sword of war will pass through your land. 7You will pursue your enemies, and they will fall before you by the sword. 8Five of you will pursue a hundred, and a hundred of you will pursue ten thousand, and your enemies will fall before you by the sword. 9I will turn to you, make you fruitful, multiply you, and maintain my covenant with you. 10You will still be eating stored produce from the previous year and will have to clean out what is stored from the previous year to make room for new.

11"'I will put my tabernacle in your midst, and I will not abhor you. 12I will walk among you, and I will be your God, and you will be my people. 13I am the LORD your God who brought you out from the land of Egypt, from being their slaves, and I broke the bars of your yoke and caused you to walk upright.

THE CONSEQUENCES OF DISOBEDIENCE

14"'If, however, you do not obey me and keep all these commandments—15if you reject my statutes and abhor my regulations so that you do not keep all my commandments and you break my covenant—16I for my part will do this to you: I will inflict horror on you, consumption and fever, which diminish eyesight and drain away the vitality of life. You will sow your seed in vain because your enemies will eat it. 17I will set my face against you. You will be struck down before your enemies; those who hate you will rule over you, and you will flee when there is no one pursuing you.

18"'If, in spite of all these things, you do not obey me, I will discipline you seven times more on account of your sins. 19I will break your strong pride and make your sky like iron and your land like bronze. 20Your strength will be used up in vain; your land will not give its yield, and the trees of the land will not produce their fruit.

21"'If you walk in hostility against me and are not willing to obey me, I will increase your affliction seven times according to your sins. 22I will send the wild animals against you, and they will bereave you of your children, annihilate your cattle, and diminish your population so that your roads will become deserted.

23"'If in spite of these things you do not allow yourselves to be disciplined and you walk in hostility against me, 24then I myself will also walk in hostility against you and strike you seven times on account of your sins. 25I will bring on you an avenging sword, a covenant vengeance. Although you will gather together into your cities, I will send pestilence among you, and

26:23–24 His righteousness exclaims, *If you come right to me, I also will come right to you; if you walk crooked, I also will walk crooked,* says the Lord of Hosts, alluding to the offenses of sinners under the name of crooked ways. For the straight way, and that according to nature, which is pointed out by the iota of Jesus, is his goodness, which is immoveable toward those who have obediently believed. For the Lord is good to the straight in the way, but those who turn aside after their crooked ways he shall lead forth with those who work iniquity.

CLEMENT OF ALEXANDRIA (C. 150–C. 215)
STROMATEIS

you will be given into enemy hands. [26]When I break off your supply of bread, ten women will bake your bread in one oven; they will ration your bread by weight, and you will eat and not be satisfied.

[27]"'If in spite of this you do not obey me but walk in hostility against me, [28]I will walk in hostile rage against you, and I myself will also discipline you seven times on account of your sins. [29]You will eat the flesh of your sons and the flesh of your daughters. [30]I will destroy your high places and cut down your incense altars, and I will stack your dead bodies on top of the lifeless bodies of your idols. I will abhor you. [31]I will lay your cities waste and make your sanctuaries desolate, and I will refuse to smell your soothing aromas. [32]I myself will make the land desolate, and your enemies who live in it will be appalled. [33]I will scatter you among the nations and unsheathe the sword after you, so your land will become desolate and your cities will become a waste.

[34]"'Then the land will make up for its Sabbaths all the days it lies desolate while you are in the land of your enemies; then the land will rest and make up its Sabbaths. [35]All the days of the desolation it will have the rest it did not have on your Sabbaths when you lived on it.

[36]"'As for the ones who remain among you, I will bring despair into their hearts in the lands of their enemies. The sound of a blowing leaf will pursue them, and they will flee as one who flees the sword and will fall down even though there is no pursuer. [37]They will stumble over each other as those who flee before a sword, though there is no pursuer, and there will be no one to take a stand for you before your enemies. [38]You will perish among the nations; the land of your enemies will consume you.

RESTORATION THROUGH CONFESSION AND REPENTANCE

[39]"'As for the ones who remain among you, they will rot away because of their iniquity in the lands of your enemies, and they will also rot away because of their ancestors' iniquities which are with them. [40]However, when they confess their iniquity and their ancestors' iniquities which they committed by trespassing against me, by which they also walked in hostility against me [41](and I myself will walk in hostility against them and bring them into the land of their enemies), and then their uncircumcised hearts become humbled and they make up for their iniquities, [42]I will remember my covenant with Jacob and also my covenant with Isaac and also my covenant with Abraham, and I will remember the land. [43]The land will be abandoned by them in order that it may make up for its Sabbaths while it is made desolate without them, and they will make up for their iniquity because they have rejected my regulations and have abhorred my statutes. [44]In spite of this, however, when they are in the land of their enemies, I will not reject them and abhor them to make a complete end of them, to break my covenant with them, for I am the LORD their God. [45]I will remember for them the covenant with their ancestors whom I brought out from the land of Egypt in the sight of the nations to be their God. I am the LORD.'"

SUMMARY COLOPHON

[46]These are the statutes, regulations, and instructions which the LORD established between himself and the Israelites at Mount Sinai through Moses.

REDEMPTION OF PERSONS GIVEN AS VOTIVE OFFERINGS

27 The LORD spoke to Moses: 2"Speak to the Israelites and tell them, 'When a man makes a special votive offering based on the conversion value of a person to the LORD, 3the conversion value of the male from twenty years old up to sixty years old is 50 shekels by the standard of the sanctuary shekel. 4If the person is a female, the conversion value is 30 shekels. 5If the person is from five years old up to twenty years old, the conversion value of the male is 20 shekels, and for the female 10 shekels. 6If the person is one month old up to five years old, the conversion value of the male is five shekels of silver, and for the female the conversion value is three shekels of silver. 7If the person is from sixty years old and older, if he is a male, the conversion value is 15 shekels, and for the female 10 shekels. 8If the person making the votive offering is too poor to pay the conversion value, he must stand the person before the priest, and the priest will establish his conversion value; according to what the man who made the votive offering can afford, the priest will establish his conversion value.

REDEMPTION OF ANIMALS GIVEN AS VOTIVE OFFERINGS

9"'If what is vowed is a kind of animal from which an offering may be presented to the LORD, anything which he gives to the LORD from this kind of animal will be holy. 10He must not replace or exchange it, good for bad or bad for good, and if he does indeed exchange one animal for another animal, then both the original animal and its substitute will be holy. 11If what is vowed is an unclean animal from which an offering must not be presented to the LORD, then he must stand the animal before the priest, 12and the priest will establish its conversion value, whether good or bad. According to the conversion value assessed by the priest, thus it will be. 13If, however, the person who made the vow redeems the animal, he must add one-fifth to its conversion value.

REDEMPTION OF HOUSES GIVEN AS VOTIVE OFFERINGS

14"'If a man consecrates his house as holy to the LORD, the priest will establish its conversion value, whether good or bad. Just as the priest establishes its conversion value, thus it will stand. 15If the one who consecrates it redeems his house, he must add to it one-fifth of its conversion value in silver, and it will belong to him.

REDEMPTION OF FIELDS GIVEN AS VOTIVE OFFERINGS

16"'If a man consecrates to the LORD some of his own landed property, the conversion value must be calculated in accordance with the amount of seed needed to sow it, a homer of barley seed being priced at 50 shekels of silver. 17If he consecrates his field in the Jubilee year, the conversion value will stand, 18but if he consecrates his field after the Jubilee, the priest will calculate the price for him according to the years that are left until the next Jubilee year, and it will be deducted from the conversion value. 19If, however, the one who consecrated the field redeems it, he must add to it one-fifth of the conversion price, and it will belong to him. 20If he does not redeem the

field, but sells the field to someone else, he may never redeem
it. [21]When it reverts in the Jubilee, the field will be holy to the
LORD like a permanently dedicated field; it will become the
priest's property.
[22]"'If he consecrates to the LORD a field he has purchased,
which is not part of his own landed property, [23]the priest will
calculate for him the amount of its conversion value until the
Jubilee year, and he must pay the conversion value on that Jubilee day as something that is holy to the LORD. [24]In the Jubilee
year the field will return to the one from whom he bought it,
the one to whom it belongs as landed property. [25]Every conversion value must be calculated by the standard of the sanctuary
shekel; 20 gerahs to the shekel.

REDEMPTION OF THE FIRSTBORN

[26]"'Surely no man may consecrate a firstborn that already belongs to the LORD as a firstborn among the animals; whether
it is an ox or a sheep, it belongs to the LORD. [27]If, however, it is
among the unclean animals, he may ransom it according to its
conversion value and must add one-fifth to it, but if it is not
redeemed, it must be sold according to its conversion value.

THINGS PERMANENTLY DEDICATED TO THE LORD

[28]"'Surely anything that a man permanently dedicates to the
LORD from all that belongs to him, whether from people,
animals, or his landed property, must be neither sold nor redeemed; anything permanently dedicated is most holy to the
LORD. [29]Any human being who is permanently dedicated to
the LORD must not be ransomed; such a person must be put
to death.

27:28–34 Upon the whole we have cause to bless God that we are not come to Mount Sinai, that we are not under the dark shadows of the law but enjoy the clear light of the gospel. The doctrine of our reconciliation to God by a mediator is not clouded with the smoke of burning sacrifices but cleared by the knowledge of Christ and him crucified. And we may praise him that we are not under the yoke of the law but under the sweet and easy instructions of the gospel, which pronounces those the true worshipers who worship the Father in spirit and in truth, by Christ only, who is our priest, temple, altar, sacrifice, purification, and all.

JOHN WESLEY (1703–1791)
EXPLANATORY NOTES ON THE BIBLE

REDEMPTION OF THE TITHE

[30]"'Any tithe of the land, from the grain of the land or from the
fruit of the trees, belongs to the LORD; it is holy to the LORD. [31]If
a man redeems part of his tithe, however, he must add one-fifth
to it. [32]All the tithe of herds or flocks, everything which passes
under the rod, the tenth one will be holy to the LORD. [33]The
owner must not examine the animals to distinguish between
good and bad, and he must not exchange it. If, however, he does
exchange it, both the original animal and its substitute will be
holy and must not be redeemed.'"

FINAL COLOPHON

[34]These are the commandments which the LORD commanded
Moses to tell the Israelites at Mount Sinai.

AUTHOR	AUDIENCE	DATE	PURPOSE	THEMES
Moses	God's chosen people, the Israelites	Between 1446 and 1406 BC	Moses wrote this book to chronicle the faithfulness of God as seen in the numerical blessing of his people, despite their faithlessness; he also wrote to recount the years Israel wandered the wilderness because of their rebellion.	Faithfulness and faithlessness; wrath and mercy; and promise and fulfillment

Portions of the fourth book of Moses called Numbers can, at times, seem like drudgery for the modern reader, given the lists of families and clans it includes. Yet the book is an important one. Moses wrote Numbers to chronicle the faithfulness of God as seen in the numerical blessing of his people despite their faithlessness. He also wrote to recount the years the Israelites wandered the wilderness because of their rebellion. Numbers serves as both a testament to God's faithfulness and a warning against rebellion.

In Genesis the Lord said to Abraham, "Gaze into the sky and count the stars—if you are able to count them! . . . So will your descendants be" (Gen 15:5). Numbers is the initial mark and fulfillment of that promise of blessing. The book launches with a census of every clan and family, "by their clans and families, counting the name of every individual male . . . who can serve in the army, those who are twenty years old or older" (Num 1:2–3)—the total number adding up to more than 600,000 fighting men. This means the total number of Israelites, including women and children, was likely in the millions! Consider that these millions came from Abraham and Sarah, whose bodies were as good "as dead," as Paul wrote in Romans 4:19, and you can see how the numbers Moses presents here are crucial to understanding the theology of this book, for they represent God's goodness and grace. John Wesley was right; the Israelites were numbered so that "the great number of the people might be known to the praise of God's faithfulness in making good his promises of multiplying them and to their own encouragement."

In Numbers this faithfulness of God is set against the faithlessness of Israel; the first generation out of Egypt, the Israelites whom God delivered and made a covenant with, grumbled and rebelled against the Lord, refused to enter the promised land, and lost their access to it. In fact Moses himself would be barred for his own rebellion, revealing the impartiality of God's judgment. Yet alongside God's wrath we see a picture of his mercy, for a second generation is counted, numbering a similar 600,000, which led John Calvin to remark:

> By continued generation the people were so renewed as that, at the conclusion of the period, their posterity equaled their former number, and that was the work of God's inestimable grace. Thus in that awful judgment wherewith God punished his sinful people, the truth of his

> promise still shone forth . . . For, whilst the people had been instructed by punishments to fear God, still they were not to lose the savor of his paternal favor. And thus does God always temper his judgments towards his church so as in the midst of his indignation to remember mercy.

Finally, Numbers is a book of promise and blessing. First we have the famed priestly blessing the Lord gave to Aaron and his sons on behalf of the people of Israel, indicating God's clear intent to fulfill his promises to his people: "The Lord bless you and protect you; the Lord make his face shine upon you, and be gracious to you; the Lord lift up his countenance upon you and give you peace" (6:24–26). Then there is the promise of the land of Canaan, which was explored at the Lord's command and found fruitful. Commenting on this promised blessing and the massive grapes brought back as proof, Clement of Alexandria offered:

> A sacred vine put forth a cluster of grapes that was prophetic. To those who had been led by the Educator to a place of rest after their wanderings it was a sign, for the great cluster of grapes is the Word crushed on our account. The Word desired that the "blood of the grape" be mixed with water as a symbol that his own blood is an integral element in salvation.

This, of course, is a reference to the ultimate promise of salvation in Christ, which the early church fathers found on the lips of the pagan prophet Balaam when he prophesied, "A star will march forth out of Jacob, and a scepter will rise out of Israel" (24:17). Chrysostom wrote, "When urged to curse the people, [Balaam] not merely did not curse them but even prophesied great and wonderful things, not merely about the people but also about the coming of the Savior."

There is within this fourth book of Moses a font of encouragement and exhortation for the communion of saints. It is a chronicle of the Lord's faithfulness, mercy, and fulfilled promises, despite the faithlessness and rebellion of his people.

ORGANIZING THE CENSUS OF THE ISRAELITES

1 Now the LORD spoke to Moses in the tent of meeting in the
desert of Sinai on the first day of the second month of the
second year after the Israelites departed from the land of Egypt.
He said: 2“Take a census of the entire Israelite community by
their clans and families, counting the name of every individual
male. 3You and Aaron are to number all in Israel who can serve
in the army, those who are twenty years old or older, by their
divisions. 4And to help you there is to be a man from each tribe,
each man the head of his family. 5Now these are the names of
the men who are to help you:
from Reuben, Elizur son of Shedeur;
6 from Simeon, Shelumiel son of Zurishaddai;
7 from Judah, Nahshon son of Amminadab;
8 from Issachar, Nethanel son of Zuar;
9 from Zebulun, Eliab son of Helon;
10 from the sons of Joseph:
from Ephraim, Elishama son of Ammihud;
from Manasseh, Gamaliel son of Pedahzur;
11 from Benjamin, Abidan son of Gideoni;
12 from Dan, Ahiezer son of Ammishaddai;
13 from Asher, Pagiel son of Ocran;
14 from Gad, Eliasaph son of Deuel;
15 from Naphtali, Ahira son of Enan.”

THE CENSUS OF THE TRIBES

16These were the ones chosen from the community, leaders of
their ancestral tribes. They were the heads of the thousands
of Israel.
17So Moses and Aaron took these men who had been mentioned specifically by name, 18and they assembled the entire
community together on the first day of the second month. Then
the people recorded their ancestry by their clans and families,
and the men who were twenty years old or older were listed by
name individually, 19just as the LORD had commanded Moses.
And so he numbered them in the desert of Sinai.
20And they were as follows:
The descendants of Reuben, the firstborn son of Israel: According to the records of their clans and families, all the males
twenty years old or older who could serve in the army were listed by name individually. 21Those of them who were numbered
from the tribe of Reuben were 46,500.
22From the descendants of Simeon: According to the records
of their clans and families, all the males numbered of them
twenty years old or older who could serve in the army were
listed by name individually. 23Those of them who were numbered from the tribe of Simeon were 59,300.
24From the descendants of Gad: According to the records of
their clans and families, all the males twenty years old or older
who could serve in the army were listed by name. 25Those of
them who were numbered from the tribe of Gad were 45,650.
26From the descendants of Judah: According to the records of
their clans and families, all the males twenty years old or older
who could serve in the army were listed by name. 27Those of
them who were numbered from the tribe of Judah were 74,600.
28From the descendants of Issachar: According to the records
of their clans and families, all the males twenty years old or older
who could serve in the army were listed by name. 29Those of them
who were numbered from the tribe of Issachar were 54,400.

30 From the descendants of Zebulun: According to the records
of their clans and families, all the males twenty years old or
older who could serve in the army were listed by name. 31 Those
of them who were numbered from the tribe of Zebulun were
57,400.
32 From the sons of Joseph:
From the descendants of Ephraim: According to the records
of their clans and families, all the males twenty years old or
older who could serve in the army were listed by name. 33 Those
of them who were numbered from the tribe of Ephraim were
40,500. 34 From the descendants of Manasseh: According to
the records of their clans and families, all the males twenty
years old or older who could serve in the army were listed by
name. 35 Those of them who were numbered from the tribe of
Manasseh were 32,200.
36 From the descendants of Benjamin: According to the records of their clans and families, all the males twenty years old or
older who could serve in the army were listed by name. 37 Those
of them who were numbered from the tribe of Benjamin were
35,400.
38 From the descendants of Dan: According to the records of
their clans and families, all the males twenty years old or older
who could serve in the army were listed by name. 39 Those of
them who were numbered from the tribe of Dan were 62,700.
40 From the descendants of Asher: According to the records of
their clans and families, all the males twenty years old or older
who could serve in the army were listed by name. 41 Those of
them who were numbered from the tribe of Asher were 41,500.
42 From the descendants of Naphtali: According to the records of their clans and families, all the males twenty years old or
older who could serve in the army were listed by name. 43 Those
of them who were numbered from the tribe of Naphtali were
53,400.
44 These were the men whom Moses and Aaron numbered
along with the twelve leaders of Israel, each of whom was from
his own family. 45 All the Israelites who were twenty years old or
older, who could serve in Israel's army, were numbered according to their families. 46 And all those numbered totaled 603,550.

THE EXEMPTION OF THE LEVITES

47 But the Levites, according to the tribe of their fathers, were
not numbered among them. 48 The LORD had said to Moses,
49 "Only the tribe of Levi you must not number or count with
the other Israelites. 50 But appoint the Levites over the tabernacle of the testimony, over all its furnishings and over everything
in it. They must carry the tabernacle and all its furnishings;
and they must attend to it and camp around it. 51 Whenever
the tabernacle is to move, the Levites must take it down, and
whenever the tabernacle is to be reassembled, the Levites
must set it up. Any unauthorized person who approaches it
must be killed.
52 "The Israelites will camp according to their divisions, each
man in his camp, and each man by his standard. 53 But the Levites must camp around the tabernacle of the testimony, so
that the LORD's anger will not fall on the Israelite community.
The Levites are responsible for the care of the tabernacle of
the testimony."
54 The Israelites did according to all that the LORD commanded Moses—that is what they did.

1:47–53 We know that the Levites are not reckoned among the rest but are preferred before all, for they are chosen out of all and are sanctified like the firstfruits and the firstlings that belong to the Lord, since the payment of vows and redemption for sin are offered by them. "Only the tribe of Levi you must not number or count with the other Israelites. But appoint the Levites over the tabernacle of the testimony, over all its furnishings and over everything in it. They must carry the tabernacle and all its furnishings; and they must attend to it and camp around it."

AMBROSE (C. 339–C. 397)
ON THE DUTIES OF THE CLERGY

2:1–4 Indeed the divine David says, "O kingdoms of the earth, sing to God. Sing praises to the Lord, to the one who rides through the sky from ancient times" (Ps 68:32–33). Moreover the scripture also says, "The LORD God planted an orchard in the east, in Eden; and there he placed the man he had formed" (Gen 2:8). And when man had transgressed his command he expelled him and made him to dwell over against the delights of paradise, which clearly is the west. So then we worship God seeking and striving after our old fatherland.

JOHN OF DAMASCUS
(C. 675–749)
AN EXACT EXPOSITION OF THE ORTHODOX FAITH

THE ARRANGEMENT OF THE TRIBES

2 The LORD spoke to Moses and to Aaron: 2"Every one of the
Israelites must camp under his standard with the emblems
of his family; they must camp at some distance around the
tent of meeting.

THE TRIBES ON THE EAST

3"Now those who will be camping on the east, toward the sunrise, are the divisions of the camp of Judah under their standard.
The leader of the people of Judah is Nahshon son of Amminadab. 4Those numbered in his division are 74,600. 5Those who
will be camping next to them are the tribe of Issachar. The
leader of the people of Issachar is Nethanel son of Zuar. 6Those
numbered in his division are 54,400. 7Next will be the tribe of
Zebulun. The leader of the people of Zebulun is Eliab son of
Helon. 8Those numbered in his division are 57,400. 9All those
numbered of the camp of Judah, according to their divisions,
are 186,400. They will travel at the front.

THE TRIBES ON THE SOUTH

10"On the south will be the divisions of the camp of Reuben
under their standard. The leader of the people of Reuben is
Elizur son of Shedeur. 11Those numbered in his division are
46,500. 12Those who will be camping next to them are the tribe
of Simeon. The leader of the people of Simeon is Shelumiel son
of Zurishaddai. 13Those numbered in his division are 59,300.
14Next will be the tribe of Gad. The leader of the people of Gad
is Eliasaph son of Deuel. 15Those numbered in his division are
45,650. 16All those numbered of the camp of Reuben, according
to their divisions, are 151,450. They will travel second.

THE TRIBE IN THE CENTER

17"Then the tent of meeting with the camp of the Levites will
travel in the middle of the camps. They will travel in the same
order as they camped, each in his own place under his standard.

THE TRIBES ON THE WEST

18"On the west will be the divisions of the camp of Ephraim
under their standard. The leader of the people of Ephraim is
Elishama son of Ammihud. 19Those numbered in his division
are 40,500. 20Next to them will be the tribe of Manasseh. The
leader of the people of Manasseh is Gamaliel son of Pedahzur.
21Those numbered in his division are 32,200. 22Next will be
the tribe of Benjamin. The leader of the people of Benjamin is
Abidan son of Gideoni. 23Those numbered in his division are
35,400. 24All those numbered of the camp of Ephraim, according
to their divisions, are 108,100. They will travel third.

THE TRIBES ON THE NORTH

25"On the north will be the divisions of the camp of Dan, under
their standards. The leader of the people of Dan is Ahiezer son
of Ammishaddai. 26Those numbered in his division are 62,700.
27Those who will be camping next to them are the tribe of Asher.
The leader of the people of Asher is Pagiel son of Ocran. 28Those
numbered in his division are 41,500. 29Next will be the tribe of
Naphtali. The leader of the people of Naphtali is Ahira son of
Enan. 30Those numbered in his division are 53,400. 31All those
numbered of the camp of Dan are 157,600. They will travel last,
under their standards."

SUMMARY

[32]These are the Israelites, numbered according to their families. All those numbered in the camps, by their divisions, are 603,550. [33]But the Levites were not numbered among the other Israelites, as the LORD commanded Moses.

[34]So the Israelites did according to all that the LORD commanded Moses; that is the way they camped under their standards, and that is the way they traveled, each with his clan and family.

THE SONS OF AARON

3 Now these are the records of Aaron and Moses when the LORD spoke with Moses on Mount Sinai. [2]These are the names of the sons of Aaron: Nadab the firstborn, Abihu, Eleazar, and Ithamar. [3]These are the names of the sons of Aaron, the anointed priests, whom he consecrated to minister as priests.

[4]Nadab and Abihu died before the LORD when they offered strange fire before the LORD in the desert of Sinai, and they had no children. So Eleazar and Ithamar ministered as priests in the presence of Aaron their father.

THE ASSIGNMENT OF THE LEVITES

[5]The LORD spoke to Moses: [6]"Bring the tribe of Levi near, and present them before Aaron the priest, that they may serve him. [7]They are responsible for his needs and the needs of the whole community before the tent of meeting, by attending to the service of the tabernacle. [8]And they are responsible for all the furnishings of the tent of meeting, and for the needs of the Israelites, as they serve in the tabernacle. [9]You are to assign the Levites to Aaron and his sons; they will be assigned exclusively to him out of all the Israelites. [10]So you are to appoint Aaron and his sons, and they will be responsible for their priesthood, but the unauthorized person who comes near must be put to death."

[11]Then the LORD spoke to Moses: [12]"Look, I myself have taken the Levites from among the Israelites instead of every firstborn who opens the womb among the Israelites. So the Levites belong to me, [13]because all the firstborn are mine. When I destroyed all the firstborn in the land of Egypt, I set apart for myself all the firstborn in Israel, both man and beast. They belong to me. I am the LORD."

THE NUMBERING OF THE LEVITES

[14]Then the LORD spoke to Moses in the desert of Sinai: [15]"Number the Levites by their clans and their families; every male from a month old and upward you are to number." [16]So Moses numbered them according to the word of the LORD, just as he had been commanded.

THE SUMMARY OF FAMILIES

[17]These were the sons of Levi by their names: Gershon, Kohath, and Merari.

[18]These are the names of the sons of Gershon by their families: Libni and Shimei. [19]The sons of Kohath by their families were: Amram, Izhar, Hebron, and Uzziel. [20]The sons of Merari by their families were Mahli and Mushi. These are the families of the Levites by their clans.

THE NUMBERING OF THE GERSHONITES

[21]From Gershon came the family of the Libnites and the family of the Shimeites; these were the families of the Gershonites.

3:1–51 There was much work belonging to the priests' office, and there were now only Aaron and his two sons to do it; God appoints the Levites to attend them. Those for whom God finds work are those for whom he will find help. All people are the Lord's by creation, and all true Christians are his by redemption. Each should know his own post and duty; nor can any service required by such a Master be rightly accounted mean or hard.

MATTHEW HENRY (1662–1714)
COMMENTARY ON THE WHOLE BIBLE

22 Those of them who were numbered, counting every male
from a month old and upward, were 7,500. 23 The families of
the Gershonites were to camp behind the tabernacle toward
the west. 24 Now the leader of the clan of the Gershonites was
Eliasaph son of Lael.
25 And the responsibilities of the Gershonites in the tent of
meeting included the tabernacle, the tent with its covering, the
curtain at the entrance of the tent of meeting, 26 the hangings
of the courtyard, the curtain at the entrance to the courtyard
that surrounded the tabernacle and the altar, and their ropes,
plus all the service connected with these things.

THE NUMBERING OF THE KOHATHITES

27 From Kohath came the family of the Amramites, the family
of the Izharites, the family of the Hebronites, and the family
of the Uzzielites; these were the families of the Kohathites.
28 Counting every male from a month old and upward, there
were 8,600. They were responsible for the care of the sanctuary.
29 The families of the Kohathites were to camp on the south side
of the tabernacle. 30 Now the leader of the clan of the families
of the Kohathites was Elizaphan son of Uzziel.
31 Their responsibilities included the ark, the table, the lampstand, the altars, and the utensils of the sanctuary with which
they ministered, the curtain, and all their service. 32 Now the
head of all the Levitical leaders was Eleazar son of Aaron the
priest. He was appointed over those who were responsible for
the sanctuary.

THE NUMBERING OF MERARI

33 From Merari came the family of the Mahlites and the family
of the Mushites; these were the families of Merari. 34 Those of
them who were numbered, counting every male from a month
old and upward, were 6,200. 35 Now the leader of the clan of the
families of Merari was Zuriel son of Abihail. These were to camp
on the north side of the tabernacle.
36 The appointed responsibilities of the Merarites included
the frames of the tabernacle, its crossbars, its posts, its sockets,
its utensils, plus all the service connected with these things,
37 and the pillars of the courtyard all around, with their sockets,
their pegs, and their ropes.
38 But those who were to camp in front of the tabernacle on
the east, in front of the tent of meeting, were Moses, Aaron,
and his sons. They were responsible for the needs of the sanctuary and for the needs of the Israelites, but the unauthorized
person who approached was to be put to death. 39 All who were
numbered of the Levites, whom Moses and Aaron numbered by
the word of the LORD, according to their families, every male
from a month old and upward, were 22,000.

THE SUBSTITUTION FOR THE FIRSTBORN

40 Then the LORD said to Moses, "Number all the firstborn males
of the Israelites from a month old and upward, and take the
number of their names. 41 And take the Levites for me—I am the
LORD—instead of all the firstborn males among the Israelites,
and the livestock of the Levites instead of all the firstborn of the
livestock of the Israelites." 42 So Moses numbered all the firstborn males among the Israelites, as the LORD had commanded
him. 43 And all the firstborn males, by the number of the names
from a month old and upward, totaled 22,273.

[44]Then the LORD spoke to Moses: [45]"Take the Levites instead of all the firstborn males among the Israelites, and the livestock of the Levites instead of their livestock. And the Levites will be mine. I am the LORD. [46]And for the redemption of the 273 firstborn males of the Israelites who exceed the number of the Levites, [47]collect five shekels for each one individually; you are to collect this amount in the currency of the sanctuary shekel (this shekel is 20 gerahs). [48]And give the money for the redemption of the excess number of them to Aaron and his sons."

[49]So Moses took the redemption money from those who were in excess of those redeemed by the Levites. [50]From the firstborn males of the Israelites he collected the money, 1,365 shekels, according to the sanctuary shekel. [51]Moses gave the redemption money to Aaron and his sons, according to the word of the LORD, as the LORD had commanded Moses.

THE SERVICE OF THE KOHATHITES

4 Then the LORD spoke to Moses and Aaron: [2]"Take a census of the Kohathites from among the Levites, by their families and by their clans, [3]from thirty years old and upward to fifty years old, all who enter the company to do the work in the tent of meeting. [4]This is the service of the Kohathites in the tent of meeting, relating to the most holy things. [5]When it is time for the camp to journey, Aaron and his sons must come and take down the screening curtain and cover the ark of the testimony with it. [6]Then they must put over it a covering of fine leather and spread over that a cloth entirely of blue, and then they must insert its poles.

[7]"On the table of the presence they must spread a blue cloth, and put on it the dishes, the pans, the bowls, and the pitchers for pouring, and the Bread of the Presence must be on it continually. [8]They must spread over them a scarlet cloth, and cover the same with a covering of fine leather; and they must insert its poles.

[9]"They must take a blue cloth and cover the lampstand of the light, with its lamps, its wick-trimmers, its trays, and all its oil vessels, with which they service it. [10]Then they must put it with all its utensils in a covering of fine leather, and put it on a carrying beam.

[11]"They must spread a blue cloth on the gold altar, and cover it with a covering of fine leather; and they must insert its poles. [12]Then they must take all the utensils of the service, with which they serve in the sanctuary, put them in a blue cloth, cover them with a covering of fine leather, and put them on a carrying beam. [13]Also, they must take away the ashes from the altar and spread a purple cloth over it. [14]Then they must place on it all its implements with which they serve there—the trays, the meat forks, the shovels, the basins, and all the utensils of the altar—and they must spread on it a covering of fine leather, and then insert its poles.

[15]"When Aaron and his sons have finished covering the sanctuary and all the furnishings of the sanctuary, when the camp is ready to journey, then the Kohathites will come to carry them; but they must not touch any holy thing, or they will die. These are the responsibilities of the Kohathites with the tent of meeting.

[16]"The appointed responsibility of Eleazar son of Aaron the priest is for the oil for the light, and the spiced incense, and the daily grain offering, and the anointing oil; he also has the

appointed responsibility over all the tabernacle with all that is in it, over the sanctuary and over all its furnishings."

17 Then the LORD spoke to Moses and Aaron: 18 "Do not allow the tribe of the families of the Kohathites to be cut off from among the Levites; 19 but in order that they will live and not die when they approach the most holy things, do this for them: Aaron and his sons will go in and appoint each man to his service and his responsibility. 20 But the Kohathites are not to go in to watch while the holy things are being covered, or they will die."

THE SERVICE OF THE GERSHONITES

21 Then the LORD spoke to Moses: 22 "Also take a census of the Gershonites also, by their clans and by their families. 23 You must number them from thirty years old and upward to fifty years old, all who enter the company to do the work of the tent of meeting. 24 This is the service of the families of Gershonites, as they serve and carry it. 25 They must carry the curtains for the tabernacle and the tent of meeting with its covering, the covering of fine leather that is over it, the curtains for the entrance of the tent of meeting, 26 the hangings for the courtyard, the curtain for the entrance of the gate of the court, which is around the tabernacle and the altar, and their ropes, along with all the furnishings for their service and everything that is made for them. So they are to serve.

27 "All the service of the Gershonites, whether carrying loads or for any of their work, will be at the direction of Aaron and his sons. You will assign them all their tasks as their responsibility. 28 This is the service of the families of the Gershonites concerning the tent of meeting. Their responsibilities will be under the authority of Ithamar son of Aaron the priest.

4:21–49 God esteems nothing small in his service, and he expects his will should be observed in the minutest circumstances. The death of the saints is represented in the taking down of the tabernacle. The immortal soul, like the most holy things, is first covered and taken away, carried by angels unseen, and care is taken also of the body, the skin and flesh, which are as the curtains, and the bones and sinews, which are as the bars and pillars. None of these shall be lost.

JOHN WESLEY (1703–1791)
EXPLANATORY NOTES ON THE BIBLE

THE SERVICE OF THE MERARITES

29 "As for the sons of Merari, you are to number them by their families and by their clans. 30 You must number them from thirty years old and upward to fifty years old, all who enter the company to do the work of the tent of meeting. 31 This is what they are responsible to carry as their entire service in the tent of meeting: the frames of the tabernacle, its crossbars, its posts, its sockets, 32 and the posts of the surrounding courtyard with their sockets, tent pegs, and ropes, along with all their furnishings and everything for their service. You are to assign by name the items that each man is responsible to carry. 33 This is the service of the families of the Merarites, their entire service concerning the tent of meeting, under the authority of Ithamar son of Aaron the priest."

SUMMARY

34 So Moses and Aaron and the leaders of the community numbered the Kohathites by their families and by clans, 35 from thirty years old and upward to fifty years old, everyone who entered the company for the work in the tent of meeting; 36 and those of them numbered by their families were 2,750. 37 These were those numbered from the families of the Kohathites, everyone who served in the tent of meeting, whom Moses and Aaron numbered according to the word of the LORD by the authority of Moses.

38 Those numbered from the Gershonites, by their families and by their clans, 39 from thirty years old and upward to fifty years old, everyone who entered the company for the work in the tent of meeting— 40 those of them numbered by their

families, by their clans, were 2,630. 41 These were those numbered from the families of the Gershonites, everyone who served in the tent of meeting, whom Moses and Aaron numbered according to the word of the LORD.

42 Those numbered from the families of the Merarites, by their families, by their clans, 43 from thirty years old and upward to fifty years old, everyone who entered the company for the work in the tent of meeting— 44 those of them numbered by their families were 3,200. 45 These are those numbered from the families of the Merarites, whom Moses and Aaron numbered according to the word of the LORD by the authority of Moses.

46 All who were numbered of the Levites, whom Moses, Aaron, and the leaders of Israel numbered by their families and by their clans, 47 from thirty years old and upward to fifty years old, everyone who entered to do the work of service and the work of carrying relating to the tent of meeting— 48 those of them numbered were 8,580. 49 According to the word of the LORD they were numbered, by the authority of Moses, each according to his service and according to what he was to carry. Thus were they numbered by him, as the LORD had commanded Moses.

SEPARATION OF THE UNCLEAN

5 Then the LORD spoke to Moses: 2 "Command the Israelites to expel from the camp every leper, everyone who has a discharge, and whoever becomes defiled by a corpse. 3 You must expel both men and women; you must put them outside the camp, so that they will not defile their camps, among which I live." 4 So the Israelites did so, and expelled them outside the camp. As the LORD had spoken to Moses, so the Israelites did.

RESTITUTION FOR SIN

5 Then the LORD spoke to Moses: 6 "Tell the Israelites, 'When a man or a woman commits any sin that people commit, thereby breaking faith with the LORD, and that person is found guilty, 7 then he must confess his sin that he has committed and must make full reparation, add one-fifth to it, and give it to whomever he wronged. 8 But if the individual has no close relative to whom reparation can be made for the wrong, the reparation for the wrong must be paid to the LORD for the priest, in addition to the ram of atonement by which atonement is made for him. 9 Every offering of all the Israelites' holy things that they bring to the priest will be his. 10 Every man's holy things will be his; whatever any man gives the priest will be his.'"

5:5–10 The law as to fraud is as follows: They must confess their sin and crave pardon from the bottom of their hearts; they must submit themselves to God knowing that they can by no means hide their sin nor by any color keep it from the sight of God. We must make satisfaction to the one we have wronged. It is not enough to make open confession to God unless also we make actual restitution to people. This is done to discourage injurious persons. For if they should only restore the principal they know, if their offenses were found out, they should be no losers.

JOSEPH EXELL (1849–1910)
NUMBERS

THE JEALOUSY ORDEAL

11 The LORD spoke to Moses: 12 "Speak to the Israelites and tell them, 'If any man's wife goes astray and behaves unfaithfully toward him, 13 and a man goes to bed with her for sexual relations without her husband knowing it, and it is undetected that she has defiled herself since there was no witness against her, nor was she caught in the act— 14 and if jealous feelings come over him and he becomes suspicious of his wife when she is defiled, or if jealous feelings come over him and he becomes suspicious of his wife, when she is not defiled— 15 then the man must bring his wife to the priest, and he must bring the offering required for her, one-tenth of an ephah of barley meal; he must not pour olive oil on it or put frankincense on it because it is a grain offering of suspicion, a grain offering for remembering, for bringing iniquity to remembrance.

16“‘Then the priest will bring her near and have her stand before the LORD. 17The priest will then take holy water in a pottery jar, and take some of the dust that is on the floor of the tabernacle, and put it into the water. 18Then the priest will have the woman stand before the LORD, and he will uncover the woman’s head and put the grain offering for remembering in her hands, which is the grain offering of suspicion. The priest will hold in his hand the bitter water that brings a curse. 19Then the priest will put the woman under oath and say to her, “If no other man has gone to bed with you, and if you have not gone astray and become defiled while under your husband’s authority, may you be free from this bitter water that brings a curse. 20But if you have gone astray while under your husband’s authority, and if you have defiled yourself and some man other than your husband has had sexual relations with you—” 21(then the priest will put the woman under the oath of the curse and will say to her) “the LORD make you an attested curse among your people if the LORD makes your thigh fall away and your abdomen swell, 22and this water that causes the curse will go into your stomach and make your abdomen swell and your thigh rot.” Then the woman must say, “Amen, amen.”

23“‘Then the priest will write these curses on a scroll and then scrape them off into the bitter water. 24He will make the woman drink the bitter water that brings a curse, and the water that brings a curse will enter her to produce bitterness. 25The priest will take the grain offering of suspicion from the woman’s hand, wave the grain offering before the LORD, and bring it to the altar. 26Then the priest will take a handful of the grain offering as its memorial portion, burn it on the altar, and afterward make the woman drink the water. 27When he has made her drink the water, then if she has defiled herself and behaved unfaithfully toward her husband, the water that brings a curse will enter her to produce bitterness—her abdomen will swell, her thigh will fall away, and the woman will become a curse among her people. 28But if the woman has not defiled herself, and is clean, then she will be free of ill effects and will be able to bear children.

29“‘This is the law for cases of jealousy, when a wife, while under her husband’s authority, goes astray and defiles herself, 30or when jealous feelings come over a man and he becomes suspicious of his wife; then he must have the woman stand before the LORD, and the priest will carry out all this law upon her. 31Then the man will be free from iniquity, but that woman will bear the consequences of her iniquity.’”

THE NAZIRITE VOW

6 Then the LORD spoke to Moses: 2“Speak to the Israelites, and tell them, ‘When someone—either a man or a woman—takes a special vow, to take a vow as a Nazirite, to separate himself to the LORD, 3he must separate himself from wine and strong drink; he must drink neither vinegar made from wine nor vinegar made from strong drink, nor may he drink any juice of grapes, nor eat fresh grapes or raisins. 4All the days of his separation he must not eat anything that is produced by the grapevine, from seed to skin.

5“‘All the days of the vow of his separation no razor may be used on his head until the time is fulfilled for which he separated himself to the LORD. He will be holy, and he must let the locks of hair on his head grow long.

6“‘All the days that he separates himself to the LORD he must not contact a dead body. 7He must not defile himself even for

his father or his mother or his brother or his sister if they die,
because the separation for his God is on his head. 8All the days
of his separation he must be holy to the LORD.

CONTINGENCIES FOR DEFILEMENT

9"'If anyone dies very suddenly beside him and he defiles his
consecrated head, then he must shave his head on the day of
his purification—on the seventh day he must shave it. 10On the
eighth day he is to bring two turtledoves or two young pigeons
to the priest, to the entrance to the tent of meeting. 11Then the
priest will offer one for a purification offering and the other as
a burnt offering, and make atonement for him, because of his
transgression in regard to the corpse. So he must reconsecrate
his head on that day. 12He must rededicate to the LORD the
days of his separation and bring a male lamb in its first year as
a reparation offering, but the former days will not be counted
because his separation was defiled.

FULFILLING THE VOWS

13"'Now this is the law of the Nazirite: When the days of his separation are fulfilled, he must be brought to the entrance of the tent
of meeting, 14and he must present his offering to the LORD: one
male lamb in its first year without blemish for a burnt offering,
one ewe lamb in its first year without blemish for a purification
offering, one ram without blemish for a peace offering, 15and a
basket of bread made without yeast, cakes of fine flour mixed
with olive oil, wafers made without yeast and smeared with olive
oil, and their grain offering and their drink offerings.

16"'Then the priest must present all these before the LORD
and offer his purification offering and his burnt offering. 17Then
he must offer the ram as a peace offering to the LORD along
with the basket of bread made without yeast; the priest must
also offer his grain offering and his drink offering.

18"'Then the Nazirite must shave his consecrated head at the
entrance to the tent of meeting and must take the hair from his
consecrated head and put it on the fire where the peace offering
is burning. 19And the priest must take the boiled shoulder of the
ram, one cake made without yeast from the basket, and one wafer
made without yeast, and put them on the hands of the Nazirite
after he has shaved his consecrated head; 20then the priest must
wave them as a wave offering before the LORD; it is a holy portion
for the priest, together with the breast of the wave offering and the
thigh of the raised offering. After this the Nazirite may drink wine.

21"'This is the law of the Nazirite who vows to the LORD his
offering according to his separation, as well as whatever else
he can provide. Thus he must fulfill his vow that he makes,
according to the law of his separation.'"

THE PRIESTLY BENEDICTION

22The LORD spoke to Moses: 23"Tell Aaron and his sons, 'This is
the way you are to bless the Israelites. Say to them:

24 "'"The LORD bless you and protect you;
25 The LORD make his face to shine upon you,
and be gracious to you;
26 The LORD lift up his countenance upon you
and give you peace."'"

27"So they will put my name on the Israelites, and I will bless
them."

6:22–27 Blessing is an act of God's genuine liberality because the abundance of all good things is derived to us from his favor as their only source. Since the main advantage of God's grace consists in our sense of it, the words "make his face to shine upon you" are added; for nothing is more desirable for the consummation of our happiness than that we should behold the serene countenance of God, that the people may perceive and taste the sweetness of God's goodness. "The LORD lift up his countenance upon you" is a common phrase of scripture meaning *May God remember his people.*

JOHN CALVIN (1509–1564)
COMPLETE COMMENTARY ON THE BIBLE

THE LEADER'S OFFERINGS

7 When Moses had completed setting up the tabernacle, he anointed it and consecrated it and all its furnishings, and he anointed and consecrated the altar and all its utensils. [2]Then the leaders of Israel, the heads of their clans, made an offering. They were the leaders of the tribes; they were the ones who had been supervising the numbering. [3]They brought their offerings before the LORD, six covered carts and twelve oxen—one cart for every two of the leaders, and an ox for each one; and they presented them in front of the tabernacle.

THE DISTRIBUTION OF THE GIFTS

[4]Then the LORD spoke to Moses: [5]"Receive these gifts from them, that they may be used in doing the work of the tent of meeting; and you must give them to the Levites, to every man as his service requires."

[6]So Moses accepted the carts and the oxen and gave them to the Levites. [7]He gave two carts and four oxen to the Gershonites, as their service required; [8]and he gave four carts and eight oxen to the Merarites, as their service required, under the authority of Ithamar son of Aaron the priest. [9]But to the Kohathites he gave none, because the service of the holy things, which they carried on their shoulders, was their responsibility.

THE TIME OF PRESENTATION

[10]The leaders offered gifts for the dedication of the altar when it was anointed. And the leaders presented their offering before the altar. [11]For the LORD said to Moses, "They must present their offering, one leader for each day, for the dedication of the altar."

THE TRIBAL OFFERINGS

[12]The one who presented his offering on the first day was Nahshon son of Amminadab, from the tribe of Judah. [13]His offering was one silver platter weighing 130 shekels, and one silver sprinkling bowl weighing 70 shekels, both according to the sanctuary shekel, each of them full of fine flour mixed with olive oil as a grain offering; [14]one gold pan weighing 10 shekels, full of incense; [15]one young bull, one ram, and one male lamb in its first year, for a burnt offering; [16]one male goat for a purification offering; [17]and for the sacrifice of peace offerings: two bulls, five rams, five male goats, and five male lambs in their first year. This was the offering of Nahshon son of Amminadab.

[18]On the second day Nethanel son of Zuar, leader of Issachar, presented an offering. [19]He offered for his offering one silver platter weighing 130 shekels and one silver sprinkling bowl weighing 70 shekels, both according to the sanctuary shekel, each of them full of fine flour mixed with olive oil as a grain offering; [20]one gold pan weighing 10 shekels, full of incense; [21]one young bull, one ram, and one male lamb in its first year, for a burnt offering; [22]one male goat for a purification offering; [23]and for the sacrifice of peace offerings: two bulls, five rams, five male goats, and five male lambs in their first year. This was the offering of Nethanel son of Zuar.

[24]On the third day Eliab son of Helon, leader of the Zebulunites, presented an offering. [25]His offering was one silver platter weighing 130 shekels and one silver sprinkling bowl weighing 70 shekels, both according to the sanctuary shekel, each of them full of fine flour mixed with olive oil as a grain

offering; [26]one gold pan weighing 10 shekels, full of incense;
[27]one young bull, one ram, and one male lamb in its first year,
for a burnt offering; [28]one male goat for a purification offering;
[29]and for the sacrifice of peace offerings: two bulls, five rams,
five male goats, and five male lambs in their first year. This was
the offering of Eliab son of Helon.
[30]On the fourth day Elizur son of Shedeur, leader of the Reubenites, presented an offering. [31]His offering was one silver
platter weighing 130 shekels and one silver sprinkling bowl
weighing 70 shekels, both according to the sanctuary shekel,
each of them full of fine flour mixed with olive oil as a grain
offering; [32]one gold pan weighing 10 shekels, full of incense;
[33]one young bull, one ram, and one male lamb in its first year,
for a burnt offering; [34]one male goat for a purification offering;
[35]and for the sacrifice of peace offerings: two bulls, five rams,
five male goats, and five lambs in their first year. This was the
offering of Elizur son of Shedeur.
[36]On the fifth day Shelumiel son of Zurishaddai, leader of the
Simeonites, presented an offering. [37]His offering was one silver
platter weighing 130 shekels and one silver sprinkling bowl
weighing 70 shekels, both according to the sanctuary shekel,
each of them full of fine flour mixed with olive oil as a grain
offering; [38]one gold pan weighing 10 shekels, full of incense;
[39]one young bull, one ram, and one male lamb in its first year,
for a burnt offering; [40]one male goat for a purification offering;
[41]and for the sacrifice of peace offerings: two bulls, five rams,
five male goats, and five lambs in their first year. This was the
offering of Shelumiel son of Zurishaddai.
[42]On the sixth day Eliasaph son of Deuel, leader of the Gadites, presented an offering. [43]His offering was one silver platter
weighing 130 shekels and one silver sprinkling bowl weighing
70 shekels, both according to the sanctuary shekel, each of
them full of fine flour mixed with olive oil as a grain offering;
[44]one gold pan weighing 10 shekels, full of incense; [45]one young
bull, one ram, and one male lamb in its first year, for a burnt
offering; [46]one male goat for a purification offering; [47]and for
the sacrifice of peace offerings: two bulls, five rams, five male
goats, and five lambs in their first year. This was the offering
of Eliasaph son of Deuel.
[48]On the seventh day Elishama son of Ammihud, leader of the
Ephraimites, presented an offering. [49]His offering was one silver
platter weighing 130 shekels and one silver sprinkling bowl
weighing 70 shekels, both according to the sanctuary shekel,
each of them full of fine flour mixed with olive oil as a grain
offering; [50]one gold pan weighing 10 shekels, full of incense;
[51]one young bull, one ram, and one male lamb in its first year,
for a burnt offering; [52]one male goat for a purification offering;
[53]and for the sacrifice of peace offerings: two bulls, five rams,
five male goats, and five lambs in their first year. This was the
offering of Elishama son of Ammihud.
[54]On the eighth day Gamaliel son of Pedahzur, leader of the
Manassehites, presented an offering. [55]His offering was one silver platter weighing 130 shekels and one silver sprinkling bowl
weighing 70 shekels, both according to the sanctuary shekel,
each of them full of fine flour mixed with olive oil as a grain
offering; [56]one gold pan weighing 10 shekels, full of incense;
[57]one young bull, one ram, and one male lamb in its first year,
for a burnt offering; [58]one male goat for a purification offering;
[59]and for the sacrifice of peace offerings: two bulls, five rams,

five male goats, and five lambs in their first year. This was the
offering of Gamaliel son of Pedahzur.
[60]On the ninth day Abidan son of Gideoni, leader of the Benjaminites, presented an offering. [61]His offering was one silver
platter weighing 130 shekels and one silver sprinkling bowl
weighing 70 shekels, both according to the sanctuary shekel,
each of them full of fine flour mixed with olive oil as a grain
offering; [62]one gold pan weighing 10 shekels, full of incense;
[63]one young bull, one ram, and one male lamb in its first year,
for a burnt offering; [64]one male goat for a purification offering;
[65]and for the sacrifice of peace offerings: two bulls, five rams,
five male goats, and five lambs in their first year. This was the
offering of Abidan son of Gideoni.
[66]On the tenth day Ahiezer son of Ammishaddai, leader of
the Danites, presented an offering. [67]His offering was one silver
platter weighing 130 shekels and one silver sprinkling bowl
weighing 70 shekels, both according to the sanctuary shekel,
each of them full of fine flour mixed with olive oil as a grain
offering; [68]one gold pan weighing 10 shekels, full of incense;
[69]one young bull, one ram, and one male lamb in its first year,
for a burnt offering; [70]one male goat for a purification offering;
[71]and for the sacrifice of peace offerings: two bulls, five rams,
five male goats, and five lambs in their first year. This was the
offering of Ahiezer son of Ammishaddai.
[72]On the eleventh day Pagiel son of Ocran, leader of the
Asherites, presented an offering. [73]His offering was one silver
platter weighing 130 shekels and one silver sprinkling bowl
weighing 70 shekels, both according to the sanctuary shekel,
each of them full of fine flour mixed with olive oil as a grain
offering; [74]one gold pan weighing 10 shekels, full of incense;
[75]one young bull, one ram, and one male lamb in its first year,
for a burnt offering; [76]one male goat for a purification offering;
[77]and for the sacrifice of peace offerings: two bulls, five rams,
five male goats, and five lambs in their first year. This was the
offering of Pagiel son of Ocran.
[78]On the twelfth day Ahira son of Enan, leader of the Naphtalites, presented an offering. [79]His offering was one silver
platter weighing 130 shekels and one silver sprinkling bowl
weighing 70 shekels, both according to the sanctuary shekel,
each of them full of fine flour mixed with olive oil as a grain
offering; [80]one gold pan weighing 10 shekels, full of incense;
[81]one young bull, one ram, and one male lamb in its first year,
for a burnt offering; [82]one male goat for a purification offering;
[83]and for the sacrifice of peace offerings: two bulls, five rams,
five male goats, and five lambs in their first year. This was the
offering of Ahira son of Enan.

SUMMARY

[84]This was the dedication for the altar from the leaders of Israel, when it was anointed: twelve silver platters, twelve silver
sprinkling bowls, and twelve gold pans. [85]Each silver platter
weighed 130 shekels, and each silver sprinkling bowl weighed
70 shekels. All the silver of the vessels weighed 2,400 shekels,
according to the sanctuary shekel. [86]The twelve gold pans full
of incense weighed 10 shekels each, according to the sanctuary
shekel; all the gold of the pans weighed 120 shekels. [87]All the
animals for the burnt offering were 12 young bulls, 12 rams, 12
male lambs in their first year, with their grain offering, and 12
male goats for a purification offering. [88]All the animals for the

sacrifice for the peace offering were 24 young bulls, 60 rams,
60 male goats, and 60 lambs in their first year. These were the
dedication offerings for the altar after it was anointed.
89 Now when Moses went into the tent of meeting to speak
with the LORD, he heard the voice speaking to him from above
the atonement lid that was on the ark of the testimony, from
between the two cherubim. Thus he spoke to him.

LIGHTING THE LAMPS

8 The LORD spoke to Moses: 2 "Speak to Aaron and tell him,
'When you set up the lamps, the seven lamps are to give light
in front of the lampstand.'"
3 And Aaron did so; he set up the lamps to face toward the
front of the lampstand, as the LORD commanded Moses. 4 This
is how the lampstand was made: It was beaten work in gold;
from its shaft to its flowers it was beaten work. According to
the pattern that the LORD had shown Moses, so he made the
lampstand.

THE SEPARATION OF THE LEVITES

5 Then the LORD spoke to Moses: 6 "Take the Levites from among
the Israelites and purify them. 7 And do this to them to purify them: Sprinkle water of purification on them; then have
them shave all their body and wash their clothes, and so purify
themselves. 8 Then they are to take a young bull with its grain
offering of fine flour mixed with olive oil; and you are to take a
second young bull for a purification offering. 9 You are to bring
the Levites before the tent of meeting and assemble the entire
community of the Israelites. 10 Then you are to bring the Levites
before the LORD, and the Israelites are to lay their hands on the
Levites; 11 and Aaron is to offer the Levites before the LORD as a
wave offering from the Israelites, that they may do the work of
the LORD. 12 When the Levites lay their hands on the heads of
the bulls, offer the one for a purification offering and the other
for a whole burnt offering to the LORD, to make atonement for
the Levites. 13 You are to have the Levites stand before Aaron
and his sons, and then offer them as a wave offering to the
LORD. 14 And so you are to separate the Levites from among
the Israelites, and the Levites will be mine.
15 "After this, the Levites will go in to do the work of the tent
of meeting. So you must cleanse them and offer them like a
wave offering. 16 For they are entirely given to me from among
the Israelites. I have taken them for myself instead of all who
open the womb, the firstborn sons of all the Israelites. 17 For
all the firstborn males among the Israelites are mine, both
humans and animals; when I destroyed all the firstborn in the
land of Egypt I set them apart for myself. 18 So I have taken the
Levites instead of all the firstborn sons among the Israelites.
19 I have given the Levites as a gift to Aaron and his sons from
among the Israelites, to do the work for the Israelites in the
tent of meeting, and to make atonement for the Israelites, so
there will be no plague among the Israelites when the Israelites
come near the sanctuary."
20 So Moses and Aaron and the entire community of the
Israelites did this with the Levites. According to all that the
LORD commanded Moses concerning the Levites, this is what
the Israelites did with them. 21 The Levites purified themselves
and washed their clothing; then Aaron presented them like a
wave offering before the LORD, and Aaron made atonement

7:89 What does it mean that Moses often entered the tabernacle and came out except that he, whose mind was raised up in contemplation, had to go out to deal with the affairs of the weak? Inside he contemplated the mysteries of God. Outside he bore the burdens of carnal persons. And Moses undoubtedly offers an example to officeholders. When in their public lives they are unsure of what to decide, they should always ponder in their minds, as in the tabernacle. Truth devoted himself to prayer on the mountain and performed miracles in the cities. Thus he showed good pastors a model to imitate. They should desire what is highest in contemplation but care for the needs of the weak by their compassion.

PATERIUS **(D. 606)**
EXPOSITION OF THE OLD AND NEW TESTAMENT

8:5–26 All who are employed for God must be dedicated to him according to the employment. Christians must be baptized, ministers must be ordained; we must first give ourselves unto the Lord and then our services. The Levites had to be cleansed. They had to be clean who bore the vessels of the Lord. Moses had to sprinkle the water of purifying upon them. This signifies the application of the blood of Christ to our souls by faith, that we may be fit to serve the living God.

MATTHEW HENRY **(1662–1714)**
COMMENTARY ON THE WHOLE BIBLE

for them to purify them. [22]After this, the Levites went in to do their work in the tent of meeting before Aaron and before his sons. As the LORD had commanded Moses concerning the Levites, so they did.

THE WORK OF THE LEVITES

[23]Then the LORD spoke to Moses: [24]"This is what pertains to the Levites: At the age of twenty-five years and upward one may begin to join the company in the work of the tent of meeting, [25]and at the age of fifty years they must retire from performing the work and may no longer work. [26]They may assist their colleagues in the tent of meeting to attend to needs, but they must do no work. This is the way you must establish the Levites regarding their duties."

PASSOVER REGULATIONS

9 The LORD spoke to Moses in the desert of Sinai, in the first month of the second year after they had come out of the land of Egypt:

[2]"The Israelites are to observe the Passover at its appointed time. [3]In the fourteenth day of this month, at twilight, you are to observe it at its appointed time; you must keep it in accordance with all its statutes and all its customs." [4]So Moses instructed the Israelites to observe the Passover. [5]And they observed the Passover on the fourteenth day of the first month at twilight in the desert of Sinai; in accordance with all that the LORD had commanded Moses, so the Israelites did.

[6]It happened that some men who were ceremonially defiled by the dead body of a man could not keep the Passover on that day, so they came before Moses and before Aaron on that day. [7]And those men said to Moses, "We are ceremonially defiled by the dead body of a man; why are we kept back from offering the LORD's offering at its appointed time among the Israelites?" [8]So Moses said to them, "Remain here and I will hear what the LORD will command concerning you."

[9]The LORD spoke to Moses: [10]"Tell the Israelites, 'If any of you or of your posterity become ceremonially defiled by touching a dead body, or are on a journey far away, then he may observe the Passover to the LORD. [11]They may observe it on the fourteenth day of the second month at twilight; they are to eat it with bread made without yeast and with bitter herbs. [12]They must not leave any of it until morning, nor break any of its bones; they must observe it in accordance with every statute of the Passover.

[13]"'But the man who is ceremonially clean, and was not on a journey, and fails to keep the Passover, that person must be cut off from his people. Because he did not bring the LORD's offering at its appointed time, that man must bear his sin. [14]If a resident foreigner lives among you and wants to keep the Passover to the LORD, he must do so according to the statute of the Passover, and according to its custom. You must have the same statute for the resident foreigner and for the one who was born in the land.'"

THE LORD LEADS THE ISRAELITES BY THE CLOUD

[15]On the day that the tabernacle was set up, the cloud covered the tabernacle—the tent of the testimony—and from evening until morning there was a fiery appearance over the tabernacle. [16]This is the way it used to be continually: The cloud

9:15–23 The tabernacle above the tent of the testimony was where the cloudy pillar stood. This was an evident token of God's special presence with and providence over them. And this cloud was easily distinguished from other clouds, both by its peculiar figure and by its constant residence in that place. "When the cloud remained" is repeated again and again because it was a constant miracle, and because it is a matter we should take particular notice of as highly significant and instructive. And the guidance of this cloud is spoken of as signifying the guidance of the blessed Spirit.

JOHN WESLEY (1703–1791)
EXPLANATORY NOTES ON THE BIBLE

would cover it by day, and there was a fiery appearance by night.
17 Whenever the cloud was taken up from the tabernacle, then
after that the Israelites would begin their journey; and in whatever place the cloud settled, there the Israelites would make
camp. 18 At the commandment of the LORD the Israelites would
begin their journey, and at the commandment of the LORD they
would make camp; as long as the cloud remained settled over
the tabernacle they would camp. 19 When the cloud remained
over the tabernacle many days, then the Israelites obeyed the
instructions of the LORD and did not journey.
20 When the cloud remained over the tabernacle a number
of days, they remained camped according to the LORD's commandment, and according to the LORD's commandment they
would journey. 21 And when the cloud remained only from evening until morning, when the cloud was taken up the following
morning, then they traveled on. Whether by day or by night,
when the cloud was taken up they traveled. 22 Whether it was
for two days, or a month, or a year that the cloud prolonged
its stay over the tabernacle, the Israelites remained camped
without traveling; but when it was taken up, they traveled on.
23 At the commandment of the LORD they camped, and at the
commandment of the LORD they traveled on; they kept the
instructions of the LORD according to the commandment of
the LORD, by the authority of Moses.

THE BLOWING OF TRUMPETS

10 The LORD spoke to Moses: 2 "Make two trumpets of silver;
you are to make them from a single hammered piece. You
will use them for assembling the community and for directing the
traveling of the camps. 3 When they blow them both, all the community must come to you to the entrance of the tent of meeting.
4 "But if they blow with one trumpet, then the leaders, the heads
of the thousands of Israel, must come to you. 5 When you blow
an alarm, then the camps that are located on the east side must
begin to travel. 6 And when you blow an alarm the second time,
then the camps that are located on the south side must begin to
travel. An alarm must be sounded for their journeys. 7 But when
you assemble the community, you must blow the trumpets, but
you must not sound an alarm. 8 The sons of Aaron, the priests,
must blow the trumpets, and they will be to you for an eternal
ordinance throughout your generations. 9 If you go to war in your
land against an adversary who opposes you, then you must sound
an alarm with the trumpets, and you will be remembered before
the LORD your God, and you will be saved from your enemies.
10 "Also, in the time when you rejoice, such as on your appointed festivals or at the beginnings of your months, you must
blow with your trumpets over your burnt offerings and over
the sacrifices of your peace offerings, so that they may become
a memorial for you before your God: I am the LORD your God."

THE JOURNEY FROM SINAI TO KADESH

11 On the twentieth day of the second month, in the second year,
the cloud was taken up from the tabernacle of the testimony.
12 So the Israelites set out on their journeys from the desert of
Sinai; and the cloud settled in the wilderness of Paran.

JUDAH BEGINS THE JOURNEY

13 This was the first time they set out on their journey according
to the commandment of the LORD, by the authority of Moses.

10:1–10 "Make two trumpets of silver; you are to make them from a single hammered piece." The army is led by two trumpets because the people are called to readiness in faith by the two commandments of charity. Scripture bids them to be made of silver so that the words of the preachers may shine with gleaming light and not confuse the minds of the hearers with any darkness of their own. They are to be hammered because those who preach the life to come grow through the blows of the present tribulations. Scripture says well, "When you blow an alarm, then the camps . . . must begin to travel."

PATERIUS **(D. 606)**
EXPOSITION OF THE OLD AND NEW TESTAMENT

[14]The standard of the camp of the Judahites set out first according to their companies, and over his company was Nahshon son of Amminadab.

[15]Over the company of the tribe of Issacharites was Nathanel son of Zuar, [16]and over the company of the tribe of the Zebulunites was Eliab son of Helon. [17]Then the tabernacle was dismantled, and the sons of Gershon and the sons of Merari set out, carrying the tabernacle.

JOURNEY ARRANGEMENTS FOR THE TRIBES

[18]The standard of the camp of Reuben set out according to their companies; over his company was Elizur son of Shedeur. [19]Over the company of the tribe of the Simeonites was Shelumiel son of Zurishaddai, [20]and over the company of the tribe of the Gadites was Eliasaph son of Deuel. [21]And the Kohathites set out, carrying the articles for the sanctuary; the tabernacle was to be set up before they arrived. [22]And the standard of the camp of the Ephraimites set out according to their companies; over his company was Elishama son of Ammihud. [23]Over the company of the tribe of the Manassehites was Gamaliel son of Pedahzur, [24]and over the company of the tribe of Benjaminites was Abidan son of Gideoni.

[25]The standard of the camp of the Danites set out, which was the rear guard of all the camps by their companies; over his company was Ahiezer son of Ammishaddai. [26]Over the company of the tribe of the Asherites was Pagiel son of Ocran, [27]and over the company of the tribe of the Naphtalites was Ahira son of Enan. [28]These were the traveling arrangements of the Israelites according to their companies when they traveled.

THE APPEAL TO HOBAB

[29]Moses said to Hobab son of Reuel, the Midianite, Moses' father-in-law, "We are journeying to the place about which the LORD said, 'I will give it to you.' Come with us and we will treat you well, for the LORD has promised good things for Israel." [30]But Hobab said to him, "I will not go, but I will go instead to my own land and to my kindred." [31]Moses said, "Do not leave us, because you know places for us to camp in the wilderness, and you could be our guide. [32]And if you come with us, it is certain that whatever good things the LORD will favor us with, we will share with you as well."

[33]So they traveled from the mountain of the LORD three days' journey; and the ark of the covenant of the LORD was traveling before them during the three days' journey, to find a resting place for them. [34]And the cloud of the LORD was over them by day, when they traveled from the camp. [35]And when the ark traveled, Moses would say, "Rise up, O LORD! May your enemies be scattered, and may those who hate you flee before you!" [36]And when it came to rest he would say, "Return, O LORD, to the many thousands of Israel!"

THE ISRAELITES COMPLAIN

11 When the people complained, it displeased the LORD. When the LORD heard it, his anger burned, and so the fire of the LORD burned among them and consumed some of the outer parts of the camp. [2]When the people cried to Moses, he prayed to the LORD, and the fire died out. [3]So he called the name of that place Taberah because there the fire of the LORD burned among them.

11:1–15 Do we not see that the Israelites got to their own hurt what their guilty lusting craved? For while manna was raining down on them from heaven, they desired to have meat to eat. They disdained what they had, and they shamelessly sought what they had not. When evil becomes our delight and good the opposite, we ought to entreat God to win us back to the love of the good rather than to grant us the evil.

AUGUSTINE **(354–430)**
TRACTATES ON THE GOSPEL OF JOHN

COMPLAINTS ABOUT FOOD

4Now the mixed multitude who were among them craved more
desirable foods, and so the Israelites wept again and said, "If
only we had meat to eat! 5We remember the fish we used to
eat freely in Egypt, the cucumbers, the melons, the leeks, the
onions, and the garlic. 6But now we are dried up, and there is
nothing at all before us except this manna!" 7(Now the manna
was like coriander seed, and its color like the color of bdellium.
8And the people went about and gathered it, and ground it with
mills or pounded it in mortars; they baked it in pans and made
cakes of it. It tasted like fresh olive oil. 9And when the dew
came down on the camp in the night, the manna fell with it.)

MOSES' COMPLAINT TO THE LORD

10Moses heard the people weeping throughout their families,
everyone at the door of his tent; and when the anger of the LORD
was kindled greatly, Moses was also displeased. 11And Moses
said to the LORD, "Why have you afflicted your servant? Why
have I not found favor in your sight, that you lay the burden of
this entire people on me? 12Did I conceive this entire people?
Did I give birth to them, that you should say to me, 'Carry them
in your arms, as a foster father bears a nursing child,' to the land
that you swore to their fathers? 13From where shall I get meat
to give to this entire people, for they cry to me, 'Give us meat,
that we may eat!' 14I am not able to bear this entire people alone,
because it is too heavy for me! 15But if you are going to deal with
me like this, then kill me immediately. If I have found favor in
your sight then do not let me see my trouble."

THE RESPONSE OF GOD

16The LORD said to Moses, "Gather to me seventy men of the
elders of Israel, whom you know are elders of the people and officials over them, and bring them to the tent of meeting; let them
take their position there with you. 17Then I will come down and
speak with you there, and I will take part of the Spirit that is on
you, and will put it on them, and they will bear some of the burden
of the people with you, so that you do not bear it all by yourself.

18"And say to the people, 'Sanctify yourselves for tomorrow,
and you will eat meat, for you have wept in the hearing of the
LORD, saying, "Who will give us meat to eat, for life was good
for us in Egypt?" Therefore the LORD will give you meat, and
you will eat. 19You will eat, not just one day, nor two days, nor
five days, nor ten days, nor twenty days, 20but a whole month,
until it comes out your nostrils and makes you sick, because
you have despised the LORD who is among you and have wept
before him, saying, "Why did we ever come out of Egypt?"'"

21Moses said, "The people around me are 600,000 on foot;
but you say, 'I will give them meat, that they may eat for a whole
month.' 22Would they have enough if the flocks and herds were
slaughtered for them? If all the fish of the sea were caught for
them, would they have enough?" 23And the LORD said to Moses,
"Is the LORD's hand shortened? Now you will see whether my
word to you will come true or not!"

24So Moses went out and told the people the words of the LORD.
He then gathered seventy men of the elders of the people and had
them stand around the tabernacle. 25And the LORD came down
in the cloud and spoke to them, and he took some of the Spirit
that was on Moses and put it on the seventy elders. When the
Spirit rested on them, they prophesied, but did not do so again.

ELDAD AND MEDAD

26 But two men remained in the camp; one's name was Eldad, and the other's name was Medad. And the Spirit rested on them. (Now they were among those in the registration, but had not gone to the tabernacle.) So they prophesied in the camp. 27 And a young man ran and told Moses, "Eldad and Medad are prophesying in the camp!" 28 Joshua son of Nun, the servant of Moses, one of his choice young men, said, "My lord Moses, stop them!" 29 Moses said to him, "Are you jealous for me? I wish that all the LORD's people were prophets, that the LORD would put his Spirit on them!" 30 Then Moses returned to the camp along with the elders of Israel.

PROVISION OF QUAIL

31 Now a wind went out from the LORD and brought quail from the sea, and let them fall near the camp, about a day's journey on this side, and about a day's journey on the other side, all around the camp, and about three feet high on the surface of the ground. 32 And the people stayed up all that day, all that night, and all the next day, and gathered the quail. The one who gathered the least gathered ten homers, and they spread them out for themselves all around the camp. 33 But while the meat was still between their teeth, before they chewed it, the anger of the LORD burned against the people, and the LORD struck the people with a very great plague.

34 So the name of that place was called Kibroth Hattaavah, because there they buried the people that craved different food. 35 The people traveled from Kibroth Hattaavah to Hazeroth, and they stayed at Hazeroth.

MIRIAM AND AARON OPPOSE MOSES

12 Then Miriam and Aaron spoke against Moses because of the Cushite woman he had married (for he had married an Ethiopian woman). 2 They said, "Has the LORD spoken only through Moses? Has he not also spoken through us?" And the LORD heard it.

3 (Now the man Moses was very humble, more so than any man on the face of the earth.)

THE RESPONSE OF THE LORD

4 The LORD spoke immediately to Moses, Aaron, and Miriam: "The three of you come to the tent of meeting." So the three of them went. 5 And the LORD came down in a pillar of cloud and stood at the entrance of the tent; he then called Aaron and Miriam, and they both came forward.

6 The LORD said, "Hear now my words: If there is a prophet among you, I the LORD will make myself known to him in a vision; I will speak with him in a dream. 7 My servant Moses is not like this; he is faithful in all my house. 8 With him I will speak face to face, openly and not in riddles, and he will see the form of the LORD. Why then were you not afraid to speak against my servant Moses?" 9 The anger of the LORD burned against them, and he departed. 10 After the cloud had departed from above the tent, there was Miriam, leprous like snow. Then Aaron turned toward Miriam, and realized that she was leprous.

THE INTERCESSION OF MOSES

11 So Aaron said to Moses, "O my lord, please do not hold this sin against us, in which we have acted foolishly and have sinned!

12:1–3 Be not a murmurer, remembering the punishment that those underwent who murmured against Moses. Be not self-willed, be not malicious, be not hard-hearted, be not passionate, be not mean-spirited; for all these things lead to blasphemy. But be meek, as was Moses, since "the meek shall inherit the earth" (Ps 37:11 KJV).

CONSTITUTIONS OF THE HOLY APOSTLES **(C. 375–390)**

12:1–16 Why was it that when these two (Aaron and Miriam) had both acted with spite toward Moses, the latter alone was adjudged punishment? Perhaps it was that Aaron was to a certain degree excusable in consideration of his being the elder brother and adorned with the dignity of high priest. Yet Miriam's punishment affected him to such an extent that no sooner did she experience it than he entreated Moses that he would by his intercession do away with the affliction. And he did not neglect to do so but at once poured forth his supplication. Upon this the Lord, who loves humankind, made him understand how he had not chastened her as a judge but as a father.

IRENAEUS **(C. 130–C. 202)**
FRAGMENTS

EUSEBIUS:

THE CHURCH'S HISTORIAN

c. 260–c. 340

Some early church leaders are known for their passionate Christian witness and martyrdom, others for their doctrine and persistent defense of the Christian faith. Eusebius of Caesarea is known for his historical accounts of the Christian faith.

Little is known about the early life of this important figure. He was born in Caesarea in Palestine around AD 260 and eventually became a bishop of the church in 313. Although Eusebius wrote works of biblical scholarship, including commentaries on the Psalms and Isaiah and a comparison of the four Gospels, his greatest legacy is his careful documentation of events of the church.

The role of church historian was a natural fit for Eusebius. One of his first works was the *Chronicle*, which is exactly what its title suggests: a two-part chronology logging the key historical events of Christianity. Integrating Christian history with significant Jewish and Greek dates, along with important historical events in the empire, the work functioned as a foundation for future works. Eusebius's follow-up was *Martyrs of Palestine*, which documented the Great Persecution launched by Emperor Diocletian against the church in 303.

These early writings were simply precursors to the groundbreaking *Ecclesiastical History*. It traced the growth of Christianity from its birth with the life of Jesus and the ministry of the apostles through the early spread of the faith in Acts beyond Jerusalem into Judea and Samaria. It described the early persecutions and covered the lives and contributions of early leaders like Justin Martyr, Polycarp, Irenaeus, and Clement of Alexandria. And it chronicled early controversies, such as Gnosticism and Marcionism. The account of the Great Persecution beginning in 303 and ending in 313 expanded upon the earlier *Martyrs of Palestine*. *Ecclesiastical History* ends with the downfall of Licinius at the hand of Constantine, whom Eusebius portrays as a "friend of God" whose very first action was "to cleanse the world from hatred of God."

Eusebius's appreciation for the changes brought by Constantine's rise to power can be seen in *The Life of Constantine*. Rather than a biography in the traditional sense, this three-part work was composed of anecdotes of the emperor's life, one of his speeches, and one speech Eusebius himself offered in praise of the man.

One person described Eusebius as "a historian in the tradition of Josephus," the famed Jewish historian. Thanks to Eusebius's commitment to preserving Christian history, many of the early events and personalities vital to the early development of the Christian faith have been accurately documented for believers today.

IMPORTANT WORKS

MARTYRS OF PALESTINE

ECCLESIASTICAL HISTORY

THE LIFE OF CONSTANTINE

12Do not let her be like a baby born dead, whose flesh is half
consumed when it comes out of its mother's womb!"
13Then Moses cried to the LORD, "Heal her now, O God."
14The LORD said to Moses, "If her father had only spit in her
face, would she not have been disgraced for seven days? Shut
her out from the camp seven days, and afterward she can be
brought back in again."
15So Miriam was shut outside of the camp for seven days, and
the people did not journey on until Miriam was brought back
in. 16After that the people moved from Hazeroth and camped
in the wilderness of Paran.

SPIES SENT OUT

13 The LORD spoke to Moses: 2"Send out men to investigate
the land of Canaan, which I am giving to the Israelites.
You are to send one man from each ancestral tribe, each one a
leader among them." 3So Moses sent them from the wilderness
of Paran at the command of the LORD. All of them were leaders
of the Israelites.
4Now these were their names: from the tribe of Reuben, Shammua son of Zaccur; 5from the tribe of Simeon, Shaphat son of Hori;
6from the tribe of Judah, Caleb son of Jephunneh; 7from the tribe
of Issachar, Igal son of Joseph; 8from the tribe of Ephraim, Hoshea
son of Nun; 9from the tribe of Benjamin, Palti son of Raphu; 10from
the tribe of Zebulun, Gaddiel son of Sodi; 11from the tribe of Joseph, namely, the tribe of Manasseh, Gaddi son of Susi; 12from the
tribe of Dan, Ammiel son of Gemalli; 13from the tribe of Asher,
Sethur son of Michael; 14from the tribe of Naphtali, Nahbi son
of Vopshi; 15from the tribe of Gad, Geuel son of Maki. 16These are
the names of the men whom Moses sent to investigate the land.
And Moses gave Hoshea son of Nun the name Joshua.

THE SPIES' INSTRUCTIONS

17When Moses sent them to investigate the land of Canaan,
he told them, "Go up through the Negev, and then go up into
the hill country 18and see what the land is like, and whether the people who live in it are strong or weak, few or many,
19and whether the land they live in is good or bad, and whether
the cities they inhabit are like camps or fortified cities, 20and
whether the land is rich or poor, and whether or not there are
forests in it. And be brave, and bring back some of the fruit of
the land." Now it was the time of year for the first ripe grapes.

THE SPIES' ACTIVITIES

21So they went up and investigated the land from the wilderness
of Zin to Rehob, at Lebo Hamath. 22When they went up through
the Negev, they came to Hebron where Ahiman, Sheshai, and
Talmai, descendants of Anak, were living. (Now Hebron had
been built seven years before Zoan in Egypt.) 23When they came
to the valley of Eshcol, they cut down from there a branch with
one cluster of grapes, and they carried it on a staff between two
men, as well as some of the pomegranates and the figs. 24That
place was called the Eshcol Valley, because of the cluster of
grapes that the Israelites cut from there. 25They returned from
investigating the land after 40 days.

THE SPIES' REPORTS

26They came back to Moses and Aaron and to the whole community of the Israelites in the wilderness of Paran at Kadesh.

13:22, 28–33 According to Caleb's faith so was it done unto him. The people were discouraged with that report of the spies that there they saw giants, the sons of Anak, and that they were in their own sight as grasshoppers. Caleb was confident that they were well able to overcome them, and therefore God gave Caleb Hebron for his possession, which was the chief seat of these giants as appears by verse 22 (Josh 11:21; 14:12, 15). God enabled Caleb himself to drive the giants thence (Josh 14:12; 15:13–14).

JONATHAN EDWARDS
(1703–1758)
SELECTIONS FROM THE UNPUBLISHED WRITINGS

They reported to the whole community and showed the fruit of the land. 27They told Moses, "We went to the land where you sent us. It is indeed flowing with milk and honey, and this is its fruit. 28But the inhabitants are strong, and the cities are fortified and very large. Moreover we saw the descendants of Anak there. 29The Amalekites live in the land of the Negev; the Hittites, Jebusites, and Amorites live in the hill country; and the Canaanites live by the sea and along the banks of the Jordan."

30Then Caleb silenced the people before Moses, saying, "Let us go up and occupy it, for we are well able to conquer it." 31But the men who had gone up with him said, "We are not able to go up against these people, because they are stronger than we are!" 32Then they presented the Israelites with a discouraging report of the land they had investigated, saying, "The land that we passed through to investigate is a land that devours its inhabitants. All the people we saw there are of great stature. 33We even saw the Nephilim there (the descendants of Anak came from the Nephilim), and we seemed like grasshoppers both to ourselves and to them."

THE ISRAELITES RESPOND IN UNBELIEF

14 Then all the community raised a loud cry, and the people wept that night. 2And all the Israelites murmured against Moses and Aaron, and the whole congregation said to them, "If only we had died in the land of Egypt, or if only we had perished in this wilderness! 3Why has the LORD brought us into this land only to be killed by the sword, that our wives and our children should become plunder? Wouldn't it be better for us to return to Egypt?" 4So they said to one another, "Let's appoint a leader and return to Egypt."

5Then Moses and Aaron fell down with their faces to the ground before the whole assembled community of the Israelites. 6And Joshua son of Nun and Caleb son of Jephunneh, two of those who had investigated the land, tore their garments. 7They said to the whole community of the Israelites, "The land we passed through to investigate is an exceedingly good land. 8If the LORD delights in us, then he will bring us into this land and give it to us—a land that is flowing with milk and honey. 9Only do not rebel against the LORD, and do not fear the people of the land, for they are bread for us. Their protection has turned aside from them, but the LORD is with us. Do not fear them!"

10However, the whole community threatened to stone them. But the glory of the LORD appeared to all the Israelites at the tent of meeting.

14:1–10 The Israelites began with weeping, which at length burst out into rage. The cause of their weeping was the fear of death, and whence did this arise except because the promised aid of God was of no account with them? Thus it appears how greatly opposed to faith is cowardice when, on the occurrence of danger, we look only to ourselves. This was the case with the Israelites who, being overwhelmed with grief, at length were stirred up by impetuosity against Moses and Aaron. We see how mad is unbelief when it gives way to itself.

JOHN CALVIN **(1509–1564)**
COMPLETE COMMENTARY ON THE BIBLE

THE PUNISHMENT FROM GOD

11The LORD said to Moses, "How long will this people despise me, and how long will they not believe in me, in spite of the signs that I have done among them? 12I will strike them with the pestilence, and I will disinherit them—I will make you into a nation that is greater and mightier than they!"

13Moses said to the LORD, "When the Egyptians hear it—for you brought up this people by your power from among them—14then they will tell it to the inhabitants of this land. They have heard that you, LORD, are among this people, that you, LORD, are seen face to face, that your cloud stands over them, and that you go before them by day in a pillar of cloud and in a pillar of fire by night. 15If you kill this entire people at once, then the nations that have heard of your fame will say,

16'Because the LORD was not able to bring this people into the
land that he swore to them, he killed them in the wilderness.'
17So now, let the power of my Lord be great, just as you have
said, 18'The LORD is slow to anger and abounding in loyal love,
forgiving iniquity and transgression, but by no means clearing
the guilty, visiting the iniquity of the fathers on the children
until the third and fourth generations.' 19Please forgive the
iniquity of this people according to your great loyal love, just
as you have forgiven this people from Egypt even until now."

20Then the LORD said, "I have forgiven them as you asked.
21But truly, as I live, all the earth will be filled with the glory of
the LORD. 22For all the people have seen my glory and my signs
that I did in Egypt and in the wilderness, and yet have tempted me now these ten times, and have not obeyed me—23they
will by no means see the land that I promised on oath to their
fathers, nor will any of them who despised me see it—24Only
my servant Caleb, because he had a different spirit and has
followed me fully—I will bring him into the land where he had
gone, and his descendants will possess it. 25(Now the Amalekites
and the Canaanites were living in the valleys.) Tomorrow, turn
and journey into the wilderness by the way of the Red Sea."

26The LORD spoke to Moses and Aaron: 27"How long must
I bear with this evil congregation that murmurs against me? I
have heard the complaints of the Israelites that they murmured
against me. 28Say to them, 'As I live, says the LORD, I will surely
do to you just what you have spoken in my hearing. 29Your dead
bodies will fall in this wilderness—all those of you who were numbered, according to your full number, from twenty years old and
upward, who have murmured against me. 30You will by no means
enter into the land where I swore to settle you. The only exceptions are Caleb son of Jephunneh and Joshua son of Nun. 31But I
will bring in your little ones, whom you said would become victims of war, and they will enjoy the land that you have despised.
32But as for you, your dead bodies will fall in this wilderness, 33and
your children will wander in the wilderness 40 years and suffer
for your unfaithfulness, until your dead bodies lie finished in
the wilderness. 34According to the number of the days you have
investigated this land, 40 days—one day for a year—you will suffer
for your iniquities, 40 years, and you will know what it means to
thwart me. 35I, the LORD, have said, "I will surely do so to all this
evil congregation that has gathered together against me. In this
wilderness they will be finished, and there they will die!"'"

36The men whom Moses sent to investigate the land, who
returned and made the whole community murmur against him
by producing an evil report about the land, 37those men who
produced the evil report about the land, died by the plague
before the LORD. 38But Joshua son of Nun and Caleb son of
Jephunneh, who were among the men who went to investigate
the land, lived. 39When Moses told these things to all the Israelites, the people mourned greatly.

40And early in the morning they went up to the crest of the
hill country, saying, "Here we are, and we will go up to the place
that the LORD commanded, for we have sinned." 41But Moses
said, "Why are you now transgressing the commandment of
the LORD? It will not succeed! 42Do not go up, for the LORD is
not among you, and you will be defeated before your enemies.
43For the Amalekites and the Canaanites are there before you,
and you will fall by the sword. Because you have turned away
from the LORD, the LORD will not be with you."

44 But they dared to go up to the crest of the hill, although
neither the ark of the covenant of the LORD nor Moses departed
from the camp. 45 So the Amalekites and the Canaanites who
lived in that hill country swooped down and attacked them as
far as Hormah.

SACRIFICIAL RULINGS

15 The LORD spoke to Moses: 2 "Speak to the Israelites and
tell them, 'When you enter the land where you are to live,
which I am giving you, 3 and you make an offering by fire to the
LORD from the herd or from the flock (whether a burnt offering
or a sacrifice for discharging a vow or as a freewill offering or
in your solemn feasts) to create a pleasing aroma to the LORD,
4 then the one who presents his offering to the LORD must bring
a grain offering of one-tenth of an ephah of finely ground flour
mixed with one-fourth of a hin of olive oil. 5 You must also prepare one-fourth of a hin of wine for a drink offering with the
burnt offering or the sacrifice for each lamb. 6 Or for a ram,
you must prepare as a grain offering two-tenths of an ephah
of finely ground flour mixed with one-third of a hin of olive oil,
7 and for a drink offering you must offer one-third of a hin of
wine as a pleasing aroma to the LORD. 8 And when you prepare
a young bull as a burnt offering or a sacrifice for discharging a
vow or as a peace offering to the LORD, 9 then a grain offering
of three-tenths of an ephah of finely ground flour mixed with
half a hin of olive oil must be presented with the young bull,
10 and you must present as the drink offering half a hin of wine
with the fire offering as a pleasing aroma to the LORD. 11 This is
what is to be done for each ox, or each ram, or each of the male
lambs or the goats. 12 You must do so for each one according to
the number that you prepare.

13 "'Every native-born person must do these things in this way
to present an offering made by fire as a pleasing aroma to the
LORD. 14 If a resident foreigner is living with you—or whoever
is among you in future generations—and prepares an offering
made by fire as a pleasing aroma to the LORD, he must do it
the same way you are to do it. 15 One statute must apply to you
who belong to the congregation and to the resident foreigner
who is living among you, as a permanent statute for your future
generations. You and the resident foreigner will be alike before
the LORD. 16 One law and one custom must apply to you and to
the resident foreigner who lives alongside you.'"

RULES FOR FIRSTFRUITS

17 The LORD spoke to Moses: 18 "Speak to the Israelites and tell
them, 'When you enter the land to which I am bringing you
19 and you eat some of the food of the land, you must offer up a
raised offering to the LORD. 20 You must offer up a cake of the
first of your finely ground flour as a raised offering; as you offer
the raised offering of the threshing floor, so you must offer it
up. 21 You must give to the LORD some of the first of your finely
ground flour as a raised offering in your future generations.

RULES FOR UNINTENTIONAL OFFENSES

22 "'If you sin unintentionally and do not observe all these commandments that the LORD has spoken to Moses—23 all that the
LORD has commanded you by the authority of Moses, from
the day that the LORD commanded Moses and continuing
through your future generations—24 then if anything is done

15:20 All the morally good emotions of your senses are the firstfruits of the threshing floor of the soul in the same manner as grain is separated on an actual barn floor. On this barn floor the wheat and the barley are separated by a winnowing process from the chaff and from other impurities while the solid parts, now rid of their lighter coating, settle on the floor. In a similar fashion our thoughts, when sifted, provide a solid food and pure nourishment for the exercise of virtue.

AMBROSE (C. 339–C. 397)
CAIN AND ABEL

unintentionally without the knowledge of the community, the whole community must prepare one young bull for a burnt offering—for a pleasing aroma to the LORD—along with its grain offering and its customary drink offering, and one male goat for a purification offering. [25]And the priest is to make atonement for the whole community of the Israelites, and they will be forgiven, because it was unintentional and they have brought their offering, an offering made by fire to the LORD, and their purification offering before the LORD, for their unintentional offense. [26]And the whole community of the Israelites and the resident foreigner who lives among them will be forgiven, since all the people were involved in the unintentional offense.

[27]"'If any person sins unintentionally, then he must bring a yearling female goat for a purification offering. [28]And the priest must make atonement for the person who sins unintentionally—when he sins unintentionally before the LORD—to make atonement for him, and he will be forgiven. [29]You must have one law for the person who sins unintentionally, both for the native-born among the Israelites and for the resident foreigner who lives among them.

DELIBERATE SIN

[30]"'But the person who acts defiantly, whether native-born or a resident foreigner, insults the LORD. That person must be cut off from among his people. [31]Because he has despised the LORD's message and has broken his commandment, that person must be completely cut off. His iniquity will be on him.'"

[32]When the Israelites were in the wilderness they found a man gathering wood on the Sabbath day. [33]Those who found him gathering wood brought him to Moses and Aaron and to the whole community. [34]They put him in custody, because there was no clear instruction about what should be done to him. [35]Then the LORD said to Moses, "The man must surely be put to death; the whole community must stone him with stones outside the camp." [36]So the whole community took him outside the camp and stoned him to death, just as the LORD commanded Moses.

RULES FOR TASSELS

[37]The LORD spoke to Moses: [38]"Speak to the Israelites and tell them to make tassels for themselves on the corners of their garments throughout their generations, and put a blue thread on the tassel of the corners. [39]You must have this tassel so that you may look at it and remember all the commandments of the LORD and obey them and so that you do not follow after your own heart and your own eyes that lead you to unfaithfulness. [40]Thus you will remember and obey all my commandments and be holy to your God. [41]I am the LORD your God, who brought you out of the land of Egypt to be your God. I am the LORD your God."

THE REBELLION OF KORAH

16 Now Korah son of Izhar, the son of Kohath, the son of Levi, and Dathan and Abiram, the sons of Eliab, and On son of Peleth, who were Reubenites, took men [2]and rebelled against Moses, along with some of the Israelites, 250 leaders of the community, chosen from the assembly, famous men. [3]And they assembled against Moses and Aaron, saying to them, "You take too much upon yourselves, seeing that the whole community is holy, every one of them, and the LORD is among them. Why then do you exalt yourselves above the community of the LORD?"

16:1–40 Let the dissidents learn to fear the agitation of the Lord and to obey the priests. Did the cleft in the earth not swallow Dathan and Abiram and Korah because of their dissension? Therefore a great dread seized all the people. Still, those guilty of the crime were singled out, and 250 men with their leaders were set apart from the body of the people. The guilty were snatched up and removed from every element of this world so that they would not contaminate the air by their breath, or the sky by their sight, or the sea by their touch, or the earth by their tombs.

AMBROSE **(C. 339–C. 397)**
LETTERS

ANDREI RUBLEV, ***THE TRINITY*** (1425)

(Blik Sergey/Shutterstock)

THOMAS COLE, ***EXPULSION FROM THE GARDEN OF EDEN*** (1828)

(Public Domain)

[4]When Moses heard it he fell down with his face to the
ground. [5]Then he said to Korah and to all his company, "In the
morning the LORD will make known who are his, and who is holy.
He will cause that person to approach him; the person he has
chosen he will cause to approach him. [6]Do this, Korah, you and
all your company: Take censers, [7]put fire in them, and set incense
on them before the LORD tomorrow, and the man whom the
LORD chooses will be holy. You take too much upon yourselves,
you sons of Levi!" [8]Moses said to Korah, "Listen now, you sons
of Levi! [9]Does it seem too small a thing to you that the God of
Israel has separated you from the community of Israel to bring
you near to himself, to perform the service of the tabernacle
of the LORD, and to stand before the community to minister
to them? [10]He has brought you near and all your brothers, the
sons of Levi, with you. Do you now seek the priesthood also?
[11]Therefore you and all your company have assembled together against the LORD! And Aaron—what is he that you murmur
against him?" [12]Then Moses summoned Dathan and Abiram, the
sons of Eliab, but they said, "We will not come up. [13]Is it a small
thing that you have brought us up out of the land that flows
with milk and honey, to kill us in the wilderness? Now do you
want to make yourself a prince over us? [14]Moreover, you have
not brought us into a land that flows with milk and honey, nor
given us an inheritance of fields and vineyards. Do you think
you can blind these men? We will not come up."

[15]Moses was very angry, and he said to the LORD, "Have no
respect for their offering! I have not taken so much as one donkey from them, nor have I harmed any one of them!"

[16]Then Moses said to Korah, "You and all your company present yourselves before the LORD—you and they, and Aaron—
tomorrow. [17]And each of you take his censer, put incense in it,
and then each of you present his censer before the LORD: 250
censers, along with you, and Aaron—each of you with his censer."
[18]So everyone took his censer, put fire in it, and set incense on
it, and stood at the entrance of the tent of meeting, with Moses
and Aaron. [19]When Korah assembled the whole community
against them at the entrance of the tent of meeting, then the
glory of the LORD appeared to the whole community.

THE JUDGMENT ON THE REBELS

[20]The LORD spoke to Moses and Aaron: [21]"Separate yourselves
from among this community, that I may consume them in an
instant." [22]Then they threw themselves down with their faces
to the ground and said, "O God, the God of the spirits of all
people, will you be angry with the whole community when
only one man sins?"

[23]So the LORD spoke to Moses: [24]"Tell the community: 'Get
away from around the homes of Korah, Dathan, and Abiram.'"
[25]Then Moses got up and went to Dathan and Abiram; and the
elders of Israel went after him. [26]And he said to the community,
"Move away from the tents of these wicked men, and do not
touch anything they have, lest you be destroyed because of all
their sins." [27]So they got away from the homes of Korah, Dathan,
and Abiram on every side, and Dathan and Abiram came out
and stationed themselves in the entrances of their tents with
their wives, their children, and their toddlers. [28]Then Moses
said, "This is how you will know that the LORD has sent me to
do all these works, for I have not done them of my own will.
[29]If these men die a natural death, or if they share the fate

of all men, then the LORD has not sent me. [30]But if the LORD
does something entirely new, and the earth opens its mouth
and swallows them up along with all that they have, and they
go down alive to the grave, then you will know that these men
have despised the LORD!"
[31]When he had finished speaking all these words, the ground
that was under them split open, [32]and the earth opened its
mouth and swallowed them, along with their households, and
all Korah's men, and all their goods. [33]They and all that they had
went down alive into the pit, and the earth closed over them. So
they perished from among the community. [34]All the Israelites
who were around them fled at their cry, for they said, "What
if the earth swallows us too?" [35]Then a fire went out from the
LORD and devoured the 250 men who offered incense.

THE ATONEMENT FOR THE REBELLION

[36]The LORD spoke to Moses: [37]"Tell Eleazar son of Aaron the
priest to pick up the censers out of the flame, for they are holy,
and then scatter the coals of fire at a distance. [38]As for the
censers of these men who sinned at the cost of their lives, they
must be made into hammered sheets for covering the altar,
because they presented them before the LORD and sanctified
them. They will become a sign to the Israelites." [39]So Eleazar
the priest took the bronze censers presented by those who
had been burned up, and they were hammered out as a covering for the altar. [40]It was a memorial for the Israelites, that no
outsider who is not a descendant of Aaron should approach to
burn incense before the LORD, that he might not become like
Korah and his company—just as the LORD had spoken by the
authority of Moses. [41]But on the next day the whole community of Israelites murmured against Moses and Aaron, saying,
"You have killed the LORD's people!" [42]When the community
assembled against Moses and Aaron, they turned toward the
tent of meeting—and the cloud covered it, and the glory of the
LORD appeared. [43]Then Moses and Aaron stood before the tent
of meeting.
[44]The LORD spoke to Moses: [45]"Get away from this community, so that I can consume them in an instant!" But they threw
themselves down with their faces to the ground. [46]Then Moses
said to Aaron, "Take the censer, put burning coals from the
altar in it, place incense on it, and go quickly into the assembly
and make atonement for them, for wrath has gone out from
the LORD—the plague has begun!" [47]So Aaron did as Moses
commanded and ran into the middle of the assembly, where
the plague was just beginning among the people. So he placed
incense on the coals and made atonement for the people.
[48]He stood between the dead and the living, and the plague
was stopped. [49]Now 14,700 people died in the plague, in addition to those who died in the event with Korah. [50]Then Aaron
returned to Moses at the entrance of the tent of meeting, and
the plague was stopped.

THE BUDDING OF AARON'S STAFF

17 The LORD spoke to Moses: [2]"Speak to the Israelites, and
receive from them a staff from each tribe, one from every
tribal leader, twelve staffs; you must write each man's name on
his staff. [3]You must write Aaron's name on the staff of Levi; for
one staff is for the head of every tribe. [4]You must place them
in the tent of meeting before the ark of the covenant where I

17:1–13 There is only one true high priest, as scripture says, of whom the high priest Aaron presented a figure. For this reason his rod blossomed. Just as Aaron's rod sprouted among the Jewish people, so the cross of Christ flowered among the Gentiles. Still, since Christ is the true high priest, he is the only one whose rod of the cross not only sprouted but also blossomed and produced the fruit of all believers. This is that priestly fruit that is promised to those "who hunger and thirst for righteousness, for they will be satisfied" (Matt 5:6).

CAESARIUS OF ARLES
(C. 468–542)
SERMONS

meet with you. 5And the staff of the man whom I choose will blossom; so I will rid myself of the complaints of the Israelites, which they murmur against you."

6So Moses spoke to the Israelites, and each of their leaders gave him a staff, one for each leader, according to their tribes—twelve staffs; the staff of Aaron was among their staffs. 7Then Moses placed the staffs before the LORD in the tent of the testimony.

8On the next day Moses went into the tent of the testimony—and the staff of Aaron for the house of Levi had sprouted, and brought forth buds, and produced blossoms, and yielded almonds! 9So Moses brought out all the staffs from before the LORD to all the Israelites. They looked at them, and each man took his staff.

THE MEMORIAL

10The LORD said to Moses, "Bring Aaron's staff back before the testimony to be preserved for a sign to the rebels, so that you may bring their murmurings to an end before me, that they will not die." 11So Moses did as the LORD commanded him—this is what he did.

12The Israelites said to Moses, "We are bound to die! We perish, we all perish! 13Anyone who even comes close to the tabernacle of the LORD will die! Are we all to die?"

RESPONSIBILITIES OF THE PRIESTS

18 The LORD said to Aaron, "You and your sons and your tribe with you must bear the iniquity of the sanctuary, and you and your sons with you must bear the iniquity of your priesthood.

2"Bring with you your brothers, the tribe of Levi, the tribe of your father, so that they may join with you and minister to you while you and your sons with you are before the tent of the testimony. 3They must be responsible to care for you and to care for the entire tabernacle. However, they must not come near the furnishings of the sanctuary and the altar, or both they and you will die. 4They must join with you, and they will be responsible for the care of the tent of meeting, for all the service of the tent, but no unauthorized person may approach you. 5You will be responsible for the care of the sanctuary and the care of the altar, so that there will be no more wrath on the Israelites. 6I myself have chosen your brothers the Levites from among the Israelites. They are given to you as a gift from the LORD, to perform the duties of the tent of meeting. 7But you and your sons with you are responsible for your priestly duties, for everything at the altar and within the curtain. And you must serve. I give you the priesthood as a gift for service, but the unauthorized person who approaches must be put to death."

THE PORTION OF THE PRIESTS

8The LORD spoke to Aaron, "See, I have given you the responsibility for my raised offerings; I have given all the holy things of the Israelites to you as your priestly portion and to your sons as a perpetual ordinance. 9Of all the most holy offerings reserved from the fire this will be yours: Every offering of theirs, whether from every grain offering or from every purification offering or from every reparation offering which they bring to me, will be most holy for you and for your sons. 10You are to eat it as a most holy offering; every male may eat it. It will be holy to you.

18:8–20 Do you wish to know what the difference was between the priests of God and the priests of Pharaoh? Pharaoh granted lands to his priests. The Lord, on the other hand, did not grant his priests a portion in the land but said to them, "I am your portion." For it is Pharaoh who wishes his priests to have possessions of lands and to work at the cultivation of the soil, not of the soul.

ORIGEN (C. 185–C. 253)
HOMILIES ON GENESIS

11“And this is yours: the raised offering of their gift, along with all the wave offerings of the Israelites. I have given them to you and to your sons and daughters with you as a perpetual ordinance. Everyone who is ceremonially clean in your household may eat of it.

12“All the best of the olive oil and all the best of the wine and of the wheat, the firstfruits of these things that they give to the LORD, I have given to you. 13And whatever first ripe fruit in their land they bring to the LORD will be yours; everyone who is ceremonially clean in your household may eat of it.

14“Everything devoted in Israel will be yours. 15The firstborn of every womb which they present to the LORD, whether human or animal, will be yours. Nevertheless, the firstborn sons you must redeem, and the firstborn males of unclean animals you must redeem. 16And those that must be redeemed you are to redeem when they are a month old, according to your estimation, for five shekels of silver according to the sanctuary shekel (which is 20 gerahs). 17But you must not redeem the firstborn of a cow or a sheep or a goat; they are holy. You must splash their blood on the altar and burn their fat for an offering made by fire for a pleasing aroma to the LORD. 18And their meat will be yours, just as the breast and the right hip of the raised offering is yours. 19All the raised offerings of the holy things that the Israelites offer to the LORD, I have given to you, and to your sons and daughters with you, as a perpetual ordinance. It is a covenant of salt forever before the LORD for you and for your descendants with you.”

DUTIES OF THE LEVITES

20The LORD spoke to Aaron, “You will have no inheritance in their land, nor will you have any portion of property among them—I am your portion and your inheritance among the Israelites. 21See, I have given the Levites all the tithes in Israel for an inheritance, for their service that they perform—the service of the tent of meeting. 22No longer may the Israelites approach the tent of meeting, or else they will bear their sin and die. 23But the Levites must perform the service of the tent of meeting, and they must bear their iniquity. It will be a perpetual ordinance throughout your generations that among the Israelites the Levites have no inheritance. 24But I have given to the Levites for an inheritance the tithes of the Israelites that are offered to the LORD as a raised offering. That is why I said to them that among the Israelites they are to have no inheritance.”

INSTRUCTIONS FOR THE LEVITES

25The LORD spoke to Moses: 26“You are to speak to the Levites, and you must tell them, ‘When you receive from the Israelites the tithe that I have given you from them as your inheritance, then you are to offer up from it as a raised offering to the LORD a tenth of the tithe. 27And your raised offering will be credited to you as though it were grain from the threshing floor or as new wine from the winepress. 28Thus you are to offer up a raised offering to the LORD of all your tithes that you receive from the Israelites; and you must give the LORD’s raised offering from it to Aaron the priest. 29From all your gifts you must offer up every raised offering due the LORD, from all the best of it, and the holiest part of it.’

30“Therefore you will say to them, ‘When you offer up the best of it, then it will be credited to the Levites as the product of the threshing floor and as the product of the winepress. [31]And you may eat it in any place, you and your household, because it is your wages for your service in the tent of meeting. [32]And you will bear no sin concerning it when you offer up the best of it. And you must not profane the holy things of the Israelites, or else you will die.'"

THE RED HEIFER RITUAL

19 The LORD spoke to Moses and Aaron: [2]"This is the ordinance of the law that the LORD has commanded: 'Instruct the Israelites to bring you a red heifer without blemish, which has no defect and has never carried a yoke. [3]You must give it to Eleazar the priest so that he can take it outside the camp, and it must be slaughtered before him. [4]Eleazar the priest is to take some of its blood with his finger, and sprinkle some of the blood seven times in the direction of the front of the tent of meeting. [5]Then the heifer must be burned in his sight—its skin, its flesh, its blood, and its offal is to be burned. [6]And the priest must take cedar wood, hyssop, and scarlet wool and throw them into the midst of the fire where the heifer is burning. [7]Then the priest must wash his clothes and bathe himself in water, and afterward he may come into the camp, but the priest will be ceremonially unclean until evening. [8]The one who burns it must wash his clothes in water and bathe himself in water. He will be ceremonially unclean until evening.

[9]"'Then a man who is ceremonially clean must gather up the ashes of the red heifer and put them in a ceremonially clean place outside the camp. They must be kept for the community of the Israelites for use in the water of purification—it is a purification for sin. [10]The one who gathers the ashes of the heifer must wash his clothes and be ceremonially unclean until evening. This will be a permanent ordinance both for the Israelites and the resident foreigner who lives among them.

PURIFICATION FROM UNCLEANNESS

[11]"'Whoever touches the corpse of any person will be ceremonially unclean seven days. [12]He must purify himself with water on the third day and on the seventh day, and so will be clean. But if he does not purify himself on the third day and the seventh day, then he will not be clean. [13]Anyone who touches the corpse of any dead person and does not purify himself defiles the tabernacle of the LORD. And that person must be cut off from Israel, because the water of purification was not sprinkled on him. He will be unclean; his uncleanness remains on him.

[14]"'This is the law: When a man dies in a tent, anyone who comes into the tent and all who are in the tent will be ceremonially unclean seven days. [15]And every open container that has no covering fastened on it is unclean. [16]And whoever touches the body of someone killed with a sword in the open fields, or the body of someone who died of natural causes, or a human bone, or a grave, will be unclean seven days.

[17]"'For a ceremonially unclean person you must take some of the ashes of the heifer burnt for purification from sin and pour fresh running water over them in a vessel. [18]Then a ceremonially clean person must take hyssop, dip it in the water, and sprinkle it on the tent, on all its furnishings, and on the people who were there, or on the one who touched a bone, or one who was killed, or one who died, or a grave. [19]And the clean person must sprinkle the unclean on the third day and on the

19:1–22 Now Moses declared that the ashes of the victims were the ashes of the heifer burnt for purification from sin, which "consecrated them and provided ritual purity" (Heb 9:13). He also understands that the sacrament of the Lord's Passion, which saves us by purifying us forever, is prefigured in these ashes. Thus the burning of a red heifer designates the actual time and event of Christ's Passion.

VENERABLE BEDE
(C. 672–735)
ON THE TABERNACLE

seventh day; and on the seventh day he must purify him, and then he must wash his clothes, and bathe in water, and he will be clean in the evening. [20]But the man who is unclean and does not purify himself, that person must be cut off from among the community, because he has polluted the sanctuary of the LORD; the water of purification was not sprinkled on him, so he is unclean.

[21]"'So this will be a perpetual ordinance for them: The one who sprinkles the water of purification must wash his clothes, and the one who touches the water of purification will be unclean until evening. [22]And whatever the unclean person touches will be unclean, and the person who touches it will be unclean until evening.'"

THE ISRAELITES COMPLAIN AGAIN

20 Then the entire community of Israel entered the wilderness of Zin in the first month, and the people stayed in Kadesh. Miriam died and was buried there.

[2]And there was no water for the community, and so they gathered themselves together against Moses and Aaron. [3]The people contended with Moses, saying, "If only we had died when our brothers died before the LORD! [4]Why have you brought up the LORD's community into this wilderness? So that we and our cattle should die here? [5]Why have you brought us up from Egypt only to bring us to this dreadful place? It is no place for grain, or figs, or vines, or pomegranates; nor is there any water to drink!"

MOSES RESPONDS

[6]So Moses and Aaron went from the presence of the assembly to the entrance to the tent of meeting. They then threw themselves down with their faces to the ground, and the glory of the LORD appeared to them. [7]Then the LORD spoke to Moses: [8]"Take the staff and assemble the community, you and Aaron your brother, and then speak to the rock before their eyes. It will pour forth its water, and you will bring water out of the rock for them, and so you will give the community and their beasts water to drink."

[9]So Moses took the staff from before the LORD, just as he commanded him. [10]Then Moses and Aaron gathered the community together in front of the rock, and he said to them, "Listen, you rebels, must we bring water out of this rock for you?" [11]Then Moses raised his hand, and struck the rock twice with his staff. And water came out abundantly. So the community drank, and their beasts drank too.

THE LORD'S JUDGMENT

[12]Then the LORD spoke to Moses and Aaron, "Because you did not trust me enough to show me as holy before the Israelites, therefore you will not bring this community into the land I have given them."

[13]These are the waters of Meribah, because the Israelites contended with the LORD, and his holiness was maintained among them.

REJECTION BY THE EDOMITES

[14]Moses sent messengers from Kadesh to the king of Edom: "Thus says your brother Israel: 'You know all the hardships we have experienced, [15]how our ancestors went down into Egypt, and we lived in Egypt a long time, and the Egyptians treated us and our

20:1–10 The people were murmuring because there was no water. Moses merely had said to his people, "Must we bring water out of this rock for you?" Thus he wavered only slightly, yet for this alone he immediately received the threat that he should not enter into the land of promise, which was at that time the chief of all the promises made to the Jews. I am fully persuaded that these words are true: "If the righteous are barely saved, what will become of the ungodly and sinners?" (1 Pet 4:18).

BASIL THE GREAT (330–379)
ASCETICAL WORKS

ancestors badly. [16]So when we cried to the LORD, he heard our
voice and sent a messenger, and has brought us up out of Egypt.
Now we are here in Kadesh, a town on the edge of your country.
[17]Please let us pass through your country. We will not pass through
the fields or through the vineyards, nor will we drink water from
any well. We will go by the King's Highway; we will not turn to
the right or the left until we have passed through your region."
[18]But Edom said to him, "You will not pass through me, or I
will come out against you with the sword." [19]Then the Israelites
said to him, "We will go along the highway, and if we or our cattle drink any of your water, we will pay for it. We will only pass
through on our feet, without doing anything else."
[20]But he said, "You may not pass through." Then Edom came
out against them with a large and powerful force. [21]So Edom
refused to give Israel passage through his border; therefore
Israel turned away from him.

AARON'S DEATH

[22]So the entire company of Israelites traveled from Kadesh
and came to Mount Hor. [23]And the LORD spoke to Moses and
Aaron at Mount Hor, by the border of the land of Edom. He
said: [24]"Aaron will be gathered to his ancestors, for he will not
enter into the land I have given to the Israelites because both of
you rebelled against my word at the waters of Meribah. [25]Take
Aaron and Eleazar his son, and bring them up on Mount Hor.
[26]Remove Aaron's priestly garments and put them on Eleazar
his son, and Aaron will be gathered to his ancestors and will
die there."
[27]So Moses did as the LORD commanded; and they went up
Mount Hor in the sight of the whole community. [28]And Moses
removed Aaron's garments and put them on his son Eleazar.
So Aaron died there on the top of the mountain. And Moses
and Eleazar came down from the mountain. [29]When all the
community saw that Aaron was dead, the whole house of Israel
mourned for Aaron thirty days.

VICTORY AT HORMAH

21 When the Canaanite king of Arad who lived in the Negev
heard that Israel was approaching along the road to Ath-
arim, he fought against Israel and took some of them prisoner.
[2]So Israel made a vow to the LORD and said, "If you will indeed
deliver this people into our hand, then we will utterly destroy
their cities." [3]The LORD listened to the voice of Israel and delivered up the Canaanites, and they utterly destroyed them
and their cities. So the name of the place was called Hormah.

FIERY SERPENTS

[4]Then they traveled from Mount Hor by the road to the Red
Sea, to go around the land of Edom, but the people became
impatient along the way. [5]And the people spoke against God
and against Moses, "Why have you brought us up from Egypt
to die in the wilderness, for there is no bread or water, and we
detest this worthless food."
[6]So the LORD sent venomous snakes among the people,
and they bit the people; many people of Israel died. [7]Then the
people came to Moses and said, "We have sinned, for we have
spoken against the LORD and against you. Pray to the LORD
that he would take away the snakes from us." So Moses prayed
for the people.

21:1–9 Now Moses was ordered by the Lord to make a bronze serpent, to raise it on a pole in the wilderness, and to admonish the people Israel that when any had been bitten by a serpent, they should look to that serpent raised up on the pole. This was done: People were bitten, and they looked and were healed. What are the biting serpents? Sins from the mortality of the flesh. What is the serpent lifted up? The Lord's death on the cross. For as death came by the serpent, it was figured by the image of a serpent. The serpent's bite was deadly; the Lord's death is life-giving. That we may be healed from sin, let us now gaze on Christ crucified; they who look in faith on Christ's death are healed from the bites of sins.

AUGUSTINE **(354–430)**
TRACTATES ON THE GOSPEL OF JOHN

[8]The LORD said to Moses, "Make a poisonous snake and set
it on a pole. When anyone who is bitten looks at it, he will live."
[9]So Moses made a bronze snake and put it on a pole, so that
if a snake had bitten someone, when he looked at the bronze
snake he lived.

THE APPROACH TO MOAB

[10]The Israelites traveled on and camped in Oboth. [11]Then they
traveled on from Oboth and camped at Iye Abarim, in the wilderness that is before Moab on the eastern side. [12]From there
they moved on and camped in the valley of Zered. [13]From there
they moved on and camped on the other side of the Arnon, in
the wilderness that extends from the regions of the Amorites,
for Arnon is the border of Moab, between Moab and the Amorites. [14]This is why it is said in the Book of the Wars of the LORD,

"Waheb in Suphah and the wadis,
the Arnon [15]and the slope of the valleys
that extends to the dwelling of Ar,
and falls off at the border of Moab."

[16]And from there they traveled to Beer; that is the well where
the LORD spoke to Moses, "Gather the people and I will give
them water." [17]Then Israel sang this song:

"Spring up, O well, sing to it!
[18] The well which the princes dug,
which the leaders of the people opened
with their scepters and their staffs."

And from the wilderness they traveled to Mattanah; [19]and
from Mattanah to Nahaliel; and from Nahaliel to Bamoth; [20]and
from Bamoth to the valley that is in the country of Moab, near
the top of Pisgah, which overlooks the wastelands.

THE VICTORY OVER SIHON AND OG

[21]Then Israel sent messengers to King Sihon of the Amorites,
saying,

[22]"Let us pass through your land; we will not turn aside into
the fields or into the vineyards, nor will we drink water from any
well, but we will go along the King's Highway until we pass your
borders." [23]But Sihon did not permit Israel to pass through his
border; he gathered all his forces together and went out against
Israel into the wilderness. When he came to Jahaz, he fought
against Israel. [24]But the Israelites defeated him in battle and
took possession of his land from the Arnon to the Jabbok, as
far as the Ammonites, for the border of the Ammonites was
strongly defended. [25]So Israel took all these cities; and Israel
settled in all the cities of the Amorites, in Heshbon, and in all
its villages. [26]For Heshbon was the city of King Sihon of the
Amorites. Now he had fought against the former king of Moab
and had taken all his land from his control, as far as the Arnon.
[27]That is why those who speak in proverbs say,

"Come to Heshbon, let it be built.
Let the city of Sihon be established!
[28] For fire went out from Heshbon,
a flame from the city of Sihon.
It has consumed Ar of Moab
and the lords of the high places of Arnon.
[29] Woe to you, Moab.
You are ruined, O people of Chemosh!

He has made his sons fugitives,
and his daughters the prisoners of King Sihon of the
Amorites.
30 We have overpowered them;
Heshbon has perished as far as Dibon.
We have shattered them as far as Nophah,
which reaches to Medeba."

[31]So the Israelites lived in the land of the Amorites. [32]Moses
sent spies to reconnoiter Jazer, and they captured its villages
and dispossessed the Amorites who were there.
[33]Then they turned and went up by the road to Bashan. And
King Og of Bashan and all his forces marched out against them
to do battle at Edrei. [34]And the LORD said to Moses, "Do not fear
him, for I have delivered him and all his people and his land
into your hand. You will do to him what you did to King Sihon
of the Amorites, who lived in Heshbon." [35]So they defeated Og,
his sons, and all his people, until there were no survivors, and
they possessed his land.

BALAAM REFUSES TO CURSE ISRAEL

22 The Israelites traveled on and camped in the rift valley
plains of Moab on the side of the Jordan River across from
Jericho. [2]Balak son of Zippor saw all that the Israelites had done
to the Amorites. [3]And the Moabites were greatly afraid of the
people, because they were so numerous. The Moabites were
sick with fear because of the Israelites.
[4]So the Moabites said to the elders of Midian, "Now this mass
of people will lick up everything around us, as the bull devours
the grass of the field." Now Balak son of Zippor was king of the
Moabites at this time. [5]And he sent messengers to Balaam son
of Beor at Pethor, which is by the Euphrates River in the land of
Amaw, to summon him, saying, "Look, a nation has come out of
Egypt. They cover the face of the earth, and they are settling next
to me. [6]So now, please come and curse this nation for me, for they
are too powerful for me. Perhaps I will prevail so that we may
conquer them and drive them out of the land. For I know that
whoever you bless is blessed, and whoever you curse is cursed."
[7]So the elders of Moab and the elders of Midian departed with
the fee for divination in their hands. They came to Balaam and
reported to him the words of Balak. [8]He replied to them, "Stay
here tonight, and I will bring back to you whatever word the LORD
may speak to me." So the princes of Moab stayed with Balaam.
[9]And God came to Balaam and said, "Who are these men with
you?" [10]Balaam said to God, "Balak son of Zippor, king of Moab,
has sent a message to me, saying, [11]'Look, a nation has come out
of Egypt, and it covers the face of the earth. Come now and put a
curse on them for me; perhaps I will be able to defeat them and
drive them out.'" [12]But God said to Balaam, "You must not go
with them; you must not curse the people, for they are blessed."
[13]So Balaam got up in the morning, and said to the princes
of Balak, "Go to your land, for the LORD has refused to permit
me to go with you." [14]So the princes of Moab departed and
went back to Balak and said, "Balaam refused to come with us."

BALAAM ACCOMPANIES THE MOABITE PRINCES

[15]Balak again sent princes, more numerous and more distinguished
than the first. [16]And they came to Balaam and said to him, "Thus

22:2–21 God said, "You must not go with them; you must not curse the people, for they are blessed." He does not hint at anything with regard to the people, for they all lay before his view, but he referred to the mystery of Christ pointed out beforehand. For as he was to be born of the fathers according to the flesh, the Spirit gives instructions to Balaam beforehand lest, going forth in ignorance, he might pronounce a curse upon the people. Not, indeed, that his curse could take any effect contrary to the will of God, but this was done as an exhibition of the providence of God that he exercised toward them on account of their forefathers.

IRENAEUS (C. 130–C. 202)
AGAINST HERESIES

says Balak son of Zippor: 'Please do not let anything hinder you
from coming to me. 17For I will honor you greatly, and whatever
you tell me I will do. So come, put a curse on this nation for me.'"
18Balaam replied to the servants of Balak, "Even if Balak
would give me his palace full of silver and gold, I could not
transgress the commandment of the LORD my God to do less
or more. 19Now therefore, please stay the night here also, that
I may know what more the LORD might say to me." 20God came
to Balaam that night, and said to him, "If the men have come to
call you, get up and go with them, but the word that I will say
to you, that you must do." 21So Balaam got up in the morning,
saddled his donkey, and went with the princes of Moab.

GOD OPPOSES BALAAM

22Then God's anger was kindled because he went, and the angel
of the LORD stood in the road to oppose him. Now he was riding
on his donkey and his two servants were with him. 23And the
donkey saw the angel of the LORD standing in the road with
his sword drawn in his hand, so the donkey turned aside from
the road and went into the field. But Balaam beat the donkey,
to make her turn back to the road.
24Then the angel of the LORD stood in a path among the vineyards, where there was a wall on either side. 25And when the donkey saw the angel of the LORD, she pressed herself into the wall,
and crushed Balaam's foot against the wall. So he beat her again.
26Then the angel of the LORD went farther, and stood in a
narrow place, where there was no way to turn either to the right
or to the left. 27When the donkey saw the angel of the LORD,
she crouched down under Balaam. Then Balaam was angry, and
he beat his donkey with a staff.
28Then the LORD opened the mouth of the donkey, and she said
to Balaam, "What have I done to you that you have beaten me these
three times?" 29And Balaam said to the donkey, "You have made
me look stupid; I wish there were a sword in my hand, for I would
kill you right now." 30The donkey said to Balaam, "Am I not your
donkey that you have ridden ever since I was yours until this day?
Have I ever attempted to treat you this way?" And he said, "No."
31Then the LORD opened Balaam's eyes, and he saw the angel of
the LORD standing in the way with his sword drawn in his hand;
so he bowed his head and threw himself down with his face to
the ground. 32The angel of the LORD said to him, "Why have you
beaten your donkey these three times? Look, I came out to oppose you because what you are doing is perverse before me. 33The
donkey saw me and turned from me these three times. If she had
not turned from me, I would have killed you but saved her alive."
34Balaam said to the angel of the LORD, "I have sinned, for I did not
know that you stood against me in the road. So now, if it is evil in
your sight, I will go back home." 35But the angel of the LORD said
to Balaam, "Go with the men, but you may only speak the word
that I will speak to you." So Balaam went with the princes of Balak.

BALAAM MEETS BALAK

36When Balak heard that Balaam was coming, he went out to
meet him at a city of Moab that was on the border of the Arnon
at the boundary of his territory. 37Balak said to Balaam, "Did I
not send again and again to you to summon you? Why did you
not come to me? Am I not able to honor you?" 38Balaam said
to Balak, "Look, I have come to you. Now, am I able to speak
just anything? I must speak only the word that God puts in my

mouth." 39 So Balaam went with Balak, and they came to Kiriath
Huzoth. 40 And Balak sacrificed bulls and sheep, and sent some
to Balaam, and to the princes who were with him. 41 Then on
the next morning Balak took Balaam, and brought him up to
Bamoth Baal. From there he saw the extent of the nation.

BALAAM BLESSES ISRAEL

23 Balaam said to Balak, "Build me seven altars here, and
prepare for me here seven bulls and seven rams." 2 So Balak did just as Balaam had said. Balak and Balaam then offered
on each altar a bull and a ram. 3 Balaam said to Balak, "Station
yourself by your burnt offering, and I will go off; perhaps the
LORD will come to meet me, and whatever he reveals to me I
will tell you." Then he went to a deserted height.

4 Then God met Balaam, who said to him, "I have prepared
seven altars, and I have offered on each altar a bull and a ram."
5 Then the LORD put a message in Balaam's mouth and said,
"Return to Balak, and speak what I tell you."

6 So he returned to him, and he was still standing by his burnt
offering, he and all the princes of Moab. 7 Then Balaam uttered
his oracle, saying,

"Balak, the king of Moab, brought me from Aram,
out of the mountains of the east, saying,
'Come, pronounce a curse on Jacob for me;
come, denounce Israel.'
8 How can I curse one whom God has not cursed,
or how can I denounce one whom the LORD has not
denounced?
9 For from the top of the rocks I see them;
from the hills I watch them.
Indeed, a nation that lives alone,
and it will not be reckoned among the nations.
10 Who can count the dust of Jacob,
or number the fourth part of Israel?
Let me die the death of the upright,
and let the end of my life be like theirs."

BALAAM RELOCATES

11 Then Balak said to Balaam, "What have you done to me? I
brought you to curse my enemies, but on the contrary you have
only blessed them!" 12 Balaam replied, "Must I not be careful
to speak what the LORD has put in my mouth?" 13 Balak said to
him, "Please come with me to another place from which you
can observe them. You will see only a part of them, but you will
not see all of them. Curse them for me from there."

14 So Balak brought Balaam to the field of Zophim, to the top
of Pisgah, where he built seven altars and offered a bull and a ram
on each altar. 15 And Balaam said to Balak, "Station yourself here
by your burnt offering, while I meet the LORD there." 16 Then the
LORD met Balaam and put a message in his mouth and said, "Return
to Balak, and speak what I tell you." 17 When Balaam came to him,
he was still standing by his burnt offering, along with the princes
of Moab. And Balak said to him, "What has the LORD spoken?"

BALAAM PROPHESIES AGAIN

18 Balaam uttered his oracle, and said,

"Rise up, Balak, and hear;
Listen to me, son of Zippor:
19 God is not a man, that he should lie,

23:13–26 "At this time it must be said of Jacob and of Israel, 'Look at what God has done!'" That is, God shall do a very strange and wonderful thing for Jacob and for Israel. "At this time," that is, what he has done at this time is a shadow and representation of it. He has now redeemed out of Egypt, and hereafter he shall send Jesus Christ to redeem them out of spiritual Egypt; with a greater strength shall he redeem them from the power of the devil.

JONATHAN EDWARDS
(1703–1758)
THE COMPLETE WORKS

nor a human being, that he should change his mind.
Has he said, and will he not do it?
Or has he spoken, and will he not make it happen?
20 Indeed, I have received a command to bless;
he has blessed, and I cannot reverse it.
21 He has not looked on iniquity in Jacob,
nor has he seen trouble in Israel.
The LORD their God is with them;
his acclamation as king is among them.
22 God brought them out of Egypt.
They have, as it were, the strength of a wild bull.
23 For there is no spell against Jacob,
nor is there any divination against Israel.
At this time it must be said of Jacob
and of Israel, 'Look at what God has done!'
24 Indeed, the people will rise up like a lioness,
and like a lion raises himself up;
they will not lie down until they eat their prey,
and drink the blood of the slain."

BALAAM RELOCATES YET AGAIN

25 Balak said to Balaam, "Neither curse them at all nor bless
them at all!" 26 But Balaam replied to Balak, "Did I not tell you,
'All that the LORD speaks, I must do'?"
27 Balak said to Balaam, "Come, please; I will take you to another place. Perhaps it will please God to let you curse them
for me from there." 28 So Balak took Balaam to the top of Peor,
that looks toward the wastelands. 29 Then Balaam said to Balak,
"Build seven altars here for me, and prepare seven bulls and
seven rams." 30 So Balak did as Balaam had said, and offered a
bull and a ram on each altar.

BALAAM PROPHESIES YET AGAIN

24 When Balaam saw that it pleased the LORD to bless Israel,
he did not go as at the other times to seek for omens, but
he set his face toward the wilderness. 2 When Balaam lifted up
his eyes, he saw Israel camped tribe by tribe; and the Spirit of
God came upon him. 3 Then he uttered this oracle:
"The oracle of Balaam son of Beor,
the oracle of the man whose eyes are open,
4 the oracle of the one who hears the words of God,
who sees a vision from the Almighty,
although falling flat on the ground with eyes open:
5 'How beautiful are your tents, O Jacob,
and your dwelling places, O Israel!
6 They are like valleys stretched forth,
like gardens by the river's side,
like aloes that the LORD has planted,
and like cedar trees beside the waters.
7 He will pour the water out of his buckets,
and their descendants will be like abundant water;
their king will be greater than Agag,
and their kingdom will be exalted.
8 God brought them out of Egypt.
They have, as it were, the strength of a young bull;
they will devour hostile people,
and will break their bones,
and will pierce them through with arrows.
9 They crouch and lie down like a lion,

24:1–10 The oracle in saying that the Lord would come into Egypt foretold the journey of our Lord Jesus Christ when he went into Egypt with his parents. Here we have the prophecy of his return from Egypt in its natural order, when he came back with his parents into the land of Israel, in the words "God brought them out of Egypt." For our Lord and Savior Jesus, the Christ of God, was the only one of the seed of Israel and of the Jewish race who has rule over many nations so that it is indisputable that he is the fulfillment of the prophecy that says, literally, that a man will come from the Jewish race and rule over many nations.

EUSEBIUS OF CAESAREA
(C. 260–339)
THE PROOF OF THE GOSPEL

and as a lioness, who can stir him?
Blessed is the one who blesses you,
and cursed is the one who curses you!'"

10Then Balak became very angry at Balaam, and he struck
his hands together. Balak said to Balaam, "I called you to curse
my enemies, and look, you have done nothing but bless them
these three times! 11So now, go back where you came from! I
said that I would greatly honor you, but now the LORD has stood
in the way of your honor."
12Balaam said to Balak, "Did I not also tell your messengers
whom you sent to me, 13'If Balak would give me his palace full
of silver and gold, I cannot go beyond the commandment of
the LORD to do either good or evil of my own will, but whatever the LORD tells me I must speak'? 14And now, I am about
to go back to my own people. Come now, and I will advise
you as to what this people will do to your people in future
days."

BALAAM PROPHESIES A FOURTH TIME

15Then he uttered this oracle:
"The oracle of Balaam son of Beor,
the oracle of the man whose eyes are open,
16 the oracle of the one who hears the words of God,
and who knows the knowledge of the Most High,
who sees a vision from the Almighty,
although falling flat on the ground with eyes open:
17 'I see him, but not now;
I behold him, but not close at hand.
A star will march forth out of Jacob,
and a scepter will rise out of Israel.
He will crush the skulls of Moab,
and the heads of all the sons of Sheth.
18 Edom will be a possession,
Seir, his enemy, will also be a possession;
but Israel will act valiantly.
19 A ruler will be established from Jacob;
he will destroy the remains of the city.'"

BALAAM'S FINAL PROPHECIES

20Then Balaam looked on Amalek and delivered this
oracle:
"Amalek was the first of the nations,
but his end will be that he will perish."

21Then he looked on the Kenites and uttered this oracle:
"Your dwelling place seems strong,
and your nest is set on a rocky cliff.
22 Nevertheless the Kenite will be consumed.
How long will Asshur take you away captive?"
23Then he uttered this oracle:
"O, who will survive when God does this!
24 Ships will come from the coast of Kittim,
and will afflict Asshur, and will afflict Eber,
and he will also perish forever."

25Balaam got up and departed and returned to his home,
and Balak also went his way.

25:1–17 I might say that those who deny Christianity on oath at the tribunals or before they have been put on trial do not worship but only bow down to idols when they take "God" from the name of the Lord God and apply it to vain and lifeless wood. Thus the people who were defiled with the daughters of Moab bowed down to idols but did not worship them. Indeed, it is written in the text itself, "These women invited the people to the sacrifices of their gods; then the people ate and bowed down to their gods." Observe that it does not say "and they worshiped their idols"; for it was not possible after such great signs and wonders in one moment of time to be persuaded by the women with whom they committed fornication to consider the idols gods.

ORIGEN (C. 185–C. 253)
EXHORTATION TO MARTYRDOM

ISRAEL'S SIN WITH THE MOABITE WOMEN

25 When Israel lived in Shittim, the people began to commit sexual immorality with the daughters of Moab. 2These women invited the people to the sacrifices of their gods; then the people ate and bowed down to their gods. 3When Israel joined themselves to Baal Peor, the anger of the LORD flared up against Israel.

GOD'S PUNISHMENT

4The LORD said to Moses, "Arrest all the leaders of the people, and hang them up before the LORD in broad daylight, so that the fierce anger of the LORD may be turned away from Israel." 5So Moses said to the judges of Israel, "Each of you must execute those of his men who were joined to Baal Peor."

6Just then one of the Israelites came and brought to his brothers a Midianite woman in the plain view of Moses and of the whole community of the Israelites, while they were weeping at the entrance of the tent of meeting. 7When Phinehas son of Eleazar, the son of Aaron the priest, saw it, he got up from among the assembly, took a javelin in his hand, 8and went after the Israelite man into the tent and thrust through the Israelite man and into the woman's abdomen. So the plague was stopped from the Israelites. 9Those that died in the plague were 24,000.

THE AFTERMATH

10The LORD spoke to Moses: 11"Phinehas son of Eleazar, the son of Aaron the priest, has turned my anger away from the Israelites, when he manifested such zeal for my sake among them, so that I did not consume the Israelites in my zeal. 12Therefore, announce: 'I am going to give to him my covenant of peace. 13So it will be to him and his descendants after him a covenant of a permanent priesthood, because he has been zealous for his God, and has made atonement for the Israelites.'"

14Now the name of the Israelite who was stabbed—the one who was stabbed with the Midianite woman—was Zimri son of Salu, a leader of a clan of the Simeonites. 15The name of the Midianite woman who was killed was Cozbi daughter of Zur. He was a leader over the people of a clan of Midian.

16Then the LORD spoke to Moses: 17"Bring trouble to the Midianites, and destroy them, 18because they bring trouble to you by their treachery with which they have deceived you in the matter of Peor, and in the matter of Cozbi, the daughter of a prince of Midian, their sister, who was killed on the day of the plague that happened as a result of Peor."

A SECOND CENSUS REQUIRED

26 After the plague the LORD said to Moses and to Eleazar son of Aaron the priest, 2"Take a census of the whole community of Israelites, from twenty years old and upward, by their clans, everyone who can serve in the army of Israel." 3So Moses and Eleazar the priest spoke with them in the rift valley plains of Moab, along the Jordan River across from Jericho. They said, 4"Number the people from twenty years old and upward, just as the LORD commanded Moses and the Israelites who went out from the land of Egypt."

REUBEN

5Reuben was the firstborn of Israel. The Reubenites: from Hanoch, the family of the Hanochites; from Pallu, the family of

the Palluites; [6]from Hezron, the family of the Hezronites; from
Carmi, the family of the Carmites. [7]These were the families
of the Reubenites; and those numbered of them were 43,730.
[8]Pallu's descendant was Eliab. [9]Eliab's descendants were Nemuel, Dathan, and Abiram. It was Dathan and Abiram who as
leaders of the community rebelled against Moses and Aaron
with the followers of Korah when they rebelled against the
LORD. [10]The earth opened its mouth and swallowed them and
Korah at the time that company died, when the fire consumed
250 men. So they became a warning. [11]But the descendants of
Korah did not die.

SIMEON

[12]The Simeonites by their families: from Nemuel, the family of
the Nemuelites; from Jamin, the family of the Jaminites; from
Jakin, the family of the Jakinites; [13]from Zerah, the family of the
Zerahites; and from Shaul, the family of the Shaulites. [14]These
were the families of the Simeonites, 22,200.

GAD

[15]The Gadites by their families: from Zephon, the family of
the Zephonites; from Haggi, the family of the Haggites; from
Shuni, the family of the Shunites; [16]from Ozni, the family of
the Oznites; from Eri, the family of the Erites; [17]from Arod,
the family of the Arodites; and from Areli, the family of the
Arelites. [18]These were the families of the Gadites according
to those numbered of them, 40,500.

JUDAH

[19]The descendants of Judah were Er and Onan, but Er and Onan
died in the land of Canaan. [20]And the Judahites by their families
were: from Shelah, the family of the Shelahites; from Perez,
the family of the Perezites; and from Zerah, the family of the
Zerahites. [21]And the Perezites were: from Hezron, the family
of the Hezronites; from Hamul, the family of the Hamulites.
[22]These were the families of Judah according to those numbered
of them, 76,500.

ISSACHAR

[23]The Issacharites by their families: from Tola, the family of
the Tolaites; from Puah, the family of the Puites; [24]from Jashub,
the family of the Jashubites; and from Shimron, the family of the
Shimronites. [25]These were the families of Issachar, according
to those numbered of them, 64,300.

ZEBULUN

[26]The Zebulunites by their families: from Sered, the family of
the Sardites; from Elon, the family of the Elonites; from Jahleel,
the family of the Jahleelites. [27]These were the families of the
Zebulunites, according to those numbered of them, 60,500.

MANASSEH

[28]The descendants of Joseph by their families: Manasseh and
Ephraim. [29]The Manassehites: from Machir, the family of the
Machirites (now Machir became the father of Gilead); from
Gilead, the family of the Gileadites. [30]These were the Gileadites:
from Iezer, the family of the Iezerites; from Helek, the family
of the Helekites; [31]from Asriel, the family of the Asrielites;
from Shechem, the family of the Shechemites; [32]from Shemida,

26:1–65 God ordered the people counted by tribe and by name, although he commanded that their family relationships should be recorded too. These words seem to say something about the blessedness of Christ, by the fact that they decree rewards proper to each virtue, and the greatest rewards go to those who are endowed with sincere hearts. For, scripture says, they will see God.

PROCOPIUS OF GAZA
(C. 465–528)
CATENA ON THE OCTATEUCH

the family of the Shemidaites; from Hepher, the family of the Hepherites. 33Now Zelophehad son of Hepher had no sons, but only daughters; and the names of the daughters of Zelophehad were Mahlah, Noah, Hoglah, Milcah, and Tirzah. 34These were the families of Manasseh; those numbered of them were 52,700.

EPHRAIM

35These are the Ephraimites by their families: from Shuthelah, the family of the Shuthelahites; from Beker, the family of the Bekerites; from Tahan, the family of the Tahanites. 36Now these were the Shuthelahites: from Eran, the family of the Eranites. 37These were the families of the Ephraimites, according to those numbered of them, 32,500. These were the descendants of Joseph by their families.

BENJAMIN

38The Benjaminites by their families: from Bela, the family of the Belaites; from Ashbel, the family of the Ashbelites; from Ahiram, the family of the Ahiramites; 39from Shupham, the family of the Shuphamites; from Hupham, the family of the Huphamites. 40The descendants of Bela were Ard and Naaman. From Ard, the family of the Ardites; from Naaman, the family of the Naamanites. 41These are the Benjaminites, according to their families, and according to those numbered of them, 45,600.

DAN

42These are the Danites by their families: from Shuham, the family of the Shuhamites. These were the families of Dan, according to their families. 43All the families of the Shuhamites according to those numbered of them were 64,400.

ASHER

44The Asherites by their families: from Imnah, the family of the Imnahites; from Ishvi, the family of the Ishvites; from Beriah, the family of the Beriahites. 45From the Beriahites: from Heber, the family of the Heberites; from Malkiel, the family of the Malkielites. 46Now the name of the daughter of Asher was Serah. 47These are the families of the Asherites, according to those numbered of them, 53,400.

NAPHTALI

48The Naphtalites by their families: from Jahzeel, the family of the Jahzeelites; from Guni, the family of the Gunites; 49from Jezer, the family of the Jezerites; from Shillem, the family of the Shillemites. 50These were the families of Naphtali according to their families; and those numbered of them were 45,400.

TOTAL NUMBER AND DIVISION OF THE LAND

51These were those numbered of the Israelites, 601,730.

52Then the LORD spoke to Moses: 53"To these the land must be divided as an inheritance according to the number of the names. 54To a larger group you will give a larger inheritance, and to a smaller group you will give a smaller inheritance. To each one its inheritance must be given according to the number of people in it. 55The land must be divided by lot; and they will inherit in accordance with the names of their ancestral tribes. 56Their inheritance must be apportioned by lot among the larger and smaller groups."

[57]And these are the Levites who were numbered according to their families: from Gershon, the family of the Gershonites; of Kohath, the family of the Kohathites; from Merari, the family of the Merarites. [58]These are the families of the Levites: the family of the Libnites, the family of the Hebronites, the family of the Mahlites, the family of the Mushites, the family of the Korahites. Kohath became the father of Amram. [59]Now the name of Amram's wife was Jochebed, daughter of Levi, who was born to Levi in Egypt. And to Amram she bore Aaron, Moses, and Miriam their sister. [60]And to Aaron were born Nadab and Abihu, Eleazar and Ithamar. [61]But Nadab and Abihu died when they offered strange fire before the LORD. [62]Those of the Levites who were numbered were 23,000, all males from a month old and upward, for they were not numbered among the Israelites; no inheritance was given to them among the Israelites.

[63]These are those who were numbered by Moses and Eleazar the priest, who numbered the Israelites in the rift valley plains of Moab along the Jordan River opposite Jericho. [64]But there was not a man among these who had been among those numbered by Moses and Aaron the priest when they numbered the Israelites in the desert of Sinai. [65]For the LORD had said of them, "They will surely die in the wilderness." And there was not left a single man of them, except Caleb son of Jephunneh and Joshua son of Nun.

SPECIAL INHERITANCE LAWS

27 Then the daughters of Zelophehad son of Hepher, the son of Gilead, the son of Machir, the son of Manasseh of the families of Manasseh, the son of Joseph came forward. Now these are the names of his daughters: Mahlah, Noah, Hoglah, Milcah, and Tirzah. [2]And they stood before Moses and Eleazar the priest and the leaders of the whole assembly at the entrance to the tent of meeting and said, [3]"Our father died in the wilderness, although he was not part of the company of those that gathered themselves together against the LORD in the company of Korah, but he died for his own sin, and he had no sons. [4]Why should the name of our father be lost from among his family because he had no son? Give us a possession among the relatives of our father."

[5]So Moses brought their case before the LORD. [6]The LORD said to Moses: [7]"The daughters of Zelophehad have a valid claim. You must indeed give them possession of an inheritance among their father's relatives, and you must transfer the inheritance of their father to them. [8]And you must tell the Israelites, 'If a man dies and has no son, then you must transfer his inheritance to his daughter; [9]and if he has no daughter, then you are to give his inheritance to his brothers; [10]and if he has no brothers, then you are to give his inheritance to his father's brothers; [11]and if his father has no brothers, then you are to give his inheritance to his relative nearest to him from his family, and he will possess it. This will be for the Israelites a legal requirement, as the LORD commanded Moses.'"

LEADERSHIP CHANGE

[12]Then the LORD said to Moses, "Go up this mountain of the Abarim range, and see the land I have given to the Israelites. [13]When you have seen it, you will be gathered to your ancestors, as Aaron your brother was gathered to his ancestors. [14]For in the wilderness of Zin when the community rebelled against me,

27:7 "The daughters of Zelophehad have a valid claim. You must indeed give them possession of an inheritance among their father's relatives"—their uncles, or rather the children of them; for it is reasonable to suppose their father's brethren, or their uncles, were dead also. "You must transfer the inheritance of their father to them"; that is, that part which would have fallen to him by lot, had he been living, these were to take, they standing in his place; and so the portion of the land he would have had was to be divided between these five daughters.

JOHN GILL (1697–1771)
EXPOSITION OF THE WHOLE BIBLE

you rebelled against my command to show me as holy before their eyes over the water—the water of Meribah in Kadesh in the wilderness of Zin."

15 Then Moses spoke to the LORD: 16 "Let the LORD, the God of the spirits of all humankind, appoint a man over the community, 17 who will go out before them, and who will come in before them, and who will lead them out, and who will bring them in, so that the community of the LORD may not be like sheep that have no shepherd."

18 The LORD replied to Moses, "Take Joshua son of Nun, a man in whom is the Spirit, and lay your hand on him; 19 set him before Eleazar the priest and before the whole community, and commission him publicly. 20 Then you must delegate some of your authority to him, so that the whole community of the Israelites will be obedient. 21 And he will stand before Eleazar the priest, who will seek counsel for him before the LORD by the decision of the Urim. At his command they will go out, and at his command they will come in, he and all the Israelites with him, the whole community."

22 So Moses did as the LORD commanded him; he took Joshua and set him before Eleazar the priest and before the whole community. 23 He laid his hands on him and commissioned him, just as the LORD commanded, by the authority of Moses.

DAILY OFFERINGS

28 The LORD spoke to Moses: 2 "Command the Israelites: 'With regard to my offering, be sure to offer my food for my offering made by fire, as a pleasing aroma to me at its appointed time.' 3 You will say to them, 'This is the offering made by fire that you must offer to the LORD: two unblemished lambs one year old each day for a continual burnt offering. 4 The first lamb you must offer in the morning, and the second lamb you must offer in the late afternoon, 5 with one-tenth of an ephah of finely ground flour as a grain offering mixed with one-quarter of a hin of pressed olive oil. 6 It is a continual burnt offering that was instituted on Mount Sinai as a pleasing aroma, an offering made by fire to the LORD.

7 "'And its drink offering must be one-quarter of a hin for each lamb. You must pour out the strong drink as a drink offering to the LORD in the Holy Place. 8 And the second lamb you must offer in the late afternoon; just as you offered the grain offering and drink offering in the morning, you must offer it as an offering made by fire, as a pleasing aroma to the LORD.

28:1–31 This is indeed a full and perfect sacrifice: "In this manner you must offer daily throughout the seven days the food of the sacrifice made by fire as a sweet aroma to the LORD. It is to be offered in addition to the continual burnt offering and its drink offering." These acts are made perfect if our souls quell the anxieties of this world and the enticements of the flesh in a victorious struggle over hedonism. Thus the soul is free from the world and dedicated to God, departing not even in the slightest way from the path of good intentions and casting aside all distractions, whether of pleasure or of toil. The wise—and no one else—celebrate with due solemnity this festal day.

AMBROSE **(C. 339–C. 397)**
CAIN AND ABEL

WEEKLY OFFERINGS

9 "'On the Sabbath day, you must offer two unblemished lambs a year old, and two-tenths of an ephah of finely ground flour as a grain offering, mixed with olive oil, along with its drink offering. 10 This is the burnt offering for every Sabbath, besides the continual burnt offering and its drink offering.

MONTHLY OFFERINGS

11 "'On the first day of each month you must offer as a burnt offering to the LORD two young bulls, one ram, and seven unblemished lambs a year old, 12 with three-tenths of an ephah of finely ground flour mixed with olive oil as a grain offering for each bull, and two-tenths of an ephah of finely ground flour mixed with olive oil as a grain offering for the ram, 13 and one-tenth of an ephah of finely ground flour mixed with olive oil as

a grain offering for each lamb, as a burnt offering for a pleasing
aroma, an offering made by fire to the LORD. 14For their drink
offerings, include half a hin of wine with each bull, one-third
of a hin for the ram, and one-fourth of a hin for each lamb. This
is the burnt offering for each month throughout the months
of the year. 15And one male goat must be offered to the LORD
as a purification offering, in addition to the continual burnt
offering and its drink offering.

THE PASSOVER

16"'On the fourteenth day of the first month is the LORD's Passover. 17And on the fifteenth day of this month is the festival.
For seven days bread made without yeast must be eaten. 18And
on the first day there is to be a holy assembly; you must do no
ordinary work on it.

19"'But you must offer to the LORD an offering made by fire,
a burnt offering of two young bulls, one ram, and seven lambs
one year old; they must all be unblemished. 20And their grain
offering is to be of finely ground flour mixed with olive oil.
For each bull you must offer three-tenths of an ephah, and
two-tenths for the ram. 21For each of the seven lambs you are
to offer one-tenth of an ephah, 22as well as one goat for a purification offering, to make atonement for you. 23You must offer
these in addition to the burnt offering in the morning that
is for a continual burnt offering. 24In this manner you must
offer daily throughout the seven days the food of the sacrifice
made by fire as a sweet aroma to the LORD. It is to be offered in
addition to the continual burnt offering and its drink offering.
25On the seventh day you are to have a holy assembly, you must
do no regular work.

FIRSTFRUITS

26"'Also, on the day of the firstfruits, when you bring a new
grain offering to the LORD during your Feast of Weeks, you
are to have a holy assembly. You must do no ordinary work.
27But you must offer as the burnt offering, as a sweet aroma to
the LORD, two young bulls, one ram, seven lambs one year old,
28with their grain offering of finely ground flour mixed with
olive oil: three-tenths of an ephah for each bull, two-tenths
for the one ram, 29with one-tenth for each of the seven lambs,
30as well as one male goat to make an atonement for you. 31You
are to offer them with their drink offerings in addition to the
continual burnt offering and its grain offering—they must be
unblemished.

BLOWING TRUMPETS

29 "'On the first day of the seventh month, you are to hold a
holy assembly. You must not do your ordinary work, for
it is a day of blowing trumpets for you. 2You must offer a burnt
offering as a sweet aroma to the LORD: one young bull, one ram,
and seven lambs one year old without blemish.

3"'Their grain offering is to be of finely ground flour mixed
with olive oil, three-tenths of an ephah for the bull, two-tenths
of an ephah for the ram, 4and one-tenth for each of the seven
lambs, 5with one male goat for a purification offering to make
an atonement for you; 6this is in addition to the monthly burnt
offering and its grain offering, and the daily burnt offering with
its grain offering and their drink offerings as prescribed, as a
sweet aroma, a sacrifice made by fire to the LORD.

29:1–11 "On the tenth day of the month" (Lev 16:29) there was the festival of atonement. Only on this day was the high priest dressed with all the pontifical garments. Then he went into that inaccessible place he can approach only once a year, that is, into the Most Holy Place. Therefore if I should consider how the true high priest, my Lord Jesus Christ, having indeed been placed in the flesh, was with the people all year, that year about which he himself says "to encourage the poor . . . to announce the year when the LORD will show his favor" (Isa 61:1–2), I perceive how once in this year, on the Day of Atonement, he goes to the Father to make atonement for the human race and prays for all those who believe in him.

ORIGEN (C. 185–C. 253)
HOMILIES ON NUMBERS

THE DAY OF ATONEMENT

7“‘On the tenth day of this seventh month you are to have a holy assembly. You must humble yourselves; you must not do any work on it. 8But you must offer a burnt offering as a pleasing aroma to the LORD, one young bull, one ram, and seven lambs one year old, all of them without blemish. 9Their grain offerings must be of finely ground flour mixed with olive oil, three-tenths of an ephah for the bull, two-tenths for the ram, 10and one-tenth for each of the seven lambs, 11along with one male goat for a purification offering, in addition to the purification offering for atonement and the continual burnt offering with its grain offering and their drink offerings.

THE FEAST OF TEMPORARY SHELTERS

12“‘On the fifteenth day of the seventh month you are to have a holy assembly; you must do no ordinary work, and you must keep a festival to the LORD for seven days. 13You must offer a burnt offering, an offering made by fire as a pleasing aroma to the LORD: thirteen young bulls, two rams, and fourteen lambs each one year old, all of them without blemish. 14Their grain offerings must be of finely ground flour mixed with olive oil, three-tenths of an ephah for each of the thirteen bulls, two-tenths of an ephah for each of the two rams, 15and one-tenth for each of the fourteen lambs, 16along with one male goat for a purification offering, in addition to the continual burnt offering with its grain offering and its drink offering.

17“‘On the second day you must offer twelve young bulls, two rams, fourteen lambs one year old, all without blemish, 18and their grain offerings and their drink offerings for the bulls, for the rams, and for the lambs, according to their number as prescribed, 19along with one male goat for a purification offering, in addition to the continual burnt offering with its grain offering and their drink offerings.

20“‘On the third day you must offer eleven bulls, two rams, fourteen lambs one year old, all without blemish, 21and their grain offerings and their drink offerings for the bulls, for the rams, and for the lambs, according to their number as prescribed, 22along with one male goat for a purification offering, in addition to the continual burnt offering with its grain offering and its drink offering.

23“‘On the fourth day you must offer ten bulls, two rams, and fourteen lambs one year old, all without blemish, 24and their grain offerings and their drink offerings for the bulls, for the rams, and for the lambs, according to their number as prescribed, 25along with one male goat for a purification offering, in addition to the continual burnt offering with its grain offering and its drink offering.

26“‘On the fifth day you must offer nine bulls, two rams, and fourteen lambs one year old, all without blemish, 27and their grain offerings and their drink offerings for the bulls, for the rams, and for the lambs, according to their number as prescribed, 28along with one male goat for a purification offering, in addition to the continual burnt offering with its grain offering and its drink offering.

29“‘On the sixth day you must offer eight bulls, two rams, and fourteen lambs one year old, all without blemish, 30and their grain offering and their drink offerings for the bulls, for the rams, and for the lambs, according to their number as prescribed, 31along with one male goat for a purification offering, in

addition to the continual burnt offering with its grain offering
and its drink offering.
32"'On the seventh day you must offer seven bulls, two rams,
and fourteen lambs one year old, all without blemish, 33and
their grain offerings and their drink offerings for the bulls,
for the rams, and for the lambs, according to their number as
prescribed, 34along with one male goat for a purification offering, in addition to the continual burnt offering with its grain
offering and its drink offering.
35"'On the eighth day you are to have a holy assembly;
you must do no ordinary work on it. 36But you must offer a
burnt offering, an offering made by fire, as a pleasing aroma
to the LORD, one bull, one ram, seven lambs one year old, all
of them without blemish, 37and with their grain offerings
and their drink offerings for the bull, for the ram, and for the
lambs, according to their number as prescribed, 38along with
one male goat for a purification offering, in addition to the
continual burnt offering with its grain offering and its drink
offering.
39"'These things you must present to the LORD at your
appointed times, in addition to your vows and your freewill
offerings, as your burnt offerings, your grain offerings, your
drink offerings, and your peace offerings.'" 40So Moses told the
Israelites everything, just as the LORD had commanded him.

VOWS MADE BY MEN

30 Moses told the leaders of the tribes concerning the Israelites, "This is what the LORD has commanded: 2If a man
makes a vow to the LORD or takes an oath of binding obligation
on himself, he must not break his word, but must do whatever
he has promised.

VOWS MADE BY SINGLE WOMEN

3"If a young woman who is still living in her father's house makes
a vow to the LORD or places herself under an obligation, 4and
her father hears of her vow or the obligation to which she has
pledged herself, and her father remains silent about her, then
all her vows will stand, and every obligation to which she has
pledged herself will stand. 5But if her father overrules her when
he hears about it, then none of her vows or her obligations that
she has pledged for herself will stand. And the LORD will release
her from it, because her father overruled her.

VOWS MADE BY MARRIED WOMEN

6"And if she marries a husband while under a vow, or she uttered anything impulsively by which she has pledged herself,
7and her husband hears about it but remains silent about her
when he hears about it, then her vows will stand and her obligations that she has pledged for herself will stand. 8But if
when her husband hears it he overrules her, then he will nullify
the vow she has taken, and whatever she uttered impulsively
that she has pledged for herself. And the LORD will release
her from it.

VOWS MADE BY OTHER WOMEN

9"But every vow of a widow or of a divorced woman which she
has pledged for herself will remain intact. 10If she made the
vow in her husband's house or put herself under obligation
with an oath, 11and her husband heard about it, but remained

30:1–16 If it is a serious matter to lie to another person, how much more to lie to God. When scripture describes his majesty, it says that God is in heaven above, and you are on the earth below. The daughter of Jephthah preferred to undergo death rather than to render her father's vow unfulfilled and mendacious. She did not know that she was the type of the saving victim, whom she prefigured in herself. For this reason Jephthah's deed was immune to guilt. It is not a model because it does not follow the law. The deed was permitted only once, as a sign, for God rejects human sacrifice.

PROCOPIUS OF GAZA
(C. 465–528)
CATENA ON THE OCTATEUCH

silent about her, and did not overrule her, then all her vows will stand, and every obligation which she pledged for herself will stand. 12But if her husband clearly nullifies them when he hears them, then whatever she says by way of vows or obligations will not stand. Her husband has made them void, and the LORD will release her from them.

13"Any vow or sworn obligation that would bring affliction to her, her husband can confirm or nullify. 14But if her husband remains completely silent about her from day to day, he thus confirms all her vows or all her obligations which she is under; he confirms them because he remained silent about her when he heard them. 15But if he should nullify them after he has heard them, then he will bear her iniquity."

16These are the statutes that the LORD commanded Moses, relating to a man and his wife, and a father and his young daughter who is still living in her father's house.

THE MIDIANITE WAR

31 The LORD spoke to Moses: 2"Exact vengeance for the Israelites from the Midianites—after that you will be gathered to your people."

3So Moses spoke to the people: "Arm men from among you for the war, to attack the Midianites and to execute the LORD's vengeance on Midian. 4You must send to the battle 1,000 men from every tribe throughout all the tribes of Israel." 5So 1,000 from every tribe, 12,000 armed for battle in all, were provided out of the thousands of Israel.

CAMPAIGN AGAINST THE MIDIANITES

6So Moses sent them to the war, 1,000 from every tribe, with Phinehas son of Eleazar the priest, who was in charge of the holy articles and the signal trumpets. 7They fought against the Midianites, as the LORD commanded Moses, and they killed every male. 8They killed the kings of Midian in addition to those slain—Evi, Rekem, Zur, Hur, and Reba—five Midianite kings. They also killed Balaam son of Beor with the sword.

9The Israelites took the women of Midian captive along with their little ones, and took all their herds, all their flocks, and all their goods as plunder. 10They burned all their towns where they lived and all their encampments. 11They took all the plunder and all the spoils, both people and animals. 12They brought the captives and the spoils and the plunder to Moses, to Eleazar the priest, and to the Israelite community, to the camp on the rift valley plains of Moab, along the Jordan River across from Jericho. 13Moses, Eleazar the priest, and all the leaders of the community went out to meet them outside the camp.

THE DEATH OF THE MIDIANITE WOMEN

14But Moses was furious with the officers of the army, the commanders over thousands and commanders over hundreds, who had come from service in the war. 15Moses said to them, "Have you allowed all the women to live? 16Look, these people through the counsel of Balaam caused the Israelites to act treacherously against the LORD in the matter of Peor—which resulted in the plague among the community of the LORD! 17Now therefore kill every boy, and kill every woman who has been intimate with a man in bed. 18But all the young women who have not experienced a man's bed will be yours.

31:1–54 How great a thing justice is can be gathered from the fact that there is no place, no person, no time with which it has nothing to do. It must even be preserved in all dealings with enemies. For instance, if the day or the spot for a battle has been agreed upon with them, it would be considered an act against justice to occupy the spot beforehand or to anticipate the time. A deeper vengeance is taken on fiercer foes and on those who are false as well as on those who have done greater wrongs, as was the case with the Midianites. For they had made many of the Jewish people to sin through their women, for which reason the anger of the Lord was poured out upon the people of our fathers. Thus it came about that Moses, when victorious, allowed none of them to live.

AMBROSE (C. 339–C. 397)
ON THE DUTIES OF THE CLERGY

PURIFICATION AFTER BATTLE

19“Any of you who has killed anyone or touched any of the dead,
remain outside the camp for seven days; purify yourselves and
your captives on the third day, and on the seventh day. 20You
must purify each garment and everything that is made of skin,
everything made of goats’ hair, and everything made of wood.”
21Then Eleazar the priest said to the men of war who had
gone into the battle, “This is the ordinance of the law that
the LORD commanded Moses: 22‘Only the gold, the silver, the
bronze, the iron, the tin, and the lead, 23everything that may
stand the fire, you are to pass through the fire, and it will be
ceremonially clean, but it must still be purified with the water
of purification. Anything that cannot withstand the fire you
must pass through the water. 24You must wash your clothes
on the seventh day, and you will be ceremonially clean, and
afterward you may enter the camp.’”

THE DISTRIBUTION OF SPOILS

25Then the LORD spoke to Moses: 26“You and Eleazar the priest,
and all the family leaders of the community, take the sum of
the plunder that was captured, both people and animals. 27Di-
vide the plunder into two parts, one for those who took part
in the war—who went out to battle—and the other for all the
community.
28“You must exact a tribute for the LORD from the fighting
men who went out to battle: one life out of 500, from the people,
the cattle, and from the donkeys and the sheep. 29You are to
take it from their half share and give it to Eleazar the priest for
a raised offering to the LORD. 30From the Israelites’ half share
you are to take one portion out of 50 of the people, the cattle,
the donkeys, and the sheep—from every kind of animal—and
you are to give them to the Levites, who are responsible for the
care of the LORD’s tabernacle.”
31So Moses and Eleazar the priest did as the LORD commanded Moses. 32The spoil that remained of the plunder that the
fighting men had gathered was 675,000 sheep, 3372,000 cattle,
3461,000 donkeys, 35and 32,000 young women who had not
experienced a man’s bed.
36The half portion of those who went to war numbered
337,500 sheep; 37the LORD’s tribute from the sheep was 675.
38The cattle numbered 36,000; the LORD’s tribute was 72. 39The
donkeys were 30,500, of which the LORD’s tribute was 61. 40The
people were 16,000, of which the LORD’s tribute was 32 people.
41So Moses gave the tribute, which was the LORD’s raised
offering, to Eleazar the priest, as the LORD commanded Moses.
42From the Israelites’ half share that Moses had separated
from the fighting men, 43there were 337,500 sheep from the
portion belonging to the community, 4436,000 cattle, 4530,500
donkeys, 46and 16,000 people.
47From the Israelites’ share Moses took one of every 50
people and animals and gave them to the Levites who were
responsible for the care of the LORD’s tabernacle, just as the
LORD commanded Moses.
48Then the officers who were over the thousands of the army,
the commanders over thousands and the commanders over
hundreds, approached Moses 49and said to him, “Your servants
have taken a count of the men who were in the battle, who
were under our authority, and not one is missing. 50So we have
brought as an offering for the LORD what each man found:

gold ornaments, armlets, bracelets, signet rings, earrings, and necklaces, to make atonement for ourselves before the LORD." [51]Moses and Eleazar the priest took the gold from them, all of it in the form of ornaments. [52]All the gold of the offering they offered up to the LORD from the commanders of thousands and the commanders of hundreds weighed 16,750 shekels. [53]Each soldier had taken plunder for himself. [54]So Moses and Eleazar the priest received the gold from the commanders of thousands and commanders of hundreds and brought it into the tent of meeting as a memorial for the Israelites before the LORD.

THE PETITION OF THE REUBENITES AND GADITES

32 Now the Reubenites and the Gadites possessed a very large number of cattle. When they saw that the lands of Jazer and Gilead were ideal for cattle, [2]the Gadites and the Reubenites came and addressed Moses, Eleazar the priest, and the leaders of the community. They said, [3]"Ataroth, Dibon, Jazer, Nimrah, Heshbon, Elealeh, Sebam, Nebo, and Beon, [4]the land that the LORD subdued before the community of Israel, is ideal for cattle, and your servants have cattle." [5]So they said, "If we have found favor in your sight, let this land be given to your servants for our inheritance. Do not have us cross the Jordan River."

32:1–15 Kindred has its obligations. The Reubenites and Gadites would have been unbrotherly if they had claimed the land that had been conquered and had left the rest of the people to fight for their portions alone. We have received much by means of the efforts and sufferings of the saints in years gone by, and if we do not make some return to the church of Christ by giving her our best energies, we are unworthy to be enrolled in her ranks. It is a cowardly pride that would choose a downy pillow and a silken couch for a soldier of the cross.

CHARLES SPURGEON
(1834–1892)
MORNING AND EVENING

MOSES' RESPONSE

[6]Moses said to the Gadites and the Reubenites, "Must your brothers go to war while you remain here? [7]Why do you frustrate the intent of the Israelites to cross over into the land that the LORD has given them? [8]Your fathers did the same thing when I sent them from Kadesh Barnea to see the land. [9]When they went up to the Eshcol Valley and saw the land, they frustrated the intent of the Israelites so that they did not enter the land that the LORD had given them. [10]So the anger of the LORD was kindled that day, and he swore, [11]'Because they have not followed me wholeheartedly, not one of the men twenty years old and upward who came from Egypt will see the land that I swore to give to Abraham, Isaac, and Jacob, [12]except Caleb son of Jephunneh the Kenizzite, and Joshua son of Nun, for they followed the LORD wholeheartedly.' [13]So the LORD's anger was kindled against the Israelites, and he made them wander in the wilderness for 40 years, until all that generation that had done wickedly before the LORD was finished. [14]Now look, you are standing in your fathers' place, a brood of sinners, to increase still further the fierce wrath of the LORD against the Israelites. [15]For if you turn away from following him, he will once again abandon them in the wilderness, and you will be the reason for their destruction."

THE OFFER OF THE REUBENITES AND GADITES

[16]Then they came very close to him and said, "We will build sheep folds here for our flocks and cities for our families, [17]but we will maintain ourselves in armed readiness and go before the Israelites until whenever we have brought them to their place. Our descendants will be living in fortified towns as a protection against the inhabitants of the land. [18]We will not return to our homes until every Israelite has his inheritance. [19]For we will not accept any inheritance on the other side of the Jordan River and beyond, because our inheritance has come to us on this eastern side of the Jordan."

[20]Then Moses replied, "If you will do this thing, and if you
will arm yourselves for battle before the LORD, [21]and if all your
armed men cross the Jordan before the LORD until he drives
out his enemies from his presence [22]and the land is subdued
before the LORD, then afterward you may return and be free of
your obligation to the LORD and to Israel. This land will then
be your possession in the LORD's sight.

[23]"But if you do not do this, then look, you will have sinned
against the LORD. And know that your sin will find you out. [24]So
build cities for your descendants and pens for your sheep, but
do what you have said you would do."

[25]So the Gadites and the Reubenites replied to Moses, "Your
servants will do as our lord commands. [26]Our children, our
wives, our flocks, and all our livestock will be there in the cities
of Gilead, [27]but your servants will cross over, every man armed
for war, to do battle in the LORD's presence, just as our lord says."

[28]So Moses gave orders about them to Eleazar the priest,
to Joshua son of Nun, and to the heads of the families of the
Israelite tribes. [29]Moses said to them: "If the Gadites and the
Reubenites cross the Jordan with you, each one equipped for
battle in the LORD's presence, and you conquer the land, then
you must allot them the territory of Gilead as their possession.
[30]But if they do not cross over with you armed, they must receive possessions among you in Canaan." [31]Then the Gadites and
the Reubenites answered, "Your servants will do what the LORD
has spoken. [32]We will cross armed in the LORD's presence into
the land of Canaan, and then the possession of our inheritance
that we inherit will be ours on this side of the Jordan River."

LAND ASSIGNMENT

[33]So Moses gave to the Gadites, the Reubenites, and to half the
tribe of Manasseh son of Joseph the realm of King Sihon of
the Amorites, and the realm of King Og of Bashan, the entire
land with its cities and the territory surrounding them. [34]The
Gadites rebuilt Dibon, Ataroth, Aroer, [35]Atroth Shophan, Jazer,
Jogbehah, [36]Beth Nimrah, and Beth Haran as fortified cities,
and constructed pens for their flocks. [37]The Reubenites rebuilt
Heshbon, Elealeh, Kiriathaim, [38]Nebo, Baal Meon (with a change
of name), and Sibmah. They renamed the cities they built.

[39]The descendants of Machir son of Manasseh went to Gilead, took it, and dispossessed the Amorites who were in it. [40]So
Moses gave Gilead to Machir, son of Manasseh, and he lived
there. [41]Now Jair son of Manasseh went and captured their
small towns and named them Havvoth Jair. [42]Then Nobah went
and captured Kenath and its villages and called it Nobah after
his own name.

WANDERINGS FROM EGYPT TO SINAI

33 These are the journeys of the Israelites, who went out of
the land of Egypt by their divisions under the authority
of Moses and Aaron. [2]Moses recorded their departures according to their journeys, by the commandment of the LORD; now
these are their journeys according to their departures. [3]They
departed from Rameses in the first month, on the fifteenth day
of the first month; on the day after the Passover the Israelites
went out defiantly in plain sight of all the Egyptians. [4]Now the
Egyptians were burying all their firstborn, whom the LORD
had killed among them; the LORD also executed judgments
on their gods.

33:1–49 You have heard that Moses wrote this down by the word of the Lord. Why did the Lord want him to write it down? Was it so that this passage in scripture about the stages the children of Israel made might benefit us in some way or that it should bring us no benefit? Who would dare to say that what is written "by the commandment of the LORD" is of no use? He wrote them down so that when we read them and see how many starting places lie ahead of us on the journey that leads to the kingdom, we may prepare ourselves for this way of life.

ORIGEN (C. 185–C. 253)
HOMILIES ON NUMBERS

5 The Israelites traveled from Rameses and camped in
Sukkoth.
6 They traveled from Sukkoth, and camped in Etham, which
is on the edge of the desert. 7 They traveled from Etham, and
turned again to Pi Hahiroth, which is before Baal Zephon; and
they camped before Migdal. 8 They traveled from Pi Hahiroth,
and passed through the middle of the sea into the wilderness,
and went three days' journey in the wilderness of Etham, and
camped in Marah. 9 They traveled from Marah and came to
Elim; in Elim there are twelve fountains of water and seventy
palm trees, so they camped there.
10 They traveled from Elim, and camped by the Red Sea.
11 They traveled from the Red Sea and camped in the wilderness of Sin. 12 They traveled from the wilderness of Sin and
camped in Dophkah. 13 And they traveled from Dophkah, and
camped in Alush.
14 They traveled from Alush and camped at Rephidim, where
there was no water for the people to drink. 15 They traveled from
Rephidim and camped in the desert of Sinai.

WANDERINGS IN THE WILDERNESS

16 They traveled from the desert of Sinai and camped at Kibroth Hattaavah. 17 They traveled from Kibroth Hattaavah and
camped at Hazeroth. 18 They traveled from Hazeroth and
camped in Rithmah. 19 They traveled from Rithmah and camped
at Rimmon Perez. 20 They traveled from Rimmon Perez and
camped in Libnah. 21 They traveled from Libnah and camped at
Rissah. 22 They traveled from Rissah and camped in Kehelathah.
23 They traveled from Kehelathah and camped at Mount Shepher. 24 They traveled from Mount Shepher and camped in Haradah. 25 They traveled from Haradah and camped in Makheloth.
26 They traveled from Makheloth and camped at Tahath. 27 They
traveled from Tahath and camped at Terah. 28 They traveled from
Terah and camped in Mithcah. 29 They traveled from Mithcah
and camped in Hashmonah. 30 They traveled from Hashmonah and camped in Moseroth. 31 They traveled from Moseroth
and camped in Bene Jaakan. 32 They traveled from Bene Jaakan
and camped at Hor Haggidgad. 33 They traveled from Hor Haggidgad and camped in Jotbathah. 34 They traveled from Jotbathah and camped in Abronah. 35 They traveled from Abronah
and camped at Ezion Geber. 36 They traveled from Ezion Geber
and camped in the wilderness of Zin, that is, Kadesh.

WANDERINGS FROM KADESH TO MOAB

37 They traveled from Kadesh and camped at Mount Hor at the
edge of the land of Edom. 38 Aaron the priest ascended Mount
Hor at the command of the LORD, and he died there in the
fortieth year after the Israelites had come out of the land of
Egypt on the first day of the fifth month. 39 Now Aaron was 123
years old when he died on Mount Hor. 40 The king of Arad, the
Canaanite king who lived in the south of the land of Canaan,
heard about the approach of the Israelites.
41 They traveled from Mount Hor and camped in Zalmonah.
42 They traveled from Zalmonah and camped in Punon. 43 They
traveled from Punon and camped in Oboth. 44 They traveled
from Oboth and camped in Iye Abarim, on the border of Moab.
45 They traveled from Iim and camped in Dibon Gad. 46 They traveled from Dibon Gad and camped in Almon Diblathaim. 47 They
traveled from Almon Diblathaim and camped in the mountains

of Abarim before Nebo. 48They traveled from the mountains of Abarim and camped in the rift valley plains by Moab along the Jordan River across from Jericho. 49They camped by the Jordan, from Beth Jeshimoth as far as Abel Shittim in the rift valley plains of Moab.

AT THE BORDER OF CANAAN

50The LORD spoke to Moses in the rift valley plains of Moab along the Jordan, across from Jericho. He said: 51"Speak to the Israelites and tell them, 'When you have crossed the Jordan into the land of Canaan, 52you must drive out all the inhabitants of the land before you. Destroy all their carved images, all their molten images, and demolish their high places. 53You must dispossess the inhabitants of the land and live in it, for I have given you the land to possess it. 54You must divide the land by lot for an inheritance among your families. To a larger group you must give a larger inheritance, and to a smaller group you must give a smaller inheritance. Everyone's inheritance must be in the place where his lot falls. You must inherit according to your ancestral tribes. 55But if you do not drive out the inhabitants of the land before you, then those whom you allow to remain will be irritants in your eyes and thorns in your side, and will cause you trouble in the land where you will be living. 56And what I intended to do to them I will do to you.'"

THE SOUTHERN BORDER OF THE LAND

34 Then the LORD spoke to Moses: 2"Give these instructions to the Israelites, and tell them: 'When you enter Canaan, the land that has been assigned to you as an inheritance, the land of Canaan with its borders, 3your southern border will extend from the wilderness of Zin along the Edomite border, and your southern border will run eastward to the extremity of the Salt Sea, 4and then the border will turn from the south to the Scorpion Ascent, continue to Zin, and then its direction will be from the south to Kadesh Barnea. Then it will go to Hazar Addar and pass over to Azmon. 5There the border will turn from Azmon to the Stream of Egypt, and then its direction is to the sea.

THE WESTERN BORDER OF THE LAND

6"'And for a western border you will have the Great Sea. This will be your western border.

THE NORTHERN BORDER OF THE LAND

7"'And this will be your northern border: From the Great Sea you will draw a line to Mount Hor; 8from Mount Hor you will draw a line to Lebo Hamath, and the direction of the border will be to Zedad. 9The border will continue to Ziphron, and its direction will be to Hazar Enan. This will be your northern border.

THE EASTERN BORDER OF THE LAND

10"'For your eastern border you will draw a line from Hazar Enan to Shepham. 11The border will run down from Shepham to Riblah, on the east side of Ain, and the border will descend and reach the eastern side of the Sea of Kinnereth. 12Then the border will continue down the Jordan River and its direction will be to the Salt Sea. This will be your land by its borders that surround it.'"

13Then Moses commanded the Israelites: "This is the land that you will inherit by lot, which the LORD has commanded to be

34:1–15 Here are directions concerning the bounds of Canaan or limits of the land beyond Jordan, which are here particularly described to direct and bind them in their wars and conquests. There was a much larger possession promised them if they were obedient, even to the river Euphrates. But this, which is properly Canaan, lay in a very little compass. But its littleness was abundantly compensated by its fruitfulness; otherwise, it could not have sustained so numerous a nation. See how little a share of the world God often gives to his own people! But they that have their portion in heaven can be content with a small pittance of this earth.

JOHN WESLEY (1703–1791)
EXPLANATORY NOTES ON THE BIBLE

given to the nine-and-a-half tribes, [14]because the tribe of the Reubenites by their families, the tribe of the Gadites by their families,
and the half-tribe of Manasseh have received their inheritance.
[15]The two-and-a-half tribes have received their inheritance on
this side of the Jordan, east of Jericho, toward the sunrise."

APPOINTED OFFICIALS

[16]The LORD said to Moses: [17]"These are the names of the men
who are to allocate the land to you as an inheritance: Eleazar the
priest and Joshua son of Nun. [18]You must take one leader from
every tribe to assist in allocating the land as an inheritance.
[19]These are the names of the men: from the tribe of Judah, Caleb
son of Jephunneh; [20]from the tribe of the Simeonites, Shemuel
son of Ammihud; [21]from the tribe of Benjamin, Elidad son of
Kislon; [22]and from the tribe of the Danites, a leader, Bukki son
of Jogli. [23]From the Josephites, Hanniel son of Ephod, a leader
from the tribe of Manasseh; [24]from the tribe of the Ephraimites,
a leader, Kemuel son of Shiphtan; [25]from the tribe of the Zebulunites, a leader, Elizaphan son of Parnach; [26]from the tribe of
the Issacharites, a leader, Paltiel son of Azzan; [27]from the tribe
of the Asherites, a leader, Ahihud son of Shelomi; [28]and from
the tribe of the Naphtalites, a leader, Pedahel son of Ammihud."
[29]These are the ones whom the LORD commanded to divide
up the inheritance among the Israelites in the land of Canaan.

THE LEVITICAL CITIES

35 Then the LORD spoke to Moses in the rift valley plains of
Moab along the Jordan near Jericho. He said: [2]"Instruct
the Israelites to give the Levites towns to live in from the inheritance the Israelites will possess. You must also give the Levites
grazing land around the towns. [3]Thus they will have towns in
which to live, and their grazing lands will be for their cattle, for
their possessions, and for all their animals. [4]The grazing lands
around the towns that you will give to the Levites must extend
to a distance of 500 yards from the town wall.

[5]"You must measure from outside the wall of the town on the
east 1,000 yards, and on the south side 1,000 yards, and on the
west side 1,000 yards, and on the north side 1,000 yards, with
the town in the middle. This territory must belong to them as
grazing land for the towns. [6]Now from these towns that you
will give to the Levites you must select six towns of refuge to
which a person who has killed someone may flee. And you must
give them 42 other towns.

[7]"So the total of the towns you will give the Levites is 48. You
must give these together with their grazing lands. [8]The towns
you will give must be from the possession of the Israelites. From
the larger tribes you must give more; and from the smaller
tribes fewer. Each must contribute some of its own towns to
the Levites in proportion to the inheritance allocated to each."

THE CITIES OF REFUGE

[9]Then the LORD spoke to Moses: [10]"Speak to the Israelites and
tell them, 'When you cross over the Jordan River into the land
of Canaan, [11]you must then designate some towns as towns
of refuge for you, to which a person who has killed someone
unintentionally may flee. [12]And they must stand as your towns
of refuge from the avenger in order that the killer may not die
until he has stood trial before the community. [13]These towns
that you must give shall be your six towns for refuge.

14"'You must give three towns on this side of the Jordan, and
you must give three towns in the land of Canaan; they must be
towns of refuge. 15These six towns will be places of refuge for
the Israelites, and for the resident foreigner, and for the settler
among them, so that anyone who kills any person accidentally
may flee there.
16"'But if he hits someone with an iron tool so that he dies, he
is a murderer. The murderer must surely be put to death. 17If he
strikes him by throwing a stone large enough that he could die,
and he dies, he is a murderer. The murderer must surely be put
to death. 18Or if he strikes him with a wooden hand weapon so
that he could die, and he dies, he is a murderer. The murderer
must surely be put to death. 19The avenger of blood himself
must kill the murderer; when he meets him, he must kill him.
20"'But if he strikes him out of hatred or throws something
at him intentionally so that he dies, 21or with enmity he strikes
him with his hand and he dies, the one who struck him must
surely be put to death, for he is a murderer. The avenger of
blood must kill the murderer when he meets him.
22"'But if he strikes him suddenly, without enmity, or throws
anything at him unintentionally, 23or with any stone large
enough that a man could die, without seeing him, and throws
it at him, and he dies, even though he was not his enemy nor
sought his harm, 24then the community must judge between
the slayer and the avenger of blood according to these decisions.
25The community must deliver the slayer out of the hand of
the avenger of blood, and the community must restore him
to the town of refuge to which he fled, and he must live there
until the death of the high priest, who was anointed with the
consecrated oil. 26But if the slayer at any time goes outside the
boundary of the town to which he had fled, 27and the avenger
of blood finds him outside the borders of the town of refuge,
and the avenger of blood kills the slayer, he will not be guilty
of blood, 28because the slayer should have stayed in his town of
refuge until the death of the high priest. But after the death of
the high priest, the slayer may return to the land of his possessions. 29So these things must be a statutory ordinance for you
throughout your generations, in all the places where you live.
30"'Whoever kills any person, the murderer must be put to
death by the testimony of witnesses, but one witness cannot testify against any person to cause him to be put to death. 31More-
over, you must not accept a ransom for the life of a murderer
who is guilty of death; he must surely be put to death. 32And you
must not accept a ransom for anyone who has fled to a town of
refuge, to allow him to return home and live on his own land
before the death of the high priest.
33"'You must not pollute the land where you live, for blood
defiles the land, and the land cannot be cleansed of the blood
that is shed there, except by the blood of the person who shed
it. 34Therefore do not defile the land that you will inhabit, in
which I live, for I the LORD live among the Israelites.'"

WOMEN AND LAND INHERITANCE

36 Then the heads of the family groups of the Gileadites,
the descendant of Machir, the descendant of Manasseh,
who were from the Josephite families, approached and spoke
before Moses and the leaders who were the heads of the Israelite families. 2They said, "The LORD commanded my lord to
give the land as an inheritance by lot to the Israelites; and my

35:26–28 After the manslayer had been received into the city of refuge, the avenger of blood could act only as prosecutor, and the magistrates, in the presence of the people, were appointed to decide the cause according to the rules here laid down. But if in the meanwhile he ventured to leave the city and the avenger met him and slew him, the avenger must not be punished. This shows that if, by the testimony of two credible witnesses, the man who had fled to the city of refuge was adjudged guilty, he must without fail be put to death.

R. A. TORREY (1856–1928)
TREASURY OF SCRIPTURE KNOWLEDGE

36:1–13 And truly Moses gave them all these precepts, being such as were observed during his own lifetime; but though he lived now in the wilderness, yet did he make provision how they might observe the same laws when they should have taken the land of Canaan. He gave them rest to the land from plowing and planting every seventh year, as he had prescribed to them to rest from working every seventh day. And he ordained that they should do the same after seven times seven years, which in all are 50 years; and that fiftieth year is called by the Hebrews the "Jubilee," wherein debtors are freed from their debts.

JOSEPHUS (C. 37–C. 100)
THE WORKS

lord was commanded by the LORD to give the inheritance of
our brother Zelophehad to his daughters. 3Now if they should
be married to one of the men from another Israelite tribe, their
inheritance would be taken from the inheritance of our fathers
and added to the inheritance of the tribe into which they marry. As a result, it will be taken from the lot of our inheritance.
4And when the Jubilee of the Israelites is to take place, their
inheritance will be added to the inheritance of the tribe into
which they marry. So their inheritance will be taken away from
the inheritance of our ancestral tribe."

MOSES' DECISION

5Then Moses gave a ruling to the Israelites by the word of the
LORD: "What the tribe of the Josephites is saying is right. 6This
is what the LORD has commanded for Zelophehad's daughters:
'Let them marry whomever they think best, only they must
marry within the family of their father's tribe. 7In this way
the inheritance of the Israelites will not be transferred from
tribe to tribe. But every one of the Israelites must retain the
ancestral heritage. 8And every daughter who possesses an inheritance from any of the tribes of the Israelites must become
the wife of a man from any family in her father's tribe, so that
every Israelite may retain the inheritance of his fathers. 9No
inheritance may pass from tribe to tribe. But every one of the
tribes of the Israelites must retain its inheritance.'"
10As the LORD had commanded Moses, so the daughters of
Zelophehad did. 11For the daughters of Zelophehad—Mahlah,
Tirzah, Hoglah, Milcah, and Noah—were married to the sons
of their uncles. 12They were married into the families of the
Manassehites, the descendants of Joseph, and their inheritance
remained in the tribe of their father's family.
13These are the commandments and the decisions that the
LORD commanded the Israelites through the authority of Moses, in the rift valley plains by Moab along the Jordan River
opposite Jericho.

AUTHOR	AUDIENCE	DATE	PURPOSE	THEMES
Moses	God's chosen people, the Israelites	Between 1446 and 1406 BC	Moses wrote this book to recount the history of God's people, outline the legal requirements of their covenant with the Lord, offer a prophetic word of future blessings and curses, and bid farewell to the nation he led.	The character of God; the covenant relationship between God and his people; and God's law

The final book of the Pentateuch, Deuteronomy, is a series of speeches by Moses recalling Israel's history and laws. It's also a prophetic announcement of future blessings and curses and a personal farewell address from Moses. Christian writers designated it the "second law" given that the book recapitulates much of the legal content from Exodus and Numbers.

As John Wesley explained,

> The Greek interpreters call this book Deuteronomy, that is, The Second Law or a second edition of the law, because it is a repetition of many of the laws, as well as much of the history contained in the three foregoing books. They to whom the first law was given were all dead, and a new generation sprung up to whom God would have it repeated by Moses himself that it might make the deeper impression upon them.

Within the original Jewish community, the book was a call to faithfulness in light of redemption. It was a reminder of the consequences the people's disobedience would bring, as well as the blessings God promised if they walked closely with him. The speeches in Deuteronomy called for the people of Israel to renew their covenant with God before entering the promised land—and they served as a call to continual renewal in the centuries that followed.

Deuteronomy is an encounter with the eternal and transcendent God, for here we meet his justice and righteousness brought together. The Lord is Judge with pronouncements of blessing and cursing (30:3–9), and he is also Redeemer, as the exodus story is recounted (6:21–23).

The name Deuteronomy signals a second giving or recounting of the law. And yet the book is more than just a collection of legal requirements. It's about a covenantal bond forged between two parties: the Lord, Yahweh, and his people, Israel. The covenant was first cut on Mount Sinai in Exodus, and it was renewed by the generation about to enter the promised land in Deuteronomy. This covenant is encapsulated in the central creed of the Jewish people, the *Shema*: "Hear, O Israel: The Lord is our God, the Lord is one! You must love the Lord your God with your whole mind, your whole being, and all your strength. These words I am commanding you today must be kept in mind" (6:4–6) The "words" are the terms of that covenant, commandments that were given to direct Israel's relationship with and worship of Yahweh, and these commandments were to

DEUTERONOMY

govern the relationships the people of Israel had with each other too. The people of Israel were called to model the character of the Lord, showing their neighbors the life he always meant for humanity to experience.

Martin Luther valued the book precisely for these commands, identifying them as the book's significance: "It teaches this people to live well according to the Ten Commandments in both spirit and body. Further, it sets up the inner rule of conscience together with secular government, then the outward manner of ceremonies with wholly divine justice and wisdom so that there is nothing in the whole range of life that is not arranged here most wisely and properly." The subsequent regulations were meant to govern and guide the Israelites' lives with God and with one another, wisely and properly.

Augustine contrasted the law as it was written upon tablets of stone under the old covenant with the Holy Spirit, "written" upon our hearts as part of the new covenant in Christ. As he explained:

> There the finger of God worked upon tables of stone: here upon the hearts of men. So there the law was set outside men to be a terror to the unjust: here it was given within them to be their justification . . . This law is not written on tables of stone but is shed abroad in our hearts through the Holy Spirit who is given to us. Therefore the law of God is charity. To it the mind of the flesh is not subject, neither indeed can be. But when, to put fear into the mind of the flesh, the works of charity are written upon tables, we have the law of works, the letter killing the transgression. When charity itself is shed abroad in the hearts of believers, we have the law of faith, the Spirit giving life to the lover.

Near the end of his life, Moses said to the Israelites: "I have set life and death, blessing and curse, before you. Therefore choose life so that you and your descendants may live!" (30:19). Caesarius of Arles exhorted the believers in his day to take Moses' words seriously, and it's a good idea for us today too: "Power is given to you through the grace of Christ: 'Stretch forth your hand to whichever you choose.' 'Choose life, that you may live'; leave the broad way on the left that drags you to death and cling to the narrow path on the right that happily leads you to life. Do not allow the wideness of that road on the left to keep you or give you pleasure."

1:1–8 And here this fact will not appear to be without significance that it is Moses who hears from God all that is written down in the law of Leviticus, whereas in Deuteronomy it is the people who are represented as listening to Moses and learning from him what they could not hear from God. This indeed is why it is called Deuteronomy, meaning "the second law." A fact that some will think points to this is that when the first law given through Moses came to an end, a second legislation was apparently composed, and this was specially delivered by Moses to his successor, Joshua. And Joshua is certainly believed to be a figure of our Savior, by whose second law, that is, by the precepts of the Gospels, all things are brought to perfection.

ORIGEN (C. 185–C. 253)
ON FIRST PRINCIPLES

THE COVENANT SETTING

1 This is what Moses said to all of Israel in the Transjordanian wilderness, the arid rift valley opposite Suph, between Paran and Tophel, Laban, Hazeroth, and Di Zahab. [2]Now it is ordinarily an eleven-day journey from Horeb to Kadesh Barnea by way of Mount Seir. [3]However, it was not until the first day of the eleventh month of the fortieth year that Moses addressed the Israelites just as the LORD had instructed him to do. [4]This took place after the defeat of King Sihon of the Amorites, whose capital was in Heshbon, and King Og of Bashan, whose capital was in Ashtaroth, specifically in Edrei. [5]So it was in the Transjordan, in Moab, that Moses began to deliver these words:

EVENTS AT HOREB

[6]The LORD our God spoke to us at Horeb and said, "You have stayed in the area of this mountain long enough. [7]Head out and resume your journey. Enter the Amorite hill country, and all its neighboring areas, including the rift valley, the hill country, the foothills, the Negev, and the coastal plain—all of Canaan and Lebanon as far as the Great River, that is, the Euphrates. [8]Look! I have already given the land to you. Go, occupy the territory that I, the LORD, promised to give to your ancestors Abraham, Isaac, and Jacob, and to their descendants." [9]I also said to you at that time, "I am no longer able to sustain you by myself. [10]The LORD your God has increased your population to the point that you are now as numerous as the very stars of the sky. [11]Indeed, may the LORD, the God of your ancestors, make you a thousand times more numerous than you are now, blessing you just as he said he would! [12]But how can I alone bear up under the burden of your hardship and strife? [13]Select wise and practical men, those known among your tribes, whom I may appoint as your leaders." [14]You replied to me that what I had said to you was good. [15]So I chose as your tribal leaders wise and well-known men, placing them over you as administrators of groups of thousands, hundreds, fifties, and tens, and also as other tribal officials. [16]I furthermore admonished your judges at that time that they should pay attention to issues among your fellow citizens and judge fairly, whether between one person and a native Israelite or a resident foreigner. [17]They must not discriminate in judgment, but hear the lowly and the great alike. Nor should they be intimidated by human beings, for judgment belongs to God. If the matter being adjudicated is too difficult for them, they should bring it before me for a hearing.

INSTRUCTIONS AT KADESH BARNEA

[18]So I instructed you at that time regarding everything you should do. [19]Then we left Horeb and passed through all that immense, forbidding wilderness that you saw on the way to the Amorite hill country as the LORD our God had commanded us to do, finally arriving at Kadesh Barnea. [20]Then I said to you, "You have come to the Amorite hill country, which the LORD our God is about to give us. [21]Look, he has placed the land in front of you! Go up, take possession of it, just as the LORD, the God of your ancestors, said to do. Do not be afraid or discouraged!" [22]So all of you approached me and said, "Let's send some men ahead of us to scout out the land and bring us back word as to how we should attack it and what the cities are like there." [23]I thought this was a good idea, so I sent twelve men from among you, one from each tribe. [24]They left and went up to the hill country, coming to the Eshcol Valley, which they scouted out.

25 Then they took some of the produce of the land and carried it back down to us. They also brought a report to us, saying, "The land that the LORD our God is about to give us is good."

DISOBEDIENCE AT KADESH BARNEA

26 You were not willing to go up, however, but instead rebelled against the LORD your God. 27 You complained among yourselves privately and said, "Because the LORD hates us he brought us from Egypt to deliver us over to the Amorites so they could destroy us! 28 What is going to happen to us? Our brothers have drained away our courage by describing people who are more numerous and taller than we are, and great cities whose defenses appear to be as high as heaven itself! Moreover, they said they saw Anakites there." 29 So I responded to you, "Do not be terrified of them! 30 The LORD your God is about to go ahead of you; he will fight for you, just as you saw him do in Egypt 31 and in the wilderness, where you saw him carrying you along like a man carries his son. This he did everywhere you went until you came to this very place." 32 However, through all this you did not have confidence in the LORD your God, 33 who would go before you on the way to find places for you to camp, appearing in a fire at night and in a cloud by day to show you the way you ought to go.

JUDGMENT AT KADESH BARNEA

34 When the LORD heard you, he became angry and made this vow: 35 "Not a single person of this evil generation will see the good land that I promised to give to your ancestors! 36 The exception is Caleb son of Jephunneh; he will see it and I will give him and his descendants the territory on which he has walked, because he has wholeheartedly followed me." 37 As for me, the LORD was also angry with me on your account. He said, "You also will not be able to go there. 38 However, Joshua son of Nun, your assistant, will go. Encourage him, because he will enable Israel to inherit the land. 39 Also, your infants, who you thought would die on the way, and your children, who as yet do not know good from bad, will go there; I will give them the land and they will possess it. 40 But as for you, turn back and head for the wilderness by the way to the Red Sea."

UNSUCCESSFUL CONQUEST OF CANAAN

41 Then you responded to me and admitted, "We have sinned against the LORD. We will now go up and fight as the LORD our God has told us to do." So you each put on your battle gear and prepared to go up to the hill country. 42 But the LORD told me: "Tell them this: 'Do not go up and fight, because I will not be with you and you will be defeated by your enemies.'" 43 I spoke to you, but you did not listen. Instead you rebelled against the LORD and recklessly went up to the hill country. 44 The Amorite inhabitants of that area confronted you and chased you like a swarm of bees, striking you down from Seir as far as Hormah. 45 Then you came back and wept before the LORD, but he paid no attention to you whatsoever. 46 Therefore, you remained at Kadesh for a long time—indeed, for the full time.

THE JOURNEY FROM KADESH BARNEA TO MOAB

2 Then we turned and set out toward the wilderness on the way to the Red Sea just as the LORD told me to do, detouring around Mount Seir for a long time. 2 At this point the LORD said to me, 3 "You have circled around this mountain long enough;

2:1–7 "All along the way I, the LORD your God, have blessed your every effort," and this deals not with people's sin but with God's blessing. As with Israel so with us; in our life the most remarkable fact has been the blessing of God. He has blessed us with all spiritual blessings in heavenly places, blessed us all ways and blessed us always; blessed us beyond conception, blessed us exceeding abundantly above what we asked or even thought, and beyond what we can now remember. He has blessed us like a God.

CHARLES SPURGEON
(1834–1892)
METROPOLITAN TABERNACLE SERMONS

now turn north. [4]Instruct these people as follows: 'You are about
to cross the border of your relatives the descendants of Esau,
who inhabit Seir. They will be afraid of you, so watch yourselves
carefully. [5]Do not be hostile toward them, because I am not
giving you any of their land, not even a footprint, for I have
given Mount Seir as an inheritance for Esau. [6]You may purchase
food to eat and water to drink from them. [7]All along the way I,
the LORD your God, have blessed your every effort. I have been
attentive to your travels through this great wilderness. These
40 years I have been with you; you have lacked nothing.'"
[8]So we turned away from our relatives the descendants of Esau,
the inhabitants of Seir, turning from the route of the rift valley
which comes up from Elat and Ezion Geber, and traveling the
way of the wilderness of Moab. [9]Then the LORD said to me, "Do
not harass Moab and provoke them to war, for I will not give you
any of their land as your territory. This is because I have given
Ar to the descendants of Lot as their possession. [10](The Emites
used to live there, a people as powerful, numerous, and tall as the
Anakites. [11]These people, as well as the Anakites, are also considered Rephaites; the Moabites call them Emites. [12]Previously the
Horites lived in Seir, but the descendants of Esau dispossessed
and destroyed them and settled in their place, just as Israel did
to the land it came to possess, the land the LORD gave them.)
[13]Now, get up and cross the Wadi Zered." So we did so. [14]Now
the length of time it took for us to go from Kadesh Barnea to the
crossing of Wadi Zered was thirty-eight years, time for all the
military men of that generation to die, just as the LORD had
vowed to them. [15]Indeed, it was the very hand of the LORD that
eliminated them from within the camp until they were all gone.

INSTRUCTIONS CONCERNING AMMON

[16]So it was that after all the military men had been eliminated
from the community, [17]the LORD said to me, [18]"Today you are
going to cross the border of Moab, that is, of Ar. [19]But when
you come close to the Ammonites, do not harass or provoke
them because I am not giving you any of the Ammonites' land
as your possession; I have already given it to Lot's descendants
as their possession."

[20](That also is considered to be a land of the Rephaites. The
Rephaites lived there originally; the Ammonites call them
Zamzummites. [21]They are a people as powerful, numerous,
and tall as the Anakites. But the LORD destroyed the Rephaites
in advance of the Ammonites, so they dispossessed them and
settled down in their place. [22]This is exactly what he did for the
descendants of Esau who lived in Seir when he destroyed the
Horites before them so that they could dispossess them and
settle in their area to this very day. [23]As for the Avvites who
lived in settlements as far west as Gaza, Caphtorites who came
from Crete destroyed them and settled down in their place.)

[24]"Get up, make your way across Wadi Arnon. Look, I have
already delivered over to you Sihon the Amorite, king of Heshbon, and his land. Go ahead—take it! Engage him in war! [25]This
very day I will begin to fill all the people of the earth with dread
and to terrify them when they hear about you. They will shiver
and shake in anticipation of your approach."

DEFEAT OF SIHON, KING OF HESHBON

[26]Then I sent messengers from the Kedemoth wilderness to
King Sihon of Heshbon with an offer of peace: [27]"Let us pass

ATHANASIUS OF ALEXANDRIA:

SAINT OF STUBBORNNESS
c. 293–373

You know you're doing something right when you are forced into exile for your stubborn defense of the Christian faith. That's the story of Athanasius, a young bishop who refused to compromise with forces inside the church seeking to transform the faith into something that it wasn't.

Around AD 293, Athanasius was born to wealthy Christian parents in the city of Alexandria in Egypt. Their wealth afforded him the kind of education that would be crucial to his later battles for the historic Christian faith. It was during the early formative years in his ministry that he first came into contact with Arius, who was eventually recognized as a heretic for compromising the divine nature of Jesus and the doctrine of the Trinity.

Athanasius's first encounters with Arius's teachings were through observing the counter-teachings of his mentor, the bishop Alexander, who led the charge condemning and refuting Arius and his false teachings. Eventually Athanasius himself would take the lead, becoming the mortal enemy of anything that smacked of Arianism.

Despite the constant accusations hurled by the Arians against him—ranging from government subversion to prostitution to murder and even sorcery—Athanasius refused to compromise his theological integrity.

The nature of the debate is complex, but it revolved around the proper understanding of the nature of Jesus Christ in relation to God the Father. Arius insisted that the Godhead—Father, Son, and Spirit—is made of three divine beings, only one of whom is truly God. The Son, Jesus Christ, was merely a creature who was made, not true God from true God. He emphasized Jesus' creatureliness and essential humanity. But he rejected the idea that Jesus shared the same essence with God the Father. This had serious ramifications: When we look at Arius's Jesus, we do not see divinity taking up our human nature and healing it. Instead, Arius's Jesus merely conformed to God's moral, divine standards, but wasn't actually himself God.

When the son of Emperor Constantine, Constantius, took over from his father and tried to end the conflict by replacing the theological phrase "of the *same* substance" with "of *similar* substance," Athanasius refused. He understood that such a redefinition of Christ's nature in favor of Arianism would have radically changed Christianity—for one means Jesus *is* God, the other that Jesus is *like* God. Our salvation depends on Christ's reconciling humans with God in his own person, by being truly God *and* truly man, not just a great creature who acted like God.

Eventually, Athanasius was forced into exile, where he remained until his death in 373. Nearly a decade after his death, Athanasius's doctrines were recognized as true orthodoxy at the Council of Constantinople in 381.

IMPORTANT WORKS

ORATIONS AGAINST THE ARIANS

THE INCARNATION OF THE WORD OF GOD

AGAINST THE HEATHENS

through your land; we will keep strictly to the roadway. We will
not turn aside to the right or the left. 28Sell us food for cash so
that we can eat and sell us water to drink. Just allow us to go
through on foot, 29just as the descendants of Esau who live at
Seir and the Moabites who live in Ar did for us, until we cross
the Jordan to the land the LORD our God is giving us." 30But
King Sihon of Heshbon was unwilling to allow us to pass near
him because the LORD our God had made him obstinate and
stubborn so that he might deliver him over to you this very day.
31The LORD said to me, "Look! I have already begun to give over
Sihon and his land to you. Start right now to take his land as
your possession." 32When Sihon and all his troops emerged to
encounter us in battle at Jahaz, 33the LORD our God delivered
him over to us and we struck him down, along with his sons and
everyone else. 34At that time we seized all his cities and put every
one of them under divine judgment, including even the women
and children; we left no survivors. 35We kept only the livestock
and plunder from the cities for ourselves. 36From Aroer, which
is at the edge of Wadi Arnon (it is the city in the wadi), all the
way to Gilead there was not a town able to resist us—the LORD
our God gave them all to us. 37However, you did not approach
the land of the Ammonites, the Wadi Jabbok, the cities of the
hill country, or any place else forbidden by the LORD our God.

DEFEAT OF OG, KING OF BASHAN

3 Next we set out on the route to Bashan, but King Og of Bashan
and his whole army came out to meet us in battle at Edrei.
2The LORD, however, said to me, "Don't be afraid of him because
I have already given him, his whole army, and his land to you.
You will do to him exactly what you did to King Sihon of the
Amorites who lived in Heshbon." 3So the LORD our God did
indeed give over to us King Og of Bashan and his whole army,
and we struck them down until not a single survivor was left.
4We captured all his cities at that time—there was not a town we
did not take from them—sixty cities, all the region of Argob, the
dominion of Og in Bashan. 5All of these cities were fortified by
high walls, gates, and locking bars; in addition there were a great
many open villages. 6We put all of these under divine judgment
just as we had done to King Sihon of Heshbon—every occupied
city, including women and children. 7But all the livestock and
plunder from the cities we kept for ourselves. 8So at that time
we took the land of the two Amorite kings in the Transjordan from Wadi Arnon to Mount Hermon 9(the Sidonians call
Hermon Sirion and the Amorites call it Senir), 10all the cities
of the plateau, all of Gilead and Bashan as far as Salecah and
Edrei, cities of the kingdom of Og in Bashan. 11Only King Og of
Bashan was left of the remaining Rephaites. (It is noteworthy
that his sarcophagus was made of iron. Does it not, indeed, still
remain in Rabbath of the Ammonites? It is 13½ feet long and
6 feet wide according to standard measure.)

DISTRIBUTION OF THE TRANSJORDANIAN ALLOTMENTS

12This is the land we brought under our control at that time: The
territory extending from Aroer by the Wadi Arnon and half the
Gilead hill country with its cities I gave to the Reubenites and
Gadites. 13The rest of Gilead and all of Bashan, the kingdom of
Og, I gave to half the tribe of Manasseh. (All the region of Argob,
that is, all Bashan, is called the land of Rephaim. 14Jair, son of

3:12–29 Moses prayed that if it were God's will, he might go before Israel over Jordan into Canaan. God's answer to this prayer had a mixture of mercy and judgment. Let it be sufficient for you to have God for your Father and heaven for your portion though you do not have everything you would want to have in the world. God promised Moses a sight of Canaan from the top of Pisgah. Though he should not have the possession of it, he should have the prospect of it. Let us submit to the Lord's will and speak no more to him of matters that he sees good to refuse us.

MATTHEW HENRY (1662–1714)
COMMENTARY ON THE WHOLE BIBLE

Manasseh, took all the Argob region as far as the border with the Geshurites and Maacathites—namely Bashan—and called it by his name, Havvoth Jair, which it retains to this very day.) [15]I gave Gilead to Machir. [16]To the Reubenites and Gadites I allocated the territory extending from Gilead as far as Wadi Arnon (the exact middle of the wadi was a boundary) all the way to the Wadi Jabbok, the Ammonite border. [17]The rift valley and the Jordan River were also a border, from the Sea of Kinnereth to the sea of the rift valley (that is, the Salt Sea), beneath the slopes of Pisgah to the east.

INSTRUCTIONS TO THE TRANSJORDANIAN TRIBES

[18]At that time I instructed you as follows: "The LORD your God has given you this land for your possession. You warriors are to cross over equipped for battle before your fellow Israelites. [19]But your wives, children, and livestock (of which I know you have many) may remain in the cities I have given you. [20]You must fight until the LORD gives your countrymen victory as he did you and they take possession of the land that the LORD your God is giving them on the other side of the Jordan River. Then each of you may return to his own territory that I have given you." [21]I also commanded Joshua at the same time, "You have seen everything the LORD your God did to these two kings; he will do the same to all the kingdoms where you are going. [22]Do not be afraid of them, for the LORD your God will personally fight for you."

DENIAL TO MOSES OF THE PROMISED LAND

[23]Moreover, at that time I pleaded with the LORD, [24]"O, Sovereign LORD, you have begun to show me your greatness and strength. (What god in heaven or earth can rival your works and mighty deeds?) [25]Let me please cross over to see the good land on the other side of the Jordan River—this good hill country and the Lebanon!" [26]But the LORD was angry at me because of you and would not listen to me. Instead, he said to me, "Enough of that! Do not speak to me anymore about this matter. [27]Go up to the top of Pisgah and take a good look to the west, north, south, and east, for you will not be allowed to cross the Jordan. [28]Commission Joshua, and encourage and strengthen him, because he will lead these people over and will enable them to inherit the land you will see." [29]So we settled down in the valley opposite Beth Peor.

THE PRIVILEGES OF THE COVENANT

4 Now, Israel, pay attention to the statutes and ordinances I am about to teach you, so that you might live and go on to enter and take possession of the land that the LORD, the God of your ancestors, is giving you. [2]Do not add a thing to what I command you nor subtract from it, so that you may keep the commandments of the LORD your God that I am delivering to you. [3]You have witnessed what the LORD did at Baal Peor, how he eradicated from your midst everyone who followed Baal Peor. [4]But you who remained faithful to the LORD your God are still alive to this very day, every one of you. [5]Look! I have taught you statutes and ordinances just as the LORD my God told me to do, so that you might carry them out in the land you are about to enter and possess. [6]So be sure to do them, because this will testify of your wise understanding to the people who will learn of all these statutes and say, "Indeed, this great nation is a very

4:1–14 The words of God are infinite. The riches of God cannot be computed or limited. If you take away water from the sea, the deficiency will be imperceptible. And if you remove sand from the seashore, its measure will not be diminished. Therefore know that, as concerning the Word of God, no one has reached or will reach its end. Therefore don't dispute about these things but say, "These things are so. That is enough."

APHRAHAT (C. 280–C. 345)
DEMONSTRATIONS

wise people." 7 In fact, what other great nation has a god so near
to them like the LORD our God whenever we call on him? 8 And
what other great nation has statutes and ordinances as just as
this whole law that I am about to share with you today?

REMINDER OF THE HOREB COVENANT

9 Again, however, pay very careful attention, lest you forget the
things you have seen and disregard them for the rest of your
life; instead teach them to your children and grandchildren.
10 You stood before the LORD your God at Horeb and he said to
me, "Assemble the people before me so that I can tell them my
commands. Then they will learn to revere me all the days they
live in the land, and they will instruct their children." 11 You
approached and stood at the foot of the mountain, a mountain
ablaze to the sky above it and yet dark with a thick cloud. 12 Then
the LORD spoke to you from the middle of the fire; you heard
speech but you could not see anything—only a voice was heard.
13 And he revealed to you the covenant he has commanded you
to keep, the Ten Commandments, writing them on two stone
tablets. 14 Moreover, at that same time the LORD commanded
me to teach you statutes and ordinances for you to keep in the
land that you are about to enter and possess.

THE NATURE OF ISRAEL'S GOD

15 Be very careful, then, because you saw no form at the time the
LORD spoke to you at Horeb from the middle of the fire. 16 I say
this so you will not corrupt yourselves by making an image in the
form of any kind of figure. This includes the likeness of a human
male or female, 17 any kind of land animal, any bird that flies in
the sky, 18 anything that crawls on the ground, or any fish in the
deep waters under the earth. 19 When you look up to the sky and
see the sun, moon, and stars—the whole heavenly creation—you
must not be seduced to worship and serve them, for the LORD
your God has assigned them to all the people of the world. 20 You,
however, the LORD has selected and brought from Egypt, that
iron-smelting furnace, to be his special people as you are today.
21 But the LORD became angry with me because of you and vowed
that I would never cross the Jordan nor enter the good land that
he is about to give you. 22 So I must die here in this land; I will
not cross the Jordan. But you are going over and will possess that
good land. 23 Be on guard so that you do not forget the covenant
of the LORD your God that he has made with you, and that you
do not make an image of any kind, just as he has forbidden you.
24 For the LORD your God is a consuming fire; he is a jealous God.

THREAT AND BLESSING FOLLOWING COVENANT DISOBEDIENCE

25 After you have produced children and grandchildren and
have been in the land a long time, if you become corrupt and
make an image of any kind and do other evil things before the
LORD your God that enrage him, 26 I invoke heaven and earth as
witnesses against you today that you will surely and swiftly be
removed from the very land you are about to cross the Jordan
to possess. You will not last long there because you will surely
be annihilated. 27 Then the LORD will scatter you among the
peoples and there will be very few of you among the nations
where the LORD will drive you. 28 There you will worship gods
made by human hands—wood and stone that can neither see,
hear, eat, nor smell. 29 But if you seek the LORD your God from

there, you will find him, if, indeed, you seek him with all your
heart and soul. 30 In your distress when all these things happen
to you in future days, if you return to the LORD your God and
obey him 31 (for he is a merciful God), he will not let you down
or destroy you, for he cannot forget the covenant with your
ancestors that he confirmed by oath to them.

THE UNIQUENESS OF ISRAEL'S GOD

32 Indeed, ask about the distant past, starting from the day God
created humankind on the earth, and ask from one end of heav-
en to the other, whether there has ever been such a great thing as
this, or even a rumor of it. 33 Have a people ever heard the voice of
God speaking from the middle of fire, as you yourselves have, and
lived to tell about it? 34 Or has God ever before tried to deliver
a nation from the middle of another nation, accompanied by
judgments, signs, wonders, war, strength, power, and other very
terrifying things like the LORD your God did for you in Egypt
before your very eyes? 35 You have been taught that the LORD
alone is God—there is no other besides him. 36 From heaven he
spoke to you in order to teach you, and on earth he showed you
his great fire from which you also heard his words. 37 Moreover,
because he loved your ancestors, he chose their descendants
who followed them and personally brought you out of Egypt
with his great power 38 to dispossess nations greater and stronger
than you and brought you here this day to give you their land as
your property. 39 Today realize and carefully consider that the
LORD is God in heaven above and on earth below—there is no
other! 40 Keep his statutes and commandments that I am setting
forth today so that it may go well with you and your descendants
and that you may enjoy longevity in the land that the LORD your
God is about to give you as a permanent possession.

THE NARRATIVE CONCERNING CITIES OF REFUGE

41 Then Moses selected three cities in the Transjordan, toward
the east. 42 Anyone who accidentally killed someone without
hating him at the time of the accident could flee to one of those
cities and be safe. 43 These cities are Bezer, in the wilderness
plateau, for the Reubenites; Ramoth in Gilead for the Gadites;
and Golan in Bashan for the Manassehites.

THE SETTING AND INTRODUCTION OF THE COVENANT

44 This is the law that Moses set before the Israelites. 45 These are
the stipulations, statutes, and ordinances that Moses spoke to
the Israelites after he had brought them out of Egypt, 46 in the
Transjordan, in the valley opposite Beth Peor, in the land of King
Sihon of the Amorites, who lived in Heshbon. (It is he whom
Moses and the Israelites attacked after they came out of Egypt.
47 They possessed his land and that of King Og of Bashan—both
of whom were Amorite kings in the Transjordan, to the east.
48 Their territory extended from Aroer at the edge of the Arnon
valley as far as Mount Siyon—that is, Hermon—49 including all
the rift valley of the Transjordan in the east to the sea of the
rift valley, beneath the slopes of Pisgah.)

THE OPENING EXHORTATION

5 Then Moses called all the people of Israel together and said
to them: "Listen, Israel, to the statutes and ordinances that
I am about to deliver to you today; learn them and be careful

to keep them! 2The LORD our God made a covenant with us at Horeb. 3He did not make this covenant with our ancestors but with us, we who are here today, all of us living now. 4The LORD spoke face to face with you at the mountain, from the middle of the fire. 5(I was standing between the LORD and you at that time to reveal the LORD's message to you, because you were afraid of the fire and would not go up the mountain.) He said:

THE TEN COMMANDMENTS

6"I am the LORD your God—he who brought you from the land of Egypt, from the place of slavery.

7"You must not have any other gods besides me.

8"You must not make for yourself an image of anything in heaven above, on earth below, or in the waters beneath. 9You must not worship or serve them, for I, the LORD your God, am a jealous God. I punish the sons, grandsons, and great-grandsons for the sin of the fathers who reject me, 10but I show covenant faithfulness to the thousands who choose me and keep my commandments.

11"You must not make use of the name of the LORD your God for worthless purposes, for the LORD will not exonerate anyone who abuses his name that way.

12"Be careful to observe the Sabbath day just as the LORD your God has commanded you. 13You are to work and do all your tasks in six days, 14but the seventh day is the Sabbath of the LORD your God. On that day you must not do any work, you, your son, your daughter, your male slave, your female slave, your ox, your donkey, any other animal, or the resident foreigner who lives with you, so that your male and female slaves, like yourself, may have rest. 15Recall that you were slaves in the land of Egypt and that the LORD your God brought you out of there by strength and power. That is why the LORD your God has commanded you to observe the Sabbath day.

16"Honor your father and your mother just as the LORD your God has commanded you to do, so that your days may be extended and that it may go well with you in the land that he is about to give you.

17"You must not murder.

18"You must not commit adultery.

19"You must not steal.

20"You must not offer false testimony against another. 21You must not desire another man's wife, nor should you crave his house, his field, his male and female servants, his ox, his donkey, or anything else he owns."

THE NARRATIVE OF THE SINAI REVELATION AND ISRAEL'S RESPONSE

22The LORD said these things to your entire assembly at the mountain from the middle of the fire, the cloud, and the darkness with a loud voice, and that was all he said. Then he inscribed the words on two stone tablets and gave them to me. 23Then, when you heard the voice from the midst of the darkness while the mountain was ablaze, all your tribal leaders and elders approached me. 24You said, "The LORD our God has shown us his great glory, and we have heard him speak from the middle of the fire. It is now clear to us that God can speak to human beings and they can keep on living. 25But now, why should we die, because this intense fire will consume us? If we keep hearing the voice of the LORD our God we will die! 26Who

5:23–33 How shall the glory of God be manifested to such fallen creatures as we are? It is clear that self must stand out of the way that there may be room for God to be exalted; and this is the reason why he brings his people oftentimes into straits and difficulties, that, being made conscious of their own folly and weakness, they may be fitted to behold the majesty of God when he comes forth to work their deliverance. Thank God then if you have been led by a rough road: It is this that has given you your experience of God's greatness and loving-kindness.

CHARLES SPURGEON
(1834–1892)
MORNING AND EVENING

is there from the entire human race who has heard the voice of
the living God speaking from the middle of the fire as we have,
and has lived? 27You go near so that you can hear everything the
LORD our God is saying and then you can tell us whatever he
says to you; then we will pay attention and do it." 28When the
LORD heard you speaking to me, he said to me, "I have heard
what these people have said to you—they have spoken well.
29If only it would really be their desire to fear me and obey all
my commandments in the future, so that it may go well with
them and their descendants forever. 30Go and tell them, 'Return
to your tents!' 31But as for you, remain here with me so I can
declare to you all the commandments, statutes, and ordinances
that you are to teach them, so that they can carry them out in
the land I am about to give them." 32Be careful, therefore, to
do exactly what the LORD your God has commanded you; do
not turn right or left! 33Walk just as he has commanded you
so that you may live, that it may go well with you, and that you
may live long in the land you are going to possess.

EXHORTATION TO KEEP THE COVENANT PRINCIPLES

6 Now these are the commandments, statutes, and ordinances
that the LORD your God instructed me to teach you so that
you may carry them out in the land where you are headed 2and
that you may so revere the LORD your God that you will keep
all his statutes and commandments that I am giving you—you,
your children, and your grandchildren—all your lives, to prolong
your days. 3Pay attention, Israel, and be careful to do this so that
it may go well with you and that you may increase greatly in
number—as the LORD, the God of your ancestors, said to you,
you will have a land flowing with milk and honey.

THE ESSENCE OF THE COVENANT PRINCIPLES

4Hear, O Israel: The LORD is our God, the LORD is one! 5You
must love the LORD your God with your whole mind, your whole
being, and all your strength.

EXHORTATION TO TEACH THE COVENANT PRINCIPLES

6These words I am commanding you today must be kept in
mind, 7and you must teach them to your children and speak of
them as you sit in your house, as you walk along the road, as you
lie down, and as you get up. 8You should tie them as a reminder
on your forearm and fasten them as symbols on your forehead.
9Inscribe them on the doorframes of your houses and gates.

EXHORTATION TO WORSHIP THE LORD EXCLUSIVELY

10Then when the LORD your God brings you to the land he
promised your ancestors Abraham, Isaac, and Jacob to give
you—a land with large, fine cities you did not build, 11houses
filled with choice things you did not accumulate, hewn-out
cisterns you did not dig, and vineyards and olive groves you did
not plant—and you eat your fill, 12be careful not to forget the
LORD who brought you out of Egypt, that place of slavery. 13You
must revere the LORD your God, serve him, and take oaths using
only his name. 14You must not go after other gods, those of the
surrounding peoples, 15for the LORD your God, who is present
among you, is a jealous God—his anger will erupt against you
and remove you from the land.

6:4 If there be but one God who is above all, then he must be loved by all. We must love him with a love of appreciation, set the highest estimate on him who is the only fountain of being and bliss. Our love to other things must be more indifferent; some drops of love may run beside to the creature, but the full stream must run toward God. Especially if God has savingly revealed himself to us, if he has given us eyes to see the light, we can never be enough thankful to God.

THOMAS WATSON
(1620–1686)
BODY OF DIVINITY

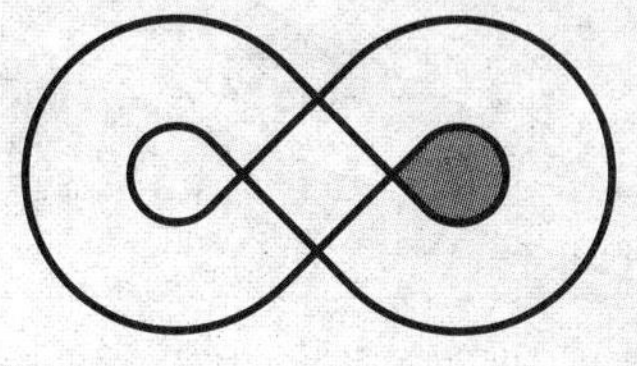

THE NICENE CREED (325)

THE NICENE CREED was produced by two ecumenical councils, the Nicaean (325) and Constantinopolitan (381). This creed is one of the most famous documents in church history because it was formulated to address questions related to the doctrine of the Trinity, then improved to strengthen the language related to the divinity of Jesus and the Holy Spirit. The Nicene Creed was further confirmed during the Councils of Ephesus following a dispute on the nature of Christ (431, 449, 475), between the teachings of Cyril of Alexandria and Nestorius.

I BELIEVE in one God, the Father Almighty, Maker of heaven and earth, and of all things visible and invisible.

AND IN one Lord Jesus Christ, the Only Begotten Son of God, begotten of the Father before all worlds; God of God, Light of Light, very God of very God; begotten, not made, being of one substance with the Father, by whom all things were made.

WHO, FOR us men for our salvation, came down from heaven, and was incarnate by the Holy Spirit of the Virgin Mary, and was made man; and was crucified also for us under Pontius Pilate; he suffered and was buried; and the third day he rose again, according to the Scriptures; and ascended into heaven, and sits on the right hand of the Father; and he shall come again, with glory, to judge the quick and the dead; whose kingdom shall have no end.

AND I believe in the Holy Ghost, the Lord and Giver of Life; who proceeds from the Father; who with the Father and the Son together is worshiped and glorified; who spoke by the prophets.

AND I believe in one holy catholic and apostolic church. I acknowledge one baptism for the remission of sins; and I look for the resurrection of the dead, and the life of the world to come. Amen.

EXHORTATION TO OBEY THE LORD EXCLUSIVELY

16You must not put the LORD your God to the test as you did
at Massah. 17Keep his commandments very carefully, as well as
the stipulations and statutes he commanded you to observe.
18Do whatever is proper and good before the LORD so that it
may go well with you and that you may enter and occupy the
good land that he promised your ancestors, 19and that you may
drive out all your enemies just as the LORD said.

EXHORTATION TO REMEMBER THE PAST

20When your children ask you later on, "What are the stipulations, statutes, and ordinances that the LORD our God commanded you?" 21you must say to them, "We were Pharaoh's
slaves in Egypt, but the LORD brought us out of Egypt in a powerful way. 22And he brought signs and great, devastating wonders
on Egypt, on Pharaoh, and on his whole family before our very
eyes. 23He delivered us from there so that he could give us the
land he had promised our ancestors. 24The LORD commanded
us to obey all these statutes and to revere him so that it may
always go well for us and he may preserve us, as he has to this
day. 25We will be innocent if we carefully keep all these commandments before the LORD our God, just as he demands."

THE DISPOSSESSION OF NONVASSALS

7 When the LORD your God brings you to the land that you are
going to occupy and forces out many nations before you—
Hittites, Girgashites, Amorites, Canaanites, Perizzites, Hivites,
and Jebusites, seven nations more numerous and powerful than
you—2and he delivers them over to you and you attack them, you
must utterly annihilate them. Make no treaty with them and
show them no mercy! 3You must not intermarry with them. Do
not give your daughters to their sons or take their daughters for
your sons, 4for they will turn your sons away from me to worship
other gods. Then the anger of the LORD will erupt against you and
he will quickly destroy you. 5Instead, this is what you must do to
them: You must tear down their altars, shatter their sacred pillars,
cut down their sacred Asherah poles, and burn up their idols. 6For
you are a people holy to the LORD your God. He has chosen you
to be his people, prized above all others on the face of the earth.

THE BASIS OF ISRAEL'S ELECTION

7It is not because you were more numerous than all the other
peoples that the LORD favored and chose you—for in fact you were
the least numerous of all peoples. 8Rather it is because of his love
for you and his faithfulness to the promise he solemnly vowed to
your ancestors that the LORD brought you out with great power,
redeeming you from the place of slavery, from the power of Pharaoh king of Egypt. 9So realize that the LORD your God is the true
God, the faithful God who keeps covenant faithfully with those
who love him and keep his commandments, to a thousand generations, 10but who pays back those who hate him as they deserve
and destroys them. He will not ignore those who hate him but
will repay them as they deserve! 11So keep the commandments,
statutes, and ordinances that I today am commanding you to do.

PROMISES OF GOOD FOR COVENANT OBEDIENCE

12If you obey these ordinances and are careful to do them, the
LORD your God will faithfully keep covenant with you as he promised your ancestors. 13He will love and bless you, and make you

7:1–11 *For by grace the Jews were saved: I chose you,* said God, *not because you were many in number, but because of your fathers.* If now they were chosen by God not for their own good deeds, it is manifest that by grace they obtained this honor. And we too all are saved by grace but not in like manner; not for the same objects, but for objects much greater and higher. The grace then that is with us is not like theirs. For not only was pardon of sins given to us (since this we have in common with them, for all have sinned), but righteousness also, and sanctification and the gift of the Spirit far more glorious and more abundant. These I say are proofs of the greatest grace and unspeakable loving-kindness.

CHRYSOSTOM **(C. 347–407)**
HOMILIES ON THE GOSPEL OF JOHN

numerous. He will bless you with many children, with the produce of your soil, your grain, your new wine, your olive oil, the
offspring of your oxen, and the young of your flocks in the land
that he promised your ancestors to give you. 14You will be blessed
beyond all peoples; there will be no barrenness among you or
your livestock. 15The LORD will protect you from all sickness, and
you will not experience any of the terrible diseases that you knew
in Egypt; instead he will inflict them on all those who hate you.

EXHORTATION TO DESTROY CANAANITE PAGANISM

16You must destroy all the people whom the LORD your God is
about to deliver over to you; you must not pity them or worship
their gods, for that will be a snare to you. 17If you think, "These
nations are more numerous than I—how can I dispossess them?"
18you must not fear them. You must carefully recall what the
LORD your God did to Pharaoh and all Egypt, 19the great judgments you saw, the signs and wonders, the strength and power
by which he brought you out—thus the LORD your God will do
to all the people you fear. 20Furthermore, the LORD your God
will release hornets among them until the very last ones who
hide from you perish. 21You must not tremble in their presence,
for the LORD your God, who is present among you, is a great
and awesome God. 22He, the God who leads you, will expel the
nations little by little. You will not be allowed to destroy them all
at once lest the wild animals overrun you. 23The LORD your God
will give them over to you; he will throw them into a great panic
until they are destroyed. 24He will hand over their kings to you,
and you will erase their very names from memory. Nobody will
be able to resist you until you destroy them. 25You must burn
the images of their gods, but do not covet the silver and gold
that covers them so much that you take it for yourself and thus
become ensnared by it; for it is abhorrent to the LORD your God.
26You must not bring any abhorrent thing into your house and
thereby become an object of divine wrath along with it. You must
absolutely detest and abhor it, for it is an object of divine wrath.

THE LORD'S PROVISION IN THE DESERT

8 You must keep carefully all these commandments I am giving
you today so that you may live, increase in number, and go in
and occupy the land that the LORD promised to your ancestors.
2Remember the whole way by which he has brought you these
40 years through the wilderness so that he might, by humbling
you, test you to see if you have it within you to keep his commandments or not. 3So he humbled you by making you hungry
and then feeding you with unfamiliar manna. He did this to
teach you that humankind cannot live by bread alone, but also
by everything that comes from the LORD's mouth. 4Your clothing
did not wear out nor did your feet swell all these 40 years. 5Be
keenly aware that just as a parent disciplines his child, so the
LORD your God disciplines you. 6So you must keep his commandments, live according to his standards, and revere him. 7For the
LORD your God is bringing you to a good land, a land of brooks,
springs, and fountains flowing forth in valleys and hills, 8a land
of wheat, barley, vines, fig trees, and pomegranates, of olive trees
and honey, 9a land where you may eat food in plenty and find no
lack of anything, a land whose stones are iron and from whose
hills you can mine copper. 10You will eat your fill and then praise
the LORD your God because of the good land he has given you.

8:1–10 Nourish your soul with the fear of God, and God will nourish your body. Do these things so that what you yourself are unable to procure may be given you by God. Take note of this: If God does not give the rain and the wind, it avails you naught, even if you are anxious. Obey God therefore, and creation will obey your needs. If God nourished the Israelites for 40 years in the desert, while they were murmuring and disbelieving, and effortlessly preserved their sandals and clothing, how much more so in the case of believers?

EPHREM THE SYRIAN
(C. 306–373)
COMMENTARY ON TATIAN'S DIATESSARON

EXHORTATION TO REMEMBER THAT BLESSING COMES FROM GOD

[11]Be sure you do not forget the LORD your God by not keeping his commandments, ordinances, and statutes that I am giving you today. [12]When you eat your fill, when you build and occupy good houses, [13]when your cattle and flocks increase, when you have plenty of silver and gold, and when you have abundance of everything, [14]be sure you do not feel self-important and forget the LORD your God who brought you from the land of Egypt, the place of slavery, [15]and who brought you through the great, fearful wilderness of venomous serpents and scorpions, an arid place with no water. He made water flow from a flint rock and [16]fed you in the wilderness with manna (which your ancestors had never before known) so that he might by humbling you test you and eventually bring good to you. [17]Be careful not to say, "My own ability and skill have gotten me this wealth." [18]You must remember the LORD your God, for he is the one who gives ability to get wealth; if you do this he will confirm his covenant that he made by oath to your ancestors, even as he has to this day. [19]Now if you forget the LORD your God at all and follow other gods, worshiping and prostrating yourselves before them, I testify to you today that you will surely be annihilated. [20]Just like the nations the LORD is about to destroy from your sight, so he will do to you because you would not obey him.

THEOLOGICAL JUSTIFICATION OF THE CONQUEST

9 Listen, Israel: Today you are about to cross the Jordan so you can dispossess the nations there, people greater and stronger than you who live in large cities with extremely high fortifications. [2]They include the Anakites, a numerous and tall people whom you know about and of whom it is said, "Who is able to resist the Anakites?" [3]Understand today that the LORD your God who goes before you is a devouring fire; he will defeat and subdue them before you. You will dispossess and destroy them quickly just as he has told you. [4]Do not think to yourself after the LORD your God has driven them out before you, "Because of my own righteousness the LORD has brought me here to possess this land." It is because of the wickedness of these nations that the LORD is driving them out ahead of you. [5]It is not because of your righteousness, or even your inner uprightness, that you have come here to possess their land. Instead, because of the wickedness of these nations, the LORD your God is driving them out ahead of you in order to confirm the promise he made on oath to your ancestors, to Abraham, Isaac, and Jacob. [6]Understand, therefore, that it is not because of your righteousness that the LORD your God is about to give you this good land as a possession, for you are a stubborn people!

THE HISTORY OF ISRAEL'S STUBBORNNESS

[7]Remember—don't ever forget—how you provoked the LORD your God in the wilderness; from the time you left the land of Egypt until you came to this place you were constantly rebelling against him. [8]At Horeb you provoked him and he was angry enough with you to destroy you. [9]When I went up the mountain to receive the stone tablets, the tablets of the covenant that the LORD made with you, I remained there 40 days and nights, eating and drinking nothing. [10]The LORD gave me the two stone tablets, written by the very finger of God, and

9:1–6 By Moses' impressing on them, for the third time, that the Israelites had not deserved the land by their righteousness, we learn that nothing is more difficult for human beings than to strip themselves of their blind arrogance whereby they detract some portion of the praise from God's mercies. They who are regenerated by God's Spirit know that they are not naturally formed unto obedience, and thus that it is only mercy that makes them to differ from the worst of human beings.

JOHN CALVIN **(1509–1564)**
COMPLETE COMMENTARY ON THE BIBLE

on them was everything he said to you at the mountain from the midst of the fire at the time of that assembly. 11Now at the end of the 40 days and nights the LORD presented me with the two stone tablets, the tablets of the covenant. 12And he said to me, "Get up, go down at once from here because your people whom you brought out of Egypt have sinned! They have quickly turned from the way I commanded them and have made for themselves a cast metal image." 13Moreover, he said to me, "I have taken note of these people; they are a stubborn lot! 14Stand aside and I will destroy them, obliterating their very name from memory, and I will make you into a stronger and more numerous nation than they are."

15So I turned and went down the mountain while it was blazing with fire; the two tablets of the covenant were in my hands. 16When I looked, you had indeed sinned against the LORD your God and had cast for yourselves a metal calf; you had quickly turned aside from the way he had commanded you! 17I grabbed the two tablets, threw them down, and shattered them before your very eyes. 18Then I again fell down before the LORD for 40 days and nights; I ate and drank nothing because of all the sin you had committed, doing such evil before the LORD as to enrage him. 19For I was terrified at the LORD's intense anger that threatened to destroy you. But he listened to me this time as well. 20The LORD was also angry enough at Aaron to kill him, but at that time I prayed for him too. 21As for your sinful thing that you had made, the calf, I took it, melted it down, ground it up until it was as fine as dust, and tossed the dust into the stream that flows down the mountain. 22Moreover, you continued to provoke the LORD at Taberah, Massah, and Kibroth Hattaavah. 23And when he sent you from Kadesh Barnea and told you, "Go up and possess the land I have given you," you rebelled against the LORD your God and would neither believe nor obey him. 24You have been rebelling against him from the very first day I knew you!

MOSES' PLEA ON BEHALF OF GOD'S REPUTATION

25I lay flat on the ground before the LORD for 40 days and nights, for he had said he would destroy you. 26I prayed to him: O, Sovereign LORD, do not destroy your people, your valued property that you have powerfully redeemed, whom you brought out of Egypt by your strength. 27Remember your servants Abraham, Isaac, and Jacob; ignore the stubbornness, wickedness, and sin of these people. 28Otherwise the people of the land from which you brought us will say, "The LORD was unable to bring them to the land he promised them, and because of his hatred for them he has brought them out to kill them in the wilderness." 29They are your people, your valued property, whom you brought out with great strength and power.

THE OPPORTUNITY TO BEGIN AGAIN

10 At that same time the LORD said to me, "Carve out for yourself two stone tablets like the first ones and come up the mountain to me; also make for yourself a wooden ark. 2I will write on the tablets the same words that were on the first tablets you broke, and you must put them into the ark." 3So I made an ark of acacia wood and carved out two stone tablets just like the first ones. Then I went up the mountain with the two tablets in my hands. 4The LORD then wrote on the tablets

10:1–11 Though the tablets were broken because they broke his commandment, they were now renewed in proof that his wrath was turned away. And thus God's writing his law in our inward parts is the surest proof of our reconciliation to him. 'Twas fit that he who had saved them from ruin by his intercession should have the conduct and command of them. And herein he was a type of Christ who, as he ever lives to make intercession for us, so has all power in heaven and in earth.

JOHN WESLEY **(1703–1791)**
EXPLANATORY NOTES ON THE BIBLE

the same words, the Ten Commandments, which he had spoken
to you at the mountain from the middle of the fire at the time
of that assembly, and he gave them to me. 5Then I turned, went
down the mountain, and placed the tablets into the ark I had
made—they are still there, just as the LORD commanded me.

CONCLUSION OF THE HISTORICAL RÉSUMÉ

6During those days the Israelites traveled from Beeroth Bene
Jaakan to Moserah. There Aaron died and was buried, and his son
Eleazar became priest in his place. 7From there they traveled to
Gudgodah, and from Gudgodah to Jotbathah, a place of flowing
streams. 8At that time the LORD set apart the tribe of Levi to
carry the ark of the LORD's covenant, to stand before the LORD
to serve him, and to formulate blessings in his name, as they do
to this very day. 9Therefore Levi has no allotment or inheritance
among his brothers; the LORD is his inheritance just as the LORD
your God told him. 10As for me, I stayed at the mountain as I
did the first time, 40 days and nights. The LORD listened to me
that time as well and decided not to destroy you. 11Then he said
to me, "Get up, set out leading the people so they may go and
possess the land I promised to give to their ancestors."

AN EXHORTATION TO LOVE BOTH GOD AND PEOPLE

12Now, Israel, what does the LORD your God require of you except
to revere him, to obey all his commandments, to love him, to serve
him with all your mind and being, 13and to keep the LORD's commandments and statutes that I am giving you today for your own
good? 14The heavens—indeed the highest heavens—belong to the
LORD your God, as does the earth and everything in it. 15However,
only to your ancestors did he show his loving favor, and he chose
you, their descendants, from all peoples—as is apparent today.
16Therefore, cleanse your hearts and stop being so stubborn!
17For the LORD your God is God of gods and Lord of lords, the
great, mighty, and awesome God who is unbiased and takes no
bribe, 18who justly treats the orphan and widow, and who loves
resident foreigners, giving them food and clothing. 19So you must
love the resident foreigner because you were foreigners in the
land of Egypt. 20Revere the LORD your God, serve him, be loyal to
him, and take oaths only in his name. 21He is the one you should
praise; he is your God, the one who has done these great and awesome things for you that you have seen. 22When your ancestors
went down to Egypt, they numbered only seventy, but now the
LORD your God has made you as numerous as the stars of the sky.

REITERATION OF THE CALL TO OBEDIENCE

11 You must love the LORD your God and do what he requires;
keep his statutes, ordinances, and commandments at all
times. 2Bear in mind today that I am not speaking to your children who have not personally experienced the judgments of
the LORD your God, which revealed his greatness, strength, and
power. 3They did not see the awesome deeds he performed in
the midst of Egypt against Pharaoh king of Egypt and his whole
land, 4or what he did to the army of Egypt, including their horses
and chariots, when he made the waters of the Red Sea overwhelm them while they were pursuing you and he annihilated
them. 5They did not see what he did to you in the wilderness
before you reached this place, 6or what he did to Dathan and
Abiram, sons of Eliab the Reubenite, when the earth opened its

11:1 This chapter is a sort of conclusion to all previous exhortations concerning the first commandment. It repeats and drives home the blessings received in Egypt and the desert and promises the land and future benefits that will be received when the people keep the commandments of God and do not worship strange gods. He is so concerned about it that he commands it to be taken to heart, to be bound as a sign on hands and eyes, and to be taught to the children . . . for it contains the whole sum and fulfillment of all the commandments that follow.

MARTIN LUTHER **(1483–1546)**
LECTURES ON DEUTERONOMY

mouth in the middle of the Israelite camp and swallowed them, their families, their tents, and all the property they brought with them. [7]I am speaking to you because you are the ones who saw with your own eyes all the great deeds of the LORD.

THE ABUNDANCE OF THE LAND OF PROMISE

[8]Now pay attention to all the commandments I am giving you today, so that you may be strong enough to enter and possess the land where you are headed, [9]and that you may enjoy long life in the land the LORD promised to give to your ancestors and their descendants, a land flowing with milk and honey. [10]For the land where you are headed is not like the land of Egypt from which you came, a land where you planted seed and which you irrigated by hand like a vegetable garden. [11]Instead, the land you are crossing the Jordan to occupy is one of hills and valleys, a land that drinks in water from the rains, [12]a land the LORD your God looks after. He is constantly attentive to it from the beginning to the end of the year. [13]Now, if you pay close attention to my commandments that I am giving you today and love the LORD your God and serve him with all your mind and being, [14]then he promises, "I will send rain for your land in its season, the autumn and the spring rains, so that you may gather in your grain, new wine, and olive oil. [15]I will provide pasture for your livestock and you will eat your fill."

EXHORTATION TO INSTRUCTION AND OBEDIENCE

[16]Make sure you do not turn away to serve and worship other gods! [17]Then the anger of the LORD will erupt against you, and he will close up the sky so that it does not rain. The land will not yield its produce, and you will soon be removed from the good land that the LORD is about to give you. [18]Fix these words of mine into your mind and being, tie them as a reminder on your hands, and let them be symbols on your forehead. [19]Teach them to your children and speak of them as you sit in your house, as you walk along the road, as you lie down, and as you get up. [20]Inscribe them on the doorframes of your houses and on your gates [21]so that your days and those of your descendants may be extended in the land that the LORD promised to give to your ancestors, like the days of heaven itself. [22]For if you carefully observe all of these commandments I am giving you and love the LORD your God, live according to his standards, and remain loyal to him, [23]then he will drive out all these nations ahead of you, and you will dispossess nations greater and stronger than you. [24]Every place you set your foot will be yours; your border will extend from the desert to Lebanon and from the River (that is, the Euphrates) as far as the Mediterranean Sea. [25]Nobody will be able to resist you; the LORD your God will spread the fear and terror of you over the whole land on which you walk, just as he promised you.

ANTICIPATION OF A BLESSING AND CURSING CEREMONY

[26]Take note—I am setting before you today a blessing and a curse: [27]the blessing if you take to heart the commandments of the LORD your God that I am giving you today, [28]and the curse if you pay no attention to his commandments and turn from the way I am setting before you today to pursue other gods you have not known. [29]When the LORD your God brings you into the land you are to possess, you must pronounce the blessing on Mount Gerizim and the curse on Mount Ebal. [30]Are they

not across the Jordan River, toward the west, in the land of
the Canaanites who live in the rift valley opposite Gilgal near
the oak of Moreh? 31 For you are about to cross the Jordan to
possess the land the LORD your God is giving you, and you will
possess and inhabit it. 32 Be certain to keep all the statutes and
ordinances that I am presenting to you today.

THE CENTRAL SANCTUARY

12 These are the statutes and ordinances you must be careful
to obey as long as you live in the land the LORD, the God of
your ancestors, has given you to possess. 2 You must by all means
destroy all the places where the nations you are about to dispossess worship their gods—on the high mountains and hills and
under every leafy tree. 3 You must tear down their altars, shatter
their sacred pillars, burn up their sacred Asherah poles, and cut
down the images of their gods; you must eliminate their very
memory from that place. 4 You must not worship the LORD your
God the way they worship. 5 But you must seek only the place he
chooses from all your tribes to establish his name as his place
of residence, and you must go there. 6 And there you must take
your burnt offerings, your sacrifices, your tithes, the personal
offerings you have prepared, your votive offerings, your freewill
offerings, and the firstborn of your herds and flocks. 7 Both you
and your families must feast there before the LORD your God and
rejoice in all the output of your labor with which he has blessed
you. 8 You must not do as we are doing here today, with everyone
doing what seems best to him, 9 for you have not yet come to
the final stop and inheritance the LORD your God is giving you.
10 When you do go across the Jordan River and settle in the land
he is granting you as an inheritance and you find relief from all
the enemies who surround you, you will live in safety. 11 Then
you must come to the place the LORD your God chooses for his
name to reside, bringing everything I am commanding you—
your burnt offerings, sacrifices, tithes, the personal offerings
you have prepared, and all your choice votive offerings that you
devote to him. 12 You shall rejoice in the presence of the LORD
your God, along with your sons, daughters, male and female
servants, and the Levites in your villages (since they have no
allotment or inheritance with you). 13 Make sure you do not offer
burnt offerings in any place you wish, 14 for you may do so only
in the place the LORD chooses in one of your tribal areas—there
you may do everything I am commanding you.

REGULATIONS FOR EATING SACRIFICIAL AND NON-SACRIFICIAL FOODS

15 On the other hand, you may slaughter and eat meat as you
please when the LORD your God blesses you in all your villages.
Both the ritually pure and impure may eat it, whether it is a
gazelle or an ibex. 16 However, you must not eat blood—pour
it out on the ground like water. 17 You will not be allowed to
eat in your villages your tithe of grain, new wine, olive oil, the
firstborn of your herd and flock, any votive offerings you have
vowed, or your freewill and personal offerings. 18 Only in the
presence of the LORD your God may you eat these, in the place
he chooses. This applies to you, your son, your daughter, your
male and female servants, and the Levites in your villages. In
that place you will rejoice before the LORD your God in all the
output of your labor. 19 Be careful not to overlook the Levites
as long as you live in the land.

12:5–14 Under the gospel, we have no temple or altar that sanctifies the gift but Christ only; and as to the places of worship, the prophets foretold that in every place the spiritual incense should be offered (Mal 1:11). Our Savior declared that those are accepted as true worshipers who worship God in sincerity and truth, without regard either to this mountain or Jerusalem (John 4:21). And a devout Israelite might honor God, keep up communion with him, and obtain mercy from him though he had no opportunity of bringing a sacrifice to his altar. Work for God should be done with holy joy and cheerfulness.

MATTHEW HENRY (1662–1714)
COMMENTARY ON THE WHOLE BIBLE

THE SANCTITY OF BLOOD

20 When the LORD your God extends your borders as he said he would do and you say, "I want to eat meat just as I please," you may do so as you wish. 21 If the place he chooses to locate his name is too far for you, you may slaughter any of your herd and flock he has given you just as I have stipulated; you may eat them in your villages just as you wish. 22 As you eat the gazelle or ibex, so you may eat these; the ritually impure and pure alike may eat them. 23 However, by no means eat the blood, for the blood is life itself—you must not eat the life with the meat. 24 You must not eat it! You must pour it out on the ground like water. 25 You must not eat it so that it may go well with you and your children after you; you will be doing what is right in the LORD's sight. 26 But the holy things and votive offerings that belong to you, you must pick up and take to the place the LORD will choose. 27 You must offer your burnt offerings, both meat and blood, on the altar of the LORD your God; the blood of your other sacrifices you must pour out on his altar while you eat the meat. 28 Pay careful attention to all these things I am commanding you so that it may always go well with you and your children after you when you do what is good and right in the sight of the LORD your God.

THE ABOMINATION OF PAGAN GODS

29 When the LORD your God eliminates the nations from the place where you are headed and you dispossess them, you will settle down in their land. 30 After they have been destroyed from your presence, be careful not to be ensnared like they are; do not pursue their gods and say, "How do these nations serve their gods? I will do the same." 31 You must not worship the LORD your God the way they do! For everything that is abhorrent to him, everything he hates, they have done when worshiping their gods. They even burn up their sons and daughters before their gods!

IDOLATRY AND FALSE PROPHETS

32 You must be careful to do everything I am commanding you.

13 Do not add to it or subtract from it! 1 Suppose a prophet or one who foretells by dreams should appear among you and show you a sign or wonder, 2 and the sign or wonder should come to pass concerning what he said to you, namely, "Let us follow other gods"—gods whom you have not previously known—"and let us serve them." 3 You must not listen to the words of that prophet or dreamer, for the LORD your God will be testing you to see if you love him with all your mind and being. 4 You must follow the LORD your God and revere only him; and you must observe his commandments, obey him, serve him, and remain loyal to him. 5 As for that prophet or dreamer, he must be executed because he encouraged rebellion against the LORD your God who brought you from the land of Egypt, redeeming you from that place of slavery, and because he has tried to entice you from the way the LORD your God has commanded you to go. In this way you must purge evil from among you.

> 13:1–18 We must clearly perceive and, according to the rules of Deuteronomy, fully understand that if at any time a teacher of the church deviates from the faith, divine providence permits this to happen in order to test and to try us. Since this is so, we may say that a true and genuine Catholic is the person who loves the truth of God, the church, and the body of Christ. Such a person does not put anything above divine religion and the Catholic faith—neither the authority, nor the affection, nor the genius, nor the eloquence, nor the philosophy of any other human being.
>
> VINCENT OF LÉRINS (C. 445)
> *COMMONITORIUM*

FALSE PROPHETS IN THE FAMILY

6 Suppose your own full brother, your son, your daughter, your beloved wife, or your closest friend should seduce you secretly and encourage you to go and serve other gods that neither you nor your ancestors have previously known, 7 the gods of the surrounding people (whether near you or far from you, from

one end of the earth to the other). 8You must not give in to him or even listen to him; do not feel sympathy for him or spare him or cover up for him. 9Instead, you must kill him without fail! Your own hand must be the first to strike him, and then the hands of the whole community. 10You must stone him to death because he tried to entice you away from the LORD your God, who delivered you from the land of Egypt, that place of slavery. 11Thus all Israel will hear and be afraid; no longer will they continue to do evil like this among you.

PUNISHMENT OF COMMUNITY IDOLATRY

12Suppose you should hear in one of your cities, which the LORD your God is giving you as a place to live, that 13some evil people have departed from among you to entice the inhabitants of their cities, saying, "Let's go and serve other gods" (whom you have not known before). 14You must investigate thoroughly and inquire carefully. If it is indeed true that such a disgraceful thing is being done among you, 15you must by all means slaughter the inhabitants of that city with the sword; annihilate with the sword everyone in it, as well as the livestock. 16You must gather all of its plunder into the middle of the plaza and burn the city and all its plunder as a whole burnt offering to the LORD your God. It will be an abandoned ruin forever—it must never be rebuilt again. 17You must not take for yourself anything that has been placed under judgment. Then the LORD will relent from his intense anger, show you compassion, have mercy on you, and multiply you as he promised your ancestors. 18Thus you must obey the LORD your God, keeping all his commandments that I am giving you today and doing what is right before him.

THE HOLY AND THE PROFANE

14 You are children of the LORD your God. Do not cut yourselves or shave your forehead bald for the sake of the dead. 2For you are a people holy to the LORD your God. He has chosen you to be his people, prized above all others on the face of the earth.

3You must not eat any forbidden thing. 4These are the animals you may eat: the ox, the sheep, the goat, 5the ibex, the gazelle, the deer, the wild goat, the antelope, the wild oryx, and the mountain sheep. 6You may eat any animal that has hooves divided into two parts and that chews the cud. 7However, you may not eat the following animals among those that chew the cud or those that have divided hooves: the camel, the hare, and the rock badger. (Although they chew the cud, they do not have divided hooves and are therefore ritually impure to you.) 8Also, the pig is ritually impure to you; though it has divided hooves, it does not chew the cud. You may not eat their meat or even touch their remains.

9These you may eat from among water creatures: anything with fins and scales you may eat, 10but whatever does not have fins and scales you may not eat; it is ritually impure to you.

11All ritually clean birds you may eat. 12These are the ones you may not eat: the eagle, the vulture, the black vulture, 13the kite, the black kite, the dayyah after its species, 14every raven after its species, 15the ostrich, the owl, the seagull, the falcon after its species, 16the little owl, the long-eared owl, the white owl, 17the jackdaw, the carrion vulture, the cormorant, 18the stork, the heron after its species, the hoopoe, and the bat.

14:3–21 Among the Jews, frugality was made a matter of precept by a very wise dispensation of the law. Christ the educator forbade them the use of innumerable things. He explained the reasons, the spiritual ones hidden, the material ones obvious, but all of which they trusted. Some animals were forbidden because they were not cloven-footed; others because they did not ruminate their food; a third class, because they, alone among all the fish of the seas, had no scales; until finally there were only a few things left fit for food. And even of those he placed a prohibition on the ones found dead or offered to idols or strangled. He imposed upon them a contrary course of action until the inclination engendered by habits of easy living be broken because it is difficult for one who indulges in pleasures to keep himself from returning to them.

CLEMENT OF ALEXANDRIA (C. 150–C. 215)
CHRIST THE EDUCATOR

19And any swarming winged thing is impure to you—they
may not be eaten. 20You may eat any winged creature that is
clean. 21You may not eat any corpse, though you may give it
to the resident foreigner who is living in your villages and he
may eat it, or you may sell it to a foreigner. You are a people
holy to the LORD your God. Do not boil a young goat in its
mother's milk.

THE OFFERING OF TITHES

22You must be certain to tithe all the produce of your seed that
comes from the field year after year. 23In the presence of the
LORD your God, in the place he chooses to locate his name,
you must eat from the tithe of your grain, your new wine, your
olive oil, and the firstborn of your herds and flocks, so that
you may learn to revere the LORD your God always. 24When he
blesses you, if the place where he chooses to locate his name
is distant, 25you may convert the tithe into money, secure the
money, and travel to the place the LORD your God chooses for
himself. 26Then you may spend the money however you wish for
cattle, sheep, wine, beer, or whatever you desire. You and your
household may eat there in the presence of the LORD your God
and enjoy it. 27As for the Levites in your villages, you must not
ignore them, for they have no allotment or inheritance along
with you. 28At the end of every three years you must bring all
the tithe of your produce, in that very year, and you must store
it up in your villages. 29Then the Levites (because they have no
allotment or inheritance with you), the resident foreigners,
the orphans, and the widows of your villages may come and
eat their fill so that the LORD your God may bless you in all
the work you do.

THE YEAR OF DEBT RELEASE

15 At the end of every seven years you must declare a cancellation of debts. 2This is the nature of the cancellation:
Every creditor must remit what he has loaned to another person; he must not force payment from his fellow Israelite, for
it is to be recognized as "the LORD's cancellation of debts."
3You may exact payment from a foreigner, but whatever your
fellow Israelite owes you, you must remit. 4However, there
should not be any poor among you, for the LORD will surely
bless you in the land that he is giving you as an inheritance, 5if
you carefully obey him by keeping all these commandments
that I am giving you today. 6For the LORD your God will bless
you just as he has promised; you will lend to many nations but
will not borrow from any, and you will rule over many nations
but they will not rule over you.

THE SPIRIT OF LIBERALITY

7If a fellow Israelite from one of your villages in the land that
the LORD your God is giving you should be poor, you must not
harden your heart or be insensitive to his impoverished condition. 8Instead, you must be sure to open your hand to him and
generously lend him whatever he needs. 9Be careful lest you
entertain the wicked thought that the seventh year, the year
of cancellation of debts, has almost arrived, and your attitude
be wrong toward your impoverished fellow Israelite and you
do not lend him anything; he will cry out to the LORD against
you, and you will be regarded as having sinned. 10You must by
all means lend to him and not be upset by doing it, for because

of this the LORD your God will bless you in all your work and in
everything you attempt. 11There will never cease to be some
poor people in the land; therefore, I am commanding you to
make sure you open your hand to your fellow Israelites who
are needy and poor in your land.

RELEASE OF DEBT SLAVES

12If your fellow Hebrew—whether male or female—is sold to you
and serves you for six years, then in the seventh year you must
let that servant go free. 13If you set them free, you must not send
them away empty-handed. 14You must supply them generously
from your flock, your threshing floor, and your winepress—as
the LORD your God has blessed you, you must give to them.
15Remember that you were a slave in the land of Egypt and
the LORD your God redeemed you; therefore, I am commanding you to do this thing today. 16However, if the servant says
to you, "I do not want to leave you," because he loves you and
your household, since he is well off with you, 17you shall take
an awl and pierce a hole through his ear to the door. Then he
will become your servant permanently (this applies to your
female servant as well). 18You should not consider it difficult
to let him go free, for he will have served you for six years, twice
the time of a hired worker; the LORD your God will bless you
in everything you do.

GIVING GOD THE BEST

19You must set apart for the LORD your God every firstborn
male born to your herds and flocks. You must not work the
firstborn of your bulls or shear the firstborn of your flocks.
20You and your household must eat them annually before the
LORD your God in the place he chooses. 21If one of them has
any kind of blemish—lameness, blindness, or anything else—
you may not offer it as a sacrifice to the LORD your God. 22You
may eat it in your villages, whether you are ritually impure
or clean, just as you would eat a gazelle or an ibex. 23Howev-
er, you must not eat its blood; you must pour it out on the
ground like water.

THE PASSOVER

16 Observe the month Abib and keep the Passover to the
LORD your God, for in that month he brought you out of
Egypt by night. 2You must sacrifice the Passover animal (from
the flock or the herd) to the LORD your God in the place where
he chooses to locate his name. 3You must not eat any yeast with
it; for seven days you must eat bread made without yeast, as
symbolic of affliction, for you came out of Egypt hurriedly. You
must do this so you will remember for the rest of your lives the
day you came out of the land of Egypt. 4There must not be a
scrap of yeast within your land for seven days, nor can any of
the meat you sacrifice on the evening of the first day remain
until the next morning. 5You may not sacrifice the Passover in
just any of your villages that the LORD your God is giving you,
6but you must sacrifice it in the evening in the place where he
chooses to locate his name, at sunset, the time of day you came
out of Egypt. 7You must cook and eat it in the place the LORD
your God chooses; you may return the next morning to your
tents. 8You must eat bread made without yeast for six days. The
seventh day you are to hold an assembly for the LORD your God;
you must not do any work on that day.

15:11 Merely to give something is not sufficient; it answers not the rule nor comes up to the holy command of God, but we must open our hand wide. What we give considering our neighbor's wants and our ability should be such as may be called a liberal gift. What is meant in the text by opening the hand wide, with respect to those who are able, is explained: "Make sure you open your hand to your fellow Israelites who are needy and poor in your land." By lending here is not only meant as lending to receive again; the word "lend" in scripture is sometimes used for giving. "Do good, and lend, expecting nothing back" (Luke 6:35).

JONATHAN EDWARDS
(1703–1758)
THE COMPLETE WORKS

THE FEAST OF WEEKS

9 You must count seven weeks; you must begin to count them
from the time you begin to harvest the standing grain. 10 Then
you are to celebrate the Feast of Weeks before the LORD your
God with the voluntary offering that you will bring, in proportion to how he has blessed you. 11 You shall rejoice before him—
you, your son, your daughter, your male and female slaves, the
Levites in your villages, the resident foreigners, the orphans,
and the widows among you—in the place where the LORD chooses to locate his name. 12 Furthermore, remember that you were
a slave in Egypt, and so be careful to observe these statutes.

THE FEAST OF TEMPORARY SHELTERS

13 You must celebrate the Feast of Shelters for seven days, at the
time of the grain and grape harvest. 14 You are to rejoice in your
festival, you, your son, your daughter, your male and female slaves,
the Levites, the resident foreigners, the orphans, and the widows
who are in your villages. 15 You are to celebrate the festival seven
days before the LORD your God in the place he chooses, for he
will bless you in all your productivity and in whatever you do; so
you will indeed rejoice! 16 Three times a year all your males must
appear before the LORD your God in the place he chooses for the
Feast of Unleavened Bread, the Feast of Weeks, and the Feast of
Shelters; and they must not appear before him empty-handed.
17 Every one of you must give as you are able, according to the
blessing of the LORD your God that he has given you.

16:18—17:13 Those who hear cases should decide them justly and not accept bribes at the expense of the innocent, "for bribes blind the eyes of the wise and distort the words of the righteous." Otherwise, while they are acquiring money, they may lose their soul. No one obtains unjust profit without a just loss. Where the gain is, there is the loss: a gain in the money coffer but a loss in the conscience.

CAESARIUS OF ARLES
(C. 468–542)
SERMONS

PROVISION FOR JUSTICE

18 You must appoint judges and civil servants for each tribe in
all your villages that the LORD your God is giving you, and they
must judge the people fairly. 19 You must not pervert justice or
show favor. Do not take a bribe, for bribes blind the eyes of the
wise and distort the words of the righteous. 20 You must pursue
justice alone so that you may live and inherit the land the LORD
your God is giving you.

EXAMPLES OF LEGAL CASES

21 You must not plant any kind of tree as a sacred Asherah pole
near the altar of the LORD your God which you build for yourself. 22 You must not erect a sacred pillar, a thing the LORD your
God detests.

17 You must not sacrifice to him a bull or sheep that has a
blemish or any other defect, because that is considered
offensive to the LORD your God. 2 Suppose a man or woman is
discovered among you in one of your villages that the LORD
your God is giving you who sins before the LORD your God and
breaks his covenant 3 by serving other gods and worshiping
them—the sun, moon, or any other heavenly bodies that I have
not permitted you to worship. 4 When it is reported to you and
you hear about it, you must investigate carefully. If it is indeed
true that such a disgraceful thing is being done in Israel, 5 you
must bring to your city gates that man or woman who has done
this wicked thing—that very man or woman—and you must
stone that person to death. 6 At the testimony of two or three
witnesses the person must be executed. They cannot be put
to death on the testimony of only one witness. 7 The witnesses
must be first to begin the execution, and then all the people
are to join in afterward. In this way you will purge the evil from
among you.

APPEAL TO A HIGHER COURT

8 If a matter is too difficult for you to judge—bloodshed, legal
claim, or assault—matters of controversy in your villages—you
must leave there and go up to the place the LORD your God chooses. 9 You will go to the Levitical priests and the judge in office in
those days and seek a solution; they will render a verdict. 10 You
must then do as they have determined at that place the LORD
chooses. Be careful to do just as you are taught. 11 You must do
what you are instructed, and the verdict they pronounce to you,
without fail. Do not deviate right or left from what they tell you.
12 The person who pays no attention to the priest currently serving the LORD your God there, or to the judge—that person must
die, so that you may purge evil from Israel. 13 Then all the people
will hear and be afraid, and not be so presumptuous again.

PROVISION FOR KINGSHIP

14 When you come to the land the LORD your God is giving you
and take it over and live in it and then say, "I will select a king
like all the nations surrounding me," 15 you must select without
fail a king whom the LORD your God chooses. From among your
fellow citizens you must appoint a king—you may not designate
a foreigner who is not one of your fellow Israelites. 16 Moreover,
he must not accumulate horses for himself or allow the people
to return to Egypt to do so, for the LORD has said you must never
again return that way. 17 Furthermore, he must not marry many
wives lest his affections turn aside, and he must not accumulate much silver and gold. 18 When he sits on his royal throne
he must make a copy of this law on a scroll given to him by the
Levitical priests. 19 It must be with him constantly, and he must
read it as long as he lives, so that he may learn to revere the
LORD his God and observe all the words of this law and these
statutes and carry them out. 20 Then he will not exalt himself
above his fellow citizens or turn from the commandments to
the right or left, and he and his descendants will enjoy many
years ruling over his kingdom in Israel.

PROVISION FOR PRIESTS AND LEVITES

18 The Levitical priests—indeed, the entire tribe of Levi—will
have no allotment or inheritance with Israel; they may eat
the burnt offerings of the LORD and of his inheritance. 2 They will
have no inheritance in the midst of their fellow Israelites; the
LORD alone is their inheritance, just as he had told them. 3 This
shall be the priests' fair allotment from the people who offer
sacrifices, whether bull or sheep—they must give to the priest
the shoulder, the jowls, and the stomach. 4 You must give them
the best of your grain, new wine, and olive oil, as well as the best
of your wool when you shear your flocks. 5 For the LORD your God
has chosen them and their sons from all your tribes to stand and
serve in his name permanently. 6 Suppose a Levite comes by his
own free will from one of your villages, from any part of Israel
where he is living, to the place the LORD chooses 7 and serves in the
name of the LORD his God like his fellow Levites who stand there
before the LORD. 8 He must eat the same share they do, despite
any profits he may gain from the sale of his family's inheritance.

PROHIBITED OCCULT PRACTICES

9 When you enter the land the LORD your God is giving you, you
must not learn the abhorrent practices of those nations. 10 There
must never be found among you anyone who sacrifices his son or

daughter in the fire, anyone who practices divination, an omen reader, a soothsayer, a sorcerer, [11]one who casts spells, one who conjures up spirits, a practitioner of the occult, or a necromancer. [12]Whoever does these things is abhorrent to the LORD, and because of these detestable things the LORD your God is about to drive them out from before you. [13]You must be blameless before the LORD your God. [14]Those nations that you are about to dispossess listen to omen readers and diviners, but the LORD your God has not given you permission to do such things.

[15]The LORD your God will raise up for you a prophet like me from among you—from your fellow Israelites; you must listen to him. [16]This accords with what happened at Horeb in the day of the assembly. You asked the LORD your God: "Please do not make us hear the voice of the LORD our God anymore or see this great fire anymore lest we die." [17]The LORD then said to me, "What they have said is good. [18]I will raise up a prophet like you for them from among their fellow Israelites. I will put my words in his mouth and he will speak to them whatever I command. [19]I will personally hold responsible anyone who then pays no attention to the words that prophet speaks in my name.

[20]"But if any prophet presumes to speak anything in my name that I have not authorized him to speak, or speaks in the name of other gods, that prophet must die. [21]Now if you say to yourselves, 'How can we tell that a message is not from the LORD?'—[22]whenever a prophet speaks in my name and the prediction is not fulfilled, then I have not spoken it; the prophet has presumed to speak it, so you need not fear him."

18:15 When in the meantime Moses perceived that the vice of sacrificing to idols had been deeply ingrained into the people from their association with the Egyptians, he allowed them indeed to sacrifice but permitted it to be done only to God, that by any means he might cut off one-half of the deeply ingrained evil, leaving the other half to be corrected by another and at a future time; by him, namely, concerning whom he said himself, "The LORD your God will raise up for you a prophet like me from among you—from your fellow Israelites; you must listen to him." Whosoever shall not hear that prophet, his soul shall be cut off from his people.

CLEMENT OF ROME **(D. 99)**
RECOGNITIONS

LAWS CONCERNING MANSLAUGHTER

19 When the LORD your God destroys the nations whose land he is about to give you and you dispossess them and settle in their cities and houses, [2]you must set apart for yourselves three cities in the middle of your land that the LORD your God is giving you as a possession. [3]You shall build a roadway and divide into thirds the whole extent of your land that the LORD your God is providing as your inheritance; anyone who kills another person should flee to the closest of these cities. [4]Now this is the law pertaining to one who flees there in order to live, if he has accidentally killed another without hating him at the time of the accident. [5]Suppose he goes with someone else to the forest to cut wood and when he raises the ax to cut the tree, the ax head flies loose from the handle and strikes his fellow worker so hard that he dies. The person responsible may then flee to one of these cities to save himself. [6]Otherwise the blood avenger will chase after the killer in the heat of his anger, eventually overtake him, and kill him, though this is not a capital case since he did not hate him at the time of the accident. [7]Therefore, I am commanding you to set apart for yourselves three cities. [8]If the LORD your God enlarges your borders as he promised your ancestors and gives you all the land he pledged to them, [9]and then you are careful to observe all these commandments I am giving you today (namely, to love the LORD your God and to always walk in his ways), then you must add three more cities to these three. [10]You must not shed innocent blood in your land that the LORD your God is giving you as an inheritance, for that would make you guilty. [11]However, suppose a person hates someone else and stalks him, attacks him, kills him, and then flees to one of these cities. [12]The elders of his own city must send for him and remove him from there to deliver him

over to the blood avenger to die. 13 You must not pity him, but purge from Israel the guilt of shedding innocent blood, so that it may go well with you.

LAWS CONCERNING WITNESSES

14 You must not encroach on your neighbor's property, which will have been defined in the inheritance you will obtain in the land the LORD your God is giving you.

15 A single witness may not testify against another person for any trespass or sin that he commits. A matter may be legally established only on the testimony of two or three witnesses. 16 If a false witness testifies against another person and accuses him of a crime, 17 then both parties to the controversy must stand before the LORD, that is, before the priests and judges who will be in office in those days. 18 The judges will thoroughly investigate the matter, and if the witness should prove to be false and to have given false testimony against the accused, 19 you must do to him what he had intended to do to the accused. In this way you will purge the evil from among you. 20 The rest of the people will hear and become afraid to keep doing such evil among you. 21 You must not show pity; the principle will be a life for a life, an eye for an eye, a tooth for a tooth, a hand for a hand, and a foot for a foot.

LAWS CONCERNING WAR WITH DISTANT ENEMIES

20 When you go to war against your enemies and see chariotry and troops who outnumber you, do not be afraid of them, for the LORD your God, who brought you up out of the land of Egypt, is with you. 2 As you move forward for battle, the priest will approach and say to the soldiers, 3 "Listen, Israel! Today you are moving forward to do battle with your enemies. Do not be fainthearted. Do not fear and tremble or be terrified because of them, 4 for the LORD your God goes with you to fight on your behalf against your enemies to give you victory." 5 Moreover, the officers are to say to the troops, "Who among you has built a new house and not dedicated it? He may go home, lest he die in battle and someone else dedicate it. 6 Or who among you has planted a vineyard and not benefited from it? He may go home, lest he die in battle and someone else benefit from it. 7 Or who among you has become engaged to a woman but has not married her? He may go home, lest he die in battle and someone else marry her." 8 In addition, the officers are to say to the troops, "Who among you is afraid and fainthearted? He may go home so that he will not make his fellow soldier's heart as fearful as his own." 9 Then, when the officers have finished speaking, they must appoint unit commanders to lead the troops.

10 When you approach a city to wage war against it, offer it terms of peace. 11 If it accepts your terms and submits to you, all the people found in it will become your slaves. 12 If it does not accept terms of peace but makes war with you, then you are to lay siege to it. 13 The LORD your God will deliver it over to you, and you must kill every single male by the sword. 14 However, the women, little children, cattle, and anything else in the city—all its plunder—you may take for yourselves as spoil. You may take from your enemies the plunder that the LORD your God has given you. 15 This is how you are to deal with all those cities located far from you, those that do not belong to these nearby nations.

19:15–21 A single witness, though he speaks truth, is not to be accepted for the condemnation of another man, but if he be convicted of false witness, this is sufficient for his own condemnation.

JOHN WESLEY **(1703–1791)**
EXPLANATORY NOTES ON THE BIBLE

20:5–7 Since it is expedient for the state that vineyards should be sown or planted and that houses should be built, while men would not address themselves to these duties with sufficient alacrity unless encouraged by the hope of enjoying them, God gives them the privilege of exemption from fighting. He makes also the same appointment as to possessors of vineyards if they have not yet tasted of the fruit of their labor, and they will not have men torn from their affianced wives until they have enjoyed their embraces.

JOHN CALVIN **(1509–1564)**
COMPLETE COMMENTARY ON THE BIBLE

LAWS CONCERNING WAR WITH CANAANITE NATIONS

16 As for the cities of these peoples that the LORD your God is going to give you as an inheritance, you must not allow a single living thing to survive. 17 Instead you must utterly annihilate them—the Hittites, Amorites, Canaanites, Perizzites, Hivites, and Jebusites—just as the LORD your God has commanded you, 18 so that they cannot teach you all the abhorrent ways they worship their gods, causing you to sin against the LORD your God. 19 If you besiege a city for a long time while attempting to capture it, you must not chop down its trees, for you may eat fruit from them and should not cut them down. A tree in the field is not human that you should besiege it! 20 However, you may chop down any tree you know is not suitable for food, and you may use it to build siege works against the city that is making war with you until that city falls.

LAWS CONCERNING UNSOLVED MURDERS

21 If a homicide victim should be found lying in a field in the land the LORD your God is giving you, and no one knows who killed him, 2 your elders and judges must go out and measure how far it is to the cities in the vicinity of the corpse. 3 Then the elders of the city nearest to the corpse must take from the herd a heifer that has not been worked—that has never pulled with the yoke—4 and bring the heifer down to a wadi with flowing water, to a valley that is neither plowed nor sown. There at the wadi they are to break the heifer's neck. 5 Then the Levitical priests will approach (for the LORD your God has chosen them to serve him and to pronounce blessings in his name, and to decide every judicial verdict), 6 and all the elders of that city nearest the corpse must wash their hands over the heifer whose neck was broken in the valley. 7 Then they must proclaim, "Our hands have not spilled this blood, nor have we witnessed the crime. 8 Do not blame your people Israel whom you redeemed, O LORD, and do not hold them accountable for the bloodshed of an innocent person." Then atonement will be made for the bloodshed. 9 In this manner you will purge the guilt of innocent blood from among you, for you must do what is right before the LORD.

LAWS CONCERNING FEMALE CAPTIVES

10 When you go out to do battle with your enemies and the LORD your God allows you to prevail and you take prisoners, 11 if you should see among them an attractive woman whom you wish to take as a wife, 12 you may bring her back to your house. She must shave her head, trim her nails, 13 discard the clothing she was wearing when captured, and stay in your house, lamenting for her father and mother for a full month. After that you may sleep with her and become her husband and she your wife. 14 If you are not pleased with her, then you must let her go where she pleases. You cannot in any case sell her; you must not take advantage of her, since you have already humiliated her.

LAWS CONCERNING CHILDREN

15 Suppose a man has two wives, one whom he loves more than the other, and they both bear him sons, with the firstborn being the child of the less-loved wife. 16 In the day he divides his inheritance he must not appoint as firstborn the son of the favorite wife in place of the other wife's son who is actually the

firstborn. 17Rather, he must acknowledge the son of the less-
loved wife as firstborn and give him the double portion of all
he has, for that son is the beginning of his father's procreative
power—to him should go the right of the firstborn.
18If a person has a stubborn, rebellious son who pays no attention to his father or mother, and they discipline him to no
avail, 19his father and mother must seize him and bring him
to the elders at the gate of his city. 20They must declare to the
elders of his city, "Our son is stubborn and rebellious and pays
no attention to what we say—he is a glutton and drunkard."
21Then all the men of his city must stone him to death. In this
way you will purge wickedness from among you, and all Israel
will hear about it and be afraid.

DISPOSITION OF A CRIMINAL'S REMAINS

22If a person commits a sin punishable by death and is executed,
and you hang the corpse on a tree, 23his body must not remain
all night on the tree; instead you must make certain you bury
him that same day, for the one who is left exposed on a tree is
cursed by God. You must not defile your land that the LORD
your God is giving you as an inheritance.

LAWS CONCERNING PRESERVATION OF LIFE

22 When you see your neighbor's ox or sheep going astray,
do not ignore it; you must return it without fail to your
neighbor. 2If the owner does not live near you or you do not
know who the owner is, then you must corral the animal at
your house and let it stay with you until the owner looks for
it; then you must return it to him. 3You shall do the same to
his donkey, his clothes, or anything else your neighbor has lost
and you have found; you must not refuse to get involved. 4When
you see your neighbor's donkey or ox fallen along the road, do
not ignore it; instead, you must be sure to help him get the
animal on its feet again.
5A woman must not wear men's clothing, nor should a man
dress up in women's clothing, for anyone who does this is offensive to the LORD your God.
6If you happen to notice a bird's nest along the road, whether
in a tree or on the ground, and there are chicks or eggs with the
mother bird sitting on them, you must not take away a mother
that is with her young. 7You must be sure to let the mother go,
but you may take the young for yourself. Do this so that it may
go well with you and you may have a long life.
8If you build a new house, you must construct a guardrail
around your roof to avoid being culpable in the event someone
should fall from it.

ILLUSTRATIONS OF THE PRINCIPLE OF PURITY

9You must not plant your vineyard with two kinds of seed; otherwise the entire yield, both of the seed you plant and the produce
of the vineyard, will be defiled. 10You must not plow with an ox
and a donkey harnessed together. 11You must not wear clothing
made with wool and linen meshed together. 12You shall make
yourselves tassels for the four corners of the clothing you wear.

PURITY IN THE MARRIAGE RELATIONSHIP

13Suppose a man marries a woman, sleeps with her, and then
rejects her, 14accusing her of impropriety and defaming her reputation by saying, "I married this woman but when I approached

---

21:22–23 If the Lord's death is the ransom of all, how would he have called us to him had he not been crucified? For it is only on the cross that a man dies with his hands spread out. Therefore it was fitting for the Lord to bear this also and to spread out his hands, that with the one he might draw the ancient people and with the other those from the Gentiles and unite both in himself. For as he offered his body to death on behalf of all, so by it he once more made ready the way up into the heavens.

ATHANASIUS **(C. 296–373)**
ON THE INCARNATION

22:13–30 It appears how greatly God abominates adultery since he proscribes capital punishment against it. And assuredly, since marriage is a covenant consecrated by God, its profanation is in no way tolerable. Those who boast themselves of the Christian name are so tender and remiss that they visit this execrable offense with a very light reproof. Although the disloyalty of husband and wife are not punished alike by human tribunals, still, since they are under mutual obligation to each other, God will take vengeance on them both.

JOHN CALVIN **(1509–1564)**
COMPLETE COMMENTARY ON THE BIBLE

her for marital relations I discovered she was not a virgin!" [15]Then
the father and mother of the young woman must produce the
evidence of virginity for the elders of the city at the gate. [16]The
young woman's father must say to the elders, "I gave my daughter
to this man and he has rejected her. [17]Moreover, he has raised
accusations of impropriety by saying, 'I discovered your daughter
was not a virgin,' but this is the evidence of my daughter's virginity!" The cloth must then be spread out before the city's elders.
[18]The elders of that city must then seize the man and punish
him. [19]They will fine him 100 shekels of silver and give them to
the young woman's father, for the man who made the accusation
ruined the reputation of an Israelite virgin. She will then become
his wife, and he may never divorce her as long as he lives.

[20]But if the accusation is true and the young woman was not
a virgin, [21]the men of her city must bring the young woman
to the door of her father's house and stone her to death, for
she has done a disgraceful thing in Israel by behaving like a
prostitute while living in her father's house. In this way you
will purge the evil from among you.

[22]If a man is discovered in bed with a married woman, both
the man lying in bed with the woman and the woman herself
must die; in this way you will purge the evil from Israel.

[23]If a virgin is engaged to a man and another man meets her
in the city and goes to bed with her, [24]you must bring the two of
them to the gate of that city and stone them to death, the young
woman because she did not cry out though in the city and the
man because he violated his neighbor's fiancée; in this way you
will purge evil from among you. [25]But if the man came across
the engaged woman in the field and overpowered her and raped
her, then only the rapist must die. [26]You must not do anything
to the young woman—she has done nothing deserving of death.
This case is the same as when someone attacks another person
and murders him, [27]for the man met her in the field and the
engaged woman cried out, but there was no one to rescue her.

[28]Suppose a man comes across a virgin who is not engaged
and takes hold of her and sleeps with her and they are discovered. [29]The man who has slept with her must pay her father 50
shekels of silver and she must become his wife. Because he has
humiliated her, he may never divorce her as long as he lives.

[30]A man may not marry his father's former wife and in this
way dishonor his father.

PURITY IN PUBLIC WORSHIP

23 A man with crushed or severed genitals may not enter the
assembly of the LORD. [2]A person of illegitimate birth may
not enter the assembly of the LORD; to the tenth generation
no one related to him may do so.

[3]No Ammonite or Moabite may enter the assembly of the
LORD; to the tenth generation none of their descendants shall
ever do so, [4]for they did not meet you with food and water
on the way as you came from Egypt, and furthermore, they
hired Balaam son of Beor of Pethor in Aram Naharaim to curse
you. [5]But the LORD your God refused to listen to Balaam and
changed the curse to a blessing, for the LORD your God loves
you. [6]You must not seek peace and prosperity for them through
all the ages to come. [7]You must not hate an Edomite, for he is
your relative; you must not hate an Egyptian, for you lived as
a foreigner in his land. [8]Children of the third generation born
to them may enter the assembly of the LORD.

PURITY IN PERSONAL HYGIENE

[9]When you go out as an army against your enemies, guard yourselves against anything impure. [10]If there is someone among you who is impure because of some nocturnal emission, he must leave the camp; he may not reenter it immediately. [11]When evening arrives he must wash himself with water, and then at sunset he may reenter the camp.

[12]You are to have a place outside the camp to serve as a latrine. [13]You must have a spade among your other equipment, and when you relieve yourself outside you must dig a hole with the spade and then turn and cover your excrement. [14]For the LORD your God walks about in the middle of your camp to deliver you and defeat your enemies for you. Therefore your camp should be holy, so that he does not see anything indecent among you and turn away from you.

PURITY IN THE TREATMENT OF THE UNPRIVILEGED

[15]You must not return an escaped slave to his master when he has run away to you. [16]Indeed, he may live among you in any place he chooses, in whichever of your villages he prefers; you must not oppress him.

CULTIC PROSTITUTION BANNED

[17]There must never be a sacred prostitute among the young women of Israel nor a sacred male prostitute among the young men of Israel. [18]You must never bring the pay of a female prostitute or the wage of a male prostitute into the temple of the LORD your God in fulfillment of any vow, for both of these are abhorrent to the LORD your God.

RESPECT FOR OTHERS' PROPERTY

[19]You must not charge interest on a loan to your fellow Israelite, whether on money, food, or anything else that has been loaned with interest. [20]You may lend with interest to a foreigner, but not to your fellow Israelite; if you keep this command the LORD your God will bless you in all you undertake in the land you are about to enter to possess. [21]When you make a vow to the LORD your God you must not delay in fulfilling it, for otherwise he will surely hold you accountable as a sinner. [22]If you refrain from making a vow, it will not be sinful. [23]Whatever you vow, you must be careful to do what you have promised, such as what you have vowed to the LORD your God as a freewill offering. [24]When you enter the vineyard of your neighbor you may eat as many grapes as you please, but you must not take away any in a container. [25]When you go into the ripe grain fields of your neighbor you may pluck off the kernels with your hand, but you must not use a sickle on your neighbor's ripe grain.

24 If a man marries a woman and she does not please him because he has found something indecent in her, then he may draw up a divorce document, give it to her, and evict her from his house. [2]When she has left him she may go and become someone else's wife. [3]If the second husband rejects her and then divorces her, gives her the papers, and evicts her from his house, or if the second husband who married her dies, [4]her first husband who divorced her is not permitted to remarry her after she has become ritually impure, for that is offensive to the LORD. You must not bring guilt on the land that the LORD your God is giving you as an inheritance.

23:19 It is a mark of kindly feeling to help one who has nothing, but it is a sign of a hard nature to extort more than one has given. If a person has need of your assistance because he has not enough of his own wherewith to repay a debt, is it not a wicked thing to demand under the guise of kindly feeling a larger sum from the one who has not the means to pay off a lesser amount? You free him from debt to another to bring him under your own hand, and you call that human kindliness what is but a further wickedness.

AMBROSE **(C. 339–C. 397)**
ON THE DUTIES OF THE CLERGY

5 When a man is newly married, he need not go into the army nor be obligated in any way; he must be free to stay at home for a full year and bring joy to the wife he has married.

6 One must not take either lower or upper millstones as security on a loan, for that is like taking a life itself as security.

7 If a man is found kidnapping a person from among his fellow Israelites, and regards him as mere property and sells him, that kidnapper must die. In this way you will purge the evil from among you.

RESPECT FOR HUMAN DIGNITY

8 Be careful during an outbreak of leprosy to follow precisely all that the Levitical priests instruct you; as I have commanded them, so you should do. 9 Remember what the LORD your God did to Miriam along the way after you left Egypt.

10 When you make any kind of loan to your neighbor, you may not go into his house to claim what he is offering as security. 11 You must stand outside and the person to whom you are making the loan will bring out to you what he is offering as security. 12 If the person is poor you may not use what he gives you as security for a covering. 13 You must by all means return to him at sunset the item he gave you as security so that he may sleep in his outer garment and bless you for it; it will be considered a just deed by the LORD your God.

14 You must not oppress a lowly and poor servant, whether one from among your fellow Israelites or from the resident foreigners who are living in your land and villages. 15 You must pay his wage that very day before the sun sets, for he is poor and his life depends on it. Otherwise he will cry out to the LORD against you, and you will be guilty of sin.

16 Fathers must not be put to death for what their children do, nor children for what their fathers do; each must be put to death for his own sin.

17 You must not pervert justice due a resident foreigner or an orphan, or take a widow's garment as security for a loan. 18 Remember that you were slaves in Egypt and that the LORD your God redeemed you from there; therefore I am commanding you to do all this. 19 Whenever you reap your harvest in your field and leave some unraked grain there, you must not return to get it; it should go to the resident foreigner, orphan, and widow so that the LORD your God may bless all the work you do. 20 When you beat your olive tree you must not repeat the procedure; the remaining olives belong to the resident foreigner, orphan, and widow. 21 When you gather the grapes of your vineyard you must not do so a second time; they should go to the resident foreigner, orphan, and widow. 22 Remember that you were slaves in the land of Egypt; therefore, I am commanding you to do all this.

25 If controversy arises between people, they should go to court for judgment. When the judges hear the case, they shall exonerate the innocent but condemn the guilty. 2 Then, if the guilty person is sentenced to a beating, the judge shall force him to lie down and be beaten in his presence with the number of blows his wicked behavior deserves. 3 The judge may sentence him to 40 blows, but no more. If he is struck with more than these, you might view your fellow Israelite with contempt.

4 You must not muzzle your ox when it is treading grain.

24:16 With us, according to our faith and the given rule of divine preaching, agrees the principle of truth that all are themselves held fast in their own sin; no one can become guilty for another since the Lord forewarns us, saying, "The person who sins is the one who will die. A son will not suffer for his father's iniquity, and a father will not suffer for his son's iniquity; the righteous person will be judged according to his righteousness, and the wicked person according to his wickedness" (Ezek 18:20). Reading and observing this we certainly think that no one is to be restrained from the fruit of satisfaction and the hope of peace since we know, according to the faith of the divine scriptures, God himself being their Author and exhorting in them both, that sinners are brought back to repentance, and that pardon and mercy are not denied to penitents.

CYPRIAN OF CARTHAGE
(C. 210–258)
THE EPISTLES

25:1–3 Every punishment should be carried out with solemnity, that those who see it may be filled with dread and be warned not to offend in like manner. And though the criminals must be shamed as well as put to pain for their warning and disgrace, yet care should be taken that they do not appear totally vile. Happy are those who are chastened of the Lord to humble them that they should not be condemned with the world to destruction.

MATTHEW HENRY **(1662–1714)**
COMMENTARY ON THE WHOLE BIBLE

RESPECT FOR THE SANCTITY OF OTHERS

[5]If brothers live together and one of them dies without having a son, the dead man's wife must not remarry someone outside the family. Instead, her late husband's brother must go to her, marry her, and perform the duty of a brother-in-law. [6]Then the first son she bears will continue the name of the dead brother, thus preventing his name from being blotted out of Israel. [7]But if the man does not want to marry his brother's widow, then she must go to the elders at the town gate and say, "My husband's brother refuses to preserve his brother's name in Israel; he is unwilling to perform the duty of a brother-in-law to me!" [8]Then the elders of his city must summon him and speak to him. If he persists, saying, "I don't want to marry her," [9]then his sister-in-law must approach him in view of the elders, remove his sandal from his foot, and spit in his face. She will then respond, "Thus may it be done to any man who does not maintain his brother's family line!" [10]His family name will be referred to in Israel as "the family of the one whose sandal was removed."

[11]If two men get into a hand-to-hand fight, and the wife of one of them gets involved to help her husband against his attacker, and she reaches out her hand and grabs his private parts, [12]then you must cut off her hand—do not pity her.

[13]You must not have in your bag different stone weights, a heavy and a light one. [14]You must not have in your house different measuring containers, a large and a small one. [15]You must have an accurate and correct stone weight and an accurate and correct measuring container, so that your life may be extended in the land the LORD your God is about to give you. [16]For anyone who acts dishonestly in these ways is abhorrent to the LORD your God.

TREATMENT OF THE AMALEKITES

[17]Remember what the Amalekites did to you on your way from Egypt, [18]how they met you along the way and cut off all your stragglers in the rear of the march when you were exhausted and tired; they were unafraid of God. [19]So when the LORD your God gives you relief from all the enemies who surround you in the land he is giving you as an inheritance, you must wipe out the memory of the Amalekites from under heaven—do not forget!

PRESENTATION OF THE FIRSTFRUITS

26 When you enter the land that the LORD your God is giving you as an inheritance, and you occupy it and live in it, [2]you must take the first of all the ground's produce you harvest from the land the LORD your God is giving you, place it in a basket, and go to the place where he chooses to locate his name. [3]You must go to the priest in office at that time and say to him, "I declare today to the LORD your God that I have come into the land that the LORD promised to our ancestors to give us." [4]The priest will then take the basket from you and set it before the altar of the LORD your God. [5]Then you must affirm before the LORD your God, "A wandering Aramean was my ancestor, and he went down to Egypt and lived there as a foreigner with a household few in number, but there he became a great, powerful, and numerous people. [6]But the Egyptians mistreated and oppressed us, forcing us to do burdensome labor. [7]So we cried out to the LORD, the God of our ancestors, and he heard us and saw our humiliation, toil, and oppression. [8]Therefore the LORD brought us out of Egypt with tremendous strength and power,

26:1–15 No branch of the ceremonial code was more reasonable and instructive than the oblation of the firstfruits to God, who has every claim of gratitude from his creatures. The Israelite dwelling in a climate the most salubrious, and on a soil the most fertile that can be conceived, would find his piety very much increased by the oblation of so small a tribute to his Maker, for reflection must accompany his gift. The Lord, conformably to his promise and oath, had preserved Jacob unhurt from a thousand dangers and then made him a great nation controlling all the east. Surely this family was in covenant with God; surely Providence had watched for their welfare; surely the strong arm of God had been their salvation, or they had never escaped from Egypt and conquered Canaan.

JOSEPH SUTCLIFFE
(1762–1856)
COMMENTARY ON THE OLD AND NEW TESTAMENT

as well as with great awe-inspiring signs and wonders. [9]Then he brought us to this place and gave us this land, a land flowing with milk and honey. [10]So now, look! I have brought the first of the ground's produce that you, LORD, have given me." Then you must set it down before the LORD your God and worship before him. [11]You will celebrate all the good things that the LORD your God has given you and your family, along with the Levites and the resident foreigners among you.

PRESENTATION OF THE THIRD-YEAR TITHE

[12]When you finish tithing all your income in the third year (the year of tithing), you must give it to the Levites, the resident foreigners, the orphans, and the widows so that they may eat to their satisfaction in your villages. [13]Then you shall say before the LORD your God, "I have removed the sacred offering from my house and given it to the Levites, the resident foreigners, the orphans, and the widows just as you have commanded me. I have not violated or forgotten your commandments. [14]I have not eaten anything when I was in mourning, or removed any of it while ceremonially unclean, or offered any of it to the dead; I have obeyed you and have done everything you have commanded me. [15]Look down from your holy dwelling place in heaven and bless your people Israel and the land you have given us, just as you promised our ancestors—a land flowing with milk and honey."

NARRATIVE INTERLUDE

[16]Today the LORD your God is commanding you to keep these statutes and ordinances, something you must do with all your heart and soul. [17]Today you have declared the LORD to be your God, and that you will walk in his ways, keep his statutes, commandments, and ordinances, and obey him. [18]And today the LORD has declared you to be his special people (as he already promised you) so you may keep all his commandments. [19]Then he will elevate you above all the nations he has made and you will receive praise, fame, and honor. You will be a people holy to the LORD your God, as he has said.

THE ASSEMBLY AT SHECHEM

27 Then Moses and the elders of Israel commanded the people: "Pay attention to all the commandments I am giving you today. [2]When you cross the Jordan River to the land the LORD your God is giving you, you must erect great stones and cover them with plaster. [3]Then you must inscribe on them all the words of this law when you cross over, so that you may enter the land the LORD your God is giving you, a land flowing with milk and honey just as the LORD, the God of your ancestors, said to you. [4]So when you cross the Jordan you must erect on Mount Ebal these stones about which I am commanding you today, and you must cover them with plaster. [5]Then you must build an altar there to the LORD your God, an altar of stones—do not use an iron tool on them. [6]You must build the altar of the LORD your God with whole stones and offer burnt offerings on it to the LORD your God. [7]Also you must offer fellowship offerings and eat them there, rejoicing before the LORD your God. [8]You must inscribe on the stones all the words of this law, making them clear."

[9]Then Moses and the Levitical priests spoke to all Israel: "Be quiet and pay attention, Israel. Today you have become the

27:1–10 Since Canaan is given only by promise, it must be held by obedience. The law is written to signify that a curse was due to the violators of it, and that no person could expect justification from the works of the law by the sentence whereof all people are justly accused as being all guilty of the transgression of it in one kind and degree or other. Here the sacrifices are to be offered to show that there is no way to be delivered from this curse but by the blood of Christ, which all these sacrifices did typify, and by Christ's being made a curse for us.

JOHN WESLEY (1703–1791)
EXPLANATORY NOTES ON THE BIBLE

people of the LORD your God. 10You must obey him and keep
his commandments and statutes that I am giving you today."
11Moreover, Moses commanded the people that day: 12"The
following tribes must stand to bless the people on Mount Gerizim when you cross the Jordan: Simeon, Levi, Judah, Issachar,
Joseph, and Benjamin. 13And these other tribes must stand for
the curse on Mount Ebal: Reuben, Gad, Asher, Zebulun, Dan,
and Naphtali.

THE COVENANT CURSES

14"The Levites will call out to every Israelite with a loud voice:
15'Cursed is the one who makes a carved or metal image—
something abhorrent to the LORD, the work of the craftsman—
and sets it up in a secret place.' Then all the people will say,
'Amen!' 16'Cursed is the one who disrespects his father and
mother.' Then all the people will say, 'Amen!' 17'Cursed is the
one who moves his neighbor's boundary marker.' Then all the
people will say, 'Amen!' 18'Cursed is the one who misleads a
blind person on the road.' Then all the people will say, 'Amen!'
19'Cursed is the one who perverts justice for the resident foreigner, the orphan, and the widow.' Then all the people will say,
'Amen!' 20'Cursed is the one who goes to bed with his father's
former wife, for he dishonors his father.' Then all the people will
say, 'Amen!' 21'Cursed is the one who commits bestiality.' Then
all the people will say, 'Amen!' 22'Cursed is the one who goes to
bed with his sister, the daughter of either his father or mother.'
Then all the people will say, 'Amen!' 23'Cursed is the one who
goes to bed with his mother-in-law.' Then all the people will say,
'Amen!' 24'Cursed is the one who kills his neighbor in private.'
Then all the people will say, 'Amen!' 25'Cursed is the one who
takes a bribe to kill an innocent person.' Then all the people
will say, 'Amen!' 26'Cursed is the one who refuses to keep the
words of this law.' Then all the people will say, 'Amen!'

THE COVENANT BLESSINGS

28 "If you indeed obey the LORD your God and are careful
to observe all his commandments I am giving you today,
the LORD your God will elevate you above all the nations of
the earth. 2All these blessings will come to you in abundance
if you obey the LORD your God: 3You will be blessed in the city
and blessed in the field. 4Your children will be blessed, as well
as the produce of your soil, the offspring of your livestock, the
calves of your herds, and the lambs of your flocks. 5Your basket and your mixing bowl will be blessed. 6You will be blessed
when you come in and blessed when you go out. 7The LORD will
cause your enemies who attack you to be struck down before
you; they will attack you from one direction but flee from you
in seven different directions. 8The LORD will decree blessing
for you with respect to your barns and in everything you do—
yes, he will bless you in the land he is giving you. 9The LORD
will designate you as his holy people just as he promised you,
if you keep his commandments and obey him. 10Then all the
peoples of the earth will see that you belong to the LORD, and
they will respect you. 11The LORD will greatly multiply your
children, the offspring of your livestock, and the produce of
your soil in the land that he promised your ancestors he would
give you. 12The LORD will open for you his good treasure house,
the heavens, to give you rain for the land in its season and to
bless all you do; you will lend to many nations but you will not

borrow from any. [13]The LORD will make you the head and not
the tail, and you will always end up at the top and not at the
bottom, if you obey his commandments that I am urging you
today to be careful to do. [14]But you must not turn away from all
the commandments I am giving you today, to either the right
or left, nor pursue other gods and worship them.

CURSES AS REVERSAL OF BLESSINGS

[15]"But if you ignore the LORD your God and are not careful to
keep all his commandments and statutes I am giving you today,
then all these curses will come upon you in full force: [16]You will
be cursed in the city and cursed in the field. [17]Your basket and
your mixing bowl will be cursed. [18]Your children will be cursed,
as well as the produce of your soil, the calves of your herds, and
the lambs of your flocks. [19]You will be cursed when you come
in and cursed when you go out.

CURSES BY DISEASE AND DROUGHT

[20]"The LORD will send on you a curse, confusing you and opposing you in everything you undertake until you are destroyed
and quickly perish because of the evil of your deeds, in that
you have forsaken me. [21]The LORD will plague you with deadly
diseases until he has completely removed you from the land you
are about to possess. [22]He will afflict you with weakness, fever,
inflammation, infection, sword, blight, and mildew; these will
attack you until you perish. [23]The sky above your heads will be
bronze and the earth beneath you iron. [24]The LORD will make
the rain of your land powder and dust; it will come down on
you from the sky until you are destroyed.

CURSES BY DEFEAT AND DEPORTATION

[25]"The LORD will allow you to be struck down before your
enemies; you will attack them from one direction but flee
from them in seven directions and will become an object of
terror to all the kingdoms of the earth. [26]Your carcasses will
be food for every bird of the sky and wild animal of the earth,
and there will be no one to chase them off. [27]The LORD will
afflict you with the boils of Egypt and with tumors, eczema,
and scabies, all of which cannot be healed. [28]The LORD will
also subject you to madness, blindness, and confusion of mind.
[29]You will feel your way along at noon like the blind person
does in darkness and you will not succeed in anything you
do; you will be constantly oppressed and continually robbed,
with no one to save you. [30]You will be engaged to a woman,
and another man will rape her. You will build a house but not
live in it. You will plant a vineyard but not even begin to use
it. [31]Your ox will be slaughtered before your very eyes, but
you will not eat of it. Your donkey will be stolen from you as
you watch and will not be returned to you. Your flock of sheep
will be given to your enemies, and there will be no one to save
you. [32]Your sons and daughters will be given to another people
while you look on in vain all day, and you will be powerless to
do anything about it. [33]As for the produce of your land and
all your labor, a people you do not know will consume it, and
you will be nothing but oppressed and crushed for the rest of
your lives. [34]You will go insane from seeing all this. [35]The LORD
will afflict you in your knees and on your legs with painful,
incurable boils—from the soles of your feet to the top of your
head. [36]The LORD will force you and your king whom you will

28:15–68 Many men and women in discontented moods are mad kinds of people, and though you may please yourself in such a mad kind of behavior, yet know that it is a curse of God on people to be given up to a kind of madness for evils that they suppose are upon them and that they fear. God here threatens to bring his curse upon them as to make them a wonder and a sign to others. Why? Because they served not the Lord with joyfulness of heart. Oh, how far are you then who has a murmuring heart from serving the Lord with joyfulness?

JEREMIAH BURROUGHS
(1599–1646)
THE RARE JEWEL OF CHRISTIAN CONTENTMENT

appoint over you to go away to a people whom you and your
ancestors have not known, and you will serve other gods of
wood and stone there. 37You will become an occasion of horror,
a proverb, and an object of ridicule to all the peoples to whom
the LORD will drive you.

THE CURSE OF REVERSED STATUS

38"You will take much seed to the field but gather little harvest, because locusts will consume it. 39You will plant vineyards
and cultivate them, but you will not drink wine or gather in
grapes, because worms will eat them. 40You will have olive trees
throughout your territory, but you will not anoint yourself with
olive oil, because the olives will drop off the trees while still
unripe. 41You will bear sons and daughters but not keep them,
because they will be taken into captivity. 42Whirring locusts
will take over every tree and all the produce of your soil. 43The
resident foreigners who reside among you will become higher and higher over you, and you will become lower and lower.
44They will lend to you, but you will not lend to them; they will
become the head, and you will become the tail!

45"All these curses will fall on you, pursuing and overtaking
you until you are destroyed, because you would not obey the
LORD your God by keeping his commandments and statutes
that he has given you. 46These curses will be a perpetual sign
and wonder with reference to you and your descendants.

THE CURSE OF MILITARY SIEGE

47"Because you have not served the LORD your God joyfully and
wholeheartedly with the abundance of everything you have,
48instead in hunger, thirst, nakedness, and poverty you will
serve your enemies whom the LORD will send against you. They
will place an iron yoke on your neck until they have destroyed
you. 49The LORD will raise up a distant nation against you, one
from the other side of the earth as the eagle flies, a nation
whose language you will not understand, 50a nation of stern
appearance that will have no regard for the elderly or pity for
the young. 51They will devour the offspring of your livestock and
the produce of your soil until you are destroyed. They will not
leave you with any grain, new wine, olive oil, calves of your herds,
or lambs of your flocks until they have destroyed you. 52They
will besiege all of your villages until all of your high and fortified
walls collapse—those in which you put your confidence throughout the land. They will besiege all your villages throughout the
land the LORD your God has given you. 53You will then eat your
own offspring, the flesh of the sons and daughters the LORD
your God has given you, because of the severity of the siege
by which your enemies will constrict you. 54The man among
you who is by nature tender and sensitive will turn against his
brother, his beloved wife, and his remaining children. 55He will
withhold from all of them his children's flesh that he is eating
(since there is nothing else left), because of the severity of the
siege by which your enemy will constrict you in your villages.
56Likewise, the most tender and delicate of your women, who
would never think of putting even the sole of her foot on the
ground because of her daintiness, will turn against her beloved
husband, her sons and daughters, 57and will secretly eat her
afterbirth and her newborn children (since she has nothing
else), because of the severity of the siege by which your enemy
will constrict you in your villages.

THE CURSE OF COVENANT TERMINATION

[58]“If you refuse to obey all the words of this law, the things written in this scroll, and refuse to fear this glorious and awesome
name, the LORD your God, [59]then the LORD will increase your
punishments and those of your descendants—great and long-
lasting afflictions and severe, enduring illnesses. [60]He will infect
you with all the diseases of Egypt that you dreaded, and they will
persistently afflict you. [61]Moreover, the LORD will bring upon you
every kind of sickness and plague not mentioned in this scroll
of commandments, until you have perished. [62]There will be very
few of you left, though at one time you were as numerous as the
stars in the sky, because you will have disobeyed the LORD your
God. [63]This is what will happen: Just as the LORD delighted to do
good for you and make you numerous, so he will also take delight
in destroying and decimating you. You will be uprooted from the
land you are about to possess. [64]The LORD will scatter you among
all nations, from one end of the earth to the other. There you will
worship other gods that neither you nor your ancestors have
known, gods of wood and stone. [65]Among those nations you will
have no rest, nor will there be a place of peaceful rest for the soles
of your feet, for there the LORD will give you an anxious heart,
failing eyesight, and a spirit of despair. [66]Your life will hang in
doubt before you; you will be terrified by night and day and will
have no certainty of surviving from one day to the next. [67]In the
morning you will say, ‘If only it were evening!’ And in the evening
you will say, ‘I wish it were morning!’ because of the things you will
fear and the things you will see. [68]Then the LORD will make you
return to Egypt by ship, over a route I said to you that you would
never see again. There you will sell yourselves to your enemies
as male and female slaves, but no one will buy you.”

NARRATIVE INTERLUDE

29 These are the words of the covenant that the LORD commanded Moses to make with the people of Israel in the
land of Moab, in addition to the covenant he had made with
them at Horeb.

29:1–21 The national covenant made with Israel not only typified the covenant of grace made with true believers, but it also represented the outward dispensation of the gospel. Those who have been enabled to consent to the Lord’s new covenant of mercy and grace in Jesus Christ and to give up themselves to be his people should embrace every opportunity of renewing their open profession of relation to him, and their obligation to him, as the God of salvation, walking according thereto.

MATTHEW HENRY **(1662–1714)**
COMMENTARY ON THE WHOLE BIBLE

THE EXODUS, WANDERING, AND CONQUEST REVIEWED

[2]Moses proclaimed to all Israel as follows: “You have seen all
that the LORD did in the land of Egypt to Pharaoh, all his servants, and his land. [3]Your eyes have seen the great judgments,
those signs and mighty wonders. [4]But to this very day the LORD
has not given you an understanding mind, perceptive eyes, or
discerning ears! [5]I have led you through the wilderness for 40
years. Your clothing has not worn out nor have your sandals
deteriorated. [6]You have eaten no bread and drunk no wine
or beer—all so that you might know that I am the LORD your
God! [7]When you came to this place King Sihon of Heshbon
and King Og of Bashan came out to make war and we defeated
them. [8]Then we took their land and gave it as an inheritance
to Reuben, Gad, and half the tribe of Manasseh.

THE PRESENT COVENANT SETTING

[9]“Therefore, keep the terms of this covenant and obey them
so that you may be successful in everything you do. [10]You are
standing today, all of you, before the LORD your God—the heads
of your tribes, your elders, your officials, every Israelite man,
[11]your infants, your wives, and the resident foreigners living in

your encampment, those who chop wood and those who carry water—[12]so that you may enter by oath into the covenant the LORD your God is making with you today. [13]Today he will affirm that you are his people and that he is your God, just as he promised you and as he swore by oath to your ancestors Abraham, Isaac, and Jacob. [14]It is not with you alone that I am making this covenant by oath, [15]but with whoever stands with us here today before the LORD our God as well as those not with us here today.

THE RESULTS OF DISOBEDIENCE

[16]"(For you know how we lived in the land of Egypt and how we crossed through the nations as we traveled. [17]You have seen their detestable things and idols of wood, stone, silver, and gold.) [18]Beware that the heart of no man, woman, clan, or tribe among you turns away from the LORD our God today to pursue and serve the gods of those nations; beware that there is among you no root producing poisonous and bitter fruit. [19]When such a person hears the words of this oath he secretly blesses himself and says, 'I will have peace though I continue to walk with a stubborn spirit.' This will destroy the watered ground with the parched. [20]The LORD will be unwilling to forgive him, and his intense anger will rage against that man; all the curses written in this scroll will fall upon him, and the LORD will obliterate his name from memory. [21]The LORD will single him out for judgment from all the tribes of Israel according to all the curses of the covenant written in this scroll of the law. [22]The generation to come—your descendants who will rise up after you, as well as the foreigner who will come from distant places—will see the afflictions of that land and the illnesses that the LORD has brought on it. [23]The whole land will be covered with brimstone, salt, and burning debris; it will not be planted nor will it sprout or produce grass. It will resemble the destruction of Sodom and Gomorrah, Admah and Zeboyim, which the LORD destroyed in his intense anger. [24]Then all the nations will ask, 'Why has the LORD done all this to this land? What is this fierce, heated display of anger all about?' [25]Then people will say, 'Because they abandoned the covenant of the LORD, the God of their ancestors, which he made with them when he brought them out of the land of Egypt. [26]They went and served other gods and worshiped them, gods they did not know and that he did not permit them to worship. [27]That is why the LORD's anger erupted against this land, bringing on it all the curses written in this scroll. [28]So the LORD has uprooted them from their land in anger, wrath, and great rage and has deported them to another land, as is clear today.' [29]The secret things belong to the LORD our God, but those that are revealed belong to us and our descendants forever, so that we might obey all the words of this law.

THE RESULTS OF COVENANT REAFFIRMATION

30 "When you have experienced all these things, both the blessings and the curses I have set before you, you will reflect upon them in all the nations where the LORD your God has banished you. [2]Then if you and your descendants turn to the LORD your God and obey him with your whole mind and being just as I am commanding you today, [3]the LORD your God will reverse your captivity and have pity on you. He will turn and gather you from all the peoples among whom he has scattered you. [4]Even if your exiles are in the most distant land, from there the LORD your God will gather you and bring you back. [5]Then he will bring you

30:1–11 If you return "to the LORD your God and obey him with your whole mind and being," you will not find God's commandment grievous. How indeed can it be too difficult when it is the precept of love? Those possess love if they do what is here enjoined on Israel by returning to the Lord their God with all their heart and with all their soul. "I give you a new commandment," said he, "to love one another" (John 13:34). "The one who loves his neighbor has fulfilled the law" (Rom 13:8).

AUGUSTINE **(354–430)**
ANTI-PELAGIAN WRITINGS

to the land your ancestors possessed and you also will possess it; he will do better for you and multiply you more than he did your ancestors. [6]The LORD your God will also cleanse your heart, and the hearts of your descendants so that you may love him with all your mind and being and so that you may live. [7]Then the LORD your God will put all these curses on your enemies, on those who hate you and persecute you. [8]You will return and obey the LORD, keeping all his commandments I am giving you today. [9]The LORD your God will make the labor of your hands abundantly successful and multiply your children, the offspring of your cattle, and the produce of your soil. For the LORD will once more rejoice over you to make you prosperous just as he rejoiced over your ancestors, [10]if you obey the LORD your God and keep his commandments and statutes that are written in this scroll of the law. But you must turn to him with your whole mind and being.

EXHORTATION TO COVENANT OBEDIENCE

[11]"This commandment I am giving you today is not too difficult for you, nor is it too remote. [12]It is not in heaven, as though one must say, 'Who will go up to heaven to get it for us and proclaim it to us so we may obey it?' [13]And it is not across the sea, as though one must say, 'Who will cross over to the other side of the sea and get it for us and proclaim it to us so we may obey it?' [14]For the thing is very near you—it is in your mouth and in your mind so that you can do it.

[15]"Look! I have set before you today life and prosperity on the one hand, and death and disaster on the other. [16]What I am commanding you today is to love the LORD your God, to walk in his ways, and to obey his commandments, his statutes, and his ordinances. Then you will live and become numerous and the LORD your God will bless you in the land that you are about to possess. [17]However, if you turn aside and do not obey, but are lured away to worship and serve other gods, [18]I declare to you this very day that you will certainly perish! You will not extend your time in the land you are crossing the Jordan to possess. [19]Today I invoke heaven and earth as witnesses against you that I have set life and death, blessing and curse, before you. Therefore choose life so that you and your descendants may live! [20]I also call on you to love the LORD your God, to obey him and be loyal to him, for he gives you life and enables you to live continually in the land the LORD promised to give to your ancestors Abraham, Isaac, and Jacob."

SUCCESSION OF MOSES BY JOSHUA

31 Then Moses went and spoke these words to all Israel. [2]He said to them, "Today I am 120 years old. I am no longer able to get about, and the LORD has said to me, 'You will not cross the Jordan.' [3]As for the LORD your God, he is about to cross over before you; he will destroy these nations before you, and you will dispossess them. As for Joshua, he is about to cross before you just as the LORD has said. [4]The LORD will do to them just what he did to Sihon and Og, the Amorite kings, and to their land, which he destroyed. [5]The LORD will deliver them over to you, and you will do to them according to the whole commandment I have given you. [6]Be strong and courageous! Do not fear or tremble before them, for the LORD your God is the one who is going with you. He will not fail you or abandon you!" [7]Then Moses called out to Joshua in the presence of all Israel, "Be strong and courageous, for you will accompany these people to the land that the LORD promised to give their ancestors, and you will enable them to inherit

it. [8]The LORD is indeed going before you—he will be with you; he will not fail you or abandon you. Do not be afraid or discouraged!"

THE DEPOSIT OF THE COVENANT TEXT

[9]Then Moses wrote down this law and gave it to the Levitical priests, who carry the ark of the LORD's covenant, and to all Israel's elders. [10]He commanded them: "At the end of seven years, at the appointed time of the cancellation of debts, at the Feast of Shelters, [11]when all Israel comes to appear before the LORD your God in the place he chooses, you must read this law before them within their hearing. [12]Gather the people—men, women, and children, as well as the resident foreigners in your villages—so they may hear and thus learn about and fear the LORD your God and carefully obey all the words of this law. [13]Then their children, who have not known this law, will also hear about and learn to fear the LORD your God for as long as you live in the land you are crossing the Jordan to possess."

THE COMMISSIONING OF JOSHUA

[14]Then the LORD said to Moses, "The day of your death is near. Summon Joshua and present yourselves in the tent of meeting so that I can commission him." So Moses and Joshua presented themselves in the tent of meeting. [15]The LORD appeared in the tent in a pillar of cloud that stood above the door of the tent. [16]Then the LORD said to Moses, "You are about to die, and then these people will begin to prostitute themselves with the foreign gods of the land into which they are going. They will reject me and break my covenant that I have made with them. [17]At that time my anger will erupt against them, and I will abandon them and hide my face from them until they are devoured. Many disasters and distresses will overcome them so that they will say at that time, 'Have not these disasters overcome us because our God is not among us?' [18]But I will certainly hide myself at that time because of all the wickedness they will have done by turning to other gods. [19]Now write down for yourselves the following song and teach it to the Israelites. Put it into their very mouths so that this song may serve as my witness against the Israelites! [20]For after I have brought them to the land I promised to their ancestors—one flowing with milk and honey—and they eat their fill and become fat, then they will turn to other gods and worship them; they will reject me and break my covenant. [21]Then when many disasters and distresses overcome them this song will testify against them, for their descendants will not forget it. I know the intentions they have in mind today, even before I bring them to the land I have promised." [22]So on that day Moses wrote down this song and taught it to the Israelites, [23]and the LORD commissioned Joshua son of Nun, "Be strong and courageous, for you will take the Israelites to the land I have promised them, and I will be with you."

ANTICIPATION OF DISOBEDIENCE

[24]When Moses finished writing on a scroll the words of this law in their entirety, [25]he commanded the Levites who carried the ark of the LORD's covenant, [26]"Take this scroll of the law and place it beside the ark of the covenant of the LORD your God. It will remain there as a witness against you, [27]for I know about your rebellion and stubbornness. Indeed, even while I have been living among you to this very day, you have rebelled against the LORD; you will be even more rebellious after my death! [28]Gather

31:20 God alone is wise, from whom comes wisdom, and alone perfect, and therefore alone worthy of praise. I say then that praise or blame, or whatever resembles praise or blame, are medicines most essential of all to people. Some are ill to cure and like iron are wrought into shape with fire, hammer, and anvil, that is, with threatening, reproof, and chastisement. Others, cleaving to faith itself as self-taught, and as acting of their own free will, grow by praise.

CLEMENT OF ALEXANDRIA (C. 150–C. 215)
THE PAEDAGOGUS

to me all your tribal elders and officials so I can speak to them
directly about these things and call the heavens and the earth
to witness against them. 29 For I know that after I die you will
totally corrupt yourselves and turn away from the path I have
commanded you to walk. Disaster will confront you in future
days because you will act wickedly before the LORD, inciting
him to anger because of your actions." 30 Then Moses recited
the words of this song from start to finish in the hearing of the
whole assembly of Israel:

INVOCATION OF WITNESSES

32 Listen, O heavens, and I will speak;
hear, O earth, the words of my mouth.
2 My teaching will drop like the rain,
my sayings will drip like the dew,
as rain drops upon the grass,
and showers upon new growth.
3 For I will proclaim the name of the LORD;
you must acknowledge the greatness of our God.
4 As for the Rock, his work is perfect,
for all his ways are just.
He is a reliable God who is never unjust,
he is fair and upright.
5 His people have been unfaithful to him;
they have not acted like his children—this is their sin.
They are a perverse and deceitful generation.
6 Is this how you repay the LORD,
you foolish, unwise people?
Is he not your father, your Creator?
He has made you and established you.
7 Remember the ancient days;
bear in mind the years of past generations.
Ask your father and he will inform you,
your elders, and they will tell you.
8 When the Most High gave the nations their inheritance,
when he divided up humankind,
he set the boundaries of the peoples,
according to the number of the heavenly assembly.
9 For the LORD's allotment is his people,
Jacob is his special possession.
10 The LORD found him in a desolate land,
in an empty wasteland where animals howl.
He continually guarded him and taught him;
he continually protected him like the pupil of his eye.
11 Like an eagle that stirs up its nest,
that hovers over its young,
so the LORD spread out his wings and took him,
he lifted him up on his pinions.
12 The LORD alone was guiding him,
no foreign god was with him.
13 He enabled him to travel over the high terrain of the
land,
and he ate of the produce of the fields.
He provided honey for him from the cliffs,
and olive oil from the hardest of rocks,
14 butter from the herd
and milk from the flock,
along with the fat of lambs,
rams and goats of Bashan,

along with the best of the kernels of wheat;
and from the juice of grapes you drank wine.

ISRAEL'S REBELLION

15 But Jeshurun became fat and kicked;
you got fat, thick, and stuffed!
Then he deserted the God who made him,
and treated the Rock who saved him with contempt.
16 They made him jealous with other gods,
they enraged him with abhorrent idols.
17 They sacrificed to demons, not God,
to gods they had not known;
to new gods who had recently come along,
gods your ancestors had not known about.
18 You forgot the Rock who fathered you,
and put out of mind the God who gave you birth.

A WORD OF JUDGMENT

19 But the LORD took note and despised them
because his sons and daughters enraged him.
20 He said, "I will reject them.
I will see what will happen to them;
for they are a perverse generation,
children who show no loyalty.
21 They have made me jealous with false gods,
enraging me with their worthless gods;
so I will make them jealous with a people they do not
recognize,
with a nation slow to learn I will enrage them.
22 For a fire has been kindled by my anger,
and it burns to lowest Sheol;
it consumes the earth and its produce,
and ignites the foundations of the mountains.
23 I will increase their disasters;
I will use up my arrows on them.
24 They will be starved by famine,
eaten by plague, and bitterly stung;
I will send the teeth of wild animals against them,
along with the poison of creatures that crawl in the dust.
25 The sword will make people childless outside,
and terror will do so inside;
they will destroy both the young man and the virgin,
the infant and the gray-haired man.

THE WEAKNESS OF OTHER GODS

26 "I said, 'I want to cut them in pieces.
I want to make people forget they ever existed.
27 But I fear the reaction of their enemies,
for their adversaries would misunderstand
and say, "Our power is great,
and the LORD has not done all this!"'
28 They are a nation devoid of wisdom,
and there is no understanding among them.
29 I wish that they were wise and could understand this,
and that they could comprehend what will happen to them."
30 How can one man chase a thousand of them,
and two pursue ten thousand,
unless their Rock had delivered them up—
and the LORD had handed them over?

31 For our enemies' rock is not like our Rock,
as even our enemies concede.
32 For their vine is from the stock of Sodom,
and from the fields of Gomorrah.
Their grapes contain venom;
their clusters of grapes are bitter.
33 Their wine is snakes' poison,
the deadly venom of cobras.
34 "Is this not stored up with me?" says the LORD,
"Is it not sealed up in my storehouses?
35 I will get revenge and pay them back
at the time their foot slips;
for the day of their disaster is near,
and the impending judgment is rushing upon them!"
36 The LORD will judge his people,
and will change his plans concerning his servants;
when he sees that their power has disappeared,
and that no one is left, whether confined or set free.
37 He will say, "Where are their gods,
the rock in whom they sought security,
38 who ate the best of their sacrifices,
and drank the wine of their drink offerings?
Let them rise and help you;
let them be your refuge!

THE VINDICATION OF THE LORD

39 "See now that I, indeed I, am he!" says the LORD,
"and there is no other god besides me.
I kill and give life,
I smash and I heal,
and none can resist my power.
40 For I raise up my hand to heaven,
and say, 'As surely as I live forever,
41 I will sharpen my lightning-like sword,
and my hand will grasp hold of the weapon of judgment;
I will execute vengeance on my foes,
and repay those who hate me!
42 I will make my arrows drunk with blood,
and my sword will devour flesh—
the blood of the slaughtered and captured,
the chief of the enemy's leaders.'"
43 Cry out, O nations, with his people,
for he will avenge his servants' blood;
he will take vengeance against his enemies,
and make atonement for his land and people.

NARRATIVE INTERLUDE

44 Then Moses went with Joshua son of Nun and recited all the
words of this song to the people. 45 When Moses finished re-
citing all these words to all Israel 46 he said to them, "Keep in
mind all the words I am solemnly proclaiming to you today;
you must command your children to observe carefully all the
words of this law. 47 For this is no idle word for you—it is your
life! By this word you will live a long time in the land you are
about to cross the Jordan to possess."

INSTRUCTIONS ABOUT MOSES' DEATH

48 Then the LORD said to Moses that same day, 49 "Go up to this
Abarim hill country, to Mount Nebo (which is in the land of

32:48–52 The words contain a reason why Moses and Aaron were shut out of Canaan. The one expression seems to imply a sin of commission: "You rebelled against me," that is, disobeyed God. The other a sin of omission, "You did not show me proper respect among the Israelites." For the first, this sin is called a rebellion against the commandment of the Lord; for the second, not sanctifying God. To sanctify God is to carry ourselves to him as to a God of such glory and power, to fear him above all, and to love him and trust him above all.

THOMAS MANTON
(1620–1677)
THE COMPLETE WORKS

Moab opposite Jericho), and look at the land of Canaan that I am giving to the Israelites as a possession. [50]You will die on the mountain that you ascend and join your deceased ancestors, just as Aaron your brother died on Mount Hor and joined his deceased ancestors, [51]for both of you rebelled against me among the Israelites at the waters of Meribah Kadesh in the wilderness of Zin when you did not show me proper respect among the Israelites. [52]You will see the land before you, but you will not enter the land that I am giving to the Israelites."

INTRODUCTION TO THE BLESSING OF MOSES

33 This is the blessing Moses the man of God pronounced upon the Israelites before his death. [2]He said:

A HISTORICAL REVIEW

"The LORD came from Sinai
and revealed himself to Israel from Seir.
He appeared in splendor from Mount Paran,
and came forth with ten thousand holy ones.
With his right hand he gave a fiery law to them.
3 Surely he loves the people;
all your holy ones are in your power.
And they sit at your feet,
each receiving your words.
4 Moses delivered to us a law,
an inheritance for the assembly of Jacob.
5 The LORD was king over Jeshurun,
when the leaders of the people assembled,
the tribes of Israel together.

BLESSING ON REUBEN

6 "May Reuben live and not die,
and may his people multiply."

BLESSING ON JUDAH

7 And this is the blessing to Judah. He said,
"Listen, O LORD, to Judah's voice,
and bring him to his people.
May his power be great,
and may you help him against his foes."

BLESSING ON LEVI

8 Of Levi he said:
"Your Thummim and Urim belong to your godly one,
whose authority you challenged at Massah,
and with whom you argued at the waters of Meribah.
9 He said to his father and mother, 'I have not seen him,'
and he did not acknowledge his own brothers
or know his own children,
for they kept your word,
and guarded your covenant.
10 They will teach Jacob your ordinances
and Israel your law;
they will offer incense as a pleasant odor,
and a whole offering on your altar.
11 Bless, O LORD, his goods,
and be pleased with his efforts;
undercut the legs of any who attack him,
and of those who hate him, so that they cannot stand."

33:1–25 "With his right hand he gave a fiery law to them." It was a light to enlighten them; it is more natural to say it is for them than if it were a fire threatening to consume them. And in this sense much the best agrees with the following verses and their evident connection with these words that speak of God's great love and grace in giving them this law, and how it was given as an inheritance to them, and with what pleasure and delight they received it: "Surely he loves the people; all your holy ones are in your power. And they sit at your feet, each receiving your words. Moses delivered to us a law, an inheritance for the assembly of Jacob."

JONATHAN EDWARDS
(1703–1758)
SELECTIONS FROM THE UNPUBLISHED WRITINGS

BLESSING ON BENJAMIN

12 Of Benjamin he said:
"The beloved of the LORD will live safely by him;
he protects him all the time,
and the LORD places him on his chest."

BLESSING ON JOSEPH

13 Of Joseph he said:
"May the LORD bless his land
with the harvest produced by the sky, by the dew,
and by the depths crouching beneath;
14 with the harvest produced by the daylight
and by the moonlight;
15 with the best of the ancient mountains
and the harvest produced by the age-old hills;
16 with the harvest of the earth and its fullness
and the pleasure of him who resided in the burning
bush.
May blessing rest on Joseph's head,
and on the top of the head of the one set apart from his
brothers.
17 May the firstborn of his bull bring him honor,
and may his horns be those of a wild ox;
with them may he gore all peoples,
all the far reaches of the earth.
They are the ten thousands of Ephraim,
and they are the thousands of Manasseh."

BLESSING ON ZEBULUN AND ISSACHAR

18 Of Zebulun he said:
"Rejoice, Zebulun, when you go outside,
and Issachar, when you are in your tents.
19 They will summon peoples to the mountain,
there they will sacrifice proper sacrifices;
for they will enjoy the abundance of the seas,
and the hidden treasures of the shores."

BLESSING ON GAD

20 Of Gad he said:
"Blessed be the one who enlarges Gad.
Like a lioness he will dwell;
he will tear at an arm—indeed, a scalp.
21 He has selected the best part for himself,
for the portion of the ruler is set aside there;
he came with the leaders of the people,
he obeyed the righteous laws of the LORD
and his ordinances with Israel."

BLESSING ON DAN

22 Of Dan he said:
"Dan is a lion's cub;
he will leap forth from Bashan."

BLESSING ON NAPHTALI

23 Of Naphtali he said:
"O Naphtali, overflowing with favor,
and full of the LORD's blessing,
possess the west and south."

BLESSING ON ASHER

24 Of Asher he said:
"Asher is blessed with children;
may he be favored by his brothers,
and may he dip his foot in olive oil.
25 The bars of your gates will be made of iron and bronze,
and may you have lifelong strength."

GENERAL PRAISE AND BLESSING

26 "There is no one like God, O Jeshurun,
who rides through the sky to help you,
on the clouds in majesty.
27 The everlasting God is a refuge,
and underneath you are his eternal arms;
he has driven out enemies before you,
and has said, 'Destroy!'
28 Israel lives in safety,
the fountain of Jacob is quite secure,
in a land of grain and new wine;
indeed, its heavens rain down dew.
29 You have joy, Israel! Who is like you?
You are a people delivered by the LORD,
your protective shield
and your exalted sword.
May your enemies cringe before you;
may you trample on their backs."

THE DEATH OF MOSES

34 Then Moses ascended from the rift valley plains of Moab
to Mount Nebo, to the summit of Pisgah, which is opposite Jericho. The LORD showed him the whole land—Gilead to
Dan, 2and all of Naphtali, the land of Ephraim and Manasseh,
all the land of Judah as far as the distant sea, 3the Negev, and
the plain of the Valley of Jericho, the city of date palm trees,
as far as Zoar. 4Then the LORD said to him, "This is the land I
promised to Abraham, Isaac, and Jacob when I said, 'I will give
it to your descendants.' I have let you see it, but you will not
cross over there."
5So Moses, the servant of the LORD, died there in the land
of Moab as the LORD had said. 6He buried him in the valley in
the land of Moab near Beth Peor, but no one knows his exact
burial place to this very day. 7Moses was 120 years old when he
died, but his eye was not dull nor had his vitality departed. 8The
Israelites mourned for Moses in the rift valley plains of Moab
for thirty days; then the days of mourning for Moses ended.

34:1–10 The ascent of Moses was equivalent to a voluntary going forth to death, for he was not ignorant of what was to happen but being called by God to die he went to meet death of his own accord. Such willing submission proceeded from no other source than faith in God's grace whereby alone all terror is mitigated and set at rest, and the bitterness of death is sweetened. He did not hesitate to offer himself without alarm. And because he was firmly persuaded that the inheritance of the people would be there set before his eyes, he cheerfully ascended to the place from which he was to behold it.

JOHN CALVIN (1509–1564)
COMPLETE COMMENTARY ON THE BIBLE

AN EPITAPH FOR MOSES

9Now Joshua son of Nun was full of the spirit of wisdom, for
Moses had placed his hands on him; and the Israelites listened
to him and did just what the LORD had commanded Moses.
10No prophet ever again arose in Israel like Moses, who knew
the LORD face to face. 11He did all the signs and wonders the
LORD had sent him to do in the land of Egypt, to Pharaoh, all
his servants, and the whole land, 12and he displayed great power
and awesome might in view of all Israel.

AUTHOR	AUDIENCE	DATE	PURPOSE	THEMES
Traditionally, Joshua	God's chosen people, the Israelites	Probably about 1390 BC	The purpose of this book is to explain how God fulfilled the central provision of his covenant with his people: the inheritance of the land of Canaan.	The land; the promises of God; the Lord's intervention; and covenant obedience

The book of Joshua continues the story of God's people beyond the death of Moses. As the book opens, Israel is on the other side of the wilderness at the doorstep of the promised land, and Joshua is about to lead the people to claim their home and defeat their enemies. It is the first in a collection of books that chronicles Israel's history as a nation.

A summary of this book is offered in 21:43–45: "So the LORD gave Israel all the land . . . and they conquered it and lived in it. The LORD made them secure . . . The LORD handed all their enemies over to them. Not one of the LORD's faithful promises to the family of Israel was left unfulfilled; every one was realized." God fulfilled the central provision of his covenant with his people: giving Israel an inheritance of land to make them a nation of his own possession and glory before the nations.

One of the most important themes running throughout the Old Testament is God's promise of "the land," which occurs about 1,600 times. Not only is there sociopolitical significance to this land—the land of Canaan—there is theological significance as well. It connects the national identity of Israel to the promises God made to Abraham, Isaac, and Jacob hundreds of years earlier in that very land. Keeping the promise of the land central, the book of Joshua can be divided in this way: 1:1—5:12, Israel's *entrance* into the land; 5:13—12:24, Israel's *conquest* of the land; 13–21, Israel's *distribution* of the land; 22–24, Israel's *covenant renewed* inside the land.

The book begins with a promise God made to Joshua: "Be strong and brave! You must lead these people in the conquest of this land that I solemnly promised their ancestors I would hand over to them" (1:6). "Although the people had already gained signal victories and become the occupants of a commodious and tolerably fertile tract of country," explained John Calvin, "the divine promise as to the land of Canaan still remained suspended." The central element of the Lord's covenant with his people was pending: "The leading article in the covenant was unaccomplished as if God, after cooping up his people in a corner, had left his work in a shapeless and mutilated form." So God intervened in their history to fulfill his promise.

JOSHUA

Although God's intervention in Israel's history through warfare is foreign to us, God's character is on full display in the conquest campaign. Through the display of his divine power on behalf of his people in fulfillment of his covenant promises, the Lord is revealed to be a warrior who fights for his people.

When the covenant was renewed after Israel entered Canaan, Joshua built an altar and sacrifices were offered. All of Israel was assembled around the ark of the covenant—a tangible reminder of the covenant. Joshua read the entire law in the presence of the people, blessings and curses and all, to remind Israel of its obligations. Before Joshua passed away there was a second ceremony of renewal at Shechem, in which he highlighted the Lord's providential intervention in the people's lives and called them to a life of obedience, declaring: "Now obey the Lord and worship him with integrity and loyalty. Put aside the gods your ancestors worshiped beyond the Euphrates and in Egypt, and worship the Lord" (24:14). Origen rightly noted, "What Joshua said to the people when he settled them in the holy land the scripture might also say now to us."

The early church fathers, as well as the Reformers, saw within Joshua a type of Christ, for Jesus' Hebrew name is itself *Yeshua* or *Joshua*. Chrysostom summarized this typology as well as how this book and its story have functioned within the communion of saints: "The name of Jesus [Joshua] was a type. For this reason then, and because of the very name, the creation reverenced him . . . He brought the people into the promised land, as Jesus into heaven; not the law, since neither did Moses [enter the promised land] but remained outside. The law has not power to bring in, but grace."

May we listen to what the saints of old can tell us about this book as we read it, and may we find greater understanding of Christ who himself leads us into the promised land. As Origen also explains, "The book does not so much indicate to us the deeds of the son of Nun as it represents for us the mysteries of Jesus our Lord."

THE LORD COMMISSIONS JOSHUA

1 After Moses the LORD's servant died, the LORD said to Joshua
son of Nun, Moses' assistant: 2“Moses my servant is dead. Get
ready! Cross the Jordan River. Lead these people into the land
that I am ready to hand over to them. 3I am handing over to you
every place you set foot, as I promised Moses. 4Your territory
will extend from the desert in the south to Lebanon in the
north. It will extend all the way to the great River Euphrates in
the east (including all Syria) and all the way to the Mediterranean Sea in the west. 5No one will be able to resist you all the
days of your life. As I was with Moses, so I will be with you. I
will not abandon you or leave you alone. 6Be strong and brave!
You must lead these people in the conquest of this land that I
solemnly promised their ancestors I would hand over to them.
7Make sure you are very strong and brave! Carefully obey all
the law my servant Moses charged you to keep. Do not swerve
from it to the right or to the left, so that you may be successful
in all you do. 8This law scroll must not leave your lips. You must
memorize it day and night so you can carefully obey all that is
written in it. Then you will prosper and be successful. 9I repeat,
be strong and brave! Don't be afraid and don't panic, for I, the
LORD your God, am with you in all you do.”

1:6 Joshua was assured of his divine call that he might have no hesitation in undertaking the office that had been divinely committed to him nor begin to waver midway on being obliged to contend with obstacles. It would not have been enough for him diligently to exert himself at the outset without being well prepared to persevere in the struggle. We may add that not once only or by one single expression were strength and constancy required of Joshua, but he was confirmed repeatedly and in various terms because he was to be engaged in many and various contests. He was told to be of strong and invincible courage.

JOHN CALVIN (1509–1564)
COMPLETE COMMENTARY ON THE BIBLE

JOSHUA PREPARES FOR THE INVASION

10Joshua instructed the leaders of the people: 11“Go through
the camp and command the people, ‘Prepare your supplies,
for within three days you will cross the Jordan River and begin
the conquest of the land the LORD your God is ready to hand
over to you.’”
12Joshua told the Reubenites, the Gadites, and the half-tribe
of Manasseh: 13“Remember what Moses the LORD's servant
commanded you. The LORD your God is giving you a place to
settle and is handing this land over to you. 14Your wives, children, and cattle may stay in the land that Moses assigned to
you east of the Jordan River. But all of you warriors must cross
over armed for battle ahead of your brothers. You must help
them 15until the LORD gives your brothers a place like yours to
settle and they conquer the land the LORD your God is ready
to hand over to them. Then you may go back to your allotted
land and occupy the land Moses the LORD's servant assigned
you east of the Jordan.”
16They told Joshua, “We will do everything you say. We will
go wherever you send us. 17Just as we obeyed Moses, so we will
obey you. But may the LORD your God be with you as he was
with Moses. 18Any man who rebels against what you say and
does not obey all your commands will be executed. But be strong
and brave!”

JOSHUA SENDS SPIES INTO THE LAND

2 Joshua son of Nun sent two spies out from Shittim secretly
and instructed them: “Find out what you can about the land,
especially Jericho.” They stopped at the house of a prostitute
named Rahab and spent the night there. 2The king of Jericho
received this report: “Note well! Israelite men have come here
tonight to spy on the land.” 3So the king of Jericho sent this order
to Rahab: “Turn over the men who came to you—the ones who
came to your house—for they have come to spy on the whole
land!” 4But the woman hid the two men and replied, “Yes, these
men were clients of mine, but I didn't know where they came

2:1–24 On account of her faith and hospitality, Rahab the prostitute was saved. She said to the spies, “Because I have shown allegiance to you, show allegiance to my family. Give me a solemn pledge that you will spare the lives of my father, mother, brothers, sisters, and all who belong to them.” And they said, “Gather together in your house your father, mother, brothers, and all who live in your father's house.” Moreover they gave her a sign to this effect, that she should hang from her house a scarlet rope. And thus they made it manifest that redemption should flow through the blood of the Lord to all those who believe and hope in God.

CLEMENT OF ROME (D. 99)
FIRST CLEMENT

from. 5When it was time to shut the city gate for the night, the men left. I don't know where they were heading. Chase after them quickly, for you have time to catch them!" 6(Now she had taken them up to the roof and had hidden them in the stalks of flax she had spread out on the roof.) 7Meanwhile, the king's men tried to find them on the road to the Jordan River near the fords. The city gate was shut as soon as they set out in pursuit of them.

8Now before the spies went to sleep, Rahab went up to the roof. 9She said to the men, "I know the LORD is handing this land over to you. We are absolutely terrified of you, and all who live in the land are cringing before you. 10For we heard how the LORD dried up the water of the Red Sea before you when you left Egypt and how you annihilated the two Amorite kings, Sihon and Og, on the other side of the Jordan. 11When we heard the news, we lost our courage, and no one could even breathe for fear of you. For the LORD your God is God in heaven above and on earth below! 12So now, promise me this with an oath sworn in the LORD's name. Because I have shown allegiance to you, show allegiance to my family. Give me a solemn pledge 13that you will spare the lives of my father, mother, brothers, sisters, and all who belong to them, and will rescue us from death." 14The men said to her, "If you die, may we die too! If you do not report what we've been up to, then we will show unswerving allegiance to you when the LORD hands the land over to us."

15Then Rahab let them down by a rope through the window. (Her house was built as part of the city wall; she lived in the wall.) 16She told them, "Head to the hill country, so the ones chasing you don't find you. Hide from them there for three days, long enough for those chasing you to return. Then you can be on your way." 17The men said to her, "We are not bound by this oath you made us swear unless the following conditions are met: 18When we invade the land, tie this red rope in the window through which you let us down, and gather together in your house your father, mother, brothers, and all who live in your father's house. 19Anyone who leaves your house will be responsible for his own death—we are innocent in that case! But if anyone with you in the house is harmed, we will be responsible. 20If you should report what we've been up to, we are not bound by this oath you made us swear." 21She said, "I agree to these conditions." She sent them on their way and then tied the red rope in the window. 22They went to the hill country and stayed there for three days, long enough for those chasing them to return. Their pursuers looked all along the way but did not find them. 23Then the two men returned—they came down from the hills, crossed the river, came to Joshua son of Nun, and reported to him all they had discovered. 24They told Joshua, "Surely the LORD is handing over all the land to us! All who live in the land are cringing before us!"

ISRAEL CROSSES THE JORDAN

3 Bright and early the next morning Joshua and the Israelites left Shittim and came to the Jordan. They camped there before crossing the river. 2After three days the leaders went through the camp 3and commanded the people: "When you see the ark of the covenant of the LORD your God being carried by the Levitical priests, you must leave here and walk behind it. 4But stay about 3,000 feet behind it. Keep your distance so you can see which way you should go, for you have not traveled this way before."

3:1–17 Let us ask God to grant us the ability to understand spiritually the crossing of the Jordan through Joshua. Paul would have said of this crossing, *I do not wish you to be ignorant, brothers and sisters, that our fathers all passed through the Jordan and all were baptized into Jesus in the Spirit and in the river* (see 1 Cor 10:1–4). Joshua, who succeeded Moses, was a type of Jesus the Christ who succeeded the dispensation through the law with the gospel proclamation. This is why, although they are all baptized into Moses in the cloud and in the sea, their baptism has a bitter and briny element, for they still fear their enemies and cry out to the Lord and to Moses, saying, "Is it because there are no graves in Egypt that you have taken us away to die in the desert?" (Exod 14:11). But baptism into Jesus in the truly sweet and fresh river has many elements superior to that baptism, since the religion has by this time been clarified and received a proper order. Joshua says to the people, "Ritually consecrate yourselves, for tomorrow the LORD will perform miraculous deeds among you."

ORIGEN (C. 185–C. 253)
COMMENTARY ON THE GOSPEL OF JOHN

ANTHONY OF THE DESERT:

INSPIRATION FOR EARLY MONASTICISM

c. 251–373

The Christian renunciation of worldly possessions in pursuit of Jesus' way of life is as old as the Christian faith itself. Anthony of the Desert can be credited with inspiring the particular form of imitating Christ known as monasticism.

Anthony was an Egyptian, born in 251 to wealthy Christian parents who died shortly after he turned eighteen. Although the inheritance left to him by his parents made Anthony extremely wealthy, he made the surprising choice to abandon a life of leisure and material comforts and move to a desert region. As tradition has it, Anthony heard a sermon one Sunday morning on Matthew 19:21, and Jesus' words cut him to the quick: "If you wish to be perfect, go sell your possessions and give the money to the poor, and you will have treasure in heaven. Then come, follow me." He promptly sold much of the estate property and most of his possessions, and donated the proceeds to service of the poor, except for a small amount to care for his orphaned sister. He left his home and became the disciple of a local hermit, learning and adopting his ascetic lifestyle.

He would eventually move to the desert to pursue a life of rigorous Christian devotion: He lived in solitude, slept on the ground, consumed nothing but bread and water, deprived himself of sleep, didn't bathe or read, and kept still and isolated. Such a lifestyle led to intense spiritual conflict full of temptations and battles with demonic influences. Here is how his biographer described the experience: "[The devil] attacked the young man, disturbing him by night and harassing him by day, so that even the onlookers saw the struggle which was going on between them." Throughout these spiritual struggles, Anthony came to rely upon the power of prayer and worship to overcome all temptation.

When he emerged after living in solitude for twenty years, he was the talk of the region. People flocked to see the famous man and learn how they could follow his example. Becoming an abbot of a monastery in the area, Anthony embraced the role of teacher and advisor as interest in the monastic way of life reached unprecedented levels. He also traveled to Alexandria twice, once to offer himself as a martyr in place of other persecuted Christians and later to defend himself against charges of Arianism.

Anthony became one of the most popular, well-known men of his era, even garnering attention from the emperor Constantine and his sons, and earning a hagiography—a biography of a saint. *The Life of St. Anthony*, penned by Athanasius, became hugely influential in popularizing monastic ideals and spurring the creation of monasteries throughout the Christian world.

After his death in 373, Anthony of the Desert's example inspired a wave of monasticism and greatly influenced the direction of Western Christianity for generations to come.

[5]Joshua told the people, "Ritually consecrate yourselves, for tomorrow the LORD will perform miraculous deeds among you." [6]Joshua told the priests, "Pick up the ark of the covenant and pass on ahead of the people." So they picked up the ark of the covenant and went ahead of the people.

[7]The LORD told Joshua, "This very day I will begin to honor you before all Israel, so they will know that I am with you just as I was with Moses. [8]Instruct the priests carrying the ark of the covenant, 'When you reach the bank of the Jordan River, wade into the water.'"

[9]Joshua told the Israelites, "Come here and listen to the words of the LORD your God!" [10]Joshua continued, "This is how you will know the living God is among you and that he will truly drive out before you the Canaanites, Hittites, Hivites, Perizzites, Girgashites, Amorites, and Jebusites. [11]Look! The ark of the covenant of the Lord of the whole earth is ready to enter the Jordan ahead of you. [12]Now select for yourselves 12 men from the tribes of Israel, one per tribe. [13]When the feet of the priests carrying the ark of the LORD, the Lord of the whole earth, touch the water of the Jordan, the water coming downstream toward you will stop flowing and pile up."

[14]So when the people left their tents to cross the Jordan, the priests carrying the ark of the covenant went ahead of them. [15]When the ones carrying the ark reached the Jordan, and the feet of the priests carrying the ark touched the surface of the water—(the Jordan is at flood stage all during harvest time)—[16]the water coming downstream toward them stopped flowing. It piled up far upstream at Adam (the city near Zarethan); there was no water at all flowing to the sea of the rift valley (the Salt Sea). The people crossed the river opposite Jericho. [17]The priests carrying the ark of the covenant of the LORD stood firmly on dry ground in the middle of the Jordan. All Israel crossed over on dry ground until the entire nation was on the other side.

ISRAEL COMMEMORATES THE CROSSING

4 When the entire nation was on the other side, the LORD told Joshua, [2]"Select for yourselves 12 men from the people, one per tribe. [3]Instruct them, 'Pick up 12 stones from the middle of the Jordan, from the very place where the priests stand firmly, and carry them over with you and put them in the place where you camp tonight.'"

[4]Joshua summoned the 12 men he had appointed from the Israelites, one per tribe. [5]Joshua told them, "Go in front of the ark of the LORD your God to the middle of the Jordan. Each of you is to put a stone on his shoulder, according to the number of the Israelite tribes. [6]The stones will be a reminder to you. When your children ask someday, 'Why are these stones important to you?' [7]tell them how the water of the Jordan stopped flowing before the ark of the covenant of the LORD. When it crossed the Jordan, the water of the Jordan stopped flowing. These stones will be a lasting memorial for the Israelites."

[8]The Israelites did just as Joshua commanded. They picked up 12 stones, according to the number of the Israelite tribes, from the middle of the Jordan as the LORD had instructed Joshua. They carried them over with them to the camp and put them there. [9]Joshua also set up 12 stones in the middle of the Jordan in the very place where the priests carrying the ark of the covenant stood. They remain there to this very day.

4:1–24 God ordered 12 stones to be taken from the Jordan and specified why, for he says, "When your children ask someday, 'Why are these stones important to you?' tell them how the water of the Jordan stopped flowing before the ark of the covenant of the LORD. When it crossed the Jordan, the water of the Jordan stopped flowing." And thus the ark was saved and all the people. Shall we not then record with images the saving passion and miracles of Christ our God, so that when my son asks me, "What is this?" I may say that God the Word became man, and that through him not only Israel passed through the Jordan, but the whole human race regained its original happiness? Through him human nature rose from the lowest depths to the most exalted heights and in him sat on the Father's throne.

JOHN OF DAMASCUS
(C. 675–749)
ON DIVINE IMAGES

10Now the priests carrying the ark of the covenant were standing in the middle of the Jordan until everything the LORD had commanded Joshua to tell the people was accomplished, in accordance with all that Moses had commanded Joshua. The people went across quickly, 11and when all the people had finished crossing, the ark of the LORD and the priests crossed as the people looked on. 12The Reubenites, the Gadites, and the half-tribe of Manasseh crossed over armed for battle ahead of the Israelites, just as Moses had instructed them. 13About 40,000 battle-ready troops marched past the LORD to fight on the rift valley plains of Jericho. 14That day the LORD brought honor to Joshua before all Israel. They respected him all his life, just as they had respected Moses.

15The LORD told Joshua, 16"Instruct the priests carrying the ark of the covenantal laws to come up from the Jordan." 17So Joshua instructed the priests, "Come up from the Jordan!" 18The priests carrying the ark of the covenant of the LORD came up from the middle of the Jordan, and as soon as they set foot on dry land, the water of the Jordan flowed again and returned to flood stage.

19The people went up from the Jordan on the tenth day of the first month and camped in Gilgal on the eastern border of Jericho. 20Now Joshua set up in Gilgal the 12 stones they had taken from the Jordan. 21He told the Israelites, "When your children someday ask their fathers, 'What do these stones represent?' 22explain to your children, 'Israel crossed the Jordan River on dry ground.' 23For the LORD your God dried up the water of the Jordan before you while you crossed over. It was just like when the LORD your God dried up the Red Sea before us while we crossed it. 24He has done this so all the nations of the earth might recognize the LORD's power and so you might always obey the LORD your God."

5 When all the Amorite kings on the west side of the Jordan and all the Canaanite kings along the seacoast heard how the LORD had dried up the water of the Jordan before the Israelites while they crossed, they lost their courage and could not even breathe for fear of the Israelites.

A NEW GENERATION IS CIRCUMCISED

2At that time the LORD told Joshua, "Make flint knives and circumcise the Israelites once again." 3So Joshua made flint knives and circumcised the Israelites at the Hill of the Foreskins. 4This is why Joshua had to circumcise them: All the men old enough to fight when they left Egypt died on the journey through the wilderness after they left Egypt. 5Now all the men who left were circumcised, but all the sons born on the journey through the wilderness after they left Egypt were uncircumcised. 6Indeed, for 40 years the Israelites traveled through the wilderness until all the men old enough to fight when they left Egypt, the ones who had disobeyed the LORD, died off. For the LORD had sworn a solemn oath to them that he would not let them see the land he had sworn by oath to their ancestors to give them, a land rich in milk and honey. 7He replaced them with their sons, whom Joshua circumcised. They were uncircumcised; their fathers had not circumcised them along the way. 8When all the men had been circumcised, they stayed there in the camp until they had healed. 9The LORD said to Joshua, "Today I have taken away the disgrace of Egypt from you." So that place is called Gilgal even to this day.

5:1–12 This was the second general circumcision of the congregation. The first was probably before the Passover they kept in Egypt while they had peace in Egypt. But before the Passover, the night before they went out of Egypt they were doubtless generally circumcised, because it was then most strictly commanded that no uncircumcised person should eat the Passover. Concerning their not circumcising the children who were born in the wilderness—considering the plainness of the precept of circumcision and the strictness of the injunction, and that no great stress was laid upon it—I say, considering these things, it is unaccountable that all the children that were born for 38 years together should not be circumcised unless it was omitted by divine direction . . . Therefore it rather seems to have been a continued token of God's displeasure against them. Circumcision was originally a seal of the promise of the land of Canaan.

JONATHAN EDWARDS
(1703–1758)
SELECTIONS FROM THE UNPUBLISHED WRITINGS

[10]So the Israelites camped in Gilgal and celebrated the Passover in the evening of the fourteenth day of the month in the
rift valley plains of Jericho. [11]They ate some of the produce
of the land the day after the Passover, including unleavened
bread and roasted grain. [12]The manna stopped appearing the
day they ate some of the produce of the land; the Israelites
never ate manna again. They ate from the produce of the land
of Canaan that year.

ISRAEL CONQUERS JERICHO

[13]When Joshua was near Jericho, he looked up and saw a man
standing in front of him holding a drawn sword. Joshua approached him and asked him, "Are you on our side or allied with
our enemies?" [14]He answered, "Truly I am the commander of
the LORD's army. Now I have arrived!" Joshua bowed down with
his face to the ground and asked, "What does my master want
to say to his servant?" [15]The commander of the LORD's army
answered Joshua, "Remove your sandals from your feet because
the place where you stand is holy." Joshua did so.

6 Now Jericho was shut tightly because of the Israelites. No one
was allowed to leave or enter. [2]The LORD told Joshua, "See,
I am about to defeat Jericho for you, along with its king and
its warriors. [3]Have all the warriors march around the city one
time; do this for six days. [4]Have seven priests carry seven rams'
horns in front of the ark. On the seventh day march around
the city seven times, while the priests blow the horns. [5]When
you hear the signal from the rams' horns, have the whole army
give a loud battle cry. Then the city wall will collapse, and the
warriors should charge straight ahead."

[6]So Joshua son of Nun summoned the priests and instructed
them, "Pick up the ark of the covenant, and seven priests must
carry seven rams' horns in front of the ark of the LORD." [7]And
he told the army, "Move ahead and march around the city, with
armed troops going ahead of the ark of the LORD."

[8]When Joshua gave the army its orders, the seven priests
carrying the seven rams' horns before the LORD moved ahead
and blew the horns as the ark of the covenant of the LORD
followed behind. [9]Armed troops marched ahead of the priests
blowing the horns, while the rear guard followed along behind
the ark blowing rams' horns. [10]Now Joshua had instructed the
army, "Do not give a battle cry or raise your voices; say nothing
until the day I tell you, 'Give the battle cry.' Then give the battle
cry!" [11]So Joshua made sure they marched the ark of the LORD
around the city one time. Then they went back to the camp
and spent the night there.

[12]Bright and early the next morning Joshua had the priests
pick up the ark of the LORD. [13]The seven priests carrying the
seven rams' horns before the ark of the LORD marched along
blowing their horns. Armed troops marched ahead of them,
while the rear guard followed along behind the ark of the LORD
blowing rams' horns. [14]They marched around the city one time
on the second day, then returned to the camp. They did this
six days in all.

[15]On the seventh day they were up at the crack of dawn and
marched around the city as before—only this time they marched
around it seven times. [16]The seventh time around, the priests
blew the rams' horns, and Joshua told the army, "Give the battle
cry, for the LORD is handing the city over to you! [17]The city and
all that is in it must be set apart for the LORD; only Rahab the

6:1–21 The manner of Jericho's destruction was thus: it was by the marching of Israel about the city seven days, and the priests going before them blowing with rams' horns—a type of God's blessing on the labors of his ministers in stirring up his people against the kingdom of sin, Satan, and antichrist. But faith must use such means as God has appointed, though to appearance they be ever so despicable. So here, by the blast of the rams' horns, the walls of this seemingly impregnable city fell flat to the ground.

THOMAS MANTON
(1620–1677)
THE COMPLETE WORKS

prostitute and all who are with her in her house will live, because she hid the spies we sent. [18]But be careful when you are setting apart the riches for God. If you take any of it, then you will make the Israelite camp subject to annihilation and cause a disaster. [19]All the silver and gold, as well as bronze and iron items, belong to the LORD. They must go into the LORD's treasury."

[20]The rams' horns sounded, and when the army heard the signal, they gave a loud battle cry. The wall collapsed, and the warriors charged straight ahead into the city and captured it. [21]They annihilated with the sword everything that breathed in the city, including men and women, young and old, as well as cattle, sheep, and donkeys. [22]Joshua told the two men who had spied on the land, "Enter the prostitute's house and bring out the woman and all who belong to her as you promised her." [23]So the young spies went and brought out Rahab, her father, mother, brothers, and all who belonged to her. They brought out her whole family and took them to a place outside the Israelite camp. [24]But they burned the city and all that was in it, except for the silver, gold, and bronze and iron items they put in the treasury of the LORD's house. [25]Yet Joshua spared Rahab the prostitute, her father's family, and all who belonged to her. She lives in Israel to this very day because she hid the messengers Joshua sent to spy on Jericho. [26]At that time Joshua made this solemn declaration: "The man who attempts to rebuild this city of Jericho will stand condemned before the LORD. He will lose his firstborn son when he lays its foundations and his youngest son when he erects its gates!" [27]The LORD was with Joshua, and he became famous throughout the land.

ACHAN SINS AND IS PUNISHED

7 But the Israelites disobeyed the command about the city's riches. Achan son of Carmi, son of Zabdi, son of Zerah, from the tribe of Judah, stole some of the riches. The LORD was furious with the Israelites.

[2]Joshua sent men from Jericho to Ai (which is located near Beth Aven, east of Bethel) and instructed them, "Go up and spy on the land." So the men went up and spied on Ai. [3]They returned and reported to Joshua, "Don't send the whole army. About two or three thousand men are adequate to defeat Ai. Don't tire out the whole army, for Ai is small."

[4]So about 3,000 men went up, but they fled from the men of Ai. [5]The men of Ai killed about thirty-six of them and chased them from in front of the city gate all the way to the fissures and defeated them on the steep slope. The people's courage melted away like water.

[6]Joshua tore his clothes; he and the leaders of Israel lay face down on the ground before the ark of the LORD until evening and threw dirt on their heads. [7]Joshua prayed, "O, Sovereign LORD! Why did you bring these people across the Jordan to hand us over to the Amorites so they could destroy us? If only we had been satisfied to live on the other side of the Jordan! [8]O Lord, what can I say now that Israel has retreated before its enemies? [9]When the Canaanites and all who live in the land hear about this, they will turn against us and destroy the very memory of us from the earth. What will you do to protect your great reputation?"

[10]The LORD responded to Joshua, "Get up! Why are you lying there face down? [11]Israel has sinned; they have violated my covenantal commandment! They have taken some of the riches; they have stolen them and deceitfully put them among their

7:1–9 Why did God punish the whole society for this one man's sin? Partly because several of them might be guilty of this sin, either by coveting what Achan actually did or by concealing his fault; or by not sorrowing for it and endeavoring to purge themselves from it, partly to make sin the more hateful as being the cause of such dreadful judgments, and partly to oblige all the members of every society to be more circumspect in ordering their own actions, and more diligent to prevent the sins of their fellow human beings, which is a great benefit to them and to the whole society.

JOHN WESLEY (1703–1791)
EXPLANATORY NOTES ON THE BIBLE

own possessions. 12The Israelites are unable to stand before their enemies; they retreat because they have become subject to annihilation. I will no longer be with you, unless you destroy what has contaminated you. 13Get up! Ritually consecrate the people and tell them this: 'Ritually consecrate yourselves for tomorrow because this is what the LORD God of Israel has said, "You are contaminated, O Israel! You will not be able to stand before your enemies until you remove what is contaminating you." 14In the morning you must approach in tribal order. The tribe the LORD selects must approach by clans. The clan the LORD selects must approach by families. The family the LORD selects must approach man by man. 15The one caught with the riches must be burned up along with all who belong to him because he violated the LORD's covenant and did such a disgraceful thing in Israel.'"

16Bright and early the next morning Joshua made Israel approach in tribal order, and the tribe of Judah was selected. 17He then made the clans of Judah approach, and the clan of the Zerahites was selected. He made the clan of the Zerahites approach, and Zabdi was selected. 18He then made Zabdi's family approach man by man and Achan son of Carmi, son of Zabdi, son of Zerah, from the tribe of Judah, was selected. 19So Joshua said to Achan, "My son, honor the LORD God of Israel and give him praise! Tell me what you did; don't hide anything from me." 20Achan told Joshua, "It is true. I have sinned against the LORD God of Israel in this way: 21I saw among the goods we seized a nice robe from Babylon, 200 silver pieces, and a bar of gold weighing 50 shekels. I wanted them, so I took them. They are hidden in the ground right in the middle of my tent, with the silver underneath."

22Joshua sent messengers who ran to the tent. The things were hidden right in his tent, with the silver underneath. 23They took it all from the middle of the tent, brought it to Joshua and all the Israelites, and placed it before the LORD. 24Then Joshua and all Israel took Achan, son of Zerah, along with the silver, the robe, the bar of gold, his sons, daughters, oxen, donkeys, sheep, tent, and all that belonged to him and brought them up to the Valley of Disaster. 25Joshua said, "Why have you brought disaster on us? The LORD will bring disaster on you today!" All Israel stoned him to death. (They also stoned and burned the others.) 26Then they erected over him a large pile of stones (it remains to this very day), and the LORD's anger subsided. So that place is called the Valley of Disaster to this very day.

ISRAEL CONQUERS AI

8 The LORD told Joshua, "Don't be afraid and don't panic! Take the whole army with you and march against Ai! See, I am handing over to you the king of Ai, along with his people, city, and land. 2Do to Ai and its king what you did to Jericho and its king, except you may plunder its goods and cattle. Set an ambush behind the city."

3Joshua and the whole army marched against Ai. Joshua selected 30,000 brave warriors and sent them out at night. 4He ordered them, "Look, set an ambush behind the city. Don't go very far from the city; all of you be ready! 5I and all the troops who are with me will approach the city. When they come out to fight us like before, we will retreat from them. 6They will attack us until we have lured them from the city, for they will say, 'They are retreating from us like before.' We will retreat

8:1–29 Since God ordered Joshua to plant an ambush behind Ai, we can learn that such treachery is not unjustly carried out by those who wage a just war. Once they have undertaken a just war, it makes no difference to the justice of the war whether they win in open warfare or by treachery. Just wars ought to be defined as those that avenge injuries, if the tribe or state that is about to be sought in war either neglected to punish a crime improperly committed by its own inhabitants or neglected to repay what had been lost through those injuries. We must consider whether every attempt at deception ought to be reckoned as a lie and, if so, whether a lie can be just when someone who should be deceived is deceived. And if not even this kind of a lie is found to be just, we must still relate what transpired with the ambush to the truth with some other meaning.

AUGUSTINE **(354–430)**
QUESTIONS ON JOSHUA

from them. 7Then you rise up from your hiding place and seize
the city. The LORD your God will hand it over to you. 8When
you capture the city, set it on fire in keeping with the LORD's
message. See, I have given you orders." 9Joshua sent them away
and they went to their hiding place west of Ai, between Bethel
and Ai. Joshua spent that night with the army.

10Bright and early the next morning Joshua gathered the
army, and he and the leaders of Israel marched at the head of
it to Ai. 11All the troops that were with him marched up and
drew near the city. They camped north of Ai on the other side
of the valley. 12He took 5,000 men and set an ambush west of
the city between Bethel and Ai. 13The army was in position—the
main army north of the city and the rear guard west of the city.
That night Joshua went into the middle of the valley.

14When the king of Ai and all his people saw Israel, they
rushed to get up early. Then the king and the men of the city
went out to meet Israel in battle, at the meeting place near
the rift valley. But he did not realize an ambush was waiting
for him behind the city. 15Joshua and all Israel pretended to
be defeated by them, and they retreated along the way to the
wilderness. 16All the reinforcements in Ai were ordered to chase
them; they chased Joshua and were lured away from the city.
17No men were left in Ai or Bethel; they all went out after Israel.
They left the city wide open and chased Israel.

18The LORD told Joshua, "Hold out toward Ai the curved sword
in your hand, for I am handing the city over to you." So Joshua
held out toward Ai the curved sword in his hand. 19When he
held out his hand, the men waiting in ambush rose up quickly
from their place and attacked. They entered the city, captured
it, and immediately set it on fire. 20When the men of Ai turned
around, they saw the smoke from the city ascending into the sky
and were so shocked they were unable to flee in any direction. In
the meantime the men who were retreating to the wilderness
turned against their pursuers. 21When Joshua and all Israel saw
that the men in ambush had captured the city and that the city
was going up in smoke, they turned around and struck down
the men of Ai. 22At the same time the men who had taken the
city came out to fight, and the men of Ai were trapped in the
middle. The Israelites struck them down, leaving no survivors
or refugees. 23But they captured the king of Ai alive and brought
him to Joshua.

24When Israel had finished killing all the men of Ai who had
chased them toward the wilderness (they all fell by the sword),
all Israel returned to Ai and put the sword to it. 25So 12,000 men
and women died that day, including all the men of Ai. 26Joshua
kept holding out his curved sword until Israel had annihilated
all who lived in Ai. 27But Israel did plunder the cattle and the
goods of the city, in keeping with the LORD's orders to Joshua.
28Joshua burned Ai and made it a permanently uninhabited
mound (it remains that way to this very day). 29He hung the king
of Ai on a tree, leaving him exposed until evening. At sunset
Joshua ordered that his corpse be taken down from the tree.
They threw it down at the entrance of the city gate and erected
over it a large pile of stones (it remains to this very day).

COVENANT RENEWAL

30Then Joshua built an altar for the LORD God of Israel on Mount
Ebal, 31just as Moses the LORD's servant had commanded the
Israelites. As described in the law scroll of Moses, it was made

with uncut stones untouched by an iron tool. On it they offered
burnt sacrifices to the LORD and sacrificed tokens of peace.
[32]There, in the presence of the Israelites, Joshua inscribed on
the stones a duplicate of the law written by Moses. [33]All the
people, rulers, leaders, and judges were standing on either side
of the ark, in front of the Levitical priests who carried the ark of
the covenant of the LORD. Both resident foreigners and native
Israelites were there. Half the people stood in front of Mount
Gerizim and the other half in front of Mount Ebal, as Moses
the LORD's servant had previously instructed them to do for
the formal blessing ceremony. [34]Then Joshua read aloud all the
words of the law, including the blessings and the curses, just
as they are written in the law scroll. [35]Joshua read aloud every
commandment Moses had given before the whole assembly of
Israel, including the women, children, and resident foreigners
who lived among them.

THE GIBEONITES DECEIVE ISRAEL

9 When the news reached all the kings on the west side of the
Jordan—in the hill country, the foothills, and all along the
Mediterranean coast as far as Lebanon (including the Hittites,
Amorites, Canaanites, Perizzites, Hivites, and Jebusites)—[2]they
formed an alliance to fight against Joshua and Israel.

[3]When the residents of Gibeon heard what Joshua did to
Jericho and Ai, [4]they did something clever. They collected some
provisions and put worn-out sacks on their donkeys, along with
worn-out wineskins that were ripped and patched. [5]They had
worn-out, patched sandals on their feet and dressed in worn-
out clothes. All their bread was dry and hard. [6]They came to
Joshua at the camp in Gilgal and said to him and the men of
Israel, "We have come from a distant land. Make a treaty with
us." [7]The men of Israel said to the Hivites, "Perhaps you live
near us. So how can we make a treaty with you?" [8]But they said
to Joshua, "We are willing to be your subjects." So Joshua said
to them, "Who are you and where do you come from?" [9]They
told him, "Your subjects have come from a very distant land
because of the reputation of the LORD your God, for we have
heard the news about all he did in Egypt [10]and all he did to
the two Amorite kings on the other side of the Jordan—King
Sihon of Heshbon and King Og of Bashan in Ashtaroth. [11]Our
leaders and all who live in our land told us, 'Take provisions for
your journey and go meet them. Tell them, "We are willing to
be your subjects. Make a treaty with us."' [12]This bread of ours
was warm when we packed it in our homes the day we started
out to meet you, but now it is dry and hard. [13]These wineskins
we filled were brand new, but look how they have ripped. Our
clothes and sandals have worn out because it has been a very
long journey." [14]The men examined some of their provisions,
but they failed to ask the LORD's advice. [15]Joshua made a peace
treaty with them and agreed to let them live. The leaders of
the community sealed it with an oath.

[16]Three days after they made the treaty with them, the Israelites found out they were from the local area and lived nearby.
[17]So the Israelites set out and on the third day arrived at their
cities—Gibeon, Kephirah, Beeroth, and Kiriath Jearim. [18]The
Israelites did not attack them because the leaders of the community had sworn an oath to them in the name of the LORD God
of Israel. The whole community criticized the leaders, [19]but all
the leaders told the whole community, "We swore an oath to

9:1–27 Then the Gibeonites came with guile, pretending that they were from a land very far away. They said too that their reason for undergoing so much labor was their desire to obtain peace and to form friendship with the Hebrews, and they began to ask Joshua to form an alliance with them. And he, being as yet ignorant of localities, did not see through their deceit, nor did he inquire of God but readily believed them. We must not blame Joshua's readiness to believe but should rather praise his goodness. This is to be innocent. And although he is cheated by another, still he thinks well of all, for he thinks there is good faith in all.

AMBROSE **(C. 339–C. 397)**
ON THE DUTIES OF THE CLERGY

them in the name of the LORD God of Israel! So now we can't
hurt them. 20We must let them live so we can escape the curse
attached to the oath we swore to them." 21The leaders then
added, "Let them live." So they became woodcutters and water
carriers for the whole community, as the leaders had decided.
22Joshua summoned the Gibeonites and said to them, "Why
did you trick us by saying, 'We live far away from you,' when
you really live nearby? 23Now you are condemned to perpetual
servitude as woodcutters and water carriers for the house of
my God." 24They said to Joshua, "It was carefully reported to
your subjects how the LORD your God commanded Moses his
servant to assign you the whole land and to destroy all who live
in the land from before you. Because of you we were terrified
we would lose our lives, so we did this thing. 25So now we are in
your power. Do to us what you think is good and appropriate."
26Joshua did as they said; he kept the Israelites from killing
them 27and that day made them woodcutters and water carriers
for the community and for the altar of the LORD at the divinely
chosen site. (They continue in that capacity to this very day.)

ISRAEL DEFEATS AN AMORITE COALITION

10 Adoni-Zedek, king of Jerusalem, heard how Joshua captured Ai and annihilated it and its king as he did Jericho
and its king. He also heard how the people of Gibeon made
peace with Israel and lived among them. 2All Jerusalem was
terrified because Gibeon was a large city, like one of the royal
cities. It was larger than Ai, and all its men were warriors. 3So
King Adoni-Zedek of Jerusalem sent this message to King Ho-
ham of Hebron, King Piram of Jarmuth, King Japhia of Lachish,
and King Debir of Eglon: 4"Come to my aid so we can attack
Gibeon, for it has made peace with Joshua and the Israelites."
5So the five Amorite kings (the kings of Jerusalem, Hebron,
Jarmuth, Lachish, and Eglon) and all their troops gathered together and advanced. They deployed their troops and fought
against Gibeon.
6The men of Gibeon sent this message to Joshua at the camp
in Gilgal, "Do not abandon your subjects! Come up here quickly
and rescue us! Help us! For all the Amorite kings living in the
hill country are attacking us." 7So Joshua and his whole army,
including the bravest warriors, marched up from Gilgal. 8The
LORD told Joshua, "Don't be afraid of them, for I am handing
them over to you. Not one of them can resist you." 9Joshua attacked them by surprise after marching all night from Gilgal.
10The LORD routed them before Israel. Israel thoroughly defeated them at Gibeon. They chased them up the road to the
pass of Beth Horon and struck them down all the way to Azekah
and Makkedah. 11As they fled from Israel on the slope leading
down from Beth Horon, the LORD threw down on them large
hailstones from the sky, all the way to Azekah. They died—in
fact, more died from the hailstones than the Israelites killed
with the sword.
12The day the LORD delivered the Amorites over to the Israelites, Joshua prayed to the LORD before Israel:

"O sun, stand still over Gibeon;
O moon, over the Valley of Aijalon!"

13The sun stood still and the moon stood motionless while
the nation took vengeance on its enemies. The event is recorded
in the Scroll of the Upright One. The sun stood motionless in

the middle of the sky and did not set for about a full day. [14]There has not been a day like it before or since. The LORD listened to a human being, for the LORD fought for Israel! [15]Then Joshua and all Israel returned to the camp at Gilgal.

[16]The five Amorite kings ran away and hid in the cave at Makkedah. [17]Joshua was told, "The five kings have been found hiding in the cave at Makkedah." [18]Joshua said, "Roll large stones over the mouth of the cave and post guards in front of it. [19]But don't you delay! Chase your enemies and catch them. Don't allow them to retreat to their cities, for the LORD your God is handing them over to you." [20]Joshua and the Israelites almost totally wiped them out, but some survivors did escape to the fortified cities. [21]Then the whole army safely returned to Joshua at the camp in Makkedah. No one dared threaten the Israelites. [22]Joshua said, "Open the cave's mouth and bring the five kings out of the cave to me." [23]They did as ordered; they brought the five kings out of the cave to him—the kings of Jerusalem, Hebron, Jarmuth, Lachish, and Eglon. [24]When they brought the kings out to Joshua, he summoned all the men of Israel and said to the commanders of the troops who accompanied him, "Come here and put your feet on the necks of these kings." So they came up and put their feet on their necks. [25]Then Joshua said to them, "Don't be afraid and don't panic! Be strong and brave, for the LORD will do the same thing to all your enemies you fight." [26]Then Joshua executed them and hung them on five trees. They were left hanging on the trees until evening. [27]At sunset Joshua ordered his men to take them down from the trees. They threw them into the cave where they had hidden and piled large stones over the mouth of the cave. (They remain to this very day.)

JOSHUA LAUNCHES A SOUTHERN CAMPAIGN

[28]That day Joshua captured Makkedah and put the sword to it and its king. He annihilated everyone who lived in it; he left no survivors. He did to its king what he had done to the king of Jericho.

[29]Joshua and all Israel marched from Makkedah to Libnah and fought against it. [30]The LORD handed it and its king over to Israel, and Israel put the sword to all who lived there; they left no survivors. They did to its king what they had done to the king of Jericho.

[31]Joshua and all Israel marched from Libnah to Lachish. He deployed his troops and fought against it. [32]The LORD handed Lachish over to Israel, and they captured it on the second day. They put the sword to all who lived there, just as they had done to Libnah. [33]Then King Horam of Gezer came up to help Lachish, but Joshua struck him down, as well as his army, until no survivors remained.

[34]Joshua and all Israel marched from Lachish to Eglon. They deployed troops and fought against it. [35]That day they captured it and put the sword to all who lived there. That day they annihilated it just as they had done to Lachish.

[36]Joshua and all Israel marched up from Eglon to Hebron and fought against it. [37]They captured it and put the sword to its king, all its surrounding cities, and all who lived in it; they left no survivors. As they had done at Eglon, they annihilated it and all who lived there.

[38]Joshua and all Israel turned to Debir and fought against it. [39]They captured it, its king, and all its surrounding cities and

10:28–42 I myself think it is better that the Israelite wars be understood in this way, and it is better that Joshua is thought to fight in this way and to destroy cities and overthrow kingdoms. For in this manner what is said will also appear more devout and more merciful when he is said to have so subverted and devastated individual cities that "he left no survivors. He annihilated everything that breathed." Would that the Lord might thus cast out and extinguish all former evils from the souls who believe in him—even those he claims for his kingdom.

ORIGEN **(C. 185–C. 253)**
HOMILIES ON JOSHUA

put the sword to them. They annihilated everyone who lived
there; they left no survivors. They did to Debir and its king what
they had done to Libnah and its king and to Hebron.
40Joshua defeated the whole land, including the hill country,
the Negev, the foothills, the slopes, and all their kings. He left
no survivors. He annihilated everything that breathed, just as
the LORD God of Israel had commanded. 41Joshua conquered
the area between Kadesh Barnea and Gaza and the whole region of Goshen, all the way to Gibeon. 42Joshua captured in one
campaign all these kings and their lands, for the LORD God of
Israel fought for Israel. 43Then Joshua and all Israel returned
to the camp at Gilgal.

ISRAEL DEFEATS A NORTHERN COALITION

11 When King Jabin of Hazor heard the news about Israel's
victories, he organized a coalition, including King Jobab
of Madon, the king of Shimron, the king of Acshaph, 2and the
northern kings who ruled in the hill country, in the rift valley
south of Kinnereth, in the foothills, and on the heights of Dor
to the west. 3Canaanites came from the east and west; Amorites, Hittites, Perizzites, and Jebusites from the hill country;
and Hivites from below Hermon in the area of Mizpah. 4These
kings came out with their armies; they were as numerous as
the sand on the seashore and had a large number of horses
and chariots. 5All these kings gathered and joined forces at the
Waters of Merom to fight Israel.
6The LORD told Joshua, "Don't be afraid of them, for about
this time tomorrow I will cause all of them to lie dead before
Israel. You must hamstring their horses and burn their chariots." 7Joshua and his whole army caught them by surprise at the
Waters of Merom and attacked them. 8The LORD handed them
over to Israel, and they struck them down and chased them all
the way to Greater Sidon, Misrephoth Maim, and the Mizpah
Valley to the east. They struck them down until no survivors
remained. 9Joshua did to them as the LORD had commanded
him; he hamstrung their horses and burned their chariots.
10At that time Joshua turned, captured Hazor, and struck
down its king with the sword, for Hazor was at that time the
leader of all these kingdoms. 11They annihilated everyone who
lived there with the sword—no one who breathed remained—
and burned Hazor.
12Joshua captured all these royal cities and all their kings
and annihilated them with the sword, as Moses the LORD's
servant had commanded. 13But Israel did not burn any of the
cities located on mounds except for Hazor; it was the only one
Joshua burned. 14The Israelites plundered all the goods of these
cities and the cattle, but they totally destroyed all the people
and allowed no one who breathed to live. 15Moses the LORD's
servant passed on the LORD's commands to Joshua, and Joshua
did as he was told. He did not ignore any of the commands the
LORD had given Moses.

A SUMMARY OF ISRAEL'S VICTORIES

16Joshua conquered the whole land, including the hill country, all the Negev, all the land of Goshen, the foothills, the rift
valley, the hill country of Israel and its foothills, 17from Mount
Halak up to Seir, as far as Baal Gad in the Lebanon Valley below
Mount Hermon. He captured all their kings and executed them.
18Joshua campaigned against these kings for quite some time.

11:16—12:24 All the southern part of the country, after the capture of Jericho and Ai, was practically brought about by one decisive battle, the battle of Beth Horon, where the Almighty thundered and sent his hailstones and where the sun stood still. Now the northern conquest was brought about by one decisive battle: When the northern tribes learned of the subjugation of the southern tribes, they saw that it was a life-and-death matter and they sent an invitation to the remnant of the tribes that had been conquered. Joshua gave them no time to rally, and when they had been thoroughly discomfited, he took the towns.

B. H. CARROLL (1843–1914)
INTERPRETATION OF THE ENGLISH BIBLE

19 No city made peace with the Israelites (except the Hivites
living in Gibeon); they had to conquer all of them, 20 for the
LORD determined to make them obstinate so they would attack
Israel. He wanted Israel to annihilate them without mercy, as
he had instructed Moses.
21 At that time Joshua attacked and eliminated the Anakites
from the hill country—from Hebron, Debir, Anab, and all the
hill country of Judah and Israel. Joshua annihilated them and
their cities. 22 No Anakites were left in Israelite territory, though
some remained in Gaza, Gath, and Ashdod. 23 Joshua conquered
the whole land, just as the LORD had promised Moses, and he assigned Israel their tribal portions. Then the land was free of war.

12 Now these are the kings of the land whom the Israelites
defeated and drove from their land on the east side of the
Jordan, from the Arnon Valley to Mount Hermon, including all
the eastern rift valley:
2 King Sihon of the Amorites who lived in Heshbon and ruled
from Aroer (on the edge of the Arnon Valley)—including the city
in the middle of the valley and half of Gilead—all the way to the
Jabbok Valley bordering Ammonite territory. 3 His kingdom
included the eastern rift valley from the Sea of Kinnereth to the
sea of the rift valley (the Salt Sea), including the route to Beth
Jeshimoth and the area southward below the slopes of Pisgah.
4 The territory of King Og of Bashan, one of the few remaining Rephaites, who lived in Ashtaroth and Edrei 5 and ruled
over Mount Hermon, Salecah, all Bashan to the border of the
Geshurites and Maacathites, and half of Gilead as far as the
border of King Sihon of Heshbon.
6 Moses the LORD's servant and the Israelites defeated them,
and Moses the LORD's servant assigned their land to Reuben,
Gad, and the half-tribe of Manasseh.
7 These are the kings of the land whom Joshua and the Israelites defeated on the west side of the Jordan, from Baal Gad in
the Lebanon Valley to Mount Halak up to Seir. Joshua assigned
this territory to the Israelite tribes, 8 including the hill country,
the foothills, the rift valley, the slopes, the wilderness, and the
Negev—the land of the Hittites, Amorites, Canaanites, Perizzites, Hivites, and Jebusites:

9 the king of Jericho (one),
the king of Ai—located near Bethel—(one),
10 the king of Jerusalem (one),
the king of Hebron (one),
11 the king of Jarmuth (one),
the king of Lachish (one),
12 the king of Eglon (one),
the king of Gezer (one),
13 the king of Debir (one),
the king of Geder (one),
14 the king of Hormah (one),
the king of Arad (one),
15 the king of Libnah (one),
the king of Adullam (one),
16 the king of Makkedah (one),
the king of Bethel (one),
17 the king of Tappuah (one),
the king of Hepher (one),
18 the king of Aphek (one),
the king of Lasharon (one),
19 the king of Madon (one),

the king of Hazor (one),
20 the king of Shimron Meron (one),
the king of Acshaph (one),
21 the king of Taanach (one),
the king of Megiddo (one),
22 the king of Kedesh (one),
the king of Jokneam near Carmel (one),
23 the king of Dor—near Naphath Dor—(one),
the king of Goyim—near Gilgal—(one),
24 the king of Tirzah (one),
a total of thirty-one kings.

13:1–7 Whatever becomes of us, however we may be laid aside as broken vessels, God will do his work in his own time. But the promise of driving their enemies out from before the children of Israel supposes that the Israelites must use their own endeavors, must go up against them. If Israel through sloth or cowardice let them alone, they were not likely to be driven out. We must go forth on our Christian warfare, and then God will go before us.

JOHN WESLEY (1703–1791)
EXPLANATORY NOTES ON THE BIBLE

THE LORD SPEAKS TO JOSHUA

13 When Joshua was very old, the LORD told him, "You are
very old, and a great deal of land remains to be conquered.
2This is the land that remains: all the territory of the Philistines
and all the Geshurites, 3from the Shihor River east of Egypt
northward to the territory of Ekron (it is regarded as Canaanite
territory), including the area belonging to the five Philistine
lords who ruled in Gaza, Ashdod, Ashkelon, Gath, and Ekron,
as well as Avvite land 4to the south; all the Canaanite territory,
from Arah in the region of Sidon to Aphek, as far as Amorite
territory; 5the territory of Byblos and all Lebanon to the east,
from Baal Gad below Mount Hermon to Lebo Hamath. 6I will
drive out before the Israelites all who live in the hill country
from Lebanon to Misrephoth Maim, all the Sidonians; you be
sure to parcel it out to Israel as I instructed you. 7Now, divide up
this land among the nine tribes and the half-tribe of Manasseh."

TRIBAL LANDS EAST OF THE JORDAN

8The other half of Manasseh, Reuben, and Gad received their
allotted tribal lands on the east side of the Jordan, just as Moses,
the LORD's servant, had assigned them. 9Their territory started
from Aroer (on the edge of the Arnon Valley), included the city
in the middle of the valley, the whole plain of Medeba as far as
Dibon, 10and all the cities of King Sihon of the Amorites who
ruled in Heshbon, and ended at the Ammonite border. 11Their
territory also included Gilead, Geshurite and Maacathite territory, all Mount Hermon, and all Bashan to Salecah—12the whole
kingdom of Og in Bashan, who ruled in Ashtaroth and Edrei. (He
was one of the few remaining Rephaites.) Moses defeated them
and took their lands. 13But the Israelites did not conquer the
Geshurites and Maacathites; Geshur and Maacah live among
Israel to this very day. 14However, Moses did not assign land as
an inheritance to the Levites; their inheritance is the sacrificial
offerings made to the LORD God of Israel, as he instructed them.
15Moses assigned land to the tribe of Reuben by its clans.
16Their territory started at Aroer (on the edge of the Arnon
Valley) and included the city in the middle of the valley, the
whole plain of Medeba, 17Heshbon and all its surrounding cities
on the plain, including Dibon, Bamoth Baal, Beth Baal Meon,
18Jahaz, Kedemoth, Mephaath, 19Kiriathaim, Sibmah, Zereth
Shahar on the hill in the valley, 20Beth Peor, the slopes of Pisgah,
and Beth Jeshimoth. 21It encompassed all the cities of the plain
and the whole realm of King Sihon of the Amorites who ruled
in Heshbon. Moses defeated him and the Midianite leaders
Evi, Rekem, Zur, Hur, and Reba (they were subjects of Sihon and
lived in his territory). 22The Israelites killed Balaam son of Beor,
the omen reader, along with the others. 23The border of the

tribe of Reuben was the Jordan. The land allotted to the tribe
of Reuben by its clans included these cities and their towns.
24 Moses assigned land to the tribe of Gad by its clans. 25 Their
territory included Jazer, all the cities of Gilead, and half the Ammonite territory as far as Aroer near Rabbah. 26 Their territory
ran from Heshbon to Ramath Mizpah and Betonim, and from
Mahanaim to the territory of Debir. 27 It included the valley of
Beth Haram, Beth Nimrah, Sukkoth, and Zaphon, and the rest of
the realm of King Sihon of Heshbon, the area east of the Jordan
to the end of the Sea of Kinnereth. 28 The land allotted to the
tribe of Gad by its clans included these cities and their towns.
29 Moses assigned land to the half-tribe of Manasseh by its
clans. 30 Their territory started at Mahanaim and encompassed
all Bashan, the whole realm of King Og of Bashan, including all
60 cities in Havvoth Jair in Bashan. 31 Half of Gilead, Ashtaroth,
and Edrei, cities in the kingdom of Og in Bashan, were assigned
to the descendants of Makir son of Manasseh, to half the descendants of Makir by their clans.
32 These are the land assignments made by Moses in the rift
valley plains of Moab east of the Jordan River opposite Jericho.
33 However, Moses did not assign land as an inheritance to the
Levites; their inheritance is the LORD God of Israel, as he instructed them.

JUDAH'S TRIBAL LANDS

14 The following is a record of the territory assigned to the
Israelites in the land of Canaan by Eleazar the priest, Joshua son of Nun, and the Israelite tribal leaders. 2 The land assignments to the nine-and-a-half tribes were made by drawing lots,
as the LORD had instructed Moses. 3 Now Moses had assigned
land to the two-and-a-half tribes east of the Jordan, but he assigned no land to the Levites. 4 The descendants of Joseph were
considered as two tribes, Manasseh and Ephraim. The Levites
were allotted no territory, though they were assigned cities in
which to live, along with the grazing areas for their cattle and
possessions. 5 The Israelites followed the LORD's instructions
to Moses and divided up the land.
6 The men of Judah approached Joshua in Gilgal, and Caleb
son of Jephunneh the Kenizzite said to him, "You know what
the LORD said about you and me to Moses, the man of God, at
Kadesh Barnea. 7 I was forty years old when Moses, the LORD's
servant, sent me from Kadesh Barnea to spy on the land and I
brought back to him an honest report. 8 My countrymen who
accompanied me frightened the people, but I remained loyal to
the LORD my God. 9 That day Moses made this solemn promise:
'Surely the land on which you walked will belong to you and
your descendants permanently, for you remained loyal to the
LORD your God.' 10 So now, look, the LORD has preserved my life,
just as he promised, these past forty-five years since the LORD
spoke these words to Moses, while Israel traveled through the
wilderness. See here, I am today eighty-five years old! 11 Today
I am still as strong as when Moses sent me out. I can fight and
go about my daily activities with the same energy I had then.
12 Now, assign me this hill country that the LORD promised
me at that time! No doubt you heard then that the Anakites
live there in large, fortified cities. But assuming the LORD is
with me, I will conquer them, as the LORD promised." 13 Joshua
asked God to empower Caleb son of Jephunneh and assigned
him Hebron. 14 So Hebron remains the assigned land of Caleb

14:6–15 The Lord said they should not come to that land that they had refused as a penalty for their unbelief. So the bodies of those of twenty years old and upward fell in the desert. The punishment of the rest was put aside. But they who had gone up with Joshua and had thought fit to dissuade the people died forthwith of a great plague. Joshua and Caleb entered the land of promise together with those who were innocent by reason of age or sex. The better part, therefore, preferred glory to safety, and the worse part safety to virtue.

AMBROSE **(C. 339–C. 397)**
ON THE DUTIES OF THE CLERGY

15:1–12 All who want to enter the portion of the children of Judah must first pass through the Salt Sea. That is to say, they must surmount the waves and billows of this life and escape from all things in this world that, by virtue of their own uncertainty and hazardousness, are compared with the waves of the sea. Then they may be able to reach the land of Judah and to approach the fountain of the sun. But what is the fountain of the sun, or of which sun? Of that sun, of course, about which it is written, "But for you who respect my name, the sun of vindication will rise" (Mal 4:2). Therefore you will find the fountain of this sun in the land of Judah if you move away from the Salt Sea.

ORIGEN (C. 185–C. 253)
HOMILIES ON JOSHUA

son of Jephunneh the Kenizzite to this very day because he remained loyal to the LORD God of Israel. [15](Hebron used to be called Kiriath Arba. Arba was a famous Anakite.) Then the land was free of war.

15 The land allotted to the tribe of Judah by its clans reached to the border of Edom, to the wilderness of Zin in the Negev far to the south. [2]Their southern border started at the southern tip of the Salt Sea, [3]extended south of the Scorpion Ascent, crossed to Zin, went up from the south to Kadesh Barnea, crossed to Hezron, went up to Addar, and turned toward Karka. [4]It then crossed to Azmon, extended to the Stream of Egypt, and ended at the Mediterranean Sea. This was their southern border.

[5]The eastern border was the Salt Sea to the mouth of the Jordan River.

The northern border started north of the Salt Sea at the mouth of the Jordan, [6]went up to Beth Hoglah, crossed north of Beth Arabah, and went up to the Stone of Bohan son of Reuben. [7]It then went up to Debir from the Valley of Achor, turning northward to Gilgal (which is opposite the Pass of Adummim south of the valley), crossed to the waters of En Shemesh, and extended to En Rogel. [8]It then went up the Valley of Ben Hinnom to the slope of the Jebusites on the south (that is, Jerusalem), going up to the top of the hill opposite the Valley of Ben Hinnom to the west, which is at the end of the Valley of the Rephaites to the north. [9]It then went from the top of the hill to the spring of the waters of Nephtoah, extended to the cities of Mount Ephron, and went to Baalah (that is, Kiriath Jearim). [10]It then turned from Baalah westward to Mount Seir, crossed to the slope of Mount Jearim on the north (that is Kesalon), descended to Beth Shemesh, and crossed to Timnah. [11]It then extended to the slope of Ekron to the north, went toward Shikkeron, crossed to Mount Baalah, extended to Jabneel, and ended at the sea.

[12]The western border was the Mediterranean Sea. These were the borders of the tribe of Judah and its clans.

[13]Caleb son of Jephunneh was assigned Kiriath Arba (that is Hebron) within the tribe of Judah, according to the LORD's instructions to Joshua. (Arba was the father of Anak.) [14]Caleb drove out from there three Anakites—Sheshai, Ahiman, and Talmai, descendants of Anak. [15]From there he attacked the people of Debir. (Debir used to be called Kiriath Sepher.) [16]Caleb said, "To the man who attacks and captures Kiriath Sepher I will give my daughter Achsah as a wife." [17]When Othniel son of Kenaz, Caleb's brother, captured it, Caleb gave Achsah his daughter to him as a wife.

[18]One time Achsah came and charmed her father so that she could ask him for some land. When she got down from her donkey, Caleb said to her, "What would you like?" [19]She answered, "Please give me a special present. Since you have given me land in the Negev, now give me springs of water." So he gave her both the upper and lower springs.

[20]This is the land assigned to the tribe of Judah by its clans: [21]These cities were located at the southern extremity of Judah's tribal land near the border of Edom: Kabzeel, Eder, Jagur, [22]Kinah, Dimonah, Adadah, [23]Kedesh, Hazor, Ithnan, [24]Ziph, Telem, Bealoth, [25]Hazor Hadattah, Kerioth Hezron (that is, Hazor), [26]Amam, Shema, Moladah, [27]Hazar Gaddah, Heshbon, Beth Pelet, [28]Hazar Shual, Beer Sheba, Biziothiah, [29]Baalah,

Iim, Ezem, 30Eltolad, Kesil, Hormah, 31Ziklag, Madmannah,
Sansannah, 32Lebaoth, Shilhim, Ain, and Rimmon—a total of
29 cities and their towns.
33These cities were in the foothills: Eshtaol, Zorah, Ashnah,
34Zanoah, En Gannim, Tappuah, Enam, 35Jarmuth, Adullam,
Socoh, Azekah, 36Shaaraim, Adithaim, and Gederah (or Gedero-
thaim)—a total of 14 cities and their towns.
37Zenan, Hadashah, Migdal Gad, 38Dilean, Mizpah, Joktheel, 39Lachish, Bozkath, Eglon, 40Cabbon, Lahmas, Kitlish,
41Gederoth, Beth Dagon, Naamah, and Makkedah—a total of
16 cities and their towns.
42Libnah, Ether, Ashan, 43Iphtah, Ashnah, Nezib, 44Keilah,
Achzib, and Mareshah—a total of nine cities and their towns.
45Ekron and its surrounding towns and settlements; 46from
Ekron westward, all those in the vicinity of Ashdod and their
towns; 47Ashdod with its surrounding towns and settlements,
and Gaza with its surrounding towns and settlements, as far as
the Stream of Egypt and the border at the Mediterranean Sea.
48These cities were in the hill country: Shamir, Jattir, Socoh,
49Dannah, Kiriath Sannah (that is, Debir), 50Anab, Eshtemoh,
Anim, 51Goshen, Holon, and Giloh—a total of eleven cities and
their towns.
52Arab, Dumah, Eshan, 53Janim, Beth Tappuah, Aphekah,
54Humtah, Kiriath Arba (that is, Hebron), and Zior—a total of
nine cities and their towns.
55Maon, Carmel, Ziph, Juttah, 56Jezreel, Jokdeam, Zanoah,
57Kain, Gibeah, and Timnah—a total of 10 cities and their towns.
58Halhul, Beth Zur, Gedor, 59Maarath, Beth Anoth, and Elte-
kon—a total of six cities and their towns.
60Kiriath Baal (that is, Kiriath Jearim) and Rabbah—a total
of two cities and their towns.
61These cities were in the wilderness: Beth Arabah, Middin,
Secacah, 62Nibshan, the City of Salt, and En Gedi—a total of six
cities and their towns.
63The men of Judah were unable to conquer the Jebusites
living in Jerusalem. The Jebusites live with the people of Judah
in Jerusalem to this very day.

JOSEPH'S TRIBAL LANDS

16 The land allotted to Joseph's descendants extended from
the Jordan at Jericho to the waters of Jericho to the east,
through the desert and on up from Jericho into the hill country
of Bethel. 2The southern border extended from Bethel to Luz,
and crossed to Arkite territory at Ataroth. 3It then descended
westward to Japhletite territory, as far as the territory of lower
Beth Horon and Gezer, and ended at the sea.
4Joseph's descendants, Manasseh and Ephraim, were assigned their land. 5The territory of the tribe of Ephraim by its
clans included the following: The border of their assigned land
to the east was Ataroth Addar as far as upper Beth Horon. 6It
then extended on to the sea, with Micmethath on the north.
It turned eastward to Taanath Shiloh and crossed it on the
east to Janoah. 7It then descended from Janoah to Ataroth
and Naarah, touched Jericho, and extended to the Jordan River. 8From Tappuah it went westward to the Valley of Kanah
and ended at the sea. This is the land assigned to the tribe of
Ephraim by its clans. 9Also included were the cities set apart
for the tribe of Ephraim within Manasseh's territory, along
with their towns.

16:1–10 "The Canaanites live among the Ephraimites to this very day." But Ephraim is interpreted as "fruitful." Therefore, although it is fruitful, it is not able to eject the Canaanite (who is of a different and cursed seed) from its territory until this day. But we can also say this concerning the church. Taken another way, there are no souls who are able to remain pure in this present life, seeking peace alone without sinning until they see Christ, the Peace of God. For no one is clean from strange or alien thinking on his own. And so, just as the Jebusites and Canaanites are always found in Jerusalem, it is also necessary to suffer for the casting out of these, but only those who call upon God are able to do so.

PROCOPIUS OF GAZA
(C. 465–528)
COMMENTARY ON JOSHUA

10The Ephraimites did not conquer the Canaanites living in
Gezer. The Canaanites live among the Ephraimites to this very
day and do hard labor as their servants.

17 The tribe of Manasseh, Joseph's firstborn son, was also
allotted land. The descendants of Makir, Manasseh's
firstborn and the father of Gilead, received land, for they were
warriors. They were assigned Gilead and Bashan. 2The rest of
Manasseh's descendants were also assigned land by their clans,
including the descendants of Abiezer, Helek, Asriel, Shechem,
Hepher, and Shemida. These are the male descendants of
Manasseh son of Joseph by their clans.

3Now Zelophehad son of Hepher, son of Gilead, son of Makir, son of Manasseh, had no sons, only daughters. These are
the names of his daughters: Mahlah, Noah, Hoglah, Milcah,
and Tirzah. 4They went before Eleazar the priest, Joshua
son of Nun, and the leaders and said, "The LORD told Moses
to assign us land among our relatives." So Joshua assigned
them land among their uncles, as the LORD had commanded. 5Manasseh was allotted 10 shares of land, in addition to
the land of Gilead and Bashan east of the Jordan, 6for the
daughters of Manasseh were assigned land among his sons.
The land of Gilead belonged to the rest of the descendants
of Manasseh.

7The border of Manasseh went from Asher to Micmethath,
which is near Shechem. It then went south toward those
who live by En Tappuah. 8(The land of Tappuah belonged to
Manasseh, but Tappuah, located on the border of Manasseh,
belonged to the tribe of Ephraim.) 9The border then descended
southward to the Valley of Kanah. Ephraim was assigned cities
there among the cities of Manasseh, but the border of Manasseh
was north of the valley and ended at the sea. 10Ephraim's territory was to the south, and Manasseh's to the north. The sea was
Manasseh's western border, and their territory touched Asher
on the north and Issachar on the east. 11Within Issachar's and
Asher's territories Manasseh was assigned Beth Shean, Ibleam,
the residents of Dor, the residents of Endor, the residents of Taanach, the residents of Megiddo, the three of Napheth, and the
towns surrounding all these cities. 12But the men of Manasseh
were unable to conquer these cities; the Canaanites managed
to remain in those areas. 13Whenever the Israelites were strong
militarily, they forced the Canaanites to do hard labor, but they
never totally conquered them.

14The descendants of Joseph said to Joshua, "Why have you
assigned us only one tribal allotment? After all, we have many
people, for until now the LORD has enabled us to increase in
number." 15Joshua replied to them, "Since you have so many
people, go up into the forest and clear out a place to live in
the land of the Perizzites and Rephaites, if the hill country
of Ephraim is too small for you." 16The descendants of Joseph
said, "The whole hill country is inadequate for us, and the Canaanites living down in the valley in Beth Shean and its surrounding towns and in the Valley of Jezreel have chariots with
iron-rimmed wheels." 17Joshua said to the family of Joseph—to
both Ephraim and Manasseh: "You have many people and great
military strength. You will not have just one tribal allotment.
18The whole hill country will be yours; though it is a forest,
you can clear it, and it will be entirely yours. You can conquer
the Canaanites, though they have chariots with iron-rimmed
wheels and are strong."

17:11–18 The habitation given to the Israelites was not a subjected one that they might immediately enjoy, but it was an inheritance treasured up in hope and founded more on heavenly promise than on actual possession. And yet their not gaining possession of those cities is attributed to their fault because the lot assigning it to them was an indubitable pledge of victory. The reason, therefore, why they could not expel the inhabitants was because they were not fully persuaded in their minds that God is true, and they stifled his agency by their own sluggishness.

JOHN CALVIN **(1509–1564)**
COMPLETE COMMENTARY ON THE BIBLE

THE TRIBES MEET AT SHILOH

18 The entire Israelite community assembled at Shiloh and
there they set up the tent of meeting. Though they had
subdued the land, 2seven Israelite tribes had not been assigned
their allotted land. 3So Joshua said to the Israelites: "How long do
you intend to put off occupying the land the LORD God of your
ancestors has given you? 4Pick three men from each tribe. I will
send them out to walk through the land and make a map of it for
me. 5Divide it into seven regions. Judah will stay in its territory
in the south and the family of Joseph in its territory in the north.
6But as for you, map out the land into seven regions and bring
it to me. I will draw lots for you here before the LORD our God.
7But the Levites will not have an allotted portion among you, for
their inheritance is to serve the LORD. Gad, Reuben, and the half-
tribe of Manasseh have already received their allotted land east
of the Jordan, which Moses the LORD's servant assigned them."
8When the men started out, Joshua told those going to map
out the land, "Go, walk through the land, map it out, and return
to me. Then I will draw lots for you before the LORD here in
Shiloh." 9The men journeyed through the land and mapped
it and its cities out into seven regions on a scroll. Then they
came to Joshua at the camp in Shiloh. 10Joshua drew lots for
them in Shiloh before the LORD and divided the land among
the Israelites according to their allotted portions.

BENJAMIN'S TRIBAL LANDS

11The first lot belonged to the tribe of Benjamin by its clans.
Their allotted territory was between Judah and Joseph. 12Their
northern border started at the Jordan, went up to the slope of
Jericho on the north, ascended westward to the hill country, and
extended to the wilderness of Beth Aven. 13It then crossed from
there to Luz, to the slope of Luz to the south (that is, Bethel), and
descended to Ataroth Addar located on the hill that is south of
lower Beth Horon. 14It then turned on the west side southward
from the hill near Beth Horon on the south and extended to
Kiriath Baal (that is, Kiriath Jearim), a city belonging to the tribe
of Judah. This is the western border. 15The southern side started
on the edge of Kiriath Jearim and extended westward to the
spring of the waters of Nephtoah. 16The border then descended
to the edge of the hill country near the Valley of Ben Hinnom
located in the Valley of the Rephaites to the north. It descended
through the Valley of Hinnom to the slope of the Jebusites to the
south and then down to En Rogel. 17It went northward, extending
to En Shemesh and Geliloth opposite the Pass of Adummim, and
descended to the Stone of Bohan son of Reuben. 18It crossed to
the slope in front of the rift valley to the north and descended
into the rift valley. 19It then crossed to the slope of Beth Hoglah
to the north and ended at the northern tip of the Salt Sea at the
mouth of the Jordan River. This was the southern border. 20The
Jordan River bordered it on the east. These were the borders of
the land assigned to the tribe of Benjamin by its clans.
21These cities belonged to the tribe of Benjamin by its clans:
Jericho, Beth Hoglah, Emek Keziz, 22Beth Arabah, Zemaraim,
Bethel, 23Avvim, Parah, Ophrah, 24Kephar Ammoni, Ophni, and
Geba—a total of 12 cities and their towns.
25Gibeon, Ramah, Beeroth, 26Mizpah, Kephirah, Mozah, 27Re-
kem, Irpeel, Taralah, 28Zelah, Haeleph, the Jebusite city (that is,
Jerusalem), Gibeah, and Kiriath—a total of 14 cities and their towns.
This was the land assigned to the tribe of Benjamin by its clans.

18:1–10 The saints who serve the Lord in this life and make a tabernacle for him in their hearts despise the proud boasting of the impious, confidently mindful that it is soon to pass away. When they are established with the Lord in the future homeland, they shall look at the perpetual punishment of the impious without any interruption of their own felicity. Consequently the elders give thanks to the Lord because they also contemplate the evil things from which he has delivered them.

VENERABLE BEDE
(C. 672–735)
ON THE TABERNACLE

SIMEON'S TRIBAL LANDS

19 The second lot belonged to the tribe of Simeon by its clans. Their assigned land was in the middle of Judah's assigned land. 2 Their assigned land included Beer Sheba, Moladah, 3 Hazar Shual, Balah, Ezem, 4 Eltolad, Bethul, Hormah, 5 Ziklag, Beth Marcaboth, Hazar Susah, 6 Beth Lebaoth, and Sharuhen—a total of 13 cities and their towns, 7 Ain, Rimmon, Ether, and Ashan—a total of four cities and their towns, 8 as well as all the towns around these cities as far as Baalath Beer (Ramah of the Negev). This was the land assigned to the tribe of Simeon by its clans. 9 Simeon's assigned land was taken from Judah's allotted portion, for Judah's territory was too large for them; so Simeon was assigned land within Judah.

ZEBULUN'S TRIBAL LANDS

10 The third lot belonged to the tribe of Zebulun by its clans. The border of their territory extended to Sarid. 11 Their border went up westward to Maralah and touched Dabbesheth and the valley near Jokneam. 12 From Sarid it turned eastward to the territory of Kisloth Tabor, extended to Daberath, and went up to Japhia. 13 From there it crossed eastward to Gath Hepher and Eth Kazin, and extended to Rimmon, turning toward Neah. 14 It then turned on the north to Hannathon and ended at the Valley of Iphtah El. 15 Their territory included Kattah, Nahalal, Shimron, Idalah, and Bethlehem; in all they had 12 cities and their towns. 16 This was the land assigned to the tribe of Zebulun by its clans, including these cities and their towns.

ISSACHAR'S TRIBAL LANDS

17 The fourth lot belonged to the tribe of Issachar by its clans. 18 Their assigned land included Jezreel, Kesulloth, Shunem, 19 Hapharaim, Shion, Anaharath, 20 Rabbith, Kishion, Ebez, 21 Remeth, En Gannim, En Haddah and Beth Pazzez. 22 Their border touched Tabor, Shahazumah, and Beth Shemesh, and ended at the Jordan. They had 16 cities and their towns. 23 This was the land assigned to the tribe of Issachar by its clans, including these cities and their towns.

ASHER'S TRIBAL LANDS

24 The fifth lot belonged to the tribe of Asher by its clans. 25 Their territory included Helkath, Hali, Beten, Acshaph, 26 Alammelech, Amad, and Mishal. Their border touched Carmel to the west and Shihor Libnath. 27 It turned eastward toward Beth Dagon, touched Zebulun and the Valley of Iphtah El to the north, as well as Beth Emek and Neiel, and extended to Cabul on the north 28 and on to Ebron, Rehob, Hammon, and Kanah, as far as Greater Sidon. 29 It then turned toward Ramah as far as the fortified city of Tyre, turned to Hosah, and ended at the sea near Hebel, Achzib, 30 Umah, Aphek, and Rehob. In all they had 22 cities and their towns. 31 This was the land assigned to the tribe of Asher by its clans, including these cities and their towns.

NAPHTALI'S TRIBAL LANDS

32 The sixth lot belonged to the tribe of Naphtali by its clans. 33 Their border started at Heleph and the oak of Zaanannim, went to Adami Nekeb, Jabneel and on to Lakkum, and ended at the Jordan River. 34 It turned westward to Aznoth Tabor, extended from there to Hukok, touched Zebulun on the south,

Asher on the west, and the Jordan on the east. 35 The fortified cities included Ziddim, Zer, Hammath, Rakkath, Kinnereth, 36 Adamah, Ramah, Hazor, 37 Kedesh, Edrei, En Hazor, 38 Yiron, Migdal El, Horem, Beth Anath, and Beth Shemesh. In all they had 19 cities and their towns. 39 This was the land assigned to the tribe of Naphtali by its clans, including these cities and their towns.

DAN'S TRIBAL LANDS

40 The seventh lot belonged to the tribe of Dan by its clans. 41 Their assigned land included Zorah, Eshtaol, Ir Shemesh, 42 Shaalabbin, Aijalon, Ithlah, 43 Elon, Timnah, Ekron, 44 Eltekeh, Gibbethon, Baalath, 45 Jehud, Bene Berak, Gath Rimmon, 46 the waters of Jarkon, and Rakkon, including the territory in front of Joppa. 47 (The Danites failed to conquer their territory, so they went up and fought with Leshem and captured it. They put the sword to it, took possession of it, and lived in it. They renamed it Dan after their ancestor.) 48 This was the land assigned to the tribe of Dan by its clans, including these cities and their towns.

JOSHUA RECEIVES LAND

49 When they finished dividing the land into its regions, the Israelites gave Joshua son of Nun some land. 50 As the LORD had instructed, they gave him the city he requested—Timnath Serah in the Ephraimite hill country. He built up the city and lived in it.

51 These are the land assignments that Eleazar the priest, Joshua son of Nun, and the Israelite tribal leaders made by drawing lots in Shiloh before the LORD at the entrance of the tent of meeting. So they finished dividing up the land.

ISRAEL DESIGNATES CITIES OF REFUGE

20 The LORD instructed Joshua: 2 "Have the Israelites select the cities of refuge that I told you about through Moses. 3 Anyone who accidentally kills someone can escape there; these cities will be a place of asylum from the avenger of blood. 4 The one who committed manslaughter should escape to one of these cities, stand at the entrance of the city gate, and present his case to the leaders of that city. They should then bring him into the city, give him a place to stay, and let him live there. 5 When the avenger of blood comes after him, they must not hand over to him the one who committed manslaughter, for he accidentally killed his fellow man without premeditation. 6 He must remain in that city until his case is decided by the assembly, and the high priest dies. Then the one who committed manslaughter may return home to the city from which he escaped."

7 So they selected Kedesh in Galilee in the hill country of Naphtali, Shechem in the hill country of Ephraim, and Kiriath Arba (that is, Hebron) in the hill country of Judah. 8 Beyond the Jordan east of Jericho they selected Bezer in the wilderness on the plain belonging to the tribe of Reuben, Ramoth in Gilead belonging to the tribe of Gad, and Golan in Bashan belonging to the tribe of Manasseh. 9 These were the cities of refuge appointed for all the Israelites and for resident foreigners living among them. Anyone who accidentally killed someone could escape there and not be executed by the avenger of blood, at least until his case was reviewed by the assembly.

19:49–50 In this the modesty of Joshua appeared, that he distributed possessions to all the people before he demanded a possession for himself, and this when he was the prince over all. Here he may be seen an example to other princes and rulers to mind the welfare of the people under them more than their own private benefit. And in this he was notably a type of Jesus, who neglected himself to enrich us with possessions in the kingdom of heaven.

JOHN MAYER **(1583–1664)**
COMMENTARY ON JOSHUA

20:1–9 With regard to the roads to the city of refuge, we are told that they were strictly preserved so that the one who fled might find an easy passage to the city. Once a year the elders went along the roads and saw to their order so that nothing might impede the flight of anyone and cause, through delay, that person to be overtaken and slain. This is a picture of the road to Christ Jesus. It is no roundabout road of the law; it is a straight road: Believe and live. No sooner did the manslayer reach the outworks of the city than he was safe. Learn then that if you do but touch the hem of Christ's garment, you shall be made whole.

CHARLES SPURGEON
(1834–1892)
MORNING AND EVENING

LEVITICAL CITIES

21 The tribal leaders of the Levites went before Eleazar the priest and Joshua son of Nun and the Israelite tribal leaders [2]in Shiloh in the land of Canaan and said, "The LORD told Moses to assign us cities in which to live along with the grazing areas for our cattle." [3]So the Israelites assigned these cities and their grazing areas to the Levites from their own holdings, as the LORD had instructed.

[4]The first lot belonged to the Kohathite clans. The Levites who were descendants of Aaron the priest were allotted 13 cities from the tribes of Judah, Simeon, and Benjamin. [5]The rest of Kohath's descendants were allotted 10 cities from the clans of the tribe of Ephraim, and from the tribe of Dan and the half-tribe of Manasseh. [6]Gershon's descendants were allotted 13 cities from the clans of the tribe of Issachar, and from the tribes of Asher and Naphtali and the half-tribe of Manasseh in Bashan. [7]Merari's descendants by their clans were allotted 12 cities from the tribes of Reuben, Gad, and Zebulun. [8]So the Israelites assigned to the Levites by lot these cities and their grazing areas, as the LORD had instructed Moses.

[9]They assigned from the tribes of Judah and Simeon the cities listed below. [10](They were assigned to the Kohathite clans of the Levites who were descendants of Aaron, for the first lot fell to them.) [11]They assigned them Kiriath Arba (Arba was the father of Anak), that is, Hebron, in the hill country of Judah, along with its surrounding grazing areas. [12](Now the city's fields and surrounding towns they had assigned to Caleb son of Jephunneh as his property.) [13]So to the descendants of Aaron the priest they assigned Hebron (a city of refuge for one who committed manslaughter), Libnah, [14]Jattir, Eshtemoa, [15]Holon, Debir, [16]Ain, Juttah, and Beth Shemesh, along with the grazing areas of each—a total of nine cities taken from these two tribes. [17]From the tribe of Benjamin they assigned Gibeon, Geba, [18]Anathoth, and Almon, along with the grazing areas of each—a total of four cities. [19]The priests descended from Aaron received 13 cities and their grazing areas.

[20]The rest of the Kohathite clans of the Levites were allotted cities from the tribe of Ephraim. [21]They assigned them Shechem (a city of refuge for one who committed manslaughter) in the hill country of Ephraim, Gezer, [22]Kibzaim, and Beth Horon, along with the grazing areas of each—a total of four cities. [23]From the tribe of Dan they assigned Eltekeh, Gibbethon, [24]Aijalon, and Gath Rimmon, along with the grazing areas of each—a total of four cities. [25]From the half-tribe of Manasseh they assigned Taanach and Gath Rimmon, along with the grazing areas of each—a total of two cities. [26]The rest of the Kohathite clans received 10 cities and their grazing areas.

[27]They assigned to the Gershonite clans of the Levites the following cities: from the half-tribe of Manasseh: Golan in Bashan (a city of refuge for one who committed manslaughter) and Beeshtarah, along with the grazing areas of each—a total of two cities; [28]from the tribe of Issachar: Kishon, Daberath, [29]Jarmuth, and En Gannim, along with the grazing areas of each—a total of four cities; [30]from the tribe of Asher: Mishal, Abdon, [31]Helkath, and Rehob, along with the grazing areas of each—a total of four cities; [32]from the tribe of Naphtali: Kedesh in Galilee (a city of refuge for one who committed manslaughter), Hammoth Dor, and Kartan, along with the grazing areas of each—a total of three cities. [33]The Gershonite clans received 13 cities and their grazing areas.

[34]They assigned to the Merarite clans (the remaining Levites) the following cities: from the tribe of Zebulun: Jokneam, Kartah, [35]Dimnah, and Nahalal, along with the grazing areas of each—a total of four cities; [36]from the tribe of Reuben: Bezer, Jahaz, [37]Kedemoth, and Mephaath, along with the grazing areas of each—a total of four cities; [38]from the tribe of Gad: Ramoth in Gilead (a city of refuge for one who committed manslaughter), Mahanaim, [39]Heshbon, and Jazer, along with the grazing areas of each—a total of four cities. [40]The Merarite clans (the remaining Levites) were allotted 12 cities.

[41]The Levites received within the land owned by the Israelites 48 cities in all and their grazing areas. [42]Each of these cities had grazing areas around it; they were alike in this regard.

[43]So the LORD gave Israel all the land he had solemnly promised to their ancestors, and they conquered it and lived in it. [44]The LORD made them secure, in fulfillment of all he had solemnly promised their ancestors. None of their enemies could resist them. The LORD handed all their enemies over to them. [45]Not one of the LORD's faithful promises to the family of Israel was left unfulfilled; every one was realized.

JOSHUA SENDS HOME THE EASTERN TRIBES

22 Then Joshua summoned the Reubenites, the Gadites, and the half-tribe of Manasseh [2]and told them: "You have carried out all the instructions of Moses the LORD's servant, and you have obeyed all I have told you. [3]You have not abandoned your fellow Israelites this entire time, right up to this very day. You have completed the task given you by the LORD your God. [4]Now the LORD your God has made your fellow Israelites secure, just as he promised them. So now you may turn around and go to your homes in your own land that Moses the LORD's servant assigned to you east of the Jordan. [5]But carefully obey the commands and instructions Moses the LORD's servant gave you. Love the LORD your God, follow all his instructions, obey his commands, be loyal to him, and serve him with all your heart and being!"

[6]Joshua rewarded them and sent them on their way; they returned to their homes. [7](Now to one half-tribe of Manasseh, Moses had assigned land in Bashan; and to the other half Joshua had assigned land on the west side of the Jordan with their fellow Israelites.) When Joshua sent them home, he rewarded them, [8]saying, "Take home great wealth, a lot of cattle, silver, gold, bronze, iron, and a lot of clothing. Divide up the goods captured from your enemies with your brothers." [9]So the Reubenites, the Gadites, and the half-tribe of Manasseh left the Israelites in Shiloh in the land of Canaan and headed home to their own land in Gilead, which they acquired by the LORD's command through Moses.

CIVIL WAR IS AVERTED

[10]The Reubenites, the Gadites, and the half-tribe of Manasseh came to Geliloth near the Jordan in the land of Canaan and built there, near the Jordan, an impressive altar. [11]The Israelites received this report: "Look, the Reubenites, the Gadites, and the half-tribe of Manasseh have built an altar at the entrance to the land of Canaan, at Geliloth near the Jordan on the Israelite side." [12]When the Israelites heard this, the entire Israelite community assembled at Shiloh to launch an attack against them.

21:43–45 The Lord gave them the right to all the land, the actual possession of the greatest part of it, and power to possess the rest as soon as it was needful for them, which was when their numbers were increased and the absolute dominion of all the people remaining in it. Such an acknowledgment as this, here subscribed by Joshua, in the name of all Israel, we afterward find made by Solomon, and all Israel did in effect say amen to it. The inviolable truth of God's promise and the performance of it to the uttermost is what all believers in Christ have been always ready to bear testimony to. And if in anything it has seemed to come short, they have been as ready to take all the blame to themselves.

JOHN WESLEY (1703–1791)
EXPLANATORY NOTES ON THE BIBLE

22:10–20 The motive for erecting the altar was right in itself. But they sinned not lightly in attempting a novelty without paying any regard to the high priest or consulting their colleagues. Seeing that the work might be deemed vicious, they ought at least, in so great and so serious a matter, to have made their fellows sharers in their counsel; more especially were they in the wrong in neglecting to consult the high priest from whose lips the divine will was to be ascertained. Therefore, let us learn to attempt nothing rashly, even should it be free from blame, and let us always give due heed to the admonition that it is necessary to attend not only to what is lawful but also to what is expedient; more especially let us sedulously beware of disturbing pious minds by the introduction of any kind of novelty.

JOHN CALVIN (1509–1564)
COMPLETE COMMENTARY ON THE BIBLE

[13]The Israelites sent Phinehas son of Eleazar, the priest, to the land of Gilead to the Reubenites, the Gadites, and the half-tribe of Manasseh. [14]He was accompanied by 10 leaders, one from each of the Israelite tribes, each one a family leader among the Israelite clans. [15]They went to the land of Gilead to the Reubenites, the Gadites, and the half-tribe of Manasseh, and said to them: [16]"The entire community of the LORD says, 'Why have you disobeyed the God of Israel by turning back today from following the LORD? You built an altar for yourselves and have rebelled today against the LORD. [17]The sin we committed at Peor was bad enough. To this very day we have not purified ourselves; it even brought a plague on the community of the LORD. [18]Now today you dare to turn back from following the LORD! You are rebelling today against the LORD; tomorrow he may break out in anger against the entire community of Israel. [19]But if your own land is impure, cross over to the LORD's own land, where the LORD himself lives, and settle down among us. But don't rebel against the LORD or us by building for yourselves an altar other than the altar of the LORD our God. [20]When Achan son of Zerah disobeyed the command about the city's riches, the entire Israelite community was judged, though only one man had sinned. He most certainly died for his sin!'"

[21]The Reubenites, the Gadites, and the half-tribe of Manasseh answered the leaders of the Israelite clans: [22]"El, God, the LORD! El, God, the LORD! He knows the truth! Israel must also know! If we have rebelled or disobeyed the LORD, don't spare us today! [23]If we have built an altar for ourselves to turn back from following the LORD by making burnt sacrifices and grain offerings on it, or by offering tokens of peace on it, the LORD himself will punish us. [24]We swear we have done this because we were worried that in the future your descendants would say to our descendants, 'What relationship do you have with the LORD God of Israel? [25]The LORD made the Jordan a boundary between us and you Reubenites and Gadites. You have no right to worship the LORD.' In this way your descendants might cause our descendants to stop obeying the LORD. [26]So we decided to build this altar, not for burnt offerings and sacrifices, [27]but as a reminder to us and you and our descendants who follow us, that we will honor the LORD in his very presence with burnt offerings, sacrifices, and tokens of peace. Then in the future your descendants will not be able to say to our descendants, 'You have no right to worship the LORD.' [28]We said, 'If in the future they say such a thing to us or to our descendants, we will reply, "See the model of the LORD's altar that our ancestors made, not for burnt offerings or sacrifices, but as a reminder to us and you."' [29]Far be it from us to rebel against the LORD by turning back today from following after the LORD by building an altar for burnt offerings, sacrifices, and tokens of peace aside from the altar of the LORD our God located in front of his dwelling place!"

[30]When Phinehas the priest and the community leaders and Israel's clan leaders who accompanied him heard the defense of the Reubenites, the Gadites, and the Manassehites, they were satisfied. [31]Phinehas son of Eleazar, the priest, said to the Reubenites, the Gadites, and the Manassehites, "Today we know that the LORD is among us because you have not disobeyed the LORD in this. Now you have rescued the Israelites from the LORD's judgment."

[32]Phinehas son of Eleazar, the priest, and the leaders left the Reubenites and Gadites in the land of Gilead and reported back

to the Israelites in the land of Canaan. [33]The Israelites were
satisfied with their report and gave thanks to God. They said
nothing more about launching an attack to destroy the land
in which the Reubenites and Gadites lived. [34]The Reubenites
and Gadites named the altar, "Surely it is a Reminder to us that
the LORD is God."

JOSHUA CHALLENGES ISRAEL TO BE FAITHFUL

23 A long time passed after the LORD made Israel secure
from all their enemies, and Joshua was very old. [2]So Joshua
summoned all Israel, including the elders, rulers, judges, and
leaders, and told them: "I am very old. [3]You saw everything the
LORD your God did to all these nations on your behalf, for the
LORD your God fights for you. [4]See, I have parceled out to your
tribes these remaining nations, from the Jordan to the Mediterranean Sea in the west, including all the nations I defeated.
[5]The LORD your God will drive them out from before you and
remove them, so you can occupy their land as the LORD your
God promised you. [6]Be very strong! Carefully obey all that is
written in the law scroll of Moses so you won't swerve from it
to the right or the left, [7]or associate with these nations that
remain near you. You must not invoke or make solemn declarations by the names of their gods! You must not worship or
bow down to them! [8]But you must be loyal to the LORD your
God, as you have been to this very day.

[9]"The LORD drove out from before you great and mighty
nations; no one has been able to resist you to this very day.
[10]One of you makes a thousand run away, for the LORD your
God fights for you, as he promised you he would. [11]Watch yourselves carefully! Love the LORD your God! [12]But if you ever turn
away and make alliances with these nations that remain near
you, and intermarry with them and establish friendly relations
with them, [13]know for certain that the LORD your God will no
longer drive out these nations from before you. They will trap
and ensnare you; they will be a whip that tears your sides and
thorns that blind your eyes until you disappear from this good
land the LORD your God gave you.

[14]"Look, today I am about to die. You know with all your
heart and being that not even one of all the faithful promises
the LORD your God made to you is left unfulfilled; every one
was realized—not one promise is unfulfilled! [15]But in the same
way that every faithful promise the LORD your God made to you
has been realized, it is just as certain that if you disobey, then
the LORD will bring on you every judgment until he destroys
you from this good land that the LORD your God gave you. [16]If
you violate the covenantal laws of the LORD your God which
he commanded you to keep, and you follow, worship, and bow
down to other gods, then the LORD will be very angry with
you and you will disappear quickly from the good land that
he gave to you."

ISRAEL RENEWS ITS COMMITMENT TO THE LORD

24 Joshua assembled all the Israelite tribes at Shechem. He
summoned Israel's elders, rulers, judges, and leaders, and
they appeared before God. [2]Joshua told all the people, "This is
what the LORD God of Israel has said: 'In the distant past your
ancestors lived beyond the Euphrates River, including Terah
the father of Abraham and Nahor. They worshiped other gods,
[3]but I took your father Abraham from beyond the Euphrates

23:1–16 If we would cleave to the Lord, we must always stand upon our guard, for many a soul is lost through carelessness. The way of sin is downhill, and those who have fellowship with sinners cannot avoid having fellowship with sin. Joshua describes the destruction he warns them of. The goodness of the heavenly Canaan, and the free and sure grant God has made of it, will add to the misery of those who shall forever be shut out from it. Nothing will make them see how wretched they are as much as to see how happy they might have been. Let us watch and pray against temptation. Let us trust in God's faithfulness, love, and power; let us plead his promises and cleave to his commandments—then we shall be happy in life, in death, and forever.

MATTHEW HENRY (1662–1714)
COMMENTARY ON THE WHOLE BIBLE

24:1–28 These words contain the holy resolution of pious Joshua, who in a most moving, affectionate discourse recounted to the Israelites what great things God had done for them. He acquaints them, in the most pressing terms, that since God had been so exceeding gracious unto them, they could do not less than out of gratitude for such uncommon favors and mercies dedicate both themselves and families to his service. "Now obey the LORD and worship him with integrity and loyalty." But then, that they might not excuse themselves (as too many might be apt to do), he tells them in the text that whatever regard they might pay to the doctrine he had been preaching, yet he was resolved to live up to and practice it himself: "Choose today whom you will worship . . . But I and my family will worship the LORD."

GEORGE WHITEFIELD
(1714–1770)
THE WORKS

and brought him into the entire land of Canaan. I made his
descendants numerous; I gave him Isaac, 4 and to Isaac I gave
Jacob and Esau. To Esau I assigned Mount Seir, while Jacob and
his sons went down to Egypt. 5 I sent Moses and Aaron, and
I struck Egypt down when I intervened in their land. Then I
brought you out. 6 When I brought your fathers out of Egypt,
you arrived at the sea. The Egyptians chased your fathers with
chariots and horsemen to the Red Sea. 7 Your fathers cried out
for help to the LORD; he made the area between you and the
Egyptians dark, and then he drowned them in the sea. You witnessed with your very own eyes what I did in Egypt. You lived in
the wilderness for a long time. 8 Then I brought you to the land
of the Amorites who lived east of the Jordan. They fought with
you, but I handed them over to you; you conquered their land,
and I destroyed them from before you. 9 Balak son of Zippor,
king of Moab, launched an attack against Israel. He summoned
Balaam son of Beor to call down judgment on you. 10 I refused
to respond to Balaam; he kept prophesying good things about
you, and I rescued you from his power. 11 You crossed the Jordan
and came to Jericho. The leaders of Jericho, as well as the Amorites, Perizzites, Canaanites, Hittites, Girgashites, Hivites, and
Jebusites, fought against you, but I handed them over to you. 12 I
sent terror ahead of you to drive out before you the two Amorite
kings. I gave you the victory; it was not by your swords or bows.
13 I gave you a land in which you had not worked hard; you took
up residence in cities you did not build, and you are eating the
produce of vineyards and olive groves you did not plant.'

14 "Now obey the LORD and worship him with integrity and
loyalty. Put aside the gods your ancestors worshiped beyond
the Euphrates and in Egypt, and worship the LORD. 15 If you
have no desire to worship the LORD, then choose today whom
you will worship, whether it be the gods whom your ancestors
worshiped beyond the Euphrates or the gods of the Amorites
in whose land you are living. But I and my family will worship
the LORD."

16 The people responded, "Far be it from us to abandon the
LORD so we can worship other gods! 17 For the LORD our God
took us and our fathers out of slavery in the land of Egypt and
performed these awesome miracles before our very eyes. He
continually protected us as we traveled and when we passed
through nations. 18 The LORD drove out from before us all the
nations, including the Amorites who lived in the land. So we
too will worship the LORD, for he is our God!"

19 Joshua warned the people, "You will not keep worshiping
the LORD, for he is a holy God. He is a jealous God who will not
forgive your rebellion or your sins. 20 If you abandon the LORD
and worship foreign gods, he will turn against you; he will bring
disaster on you and destroy you, though he once treated you
well."

21 The people said to Joshua, "No! We really will worship the
LORD." 22 Joshua said to the people, "Do you agree to be witnesses
against yourselves that you have chosen to worship the LORD?"
They replied, "We are witnesses!" 23 Joshua said, "Now put aside
the foreign gods that are among you and submit to the LORD
God of Israel."

24 The people said to Joshua, "We will worship the LORD our
God and obey him."

25 That day Joshua drew up an agreement for the people, and
he established rules and regulations for them in Shechem.

[26]Joshua wrote these words in the Law Scroll of God. He then took a large stone and set it up there under the oak tree near the LORD's sanctuary. [27]Joshua said to all the people, "Look, this stone will be a witness against us, for it has heard everything the LORD said to us. It will be a witness against you if you deny your God." [28]When Joshua dismissed the people, they went to their allotted portions of land.

AN ERA ENDS

[29]After all this Joshua son of Nun, the LORD's servant, died at the age of 110. [30]They buried him in his allotted territory in Timnath Serah in the hill country of Ephraim, north of Mount Gaash. [31]Israel worshiped the LORD throughout Joshua's lifetime and as long as the elderly men who outlived him remained alive. These men had experienced firsthand everything the LORD had done for Israel.

[32]The bones of Joseph, which the Israelites had brought up from Egypt, were buried at Shechem in the part of the field that Jacob bought from the sons of Hamor, the father of Shechem, for 100 pieces of money. So it became the inheritance of the tribe of Joseph.

[33]Eleazar son of Aaron died, and they buried him in Gibeah in the hill country of Ephraim, where his son Phinehas had been assigned land.

AUTHOR	AUDIENCE	DATE	PURPOSE	THEMES
Traditionally, Samuel	God's chosen people, the Israelites	Probably about 1000 BC	The book of Judges was written to show how the Israelites failed to live up to the terms of the covenant with the Lord and the consequences of their faithlessness.	Idolatry and apostasy; sin and disobedience; judgment and discipline; repentance and confession; and redemption and restoration

The book of Judges recounts the history of Israel after the death of Joshua. The state of the nation during that time can be properly summed up in a single passage: "That entire generation passed away; a new generation grew up that had not personally experienced the LORD's presence or seen what he had done for Israel." As a consequence, "the Israelites did evil before the LORD BY worshiping the Baals" (2:10–11). Tertullian summarizes this tragic book in this way:

> After the death of Joshua, they forsook the God of their fathers and served idols, Baal and Ashtaroth; and the Lord in anger delivered them up to the hands of plunderers, and they continued to be plundered by them and to be sold to their adversaries, and [they] could not at all stand before their enemies. Wherever they went forth, his hand was upon them for evil, and they were greatly distressed. And after this God sets judges over them. But not even these did they continue steadfastly to obey. So soon as one of the judges died, they proceeded to transgress more than their fathers had done by going after the gods of others and serving and worshiping them. Therefore the Lord was angry.

Over the course of the book, a cycle of judges led Israel through a downward spiral of ever-increasing wickedness. In chapter 6, "the Israelites did evil in the LORD's sight, so the LORD turned them over to Midian for seven years." In response "the Israelites cried out to the LORD for help because of Midian," so he sent them the prophet Gideon. The Lord promised him, "I will be with you! You will strike down the whole Midianite army" (6:1, 7, 16). He was, and Gideon did; and the cycle of God's faithfulness despite Israel's faithlessness was complete.

JUDGES

Commenting on this passage, Matthew Henry illuminated this pattern and how it has served as a warning to believers in every generation:

> Israel's sin was renewed, and Israel's troubles were repeated. Let all that sin expect to suffer. The Israelites hid themselves in dens and caves; such was the effect of a guilty conscience. Sin dispirits men. The invaders left no food for Israel, except what was taken into the caves. They prepared that for Baal what God should have been served, now God justly sends an enemy to take it away in the season thereof. They cried to God for a deliverer, and he sent them a prophet to teach them. When God furnishes a land with faithful ministers, it is a token that he has mercy in store for it. He charges them with rebellion against the Lord; he intends to bring them to repentance. Repentance is real when the sinfulness of sin, as disobedience to God, is chiefly lamented.

For generations the book of Judges has stood as a clarion call to the communion of saints. As Matthew Henry commented, "The history exemplifies the frequent warnings and predictions of Moses and should have close attention. The whole is full of important instruction." Through its negative cycle of apostasy and oppression, this book offers a warning against falling away as well as sound instruction and should be carefully attended to in order that we may avoid the same fate as Israel. But thanks be to the God and Father of our Lord and Savior, Jesus Christ, that we, and the whole communion of saints, will experience the same faithful deliverance that Israel experienced.

JUDGES

JUDAH TAKES THE LEAD

1 After Joshua died, the Israelites asked the LORD, "Who should lead the invasion against the Canaanites and launch the attack?" 2The LORD said, "The men of Judah should take the lead. Be sure of this! I am handing the land over to them." 3The men of Judah said to their relatives, the men of Simeon, "Invade our allotted land with us and help us attack the Canaanites. Then we will go with you into your allotted land." So the men of Simeon went with them.

4The men of Judah attacked, and the LORD handed the Canaanites and Perizzites over to them. They killed 10,000 men at Bezek. 5They met Adoni-Bezek at Bezek and fought him. They defeated the Canaanites and Perizzites. 6When Adoni-Bezek ran away, they chased him and captured him. Then they cut off his thumbs and big toes. 7Adoni-Bezek said, "Seventy kings, with thumbs and big toes cut off, used to lick up food scraps under my table. God has repaid me for what I did to them." They brought him to Jerusalem, where he died. 8The men of Judah attacked Jerusalem and captured it. They put the sword to it and set the city on fire.

9Later the men of Judah went down to attack the Canaanites living in the hill country, the Negev, and the foothills. 10The men of Judah attacked the Canaanites living in Hebron. (Hebron used to be called Kiriath Arba.) They killed Sheshai, Ahiman, and Talmai. 11From there they attacked the people of Debir. (Debir used to be called Kiriath Sepher.) 12Caleb said, "To the man who attacks and captures Kiriath Sepher I will give my daughter Achsah as a wife." 13When Othniel son of Kenaz, Caleb's younger brother, captured it, Caleb gave him his daughter Achsah as a wife.

14One time Achsah came and charmed her father so she could ask him for some land. When she got down from her donkey, Caleb said to her, "What would you like?" 15She answered, "Please give me a special present. Since you have given me land in the Negev, now give me springs of water." So Caleb gave her both the upper and lower springs.

16Now the descendants of the Kenite, Moses' father-in-law, went up with the people of Judah from the city of date palm trees to Arad in the wilderness of Judah, located in the Negev. They went and lived with the people of Judah.

17The men of Judah went with their brothers the men of Simeon and defeated the Canaanites living in Zephath. They wiped out Zephath. So people now call the city Hormah. 18The men of Judah captured Gaza, Ashkelon, Ekron, and the territory surrounding each of these cities.

19The LORD was with the men of Judah. They conquered the hill country, but they could not conquer the people living in the coastal plain because they had chariots with iron-rimmed wheels. 20Caleb received Hebron, just as Moses had promised. He drove out the three Anakites. 21The men of Benjamin, however, did not conquer the Jebusites living in Jerusalem. The Jebusites live with the people of Benjamin in Jerusalem to this very day.

PARTIAL SUCCESS

22When the men of Joseph attacked Bethel, the LORD was with them. 23When the men of Joseph spied out Bethel (it used to be called Luz), 24the spies spotted a man leaving the city. They said to him, "If you show us a secret entrance into the city, we will reward you." 25He showed them a secret entrance into the city, and they put the city to the sword. But they let the man and his extended family leave safely. 26He moved to Hittite

1:1–26 In the book of Joshua, when the land of promise was divided by lot among the other tribes, the tribe of Judah took its own portion of the land first and without casting lots. And moreover, "after Joshua died, the Israelites asked the LORD, 'Who shall lead the invasion against the Canaanites and launch the attack?' The LORD said, 'The men of Judah should take the lead. Be sure of this! I am handing the land over to them.'" These words then make it clear that God ordained the tribe of Judah to be the head of all Israel, and the account goes on. In the book of Judges, when different persons at different times were at the head of the people, speaking generally the tribe of Judah was head of the whole people.

EUSEBIUS OF CAESAREA
(C. 260–339)
THE PROOF OF THE GOSPEL

country and built a city. He named it Luz, and it has kept that
name to this very day.
27 The men of Manasseh did not conquer Beth Shean, Taanach, or their surrounding towns. Nor did they conquer the
people living in Dor, Ibleam, Megiddo, or their surrounding
towns. The Canaanites managed to remain in those areas.
28 Whenever Israel was strong militarily, they forced the Canaanites to do hard labor, but they never totally conquered them.
29 The men of Ephraim did not conquer the Canaanites living
in Gezer. The Canaanites lived among them in Gezer.
30 The men of Zebulun did not conquer the people living in
Kitron and Nahalol. The Canaanites lived among them and
were forced to do hard labor.
31 The men of Asher did not conquer the people living in Acco
or Sidon, nor did they conquer Ahlab, Achzib, Helbah, Aphek,
or Rehob. 32 The people of Asher live among the Canaanites
residing in the land because they did not conquer them.
33 The men of Naphtali did not conquer the people living in
Beth Shemesh or Beth Anath. They live among the Canaanites
residing in the land. The Canaanites living in Beth Shemesh
and Beth Anath were forced to do hard labor for them.
34 The Amorites forced the people of Dan to live in the hill
country. They did not allow them to live in the coastal plain.
35 The Amorites managed to remain in Har Heres, Aijalon, and
Shaalbim. Whenever the tribe of Joseph was strong militarily,
the Amorites were forced to do hard labor. 36 The border of Amorite territory ran from the Scorpion Ascent to Sela and on up.

CONFRONTATION AND REPENTANCE AT BOKIM

2 The angel of the LORD went up from Gilgal to Bokim. He
said, "I brought you up from Egypt and led you into the land
I had solemnly promised to give to your ancestors. I said, 'I will
never break my covenant with you, 2 but you must not make an
agreement with the people who live in this land. You should tear
down the altars where they worship.' But you have disobeyed
me. Why would you do such a thing? 3 At that time I also warned
you, 'If you disobey, I will not drive out the Canaanites before
you. They will ensnare you and their gods will lure you away.'"
4 When the angel of the LORD finished speaking these words
to all the Israelites, the people wept loudly. 5 They named that
place Bokim and offered sacrifices to the LORD there.

2:1–6 We read in the book of Judges that when the angel came and preached repentance to the people, saying, *You have abandoned the Lord, and the Lord shall abandon you*, the Israelites wept aloud, and that place was called the Valley of Tears. We have called attention to ancient history in order to avoid heresy. The Valley of Tears, moreover, we may understand allegorically as this world, for we are not on the mountain, that is, in the kingdom of heaven, but in the valley, in the darknesses of this world; through a fault, we have been cast out of paradise with Adam into a lowly vale of tears where there are repentance and weeping.

JEROME (C. 342–420)
HOMILIES ON THE PSALMS

THE END OF AN ERA

6 When Joshua dismissed the people, the Israelites went to their
allotted portions of territory, intending to take possession of
the land. 7 The people worshiped the LORD throughout Joshua's lifetime and as long as the elderly men who outlived him
remained alive. These men had witnessed all the great things
the LORD had done for Israel. 8 Joshua son of Nun, the LORD's
servant, died at the age of 110. 9 The people buried him in his
allotted land in Timnath Heres in the hill country of Ephraim,
north of Mount Gaash. 10 That entire generation passed away; a
new generation grew up that had not personally experienced
the LORD's presence or seen what he had done for Israel.

A MONOTONOUS CYCLE

11 The Israelites did evil before the LORD by worshiping the
Baals. 12 They abandoned the LORD God of their ancestors who
brought them out of the land of Egypt. They followed other

EPHREM THE SYRIAN:

THE HARP OF THE HOLY SPIRIT
306–373

While Egypt was the hub of fourth-century monasticism, particularly in the West, Eastern monasticism was popular in two locales: Caesarea and Syria. Ephrem the Syrian was the most notable monastic of this Eastern movement.

Little is known about the man's life other than that he was born in 306 and lived in the city of Nisibis in modern-day Turkey. Scholars conjecture that he likely grew up in a Christian household since the Christian faith had spread to the region in which he lived. What *is* known is his devotion to the monastic way of life. His literary output is also noteworthy: Ephrem churned out a cornucopia of written works across a spectrum of genres, including theological treatises and a collection of magisterial hymns and poems. Ephrem penned over 400 hymns and 300,000 verses in such works, despite no formal training in literature or poetry.

His poems were known for ushering the reader into a posture of reverence and worship of Christ: "I will run in my affections to him who heals freely / He who healed my sorrows, the first and the second, he who cured the third, he will heal the fourth / Heal me, thou Son the first born!"

One of Ephrem's more influential works was *Hymns Against Heresies*, a collection of hymns instructing Christians in orthodoxy and warning against the false teachings roiling the early church. Embedding doctrine in his hymns, he was able to teach against such heresies as Docetism (the teaching that Christ only appeared to be human but was really just a divine spirit) while simultaneously teaching positively about the orthodox position regarding Christ's incarnation and his divine and human natures.

Ephrem's emphasis on right thinking extended from the mind to the heart. His orthodoxy impacted his behavior, as evidenced by Ephrem's ascetic lifestyle and care for the poor. He regularly denied himself food and possessions in order to be generous toward others. One prime example comes from the end of his life. During the famine of 373, the poor of his town of Edessa were ravaged by starvation and plague. He took it upon himself to appeal to the wealthy of the region for help, rebuking the rich and well-fed for their greed and lack of generosity. He traveled around taking up a collection, raising enough to purchase hundreds of beds to provide relief and recovery. He then attended the sick personally until the plague passed.

Ephrem literally spent his life for the sake of selfless service. He died in 373 as the famine came to an end while caring for the sick of his town. As one person said, he was "a victim of his own compassion." Because of both the conduct of his life and the product of his pen he was called "Harp of the Holy Spirit"—a fruitful instrument for the Spirit's harmonies.

IMPORTANT WORKS

HYMNS AGAINST HERESIES

COMMENTARY ON TATIAN'S DIATESSARON

COMMENTARY ON GENESIS AND EXODUS

gods—the gods of the nations who lived around them. They
worshiped them and made the LORD angry. [13]They abandoned
the LORD and worshiped Baal and the Ashtoreths.

[14]The LORD was furious with Israel and handed them over
to robbers who plundered them. He turned them over to their
enemies who lived around them. They could no longer withstand their enemies' attacks. [15]Whenever they went out to fight,
the LORD did them harm, just as he had warned and solemnly
vowed he would do. They suffered greatly.

[16]The LORD raised up leaders who delivered them from these
robbers. [17]But they did not obey their leaders. Instead they
prostituted themselves to other gods and worshiped them.
They quickly turned aside from the path their ancestors had
walked. Their ancestors had obeyed the LORD's commands, but
they did not. [18]When the LORD raised up leaders for them, the
LORD was with each leader and delivered the people from their
enemies while the leader remained alive. The LORD felt sorry
for them when they cried out in agony because of what their
harsh oppressors did to them. [19]When a leader died, the next
generation would again act more wickedly than the previous
one. They would follow after other gods, worshiping them and
bowing down to them. They did not give up their practices or
their stubborn ways.

A DIVINE DECISION

[20]The LORD was furious with Israel. He said, "This nation has
violated the terms of the covenant I made with their ancestors
by disobeying me. [21]So I will no longer remove before them
any of the nations that Joshua left unconquered when he died,
[22]in order to test Israel. I want to see whether or not the people will carefully walk in the path marked out by the LORD,
as their ancestors were careful to do." [23]This is why the LORD
permitted these nations to remain and did not conquer them
immediately; he did not hand them over to Joshua.

3 These were the nations the LORD permitted to remain so
he could use them to test Israel—he wanted to test all those
who had not experienced battle against the Canaanites. [2]He
left those nations simply because he wanted to teach the subsequent generations of Israelites, who had not experienced
the earlier battles, how to conduct holy war. [3]These were the
nations: the five lords of the Philistines, all the Canaanites,
the Sidonians, and the Hivites living in Mount Lebanon, from
Mount Baal Hermon to Lebo Hamath. [4]They were left to test
Israel, so the LORD would know if his people would obey the
commands he gave their ancestors through Moses.

[5]The Israelites lived among the Canaanites, Hittites, Amorites, Perizzites, Hivites, and Jebusites. [6]They took the Canaanites' daughters as wives and gave their daughters to the
Canaanites; they worshiped their gods as well.

OTHNIEL: A MODEL LEADER

[7]The Israelites did evil in the LORD's sight. They forgot the LORD
their God and worshiped the Baals and the Asherahs. [8]The LORD
was furious with Israel and turned them over to King Cushan
Rishathaim of Armon Haraim. They were Cushan Rishathaim's
subjects for eight years. [9]When the Israelites cried out for help
to the LORD, he raised up a deliverer for the Israelites who rescued them. His name was Othniel son of Kenaz, Caleb's younger
brother. [10]The LORD's Spirit empowered him and he led Israel.

3:1–6 **God did not begrudge Israelites their peace or look with malice upon them, but he planned this conflict in the knowledge that it would be beneficial. Thus, constantly oppressed by the onslaught of the nations, they would never feel that they did not need the Lord's help. Then they would always meditate on him and cry out to him, and they would neither lapse into sluggish inactivity nor lose their ability to fight and their training in virtue. For frequently security and prosperity have brought low those whom adversities cannot overcome.**

JOHN CASSIAN
(C. 360–C. 435)
THE CONFERENCES

When he went to do battle, the LORD handed over to him King Cushan Rishathaim of Armon, and Othniel overpowered him. 11 The land had rest for 40 years; then Othniel son of Kenaz died.

DECEIT, ASSASSINATION, AND DELIVERANCE

12 The Israelites again did evil in the LORD's sight. The LORD gave King Eglon of Moab control over Israel because they had done evil in the LORD's sight. 13 Eglon formed alliances with the Ammonites and Amalekites. He came and defeated Israel, and they seized the city of date palm trees. 14 The Israelites were subject to King Eglon of Moab for 18 years.

15 When the Israelites cried out for help to the LORD, he raised up a deliverer for them. His name was Ehud son of Gera the Benjaminite, a left-handed man. The Israelites sent him to King Eglon of Moab with their tribute payment. 16 Ehud made himself a sword—it had two edges and was 18 inches long. He strapped it under his coat on his right thigh. 17 He brought the tribute payment to King Eglon of Moab. (Now Eglon was a very fat man.)

18 After Ehud brought the tribute payment, he dismissed the people who had carried it. 19 But he went back once he reached the carved images at Gilgal. He said to Eglon, "I have a secret message for you, O king." Eglon said, "Be quiet!" All his attendants left. 20 When Ehud approached him, he was sitting in his well-ventilated upper room all by himself. Ehud said, "I have a message from God for you." When Eglon rose up from his seat, 21 Ehud reached with his left hand, pulled the sword from his right thigh, and drove it into Eglon's belly. 22 The handle went in after the blade, and the fat closed around the blade, for Ehud did not pull the sword out of his belly. 23 As Ehud went out into the vestibule, he closed the doors of the upper room behind him and locked them.

24 When Ehud had left, Eglon's servants came and saw the locked doors of the upper room. They said, "He must be relieving himself in the well-ventilated inner room." 25 They waited so long they were embarrassed, but he still did not open the doors of the upper room. Finally they took the key and opened the doors. Right before their eyes was their master, sprawled out dead on the floor! 26 Now Ehud had escaped while they were delaying. When he passed the carved images, he escaped to Seirah. 27 When he reached Seirah, he blew a trumpet in the Ephraimite hill country. The Israelites went down with him from the hill country, with Ehud in the lead. 28 He said to them, "Follow me, for the LORD is about to defeat your enemies, the Moabites!" They followed him, captured the fords of the Jordan River opposite Moab, and did not let anyone cross. 29 That day they killed about 10,000 Moabites—all strong, capable warriors; not one escaped. 30 Israel humiliated Moab that day, and the land had rest for 80 years.

31 After Ehud came Shamgar son of Anath. He killed 600 Philistines with an oxgoad. So he also delivered Israel.

DEBORAH SUMMONS BARAK

4 The Israelites again did evil in the LORD's sight after Ehud's death. 2 The LORD turned them over to King Jabin of Canaan, who ruled in Hazor. The general of his army was Sisera, who lived in Harosheth Haggoyim. 3 The Israelites cried out for help to the LORD because Sisera had 900 chariots with iron-rimmed wheels, and he cruelly oppressed the Israelites for 20 years.

4:1–23 Deborah showed that women have no need of the help of a man inasmuch as she, not at all restrained by her gender, undertook to perform the duties of a man and did even more than she had undertaken. And at last, when the Jews were being ruled under the leadership of the judges, they chose Deborah, by whose judgment they might be ruled. And so one woman both ruled many thousands of men in peace and defended them from the enemy. A woman, she governs the people; a woman, she leads armies; a woman, she chooses generals; a woman, she determines wars and orders triumphs. So, then, it is not gender but valor that makes strong.

AMBROSE **(C. 339–C. 397)**
CONCERNING WIDOWS

4 Now Deborah, a prophetess, wife of Lappidoth, was leading
Israel at that time. 5 She would sit under the Date Palm Tree of Deborah between Ramah and Bethel in the Ephraimite hill country.
The Israelites would come up to her to have their disputes settled.
6 She summoned Barak son of Abinoam from Kedesh in Naphtali. She said to him, "Is it not true that the LORD God of Israel
is commanding you? Go, march to Mount Tabor! Take with you
10,000 men from Naphtali and Zebulun. 7 I will bring Sisera, the
general of Jabin's army, to you at the Kishon River, along with his
chariots and huge army. I will hand him over to you." 8 Barak said
to her, "If you go with me, I will go. But if you do not go with me,
I will not go." 9 She said, "I will indeed go with you. But you will
not gain fame on the expedition you are undertaking, for the
LORD will turn Sisera over to a woman." Deborah got up and went
with Barak to Kedesh. 10 Barak summoned men from Zebulun
and Naphtali to Kedesh, and 10,000 men followed him; Deborah
went up with him as well. 11 Now Heber the Kenite had moved
away from the Kenites, the descendants of Hobab, Moses' father-
in-law. He lived near the great tree in Zaanannim near Kedesh.
12 When Sisera heard that Barak son of Abinoam had gone
up to Mount Tabor, 13 he ordered all his chariotry—900 chariots
with iron-rimmed wheels—and all the troops he had with him
to go from Harosheth Haggoyim to the Kishon River. 14 Deborah
said to Barak, "Spring into action, for this is the day the LORD is
handing Sisera over to you! Has the LORD not taken the lead?"
So Barak went down from Mount Tabor with 10,000 men following him. 15 The LORD routed Sisera, all his chariotry, and all
his army with the edge of the sword. Sisera jumped out of his
chariot and ran away on foot. 16 Now Barak chased the chariots
and the army all the way to Harosheth Haggoyim. Sisera's whole
army died by the edge of the sword; not even one survived!
17 Now Sisera ran away on foot to the tent of Jael, wife of
Heber the Kenite, for King Jabin of Hazor and the family of
Heber the Kenite had made a peace treaty. 18 Jael came out to
welcome Sisera. She said to him, "Stop and rest, my lord. Stop
and rest with me. Don't be afraid." So Sisera stopped to rest in
her tent, and she put a blanket over him. 19 He said to her, "Give
me a little water to drink because I'm thirsty." She opened a
goatskin container of milk and gave him some milk to drink.
Then she covered him up again. 20 He said to her, "Stand watch
at the entrance to the tent. If anyone comes along and asks
you, 'Is there a man here?' say, 'No.'" 21 Then Jael wife of Heber
took a tent peg in one hand and a hammer in the other. She
crept up on him, drove the tent peg through his temple into
the ground while he was asleep from exhaustion, and he died.
22 Now Barak was chasing Sisera. Jael went out to welcome him.
She said to him, "Come here and I will show you the man you are
searching for." He went with her into the tent, and there he saw
Sisera sprawled out dead with the tent peg through his temple.
23 That day God humiliated King Jabin of Canaan before the
Israelites. 24 Israel's power continued to overwhelm King Jabin
of Canaan until they did away with him.

CELEBRATING THE VICTORY IN SONG

5 On that day Deborah and Barak son of Abinoam sang this
victory song:

2 "When the leaders took the lead in Israel,
When the people answered the call to war—
Praise the LORD!

5:1–12 "Wake up, wake up, Deborah!" Increase righteousness, establish the people, and arise for the glory of God and the salvation of the people. But also, Deborah, strengthen Barak. For the saints also give courage to us in the power of the Lord, instructing our souls against our enemies. But every mind should be held captive to the obedience of Christ. And if, Deborah, you should fall in your work, like what happened to Jonathan when he tasted the honey, may your soul be strengthened by the sweet taste of prophecy.

PROCOPIUS OF GAZA
(C. 465–528)
COMMENTARY ON JUDGES

3 Hear, O kings!
Pay attention, O rulers!
I will sing to the LORD!
I will sing to the LORD God of Israel!

4 "O LORD, when you departed from Seir,
when you marched from Edom's plains,
the earth shook, the heavens poured down,
the clouds poured down rain.
5 The mountains trembled before the LORD, the God of
Sinai;
before the LORD God of Israel.

6 "In the days of Shamgar son of Anath,
in the days of Jael caravans disappeared;
travelers had to go on winding side roads.
7 Warriors were scarce;
they were scarce in Israel,
until you arose, Deborah,
until you arose as a motherly protector in Israel.
8 God chose new leaders,
then fighters appeared in the city gates;
but, I swear, not a shield or spear could be found
among 40 military units in Israel.
9 My heart went out to Israel's leaders,
to the people who answered the call to war.
Praise the LORD!

10 "You who ride on light-colored female donkeys,
who sit on saddle blankets,
you who walk on the road, pay attention!
11 Hear the sound of those who divide the sheep among
the watering places;
there they tell of the LORD's victorious deeds,
the victorious deeds of his warriors in Israel.
Then the LORD's people went down to the city gates—

12 "Wake up, wake up, Deborah!
Wake up, wake up, sing a song!
Get up, Barak!
Capture your prisoners of war, son of Abinoam!
13 Then the survivors came down to the mighty ones;
the LORD's people came down to me as warriors.
14 They came from Ephraim, who uprooted Amalek;
they follow after you, Benjamin, with your soldiers.
From Makir leaders came down,
from Zebulun came the ones who march carrying an
officer's staff.
15 Issachar's leaders were with Deborah;
the men of Issachar supported Barak;
into the valley they were sent under Barak's command.
Among the clans of Reuben there was intense heart
searching.
16 Why do you remain among the sheepfolds,
listening to the shepherds playing their pipes for their
flocks?
As for the clans of Reuben—there was intense searching
of heart.
17 Gilead stayed put beyond the Jordan River.

As for Dan—why did he seek temporary employment in
the shipyards?
Asher remained on the seacoast;
he stayed by his harbors.
18 The men of Zebulun were not concerned about their
lives;
Naphtali charged onto the battlefields.

19 "Kings came, they fought;
the kings of Canaan fought
at Taanach by the waters of Megiddo,
but they took no silver as plunder.
20 From the sky the stars fought,
from their paths in the heavens they fought against
Sisera.
21 The Kishon River carried them off;
the river confronted them—the Kishon River.
Step on the necks of the strong!

22 "The horses' hooves pounded the ground;
the stallions galloped madly.
23 'Call judgment down on Meroz,' says the angel of the
LORD;
'Be sure to call judgment down on those who live there,
because they did not come to help in the LORD's battle,
to help in the LORD's battle against the warriors.'

24 "The most rewarded of women should be Jael,
the wife of Heber the Kenite!
She should be the most rewarded of women who live in
tents.
25 He asked for water,
and she gave him milk;
in a bowl fit for a king,
she served him curds.
26 Her left hand reached for the tent peg,
her right hand for the workmen's hammer.
She 'hammered' Sisera,
she shattered his skull,
she smashed his head,
she drove the tent peg through his temple.
27 Between her feet he collapsed,
he fell limp and was lifeless;
between her feet he collapsed and fell,
in the spot where he collapsed,
there he fell—violently killed!

28 "Through the window she looked;
Sisera's mother cried out through the lattice:
'Why is his chariot so slow to return?
Why are the hoofbeats of his chariot horses delayed?'
29 The wisest of her ladies answer;
indeed she even thinks to herself,
30 'No doubt they are gathering and dividing the plunder—
a girl or two for each man to rape!
Sisera is grabbing up colorful cloth,
he is grabbing up colorful embroidered cloth,
two pieces of colorful embroidered cloth,
for the neck of the plunderer!'

31 "May all your enemies perish like this, O LORD!
But may those who love you shine
like the rising sun at its brightest."

And the land had rest for forty years.

OPPRESSION AND CONFRONTATION

6 The Israelites did evil in the LORD's sight, so the LORD turned
them over to Midian for seven years. 2The Midianites overwhelmed Israel. Because of Midian the Israelites made shelters
for themselves in the hills, caves, and strongholds. 3Whenever the
Israelites planted their crops, the Midianites, Amalekites, and the
people from the east would attack them. 4They invaded the land
and devoured its crops all the way to Gaza. They left nothing for
the Israelites to eat, and they took away the sheep, oxen, and donkeys. 5When they invaded with their cattle and tents, they were as
thick as locusts. Neither they nor their camels could be counted.
They came to devour the land. 6Israel was so severely weakened
by Midian that the Israelites cried out to the LORD for help.
7When the Israelites cried out to the LORD for help because
of Midian, 8the LORD sent a prophet to the Israelites. He said to
them, "This is what the LORD God of Israel has said: 'I brought
you up from Egypt and took you out of that place of slavery.
9I rescued you from Egypt's power and from the power of all
who oppressed you. I drove them out before you and gave their
land to you. 10I said to you, "I am the LORD your God! Do not
worship the gods of the Amorites, in whose land you are now
living." But you have disobeyed me.'"

GIDEON MEETS SOME VISITORS

11The angel of the LORD came and sat down under the oak
tree in Ophrah owned by Joash the Abiezrite. He arrived while
Joash's son Gideon was threshing wheat in a winepress so he
could hide it from the Midianites. 12The angel of the LORD
appeared and said to him, "The LORD is with you, courageous
warrior!" 13Gideon said to him, "Pardon me, but if the LORD is
with us, why has such disaster overtaken us? Where are all his
miraculous deeds our ancestors told us about? They said, 'Did
the LORD not bring us up from Egypt?' But now the LORD has
abandoned us and handed us over to Midian." 14Then the LORD
himself turned to him and said, "You have the strength. Deliver
Israel from the power of the Midianites! Have I not sent you?"
15Gideon said to him, "But Lord, how can I deliver Israel? Just
look! My clan is the weakest in Manasseh, and I am the youngest
in my family." 16The LORD said to him, "Ah, but I will be with you!
You will strike down the whole Midianite army." 17Gideon said
to him, "If you really are pleased with me, then give me a sign
as proof that it is really you speaking with me. 18Do not leave
this place until I come back with a gift and present it to you."
The LORD said, "I will stay here until you come back."
19Gideon went and prepared a young goat, along with unleavened bread made from an ephah of flour. He put the meat
in a basket and the broth in a pot. He brought the food to him
under the oak tree and presented it to him. 20God's angel said
to him, "Put the meat and unleavened bread on this rock, and
pour out the broth." Gideon did as instructed. 21The angel of the
LORD touched the meat and the unleavened bread with the tip
of his staff. Fire flared up from the rock and consumed the meat
and unleavened bread. The angel of the LORD then disappeared.

6:11–35 Gideon was a man of a brave, active spirit yet in obscurity; he is here stirred up to undertake something great. It was very sure that the Lord was with him when his angel was with him. While God called Gideon "courageous," he made him so. God delights to advance the humble. Gideon desired to have his faith confirmed. Now, under the influence of the Spirit, we are not to expect signs before our eyes such as Gideon here desired but must earnestly pray to God that if we have found grace in his sight, he will show us a sign in our heart by the powerful working of his Spirit there. Gideon's courage failed him. But God spoke peace to him.

MATTHEW HENRY **(1662–1714)**
COMMENTARY ON THE WHOLE BIBLE

[22]When Gideon realized that it was the angel of the LORD, he said, "Oh no! Sovereign LORD! I have seen the angel of the LORD face-to-face!" [23]The LORD said to him, "You are safe! Do not be afraid. You are not going to die!" [24]Gideon built an altar for the LORD there, and named it "The LORD is on friendly terms with me." To this day it is still there in Ophrah of the Abiezrites.

GIDEON DESTROYS THE ALTAR

[25]That night the LORD said to him, "Take the bull from your father's herd, as well as a second bull, one that is seven years old. Pull down your father's Baal altar and cut down the nearby Asherah pole. [26]Then build an altar for the LORD your God on the top of this stronghold according to the proper pattern. Take the second bull and offer it as a burnt sacrifice on the wood from the Asherah pole that you cut down." [27]So Gideon took 10 of his servants and did just as the LORD had told him. He was too afraid of his father's family and the men of the city to do it in broad daylight, so he waited until nighttime.

[28]When the men of the city got up the next morning, they saw the Baal altar pulled down, the nearby Asherah pole cut down, and the second bull sacrificed on the newly built altar. [29]They said to one another, "Who did this?" They investigated the matter thoroughly and concluded that Gideon son of Joash had done it. [30]The men of the city said to Joash, "Bring out your son, so we can execute him! He pulled down the Baal altar and cut down the nearby Asherah pole." [31]But Joash said to all those who confronted him, "Must you fight Baal's battles? Must you rescue him? Whoever takes up his cause will die by morning! If he really is a god, let him fight his own battles! After all, it was his altar that was pulled down." [32]That very day Gideon's father named him Jerub Baal, because he had said, "Let Baal fight with him, for it was his altar that was pulled down."

GIDEON SUMMONS AN ARMY AND SEEKS CONFIRMATION

[33]All the Midianites, Amalekites, and the people from the east assembled. They crossed the Jordan River and camped in the Jezreel Valley. [34]The LORD's Spirit took control of Gideon. He blew a trumpet, summoning the Abiezrites to follow him. [35]He sent messengers throughout Manasseh and summoned them to follow him as well. He also sent messengers throughout Asher, Zebulun, and Naphtali, and they came up to meet him.

[36]Gideon said to God, "If you really intend to use me to deliver Israel, as you promised, then give me a sign as proof. [37]Look, I am putting a wool fleece on the threshing floor. If there is dew only on the fleece, and the ground around it is dry, then I will be sure that you will use me to deliver Israel, as you promised." [38]The LORD did as he asked. When he got up the next morning, he squeezed the fleece, and enough dew dripped from it to fill a bowl. [39]Gideon said to God, "Please do not get angry at me, when I ask for just one more sign. Please allow me one more test with the fleece. This time make only the fleece dry, while the ground around it is covered with dew." [40]That night God did as he asked. Only the fleece was dry and the ground around it was covered with dew.

GIDEON REDUCES THE RANKS

7 Jerub Baal (that is, Gideon) and his men got up the next morning and camped near the spring of Harod. The Midianites were camped north of them near the hill of Moreh in the valley.

7:1–25 Gideon does precisely what all Christians must do. First you must shine; break the pitcher that conceals your light, throw aside the bushel that has been hiding your candle, and shine. Then there must be the sound, the blowing of the trumpet. There must be active exertions for the ingathering of sinners by proclaiming Christ crucified. Remember that the true war cry of the church is Gideon's watchword, "For the LORD and for Gideon!" God must do it, it is his own work. We can do nothing of ourselves, but we can do everything by the help of our God.

CHARLES SPURGEON
(1834–1892)
MORNING AND EVENING

2The LORD said to Gideon, "You have too many men for me to
hand Midian over to you. Israel might brag, 'Our own strength
has delivered us.' 3Now, announce to the men, 'Whoever is
shaking with fear may turn around and leave Mount Gilead.'"
Twenty-two thousand men went home; 10,000 remained. 4The
LORD spoke to Gideon again, "There are still too many men.
Bring them down to the water, and I will thin the ranks some
more. When I say, 'This one should go with you,' pick him to go;
when I say, 'This one should not go with you,' do not take him."
5So he brought the men down to the water. Then the LORD said
to Gideon, "Separate those who lap the water as a dog laps from
those who kneel to drink." 6Only 300 men lapped with their
hands to their mouths; the rest of the men kneeled to drink
water. 7The LORD said to Gideon, "With the 300 men who lapped
I will deliver the whole army, and I will hand Midian over to
you. The rest of the men should go home." 8The men who were
chosen took supplies and their trumpets. Gideon sent all the
men of Israel back to their homes; he kept only 300 men. Now
the Midianites were camped down below in the valley.

GIDEON REASSURED OF VICTORY

9That night the LORD said to Gideon, "Get up! Attack the camp,
for I am handing it over to you. 10But if you are afraid to attack,
go down to the camp with Purah your servant 11and listen to
what they are saying. Then you will be brave and attack the
camp." So he went down with Purah his servant to where the
sentries were guarding the camp. 12Now the Midianites, Amalekites, and the people from the east covered the valley like a
swarm of locusts. Their camels could not be counted; they were
as innumerable as the sand on the seashore. 13When Gideon
arrived, he heard a man telling another man about a dream
he had. The man said, "Look! I had a dream. I saw a stale cake
of barley bread rolling into the Midianite camp. It hit a tent
so hard it knocked it over and turned it upside down. The tent
just collapsed." 14The other man said, "Without a doubt this
symbolizes the sword of Gideon son of Joash, the Israelite. God
is handing Midian and all the army over to him."

GIDEON ROUTS THE ENEMY

15When Gideon heard the report of the dream and its interpretation, he praised God. Then he went back to the Israelite camp
and said, "Get up, for the LORD is handing the Midianite army
over to you!" 16He divided the 300 men into three units. He gave
them all trumpets and empty jars with torches inside them.
17He said to them, "Watch me and do as I do. Watch closely! I am
going to the edge of the camp. Do as I do! 18When I and all who
are with me blow our trumpets, you also blow your trumpets
all around the camp. Then say, 'For the LORD and for Gideon!'"
19Gideon took 100 men to the edge of the camp at the beginning of the middle watch, just after they had changed the
guards. They blew their trumpets and broke the jars they were
carrying. 20All three units blew their trumpets and broke their
jars. They held the torches in their left hand and the trumpets
in their right. Then they yelled, "A sword for the LORD and for
Gideon!" 21They stood in order all around the camp. The whole
Midianite army ran away; they shouted as they scrambled away.
22When the 300 men blew their trumpets, the LORD caused the
Midianites to attack one another with their swords throughout
the camp. The army fled to Beth Shittah on the way to Zererah.

7:1–25 Gideon does precisely what all Christians must do. First, you must shine: break the pitcher that conceals your light, throw aside the bushel that has been hiding your candle, and shine. Then there must be the sound, the blowing of the trumpet. There must be active exertions for the ingathering of sinners by proclaiming Christ crucified. Remember that the true war cry of the church is Gideon's watchword, "For the LORD and for Gideon!" God must do it; it is his own work. We can do nothing of ourselves, but we can do everything by the help of our God.

CHARLES SPURGEON
(1834–1892)
MORNING AND EVENING

They went to the border of Abel Meholah near Tabbath. 23Isra-
elites from Naphtali, Asher, and Manasseh answered the call
and chased the Midianites.

GIDEON APPEASES THE EPHRAIMITES

24Now Gideon sent messengers throughout the Ephraimite hill
country who announced, "Go down and head off the Midianites.
Take control of the fords of the streams all the way to Beth
Barah and the Jordan River." When all the Ephraimites had
assembled, they took control of the fords all the way to Beth
Barah and the Jordan River. 25They captured the two Midianite generals, Oreb and Zeeb. They executed Oreb on the rock
of Oreb and Zeeb in the winepress of Zeeb. They chased the
Midianites and brought the heads of Oreb and Zeeb to Gideon,
who was now on the other side of the Jordan River.
8 The Ephraimites said to him, "Why have you done such a
thing to us? You did not summon us when you went to fight
the Midianites!" They argued vehemently with him. 2He said
to them, "Now what have I accomplished compared to you?
Even Ephraim's leftover grapes are better quality than Abiezer's
harvest! 3It was to you that God handed over the Midianite
generals, Oreb and Zeeb! What did I accomplish to rival that?"
When he said this, they calmed down.

GIDEON TRACKS DOWN THE MIDIANITE KINGS

4Now Gideon and his 300 men had crossed over the Jordan
River, and even though they were exhausted, they were still
chasing the Midianites. 5He said to the men of Sukkoth, "Give
some loaves of bread to the men who are following me because
they are exhausted. I am chasing Zebah and Zalmunna, the
kings of Midian." 6The officials of Sukkoth said, "You have not
yet overpowered Zebah and Zalmunna. So why should we give
bread to your army?" 7Gideon said, "Since you will not help,
after the LORD hands Zebah and Zalmunna over to me, I will
thresh your skin with desert thorns and briers." 8He went up
from there to Penuel and made the same request. The men of
Penuel responded the same way the men of Sukkoth had. 9He
also threatened the men of Penuel, warning, "When I return
victoriously, I will tear down this tower."

10Now Zebah and Zalmunna were in Karkor with their armies.
There were about 15,000 survivors from the army of the eastern
peoples; 120,000 sword-wielding soldiers had been killed. 11Gide-
on went up the road of the nomads east of Nobah and Jogbehah
and ambushed the surprised army. 12When Zebah and Zalmunna
ran away, Gideon chased them and captured the two Midianite
kings, Zebah and Zalmunna. He had surprised their entire army.

13Gideon son of Joash returned from the battle by the pass
of Heres. 14He captured a young man from Sukkoth and inter-
rogated him. The young man wrote down for him the names
of Sukkoth's officials and city leaders—77 men in all. 15He approached the men of Sukkoth and said, "Look what I have! Zebah and Zalmunna! You insulted me, saying, 'You have not yet
overpowered Zebah and Zalmunna. So why should we give bread
to your exhausted men?'" 16He seized the leaders of the city,
along with some desert thorns and briers; he then "threshed"
the men of Sukkoth with them. 17He also tore down the tower
of Penuel and executed the city's men.

18He said to Zebah and Zalmunna, "Describe for me the men
you killed at Tabor." They said, "They were like you. Each one

looked like a king's son." [19]He said, "They were my brothers, the sons of my mother. I swear, as surely as the LORD is alive, if you had let them live, I would not kill you." [20]He ordered Jether his firstborn son, "Come on! Kill them!" But Jether was too afraid to draw his sword because he was still young. [21]Zebah and Zalmunna said to Gideon, "Come on, you strike us, for a man is judged by his strength." So Gideon killed Zebah and Zalmunna, and he took the crescent-shaped ornaments that were on the necks of their camels.

GIDEON REJECTS A CROWN BUT MAKES AN EPHOD

[22]The men of Israel said to Gideon, "Rule over us—you, your son, and your grandson. For you have delivered us from Midian's power." [23]Gideon said to them, "I will not rule over you, nor will my son rule over you. The LORD will rule over you." [24]Gideon continued, "I would like to make one request. Each of you give me an earring from the plunder you have taken." (The Midianites had gold earrings because they were Ishmaelites.) [25]They said, "We are happy to give you earrings." So they spread out a garment, and each one threw an earring from his plunder onto it. [26]The total weight of the gold earrings he requested came to 1,700 gold shekels. This was in addition to the crescent-shaped ornaments, jewelry, purple clothing worn by the Midianite kings, and the necklaces on the camels. [27]Gideon used all this to make an ephod, which he put in his hometown of Ophrah. All the Israelites prostituted themselves to it by worshiping it there. It became a snare to Gideon and his family.

8:22–28 We read that the children of Israel said to Gideon, "Rule over us." Yet God cannot permit any authority to usurp his own among his people. The sin consisted in the fact that, not content with God's government, they chose human government instead. Gideon and the holy kings did not extend their authority as rulers a hairsbreadth farther than God's command warranted, and they did not regard themselves in any other light than as servants and ministers of God; that is, they ruled according to God's direction and not according to their own.

MARTIN LUTHER **(1483–1546)**
ANNOTATIONS ON JUDGES

GIDEON'S STORY ENDS

[28]The Israelites humiliated Midian; the Midianites' fighting spirit was broken. The land had rest for 40 years during Gideon's time. [29]Then Jerub Baal son of Joash went home and settled down. [30]Gideon fathered 70 sons through his many wives. [31]His concubine, who lived in Shechem, also gave him a son, whom he named Abimelech. [32]Gideon son of Joash died at a very old age and was buried in the tomb of his father Joash located in Ophrah of the Abiezrites.

ISRAEL RETURNS TO BAAL WORSHIP

[33]After Gideon died, the Israelites again prostituted themselves to the Baals. They made Baal Berith their god. [34]The Israelites did not remain true to the LORD their God, who had delivered them from all the enemies who lived around them. [35]They did not treat the family of Jerub Baal (that is, Gideon) fairly in return for all the good he had done for Israel.

ABIMELECH MURDERS HIS BROTHERS

9 Now Abimelech son of Jerub Baal went to Shechem to see his mother's relatives. He said to them and to his mother's entire extended family, [2]"Tell all the leaders of Shechem this: 'Why would you want to have 70 men, all Jerub Baal's sons, ruling over you when you can have just one ruler? Recall that I am your own flesh and blood.'" [3]His mother's relatives spoke on his behalf to all the leaders of Shechem and reported his proposal. The leaders were drawn to Abimelech; they said, "He is our close relative." [4]They paid him 70 silver shekels out of the temple of Baal Berith. Abimelech then used the silver to hire some lawless, dangerous men as his followers. [5]He went to his

father's home in Ophrah and murdered his half brothers, the 70
legitimate sons of Jerub Baal, on one stone. Only Jotham, Jerub
Baal's youngest son, escaped because he hid. 6 All the leaders of
Shechem and Beth Millo assembled and then went and made
Abimelech king by the oak near the pillar in Shechem.

JOTHAM'S PARABLE

7 When Jotham heard the news, he went and stood on the top of
Mount Gerizim. He spoke loudly to the people below, "Listen to
me, leaders of Shechem, so that God may listen to you!
8 "The trees were determined to go out and choose a king for
themselves. They said to the olive tree, 'Be our king!' 9 But the
olive tree said to them, 'I am not going to stop producing my
oil, which is used to honor gods and men, just to sway above
the other trees!'

10 "So the trees said to the fig tree, 'You come and be our
king!' 11 But the fig tree said to them, 'I am not going to stop
producing my sweet figs, my excellent fruit, just to sway above
the other trees!'

12 "So the trees said to the grapevine, 'You come and be our
king!' 13 But the grapevine said to them, 'I am not going to stop
producing my wine, which makes gods and men so happy, just
to sway above the other trees!'

14 "So all the trees said to the thornbush, 'You come and be
our king!' 15 The thornbush said to the trees, 'If you really want
to choose me as your king, then come along, find safety under
my branches. Otherwise may fire blaze from the thornbush
and consume the cedars of Lebanon!'

16 "Now, if you have shown loyalty and integrity when you
made Abimelech king, if you have done right to Jerub Baal and
his family, if you have properly repaid him— 17 my father fought
for you; he risked his life and delivered you from Midian's power.
18 But you have attacked my father's family today. You murdered
his 70 legitimate sons on one stone and made Abimelech, the
son of his female slave, king over the leaders of Shechem just
because he is your close relative. 19 So if you have shown loyalty
and integrity to Jerub Baal and his family today, then may Abimelech bring you happiness and may you bring him happiness!
20 But if not, may fire blaze from Abimelech and consume the
leaders of Shechem and Beth Millo! May fire also blaze from the
leaders of Shechem and Beth Millo and consume Abimelech!"
21 Then Jotham ran away to Beer and lived there to escape from
Abimelech his half-brother.

GOD FULFILLS JOTHAM'S CURSE

22 Abimelech commanded Israel for three years. 23 God sent
a spirit to stir up hostility between Abimelech and the leaders of Shechem. He made the leaders of Shechem disloyal to
Abimelech. 24 He did this so the violent deaths of Jerub Baal's
70 sons might be avenged and Abimelech, their half-brother
who murdered them, might have to pay for their spilled blood,
along with the leaders of Shechem who helped him murder
them. 25 The leaders of Shechem rebelled against Abimelech by
putting bandits in the hills, who robbed everyone who traveled
by on the road. But Abimelech found out about it.

26 Gaal son of Ebed came through Shechem with his brothers. The leaders of Shechem transferred their loyalty to him.
27 They went out to the field, harvested their grapes, squeezed
out the juice, and celebrated. They came to the temple of their

9:22–57 Abimelech killed the seventy legitimate sons and, thinking he had hit upon a ruse for securing his grasp on the royal power, he destroyed his accomplices in the crime. He, however, was in turn destroyed by them and in the end was slain with a stone cast by a woman's hand. Countless examples teach us that the profit of human wisdom is illusory, for it is a meager and lowly thing and not a great and preeminent good.

BASIL THE GREAT **(330-379)**
ON HUMILITY

god and ate, drank, and cursed Abimelech. [28]Gaal son of Ebed
said, "Who is Abimelech and who is Shechem, that we should
serve him? Is he not the son of Jerub Baal, and is not Zebul the
deputy he appointed? Serve the sons of Hamor, the father of
Shechem! But why should we serve Abimelech? [29]If only these
men were under my command, I would get rid of Abimelech!"
He challenged Abimelech, "Muster your army and come out
for battle!"

[30]When Zebul, the city commissioner, heard the words of
Gaal son of Ebed, he was furious. [31]He sent messengers to Abimelech, who was in Arumah, reporting, "Beware! Gaal son of Ebed
and his brothers are coming to Shechem and inciting the city to
rebel against you. [32]Now, come up at night with your men and
set an ambush in the field outside the city. [33]In the morning
at sunrise quickly attack the city. When he and his men come
out to fight you, do what you can to him."

[34]So Abimelech and all his men came up at night and set an
ambush outside Shechem; they divided into four units. [35]When
Gaal son of Ebed came out and stood at the entrance to the city's
gate, Abimelech and his men got up from their hiding places.
[36]Gaal saw the men and said to Zebul, "Look, men are coming
down from the tops of the hills." But Zebul said to him, "You are
seeing the shadows on the hills—it just looks like men." [37]Gaal
again said, "Look, men are coming down from the very center of
the land. A unit is coming by way of the Oak Tree of the Diviners." [38]Zebul said to him, "Where now are your bragging words,
'Who is Abimelech that we should serve him?' Are these not the
men you insulted? Go out now and fight them!" [39]So Gaal led
the leaders of Shechem out and fought Abimelech. [40]Abimelech
chased him, and Gaal ran from him. Many Shechemites fell
wounded at the entrance of the gate. [41]Abimelech went back
to Arumah; Zebul drove Gaal and his brothers out of Shechem.

[42]The next day the Shechemites came out to the field. When
Abimelech heard about it, [43]he took his men and divided them
into three units and set an ambush in the field. When he saw
the people coming out of the city, he attacked and struck them
down. [44]Abimelech and his units attacked and blocked the entrance to the city's gate. Two units then attacked all the people
in the field and struck them down. [45]Abimelech fought against
the city all that day. He captured the city and killed all the
people in it. Then he leveled the city and spread salt over it.

[46]When all the leaders of the Tower of Shechem heard the
news, they went to the stronghold of the temple of El Berith.
[47]Abimelech heard that all the leaders of the Tower of Shechem
were in one place. [48]He and all his men went up on Mount
Zalmon. He took an ax in his hand and cut off a tree branch.
He put it on his shoulder and said to his men, "Quickly, do what
you have just seen me do!" [49]So each of his men also cut off a
branch and followed Abimelech. They put the branches against
the stronghold and set fire to it. All the people of the Tower of
Shechem died—about 1,000 men and women.

[50]Abimelech moved on to Thebez; he besieged and captured
it. [51]There was a fortified tower in the center of the city, so all
the men and women, as well as the city's leaders, ran into it and
locked the entrance. Then they went up to the roof of the tower.
[52]Abimelech came and attacked the tower. When he approached
the entrance of the tower to set it on fire, [53]a woman threw
an upper millstone down on his head and shattered his skull.
[54]He quickly called to the young man who carried his weapons,

"Draw your sword and kill me, so they will not say, 'A woman
killed him.'" So the young man stabbed him and he died. 55When
the Israelites saw that Abimelech was dead, they went home.
56God repaid Abimelech for the evil he did to his father by
murdering his 70 half brothers. 57God also repaid the men of
Shechem for their evil deeds. The curse spoken by Jotham son
of Jerub Baal fell on them.

STABILITY RESTORED

10 After Abimelech's death, Tola son of Puah, grandson of
Dodo, from the tribe of Issachar, rose up to deliver Israel.
He lived in Shamir in the Ephraimite hill country. 2He led Israel
for 23 years, then died and was buried in Shamir.
3Jair the Gileadite rose up after him; he led Israel for 22 years.
4He had 30 sons who rode on 30 donkeys and possessed 30 cities.
To this day these towns are called Havvoth Jair—they are in the
land of Gilead. 5Jair died and was buried in Kamon.

THE LORD'S PATIENCE RUNS SHORT

6The Israelites again did evil in the LORD's sight. They worshiped the Baals and the Ashtoreths, as well as the gods of
Syria, Sidon, Moab, the Ammonites, and the Philistines. They
abandoned the LORD and did not worship him. 7The LORD was
furious with Israel and turned them over to the Philistines and
Ammonites. 8They ruthlessly oppressed the Israelites that
eighteenth year—that is, all the Israelites living east of the Jordan in Amorite country in Gilead. 9The Ammonites crossed
the Jordan to fight with Judah, Benjamin, and Ephraim. Israel
suffered greatly.
10The Israelites cried out for help to the LORD: "We have
sinned against you. We abandoned our God and worshiped the
Baals." 11The LORD said to the Israelites, "Did I not deliver you
from Egypt, the Amorites, the Ammonites, the Philistines, 12the
Sidonians, Amalek, and Midian when they oppressed you? You
cried out for help to me, and I delivered you from their power.
13But since you abandoned me and worshiped other gods, I will
not deliver you again. 14Go and cry for help to the gods you have
chosen! Let them deliver you from trouble!" 15But the Israelites
said to the LORD, "We have sinned. You do to us as you see fit,
but deliver us today!" 16They threw away the foreign gods they
owned and worshiped the LORD. Finally the LORD grew tired
of seeing Israel suffer so much.

AN OUTCAST BECOMES A GENERAL

17The Ammonites assembled and camped in Gilead; the Israelites gathered together and camped in Mizpah. 18The leaders
of Gilead said to one another, "Who is willing to lead the charge
against the Ammonites? He will become the leader of all who
live in Gilead!"

11 Now Jephthah the Gileadite was a brave warrior. His mother was a prostitute, but Gilead was his father. 2Gilead's wife
also gave him sons. When his wife's sons grew up, they made
Jephthah leave and said to him, "You are not going to inherit
any of our father's wealth because you are another woman's
son." 3So Jephthah left his half brothers and lived in the land of
Tob. Lawless men joined Jephthah's gang and traveled with him.
4It was some time after this when the Ammonites fought with
Israel. 5When the Ammonites attacked, the leaders of Gilead
asked Jephthah to come back from the land of Tob. 6They said,

10:6–18 The one chapter and the whole history of Judges is an example that illustrates the repentance of the Israelites who, having deserted faith and obedience to the only true God, lapsed into sin, idolatry, and other shameful crimes; and having with calamities and divine afflictions laid on them from the wrath of God against sin, turned back to God in true repentance and faith. Indeed, true repentance, or conversion to God, is contrition, faith, and good intention. Contrition is to grieve earnestly that we offended God with our sins, to tremble at the knowledge of the wrath of God against our sins, and to beg for pardon and forgiveness on account of Christ, as the Israelites did in this passage.

DAVID CHYTRAEUS
(1530–1600)
COMMENTARY ON JUDGES

11:1–28 We may note those especial endowments that God granted to sundry persons for the accomplishment of some special design. He came upon Jephthah to anoint him for the work of delivering the people from their adversaries in battle. This coming of the Spirit of God upon them and clothing of Jephthah was his special excitation of their courage and his fortifying of Jephthah against those dangers they were to inflict withal. And this God did by such efficacious impression of his power upon Jephthah that he received confirmation of his call, and others might discern the presence of God with him.

JOHN OWEN **(1616–1683)**
THE WORKS

"Come, be our commander, so we can fight with the Ammonites." 7Jephthah said to the leaders of Gilead, "But you hated me and made me leave my father's house. Why do you come to me now, when you are in trouble?" 8The leaders of Gilead said to Jephthah, "That may be true, but now we pledge to you our loyalty. Come with us and fight with the Ammonites. Then you will become the leader of all who live in Gilead." 9Jephthah said to the leaders of Gilead, "All right. If you take me back to fight with the Ammonites and the LORD gives them to me, I will be your leader." 10The leaders of Gilead said to Jephthah, "The LORD will judge any grievance you have against us if we do not do as you say." 11So Jephthah went with the leaders of Gilead. The people made him their leader and commander. Jephthah repeated the terms of the agreement before the LORD in Mizpah.

JEPHTHAH GIVES A HISTORY LESSON

12Jephthah sent messengers to the Ammonite king, saying, "Why have you come against me to attack my land?" 13The Ammonite king said to Jephthah's messengers, "Because Israel stole my land when they came up from Egypt—from the Arnon River in the south to the Jabbok River in the north, and as far west as the Jordan. Now return it peaceably!"

14Jephthah sent messengers back to the Ammonite king 15and said to him, "This is what Jephthah says, 'Israel did not steal the land of Moab and the land of the Ammonites. 16When they left Egypt, Israel traveled through the desert as far as the Red Sea and then came to Kadesh. 17Israel sent messengers to the king of Edom, saying, "Please allow us to pass through your land." But the king of Edom rejected the request. Israel sent the same request to the king of Moab, but he was unwilling to cooperate. So Israel stayed at Kadesh. 18Then Israel went through the wilderness and bypassed the land of Edom and the land of Moab. They traveled east of the land of Moab and camped on the other side of the Arnon River; they did not go through Moabite territory (the Arnon was Moab's border). 19Israel sent messengers to King Sihon, the Amorite king who ruled in Heshbon, and said to him, "Please allow us to pass through your land to our land." 20But Sihon did not trust Israel to pass through his territory. He assembled his whole army, camped in Jahaz, and fought with Israel. 21The LORD God of Israel handed Sihon and his whole army over to Israel, and they defeated them. Israel took all the land of the Amorites who lived in that land. 22They took all the Amorite territory from the Arnon River on the south to the Jabbok River on the north, from the desert in the east to the Jordan in the west. 23Since the LORD God of Israel has driven out the Amorites before his people Israel, do you think you can just take it from them? 24You have the right to take what Chemosh your god gives you, but we will take the land of all whom the LORD our God has driven out before us. 25Are you really better than Balak son of Zippor, king of Moab? Did he dare to quarrel with Israel? Did he dare to fight with them? 26Israel has been living in Heshbon and its nearby towns, in Aroer and its nearby towns, and in all the cities along the Arnon for 300 years! Why did you not reclaim them during that time? 27I have not done you wrong, but you are doing wrong by attacking me. May the LORD, the Judge, judge this day between the Israelites and the Ammonites!'" 28But the Ammonite king disregarded the message sent by Jephthah.

A FOOLISH VOW SPELLS DEATH FOR A DAUGHTER

29 The LORD's Spirit empowered Jephthah. He passed through Gilead and Manasseh and went to Mizpah in Gilead. From there he approached the Ammonites. 30 Jephthah made a vow to the LORD, saying, "If you really do hand the Ammonites over to me, 31 then whoever is the first to come through the doors of my house to meet me when I return safely from fighting the Ammonites—he will belong to the LORD, and I will offer him up as a burnt sacrifice." 32 Jephthah approached the Ammonites to fight with them, and the LORD handed them over to him. 33 He defeated them from Aroer all the way to Minnith—20 cities in all, even as far as Abel Keramim. He wiped them out! The Israelites humiliated the Ammonites.

34 When Jephthah came home to Mizpah, there was his daughter hurrying out to meet him, dancing to the rhythm of tambourines. She was his only child; except for her he had no son or daughter. 35 When he saw her, he ripped his clothes and said, "Oh no! My daughter! You have completely ruined me! You have brought me disaster! I made an oath to the LORD, and I cannot break it." 36 She said to him, "My father, since you made an oath to the LORD, do to me as you promised. After all, the LORD vindicated you before your enemies, the Ammonites." 37 She then said to her father, "Please grant me this one wish. For two months allow me to walk through the hills with my friends and mourn my virginity." 38 He said, "You may go." He permitted her to leave for two months. She went with her friends and mourned her virginity as she walked through the hills. 39 After two months she returned to her father, and he did to her as he had vowed. She died a virgin. Her tragic death gave rise to a custom in Israel. 40 Every year Israelite women commemorate the daughter of Jephthah the Gileadite for four days.

CIVIL STRIFE MARS THE VICTORY

12 The Ephraimites assembled and crossed over to Zaphon. They said to Jephthah, "Why did you go and fight with the Ammonites without asking us to go with you? We will burn your house down right over you!"

2 Jephthah said to them, "My people and I were in a struggle, and the Ammonites were oppressing me greatly. I asked for your help, but you did not deliver me from their power. 3 When I saw that you were not going to help, I risked my life and advanced against the Ammonites, and the LORD handed them over to me. Why have you come up to fight with me today?" 4 Jephthah assembled all the men of Gilead and they fought with Ephraim. The men of Gilead defeated Ephraim because the Ephraimites insulted them, saying, "You Gileadites are refugees in Ephraim, living within Ephraim's and Manasseh's territory." 5 The Gileadites captured the fords of the Jordan River opposite Ephraim. Whenever an Ephraimite fugitive said, "Let me cross over," the men of Gilead asked him, "Are you an Ephraimite?" If he said, "No," 6 then they said to him, "Say 'Shibboleth!'" If he said, "Sibboleth" (and could not pronounce the word correctly), they grabbed him and executed him right there at the fords of the Jordan. On that day 42,000 Ephraimites fell dead.

7 Jephthah led Israel for six years; then he died and was buried in his town in Gilead.

12:1 The Ephraimites quarreled with Jephthah just in the same manner as they did with Gideon: These Ephraimites were a proud and turbulent people and especially were very jealous of the tribe of Manasseh, of which both Gideon and Jephthah were—the one of the half tribe on this side of the Jordan, and the other of the half that was on the other side. And they were jealous of both, lest any honor and glory should accrue to them and they should get any superiority in any respect over them, since Jacob their father had given the preference to Ephraim; and this seems to lie at the bottom of all their proceedings.

JOHN GILL (1697–1771)
EXPOSITION OF THE WHOLE BIBLE

ORDER RESTORED

[8]After him Ibzan of Bethlehem led Israel. [9]He had 30 sons.
He arranged for 30 of his daughters to be married outside his
extended family, and he arranged for 30 young women to be
brought from outside as wives for his sons. Ibzan led Israel
for seven years; [10]then he died and was buried in Bethlehem.
[11]After him Elon the Zebulunite led Israel for 10 years. [12]Then
Elon the Zebulunite died and was buried in Aijalon in the land
of Zebulun.
[13]After him Abdon son of Hillel the Pirathonite led Israel.
[14]He had 40 sons and 30 grandsons who rode on 70 donkeys.
He led Israel for eight years. [15]Then Abdon son of Hillel the
Pirathonite died and was buried in Pirathon in the land of
Ephraim, in the hill country of the Amalekites.

SAMSON'S BIRTH

13 The Israelites again did evil in the LORD's sight, so the
LORD handed them over to the Philistines for 40 years.
[2]There was a man named Manoah from Zorah, from the
Danite tribe. His wife was infertile and childless. [3]The angel
of the LORD appeared to the woman and said to her, "You are
infertile and childless, but you will conceive and have a son.
[4]Now be careful! Do not drink wine or beer, and do not eat any
food that will make you ritually unclean. [5]Look, you will conceive and have a son. You must never cut his hair, for the child
will be dedicated to God from birth. He will begin to deliver
Israel from the power of the Philistines."
[6]The woman went and said to her husband, "A man sent from
God came to me! He looked like God's angel—he was very awesome. I did not ask him where he came from, and he did not
tell me his name. [7]He said to me, 'Look, you will conceive and
have a son. So now, do not drink wine or beer and do not eat
any food that will make you ritually unclean. For the child will
be dedicated to God from birth till the day he dies.'"
[8]Manoah prayed to the LORD, "Please, Lord, allow the man
sent from God to visit us again, so he can teach us how we
should raise the child who will be born." [9]God answered Manoah's prayer. God's angel visited the woman again while she was
sitting in the field. But her husband Manoah was not with her.
[10]The woman ran at once and told her husband, "Come quickly,
the man who visited me the other day has appeared to me!"
[11]So Manoah got up and followed his wife. When he met the
man, he said to him, "Are you the man who spoke to my wife?"
He said, "Yes." [12]Manoah said, "Now, when your announcement
comes true, how should the child be raised and what should he
do?" [13]The angel of the LORD told Manoah, "Your wife should
pay attention to everything I told her. [14]She should not drink
anything that the grapevine produces. She must not drink wine
or beer, and she must not eat any food that will make her ritually unclean. She should obey everything I commanded her
to do." [15]Manoah said to the angel of the LORD, "Please stay
here awhile, so we can prepare a young goat for you to eat."
[16]The angel of the LORD said to Manoah, "If I stay, I will not
eat your food. But if you want to make a burnt sacrifice to the
LORD, you should offer it." (He said this because Manoah did
not know that he was the angel of the LORD.) [17]Manoah said
to the angel of the LORD, "Tell us your name, so we can honor
you when your announcement comes true." [18]The angel of the
LORD said to him, "You should not ask me my name because

13:1–7 Thus Jacob, the patriarch Joseph, Samson, who was the bravest of the chieftains, and Samuel, who was the most distinguished of the prophets—all had as their progenitors mothers who were for a long time barren in body but always fruitful in virtues. In this way their dignity would be known from the miraculous nativity of those who were born, and it might be proven that they would be famous in their lives, since at the very outset of their lives they transcended the norms of the human condition.

VENERABLE BEDE
(C. 672–735)
HOMILIES ON THE GOSPELS

you cannot comprehend it." [19]Manoah took a young goat and
a grain offering and offered them on a rock to the LORD. The
LORD's messenger did an amazing thing as Manoah and his wife
watched. [20]As the flame went up from the altar toward the sky,
the angel of the LORD went up in it while Manoah and his wife
watched. They fell facedown to the ground.
[21]The angel of the LORD did not appear again to Manoah
and his wife. After all this happened Manoah realized that the
visitor had been the angel of the LORD. [22]Manoah said to his
wife, "We will certainly die because we have seen a supernatural
being!" [23]But his wife said to him, "If the LORD wanted to kill
us, he would not have accepted the burnt offering and the grain
offering from us. He would not have shown us all these things
or have spoken to us like this just now."
[24]Manoah's wife gave birth to a son and named him Samson.
The child grew and the LORD empowered him. [25]The LORD's
Spirit began to control him in Mahaneh Dan between Zorah
and Eshtaol.

SAMSON'S UNCONSUMMATED MARRIAGE

14 Samson went down to Timnah, where a Philistine girl
caught his eye. [2]When he got home, he told his father and
mother, "A Philistine girl in Timnah has caught my eye. Now
get her for my wife." [3]But his father and mother said to him,
"Certainly you can find a wife among your relatives or among
all our people! You should not have to go and get a wife from the
uncircumcised Philistines." But Samson said to his father, "Get
her for me because she is the right one for me." [4]Now his father
and mother did not realize this was the LORD's doing because
he was looking for an opportunity to stir up trouble with the
Philistines (for at that time the Philistines were ruling Israel).
[5]Samson went down to Timnah. When he approached the
vineyards of Timnah, he saw a roaring young lion attacking
him. [6]The LORD's Spirit empowered him, and he tore the lion
in two with his bare hands as easily as one would tear a young
goat. But he did not tell his father or mother what he had done.
[7]Samson continued on down to Timnah and spoke to the
girl. In his opinion, she was just the right one. [8]Sometime later,
when he went back to marry her, he turned aside to see the lion's
remains. He saw a swarm of bees in the lion's carcass, as well as
some honey. [9]He scooped it up with his hands and ate it as he
walked along. When he returned to his father and mother,
he offered them some and they ate it. But he did not tell them
he had scooped the honey out of the lion's carcass.
[10]Then Samson's father accompanied him to Timnah for the
marriage. Samson hosted a party there, for this was customary
for bridegrooms to do. [11]When the Philistines saw he had no
attendants, they gave him 30 groomsmen who kept him company. [12]Samson said to them, "I will give you a riddle. If you really
can solve it during the seven days the party lasts, I will give
you 30 linen robes and 30 sets of clothes. [13]But if you cannot
solve it, you will give me 30 linen robes and 30 sets of clothes."
They said to him, "Let us hear your riddle." [14]He said to them,
"Out of the one who eats came something to eat;
out of the strong one came something sweet."
They could not solve the riddle for three days.
[15]On the fourth day they said to Samson's bride, "Trick your
husband into giving the solution to the riddle. If you refuse, we
will burn up you and your father's family. Did you invite us here

14:1–20 The strength that Samson possessed came from the grace of God rather than by nature, for if he had been naturally strong his power would not have been taken away when his hair was cut. Where then was that most powerful strength except in what the scripture says: "The LORD's Spirit empowered him"? Therefore his strength belonged to the Spirit of the Lord. In Samson was the vessel, but the fullness was in the Spirit. A vessel can be filled and emptied. Moreover, every vessel has its perfection from something else.

CAESARIUS OF ARLES
(C. 468–542)
SERMONS

to make us poor?" [16]So Samson's bride cried on his shoulder and said, "You must hate me; you do not love me! You told the young men a riddle, but you have not told me the solution." He said to her, "Look, I have not even told my father or mother. Do you really expect me to tell you?" [17]She cried on his shoulder until the party was almost over. Finally, on the seventh day, he told her because she had nagged him so much. Then she told the young men the solution to the riddle. [18]On the seventh day, before the sun set, the men of the city said to him,

"What is sweeter than honey?
What is stronger than a lion?"

He said to them,

"If you had not plowed with my heifer,
you would not have solved my riddle!"

[19]The LORD's Spirit empowered him. He went down to Ashkelon and killed 30 men. He took their clothes and gave them to the men who had solved the riddle. He was furious as he went back home. [20]Samson's bride was then given to his best man.

SAMSON VERSUS THE PHILISTINES

15 Sometime later, during the wheat harvest, Samson took a young goat as a gift and went to visit his bride. He said to her father, "I want to sleep with my bride in her bedroom!" But her father would not let him enter. [2]Her father said, "I really thought you absolutely despised her, so I gave her to your best man. Her younger sister is more attractive than she is. Take her instead!" [3]Samson said to them, "This time I am justified in doing the Philistines harm!" [4]Samson went and captured 300 jackals and got some torches. He tied the jackals in pairs by their tails and then tied a torch to each pair. [5]He lit the torches and set the jackals loose in the Philistines' standing grain. He burned up the grain heaps and the standing grain, as well as the vineyards and olive groves. [6]The Philistines asked, "Who did this?" They were told, "Samson, the Timnite's son-in-law, because the Timnite took Samson's bride and gave her to his best man." So the Philistines went up and burned her and her father. [7]Samson said to them, "Because you did this, I will get revenge against you before I quit fighting." [8]He struck them down and defeated them. Then he went down and lived for a time in the cave in the cliff of Etam.

[9]The Philistines went up and invaded Judah. They arrayed themselves for battle in Lehi. [10]The men of Judah said, "Why are you attacking us?" The Philistines said, "We have come up to take Samson prisoner so we can do to him what he has done to us." [11]So 3,000 men of Judah went down to the cave in the cliff of Etam and said to Samson, "Do you not know that the Philistines rule over us? Why have you done this to us?" He said to them, "I have only done to them what they have done to me." [12]They said to him, "We have come down to take you prisoner so we can hand you over to the Philistines." Samson said to them, "Promise me you will not kill me." [13]They said to him, "We promise! We will only take you prisoner and hand you over to them. We promise not to kill you." They tied him up with two brand new ropes and led him up from the cliff. [14]When he arrived in Lehi, the Philistines shouted as they approached him. But the LORD's Spirit empowered him. The ropes around his arms were like flax dissolving in fire, and they melted away from his hands. [15]He happened to see a solid

15:1–20 Samson had slain a thousand Philistines and piled them up in heaps, then fainted for a little water! Strange that there must be a shrinking of the sinew whenever we win the day—as if the Lord must teach us our littleness, our nothingness, in order to keep us within bounds. Samson boasted right loudly when he said, "I have struck down a thousand men!" His boastful throat soon grew hoarse with thirst, and he took himself to prayer. God has many ways of humbling his people. Dear child of God, if after great mercy you are laid very low, your case is not an unusual one. You must expect to feel weakest when you are enjoying your greatest triumph. The Lord will not let you faint or suffer the offspring of the uncircumcised to triumph over you.

CHARLES SPURGEON
(1834–1892)
MORNING AND EVENING

jawbone of a donkey. He grabbed it and struck down 1,000 men.
16 Samson then said,

"With the jawbone of a donkey
I have left them in heaps;
with the jawbone of a donkey
I have struck down a thousand men!"

17 When he finished speaking, he threw the jawbone down
and named that place Ramath Lehi.
18 He was very thirsty, so he cried out to the LORD and
said, "You have given your servant this great victory. But
now must I die of thirst and fall into the hands of these
uncircumcised Philistines?" 19 So God split open the basin
at Lehi, and water flowed out from it. When he took a drink,
his strength was restored and he revived. For this reason
he named the spring En Hakkore. It remains in Lehi to this
very day. 20 Samson led Israel for 20 years during the days
of Philistine prominence.

SAMSON'S DOWNFALL

16 Samson went to Gaza. There he saw a prostitute and slept
with her. 2 The Gazites were told, "Samson has come here!"
So they surrounded the town and hid all night at the city gate,
waiting for him to leave. They relaxed all night, thinking, "He
will not leave until morning comes; then we will kill him!" 3 Samson spent half the night with the prostitute; then he got up in
the middle of the night and left. He grabbed the doors of the
city gate, as well as the two posts, and pulled them right off, bar
and all. He put them on his shoulders and carried them up to
the top of a hill east of Hebron.
4 After this Samson fell in love with a woman named Delilah,
who lived in the Sorek Valley. 5 The rulers of the Philistines went
up to visit her and said to her, "Trick him! Find out what makes
him so strong and how we can subdue him and humiliate him.
Each one of us will give you 1,100 silver pieces."
6 So Delilah said to Samson, "Tell me what makes you so
strong and how you can be subdued and humiliated." 7 Samson
said to her, "If they tie me up with seven fresh bowstrings that
have not been dried, I will become weak and be just like any
other man." 8 So the rulers of the Philistines brought her seven
fresh bowstrings that had not been dried, and she tied him up
with them. 9 They hid in the bedroom and then she said to him,
"The Philistines are here, Samson!" He snapped the bowstrings
as easily as a thread of yarn snaps when it is put close to fire.
The secret of his strength was not discovered.
10 Delilah said to Samson, "Look, you deceived me and told
me lies! Now tell me how you can be subdued." 11 He said to her,
"If they tie me tightly with brand new ropes that have never
been used, I will become weak and be just like any other man."
12 So Delilah took new ropes and tied him with them and said
to him, "The Philistines are here, Samson!" (The Philistines
were hiding in the bedroom.) But he tore the ropes from his
arms as if they were a piece of thread.
13 Delilah said to Samson, "Up to now you have deceived me
and told me lies. Tell me how you can be subdued." He said to
her, "If you weave the seven braids of my hair into the fabric on
the loom and secure it with the pin, I will become weak and be
like any other man." 14 So she made him go to sleep, wove the
seven braids of his hair into the fabric on the loom, fastened it

16:1–22 When we sleep, our spiritual enemies do not. Samson's eyes were the inlets of his sin, and now his punishment began there. Take warning by his fall to watch carefully against all fleshly lusts, for all our glory is gone and our defense departed from us when our separation to God, as spiritual Nazirites, is profaned. Samson's afflictions were the means of bringing him to deep repentance. By the loss of his bodily sight, the eyes of his understanding were opened; and by depriving him of bodily strength, the Lord was pleased to renew his spiritual strength.

MATTHEW HENRY (1662–1714)
COMMENTARY ON THE WHOLE BIBLE

with the pin, and said to him, "The Philistines are here, Samson!"
He woke up and tore away the pin of the loom and the fabric.
[15]She said to him, "How can you say, 'I love you,' when you
will not share your secret with me? Three times you have deceived me and have not told me what makes you so strong."
[16]She nagged him every day and pressured him until he was
sick to death of it. [17]Finally he told her his secret. He said to
her, "My hair has never been cut, for I have been dedicated to
God from the time I was conceived. If my head were shaved,
my strength would leave me; I would become weak and be just
like all other men." [18]When Delilah saw that he had told her his
secret, she sent for the rulers of the Philistines, saying, "Come
up here again, for he has told me his secret." So the rulers of
the Philistines went up to visit her, bringing the silver in their
hands. [19]She made him go to sleep on her lap and then called a
man in to shave off the seven braids of his hair. She made him
vulnerable and his strength left him. [20]She said, "The Philistines
are here, Samson!" He woke up and thought, "I will do as I did
before and shake myself free." But he did not realize that the
LORD had left him. [21]The Philistines captured him and gouged
out his eyes. They brought him down to Gaza and bound him
in bronze chains. He became a grinder in the prison. [22]His hair
began to grow back after it had been shaved off.

SAMSON'S DEATH AND BURIAL

[23]The rulers of the Philistines gathered to offer a great sacrifice
to Dagon their god and to celebrate. They said, "Our god has
handed Samson, our enemy, over to us." [24]When the people
saw him, they praised their god, saying, "Our god has handed
our enemy over to us, the one who ruined our land and killed
so many of us!"
[25]When they really started celebrating, they said, "Call for
Samson so he can entertain us!" So they summoned Samson
from the prison and he entertained them. They made him stand
between two pillars. [26]Samson said to the young man who held
his hand, "Position me so I can touch the pillars that support the
temple. Then I can lean on them." [27]Now the temple was filled
with men and women, and all the rulers of the Philistines were
there. There were 3,000 men and women on the roof watching
Samson entertain. [28]Samson called to the LORD, "O Sovereign
LORD, remember me! Strengthen me just one more time, O God,
so I can get swift revenge against the Philistines for my two
eyes!" [29]Samson took hold of the two middle pillars that supported the temple and he leaned against them, with his right
hand on one and his left hand on the other. [30]Samson said, "Let
me die with the Philistines!" He pushed hard, and the temple
collapsed on the rulers and all the people in it. He killed many
more people in his death than he had killed during his life. [31]His
brothers and all his family went down and brought him back.
They buried him between Zorah and Eshtaol in the tomb of
Manoah his father. He had led Israel for 20 years.

MICAH MAKES HIS OWN RELIGION

17 There was a man named Micah from the Ephraimite hill
country. [2]He said to his mother, "You know the 1,100 pieces
of silver which were stolen from you, about which I heard you
pronounce a curse? Look here, I have the silver. I stole it, but
now I am giving it back to you." His mother said, "May the LORD
reward you, my son!" [3]When he gave back to his mother the

17:1–13 Micah appropriated to the idols an apartment of his house for a temple and consecrated someone "like a son" to be a priest, to officiate before them with an ephod that was made for his use. It is not of idolatry in general that I speak, but only of that particular modification of it that Micah established, and of the confidence he expressed when his newly invented religion was made to bear some faint resemblance to the Mosaic ritual. This so exactly represents the false confidences to which ungodly people of every age resort. Was this justified by facts? Could his idols help him in the day of adversity? And when he complained of the spoilers who had robbed him, his pathetic expostulations were of no avail, and he was constrained to submit in silence to the loss of all wherein he had put his trust.

CHARLES SIMEON
(1759–1836)
HORAE HOMILETICAE

1,100 pieces of silver, his mother said, "I solemnly dedicate this
silver to the LORD. It will be for my son's benefit. We will use
it to make a carved image and a metal image." [4]When he gave
the silver back to his mother, she took 200 pieces of silver to a
silversmith, who made them into a carved image and a metal
image. She then put them in Micah's house. [5]Now this man
Micah owned a shrine. He made an ephod and some personal
idols and hired one of his sons to serve as a priest. [6]In those days
Israel had no king. Each man did what he considered to be right.

MICAH HIRES A PROFESSIONAL

[7]There was a young man from Bethlehem in Judah. He was a
Levite who had been temporarily residing among the tribe of
Judah. [8]This man left the town of Bethlehem in Judah to find
another place to live. He came to the Ephraimite hill country
and made his way to Micah's house. [9]Micah said to him, "Where
do you come from?" He replied, "I am a Levite from Bethlehem
in Judah. I am looking for a new place to live." [10]Micah said to
him, "Stay with me. Become my adviser and priest. I will give
you 10 pieces of silver per year, plus clothes and food." [11]So
the Levite agreed to stay with the man; the young man was
like a son to Micah. [12]Micah paid the Levite; the young man
became his priest and lived in Micah's house. [13]Micah said,
"Now I know the LORD will make me rich because I have this
Levite as my priest."

THE TRIBE OF DAN FINDS AN INHERITANCE

18 In those days Israel had no king. And in those days the
Danite tribe was looking for a place to settle because at
that time they did not yet have a place to call their own among
the tribes of Israel. [2]The Danites sent out from their whole
tribe five representatives, capable men from Zorah and Eshtaol, to spy out the land and explore it. They said to them, "Go,
explore the land." They came to the Ephraimite hill country and
spent the night at Micah's house. [3]As they approached Micah's
house, they recognized the accent of the young Levite. So they
stopped there and said to him, "Who brought you here? What
are you doing in this place? What is your business here?" [4]He
told them what Micah had done for him, saying, "He hired me,
and I became his priest." [5]They said to him, "Seek a divine oracle
for us, so we can know if we will be successful on our mission."
[6]The priest said to them, "Go with confidence. The LORD will
be with you on your mission."

[7]So the five men journeyed on and arrived in Laish. They
noticed that the people there were living securely, like the Sidonians do, undisturbed and unsuspecting. No conqueror was
troubling them in any way. They lived far from the Sidonians
and had no dealings with anyone. [8]When the Danites returned
to their tribe in Zorah and Eshtaol, their kinsmen asked them,
"How did it go?" [9]They said, "Come on, let's attack them, for we
saw their land and it is very good. You seem lethargic, but don't
hesitate to invade and conquer the land. [10]When you invade,
you will encounter unsuspecting people. The land is wide! God
is handing it over to you—a place that lacks nothing on earth!"

[11]So 600 Danites, fully armed, set out from Zorah and Eshtaol. [12]They went up and camped in Kiriath Jearim in Judah. (To
this day that place is called Camp of Dan. It is west of Kiriath
Jearim.) [13]From there they traveled through the Ephraimite
hill country and arrived at Micah's house. [14]The five men who

had gone to spy out the land of Laish said to their kinsmen,
"Do you realize that inside these houses are an ephod, some
personal idols, a carved image, and a metal image? Decide now
what you want to do." 15They stopped there, went inside the
young Levite's house (which belonged to Micah), and asked
him how he was doing. 16Meanwhile the 600 Danites, fully
armed, stood at the entrance to the gate. 17The five men who
had gone to spy out the land broke in and stole the carved image,
the ephod, the personal idols, and the metal image, while the
priest was standing at the entrance to the gate with the 600
fully armed men. 18When these men broke into Micah's house
and stole the carved image, the ephod, the personal idols, and
the metal image, the priest said to them, "What are you doing?"
19They said to him, "Shut up! Put your hand over your mouth
and come with us! You can be our adviser and priest. Wouldn't
it be better to be a priest for a whole Israelite tribe than for just
one man's family?" 20The priest was happy. He took the ephod,
the personal idols, and the carved image and joined the group.
21They turned and went on their way, but they walked behind
the children, the cattle, and their possessions. 22After they had
gone a good distance from Micah's house, Micah's neighbors
gathered together and caught up with the Danites. 23When they
called out to the Danites, the Danites turned around and said
to Micah, "Why have you gathered together?" 24He said, "You
stole my gods that I made, as well as this priest, and then went
away. What do I have left? How can you have the audacity to say
to me, 'What do you want?'" 25The Danites said to him, "Don't
say another word to us, or some very angry men will attack
you, and you and your family will die." 26The Danites went on
their way; when Micah realized they were too strong to resist,
he turned around and went home.

27Now the Danites took what Micah had made, as well as his
priest, and came to Laish, where the people were undisturbed
and unsuspecting. They struck them down with the sword and
burned the city. 28No one came to the rescue because the city
was far from Sidon and they had no dealings with anyone. The
city was in a valley near Beth Rehob. The Danites rebuilt the
city and occupied it. 29They named it Dan after their ancestor,
who was one of Israel's sons. But the city's name used to be
Laish. 30The Danites worshiped the carved image. Jonathan,
descendant of Gershom, son of Moses, and his descendants
served as priests for the tribe of Dan until the time of the exile.
31They worshiped Micah's carved image the whole time God's
authorized shrine was in Shiloh.

SODOM AND GOMORRAH REVISITED

19 In those days Israel had no king. There was a Levite living
temporarily in the remote region of the Ephraimite hill
country. He acquired a concubine from Bethlehem in Judah.
2However, she got angry at him and went home to her father's
house in Bethlehem in Judah. When she had been there four
months, 3her husband came after her, hoping he could convince
her to return. He brought with him his servant and a pair of
donkeys. When she brought him into her father's house and the
girl's father saw him, he greeted him warmly. 4His father-in-law,
the girl's father, persuaded him to stay with him for three days,
and they ate and drank together, and spent the night there. 5On
the fourth day they woke up early and the Levite got ready to
leave. But the girl's father said to his son-in-law, "Have a bite

18:27–31 It seems almost certain that this Jonathan, the grandson of Moses, was the same who had been Micah's priest. And how touchingly does it speak for the magnanimous disinterestedness of that truly great man that not only did he twice decline the offer of the aggrandizement of his own family, when the Lord proposed to make of him "a great nation" (Ex 32:10), rejecting the Israelites for their rebellions—but that, neglecting all opportunities of enriching his descendants, he left his sons undistinguished from common Levites by rank or patrimony and so poor that one of his grandsons was glad to accept a situation that afforded only his victuals, with a suit of clothes and a salary of less than twenty-five shillings by the year!

JOHN KITTO **(1804–1854)**
THE PICTORIAL BIBLE

to eat for some energy, then you can go." [6]So the two of them
sat down and had a meal together. Then the girl's father said to
the man, "Why not stay another night and have a good time?"
[7]When the man got ready to leave, his father-in-law convinced
him to stay another night. [8]He woke up early in the morning
on the fifth day so he could leave, but the girl's father said, "Get
some energy! Wait until later in the day to leave." So they ate
a meal together. [9]When the man got ready to leave with his
concubine and his servant, his father-in-law, the girl's father,
said to him, "Look! The day is almost over. Stay another night!
Since the day is over, stay another night here and have a good
time. You can get up early tomorrow and start your trip home."
[10]But the man did not want to stay another night. He left and
traveled as far as Jebus (that is, Jerusalem). He had with him a
pair of saddled donkeys and his concubine.

[11]When they got near Jebus, it was getting quite late and the
servant said to his master, "Come on, let's stop at this Jebusite
city and spend the night in it." [12]But his master said to him,
"We should not stop at a foreign city where non-Israelites live.
We will travel on to Gibeah." [13]He said to his servant, "Come
on, we will go into one of the other towns and spend the night
in Gibeah or Ramah." [14]So they traveled on, and the sun went
down when they were near Gibeah in the territory of Benjamin.
[15]They stopped there and decided to spend the night in Gibeah.
They came into the city and sat down in the town square, but
no one invited them to spend the night.

[16]But then an old man passed by, returning at the end of the
day from his work in the field. The man was from the Ephraimite
hill country; he was living temporarily in Gibeah. (The residents
of the town were Benjaminites.) [17]When he looked up and saw
the traveler in the town square, the old man said, "Where are
you heading? Where do you come from?" [18]The Levite said to
him, "We are traveling from Bethlehem in Judah to the remote
region of the Ephraimite hill country. That's where I'm from. I
had business in Bethlehem in Judah, but now I'm heading home.
But no one has invited me into their home. [19]We have enough
straw and grain for our donkeys, and there is enough food and
wine for me, your female servant, and the young man who is with
your servants. We lack nothing." [20]The old man said, "Everything
is just fine. I will take care of all your needs. But don't spend the
night in the town square." [21]So he brought him to his house and
fed the donkeys. They washed their feet and had a meal.

[22]They were having a good time, when suddenly some men
of the city, some good-for-nothings, surrounded the house and
kept beating on the door. They said to the old man who owned
the house, "Send out the man who came to visit you so we can
take carnal knowledge of him." [23]The man who owned the house
went outside and said to them, "No, my brothers! Don't do this
wicked thing! After all, this man is a guest in my house. Don't
do such a disgraceful thing! [24]Here are my virgin daughter and
my guest's concubine. I will send them out, and you can abuse
them and do to them whatever you like. But don't do such a
disgraceful thing to this man!" [25]The men refused to listen
to him, so the Levite grabbed his concubine and made her go
outside. They raped her and abused her all night long until
morning. They let her go at dawn. [26]The woman arrived back
at daybreak and was sprawled out on the doorstep of the house
where her master was staying until it became light. [27]When her
master got up in the morning, opened the doors of the house,

19:22—20:11 It happened that a certain Levite was injured in the person of his concubine, and being astounded at the outrage, he divided his concubine's body and sent a part of it to every tribe in Israel. So every tribe of Israel was moved, and all came together against the offenders. Compare those ancient transactions with what has happened to us now. For the treatment we have undergone surpasses the bitterness of any persecution, and the calamity of the Levite was but small when compared with the enormities that have now been committed against the church. For ecclesiastical canons and the faith of the church are in danger unless God shall speedily by your hands amend what has been done amiss and the church be avenged on its enemies.

ATHANASIUS (C. 296–373)
ENCYCLICAL LETTER

and went outside to start on his journey, there was the woman, his concubine, sprawled out on the doorstep of the house
with her hands on the threshold. 28He said to her, "Get up, let's
leave." But there was no response. He put her on the donkey
and went home. 29When he got home, he took a knife, grasped
his concubine, and carved her up into twelve pieces. Then he
sent the pieces throughout Israel. 30Everyone who saw the sight
said, "Nothing like this has happened or been witnessed during
the entire time since the Israelites left the land of Egypt! Take
careful note of it! Discuss it and speak!"

CIVIL WAR BREAKS OUT

20 All the Israelites from Dan to Beer Sheba and from the
land of Gilead left their homes and assembled together before the LORD at Mizpah. 2The leaders of all the people
from all the tribes of Israel took their places in the assembly
of God's people, which numbered 400,000 sword-wielding foot
soldiers. 3The Benjaminites heard that the Israelites had gone
up to Mizpah. Then the Israelites said, "Explain how this wicked
thing happened!" 4The Levite, the husband of the murdered
woman, spoke up, "I and my concubine stopped in Gibeah in
the territory of Benjamin to spend the night. 5The leaders of
Gibeah attacked me and at night surrounded the house where
I was staying. They wanted to kill me; instead they abused my
concubine so badly that she died. 6I took hold of my concubine
and carved her up and sent the pieces throughout the territory
occupied by Israel because they committed such an unthink-
able atrocity in Israel. 7All you Israelites, make a decision here!"
8All Israel rose up in unison and said, "Not one of us will go
home! Not one of us will return to his house! 9Now this is what
we will do to Gibeah: We will attack the city as the lot dictates.
10We will take ten of every group of a hundred men from all the
tribes of Israel (and a hundred of every group of a thousand,
and a thousand of every group of ten thousand) to get supplies
for the army. When they arrive in Gibeah of Benjamin, they will
punish them for the atrocity that they committed in Israel."
11So all the men of Israel gathered together at the city as allies.
12The tribes of Israel sent men throughout the tribe of Benjamin, saying, "How could such a wicked thing take place? 13Now,
hand over the good-for-nothings in Gibeah, so we can execute
them and purge Israel of wickedness." But the Benjaminites
refused to listen to their Israelite brothers. 14The Benjaminites
came from their cities and assembled at Gibeah to make war
against the Israelites. 15That day the Benjaminites mustered
from their cities 26,000 sword-wielding soldiers, besides 700
well-trained soldiers from Gibeah. 16Among this army were 700
specially trained left-handed soldiers. Each one could sling a
stone and hit even the smallest target. 17The men of Israel (not
counting Benjamin) had mustered 400,000 sword-wielding
soldiers, every one an experienced warrior.
18The Israelites went up to Bethel and asked God, "Who
should lead the charge against the Benjaminites?" The LORD
said, "Judah should lead." 19The Israelites got up the next morning and moved against Gibeah. 20The men of Israel marched
out to fight Benjamin; they arranged their battle lines against
Gibeah. 21The Benjaminites attacked from Gibeah and struck
down 22,000 Israelites that day.
22The Israelite army took heart and once more arranged
their battle lines, in the same place where they had taken their

19:22—20:11 It happened that a certain Levite was injured in the person of his concubine, and being astounded at the outrage, he divided his concubine's body and sent a part of it to every tribe in Israel. So every tribe of Israel was moved and all came together against the offenders. Compare those ancient transactions with what has happened to us now, for the treatment we have undergone surpasses the bitterness of any persecution, and the calamity of the Levite was but small when compared with the enormities that have now been committed against the church. For ecclesiastical canons and the faith of the church are in danger, unless God shall speedily by your hands amend what has been done amiss, and the church be avenged on its enemies.

ATHANASIUS (c. 296–373)
ENCYCLICAL LETTER

positions the day before. [23]The Israelites went up and wept
before the LORD until evening. They asked the LORD, "Should
we again march out to fight the Benjaminites, our brothers?"
The LORD said, "Attack them." [24]So the Israelites marched toward the Benjaminites the next day. [25]The Benjaminites again
attacked them from Gibeah and struck down 18,000 sword-
wielding Israelite soldiers.

[26]So all the Israelites, the whole army, went up to Bethel.
They wept and sat there before the LORD; they did not eat anything that day until evening. They offered up burnt sacrifices
and tokens of peace to the LORD. [27]The Israelites asked the
LORD (for the ark of God's covenant was there in those days;
[28]Phinehas son of Eleazar, son of Aaron, was serving the LORD
in those days), "Should we once more march out to fight the
Benjaminites our brothers, or should we quit?" The LORD said,
"Attack, for tomorrow I will hand them over to you."

[29]So Israel hid men in ambush outside Gibeah. [30]The Israelites attacked the Benjaminites the next day; they took their
positions against Gibeah just as they had done before. [31]The
Benjaminites attacked the army, leaving the city unguarded.
They began to strike down their enemy just as they had done
before. On the main roads (one leads to Bethel, the other to
Gibeah) and in the field, they struck down about 30 Israelites.
[32]Then the Benjaminites said, "They are defeated just as before."
But the Israelites said, "Let's retreat and lure them away from
the city into the main roads." [33]All the men of Israel got up from
their places and took their positions at Baal Tamar, while the
Israelites hiding in ambush jumped out of their places west
of Gibeah. [34]Then 10,000 men, well-trained soldiers from all
Israel, made a frontal assault against Gibeah; the battle was
fierce. But the Benjaminites did not realize that disaster was
at their doorstep. [35]The LORD annihilated Benjamin before
Israel; the Israelites struck down that day 25,100 sword-wielding
Benjaminites. [36]Then the Benjaminites saw they were defeated.

The Israelites retreated before Benjamin because they had
confidence in the men they had hidden in ambush outside
Gibeah. [37]The men hiding in ambush made a mad dash to Gibeah. They attacked and put the sword to the entire city. [38]The
Israelites and the men hiding in ambush had arranged a signal.
When the men hiding in ambush sent up a smoke signal from
the city, [39]the Israelites counterattacked. Benjamin had begun
to strike down the Israelites; they struck down about 30 men.
They said, "There's no doubt about it! They are totally defeated
as in the earlier battle." [40]But when the signal, a pillar of smoke,
began to rise up from the city, the Benjaminites turned around
and saw the whole city going up in a cloud of smoke that rose
high into the sky. [41]When the Israelites turned around, the
Benjaminites panicked because they could see that disaster
was on their doorstep. [42]They retreated before the Israelites,
taking the road to the wilderness. But the battle overtook them
as men from the surrounding cities struck them down. [43]They
surrounded the Benjaminites, chased them from Nohah, and
annihilated them all the way to a spot east of Geba. [44]So 18,000
Benjaminites, all of them capable warriors, fell dead. [45]The rest
turned and ran toward the wilderness, heading toward the cliff
of Rimmon. But the Israelites caught 5,000 of them on the main
roads. They stayed right on their heels all the way to Gidom and
struck down 2,000 more. [46]That day 25,000 sword-wielding
Benjaminites fell in battle, all of them capable warriors. [47]But

600 survivors turned and ran away to the wilderness, to the cliff of Rimmon. They stayed there four months. [48]The Israelites returned to the Benjaminite towns and put the sword to them. They wiped out the cities, the animals, and everything they could find. They set fire to every city in their path.

SIX HUNDRED BRIDES FOR SIX HUNDRED BROTHERS

21 The Israelites had taken an oath in Mizpah, saying, "Not one of us will allow his daughter to marry a Benjaminite." [2]So the people came to Bethel and sat there before God until evening, weeping loudly and uncontrollably. [3]They said, "Why, O LORD God of Israel, has this happened in Israel? An entire tribe has disappeared from Israel today!"

[4]The next morning the people got up early and built an altar there. They offered up burnt sacrifices and tokens of peace. [5]The Israelites asked, "Who from all the Israelite tribes has not assembled before the LORD?" They had made a solemn oath that whoever did not assemble before the LORD at Mizpah must certainly be executed. [6]The Israelites regretted what had happened to their brother Benjamin. They said, "Today we cut off an entire tribe from Israel! [7]How can we find wives for those who are left? After all, we took an oath in the LORD's name not to give them our daughters as wives." [8]So they asked, "Who from all the Israelite tribes did not assemble before the LORD at Mizpah?" Now it just so happened no one from Jabesh Gilead had come to the gathering. [9]When they took roll call, they noticed none of the inhabitants of Jabesh Gilead were there. [10]So the assembly sent 12,000 capable warriors against Jabesh Gilead. They commanded them, "Go and kill with your swords the inhabitants of Jabesh Gilead, including the women and little children. [11]Do this: Exterminate every male, as well as every woman who has experienced a man's bed. But spare the lives of any virgins." So they did as instructed. [12]They found among the inhabitants of Jabesh Gilead 400 young girls who were virgins who had never been intimate with a man in bed. They brought them back to the camp at Shiloh in the land of Canaan.

[13]The entire assembly sent messengers to the Benjaminites at the cliff of Rimmon and assured them they would not be harmed. [14]The Benjaminites returned at that time, and the Israelites gave to them the women they had spared from Jabesh Gilead. But there were not enough to go around.

[15]The people regretted what had happened to Benjamin because the LORD had weakened the Israelite tribes. [16]The leaders of the assembly said, "How can we find wives for those who are left? After all, the Benjaminite women have been wiped out. [17]The remnant of Benjamin must be preserved. An entire Israelite tribe should not be wiped out. [18]But we can't allow our daughters to marry them, for the Israelites took an oath, saying, 'Whoever gives a woman to a Benjaminite will be destroyed.' [19]However, there is an annual festival to the LORD in Shiloh, which is north of Bethel (east of the main road that goes up from Bethel to Shechem) and south of Lebonah." [20]So they commanded the Benjaminites, "Go hide in the vineyards, [21]and keep your eyes open. When you see the daughters of Shiloh coming out to dance in the celebration, jump out from the vineyards. Each one of you, catch yourself a wife from among the daughters of Shiloh and then go home to the land of Benjamin. [22]When their fathers or brothers come and protest to us, we'll say to them,

21:1–25 "In those days Israel had no king. Each man did what he considered to be right." The explanation of these words applied also to the present circumstances, incredible and frightening as it may be, is quite truly pertinent when it is understood; for never before has there arisen such discord and quarreling as now among the members of the church in consequence of their turning away from the one great and true God and only King of the universe. People abandon the teachings of our Lord Jesus Christ and assume authority in dealing with certain questions, making their own private rules and preferring to exercise leadership in opposition to being led by the Lord.

BASIL THE GREAT (330–379)
ASCETICAL WORKS

'Do us a favor and let them be, for we could not get each one a
wife through battle. Don't worry about breaking your oath! You
would only be guilty if you had voluntarily given them wives.'"
[23]The Benjaminites did as instructed. They abducted 200 of
the dancing girls to be their wives. They went home to their
own territory, rebuilt their cities, and settled down. [24]Then
the Israelites dispersed from there to their respective tribal
and clan territories. Each went from there to his own property. [25]In those days Israel had no king. Each man did what he
considered to be right.

AUTHOR	AUDIENCE	DATE	PURPOSE	THEMES
Unknown	God's chosen people, the Israelites	Ruth lived during the time of the judges; the book was written sometime after David became king in about 1010 BC.	This book was written to showcase an example of faith and the faithfulness of God.	Hardship and suffering; God's faithfulness; and redemption

"This short history fitly follows the book of Judges," explained John Wesley. "The design of it is to lead us to Providence, acknowledging God in all our ways; to lead to Christ, who descended from Ruth, and part of whose genealogy concludes the book." Both of these themes, the providence of God and the person of Christ, have been central to the reading of Ruth down through the centuries.

This book was written to provide an important contrast to the book of Judges: It showcases an example of faithfulness (and by a non-Jew, no less) and the resulting faithfulness of God. Occurring "during the time of the judges" (1:1), the story opens with a massive reversal of fortunes in the land of Israel: a famine. A Jew named Elimelech has left the promised land with his wife, Naomi, and their two sons to seek a better life. But in the land of Moab, Elimelech and his sons die, leaving Naomi and her Moabite daughter-in-law Ruth desperate. It is through Ruth's faithfulness to Naomi that the faithfulness of God shines through.

Matthew Henry highlighted an important theme in this book: "We see the special care which God's providence takes of our smallest concerns, encouraging us to full trust therein." And we can trust God because he is presented time and again throughout the scriptures as our Redeemer, the one who comes to free and help us, rescue and restore us. This is, in fact, the central organizing theme of the book of Ruth: redemption. For at critical junctures in the narrative, a highly significant term of redemption is used to frame the story and infuse it with meaning.

While sometimes translated "guardian" (see 2:20; 3:9, 12; 4:1, 3, 6, 8, 14) the term can also mean "guardian-redeemer," a concept that mirrors God's own posture toward his people. He is their *go'el*—Redeemer. God first reveals himself to us in this way in the book of Exodus, and the Israelites were to follow his example taking up this role for each other, especially in the context of family. "Guardian-redeemer" is a legal term for one who is obligated to redeem a relative who has fallen on hard times, as Leviticus 25:25–55 commands. Boaz becomes a redeemer to Ruth and Naomi.

RUTH

In relating the story of Ruth to the story of Christ, the early church father Ambrose of Milan asked some important questions and revealed some important answers:

> For how did Ruth, when she was a foreigner, marry a Jew? And for what reason did the Evangelist believe that this marriage, which was forbidden by the weight of the law, should be included in the genealogy of Christ? Did the Savior therefore descend from an illegitimate heritage? Unless you return to the apostolic principle that the law was not given for the just but for the unjust, then his genealogy would seem to be deformed, given that Ruth was a foreigner and a Moabite . . . Hence, how did she enter the church unless because she was made holy and immaculate by deeds [*moribus*] that go beyond the law? For if the law was given for the irreverent and sinners, then surely Ruth, who exceeded the limits of the law and entered the church and was made an Israelite and deserved to be counted among the honored figures in the Lord's genealogy, chosen for kinship of mind, not of body, is a great example for us, because she prefigures all of us who were gathered from the nations for the purpose of joining the church of the Lord.

Although Gentiles were strangers to the original promises of blessing given to the Jewish people, God had always intended those blessings to extend to all the nations, and he has accomplished this purpose through Christ "who made both groups into one and who destroyed the middle wall of partition, the hostility, when he nullified in his flesh the law of commandments in decrees" (Eph 2:14–15). And when the promises of God feel far and foreign, as if he hadn't offered them in the first place, the book of Ruth is a perennial reminder that God does not leave us without a Guardian-Redeemer, for "he will encourage you and provide for you when you are old" (4:15).

A FAMILY TRAGEDY: FAMINE AND DEATH

1 During the time of the judges, there was a famine in the
land of Judah. So a man from Bethlehem in Judah went to
live as a resident foreigner in the region of Moab, along with
his wife and two sons. 2(Now the man's name was Elimelech,
his wife was Naomi, and his two sons were Mahlon and Kilion.
They were of the clan of Ephrath from Bethlehem in Judah.)
They entered the region of Moab and settled there. 3Some-
time later Naomi's husband Elimelech died, so she and her
two sons were left alone. 4Both her sons married Moabite
women. (One was named Orpah and the other Ruth.) And they
continued to live there about 10 years. 5Then Naomi's two
sons, Mahlon and Kilion, also died. So the woman was left all
alone—bereaved of her two children as well as her husband!
6So she decided to return home from the region of Moab,
accompanied by her daughters-in-law, because while she
was living in Moab she had heard that the LORD had shown
concern for his people, reversing the famine by providing
abundant crops.

1:6–22 Now let us look at Ruth, for she is a type of the church. First she is a type because she is a stranger from the Gentile people who renounced her native land and all things belonging to it. She made her way to the land of Israel. And when her mother-in-law forbade her to come with her, she persisted. The church was called to God from the Gentiles in just this way: Leaving her native land (which was idolatry) and giving up all earthly associations, she confessed that he in whom the saints believed is the Lord God, and that she herself would go where the flesh of Christ ascended after his Passion; and that on account of his name she would suffer in this world unto death, and that she would unite with the community of the saints, that is, the patriarchs and the prophets.

ISIDORE OF SEVILLE
(C. 560–636)
ON RUTH

RUTH RETURNS WITH NAOMI

7Now as she and her two daughters-in-law began to leave the
place where she had been living to return to the land of Judah,
8Naomi said to her two daughters-in-law, "Listen to me! Each of
you should return to your mother's home. May the LORD show
you the same kind of devotion that you have shown to your
deceased husbands and to me. 9May the LORD enable each of
you to find security in the home of a new husband." Then she
kissed them goodbye, and they wept loudly. 10But they said to
her, "No! We will return with you to your people."
11But Naomi replied, "Go back home, my daughters! There
is no reason for you to return to Judah with me. I am no longer capable of giving birth to sons who might become your
husbands! 12Go back home, my daughters! For I am too old
to get married again. Even if I thought that there was hope
that I could get married tonight and conceive sons, 13surely
you would not want to wait until they were old enough to
marry. Surely you would not remain unmarried all that time!
No, my daughters, you must not return with me. For my intense suffering is too much for you to bear. For the LORD is
afflicting me!"
14Again they wept loudly. Then Orpah kissed her mother-
in-law goodbye, but Ruth clung tightly to her. 15So Naomi
said, "Look, your sister-in-law is returning to her people and
to her god. Follow your sister-in-law back home!" 16But Ruth
replied,

"Stop urging me to abandon you!
For wherever you go, I will go.
Wherever you live, I will live.
Your people will become my people,
and your God will become my God.
17 Wherever you die, I will die—and there I will be buried.
May the LORD punish me severely if I do not keep my
promise!
Only death will be able to separate me from you!"

18When Naomi realized that Ruth was determined to go with
her, she stopped trying to dissuade her. 19So the two of them
journeyed together until they arrived in Bethlehem.

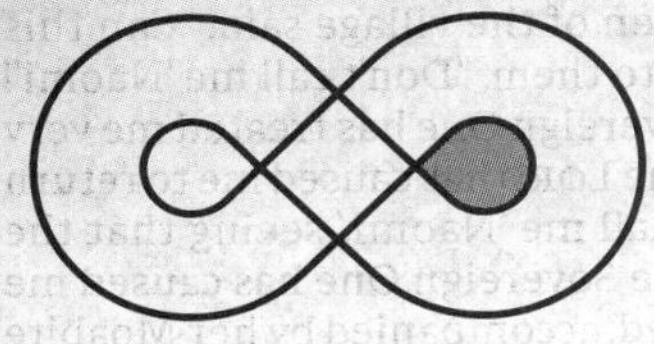

THE CHALCEDONIAN DEFINITION (451)

FOLLOWING THE COUNCIL of Ephesus's discussions on the nature of Christ, the Council of Chalcedon convened to articulate a clear and concise statement on the person and nature of Jesus Christ. When the more than 500 bishops gathered, the largest council thus far, they developed what would become the most significant Christological statement in church history. In a sense, the Chalcedonian Definition is an affirmation of the Nicene Creed along with noteworthy clarifications heavily influenced by the theology of Cyril of Alexandria and the Tome by Pope Leo.

WE, THEN, following the holy Fathers, all with one consent, teach men to confess one and the same Son, our Lord Jesus Christ, the same perfect in Godhead and also perfect in manhood; truly God and truly man, of a reasonable soul and body; consubstantial with the Father according to the Godhead, and consubstantial with us according to the Manhood; in all things like unto us, without sin; begotten before all ages of the Father according to the Godhead, and in these latter days, for us and for our salvation, born of the Virgin Mary, the Mother of God, according to the Manhood; one and the same Christ, Son, Lord, only begotten, to be acknowledged in two natures, unconfusedly, unchangeably, indivisibly, inseparably; the distinction of natures being by no means taken away by the union, but rather the property of each nature being preserved, and concurring in one person and one Subsistence, not parted or divided into two persons, but one and the same Son, and only begotten, God the Word, the Lord Jesus Christ; as the prophets from the beginning have declared concerning him, and the Lord Jesus Christ himself has taught us, and the creed of the holy Fathers has handed down to us.

NAOMI AND RUTH ARRIVE IN BETHLEHEM

When they entered Bethlehem, the whole village was excited about their arrival. The women of the village said, "Can this be Naomi?" [20]But she replied to them, "Don't call me 'Naomi'! Call me 'Mara' because the Sovereign One has treated me very harshly. [21]I left here full, but the LORD has caused me to return empty-handed. Why do you call me 'Naomi,' seeing that the LORD has opposed me, and the Sovereign One has caused me to suffer?" [22]So Naomi returned, accompanied by her Moabite daughter-in-law Ruth, who came back with her from the region of Moab. (Now they arrived in Bethlehem at the beginning of the barley harvest.)

> 2:1–16 Does the widow Naomi seem to you of small account, who supported her widowhood on the gleanings from another's harvest and who, when heavy with age, was supported by her daughter-in-law? It is a great benefit both for the support and for the advantage of widows that they so train their daughters-in-law as to have in them a support in full old age and, as it were, payment for their teaching and reward for their training. So that Naomi, deprived of her husband and her two sons, having lost the offspring of her fruitfulness, lost not the reward of her pious care, for she found both a comfort in sorrow and a support in poverty.
>
> AMBROSE (C. 339–C. 397)
> *CONCERNING WIDOWS*

RUTH WORKS IN THE FIELD OF BOAZ

2 Now Naomi had a relative on her husband's side of the family named Boaz. He was a wealthy, prominent man from the clan of Elimelech. [2]One day Ruth the Moabite said to Naomi, "Let me go to the fields so I can gather grain behind whoever permits me to do so." Naomi replied, "You may go, my daughter." [3]So Ruth went and gathered grain in the fields behind the harvesters. Now she just happened to end up in the portion of the field belonging to Boaz, who was from the clan of Elimelech.

BOAZ AND RUTH MEET

[4]Now at that very moment, Boaz arrived from Bethlehem and greeted the harvesters, "May the LORD be with you!" They replied, "May the LORD bless you!" [5]Boaz asked his servant in charge of the harvesters, "To whom does this young woman belong?" [6]The servant in charge of the harvesters replied, "She's the young Moabite woman who came back with Naomi from the region of Moab. [7]She asked, 'May I follow the harvesters and gather grain among the bundles?' Since she arrived she has been working hard from this morning until now—except for sitting in the resting hut a short time."

[8]So Boaz said to Ruth, "Listen carefully, my dear! Do not leave to gather grain in another field. You need not go beyond the limits of this field. You may go along beside my female workers. [9]Take note of the field where the men are harvesting and follow behind with the female workers. I will tell the men to leave you alone. When you are thirsty, you may go to the water jars and drink some of the water the servants draw."

[10]Ruth knelt before him with her forehead to the ground and said to him, "Why are you so kind and so attentive to me, even though I am a foreigner?" [11]Boaz replied to her, "I have been given a full report of all that you have done for your mother-in-law following the death of your husband—how you left your father and your mother, as well as your homeland, and came to live among people you did not know previously. [12]May the LORD reward your efforts! May your acts of kindness be repaid fully by the LORD God of Israel, from whom you have sought protection." [13]She said, "You really are being kind to me, sir, for you have reassured and encouraged me, your servant, even though I will never be like one of your servants."

[14]Later during the mealtime Boaz said to her, "Come here and have some food! Dip your bread in the vinegar." So she sat down beside the harvesters. Then he handed her some roasted grain. She ate until she was full and saved the rest. [15]When she got up to gather grain, Boaz told his male servants, "Let her gather grain even among the bundles. Don't chase her off!

[16]Make sure you pull out ears of grain for her and drop them so
she can gather them up. Don't tell her not to!" [17]So she gathered
grain in the field until evening. When she threshed what she
had gathered, it came to about 30 pounds of barley.

RUTH RETURNS TO NAOMI

[18]She carried it back to town, and her mother-in-law saw how
much grain she had gathered. Then Ruth gave her the roasted
grain she had saved from mealtime. [19]Her mother-in-law asked
her, "Where did you gather grain today? Where did you work?
May the one who took notice of you be rewarded!" So Ruth told
her mother-in-law with whom she had worked. She said, "The
name of the man with whom I worked today is Boaz." [20]Naomi
said to her daughter-in-law, "May he be rewarded by the LORD
because he has shown loyalty to the living on behalf of the
dead!" Then Naomi said to her, "This man is a close relative of
ours; he is our guardian." [21]Ruth the Moabite replied, "He even
told me, 'You may go along beside my servants until they have
finished gathering all my harvest!'" [22]Naomi then said to her
daughter-in-law Ruth, "It is good, my daughter, that you should
go out to work with his female servants. That way you will not
be harmed, which could happen in another field." [23]So Ruth
worked beside Boaz's female servants, gathering grain until
the end of the barley harvest as well as the wheat harvest. After
that she stayed home with her mother-in-law.

NAOMI INSTRUCTS RUTH

3 At that time, Naomi, her mother-in-law, said to her, "My
daughter, I must find a home for you so you will be secure.
[2]Now Boaz, with whose female servants you worked, is our close
relative. Look, tonight he is winnowing barley at the threshing
floor. [3]So bathe yourself, rub on some perfumed oil, and get
dressed up. Then go down to the threshing floor. But don't let
the man know you're there until he finishes his meal. [4]When he
gets ready to go to sleep, take careful notice of the place where
he lies down. Then go, uncover his legs, and lie down beside him.
He will tell you what you should do." [5]Ruth replied to Naomi,
"I will do everything you have told me to do."

RUTH VISITS BOAZ

[6]So she went down to the threshing floor and did everything
her mother-in-law had instructed her to do. [7]When Boaz had
finished his meal and was feeling satisfied, he lay down to sleep
at the far end of the grain heap. Then Ruth crept up quietly,
uncovered his legs, and lay down beside him. [8]In the middle of
the night he was startled and turned over. Now he saw a woman
lying beside him! [9]He said, "Who are you?" She replied, "I am
Ruth, your servant. Marry your servant, for you are a guardian
of the family interests." [10]He said, "May you be rewarded by the
LORD, my dear! This act of devotion is greater than what you did
before. For you have not sought to marry one of the young men,
whether rich or poor. [11]Now, my dear, don't worry! I intend to
do for you everything you propose, for everyone in the village
knows that you are a worthy woman. [12]Now yes, it is true that
I am a guardian, but there is another guardian who is a closer
relative than I am. [13]Remain here tonight. Then in the morning,
if he agrees to marry you, fine, let him do so. But if he does not
want to do so, I promise, as surely as the LORD lives, to marry
you. Sleep here until morning." [14]So she slept beside him until

3:1–18 Unless God's inspiration had been in Ruth, she would not have said what she said or done what she did. What is praised in her first? A love of the tribe of Israel, or obedience, or faith? She desired to have sons out of the seed of Israel and become one of the people of God. Simplicity is praised also because she came in under Boaz's coverlet voluntarily. She feared neither that he would perhaps spurn her, as a just man might spurn a lascivious woman, or that he might deceive her and worse, despise a deceived woman, as many men might have done. Obeying her mother-in-law's plans, she confidently believed that God would prosper her action, knowing her conscience, because lust did not push her to it but rather religion was her encouragement.

***INCOMPLETE WORK ON MATTHEW* (C. 400)**

morning. She woke up while it was still dark. Boaz thought, "No
one must know that a woman visited the threshing floor." 15Then
he said, "Hold out the shawl you are wearing and grip it tightly."
As she held it tightly, he measured out about 60 pounds of barley
into the shawl and put it on her shoulders. Then he went into
town, 16and she returned to her mother-in-law.

RUTH RETURNS TO NAOMI

When Ruth returned to her mother-in-law, Naomi asked, "How
did things turn out for you, my daughter?" Ruth told her about
all the man had done for her. 17She said, "He gave me these 60
pounds of barley, for he said to me, 'Do not go to your mother-in-
law empty-handed.'" 18Then Naomi said, "Stay put, my daughter,
until you know how the matter turns out. For the man will not
rest until he has taken care of the matter today."

4:1–12 Ruth was an outsider and had fallen into extreme poverty, but Boaz, seeing her, did not despise her on account of her poverty, nor was he horrified on account of her impiety; even as Christ received the church, who was both a stranger and laboring in need of great good things. Ruth is not joined with her consort before forsaking her parents and her nation and her native land: Never was anyone so much ennobled by marriage.

CHRYSOSTOM **(C. 347–407)**
HOMILIES ON THE GOSPEL OF MATTHEW

BOAZ SETTLES THE MATTER

4 Now Boaz went up to the village gate and sat there. Then
along came the guardian whom Boaz had mentioned to Ruth.
Boaz said, "Come here, what's-your-name, and sit down." So he
came and sat down. 2Boaz chose 10 of the village leaders and
said, "Sit down here!" So they sat down. 3Then Boaz said to the
guardian, "Naomi, who has returned from the region of Moab,
is selling the portion of land that belongs to our relative Elimelech. 4So I am legally informing you: Acquire it before those
sitting here and before the leaders of my people. If you want to
exercise your right to redeem it, then do so. But if not, then tell
me so I will know. For you possess the first option to redeem it;
I am next in line after you." He replied, "I will redeem it." 5Then
Boaz said, "When you acquire the field from Naomi, you must
also acquire Ruth the Moabite, the wife of our deceased relative,
in order to preserve his family name by raising up a descendant
who will inherit his property." 6The guardian said, "Then I am
unable to redeem it, for I would ruin my own inheritance in
that case. You may exercise my redemption option, for I am
unable to redeem it." 7(Now this used to be the customary way
to finalize a transaction involving redemption in Israel: A man
would remove his sandal and give it to the other party. This was
a legally binding act in Israel.) 8So the guardian said to Boaz,
"You may acquire it," and he removed his sandal. 9Then Boaz
said to the leaders and all the people, "You are witnesses today
that I have acquired from Naomi all that belonged to Elimelech,
Kilion, and Mahlon. 10I have also acquired Ruth the Moabite,
the wife of Mahlon, as my wife to raise up a descendant who
will inherit his property so the name of the deceased might
not disappear from among his relatives and from his village.
You are witnesses today." 11All the people who were at the gate
and the elders replied, "We are witnesses. May the LORD make
the woman who is entering your home like Rachel and Leah,
both of whom built up the house of Israel! May you prosper
in Ephrathah and become famous in Bethlehem. 12May your
family become like the family of Perez—whom Tamar bore to
Judah—through the descendants the LORD gives you by this
young woman."

A GRANDSON IS BORN TO NAOMI

13So Boaz married Ruth and slept with her. The LORD enabled
her to conceive and she gave birth to a son. 14The village women
said to Naomi, "May the LORD be praised because he has not

left you without a guardian today! May he become famous in
Israel! [15]He will encourage you and provide for you when you
are old, for your daughter-in-law, who loves you, has given him
birth. She is better to you than seven sons!" [16]Naomi took the
child and placed him on her lap; she became his caregiver. [17]The
neighbor women gave him a name, saying, "A son has been born
to Naomi." They named him Obed. Now he became the father
of Jesse—David's father.

EPILOGUE: OBED IN THE GENEALOGY OF DAVID

[18]These are the descendants of Perez: Perez was the father of
Hezron, [19]Hezron was the father of Ram, Ram was the father
of Amminadab, [20]Amminadab was the father of Nachshon,
Nachshon was the father of Salmah, [21]Salmon was the father
of Boaz, Boaz was the father of Obed, [22]Obed was the father of
Jesse, and Jesse was the father of David.

AUTHOR	AUDIENCE	DATE	PURPOSE	THEMES
Unknown	God's chosen people, the Israelites	Sometime after Israel was divided into the northern and southern kingdoms in about 930 BC	This book was written to tell the story of how Israel's king arose and how the line of David and the Davidic covenant were established.	Leadership; God's covenant; sin and consequences; and faithfulness and obedience

First Samuel is the beginning of the story of how Israel first received a king, Saul; how David, the shepherd boy, rose to power to replace him; and how God established his covenant with the shepherd-king and his line. The marginal notes in the Geneva Bible, the version of Holy scripture used by many sixteenth-century Protestants, offered this insight into the broad purpose and themes of the book:

> According to Deuteronomy 17:14, God ordained that when the Israelites should reside in the land of Canaan, he would appoint them a king. Consequently, this first book of Samuel narrates the state of this people under their first king, King Saul. However, contrary to God's timing, the people were not content with the current government God had erected and they demanded a king so that the Israelites might be like the other nations, which the Israelites believed to be safer since they had kings. The Israelites did not ask for a king so that they could better serve God under a godly person who represented Jesus Christ, the true deliverer. Therefore God gave them a tyrant and a hypocrite to rule over them so they might learn that a human king is not sufficient to defend them—rather, only a ruler who was empowered and helped by God to do so. Therefore God punished the ingratitude of his people and sent them continual wars both at home and abroad. And because Saul, who was not truly worthy of the office of king, did not acknowledge God's mercy toward him but rather disposed of the word of God and was not zealous for God's glory, he was put down by the voice of God. In his place, David, the true figure of the Messiah, was placed on the throne.

Both Saul and David were anointed by this book's namesake, Samuel. After being born under the Lord's special providence, the boy Samuel ministered in the temple of the Lord under the direction of Eli. "Receiving a message from the Lord was rare in those days; revelatory visions were infrequent" (3:1). Part of the reason is indicated in the opening: The priest sons of Eli treated the sacrifice of the Lord with contempt. But the answer may also be found in the people's request for a king. While their request wasn't

1 SAMUEL

wrong in and of itself, the spirit behind their request was: "We will be like all the other nations. Our king will judge us and lead us and fight our battles" (8:20).

If it wasn't enough that the Israelites wanted to "be like all the other nations," they also wanted a king to fight for them and secure their future. God was their King. He was the one who had delivered them from Egypt and fought for them. The Lord said this rejection was consistent with their idolatry, a sin that had ensnared them since their first days in the wilderness under Moses. As Reformer Andrew Willet explained, "It is not quite true to say that the government under kings is a shaking off of the Lord's yoke . . . Yet the people rejected the Lord's government because they disliked the form of administration the Lord had set on them. They desired change and innovation without any direction from God."

Deuteronomy 17 tells us that God had made provision for a king—that the man who would serve in that role would be someone who would model for Israel and the world the Lord's own kingship. Through purity, charity, and wholehearted obedience to the law, the king was meant to be a man after the Lord's own heart. Instead Samuel told the people what they would receive for their rejection of God: a tyrant. Saul would prove those prophetic words true.

After the Lord rejected Saul as king, he sent Samuel to find his replacement in the tribe of Judah, from the family of Jesse. The Lord did not choose the oldest son or even the most accomplished. Instead he told Samuel to anoint David, the youngest son of Jesse, a shepherd. But David would prove to be a tremendous king. Relating King David to our own situation in Christ, the Geneva Bible tells us, "David's patience, modesty, constancy, persecution by open enemies, false friends, and lying flatterers are left to the church, and to every member of the body of Christ, as a template for their vocation as God's people."

HANNAH IS CHILDLESS

1 There was a man from Ramathaim Zophim, from the hill country of Ephraim. His name was Elkanah. He was the son of Jeroham, the son of Elihu, the son of Tohu, the son of Zuph, an Ephraimite. 2 He had two wives; the name of the first was Hannah and the name of the second was Peninnah. Peninnah had children, but Hannah had no children. 3 This man would go up from his city year after year to worship and to sacrifice to the LORD of Heaven's Armies at Shiloh. (It was there that the two sons of Eli, Hophni and Phinehas, served as the LORD's priests.) 4 The day came, and Elkanah sacrificed.

(Now he used to give meat portions to his wife Peninnah and to all her sons and daughters. 5 But to Hannah he would give a double portion because he loved Hannah, although the LORD had not enabled her to have children. 6 Her rival used to aggravate her to the point of exasperation, just to irritate her, since the LORD had not enabled her to have children. 7 This is how it would go year after year. As often as she went up to the LORD's house, Peninnah would offend her in that way.)

So she cried and refused to eat. 8 Then her husband Elkanah said to her, "Hannah, why are you crying and why won't you eat? Why are you so upset? Am I not better to you than 10 sons?" 9 So Hannah got up after they had finished eating and drinking in Shiloh.

At the time Eli the priest was sitting in his chair by the doorpost of the LORD's sanctuary. 10 As for Hannah, she was very distressed. She prayed to the LORD and was, in fact, weeping. 11 She made a vow saying, "O LORD of Heaven's Armies, if you would truly look on the suffering of your servant, and would keep me in mind and not neglect your servant, and give your servant a male child, then I will dedicate him to the LORD all the days of his life. His hair will never be cut."

1:8–19 A godly heart is like a flower. Flowers shut when the sun sets and the night comes but open again when the sun returns and shines on them. If God withdraws his favor and sends a night of affliction, they shut up themselves as well as their thoughts in silence. But if he shines again and sheds abroad the light and sense of his love on them, then their heart and mouth are wide open toward heaven in lifting up praises to God. Hannah prayed silently as long as she was in bitterness of soul and of a sorrowful spirit. But as soon as God answered her prayers and filled her heart with joy in him, her mouth immediately opened into a song of thanksgiving.

EDWARD REYNOLDS
(1599–1676)
SEVEN SERMONS ON FOURTEENTH CHAPTER OF HOSEA

12 It turned out that she did a great deal of praying before the LORD. Meanwhile Eli was watching her mouth. 13 As for Hannah, she was speaking in her mind. Only her lips were moving; her voice could not be heard. So Eli thought she was a drunkard.

14 Then he said to her, "How much longer do you intend to get drunk? Put away your wine!" 15 But Hannah replied, "Not so, my lord! I am a woman under a great deal of stress. I haven't drunk wine or beer. But I have poured out my soul before the LORD. 16 Don't consider your servant a wicked woman. It's just that, to this point, I have spoken from my deep pain and anguish."

17 Eli replied, "Go in peace, and may the God of Israel grant the request that you have asked of him." 18 She said, "May I, your servant, find favor in your sight." So the woman went her way and got something to eat. Her face no longer looked sad.

19 They got up early the next morning. Then they worshiped the LORD and returned to their home at Ramathaim. Elkanah was intimate with his wife Hannah, and the LORD called her to mind. 20 Then Hannah became pregnant.

HANNAH DEDICATES SAMUEL TO THE LORD

In the course of time she gave birth to a son. And she named him Samuel, thinking, "I asked the LORD for him." 21 Then the man Elkanah and all his family went up to make the yearly sacrifice to the LORD and to keep his vow. 22 But Hannah did not go up with them, because she had told her husband, "Not until the boy is weaned. Then I will bring him so that he may appear before the LORD. And he will remain there from then on."

23 Then her husband Elkanah said to her, "Do what you think
best. Stay until you have weaned him. Only may the LORD fulfill
his promise."

So the woman stayed and nursed her son until she had weaned
him. 24 Then she took him up with her as soon as she had weaned
him, along with three bulls, an ephah of flour, and a container of
wine. She came to the LORD's house at Shiloh, and the boy was
with them. 25 They slaughtered the bull, then brought the boy to
Eli. 26 She said, "My lord. Just as surely as you are alive, my lord,
I am the woman who previously stood here with you in order
to pray to the LORD. 27 For this boy I prayed, and the LORD has
given me the request that I asked of him. 28 So I also dedicate
him to the LORD. For all the days of his life he is dedicated to
the LORD." Then he bowed down there in worship to the LORD.

HANNAH EXALTS THE LORD IN PRAYER

2 Hannah prayed,
"My heart has rejoiced in the LORD;
my horn has been raised high because of the LORD.
I have loudly denounced my enemies.
Indeed I rejoice in your deliverance.
2 No one is holy like the LORD!
There is no one other than you!
There is no rock like our God!
3 Don't keep speaking so arrogantly.
Proud talk should not come out of your mouth,
for the LORD is a God who knows;
he evaluates what people do.
4 The bows of warriors are shattered,
but those who stumbled have taken on strength.
5 The well fed hire themselves out to earn food,
but the hungry no longer lack.
Even the barren woman has given birth to seven,
but the one with many children has declined.
6 The LORD both kills and gives life;
he brings down to the grave and raises up.
7 The LORD impoverishes and makes wealthy;
he humbles and he exalts.
8 He lifts the weak from the dust;
he raises the poor from the ash heap
to seat them with princes—
he bestows on them an honored position.
The foundations of the earth belong to the LORD—
he placed the world on them.
9 He watches over his holy ones,
but the wicked are made speechless in the darkness,
for it is not by one's own strength that one prevails.
10 The LORD shatters his adversaries;
he thunders against them from the heavens.
The LORD executes judgment to the ends of the earth.
He will strengthen his king
and exalt the power of his anointed one."

11 Then Elkanah went back home to Ramah.

ELI'S SONS MISUSE THEIR SACRED OFFICE

The boy Samuel was serving the LORD with the favor of Eli
the priest. 12 But the sons of Eli were wicked men. They did
not acknowledge the LORD's authority. 13 This was the priests'

2:1–11 I have often seen excellent people horribly vexed by terrors, afflictions, and the severest persecutions, so much so that they nearly experienced despair of heart. For God leads down to hell and brings back. Now you see his back, and God seems to be shunning you, but sometime later you will see his front and his face. This is what it means for him to love those whom he chastises. This love must be learned from experience, nor should chastisement be avoided and shunned. The story is told of a peasant who, when he heard this consolation from his pastor, that the afflictions and troubles by which God afflicts us are signs of his love, replied: "Ah, how I would like him to love others and not me!"

MARTIN LUTHER **(1483–1546)**
COMMENTARY ON GALATIANS

JOHN CASSIAN:

FATHER OF WESTERN MONASTICISM

c. 360–c. 432

Born near modern-day Romania around 360, John Cassian pursued a calling to the monastic life in Bethlehem, Palestine, and in Egypt. Although he was later dismissed from these monasteries for doctrinal controversies, he would go on to found separate monasteries for men and women in Marseilles, modern-day France.

Two of John's works would become incredibly influential, broadcasting his theology of monasticism, organizational principles for monastic communities, and outlines for monastic discipline. His systemization of Western monasticism eventually impacted the more well-known monastic Benedict of Nursia, with John's ideals making their way into the *Rule of Saint Benedict*.

In one work, *Institutes of the Coenobia*, John outlined the manner in which such communities should be governed, providing rules for life under monastic conditions. In a second work, *Conferences of the Desert Fathers*, John recorded a number of conversations he had with some of the famed desert monks, outlining their moral and devotional lives with God. He understood that life unfolded in a threefold progression: Intentional *purgation* combined with a life of *contemplation* would lead to *unity* with God.

John suggested there were shortcomings with a certain theologian at the time, Augustine of Hippo. Augustine had been confronting a controversial view of salvation known as Pelagianism. John offered his own view as a rebuttal. His monasteries became hotbeds of opposition against Augustine's view of divine predestination. Because their opposition was labeled semi-Pelagianism, placing them in a heterodox camp that skirted the unorthodox line, John and his Marseilles colleagues had to work out an orthodox synergism in contrast to Augustine's monergism while taking care to avoid falling into the Pelagian heresy.

The Eastern Church had long held a synergistic view of God's divine grace and human decision and effort in the matter of salvation. Augustine departed from this view, insisting it was God's grace all the way down. John and his monastery companions tried to forge a third way for orthodox synergism. They argued that God's assisting grace was absolutely necessary, even endorsing Augustine's vision of God's necessary, all-sufficient grace for salvation. Yet they also believed individuals played a role in the unfolding of salvation through free will and personal choice. Their attempt at charting a third way was not accepted. After their deaths, John and his theology were condemned in 529 by the Synod of Orange, where a supermajority of church leaders deemed his views too close to the heresy of Pelagianism.

Although John Cassian is not as well known as his contemporary Benedict of Nursia, he is appropriately honored as the father of Western monasticism. Through his commitment to purgation and contemplation, the monastic way of life extended from the East to the early medieval Western church.

IMPORTANT WORKS

INSTITUTES OF THE COENOBIA
CONFERENCES OF THE DESERT FATHERS

routine with the people. Whenever anyone was making a sacrifice, the priest's attendant would come with a three-pronged fork in his hand, just as the meat was boiling. 14He would jab it into the basin, kettle, cauldron, or pot. Everything that the fork would bring up the priest would take for himself. This is how they used to treat all the Israelites who came there to Shiloh.

15Also, before they burned the fat the priest's attendant would come and say to the person who was making the sacrifice, "Give some meat for the priest to roast! He won't accept boiled meat from you, but only raw." 16If the individual said to him, "They should certainly burn the fat away first, then take for yourself whatever you wish," then he would say, "No! Give it now! If not, I'll take it by force!" 17The sin of these young men was very great in the LORD's sight, for they treated the LORD's offering with contempt.

18Now Samuel was ministering with the favor of the LORD. The boy was dressed in a linen ephod. 19His mother used to make him a small robe and bring it to him from time to time when she would go up with her husband to make the annual sacrifice. 20Eli would bless Elkanah and his wife saying, "May the LORD establish descendants for you from this woman in place of the one that she dedicated to the LORD." Then they would go to their home. 21And indeed the LORD attended to Hannah. She got pregnant and gave birth to three sons and two daughters. But the boy Samuel grew up before the LORD.

22Eli was very old. And he would hear about everything that his sons used to do to all the people of Israel and how they used to go to bed with the women who were stationed at the entrance to the tent of meeting. 23So he said to them, "Why do you do these things, these evil things that I hear about from all these people? 24No, my sons! For the report that I hear circulating among the LORD's people is not good. 25If a man sins against a man, one may appeal to God on his behalf. But if a man sins against the LORD, who can intercede for him?" But Eli's sons would not listen to their father. Indeed the LORD had decided to kill them. 26However, the boy Samuel was growing up and finding favor both with the LORD and with people.

THE LORD JUDGES THE HOUSE OF ELI

27Then a man of God came to Eli and said to him, "This is what the LORD has said: 'I plainly revealed myself to your ancestor's house when they were slaves to the house of Pharaoh in Egypt. 28I chose your ancestor from all the tribes of Israel to be my priest, to offer sacrifice on my altar, to burn incense, and to bear the ephod before me. I gave to your ancestor's house all the fire offerings made by the Israelites. 29Why are you scorning my sacrifice and my offering that I commanded for my dwelling place? You have honored your sons more than you have me by having made yourselves fat from the best parts of all the offerings of my people Israel.'

30"Therefore the LORD, the God of Israel, says, 'I really did say that your house and your ancestor's house would serve me forever.' But now the LORD says, 'May it never be! For I will honor those who honor me, but those who despise me will be cursed! 31In fact, days are coming when I will remove your strength and the strength of your father's house. There will not be an old man in your house! 32You will see trouble in my dwelling place! Israel will experience blessings, but there will not be an old man in your house for all time. 33Any man of yours that I do not cut off from my altar, I will cause his eyes to fail and will

cause him grief. All those born to your family will die by the
sword of man. 34This will be a confirming sign for you that will
be fulfilled through your two sons, Hophni and Phinehas: in a
single day they both will die! 35Then I will raise up for myself
a faithful priest. He will do what is in my heart and soul. I will
build for him a lasting dynasty, and he will serve my chosen
one for all time. 36Everyone who remains in your house will
come to bow before him for a little money and for a scrap of
bread. Each will say, "Assign me to a priestly task so I can eat
a scrap of bread."'"

THE CALL OF SAMUEL

3 Now the boy Samuel continued serving the LORD under Eli's
supervision. Receiving a message from the LORD was rare in
those days; revelatory visions were infrequent.
2Eli's eyes had begun to fail, so that he was unable to see well.
At that time he was lying down in his place, 3and the lamp of
God had not yet been extinguished. Samuel was lying down in
the temple of the LORD as well; the ark of God was also there.
4The LORD called to Samuel, and he replied, "Here I am!" 5Then
he ran to Eli and said, "Here I am, for you called me." But Eli
said, "I didn't call you. Go back and lie down." So he went back
and lay down. 6The LORD again called, "Samuel!" So Samuel
got up and went to Eli and said, "Here I am, for you called me."
But Eli said, "I didn't call you, my son. Go back and lie down."
7Now Samuel did not yet know the LORD; the LORD's messages had not yet been revealed to him. 8Then the LORD called
Samuel a third time. So he got up and went to Eli and said, "Here
I am, for you called me!" Eli then realized that it was the LORD
who was calling the boy. 9So Eli said to Samuel, "Go back and
lie down. When he calls you, say, 'Speak, LORD, for your servant
is listening.'" So Samuel went back and lay down in his place.
10Then the LORD came and stood nearby, calling as he had
previously done, "Samuel! Samuel!" Samuel replied, "Speak,
for your servant is listening!" 11The LORD said to Samuel,
"Look! I am about to do something in Israel; when anyone
hears about it, both of his ears will tingle. 12On that day I
will carry out against Eli everything that I spoke about his
house—from start to finish! 13You should tell him that I am
about to judge his house forever because of the sin that he
knew about. For his sons were cursing God, and he did not
rebuke them. 14Therefore I swore an oath to the house of Eli,
'The sin of the house of Eli can never be forgiven by sacrifice
or by grain offering.'"
15So Samuel lay down until morning. Then he opened the
doors of the LORD's house. But Samuel was afraid to tell Eli
about the vision. 16However, Eli called Samuel and said, "Samuel, my son!" He replied, "Here I am." 17Eli said, "What message
did he speak to you? Don't conceal it from me. God will judge you
severely if you conceal from me anything that he said to you!"
18So Samuel told him everything. He did not hold back anything from him. Eli said, "The LORD will do what he pleases."
19Samuel continued to grow, and the LORD was with him. None
of his prophecies fell to the ground unfulfilled. 20All Israel from
Dan to Beer Sheba realized that Samuel was confirmed as a
prophet of the LORD. 21Then the LORD again appeared in Shiloh, for it was in Shiloh that the LORD had revealed himself to
Samuel through a message from the LORD. 1Samuel revealed
4 the word of the LORD to all Israel.

3:1–21 The study of scripture was neglected when Samuel came along, and he roused and illuminated the study of it again. And just as the supreme good of any church is the preservation of the true doctrine of God, so the worst thing that can happen to a church is to have a famine not of bread, but of the Word of God. Whenever the Word is lost or obscured, a horrible darkness concerning the benefits of Christ, concerning true prayer, and concerning faith must inevitably follow. Therefore we give thanks to God because his Word desires to dwell among us abundantly with all wisdom.

VIKTORIN STRIGEL
(C. 1524–1569)
BOOK OF SAMUEL

THE ARK OF THE COVENANT IS LOST TO THE PHILISTINES

Then the Israelites went out to fight the Philistines. They
camped at Ebenezer, and the Philistines camped at Aphek.
[2]The Philistines arranged their forces to fight Israel. As the
battle spread out, Israel was defeated by the Philistines, who
killed about 4,000 men in the battle line in the field.
[3]When the army came back to the camp, the elders of Israel
said, "Why did the LORD let us be defeated today by the Philistines? Let's take with us the ark of the covenant of the LORD
from Shiloh. When it is with us, it will save us from the hand
of our enemies."
[4]So the army sent to Shiloh, and they took from there the
ark of the covenant of the LORD of Heaven's Armies, who sits
between the cherubim. Now the two sons of Eli, Hophni and
Phinehas, were there with the ark of the covenant of God.
[5]When the ark of the covenant of the LORD arrived at the camp,
all Israel shouted so loudly that the ground shook.
[6]When the Philistines heard the sound of the shout, they
said, "What is this loud shout in the camp of the Hebrews?"
Then they realized that the ark of the LORD had arrived at
the camp. [7]The Philistines were scared because they thought
that gods had come to the camp. They said, "Woe to us! We've
never seen anything like this! [8]Woe to us! Who can deliver us
from the hand of these mighty gods? These are the gods who
struck the Egyptians with all sorts of plagues in the desert! [9]Be
strong and act like men, you Philistines, or else you will wind
up serving the Hebrews the way they have served you! Act like
men and fight!"
[10]So the Philistines fought. Israel was defeated; they all ran
home. The slaughter was very great; 30,000 foot soldiers from
Israel fell in battle. [11]The ark of God was taken, and the two
sons of Eli, Hophni and Phinehas, were killed.

ELI DIES

[12]On that day a Benjaminite ran from the battle lines and
came to Shiloh. His clothes were torn, and dirt was on his head.
[13]When he arrived in Shiloh, Eli was sitting in his chair on the
lookout by the side of the road, for he was very worried about
the ark of God. As the man entered the city to give his report,
the whole city cried out.
[14]When Eli heard the outcry, he said, "What's this commotion?" The man quickly came and told Eli. [15]Now Eli was
ninety-eight years old and his eyes looked straight ahead; he
was unable to see.
[16]The man said to Eli, "I am the one who came from the
battle lines! Just today I fled from the battle lines!" Eli asked,
"How did things go, my son?" [17]The messenger replied, "Israel
has fled from the Philistines! The army has suffered a great
defeat! Your two sons, Hophni and Phinehas, are dead! The ark
of God has been captured!"
[18]When he mentioned the ark of God, Eli fell backward from
his chair beside the gate. He broke his neck and died, for he was
old and heavy. He had judged Israel for 40 years.
[19]His daughter-in-law, the wife of Phinehas, was pregnant and
close to giving birth. When she heard that the ark of God was
captured and that her father-in-law and her husband were dead,
she doubled over and gave birth. But her labor pains were too
much for her. [20]As she was dying, the women who were there

4:1–11 Whoever goes to war without the word of God and trusts in their own strength will fail because victory is the Lord's. The self-appointed masters Hophni and Phinehas show that they did not have this word of God. You will not remain standing against "the Philistines," whether that means people of God or enemies of the faith, unless the spiritual word guards your heart. This is what is meant that the Israelites hoped for salvation from the ark. Without the word of God, that is, without faith in their hearts, the ark was nothing but that death that they simply brought on themselves.

JOHANNES BUGENHAGEN
(1485–1558)
COMMENTARY ON FIRST SAMUEL

with her said, "Don't be afraid! You have given birth to a son!"
But she did not reply or pay any attention.
21She named the boy Ichabod, saying, "The glory has departed from Israel," referring to the capture of the ark of God and
the deaths of her father-in-law and her husband. 22She said,
"The glory has departed from Israel, because the ark of God
has been captured."

GOD SENDS TROUBLE FOR THE PHILISTINES WHO HAVE THE ARK

5 Now the Philistines had captured the ark of God and brought
it from Ebenezer to Ashdod. 2The Philistines took the ark of
God and brought it into the temple of Dagon, where they positioned it beside Dagon. 3When the residents of Ashdod got up
early the next day, Dagon was lying on the ground before the ark
of the LORD. So they took Dagon and set him back in his place.
4But when they got up early the following day, Dagon was again
lying on the ground before the ark of the LORD. The head of
Dagon and his two hands were sheared off and were lying at the
threshold. Only Dagon's body was left intact. 5(For this reason,
to this very day, neither Dagon's priests nor anyone else who
enters Dagon's temple steps on Dagon's threshold in Ashdod.)
6The LORD attacked the residents of Ashdod severely, bringing devastation on them. He struck the people of both Ashdod
and the surrounding area with sores. 7When the people of Ashdod saw what was happening, they said, "The ark of the God of
Israel should not remain with us, for he has attacked both us
and our god Dagon!"

8So they assembled all the leaders of the Philistines and
asked, "What should we do with the ark of the God of Israel?"
They replied, "The ark of the God of Israel should be moved to
Gath." So they moved the ark of the God of Israel.

9But after it had been moved the LORD attacked that city
as well, causing a great deal of panic. He struck all the people
of that city with sores. 10So they sent the ark of God to Ekron.

But when the ark of God arrived at Ekron, the residents of
Ekron cried out saying, "They have brought the ark of the God
of Israel here to kill our people!" 11So they assembled all the
leaders of the Philistines and said, "Get the ark of the God of
Israel out of here! Let it go back to its own place so that it won't
kill us and our people!" The terror of death was throughout the
entire city; God was attacking them very severely there. 12The
people who did not die were struck with sores; the city's cry
for help went all the way up to heaven.

THE PHILISTINES RETURN THE ARK

6 When the ark of the LORD had been in the land of the Philistines for seven months, 2the Philistines called the priests
and the omen readers, saying, "What should we do with the
ark of the LORD? Advise us as to how we should send it back
to its place."

3They replied, "If you are going to send the ark of the God of
Israel back, don't send it away empty. Be sure to return it with a
guilt offering. Then you will be healed, and you will understand
why his hand has not been removed from you." 4They inquired,
"What is the guilt offering that we should send to him?"

They replied, "The Philistine leaders number five. So send five
gold sores and five gold mice, for it is the same plague that has
afflicted both you and your leaders. 5You should make images

5:1–12 The Philistines set the ark beside Dagon, evidently as if in triumph about taking captive the God of Israel, whose captured ark was taken into their idol's temple like spoils of war. For it was the custom to be arrogant in such victories, especially when enemies conquered God's people. But God did not let a day go by without avenging their insults against him. Then "when they got up early the following day, Dagon was again lying before the ark of the LORD," as if adoring the ark in veneration. For when an act of true religion is seen, then God begins to bring a great number of people to himself. Quite sensibly, then, from this miracle the Philistines recognized the Israelites' religion as truth and their idol Dagon as vanity. But with blinded minds, they did not totally comprehend it.

LUCAS OSIANDER
(1534–1604)
ANNOTATIONS ON FIRST SAMUEL

6:1–19 Seven months the Philistines were punished with the presence of the ark because they would not send it home sooner. Sinners lengthen their own miseries by refusing to part with their sins. The Israelites made no effort to recover the ark. Alas! Where shall we find concern for religion prevailing above all other matters? In times of public calamity, we fear for ourselves, for our families, and for our country; but who cares for the ark of God? We are favored with the gospel, but it is treated with neglect or contempt. There are those who value the house, the Word, and the ministry of God above their richest possessions, who dread the loss of these blessings more than death. How willing bad people are to shift off their convictions, and when they are in trouble, to believe it is a chance that happens, and that the rod has no voice which they should hear or heed!

MATTHEW HENRY **(1662–1714)**
COMMENTARY ON THE WHOLE BIBLE

of the sores and images of the mice that are destroying the land.
You should honor the God of Israel. Perhaps he will release his
grip on you, your gods, and your land. [6]Why harden your hearts
like the Egyptians and Pharaoh did? When God treated them
harshly, didn't the Egyptians send the Israelites on their way?
[7]So now go and make a new cart. Get two cows that have calves
and that have never had a yoke placed on them. Harness the
cows to the cart, and take their calves from them back to their
stalls. [8]Then take the ark of the LORD and place it on the cart,
and put in a chest beside it the gold objects you are sending to
him as a guilt offering. You should then send it on its way. [9]But
keep an eye on it. If it should go up by the way of its own border
to Beth Shemesh, then he has brought this great calamity on us.
But if that is not the case, then we will know that it was not his
hand that struck us; rather, it just happened to us by accident."
[10]So the men did as instructed. They took two cows that had
calves and harnessed the cows to a cart; they also removed their
calves to their stalls. [11]They put the ark of the LORD on the cart,
along with the chest, the gold mice, and the images of the sores.
[12]Then the cows went directly on the road to Beth Shemesh.
They went along that route, bellowing more and more; they
turned neither to the right nor to the left. The leaders of the
Philistines were walking along behind them all the way to the
border of Beth Shemesh.
[13]Now the residents of Beth Shemesh were harvesting wheat
in the valley. When they looked up and saw the ark, they were
pleased at the sight. [14]The cart was coming to the field of Joshua,
who was from Beth Shemesh. It paused there near a big stone.
Then they cut up the wood of the cart and offered the cows as a
burnt offering to the LORD. [15]The Levites took down the ark of
the LORD and the chest that was with it, which contained the gold
objects. They placed them near the big stone. At that time the
people of Beth Shemesh offered burnt offerings and made sacrifices to the LORD. [16]The five leaders of the Philistines watched
what was happening and then returned to Ekron on the same day.
[17]These are the gold sores that the Philistines brought as a
guilt offering to the LORD—one for each of the following cities: Ashdod, Gaza, Ashkelon, Gath, and Ekron. [18]The gold mice
corresponded in number to all the Philistine cities of the five
leaders, from the fortified cities to hamlet villages, to greater
Abel. They positioned the ark of the LORD on a rock until this
very day in the field of Joshua who was from Beth Shemesh.
[19]But the LORD struck down some of the people of Beth
Shemesh because they had looked into the ark of the LORD;
he struck down 50,070 of the men. The people grieved because
the LORD had struck the people with a hard blow. [20]The residents of Beth Shemesh asked, "Who is able to stand before the
LORD, this holy God? To whom will the ark go up from here?"
[21]So they sent messengers to the residents of Kiriath Jearim,
saying, "The Philistines have returned the ark of the LORD.
Come down here and take it back home with you."

7 Then the people of Kiriath Jearim came and took the ark of the
LORD; they brought it to the house of Abinadab located on the
hill. They consecrated Eleazar his son to guard the ark of the LORD.

FURTHER CONFLICT WITH THE PHILISTINES

[2]It was quite a long time—some 20 years in all—that the ark
stayed at Kiriath Jearim. All the people of Israel longed for the
LORD. [3]Samuel said to all the people of Israel, "If you are really

7:1–17 "Up to here the LORD has helped us." Look down the long aisles of your years at the green boughs of mercy overhead and the strong pillars of lovingkindness and faithfulness that bear up your joys. The phrase also points forward. There is more yet—awakening in Jesus' likeness, thrones, harps, songs, psalms, white raiment, the face of Jesus, the society of saints, the glory of God, the fullness of eternity, and the infinity of bliss. O be of good courage, believer, for he who has helped you thus far will help you all your journey through.

CHARLES SPURGEON
(1834–1892)
MORNING AND EVENING

turning to the LORD with all your hearts, remove from among you the foreign gods and the images of Ashtoreth. Give your hearts to the LORD and serve only him. Then he will deliver you from the hand of the Philistines." [4]So the Israelites removed the Baals and images of Ashtoreth. They served only the LORD.

[5]Then Samuel said, "Gather all Israel to Mizpah, and I will pray to the LORD on your behalf." [6]After they had assembled at Mizpah, they drew water and poured it out before the LORD. They fasted on that day, and they confessed there, "We have sinned against the LORD." So Samuel led the people of Israel at Mizpah.

[7]When the Philistines heard that the Israelites had gathered at Mizpah, the leaders of the Philistines went up against Israel. When the Israelites heard about this, they were afraid of the Philistines. [8]The Israelites said to Samuel, "Keep crying out to the LORD our God so that he may save us from the hand of the Philistines!" [9]So Samuel took a nursing lamb and offered it as a whole burnt offering to the LORD. Samuel cried out to the LORD on Israel's behalf, and the LORD answered him.

[10]As Samuel was offering burnt offerings, the Philistines approached to do battle with Israel. But on that day the LORD thundered loudly against the Philistines. He caused them to panic, and they were defeated by Israel. [11]Then the men of Israel left Mizpah and chased the Philistines, striking them down all the way to an area below Beth Car.

[12]Samuel took a stone and placed it between Mizpah and Shen. He named it Ebenezer, saying, "Up to here the LORD has helped us." [13]So the Philistines were defeated; they did not invade Israel again. The hand of the LORD was against the Philistines all the days of Samuel.

[14]The cities that the Philistines had captured from Israel were returned to Israel, from Ekron to Gath. Israel also delivered their territory from the control of the Philistines. There was also peace between Israel and the Amorites. [15]So Samuel led Israel all the days of his life. [16]Year after year he used to travel the circuit of Bethel, Gilgal, and Mizpah; he used to judge Israel in all these places. [17]Then he would return to Ramah, because his home was there. He also judged Israel there and built an altar to the LORD there.

ISRAEL SEEKS A KING

8 In his old age Samuel appointed his sons as judges over Israel. [2]The name of his firstborn son was Joel, and the name of his second son was Abijah. They were judges in Beer Sheba. [3]But his sons did not follow his ways. Instead, they made money dishonestly, accepted bribes, and perverted justice.

[4]So all the elders of Israel gathered together and approached Samuel at Ramah. [5]They said to him, "Look, you are old, and your sons don't follow your ways. So now appoint over us a king to lead us, just like all the other nations have."

[6]But this request displeased Samuel, for they said, "Give us a king to lead us." So Samuel prayed to the LORD. [7]The LORD said to Samuel, "Do everything the people request of you. For it is not you that they have rejected, but it is me that they have rejected as their king. [8]Just as they have done from the day that I brought them up from Egypt until this very day, they have rejected me and have served other gods. This is what they are also doing to you. [9]So now do as they say. But you must warn them and make them aware of the policies of the king who will rule over them."

8:1–22 The Lord is with kings and he rules his people through them: They are the ordinance of God. Wisdom says, "By [the Lord] kings reign." Yet the people rejected the Lord's government because they disliked the form of administration the Lord had set on them. They desired change and innovation without any direction from God. Did God also reign with bad kings? Yes. Even the authority of wicked kings is of God, which they abuse to tyranny. And for their evil and abuse of the government they shall give account to God. But although the people are evil who govern, yet the authority they possess is lawful and good. For even under tyrants there are many good things, such as the enacting of political laws, the administration of justice, and the punishment of lawbreakers.

ANDREW WILLET (1562–1621)
A HARMONY UPON THE FIRST BOOK OF SAMUEL

10 So Samuel spoke all the LORD's words to the people who
were asking him for a king. 11 He said, "Here are the policies of
the king who will rule over you: He will conscript your sons and
put them in his chariot forces and in his cavalry; they will run
in front of his chariot. 12 He will appoint for himself leaders of
thousands and leaders of fifties, as well as those who plow his
ground, reap his harvest, and make his weapons of war and
his chariot equipment. 13 He will take your daughters to be
ointment makers, cooks, and bakers. 14 He will take your best
fields, vineyards, and olive groves, and give them to his own
servants. 15 He will demand a tenth of your seed and of the
produce of your vineyards and give it to his administrators and
his servants. 16 He will take your male and female servants, as
well as your best cattle and your donkeys, and assign them for
his own use. 17 He will demand a tenth of your flocks, and you
yourselves will be his servants. 18 In that day you will cry out
because of your king whom you have chosen for yourselves, but
the LORD won't answer you in that day."

19 But the people refused to heed Samuel's warning. Instead
they said, "No! There will be a king over us! 20 We will be like
all the other nations. Our king will judge us and lead us and
fight our battles."

21 So Samuel listened to everything the people said and then
reported it to the LORD. 22 The LORD said to Samuel, "Do as they
say and install a king over them." Then Samuel said to the men
of Israel, "Each of you go back to his own city."

SAMUEL MEETS WITH SAUL

9 There was a Benjaminite man named Kish son of Abiel, the
son of Zeror, the son of Becorath, the son of Aphiah of Benjamin. Kish was a prominent person. 2 He had a son named Saul, a
handsome young man. There was no one among the Israelites
more handsome than he was; he stood head and shoulders
above all the people.

3 The donkeys of Saul's father Kish wandered off, so Kish said
to his son Saul, "Take one of the servants with you and go look
for the donkeys." 4 So Saul crossed through the hill country of
Ephraim, passing through the land of Shalisha, but they did
not find them. So they crossed through the land of Shaalim,
but they were not there. Then he crossed through the land of
Benjamin, and still they did not find them.

5 When they came to the land of Zuph, Saul said to his servant who was with him, "Come on, let's head back before my
father quits worrying about the donkeys and becomes anxious about us!" 6 But the servant said to him, "Look, there is a
man of God in this town. He is highly respected. Everything
that he says really happens. Now let's go there. Perhaps he
will tell us where we should go from here." 7 So Saul said to
his servant, "All right, we can go. But what can we bring the
man, since the food in our bags is used up? We have no gift
to take to the man of God. What do we have?" 8 The servant
went on to answer Saul, "Look, I happen to have in my hand a
quarter shekel of silver. I will give it to the man of God and he
will tell us where we should go." 9 (Now it used to be in Israel
that whenever someone went to inquire of God he would say,
"Come on, let's go to the seer." For today's prophet used to
be called a seer.) 10 So Saul said to his servant, "That's a good
idea! Come on. Let's go." So they went to the town where the
man of God was.

9:6–26 The straying donkeys, in search of which Saul had left his father's house, show clearly enough that they went astray at the ordination of God, since the son sought donkeys and found the kingdom that he had not sought, and the father got not only the donkeys he was concerned about but also a king for a son, which he had never anticipated. In this we see that everywhere the things we say occur by accident are done and regulated by Providence.

ULRICH ZWINGLI **(1484–1531)**
ON THE PROVIDENCE OF GOD

[11]As they were going up the ascent to the town, they met some girls coming out to draw water. They said to them, "Is this where the seer is?" [12]They replied, "Yes, straight ahead! But hurry now, for he came to the town today, and the people are making a sacrifice at the high place. [13]When you enter the town, you can find him before he goes up to the high place to eat. The people won't eat until he arrives, for he must bless the sacrifice. Once that happens, those who have been invited will eat. Now go on up, for this is the time when you can find him." [14]So they went up to the town. As they were heading for the middle of the town, Samuel was coming in their direction to go up to the high place. [15]Now the day before Saul arrived, the LORD had told Samuel: [16]"At this time tomorrow I will send to you a man from the land of Benjamin. You must consecrate him as a leader over my people Israel. He will save my people from the hand of the Philistines. For I have looked with favor on my people. Their cry has reached me."

[17]When Samuel saw Saul, the LORD said, "Here is the man that I told you about. He will rule over my people." [18]As Saul approached Samuel in the middle of the gate, he said, "Please tell me where the seer's house is."

[19]Samuel replied to Saul, "I am the seer! Go up in front of me to the high place! Today you will eat with me and in the morning I will send you away. I will tell you everything that you are thinking. [20]Don't be concerned about the donkeys that you lost three days ago, for they have been found. Whom does all Israel desire? Is it not you, and all your father's family?"

[21]Saul replied, "Am I not a Benjaminite, from the smallest of Israel's tribes, and is not my family clan the smallest of all the clans in the tribe of Benjamin? Why do you speak to me in this way?"

[22]Then Samuel brought Saul and his servant into the room and gave them a place at the head of those who had been invited. There were about thirty people present. [23]Samuel said to the cook, "Give me the portion of meat that I gave to you—the one I asked you to keep with you."

[24]So the cook picked up the leg and brought it and set it in front of Saul. Samuel said, "What was kept is now set before you! Eat, for it has been kept for you for this meeting time, from the time I said, 'I have invited the people.'" So Saul ate with Samuel that day.

[25]When they came down from the high place to the town, Samuel spoke with Saul on the roof. [26]They got up at dawn and Samuel called to Saul on the roof, "Get up, so I can send you on your way." So Saul got up and the two of them—he and Samuel—went outside. [27]While they were going down to the edge of town, Samuel said to Saul, "Tell the servant to go on ahead of us." So he did. Samuel then said, "You remain here awhile, so I can inform you of God's message."

SAMUEL ANOINTS SAUL

10 Then Samuel took a small container of olive oil and poured it on Saul's head. Samuel kissed him and said, "The LORD has chosen you to lead his people Israel! You will rule over the LORD's people and you will deliver them from the power of the enemies who surround them. This will be your sign that the LORD has chosen you as leader over his inheritance. [2]When you leave me today, you will find two men near Rachel's tomb at Zelzah on Benjamin's border. They will say to

10:1–16 Here Samuel did not set forth one single work but he sent a man, changed by the Spirit, as into a forest of works. Because he had become another man, other works followed. Our opponents do not understand this theology but turn it upside down. They prescribe and teach that people should do works until they are changed and become different. But a person must first be changed. Afterward everything will be made right. Everything now pleases God because the person pleases God, not for his or her own sake but for the sake of the sacrifice of Christ and the mercy that faith grasps.

MARTIN LUTHER **(1483–1546)**
COMMENTS ON PSALM 51

you, 'The donkeys you have gone looking for have been found. Your father is no longer concerned about the donkeys but has become anxious about you two! He is asking, "What should I do about my son?"'

3"As you continue on from there, you will come to the tall tree of Tabor. At that point three men who are going up to God at Bethel will meet you. One of them will be carrying three young goats, one of them will be carrying three round loaves of bread, and one of them will be carrying a container of wine. 4They will ask you how you're doing and will give you two loaves of bread. You will accept them. 5Afterward you will go to Gibeah of God, where there are Philistine officials. When you enter the town, you will meet a company of prophets coming down from the high place. They will have harps, tambourines, flutes, and lyres, and they will be prophesying. 6Then the Spirit of the LORD will rush upon you and you will prophesy with them. You will be changed into a different person.

7"When these signs have taken place, do whatever your hand finds to do, for God will be with you. 8You will go down to Gilgal before me. I am going to join you there to offer burnt offerings and to make peace offerings. You should wait for seven days until I arrive and tell you what to do."

SAUL BECOMES KING

9As Saul turned to leave Samuel, God changed his inmost person. All these signs happened on that very day. 10When Saul and his servant arrived at Gibeah, a company of prophets was coming out to meet him. Then the Spirit of God rushed upon Saul and he prophesied among them. 11When everyone who had known him previously saw him prophesying with the prophets, the people asked one another, "What on earth has happened to the son of Kish? Does even Saul belong with the prophets?"

12A man who was from there replied, "And who is their father?" Therefore this became a proverb: "Is even Saul among the prophets?" 13When Saul had finished prophesying, he went to the high place.

14Saul's uncle asked him and his servant, "Where did you go?" Saul replied, "To look for the donkeys. But when we realized they were lost, we went to Samuel." 15Saul's uncle said, "Tell me what Samuel said to you." 16Saul said to his uncle, "He assured us that the donkeys had been found." But Saul did not tell him what Samuel had said about the matter of kingship.

17Then Samuel called the people together before the LORD at Mizpah. 18He said to the Israelites, "This is what the LORD God of Israel has said, 'I brought Israel up from Egypt and I delivered you from the power of the Egyptians and from the power of all the kingdoms that oppressed you. 19But today you have rejected your God who saves you from all your trouble and distress. You have said, "No! Appoint a king over us." Now take your positions before the LORD by your tribes and by your clans.'"

20Then Samuel brought all the tribes of Israel near, and the tribe of Benjamin was chosen by lot. 21Then he brought the tribe of Benjamin near by its families, and the family of Matri was chosen by lot. At last Saul son of Kish was chosen by lot. But when they looked for him, he was nowhere to be found. 22So they inquired again of the LORD, "Has the man arrived here yet?" The LORD said, "He has hidden himself among the equipment."

[23]So they ran and brought him from there. When he took
his position among the people, he stood head and shoulders
above them all. [24]Then Samuel said to all the people, "Do you
see the one whom the LORD has chosen? Indeed, there is no
one like him among all the people." All the people shouted out,
"Long live the king!"
[25]Then Samuel talked to the people about how the kingship
would work. He wrote it all down on a scroll and set it before
the LORD. Then Samuel sent all the people away to their homes.
[26]Even Saul went to his home in Gibeah. With him went some
brave men whose hearts God had touched. [27]But some wicked
men said, "How can this man save us?" They despised him and
did not even bring him a gift. But Saul said nothing about it.

SAUL COMES TO THE AID OF JABESH

11 Nahash the Ammonite marched against Jabesh Gilead. All
the men of Jabesh Gilead said to Nahash, "Make a treaty
with us and we will serve you."
[2]But Nahash the Ammonite said to them, "The only way I
will make a treaty with you is if you let me gouge out the right
eye of every one of you and in so doing humiliate all Israel!"
[3]The elders of Jabesh said to him, "Leave us alone for seven
days so that we can send messengers throughout the territory
of Israel. If there is no one who can deliver us, we will come out
voluntarily to you."
[4]When the messengers went to Gibeah (where Saul lived)
and informed the people of these matters, all the people wept
loudly. [5]Now Saul was walking behind the oxen as he came
from the field. Saul asked, "What has happened to the people?
Why are they weeping?" So they told him about the men of
Jabesh.
[6]The Spirit of God rushed upon Saul when he heard these
words, and he became very angry. [7]He took a pair of oxen and
cut them up. Then he sent the pieces throughout the territory
of Israel by the hand of messengers, who said, "Whoever does
not go out after Saul and after Samuel should expect this to
be done to his oxen!" Then the terror of the LORD fell on the
people, and they went out as one army. [8]When Saul counted
them at Bezek, the Israelites were 300,000 strong and the men
of Judah numbered 30,000.
[9]They said to the messengers who had come, "Here's what
you should say to the men of Jabesh Gilead: 'Tomorrow deliverance will come to you when the sun is fully up.'" When the
messengers went and told the men of Jabesh Gilead, they were
happy. [10]The men of Jabesh said, "Tomorrow we will come out
to you and you can do with us whatever you wish."
[11]The next day Saul placed the people in three groups. They
went to the Ammonite camp during the morning watch and
struck them down until the hottest part of the day. The survivors scattered; no two of them remained together.

11:6–8 As Moses at the Red Sea got courage to go forward, as Caleb, the faithful spy, was able to resist all the clamor of his colleagues and the people, so on this occasion the Spirit who rises above the storm and flings defiance even on the strongest enemies came mightily on one man—Saul. His conduct at this time is another evidence of how well he conducted himself in the opening period of his reign. "The Spirit of God rushed upon Saul when he heard these words, and he became very angry." The "Spirit of God" evidently means here that spirit of courage, of noble energy, of dauntless resolution that was needed to meet the emergency that had arisen . . . O Saul, Saul, how well it would have been for you had you maintained this spirit! For then God would not have had to reject you from being king and to seek among the sheepfolds of Bethlehem a man after his own heart to be the leader of his people!

WILLIAM GARDEN BLAIKIE
(1820–1899)
THE FIRST BOOK OF SAMUEL

SAUL IS ESTABLISHED AS KING

[12]Then the people said to Samuel, "Who were the ones asking, 'Will Saul reign over us?' Hand over those men so we may
execute them!" [13]But Saul said, "No one will be killed on this
day. For today the LORD has given Israel a victory!" [14]Samuel
said to the people, "Come on! Let's go to Gilgal and renew the
kingship there." [15]So all the people went to Gilgal, where they
established Saul as king in the LORD's presence. They offered

up peace offerings there in the LORD's presence. Saul and all
the Israelites were very happy.
12 Samuel said to all Israel, "I have done everything you requested. I have given you a king. 2Now look! This king
walks before you. As for me, I am old and gray, and my sons are
here with you. I have walked before you from the time of my
youth till the present day. 3Here I am. Bring a charge against
me before the LORD and before his chosen king. Whose ox have
I taken? Whose donkey have I taken? Whom have I wronged?
Whom have I oppressed? From whose hand have I taken a bribe
so that I would overlook something? Tell me, and I will return
it to you!"
4They replied, "You have not wronged us or oppressed us. You
have not taken anything from the hand of anyone." 5He said to
them, "The LORD is witness against you, and his chosen king is
witness this day, that you have not found any reason to accuse
me." They said, "He is witness!"
6Samuel said to the people, "The LORD is the one who chose
Moses and Aaron and who brought your ancestors up from the
land of Egypt. 7Now take your positions, so I may confront you
before the LORD regarding all the LORD's just actions toward
you and your ancestors. 8When Jacob entered Egypt, your ancestors cried out to the LORD. The LORD sent Moses and Aaron,
and they led your ancestors out of Egypt and settled them in
this place.
9"But they forgot the LORD their God, so he gave them into
the hand of Sisera, the general in command of Hazor's army,
and into the hands of the Philistines and the king of Moab,
and they fought against them. 10Then they cried out to the
LORD and admitted, 'We have sinned, for we have forsaken the
LORD and have served the Baals and the images of Ashtoreth.
Now deliver us from the hands of our enemies so that we may
serve you.' 11So the LORD sent Jerub Baal, Barak, Jephthah, and
Samuel, and he delivered you from the hands of the enemies
all around you, and you were able to live securely.
12"When you saw that King Nahash of the Ammonites was
advancing against you, you said to me, 'No! A king will rule over
us'—even though the LORD your God is your king. 13Now look!
Here is the king you have chosen—the one that you asked for!
Look, the LORD has given you a king. 14If you fear the LORD,
serving him and obeying him and not rebelling against what
he says, and if both you and the king who rules over you follow
the LORD your God, all will be well. 15But if you don't obey the
LORD and rebel against what the LORD says, the hand of the
LORD will be against both you and your king.
16"So now, take your positions and watch this great thing
that the LORD is about to do in your sight. 17Is this not the time
of the wheat harvest? I will call on the LORD so that he makes
it thunder and rain. Realize and see what a great sin you have
committed before the LORD by asking for a king for yourselves."
18So Samuel called to the LORD, and the LORD made it thunder and rain that day. All the people were very afraid of both
the LORD and Samuel. 19All the people said to Samuel, "Pray
to the LORD your God on behalf of us—your servants—so we
won't die, for we have added to all our sins by asking for a king."
20Then Samuel said to the people, "Don't be afraid. You have
indeed sinned. However, don't turn aside from the LORD. Serve
the LORD with all your heart. 21You should not turn aside after
empty things that can't profit and can't deliver, since they are

12:5–12 Samuel confronted their sins with this biting address about God's clearly extensive works; he retold the whole story in only a few words. By telling this history Samuel declared that God had ruled the people to this point and that the people had confidently lived under God. He showed how for so long God had been a king and continuously raised up good leaders in those days. He did this so that the people would acknowledge what they had done. And by a clear miracle of God, Samuel conquered their hardened hearts. He led them to confess the sin, and they judged his wisdom to be real, useful, necessary, and salutary.

JOHANNES BUGENHAGEN
(1485–1558)
COMMENTARY ON FIRST SAMUEL

empty. [22]The LORD will not abandon his people because he wants to uphold his great reputation. The LORD was pleased to make you his own people. [23]As far as I am concerned, far be it from me to sin against the LORD by ceasing to pray for you! I will instruct you in the way that is good and upright. [24]However, fear the LORD and serve him faithfully with all your heart. Just look at the great things he has done for you! [25]But if you continue to do evil, both you and your king will be swept away."

SAUL FAILS THE LORD

13 Saul was [thirty]* years old when he began to reign; he ruled over Israel for [forty]† years. [2]Saul selected for himself 3,000 men from Israel. Of these 2,000 were with Saul at Micmash and in the hill country of Bethel; the remaining 1,000 were with Jonathan at Gibeah in the territory of Benjamin. He sent all the rest of the people back home.

[3]Jonathan attacked the Philistine outpost that was at Geba and the Philistines heard about it. Then Saul alerted all the land saying, "Let the Hebrews pay attention!" [4]All Israel heard this message, "Saul has attacked the Philistine outpost, and now Israel is repulsive to the Philistines!" So the people were summoned to join Saul at Gilgal.

[5]Meanwhile the Philistines gathered to battle with Israel. Then they went up against Israel with 3,000 chariots, 6,000 horsemen, and an army as numerous as the sand on the seashore. They went up and camped at Micmash, east of Beth Aven. [6]The men of Israel realized they had a problem because their army was hard pressed. So the army hid in caves, thickets, cliffs, strongholds, and cisterns. [7]Some of the Hebrews crossed over the Jordan River to the land of Gad and Gilead. But Saul stayed at Gilgal; the entire army that was with him was terrified. [8]He waited for seven days, the time period indicated by Samuel. But Samuel did not come to Gilgal, and the army began to abandon Saul.

[9]So Saul said, "Bring me the burnt offering and the peace offerings." Then he offered a burnt offering. [10]Just when he had finished offering the burnt offering, Samuel appeared on the scene. Saul went out to meet him and to greet him.

[11]But Samuel said, "What have you done?" Saul replied, "When I saw that the army had started to abandon me, and that you didn't come at the appointed time, and that the Philistines had assembled at Micmash, [12]I thought, 'Now the Philistines will come down on me at Gilgal and I have not sought the LORD's favor.' So I felt obligated to offer the burnt offering."

[13]Then Samuel said to Saul, "You have made a foolish choice! You have not obeyed the commandment that the LORD your God gave you. Had you done that, the LORD would have established your kingdom over Israel forever. [14]But now your kingdom will not continue. The LORD has sought out for himself a man who is loyal to him, and the LORD has appointed him to be leader over his people, for you have not obeyed what the LORD commanded you."

[15]Then Samuel set out and went up from Gilgal to Gibeah in the territory of Benjamin. Saul mustered the army that remained with him; there were about 600 men. [16]Saul, his son Jonathan, and the army that remained with them stayed in Gibeah in the territory of Benjamin, while the Philistines camped in Micmash. [17]Raiding bands went out from the camp of the Philistines in three groups. One band turned toward

13:1–16 If someone had asked all the people in the time of Saul, "Do you want to seek God?" each one would've replied, "Yes, this is my intention." But so what? God disdained their talk and declared that they were despising and rejecting him, and in fact denying him. Why? Because they had no zeal and no pure and true affection for him. Let us therefore be careful not to seek God halfway. On the contrary, let us earnestly seek his face, driving ourselves forward as we realize that he is the mainspring of our whole life, on whom we must concentrate all our thoughts and study in order to be pleasing to him.

JOHN CALVIN (1509–1564)
COMPLETE COMMENTARY ON THE BIBLE

the road leading to Ophrah by the land of Shual; [18]another band turned toward the road leading to Beth Horon; and yet another band turned toward the road leading to the border that overlooks the valley of Zeboyim in the direction of the desert.

[19]A blacksmith could not be found in all the land of Israel, for the Philistines had said, "This will prevent the Hebrews from making swords and spears." [20]So all Israel had to go down to the Philistines in order to get their plowshares, cutting instruments, axes, and sickles sharpened. [21]They charged two-thirds of a shekel to sharpen plowshares and cutting instruments, and one-third of a shekel to sharpen picks and axes, and to set ox goads. [22]So on the day of the battle no sword or spear was to be found in the hand of anyone in the army that was with Saul and Jonathan. No one but Saul and his son Jonathan had them.

JONATHAN IGNITES A BATTLE

[23]A garrison of the Philistines had gone out to the pass at Micmash.

14 Then one day Jonathan son of Saul said to his armor-bearer, "Come on, let's go over to the Philistine garrison that is opposite us." But he did not let his father know.

[2]Now Saul was sitting under a pomegranate tree in Migron, on the outskirts of Gibeah. The army that was with him numbered about 600 men. [3]Now Ahijah was carrying an ephod. He was the son of Ahitub, who was the brother of Ichabod and a son of Phinehas, son of Eli, the priest of the LORD in Shiloh. The army was unaware that Jonathan had left.

[4]Now there was a steep cliff on each side of the pass through which Jonathan intended to go to reach the Philistine garrison. One cliff was named Bozez, the other Seneh. [5]The cliff to the north was closer to Micmash, the one to the south closer to Geba.

[6]Jonathan said to his armor-bearer, "Come on, let's go over to the garrison of these uncircumcised men. Perhaps the LORD will intervene for us. Nothing can prevent the LORD from delivering, whether by many or by a few." [7]His armor-bearer said to him, "Do everything that is on your mind. Do as you're inclined. I'm with you all the way!"

[8]Jonathan replied, "All right. We'll go over to these men and fight them. [9]If they say to us, 'Stay put until we approach you,' we will stay right there and not go up to them. [10]But if they say, 'Come up against us,' we will go up. For in that case the LORD has given them into our hand—it will be a sign to us."

[11]When they made themselves known to the Philistine garrison, the Philistines said, "Look! The Hebrews are coming out of the holes in which they hid themselves." [12]Then the men of the garrison said to Jonathan and his armor-bearer, "Come on up to us so we can teach you a thing or two!" Then Jonathan said to his armor-bearer, "Come up behind me, for the LORD has given them into the hand of Israel!"

[13]Jonathan crawled up on his hands and feet, with his armor-bearer following behind him. Jonathan struck down the Philistines, while his armor-bearer came along behind him and killed them. [14]In this initial skirmish Jonathan and his armor-bearer struck down about 20 men in an area that measured half an acre.

[15]Then fear overwhelmed those who were in the camp, those who were in the field, all the army in the garrison, and the raiding bands. They trembled and the ground shook. This fear was caused by God.

14:6 "These uncircumcised men": so Jonathan called them, partly in contempt and principally to strengthen his faith by this consideration that his enemies were enemies to God and without any hope in God or help from him, whereas he was circumcised and therefore in covenant with God, who was both able and engaged to assist his people. It may be he spoke doubtfully, for though he found and felt himself stirred up by God to this exploit and was assured that God would deliver his people, yet he was not certain that he would do it at this time and in this way. The Lord will work, to wit, great and wonderful things. There is no restraint to the Lord; there is no person or thing that can hinder God from thus doing.

MATTHEW POOLE **(1624–1679)**
ENGLISH ANNOTATIONS ON THE HOLY BIBLE

[16]Saul's watchmen at Gibeah in the territory of Benjamin
looked on as the crowd of soldiers seemed to melt away first in
one direction and then in another. [17]So Saul said to the army
that was with him, "Muster the troops and see who is no longer
with us." When they mustered the troops, Jonathan and his
armor-bearer were not there. [18]So Saul said to Ahijah, "Bring
near the ephod," for he was at that time wearing the ephod in
front of the Israelites. [19]While Saul spoke to the priest, the panic
in the Philistines' camp was becoming greater and greater. So
Saul said to the priest, "Withdraw your hand."

[20]Saul and all the army assembled and marched into battle,
where they found the Philistines in total panic killing one another with their swords. [21]The Hebrews who had earlier gone
over to the Philistine side joined the Israelites who were with
Saul and Jonathan. [22]When all the Israelites who had hidden
themselves in the hill country of Ephraim heard that the Philistines had fled, they too pursued them in battle. [23]So the LORD
delivered Israel that day, and the battle shifted over to Beth
Aven.

JONATHAN VIOLATES SAUL'S OATH

[24]Now the men of Israel were hard pressed that day, for Saul had
made the army agree to this oath: "Cursed be the man who eats
food before evening. I will get my vengeance on my enemies!"
So no one in the army ate anything.

[25]Now the whole army entered the forest, and there was honey on the ground. [26]When the army entered the forest, they
saw the honey flowing, but no one ate any of it, for the army
was afraid of the oath. [27]But Jonathan had not heard about the
oath his father had made the army take. He extended the end
of his staff that was in his hand and dipped it in the honeycomb.
When he ate it, his eyes gleamed. [28]Then someone from the
army informed him, "Your father put the army under a strict
oath saying, 'Cursed be the man who eats food today.' That is why
the army is tired." [29]Then Jonathan said, "My father has caused
trouble for the land. See how my eyes gleamed when I tasted
just a little of this honey. [30]Certainly if the army had eaten some
of the enemies' provisions that they came across today, would
not the slaughter of the Philistines have been even greater?"

[31]On that day the army struck down the Philistines from
Micmash to Aijalon, and they became very tired. [32]So the army
rushed greedily on the plunder, confiscating sheep, cattle, and
calves. They slaughtered them right on the ground, and the
army ate them, blood and all.

[33]Now it was reported to Saul, "Look, the army is sinning
against the LORD by eating even the blood." He said, "All of you
have broken the covenant! Roll a large stone over here to me."
[34]Then Saul said, "Scatter out among the army and say to them,
'Each of you bring to me your ox and sheep and slaughter them
in this spot and eat. But don't sin against the LORD by eating the
blood.'" So that night each one brought his ox and slaughtered
it there. [35]Then Saul built an altar for the LORD; it was the first
time he had built an altar for the LORD.

[36]Saul said, "Let's go down after the Philistines at night; we
will rout them until the break of day. We won't leave any of
them alive!" They replied, "Do whatever seems best to you." But
the priest said, "Let's approach God here." [37]So Saul asked God,
"Should I go down after the Philistines? Will you deliver them
into the hand of Israel?" But he did not answer him that day.

38 Then Saul said, "All you leaders of the army come here. Find
out how this sin occurred today. 39 For as surely as the LORD,
the deliverer of Israel, lives, even if it turns out to be my own
son Jonathan, he will certainly die!" But no one from the army
said anything.

40 Then he said to all Israel, "You will be on one side, and I and
my son Jonathan will be on the other side." The army replied
to Saul, "Do whatever you think is best."

41 Then Saul said, "O LORD God of Israel! If this sin has been
committed by me or by my son Jonathan, then, O LORD God of
Israel, respond with Urim. But if this sin has been committed
by your people Israel, respond with Thummim." Then Jonathan
and Saul were indicated by lot, while the army was exonerated.
42 Then Saul said, "Cast the lot between me and my son Jonathan!" Jonathan was indicated by lot.

43 So Saul said to Jonathan, "Tell me what you have done."
Jonathan told him, "I used the end of the staff that was in my
hand to taste a little honey. I must die!" 44 Saul said, "God will
punish me severely if Jonathan doesn't die!"

45 But the army said to Saul, "Should Jonathan, who won this
great victory in Israel, die? May it never be! As surely as the
LORD lives, not a single hair of his head will fall to the ground,
for it is with the help of God that he has acted today." So the
army rescued Jonathan from death.

46 Then Saul stopped chasing the Philistines, and the Philistines went back home. 47 After Saul had secured his royal
position over Israel, he fought against all their enemies on all
sides—the Moabites, Ammonites, Edomites, the kings of Zobah,
and the Philistines. In every direction that he turned, he was
victorious. 48 He fought bravely, striking down the Amalekites
and delivering Israel from the hand of its enemies.

MEMBERS OF SAUL'S FAMILY

49 The sons of Saul were Jonathan, Ishvi, and Malki-Shua. He
had two daughters; the older one was named Merab and the
younger Michal. 50 The name of Saul's wife was Ahinoam, the
daughter of Ahimaaz. The name of the general in command
of his army was Abner son of Ner, Saul's uncle. 51 Kish was the
father of Saul, and Ner the father of Abner was the son of
Abiel.

52 There was fierce war with the Philistines all the days of
Saul. So whenever Saul saw anyone who was a warrior or a brave
individual, he would conscript him.

SAUL IS REJECTED AS KING

15 Then Samuel said to Saul, "I was the one the LORD sent
to anoint you as king over his people Israel. Now listen to
what the LORD says. 2 Here is what the LORD of Heaven's Armies
has said: 'I carefully observed how the Amalekites opposed
Israel along the way when Israel came up from Egypt. 3 So go
now and strike down the Amalekites. Destroy everything they
have. Don't spare them. Put them to death—man, woman, child,
infant, ox, sheep, camel, and donkey alike.'"

4 So Saul assembled the army and mustered them at Telaim.
There were 200,000 foot soldiers and 10,000 men of Judah.
5 Saul proceeded to the city of Amalek, where he set an ambush
in the wadi. 6 Saul said to the Kenites, "Go on and leave! Go down
from among the Amalekites. Otherwise I will sweep you away
with them. After all, you were kind to all the Israelites when

15:1–9 Observe how severely and frequently God has punished human inventions they considered holy transactions and religion! Saul had mercy on Agag, the king of the Amalekites, and prompted by his invention he spared the best and fattest sheep and oxen to sacrifice to the Lord, contrary to the word of the prophet. That act of would-be mercy and illustrious zeal was punished as a sin of witchcraft and idolatry because he acted according to his own invention and not according to the word of the prophet. He was reproved by the prophet, smitten with pestilence, and his kingdom was taken from him and given to a more faithful man.

MENNO SIMONS **(1496–1561)**
TRUE CHRISTIAN FAITH

they came up from Egypt." So the Kenites withdrew from among
the Amalekites.
7 Then Saul struck down the Amalekites all the way from
Havilah to Shur, which is next to Egypt. 8 He captured King Agag
of the Amalekites alive, but he executed all Agag's people with
the sword. 9 However, Saul and the army spared Agag, along with
the best of the flock, the cattle, the fatlings, and the lambs, as
well as everything else that was of value. They were not willing
to slaughter them. But they did slaughter everything that was
despised and worthless.
10 Then the LORD's message came to Samuel: 11 "I regret that
I have made Saul king, for he has turned away from me and has
not done what I told him to do." Samuel became angry and he
cried out to the LORD all that night.
12 Then Samuel got up early to meet Saul the next morning.
But Samuel was informed, "Saul has gone to Carmel where he
is setting up a monument for himself." Then Samuel left and
went down to Gilgal. 13 When Samuel came to Saul, Saul said
to him, "May the LORD bless you! I have fulfilled the LORD's
orders."
14 Samuel replied, "If that is the case, then what is this sound
of sheep in my ears and the sound of cattle that I hear?" 15 Saul
said, "They were brought from the Amalekites; the army spared
the best of the flocks and cattle to sacrifice to the LORD our
God. But everything else we slaughtered."
16 Then Samuel said to Saul, "Wait a minute! Let me tell you
what the LORD said to me last night." Saul said to him, "Tell
me." 17 Samuel said, "Is it not true that when you were insignificant in your own eyes, you became head of the tribes of Israel?
The LORD chose you as king over Israel. 18 The LORD sent you
on a campaign saying, 'Go and exterminate those sinful Amalekites! Fight against them until you have destroyed them.'
19 Why haven't you obeyed the LORD? Instead you have greedily
rushed upon the plunder! You have done what is wrong in the
LORD's estimation."
20 Then Saul said to Samuel, "But I have obeyed the LORD! I
went on the campaign the LORD sent me on. I brought back King
Agag of the Amalekites after exterminating the Amalekites.
21 But the army took from the plunder some of the sheep and
cattle—the best of what was to be slaughtered—to sacrifice to
the LORD your God in Gilgal."
22 Then Samuel said,

"Does the LORD take pleasure in burnt offerings and
sacrifices
as much as he does in obedience?
Certainly, obedience is better than sacrifice;
paying attention is better than the fat of rams.
23 For rebellion is like the sin of divination,
and presumption is like the evil of idolatry.
Because you have rejected the LORD's orders,
he has rejected you from being king."

24 Then Saul said to Samuel, "I have sinned, for I have disobeyed what the LORD commanded and your words as well. For
I was afraid of the army, and I obeyed their voice. 25 Now please
forgive my sin. Go back with me so I can worship the LORD."
26 Samuel said to Saul, "I will not go back with you, for you
have rejected the LORD's orders, and the LORD has rejected you
from being king over Israel!"

27 When Samuel turned to leave, Saul grabbed the edge of his robe and it tore. 28 Samuel said to him, "The LORD has torn the kingdom of Israel from you this day and has given it to one of your colleagues who is better than you! 29 The Preeminent One of Israel does not go back on his word or change his mind, for he is not a human being who changes his mind." 30 Saul again replied, "I have sinned. But please honor me before the elders of my people and before Israel. Go back with me so I may worship the LORD your God." 31 So Samuel followed Saul back, and Saul worshiped the LORD.

SAMUEL PUTS AGAG TO DEATH

32 Then Samuel said, "Bring me King Agag of the Amalekites." So Agag came to him trembling, thinking to himself, "Surely death is bitter!" 33 Samuel said, "Just as your sword left women childless, so your mother will be the most bereaved among women." Then Samuel hacked Agag to pieces there in Gilgal before the LORD.

34 Then Samuel went to Ramah, while Saul went up to his home in Gibeah of Saul. 35 Until the day he died, Samuel did not see Saul again. Samuel did, however, mourn for Saul, but the LORD regretted that he had made Saul king over Israel.

SAMUEL ANOINTS DAVID AS KING

16 The LORD said to Samuel, "How long do you intend to mourn for Saul? I have rejected him as king over Israel. Fill your horn with olive oil and go. I am sending you to Jesse in Bethlehem, for I have selected a king for myself from among his sons."

2 Samuel replied, "How can I go? Saul will hear about it and kill me!" But the LORD said, "Take a heifer with you and say, 'I have come to sacrifice to the LORD.' 3 Then invite Jesse to the sacrifice, and I will show you what you should do. You will anoint for me the one I point out to you."

4 Samuel did what the LORD told him. When he arrived in Bethlehem, the elders of the city were afraid to meet him. They said, "Do you come in peace?" 5 He replied, "Yes, in peace. I have come to sacrifice to the LORD. Consecrate yourselves and come with me to the sacrifice." So he consecrated Jesse and his sons and invited them to the sacrifice.

6 When they arrived, Samuel noticed Eliab and said to himself, "Surely, here before the LORD stands his chosen king." 7 But the LORD said to Samuel, "Don't be impressed by his appearance or his height, for I have rejected him. God does not view things the way people do. People look on the outward appearance, but the LORD looks at the heart."

8 Then Jesse called Abinadab and presented him to Samuel. But Samuel said, "The LORD has not chosen this one either." 9 Then Jesse presented Shammah. But Samuel said, "The LORD has not chosen this one either." 10 Jesse presented seven of his sons to Samuel. But Samuel said to Jesse, "The LORD has not chosen any of these." 11 Then Samuel asked Jesse, "Is that all the young men?" Jesse replied, "There is still the youngest one, but he's taking care of the flock." Samuel said to Jesse, "Send and get him, for we cannot turn our attention to other things until he comes here."

12 So Jesse had him brought in. Now he was ruddy, with attractive eyes and a handsome appearance. The LORD said, "Go and anoint him. This is the one." 13 So Samuel took the horn full of olive oil and anointed him in the presence of his brothers. The Spirit of the LORD rushed upon David from that day onward. Then Samuel got up and went to Ramah.

16:14–15 When people fall from the Spirit for any wickedness, if they repent after their fall, the grace remains irrevocably to those who are willing; otherwise they who have fallen are no longer in God (because that Holy Spirit and Paraclete who are in God have deserted him). These sinners shall be in him to whom they have subjected themselves as took place in Saul's instance, for the Spirit of God departed from him and an evil spirit was afflicting him.

ATHANASIUS (C. 296–373)
FOUR DISCOURSES AGAINST THE ARIANS

DAVID APPEARS BEFORE SAUL

14 Now the Spirit of the LORD had turned away from Saul, and an evil spirit from the LORD tormented him. 15 Then Saul's servants said to him, "Look, an evil spirit from God is tormenting you. 16 Let our lord instruct his servants who are here before you to look for a man who knows how to play the lyre. Then whenever the evil spirit from God comes upon you, he can play the lyre and you will feel better." 17 So Saul said to his servants, "Find me a man who plays well and bring him to me." 18 One of his attendants replied, "I have seen a son of Jesse in Bethlehem who knows how to play the lyre. He is a brave warrior and is articulate and handsome, for the LORD is with him."

19 So Saul sent messengers to Jesse and said, "Send me your son David, who is out with the sheep." 20 So Jesse took a donkey loaded with bread, a container of wine, and a young goat and sent them to Saul with his son David. 21 David came to Saul and stood before him. Saul liked him a great deal, and he became his armor-bearer. 22 Then Saul sent word to Jesse saying, "Let David be my servant, for I am very pleased with him."

23 So whenever the spirit from God would come upon Saul, David would take his lyre and play it. This would bring relief to Saul and make him feel better. Then the evil spirit would leave him alone.

17:1–37 Goliath, lord of the Philistines, was the ruler of the world. David was Christ and anyone who has a firm spirit in Christ. Here you see David's marvelous faith and zeal for his people against the blasphemy of their enemies as he blazed—carried by the Spirit—for the glory of God. These are Christ's benefits presented to us so that from the beginning of his anointing David might show through God what the kingdom itself would produce through Christ, David's son. This is also the result of all faith fighting against Satan's cunning and against worldly wisdom and power. These are not the weapons of the flesh but the armor of God.

JOHANNES BUGENHAGEN
(1485–1558)
COMMENTARY ON FIRST SAMUEL

DAVID KILLS GOLIATH

17 The Philistines gathered their troops for battle. They assembled at Socoh in Judah. They camped in Ephes Dammim, between Socoh and Azekah. 2 Saul and the Israelite army assembled and camped in the valley of Elah, where they arranged their battle lines to fight against the Philistines. 3 The Philistines were standing on one hill, and the Israelites on another hill, with the valley between them.

4 Then a champion came out from the camp of the Philistines. His name was Goliath; he was from Gath. He was close to seven feet tall. 5 He had a bronze helmet on his head and was wearing scale body armor. The weight of his bronze body armor was 5,000 shekels. 6 He had bronze shin guards on his legs, and a bronze javelin was slung over his shoulders. 7 The shaft of his spear was like a weaver's beam, and the iron point of his spear weighed 600 shekels. His shield bearer was walking before him. 8 Goliath stood and called to Israel's troops, "Why do you come out to prepare for battle? Am I not the Philistine, and are you not the servants of Saul? Choose for yourselves a man so he may come down to me! 9 If he is able to fight with me and strike me down, we will become your servants. But if I prevail against him and strike him down, you will become our servants and will serve us." 10 Then the Philistine said, "I defy Israel's troops this day! Give me a man so we can fight each other!" 11 When Saul and all the Israelites heard these words of the Philistine, they were upset and very afraid.

12 Now David was the son of an Ephrathite named Jesse from Bethlehem in Judah. He had eight sons, and in Saul's days he was old and well advanced in years. 13 Jesse's three oldest sons had followed Saul to war. The names of the three sons who went to war were Eliab, his firstborn; Abinadab, the second oldest; and Shammah, the third oldest. 14 Now David was the youngest. While the three oldest sons followed Saul, 15 David was going back and forth from Saul in order to care for his father's sheep in Bethlehem.

16 Meanwhile for 40 days the Philistine approached every
morning and evening and took his position. 17 Jesse said to his
son David, "Take your brothers this ephah of roasted grain and
these 10 loaves of bread; go quickly to the camp to your brothers.
18 Also take these 10 portions of cheese to their commanding
officer. Find out how your brothers are doing and bring back
their pledge that they received the goods. 19 They are with Saul
and the whole Israelite army in the valley of Elah, fighting with
the Philistines."

20 So David got up early in the morning and entrusted the
flock to someone else who would watch over it. After loading
up, he went just as Jesse had instructed him. He arrived at the
camp as the army was going out to the battle lines shouting its
battle cry. 21 Israel and the Philistines drew up their battle lines
opposite one another. 22 After David had entrusted his cargo to
the care of the supply officer, he ran to the battlefront. When
he arrived, he asked his brothers how they were doing. 23 As
he was speaking with them, the champion named Goliath, the
Philistine from Gath, was coming up from the battle lines of the
Philistines. He spoke the way he usually did, and David heard
it. 24 When all the men of Israel saw this man, they retreated
from his presence and were very afraid.

25 The men of Israel said, "Have you seen this man who is
coming up? He does so to defy Israel. But the king will make
the man who can strike him down very wealthy! He will give
him his daughter in marriage, and he will make his father's
house exempt from tax obligations in Israel."

26 David asked the men who were standing near him, "What
will be done for the man who strikes down this Philistine
and frees Israel from this humiliation? For who is this uncircumcised Philistine, that he defies the armies of the living
God?" 27 The soldiers told him what had been promised, saying, "This is what will be done for the man who can strike him
down."

28 When David's oldest brother Eliab heard him speaking to
the men, he became angry with David and said, "Why have you
come down here? To whom did you entrust those few sheep in
the wilderness? I am familiar with your pride and deceit! You
have come down here to watch the battle."

29 David replied, "What have I done now? Can't I say anything?" 30 Then he turned from those who were nearby to someone else and asked the same question, but they gave him the
same answer as before. 31 When David's words were overheard
and reported to Saul, he called for him.

32 David said to Saul, "Don't let anyone be discouraged. Your
servant will go and fight this Philistine!" 33 But Saul replied to
David, "You aren't able to go against this Philistine and fight
him. You're just a boy! He has been a warrior from his youth."

34 David replied to Saul, "Your servant has been a shepherd
for his father's flock. Whenever a lion or bear would come and
carry off a sheep from the flock, 35 I would go out after it, strike it
down, and rescue the sheep from its mouth. If it rose up against
me, I would grab it by its jaw, strike it, and kill it. 36 Your servant
has struck down both the lion and the bear. This uncircumcised
Philistine will be just like one of them, for he has defied the
armies of the living God." 37 David went on to say, "The LORD
who delivered me from the lion and the bear will also deliver
me from the hand of this Philistine." Then Saul said to David,
"Go! The LORD will be with you."

38 Then Saul clothed David with his own fighting attire and
put a bronze helmet on his head. He also put body armor on
him. 39 David strapped on his sword over his fighting attire and
tried to walk around, but he was not used to them. David said to
Saul, "I can't walk in these things, for I'm not used to them." So
David removed them. 40 He took his staff in his hand, picked out
five smooth stones from the stream, placed them in the pouch
of his shepherd's bag, took his sling in hand, and approached
the Philistine.

41 The Philistine, with his shield bearer walking in front of
him, kept coming closer to David. 42 When the Philistine looked
carefully at David, he despised him, for he was only a ruddy
and handsome boy. 43 The Philistine said to David, "Am I a dog,
that you are coming after me with sticks?" Then the Philistine
cursed David by his gods. 44 The Philistine said to David, "Come
here to me, so I can give your flesh to the birds of the sky and
the wild animals of the field!"

45 But David replied to the Philistine, "You are coming against
me with sword and spear and javelin. But I am coming against
you in the name of the LORD of Heaven's Armies, the God of
Israel's armies, whom you have defied! 46 This very day the LORD
will deliver you into my hand. I will strike you down and cut
off your head. This day I will give the corpses of the Philistine
army to the birds of the sky and the wild animals of the land.
Then all the land will realize that Israel has a God, 47 and all
this assembly will know that it is not by sword or spear that
the LORD saves! For the battle is the LORD's, and he will deliver
you into our hand."

48 The Philistine drew steadily closer to David to attack him,
while David quickly ran toward the battle line to attack the
Philistine. 49 David reached his hand into the bag and took out
a stone. He slung it, striking the Philistine on the forehead. The
stone sank deeply into his forehead, and he fell down with his
face to the ground.

50 David prevailed over the Philistine with just the sling and
the stone. He struck down the Philistine and killed him. David
did not even have a sword in his hand. 51 David ran and stood
over the Philistine. He grabbed Goliath's sword, drew it from
its sheath, and after killing him, he cut off his head with it.
When the Philistines saw their champion was dead, they ran
away.

52 Then the men of Israel and Judah charged forward, shouting a battle cry. They chased the Philistines to the valley and
to the very gates of Ekron. The Philistine corpses lay fallen
along the Shaaraim road to Gath and Ekron. 53 When the Israelites returned from their hot pursuit of the Philistines, they
looted their camp. 54 David took the head of the Philistine and
brought it to Jerusalem, and he put Goliath's weapons in his
tent.

55 Now as Saul watched David going out to fight the Philistine,
he asked Abner, the general in command of the army, "Whose
son is that young man, Abner?" Abner replied, "As surely as
you live, O king, I don't know." 56 The king said, "Find out whose
son this boy is."

57 So when David returned from striking down the Philistine,
Abner took him and brought him before Saul. He still had the
head of the Philistine in his hand. 58 Saul said to him, "Whose
son are you, young man?" David replied, "I am the son of your
servant Jesse in Bethlehem."

SAUL COMES TO FEAR DAVID

18 When David had finished talking with Saul, Jonathan and David became bound together in close friendship. Jonathan loved David as much as he did his own life. [2]Saul retained David on that day and did not allow him to return to his father's house. [3]Jonathan made a covenant with David, for he loved him as much as he did his own life. [4]Jonathan took off the robe he was wearing and gave it to David, along with the rest of his gear including his sword, his bow, and even his belt.

[5]On every mission on which Saul sent him, David achieved success. So Saul appointed him over the men of war. This pleased not only all the army, but also Saul's servants.

[6]When the men arrived after David returned from striking down the Philistine, the women from all the cities of Israel came out singing and dancing to meet King Saul. They were happy as they played their tambourines and three-stringed instruments. [7]The women who were playing the music sang,

"Saul has struck down his thousands,
but David his tens of thousands!"

[8]This made Saul very angry. The statement displeased him and he thought, "They have attributed to David tens of thousands, but to me they have attributed only thousands. What does he lack, except the kingdom?" [9]So Saul was keeping an eye on David from that day onward.

[10]The next day an evil spirit from God rushed upon Saul and he prophesied within his house. Now David was playing the lyre as usual. There was a spear in Saul's hand, [11]and Saul threw the spear, thinking, "I'll nail David to the wall!" But David escaped from him on two different occasions.

[12]So Saul feared David, because the LORD was with David but had departed from Saul. [13]Saul removed David from his presence and made him a commanding officer. David led the army out to battle and back. [14]Now David achieved success in all he did, for the LORD was with him. [15]When Saul saw how very successful he was, he was afraid of him. [16]But all Israel and Judah loved David, for he was the one leading them out to battle and back.

[17]Then Saul said to David, "Here's my oldest daughter, Merab. I want to give her to you in marriage. Only be a brave warrior for me and fight the battles of the LORD." For Saul thought, "There's no need for me to raise my hand against him. Let it be the hand of the Philistines!"

[18]David said to Saul, "Who am I? Who are my relatives or the clan of my father in Israel that I should become the king's son-in-law?" [19]When the time came for Merab, Saul's daughter, to be given to David, she instead was given in marriage to Adriel, who was from Meholah.

[20]Now Michal, Saul's daughter, loved David. When they told Saul about this, it pleased him. [21]Saul said, "I will give her to him so that she may become a snare to him and so the hand of the Philistines may be against him." So Saul said to David, "Today is the second time for you to become my son-in-law."

[22]Then Saul instructed his servants, "Tell David secretly, 'The king is pleased with you, and all his servants like you. So now become the king's son-in-law.'" [23]So Saul's servants spoke these words privately to David. David replied, "Is becoming the king's son-in-law something insignificant to you? I'm just a poor and lightly esteemed man!"

18:1–16 The ground and foundation of true Christian friendship is the admiration of virtue or of some special gift of God that resides in another—the praise or use of which respects either God himself or a person. This moved Jonathan to knit himself in most firm friendship with David, whom for his valiant heart and noble courage in vanquishing proud Goliath he highly esteemed, honored, and entirely loved. Such persons—as either some singular gift of true godliness or some special praise of some moral virtue—excel others and are therefore worthily invested with the title of deserved commendation; these people we thoroughly love, entirely reverence, and heartily favor. For all true and holy friendship has its ground from God, in whom it is firmly established and by whom alone it continues sure, steadfast, and permanent.

LAMBERT DANEAU
(C. 1530–C. 1590)
TRUE AND CHRISTIAN FRIENDSHIP

24When Saul's servants reported what David had said, 25Saul
replied, "Here is what you should say to David: 'There is nothing
that the king wants as a price for the bride except 100 Philistine foreskins, so that he can be avenged of his enemies.'" (Now
Saul was thinking that he could kill David by the hand of the
Philistines.)
26So his servants told David these things and David agreed
to become the king's son-in-law. Now the specified time had
not yet expired 27when David, along with his men, went out and
struck down 200 Philistine men. David brought their foreskins
and presented all of them to the king so that he could become
the king's son-in-law. Saul then gave him his daughter Michal
in marriage.
28When Saul realized that the LORD was with David and that
his daughter Michal loved David, 29Saul became even more
afraid of him. Saul continued to be at odds with David from
then on. 30The leaders of the Philistines would march out, and
as often as they did so, David achieved more success than all of
Saul's servants. His name was held in high esteem.

SAUL REPEATEDLY ATTEMPTS TO TAKE DAVID'S LIFE

19 Then Saul told his son Jonathan and all his servants to
kill David. But Saul's son Jonathan liked David very much.
2So Jonathan told David, "My father Saul is trying to kill you.
So be careful tomorrow morning. Find a hiding place and stay
in seclusion. 3I will go out and stand beside my father in the
field where you are. I will speak to my father about you. When
I find out what the problem is, I will let you know."
4So Jonathan spoke on David's behalf to his father Saul. He
said to him, "The king should not sin against his servant David,
for he has not sinned against you. On the contrary, his actions
have been very beneficial for you. 5He risked his life when he
struck down the Philistine, and the LORD gave all Israel a great
victory. When you saw it, you were happy. So why would you
sin against innocent blood by putting David to death for no
reason?"
6Saul accepted Jonathan's advice and took an oath, "As surely
as the LORD lives, he will not be put to death." 7Then Jonathan
called David and told him all these things. Jonathan brought
David to Saul, and he served him as he had done formerly.
8Now once again there was war. So David went out to fight
the Philistines. He defeated them thoroughly, and they ran away
from him. 9Then an evil spirit from the LORD came upon Saul.
He was sitting in his house with his spear in his hand, while
David was playing the lyre. 10Saul tried to nail David to the wall
with the spear, but he escaped from Saul's presence, and the
spear drove into the wall. David escaped quickly that night.
11Saul sent messengers to David's house to guard it and to
kill him in the morning. Then David's wife Michal told him, "If
you do not save yourself tonight, tomorrow you will be dead!"
12So Michal lowered David through the window, and he ran
away and escaped.
13Then Michal took a household idol and put it on the bed.
She put a quilt made of goats' hair over its head and then covered the idol with a garment. 14When Saul sent messengers to
arrest David, she said, "He's sick."
15Then Saul sent the messengers back to see David, saying,
"Bring him up to me on his bed so I can kill him." 16When the

19:1–24 The notion that God delivers his chosen from their enemies is not written for David only, but also for all those who suffer tribulation. For I, John Knox—let this be said to the acclaim and praise of God alone—in anguish of mind and vehement tribulation and affliction called on the Lord when not only the ungodly but even my faithful brothers judged my case to be irremediable. And yet, in my greatest calamity, and when my pains were most cruel, God's eternal wisdom willed that I should be a writer, which his mercy has proved true, blessed be his holy name. And therefore I dare to be bold in the truth of God's Word to promise that—notwithstanding the vehemence of trouble, the long continuance of it, the despair of all people and the fearfulness, danger, pain, and anguish of our own hearts—yet if we call constantly to God, even beyond all human expectation, he shall deliver.

JOHN KNOX (C. 1514–1572)
A TREATISE ON PRAYER

messengers came, they found only the idol on the bed and the quilt made of goats' hair at its head.

[17]Saul said to Michal, "Why have you deceived me this way by sending my enemy away? Now he has escaped!" Michal replied to Saul, "He said to me, 'Help me get away or else I will kill you!'"

[18]Now David had run away and escaped. He went to Samuel in Ramah and told him everything that Saul had done to him. Then he and Samuel went and stayed at Naioth. [19]It was reported to Saul saying, "David is at Naioth in Ramah." [20]So Saul sent messengers to capture David. When they saw a company of prophets prophesying with Samuel standing there as their leader, the Spirit of God came upon Saul's messengers, and they also prophesied. [21]When it was reported to Saul, he sent more messengers, but they prophesied too. So Saul sent messengers a third time, but they also prophesied. [22]Finally Saul himself went to Ramah. When he arrived at the large cistern that is in Secu, he asked, "Where are Samuel and David?" They said, "At Naioth in Ramah."

[23]So Saul went to Naioth in Ramah. The Spirit of God came upon him as well, and he walked along prophesying until he came to Naioth in Ramah. [24]He even stripped off his clothes and prophesied before Samuel. He lay there naked all that day and night. (For that reason it is asked, "Is Saul also among the prophets?")

JONATHAN SEEKS TO PROTECT DAVID

20 David fled from Naioth in Ramah. He came to Jonathan and asked, "What have I done? What is my offense? How have I sinned before your father, that he is seeking my life?"

[2]Jonathan said to him, "By no means are you going to die! My father does nothing large or small without making me aware of it. Why would my father hide this matter from me? It just won't happen!"

[3]Taking an oath, David again said, "Your father is very much aware of the fact that I have found favor with you, and he has thought, 'Don't let Jonathan know about this, or he will be upset.' But as surely as the LORD lives and you live, there is about one step between me and death!" [4]Jonathan replied to David, "Tell me what I can do for you."

[5]David said to Jonathan, "Tomorrow is the new moon, and I am certainly expected to join the king for a meal. You must send me away so I can hide in the field until the third evening from now. [6]If your father happens to miss me, you should say, 'David urgently requested me to let him go to his town Bethlehem, for there is an annual sacrifice there for his entire family.' [7]If he should then say, 'That's fine,' then your servant is safe. But if he becomes very angry, be assured that he has decided to harm me. [8]You must be loyal to your servant, for you have made a covenant with your servant in the LORD's name. If I am guilty, you yourself kill me! Why bother taking me to your father?"

[9]Jonathan said, "Far be it from you to suggest this! If I were at all aware that my father had decided to harm you, wouldn't I tell you about it?" [10]David said to Jonathan, "Who will tell me if your father answers you harshly?" [11]Jonathan said to David, "Come on. Let's go out to the field."

When the two of them had gone out into the field, [12]Jonathan said to David, "The LORD God of Israel is my witness! I will feel out my father about this time the day after tomorrow. If he is favorably inclined toward David, will I not

20:1–16 David began to doubt even most faithful Jonathan's friendship, loyalty, and help. These words reveal David's mistrustful mind. We focus on how plainly hopeless perfection is; we will never be able to achieve it. For who will dare to boast of their perfection when they see David's weak faith and elsewhere that he falls into such stupid and shameful deeds—and not only when we regard this one man but also so great a host of God's saints? So then, let us consider the saints' weakness and sin so that, firm in the faith, even when we fail through our weakness, we would always fear, trust, and pray to God; so that when we stand firm, God would guard us through his grace, not desert us, and when we fail, through his mercy he would lift us up and sustain us.

JUSTUS MENIUS **(1499–1558)**
COMMENTARY ON FIRST SAMUEL

then send word to you and let you know? 13 But if my father
intends to do you harm, may the LORD do all this and more
to Jonathan if I don't let you know and send word to you, so
you can go safely on your way. May the LORD be with you, as
he was with my father. 14 While I am still alive, extend to me
the loyalty of the LORD, or else I will die. 15 Don't ever cut off
your loyalty to my family, not even when the LORD has cut
off every one of David's enemies from the face of the earth
16 and called David's enemies to account." So Jonathan made a
covenant with the house of David. 17 Jonathan once again took
an oath with David, because he loved him. In fact Jonathan
loved him as much as he did his own life. 18 Jonathan said to
him, "Tomorrow is the new moon, and you will be missed,
for your seat will be empty. 19 On the third day you should go
down quickly and come to the place where you hid yourself
the day this all started. Stay near the stone Ezel. 20 I will shoot
three arrows near it, as though I were shooting at a target.
21 When I send a boy after them, I will say, 'Go and find the
arrows.' If I say to the boy, 'Look, the arrows are on this side
of you; get them,' then come back. For as surely as the LORD
lives, you will be safe and there will be no problem. 22 But if I
say to the boy, 'Look, the arrows are on the other side of you,'
then get away. For in that case the LORD has sent you away.
23 With regard to the matter that you and I discussed, the
LORD is the witness between us forever."

24 So David hid in the field. When the new moon came, the
king sat down to eat his meal. 25 The king sat down in his usual
place by the wall, with Jonathan opposite him and Abner at his
side. But David's place was vacant. 26 However, Saul said nothing
about it that day, for he thought, "Something has happened to
make him ceremonially unclean. Yes, he must be unclean." 27 But
the next morning, the second day of the new moon, David's
place was still vacant. So Saul said to his son Jonathan, "Why
has Jesse's son not come to the meal yesterday or today?"

28 Jonathan replied to Saul, "David urgently requested that
he be allowed to go to Bethlehem. 29 He said, 'Permit me to go,
for we are having a family sacrifice in the town, and my brother
urged me to be there. So now, if I have found favor with you,
let me go to see my brothers.' For that reason he has not come
to the king's table."

30 Saul became angry with Jonathan and said to him, "You
stupid traitor! Don't I realize that to your own disgrace and
to the disgrace of your mother's nakedness you have chosen
this son of Jesse? 31 For as long as this son of Jesse is alive on
the earth, you and your kingdom will not be established. Now,
send some men and bring him to me. For he is as good as dead!"

32 Jonathan responded to his father Saul, "Why should he
be put to death? What has he done?" 33 Then Saul threw his
spear at Jonathan in order to strike him down. So Jonathan was
convinced that his father had decided to kill David. 34 Jonathan
got up from the table enraged. He did not eat any food on that
second day of the new moon, for he was upset that his father
had humiliated David.

35 The next morning Jonathan, along with a young servant,
went out to the field to meet David. 36 He said to his servant, "Run,
find the arrows that I am about to shoot." As the servant ran,
Jonathan shot the arrow beyond him. 37 When the servant
came to the place where Jonathan had shot the arrow, Jonathan called out to the servant, "Isn't the arrow farther beyond

you?" 38Jonathan called out to the servant, "Hurry! Go faster! Don't delay!" Jonathan's servant retrieved the arrow and came back to his master. 39(Now the servant did not understand any of this. Only Jonathan and David knew what was going on.) 40Then Jonathan gave his equipment to the servant who was with him. He said to him, "Go, take these things back to the town."

41When the servant had left, David got up from beside the mound, knelt with his face to the ground, and bowed three times. Then they kissed each other and they both wept, especially David. 42Jonathan said to David, "Go in peace, for the two of us have sworn together in the name of the LORD saying, 'The LORD will be between me and you and between my descendants and your descendants forever.'"

DAVID GOES TO NOB

Then David got up and left, while Jonathan went back to the

21 town of Naioth. 1David went to Ahimelech the priest in Nob. Ahimelech was shaking with fear when he met David, and said to him, "Why are you by yourself with no one accompanying you?" 2David replied to Ahimelech the priest, "The king instructed me to do something, but he said to me, 'Don't let anyone know the reason I am sending you or the instructions I have given you.' I have told my soldiers to wait at a certain place. 3Now what do you have at your disposal? Give me five loaves of bread, or whatever can be found."

4The priest replied to David, "I don't have any ordinary bread at my disposal. Only holy bread is available, and then only if your soldiers have abstained from relations with women." 5David said to the priest, "Certainly women have been kept away from us, just as on previous occasions when I have set out. The soldiers' equipment is holy, even on an ordinary journey. How much more so will they be holy today, along with their equipment!"

6So the priest gave him holy bread, for there was no bread there other than the Bread of the Presence. It had been removed from before the LORD in order to replace it with hot bread on the day it had been taken away. 7(One of Saul's servants was there that day, detained before the LORD. His name was Doeg the Edomite, who was in charge of Saul's shepherds.) 8David said to Ahimelech, "Is there no sword or spear here at your disposal? I don't have my own sword or equipment in hand due to the urgency of the king's instructions."

DAVID GOES TO GATH

9The priest replied, "The sword of Goliath the Philistine, whom you struck down in the valley of Elah, is wrapped in a garment behind the ephod. If you wish, take it for yourself. Other than that one, there's no sword here." David said, "There's nothing like it. Give it to me." 10So on that day David arose and fled from Saul. He went to King Achish of Gath. 11The servants of Achish said to him, "Isn't this David, the king of the land? Isn't he the one that they sing about when they dance, saying,

"'Saul struck down his thousands,
but David his tens of thousands'?"

12David thought about what they said and was very afraid of King Achish of Gath. 13He altered his behavior in their presence. Since he was in their power, he pretended to be insane,

21:1–9 In many other testimonies of the divine scriptures Christ appears both as king and as priest. With good reason therefore he is declared to be David's son more frequently than he is said to be Abraham's son. Matthew and Luke both affirmed this: the one viewing David as the person from whom, through Solomon, Jesus' lineage can be traced down, and the other taking David for the person to whom, through Nathan, Jesus' genealogy can be carried up. So David did represent the role of a priest, although he was patently a king, when he ate the Bread of the Presence. For it was not lawful for anyone to eat that except the priests alone.

AUGUSTINE **(354–430)**
HARMONY OF THE GOSPELS

making marks on the doors of the gate and letting his saliva run down his beard.
[14]Achish said to his servants, "Look at this madman! Why did you bring him to me? [15]Do I have a shortage of fools so that you have brought me this man to display his insanity in front of me? Should this man enter my house?"

DAVID GOES TO ADULLAM AND MIZPAH

22 So David left there and escaped to the cave of Adullam. When his brothers and the rest of his father's family learned about it, they went down there to him. [2]All those who were in trouble or owed someone money or were discontented gathered around him, and he became their leader. He had about 400 men with him.

[3]Then David went from there to Mizpah in Moab, where he said to the king of Moab, "Please let my father and mother stay with you until I know what God is going to do for me." [4]So he had them stay with the king of Moab; they stayed with him the whole time that David was in the stronghold. [5]Then Gad the prophet said to David, "Don't stay in the stronghold. Go to the land of Judah." So David left and went to the forest of Hereth.

SAUL EXECUTES THE PRIESTS

[6]But Saul found out the whereabouts of David and the men who were with him. Now Saul was sitting at Gibeah under the tamarisk tree at an elevated location with his spear in hand and all his servants stationed around him. [7]Saul said to his servants, "Listen up, you Benjaminites! Is Jesse's son giving fields and vineyards to all of you? Or is he making all of you commanders and officers? [8]For all of you have conspired against me! No one informs me when my own son makes an agreement with the son of Jesse. Not one of you feels sorry for me or informs me that my own son has commissioned my own servant to hide in ambush against me, as is the case today!"

[9]But Doeg the Edomite, who had stationed himself with the servants of Saul, replied, "I saw this son of Jesse come to Ahimelech son of Ahitub at Nob. [10]He inquired of the LORD for him and gave him provisions. He also gave him the sword of Goliath the Philistine."

[11]Then the king arranged for a meeting with the priest Ahimelech son of Ahitub and all the priests of his father's house who were at Nob. They all came to the king. [12]Then Saul said, "Listen, son of Ahitub." He replied, "Here I am, my lord." [13]Saul said to him, "Why have you conspired against me, you and this son of Jesse? You gave him bread and a sword and inquired of God on his behalf, so that he opposes me and waits in ambush, as is the case today!"

[14]Ahimelech replied to the king, "Who among all your servants is faithful like David? He is the king's son-in-law, the leader of your bodyguard, and honored in your house. [15]Was it just today that I began to inquire of God on his behalf? Far be it from me! The king should not accuse his servant or any of my father's house, for your servant is not aware of all this—not in whole or in part!"

[16]But the king said, "You will surely die, Ahimelech, you and all your father's house!" [17]Then the king said to the messengers who were stationed beside him, "Turn and kill the priests of the LORD, for they too have sided with David. They knew he was

22:1–5 God promised David a kingdom but immediately stirred up King Saul against him to persecute him, to hunt him as hunters do hares with greyhounds, and to ferret him out of every hole. And God did this for the space of many years to tame David, to make him meek, to kill his lusts, to make him feel other people's infirmities, to make him merciful, and to make him understand that he was made king to minister and serve. In short, he was persecuted so that he should not think his subjects were made to minister to his lusts, or that it was lawful for him to take away from them life and goods at his pleasure.

WILLIAM TYNDALE
(C. 1494–C. 1536)
DOCTRINAL TREATISES AND INTRODUCTIONS TO OTHER PORTIONS OF HOLY SCRIPTURES

fleeing, but they did not inform me." But the king's servants
refused to harm the priests of the LORD.
18Then the king said to Doeg, "You turn and strike down
the priests!" So Doeg the Edomite turned and struck down the
priests. He killed on that day 85 men who wore the linen ephod.
19As for Nob, the city of the priests, Doeg struck down men and
women, children and infants, oxen, donkeys, and sheep—all
with the sword.
20But one of the sons of Ahimelech son of Ahitub escaped
and fled to David. His name was Abiathar. 21Abiathar told David
that Saul had killed the priests of the LORD. 22Then David said
to Abiathar, "I knew that day when Doeg the Edomite was there
that he would certainly tell Saul! I am guilty of all the deaths in
your father's house. 23Stay with me. Don't be afraid. Whoever
seeks my life is seeking your life as well. You are secure with me."

DAVID DELIVERS THE CITY OF KEILAH

23 They told David, "The Philistines are fighting in Keilah
and are looting the threshing floors." 2So David asked the
LORD, "Should I go and strike down these Philistines?" The LORD
said to David, "Go, strike down the Philistines and deliver Keilah."
3But David's men said to him, "We are afraid while we are
still here in Judah. What will it be like if we go to Keilah against
the armies of the Philistines?" 4So David asked the LORD once
again. But again the LORD replied, "Arise, go down to Keilah,
for I will give the Philistines into your hand."
5So David and his men went to Keilah and fought the Philistines. He took away their cattle and thoroughly defeated them.
David delivered the inhabitants of Keilah.

DAVID ELUDES SAUL AGAIN

6Now when Abiathar son of Ahimelech had fled to David at
Keilah, he had brought with him an ephod. 7When Saul was told
that David had come to Keilah, Saul said, "God has delivered
him into my hand, for he has boxed himself into a corner by
entering a city with two barred gates." 8So Saul mustered all
his army to go down to Keilah and besiege David and his men.
9When David realized that Saul was planning to harm him,
he told Abiathar the priest, "Bring the ephod." 10Then David
said, "O LORD God of Israel, your servant has clearly heard that
Saul is planning to come to Keilah to destroy the city because
of me. 11Will the leaders of Keilah deliver me into his hand?
Will Saul come down as your servant has heard? O LORD God
of Israel, please inform your servant."
Then the LORD said, "He will come down." 12David asked,
"Will the leaders of Keilah deliver me and my men into Saul's
hand?" The LORD said, "They will deliver you over."
13So David and his men, who numbered about 600, set out
and left Keilah; they moved around from one place to another.
When told that David had escaped from Keilah, Saul called a halt
to his expedition. 14David stayed in the strongholds that were in
the desert and in the hill country of the wilderness of Ziph. Saul
looked for him all the time, but God did not deliver David into
his hands. 15David realized that Saul had come out to seek his
life; at that time David was in Horesh in the wilderness of Ziph.
16Then Jonathan son of Saul left and went to David at Horesh.
He encouraged him through God. 17He said to him, "Don't be
afraid! For the hand of my father Saul cannot find you. You
will rule over Israel, and I will be your second-in-command.

23:14–29 Friendship does not cease or utterly perish even when absent because it grows on just and reasonable causes. As we may see in David and Jonathan, the whole friendship continued and lasted despite the one being absent from the other, for such deep-rooted goodwill and such ardent affection cannot be easily quenched. Therefore friendship—being strongly and surely grounded between persons present—continues still between them when they are absent. And the further they are separated, the greater is the longing desire of one for the other and the more vehemently their inflamed hearts increase.

LAMBERT DANEAU
(C. 1530–C. 1590)
TRUE AND CHRISTIAN FRIENDSHIP

Even my father Saul realizes this.” 18When the two of them had
made a covenant before the LORD, David stayed at Horesh, but
Jonathan went to his house.
19Then the Ziphites went up to Saul at Gibeah and said, “Isn’t
David hiding among us in the strongholds at Horesh on the hill
of Hakilah, south of Jeshimon? 20Now at your own discretion,
O king, come down. Delivering him into the king’s hand will
be our responsibility.”
21Saul replied, “May you be blessed by the LORD, for you have
had compassion on me. 22Go and make further arrangements.
Determine precisely where he is and who has seen him there,
for I am told that he is extremely cunning. 23Locate precisely
all the places where he hides and return to me with dependable
information. Then I will go with you. If he is in the land, I will
find him among all the thousands of Judah.”
24So they left and went to Ziph ahead of Saul. Now David
and his men were in the wilderness of Maon, in the rift valley
to the south of Jeshimon. 25Saul and his men went to look for
him. But David was informed and went down to the rock and
stayed in the wilderness of Maon. When Saul heard about it,
he pursued David in the wilderness of Maon. 26Saul went on
one side of the mountain, while David and his men went on
the other side of the mountain. David was hurrying to get away
from Saul, but Saul and his men were surrounding David and his
men to capture them. 27But a messenger came to Saul saying,
“Come quickly, for the Philistines have raided the land!”
28So Saul stopped pursuing David and went to confront the
Philistines. Therefore that place is called Sela Hammahlekoth.
29Then David went up from there and stayed in the strongholds
of En Gedi.

DAVID SPARES SAUL’S LIFE

24 When Saul returned from pursuing the Philistines, he was
told, “Look, David is in the desert of En Gedi.” 2So Saul
took 3,000 select men from all Israel and went to find David
and his men in the region of the rocks of the mountain goats.
3He came to the sheepfolds by the road, where there was a cave.
Saul went into it to relieve himself.
Now David and his men were sitting in the recesses of the
cave. 4David’s men said to him, “This is the day about which the
LORD said to you, ‘I will give your enemy into your hand, and you
can do to him whatever seems appropriate to you.’” So David
got up and quietly cut off an edge of Saul’s robe. 5Afterward
David’s conscience bothered him because he had cut off an
edge of Saul’s robe. 6He said to his men, “May the LORD keep me
far away from doing such a thing to my lord, who is the LORD’s
chosen one, by extending my hand against him. After all, he is
the LORD’s chosen one.” 7David restrained his men with these
words and did not allow them to rise up against Saul. Then Saul
left the cave and started down the road.
8Afterward David got up and went out of the cave. He called
out to Saul, “My lord, O king!” When Saul looked behind him,
David kneeled down and bowed with his face to the ground.
9David said to Saul, “Why do you pay attention when men say,
‘David is seeking to do you harm’? 10Today your own eyes see
how the LORD delivered you—this very day—into my hands in
the cave. Some told me to kill you, but I had pity on you and
said, ‘I will not extend my hand against my lord, for he is the
LORD’s chosen one.’ 11Look, my father, and see the edge of your

24:1–22 The one who forbears conquers the very malice of his enemy. For when two competitors are in contention and conflict, the one who draws the other into similarity with itself conquers, and the one who is drawn and changed by the other is conquered. We say water is overcome by fire when it becomes warm, and on the contrary to have overcome it if, retaining its own cold, it can subdue the fire. We see a beautiful example of this here where David, by forbearing and refraining from revenge, so mollified and changed Saul from breathing blood and slaughter that he melted into tears and entreaties, confessed his fault, and was compelled to acknowledge and extol David’s innocence and meekness. Who does not here see the malice of Saul overcome and the patience of David triumphant?

JOHN DAVENANT (1572–1641)
EXPOSITION ON COLOSSIANS

robe in my hand! When I cut off the edge of your robe, I didn't
kill you. So realize and understand that I am not planning evil
or rebellion. Even though I have not sinned against you, you
are waiting in ambush to take my life. 12May the LORD judge
between the two of us, and may the LORD vindicate me over you,
but my hand will not be against you. 13It's like the old proverb
says: 'From evil people evil proceeds.' But my hand will not be
against you. 14Who has the king of Israel come out after? Who
is it that you are pursuing? A dead dog? A single flea? 15May
the LORD be our judge and arbiter. May he see and arbitrate
my case and deliver me from your hands."
16When David finished speaking these words to Saul, Saul
said, "Is that your voice, my son David?" Then Saul wept loudly.
17He said to David, "You are more innocent than I, for you have
treated me well, even though I have tried to harm you. 18You
have explained today how you have treated me well. The LORD
delivered me into your hand, but you did not kill me. 19Now
if a man finds his enemy, does he send him on his way in good
shape? May the LORD repay you with good this day for what
you have done to me. 20Now look, I realize that you will in fact
be king and that the kingdom of Israel will be established in
your hands. 21So now swear to me in the LORD's name that you
will not kill my descendants after me or destroy my name from
the house of my father."
22David promised Saul this on oath. Then Saul went to his
house, and David and his men went up to the stronghold.

THE DEATH OF SAMUEL

25 Samuel died, and all Israel assembled and mourned him.
They buried him at his home in Ramah. Then David left
and went down to the wilderness of Paran.

DAVID MARRIES ABIGAIL THE WIDOW OF NABAL

2There was a man in Maon whose business was in Carmel. This
man was very wealthy; he owned 3,000 sheep and 1,000 goats.
At that time he was shearing his sheep in Carmel. 3The man's
name was Nabal, and his wife's name was Abigail. She was both
wise and beautiful, but the man was harsh and his deeds were
evil. He was a Calebite.
4When David heard in the wilderness that Nabal was shearing his sheep, 5he sent 10 servants, saying to them, "Go up to
Carmel to see Nabal and give him greetings in my name. 6Then
you will say to my brother, 'Peace to you and your house! Peace
to all that is yours! 7Now I hear that they are shearing sheep for
you. When your shepherds were with us, we neither insulted
them nor harmed them the whole time they were in Carmel.
8Ask your own servants; they can tell you! May my servants find
favor in your sight, for we have come at the time of a holiday.
Please provide us—your servants and your son David—with
whatever you can spare.'"
9So David's servants went and spoke all these words to Nabal
in David's name. Then they paused. 10But Nabal responded to
David's servants, "Who is David, and who is this son of Jesse?
This is a time when many servants are breaking away from their
masters! 11Should I take my bread and my water and my meat
that I have slaughtered for my shearers and give them to these
men? I don't even know where they came from!"
12So David's servants went on their way. When they had
returned, they came and told David all these things. 13Then

David instructed his men, "Each of you strap on your sword!" So each one strapped on his sword, and David also strapped on his sword. About 400 men followed David, while 200 stayed behind with the equipment.

14But one of the servants told Nabal's wife Abigail, "David sent messengers from the wilderness to greet our lord, but he screamed at them. 15These men were very good to us. They did not insult us, nor did we sustain any loss during the entire time we were together in the field. 16Both night and day they were a protective wall for us the entire time we were with them, while we were tending our flocks. 17Now be aware of this, and see what you can do. For disaster has been planned for our lord and his entire household. He is such a wicked person that no one tells him anything!"

18So Abigail quickly took 200 loaves of bread, two containers of wine, five prepared sheep, five seahs of roasted grain, 100 bunches of raisins, and 200 lumps of pressed figs. She loaded them on donkeys 19and said to her servants, "Go on ahead of me. I will come after you." But she did not tell her husband Nabal. 20Riding on her donkey, she went down under cover of the mountain. David and his men were coming down to meet her, and she encountered them. 21Now David had been thinking, "In vain I guarded everything that belonged to this man in the wilderness. I didn't take anything from him. But he has repaid my good with evil. 22God will severely punish David, if I leave alive until morning even one male from all those who belong to him!"

25:23–31 David already before this had in his indignation held back his armed hand. How much greater a thing it is not to revile again than not to avenge oneself! The warriors prepared to take vengeance against Nabal, Abigail restrained by her prayers. Thus we perceive that we ought not only to yield to timely entreaties but also to be pleased with them. So much was David pleased that he blessed her who intervened because he was restrained from his desire for revenge.

AMBROSE **(C. 339–C. 397)**
ON THE DUTIES OF THE CLERGY

23When Abigail saw David, she got down quickly from the donkey, threw herself facedown before David, and bowed to the ground. 24Falling at his feet, she said, "My lord, I accept all the guilt! But please let your female servant speak to you! Please listen to the words of your servant! 25My lord should not pay attention to this wicked man Nabal. He simply lives up to his name! His name means 'fool,' and he is indeed foolish! But I, your servant, did not see the servants my lord sent.

26"Now, my lord, as surely as the LORD lives and as surely as you live, it is the LORD who has kept you from shedding blood and taking matters into your own hands. Now may your enemies and those who seek to harm my lord be like Nabal. 27Now let this present that your servant has brought to my lord be given to the servants who follow my lord. 28Please forgive the sin of your servant, for the LORD will certainly establish a lasting dynasty for my lord, because my lord fights the battles of the LORD. May no evil be found in you all your days! 29When someone sets out to chase you and to take your life, the life of my lord will be wrapped securely in the bag of the living by the LORD your God. But he will sling away the lives of your enemies from the sling's pocket! 30The LORD will do for my lord everything that he promised you, and he will make you a leader over Israel. 31Your conscience will not be overwhelmed with guilt for having poured out innocent blood and for having taken matters into your own hands. When the LORD has granted my lord success, please remember your servant."

32Then David said to Abigail, "Praised be the LORD, the God of Israel, who has sent you this day to meet me! 33Praised be your good judgment! May you yourself be rewarded for having prevented me this day from shedding blood and taking matters into my own hands! 34Otherwise, as surely as the LORD, the God of Israel, lives—he who has prevented me from harming you—if

you had not come so quickly to meet me, by morning's light not
even one male belonging to Nabal would have remained alive!"
35Then David took from her hand what she had brought to him.
He said to her, "Go back to your home in peace. Be assured that
I have listened to you and responded favorably."
36When Abigail went back to Nabal, he was holding a banquet
in his house like that of the king. Nabal was having a good time
and was very intoxicated. She told him absolutely nothing until
morning's light. 37In the morning, when Nabal was sober, his
wife told him about these matters. He had a stroke and was
paralyzed. 38After about 10 days the LORD struck Nabal down
and he died.
39When David heard that Nabal had died, he said, "Praised be
the LORD who has vindicated me and avenged the insult that I
suffered from Nabal! The LORD has kept his servant from doing
evil, and he has repaid Nabal for his evil deeds." Then David sent
word to Abigail and asked her to become his wife.
40So the servants of David went to Abigail at Carmel and said
to her, "David has sent us to you to bring you back to be his wife."
41She arose, bowed her face toward the ground, and said, "Your
female servant, like a lowly servant, will wash the feet of the
servants of my lord." 42Then Abigail quickly went and mounted
her donkey, with five of her female servants accompanying her.
She followed David's messengers and became his wife.
43David had also married Ahinoam from Jezreel; the two of
them became his wives. 44(Now Saul had given his daughter Michal,
David's wife, to Paltiel son of Laish, who was from Gallim.)

DAVID SPARES SAUL'S LIFE AGAIN

26 The Ziphites came to Saul at Gibeah and said, "Isn't David
hiding on the hill of Hakilah near Jeshimon?" 2So Saul
arose and went down to the wilderness of Ziph, accompanied
by 3,000 select men of Israel, to look for David in the wilderness of Ziph. 3Saul camped by the road on the hill of Hakilah
near Jeshimon, but David was staying in the wilderness. When
he realized that Saul had come to the wilderness to find him,
4David sent scouts and verified that Saul had indeed arrived.
5So David set out and went to the place where Saul was
camped. David saw the place where Saul and Abner son of Ner,
the general in command of his army, were sleeping. Now Saul
was lying in the entrenchment, and the army was camped all
around him. 6David said to Ahimelech the Hittite and Abishai
son of Zeruiah, Joab's brother, "Who will go down with me to
Saul in the camp?" Abishai replied, "I will go down with you."
7So David and Abishai approached the army at night and
found Saul lying asleep in the entrenchment with his spear
stuck in the ground by his head. Abner and the army were lying
all around him. 8Abishai said to David, "Today God has delivered
your enemy into your hands. Now let me drive the spear right
through him into the ground with one swift jab! A second jab
won't be necessary!"
9But David said to Abishai, "Don't kill him! Who can extend
his hand against the LORD's chosen one and remain guiltless?"
10David went on to say, "As the LORD lives, the LORD himself
will strike him down. Either his day will come and he will die,
or he will go down into battle and be swept away. 11But may the
LORD prevent me from extending my hand against the LORD's
chosen one! Now take the spear by Saul's head and the jug of
water, and let's get out of here!" 12So David took the spear and

26:1–25 All things are possible to the one who believes. And therefore in our prayers desperation is always to be expelled. Trouble and fear are the very spurs to prayer. For when a person, encircled with vehement calamities and vexed with continual anxiety—having no hope of deliverance with an oppressed and punished heart—calls to God for comfort and support, such prayer ascends to God's presence and does not return in vain. This is seen, for instance, in Saul's vehement persecution of David, as the latter was hunted and chased from every hole, fearing that one day or other he should fall into the hands of his persecutors. After that he complained that no place of rest was left to him. In the midst of these anguishes, the goodness of God sustained David so that the present tribulation was tolerable. And the infallible promises of God so assured him of deliverance that fear was partially mitigated and gone, as plainly appears to those who diligently observe the process of his prayer.

JOHN KNOX **(C. 1514–1572)**
A TREATISE ON PRAYER

the jug of water by Saul's head, and they got out of there. No one saw them or was aware of their presence or woke up. All of them were asleep, for the LORD had caused a deep sleep to fall on them.

[13]Then David crossed to the other side and stood on the top of the hill some distance away; there was a considerable distance between them. [14]David called to the army and to Abner son of Ner, "Won't you answer, Abner?" Abner replied, "Who are you, that you have called to the king?" [15]David said to Abner, "Aren't you a man? After all, who is like you in Israel? Why then haven't you protected your lord the king? One of the soldiers came to kill your lord the king. [16]This failure on your part isn't good! As surely as the LORD lives, you people who have not protected your lord, the LORD's chosen one, are as good as dead! Now look where the king's spear and the jug of water that was by his head are!"

[17]When Saul recognized David's voice, he said, "Is that your voice, my son David?" David replied, "Yes, it's my voice, my lord the king." [18]He went on to say, "Why is my lord chasing his servant? What have I done? What wrong have I done? [19]So let my lord the king now listen to the words of his servant. If the LORD has incited you against me, may he take delight in an offering. But if men have instigated this, may they be cursed before the LORD! For they have driven me away this day from being united with the LORD's inheritance, saying, 'Go on, serve other gods!' [20]Now don't let my blood fall to the ground away from the LORD's presence, for the king of Israel has gone out to look for a flea the way one looks for a partridge in the hill country."

[21]Saul replied, "I have sinned. Come back, my son David. I won't harm you anymore, for you treated my life with value this day. I have behaved foolishly and have made a very terrible mistake!" [22]David replied, "Here is the king's spear! Let one of your servants cross over and get it. [23]The LORD rewards each man for his integrity and loyalty. Even though today the LORD delivered you into my hand, I was not willing to extend my hand against the LORD's chosen one. [24]In the same way that I valued your life this day, may the LORD value my life and deliver me from all danger." [25]Saul replied to David, "May you be rewarded, my son David! You will without question be successful!" So David went on his way, and Saul returned to his place.

DAVID ALIGNS HIMSELF WITH THE PHILISTINES

27 David thought to himself, "One of these days I'm going to be swept away by the hand of Saul! There is nothing better for me than to escape to the land of the Philistines. Then Saul will despair of searching for me through all the territory of Israel and I will escape from his hand."

[2]So David left and crossed over to King Achish son of Maoch of Gath accompanied by his 600 men. [3]David settled with Achish in Gath, along with his men and their families. David had with him his two wives, Ahinoam the Jezreelite and Abigail the Carmelite, Nabal's widow. [4]When Saul learned that David had fled to Gath, he did not mount a new search for him.

[5]David said to Achish, "If I have found favor with you, let me be given a place in one of the country towns so that I can live there. Why should your servant settle in the royal city with you?" [6]So Achish gave him Ziklag on that day. (For that reason Ziklag has belonged to the kings of Judah until this very day.)

27:1—28:2 "One of these days I'm going to swept away by the hand of Saul!" The thought of David's heart at this time was a false thought. On no one occasion had the Lord deserted his servant. David should have argued from what God had done for him that God would be his defender still. But is it not just in the same way that we doubt God's help? Is it not mistrust without a cause? Have we ever had the shadow of a reason to doubt our Father's goodness? Have not his loving-kindnesses been marvelous? Has he once failed to justify our trust? Ah, no! Our God has not left us at any time. We have had dark nights, but the star of love has shone forth amid the blackness; we have been in stern conflicts, but over our head he has held aloft the shield of our defense. What we have known of our faithful God proves that he will keep us to the end. Let us not, then, reason contrary to evidence.

CHARLES SPURGEON
(1834–1892)
MORNING AND EVENING

[7]The length of time that David lived in the Philistine countryside was a year and four months.

[8]Then David and his men went up and raided the Geshurites, the Girzites, and the Amalekites. (They had been living in that land for a long time, from the approach to Shur as far as the land of Egypt.) [9]When David would attack a district, he would leave neither man nor woman alive. He would take sheep, cattle, donkeys, camels, and clothing and would then go back to Achish. [10]When Achish would ask, "Where did you raid today?" David would say, "The Negev of Judah" or "The Negev of Jerahmeel" or "The Negev of the Kenites." [11]Neither man nor woman would David leave alive so as to bring them back to Gath. He was thinking, "This way they can't tell on us, saying, 'This is what David did.'" Such was his practice the entire time that he lived in the country of the Philistines. [12]So Achish trusted David, thinking to himself, "He is really hated among his own people in Israel! From now on he will be my servant."

THE WITCH OF ENDOR

28 In those days the Philistines gathered their troops for war in order to fight Israel. Achish said to David, "You should fully understand that you and your men must go with me into the battle." [2]David replied to Achish, "That being the case, you will come to know what your servant can do!" Achish said to David, "Then I will make you my bodyguard from now on."

[3]Now Samuel had died, and all Israel had lamented over him and had buried him in Ramah, his hometown. In the meantime Saul had removed the mediums and magicians from the land. [4]The Philistines assembled; they came and camped at Shunem. Saul mustered all Israel and camped at Gilboa. [5]When Saul saw the camp of the Philistines, he was absolutely terrified. [6]So Saul inquired of the LORD, but the LORD did not answer him—not by dreams nor by Urim nor by the prophets. [7]So Saul instructed his servants, "Find me a woman who is a medium, so that I may go to her and inquire of her." His servants replied to him, "There is a woman who is a medium in Endor."

[8]So Saul disguised himself and put on other clothing and left, accompanied by two of his men. They came to the woman at night and said, "Use your ritual pit to conjure up for me the one I tell you."

[9]But the woman said to him, "Look, you are aware of what Saul has done; he has removed the mediums and magicians from the land! Why are you trapping me so you can put me to death?" [10]But Saul swore an oath to her by the LORD, "As surely as the LORD lives, you will not incur guilt in this matter!" [11]The woman replied, "Who is it that I should bring up for you?" He said, "Bring up for me Samuel."

[12]When the woman saw Samuel, she cried out loudly. The woman said to Saul, "Why have you deceived me? You are Saul!" [13]The king said to her, "Don't be afraid! But what have you seen?" The woman replied to Saul, "I have seen a divine being coming up from the ground!" [14]He said to her, "What about his appearance?" She said, "An old man is coming up! He is wrapped in a robe!"

Then Saul realized it was Samuel, and he bowed his face toward the ground and kneeled down. [15]Samuel said to Saul, "Why have you disturbed me by bringing me up?" Saul replied, "I am terribly troubled! The Philistines are fighting against me and God has turned away from me. He does not answer me

anymore—not by the prophets nor by dreams. So I have called
on you to tell me what I should do."
16Samuel said, "Why are you asking me, now that the LORD
has turned away from you and has become your enemy? 17The
LORD has done exactly as I prophesied! The LORD has torn the
kingdom from your hand and has given it to your neighbor David!
18Since you did not obey the LORD and did not carry out his fierce
anger against the Amalekites, the LORD has done this thing to
you today. 19The LORD will hand you and Israel over to the Philistines! Tomorrow both you and your sons will be with me. The
LORD will also hand the army of Israel over to the Philistines!"
20Saul quickly fell full length on the ground and was very
afraid because of Samuel's words. He was completely drained
of energy, having not eaten anything all that day and night.
21When the woman came to Saul and saw how terrified he was,
she said to him, "Your servant has done what you asked. I took
my life into my own hands and did what you told me. 22Now it's
your turn to listen to your servant! Let me set before you a bit
of bread so that you can eat. When you regain your strength,
you can go on your way."
23But he refused, saying, "I won't eat!" Both his servants and
the woman urged him to eat, so he gave in. He got up from
the ground and sat down on the bed. 24Now the woman had a
well-fed calf at her home that she quickly slaughtered. Taking
some flour, she kneaded it and baked bread without leaven.
25She brought it to Saul and his servants, and they ate. Then
they arose and left that same night.

DAVID IS REJECTED BY THE PHILISTINE LEADERS

29 The Philistines assembled all their troops at Aphek, while
Israel camped at the spring that is in Jezreel. 2When the
leaders of the Philistines were passing in review at the head
of their units of hundreds and thousands, David and his men
were passing in review in the rear with Achish.
3The leaders of the Philistines asked, "What about these
Hebrews?" Achish said to the leaders of the Philistines, "Isn't
this David, the servant of King Saul of Israel, who has been with
me for quite some time? I have found no fault with him from
the day of his defection until the present time!"
4But the leaders of the Philistines became angry with him
and said to him, "Send the man back! Let him return to the place
that you assigned him! Don't let him go down with us into the
battle, for he might become our adversary in the battle. What
better way to please his lord than with the heads of these men?
5Isn't this David, of whom they sang as they danced,

"'Saul has struck down his thousands,
but David his tens of thousands'?"

6So Achish summoned David and said to him, "As surely as
the LORD lives, you are an honest man, and I am glad to have
you serving with me in the army. I have found no fault with you
from the day that you first came to me until the present time.
But in the opinion of the leaders, you are not reliable. 7So turn
and leave in peace. You must not do anything that the leaders
of the Philistines consider improper!"
8But David said to Achish, "What have I done? What have you
found in your servant from the day that I first came into your
presence until the present time, that I shouldn't go and fight the
enemies of my lord the king?" 9Achish replied to David, "I am

29:1–11 The lords of the Philistines said, "What about these Hebrews?" They saw the inconsistency if David and his men did not. They were sharp to detect it, and David and his band did not rise in their opinion but decidedly went down when the Philistines saw them marching in such an unnatural place as "in the rear with Achish" and ready to flesh their swords in the blood of their brethren. So let me tell you, you will neither recommend your religion nor yourself to people of the world by inconsistently trying to identify yourselves with them. Do you think that the world respects those Christians or regards their religion as the kind of thing to be admired? No; the question that they fling at such people is the question that David was humiliated by having pitched at his head—"What about these Hebrews?" Let them go back to their mountains. This is no place for them. The world respects an out-and-out Christian, but neither God nor the world respects an inconsistent one.

ALEXANDER MACLAREN
(1826–1910)
EXPOSITIONS OF THE HOLY SCRIPTURES

convinced that you are as reliable as the angel of God! However, the leaders of the Philistines have said, 'He must not go up with us in the battle.' [10]So get up early in the morning along with the servants of your lord who have come with you. When you get up early in the morning, as soon as it is light enough to see, leave."

[11]So David and his men got up early in the morning to return to the land of the Philistines, but the Philistines went up to Jezreel.

DAVID DEFEATS THE AMALEKITES

30 On the third day David and his men came to Ziklag. Now the Amalekites had raided the Negev and Ziklag. They attacked Ziklag and burned it. [2]They took captive the women and all who were in it, from the youngest to the oldest, but they did not kill anyone. They simply carried them off and went on their way.

[3]When David and his men came to the city, they found it burned. Their wives, sons, and daughters had been taken captive. [4]Then David and the men who were with him wept loudly until they could weep no more. [5]David's two wives had been taken captive—Ahinoam the Jezreelite and Abigail the Carmelite, Nabal's widow. [6]David was very upset, for the men were thinking of stoning him; each man grieved bitterly over his sons and daughters. But David drew strength from the LORD his God.

[7]Then David said to the priest Abiathar son of Ahimelech, "Bring me the ephod." So Abiathar brought the ephod to David. [8]David inquired of the LORD, saying, "Should I pursue this raiding band? Will I overtake them?" He said to him, "Pursue, for you will certainly overtake them and carry out a rescue!"

[9]So David went, accompanied by his 600 men. When he came to the Wadi Besor, those who were in the rear stayed there. [10]David and 400 men continued the pursuit, but 200 men who were too exhausted to cross the Wadi Besor stayed there.

[11]Then they found an Egyptian in the field and brought him to David. They gave him bread to eat and water to drink. [12]They gave him a slice of pressed figs and two bunches of raisins to eat. This greatly refreshed him, for he had not eaten food or drunk water for three days and three nights. [13]David said to him, "To whom do you belong, and where are you from?" The young man said, "I am an Egyptian, the servant of an Amalekite man. My master abandoned me when I was ill for three days. [14]We conducted a raid on the Negev of the Kerethites, on the area of Judah, and on the Negev of Caleb. We burned Ziklag." [15]David said to him, "Can you take us down to this raiding party?" He said, "Swear to me by God that you will not kill me or hand me over to my master, and I will take you down to this raiding party."

[16]So he took David down, and they found them spread out over the land. They were eating and drinking and enjoying themselves because of all the loot they had taken from the land of the Philistines and from the land of Judah. [17]But David struck them down from twilight until the following evening. None of them escaped, with the exception of 400 young men who got away on camels. [18]David retrieved everything the Amalekites had taken; he also rescued his two wives. [19]There was nothing missing, whether small or great. He retrieved sons and daughters, the plunder, and everything else they had taken. David brought everything back. [20]David took all the flocks and

30:1–31 If in all our ways, even when as in this case there can be no doubt they are just, we acknowledge God, we may expect that he will direct our steps as he did those of David. David, in tenderness to his men, would by no means urge them beyond their strength. The Son of David thus considers the frames of his followers, who are not all alike strong and vigorous in their spiritual pursuits and conflicts. But where we are weak, there he is kind; more, there he is strong. A poor Egyptian lad, scarcely alive, is made the means of a great deal of good to David. Justly did Providence make this poor servant, who was basely used by his master, an instrument in the destruction of the Amalekites, for God hears the cry of the oppressed. Those are unworthy of the name of true Israelites who shut up their compassion from persons in distress. We should neither do an injury nor deny a kindness to any person; sometime or other it may be in the power of the lowest to return a kindness or an injury.

MATTHEW HENRY (1662–1714)
COMMENTARY ON THE WHOLE BIBLE

herds and drove them in front of the rest of the animals. People
were saying, "This is David's plunder!"
21 Then David approached the 200 men who had been too
exhausted to go with him, those whom they had left at the Wadi
Besor. They went out to meet David and the people who were
with him. When David approached the people, he asked how
they were doing. 22 But all the evil and worthless men among
those who had gone with David said, "Since they didn't go with
us, we won't give them any of the loot we retrieved! They may
take only their wives and children. Let them lead them away
and be gone!"
23 But David said, "No! You shouldn't do this, my brothers.
Look at what the LORD has given us! He has protected us and
has delivered into our hands the raiding party that came against
us. 24 Who will listen to you in this matter? The portion of the
one who went down into the battle will be the same as the
portion of the one who remained with the equipment! Let their
portions be the same!"
25 From that time onward it was a binding ordinance for Israel, right up to the present time.
26 When David came to Ziklag, he sent some of the plunder
to the elders of Judah who were his friends, saying, "Here's a
gift for you from the looting of the LORD's enemies!" 27 The gift
was for those in the following locations: for those in Bethel,
Ramoth Negev, and Jattir; 28 for those in Aroer, Siphmoth, Eshtemoa, 29 and Racal; for those in the cities of the Jerahmeelites
and Kenites; 30 for those in Hormah, Bor Ashan, Athach, 31 and
Hebron; and for those in whatever other places David and his
men had traveled.

THE DEATH OF SAUL

31 Now the Philistines were fighting against Israel. The men
of Israel fled from the Philistines and many of them fell
dead on Mount Gilboa. 2 The Philistines stayed right on the
heels of Saul and his sons. They struck down Saul's sons Jonathan, Abinadab, and Malki-Shua. 3 Saul himself was in the
thick of the battle; the archers spotted him and wounded him
severely.
4 Saul said to his armor-bearer, "Draw your sword and stab
me with it! Otherwise these uncircumcised people will come,
stab me, and torture me." But his armor-bearer refused to do
it, because he was very afraid. So Saul took his sword and fell
on it. 5 When his armor-bearer saw that Saul was dead, he also
fell on his own sword and died with him. 6 So Saul, his three
sons, his armor-bearer, and all his men died together that day.
7 When the men of Israel who were in the valley and across
the Jordan saw that the men of Israel had fled and that Saul
and his sons were dead, they abandoned the cities and fled. The
Philistines came and occupied them.
8 The next day, when the Philistines came to strip loot from
the corpses, they discovered Saul and his three sons lying dead
on Mount Gilboa. 9 They cut off Saul's head and stripped him
of his armor. They sent messengers to announce the news in
the temple of their idols and among their people throughout
the surrounding land of the Philistines. 10 They placed Saul's
armor in the temple of the Ashtoreths and hung his corpse on
the city wall of Beth Shan.
11 When the residents of Jabesh Gilead heard what the Philistines had done to Saul, 12 all their warriors set out and traveled

31:1–13 It is written in the Psalms: "The LORD values the lives of his faithful followers" (Ps 116:15). This is no less true for the righteous Jonathan, who died fighting for the Lord's inheritance. But against others it says in the song, "Those who hate the godly are punished" (Ps 34:21). You read that here as it applies to Saul, who did not hope in the God of Israel and instead consulted the medium. Therefore, when pressed by his enemies while desperately leading in battle, Saul perished like the apostle Judas, who also perished as one who had earlier been greatly blessed by God. In the end Saul was a blasphemer of the God of Israel among the Gentiles and those who exalt God in the holy places. This is how hypocrites meet their end. They reign gloriously and appear to be wise, righteous, and the savior of others, but their end reveals them to be in disgrace and blasphemy of God.

JOHANNES BUGENHAGEN
(1485–1558)
COMMENTARY ON FIRST SAMUEL

throughout the night. They took Saul's corpse and the corpses
of his sons from the city wall of Beth Shan and went to Jabesh,
where they burned them. 13They took the bones and buried
them under the tamarisk tree at Jabesh; then they fasted for
seven days.

AUTHOR	AUDIENCE	DATE	PURPOSE	THEMES
Unknown	God's chosen people, the Israelites	Sometime after Israel was divided into the northern and southern kingdoms in about 930 BC	This book continues the story of David: the establishment of his monarchy, his virtues and vices, and the reformation of Israel's religious life under his reign.	Establishment of David's monarchy; virtuous character; sin, repentance, and consequences; and the character of God

The second book of Samuel continues the story of David, who became king over Judah after the death of Saul. Anglican priest and Bible expositor Andrew Willet offered this summation of the book:

> The first [part] includes the beginning, increase, and flourishing of David's reign, and then the many troubles, treasons, and oppositions against his kingdom. It also includes the story of David's fall and his rise again and reconciliation with God. The second part includes a notable difference between the reign of Saul and of David. For Saul's kingdom began with great glory and renown but ended in shame. Conversely, David's kingdom had but small beginnings yet increased more and more. The final part demonstrates how David was a lively type of Christ who found many enemies in the world who sought to suppress his kingdom from its infancy. But his dominion prevailed, and from a corner of the earth it has overtaken the world.

One of the ways the church has read this book over the generations is as a character profile on the life of David. On this approach Matthew Henry commented, "We here meet with many things worthy of imitation and many that are written for our warning. The history of King David is given in scripture with much faithfulness, and from it he appears, to those who fairly balance his many virtues and excellent qualities against his faults, to have been a great and good man." One virtue was the manner in which David inquired of the Lord. At nearly every turn in his story, he sought direction and permission from God, not wanting to take a step without his blessing.

Of course there was the infamous episode in which David committed adultery with the wife of one of his soldiers before having that loyal soldier murdered. Lessons using his example have abounded over the years. Cyril of Jerusalem offered a homily that typifies how the church has often handled this passage:

> Come then to the blessed David, and take him for your example of repentance. Great as he was, he suffered a fall. It was in the afternoon, after his siesta, that he took a turn on the housetop and saw by chance what stirred his human passion. He fulfilled the sinful deed, but his nobility, when it came to confessing the lapse, had not perished with the doing of the deed . . . The sinner confesses his wicked deed, and as it was a full and frank confession, he had the swiftest healing.

FRANCIS DANBY, ***THE DELUGE*** (1840)

(Public Domain)

PIETER BRUEGEL THE ELDER, ***THE TOWER OF BABEL*** (c. 1563)

(Public Domain)

2 SAMUEL

While God's promises to Israel are a dominant theme throughout the Old Testament, here they are tied to David and his line. While King David had wanted to build a house for the Lord, the prophet Nathan revealed the Lord had other plans: "When the time comes for you to die, I will raise up your descendant, one of your own sons, to succeed you, and I will establish his kingdom. He will build a house for my name, and I will make his dynasty permanent" (7:12–13). The Lord would build David's house, and it would have no end.

Commenting on this promise, Basil the Great wrote, "Now, if you explain this simply of Solomon, you will send me into a fit of laughter. For David will evidently have brought forth Solomon! But is not Christ here designated the seed of David as of that womb that was derived from David, that is, Mary's?" The Reformers understood this promise in the same way, finding in this blessing of longevity the promised Messiah. Martin Luther argued, "We do not deny that word for word this text can be understood as referring both to Solomon and to Christ." And consider the conclusion of Heinrich Bullinger: "It is certain that scripture draws the lineal descent of Christ very diligently from the loins of Abraham to Jacob, from Jacob to Judah, and from Judah to David. And to David are renewed the promises about the incarnation of the Son of God."

Near the end of the second book of Samuel, David offers a song of praise to the Lord that mirrors Psalm 18 in structure and composition. He extols the Lord's deliverance and protection: "The Lord is my high ridge, my stronghold, my deliverer. My God is my rocky summit where I take shelter, my shield, the horn that saves me, my stronghold, my refuge, my savior" (22:1–3). The psalm speaks of the character of God reflected throughout this narrative account of Israel's history. It reveals a God who hears us when we cry, then does something about it by rescuing us; who shows himself faithful, blameless, pure, and shrewd.

Commenting on this song, Viktorin Strigel remarked, "Just as the swan dies with a song, so David and all pious people on their migration out of this life glorify God with invocation, thanksgiving, and confession." This song marks the end of an important series of historical events in the life of Israel that rightly deserve a moment of praise.

DAVID LEARNS OF THE DEATHS OF SAUL AND JONATHAN

1 After the death of Saul, when David had returned from defeating the Amalekites, he stayed at Ziklag for two days. 2On
the third day a man arrived from the camp of Saul with his
clothes torn and dirt on his head. When he approached David,
the man threw himself to the ground.
3David asked him, "Where are you coming from?" He replied,
"I have escaped from the camp of Israel." 4David inquired, "How
were things going? Tell me!" He replied, "The people fled from
the battle and many of them fell dead. Even Saul and his son
Jonathan are dead!" 5David said to the young man who was
telling him this, "How do you know that Saul and his son Jonathan are dead?" 6The young man said, "I just happened to be
on Mount Gilboa and came across Saul leaning on his spear
for support. The chariots and leaders of the horsemen were in
hot pursuit of him. 7When he turned around and saw me, he
called out to me. I answered, 'Here I am!' 8He asked me, 'Who
are you?' I told him, 'I'm an Amalekite.' 9He said to me, 'Stand
over me and finish me off! I'm very dizzy, even though I'm still
alive.' 10So I stood over him and put him to death, since I knew
that he couldn't live in such a condition. Then I took the crown
which was on his head and the bracelet which was on his arm.
I have brought them here to my lord."
11David then grabbed his own clothes and tore them, as did
all the men who were with him. 12They lamented and wept
and fasted until evening because Saul, his son Jonathan, the
LORD's army, and the house of Israel had fallen by the sword.
13David said to the young man who told this to him, "Where
are you from?" He replied, "I am an Amalekite, the son of a
resident foreigner." 14David replied to him, "How is it that you
were not afraid to reach out your hand to destroy the LORD's
anointed?" 15Then David called one of the soldiers and said,
"Come here and strike him down!" So he struck him down, and
he died. 16David said to him, "Your blood be on your own head!
Your own mouth has testified against you, saying 'I have put
the LORD's anointed to death.'"

DAVID'S TRIBUTE TO SAUL AND JONATHAN

17Then David chanted this lament over Saul and his son Jonathan. 18(He gave instructions that the people of Judah should
be taught "The Bow." Indeed, it is written down in the Scroll
of the Upright One.)

19 "The beauty of Israel lies slain on your high places!
How the mighty have fallen!
20 Don't report it in Gath,
don't spread the news in the streets of Ashkelon,
or the daughters of the Philistines will rejoice,
the daughters of the uncircumcised will celebrate!
21 O mountains of Gilboa,
may there be no dew or rain on you, nor fields of grain
offerings!
For it was there that the shield of warriors was defiled;
the shield of Saul lies neglected without oil.
22 From the blood of the slain, from the fat of warriors,
the bow of Jonathan was not turned away.
The sword of Saul never returned empty.
23 Saul and Jonathan were greatly loved during their lives,
and not even in their deaths were they separated.

1:1–16 Let us remember David's grief over Saul's death when the Lord multiplies our sadness. For we may be expecting him to reassure us. Indeed, he may give us the opportunity to feel his grace, and yet at the same time we may have the opposite experience of being angered and frustrated. Since this happened to David, we will by no means find it a new experience. So when God does not put an end to our distress and anxieties, we will not complain at all. In fact, when he withdraws one perplexity from us, he sends something else on us from which we were desperately fleeing! Thus our faith and our patience have to be tried in various conditions. Let us humble ourselves and submit ourselves to what God knows to be just and expedient. Above all, let us benefit from the example of David so that we will not be dismayed when we experience what God was doing in him.

JOHN CALVIN (1509–1564)
COMPLETE COMMENTARY ON THE BIBLE

They were swifter than eagles, stronger than lions.
24 O daughters of Israel, weep over Saul,
who clothed you in scarlet as well as jewelry,
who put gold jewelry on your clothes.
25 How the warriors have fallen
in the midst of battle!
Jonathan lies slain on your high places!
26 I grieve over you, my brother Jonathan.
You were very dear to me.
Your love was more special to me than the love of
women.
27 How the warriors have fallen!
The weapons of war are destroyed!"

DAVID IS ANOINTED KING

2 Afterward David inquired of the LORD, "Should I go up to one
of the cities of Judah?" The LORD told him, "Go up." David
asked, "Where should I go?" The LORD replied, "To Hebron."
2So David went up, along with his two wives, Ahinoam the Jezreelite and Abigail, formerly the wife of Nabal the Carmelite.
3David also brought along the men who were with him, each
with his family. They settled in the cities of Hebron. 4The men
of Judah came and there they anointed David as king over the
people of Judah.
David was told, "The people of Jabesh Gilead are the ones
who buried Saul." 5So David sent messengers to the people
of Jabesh Gilead and told them, "May you be blessed by the
LORD because you have shown this kindness to your lord Saul
by burying him. 6Now may the LORD show you true kindness! I
also will reward you, because you have done this deed. 7Now be
courageous and prove to be valiant warriors, for your lord Saul is
dead. The people of Judah have anointed me as king over them."

DAVID'S ARMY CLASHES WITH THE ARMY OF SAUL

8Now Abner son of Ner, the general in command of Saul's army,
had taken Saul's son Ish Bosheth and had brought him to Mahanaim. 9He appointed him king over Gilead, the Geshurites,
Jezreel, Ephraim, Benjamin, and all Israel. 10Ish Bosheth son of
Saul was forty years old when he began to rule over Israel. He
ruled two years. However, the people of Judah followed David.
11David was king in Hebron over the people of Judah for seven-
and-a-half years.
12Then Abner son of Ner and the servants of Ish Bosheth
son of Saul went out from Mahanaim to Gibeon. 13Joab son of
Zeruiah and the servants of David also went out and confronted
them at the pool of Gibeon. One group stationed themselves
on one side of the pool, and the other group on the other side
of the pool. 14Abner said to Joab, "Let the soldiers get up and
fight before us." Joab said, "So be it!"
15So they got up and crossed over by number: 12 belonging
to Benjamin and to Ish Bosheth son of Saul, and 12 from the
servants of David. 16As they grappled with one another, each
one stabbed his opponent with his sword and they fell dead
together. So that place is called the Field of Flints; it is in Gibeon.
17Now the battle was very severe that day; Abner and the
men of Israel were overcome by David's soldiers. 18The three
sons of Zeruiah were there—Joab, Abishai, and Asahel. (Now
Asahel was as quick on his feet as one of the gazelles in the

2:1–7 The end of Saul's reign was the beginning of David's. David was first inaugurated as king secretly and separately by Samuel. Then two confirmations followed this. The first confirmation occurred so that David would be received in some part of the land of Judah, which was the tribe from which he came; the second confirmation then occurred before the entire kingdom. In this way we see that God does not fulfill his promises immediately but gradually. For instance, God initially gave Abraham a promise in the form of a seed, then as the land of Canaan, and finally as Christ, through whom he blessed the whole world. But none of these things came about quickly. David fulfilled the promises of the kingdom, and although it was interrupted and there were gaps in successive reigns, it endured in a certain way until the time of Christ.

PETER VERMIGLI **(1499–1562)**
COMMENTARY ON SECOND SAMUEL

field.) 19Asahel chased Abner, without turning to the right or
to the left as he followed Abner.
20Then Abner turned and asked, "Is that you, Asahel?" He
replied, "Yes it is!" 21Abner said to him, "Turn aside to your
right or to your left. Capture one of the soldiers and take his
equipment for yourself!" But Asahel was not willing to turn
aside from following him. 22So Abner spoke again to Asahel,
"Turn aside from following me! I do not want to strike you to
the ground. How then could I show my face in the presence of
Joab your brother?" 23But Asahel refused to turn aside. So Abner struck him in the abdomen with the back end of his spear.
The spear came out his back; Asahel collapsed on the spot and
died there right before Abner. Everyone who came to the place
where Asahel fell dead paused in respect.
24So Joab and Abishai chased Abner. At sunset they came to
the hill of Ammah near Giah on the way to the wilderness of
Gibeon. 25The Benjaminites formed their ranks behind Abner
and were like a single army, standing at the top of a certain hill.
26Then Abner called out to Joab, "Must the sword devour
forever? Don't you realize that this will turn bitter in the end?
When will you tell the people to turn aside from pursuing their
brothers?" 27Joab replied, "As surely as God lives, if you had not
said this, it would have been morning before the people would
have abandoned pursuit of their brothers." 28Then Joab blew
the ram's horn and all the people stopped in their tracks. They
stopped chasing Israel and ceased fighting. 29Abner and his
men went through the rift valley all that night. They crossed
the Jordan River and went through the whole region of Bitron
and came to Mahanaim.
30Now Joab returned from chasing Abner and assembled
all the people. Nineteen of David's soldiers were missing, in
addition to Asahel. 31But David's soldiers had slaughtered
the Benjaminites and Abner's men—in all, 360 men had died!
32They took Asahel's body and buried him in his father's tomb
at Bethlehem. Joab and his men then traveled all that night
3 and reached Hebron by dawn. 1However, the war was prolonged between the house of Saul and the house of David.
David was becoming steadily stronger, while the house of Saul
was becoming increasingly weaker.
2Now sons were born to David in Hebron. His firstborn was
Amnon, born to Ahinoam the Jezreelite. 3His second son was
Kileab, born to Abigail the widow of Nabal the Carmelite. His
third son was Absalom, the son of Maacah daughter of King
Talmai of Geshur. 4His fourth son was Adonijah, the son of
Haggith. His fifth son was Shephatiah, the son of Abital. 5His
sixth son was Ithream, born to David's wife Eglah. These sons
were all born to David in Hebron.

ABNER DEFECTS TO DAVID'S CAMP

6As the war continued between the house of Saul and the house
of David, Abner was becoming more influential in the house
of Saul. 7Now Saul had a concubine named Rizpah daughter of
Aiah. Ish Bosheth said to Abner, "Why did you sleep with my
father's concubine?"
8These words of Ish Bosheth really angered Abner and he
said, "Am I the head of a dog that belongs to Judah? This very
day I am demonstrating loyalty to the house of Saul your father
and to his relatives and his friends! I have not betrayed you into
the hand of David. Yet you have accused me of sinning with this

woman today! [9]God will severely judge Abner if I do not do for
David exactly what the LORD has promised him, [10]namely, to
transfer the kingdom from the house of Saul and to establish
the throne of David over Israel and over Judah all the way from
Dan to Beer Sheba!" [11]Ish Bosheth was unable to answer Abner
with even a single word because he was afraid of him.

[12]Then Abner sent messengers to David saying, "To whom
does the land belong? Make an agreement with me, and I will
do whatever I can to cause all Israel to turn to you." [13]So David
said, "Good! I will make an agreement with you. I ask only one
thing from you. You will not see my face unless you bring Saul's
daughter Michal when you come to visit me."

[14]David sent messengers to Ish Bosheth son of Saul with
this demand: "Give me my wife Michal whom I acquired for
100 Philistine foreskins." [15]So Ish Bosheth took her from her
husband Paltiel son of Laish. [16]Her husband went along behind
her, weeping all the way to Bahurim. Finally Abner said to him,
"Go back!" So he returned home.

[17]Abner advised the elders of Israel, "Previously you were
wanting David to be your king. [18]Act now! For the LORD has
said to David, 'By the hand of my servant David I will save my
people Israel from the Philistines and from all their enemies.'"

[19]Then Abner spoke privately with the Benjaminites. Abner
also went to Hebron to inform David privately of all that Israel
and the entire house of Benjamin had agreed to. [20]When Abner, accompanied by 20 men, came to David in Hebron, David
prepared a banquet for Abner and the men who were with him.
[21]Abner said to David, "Let me leave so that I may go and gather
all Israel to my lord the king so that they may make an agreement with you. Then you will rule over all that you desire." So
David sent Abner away, and he left in peace.

ABNER IS KILLED

[22]Now David's soldiers and Joab were coming back from a raid,
bringing a great deal of plunder with them. Abner was no longer
with David in Hebron, for David had sent him away and he had
left in peace. [23]When Joab and all the army that was with him
arrived, Joab was told: "Abner the son of Ner came to the king;
he sent him away, and he left in peace!"

[24]So Joab went to the king and said, "What have you done?
Abner has come to you. Why would you send him away? Now
he's gone on his way! [25]You know Abner the son of Ner. Surely he
came here to spy on you and to determine when you leave and
when you return and to discover everything that you are doing!"

[26]Then Joab left David and sent messengers after Abner.
They brought him back from the well of Sirah. (But David was
not aware of it.) [27]When Abner returned to Hebron, Joab took
him aside at the gate as if to speak privately with him. Joab then
stabbed him in the abdomen and killed him, avenging the shed
blood of his brother Asahel.

[28]When David later heard about this, he said, "I and my kingdom are forever innocent before the LORD of the shed blood
of Abner son of Ner. [29]May his blood whirl over the head of
Joab and the entire house of his father! May the males of Joab's
house never cease to have someone with a running sore or a
skin disease or one who works at the spindle or one who falls
by the sword or one who lacks food!"

[30]So Joab and his brother Abishai killed Abner, because he
had killed their brother Asahel in Gibeon during the battle.

3:20–28 **David had bound the people to himself freely in doing his duty—first, when during the division among the people he preferred to live like an exile at Hebron rather than to reign at Jerusalem; next, when he showed that he loved valor even in an enemy. He had also thought that justice should be shown to those who had borne arms against himself the same as to his own men. Again, he admired Abner, the bravest champion of the opposing side, while he was their leader and was yet waging war. Nor did David despise him when suing for peace but honored him by a banquet. When Abner was killed by treachery, David mourned and wept for him. He honored his funeral rituals and evinced his good faith in desiring vengeance for the murder.**

AMBROSE **(C. 339–C. 397)**
ON THE DUTIES OF THE CLERGY

[31]David instructed Joab and all the people who were with him, "Tear your clothes. Put on sackcloth. Lament before Abner!" Now King David followed behind the funeral pallet. [32]So they buried Abner in Hebron. The king cried loudly over Abner's grave, and all the people wept too. [33]The king chanted the following lament for Abner:

"Should Abner have died like a fool?
[34] Your hands were not bound,
and your feet were not put into irons.
You fell the way one falls before criminals."

All the people wept over him again. [35]Then all the people came and encouraged David to eat food while it was still day. But David took an oath saying, "God will punish me severely if I taste bread or anything whatsoever before the sun sets!"

[36]All the people noticed this and it pleased them. In fact, everything the king did pleased all the people. [37]All the people and all Israel realized on that day that the killing of Abner son of Ner was not done at the king's instigation.

[38]Then the king said to his servants, "Do you not realize that a great leader has fallen this day in Israel? [39]Today I am weak, even though I am anointed as king. These men, the sons of Zeruiah, are too much for me to bear! May the LORD punish appropriately the one who has done this evil thing!"

ISH BOSHETH IS KILLED

4 When Ish Bosheth the son of Saul heard that Abner had died in Hebron, he was very disheartened, and all Israel was afraid. [2]Now Saul's son had two men who were in charge of raiding units; one was named Baanah and the other Recab. They were sons of Rimmon the Beerothite, who was a Benjaminite. (Beeroth is regarded as belonging to Benjamin, [3]for the Beerothites fled to Gittaim and have remained there as resident foreigners until the present time.)

[4]Now Saul's son Jonathan had a son who was crippled in both feet. He was five years old when the news about Saul and Jonathan arrived from Jezreel. His nurse picked him up and fled, but in her haste to get away, he fell and was injured. Mephibosheth was his name.

[5]Now the sons of Rimmon the Beerothite—Recab and Baanah—went at the hottest part of the day to the home of Ish Bosheth, as he was enjoying his midday rest. [6]They entered the house under the pretense of getting wheat and mortally wounded him in the stomach. Then Recab and his brother Baanah escaped.

[7]They had entered the house while Ish Bosheth was resting on his bed in his bedroom. They mortally wounded him and then cut off his head. Taking his head, they traveled on the way of the rift valley all that night. [8]They brought the head of Ish Bosheth to David in Hebron, saying to the king, "Look! The head of Ish Bosheth son of Saul, your enemy who sought your life! The LORD has granted vengeance to my lord the king this day against Saul and his descendants!"

[9]David replied to Recab and his brother Baanah, the sons of Rimmon the Beerothite, "As surely as the LORD lives, who has delivered my life from all adversity, [10]when someone told me that Saul was dead—even though he thought he was bringing good news—I seized him and killed him in Ziklag. That was the good news I gave to him! [11]Surely when wicked men have

4:4–12 This history is inserted as that which encouraged these men to this wicked murder, because Saul's family was now reduced to a low ebb. If Ish Bosheth was dispatched, there would be none left but a lame child who was altogether unfit to manage the kingdom, and therefore the crown must necessarily come to David by their act and deed—for which they promised themselves no small recompense. But what a disappointment to Baanah and Recab was the sentence that David passed upon them! And such they will meet with who think to serve the Son of David by cruelty or injustice, who, when under color of religion, outrage or murder their brethren, think they do God service.

JOHN WESLEY (1703–1791)
EXPLANATORY NOTES ON THE BIBLE

BASIL THE GREAT:

THEOLOGIAN OF THE HOLY SPIRIT

c. 330–379

Basil the Great is known for many things, but his most enduring contribution to the communion of saints may well be his development of the theology of the Holy Spirit.

Having been raised a Christian in a wealthy family in Cappadocia, Basil found his studies during his youth led him into law and rhetoric. But at twenty-eight he had a spiritual conversion that led him to give his possessions to the poor and live a life of ascetic solitude outside Alexandria. Basil soon discovered that while he was drawn to an ascetic lifestyle focused on prayer and piety, a life of solitude wasn't for him. Having been influenced by the spirituality of his sister Macrina, who had taken vows as a nun, he founded a monastic community along with his brother Gregory of Nyssa on their family property. Basil's emphasis on the communal aspects of monasticism proved vital in the development of the monastic traditions of the East, particularly his emphasis on caring for the poor through hospitals, soup kitchens, and shelters.

In 365 Basil was made a presbyter, and in 370 he became bishop of Caesarea, taking over for the famed Eusebius after his death. In his capacity as an ecclesial leader, Basil led from a pastoral heart and fiery commitment to orthodoxy. He quickly garnered a reputation as an able church administrator and pastoral counselor in addition to being a fierce defender of the historic Christian faith against Arianism. He worked to bring about a new ecumenical council that would ratify and formally adopt the acts of the Council of Nicea and Trinitarian orthodoxy. But his doctrinal work on the third person of the Trinity proved to be especially significant.

In writing *On the Holy Spirit*, Basil became one of a small group of Christian teachers and theologians during the years between the Council of Nicea (325) and the Council of Constantinople (381) who focused especially on the Holy Spirit. *On the Holy Spirit* influenced the revision of the Nicene Creed to add a greater emphasis on the person and work of the Holy Spirit. One of Basil's concerns was how the Spirit had been ignored during the height of the Arian controversy, which tended to focus solely on the natures and persons of the Father and the Son. He worked tirelessly to maintain a proper spotlight on the third person during the controversy as well as respond to an unorthodox development among some pastors. The *pneumatomachians*, as they were known, denied the divinity of the Holy Spirit and thus espoused a "binity" view of God instead of the orthodox view of God as Trinity. Because of Basil's significant work, he rightly became known as a theologian of the Holy Spirit.

Dying in 379, Basil was remembered as a monastic leader, ecclesial administrator, pastor of pastors, defender of orthodoxy, and theologian of the Holy Spirit who would have a lasting influence upon the development of Eastern Orthodoxy.

IMPORTANT WORKS

ON THE HOLY SPIRIT

REFUTATION OF THE APOLOGY OF THE IMPIOUS EUNOMIUS

killed an innocent man as he slept in his own house, should I not now require his blood from your hands and remove you from the earth?"

12So David issued orders to the soldiers and they put them to death. Then they cut off their hands and feet and hung them near the pool in Hebron. But they took the head of Ish Bosheth and buried it in the tomb of Abner in Hebron.

DAVID IS ANOINTED KING OVER ISRAEL

5 All the tribes of Israel came to David at Hebron saying, "Look, we are your very flesh and blood! 2In the past, when Saul was our king, you were the real leader in Israel. The LORD said to you, 'You will shepherd my people Israel; you will rule over Israel.'"

3When all the leaders of Israel came to the king at Hebron, King David made an agreement with them in Hebron before the LORD. They designated David as king over Israel. 4David was thirty years old when he began to reign, and he reigned for forty years. 5In Hebron he reigned over Judah for seven years and six months, and in Jerusalem he reigned for thirty-three years over all Israel and Judah.

DAVID OCCUPIES JERUSALEM

6Then the king and his men advanced to Jerusalem against the Jebusites who lived in the land. The Jebusites said to David, "You cannot invade this place! Even the blind and the lame will turn you back, saying, 'David cannot invade this place!'"

7But David captured the fortress of Zion (that is, the City of David). 8David said on that day, "Whoever attacks the Jebusites must approach the 'lame' and the 'blind' who are David's enemies by going through the water tunnel." For this reason it is said, "The blind and the lame cannot enter the palace."

9So David lived in the fortress and called it the City of David. David built all around it, from the terrace inwards. 10David's power grew steadily, for the LORD God of Heaven's Armies was with him.

11King Hiram of Tyre sent messengers to David, along with cedar logs, carpenters, and stonemasons. They built a palace for David. 12David realized that the LORD had established him as king over Israel and that he had elevated his kingdom for the sake of his people Israel. 13David married more concubines and wives from Jerusalem after he arrived from Hebron. Even more sons and daughters were born to David. 14These are the names of children born to him in Jerusalem: Shammua, Shobab, Nathan, Solomon, 15Ibhar, Elishua, Nepheg, Japhia, 16Elishama, Eliada, and Eliphelet.

CONFLICT WITH THE PHILISTINES

17When the Philistines heard that David had been designated king over Israel, they all went up to search for David. When David heard about it, he went down to the fortress. 18Now the Philistines had arrived and spread out in the valley of Rephaim. 19So David asked the LORD, "Should I march up against the Philistines? Will you hand them over to me?" The LORD said to David, "March up, for I will indeed hand the Philistines over to you."

20So David marched against Baal Perazim and defeated them there. Then he said, "The LORD has burst out against my enemies like water bursts out." So he called the name of that place Baal Perazim. 21The Philistines abandoned their idols there, and David and his men picked them up.

5:17–25 **David had gained one battle by the strength of the Lord; he would not venture upon another until he had insured the same. He inquired, "Should I march up against the Philistines?" He waited until God's sign was given. Learn from David to take no step without God. Christian, if you would know the path of duty, take God for your compass; if you would steer your ship through the dark billows, put the tiller into the hand of the Almighty. Many a rock might be escaped if we would let our Father take the helm. Let us then take all our perplexities to him and say, "Lord, what will you have me do?" Leave not your room this morning without inquiring of the Lord.**

CHARLES SPURGEON
(1834–1892)
MORNING AND EVENING

22The Philistines again came up and spread out in the valley of Rephaim. 23So David asked the LORD what he should do. This time the LORD said to him, "Don't march straight up. Instead, circle around behind them and come against them opposite the trees. 24When you hear the sound of marching in the tops of the trees, act decisively. For at that moment the LORD is going before you to strike down the army of the Philistines." 25David did just as the LORD commanded him, and he struck down the Philistines from Gibeon all the way to Gezer.

DAVID BRINGS THE ARK TO JERUSALEM

6 David again assembled all the best men in Israel, 30,000 in number. 2David and all the men who were with him traveled to Baalah in Judah to bring up from there the ark of God which is called by the name of the LORD of Heaven's Armies, who sits enthroned between the cherubim that are on it. 3They loaded the ark of God on a new cart and carried it from the house of Abinadab, which was on the hill. Uzzah and Ahio, the sons of Abinadab, were guiding the new cart. 4They brought it with the ark of God from the house of Abinadab on the hill. Ahio was walking in front of the ark, 5while David and all Israel were energetically celebrating before the LORD, singing and playing various stringed instruments, tambourines, rattles, and cymbals.

6When they arrived at the threshing floor of Nacon, Uzzah reached out and grabbed hold of the ark of God, because the oxen stumbled. 7The LORD was so furious with Uzzah, he killed him on the spot for his negligence. He died right there beside the ark of God.

8David was angry because the LORD attacked Uzzah; so he called that place Perez Uzzah, which remains its name to this very day. 9David was afraid of the LORD that day and said, "How will the ark of the LORD ever come to me?" 10So David was no longer willing to bring the ark of the LORD to be with him in the City of David. David left it in the house of Obed-Edom the Gittite. 11The ark of the LORD remained in the house of Obed-Edom the Gittite for three months. The LORD blessed Obed-Edom and all his family. 12King David was told, "The LORD has blessed the family of Obed-Edom and everything he owns because of the ark of God." So David went and joyfully brought the ark of God from the house of Obed-Edom to the City of David. 13Those who carried the ark of the LORD took six steps and then David sacrificed an ox and a fatling calf. 14Now David, wearing a linen ephod, was dancing with all his strength before the LORD. 15David and all Israel were bringing up the ark of the LORD, shouting and blowing trumpets.

16As the ark of the LORD entered the City of David, Saul's daughter Michal looked out the window. When she saw King David leaping and dancing before the LORD, she despised him. 17They brought the ark of the LORD and put it in its place in the middle of the tent that David had pitched for it. Then David offered burnt sacrifices and peace offerings before the LORD. 18When David finished offering the burnt sacrifices and peace offerings, he pronounced a blessing over the people in the name of the LORD of Heaven's Armies. 19He then handed out to each member of the entire assembly of Israel, both men and women, a portion of bread, a date cake, and a raisin cake. Then all the people went home. 20When David went home to pronounce a blessing on his own house, Michal, Saul's daughter, came out to

6:12–23 **If you wish to demonstrate in your deeds that God alone is everything, you must become nothing in your heart. You must be as David when Michal despised him and he danced before the seat of grace and said, "I am willing to shame and humiliate myself even more than this." The one who wishes to be something is the material out of which God makes nothing. But those who wish to be nothing and consider themselves as nothing are the material out of which God makes something.**

JOHANN ARNDT **(1555–1621)**
TRUE CHRISTIANITY

meet him. She said, "How the king of Israel has distinguished himself this day! He has exposed himself today before his servants' slave girls the way a vulgar fool might do!"

[21]David replied to Michal, "It was before the LORD! I was celebrating before the LORD, who chose me over your father and his entire family and appointed me as leader over the LORD's people Israel. [22]I am willing to shame and humiliate myself even more than this. But with the slave girls whom you mentioned, let me be distinguished." [23]Now Michal, Saul's daughter, had no children to the day of her death.

THE LORD ESTABLISHES A COVENANT WITH DAVID

7 The king settled into his palace, for the LORD gave him relief from all his enemies on all sides. [2]The king said to Nathan the prophet, "Look! I am living in a palace made from cedar, while the ark of God sits in the middle of a tent." [3]Nathan replied to the king, "You should go and do whatever you have in mind, for the LORD is with you." [4]That night the LORD's message came to Nathan, [5]"Go, tell my servant David, 'This is what the LORD has said: Do you really intend to build a house for me to live in? [6]I have not lived in a house from the time I brought the Israelites up from Egypt to the present day. Instead, I was traveling with them and living in a tent. [7]Wherever I moved among all the Israelites, I did not say to any of their leaders whom I appointed to care for my people Israel, "Why have you not built me a house made from cedar?"'

[8]"So now, say this to my servant David, 'This is what the LORD of Heaven's Armies has said: I took you from the pasture and from your work as a shepherd to make you leader of my people Israel. [9]I was with you wherever you went, and I defeated all your enemies before you. Now I will make you as famous as the great men of the earth. [10]I will establish a place for my people Israel and settle them there; they will live there and not be disturbed anymore. Violent men will not oppress them again, as they did in the beginning [11]and during the time when I appointed judges to lead my people Israel. Instead, I will give you relief from all your enemies. The LORD declares to you that he himself will build a dynastic house for you. [12]When the time comes for you to die, I will raise up your descendant, one of your own sons, to succeed you, and I will establish his kingdom. [13]He will build a house for my name, and I will make his dynasty permanent. [14]I will become his father and he will become my son. When he sins, I will correct him with the rod of men and with wounds inflicted by human beings. [15]But my loyal love will not be removed from him as I removed it from Saul, whom I removed from before you. [16]Your house and your kingdom will stand before me permanently; your dynasty will be permanent.'" [17]Nathan told David all these words that were revealed to him.

7:1–17 The prophet Nathan made a promise to David for his seed, "which shall proceed," says he, "out of thy bowels" (KJV). Is not Christ here designated the Seed of David as of that womb that was derived from David, that is, Mary's? Now, because Christ rather than any other (such as Solomon) was to build the temple of God, that is to say, a holy personhood wherein God's Spirit might dwell as in a better temple, Christ rather than David's son Solomon was to be looked for as the Son of God. From Christ too God's mercy did not depart, whereas on Solomon God's anger alighted after his luxury and idolatry. Since therefore nothing of these things is compatible with Solomon but only with Christ, the method of our interpretations will certainly be true, and the very issue of the facts shows that they were clearly predicted of Christ.

TERTULLIAN (155–C. 220)
AGAINST MARCION

DAVID OFFERS A PRAYER TO GOD

[18]King David went in, sat before the LORD, and said, "Who am I, O Sovereign LORD, and what is my family, that you should have brought me to this point? [19]And you didn't stop there, O LORD God! You have also spoken about the future of your servant's family. Is this your usual way of dealing with men, O Sovereign LORD? [20]What more can David say to you? You have given your servant special recognition, O Sovereign LORD! [21]For the sake of

your promise and according to your purpose you have done this
great thing in order to reveal it to your servant. 22Therefore you
are great, O Sovereign LORD, for there is none like you. There
is no God besides you! What we have heard is true. 23Who is
like your people, Israel, a unique nation on the earth? Their
God went to claim a nation for himself and to make a name for
himself! You did great and awesome acts for your land, before
your people whom you delivered for yourself from the Egyptian
empire and its gods. 24You made Israel your very own people for
all time. You, O LORD, became their God. 25So now, O LORD God,
make this promise you have made about your servant and his
family a permanent reality. Do as you promised, 26so you may
gain lasting fame, as people say, 'The LORD of Heaven's Armies
is God over Israel!' The dynasty of your servant David will be
established before you, 27for you, O LORD of Heaven's Armies,
the God of Israel, have told your servant, 'I will build you a dynastic house.' That is why your servant has had the courage to
pray this prayer to you. 28Now, O Sovereign LORD, you are the
true God. May your words prove to be true! You have made this
good promise to your servant. 29Now be willing to bless your
servant's dynasty so that it may stand permanently before you,
for you, O Sovereign LORD, have spoken. By your blessing may
your servant's dynasty be blessed from now on into the future!"

DAVID SUBJUGATES NEARBY NATIONS

8 Later David defeated the Philistines and subdued them. David
took Metheg Ammah from the Philistines. 2He defeated the
Moabites. He made them lie on the ground and then used a rope
to measure them off. He put two-thirds of them to death and
spared the other third. The Moabites became David's subjects and
brought tribute. 3David defeated King Hadadezer son of Rehob of
Zobah when he came to reestablish his authority over the Euphrates River. 4David seized from him 1,700 charioteers and 20,000
infantrymen. David cut the hamstrings of all but 100 of the chariot
horses. 5The Arameans of Damascus came to help King Hadadezer
of Zobah, but David killed 22,000 of the Arameans. 6David placed
garrisons in the territory of the Arameans of Damascus; the Arameans became David's subjects and brought tribute. The LORD
protected David wherever he campaigned. 7David took the golden
shields that belonged to Hadadezer's servants and brought them
to Jerusalem. 8From Tebah and Berothai, Hadadezer's cities, King
David took a great deal of bronze.

9When King Toi of Hamath heard that David had defeated
the entire army of Hadadezer, 10he sent his son Joram to King
David to extend his best wishes and to pronounce a blessing
on him for his victory over Hadadezer, for Toi had been at war
with Hadadezer. He brought with him various items made of
silver, gold, and bronze. 11King David dedicated these things to
the LORD, along with the dedicated silver and gold that he had
taken from all the nations that he had subdued, 12including
Edom, Moab, the Ammonites, the Philistines, and Amalek. This
also included some of the plunder taken from King Hadadezer
son of Rehob of Zobah.

13David became famous when he returned from defeating
the Edomites in the Valley of Salt; he defeated 18,000 in all.
14He placed garrisons throughout Edom, and all the Edomites
became David's subjects. The LORD protected David wherever
he campaigned. 15David reigned over all Israel; he guaranteed
justice for all his people.

8:1–14 Having accepted the promises of an eternal kingdom, the earthly kingdom gets confirmed in the subjection of the Philistines, Moabites, Edomites, Mennonites, Syrians, and others all the way to the Euphrates. Up to this point the Jews had been vexed with many evils on earth because of God's promises. But now the impious people who thought they were seeing the illusions of God might see them as God's promises. Seeing God's promises in all things is a work of strong faith because things can take on such divergent appearances. Thus through King David and then Solomon the promised borders described in Numbers 34 could come about and the truth of God's word could be seen by all. But then the people lost it, a sign that the Lord gives his promises only to those who believe. These things clearly signify how Christ's kingdom would be expanded to the Gentiles, just as he began to reign through his gospel in Judea and then expanded its edges to the ends of the earth.

JOHANNES BUGENHAGEN
(1485–1558)
COMMENTARY ON SECOND SAMUEL

DAVID'S CABINET

[16]Joab son of Zeruiah was general in command of the army;
Jehoshaphat son of Ahilud was secretary; [17]Zadok son of Ahitub
and Ahimelech son of Abiathar were priests; Seraiah was scribe;
[18]Benaiah son of Jehoiada supervised the Kerethites and Pelethites; and David's sons were priests.

DAVID FINDS MEPHIBOSHETH

9 Then David asked, "Is anyone still left from the family of
Saul, so that I may extend kindness to him for the sake of
Jonathan?"
[2]Now there was a servant from Saul's house named Ziba,
so he was summoned to David. The king asked him, "Are you
Ziba?" He replied, "At your service." [3]The king asked, "Is there
not someone left from Saul's family that I may extend God's
kindness to him?" Ziba said to the king, "One of Jonathan's
sons is left; both of his feet are crippled." [4]The king asked him,
"Where is he?" Ziba told the king, "He is at the house of Makir
son of Ammiel in Lo Debar."
[5]So King David had him brought from the house of Makir
son of Ammiel in Lo Debar. [6]When Mephibosheth son of Jonathan, the son of Saul, came to David, he bowed low with his face
toward the ground. David said, "Mephibosheth?" He replied,
"Yes, at your service."
[7]David said to him, "Don't be afraid, because I will certainly
extend kindness to you for the sake of Jonathan your father. I
will give back to you all the land that belonged to your grandfather Saul, and you will be a regular guest at my table." [8]Then
Mephibosheth bowed and said, "Of what importance am I, your
servant, that you show regard for a dead dog like me?"
[9]Then the king summoned Ziba, Saul's attendant, and said to
him, "Everything that belonged to Saul and to his entire house
I hereby give to your master's grandson. [10]You will cultivate
the land for him—you and your sons and your servants. You will
bring its produce and it will be food for your master's grandson
to eat. But Mephibosheth, your master's grandson, will be a regular guest at my table." (Now Ziba had 15 sons and 20 servants.)
[11]Ziba said to the king, "Your servant will do everything that
my lord the king has instructed his servant to do." So Mephibosheth was a regular guest at David's table, just as though he
were one of the king's sons.
[12]Now Mephibosheth had a young son whose name was Mica.
All the members of Ziba's household were Mephibosheth's
servants. [13]Mephibosheth was living in Jerusalem, for he was a
regular guest at the king's table. But both his feet were crippled.

DAVID AND THE AMMONITES

10 Later the king of the Ammonites died and his son Hanun
succeeded him. [2]David said, "I will express my loyalty to
Hanun son of Nahash just as his father was loyal to me." So
David sent his servants with a message expressing sympathy
over his father's death. When David's servants entered the land
of the Ammonites, [3]the Ammonite officials said to their lord
Hanun, "Do you really think David is trying to honor your father by sending these messengers to express his sympathy? No,
David has sent his servants to you to get information about the
city and spy on it so they can overthrow it!"
[4]So Hanun seized David's servants and shaved off half of
each one's beard. He cut the lower part of their robes off so

---

9:1–13 Now Mephibosheth had come to David, to his court and palace in Jerusalem, being thither brought, for he could not go of himself, being lame. And David said unto him, "Don't be afraid." He might observe a dejection in Mephibosheth's countenance, a trembling in his limbs, he might discover signs of fear that David would cut him off because he was of the seed royal. But David had sworn that he would not cut off his kindness from his house forever, and now remembering his oath to Jonathan he was determined to observe it. David gave Mephibosheth an apartment in the court, a place at his table, and admitted him to be a guest with him as long as he should live. This was the kindness of God David meant to show to him.

JOHN GILL (1697–1771)
EXPOSITION OF THE WHOLE BIBLE

10:1–19 There are two bases for a just war among humankind: for the honor and worship of God and for the safety of all the people. Here are the two considerations that all those who rule and whom God has chosen to bear his sword should have: first, that the honor of God be maintained and religion kept in its purity, and second, that the people be maintained in peace. Those who are seated on the tribunal of justice and have superiority are ordained as officers of God for the protection of his subjects. But they must not forget the main thing—namely, that God is to have his sovereign empire and all people are to give homage to him. That is how wars can be legitimate, namely, if the honor of God is procured and if the rulers have regard for the peace and welfare of the people.

JOHN CALVIN (1509–1564)
COMPLETE COMMENTARY ON THE BIBLE

that their buttocks were exposed, and then sent them away.
[5]Messengers told David what had happened, so he sent them
to the men who were thoroughly humiliated. The king said,
"Stay in Jericho until your beards have grown again; then you
may come back."
[6]When the Ammonites realized that David was disgusted
with them, they sent and hired 20,000 foot soldiers from Aram
Beth Rehob and Aram Zobah, in addition to 1,000 men from
the king of Maacah and 12,000 men from Ish Tob.
[7]When David heard the news, he sent Joab and the entire
army to meet them. [8]The Ammonites marched out and were
deployed for battle at the entrance of the city gate, while the
men from Aram Zobah, Rehob, Ish Tob, and Maacah were by
themselves in the field.
[9]When Joab saw that the battle would be fought on two fronts,
he chose some of Israel's best men and deployed them against
the Arameans. [10]He put his brother Abishai in charge of the rest
of the army and they were deployed against the Ammonites.
[11]Joab said, "If the Arameans start to overpower me, you come
to my rescue. If the Ammonites start to overpower you, I will
come to your rescue. [12]Be strong! Let's fight bravely for the
sake of our people and the cities of our God! The LORD will do
what he decides is best!"
[13]So Joab and his men marched out to do battle with the
Arameans, and they fled before him. [14]When the Ammonites
saw the Arameans flee, they fled before his brother Abishai and
went into the city. Joab withdrew from fighting the Ammonites
and returned to Jerusalem.
[15]When the Arameans realized that they had been defeated
by Israel, they consolidated their forces. [16]Then Hadadezer sent
for Arameans from beyond the Euphrates River, and they came
to Helam. Shobach, the general in command of Hadadezer's
army, led them.
[17]When David was informed, he gathered all Israel, crossed
the Jordan River, and came to Helam. The Arameans deployed
their forces against David and fought with him. [18]The Arameans fled before Israel. David killed 700 Aramean charioteers and 40,000 foot soldiers. He also struck down Shobach,
the general in command of the army, who died there. [19]When
all the kings who were subject to Hadadezer saw they were
defeated by Israel, they made peace with Israel and became
subjects of Israel. The Arameans were no longer willing to
help the Ammonites.

DAVID COMMITS ADULTERY WITH BATHSHEBA

11 In the spring of the year, at the time when kings normally
conduct wars, David sent out Joab with his officers and
the entire Israelite army. They defeated the Ammonites and
besieged Rabbah. But David stayed behind in Jerusalem. [2]One
evening David got up from his bed and walked around on the
roof of his palace. From the roof he saw a woman bathing. Now
this woman was very attractive. [3]So David sent someone to
inquire about the woman. The messenger said, "Isn't this Bathsheba, the daughter of Eliam, the wife of Uriah the Hittite?"
[4]David sent some messengers to get her. She came to him
and he went to bed with her. (Now at that time she was in the
process of purifying herself from her menstrual uncleanness.)
Then she returned to her home. [5]The woman conceived and
then sent word to David saying, "I'm pregnant."

11:1–27 **David should have been engaged in fighting the Lord's battles instead of tarrying at Jerusalem and giving himself up to luxurious repose, for he arose from his bed at eventide. Idleness and luxury are the devil's jackals and find him abundant prey. When I see the king of Israel sluggishly leaving his couch at the close of the day and falling at once into temptation, let me take warning and set holy watchfulness to guard the door. Our own corruptions are enough to work our ruin unless grace prevents. Reader, be not secure. O blessed Spirit, keep us from all evil.**

JOHN CALVIN **(1509–1564)**
COMPLETE COMMENTARY ON THE BIBLE

[6]So David sent a message to Joab that said, "Send me Uriah the Hittite." So Joab sent Uriah to David. [7]When Uriah came to him, David asked about how Joab and the army were doing and how the campaign was going. [8]Then David said to Uriah, "Go down to your home and relax." When Uriah left the palace, the king sent a gift to him. [9]But Uriah stayed at the door of the palace with all the servants of his lord. He did not go down to his house.

[10]So they informed David, "Uriah has not gone down to his house." So David said to Uriah, "Haven't you just arrived from a journey? Why haven't you gone down to your house?" [11]Uriah replied to David, "The ark and Israel and Judah reside in temporary shelters, and my lord Joab and my lord's soldiers are camping in the open field. Should I go to my house to eat and drink and go to bed with my wife? As surely as you are alive, I will not do this thing!" [12]So David said to Uriah, "Stay here another day. Tomorrow I will send you back." So Uriah stayed in Jerusalem both that day and the following one. [13]Then David summoned him. He ate and drank with him, and got him drunk. But in the evening he went out to sleep on his bed with the servants of his lord; he did not go down to his own house.

[14]In the morning David wrote a letter to Joab and sent it with Uriah. [15]In the letter he wrote: "Station Uriah at the front in the thick of the battle and then withdraw from him so he will be cut down and killed."

[16]So as Joab kept watch on the city, he stationed Uriah at the place where he knew the best enemy soldiers were. [17]When the men of the city came out and fought with Joab, some of David's soldiers fell in battle. Uriah the Hittite also died.

[18]Then Joab sent a full battle report to David. [19]He instructed the messenger as follows: "When you finish giving the battle report to the king, [20]if the king becomes angry and asks you, 'Why did you go so close to the city to fight? Didn't you realize they would shoot from the wall? [21]Who struck down Abimelech the son of Jerub-Besheth? Didn't a woman throw an upper millstone down on him from the wall so that he died in Thebez? Why did you go so close to the wall?' just say to him, 'Your servant Uriah the Hittite is also dead.'"

[22]So the messenger departed. When he arrived, he informed David of all the news that Joab had sent with him. [23]The messenger said to David, "The men overpowered us and attacked us in the field. But we forced them to retreat all the way to the door of the city gate. [24]Then the archers shot at your servants from the wall and some of the king's soldiers died. Your servant Uriah the Hittite is also dead." [25]David said to the messenger, "Tell Joab, 'Don't let this thing upset you. There is no way to anticipate whom the sword will cut down. Press the battle against the city and conquer it.' Encourage him with these words."

[26]When Uriah's wife heard that her husband Uriah was dead, she mourned for him. [27]When the time of mourning passed, David had her brought to his palace. She became his wife and she bore him a son. But what David had done upset the LORD.

NATHAN THE PROPHET CONFRONTS DAVID

12 So the LORD sent Nathan to David. When he came to David, Nathan said, "There were two men in a certain city, one rich and the other poor. [2]The rich man had a great many flocks and herds. [3]But the poor man had nothing except for a little lamb he had acquired. He raised it, and it grew up alongside

12:1–15 In truth there are some smooth people, if you please, who seem to make adultery into a sport. They believe that David's adultery is made on their side, and that our Lord was favorable to the adulteress who was taken away for the act of adultery. Why don't these people consider how severely David was punished for the offense? The calamitous house of David was soon polluted by filthy incest, for Amnon raped his sister Tamar. And David's house was crudely defamed by murder, as Absalom murdered his brother Amnon while he was at a banquet. The same Absalom corrupted and defiled his father and David's wives—in the open—putting aside all sense of shame. He drove his father from the kingdom and hastened to shorten his days. David acknowledged that all these calamities were fair punishments for his crimes of adultery and murder.

HEINRICH BULLINGER
(1504–1575)
DECADES

him and his children. It used to eat his food, drink from his
cup, and sleep in his arms. It was just like a daughter to him.
4“When a traveler arrived at the rich man’s home, he did not
want to use one of his own sheep or cattle to feed the traveler
who had come to visit him. Instead, he took the poor man’s
lamb and cooked it for the man who had come to visit him.”
5Then David became very angry at this man. He said to Nathan, “As surely as the LORD lives, the man who did this deserves
to die! 6Because he committed this cold-hearted crime, he must
pay for the lamb four times over!”
7Nathan said to David, “You are that man! This is what the
LORD God of Israel has said: ‘I chose you to be king over Israel
and I rescued you from the hand of Saul. 8I gave you your master’s house, and put your master’s wives into your arms. I also
gave you the house of Israel and Judah. And if all that somehow
seems insignificant, I would have given you so much more as
well! 9Why have you shown contempt for the LORD’s decrees by
doing evil in my sight? You have struck down Uriah the Hittite
with the sword and you have taken his wife to be your own
wife! You have killed him with the sword of the Ammonites.
10So now the sword will never depart from your house. For
you have despised me by taking the wife of Uriah the Hittite
as your own!’ 11This is what the LORD has said: ‘I am about to
bring disaster on you from inside your own household! Right
before your eyes I will take your wives and hand them over to
your companion. He will go to bed with your wives in broad
daylight! 12Although you have acted in secret, I will do this
thing before all Israel, and in broad daylight.’”
13Then David exclaimed to Nathan, “I have sinned against the
LORD!” Nathan replied to David, “Yes, and the LORD has forgiven
your sin. You are not going to die. 14Nonetheless, because you
have treated the LORD with such contempt in this matter, the
son who has been born to you will certainly die.”
15Then Nathan went to his home. The LORD struck the child
that Uriah’s wife had borne to David, and the child became very
ill. 16Then David prayed to God for the child and fasted. He
would even go and spend the night lying on the ground. 17The
elders of his house stood over him and tried to lift him from
the ground, but he was unwilling, and refused to eat food with
them.
18On the seventh day the child died. But the servants of David
were afraid to inform him that the child had died, for they said,
“While the child was still alive he would not listen to us when
we spoke to him. How can we tell him that the child is dead?
He will do himself harm!”
19When David saw that his servants were whispering to one
another, he realized that the child was dead. So David asked his
servants, “Is the child dead?” They replied, “Yes, he’s dead.” 20So
David got up from the ground, bathed, put on oil, and changed
his clothes. He went to the house of the LORD and worshiped.
Then, when he entered his palace, he requested that food be
brought to him, and he ate.
21His servants said to him, “What is this that you have done?
While the child was still alive, you fasted and wept. Once the
child was dead you got up and ate food!” 22He replied, “While
the child was still alive, I fasted and wept because I thought,
‘Perhaps the LORD will show pity and the child will live.’ 23But
now he is dead. Why should I fast? Am I able to bring him back
at this point? I will go to him, but he cannot return to me!”

24So David comforted his wife Bathsheba. He came to her and
went to bed with her. Later she gave birth to a son, and David
named him Solomon. Now the LORD loved the child 25and sent
word through Nathan the prophet that he should be named
Jedidiah for the LORD's sake.

DAVID'S FORCES DEFEAT THE AMMONITES

26So Joab fought against Rabbah of the Ammonites and captured the royal city. 27Joab then sent messengers to David, saying, "I have fought against Rabbah and have captured the water
supply of the city. 28So now assemble the rest of the army and
besiege the city and capture it. Otherwise I will capture the
city and it will be named for me."

29So David assembled all the army and went to Rabbah and
fought against it and captured it. 30He took the crown of their
king from his head—it was gold, weighed about 75 pounds, and
held a precious stone—and it was placed on David's head. He
also took from the city a great deal of plunder. 31He removed
the people who were in it and made them labor with saws, iron
picks, and iron axes, putting them to work at the brick kiln. This
was his policy with all the Ammonite cities. Then David and all
the army returned to Jerusalem.

THE RAPE OF TAMAR

13 Now David's son Absalom had a beautiful sister named
Tamar. In the course of time David's son Amnon fell madly
in love with her. 2But Amnon became frustrated because he
was so lovesick over his sister Tamar. For she was a virgin, and
to Amnon it seemed out of the question to do anything to her.

3Now Amnon had a friend named Jonadab, the son of David's
brother Shimeah. Jonadab was a very crafty man. 4He asked
Amnon, "Why are you, the king's son, so depressed every morning? Can't you tell me?" So Amnon said to him, "I'm in love with
Tamar the sister of my brother Absalom." 5Jonadab replied to
him, "Lie down on your bed and pretend to be sick. When your
father comes in to see you, say to him, 'Please let my sister Tamar come in so she can fix some food for me. Let her prepare the
food in my sight so I can watch. Then I will eat from her hand.'"

6So Amnon lay down and pretended to be sick. When the
king came in to see him, Amnon said to the king, "Please let
my sister Tamar come in so she can make a couple of cakes in
my sight. Then I will eat from her hand."

7So David sent Tamar to the house saying, "Please go to the
house of Amnon your brother and prepare some food for him."
8So Tamar went to the house of Amnon her brother, who was
lying down. She took the dough, kneaded it, made some cakes
while he watched, and baked them. 9But when she took the pan
and set it before him, he refused to eat. Instead Amnon said,
"Get everyone out of here!" So everyone left.

10Then Amnon said to Tamar, "Bring the cakes into the
bedroom; then I will eat from your hand." So Tamar took the
cakes that she had prepared and brought them to her brother
Amnon in the bedroom. 11As she brought them to him to eat,
he grabbed her and said to her, "Come on! Get in bed with me,
my sister!"

12But she said to him, "No, my brother! Don't humiliate me!
This just isn't done in Israel! Don't do this foolish thing! 13How
could I ever be rid of my humiliation? And you would be considered one of the fools in Israel! Just speak to the king, for he

13:1–22 This passage warns us to fight against temptations. If we begin to consider the moral consequences of our actions, do we profit from it? When we are tempted to fornication and God sends us a good thought, how will we use it? We can say the same thing about theft and every other vice. Let us bear in mind that this is accursed and ask, *If I do this, am I an abomination to God?* For this is the goal to which the law leads us, to flee evil and to pursue good. If that thought enters our mind, we should immediately make a shield out of the will of God and arm ourselves with prayer in order to break down the cursed temptation, which is doing its uttermost to drag us down.

JOHN CALVIN **(1509–1564)**
COMPLETE COMMENTARY ON THE BIBLE

will not withhold me from you." [14]But he refused to listen to
her. He overpowered her and humiliated her by raping her.
[15]Then Amnon greatly despised her. His disdain toward her
surpassed the love he had previously felt toward her. Amnon
said to her, "Get up and leave!"
[16]But she said to him, "No I won't, for sending me away now
would be worse than what you did to me earlier!" But he refused to listen to her. [17]He called his personal attendant and
said to him, "Take this woman out of my sight and lock the
door behind her!" [18](Now she was wearing a long robe, for this
is what the king's virgin daughters used to wear.) So Amnon's
attendant removed her and bolted the door behind her. [19]Then
Tamar put ashes on her head and tore the long robe she was
wearing. She put her hands on her head and went on her way,
wailing as she went.
[20]Her brother Absalom said to her, "Was Amnon your brother
with you? Now be quiet, my sister. He is your brother. Don't
take it so seriously!" Tamar, devastated, lived in the house of
her brother Absalom.
[21]Now King David heard about all these things and was very
angry. [22]But Absalom said nothing to Amnon, either bad or
good, yet Absalom hated Amnon because he had humiliated
his sister Tamar.

ABSALOM HAS AMNON PUT TO DEATH

[23]Two years later Absalom's sheepshearers were in Baal Hazor,
near Ephraim. Absalom invited all the king's sons. [24]Then Absalom went to the king and said, "My shearers have begun their
work. Let the king and his servants go with me."
[25]But the king said to Absalom, "No, my son. We shouldn't
all go. We shouldn't burden you in that way." Though Absalom
pressed him, the king was not willing to go. Instead, David
blessed him.
[26]Then Absalom said, "If you will not go, then let my brother
Amnon go with us." The king replied to him, "Why should he go
with you?" [27]But when Absalom pressed him, he sent Amnon
and all the king's sons along with him.
[28]Absalom instructed his servants, "Look! When Amnon is
drunk and I say to you, 'Strike Amnon down,' kill him then and
there. Don't fear! Is it not I who have given you these instructions? Be strong and courageous!" [29]So Absalom's servants did
to Amnon exactly what Absalom had instructed. Then all the
king's sons got up; each one rode away on his mule and fled.
[30]While they were still on their way, the following report
reached David: "Absalom has killed all the king's sons; not one
of them is left!" [31]Then the king stood up and tore his garments
and lay down on the ground. All his servants were standing
there with torn garments as well.
[32]Jonadab, the son of David's brother Shimeah, said, "My lord
should not say, 'They have killed all the young men who are the
king's sons.' For only Amnon is dead. This is what Absalom has
talked about from the day that Amnon humiliated his sister
Tamar. [33]Now don't let my lord the king be concerned about
the report that has come saying, 'All the king's sons are dead.'
It is only Amnon who is dead."
[34]In the meantime Absalom fled. When the servant who was
the watchman looked up, he saw many people coming from the
west on a road beside the hill. [35]Jonadab said to the king, "Look!
The king's sons have come! It's just as I said."

[36]Just as he finished speaking, the king's sons arrived, wailing and weeping. The king and all his servants wept loudly as well. [37]But Absalom fled and went to King Talmai son of Ammihud of Geshur. And David grieved over his son every day.

[38]After Absalom fled and went to Geshur, he remained there for three years. [39]The king longed to go to Absalom, for he had since been consoled over the death of Amnon.

DAVID PERMITS ABSALOM TO RETURN TO JERUSALEM

14 Now Joab son of Zeruiah realized that the king longed to see Absalom. [2]So Joab sent to Tekoa and brought from there a wise woman. He told her, "Pretend to be in mourning and put on garments for mourning. Don't anoint yourself with oil. Instead, act like a woman who has been mourning for the dead for some time. [3]Go to the king and speak to him in the following fashion." Then Joab told her what to say.

[4]So the Tekoan woman went to the king. She bowed down with her face to the ground in deference to him and said, "Please help me, O king!" [5]The king replied to her, "What do you want?" She answered, "I am a widow; my husband is dead. [6]Your servant has two sons. When the two of them got into a fight in the field, there was no one present who could intervene. One of them struck the other and killed him. [7]Now the entire family has risen up against your servant, saying, 'Turn over the one who struck down his brother, so that we can execute him and avenge the death of his brother whom he killed. In so doing we will also destroy the heir.' They want to extinguish my remaining coal, leaving no one on the face of the earth to carry on the name of my husband."

[8]Then the king told the woman, "Go to your home. I will give instructions concerning your situation." [9]The Tekoan woman said to the king, "My lord the king, let any blame fall on me and on the house of my father. But let the king and his throne be innocent!"

[10]The king said, "Bring to me whoever speaks to you, and he won't bother you again!" [11]She replied, "In that case, let the king invoke the name of the LORD your God so that the avenger of blood may not add to the killing! Then they will not destroy my son!" He replied, "As surely as the LORD lives, not a single hair of your son's head will fall to the ground."

[12]Then the woman said, "Please permit your servant to speak to my lord the king about another matter." He replied, "Tell me." [13]The woman said, "Why have you devised something like this against God's people? When the king speaks in this fashion, he makes himself guilty, for the king has not brought back the one he has banished. [14]Certainly we must die, and are like water spilled on the ground that cannot be gathered up again. But God does not take away life; instead he devises ways for the banished to be restored. [15]I have now come to speak with my lord the king about this matter, because the people have made me fearful. But your servant said, 'I will speak to the king! Perhaps the king will do what his female servant asks. [16]Yes! The king may listen and deliver his female servant from the hand of the man who seeks to remove both me and my son from the inheritance God has given us!' [17]So your servant said, 'May the word of my lord the king be my security, for my lord the king is like the angel of God when it comes to deciding between right and wrong! May the LORD your God be with you!'"

14:1–33 People may be angry with their spouse, children, or friend even though they dearly love them. And God is said to be angry with his people in a similar way when the effects of displeasure are discovered in them. Upon our repentance and conversion, God promises not only to love us freely but also to clear up his countenance toward us. He promises to make us, by the removal of judgment, to see and know the fruits of his free love and bounty to us. When David called Absalom home for banishment, this was the result of love. But when David said, "He may not see my face," this was the continuation of anger. But at last when he admitted Absalom into his presence and kissed him, that anger was turned away.

EDWARD REYNOLDS
(1599–1676)
SEVEN SERMONS ON FOURTEENTH CHAPTER OF HOSEA

18 Then the king replied to the woman, "Don't hide any information from me when I question you." The woman said,
"Let my lord the king speak." 19 The king said, "Did Joab put you
up to all of this?" The woman answered, "As surely as you live,
my lord the king, there is no deviation to the right or to the
left from all that my lord the king has said. For your servant
Joab gave me instructions. He has put all these words in your
servant's mouth. 20 Your servant Joab did this so as to change
this situation. But my lord has wisdom like that of the angel
of God, and knows everything that is happening in the land."
21 Then the king said to Joab, "All right! I will do this thing. Go
and bring back the young man Absalom!" 22 Then Joab bowed
down with his face toward the ground and thanked the king.
Joab said, "Today your servant knows that I have found favor
in your sight, my lord the king, because the king has granted
the request of your servant!"
23 So Joab got up and went to Geshur and brought Absalom
back to Jerusalem. 24 But the king said, "Let him go over to his
own house. He may not see my face." So Absalom went over to
his own house; he did not see the king's face.
25 Now in all Israel everyone acknowledged that there was
no man as handsome as Absalom. From the soles of his feet
to the top of his head he was perfect in appearance. 26 When
he would shave his head—at the end of every year he used to
shave his head, for it grew too long and he would shave it—he
used to weigh the hair of his head at three pounds according to
the king's weight. 27 Absalom had three sons and one daughter,
whose name was Tamar. She was a very attractive woman.
28 Absalom lived in Jerusalem for two years without seeing
the king's face. 29 Then Absalom sent a message to Joab asking
him to send him to the king, but Joab was not willing to come
to him. So he sent a second message to him, but he still was not
willing to come. 30 So he said to his servants, "Look, Joab has a
portion of field adjacent to mine and he has some barley there.
Go and set it on fire." So Absalom's servants set Joab's portion
of the field on fire.
31 Then Joab got up and came to Absalom's house. He said to
him, "Why did your servants set my portion of field on fire?"
32 Absalom said to Joab, "Look, I sent a message to you saying,
'Come here so that I can send you to the king with this message:
"Why have I come from Geshur? It would be better for me if I
were still there."' Let me now see the face of the king. If I am
at fault, let him put me to death!"
33 So Joab went to the king and informed him. The king summoned Absalom, and he came to the king. Absalom bowed down
before the king with his face toward the ground and the king
kissed him.

ABSALOM LEADS AN INSURRECTION AGAINST DAVID

15 Some time later Absalom managed to acquire a chariot
and horses, as well as 50 men to serve as his royal guard.
2 Now Absalom used to get up early and stand beside the road
that led to the city gate. Whenever anyone came by who had a
complaint to bring to the king for arbitration, Absalom would
call out to him, "What city are you from?" The person would
answer, "I, your servant, am from one of the tribes of Israel."
3 Absalom would then say to him, "Look, your claims are legitimate and appropriate. But there is no representative of the

king who will listen to you." 4Absalom would then say, "If only they would make me a judge in the land! Then everyone who had a judicial complaint could come to me and I would make sure he receives a just settlement."

5When someone approached to bow before him, Absalom would extend his hand and embrace him and kiss him. 6Absalom acted this way toward everyone in Israel who came to the king for justice. In this way Absalom won the loyalty of the citizens of Israel.

7After four years Absalom said to the king, "Let me go and repay my vow that I made to the LORD while I was in Hebron. 8For I made this vow when I was living in Geshur in Aram: 'If the LORD really does allow me to return to Jerusalem, I will serve the LORD.'" 9The king replied to him, "Go in peace." So Absalom got up and went to Hebron.

10Then Absalom sent spies through all the tribes of Israel who said, "When you hear the sound of the horn, you may assume that Absalom rules in Hebron." 11Now 200 men had gone with Absalom from Jerusalem. Since they were invited, they went naively and were unaware of what Absalom was planning. 12While he was offering sacrifices, Absalom sent for Ahithophel the Gilonite, David's adviser, to come from his city, Giloh. The conspiracy was gaining momentum, and the people were starting to side with Absalom.

DAVID FLEES FROM JERUSALEM

13Then a messenger came to David and reported, "The men of Israel are loyal to Absalom!" 14So David said to all his servants who were with him in Jerusalem, "Come on! Let's escape! Otherwise no one will be delivered from Absalom! Go immediately, or else he will quickly overtake us and bring disaster on us and kill the city's residents with the sword." 15The king's servants replied to the king, "We will do whatever our lord the king decides."

16So the king and all the members of his royal court set out on foot, though the king left behind 10 concubines to attend to the palace. 17The king and all the people set out on foot, pausing at a spot some distance away. 18All his servants were leaving with him, along with all the Kerethites, all the Pelethites, and all the Gittites—some 600 men who had come on foot from Gath. They were leaving with the king.

19Then the king said to Ittai the Gittite, "Why should you come with us? Go back and stay with the new king, for you are a foreigner and an exile from your own country. 20It seems as if you arrived just yesterday. Today should I make you wander around by going with us? I go where I must go. But as for you, go back and take your men with you. May genuine loyal love protect you!"

21But Ittai replied to the king, "As surely as the LORD lives and as my lord the king lives, wherever my lord the king is, whether it means death or life, there I will be as well!" 22So David said to Ittai, "Come along then." So Ittai the Gittite went along, accompanied by all his men and all the dependents who were with him.

23All the land was weeping loudly as all these people were leaving. As the king was crossing over the Kidron Valley, all the people were leaving on the road that leads to the desert. 24Zadok and all the Levites who were with him were carrying the ark of the covenant of God. When they positioned the ark of God, Abiathar offered sacrifices until all the people had finished leaving the city.

15:13–37 Either David is persecuted by people for his desire to pursue justice and right religion, or he suffers on account of his sins and offenses. Let the one who suffers persecution on account of justice give joy and thanks to God. For just as the apostles rejoiced for being persecuted, so should these individuals rejoice and give thanks for being found worthy to suffer the name of Christ. But if people experience the punishment of God for their own sins, let them follow the example of David who, after he was forced to flee and go into exile, said to the priest who was carrying the ark: "Take the ark of God back to the city. If I find favor in the LORD's sight, he will bring me back and enable me to see both it and his dwelling place again. However, if he should say, 'I do not take pleasure in you,' then he will deal with me in a way that he considers appropriate."

HEINRICH BULLINGER
(1504–1575)
DECADES

[25]Then the king said to Zadok, "Take the ark of God back
to the city. If I find favor in the LORD's sight he will bring me
back and enable me to see both it and his dwelling place again.
[26]However, if he should say, 'I do not take pleasure in you,' then
he will deal with me in a way that he considers appropriate."
[27]The king said to Zadok the priest, "Are you a seer? Go back
to the city in peace! Your son Ahimaaz and Abiathar's son Jonathan may go with you and Abiathar. [28]Look, I will be waiting at
the fords of the desert until word from you reaches me." [29]So
Zadok and Abiathar took the ark of God back to Jerusalem and
remained there.
[30]As David was going up the Mount of Olives, he was weeping
as he went; his head was covered and his feet were bare. All the
people who were with him also had their heads covered and
were weeping as they went up. [31]Now David had been told,
"Ahithophel has sided with the conspirators who are with
Absalom." So David prayed, "Make the advice of Ahithophel
foolish, O LORD."
[32]When David reached the summit, where he used to worship
God, Hushai the Arkite met him with his clothes torn and dirt
on his head. [33]David said to him, "If you leave with me you will
be a burden to me. [34]But you will be able to counter the advice of
Ahithophel if you go back to the city and say to Absalom, 'I will
be your servant, O king! Previously I was your father's servant,
and now I will be your servant.' [35]Zadok and Abiathar the priests
will be there with you. Everything you hear in the king's palace
you must tell Zadok and Abiathar the priests. [36]Furthermore,
their two sons are there with them, Zadok's son Ahimaaz and
Abiathar's son Jonathan. You must send them to me with any
information you hear."
[37]So David's friend Hushai arrived in the city, just as Absalom
was entering Jerusalem.

DAVID RECEIVES GIFTS FROM ZIBA

16 When David had gone a short way beyond the summit, Ziba
the servant of Mephibosheth was there to meet him. He
had a couple of donkeys that were saddled, and on them were
200 loaves of bread, 100 raisin cakes, 100 baskets of summer
fruit, and a container of wine.
[2]The king asked Ziba, "Why did you bring these things?" Ziba
replied, "The donkeys are for the king's family to ride on, the
loaves of bread and the summer fruit are for the attendants
to eat, and the wine is for those who get exhausted in the desert." [3]The king asked, "Where is your master's grandson?" Ziba
replied to the king, "He remains in Jerusalem, for he said, 'Today the house of Israel will give back to me my grandfather's
kingdom.'" [4]The king said to Ziba, "Everything that was Mephibosheth's now belongs to you." Ziba replied, "I bow before you.
May I find favor in your sight, my lord the king."

SHIMEI CURSES DAVID AND HIS MEN

[5]Then King David reached Bahurim. There a man from Saul's
extended family named Shimei son of Gera came out, yelling
curses as he approached. [6]He threw stones at David and all
of King David's servants, as well as all the people and the soldiers who were on his right and on his left. [7]As he yelled curses,
Shimei said, "Leave! Leave! You man of bloodshed, you wicked
man! [8]The LORD has punished you for all the spilled blood of
the house of Saul, in whose place you rule. Now the LORD has

given the kingdom into the hand of your son Absalom. Disaster has overtaken you, for you are a man of bloodshed!"

9Then Abishai son of Zeruiah said to the king, "Why should this dead dog curse my lord the king? Let me go over and cut off his head!" 10But the king said, "What do we have in common, you sons of Zeruiah? If he curses because the LORD has said to him, 'Curse David!,' who can say to him, 'Why have you done this?'" 11Then David said to Abishai and to all his servants, "My own son, my very own flesh and blood, is trying to take my life. So also now this Benjaminite! Leave him alone so that he can curse, for the LORD has spoken to him. 12Perhaps the LORD will notice my affliction and this day grant me good in place of his curse."

13So David and his men went on their way. But Shimei kept going along the side of the hill opposite him, yelling curses as he threw stones and dirt at them. 14The king and all the people who were with him arrived exhausted at their destination, where David refreshed himself.

16:15—17:14 When it pleases God to remove persons from the world, he allows them to shut their eyes to all the light of reason and prudence and to cast themselves headlong into the most apparent danger. Just as when he deigned to destroy Absalom and to cut him off, he caused him to be led away by evil counsel and to disregard the discreet and prudent advice of Ahithophel. Therefore since God has appointed or foreordained before the creation of humankind the time and manner of our deaths—at what hour, in what place, and by what means whatsoever God calls away our friends or strikes at our person—it is always our duty to possess our souls with patience and not to allow the least disparaging or despairing word to proceed out of our mouths.

CHARLES DRELINCOURT
(1595–1669)
CHRISTIAN DEFENSE AGAINST THE FEAR OF DEATH

THE ADVICE OF AHITHOPHEL

15Now when Absalom and all the men of Israel arrived in Jerusalem, Ahithophel was with him. 16When David's friend Hushai the Arkite came to Absalom, Hushai said to him, "Long live the king! Long live the king!"

17Absalom said to Hushai, "Do you call this loyalty to your friend? Why didn't you go with your friend?" 18Hushai replied to Absalom, "No, I will be loyal to the one whom the LORD, these people, and all the men of Israel have chosen. 19Moreover, whom should I serve? Should it not be his son? Just as I served your father, so I will serve you."

20Then Absalom said to Ahithophel, "Give us your advice. What should we do?" 21Ahithophel replied to Absalom, "Sleep with your father's concubines whom he left to care for the palace. All Israel will hear that you have made yourself repulsive to your father. Then your followers will be motivated to support you." 22So they pitched a tent for Absalom on the roof, and Absalom slept with his father's concubines in the sight of all Israel.

23In those days Ahithophel's advice was considered as valuable as a prophetic revelation. Both David and Absalom highly regarded the advice of Ahithophel.

THE DEATH OF AHITHOPHEL

17 Ahithophel said to Absalom, "Let me pick out 12,000 men. Then I will go and pursue David this very night. 2When I catch up with him he will be exhausted and worn out. I will rout him, and the entire army that is with him will flee. I will kill only the king 3and will bring the entire army back to you. In exchange for the life of the man you are seeking, you will get back everyone. The entire army will return unharmed."

4This seemed like a good idea to Absalom and to all the leaders of Israel. 5But Absalom said, "Call for Hushai the Arkite, and let's hear what he has to say." 6So Hushai came to Absalom. Absalom said to him, "Here is what Ahithophel has advised. Should we follow his advice? If not, what would you recommend?"

7Hushai replied to Absalom, "Ahithophel's advice is not sound this time." 8Hushai went on to say, "You know your father and his men—they are soldiers and are as dangerous as a bear out in the wild that has been robbed of her cubs. Your father is an experienced soldier; he will not stay overnight with the army. 9At this very moment he is hiding out in one of the

caves or in some other similar place. If it should turn out that
he attacks our troops first, whoever hears about it will say, 'Absalom's army has been slaughtered!' 10If that happens even the
bravest soldier—one who is lion-hearted—will virtually melt
away. For all Israel knows that your father is a warrior and that
those who are with him are brave. 11My advice therefore is this:
Let all Israel from Dan to Beer Sheba—in number like the sand
by the sea—be mustered to you, and you lead them personally
into battle. 12We will come against him wherever he happens
to be found. We will descend on him like the dew falls on the
ground. Neither he nor any of the men who are with him will
be spared alive—not one of them! 13If he regroups in a city, all
Israel will take up ropes to that city and drag it down to the
valley, so that not a single pebble will be left there!"

14Then Absalom and all the men of Israel said, "The advice of
Hushai the Arkite sounds better than the advice of Ahithophel."
Now the LORD had decided to frustrate the sound advice of
Ahithophel, so that the LORD could bring disaster on Absalom.

15Then Hushai reported to Zadok and Abiathar the priests,
"Here is what Ahithophel has advised Absalom and the leaders
of Israel to do, and here is what I have advised. 16Now send word
quickly to David and warn him, "Don't spend the night at the fords
of the wilderness tonight. Instead, be sure you cross over, or else
the king and everyone who is with him may be overwhelmed."

17Now Jonathan and Ahimaaz were staying in En Rogel. A female servant would go and inform them, and they would then go
and inform King David. It was not advisable for them to be seen
going into the city. 18But a young man saw them on one occasion
and informed Absalom. So the two of them quickly departed
and went to the house of a man in Bahurim. There was a well in
his courtyard, and they got down in it. 19His wife then took the
covering and spread it over the top of the well and scattered some
grain over it. No one was aware of what she had done.

20When the servants of Absalom approached the woman
at her home, they asked, "Where are Ahimaaz and Jonathan?"
The woman replied to them, "They crossed over the stream."
Absalom's men searched but did not find them, so they returned
to Jerusalem.

21After the men had left, Ahimaaz and Jonathan climbed out
of the well. Then they left and informed King David. They advised David, "Get up and cross the stream quickly, for Ahithophel
has devised a plan to catch you." 22So David and all the people
who were with him got up and crossed the Jordan River. By dawn
there was not one person left who had not crossed the Jordan.

23When Ahithophel realized that his advice had not been
followed, he saddled his donkey and returned to his house in
his hometown. After setting his household in order, he hanged
himself. So he died and was buried in the grave of his father.

24Meanwhile David had gone to Mahanaim, while Absalom
and all the men of Israel had crossed the Jordan River. 25Absa-
lom had made Amasa general in command of the army in place
of Joab. (Now Amasa was the son of an Israelite man named
Jether, who had married Abigail the daughter of Nahash and
sister of Zeruiah, Joab's mother.) 26The army of Israel and Absalom camped in the land of Gilead.

27When David came to Mahanaim, Shobi the son of Nahash
from Rabbah of the Ammonites, Makir the son of Ammiel from
Lo Debar, and Barzillai the Gileadite from Rogelim 28brought
bedding, basins, and pottery utensils. They also brought food

18:1–18 Absalom was punished for what he most delighted in and in what he had the most pride. He was hanged by the hair of his head, which he nourished and kept long in order to glory in it. God's justice takes place when it punishes people for their sins. In this passage even nature itself conspires to take vengeance on this wicked man, for even the oak that holds on above and the mule walking away under him worked together to punish Absalom's wickedness. The oak had boughs winding and wrapping one within another, like a bramble or a bush. Absalom was caught by the hair in the oak, as the ram had been by its horns in the bush in Genesis 22:13. In this passage the same word is used to refer to this entanglement. Absalom hanged between heaven and earth as accursed by God. For this kind of death was accursed by the law of God. The same shameful death came to Ahithophel for his similar sin of rebellion and disobedience. In the same way, Judas afterward, whom Ahithophel resembled in many ways, hanged himself after he had betrayed Christ.

ANDREW WILLET **(1562–1621)**
A HARMONY UPON THE SECOND BOOK OF SAMUEL

for David and all who were with him, including wheat, barley,
flour, roasted grain, beans, lentils, [29]honey, curds, flocks, and
cheese. For they said, "The people are no doubt hungry, tired,
and thirsty there in the desert."

THE DEATH OF ABSALOM

18 David assembled the army that was with him. He appointed leaders of thousands and leaders of hundreds. [2]David
then sent out the army—a third under the leadership of Joab,
a third under the leadership of Joab's brother Abishai son of
Zeruiah, and a third under the leadership of Ittai the Gittite.
The king said to the troops, "I too will indeed march out with
you."

[3]But the soldiers replied, "You should not do this! For if we
should have to make a rapid retreat, they won't be concerned
about us. Even if half of us should die, they won't be concerned.
But you are like 10,000 of us! So it is better if you remain in
the city for support." [4]Then the king said to them, "I will do
whatever seems best to you."

So the king stayed beside the city gate, while all the army
marched out by hundreds and by thousands. [5]The king gave this
order to Joab, Abishai, and Ittai: "For my sake deal gently with the
young man Absalom." Now the entire army was listening when
the king gave all the leaders this order concerning Absalom.

[6]Then the army marched out to the field to fight against
Israel. The battle took place in the forest of Ephraim. [7]The
army of Israel was defeated there by David's men. The slaughter there was great that day—20,000 soldiers were killed. [8]The
battle there was spread out over the whole area, and the forest
consumed more soldiers than the sword devoured that day.

[9]Then Absalom happened to come across David's men. Now as
Absalom was riding on his mule, it went under the branches of
a large oak tree. His head got caught in the oak and he was suspended in midair, while the mule he had been riding kept going.
[10]When one of the men saw this, he reported it to Joab saying,
"I saw Absalom hanging in an oak tree." [11]Joab replied to the
man who was telling him this, "What! You saw this? Why didn't
you strike him down right on the spot? I would have given you
10 pieces of silver and a commemorative belt!"

[12]The man replied to Joab, "Even if I were receiving 1,000
pieces of silver, I would not strike the king's son! In our very
presence the king gave this order to you and Abishai and Ittai,
'Protect the young man Absalom for my sake.' [13]If I had acted at
risk of my own life—and nothing is hidden from the king—you
would have abandoned me."

[14]Joab replied, "I will not wait around like this for you!" He
took three spears in his hand and thrust them into the middle
of Absalom while he was still alive in the middle of the oak
tree. [15]Then 10 soldiers who were Joab's armor-bearers struck
Absalom and finished him off.

[16]Then Joab blew the trumpet and the army turned back
from chasing Israel, for Joab had called for the army to halt.
[17]They took Absalom, threw him into a large pit in the forest,
and stacked a huge pile of stones over him. In the meantime
all the Israelite soldiers fled to their homes.

[18]Before this Absalom had set up a monument and dedicated
it to himself in the King's Valley, reasoning, "I have no son who
will carry on my name." He named the monument after himself,
and to this day it is known as Absalom's Memorial.

DAVID LEARNS OF ABSALOM'S DEATH

19 Then Ahimaaz the son of Zadok said, "Let me run and give the king the good news that the LORD has vindicated him before his enemies." 20 But Joab said to him, "You will not be a bearer of good news today. You will bear good news some other day, but not today, for the king's son is dead."

21 Then Joab said to the Cushite, "Go and tell the king what you have seen." After bowing to Joab, the Cushite ran off. 22 Ahimaaz the son of Zadok again spoke to Joab, "Whatever happens, let me go after the Cushite." But Joab said, "Why is it that you want to go, my son? You have no good news that will bring you a reward." 23 But he said, "Whatever happens, I want to go!" So Joab said to him, "Then go!" So Ahimaaz ran by the way of the Jordan plain, and he passed the Cushite.

24 Now David was sitting between the inner and outer gates, and the watchman went up to the roof over the gate at the wall. When he looked, he saw a man running by himself. 25 So the watchman called out and informed the king. The king said, "If he is by himself, he brings good news." The runner came ever closer.

26 Then the watchman saw another man running. The watchman called out to the gatekeeper, "There is another man running by himself." The king said, "This one also is bringing good news." 27 The watchman said, "It appears to me that the first runner is Ahimaaz son of Zadok." The king said, "He is a good man, and he comes with good news."

28 Then Ahimaaz called out and said to the king, "Greetings!" He bowed down before the king with his face toward the ground and said, "May the LORD your God be praised because he has defeated the men who opposed my lord the king!"

29 The king replied, "How is the young man Absalom?" Ahimaaz replied, "I saw a great deal of confusion when Joab was sending the king's servant and me, your servant, but I don't know what it was all about." 30 The king said, "Turn aside and take your place here." So he turned aside and waited.

31 Then the Cushite arrived and said, "May my lord the king now receive the good news! The LORD has vindicated you today and delivered you from the hand of all who have rebelled against you!" 32 The king asked the Cushite, "How is the young man Absalom?" The Cushite replied, "May the enemies of my lord the king and all who have plotted against you be like that young man!"

33 The king then became very upset. He went up to the upper room over the gate and wept. As he went he said, "My son, Absalom! My son, my son, Absalom! If only I could have died in your place! Absalom, my son, my son!"

19 Joab was told, "The king is weeping and mourning over Absalom." 2 So the victory of that day was turned to mourning as far as all the people were concerned. For the people heard on that day, "The king is grieved over his son." 3 That day the people stole away to go to the city the way people who are embarrassed steal away in fleeing from battle. 4 The king covered his face and cried out loudly, "My son, Absalom! Absalom, my son, my son!"

5 So Joab visited the king at his home. He said, "Today you have embarrassed all your servants who have saved your life this day, as well as the lives of your sons, your daughters, your wives, and your concubines. 6 You seem to love your enemies and hate your friends! For you have as much as declared today that leaders and servants don't matter to you. I realize now that if Absalom were alive and all of us were dead today, it would be all right with you.

19:1–8 When King David had suffered injury at the hands of his impious and unnatural son, he not only bore with him in his mad passion but mourned over him in his death. He certainly was not caught in the meshes of carnal jealousy, seeing that it was not his own injuries but the sins of his son that moved him. For it was on this account he had given orders that his son should not be slain if he were conquered in battle, that he might have a place of repentance after he was subdued. When he was baffled in this design, he mourned over his son's death, not because of his own loss but because he knew to what punishment so impious an adulterer and parricide had been hurried.

AUGUSTINE **(354–430)**
ON CHRISTIAN DOCTRINE

7So get up now and go out and give some encouragement to your
servants. For I swear by the LORD that if you don't go out there,
not a single man will stay here with you tonight! This disaster
will be worse for you than any disaster that has overtaken you
from your youth right to the present time!"

8So the king got up and sat at the city gate. When all the
people were informed that the king was sitting at the city gate,
they all came before him.

DAVID GOES BACK TO JERUSALEM

But the Israelite soldiers had all fled to their own homes. 9All
the people throughout all the tribes of Israel were arguing
among themselves saying, "The king delivered us from the hand
of our enemies. He rescued us from the hand of the Philistines,
but now he has fled from the land because of Absalom. 10But
Absalom, whom we anointed as our king, has died in battle. So
now why do you hesitate to bring the king back?"

11Then King David sent a message to Zadok and Abiathar the
priests saying, "Tell the elders of Judah, 'Why should you delay
any further in bringing the king back to his palace, when everything Israel is saying has come to the king's attention. 12You
are my brothers—my very own flesh and blood! Why should you
delay any further in bringing the king back?' 13Say to Amasa,
'Are you not my flesh and blood? God will punish me severely,
if from this time on you are not the commander of my army
in place of Joab!'"

14He won over the hearts of all the men of Judah as though
they were one man. Then they sent word to the king saying, "Return, you and all your servants as well." 15So the king returned
and came to the Jordan River.

Now the people of Judah had come to Gilgal to meet the
king and to help him cross the Jordan. 16Shimei son of Gera
the Benjaminite from Bahurim came down quickly with the
men of Judah to meet King David. 17There were 1,000 men from
Benjamin with him, along with Ziba the servant of Saul's household, and with him his 15 sons and 20 servants. They hurriedly
crossed the Jordan within sight of the king. 18They crossed at
the ford in order to help the king's household cross and to do
whatever he thought appropriate.

Now after he had crossed the Jordan, Shimei son of Gera
threw himself down before the king. 19He said to the king,
"Don't think badly of me, my lord, and don't recall the sin of
your servant on the day when you, my lord the king, left Jerusalem! Please don't call it to mind! 20For I, your servant, know
that I sinned, and I have come today as the first of all the house
of Joseph to come down to meet my lord the king."

21Abishai son of Zeruiah replied, "For this should not Shimei
be put to death? After all, he cursed the LORD's anointed!" 22But
David said, "What do we have in common, you sons of Zeruiah?
You are like my enemy today! Should anyone be put to death
in Israel today? Don't I know that today I am king over Israel?"
23The king said to Shimei, "You won't die." The king vowed an
oath concerning this.

24Now Mephibosheth, Saul's grandson, came down to meet
the king. From the day the king had left until the day he safely
returned, Mephibosheth had not cared for his feet nor trimmed
his mustache nor washed his clothes.

25When he came from Jerusalem to meet the king, the king
asked him, "Why didn't you go with me, Mephibosheth?" 26He

replied, "My lord the king, my servant deceived me! I said, 'Let me get my donkey saddled so that I can ride on it and go with the king,' for I am lame. 27But my servant has slandered me to my lord the king. But my lord the king is like an angel of God. Do whatever seems appropriate to you. 28After all, there was no one in the entire house of my grandfather who did not deserve death from my lord the king. But instead you allowed me to eat at your own table! What further claim do I have to ask the king for anything?"

29Then the king replied to him, "Why should you continue speaking like this? You and Ziba will inherit the field together." 30Mephibosheth said to the king, "Let him have the whole thing! My lord the king has returned safely to his house!"

31Now when Barzillai the Gileadite had come down from Rogelim, he crossed the Jordan with the king so he could send him on his way from there. 32But Barzillai was very old—eighty years old, in fact—and he had taken care of the king when he stayed in Mahanaim, for he was a very rich man. 33So the king said to Barzillai, "Cross over with me, and I will take care of you while you are with me in Jerusalem."

34Barzillai replied to the king, "How many days do I have left to my life, that I should go up with the king to Jerusalem? 35I am now eighty years old. Am I able to discern good and bad? Can I taste what I eat and drink? Am I still able to hear the voices of male and female singers? Why should I continue to be a burden to my lord the king? 36I will cross the Jordan with the king and go a short distance. Why should the king reward me in this way? 37Let me return so that I may die in my own town near the grave of my father and my mother. But look, here is your servant Kimham. Let him cross over with my lord the king. Do for him whatever seems appropriate to you."

38The king replied, "Kimham will cross over with me, and I will do for him whatever I deem appropriate. And whatever you choose, I will do for you."

39So all the people crossed the Jordan, as did the king. After the king had kissed him and blessed him, Barzillai returned to his home. 40When the king crossed over to Gilgal, Kimham crossed over with him. Now all the soldiers of Judah along with half the soldiers of Israel had helped the king cross over.

41Then all the men of Israel began coming to the king. They asked the king, "Why did our brothers, the men of Judah, sneak the king away and help the king and his household cross the Jordan—and not only him but all of David's men as well?" 42All the men of Judah replied to the men of Israel, "Because the king is our close relative! Why are you so upset about this? Have we eaten at the king's expense? Or have we misappropriated anything for our own use?" 43The men of Israel replied to the men of Judah, "We have 10 shares in the king, and we have a greater claim on David than you do! Why do you want to curse us? Weren't we the first to suggest bringing back our king?" But the comments of the men of Judah were more severe than those of the men of Israel.

SHEBA'S REBELLION

20 Now a wicked man named Sheba son of Bikri, a Benjaminite, happened to be there. He blew the trumpet and said,
"We have no share in David;
we have no inheritance in this son of Jesse!
Every man go home, O Israel!"

20:1–22 Those who rise up against kings are worthy of punishment, even though they are sons or friends. Neither Absalom nor Sheba, who rose against David and strove concerning the kingdom, escaped without punishment. They spoke evil: Absalom of his father, David, as of an unjust judge, saying to everyone, "Your claims are legitimate and appropriate. But there is no representative of the king who will listen to you . . . If only they would make me a judge in the land!" (2 Sam 15:3–4); and Sheba, "We have no share in David; we have no inheritance in this son of Jesse!" It is plain that he could not endure to be under the government of David, of whom God said, "I have found David the son of Jesse to be a man after my heart, who will accomplish everything I want him to do" (Acts 13:22).

CONSTITUTIONS OF THE HOLY FATHERS **(C. 375)**

2 So all the men of Israel deserted David and followed Sheba
son of Bikri. But the men of Judah stuck by their king all the
way from the Jordan River to Jerusalem.
3 Then David went to his palace in Jerusalem. The king took
the 10 concubines he had left to care for the palace and placed
them under confinement. Though he provided for their needs,
he did not sleep with them. They remained under restriction
until the day they died, living out the rest of their lives as
widows.
4 Then the king said to Amasa, "Call the men of Judah together
for me in three days, and you be present here with them too."
5 So Amasa went out to call Judah together. But in doing so he
took longer than the time that the king had allotted him.
6 Then David said to Abishai, "Now Sheba son of Bikri will
cause greater disaster for us than Absalom did! Take your lord's
servants and pursue him. Otherwise he will secure fortified
cities for himself and get away from us." 7 So Joab's men, accompanied by the Kerethites, the Pelethites, and all the warriors,
left Jerusalem to pursue Sheba son of Bikri.
8 When they were near the big rock that is in Gibeon, Amasa
came to them. Now Joab was dressed in military attire and had
a dagger in its sheath belted to his waist. When he advanced,
it fell out.
9 Joab said to Amasa, "How are you, my brother?" With his
right hand Joab took hold of Amasa's beard as if to greet him
with a kiss. 10 Amasa did not protect himself from the knife in
Joab's other hand, and Joab stabbed him in the abdomen, causing Amasa's intestines to spill out on the ground. There was no
need to stab him again; the first blow was fatal. Then Joab and
his brother Abishai pursued Sheba son of Bikri.
11 One of Joab's soldiers who stood over Amasa said, "Whoever
is for Joab and whoever is for David, follow Joab!" 12 Amasa was
squirming in his own blood in the middle of the path, and this
man had noticed that all the soldiers stopped. Having noticed
that everyone who came across Amasa stopped, the man pulled
him away from the path and into the field and threw a garment
over him. 13 Once he had removed Amasa from the path, everyone followed Joab to pursue Sheba son of Bikri.
14 Sheba traveled through all the tribes of Israel to Abel of
Beth Maacah and all the Berite region. When they had assembled, they too joined him. 15 So Joab's men came and laid siege
against him in Abel of Beth Maacah. They prepared a siege ramp
outside the city that stood against its outer rampart. As all of
Joab's soldiers were trying to break through the wall so that it
would collapse, 16 a wise woman called out from the city, "Listen
up! Listen up! Tell Joab, 'Come near so that I may speak to you.'"
17 When he approached her, the woman asked, "Are you Joab?"
He replied, "I am." She said to him, "Listen to the words of your
servant." He said, "Go ahead. I'm listening." 18 She said, "In the
past they would always say, 'Let them inquire in Abel,' and that is
how they settled things. 19 I represent the peaceful and the faithful in Israel. You are attempting to destroy an important city
in Israel. Why should you swallow up the LORD's inheritance?"
20 Joab answered, "Not at all! I don't intend to swallow up or
destroy anything! 21 That's not the way things are. There is a man
from the hill country of Ephraim named Sheba son of Bikri. He
has rebelled against King David. Give me just this one man, and
I will leave the city." The woman said to Joab, "This very minute
his head will be thrown over the wall to you!"

22Then the woman went to all the people with her wise advice and they cut off Sheba's head and threw it out to Joab. Joab
blew the trumpet, and his men dispersed from the city, each
going to his own home. Joab returned to the king in Jerusalem.
23Now Joab was the general in command of all the army of
Israel. Benaiah the son of Jehoiada was over the Kerethites and
the Perethites. 24Adoniram was supervisor of the work crews.
Jehoshaphat son of Ahilud was the secretary. 25Sheva was the
scribe, and Zadok and Abiathar were the priests. 26Ira the Jairite
was David's personal priest.

THE GIBEONITES DEMAND REVENGE

21 During David's reign there was a famine for three con-
secutive years. So David inquired of the LORD. The LORD
said, "It is because of Saul and his bloodstained family, because
he murdered the Gibeonites."
2So the king summoned the Gibeonites and spoke with them.
(Now the Gibeonites were not descendants of Israel; they were
a remnant of the Amorites. The Israelites had made a promise
to them, but Saul tried to kill them because of his zeal for the
people of Israel and Judah.) 3David said to the Gibeonites, "What
can I do for you, and how can I make amends so that you will
bless the LORD's inheritance?"
4The Gibeonites said to him, "We have no claim to silver or
gold from Saul or from his family, nor would we be justified in
putting to death anyone in Israel." David asked, "What then are
you asking me to do for you?" 5They replied to the king, "As for
this man who exterminated us and who schemed against us
so that we were destroyed and left without status throughout
all the borders of Israel—6let seven of his male descendants be
turned over to us, and we will execute them before the LORD
in Gibeah of Saul, who was the LORD's chosen one." The king
replied, "I will turn them over."
7The king had mercy on Mephibosheth son of Jonathan, the
son of Saul, in light of the LORD's oath that had been taken between David and Jonathan son of Saul. 8So the king took Armoni
and Mephibosheth, the two sons of Aiah's daughter Rizpah
whom she had born to Saul, and the five sons of Saul's daughter
Merab whom she had born to Adriel the son of Barzillai the
Meholathite. 9He turned them over to the Gibeonites, and they
executed them on a hill before the LORD. The seven of them
died together; they were put to death during harvest time—
during the first days of the beginning of the barley harvest.
10Rizpah the daughter of Aiah took sackcloth and spread it
out for herself on a rock. From the beginning of the harvest
until the rain fell on them, she did not allow the birds of the air
to feed on them by day, nor the wild animals by night. 11When
David was told what Rizpah daughter of Aiah, Saul's concubine, had done, 12he went and took the bones of Saul and of
his son Jonathan from the leaders of Jabesh Gilead. (They had
secretly taken them from the plaza at Beth Shan. It was there
that Philistines publicly exposed their corpses after they had
killed Saul at Gilboa.) 13David brought the bones of Saul and of
Jonathan his son from there; they also gathered up the bones
of those who had been executed.
14They buried the bones of Saul and his son Jonathan in the
land of Benjamin at Zela in the grave of his father Kish. After
they had done everything that the king had commanded, God
responded to their prayers for the land.

21:1–14 Both the prayers and imprecations of the saints are efficacious—a very eminent example of this is displayed here in the Gibeonites who did not plead with the people of Israel but entreated God to consider them, oppressed and wretched, and to vindicate the injustice inflicted on them. By their groans and tears they caused God to punish the people of Israel with famine because they would not punish Saul's descendants. Yes, as soon as Saul's descendants were executed—the Gibeonites had begun to bless the heritage of the Lord—the famine ceased. So also as soon as Abraham had begun to pray on behalf of King Abimelech, who had returned to Abraham his wife, Sarah, whom he had taken away, the plague with which God had stricken Abimelech's entire family was removed. And the moment Samuel stopped praying on behalf of Saul, Saul had no success afterward.

HIERONYMUS WELLER VON MOLSDORF (1499–1572)
ANNOTATIONS ON 2 SAMUEL

ISRAEL ENGAGES IN VARIOUS BATTLES WITH THE PHILISTINES

15 Another battle was fought between the Philistines and Israel. So David went down with his soldiers and fought the
Philistines. David became exhausted. 16 Now Ishbi-Benob, one
of the descendants of Rapha, had a spear that weighed 300
bronze shekels, and he was armed with a new weapon. He
had said that he would kill David. 17 But Abishai the son of
Zeruiah came to David's aid, striking the Philistine down and
killing him. Then David's men took an oath saying, "You will
not go out to battle with us again! You must not extinguish
the lamp of Israel!"

18 Later there was another battle with the Philistines, this
time in Gob. On that occasion Sibbekai the Hushathite killed
Saph, who was one of the descendants of Rapha. 19 Yet another
battle occurred with the Philistines in Gob. On that occasion
Elhanan the son of Jair the Bethlehemite killed the brother of
Goliath the Gittite, the shaft of whose spear was like a weaver's
beam. 20 Yet another battle occurred in Gath. On that occasion
there was a large man who had six fingers on each hand and
six toes on each foot, twenty-four in all! He too was a descendant of Rapha. 21 When he taunted Israel, Jonathan, the son
of David's brother Shimeah, killed him. 22 These four were the
descendants of Rapha who lived in Gath; they were killed by
David and his soldiers.

22:1–51 In scripture the horn often denotes royal power as the chief power, therefore the church is called the horn of Christ. Christ fights and vanquishes the world and its prince through the church, which is his exceedingly strong and invincible horn. The church, on the contrary, calls Christ her horn because Christ is the strength of his church through whom it triumphs over the world. He himself is strength and wisdom for all who believe in him. David says here "the horn that saves me," for God is the victorious might of Christ for salvation. Therefore, just as the church is Christ's, Christ is God's and, on the contrary, God is also Christ's, and Christ is the church's; so the church is the horn of Christ, Christ is the horn of God, and on the contrary, God is the horn of Christ, and Christ is the horn of the church. For here there is reciprocal power, and it is united in one.

MARTIN LUTHER **(1483–1546)**
SCHOLIA ON PSALM 18:2

DAVID SINGS TO THE LORD

22 David sang to the LORD the words of this song when the
LORD rescued him from the power of all his enemies,
including Saul. 2 He said:

"The LORD is my high ridge, my stronghold, my
deliverer.
3 My God is my rocky summit where I take shelter,
my shield, the horn that saves me, my stronghold,
my refuge, my savior. You save me from violence!
4 I called to the LORD, who is worthy of praise,
and I was delivered from my enemies.
5 The waves of death engulfed me;
the currents of chaos overwhelmed me.
6 The ropes of Sheol tightened around me;
the snares of death trapped me.
7 In my distress I called to the LORD;
I called to my God.
From his heavenly temple he heard my voice;
he listened to my cry for help.
8 The earth heaved and shook;
the foundations of the sky trembled.
They heaved because he was angry.
9 Smoke ascended from his nose;
fire devoured as it came from his mouth;
he hurled down fiery coals.
10 He made the sky sink as he descended;
a thick cloud was under his feet.
11 He mounted a winged angel and flew;
he glided on the wings of the wind.
12 He shrouded himself in darkness,
in thick rain clouds.
13 From the brightness in front of him
came coals of fire.

14 The LORD thundered from the sky;
the Most High shouted loudly.
15 He shot arrows and scattered them,
lightning and routed them.
16 The depths of the sea were exposed;
the inner regions of the world were uncovered
by the LORD's battle cry,
by the powerful breath from his nose.
17 He reached down from above and grabbed me;
he pulled me from the surging water.
18 He rescued me from my strong enemy,
from those who hate me,
for they were too strong for me.
19 They confronted me in my day of calamity,
but the LORD helped me.
20 He brought me out into a wide open place;
he delivered me because he was pleased with me.
21 The LORD repaid me for my godly deeds;
he rewarded my blameless behavior.
22 For I have obeyed the LORD's commands;
I have not rebelled against my God.
23 For I am aware of all his regulations,
and I do not reject his rules.
24 I was blameless before him;
I kept myself from sinning.
25 The LORD rewarded me for my godly deeds;
he took notice of my blameless behavior.
26 You prove to be loyal to one who is faithful;
you prove to be trustworthy to one who is innocent.
27 You prove to be reliable to one who is blameless,
but you prove to be deceptive to one who is
perverse.
28 You deliver oppressed people,
but you watch the proud and bring them down.
29 Indeed, you are my lamp, LORD.
The LORD illumines the darkness around me.
30 Indeed, with your help I can charge against an
army;
by my God's power I can jump over a wall.
31 The one true God acts in a faithful manner;
the LORD's promise is reliable;
he is a shield to all who take shelter in him.
32 Indeed, who is God besides the LORD?
Who is a protector besides our God?
33 The one true God is my mighty refuge;
he removes the obstacles in my way.
34 He gives me the agility of a deer;
he enables me to negotiate the rugged terrain.
35 He trains my hands for battle;
my arms can bend even the strongest bow.
36 You give me your protective shield;
your willingness to help enables me to prevail.
37 You widen my path;
my feet do not slip.
38 I chase my enemies and destroy them;
I do not turn back until I wipe them out.
39 I wipe them out and beat them to death;
they cannot get up;
they fall at my feet.

40 You give me strength for battle;
you make my foes kneel before me.
41 You make my enemies retreat;
I destroy those who hate me.
42 They cry out, but there is no one to help them;
they cry out to the LORD, but he does not answer
them.
43 I grind them as fine as the dust of the ground;
I crush them and stomp them like clay in the streets.
44 You rescue me from a hostile army;
you preserve me as a leader of nations;
people over whom I had no authority are now my
subjects.
45 Foreigners are powerless before me;
when they hear of my exploits, they submit to me.
46 Foreigners lose their courage;
they shake with fear as they leave their strongholds.
47 The LORD is alive!
My Protector is praiseworthy!
The God who delivers me is exalted as king!
48 The one true God completely vindicates me;
he makes nations submit to me.
49 He delivers me from my enemies;
you snatch me away from those who attack me;
you rescue me from violent men.
50 So I will give you thanks, O LORD, before the nations!
I will sing praises to you.
51 He gives his king magnificent victories;
he is faithful to his chosen ruler,
to David and to his descendants forever!"

DAVID'S FINAL WORDS

23 These are the final words of David:
"The oracle of David son of Jesse,
the oracle of the man raised up as
the ruler chosen by the God of Jacob,
Israel's beloved singer of songs:
2 The LORD's Spirit spoke through me;
his word was on my tongue.
3 The God of Israel spoke,
the Protector of Israel spoke to me.
The one who rules fairly among men,
the one who rules in the fear of God,
4 is like the light of morning when the sun comes up,
a morning in which there are no clouds.
He is like the brightness after rain
that produces grass from the earth.
5 My dynasty is approved by God,
for he has made a perpetual covenant with me,
arranged in all its particulars and secured.
He always delivers me,
and brings all I desire to fruition.
6 But evil people are like thorns—
all of them are tossed away,
for they cannot be held in the hand.
7 The one who touches them
must use an iron instrument
or the wooden shaft of a spear.
They are completely burned up right where they lie!"

23:1–7 When storms arise, there is no hope but in our anchor, no stay or relief but in God's promises, which are settled and sure, established in heaven, and therefore never reversed or canceled on the earth. And if this faithful and sure word had not been David's delight and comfort; if he had not, in all the changes and chances of his own life, remembered that all God's promises are made in heaven where there is no inconsistency or repentance, he would have perished in his affliction. Though David, by a prophetical spirit, foresaw that God would not make his house to grow but to become a dry and withered stock of Jesse, yet herein was the ground of all his salvation and of all desire: The Lord had made a covenant with him, ordered in all things and sure; he had sworn by his holiness that he would not fail David. So it was as impossible for God to be unholy as for the word of promise made to David to fall in the ground and be untrue.

EDWARD REYNOLDS
(1599–1676)
THE SINFULNESS OF SIN

DAVID'S WARRIORS

8These are the names of David's warriors:
Josheb Basshebeth, a Tahkemonite, was head of the officers.
He killed 800 men with his spear in one battle. 9Next in command was Eleazar son of Dodo, the son of Ahohi. He was one
of the three warriors who were with David when they defied
the Philistines who were assembled there for battle. When the
men of Israel retreated, 10he stood his ground and fought the
Philistines until his hand grew so tired that it seemed stuck to
his sword. The LORD gave a great victory on that day. When the
army returned to him, the only thing left to do was to plunder
the corpses.

11Next in command was Shammah son of Agee the Hararite.
When the Philistines assembled at Lehi, where there happened
to be an area of a field that was full of lentils, the army retreated
before the Philistines. 12But he made a stand in the middle of
that area. He defended it and defeated the Philistines; the LORD
gave them a great victory.

13At the time of the harvest three of the thirty leaders
went down to David at the cave of Adullam. A band of Philistines was camped in the valley of Rephaim. 14David was in
the stronghold at the time, while a Philistine garrison was in
Bethlehem. 15David was thirsty and said, "How I wish someone would give me some water to drink from the cistern in
Bethlehem near the gate!" 16So the three elite warriors broke
through the Philistine forces and drew some water from the
cistern in Bethlehem near the gate. They carried it back to
David, but he refused to drink it. He poured it out as a drink
offering to the LORD 17and said, "O LORD, I will not do this! It
is equivalent to the blood of the men who risked their lives
by going." So he refused to drink it. Such were the exploits of
the three elite warriors.

18Abishai son of Zeruiah, the brother of Joab, was head of
the three. He killed 300 men with his spear and gained fame
among the three. 19From the three he was given honor and
he became their officer, even though he was not one of the
three.

20Benaiah son of Jehoiada was a brave warrior from Kabzeel
who performed great exploits. He struck down the two sons of
Ariel of Moab. He also went down and killed a lion in a cistern
on a snowy day. 21He also killed an impressive-looking Egyptian. The Egyptian wielded a spear, while Benaiah attacked him
with a club. He grabbed the spear out of the Egyptian's hand
and killed him with his own spear. 22Such were the exploits of
Benaiah son of Jehoiada, who gained fame among the three elite
warriors. 23He received honor from the 30 warriors, though he
was not one of the three elite warriors. David put him in charge
of his bodyguard.

24Included with the 30 were the following: Asahel the brother of Joab, Elhanan son of Dodo from Bethlehem, 25Shammah
the Harodite, Elika the Harodite, 26Helez the Paltite, Ira son
of Ikkesh from Tekoa, 27Abiezer the Anathothite, Mebunnai
the Hushathite, 28Zalmon the Ahohite, Maharai the Netophathite, 29Heled son of Baanah the Netophathite, Ittai son of
Ribai from Gibeah in Benjamin, 30Benaiah the Pirathonite,
Hiddai from the wadis of Gaash, 31Abi-Albon the Arbathite,
Azmaveth the Barhumite, 32Eliahba the Shaalbonite, the sons
of Jashen, Jonathan 33son of Shammah the Hararite, Ahiam
son of Sharar the Hararite, 34Eliphelet son of Ahasbai the

Maacathite, Eliam son of Ahithophel the Gilonite, 35 Hezrai the Carmelite, Paarai the Arbite, 36 Igal son of Nathan from Zobah, Bani the Gadite, 37 Zelek the Ammonite, Naharai the Beerothite (the armor-bearer of Joab son of Zeruiah), 38 Ira the Ithrite, Gareb the Ithrite, 39 and Uriah the Hittite. Altogether there were 37.

DAVID DISPLEASES THE LORD BY TAKING A CENSUS

24 The LORD's anger again raged against Israel, and he incited David against them, saying, "Go count Israel and Judah." 2 The king told Joab, the general in command of his army, "Go through all the tribes of Israel from Dan to Beer Sheba and muster the army, so I may know the size of the army."

3 Joab replied to the king, "May the LORD your God make the army a hundred times larger right before the eyes of my lord the king! But why does my master the king want to do this?"

4 But the king's edict stood, despite the objections of Joab and the leaders of the army. So Joab and the leaders of the army left the king's presence in order to muster the Israelite army.

5 They crossed the Jordan and camped at Aroer, on the south side of the city, at the wadi of Gad, near Jazer. 6 Then they went on to Gilead and to the region of Tahtim Hodshi, coming to Dan Jaan and on around to Sidon. 7 Then they went to the fortress of Tyre and all the cities of the Hivites and the Canaanites. Then they went on to the Negev of Judah, to Beer Sheba. 8 They went through all the land and after nine months and twenty days came back to Jerusalem.

9 Joab reported the number of warriors to the king. In Israel there were 800,000 sword-wielding warriors, and in Judah there were 500,000 soldiers.

10 David felt guilty after he had numbered the army. David said to the LORD, "I have sinned greatly by doing this! Now, O LORD, please remove the guilt of your servant, for I have acted very foolishly."

11 When David got up the next morning, the LORD's message had already come to the prophet Gad, David's seer: 12 "Go, tell David, 'This is what the LORD has said: I am offering you three forms of judgment. Pick one of them and I will carry it out against you.'"

13 Gad went to David and told him, "Shall seven years of famine come upon your land? Or shall you flee for three months from your enemies with them in hot pursuit? Or shall there be three days of plague in your land? Now decide what I should tell the one who sent me." 14 David said to Gad, "I am very upset! I prefer that we be attacked by the LORD, for his mercy is great; I do not want to be attacked by human hands!"

15 So the LORD sent a plague through Israel from the morning until the completion of the appointed time, and 70,000 people died from Dan to Beer Sheba. 16 When the angel extended his hand to destroy Jerusalem, the LORD relented from his judgment. He told the angel who was killing the people, "That's enough! Stop now!" (Now the angel of the LORD was near the threshing floor of Araunah the Jebusite.)

17 When he saw the angel who was destroying the people, David said to the LORD, "Look, it is I who have sinned and done this evil thing! As for these sheep—what have they done? Attack me and my family."

24:1–17 We poor human beings desire to be continuously strutting about, which is very distasteful to God, as we can see when David took a census of the children of Israel in order to see how powerful he was, doubtlessly ascribing all credit for the might of the nation to himself. Therefore God became angry and offered David the choice of three plagues, one of which he had to select as punishment for having counted the people. David selected the bubonic plague so that he himself might be stricken. Note that when David wished to brag and count his force, he showed that he desired to know the extent of that power which was not his, but God's. For this David was severely punished.

ULRICH ZWINGLI **(1484–1531)**
WARNING AGAINST CONTROL OF FOREIGN LANDS

DAVID ACQUIRES A THRESHING FLOOR AND CONSTRUCTS AN ALTAR THERE

18So Gad went to David that day and told him, "Go up and build
an altar for the LORD on the threshing floor of Araunah the
Jebusite." 19So David went up as Gad instructed him to do, according to the LORD's instructions.

20When Araunah looked out and saw the king and his servants approaching him, he went out and bowed to the king with
his face to the ground. 21Araunah said, "Why has my lord the
king come to his servant?" David replied, "To buy from you the
threshing floor so I can build an altar for the LORD, so that
the plague may be removed from the people." 22Araunah told
David, "My lord the king may take whatever he wishes and offer
it. Look! Here are oxen for burnt offerings, and threshing sledges
and harnesses for wood. 23I, the servant of my lord the king, give
it all to the king!" Araunah also told the king, "May the LORD
your God show you favor!" 24But the king said to Araunah, "No,
I insist on buying it from you! I will not offer to the LORD my
God burnt sacrifices that cost me nothing."

So David bought the threshing floor and the oxen for 50
pieces of silver. 25Then David built an altar for the LORD there
and offered burnt sacrifices and peace offerings. And the LORD
accepted prayers for the land, and the plague was removed
from Israel.

AUTHOR	AUDIENCE	DATE	PURPOSE	THEMES
Unknown	God's chosen people, the Israelites	Probably around 550 BC, during the Babylonian exile	This book was written to chronicle the continuation of the Davidic monarchy and its collapse through disobedience, in order to remind the children of Israel of their covenantal responsibilities to God.	The failure of David's line; the division of Israel; ungodly leadership; and virtuous living

The first book of the Kings opens with David's transition of his kingship to the next in a long line of descendants, beginning with Solomon. Traditionally, this book is thought to have been written by Jeremiah during Israel's exile as a way to explain how God's chosen people could have lost the promised land and been ruled by pagan nations. Both this book and the second book of the Kings chronicle that failure.

Solomon's reign begins with a charge from his father, David: "Be strong and become a man! Do the job the Lord your God has assigned you by following his instructions and obeying his rules, commandments, regulations, and laws as written in the law of Moses Then you will succeed in all you do and seek to accomplish, and the Lord will fulfill his promise to me" (2:2–4). Although Solomon appealed to the Davidic covenant during the dedication of the glorious temple of the Lord, eventually he negated the terms of that same covenant by taking for himself foreign wives. "His wives shifted his allegiance to other gods; he was not wholeheartedly devoted to the Lord his God, as his father David had been . . . Solomon did evil in the Lord's sight; he did not remain loyal to the Lord, as his father David had" (11:4, 6).

The consequence was the dissolution of his kingdom, yet not right away and not entirely. "We are here given an example of God's kindness but also God's truth and truthfulness," wrote Reformer Johannes Piscator.

> For even though Solomon had sinned greatly, God refused to tear away the kingdom from Solomon while he lived. Similarly, God refused to tear not only the kingdom away from Solomon but even away from his ancestors, for God decided to allow one tribe to remain of his sons. And this was due to God's former promise to David that he would leave him an everlasting dynasty.

This mercy is one of many aspects of the character of God that can be glimpsed throughout this book. The Lord is also revealed as sovereign, directing the course of redemptive history, the one who "is the only genuine God" (8:60). He is transcendent and imminent, omnipresent, omnipotent, and omniscient. He is a God of love, righteousness, and justice. Perhaps above all he is a God of grace, which would have been a comfort to the people of Judah during their exile.

1 KINGS

The circumstances of exile were connected to the failure of God's people to live up to their covenantal responsibilities. Solomon reminded the people of this covenant when he dedicated the temple, referencing both the promises and requirements of that relationship: "The Lord is worthy of praise because he has made Israel his people secure just as he promised! Not one of all the faithful promises he made through his servant Moses is left unfulfilled! May the Lord our God . . . make us submissive, so we can follow all his instructions and obey the commandments, rules, and regulations he commanded our ancestors" (8:56–58).

Yet the people's hearts were turned as Solomon's was, for eventually the kingdom split as a consequence of his sin, and wicked kings led them into idolatry. "Blessed Lord," Matthew Henry offered in response to this offense, "give us grace to reverence your temple, your ordinances, your house of prayer, your Sabbaths, and never more, like Jeroboam, to set up in our hearts any idol of abomination. Be to us everything precious; reign and rule in our hearts, the hope of glory."

Like the other historical books of the Bible, the church has often viewed the events recorded as examples and warnings. Figures such as Solomon show how a life devoted to the Lord can quickly devolve into disobedience and apostasy. Further, the account of Jeroboam's reign illustrates how people can be influenced by the evil ways of their leaders. Thus the first book of the Kings is a clarion call to faithful living. The Geneva Bible provides an apt summation:

> This book declares how kingdoms will only flourish if they are preserved by God's protection. In other words, God protects his people when his Word is set forth, virtue is esteemed, vice is punished, and harmony is maintained. Otherwise the kingdom will fall into corruption and division as appears at the dividing of the kingdom under Rehoboam and Jeroboam.

1:1–53 Six sons were born to David in Hebron. Amnon and Absalom had died and nothing is recorded of Chileab, so that Adonijah was now the greatest among the surviving brothers. The rest of David's sons, including Solomon, were born later in Jerusalem. Adonijah put his faith in this, that no one sought to be king after David's death but him. Without a command, without a call, without the word of God, Adonijah wanted to occupy the kingship as if it were owed him by right. He put his trust in this: that he was born first; that he was loved by his father; that he marched with glorious chariots and horsemen; and that Joab the commander of the army, Abiathar the priest, and all his brothers and David's sons besides Solomon were under this impression too. This was the impious feeling as long as the strength of the flesh was secure, trusting in its own cause and not fearing God.

JOHANNES BUGENHAGEN
(1485–1558)
COMMENTARY ON FIRST KINGS

ADONIJAH TRIES TO SEIZE THE THRONE

1 King David was very old; even when they covered him with
blankets, he could not get warm. 2His servants advised him,
"A young virgin must be found for our master, the king, to take
care of the king's needs and serve as his nurse. She can also
sleep with you and keep our master, the king, warm." 3So they
looked through all Israel for a beautiful young woman and
found Abishag, a Shunammite, and brought her to the king.
4The young woman was very beautiful; she became the king's
nurse and served him, but the king was not intimate with her.
5Now Adonijah, son of David and Haggith, was promoting
himself, boasting, "I will be king!" He managed to acquire chariots and horsemen, as well as 50 men to serve as his royal guard.
6(Now his father had never corrected him by saying, "Why do
you do such things?" He was also very handsome and had been
born right after Absalom.) 7He collaborated with Joab son of
Zeruiah and with Abiathar the priest, and they supported him.
8But Zadok the priest, Benaiah son of Jehoiada, Nathan the
prophet, Shimei, Rei, and David's elite warriors did not ally
themselves with Adonijah. 9Adonijah sacrificed sheep, cattle,
and fattened steers at the Stone of Zoheleth near En Rogel. He
invited all his brothers, the king's sons, as well as all the men of
Judah, the king's servants. 10But he did not invite Nathan the
prophet, Benaiah, the elite warriors, or his brother Solomon.
11Nathan said to Bathsheba, Solomon's mother, "Has it been
reported to you that Haggith's son Adonijah has become king
behind our master David's back? 12Now let me give you some
advice as to how you can save your life and your son Solomon's
life. 13Visit King David and say to him, 'My master, O king, did
you not solemnly promise your servant, "Surely your son Solomon will be king after me; he will sit on my throne"? So why
has Adonijah become king?' 14While you are still there speaking
to the king, I will arrive and verify your report."
15So Bathsheba visited the king in his private quarters. (The
king was very old, and Abishag the Shunammite was serving
the king.) 16Bathsheba bowed down on the floor before the
king. The king said, "What do you want?" 17She replied to him,
"My master, you swore an oath to your servant by the LORD
your God, 'Solomon your son will be king after me and he will
sit on my throne.' 18But now, look, Adonijah has become king!
But you, my master the king, are not even aware of it! 19He has
sacrificed many cattle, steers, and sheep and has invited all the
king's sons, Abiathar the priest, and Joab, the commander of
the army, but he has not invited your servant Solomon. 20Now,
my master, O king, all Israel is watching anxiously to see who
is named to succeed my master the king on the throne. 21If a
decision is not made, when my master the king is buried with
his ancestors, my son Solomon and I will be considered state
criminals."
22Just then, while she was still speaking to the king, Nathan
the prophet arrived. 23The king was told, "Nathan the prophet
is here." Nathan entered and bowed before the king with his
face to the floor. 24Nathan said, "My master, O king, did you
announce, 'Adonijah will be king after me; he will sit on my
throne'? 25For today he has gone down and sacrificed many
cattle, steers, and sheep and has invited all the king's sons, the
army commanders, and Abiathar the priest. At this moment
they are having a feast in his presence, and they have declared,
'Long live King Adonijah!' 26But he did not invite me—your

servant—or Zadok the priest, or Benaiah son of Jehoiada, or
your servant Solomon. 27Has my master the king authorized
this without informing your servants who should succeed my
master the king on his throne?"

DAVID PICKS SOLOMON AS HIS SUCCESSOR

28King David responded, "Summon Bathsheba!" She came and
stood before the king. 29The king swore an oath: "As certainly
as the LORD lives (he who has rescued me from every danger),
30I will keep today the oath I swore to you by the LORD God of
Israel: 'Surely Solomon your son will be king after me; he will
sit in my place on my throne.'" 31Bathsheba bowed down to the
king with her face to the floor and said, "May my master, King
David, live forever!"

32King David said, "Summon Zadok the priest, Nathan the
prophet, and Benaiah son of Jehoiada." They came before the
king, 33and he told them, "Take your master's servants with
you, put my son Solomon on my mule, and lead him down to
Gihon. 34There Zadok the priest and Nathan the prophet will
anoint him king over Israel; then blow the trumpet and declare,
'Long live King Solomon!' 35Then follow him up as he comes and
sits on my throne. He will be king in my place; I have decreed
that he will be ruler over Israel and Judah." 36Benaiah son of
Jehoiada responded to the king: "So be it! May the LORD God of
my master the king confirm it! 37As the LORD is with my master
the king, so may he be with Solomon, and may he make him an
even greater king than my master King David!"

38So Zadok the priest, Nathan the prophet, Benaiah son of
Jehoiada, the Kerethites, and the Pelethites went down, put
Solomon on King David's mule, and led him to Gihon. 39Zadok
the priest took a horn filled with olive oil from the tent and
poured it on Solomon; the trumpet was blown and all the people
declared, "Long live King Solomon!" 40All the people followed
him up, playing flutes and celebrating so loudly they made the
ground shake.

41Now Adonijah and all his guests heard the commotion just
as they had finished eating. When Joab heard the sound of the
trumpet, he asked, "Why is there such a noisy commotion in
the city?" 42As he was still speaking, Jonathan son of Abiathar
the priest arrived. Adonijah said, "Come in, for an important
man like you must be bringing good news." 43Jonathan replied to
Adonijah: "No! Our master King David has made Solomon king.
44The king sent with him Zadok the priest, Nathan the prophet,
Benaiah son of Jehoiada, the Kerethites, and the Pelethites and
they put him on the king's mule. 45Then Zadok the priest and
Nathan the prophet anointed him king in Gihon. They went
up from there rejoicing, and the city is in an uproar. That is the
sound you hear. 46Furthermore, Solomon has assumed the royal
throne. 47The king's servants have even come to congratulate
our master King David, saying, 'May your God make Solomon
more famous than you and make him an even greater king than
you!' Then the king leaned on the bed 48and said this: 'The LORD
God of Israel is worthy of praise because today he has placed a
successor on my throne and allowed me to see it.'"

49All of Adonijah's guests panicked; they jumped up and
rushed off their separate ways. 50Adonijah feared Solomon,
so he got up and went and grabbed hold of the horns of the
altar. 51Solomon was told, "Look, Adonijah fears you; see, he has
taken hold of the horns of the altar, saying, 'May King Solomon

solemnly promise me today that he will not kill his servant with the sword.'" [52]Solomon said, "If he is a loyal subject, not a hair of his head will be harmed, but if he is found to be a traitor, he will die." [53]King Solomon sent men to bring him down from the altar. He came and bowed down to King Solomon, and Solomon told him, "Go home."

DAVID'S FINAL WORDS TO SOLOMON

2 When David was close to death, he told Solomon his son: [2]"I am about to die. Be strong and become a man! [3]Do the job the LORD your God has assigned you by following his instructions and obeying his rules, commandments, regulations, and laws as written in the law of Moses. Then you will succeed in all you do and seek to accomplish, [4]and the LORD will fulfill his promise to me, 'If your descendants watch their step and live faithfully in my presence with all their heart and being, then,' he promised, 'you will not fail to have a successor on the throne of Israel.'

[5]"You know what Joab son of Zeruiah did to me—how he murdered two commanders of the Israelite armies, Abner son of Ner and Amasa son of Jether. During peacetime he struck them down as if in battle; when he shed their blood, he stained the belt on his waist and the sandals on his feet. [6]Do to him what you think is appropriate, but don't let him live long and die a peaceful death.

[7]"Treat fairly the sons of Barzillai of Gilead and provide for their needs, because they helped me when I had to flee from your brother Absalom.

[8]"Note well, you still have to contend with Shimei son of Gera, the Benjaminite from Bahurim, who tried to call down upon me a horrible judgment when I went to Mahanaim. He came down and met me at the Jordan, and I solemnly promised him by the LORD, 'I will not strike you down with the sword.' [9]But now don't treat him as if he were innocent. You are a wise man and you know how to handle him; make sure he has a bloody death."

[10]Then David passed away and was buried in the City of David. [11]David reigned over Israel forty years; he reigned in Hebron seven years, and in Jerusalem thirty-three years.

SOLOMON SECURES THE THRONE

[12]Solomon sat on his father David's throne, and his royal authority was firmly solidified.

[13]Haggith's son Adonijah visited Bathsheba, Solomon's mother. She asked, "Do you come in peace?" He answered, "Yes." [14]He added, "I have something to say to you." She replied, "Speak." [15]He said, "You know that the kingdom was mine and all Israel considered me king. But then the kingdom was given to my brother, for the LORD decided it should be his. [16]Now I'd like to ask you for just one thing. Please don't refuse me." She said, "Go ahead and ask." [17]He said, "Please ask King Solomon if he would give me Abishag the Shunammite as a wife, for he won't refuse you." [18]Bathsheba replied, "That's fine; I'll speak to the king on your behalf."

[19]So Bathsheba visited King Solomon to speak to him on Adonijah's behalf. The king got up to greet her, bowed to her, and then sat on his throne. He ordered a throne to be brought for the king's mother, and she sat at his right hand. [20]She said, "I would like to ask you for just one small favor. Please don't refuse me." He said, "Go ahead and ask, my mother, for I would not refuse you." [21]She said, "Allow Abishag the Shunammite to

---

2:1–12 The fathers concluded that another life remains in that the saints do not perish like cattle but are gathered to the people in the land of the living. Accordingly this serves to comfort us lest we, like others who have no hope, be frightened by or shudder at death. For in Christ death is not bitter as it is for the ungodly, it is a change of this wretched and unhappy life into a life that is quiet and blessed. This statement—"David rested with his fathers" (NKJV)—should convince us fully that we do not pass from a pleasant life into a life that is unhappy, but that we pass from afflictions into tranquility. For since the fathers had this comfort from these passages long before Christ, how much more reasonable it is for us to guard and preserve the same comfort! We have it in far greater abundance.

MARTIN LUTHER **(1483–1546)**
LECTURES ON GENESIS

be given to your brother Adonijah as a wife." [22]King Solomon answered his mother, "Why just request Abishag the Shunammite for him? Since he is my older brother, you should also request the kingdom for him, for Abiathar the priest, and for Joab son of Zeruiah!"

[23]King Solomon then swore an oath by the LORD, "May God judge me severely, if Adonijah does not pay for this request with his life! [24]Now, as certainly as the LORD lives (he who made me secure, allowed me to sit on my father David's throne, and established a dynasty for me as he promised), Adonijah will be executed today!" [25]King Solomon then sent Benaiah son of Jehoiada, and he killed Adonijah.

[26]The king then told Abiathar the priest, "Go back to your property in Anathoth. You deserve to die, but today I will not kill you because you did carry the ark of the Sovereign LORD before my father David and you suffered with my father through all his difficult times." [27]Solomon removed Abiathar from being a priest for the LORD, fulfilling the LORD's message that he had pronounced against the family of Eli in Shiloh.

[28]When the news reached Joab (for Joab had supported Adonijah, although he had not supported Absalom), he ran to the tent of the LORD and grabbed hold of the horns of the altar. [29]When King Solomon heard that Joab had run to the tent of the LORD and was right there beside the altar, he ordered Benaiah son of Jehoiada, "Go, strike him down." [30]When Benaiah arrived at the tent of the LORD, he said to him, "The king says, 'Come out!'" But he replied, "No, I will die here!" So Benaiah sent word to the king and reported Joab's reply. [31]The king told him, "Do as he said! Strike him down and bury him. Take away from me and from my father's family the guilt of Joab's murderous, bloody deeds. [32]May the LORD punish him for the blood he shed; behind my father David's back he struck down and murdered with the sword two men who were more innocent and morally upright than he—Abner son of Ner, commander of Israel's army, and Amasa son of Jether, commander of Judah's army. [33]May Joab and his descendants be perpetually guilty of their shed blood, but may the LORD give perpetual peace to David, his descendants, his family, and his dynasty." [34]So Benaiah son of Jehoiada went up and executed Joab; he was buried at his home in the wilderness. [35]The king appointed Benaiah son of Jehoiada to take his place at the head of the army, and the king appointed Zadok the priest to take Abiathar's place.

[36]Next the king summoned Shimei and told him, "Build yourself a house in Jerusalem and live there, but you may not leave there to go anywhere. [37]If you ever do leave and cross the Kidron Valley, know for sure that you will certainly die. You will be responsible for your own death." [38]Shimei said to the king, "My master the king's proposal is acceptable. Your servant will do as you say." So Shimei lived in Jerusalem for a long time.

[39]Three years later two of Shimei's servants ran away to King Achish son of Maacah of Gath. Shimei was told, "Look, your servants are in Gath." [40]So Shimei got up, saddled his donkey, and went to Achish at Gath to find his servants; Shimei went and brought back his servants from Gath. [41]When Solomon was told that Shimei had gone from Jerusalem to Gath and had then returned, [42]the king summoned Shimei and said to him, "You will recall that I made you take an oath by the LORD, and I solemnly warned you, 'If you ever leave and go anywhere, know for sure that you will certainly die.' You said to me, 'The

proposal is acceptable; I agree to it.' 43Why then have you broken
the oath you made before the LORD and disobeyed the order I
gave you?" 44Then the king said to Shimei, "You are well aware of
the way you mistreated my father David. The LORD will punish
you for what you did. 45But King Solomon will be empowered,
and David's dynasty will endure permanently before the LORD."
46The king then gave the order to Benaiah son of Jehoiada who
went and executed Shimei.

So Solomon took firm control of the kingdom.

THE LORD GIVES SOLOMON WISDOM

3 Solomon made an alliance by marriage with Pharaoh, king of
Egypt; he married Pharaoh's daughter. He brought her to the
City of David until he could finish building his residence and
the temple of the LORD and the wall around Jerusalem. 2Now
the people were offering sacrifices at the high places, because in
those days a temple had not yet been built to honor the LORD.
3Solomon demonstrated his loyalty to the LORD by following
the practices of his father David, except that he offered sacrifices and burned incense on the high places.

4The king went to Gibeon to offer sacrifices, for it had the
most prominent of the high places. Solomon would offer up
1,000 burnt sacrifices on the altar there. 5One night in Gibeon
the LORD appeared to Solomon in a dream. God said, "Tell me
what I should give you." 6Solomon replied, "You demonstrated
great loyalty to your servant, my father David, as he served you
faithfully, properly, and sincerely. You have maintained this
great loyalty to this day by allowing his son to sit on his throne.
7Now, O LORD my God, you have made your servant king in my
father David's place, even though I am only a young man and
am inexperienced. 8Your servant stands among your chosen
people; they are a great nation that is too numerous to count or
number. 9So give your servant a discerning mind so he can make
judicial decisions for your people and distinguish right from
wrong. Otherwise no one is able to make judicial decisions for
this great nation of yours." 10The Lord was pleased that Solomon
made this request. 11God said to him, "Because you asked for
the ability to make wise judicial decisions, and not for long life,
or riches, or vengeance on your enemies, 12I grant your request
and give you a wise and discerning mind superior to that of
anyone who has preceded or will succeed you. 13Furthermore,
I am giving you what you did not request—riches and honor so
that you will be the greatest king of your generation. 14If you
follow my instructions by obeying my rules and regulations,
just as your father David did, then I will grant you long life."
15Solomon then woke up and realized it was a dream. He went to
Jerusalem, stood before the ark of the Lord's covenant, offered
up burnt sacrifices, presented peace offerings, and held a feast
for all his servants.

SOLOMON DEMONSTRATES HIS WISDOM

16Then two prostitutes came to the king and stood before him.
17One of the women said, "My master, this woman and I live
in the same house. I had a baby while she was with me in the
house. 18Then three days after I had my baby, this woman also
had a baby. We were alone; there was no one else in the house
except the two of us. 19This woman's child suffocated during
the night when she rolled on top of him. 20She got up in the
middle of the night and took my son from my side, while your

3:1–15 If people are to govern beneficially and not be tyrants, it is necessary that they be elected by God and from among the people of God. That is to say, they must be true believers who have not themselves stepped forward for the office but have been called to it. Christian officials, recognizing themselves as under-shepherds of sheep that are not their own but God's, think to govern them not as it seems good to them but according to the law of God to whom the sheep belong. This Solomon observed. He asked God to give him a teachable heart before all things, so that he might judge his people and know the difference between good and evil. He also confessed that human reason did not have the power of distinguishing between evil and the true good, of judging rightly, but needed to learn such things from God.

MARTIN BUCER (1491–1551)
INSTRUCTIONS ON CHRISTIAN LOVE

servant was sleeping. She put him in her arms, and put her dead
son in my arms. [21]I got up in the morning to nurse my son, and
there he was, dead! But when I examined him carefully in the
morning, I realized it was not my baby." [22]The other woman
said, "No! My son is alive; your son is dead!" But the first woman
replied, "No, your son is dead; my son is alive." Each presented
her case before the king.
[23]The king said, "One says, 'My son is alive; your son is dead,'
while the other says, 'No, your son is dead; my son is alive.'"
[24]The king ordered, "Get me a sword." So they placed a sword
before the king. [25]The king then said, "Cut the living child in two,
and give half to one and half to the other!" [26]The real mother
spoke up to the king, for her motherly instincts were awakened.
She said, "My master, give her the living child! Whatever you
do, don't kill him!" But the other woman said, "Neither one
of us will have him. Let them cut him in two!" [27]The king responded, "Give the first woman the living child; don't kill him.
She is the mother." [28]When all Israel heard about the judicial
decision which the king had rendered, they respected the king,
for they realized that he possessed divine wisdom to make
judicial decisions.

SOLOMON'S ROYAL COURT AND ADMINISTRATORS

4 King Solomon ruled over all Israel. [2]These were his officials:
Azariah son of Zadok was the priest.
[3]Elihoreph and Ahijah, the sons of Shisha, wrote down what
happened.
Jehoshaphat son of Ahilud was in charge of the records.
[4]Benaiah son of Jehoiada was commander of the army.
Zadok and Abiathar were priests.
[5]Azariah son of Nathan was supervisor of the district
governors.
Zabud son of Nathan was a priest and adviser to the king.
[6]Ahishar was supervisor of the palace.
Adoniram son of Abda was supervisor of the work crews.
[7]Solomon had 12 district governors appointed throughout
Israel who acquired supplies for the king and his palace. Each
was responsible for one month in the year. [8]These were their
names:
Ben Hur was in charge of the hill country of Ephraim.
[9]Ben Deker was in charge of Makaz, Shaalbim, Beth Shemesh,
and Elon Beth Hanan.
[10]Ben Hesed was in charge of Arubboth; he controlled Socoh
and all the territory of Hepher.
[11]Ben Abinadab was in charge of Naphath Dor. (He was married to Solomon's daughter Taphath.)
[12]Baana son of Ahilud was in charge of Taanach and Megiddo,
as well as all of Beth Shean next to Zarethan below Jezreel, from
Beth Shean to Abel Meholah and on past Jokmeam.
[13]Ben Geber was in charge of Ramoth Gilead; he controlled
the villages of Jair son of Manasseh in Gilead, as well as the
region of Argob in Bashan, including 60 large walled cities with
bronze bars locking their gates.
[14]Ahinadab son of Iddo was in charge of Mahanaim.
[15]Ahimaaz was in charge of Naphtali. (He married Solomon's
daughter Basemath.)
[16]Baana son of Hushai was in charge of Asher and Aloth.
[17]Jehoshaphat son of Paruah was in charge of Issachar.

18 Shimei son of Ela was in charge of Benjamin.
19 Geber son of Uri was in charge of the land of Gilead (the
territory which had once belonged to King Sihon of the Amorites and to King Og of Bashan). He was sole governor of the area.

SOLOMON'S WEALTH AND FAME

20 The people of Judah and Israel were as innumerable as the
sand on the seashore; they had plenty to eat and drink and were
happy. 21 Solomon ruled all the kingdoms from the Euphrates
River to the land of the Philistines, as far as the border of Egypt.
These kingdoms paid tribute as Solomon's subjects throughout
his lifetime. 22 Each day Solomon's royal court consumed 30 cors
of finely milled flour, 60 cors of cereal, 23 10 calves fattened in the
stall, 20 calves from the pasture, and 100 sheep, not to mention
rams, gazelles, deer, and well-fed birds. 24 His royal court was so
large because he ruled over all the kingdoms west of the Euphrates
River from Tiphsah to Gaza; he was at peace with all his neighbors.
25 All the people of Judah and Israel had security; everyone from
Dan to Beer Sheba enjoyed the produce of their vines and fig trees
throughout Solomon's lifetime. 26 Solomon had 4,000 stalls for
his chariot horses and 12,000 horses. 27 The district governors
acquired supplies for King Solomon and all who ate in his royal
palace. Each was responsible for one month in the year; they made
sure nothing was lacking. 28 Each one also brought to the assigned
location his quota of barley and straw for the various horses.
29 God gave Solomon wisdom and very great discernment;
the breadth of his understanding was as infinite as the sand
on the seashore. 30 Solomon was wiser than all the men of the
east and all the sages of Egypt. 31 He was wiser than any man,
including Ethan the Ezrahite or Heman, Calcol, and Darda, the
sons of Mahol. He was famous in all the neighboring nations.
32 He composed 3,000 proverbs and 1,005 songs. 33 He produced
manuals on botany, describing every kind of plant, from the
cedars of Lebanon to the hyssop that grows on walls. He also
produced manuals on biology, describing animals, birds, insects,
and fish. 34 People from all nations came to hear Solomon's display of wisdom; they came from all the kings of the earth who
heard about his wisdom.

> **4:20–34** God gives wisdom, prudence, and intelligence where he is acknowledged and where others are directed to him. God also gives latitude to people's hearts, that is, a free soul, which is a conscience led into all freedom with respect to God. A person cannot be given anything greater than this. It is rarely accepted.
>
> JOHANNES BUGENHAGEN
> (1485–1558)
> *COMMENTARY ON FIRST KINGS*

SOLOMON GATHERS BUILDING MATERIALS FOR THE TEMPLE

5 King Hiram of Tyre sent messengers to Solomon when he heard
that he had been anointed king in his father's place. (Hiram had
always been an ally of David.) 2 Solomon then sent this message
to Hiram: 3 "You know that my father David was unable to build
a temple to honor the LORD his God, for he was busy fighting
battles on all fronts while the LORD subdued his enemies. 4 But
now the LORD my God has made me secure on all fronts; there
is no adversary or dangerous threat. 5 So I have decided to build
a temple to honor the LORD my God, as the LORD instructed my
father David, 'Your son, whom I will put on your throne in your
place, is the one who will build a temple to honor me.' 6 So now
order some cedars of Lebanon to be cut for me. My servants will
work with your servants. I will pay your servants whatever you
say is appropriate, for you know that we have no one among us
who knows how to cut down trees like the Sidonians."
7 When Hiram heard Solomon's message, he was very happy.
He said, "The LORD is worthy of praise today because he has given
David a wise son to rule over this great nation." 8 Hiram then sent

> **5:1–18** The reasons why Solomon sought Hiram for the cedars rather than any other king were several. First, there was a great friendship between them, as well as between Hiram and Solomon's father, David. Second, Hiram had sent Solomon ambassadors congratulating him. Third, the skillfulness of the men of Tyre was well known in comparison to that of other nations. Finally, it is held that God was disposed to use the people of Tyre, that is, Gentiles, to be employed in doing this work for the temple to prefigure the vocation of the Gentiles in their future in building the spiritual temple.
>
> JOHN MAYER (1583–1664)
> *COMMENTARY ON FIRST KINGS*

GREGORY OF NAZIANZUS:

THE HUMBLE THEOLOGIAN
c. 329–390

The best friend of Basil the Great and one of the three so-called Cappadocian Fathers, Gregory of Nazianzus is known as a humble theologian who fiercely defended the Christian faith against false teachings that threatened the established orthodox position regarding the nature of God and Christ.

Born to a wealthy Cappadocian family in 329, Gregory found Christ through his mother and was raised to follow Christ by his father, who was bishop of the Nazianzus church. Although he explored monasticism as a young man at the urging of Basil, he decided against it. In 364 he joined the priesthood and eventually became bishop of the small town of Sasima at his friend Basil's request. Sadly, this season in Gregory's life ultimately soured his relationship with Basil. As presiding bishop over the region, Basil was tasked with placing people over local parishes. Gregory felt pressure to agree to Basil's request, which created a breach in their friendship that apparently never healed. The tasks of the bishopric wearied Gregory. He was ill-suited for the more administrative demands of the role, and it sidetracked him from his preferred activities of studying, writing, and pastoral work.

Even so, he quickly gained a reputation as a fierce, capable defender of Trinitarian doctrine without ever abandoning his posture of humility. The work that established him as such a person was *Theological Orations*. It stemmed from a number of sermons he first preached in his parish in Constantinople after he was moved there in 380. His goal was to summarize for his local church the essence of accepted Trinitarian doctrine, arguing against the Arians.

His work played a role in paving the way for the second ecumenical council, the Council of Constantinople, where he was appointed by Emperor Theodosius as both patriarch of the city and presider over the council. Unfortunately, it proved too much for the mild-mannered bishop. He tried to fit into his role, serving the best he could, but ultimately he resigned both posts and retired to his home city of Nazianzus. It isn't clear what drove him to such retirement, but it was probably because of political problems, and it is possible his life was threatened by Arian detractors. It is also thought that Arians brought trumped-up charges against him of lewd, lascivious, and illegal acts. Shy, humble Gregory couldn't handle the pressure.

Gregory's sermons, *Theological Orations*, and contribution to the Council of Constantinople define this theologian from Nazianzus as someone who deftly and humbly confronted and resolved theological controversies for the sake of the church.

IMPORTANT WORK

THEOLOGICAL ORATIONS

this message to Solomon: "I received the message you sent to me. I will give you all the cedars and evergreens you need. [9]My servants will bring the timber down from Lebanon to the sea. I will send it by sea in raft-like bundles to the place you designate. There I will separate the logs and you can carry them away. In exchange you will supply the food I need for my royal court."

[10]So Hiram supplied the cedars and evergreens Solomon needed, [11]and Solomon supplied Hiram annually with 20,000 cors of wheat as provision for his royal court, as well as 120,000 gallons of pure olive oil. [12]So the LORD gave Solomon wisdom, as he had promised him. And Hiram and Solomon were at peace and made a treaty.

[13]King Solomon conscripted work crews from throughout Israel, 30,000 men in all. [14]He sent them to Lebanon in shifts of 10,000 men per month. They worked in Lebanon for one month, and then spent two months at home. Adoniram was supervisor of the work crews. [15]Solomon also had 70,000 common laborers and 80,000 stonecutters in the hills, [16]besides 3,300 officials who supervised the workers. [17]By royal order they supplied large valuable stones in order to build the temple's foundation with chiseled stone. [18]Solomon's and Hiram's construction workers, along with men from Byblos, did the chiseling and prepared the wood and stones for the building of the temple.

THE BUILDING OF THE TEMPLE

6 In the four hundred and eightieth year after the Israelites left Egypt, in the fourth year of Solomon's reign over Israel, during the month Ziv (the second month), he began building the LORD's temple. [2]The temple King Solomon built for the LORD was 90 feet long, 30 feet wide, and 45 feet high. [3]The porch in front of the main hall of the temple was 30 feet long, corresponding to the width of the temple. It was 15 feet wide, extending out from the front of the temple. [4]He made framed windows for the temple. [5]He built an extension all around the walls of the temple's main hall and Holy Place and constructed side rooms in it. [6]The bottom floor of the extension was 7½ feet wide, the middle floor 9 feet wide, and the third floor 10½ feet wide. He made ledges on the temple's outer walls so the beams would not have to be inserted into the walls. [7]As the temple was being built, only stones shaped at the quarry were used; the sound of hammers, pickaxes, or any other iron tool was not heard at the temple while it was being built. [8]The entrance to the bottom level of side rooms was on the south side of the temple; stairs went up to the middle floor and then on up to the third floor. [9]He finished building the temple and covered it with rafters and boards made of cedar. [10]He built an extension all around the temple; it was 7½ feet high and it was attached to the temple by cedar beams.

[11]The LORD's message came to Solomon: [12]"As for this temple you are building, if you follow my rules, observe my regulations, and obey all my commandments, I will fulfill through you the promise I made to your father David. [13]I will live among the Israelites and will not abandon my people Israel."

[14]So Solomon finished building the temple. [15]He constructed the walls inside the temple with cedar planks; he paneled the inside with wood from the floor of the temple to the rafters of the ceiling. He covered the temple floor with boards made from the wood of evergreens. [16]He built a wall 30 feet in from the rear of the temple as a partition for an inner sanctuary that

6:7 The temple was built in silence. It rose like an exhalation. No hammer fell, no ponderous axes rang. Like some tall palm the mystic fabric sprung. Perhaps it was merely for convenience of transport and to save time that the stones were dressed in the quarries, but more probably the silence was due to an instinct of reverence. Silence is needed for that. There must be much still communion and quiet reflection. Surely nothing is more needed in these days of noisy advertisement and measurement of the importance of things by the noise that they can make than this lesson of the place of silence in Christian progress, both for individuals and for the Christian church as a whole.

ALEXANDER MACLAREN
(1826–1910)
EXPOSITIONS OF THE HOLY SCRIPTURES

would be the Most Holy Place. He paneled the wall with cedar planks from the floor to the rafters. [17]The main hall in front of the inner sanctuary was 60 feet long. [18]The inside of the temple was all cedar and was adorned with carvings of round ornaments and of flowers in bloom. Everything was cedar; no stones were visible.

[19]He prepared the inner sanctuary inside the temple so that the ark of the covenant of the LORD could be placed there. [20]The inner sanctuary was 30 feet long, 30 feet wide, and 30 feet high. He plated it with gold, as well as the cedar altar. [21]Solomon plated the inside of the temple with gold. He hung golden chains in front of the inner sanctuary and plated the inner sanctuary with gold. [22]He plated the entire inside of the temple with gold, as well as the altar inside the inner sanctuary.

[23]In the inner sanctuary he made two cherubim of olive wood; each stood 15 feet high. [24]Each of the first cherub's wings was 7½ feet long; its entire wingspan was 15 feet. [25]The second cherub also had a wingspan of 15 feet; it was identical to the first in measurements and shape. [26]Each cherub stood 15 feet high. [27]He put the cherubim in the inner sanctuary of the temple. Their wings were spread out. One of the first cherub's wings touched one wall and one of the other cherub's wings touched the opposite wall. The first cherub's other wing touched the second cherub's other wing in the middle of the room. [28]He plated the cherubim with gold.

[29]On all the walls around the temple, inside and out, he carved cherubim, palm trees, and flowers in bloom. [30]He plated the floor of the temple with gold, inside and out. [31]He made doors of olive wood at the entrance to the inner sanctuary; the pillar on each doorpost was five sided. [32]On the two doors made of olive wood he carved cherubim, palm trees, and flowers in bloom, and he plated them with gold. He plated the cherubim and the palm trees with hammered gold. [33]In the same way he made doorposts of olive wood for the entrance to the main hall, only with four-sided pillars. [34]He also made two doors out of wood from evergreens; each door had two folding leaves. [35]He carved cherubim, palm trees, and flowers in bloom and plated them with gold, leveled out over the carvings. [36]He built the inner courtyard with three rows of chiseled stones and a row of cedar beams.

[37]In the month of Ziv in the fourth year of Solomon's reign the foundation was laid for the LORD's temple. [38]In the eleventh year, in the month of Bul (the eighth month) the temple was completed in accordance with all its specifications and blueprints. It took seven years to build.

THE BUILDING OF THE ROYAL PALACE

7 Solomon took 13 years to build his palace. [2]He named it "The Palace of the Lebanon Forest"; it was 150 feet long, 75 feet wide, and 45 feet high. It had four rows of cedar pillars and cedar beams above the pillars. [3]The roof above the beams supported by the pillars was also made of cedar; there were 45 beams, 15 per row. [4]There were three rows of windows arranged in sets of three. [5]All the entrances were rectangular in shape and they were arranged in sets of three. [6]He made a colonnade 75 feet long and 45 feet wide. There was a porch in front of this and pillars and a roof in front of the porch. [7]He also made a throne room, called "The Hall of Judgment," where he made judicial decisions. It was paneled with cedar from the floor

to the rafters. [8]The palace where he lived was constructed in a similar way. He also constructed a palace like this hall for Pharaoh's daughter, whom he had married. [9]All these were built with the best stones, chiseled to the right size and cut with a saw on all sides, from the foundation to the edge of the roof and from the outside to the great courtyard. [10]The foundation was made of large valuable stones, measuring either 15 feet or 12 feet. [11]Above the foundation the best stones, chiseled to the right size, were used along with cedar. [12]Around the great courtyard were three rows of chiseled stones and one row of cedar beams, like the inner courtyard of the LORD's temple and the hall of the palace.

SOLOMON COMMISSIONS HIRAM TO SUPPLY THE TEMPLE

[13]King Solomon sent for Hiram of Tyre. [14]He was the son of a widow from the tribe of Naphtali, and his father was a craftsman in bronze from Tyre. He had the skill and knowledge to make all kinds of works of bronze. He reported to King Solomon and did all the work he was assigned.

[15]He fashioned two bronze pillars; each pillar was 27 feet high and 18 feet in circumference. [16]He made two bronze tops for the pillars; each was 7½ feet high. [17]The latticework on the tops of the pillars was adorned with ornamental wreaths and chains; the top of each pillar had seven groupings of ornaments. [18]When he made the pillars, there were two rows of pomegranate-shaped ornaments around the latticework covering the top of each pillar. [19]The tops of the two pillars in the porch were shaped like lilies and were six feet high. [20]On the top of each pillar, right above the bulge beside the latticework, there were 200 pomegranate-shaped ornaments arranged in rows all the way around. [21]He set up the pillars on the porch in front of the main hall. He erected one pillar on the right side and called it Yakin; he erected the other pillar on the left side and called it Boaz. [22]The tops of the pillars were shaped like lilies. So the construction of the pillars was completed.

[23]He also made the large bronze basin called "The Sea." It measured 15 feet from rim to rim, was circular in shape, and stood 7½ feet high. Its circumference was 45 feet. [24]Under the rim all the way around it were round ornaments arranged in settings 15 feet long. The ornaments were in two rows and had been cast with "The Sea." [25]"The Sea" stood on top of twelve bulls. Three faced northward, three westward, three southward, and three eastward. "The Sea" was placed on top of them, and they all faced outward. [26]It was four fingers thick and its rim was like that of a cup shaped like a lily blossom. It could hold about 12,000 gallons.

[27]He also made 10 bronze movable stands. Each stand was 6 feet long, 6 feet wide, and 4½ feet high. [28]The stands were constructed with frames between the joints. [29]On these frames and joints were ornamental lions, bulls, and cherubim. Under the lions and bulls were decorative wreaths. [30]Each stand had four bronze wheels with bronze axles and four supports. Under the basin the supports were fashioned on each side with wreaths. [31]Inside the stand was a round opening that was 18 inches deep; it had a support that was 27 inches long. On the edge of the opening were carvings in square frames. [32]The four wheels were under the frames, and the crossbars of the axles were connected to the stand. Each wheel was 27 inches high. [33]The wheels were

7:13–51 The two bronze pillars in the porch of the temple, some think, were to teach those who came to worship to depend upon God only for strength and establishment in all their religious exercises. Spiritual strength and stability are found at the door of God's temple, where we must wait for the gifts of grace in use of the means of grace. Spiritual priests and spiritual sacrifices must be washed in the basin of Christ's blood and of regeneration. We must wash often, for we daily contract pollution. Let us bless God for the fountain opened by the sacrifice of Christ for sin and for uncleanness. Christ is now the temple and the builder, the altar and the sacrifice, the light of our souls, and the bread of life. Let us go to him and wash away our sins in his blood. Being strengthened by him, we shall be accepted, useful, and happy.

MATTHEW HENRY (1662–1714)
COMMENTARY ON THE WHOLE BIBLE

constructed like chariot wheels; their crossbars, rims, spokes, and hubs were made of cast metal. 34Each stand had four supports, one per side projecting out from the stand. 35On top of each stand was a round opening three-quarters of a foot deep; there were also supports and frames on top of the stands. 36He engraved ornamental cherubim, lions, and palm trees on the plates of the supports and frames wherever there was room, with wreaths all around. 37He made the 10 stands in this way. All of them were cast in one mold and were identical in measurements and shape.

38He also made 10 bronze basins, each of which could hold about 240 gallons. Each basin was 6 feet in diameter; there was one basin for each stand. 39He put five basins on the south side of the temple and five on the north side. He put "The Sea" on the south side, in the southeast corner.

40Hiram also made basins, shovels, and bowls. He finished all the work on the LORD's temple he had been assigned by King Solomon. 41He made the two pillars, the two bowl-shaped tops of the pillars, the latticework for the bowl-shaped tops of the two pillars, 42the 400 pomegranate-shaped ornaments for the latticework of the two pillars (each latticework had two rows of these ornaments at the bowl-shaped top of the pillar), 43the 10 movable stands with their 10 basins, 44the big bronze basin called "The Sea" with its 12 bulls underneath, 45and the pots, shovels, and bowls. All these items King Solomon assigned Hiram to make for the LORD's temple were made from polished bronze. 46The king had them cast in earth foundries in the region of the Jordan between Sukkoth and Zarethan. 47Solomon left all these items unweighed; there were so many of them they did not weigh the bronze.

48Solomon also made all these items for the LORD's temple: the gold altar; the gold table on which was kept the Bread of the Presence; 49the pure gold lampstands at the entrance to the inner sanctuary (five on the right and five on the left); the gold flower-shaped ornaments, lamps, and tongs; 50the pure gold bowls, trimming shears, basins, pans, and censers; and the gold door sockets for the inner sanctuary (the Most Holy Place) and for the doors of the main hall of the temple. 51When King Solomon finished constructing the LORD's temple, he put the holy items that belonged to his father David (the silver, gold, and other articles) in the treasuries of the LORD's temple.

SOLOMON MOVES THE ARK INTO THE TEMPLE

8 Then Solomon convened in Jerusalem Israel's elders, all the leaders of the Israelite tribes and families, so they could witness the transferal of the ark of the LORD's covenant from the City of David (that is, Zion). 2All the men of Israel assembled before King Solomon during the festival in the month of Ethanim (the seventh month). 3When all Israel's elders had arrived, the priests lifted the ark. 4The priests and Levites carried the ark of the LORD, the tent of meeting, and all the holy items in the tent. 5Now King Solomon and all the Israelites who had assembled with him went on ahead of the ark and sacrificed more sheep and cattle than could be counted or numbered.

6The priests brought the ark of the LORD's covenant to its assigned place in the inner sanctuary of the temple, in the Most Holy Place, under the wings of the cherubim. 7The cherubim's wings extended over the place where the ark sat; the cherubim overshadowed the ark and its poles. 8The poles were so long their ends were visible from the Holy Place in front of the inner

sanctuary, but they could not be seen from beyond that point.
They have remained there to this very day. [9]There was nothing
in the ark except the two stone tablets Moses had placed there
in Horeb. It was there that the LORD made a covenant with
the Israelites after he brought them out of the land of Egypt.
[10]Once the priests left the Holy Place, a cloud filled the LORD's
temple. [11]The priests could not carry out their duties because
of the cloud; the LORD's glory filled his temple.
[12]Then Solomon said, "The LORD has said that he lives in thick
darkness. [13]O LORD, truly I have built a lofty temple for you, a
place where you can live permanently." [14]Then the king turned
around and pronounced a blessing over the whole Israelite assembly as they stood there. [15]He said, "The LORD God of Israel
is worthy of praise because he has fulfilled what he promised
my father David. [16]He told David, 'Since the day I brought my
people Israel out of Egypt, I have not chosen a city from all the
tribes of Israel to build a temple in which to live. But I have
chosen David to lead my people Israel.' [17]Now my father David
had a strong desire to build a temple to honor the LORD God
of Israel. [18]The LORD told my father David, 'It is right for you to
have a strong desire to build a temple to honor me. [19]But you will
not build the temple; your very own son will build the temple
for my honor.' [20]The LORD has kept the promise he made. I have
taken my father David's place and have occupied the throne of
Israel, as the LORD promised. I have built this temple for the
honor of the LORD God of Israel [21]and set up in it a place for the
ark containing the covenant the LORD made with our ancestors
when he brought them out of the land of Egypt."

SOLOMON PRAYS FOR ISRAEL

[22]Solomon stood before the altar of the LORD in front of the
entire assembly of Israel and spread out his hands toward the
sky. [23]He prayed: "O LORD, God of Israel, there is no god like you
in heaven above or on earth below! You maintain covenantal
loyalty to your servants who obey you with sincerity. [24]You have
kept your word to your servant, my father David; this very day
you have fulfilled what you promised. [25]Now, O LORD, God of
Israel, keep the promise you made to your servant, my father
David, when you said, 'You will never fail to have a successor
ruling before me on the throne of Israel, provided that your
descendants watch their step and serve me as you have done.'
[26]Now, O God of Israel, may the promise you made to your servant, my father David, be realized.
[27]"God does not really live on the earth! Look, if the sky and
the highest heaven cannot contain you, how much less this temple I have built! [28]But respond favorably to your servant's prayer
and his request for help, O LORD my God. Answer the desperate
prayer your servant is presenting to you today. [29]Night and day
may you watch over this temple, the place where you promised
you would live. May you answer your servant's prayer for this
place. [30]Respond to the request of your servant and your people
Israel for this place. Hear from inside your heavenly dwelling
place and respond favorably.
[31]"When someone is accused of sinning against his neighbor
and the latter pronounces a curse on the alleged offender before
your altar in this temple, be willing to forgive the accused if the
accusation is false. [32]Listen from heaven and make a just decision
about your servants' claims. Condemn the guilty party, declare
the other innocent, and give both of them what they deserve.

8:22–53 Solomon the son of David said expressly, "But will God indeed dwell on the earth?" (KJV). He dwelled on the earth clothed in flesh, and his abode with humans was effected by the conjunction and harmony that obtain among the righteous and that build a new temple. The blessed Peter did not hesitate to say, "You yourselves, as living stones, are built up as a spiritual house to be a holy priesthood" (1 Pet 2:5). And with reference to the body, which by circumscription Jesus consecrated as a hallowed place for himself on earth, he said, "'Destroy this temple and in three days I will raise it up again.'" (John 2:19).

CLEMENT OF ALEXANDRIA
(C. 150–C. 215)
FRAGMENTS

33“The time will come when your people Israel are defeated
by an enemy because they sinned against you. If they come
back to you, renew their allegiance to you, and pray for your
help in this temple, 34then listen from heaven, forgive the sin
of your people Israel, and bring them back to the land you gave
to their ancestors.
35“The time will come when the skies are shut up tightly and
no rain falls because your people sinned against you. When they
direct their prayers toward this place, renew their allegiance
to you, and turn away from their sin because you punish them,
36then listen from heaven and forgive the sin of your servants,
your people Israel. Certainly you will then teach them the right
way to live and send rain on your land that you have given your
people to possess.
37“The time will come when the land suffers from a famine,
a plague, blight and disease, or a locust invasion, or when their
enemy lays siege to the cities of the land, or when some other
type of plague or epidemic occurs. 38When all your people Israel pray and ask for help, as they acknowledge their pain and
spread out their hands toward this temple, 39then listen from
your heavenly dwelling place, forgive their sin, and act favorably toward each one based on your evaluation of his motives.
(Indeed you are the only one who can correctly evaluate the
motives of all people.) 40Then they will obey you throughout
their lifetimes as they live on the land you gave to our ancestors.
41“Foreigners, who do not belong to your people Israel, will
come from a distant land because of your reputation. 42When they
hear about your great reputation and your ability to accomplish
mighty deeds, they will come and direct their prayers toward this
temple. 43Then listen from your heavenly dwelling place and answer all the prayers of the foreigners. Then all the nations of the
earth will acknowledge your reputation, obey you as your people
Israel do, and recognize that this temple I built belongs to you.
44“When you direct your people to march out and fight their
enemies, and they direct their prayers to the LORD toward his
chosen city and this temple I built for your honor, 45then listen
from heaven to their prayers for help and vindicate them.

46“The time will come when your people will sin against you (for
there is no one who is sinless!) and you will be angry with them
and deliver them over to their enemies, who will take them as
prisoners to their own land, whether far away or close by. 47When
your people come to their senses in the land where they are held
prisoner, they will repent and beg for your mercy in the land of
their imprisonment, admitting, ‘We have sinned and gone astray;
we have done evil.’ 48When they return to you with all their heart
and being in the land where they are held prisoner, and direct their
prayers to you toward the land you gave to their ancestors, your
chosen city, and the temple I built for your honor, 49then listen
from your heavenly dwelling place to their prayers for help and
vindicate them. 50Forgive all the rebellious acts of your sinful people and cause their captors to have mercy on them. 51After all, they
are your people and your special possession whom you brought
out of Egypt, from the middle of the iron-smelting furnace.

52“May you be attentive to your servant’s and your people Israel’s requests for help and may you respond to all their prayers
to you. 53After all, you picked them out of all the nations of
the earth to be your special possession, just as you, O Sovereign LORD, announced through your servant Moses when you
brought our ancestors out of Egypt.”

54When Solomon finished presenting all these prayers and
requests to the LORD, he got up from before the altar of the LORD
where he had kneeled and spread out his hands toward the sky.
55When he stood up, he pronounced a blessing over the entire
assembly of Israel, saying in a loud voice: 56"The LORD is worthy
of praise because he has made Israel his people secure just as he
promised! Not one of all the faithful promises he made through
his servant Moses is left unfulfilled! 57May the LORD our God be
with us, as he was with our ancestors. May he not abandon us or
leave us. 58May he make us submissive, so we can follow all his
instructions and obey the commandments, rules, and regulations
he commanded our ancestors. 59May the LORD our God be constantly aware of these requests of mine I have presented to him,
so that he might vindicate his servant and his people Israel as
the need arises. 60Then all the nations of the earth will recognize
that the LORD is the only genuine God. 61May you demonstrate
wholehearted devotion to the LORD our God by following his
rules and obeying his commandments, as you are now doing."

SOLOMON DEDICATES THE TEMPLE

62The king and all Israel with him were presenting sacrifices
to the LORD. 63Solomon offered as peace offerings to the LORD
22,000 cattle and 120,000 sheep. Then the king and all the Israelites dedicated the LORD's temple. 64That day the king consecrated the middle of the courtyard that is in front of the LORD's
temple. He offered there burnt sacrifices, grain offerings, and
the fat from the peace offerings, because the bronze altar that
stood before the LORD was too small to hold all these offerings.
65At that time Solomon and all Israel with him celebrated a
festival before the LORD our God for two entire weeks. This
great assembly included people from all over the land, from
Lebo Hamath in the north to the Stream of Egypt in the south.
66On the fifteenth day after the festival started, he dismissed
the people. They asked God to empower the king and then went
to their homes, happy and content because of all the good the
LORD had done for his servant David and his people Israel.

THE LORD GIVES SOLOMON A PROMISE AND A WARNING

9:1–9 God not only promised grace and his enduring presence to the people, he also promised Solomon personally a long-lasting and perpetual kingdom for his descendants. They would be preserved in the law of the Lord if they walked in David's way of faith and devotion. If their sins made it impossible for this to be fulfilled or only imperfectly fulfilled, then they should be restored in this way: In Christ the Messiah, the true Seed of David and Abraham, what was promised has been fulfilled, fulfilling the promise once and for all.

KONRAD PELLIKAN
(1478–1556)
COMMENTARY ON FIRST KINGS

9 After Solomon finished building the LORD's temple, the
royal palace, and all the other construction projects he had
planned, 2the LORD appeared to Solomon a second time, in the
same way he had appeared to him at Gibeon. 3The LORD said
to him, "I have answered your prayer and your request for help
that you made to me. I have consecrated this temple you built
by making it my permanent home; I will be constantly present
there. 4You must serve me with integrity and sincerity, just as
your father David did. Do everything I commanded and obey
my rules and regulations. 5Then I will allow your dynasty to rule
over Israel permanently, just as I promised your father David,
'You will not fail to have a successor on the throne of Israel.'
6"But if you or your sons ever turn away from me, fail to obey
the regulations and rules I instructed you to keep, and decide
to serve and worship other gods, 7then I will remove Israel from
the land I have given them, I will abandon this temple I have
consecrated with my presence, and Israel will be mocked and
ridiculed among all the nations. 8This temple will become a heap
of ruins; everyone who passes by it will be shocked and will hiss
out their scorn, saying, 'Why did the LORD do this to this land and

this temple?' [9]Others will then answer, 'Because they abandoned
the LORD their God, who led their ancestors out of Egypt. They
embraced other gods whom they worshiped and served. That
is why the LORD has brought all this disaster down on them.'"

FOREIGN AFFAIRS AND BUILDING PROJECTS

[10]After 20 years, during which Solomon built the LORD's temple
and the royal palace, [11]King Solomon gave King Hiram of Tyre
20 towns in the region of Galilee, because Hiram had supplied
Solomon with cedars, evergreens, and all the gold he wanted.
[12]When Hiram went out from Tyre to inspect the towns Solomon had given him, he was not pleased with them. [13]Hiram
asked, "Why did you give me these towns, my friend?" He called
that area the region of Cabul, a name which it has retained to
this day. [14]Hiram had sent to the king 120 talents of gold.
[15]Here are the details concerning the work crews King Solomon conscripted to build the LORD's temple, his palace, the
terrace, the wall of Jerusalem, and the cities of Hazor, Megiddo,
and Gezer. [16](Pharaoh, king of Egypt, had attacked and captured Gezer. He burned it and killed the Canaanites who lived
in the city. He gave it as a wedding present to his daughter, who
had married Solomon.) [17]Solomon built up Gezer, lower Beth
Horon, [18]Baalath, Tadmor in the wilderness, [19]all the storage
cities that belonged to him, and the cities where chariots and
horses were kept. He built whatever he wanted in Jerusalem,
Lebanon, and throughout his entire kingdom. [20]Now several
non-Israelite peoples were left in the land after the conquest
of Joshua, including the Amorites, Hittites, Perizzites, Hivites,
and Jebusites. [21]Their descendants remained in the land (the
Israelites were unable to wipe them out completely). Solomon
conscripted them for his work crews, and they continue in that
role to this very day. [22]Solomon did not assign Israelites to these
work crews; the Israelites served as his soldiers, attendants,
officers, charioteers, and commanders of his chariot forces.
[23]These men were also in charge of Solomon's work projects;
there were a total of 550 men who supervised the workers. [24]Sol-
omon built the terrace as soon as Pharaoh's daughter moved
up from the City of David to the palace Solomon built for her.
[25]Three times a year Solomon offered burnt offerings and
peace offerings on the altar he had built for the LORD, burning
incense along with them before the LORD. He made the temple
his official worship place.
[26]King Solomon also built ships in Ezion Geber, which is
located near Elat in the land of Edom, on the shore of the Red
Sea. [27]Hiram sent his fleet and some of his sailors, who were well
acquainted with the sea, to serve with Solomon's men. [28]They
sailed to Ophir, took from there 420 talents of gold, and then
brought them to King Solomon.

SOLOMON ENTERTAINS A QUEEN

10 When the queen of Sheba heard about Solomon, she
came to challenge him with difficult questions. [2]She arrived in Jerusalem with a great display of pomp, bringing with
her camels carrying spices, a very large quantity of gold, and
precious gems. She visited Solomon and discussed with him
everything that was on her mind. [3]Solomon answered all her
questions; there was no question too complex for the king.
[4]When the queen of Sheba saw for herself Solomon's extensive
wisdom, the palace he had built, [5]the food in his banquet hall,

10:1–13 In the queen of Sheba we are given an example of the pursuit of wisdom. Indeed, she had come to hear Solomon from a very long distance. It would be shameful for us therefore if we did not studiously and regularly attend sacred assemblies that are nearby to listen to the sermons coming from the mouths of God's ministers. And if we do not, "The queen of the South will rise up at the judgment with this generation and condemn it because she came from the ends of the earth to hear the wisdom of Solomon—and now, something greater than Solomon is here!" (Matt 12:42).

JOHANNES PISCATOR
(1546–1625)
COMMENTARY ON FIRST KINGS

his servants and attendants, their robes, his cupbearers, and his
burnt offerings which he presented in the LORD's temple, she
was amazed. 6She said to the king, "The report I heard in my
own country about your wise sayings and insight was true! 7I
did not believe these things until I came and saw them with my
own eyes. Indeed, I didn't hear even half the story! Your wisdom
and wealth surpass what was reported to me. 8Your attendants,
who stand before you at all times and hear your wise sayings,
are truly happy! 9May the LORD your God be praised because
he favored you by placing you on the throne of Israel! Because
of the LORD's eternal love for Israel, he made you king so you
could make just and right decisions." 10She gave the king 120
talents of gold, a very large quantity of spices, and precious
gems. The quantity of spices the queen of Sheba gave King Solomon has never been matched. 11(Hiram's fleet, which carried
gold from Ophir, also brought from Ophir a very large quantity
of fine timber and precious gems. 12With the timber the king
made supports for the LORD's temple and for the royal palace
and stringed instruments for the musicians. No one has seen
so much of this fine timber to this very day.) 13King Solomon
gave the queen of Sheba everything she requested, besides
what he had freely offered her. Then she left and returned to
her homeland with her attendants.

SOLOMON'S WEALTH

14Solomon received 666 talents of gold per year, 15besides what
he collected from the merchants, traders, Arabian kings, and
governors of the land. 16King Solomon made 200 large shields
of hammered gold; 600 measures of gold were used for each
shield. 17He also made 300 small shields of hammered gold;
three minas of gold were used for each of these shields. The
king placed them in the Palace of the Lebanon Forest.

18The king made a large throne decorated with ivory and
overlaid it with pure gold. 19There were six steps leading up to
the throne, and the back of it was rounded on top. The throne
had two armrests with a statue of a lion standing on each side.
20There were 12 statues of lions on the six steps, one lion at each
end of each step. There was nothing like it in any other kingdom.

21All of King Solomon's cups were made of gold, and all the
household items in the Palace of the Lebanon Forest were made
of pure gold. There were no silver items, for silver was not considered very valuable in Solomon's time. 22Along with Hiram's
fleet, the king had a fleet of large merchant ships that sailed
the sea. Once every three years the fleet came into port with
cargoes of gold, silver, ivory, apes, and peacocks.

23King Solomon was wealthier and wiser than any of the
kings of the earth. 24Everyone in the world wanted to visit Solomon to see him display his God-given wisdom. 25Year after year
visitors brought their gifts, which included items of silver, items
of gold, clothes, perfume, spices, horses, and mules.

26Solomon accumulated chariots and horses. He had 1,400
chariots and 12,000 horses. He kept them in assigned cities and
in Jerusalem. 27The king made silver as plentiful in Jerusalem
as stones; cedar was as plentiful as sycamore fig trees are in the
foothills. 28Solomon acquired his horses from Egypt and from
Que; the king's traders purchased them from Que. 29They paid
600 silver pieces for each chariot from Egypt and 150 silver
pieces for each horse. They also sold chariots and horses to all
the kings of the Hittites and to the kings of Syria.

THE LORD PUNISHES SOLOMON FOR IDOLATRY

11 King Solomon fell in love with many foreign women (besides Pharaoh's daughter), including Moabites, Ammonites, Edomites, Sidonians, and Hittites. 2They came from nations about which the LORD had warned the Israelites, "You must not establish friendly relations with them! If you do, they will surely shift your allegiance to their gods." But Solomon was irresistibly attracted to them.

3He had 700 royal wives and 300 concubines; his wives had a powerful influence over him. 4When Solomon became old, his wives shifted his allegiance to other gods; he was not wholeheartedly devoted to the LORD his God, as his father David had been. 5Solomon worshiped the Sidonian goddess Astarte and the detestable Ammonite god Milcom. 6Solomon did evil in the LORD's sight; he did not remain loyal to the LORD, as his father David had. 7Furthermore, on the hill east of Jerusalem Solomon built a high place for the detestable Moabite god Chemosh and for the detestable Ammonite god Milcom. 8He built high places for all his foreign wives so they could burn incense and make sacrifices to their gods.

9The LORD was angry with Solomon because he had shifted his allegiance away from the LORD, the God of Israel, who had appeared to him on two occasions 10and had warned him about this very thing, so that he would not follow other gods. But he did not obey the LORD's command. 11So the LORD said to Solomon, "Because you insist on doing these things and have not kept the covenantal rules I gave you, I will surely tear the kingdom away from you and give it to your servant. 12However, for your father David's sake I will not do this while you are alive. I will tear it away from your son's hand instead. 13But I will not tear away the entire kingdom; I will leave your son one tribe for my servant David's sake and for the sake of my chosen city Jerusalem."

14The LORD brought against Solomon an enemy, Hadad the Edomite, a descendant of the Edomite king. 15During David's campaign against Edom, Joab, the commander of the army, while on a mission to bury the dead, killed every male in Edom. 16For Joab and the entire Israelite army stayed there six months until they had exterminated every male in Edom. 17Hadad, who was only a small boy at the time, escaped with some of his father's Edomite servants and headed for Egypt. 18They went from Midian to Paran; they took some men from Paran and went to Egypt. Pharaoh, king of Egypt, gave him a house and some land and supplied him with food. 19Pharaoh liked Hadad so well he gave him his sister-in-law (Queen Tahpenes' sister) as a wife. 20Tahpenes' sister gave birth to his son, named Genubath. Tahpenes raised him in Pharaoh's palace; Genubath grew up in Pharaoh's palace among Pharaoh's sons. 21While in Egypt Hadad heard that David had passed away and that Joab, the commander of the army, was dead. So Hadad asked Pharaoh, "Give me permission to leave so I can return to my homeland." 22Pharaoh said to him, "What do you lack here that makes you want to go to your homeland?" Hadad replied, "Nothing, but please give me permission to leave."

23God also brought against Solomon another enemy, Rezon son of Eliada who had run away from his master, King Hadadezer of Zobah. 24He gathered some men and organized a raiding band. When David tried to kill them, they went to Damascus, where they settled down and gained control of the city.

11:15–40 Since Jeroboam later set up golden calves to be worshiped (1 Kgs 12:25–32), why did God not only allow but also order him to seize the kingdom? So that we might see that things are done according to God's will and not according to our decisions. For what wondering admiration do you think enters the pious heart when it considers the aforesaid Jeroboam, who was ordained by God to separate Israel into two kingdoms and presently abandoned Solomon whom God had installed, after he had set up golden calves to be worshiped! This thing first brought Israel and then Judah to destruction, for it was an unworthy deed to lead people away from the true God to idolatry, but it would have been an ill-considered plan on God's part to raise a person like this to the throne who was going to revolt against him unless God had determined to use his treachery for the things he was preparing.

ULRICH ZWINGLI **(1484–1531)**
ON THE PROVIDENCE OF GOD

25 He was Israel's enemy throughout Solomon's reign and, like
Hadad, caused trouble. He loathed Israel and ruled over Syria.
26 Jeroboam son of Nebat, one of Solomon's servants, rebelled
against the king. He was an Ephraimite from Zeredah whose
mother was a widow named Zeruah. 27 This is what prompted
him to rebel against the king: Solomon built a terrace, and he
closed up a gap in the wall of the city of his father David. 28 Jeroboam was a talented man; when Solomon saw that the young
man was an accomplished worker, he made him the leader of
the work crew from the tribe of Joseph. 29 At that time, when
Jeroboam had left Jerusalem, the prophet Ahijah the Shilonite
met him on the road; the two of them were alone in the open
country. Ahijah was wearing a brand new robe, 30 and he grabbed
the robe and tore it into 12 pieces. 31 Then he told Jeroboam,
"Take 10 pieces, for this is what the LORD God of Israel has said:
'Look, I am about to tear the kingdom from Solomon's hand
and I will give 10 tribes to you. 32 He will retain one tribe, for my
servant David's sake and for the sake of Jerusalem, the city I have
chosen out of all the tribes of Israel. 33 I am taking the kingdom
from him because they have abandoned me and worshiped the
Sidonian goddess Astarte, the Moabite god Chemosh, and the
Ammonite god Milcom. They have not followed my instructions
by doing what I approve and obeying my rules and regulations,
as Solomon's father David did. 34 I will not take the whole kingdom from his hand. I will allow him to be ruler for the rest of
his life for the sake of my chosen servant David who kept my
commandments and rules. 35 I will take the kingdom from the
hand of his son and give 10 tribes to you. 36 I will leave his son
one tribe so my servant David's dynasty may continue to serve
me in Jerusalem, the city I have chosen as my home. 37 I will
select you; you will rule over all you desire to have and you will
be king over Israel. 38 You must obey all I command you to do,
follow my instructions, do what I approve, and keep my rules and
commandments, as my servant David did. Then I will be with you
and establish for you a lasting dynasty, as I did for David; I will
give you Israel. 39 I will humiliate David's descendants because
of this, but not forever.'" 40 Solomon tried to kill Jeroboam, but
Jeroboam escaped to Egypt and found refuge with King Shishak
of Egypt. He stayed in Egypt until Solomon died.

SOLOMON'S REIGN ENDS

41 The rest of the events of Solomon's reign, including all his
accomplishments and his wise decisions, are recorded in the
scroll called the Annals of Solomon. 42 Solomon ruled over all
Israel from Jerusalem for 40 years. 43 Then Solomon passed
away and was buried in the city of his father David. His son
Rehoboam replaced him as king.

REHOBOAM LOSES HIS KINGDOM

12 Rehoboam traveled to Shechem, for all Israel had gathered
in Shechem to make Rehoboam king. 2 When Jeroboam
son of Nebat heard the news, he was still in Egypt, where he
had fled from King Solomon and had been living ever since.
3 They sent for him, and Jeroboam and the whole Israelite assembly came and spoke to Rehoboam, saying, 4 "Your father
made us work too hard. Now if you lighten the demands he
made and don't make us work as hard, we will serve you." 5 He
said to them, "Go away for three days, then return to me." So
the people went away.

12:1–15 Rehoboam's weakness was that, by passionate and foolish councils, he allowed his honor to be stained, his interest to be weakened, and his conscience to be defiled with resolutions of violence and injustice. Now there is no counsel like God's Word: It enlightens the eyes, makes wise the simple, and is able to make people wise for themselves and also for salvation. No other counsel can do this. There is no case—even one of great intricacy and complexity—that can stump it. There is no difficulty or temptation so knotty and involved that it cannot resolve it. There is no condition where a person can be brought to desperation and not be brought back with it. There is no employment so dark and uncouth that it cannot rescue a person. And there is no discouragement so great that God's Word cannot offer greater encouragement. In all this it is clear that people ought to run to God's Word. For if people have any judgment or spiritual sense, they will earnestly search God's Word.

EDWARD REYNOLDS
(1599–1676)
SEVEN SERMONS ON FOURTEENTH CHAPTER OF HOSEA

6 King Rehoboam consulted with the older advisers who had served his father Solomon when he had been alive. He asked them, "How do you advise me to answer these people?" 7 They said to him, "Today if you will be a servant to these people and grant their request, speaking kind words to them, they will be your servants from this time forward." 8 But Rehoboam rejected their advice and consulted the young advisers who served him, with whom he had grown up. 9 He asked them, "How do you advise me to respond to these people who said to me, 'Lessen the demands your father placed on us'?" 10 The young advisers with whom Rehoboam had grown up said to him, "Say this to these people who have said to you, 'Your father made us work hard, but now lighten our burden.' Say this to them: 'I am a lot harsher than my father! 11 My father imposed heavy demands on you; I will make them even heavier. My father punished you with ordinary whips; I will punish you with whips that really sting your flesh.'"

12 Jeroboam and all the people reported to Rehoboam on the third day, just as the king had ordered when he said, "Return to me on the third day." 13 The king responded to the people harshly. He rejected the advice of the older men 14 and followed the advice of the younger ones. He said, "My father imposed heavy demands on you; I will make them even heavier. My father punished you with ordinary whips; I will punish you with whips that really sting your flesh." 15 The king refused to listen to the people, because the LORD was instigating this turn of events so that he might bring to pass the prophetic announcement he had made through Ahijah the Shilonite to Jeroboam son of Nebat.

16 When all Israel saw that the king refused to listen to them, the people answered the king, "We have no portion in David, no share in the son of Jesse! Return to your homes, O Israel! Now, look after your own dynasty, O David!" So Israel returned to their homes. 17 (Rehoboam continued to rule over the Israelites who lived in the cities of Judah.) 18 King Rehoboam sent Adoniram, the supervisor of the work crews, out after them, but all Israel stoned him to death. King Rehoboam managed to jump into his chariot and escape to Jerusalem. 19 So Israel has been in rebellion against the Davidic dynasty to this very day. 20 When all Israel heard that Jeroboam had returned, they summoned him to the assembly and made him king over all Israel. No one except the tribe of Judah remained loyal to the Davidic dynasty.

21 When Rehoboam arrived in Jerusalem, he summoned 180,000 skilled warriors from all Judah and the tribe of Benjamin to attack Israel and restore the kingdom to Rehoboam son of Solomon. 22 But God told Shemaiah the prophet, 23 "Say this to King Rehoboam son of Solomon of Judah, and to all Judah and Benjamin, as well as the rest of the people, 24 'This is what the LORD has said: "Do not attack and make war with your brothers, the Israelites. Each of you go home. Indeed this thing has happened because of me."'" So they obeyed the LORD's message. They went home in keeping with the LORD's message.

JEROBOAM MAKES GOLDEN CALVES

25 Jeroboam built up Shechem in the Ephraimite hill country and lived there. From there he went out and built up Penuel. 26 Jeroboam then thought to himself: "Now the Davidic dynasty could regain the kingdom. 27 If these people go up to offer sacrifices in the LORD's temple in Jerusalem, their loyalty could

shift to their former master, King Rehoboam of Judah. They
might kill me and return to King Rehoboam of Judah." 28After
the king had consulted with his advisers, he made two golden
calves. Then he said to the people, "It is too much trouble for
you to go up to Jerusalem. Look, Israel, here are your gods who
brought you up from the land of Egypt." 29He put one in Bethel
and the other in Dan. 30This caused Israel to sin; the people
went to Bethel and Dan to worship the calves.
31He built temples on the high places and appointed as
priests common people who were not Levites. 32Jeroboam inaugurated a festival on the fifteenth day of the eighth month,
like the festival celebrated in Judah. On the altar in Bethel he
offered sacrifices to the calves he had made. In Bethel he also
appointed priests for the high places he had made.

A PROPHET FROM JUDAH VISITS BETHEL

33On the fifteenth day of the eighth month (a date he had arbi-
trarily chosen) Jeroboam offered sacrifices on the altar he had
made in Bethel. He inaugurated a festival for the Israelites and
13 went up to the altar to offer sacrifices. 1Just then a prophet
arrived from Judah with the LORD's message for Bethel, as
Jeroboam was standing near the altar ready to offer a sacrifice.
2He cried out against the altar with the LORD's message, "O altar,
altar! This is what the LORD has said, 'Look, a son named Josiah
will be born to the Davidic dynasty. He will sacrifice on you the
priests of the high places who offer sacrifices on you. Human
bones will be burned on you.'" 3That day he had also given a
sign, saying, "This is the sign that the LORD has declared: The
altar will split open and the ashes on it will pour out." 4When
the king heard the prophet's message that he had cried out
against the altar in Bethel, Jeroboam took his hand from the
altar and pointed it saying, "Seize him!" Then the hand that he
had pointed at him stiffened up, and he could not pull it back.
5Meanwhile the altar split open, and the ashes poured from the
altar in fulfillment of the sign the prophet had given with
the LORD's message. 6The king responded to the prophet, "Seek
the favor of the LORD your God and pray for me, so that my hand
may be restored." So the prophet sought the LORD's favor and
the king's hand was restored as it was at first. 7The king then
said to the prophet, "Come home with me and have something
to eat, so that I may give you a gift." 8But the prophet said to
the king, "Even if you were to give me half your possessions, I
would not go with you. I am not allowed to eat food or drink
water in this place. 9For this is how I was commanded in the
LORD's message, 'Eat no food. Drink no water. And do not return
by the way you came.'" 10So he started back on another road; he
did not travel back on the same road he had taken to Bethel.
11Now there was an old prophet living in Bethel. When his
sons came home, they told him everything the prophet had
done in Bethel that day. And they told their father all the words
that he had spoken to the king. 12Their father asked them,
"Which road did he take?" His sons showed him the road the
prophet from Judah had taken. 13He then told his sons, "Saddle
the donkey for me." When they had saddled the donkey for him,
he mounted it 14and took off after the prophet, whom he found
sitting under an oak tree. He asked him, "Are you the prophet
from Judah?" He answered, "Yes, I am." 15He then said to him,
"Come home with me and eat something." 16But he replied, "I
can't go back with you. I am not allowed to eat food or to drink

13:1–10 When in the temple of our God that wicked king Jeroboam took away the gifts that his father had laid up and offered them to idols on the holy altar, did not his right hand wither, and the idols that he called on were not able to help him? Then, turning to the Lord, he asked for pardon and at once his hand, which had withered by sacrilege, was healed by true religion. So complete an example was there set forth in one person both of divine mercy and wrath, when he who was sacrificing suddenly lost his right hand but when penitent received forgiveness.

AMBROSE (C. 339–C. 397)
CONCERNING VIRGINS

water with you in this place. 17For an order came to me in the LORD's message, 'Eat no food. Drink no water there. And do not return by the way you came.'" 18Then the old prophet said, "I too am a prophet like you. And an angel has told me in a message from the LORD, 'Bring him back with you to your house so he can eat food and drink water.'" But he had lied to him. 19So the prophet went back with him. He ate food in his house and he drank water.

20While they were sitting at the table, the LORD's message came to the old prophet who had brought him back. 21So he cried out to the prophet who had come from Judah, "This is what the LORD has said, 'You have rebelled against the LORD's instruction and have not obeyed the command the LORD your God gave you. 22You went back. You ate food. And you drank water in the place of which he had said to you, "Eat no food. Drink no water." Therefore your corpse will not be buried in your ancestral tomb.'"

23So this is what happened after he had eaten food and drunk water. The old prophet saddled the donkey for the prophet whom he had brought back. 24So the prophet from Judah travelled on. Then a lion attacked him on the road and killed him.

There was his body lying on the road, with the donkey standing next to it, and the lion just standing there by the body. 25Then some men came passing by and saw the body lying in the road with the lion standing next to the body. They went and reported what they had seen in the city where the old prophet lived. 26When the old prophet who had invited him to his house heard the news, he said, "It is the prophet who rebelled against the LORD. The LORD delivered him over to the lion and it tore him up and killed him, in keeping with the LORD's message that he had spoken to him." 27He told his sons, "Saddle my donkey." So they saddled it. 28He went and found the body lying in the road with the donkey and the lion standing beside it; the lion had neither eaten the body nor attacked the donkey. 29The old prophet picked up the prophet's body, put it on the donkey, and brought it back. The old prophet then entered the city to mourn him and to bury him. 30He put the body into his own tomb, and they mourned over him, saying, "Ah, my brother!" 31After he buried him, he said to his sons, "When I die, bury me in the tomb where the prophet is buried; put my bones right beside his bones, 32because the message that he announced as the LORD's message against the altar in Bethel and against all the temples on the high places in the cities of the north will certainly be fulfilled."

A PROPHET ANNOUNCES THE END OF JEROBOAM'S DYNASTY

33After this happened, Jeroboam still did not change his evil ways; he continued to appoint common people as priests at the high places. Anyone who wanted the job he consecrated as a priest. 34This sin caused Jeroboam's dynasty to come to an end and to be destroyed from the face of the earth.

14 At that time Jeroboam's son Abijah became sick. 2Jeroboam told his wife, "Disguise yourself so that people cannot recognize you are Jeroboam's wife. Then go to Shiloh; Ahijah the prophet, who told me I would rule over this nation, lives there. 3Take 10 loaves of bread, some small cakes, and a container of honey and visit him. He will tell you what will happen to the boy."

14:1–18 In Jeroboam's consultation of the prophet Ahijah regarding his son's possible death, an example of hypocrisy was set forth in two ways. First, Jeroboam consulted God through the prophet even though he had despised God by insolently persevering in idolatry, which was a great perversity. Second, Jeroboam attempted to deceive the prophet who nevertheless could see through his deceit, for the death of Jeroboam's son had been revealed to the prophet beforehand. Jeroboam's attempt was simultaneously tricky and foolish. From this we learn the lesson that trickery never aids hypocrites. For God detects frauds, as this passage indicates concerning the concealing of Jeroboam's wife to Ahijah, and God makes come to pass that which individuals feared despite their deceitful attempts at aversion. In this way it came to pass that Ahijah gravely reprimanded Jeroboam on account of his idolatry.

JOHANNES PISCATOR
(1546–1625)
COMMENTARY ON FIRST KINGS

[4]Jeroboam's wife did as she was told. She went to Shiloh
and visited Ahijah. Now Ahijah could not see; he had lost his
eyesight in his old age. [5]But the LORD had told Ahijah, "Look,
Jeroboam's wife is coming to find out from you what will happen to her son, for he is sick. Tell her such and such. When she
comes, she will be in a disguise." [6]When Ahijah heard the sound
of her footsteps as she came through the door, he said, "Come
on in, wife of Jeroboam! Why are you pretending to be someone
else? I have been commissioned to give you bad news. [7]Go, tell
Jeroboam, 'This is what the LORD God of Israel has said: "I raised
you up from among the people and made you ruler over my people Israel. [8]I tore the kingdom away from the Davidic dynasty
and gave it to you. But you are not like my servant David, who
kept my commandments and followed me wholeheartedly by
doing only what I approve. [9]You have sinned more than all who
came before you. You went and angered me by making other
gods, formed out of metal; you have completely disregarded me.
[10]So I am ready to bring disaster on the dynasty of Jeroboam.
I will cut off every last male belonging to Jeroboam in Israel,
including even the weak and incapacitated. I will burn up the
dynasty of Jeroboam, just as one burns manure until it is completely consumed. [11]Dogs will eat the members of your family
who die in the city, and the birds of the sky will eat the ones
who die in the country."' Indeed, the LORD has announced it!
[12]"As for you, get up and go home. When you set foot in the
city, the boy will die. [13]All Israel will mourn him and bury him.
He is the only one in Jeroboam's family who will receive a decent
burial, for he is the only one in whom the LORD God of Israel
found anything good. [14]The LORD will raise up a king over Israel
who will cut off Jeroboam's dynasty. It is ready to happen! [15]The
LORD will attack Israel, making it like a reed that sways in the
water. He will remove Israel from this good land he gave to
their ancestors and scatter them beyond the Euphrates River,
because they angered the LORD by making Asherah poles. [16]He
will hand Israel over to their enemies because of the sins which
Jeroboam committed and which he made Israel commit."
[17]So Jeroboam's wife got up and went back to Tirzah. As she
crossed the threshold of the house, the boy died. [18]All Israel
buried him and mourned for him, in keeping with the LORD's
message that he had spoken through his servant, the prophet
Ahijah.

JEROBOAM'S REIGN ENDS

[19]The rest of the events of Jeroboam's reign, including the details of his battles and rule, are recorded in the scroll called the
Annals of the Kings of Israel. [20]Jeroboam ruled for 22 years; then
he passed away. His son Nadab replaced him as king.

REHOBOAM'S REIGN OVER JUDAH

[21]Now Rehoboam son of Solomon ruled in Judah. He was forty-
one years old when he became king, and he ruled for 17 years
in Jerusalem, the city the LORD chose from all the tribes of
Israel to be his home. His mother was an Ammonite woman
named Naamah.
[22]Judah did evil in the sight of the LORD. They made him
more jealous by their sins than their ancestors had done. [23]They
even built for themselves high places, sacred pillars, and Asherah poles on every high hill and under every green tree. [24]There
were also male cultic prostitutes in the land. They committed

the same horrible sins as the nations that the LORD had driven
out from before the Israelites.
25 In King Rehoboam's fifth year, King Shishak of Egypt attacked Jerusalem. 26 He took away the treasures of the LORD's
temple and of the royal palace; he took everything, including all
the golden shields that Solomon had made. 27 King Rehoboam
made bronze shields to replace them and assigned them to the
officers of the royal guard who protected the entrance to the
royal palace. 28 Whenever the king visited the LORD's temple,
the royal guard carried them and then brought them back to
the guardroom.
29 The rest of the events of Rehoboam's reign, including his
accomplishments, are recorded in the scroll called the Annals
of the Kings of Judah. 30 Rehoboam and Jeroboam were continually at war with each other. 31 Rehoboam passed away and
was buried with his ancestors in the City of David. His mother
was an Ammonite named Naamah. His son Abijah replaced
him as king.

ABIJAH'S REIGN OVER JUDAH

15 In the eighteenth year of the reign of Jeroboam son of
Nebat, Abijah became king over Judah. 2 He ruled for three
years in Jerusalem. His mother was Maacah, the daughter of
Abishalom. 3 He followed all the sinful practices of his father
before him. He was not wholeheartedly devoted to the LORD his
God, as his ancestor David had been. 4 Nevertheless for David's
sake the LORD his God maintained his dynasty in Jerusalem by
giving him a son to succeed him and by protecting Jerusalem.
5 He did this because David had done what he approved and had
not disregarded any of his commandments his entire lifetime,
except for the incident involving Uriah the Hittite. 6 Rehoboam
and Jeroboam were continually at war with each other throughout Abijah's lifetime. 7 The rest of the events of Abijah's reign,
including all his accomplishments, are recorded in the scroll
called the Annals of the Kings of Judah. Abijah and Jeroboam
had been at war with each other. 8 Abijah passed away and was
buried in the City of David. His son Asa replaced him as king.

ASA'S REIGN OVER JUDAH

9 In the twentieth year of Jeroboam's reign over Israel, Asa became the king of Judah. 10 He ruled for 41 years in Jerusalem.
His grandmother was Maacah daughter of Abishalom. 11 Asa
did what the LORD approved as his ancestor David had done.
12 He removed the male cultic prostitutes from the land and
got rid of all the disgusting idols his ancestors had made. 13 He
also removed Maacah his grandmother from her position as
queen mother because she had made a loathsome Asherah
pole. Asa cut down her loathsome pole and burned it in the
Kidron Valley. 14 The high places were not eliminated, yet Asa
was wholeheartedly devoted to the LORD throughout his lifetime. 15 He brought the holy items that he and his father had
made into the LORD's temple, including the silver, gold, and
other articles.
16 Now Asa and King Baasha of Israel were continually at war
with each other. 17 King Baasha of Israel attacked Judah and
established Ramah as a military outpost to prevent anyone
from leaving or entering the land of King Asa of Judah. 18 Asa
took all the silver and gold that was left in the treasuries of
the LORD's temple and of the royal palace and handed it to his

15:1–8 The heart of the wicked is deceitful with a full, strong, and reigning deceitfulness. The deceitfulness in the heart of the godly is weaker, for it can be discerned as evil and fought against. The hearts of wicked people show their deceitfulness in the whole course of their lives, while the hearts of the godly show their deceitfulness only in some particular actions. As it is said of David, he was upright in all things "except for the incident involving Uriah the Hittite." The general current of his life was free from deceitfulness, though not that particular action. This is proper only to the godly—that they are upright in their way, that is, in the constant tenor of their conversation.

DANIEL DYKE (D. 1614)
THE MYSTERY OF SELF-DECEIVING

servants. He then told them to deliver it to Ben Hadad son of
Tabrimmon, the son of Hezion, king of Syria, ruler in Damascus,
along with this message: 19"I want to make a treaty with you, like
the one our fathers made. See, I have sent you silver and gold
as a present. Break your treaty with King Baasha of Israel, so
he will retreat from my land." 20Ben Hadad accepted King Asa's
offer and ordered his army commanders to attack the cities of
Israel. They conquered Ijon, Dan, Abel Beth Maacah, and all
the territory of Naphtali, including the region of Kinnereth.
21When Baasha heard the news, he stopped fortifying Ramah
and settled down in Tirzah. 22King Asa ordered all the men of
Judah (no exemptions were granted) to carry away the stones
and wood that Baasha had used to build Ramah. King Asa used
the materials to build up Geba (in Benjamin) and Mizpah.
23The rest of the events of Asa's reign, including all his successes and accomplishments, as well as a record of the cities he
built, are recorded in the scroll called the Annals of the Kings
of Judah. Yet when he was very old he developed a foot disease.
24Asa passed away and was buried with his ancestors in the city
of his ancestor David. His son Jehoshaphat replaced him as king.

NADAB'S REIGN OVER ISRAEL

25In the second year of Asa's reign over Judah, Jeroboam's son
Nadab became the king of Israel; he ruled Israel for two years.
26He did evil in the sight of the LORD. He followed in his father's
footsteps and encouraged Israel to sin.
27Baasha son of Ahijah, from the tribe of Issachar, conspired
against Nadab and assassinated him in Gibbethon, which was
in Philistine territory. This happened while Nadab and all the
Israelite army were besieging Gibbethon. 28Baasha killed him
in the third year of Asa's reign over Judah and replaced him as
king. 29When he became king, he executed Jeroboam's entire
family. He wiped out everyone who breathed, in keeping with
the LORD's message that he had spoken through his servant
Ahijah the Shilonite. 30This happened because of the sins which
Jeroboam committed and which he made Israel commit. These
sins angered the LORD God of Israel.
31The rest of the events of Nadab's reign, including all his
accomplishments, are recorded in the scroll called the Annals
of the Kings of Israel. 32Asa and King Baasha of Israel were
continually at war with each other.

BAASHA'S REIGN OVER ISRAEL

33In the third year of Asa's reign over Judah, Baasha son of Ahijah became king over all Israel in Tirzah; he ruled for 24 years.
34He did evil in the sight of the LORD; he followed in Jeroboam's
footsteps and encouraged Israel to sin.
16 The LORD's message against Baasha came to Jehu son of
Hanani: 2"I raised you up from the dust and made you
ruler over my people Israel. Yet you followed in Jeroboam's
footsteps and encouraged my people Israel to sin; their sins
have made me angry. 3So I am ready to burn up Baasha and his
family, and make your family like the family of Jeroboam son
of Nebat. 4Dogs will eat the members of Baasha's family who
die in the city, and the birds of the sky will eat the ones who
die in the country."
5The rest of the events of Baasha's reign, including his accomplishments and successes, are recorded in the scroll called
the Annals of the Kings of Israel. 6Baasha passed away and was

16:1–7 Though invading the kingdom was from himself and his own wicked heart, yet the translation of the kingdom from Nadab to Baasha, simply considered, was from God, who by his providence disposed of all occasions and of the hearts of the soldiers and people so that Baasha should have opportunity of executing God's judgment upon Nadab. No, the very act of Baasha's killing his master Nadab was an act of divine justice. And if Baasha had done this in obedience to God's command and with a single design to execute God's vengeance threatened against him, it had been no more a sin than Jehu's act in killing his master King Joram upon the same account in 2 Kings 9.

JOHN WESLEY (1703–1791)
EXPLANATORY NOTES ON THE BIBLE

buried in Tirzah. His son Elah replaced him as king. 7And so it was the LORD's message came through the prophet Jehu son of Hanani against Baasha and his family. This was because of all the evil he had done in the LORD's view, by angering him with his deeds and becoming like Jeroboam's dynasty, and because of how he had destroyed Jeroboam's dynasty.

ELAH'S REIGN OVER ISRAEL

8In the twenty-sixth year of Asa's reign over Judah, Baasha's son Elah became king over Israel; he ruled in Tirzah for two years. 9His servant Zimri, a commander of half of his chariot force, conspired against him. While Elah was in Tirzah drinking heavily at the house of Arza, who supervised the palace in Tirzah, 10Zimri came in and struck him dead. (This happened in the twenty-seventh year of Asa's reign over Judah.) Zimri replaced Elah as king. 11When he became king and occupied the throne, he killed Baasha's entire family. He did not spare any male belonging to him; he killed his relatives and his friends. 12Zimri destroyed Baasha's entire family, in keeping with the LORD's message which he had spoken against Baasha through Jehu the prophet. 13This happened because of all the sins which Baasha and his son Elah committed and which they made Israel commit. They angered the LORD God of Israel with their worthless idols.

14The rest of the events of Elah's reign, including all his accomplishments, are recorded in the scroll called the Annals of the Kings of Israel.

ZIMRI'S REIGN OVER ISRAEL

15In the twenty-seventh year of Asa's reign over Judah, Zimri became king over Israel; he ruled for seven days in Tirzah. Zimri's revolt took place while the army was deployed in Gibbethon, which was in Philistine territory. 16While deployed there, the army received this report: "Zimri has conspired against the king and assassinated him." So all Israel made Omri, the commander of the army, king over Israel that very day in the camp. 17Omri and all Israel went up from Gibbethon and besieged Tirzah. 18When Zimri saw that the city was captured, he went into the fortified area of the royal palace. He set the palace on fire and died in the flames. 19This happened because of the sins he committed. He did evil in the sight of the LORD and followed in Jeroboam's footsteps and encouraged Israel to continue sinning.

20The rest of the events of Zimri's reign, including the details of his revolt, are recorded in the scroll called the Annals of the Kings of Israel.

OMRI'S REIGN OVER ISRAEL

21At that time the people of Israel were divided in their loyalties. Half the people supported Tibni son of Ginath and wanted to make him king; the other half supported Omri. 22Omri's supporters were stronger than those who supported Tibni son of Ginath. Tibni died; Omri became king.

23In the thirty-first year of Asa's reign over Judah, Omri became king over Israel. He ruled for twelve years, six of them in Tirzah. 24He purchased the hill of Samaria from Shemer for two talents of silver. He launched a construction project there and named the city he built after Shemer, the former owner of the hill of Samaria. 25Omri did more evil in the sight of the LORD than all who were before him. 26He followed in the footsteps

of Jeroboam son of Nebat and encouraged Israel to sin; they
angered the LORD God of Israel with their worthless idols.
27 The rest of the events of Omri's reign, including his accomplishments and successes, are recorded in the scroll called the
Annals of the Kings of Israel. 28 Omri passed away and was buried
in Samaria. His son Ahab replaced him as king.

AHAB PROMOTES IDOLATRY

29 In the thirty-eighth year of Asa's reign over Judah, Omri's son
Ahab became king over Israel. Ahab son of Omri ruled over
Israel for 22 years in Samaria. 30 Ahab son of Omri did more
evil in the sight of the LORD than all who were before him. 31 As
if following in the sinful footsteps of Jeroboam son of Nebat
were not bad enough, he married Jezebel the daughter of King
Ethbaal of the Sidonians. Then he worshiped and bowed to Baal.
32 He set up an altar for Baal in the temple of Baal he had built
in Samaria. 33 Ahab also made an Asherah pole; he did more to
anger the LORD God of Israel than all the kings of Israel who
were before him.
34 During Ahab's reign, Hiel the Bethelite rebuilt Jericho.
Abiram, his firstborn son, died when he laid the foundation;
Segub, his youngest son, died when he erected its gates, in
keeping with the LORD's message that he had spoken through
Joshua son of Nun.

ELIJAH VISITS A WIDOW IN SIDONIAN TERRITORY

17 Elijah the Tishbite, from Tishbe in Gilead, said to Ahab, "As
certainly as the LORD God of Israel lives (whom I serve),
there will be no dew or rain in the years ahead unless I give the
command." 2 The LORD's message came to him: 3 "Leave here
and travel eastward. Hide out in the Kerith Valley near the
Jordan. 4 Drink from the stream; I have already told the ravens
to bring you food there." 5 So he carried out the LORD's message;
he went and lived in the Kerith Valley near the Jordan. 6 The
ravens would bring him bread and meat each morning and
evening, and he would drink from the stream.
7 After a while, the stream dried up because there had been
no rain in the land. 8 The LORD's message came to him, 9 "Get
up, go to Zarephath in Sidonian territory, and live there. I have
already told a widow who lives there to provide for you." 10 So
he got up and went to Zarephath. When he went through the
city gate, there was a widow gathering wood. He called out to
her, "Please give me a little water in a cup, so I can take a drink."
11 As she went to get it, he called out to her, "Please bring me a
piece of bread." 12 She said, "As certainly as the LORD your God
lives, I have no food, except for a handful of flour in a jar and
a little olive oil in a jug. Right now I am gathering a couple of
sticks for a fire. Then I'm going home to make one final meal
for my son and myself. After we have eaten that, we will die of
starvation." 13 Elijah said to her, "Don't be afraid. Go and do as
you planned. But first make me a small cake and bring it to me;
then make something for yourself and your son. 14 For this is
what the LORD God of Israel has said: 'The jar of flour will not
be empty and the jug of oil will not run out until the day the
LORD makes it rain on the surface of the ground.'" 15 She went
and did as Elijah told her; there was always enough food for
Elijah and for her and her family. 16 The jar of flour was never
empty and the jug of oil never ran out, in keeping with the
LORD's message that he had spoken through Elijah.

17:1–24 Elijah was truly great in spirit. He can even be called the foremost of the prophets. James made his argument about the prayer of faith from this history of Elijah, saying, "The prayer of a righteous person has great effectiveness. Elijah was a human being like us, and he prayed earnestly" (Jas 5:16–17). No doubt he had been moved by the king's shamelessness to pray against the king and the kingdom, as God denies those who despise his gifts. But this prophet who could make the heavens stop or start raining was in the meantime afflicted by nearly dying of hunger, so that you see how God brings such affliction on his holy ones. For God the Father always wants to be acknowledged as the one who blessedly supplies what is necessary for growth, that we might depend on him and commit all our needs in life to him alone. You truly see how God provided for Elijah so that where human help was nothing, there the ravens fed him.

JOHANNES BUGENHAGEN
(1485–1558)
COMMENTARY ON FIRST KINGS

17 After this the son of the woman who owned the house got sick. His illness was so severe he could no longer breathe. 18 She asked Elijah, "Why, prophet, have you come to me to confront me with my sin and kill my son?" 19 He said to her, "Hand me your son." He took him from her arms, carried him to the upper room where he was staying, and laid him down on his bed. 20 Then he called out to the LORD, "O LORD, my God, are you also bringing disaster on this widow I am staying with by killing her son?" 21 He stretched out over the boy three times and called out to the LORD, "O LORD, my God, please let this boy's breath return to him." 22 The LORD answered Elijah's prayer; the boy's breath returned to him and he lived. 23 Elijah took the boy, brought him down from the upper room to the house, and handed him to his mother. Elijah then said, "See, your son is alive!" 24 The woman said to Elijah, "Now I know that you are a prophet and that the LORD's message really does come through you."

ELIJAH MEETS THE KING'S SERVANT

18 Some time later, in the third year of the famine, the LORD's message came to Elijah, "Go, make an appearance before Ahab, so I may send rain on the surface of the ground." 2 So Elijah went to make an appearance before Ahab.

Now the famine was severe in Samaria. 3 So Ahab summoned Obadiah, who supervised the palace. (Now Obadiah was a very loyal follower of the LORD. 4 When Jezebel was killing the LORD's prophets, Obadiah took 100 prophets and hid them in two caves in two groups of 50. He also brought them food and water.) 5 Ahab told Obadiah, "Go through the land to all the springs and valleys. Maybe we can find some grazing areas so we can keep the horses and mules alive and not have to kill some of the animals." 6 They divided up the land between them to search it; Ahab went one way by himself and Obadiah went the other way by himself.

7 As Obadiah was traveling along, Elijah met him. When he recognized him, he fell facedown to the ground and said, "Is it really you, my master, Elijah?" 8 He replied, "Yes, go and say to your master, 'Elijah is back.'" 9 Obadiah said, "What sin have I committed that you are ready to hand your servant over to Ahab for execution? 10 As certainly as the LORD your God lives, my master has sent to every nation and kingdom in an effort to find you. When they say, 'He's not here,' he makes them swear an oath that they could not find you. 11 Now you say, 'Go and say to your master, "Elijah is back."' 12 But when I leave you, the LORD's Spirit will carry you away so I can't find you. If I go tell Ahab I've seen you, he won't be able to find you and he will kill me. That would not be fair, because your servant has been a loyal follower of the LORD from my youth. 13 Certainly my master is aware of what I did when Jezebel was killing the LORD's prophets. I hid 100 of the LORD's prophets in two caves in two groups of 50 and I brought them food and water. 14 Now you say, 'Go and say to your master, "Elijah is back,"' but he will kill me." 15 But Elijah said, "As certainly as the LORD of Heaven's Armies lives (whom I serve), I will make an appearance before him today."

ELIJAH CONFRONTS BAAL'S PROPHETS

16 When Obadiah went and informed Ahab, the king went to meet Elijah. 17 When Ahab saw Elijah, he said to him, "Is it really you, the one who brings disaster on Israel?" 18 Elijah replied, "I have not brought disaster on Israel. But you and your father's

18:1–16 Let no one think anyplace is so profane that the Lord does not have his church there. The wealthy members of society, including the politicians, work in places that are full of pride, pleasure, ease, and abundance of all things. This type of people commonly choke the Word in them so that it is unfruitful. In great cities likewise sins rage and reign in all places. In these places lewdness and wickedness are so grievous and abominable that sin overflows. Yet in all these places the Lord has his people; the Lord has those who know him and believe in his holy name. Even in Jezebel's court he had an Obadiah to hide and feed his prophets. Far be it from us therefore to condemn where the Lord has not condemned. Only God knows who are his, but there are people loyal to him in every place of the world.

HENRY AIRAY (C. 1560–1616)
LECTURES ON PHILIPPIANS

dynasty have, by abandoning the LORD's commandments and
following the Baals. 19 Now send out messengers and assemble
all Israel before me at Mount Carmel, as well as the 450 prophets
of Baal and 400 prophets of Asherah whom Jezebel supports."
20 Ahab sent messengers to all the Israelites and had the
prophets assemble at Mount Carmel. 21 Elijah approached all
the people and said, "How long are you going to be paralyzed
by indecision? If the LORD is the true God, then follow him,
but if Baal is, follow him!" But the people did not say a word.
22 Elijah said to them: "I am the only prophet of the LORD who
is left, but there are 450 prophets of Baal. 23 Let them bring us
two bulls. Let them choose one of the bulls for themselves, cut
it up into pieces, and place it on the wood. But they must not
set it on fire. I will do the same to the other bull and place it
on the wood. But I will not set it on fire. 24 Then you will invoke
the name of your god, and I will invoke the name of the LORD.
The god who responds with fire will demonstrate that he is the
true God." All the people responded, "This will be a fair test."

25 Elijah told the prophets of Baal, "Choose one of the bulls
for yourselves and go first, for you are the majority. Invoke the
name of your god, but do not light a fire." 26 So they took a bull,
as he had suggested, and prepared it. They invoked the name
of Baal from morning until noon, saying, "Baal, answer us." But
there was no sound and no answer. They jumped around on the
altar they had made. 27 At noon Elijah mocked them, "Yell louder!
After all, he is a god; he may be deep in thought, or perhaps he
stepped out for a moment or has taken a trip. Perhaps he is
sleeping and needs to be awakened." 28 So they yelled louder and,
in accordance with their prescribed ritual, mutilated themselves
with swords and spears until their bodies were covered with
blood. 29 Throughout the afternoon they were in an ecstatic
frenzy, but there was no sound, no answer, and no response.

30 Elijah then told all the people, "Approach me." So all the
people approached him. He repaired the altar of the LORD that
had been torn down. 31 Then Elijah took 12 stones, corresponding to the number of tribes that descended from Jacob, to whom
the LORD's message had come, "Israel will be your name." 32 With
the stones he constructed an altar for the LORD. Around the
altar he made a trench large enough to contain two seahs of
seed. 33 He arranged the wood, cut up the bull, and placed it on
the wood. Then he said, "Fill four water jars and pour the water
on the offering and the wood." 34 When they had done so, he said,
"Do it again." So they did it again. Then he said, "Do it a third
time." So they did it a third time. 35 The water flowed down all
sides of the altar and filled the trench. 36 When it was time for
the evening offering, Elijah the prophet approached the altar
and prayed: "O LORD God of Abraham, Isaac, and Israel, prove
today that you are God in Israel and that I am your servant and
have done all these things at your command. 37 Answer me,
O LORD, answer me, so these people will know that you, O LORD,
are the true God and that you are winning back their allegiance."
38 Then fire from the LORD fell from the sky. It consumed the
offering, the wood, the stones, and the dirt, and licked up the
water in the trench. 39 When all the people saw this, they threw
themselves down with their faces to the ground and said, "The
LORD is the true God! The LORD is the true God!" 40 Elijah told
them, "Seize the prophets of Baal! Don't let even one of them
escape!" So they seized them, and Elijah led them down to the
Kishon Valley and executed them there.

[41]Then Elijah told Ahab, "Go on up and eat and drink, for the sound of a heavy rainstorm can be heard." [42]So Ahab went on up to eat and drink, while Elijah climbed to the top of Carmel. He bent down toward the ground and put his face between his knees. [43]He told his servant, "Go on up and look in the direction of the sea." So he went on up, looked, and reported, "There is nothing." Seven times Elijah sent him to look. [44]The seventh time the servant said, "Look, a small cloud, the size of the palm of a man's hand, is rising up from the sea." Elijah then said, "Go and tell Ahab, 'Hitch up the chariots and go down, so that the rain won't overtake you.'" [45]Meanwhile the sky was covered with dark clouds, the wind blew, and there was a heavy rainstorm. Ahab rode toward Jezreel. [46]Now the LORD energized Elijah with power; he tucked his robe into his belt and ran ahead of Ahab all the way to Jezreel.

ELIJAH RUNS FOR HIS LIFE

19 Ahab told Jezebel all that Elijah had done, including a detailed account of how he killed all the prophets with the sword. [2]Jezebel sent a messenger to Elijah with this warning, "May the gods judge me severely if by this time tomorrow I do not take your life as you did theirs!"

[3]Elijah was afraid, so he got up and fled for his life to Beer Sheba in Judah. He left his servant there, [4]while he went a day's journey into the wilderness. He went and sat down under a shrub and asked the LORD to take his life: "I've had enough! Now, O LORD, take my life. After all, I'm no better than my ancestors." [5]He stretched out and fell asleep under the shrub. Suddenly an angelic messenger touched him and said, "Get up and eat." [6]He looked and right there by his head was a cake baking on hot coals and a jug of water. He ate and drank and then slept some more. [7]The angel of the LORD came back again, touched him, and said, "Get up and eat, for otherwise you won't be able to make the journey." [8]So he got up and ate and drank. That meal gave him the strength to travel 40 days and 40 nights until he reached Horeb, the mountain of God.

[9]He went into a cave there and spent the night. Suddenly the LORD's message came to him, "Why are you here, Elijah?" [10]He answered, "I have been absolutely loyal to the LORD God of Heaven's Armies, even though the Israelites have abandoned the covenant they made with you, torn down your altars, and killed your prophets with the sword. I alone am left and now they want to take my life." [11]The LORD said, "Go out and stand on the mountain before the LORD. Look, the LORD is ready to pass by."

A very powerful wind went before the LORD, digging into the mountain and causing landslides, but the LORD was not in the wind. After the windstorm there was an earthquake, but the LORD was not in the earthquake. [12]After the earthquake, there was a fire, but the LORD was not in the fire. After the fire, there was a soft whisper. [13]When Elijah heard it, he covered his face with his robe and went out and stood at the entrance to the cave. Suddenly a voice asked him, "Why are you here, Elijah?" [14]He answered, "I have been absolutely loyal to the LORD God of Heaven's Armies, even though the Israelites have abandoned the covenant they made with you, torn down your altars, and killed your prophets with the sword. I alone am left and now they want to take my life." [15]The LORD said to him, "Go back the way you came and then head for the wilderness of Damascus. Go and anoint Hazael king over Syria. [16]You must

19:1–18 All the strength supplied to us by our gracious God is meant for service. When the prophet Elijah found the cake baked on the coals and the pot of water placed at his head, he was commissioned to go forty days and forty nights in the strength of it, journeying toward Horeb, the mount of God. When the Master invited the disciples, "Come, have breakfast" with him, after the feast was concluded he said to Peter, "Feed my sheep," further adding, "Follow me" (John 21:12, 17, 19). Even thus it is with us; we eat the bread of heaven that we may expend our strength in the Master's service. Believer, in the strength you daily gain from Christ, labor for him.

CHARLES SPURGEON
(1834–1892)
MORNING AND EVENING

anoint Jehu son of Nimshi king over Israel, and Elisha son of Shaphat from Abel Meholah to take your place as prophet. 17Jehu will kill anyone who escapes Hazael's sword, and Elisha will kill anyone who escapes Jehu's sword. 18I still have left in Israel 7,000 followers who have not bowed their knees to Baal or kissed the images of him."

19Elijah went from there and found Elisha son of Shaphat. He was plowing with twelve pairs of oxen; he was near the twelfth pair. Elijah passed by him and threw his robe over him. 20He left the oxen, ran after Elijah, and said, "Please let me kiss my father and mother goodbye, then I will follow you." Elijah said to him, "Go back! Indeed, what have I done to you?" 21Elisha went back and took his pair of oxen and slaughtered them. He cooked the meat over a fire that he made by burning the harness and yoke. He gave the people meat and they ate. Then he got up and followed Elijah and became his assistant.

BEN HADAD INVADES ISRAEL

20 Now King Ben Hadad of Syria assembled all his army, along with 32 other kings with their horses and chariots. He marched against Samaria and besieged and attacked it. 2He sent messengers to King Ahab of Israel, who was in the city. He said to him, "This is what Ben Hadad says: 3'Your silver and your gold are mine, as well as the best of your wives and sons.'" 4The king of Israel replied, "It is just as you say, my master, O king. I and all I own belong to you."

5The messengers came again and said, "This is what Ben Hadad says: 'I sent this message to you, "You must give me your silver, gold, wives, and sons." 6But now at this time tomorrow I will send my servants to you and they will search through your palace and your servants' houses. They will carry away all your valuables.'" 7The king of Israel summoned all the leaders of the land and said, "Notice how this man is looking for trouble. Indeed, he demanded my wives, sons, silver, and gold, and I did not resist him." 8All the leaders and people said to him, "Do not give in or agree to his demands." 9So he said to the messengers of Ben Hadad, "Say this to my master, the king: 'I will give you everything you demanded at first from your servant, but I am unable to agree to this latest demand.'" So the messengers went back and gave their report.

10Ben Hadad sent another message to him, "May the gods judge me severely if there is enough dirt left in Samaria for all my soldiers to scoop up in their hands." 11The king of Israel replied, "Tell him the one who puts on his battle gear should not boast like one who is taking it off." 12When Ben Hadad received this reply, he and the other kings were drinking in their quarters. He ordered his servants, "Get ready to attack!" So they got ready to attack the city.

THE LORD DELIVERS ISRAEL

13Now a prophet visited King Ahab of Israel and said, "This is what the LORD has said: 'Do you see this huge army? Look, I am going to hand it over to you this very day. Then you will know that I am the LORD.'" 14Ahab asked, "By whom will this be accomplished?" He answered, "This is what the LORD has said, 'By the servants of the district governors.'" Ahab asked, "Who will launch the attack?" He answered, "You will."

15So Ahab assembled the 232 servants of the district governors. After that he assembled all the Israelite army, numbering

7,000. [16]They marched out at noon, while Ben Hadad and the 32
kings allied with him were drinking heavily in their quarters.
[17]The servants of the district governors led the march. When
Ben Hadad sent messengers, they reported back to him, "Men
are marching out of Samaria." [18]He ordered, "Whether they
come in peace or to do battle, take them alive." [19]They marched
out of the city with the servants of the district governors in the
lead and the army behind them. [20]Each one struck down an
enemy soldier; the Syrians fled and Israel chased them. King
Ben Hadad of Syria escaped on horseback with some horsemen.
[21]Then the king of Israel marched out and struck down the
horses and chariots; he thoroughly defeated Syria.

THE LORD GIVES ISRAEL ANOTHER VICTORY

[22]The prophet visited the king of Israel and instructed him,
"Go, fortify your defenses. Determine what you must do, for in
the spring the king of Syria will attack you." [23]Now the advisers of the king of Syria said to him: "Their God is a god of the
mountains. That's why they overpowered us. But if we fight
them in the plains, we will certainly overpower them. [24]So do
this: Dismiss the kings from their command, and replace them
with military commanders. [25]Muster an army like the one you
lost, with the same number of horses and chariots. Then we will
fight them in the plains; we will certainly overpower them." He
approved their plan and did as they advised.

[26]In the spring Ben Hadad mustered the Syrian army and
marched to Aphek to fight Israel. [27]When the Israelites had
mustered and received their supplies, they marched out to
face them in battle. When the Israelites deployed opposite
them, they were like two small flocks of goats, but the Syrians
filled the land. [28]The prophet visited the king of Israel and said,
"This is what the LORD has said: 'Because the Syrians said, "The
LORD is a god of the mountains and not a god of the valleys,"
I will deliver this entire huge army into to your control. Then
you will know that I am the LORD.'"

[29]The armies were deployed opposite each other for seven
days. On the seventh day the battle began, and the Israelites
killed 100,000 Syrian foot soldiers in one day. [30]The remaining
27,000 ran to Aphek and went into the city, but the wall fell
on them. Now Ben Hadad ran into the city and hid in an inner
room. [31]His advisers said to him, "Look, we have heard that the
kings of the Israelite dynasty are kind. Allow us to put sackcloth
around our waists and ropes on our heads and surrender to
the king of Israel. Maybe he will spare our lives." [32]So they put
sackcloth around their waists and ropes on their heads and
went to the king of Israel. They said, "Your servant Ben Hadad
says, 'Please let me live!'" Ahab replied, "Is he still alive? He is
my brother." [33]The men took this as a good omen and quickly
accepted his offer, saying, "Ben Hadad is your brother." Ahab
then said, "Go, get him." So Ben Hadad came out to him, and
Ahab pulled him up into his chariot. [34]Ben Hadad said, "I will
return the cities my father took from your father. You may set
up markets in Damascus, just as my father did in Samaria." Ahab
then said, "I want to make a treaty with you before I dismiss
you." So he made a treaty with him and then dismissed him.

A PROPHET DENOUNCES AHAB'S ACTIONS

[35]One of the members of the prophetic guild told his companion a message from the LORD, "Please wound me!" But the man

20:23–43 The king of the Syrians, thinking of the loving-kindness of the kings of Israel, assumed the form of a suppliant and failed not to obtain his petition. Remember therefore the divine wrath. God delivered Ahab to utter destruction for using mercy and delivered his sentence through the mouth of the prophet, saying "You will pay with your life, and your people will suffer instead of his people." We are thus commanded to temper mercy with justice, since not every kind of mercy is pleasing to the God of all.

THEODORET OF CYR
(C. 393–C. 458)
QUESTIONS ON KINGS AND CHRONICLES

refused to wound him. 36So the prophet said to him, "Because you have disobeyed the LORD, as soon as you leave me a lion will kill you." When he left him, a lion attacked and killed him. 37He found another man and said, "Wound me!" So the man wounded him severely. 38The prophet then went and stood by the road, waiting for the king. He also disguised himself by putting a bandage down over his eyes. 39When the king passed by, he called out to the king, "Your servant went out into the heat of the battle, and then a man turned aside and brought me a prisoner. He told me, 'Guard this prisoner. If he ends up missing for any reason, you will pay with your life or with a talent of silver.' 40Well, it just so happened that while your servant was doing this and that, he disappeared." The king of Israel said to him, "Your punishment is already determined by your own testimony." 41The prophet quickly removed the bandage from his eyes, and the king of Israel recognized he was one of the prophets. 42The prophet then said to him, "This is what the LORD has said: 'Because you released a man I had determined should die, you will pay with your life, and your people will suffer instead of his people.'" 43The king of Israel went home to Samaria bitter and angry.

AHAB MURDERS NABOTH

21 After this the following episode took place. Naboth the Jezreelite owned a vineyard in Jezreel adjacent to the palace of King Ahab of Samaria. 2Ahab said to Naboth, "Give me your vineyard so I can make a vegetable garden out of it, for it is adjacent to my palace. I will give you an even better vineyard in its place, or if you prefer, I will pay you silver for it." 3But Naboth replied to Ahab, "The LORD forbid that I should sell you my ancestral inheritance."

4So Ahab went into his palace, bitter and angry that Naboth the Jezreelite had said, "I will not sell to you my ancestral inheritance." He lay down on his bed, pouted, and would not eat. 5Then his wife Jezebel came in and said to him, "Why do you have a bitter attitude and refuse to eat?" 6He answered her, "While I was talking to Naboth the Jezreelite, I said to him, 'Sell me your vineyard for silver, or if you prefer, I will give you another vineyard in its place.' But he said, 'I will not sell you my vineyard.'" 7His wife Jezebel said to him, "You are the king of Israel! Get up, eat some food, and have a good time. I will get the vineyard of Naboth the Jezreelite for you."

8She wrote out orders, signed Ahab's name to them, and sealed them with his seal. She then sent the orders to the leaders and to the nobles who lived in Naboth's city. 9This is what she wrote: "Observe a time of fasting and seat Naboth in front of the people. 10Also seat two villains opposite him and have them testify, 'You cursed God and the king.' Then take him out and stone him to death."

11The men of the city, the leaders, and the nobles who lived there followed the written orders Jezebel had sent them. 12They observed a time of fasting and put Naboth in front of the people. 13The two villains arrived and sat opposite him. Then the villains testified against Naboth right before the people, saying, "Naboth cursed God and the king." So they dragged him outside the city and stoned him to death. 14Then they reported to Jezebel, "Naboth has been stoned to death."

15When Jezebel heard that Naboth had been stoned to death, she said to Ahab, "Get up, take possession of the vineyard

Naboth the Jezreelite refused to sell you for silver, for Naboth
is no longer alive; he's dead." 16When Ahab heard that Naboth
was dead, he got up and went down to take possession of the
vineyard of Naboth the Jezreelite.
17The LORD's message came to Elijah the Tishbite: 18"Get up,
go down and meet King Ahab of Israel who lives in Samaria. He
is at the vineyard of Naboth; he has gone down there to take
possession of it. 19Say to him, 'This is what the LORD has said:
"Haven't you committed murder and taken possession of the
property of the deceased?"' Then say to him, 'This is what the
LORD has said: "In the spot where dogs licked up Naboth's blood
they will also lick up your blood—yes, yours!"'"
20When Elijah arrived, Ahab said to him, "So, you have found
me, my enemy!" Elijah replied, "I have found you, because you
are committed to doing evil in the sight of the LORD. 21The
LORD says, 'Look, I am ready to bring disaster on you. I will
destroy you and cut off every last male belonging to Ahab in
Israel, including even the weak and incapacitated. 22I will make
your dynasty like those of Jeroboam son of Nebat and Baasha
son of Ahijah because you angered me and made Israel sin.'
23The LORD says this about Jezebel, 'Dogs will devour Jezebel
by the outer wall of Jezreel.' 24As for Ahab's family, dogs will eat
the ones who die in the city, and the birds of the sky will eat the
ones who die in the country." 25(There had never been anyone
like Ahab, who was firmly committed to doing evil in the sight
of the LORD, urged on by his wife Jezebel. 26He was so wicked
he worshiped the disgusting idols, just as the Amorites whom
the LORD had driven out from before the Israelites.)
27When Ahab heard these words, he tore his clothes, put on
sackcloth, and fasted. He slept in sackcloth and walked around
dejected. 28The LORD's message came to Elijah the Tishbite,
29"Have you noticed how Ahab shows remorse before me? Because he shows remorse before me, I will not bring disaster on
his dynasty during his lifetime, but during the reign of his son."

AHAB DIES IN BATTLE

22 There was no war between Syria and Israel for three years.
2In the third year King Jehoshaphat of Judah came down
to visit the king of Israel. 3The king of Israel said to his servants,
"Surely you recognize that Ramoth Gilead belongs to us, though
we are hesitant to reclaim it from the king of Syria." 4Then he
said to Jehoshaphat, "Will you go with me to attack Ramoth
Gilead?" Jehoshaphat replied to the king of Israel, "I will support you; my army and horses are at your disposal." 5But then
Jehoshaphat said to Israel's king, "Please seek a message from
the LORD this very day." 6So the king of Israel assembled about
400 prophets and asked them, "Should I attack Ramoth Gilead
or not?" They said, "Attack! The Sovereign One will hand it over
to the king." 7But Jehoshaphat asked, "Is there not a prophet of
the LORD still here, that we may ask him?" 8The king of Israel
answered Jehoshaphat, "There is still one man through whom
we can seek the LORD's will. But I despise him because he does
not prophesy prosperity for me, but disaster. His name is Micaiah son of Imlah." Jehoshaphat said, "The king should not say
such things." 9The king of Israel summoned an official and said,
"Quickly bring Micaiah son of Imlah."
10Now the king of Israel and King Jehoshaphat of Judah were
sitting on their respective thrones, dressed in their robes, at
the threshing floor at the entrance of the gate of Samaria. All

21:17–29 Ahab's response offers three notable things for our consideration. See first how far a hypocrite, a castaway, may go in outward performance of holy duty and particularly in the practice of repentance. Here is Ahab humbled—such a man and yet so penitent. See again, second, how deep God's word, though in the mouth but of weak instruments, when he is pleased to give strength to it, pierces into the conscience of obstinate sinners and brings the proudest of them to their knees despite their wicked hearts. Here is Ahab quelled by Elijah—such a great one by such a weak one. See yet again, third, how prone God is to mercy and how ready to take any advantage, as it were, any occasion to show compassion. Here is Ahab humbled and his judgment adjourned—such a real substantial favor, and yet on such an empty shadow of repentance.

ROBERT SANDERSON
(1587–1663)
TO THE PEOPLE

the prophets were prophesying before them. 11Zedekiah son of
Kenaanah made iron horns and said, "This is what the LORD has
said, 'With these you will gore Syria until they are destroyed.'"
12All the prophets were prophesying the same, saying, "Attack
Ramoth Gilead! You will succeed; the LORD will hand it over to
the king." 13Now the messenger who went to summon Micaiah
said to him, "Look, the prophets are in complete agreement that
the king will succeed. Your words must agree with theirs; you
must predict success." 14But Micaiah said, "As certainly as the
LORD lives, I will say what the LORD tells me to say."
15When he came before the king, the king asked him, "Micaiah, should we attack Ramoth Gilead or not?" He answered
him, "Attack! You will succeed; the LORD will hand it over to the
king." 16The king said to him, "How many times must I make
you solemnly promise in the name of the LORD to tell me only
the truth?" 17Micaiah said, "I saw all Israel scattered on the
mountains like sheep that have no shepherd. Then the LORD
said, 'They have no master. They should go home in peace.'"
18The king of Israel said to Jehoshaphat, "Didn't I tell you he
does not prophesy prosperity for me, but disaster?" 19Micaiah
said, "That being the case, listen to the LORD's message. I saw
the LORD sitting on his throne, with all the heavenly assembly
standing beside him on his right and on his left. 20The LORD
said, 'Who will deceive Ahab, so he will attack Ramoth Gilead
and die there?' One said this and another that. 21Then a spirit
stepped forward and stood before the LORD. He said, 'I will
deceive him.' 22The LORD asked him, 'How?' He replied, 'I will
go out and be a lying spirit in the mouths of all his prophets.'
The LORD said, 'Deceive and overpower him. Go out and do
as you have proposed.' 23So now, look, the LORD has placed a
lying spirit in the mouths of all these prophets of yours, but
the LORD has decreed disaster for you." 24Zedekiah son of Kenaanah approached, hit Micaiah on the jaw, and said, "Which
way did the LORD's Spirit go when he went from me to speak
to you?" 25Micaiah replied, "Look, you will see in the day when
you go into an inner room to hide." 26Then the king of Israel
said, "Take Micaiah and return him to Amon the city official
and Joash the king's son. 27Say, 'This is what the king says, "Put
this man in prison. Give him only a little bread and water until
I safely return."'" 28Micaiah said, "If you really do safely return,
then the LORD has not spoken through me." Then he added,
"Take note, all you people."
29The king of Israel and King Jehoshaphat of Judah attacked
Ramoth Gilead. 30The king of Israel said to Jehoshaphat, "I
will disguise myself and then enter into the battle, but you
wear your royal robes." So the king of Israel disguised himself
and then entered into the battle. 31Now the king of Syria had
ordered his 32 chariot commanders, "Do not fight common
soldiers or high-ranking officers; fight only the king of Israel."
32When the chariot commanders saw Jehoshaphat, they said,
"He must be the king of Israel." So they turned and attacked him,
but Jehoshaphat cried out. 33When the chariot commanders
realized he was not the king of Israel, they turned away from
him. 34Now an archer shot an arrow at random, and it struck
the king of Israel between the plates of his armor. The king
ordered his charioteer, "Turn around and take me from the
battle line, because I'm wounded." 35While the battle raged
throughout the day, the king stood propped up in his chariot
opposite the Syrians. He died in the evening; the blood from

the wound ran down into the bottom of the chariot. [36]As the
sun was setting, a cry went through the camp, "Each one should
return to his city and to his homeland." [37]So the king died and
was taken to Samaria, where they buried him. [38]They washed
off the chariot at the pool of Samaria. Then the dogs licked his
blood, while the prostitutes bathed, in keeping with the LORD's
message that he had spoken.

[39]The rest of the events of Ahab's reign, including a record
of his accomplishments and how he built a luxurious palace
and various cities, are recorded in the scroll called the Annals
of the Kings of Israel. [40]Ahab passed away. His son Ahaziah
replaced him as king.

JEHOSHAPHAT'S REIGN OVER JUDAH

[41]In the fourth year of Ahab's reign over Israel, Asa's son Jehoshaphat became king over Judah. [42]Jehoshaphat was thirty-
five years old when he became king, and he reigned for 25 years
in Jerusalem. His mother was Azubah, the daughter of Shilhi.
[43]He followed in his father Asa's footsteps and was careful to
do what the LORD approved. However, the high places were not
eliminated; the people continued to offer sacrifices and burn
incense on the high places. [44]Jehoshaphat was also at peace
with the king of Israel.

[45]The rest of the events of Jehoshaphat's reign, including
his successes and military exploits, are recorded in the scroll
called the Annals of the Kings of Judah. [46]He removed from the
land any male cultic prostitutes who had managed to survive
the reign of his father Asa. [47]There was no king in Edom at this
time; a governor ruled. [48]Jehoshaphat built a fleet of large merchant ships to travel to Ophir for gold, but they never made the
voyage because they were shipwrecked in Ezion Geber. [49]Then
Ahaziah son of Ahab said to Jehoshaphat, "Let my sailors join
yours in the fleet," but Jehoshaphat refused.

[50]Jehoshaphat passed away and was buried with his ancestors
in the city of his ancestor David. His son Jehoram replaced
him as king.

AHAZIAH'S REIGN OVER ISRAEL

[51]In the seventeenth year of Jehoshaphat's reign over Judah,
Ahab's son Ahaziah became king over Israel in Samaria. He
ruled for two years over Israel. [52]He did evil in the sight of the
LORD and followed in the footsteps of his father and mother;
like Jeroboam son of Nebat, he encouraged Israel to sin. [53]He
worshiped and bowed down to Baal, angering the LORD God of
Israel just as his father had done.

22:41–53 Jehoshaphat's reign appears to have been one of the best, both as to piety and prosperity. He pleased God, and God blessed him. Ahaziah's reign was very short, not two years; some sinners God makes quick work with. A very bad character is given of him: He listened not to instruction, took no warning, but followed the example of his wicked father and the counsel of his more wicked mother, Jezebel, who was still living. Miserable are the children who not only derive a sinful nature from their parents but are taught by them to increase it, and most unhappy parents are they who help to damn their children's souls. Hardened sinners rush forward, unawed and unmoved in the ways from which others before them have been driven into everlasting misery.

MATTHEW HENRY (1662–1714)
COMMENTARY ON THE WHOLE BIBLE

AUTHOR	AUDIENCE	DATE	PURPOSE	THEMES
Unknown	God's chosen people, the Israelites	Probably around 550 BC, during the Babylonian exile	This book continues the story begun in 1 Kings, recounting the history of the divided kingdoms and the people's rebellion against the Lord, which led to invasion and exile.	Faithfulness and obedience; disobedience and evil; and sin's consequences

The second book of the Kings opens with Elijah the Tishbite condemning King Ahaziah of Israel for turning away from the Lord. From there the book recounts the ongoing sin of the two kingdoms, Israel and Judah, and their kings with the refrain: "He did evil in the sight of the Lord" (2 Kgs 3:2). Though the book is technically anonymous, traditional thought attributes the work to Jeremiah, who may have written it during Judah's exile as a way of explaining how God's chosen people lost the promised land. Both this book and 1 Kings chronicle the people's failure, which Giovanni Diodati explained in this way:

> As for the kingdom of the ten tribes, the history sets down how the corruption of God's service was never amended by the successors of Jeroboam, who was the first in that line to follow idolatry and pagan abominations. This refusal to mend its ways caused God to punish the kingdom. There were frequent murders of kings, treasons, changes of royal lines, wars, and other accidents that happened on account of God's express command and calling and sometimes through the ambition and evil motions of people's attempts.
>
> As for the kingdom of Judah, the history declares that idolatry was rampant even though the church—and, consequently, God's Word, sacraments, grace, presence, and the spirit—were preserved. Indeed, the kingdom of Judah was infected by the idolatry and sin of the kingdom of Israel, for they violated both tables of the law. At the same time, the kingdom was not able to completely root out God's presence and his words of prophecy. And there were occasionally kings who excelled in piety and virtue whom God raised up from time to time to repair the breaches and hold up the coming ruin. Nevertheless the holy endeavors of these righteous kings were almost always overthrown by their successors' boundless impiety.

Although God's promises found their fulfillment in David's reign in the previous book, the blessings of Israel fell apart in the end, and the people continued their downward trajectory toward judgment. The present book culminates with the destruction of both kingdoms at the hands of foreign powers and the subsequent exile of God's people. Consider this description of the Assyrian invasion offered in 2 Kings: "This happened because the Israelites sinned against the Lord their God . . . The Israelites said things about

2 KINGS

the LORD their God that were not right . . . Their evil practices made the LORD angry. They worshiped the disgusting idols in blatant disregard of the LORD's command" (17:7, 9, 11–12).

In response "the LORD was furious with Israel and rejected them" (17:18). Several years later the same fate befell the nation of Judah, for Jehoiakim "did evil in the sight of the LORD as his ancestors had done" (23:37). As with Israel the Lord used foreign armies to conquer and plunder: "The LORD sent against him Babylonian, Syrian, Moabite, and Ammonite raiding bands; he sent them to destroy Judah, just as in the LORD's message that he announced through his servants the prophets" (24:2). Both accounts make plain that God allows his people to reap the full measure of sins' consequences in due time. In fact it was God himself who brought about their destruction.

There were, however, bright spots, a faithful remnant that included kings like Joash of Judah, who did "what the LORD approved all his days when Jehoiada the priest taught him" (12:2). Similarly, eight-year-old Josiah "did what the LORD approved and followed in his ancestor David's footsteps; he did not deviate to the right or the left" (22:2). After the pagan reign of Manasseh, Josiah set about renovating the temple. During those renovations, the scroll of the law was discovered, and the find sparked an unprecedented spiritual renewal. "Whether this was the only copy in being or not," Matthew Henry explains, "the things contained in it were new, both to the king and to the high priest." This is remarkable, because many believe the "scroll of the law" (22:8) to be the book of Deuteronomy, the cornerstone document for the religious commitment of God's people. And it had been missing and unknown for generations! Immediately Josiah called together all of Judah to read the book and renew the terms of the covenant contained within it. Then he reinstated the Passover, the central religious ceremony of God's people, an act that showed just how far they had strayed from the Lord.

Although Judah eventually fell, Josiah stands as a rock of faithfulness and obedience in a sea of sin and evil, for "no king before or after repented before the LORD as he did, with his whole heart, soul, and being in accordance with the whole law of Moses" (23:25). In every era of the church, men and women have looked to these portraits of disobedience and obedience, learning what happens when God's people stray from the Lord. May we continue to listen to what God is telling us through 2 Kings.

1:1–15 It is clear that we ought to have no fellowship with Satan, whether it be directly and mediately or else indirectly and immediately, as some term it. Neither ought we to seek any relief by his help, aid, or counsel. We must make recourse in all our afflictions to our only true God. Why would we seek help and assistance from Baal Zebub since there is a God in Israel, as the prophet Elijah worthily grieved and retorted? Therefore we ought to cleave to God, to depend on him, and by no means should we allow, condone, or seek out Satan himself or his ministers (as sorcerers certainly are). For we cannot serve two masters, namely, God and the devil. We must utterly forsake the devil so that we may entirely cleave to God.

LAMBERT DANEAU
(C. 1530–C. 1590)
DIALOGUE OF WITCHES

ELIJAH CONFRONTS THE KING AND HIS COMMANDERS

1 After Ahab died, Moab rebelled against Israel. 2Ahaziah
fell through a window lattice in his upper chamber in Samaria and was injured. He sent messengers with these orders,
"Go, ask Baal Zebub, the god of Ekron, if I will survive this
injury."
3But the angel of the LORD told Elijah the Tishbite, "Get up;
go to meet the messengers from the king of Samaria. Say this to
them: 'You must think there is no God in Israel! That explains
why you are on your way to seek an oracle from Baal Zebub the
god of Ekron. 4Therefore this is what the LORD has said, "You
will not leave the bed you lie on, for you will certainly die!"'"
So Elijah went on his way.
5When the messengers returned to the king, he asked them,
"Why have you returned?" 6They replied, "A man came up to
meet us. He told us, 'Go back to the king who sent you and tell
him, "This is what the LORD has said: 'You must think there
is no God in Israel! That explains why you are sending for an
oracle from Baal Zebub, the god of Ekron. Therefore you will not
leave the bed you lie on, for you will certainly die.'"'" 7The king
asked them, "Describe the appearance of this man who came
up to meet you and told you these things." 8They replied, "He
was a hairy man and had a leather belt tied around his waist."
The king said, "He is Elijah the Tishbite."
9The king sent a captain and his 50 soldiers to retrieve Elijah.
The captain went up to him while he was sitting on the top
of a hill. He told him, "Prophet, the king says, 'Come down!'"
10Elijah replied to the captain, "If I am indeed a prophet, may
fire come down from the sky and consume you and your 50
soldiers!" Fire then came down from the sky and consumed
him and his 50 soldiers.
11The king sent another captain and his 50 soldiers to retrieve Elijah. He went up and told him, "Prophet, this is what
the king says, 'Come down at once!'" 12Elijah replied to them, "If
I am indeed a prophet, may fire come down from the sky and
consume you and your 50 soldiers!" Fire from God came down
from the sky and consumed him and his 50 soldiers.
13The king sent a third captain and his 50 soldiers. This third
captain went up and fell on his knees before Elijah. He begged
for mercy, "Prophet, please have respect for my life and for the
lives of these 50 servants of yours. 14Indeed, fire came down
from the sky and consumed the two captains who came before
me, along with their men. So now, please have respect for my
life." 15The angel of the LORD said to Elijah, "Go down with him.
Don't be afraid of him." So he got up and went down with him
to the king.
16Elijah said to the king, "This is what the LORD has said, 'You
sent messengers to seek an oracle from Baal Zebub, the god of
Ekron. Is it because there is no God in Israel from whom you
can seek a message? Therefore you will not leave the bed you
lie on, for you will certainly die.'"
17And he did die in keeping with the LORD's message that he
had spoken through Elijah. In the second year of the reign of
King Jehoram son of Jehoshaphat over Judah, Ahaziah's brother Jehoram replaced him as king of Israel, because he had no
son. 18The rest of the events of Ahaziah's reign, including his
accomplishments, are recorded in the scroll called the Annals
of the Kings of Israel.

ELIJAH MAKES A SWIFT DEPARTURE

2 Just before the LORD took Elijah up to heaven in a windstorm, Elijah and Elisha were traveling from Gilgal. 2 Elijah told Elisha, "Stay here, for the LORD has sent me to Bethel." But Elisha said, "As certainly as the LORD lives and as you live, I will not leave you." So they went down to Bethel. 3 Some members of the prophetic guild in Bethel came out to Elisha and said, "Do you know that today the LORD is going to take your master from you?" He answered, "Yes, I know. Be quiet."

4 Elijah said to him, "Elisha, stay here, for the LORD has sent me to Jericho." But he replied, "As certainly as the LORD lives and as you live, I will not leave you." So they went to Jericho. 5 Some members of the prophetic guild in Jericho approached Elisha and said, "Do you know that today the LORD is going to take your master from you?" He answered, "Yes, I know. Be quiet."

6 Elijah said to him, "Stay here, for the LORD has sent me to the Jordan." But he replied, "As certainly as the LORD lives and as you live, I will not leave you." So they traveled on together. 7 The 50 members of the prophetic guild went and stood opposite them at a distance, while Elijah and Elisha stood by the Jordan. 8 Elijah took his cloak, folded it up, and hit the water with it. The water divided, and the two of them crossed over on dry ground. 9 When they had crossed over, Elijah said to Elisha, "What can I do for you, before I am taken away from you?" Elisha answered, "May I receive a double portion of the prophetic spirit that energizes you?" 10 Elijah replied, "That's a difficult request! If you see me taken from you, may it be so, but if you don't, it will not happen."

11 As they were walking along and talking, suddenly a fiery chariot pulled by fiery horses appeared. They went between Elijah and Elisha, and Elijah went up to heaven in a windstorm. 12 While Elisha was watching, he was crying out, "My father, my father! The chariot and horsemen of Israel!" Then he could no longer see him. He grabbed his clothes and tore them in two. 13 He picked up Elijah's cloak, which had fallen off him, and went back and stood on the shore of the Jordan. 14 He took the cloak that had fallen off Elijah, hit the water with it, and said, "Where is the LORD, the God of Elijah?" When he hit the water, it divided and Elisha crossed over.

15 When the members of the prophetic guild in Jericho, who were standing at a distance, saw him do this, they said, "The spirit that energized Elijah rests upon Elisha." They went to meet him and bowed down to the ground before him. 16 They said to him, "Look, there are 50 capable men with your servants. Let them go and look for your master, for the wind sent from the LORD may have carried him away and dropped him on one of the hills or in one of the valleys." But Elisha replied, "Don't send them out." 17 But they were so insistent that he became embarrassed. So he said, "Send them out." They sent the 50 men out, and they looked for three days, but could not find Elijah. 18 When they came back, Elisha was staying in Jericho. He said to them, "Didn't I tell you, 'Don't go'?"

ELISHA DEMONSTRATES HIS AUTHORITY

19 The men of the city said to Elisha, "Look, the city has a good location, as our master can see. But the water is bad and the land doesn't produce crops." 20 Elisha said, "Get me a new jar and put some salt in it." So they got it. 21 He went out to the spring and threw the salt in. Then he said, "This is what the LORD has

2:1–18 The Lord had let Elijah know that his time was at hand. He therefore went to the different schools of the prophets to give them his last exhortations and blessings. The removal of Elijah was a type and figure of the ascension of Christ and the opening of the kingdom of heaven to all believers. Elisha had long followed Elijah, and he would not leave him now when he hoped for the parting blessing. Let not those who follow Christ come short by tiring at last. The waters of Jordan of old yielded to the ark, now to the prophet's mantle as a token of God's presence. When God will take up his faithful ones to heaven, death is the Jordan they must pass through, and they find a way through it. The death of Christ has divided those waters, that the ransomed of the Lord may pass over. O death, where is thy sting, thy hurt, thy terror!

MATTHEW HENRY **(1662–1714)**
COMMENTARY ON THE WHOLE BIBLE

3:1–27 "When the musician played, the LORD energized him." Next to the Word of God, music deserves the highest praise. For whether you wish to comfort the sad, to terrify the happy, to encourage the despairing, to humble the proud, to calm the passionate, or to appease those full of hate—what more effective means than music could you find? The Holy Ghost himself honors her as an instrument for his proper work when in his holy scriptures he asserts that through her his gifts were instilled in the holy prophets, as can be seen in Elisha. Thus it was not without reason that the fathers and prophets wanted nothing else to be associated so closely with the Word of God as music.

MARTIN LUTHER (1483–1546)
PREFACE TO THE GEORG RHAU SYMPHONIAE

said, 'I have purified this water. It will no longer cause death or
fail to produce crops.'" [22]The water has been pure to this very
day, just as Elisha prophesied.
[23]He went up from there to Bethel. As he was traveling up
the road, some young boys came out of the city and made fun
of him, saying, "Go on up, baldy! Go on up, baldy!" [24]When he
turned around and saw them, he called God's judgment down
on them. Two female bears came out of the woods and ripped
42 of the boys to pieces. [25]From there he traveled to Mount
Carmel and then back to Samaria.

MOAB FIGHTS WITH ISRAEL

3 In the eighteenth year of King Jehoshaphat's reign over Judah, Ahab's son Jehoram became king over Israel in Samaria;
he ruled for 12 years. [2]He did evil in the sight of the LORD, but
not to the same degree as his father and mother. He did remove
the sacred pillar of Baal that his father had made. [3]Yet he persisted in the sins of Jeroboam son of Nebat, who encouraged
Israel to sin; he did not turn from them.
[4]Now King Mesha of Moab was a sheep breeder. He would
send as tribute to the king of Israel 100,000 male lambs and
the wool of 100,000 rams. [5]When Ahab died, the king of Moab
rebelled against the king of Israel. [6]At that time King Jehoram left
Samaria and assembled all Israel for war. [7]He sent this message
to King Jehoshaphat of Judah: "The king of Moab has rebelled
against me. Will you fight with me against Moab?" Jehoshaphat
replied, "I will join you in the campaign; my army and horses
are at your disposal." [8]He then asked, "Which invasion route are
we going to take?" Jehoram answered, "By the road through the
wilderness of Edom." [9]So the kings of Israel, Judah, and Edom set
out together. They wandered around on the road for seven days
and finally ran out of water for the men and animals they had
with them. [10]The king of Israel said, "Oh no! Certainly the LORD
has summoned these three kings so that he can hand them over
to the king of Moab!" [11]Jehoshaphat asked, "Is there no prophet of the LORD here that we might seek the LORD's direction?"
One of the servants of the king of Israel answered, "Elisha son
of Shapat is here; he used to be Elijah's servant." [12]Jehoshaphat
said, "Yes, he receives the LORD's messages." So the king of Israel
and Jehoshaphat and the king of Edom went down to visit him.
[13]Elisha said to the king of Israel, "Why are you here? Go
to your father's prophets or your mother's prophets!" The
king of Israel replied to him, "No, for the LORD is the one who
summoned these three kings so that he can hand them over
to Moab." [14]Elisha said, "As certainly as the LORD of Heav-
en's Armies lives (whom I serve), if I did not respect King
Jehoshaphat of Judah, I would not pay attention to you or
acknowledge you. [15]But now, get me a musician." When the
musician played, the LORD energized him, [16]and he said, "This
is what the LORD has said, 'Make many cisterns in this valley,'
[17]for this is what the LORD has said, 'You will not feel any wind
or see any rain, but this valley will be full of water, and you and
your cattle and animals will drink.' [18]This is an easy task for the
LORD; he will also hand Moab over to you. [19]You will defeat every
fortified city and every important city. You must chop down
every productive tree, stop up all the springs, and cover all the
cultivated land with stones."
[20]Sure enough, the next morning, at the time of the morning
sacrifice, water came flowing down from Edom and filled the

land. [21]Now all Moab had heard that the kings were attacking, so everyone old enough to fight was mustered and placed at the border. [22]When they got up early the next morning, the sun was shining on the water. To the Moabites, who were some distance away, the water looked red like blood. [23]The Moabites said, "It's blood! The kings must have fought one another! The soldiers have struck one another down! Now, Moab, seize the plunder!" [24]When they approached the Israelite camp, the Israelites rose up and struck down the Moabites, who then ran from them. The Israelites thoroughly defeated Moab. [25]They tore down the cities, and each man threw a stone into every cultivated field until they were covered. They stopped up every spring and chopped down every productive tree.

Only Kir Hareseth was left intact, but the soldiers armed with slings surrounded it and attacked it. [26]When the king of Moab realized he was losing the battle, he and 700 swordsmen tried to break through and attack the king of Edom, but they failed. [27]So he took his firstborn son, who was to succeed him as king, and offered him up as a burnt sacrifice on the wall. There was an outburst of divine anger against Israel, so they broke off the attack and returned to their homeland.

ELISHA HELPS A WIDOW AND HER SONS

4 Now a wife of one of the prophets appealed to Elisha for help, saying, "Your servant, my husband is dead. You know that your servant was a loyal follower of the LORD. Now the creditor is coming to take away my two boys to be his servants." [2]Elisha said to her, "What can I do for you? Tell me, what do you have in the house?" She answered, "Your servant has nothing in the house except a small jar of olive oil." [3]He said, "Go and ask all your neighbors for empty containers. Get as many as you can. [4]Go and close the door behind you and your sons. Pour the olive oil into all the containers; set aside each one when you have filled it." [5]So she left him and closed the door behind her and her sons. As they were bringing the containers to her, she was pouring the olive oil. [6]When the containers were full, she said to one of her sons, "Bring me another container." But he answered her, "There are no more." Then the olive oil stopped flowing. [7]She went and told the prophet. He said, "Go, sell the olive oil. Repay your creditor, and then you and your sons can live off the rest of the profit."

ELISHA GIVES LIFE TO A BOY

[8]One day Elisha traveled to Shunem, where a prominent woman lived. She insisted that he stop for a meal. So whenever he was passing through, he would stop in there for a meal. [9]She said to her husband, "Look, I'm sure that the man who regularly passes through here is a very special prophet. [10]Let's make a small, private upper room and furnish it with a bed, table, chair, and lamp. When he visits us, he can stay there."

[11]One day Elisha came for a visit; he went into the upper room and rested. [12]He told his servant Gehazi, "Ask the Shunammite woman to come here." So he did so and she came to him. [13]Elisha said to Gehazi, "Tell her, 'Look, you have treated us with such great respect. What can I do for you? Can I put in a good word for you with the king or the commander of the army?'" She replied, "I'm quite secure." [14]So he asked Gehazi, "What can I do for her?" Gehazi replied, "She has no son, and her husband is old." [15]Elisha told him, "Ask her to come here."

4:8–37 Scripture gives an example of how a holy woman rightly used her great wealth. These resources and blessings have been given by God not for the sake of luxury or inane ornamentation but to care for one's needs, assist the ministry of the gospel, serve the state, and redress the suffering of the poor. This wealthy Shunammite woman was offering much kindness to the prophet Elisha. She overlooked nothing in how to care for this man of God. Remember the promise of Christ: Whoever gives a cup of water in the name of God will not lose their reward. Therefore pious wanderers are imitators of Elisha, who conducted himself in such a way that true and holy acts of hospitality might increase.

VIKTORIN STRIGEL
(C. 1524–1569)
BOOK OF KINGS

GREGORY OF NYSSA:

DEFENDER OF TRINITARIAN ORTHODOXY

c. 335–c. 395

During the fourth century, the early leaders of the church were in a fight for the faith that had as much to do with the nature of God and Jesus Christ as it did the nature of salvation. Leading the charge was Gregory of Nyssa.

We know little about his life other than that he was the younger brother of Basil the Great and was largely raised and taught by his sister Macrina. He excelled in rhetoric like his brother and in Greek philosophy. He was known to be more mystical than the other Cappadocian Fathers, having had dreams, visions, and spiritual experiences. After having been converted to the faith through a vision and then baptized in the faith, he briefly withdrew into an ascetic life of monasticism with his brother and sister. But such a life wasn't for him.

Much of Gregory's activity centered around reading and studying Platonic and Neoplatonic philosophy, seeking to inform Christian concepts of God's character and the nature of the Trinity with the best of his ideas. In 372 Gregory put his passions to work by becoming the bishop of Nyssa, a miserable experience as he was consumed by controversies and suffered persecution for his Trinitarian orthodoxy.

When Basil died, Gregory assumed the role for which he would most be known: defender of the Christian faith through anti-Arian lobbying. One of his greatest contributions was participating in the Council of Constantinople, where he offered the opening address and helped steer the council toward affirming and ratifying Nicene Trinitarian beliefs. He leveraged his knowledge and insight into Greek philosophy to inform his commentary on God's nature and transcendence.

Borrowing from Greek metaphysics, Gregory described the nature of God's unity and threeness in ways that mirrored the Platonic notion of "forms." Elsewhere his writings carried shades of Origen's speculative flair, though with less of his problematic doctrine. For instance, he agreed that God was ineffable and beyond our ability to know except through spiritual experience. His most important writings include: *On the Holy Trinity; On Not Three Gods;* and *Against Eunomius*. All three share the same goal of offering an account of the Trinity that would answer the distortions and denials of challengers to orthodoxy.

Though revered as a saint, Gregory was largely overshadowed by his brother Basil the Great and their friend Gregory of Nazianzus. His work languished in relative obscurity until the mid-1900s when a surge of interest in his theological writings raised awareness of the significant role he played as a true defender of Trinitarian orthodoxy.

IMPORTANT WORKS

ON THE HOLY TRINITY
ON NOT THREE GODS
AGAINST EUNOMIUS

So he did so and she came and stood in the doorway. 16He said, "About this time next year you will be holding a son." She said, "No, my master! O prophet, do not lie to your servant!" 17The woman did conceive, and at the specified time the next year she gave birth to a son, just as Elisha had told her.

18The boy grew and one day he went out to see his father who was with the harvest workers. 19He said to his father, "My head! My head!" His father told a servant, "Carry him to his mother." 20So he picked him up and took him to his mother. He sat on her lap until noon and then died. 21She went up and laid him down on the prophet's bed. She shut the door behind her and left. 22She called to her husband, "Send me one of the servants and one of the donkeys, so I can go see the prophet quickly and then return." 23He said, "Why do you want to go see him today? It is not the new moon or the Sabbath." She said, "Everything's fine." 24She saddled the donkey and told her servant, "Lead on. Do not stop unless I say so."

25So she went to visit the prophet at Mount Carmel. When he saw her at a distance, he said to his servant Gehazi, "Look, it's the Shunammite woman. 26Now, run to meet her and ask her, 'Are you well? Are your husband and the boy well?'" She told Gehazi, "Everything's fine." 27But when she reached the prophet on the mountain, she grabbed hold of his feet. Gehazi came near to push her away, but the prophet said, "Leave her alone, for she is very upset. The LORD has kept the matter hidden from me; he didn't tell me about it." 28She said, "Did I ask my master for a son? Didn't I say, 'Don't mislead me?'" 29Elisha told Gehazi, "Tuck your robes into your belt, take my staff, and go! Don't stop to exchange greetings with anyone! Place my staff on the child's face." 30The mother of the child said, "As certainly as the LORD lives and as you live, I will not leave you." So Elisha got up and followed her back.

31Now Gehazi went on ahead of them. He placed the staff on the child's face, but there was no sound or response. When he came back to Elisha he told him, "The child did not wake up." 32When Elisha arrived at the house, there was the child lying dead on his bed. 33He went in by himself and closed the door. Then he prayed to the LORD. 34He got up on the bed and spread his body out over the boy; he put his mouth on the boy's mouth, his eyes over the boy's eyes, and the palms of his hands against the boy's palms. As he bent down across him, the boy's skin grew warm. 35Elisha went back and walked around in the house. Then he got up on the bed again and bent down over him. The child sneezed seven times and opened his eyes. 36Elisha called to Gehazi and said, "Get the Shunammite woman." So he did so and she came to him. He said to her, "Take your son." 37She came in, fell at his feet, and bowed down. Then she picked up her son and left.

ELISHA MAKES A MEAL EDIBLE

38Now Elisha went back to Gilgal, while there was a famine in the land. Some of the prophets were visiting him and he told his servant, "Put the big pot on the fire and boil some stew for the prophets." 39Someone went out to the field to gather some herbs and found a wild vine. He picked some of its fruit, enough to fill up the fold of his robe. He came back, cut it up, and threw the slices into the stew pot, not knowing they were harmful. 40The stew was poured out for the men to eat. When they ate some of the stew, they cried out, "Death is in the pot,

O prophet!" They could not eat it. 41 He said, "Get some flour."
Then he threw it into the pot and said, "Now pour some out
for the men so they may eat." There was no longer anything
harmful in the pot.

ELISHA MIRACULOUSLY FEEDS A HUNDRED PEOPLE

42 Now a man from Baal Shalisha brought some food for the
prophet—20 loaves of bread made from the firstfruits of the
barley harvest, as well as fresh ears of grain. Elisha said, "Set it
before the people so they may eat." 43 But his attendant said,
"How can I feed a hundred men with this?" He replied, "Set it
before the people so they may eat, for this is what the LORD
has said, 'They will eat and have some left over.'" 44 So he set
it before them; they ate and had some left over, just as in the
LORD's message.

ELISHA HEALS A SYRIAN GENERAL

5 Now Naaman, the commander of the king of Syria's army, was
esteemed and respected by his master, for through him the
LORD had given Syria military victories. But this great warrior
had a skin disease. 2 Raiding parties went out from Syria and
took captive from the land of Israel a young girl, who became
a servant to Naaman's wife. 3 She told her mistress, "If only my
master were in the presence of the prophet who is in Samaria!
Then he would cure him of his skin disease."

4 Naaman went and told his master what the girl from the
land of Israel had said. 5 The king of Syria said, "Go! I will send
a letter to the king of Israel." So Naaman went, taking with
him 10 talents of silver, 6,000 shekels of gold, and 10 suits of
clothes. 6 He brought the letter to the king of Israel. It read:
"This is a letter of introduction for my servant Naaman, whom
I have sent to be cured of his skin disease." 7 When the king of
Israel read the letter, he tore his clothes and said, "Am I God?
Can I kill or restore life? Why does he ask me to cure a man of
his skin disease? Certainly you must see that he is looking for
an excuse to fight me!"

8 When Elisha the prophet heard that the king of Israel had
torn his clothes, he sent this message to the king, "Why did
you tear your clothes? Send him to me so he may know there
is a prophet in Israel." 9 So Naaman came with his horses and
chariots and stood in the doorway of Elisha's house. 10 Elisha
sent out a messenger who told him, "Go and wash seven times
in the Jordan; your skin will be restored and you will be healed."
11 Naaman went away angry. He said, "Look, I thought for sure
he would come out, stand there, invoke the name of the LORD
his God, wave his hand over the area, and cure the skin disease.
12 The rivers of Damascus, the Abana and Pharpar, are better
than any of the waters of Israel! Could I not wash in them and
be healed?" So he turned around and went away angry. 13 His
servants approached and said to him, "O master, if the prophet
had told you to do some difficult task, you would have been willing to do it. It seems you should be happy that he simply said,
'Wash and you will be healed.'" 14 So he went down and dipped
in the Jordan seven times, as the prophet had instructed. His
skin became as smooth as a young child's and he was healed.

15 He and his entire entourage returned to the prophet.
Naaman came and stood before him. He said, "For sure I know
that there is no God in all the earth except in Israel! Now, please

5:1–19 Holy Elisha typified our Lord and Savior while Naaman prefigured the Gentiles. Naaman believed he would recover his health as the result of his own rivers: The human race presumes on its free will and its own merits, but without the grace of Christ its own merits cannot possess health. "Wash seven times in the Jordan," Elisha said because of the sevenfold grace of the Holy Spirit that reposed in Christ our Lord. Moreover, when our Lord was baptized in this river, the Holy Spirit came on him in the form of a dove. When Naaman descended into the river as a figure of baptism, "his skin became as smooth as a young child's." Notice, beloved, that this likeness was perfected in the Christian people. Following the example of Naaman, they are renewed like little children by salutary baptism, although they have always been bent down under the weight of sins.

CAESARIUS OF ARLES
(C. 468–542)
SERMONS

accept a gift from your servant." 16But Elisha replied, "As certainly as the LORD lives (whom I serve), I will take nothing from
you." Naaman insisted that he take it, but he refused. 17Naaman
said, "If not, then please give your servant a load of dirt, enough
for a pair of mules to carry, for your servant will never again
offer a burnt offering or sacrifice to a god other than the LORD.
18May the LORD forgive your servant for this one thing: When
my master enters the temple of Rimmon to worship, and he
leans on my arm and I bow down in the temple of Rimmon,
may the LORD forgive your servant for this." 19Elisha said to
him, "Go in peace."

When he had gone a short distance, 20Gehazi, the prophet
Elisha's servant, thought, "Look, my master did not accept what
this Syrian Naaman offered him. As certainly as the LORD lives, I
will run after him and accept something from him." 21So Gehazi
ran after Naaman. When Naaman saw someone running after
him, he got down from his chariot to meet him and asked, "Is
everything all right?" 22He answered, "Everything is fine. My
master sent me with this message, 'Look, two servants of the
prophets just arrived from the Ephraimite hill country. Please
give them a talent of silver and two suits of clothes.'" 23Naaman
said, "Please accept two talents of silver." He insisted, and tied
up two talents of silver in two bags, along with two suits of
clothes. He gave them to two of his servants and they carried
them for Gehazi. 24When he arrived at the hill, he took them
from the servants and put them in the house. Then he sent
the men on their way.

25When he came and stood before his master, Elisha asked
him, "Where have you been, Gehazi?" He answered, "Your servant hasn't been anywhere." 26Elisha replied, "I was there in
spirit when a man turned and got down from his chariot to
meet you. This is not the proper time to accept silver or to
accept clothes, olive groves, vineyards, sheep, cattle, and male
and female servants. 27Therefore Naaman's skin disease will
afflict you and your descendants forever!" When Gehazi went
out from his presence, his skin was as white as snow.

ELISHA MAKES AN AX HEAD FLOAT

6 Some of the prophets said to Elisha, "Look, the place where we
meet with you is too cramped for us. 2Let's go to the Jordan.
Each of us will get a log from there, and we will build a meeting place for ourselves there." He said, "Go." 3One of them said,
"Please come along with your servants." He replied, "All right, I'll
come." 4So he went with them. When they arrived at the Jordan,
they started cutting down trees. 5As one of them was felling
a tree, the ax head dropped into the water. He shouted, "Oh
no, my master! It was borrowed!" 6The prophet asked, "Where
did it drop in?" When he showed him the spot, Elisha cut off
a branch, threw it in at that spot, and made the ax head float.
7He said, "Lift it out." So he reached out his hand and grabbed it.

ELISHA DEFEATS AN ARMY

8Now the king of Syria was at war with Israel. He consulted his
advisers, who said, "Invade at such and such a place." 9But the
prophet sent this message to the king of Israel, "Make sure you
don't pass through this place because Syria is invading there."
10So the king of Israel sent a message to the place the prophet
had pointed out, warning it to be on its guard. This happened
on several occasions. 11This made the king of Syria upset. So

he summoned his advisers and said to them, “One of us must be helping the king of Israel.” [12]One of his advisers said, “No, my master, O king. The prophet Elisha who lives in Israel keeps telling the king of Israel the things you say in your bedroom.” [13]The king ordered, “Go, find out where he is, so I can send some men to capture him.” The king was told, “He is in Dothan.” [14]So he sent horses and chariots there, along with a good-sized army. They arrived during the night and surrounded the city.

[15]The prophet’s attendant got up early in the morning. When he went outside there was an army surrounding the city, along with horses and chariots. He said to Elisha, “Oh no, my master! What will we do?” [16]He replied, “Don’t be afraid, for our side outnumbers them.” [17]Then Elisha prayed, “O LORD, open his eyes so he can see.” The LORD opened the servant’s eyes, and he saw that the hill was full of horses and chariots of fire all around Elisha. [18]As the army approached him, Elisha prayed to the LORD, “Strike these people with blindness.” The LORD struck them with blindness as Elisha requested. [19]Then Elisha said to them, “This is not the right road or city. Follow me, and I will lead you to the man you’re looking for.” He led them to Samaria.

[20]When they had entered Samaria, Elisha said, “O LORD, open their eyes, so they can see.” The LORD opened their eyes, and they saw that they were in the middle of Samaria. [21]When the king of Israel saw them, he asked Elisha, “Should I strike them down, my master?” [22]He replied, “Do not strike them down! You did not capture them with your sword or bow, so what gives you the right to strike them down? Give them some food and water, so they can eat and drink and then go back to their master.” [23]So he threw a big banquet for them and they ate and drank. Then he sent them back to their master. After that no Syrian raiding parties again invaded the land of Israel.

THE LORD SAVES SAMARIA

[24]Later King Ben Hadad of Syria assembled his entire army and attacked and besieged Samaria. [25]Samaria’s food supply ran out. They laid siege to it so long that a donkey’s head was selling for eighty shekels of silver and a quarter of a kab of dove’s droppings for five shekels of silver.

[26]While the king of Israel was passing by on the city wall, a woman shouted to him, “Help us, my master, O king!” [27]He replied, “No, let the LORD help you. How can I help you? The threshing floor and winepress are empty.” [28]Then the king asked her, “What’s your problem?” She answered, “This woman said to me, ‘Hand over your son; we’ll eat him today and then eat my son tomorrow.’ [29]So we boiled my son and ate him. Then I said to her the next day, ‘Hand over your son and we’ll eat him.’ But she hid her son!” [30]When the king heard what the woman said, he tore his clothes. As he was passing by on the wall, the people could see he was wearing sackcloth under his clothes. [31]Then he said, “May God judge me severely if Elisha son of Shaphat still has his head by the end of the day!”

[32]Now Elisha was sitting in his house with the community leaders. The king sent a messenger on ahead, but before he arrived, Elisha said to the leaders, “Do you realize this assassin intends to cut off my head? Look, when the messenger arrives, shut the door and lean against it. His master will certainly be right behind him.” [33]He was still talking to them when the messenger approached and said, “Look, the LORD is responsible for this disaster! Why should I continue to wait for the LORD

6:24—7:3 A famine is described that neither the word of the Lord nor the prophet could address unless the people cried out for the Lord’s blessing in this time of great calamity. But the glorious prophet Elisha had been rejected by those who knew him so that they did not send for him to implore God’s grace on their behalf. Neither did they request his counsel because they hated the Lord and blamed his servant for these problems. In their ignorance they would not suffer his presence. And so where the prophets of the Lord are not received, there they can give no prosperity. The head of a large donkey is desired as if it were the word of God and the face of the prophet. They desperately sought out dove’s dung, disregarding the manna from above, the food of angels.

JOHANNES PISCATOR
(1546–1625)
COMMENTARY ON SECOND KINGS

7 to help?” 1 Elisha replied, “Listen to the LORD’s message. This
is what the LORD has said, ‘About this time tomorrow a seah
of finely milled flour will sell for a shekel and two seahs of barley
for a shekel at the gate of Samaria.’” 2 An officer who was the
king’s right-hand man responded to the prophet, “Look, even
if the LORD made it rain by opening holes in the sky, could this
happen so soon?” Elisha said, “Look, you will see it happen with
your own eyes, but you will not eat any of the food!”
3 Now four men with a skin disease were sitting at the entrance of the city gate. They said to one another, “Why are we
just sitting here waiting to die? 4 If we go into the city, we’ll die
of starvation, and if we stay here we’ll die! So come on, let’s
defect to the Syrian camp! If they spare us, we’ll live; if they kill
us—well, we were going to die anyway.” 5 So they started toward
the Syrian camp at dusk. When they reached the edge of the
Syrian camp, there was no one there. 6 The Lord had caused
the Syrian camp to hear the sound of chariots and horses and
a large army. Then they said to one another, “Look, the king of
Israel has paid the kings of the Hittites and Egyptians to attack
us!” 7 So they got up and fled at dusk, leaving behind their tents,
horses, and donkeys. They left the camp as it was and ran for
their lives. 8 When the men with a skin disease reached the edge
of the camp, they entered a tent and had a meal. They also took
some silver, gold, and clothes and went and hid it all. Then they
went back and entered another tent. They looted it and went
and hid what they had taken. 9 Then they said to one another,
“It’s not right what we’re doing! This is a day to celebrate, but
we haven’t told anyone. If we wait until dawn, we’ll be punished.
So come on, let’s go and inform the royal palace.” 10 So they went
and called out to the gatekeepers of the city. They told them,
“We entered the Syrian camp and there was no one there. We
didn’t even hear a man’s voice. But the horses and donkeys are
still tied up, and the tents remain up.” 11 The gatekeepers relayed
the news to the royal palace.
12 The king got up in the night and said to his advisers, “I will tell
you what the Syrians have done to us. They know we are starving,
so they left the camp and hid in the field, thinking, ‘When they
come out of the city, we will capture them alive and enter the
city.’” 13 One of his advisers replied, “Pick some men and have them
take five of the horses that are left in the city. (Even if they are
killed, their fate will be no different than that of all the Israelite
people—we’re all going to die!) Let’s send them out so we can know
for sure what’s going on.” 14 So they picked two horsemen and the
king sent them out to track the Syrian army. He ordered them,
“Go and find out what’s going on.” 15 So they tracked them as far
as the Jordan. The road was filled with clothes and equipment
that the Syrians had discarded in their haste. The scouts went
back and told the king. 16 Then the people went out and looted
the Syrian camp. A seah of finely milled flour sold for a shekel,
and two seahs of barley for a shekel, just as in the LORD’s message.
17 Now the king had placed the officer who was his right-hand
man at the city gate. When the people rushed out, they trampled him to death in the gate. This fulfilled the prophet’s word
which he had spoken when the king tried to arrest him. 18 The
prophet had told the king, “Two seahs of barley will sell for a
shekel, and a seah of finely milled flour for a shekel; this will
happen about this time tomorrow in the gate of Samaria.” 19 But
the officer had replied to the prophet, “Look, even if the LORD
made it rain by opening holes in the sky, could this happen so

soon?" Elisha had said, "Look, you will see it happen with your own eyes, but you will not eat any of the food!" [20]This is exactly what happened to him. The people trampled him to death in the city gate.

ELISHA AGAIN HELPS THE SHUNAMMITE WOMAN

8 Now Elisha advised the woman whose son he had brought back to life, "You and your family should go and live somewhere else for a while, for the LORD has decreed that a famine will overtake the land for seven years." [2]So the woman did as the prophet said. She and her family went and lived in the land of the Philistines for seven years. [3]After seven years the woman returned from the land of the Philistines and went to ask the king to give her back her house and field. [4]Now the king was talking to Gehazi, the prophet's servant, and said, "Tell me all the great things that Elisha has done." [5]While Gehazi was telling the king how Elisha had brought the dead back to life, the woman whose son he had brought back to life came to ask the king for her house and field. Gehazi said, "My master, O king, this is the very woman, and this is her son whom Elisha brought back to life!" [6]The king asked the woman about it, and she gave him the details. The king assigned a eunuch to take care of her request and ordered him, "Give her back everything she owns, as well as the amount of crops her field produced from the day she left the land until now."

8:1–6 This is the Shunammite woman who had received Elisha in her home. And the prophet had taken care of her son too, who had died, by reviving him. Elisha predicted to her that a seven-year famine would occur and invited her to find a new home by immigrating. He chose for her the Holy Land, a close and fertile region where the inhabitants were rich thanks to their maritime commerce. From the allegorical point of view, the Holy Land, which received the righteous who were in exile and symbolically far from the Lord, was a figure of the world. The world hates the saints and constantly persecutes them. And even after our Lord has defeated it and its prince (the devil) has been thrown out, these two never cease from fighting against his servants, grabbing and destroying the idle and the ignorant.

EPHREM THE SYRIAN
(C. 306–373)
COMMENTARY ON THE SECOND BOOK OF KINGS

ELISHA MEETS WITH HAZAEL

[7]Elisha traveled to Damascus while King Ben Hadad of Syria was sick. The king was told, "The prophet has come here." [8]So the king told Hazael, "Take a gift and go visit the prophet. Request from him an oracle from the LORD. Ask him, 'Will I recover from this sickness?'" [9]So Hazael went to visit Elisha. He took along a gift, as well as 40 camel-loads of all the fine things of Damascus. When he arrived, he stood before him and said, "Your son, King Ben Hadad of Syria, has sent me to you with this question, 'Will I recover from this sickness?'" [10]Elisha said to him, "Go and tell him, 'You will surely recover,' but the LORD has revealed to me that he will surely die." [11]Elisha just stared at him until Hazael became uncomfortable. Then the prophet started crying. [12]Hazael asked, "Why are you crying, my master?" He replied, "Because I know the trouble you will cause the Israelites. You will set fire to their fortresses, kill their young men with the sword, smash their children to bits, and rip open their pregnant women." [13]Hazael said, "How could your servant, who is as insignificant as a dog, accomplish this great military victory?" Elisha answered, "The LORD has revealed to me that you will be the king of Syria." [14]He left Elisha and went to his master. Ben Hadad asked him, "What did Elisha tell you?" Hazael replied, "He told me you would surely recover." [15]The next day Hazael took a piece of cloth, dipped it in water, and spread it over Ben Hadad's face until he died. Then Hazael replaced him as king.

JEHORAM'S REIGN OVER JUDAH

[16]In the fifth year of the reign of Israel's King Joram, son of Ahab, Jehoshaphat's son Jehoram became king over Judah. [17]He was thirty-two years old when he became king, and he reigned for eight years in Jerusalem. [18]He followed in the footsteps of the kings of Israel, just as Ahab's dynasty had done, for he married Ahab's daughter. He did evil in the sight of the LORD. [19]But

the LORD was unwilling to destroy Judah. He preserved Judah
for the sake of his servant David to whom he had promised a
perpetual dynasty.
[20]During his reign Edom freed themselves from Judah's control and set up their own king. [21]Jehoram crossed over to Zair
with all his chariots. The Edomites, who had surrounded him,
attacked at night and defeated him and his chariot officers.
The Israelite army retreated to their homeland. [22]So Edom
has remained free from Judah's control to this very day. At that
same time Libnah also rebelled.
[23]The rest of the events of Jehoram's reign, including a record
of his accomplishments, are recorded in the scroll called the
Annals of the Kings of Judah. [24]Jehoram passed away and was
buried with his ancestors in the City of David. His son Ahaziah
replaced him as king.

AHAZIAH TAKES THE THRONE OF JUDAH

[25]In the twelfth year of the reign of Israel's King Joram, son of
Ahab, Jehoram's son Ahaziah became king over Judah. [26]Aha-
ziah was twenty-two years old when he became king, and he
reigned for one year in Jerusalem. His mother was Athaliah,
the granddaughter of King Omri of Israel. [27]He followed in the
footsteps of Ahab's dynasty and did evil in the sight of the LORD,
as Ahab's dynasty had done, for he was related to Ahab's family.
[28]He joined Ahab's son Joram in a battle against King Hazael
of Syria at Ramoth Gilead in which the Syrians defeated Joram.
[29]King Joram returned to Jezreel to recover from the wounds
he received from the Syrians in Ramah when he fought against
King Hazael of Syria. King Ahaziah son of Jehoram of Judah
went down to visit Joram son of Ahab in Jezreel, for he was ill.

JEHU BECOMES KING

9 Now Elisha the prophet summoned a member of the prophetic guild and told him, "Tuck your robes into your belt,
take this container of olive oil in your hand, and go to Ramoth
Gilead. [2]When you arrive there, look for Jehu son of Jehoshaphat
son of Nimshi and take him aside into an inner room. [3]Take
the container of olive oil, pour it over his head, and say, 'This
is what the LORD has said, "I have designated you as king over
Israel."' Then open the door and run away quickly!"
[4]So the young prophet went to Ramoth Gilead. [5]When he
arrived, the officers of the army were sitting there. So he said,
"I have a message for you, O officer." Jehu asked, "For which one
of us?" He replied, "For you, O officer." [6]So Jehu got up and went
inside. Then the prophet poured the olive oil on his head and
said to him, "This is what the LORD God of Israel has said, 'I
have designated you as king over the LORD's people Israel. [7]You
will destroy the family of your master Ahab. I will get revenge
against Jezebel for the shed blood of my servants the prophets
and for the shed blood of all the LORD's servants. [8]Ahab's entire
family will die. I will cut off every last male belonging to Ahab
in Israel, including even the weak and incapacitated. [9]I will
make Ahab's dynasty like those of Jeroboam son of Nebat and
Baasha son of Ahijah. [10]Dogs will devour Jezebel on the plot of
ground in Jezreel; she will not be buried.'" Then he opened the
door and ran away.
[11]When Jehu rejoined his master's servants, they asked him,
"Is everything all right? Why did this madman visit you?" He
replied, "Ah, it's not important. You know what kind of man

he is and the kinds of things he says." [12]But they said, "You're
lying! Tell us what he said." So he told them what he had said.
He also related how he had said, "This is what the LORD has
said, 'I have designated you as king over Israel.'" [13]Each of them
quickly took off his cloak, and they spread them out at Jehu's
feet on the steps. The trumpet was blown and they shouted,
"Jehu is king!" [14]Then Jehu son of Jehoshaphat son of Nimshi
conspired against Joram.

JEHU THE ASSASSIN

Now Joram had been in Ramoth Gilead with the whole Israelite
army, guarding against an invasion by King Hazael of Syria.
[15]But King Joram had returned to Jezreel to recover from the
wounds he received from the Syrians when he fought against
King Hazael of Syria. Jehu told his supporters, "If you really
want me to be king, then don't let anyone escape from the city
to go and warn Jezreel." [16]Jehu drove his chariot to Jezreel, for
Joram was recuperating there. (Now King Ahaziah of Judah had
come down to visit Joram.)
[17]Now the watchman was standing on the tower in Jezreel
and saw Jehu's troops approaching. He said, "I see troops!" Joram
ordered, "Send a rider out to meet them and have him ask, 'Is
everything all right?'" [18]So the horseman went to meet him and
said, "This is what the king says, 'Is everything all right?'" Jehu
replied, "None of your business! Follow me." The watchman
reported, "The messenger reached them, but hasn't started
back." [19]So he sent a second horseman out to them and he
said, "This is what the king says, 'Is everything all right?'" Jehu
replied, "None of your business! Follow me." [20]The watchman
reported, "He reached them, but hasn't started back. The one
who drives the lead chariot drives like Jehu son of Nimshi; he
drives recklessly." [21]Joram ordered, "Hitch up my chariot." When
his chariot had been hitched up, King Joram of Israel and King
Ahaziah of Judah went out in their respective chariots to meet
Jehu. They met up with him in the plot of land that had once
belonged to Naboth of Jezreel.
[22]When Joram saw Jehu, he asked, "Is everything all right,
Jehu?" He replied, "How can everything be all right as long as
your mother Jezebel promotes idolatry and pagan practices?"
[23]Joram turned his chariot around and took off. He said to Ahaziah, "It's a trap, Ahaziah!" [24]Jehu aimed his bow and shot an
arrow right between Joram's shoulders. The arrow went through
his heart and he fell to his knees in his chariot. [25]Jehu ordered
his officer Bidkar, "Pick him up and throw him into the part of
the field that once belonged to Naboth of Jezreel. Remember,
you and I were riding together behind his father, Ahab, when
the LORD pronounced this oracle against him, [26]'"Know for sure
that I saw the shed blood of Naboth and his sons yesterday,"
says the LORD, "and that I will give you what you deserve right
here in this plot of land," says the LORD.' So now pick him up and
throw him into this plot of land, just as in the LORD's message."
[27]When King Ahaziah of Judah saw what happened, he took
off up the road to Beth Haggan. Jehu chased him and ordered,
"Shoot him too." They shot him while he was driving his chariot up the ascent of Gur near Ibleam. He fled to Megiddo and
died there. [28]His servants took his body back to Jerusalem and
buried him in his tomb with his ancestors in the City of David.
[29]Ahaziah had become king over Judah in the eleventh year of
Joram son of Ahab.

9:14–29 When Joram inquired of Jehu, "Is everything all right, Jehu?" he replied, "How can everything be all right as long as your mother Jezebel promotes idolatry and pagan practices?" So do those of the true religion reply, and justly too, to those who maintain a false religion, *What peace while the errors and corrections of the church, which you acknowledge as your mother, are so many?*

JOHN DAVENANT **(1572–1641)**
EXPOSITION ON COLOSSIANS

30 Jehu approached Jezreel. When Jezebel heard the news, she put on some eye liner, fixed up her hair, and leaned out the window. 31 When Jehu came through the gate, she said, "Is everything all right, Zimri, murderer of his master?" 32 He looked up at the window and said, "Who is on my side? Who?" Two or three eunuchs looked down at him. 33 He said, "Throw her down!" So they threw her down, and when she hit the ground, her blood splattered against the wall and the horses, and Jehu drove his chariot over her. 34 He went inside and had a meal. Then he said, "Dispose of this accursed woman's corpse. Bury her, for after all, she was a king's daughter." 35 But when they went to bury her, they found nothing left but the skull, feet, and palms of the hands. 36 So they went back and told him. Then he said, "It is the fulfillment of the LORD's message that he had spoken through his servant, Elijah the Tishbite, 'In the plot of land at Jezreel, dogs will devour Jezebel's flesh. 37 Jezebel's corpse will be like manure on the surface of the ground in the plot of land at Jezreel. People will not be able to even recognize her.'"

JEHU WIPES OUT AHAB'S FAMILY

10 Ahab had 70 sons living in Samaria. So Jehu wrote letters and sent them to Samaria to the leading officials of Jezreel and to the guardians of Ahab's dynasty. This is what the letters said, 2 "You have with you the sons of your master, chariots and horses, a fortified city, and weapons. So when this letter arrives, 3 pick the best and most capable of your master's sons, place him on his father's throne, and defend your master's dynasty."

4 They were absolutely terrified and said, "Look, two kings could not stop him! How can we?" 5 So the palace supervisor, the city commissioner, the leaders, and the guardians sent this message to Jehu, "We are your subjects! Whatever you say, we will do. We will not make anyone king. Do what you consider proper."

6 He wrote them a second letter, saying, "If you are really on my side and are willing to obey me, then take the heads of your master's sons and come to me in Jezreel at this time tomorrow." Now the king had 70 sons, and the prominent men of the city were raising them. 7 When they received the letter, they seized the king's sons and executed all 70 of them. They put their heads in baskets and sent them to him in Jezreel. 8 The messenger came and told Jehu, "They have brought the heads of the king's sons." Jehu said, "Stack them in two piles at the entrance of the city gate until morning." 9 In the morning he went out and stood there. Then he said to all the people, "You are innocent. I conspired against my master and killed him. But who struck down all of these men? 10 Therefore take note that not one of the LORD's words which he pronounced against Ahab's dynasty will fail to materialize. The LORD has done what he announced through his servant Elijah." 11 Then Jehu killed all who were left of Ahab's family in Jezreel, and all his nobles, close friends, and priests. He left no survivors.

12 Jehu then left there and set out for Samaria. While he was traveling through Beth Eked of the Shepherds, 13 Jehu encountered the relatives of King Ahaziah of Judah. He asked, "Who are you?" They replied, "We are Ahaziah's relatives. We have come down to see how the king's sons and the queen mother's sons are doing." 14 He said, "Capture them alive!" So they captured them alive and then executed all 42 of them by the cistern at Beth Eked. He left no survivors.

10:1–32 Jehu was commanded to destroy the house of Ahab. He did so, yet his heart and God's heart were far apart. God wanted Ahab's house destroyed because of justice, while Jehu wanted it destroyed because of policy. Therefore, although Jehu esteemed his destruction as zeal, God considered it murder in the shedding of blood. And although God rewarded Jehu for doing what he commanded him to do, he still threatened to avenge himself since Jehu's execution of God's commandment was excessive. What then, is Jehu to commit murder? God forbid, and yet wasn't he commanded to commit murder? Yes, for God required it. So therefore he was to perform God's command, but he was not therefore to work out his own agenda: God commanded him to execute his justice but not his own revenge.

EDWARD REYNOLDS
(1599–1676)
THE SINFULNESS OF SIN

15When he left there, he met Jehonadab son of Rekab who had been looking for him. Jehu greeted him and asked, "Are you as committed to me as I am to you?" Jehonadab answered, "I am!" Jehu replied, "If so, give me your hand." So he offered his hand and Jehu pulled him up into the chariot. 16Jehu said, "Come with me and see how zealous I am for the LORD's cause." So he took him along in his chariot. 17He went to Samaria and killed each of Ahab's remaining family members who were in Samaria until he destroyed them, in keeping with the LORD's message which he had announced to Elijah.

JEHU EXECUTES THE PROPHETS AND PRIESTS OF BAAL

18Jehu assembled all the people and said to them, "Ahab worshiped Baal a little; Jehu will worship him with great devotion. 19So now, bring to me all the prophets of Baal, as well as all his servants and priests. None of them must be absent, for I am offering a great sacrifice to Baal. Any of them who fails to appear will lose his life." But Jehu was tricking them so he could destroy the servants of Baal. 20Then Jehu ordered, "Make arrangements for a celebration for Baal." So they announced it. 21Jehu sent invitations throughout Israel, and all the servants of Baal came; not one was absent. They arrived at the temple of Baal and filled it up from end to end. 22Jehu ordered the one who was in charge of the wardrobe, "Bring out robes for all the servants of Baal." So he brought out robes for them. 23Then Jehu and Jehonadab son of Rekab went to the temple of Baal. Jehu said to the servants of Baal, "Make sure there are no servants of the LORD here with you; there must be only servants of Baal." 24They went inside to offer sacrifices and burnt offerings. Now Jehu had stationed 80 men outside. He had told them, "If any of the men inside gets away, you will pay with your lives!"

25When he finished offering the burnt sacrifice, Jehu ordered the royal guard and officers, "Come in and strike them down! Don't let any escape!" So the royal guard and officers struck them down with the sword and left their bodies lying there. Then they entered the inner sanctuary of the temple of Baal. 26They hauled out the sacred pillar of the temple of Baal and burned it. 27They demolished the sacred pillar of Baal and the temple of Baal; it is used as a latrine to this very day. 28So Jehu eradicated Baal worship from Israel.

A SUMMARY OF JEHU'S REIGN

29However, Jehu did not repudiate the sins that Jeroboam son of Nebat had encouraged Israel to commit; the golden calves remained in Bethel and Dan. 30The LORD said to Jehu, "You have done well. You have accomplished my will and carried out my wishes with regard to Ahab's dynasty. Therefore four generations of your descendants will rule over Israel." 31But Jehu did not carefully and wholeheartedly obey the law of the LORD God of Israel. He did not repudiate the sins which Jeroboam had encouraged Israel to commit.

32In those days the LORD began to reduce the size of Israel's territory. Hazael attacked their eastern border. 33He conquered all the land of Gilead, including the territory of Gad, Reuben, and Manasseh, extending all the way from the Aroer in the Arnon Valley through Gilead to Bashan.

34The rest of the events of Jehu's reign, including all his accomplishments and successes, are recorded in the scroll called the Annals of the Kings of Israel. [35]Jehu passed away and was buried in Samaria. His son Jehoahaz replaced him as king. [36]Jehu reigned over Israel for 28 years in Samaria.

ATHALIAH IS ELIMINATED

11 When Athaliah, the mother of Ahaziah, saw that her son was dead, she was determined to destroy the entire royal line. [2]So Jehosheba, the daughter of King Jehoram and sister of Ahaziah, took Ahaziah's son Joash and stole him away from the rest of the royal descendants who were to be executed. She hid him and his nurse in the room where the bed covers were stored. So he was hidden from Athaliah and escaped execution. [3]He hid out with his nurse in the LORD's temple for six years, while Athaliah was ruling over the land.

[4]In the seventh year Jehoiada summoned the officers of the units of hundreds of the Carians and the royal bodyguard. He met with them in the LORD's temple. He made an agreement with them and made them swear an oath of allegiance in the LORD's temple. Then he showed them the king's son. [5]He ordered them, "This is what you must do. One-third of the unit that is on duty during the Sabbath will guard the royal palace. [6]Another third of you will be stationed at the Foundation Gate. Still another third of you will be stationed at the gate behind the royal guard. You will take turns guarding the palace. [7]The two units who are off duty on the Sabbath will guard the LORD's temple and protect the king. [8]You must surround the king. Each of you must hold his weapon in his hand. Whoever approaches your ranks must be killed. You must accompany the king wherever he goes."

[9]The officers of the units of hundreds did just as Jehoiada the priest ordered. Each of them took his men, those who were on duty during the Sabbath as well as those who were off duty on the Sabbath, and reported to Jehoiada the priest. [10]The priest gave to the officers of the units of hundreds King David's spears and the shields that were kept in the LORD's temple. [11]The royal bodyguard took their stations, each holding his weapon in his hand. They lined up from the south side of the temple to the north side and stood near the altar and the temple, surrounding the king. [12]Jehoiada led out the king's son and placed on him the crown and the royal insignia. They proclaimed him king and poured olive oil on his head. They clapped their hands and cried out, "Long live the king!"

[13]When Athaliah heard the royal guard shout, she joined the crowd at the LORD's temple. [14]Then she saw the king standing by the pillar, according to custom. The officers stood beside the king with their trumpets, and all the people of the land were celebrating and blowing trumpets. Athaliah tore her clothes and screamed, "Treason, treason!" [15]Jehoiada the priest ordered the officers of the units of hundreds, who were in charge of the army, "Bring her outside the temple to the guards. Put to death by the sword anyone who follows her." The priest gave this order because he had decided she should not be executed in the LORD's temple. [16]They seized her and took her into the precincts of the royal palace through the horses' entrance. There she was executed.

[17]Jehoiada then drew up a covenant between the LORD and the king and people, stipulating that they should be loyal to the LORD. [18]All the people of the land went and demolished the temple of Baal. They smashed its altars and idols to bits. They

11:1–20 Enemies can be loved in such a way that does not dishonor the righteousness of God through punishment. Thus righteousness is honored in a punishment that does not come from an evil judge but from a good judge. So it was in this case. We may rejoice about the destruction of this tyrannical Athaliah for two reasons. First, this death conforms to the rule: "Whoever sheds human blood, by other humans must his blood be shed" (Gen 9:6). Second, there is the admonishment to repentance as the Lord said in Luke 13: "Unless you repent, you will all perish" (Luke 13:3). Therefore let us wash our hands of Athaliah's blood. That is, we ought first to give praise to God's righteousness for punishing tyranny and second to exclaim with the psalm: "Yes indeed, the godly are rewarded. Yes indeed, there is a God who judges in the earth" (Ps 58:11). Then, having been thus admonished, we should learn righteousness and not despise the things of God.

VIKTORIN STRIGEL
(C. 1524–1569)
BOOK OF KINGS

killed Mattan the priest of Baal in front of the altar. Jehoiada the priest then placed guards at the LORD's temple. [19]He took the officers of the units of hundreds, the Carians, the royal bodyguard, and all the people of the land, and together they led the king down from the LORD's temple. They entered the royal palace through the Gate of the Royal Bodyguard, and the king sat down on the royal throne. [20]All the people of the land celebrated, for the city had rest now that they had killed Athaliah with the sword in the royal palace.

JOASH'S REIGN OVER JUDAH

12 [21]Jehoash was seven years old when he began to reign. [1]In Jehu's seventh year Jehoash became king; he reigned for 40 years in Jerusalem. His mother was Zibiah, who was from Beer Sheba. [2]Jehoash did what the LORD approved all his days when Jehoiada the priest taught him. [3]But the high places were not eliminated; the people continued to offer sacrifices and burn incense on the high places.

[4]Jehoash said to the priests, "I place at your disposal all the consecrated silver that has been brought to the LORD's temple, including the silver collected from the census tax, the silver received from those who have made vows, and all the silver that people have voluntarily contributed to the LORD's temple. [5]The priests should receive the silver they need from the treasurers and repair any damage to the temple they discover."

[6]By the twenty-third year of King Jehoash's reign the priests had still not repaired the damage to the temple. [7]So King Jehoash summoned Jehoiada the priest along with the other priests, and said to them, "Why have you not repaired the damage to the temple? Now, take no more silver from your treasurers unless you intend to use it to repair the damage." [8]The priests agreed not to collect silver from the people and relieved themselves of personal responsibility for the temple repairs.

[9]Jehoiada the priest took a chest and drilled a hole in its lid. He placed it on the right side of the altar near the entrance of the LORD's temple. The priests who guarded the entrance would put into it all the silver brought to the LORD's temple. [10]When they saw the chest was full of silver, the royal secretary and the high priest counted the silver that had been brought to the LORD's temple and bagged it up. [11]They would then hand over the silver that had been weighed to the construction foremen assigned to the LORD's temple. They hired carpenters and builders to work on the LORD's temple, [12]as well as masons and stonecutters. They bought wood and chiseled stone to repair the damage to the LORD's temple and also paid for all the other expenses. [13]The silver brought to the LORD's temple was not used for silver bowls, trimming shears, basins, trumpets, or any kind of gold or silver implements. [14]It was handed over to the foremen who used it to repair the LORD's temple. [15]They did not audit the treasurers who disbursed the funds to the foremen, for they were honest. [16](The silver collected in conjunction with reparation offerings and sin offerings was not brought to the LORD's temple; it belonged to the priests.)

[17]At that time King Hazael of Syria attacked Gath and captured it. Hazael then decided to attack Jerusalem. [18]King Jehoash of Judah collected all the sacred items that his ancestors Jehoshaphat, Jehoram, and Ahaziah, kings of Judah, had consecrated, as well as his own sacred items and all the gold that could be found in the treasuries of the LORD's temple and the

12:1–16 We are given a good example in the life of Joash. For after he was forced to pay tribute to the king of Syria, he was later taken by force at the hands of two of his servants. All of this occurred because after being subdued he returned to idolatry, as we read in 2 Chronicles 24:17–18. This should serve as a warning to all princes and leaders: If they do not constantly preserve the pure worship of God, they will often be punished by God.

JOHANNES PISCATOR
(1546–1625)
COMMENTARY ON SECOND KINGS

royal palace. He sent it all to King Hazael of Syria, who then withdrew from Jerusalem.

[19]The rest of the events of Joash's reign, including all his accomplishments, are recorded in the scroll called the Annals of the Kings of Judah. [20]His servants conspired against him and murdered Joash at Beth Millo, on the road that goes down to Silla. [21]His servants Jozabad son of Shimeath and Jehozabad son of Shomer murdered him. He was buried with his ancestors in the City of David. His son Amaziah replaced him as king.

JEHOAHAZ'S REIGN OVER ISRAEL

13 In the twenty-third year of the reign of Judah's King Joash son of Ahaziah, Jehu's son Jehoahaz became king over Israel. He reigned in Samaria for 17 years. [2]He did evil in the sight of the LORD. He continued in the sinful ways of Jeroboam son of Nebat who had encouraged Israel to sin; he did not repudiate those sins. [3]The LORD was furious with Israel and handed them over to King Hazael of Syria and to Hazael's son Ben Hadad for many years.

[4]Jehoahaz asked for the LORD's mercy, and the LORD responded favorably, for he saw that Israel was oppressed by the king of Syria. [5]The LORD provided a deliverer for Israel, and they were freed from Syria's power. The Israelites once more lived in security. [6]But they did not repudiate the sinful ways of the family of Jeroboam, who encouraged Israel to sin; they continued in those sins. There was even an Asherah pole standing in Samaria. [7]Jehoahaz had no army left except for 50 horsemen, 10 chariots, and 10,000 foot soldiers. The king of Syria had destroyed his troops and trampled on them as dust.

[8]The rest of the events of Jehoahaz's reign, including all his accomplishments and successes, are recorded in the scroll called the Annals of the Kings of Israel. [9]Jehoahaz passed away and was buried in Samaria. His son Jehoash replaced him as king.

JEHOASH'S REIGN OVER ISRAEL

[10]In the thirty-seventh year of King Jehoash's reign over Judah, Jehoahaz's son Jehoash became king over Israel. He reigned in Samaria for 16 years. [11]He did evil in the sight of the LORD. He did not repudiate the sinful ways of Jeroboam son of Nebat who encouraged Israel to sin; he continued in those sins. [12]The rest of the events of Jehoash's reign, including all his accomplishments and his successful war with King Amaziah of Judah, are recorded in the scroll called the Annals of the Kings of Israel. [13]Jehoash passed away and Jeroboam succeeded him on the throne. Jehoash was buried in Samaria with the kings of Israel.

ELISHA MAKES ONE FINAL PROPHECY

[14]Now Elisha had a terminal illness. King Jehoash of Israel went down to visit him. He wept before him and said, "My father, my father! The chariot and horsemen of Israel!" [15]Elisha told him, "Take a bow and some arrows," and he did so. [16]Then Elisha told the king of Israel, "Aim the bow." He did so, and Elisha placed his hands on the king's hands. [17]Elisha said, "Open the east window," and he did so. Elisha said, "Shoot!" and he did so. Elisha said, "This arrow symbolizes the victory the LORD will give you over Syria. You will annihilate Syria in Aphek!" [18]Then Elisha said, "Take the arrows," and he did so. He told the king of Israel, "Strike the ground!" He struck the ground three times and stopped. [19]The prophet got angry at him and said, "If you

13:1–9 Although in the past a great multitude would have been raised to go to war out of Israel, now there were left only 50 horsemen, 10 chariots, and 10,000 soldiers. This is set down to show how deeply grounded wickedness was in them by a continual accustoming themselves to sin so that we may beware of sinful customs. We are to so magnify the goodness of God that he would be entreated to help us and use his power to give great victories to Israel. But God did not merely help the people because they sought him with their lips while their hearts were far away from him. Rather God acted to maintain his covenant with Abraham, Isaac, and Jacob. Moreover, God had already predetermined a longer time for them before he would destroy them. This is so that his exceedingly great patience would be admired by all people who still upheld their state when they were so near to utter ruin. God also helped them so that when they would later abuse the help he gave them and were eventually destroyed by the Assyrians, they might acknowledge his judgments to be most just.

JOHN MAYER **(1583–1664)**
COMMENTARY ON SECOND KINGS

had struck the ground five or six times, you would have annihilated Syria! But now, you will defeat Syria only three times."
20 Elisha died and was buried. Moabite raiding parties invaded the land at the beginning of the year. 21 One day some men
were burying a man when they spotted a raiding party. So they
threw the dead man into Elisha's tomb. When the body touched
Elisha's bones, the dead man came to life and stood on his feet.
22 Now King Hazael of Syria oppressed Israel throughout
Jehoahaz's reign. 23 But the LORD had mercy on them and felt
pity for them. He extended his favor to them because of the
promise he had made to Abraham, Isaac, and Jacob. He has been
unwilling to destroy them or remove them from his presence
to this very day. 24 When King Hazael of Syria died, his son Ben
Hadad replaced him as king. 25 Jehoahaz's son Jehoash took back
from Ben Hadad son of Hazael the cities that he had taken from
his father Jehoahaz in war. Jehoash defeated him three times
and recovered the Israelite cities.

AMAZIAH'S REIGN OVER JUDAH

14 In the second year of the reign of Israel's King Joash son
of Joahaz, Joash's son Amaziah became king over Judah.
2 He was twenty-five years old when he began to reign, and he
reigned for twenty-nine years in Jerusalem. His mother was
Jehoaddan, who was from Jerusalem. 3 He did what the LORD
approved, but not like David his ancestor had done. He followed
the example of his father Joash. 4 But the high places were not
eliminated; the people continued to offer sacrifices and burn
incense on the high places.
5 When he had secured control of the kingdom, he executed the servants who had assassinated his father. 6 But he did
not execute the sons of the assassins. He obeyed the LORD's
commandment as recorded in the scroll of the law of Moses,
"Fathers must not be put to death for what their sons do, and
sons must not be put to death for what their fathers do. A man
must be put to death only for his own sin."
7 He defeated 10,000 Edomites in the Salt Valley; he captured
Sela in battle and renamed it Joktheel, a name it has retained
to this very day. 8 Then Amaziah sent messengers to Jehoash
son of Jehoahaz son of Jehu, king of Israel. He said, "Come, let's
meet face to face." 9 King Jehoash of Israel sent this message back
to King Amaziah of Judah, "A thornbush in Lebanon sent this
message to a cedar in Lebanon, 'Give your daughter to my son
as a wife.' Then a wild animal of Lebanon came by and trampled down the thorn. 10 You thoroughly defeated Edom, and
it has gone to your head! Gloat over your success, but stay in
your palace. Why bring calamity on yourself? Why bring down
yourself and Judah along with you?" 11 But Amaziah would not
heed the warning, so King Jehoash of Israel attacked. He and
King Amaziah of Judah met face to face in Beth Shemesh of
Judah. 12 Judah was defeated by Israel, and each man ran back
home. 13 King Jehoash of Israel captured King Amaziah of Judah,
son of Jehoash son of Ahaziah, in Beth Shemesh. He attacked
Jerusalem and broke down the wall of Jerusalem from the Gate
of Ephraim to the Corner Gate—a distance of about 600 feet.
14 He took away all the gold and silver, all the items found in
the LORD's temple and in the treasuries of the royal palace, and
some hostages. Then he went back to Samaria.
15 The rest of the events of Jehoash's reign, including all his
accomplishments and his successful war with King Amaziah of

14:1–22 The history of Amaziah is entirely similar to that of his father, Joash. For at first he was seen as doing that which was right and he listened to the prophet, as you see in Chronicles. The Lord gave him a sign of victory against the Edomites, but that resulted only in showing him to be a hypocrite. For where he had a chance to give thanks to God for the victory, he blasphemously worshiped the gods of the Edomites instead. Therefore the judgment of God was raised up against him so that in his pride he provoked Joash the king of Israel. Unlike his father David but like his own father, Joash, he did not remove the high places, which reveals his hypocrisy. For though his works may have been similar to David's, his fate was not. As Chronicles says, "He did what the LORD approved, but not with wholehearted devotion" (2 Chr 25:2).

JOHANNES BUGENHAGEN
(1485–1558)
COMMENTARY ON SECOND KINGS

Judah, are recorded in the scroll called the Annals of the Kings
of Israel. 16Jehoash passed away and was buried in Samaria
with the kings of Israel. His son Jeroboam replaced him as king.
17King Amaziah son of Joash of Judah lived for 15 years after the death of King Jehoash son of Jehoahaz of Israel. 18The
rest of the events of Amaziah's reign are recorded in the scroll
called the Annals of the Kings of Judah. 19Conspirators plotted
against him in Jerusalem, so he fled to Lachish. But they sent
assassins after him, and they killed him there. 20His body was
carried back by horses, and he was buried in Jerusalem with his
ancestors in the City of David. 21All the people of Judah took
Azariah, who was sixteen years old, and made him king in his
father Amaziah's place. 22Azariah built up Elat and restored it
to Judah after the king had passed away.

JEROBOAM II'S REIGN OVER ISRAEL

23In the fifteenth year of the reign of Judah's King Amaziah son
of Joash, Jeroboam son of Joash became king over Israel. He
reigned for 41 years in Samaria. 24He did evil in the sight of the
LORD; he did not repudiate the sinful ways of Jeroboam son of
Nebat who encouraged Israel to sin. 25He restored the border
of Israel from Lebo Hamath in the north to the sea of the rift
valley in the south, just as in the message from the LORD God
of Israel that he had announced through his servant Jonah son
of Amittai, the prophet from Gath Hepher. 26The LORD saw
Israel's intense suffering; everyone was weak and incapacitated
and Israel had no deliverer. 27The LORD had not decreed that
he would blot out Israel's memory from under heaven, so he
delivered them through Jeroboam son of Joash.
28The rest of the events of Jeroboam's reign, including all his
accomplishments, his military success in restoring Israelite
control over Damascus and Hamath, are recorded in the scroll
called the Annals of the Kings of Israel. 29Jeroboam passed away
and was buried in Samaria with the kings of Israel. His son
Zechariah replaced him as king.

AZARIAH'S REIGN OVER JUDAH

15 In the twenty-seventh year of King Jeroboam's reign over
Israel, Amaziah's son Azariah became king over Judah. 2He
was sixteen years old when he began to reign, and he reigned
for 52 years in Jerusalem. His mother's name was Jecholiah,
who was from Jerusalem. 3He did what the LORD approved,
just as his father Amaziah had done. 4But the high places were
not eliminated; the people continued to offer sacrifices and
burn incense on the high places. 5The LORD afflicted the king
with an illness; he suffered from a skin disease until the day he
died. He lived in separate quarters, while his son Jotham was
in charge of the palace and ruled over the people of the land.
6The rest of the events of Azariah's reign, including all his
accomplishments, are recorded in the scroll called the Annals
of the Kings of Judah. 7Azariah passed away and was buried
with his ancestors in the City of David. His son Jotham replaced
him as king.

ZECHARIAH'S REIGN OVER ISRAEL

8In the thirty-eighth year of King Azariah's reign over Judah,
Jeroboam's son Zechariah became king over Israel. He reigned
in Samaria for six months. 9He did evil in the sight of the LORD,
as his ancestors had done. He did not repudiate the sinful ways

of Jeroboam son of Nebat who encouraged Israel to sin. [10]Shal-
lum son of Jabesh conspired against him; he assassinated him
in Ibleam and took his place as king. [11]The rest of the events of
Zechariah's reign are recorded in the scroll called the Annals
of the Kings of Israel. [12]His assassination fulfilled the LORD's
message to Jehu, "Four generations of your descendants will
rule on Israel's throne." And that is how it happened.
[13]Shallum son of Jabesh became king in the thirty-ninth year
of King Uzziah's reign over Judah. He reigned for one month
in Samaria. [14]Menahem son of Gadi went up from Tirzah to
Samaria and attacked Shallum son of Jabesh. He killed him
and took his place as king. [15]The rest of the events of Shallum's
reign, including the conspiracy he organized, are recorded in
the scroll called the Annals of the Kings of Israel. [16]At that time
Menahem came from Tirzah and attacked Tiphsah. He struck
down all who lived in the city and the surrounding territory,
because they would not surrender. He even ripped open the
pregnant women.

MENAHEM'S REIGN OVER ISRAEL

[17]In the thirty-ninth year of King Azariah's reign over Judah,
Menahem son of Gadi became king over Israel. He reigned for
10 years in Samaria. [18]He did evil in the sight of the LORD; he
did not repudiate the sinful ways of Jeroboam son of Nebat,
who encouraged Israel to sin.
During his reign, [19]Pul king of Assyria invaded the land, and
Menahem paid him 1,000 talents of silver to gain his support
and to solidify his control of the kingdom. [20]Menahem got this
silver by taxing all the wealthy men in Israel; he took 50 shekels
of silver from each one of them and paid it to the king of Assyria.
Then the king of Assyria left; he did not stay there in the land.
[21]The rest of the events of Menahem's reign, including all
his accomplishments, are recorded in the scroll called the Annals of the Kings of Israel. [22]Menahem passed away and his son
Pekahiah replaced him as king.

PEKAHIAH'S REIGN OVER ISRAEL

[23]In the fiftieth year of King Azariah's reign over Judah, Menahem's son Pekahiah became king over Israel. He reigned in
Samaria for two years. [24]He did evil in the sight of the LORD;
he did not repudiate the sinful ways of Jeroboam son of Nebat
who encouraged Israel to sin. [25]His officer Pekah son of Remaliah conspired against him. He and 50 Gileadites assassinated
Pekahiah, as well as Argob and Arieh, in Samaria in the fortress
of the royal palace. Pekah then took his place as king.
[26]The rest of the events of Pekahiah's reign, including all his
accomplishments, are recorded in the scroll called the Annals
of the Kings of Israel.

PEKAH'S REIGN OVER ISRAEL

[27]In the fifty-second year of King Azariah's reign over Judah,
Pekah son of Remaliah became king over Israel. He reigned
in Samaria for twenty years. [28]He did evil in the sight of the
LORD; he did not repudiate the sinful ways of Jeroboam son of
Nebat who encouraged Israel to sin. [29]During Pekah's reign over
Israel, King Tiglath-Pileser of Assyria came and captured Ijon,
Abel Beth Maacah, Janoah, Kedesh, Hazor, Gilead, and Galilee,
including all the territory of Naphtali. He deported the people
to Assyria. [30]Hoshea son of Elah conspired against Pekah son

of Remaliah. He assassinated him and took his place as king, in the twentieth year of the reign of Jotham son of Uzziah.

[31]The rest of the events of Pekah's reign, including all his accomplishments, are recorded in the scroll called the Annals of the Kings of Israel.

JOTHAM'S REIGN OVER JUDAH

[32]In the second year of the reign of Israel's King Pekah son of Remaliah, Uzziah's son Jotham became king over Judah. [33]He was twenty-five years old when he began to reign, and he reigned for sixteen years in Jerusalem. His mother was Jerusha the daughter of Zadok. [34]He did what the LORD approved, just as his father Uzziah had done. [35]But the high places were not eliminated; the people continued to offer sacrifices and burn incense on the high places. He built the Upper Gate to the LORD's temple.

[36]The rest of the events of Jotham's reign, including his accomplishments, are recorded in the scroll called the Annals of the Kings of Judah. [37]In those days the LORD prompted King Rezin of Syria and Pekah son of Remaliah to attack Judah. [38]Jotham passed away and was buried with his ancestors in the city of his ancestor David. His son Ahaz replaced him as king.

AHAZ'S REIGN OVER JUDAH

16 In the seventeenth year of the reign of Pekah son of Remaliah, Jotham's son Ahaz became king over Judah. [2]Ahaz was twenty years old when he began to reign, and he reigned for sixteen years in Jerusalem. He did not do what pleased the LORD his God, in contrast to his ancestor David. [3]He followed in the footsteps of the kings of Israel. He passed his son through the fire, a horrible sin practiced by the nations whom the LORD drove out from before the Israelites. [4]He offered sacrifices and burned incense on the high places, on the hills, and under every green tree.

[5]At that time King Rezin of Syria and King Pekah son of Remaliah of Israel attacked Jerusalem. They besieged Ahaz, but were unable to conquer him. [6](At that time King Rezin of Syria recovered Elat for Syria; he drove the Judahites from there. Syrians arrived in Elat and live there to this very day.) [7]Ahaz sent messengers to King Tiglath-Pileser of Assyria, saying, "I am your servant and your dependent. March up and rescue me from the power of the king of Syria and the king of Israel, who have attacked me." [8]Then Ahaz took the silver and gold that were in the LORD's temple and in the treasuries of the royal palace and sent it as tribute to the king of Assyria. [9]The king of Assyria responded favorably to his request; he attacked Damascus and captured it. He deported the people to Kir and executed Rezin.

[10]When King Ahaz went to meet with King Tiglath-Pileser of Assyria in Damascus, he saw the altar there. King Ahaz sent to Uriah the priest a drawing of the altar and a blueprint for its design. [11]Uriah the priest built an altar in conformity to the plans King Ahaz had sent from Damascus. Uriah the priest finished it before King Ahaz arrived back from Damascus. [12]When the king arrived back from Damascus and saw the altar, he approached it and offered a sacrifice on it. [13]He offered his burnt sacrifice and his grain offering. He poured out his libation and sprinkled the blood from his peace offerings on the altar. [14]He moved the bronze altar that stood in the LORD's presence from the front

15:32–36 "In the second year of the reign of Israel's King Pekah son of Remaliah, Uzziah's son Jotham became king over Judah." After rising to power in that year, Jotham administered the government of Judah for 16 years, earning great praise. Scripture never reproaches him in this passage for any error except his toleration of the high places, which was a fault common to all the most-praised kings of Judah. He strengthened Jerusalem with new fortifications and built towers and castles in desert places. He conquered the Ammonites, who were perpetual enemies of the Jews, and ordered them for the future to pay the kings of Judah an annual tribute.

EPHREM THE SYRIAN
(C. 306–373)
COMMENTARY ON THE SECOND BOOK OF KINGS

16:15 Whatsoever is offered to the true God, either in King Ahaz's name (for possibly he did not yet utterly forsake God but worshiped idols with him) or on the behalf of the people, shall be offered on this new altar. This new altar shall be reserved for King Ahaz's proper use to inquire by, at which he may seek God or inquire of his will, by sacrifices joined with prayer, when he shall see fit. Having thrust it out from the use for which it was instituted, which was to sanctify the gifts offered upon it, he pretended to advance it above its institution, which it was common for superstitious people to do. But to overdo is to underdo. Our wisdom is to do just what God has commanded.

JOHN WESLEY **(1703–1791)**
EXPLANATORY NOTES ON THE BIBLE

17:5–23 God had now been greatly provoked in that kingdom. And even though Hoshea was not as bad as his predecessors, his kingdom was completely tainted with idolatry, and he was as guilty as the rest of them. For he did not seek to reform the kingdom as he should have done. God would now spare him no longer. He would first bring them into servitude and thereafter into miserable captivity. Just because we are not as wicked as another, this does not merit God's mercy, which spares us from his most severe judgments. Whoever does evil, despite how small and seemingly inconsequential, is in danger of God's wrath. And certainly those who sin greatly are much more likely in danger. We must learn not to abhor evil in relation to someone's worse evil, but to hate any evil at all.

JOHN MAYER **(1583–1664)**
COMMENTARY ON SECOND KINGS

of the temple (between the altar and the LORD's temple) and put it on the north side of the new altar. 15King Ahaz ordered Uriah the priest, "On the large altar offer the morning burnt sacrifice, the evening grain offering, the royal burnt sacrifices and grain offering, the burnt sacrifice for all the people of the land, their grain offering, and their libations. Sprinkle all the blood of the burnt sacrifice and other sacrifices on it. The bronze altar will be for my personal use." 16So Uriah the priest did exactly as King Ahaz ordered.

17King Ahaz took off the frames of the movable stands, and removed the basins from them. He took "The Sea" down from the bronze bulls that supported it and put it on the stone pavement. 18He also removed the Sabbath awning that had been built in the temple and the king's outer entranceway to the LORD's temple, on account of the king of Assyria.

19The rest of the events of Ahaz's reign, including his accomplishments, are recorded in the scroll called the Annals of the Kings of Judah. 20Ahaz passed away and was buried with his ancestors in the City of David. His son Hezekiah replaced him as king.

HOSHEA'S REIGN OVER ISRAEL

17 In the twelfth year of King Ahaz's reign over Judah, Hoshea son of Elah became king over Israel. He reigned in Samaria for nine years. 2He did evil in the sight of the LORD, but not to the same degree as the Israelite kings who preceded him. 3King Shalmaneser of Assyria marched up to attack him; so Hoshea became his subject and paid him tribute. 4The king of Assyria discovered that Hoshea was planning a revolt. Hoshea had sent messengers to King So of Egypt and had not sent his annual tribute to the king of Assyria. So the king of Assyria arrested him and imprisoned him. 5The king of Assyria marched through the whole land. He attacked Samaria and besieged it for three years. 6In the ninth year of Hoshea's reign, the king of Assyria captured Samaria and deported the people of Israel to Assyria. He settled them in Halah, along the Habor (the river of Gozan), and in the cities of the Medes.

A SUMMARY OF ISRAEL'S SINFUL HISTORY

7This happened because the Israelites sinned against the LORD their God, who brought them up from the land of Egypt and freed them from the power of Pharaoh king of Egypt. They worshiped other gods; 8they observed the practices of the nations whom the LORD had driven out from before them, and followed the example of the kings of Israel. 9The Israelites said things about the LORD their God that were not right. They built high places in all their towns, from watchtower to fortified city. 10They set up sacred pillars and Asherah poles on every high hill and under every green tree. 11They burned incense on all the high places just like the nations whom the LORD had driven away before them did. Their evil practices made the LORD angry. 12They worshiped the disgusting idols in blatant disregard of the LORD's command.

13The LORD solemnly warned Israel and Judah through all his prophets and all the seers, "Turn back from your evil ways; obey my commandments and rules that are recorded in the law. I ordered your ancestors to keep this law and sent my servants the prophets to remind you of its demands." 14But they did not pay attention and were as stubborn as their ancestors, who had

not trusted the LORD their God. 15They rejected his rules, the
covenant he had made with their ancestors, and the laws he had
commanded them to obey. They paid allegiance to worthless
idols, and so became worthless to the LORD. They copied the
practices of the surrounding nations in blatant disregard of the
LORD's command. 16They abandoned all the commandments of
the LORD their God; they made two metal calves and an Asherah pole, bowed down to all the stars in the sky, and worshiped
Baal. 17They passed their sons and daughters through the fire,
and practiced divination and omen reading. They committed
themselves to doing evil in the sight of the LORD and made
him angry.

18So the LORD was furious with Israel and rejected them;
only the tribe of Judah was left. 19Judah also failed to keep the
commandments of the LORD their God; they followed Israel's
example. 20So the LORD rejected all of Israel's descendants; he
humiliated them and handed them over to robbers, until he
had thrown them from his presence. 21He tore Israel away from
David's dynasty, and Jeroboam son of Nebat became their king.
Jeroboam drove Israel away from the LORD and encouraged
them to commit a serious sin. 22The Israelites followed in the
sinful ways of Jeroboam and did not repudiate them. 23Finally
the LORD rejected Israel just as he had warned he would do
through all his servants the prophets. Israel was deported from
its land to Assyria and remains there to this very day.

THE KING OF ASSYRIA POPULATES ISRAEL WITH FOREIGNERS

24The king of Assyria brought foreigners from Babylon, Cuthah,
Avva, Hamath, and Sepharvaim and settled them in the cities
of Samaria in place of the Israelites. They took possession of
Samaria and lived in its cities. 25When they first moved in, they
did not worship the LORD. So the LORD sent lions among them
and the lions were killing them. 26The king of Assyria was told,
"The nations whom you deported and settled in the cities of
Samaria do not know the requirements of the God of the land,
so he has sent lions among them. They are killing the people
because they do not know the requirements of the God of the
land." 27So the king of Assyria ordered, "Take back one of the
priests whom you deported from there. He must settle there
and teach them the requirements of the God of the land." 28So
one of the priests whom they had deported from Samaria went
back and settled in Bethel. He taught them how to worship
the LORD.

29But each of these nations made its own gods and put them
in the shrines on the high places that the people of Samaria
had made. Each nation did this in the cities where they lived.
30The people from Babylon made Sukkoth Benoth, the people
from Cuth made Nergal, the people from Hamath made Ashima,
31the Avvites made Nibhaz and Tartak, and the Sepharvites
burned their sons in the fire as an offering to Adrammelech
and Anammelech, the gods of Sepharvaim. 32At the same time
they worshiped the LORD. They appointed some of their own
people to serve as priests in the shrines on the high places.
33They were worshiping the LORD and at the same time serving
their own gods in accordance with the practices of the nations
from which they had been deported.

34To this very day they observe their earlier practices.
They do not worship the LORD; they do not obey the rules,

regulations, law, and commandments that the LORD gave the
descendants of Jacob, whom he renamed Israel. 35 The LORD
made a covenant with them and instructed them, "You must
not worship other gods. Do not bow down to them, serve them,
or offer sacrifices to them. 36 Instead you must worship the
LORD, who brought you up from the land of Egypt by his great
power and military ability; bow down to him and offer sacrifices to him. 37 You must carefully obey at all times the rules,
regulations, law, and commandments he wrote down for you.
You must not worship other gods. 38 You must never forget the
covenant I made with you, and you must not worship other
gods. 39 Instead you must worship the LORD your God; then he
will rescue you from the power of all your enemies." 40 But they
paid no attention; instead they observed their earlier practices.
41 These nations were worshiping the LORD and at the same
time serving their idols; their sons and grandsons are doing
just as their fathers have done, to this very day.

HEZEKIAH BECOMES KING OF JUDAH

18 In the third year of the reign of Israel's King Hoshea son
of Elah, Ahaz's son Hezekiah became king over Judah.
2 He was twenty-five years old when he began to reign, and he
reigned twenty-nine years in Jerusalem. His mother was Abi,
the daughter of Zechariah. 3 He did what the LORD approved,
just as his ancestor David had done. 4 He eliminated the high
places, smashed the sacred pillars to bits, and cut down the
Asherah pole. He also demolished the bronze serpent that
Moses had made, for up to that time the Israelites had been
offering incense to it; it was called Nehushtan. 5 He trusted
in the LORD God of Israel; in this regard there was none like
him among the kings of Judah either before or after. 6 He was
loyal to the LORD and did not abandon him. He obeyed the
commandments that the LORD had given to Moses. 7 The LORD
was with him; he succeeded in all his endeavors. He rebelled
against the king of Assyria and refused to submit to him. 8 He
defeated the Philistines as far as Gaza and its territory, from
watchtower to fortified city.

9 In the fourth year of King Hezekiah's reign (it was the seventh year of the reign of Israel's King Hoshea, son of Elah), King
Shalmaneser of Assyria marched up against Samaria and besieged it. 10 After three years he captured it (in the sixth year of
Hezekiah's reign); in the ninth year of King Hoshea's reign over
Israel, Samaria was captured. 11 The king of Assyria deported the
people of Israel to Assyria. He settled them in Halah, along the
Habor (the river of Gozan), and in the cities of the Medes. 12 This
happened because they did not obey the LORD their God and
broke his covenant with them. They did not pay attention to
and obey all that Moses, the LORD's servant, had commanded.

SENNACHERIB INVADES JUDAH

13 In the fourteenth year of King Hezekiah's reign, King Sennacherib of Assyria marched up against all the fortified cities
of Judah and captured them. 14 King Hezekiah of Judah sent
this message to the king of Assyria, who was at Lachish, "I have
violated our treaty. If you leave, I will do whatever you demand."
So the king of Assyria demanded that King Hezekiah of Judah
pay 300 talents of silver and 30 talents of gold. 15 Hezekiah gave
him all the silver in the LORD's temple and in the treasuries of
the royal palace. 16 At that time King Hezekiah of Judah stripped

the metal overlays from the doors of the LORD's temple and from the posts that he had plated and gave them to the king of Assyria.

17The king of Assyria sent his commanding general, the chief eunuch, and the chief adviser from Lachish to King Hezekiah in Jerusalem, along with a large army. They went up and arrived at Jerusalem. They went and stood at the conduit of the upper pool which is located on the road to the field where they wash and dry cloth. 18They summoned the king, so Eliakim son of Hilkiah, the palace supervisor, accompanied by Shebna, the scribe, and Joah son of Asaph, the secretary, went out to meet them.

19The chief adviser said to them, "Tell Hezekiah: 'This is what the great king, the king of Assyria, says: "What is your source of confidence? 20Your claim to have a strategy and military strength is just empty talk. In whom are you trusting that you would dare to rebel against me? 21Now look, you must be trusting in Egypt, that splintered reed staff. If a man leans for support on it, it punctures his hand and wounds him. That is what Pharaoh king of Egypt does to all who trust in him. 22Perhaps you will tell me, 'We are trusting in the LORD our God.' But Hezekiah is the one who eliminated his high places and altars and then told the people of Judah and Jerusalem, 'You must worship at this altar in Jerusalem.' 23Now make a deal with my master the king of Assyria, and I will give you 2,000 horses, provided you can find enough riders for them. 24Certainly you will not refuse one of my master's minor officials and trust in Egypt for chariots and horsemen. 25Furthermore it was by the command of the LORD that I marched up against this place to destroy it. The LORD told me, 'March up against this land and destroy it.'"'"

26Eliakim son of Hilkiah, Shebna, and Joah said to the chief adviser, "Speak to your servants in Aramaic, for we understand it. Don't speak with us in the Judahite dialect in the hearing of the people who are on the wall." 27But the chief adviser said to them, "My master did not send me to speak these words only to your master and to you. His message is also for the men who sit on the wall, for they will eat their own excrement and drink their own urine along with you."

28The chief adviser then stood there and called out loudly in the Judahite dialect, "Listen to the message of the great king, the king of Assyria. 29This is what the king says: 'Don't let Hezekiah mislead you, for he is not able to rescue you from my hand! 30Don't let Hezekiah talk you into trusting in the LORD when he says, "The LORD will certainly rescue us; this city will not be handed over to the king of Assyria." 31Don't listen to Hezekiah!' For this is what the king of Assyria says, 'Send me a token of your submission and surrender to me. Then each of you may eat from his own vine and fig tree and drink water from his own cistern, 32until I come and take you to a land just like your own—a land of grain and new wine, a land of bread and vineyards, a land of olive oil and honey. Then you will live and not die. Don't listen to Hezekiah, for he is misleading you when he says, "The LORD will rescue us." 33Have any of the gods of the nations actually rescued his land from the power of the king of Assyria? 34Where are the gods of Hamath and Arpad? Where are the gods of Sepharvaim, Hena, and Ivvah? Indeed, did any gods rescue Samaria from my power? 35Who among all the gods of the lands has rescued their lands from my power? So how can the LORD rescue Jerusalem from my power?'"

18:17–37 We see how Sennacherib talked when he came to besiege Jerusalem. His chief adviser stated, *Do not think that God must help you, for he has sent me here.* Here was Sennacherib, who was notoriously fighting against God, and still his chief adviser did not fail to boast that God sent him there. That is how the wicked always falsify the name of God and harden themselves in order to give themselves license to do all the more evil—as if God must excuse them, or as though he were constrained to take part of their guilt on himself. When we see that let us not be surprised, seeing that it has always been this way.

JOHN CALVIN (1509–1564)
COMPLETE COMMENTARY ON THE BIBLE

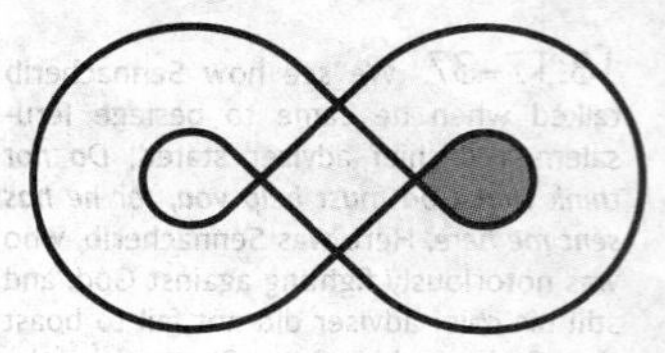

THE ATHANASIAN CREED (LATE 400s TO EARLY 500s)

WHILE THE ORIGIN of the Athanasian Creed is unknown, its name implies that it was authored by Athanasius of Alexandria, though it first appeared a century after his death. In three parts this creed addresses the doctrine of the Trinity and the nature of Christ and finally issues a warning of condemnation for those who reject the tenets of biblical faith summarized in this creed. Here is a summary selection from the creed.

WHOEVER DESIRES to be saved should above all hold to the catholic faith. Anyone who does not keep it whole and unbroken will doubtless perish eternally. Now this is the catholic faith: that we worship one God in Trinity and the Trinity in unity, neither blending their persons nor dividing their essence. For the person of the Father is a distinct person, the person of the Son is another, and that of the Holy Spirit still another. But the divinity of the Father, Son, and Holy Spirit is one, their glory equal, their majesty coeternal. What quality the Father has, the Son has, and the Holy Spirit has . . . Thus the Father is God, the Son is God, the Holy Spirit is God. Yet there are not three gods; there is but one God . . . Just as Christian truth compels us to confess each person individually as both God and Lord, so catholic religion forbids us to say that there are three gods or lords . . .

NOTHING IN this Trinity is before or after, nothing is greater or smaller; in their entirety the three persons are coeternal and coequal with each other. We must worship their Trinity in their unity and their unity in their Trinity. Anyone then who desires to be saved should think thus about the Trinity.

BUT IT is necessary for eternal salvation that one also believe in the incarnation of our Lord Jesus Christ faithfully. Now this is the true faith: that we believe and confess that our Lord Jesus Christ, God's Son, is both God and human, equally . . . Although he is God and human, yet Christ is not two but one. He is one, however, not by his divinity being turned into flesh, but by God's taking humanity to himself . . .

For just as one human is both rational soul and flesh, so too the one Christ is both God and human.

HE SUFFERED for our salvation; he descended to hell; he arose from the dead; he ascended to heaven; he is seated at the Father's right hand; from there he will come to judge the living and the dead. At his coming all people will arise bodily and give an accounting of their own deeds. Those who have done good will enter eternal life, and those who have done evil will enter eternal fire. This is the catholic faith: one cannot be saved without believing it firmly and faithfully.

36The people were silent and did not respond, for the king had
ordered, "Don't respond to him."
37Eliakim son of Hilkiah, the palace supervisor, accompanied
by Shebna the scribe and Joah son of Asaph, the secretary, went
to Hezekiah with their clothes torn and reported to him what
19 the chief adviser had said. 1When King Hezekiah heard
this, he tore his clothes, put on sackcloth, and went to the
LORD's temple. 2He sent Eliakim the palace supervisor, Shebna
the scribe, and the leading priests, clothed in sackcloth, to the
prophet Isaiah son of Amoz. 3They told him, "This is what Hezekiah says: 'This is a day of distress, insults, and humiliation, as
when a baby is ready to leave the birth canal, but the mother
lacks the strength to push it through. 4Perhaps the LORD your
God will hear all these things the chief adviser has spoken on
behalf of his master, the king of Assyria, who sent him to taunt
the living God. When the LORD your God hears, perhaps he will
punish him for the things he has said. So pray for this remnant
that remains.'"
5When King Hezekiah's servants came to Isaiah, 6Isaiah said
to them, "Tell your master this: 'This is what the LORD has said:
"Don't be afraid because of the things you have heard, because
the Assyrian king's officers have insulted me. 7Look, I will take
control of his mind; he will receive a report and return to his
own land. I will cut him down with a sword in his own land."'"
8When the chief adviser heard the king of Assyria had departed from Lachish, he left and went to Libnah, where the king was
campaigning. 9The king heard that King Tirhakah of Ethiopia
was marching out to fight him. He again sent messengers to
Hezekiah, ordering them: 10"Tell King Hezekiah of Judah this:
'Don't let your God in whom you trust mislead you when he
says, "Jerusalem will not be handed over to the king of Assyria." 11Certainly you have heard how the kings of Assyria have
annihilated all lands. Do you really think you will be rescued?
12Were the nations whom my ancestors destroyed—the nations
of Gozan, Haran, Rezeph, and the people of Eden in Telassar—
rescued by their gods? 13Where are the king of Hamath, the king
of Arpad, and the kings of Lair, Sepharvaim, Hena, and Ivvah?'"
14Hezekiah took the letter from the messengers and read it.
Then Hezekiah went up to the LORD's temple and spread it out

19:1–19 The example of Hezekiah testifies to the fact that God is near to those whose hearts are troubled and saves those of humble spirit. God consoles those who are caught up in the highest anguish so that the voice of the prophet not only promises freedom to the church but also denounces the destruction of blasphemous tyrants. It is as if the prophet then says, *Do not fear the foolish and baseless words of the tyrant. For because his speech is foolish, I will prove his results to also be foolish. I will strike such fear in him that he will not attack anyone. Thus I will restrain him from being able to make any more trouble for you.*

VIKTORIN STRIGEL
(C. 1524–1569)
BOOK OF KINGS

before the LORD. 15 Hezekiah prayed before the LORD: "LORD
God of Israel, who is enthroned above the cherubim! You alone
are God over all the kingdoms of the earth. You made the sky
and the earth. 16 Pay attention, LORD, and hear! Open your eyes,
LORD, and observe! Listen to the message Sennacherib sent
and how he taunts the living God! 17 It is true, LORD, that the
kings of Assyria have destroyed the nations and their lands.
18 They have burned the gods of the nations, for they are not
really gods, but only the product of human hands manufactured
from wood and stone. That is why the Assyrians could destroy
them. 19 Now, O LORD our God, rescue us from his power, so
that all the kingdoms of the earth will know that you, LORD,
are the only God."

20 Isaiah son of Amoz sent this message to Hezekiah: "This is
what the LORD God of Israel has said: 'I have heard your prayer
concerning King Sennacherib of Assyria. 21 This is what the
LORD says about him:

"'"The virgin daughter Zion
despises you, she makes fun of you;
Daughter Jerusalem
shakes her head after you.
22 Whom have you taunted and hurled insults at?
At whom have you shouted,
and looked so arrogantly?
At the Holy One of Israel!
23 Through your messengers you taunted the Sovereign
Master,
'With my many chariots
I climbed up the high mountains,
the slopes of Lebanon.
I cut down its tall cedars
and its best evergreens.
I invaded its most remote regions,
its thickest woods.
24 I dug wells and drank
water in foreign lands.
With the soles of my feet I dried up
all the rivers of Egypt.'
25 Certainly you must have heard!
Long ago I worked it out.
In ancient times I planned it;
and now I am bringing it to pass.
The plan is this:
Fortified cities will crash
into heaps of ruins.
26 Their residents are powerless,
they are terrified and ashamed.
They are as short-lived as plants in the field,
or green vegetation.
They are as short-lived as grass on the rooftops
when it is scorched by the east wind.
27 I know where you live
and everything you do.
28 Because you rage against me,
and the uproar you create has reached my ears,
I will put my hook in your nose,
and my bridle between your lips,
and I will lead you back the way
you came."

[29]"'This will be your confirmation that I have spoken the
truth: This year you will eat what grows wild, and next year
what grows on its own from that. But in the third year you will
plant seed and harvest crops; you will plant vines and consume
their produce. [30]Those who remain in Judah will take root in
the ground and bear fruit.

[31] "'For a remnant will leave Jerusalem;
survivors will come out of Mount Zion.
The zeal of the LORD of Heaven's Armies will
accomplish this.
[32] So this is what the LORD has said about the king of
Assyria:
"He will not enter this city,
nor will he shoot an arrow here.
He will not attack it with his shield-carrying
warriors,
nor will he build siege works against it.
[33] He will go back the way he came.
He will not enter this city," says the LORD.

[34]"'I will shield this city and rescue it for the sake of my reputation and because of my promise to David my servant.'"

[35]That very night the angel of the LORD went out and killed
185,000 in the Assyrian camp. When they got up early the next
morning, there were all the corpses. [36]So King Sennacherib
of Assyria broke camp and went on his way. He went home
and stayed in Nineveh. [37]One day, as he was worshiping in the
temple of his god Nisroch, his sons Adrammelech and Sharezer
struck him down with the sword. They escaped to the land of
Ararat; his son Esarhaddon replaced him as king.

HEZEKIAH IS HEALED

20 In those days Hezekiah was stricken with a terminal illness. The prophet Isaiah son of Amoz visited him and
told him, "This is what the LORD has said, 'Give your household
instructions, for you are about to die; you will not get well.'" [2]He
turned his face to the wall and prayed to the LORD, [3]"Please,
LORD. Remember how I have served you faithfully and with
wholehearted devotion, and how I have carried out your will."
Then Hezekiah wept bitterly.

[4]Isaiah had not yet left the middle courtyard when the LORD's
message came to him, [5]"Go back and tell Hezekiah, the leader of
my people: 'This is what the LORD God of your ancestor David
has said: "I have heard your prayer; I have seen your tears. Look,
I will heal you. The day after tomorrow you will go up to the
LORD's temple. [6]I will add 15 years to your life and rescue you
and this city from the king of Assyria. I will shield this city for
the sake of my reputation and because of my promise to David
my servant."'" [7]Isaiah ordered, "Get a fig cake." So they did as he
ordered and placed it on the ulcerated sore, and he recovered.

[8]Hezekiah had said to Isaiah, "What is the confirming sign
that the LORD will heal me and that I will go up to the LORD's
temple the day after tomorrow?" [9]Isaiah replied, "This is your
sign from the LORD confirming that the LORD will do what he
has said. Do you want the shadow to move ahead 10 steps or
to go back 10 steps?" [10]Hezekiah answered, "It is easy for the
shadow to lengthen 10 steps, but not for it to go back 10 steps."
[11]Isaiah the prophet called out to the LORD, and the LORD made
the shadow go back 10 steps on the stairs of Ahaz.

20:1–11 Death and the cutting of the thread of life are just as much ordained as creation in the course of life is. For this is properly one's fate. Hence it is to be inferred that no one dies in infancy whose fate has not been determined from eternity, and that no power can cause someone to elude the end, whenever it might be, that has been assigned. The 15 years that the Lord granted to Hezekiah as an addition to his life have been put down as an addition before the establishment of the world. For what has once been arranged remains fixed forever. Hezekiah's fate therefore had been so arranged that the years should be added in this way, and only after them should Atropos really cut the thread she had only threatened to cut before.

ULRICH ZWINGLI (1484–1531)
ON THE PROVIDENCE OF GOD

MESSENGERS FROM BABYLON VISIT HEZEKIAH

[12]At that time Merodach Baladan son of Baladan, king of Babylon, sent messengers with letters and a gift to Hezekiah, for he had heard that Hezekiah was ill. [13]Hezekiah welcomed them and showed them his whole storehouse, with its silver, gold, spices, and high quality olive oil, as well as his armory and everything in his treasuries. Hezekiah showed them everything in his palace and in his whole kingdom. [14]Isaiah the prophet visited King Hezekiah and asked him, "What did these men say? Where do they come from?" Hezekiah replied, "They come from the distant land of Babylon." [15]Isaiah asked, "What have they seen in your palace?" Hezekiah replied, "They have seen everything in my palace. I showed them everything in my treasuries." [16]Isaiah said to Hezekiah, "Listen to the LORD's message, [17]'Look, a time is coming when everything in your palace and the things your ancestors have accumulated to this day will be carried away to Babylon; nothing will be left,' says the LORD. [18]'Some of your very own descendants whom you father will be taken away and will be made eunuchs in the palace of the king of Babylon.'" [19]Hezekiah said to Isaiah, "The LORD's message which you have announced is appropriate." Then he added, "At least there will be peace and stability during my lifetime."

[20]The rest of the events of Hezekiah's reign and all his accomplishments, including how he built a pool and conduit to bring water into the city, are recorded in the scroll called the Annals of the Kings of Judah. [21]Hezekiah passed away and his son Manasseh replaced him as king.

MANASSEH'S REIGN OVER JUDAH

21 Manasseh was twelve years old when he became king, and he reigned for fifty-five years in Jerusalem. His mother was Hephzibah. [2]He did evil in the sight of the LORD and committed the same horrible sins practiced by the nations whom the LORD drove out before the Israelites. [3]He rebuilt the high places that his father Hezekiah had destroyed; he set up altars for Baal and made an Asherah pole just as King Ahab of Israel had done. He bowed down to all the stars in the sky and worshiped them. [4]He built altars in the LORD's temple, about which the LORD had said, "Jerusalem will be my home." [5]In the two courtyards of the LORD's temple he built altars for all the stars in the sky. [6]He passed his son through the fire and practiced divination and omen reading. He set up a ritual pit to conjure up underworld spirits and appointed magicians to supervise it. He did a great amount of evil in the sight of the LORD, provoking him to anger. [7]He put an idol of Asherah he had made in the temple, about which the LORD had said to David and to his son Solomon, "This temple in Jerusalem, which I have chosen out of all the tribes of Israel, will be my permanent home. [8]I will not make Israel again leave the land I gave to their ancestors, provided that they carefully obey all I commanded them, the whole law my servant Moses ordered them to obey." [9]But they did not obey, and Manasseh misled them so that they sinned more than the nations whom the LORD had destroyed from before the Israelites.

[10]So the LORD announced through his servants the prophets: [11]"King Manasseh of Judah has committed horrible sins. He has sinned more than the Amorites before him and has encouraged Judah to sin by worshiping his disgusting idols. [12]So this

21:1–18 Immediately upon the death of Hezekiah, God sent an operation of delusion through Manasseh so that with debased minds the people and the king sinned in all the ways that had been handed down to them. In this they even surpassed the impiety of the Canaanites and the idolatry of the Israelites, not frightened by the judgment that they saw carried out on each of those peoples. No one was affected by or feared the law of God; they omitted no impieties. The holy city that God had chosen and the holy temple that had been consecrated for worship became nothing. The promises of God were despised. The prophets were not listened to; rather they were killed with other officials who were doubtless confessors of the truth, a remnant of those who had been consecrated to God under Hezekiah.

JOHANNES BUGENHAGEN
(1485–1558)
COMMENTARY ON SECOND KINGS

is what the LORD God of Israel has said, 'I am about to bring
disaster on Jerusalem and Judah. The news will reverberate in
the ears of those who hear about it. 13I will destroy Jerusalem
the same way I did Samaria and the dynasty of Ahab. I will wipe
Jerusalem clean, just as one wipes a plate on both sides. 14I will
abandon this last remaining tribe among my people and hand
them over to their enemies; they will be plundered and robbed
by all their enemies, 15because they have done evil in my sight
and have angered me from the time their ancestors left Egypt
right up to this very day!'"

16Furthermore Manasseh killed so many innocent people,
he stained Jerusalem with their blood from end to end, in addition to encouraging Judah to sin by doing evil in the sight
of the LORD.

17The rest of the events of Manasseh's reign and all his accomplishments, as well as the sinful acts he committed, are
recorded in the scroll called the Annals of the Kings of Judah.
18Manasseh passed away and was buried in his palace garden,
the garden of Uzzah, and his son Amon replaced him as king.

AMON'S REIGN OVER JUDAH

19Amon was twenty-two years old when he became king, and he
reigned for two years in Jerusalem. His mother was Meshulle-
meth, the daughter of Haruz, from Jotbah. 20He did evil in the
sight of the LORD, just as his father Manasseh had done. 21He
followed in the footsteps of his father and worshiped and bowed
down to the disgusting idols that his father had worshiped. 22He
abandoned the LORD, God of his ancestors, and did not follow
the LORD's instructions. 23Amon's servants conspired against
him and killed the king in his palace. 24The people of the land
executed all those who had conspired against King Amon, and
they made his son Josiah king in his place.

25The rest of Amon's accomplishments are recorded in the
scroll called the Annals of the Kings of Judah. 26He was buried
in his tomb in the garden of Uzzah, and his son Josiah replaced
him as king.

JOSIAH REPENTS

22 Josiah was eight years old when he became king, and he
reigned for thirty-one years in Jerusalem. His mother was
Jedidah, daughter of Adaiah, from Bozkath. 2He did what the
LORD approved and followed in his ancestor David's footsteps;
he did not deviate to the right or the left.

3In the eighteenth year of King Josiah's reign, the king sent
the scribe Shaphan son of Azaliah, son of Meshullam, to the
LORD's temple with these orders: 4"Go up to Hilkiah the high
priest and have him melt down the silver that has been brought
by the people to the LORD's temple and has been collected by
the guards at the door. 5Have them hand it over to the construction foremen assigned to the LORD's temple. They in
turn should pay the temple workers to repair it, 6including
craftsmen, builders, and masons, and should buy wood and
chiseled stone for the repair work. 7Do not audit the foremen
who disburse the silver, for they are honest."

8Hilkiah the high priest informed Shaphan the scribe, "I
found the scroll of the law in the LORD's temple." Hilkiah gave
the scroll to Shaphan and he read it. 9Shaphan the scribe went
to the king and reported, "Your servants melted down the silver
in the temple and handed it over to the construction foremen

22:1–20 From the example of Josiah, a pious king, other kings and leaders should learn that they must rightly establish the worship of God. And they must not break the commandments of the divine Word, turning aside to the right or to the left. Similarly, when doubt comes they must consult God through ministers of the Word who are acquainted with the will of God through the Word, and they will bring God's will to light. In the same way they must command that the buildings for the worship of God be established and that they are watched over and maintained.

JOHANNES PISCATOR
(1546–1625)
COMMENTARY ON SECOND KINGS

assigned to the LORD's temple." 10Then Shaphan the scribe told
the king, "Hilkiah the priest has given me a scroll." Shaphan read
it out loud before the king. 11When the king heard the words of
the law scroll, he tore his clothes. 12The king ordered Hilkiah
the priest, Ahikam son of Shaphan, Achbor son of Micaiah,
Shaphan the scribe, and Asaiah the king's servant, 13"Go, seek
an oracle from the LORD for me and the people—for all Judah.
Find out about the words of this scroll that has been discovered.
For the LORD's great fury has been ignited against us, because
our ancestors have not obeyed the words of this scroll by doing
all that it instructs us to do."

14So Hilkiah the priest, Ahikam, Achbor, Shaphan, and Asaiah went to Huldah the prophetess, the wife of Shullam son
of Tikvah, the son of Harhas, the supervisor of the wardrobe.
(She lived in Jerusalem in the Mishneh district.) They stated
their business, 15and she said to them: "This is what the LORD
God of Israel has said: 'Say this to the man who sent you to me:
16"This is what the LORD has said: 'I am about to bring disaster
on this place and its residents, all the things in the scroll that
the king of Judah has read. 17This will happen because they have
abandoned me and offered sacrifices to other gods, angering me
with all the idols they have made. My anger will ignite against
this place and will not be extinguished!'" 18Say this to the king
of Judah, who sent you to seek an oracle from the LORD: "This
is what the LORD God of Israel has said concerning the words
you have heard: 19'You displayed a sensitive spirit and humbled
yourself before the LORD when you heard how I intended to
make this place and its residents into an appalling example of
an accursed people. You tore your clothes and wept before me,
and I have heard you,' says the LORD. 20'Therefore I will allow
you to die and be buried in peace. You will not have to witness
all the disaster I will bring on this place.'"'" Then they reported
back to the king.

THE KING INSTITUTES RELIGIOUS REFORM

23 The king summoned all the leaders of Judah and Jerusalem. 2The king went up to the LORD's temple, accompanied by all the people of Judah, all the residents of Jerusalem,
the priests, and the prophets. All the people were there, from
the youngest to the oldest. He read aloud all the words of the
scroll of the covenant that had been discovered in the LORD's
temple. 3The king stood by the pillar and renewed the covenant
before the LORD, agreeing to follow the LORD and to obey his
commandments, laws, and rules with all his heart and being, by
carrying out the terms of this covenant recorded on this scroll.
All the people agreed to keep the covenant.

4The king ordered Hilkiah the high priest, the high-ranking
priests, and the guards to bring out of the LORD's temple all the
items that were used in the worship of Baal, Asherah, and all the
stars of the sky. The king burned them outside of Jerusalem in
the terraces of Kidron, and carried their ashes to Bethel. 5He
eliminated the pagan priests whom the kings of Judah had
appointed to offer sacrifices on the high places in the cities of
Judah and in the area right around Jerusalem. (They offered
sacrifices to Baal, the sun god, the moon god, the constellations,
and all the stars in the sky.) 6He removed the Asherah pole
from the LORD's temple and took it outside Jerusalem to the
Kidron Valley, where he burned it. He smashed it to dust and
then threw the dust in the public graveyard. 7He tore down the

23:1–27 Observe what kind of faith Josiah had. He heard the Word of the Lord and believed it. He rent his clothes, inquired of the Lord, and renewed the covenant. He was strong in the Lord and acted valiantly in all his doings. For he believed and trusted God with all his strength, and with earnest zeal he tore down all that his forefathers and the former kings out of their own imaginations and choice had introduced and established as holy service. He destroyed all that was opposed to and contrary to the law of God. He kept the Passover of the Lord in such a glorious manner as no judge or king had kept it before. He also swept away all soothsayers and necromancers, all images and idols, and all the abominations that were seen in the land of Judea and Jerusalem, in order that they might perform the words of the Lord that were written in the book that Hilkiah, the high priest, had found in the house of the Lord. There was no king like him who turned to the Lord with all his heart.

MENNO SIMONS **(1496–1561)**
TRUE CHRISTIAN FAITH

quarters of the male cultic prostitutes in the LORD's temple,
where women were weaving shrines for Asherah.
8He brought all the priests from the cities of Judah and ruined the high places where the priests had offered sacrifices,
from Geba to Beer Sheba. He tore down the high place of the
goat idols situated at the entrance of the gate of Joshua, the
city official, on the left side of the city gate. 9(Now the priests
of the high places did not go up to the altar of the LORD in
Jerusalem, but they did eat unleavened cakes among their
fellow priests.) 10The king ruined Topheth in the Valley of Ben
Hinnom so that no one could pass his son or his daughter
through the fire to Molech. 11He removed from the entrance
to the LORD's temple the statues of horses that the kings of
Judah had placed there in honor of the sun god. (They were
kept near the room of Nathan Melech the eunuch, which was
situated among the courtyards.) He burned up the chariots
devoted to the sun god. 12The king tore down the altars the
kings of Judah had set up on the roof of Ahaz's upper room, as
well as the altars Manasseh had set up in the two courtyards
of the LORD's temple. He crushed them and threw the dust
in the Kidron Valley. 13The king ruined the high places east
of Jerusalem, south of the Mount of Destruction, that King
Solomon of Israel had built for the detestable Sidonian goddess Astarte, the detestable Moabite god Chemosh, and the
horrible Ammonite god Milcom. 14He smashed the sacred
pillars to bits, cut down the Asherah poles, and filled those
shrines with human bones.
15He also tore down the altar in Bethel at the high place
made by Jeroboam son of Nebat, who encouraged Israel to sin.
He burned all the combustible items at that high place and
crushed them to dust, including the Asherah pole. 16When
Josiah turned around, he saw the tombs there on the hill. So
he ordered the bones from the tombs to be brought; he burned
them on the altar and defiled it, just as in the LORD's message
that was announced by the prophet while Jeroboam stood by
the altar during a festival. Then the king turned and saw the
grave of the prophet who had foretold this. 17He asked, "What
is this grave marker I see?" The men from the city replied, "It's
the grave of the prophet who came from Judah and foretold
these very things you have done to the altar of Bethel." 18The
king said, "Leave it alone! No one must touch his bones." So they
left his bones undisturbed, as well as the bones of the Israelite
prophet buried beside him.
19Josiah also removed all the shrines on the high places in
the cities of Samaria. The kings of Israel had made them and
angered the LORD. He did to them what he had done to the
high place in Bethel. 20He sacrificed all the priests of the high
places on the altars located there, and burned human bones
on them. Then he returned to Jerusalem.
21The king ordered all the people, "Observe the Passover
of the LORD your God, as prescribed in this scroll of the covenant." 22He issued this edict because a Passover like this had
not been observed since the days of the judges who led Israel;
it was neglected for the entire period of the kings of Israel and
Judah. 23But in the eighteenth year of King Josiah's reign, such
a Passover of the LORD was observed in Jerusalem.
24Josiah also got rid of the ritual pits used to conjure up spirits, the magicians, personal idols, disgusting images, and all the
detestable idols that had appeared in the land of Judah and

in Jerusalem. In this way he carried out the terms of the law
recorded on the scroll that Hilkiah the priest had discovered
in the LORD's temple. [25]No king before or after repented before
the LORD as he did, with his whole heart, soul, and being in
accordance with the whole law of Moses.
[26]Yet the LORD's great anger against Judah did not subside; he
was still infuriated by all the things Manasseh had done. [27]The
LORD announced, "I will also spurn Judah, just as I spurned
Israel. I will reject this city that I chose—both Jerusalem and
the temple, about which I said, 'I will live there.'"
[28]The rest of the events of Josiah's reign and all his accomplishments are recorded in the scroll called the Annals of the
Kings of Judah. [29]During Josiah's reign Pharaoh Necho king of
Egypt marched toward the Euphrates River to help the king of
Assyria. King Josiah marched out to fight him, but Necho killed
him at Megiddo when he saw him. [30]His servants transported
his dead body from Megiddo in a chariot and brought it to
Jerusalem, where they buried him in his tomb. The people of
the land took Josiah's son Jehoahaz, poured olive oil on his head,
and made him king in his father's place.

JEHOAHAZ'S REIGN OVER JUDAH

[31]Jehoahaz was twenty-three years old when he became king,
and he reigned three months in Jerusalem. His mother was
Hamutal the daughter of Jeremiah, from Libnah. [32]He did evil
in the sight of the LORD as his ancestors had done. [33]Pharaoh
Necho imprisoned him in Riblah in the land of Hamath and
prevented him from ruling in Jerusalem. He imposed on the
land a special tax of 100 talents of silver and a talent of gold.
[34]Pharaoh Necho made Josiah's son Eliakim king in Josiah's
place, and changed his name to Jehoiakim. He took Jehoahaz
to Egypt, where he died. [35]Jehoiakim paid Pharaoh the required
amount of silver and gold, but to meet Pharaoh's demands Jehoiakim had to tax the land. He collected an assessed amount
from each man among the people of the land in order to pay
Pharaoh Necho.

JEHOIAKIM'S REIGN OVER JUDAH

[36]Jehoiakim was twenty-five years old when he became king,
and he reigned for eleven years in Jerusalem. His mother was
Zebidah the daughter of Pedaiah, from Rumah. [37]He did evil in
the sight of the LORD as his ancestors had done.

24 During Jehoiakim's reign, King Nebuchadnezzar of Babylon attacked. Jehoiakim was his subject for three years,
but then he rebelled against him. [2]The LORD sent against him
Babylonian, Syrian, Moabite, and Ammonite raiding bands; he
sent them to destroy Judah, just as in the LORD's message that
he had announced through his servants the prophets. [3]Just as
the LORD had announced, he rejected Judah because of all the
sins that Manasseh had committed. [4]Because he killed innocent
people and stained Jerusalem with their blood, the LORD was
unwilling to forgive them.
[5]The rest of the events of Jehoiakim's reign and all his accomplishments, are recorded in the scroll called the Annals of the
Kings of Judah. [6]He passed away and his son Jehoiachin replaced
him as king. [7]The king of Egypt did not march out from his land
again, for the king of Babylon conquered all the territory that
the king of Egypt had formerly controlled between the Stream
of Egypt and the Euphrates River.

24:1–10 The adversary has no power against us unless God has previously permitted it in order that all our fear and devotion and obedience may be turned to God, since in temptations nothing evil is permitted unless the power is granted by him. Scripture proves this when it says, "The generals of King Nebuchadnezzar of Babylon marched to Jerusalem and besieged the city." Moreover, power is given to evil against us according to our sins; as it is written, "Who handed Jacob over to the robber? Who handed Israel over to the looters? Was it not the LORD, against whom we sinned? They refused to follow his commands . . . So he poured out his fierce anger on them" (Isa 42:24–25).

CYPRIAN OF CARTHAGE
(C. 210–258)
THE LORD'S PRAYER

JEHOIACHIN'S REIGN OVER JUDAH

8 Jehoiachin was eighteen years old when he became king, and he
reigned three months in Jerusalem. His mother was Nehushta
the daughter of Elnathan, from Jerusalem. 9 He did evil in the
sight of the LORD as his ancestors had done.
10 At that time the generals of King Nebuchadnezzar of Babylon marched to Jerusalem and besieged the city. 11 King Nebuchadnezzar of Babylon came to the city while his generals were
besieging it. 12 King Jehoiachin of Judah, along with his mother,
his servants, his officials, and his eunuchs surrendered to the
king of Babylon. The king of Babylon, in the eighth year of his
reign, took Jehoiachin prisoner. 13 Nebuchadnezzar took from
there all the riches in the treasuries of the LORD's temple and
of the royal palace. He removed all the gold items that King
Solomon of Israel had made for the LORD's temple, just as the
LORD had warned. 14 He deported all the residents of Jerusalem,
including all the officials and all the soldiers (10,000 people
in all). This included all the craftsmen and those who worked
with metal. No one was left except for the poorest among the
people of the land. 15 He deported Jehoiachin from Jerusalem to
Babylon, along with the king's mother and wives, his eunuchs,
and the high-ranking officials of the land. 16 The king of Babylon
deported to Babylon all the soldiers (there were 7,000), as well
as 1,000 craftsmen and metal workers. This included all the best
warriors. 17 The king of Babylon made Mattaniah, Jehoiachin's
uncle, king in Jehoiachin's place. He renamed him Zedekiah.

ZEDEKIAH'S REIGN OVER JUDAH

18 Zedekiah was twenty-one years old when he became king,
and he ruled for eleven years in Jerusalem. His mother was
Hamutal, the daughter of Jeremiah, from Libnah. 19 He did evil
in the sight of the LORD, as Jehoiakim had done.
20 What follows is a record of what happened to Jerusalem and
Judah because of the LORD's anger; he finally threw them out
of his presence. Zedekiah rebelled against the king of Babylon.

25 1 So King Nebuchadnezzar of Babylon came against Jerusalem with his whole army and set up camp outside it.
They built siege ramps all around it. He arrived on the tenth
day of the tenth month in the ninth year of Zedekiah's reign.
2 The city remained under siege until King Zedekiah's eleventh year. 3 By the ninth day of the fourth month the famine in
the city was so severe the residents had no food. 4 The enemy
broke through the city walls, and all the soldiers tried to escape.
They left the city during the night. They went through the gate
between the two walls, which is near the king's garden. (The
Babylonians were all around the city.) Then they headed for
the rift valley. 5 But the Babylonian army chased after the king.
They caught up with him in the rift valley plains of Jericho,
and his entire army deserted him. 6 They captured the king
and brought him up to the king of Babylon at Riblah, where
he passed sentence on him. 7 Zedekiah's sons were executed
while Zedekiah was forced to watch. The king of Babylon then
had Zedekiah's eyes put out, bound him in bronze chains, and
carried him off to Babylon.

NEBUCHADNEZZAR DESTROYS JERUSALEM

8 On the seventh day of the fifth month, in the nineteenth year
of King Nebuchadnezzar of Babylon, Nebuzaradan, the captain
of the royal guard, who served the king of Babylon, arrived in

25:1–21 The entire history of the fall of Jerusalem is full of many lessons. The wrath of God is seen in the punishment of the ungodly. On the other hand mercy is also revealed because amid such calamity God wonderfully preserved a remnant of the church. For King Zedekiah commanded that Jeremiah be spared and permitted him to stay in the land with a remnant of the people (see Jer 38–39). This example agrees with the saying, "The LORD's loyal kindness never ceases; his compassions never end" (Lam 3:22). But we ourselves see this time of the ruin of the empire and other calamities. Therefore we should recognize God's wrath and pray that we be turned back to God. And we should hope that punishment might be alleviated and the church be preserved.

VIKTORIN STRIGEL
(C. 1524–1569)
BOOK OF KINGS

Jerusalem. [9]He burned down the LORD's temple, the royal palace, and all the houses in Jerusalem, including every large house. [10]The whole Babylonian army that came with the captain of the royal guard tore down the walls that surrounded Jerusalem. [11]Nebuzaradan, the captain of the royal guard, deported the rest of the people who were left in the city, those who had deserted to the king of Babylon, and the rest of the craftsmen. [12]But he left behind some of the poor of the land and gave them fields and vineyards.

[13]The Babylonians broke the two bronze pillars in the LORD's temple, as well as the movable stands and the big bronze basin called "The Sea." They took the bronze to Babylon. [14]They also took the pots, shovels, trimming shears, pans, and all the bronze utensils used by the priests. [15]The captain of the royal guard took the golden and silver censers and basins. [16]The bronze of the items that King Solomon made for the LORD's temple—including the two pillars, the big bronze basin called "The Sea," the twelve bronze bulls under "The Sea," and the movable stands—was too heavy to be weighed. [17]Each of the pillars was about 27 feet high. The bronze top of one pillar was about 4½ feet high and had bronze latticework and pomegranate-shaped ornaments all around it. The second pillar with its latticework was like it.

[18]The captain of the royal guard took Seraiah, the chief priest, and Zephaniah, the priest who was second in rank, and the three doorkeepers. [19]From the city he took a eunuch who was in charge of the soldiers, five of the king's advisers who were discovered in the city, an official army secretary who drafted citizens for military service, and 60 citizens from the people of the land who were discovered in the city. [20]Nebuzaradan, captain of the royal guard, took them and brought them to the king of Babylon at Riblah. [21]The king of Babylon ordered them to be executed at Riblah in the territory of Hamath. So Judah was deported from its land.

GEDALIAH APPOINTED GOVERNOR

[22]Now King Nebuchadnezzar of Babylon appointed Gedaliah son of Ahikam, son of Shaphan, as governor over the people whom he allowed to remain in the land of Judah. [23]All the officers of the Judahite army and their troops heard that the king of Babylon had appointed Gedaliah to govern. So they came to Gedaliah at Mizpah. The officers who came were Ishmael son of Nethaniah, Johanan son of Kareah, Seraiah son of Tanhumeth the Netophathite, and Jaazaniah son of the Maacathite. [24]Gedaliah took an oath so as to give them and their troops some assurance of safety. He said, "You don't need to be afraid to submit to the Babylonian officials. Settle down in the land and submit to the king of Babylon. Then things will go well for you." [25]But in the seventh month Ishmael son of Nethaniah, son of Elishama, who was a member of the royal family, came with 10 of his men and murdered Gedaliah, as well as the Judeans and Babylonians who were with him at Mizpah. [26]Then all the people, from the youngest to the oldest, as well as the army officers, left for Egypt, because they were afraid of what the Babylonians might do.

JEHOIACHIN IN BABYLON

[27]In the thirty-seventh year of the exile of King Jehoiachin of Judah, on the twenty-seventh day of the twelfth month, King

Evil Merodach of Babylon, in the first year of his reign, pardoned
King Jehoiachin of Judah and released him from prison. [28]He
spoke kindly to him and gave him a more prestigious position
than the other kings who were with him in Babylon. [29]Jehoia-
chin took off his prison clothes and ate daily in the king's presence for the rest of his life. [30]He was given daily provisions by
the king for the rest of his life until the day he died.

AUTHOR	AUDIENCE	DATE	PURPOSE	THEMES
Unknown; possibly Ezra	The people of Judah who had returned from exile in Babylon	Between 450 and 400 BC	This book was written to chronicle the faithfulness of God in the hopes that it would provoke God's people to seek the Lord and rest in his promises.	God's faithfulness, past and present; importance of religious leadership; promises of the Messiah; and hope for the future

The first book of Chronicles overlaps in many ways with the history 1 Samuel and the beginning of 1 Kings reveal as it tells the history of Saul, the rise of David as king over all Israel, and the exaltation of Solomon to the throne. Originally one literary work along with the second book of Chronicles, 1 Chronicles was written during the postexilic period, after King Cyrus of Persia allowed the people of Judah to return home from captivity in Babylon.

The book isn't merely a history lesson, though. The political and religious material has been arranged in such a way as to communicate a specific message. The purpose was to chronicle the faithfulness of God in the hopes that it would provoke God's people to seek the Lord and rest in his promises. The book is also an exhortation to covenant renewal, a call to live as God intended his people to live.

Within the books of Chronicles, the Reformers found the promise of Christ. Viktorin Strigel explained:

> Just as Xenophon wrote the events that were left over from the Peloponnesian War originally set forth by Thucydides, so Ezra compiled these two books of Chronicles from what was left over and lacking in the history of the kings of Judah and Israel. This first book of Chronicles contains a genealogy of Christ from Adam to David, and it chiefly touches on the things that David did in his old age in the ordering of the priests, Levites, musicians, and in preparing everything that was needed for the operation of the temple. This book also repeats the extraordinary promise of a Messiah bound to the seed of David.

One of the ways that the chronicler communicated his message was by weaving together threads from Israel's past and present. He opened the book by taking Israel back into her past. While the nation officially began with Abraham, Isaac, and Jacob, the chronicler went further to Noah and Adam, recalling the faithfulness of God as creator and sustainer. From there he recalled Israel's sons and clans and the kings of the divided kingdom. In recalling Abraham and David and their descendants, the chronicler recalled the promises God gave to them.

1 CHRONICLES

Of course, at the center of God's promises was the covenant he made with his people, which is why the Chronicler makes it central to his account. David vowed to bring back the ark of the covenant, "for we did not seek his will throughout Saul's reign" (13:3). He prepared a place for it in Jerusalem, and Israel celebrated its arrival with dancing, singing, and sacrifices. David led the priests and the people in a song of praise extoling the faithfulness of the Lord: "Remember continually his covenantal decree, the promise he made to a thousand generations—the promise he made to Abraham, the promise he made by oath to Isaac! He gave it to Jacob as a decree, to Israel as a lasting promise, saying, 'To you I will give the land of Canaan as the portion of your inheritance'" (16:15–18).

Afterward the Lord gave a promise to David that the communion of saints have recognized as the messianic promise of Christ: "I will raise up your descendant, one of your own sons, to succeed you, and I will establish his kingdom . . . I will become his father and he will become my son. I will never withhold my loyal love from him, as I withheld it from the one who ruled before you. I will put him in permanent charge of my house and my kingdom; his dynasty will be permanent" (17:11–14). As Martin Luther explained: "This house, to be built by Messiah, the Son of David and of God . . . is the holy Christian church, which extends to the ends of the earth. Furthermore it is an everlasting house, a house that will endure and live forever, a house in which God remains and lives and keeps house forever."

This chronicling of the Lord's past promises was meant to give the Israelites hope for the future as they left their captivity and regained Jerusalem in much the same way that Deuteronomy functioned for the generation of Israelites waiting to enter the promised land. Before he died, David assembled the leaders of Israel and reminded them of the nation's history and its obligations to the Lord, saying: "The Lord your God is with you! He has made you secure on every side, for he handed over to me the inhabitants of the region and the region is subdued before the Lord and his people. Now seek the Lord your God wholeheartedly and with your entire being!" (22:18–19). May we too remember the faithfulness of the Lord in order to be strengthened in our own obedience and hope.

1:1–42 In the time of Peleg arose the dispersion of nations. Now these nations were 72, corresponding with the number of Abraham's children. And the reason for our particularity is our desire to manifest to those who are of a studious disposition the love we cherish toward the divinity, and the indubitable knowledge respecting the truth, which in the course of our labors we have acquired possession of. Arphaxad was a son of Shem and a grandson of Noah. And in Noah's time there occurred a flood throughout the entire world that neither Egyptians, nor Chaldeans, nor Greeks recollect. This Noah, inasmuch as he was a most religious and God-loving man, with wife and children and the three wives of these, escaped the flood that ensued. It is then possible for those who are disposed to investigate the subject industriously to perceive how clearly has been demonstrated the existence of a nation of worshipers of the true God, more ancient than all the Chaldeans, Egyptians, and Greeks.

HIPPOLYTUS OF ROME
(C. 170–C. 235)
THE REFUTATION OF ALL HERESIES

ADAM'S DESCENDANTS

1 Adam, Seth, Enosh, 2Kenan, Mahalalel, Jered, 3Enoch, Methuselah, Lamech, 4Noah, Shem, Ham, and Japheth.

JAPHETH'S DESCENDANTS

5The sons of Japheth: Gomer, Magog, Madai, Javan, Tubal,
Meshech, and Tiras.
6The sons of Gomer: Ashkenaz, Riphath, and Togarmah.
7The sons of Javan: Elishah, Tarshish, the Kittites, and the
Rodanites.

HAM'S DESCENDANTS

8The sons of Ham: Cush, Mizraim, Put, and Canaan.
9The sons of Cush: Seba, Havilah, Sabta, Raamah, and Sabteca.
The sons of Raamah: Sheba and Dedan.
10Cush was the father of Nimrod, who established himself
as a mighty warrior on earth.
11Mizraim was the father of the Ludites, Anamites, Leha-
bites, Naphtuhites, 12Pathrusites, Casluhites (from whom the
Philistines descended), and the Caphtorites.
13Canaan was the father of Sidon—his firstborn—and Heth,
14as well as the Jebusites, Amorites, Girgashites, 15Hivites,
Arkites, Sinites, 16Arvadites, Zemarites, and Hamathites.

SHEM'S DESCENDANTS

17The sons of Shem: Elam, Asshur, Arphaxad, Lud, and Aram.
The sons of Aram: Uz, Hul, Gether, and Meshech.
18Arphaxad was the father of Shelah, and Shelah was the
father of Eber. 19Two sons were born to Eber: The first was
named Peleg, for during his lifetime the earth was divided; his
brother's name was Joktan.
20Joktan was the father of Almodad, Sheleph, Hazarmaveth,
Jerah, 21Hadoram, Uzal, Diklah, 22Ebal, Abimael, Sheba, 23Ophir,
Havilah, and Jobab. All these were the sons of Joktan.
24Shem, Arphaxad, Shelah, 25Eber, Peleg, Reu, 26Serug, Nahor,
Terah, 27Abram (that is, Abraham).
28The sons of Abraham: Isaac and Ishmael.
29These were their descendants:

ISHMAEL'S DESCENDANTS

Ishmael's firstborn son was Nebaioth; the others were Kedar,
Adbeel, Mibsam, 30Mishma, Dumah, Massa, Hadad, Tema, 31Je-
tur, Naphish, and Kedemah. These were the sons of Ishmael.

KETURAH'S DESCENDANTS

32The sons to whom Keturah, Abraham's concubine, gave birth:
Zimran, Jokshan, Medan, Midian, Ishbak, Shuah.
The sons of Jokshan: Sheba and Dedan.
33The sons of Midian: Ephah, Epher, Hanoch, Abida, and Eldaah. All these were the sons of Keturah.

ISAAC'S DESCENDANTS

34Abraham was the father of Isaac. The sons of Isaac: Esau and Israel.

ESAU'S DESCENDANTS

35The sons of Esau: Eliphaz, Reuel, Jeush, Jalam, and Korah.
36The sons of Eliphaz: Teman, Omar, Zephi, Gatam, Kenaz,
and (by Timna) Amalek.
37The sons of Reuel: Nahath, Zerah, Shammah, and Mizzah.

THE DESCENDANTS OF SEIR

38 The sons of Seir: Lotan, Shobal, Zibeon, Anah, Dishon, Ezer, and Dishan.

39 The sons of Lotan: Hori and Homam. (Timna was Lotan's sister.)

40 The sons of Shobal: Alyan, Manahath, Ebal, Shephi, and Onam.

The sons of Zibeon: Aiah and Anah.

41 The son of Anah: Dishon.

The sons of Dishon: Hamran, Eshban, Ithran, and Keran.

42 The sons of Ezer: Bilhan, Zaavan, Jaakan.

The sons of Dishan: Uz and Aran.

KINGS OF EDOM

43 These were the kings who reigned in the land of Edom before any king ruled over the Israelites: Bela son of Beor; the name of his city was Dinhabah.

44 When Bela died, Jobab son of Zerah from Bozrah succeeded him.

45 When Jobab died, Husham from the land of the Temanites succeeded him.

46 When Husham died, Hadad son of Bedad succeeded him. He struck down the Midianites in the plains of Moab; the name of his city was Avith.

47 When Hadad died, Samlah from Masrekah succeeded him.

48 When Samlah died, Shaul from Rehoboth on the River succeeded him.

49 When Shaul died, Baal Hanan son of Achbor succeeded him.

50 When Baal Hanan died, Hadad succeeded him; the name of his city was Pai. His wife was Mehetabel, daughter of Matred, daughter of Me-Zahab.

51 Hadad died.

TRIBAL CHIEFS OF EDOM

The tribal chiefs of Edom were: Timna, Alvah, Jetheth, 52 Oholibamah, Elah, Pinon, 53 Kenaz, Teman, Mibzar, 54 Magdiel, and Iram. These were the tribal chiefs of Edom.

ISRAEL'S DESCENDANTS

2 These were the sons of Israel: Reuben, Simeon, Levi, and Judah; Issachar and Zebulun;

2 Dan, Joseph, and Benjamin;

Naphtali, Gad, and Asher.

JUDAH'S DESCENDANTS

3 The sons of Judah: Er, Onan, and Shelah. These three were born to him by Bathshua, a Canaanite woman. Er, Judah's firstborn, displeased the LORD, so the LORD killed him.

4 Tamar, Judah's daughter-in-law, bore to him Perez and Zerah. Judah had five sons in all.

5 The sons of Perez: Hezron and Hamul.

6 The sons of Zerah: Zimri, Ethan, Heman, Kalkol, Dara—five in all.

7 The son of Carmi: Achan, who brought the disaster on Israel when he stole what was devoted to God.

8 The son of Ethan: Azariah.

9 The sons born to Hezron: Jerahmeel, Ram, and Caleb.

2:1–17 Just as the succession from Adam to Jacob, who was also called Israel, is recounted in the first chapter, so this chapter is concerned with that succession from Jacob to David. God wished that from this succession we would know that God willed for the Messiah to be born from this stock, which we would hope and expect. To see this succession is most pleasing, since the church after the flood was governed and survived. For the mystery of all the scriptures is Christ and the church.

VIKTORIN STRIGEL
(C. 1524–1569)
BOOK OF CHRONICLES

RAM'S DESCENDANTS

10 Ram was the father of Amminadab, and Amminadab was the
father of Nahshon, the tribal chief of Judah. 11 Nahshon was the
father of Salma, and Salma was the father of Boaz. 12 Boaz was
the father of Obed, and Obed was the father of Jesse.
13 Jesse was the father of Eliab, his firstborn; Abinadab was
born second, Shimea third, 14 Nethanel fourth, Raddai fifth,
15 Ozem sixth, and David seventh. 16 Their sisters were Zeruiah
and Abigail. Zeruiah's three sons were Abshai, Joab, and Asahel.
17 Abigail bore Amasa, whose father was Jether the Ishmaelite.

CALEB'S DESCENDANTS

18 Caleb son of Hezron fathered sons by his wife Azubah (also
known as Jerioth). Her sons were Jesher, Shobab, and Ardon.
19 When Azubah died, Caleb married Ephrath, who bore him Hur.
20 Hur was the father of Uri, and Uri was the father of Bezalel.
21 Later Hezron slept with the daughter of Makir, the father
of Gilead. (He had married her when he was sixty years old.)
She bore him Segub. 22 Segub was the father of Jair, who owned
twenty-three cities in the land of Gilead. 23 (Geshur and Aram
captured the towns of Jair, along with Kenath and its sixty
surrounding towns.) All these were descendants of Makir, the
father of Gilead.
24 After Hezron's death, Caleb slept with Ephrath, his father
Hezron's widow, and she bore to him Ashhur the father of Tekoa.

JERAHMEEL'S DESCENDANTS

25 The sons of Jerahmeel, Hezron's firstborn, were Ram, the
firstborn, Bunah, Oren, Ozem, and Ahijah. 26 Jerahmeel had
another wife named Atarah; she was Onam's mother.
27 The sons of Ram, Jerahmeel's firstborn, were Maaz, Jamin,
and Eker.
28 The sons of Onam were Shammai and Jada.
The sons of Shammai: Nadab and Abishur.
29 Abishur's wife was Abihail, who bore him Ahban and Molid.
30 The sons of Nadab: Seled and Appaim. (Seled died without
having sons.)
31 The son of Appaim: Ishi.
The son of Ishi: Sheshan.
The son of Sheshan: Ahlai.
32 The sons of Jada, Shammai's brother: Jether and Jonathan.
(Jether died without having sons.)
33 The sons of Jonathan: Peleth and Zaza.
These were the descendants of Jerahmeel.
34 Sheshan had no sons, only daughters. Sheshan had an Egyptian servant named Jarha. 35 Sheshan gave his daughter to his
servant Jarha as a wife; she bore him Attai.
36 Attai was the father of Nathan, and Nathan was the father
of Zabad. 37 Zabad was the father of Ephlal, and Ephlal was the
father of Obed. 38 Obed was the father of Jehu, and Jehu was the
father of Azariah. 39 Azariah was the father of Helez, and Helez
was the father of Eleasah. 40 Eleasah was the father of Sismai,
and Sismai was the father of Shallum. 41 Shallum was the father
of Jekamiah, and Jekamiah was the father of Elishama.

MORE OF CALEB'S DESCENDANTS

42 The sons of Caleb, Jerahmeel's brother: his firstborn Mesha,
the father of Ziph, and his second son Mareshah, the father
of Hebron.

AMBROSE OF MILAN:

FATHER OF CHURCH HYMNODY

c. 339–397

Out of northern Italy arose a church father who made important contributions to ecclesial and devotional life and became known as one of the four great Doctors of the Church in the West (along with Gregory the Great, Augustine, and Jerome). Ambrose was born in 339 and raised by Christian parents. Initially he practiced law and became governor of his childhood region. But after the local Arian bishop died in 374, Ambrose's work in moderating between two sides clamoring for control led to the town's insistence that he be their bishop.

During the course of his ministry as the bishop of Milan, Ambrose wrote several volumes of sermons and treatises on the Christian faith. He was highly devoted to ministering to and caring for the poor, believing it "better to preserve for the Lord souls rather than gold." He venerated Mary, one of the first such Christian leaders to do so, in light of her example of virtue and chastity. And he shocked the world by boldly confronting the emperor Theodosius after Theodosius punished a rebellious town by indiscriminately killing 7,000 civilians. Ambrose publicly refused the emperor entry to his church and communion and eventually brought him to repentance and restoration. Ambrose even baptized the great Augustine, who came to faith in part through Ambrose's preaching.

Ambrose is especially notable for his commitment to bringing hymnody into the life of the Western church. The arts of singing and composing hymns were important developments in the early era of the church, with Ignatius of Antioch introducing Greek antiphonal chants—a Psalm-based refrain often with a call-and-response element. Ambrose introduced this type of hymn singing to his church, and his collection of hymns remain in use by the Roman Catholic Church to this day. According to Augustine, Ambrose was the first to incorporate rhymes and meter into his songs and worship, utilizing the cadences from common soldiers' marches to assist people with singing the hymns. His hymnody was deeply theological, reflecting his desire to combat heresy, particularly Arianism, by centering his flock's thinking upon sound doctrine.

Ambrose's musical innovation was rooted in the doctrines of the church and utilized the popular styles of his time, significantly impacting Western hymnody and worship. In fact, it's reported that when he was locked in his church along with his congregants after taking a stand against Arianism, he passed the time by leading them in singing hymns together. It's no wonder that he's known as the father of church hymnody.

IMPORTANT WORKS

ON THE DUTIES OF THE CLERGY

ON THE HOLY SPIRIT

EXPOSITION OF THE CHRISTIAN FAITH

[43]The sons of Hebron: Korah, Tappuah, Rekem, and Shema.
[44]Shema was the father of Raham, the father of Jorkeam.
Rekem was the father of Shammai. [45]Shammai's son was Maon,
who was the father of Beth Zur.
[46]Caleb's concubine Ephah bore Haran, Moza, and Gazez.
Haran was the father of Gazez.
[47]The sons of Jahdai: Regem, Jotham, Geshan, Pelet, Ephah,
and Shaaph.
[48]Caleb's concubine Maacah bore Sheber and Tirhanah. [49]She
also bore Shaaph the father of Madmannah and Sheva the father of Machbenah and Gibea. Caleb's daughter was Achsah.
[50]These were the descendants of Caleb.
The sons of Hur, the firstborn of Ephrath: Shobal, the father
of Kiriath Jearim, [51]Salma, the father of Bethlehem, and Hareph,
the father of Beth Gader.
[52]The sons of Shobal, the father of Kiriath Jearim, were
Haroeh, half the Manahathites, [53]the clans of Kiriath Jearim—
the Ithrites, Puthites, Shumathites, and Mishraites. (The
Zorathites and Eshtaolites descended from these groups.)
[54]The sons of Salma: Bethlehem, the Netophathites, Atroth
Beth Joab, half the Manahathites, the Zorites, [55]and the clans
of the scribes who lived in Jabez: the Tirathites, Shimeathites,
and Sucathites. These are the Kenites who descended from
Hammath, the father of Beth Rechab.

DAVID'S DESCENDANTS

3 These were the sons of David who were born to him in
Hebron:
The firstborn was Amnon, whose mother was Ahinoam from
Jezreel;
the second was Daniel, whose mother was Abigail from
Carmel;
[2]the third was Absalom, whose mother was Maacah, daughter
of King Talmai of Geshur;
the fourth was Adonijah, whose mother was Haggith;
[3]the fifth was Shephatiah, whose mother was Abital;
the sixth was Ithream, whose mother was Eglah, David's wife.
[4]These six were born to David in Hebron, where he ruled for
seven years and six months.
He ruled thirty-three years in Jerusalem. [5]These were the
sons born to him in Jerusalem:
Shimea, Shobab, Nathan, and Solomon—the mother of these
four was Bathsheba the daughter of Ammiel.
[6]The other nine were Ibhar, Elishua, Elpelet, [7]Nogah, Nepheg,
Japhia, [8]Elishama, Eliada, and Eliphelet.
[9]These were all the sons of David, not counting the sons of
his concubines. Tamar was their sister.

3:1–24 Here we have enumerated those kings who ruled in Judah from David to the exile of Babylon according to the promise of God. Among these kings there were some who were good, such as David, Jehoshaphat, Jotham, Hezekiah, and Josiah. There were some whose reigns began well but ended poorly, such as Solomon, Rehoboam, Asa, Joash, Amaziah, and Azariah. Then there were some whose reigns began poorly but ended well, such as Manasseh and Jeconiah. Finally, there were others who were always evil and tyrannical, such as Joram, Ahaziah, Ahaz, Amon, and the sons of Josiah who did not grieve over their evil condition. We see from these kings all the vicissitudes of humanity, for today we have leaders who also have good, mediocre, and bad reigns.

LUDWIG LAVATER **(1527–1586)**
COMMENTARY ON FIRST CHRONICLES

SOLOMON'S DESCENDANTS

[10]Solomon's son was Rehoboam,
followed by Abijah his son,
Asa his son,
Jehoshaphat his son,
[11]Joram his son,
Ahaziah his son,
Joash his son,
[12]Amaziah his son,
Azariah his son,
Jotham his son,

13 Ahaz his son,
Hezekiah his son,
Manasseh his son,
14 Amon his son,
Josiah his son.
15 The sons of Josiah: Johanan was the firstborn; Jehoiakim
was born second; Zedekiah third, and Shallum fourth.
16 The sons of Jehoiakim: his son Jehoiachin and his son
Zedekiah.
17 The sons of Jehoiachin the exile: Shealtiel his son, 18 Malki-
ram, Pedaiah, Shenazzar, Jekamiah, Hoshama, and Nedabiah.
19 The sons of Pedaiah: Zerubbabel and Shimei.
The sons of Zerubbabel: Meshullam and Hananiah. Shelomith was their sister.
20 The five others were Hashubah, Ohel, Berechiah, Hasadiah,
and Jushab Hesed.
21 The descendants of Hananiah: Pelatiah, Jeshaiah, the sons
of Rephaiah, of Arnan, of Obadiah, and of Shecaniah.
22 The descendants of Shecaniah: Shemaiah and his sons:
Hattush, Igal, Bariah, Neariah, and Shaphat—six in all.
23 The sons of Neariah: Elioenai, Hizkiah, and Azrikam—three
in all.
24 The sons of Elioenai: Hodaviah, Eliashib, Pelaiah, Akkub,
Johanan, Delaiah, and Anani—seven in all.

JUDAH'S DESCENDANTS

4 The descendants of Judah: Perez, Hezron, Carmi, Hur, and
Shobal.
2 Reaiah the son of Shobal was the father of Jahath, and Jahath
was the father of Ahumai and Lahad. These were the clans of
the Zorathites.
3 These were the sons of Etam: Jezreel, Ishma, and Idbash.
Their sister was Hazzelelponi.
4 Penuel was the father of Gedor, and Ezer was the father of
Hushah. These were the descendants of Hur, the firstborn of
Ephrathah and the father of Bethlehem.
5 Ashhur the father of Tekoa had two wives, Helah and Naarah. 6 Naarah bore him Ahuzzam, Hepher, Temeni, and Haa-
hashtari. These were the sons of Naarah. 7 The sons of Helah:
Zereth, Zohar, Ethnan, 8 and Koz, who was the father of Anub,
Hazzobebah, and the clans of Aharhel the son of Harum.
9 Jabez was more respected than his brothers. His mother had
named him Jabez, for she said, "I experienced pain when I gave
birth to him." 10 Jabez called out to the God of Israel, "If only
you would greatly bless me and expand my territory. May your
hand be with me! Keep me from harm so I might not endure
pain." God answered his prayer.
11 Kelub, the brother of Shuhah, was the father of Mehir, who
was the father of Eshton. 12 Eshton was the father of Beth Rapha,
Paseah, and Tehinnah, the father of Ir Nahash. These were the
men of Recah.
13 The sons of Kenaz: Othniel and Seraiah.
The sons of Othniel: Hathath and Meonothai. 14 Meonothai
was the father of Ophrah.
Seraiah was the father of Joab, the father of those who live
in the Valley of the Craftsmen, for they were craftsmen.
15 The sons of Caleb son of Jephunneh: Iru, Elah, and Naam.
The son of Elah: Kenaz.
16 The sons of Jehallelel: Ziph, Ziphah, Tiria, and Asarel.

4:1–43 The most remarkable person in this chapter is Jabez. We find that he was a praying man. The way to be truly great is to seek to do God's will and to pray earnestly. Four things Jabez prayed for: (1) That God would bless him indeed. Spiritual blessings are the best blessings—God's blessings are real things and produce real effects. (2) That he would enlarge his coast. (3) That God's hand might be with him. (4) That he would keep him from evil, the evil of sin, the evil of trouble, and all the evil designs of his enemies, that they might not hurt or make him a Jabez indeed, a man of sorrow. God granted what he requested. God is ever ready to hear prayer: His ear is not now heavy.

MATTHEW HENRY (1662–1714)
COMMENTARY ON THE WHOLE BIBLE

17 The sons of Ezrah: Jether, Mered, Epher, and Jalon.
Mered's wife Bithiah gave birth to Miriam, Shammai, and
Ishbah, the father of Eshtemoa. 18 (His Judahite wife gave birth
to Jered the father of Gedor, Heber the father of Soco, and Je-
kuthiel the father of Zanoah.) These were the sons of Pharaoh's
daughter Bithiah, whom Mered married.
19 The sons of Hodiah's wife, the sister of Naham: the father
of Keilah the Garmite, and Eshtemoa the Maacathite.
20 The sons of Shimon: Amnon, Rinnah, Ben Hanan, and Tilon.
The descendants of Ishi: Zoheth and Ben Zoheth.
21 The sons of Shelah son of Judah: Er the father of Lecah, Laa-
dah the father of Mareshah, the clans of the linen workers at Beth
Ashbea, 22 Jokim, the men of Cozeba, and Joash and Saraph, both
of whom ruled in Moab and Jashubi Lehem. (This information
is from ancient records.) 23 They were the potters who lived in
Netaim and Gederah; they lived there and worked for the king.

SIMEON'S DESCENDANTS

24 The descendants of Simeon: Nemuel, Jamin, Jarib, Zerah,
Shaul, 25 his son Shallum, his son Mibsam, and his son Mishma.
26 The descendants of Mishma: his son Hammuel, his son
Zaccur, and his son Shimei.
27 Shimei had sixteen sons and six daughters. But his brothers
did not have many sons, so their whole clan was not as numerous as the sons of Judah. 28 They lived in Beer Sheba, Moladah,
Hazar Shual, 29 Bilhah, Ezem, Tolad, 30 Bethuel, Hormah, Ziklag,
31 Beth Marcaboth, Hazar Susim, Beth Biri, and Shaaraim. These
were their towns until the reign of David. 32 Their settlements
also included Etam, Ain, Rimmon, Tochen, and Ashan—five
towns, 33 along with all their settlements that surrounded these
towns as far as Baal. These were the places where they lived;
they kept genealogical records.
34 Their clan leaders were: Meshobab, Jamlech, Joshah son of
Amaziah, 35 Joel, Jehu son of Joshibiah (son of Seraiah, son of
Asiel), 36 Eleoenai, Jaakobah, Jeshohaiah, Asaiah, Adiel, Jesimiel,
Benaiah, 37 Ziza son of Shipi (son of Allon, son of Jedaiah, son of
Shimri, son of Shemaiah). 38 These who are named above were
the leaders of their clans.
Their extended families increased greatly in numbers. 39 They
went to the entrance of Gedor, to the east of the valley, looking
for pasture for their sheep. 40 They found fertile and rich pasture; the land was very broad, undisturbed, and peaceful. Indeed
some Hamites had been living there before that. 41 The men
whose names are listed came during the time of King Hezekiah
of Judah and attacked the Hamites' settlements, as well as the
Meunites they discovered there, and they wiped them out, as
can be seen to this very day. They dispossessed them, for they
found pasture for their sheep there. 42 Five hundred men of
Simeon, led by Pelatiah, Neariah, Rephaiah, and Uzziel, the
sons of Ishi, went to the hill country of Seir 43 and defeated the
rest of the Amalekite refugees; they live there to this very day.

REUBEN'S DESCENDANTS

5 The sons of Reuben, Israel's firstborn—
(Now he was the firstborn, but when he defiled his father's
bed, his rights as firstborn were given to the sons of Joseph, Israel's
son. So Reuben is not listed as firstborn in the genealogical records.
2 Though Judah was the strongest among his brothers and a leader
descended from him, the right of the firstborn belonged to Joseph.)

5:1–26 Warrior, fighting under the banner of the Lord Jesus, observe this passage with holy joy, for as it was in the days of old so is it now, if the war is of God the victory is sure. The sons of Reuben, the Gadites, and the half tribe of Manasseh could barely muster 45,000 fighting men, and yet in their war with the Hagrites they captured "100,000 people" for "they cried out to God during the battle; he responded to their prayers because they trusted in him." The Lord saves not by many or by few; it is ours to go forth in Jehovah's name if we be but a handful of warriors, for the Lord of Hosts is with us for our captain. Our confidence must rest in the Lord alone, for he is the sword and the shield of his people. The battle is the Lord's, and he will deliver his enemies into our hands.

CHARLES SPURGEON
(1834–1892)
MORNING AND EVENING

[3]The sons of Reuben, Israel's firstborn: Hanoch, Pallu, Hezron, and Carmi.
[4]The descendants of Joel: his son Shemaiah, his son Gog, his
son Shimei, [5]his son Micah, his son Reaiah, his son Baal, [6]and
his son Beerah, whom King Tiglath-Pileser of Assyria carried
into exile. Beerah was the tribal leader of Reuben.
[7]His brothers by their clans, as listed in their genealogical
records:
The leader Jeiel, Zechariah, [8]and Bela son of Azaz, son of
Shema, son of Joel.
They lived in Aroer as far as Nebo and Baal Meon. [9]In the
east they settled as far as the entrance to the wilderness that
stretches to the Euphrates River, for their cattle had increased
in numbers in the land of Gilead. [10]During the time of Saul they
attacked the Hagrites and defeated them. They took over their
territory in the entire eastern region of Gilead.

GAD'S DESCENDANTS

[11]The descendants of Gad lived near them in the land of Bashan,
as far as Salecah.
[12]They included Joel the leader, Shapham the second-in-
command, Janai, and Shaphat in Bashan. [13]Their relatives, listed according to their families, included Michael, Meshullam,
Sheba, Jorai, Jacan, Zia, and Eber—seven in all.
[14]These were the sons of Abihail son of Huri, son of Jaroah,
son of Gilead, son of Michael, son of Jeshishai, son of Jahdo, son
of Buz. [15]Ahi son of Abdiel, son of Guni, was the leader of the
family. [16]They lived in Gilead, in Bashan and its surrounding
settlements, and in the pasturelands of Sharon to their very
borders. [17]All of them were listed in the genealogical records
in the time of King Jotham of Judah and in the time of King
Jeroboam of Israel.
[18]The Reubenites, Gadites, and the half-tribe of Manasseh
had 44,760 men in their combined armies, warriors who carried
shields and swords, were equipped with bows, and were trained
for war. [19]They attacked the Hagrites, Jetur, Naphish, and No-
dab. [20]They received divine help in fighting them, and the Hagrites and all their allies were handed over to them. They cried
out to God during the battle; he responded to their prayers because they trusted in him. [21]They seized the Hagrites' animals,
including 50,000 camels, 250,000 sheep, and 2,000 donkeys.
They also took captive 100,000 people. [22]Because God fought
for them, they killed many of the enemy. They dispossessed the
Hagrites and lived in their land until the exile.

THE HALF-TRIBE OF MANASSEH

[23]The half-tribe of Manasseh settled in the land from Bashan
as far as Baal Hermon, Senir, and Mount Hermon. They grew
in number.
[24]These were the leaders of their families:
Epher, Ishi, Eliel, Azriel, Jeremiah, Hodaviah, and Jahdiel.
They were skilled warriors, men of reputation, and leaders of
their families. [25]But they were unfaithful to the God of their
ancestors and worshiped instead the gods of the native peoples
whom God had destroyed before them. [26]So the God of Israel
stirred up King Pul of Assyria (that is, King Tiglath-Pileser of
Assyria), and he carried away the Reubenites, Gadites, and half-
tribe of Manasseh and took them to Halah, Habor, Hara, and
the river of Gozan, where they remain to this very day.

6:1–53 Aaron and the high priests who succeeded him were types of Christ to the extent that they made sacrifices and expiation on behalf of the people of God. For they made atonement of death in a ceremonial way, but the true and real atonement was made by the sacrifice of Christ on the altar of the cross when he was executed. As Hebrews says, "For it is indeed fitting for us to have such a high priest: holy, innocent, undefiled, separate from sinners, and exalted above the heavens. He has no need to do every day what those priests do, to offer sacrifices first for their own sins and then for the sins of the people, since he did this in offering himself once for all" (Heb 7:26–27).

JOHANNES PISCATOR
(1546–1625)
COMMENTARY ON FIRST CHRONICLES

LEVI'S DESCENDANTS

6 The sons of Levi: Gershon, Kohath, and Merari.
2The sons of Kohath: Amram, Izhar, Hebron, and Uzziel.
3The children of Amram: Aaron, Moses, and Miriam.
The sons of Aaron: Nadab, Abihu, Eleazar, and Ithamar.
4Eleazar was the father of Phinehas, and Phinehas was the
father of Abishua. 5Abishua was the father of Bukki, and Bukki
was the father of Uzzi. 6Uzzi was the father of Zerahiah, and
Zerahiah was the father of Meraioth. 7Meraioth was the father
of Amariah, and Amariah was the father of Ahitub. 8Ahitub
was the father of Zadok, and Zadok was the father of Ahimaaz.
9Ahimaaz was the father of Azariah, and Azariah was the father
of Johanan. 10Johanan was the father of Azariah, who served as a
priest in the temple Solomon built in Jerusalem. 11Azariah was
the father of Amariah, and Amariah was the father of Ahitub.
12Ahitub was the father of Zadok, and Zadok was the father of
Shallum. 13Shallum was the father of Hilkiah, and Hilkiah was
the father of Azariah. 14Azariah was the father of Seraiah, and
Seraiah was the father of Jehozadak. 15Jehozadak went into
exile when the LORD sent the people of Judah and Jerusalem
into exile by the hand of Nebuchadnezzar.
16The sons of Levi: Gershom, Kohath, and Merari.
17These are the names of the sons Gershom: Libni and
Shimei.
18The sons of Kohath: Amram, Izhar, Hebron, and Uzziel.
19The sons of Merari: Mahli and Mushi.
These are the clans of the Levites by their families.
20To Gershom: his son Libni, his son Jahath, his son Zimmah,
21his son Joah, his son Iddo, his son Zerah, and his son Jeatherai.
22The sons of Kohath: his son Amminadab, his son Korah, his
son Assir, 23his son Elkanah, his son Ebiasaph, his son Assir, 24his
son Tahath, his son Uriel, his son Uzziah, and his son Shaul.
25The sons of Elkanah: Amasai, Ahimoth, 26his son Elkanah,
his son Zophai, his son Nahath, 27his son Eliab, his son Jeroham,
and his son Elkanah.
28The sons of Samuel: Joel the firstborn and Abijah the second oldest.
29The descendants of Merari: Mahli, his son Libni, his son
Shimei, his son Uzzah, 30his son Shimea, his son Haggiah, and
his son Asaiah.

PROFESSIONAL MUSICIANS

31These are the men David put in charge of music in the LORD's
sanctuary, after the ark was placed there. 32They performed
music before the sanctuary of the meeting tent until Solomon
built the LORD's temple in Jerusalem. They carried out their
tasks according to regulations.
33These are the ones who served along with their sons:
From the Kohathites: Heman the musician, son of Joel, son
of Samuel, 34son of Elkanah, son of Jeroham, son of Eliel, son
of Toah, 35son of Zuph, son of Elkanah, son of Mahath, son of
Amasai, 36son of Elkanah, son of Joel, son of Azariah, son of
Zephaniah, 37son of Tahath, son of Assir, son of Ebiasaph, son
of Korah, 38son of Izhar, son of Kohath, son of Levi, son of Israel.
39Serving beside him was his fellow Levite Asaph, son of
Berechiah, son of Shimea, 40son of Michael, son of Baaseiah,
son of Malkijah, 41son of Ethni, son of Zerah, son of Adaiah,
42son of Ethan, son of Zimmah, son of Shimei, 43son of Jahath,
son of Gershom, son of Levi.

[44]Serving beside them were their fellow Levites, the descendants of Merari, led by Ethan, son of Kishi, son of Abdi, son of
Malluch, [45]son of Hashabiah, son of Amaziah, son of Hilkiah,
[46]son of Amzi, son of Bani, son of Shemer, [47]son of Mahli, son
of Mushi, son of Merari, son of Levi.

[48]The rest of their fellow Levites were assigned to perform
the remaining tasks at God's sanctuary. [49]But Aaron and his
descendants offered sacrifices on the altar for burnt offerings
and on the altar for incense as they had been assigned to do
in the Most Holy Sanctuary. They made atonement for Israel,
just as God's servant Moses had ordered.

[50]These were the descendants of Aaron:

His son Eleazar, his son Phinehas, his son Abishua, [51]his son
Bukki, his son Uzzi, his son Zerahiah, [52]his son Meraioth, his son
Amariah, his son Ahitub, [53]his son Zadok, and his son Ahimaaz.

[54]These were the areas where Aaron's descendants lived:

The following belonged to the Kohathite clan, for they received the first allotment:

[55]They were allotted Hebron in the territory of Judah, as
well as its surrounding pasturelands. [56](But the city's land and
nearby towns were allotted to Caleb son of Jephunneh.) [57]The
descendants of Aaron were also allotted as cities of refuge
Hebron, Libnah and its pasturelands, Jattir, Eshtemoa and its
pasturelands, [58]Hilez and its pasturelands, Debir and its pasturelands, [59]Ashan and its pasturelands, and Beth Shemesh
and its pasturelands.

[60]Within the territory of the tribe of Benjamin, they were allotted Geba and its pasturelands, Alemeth and its pasturelands,
and Anathoth and its pasturelands. Their clans were allotted
thirteen cities in all. [61]The rest of Kohath's descendants were
allotted ten cities in the territory of the half-tribe of Manasseh.

[62]The clans of Gershom's descendants received thirteen cities within the territory of the tribes of Issachar, Asher, Naphtali,
and Manasseh (in Bashan).

[63]The clans of Merari's descendants were allotted twelve
cities within the territory of the tribes of Reuben, Gad, and
Zebulun.

[64]So the Israelites gave to the Levites these cities and their
pasturelands. [65]They allotted these previously named cities
from the territory of the tribes of Judah, Simeon, and Benjamin.

[66]The clans of Kohath's descendants also received cities
as their territory within the tribe of Ephraim. [67]They were
allotted as cities of refuge Shechem and its pasturelands
(in the hill country of Ephraim), Gezer and its pasturelands,
[68]Jokmeam and its pasturelands, Beth Horon and its pasturelands, [69]Aijalon and its pasturelands, and Gath Rimmon and
its pasturelands.

[70]Within the territory of the half-tribe of Manasseh, the rest
of Kohath's descendants received Aner and its pasturelands
and Bileam and its pasturelands.

[71]The following belonged to Gershom's descendants:

Within the territory of the half-tribe of Manasseh: Golan in
Bashan and its pasturelands and Ashtaroth and its pasturelands.

[72]Within the territory of the tribe of Issachar: Kedesh and
its pasturelands, Daberath and its pasturelands, [73]Ramoth and
its pasturelands, and Anem and its pasturelands.

[74]Within the territory of the tribe of Asher: Mashal and its
pasturelands, Abdon and its pasturelands, [75]Hukok and its pasturelands, and Rehob and its pasturelands.

[76]Within the territory of the tribe of Naphtali: Kedesh in
Galilee and its pasturelands, Hammon and its pasturelands,
and Kiriathaim and its pasturelands.
[77]The following belonged to the rest of Merari's descendants:
Within the territory of the tribe of Zebulun: Rimmono and
its pasturelands and Tabor and its pasturelands.
[78]Within the territory of the tribe of Reuben across the
Jordan River east of Jericho: Bezer in the wilderness and its
pasturelands, Jahzah and its pasturelands, [79]Kedemoth and its
pasturelands, and Mephaath and its pasturelands.
[80]Within the territory of the tribe of Gad: Ramoth in Gilead
and its pasturelands, Mahanaim and its pasturelands, [81]Hesh-
bon and its pasturelands, and Jazer and its pasturelands.

ISSACHAR'S DESCENDANTS

7 The sons of Issachar: Tola, Puah, Jashub, and Shimron—four
in all.
[2]The sons of Tola: Uzzi, Rephaiah, Jeriel, Jahmai, Jibsam, and
Samuel. They were leaders of their families. In the time of David
there were 22,600 warriors listed in Tola's genealogical records.
[3]The son of Uzzi: Izrahiah.
The sons of Izrahiah: Michael, Obadiah, Joel, and Isshiah.
All five were leaders.
[4]According to the genealogical records of their families, they
had 36,000 warriors available for battle, for they had numerous
wives and sons. [5]Altogether the genealogical records of the clans
of Issachar listed 87,000 warriors.

BENJAMIN'S DESCENDANTS

[6]The sons of Benjamin: Bela, Beker, and Jediael—three in all.
[7]The sons of Bela: Ezbon, Uzzi, Uzziel, Jerimoth, and Iri. The
five of them were leaders of their families. There were 22,034
warriors listed in their genealogical records.
[8]The sons of Beker: Zemirah, Joash, Eliezer, Elioenai, Omri,
Jeremoth, Abijah, Anathoth, and Alemeth. All these were the
sons of Beker. [9]There were 20,200 family leaders and warriors
listed in their genealogical records.
[10]The son of Jediael: Bilhan.
The sons of Bilhan: Jeush, Benjamin, Ehud, Kenaanah, Zethan,
Tarshish, and Ahishahar. [11]All these were the sons of Jediael.
There were 17,200 family leaders and warriors who were capable
of marching out to battle.
[12]The Shuppites and Huppites were descendants of Ir; the
Hushites were descendants of Aher.

NAPHTALI'S DESCENDANTS

[13]The sons of Naphtali: Jahziel, Guni, Jezer, and Shallum—sons
of Bilhah.

MANASSEH'S DESCENDANTS

[14]The sons of Manasseh: Asriel, who was born to Manasseh's
Aramean concubine. She also gave birth to Makir the father
of Gilead. [15]Now Makir married a wife from the Huppites and
Shuppites. (His sister's name was Maacah.)
Zelophehad was Manasseh's second son; he had only
daughters.
[16]Maacah, Makir's wife, gave birth to a son, whom she named
Peresh. His brother was Sheresh, and his sons were Ulam and
Rekem.

[17]The son of Ulam: Bedan.
These were the sons of Gilead, son of Makir, son of Manasseh.
[18]His sister Hammoleketh gave birth to Ishhod, Abiezer, and
Mahlah.
[19]The sons of Shemida were Ahian, Shechem, Likhi, and
Aniam.

EPHRAIM'S DESCENDANTS

[20]The descendants of Ephraim: Shuthelah, his son Bered, his
son Tahath, his son Eleadah, his son Tahath, [21]his son Zabad,
his son Shuthelah (Ezer and Elead were killed by the men of
Gath, who were natives of the land, when they went down to
steal their cattle. [22]Their father Ephraim mourned for them
many days and his brothers came to console him. [23]He slept
with his wife; she became pregnant and gave birth to a son.
Ephraim named him Beriah because tragedy had come to his
family. [24]His daughter was Sheerah, who built Lower and Upper
Beth Horon, as well as Uzzen Sheerah),
[25]his son Rephah, his son Resheph, his son Telah, his son
Tahan, [26]his son Ladan, his son Ammihud, his son Elishama,
[27]his son Nun, and his son Joshua.
[28]Their property and settlements included Bethel and its
surrounding towns, Naaran to the east, Gezer and its surrounding towns to the west, and Shechem and its surrounding towns
as far as Ayyah and its surrounding towns. [29]On the border of
Manasseh's territory were Beth Shean and its surrounding
towns, Taanach and its surrounding towns, Megiddo and its
surrounding towns, and Dor and its surrounding towns. The
descendants of Joseph, Israel's son, lived here.

ASHER'S DESCENDANTS

[30]The sons of Asher: Imnah, Ishvah, Ishvi, and Beriah. Serah
was their sister.
[31]The sons of Beriah: Heber and Malkiel, who was the father
of Birzaith.
[32]Heber was the father of Japhlet, Shomer, Hotham, and
Shua their sister.
[33]The sons of Japhlet: Pasach, Bimhal, and Ashvath. These
were Japhlet's sons.
[34]The sons of his brother Shemer: Rohgah, Hubbah, and
Aram.
[35]The sons of his brother Helem: Zophah, Imna, Shelesh,
and Amal.
[36]The sons of Zophah: Suah, Harnepher, Shual, Beri, Imrah,
[37]Bezer, Hod, Shamma, Shilshah, Ithran, and Beera.
[38]The sons of Jether: Jephunneh, Pispah, and Ara.
[39]The sons of Ulla: Arah, Hanniel, and Rizia.
[40]All these were the descendants of Asher. They were the
leaders of their families, the most capable men, who were warriors and served as head chiefs. There were 26,000 warriors
listed in their genealogical records as capable of doing battle.

BENJAMIN'S DESCENDANTS (CONTINUED)

8 Benjamin was the father of Bela, his firstborn; Ashbel was
born second, Aharah third, [2]Nohah fourth, and Rapha fifth.
[3]Bela's sons were Addar, Gera, Abihud, [4]Abishua, Naaman,
Ahoah, [5]Gera, Shephuphan, and Huram.
[6]These were the descendants of Ehud who were leaders of the
families living in Geba who were forced to move to Manahath:

7:23 His grief was in some measure repaired by the addition of another son in Ephraim's old age. When God thus restores comfort to his mourners, he makes glad according to the days wherein he afflicted. Setting the mercies against the crosses, we ought to observe the kindness of his providence. Yet the joy that a man was born into Ephraim's family could not make him forget his grief. For he gave a melancholy name to his son, Beriah, that is, "in trouble": For he was born when the family was in mourning. It is good to have in remembrance the affliction and the misery that are past, that our souls may be humbled within us.

JOHN WESLEY **(1703–1791)**
EXPLANATORY NOTES ON THE BIBLE

8:1—9:2 In this chapter is recounted the genealogy of the tribe of Benjamin and especially that of Saul, the first king of the people of God, and of his son Jonathan. The image of Saul is very sad. After his army was lost, he approved of killing himself and fell into eternal punishment. This should often be considered so that we may recognize the magnitude of the wrath of God against sin. Yet in Saul's son Jonathan we are given a meek example of one who had a mild and modest spirit. He is set forth as an example for all generations of people to imitate.

VIKTORIN STRIGEL
(C. 1524–1569)
BOOK OF CHRONICLES

7 Naaman, Ahijah, and Gera, who moved them. Gera was the
father of Uzzah and Ahihud.
8 Shaharaim fathered sons in Moab after he divorced his
wives Hushim and Baara. 9 By his wife Hodesh he fathered Jobab,
Zibia, Mesha, Malkam, 10 Jeuz, Sakia, and Mirmah. These were
his sons; they were family leaders. 11 By Hushim he fathered
Abitub and Elpaal.
12 The sons of Elpaal: Eber, Misham, Shemed (who built Ono
and Lod, as well as its surrounding towns), 13 Beriah, and Shema.
They were leaders of the families living in Aijalon and chased
out the inhabitants of Gath.
14 Ahio, Shashak, Jeremoth, 15 Zebadiah, Arad, Eder, 16 Michael,
Ishpah, and Joha were the sons of Beriah.
17 Zebadiah, Meshullam, Hizki, Heber, 18 Ishmerai, Izliah, and
Jobab were the sons of Elpaal.
19 Jakim, Zikri, Zabdi, 20 Elienai, Zillethai, Eliel, 21 Adaiah, Ber-
aiah, and Shimrath were the sons of Shimei.
22 Ishpan, Eber, Eliel, 23 Abdon, Zikri, Hanan, 24 Hananiah, Elam,
Anthothijah, 25 Iphdeiah, and Penuel were the sons of Shashak.
26 Shamsherai, Shechariah, Athaliah, 27 Jaareshiah, Elijah, and
Zikri were the sons of Jeroham. 28 These were the family leaders
listed in the genealogical records; they lived in Jerusalem.
29 The father of Gibeon lived in Gibeon; his wife's name was
Maacah. 30 His firstborn son was Abdon, followed by Zur, Kish,
Baal, Nadab, 31 Gedor, Ahio, Zeker, and Mikloth.
32 Mikloth was the father of Shimeah. They also lived near
their relatives in Jerusalem.
33 Ner was the father of Kish, and Kish was the father of Saul. Saul
was the father of Jonathan, Malki-Shua, Abinadab, and Eshbaal.
34 The son of Jonathan: Meribbaal.
Meribbaal was the father of Micah.
35 The sons of Micah: Pithon, Melech, Tarea, and Ahaz.
36 Ahaz was the father of Jehoaddah, and Jehoaddah was the
father of Alemeth, Azmaveth, and Zimri. Zimri was the father of
Moza, 37 and Moza was the father of Binea. His son was Raphah,
whose son was Eleasah, whose son was Azel.
38 Azel had six sons: Azrikam his firstborn, followed by Ishmael, Sheariah, Obadiah, and Hanan. All these were the sons
of Azel.
39 The sons of his brother Eshek:
Ulam was his firstborn, Jeush second, and Eliphelet third.
40 The sons of Ulam were warriors who were adept archers. They
had many sons and grandsons, a total of 150.
All these were the descendants of Benjamin.

9 Genealogical records were kept for all Israel; they are recorded in the Scroll of the Kings of Israel.

EXILES WHO RESETTLED IN JERUSALEM

The people of Judah were carried away to Babylon because of
their unfaithfulness. 2 The first to resettle on their property
and in their cities were some Israelites, priests, Levites, and
temple servants. 3 Some from the tribes of Judah, Benjamin,
and Ephraim and Manasseh settled in Jerusalem.
4 The settlers included: Uthai son of Ammihud, son of Omri,
son of Imri, son of Bani, who was a descendant of Perez son of
Judah.
5 From the Shilonites: Asaiah the firstborn and his sons.
6 From the descendants of Zerah: Jeuel.
Their relatives numbered 690.

7From the descendants of Benjamin:
Sallu son of Meshullam, son of Hodaviah, son of Hassenuah;
8Ibneiah son of Jeroham; Elah son of Uzzi, son of Mikri; and
Meshullam son of Shephatiah, son of Reuel, son of Ibnijah.
9Their relatives, listed in their genealogical records, numbered 956. All these men were leaders of their families.
10From the priests:
Jedaiah; Jehoiarib; Jakin; 11Azariah son of Hilkiah, son of
Meshullam, son of Zadok, son of Meraioth, son of Ahitub the
leader in God's temple; 12Adaiah son of Jeroham, son of Pashhur,
son of Malkijah; and Maasai son of Adiel, son of Jahzerah, son
of Meshullam, son of Meshillemith, son of Immer.
13Their relatives, who were leaders of their families, numbered 1,760. They were capable men who were assigned to carry
out the various tasks of service in God's temple.
14From the Levites:
Shemaiah son of Hasshub, son of Azrikam, son of Hashabiah a
descendant of Merari; 15Bakbakkar; Heresh; Galal; Mattaniah son
of Mika, son of Zikri, son of Asaph; 16Obadiah son of Shemaiah,
son of Galal, son of Jeduthun; and Berechiah son of Asa, son of
Elkanah, who lived among the settlements of the Netophathites.
17The gatekeepers were:
Shallum, Akkub, Talmon, Ahiman, and their brothers. Shallum was the leader; 18he serves to this day at the King's Gate
on the east. These were the gatekeepers from the camp of the
descendants of Levi.
19Shallum son of Kore, son of Ebiasaph, son of Korah, and his
relatives from his family (the Korahites) were assigned to guard
the entrance to the sanctuary. Their ancestors had guarded
the entrance to the LORD's dwelling place. 20Phinehas son of
Eleazar had been their leader in earlier times, and the LORD
was with him. 21Zechariah son of Meshelemiah was the guard
at the entrance to the meeting tent.
22All those selected to be gatekeepers at the entrances numbered 212. Their names were recorded in the genealogical records
of their settlements. David and Samuel the prophet had appointed them to their positions. 23They and their descendants were
assigned to guard the gates of the LORD's sanctuary (that is, the
tabernacle). 24The gatekeepers were posted on all four sides—
east, west, north, and south. 25Their relatives, who lived in their
settlements, came from time to time and served with them for
seven-day periods. 26The four head gatekeepers, who were Levites,
were assigned to guard the storerooms and treasuries in God's
sanctuary. 27They would spend the night in their posts all around
God's sanctuary, for they were assigned to guard it and would open
it with the key every morning. 28Some of them were in charge of
the articles used by those who served; they counted them when
they brought them in and when they brought them out. 29Some
of them were in charge of the equipment and articles of the sanctuary, as well as the flour, wine, olive oil, incense, and spices. 30(But
some of the priests mixed the spices.) 31Mattithiah, a Levite, the
firstborn son of Shallum the Korahite, was in charge of baking the
bread for offerings. 32Some of the Kohathites, their relatives, were
in charge of preparing the bread that is displayed each Sabbath.
33The musicians and Levite family leaders stayed in rooms at
the sanctuary and were exempt from other duties, for day and
night they had to carry out their assigned tasks. 34These were
the family leaders of the Levites, as listed in their genealogical
records. They lived in Jerusalem.

JEIEL'S DESCENDANTS

35Jeiel (the father of Gibeon) lived in Gibeon. His wife was
Maacah. 36His firstborn son was Abdon, followed by Zur, Kish,
Baal, Ner, Nadab, 37Gedor, Ahio, Zechariah, and Mikloth. 38Mik-
loth was the father of Shimeam. They also lived near their relatives in Jerusalem.

39Ner was the father of Kish, and Kish was the father of Saul.
Saul was the father of Jonathan, Malki-Shua, Abinadab, and
Eshbaal.

40The son of Jonathan:
Meribbaal, who was the father of Micah.
41The sons of Micah:
Pithon, Melech, Tahrea, and Ahaz.

42Ahaz was the father of Jarah, and Jarah was the father of
Alemeth, Azmaveth, and Zimri. Zimri was the father of Moza,
43and Moza was the father of Binea. His son was Rephaiah,
whose son was Eleasah, whose son was Azel.

44Azel had six sons: Azrikam his firstborn, followed by Ishmael, Sheariah, Obadiah, and Hanan. These were the sons of Azel.

SAUL'S DEATH

10 Now the Philistines fought against Israel. The Israelites
fled before the Philistines and many of them fell dead
on Mount Gilboa. 2The Philistines stayed right on the heels
of Saul and his sons. They struck down Saul's sons Jonathan,
Abinadab, and Malki-Shua. 3The battle was thick around Saul;
the archers spotted him and wounded him. 4Saul told his armor-
bearer, "Draw your sword and stab me with it. Otherwise these
uncircumcised people will come and torture me." But his armor-
bearer refused to do it because he was very afraid. So Saul took
the sword and fell on it. 5When his armor-bearer saw that Saul
was dead, he also fell on his sword and died. 6So Saul and his
three sons died; his whole household died together. 7When all
the Israelites who were in the valley saw that the army had fled
and that Saul and his sons were dead, they abandoned their
cities and fled. The Philistines came and occupied them.

8The next day, when the Philistines came to strip loot from
the corpses, they discovered Saul and his sons lying dead on
Mount Gilboa. 9They stripped his corpse and then carried off
his head and his armor. They sent messengers throughout the
land of the Philistines proclaiming the news to their idols and
their people. 10They placed his armor in the temple of their
gods and hung his head in the temple of Dagon. 11When all the
residents of Jabesh Gilead heard about everything the Philistines had done to Saul, 12all the warriors went and recovered
the bodies of Saul and his sons and brought them to Jabesh.
They buried their remains under the oak tree in Jabesh and
fasted for seven days.

13So Saul died because he was unfaithful to the LORD and
did not obey the LORD's instructions; he even tried to conjure
up underworld spirits. 14He did not seek the LORD's guidance,
so the LORD killed him and transferred the kingdom to David
son of Jesse.

10:1–14 Saul broke faith with the Lord, for he did not await the sacrifice of the prophet Samuel as he had been commanded, and he did not completely obliterate the Amalekites with the due severity that the Lord had commanded, he persecuted the innocent David with a most bitter hatred, and he massacred the priests of the Lord. Above all that he rushed into a terrible sin that led to his miserable death when he consulted the witch about the outcome of the war because he did not hope in the Lord. Therefore we ought to seriously learn the fear of God, trusting in him to prosper us even in times of adversity. In this way we will have a helper and protector in God and not ever be cast away from God's face as happened to Saul.

LUCAS OSIANDER
(1534–1604)
ANNOTATIONS ON FIRST CHRONICLES

DAVID BECOMES KING

11 All Israel joined David at Hebron and said, "Look, we are
your very flesh and blood! 2In the past, even when Saul was
king, you were Israel's commanding general. The LORD your God
said to you, 'You will shepherd my people Israel; you will rule

over my people Israel.'" 3When all the leaders of Israel came to the king at Hebron, David made a covenant with them in Hebron before the LORD. They anointed David king over Israel, in keeping with the LORD's message that came through Samuel.

DAVID CONQUERS JERUSALEM

4David and the whole Israelite army advanced to Jerusalem (that is, Jebus). (The Jebusites, the land's original inhabitants, lived there.) 5The residents of Jebus said to David, "You cannot invade this place!" But David captured the fortress of Zion (that is, the City of David). 6David said, "Whoever attacks the Jebusites first will become commanding general!" So Joab son of Zeruiah attacked first and became commander. 7David lived in the fortress; for this reason it is called the City of David. 8He built up the city around it, from the terrace to the surrounding walls; Joab restored the rest of the city. 9David's power steadily grew, for the LORD of Heaven's Armies was with him.

DAVID'S WARRIORS

10These were the leaders of David's warriors who, together with all Israel, stood courageously with him in his kingdom by installing him as king, in keeping with the LORD's message concerning Israel. 11This is the list of David's warriors:

Jashobeam, a Hacmonite, was head of the officers. He killed 300 men with his spear in a single battle.

12Next in command was Eleazar son of Dodo the Ahohite. He was one of the three elite warriors. 13He was with David in Pas Dammim when the Philistines assembled there for battle. In an area of the field that was full of barley, the army retreated before the Philistines, 14but then they made a stand in the middle of that area. They defended it and defeated the Philistines; the LORD gave them a great victory.

15Three of the thirty leaders went down to David at the rocky cliff at the cave of Adullam, while a Philistine force was camped in the Valley of Rephaim. 16David was in the stronghold at the time, while a Philistine garrison was in Bethlehem. 17David was thirsty and said, "How I wish someone would give me some water to drink from the cistern in Bethlehem near the city gate!" 18So the three elite warriors broke through the Philistine forces and drew some water from the cistern in Bethlehem near the city gate. They carried it back to David, but David refused to drink it. He poured it out as a drink offering to the LORD 19and said, "God forbid that I should do this! Should I drink the blood of these men who risked their lives?" Because they risked their lives to bring it to him, he refused to drink it. Such were the exploits of the three elite warriors.

20Abishai the brother of Joab was head of the three elite warriors. He killed 300 men with his spear and gained fame along with the three elite warriors. 21From the three he was given double honor and he became their officer, even though he was not one of them.

22Benaiah son of Jehoiada was a brave warrior from Kabzeel who performed great exploits. He struck down the two sons of Ariel of Moab; he also went down and killed a lion inside a cistern on a snowy day. 23He even killed an Egyptian who was 7½ feet tall. The Egyptian had a spear in his hand as big as the crossbeam of a weaver's loom; Benaiah attacked him with a club. He grabbed the spear out of the Egyptian's hand and killed him with his own spear. 24Such were the exploits of Benaiah son of Jehoiada, who

11:1–9 The example of David admonishes us to await a divine calling. For even though David had been promised the kingdom of Israel by the words of Samuel, he did not seek to occupy the throne either when Saul was living or right after he died. But after the death of Saul, David remained in Hebron, and only the tribe of Judah came to him. Then later the remaining eleven tribes of Israel came freely and joined together with David by divine instinct. Afterward all of Israel offered him the crown of the kingdom without any deceit or compulsion.

VIKTORIN STRIGEL
(C. 1524–1569)
BOOK OF CHRONICLES

gained fame along with the three elite warriors. 25 He received
honor from the thirty warriors, though he was not one of the
three elite warriors. David put him in charge of his bodyguard.

26 The mighty warriors were:
Asahel the brother of Joab,
Elhanan son of Dodo, from Bethlehem,
27 Shammoth the Harorite,
Helez the Pelonite,
28 Ira son of Ikkesh the Tekoite,
Abiezer the Anathothite,
29 Sibbekai the Hushathite,
Ilai the Ahohite,
30 Maharai the Netophathite,
Heled son of Baanah the Netophathite,
31 Ithai son of Ribai from Gibeah in Benjaminite territory,
Benaiah the Pirathonite,
32 Hurai from the valleys of Gaash,
Abiel the Arbathite,
33 Azmaveth the Baharumite,
Eliahba the Shaalbonite,
34 the sons of Hashem the Gizonite,
Jonathan son of Shageh the Hararite,
35 Ahiam son of Sakar the Hararite,
Eliphal son of Ur,
36 Hepher the Mekerathite,
Ahijah the Pelonite,
37 Hezro the Carmelite,
Naarai son of Ezbai,
38 Joel the brother of Nathan,
Mibhar son of Hagri,
39 Zelek the Ammonite,
Naharai the Beerothite, the armor-bearer of Joab son of Zeruiah,
40 Ira the Ithrite,
Gareb the Ithrite,
41 Uriah the Hittite,
Zabad son of Achli,
42 Adina son of Shiza the Reubenite, leader of the Reubenites and the thirty warriors with him,
43 Hanan son of Maacah,
Joshaphat the Mithnite,
44 Uzzia the Ashterathite,
Shama and Jeiel, the sons of Hotham the Aroerite,
45 Jediael son of Shimri,
and Joha his brother, the Tizite,
46 Eliel the Mahavite,
and Jeribai and Joshaviah, the sons of Elnaam,
and Ithmah the Moabite,
47 Eliel,
and Obed,
and Jaasiel the Mezobaite.

WARRIORS WHO JOINED DAVID AT ZIKLAG

12 These were the men who joined David in Ziklag, when he
was banished from the presence of Saul son of Kish. (They
were among the warriors who assisted him in battle. 2 They
were armed with bows and could shoot arrows or sling stones
right- or left-handed. They were fellow tribesmen of Saul from
Benjamin.) These were:

12:1–40 People's wills cannot withstand the will of God. For this reason David continued to increase and was magnified, and the Lord was with him. Could human beings withstand the will of God and not do the will of him who worked in David's heart by his Spirit, with which he was clothed to will, speak, and do thus? By their own will certainly they appointed David king. They did it with a peaceful heart. And yet he wrought this in them who works what he will in the hearts of humankind: "David's power steadily grew, for the LORD of Heaven's Armies was with him" (1 Chr 11:9). And thus the Lord Omnipotent induced these men to appoint him king. He stirred their hearts and drew them by their own wills, which he himself wrought in them. If so, when God wills to set up kings in the earth, he has the wills of human beings more in his power than they themselves have.

AUGUSTINE (354–430)
ANTI-PELAGIAN WRITINGS

[3]Ahiezer, the leader, and Joash, the sons of Shemaah the Gibeathite; Jeziel and Pelet, the sons of Azmaveth; Berachah, Jehu the Anathothite,

[4]Ishmaiah the Gibeonite, one of the thirty warriors and their leader, Jeremiah, Jahaziel, Johanan, Jozabad the Gederathite,

[5]Eluzai, Jerimoth, Bealiah, Shemariah, Shephatiah the Haruphite,

[6]Elkanah, Isshiah, Azarel, Joezer, and Jashobeam, who were Korahites,

[7]and Joelah and Zebadiah, the sons of Jeroham from Gedor.

[8]Some of the Gadites joined David at the stronghold in the wilderness. They were warriors who were trained for battle; they carried shields and spears. They were as fierce as lions and could
run as quickly as gazelles across the hills. [9]Ezer was the leader,
Obadiah the second-in-command, Eliab the third, [10]Mishman-
nah the fourth, Jeremiah the fifth, [11]Attai the sixth, Eliel the
seventh, [12]Johanan the eighth, Elzabad the ninth, [13]Jeremiah
the tenth, and Machbannai the eleventh. [14]These Gadites were
military leaders; the least led a hundred men, the greatest a
thousand. [15]They crossed the Jordan River in the first month,
when it was overflowing its banks, and routed those living in
all the valleys to the east and west.

[16]Some from Benjamin and Judah also came to David's
stronghold. [17]David went out to meet them and said, "If you
come to me in peace and want to help me, then I will make an
alliance with you. But if you come to betray me to my enemies
when I have not harmed you, may the God of our ancestors
take notice and judge!" [18]But a spirit empowered Amasai, the
leader of the group of warriors known as the Thirty, and he said:

"We are yours, O David!
We support you, O son of Jesse!
May you greatly prosper.
May those who help you prosper.
Indeed your God helps you!"

So David accepted them and made them leaders of raiding bands.

[19]Some men from Manasseh joined David when he went with
the Philistines to fight against Saul. (But in the end they did not
help the Philistines because, after taking counsel, the Philistine
lords sent David away, saying, "It would be disastrous for us if he
deserts to his master Saul.") [20]When David went to Ziklag, the men
of Manasseh who joined him were Adnach, Jozabad, Jediael, Michael, Jozabad, Elihu, and Zillethai, leaders of 1,000 soldiers each
in the tribe of Manasseh. [21]They helped David fight against raiding
bands, for all of them were warriors and leaders in the army. [22]Each
day men came to help David until his army became very large.

SUPPORT FOR DAVID IN HEBRON

[23]The following is a record of the armed warriors who came with their leaders and joined David in Hebron in order to make David king in Saul's place, in accordance with the LORD's decree:

[24]From Judah came 6,800 trained warriors carrying shields and spears.

[25]From Simeon there were 7,100 warriors.

[26]From Levi there were 4,600. [27]Jehoiada, the leader of Aaron's descendants, brought 3,700 men with him, [28]along with
Zadok, a young warrior, and 22 leaders from his family.

[29]From Benjamin, Saul's tribe, there were 3,000, most of whom, up to that time, had been loyal to Saul.

[30]From Ephraim there were 20,800 warriors, who had brought fame to their families.

[31]From the half-tribe of Manasseh there were 18,000 who had been designated by name to come and make David king.

[32]From Issachar there were 200 leaders and all their relatives at their command—they understood the times and knew what Israel should do.

[33]From Zebulun there were 50,000 warriors who were prepared for battle, equipped with all kinds of weapons, and ready to give their undivided loyalty.

[34]From Naphtali there were 1,000 officers, along with 37,000 men carrying shields and spears.

[35]From Dan there were 28,600 men prepared for battle.

[36]From Asher there were 40,000 warriors prepared for battle.

[37]From the other side of the Jordan, from Reuben, Gad, and the half-tribe of Manasseh, there were 120,000 men armed with all kinds of weapons.

[38]All these men were warriors who were ready to march. They came to Hebron to make David king over all Israel by acclamation; all the rest of the Israelites also were in agreement that David should become king. [39]They spent three days feasting there with David, for their relatives had given them provisions. [40]Also their neighbors, from as far away as Issachar, Zebulun, and Naphtali, were bringing food on donkeys, camels, mules, and oxen. There were large supplies of flour, fig cakes, raisins, wine, olive oil, beef, and lamb, for Israel was celebrating.

UZZAH MEETS DISASTER

13 David consulted with his military officers, including those who led groups of a thousand and those who led groups of a hundred. [2]David said to the whole Israelite assembly, "If you so desire and the LORD our God approves, let's spread the word to our brothers who remain in all the regions of Israel, and to the priests and Levites in their cities, so they may join us. [3]Let's move the ark of our God back here, for we did not seek his will throughout Saul's reign." [4]The whole assembly agreed to do this, for the proposal seemed right to all the people. [5]So David assembled all Israel from the Shihor River in Egypt to Lebo Hamath, to bring the ark of God from Kiriath Jearim. [6]David and all Israel went up to Baalah (that is, Kiriath Jearim) in Judah to bring up from there the ark of God the LORD, who sits enthroned between the cherubim—the ark that is called by his Name.

[7]They transported the ark of God on a new cart from the house of Abinadab; Uzzah and Ahio were guiding the cart, [8]while David and all Israel were energetically celebrating before God, singing and playing various stringed instruments, tambourines, cymbals, and trumpets. [9]When they arrived at the threshing floor of Kidon, Uzzah reached out his hand to take hold of the ark because the oxen stumbled. [10]The LORD was so furious with Uzzah, he killed him, because he reached out his hand and touched the ark. He died right there before God.

[11]David was angry because the LORD attacked Uzzah; so he called that place Perez Uzzah, which remains its name to this very day. [12]David was afraid of God that day and said, "How will I ever be able to bring the ark of God up here?" [13]So David did not move the ark to the City of David; he left it in the house of Obed-Edom the Gittite. [14]The ark of God remained in Obed-Edom's house for three months; the LORD blessed Obed-Edom's family and everything that belonged to him.

13:1–14 After David was settled in his kingdom, that is, after he had taken Zion and built his city, he was resolved to bring the ark to Jerusalem. This reveals David's piety to God and his desire for God's presence and blessing to accompany him. And because this was a great and solemn work to be performed, David consulted with others to ensure that it could be solemnly performed.

***THE WESTMINSTER ANNOTATIONS* (1683)**

DAVID'S PRESTIGE GROWS

14 King Hiram of Tyre sent messengers to David, along with cedar logs, stonemasons, and carpenters to build a palace for him. 2 David realized that the LORD had established him as king over Israel and that he had elevated his kingdom for the sake of his people Israel.

3 In Jerusalem David married more wives and fathered more sons and daughters. 4 These are the names of children born to him in Jerusalem: Shammua, Shobab, Nathan, Solomon, 5 Ibhar, Elishua, Elpelet, 6 Nogah, Nepheg, Japhia, 7 Elishama, Beeliada, and Eliphelet.

8 When the Philistines heard that David had been anointed king of all Israel, all the Philistines marched up to confront him. When David heard about it, he marched out against them. 9 Now the Philistines had come and raided the Valley of Rephaim. 10 David asked God, "Should I march up against the Philistines? Will you hand them over to me?" The LORD said to him, "March up! I will hand them over to you!" 11 So they marched against Baal Perazim and David defeated them there. David said, "Using me as his instrument, God has burst out against my enemies like water bursts out." So that place is called Baal Perazim. 12 The Philistines left their idols there, so David ordered that they be burned.

13 The Philistines again raided the valley. 14 So David again asked God what he should do. This time God told him, "Don't march up after them; circle around them and come against them in front of the trees. 15 When you hear the sound of marching in the tops of the trees, then attack. For at that moment God is going before you to strike down the army of the Philistines." 16 David did just as God commanded him, and they struck down the Philistine army from Gibeon to Gezer.

17 So David became famous in all the lands; the LORD caused all the nations to fear him.

14:8–17 Even after being defeated by the Israelites the first time, the Philistines once more advanced against Israel for battle. This is an example of foolish and ungodly persistence, for the Philistines were guilty of scorning the judgment of God. Indeed God was fighting on behalf of the Israelites by means of his holy angels.

JOHANNES PISCATOR
(1546–1625)
COMMENTARY ON FIRST CHRONICLES

DAVID BRINGS THE ARK TO JERUSALEM

15 David constructed buildings in the City of David; he then prepared a place for the ark of God and pitched a tent for it. 2 Then David said, "Only the Levites may carry the ark of God, for the LORD chose them to carry the ark of the LORD and to serve before him perpetually." 3 David assembled all Israel at Jerusalem to bring the ark of the LORD up to the place he had prepared for it. 4 David gathered together the descendants of Aaron and the Levites:

5 From the descendants of Kohath: Uriel the leader and 120 of his relatives.

6 From the descendants of Merari: Asaiah the leader and 220 of his relatives.

7 From the descendants of Gershom: Joel the leader and 130 of his relatives.

8 From the descendants of Elizaphan: Shemaiah the leader and 200 of his relatives.

9 From the descendants of Hebron: Eliel the leader and 80 of his relatives.

10 From the descendants of Uzziel: Amminadab the leader and 112 of his relatives.

11 David summoned the priests Zadok and Abiathar, along with the Levites Uriel, Asaiah, Joel, Shemaiah, Eliel, and Amminadab. 12 He told them: "You are the leaders of the Levites' families. You and your relatives must consecrate yourselves and

15:1–29 Although there will doubtlessly be many Michals among us, let us rejoice and praise God for the discovery of them, assuring ourselves that they were never of us. We should consider all those to be against us who either rejoice at the prosperity of our enemies or do not rejoice with us on account of our miraculous deliverance. Let us bring in the ark among us in two respects. Since we have already received the gospel, first, be constant, remaining in the purity of the truth, which is our most certain covenant of salvation in the merits of our Savior alone. And second, let us so reform our daily lives as becomes regenerate Christians: the great glory of our God.

KING JAMES VI **(1566–1625)**
A MEDITATION ON 1 CHRONICLES

bring the ark of the LORD God of Israel up to the place I have
prepared for it. 13The first time you did not carry it; that is why
the LORD God attacked us, because we did not ask him about the
proper way to carry it." 14The priests and Levites consecrated
themselves so they could bring up the ark of the LORD God
of Israel. 15The descendants of Levi carried the ark of God on
their shoulders with poles, just as Moses had commanded in
keeping with the LORD's instruction.

16David told the leaders of the Levites to appoint some of
their relatives as musicians; they were to play various instruments, including stringed instruments and cymbals, and to
sing loudly and joyfully. 17So the Levites appointed Heman
son of Joel; one of his relatives, Asaph son of Berechiah; one
of the descendants of Merari, Ethan son of Kushaiah; 18along
with some of their relatives who were second in rank, including
Zechariah, Jaaziel, Shemiramoth, Jehiel, Unni, Eliab, Benaiah,
Maaseiah, Mattithiah, Eliphelehu, Mikneiah, Obed-Edom, and
Jeiel, the gatekeepers.

19The musicians Heman, Asaph, and Ethan were to sound the
bronze cymbals; 20Zechariah, Aziel, Shemiramoth, Jehiel, Unni,
Eliab, Maaseiah, and Benaiah were to play the harps according to the *alamoth* style; 21Mattithiah, Eliphelehu, Mikneiah,
Obed-Edom, Jeiel, and Azaziah were to play the lyres according
to the *sheminith* style, as led by the director; 22Kenaniah, the
leader of the Levites, was in charge of transport, for he was
well-informed on this matter; 23Berechiah and Elkanah were
guardians of the ark; 24Shebaniah, Joshaphat, Nethanel, Amasai,
Zechariah, Benaiah, and Eliezer the priests were to blow the
trumpets before the ark of God; Obed-Edom and Jehiel were
also guardians of the ark.

25So David, the leaders of Israel, and the commanders of units
of a thousand went to bring up the ark of the LORD's covenant
from the house of Obed-Edom with celebration. 26When God
helped the Levites who were carrying the ark of the LORD's
covenant, they sacrificed seven bulls and seven rams. 27David
was wrapped in a linen robe, as were all the Levites carrying the
ark, the musicians, and Kenaniah the supervisor of transport
and the musicians; David also wore a linen ephod. 28All Israel
brought up the ark of the LORD's covenant; they were shouting,
blowing trumpets, sounding cymbals, and playing stringed instruments. 29As the ark of the LORD's covenant entered the City
of David, Michal, Saul's daughter, looked out the window. When
she saw King David jumping and celebrating, she despised him.

DAVID LEADS IN WORSHIP

16 They brought the ark of God and put it in the middle of
the tent David had pitched for it. Then they offered burnt
sacrifices and peace offerings before God. 2When David finished
offering burnt sacrifices and peace offerings, he pronounced a
blessing over the people in the LORD's name. 3He then handed
out to each Israelite man and woman a loaf of bread, a date
cake, and a raisin cake. 4He appointed some of the Levites to
serve before the ark of the LORD, to offer prayers, songs of
thanks, and hymns to the LORD God of Israel. 5Asaph was the
leader and Zechariah second-in-command, followed by Jeiel,
Shemiramoth, Jehiel, Mattithiah, Eliab, Benaiah, Obed-Edom,
and Jeiel. They were to play stringed instruments, Asaph was to
sound the cymbals, 6and the priests Benaiah and Jahaziel were
to blow trumpets regularly before the ark of God's covenant.

DAVID THANKS GOD

7 That day David first gave to Asaph and his colleagues this song of thanks to the LORD.

8 Give thanks to the LORD!
Call on his name!
Make known his accomplishments among the nations.
9 Sing to him! Make music to him!
Tell about all his miraculous deeds.
10 Boast about his holy name.
Let the hearts of those who seek the LORD rejoice.
11 Seek the LORD and the strength he gives.
Seek his presence continually!
12 Recall the miraculous deeds he performed,
his mighty acts and the judgments he decreed,
13 O children of Israel, God's servant,
you descendants of Jacob, God's chosen ones!
14 He is the LORD our God;
he carries out judgment throughout the earth.
15 Remember continually his covenantal decree,
the promise he made to a thousand generations—
16 the promise he made to Abraham,
the promise he made by oath to Isaac!
17 He gave it to Jacob as a decree,
to Israel as a lasting promise,
18 saying, "To you I will give the land of Canaan
as the portion of your inheritance."
19 When they were few in number,
just a very few, and foreign residents within it,
20 they wandered from nation to nation,
and from one kingdom to another.
21 He let no one oppress them;
he disciplined kings for their sake,
22 saying, "Don't touch my anointed ones!
Don't harm my prophets!"
23 Sing to the LORD, all the earth!
Announce every day how he delivers.
24 Tell the nations about his splendor,
tell all the nations about his miraculous deeds.
25 For the LORD is great and certainly worthy of praise,
he is more awesome than all gods.
26 For all the gods of the nations are worthless,
but the LORD made the heavens.
27 Majestic splendor emanates from him,
he is the source of strength and joy.
28 Ascribe to the LORD, O families of the nations,
ascribe to the LORD splendor and strength!
29 Ascribe to the LORD the splendor he deserves!
Bring an offering and enter his presence!
Worship the LORD in holy attire!
30 Tremble before him, all the earth!
The world is established, it cannot be moved.
31 Let the heavens rejoice, and the earth be happy!
Let the nations say, "The LORD reigns!"
32 Let the sea and everything in it shout!
Let the fields and everything in them celebrate!
33 Then let the trees of the forest shout with joy before the LORD,
for he comes to judge the earth!

16:7–43 On the occasion of the ark's entry, David first established that God be praised through the hand of Asaph and his brothers. That is, after this time it was usual for God to be celebrated through psalms and sacred music led by people who were appointed to do so. This is the same as when our Lord God is celebrated for his immense goodness to us either individually in private or publicly in the church, especially in the language of the people. In this way God's glory is spread widely, and remembrance of God's righteousness and goodness might inspire in many more people the fear of God and faith in God. The Psalms are sung in the common language among us for precisely this reason.

LUCAS OSIANDER
(1534–1604)
ANNOTATIONS ON FIRST CHRONICLES

34 Give thanks to the LORD, for he is good
and his loyal love endures.
35 Say this prayer: “Deliver us, O God who delivers us!
Gather us! Rescue us from the nations!
Then we will give thanks to your holy name,
and boast about your praiseworthy deeds.”
36 May the LORD God of Israel be praised,
in the future and forevermore.
Then all the people said, “We agree! Praise the LORD.”

DAVID APPOINTS WORSHIP LEADERS

[37]David left Asaph and his colleagues there before the ark of
the LORD’s covenant to serve before the ark regularly and fulfill
each day’s requirements, [38]including Obed-Edom and sixty-
eight colleagues. Obed-Edom son of Jeduthun and Hosah were
gatekeepers. [39]Zadok the priest and his fellow priests served
before the LORD’s tabernacle at the worship center in Gibeon,
[40]regularly offering burnt sacrifices to the LORD on the altar
for burnt sacrifice, morning and evening, according to what is
prescribed in the law of the LORD which he charged Israel to
observe. [41]Joining them were Heman, Jeduthun, and the rest
of those chosen and designated by name to give thanks to the
LORD. (For his loyal love endures!) [42]Heman and Jeduthun were
in charge of the music, including the trumpets, cymbals, and
the other musical instruments used in praising God. The sons
of Jeduthun guarded the entrance.
[43]Then all the people returned to their homes, and David
went to pronounce a blessing on his family.

GOD MAKES A PROMISE TO DAVID

17 When David had settled into his palace, he said to Nathan
the prophet, “Look, I am living in a palace made from cedar,
while the ark of the LORD’s covenant is under a tent.” [2]Nathan
said to David, “You should do whatever you have in mind, for
God is with you.”
[3]That night God told Nathan, [4]“Go, tell my servant David:
‘This is what the LORD says: “You must not build me a house
in which to live. [5]For I have not lived in a house from the time
I brought Israel up from Egypt to the present day. I have lived
in a tent that has been in various places. [6]Wherever I moved
throughout Israel, I did not say to any of the leaders whom I
appointed to care for my people Israel, ‘Why have you not built
me a house made from cedar?’”’
[7]“So now, say this to my servant David: ‘This is what the LORD
of Heaven’s Armies says: “I took you from the pasture and from
your work as a shepherd to make you a leader of my people Israel. [8]I was with you wherever you went, and I defeated all your
enemies before you. Now I will make you as famous as the great
men of the earth. [9]I will establish a place for my people Israel
and settle them there; they will live there and not be disturbed
anymore. Violent men will not oppress them again, as they
did in the beginning [10]and during the time when I appointed
judges to lead my people Israel. I will subdue all your enemies.
“‘“I declare to you that the LORD will build a dynastic house
for you! [11]When the time comes for you to die, I will raise up
your descendant, one of your own sons, to succeed you, and I
will establish his kingdom. [12]He will build me a house, and I will
make his dynasty permanent. [13]I will become his father, and he
will become my son. I will never withhold my loyal love from

17:1–15 There is no doubt that Solomon was the son of David and his successor in the kingdom. And he first built the temple of God at Jerusalem, and perhaps the Jews understand him to be the subject of the prophecy. But we may fairly ask them whether the oracle applies to Solomon that says “his dynasty will be permanent,” and also where God swore with the affirmation of an oath by his holy one, “Your house and your kingdom will stand before me permanently; your dynasty will be permanent” (2 Sam 7:16). And the words, “I will become his father and he will become my son” (2 Sam 7:14), how can they refer to Solomon? We require someone else, here revealed to arise from the seed of David. But there was no other born of him, save only our Lord and Savior Jesus the Christ of God, who alone is called through the whole world the Son of David, and whose kingdom continues and will continue, lasting for endless time.

EUSEBIUS OF CAESAREA
(C. 260–339)
THE PROOF OF THE GOSPEL

him, as I withheld it from the one who ruled before you. 14 I will put him in permanent charge of my house and my kingdom; his dynasty will be permanent.'" 15 Nathan told David all these words that were revealed to him.

DAVID PRAISES GOD

16 King David went in, sat before the LORD, and said: "Who am I, O LORD God, and what is my family, that you should have brought me to this point? 17 And you did not stop there, O God! You have also spoken about the future of your servant's family. You have revealed to me what men long to know, O LORD God. 18 What more can David say to you? You have honored your servant; you have given your servant special recognition. 19 O LORD, for the sake of your servant and according to your will, you have done this great thing in order to reveal your greatness. 20 O LORD, there is none like you; there is no God besides you! What we heard is true! 21 And who is like your people, Israel, a unique nation in the earth? Their God went to claim a nation for himself! You made a name for yourself by doing great and awesome deeds when you drove out nations before your people whom you had delivered from the Egyptian empire and its gods. 22 You made Israel your very own nation for all time. You, O LORD, became their God. 23 So now, O LORD, may the promise you made about your servant and his family become a permanent reality! Do as you promised, 24 so it may become a reality and you may gain lasting fame, as people say, 'The LORD of Heaven's Armies is the God of Israel.' The dynasty of your servant David will be established before you, 25 for you, my God, have revealed to your servant that you will build a dynasty for him. That is why your servant has had the courage to pray to you. 26 Now, O LORD, you are the true God; you have made this good promise to your servant. 27 Now you are willing to bless your servant's dynasty so that it may stand permanently before you, for you, O LORD, have blessed it and it will be blessed from now on into the future."

DAVID CONQUERS THE NEIGHBORING NATIONS

18 Later David defeated the Philistines and subdued them. He took Gath and its surrounding towns away from the Philistines.

2 He defeated the Moabites; the Moabites became David's subjects and brought tribute.

3 David defeated King Hadadezer of Zobah as far as Hamath, when he went to extend his authority to the Euphrates River. 4 David seized from him 1,000 chariots, 7,000 charioteers, and 20,000 infantrymen. David cut the hamstrings of all but 100 of Hadadezer's chariot horses. 5 The Arameans of Damascus came to help King Hadadezer of Zobah, but David killed 22,000 of the Arameans. 6 David placed garrisons in the territory of the Arameans of Damascus; the Arameans became David's subjects and brought tribute. The LORD protected David wherever he campaigned. 7 David took the golden shields which Hadadezer's servants had carried and brought them to Jerusalem. 8 From Tibhath and Kun, Hadadezer's cities, David took a great deal of bronze. (Solomon used it to make the big bronze basin called "The Sea," the pillars, and other bronze items.)

9 When King Tou of Hamath heard that David had defeated the entire army of King Hadadezer of Zobah, 10 he sent his son Hadoram to King David to extend his best wishes and to

18:1–17 David is set forth as an example of a victorious, godly, just, and wise king. He was an example of a victorious king since he achieved four military victories, which were reported in a brief time period from among different enemies. He was an example of godliness because he manifested himself as one who was not confident in a multitude of horses for battle and as one who consecrated the precious vessels he confiscated in battle. He was an example of justice since his governance was praised as being fair to all. Finally, David was an example of wisdom because he had regard for ordering the many different officials in his kingdom.

JOHANNES PISCATOR
(1546–1625)
COMMENTARY ON FIRST CHRONICLES

pronounce a blessing on him for his victory over Hadadezer,
for Tou had been at war with Hadadezer. He also sent various
items made of gold, silver, and bronze. [11]King David dedicated
these things to the LORD, along with the silver and gold which
he had carried off from all the nations, including Edom, Moab,
the Ammonites, the Philistines, and Amalek.

[12]Abishai son of Zeruiah killed 18,000 Edomites in the Valley
of Salt. [13]He placed garrisons in Edom, and all the Edomites
became David's subjects. The LORD protected David wherever
he campaigned.

DAVID'S OFFICIALS

[14]David reigned over all Israel; he guaranteed justice for all his
people. [15]Joab son of Zeruiah was commanding general of the
army; Jehoshaphat son of Ahilud was secretary; [16]Zadok son of
Ahitub and Abimelech son of Abiathar were priests; Shavsha
was scribe; [17]Benaiah son of Jehoiada supervised the Kerethites
and Pelethites; and David's sons were the king's leading officials.

DAVID'S CAMPAIGN AGAINST THE AMMONITES

19 Later King Nahash of the Ammonites died and his son
succeeded him. [2]David said, "I will express my loyalty to
Hanun son of Nahash, for his father was loyal to me." So David sent messengers to express his sympathy over his father's
death. When David's servants entered Ammonite territory to
visit Hanun and express the king's sympathy, [3]the Ammonite
officials said to Hanun, "Do you really think David is trying to
honor your father by sending these messengers to express his
sympathy? No, his servants have come to you so they can get
information and spy out the land!" [4]So Hanun seized David's
servants and shaved their beards off. He cut off the lower part
of their robes so that their buttocks were exposed and then sent
them away. [5]People came and told David what had happened
to the men, so he sent messengers to meet them, for the men
were thoroughly humiliated. The king said, "Stay in Jericho until
your beards grow again; then you may come back."

[6]When the Ammonites realized that David was disgusted
with them, Hanun and the Ammonites sent 1,000 talents of
silver to hire chariots and charioteers from Aram Naharaim,
Aram Maacah, and Zobah. [7]They hired 32,000 chariots, along
with the king of Maacah and his army, who came and camped
in front of Medeba. The Ammonites also assembled from their
cities and marched out to do battle.

[8]When David heard the news, he sent Joab and the entire
army to meet them. [9]The Ammonites marched out and were
deployed for battle at the entrance to the city, while the kings
who had come were by themselves in the field. [10]When Joab saw
that the battle would be fought on two fronts, he chose some
of Israel's best men and deployed them against the Arameans.
[11]He put his brother Abishai in charge of the rest of the army,
and they were deployed against the Ammonites. [12]Joab said, "If
the Arameans start to overpower me, you come to my rescue.
If the Ammonites start to overpower you, I will come to your
rescue. [13]Be strong! Let's fight bravely for the sake of our people
and the cities of our God! The LORD will do what he decides is
best!" [14]So Joab and his men marched toward the Arameans to
do battle, and they fled before him. [15]When the Ammonites saw
the Arameans flee, they fled before Joab's brother Abishai and
withdrew into the city. Joab went back to Jerusalem.

19:1—20:8 This story should serve as an instructive, exemplary warning against this thoroughly perverse vice of distrust. For the counselors of King Hanun distrusted David, and thereby they were the cause of ruining both their master and the whole country. Hence let us learn not to be influenced by our own malice to put a bad interpretation on what could be taken as good. God will certainly punish us at once for such an attitude. What therefore happened to the people of Ammon reminds us to take things in good part and not to let our spirits be poised with suspicion and distrust when it is not necessary.

JOHN CALVIN (1509–1564)
COMPLETE COMMENTARY ON THE BIBLE

[16]When the Arameans realized they had been defeated by
Israel, they sent for reinforcements from beyond the Euphrates River, led by Shophach the commanding general of Hadadezer's army. [17]When David was informed, he gathered all
Israel, crossed the Jordan River, and marched against them.
David deployed his army against the Arameans for battle and
they fought against him. [18]The Arameans fled before Israel.
David killed 7,000 Aramean charioteers and 40,000 infantrymen; he also killed Shophach the commanding general. [19]When
Hadadezer's subjects saw they were defeated by Israel, they
made peace with David and became his subjects. The Arameans
were no longer willing to help the Ammonites.

20 In the spring, at the time when kings normally conduct
wars, Joab led the army into battle and devastated the
land of the Ammonites. He went and besieged Rabbah, while David stayed in Jerusalem. Joab defeated Rabbah and tore it down.
[2]David took the crown from the head of their king and wore
it (its weight was a talent of gold, and it was set with precious
stones). He took a large amount of plunder from the city. [3]He
removed the city's residents and made them labor with saws,
iron picks, and axes. This was his policy with all the Ammonite
cities. Then David and all the army returned to Jerusalem.

BATTLES WITH THE PHILISTINES

[4]Later there was a battle with the Philistines in Gezer. At that
time Sibbekai the Hushathite killed Sippai, one of the descendants of the Rephaim, and the Philistines were subdued.
[5]There was another battle with the Philistines in which Elhanan son of Jair the Bethlehemite killed the brother of Goliath
the Gittite, whose spear had a shaft as big as the crossbeam of
a weaver's loom.
[6]In a battle in Gath there was a large man who had six fingers
on each hand and six toes on each foot—twenty-four in all! He
too was a descendant of Rapha. [7]When he taunted Israel, Jonathan son of Shimea, David's brother, killed him.
[8]These were the descendants of Rapha who lived in Gath;
they were killed by the hand of David and his soldiers.

THE LORD SENDS A PLAGUE AGAINST ISRAEL

21 An adversary opposed Israel, inciting David to count how
many warriors Israel had. [2]David told Joab and the leaders of the army, "Go, count the number of warriors from Beer
Sheba to Dan. Then bring back a report to me so I may know
how many we have." [3]Joab replied, "May the LORD make his
army a hundred times larger! My master, O king, do not all of
them serve my master? Why does my master want to do this?
Why bring judgment on Israel?"
[4]But the king's edict stood, despite Joab's objections. So
Joab left and traveled throughout Israel before returning to
Jerusalem. [5]Joab reported to David the number of warriors. In
all Israel there were 1,100,000 sword-wielding soldiers; Judah
alone had 470,000 sword-wielding soldiers. [6]Now Joab did not
number Levi and Benjamin, for the king's edict disgusted him.
[7]God was also offended by it, so he attacked Israel.
[8]David said to God, "I have sinned greatly by doing this! Now,
please remove the guilt of your servant, for I have acted very
foolishly." [9]The LORD told Gad, David's prophet, [10]"Go, tell David,
'This is what the LORD says: "I am offering you three forms of
judgment from which to choose. Pick one of them."'" [11]Gad went

21:1–30 When it is said, "An adversary opposed Israel, inciting David to count how many warriors Israel had," it must be explained that for wise and holy ends, God permitted the devil to do it. That Satan, the enemy of God and all good, should stand up against Israel is not strange. But that he should influence David, the man of God's own heart, to do a wrong thing may well be wondered at. One would think him one of those whom the wicked one touches not. No, even the best saints, till they come to heaven, must never think themselves out of the reach of Satan's temptations. Now, when Satan meant to do the Israelites a mischief, he provoked David, the best friend they had, to number them and so to offend God and set him against them.

MATTHEW HENRY **(1662–1714)**
COMMENTARY ON THE WHOLE BIBLE

to David and told him, "This is what the LORD says: 'Pick one of these: [12]three years of famine, or three months being chased by your enemies and struck down by their swords, or three days being struck down by the LORD, during which a plague will invade the land and the angel of the LORD will destroy throughout Israel's territory.' Now, decide what I should tell the one who sent me." [13]David said to Gad, "I am very upset! I prefer to be attacked by the LORD, for his mercy is very great; I do not want to be attacked by men!" [14]So the LORD sent a plague through Israel, and 70,000 Israelite men died.

[15]God sent an angel to ravage Jerusalem. As he was doing so, the LORD watched and relented from his judgment. He told the angel who was destroying, "That's enough! Stop now!"

Now the angel of the LORD was standing near the threshing floor of Ornan the Jebusite. [16]David looked up and saw the angel of the LORD standing between the earth and sky with his sword drawn and in his hand, stretched out over Jerusalem. David and the leaders, covered with sackcloth, threw themselves down with their faces to the ground. [17]David said to God, "Was I not the one who decided to number the army? I am the one who sinned and committed this awful deed! As for these sheep—what have they done? O LORD my God, attack me and my family, but remove the plague from your people!"

[18]So the angel of the LORD told Gad to instruct David to go up and build an altar for the LORD on the threshing floor of Ornan the Jebusite. [19]So David went up as Gad instructed him to do in the name of the LORD. [20]While Ornan was threshing wheat, he turned and saw the messenger, and he and his four sons hid themselves. [21]When David came to Ornan, Ornan looked and saw David; he came out from the threshing floor and bowed to David with his face to the ground. [22]David said to Ornan, "Sell me the threshing floor so I can build on it an altar for the LORD—I'll pay top price—so that the plague may be removed from the people." [23]Ornan told David, "You can have it! My master, the king, may do what he wants. Look, I am giving you the oxen for burnt sacrifices, the threshing sledges for wood, and the wheat for an offering. I give it all to you." [24]King David replied to Ornan, "No, I insist on buying it for top price. I will not offer to the LORD what belongs to you or offer a burnt sacrifice that cost me nothing. [25]So David bought the place from Ornan for 600 pieces of gold. [26]David built there an altar to the LORD and offered burnt sacrifices and peace offerings. He called out to the LORD, and the LORD responded by sending fire from the sky and consuming the burnt sacrifice on the altar. [27]The LORD ordered the messenger to put his sword back into its sheath.

[28]At that time, when David saw that the LORD responded to him at the threshing floor of Ornan the Jebusite, he sacrificed there. [29]Now the LORD's tabernacle (which Moses had made in the wilderness) and the altar for burnt sacrifices were at that time at the worship center in Gibeon. [30]But David could not go before it to seek God's will, for he was afraid of the sword of

22 the angel of the LORD. [1]David then said, "This is the place where the temple of the LORD God will be, along with the altar for burnt sacrifices for Israel."

DAVID ORDERS A TEMPLE TO BE BUILT

[2]David ordered the resident foreigners in the land of Israel to be called together. He appointed some of them to be stonecutters to chisel stones for the building of God's temple. [3]David supplied

22:1–19 Now the temple of the Lord, to be sure, was prepared by David but built by Solomon. The intended location of the temple was given to David by an angel. It is where David first made a sacrifice and also added these words: "This is the place where the temple of the LORD God will be, along with the altar for burnt sacrifices for Israel." For all the interpreters of the sacred scriptures here consent that the place was Jerusalem, on Mount Moriah, where Abraham would have sacrificed his son Isaac. And in this fateful location the temple was placed, where the hill of Golgotha, or Calvary, was not far away. The holy Gospels testified that on top of Mount Moriah, the place of the holy hill, Christ was sacrificed for the sins of the entire world. Now, in Christ all the sacrifices, both of the temple and of the ancients, were prefigured. The use and purpose of the temple was none other than the use and purpose of the tabernacle beforehand.

HEINRICH BULLINGER
(1504–1575)
DECADES

a large amount of iron for the nails of the doors of the gates
and for braces, more bronze than could be weighed, [4]and more
cedar logs than could be counted. (The Sidonians and Tyrians
had brought a large amount of cedar logs to David.)
[5]David said, "My son Solomon is just an inexperienced young
man, and the temple to be built for the LORD must be especially magnificent so it will become famous and be considered
splendid by all the nations. Therefore I will make preparations
for its construction." So David made extensive preparations
before he died.
[6]He summoned his son Solomon and charged him to build a
temple for the LORD God of Israel. [7]David said to Solomon: "My
son, I really wanted to build a temple to honor the LORD my
God. [8]But this was the LORD's message to me: 'You have spilled a
great deal of blood and fought many battles. You must not build
a temple to honor me, for you have spilled a great deal of blood
on the ground before me. [9]Look, you will have a son, who will
be a peaceful man. I will give him rest from all his enemies on
every side. Indeed, Solomon will be his name; I will give Israel
peace and quiet during his reign. [10]He will build a temple to
honor me; he will become my son, and I will become his father.
I will grant to his dynasty permanent rule over Israel.'
[11]"Now, my son, may the LORD be with you! May you succeed
and build a temple for the LORD your God, just as he announced
you would. [12]Only may the LORD give you insight and understanding when he places you in charge of Israel, so you may
obey the law of the LORD your God. [13]Then you will succeed, if
you carefully obey the rules and regulations which the LORD
ordered Moses to give to Israel. Be strong and brave! Don't be
afraid and don't panic! [14]Now, look, I have made every effort to
supply what is needed to build the LORD's temple. I have stored
up 100,000 talents of gold, 1,000,000 talents of silver, and so
much bronze and iron it cannot be weighed, as well as wood and
stones. Feel free to add more! [15]You also have available many
workers, including stonecutters, masons, carpenters, and an
innumerable array of workers who are skilled [16]in using gold,
silver, bronze, and iron. Get up and begin the work! May the
LORD be with you!"
[17]David ordered all the officials of Israel to support his son
Solomon. [18]He told them, "The LORD your God is with you!
He has made you secure on every side, for he handed over to
me the inhabitants of the region and the region is subdued
before the LORD and his people. [19]Now seek the LORD your
God wholeheartedly and with your entire being! Get up and
build the sanctuary of the LORD God! Then you can bring the
ark of the LORD's covenant and the holy items dedicated to
God's service into the temple that is built to honor the LORD."

DAVID ORGANIZES THE LEVITES

23 When David was old and approaching the end of his life,
he made his son Solomon king over Israel.
[2]David assembled all the leaders of Israel, along with the
priests and the Levites. [3]The Levites who were thirty years old
and up were counted; there were 38,000 men. [4]David said, "Of
these, 24,000 are to direct the work of the LORD's temple; 6,000
are to be officials and judges; [5]4,000 are to be gatekeepers; and
4,000 are to praise the LORD with the instruments I supplied
for worship." [6]David divided them into groups corresponding
to the sons of Levi: Gershon, Kohath, and Merari.

23:1–32 It may be asked whether the way David distributed the holy Levites in this passage can be used to defend the current practice of some churches to order their priests. I respond that it is not. The reason is because the ministry of the Levites pertained to the shadow of the Old Testament to prefigure the sacrifice of Christ. But now that Christ has made his offering, the shadow has been abolished. What's more, in the New Testament Christ has instituted new orders for ministers: "And he himself gave some as apostles, some as prophets, some as evangelists, and some as pastors and teachers" (Eph 4:11).

JOHANNES PISCATOR
(1546–1625)
COMMENTARY ON FIRST CHRONICLES

[7]The Gershonites included Ladan and Shimei.
[8]The sons of Ladan: Jehiel the oldest, Zetham, and Joel—three
in all.
[9]The sons of Shimei: Shelomoth, Haziel, and Haran—three
in all.
These were the leaders of the family of Ladan.
[10]The sons of Shimei: Jahath, Zina, Jeush, and Beriah. These
were Shimei's sons—four in all. [11]Jahath was the oldest and Zizah
the second oldest. Jeush and Beriah did not have many sons,
so they were considered one family with one responsibility.
[12]The sons of Kohath: Amram, Izhar, Hebron, and Uzziel—
four in all.
[13]The sons of Amram: Aaron and Moses.
Aaron and his descendants were chosen on a permanent
basis to consecrate the most holy items, to offer sacrifices
before the LORD, to serve him, and to praise his name. [14]The
descendants of Moses the man of God were considered Levites.
[15]The sons of Moses: Gershom and Eliezer.
[16]The son of Gershom: Shebuel the oldest.
[17]The son of Eliezer was Rehabiah, the oldest. Eliezer had no
other sons, but Rehabiah had many descendants.
[18]The son of Izhar: Shelomith the oldest.
[19]The sons of Hebron: Jeriah the oldest, Amariah the second,
Jahaziel the third, and Jekameam the fourth.
[20]The sons of Uzziel: Micah the oldest, and Isshiah the second.
[21]The sons of Merari: Mahli and Mushi.
The sons of Mahli: Eleazar and Kish.
[22]Eleazar died without having sons; he had only daughters.
The sons of Kish, their cousins, married them.
[23]The sons of Mushi: Mahli, Eder, and Jeremoth—three in all.
[24]These were the descendants of Levi according to their families, that is, the leaders of families as counted and individually
listed who carried out assigned tasks in the LORD's temple and
were twenty years old and up. [25]For David said, "The LORD God
of Israel has given his people rest and has permanently settled
in Jerusalem. [26]So the Levites no longer need to carry the tabernacle or any of the items used in its service." [27]According to
David's final instructions, the Levites twenty years old or older
were counted.
[28]Their job was to help Aaron's descendants in the service
of the LORD's temple. They were to take care of the courtyards,
the rooms, ceremonial purification of all holy items, and other
jobs related to the service of God's temple. [29]They also took
care of the bread that is displayed, the flour for offerings, the
unleavened wafers, the round cakes, the mixing, and all the measuring. [30]They also stood in a designated place every morning
and offered thanks and praise to the LORD. They also did this in
the evening [31]and whenever burnt sacrifices were offered to the
LORD on the Sabbath and at new moon festivals and assemblies.
A designated number were to serve before the LORD regularly
in accordance with regulations. [32]They were in charge of the
meeting tent and the Holy Place, and helped their relatives,
the descendants of Aaron, in the service of the LORD's temple.

DAVID ORGANIZES THE PRIESTS

24 The divisions of Aaron's descendants were as follows:
The sons of Aaron: Nadab, Abihu, Eleazar, and Ithamar.
[2]Nadab and Abihu died before their father did; they had no
sons. Eleazar and Ithamar served as priests.

24:1–31 David arranged for singers to chant psalms daily at the time of sacrifice to the tune of musical instruments. This was to arouse the minds of the people in attendance to remembrance and love of heavenly matters. David called together all the descendants of the sons of Aaron, and he divided them into 24 sections, choosing individuals from each section as high priests. David set up these sections in such a way that the individual high priests, along with the priests who were under them, should minister for eight successive days, that is, from Sabbath to Sabbath.

VENERABLE BEDE
(C. 672–735)
HOMILIES ON THE GOSPELS

[3]David, Zadok (a descendant of Eleazar), and Ahimelech (a
descendant of Ithamar) divided them into groups to carry out
their assigned responsibilities. [4]The descendants of Eleazar
had more leaders than the descendants of Ithamar, so they
divided them up accordingly; the descendants of Eleazar
had sixteen leaders, while the descendants of Ithamar had
eight. [5]They divided them by lots, for there were officials of
the Holy Place and officials designated by God among the
descendants of both Eleazar and Ithamar. [6]The scribe Shemaiah son of Nethanel, a Levite, wrote down their names
before the king, the officials, Zadok the priest, Ahimelech
son of Abiathar, and the leaders of the priestly and Levite
families. One family was drawn by lot from Eleazar, and then
the next from Ithamar.

[7]The first lot went to Jehoiarib,
the second to Jedaiah,
[8]the third to Harim,
the fourth to Seorim,
[9]the fifth to Malkijah,
the sixth to Mijamin,
[10]the seventh to Hakkoz,
the eighth to Abijah,
[11]the ninth to Jeshua,
the tenth to Shecaniah,
[12]the eleventh to Eliashib,
the twelfth to Jakim,
[13]the thirteenth to Huppah,
the fourteenth to Jeshebeab,
[14]the fifteenth to Bilgah,
the sixteenth to Immer,
[15]the seventeenth to Hezir,
the eighteenth to Happizzez,
[16]the nineteenth to Pethahiah,
the twentieth to Jehezkel,
[17]the twenty-first to Jakin,
the twenty-second to Gamul,
[18]the twenty-third to Delaiah,
the twenty-fourth to Maaziah.

[19]This was the order in which they carried out their
assigned responsibilities when they entered the LORD's
temple, according to the regulations given them by their
ancestor Aaron, just as the LORD God of Israel had instructed
him.

REMAINING LEVITES

[20]The rest of the Levites included:
Shubael from the sons of Amram,
Jehdeiah from the sons of Shubael,
[21]the firstborn Isshiah from Rehabiah and the sons of
Rehabiah,
[22]Shelomoth from the Izharites,
Jahath from the sons of Shelomoth.
[23]The sons of Hebron: Jeriah, Amariah the second, Jahaziel
the third, and Jekameam the fourth.
[24]The son of Uzziel: Micah;
Shamir from the sons of Micah.
[25]The brother of Micah: Isshiah.
Zechariah from the sons of Isshiah.
[26]The sons of Merari: Mahli and Mushi.

The son of Jaaziah: Beno.
[27]The sons of Merari, from Jaaziah: Beno, Shoham, Zaccur, and Ibri.
[28]From Mahli: Eleazar, who had no sons.
[29]From Kish: Jerahmeel.
[30]The sons of Mushi: Mahli, Eder, and Jerimoth.
These were the Levites, listed by their families.
[31]Like their relatives, the descendants of Aaron, they also cast lots before King David, Zadok, Ahimelech, the leaders of families, the priests, and the Levites. The families of the oldest son cast lots along with those of the youngest.

DAVID ORGANIZES THE MUSICIANS

25 David and the army officers selected some of the sons of Asaph, Heman, and Jeduthun to prophesy as they played stringed instruments and cymbals. The following men were assigned this responsibility:
[2]From the sons of Asaph: Zaccur, Joseph, Nethaniah, and Asarelah. The sons of Asaph were supervised by Asaph, who prophesied under the king's supervision.
[3]From the sons of Jeduthun: Gedaliah, Zeri, Jeshaiah, Hashabiah, and Mattithiah—six in all, under supervision of their father Jeduthun, who prophesied as he played a harp, giving thanks and praise to the LORD.
[4]From the sons of Heman: Bukkiah, Mattaniah, Uzziel, Shebuel, Jerimoth, Hananiah, Hanani, Eliathah, Giddalti, Romamti-Ezer, Joshbekashah, Mallothi, Hothir, and Mahazioth.
[5]All these were the sons of Heman, the king's prophet. God had promised him these sons in order to make him prestigious. God gave Heman fourteen sons and three daughters.
[6]All these were under the supervision of their fathers; they were musicians in the LORD's temple, playing cymbals and stringed instruments as they served in God's temple. Asaph, Jeduthun, and Heman were under the supervision of the king.
[7]They and their relatives, all of them skilled and trained to make music to the LORD, numbered 288.
[8]They cast lots to determine their responsibilities—oldest as well as youngest, teacher as well as student.
[9]The first lot went to Asaph's son Joseph and his relatives and sons—twelve in all,
the second to Gedaliah and his relatives and sons—twelve in all,
[10]the third to Zaccur and his sons and relatives—twelve in all,
[11]the fourth to Izri and his sons and relatives—twelve in all,
[12]the fifth to Nethaniah and his sons and relatives—twelve in all,
[13]the sixth to Bukkiah and his sons and relatives—twelve in all,
[14]the seventh to Jesharelah and his sons and relatives—twelve in all,
[15]the eighth to Jeshaiah and his sons and relatives—twelve in all,
[16]the ninth to Mattaniah and his sons and relatives—twelve in all,
[17]the tenth to Shimei and his sons and relatives—twelve in all,
[18]the eleventh to Azarel and his sons and relatives—twelve in all,
[19]the twelfth to Hashabiah and his sons and relatives—twelve in all,

25:1–31 When the prophet David grew old in years devoted to the Lord, he chose 4,000 young men from the people of Israel to render the psalms, which he had composed through the Lord's inspiration, so as to attain the great sweetness of heavenly grace by means of pipes, lyres, harps, timbrels, cymbals, trumpets, and their own voices. This sweet harmony clearly comprised a threefold division: a rational part consisting of the human voice, an irrational part comprising musical instruments, and a common part resulting from the fusion of the two, such that the human voice issued forth in fixed melody and the tune of the instruments joined in harmonious accompaniment. With this performance the sweet and pleasant music presaged the catholic church, which by the Lord's gift was to believe with varied tongues and diverse blending in the single harmony of faith.

CASSIODORUS (C. 485–C. 585)
EXPLANATION OF THE PSALMS

[20]the thirteenth to Shubael and his sons and relatives—
twelve in all,
[21]the fourteenth to Mattithiah and his sons and relatives—
twelve in all,
[22]the fifteenth to Jerimoth and his sons and relatives—twelve
in all,
[23]the sixteenth to Hananiah and his sons and relatives—
twelve in all,
[24]the seventeenth to Joshbekashah and his sons and
relatives—twelve in all,
[25]the eighteenth to Hanani and his sons and relatives—
twelve in all,
[26]the nineteenth to Mallothi and his sons and relatives—
twelve in all,
[27]the twentieth to Eliathah and his sons and relatives—twelve
in all,
[28]the twenty-first to Hothir and his sons and relatives—
twelve in all,
[29]the twenty-second to Giddalti and his sons and relatives—
twelve in all,
[30]the twenty-third to Mahazioth and his sons and relatives—
twelve in all,
[31]the twenty-fourth to Romamti-Ezer and his sons and
relatives—twelve in all.

DIVISIONS OF GATEKEEPERS

26 The divisions of the gatekeepers:
From the Korahites: Meshelemiah, son of Kore, one
of the sons of Asaph.
[2]Meshelemiah's sons:
The firstborn Zechariah, the second Jediael, the third Zebadiah, the fourth Jathniel, [3]the fifth Elam, the sixth Jehohanan,
and the seventh Elihoenai.
[4]Obed-Edom's sons:
The firstborn Shemaiah, the second Jehozabad, the third
Joah, the fourth Sakar, the fifth Nethanel, [5]the sixth Ammiel,
the seventh Issachar, and the eighth Peullethai. (Indeed, God
blessed Obed-Edom.)
[6]His son Shemaiah also had sons, who were leaders of their
families, for they were highly respected. [7]The sons of Shemaiah:
Othni, Rephael, Obed, and Elzabad. His relatives Elihu and
Semakiah were also respected.
[8]All these were the descendants of Obed-Edom. They and
their sons and relatives were respected men, capable of doing
their responsibilities. There were sixty-two of them related
to Obed-Edom.
[9]Meshelemiah had sons and relatives who were respected—
eighteen in all.
[10]Hosah, one of the descendants of Merari, had sons:
The firstborn Shimri (he was not actually the firstborn, but
his father gave him that status), [11]the second Hilkiah, the third
Tebaliah, and the fourth Zechariah. All Hosah's sons and relatives numbered thirteen.
[12]These divisions of the gatekeepers, corresponding to their
leaders, had assigned responsibilities, like their relatives, as
they served in the LORD's temple.
[13]They cast lots, both young and old, according to their
families, to determine which gate they would be responsible
for. [14]The lot for the east gate went to Shelemiah. They then

26:1–19 The gatekeepers were officials who took care that no human profanity entered the temple or that it was polluted, violated, or otherwise desecrated by disgraceful acts or sacrilege. Ministers today are janitors of the spiritual temple, the church, and they take care that the temple of God might not become a place where believers are polluted by disgraceful things, as it is written in Colossians: "Be careful not to allow anyone to captivate you through an empty, deceitful philosophy" (Col 2:8). Instead be kept whole in the wonderful heavenly teaching and sacraments.

LUCAS OSIANDER
(1534–1604)
ANNOTATIONS ON FIRST CHRONICLES

cast lots for his son Zechariah, a wise adviser, and the lot for
the north gate went to him. [15]Obed-Edom was assigned the
south gate, and his sons were assigned the storehouses. [16]Shup-
pim and Hosah were assigned the west gate, along with the
Shalleketh gate on the upper road. One guard was adjacent to
another. [17]Each day there were six Levites posted on the east,
four on the north, and four on the south. At the storehouses
they were posted in pairs. [18]At the court on the west there
were four posted on the road and two at the court. [19]These
were the divisions of the gatekeepers who were descendants
of Korah and Merari.

SUPERVISORS OF THE STOREHOUSES

[20]Their fellow Levites were in charge of the storehouses in God's
temple and the storehouses containing consecrated items.
[21]The descendants of Ladan, who were descended from Gershon
through Ladan and were leaders of the families of Ladan the
Gershonite, included Jehieli [22]and the sons of Jehieli, Zetham
and his brother Joel. They were in charge of the storehouses
in the LORD's temple.

[23]As for the Amramites, Izharites, Hebronites, and Uzzielites:
[24]Shebuel son of Gershom, the son of Moses, was the supervisor of the storehouses. [25]His relatives through Eliezer included: Rehabiah his son, Jeshaiah his son, Joram his son, Zikri
his son, and Shelomith his son. [26]Shelomith and his relatives
were in charge of all the storehouses containing the consecrated items dedicated by King David, the family leaders who
led units of a thousand and a hundred, and the army officers.
[27]They had dedicated some of the plunder taken in battles
to be used for repairs on the LORD's temple. [28]They were also
in charge of everything dedicated by Samuel the prophet,
Saul son of Kish, Abner son of Ner, and Joab son of Zeruiah;
Shelomith and his relatives were in charge of everything that
had been dedicated.

[29]As for the Izharites: Kenaniah and his sons were given responsibilities outside the temple as officers and judges over
Israel.

[30]As for the Hebronites: Hashabiah and his relatives, 1,700
respected men, were assigned responsibilities in Israel west
of the Jordan; they did the LORD's work and the king's service.

[31]As for the Hebronites: Jeriah was the leader of the Hebronites according to the genealogical records. In the fortieth
year of David's reign, they examined the records and discovered
there were highly respected men in Jazer in Gilead. [32]Jeriah had
2,700 relatives who were respected family leaders. King David
placed them in charge of the Reubenites, the Gadites, and the
half-tribe of Manasseh; they took care of all matters pertaining
to God and the king.

LEADERS OF THE ARMY

27 What follows is a list of Israelite family leaders and commanders of units of a thousand and a hundred, as well
as their officers who served the king in various matters. Each
division was assigned to serve for one month during the year;
each consisted of 24,000 troops.

[2]Jashobeam son of Zabdiel was in charge of the first division,
which was assigned the first month. His division consisted of
24,000 troops. [3]He was a descendant of Perez; he was in charge
of all the army officers for the first month.

27:1–15 **In the kingdoms of this world, readiness for war forms a security for peace; in like manner, nothing so much encourages Satan's assaults as to be unwatchful. As long as we stand armed with the whole armor of God, in the exercise of faith and preparation of heart for the conflict, we shall certainly be safe and probably enjoy inward peace.**

MATTHEW HENRY **(1662–1714)**
COMMENTARY ON THE WHOLE BIBLE

[4]Dodai the Ahohite was in charge of the division assigned
the second month; Mikloth was the next in rank. His division
consisted of 24,000 troops.
[5]The third army commander, assigned the third month,
was Benaiah son of Jehoiada the priest. He was the leader of
his division, which consisted of 24,000 troops. [6]Benaiah was
the leader of the thirty warriors and his division; his son was
Ammizabad.
[7]The fourth, assigned the fourth month, was Asahel, brother
of Joab; his son Zebadiah succeeded him. His division consisted
of 24,000 troops.
[8]The fifth, assigned the fifth month, was the commander
Shamhuth the Izrahite. His division consisted of 24,000 troops.
[9]The sixth, assigned the sixth month, was Ira son of Ikkesh
the Tekoite. His division consisted of 24,000 troops.
[10]The seventh, assigned the seventh month, was Helez the
Pelonite, an Ephraimite. His division consisted of 24,000 troops.
[11]The eighth, assigned the eighth month, was Sibbekai the
Hushathite, a Zerahite. His division consisted of 24,000 troops.
[12]The ninth, assigned the ninth month, was Abiezer the Anathothite, a Benjaminite. His division consisted of 24,000 troops.
[13]The tenth, assigned the tenth month, was Maharai the Netophathite, a Zerahite. His division consisted of 24,000 troops.
[14]The eleventh, assigned the eleventh month, was Benaiah the Pirathonite, an Ephraimite. His division consisted of
24,000 troops.
[15]The twelfth, assigned the twelfth month, was Heldai the
Netophathite, a descendant of Othniel. His division consisted
of 24,000 troops.
[16]The officers of the Israelite tribes:
Eliezer son of Zikri was the leader of the Reubenites,
Shephatiah son of Maacah led the Simeonites,
[17]Hashabiah son of Kemuel led the Levites,
Zadok led the descendants of Aaron,
[18]Elihu, a brother of David, led Judah,
Omri son of Michael led Issachar,
[19]Ishmaiah son of Obadiah led Zebulun,
Jerimoth son of Azriel led Naphtali,
[20]Hoshea son of Azaziah led the Ephraimites,
Joel son of Pedaiah led the half-tribe of Manasseh,
[21]Iddo son of Zechariah led the half-tribe of Manasseh in
Gilead,
Jaasiel son of Abner led Benjamin,
[22]Azarel son of Jeroham led Dan.
These were the commanders of the Israelite tribes.
[23]David did not count the males twenty years old and under,
for the LORD had promised to make Israel as numerous as the
stars in the sky. [24]Joab son of Zeruiah started to count the men
but did not finish. God was angry with Israel because of this, so
the number was not recorded in the scroll called The Annals
of King David.

ROYAL OFFICIALS

[25]Azmaveth son of Adiel was in charge of the king's storehouses;
Jonathan son of Uzziah was in charge of the storehouses in
the field, in the cities, in the towns, and in the towers.
[26]Ezri son of Kelub was in charge of the field workers who
farmed the land.
[27]Shimei the Ramathite was in charge of the vineyards;

Zabdi the Shiphmite was in charge of the wine stored in the vineyards.

28 Baal Hanan the Gederite was in charge of the olive and sycamore trees in the foothills;

Joash was in charge of the storehouses of olive oil.

29 Shitrai the Sharonite was in charge of the cattle grazing in Sharon;

Shaphat son of Adlai was in charge of the cattle in the valleys.

30 Obil the Ishmaelite was in charge of the camels;

Jehdeiah the Meronothite was in charge of the donkeys.

31 Jaziz the Hagrite was in charge of the sheep.

All these were the officials in charge of King David's property.

32 Jonathan, David's uncle, was a wise adviser and scribe;

Jehiel son of Hacmoni cared for the king's sons.

33 Ahithophel was the king's adviser;

Hushai the Arkite was the king's confidant.

34 Ahithophel was succeeded by Jehoiada son of Benaiah and by Abiathar.

Joab was the commanding general of the king's army.

DAVID COMMISSIONS SOLOMON TO BUILD THE TEMPLE

28:1–21 The Holy Spirit puts little difference between the will and the deed, especially as the will is inclined to that which is good. An example of this is found in David's willingness and desire to build a temple for the Lord. He did not end up building it, yet his purpose and desire to build it were acceptable to God. And generally this is true: that God accepts the will and desire as the deed so that the will, desire, and endeavor to walk in the ways of God clearly reveal to us that we are the children of God and are accepted by God as if we are walking holy and without blame.

HENRY AIRAY (C. 1560–1616)
LECTURES ON PHILIPPIANS

28 David assembled in Jerusalem all the officials of Israel,
including the commanders of the tribes, the commanders
of the army divisions that served the king, the commanders
of units of a thousand and a hundred, the officials who were
in charge of all the property and livestock of the king and his
sons, the eunuchs, and the warriors, including the most skilled
of them.
2 King David rose to his feet and said: "Listen to me, my
brothers and my people. I wanted to build a temple where
the ark of the LORD's covenant could be placed as a footstool
for our God. I have made the preparations for building it. 3 But
God said to me, 'You must not build a temple to honor me,
for you are a warrior and have spilled blood.' 4 The LORD God
of Israel chose me out of my father's entire family to become
king over Israel and have a permanent dynasty. Indeed, he
chose Judah as leader, and my father's family within Judah,
and then he picked me out from among my father's sons and
made me king over all Israel. 5 From all the many sons the LORD
has given me, he chose Solomon my son to rule on his behalf
over Israel. 6 He said to me, 'Solomon your son is the one who
will build my temple and my courts, for I have chosen him to
become my son and I will become his father. 7 I will establish
his kingdom permanently, if he remains committed to obeying my commands and regulations, as you are doing this day.'
8 So now, in the sight of all Israel, the LORD's assembly, and in
the hearing of our God, I say this: Carefully observe all the
commands of the LORD your God, so that you may possess
this good land and may leave it as a permanent inheritance
for your children after you.
9 "And you, Solomon my son, obey the God of your father and
serve him with a submissive attitude and a willing spirit, for
the LORD examines all minds and understands every motive
of one's thoughts. If you seek him, he will let you find him, but
if you abandon him, he will reject you permanently. 10 Realize
now that the LORD has chosen you to build a temple as his
sanctuary. Be strong and do it!"

11 David gave to his son Solomon the blueprints for the temple porch, its buildings, its treasuries, its upper areas, its inner rooms, and the room for atonement. 12 He gave him the blueprints of all he envisioned for the courts of the LORD's temple, all the surrounding rooms, the storehouses of God's temple, and the storehouses for the holy items.

13 He gave him the regulations for the divisions of priests and Levites, for all the assigned responsibilities within the LORD's temple, and for all the items used in the service of the LORD's temple.

14 He gave him the prescribed weight for all the gold items to be used in various types of service in the LORD's temple, for all the silver items to be used in various types of service; 15 for the gold lampstands and their gold lamps, including the weight of each lampstand and its lamps; for the silver lampstands, including the weight of each lampstand and its lamps, according to the prescribed use of each lampstand; 16 for the gold used in the display tables, including the amount to be used in each table; for the silver to be used in the silver tables; 17 for the pure gold used for the meat forks, bowls, and jars; for the small gold bowls, including the weight for each bowl; for the small silver bowls, including the weight for each bowl; 18 and for the refined gold of the incense altar.

He gave him the blueprint for the seat of the gold cherubim that spread their wings and provide shelter for the ark of the LORD's covenant.

19 David said, "All this I put in writing as the LORD directed me and gave me insight regarding the details of the blueprints."

20 David said to his son Solomon: "Be strong and brave! Do it! Don't be afraid and don't panic! For the LORD God, my God, is with you. He will not leave you or abandon you before all the work for the service of the LORD's temple is finished. 21 Here are the divisions of the priests and Levites who will perform all the service of God's temple. All the willing and skilled men are ready to assist you in all the work and perform their service. The officials and all the people are ready to follow your instructions."

THE PEOPLE CONTRIBUTE TO THE PROJECT

29 King David said to the entire assembly: "My son Solomon, the one whom God has chosen, is just an inexperienced young man, and the task is great, for this palace is not for man, but for the LORD God. 2 So I have made every effort to provide what is needed for the temple of my God, including the gold, silver, bronze, iron, wood, as well as a large amount of onyx, settings of antimony and other stones, all kinds of precious stones, and alabaster. 3 Now, to show my commitment to the temple of my God, I donate my personal treasure of gold and silver to the temple of my God, in addition to all that I have already supplied for this holy temple. 4 This includes 3,000 talents of gold from Ophir and 7,000 talents of refined silver for overlaying the walls of the buildings, 5 for gold and silver items, and for all the work of the craftsmen. Who else wants to contribute to the LORD today?"

6 The leaders of the families, the leaders of the Israelite tribes, the commanders of units of a thousand and a hundred, and the supervisors of the king's work contributed willingly. 7 They donated for the service of God's temple 5,000 talents and 10,000 darics of gold, 10,000 talents of silver, 18,000

29:1–9 We give God nothing of our own, but only what we have received from him. For whether the gifts are physical or spiritual, we receive them all of God and therefore we must give him the glory.

GENEVA BIBLE **(1560)**

talents of bronze, and 100,000 talents of iron. 8 All who pos-
sessed precious stones donated them to the treasury of the
LORD's temple, which was under the supervision of Jehiel the
Gershonite. 9 The people were delighted with their donations,
for they contributed to the LORD with a willing attitude; King
David was also very happy.

DAVID PRAISES THE LORD

10 David praised the LORD before the entire assembly:
"O LORD God of our father Israel, you deserve praise forevermore! 11 O LORD, you are great, mighty, majestic, magnificent, glorious, and sovereign over all the sky and earth! You,
LORD, have dominion and exalt yourself as the ruler of all.
12 You are the source of wealth and honor; you rule over all.
You possess strength and might to magnify and give strength
to all. 13 Now, our God, we give thanks to you and praise your
majestic name!
14 "But who am I and who are my people that we should be in
a position to contribute this much? Indeed, everything comes
from you, and we have simply given back to you what is yours.
15 For we are resident foreigners and temporary settlers in your
presence, as all our ancestors were; our days are like a shadow on
the earth, without security. 16 O LORD our God, all this wealth,
which we have collected to build a temple for you to honor
your holy name, comes from you; it all belongs to you. 17 I know,
my God, that you examine thoughts and are pleased with integrity. With pure motives I contribute all this; and now I look
with joy as your people who have gathered here contribute to
you. 18 O LORD God of our ancestors Abraham, Isaac, and Israel,
always maintain these motives of your people and keep them
devoted to you. 19 Make my son Solomon willing to obey your
commands, rules, and regulations, and to complete building
the palace for which I have made preparations."
20 David told the entire assembly: "Praise the LORD your God!"
So the entire assembly praised the LORD God of their ancestors;
they bowed down and stretched out flat on the ground before
the LORD and the king.

DAVID DESIGNATES SOLOMON KING

21 The next day they made sacrifices and offered burnt sacrifices
to the LORD (1,000 bulls, 1,000 rams, 1,000 lambs), along with
their accompanying drink offerings and many other sacrifices
for all Israel. 22 They held a feast before the LORD that day and
celebrated.
Then they designated Solomon, David's son, as king a second time; before the LORD they anointed him as ruler and Zadok as priest. 23 Solomon sat on the LORD's throne as king in
place of his father David; he was successful and all Israel was
loyal to him. 24 All the officers and warriors, as well as all of
King David's sons, pledged their allegiance to King Solomon.
25 The LORD greatly magnified Solomon before all Israel and
bestowed on him greater majesty than any king of Israel before
him.

29:1–9 We give God nothing of our own, but only what we have received from him. For whether the gifts are physical or spiritual, we receive them all of God and therefore we must give him the glory.

GENEVA BIBLE (1560)

DAVID'S REIGN COMES TO AN END

26 David son of Jesse reigned over all Israel. 27 He reigned over
Israel forty years; he reigned in Hebron seven years and in Jerusalem thirty-three years. 28 He died at a good old age, having
enjoyed long life, wealth, and honor. His son Solomon succeeded

him. 29 King David's accomplishments, from start to finish, are
recorded in the Annals of Samuel the prophet, the Annals of
Nathan the prophet, and the Annals of Gad the prophet. 30 Recorded there are all the facts about his reign and accomplishments, and an account of the events that involved him, Israel,
and all the neighboring kingdoms.

AUTHOR	AUDIENCE	DATE	PURPOSE	THEMES
Unknown; possibly Ezra	The people of Judah who had returned from exile in Babylon	Between 450 and 400 BC	This book was written to showcase the rise and fall of the Davidic kingdom, emphasizing the role of blessings for obedience and destruction for disobedience, and the hope God's sovereignty brings.	God's sovereignty; blessings and obedience; and destruction and disobedience

The second book of Chronicles picks up the events of Israel's story where the first book ended: the establishment of Solomon as king over David's kingdom. The book was written for the people of Israel after their captivity. Although it covers much the same content as 1 and 2 Kings, the Chronicler arranged the material so that the children of Israel would see their postexilic situation as one of hope and impending redemption. Unlike the books of Kings, which focused on Israel's failures, this book showcases Israel's reforms and ends with their redemption.

The Geneva Bible outlined three considerations for reading 2 Chronicles, highlighting the Lord's providential deliverance:

> First, the people made recourse to the Lord and by earnest prayer were heard; therefore the plagues were removed. Second, it is a great offense against God for those who fear him and profess his religion to join into relationship with the wicked. Third, good rulers always loved God's prophets, and they were very zealous to set forth his religion throughout all their dominion. But, on the contrary, evil rulers always hated God's ministers, deposed them, and—in exchange for the true religion and Word of God—set up idolatry and served God according to human fantasy.

From the start, this book is oriented by Solomon's building and dedication of the temple, which anchors Israel's past and future in the Lord's continued presence with his people. When the Lord appeared to Solomon, he exhorted him to obey his commands and observe his decrees as his father David had, promising blessing and the preservation of his kingdom. But he warned: "If you people ever turn away from me, fail to obey the regulations and rules I instructed you to keep, and decide to serve and worship other gods, then I will remove you from my land I have given you, I will abandon this temple I have consecrated with my presence, and I will make you an object of mockery and ridicule among all the nations" (7:19–20). Unfortunately, Solomon and his successors chose the latter.

During Solomon's reign a number of pagan nations still inhabited the land—"The Israelites were unable to wipe them out" (8:8). This may seem like an act of mercy on the part of Israel, but it was instead an act of disobedience that led to idolatry and rebellious living. Eventually the kingdom split into two, and a number of kings ascended to

2 CHRONICLES

the thrones of Israel and Judah, kings who "did evil in the sight of the LORD" (21:16). The eventual consequence for both nations was judgment at the hands of their enemies.

The Chronicler explained how it was the Lord who "brought against them the king of the Babylonians . . . God handed everyone over to him" (36:17). In response to wickedness of his people, God directed the pagan king Nebuchadnezzar to wage war against Judah, delivering God's people into the hands of the Babylonians. John Wesley made an important connection between Judah's wickedness and God's promises: "Abraham was called out of Ur of the Chaldees [Babylonians], when God took him into covenant with himself. And now his degenerate seed are carried into that country again, to signify that they had forfeited all that kindness wherewith they had been loved for their father's sake, and the benefit of the covenant into which he was called." The Lord made good on his promises of judgment for his people's willful rebellion.

Yet this book isn't merely about disobedience and destruction. The second book of Chronicles also highlights the hope of deliverance through a renewed commitment to obedience. "Asa did what the LORD his God desired and approved" (14:2) as did Jehoshaphat, Uzziah, Hezekiah, and Josiah. Not only did they obey God, but they also put the covenant at the center of national life by purifying the temple and instituting religious reform. This emphasis on reform and obedience is meant to offer a word of hope for a people devastated by exile, a note upon which the book itself ends.

The book concludes with the Lord's sovereignly directing the heart of another king—Cyrus of Persia—to allow Judah to go back to the promised land. Matthew Henry offered profound insight into this hopeful theme of redemption:

> God had promised the restoring of the captives and the rebuilding of Jerusalem at the end of 70 years; that time to favor Zion, that set time, came at last. Though God's church be cast down, it is not cast off; though his people be corrected, they are not abandoned; though thrown into the furnace, they are not lost there, nor left there any longer than till the dross be separated. Though God contend long, he will not contend always.

1:1–17 Some think that Solomon asked for all kinds of wisdom not only to govern but also to understand all divine mysteries and all natural things. That's because his understanding was enlarged in these areas. But the text is plain: It says that he asked only for wisdom to govern and manage the great affairs committed to him. But God, who is wont to give more to his faithful servants than they ask, gave him a most large understanding in all other things also.

JOHN MAYER (1583–1664)
COMMENTARY ON SECOND CHRONICLES

THE LORD GIVES SOLOMON WISDOM

1 Solomon son of David solidified his royal authority, for the
LORD his God was with him and magnified him greatly.
[2]Solomon addressed all Israel, including those who commanded units of a thousand and a hundred, the judges, and all
the leaders of all Israel who were heads of families. [3]Solomon
and the entire assembly went to the worship center in Gibeon,
for the tent where they met God was located there, which Moses
the LORD's servant had made in the wilderness. [4](Now David
had brought up the ark of God from Kiriath Jearim to the place
he had prepared for it, for he had pitched a tent for it in Jerusalem. [5]But the bronze altar made by Bezalel son of Uri, son of
Hur, was in front of the LORD's tabernacle. Solomon and the
entire assembly prayed to him there.) [6]Solomon went up to the
bronze altar before the LORD which was at the meeting tent,
and he offered up 1,000 burnt sacrifices.
[7]That night God appeared to Solomon and said to him,
"Tell me what I should give you." [8]Solomon replied to God,
"You demonstrated great loyalty to my father David and have
made me king in his place. [9]Now, LORD God, may your promise
to my father David be realized, for you have made me king over
a great nation as numerous as the dust of the earth. [10]Now
give me wisdom and discernment so I can effectively lead this
nation. Otherwise no one is able to make judicial decisions for
this great nation of yours."
[11]God said to Solomon, "Because you desire this, and did not
ask for riches, wealth, and honor, or for vengeance on your enemies, and because you did not ask for long life, but requested
wisdom and discernment so you can make judicial decisions for
my people over whom I have made you king, [12]you are granted
wisdom and discernment. Furthermore I am giving you riches,
wealth, and honor surpassing that of any king before or after you."
[13]Solomon left the meeting tent at the worship center in
Gibeon and went to Jerusalem, where he reigned over Israel.

SOLOMON'S WEALTH

[14]Solomon accumulated chariots and horses. He had 1,400
chariots and 12,000 horses. He kept them in assigned cities
and in Jerusalem. [15]The king made silver and gold as plentiful
in Jerusalem as stones; cedar was as plentiful as sycamore fig
trees are in the foothills. [16]Solomon acquired his horses from
Egypt and from Que; the king's traders purchased them from
Que. [17]They paid 600 silver pieces for each chariot from Egypt
and 150 silver pieces for each horse. They also sold chariots and
horses to all the kings of the Hittites and to the kings of Syria.

SOLOMON GATHERS BUILDING MATERIALS FOR THE TEMPLE

2 Solomon ordered a temple to be built to honor the LORD,
as well as a royal palace for himself. [2]Solomon had 70,000
common laborers and 80,000 stonecutters in the hills, in addition to 3,600 supervisors.
[3]Solomon sent a message to King Huram of Tyre: "Help me as
you did my father David, when you sent him cedar logs for the
construction of his palace. [4]Look, I am ready to build a temple
to honor the LORD my God and to dedicate it to him in order
to burn fragrant incense before him, to set out the bread that is
regularly displayed, and to offer burnt sacrifices each morning
and evening, and on Sabbaths, new moon festivals, and at other

2:1–16 When people are converted to God, it is rightly said that they are holy temples of God, for God lives in them. A temple made of stones, however, can be truly said to be holy when it is dedicated to the service of God. Yet if God were to be in any one place, then God would not be God, which Solomon himself means when he says, "The highest heavens cannot contain him." Why then did Solomon, who taught about the spiritual temple, build a temple if God does not live in a temple made of human hands? Solomon posed this question to make clear to the people that they would gather at the temple for preaching, prayer, and public ceremonies.

VIKTORIN STRIGEL
(C. 1524–1569)
BOOK OF CHRONICLES

times appointed by the LORD our God. This is something Israel
must do on a permanent basis. 5I will build a great temple, for
our God is greater than all gods. 6Of course, who can really build
a temple for him, since the sky and the highest heavens cannot
contain him? Who am I that I should build him a temple! It will
really be only a place to offer sacrifices before him.
7"Now send me a man who is skilled in working with gold,
silver, bronze, and iron, as well as purple-, crimson-, and blue-
colored fabrics, and who knows how to engrave. He will work with
my skilled craftsmen here in Jerusalem and Judah, whom my
father David provided. 8Send me cedars, evergreens, and algum
trees from Lebanon, for I know your servants are adept at cutting
down trees in Lebanon. My servants will work with your servants
9to supply me with large quantities of timber, for I am building a
great, magnificent temple. 10Look, I will pay your servants who
cut the timber 20,000 cors of ground wheat, 20,000 cors of barley,
120,000 gallons of wine, and 120,000 gallons of olive oil."
11King Huram of Tyre sent this letter to Solomon: "Because
the LORD loves his people, he has made you their king." 12Huram
also said, "Worthy of praise is the LORD God of Israel, who made
the sky and the earth! He has given King David a wise son who
has discernment and insight and will build a temple for the
LORD, as well as a royal palace for himself. 13Now I am sending
you Huram Abi, a skilled and capable man, 14whose mother is
a Danite and whose father is a Tyrian. He knows how to work
with gold, silver, bronze, iron, stones, and wood, as well as purple,
blue, white, and crimson fabrics. He knows how to do all kinds
of engraving and understands any design given to him. He will
work with your skilled craftsmen and the skilled craftsmen of
my lord David your father. 15Now let my lord send to his servants
the wheat, barley, olive oil, and wine he has promised; 16we will
get all the timber you need from Lebanon and bring it in raft-like
bundles by sea to Joppa. You can then haul it on up to Jerusalem."
17Solomon took a census of all the male resident foreigners
in the land of Israel, after the census his father David had taken.
There were 153,600 in all. 18He designated 70,000 as common
laborers, 80,000 as stonecutters in the hills, and 3,600 as supervisors to make sure the people completed the work.

THE BUILDING OF THE TEMPLE

3 Solomon began building the LORD's temple in Jerusalem on
Mount Moriah, where the LORD had appeared to his father
David. This was the place that David prepared at the threshing
floor of Ornan the Jebusite. 2He began building on the second
day of the second month of the fourth year of his reign.
3Solomon laid the foundation for God's temple; its length (determined according to the old standard of measure) was 90 feet,
and its width 30 feet. 4The porch in front of the main hall was 30
feet long, corresponding to the width of the temple, and its height
was 30 feet. He plated the inside with pure gold. 5He paneled the
main hall with boards made from evergreen trees and plated it
with fine gold, decorated with palm trees and chains. 6He decorated the temple with precious stones; the gold he used came
from Parvaim. 7He overlaid the temple's rafters, thresholds, walls
and doors with gold; he carved decorative cherubim on the walls.
8He made the Most Holy Place; its length was 30 feet, corresponding to the width of the temple, and its width 30 feet. He
plated it with 600 talents of fine gold. 9The gold nails weighed
50 shekels; he also plated the upper areas with gold. 10In the

3:1–17 For this was the temple in which were sacrifices and prayers and services. This was the temple where was the Most Holy Place, and the cherubim, the covenant, and the golden pot—the great symbols of God's providence toward that people. This was the temple where oracles from heaven were constantly being received, where prophets became inspired, where the fashioning was not the work of human art but proceeded from the wisdom of God, where the walls were on every side resplendent with much gold and where, in surpassing excellence, costliness of material and perfection of art met together and demonstrated that there was no other temple like this upon earth! Not only the perfection of art, but also the wisdom of God assisted in that building. For Solomon had learned all, not intuitively and from himself but from God, and having received the design of it from the heavens, he then marked it out and erected it.

CHRYSOSTOM (C. 347–407)
HOMILIES ON STATUTES

JEROME:

FATHER OF THE COMMON BIBLE

c. 347–420

Jerome had a singular and lasting impact on the church's experience of the Bible, even though his personal life was at times marked by less than ideal choices. Born in the region known as Slovenia around 347, he traveled to Rome as a young man to receive a classical education in Latin, Greek, rhetoric, and philosophy. As a student in Rome, he engaged in a lifestyle of drinking and sexual promiscuity, which began to nag at his conscience. Beset by pangs of guilt, Jerome took to visiting the burial crypts of early Christians in the Roman catacombs, where he experienced vivid fears of judgment. He explored desert monasticism as a way to leave behind his life of sin but was unable to part with his favorite Greek and Roman authors.

On a journey to Jerusalem, Jerome experienced a life change: He fell ill and had a vision of Jesus, who chastised him for seemingly loving the Roman philosopher Cicero more than his Savior Christ. After the experience he vowed to make studying the Bible his vocation. He lived up to the vow, becoming the most prolific biblical scholar and writer of his generation.

A few years later he traveled from Rome to Constantinople to study under the Cappadocian father Gregory of Nazianzus only to return again as secretary to Pope Damasus I. The two became close, and Damasus chose Jerome for one of the most important developments in the life of the church: creating a unified translation of the Bible into Latin, the language of the people.

While there had been other similar translations, Jerome's work stood out for several reasons, perhaps most notably the fact that he translated the Old Testament into Latin from the original Hebrew. All previous translations had used a Greek translation of the Old Testament known as the Septuagint. Jerome started with the Gospels, finishing that initial translation work in 384; then he completed his revision of the rest of the New Testament from existing Latin translations, finishing in 390. He then spent 15 years on the Old Testament, translating the 39 books of the Hebrew scriptures considered to be canon and choosing to forego the Apocrypha. His translation was literal yet maintained an everyday style. This Bible was the standard of the entire Western church for hundreds of years and was known in the Middle Ages as *versio vulgata*—translated "common version"—or simply the Vulgate.

Jerome is reported to have spent the last 34 years of his life living and working in a cave near Bethlehem—supposedly the cave in which Jesus was born. He left behind an astonishing collection of scriptural commentaries, theological and polemical writings, and of course his translation of the Bible. As the father of the common Bible, Jerome played a key role in bringing the message of God's love into a language that all people could read and understand.

IMPORTANT WORKS

THE LETTERS OF ST. JEROME

AGAINST THE LUCIFERIANS

AGAINST THE PELAGIANS

Most Holy Place he made two images of cherubim and plated
them with gold. [11]The combined wing span of the cherubim
was 30 feet. One of the first cherub's wings was 7½ feet long and
touched one wall of the temple; its other wing was also 7½ feet
long and touched one of the second cherub's wings. [12]Likewise
one of the second cherub's wings was 7½ feet long and touched
the other wall of the temple; its other wing was also 7½ feet long
and touched one of the first cherub's wings. [13]The combined
wingspan of these cherubim was 30 feet. They stood upright, facing inward. [14]He made the curtain out of blue, purple, crimson,
and white fabrics, and embroidered on it decorative cherubim.
[15]In front of the temple he made two pillars which had a
combined length of 52½ feet, with each having a plated capital 7½ feet high. [16]He made ornamental chains and put them
on top of the pillars. He also made 100 pomegranate-shaped
ornaments and arranged them within the chains. [17]He set up
the pillars in front of the temple, one on the right side and the
other on the left. He named the one on the right Yakin and the
one on the left Boaz.

4 He made a bronze altar, 30 feet long, 30 feet wide, and 15 feet
high. [2]He also made the big bronze basin called "The Sea."
It measured 15 feet from rim to rim, was circular in shape, and
stood 7½ feet high. Its circumference was 45 feet. [3]Images of
bulls were under it all the way around, ten every 18 inches all
the way around. The bulls were in two rows and had been cast
with "The Sea." [4]"The Sea" stood on top of twelve bulls. Three
faced northward, three westward, three southward, and three
eastward. "The Sea" was placed on top of them, and they all faced
outward. [5]It was four fingers thick, and its rim was like that of
a cup shaped like a lily blossom. It could hold 18,000 gallons.
[6]He made ten washing basins; he put five on the south side and
five on the north side. In them they rinsed the items used for
burnt sacrifices; the priests washed in "The Sea."
[7]He made ten gold lampstands according to specifications
and put them in the temple, five on the right and five on the
left. [8]He made ten tables and set them in the temple, five on
the right and five on the left. He also made 100 gold bowls. [9]He
made the courtyard of the priests and the large enclosure and
its doors; he plated their doors with bronze. [10]He put "The Sea"
on the south side, in the southeast corner.
[11]Huram Abi made the pots, shovels, and bowls. He finished
all the work on God's temple he had been assigned by King Solomon. [12]He made the two pillars, the two bowl-shaped tops
of the pillars, the latticework for the bowl-shaped tops of the
two pillars, [13]the 400 pomegranate-shaped ornaments for the
latticework of the two pillars (each latticework had two rows
of these ornaments at the bowl-shaped top of the pillar), [14]the
ten movable stands with their ten basins, [15]the big bronze basin
called "The Sea" with its twelve bulls underneath, [16]and the pots,
shovels, and meat forks. All the items King Solomon assigned
Huram Abi to make for the LORD's temple were made from polished bronze. [17]The king had them cast in earth foundries in the
region of the Jordan between Sukkoth and Zarethan. [18]Solomon
made so many of these items they did not weigh the bronze.
[19]Solomon also made these items for God's temple: the gold
altar, the tables on which the Bread of the Presence was kept,
[20]the pure gold lampstands and their lamps which burned as
specified at the entrance to the inner sanctuary, [21]the pure
gold flower-shaped ornaments, lamps, and tongs, [22]the pure

4:1—5:1 Frequent mention is made of this altar in Solomon's time and of the offerings made on it. But in the book of Kings there is no mention of making it. This altar of burnt offerings far exceeded that altar in the book of Exodus, for the temple far exceeded the tabernacle. The altar's twenty cubits in length and width was at least ten yards squared. It was so large because the priests offered so many oxen and other great beasts on it. The altar's height was at least fifteen feet high, and there was a plain ascent like a hill to go up and make offerings on it. In this respect the priest is said to "come down" from the altar. The reason that it was so high was so that the people in the courts could all see the offerings laid on the altar and, by the sight of the smoke and the flames ascending, they could be moved to raise up their hearts to heaven. And by the sight of the burnt offerings, they could remember their sins and of the sacrifice of Christ to expiate these sins.

THE WESTMINSTER ANNOTATIONS
(1683)

gold trimming shears, basins, pans, and censers, and the gold
door sockets for the inner sanctuary (the Most Holy Place) and
for the doors of the main hall of the temple.
5 1When Solomon
had finished constructing the LORD's temple, he put the holy
items that belonged to his father David (the silver, gold, and all
the other articles) in the treasuries of God's temple.

SOLOMON MOVES THE ARK INTO THE TEMPLE

2Then Solomon convened Israel's elders—all the leaders of
the Israelite tribes and families—in Jerusalem, so they could
witness the transferal of the ark of the covenant of the LORD
from the City of David (that is, Zion). 3All the men of Israel
assembled before the king during the festival in the seventh
month. 4When all Israel's elders had arrived, the Levites lifted
the ark. 5The priests and Levites carried the ark, the tent where
God appeared to his people, and all the holy items in the tent.
6Now King Solomon and all the Israelites who had assembled
with him went on ahead of the ark and sacrificed more sheep
and cattle than could be counted or numbered.

7The priests brought the ark of the covenant of the LORD
to its assigned place in the inner sanctuary of the temple, in
the Most Holy Place under the wings of the cherubim. 8The
cherubim's wings extended over the place where the ark sat;
the cherubim overshadowed the ark and its poles. 9The poles
were so long their ends extending out from the ark were visible from in front of the inner sanctuary, but they could not be
seen from beyond that point. They have remained there to this
very day. 10There was nothing in the ark except the two tablets
Moses had placed there in Horeb. (It was there that the LORD
made a covenant with the Israelites after he brought them out
of the land of Egypt.)

11The priests left the Holy Place. All the priests who participated had consecrated themselves, no matter which division
they represented. 12All the Levites who were musicians, including Asaph, Heman, Jeduthun, and their sons and relatives, wore
linen. They played cymbals and stringed instruments as they
stood east of the altar. They were accompanied by 120 priests
who blew trumpets. 13The trumpeters and musicians played
together, praising and giving thanks to the LORD. Accompanied by trumpets, cymbals, and other instruments, they loudly
praised the LORD, singing: "Certainly he is good; certainly his
loyal love endures!" Then a cloud filled the LORD's temple. 14The
priests could not carry out their duties because of the cloud;
the LORD's splendor filled God's temple.

6 Then Solomon said, "The LORD has said that he lives in thick
darkness. 2O LORD, I have built a lofty temple for you, a place
where you can live permanently." 3Then the king turned around
and pronounced a blessing over the whole Israelite assembly as
they stood there. 4He said, "The LORD God of Israel is worthy
of praise because he has fulfilled what he promised my father
David. 5He told David, 'Since the day I brought my people out
of the land of Egypt, I have not chosen a city from all the tribes
of Israel to build a temple in which to live. Nor did I choose
a man as leader of my people Israel. 6But now I have chosen
Jerusalem as a place to live, and I have chosen David to lead
my people Israel.' 7Now my father David had a strong desire
to build a temple to honor the LORD God of Israel. 8The LORD
told my father David, 'It is right for you to have a strong desire to build a temple to honor me. 9But you will not build the

6:3–11 God was not worshiped except through types in this temple of Solomon. Hence let us conclude that, as God is spirit and truth (see John 4:24), there must also be a temple that corresponds to his nature. Thus we are bound to glorify God because his promise has finally been fulfilled in us who deserved only to be built into a pigsty since we were so full of infection and rot! Yet our Lord Jesus Christ has purified us and willed that we be built into a house set apart for him. Furthermore we see that this promise was not restricted to the Jews, but that it had its extension in all nations of the earth when it pleased God to manifest his mercy everywhere.

JOHN CALVIN (1509–1564)
COMPLETE COMMENTARY ON THE BIBLE

temple; your very own son will build the temple for my honor.'
[10]The LORD has kept the promise he made. I have taken my
father David's place and have occupied the throne of Israel,
as the LORD promised. I have built this temple for the honor
of the LORD God of Israel [11]and set up in it a place for the ark
containing the covenant the LORD made with the Israelites."
[12]He stood before the altar of the LORD in front of the entire
assembly of Israel and spread out his hands. [13]Solomon had
made a bronze platform and had placed it in the middle of the
enclosure. It was 7½ feet long, 7½ feet wide, and 4½ feet high. He
stood on it and then got down on his knees in front of the entire
assembly of Israel. He spread out his hands toward the sky, [14]and
prayed: "O LORD God of Israel, there is no god like you in heaven
or on earth! You maintain covenantal loyalty to your servants
who obey you with sincerity. [15]You have kept your word to your
servant, my father David; this very day you have fulfilled what
you promised. [16]Now, O LORD God of Israel, keep the promise
you made to your servant, my father David, when you said, 'You
will never fail to have a successor ruling before me on the throne
of Israel, provided that your descendants watch their step and
obey my law as you have done.' [17]Now, O LORD God of Israel,
may the promise you made to your servant David be realized.
[18]"God does not really live with humankind on the earth!
Look, if the sky and the highest heaven cannot contain you,
how much less this temple I have built! [19]But respond favorably
to your servant's prayer and his request for help, O LORD my
God. Answer the desperate prayer your servant is presenting
to you. [20]Night and day may you watch over this temple, the
place where you promised you would live. May you answer your
servant's prayer for this place. [21]Respond to the requests of
your servant and your people Israel for this place. Hear from
your heavenly dwelling place and respond favorably and forgive.
[22]"When someone is accused of sinning against his neighbor
and the latter pronounces a curse on the alleged offender before your altar in this temple, [23]listen from heaven and make a
just decision about your servants' claims. Condemn the guilty
party, declare the other innocent, and give both of them what
they deserve.
[24]"If your people Israel are defeated by an enemy because
they sinned against you, then if they come back to you, renew
their allegiance to you, and pray for your help before you in
this temple, [25]then listen from heaven, forgive the sin of your
people Israel, and bring them back to the land you gave to them
and their ancestors.
[26]"The time will come when the skies are shut up tightly and
no rain falls because your people sinned against you. When they
direct their prayers toward this place, renew their allegiance
to you, and turn away from their sin because you punish them,
[27]then listen from heaven and forgive the sin of your servants,
your people Israel. Certainly you will then teach them the right
way to live and send rain on your land that you have given your
people to possess.
[28]"The time will come when the land suffers from a famine,
a plague, blight, and disease, or a locust invasion, or when their
enemy lays siege to the cities of the land, or when some other
type of plague or epidemic occurs. [29]When all your people Israel
pray and ask for help, as they acknowledge their intense pain and
spread out their hands toward this temple, [30]then listen from your
heavenly dwelling place, forgive their sin, and act favorably toward

each one based on your evaluation of their motives. (Indeed you
are the only one who can correctly evaluate the motives of all
people.) [31]Then they will honor you by obeying you throughout
their lifetimes as they live on the land you gave to our ancestors.
[32]"Foreigners who do not belong to your people Israel will
come from a distant land because of your great reputation and
your ability to accomplish mighty deeds; they will come and
direct their prayers toward this temple. [33]Then listen from
your heavenly dwelling place and answer all the prayers of the
foreigners. Then all the nations of the earth will acknowledge
your reputation, obey you as your people Israel do, and recognize that this temple I built belongs to you.
[34]"When you direct your people to march out and fight their
enemies, and they direct their prayers to you toward this chosen
city and this temple I built for your honor, [35]then listen from
heaven to their prayers for help and vindicate them.
[36]"The time will come when your people will sin against you
(for there is no one who is sinless!) and you will be angry at
them and deliver them over to their enemies, who will take
them as prisoners to their land, whether far away or close by.
[37]When your people come to their senses in the land where
they are held prisoner, they will repent and beg for your mercy
in the land of their imprisonment, admitting, 'We have sinned
and gone astray, we have done evil!' [38]When they return to you
with all their heart and being in the land where they are held
prisoner and direct their prayers toward the land you gave to
their ancestors, your chosen city, and the temple I built for your
honor, [39]then listen from your heavenly dwelling place to their
prayers for help, vindicate them, and forgive your sinful people.
[40]"Now, my God, may you be attentive and responsive to the
prayers offered in this place. [41]Now ascend, O LORD God, to
your resting place, you and the ark of your strength! May your
priests, O LORD God, experience your deliverance. May your
loyal followers rejoice in the prosperity you give. [42]O LORD
God, do not reject your chosen ones! Remember the faithful
promises you made to your servant David!"

SOLOMON DEDICATES THE TEMPLE

7 When Solomon finished praying, fire came down from heaven
and consumed the burnt offering and the sacrifices, and the
LORD's splendor filled the temple. [2]The priests were unable to
enter the LORD's temple because the LORD's splendor filled the
LORD's temple. [3]When all the Israelites saw the fire come down
and the LORD's splendor over the temple, they got on their
knees with their faces downward toward the pavement. They
worshiped and gave thanks to the LORD, saying, "Certainly he
is good; certainly his loyal love endures!"
[4]The king and all the people were presenting sacrifices to the
LORD. [5]King Solomon sacrificed 22,000 cattle and 120,000 sheep.
Then the king and all the people dedicated God's temple. [6]The
priests stood in their assigned spots, along with the Levites who
had the musical instruments used for praising the LORD. (These
were the ones King David made for giving thanks to the LORD and
which were used by David when he offered praise, saying, "Certainly his loyal love endures.") Opposite the Levites, the priests
were blowing the trumpets, while all Israel stood there. [7]Solomon
consecrated the middle of the courtyard that is in front of the
LORD's temple. He offered burnt sacrifices, grain offerings, and the
fat from the peace offerings there because the bronze altar that

7:1 The surest evidence of God's acceptance of our prayers is the descent of his holy fire upon us. As a further token that God accepted Solomon's prayer, the glory of the Lord filled the house; the heart that is filled with a holy awe and reverence of the divine glory, to which God manifests his greatness and (which is no less his glory) his goodness, is thereby owned as a living temple.

JOHN WESLEY (1703–1791)
EXPLANATORY NOTES ON THE BIBLE

Solomon had made was too small to hold all these offerings. [8]At
that time Solomon and all Israel with him celebrated a festival
for seven days. This great assembly included people from Lebo
Hamath in the north to the Stream of Egypt in the south. [9]On the
eighth day they held an assembly, for they had dedicated the altar
for seven days and celebrated the festival for seven more days.
[10]On the twenty-third day of the seventh month, Solomon sent
the people home. They left happy and contented because of the
good the LORD had done for David, Solomon, and his people Israel.

THE LORD GIVES SOLOMON A PROMISE AND A WARNING

[11]After Solomon finished building the LORD's temple and the
royal palace and accomplished all his plans for the LORD's temple
and his royal palace, [12]the LORD appeared to Solomon at night
and said to him: "I have answered your prayer and chosen this
place to be my temple where sacrifices are to be made. [13]When
I close up the sky so that it doesn't rain, or command locusts to
devour the land's vegetation, or send a plague among my people,
[14]if my people, who belong to me, humble themselves, pray,
seek to please me, and repudiate their sinful practices, then I
will respond from heaven, forgive their sin, and heal their land.
[15]Now I will be attentive and responsive to the prayers offered
in this place. [16]Now I have chosen and consecrated this temple
by making it my permanent home; I will be constantly present
there. [17]You must serve me as your father David did. Do everything I commanded and obey my rules and regulations. [18]Then I
will establish your dynasty, just as I promised your father David,
'You will not fail to have a successor ruling over Israel.'

[19]"But if you people ever turn away from me, fail to obey the
regulations and rules I instructed you to keep, and decide to
serve and worship other gods, [20]then I will remove you from
my land I have given you, I will abandon this temple I have
consecrated with my presence, and I will make you an object of
mockery and ridicule among all the nations. [21]As for this temple, which was once majestic, everyone who passes by it will be
shocked and say, 'Why did the LORD do this to this land and this
temple?' [22]Others will then answer, 'Because they abandoned
the LORD God of their ancestors, who led them out of Egypt.
They embraced other gods whom they worshiped and served.
That is why he brought all this disaster down on them.'"

BUILDING PROJECTS AND COMMERCIAL EFFORTS

8 After twenty years, during which Solomon built the LORD's
temple and his royal palace, [2]Solomon rebuilt the cities that
Huram had given him and settled Israelites there. [3]Solomon
went to Hamath Zobah and seized it. [4]He built up Tadmor in
the wilderness and all the storage cities he had built in Hamath.
[5]He made upper Beth Horon and lower Beth Horon fortified
cities with walls and barred gates, [6]and built up Baalath, all the
storage cities that belonged to him, and all the cities where
chariots and horses were kept. He built whatever he wanted
in Jerusalem, Lebanon, and throughout his entire kingdom.

[7]Now several non-Israelite peoples were left in the land after
the conquest of Joshua, including the Hittites, Amorites, Perizzites, Hivites, and Jebusites. [8]Their descendants remained in
the land (the Israelites were unable to wipe them out). Solomon
conscripted them for his work crews, and they continue in that
role to this very day. [9]Solomon did not assign Israelites to these

8:1–18 The only mention made of the daughter of Pharaoh in Chronicles is in this chapter. He married her in the beginning of the reign. Her removal to the house Solomon had built for her now took place. The worship in the house was then carried on in a perfect way. At the appointed times all was done and all David, the man of God, had commanded was carried out. There was no departure from the commandment of the king, so the house of the Lord was perfected. It foreshadows a perfect obedience and worship that the earth will see when the true King has come. Then, as it was in Solomon's day, the King's commandment will be the absolute rule for everything.

ARNO C. GAEBELEIN
(1861–1945)
THE ANNOTATED BIBLE

work crews; the Israelites served as his soldiers, officers, charioteers, and commanders of his chariot forces. 10These men
worked for King Solomon as supervisors; there were a total of
250 of them who were in charge of the people.
11Solomon moved Pharaoh's daughter up from the City of
David to the palace he had built for her, for he said, "My wife
must not live in the palace of King David of Israel, for the places
where the ark of the LORD has entered are holy."
12Then Solomon offered burnt sacrifices to the LORD on the
altar of the LORD which he had built in front of the temple's
porch. 13He observed the daily requirements for sacrifices that
Moses had specified for Sabbaths, new moon festivals, and the
three annual celebrations—the Feast of Unleavened Bread, the
Feast of Weeks, and the Feast of Shelters. 14As his father David
had decreed, Solomon appointed the divisions of the priests to
do their assigned tasks, the Levitical orders to lead worship and
help the priests with their daily tasks, and the divisions of the
gatekeepers to serve at their assigned gates. This was what David
the man of God had ordered. 15They did not neglect any detail of
the king's orders pertaining to the priests, Levites, and treasuries.
16All the work ordered by Solomon was completed, from the
day the foundation of the LORD's temple was laid until it was
finished; the LORD's temple was completed.
17Then Solomon went to Ezion Geber and to Elat on the coast
in the land of Edom. 18Huram sent him ships and some of his
sailors, men who were well acquainted with the sea. They sailed
with Solomon's men to Ophir and took from there 450 talents
of gold, which they brought back to King Solomon.

SOLOMON ENTERTAINS A QUEEN

9 When the queen of Sheba heard about Solomon, she came
to challenge him with difficult questions. She arrived in Jerusalem with a great display of pomp, bringing with her camels
carrying spices, a very large quantity of gold, and precious gems.
She visited Solomon and discussed with him everything that
was on her mind. 2Solomon answered all her questions; there
was no question too complex for the king. 3When the queen of
Sheba saw for herself Solomon's wisdom, the palace he had built,
4the food in his banquet hall, his servants and attendants in their
robes, his cupbearers in their robes, and his burnt sacrifices
which he presented in the LORD's temple, she was amazed. 5She
said to the king, "The report I heard in my own country about
your wise sayings and insight was true! 6I did not believe these
things until I came and saw them with my own eyes. Indeed, I
didn't hear even half the story! Your wisdom surpasses what
was reported to me. 7Your attendants, who stand before you at
all times and hear your wise sayings, are truly happy! 8May the
LORD your God be praised because he favored you by placing
you on his throne as the one ruling on his behalf. Because of
your God's love for Israel and his lasting commitment to them,
he made you king over them so you could make just and right
decisions." 9She gave the king 120 talents of gold and a very large
quantity of spices and precious gems. The quantity of spices the
queen of Sheba gave King Solomon has never been matched.
10(Huram's servants, aided by Solomon's servants, brought gold
from Ophir, as well as fine timber and precious gems. 11With
the timber the king made steps for the LORD's temple and royal
palace as well as stringed instruments for the musicians. No
one had seen anything like them in the land of Judah before

9:1–7 The queen of Sheba came from the end of the earth to listen to the wisdom of Solomon. The sending by the Ethiopian queen of the treasures of the nations to Jerusalem signifies that the church would bring gifts of virtue and of faith to the Lord. In the scriptures it is she to whom it was said, "Listen, O princess. Observe and pay attention! Forget your homeland and your family" (Ps 45:10).

VENERABLE BEDE
(C. 672–735)
COMMENTARY ON THE ACTS OF THE APOSTLES

that.) 12King Solomon gave the queen of Sheba everything she
requested, more than what she had brought him. Then she left
and returned to her homeland with her attendants.

SOLOMON'S WEALTH

13Solomon received 666 talents of gold per year, 14besides what
he collected from the merchants and traders. All the Arabian kings and the governors of the land also brought gold and
silver to Solomon. 15King Solomon made 200 large shields of
hammered gold; 600 measures of hammered gold were used
for each shield. 16He also made 300 small shields of hammered
gold; 300 measures of gold were used for each of those shields.
The king placed them in the Palace of the Lebanon Forest.
17The king made a large throne decorated with ivory and
overlaid it with pure gold. 18There were six steps leading up
to the throne, and a gold footstool was attached to the throne.
The throne had two armrests with a statue of a lion standing
on each side. 19There were twelve statues of lions on the six
steps, one lion at each end of each step. There was nothing like
it in any other kingdom.
20All of King Solomon's cups were made of gold, and all the
household items in the Palace of the Lebanon Forest were made
of pure gold. There were no silver items, for silver was not considered very valuable in Solomon's time. 21The king had a fleet
of large merchant ships manned by Huram's men that sailed
the sea. Once every three years the fleet came into port with
cargoes of gold, silver, ivory, apes, and peacocks.
22King Solomon was wealthier and wiser than any of the
kings of the earth. 23All the kings of the earth wanted to visit
Solomon to see him display his God-given wisdom. 24Year after
year visitors brought their gifts, which included items of silver,
items of gold, clothes, perfume, spices, horses, and mules.
25Solomon had 4,000 stalls for his chariot horses and 12,000
horses. He kept them in assigned cities and also with him in
Jerusalem. 26He ruled all the kingdoms from the Euphrates
River to the land of the Philistines as far as the border of Egypt.
27The king made silver as plentiful in Jerusalem as stones; cedar was as plentiful as sycamore fig trees are in the foothills.
28Solomon acquired horses from Egypt and from all the lands.

SOLOMON'S REIGN ENDS

29The rest of the events of Solomon's reign, from start to finish,
are recorded in the Annals of Nathan the Prophet, the Prophecy of Ahijah the Shilonite, and the Vision of Iddo the Seer
pertaining to Jeroboam son of Nebat. 30Solomon ruled over all
Israel from Jerusalem for forty years. 31Then Solomon passed
away and was buried in the city of his father David. His son
Rehoboam replaced him as king.

THE NORTHERN TRIBES REBEL

10 Rehoboam traveled to Shechem, for all Israel had gathered
in Shechem to make Rehoboam king. 2When Jeroboam son
of Nebat heard the news, he was still in Egypt, where he had
fled from King Solomon. Jeroboam returned from Egypt. 3They
sent for him, and Jeroboam and all Israel came and spoke to
Rehoboam, saying, 4"Your father made us work too hard! Now
if you lighten the demands he made and don't make us work
as hard, we will serve you." 5He said to them, "Go away for three
days, then return to me." So the people went away.

10:1—11:4 Solomon did not act entirely wise with his son, for he delayed in setting his son on the throne during his lifetime. And this is despite the fact that Solomon otherwise saw that Jeroboam would be a threat to the kingdom of his son. What's more, Solomon himself had been given an example of how a king is supposed to establish his son as his successor given that David had done this for him. Either Solomon saw Rehoboam's foolishness and was therefore careless in establishing him as king, or Solomon did not think it proper to establish Rehoboam as king while he lived. As it is said in Sirach: "Solomon rested with his ancestors, and left behind him one of his sons, broad in folly and lacking in sense, Rehoboam, whose policy drove the people to revolt" (Sir 47:23 NRSV). Yet in all these things we must recognize a higher hand at play that intervened to bring about the punishment that God had decreed for the punishment of Solomon.

JOHN MAYER (1583–1664)
COMMENTARY ON SECOND CHRONICLES

6King Rehoboam consulted with the older advisers who had
served his father Solomon when he had been alive. He asked
them, “How do you advise me to answer these people?” 7They
said to him, “If you are fair to these people, grant their request,
and are cordial to them, they will be your servants from this
time forward.” 8But Rehoboam rejected their advice and consulted the young advisers who served him, with whom he had
grown up. 9He asked them, “How do you advise me to respond to
these people who said to me, ‘Lessen the demands your father
placed on us’?” 10The young advisers with whom Rehoboam had
grown up said to him, “Say this to these people who have said
to you, ‘Your father made us work hard, but now lighten our
burden’—say this to them: ‘I am a lot harsher than my father!
11My father imposed heavy demands on you; I will make them
even heavier. My father punished you with ordinary whips; I
will punish you with whips that really sting your flesh.’”

12Jeroboam and all the people reported to Rehoboam on the
third day, just as the king had ordered when he said, “Return
to me on the third day.” 13The king responded to the people
harshly. He rejected the advice of the older men 14and followed
the advice of the younger ones. He said, “My father imposed
heavy demands on you; I will make them even heavier. My father punished you with ordinary whips; I will punish you with
whips that really sting your flesh.” 15The king refused to listen
to the people, because God was instigating this turn of events so
that he might bring to pass the prophetic announcement he had
made through Ahijah the Shilonite to Jeroboam son of Nebat.

16When all Israel saw that the king refused to listen to them,
the people answered the king, “We have no portion in David—no
share in the son of Jesse! Return to your homes, O Israel! Now,
look after your own dynasty, O David!” So all Israel returned
to their homes. 17(Rehoboam continued to rule over the Israelites who lived in the cities of Judah.) 18King Rehoboam sent
Hadoram, the supervisor of the work crews, out after them, but
the Israelites stoned him to death. King Rehoboam managed to
jump into his chariot and escape to Jerusalem. 19So Israel has
been in rebellion against the Davidic dynasty to this very day.

11 When Rehoboam arrived in Jerusalem, he summoned
180,000 skilled warriors from Judah and Benjamin to attack Israel and restore the kingdom to Rehoboam. 2But the
LORD's message came to the prophet Shemaiah, 3“Say this to
King Rehoboam son of Solomon of Judah and to all the Israelites
in Judah and Benjamin, 4‘The LORD says this: “Do not attack and
make war with your brothers. Each of you go home, for I have
caused this to happen.”’” They obeyed the LORD and called off
the attack against Jeroboam.

REHOBOAM'S REIGN

5Rehoboam lived in Jerusalem; he built up these fortified cities
throughout Judah: 6Bethlehem, Etam, Tekoa, 7Beth Zur, Soco,
Adullam, 8Gath, Mareshah, Ziph, 9Adoraim, Lachish, Azekah,
10Zorah, Aijalon, and Hebron. These were the fortified cities
in Judah and Benjamin. 11He fortified these cities and placed
officers in them, as well as storehouses of food, olive oil, and
wine. 12In each city there were shields and spears; he strongly
fortified them. Judah and Benjamin belonged to him.

13The priests and Levites who lived throughout Israel supported him, no matter where they resided. 14The Levites even
left their pasturelands and their property behind and came

to Judah and Jerusalem, for Jeroboam and his sons prohibited
them from serving as the LORD's priests. 15Jeroboam appointed his own priests to serve at the worship centers and to lead
in the worship of the goat idols and calf idols he had made.
16Those among all the Israelite tribes who were determined to
worship the LORD God of Israel followed them to Jerusalem to
sacrifice to the LORD God of their ancestors. 17They supported the kingdom of Judah and were loyal to Rehoboam son of
Solomon for three years; they followed the edicts of David and
Solomon for three years.
18Rehoboam married Mahalath the daughter of David's son
Jerimoth and of Abihail, the daughter of Jesse's son Eliab. 19She
bore him sons named Jeush, Shemariah, and Zaham. 20He later
married Maacah the daughter of Absalom. She bore to him
Abijah, Attai, Ziza, and Shelomith. 21Rehoboam loved Maacah
daughter of Absalom more than his other wives and concubines. He had eighteen wives and sixty concubines; he fathered
twenty-eight sons and sixty daughters.
22Rehoboam appointed Abijah son of Maacah as the leader
over his brothers, for he intended to name him his successor.
23He wisely placed some of his many sons throughout the regions of Judah and Benjamin in the various fortified cities. He
supplied them with abundant provisions and acquired many
wives for them.

12 After Rehoboam's rule was established and solidified, he
and all Israel rejected the law of the LORD. 2Because they
were unfaithful to the LORD, in King Rehoboam's fifth year, King
Shishak of Egypt attacked Jerusalem. 3He had 1,200 chariots,
60,000 horsemen, and an innumerable number of soldiers who
accompanied him from Egypt, including Libyans, Sukkites,
and Cushites. 4He captured the fortified cities of Judah and
marched against Jerusalem.
5Shemaiah the prophet visited Rehoboam and the leaders of
Judah who were assembled in Jerusalem because of Shishak. He
said to them, "This is what the LORD says: 'You have rejected me,
so I have rejected you and will hand you over to Shishak.'" 6The
leaders of Israel and the king humbled themselves and said, "The
LORD is just." 7When the LORD saw that they humbled themselves,
the LORD's message came to Shemaiah: "They have humbled
themselves, so I will not destroy them. I will deliver them soon. My
anger will not be unleashed against Jerusalem through Shishak.
8Yet they will become his subjects, so they can experience how
serving me differs from serving the surrounding nations."
9King Shishak of Egypt attacked Jerusalem and took away
the treasures of the LORD's temple and of the royal palace; he
took everything, including the gold shields that Solomon had
made. 10King Rehoboam made bronze shields to replace them
and assigned them to the officers of the royal guard who protected the entrance to the royal palace. 11Whenever the king
visited the LORD's temple, the royal guards carried them and
then brought them back to the guardroom.
12So when Rehoboam humbled himself, the LORD relented
from his anger and did not annihilate him; Judah experienced
some good things. 13King Rehoboam solidified his rule in Jerusalem; he was forty-one years old when he became king, and he
ruled for seventeen years in Jerusalem, the city the LORD chose
from all the tribes of Israel to be his home. Rehoboam's mother
was an Ammonite named Naamah. 14He did evil because he
was not determined to follow the LORD.

12:1–12 **Rehoboam and his subjects walked in the way of David for three years. But in the fourth year they revolted against the law of the Lord. By doing so they provoked the Lord's wrath against them. And in the fifth year of Rehoboam's reign, the Lord therefore stirred up the spirit of the king of Egypt against them. But had God been with Judah, Shishak could no more have prevailed against Rehoboam than Zerah did against Asa. But once the Lord left them, they soon fell into Shishak's power. This shows us how dangerous it is to forsake the Lord.**

***THE WESTMINSTER ANNOTATIONS* (1683)**

[15]The events of Rehoboam's reign, from start to finish, are
recorded in the Annals of Shemaiah the Prophet and of Iddo
the Seer that include genealogical records. There were wars between Rehoboam and Jeroboam continually. [16]Then Rehoboam
passed away and was buried in the City of David. His son Abijah
replaced him as king.

ABIJAH'S REIGN

13 In the eighteenth year of the reign of King Jeroboam, Abijah became king over Judah. [2]He ruled for three years in
Jerusalem. His mother was Michaiah, the daughter of Uriel
from Gibeah.

There was war between Abijah and Jeroboam. [3]Abijah
launched the attack with 400,000 well-trained warriors, while
Jeroboam deployed against him 800,000 well-trained warriors.
[4]Abijah ascended Mount Zemaraim, in the Ephraimite hill
country, and said: "Listen to me, Jeroboam and all Israel! [5]Don't
you realize that the LORD God of Israel has given David and his
dynasty lasting dominion over Israel by a formal covenant?
[6]Jeroboam son of Nebat, a servant of Solomon son of David, rose
up and rebelled against his master. [7]Lawless good-for-nothing
men gathered around him and conspired against Rehoboam son
of Solomon, when Rehoboam was an inexperienced young man
and could not resist them. [8]Now you are declaring that you will
resist the LORD's rule through the Davidic dynasty. You have a
huge army and bring with you the gold calves that Jeroboam
made for you as gods. [9]But you banished the LORD's priests,
Aaron's descendants, and the Levites, and appointed your own
priests just as the surrounding nations do! Anyone who comes
to consecrate himself with a young bull or seven rams becomes
a priest of these fake gods! [10]But as for us, the LORD is our God
and we have not rejected him. Aaron's descendants serve as
the LORD's priests, and the Levites assist them with the work.
[11]They offer burnt sacrifices to the LORD every morning and
every evening, along with fragrant incense. They arrange the
Bread of the Presence on a ritually clean table and light the
lamps on the gold lampstand every evening. Certainly we are
observing the LORD our God's regulations, but you have rejected
him. [12]Now look, God is with us as our leader. His priests are
ready to blow the trumpets to signal the attack against you. You
Israelites, don't fight against the LORD God of your ancestors,
for you will not win!"

[13]Now Jeroboam had sent some men to ambush the Judahite
army from behind. The main army was in front of the Judahite
army; the ambushers were behind it. [14]The men of Judah turned
around and realized they were being attacked from the front
and the rear. So they cried out to the LORD for help. The priests
blew their trumpets, [15]and the men of Judah gave the battle
cry. As the men of Judah gave the battle cry, God struck down
Jeroboam and all Israel before Abijah and Judah. [16]The Israelites
fled from before the Judahite army, and God handed them over
to the men of Judah. [17]Abijah and his army thoroughly defeated them; 500,000 well-trained Israelite men fell dead. [18]That
day the Israelites were defeated; the men of Judah prevailed
because they relied on the LORD God of their ancestors.

[19]Abijah chased Jeroboam; he seized from him these cities:
Bethel and its surrounding towns, Jeshanah and its surrounding
towns, and Ephron and its surrounding towns. [20]Jeroboam did
not regain power during the reign of Abijah. The LORD struck

13:1—14:1 Jeroboam and his people, by apostasy and idolatry, merited the severe punishment Abijah was permitted to execute upon them. It appears from the character of Abijah that he was not himself truly religious, yet he encouraged himself from the religion of his people. It is common for those who deny the power of godliness to boast of the form of it. Many who have little religion themselves value it in others. But it was true that there were numbers of pious worshipers in Judah and that theirs was the more righteous cause. In their distress, when danger was on every side, which way should they look for deliverance unless upward? It is an unspeakable comfort that our way is always open. They cried unto the Lord. Earnest prayer is crying. To the cry of prayer they added the shout of faith and became more than conquerors. Jeroboam escaped the sword of Abijah, but God struck him; there is no escaping his sword.

MATTHEW HENRY (1662–1714)
COMMENTARY ON THE WHOLE BIBLE

him down and he died. 21 Abijah's power grew; he had fourteen
wives and fathered twenty-two sons and sixteen daughters.
22The rest of the events of Abijah's reign, including his deeds
and sayings, are recorded in the writings of the prophet Iddo.
14 Abijah passed away and was buried in the City of David.
His son Asa replaced him as king. During his reign the
land had rest for ten years.

ASA'S RELIGIOUS AND MILITARY ACCOMPLISHMENTS

2Asa did what the LORD his God desired and approved. 3He
removed the pagan altars and the high places, smashed the
sacred pillars, and cut down the Asherah poles. 4He ordered
Judah to seek the LORD God of their ancestors and to observe
his law and commands. 5He removed the high places and the
incense altars from all the towns of Judah. The kingdom had
rest under his rule.
6He built fortified cities throughout Judah, for the land was
at rest and there was no war during those years; the LORD gave
him peace. 7He said to the people of Judah: "Let's build these
cities and fortify them with walls, towers, and barred gates. The
land remains ours because we have followed the LORD our God;
we have followed him, and he has made us secure on all sides."
So they built the cities and prospered.
8Asa had an army of 300,000 men from Judah, equipped with
large shields and spears. He also had 280,000 men from Benjamin who carried small shields and were adept archers; they
were all skilled warriors. 9Zerah the Cushite marched against
them with an army of a million men and 300 chariots. He arrived at Mareshah, 10and Asa went out to oppose him. They
deployed for battle in the Valley of Zephathah near Mareshah.
11Asa prayed to the LORD his God: "O LORD, there is no one
but you who can help the weak when they are vastly outnum-
bered. Help us, O LORD our God, for we rely on you and have
marched on your behalf against this huge army. O LORD, you
are our God; don't let men prevail against you!" 12The LORD
struck down the Cushites before Asa and Judah. The Cushites
fled, 13and Asa and his army chased them as far as Gerar. The
Cushites were wiped out; they were shattered before the LORD
and his army. The men of Judah carried off a huge amount of
plunder. 14They defeated all the towns surrounding Gerar, for
the LORD caused them to panic. The men of Judah looted all the
towns, for they contained a huge amount of goods. 15They also
attacked the tents of the herdsmen in charge of the livestock.
They carried off many sheep and camels and then returned
to Jerusalem.
15 God's Spirit came upon Azariah son of Oded. 2He met
Asa and told him, "Listen to me, Asa and all Judah and
Benjamin! The LORD is with you when you are loyal to him. If
you seek him, he will respond to you, but if you reject him, he
will reject you. 3For a long time Israel had not sought the one
true God, or a priest to instruct them, or the law. 4Because of
their distress, they turned back to the LORD God of Israel. They
sought him, and he responded to them. 5In those days no one
could travel safely, for total chaos had overtaken all the people
of the surrounding lands. 6One nation was crushed by another,
and one city by another, for God caused them to be in great
turmoil. 7But as for you, be strong and don't get discouraged,
for your work will be rewarded."

15:1–19 The passage shows the impiety of the ten tribes: "For a long time Israel had not sought the one true God, or a priest to instruct them, or the law. Because of their distress, they turned back to the LORD God of Israel. They sought him and he responded to them." Do not imitate, the scripture says, the impiety of others who do not preach the true God but pursue false idols. For this reason they have been deprived of the priests and the teachers who could teach them the law of God. Experience therefore becomes our guide in showing the damages of impiety. For after being afflicted by any kind of calamity, they implore now the help of God, giving themselves entirely to the indescribable goodness of the Lord.

THEODORET OF CYR
(C. 393–C. 458)
QUESTIONS ON KINGS AND CHRONICLES

[8]When Asa heard these words and the prophecy of Oded the
prophet, he was encouraged. He removed the detestable idols
from the entire land of Judah and Benjamin and from the cities
he had seized in the Ephraimite hill country. He repaired the
altar of the LORD in front of the porch of the LORD's temple.
[9]He assembled all Judah and Benjamin, as well as the settlers
from Ephraim, Manasseh, and Simeon who had come to live with
them. Many people from Israel had come there to live when they
saw that the LORD his God was with him. [10]They assembled in Jerusalem in the third month of the fifteenth year of Asa's reign. [11]At
that time they sacrificed to the LORD some of the plunder they
had brought back, including 700 head of cattle and 7,000 sheep.
[12]They solemnly agreed to seek the LORD God of their ancestors
with their whole heart and being. [13]Anyone who would not seek
the LORD God of Israel would be executed, whether they were
young or old, male or female. [14]They swore their allegiance to the
LORD, shouting their approval loudly and sounding trumpets and
horns. [15]All Judah was happy about the oath because they made
the vow with their whole heart. They willingly sought the LORD
and he responded to them. He made them secure on every side.
[16]King Asa also removed Maacah his grandmother from her
position as queen mother because she had made a loathsome
Asherah pole. Asa cut down her loathsome pole and crushed
and burned it in the Kidron Valley. [17]The high places were not
eliminated from Israel, yet Asa was wholeheartedly devoted to
the LORD throughout his lifetime. [18]He brought the holy items
that his father and he had made into God's temple, including
the silver, gold, and other articles.

ASA'S FAILURES

[19]There was no more war until the thirty-fifth year of Asa's reign.
16 [1]In the thirty-sixth year of Asa's reign, King Baasha of Israel
attacked Judah, and he established Ramah as a military
outpost to prevent anyone from leaving or entering the land
of King Asa of Judah. [2]Asa took all the silver and gold that was
left in the treasuries of the LORD's temple and of the royal palace and sent it to King Ben Hadad of Syria, ruler in Damascus,
along with this message: [3]"I want to make a treaty with you, like
the one our fathers made. See, I have sent you silver and gold.
Break your treaty with King Baasha of Israel, so he will retreat
from my land." [4]Ben Hadad accepted King Asa's offer and ordered his army commanders to attack the cities of Israel. They
conquered Ijon, Dan, Abel Maim, and all the storage cities of
Naphtali. [5]When Baasha heard the news, he stopped fortifying
Ramah and abandoned the project. [6]King Asa ordered all the
men of Judah to carry away the stones and wood that Baasha
had used to build Ramah. He used the materials to build up
Geba and Mizpah.
[7]At that time Hanani the prophet visited King Asa of Judah
and said to him: "Because you relied on the king of Syria and did
not rely on the LORD your God, the army of the king of Syria has
escaped from your hand. [8]Did not the Cushites and Libyans have
a huge army with chariots and a very large number of horsemen? But when you relied on the LORD, he handed them over
to you! [9]Certainly the LORD watches the whole earth carefully
and is ready to strengthen those who are devoted to him. You
have acted foolishly in this matter; from now on you will have
war." [10]Asa was so angry at the prophet, he put him in jail. Asa
also oppressed some of the people at that time.

16:7–14 The Spirit of God does not blame this prince because he desired the assistance of physicians. He blames him because he neglected to seek the help of God or to implore his aid in the day of his distress. The one who is sick may as freely take medicine as the one who is well may eat and drink; yet we must not altogether relax our confidence and trust in the remedies. Rather we must put our confidence in the God who sends both sickness and health. Just as a person does not live by bread alone but by every word that proceeds from the mouth of God, so it is not by medicine alone that a patient is cured of his sickness. Rather it is by the blessing and power of him who both gives the sickness and cures it, that is, of him who strikes and heals as he pleases.

CHARLES DRELINCOURT
(1595–1669)
CHRISTIAN DEFENSE AGAINST THE FEAR OF DEATH

ASA'S REIGN ENDS

[11]The events of Asa's reign, from start to finish, are recorded in
the Scroll of the Kings of Judah and Israel. [12]In the thirty-ninth
year of his reign, Asa developed a foot disease, and his disease
became severe. Yet even in his disease, he did not seek the LORD,
but only the doctors. [13]Asa passed away in the forty-first year
of his reign. [14]He was buried in the tomb he had carved out in
the City of David. They laid him to rest on a platform covered
with spices and assorted mixtures of ointments. They made a
huge bonfire to honor him.

JEHOSHAPHAT BECOMES KING

17 His son Jehoshaphat replaced him as king and solidified
his rule over Israel. [2]He placed troops in all Judah's fortified cities and posted garrisons throughout the land of Judah
and in the cities of Ephraim that his father Asa had seized.

[3]The LORD was with Jehoshaphat because he followed in
his ancestor David's footsteps at the beginning of his reign.
He did not seek the Baals, [4]but instead sought the God of his
ancestors and obeyed his commands, unlike the Israelites. [5]The
LORD made his kingdom secure; all Judah brought tribute to
Jehoshaphat, and he became very wealthy and greatly respected.
[6]He was committed to following the LORD; he even removed
the high places and Asherah poles from Judah.

[7]In the third year of his reign he sent his officials Ben Hail,
Obadiah, Zechariah, Nethanel, and Micaiah to teach in the cities
of Judah. [8]They were accompanied by the Levites Shemaiah,
Nethaniah, Zebadiah, Asahel, Shemiramoth, Jehonathan, Adonijah, Tobijah, and Tob-Adonijah, and by the priests Elishama
and Jehoram. [9]They taught throughout Judah, taking with them
the scroll of the law of the LORD. They traveled to all the cities
of Judah and taught the people.

[10]The LORD put fear into all the kingdoms surrounding Judah; they did not make war with Jehoshaphat. [11]Some of the
Philistines brought Jehoshaphat tribute, including a load of
silver. The Arabs brought him 7,700 rams and 7,700 goats from
their flocks.

[12]Jehoshaphat's power kept increasing. He built fortresses
and storage cities throughout Judah. [13]He had many supplies
stored in the cities of Judah and an army of skilled warriors
stationed in Jerusalem. [14]These were their divisions by families:

There were 1,000 officers from Judah. Adnah the commander
led 300,000 skilled warriors, [15]Jehochanan the commander led
280,000, [16]and Amasiah son of Zikri, who volunteered to serve
the LORD, led 200,000 skilled warriors.

[17]From Benjamin, Eliada, a skilled warrior, led 200,000 men
who were equipped with bows and shields, [18]and Jehozabad led
180,000 trained warriors.

[19]These were the ones who served the king, besides those
whom the king placed in the fortified cities throughout Judah.

JEHOSHAPHAT ALLIES WITH AHAB

18 Jehoshaphat was very wealthy and greatly respected. He
made an alliance by marriage with Ahab, [2]and after several
years went down to visit Ahab in Samaria. Ahab slaughtered
many sheep and cattle to honor Jehoshaphat and those who
came with him. He persuaded him to join in an attack against
Ramoth Gilead. [3]King Ahab of Israel said to King Jehoshaphat
of Judah, "Will you go with me to attack Ramoth Gilead?" He

17:1–19 "The LORD," says scripture, "was with Jehoshaphat." Why? Because he did what was right in the sight of the Lord. What is pleasing to the Lord? When you want to see into God's heart and discover God's goodwill, you must keep his Word, commands, and prohibitions under your eyes. For what God commands pleases him, and he forbids what displeases him.

JOHANNES BRENZ
(1499–1570)
HISTORY OF JEHOSHAPHAT

18:1–27 When Ahab did not want to listen to the Lord's prophet Micaiah, he was punished for his ingratitude and deceived by false prophets who invented lies. The false prophets would not have any authority with the king unless they preached something other than what would actually happen. Therefore such creatures were instruments of Satan, not preaching any future revealed by the Spirit of God but instead they were advised by the devil, who covers his ministers with a veneer of truth, getting them used to hiding under such curtains. Relying not on the Word of God alone but on the whims of King Ahab, the false prophets promised victory and joined in making proud the arrogant insults against the prophet Micaiah.

VIKTORIN STRIGEL
(C. 1524–1569)
BOOK OF CHRONICLES

replied, "I will support you; my army is at your disposal and
will support you in battle." [4]Then Jehoshaphat said further to
the king of Israel, "First, please seek an oracle from the LORD."
[5]So the king of Israel assembled 400 prophets and asked them,
"Should we attack Ramoth Gilead or not?" They said, "Attack!
God will hand it over to the king." [6]But Jehoshaphat asked, "Is
there not a prophet of the LORD still here that we may ask him?"
[7]The king of Israel answered Jehoshaphat, "There is still one
man through whom we can seek the LORD's will, but I despise
him because he does not prophesy prosperity for me, but always
disaster—Micaiah son of Imlah." Jehoshaphat said, "The king
should not say such things!" [8]The king of Israel summoned an
officer and said, "Quickly bring Micaiah son of Imlah."
[9]Now the king of Israel and King Jehoshaphat of Judah were
sitting on their respective thrones, dressed in their royal robes,
at the threshing floor at the entrance of the gate of Samaria. All
the prophets were prophesying before them. [10]Zedekiah son
of Kenaanah made iron horns and said, "This is what the LORD
says, 'With these you will gore Syria until they are destroyed.'"
[11]All the prophets were prophesying the same, saying, "Attack
Ramoth Gilead! You will succeed; the LORD will hand it over to
the king." [12]Now the messenger who went to summon Micaiah
said to him, "Look, the prophets are in complete agreement that
the king will succeed. Your words must agree with theirs; you
must predict success!" [13]But Micaiah said, "As certainly as the
LORD lives, I will say what my God tells me to say!"
[14]Micaiah came before the king and the king asked him,
"Micaiah, should we attack Ramoth Gilead or not?" He answered him, "Attack! You will succeed; they will be handed over
to you." [15]The king said to him, "How many times must I make
you solemnly promise in the name of the LORD to tell me only
the truth?" [16]Micaiah replied, "I saw all Israel scattered on the
mountains like sheep that have no shepherd. Then the LORD
said, 'They have no master. They should go home in peace.'" [17]The
king of Israel said to Jehoshaphat, "Didn't I tell you he does not
prophesy prosperity for me, but disaster?" [18]Micaiah said, "That
being the case, listen to the LORD's message. I saw the LORD
sitting on his throne, with all the heavenly assembly standing on
his right and on his left. [19]The LORD said, 'Who will deceive King
Ahab of Israel, so he will attack Ramoth Gilead and die there?'
One said this and another that. [20]Then a spirit stepped forward
and stood before the LORD. He said, 'I will deceive him.' The
LORD asked him, 'How?' [21]He replied, 'I will go out and be a lying
spirit in the mouths of all his prophets.' The LORD said, 'Deceive
and overpower him. Go out and do as you have proposed.' [22]So
now, look, the LORD has placed a lying spirit in the mouths of all
these prophets of yours, but the LORD has decreed disaster for
you." [23]Zedekiah son of Kenaanah approached, hit Micaiah on
the jaw, and said, "Which way did the LORD's Spirit go when he
went from me to speak to you?" [24]Micaiah replied, "Look, you will
see in the day when you go into an inner room to hide." [25]Then
the king of Israel said, "Take Micaiah and return him to Amon
the city official and Joash the king's son. [26]Say, 'This is what the
king says: "Put this man in prison. Give him only a little bread
and water until I return safely."'" [27]Micaiah said, "If you really
do return safely, then the LORD has not spoken through me!"
Then he added, "Take note, all you people."
[28]The king of Israel and King Jehoshaphat of Judah attacked
Ramoth Gilead. [29]The king of Israel said to Jehoshaphat, "I will

disguise myself and then enter the battle, but you wear your
royal attire." So the king of Israel disguised himself and they
entered the battle. 30 Now the king of Syria had ordered his chariot commanders, "Do not fight common soldiers or high rank-
ing officers; fight only the king of Israel!" 31 When the chariot
commanders saw Jehoshaphat, they said, "He must be the king
of Israel!" So they turned and attacked him, but Jehoshaphat
cried out. The LORD helped him; God lured them away from
him. 32 When the chariot commanders realized he was not the
king of Israel, they turned away from him. 33 Now an archer shot
an arrow at random, and it struck the king of Israel between
the plates of his armor. The king ordered his charioteer, "Turn
around and take me from the battle line, for I am wounded."
34 While the battle raged throughout the day, the king of Israel
stood propped up in his chariot opposite the Syrians. He died
in the evening as the sun was setting.

19 When King Jehoshaphat of Judah returned home safely to
Jerusalem, 2 the prophet Jehu son of Hanani confronted
him; he said to King Jehoshaphat, "Is it right to help the wicked
and be an ally of those who oppose the LORD? Because you have
done this, the LORD is angry with you! 3 Nevertheless you have
done some good things; you removed the Asherah poles from
the land, and you were determined to follow God."

JEHOSHAPHAT APPOINTS JUDGES

4 Jehoshaphat lived in Jerusalem. He went out among the people
from Beer Sheba to the hill country of Ephraim and encouraged
them to follow the LORD God of their ancestors. 5 He appointed
judges throughout the land and in each of the fortified cities
of Judah. 6 He told the judges, "Be careful what you do, for you
are not judging for men, but for the LORD, who will be with
you when you make judicial decisions. 7 Respect the LORD and
make careful decisions, for the LORD our God disapproves of
injustice, partiality, and bribery."

8 In Jerusalem Jehoshaphat appointed some Levites, priests,
and Israelite family leaders to judge on behalf of the LORD
and to settle disputes among the residents of Jerusalem. 9 He
commanded them: "Carry out your duties with respect for
the LORD, with honesty, and with pure motives. 10 Whenever
your countrymen who live in the cities bring a case before you
(whether it involves a violent crime or other matters related
to the law, commandments, rules, and regulations), warn them
that they must not sin against the LORD. If you fail to do so,
God will be angry with you and your colleagues, but if you obey,
you will be free of guilt. 11 Take note, Amariah the chief priest
will oversee you in every matter pertaining to the LORD and
Zebadiah son of Ishmael, the leader of the family of Judah, in
every matter pertaining to the king. The Levites will serve as
officials before you. Act courageously, and may the LORD be
with those who do well!"

THE LORD GIVES JEHOSHAPHAT MILITARY SUCCESS

20 Later the Moabites and Ammonites, along with some
of the Meunites, attacked Jehoshaphat. 2 Messengers arrived and reported to Jehoshaphat, "A huge army is attacking
you from the other side of the Dead Sea, from the direction of
Edom. Look, they are in Hazazon Tamar (that is, En Gedi)." 3 Jehoshaphat was afraid, so he decided to seek the LORD's advice.

19:1–11 When Jehoshaphat returned from the war in which Ahab was killed, this prophet came to him. And though his message was very sad, and he had to deliver it to a king of all people, he boldly declared the mind of the Lord to Jehoshaphat. By the help Jehoshaphat afforded Ahab, he seemed to give tolerance to his idolatry. Now, revolters are to be detested. And in this respect two circumstances plainly demonstrate that Jehoshaphat had sinned and even aggravated his sin. First, Jehoshaphat loved the ungodly. He did this not only with a political respect, but with an inward entity of affection. Second, the ungodly are so detestable to the Lord that it is as if those who love the ungodly actually profess a hatred of the Lord.

***THE WESTMINSTER ANNOTATIONS* (1683)**

20:1–30 In all dangers, public or personal, our first business should be to seek help from God. We must approach him with humiliation for our sins, trusting only in his mercy and power. Jehoshaphat acknowledged the sovereign dominion of the divine Providence. Though the king had a great army, he said, "We are powerless against this huge army that attacks us. We don't know what we should do; we look to you for help." Jehoshaphat exhorted his troops to firm faith in God. Faith inspires true courage; nor will anything help more the establishing of the heart in shaking times than a firm belief in the power and mercy and promise of God. In all our trust in the Lord and our praises of him, let us especially look at his everlasting mercy to sinners through Jesus Christ.

MATTHEW HENRY **(1662–1714)**
COMMENTARY ON THE WHOLE BIBLE

He decreed that all Judah should observe a fast. 4The people of
Judah assembled to ask for the LORD's help; they came from all
the cities of Judah to ask for the LORD's help.

5Jehoshaphat stood before the assembly of Judah and Jerusalem at the LORD's temple, in front of the new courtyard. 6He
prayed: "O LORD God of our ancestors, you are the God who lives
in heaven and rules over all the kingdoms of the nations. You possess strength and power; no one can stand against you. 7Our God,
you drove out the inhabitants of this land before your people
Israel and gave it as a permanent possession to the descendants
of your friend Abraham. 8They settled down in it and built in it
a temple to honor you, saying, 9'If disaster comes on us in the
form of military attack, judgment, plague, or famine, we will
stand in front of this temple before you, for you are present in
this temple. We will cry out to you for help in our distress, so that
you will hear and deliver us.' 10Now the Ammonites, Moabites,
and men from Mount Seir are coming! When Israel came from
the land of Egypt, you did not allow them to invade these lands.
They bypassed them and did not destroy them. 11Look how they
are repaying us! They come to drive us out of our allotted land
which you assigned to us! 12Our God, will you not judge them?
For we are powerless against this huge army that attacks us. We
don't know what we should do; we look to you for help."

13All the men of Judah were standing before the LORD, along
with their infants, wives, and children. 14Then in the midst of
the assembly, the LORD's Spirit came upon Jachaziel son of
Zechariah, son of Benaiah, son of Jeiel, son of Mattaniah, a Levite and descendant of Asaph. 15He said: "Pay attention, all you
people of Judah, residents of Jerusalem, and King Jehoshaphat!
This is what the LORD says to you: 'Don't be afraid and don't
panic because of this huge army! For the battle is not yours, but
God's. 16Tomorrow march down against them as they come up
the Ascent of Ziz. You will find them at the end of the ravine
in front of the wilderness of Jeruel. 17You will not fight in this
battle. Take your positions, stand, and watch the LORD deliver
you, O Judah and Jerusalem. Don't be afraid and don't panic!
Tomorrow march out toward them; the LORD is with you!'"

18Jehoshaphat bowed down with his face toward the ground,
and all the people of Judah and the residents of Jerusalem fell
down before the LORD and worshiped him. 19Then some Levites,
from the Kohathites and Korahites, got up and loudly praised
the LORD God of Israel.

20Early the next morning they marched out to the wilderness
of Tekoa. When they were ready to march, Jehoshaphat stood
up and said: "Listen to me, you people of Judah and residents
of Jerusalem! Trust in the LORD your God and you will be safe!
Trust in the message of his prophets and you will win." 21He
met with the people and appointed musicians to play before
the LORD and praise his majestic splendor. As they marched
ahead of the warriors they said: "Give thanks to the LORD, for
his loyal love endures."

22When they began to shout and praise, the LORD suddenly attacked the Ammonites, Moabites, and men from Mount
Seir who were invading Judah, and they were defeated. 23The
Ammonites and Moabites attacked the men from Mount Seir
and annihilated them. When they had finished off the men
of Seir, they attacked and destroyed one another. 24When the
men of Judah arrived at the observation post overlooking the
wilderness and looked at the huge army, they saw dead bodies

on the ground; there were no survivors. 25Jehoshaphat and his
men went to gather the plunder; they found a huge amount of
supplies, clothing, and valuable items. They carried away everything they could. There was so much plunder, it took them
three days to haul it off.
26On the fourth day they assembled in the Valley of Berachah,
where they praised the LORD. So that place is called the Valley of
Berachah to this very day. 27Then all the men of Judah and Jerusalem returned joyfully to Jerusalem with Jehoshaphat leading
them; the LORD had given them reason to rejoice over their
enemies. 28They entered Jerusalem to the sound of stringed
instruments and trumpets and proceeded to the temple of
the LORD. 29All the kingdoms of the surrounding lands were
afraid of God when they heard how the LORD had fought against
Israel's enemies. 30Jehoshaphat's kingdom enjoyed peace; his
God made him secure on every side.

JEHOSHAPHAT'S REIGN ENDS

31Jehoshaphat reigned over Judah. He was thirty-five years old
when he became king, and he reigned for twenty-five years
in Jerusalem. His mother was Azubah, the daughter of Shilhi.
32He followed in his father Asa's footsteps and was careful to
do what the LORD approved. 33However, the high places were
not eliminated; the people were still not devoted to the God
of their ancestors.
34The rest of the events of Jehoshaphat's reign, from start to
finish, are recorded in the Annals of Jehu son of Hanani, which
are included in the Scroll of the Kings of Israel.
35Later King Jehoshaphat of Judah made an alliance with
King Ahaziah of Israel, who did evil. 36They agreed to make large
seagoing merchant ships; they built the ships in Ezion Geber.
37Eliezer son of Dodavahu from Mareshah prophesied against
Jehoshaphat, "Because you made an alliance with Ahaziah, the
LORD will shatter what you have made." The ships were wrecked
and unable to go to sea.

21 Jehoshaphat passed away and was buried with his ancestors in the City of David. His son Jehoram replaced
him as king.

JEHORAM'S REIGN

2His brothers, Jehoshaphat's sons, were Azariah, Jechiel, Zechariah, Azariahu, Michael, and Shephatiah. All these were sons
of King Jehoshaphat of Israel. 3Their father gave them many
presents, including silver, gold, and other precious items, along
with fortified cities in Judah. But he gave the kingdom to Jehoram because he was the firstborn.
4Jehoram took control of his father's kingdom and became
powerful. Then he killed all his brothers, as well as some of the
officials of Israel. 5Jehoram was thirty-two years old when he
became king, and he reigned for eight years in Jerusalem. 6He
followed in the footsteps of the kings of Israel, just as Ahab's
dynasty had done, for he married Ahab's daughter. He did evil
in the sight of the LORD. 7But the LORD was unwilling to destroy
David's dynasty because of the promise he had made to give
David a perpetual dynasty.
8During Jehoram's reign Edom freed themselves from Judah's control and set up their own king. 9Jehoram crossed over
with his officers and all his chariots. The Edomites, who had
surrounded him, attacked at night and defeated him and his

21:1–20 Here we have a clear indication of how God stirs up enemies to lay waste those countries that he judges to be deserving of such punishment. And yet was it not of their own will that the Philistines and Arabs came to lay waste the country of Judah? Or did they so come of their own will that the scripture lies where it tells us that the Lord stirred up their spirit to do so? On the contrary, both statements are true because they did come of their own will, and God did stir up their spirit. For the Almighty, who cannot possibly will anything unjust, is able to set in motion even the inclinations of their will in human hearts in order to accomplish through these people whatever he wishes to achieve through their agency.

AUGUSTINE **(354–430)**
ON GRACE AND FREE WILL

chariot officers. 10So Edom has remained free from Judah's
control to this very day. At that same time Libnah also rebelled
and freed themselves from Judah's control because Jehoram
rejected the LORD God of his ancestors. 11He also built high
places on the hills of Judah; he encouraged the residents of
Jerusalem to be unfaithful to the LORD and led Judah away
from the LORD.
12Jehoram received this letter from Elijah the prophet: "This
is what the LORD God of your ancestor David says: 'You have
not followed in the footsteps of your father Jehoshaphat and
of King Asa of Judah, 13but have instead followed in the footsteps of the kings of Israel. You encouraged the people of Judah
and the residents of Jerusalem to be unfaithful to the LORD,
just as the family of Ahab does in Israel. You also killed your
brothers, members of your father's family, who were better
than you. 14So look, the LORD is about to severely afflict your
people, your sons, your wives, and all you own. 15And you will
get a serious, chronic intestinal disease which will cause your
intestines to come out.'"
16The LORD stirred up against Jehoram the Philistines and the
Arabs who lived beside the Cushites. 17They attacked Judah and
swept through it. They carried off everything they found in the
royal palace, including his sons and wives. None of his sons was
left, except for his youngest, Ahaziah. 18After all this happened,
the LORD afflicted him with an incurable intestinal disease.
19After about two years his intestines came out because of the
disease, so that he died a very painful death. His people did not
make a bonfire to honor him, as they had done for his ancestors.
20Jehoram was thirty-two years old when he became king, and
he reigned eight years in Jerusalem. No one regretted his death;
he was buried in the City of David, but not in the royal tombs.

AHAZIAH'S REIGN

22 The residents of Jerusalem made his youngest son Ahaziah king in his place, for the raiding party that invaded the
camp with the Arabs had killed all the older sons. So Ahaziah
son of Jehoram became king of Judah. 2Ahaziah was twenty-two
years old when he became king, and he reigned for one year
in Jerusalem. His mother was Athaliah, the granddaughter of
Omri. 3He followed in the footsteps of Ahab's dynasty, for his
mother gave him evil advice. 4He did evil in the sight of the
LORD like Ahab's dynasty because, after his father's death, they
gave him advice that led to his destruction. 5He followed their
advice and joined Ahab's son King Joram of Israel in a battle
against King Hazael of Syria at Ramoth Gilead in which the
Syrians defeated Joram. 6Joram returned to Jezreel to recover
from the wounds he received from the Syrians in Ramah when
he fought against King Hazael of Syria. Ahaziah son of King Jehoram of Judah went down to visit Joram son of Ahab in Jezreel,
because he had been wounded.
7God brought about Ahaziah's downfall through his visit to
Joram. When Ahaziah arrived, he went out with Joram to meet
Jehu son of Nimshi, whom the LORD had commissioned to wipe
out Ahab's family. 8While Jehu was dishing out punishment
to Ahab's family, he discovered the officials of Judah and the
sons of Ahaziah's relatives who were serving Ahaziah and killed
them. 9He looked for Ahaziah, who was captured while hiding
in Samaria. They brought him to Jehu and then executed him.
They did give him a burial, for they reasoned, "He is the son of

22:8–9 The Lord established the kingdom in Jehoshaphat's hand, and all Judah brought presents to him. And he acquired immense wealth and riches and much glory. And, lest we suppose that the justice he possessed in the past was destroyed by the fact that he committed this sin and was reproved by the prophet, it is written subsequently of Ahaziah, his descendant, that Jehu found him lying in Samaria and, when he was brought in, he killed him: "They did give him a burial," he says, "for they reasoned, 'He is the son of Jehoshaphat, who sought the LORD with his whole heart.'"

JEROME **(C. 342–420)**
AGAINST THE PELAGIANS

Jehoshaphat, who sought the LORD with his whole heart." There
was no one in Ahaziah's family strong enough to rule in his place.

ATHALIAH IS ELIMINATED

10When Athaliah the mother of Ahaziah saw that her son was
dead, she was determined to destroy the entire royal line of
Judah. 11So Jehoshabeath, the daughter of King Jehoram, took
Ahaziah's son Joash and stole him away from the rest of the
royal descendants who were to be executed. She hid him and
his nurse in the room where the bed covers were stored. So
Jehoshabeath the daughter of King Jehoram, wife of Jehoiada
the priest and sister of Ahaziah, hid him from Athaliah so she
could not execute him. 12He remained in hiding in God's temple
for six years while Athaliah was ruling over the land.

23 In the seventh year Jehoiada made a bold move. He made
a pact with the officers of the units of hundreds: Azariah
son of Jehoram, Ishmael son of Jehochanan, Azariah son of
Obed, Maaseiah son of Adaiah, and Elishaphat son of Zikri.
2They traveled throughout Judah and assembled the Levites
from all the cities of Judah, as well as the Israelite family leaders.

They came to Jerusalem, 3and the whole assembly made a
covenant with the king in the temple of God. Jehoiada said to
them, "The king's son will rule, just as the LORD promised David's
descendants. 4This is what you must do. One-third of you priests
and Levites who are on duty during the Sabbath will guard the
doors. 5Another third of you will be stationed at the royal palace
and still another third at the Foundation Gate. All the others
will stand in the courtyards of the LORD's temple. 6No one must
enter the LORD's temple except the priests and Levites who are
on duty. They may enter because they are ceremonially pure.
All the others should carry out their assigned service to the
LORD. 7The Levites must surround the king. Each of you must
hold his weapon in his hand. Whoever tries to enter the temple
must be killed. You must accompany the king wherever he goes."

8The Levites and all the men of Judah did just as Jehoiada the
priest ordered. Each of them took his men, those who were on
duty during the Sabbath as well as those who were off duty on
the Sabbath. Jehoiada the priest did not release his divisions
from their duties. 9Jehoiada the priest gave to the officers of
the units of hundreds King David's spears and shields that were
kept in God's temple. 10He placed the men at their posts, each
holding his weapon in his hand. They lined up from the south
side of the temple to the north side and stood near the altar
and the temple, surrounding the king. 11Jehoiada and his sons
led out the king's son and placed on him the crown and the
royal insignia. They proclaimed him king and poured olive oil
on his head. They declared, "Long live the king!"

12When Athaliah heard the royal guard shouting and praising
the king, she joined the crowd at the LORD's temple. 13Then she
saw the king standing by his pillar at the entrance. The officers
and trumpeters stood beside the king and all the people of the
land were celebrating and blowing trumpets, and the musicians
with various instruments were leading the celebration. Athaliah tore her clothes and yelled, "Treason! Treason!" 14Jehoiada
the priest sent out the officers of the units of hundreds, who
were in charge of the army, and ordered them, "Bring her outside the temple to the guards. Put the sword to anyone who
follows her." The priest gave this order because he had decided
she should not be executed in the LORD's temple. 15They seized

23:1–21 In order to display more fully his own truth and faithfulness, God often permits events to arise that seem to render the accomplishment of his promises almost, if not altogether, hopeless. The descendants of David, to whom God had promised that his seed should continue to sit upon the throne of Judah, had more than once been in imminent danger of utter excision. Joash, the youngest son of Ahaziah, was actually with his brethren when they all were slain and by some means, being only an infant, was hid among them so as to escape the general slaughter. From that state he was rescued by his aunt and was hid, together with his nurse, in a bedchamber till he was seven years old. At that time Jehoiada the priest established Joash on his father's throne.

CHARLES SIMEON
(1759–1836)
HORAE HOMILETICAE

her and took her into the precincts of the royal palace through the horses' entrance. There they executed her.

16 Jehoiada then drew up a covenant stipulating that he, all the people, and the king should be loyal to the LORD. 17 All the people went and demolished the temple of Baal. They smashed its altars and idols. They killed Mattan the priest of Baal in front of the altars. 18 Jehoiada then assigned the duties of the LORD's temple to the priests, the Levites whom David had assigned to the LORD's temple. They were responsible for offering burnt sacrifices to the LORD with joy and music, according to the law of Moses and the edict of David. 19 He posted guards at the gates of the LORD's temple, so no one who was ceremonially unclean in any way could enter. 20 He summoned the officers of the units of hundreds, the nobles, the rulers of the people, and all the people of the land, and he then led the king down from the LORD's temple. They entered the royal palace through the Upper Gate and seated the king on the royal throne. 21 All the people of the land celebrated, for the city had rest now that they had killed Athaliah.

JOASH'S REIGN

24 Joash was seven years old when he began to reign. He reigned for forty years in Jerusalem. His mother was Zibiah, who was from Beer Sheba. 2 Joash did what the LORD approved throughout the lifetime of Jehoiada the priest. 3 Jehoiada chose two wives for him who gave him sons and daughters.

4 Later, Joash was determined to repair the LORD's temple. 5 He assembled the priests and Levites and ordered them, "Go out to the cities of Judah and collect the annual quota of silver from all Israel for repairs on the temple of your God. Be quick about it!" But the Levites delayed.

6 So the king summoned Jehoiada the chief priest, and said to him, "Why have you not made the Levites collect from Judah and Jerusalem the tax authorized by Moses the LORD's servant and by the assembly of Israel at the tent containing the tablets of the law?" 7 (Wicked Athaliah and her sons had broken into God's temple and used all the holy items of the LORD's temple in their worship of the Baals.) 8 The king ordered a chest to be made and placed outside the gate of the LORD's temple. 9 An edict was sent throughout Judah and Jerusalem requiring the people to bring to the LORD the tax that Moses, God's servant, imposed on Israel in the wilderness. 10 All the officials and all the people gladly brought their silver and threw it into the chest until it was full. 11 Whenever the Levites brought the chest to the royal accountant and they saw there was a lot of silver, the royal scribe and the accountant of the high priest emptied the chest and then took it back to its place. They went through this routine every day and collected a large amount of silver.

12 The king and Jehoiada gave it to the construction foremen assigned to the LORD's temple. They hired carpenters and craftsmen to repair the LORD's temple, as well as those skilled in working with iron and bronze to restore the LORD's temple. 13 They worked hard and made the repairs. They followed the measurements specified for God's temple and restored it. 14 When they were finished, they brought the rest of the silver to the king and Jehoiada. They used it to make items for the LORD's temple, including items used in the temple service and for burnt sacrifices, pans, and various other gold and silver items. Throughout Jehoiada's lifetime, burnt sacrifices were offered regularly in the LORD's temple.

[15]Jehoiada grew old and died at the age of 130. [16]He was buried in the City of David with the kings, because he had accomplished good in Israel and for God and his temple.

[17]After Jehoiada died, the officials of Judah visited the king and declared their loyalty to him. The king listened to their advice. [18]They abandoned the temple of the LORD God of their ancestors and worshiped the Asherah poles and idols. Because of this sinful activity, God was angry with Judah and Jerusalem. [19]The LORD sent prophets among them to lead them back to him. They warned the people, but they would not pay attention. [20]God's Spirit energized Zechariah son of Jehoiada the priest. He stood up before the people and said to them, "This is what God says: 'Why are you violating the commands of the LORD? You will not be prosperous. Because you have rejected the LORD, he has rejected you!'" [21]They plotted against him and by royal decree stoned him to death in the courtyard of the LORD's temple. [22]King Joash disregarded the loyalty Zechariah's father Jehoiada had shown him and killed Jehoiada's son. As Zechariah was dying, he said, "May the LORD take notice and seek vengeance!"

[23]At the beginning of the year the Syrian army attacked Joash and invaded Judah and Jerusalem. They wiped out all the leaders of the people and sent all the plunder they gathered to the king of Damascus. [24]Even though the invading Syrian army was relatively weak, the LORD handed over to them Judah's very large army, for the people of Judah had abandoned the LORD God of their ancestors. The Syrians gave Joash what he deserved. [25]When they withdrew, they left Joash badly wounded. His servants plotted against him because of what he had done to the son of Jehoiada the priest. They murdered him on his bed. Thus he died and was buried in the City of David, but not in the tombs of the kings. [26]The conspirators were Zabad son of Shimeath (an Ammonite woman) and Jehozabad son of Shimrith (a Moabite woman).

[27]The list of Joash's sons, the many prophetic oracles about him, and the account of his building project on God's temple are included in the record of the Scroll of the Kings. His son Amaziah replaced him as king.

24:15–22 We may note the following things: First, we have great need always to pray so that we may be upheld in the truth, seeing that Joash was godly for so long, yet, finally destitute of his tutor, he quickly fell into sin. Second, it is of great avail to commit youth to good tutors and overseers. Third, there is not a more pestilent way of corrupting princes or leaders than by flattery. By showing ourselves hateful of flattery at all times, we may keep out of danger. Finally, to tolerate a false religion is the very way for kings to overthrow themselves and their kingdoms. For even if leaders do not embrace false religion themselves, they will fall into ruin.

JOHN MAYER **(1583–1664)**
COMMENTARY ON SECOND CHRONICLES

AMAZIAH'S REIGN

25 Amaziah was twenty-five years old when he began to reign, and he reigned for twenty-nine years in Jerusalem. His mother was Jehoaddan, who was from Jerusalem. [2]He did what the LORD approved, but not with wholehearted devotion.

[3]When he had secured control of the kingdom, he executed the servants who had assassinated his father the king. [4]However, he did not execute their sons. He obeyed the LORD's commandment as recorded in the law scroll of Moses, "Fathers must not be executed for what their sons do, and sons must not be executed for what their fathers do. A man must be executed only for his own sin."

[5]Amaziah assembled the people of Judah and assigned them by families to the commanders of units of 1,000 and the commanders of units of 100 for all Judah and Benjamin. He counted those twenty years old and up and discovered there were 300,000 young men of fighting age equipped with spears and shields. [6]He hired 100,000 Israelite warriors for 100 talents of silver.

[7]But a prophet visited him and said: "O king, the Israelite troops must not go with you, for the LORD is not with Israel or any of the Ephraimites. [8]Even if you go and fight bravely in battle, God will defeat you before the enemy. God is capable of helping or defeating." [9]Amaziah asked the prophet: "But what

25:1–28 How does the power of God help some in war by giving them confidence and put others to flight by injecting fear into them except it be that he who has made all things according to his own will, in heaven and on earth, also works in the hearts of human beings? We read also what Joash, king of Israel, said when he sent a message to Amaziah, king of Judah, who wanted to fight with him: "Gloat over your success, but stay in your palace. Why bring calamity on yourself? Why bring down yourself and Judah along with you?" Then the scripture has added this sequel: "But Amaziah did not heed the warning, for God wanted to hand them over to Joash because they followed the gods of Edom." Behold now how God, wishing to punish the sin of idolatry, wrought this in the heart of this man with whom he was indeed justly angry not to listen to sound advice but to despise it and go to the battle in which he with his army was routed.

AUGUSTINE **(354–430)**
ON GRACE AND FREE WILL

should I do about the 100 talents of silver I paid the Israelite
troops?" The prophet replied, "The LORD is capable of giving
you more than that." [10]So Amaziah dismissed the troops that
had come to him from Ephraim and sent them home. They were
very angry at Judah and returned home incensed. [11]Amaziah
boldly led his army to the Valley of Salt, where he defeated
10,000 Edomites. [12]The men of Judah captured 10,000 men
alive. They took them to the top of a cliff and threw them over.
All the captives fell to their death. [13]Now the troops Amaziah
had dismissed and had not allowed to fight in the battle raided
the cities of Judah from Samaria to Beth Horon. They killed
3,000 people and carried off a large amount of plunder.

[14]When Amaziah returned from defeating the Edomites, he
brought back the gods of the people of Seir and made them his
personal gods. He bowed down before them and offered them
sacrifices. [15]The LORD was angry at Amaziah and sent a prophet
to him, who said, "Why are you following these gods that could
not deliver their own people from your power?" [16]While he was
speaking, Amaziah said to him, "Did we appoint you to be a royal
counselor? Stop prophesying or else you will be killed!" So the
prophet stopped, but added, "I know that God has decided to
destroy you because you have done this thing and refused to
listen to my advice."

[17]After King Amaziah of Judah consulted with his advisers,
he sent this message to the king of Israel, Joash son of Jehoahaz,
the son of Jehu, "Come, face me on the battlefield." [18]King Joash
of Israel sent this message back to King Amaziah of Judah, "A
thorn bush in Lebanon sent this message to a cedar in Lebanon,
'Give your daughter to my son as a wife.' Then a wild animal of
Lebanon came by and trampled down the thorn bush. [19]You
defeated Edom and it has gone to your head. Gloat over your
success, but stay in your palace. Why bring calamity on yourself?
Why bring down yourself and Judah along with you?"

[20]But Amaziah did not heed the warning, for God wanted
to hand them over to Joash because they followed the gods of
Edom. [21]So King Joash of Israel attacked. He and King Amaziah
of Judah faced each other on the battlefield in Beth Shemesh of
Judah. [22]Judah was defeated by Israel, and each man ran back
home. [23]King Joash of Israel captured King Amaziah of Judah,
son of Joash son of Jehoahaz, in Beth Shemesh and brought him
to Jerusalem. He broke down the wall of Jerusalem from the Gate
of Ephraim to the Corner Gate—a distance of about 600 feet.
[24]He took away all the gold and silver, all the items found in God's
temple that were in the care of Obed-Edom, the riches in the
royal palace, and some hostages. Then he went back to Samaria.

[25]King Amaziah son of Joash of Judah lived for fifteen years after
the death of King Joash son of Jehoahaz of Israel. [26]The rest of the
events of Amaziah's reign, from start to finish, are recorded in the
Scroll of the Kings of Judah and Israel. [27]From the time Amaziah
turned from following the LORD, conspirators plotted against him
in Jerusalem, so he fled to Lachish. But they sent assassins after
him, and they killed him there. [28]His body was carried back by
horses, and he was buried with his ancestors in the City of David.

UZZIAH'S REIGN

26 All the people of Judah took Uzziah, who was sixteen
years old, and made him king in his father Amaziah's
place. [2]Uzziah built up Elat and restored it to Judah after King
Amaziah had passed away.

26:1–23 People are prone to abuse God's blessings, giving them a power that eventually leads to pride and self-confidence. Pride is the forerunner of ruin. It makes people attempt such things as provoke God's wrath on them. Uzziah's act of entering the temple was expressly forbidden. And this was an aggravation of his sin, given that God had shown himself faithful to Uzziah in so many ways. The golden altar was set close to the entrance in the Most Holy Place. This shows the height of Uzziah's impiety and monstrous presumption. He went through the priests' court, the high court, and the holy place, even to the uppermost part of it, where he was not allowed to be.

THE WESTMINSTER ANNOTATIONS
(1683)

3Uzziah was sixteen years old when he began to reign, and
he reigned for fifty-two years in Jerusalem. His mother's name
was Jecholiah, who was from Jerusalem. 4He did what the LORD
approved, just as his father Amaziah had done. 5He followed God
during the lifetime of Zechariah, who taught him how to honor
God. As long as he followed the LORD, God caused him to succeed.
6Uzziah attacked the Philistines and broke down the walls
of Gath, Jabneh, and Ashdod. He built cities in the region of
Ashdod and throughout Philistine territory. 7God helped him
in his campaigns against the Philistines, the Arabs living in Gur
Baal, and the Meunites. 8The Ammonites paid tribute to Uzziah,
and his fame reached the border of Egypt, for he grew in power.
9Uzziah built and fortified towers in Jerusalem at the Corner
Gate, Valley Gate, and at the Angle. 10He built towers in the
wilderness and dug many cisterns, for he owned many herds in
the foothills and on the plain. He had workers in the fields and
vineyards in the hills and in Carmel, for he loved agriculture.
11Uzziah had an army of skilled warriors trained for battle.
They were organized by divisions according to the muster rolls
made by Jeiel the scribe and Maaseiah the officer under the
authority of Hananiah, a royal official. 12The total number of
family leaders who led warriors was 2,600. 13They commanded
an army of 307,500 skilled and able warriors who were ready to
defend the king against his enemies. 14Uzziah supplied shields,
spears, helmets, breastplates, bows, and slingstones for the
entire army. 15In Jerusalem he made war machines carefully
designed to shoot arrows and large stones from the towers and
corners of the walls. He became very famous, for he received
tremendous support and became powerful.
16But once he became powerful, his pride destroyed him. He
disobeyed the LORD his God. He entered the LORD's temple
to offer incense on the incense altar. 17Azariah the priest and
eighty other brave priests of the LORD followed him in. 18They
confronted King Uzziah and said to him, "It is not proper for you,
Uzziah, to offer incense to the LORD. That is the responsibility
of the priests, the descendants of Aaron, who are consecrated to
offer incense. Leave the sanctuary, for you have disobeyed and
the LORD God will not honor you!" 19Uzziah, who had an incense
censer in his hand, became angry. While he was ranting and
raving at the priests, a skin disease appeared on his forehead
right there in front of the priests in the LORD's temple near the
incense altar. 20When Azariah the high priest and the other
priests looked at him, there was a skin disease on his forehead.
They hurried him out of there; even the king himself wanted to
leave quickly because the LORD had afflicted him. 21King Uzziah
suffered from a skin disease until the day he died. He lived in
separate quarters, afflicted by a skin disease and banned from
the LORD's temple. His son Jotham was in charge of the palace
and ruled over the people of the land.
22The rest of the events of Uzziah's reign, from start to finish,
were recorded by the prophet Isaiah son of Amoz. 23Uzziah
passed away and was buried near his ancestors in a cemetery
belonging to the kings. (This was because he had a skin disease.)
His son Jotham replaced him as king.

JOTHAM'S REIGN

27 Jotham was twenty-five years old when he began to reign,
and he reigned for sixteen years in Jerusalem. His mother
was Jerusha the daughter of Zadok. 2He did what the LORD

27:1–9 If people's ways are prepared before the Lord their God, they will be mighty not only against their foes but in the midst of their own people. Even though Jotham's subjects would not follow him in all respects, they respected him, loved him, and made great lamentation over him when he died. If you want to have influence over others, do not take to flattering them, and never try to show them how great your talents are or to make them believe you are somebody of importance. We have seen plenty of flashes in the pan, but the darkness has been just as great afterward. Believe me, there is no building up of character except upon sound principles, and there is no building up of influence except upon good character. You must seek, God helping you by his Spirit, to prepare and establish your ways before him, and then such influence as you ought to have will come to you.

CHARLES SPURGEON
(1834–1892)
METROPOLITAN TABERNACLE SERMONS

approved, just as his father Uzziah had done. (He did not, however, have the audacity to enter the temple.) Yet the people were still sinning.

3He built the Upper Gate to the LORD's temple and did a lot of work on the wall in the area known as Ophel. 4He built cities in the hill country of Judah and fortresses and towers in the forests.

5He launched a military campaign against the king of the Ammonites and defeated them. That year the Ammonites paid him 100 talents of silver, 10,000 cors of wheat, and 10,000 cors of barley. The Ammonites also paid this same amount of annual tribute the next two years.

6Jotham grew powerful because he was determined to please the LORD his God. 7The rest of the events of Jotham's reign, including all his military campaigns and his accomplishments, are recorded in the Scroll of the Kings of Israel and Judah. 8He was twenty-five years old when he began to reign, and he reigned for sixteen years in Jerusalem. 9Jotham passed away and was buried in the City of David. His son Ahaz replaced him as king.

AHAZ'S REIGN

28 Ahaz was twenty years old when he began to reign, and he reigned for sixteen years in Jerusalem. He did not do what pleased the LORD, in contrast to his ancestor David. 2He followed in the footsteps of the kings of Israel; he also made images of the Baals. 3He offered sacrifices in the Valley of Ben Hinnom and passed his sons through the fire, a horrible sin practiced by the nations whom the LORD drove out before the Israelites. 4He offered sacrifices and burned incense on the high places, on the hills, and under every green tree.

5The LORD his God handed him over to the king of Syria. The Syrians defeated him and deported many captives to Damascus. He was also handed over to the king of Israel, who thoroughly defeated him. 6In one day Pekah son of Remaliah killed 120,000 warriors in Judah because they had abandoned the LORD God of their ancestors. 7Zikri, an Ephraimite warrior, killed the king's son Maaseiah, Azrikam, the supervisor of the palace, and Elkanah, the king's second-in-command. 8The Israelites seized from their brothers 200,000 wives, sons, and daughters. They also carried off a huge amount of plunder and took it back to Samaria.

9Oded, a prophet of the LORD, was there. He went to meet the army as they arrived in Samaria and said to them: "Look, because the LORD God of your ancestors was angry with Judah, he handed them over to you. You have killed them so mercilessly that God has taken notice. 10And now you are planning to enslave the people of Judah and Jerusalem. Yet are you not also guilty before the LORD your God? 11Now listen to me! Send back those you have seized from your brothers, for the LORD is very angry at you!" 12So some of the Ephraimite family leaders, Azariah son of Jehochanan, Berechiah son of Meshillemoth, Jechizkiah son of Shallum, and Amasa son of Hadlai confronted those returning from the battle. 13They said to them, "Don't bring those captives here! Are you planning on making us even more sinful and guilty before the LORD? Our guilt is already great, and the LORD is very angry at Israel." 14So the soldiers released the captives and the plunder before the officials and the entire assembly. 15Men were assigned to take the prisoners and find clothes among the plunder for those who were naked.

28:1–27 Chronicles reads, "During his time of trouble King Ahaz was even more unfaithful to the LORD. He offered sacrifices to the gods of Damascus whom he thought had defeated him." He also "gathered the items in God's temple and removed them. He shut the doors of the LORD's temple and erected altars on every street corner in Jerusalem." He did these and other similar things; he removed the genuine altar of bronze, which Solomon had built, and put in its place another one recently made. And he even dared to commit another act of impiety: He moved the entrance of the royal house into the divine temple, transforming the sacred enclosure into a thoroughfare.

THEODORET OF CYR
(C. 393–C. 458)
QUESTIONS ON KINGS AND CHRONICLES

So they clothed them, supplied them with sandals, gave them
food and drink, and provided them with oil to rub on their skin.
They put the ones who couldn't walk on donkeys. They brought
them back to their brothers at Jericho, the city of date palm
trees, and then returned to Samaria.
[16]At that time King Ahaz asked the king of Assyria for help.
[17]The Edomites had again invaded and defeated Judah and
carried off captives. [18]The Philistines had raided the cities of
Judah in the foothills and the Negev. They captured and settled
in Beth Shemesh, Aijalon, Gederoth, Soco and its surrounding
villages, Timnah and its surrounding villages, and Gimzo and its
surrounding villages. [19]The LORD humiliated Judah because of
King Ahaz of Israel, for he encouraged Judah to sin and was very
unfaithful to the LORD. [20]King Tiglath-Pileser of Assyria came,
but he gave him more trouble than support. [21]Ahaz gathered
riches from the LORD's temple, the royal palace, and the officials
and gave them to the king of Assyria, but that did not help.
[22]During his time of trouble King Ahaz was even more
unfaithful to the LORD. [23]He offered sacrifices to the gods of
Damascus whom he thought had defeated him. He reasoned,
"Since the gods of the kings of Syria helped them, I will sacrifice to them so they will help me." But they caused him and all
Israel to stumble. [24]Ahaz gathered the items in God's temple
and removed them. He shut the doors of the LORD's temple and
erected altars on every street corner in Jerusalem. [25]In every
city throughout Judah he set up high places to offer sacrifices
to other gods. He angered the LORD God of his ancestors.
[26]The rest of the events of Ahaz's reign, including his accomplishments from start to finish, are recorded in the Scroll of the
Kings of Judah and Israel. [27]Ahaz passed away and was buried
in the city of Jerusalem; they did not bring him to the tombs
of the kings of Israel. His son Hezekiah replaced him as king.

HEZEKIAH CONSECRATES THE TEMPLE

29 Hezekiah was twenty-five years old when he began to
reign, and he reigned twenty-nine years in Jerusalem.
His mother was Abijah, the daughter of Zechariah. [2]He did
what the LORD approved, just as his ancestor David had done.
[3]In the first month of the first year of his reign, he opened
the doors of the LORD's temple and repaired them. [4]He brought
in the priests and Levites and assembled them in the square
on the east side. [5]He said to them: "Listen to me, you Levites!
Now consecrate yourselves, so you can consecrate the temple
of the LORD God of your ancestors. Remove from the sanctuary
what is ceremonially unclean. [6]For our fathers were unfaithful; they did what is evil in the sight of the LORD our God and
abandoned him. They turned away from the LORD's dwelling
place and rejected him. [7]They closed the doors of the temple
porch and put out the lamps; they did not offer incense or burnt
sacrifices in the sanctuary of the God of Israel. [8]The LORD was
angry at Judah and Jerusalem and made them an appalling
object of horror at which people hiss out their scorn, as you
can see with your own eyes. [9]Look, our fathers died violently,
and our sons, daughters, and wives were carried off because of
this. [10]Now I intend to make a covenant with the LORD God
of Israel, so that he may relent from his raging anger. [11]My
sons, do not be negligent now, for the LORD has chosen you to
stand in his presence, to minister to him, to be his ministers,
and offer sacrifices."

29:1–36 The impious father closed the temple and contaminated the entire kingdom with idols. As a sign of his piety, the son opened the temple, destroyed his father's idols, and reinstituted the devotion and positions of the priests and Levites. Hezekiah's zeal was such that he delayed hardly a day to make these religious changes but resolutely started them in the first month of the first year of his reign. This was no small business. The pious and zealous king ardently sought first the kingdom of God, and shortly afterward all good things were added. The cleansing of the temple is an image for reforming doctrine. Such work requires three things: a mind big enough to handle the mysteries of God, a fearless spirit, and eloquence of speech. For just as a dirty mirror cannot show a clear image, so a soul that is tangled up in this life and made sluggish by physical cares is not capable of light and spiritual wisdom.

VIKTORIN STRIGEL
(C. 1524–1569)
BOOK OF CHRONICLES

[12]The following Levites prepared to carry out the king's
orders:

From the Kohathites: Mahath son of Amasai and Joel son
of Azariah;

from the Merarites: Kish son of Abdi and Azariah son of
Jehallelel;

from the Gershonites: Joah son of Zimmah and Eden son
of Joah;

[13]from the descendants of Elizaphan: Shimri and Jeiel;

from the descendants of Asaph: Zechariah and Mattaniah;

[14]from the descendants of Heman: Jehiel and Shimei;

from the descendants of Jeduthun: Shemaiah and Uzziel.

[15]They assembled their brothers and consecrated themselves. Then they went in to purify the LORD's temple, just
as the king had ordered, in accordance with the word of the
LORD. [16]The priests then entered the LORD's temple to purify it; they brought out to the courtyard of the LORD's temple
every ceremonially unclean thing they discovered inside. The
Levites took them out to the Kidron Valley. [17]On the first day
of the first month they began consecrating; by the eighth day
of the month they reached the porch of the LORD's temple. For
eight more days they consecrated the LORD's temple. On the
sixteenth day of the first month they were finished. [18]They
went to King Hezekiah and said: "We have purified the entire
temple of the LORD, including the altar of burnt sacrifice and
all its equipment, and the table for the Bread of the Presence
and all its equipment. [19]We have prepared and consecrated all
the items that King Ahaz removed during his reign when he
acted unfaithfully. They are in front of the altar of the LORD."

[20]Early the next morning King Hezekiah assembled the city officials and went up to the LORD's temple. [21]They brought seven bulls,
seven rams, seven lambs, and seven goats as a sin offering for the
kingdom, the sanctuary, and Judah. The king told the priests, the
descendants of Aaron, to offer burnt sacrifices on the altar of
the LORD. [22]They slaughtered the bulls, and the priests took the
blood and splashed it on the altar. Then they slaughtered the rams
and splashed the blood on the altar; next they slaughtered the
lambs and splashed the blood on the altar. [23]Finally they brought
the goats for the sin offering before the king and the assembly, and
they placed their hands on them. [24]Then the priests slaughtered
them. They offered their blood as a sin offering on the altar to
make atonement for all Israel because the king had decreed that
the burnt sacrifice and sin offering were for all Israel.

[25]Hezekiah stationed the Levites in the LORD's temple with
cymbals and stringed instruments just as David, Gad the king's
prophet, and Nathan the prophet had ordered. (The LORD had
actually given these orders through his prophets.) [26]The Levites
had David's musical instruments and the priests had trumpets.
[27]Hezekiah ordered the burnt sacrifice to be offered on the
altar. As they began to offer the sacrifice, they also began to
sing to the LORD, accompanied by the trumpets and the musical instruments of King David of Israel. [28]The entire assembly
worshiped, as the singers sang and the trumpeters played. They
continued until the burnt sacrifice was completed.

[29]When the sacrifices were completed, the king and all who
were with him bowed down and worshiped. [30]King Hezekiah
and the officials told the Levites to praise the LORD, using the
psalms of David and Asaph the prophet. So they joyfully offered
praise and bowed down and worshiped. [31]Hezekiah said, "Now

you have consecrated yourselves to the LORD. Come and bring
sacrifices and thank offerings to the LORD's temple." So the
assembly brought sacrifices and thank offerings, and whoever
desired to do so brought burnt sacrifices.
32The assembly brought a total of 70 bulls, 100 rams, and
200 lambs as burnt sacrifices to the LORD, 33and 600 bulls and
3,000 sheep were consecrated. 34But there were not enough
priests to skin all the animals, so their brothers, the Levites,
helped them until the work was finished and the priests could
consecrate themselves. (The Levites had been more conscientious about consecrating themselves than the priests.) 35There
was a large number of burnt sacrifices, as well as fat from the
peace offerings and drink offerings that accompanied the burnt
sacrifices. So the service of the LORD's temple was reinstituted.
36Hezekiah and all the people were happy about what God had
done for them, for it had been done quickly.

HEZEKIAH OBSERVES THE PASSOVER

30 Hezekiah sent messages throughout Israel and Judah; he
even wrote letters to Ephraim and Manasseh, summoning
them to come to the LORD's temple in Jerusalem and observe
a Passover celebration for the LORD God of Israel. 2The king,
his officials, and the entire assembly in Jerusalem decided to
observe the Passover in the second month. 3They were unable
to observe it at the regular time because not enough priests had
consecrated themselves and the people had not assembled in
Jerusalem. 4The proposal seemed appropriate to the king and
the entire assembly. 5So they sent an edict throughout Israel
from Beer Sheba to Dan, summoning the people to come and
observe a Passover for the LORD God of Israel in Jerusalem, for
they had not observed it on a nationwide scale as prescribed in
the law. 6Messengers delivered the letters from the king and
his officials throughout Israel and Judah.

This royal edict read: "O Israelites, return to the LORD God
of Abraham, Isaac, and Israel, so he may return to you who
have been spared from the kings of Assyria. 7Don't be like your
fathers and brothers who were unfaithful to the LORD God of
their ancestors, provoking him to destroy them, as you can
see. 8Now, don't be stubborn like your fathers. Submit to the
LORD and come to his sanctuary which he has permanently
consecrated. Serve the LORD your God so that he might relent from his raging anger. 9For if you return to the LORD,
your brothers and sons will be shown mercy by their captors
and return to this land. The LORD your God is merciful and
compassionate; he will not reject you if you return to him."
10The messengers journeyed from city to city through the
land of Ephraim and Manasseh as far as Zebulun, but people
mocked and ridiculed them. 11But some men from Asher,
Manasseh, and Zebulun humbled themselves and came to Jerusalem. 12In Judah God moved the people to unite and carry
out the edict of the king and the officers in keeping with the
LORD's message. 13A huge crowd assembled in Jerusalem to
observe the Feast of Unleavened Bread in the second month.
14They removed the altars in Jerusalem; they also removed
all the incense altars and threw them into the Kidron Valley.
15They slaughtered the Passover lamb on the fourteenth day
of the second month. The priests and Levites were ashamed,
so they consecrated themselves and brought burnt sacrifices
to the LORD's temple. 16They stood at their posts according to

30:1–12 There are few who are wise to salvation and who seriously attend and manage the ministry of the Word to that end. Hezekiah sent messengers to all Israel to invite them to the true worship of God at Jerusalem. But they were mocked and laughed to scorn. Only a remnant humbled itself and went to Jerusalem. Though a net is spread over the whole pond, only a few fish are caught. The basest creatures are usually the most numerous, such as flies and vermin. Those that are nobler are rare. The people of the God of Abraham are, as far as scripture is concerned, princes and nobles; but there are very few compared with the rest of the world.

EDWARD REYNOLDS
(1599–1676)
THE SINFULNESS OF SIN

the regulations outlined in the law of Moses, the man of God. The priests were splashing the blood as the Levites handed it to them. 17Because many in the assembly had not consecrated themselves, the Levites slaughtered the Passover lambs of all who were ceremonially unclean and could not consecrate their sacrifice to the LORD. 18The majority of the many people from Ephraim, Manasseh, Issachar, and Zebulun were ceremonially unclean, yet they ate the Passover in violation of what is prescribed in the law. For Hezekiah prayed for them, saying: "May the LORD, who is good, forgive 19everyone who has determined to follow God, the LORD God of his ancestors, even if he is not ceremonially clean according to the standards of the temple." 20The LORD responded favorably to Hezekiah and forgave the people.

21The Israelites who were in Jerusalem observed the Feast of Unleavened Bread for seven days with great joy. The Levites and priests were praising the LORD every day with all their might. 22Hezekiah expressed his appreciation to all the Levites, who demonstrated great skill in serving the LORD. They feasted for the seven days of the festival and were making peace offerings and giving thanks to the LORD God of their ancestors.

23The entire assembly then decided to celebrate for seven more days; so they joyfully celebrated for seven more days. 24King Hezekiah of Judah supplied 1,000 bulls and 7,000 sheep for the assembly, while the officials supplied them with 1,000 bulls and 10,000 sheep. Many priests consecrated themselves. 25The celebration included the entire assembly of Judah, the priests, the Levites, the entire assembly of those who came from Israel, the resident foreigners who came from the land of Israel, and those who were residents of Judah. 26There was a great celebration in Jerusalem, unlike anything that had occurred in Jerusalem since the time of King Solomon son of David of Israel. 27The priests and Levites got up and pronounced blessings on the people. The LORD responded favorably to them as their prayers reached his holy dwelling place in heaven.

31 When all this was over, the Israelites who were in the cities of Judah went out and smashed the sacred pillars, cut down the Asherah poles, and demolished all the high places and altars throughout Judah, Benjamin, Ephraim, and Manasseh. Then all the Israelites returned to their own homes in their cities.

THE PEOPLE CONTRIBUTE TO THE TEMPLE

2Hezekiah appointed the divisions of the priests and Levites to do their assigned tasks—to offer burnt sacrifices and present offerings and to serve, give thanks, and offer praise in the gates of the LORD's sanctuary.

3The king contributed some of what he owned for burnt sacrifices, including the morning and evening burnt sacrifices and the burnt sacrifices made on Sabbaths, new moon festivals, and at other appointed times prescribed in the law of the LORD. 4He ordered the people living in Jerusalem to contribute the portion prescribed for the priests and Levites so they might be obedient to the law of the LORD. 5When the edict was issued, the Israelites freely contributed the initial portion of their grain, wine, olive oil, honey, and all the produce of their fields. They brought a tenth of everything, which added up to a huge amount. 6The Israelites and people of Judah who lived in the cities of Judah also contributed a tenth of their cattle and sheep, as well as a tenth of the holy items consecrated to the LORD their God. They brought them and placed them in many heaps.

[7]In the third month they began piling their contributions in
heaps and finished in the seventh month. [8]When Hezekiah and
the officials came and saw the heaps, they praised the LORD
and pronounced blessings on his people Israel.
[9]When Hezekiah asked the priests and Levites about the
heaps, [10]Azariah, the head priest from the family of Zadok, said
to him, "Since the contributions began arriving in the LORD's
temple, we have had plenty to eat and have a large quantity left
over. For the LORD has blessed his people, and this large amount
remains." [11]Hezekiah ordered that storerooms be prepared in
the LORD's temple. When this was done, [12]they brought in the
contributions, tithes, and consecrated items that had been
offered. Konaniah, a Levite, was in charge of all this, assisted by
his brother Shimei. [13]Jehiel, Azaziah, Nahath, Asahel, Jerimoth,
Jozabad, Eliel, Ismakiah, Mahath, and Benaiah worked under
the supervision of Konaniah and his brother Shimei, as directed
by King Hezekiah and Azariah, the supervisor of God's temple.
[14]Kore son of Imnah, a Levite and the guard on the east side,
was in charge of the voluntary offerings made to God and disbursed the contributions made to the LORD and the consecrated
items. [15]In the cities of the priests, Eden, Miniamin, Jeshua,
Shemaiah, Amariah, and Shecaniah faithfully assisted him in
making disbursements to their fellow priests according to their
divisions, regardless of age. [16]They made disbursements to all
the males three years old and up who were listed in the genealogical records—to all who would enter the LORD's temple to
serve on a daily basis and fulfill their duties as assigned to their
divisions. [17]They made disbursements to the priests listed in the
genealogical records by their families, and to the Levites twenty
years old and up, according to their duties as assigned to their
divisions, [18]and to all the infants, wives, sons, and daughters of
the entire assembly listed in the genealogical records, for they
faithfully consecrated themselves. [19]As for the descendants of
Aaron, the priests who lived in the outskirts of all their cities,
men were assigned to disburse portions to every male among
the priests and to every Levite listed in the genealogical records.
[20]This is what Hezekiah did throughout Judah. He did what
the LORD his God considered good and right and faithful. [21]He
wholeheartedly and successfully reinstituted service in God's
temple and obedience to the law, in order to follow his God.

SENNACHERIB INVADES JUDAH

32 After these faithful deeds were accomplished, King Sennacherib of Assyria invaded Judah. He besieged the fortified cities, intending to seize them. [2]When Hezekiah saw that
Sennacherib had invaded and intended to attack Jerusalem, [3]he
consulted with his advisers and military officers about stopping
up the springs outside the city, and they supported him. [4]A
large number of people gathered together and stopped up all
the springs and the stream that flowed through the district.
They reasoned, "Why should the kings of Assyria come and find
plenty of water?" [5]Hezekiah energetically rebuilt every broken
wall. He erected towers and an outer wall and fortified the terrace of the City of David. He made many weapons and shields.
[6]He appointed military officers over the army and assembled them in the square at the city gate. He encouraged them,
saying, [7]"Be strong and brave! Don't be afraid and don't panic
because of the king of Assyria and this huge army that is with
him. We have with us one who is stronger than those who are

31:14–21 Let us then draw near to him with holiness of spirit, lifting up pure and undefiled hands to him, loving our gracious and merciful Father, who has made us partakers in the blessings of his elect.

CLEMENT OF ROME **(D. 99)**
FIRST CLEMENT

with him. [8]He has with him mere human strength, but the LORD our God is with us to help us and fight our battles!" The army was encouraged by the words of King Hezekiah of Judah.

[9]Afterward King Sennacherib of Assyria, while attacking Lachish with all his military might, sent his messengers to Jerusalem. The message was for King Hezekiah of Judah and all the people of Judah who were in Jerusalem. It read: [10]"This is what King Sennacherib of Assyria says: 'Why are you so confident that you remain in Jerusalem while it is under siege? [11]Hezekiah says, "The LORD our God will rescue us from the power of the king of Assyria." But he is misleading you, and you will die of hunger and thirst! [12]Hezekiah is the one who eliminated the LORD's high places and altars and then told Judah and Jerusalem, "At one altar you must worship and offer sacrifices." [13]Are you not aware of what I and my predecessors have done to all the nations of the surrounding lands? Have the gods of the surrounding lands actually been able to rescue their lands from my power? [14]Who among all the gods of these nations whom my predecessors annihilated was able to rescue his people from my power that your God would be able to rescue you from my power? [15]Now don't let Hezekiah deceive you or mislead you like this. Don't believe him, for no god of any nation or kingdom has been able to rescue his people from my power or the power of my predecessors. So how can your gods rescue you from my power?'"

[16]Sennacherib's servants further insulted the LORD God and his servant Hezekiah. [17]He wrote letters mocking the LORD God of Israel and insulting him with these words: "The gods of the surrounding nations could not rescue their people from my power. Neither can Hezekiah's god rescue his people from my power." [18]They called out loudly in the Judahite dialect to the people of Jerusalem who were on the wall, trying to scare and terrify them so they could seize the city. [19]They talked about the God of Jerusalem as if he were one of the man-made gods of the nations of the earth.

[20]King Hezekiah and the prophet Isaiah son of Amoz prayed about this and cried out to heaven. [21]The LORD sent a messenger and he wiped out all the soldiers, princes, and officers in the army of the king of Assyria. So Sennacherib returned home humiliated. When he entered the temple of his god, some of his own sons struck him down with the sword. [22]The LORD delivered Hezekiah and the residents of Jerusalem from the power of King Sennacherib of Assyria and from all the other nations. He made them secure on every side. [23]Many were bringing presents to the LORD in Jerusalem and precious gifts to King Hezekiah of Judah. From that time on he was respected by all the nations.

HEZEKIAH'S SHORTCOMINGS AND ACCOMPLISHMENTS

[24]In those days Hezekiah was stricken with a terminal illness. He prayed to the LORD, who answered him and gave him a sign confirming that he would be healed. [25]But Hezekiah was ungrateful; he had a proud attitude, provoking God to be angry at him, as well as Judah and Jerusalem. [26]But then Hezekiah and the residents of Jerusalem humbled themselves and abandoned their pride, and the LORD was not angry with them for the rest of Hezekiah's reign.

[27]Hezekiah was very wealthy and greatly respected. He made storehouses for his silver, gold, precious stones, spices, shields, and all his other valuable possessions. [28]He made storerooms for the harvest of grain, wine, and olive oil, and stalls for all his various kinds of livestock and his flocks. [29]He built royal cities

32:24–26 How dangerous, how terrible is the malady of vanity! So much goodness, so many virtues, faith and devotion great enough to prevail to change nature itself and the laws of the whole world—all destroyed by a single act of pride! The result would have been that all Hezekiah's good deeds would have been forgotten as if they had never existed, and he would at once have been subject to the wrath of the Lord unless he had appeased him by recovering his humility. Thus he who, at the suggestion of pride, had fallen from so great a height of excellence could only mount again to the height he had lost by the same steps of humility.

JOHN CASSIAN
(C. 360–C. 435)
INSTITUTES

and owned a large number of sheep and cattle, for God gave him a huge amount of possessions.

30 Hezekiah dammed up the source of the waters of the Upper Gihon and directed them down to the west side of the City of David. Hezekiah succeeded in all that he did. 31 So when the envoys arrived from the Babylonian officials to visit him and inquire about the sign that occurred in the land, God left him alone to test him in order to know his true motives.

32 The rest of the events of Hezekiah's reign, including his faithful deeds, are recorded in the vision of the prophet Isaiah son of Amoz, included in the Scroll of the Kings of Judah and Israel. 33 Hezekiah passed away and was buried on the ascent of the tombs of the descendants of David. All the people of Judah and the residents of Jerusalem buried him with great honor. His son Manasseh replaced him as king.

MANASSEH'S REIGN

33 Manasseh was twelve years old when he became king, and he reigned for fifty-five years in Jerusalem. 2 He did evil in the sight of the LORD and committed the same horrible sins practiced by the nations whom the LORD drove out ahead of the Israelites. 3 He rebuilt the high places that his father Hezekiah had destroyed; he set up altars for the Baals and made Asherah poles. He bowed down to all the stars in the sky and worshiped them. 4 He built altars in the LORD's temple, about which the LORD had said, "Jerusalem will be my permanent home." 5 In the two courtyards of the LORD's temple, he built altars for all the stars in the sky. 6 He passed his sons through the fire in the Valley of Ben Hinnom and practiced divination, omen reading, and sorcery. He set up a ritual pit to conjure up underworld spirits and appointed magicians to supervise it. He did a great amount of evil in the sight of the LORD and angered him. 7 He put an idolatrous image he had made in God's temple, about which God had said to David and to his son Solomon, "This temple in Jerusalem, which I have chosen out of all the tribes of Israel, will be my permanent home. 8 I will not make Israel again leave the land I gave to their ancestors provided that they carefully obey all I commanded them, the whole law, the rules and regulations given through Moses." 9 But Manasseh misled the people of Judah and the residents of Jerusalem so that they sinned more than the nations whom the LORD had destroyed ahead of the Israelites.

10 The LORD confronted Manasseh and his people, but they paid no attention. 11 So the LORD brought against them the commanders of the army of the king of Assyria. They seized Manasseh, put hooks in his nose, bound him with bronze chains, and carried him away to Babylon. 12 In his pain Manasseh asked the LORD his God for mercy and truly humbled himself before the God of his ancestors. 13 When he prayed to the LORD, the LORD responded to him and answered favorably his cry for mercy. The LORD brought him back to Jerusalem to his kingdom. Then Manasseh realized that the LORD is the true God.

14 After this Manasseh built up the outer wall of the City of David on the west side of the Gihon in the valley to the entrance of the Fish Gate and all around the terrace; he made it much higher. He placed army officers in all the fortified cities in Judah.

15 He removed the foreign gods and images from the LORD's temple and all the altars he had built on the hill of the LORD's temple and in Jerusalem; he threw them outside the city. 16 He erected the altar of the LORD and offered on it peace offerings

33:1–20 We have seen Manasseh's wickedness; here we have his repentance, and a memorable instance it is of the riches of God's pardoning mercy and the power of his renewing grace. Deprived of his liberty, separated from his evil counselors and companions, without any prospect but of ending his days in a wretched prison, Manasseh thought upon what had passed; he began to cry for mercy and deliverance. He confessed his sins, condemned himself, and was humbled before God, loathing himself as a monster of impiety and wickedness. Yet he hoped to be pardoned through the abundant mercy of the Lord. Then Manasseh knew that Jehovah was God, able to deliver. He knew him as a God of salvation; he learned to fear, trust in, love, and obey him. From this time he bore a new character and walked in newness of life. Say the worst against yourself, here is one as bad who finds the way to repentance. Deny not to yourself what God has not denied to you; it is not your sin, but your failure to repent, that bars heaven against you.

MATTHEW HENRY **(1662–1714)**
COMMENTARY ON THE WHOLE BIBLE

and thank offerings. He told the people of Judah to serve the
LORD God of Israel. [17]However, the people continued to offer
sacrifices at the high places, but only to the LORD their God.
[18]The rest of the events of Manasseh's reign, including his
prayer to his God and the words the prophets spoke to him in
the name of the LORD God of Israel, are recorded in the Annals
of the Kings of Israel. [19]The Annals of the Prophets include his
prayer, give an account of how the LORD responded to it, record
all his sins and unfaithful acts, and identify the sites where he
built high places and erected Asherah poles and idols before
he humbled himself. [20]Manasseh passed away and was buried
in his palace. His son Amon replaced him as king.

AMON'S REIGN

[21]Amon was twenty-two years old when he became king, and he
reigned for two years in Jerusalem. [22]He did evil in the sight of
the LORD, just as his father Manasseh had done. Amon offered
sacrifices to all the idols his father Manasseh had made and
worshiped them. [23]He did not humble himself before the LORD
as his father Manasseh had done. Amon was guilty of great sin.
[24]His servants conspired against him and killed him in his palace.
[25]The people of the land executed all who had conspired against
King Amon, and they made his son Josiah king in his place.

JOSIAH INSTITUTES RELIGIOUS REFORMS

34 Josiah was eight years old when he became king, and he
reigned for thirty-one years in Jerusalem. [2]He did what
the LORD approved and followed in his ancestor David's footsteps; he did not deviate to the right or the left.
[3]In the eighth year of his reign, while he was still young,
he began to seek the God of his ancestor David. In his twelfth
year he began ridding Judah and Jerusalem of the high places,
Asherah poles, idols, and images. [4]He ordered the altars of the
Baals to be torn down and broke the incense altars that were
above them. He smashed the Asherah poles, idols, and images,
crushed them, and sprinkled the dust over the tombs of those
who had sacrificed to them. [5]He burned the bones of the pagan
priests on their altars; he purified Judah and Jerusalem. [6]In the
cities of Manasseh, Ephraim, and Simeon, as far as Naphtali, and
in the ruins around them, [7]he tore down the altars and Asherah
poles, demolished the idols, and smashed all the incense altars
throughout the land of Israel. Then he returned to Jerusalem.
[8]In the eighteenth year of his reign, he continued his policy
of purifying the land and the temple. He sent Shaphan son of
Azaliah, Maaseiah the city official, and Joah son of Joahaz the
secretary to repair the temple of the LORD his God. [9]They went
to Hilkiah the high priest and gave him the silver that had been
brought to God's temple. The Levites who guarded the door
had collected it from the people of Manasseh and Ephraim and
from all who were left in Israel, as well as from all the people
of Judah and Benjamin and the residents of Jerusalem. [10]They
handed it over to the construction foremen assigned to the
LORD's temple. They in turn paid the temple workers to restore
and repair it. [11]They gave money to the craftsmen and builders
to buy chiseled stone and wood for the braces and rafters of
the buildings that the kings of Judah had allowed to fall into
disrepair. [12]The men worked faithfully. Their supervisors were
Jahath and Obadiah (Levites descended from Merari), as well
as Zechariah and Meshullam (descendants of Kohath). The

Levites, all of whom were skilled musicians, [13]supervised the laborers and all the foremen on their various jobs. Some of the Levites were scribes, officials, and guards.

[14]When they took out the silver that had been brought to the LORD's temple, Hilkiah the priest found the law scroll the LORD had given to Moses. [15]Hilkiah informed Shaphan the scribe, "I found the law scroll in the LORD's temple." Hilkiah gave the scroll to Shaphan. [16]Shaphan brought the scroll to the king and reported, "Your servants are doing everything assigned to them. [17]They melted down the silver in the LORD's temple and handed it over to the supervisors and the construction foremen." [18]Then Shaphan the scribe told the king, "Hilkiah the priest has given me a scroll." Shaphan read it out loud before the king. [19]When the king heard the words of the law, he tore his clothes. [20]The king ordered Hilkiah, Ahikam son of Shaphan, Abdon son of Micah, Shaphan the scribe, and Asaiah the king's servant, [21]"Go, ask the LORD for me and for those who remain in Israel and Judah about the words of this scroll that has been discovered. For the LORD's great fury has been ignited against us because our ancestors did not obey the word of the LORD by living according to all that is written in this scroll."

[22]So Hilkiah and the others sent by the king went to Huldah the prophetess, the wife of Shallum son of Tokhath, the son of Hasrah, the supervisor of the wardrobe. (She lived in Jerusalem in the Mishneh district.) They stated their business, [23]and she said to them: "This is what the LORD God of Israel says: 'Say this to the man who sent you to me: [24]"This is what the LORD says: 'I am about to bring disaster on this place and its residents, all the curses that are recorded in the scroll which they read before the king of Judah. [25]This will happen because they have abandoned me and offered sacrifices to other gods, angering me with all the idols they have made. My anger will ignite against this place and will not be extinguished!'" [26]Say this to the king of Judah, who sent you to seek an oracle from the LORD: "This is what the LORD God of Israel says concerning the words you have heard: [27]'You displayed a sensitive spirit and humbled yourself before God when you heard his words concerning this place and its residents. You humbled yourself before me, tore your clothes, and wept before me, and I have heard you,' says the LORD. [28]'Therefore I will allow you to die and be buried in peace. You will not have to witness all the disaster I will bring on this place and its residents.'"'" Then they reported back to the king.

[29]The king summoned all the leaders of Judah and Jerusalem. [30]The king went up to the LORD's temple, accompanied by all the people of Judah, the residents of Jerusalem, the priests, and the Levites. All the people were there, from the oldest to the youngest. He read aloud all the words of the scroll of the covenant that had been discovered in the LORD's temple. [31]The king stood by his pillar and renewed the covenant before the LORD, agreeing to follow the LORD and to obey his commandments, laws, and rules with all his heart and being, by carrying out the terms of this covenant recorded on this scroll. [32]He made all who were in Jerusalem and Benjamin agree to it. The residents of Jerusalem acted in accordance with the covenant of God, the God of their ancestors. [33]Josiah removed all the detestable idols from all the areas belonging to the Israelites and encouraged all who were in Israel to worship the LORD their God. Throughout the rest of his reign they did not turn aside from following the LORD God of their ancestors.

34:22–24 Of Josiah it is written, "He did what the LORD approved and followed in his ancestor David's footsteps; he did not deviate to the right or the left" (2 Kgs 22:2). And although he was a just man, in a time of need and dire necessity, he sent Hilkiah to Huldah the prophet. She told them, "This is what the LORD says: 'I am about to bring disaster on this place and its residents, all the curses that are recorded in the scroll which they read before the king of Judah.'" There is contained in these words a secret reproof of the king and priests and all people because never was there any saint found among people who could predict the future.

JEROME (C. 342–420)
HEBREW QUESTIONS ON CHRONICLES

35:1–19 To the conservation of public ministry belong the tasks of gathering the people and using the signs of faith. The voice of God's doctrines is passed on through upright public gatherings, which give their clear and shared consent through confession and thanksgiving. To strengthen the will of the collective assembly, there are always external signs that reveal this congregation is bound together in one worship, doctrine, and invocation. Such was the Passover, which Josiah took care to celebrate regularly so that it might be an external sign of mutual affection and public ministry. He reinstituted the various levels of priests and admonished his people to serve the Lord and the people. Whoever rightly observes Josiah's admonition serves God not with an imaginary faith but with a firm hope and sincere love, considering all matters in terms of building up the church.

VIKTORIN STRIGEL
(C. 1524–1569)
BOOK OF CHRONICLES

JOSIAH OBSERVES THE PASSOVER

35 Josiah observed a Passover festival for the LORD in Jerusalem. They slaughtered the Passover lambs on the fourteenth day of the first month. 2 He appointed the priests to fulfill their duties and encouraged them to carry out their service in the LORD's temple. 3 He told the Levites, who instructed all Israel about things consecrated to the LORD, "Place the holy ark in the temple which King Solomon son of David of Israel built. Don't carry it on your shoulders. Now serve the LORD your God and his people Israel! 4 Prepare yourselves by your families according to your divisions, as instructed in writing by King David of Israel and his son Solomon. 5 Stand in the sanctuary and, together with the Levites, represent the family divisions of your countrymen. 6 Slaughter the Passover lambs, consecrate yourselves, and make preparations for your countrymen to celebrate according to the LORD's message which came through Moses."

7 From his own royal flocks and herds, Josiah supplied the people with 30,000 lambs and goats for the Passover sacrifice, as well as 3,000 cattle. 8 His officials also willingly contributed to the people, priests, and Levites. Hilkiah, Zechariah, and Jehiel, the leaders of God's temple, gave the priests 2,600 Passover sacrifices and 300 cattle. 9 Konaniah and his brothers Shemaiah and Nethanel, along with Hashabiah, Jeiel, and Jozabad, the officials of the Levites, supplied the Levites with 5,000 Passover sacrifices and 500 cattle. 10 Preparations were made, and the priests stood at their posts and the Levites in their divisions as prescribed by the king. 11 They slaughtered the Passover lambs and the priests splashed the blood, while the Levites skinned the animals. 12 They reserved the burnt offerings and the cattle for the family divisions of the people to present to the LORD, as prescribed in the scroll of Moses. 13 They cooked the Passover sacrifices over the open fire as prescribed and cooked the consecrated offerings in pots, kettles, and pans. They quickly served them to all the people. 14 Afterward they made preparations for themselves and for the priests, because the priests, the descendants of Aaron, were offering burnt sacrifices and fat portions until evening. The Levites made preparations for themselves and for the priests, the descendants of Aaron. 15 The musicians, the descendants of Asaph, manned their posts, as prescribed by David, Asaph, Heman, and Jeduthun the king's prophet. The guards at the various gates did not need to leave their posts, for their fellow Levites made preparations for them. 16 So all the preparations for the LORD's service were made that day, as the Passover was observed and the burnt sacrifices were offered on the altar of the LORD, as prescribed by King Josiah. 17 So the Israelites who were present observed the Passover at that time, as well as the Feast of Unleavened Bread for seven days. 18 A Passover like this had not been observed in Israel since the days of Samuel the prophet. None of the kings of Israel had observed a Passover like the one celebrated by Josiah, the priests, the Levites, all the people of Judah and Israel who were there, and the residents of Jerusalem. 19 This Passover was observed in the eighteenth year of Josiah's reign.

JOSIAH'S REIGN ENDS

20 After Josiah had done all this for the temple, King Necho of Egypt marched up to do battle at Carchemish on the Euphrates River. Josiah marched out to oppose him. 21 Necho sent messengers to him, saying, "Why are you opposing me, O king of Judah? I am not attacking you today, but the kingdom with

CARAVAGGIO, ***SACRIFICE OF ISAAC*** (1603)

(Public Domain)

REMBRANDT, ***MOSES BREAKING THE TABLETS OF LAW*** (1659)

(Public Domain)

which I am at war. God told me to hurry. Stop opposing God,
who is with me, or else he will destroy you." 22But Josiah did not
turn back from him; he disguised himself for battle. He did not
take seriously the words of Necho that he had received from
God; he went to fight him in the Plain of Megiddo. 23Archers
shot King Josiah; the king ordered his servants, "Take me out
of this chariot, for I am seriously wounded." 24So his servants
took him out of the chariot, put him in another chariot that he
owned, and brought him to Jerusalem, where he died. He was
buried in the tombs of his ancestors; all the people of Judah
and Jerusalem mourned Josiah. 25Jeremiah composed laments
for Josiah which all the male and female singers use to mourn
Josiah to this very day. It has become customary in Israel to sing
these; they are recorded in the Book of Laments.

26The rest of the events of Josiah's reign, including the faithful acts he did in obedience to what is written in the law of
the LORD 27and his accomplishments, from start to finish, are
recorded in the Scroll of the Kings of Israel and Judah.

JEHOAHAZ'S REIGN

36 The people of the land took Jehoahaz son of Josiah and
made him king in his father's place in Jerusalem. 2Jeho-
ahaz was twenty-three years old when he became king, and he
reigned three months in Jerusalem. 3The king of Egypt prevented him from ruling in Jerusalem and imposed on the land a
special tax of 100 talents of silver and a talent of gold. 4The king
of Egypt made Jehoahaz's brother Eliakim king over Judah and
Jerusalem, and changed his name to Jehoiakim. Necho seized
his brother Jehoahaz and took him to Egypt.

JEHOIAKIM'S REIGN

5Jehoiakim was twenty-five years old when he became king,
and he reigned for eleven years in Jerusalem. He did evil in the
sight of the LORD his God. 6King Nebuchadnezzar of Babylon
attacked him, bound him with bronze chains, and carried him
away to Babylon. 7Nebuchadnezzar took some of the items in
the LORD's temple to Babylon and put them in his palace there.

8The rest of the events of Jehoiakim's reign, including the
horrible sins he committed and his shortcomings, are recorded
in the Scroll of the Kings of Israel and Judah. His son Jehoiachin
replaced him as king.

JEHOIACHIN'S REIGN

9Jehoiachin was eighteen years old when he became king, and
he reigned three months and ten days in Jerusalem. He did
evil in the sight of the LORD. 10At the beginning of the year
King Nebuchadnezzar ordered him to be brought to Babylon,
along with the valuable items in the LORD's temple. In his place
Nebuchadnezzar made Jehoiachin's relative Zedekiah king over
Judah and Jerusalem.

ZEDEKIAH'S REIGN

11Zedekiah was twenty-one years old when he became king, and
he ruled for eleven years in Jerusalem. 12He did evil in the sight
of the LORD his God. He did not humble himself before Jeremiah
the prophet, the LORD's spokesman. 13He also rebelled against
King Nebuchadnezzar, who had made him vow allegiance in
the name of God. He was stubborn and obstinate and refused
to return to the LORD God of Israel. 14All the leaders of the

AUGUSTINE:

A THEOLOGICAL GIANT
354–430

It is hard to encapsulate the legacy of Augustine of Hippo into a brief portrait, given how consequential his impact has been upon the Christian faith. Born in 354 in Hippo, which is in modern-day Algeria, Augustine moved to Carthage when he was eighteen. There, he fell in love with rhetoric and Greek philosophy. He was a natural at both and had a burning desire to discover truth, which led him to begin studying the scriptures. For a time he became enamored with *Manichaeism*, a major religious movement that bore some similarities to Gnosticism; but the Manichaeans' teachings never satiated his soul and he eventually renounced them.

After becoming a professor of rhetoric and moving to Rome, he frequented Ambrose's parish in Milan to listen to his messages. Ambrose became like a father to him and began influencing his spiritual development. But Augustine was unconvinced of the Christian worldview and not ready to commit, though he had deep inner spiritual struggles. His autobiography *Confessions* details this struggle and his eventual conversion. While reflecting with a friend on spiritual matters, he retreated to a garden in bitter contrition where he heard the voice of a child coming over the garden wall: "Take up and read!" Augustine had a Bible with him, which he opened and read the first passage he came to, Romans 13:13–14. As he reported, "No further would I read, nor did I need; for instantly, as the sentence ended—by a light, as it were, of security infused into my heart—all the gloom of doubt vanished away."

Shortly thereafter he was baptized by Ambrose, then moved back to Hippo and became a presbyter and eventually the bishop in 395. His greatest impact has certainly been through his theological work. Augustine emphasized the absolute sovereignty of God in human salvation and absolute dependency of humanity upon God's grace. This view is sometimes called *monergism*. While Augustine's writings clearly affirm the reality of human freedom, he also affirms the utter priority of God's grace in all things, particularly in the human will to do good or to put faith in God for salvation. Augustine's increasing emphasis on divine grace was motivated especially by his arguments with Pelagius, a British-born Christian thinker in Palestine who wrote on sin, free will, and grace.

Pelagius denied that humans possessed an original sin nature, arguing that the event of the fall described in Genesis 3 does not predispose humans to sin. Instead, he argued, we are born sinless and then go on to sin through ignorance, bad examples, and habits that corrupt the individual and society. He further taught that by our own effort and initiative we can ask God for salvation, both because of God's available Word and our own intellect. Augustine responded with a strong theology of human depravity and God's grace influenced by Romans 5. He believed it taught the all-consuming effects of sin, so that for all humans after Adam and Eve, it is "not possible not to sin." God's power and sovereignty are thus key to Augustine's theology of grace, freedom, and salvation.

Augustine's impact on Christian thinking—especially on Christian understandings of good and evil, the church and sacraments, human depravity, and God's sovereignty—can hardly be overstated. He stands with Thomas Aquinas of the Middle Ages, Martin Luther and John Calvin of the Reformation, and Karl Barth of the Modern era as a true theological giant rivaled by few.

IMPORTANT WORKS

CONCERNING THE NATURE OF GOOD
CONFESSIONS
THE CITY OF GOD
ON NATURE AND GRACE
ON GRACE AND FREE WILL

priests and people became more unfaithful and committed the
same horrible sins practiced by the nations. They defiled the
LORD's temple which he had consecrated in Jerusalem.

THE BABYLONIANS DESTROY JERUSALEM

15The LORD God of their ancestors continually warned them
through his messengers, for he felt compassion for his people
and his dwelling place. 16But they mocked God's messengers,
despised his warnings, and ridiculed his prophets. Finally the
LORD got very angry at his people and there was no one who
could prevent his judgment. 17He brought against them the
king of the Babylonians, who slaughtered their young men in
their temple. He did not spare young men or women, or even the
old and aging. God handed everyone over to him. 18He carried
away to Babylon all the items in God's temple, whether large or
small, as well as what was in the treasuries of the LORD's temple
and in the treasuries of the king and his officials. 19They burned
down God's temple and tore down the wall of Jerusalem. They
burned all its fortified buildings and destroyed all its valuable
items. 20He deported to Babylon all who escaped the sword.
They served him and his sons until the Persian kingdom rose
to power. 21This took place to fulfill the LORD's message spoken
through Jeremiah and lasted until the land experienced its
sabbatical years. All the time of its desolation the land rested
in order to fulfill the seventy years.

CYRUS ALLOWS THE EXILES TO GO HOME

22In the first year of King Cyrus of Persia, in fulfillment of the
LORD's message spoken through Jeremiah, the LORD motivated
King Cyrus of Persia to issue a proclamation throughout his
kingdom and also to put it in writing. It read:
23"This is what King Cyrus of Persia says:
'The LORD God of heaven has given me all the kingdoms
of the earth. He has appointed me to build a temple for him
in Jerusalem, which is in Judah. Anyone of his people among
you may go up there, and may the LORD his God be with him.'"

36:15–21 God's wrath is not easily incensed. Yet here we see four causes: first, there was a conspiracy among the people against the Lord; second, there was a multiplication of transgressions; third, there were monstrous abominations; and fourth, there were great profanities and contempt for God's messengers. By all these and many other things, the people of Judah provoked the wrath of the Lord. And the last means that is ordinarily used to reclaim people is God's messengers, to tell the people of their sins to their faces and to pronounce judgment against them. If this does not prevail, nothing remains but an expectation of God's judgment and wrath.

***THE WESTMINSTER ANNOTATIONS* (1683)**

AUTHOR	AUDIENCE	DATE	PURPOSE	THEMES
Unknown; possibly Ezra	The people of Judah who had returned from exile in Babylon	Sometime after 440 BC	This book was written to recount the Lord's faithfulness to protect and deliver his people, showing how he acts through world events to sanctify his people.	God's providence and sovereignty; repentance and restoration; and sanctification

The book of Ezra begins with the return of exiles to their promised land. The first series of verses of Ezra mirror the last set of verses in 2 Chronicles, so much so that some believe that both books were once part of the same volume of work. Ezra offers a similarly hopeful outlook on the future as the Chronicler: He wrote to showcase the Lord's providential protection and faithful deliverance of his people, showing how he acts through world events to sanctify his people. The book could be summarized by this verse near the end of the book: "We have been unfaithful to our God . . . Nonetheless, there is still hope for Israel in this regard" (10:2). Through his gracious providence, the Lord brings us to repentance and offers us hopeful deliverance.

One of the clearest themes running through this book is God's providence—how he reigns over the affairs of the universe, shaping world events according to his perfect plan. What's remarkable is that God executes this plan through human rulers and pagan powers: "The LORD motivated King Cyrus of Persia to issue a proclamation throughout his kingdom" (1:1) to release Israel from captivity, sending the people back to their land stocked with supplies to rebuild the temple.

John Wesley commented, "God can, when he pleases, incline the hearts of strangers to be kind to his people. In fact, he can make those strengthen their hands who formerly weakened them." Even when opposition rose to thwart the people, the providential hand of God can be seen assisting them, sustaining them, and providing for them by sovereignly directing events. And the people recognized this: "They observed the Feast of Unleavened Bread for seven days with joy, for the LORD had given them joy and had changed the opinion of the king of Assyria toward them so that he assisted them in the work on the temple of God, the God of Israel" (6:22).

The book also offers an important lesson on the Lord's sanctifying work in our lives, his voice calling us to repentance and restoration after we have sinned against him. Ezra recognized that Judah's exile and suffering were due to their sin: "From the days of our fathers until this very day our guilt has been great. Because of our iniquities we, along with our kings and priests, have been delivered over by the local kings to sword, captivity, plunder, and embarrassment—right up to the present time." Ezra saw that

"everything that has happened to us has come about because of our wicked actions and our great guilt" (9:7, 13).

And yet the book of Ezra ends on a hopeful note: the promise of restoration through the repentance of sins. Leaders had come to Ezra and confessed the fact that neither Israel's people nor her leaders had "separated themselves from the local residents who practice detestable things . . . Indeed, they have taken some of their daughters as wives for themselves and for their sons, so that the holy race has become intermingled with the local residents" (9:1–2). As a result they had broken their covenantal relationship with the Lord and their hearts were far from him.

Ezra tore his clothes, wept, and prayed over the nation's sin, and soon a large number of Israelites did as well. They admitted, "We have been unfaithful to our God by marrying foreign women from the local peoples." But Ezra didn't stop there, declaring, "Nonetheless, there is still hope for Israel in this regard" (10:2). God's people could find deliverance by renewing their covenant with the Lord and separating themselves from the nations. The Venerable Bede commented on the results of their repentance: "Once they expelled the baseness of self-indulgence, the beauty of chasteness returned; once they cast out the debris of the vices, the flowers and spices of the virtues were strewn in the Lord's city."

John Wesley likened Ezra and its message of deliverance to the New Testament book of Revelation, saying the book was "a type of the accomplishment of the prophecies in the Revelation, touching the deliverance of the gospel church from spiritual Babylon." As is true of Revelation, the book of Ezra reveals the glory of God's sovereignty and providence working on behalf of his people to preserve them, sanctify them, and ultimately rescue them. May we respond to its message as the people of Israel themselves did: by recognizing our sin, repenting of it, and then resting in the hope of God's grace.

1:1–11 The Lord stirred up the spirit of Cyrus. God governs the world by his influence on the spirits of human beings; whatever good they do, God stirs up their spirits to do it. It was during the captivity of the Jews that God principally employed them as the means of calling the attention of the heathen to him. The same God who raised up the spirit of Cyrus to proclaim liberty to the Jews raised up their spirits to take the benefit. The temptation was for some to stay in Babylon, but some did not fear to return, and they were those whose spirits God raised by his Spirit and grace. Whatever good we do is owing to the grace of God. Our spirits naturally bow down to this earth and the things of it; if they move upward in any good affections or good actions, it is God who raises them.

MATTHEW HENRY **(1662–1714)**
COMMENTARY ON THE WHOLE BIBLE

THE DECREE OF CYRUS

1 In the first year of King Cyrus of Persia, in fulfillment of the
LORD's message spoken through Jeremiah, the LORD motivated King Cyrus of Persia to issue a proclamation throughout
his kingdom and also to put it in writing. It read:
2"This is what King Cyrus of Persia says:
"'The LORD God of heaven has given me all the kingdoms of
the earth. He has appointed me to build a temple for him in
Jerusalem, which is in Judah. 3Anyone of his people among you
(may his God be with him!) may go up to Jerusalem, which is in
Judah, and may build the temple of the LORD God of Israel—he
is the God who is in Jerusalem. 4Anyone who survives in any of
those places where he is a resident foreigner must be helped
by his neighbors with silver, gold, equipment, and animals,
along with voluntary offerings for the temple of God which
is in Jerusalem.'"

THE EXILES PREPARE TO RETURN TO JERUSALEM

5Then the leaders of Judah and Benjamin, along with the priests
and the Levites—all those whose mind God had stirred—got
ready to go up in order to build the temple of the LORD in Jerusalem. 6All their neighbors assisted them with silver utensils,
gold, equipment, animals, and expensive gifts, not to mention
all the voluntary offerings.
7Then King Cyrus brought out the vessels of the LORD's temple which Nebuchadnezzar had brought from Jerusalem and
had displayed in the temple of his gods. 8King Cyrus of Persia
entrusted them to Mithredath the treasurer, who counted them
out to Sheshbazzar the leader of the Judahite exiles.
9The inventory of these items was as follows:
30 gold basins,
1,000 silver basins,
29 silver utensils,
10 30 gold bowls,
410 other silver bowls,
and 1,000 other vessels.

11All these gold and silver vessels totaled 5,400. Sheshbazzar
brought them all along when the captives were brought up from
Babylon to Jerusalem.

2:1–70 The Jews were generally very exact in their genealogies from their own choice and interest, that they might preserve the distinctions of the several tribes and families. This was necessary both to make out their titles to offices or inheritances and to govern themselves thereby in the matter of marriages; and, from the special providence of God, so it might be certainly known of what tribe and family the Messiah was born.

JOHN WESLEY **(1703–1791)**
EXPLANATORY NOTES ON THE BIBLE

THE NAMES OF THE RETURNING EXILES

2 These are the people of the province who were going up,
from the captives of the exile whom King Nebuchadnezzar
of Babylon had forced into exile in Babylon. They returned to
Jerusalem and Judah, each to his own city. 2They came with
Zerubbabel, Jeshua, Nehemiah, Seraiah, Reelaiah, Mordecai,
Bilshan, Mispar, Bigvai, Rehum, and Baanah.
The number of Israelites was as follows:
3the descendants of Parosh: 2,172;
4the descendants of Shephatiah: 372;
5the descendants of Arah: 775;
6the descendants of Pahath Moab (from the line of Jeshua
and Joab): 2,812;
7the descendants of Elam: 1,254;
8the descendants of Zattu: 945;
9the descendants of Zaccai: 760;
10the descendants of Bani: 642;
11the descendants of Bebai: 623;

[12]the descendants of Azgad: 1,222;
[13]the descendants of Adonikam: 666;
[14]the descendants of Bigvai: 2,056;
[15]the descendants of Adin: 454;
[16]the descendants of Ater (through Hezekiah): 98;
[17]the descendants of Bezai: 323;
[18]the descendants of Jorah: 112;
[19]the descendants of Hashum: 223;
[20]the descendants of Gibbar: 95.
[21]The men of Bethlehem: 123;
[22]the men of Netophah: 56;
[23]the men of Anathoth: 128;
[24]the men of the family of Azmaveth: 42;
[25]the men of Kiriath Jearim, Kephirah and Beeroth: 743;
[26]the men of Ramah and Geba: 621;
[27]the men of Micmash: 122;
[28]the men of Bethel and Ai: 223;
[29]the descendants of Nebo: 52;
[30]the descendants of Magbish: 156;
[31]the descendants of the other Elam: 1,254;
[32]the descendants of Harim: 320;
[33]the men of Lod, Hadid, and Ono: 725;
[34]the men of Jericho: 345;
[35]the descendants of Senaah: 3,630.
[36]The priests: the descendants of Jedaiah (through the family
of Jeshua): 973;
[37]the descendants of Immer: 1,052;
[38]the descendants of Pashhur: 1,247;
[39]the descendants of Harim: 1,017.
[40]The Levites: the descendants of Jeshua and Kadmiel
(through the line of Hodaviah): 74.
[41]The singers: the descendants of Asaph: 128.
[42]The gatekeepers: the descendants of Shallum, the descendants of Ater, the descendants of Talmon, the descendants
of Akkub, the descendants of Hatita, and the descendants of
Shobai: 139.
[43]The temple servants: the descendants of Ziha, the descendants of Hasupha, the descendants of Tabbaoth, [44]the descendants of Keros, the descendants of Siaha, the descendants of
Padon, [45]the descendants of Lebanah, the descendants of Hagabah, the descendants of Akkub, [46]the descendants of Hagab,
the descendants of Shalmai, the descendants of Hanan, [47]the
descendants of Giddel, the descendants of Gahar, the descendants of Reaiah, [48]the descendants of Rezin, the descendants
of Nekoda, the descendants of Gazzam, [49]the descendants of
Uzzah, the descendants of Paseah, the descendants of Besai,
[50]the descendants of Asnah, the descendants of Meunim, the
descendants of Nephussim, [51]the descendants of Bakbuk,
the descendants of Hakupha, the descendants of Harhur, [52]the
descendants of Bazluth, the descendants of Mehida, the descendants of Harsha, [53]the descendants of Barkos, the descendants
of Sisera, the descendants of Temah, [54]the descendants of Neziah, and the descendants of Hatipha.
[55]The descendants of the servants of Solomon: the descendants of Sotai, the descendants of Hassophereth, the descendants of Peruda, [56]the descendants of Jaala, the descendants
of Darkon, the descendants of Giddel, [57]the descendants of
Shephatiah, the descendants of Hattil, the descendants of Pokereth Hazzebaim, and the descendants of Ami.

[58]All the temple servants and the descendants of the servants of Solomon: 392.

[59]These are the ones that came up from Tel Melah, Tel Harsha, Kerub, Addon, and Immer (although they were unable to certify their family connection or their ancestry, as to whether they really were from Israel):

[60]the descendants of Delaiah, the descendants of Tobiah, and the descendants of Nekoda: 652.

[61]And from among the priests: the descendants of Hobaiah, the descendants of Hakkoz, and the descendants of Barzillai (who had taken a wife from the daughters of Barzillai the Gileadite and was called by that name). [62]They searched for their records in the genealogical materials, but did not find them. They were therefore excluded from the priesthood. [63]The governor instructed them not to eat any of the sacred food until there was a priest who could consult the Urim and Thummim.

[64]The entire group numbered 42,360, [65]not counting their male and female servants, who numbered 7,337. They also had 200 male and female singers [66]and 736 horses, 245 mules, [67]435 camels, and 6,720 donkeys. [68]When they came to the LORD's temple in Jerusalem, some of the family leaders offered voluntary offerings for the temple of God in order to rebuild it on its site. [69]As they were able, they gave to the treasury for this work 61,000 drachmas of gold, 5,000 minas of silver, and 100 priestly robes.

[70]The priests, the Levites, some of the people, the singers, the gatekeepers, and the temple servants lived in their towns, and all the rest of Israel lived in their towns.

THE ALTAR IS REBUILT

3 When the seventh month arrived and the Israelites were living in their towns, the people assembled in Jerusalem. [2]Then Jeshua the son of Jozadak and his priestly colleagues and Zerubbabel son of Shealtiel and his colleagues started to build the altar of the God of Israel so they could offer burnt offerings on it as required by the law of Moses the man of God. [3]They established the altar on its foundations, even though they were in terror of the local peoples, and they offered burnt offerings on it to the LORD, both the morning and the evening offerings. [4]They observed the Feast of Shelters as required and offered the proper number of daily burnt offerings according to the requirement for each day. [5]Afterward they offered the continual burnt offerings and those for the new moons and those for all the holy assemblies of the LORD and all those that were being voluntarily offered to the LORD. [6]From the first day of the seventh month they began to offer burnt offerings to the LORD. However, the LORD's temple was not at that time established.

PREPARATIONS FOR REBUILDING THE TEMPLE

[7]So they provided money for the masons and carpenters, and food, beverages, and olive oil for the people of Sidon and Tyre, so that they would bring cedar timber from Lebanon to the seaport at Joppa, in accord with the edict of King Cyrus of Persia. [8]In the second year after they had come to the temple of God in Jerusalem, in the second month, Zerubbabel the son of Shealtiel and Jeshua the son of Jozadak initiated the work, along with the rest of their associates, the priests and the Levites, and all those who were coming to Jerusalem from the exile. They appointed the Levites who were at least twenty years old to take charge

3:1–13 Jeshua, Zerubbabel, and Ezra the priest and scribe of the law—as the temple was being built after the captivity, the Feast of Shelters being at hand—gathered the people together in the great court and prepared the altar to God, and there they offered their gifts and kept the feast. And so afterward they brought hither their sacrifices on the Sabbaths and the new moons, and the people offered up their prayers. And yet the scripture says expressly that when these things were done, the temple of God was not yet built; but rather while they thus prayed, the building of the house was advancing. So neither were their prayers deferred in expectation of the dedication, nor was the dedication prevented by the assemblies held for the sake of prayer. But the people thus continued to pray; and when the house was entirely finished, they celebrated the dedication and brought their gifts for that purpose, and all kept the feast for the completion of the work.

ATHANASIUS (C. 296–373)
DEFENSE BEFORE CONSTANTIUS

of the work on the LORD's temple. [9]So Jeshua appointed both
his sons and his relatives, Kadmiel and his sons (the sons of
Yehudah), to take charge of the workers in the temple of God,
along with the sons of Henadad, their sons, and their relatives
the Levites. [10]When the builders established the LORD's temple, the priests, ceremonially attired and with their clarions,
and the Levites (the sons of Asaph) with their cymbals, stood
to praise the LORD according to the instructions left by King
David of Israel. [11]With antiphonal response they sang, praising
and glorifying the LORD:

"For he is good;
his loyal love toward Israel is forever."

All the people gave a loud shout as they praised the LORD
when the temple of the LORD was established. [12]Many of the
priests, the Levites, and the leaders—older people who had
seen with their own eyes the former temple while it was still
established—were weeping loudly, and many others raised their
voice in a joyous shout. [13]People were unable to tell the difference between the sound of joyous shouting and the sound of
the people's weeping, for the people were shouting so loudly
that the sound was heard a long way off.

OPPOSITION TO THE BUILDING EFFORTS

4 When the enemies of Judah and Benjamin learned that the
former exiles were building a temple for the LORD God of
Israel, [2]they came to Zerubbabel and the leaders and said to
them, "Let us help you build, for like you we seek your God and
we have been sacrificing to him from the time of King Esarhaddon of Assyria, who brought us here." [3]But Zerubbabel, Jeshua,
and the rest of the leaders of Israel said to them, "You have no
right to help us build the temple of our God. We will build it
by ourselves for the LORD God of Israel, just as King Cyrus, the
king of Persia, has commanded us." [4]Then the local people began to discourage the people of Judah and to dishearten them
from building. [5]They were hiring advisers to oppose them, so
as to frustrate their plans, throughout the time of King Cyrus
of Persia until the reign of King Darius of Persia.

OFFICIAL COMPLAINTS ARE LODGED AGAINST THE JEWS

[6]At the beginning of the reign of Ahasuerus they filed an accusation against the inhabitants of Judah and Jerusalem. [7]And
during the reign of Artaxerxes, Bishlam, Mithredath, Tabeel,
and the rest of their colleagues wrote to King Artaxerxes of Persia. This letter was first written in Aramaic but then translated.
[What follows is in Aramaic.]‡
[8]Rehum the commander and Shimshai the scribe wrote
a letter concerning Jerusalem to King Artaxerxes as follows:
[9]From Rehum the commander, Shimshai the scribe, and the
rest of their colleagues—the judges, the rulers, the officials,
the secretaries, the Erechites, the Babylonians, the people of
Susa (that is, the Elamites), [10]and the rest of the nations whom
the great and noble Ashurbanipal deported and settled in the
cities of Samaria and other places in Trans-Euphrates. [11](This
is a copy of the letter they sent to him.)
"To King Artaxerxes, from your servants in Trans-Euphrates:
[12]Now let the king be aware that the Jews who came up to us
from you have gone to Jerusalem. They are rebuilding that

4:1–24 Opposition began as soon as the foundations were laid, as is usually the case with all great attempts to build God's house. It came from the Samaritans. The writer calls the Samaritans "the enemies," though they began with offers of friendship and alliance. The proposal to unite in building the temple was a political move for, the calculation was that if the returning exiles could be united with the much more numerous Samaritans, they would soon be absorbed in them. The insincere request was based on an untruth, for the Samaritans did not worship Jehovah as the Jews did, but they worshiped him along with their own gods. To divide his dominion with others was to dethrone him altogether. It therefore became an act of faithfulness to Jehovah to reject the entangling alliance. To have accepted it would have been tantamount to frustrating the very purpose of the return and consenting to be muzzled about the sin of idolatry.

ALEXANDER MACLAREN
(1826–1910)
EXPOSITIONS OF THE HOLY SCRIPTURES

rebellious and odious city. They are completing its walls and
repairing its foundations. [13]Let the king also be aware that if
this city is built and its walls are completed, no more tax, custom, or toll will be paid, and the royal treasury will suffer loss.
[14]In light of the fact that we are loyal to the king, and since it
does not seem appropriate to us that the king should sustain
damage, we are sending the king this information [15]so that he
may initiate a search of the records of his predecessors and discover in those records that this city is rebellious and injurious
to both kings and provinces, producing internal revolts from
long ago. It is for this very reason that this city was destroyed.
[16]We therefore are informing the king that if this city is rebuilt
and its walls are completed, you will not retain control of this
portion of Trans-Euphrates."
[17]The king sent the following response:
"To Rehum the commander, Shimshai the scribe, and the
rest of their colleagues who live in Samaria and other parts of
Trans-Euphrates: Greetings! [18]The letter you sent to us has been
translated and read in my presence. [19]So I gave orders, and it
was determined that this city from long ago has been engaging
in insurrection against kings. It has continually engaged in rebellion and revolt. [20]Powerful kings have been over Jerusalem
who ruled throughout the entire Trans-Euphrates and who
were the beneficiaries of tribute, custom, and toll. [21]Now give
orders that these men cease their work and that this city not be
rebuilt until such time as I so instruct. [22]Exercise appropriate
caution so that there is no negligence in this matter. Why should
danger increase to the point that the king sustains damage?"
[23]Then, as soon as the copy of the letter from King Artaxerxes
was read in the presence of Rehum, Shimshai the scribe, and
their colleagues, they proceeded promptly to the Jews in Jerusalem and stopped them with threat of armed force.
[24]So the work on the temple of God in Jerusalem came to a
halt. It remained halted until the second year of the reign of
King Darius of Persia.

TATTENAI APPEALS TO DARIUS

5 Then the prophets Haggai and Zechariah son of Iddo prophesied concerning the Jews who were in Judah and Jerusalem
in the name of the God of Israel who was over them. [2]Then
Zerubbabel the son of Shealtiel and Jeshua the son of Jozadak
began to rebuild the temple of God in Jerusalem. The prophets
of God were with them, supporting them.

5:1–17 The leaders of the Jews, strengthened by the prophets' words, could not be hindered by the harrying of the enemies from the holy work from which they had ceased out of fear of the enemies when the prophets still remained silent. This occurs in the same way in the holy church now when those who have been held back by the attacks of wicked people or spirits and have remained for a while rather lax with respect to good deeds are suddenly set straight by the words either of faithful teachers or of the divine scriptures. Then they begin to burn so greatly for righteous pursuits that they cannot be overcome by any wiles of temptations or be called back from what they intended to do.

VENERABLE BEDE
(C. 672–735)
ON EZRA AND NEHEMIAH

[3]At that time Tattenai governor of Trans-Euphrates, Shethar-
Bozenai, and their colleagues came to them and asked, "Who
gave you authority to rebuild this temple and to complete this
structure?" [4]They also asked them, "What are the names of the
men who are building this edifice?" [5]But God was watching over
the elders of Judah, and they were not stopped until a report
could be dispatched to Darius and a letter could be sent back
concerning this.
[6]This is a copy of the letter that Tattenai governor of Trans-
Euphrates, Shethar-Bozenai, and his colleagues (who were the
officials of Trans-Euphrates) sent to King Darius. [7]The report
they sent to him was written as follows:
"To King Darius: All greetings! [8]Let it be known to the king
that we have gone to the province of Judah, to the temple of
the great God. It is being built with large stones, and timbers
are being placed in the walls. This work is being done with all

diligence and is prospering in their hands. [9]We inquired of those
elders, asking them, 'Who gave you the authority to rebuild this
temple and to complete this structure?' [10]We also inquired of
their names in order to inform you, so that we might write the
names of the men who were their leaders. [11]They responded to
us in the following way: 'We are servants of the God of heaven
and earth. We are rebuilding the temple which was previously
built many years ago. A great king of Israel built it and completed it. [12]But after our ancestors angered the God of heaven,
he delivered them into the hands of King Nebuchadnezzar of
Babylon, the Chaldean, who destroyed this temple and exiled
the people to Babylon. [13]But in the first year of King Cyrus of
Babylon, King Cyrus enacted a decree to rebuild this temple of
God. [14]Even the gold and silver vessels of the temple of God that
Nebuchadnezzar had taken from the temple in Jerusalem and
had brought to the palace of Babylon—even those things King
Cyrus brought from the palace of Babylon and presented to a
man by the name of Sheshbazzar whom he had appointed as
governor. [15]He said to him, "Take these vessels and go deposit
them in the temple in Jerusalem, and let the house of God be
rebuilt in its proper location." [16]Then this Sheshbazzar went
and laid the foundations of the temple of God in Jerusalem.
From that time to the present moment it has been in the process of being rebuilt, although it is not yet finished.'
[17]"Now if the king is so inclined, let a search be conducted
in the royal archives there in Babylon in order to determine
whether King Cyrus did in fact issue orders for this temple
of God to be rebuilt in Jerusalem. Then let the king send us a
decision concerning this matter."

DARIUS ISSUES A DECREE

6 So Darius the king issued orders, and they searched in the
archives of the treasury which were deposited there in Babylon. [2]A scroll was found in the citadel of Ecbatana which is in
the province of Media, and it was inscribed as follows:
"Memorandum: [3]In the first year of his reign, King Cyrus
gave orders concerning the temple of God in Jerusalem: 'Let
the temple be rebuilt as a place where sacrifices are offered.
Let its foundations be set in place. Its height is to be 90 feet
and its width 90 feet, [4]with three layers of large stones and
one layer of timber. The expense is to be subsidized by the
royal treasury. [5]Furthermore, let the gold and silver vessels of
the temple of God, which Nebuchadnezzar brought from the
temple in Jerusalem and carried to Babylon, be returned and
brought to their proper place in the temple in Jerusalem. Let
them be deposited in the temple of God.'
[6]"Now Tattenai governor of Trans-Euphrates, Shethar-
Bozenai, and their colleagues, the officials of Trans-Euphrates—
all of you stay far away from there. [7]Leave the work on this
temple of God alone. Let the governor of the Jews and the elders
of the Jews rebuild this temple of God in its proper place.
[8]"I also hereby issue orders as to what you are to do with
those elders of the Jews in order to rebuild this temple of God.
From the royal treasury, from the taxes of Trans-Euphrates, the
complete costs are to be given to these men so that there may
be no interruption of the work. [9]Whatever is needed—whether
oxen or rams or lambs for burnt offerings for the God of heaven
or wheat or salt or wine or oil, as required by the priests who are
in Jerusalem—must be given to them daily without any neglect,

6:1–22 These prophets had predicted that if they persisted in building the temple, soon, with the Lord's assistance, they would have a more abundant supply of all good things as a reward for their devotion. For divine help will be present, by which the Lord's house that has been begun may be brought to completion in the hearts of their listeners by their believing and living well. And to the architects themselves will come the blessing of crops, the vine, the fig tree, the pomegranate, and the olive (i.e., more abundance of spiritual gifts), which without any doubt will be more copiously granted to us by the Lord the more diligently we have endeavored to establish the abode of his glory either in ourselves or in the hearts of our neighbors.

VENERABLE BEDE
(C. 672–735)
ON EZRA AND NEHEMIAH

10 so that they may be offering incense to the God of heaven and
may be praying for the good fortune of the king and his family.
11 "I hereby give orders that if anyone changes this directive a
beam is to be pulled out from his house and he is to be raised up
and impaled on it, and his house is to be reduced to a rubbish heap
for this indiscretion. 12 May God who makes his name to reside
there overthrow any king or nation who reaches out to cause
such change so as to destroy this temple of God in Jerusalem. I,
Darius, have given orders. Let them be carried out with precision!"

THE TEMPLE IS FINALLY DEDICATED

13 Then Tattenai governor of Trans-Euphrates, Shethar-Bozenai,
and their colleagues acted accordingly—with precision, just as
Darius the king had given instructions. 14 The elders of the Jews
continued building and prospering, while at the same time
Haggai the prophet and Zechariah the son of Iddo continued
prophesying. They built and brought it to completion by the
command of the God of Israel and by the command of Cyrus
and Darius and Artaxerxes king of Persia. 15 They finished this
temple on the third day of the month Adar, which is the sixth
year of the reign of King Darius.
16 The people of Israel—the priests, the Levites, and the rest of
the exiles—observed the dedication of this temple of God with
joy. 17 For the dedication of this temple of God they offered 100
bulls, 200 rams, 400 lambs, and 12 male goats for the sin of all
Israel, according to the number of the tribes of Israel. 18 They
appointed the priests by their divisions and the Levites by their
divisions over the worship of God at Jerusalem, in accord with
the book of Moses. 19 The exiles observed the Passover on the
fourteenth day of the first month. 20 The priests and the Levites
had purified themselves, every last one, and they all were ceremonially pure. They sacrificed the Passover lamb for all the exiles, for
their colleagues the priests, and for themselves. 21 The Israelites
who were returning from the exile ate it, along with all those who
had joined them in separating themselves from the uncleanness
of the nations of the land to seek the LORD God of Israel. 22 They
observed the Feast of Unleavened Bread for seven days with joy,
for the LORD had given them joy and had changed the opinion
of the king of Assyria toward them so that he assisted them in
the work on the temple of God, the God of Israel.

THE ARRIVAL OF EZRA

7 Now after these things had happened, during the reign of King
Artaxerxes of Persia, Ezra came up from Babylon. Ezra was the
son of Seraiah, who was the son of Azariah, who was the son of
Hilkiah, 2 who was the son of Shallum, who was the son of Zadok,
who was the son of Ahitub, 3 who was the son of Amariah, who was
the son of Azariah, who was the son of Meraioth, 4 who was the son
of Zerahiah, who was the son of Uzzi, who was the son of Bukki,
5 who was the son of Abishua, who was the son of Phinehas, who
was the son of Eleazar, who was the son of Aaron the chief priest.
6 This Ezra is the one who came up from Babylon. He was a scribe
who was skilled in the law of Moses which the LORD God of Israel
had given. The king supplied him with everything he requested,
for the hand of the LORD his God was on him. 7 In the seventh
year of King Artaxerxes, Ezra brought up to Jerusalem some of
the Israelites and some of the priests, the Levites, the attendants,
the gatekeepers, and the temple servants. 8 He entered Jerusalem
in the fifth month of the seventh year of the king. 9 On the first

7:1–28 Salt was used in every offering made by fire to the Lord, and from its preserving and purifying properties it was the grateful emblem of divine grace in the soul. It is worthy of our attentive regard that, when Artaxerxes gave salt to Ezra the priest, he set no limit to the quantity, and we may be quite certain that when the King of kings distributes grace among his royal priesthood, the supply is not cut short by him. Often are we impoverished in ourselves, but never in the Lord. Believer, go to the throne for a large supply of heavenly salt. It will season your afflictions that are unsavory without salt, it will preserve your heart that corrupts if salt is absent, and it will kill your sins even as salt kills reptiles. You need much; seek much, and have much.

CHARLES SPURGEON
(1834–1892)
MORNING AND EVENING

day of the first month he had determined to make the ascent
from Babylon, and on the first day of the fifth month he arrived
at Jerusalem, for the good hand of his God was on him. [10]Now Ezra
had dedicated himself to the study of the law of the LORD, to its
observance, and to teaching its statutes and judgments in Israel.

ARTAXERXES GIVES OFFICIAL ENDORSEMENT TO EZRA'S MISSION

[11]What follows is a copy of the letter that King Artaxerxes gave
to Ezra the priestly scribe. Ezra was a scribe in matters pertaining to the commandments of the LORD and his statutes over Israel:

[12]"Artaxerxes, king of kings, to Ezra the priest, a scribe of the
law of the God of heaven: [13]I have now issued a decree that anyone
in my kingdom from the people of Israel—even the priests and Levites—who wishes to do so may go up with you to Jerusalem.
[14]You are authorized by the king and his seven advisers to inquire
concerning Judah and Jerusalem, according to the law of your God
which is in your possession, [15]and to bring silver and gold which
the king and his advisers have freely contributed to the God of
Israel, who resides in Jerusalem, [16]along with all the silver and
gold that you may collect throughout all the province of Babylon and the contributions of the people and the priests for the
temple of their God which is in Jerusalem. [17]With this money you
should be sure to purchase bulls, rams, and lambs, along with the appropriate meal offerings and libations. You should bring them
to the altar of the temple of your God which is in Jerusalem. [18]You
may do whatever seems appropriate to you and your colleagues with the rest of the silver and the gold, in keeping with the will
of your God. [19]Deliver to the God of Jerusalem the vessels that
are given to you for the service of the temple of your God. [20]The
rest of the needs for the temple of your God that you may have to supply, you may do so from the royal treasury.

[21]"I, King Artaxerxes, hereby issue orders to all the treasurers of Trans-Euphrates that you precisely execute all that Ezra the priestly scribe of the law of the God of heaven may request of
you—[22]up to 100 talents of silver, 100 cors of wheat, 100 baths
of wine, 100 baths of olive oil, and unlimited salt. [23]Everything
that the God of heaven has required should be precisely done for the temple of the God of heaven. Why should there be wrath
against the empire of the king and his sons? [24]Furthermore,
be aware of the fact that you have no authority to impose tax, tribute, or toll on any of the priests, the Levites, the musicians, the doorkeepers, the temple servants, or the attendants at the temple of this God.

[25]"Now you, Ezra, in keeping with the wisdom of your God which you possess, appoint judges and court officials who can arbitrate cases on behalf of all the people who are in Trans-Euphrates who know the laws of your God. Those who do not
know this law should be taught. [26]Everyone who does not observe
both the law of your God and the law of the king will be completely liable to the appropriate penalty, whether it is death or banishment or confiscation of property or detainment in prison."

[27]Blessed be the LORD God of our fathers, who so moved in the heart of the king to so honor the temple of the LORD which
is in Jerusalem! [28]He has also conferred his favor on me before
the king, his advisers, and all the influential leaders of the king. I gained strength as the hand of the LORD my God was on me, and I gathered leaders from Israel to go up with me.

THE LEADERS WHO RETURNED WITH EZRA

8 These are the leaders and those enrolled with them by genealogy who were coming up with me from Babylon during
the reign of King Artaxerxes:
2from the descendants of Phinehas, Gershom;
from the descendants of Ithamar, Daniel;
from the descendants of David, Hattush 3the son of
Shecaniah;
from the descendants of Parosh, Zechariah, and with him
were enrolled by genealogy 150 men;
4from the descendants of Pahath Moab, Eliehoenai son of
Zerahiah, and with him 200 men;
5from the descendants of Zattu, Shecaniah son of Jahaziel,
and with him 300 men;
6from the descendants of Adin, Ebed son of Jonathan, and
with him 50 men;
7from the descendants of Elam, Jeshaiah son of Athaliah,
and with him 70 men;
8from the descendants of Shephatiah, Zebadiah son of Michael, and with him 80 men;
9from the descendants of Joab, Obadiah son of Jehiel, and
with him 218 men;
10from the descendants of Bani, Shelomith son of Josiphiah,
and with him 160 men;
11from the descendants of Bebai, Zechariah son of Bebai,
and with him 28 men;
12from the descendants of Azgad, Johanan son of Hakkatan,
and with him 110 men;
13from the descendants of Adonikam there were the latter
ones. Their names were Eliphelet, Jeuel, and Shemaiah, and
with them 60 men;
14from the descendants of Bigvai, Uthai, and Zaccur, and
with them 70 men.

THE EXILES TRAVEL TO JERUSALEM

15I had them assemble at the canal that flows toward Ahava,
and we camped there for three days. I observed that the people
and the priests were present, but I found no Levites there. 16So
I sent for Eliezer, Ariel, Shemaiah, Elnathan, Jarib, Elnathan, Nathan, Zechariah, and Meshullam, who were leaders, and Joiarib
and Elnathan, who were teachers. 17I sent them to Iddo, who
was the leader in the place called Casiphia. I told them what
to say to Iddo and his relatives, who were the temple servants
in Casiphia, so they would bring us attendants for the temple
of our God.
18Due to the fact that the good hand of our God was on us,
they brought us a skilled man, from the descendants of Mahli
the son of Levi son of Israel. This man was Sherebiah, who was
accompanied by his sons and brothers, 18 men; 19and Hashabiah,
along with Jeshaiah from the descendants of Merari, with his
brothers and their sons, 20 men; 20and some of the temple servants that David and his officials had established for the work
of the Levites—220 of them. They were all designated by name.
21I called for a fast there by the Ahava Canal, so that we might
humble ourselves before our God and seek from him a safe journey for us, our children, and all our property. 22I was embarrassed
to request soldiers and horsemen from the king to protect us
from the enemy along the way, because we had said to the king,
"The good hand of our God is on everyone who is seeking him,

8:21–35 Public prayers must be made that all who are to share in the comfort may share in the requests for it. We must afflict ourselves for our sins and so be qualified for the pardon of them. When we are entering into any new condition of life, our care should be to bring into it none of the guilt of the sins of our former condition. When we are in any imminent danger, let us make our peace with God, and then nothing can hurt us. For it is the atonement that secures every mercy to us, which will not be truly comfortable unless iniquity be taken away and our peace made with God.

JOHN WESLEY (1703–1791)
EXPLANATORY NOTES ON THE BIBLE

but his great anger is against everyone who forsakes him." [23]So
we fasted and prayed to our God about this, and he answered us.
[24]Then I set apart 12 of the leading priests, together with
Sherebiah, Hashabiah, and 10 of their brothers, [25]and I weighed
out to them the silver, the gold, and the vessels intended for
the temple of our God—items that the king, his advisers, his
officials, and all Israel who were present had contributed. [26]I
weighed out to them: 650 talents of silver, silver vessels worth
100 talents, 100 talents of gold, [27]20 gold bowls worth 1,000
darics, and 2 exquisite vessels of gleaming bronze, as valuable
as gold. [28]Then I said to them, "You are holy to the LORD, just
as these vessels are holy. The silver and the gold are a voluntary
offering to the LORD, the God of your fathers. [29]Be careful with
them and protect them, until you weigh them out before the
leading priests and the Levites and the family leaders of Israel
in Jerusalem, in the storerooms of the temple of the LORD.
[30]Then the priests and the Levites took charge of the silver,
the gold, and the vessels that had been weighed out, to transport
them to Jerusalem to the temple of our God.
[31]On the twelfth day of the first month we began traveling
from the Ahava Canal to go to Jerusalem. The hand of our God
was on us, and he delivered us from our enemies and from bandits along the way. [32]So we came to Jerusalem, and we stayed
there for three days. [33]On the fourth day we weighed out the
silver, the gold, and the vessels in the house of our God into
the care of Meremoth son of Uriah, the priest, and Eleazar son
of Phinehas, who were accompanied by Jozabad son of Jeshua
and Noadiah son of Binnui, who were Levites. [34]Everything
was verified by number and by weight, and the total weight
was written down at that time.
[35]The exiles who were returning from the captivity offered
burnt offerings to the God of Israel—12 bulls for all Israel, 96
rams, 77 male lambs, along with 12 male goats as a sin offering.
All this was a burnt offering to the LORD. [36]Then they presented
the decrees of the king to the king's satraps and to the governors of Trans-Euphrates, who assisted the people and the
temple of God.

A PRAYER OF EZRA

9 Now when these things had been completed, the leaders
approached me and said, "The people of Israel, the priests,
and the Levites have not separated themselves from the local
residents who practice detestable things similar to those of
the Canaanites, the Hittites, the Perizzites, the Jebusites, the
Ammonites, the Moabites, the Egyptians, and the Amorites.
[2]Indeed, they have taken some of their daughters as wives for
themselves and for their sons, so that the holy race has become intermingled with the local residents. Worse still, the
leaders and the officials have been at the forefront of all this
unfaithfulness!"
[3]When I heard this report, I tore my tunic and my robe and
ripped out some of the hair from my head and beard. Then I
sat down, quite devastated. [4]Everyone who held the words of
the God of Israel in awe gathered around me because of the unfaithful acts of the people of the exile. Devastated, I continued
to sit there until the evening offering.
[5]At the time of the evening offering I got up from my self-
abasement, with my tunic and robe torn, and then dropped to
my knees and spread my hands to the LORD my God. [6]I prayed:

9:1–15 Ezra's address is a penitent confession of the sin of his people. But let this be the comfort of true penitents, that though their sins reach to the heavens, God's mercy is in the heavens. Ezra, speaking of sin, spoke as one much ashamed. Holy shame is as necessary in true repentance as holy sorrow. Ezra spoke as much amazed. The discoveries of guilt cause amazement; the more we think of sin, the worse it looks. Say, *God be merciful to me, a sinner.* Ezra spoke as one much afraid. There is not a surer or sadder presage of ruin than turning to sin after great judgments and great deliverances. People in the church of God have to wonder that they have not wearied the Lord's patience and brought destruction upon themselves. What then must be the case of the ungodly? But though true penitents have nothing to plead in their own behalf, the heavenly Advocate pleads most powerfully for them.

MATTHEW HENRY **(1662–1714)**
COMMENTARY ON THE WHOLE BIBLE

"O my God, I am ashamed and embarrassed to lift my face to
you, my God! For our iniquities have climbed higher than our
heads, and our guilt extends to the heavens. [7]From the days of
our fathers until this very day our guilt has been great. Because
of our iniquities we, along with our kings and priests, have been
delivered over by the local kings to sword, captivity, plunder,
and embarrassment—right up to the present time.

[8]"But now briefly we have received mercy from the LORD our
God, in that he has left us a remnant and has given us a secure
position in his holy place. Thus our God has enlightened our
eyes and has given us a little relief in our time of servitude.
[9]Although we are slaves, our God has not abandoned us in our
servitude. He has extended kindness to us in the sight of the
kings of Persia, in that he has revived us to restore the temple
of our God and to raise up its ruins and to give us a protective
wall in Judah and Jerusalem.

[10]"And now what are we able to say after this, our God? For we
have forsaken your commandments [11]which you commanded
us through your servants the prophets with these words: 'The
land that you are entering to possess is a land defiled by the
impurities of the local residents! With their abominations they
have filled it from one end to the other with their filthiness.
[12]Therefore do not give your daughters in marriage to their
sons, and do not take their daughters in marriage for your sons.
Do not ever seek their peace or welfare, so that you may be
strong and may eat the good of the land and may leave it as an
inheritance for your children forever.'

[13]"Everything that has happened to us has come about because of our wicked actions and our great guilt. Even so, our God,
you have exercised restraint toward our iniquities and have
given us a remnant such as this. [14]Shall we once again break
your commandments and intermarry with these abominable
peoples? Would you not be so angered by us that you would
wipe us out, with no survivor or remnant? [15]O LORD God of
Israel, you are righteous, for we are left as a remnant this day.
Indeed, we stand before you in our guilt. However, because of
this guilt no one can really stand before you."

THE PEOPLE CONFESS THEIR SINS

10 While Ezra was praying and confessing, weeping and
throwing himself to the ground before the temple of God, a
very large crowd of Israelites—men, women, and children alike—
gathered around him. The people wept loudly. [2]Then Shecaniah son of Jehiel, from the descendants of Elam, addressed
Ezra:

"We have been unfaithful to our God by marrying foreign
women from the local peoples. Nonetheless, there is still hope
for Israel in this regard. [3]Therefore let us enact a covenant with
our God to send away all these women and their offspring, in
keeping with your counsel, my lord, and that of those who respect the commandments of our God. And let it be done according to the law. [4]Get up, for this matter concerns you. We
are with you, so be strong and act decisively!"

[5]So Ezra got up and made the leading priests and Levites and
all Israel take an oath to carry out this plan. And they all took a
solemn oath. [6]Then Ezra got up from in front of the temple of
God and went to the room of Jehohanan son of Eliashib. While
he stayed there, he did not eat food or drink water, for he was
in mourning over the infidelity of the exiles.

10:1–44 Consider how those who could not be overcome by misfortunes were overcome by enticements; they conquered their public enemies when the Lord's temple was built and dedicated but were conquered by a desire for Gentile women so that they did not keep the temples of their own hearts and bodies worthy for God to inhabit. Very clearly there is a complete allegorical interpretation of this for our own times. For we see that the minds of the faithful are tempted inwardly with much greater danger now when they are seduced and enticed by their own lust than when they were previously tempted outwardly when their brutal opponent was raging against their constancy by sword and fire. But the mercy of the Lord will be present, so that just as it then endowed those people with the virtue of patience against open battles of those who raged against them, in the same way it may also give us the protection of caution against the snares of enticements that catch us unawares.

VENERABLE BEDE
(C. 672–735)
ON EZRA AND NEHEMIAH

[7]A proclamation was circulated throughout Judah and Jerusalem that all the exiles were to be assembled in Jerusalem.
[8]Everyone who did not come within three days would thereby
forfeit all his property, in keeping with the counsel of the officials and the elders. Furthermore, he himself would be excluded
from the assembly of the exiles.
[9]All the men of Judah and Benjamin were gathered in Jerusalem within the three days. (It was in the ninth month, on the
twentieth day of that month.) All the people sat in the square
at the temple of God, trembling because of this matter and
because of the rains.

[10]Then Ezra the priest stood up and said to them, "You have
behaved in an unfaithful manner by taking foreign wives! This
has contributed to the guilt of Israel. [11]Now give praise to the
LORD God of your fathers, and do his will. Separate yourselves
from the local residents and from these foreign wives."

[12]All the assembly replied in a loud voice: "We will do just as
you have said! [13]However, the people are numerous and it is the
rainy season. We are unable to stand here outside. Furthermore,
this business cannot be resolved in a day or two, for we have
sinned greatly in this matter. [14]Let our leaders take steps on
behalf of all the assembly. Let all those in our towns who have
married foreign women come at an appointed time, and with
them the elders of each town and its judges, until the hot anger
of our God is turned away from us in this matter."

[15]Only Jonathan son of Asahel and Jahzeiah son of Tikvah
were against this, assisted by Meshullam and Shabbethai the
Levite. [16]So the exiles proceeded accordingly. Ezra the priest
separated out by name men who were leaders in their family
groups. They sat down to consider this matter on the first day
of the tenth month, [17]and on the first day of the first month
they finished considering all the men who had married foreign wives.

THOSE WHO HAD TAKEN FOREIGN WIVES

[18]It was determined that from the descendants of the priests,
the following had taken foreign wives: from the descendants of
Jeshua son of Jozadak, and his brothers: Maaseiah, Eliezer, Jarib,
and Gedaliah. [19](They gave their word to send away their wives;
their guilt offering was a ram from the flock for their guilt.)

[20]From the descendants of Immer: Hanani and Zebadiah.

[21]From the descendants of Harim: Maaseiah, Elijah, Shemaiah, Jehiel, and Uzziah.

[22]From the descendants of Pashhur: Elioenai, Maaseiah,
Ishmael, Nethanel, Jozabad, and Elasah.

[23]From the Levites: Jozabad, Shimei, Kelaiah (also known as
Kelita), Pethahiah, Judah, and Eliezer.

[24]From the singers: Eliashib. From the gatekeepers: Shallum,
Telem, and Uri.

[25]From the Israelites: from the descendants of Parosh: Rami-
ah, Izziah, Malkijah, Mijamin, Eleazar, Malkijah, and Benaiah.

[26]From the descendants of Elam: Mattaniah, Zechariah,
Jehiel, Abdi, Jeremoth, and Elijah.

[27]From the descendants of Zattu: Elioenai, Eliashib, Mattaniah, Jeremoth, Zabad, and Aziza.

[28]From the descendants of Bebai: Jehohanan, Hananiah,
Zabbai, and Athlai.

[29]From the descendants of Bani: Meshullam, Malluch,
Adaiah, Jashub, Sheal, and Jeremoth.

[30]From the descendants of Pahath Moab: Adna, Kelal, Benaiah, Maaseiah, Mattaniah, Bezalel, Binnui, and Manasseh.
[31]From the descendants of Harim: Eliezer, Ishijah, Malkijah,
Shemaiah, Shimeon, [32]Benjamin, Malluch, and Shemariah.
[33]From the descendants of Hashum: Mattenai, Mattattah,
Zabad, Eliphelet, Jeremai, Manasseh, and Shimei.
[34]From the descendants of Bani: Maadai, Amram, Uel, [35]Be-
naiah, Bedeiah, Keluhi, [36]Vaniah, Meremoth, Eliashib, [37]Mat-
taniah, Mattenai, and Jaasu.
[38]From the descendants of Binnui: Shimei, [39]Shelemiah,
Nathan, Adaiah, [40]Machnadebai, Shashai, Sharai, [41]Azarel, Shelemiah, Shemariah, [42]Shallum, Amariah, and Joseph.
[43]From the descendants of Nebo: Jeiel, Mattithiah, Zabad,
Zebina, Jaddai, Joel, and Benaiah.
[44]All these had taken foreign wives, and some of them also
had children by these women.

AUTHOR	AUDIENCE	DATE	PURPOSE	THEMES
Unknown, possibly Ezra appropriating Nehemiah's memoirs	The people of Judah who had returned from exile in Babylon	Sometime after 420 BC	This book shows how the Lord restored his people to the promised land—delivering them, protecting them, and providing for them. Nehemiah serves as a portrait of godly leadership and religious dedication.	Godly leadership, religious dedication, prayer and God's deliverance and restoration

Like the book of Ezra, the book of Nehemiah was written to Jews returning from exile. At one point the two separate books had been one volume that chronicled God's faithful restoration of the nation. The later division can be traced to Origen and was later perpetuated by Jerome when he created the Latin Vulgate translation of the Bible. Since then the two books have been set apart from one another. Although the early church fathers mostly neglected the book of Nehemiah, the patristic thinker the Venerable Bede authored an extensive commentary on the book, applying it in an allegorical fashion, which was typical for the time. Consider how he described its scope:

> Nehemiah is interpreted in Latin as "my consoler is the Lord," or "the consoler from the Lord." For when Nehemiah restored Jerusalem's walls and, after delivering them from the disdain of their enemies, raised up the people of God to the observance of the divine law, it is surely clear that by his word and deed and person he not unfittingly designates the mediator of God and people, the man Christ Jesus, who indicates that he was sent to console the poor in spirit when he said to his disciples as he was about to ascend to heaven: "I will ask the Father, and he will give you another Advocate" (John 14:16), that is, a Consoler, by whom the psalmist showed that God's holy city (namely the church) would be rebuilt and also those who in it would be consoled when he said, "The Lord builds Jerusalem, and gathers the exiles of Israel. He heals the brokenhearted," and so on (Ps 147:2–3).

This interpretation of Nehemiah's name is fitting, for the book that bears his moniker showcases the hand of the Lord providing consolation and renewal for his people after their exile. Nehemiah, a cupbearer for King Artaxerxes, heard a report about Jerusalem from the exiles who had already returned. Things were so bad that the walls were in ruins, making the city vulnerable to attack. He recognized this destruction was the result of sin, and he prayed: "We have behaved corruptly against you, not obeying the commandments, the statutes, and the judgments that you commanded your servant Moses" (1:7).

Yet Nehemiah appealed to the Lord's promises:

> Please recall the word you commanded your servant Moses: "If you act unfaithfully, I will scatter you among the nations, but if you repent and obey my commandments and do them, then even if your dispersed

AUTHOR	AUDIENCE	DATE	PURPOSE	THEMES
Unknown; possibly Ezra appropriating Nehemiah's memoirs	The people of Judah who had returned from exile in Babylon	Sometime after 430 BC	This book shows how the Lord restored his people to the promised land—delivering them, protecting them, and providing for them. Nehemiah serves as a portrait of godly leadership and religious dedication.	Godly leadership; religious dedication; prayer; and God's deliverance and restoration

Like the book of Ezra, the book of Nehemiah was written to Jews returning from exile. At one point the two separate books had been one volume that chronicled God's faithful restoration of the nation. The later division can be traced to Origen and was later perpetuated by Jerome when he created the Latin Vulgate translation of the Bible. Since then the two books have been set apart from one another. Although the early church fathers mostly neglected the book of Nehemiah, the patristic thinker the Venerable Bede authored an extensive commentary on the book, applying it in an allegorical fashion, which was typical for the time. Consider how he described its scope:

> Nehemiah is interpreted in Latin as "My consoler is the Lord" or "the consoler from the Lord." For when Nehemiah restored Jerusalem's walls and, after delivering them from the disdain of their enemies, raised up the people of God to the observance of the divine law, it is surely clear that by his word and deed and person he not unsuitably designates the mediator of God and people, the man Christ Jesus, who indicates that he was sent to console the poor in spirit when he said to his disciples as he was about to ascend to heaven: "I will ask the Father, and he will give you another Advocate" (John 14:16). That is, a Consoler, by whom the psalmist showed that God's holy city (namely the church) would be rebuilt and also those who mourn would be consoled when he said, "The LORD rebuilds Jerusalem, and gathers the exiles of Israel. He heals the brokenhearted," and so on (Ps 147:2–3).

This interpretation of Nehemiah's name is fitting, for the book that bears his moniker showcases the hand of the Lord providing consolation and renewal for his people after their exile. Nehemiah, a cupbearer for King Artaxerxes, heard a report about Jerusalem from the exiles who had already returned. Things were so bad that the walls were in ruins, making the city vulnerable to attack. He recognized this destruction was the result of sin, and he prayed, "We have behaved corruptly against you, not obeying the commandments, the statutes, and the judgments that you commanded your servant Moses" (1:7).

Yet Nehemiah appealed to the Lord's promises:

> Please recall the word you commanded your servant Moses: "If you act unfaithfully, I will scatter you among the nations. But if you repent and obey my commandments and do them, then even if your dispersed

NEHEMIAH

> people are in the most remote location, I will gather them from there and bring them to the place I have chosen for my name to reside." They are your servants and your people, whom you have redeemed by your mighty strength and by your powerful hand. (1:8–10)

This gathering had already begun by the Lord's grace and mercy, but the time of rebuilding was now at hand. Nehemiah volunteered to lead that rebuilding, casting a vision and appealing to the Lord for guidance and help.

The book of Nehemiah is steeped in prayer. At several important junctures, Nehemiah pauses to offer petitions to the Lord. When he first heard the city of Jerusalem lay in ruins, Nehemiah said, "I sat down abruptly, crying and mourning for several days. I continued fasting and praying before the God of heaven" (1:4). Then, when he was waiting upon the needs of King Artaxerxes, and the king asked Nehemiah what he wanted for Jerusalem, he "prayed to the God of heaven" (2:4). And later, when he faced opposition to rebuilding the wall, Nehemiah prayed, "So now, strengthen my hands" (6:9). Matthew Henry made an important observation concerning these prayers: "Nehemiah's first application was to God, that he might have the fuller confidence in his application to the king. Our best pleas in prayer are taken from the promise of God, the Word on which he has caused us to hope. Other means must be used, but the effectual fervent prayer of a righteous man avails most."

When the wall had been repaired, there was a ceremony of dedication that involved the full leadership of the priests, who performed the services of God for purification. The book of Moses was also read, and the people brought their tithes and offerings. Nehemiah closes his book with these words: "Please remember me for good, O my God" (13:30). Again Matthew Henry offered an apt comment on Nehemiah's conclusion:

> This may well be the summary of our petitions; we need no more to make us happy than this; *Remember me, O my God, for good*. We may humbly hope that the Lord will remember us and our services although, after lives of unwearied activity and usefulness, we shall still see cause to abhor ourselves and repent in dust and ashes and to cry out with Nehemiah, "Have pity on me in keeping with your great love" (13:22).

1:1–11 For Israel was once "the LORD's allotment" (Deut 32:9), but their enemies made the Israelites turn from their God in sin, and because of their sins God said to them, *Because of your sins you have been scattered under the whole heaven.* But then he said to them, "Even if your dispersed people are in the most remote location, I will gather them from there and bring them to the place I have chosen for my name to reside." Because "the rulers of this age" (1 Cor 2:8) had first invaded "the LORD's allotment," "the good shepherd" (John 10:11) had necessarily to descend to the lands and seek the one sheep that was lost, and when it was found and carried back on his shoulders, to recall it to the sheepfold of perfection on high.

ORIGEN **(C. 185–C. 253)**
HOMILIES ON GENESIS

A PRAYER OF NEHEMIAH

1 These are the words of Nehemiah son of Hacaliah:

It so happened that in the month of Kislev, in the twentieth year, I was in Susa the citadel. 2Hanani, who was one of my relatives, along with some of the men from Judah, came to me, and I asked them about the Jews who had escaped and had survived the exile, and about Jerusalem.

3They said to me, "The remnant that remains from the exile there in the province are experiencing considerable adversity and reproach. The wall of Jerusalem lies breached, and its gates have been burned down!"

4When I heard these things I sat down abruptly, crying and mourning for several days. I continued fasting and praying before the God of heaven. 5Then I said, "Please, O LORD God of heaven, great and awesome God, who keeps his loving covenant with those who love him and obey his commandments, 6may your ear be attentive and your eyes be open to hear the prayer of your servant that I am praying to you today throughout both day and night on behalf of your servants the Israelites. I am confessing the sins of the Israelites that we have committed against you—both I myself and my family have sinned. 7We have behaved corruptly against you, not obeying the commandments, the statutes, and the judgments that you commanded your servant Moses. 8Please recall the word you commanded your servant Moses: 'If you act unfaithfully, I will scatter you among the nations. 9But if you repent and obey my commandments and do them, then even if your dispersed people are in the most remote location, I will gather them from there and bring them to the place I have chosen for my name to reside.' 10They are your servants and your people, whom you have redeemed by your mighty strength and by your powerful hand. 11Please, Lord, listen attentively to the prayer of your servant and to the prayer of your servants who take pleasure in showing respect to your name. Grant your servant success today and show compassion to me in the presence of this man."

Now I was cupbearer for the king.

NEHEMIAH IS PERMITTED TO GO TO JERUSALEM

2 Then in the month of Nisan, in the twentieth year of King Artaxerxes, when wine was brought to me, I took the wine and gave it to the king. Previously I had not been depressed in the king's presence. 2So the king said to me, "Why do you appear to be depressed when you aren't sick? What can this be other than sadness of heart?" This made me very fearful.

3I replied to the king, "O king, live forever! Why would I not appear dejected when the city with the graves of my ancestors lies desolate and its gates destroyed by fire?" 4The king responded, "What is it you are seeking?" Then I quickly prayed to the God of heaven 5and said to the king, "If the king is so inclined and if your servant has found favor in your sight, dispatch me to Judah, to the city with the graves of my ancestors, so that I can rebuild it." 6Then the king, with his consort sitting beside him, replied, "How long would your trip take, and when would you return?" Since the king was pleased to send me, I gave him a time. 7I said to the king, "If the king is so inclined, let him give me letters for the governors of Trans-Euphrates that will enable me to travel safely until I reach Judah, 8and a letter for Asaph the keeper of the king's nature preserve, so that he will give me timber for beams for the gates of the fortress adjacent

to the temple and for the city wall and for the house to which I
go." So the king granted me these requests, for the good hand
of my God was on me. 9Then I went to the governors of Trans-
Euphrates, and I presented to them the letters from the king.
The king had sent with me officers of the army and horsemen.
10When Sanballat the Horonite and Tobiah the Ammonite
official heard all this, they were very displeased that someone
had come to seek benefit for the Israelites.

NEHEMIAH ARRIVES IN JERUSALEM

11So I came to Jerusalem. When I had been there for three days,
12I got up during the night, along with a few men who were with
me. But I did not tell anyone what my God was putting on my
heart to do for Jerusalem. There were no animals with me, except
for the one I was riding. 13I proceeded through the Valley Gate by
night, in the direction of the Well of the Dragons and the Dung
Gate, inspecting the walls of Jerusalem that had been breached
and its gates that had been destroyed by fire. 14I passed on to the
Gate of the Well and the King's Pool, where there was not enough
room for my animal to pass with me. 15I continued up the valley
during the night, inspecting the wall. Then I turned back and
came to the Valley Gate, and so returned. 16The officials did not
know where I had gone or what I had been doing, for up to this
point I had not told any of the Jews or the priests or the nobles
or the officials or the rest of the workers. 17Then I said to them,
"You see the problem that we have—Jerusalem is desolate and its
gates are burned. Come on! Let's rebuild the wall of Jerusalem so
that this reproach will not continue." 18Then I related to them
how the good hand of my God was on me and what the king
had said to me. Then they replied, "Let's begin rebuilding right
away!" So they readied themselves for this good project. 19But
when Sanballat the Horonite, Tobiah the Ammonite official, and
Geshem the Arab heard all this, they derided us and expressed
contempt toward us. They said, "What is this you are doing? Are
you rebelling against the king?" 20I responded to them by saying,
"The God of heaven will prosper us. We his servants will start the
rebuilding. But you have no just or ancient right in Jerusalem."

THE NAMES OF THE BUILDERS

3 Then Eliashib the high priest and his priestly colleagues
arose and built the Sheep Gate. They dedicated it and erected
its doors, working as far as the Tower of the Hundred and the
Tower of Hananel. 2The men of Jericho built adjacent to it, and
Zaccur son of Imri built adjacent to them.

3The sons of Hassenaah rebuilt the Fish Gate. They laid its
beams and positioned its doors, its bolts, and its bars. 4Mere-
moth son of Uriah, the son of Hakoz, worked on the section
adjacent to them. Meshullam son of Berechiah the son of
Meshezabel worked on the section next to them. And Zadok
son of Baana worked on the section adjacent to them. 5The men
of Tekoa worked on the section adjacent to them, but their
town leaders would not assist with the work of their master.
6Joiada son of Paseah and Meshullam son of Besodeiah
worked on the Jeshanah Gate. They laid its beams and positioned its doors, its bolts, and its bars. 7Adjacent to them worked
Melatiah the Gibeonite and Jadon the Meronothite, who were
men of Gibeon and Mizpah. These towns were under the jurisdiction of the governor of Trans-Euphrates. 8Uzziel son of
Harhaiah, a member of the goldsmiths' guild, worked on the

2:20 With much spirit and boldness, not at all intimidated by scoffs or threats, Nehemiah proclaimed, *The God of heaven, he will prosper us: Him we serve, and under his protection we are, and we will succeed in this undertaking. It's in his name we engage in it and on him we depend.* The opposition had no portion, nor right, nor memorial in Jerusalem. No part of the city belonged to them. They had no jurisdiction there. They had no name there, nor their ancestors, in times past; nor had they done anything to perpetuate their memory in it. In short, they had nothing to do with the Israelites, neither in religious nor in civil things; and it was best for them to mind their own affairs where they presided and not trouble themselves about others' affairs.

JOHN GILL **(1697–1771)**
EXPOSITION OF THE WHOLE BIBLE

3:1–32 Cities well fortified have broad walls, and so had Jerusalem in her glory. The New Jerusalem must, in like manner, be surrounded and preserved by a broad wall of nonconformity to the world and separation from its customs and spirit. The tendency of these days is to break down the holy barrier and make the distinction between the church and the world merely nominal. Professors are no longer strict and Puritanical, questionable literature is read on all hands, frivolous pastimes are currently indulged, and a general laxity threatens to deprive the Lord's peculiar people of those sacred singularities that separate them from sinners. It will be an ill day for the church and the world when the proposed amalgamation shall be complete, and the people of God and the people of men shall be as one: Then shall another deluge of wrath be ushered in.

CHARLES SPURGEON
(1834–1892)
MORNING AND EVENING

section adjacent to him. Hananiah, a member of the perfumers'
guild, worked on the section adjacent to him. They plastered the
city wall of Jerusalem as far as the Broad Wall. [9]Rephaiah son of
Hur, head of a half district of Jerusalem, worked on the section
adjacent to them. [10]Jedaiah son of Harumaph worked on the
section adjacent to them opposite his house, and Hattush son
of Hashabneiah worked on the section adjacent to him. [11]Mal-
kijah son of Harim and Hasshub son of Pahath Moab worked on
another section and the Tower of the Ovens. [12]Shallum son of
Hallohesh, head of a half district of Jerusalem, worked on the
section adjacent to him, assisted by his daughters.

[13]Hanun and the residents of Zanoah worked on the Valley
Gate. They rebuilt it and positioned its doors, its bolts, and its
bars, in addition to working on 1,500 feet of the wall as far as
the Dung Gate.

[14]Malkijah son of Recab, head of the district of Beth Hakkerem, worked on the Dung Gate. He rebuilt it and positioned
its doors, its bolts, and its bars.

[15]Shallun son of Col-Hozeh, head of the district of Mizpah,
worked on the Fountain Gate. He rebuilt it, put on its roof,
and positioned its doors, its bolts, and its bars. In addition, he
rebuilt the wall of the Pool of Siloam, by the royal garden, as far
as the steps that go down from the City of David. [16]Nehemiah
son of Azbuk, head of a half district of Beth Zur, worked after
him as far as the tombs of David and the artificial pool and the
House of the Warriors.

[17]After him the Levites worked—Rehum son of Bani and
after him Hashabiah, head of half the district of Keilah, for
his district. [18]After him their relatives worked—Binnui son of
Henadad, head of a half district of Keilah. [19]Adjacent to him
Ezer son of Jeshua, head of Mizpah, worked on another section,
opposite the ascent to the armory at the buttress. [20]After him
Baruch son of Zabbai worked on another section, from the buttress to the door of the house of Eliashib the high priest. [21]After
him Meremoth son of Uriah, the son of Hakkoz, worked on another section from the door of Eliashib's house to the end of it.

[22]After him the priests worked, men of the nearby district. [23]Af-
ter them Benjamin and Hasshub worked opposite their house.
After them Azariah son of Maaseiah, the son of Ananiah, worked
near his house. [24]After him Binnui son of Henadad worked on
another section, from the house of Azariah to the buttress and
the corner. [25]After him Palal son of Uzai worked opposite the
buttress and the tower that protrudes from the upper palace of
the court of the guard. After him Pedaiah son of Parosh [26]and
the temple servants who were living on Ophel worked up to the
area opposite the Water Gate toward the east and the protruding
tower. [27]After them the men of Tekoa worked on another section,
from opposite the great protruding tower to the wall of Ophel.

[28]Above the Horse Gate the priests worked, each in front of
his house. [29]After them Zadok son of Immer worked opposite
his house, and after him Shemaiah son of Shecaniah, guard at
the East Gate, worked. [30]After him Hananiah son of Shelemiah,
and Hanun, the sixth son of Zalaph, worked on another section.
After them Meshullam son of Berechiah worked opposite his
quarters. [31]After him Malkijah, one of the goldsmiths, worked
as far as the house of the temple servants and the traders, opposite the Inspection Gate, and up to the room above the corner.
[32]And between the room above the corner and the Sheep Gate
the goldsmiths and traders worked.

OPPOSITION TO THE WORK CONTINUES

4 Now when Sanballat heard that we were rebuilding the wall
he became angry and was quite upset. He derided the Jews,
2and in the presence of his colleagues and the army of Samaria
he said, "What are these feeble Jews doing? Will they be left to
themselves? Will they again offer sacrifice? Will they finish
this in a day? Can they bring these burnt stones to life again
from piles of dust?"
3Then Tobiah the Ammonite, who was close by, said, "If even
a fox were to climb up on what they are building, it would break
down their wall of stones!"
4Hear, O our God, for we are despised. Return their reproach
on their own head. Reduce them to plunder in a land of exile!
5Do not cover their iniquity, and do not wipe out their sin from
your sight, for they have bitterly offended the builders.
6So we rebuilt the wall, and the entire wall was joined together up to half its height. The people were enthusiastic in
their work.
7When Sanballat, Tobiah, the Arabs, the Ammonites, and
the people of Ashdod heard that the restoration of the walls of
Jerusalem had moved ahead and that the breaches had begun to
be closed, they were very angry. 8All of them conspired together
to move with armed forces against Jerusalem and to create
a disturbance in it. 9So we prayed to our God and stationed
a guard to protect against them both day and night. 10Then
those in Judah said, "The strength of the laborers has failed!
The debris is so great that we are unable to rebuild the wall."
11Our adversaries also boasted, "Before they are aware or
anticipate anything, we will come in among them and kill them,
and we will bring this work to a halt!"
12So it happened that the Jews who were living near them
came and warned us repeatedly about all the schemes they
were plotting against us.
13So I stationed people at the lower places behind the wall in
the exposed places. I stationed the people by families, with their
swords, spears, and bows. 14When I had made an inspection, I
stood up and said to the nobles, the officials, and the rest of
the people, "Don't be afraid of them. Remember the great and
awesome Lord, and fight on behalf of your brothers, your sons,
your daughters, your wives, and your families!"
15It so happened that when our adversaries heard that we
were aware of these matters, God frustrated their intentions.
Then all of us returned to the wall, each to his own work. 16From
that day forward, half my men were doing the work and half
were taking up spears, shields, bows, and body armor. Now the
officers were behind all the people of Judah 17who were rebuilding the wall. Those who were carrying loads did so by keeping
one hand on the work and the other on their weapon. 18The
builders, to a man, had their swords strapped to their sides
while they were building. But the trumpeter remained with me.
19I said to the nobles, the officials, and the rest of the people,
"The work is demanding and extensive, and we are spread out
on the wall, far removed from one another. 20Wherever you
hear the sound of the trumpet, gather there with us. Our God
will fight for us!"
21So we worked on, with half holding spears, from dawn till
dusk. 22At that time I instructed the people, "Let every man
and his coworker spend the night in Jerusalem and let them
be guards for us by night and workers by day." 23We did not

4:1–23 Now it is well said that Nehemiah stationed the people "at the lower places behind the wall in the exposed places" with weapons so that, surrounded by a troop of armed men, the builders might press on in building the wall with a freer and securer hand. For the grades of the faithful are divided up: Some build up the church by adorning it with good works on the inside, while others, armed with the weapons of sacred reading, keep vigilant for heretics who attack the same church. The former in religious devotion strengthen their neighbors in the truth of the faith, while the latter wage a necessary battle against the weapons of the devil or of the vices with which they struggle to assault this same faith and with pastoral solicitude repel the wolves lying in ambush for the Lord's sheepfold.

VENERABLE BEDE
(C. 672–735)
ON EZRA AND NEHEMIAH

change clothes—not I, nor my relatives, nor my workers, nor the watchmen who were with me. Each had his weapon, even when getting a drink of water.

NEHEMIAH INTERVENES ON BEHALF OF THE OPPRESSED

5 Then there was a great outcry from the people and their wives
against their fellow Jews. [2]There were those who said, "With
our sons and daughters, we are many. We must obtain grain in
order to eat and stay alive." [3]There were others who said, "We are
putting up our fields, our vineyards, and our houses as collateral
in order to obtain grain during the famine." [4]Then there were
those who said, "We have borrowed money to pay our taxes to
the king on our fields and our vineyards. [5]And now, though we
share the same flesh and blood as our fellow countrymen and
our children are just like their children, still we have found it
necessary to subject our sons and daughters to slavery. Some
of our daughters have been subjected to slavery, while we are
powerless to help, since our fields and vineyards now belong
to other people."
[6]I was very angry when I heard their outcry and these complaints. [7]I considered these things carefully and then registered a
complaint with the wealthy and the officials. I said to them, "Each
one of you is seizing the collateral from your own countrymen!"
Because of them I called for a great public assembly. [8]I said to
them, "To the extent possible we have bought back our fellow
Jews who had been sold to the Gentiles. But now you yourselves
want to sell your own countrymen, so that we can then buy them
back!" They were utterly silent, and could find nothing to say.
[9]Then I said, "The thing that you are doing is wrong! Should
you not conduct yourselves in the fear of our God in order to
avoid the reproach of the Gentiles who are our enemies? [10]Even
I and my relatives and my associates are lending them money
and grain. But let us abandon this practice of seizing collateral!
[11]This very day return to them their fields, their vineyards,
their olive trees, and their houses, along with the interest that
you are exacting from them on the money, the grain, the new
wine, and the olive oil."
[12]They replied, "We will return these things, and we will no
longer demand anything from them. We will do just as you say."
Then I called the priests and made the wealthy and the officials
swear to do what had been promised. [13]I also shook out my
garment, and I said, "In this way may God shake out from his
house and his property every person who does not carry out
this matter. In this way may he be shaken out and emptied!"
All the assembly replied, "So be it!" and they praised the LORD.
Then the people did as they had promised.
[14]From the day that I was appointed governor in the land of
Judah, that is, from the twentieth year until the thirty-second
year of King Artaxerxes—twelve years in all—neither I nor my
relatives ate the food allotted to the governor. [15]But the former
governors who preceded me had burdened the people and had
taken food and wine from them, in addition to 40 shekels of
silver. Their associates were also domineering over the people.
But I did not behave in this way, due to my fear of God. [16]I gave
myself to the work on this wall, without even purchasing a field.
All my associates were gathered there for the work.
[17]There were 150 Jews and officials who dined with me rou-
tinely, in addition to those who came to us from the nations all

5:15 When Nehemiah kept aloof from the evil ways of others, he gave his reason: "I did not behave in this way, due to my fear of God." Of the righteous it is said, *The fear of God is before their eyes.* It was this that operated and influenced all Nehemiah's proceedings. He was conscientious, not only as to actual duties, but as to responsibilities. It is conscientiousness arising from the sense of God's presence, the wish to please him, the fear of offending him, the desire to do all that is well pleasing in his sight. As the love of Christ constrains, so the fear of God makes conscientious.

HORATIUS BONAR
(1808–1889)
DIVERSE KINDS OF CONSCIENCE

around us. [18]Every day one ox, six select sheep, and some birds were prepared for me, and every ten days all kinds of wine in abundance. Despite all this I did not require the food allotted to the governor, for the work was demanding on this people.

[19]Please remember me for good, O my God, for all that I have done for this people.

OPPOSITION TO THE REBUILDING EFFORTS CONTINUES

6 When Sanballat, Tobiah, Geshem the Arab, and the rest of our enemies heard that I had rebuilt the wall and no breach remained in it (even though up to that time I had not positioned doors in the gates), [2]Sanballat and Geshem sent word to me saying, "Come on! Let's set up a time to meet together at Kephirim in the plain of Ono." Now they intended to do me harm.

[3]So I sent messengers to them saying, "I am engaged in an important work, and I am unable to come down. Why should the work come to a halt when I leave it to come down to you?" [4]They contacted me four times in this way, and I responded the same way each time.

[5]The fifth time that Sanballat sent his assistant to me in this way, he had an open letter in his hand. [6]Written in it were the following words:

"Among the nations it is rumored (and Geshem has substantiated this) that you and the Jews have intentions of revolting, and for this reason you are building the wall. Furthermore, according to these rumors you are going to become their king. [7]You have also established prophets to announce in Jerusalem on your behalf, 'We have a king in Judah!' Now the king is going to hear about these rumors. So come on, let's talk about this."

[8]I sent word back to him, "We are not engaged in these activities you are describing. All of this is a figment of your imagination."

[9]All of them were wanting to scare us, supposing, "Their hands will grow slack from the work, and it won't get done."

So now, strengthen my hands!

[10]Then I went to the house of Shemaiah son of Delaiah, the son of Mehetabel. He was confined to his home. He said, "Let's set up a time to meet in the house of God, within the temple. Let's close the doors of the temple, for they are coming to kill you. It will surely be at night that they will come to kill you."

[11]But I replied, "Should a man like me run away? Would someone like me flee to the temple in order to save his life? I will not go!" [12]I recognized the fact that God had not sent him, for he had spoken the prophecy against me as a hired agent of Tobiah and Sanballat. [13]He had been hired to scare me so that I would do this and thereby sin. They would thus bring reproach on me and I would be discredited.

[14]Remember, O my God, Tobiah and Sanballat in light of these actions of theirs—also Noadiah the prophetess and the other prophets who have been trying to scare me!

THE REBUILDING OF THE WALL IS FINALLY COMPLETED

[15]So the wall was completed on the twenty-fifth day of Elul, in just fifty-two days. [16]When all our enemies heard and all the nations who were around us saw this, they were greatly disheartened. They knew that this work had been accomplished with the help of our God.

6:1–14 The greatest mischief our enemies can do us is to frighten us from our duty and to lead us to do what is sinful. Let us never decline a good work, and never do a bad one. We ought to test all advice and to reject what is contrary to the Word of God. Every person should study to be consistent. All that God has done for us or by us or given to us should lead us to watchfulness, self-denial, and diligence. Next to the sinfulness of sin, we should dread the scandal.

MATTHEW HENRY **(1662–1714)**
COMMENTARY ON THE WHOLE BIBLE

[17]In those days the aristocrats of Judah repeatedly sent letters to Tobiah, and responses from Tobiah were repeatedly
coming to them. [18]For many in Judah had sworn allegiance to
him, because he was the son-in-law of Shecaniah son of Arah.
His son Jonathan had married the daughter of Meshullam son
of Berechiah. [19]They were telling me about his good deeds and
then taking back to him the things I said. Tobiah, on the other
hand, sent letters in order to scare me.

7 When the wall had been rebuilt and I had positioned the
doors, and the gatekeepers, the singers, and the Levites
had been appointed, [2]I then put in charge over Jerusalem my
brother Hanani and Hananiah the chief of the citadel, for he
was a faithful man and feared God more than many do. [3]I said
to them, "The gates of Jerusalem must not be opened in the
early morning, until those who are standing guard close the
doors and lock them. Position residents of Jerusalem as guards,
some at their guard stations and some near their homes." [4]Now
the city was spread out and large, and there were not a lot of
people in it. At that time houses had not been rebuilt. [5]My God
placed it on my heart to gather the leaders, the officials, and
the ordinary people so they could be enrolled on the basis of
genealogy. I found the genealogical records of those who had
formerly returned. Here is what I found written in that record:

[6]These are the people of the province who returned from the
captivity of the exiles, whom King Nebuchadnezzar of Babylon
had forced into exile. They returned to Jerusalem and to Judah, each to his own city. [7]They came with Zerubbabel, Jeshua,
Nehemiah, Azariah, Raamiah, Nahamani, Mordecai, Bilshan,
Mispereth, Bigvai, Nehum, and Baanah.

The number of Israelite men was as follows:

[8]the descendants of Parosh: 2,172;
[9]the descendants of Shephatiah: 372;
[10]the descendants of Arah: 652;
[11]the descendants of Pahath Moab (from the line of Jeshua
and Joab): 2,818;
[12]the descendants of Elam: 1,254;
[13]the descendants of Zattu: 845;
[14]the descendants of Zaccai: 760;
[15]the descendants of Binnui: 648;
[16]the descendants of Bebai: 628;
[17]the descendants of Azgad: 2,322;
[18]the descendants of Adonikam: 667;
[19]the descendants of Bigvai: 2,067;
[20]the descendants of Adin: 655;
[21]the descendants of Ater (through Hezekiah): 98;
[22]the descendants of Hashum: 328;
[23]the descendants of Bezai: 324;
[24]the descendants of Harif: 112;
[25]the descendants of Gibeon: 95;
[26]The men of Bethlehem and Netophah: 188;
[27]the men of Anathoth: 128;
[28]the men of the family of Azmaveth: 42;
[29]the men of Kiriath Jearim, Kephirah, and Beeroth: 743;
[30]the men of Ramah and Geba: 621;
[31]the men of Micmash: 122;
[32]the men of Bethel and Ai: 123;
[33]the men of the other Nebo: 52;
[34]the descendants of the other Elam: 1,254;
[35]the descendants of Harim: 320;

36 the descendants of Jericho: 345;
37 the descendants of Lod, Hadid, and Ono: 721;
38 the descendants of Senaah: 3,930;
39 The priests: the descendants of Jedaiah (through the family
of Jeshua): 973;
40 the descendants of Immer: 1,052;
41 the descendants of Pashhur: 1,247;
42 the descendants of Harim: 1,017.
43 The Levites: the descendants of Jeshua (through Kadmiel,
through the line of Hodaviah): 74.
44 The singers: the descendants of Asaph: 148.
45 The gatekeepers: the descendants of Shallum, the descendants of Ater, the descendants of Talmon, the descendants
of Akkub, the descendants of Hatita, and the descendants of
Shobai: 138.
46 The temple servants: the descendants of Ziha, the descendants of Hasupha, the descendants of Tabbaoth, 47 the
descendants of Keros, the descendants of Sia, the descendants
of Padon, 48 the descendants of Lebanah, the descendants of
Hagabah, the descendants of Shalmai, 49 the descendants of
Hanan, the descendants of Giddel, the descendants of Gahar,
50 the descendants of Reaiah, the descendants of Rezin, the
descendants of Nekoda, 51 the descendants of Gazzam, the de-
scendants of Uzzah, the descendants of Paseah, 52 the descen-
dants of Besai, the descendants of Meunim, the descendants
of Nephussim, 53 the descendants of Bakbuk, the descendants
of Hakupha, the descendants of Harhur, 54 the descendants of
Bazluth, the descendants of Mehida, the descendants of Harsha,
55 the descendants of Barkos, the descendants of Sisera, the
descendants of Temah, 56 the descendants of Neziah, the descendants of Hatipha.
57 The descendants of the servants of Solomon: the descendants of Sotai, the descendants of Sophereth, the descendants
of Perida, 58 the descendants of Jaala, the descendants of Darkon,
the descendants of Giddel, 59 the descendants of Shephatiah, the
descendants of Hattil, the descendants of Pokereth Hazzebaim,
and the descendants of Amon.
60 All the temple servants and the descendants of the servants
of Solomon, 392.
61 These are the ones who came up from Tel Melah, Tel
Harsha, Kerub, Addon, and Immer (although they were unable to certify their family connection or their ancestry, as to
whether they were really from Israel):
62 the descendants of Delaiah, the descendants of Tobiah,
and the descendants of Nekoda, 642.
63 And from among the priests: the descendants of Hobaiah,
the descendants of Hakkoz, and the descendants of Barzillai
(who had married a woman from the daughters of Barzillai
the Gileadite and was called by that name). 64 They searched
for their records in the genealogical materials, but none were
found. They were therefore excluded from the priesthood. 65 The
governor instructed them not to eat any of the sacred food until
there was a priest who could consult the Urim and Thummim.
66 The entire group numbered 42,360— 67 not counting their
7,337 male and female servants. They also had 245 male and
female singers. 68 They had 736 horses, 245 mules, 69 435 camels,
and 6,720 donkeys. 70 Some of the family leaders contributed
to the work. The governor contributed to the treasury 1,000
gold drachmas, 50 bowls, and 530 priestly garments. 71 Some

7:64 Men who were called to be God's priests dropped out of the register of those who served before him. It may be they were not sure of their genealogy and had lost the assurance of sonship; their spirit was no longer filled with the blessed cowitness of the Holy Spirit. God was far from them and, being out of harmony with him, they were out of sympathy with their fellows. They were therefore rightly put out of the priesthood. Now trace this matter back to its beginning. As likely as not you will find it originated in some worldly alliance. Those who will be friends of the world are necessarily enemies of God.

F. B. MEYER **(1847–1929)**
OUR DAILY HOMILY

CYRIL OF ALEXANDRIA:

DEFENDER OF CHRIST'S DUAL NATURES

c. 376–444

Little is known about Cyril's early background beyond his birth in the small Egyptian city of Theodosius around 376. We do know he was the nephew of Theophilus, the bishop and patriarch of Alexandria. This detail would prove to be important, for Cyril eventually took over his uncle's role as bishop of Alexandria in 412, setting Cyril up for a major role in defending the deity and humanity of Christ against the false teachings of Nestorius, bishop in the city of Constantinople.

Nestorius is integral to the story of Cyril. Rising to the position of bishop and patriarch of Constantinople in 428, Nestorius became extremely influential in the East. Shortly after his arrival, a close associate of his, Anastasius, gave a sermon that would send shock waves through the church. In November of that year, Anastasius preached a sermon that contained this controversial line: "Let no one call Mary *Theotokos*: for Mary was but a woman, and it is impossible that God should be born of a woman."

Theotokos means "God-bearer," reflecting the belief in Jesus Christ's true and complete divinity. Mary gave birth not merely to a boy, but to God himself. Understandably, Anastasius created confusion in the congregation and conflict among the churches. Nestorius, however, defended his friend by launching a series of sermons on Christmas morning of that year, similarly condemning the *Theotokos* title. Nestorius said one could call Mary *Christikos*, "Christ-bearer," for Christ was born of a woman. But he argued it was impossible for God to be born—one must not say that Mary gave birth to God. It's not difficult to see why Nestorius was concerned: The incarnation is an extraordinarily challenging, even dangerous doctrine, and it seems shockingly irreverent to say that a human woman gave birth to God! Nestorius understood that when Christians claim that Jesus is both God and man, we must be very precise: The divinity and humanity didn't mix or change. What Nestorius failed to understand was how these unchanged, unmixed natures were united in one divine person. The incarnation changes how we can talk about God. We now say that the Logos, the Son of God, the second person of the Trinity, was literally born to Mary—and he was able to do this because he assumed a human nature.

But at this point in church history, the doctrine's impact on how we should talk about God remained contested. Nestorius represented those who were specially concerned to keep Christ's natures distinct. But others emphasized the unity of Christ's person. Led by Cyril, the Alexandrian church leaders launched a campaign to discredit Nestorius and debate his ideas. Cyril argued for the *hypostatic*, or personal, union of the divine and human natures. This union meant that it was right to say that the eternal Son of God, who is God and who was present at creation, is also the one who walked the earth and died; the one who walked on water, forgave sins, and rose from the dead. Everything we can say about humanity or divinity can properly be said of the one person, Jesus Christ.

Eventually, the Council of Ephesus was convened in 431 to settle the issue. The result was the ratification of Cyril's formula, and the confirmation that the eternal Son and Mary's son are one and the same person; Mary truly was the God-bearer.

Cyril's unrelenting emphasis on the unity of Christ's divine and human natures moved forward the church's ongoing struggle to understand and apply scripture's teachings about Jesus—the one who is both God and man, who heals humanity's brokenness and reconciles us with God in his own person (2 Cor 5:18–19; Col 2:9).

IMPORTANT WORKS

FIVE TOMES AGAINST NESTORIUS

THAT CHRIST IS ONE

of the family leaders gave to the project treasury 20,000 gold drachmas and 2,200 silver minas. [72]What the rest of the people gave amounted to 20,000 gold drachmas, 2,000 silver minas, and 67 priestly garments.

[73]The priests, the Levites, the gatekeepers, the singers, some of the people, the temple servants, and all the rest of Israel lived in their cities.

THE PEOPLE RESPOND TO THE READING OF THE LAW

When the seventh month arrived and the Israelites were settled
8 in their towns, [1]all the people gathered together in the plaza
which was in front of the Water Gate. They asked Ezra the
scribe to bring the book of the law of Moses which the LORD
had commanded Israel. [2]So Ezra the priest brought the law
before the assembly which included men and women and all
those able to understand what they heard. (This happened on
the first day of the seventh month.) [3]So he read it before the
plaza in front of the Water Gate from dawn till noon before the
men and women and those children who could understand. All
the people were eager to hear the book of the law.
[4]Ezra the scribe stood on a towering wooden platform constructed for this purpose. Standing near him on his right were
Mattithiah, Shema, Anaiah, Uriah, Hilkiah, and Masseiah. On
his left were Pedaiah, Mishael, Malkijah, Hashum, Hashbad-
danah, Zechariah, and Meshullam. [5]Ezra opened the book in
plain view of all the people, for he was elevated above all the
people. When he opened the book, all the people stood up. [6]Ezra
blessed the LORD, the great God, and all the people replied
"Amen! Amen!" as they lifted their hands. Then they bowed
down and worshiped the LORD with their faces to the ground.
[7]Jeshua, Bani, Sherebiah, Jamin, Akkub, Shabbethai, Hodiah,
Maaseiah, Kelita, Azariah, Jozabad, Hanan, and Pelaiah—all of
whom were Levites—were teaching the people the law, as the
people remained standing. [8]They read from the book of God's
law, explaining it and imparting insight. Thus the people gained
understanding from what was read.
[9]Then Nehemiah the governor, Ezra the priestly scribe, and
the Levites who were imparting understanding to the people
said to all of them, "This day is holy to the LORD your God. Do

8:1–18 There has come a time in Nehemiah's great enterprise when the law, long forgotten, long broken by the captives, is now to be established again as the rule of the newly founded commonwealth. Naturally enough there comes a remembrance of many sins in the past history of the people, and tears naturally mingle with the thankfulness that again they are a nation having a divine worship and a divine law in their midst. Their leader, knowing that if the spirits of his people once began to flag, they could not face nor conquer the difficulties of their position, said to them, "This day is holy to the LORD your God. Do not mourn or weep." *You will have no more power for obedience, you will not be fit for your work, if you fall into a desponding state. Be thankful and glad, and remember that the purest worship is the worship of God-fixed joy*: "the joy of the LORD is your strength."

ALEXANDER MACLAREN
(1826–1910)
EXPOSITIONS OF THE HOLY SCRIPTURES

not mourn or weep." For all the people had been weeping when they heard the words of the law. [10]He said to them, "Go and eat delicacies and drink sweet drinks and send portions to those for whom nothing is prepared. For this day is holy to our Lord. Do not grieve, for the joy of the LORD is your strength."

[11]Then the Levites quieted all the people saying, "Be quiet, for this day is holy. Do not grieve." [12]So all the people departed to eat and drink and to share their food with others and to enjoy tremendous joy, for they had gained insight in the matters that had been made known to them.

[13]On the second day of the month the family leaders met with Ezra the scribe, together with all the people, the priests, and the Levites, to consider the words of the law. [14]They discovered written in the law that the LORD had commanded through Moses that the Israelites should live in temporary shelters during the festival of the seventh month, [15]and that they should make a proclamation and disseminate this message in all their cities and in Jerusalem: "Go to the hill country and bring back olive branches and branches of wild olive trees, myrtle trees, date palms, and other leafy trees to construct temporary shelters, as it is written."

[16]So the people went out and brought these things back and constructed temporary shelters for themselves, each on his roof and in his courtyard and in the courtyards of the temple of God and in the plaza of the Water Gate and the plaza of the Ephraim Gate. [17]So all the assembly which had returned from the exile constructed temporary shelters and lived in them. The Israelites had not done so from the days of Joshua son of Nun until that day. Everyone experienced very great joy. [18]Ezra read in the book of the law of God day by day, from the first day to the last. They observed the festival for seven days, and on the eighth day they held an assembly as was required.

THE PEOPLE ACKNOWLEDGE THEIR SIN BEFORE GOD

9 On the twenty-fourth day of this same month the Israelites assembled; they were fasting and wearing sackcloth, their heads covered with dust. [2]Those truly of Israelite descent separated from all the foreigners, standing and confessing their sins and the iniquities of their ancestors. [3]For one-fourth of the day they stood in their place and read from the book of the law of the LORD their God, and for another fourth they were confessing their sins and worshiping the LORD their God. [4]Then the Levites—Jeshua, Binnui, Kadmiel, Shebaniah, Bunni, Sherebiah, Bani, and Kenani—stood on the steps and called out loudly to the LORD their God. [5]The Levites—Jeshua, Kadmiel, Bani, Hashabneiah, Sherebiah, Hodiah, Shebaniah, and Pethahiah—said, "Stand up and bless the LORD your God!"

"May you be blessed, O LORD our God, from age to age. May your glorious name be blessed; may it be lifted up above all blessing and praise. [6]You alone are the LORD. You made the heavens, even the highest heavens, along with all their multitude of stars, the earth and all that is on it, the seas and all that is in them. You impart life to them all, and the multitudes of heaven worship you.

[7]"You are the LORD God who chose Abram and brought him forth from Ur of the Chaldeans. You changed his name to Abraham. [8]When you perceived that his heart was faithful toward you, you established a covenant with him to give his

9:1–38 "Because of all this we are entering into a binding covenant in written form." There are many occasions in our experience when we may very rightly, and with benefit, renew our covenant with God. After recovery from sickness when, like Hezekiah, we have had a new term of years added to our life, we may fitly do it. After any deliverance from trouble, when our joys bud forth anew, let us renew our consecration. Especially let us do this after any sin that has grieved the Holy Spirit; let us again offer ourselves to the Lord. We should not only let our troubles confirm our dedication to God, but also our prosperity should do the same. Surely if he has crowned us, we ought also to crown our God.

CHARLES SPURGEON
(1834–1892)
MORNING AND EVENING

descendants the land of the Canaanites, the Hittites, the Amorites, the Perizzites, the Jebusites, and the Girgashites. You
have fulfilled your promise, for you are righteous.
9"You saw the affliction of our ancestors in Egypt, and you
heard their cry at the Red Sea. 10You performed awesome signs
against Pharaoh, against his servants, and against all the people
of his land, for you knew that the Egyptians had acted presumptuously against them. You made for yourself a name that
is celebrated to this day. 11You split the sea before them, and
they crossed through the sea on dry ground. But you threw their
pursuers into the depths, like a stone into surging waters. 12You
guided them with a pillar of cloud by day and with a pillar of
fire by night to illumine for them the path they were to travel.
13"You came down on Mount Sinai and spoke with them
from heaven. You provided them with just judgments, true laws,
and good statutes and commandments. 14You made known to
them your holy Sabbath; you issued commandments, statutes,
and laws to them through Moses your servant. 15You provided
bread from heaven for them in their time of hunger, and you
brought forth water from the rock for them in their time of
thirst. You told them to enter in order to possess the land that
you had sworn to give them.
16"But they—our ancestors—behaved presumptuously; they
rebelled and did not obey your commandments. 17They refused to obey and did not recall your miracles that you had
performed among them. Instead, they rebelled and appointed
a leader to return to their bondage in Egypt. But you are a God
of forgiveness, merciful and compassionate, slow to get angry
and unfailing in your loyal love. You did not abandon them,
18even when they made a cast image of a calf for themselves
and said, 'This is your God who brought you up from Egypt,' or
when they committed atrocious blasphemies.
19"Due to your great compassion you did not abandon them
in the wilderness. The pillar of cloud did not stop guiding them
in the path by day, nor did the pillar of fire stop illuminating
for them by night the path on which they should travel. 20You
imparted your good Spirit to instruct them. You did not withhold your manna from their mouths; you provided water for
their thirst. 21For 40 years you sustained them. Even in the
wilderness they never lacked anything. Their clothes did not
wear out and their feet did not swell.
22"You gave them kingdoms and peoples, and you allocated
them to every corner of the land. They inherited the land of
King Sihon of Heshbon and the land of King Og of Bashan.
23You multiplied their descendants like the stars of the sky.
You brought them to the land you had told their ancestors to
enter in order to possess. 24Their descendants entered and
possessed the land. You subdued before them the Canaanites
who were the inhabitants of the land. You delivered them into
their hand, together with their kings and the peoples of the
land, to deal with as they pleased. 25They captured fortified
cities and fertile land. They took possession of houses full of
all sorts of good things—wells previously dug, vineyards, olive
trees, and fruit trees in abundance. They ate until they were
full and grew fat. They enjoyed to the full your great goodness.
26"Nonetheless they grew disobedient and rebelled against
you; they disregarded your law. They killed your prophets
who had solemnly admonished them in order to cause them
to return to you. They committed atrocious blasphemies.

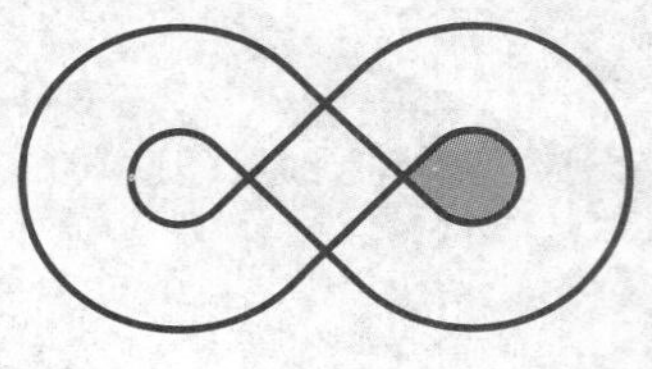

THE AUGSBURG CONFESSION (1530)

EARLY IN THE Protestant Reformation, the Augsburg Confession was written to address Charles V in order to gain imperial approval for the Protestant movement and to refute the doctrinal errors of the Roman Catholic Church. This significant Confession was primarily prepared by Philip Melanchthon in conjunction with the council in Augsburg, Germany, and in the wake of Martin Luther's publication of *The Ninety-Five Theses* (1517). Here are selections from the Augsburg Confession.

ARTICLE II. OF ORIGINAL SIN

[OUR CHURCHES] teach that since the fall of Adam all men begotten in the natural way are born with sin, that is, without the fear of God, without trust in God, and with concupiscence; and that this disease, or vice of origin, is truly sin, even now condemning and bringing eternal death upon those not born again through baptism and the Holy Ghost. They condemn the Pelagians and others who deny that original depravity is sin, and who, to obscure the glory of Christ's merit and benefits, argue that man can be justified before God by his own strength and reason.

ARTICLE IV. OF JUSTIFICATION

[OUR CHURCHES] teach that men cannot be justified before God by their own strength, merits, or works but are freely justified for Christ's sake, through faith, when they believe that they are received into favor, and that their sins are forgiven for Christ's sake, who, by his death, has made satisfaction for our sins. This faith God imputes for righteousness in his sight (Romans 3–4).

ARTICLE VI. OF NEW OBEDIENCE

[OUR CHURCHES] teach that this faith is bound to bring forth good fruits, and that it is necessary to do good works commanded by God, because of God's will, but that we should not rely on those works to merit justification before God. For remission of sins and justification is apprehended by faith, as also the voice of Christ attests: "When ye shall have done all those things . . . say, We are unprofitable servants" (Luke 17:10). The same is also taught by the Fathers. For Ambrose says: It is ordained of God that he who believes in Christ is saved, freely receiving remission of sins, without works, by faith alone.

27 Therefore you delivered them into the hand of their adversaries, who oppressed them. But in the time of their distress they called to you, and you heard from heaven. In your abundant compassion you provided them with deliverers to rescue them from their adversaries.

28 "Then, when they were at rest again, they went back to
doing evil before you. Then you abandoned them to their enemies, and they gained dominion over them. When they again
cried out to you, in your compassion you heard from heaven and
rescued them time and again. 29 And you solemnly admonished
them in order to return them to your law, but they behaved
presumptuously and did not obey your commandments. They
sinned against your ordinances—those by which an individual,
if he obeys them, will live. They boldly turned from you; they
rebelled and did not obey. 30 You prolonged your kindness with
them for many years, and you solemnly admonished them by
your Spirit through your prophets. Still they paid no attention, so you delivered them into the hands of the neighboring
peoples. 31 However, due to your abundant mercy you did not
do away with them altogether; you did not abandon them. For
you are a merciful and compassionate God.

32 "So now, our God—the great, powerful, and awesome God,
who keeps covenant fidelity—do not regard as inconsequential
all the hardship that has befallen us—our kings, our leaders,
our priests, our prophets, our ancestors, and all your people—
from the days of the kings of Assyria until this very day. 33 You
are righteous with regard to all that has happened to us, for
you have acted faithfully. It is we who have been in the wrong!
34 Our kings, our leaders, our priests, and our ancestors have
not kept your law. They have not paid attention to your commandments or your testimonies by which you have solemnly
admonished them. 35 Even when they were in their kingdom
and benefiting from your incredible goodness that you had
lavished on them in the spacious and fertile land you had set
before them, they did not serve you, nor did they turn from
their evil practices.

36 "So today we are slaves! In the very land you gave to our
ancestors to eat its fruit and to enjoy its good things—we are
slaves. 37 Its abundant produce goes to the kings you have placed
over us due to our sins. They rule over our bodies and our livestock as they see fit, and we are in great distress!

THE PEOPLE PLEDGE TO BE FAITHFUL

38 "Because of all this we are entering into a binding covenant in written form; our leaders, our Levites, and our priests have affixed their names on the sealed document."

10 On the sealed documents were the following names:
Nehemiah the governor, son of Hacaliah, along with
Zedekiah,
2 Seraiah, Azariah, Jeremiah,
3 Pashhur, Amariah, Malkijah,
4 Hattush, Shebaniah, Malluch,
5 Harim, Meremoth, Obadiah,
6 Daniel, Ginnethon, Baruch,
7 Meshullam, Abijah, Mijamin,
8 Maaziah, Bilgai, and Shemaiah. These were the priests.
9 The Levites were as follows:
Jeshua son of Azaniah, Binnui of the sons of Henadad,
Kadmiel.
10 Their colleagues were as follows:
Shebaniah, Hodiah, Kelita, Pelaiah, Hanan,
11 Mica, Rehob, Hashabiah,
12 Zaccur, Sherebiah, Shebaniah,
13 Hodiah, Bani, and Beninu.
14 The leaders of the people were as follows:
Parosh, Pahath Moab, Elam, Zattu, Bani,
15 Bunni, Azgad, Bebai,
16 Adonijah, Bigvai, Adin,
17 Ater, Hezekiah, Azzur,
18 Hodiah, Hashum, Bezai,
19 Hariph, Anathoth, Nebai,
20 Magpiash, Meshullam, Hezir,
21 Meshezabel, Zadok, Jaddua,
22 Pelatiah, Hanan, Anaiah,
23 Hoshea, Hananiah, Hasshub,
24 Hallohesh, Pilha, Shobek,
25 Rehum, Hashabnah, Maaseiah,
26 Ahiah, Hanan, Anan,
27 Malluch, Harim, and Baanah.
28 "Now the rest of the people—the priests, the Levites, the
gatekeepers, the singers, the temple attendants, and all those
who have separated themselves from the neighboring peoples
because of the law of God, along with their wives, their sons, and
their daughters, all of whom are able to understand—29 hereby
participate with their colleagues the town leaders and enter
into a curse and an oath to adhere to the law of God which was
given through Moses the servant of God, and to obey carefully
all the commandments of the LORD our Lord, along with his
ordinances and his statutes.
30 "We will not give our daughters in marriage to the neighboring peoples, and we will not take their daughters in marriage
for our sons. 31 We will not buy on the Sabbath or on a holy day
from the neighboring peoples who bring their wares and all
kinds of grain to sell on the Sabbath day. We will let the fields
lie fallow every seventh year, and we will cancel every loan.
32 We accept responsibility for fulfilling the commands to give
one-third of a shekel each year for the work of the temple of
our God, 33 for the loaves of presentation and for the regular
grain offerings and regular burnt offerings, for the Sabbaths,
for the new moons, for the appointed meetings, for the holy
offerings, for the sin offerings to make atonement for Israel,
and for all the work of the temple of our God.
34 "We—the priests, the Levites, and the people—have cast lots
concerning the wood offerings, to bring them to the temple of
our God according to our families at the designated times year

10:28–39 All the matters in this chapter are relevant to the care of the Lord's house and his ministers and services. This excellent order of religious life ought to be imitated by us in a spiritual manner today—namely, that first the descendants of the exiles purified themselves from the pollution caused by the Gentiles, then they were sanctified by keeping the Sabbath (which stood prominently among the first commandments of the law), and only then did they turn all their attention to carrying out the observance of divine worship in other respects. For we must first be cleansed from evils and only then equip ourselves for good works.

VENERABLE BEDE
(C. 672–735)
ON EZRA AND NEHEMIAH

by year to burn on the altar of the LORD our God, as is written in the law. [35]We also accept responsibility for bringing the firstfruits of our land and the firstfruits of every fruit tree year by year to the temple of the LORD. [36]We also accept responsibility, as is written in the law, for bringing the firstborn of our sons and our cattle and the firstborn of our herds and of our flocks to the temple of our God, to the priests who are ministering in the temple of our God. [37]We will also bring the first of our coarse meal, of our contributions, of the fruit of every tree, of new wine, and of olive oil to the priests at the storerooms of the temple of our God, along with a tenth of the produce of our land to the Levites, for the Levites are the ones who collect the tithes in all the cities where we work. [38]A priest of Aaron's line will be with the Levites when the Levites collect the tithes, and the Levites will bring up a tenth of the tithes to the temple of our God, to the storerooms of the treasury. [39]The Israelites and the Levites will bring the contribution of the grain, the new wine, and the olive oil to the storerooms where the utensils of the sanctuary are kept, and where the priests who minister stay, along with the gatekeepers and the singers. We will not neglect the temple of our God."

THE POPULATION OF JERUSALEM

11 So the leaders of the people settled in Jerusalem, while the rest of the people cast lots to bring one out of every ten to settle in Jerusalem, the holy city, while the other nine remained in other cities. [2]The people gave their blessing on all the men who volunteered to settle in Jerusalem.

[3]These are the provincial leaders who settled in Jerusalem. (While other Israelites, the priests, the Levites, the temple attendants, and the sons of the servants of Solomon settled in the cities of Judah, each on his own property in their cities, [4]some of the descendants of Judah and some of the descendants of Benjamin settled in Jerusalem.)

Of the descendants of Judah:

Athaiah son of Uzziah, the son of Zechariah, the son of Amariah, the son of Shephatiah, the son of Mahalalel, from the descendants of Perez; [5]and Maaseiah son of Baruch, the son of Col-Hozeh, the son of Hazaiah, the son of Adaiah, the son of Joiarib, the son of Zechariah, from the descendants of Shelah. [6]The sum total of the descendants of Perez who were settling in Jerusalem was 468 exceptional men.

[7]These are the descendants of Benjamin:

Sallu son of Meshullam, the son of Joed, the son of Pedaiah, the son of Kolaiah, the son of Maaseiah, the son of Ithiel, the son of Jeshaiah, [8]and his followers, Gabbai and Sallai—928 in all. [9]Joel son of Zicri was the officer in charge of them, and Judah son of Hassenuah was second-in-command over the city.

[10]From the priests:

Jedaiah son of Joiarib, Jakin, [11]Seraiah son of Hilkiah, the son of Meshullam, the son of Zadok, the son of Meraioth, the son of Ahitub, supervisor in the temple of God, [12]and their colleagues who were carrying out work for the temple—822; and Adaiah son of Jeroham, the son of Pelaliah, the son of Amzi, the son of Zechariah, the son of Pashhur, the son of Malkijah, [13]and his colleagues who were heads of families—242; and Amashsai son of Azarel, the son of Ahzai, the son of Meshillemoth, the son of Immer, [14]and his colleagues who were exceptional men—128. The officer over them was Zabdiel the son of Haggedolim.

11:1–36 The eleventh chapter opens with a grievous mark of Jerusalem's degradation. She is a witness against herself that she is not as the Lord will have her in the days of coming glory. What a sign that restoration was not glory! Jerusalem is still trodden down; the times of the Gentiles are still unfulfilled. Surely the daughter of Zion has not arisen, shaken herself from the dust, and put on her strength and her beautiful garments. Still, she must be inhabited; she must have her citizens within her. The land must have its people, for Messiah is soon to walk among them; the city must have its inhabitants, for her King is soon to be offered to her.

J. G. BELLETT **(1795–1864)**
THE CAPTIVES RETURNED TO JERUSALEM

15From the Levites:

Shemaiah son of Hasshub, the son of Azrikam, the son of Hashabiah, the son of Bunni; 16Shabbethai and Jozabad, leaders of the Levites, were in charge of the external work for the temple of God; 17Mattaniah son of Mica, the son of Zabdi, the son of Asaph, the praise leader who led in thanksgiving and prayer; Bakbukiah, second among his colleagues; and Abda son of Shammua, the son of Galal, the son of Jeduthun. 18The sum total of the Levites in the holy city was 284.

19And the gatekeepers:

Akkub, Talmon, and their colleagues who were guarding the gates—172.

20And the rest of the Israelites, with the priests and the Levites, were in all the cities of Judah, each on his own property. 21The temple attendants were living on Ophel, and Ziha and Gishpa were over them.

22The overseer of the Levites in Jerusalem was Uzzi son of Bani, the son of Hashabiah, the son of Mattaniah, the son of Mica. He was one of Asaph's descendants, who were the singers responsible for the service of the temple of God. 23For they were under royal orders which determined their activity day by day.

24Pethahiah son of Meshezabel, one of the descendants of Zerah son of Judah, was an adviser to the king in every matter pertaining to the people.

25As for the settlements with their fields, some of the people of Judah settled in Kiriath Arba and its neighboring villages, in Dibon and its villages, in Jekabzeel and its settlements, 26in Jeshua, in Moladah, in Beth Pelet, 27in Hazar Shual, in Beer Sheba and its villages, 28in Ziklag, in Meconah and its villages, 29in En Rimmon, in Zorah, in Jarmuth, 30Zanoah, Adullam and their settlements, in Lachish and its fields, and in Azekah and its villages. So they were encamped from Beer Sheba to the Valley of Hinnom.

31Some of the descendants of Benjamin settled in Geba, Micmash, Aija, Bethel and its villages, 32in Anathoth, Nob, and Ananiah, 33in Hazor, Ramah, and Gittaim, 34in Hadid, Zeboyim, and Neballat, 35in Lod, Ono, and the Valley of the Craftsmen. 36Some of the Judean divisions of the Levites settled in Benjamin.

THE PRIESTS AND THE LEVITES WHO RETURNED TO JERUSALEM

12 These are the priests and Levites who returned with Zerubbabel son of Shealtiel and Jeshua: Seraiah, Jeremiah, Ezra, 2Amariah, Malluch, Hattush, 3Shecaniah, Rehum, Meremoth, 4Iddo, Ginnethon, Abijah, 5Mijamin, Moadiah, Bilgah, 6Shemaiah, Joiarib, Jedaiah, 7Sallu, Amok, Hilkiah, and Jedaiah. These were the leaders of the priests and their colleagues in the days of Jeshua.

8And the Levites: Jeshua, Binnui, Kadmiel, Sherebiah, Judah, and Mattaniah, who together with his colleagues was in charge of the songs of thanksgiving. 9Bakbukiah and Unni, their colleagues, stood opposite them in the services.

10Jeshua was the father of Joiakim, Joiakim was the father of Eliashib, Eliashib was the father of Joiada, 11Joiada was the father of Jonathan, and Jonathan was the father of Jaddua.

12In the days of Joiakim, these were the priests who were leaders of the families: of Seraiah, Meraiah; of Jeremiah, Hananiah; 13of Ezra, Meshullam; of Amariah, Jehohanan; 14of Malluch, Jonathan; of Shecaniah, Joseph; 15of Harim, Adna; of Meremoth, Helkai; 16of Iddo, Zechariah; of Ginnethon, Meshullam; 17of

Abijah, Zicri; of Miniamin and of Moadiah, Piltai; [18]of Bilgah, Shammua; of Shemaiah, Jehonathan; [19]of Joiarib, Mattenai; of Jedaiah, Uzzi; [20]of Sallu, Kallai; of Amok, Eber; [21]of Hilkiah, Hashabiah; of Jedaiah, Nethanel.

[22]As for the Levites, in the days of Eliashib, Joiada, Johanan, and Jaddua the heads of families were recorded, as were the priests during the reign of Darius the Persian. [23]The descendants of Levi were recorded in the Book of the Chronicles as heads of families up to the days of Johanan son of Eliashib. [24]And the leaders of the Levites were Hashabiah, Sherebiah, Jeshua son of Kadmiel, and their colleagues, who stood opposite them to offer praise and thanks, one contingent corresponding to the other, as specified by David the man of God.

[25]Mattaniah, Bakbukiah, Obadiah, Meshullam, Talmon, and Akkub were gatekeepers who were guarding the storerooms at the gates. [26]These all served in the days of Joiakim son of Jeshua, the son of Jozadak, and in the days of Nehemiah the governor and of Ezra the priestly scribe.

THE WALL OF JERUSALEM IS DEDICATED

[27]At the dedication of the wall of Jerusalem, they sought out the Levites from all the places they lived to bring them to Jerusalem to celebrate the dedication joyfully with songs of thanksgiving and songs accompanied by cymbals, harps, and lyres. [28]The singers were also assembled from the district around Jerusalem and from the settlements of the Netophathites [29]and from Beth Gilgal and from the fields of Geba and Azmaveth, for the singers had built settlements for themselves around Jerusalem. [30]When the priests and Levites had purified themselves, they purified the people, the gates, and the wall.

[31]I brought the leaders of Judah up on top of the wall, and I appointed two large choirs to give thanks. One was to proceed on the top of the wall southward toward the Dung Gate. [32]Going after them were Hoshaiah, half the leaders of Judah, [33]Azariah, Ezra, Meshullam, [34]Judah, Benjamin, Shemaiah, Jeremiah, [35]some of the priests with trumpets, Zechariah son of Jonathan, the son of Shemaiah, the son of Mattaniah, the son of Micaiah, the son of Zaccur, the son of Asaph, [36]and his colleagues—Shemaiah, Azarel, Milalai, Gilalai, Maai, Nethanel, Judah, and Hanani—with musical instruments of David the man of God. (Ezra the scribe led them.) [37]They went over the Fountain Gate and continued directly up the steps of the City of David on the ascent to the wall. They passed the house of David and continued on to the Water Gate toward the east.

[38]The second choir was proceeding in the opposite direction. I followed them, along with half the people, on top of the wall, past the Tower of the Ovens to the Broad Wall, [39]over the Ephraim Gate, the Jeshanah Gate, the Fish Gate, the Tower of Hananel, and the Tower of the Hundred, to the Sheep Gate. They stopped at the Gate of the Guard.

[40]Then the two choirs that gave thanks took their stations in the temple of God. I did also, along with half the officials with me, [41]and the priests—Eliakim, Maaseiah, Miniamin, Micaiah, Elioenai, Zechariah, and Hananiah, with their trumpets—[42]and also Maaseiah, Shemaiah, Eleazar, Uzzi, Jehohanan, Malkijah, Elam, and Ezer. The choirs sang loudly under the direction of Jezrahiah. [43]And on that day they offered great sacrifices and rejoiced, for God had given them great joy. The women and children also rejoiced. The rejoicing in Jerusalem could be heard from far away.

12:27–47 Believers should undertake nothing that they do not dedicate to the Lord. We are concerned to cleanse our hands and purify our hearts when any work for God is to pass through them. Those who would be employed to sanctify others must set themselves apart for God. To those who are sanctified, all their creature comforts and enjoyments are made holy. We read that the people greatly rejoiced. All who share in public mercies ought to join in public thanksgivings. When the solemnities of a thanksgiving day leave such impressions on ministers and people that both are more careful and cheerful in doing their duty, they are indeed acceptable to the Lord and turn to good account. And whatever we do must be purified by the blood of sprinkling and by the grace of the Holy Spirit, or it cannot be acceptable to God.

MATTHEW HENRY **(1662-1714)**
COMMENTARY ON THE WHOLE BIBLE

[44]On that day men were appointed over the storerooms for the contributions, firstfruits, and tithes, to gather into them from the fields of the cities the portions prescribed by the law for the priests and the Levites, for the people of Judah took delight in the priests and Levites who were ministering. [45]They performed the service of their God and the service of purification, along with the singers and gatekeepers, according to the commandment of David and his son Solomon. [46]For long ago, in the days of David and Asaph, there had been directors for the singers and for the songs of praise and thanks to God. [47]So in the days of Zerubbabel and in the days of Nehemiah, all Israel was contributing the portions for the singers and gatekeepers, according to the daily need. They also set aside the portion for the Levites, and the Levites set aside the portion for the descendants of Aaron.

FURTHER REFORMS BY NEHEMIAH

13 On that day the book of Moses was read aloud in the hearing of the people. They found written in it that no Ammonite or Moabite may ever enter the assembly of God, [2]for they had not met the Israelites with food and water, but instead had hired Balaam to curse them. (Our God, however, turned the curse into blessing.) [3]When they heard the law, they removed from Israel all who were of mixed ancestry.

[4]But before this time, Eliashib the priest, a relative of Tobiah, had been appointed over the storerooms of the temple of our God. [5]He made for him a large storeroom where previously they had been keeping the grain offering, the incense, and the vessels, along with the tithes of the grain, the new wine, and the olive oil as commanded for the Levites, the singers, the gatekeepers, and the offering for the priests.

[6]During all this time I was not in Jerusalem, for in the thirty-second year of King Artaxerxes of Babylon, I had gone back to the king. After some time I had requested leave of the king, [7]and I returned to Jerusalem. Then I discovered the evil that Eliashib had done for Tobiah by supplying him with a storeroom in the courts of the temple of God. [8]I was very upset, and I threw all of Tobiah's household possessions out of the storeroom. [9]Then I gave instructions that the storerooms should be purified, and I brought back the equipment of the temple of God, along with the grain offering and the incense.

[10]I also discovered that the portions for the Levites had not been provided, and that as a result the Levites and the singers who performed this work had all gone off to their fields. [11]So I registered a complaint with the leaders, asking, "Why is the temple of God neglected?" Then I gathered them and reassigned them to their positions.

[12]Then all of Judah brought the tithe of the grain, the new wine, and the olive oil to the storerooms. [13]I gave instructions that Shelemiah the priest, Zadok the scribe, and a certain Levite named Pedaiah be put in charge of the storerooms, and that Hanan son of Zaccur, the son of Mattaniah, be their assistant, for they were regarded as trustworthy. It was then their responsibility to oversee the distribution to their colleagues.

[14]Please remember me for this, O my God, and do not wipe out the kindness that I have done for the temple of my God and for its services!

[15]In those days I saw people in Judah treading winepresses on the Sabbath, bringing in heaps of grain and loading them onto

13:1–30 It is in all respects an apt and appropriate end to the work of building the holy city and the temple of the Lord that when the citizens had been purified by God from all the filth of foreign pollution, the orders of the priests and the Levites should be duly preserved in their own ministry in order that the teachers of the church who have been instructed according to rule may continually exhort the people now cleansed from all sin to remain henceforth in goodness and to grow. Among other things, the people offered wood to the Lord to feed the fire of the altar when they performed works of virtues that were assuredly worthy of divine consecration. For if wood did not sometimes symbolize something good, the prophet would not have said, "Let the trees of the forest shout with joy" (Ps 96:12). Now the wood burned and was consumed in the altar of the burnt offering when in the hearts of the elect works of righteousness were perfected in the flame of love.

VENERABLE BEDE
(C. 672–735)
ON EZRA AND NEHEMIAH

donkeys, along with wine, grapes, figs, and all kinds of loads, and bringing them to Jerusalem on the Sabbath day. So I warned
them on the day that they sold these provisions. 16The people from Tyre who lived there were bringing fish and all kinds of merchandise and were selling it on the Sabbath to the people
of Judah—and in Jerusalem, of all places! 17So I registered a complaint with the nobles of Judah, saying to them, "What is this evil thing that you are doing, profaning the Sabbath day?
18Isn't this the way your ancestors acted, causing our God to bring on them and on this city all this misfortune? And now you are causing even more wrath on Israel, profaning the Sabbath like this!"

19When the evening shadows began to fall on the gates of Jerusalem before the Sabbath, I ordered the doors to be closed. I further directed that they were not to be opened until after the Sabbath. I positioned some of my young men at the gates
so that no load could enter on the Sabbath day. 20The traders and sellers of all kinds of merchandise spent the night outside
Jerusalem once or twice. 21But I warned them and said, "Why do you spend the night by the wall? If you repeat this, I will forcibly remove you!" From that time on they did not show up on the
Sabbath. 22Then I directed the Levites to purify themselves and come and guard the gates in order to keep the Sabbath day holy.

For this please remember me, O my God, and have pity on me in keeping with your great love.

23Also in those days I saw the men of Judah who had married
women from Ashdod, Ammon, and Moab. 24Half their children spoke the language of Ashdod (or the language of one of the other peoples mentioned) and were unable to speak the lan-
guage of Judah. 25So I entered a complaint with them. I called down a curse on them, and I struck some of the men and pulled out their hair. I had them swear by God saying, "You will not marry off your daughters to their sons, and you will not take any of their daughters as wives for your sons or for yourselves.
26Was it not because of things like these that King Solomon of Israel sinned? Among the many nations there was no king like him. He was loved by his God, and God made him king over all
Israel. But the foreign wives made even him sin! 27Should we then in your case hear that you do all this great evil, thereby being unfaithful to our God by marrying foreign wives?"

28Now one of the sons of Joiada son of Eliashib the high priest was a son-in-law of Sanballat the Horonite. So I banished him from my sight.

29Please remember them, O my God, because they have defiled the priesthood, the covenant of the priesthood, and the Levites.

30So I purified them of everything foreign, and I assigned
specific duties to the priests and the Levites. 31I also provided for the wood offering at the appointed times and also for the firstfruits.

Please remember me for good, O my God.

AUTHOR	AUDIENCE	DATE	PURPOSE	THEMES
Unknown	The Jewish people	Sometime after 460 BC	The book of Esther reveals the hand of God that works behind the scenes of history to accomplish his sovereign plan, protect his people, and exact justice.	God's sovereignty; justice and activism; and prayer and faith

The book of Esther has been somewhat neglected over the course of church history. The first known complete commentary on the book was written by Rabanus Maurus 700 years into the life of the church. When the early church fathers did comment on the book, they relied on an allegorical or typological reading, raising Esther up to be a type of moral heroine to be emulated. Apparently John Calvin neither wrote a commentary on the book nor preached from it. And Martin Luther once wished it had never been part of the canon of scripture in the first place! Yet the book of Esther is an important work because it reveals God's working behind the scenes of history to accomplish his sovereign plan, protect his people, and exact justice.

One of the interesting features of Esther is what's missing: direct mention of God, for he is never named in the book. Esther is the only book in the Bible in which this is the case. Yet God is not absent—not in the least. Matthew Henry explained: "We find in this book, that even those Jews who were scattered in the province of the heathen were taken care of and were wonderfully preserved when threatened with destruction. Though the name of God be not in this book, the finger of God is shown by minute events for bringing about his people's deliverance." For generations this book has stood as a testimony to God's unseen hand attending to the affairs of his people—directing their circumstances, providing for and protecting them at every turn.

Although God is not explicitly mentioned in this book, he is there and he is not silent: "King Ahasuerus sat on his royal throne" (1:2) because the Lord put him there; he also put it in the king's heart to have a banquet and for the queen to defy him. The Lord strategically placed Mordecai and his niece Esther in Susa so that she would eventually find favor with Ahasuerus and be made queen. Through the Lord's hand, Mordecai overheard a plan to assassinate the king. "King Ahasuerus promoted Haman" (3:1) according to God's sovereign plan, which led to his people's being threatened with destruction. The Lord ordained that Ahasuerus couldn't sleep one night, and so he learned of Mordecai's deed that saved his life. And by providence Esther exposed Haman's treacherous plot to destroy God's people, which ultimately ensured their safety.

Before Esther saved her people from annihilation, Mordecai had suggested, "It may very well be that you have achieved royal status for such a time as this!" (4:14). Embedded in this statement is an implicit understanding of God's sovereignty, for it was the Lord who placed Esther in that lofty position. Mordecai also said to Esther, "If you keep quiet at this time, liberation and protection for the Jews will appear from another source" (4:14). This honest assessment recognized that Esther had a responsibility to act as God's agent of justice, but even if she didn't the Lord would still come to his people's aid.

In commenting on this passage, John Wesley offered an exhortation for our own agency in the Lord's sovereign plan of justice: "*It is probable God has raised you to this honor for this very season*. We should every one of us consider for what end God has put us in the place where we are? And when an opportunity offers of serving God and our generation, we must take care not to let it slip." Mordecai himself fits this description, for he is remembered as one who "worked enthusiastically for the good of his people and was an advocate for the welfare of all his descendants" (10:3).

Finally, the book illustrates the power and necessity of faith and prayer amid calamitous life circumstances. When Mordecai learned about the edict condemning the Jewish people to destruction, "he tore his garments and put on sackcloth and ashes. He went out into the city, crying out in a loud and bitter voice" (4:1). The rest of his people joined him: "There was considerable mourning among the Jews, along with fasting, weeping, and sorrow. Sackcloth and ashes were characteristic of many" (4:3). This is the language of divine petition. Athanasius commented, "When the whole nation of Israel was about to perish, blessed Esther defeated the tyrant's anger simply by fasting and praying to God. By faith she changed the ruin of her people into safety." We are similarly called to petition the Lord through fasting and prayer, believing in faith that he will come to our aid.

May we glean from Esther's example to trust in God's providential care and to have the courage to fight injustice, so that we too might be used of God for such a time as this.

1:1–22 The feast in the palace of the king was characterized by all the gorgeousness peculiar to the East. It resolved itself into a debauch of drunken revelry. In the midst of this, the king commanded Vashti, his queen, to his presence and to that of his drunken nobles. She refused to come. She paid the price of her loyalty to her womanhood in being deposed. Incidentally, the story reveals the place that women occupied outside the covenant of the chosen people; it was that of being the plaything and the slave of man. It also reminds us that in the midst of the grossest darkness, the human soul is not without some consciousness of higher things; and that among the least favored we may at times discover things of real value and beauty. Let the name of Vashti be held in everlasting honor for her refusal.

G. CAMPBELL MORGAN
(1883–1945)
LIVING MESSAGES OF THE BOOKS OF THE BIBLE

THE KING THROWS A LAVISH PARTY

1 The following events happened in the days of Ahasuerus. (I am
referring to that Ahasuerus who used to rule over 127 provinces extending all the way from India to Ethiopia.) 2In those days,
as King Ahasuerus sat on his royal throne in Susa the citadel,
3in the third year of his reign he provided a banquet for all his
officials and his servants. The army of Persia and Media was
present, as well as the nobles and the officials of the provinces.
4He displayed the riches of his royal glory and the splendor of
his majestic greatness for a lengthy period of time—180 days, to
be exact! 5When those days were completed, the king then provided a seven-day banquet for all the people who were present
in Susa the citadel, for those of highest standing to the most
lowly. It was held in the court located in the garden of the royal
palace. 6The furnishings included white linen and blue curtains
hung by cords of the finest linen and purple wool on silver
rings, alabaster columns, gold and silver couches displayed on
a floor made of valuable stones of alabaster, mother-of-pearl,
and mineral stone. 7Drinks were served in golden containers,
all of which differed from one another. Royal wine was available
in abundance at the king's expense. 8There were no restrictions
on the drinking, for the king had instructed all his supervisors
that they should do as everyone so desired. 9Queen Vashti also
gave a banquet for the women in King Ahasuerus' royal palace.

QUEEN VASHTI IS REMOVED FROM HER ROYAL POSITION

10On the seventh day, as King Ahasuerus was feeling the effects
of the wine, he ordered Mehuman, Biztha, Harbona, Bigtha,
Abagtha, Zethar, and Carcas, the seven eunuchs who attended
him, 11to bring Queen Vashti into the king's presence wearing
her royal high turban. He wanted to show the people and the
officials her beauty, for she was very attractive. 12But Queen
Vashti refused to come at the king's bidding conveyed through
the eunuchs. Then the king became extremely angry, and his
rage consumed him.
13The king then inquired of the wise men who were discern-
ers of the times—for it was the royal custom to confer with all
those who were proficient in laws and legalities. 14Those who
were closest to him were Carshena, Shethar, Admatha, Tarshish,
Meres, Marsena, and Memucan. These men were the seven officials of Persia and Media who saw the king on a regular basis
and had the most prominent offices in the kingdom. 15The king
asked, "By law, what should be done to Queen Vashti in light
of the fact that she has not obeyed the instructions of King
Ahasuerus conveyed through the eunuchs?"
16Memucan then replied to the king and the officials, "The
wrong of Queen Vashti is not against the king alone, but against
all the officials and all the people who are throughout all the
provinces of King Ahasuerus. 17For the matter concerning the
queen will spread to all the women, leading them to treat their
husbands with contempt, saying, 'When King Ahasuerus gave
orders to bring Queen Vashti into his presence, she would not
come.' 18And this very day the noble ladies of Persia and Media
who have heard the matter concerning the queen will respond
in the same way to all the royal officials, and there will be more
than enough contempt and anger. 19If the king is so inclined,
let a royal edict go forth from him, and let it be written in the
laws of Persia and Media that cannot be repealed that Vashti

may not come into the presence of King Ahasuerus, and let
the king convey her royalty to another who is more deserving
than she. [20]And let the king's decision that he will enact be
disseminated throughout all his kingdom, vast though it is.
Then all the women will give honor to their husbands, from
the most prominent to the lowly."

[21]The matter seemed appropriate to the king and the officials. So the king acted on the advice of Memucan. [22]He sent
letters throughout all the royal provinces, to each province
according to its own script and to each people according to their
own language, that every man should be ruling his family and
should be speaking the language of his own people.

ESTHER BECOMES QUEEN IN VASHTI'S PLACE

2 When these things had been accomplished and the rage of
King Ahasuerus had diminished, he remembered Vashti and
what she had done and what had been decided against her.
[2]The king's servants who attended him said, "Let a search be
conducted on the king's behalf for attractive young women.
[3]And let the king appoint officers throughout all the provinces
of his kingdom to gather all the attractive young women to
Susa the citadel, to the harem under the authority of Hegai,
the king's eunuch who oversees the women, and let him provide whatever cosmetics they desire. [4]Let the young woman
whom the king finds most attractive become queen in place
of Vashti." This seemed like a good idea to the king, so he
acted accordingly.

[5]Now there happened to be a Jewish man in Susa the citadel
whose name was Mordecai. He was the son of Jair, the son of
Shimei, the son of Kish, a Benjaminite, [6]who had been taken
into exile from Jerusalem with the captives who had been carried into exile with Jeconiah king of Judah, whom Nebuchadnezzar king of Babylon had taken into exile. [7]Now he was acting
as the guardian of Hadassah (that is, Esther), the daughter of
his uncle, for neither her father nor her mother was alive. This
young woman was very attractive and had a beautiful figure.
When her father and mother died, Mordecai had raised her as
if she were his own daughter.

[8]It so happened that when the king's edict and his law became known many young women were taken to Susa the citadel to be placed under the authority of Hegai. Esther also was
taken to the royal palace to be under the authority of Hegai,
who was overseeing the women. [9]This young woman pleased
him, and she found favor with him. He quickly provided her
with her cosmetics and her rations; he also provided her with
the seven specially chosen young women who were from the
palace. He then transferred her and her young women to the
best quarters in the harem.

[10]Now Esther had not disclosed her people or her lineage,
for Mordecai had instructed her not to do so. [11]And day after
day Mordecai used to walk back and forth in front of the court
of the harem in order to learn how Esther was doing and what
might happen to her.

[12]At the end of the twelve months that were required for
the women, when the turn of each young woman arrived to
go to King Ahasuerus—for in this way they had to fulfill their
time of cosmetic treatment: six months with oil of myrrh,
and six months with perfume and various ointments used by
women—[13]the woman would go to the king in the following

2:1–9 The worldly philosophers drive out an old passion by instilling a new one; they hammer out one nail by hammering in another. It was on this principle that the seven princes of Persia acted toward Ahasuerus, for they subdued his regret for Vashti by inducing him to love other maidens. But whereas they cured one fault by another fault and one sin by another sin, we must overcome our faults by learning to love the opposite virtues. "Turn away from evil," says the psalmist, "and do what is right. Strive for peace and promote it" (Ps 34:14).

JEROME (C. 342–420)
EXPLANATION ON THE BOOK OF ESTHER

way: Whatever she asked for would be provided for her to take
with her from the harem to the royal palace. 14In the evening
she went, and in the morning she returned to a separate part
of the harem, to the authority of Shaashgaz, the king's eunuch
who was overseeing the concubines. She would not go back
to the king unless the king was pleased with her and she was
requested by name.
15When it became the turn of Esther, daughter of Abihail,
the uncle of Mordecai (who had raised her as if she were his
own daughter), to go to the king, she did not request anything
except what Hegai the king's eunuch, who was overseer of the
women, had recommended. Yet Esther met with the approval
of all who saw her. 16Then Esther was taken to King Ahasuerus
at his royal residence in the tenth month (that is, the month of
Tebeth) in the seventh year of his reign. 17And the king loved
Esther more than all the other women, and she met with his
loving approval more than all the other young women. So he
placed the royal high turban on her head and appointed her
queen in place of Vashti. 18Then the king prepared a large banquet for all his officials and his servants—it was actually Esther's
banquet. He also set aside a holiday for the provinces, and he
provided for offerings at the king's expense.

MORDECAI LEARNS OF A PLOT AGAINST THE KING

19Now when the young women were being gathered again,
Mordecai was sitting at the king's gate. 20Esther was still not
divulging her lineage or her people, just as Mordecai had instructed her. Esther continued to do whatever Mordecai said,
just as she had done when he was raising her.
21In those days while Mordecai was sitting at the king's gate,
Bigthan and Teresh, two of the king's eunuchs who protected
the entrance, became angry and plotted to assassinate King
Ahasuerus. 22When Mordecai learned of the conspiracy, he
informed Queen Esther, and Esther told the king in Mordecai's
name. 23The king then had the matter investigated and, finding
it to be so, had the two conspirators hanged on a gallows. It was
then recorded in the daily chronicles in the king's presence.

HAMAN CONSPIRES TO DESTROY THE JEWS

3 Some time later King Ahasuerus promoted Haman the
son of Hammedatha, the Agagite, exalting him and setting
his position above that of all the officials who were with him.
2As a result, all the king's servants who were at the king's gate
were bowing and paying homage to Haman, for the king had
so commanded. However, Mordecai did not bow, nor did he
pay him homage.
3Then the servants of the king who were at the king's gate
asked Mordecai, "Why are you violating the king's commandment?" 4And after they had spoken to him day after day without
his paying any attention to them, they informed Haman to see
whether this attitude on Mordecai's part would be permitted.
Furthermore, he had disclosed to them that he was a Jew.
5When Haman saw that Mordecai was not bowing or paying
homage to him, he was filled with rage. 6But the thought of
striking out against Mordecai alone was repugnant to him, for
he had been informed of the identity of Mordecai's people. So
Haman sought to destroy all the Jews (that is, the people of
Mordecai) who were in all the kingdom of Ahasuerus.

3:1–15 Nothing else is symbolized by the arrogant Haman than the opulence of the powerful of this world who take advantage of the benefits conceded to them by divine mercy. They despise allowing their neighbors, who are given to them as companions by nature, to have as sharers of such grace. Therefore they are guilty of striving to transfer to themselves the honor and reverence that are rightly due to God alone. And so they pursue with hatred all those who do not want to act according to such behavior or comply with it. They persecute them with afflictions and endeavor to put them to death.

RABANUS MAURUS
(C. 780–856)
EXPLANATION ON THE BOOK OF ESTHER

7In the first month (that is, the month of Nisan), in the twelfth year of King Ahasuerus' reign, *pur* (that is, the lot) was cast before Haman in order to determine a day and a month. It turned out to be the twelfth month (that is, the month of Adar).

8Then Haman said to King Ahasuerus, "There is a particular people that is dispersed and spread among the inhabitants throughout all the provinces of your kingdom whose laws differ from those of all other peoples. Furthermore, they do not observe the king's laws. It is not appropriate for the king to provide a haven for them. 9If the king is so inclined, let an edict be issued to destroy them. I will pay 10,000 talents of silver to be conveyed to the king's treasuries for the officials who carry out this business."

10So the king removed his signet ring from his hand and gave it to Haman the son of Hammedatha, the Agagite, who was hostile toward the Jews. 11The king replied to Haman, "Keep your money, and do with those people whatever you wish."

12So the royal scribes were summoned in the first month, on the thirteenth day of the month. Everything Haman commanded was written to the king's satraps and governors who were in every province and to the officials of every people, province by province according to its script and people by people according to their language. In the name of King Ahasuerus it was written and sealed with the king's signet ring. 13Letters were sent by the runners to all the king's provinces stating that they should destroy, kill, and annihilate all the Jews, from youth to elderly, both women and children, on a particular day, namely the thirteenth day of the twelfth month (that is, the month of Adar), and to loot and plunder their possessions. 14A copy of this edict was to be presented as law throughout every province; it was to be made known to all the inhabitants, so that they would be prepared for this day. 15The messengers scurried forth with the king's order. The edict was issued in Susa the citadel. While the king and Haman sat down to drink, the city of Susa was in an uproar.

ESTHER DECIDES TO RISK EVERYTHING IN ORDER TO HELP HER PEOPLE

4 Now when Mordecai became aware of all that had been done, he tore his garments and put on sackcloth and ashes. He went out into the city, crying out in a loud and bitter voice. 2But he went no farther than the king's gate, for no one was permitted to enter the king's gate clothed in sackcloth. 3Throughout each and every province where the king's edict and law were announced there was considerable mourning among the Jews, along with fasting, weeping, and sorrow. Sackcloth and ashes were characteristic of many. 4When Esther's female attendants and her eunuchs came and informed her about Mordecai's behavior, the queen was overcome with anguish. Although she sent garments for Mordecai to put on so that he could remove his sackcloth, he would not accept them. 5So Esther called for Hathach, one of the king's eunuchs who had been placed at her service, and instructed him to find out the cause and reason for Mordecai's behavior. 6So Hathach went to Mordecai at the plaza of the city in front of the king's gate. 7Then Mordecai related to him everything that had happened to him, even the specific amount of money that Haman had offered to pay to the king's treasuries for the Jews to be destroyed. 8He also gave him a written copy of the law that had been disseminated in

4:1–17 Many women, fortified by the grace of God, have accomplished many heroic actions. To no less danger did Esther, who was perfect in faith, expose herself in order to save the twelve tribes of Israel that were to be destroyed. For by fasting and humiliation, she begged the all-seeing Master of the ages, and he, seeing the meekness of her soul, rescued the people for whose sake she had faced danger.

CLEMENT OF ROME (D. 99)
FIRST CLEMENT

Susa for their destruction so that he could show it to Esther and
talk to her about it. He also gave instructions that she should
go to the king to implore him and petition him on behalf of
her people. 9So Hathach returned and related Mordecai's instructions to Esther.
10Then Esther replied to Hathach with instructions for Mordecai: 11"All the servants of the king and the people of the king's
provinces know that there is only one law applicable to any
man or woman who comes uninvited to the king in the inner
court—that person will be put to death, unless the king extends
to him the gold scepter, permitting him to be spared. Now I
have not been invited to come to the king for some 30 days."
12When Esther's reply was conveyed to Mordecai, 13he said
to take back this answer to Esther: "Don't imagine that because
you are part of the king's household you will be the one Jew
who will escape. 14If you keep quiet at this time, liberation and
protection for the Jews will appear from another source, while
you and your father's household perish. It may very well be that
you have achieved royal status for such a time as this!"
15Then Esther sent this reply to Mordecai: 16"Go, assemble
all the Jews who are found in Susa, and fast on my behalf. Don't
eat and don't drink for three days, night or day. My female attendants and I will also fast in the same way. Afterward I will go
to the king, even though it violates the law. If I perish, I perish."
17So Mordecai set out to do everything that Esther had instructed him.

ESTHER APPEALS TO THE KING FOR HELP

5 It so happened that on the third day Esther put on her royal
attire and stood in the inner court of the palace, opposite
the king's quarters. The king was sitting on his royal throne in
the palace, opposite the entrance. 2When the king saw Queen
Esther standing in the court, she met with his approval. The
king extended to Esther the gold scepter that was in his hand,
and Esther approached and touched the end of the scepter.
3The king said to her, "What is on your mind, Queen Esther?
What is your request? Even as much as half the kingdom will
be given to you."
4Esther replied, "If the king is so inclined, let the king and
Haman come today to the banquet that I have prepared for the
king." 5The king replied, "Find Haman quickly so that we can
do as Esther requests."
So the king and Haman went to the banquet that Esther
had prepared. 6While at the banquet of wine, the king said to
Esther, "What is your request? It shall be given to you. What
is your petition? Ask for as much as half the kingdom, and it
shall be done."
7Esther responded, "My request and my petition is this: 8If
I have found favor in the king's sight and if the king is inclined
to grant my request and approve my petition, let the king and
Haman come tomorrow to the banquet that I will prepare for
them. At that time I will do as the king wishes."

HAMAN EXPRESSES HIS HATRED OF MORDECAI

9Now Haman went forth that day pleased and very much encouraged. But when Haman saw Mordecai at the king's gate,
and he did not rise or tremble in his presence, Haman was filled
with rage toward Mordecai. 10But Haman restrained himself
and went on to his home.

5:1–14 Esther, having had power with God and prevailing, like Jacob, had power with men too. He who will lose his life for God shall save it or find it in a better life. The king encouraged her. Let us from this be encouraged to pray always to our God and not to faint. Esther came to a proud, imperious man, but we come to the God of love and grace. She was not called, but we are; the Spirit says, *Come*, and the Bride says, *Come*. She had a law against her; we have a promise, many a promise, in favor of us. Ask, and it shall be given you. She had no friend to go with her or to plead for her; on the contrary, he who was then the king's favorite was her enemy. But we have an Advocate with the Father in whom he is well pleased. Let us therefore come boldly to the throne of grace. God put it into Esther's heart to delay her petition a day longer; she knew not, but God did, what was to happen on that very night.

MATTHEW HENRY (1662–1714)
COMMENTARY ON THE WHOLE BIBLE

He then sent for his friends to join him, along with his wife
Zeresh. [11]Haman then recounted to them his fabulous wealth,
his many sons, and how the king had magnified him and exalted
him over the king's other officials and servants. [12]Haman said,
"Furthermore, Queen Esther invited only me to accompany the
king to the banquet that she prepared. And also tomorrow I am
invited along with the king. [13]Yet all this fails to satisfy me so
long as I have to see Mordecai the Jew sitting at the king's gate."
[14]Haman's wife Zeresh and all his friends said to him, "Have
a gallows 75 feet high built, and in the morning tell the king
that Mordecai should be hanged on it. Then go with the king
to the banquet contented."

It seemed like a good idea to Haman, so he had the gallows built.

THE TURNING POINT: THE KING HONORS MORDECAI

6 Throughout that night the king was unable to sleep, so he
asked for the book containing the historical records to be
brought. As the records were being read in the king's presence,
[2]it was found written that Mordecai had disclosed that Bigthana
and Teresh, two of the king's eunuchs who guarded the entrance, had plotted to assassinate King Ahasuerus.
[3]The king asked, "What great honor was bestowed on Mordecai because of this?" The king's attendants who served him
responded, "Not a thing was done for him."
[4]Then the king said, "Who is that in the courtyard?" Now Haman had come to the outer courtyard of the palace to suggest that
the king hang Mordecai on the gallows that he had constructed
for him. [5]The king's attendants said to him, "It is Haman who is
standing in the courtyard." The king said, "Let him enter."
[6]So Haman came in, and the king said to him, "What should
be done for the man whom the king wishes to honor?" Haman
thought to himself, "Who is it that the king would want to honor
more than me?" [7]So Haman said to the king, "For the man whom
the king wishes to honor, [8]let them bring royal attire which the
king himself has worn and a horse on which the king himself has
ridden—one bearing the royal insignia. [9]Then let this clothing and
this horse be given to one of the king's noble officials. Let him then
clothe the man whom the king wishes to honor, and let him lead
him about through the plaza of the city on the horse, calling before
him, 'So shall it be done to the man whom the king wishes to honor!'"
[10]The king then said to Haman, "Go quickly! Take the clothing
and the horse, just as you have described, and do as you just
indicated to Mordecai the Jew, who sits at the king's gate. Don't
neglect a single thing of all that you have said."
[11]So Haman took the clothing and the horse, and he clothed
Mordecai. He led him about on the horse throughout the plaza
of the city, calling before him, "So shall it be done to the man
whom the king wishes to honor!"
[12]Then Mordecai again sat at the king's gate, while Haman
hurried away to his home, mournful and with a veil over his
head. [13]Haman then related to his wife Zeresh and to all his
friends everything that had happened to him. These wise men,
along with his wife Zeresh, said to him, "If indeed this Mordecai before whom you have begun to fall is Jewish, you will not
prevail against him. No, you will surely fall before him!"
[14]While they were still speaking with him, the king's eunuchs
arrived. They quickly brought Haman to the banquet that Esther had prepared.

6:1–14 **Sleep was removed from the eyes of Ahasuerus, whom the Seventy call Artaxerxes, that he might turn over the memoirs of his faithful ministers and come on Mordecai, by whose evidence he was delivered from a conspiracy; and that thus Esther might be more acceptable and the whole people of the Jews escape imminent death. There is no doubt that the mighty sovereign to whom belonged the whole East, from India to the north and to Ethiopia, after feasting sumptuously on delicacies gathered from every part of the world would have desired to sleep, to take his rest, and to gratify his free choice of sleep had not the Lord, the provider of all good things, hindered the course of nature so that in defiance of nature the tyrant's cruelty might be overcome.**

JEROME **(C. 342–420)**
AGAINST THE PELAGIANS

7:1–10 Haman's appeal to Queen Esther was considered by King Ahasuerus to be an act of deceit. Indeed, when the day of judgment is about to come, the petition of the wicked is no longer a prayer but a source of irritation. Therefore the request is made for the oppression of those who previously oppressed the humble because the time of retribution has come. Haman was forced to support the cross that he had prepared for Mordecai.

RABANUS MAURUS
(C. 780–856)
EXPLANATION ON THE BOOK OF ESTHER

THE KING HAS HAMAN EXECUTED

7 So the king and Haman came to dine with Queen Esther. [2]On the second day of the banquet of wine the king asked Esther, "What is your request, Queen Esther? It shall be granted to you. And what is your petition? Ask for up to half the kingdom, and it shall be done."

[3]Queen Esther replied, "If I have met with your approval, O king, and if the king is so inclined, grant me my life as my request, and my people as my petition. [4]For we have been sold—both I and my people—to destruction and to slaughter and to annihilation. If we had simply been sold as male and female slaves, I would have remained silent, for such distress would not have been sufficient for troubling the king."

[5]Then King Ahasuerus responded to Queen Esther, "Who is this individual? Where is this person to be found who is presumptuous enough to act in this way?"

[6]Esther replied, "The oppressor and enemy is this evil Haman!"

Then Haman became terrified in the presence of the king and queen. [7]In rage the king arose from the banquet of wine and withdrew to the palace garden. Meanwhile, Haman stood to beg Queen Esther for his life, for he realized that the king had now determined a catastrophic end for him.

[8]When the king returned from the palace garden to the banquet of wine, Haman was throwing himself down on the couch where Esther was lying. The king exclaimed, "Will he also attempt to rape the queen while I am still in the building?"

As these words left the king's mouth, they covered Haman's face. [9]Harbona, one of the king's eunuchs, said, "Indeed, there is the gallows that Haman made for Mordecai, who spoke out on the king's behalf. It stands near Haman's home and is 75 feet high."

The king said, "Hang him on it!" [10]So they hanged Haman on the very gallows that he had prepared for Mordecai. The king's rage then abated.

8:1–17 The fact that Esther fell at the feet of the king and entreated him for the salvation of the people plainly symbolizes the holy church that humbly implores the almighty Lord every day for the rescue of her children through the faith and the mystery of the incarnation of the only begotten Son, so that the arrogance of her enemies may be restrained by the Lord's grace, and the innocence of the faithful may be freed from the clutches of the wicked. The heavenly king held out his golden scepter to the pleading queen because he abundantly bestowed the clemency of his mercy upon her. She asked that the old decree of the most wicked Haman be changed into a new decree. Indeed this is the interest of the true queen, namely that any sect that is in error, any hostile plot that the ancient enemy prepares through his ministers for the extinction of the people of God, may be repelled and destroyed through the saving documents of the gospel.

RABANUS MAURUS
(C. 780–856)
EXPLANATION ON THE BOOK OF ESTHER

THE KING ACTS TO PROTECT THE JEWS

8 On that same day King Ahasuerus gave the estate of Haman, that adversary of the Jews, to Queen Esther. Now Mordecai had come before the king, for Esther had revealed how he was related to her. [2]The king then removed his signet ring (the very one he had taken back from Haman) and gave it to Mordecai. And Esther designated Mordecai to be in charge of Haman's estate.

[3]Then Esther again spoke with the king, falling at his feet. She wept and begged him for mercy that he might nullify the evil of Haman the Agagite and the plot that he had intended against the Jews. [4]When the king extended to Esther the gold scepter, she arose and stood before the king.

[5]She said, "If the king is so inclined, and if I have met with his approval, and if the matter is agreeable to the king, and if I am attractive to him, let an edict be written rescinding those recorded intentions of Haman the son of Hammedatha, the Agagite, which he wrote in order to destroy the Jews who are throughout all the king's provinces. [6]For how can I watch the calamity that will befall my people, and how can I watch the destruction of my relatives?"

[7]King Ahasuerus replied to Queen Esther and to Mordecai the Jew, "Look, I have already given Haman's estate to Esther, and he has been hanged on the gallows because he took hostile

action against the Jews. 8Now write in the king's name whatever in your opinion is appropriate concerning the Jews and
seal it with the king's signet ring. Any decree that is written in
the king's name and sealed with the king's signet ring cannot
be rescinded."
9The king's scribes were quickly summoned—in the third
month (that is, the month of Sivan), on the twenty-third day.
They wrote out everything that Mordecai instructed to the
Jews, and to the satraps, and the governors, and the officials of
the provinces all the way from India to Ethiopia—127 provinces
in all—to each province in its own script and to each people
in their own language, and to the Jews according to their own
script and their own language. 10Mordecai wrote in the name
of King Ahasuerus and sealed it with the king's signet ring. He
then sent letters by couriers, who rode royal horses that were
very swift.
11The king thereby allowed the Jews who were in every city
to assemble and to stand up for themselves—to destroy, to kill,
and to annihilate any army of whatever people or province
that should become their adversaries, including their wom-
en and children, and to confiscate their property. 12This was
to take place on a certain day throughout all the provinces of
King Ahasuerus—namely, on the thirteenth day of the twelfth
month (that is, the month of Adar). 13A copy of the edict was to
be presented as law throughout each and every province and
made known to all peoples, so that the Jews might be prepared
on that day to avenge themselves on their enemies.
14The couriers who were riding the royal horses went forth
with the king's edict without delay. And the law was presented
in Susa the citadel as well.
15Now Mordecai went out from the king's presence in blue
and white royal attire, with a large golden crown and a purple
linen mantle. The city of Susa shouted with joy. 16For the Jews
there was radiant happiness and joyous honor. 17Throughout
every province and throughout every city where the king's edict
and his law arrived, the Jews experienced happiness and joy,
banquets and holidays. Many of the resident peoples pretended
to be Jews, because the fear of the Jews had overcome them.

THE JEWS PREVAIL OVER THEIR ENEMIES

9 In the twelfth month (that is, the month of Adar), on its
thirteenth day, the edict of the king and his law were to be
executed. It was on this day that the enemies of the Jews had
supposed that they would gain power over them. But contrary
to expectations, the Jews gained power over their enemies.
2The Jews assembled themselves in their cities throughout
all the provinces of King Ahasuerus to strike out against those
who were seeking their harm. No one was able to stand before
them, for dread of them fell on all the peoples. 3All the officials
of the provinces, the satraps, the governors, and those who
performed the king's business were assisting the Jews, for the
dread of Mordecai had fallen on them. 4Mordecai was of high
rank in the king's palace, and word about him was spreading
throughout all the provinces. His influence continued to become greater and greater.
5The Jews struck all their enemies with the sword, bringing
death and destruction, and they did as they pleased with their
enemies. 6In Susa the citadel the Jews killed and destroyed
500 men. 7In addition, they also killed Parshandatha, Dalphon,

Aspatha, [8]Poratha, Adalia, Aridatha, [9]Parmashta, Arisai, Aridai,
and Vaizatha, [10]the 10 sons of Haman son of Hammedatha, the
enemy of the Jews. But they did not confiscate their property.
[11]On that same day the number of those killed in Susa the
citadel was brought to the king's attention. [12]Then the king
said to Queen Esther, "In Susa the citadel the Jews have killed
and destroyed 500 men and the 10 sons of Haman. What then
have they done in the rest of the king's provinces? What is your
request? It shall be given to you. What other petition do you
have? It shall be done."
[13]Esther replied, "If the king is so inclined, let the Jews who
are in Susa be permitted to act tomorrow also according to
today's law, and let them hang the 10 sons of Haman on the
gallows."
[14]So the king issued orders for this to be done. A law was
passed in Susa, and the ten sons of Haman were hanged. [15]The
Jews who were in Susa then assembled on the fourteenth day of
the month of Adar, and they killed 300 men in Susa. But they
did not confiscate their property.
[16]The rest of the Jews who were throughout the provinces
of the king assembled in order to stand up for themselves and
to have rest from their enemies. They killed 75,000 of their
adversaries, but they did not confiscate their property. [17]All
this happened on the thirteenth day of the month of Adar.
They then rested on the fourteenth day and made it a day for
banqueting and happiness.

THE ORIGINS OF THE FEAST OF PURIM

[18]But the Jews who were in Susa assembled on the thirteenth
and fourteenth days, and rested on the fifteenth, making it a
day for banqueting and happiness. [19]This is why the Jews who
are in the rural country—those who live in rural villages—set
aside the fourteenth day of the month of Adar for happiness,
banqueting, a holiday, and sending gifts to one another.
[20]Mordecai wrote these matters down and sent letters to
all the Jews who were throughout all the provinces of King
Ahasuerus, both near and far, [21]to have them observe the fourteenth and the fifteenth days of the month of Adar each year
[22]as the time when the Jews gave themselves rest from their
enemies—the month when their trouble was turned to happiness and their mourning to a holiday. These were to be days
of banqueting, happiness, sending gifts to one another, and
providing for the poor.
[23]So the Jews committed themselves to continuing what
they had begun to do and to what Mordecai had written to
them. [24]For Haman the son of Hammedatha, the Agagite, the
enemy of all the Jews, had devised plans against the Jews to
destroy them. He had cast *pur* (that is, the lot) in order to afflict
and destroy them. [25]But when the matter came to the king's
attention, the king gave written orders that Haman's evil intentions that he had devised against the Jews should fall on his
own head. He and his sons were hanged on the gallows. [26]For
this reason these days are known as *Purim,* after the name of
pur. Therefore, because of the account found in this letter and
what they had faced in this regard and what had happened to
them, [27]the Jews established as binding on themselves, their
descendants, and all who joined their company that they should
observe these two days without fail, just as written and at the
appropriate time on an annual basis. [28]These days were to be

9:18–25 The Israelites, coming out of affliction to a state of rest, sang a song of praise for the victory as they kept the feast. And in the time of Esther the people kept a feast to the Lord because they had been delivered from a deadly decree. They called a feast, thanking and praising the Lord because he had changed the situation for them. Therefore let us keep our promises to the Lord, confess our sins, and keep the feast to him—in behavior, moral conduct, and way of life. Let us keep it by praising the Lord, who has disciplined us so lightly but has never failed us nor forsaken us nor stopped speaking to us.

ATHANASIUS (C. 296–373)
FESTAL LETTERS

remembered and to be celebrated in every generation and in every family, every province, and every city. The Jews were not to fail to observe these days of Purim; the remembrance of them was not to cease among their descendants.
29 So Queen Esther, the daughter of Abihail, and Mordecai the Jew wrote with full authority to confirm this second letter about
Purim. 30 Letters were sent to all the Jews in the 127 provinces of
the empire of Ahasuerus—words of true peace—31 to establish
these days of Purim in their proper times, just as Mordecai the Jew and Queen Esther had established, and just as they had established both for themselves and their descendants,
matters pertaining to fasting and lamentation. 32 Esther's com-
mand established these matters of Purim, and the matter was officially recorded.

MORDECAI'S FAME INCREASES

10 King Ahasuerus then imposed forced labor on the land
and on the coastlands of the sea. 2 Now all the actions car-
ried out under his authority and his great achievements, along with an exact statement concerning the greatness of Mordecai, whom the king promoted, are they not written in the Book of
the Chronicles of the Kings of Media and Persia? 3 Mordecai the
Jew was second only to King Ahasuerus. He was the highest-ranking Jew, and he was admired by his numerous relatives. He worked enthusiastically for the good of his people and was an advocate for the welfare of all his descendants.

10:1–3 Mordecai was a true patriot, and therefore being exalted to the highest position under Ahasuerus, he used his eminence to promote the prosperity of Israel. In this he was a type of Jesus who, upon his throne of glory, seeks not his own but spends his power for his people. It were well if every Christian would be a Mordecai to the church, striving according to his ability for its prosperity . . . It is at once the most Christlike and the happiest course for believers to cease from living for themselves. He who blesses others cannot fail to be blessed himself.

CHARLES SPURGEON
(1834–1892)
MORNING AND EVENING

AUTHOR	AUDIENCE	DATE	PURPOSE	THEMES
Unknown	God's people	Unknown, though Job himself probably lived during the patriarchal period	The book of Job explores the nature of human suffering and its connection to divine justice, provoking us to consider God's sovereignty over our lives and trust him without exception.	Human suffering; God's character; and God's sovereignty

The question "Why do bad things happen to good, godly people?" is one with which every generation of saints must wrestle. While the book of Job does not offer a concrete answer to this complex question, it does offer direction for our wrestling. It tells the story of Job, a righteous man who feared God yet experienced tremendous calamity—the kind of loss many of us fear and few of us experience. The book shows how Job engaged the struggle, even questioning God and his sovereign plan. The book is wisdom literature, for it explores the nature of human suffering and its connection to divine justice and provokes us to consider God's sovereignty over our lives and trust him no matter what. Church teachers from the early fathers through the Reformation to today have emphasized Job's piety as a model for the Christian life.

Job was a man who seemed to be doing everything right. After all, Job "was blameless and upright, one who feared God and turned away from evil" (1:1), and he appeared to be blessed by God for his piety, so much so that he was considered "the greatest of all the people in the east" (1:3). Then suddenly all of his possessions were taken away, stolen, or slaughtered; his ten children died, killed by a windstorm; and his own body was afflicted by a crippling ailment. And the Lord allowed it all, granting Satan permission to bring these calamities to his servant. Yet through it all, "Job did not sin, nor did he charge God with moral impropriety" (1:22). Even after his own wife urged him to "curse God, and die!" (2:9), he did not sin.

Job's response is a noteworthy one, for often people accuse God of neglect or blame him for their troubles. Instead, as one early church teacher said, initially Job "was pure from sins committed with his tongue or in his thoughts, and he praised God by means of words in accordance with his thoughts." Further, "Job does not accuse the will of God or scorn the economy of the Creator, and he does not perceive insanity in the events that had occurred. He did not believe that the righteous are abandoned into the hands of sinners." Hesychius of Jerusalem's comments reveal important truths about how we ourselves should respond to our own suffering—we ought to join Job in praise and worship. Although Job does address God with questions about his suffering, even appearing a bit too confrontational at times, he eventually recognizes that he "declared without understanding things too wonderful for me to know" (42:3).

"Another great doctrine of the faith, particularly set forth in the book of Job," Matthew Henry explained, "is that of Providence. It is plain from this history that the Lord watched over his servant Job with the affection of a wise and loving Father." *Theodicy* is a term used to describe the apparent contradiction between God's goodness and God's sovereignty in light of human suffering. The Bible doesn't neatly reconcile this apparent conflict. Job's friends tried, accusing Job of egregious sin against God as if there were a tit-for-tat relationship between a sin and a curse, a righteous deed and a blessing.

Job himself can't reconcile the contradiction. Not only does he question God's motives but he also accuses God of perverting justice. He wants to speak with God directly and argue his case. While this sort of honesty with God is, in one sense, admirable and something to be emulated, there is another sense in which Job is essentially putting God on trial. In turn God responds:

> Who is this who darkens counsel with words without knowledge? Get ready for a difficult task like a man; I will question you and you will inform me . . . Will the one who contends with the Almighty correct him? Let the person who accuses God give him an answer! . . . Would you indeed annul my justice? Would you declare me guilty so that you might be right? Do you have an arm as powerful as God's? (38:2–3; 40:2, 8–9).

God rightly confronts questions about his goodness with a series of questions designed to reveal the depths of his sovereignty. "He shows that he does everything with wisdom and intelligence," Chrysostom explained, "and therefore it would have been inconsistent with God, who did so many things with wisdom and intelligence, to neglect the human beings for whom he has created everything, even when they are wretched as in this case." Job himself finally understood this, recognizing the answer to human suffering is God's sovereignty: "I know that you can do all things; no purpose of yours can be thwarted" (42:2).

John Wesley wrote of Job,

> We have here much of God, his infinite perfections, and his government both of the world and of the church . . . Here is what may enlighten our understandings and acquaint us with the deep things of God. And this divine light may bring into the soul a divine fire, which will kindle and inflame devout affections on which wings we may soar upwards, until we enter into the holiest.

1:1–12 "Is it for nothing that Job fears God?" This was the wicked question of Satan concerning that upright man of old, but there are many in the present day concerning whom it might be asked with justice, for they love God after a fashion because he prospers them; but if things went ill with them, they would give up all their boasted faith in God. Their love is the love of the table, not of the host; a love to the cupboard, not to the master of the house. As for true Christians, they expect to have their reward in the next life and to endure hardness in this. Fear not, but rather rejoice that such fruitful times are in store for you, for in them you will be weaned from earth and made suitable for heaven.

CHARLES SPURGEON
(1834–1892)
MORNING AND EVENING

I. THE PROLOGUE (1:1–2:13)

JOB'S GOOD LIFE

1 There was a man in the land of Uz whose name was Job. And that man was blameless and upright, one who feared God and turned away from evil. 2 Seven sons and three daughters were born to him. 3 His possessions included 7,000 sheep, 3,000 camels, 500 yoke of oxen, and 500 female donkeys; in addition he had a very great household. Thus he was the greatest of all the people in the east.

4 Now his sons used to go and hold a feast in the house of each one in turn, and they would send and invite their three sisters to eat and to drink with them. 5 When the days of their feasting were finished, Job would send for them and sanctify them; he would get up early in the morning and offer burnt offerings according to the number of them all. For Job thought, "Perhaps my children have sinned and cursed God in their hearts." This was Job's customary practice.

SATAN'S ACCUSATION OF JOB

6 Now the day came when the sons of God came to present themselves before the LORD—and Satan also arrived among them. 7 The LORD said to Satan, "Where have you come from?" And Satan answered the LORD, "From roving about on the earth, and from walking back and forth across it." 8 So the LORD said to Satan, "Have you considered my servant Job? There is no one like him on the earth, a blameless and upright man, one who fears God and turns away from evil."

9 Then Satan answered the LORD, "Is it for nothing that Job fears God? 10 Have you not made a hedge around him and his household and all that he has on every side? You have blessed the work of his hands, and his livestock have increased in the land. 11 But extend your hand and strike everything he has, and he will no doubt curse you to your face!"

12 So the LORD said to Satan, "All right then, everything he has is in your power. Only do not extend your hand against the man himself!" So Satan went out from the presence of the LORD.

JOB'S INTEGRITY IN ADVERSITY

13 Now the day came when Job's sons and daughters were eating and drinking wine in their oldest brother's house, 14 and a messenger came to Job, saying, "The oxen were plowing and the donkeys were grazing beside them, 15 and the Sabeans swooped down and carried them all away, and they killed the servants with the sword! And I—only I alone—escaped to tell you!"

16 While this one was still speaking, another messenger arrived and said, "The fire of God has fallen from heaven and has burned up the sheep and the servants—it has consumed them! And I—only I alone—escaped to tell you!"

17 While this one was still speaking another messenger arrived and said, "The Chaldeans formed three bands and made a raid on the camels and carried them all away, and they killed the servants with the sword! And I—only I alone—escaped to tell you!"

18 While this one was still speaking another messenger arrived and said, "Your sons and your daughters were eating and drinking wine in their oldest brother's house, 19 and suddenly a great wind swept across the wilderness and struck the four corners of the house, and it fell on the young people, and they died! And I—only I alone—escaped to tell you!"

[20]Then Job got up and tore his robe. He shaved his head, and
then he threw himself down with his face to the ground. [21]He
said, "Naked I came from my mother's womb, and naked I will
return there. The LORD gives, and the LORD takes away. May
the name of the LORD be blessed!" [22]In all this Job did not sin,
nor did he charge God with moral impropriety.

SATAN'S ADDITIONAL CHARGE

2 Again the day came when the sons of God came to present
themselves before the LORD, and Satan also arrived among
them to present himself before the LORD. [2]And the LORD said
to Satan, "Where have you come from?" Satan answered the
LORD, "From roving about on the earth, and from walking back
and forth across it." [3]Then the LORD said to Satan, "Have you
considered my servant Job? For there is no one like him on the
earth, a pure and upright man, one who fears God and turns
away from evil. And he still holds firmly to his integrity, so that
you stirred me up to destroy him without reason."
[4]But Satan answered the LORD, "Skin for skin! Indeed, a man
will give up all that he has to save his life. [5]But extend your
hand and strike his bone and his flesh, and he will no doubt
curse you to your face!"
[6]So the LORD said to Satan, "All right, he is in your power;
only preserve his life."

JOB'S INTEGRITY IN SUFFERING

[7]So Satan went out from the presence of the LORD, and he
afflicted Job with a malignant ulcer from the soles of his feet
to the top of his head. [8]Job took a shard of broken pottery to
scrape himself with while he was sitting among the ashes.
[9]Then his wife said to him, "Are you still holding firmly to
your integrity? Curse God, and die!" [10]But he replied, "You're
talking like one of the godless women would do! Should we
receive what is good from God, and not also receive what is
evil?" In all this Job did not sin by what he said.

THE VISIT OF JOB'S FRIENDS

[11]When Job's three friends heard about all this calamity that had
happened to him, each of them came from his own country—
Eliphaz the Temanite, Bildad the Shuhite, and Zophar the
Naamathite. They met together to come to show sympathy
for him and to console him. [12]But when they gazed intently
from a distance but did not recognize him, they began to weep
loudly. Each of them tore his robes, and they threw dust into
the air over their heads. [13]Then they sat down with him on the
ground for seven days and seven nights, yet no one spoke a word
to him, for they saw that his pain was very great.

2:1–13 The present season is one for tears, not for words; for lamentation, not for discourse; for prayer, not for preaching. For even as the devil then killed violently the flocks, and herds, and all the substance of the just man, so now has he raged against this whole city. But then, as well as now, God permitted it; then indeed that he might make the just man more illustrious by the greatness of his trials, and now he may make us more sober-minded by the extremity of this tribulation.

CHRYSOSTOM (C. 347–407)
HOMILIES ON STATUTES

II. JOB'S DIALOGUE WITH HIS FRIENDS (3:1–27:23)

JOB REGRETS HIS BIRTH

3 After this Job opened his mouth and cursed the day he was
born. [2]Job spoke up and said:

3 "Let the day on which I was born perish,
and the night that said,
'A man has been conceived!'
4 That day—let it be darkness;
let not God on high regard it,
nor let light shine on it!

3:1–26 Human beings are apt to curse and grumble against the misfortunes that befall them. God, in fact, does not expect insensitivity on our part. But when we are in tribulations and suffer those afflictions that strike us, God expects that we not abandon ourselves to blasphemous words but use those that demonstrate our grief and express the seriousness of our misery.

ISHODAD OF MERV (850)
COMMENTARY ON JOB

5 Let darkness and the deepest shadow claim it;
let a cloud settle on it;
let whatever blackens the day terrify it.
6 That night—let darkness seize it;
let it not be included among the days of the year;
let it not enter among the number of the months!
7 Indeed, let that night be barren;
let no shout of joy penetrate it!
8 Let those who curse the day curse it—
those who are prepared to rouse Leviathan.
9 Let its morning stars be darkened;
let it wait for daylight but find none,
nor let it see the first rays of dawn,
10 because it did not shut the doors of my mother's womb
on me,
nor did it hide trouble from my eyes.

JOB WISHES HE HAD DIED AT BIRTH

11 "Why did I not die at birth,
and why did I not expire
as I came out of the womb?
12 Why did the knees welcome me,
and why were there two breasts
that I might nurse at them?
13 For now I would be lying down
and would be quiet,
I would be asleep and then at peace
14 with kings and counselors of the earth
who built for themselves places now desolate,
15 or with princes who possessed gold,
who filled their palaces with silver.
16 Or why was I not buried
like a stillborn infant,
like infants who have never seen the light?
17 There the wicked cease from turmoil,
and there the weary are at rest.
18 There the prisoners relax together;
they do not hear the voice of the oppressor.
19 Small and great are there,
and the slave is free from his master.

LONGING FOR DEATH

20 "Why does God give light to one who is in misery,
and life to those whose soul is bitter,
21 to those who wait for death that does not come,
and search for it
more than for hidden treasures,
22 who rejoice even to jubilation,
and are exultant when they find the grave?
23 Why is light given to a man
whose way is hidden,
and whom God has hedged in?
24 For my sighing comes in place of my food,
and my groanings flow forth like water.
25 For the very thing I dreaded has happened
to me,
and what I feared has come upon me.
26 I have no ease; I have no quietness;
I cannot rest; turmoil has come upon me."

ELIPHAZ BEGINS TO SPEAK

4 Then Eliphaz the Temanite answered:
2 "If someone should attempt a word with you,
will you be impatient?
But who can refrain from speaking?
3 Look, you have instructed many;
you have strengthened feeble hands.
4 Your words have supported those
who stumbled,
and you have strengthened the knees
that gave way.
5 But now the same thing comes to you,
and you are discouraged;
it strikes you,
and you are terrified.
6 Is not your piety your confidence,
and your blameless ways your hope?
7 Call to mind now:
Who, being innocent, ever perished?
And where were upright people ever destroyed?
8 Even as I have seen, those who plow iniquity
and those who sow trouble reap the same.
9 By the breath of God they perish,
and by the blast of his anger they are consumed.
10 There is the roaring of the lion
and the growling of the young lion,
but the teeth of the young lions are broken.
11 The mighty lion perishes for lack of prey,
and the cubs of the lioness are scattered.

UNGODLY COMPLAINERS PROVOKE GOD'S WRATH

12 "Now a word was stealthily brought to me,
and my ear caught a whisper of it.
13 In the troubling thoughts of the dreams in the night
when a deep sleep falls on men,
14 dread gripped me and trembling,
which made all my bones shake.
15 Then a breath of air passes by my face;
it makes the hair of my flesh stand up.
16 It stands still,
but I cannot recognize its appearance;
an image is before my eyes,
and I hear a murmuring voice:
17 'Is a mortal man righteous before God?
Or a man pure before his Creator?
18 If God puts no trust in his servants
and attributes folly to his angels,
19 how much more to those who live in houses of clay,
whose foundation is in the dust,
who are crushed like a moth?
20 They are destroyed between morning and evening;
they perish forever without anyone regarding it.
21 Is not their excess wealth taken away from them?
They die, yet without attaining wisdom.'

5 "Call now! Is there anyone who will answer you?
To which of the holy ones will you turn?
2 For wrath kills the foolish person,

4:1–21 They are genuinely righteous who produce the love of the heavenly country to meet all the ills of the present life. For all who fear enduring ills in this life are clearly not righteous people. They have forgotten they suffer for the sake of eternal blessings. But Eliphaz does not take into account either that the righteous are cut off or that the innocent perish here. For people often serve God not in the hope of heavenly glory but for an earthly recompense. They make a fiction in their own head of that which they are seeking.

GREGORY THE GREAT
(C. 540–604)
MORALS ON THE BOOK OF JOB

5:1–16 Look! This is what God does so the weak may hope for happiness and the powerful may not become proud. In fact Eliphaz said, "Call now! Is there anyone who will answer you?" so that you may not think that there are things that escape Providence. Eliphaz dedicates the beginning of his speech to the defeat of Job. Indeed, God is accustomed to exalt the weak, to bring down the powerful, and to confound the cunning. Now draw your own conclusions.

CHRYSOSTOM **(C. 347–407)**
COMMENTARY ON JOB

and anger slays the silly one.
3 I myself have seen the fool taking root,
but suddenly I cursed his place of residence.
4 His children are far from safety,
and they are crushed at the place where judgment is
rendered,
nor is there anyone to deliver them.
5 The hungry eat up his harvest,
and take it even from behind the thorns,
and the thirsty pant for their wealth.
6 For evil does not come up from the dust,
nor does trouble spring up from the ground,
7 but people are born to trouble,
as surely as the sparks fly upward.

BLESSINGS FOR THE ONE WHO SEEKS GOD

8 "But as for me, I would seek God,
and to God I would set forth my case.
9 He does great and unsearchable things,
marvelous things without number;
10 he gives rain on the earth,
and sends water on the fields;
11 he sets the lowly on high,
that those who mourn are raised to safety.
12 He frustrates the plans of the crafty
so that their hands cannot accomplish
what they had planned.
13 He catches the wise in their own craftiness,
and the counsel of the cunning is brought to a quick end.
14 They meet with darkness in the daytime,
and grope about in the noontime as if it were night.
15 So he saves from the sword that comes from their mouth,
even the poor from the hand of the powerful.
16 Thus the poor have hope,
and iniquity shuts its mouth.

17 "Therefore, blessed is the man whom God corrects,
so do not despise the discipline of the Almighty.
18 For he wounds, but he also bandages;
he strikes, but his hands also heal.
19 He will deliver you from six calamities;
yes, in seven no evil will touch you.
20 In time of famine he will redeem you from death,
and in time of war from the power of the sword.
21 You will be protected from malicious gossip
and will not be afraid of the destruction when it comes.
22 You will laugh at destruction and famine
and need not be afraid of the beasts of the earth.
23 For you will have a pact with the stones of the field,
and the wild animals will be at peace with you.
24 And you will know that your home will be secure,
and when you inspect your domains,
you will not be missing anything.
25 You will also know that your children will be numerous
and your descendants like the grass of the earth.
26 You will come to your grave in a full age,
As stacks of grain are harvested in their season.
27 Look, we have investigated this, so it is true.
Hear it, and apply it for your own good."

JOB REPLIES TO ELIPHAZ

6 Then Job responded:
2 "Oh, if only my grief could be weighed,
and my misfortune laid on the scales too!
3 But because it is heavier than the sand of the sea,
that is why my words have been wild.
4 For the arrows of the Almighty are within me;
my spirit drinks their poison;
God's sudden terrors are arrayed against me.

COMPLAINTS REFLECT SUFFERING

5 "Does the wild donkey bray when it is near grass?
Or does the ox bellow over its fodder?
6 Can food that is tasteless be eaten without salt?
Or is there any taste in the white of an egg?
7 I have refused to touch such things;
they are like loathsome food to me.

A CRY FOR DEATH

8 "Oh that my request would be realized,
and that God would grant me what I long for!
9 And that God would be willing to crush me,
that he would let loose his hand
and kill me.
10 Then I would yet have my comfort,
then I would rejoice,
in spite of pitiless pain,
for I have not concealed the words of the Holy One.
11 What is my strength, that I should wait?
And what is my end,
that I should prolong my life?
12 Is my strength like that of stones?
Or is my flesh made of bronze?
13 Is not my power to help myself nothing,
and has not every resource been driven from me?

DISAPPOINTING FRIENDS

14 "To the one in despair, kindness should come from his friend
even if he forsakes the fear of the Almighty.
15 My brothers have been as treacherous as a seasonal stream,
and as the riverbeds of the intermittent streams
that flow away.
16 They are dark because of ice;
snow is piled up over them.
17 When they are scorched, they dry up,
when it is hot, they vanish from their place.
18 Caravans turn aside from their routes;
they go into the wasteland and perish.
19 The caravans of Tema looked intently for these streams;
the traveling merchants of Sheba hoped for them.
20 They were distressed
because each one had been so confident;
they arrived there, but were disappointed.
21 For now you have become like these streams that are no help;
you see a terror and are afraid.

6:2–3 And when Job says in 9:17 concerning the Lord, "he who crushes me with a tempest and multiplies my wounds for no reason," observe that it was not because of his manifold sins that these many bruises were inflicted on him, but in order to make trial of his patience. For on account of his sins, indeed, without which, as he acknowledges in another passage, he was certainly not, yet he judges that he ought to have suffered less.

AUGUSTINE (354–430)
ANTI-PELAGIAN WRITINGS

FRIENDS' FEARS

22 "Have I ever said, 'Give me something,
and from your fortune make gifts in my favor'?
23 Or, 'Deliver me from the enemy's power,
and from the hand of tyrants ransom me'?

NO SIN DISCOVERED

24 "Teach me, and I, for my part, will be silent;
explain to me how I have been mistaken.
25 How painful are honest words!
But what does your reproof prove?
26 Do you intend to criticize mere words,
and treat the words of a despairing man as wind?
27 Yes, you would gamble for the fatherless,
and auction off your friend.

OTHER EXPLANATION

28 "Now then, be good enough to look at me;
and I will not lie to your face!
29 Relent, let there be no falsehood;
reconsider, for my righteousness is intact!
30 Is there any falsehood on my lips?
Can my mouth not discern evil things?

THE BREVITY OF LIFE

7 "Does not humanity have hard service on earth?
Are not their days also like the days of a hired man?
2 Like a servant longing for the evening shadow,
and like a hired man looking for his wages,
3 thus I have been made to inherit
months of futility,
and nights of sorrow
have been appointed to me.
4 If I lie down, I say, 'When will I arise?'
And the night stretches on,
and I toss and turn restlessly
until the day dawns.
5 My body is clothed with worms and dirty scabs;
my skin is broken and festering.
6 My days are swifter than a weaver's shuttle,
and they come to an end without hope.
7 Remember that my life is but a breath,
that my eyes will never again see happiness.
8 The eye of him who sees me now will see me no more;
your eyes will look for me, but I will be gone.
9 As a cloud is dispersed and then disappears,
so the one who goes down to the grave
does not come up again.
10 He returns no more to his house,
nor does his place of residence know him anymore.

JOB REMONSTRATES WITH GOD

11 "Therefore, I will not refrain my mouth;
I will speak in the anguish of my spirit;
I will complain in the bitterness of my soul.
12 Am I the sea, or the creature of the deep,
that you must put me under guard?
13 If I say, 'My bed will comfort me,
my couch will ease my complaint,'

7:1–16 Job might have drawn a better conclusion than "I will complain." When we have but a few breaths to draw, we should spend them in the holy, gracious breathings of faith and prayer, not in the noisome, noxious breathings of sin and corruption. We have much reason to pray that he who keeps Israel and neither slumbers nor sleeps may keep us when we slumber and sleep. Job covets to rest in his grave. Doubtless this was his infirmity; for though a good man would choose death rather than sin, yet he should be content to live as long as God pleases because life is our opportunity of glorifying him and preparing for heaven.

MATTHEW HENRY **(1662–1714)**
COMMENTARY ON THE WHOLE BIBLE

14 then you scare me with dreams
and terrify me with visions,
15 so that I would prefer strangling
and death more than life.
16 I loathe it; I do not want to live forever;
leave me alone, for my days are a vapor!

INSIGNIFICANCE OF HUMANS

17 "What is mankind that you make so much of them,
and that you pay attention to them?
18 And that you visit them every morning,
and try them every moment?
19 Will you never look away from me,
will you not let me alone
long enough to swallow my spittle?
20 If I have sinned—what have I done to you,
O watcher of men?
Why have you set me as your target?
Have I become a burden to you?
21 And why do you not pardon my transgression
and take away my iniquity?
For now I will lie down in the dust,
and you will seek me diligently,
but I will be gone."

BILDAD'S FIRST SPEECH TO JOB

8 Then Bildad the Shuhite spoke up and said:
2 "How long will you speak these things,
seeing that the words of your mouth
are like a great wind?
3 Does God pervert justice?
Or does the Almighty pervert what is right?
4 If your children sinned against him,
he gave them over to the penalty of their sin.
5 But if you will look to God
and make your supplication to the Almighty,
6 if you become pure and upright,
even now he will rouse himself for you
and will restore your righteous home.
7 Your beginning will seem so small,
since your future will flourish.

8 "For inquire now of the former generation,
and pay attention to the findings
of their ancestors;
9 For we were born yesterday and do not have knowledge,
since our days on earth are but a shadow.
10 Will they not instruct you and speak to you,
and bring forth words
from their understanding?
11 Can the papyrus plant grow tall where there is no
marsh?
Can reeds flourish without water?
12 While they are still beginning to flower
and not ripe for cutting,
they can wither away
faster than any grass.
13 Such is the destiny of all who forget God;
the hope of the godless perishes,

8:11–22 Those who lived in Job's time had doubtless abundance of traditions from the antediluvians, who might have been instructed from Adam himself and who, through their vast age, had abundant opportunity to acquire great knowledge and experience. It is very probable that much of the learning that was in the heathen world was the corrupted remains of what was declared to humankind by those who came out of the ark. Job lived in early days after the flood, and there is abundance of philosophy in this book, which in all probability they derived by tradition from their fathers. In this book, as here in this place, there is a plain referring to tradition from the beginning of the world, or from the second beginning after the flood.

JONATHAN EDWARDS
(1703–1758)
THE COMPLETE WORKS

BOETHIUS:

TRAILBLAZER OF INTROSPECTION

c. 480–524

Boethius was born in 480 to a leading Roman family with wealth and power. Though later orphaned, he became a high-ranking official within the Italian court of Theodoric, king of the Ostrogoths and sole ruler of Italy. But shortly thereafter Boethius fell out of favor through the treacherous machinations of political rivals and came under suspicion of being a spy. He was eventually imprisoned, and it was while in prison that he wrote his most famous and enduring work: *Consolation of Philosophy*.

This philosophical work confronted with groundbreaking brilliance the big questions of life: how a good God can allow so much evil, the nature of life, the nature and purpose of human beings, the virtuous life, good and ill fortune, and the dynamic of human free will and God's sovereignty. The work cast its author in dialogue with an allegorical personification of philosophy: Boethius, sorrowful and morose, converses with Lady Philosophy through his meaningful questions.

One finds in *Consolation of Philosophy* a man wrestling with God and his will. He is trying to come to grips with life as it is influenced by God and his sovereignty, foreknowledge, and divine grace. In many ways, the introspective search is similar to David's journey we find in the Psalms as he wrestled with the nature of life and Yahweh, the God of Israel. Boethius questions and prods the Almighty, but ultimately he praises God and submits to his sovereign authority—acknowledging the goodness of God over the affairs of the world.

Though Boethius was a Christian, *Consolation of Philosophy* wasn't obviously so. Where one would expect references to Christ or the specific hope of his gospel, we see rather general philosophical comments about the divine or the good. This was intentional: Boethius was committed to the idea that faith and reason are complementary, and that the truths of Christianity could be confirmed by good philosophy. Thus *Consolation* is a classical philosophical work by a Christian wrestling with major questions of life, seeking wisdom and understanding.

Boethius was eventually put to death by the state in 524, but his *Consolation of Philosophy* proved to be pivotal in Western thought and life. Indeed, its popularity and influence were such that Dante called Boethius the "last of the Romans and the first of the Scholastics."

IMPORTANT WORKS

CONSOLATION OF PHILOSOPHY

THEOLOGICAL TRACTATES

TRINITY IS ONE GOD NOT THREE GODS

14 whose trust is in something futile,
whose security is a spider's web.
15 He leans against his house, but it does not
hold up;
he takes hold of it, but it does not stand.
16 He is a well-watered plant in the sun;
its shoots spread over its garden.
17 It wraps its roots around a heap of stones,
and it looks for a place among stones.

18 If he is uprooted from his place,
then that place will disown him, saying,
'I have never seen you!'
19 Indeed, this is the joy of his way,
and out of the earth others spring up.

20 "Surely, God does not reject a blameless man,
nor does he grasp the hand
of the evildoers.
21 He will yet fill your mouth with laughter
and your lips with gladness.
22 Those who hate you will be clothed with shame,
and the tent of the wicked will be no more."

JOB'S REPLY TO BILDAD

9 Then Job answered:
2 "Truly, I know that this is so.
But how can a human be just before God?
3 If someone wishes to contend with him,
he cannot answer him one time in a thousand.
4 He is wise in heart and mighty in strength—
who has resisted him and remained safe?
5 He who removes mountains suddenly,
who overturns them in his anger,
6 he who shakes the earth out of its place
so that its pillars tremble,
7 he who commands the sun, and it does not shine
and seals up the stars,
8 he alone spreads out the heavens
and treads on the waves of the sea.
9 He makes the Bear, Orion, and the Pleiades,
and the constellations of the southern sky;
10 he does great and unsearchable things,
and wonderful things without number.
11 If he passes by me, I cannot see him;
if he goes by, I cannot perceive him.
12 If he snatches away, who can turn him back?
Who dares to say to him, 'What are you doing?'
13 God does not restrain his anger;
under him the helpers of Rahab lie crushed.

THE IMPOSSIBILITY OF FACING GOD IN COURT

14 "How much less, then, can I answer him
and choose my words to argue with him.
15 Although I am innocent,
I could not answer him;
I could only plead with my judge for mercy.
16 If I summoned him and he answered me,

9:1–13 Whoever is great necessarily does great things. But the one who does great things is not necessarily great. Job demonstrates regarding greatness that only the one who is great makes great the things he does. He says this, however, so that his friends—who think there is only one reason for hardship—may consider that he who does great and dreadful things also has deep and unfathomable resolutions that are glorious. These things are filled with glory, so to speak. Paul wrote something similar when he said, "Oh, the depth of the riches and wisdom and knowledge of God! How unsearchable are his judgments and how unfathomable his ways! For who has known the mind of the Lord?" (Rom 11:33–34).

DIDYMUS THE BLIND
(C. 313–398)
COMMENTARY ON JOB

I would not believe
that he would be listening to my voice—
17 he who crushes me with a tempest
and multiplies my wounds for no reason.
18 He does not allow me to recover my breath,
for he fills me with bitterness.
19 If it is a matter of strength,
most certainly he is the strong one!
And if it is a matter of justice,
he will say, 'Who will summon me?'
20 Although I am innocent,
my mouth would condemn me;
although I am blameless,
it would declare me perverse.
21 I am blameless. I do not know myself.
I despise my life.

ACCUSATION OF GOD'S JUSTICE

22 "It is all one! That is why I say,
'He destroys the blameless and the guilty.'
23 If a scourge brings sudden death,
he mocks at the despair of the innocent.
24 If a land has been given
into the hand of a wicked man,
he covers the faces of its judges;
if it is not he, then who is it?

RENEWED COMPLAINT

25 "My days are swifter than a runner,
they speed by without seeing happiness.
26 They glide by like reed boats,
like an eagle that swoops down on its prey.
27 If I say, 'I will forget my complaint,
I will change my expression and be cheerful,'
28 I dread all my sufferings,
for I know that you do not hold me blameless.
29 If I am guilty,
why then weary myself in vain?
30 If I wash myself with snow-melt water
and make my hands clean with lye,
31 then you plunge me into a slimy pit
and my own clothes abhor me.
32 For he is not a human being like I am,
that I might answer him,
that we might come together in judgment.
33 Nor is there an arbiter between us,
who might lay his hand on us both,
34 who would take his rod away from me
so that his terror would not make me afraid.
35 Then would I speak and not fear him,
but it is not so with me.

AN APPEAL FOR REVELATION

10 "I am weary of my life;
I will complain freely without restraint;
I will speak in the bitterness of my soul.
2 I will say to God, 'Do not condemn me;
tell me why you are contending with me.'
3 Is it good for you to oppress,

9:14–17 And when Job says in 9:17 concerning the Lord, "he who crushes me with a tempest, and multiplies my wounds for no reason," observe that it was not because of his manifold sins that these many bruises were inflicted on him, but in order to make trial of his patience. For on account of his sins, indeed, without which, as he acknowledges in another passage, he was certainly not, he yet judges that he ought to have suffered less.

AUGUSTINE (354–430)
ANTI-PELAGIAN WRITINGS

10:1–22 "Tell me why you are contending with me." *How can you know that you have faith until your faith is exercised?* God often takes away our comforts and our privileges in order to make us better Christians. He trains his soldiers, not in tents of ease and luxury, but by turning them out and using them in forced marches and hard service. He makes them ford through streams, swim through rivers, climb mountains, and walk many a long mile with heavy knapsacks of sorrow on their backs. Well, Christian, may not this account for the troubles through which you are passing? Is not the Lord bringing out your graces and making them grow? Is not this the reason why he is contending with you?

CHARLES SPURGEON
(1834–1892)
MORNING AND EVENING

to despise the work of your hands,
while you smile
on the schemes of the wicked?

MOTIVATIONS OF GOD

4 "Do you have eyes of flesh,
or do you see as a human being sees?
5 Are your days like the days of a mortal,
or your years like the years of a mortal,
6 that you must search out my iniquity
and inquire about my sin,
7 although you know that I am not guilty,
and that there is no one who can deliver
out of your hand?

CONTRADICTIONS IN GOD'S DEALINGS

8 "Your hands have shaped me and made me,
but now you destroy me completely.
9 Remember that you have made me as with the clay;
will you return me to dust?
10 Did you not pour me out like milk
and curdle me like cheese?
11 You clothed me with skin and flesh
and knit me together with bones and sinews.
12 You gave me life and favor,
and your intervention watched over my spirit.

13 "But these things you have concealed in your heart;
I know that this is with you:
14 If I sinned, then you would watch me,
and you would not acquit me of my iniquity.
15 If I am guilty, woe to me,
and if I am innocent, I cannot lift my head;
I am full of shame
and satiated with my affliction.
16 If I lift myself up,
you hunt me as a fierce lion,
and again you display your power against me.
17 You bring new witnesses against me
and increase your anger against me;
relief troops come against me.

AN APPEAL FOR RELIEF

18 "Why then did you bring me out from the womb?
I should have died,
and no eye would have seen me!
19 I should have been as though I had never existed;
I should have been carried
right from the womb to the grave!
20 Are not my days few?
Cease, then, and leave me alone
that I may find a little comfort,
21 before I depart, never to return,
to the land of darkness
and the deepest shadow,
22 to the land of utter darkness,
like the deepest darkness,
and the deepest shadow and disorder,
where even the light is like darkness."

ZOPHAR'S FIRST SPEECH TO JOB

11 Then Zophar the Naamathite spoke up and said:
2 "Should not this abundance of words be answered,
or should this talkative man
be vindicated?
3 Should people remain silent at your idle talk,
and should no one rebuke you when you mock?
4 For you have said, 'My teaching is flawless,
and I am pure in your sight.'
5 But if only God would speak,
if only he would open his lips against you
6 and reveal to you the secrets of wisdom—
for true wisdom has two sides—
so that you would know
that God has forgiven some of your sins.

7 "Can you discover the essence of God?
Can you find out the perfection of the Almighty?
8 It is higher than the heavens—what can you do?
It is deeper than Sheol—what can you know?
9 Its measure is longer than the earth
and broader than the sea.
10 If he comes by and confines you
and convenes a court,
then who can prevent him?
11 For he knows deceitful men;
when he sees evil, will he not consider it?
12 But an empty man will become wise,
when a wild donkey's colt is born a human being.

13 "As for you, if you prove faithful,
and if you stretch out your hands toward him,
14 if iniquity is in your hand—put it far away,
and do not let evil reside in your tents.
15 For then you will lift up your face
without blemish;
you will be securely established
and will not fear.
16 For you will forget your trouble;
you will remember it
like water that has flowed away.
17 And life will be brighter than the noonday;
though there be darkness,
it will be like the morning.
18 And you will be secure because there is hope;
you will be protected
and will take your rest in safety.
19 You will lie down with no one to make you afraid,
and many will seek your favor.
20 But the eyes of the wicked fail,
and escape eludes them;
their one hope is to breathe their last."

11:7–12 "Can you discover the essence of God?" These words mean, *Do you know what the Almighty will do at the end of his works?* I certainly grant that we have experience of things that are otherwise evident and manifest, but they only disclose to us the loftiness of heaven and all divine things.

EPHREM THE SYRIAN
(C. 306–373)
COMMENTARY ON JOB

JOB'S REPLY TO ZOPHAR

12 Then Job answered:
2 "Without a doubt you are the people,
and wisdom will die with you.
3 I also have understanding as well as you;
I am not inferior to you.

Who does not know such things as these?
4 I am a laughingstock to my friends,
I, who called on God and whom he answered—
a righteous and blameless man
is a laughingstock!
5 For calamity, there is derision
(according to the ideas of the fortunate)—
a fate for those whose feet slip.
6 But the tents of robbers are peaceful,
and those who provoke God are confident—
who carry their god in their hands.

KNOWLEDGE OF GOD'S WISDOM

7 "But now, ask the animals and they will
teach you,
or the birds of the sky and they will tell you.
8 Or speak to the earth and it will teach you,
or let the fish of the sea declare to you.
9 Which of all these does not know
that the hand of the LORD has done this?
10 In his hand is the life of every creature
and the breath of all the human race.
11 Does not the ear test words,
as the tongue tastes food?
12 Is not wisdom found among the aged?
Does not long life bring understanding?
13 With God are wisdom and power;
counsel and understanding are his.
14 If he tears down, it cannot be rebuilt;
if he imprisons a person, there is no
escape.
15 If he holds back the waters, then they
dry up;
if he releases them, they destroy the land.
16 With him are strength and prudence;
both the one who goes astray
and the one who misleads are his.
17 He leads counselors away stripped
and makes judges into fools.
18 He loosens the bonds of kings
and binds a loincloth around their waist.
19 He leads priests away stripped
and overthrows the potentates.
20 He deprives the trusted advisers of speech
and takes away the discernment of elders.
21 He pours contempt on noblemen
and disarms the powerful.
22 He reveals the deep things of darkness
and brings deep shadows into the light.
23 He makes nations great and destroys them;
he extends the boundaries of nations
and disperses them.
24 He deprives the leaders of the earth
of their understanding;
he makes them wander
in a trackless desert waste.
25 They grope about in darkness without
light;
he makes them stagger like drunkards.

12:1–12 **Job speaks in an admirable way: "Without a doubt you are the people, and wisdom will die with you." This means, *Is the honor of rational beings really intact within you? Do you know the decisions that God forms with regard to sinners and righteous people?* Know that God tests the righteous and shows tolerance with sinners. That is why the latter are wealthy and the former in the ordeal because for sinners God's long tolerance will be the reason for a return to repentance, while to the righteous the long battle will offer the occasion to be crowned. If you knew that, you would not condemn the righteous person who is in the ordeal, and you would not consider the sinner who is wealthy as the righteous.**

HESYCHIUS OF JERUSALEM **(C. 450)**
HOMILIES ON JOB

JOB PLEADS HIS CAUSE TO GOD

13 "Indeed, my eyes have seen all this;
my ears have heard and understood it.
2 What you know, I know also;
I am not inferior to you!
3 But I wish to speak to the Almighty,
and I desire to argue my case with God.
4 But you, however, are inventors of lies;
all of you are worthless physicians!
5 If only you would keep completely silent!
For you, that would be wisdom.
6 Listen now to my argument,
and be attentive to my lips' contentions.
7 Will you speak wickedly on God's behalf?
Will you speak deceitfully for him?
8 Will you show him partiality?
Will you argue the case for God?
9 Would it turn out well if he would examine you?
Or as one deceives a man would you deceive him?
10 He would certainly rebuke you
if you secretly showed partiality.
11 Would not his splendor terrify you
and the fear he inspires fall on you?
12 Your maxims are proverbs of ashes;
your defenses are defenses of clay.

13 "Refrain from talking with me so that I may speak;
then let come to me what may.
14 Why do I put myself in peril,
and take my life in my hands?
15 Even if he slays me, I will hope in him;
I will surely defend my ways to his face.
16 Moreover, this will become my deliverance,
for no godless person would come before him.
17 Listen carefully to my words;
let your ears be attentive to my explanation.
18 See now, I have prepared my case;
I know that I am right.
19 Who will contend with me?
If anyone can, I will be silent and die.
20 Only in two things spare me, O God,
and then I will not hide from your face:
21 Remove your hand far from me
and stop making me afraid with your terror.
22 Then call, and I will answer,
or I will speak, and you respond to me.
23 How many are my iniquities and sins?
Show me my transgression and my sin.
24 Why do you hide your face
and regard me as your enemy?
25 Do you wish to torment a windblown leaf
and chase after dry chaff?
26 For you write down bitter things against me
and cause me to inherit the sins of my youth.
27 And you put my feet in the stocks
and you watch all my movements;
you put marks on the soles of my feet.
28 So I waste away like something rotten,
like a garment eaten by moths.

13:20—14:22 **Job complains sorrowfully of God's severe dealings with him. Time does not wear out the guilt of sin. When God writes bitter things against us, his design is to make us bring forgotten sins to mind and so to bring us to repent of them, as to break us off from them. Job also complains that his present mistakes are strictly noticed. This was the language of Job's melancholy views. If God marks our steps and narrowly examines our paths in judgment, both body and soul feel his righteous vengeance. Here is a clear proof that Job understood and believed the doctrine of original sin. He seems to have intended it as a plea why the Lord should not deal with him according to his own works, but according to his mercy and grace. We should humble ourselves before God and cast ourselves wholly on the mercy of God through our divine surety. We should daily seek the renewing of the Holy Spirit and look to heaven as the only place of perfect holiness and happiness.**

MATTHEW HENRY **(1662–1714)**
COMMENTARY ON THE WHOLE BIBLE

THE BREVITY OF LIFE

14 "Man, born of woman,
lives but a few days, and they are full of trouble.
2 He grows up like a flower and then withers away;
he flees like a shadow and does not remain.
3 Do you fix your eye on such a one?
And do you bring me before you for judgment?
4 Who can make a clean thing come from an unclean?
No one!
5 Since man's days are determined,
the number of his months is under your control;
you have set his limit, and he cannot pass it.
6 Look away from him and let him desist,
until he fulfills his time like a hired man.

THE INEVITABILITY OF DEATH

7 "But there is hope for a tree:
If it is cut down, it will sprout again,
and its new shoots will not fail.
8 Although its roots may grow old in the ground
and its stump begins to die in the soil,
9 at the scent of water it will flourish
and put forth shoots like a new plant.
10 But man dies and is powerless;
he expires—and where is he?
11 As water disappears from the sea,
or a river drains away and dries up,
12 so man lies down and does not rise;
until the heavens are no more,
they will not awake
nor arise from their sleep.

THE POSSIBILITY OF ANOTHER LIFE

13 "O that you would hide me in Sheol,
and conceal me till your anger has passed!
O that you would set me a time
and then remember me!
14 If a man dies, will he live again?
All the days of my hard service I will wait
until my release comes.
15 You will call and I—I will answer you;
you will long for the creature you have made.

THE PRESENT CONDITION

16 "Surely now you count my steps;
then you would not mark my sin.
17 My offenses would be sealed up in a bag;
you would cover over my sin.
18 But as a mountain falls away and crumbles,
and as a rock will be removed from its place,
19 as water wears away stones,
and torrents wash away the soil,
so you destroy man's hope.
20 You overpower him once for all,
and he departs;
you change his appearance
and send him away.
21 If his sons are honored,
he does not know it;

if they are brought low,
he does not see it.
22 His flesh only has pain for him,
and he mourns for himself."

ELIPHAZ'S SECOND SPEECH

15 Then Eliphaz the Temanite answered:
2 "Does a wise man answer with blustery knowledge,
or fill his belly with the east wind?
3 Does he argue with useless talk,
with words that have no value in them?
4 But you even break off piety
and hinder meditation before God.
5 Your sin inspires your mouth;
you choose the language of the crafty.
6 Your own mouth condemns you, not I;
your own lips testify against you.

7 "Were you the first man ever born?
Were you brought forth before the hills?
8 Do you listen in on God's secret council?
Do you limit wisdom to yourself?
9 What do you know that we don't know?
What do you understand that we don't understand?
10 The gray-haired and the aged are on our side,
men far older than your father.
11 Are God's consolations too trivial for you,
or a word spoken in gentleness to you?
12 Why has your heart carried you away,
and why do your eyes flash,
13 when you turn your rage against God
and allow such words to escape from your mouth?
14 What is man that he should be pure,
or one born of woman, that he should be righteous?
15 If God places no trust in his holy ones,
if even the heavens are not pure in his eyes,
16 how much less man, who is abominable and corrupt,
who drinks in evil like water!
17 I will explain to you;
listen to me,
and what I have seen, I will declare,
18 what wise men declare,
hiding nothing,
from the tradition of their ancestors,
19 to whom alone the land was given
when no foreigner passed among them.
20 All his days the wicked man suffers torment,
throughout the number of the years
that are stored up for the tyrant.
21 Terrifying sounds fill his ears;
in a time of peace marauders attack him.
22 He does not expect to escape from darkness;
he is marked for the sword;
23 he wanders about—food for vultures—
he knows that the day of darkness is at hand.
24 Distress and anguish terrify him;
they prevail against him
like a king ready to launch an attack,
25 for he stretches out his hand against God,

15:4 **We should, before prayer, meditate upon him to whom it is to be addressed. Let our thoughts be directed to the living and true God. Let me remember that he is omnipotent, then I shall ask large things. Let me remember that he is very tender and full of compassion, then I shall ask little things and be minute in my supplication. Let me remember the greatness of his covenant, then I shall ask very boldly. Let me remember also that his faithfulness is like the great mountains, that his promises are sure to all the seed; then I shall ask very confidently, for I shall be persuaded that he will do as he has said. Let me fill my soul with the reflection of the greatness of his majesty, then I shall be struck with awe, with the equal greatness of his love, then I shall be filled with delight.**

CHARLES SPURGEON
(1834–1892)
METROPOLITAN TABERNACLE SERMONS

and vaunts himself against the Almighty,
26 defiantly charging against him
with a thick, strong shield!
27 Because he covered his face with fat
and made his hips bulge with fat,
28 he lived in ruined towns
and in houses where no one lives,
where they are ready to crumble into heaps.
29 He will not grow rich,
and his wealth will not endure,
nor will his possessions spread over the land.
30 He will not escape the darkness;
a flame will wither his shoots,
and he will depart
by the breath of God's mouth.
31 Let him not trust in what is worthless,
deceiving himself;
for worthlessness will be his reward.
32 Before his time he will be paid in full,
and his branches will not flourish.
33 Like a vine he will let his sour grapes fall,
and like an olive tree
he will shed his blossoms.
34 For the company of the godless is barren,
and fire consumes the tents of those who accept bribes.
35 They conceive trouble and bring forth evil;
their belly prepares deception."

JOB'S REPLY TO ELIPHAZ

16 Then Job replied:
2 "I have heard many things like these before.
What miserable comforters are you all!
3 Will there be an end to your windy words?
Or what provokes you that you answer?
4 I also could speak like you,
if you were in my place;
I could pile up words against you,
and I could shake my head at you.
5 But I would strengthen you with my words;
comfort from my lips would bring you relief.

ABANDONMENT BY GOD AND MAN

6 "But if I speak, my pain is not relieved,
and if I refrain from speaking,
how much of it goes away?
7 Surely now he has worn me out;
you have devastated my entire household.
8 You have seized me,
and it has become a witness;
my leanness has risen up against me
and testifies against me.
9 His anger has torn me and persecuted me;
he has gnashed at me with his teeth;
my adversary locks his eyes on me.
10 People have opened their mouths against me;
they have struck my cheek in scorn;
they unite together against me.
11 God abandons me to evil men,
and throws me into the hands of wicked men.

16:8–17 For who can justly accuse the man who wishes evil to no one, who faithfully does good to all he can, who never cherishes a wish to avenge himself on any man who does him wrong so that he can truly say, "for we also forgive everyone who sins against us" (Luke 11:4)? And yet by the very fact that he truly says, "Forgive, as we also forgive," he plainly admits that he is not without sin. Hence the force of the statement: "There is no violence in my hands and my prayer is pure." For the purity of his prayer arose from this circumstance, that it was not improper for him to ask forgiveness in prayer when he really bestowed forgiveness himself.

AUGUSTINE (354–430)
ANTI-PELAGIAN WRITINGS

12 I was in peace, and he has shattered me.
He has seized me by the neck and crushed me.
He has made me his target;
13 his archers surround me.
Without pity he pierces my kidneys
and pours out my gall on the ground.
14 He breaks through against me, time and time again;
he rushes against me like a warrior.
15 I have sewed sackcloth on my skin
and buried my horn in the dust;
16 my face is reddened because of weeping,
and on my eyelids there is a deep darkness,
17 although there is no violence in my hands
and my prayer is pure.

AN APPEAL TO GOD AS WITNESS

18 "O earth, do not cover my blood,
nor let there be a secret place for my cry.
19 Even now my witness is in heaven;
my advocate is on high.
20 My intercessor is my friend
as my eyes pour out tears to God;
21 and he contends with God on behalf of man
as a man pleads for his friend.
22 For the years that lie ahead are few,
and then I will go on the way of no return.
17 My spirit is broken,
my days have faded out;
the grave awaits me.
2 Surely mockery is with me;
my eyes must dwell on their hostility.
3 Set my pledge beside you.
Who else will put up security for me?
4 Because you have closed their minds to understanding,
therefore you will not exalt them.
5 If a man denounces his friends for personal gain,
the eyes of his children will fail.
6 He has made me a byword to people;
I am the one in whose face they spit.
7 My eyes have grown dim with grief;
my whole frame is but a shadow.
8 Upright men are appalled at this;
the innocent man is troubled with the godless.
9 But the righteous man holds to his way,
and the one with clean hands grows stronger.

ANTICIPATION OF DEATH

10 "But turn, all of you, and come now!
I will not find a wise man among you.
11 My days have passed; my plans are shattered,
even the desires of my heart.
12 These men change night into day;
they say, 'The light is near
in the face of darkness.'
13 If I hope for the grave to be my home,
if I spread out my bed in darkness,
14 if I cry out to corruption, 'You are my father,'
and to the worm, 'My mother,' or 'My sister,'
15 where then is my hope?

17:8 Ah, the depth and mysteriousness of God's judgments that fall on innocent people while the worst of people prosper. Notwithstanding all these sufferings of good folk and the astonishment they cause, God shall the more zealously oppose those hypocrites who make these strange providences of God an objection to religion.

JOHN WESLEY (1703–1791)
EXPLANATORY NOTES ON THE BIBLE

And my hope, who sees it?
16 Will it go down to the barred gates of death?
Will we descend together into the dust?"

BILDAD'S SECOND SPEECH

18 Then Bildad the Shuhite answered:
2 "How long until you make an end of words?
You must consider, and then we can talk.
3 Why should we be regarded as beasts,
and considered stupid in your sight?
4 You who tear yourself to pieces in your anger,
will the earth be abandoned for your sake?
Or will a rock be moved from its place?

5 "Yes, the lamp of the wicked is extinguished;
his flame of fire does not shine.
6 The light in his tent grows dark;
his lamp above him is extinguished.
7 His vigorous steps are restricted,
and his own counsel throws him down.
8 For he has been thrown into a net by his feet,
and he wanders into a mesh.
9 A trap seizes him by the heel;
a snare grips him.
10 A rope is hidden for him on the ground,
and a trap for him lies on the path.
11 Terrors frighten him on all sides
and dog his every step.
12 Calamity is hungry for him,
and misfortune is ready at his side.
13 It eats away parts of his skin;
the most terrible death devours his limbs.
14 He is dragged from the security of his tent,
and marched off to the king of terrors.
15 Fire resides in his tent;
over his residence burning sulfur is scattered.
16 Below his roots dry up,
and his branches wither above.
17 His memory perishes from the earth
he has no name in the land.
18 He is driven from light into darkness
and is banished from the world.
19 He has neither children nor descendants among his people,
no survivor in those places he once stayed.
20 People of the west are appalled at his fate;
people of the east are seized with horror, saying,
21 'Surely such is the residence of an evil man;
and this is the place of one who has not known God.'"

JOB'S REPLY TO BILDAD

19 Then Job answered:
2 "How long will you torment me
and crush me with your words?
3 These ten times you have been reproaching me;
you are not ashamed to attack me.
4 But even if it were true that I have erred,
my error remains solely my concern!
5 If indeed you would exalt yourselves above me

18:1–21 "He is driven from light into darkness and is banished from the world." For of old, before the divine sojourn of the Savior took place, even to the saints death was terrible and all wept for the dead as though they perished. But now that the Savior has raised his body, death is no longer terrible; for all who believe in Christ choose rather to die than to deny their faith in Christ. They know that when they die they are not destroyed but actually begin to live and become incorruptible through the resurrection. Death having been conquered and exposed by the Savior on the cross and bound hand and foot, all they who are in Christ trample on it, and witnessing to Christ scoff at death, jesting at it, and saying what has been written against it of old: "Where, O death, is your victory? Where, O death, is your sting?" (1 Cor 15:55).

ATHANASIUS (C. 296–373)
ON THE INCARNATION

19:1–29 The marrow of Job's comfort lies in that little word "my"—"my Redeemer"—and in the fact that the Redeemer lives. Rest not content until by faith you can say, *Yes, I cast myself upon my living Lord, and he is mine.* It may be you hold him with a feeble hand; you half think it presumption to say like Job, "I know that my Redeemer lives," yet remember if you have but faith as a grain of mustard seed, that little faith entitles you to say it. But to reach the essence of consolation you must say like Job, "I know." If I know that Jesus lives for me, then darkness is not dark: even the night is light about me. Surely if Job, in those ages before the coming and advent of Christ, could say, "I know," we should not speak less positively.

CHARLES SPURGEON
(1834–1892)
MORNING AND EVENING

and plead my disgrace against me,
6 know then that God has wronged me
and encircled me with his net.

JOB'S ABANDONMENT AND AFFLICTION

7 "If I cry out, 'Violence!'
I receive no answer;
I cry for help,
but there is no justice.
8 He has blocked my way so I cannot pass
and has set darkness over my paths.
9 He has stripped me of my honor
and has taken the crown off my head.
10 He tears me down on every side until I perish;
he uproots my hope like an uprooted tree.
11 Thus his anger burns against me,
and he considers me among his enemies.
12 His troops advance together;
they throw up a siege ramp against me,
and they camp around my tent.

JOB'S FORSAKEN STATE

13 "He has put my relatives far from me;
my acquaintances only turn away from me.
14 My kinsmen have failed me;
my friends have forgotten me.
15 My guests and my servant girls
consider me a stranger;
I am a foreigner in their eyes.
16 I summon my servant, but he does not respond,
even though I implore him with my own mouth.
17 My breath is repulsive to my wife;
I am loathsome to my brothers.
18 Even youngsters have scorned me;
when I get up, they scoff at me.
19 All my closest friends detest me;
and those whom I love have turned against me.
20 My bones stick to my skin and my flesh;
I have escaped alive with only the skin of my teeth.
21 Have pity on me, my friends, have pity on me,
for the hand of God has struck me.
22 Why do you pursue me like God does?
Will you never be satiated with my flesh?

JOB'S ASSURANCE OF VINDICATION

23 "O that my words were written down!
O that they were written on a scroll!
24 O that with an iron chisel and with lead
they were engraved in a rock forever!
25 As for me, I know that my Redeemer lives,
and that as the last
he will stand upon the earth.
26 And after my skin has been destroyed,
yet in my flesh I will see God,
27 whom I will see for myself,
and whom my own eyes will behold,
and not another.
My heart grows faint within me.
28 If you say, 'How we will pursue him,

since the root of the trouble is found in him!'
29 Fear the sword yourselves,
for wrath brings the punishment by the sword,
so that you may know
that there is judgment."

ZOPHAR'S SECOND SPEECH

20 Then Zophar the Naamathite answered:
2 "This is why my troubled thoughts bring me back—
because of my feelings within me.
3 When I hear a reproof that dishonors me,
then my understanding prompts me to answer.

4 "Surely you know that it has been from old,
ever since humankind was placed on the earth,
5 that the elation of the wicked is brief,
the joy of the godless lasts but a moment.
6 Even though his stature reaches to the heavens
and his head touches the clouds,
7 he will perish forever, like his own excrement;
those who used to see him will say, 'Where is he?'
8 Like a dream he flies away, never again to be found,
and like a vision of the night he is put to flight.
9 People who had seen him will not see him again,
and the place where he was
will recognize him no longer.
10 His sons must recompense the poor;
his own hands must return his wealth.
11 His bones were full of his youthful vigor,
but that vigor will lie down with him in the dust.

12 "If evil is sweet in his mouth
and he hides it under his tongue,
13 if he retains it for himself
and does not let it go,
and holds it fast in his mouth,
14 his food is turned sour in his stomach;
it becomes the venom of serpents within him.
15 The wealth that he consumed he vomits up,
God will make him throw it out of his stomach.
16 He sucks the poison of serpents;
the fangs of a viper kill him.
17 He will not look on the streams,
the rivers that are the torrents
of honey and butter.
18 He gives back the ill-gotten gain
without assimilating it;
he will not enjoy the wealth from his commerce.
19 For he has oppressed the poor and abandoned them;
he has seized a house which he did not build.
20 For he knows no satisfaction in his appetite;
he does not let anything he desires escape.
21 Nothing is left for him to devour;
that is why his prosperity does not last.
22 In the fullness of his sufficiency,
distress overtakes him.
The full force of misery will come upon him.
23 While he is filling his belly,
God sends his burning anger against him

20:1–29 The pride of the hypocrite "reaches to the heavens" when his high-mindedness has the appearance of leading a heavenly life. And his "head touches the clouds" when the leading part, that is, his intellect, is thought to equal the merits of the saints who have gone before. Yet "he will perish forever, like his own excrement" because at his death, when he is led to torments, being full of the dung of evil habits, he is trampled underfoot by evil spirits. Concerning the brevity of the hypocrite's life, it is yet further added fittingly, "Like a dream he flies away, never again to be found, and like a vision of the night he is put to flight." What else is the life of the hypocrite but the vision of a phantom that exhibits the facade that it does not possess in truth?

GREGORY THE GREAT
(C. 540–604)
MORALS ON THE BOOK OF JOB

and rains down his blows upon him.
24 If he flees from an iron weapon,
then an arrow from a bronze bow pierces him.
25 When he pulls it out and it comes out of his back,
the gleaming point out of his liver,
terrors come over him.
26 Total darkness waits to receive his treasures;
a fire that has not been kindled
will consume him and devour what is left in his tent.
27 The heavens reveal his iniquity;
the earth rises up against him.
28 A flood will carry off his house,
rushing waters on the day of God's wrath.
29 Such is the lot God allots the wicked,
and the heritage of his appointment from God."

JOB'S REPLY TO ZOPHAR

21 Then Job answered:
2 "Listen carefully to my words;
let this be the consolation you offer me.
3 Bear with me and I will speak,
and after I have spoken you may mock.
4 Is my complaint against a man?
If so, why should I not be impatient?
5 Look at me and be appalled;
put your hands over your mouths.
6 For, when I think about this, I am terrified
and my body feels a shudder.

THE WICKED PROSPER

7 "Why do the wicked go on living,
grow old, even increase in power?
8 Their children are firmly established in their presence,
their offspring before their eyes.
9 Their houses are safe and without fear;
and no rod of punishment from God is upon them.
10 Their bulls breed without fail;
their cows calve and do not miscarry.
11 They allow their children to run like a flock;
their little ones dance about.
12 They sing to the accompaniment of tambourine and harp,
and make merry to the sound of the flute.
13 They live out their years in prosperity
and go down to the grave in peace.
14 So they say to God, 'Turn away from us!
We do not want to know your ways.
15 Who is the Almighty, that we should serve him?
What would we gain
if we were to pray to him?'
16 But their prosperity is not their own doing.
The counsel of the wicked is far from me!

HOW OFTEN DO THE WICKED SUFFER?

17 "How often is the lamp of the wicked extinguished?
How often does their misfortune come upon them?
How often does God apportion pain to them in his anger?
18 How often are they like straw before the wind
and like chaff swept away by a whirlwind?

21:1–21 "How can you console me with your futile words?" In these days, the thoughts of religion were very grievous to me; I could neither endure it myself nor that any other should. Then I said unto God, "Turn away from us! We do not want to know your ways." I was now void of all good consideration, heaven and hell were both out of sight and mind, and as for saving and damning, they were least in my thoughts. *O Lord, you know my life, and my ways were not hid from you.* As once above all the rest when I was in my height of vanity, yet hearing one to swear that I was reckoned for a religious man, it had so great a stroke upon my spirit that it made my heart to ache. Yet God did not utterly leave me but followed me still, not now with convictions but judgments, yet such as were mixed with mercy.

JOHN BUNYAN **(1628–1688)**
GRACE ABOUNDING TO THE CHIEF OF SINNERS

19 You may say, 'God stores up a man's punishment for his
children!'
Instead let him repay the man himself
so that he may be humbled!
20 Let his own eyes see his destruction;
let him drink of the anger of the Almighty.
21 For what is his interest in his home
after his death,
when the number of his months
has been broken off?
22 Can anyone teach God knowledge,
since he judges those that are on high?

DEATH LEVELS EVERYTHING

23 "One man dies in his full vigor,
completely secure and prosperous,
24 his body well nourished,
and the marrow of his bones moist.
25 And another man dies in bitterness of soul,
never having tasted anything good.
26 Together they lie down in the dust,
and worms cover over them both.

FUTILE WORDS, DECEPTIVE ANSWERS

27 "Yes, I know what you are thinking,
the schemes by which you would wrong me.
28 For you say,
'Where now is the nobleman's house,
and where are the tents in which the wicked lived?'
29 Have you never questioned those who travel
the roads?
Do you not recognize their accounts—
30 that the evil man is spared
from the day of his misfortune,
that he is delivered
from the day of God's wrath?
31 No one denounces his conduct to his face;
no one repays him for what he has done.
32 And when he is carried to the tombs
and watch is kept over the funeral mound,
33 the clods of the torrent valley are sweet to him;
behind him everybody follows in procession,
and before him goes a countless throng.
34 So how can you console me with your futile
words?
Nothing is left of your answers but deception!"

ELIPHAZ'S THIRD SPEECH

22 Then Eliphaz the Temanite answered:
2 "Is it to God that a strong man is of benefit?
Is it to him that even a wise man is profitable?
3 Is it of any special benefit to the Almighty
that you should be righteous,
or is it any gain to him
that you make your ways blameless?
4 Is it because of your piety that he rebukes you
and goes to judgment with you?
5 Is not your wickedness great
and is there no end to your iniquity?

22:1–30 Eliphaz brought heavy charges against Job without reason for his accusations, except that Job was visited as he supposed God always visited every wicked man. He charged him with oppression and that he did harm with his wealth and power in the time of his prosperity. But if others are consumed and we are not, instead of blaming them and lifting up ourselves, as Eliphaz did here, we ought to be thankful to God and take it for a warning. The answer of Eliphaz wrongly implied that Job had hitherto not known God and that prosperity in this life would follow his sincere conversion. The counsel Eliphaz here gives is good, though, as to Job, it was built upon a false supposition that he was a stranger and enemy to God. Let us beware of slandering our brethren, and if it be our lot to suffer in this manner, let us remember how Job was treated—yes, how Jesus was reviled, that we may be patient.

MATTHEW HENRY **(1662–1714)**
COMMENTARY ON THE WHOLE BIBLE

6 "For you took pledges from your brothers
for no reason,
and you stripped the clothing from the naked.
7 You gave the weary no water to drink
and from the hungry you withheld food.
8 Although you were a powerful man, owning land,
an honored man living on it,
9 you sent widows away empty-handed,
and the arms of the orphans you crushed.
10 That is why snares surround you,
and why sudden fear terrifies you,
11 why it is so dark you cannot see,
and why a flood of water covers you.

12 "Is not God on high in heaven?
And see the lofty stars, how high they are!
13 But you have said, 'What does God know?
Does he judge through such deep darkness?
14 Thick clouds are a veil for him, so he does not see us,
as he goes back and forth
in the vault of heaven.'
15 Will you keep to the old path
that evil men have walked—
16 men who were carried off before their time,
when the flood was poured out
on their foundations?
17 They were saying to God, 'Turn away from us,'
and, 'What can the Almighty do to us?'
18 But it was he who filled their houses
with good things—
yet the counsel of the wicked
was far from me.
19 The righteous see their destruction and rejoice;
the innocent mock them scornfully, saying,
20 'Surely our enemies are destroyed,
and fire consumes their wealth.'

21 "Reconcile yourself with God,
and be at peace with him;
in this way your prosperity will be good.
22 Accept instruction from his mouth
and store up his words in your heart.
23 If you return to the Almighty, you will be built up;
if you remove wicked behavior far from your tent,
24 and throw your gold in the dust—
your gold of Ophir
among the rocks in the ravines—
25 then the Almighty himself will be your gold,
and the choicest silver for you.
26 Surely then you will delight yourself in the Almighty
and will lift up your face toward God.
27 You will pray to him, and he will hear you,
and you will fulfill your vows to him.
28 Whatever you decide on a matter,
it will be established for you,
and light will shine on your ways.
29 When people are brought low and you say,
'Lift them up!'
then he will save the downcast;

30 he will deliver even someone who is not innocent,
who will escape through the cleanness of your hands."

JOB'S REPLY TO ELIPHAZ

23 Then Job answered:
2 "Even today my complaint is still bitter;
his hand is heavy despite my groaning.
3 O that I knew where I might find him,
that I could come to his place of residence!
4 I would lay out my case before him
and fill my mouth with arguments.
5 I would know with what words he would answer me
and understand what he would say to me.
6 Would he contend with me with great power?
No, he would only pay attention to me.
7 There an upright person
could present his case before him,
and I would be delivered forever from my judge.

THE INACCESSIBILITY AND POWER OF GOD

8 "If I go to the east, he is not there,
and to the west, yet I do not perceive him.
9 In the north when he is at work,
I do not see him;
when he turns to the south,
I see no trace of him.
10 But he knows the pathway that I take;
if he tested me, I would come forth like gold.
11 My feet have followed his steps closely;
I have kept to his way and have not turned aside.
12 I have not departed from the commands of his lips;
I have treasured the words of his mouth more than my allotted portion.
13 But he is unchangeable, and who can change him?
Whatever he has desired, he does.
14 For he fulfills his decree against me,
and many such things are his plans.
15 That is why I am terrified in his presence;
when I consider, I am afraid because of him.
16 Indeed, God has made my heart faint;
the Almighty has terrified me.
17 Yet I have not been silent because of the darkness,
because of the thick darkness
that covered my face.

THE APPARENT INDIFFERENCE OF GOD

24 "Why are times not appointed by the Almighty?
Why do those who know him not see his days?
2 Men move boundary stones;
they seize the flock and pasture them.
3 They drive away the orphan's donkey;
they take the widow's ox as a pledge.
4 They turn the needy from the pathway,
and the poor of the land hide themselves together.
5 Like wild donkeys in the wilderness,
they go out to their labor seeking diligently for food;
the arid rift valley provides food for them and for their children.
6 They reap fodder in the field

23:1–17 In Job's uttermost extremity he cried after the Lord. "O, that I knew where I might find him [who is my God!], that I could come to his place of residence!" God's children run home when the storm comes on. It is the heaven-born instinct of a gracious soul to seek shelter from all ills beneath the wings of Jehovah. "The one who lives in the shelter of the Most High" (Ps 91:1) might serve as the title of a true believer. Job's desire to commune with God was intensified by the failure of all other sources of consolation. The patriarch turned away from his sorry friends and looked up to the celestial throne. Nothing teaches us so much the preciousness of the Creator as when we learn the emptiness of all besides. In every trouble we should first seek to realize God's presence with us. Only let us enjoy his smile, and we can bear our daily cross with a willing heart for his dear sake.

CHARLES SPURGEON
(1834–1892)
MORNING AND EVENING

24:1–25 Job pursued the crimes of the wicked to the end of his speech. "Times are not hidden," he said, "from the Almighty" (NKJV), that is, in his knowledge dwells a full awareness of all our moments. It is as if he said, *God does not ignore any time of our actions even as we change them constantly,* yet we who touch him with the devotion of our mind ignore how many days of patience and deferment he hangs on our judgment . . . It must be noticed in this reproof of human vices that they are weighed more lightly or more seriously according to their effect on the virtue of soul. Thus Job and his friends are affected in different ways by different vices; the friends accuse only the acts of inhumanity, whereas Job describes the crimes of iniquity, violence, robbery, lewdness, pride, and impiety.

JULIAN OF ECLANUM
(C. 386–C. 455)
EXPOSITION ON THE BOOK OF JOB

and glean in the vineyard of the wicked.
7 They spend the night naked because they lack clothing;
they have no covering against the cold.
8 They are soaked by mountain rains
and huddle in the rocks because they lack shelter.
9 The fatherless child is snatched from the breast;
the infant of the poor is taken as a pledge.
10 They go about naked, without clothing,
and go hungry while they carry the sheaves.
11 They press out the olive oil between the rows of olive
trees;
they tread the winepresses while they are thirsty.
12 From the city the dying groan,
and the wounded cry out for help,
but God charges no one with wrongdoing.
13 There are those who rebel against the light;
they do not know its ways,
and they do not stay on its paths.
14 Before daybreak the murderer rises up;
he kills the poor and the needy;
in the night he is like a thief.
15 And the eye of the adulterer watches for the twilight,
thinking, 'No eye can see me,'
and covers his face with a mask.
16 In the dark the robber breaks into houses,
but by day they shut themselves in;
they do not know the light.
17 For all of them, the morning is to them like deep darkness;
they are friends with the terrors of darkness.

18 "You say, 'He is foam on the face of the waters;
their portion of the land is cursed
so that no one goes to their vineyard.
19 The drought as well as the heat
snatch up the melted snow;
so the grave snatches up the sinner.
20 The womb forgets him,
the worm feasts on him,
no longer will he be remembered.
Like a tree, wickedness will be broken down.
21 He preys on the barren and childless woman
and does not treat the widow well.
22 But God drags off the mighty by his power;
when God rises up against him, he has no faith in his
life.
23 God may let them rest in a feeling of security,
but he is constantly watching all their ways.
24 They are exalted for a little while, and then they are
gone;
they are brought low like all others and gathered in,
and like a head of grain they are cut off.'

25 "If this is not so, who can prove me a liar
and reduce my words to nothing?"

BILDAD'S THIRD SPEECH

25 Then Bildad the Shuhite answered:
2 "Dominion and awesome might belong to God;
he establishes peace in his heights.

3 Can his armies be numbered?
On whom does his light not rise?
4 How then can a human being be righteous before God?
How can one born of a woman be pure?
5 If even the moon is not bright,
and the stars are not pure as far as he is concerned,
6 how much less a mortal man, who is but a maggot—
a son of man, who is only a worm!"

JOB'S REPLY TO BILDAD

26 Then Job replied:
2 "How you have helped the powerless!
How you have saved the person who has no strength!
3 How you have advised the one without wisdom,
and abundantly revealed your insight!
4 To whom did you utter these words?
And whose spirit has come forth from your mouth?

A BETTER DESCRIPTION OF GOD'S GREATNESS

5 "The dead tremble—
those beneath the waters
and all that live in them.
6 The underworld is naked before God;
the place of destruction lies uncovered.
7 He spreads out the northern skies over empty space;
he suspends the earth on nothing.
8 He locks the waters in his clouds,
and the clouds do not burst with the weight of them.
9 He conceals the face of the full moon,
shrouding it with his clouds.
10 He marks out the horizon on the surface of the waters
as a boundary between light and darkness.
11 The pillars of the heavens tremble
and are amazed at his rebuke.
12 By his power he stills the sea;
by his wisdom he cut Rahab the great sea monster to pieces.
13 By his breath the skies became fair;
his hand pierced the fleeing serpent.
14 Indeed, these are but the outer fringes of his ways!
How faint is the whisper we hear of him!
But who can understand the thunder of his power?"

A PROTEST OF INNOCENCE

27 And Job took up his discourse again:
2 "As surely as God lives, who has denied me justice,
the Almighty, who has made my life bitter—
3 for while my spirit is still in me,
and the breath from God is in my nostrils,
4 my lips will not speak wickedness,
and my tongue will whisper no deceit.
5 I will never declare that you three are in the right;
until I die, I will not set aside my integrity!
6 I will maintain my righteousness
and never let it go;
my conscience will not reproach me
for as long as I live.

25:4–5 Bildad appears to assert that not only may the stars be subject to sin, but even that they are actually not clean from the contagion of it: "The stars are not pure as far as he is concerned." Nor is this to be understood of the splendor of their physical substance as if one were to say, for example, of a garment that it is not clean; for if such were the meaning, then the accusation of a want of cleanness in the splendor of their bodily substance would imply an injurious reflection upon their Creator. For if they are unable through their own diligent efforts either to acquire for themselves a body of greater brightness or through their sloth to make the one they have less pure, how should they incur censure for being stars that are not clean if they receive no praise because they are so?

ORIGEN (C. 185–C. 253)
ON FIRST PRINCIPLES

26:1–14 "He locks the water in his clouds, and the clouds do not burst with the weight of them." In fact, if he does not order the clouds to rain, they do not release rain on earth in the quantity that has been ordered by him. "He covers the face of His throne, and spreads His cloud over it" (NKJV). Heaven is often called "the throne of God" in holy scripture. Air (or elements) is placed before the face of heaven. Therefore he says that God, by containing the air (or elements) and expanding the clouds, does not allow them to release rain if not in the measure that he knows to be convenient and useful.

OLYMPIODORUS (C. 470–520)
COMMENTARY ON JOB

27:1–13 Job's three friends, in their speeches to him, insisted much that he was a hypocrite. But in this chapter Job asserted his sincerity and integrity. Particularly he declared his steadfast and immoveable resolution of persevering and holding out in the ways of religion and righteousness to the end. In the text he showed how contrary to this steadfastness and perseverance the character of the hypocrite is who is not determined thus to hold out in religion.

JONATHAN EDWARDS
(1703–1758)
THE COMPLETE WORKS

THE CONDITION OF THE WICKED

7 "May my enemy be like the wicked,
my adversary like the unrighteous.
8 For what hope does the godless have when he is cut off,
when God takes away his life?
9 Does God listen to his cry
when distress overtakes him?
10 Will he find delight in the Almighty?
Will he call out to God at all times?
11 I will teach you about the power of God;
what is on the Almighty's mind I will not conceal.
12 If you yourselves have all seen this,
Why in the world do you continue this meaningless talk?
13 This is the portion of the wicked man
allotted by God,
the inheritance that evildoers receive
from the Almighty.
14 If his children increase—it is for the sword!
His offspring never have enough to eat.
15 Those who survive him are buried by the plague,
and their widows do not mourn for them.
16 If he piles up silver like dust
and stores up clothing like mounds of clay,
17 what he stores up a righteous man will wear,
and an innocent man will inherit his silver.
18 The house he builds is as fragile as a moth's cocoon,
like a hut that a watchman has made.
19 He goes to bed wealthy, but will do so no more.
When he opens his eyes, it is all gone.
20 Terrors overwhelm him like a flood;
at night a whirlwind carries him off.
21 The east wind carries him away, and he is gone;
it sweeps him out of his place.
22 It hurls itself against him without pity
as he flees headlong from its power.
23 It claps its hands at him in derision
and hisses him away from his place.

III. JOB'S SEARCH FOR WISDOM (28:1–28)

NO KNOWN ROAD TO WISDOM

28 "Surely there is a mine for silver
and a place where gold is refined.
2 Iron is taken from the ground,
and rock is poured out as copper.
3 Man puts an end to the darkness;
he searches the farthest recesses
for the ore in the deepest darkness.
4 Far from where people live he sinks a shaft,
in places travelers have long forgotten,
far from other people he dangles and sways.
5 The earth, from which food comes,
is overturned below as though by fire;
6 a place whose stones are sapphires
that contain dust of gold;
7 a hidden path no bird of prey knows—
no falcon's eye has spotted it.
8 Proud beasts have not set foot on it,
and no lion has passed along it.

28:1–28 Job having showed that God does sometimes prosper the wicked all their days so they live and die without any visible token of God's displeasure, when on the contrary, good people are exercised with many calamities; in this chapter he declares that this is one of the depths of divine wisdom, not discoverable by any mortal, that this was a wisdom of a higher nature and out of humans' reach. The caverns of the earth they may discover but not the counsels of heaven . . . By a diligent inquiry we find at length that there is a twofold wisdom: one hid in God, which belongs not to us, the other revealed to humanity, which belongs to us and to our children. The line and plummet of human reason can never fathom the abyss of the divine counsels.

JOHN WESLEY (1703–1791)
EXPLANATORY NOTES ON THE BIBLE

9 On the flinty rock man has set to work with his hand;
he has overturned mountains at their bases.
10 He has cut out channels through the rocks;
his eyes have spotted every precious thing.
11 He has searched the sources of the rivers,
and what was hidden he has brought into the light.

NO PRICE CAN BUY WISDOM

12 "But wisdom—where can it be found?
Where is the place of understanding?
13 Mankind does not know its place;
it cannot be found in the land of the living.
14 The deep says, 'It is not with me.'
And the sea says, 'It is not with me.'
15 Fine gold cannot be given in exchange for it,
nor can its price be weighed out in silver.
16 It cannot be measured out for purchase with the gold of Ophir,
with precious onyx or sapphires.
17 Neither gold nor crystal can be compared with it,
nor can a vase of gold match its worth.
18 Of coral and jasper no mention will be made;
the price of wisdom is more than pearls.
19 The topaz of Cush cannot be compared with it;
it cannot be purchased with pure gold.

GOD ALONE HAS WISDOM

20 "But wisdom—where does it come from?
Where is the place of understanding?
21 For it has been hidden
from the eyes of every living creature,
and from the birds of the sky it has been concealed.
22 Destruction and Death say,
'With our ears we have heard a rumor about where it can be found.'
23 God understands the way to it,
and he alone knows its place.
24 For he looks to the ends of the earth
and observes everything under the heavens.
25 When he made the force of the wind
and measured the waters with a gauge,
26 when he imposed a limit for the rain,
and a path for the thunderstorm,
27 then he looked at wisdom and assessed its value;
he established it and examined it closely.
28 And he said to mankind,
'The fear of the Lord—that is wisdom,
and to turn away from evil is understanding.'"

IV. JOB'S CONCLUDING SOLILOQUY (29:1–31:40)

JOB RECALLS HIS FORMER CONDITION

29 Then Job continued his speech:
2 "O that I could be as I was
in the months now gone,
in the days when God watched over me,
3 when he caused his lamp
to shine upon my head,
and by his light

29:1–25 Christian, if you are not now as you were "in the months now gone," do not rest satisfied with wishing for a return of former happiness, but go at once to seek your Master and tell him your sad state. Ask his grace and strength to help you to walk more closely with him; humble yourself before him, and he will lift you up and give you yet again to enjoy the light of his countenance. Do not sit down to sigh and lament; while the beloved Physician lives there is hope, there is a certainty of recovery for the worst cases.

CHARLES SPURGEON
(1834–1892)
MORNING AND EVENING

I walked through darkness;
4 just as I was in my most productive time,
when God's intimate friendship was experienced in my tent,
5 when the Almighty was still with me
and my children were around me;
6 when my steps were bathed with butter
and the rock poured out for me streams of olive oil!
7 When I went out to the city gate
and secured my seat in the public square,
8 the young men would see me and step aside,
and the old men would get up and remain standing;
9 the chief men refrained from talking
and covered their mouths with their hands;
10 the voices of the nobles fell silent,
and their tongues stuck to the roof of their mouths.

JOB'S BENEVOLENCE

11 "As soon as the ear heard these things, it blessed me,
and when the eye saw them, it bore witness to me;
12 for I rescued the poor who cried out for help,
and the orphan who had no one to assist him;
13 the blessing of the dying man descended on me,
and I made the widow's heart rejoice;
14 I put on righteousness and it clothed me;
my just dealing was like a robe and a turban;
15 I was eyes for the blind
and feet for the lame;
16 I was a father to the needy,
and I investigated the case of the person I did not know;
17 I broke the fangs of the wicked,
and made him drop his prey from his teeth.

JOB'S CONFIDENCE

18 "Then I thought, 'I will die in my own home,
my days as numerous as the grains of sand.
19 My roots reach the water,
and the dew lies on my branches all night long.
20 My glory will always be fresh in me,
and my bow ever new in my hand.'

JOB'S REPUTATION

21 "People listened to me and waited silently;
they kept silent for my advice.
22 After I had spoken, they did not respond;
my words fell on them drop by drop.
23 They waited for me as people wait for the rain,
and they opened their mouths as for the spring rains.
24 If I smiled at them, they hardly believed it;
and they did not cause the light of my face to darken.
25 I chose the way for them
and sat as their chief;
I lived like a king among his troops;
I was like one who comforts mourners.

JOB'S PRESENT MISERY

30 "But now they mock me, those who are younger than I,
whose fathers I disdained too much
to put with my sheep dogs.

2 Moreover, the strength of their hands—
what use was it to me?
Those whose strength had perished,
3 gaunt with want and hunger,
they would roam the parched land,
by night a desolate waste.
4 By the brush they would gather herbs from the salt
marshes,
and the root of the broom tree was their food.
5 They were banished from the community—
people shouted at them
as they would shout at thieves—
6 so that they had to live
in the dry stream beds,
in the holes of the ground, and among the rocks.
7 They brayed like animals among the bushes
and were huddled together under the nettles.
8 Sons of senseless and nameless people,
they were driven out of the land with whips.

JOB'S INDIGNITIES

9 "And now I have become their taunt song;
I have become a byword among them.
10 They detest me and maintain their distance;
they do not hesitate to spit in my face.
11 Because God has untied my tent cord and
afflicted me,
people throw off all restraint in my presence.
12 On my right the young rabble rise up;
they drive me from place to place
and build up siege ramps against me.
13 They destroy my path;
they succeed in destroying me
without anyone assisting them.
14 They come in as through a wide breach;
amid the crash they come rolling in.
15 Terrors are turned loose on me;
they drive away my honor like the wind,
and as a cloud my deliverance has passed
away.

JOB'S DESPONDENCY

16 "And now my soul pours itself out within me;
days of suffering take hold of me.
17 Night pierces my bones;
my gnawing pains never cease.
18 With great power God grasps my clothing;
he binds me like the collar of my tunic.
19 He has flung me into the mud,
and I have come to resemble dust and ashes.
20 I cry out to you, but you do not answer me;
I stand up, and you only look at me.
21 You have become cruel to me;
with the strength of your hand you attack me.
22 You pick me up on the wind and make me ride
on it;
you toss me about in the storm.
23 I know that you are bringing me to death,
to the meeting place for all the living.

30:1–31 Job contrasted his present condition with his former honor and authority. Job complained a great deal. Harboring hard thoughts of God was the sin that did, at this time, most easily beset him. When inward temptations join with outward calamities, the soul is harried as in a tempest and is filled with confusion. If none pity us, yet our God who corrects pities us, even as a father pities his own children. And let us look more to the things of eternity: Then the believer will cease from mourning and joyfully praise redeeming love.

MATTHEW HENRY (1662–1714)
COMMENTARY ON THE WHOLE BIBLE

THE CONTRAST WITH THE PAST

24 "Surely one does not stretch out his hand
against a broken man
when he cries for help in his distress.
25 Have I not wept for the unfortunate?
Was not my soul grieved for the poor?
26 But when I hoped for good, trouble came;
when I expected light, then darkness came.
27 My heart is in turmoil unceasingly;
the days of my affliction confront me.
28 I go about blackened, but not by the sun;
in the assembly I stand up and cry for help.
29 I have become a brother to jackals
and a companion of ostriches.
30 My skin has turned dark on me;
my body is hot with fever.
31 My harp is used for mourning
and my flute for the sound of weeping.

JOB VINDICATES HIMSELF

31 "I made a covenant with my eyes;
how then could I entertain thoughts against a virgin?
2 What then would be one's lot from God above,
one's heritage from the Almighty on high?
3 Is it not misfortune for the unjust
and disaster for those who work iniquity?
4 Does he not see my ways
and count all my steps?
5 If I have walked in falsehood
and if my foot has hastened to deceit—
6 let him weigh me with honest scales;
then God will discover my integrity.
7 If my footsteps have strayed from the way,
if my heart has gone after my eyes,
or if anything has defiled my hands,
8 then let me sow and let another eat,
and let my crops be uprooted.
9 If my heart has been enticed by a woman,
and I have lain in wait at my neighbor's door,
10 then let my wife turn the millstone for another man,
and may other men commit adultery with her.
11 For I would have committed a shameful act,
an iniquity to be judged.
12 For it is a fire that devours even to Destruction,
and it would uproot all my harvest.

13 "If I have disregarded the right of my male servants
or my female servants
when they disputed with me,
14 then what will I do when God confronts me in judgment;
when he intervenes,
how will I respond to him?
15 Did not the one who made me in the womb make them?
Did not the same one form us in the womb?
16 If I have refused to give the poor what they desired,
or caused the eyes of the widow to fail,
17 if I ate my morsel of bread myself,
and did not share any of it with orphans—
18 but from my youth I raised the orphan like a father,

31:1–12 Desire is a fire, and the flesh is like a garment. The latter is an easy prey, and the former is a tyrant. And when anything harmful is not only taken within but also held fast, it will not go forth again until it has made an exit for itself. For he who looks upon a woman, even though he escapes the temptation, does not come away pure of all lust. And why should one have trouble if he can be chaste and free of trouble? See what Job said: "I made a covenant with my eyes; how then could I entertain thoughts against a virgin?" Thus well did he know the power of abuse. And figuratively speaking, he keeps a fire in his breast who permits an impure thought to dwell in his heart. And he walks upon coals who, by sinning in act, destroys his own soul.

HIPPOLYTUS OF ROME
(C. 170–C. 235)
THE REFUTATION OF ALL HERESIES

and from my mother's womb I guided the widow—
19 if I have seen anyone about to perish for lack of clothing,
or a poor man without a coat,
20 whose heart did not bless me
as he warmed himself with the fleece of my sheep,
21 if I have raised my hand to vote against the orphan,
when I saw my support in the court,
22 then let my arm fall from the shoulder,
let my arm be broken off at the socket.
23 For the calamity from God was a terror to me,
and by reason of his majesty I was powerless.

24 "If I have put my confidence in gold
or said to pure gold,
'You are my security!'
25 if I have rejoiced because of the extent of my wealth,
or because of the great wealth my hand had gained,
26 if I looked at the sun when it was shining,
and the moon advancing as a precious thing,
27 so that my heart was secretly enticed,
and my hand threw them a kiss from my mouth,
28 then this also would be iniquity to be judged,
for I would have been false to God above.
29 If I have rejoiced over the misfortune of my enemy
or exulted because calamity found him—
30 I have not even permitted my mouth to sin
by asking for his life through a curse—
31 if the members of my household have never said,
'If only there were someone
who has not been satisfied from Job's meat!'—
32 but no stranger had to spend the night outside,
for I opened my doors to the traveler—
33 if I have covered my transgressions as men do,
by hiding iniquity in my heart,
34 because I was terrified of the great multitude,
and the contempt of families terrified me,
so that I remained silent
and would not go outdoors—

JOB'S APPEAL

35 "If only I had someone to hear me!
Here is my signature—
let the Almighty answer me!
If only I had an indictment
that my accuser had written.
36 Surely I would wear it proudly on my shoulder,
I would bind it on me like a crown;
37 I would give him an accounting of my steps;
like a prince I would draw near to him."

JOB'S FINAL SOLEMN OATH

38 "If my land cried out against me
and all its furrows wept together,
39 if I have eaten its produce without paying,
or caused the death of its owners,
40 then let thorns sprout up in place of wheat,
and in place of barley, noxious weeds."

The words of Job are ended.

32:1–6 Elihu is inflamed, not because Job declared himself to be righteous but because he thought that Job brought an action against God. In fact, to justify oneself has no great importance in itself, but to do that with the intention of bringing an action against God is absolutely unsuitable. Now, if this is true, what an extreme act of impiety on the part of Job if he believed himself to be more righteous than God. What really happened? This was not Job's thought at all. It is Elihu who believed so. Job did not speak with the idea that he was more righteous than God but with the idea that God was responsible for his afflictions. Therefore he did not reproach God for any injustice: It is Elihu who understood it so.

CHRYSOSTOM (C. 347-407)
COMMENTARY ON JOB

V. THE SPEECHES OF ELIHU (32:1–37:24)

ELIHU'S FIRST SPEECH

32 So these three men refused to answer Job further, because he was righteous in his own eyes. [2]Then Elihu son
of Barakel the Buzite, of the family of Ram, became very angry.
He was angry with Job for justifying himself rather than God.
[3]With Job's three friends he was also angry because they could
not find an answer, and so declared Job guilty. [4]Now Elihu had
waited before speaking to Job because the others were older
than he was. [5]But when Elihu saw that the three men had no
further reply, he became very angry.

ELIHU CLAIMS WISDOM

[6]So Elihu son of Barakel the Buzite spoke up:
"I am young, but you are elderly;
that is why I was fearful
and afraid to explain to you what I know.
7 I said to myself, 'Age should speak,
and length of years should make wisdom known.'
8 But it is a spirit in people,
the breath of the Almighty,
that makes them understand.
9 It is not the aged who are wise,
nor old men who understand what is right.
10 Therefore I say, 'Listen to me.
I, even I, will explain what I know.'
11 Look, I waited for you to speak;
I listened closely to your wise thoughts, while you were searching for words.
12 Now I was paying you close attention,
yet there was no one proving Job wrong,
not one of you was answering his statements.
13 So do not say, 'We have found wisdom.
God will refute him, not man.'
14 Job has not directed his words to me,
and so I will not reply to him with your arguments.

JOB'S FRIENDS FAILED TO ANSWER

15 "They are dismayed and cannot answer anymore;
they have nothing left to say.
16 And I have waited. But because they do not speak,
because they stand there and answer no more,
17 I too will answer my part;
I too will explain what I know.
18 For I am full of words,
and the spirit within me constrains me.
19 Inside I am like wine that has no outlet,
like new wineskins ready to burst!
20 I will speak, so that I may find relief;
I will open my lips, so that I may answer.
21 I will not show partiality to any person,
nor will I confer a title on anyone.
22 For I do not know how to give honorary titles;
if I did, my Creator would quickly do away with me.

ELIHU INVITES JOB'S ATTENTION

33 "But now, O Job, listen to my words,
and hear everything I have to say.
2 See now, I have opened my mouth;

my tongue in my mouth has spoken.
3 My words come from the uprightness of my heart,
and my lips will utter knowledge sincerely.
4 The Spirit of God has made me,
and the breath of the Almighty gives me life.
5 Reply to me, if you can;
set your arguments in order before me
and take your stand.
6 Look, I am just like you in relation to God;
I too have been molded from clay.
7 Therefore no fear of me should terrify you,
nor should my pressure be heavy on you.

ELIHU REJECTS JOB'S PLEA OF INNOCENCE

8 "Indeed, you have said in my hearing
(I heard the sound of the words!):
9 'I am pure, without transgression;
I am clean and have no iniquity.
10 Yet God finds occasions with me;
he regards me as his enemy.
11 He puts my feet in shackles;
he watches closely all my paths.'
12 Now in this, you are not right—I answer you,
for God is greater than a human being.
13 Why do you contend against him,
that he does not answer all a person's words?

ELIHU DISAGREES WITH JOB'S VIEW OF GOD

14 "For God speaks, the first time in one way,
the second time in another,
though a person does not perceive it.
15 In a dream, a night vision,
when deep sleep falls on people
as they sleep in their beds,
16 then he gives a revelation to people
and terrifies them with warnings,
17 to turn a person from his sin,
and to cover a person's pride.
18 He spares a person's life from corruption,
his very life from crossing over the river.
19 Or a person is chastened by pain on his bed
and with the continual strife of his bones,
20 so that his life loathes food
and his soul rejects appetizing fare.
21 His flesh wastes away from sight,
and his bones, which were not seen,
are easily visible.
22 He draws near to the place of corruption,
and his life to the messengers of death.
23 If there is an angel beside him,
one mediator out of a thousand,
to tell a person what constitutes his
uprightness,
24 and if God is gracious to him and says,
'Spare him from going down
to the place of corruption,
I have found a ransom for him,'
25 then his flesh is restored like a youth's;
he returns to the days of his youthful vigor.

33:4 How is it that Job plainly set forth the Spirit as his Creator, saying, "The Spirit of God has made me"? In one short verse he showed him to be both divine and Creator. If then the Spirit is Creator, he is certainly not a creature, for the apostle Paul separated the Creator and the creature, saying: "They . . . served the creation rather than the Creator" (Rom 1:25).

AMBROSE (C. 339–C. 397)
ON THE HOLY SPIRIT

26 He entreats God, and God delights in him;
he sees God's face with rejoicing,
and God restores to him his righteousness.
27 That person sings to others, saying:
'I have sinned and falsified what is right,
but I was not punished according to what
I deserved.
28 He redeemed my life
from going down to the place of corruption,
and my life sees the light!'

ELIHU'S APPEAL TO JOB

29 "Indeed, God does all these things,
twice, three times, in his dealings with a person,
30 to turn back his life from the place of corruption,
that he may be enlightened with the light of life.
31 Pay attention, Job—listen to me;
be silent, and I will speak.
32 If you have any words, reply to me;
speak, for I want to justify you.
33 If not, you listen to me;
be silent, and I will teach you wisdom."

ELIHU'S SECOND SPEECH

34 Elihu answered:
2 "Listen to my words, you wise men;
hear me, you learned men.
3 For the ear assesses words
as the mouth tastes food.
4 Let us evaluate for ourselves what is right;
let us come to know among ourselves what is good.
5 For Job says, 'I am innocent,
but God turns away my right.
6 Concerning my right, should I lie?
My wound is incurable,
although I am without transgression.'
7 Who is there like Job,
who drinks derision like water?
8 He goes about in company with evildoers;
he goes along with wicked men.
9 For he says, 'It does not profit a man
when he makes his delight with God.'

GOD IS NOT UNJUST

10 "Therefore, listen to me, you men of
understanding.
Far be it from God to do wickedness,
from the Almighty to do evil.
11 For he repays a person for his work,
and according to the conduct of a person,
he causes the consequences to find him.
12 Indeed, in truth, God does not act wickedly,
and the Almighty does not pervert justice.
13 Who entrusted to him the earth?
And who put him over the whole world?
14 If God were to set his heart on it,
and gather in his spirit and his breath,
15 all flesh would perish together,
and human beings would return to dust.

34:1–37 Elihu said, "Far be it from God to do wickedness, from the Almighty to do evil" and "the Almighty does not pervert justice." To condemn is one thing, to afflict another. He afflicts therefore in some respect without cause but does not condemn without cause. Nor does Almighty God pervert justice because, although our sufferings seem to be unjust, yet they are rightly inflicted in his secret judgment. It follows, "Who entrusted to him the earth? And who put him over the whole world?" No one. For he governs indeed by himself the world that he created by himself. Almighty God governs correctly that which he created correctly. He does not order in heartlessness that which he fashioned in mercy. And he who provided for their being before they were made does not forsake them after their creation. He therefore does not omit to take care of us.

GREGORY THE GREAT
(C. 540–604)
MORALS ON THE BOOK OF JOB

GOD IS IMPARTIAL AND OMNISCIENT

16 "If you have understanding, listen to this,
hear what I have to say.
17 Do you really think
that one who hates justice can govern?
And will you declare guilty
the supremely Righteous One,
18 who says to a king, 'Worthless man,'
and to nobles, 'Wicked men,'
19 who shows no partiality to princes,
and does not take note of the rich more than
the poor
because all of them are the work of his hands?
20 In a moment they die, in the middle of the night;
people are shaken, and they pass away.
The mighty are removed effortlessly.
21 For his eyes are on the ways of an individual;
he observes all a person's steps.
22 There is no darkness, and no deep darkness,
where evildoers can hide themselves.
23 For he does not still consider a person,
that he should come before God in judgment.
24 He shatters the great without inquiry
and sets up others in their place.
25 Therefore, he knows their deeds;
he overthrows them in the night,
and they are crushed.
26 He strikes them for their wickedness
in a place where people can see,
27 because they have turned away from following him
and have not understood any of his ways,
28 so that they caused the cry of the poor
to come before him,
so that he hears the cry of the needy.
29 But if God is quiet, who can condemn him?
If he hides his face, then who can see him?
Yet he is over the individual and the nation alike,
30 so that the godless man should not rule
and not lay snares for the people.

JOB IS FOOLISH TO REBEL

31 "Has anyone said to God,
'I have endured chastisement,
but I will not act wrongly any more;
32 teach me what I cannot see;
if I have done evil, I will do so no more'?
33 Is it your opinion that God should recompense it,
because you reject this?
But you must choose, and not I,
so tell us what you know.
34 Men of understanding say to me—
any wise man listening to me says—
35 that Job speaks without knowledge
and his words are without understanding.
36 But Job will be tested to the end,
because his answers are like those of wicked men.
37 For he adds transgression to his sin;
in our midst he claps his hands
and multiplies his words against God."

35:1–16 "Gaze at the heavens and see; consider the clouds, which are higher than you." The one who looks at the heavens is not he who raises his physical eyes and observes the heavens. Indeed, dogs and donkeys look at the heavens in this manner. No one who loves the world looks at the heavens, but only he who does not love the world and the things that are in it. If we love the things that are here, we do not look to the heavens.

ORIGEN (C. 185–C. 253)
FRAGMENTS ON JOB

ELIHU'S THIRD SPEECH

35 Then Elihu answered:
2 "Do you think this to be just
when you say, 'My right before God'?
3 But you say, 'What will it profit you,'
and, 'What do I gain by not sinning?'
4 I will reply to you,
and to your friends with you.
5 Gaze at the heavens and see;
consider the clouds, which are higher than you.
6 If you sin, how does it affect God?
If your transgressions are many,
what does it do to him?
7 If you are righteous, what do you give to God,
or what does he receive from your hand?
8 Your wickedness affects only a person like yourself,
and your righteousness only other people.

9 "People cry out
because of the excess of oppression;
they cry out for help
because of the power of the mighty.
10 But no one says, 'Where is God, my Creator,
who gives songs in the night,
11 who teaches us more than the wild animals of the earth,
and makes us wiser than the birds of the sky?'
12 Then they cry out—but he does not answer—
because of the arrogance of the wicked.
13 Surely it is an empty cry—God does not hear it;
the Almighty does not take notice of it.
14 How much less, then,
when you say that you do not perceive him,
that the case is before him
and you are waiting for him!
15 And further, when you say
that his anger does not punish,
and that he does not know transgression!
16 So Job opens his mouth to no purpose;
without knowledge he multiplies words."

36:5–33 "Yes, God is great—beyond our knowledge!" God is infinitely wise, and as none can work like him, so none can teach like him. Therefore do not presume to teach him how to govern the world. No one teaches with such authority and convincing evidence, with such condescension and compassion, with such power and efficacy as God does. The power, wisdom, and greatness of God are so manifest in all his works that all who are not stupid must see and acknowledge them. He is eternal, as in his being, so in all his counsels, which therefore must be infinitely above the comprehension of short-lived human beings.

JOHN WESLEY (1703–1791)
EXPLANATORY NOTES ON THE BIBLE

ELIHU'S FOURTH SPEECH

36 Elihu said further:
2 "Be patient with me a little longer,
and I will instruct you,
for I still have words to speak on God's behalf.
3 With my knowledge I will speak comprehensively,
and to my Creator I will ascribe righteousness.
4 For in truth, my words are not false;
it is one complete in knowledge
who is with you.
5 Indeed, God is mighty, and he does not despise people;
he is mighty, and firm in his intent.
6 He does not allow the wicked to live,
but he gives justice to the poor.
7 He does not take his eyes off the righteous;
but with kings on the throne
he seats the righteous and exalts them forever.
8 But if they are bound in chains
and held captive by the cords of affliction,

9 then he reveals to them what they have done
and their transgressions,
that they were behaving proudly.
10 And he reveals this for correction
and says that they must turn from evil.
11 If they obey and serve him,
they live out their days in prosperity
and their years in pleasantness.
12 But if they refuse to listen,
they pass over the river of death
and expire without knowledge.
13 The godless at heart nourish anger;
they do not cry out even when he binds them.
14 They die in their youth,
and their life ends among the male cultic prostitutes.
15 He delivers the afflicted by their afflictions;
he reveals himself to them by their suffering.
16 And surely, he drew you from the mouth of distress,
to a wide place, unrestricted,
and to the comfort of your table
filled with rich food.
17 But now you are preoccupied with the judgment due
the wicked;
judgment and justice take hold of you.
18 Be careful that no one entices you with riches;
do not let a large bribe turn you aside.
19 Would your wealth sustain you,
so that you would not be in distress,
even all your mighty efforts?
20 Do not long for the cover of night
to drag people away from their homes.
21 Take heed; do not turn to evil,
for because of this you have been tested by affliction.
22 Indeed, God is exalted in his power;
who is a teacher like him?
23 Who has prescribed his ways for him?
Or said to him, 'You have done what is wicked'?
24 Remember to extol his work,
which people have praised in song.
25 All humanity has seen it;
people gaze on it from afar.

THE WORK AND WISDOM OF GOD

26 "Yes, God is great—beyond our knowledge!
The number of his years is unsearchable.
27 He draws up drops of water;
they distill the rain into its mist,
28 which the clouds pour down
and shower on humankind abundantly.
29 Who can understand the spreading of the clouds,
the thunderings of his pavilion?
30 See how he scattered his lightning about him;
he has covered the depths of the sea.
31 It is by these that he judges the nations
and supplies food in abundance.
32 With his hands he covers the lightning
and directs it against its target.
33 His thunder announces the coming storm,
the cattle also, concerning the storm's approach.

37:1–13 "He does great things beyond our understanding." This is the reason, Elihu said, for the grandiosity of his creations, the reason for the cold and the heat, the reason for the irregularity of the winds. Was it impossible to produce a harmonious blend? If God does not do that, it is because he wants to prevent by any means the pride and arrogance of thought. Since pride first of all drove away from us our trust in God, for this reason God has organized everything in view of its contrary, either the creation, the fashioning of our body, or the course of our life, so that all this exists for humility in order that we may learn to act with moderation and recognize our own weakness.

CHRYSOSTOM (C. 347–407)
COMMENTARY ON JOB

37 At this also my heart pounds
and leaps from its place.
2 Listen carefully to the thunder of his voice,
to the rumbling that proceeds from his mouth.
3 Under the whole heaven he lets it go,
even his lightning to the far corners of the earth.
4 After that a voice roars;
he thunders with an exalted voice,
and he does not hold back his lightning bolts
when his voice is heard.
5 God thunders with his voice in marvelous ways;
he does great things beyond our understanding.
6 For to the snow he says, 'Fall to earth,'
and to the torrential rains, 'Pour down.'
7 He causes everyone to stop working,
so that all people may know his work.
8 The wild animals go to their lairs,
and in their dens they remain.
9 A tempest blows out from its chamber,
icy cold from the driving winds.
10 The breath of God produces ice,
and the breadth of the waters freeze solid.
11 He loads the clouds with moisture;
he scatters his lightning through the clouds.
12 The clouds go round in circles,
wheeling about according to his plans,
to carry out all that he commands them
over the face of the whole inhabited world.
13 Whether it is for punishment,
or for his land,
or for mercy,
he causes it to find its mark.

14 "Pay attention to this, Job!
Stand still and consider the wonders God works.
15 Do you know how God commands them,
how he makes lightning flash in his storm cloud?
16 Do you know about the balancing of the clouds,
that wondrous activity of him who is perfect in knowledge?
17 You, whose garments are hot
when the earth is still because of the south wind,
18 will you, with him, spread out the clouds,
solid as a mirror of molten metal?
19 Tell us what we should say to him.
We cannot prepare a case
because of the darkness.
20 Should he be informed that I want to speak?
If a man speaks, surely he will be swallowed up!
21 But now, the sun cannot be looked at—
it is bright in the skies—
after a wind passed and swept the clouds away.
22 From the north he comes in golden splendor;
around God is awesome majesty.
23 As for the Almighty, we cannot attain to him!
He is great in power,
but justice and abundant righteousness he does not
oppress.
24 Therefore people fear him,
for he does not regard all the wise in heart."

VI. THE DIVINE SPEECHES (38:1–42:6)

THE LORD'S FIRST SPEECH

38 Then the LORD answered Job out of the whirlwind:
2 "Who is this who darkens counsel
with words without knowledge?
3 Get ready for a difficult task like a man;
I will question you,
and you will inform me.

GOD'S QUESTIONS TO JOB

4 "Where were you
when I laid the foundation of the earth?
Tell me, if you possess understanding.
5 Who set its measurements—if you know—
or who stretched a measuring line across it?
6 On what were its bases set,
or who laid its cornerstone—
7 when the morning stars sang in chorus,
and all the sons of God shouted for joy?

8 "Who shut up the sea with doors
when it burst forth, coming out of the womb,
9 when I made the storm clouds its garment
and thick darkness its swaddling band,
10 when I prescribed its limits
and set in place its bolts and doors,
11 when I said, 'To here you may come
and no farther,
here your proud waves will be confined'?
12 Have you ever in your life commanded the morning,
or made the dawn know its place,
13 that it might seize the corners of the earth
and shake the wicked out of it?
14 The earth takes shape like clay under a seal;
its features are dyed like a garment.
15 Then from the wicked the light is withheld,
and the arm raised in violence is broken.
16 Have you gone to the springs that fill the sea
or walked about in the recesses of the deep?
17 Have the gates of death been revealed to you?
Have you seen the gates of deepest darkness?
18 Have you considered the vast expanses of
the earth?
Tell me, if you know it all.

19 "In what direction does light reside,
and darkness, where is its place,
20 that you may take them to their borders
and perceive the pathways to their homes?
21 You know, for you were born before them;
and the number of your days is great!
22 Have you entered the storehouse of the snow
or seen the armory of the hail,
23 which I reserve for the time of trouble,
for the day of war and battle?
24 In what direction is lightning dispersed,
or the east winds scattered over the earth?
25 Who carves out a channel for the heavy rains
and a path for the rumble of thunder,

38:1–41 "Have you ever in your life commanded the morning, or made the dawn know its place?" The heavens, revolving under his government, are subject to him in peace. Day and night run the course appointed by him, in no way hindering each other. The fruitful earth, according to his will, brings forth food in abundance at the proper seasons for all the living beings upon it. The vast, immeasurable sea never passes beyond the bounds placed around it but does as he has commanded. The seasons of spring, summer, autumn, and winter peacefully give place to one another. The very smallest of living beings meet together in peace and concord. All these the great Creator and Lord of all has appointed to exist in peace and harmony while he does good to all, but most abundantly to us who have fled for refuge to his compassions through Jesus Christ our Lord, to whom be glory and majesty forever and ever. Amen.

CLEMENT OF ROME (D. 99)
FIRST CLEMENT

26 to cause it to rain on an uninhabited land,
a wilderness where there are no human beings,
27 to satisfy a devastated and desolate land,
and to cause it to sprout with vegetation?
28 Does the rain have a father,
or who has fathered the drops of the dew?
29 From whose womb does the ice emerge,
and the frost from the sky, who gives birth to it,
30 when the waters become hard like stone,
when the surface of the deep is frozen solid?
31 Can you tie the bands of the Pleiades
or release the cords of Orion?
32 Can you lead out
the constellations in their seasons
or guide the Bear with its cubs?
33 Do you know the laws of the heavens,
or can you set up their rule over the earth?
34 Can you raise your voice to the clouds
so that a flood of water covers you?
35 Can you send out lightning bolts, and they go?
Will they say to you, 'Here we are'?
36 Who has put wisdom in the heart
or has imparted understanding to the mind?
37 Who by wisdom can count the clouds,
and who can tip over the water jars of heaven,
38 when the dust hardens into a mass,
and the clumps of earth stick together?

39 "Do you hunt prey for the lioness
and satisfy the appetite of the lions
40 when they crouch in their dens,
when they wait in ambush in the thicket?
41 Who prepares prey for the raven,
when its young cry out to God
and wander about for lack of food?

39 "Are you acquainted with the way
the mountain goats give birth?
Do you watch as the wild deer give birth to their young?
2 Do you count the months they must fulfill,
and do you know the time they give birth?
3 They crouch; they bear their young;
they bring forth the offspring they have carried.
4 Their young grow strong and grow up in the open;
they go off and do not return to them.
5 Who let the wild donkey go free?
Who released the bonds of the donkey,
6 to whom I appointed the arid rift valley for its home,
the salt wastes as its dwelling place?
7 It scorns the tumult in the town;
it does not hear the shouts of a driver.
8 It ranges the hills as its pasture
and searches after every green plant.
9 Is the wild ox willing to be your servant?
Will it spend the night at your feeding trough?
10 Can you bind the wild ox to a furrow with its rope;
will it till the valleys, following after you?
11 Will you rely on it because its strength is great?
Will you commit your labor to it?

39:1–30 "Is it by your understanding that the hawk soars?" Who can discern the nature of the birds of the air? Some carry with them a voice of melody, and others are variegated with all manner of painting on their wings, and others fly up into mid-air and float motionless, as the hawk: For by the divine command the hawk spreads out his wings and floats motionless, looking toward the south. What person can behold the eagle's lofty flight? If then you cannot discern the soaring of the most senseless of the birds, how would you understand the Maker of all?

CYRIL OF JERUSALEM
(C. 313–386)
CATECHETICAL LECTURES

12 Can you count on it to bring in your grain
and gather the grain to your threshing floor?

13 "The wings of the ostrich flap with joy,
but are they the pinions and plumage of a stork?
14 For she leaves her eggs on the ground
and lets them be warmed on the soil.
15 She forgets that a foot might crush them
or that a wild animal might trample them.
16 She is harsh with her young,
as if they were not hers;
she is unconcerned about the uselessness of her labor.
17 For God deprived her of wisdom
and did not impart understanding to her.
18 But as soon as she springs up,
she laughs at the horse and its rider.

19 "Do you give the horse its strength?
Do you clothe its neck with a mane?
20 Do you make it leap like a locust?
Its proud neighing is terrifying!
21 It paws the ground in the valley,
exulting mightily;
it goes out to meet the weapons.
22 It laughs at fear and is not dismayed;
it does not shy away from the sword.
23 On it the quiver rattles;
the lance and javelin flash.
24 In excitement and impatience it consumes the ground;
it cannot stand still when the trumpet is blown.
25 At the sound of the trumpet, it says, 'Aha!'
And from a distance it catches the scent of battle,
the thunderous shouting of commanders,
and the battle cries.

26 "Is it by your understanding that the hawk soars
and spreads its wings toward the south?
27 Is it at your command that the eagle soars
and builds its nest on high?
28 It lives on a rock and spends the night there,
on a rocky crag and a fortress.
29 From there it spots its prey;
its eyes gaze intently from a distance.
30 And its young ones devour the blood,
and where the dead carcasses are,
there it is."

JOB'S REPLY TO GOD'S CHALLENGE

40 Then the LORD answered Job:
2 "Will the one who contends with the Almighty
correct him?
Let the person who accuses God give him an answer!"

3 Then Job answered the LORD:
4 "Indeed, I am completely unworthy—how could I reply
to you?
I put my hand over my mouth to silence myself.
5 I have spoken once, but I cannot answer;
twice, but I will say no more."

40:1–5 If Job felt obliged to say, "I am completely unworthy," oh, poor sinner, will you be ashamed to join in the same confession? If divine grace does not eradicate all sin from the believer, how do you hope to do it yourself? And if God loves his people while they are yet vile, do you think your vileness will prevent his loving you? Believe on Jesus, you outcast of the world's society! Jesus calls you and such as you are. Even now say, "You have died for sinners; I am a sinner, Lord Jesus, sprinkle your blood on me"; if you will confess your sin you will find pardon. If now with all your heart you will say, "I am completely unworthy, wash me," you shall be washed now.

CHARLES SPURGEON
(1834–1892)
MORNING AND EVENING

40:6—41:34 God, for the further proving of his own power, describes two vast animals, far exceeding humans in bulk and strength. "Behemoth" signifies beasts. This vast animal is noticed as an argument to humble ourselves before the great God. Whatever strength this or any other creature has, it is derived from God. The description of the "Leviathan" is yet further to convince Job of his own weakness and of God's almighty power. The Lord sets forth his own power in that mighty creature. If such language describes the terrible force of Leviathan, what words can express the power of God's wrath? Under a humbling sense of our own vileness, let us revere the divine majesty, take and fill our allotted place, cease from our own wisdom, and give all glory to our gracious God and Savior.

MATTHEW HENRY **(1662–1714)**
COMMENTARY ON THE WHOLE BIBLE

THE LORD'S SECOND SPEECH

6 Then the LORD answered Job from the whirlwind:
7 "Get ready for a difficult task like a man.
I will question you, and you will inform me.
8 Would you indeed annul my justice?
Would you declare me guilty so that you might be right?
9 Do you have an arm as powerful as God's,
and can you thunder with a voice like his?
10 Adorn yourself, then, with majesty and excellency,
and clothe yourself with glory and honor.
11 Scatter abroad the abundance of your anger.
Look at every proud man and bring him low.
12 Look at every proud man and abase him;
crush the wicked on the spot.
13 Hide them in the dust together;
imprison them in the grave.
14 Then I myself will acknowledge to you
that your own right hand can save you.

THE DESCRIPTION OF BEHEMOTH

15 "Look now at Behemoth, which I made as
I made you;
it eats grass like the ox.
16 Look at its strength in its loins
and its power in the muscles of its belly.
17 It makes its tail stiff like a cedar;
the sinews of its thighs are tightly wound.
18 Its bones are tubes of bronze,
its limbs like bars of iron.
19 It ranks first among the works of God;
the One who made it
has furnished it with a sword.
20 For the hills bring it food,
where all the wild animals play.
21 Under the lotus trees it lies,
in the secrecy of the reeds and the marsh.
22 The lotus trees conceal it in their shadow;
the poplars by the stream conceal it.
23 If the river rages, it is not disturbed;
it is secure, though the Jordan
should surge up to its mouth.
24 Can anyone catch it by its eyes
or pierce its nose with a snare?

THE DESCRIPTION OF LEVIATHAN

41 "Can you pull in Leviathan with a hook
and tie down its tongue with a rope?
2 Can you put a cord through its nose
or pierce its jaw with a hook?
3 Will it make numerous supplications to you;
will it speak to you with tender words?
4 Will it make a pact with you,
so you could take it as your slave for life?
5 Can you play with it, like a bird,
or tie it on a leash for your girls?
6 Will partners bargain for it?
Will they divide it up among the merchants?
7 Can you fill its hide with harpoons
or its head with fishing spears?

8 If you lay your hand on it,
you will remember the fight.
Do not do it again!
9 See, his expectation is wrong;
he is laid low even at the sight of it.
10 Is it not fierce when it is awakened?
Who is he, then, who can stand before it?
11 Who has confronted me that I should repay?
Everything under heaven belongs to me!
12 I will not keep silent about its limbs,
and the extent of its might,
and the grace of its arrangement.
13 Who can uncover its outer covering?
Who can penetrate to the inside of its armor?
14 Who can open the doors of its mouth?
Its teeth all around are fearsome.
15 Its back has rows of shields,
shut up closely together as with a seal;
16 each one is so close to the next
that no air can come between them.
17 They lock tightly together, one to the next;
they cling together and cannot be separated.
18 Its snorting throws out flashes of light;
its eyes are like the red glow of dawn.
19 Out of its mouth go flames;
sparks of fire shoot forth!
20 Smoke streams from its nostrils
as from a boiling pot over burning rushes.
21 Its breath sets coals ablaze,
and a flame shoots from its mouth.
22 Strength lodges in its neck,
and despair runs before it.
23 The folds of its flesh are tightly joined;
they are firm on it, immovable.
24 Its heart is hard as rock,
hard as a lower millstone.
25 When it rises up, the mighty are terrified;
at its thrashing about they withdraw.
26 Whoever strikes it with a sword
will have no effect,
nor with the spear, arrow, or dart.
27 It regards iron as straw
and bronze as rotten wood.
28 Arrows do not make it flee;
slingstones become like chaff to it.
29 A club is counted as a piece of straw;
it laughs at the rattling of the lance.
30 Its underparts are the sharp points of potsherds;
it leaves its mark in the mud
like a threshing sledge.
31 It makes the deep boil like a cauldron
and stirs up the sea like a pot of ointment,
32 It leaves a glistening wake behind it;
one would think the deep had a head of
white hair.
33 The likes of it is not on earth,
a creature without fear.
34 It looks on every haughty being;
it is king over all that are proud."

41:11 "Who has confronted me that I should repay?" These words are a great evidence that Leviathan is here spoken of as a type of the devil. For no other Leviathan was ever subject to God's moral government or ever rebelled against him that God should repay him.

JONATHAN EDWARDS
(1703–1758)
SELECTIONS FROM THE UNPUBLISHED WRITINGS

JOB'S CONFESSION

42 Then Job answered the LORD:
2 "I know that you can do all things;
no purpose of yours can be thwarted;
3 you asked, 'Who is this who darkens counsel without
knowledge?'
But I have declared without understanding
things too wonderful for me to know.
4 You said, 'Pay attention, and I will speak;
I will question you, and you will answer me.'
5 I had heard of you by the hearing of the ear,
but now my eye has seen you.
6 Therefore I despise myself,
and I repent in dust and ashes!"

VII. THE EPILOGUE (42:7–17)

JOB'S RESTORATION

7 After the LORD had spoken these things to Job, he said to
Eliphaz the Temanite, "My anger is stirred up against you and
your two friends because you have not spoken about me what
is right, as my servant Job has. 8 So now take seven bulls and
seven rams and go to my servant Job and offer a burnt offering
for yourselves. And my servant Job will intercede for you, and
I will respect him, so that I do not deal with you according to
your folly, because you have not spoken about me what is right,
as my servant Job has."
9 So they went, Eliphaz the Temanite, Bildad the Shuhite,
and Zophar the Naamathite, and did just as the LORD had told
them; and the LORD had respect for Job.
10 So the LORD restored what Job had lost after he prayed for
his friends, and the LORD doubled all that had belonged to Job.
11 So they came to him, all his brothers and sisters and all who
had known him before, and they dined with him in his house.
They comforted him and consoled him for all the trouble the
LORD had brought on him, and each one gave him a piece of
silver and a gold ring.
12 So the LORD blessed the second part of Job's life more than
the first. He had 14,000 sheep, 6,000 camels, 1,000 yoke of oxen,
and 1,000 female donkeys. 13 And he also had seven sons and
three daughters. 14 The first daughter he named Jemimah, the
second Keziah, and the third Keren-Happuch. 15 Nowhere in
all the land could women be found who were as beautiful as
Job's daughters, and their father granted them an inheritance
alongside their brothers.
16 After this Job lived 140 years; he saw his children and their
children to the fourth generation. 17 And so Job died, old and
full of days.

42:7–16 "So the LORD restored what Job had lost after he prayed for his friends, and the LORD doubled all that had belonged to Job"—not only with spiritual but also with temporal blessings, just double to what they were. This is a remarkable instance of the extent of the divine providence to things that seem minute as this, the exact number of a man's cattle; as also of the harmony of providence and the reference of one event to another: For known to God are all his works, from the beginning to the end.

JOHN WESLEY (1703–1791)
EXPLANATORY NOTES ON THE BIBLE

AUTHOR	AUDIENCE	DATE	PURPOSE	THEMES
David, Asaph, the sons of Korah, Solomon, Heman, Ethan, Moses, and unknown authors	God's people	Between the time of Moses (probably about 1440 BC) and the time following the Babylonian exile (after 538 BC)	The book of Psalms, a collection of poetry, expresses the full range of human emotion through songs, laments, prayers, and poems, and serves as a guide into the heart of wisdom and the character of God	The human experience, salvation and deliverance, the reign of God, the promise of Messiah, and the character of God

Poetry is powerful. With it we can express our fears and frustrations, give voice to our doubts and expectations, and offer up praise and adoration. The book of Psalms, being a volume of poetry, puts this variety of human experience and honest emotion on display through songs, laments, and prayers. It serves as the believer's guide into the heart of wisdom. Thomas Aquinas wrote: "[David] teaches how to praise God with exultation . . . The end and purpose therefore is for the soul to be joined with God as the Holy and Most High."

This book of wisdom poetry is chiefly the product of David. In verse he expressed the longings of his heart during the varied seasons of his life. Also featured are praise choruses written by temple attendants that tell of the glory and majesty of the Lord. Psalms is divided into five smaller books, which some have said mirror the five books of Moses—Genesis, Exodus, Leviticus, Numbers, and Deuteronomy. Its content magnifies God and his character, laments and warns against sin, and points readers toward the way of righteousness.

Athanasius, bishop of Alexandria, extolled the virtue of the book of Psalms, believing it to be a special book within God's Word:

> My child, all the books of Scripture, both old and new, are inspired by God and useful for instruction, as it is written. But to those who really study it, the Psalter yields special treasure. Each book of the Bible has, of course, its own particular message . . . Each of these books, you see, is like a garden that grows one particular kind of fruit; by contrast, the Psalter is a garden which, besides its particular fruit, grows also those of all the rest.

Many saints have taken their cues from Athanasius, recognizing Psalms' riches. In particular the Reformers found in these pages the promises of Christ.

Reading through the book of Psalms, we find it impossible to escape the many emotions on display. Whether fear of enemies and denouncement for wickedness and evildoers, pleas for deliverance and salvation, the book expresses it all. It's no wonder John Calvin called the book "an anatomy of all the parts of the soul; for there is not an emotion of which any one can be conscious that is not here represented as in a mirror. Or rather, the Holy Spirit has here drawn to the life all the griefs, sorrows, fears, doubts, hopes, cares, perplexities, in short, all the distracting emotions with which the minds of men are wont to be agitated."

Yet the Psalms don't merely express emotions of the soul as ends unto themselves; they offer hope. Again, John Calvin: "It is by perusing these inspired compositions that men

AUTHOR	AUDIENCE	DATE	PURPOSE	THEMES
David, Asaph, the Korahites, Solomon, Heman, Ethan, Moses, and unknown authors	God's people	Between the time of Moses (probably about 1440 BC) and the time following the Babylonian exile (after 538 BC)	The book of Psalms is a collection of poetry that expresses honest human emotion through songs and laments, prayers and poems, and serves as a guide into the heart of wisdom and the character of God.	The human experience; salvation and deliverance; the reign of God; the promise of Messiah; and the character of God

Poetry is powerful. With it we can express our fears and frustrations, give voice to our doubts and expectations, and offer up praise and adoration. The book of Psalms, being a volume of poetry, puts this variety of human experience and honest emotion on display through songs, laments, and prayers. It serves as the believer's guide into the heart of wisdom. Thomas Aquinas wrote: "[David] teaches how to praise God with exultation . . . The end purpose therefore is for the soul to be joined with God, as the Holy and Most High."

This book of wisdom poetry is chiefly the product of David. In verse he expressed the longings of his heart during the varied seasons of his life. Also featured are praise choruses written by temple attendants that tell of the glory and majesty of the Lord. Psalms is divided into five smaller books, which some have said mirror the five books of Moses—Genesis, Exodus, Leviticus, Numbers, and Deuteronomy. Its content magnifies God and his character, laments and warns against sin, and points readers toward the way of righteousness.

Athanasius, bishop of Alexandria, extolled the virtue of the book of Psalms, believing it to be a special book within God's Word:

> My child, all the books of scripture, both old and new, are inspired by God and useful for instruction, as it is written. But to those who really study it, the Psalter yields special treasure. Each book of the Bible has, of course, its own particular message . . . Each of these books, you see, is like a garden that grows one particular kind of fruit; by contrast the Psalter is a garden, which, besides its particular fruit, grows also those of all the rest.

Many saints have taken their cues from Athanasius, recognizing Psalms' riches. In particular the Reformers found in these pages the promises of Christ.

Reading through the book of Psalms, we find it impossible to escape the raw emotions on display. Whether fear of enemies and death, lament for wickedness and evildoers, pleas for deliverance and salvation, the book expresses it all. It's no wonder John Calvin called the book "an anatomy of all the parts of the soul" for he believed "there is not an emotion of which any one can be conscious that is not here represented as in a mirror. Or rather the Holy Spirit has here drawn to the life all the griefs, sorrows, fears, doubts, hopes, cares, perplexities; in short, all the distracting emotions with which the minds of men are wont to be agitated."

Yet the Psalms don't merely express emotions of the soul as ends unto themselves; they offer hope. Again, John Calvin: "It is by perusing these inspired compositions that men will be most effectually awakened to a sense of their maladies, and at the same time instructed in seeking remedies for their cure . . . In a word, whatever may serve to encourage us when we are about to pray to God is taught us in this book." These poems encourage us by reminding us of our source for the cure we need: The Lord is our rock, our fortress, our refuge, our shield; the Lord is our shepherd who refreshes us, guides us, guards us; and the Lord's legacy of faithfulness assures us of a future hope.

The reign of God is an anchoring theme for the entire corpus of wisdom poetry. He is the Most High, the Almighty who stands sovereignly above the affairs of his creation. "The LORD reigns," says Psalm 97. "Equity and justice are the foundation of his throne." His power is all-consuming so that "the earth sees and trembles. The mountains melt like wax before the LORD, before the Lord of the whole earth." He is awe-inspiring so that "all the nations see his splendor" (Ps 97:1–2, 4–6). By virtue of his might and power, the Lord is able to provide and protect us, deliver and save us.

There is another reason: "For the LORD is good. His loyal love endures, and he is faithful through all generations" (100:5). The psalms are a lesson on the character of God, expressing not only his might and power but also his love and mercy, his goodness and faithfulness, his justice and wrath. Several recount the history of the Israelites and how God formed them into a people, redeemed and delivered them from oppression, gave them an inheritance of blessing, and preserved them. David recognized that the Lord had been intimately involved in the affairs of his own life. His response was simply to praise the Lord.

In his preface to his commentary on the Psalms, Martin Luther offered a sturdy summation of all that the book has to offer:

> The Psalter ought to be a precious and beloved book because it promises Christ's death and resurrection so clearly—and depicts his kingdom and the condition and nature of all Christendom—that it might well be called a little Bible . . . In sum, do you want to see the holy Christian church painted in living color and form comprised of one little picture? Then pick up the Psalter! There you have a fine, bright, pure mirror that will show you what Christendom is. Yes, you will even find yourself in it . . . as well as God himself and all creatures.

BOOK 1 (PSALMS 1–41)

PSALM 1

1 How blessed is the one who does not follow the advice
of the wicked,
or stand in the pathway with sinners,
or sit in the assembly of scoffers.
2 Instead he finds pleasure in obeying the LORD's
commands;
he meditates on his commands day and night.
3 He is like a tree planted by flowing streams;
it yields its fruit at the proper time,
and its leaves never fall off.
He succeeds in everything he attempts.
4 Not so with the wicked!
Instead they are like wind-driven chaff.
5 For this reason the wicked cannot withstand judgment,
nor can sinners join the assembly of the godly.
6 Certainly the LORD guards the way of the godly,
but the way of the wicked ends in destruction.

1:1–2 The gracious man does not walk in the counsel of the ungodly. He takes wiser counsel and walks in the commandments of the Lord his God. To him the ways of piety are paths of peace and pleasantness. His footsteps are ordered by the Word of God, not by the cunning and wicked devices of carnal human beings. "He finds pleasure in obeying the LORD's commands." He is not under the law as a curse and condemnation but he is in it, and he delights to be in it as his rule of life; he delights, moreover, to meditate in it, to read it by day, and to think upon it by night.

CHARLES SPURGEON
(1834–1892)
THE TREASURY OF DAVID

PSALM 2

1 Why do the nations rebel?
Why are the countries devising plots that will fail?
2 The kings of the earth form a united front;
the rulers collaborate
against the LORD and his anointed king.
3 They say, "Let's tear off the shackles they've put on us.
Let's free ourselves from their ropes."
4 The one enthroned in heaven laughs in disgust;
the Lord taunts them.
5 Then he angrily speaks to them
and terrifies them in his rage, saying,
6 "I myself have installed my king
on Zion, my holy hill."
7 The king says, "I will announce the LORD's decree. He
said to me:
'You are my son. This very day I have become your
father.
8 Ask me,
and I will give you the nations as your inheritance,
the ends of the earth as your personal property.
9 You will break them with an iron scepter;
you will smash them like a potter's jar.'"
10 So now, you kings, do what is wise;
you rulers of the earth, submit to correction.
11 Serve the LORD in fear.
Repent in terror.
12 Give sincere homage.
Otherwise he will be angry,
and you will die because of your behavior,
when his anger quickly ignites.
How blessed are all who take shelter in him!

2:1–12 Now Psalm 2, as we learn from Acts, supplied the first prayers and words of thanksgiving to God in the church of the new covenant. The new covenant or the kingdom of Christ will be a spiritual kingdom; Christ is an eternal King who will have no successor. For it is added that Satan and the world with all their powers and might can achieve nothing more than to move God to laughter and finally stir up in him such indignation that for opposing this kingdom they must perish. Knowing this is useful and comforting and belongs to a proper conception of this kingdom, lest we, troubled by the offenses with which this kingdom is assaulted, become despondent and dispirited.

MARTIN LUTHER **(1483–1546)**
COMMENTARY ON PSALM 2

PSALM 3

A psalm of David, written when he fled from his son Absalom.

1 LORD, how numerous are my enemies!
Many attack me.
2 Many say about me,

"God will not deliver him." *Selah*
3 But you, LORD, are a shield that protects me;
you are my glory and the one who restores me.
4 To the LORD I cried out,
and he answered me from his holy hill. *Selah*
5 I rested and slept;
I awoke, for the LORD protects me.
6 I am not afraid of the multitude of people
who attack me from all directions.
7 Rise up, LORD!
Deliver me, my God!
Yes, you will strike all my enemies on the jaw;
you will break the teeth of the wicked.
8 The LORD delivers;
you show favor to your people. *Selah*

PSALM 4

For the music director, to be accompanied by stringed instruments; a psalm of David.

1 When I call out, answer me,
O God who vindicates me.
Though I am hemmed in, you will lead me into a wide, open place.
Have mercy on me and respond to my prayer.
2 You men, how long will you try to turn my honor into shame?
How long will you love what is worthless
and search for what is deceptive? *Selah*
3 Realize that the LORD shows the godly special favor;
the LORD responds when I cry out to him.
4 Tremble with fear and do not sin.
Meditate as you lie in bed, and repent of your ways. *Selah*
5 Offer the prescribed sacrifices
and trust in the LORD.
6 Many say, "Who can show us anything good?"
Smile upon us, LORD!
7 You make me happier
than those who have abundant grain and wine.
8 I will lie down and sleep peacefully,
for you, LORD, make me safe and secure.

PSALM 5

For the music director, to be accompanied by wind instruments; a psalm of David.

1 Listen to what I say, LORD!
Carefully consider my complaint!
2 Pay attention to my cry for help,
my King and my God,
for I am praying to you!
3 LORD, in the morning you will hear me;
in the morning I will present my case to you and then wait expectantly for an answer.
4 Certainly you are not a God who approves of evil;
evil people cannot dwell with you.
5 Arrogant people cannot stand in your presence;
you hate all who behave wickedly.
6 You destroy liars;
the LORD despises violent and deceitful people.

3:1–8 "You, LORD, are a shield that protects me; you are my glory and the one who restores me." He begins the petition by an argument from the power and will of God whom he calls on. *I call on you only because you are my shield, that is, you have commanded that you are to be called on, you have given promises that you are willing to hear and help, and you have declared this so many times by your deeds. Save me, the one who calls on you.* He encompasses all these points when he signifies the reasons why he takes refuge in God. Moreover, it is evident from the petitions that the chief arguments are taken up from the means: *You are able and willing to help me, and you have often saved me previously; therefore to you alone do I flee.* These are ardent passions when in true sorrows we raise ourselves by this consolation, namely, that when this light still remains in our heart, we are not cast away from God but are truly received, heard, and will experience divine help, comfort, and liberation.

PHILIP MELANCHTHON
(1497–1560)
COMMENTS ON THE PSALMS

4:1–8 "When I call out, answer me, O God who vindicates me. Though I am hemmed in, you will lead me into a wide, open place." May the God and Father of our Lord Jesus Christ, and Jesus Christ himself, who is the Son of God and our everlasting High Priest, build you up in faith and truth, and in all meekness, gentleness, patience, and long-suffering. Pray also for those who persecute and hate you, and for the enemies of the cross, that your fruit may be manifest to all, and that you may be perfect in him.

POLYCARP **(69–155)**
EPISTLE TO THE PHILIPPIANS

7 But as for me, because of your great faithfulness I will
enter your house;
I will bow down toward your holy temple as I worship you.
8 LORD, lead me in your righteousness
because of those who wait to ambush me,
remove the obstacles in the way in which you are
guiding me.
9 For they do not speak the truth;
their stomachs are like the place of destruction,
their throats like an open grave,
their tongues like a steep slope leading into it.
10 Condemn them, O God!
May their own schemes be their downfall.
Drive them away because of their many acts of
insurrection,
for they have rebelled against you.
11 But may all who take shelter in you be happy.
May they continually shout for joy.
Shelter them so that those who are loyal to you may
rejoice.
12 Certainly you reward the godly, LORD.
Like a shield you protect them in your good favor.

5:11–12 "May all who take shelter in you be happy." If I am to love God, I must be quite sure that God loves me. My love can never be anything else than an answer to his. Knowledge of the acts of God brings people to love him. And there is no way of getting that knowledge but through the faith that must precede love, for faith realizes the fact that God loves. And so faith is the only possible means by which any of us can ever experience, as well as realize, the love that kindles ours.

ALEXANDER MACLAREN
(1826–1910)
EXPOSITIONS OF THE HOLY SCRIPTURES

PSALM 6

For the music director, to be accompanied by stringed instruments, according to the sheminith *style; a psalm of David.*

1 LORD, do not rebuke me in your anger.
Do not discipline me in your raging fury.
2 Have mercy on me, LORD, for I am frail.
Heal me, LORD, for my bones are shaking.
3 I am absolutely terrified,
and you, LORD—how long will this continue?
4 Relent, LORD, rescue me!
Deliver me because of your faithfulness.
5 For no one remembers you in the realm of death.
In Sheol who gives you thanks?
6 I am exhausted as I groan.
All night long I drench my bed in tears;
my tears saturate the cushion beneath me.
7 My eyes grow dim from suffering;
they grow weak because of all my enemies.
8 Turn back from me, all you who behave wickedly,
for the LORD has heard the sound of my weeping.
9 The LORD has heard my appeal for mercy;
the LORD has accepted my prayer.
10 They will be humiliated and absolutely terrified.
All my enemies will turn back and be suddenly
humiliated.

6:1–10 "Deliver me because of your faithfulness." The children of God know both prosperity and adversity to be the gifts of God alone. Therefore in prosperity they commonly are not insolent or proud, but even in the day of joy and rest they look for trouble and sorrow. And yet, in the time of adversity, they are not altogether left without comfort, but by one way or another, God shows them that their trouble will have an end. On the other hand the reprobates, either taking all things of chance or else making an idol of their own wisdom, in prosperity are so puffed up that they forget God without any care that trouble should follow. And in adversity they are so dejected that they look for nothing but hell.

JOHN KNOX (C. 1514–1572)
A FORT FOR THE AFFLICTED

PSALM 7

A musical composition by David, which he sang to the LORD concerning a Benjaminite named Cush.

1 O LORD my God, in you I have taken shelter.
Deliver me from all who chase me. Rescue me!
2 Otherwise they will rip me to shreds like a lion;
they will tear me to bits and no one will be able to
rescue me.
3 O LORD my God, if I have done what they say,
or am guilty of unjust actions,

4 or have wronged my ally,
or helped his lawless enemy,
5 may an enemy relentlessly chase me and catch me;
may he trample me to death
and leave me lying dishonored in the dust. *Selah*
6 Stand up angrily, LORD.
Rise up with raging fury against my enemies.
Wake up for my sake, and execute the judgment you
have decreed for them.
7 The countries are assembled all around you;
take once more your rightful place over them.
8 The LORD judges the nations.
Vindicate me, LORD, because I am innocent,
because I am blameless, O Exalted One.
9 May the evil deeds of the wicked come to an end.
But make the innocent secure,
O righteous God,
you who examine inner thoughts and motives.
10 The Exalted God is my shield,
the one who delivers the morally upright.
11 God is a just judge;
he is angry throughout the day.
12 If a person does not repent, God will wield his sword.
He has prepared to shoot his bow.
13 He has prepared deadly weapons to use against him;
he gets ready to shoot flaming arrows.
14 See the one who is pregnant with wickedness,
who conceives destructive plans,
and gives birth to harmful lies—
15 he digs a pit
and then falls into the hole he has made.
16 He becomes the victim of his own destructive plans—
and the violence he intended for others falls on his own
head.
17 I will thank the LORD for his justice;
I will sing praises to the LORD Most High!

PSALM 8

For the music director, according to the gittith *style; a psalm of David.*

1 O LORD, our Lord,
how magnificent is your reputation throughout the
earth!
You reveal your majesty in the heavens above.
2 From the mouths of children and nursing babies
you have ordained praise on account of your
adversaries,
so that you might put an end to the vindictive enemy.
3 When I look up at the heavens, which your fingers
made,
and see the moon and the stars, which you set in place,
4 Of what importance is the human race, that you should
notice them?
Of what importance is mankind, that you should pay
attention to them?
5 You made them a little less than the heavenly beings.
You crowned mankind with honor and majesty.
6 you appoint them to rule over your creation;
you have placed everything under their authority,

7:1–17 When human beings become accustomed to being harassed with reproachful slanders, so that it is difficult for them to bridle their rage and its consequent evils—we are taught in this psalm to seek defense in the presence of God and to oppose human beings. But even so, without any wild feelings let us entrust our innocence to God alone, the most severe punisher of slanderous tongues. "May the evil deeds of the wicked come to an end. But make the innocent secure, O righteous God."

THEODORE BEZA (1519–1605)
THE PSALMS OF DAVID

8:1–9 The psalmist seeks to give to God the glory due to his name. He is ours, for he made us, protects us, and takes special care of us. [We see this through] the birth, life, preaching, miracles, suffering, death, resurrection, and ascension of Jesus. No name is so universal, no power and influence so generally felt, as those of the Savior of mankind. The greatest favor ever showed to the human race and the greatest honor ever put on human nature were exemplified in the Lord Jesus. With good reason does the psalmist conclude as he began, "O LORD, our Lord, how magnificent is your reputation throughout the earth!"

MATTHEW HENRY (1662–1714)
COMMENTARY ON THE WHOLE BIBLE

7 including all the sheep and cattle,
as well as the wild animals,
8 the birds in the sky, the fish in the sea,
and everything that moves through the currents of the seas.
9 O LORD, our Lord,
how magnificent is your reputation throughout the earth!

PSALM 9

For the music director, according to the alumoth-labben *style; a psalm of David.*

1 I will thank the LORD with all my heart!
I will tell about all your amazing deeds.
2 I will be happy and rejoice in you.
I will sing praises to you, O Most High.
3 When my enemies turn back,
they trip and are defeated before you.
4 For you defended my just cause;
from your throne you pronounced a just decision.
5 You terrified the nations with your battle cry.
You destroyed the wicked;
you permanently wiped out all memory of them.
6 The enemy's cities have been reduced to permanent ruins.
You destroyed their cities;
all memory of the enemies has perished.
7 But the LORD rules forever;
he reigns in a just manner.
8 He judges the world fairly;
he makes just legal decisions for the nations.
9 Consequently the LORD provides safety for the oppressed;
he provides safety in times of trouble.
10 Your loyal followers trust in you,
for you, LORD, do not abandon those who seek your help.
11 Sing praises to the LORD, who rules in Zion.
Tell the nations what he has done.
12 For the one who takes revenge against murderers took notice of the oppressed;
he did not overlook their cry for help
13 when they prayed:
"Have mercy on me, LORD!
See how I am oppressed by those who hate me,
O one who can snatch me away from the gates of death!
14 Then I will tell about all your praiseworthy acts;
in the gates of Daughter Zion I will rejoice because of your deliverance."
15 The nations fell into the pit they had made;
their feet were caught in the net they had hidden.
16 The LORD revealed himself;
he accomplished justice.
The wicked were ensnared by their own actions.
Higgaion. Selah
17 The wicked are turned back and sent to Sheol;
this is the destiny of all the nations that ignore God,
18 for the needy are not permanently ignored,
the hopes of the oppressed are not forever dashed.

9:1–2 "I will tell about all your amazing deeds." David tells all God's marvels to him who sees them performed not only openly on the body, but invisibly indeed too in the soul, but far more sublimely and excellently. For people earthly and led wholly by the eye marvel more that the dead Lazarus rose again in the body than that Paul the persecutor rose again in soul. But since the visible miracle calls the soul to the light, and the invisible enlightens the soul that comes when called, he tells all God's marvels to him who, by believing the visible, passes on to the understanding of the invisible.

AUGUSTINE (354–430)
EXPOSITIONS ON THE PSALMS

19 Rise up, LORD!
Don't let men be defiant.
May the nations be judged in your presence.
20 Terrify them, LORD.
Let the nations know they are mere mortals. *Selah*

PSALM 10

1 Why, LORD, do you stand far off?
Why do you pay no attention during times of trouble?
2 The wicked arrogantly chase the oppressed;
the oppressed are trapped by the schemes the wicked have dreamed up.
3 Yes, the wicked man boasts because he gets what he wants;
the one who robs others curses and rejects the LORD.
4 The wicked man is so arrogant he always thinks,
"God won't hold me accountable; he doesn't care."
5 He is secure at all times.
He has no regard for your commands;
he disdains all his enemies.
6 He says to himself,
"I will never be shaken,
because I experience no calamity."
7 His mouth is full of curses and deceptive, harmful words;
his tongue injures and destroys.
8 He waits in ambush near the villages;
in hidden places he kills the innocent.
His eyes look for some unfortunate victim.
9 He lies in ambush in a hidden place, like a lion in a thicket.
He lies in ambush, waiting to catch the oppressed;
he catches the oppressed by pulling in his net.
10 His victims are crushed and beaten down;
they are trapped in his sturdy nets.
11 He says to himself,
"God overlooks it;
he does not pay attention;
he never notices."
12 Rise up, LORD!
O God, strike him down.
Do not forget the oppressed.
13 Why does the wicked man reject God?
He says to himself, "You will not hold me accountable."
14 You have taken notice,
for you always see one who inflicts pain and suffering.
The unfortunate victim entrusts his cause to you;
you deliver the fatherless.
15 Break the arm of the wicked and evil man.
Hold him accountable for his wicked deeds,
which he thought you would not discover.
16 The LORD rules forever!
The nations are driven out of his land.
17 LORD, you have heard the request of the oppressed;
you make them feel secure because you listen to their prayer.
18 You defend the fatherless and oppressed,
so that mere mortals may no longer terrorize them.

10:1–18 The faithful promise themselves security in God and nowhere else, yet while they do this, they know that they are exposed to all the storms of affliction and patiently submit to them. There is a very great difference between despisers of God and godly persons. Godly persons know that their lives hang only by a thread, that they are encompassed by a thousand deaths, and they are ready to endure any kind of afflictions that shall be sent on them. These persons live in the world as if they were sailing on a tempestuous and dangerous sea; nevertheless they bear patiently all their troubles and sorrows and comfort themselves in their afflictions because they lean wholly on the grace of God and entirely have confidence in it.

JOHN CALVIN (1509–1564)
COMPLETE COMMENTARY ON THE BIBLE

11:1–7 Great is the power of hope in the Lord. Do you see a ready ally, a well-prepared aid, present everywhere, seeing everything, gazing on all things, having as his particular role to exercise providence and care, to pursue wrongdoers, to assist the wronged, to award recompense to the virtuous, to assign punishment to sinners? He is therefore ignorant of nothing; his eyes in fact look attentively on the whole world. If, in fact, he is righteous, he will not simply overlook these happenings. He rebuffs the wicked; he praises the righteous.

CHRYSOSTOM (C. 347–407)
COMMENTARY ON THE PSALMS

12:1–8 "Deliver, LORD!" The prayer itself is remarkable, for it is short but seasonable, sententious, and suggestive. David mourned the fewness of faithful men and therefore lifted up his heart in supplication—when the creature failed, he flew to the Creator. He evidently felt his own weakness, or he would not have cried for help. "Deliver, LORD!" will suit us living and dying, suffering or laboring, rejoicing or sorrowing. In him our help is found, so let us not be slack to cry to him. The Lord's character assures us that he will not leave his people; his relationship as Father and Husband guarantees us his aid; his gift of Jesus is a pledge of every good thing; and his sure promise stands, "Don't be afraid . . . I [will] help you" (Isa 41:10).

CHARLES SPURGEON
(1834–1892)
MORNING AND EVENING

PSALM 11

For the music director, by David.

1 In the LORD I have taken shelter.
How can you say to me,
"Flee to a mountain like a bird.
2 For look, the wicked prepare their bows,
they put their arrows on the strings,
to shoot in the darkness at the morally upright.
3 When the foundations are destroyed,
what can the godly accomplish?"
4 The LORD is in his holy temple;
the LORD's throne is in heaven.
His eyes watch;
his eyes examine all people.
5 The LORD approves of the godly,
but he hates the wicked and those who love to do
violence.
6 May he rain down burning coals and brimstone on the
wicked!
A whirlwind is what they deserve.
7 Certainly the LORD is just;
he rewards godly deeds.
The upright will experience his favor.

PSALM 12

For the music director, according to the sheminith *style; a psalm of David.*

1 Deliver, LORD!
For the godly have disappeared;
people of integrity have vanished.
2 People lie to one another;
they flatter and deceive.
3 May the LORD cut off all flattering lips,
and the tongue that boasts!
4 They say, "We speak persuasively;
we know how to flatter and boast.
Who is our master?"
5 "Because of the violence done to the oppressed,
because of the painful cries of the needy,
I will spring into action," says the LORD.
"I will provide the safety they so desperately desire."
6 The LORD's words are absolutely reliable.
They are as untainted as silver purified in a furnace on
the ground,
where it is thoroughly refined.
7 You, LORD, will protect them;
you will continually shelter each one from these evil
people,
8 for the wicked seem to be everywhere,
when people promote evil.

PSALM 13

For the music director, a psalm of David.

1 How long, LORD, will you continue to ignore me?
How long will you pay no attention to me?
2 How long must I worry,
and suffer in broad daylight?
How long will my enemy gloat over me?
3 Look at me! Answer me, O LORD my God!

Revive me, or else I will die.
4 Then my enemy will say, "I have defeated him."
Then my foes will rejoice because I am shaken.
5 But I trust in your faithfulness.
May I rejoice because of your deliverance.
6 I will sing praises to the LORD
when he vindicates me.

PSALM 14

For the music director, by David.

1 Fools say to themselves, "There is no God."
They sin and commit evil deeds;
none of them does what is right.
2 The LORD looks down from heaven at the human race,
to see if there is anyone who is wise and seeks God.
3 Everyone rejects God;
they are all morally corrupt.
None of them does what is right,
not even one.
4 All those who behave wickedly do not understand—
those who devour my people as if they were eating
bread
and do not call out to the LORD.
5 They are absolutely terrified,
for God defends the godly.
6 You want to humiliate the oppressed,
even though the LORD is their shelter.
7 I wish the deliverance of Israel would come from Zion!
When the LORD restores the well-being of his people,
may Jacob rejoice,
may Israel be happy!

PSALM 15

A psalm of David.

1 LORD, who may be a guest in your home?
Who may live on your holy hill?
2 Whoever lives a blameless life,
does what is right,
and speaks honestly.
3 He does not slander,
or do harm to others,
or insult his neighbor.
4 He despises a reprobate,
but honors the LORD's loyal followers.
He makes firm commitments and does not renege on
his promise.
5 He does not charge interest when he lends his money.
He does not take bribes to testify against the innocent.
The one who lives like this will never be shaken.

PSALM 16

A prayer of David.

1 Protect me, O God, for I have taken shelter in you.
2 I say to the LORD, "You are the Lord,
my only source of well-being."
3 As for God's chosen people who are in the land,
and the leading officials I admired so much—
4 their troubles multiply;
they desire other gods.

13:1–6 "I will sing praises to the LORD when he vindicates me." The love of God is a spring shower of virtues under which a blessed desire begins to bud and holy action bears fruit. This love is patient under adversities in this life, temperate in prosperity, powerful in its humility, joyful in affliction, benevolent toward enemies, and overcomes the wicked by its goodness. From this source even heavenly creatures are constantly ignited by God's love as a restoring flame, a growing desire for salvation. To summarize all of this with a phrase from the apostle: "God is love" (1 John 4:8).

CASSIODORUS **(C. 485–C. 585)**
EXPLANATION OF THE PSALMS

14:1 There is in people's hearts an abundance of false principles that are the root of all other false reasoning. These possess their judgments—all those vain arguments whereby people sheath themselves in their evil ways. The first of them is my text: "Fools say to themselves, 'There is no God.' They sin and commit evil deeds; none of them does what is right." This is the fundamental principle of all. As all being depends on God, so the belief in a God is the upholder of all. This is the ground of all impiety in their lives. This text lays open unto us the unbelief in human hearts and the false principles that are in them that break forth into action. In all human hearts there is a principle of unbelief and so consequently of corruption of manners in their lives.

THOMAS GOODWIN
(1600–1680)
THE WORKS

15:1–5 Some think that David wrote this song when he led God's ark of the covenant into Jerusalem so that he could promulgate to the entire people what they should do if they longed to remain in God's protection and to enjoy the presence of his mercy at all times. Yet he presents a general lesson that demonstrates what true good works are. All who want to be true members of God's church and in the end to possess the heavenly fatherland should diligently strive to do such good works. And notice that here he does not talk about the first cause and the basis for our salvation—which is the mercy of God, in which we have become participants through faith in Christ—rather he talks about the fruits of faith that all who present themselves as believers bear.

RUDOLF GWALTHER
(1519–1586)
THE PSALTER

16:1–11 "You are the Lord, my only source of well-being." You will raise me from the grave and conduct me to the place and state of everlasting felicity. In that heavenly paradise, where you are gloriously present, where we will clearly and fully behold the light of your countenance while in this life you hide your face and show us only your back. In this life all our joys are empty and defective, but in heaven there is fullness of joy. Our pleasures here are transient and momentary, but those at God's right hand are pleasures forevermore. For they are the pleasures of immortal souls in the enjoyment of an eternal God.

JOHN WESLEY **(1703–1791)**
EXPLANATORY NOTES ON THE BIBLE

I will not pour out drink offerings of blood to their gods,
nor will I make vows in the name of their gods.
5 LORD, you give me stability and prosperity;
you make my future secure.
6 It is as if I have been given fertile fields
or received a beautiful tract of land.
7 I will praise the LORD who guides me;
yes, during the night I reflect and learn.
8 I constantly trust in the LORD;
because he is at my right hand, I will not be shaken.
9 So my heart rejoices
and I am happy;
my life is safe.
10 You will not abandon me to Sheol;
you will not allow your faithful follower to see the Pit.
11 You lead me in the path of life.
I experience absolute joy in your presence;
you always give me sheer delight.

PSALM 17

A prayer of David.

1 LORD, consider my just cause.
Pay attention to my cry for help.
Listen to the prayer
I sincerely offer.
2 Make a just decision on my behalf.
Decide what is right.
3 You have scrutinized my inner motives;
you have examined me during the night.
You have carefully evaluated me, but you find no sin.
I am determined I will say nothing sinful.
4 As for the actions of people—
just as you have commanded,
I have not followed in the footsteps of violent men.
5 I carefully obey your commands;
I do not deviate from them.
6 I call to you because you will answer me, O God.
Listen to me!
Hear what I say!
7 Accomplish awesome, faithful deeds,
you who powerfully deliver those who look to you for protection from their enemies.
8 Protect me as you would protect the pupil of your eye.
Hide me in the shadow of your wings.
9 Protect me from the wicked men who attack me,
my enemies who crowd around me for the kill.
10 They are calloused;
they speak arrogantly.
11 They attack me, now they surround me;
they intend to throw me to the ground.
12 He is like a lion that wants to tear its prey to bits,
like a young lion crouching in hidden places.
13 Rise up, LORD!
Confront him. Knock him down.
Use your sword to rescue me from the wicked man.
14 LORD, use your power to deliver me from these murderers,
from the murderers of this world.
They enjoy prosperity;

you overwhelm them with the riches they desire.
They have many children,
and leave their wealth to their offspring.
15 As for me, because I am innocent I will see your face;
when I awake you will reveal yourself to me.

PSALM 18

For the music director, by the LORD's servant David, who sang to the LORD the words of this song when the LORD rescued him from the power of all his enemies, including Saul.

1 He said:
"I love you, LORD, my source of strength!
2 The LORD is my high ridge, my stronghold, my deliverer.
My God is my rocky summit where I take shelter,
my shield, the horn that saves me, and my refuge.
3 I called to the LORD, who is worthy of praise,
and I was delivered from my enemies.
4 The waves of death engulfed me,
the currents of chaos overwhelmed me.
5 The ropes of Sheol tightened around me,
the snares of death trapped me.
6 In my distress I called to the LORD;
I cried out to my God.
From his heavenly temple he heard my voice;
he listened to my cry for help.
7 The earth heaved and shook.
The roots of the mountains trembled;
they heaved because he was angry.
8 Smoke ascended from his nose;
fire devoured as it came from his mouth.
He hurled down fiery coals.
9 He made the sky sink as he descended;
a thick cloud was under his feet.
10 He mounted a winged angel and flew;
he glided on the wings of the wind.
11 He shrouded himself in darkness,
in thick rain clouds.
12 From the brightness in front of him came
hail and fiery coals.
13 The LORD thundered in the sky;
the Most High shouted.
14 He shot his arrows and scattered them,
many lightning bolts and routed them.
15 The depths of the sea were exposed;
the inner regions of the world were uncovered
by your battle cry, LORD,
by the powerful breath from your nose.
16 He reached down from above and took hold of me;
he pulled me from the surging water.
17 He rescued me from my strong enemy,
from those who hate me,
for they were too strong for me.
18 They confronted me in my day of calamity,
but the LORD helped me.
19 He brought me out into a wide open place;
he delivered me because he was pleased with me.
20 The LORD repaid me for my godly deeds;
he rewarded my blameless behavior.
21 For I have obeyed the LORD's commands;

17:15 The righteous alone . . . shall be satisfied, saying, "Because I am innocent I will see your face; when I awake you will reveal yourself to me." Those who partake of divine bread always hunger with desire, and they who thus hunger have a never-failing gift, as he promises: "I will abundantly supply what she needs; I will give her poor all the food they need" (Ps 132:15). We may also hear our Savior saying, "Blessed are those who hunger and thirst for righteousness, for they will be satisfied" (Matt 5:6). Well then do the saints and those who love the life that is in Christ raise themselves to a longing after this food. "O God, you are my God. I long for you . . . my flesh yearns for you, in a dry and parched land where there is no water" (Ps 63:1).

ATHANASIUS **(C. 296–373)**
FESTAL LETTERS

18:16–27 "He delivered me because he was pleased with me"; indeed, it was not that I had repented or been convicted concerning my sin or had a prophet sent to me, but it was because he took pleasure to deliver me. And I know and I am absolutely persuaded that in the day of his judgment of the righteous, no mention will be made of my sin and the crimes that I committed in the day of my misery.

EUSEBIUS OF CAESAREA
(C. 260–339)
COMMENTARY ON THE PSALMS

I have not rebelled against my God.
22 For I am aware of all his regulations,
and I do not reject his rules.
23 I was innocent before him,
and kept myself from sinning.
24 The LORD rewarded me for my godly deeds;
he took notice of my blameless behavior.
25 You prove to be loyal to one who is faithful;
you prove to be trustworthy to one who is innocent.
26 You prove to be reliable to one who is blameless,
but you prove to be deceptive to one who is perverse.
27 For you deliver oppressed people,
but you bring down those who have a proud look.
28 Indeed, you light my lamp, LORD.
My God illuminates the darkness around me.
29 Indeed, with your help I can charge against an army;
by my God's power I can jump over a wall.
30 The one true God acts in a faithful manner;
the LORD's promise is reliable.
He is a shield to all who take shelter in him.
31 Indeed, who is God besides the LORD?
Who is a protector besides our God?
32 The one true God gives me strength;
he removes the obstacles in my way.
33 He gives me the agility of a deer;
he enables me to negotiate the rugged terrain.
34 He trains my hands for battle;
my arms can bend even the strongest bow.
35 You give me your protective shield;
your right hand supports me.
Your willingness to help enables me to prevail.
36 You widen my path;
my feet do not slip.
37 I chase my enemies and catch them;
I do not turn back until I wipe them out.
38 I beat them to death;
they fall at my feet.
39 You give me strength for battle;
you make my foes kneel before me.
40 You make my enemies retreat;
I destroy those who hate me.
41 They cry out, but there is no one to help them;
they cry out to the LORD, but he does not answer them.
42 I grind them as fine windblown dust;
I beat them underfoot like clay in the streets.
43 You rescue me from a hostile army.
You make me a leader of nations;
people over whom I had no authority are now my subjects.
44 When they hear of my exploits, they submit to me.
Foreigners are powerless before me.
45 Foreigners lose their courage;
they shake with fear as they leave their strongholds.
46 The LORD is alive!
My Protector is praiseworthy.
The God who delivers me is exalted as king.
47 The one true God completely vindicates me;
he makes nations submit to me.
48 He delivers me from my enemies.
You snatch me away from those who attack me;

you rescue me from violent men.
49 So I will give you thanks before the nations, O LORD.
I will sing praises to you.
50 He gives his king magnificent victories;
he is faithful to his chosen ruler,
to David and his descendants forever."

PSALM 19

For the music director, a psalm of David.

1 The heavens declare the glory of God;
the sky displays his handiwork.
2 Day after day it speaks out;
night after night it reveals his greatness.
3 There is no actual speech or word,
nor is its voice literally heard.
4 Yet its voice echoes throughout the earth;
its words carry to the distant horizon.
In the sky he has pitched a tent for the sun.
5 Like a bridegroom it emerges from its chamber;
like a strong man it enjoys running its course.
6 It emerges from the distant horizon,
and goes from one end of the sky to the other;
nothing can escape its heat.
7 The law of the LORD is perfect
and preserves one's life.
The rules set down by the LORD are reliable
and impart wisdom to the inexperienced.
8 The LORD's precepts are fair
and make one joyful.
The LORD's commands are pure
and give insight for life.
9 The commands to fear the LORD are right
and endure forever.
The judgments given by the LORD are trustworthy
and absolutely just.
10 They are of greater value than gold,
than even a great amount of pure gold;
they bring greater delight than honey,
than even the sweetest honey from a honeycomb.
11 Yes, your servant finds moral guidance there;
those who obey them receive a rich reward.
12 Who can know all his errors?
Please do not punish me for sins I am unaware of.
13 Moreover, keep me from committing flagrant sins;
do not allow such sins to control me.
Then I will be blameless
and innocent of blatant rebellion.
14 May my words and my thoughts
be acceptable in your sight,
O LORD, my sheltering rock and my redeemer.

PSALM 20

For the music director, a psalm of David.

1 May the LORD answer you when you are in trouble;
may the God of Jacob make you secure.
2 May he send you help from his temple;
from Zion may he give you support.
3 May he take notice of all your offerings;
may he accept your burnt sacrifice. *Selah*

19:1–14 The heavens are as a legible book. Every day and night repeat these demonstrations of God's glory. Their magnificent structure, their exquisite order, and their most regular course declare their author no less than people declare their minds by their words. He then proceeds to another demonstration of God's glory (his law), which he compares with and prefers before the former. The creation, although it did declare so much of God as left all men without excuse, yet it did not fully manifest the will of God or bring humanity to eternal salvation. His law is a witness between God and humankind of what God requires of us and what upon the performance of that condition he will do for us.

JOHN WESLEY **(1703–1791)**
EXPLANATORY NOTES ON THE BIBLE

20:1–9 It is abundantly obvious that this psalm is true of the Messiah alone: "May the LORD grant all your requests." There is no king except the Messiah about whom David prophesied that he will help in our day of trouble, especially because David counted himself among those crying out, saying, "He will answer us when we call to him for help!" So, because the words in this psalm surpassed David—and how much more the other kings, indeed even the people!—they fit the Messiah. It must be concluded that this psalm, according to the letter, is about the exaltation of the Messiah as a result of the merit of his Passion by which he subjected the world to the yoke of faith.

THOMAS CAJETAN
(1469–1534)
COMMENTARY ON THE PSALMS

4 May he grant your heart's desire;
may he bring all your plans to pass.
5 Then we will shout for joy over your victory;
we will rejoice in the name of our God.
May the LORD grant all your requests.
6 Now I am sure that the LORD will deliver his chosen
king;
he will intervene for him from his holy, heavenly
temple,
and display his mighty ability to deliver.
7 Some trust in chariots and others in horses,
but we depend on the LORD our God.
8 They will fall down,
but we will stand firm.
9 The LORD will deliver the king;
he will answer us when we call to him for help!

PSALM 21

For the music director, a psalm of David.

1 O LORD, the king rejoices in the strength you give;
he takes great delight in the deliverance you provide.
2 You grant him his heart's desire;
you do not refuse his request. *Selah*
3 For you bring him rich blessings;
you place a golden crown on his head.
4 He asked you to sustain his life,
and you have granted him long life and an enduring
dynasty.
5 Your deliverance brings him great honor;
you give him majestic splendor.
6 For you grant him lasting blessings;
you give him great joy by allowing him into your
presence.
7 For the king trusts in the LORD,
and because of the Most High's faithfulness he is not
shaken.
8 You prevail over all your enemies;
your power is too great for those who hate you.
9 You burn them up like a fiery furnace when you appear.
The LORD angrily devours them;
the fire consumes them.
10 You destroy their offspring from the earth,
their descendants from among the human race.
11 Yes, they intend to do you harm;
they dream up a scheme, but they do not succeed.
12 For you make them retreat
when you aim your arrows at them.
13 Rise up, O LORD, in strength!
We will sing and praise your power.

PSALM 22

For the music director, according to the tune "Morning Doe"; a psalm of David.

1 My God, my God, why have you abandoned me?
I groan in prayer, but help seems far away.
2 My God, I cry out during the day,
but you do not answer,
and during the night my prayers do not let up.
3 You are holy;

21:1–13 The psalmist considers a twofold kind of joy in this passage. By the joy of the flesh, we rejoice in many kindnesses and great affection. About this joy the pious do not speak here. The other is the joy by which the pious rejoice, not because of kindness alone but rather because of a sense of the grace and favor of God. At such joy these singers gaze because they do not say, "You have made him joyful with your kindness," but "You give him great joy by allowing him into your presence." Those who love sincerely are affected by this kind of joy, and they care for nothing more than gaining the favor of him whom they love.

WOLFGANG MUSCULUS
(1497–1563)
COMMENTARY ON THE PSALMS

you sit as king receiving the praises of Israel.
4 In you our ancestors trusted;
they trusted in you and you rescued them.
5 To you they cried out, and they were saved;
in you they trusted and they were not disappointed.
6 But I am a worm, not a man;
people insult me and despise me.
7 All who see me taunt me;
they mock me and shake their heads.
8 They say,
"Commit yourself to the LORD!
Let the LORD rescue him!
Let the LORD deliver him, for he delights in him."
9 Yes, you are the one who brought me out from the womb
and made me feel secure on my mother's breasts.
10 I have been dependent on you since birth;
from the time I came out of my mother's womb you
have been my God.
11 Do not remain far away from me,
for trouble is near and I have no one to help me.
12 Many bulls surround me;
powerful bulls of Bashan hem me in.
13 They open their mouths to devour me
like a roaring lion that rips its prey.
14 My strength drains away like water;
all my bones are dislocated.
My heart is like wax;
it melts away inside me.
15 The roof of my mouth is as dry as a piece of pottery;
my tongue sticks to my gums.
You set me in the dust of death.
16 Yes, wild dogs surround me—
a gang of evil men crowd around me;
like a lion they pin my hands and feet.
17 I can count all my bones;
my enemies are gloating over me in triumph.
18 They are dividing up my clothes among themselves;
they are rolling dice for my garments.
19 But you, O LORD, do not remain far away.
You are my source of strength. Hurry and help me!
20 Deliver me from the sword.
Save my life from the claws of the wild dogs.
21 Rescue me from the mouth of the lion
and from the horns of the wild oxen.
You have answered me.
22 I will declare your name to my countrymen.
In the middle of the assembly I will praise you.
23 You loyal followers of the LORD, praise him.
All you descendants of Jacob, honor him.
All you descendants of Israel, stand in awe of him.
24 For he did not despise or detest the suffering of the
oppressed.
He did not ignore him;
when he cried out to him, he responded.
25 You are the reason I offer praise in the great assembly;
I will fulfill my promises before the LORD's loyal followers.
26 Let the oppressed eat and be filled.
Let those who seek his help praise the LORD.
May you live forever!

22:1–31 "My God, my God, why have you abandoned me?" At this moment physical weakness was united with acute mental torture from the shame and ignominy through which Jesus had to pass. This was the black midnight of his horror; then it was that he descended into the abyss of suffering. No human being can perceive the full meaning of these words. We grieve at a little withdrawal of our Father's love, but the real turning away of God's face from his Son—who shall calculate how deep the agony it caused him? O you poor, distressed soul who once lived in the sunshine of God's face but are now in darkness, remember that he has not really forsaken you. God in the clouds is as much our God as when he shines forth in all the luster of his grace.

CHARLES SPURGEON
(1834–1892)
MORNING AND EVENING

27 Let all the people of the earth acknowledge the LORD
and turn to him.
Let all the nations worship you.
28 For the LORD is king
and rules over the nations.
29 All the thriving people of the earth will join the
celebration and worship;
all those who are descending into the grave will bow
before him,
including those who cannot preserve their lives.
30 A whole generation will serve him;
they will tell the next generation about the Lord.
31 They will come and tell about his saving deeds;
they will tell a future generation what he has
accomplished.

PSALM 23

A psalm of David.

1 The LORD is my shepherd,
I lack nothing.
2 He takes me to lush pastures,
he leads me to refreshing water.
3 He restores my strength.
He leads me down the right paths
for the sake of his reputation.
4 Even when I must walk through the darkest valley,
I fear no danger,
for you are with me;
your rod and your staff reassure me.
5 You prepare a feast before me
in plain sight of my enemies.
You refresh my head with oil;
my cup is completely full.
6 Surely your goodness and faithfulness will pursue me
all my days,
and I will live in the LORD's house for the rest of my life.

PSALM 24

A psalm of David.

1 The LORD owns the earth and all it contains,
the world and all who live in it.
2 For he set its foundation upon the seas,
and established it upon the ocean currents.
3 Who is allowed to ascend the mountain of the LORD?
Who may go up to his holy dwelling place?
4 The one whose deeds are blameless
and whose motives are pure,
who does not lie,
or make promises with no intention of keeping them.
5 Such godly people are rewarded by the LORD,
and vindicated by the God who delivers them.
6 Such purity characterizes the people who seek his favor,
Jacob's descendants, who pray to him. *Selah*
7 Look up, you gates.
Rise up, you eternal doors.
Then the majestic king will enter.
8 Who is this majestic king?
The LORD who is strong and mighty.
The LORD who is mighty in battle.

23:1–6 A sheep must live entirely by its shepherd's help, protection, and care. It is a poor, weak, simple little beast that can neither feed nor rule itself, nor find the right way, nor protect itself against any kind of danger or misfortune. Moreover, it is by nature timid, shy, and likely to go astray. When it does go a bit astray and leaves its shepherd, it is unable to find its way back to him; indeed, it merely runs farther away from him. It is the function of a faithful shepherd not only to supply his sheep with good pasture and other related things but also to keep them from suffering harm. He takes good care not to lose any of them, but if one of them should go astray, he seeks it and returns it. He looks after the young, the weak, and the sick very carefully, waits on them, lifts them up, and carries them in his arms until they are grown and strong and well.

MARTIN LUTHER **(1483–1546)**
EXEGESIS OF PSALM 23

24:1–10 He speaks here of the gates and doors of the temple, which by faith and the spirit of prophecy he beheld as already built. These gates he bids lift up their heads by allusion to those gates that have a portcullis that may be let down or taken up. And as the temple was a type of Christ, of his church, and of heaven itself, so this place may also contain a representation of Christ's entrance either into his church or into the hearts of his faithful people, who are here commanded to set open their hearts and souls for his reception; or of his ascension into heaven, where the saints or angels are poetically introduced as preparing the way and opening the heavenly gates to receive their Lord and King returning to his royal habitation with triumph and glory.

JOHN WESLEY **(1703–1791)**
EXPLANATORY NOTES ON THE BIBLE

9 Look up, you gates.
Rise up, you eternal doors.
Then the majestic king will enter.
10 Who is this majestic king?
The LORD of Heaven's Armies.
He is the majestic king. *Selah*

PSALM 25

By David.

1 O LORD, I come before you in prayer.
2 My God, I trust in you.
Please do not let me be humiliated;
do not let my enemies triumphantly rejoice over me.
3 Certainly none who rely on you will be humiliated.
Those who deal in treachery will be thwarted and humiliated.
4 Make me understand your ways, O LORD.
Teach me your paths.
5 Guide me into your truth and teach me.
For you are the God who delivers me;
on you I rely all day long.
6 Remember your compassionate and faithful deeds, O LORD,
for you have always acted in this manner.
7 Do not hold against me the sins of my youth or my rebellious acts.
Because you are faithful to me, extend to me your favor, O LORD.
8 The LORD is both kind and fair;
that is why he teaches sinners the right way to live.
9 May he show the humble what is right.
May he teach the humble his way.
10 The LORD always proves faithful and reliable
to those who follow the demands of his covenant.
11 For the sake of your reputation, O LORD,
forgive my sin, because it is great.
12 The LORD shows his faithful followers
the way they should live.
13 They experience his favor;
their descendants inherit the land.
14 The LORD's loyal followers receive his guidance,
and he reveals his covenantal demands to them.
15 I continually look to the LORD for help,
for he will free my feet from the enemy's net.
16 Turn toward me and have mercy on me,
for I am alone and oppressed.
17 Deliver me from my distress;
rescue me from my suffering.
18 See my pain and suffering.
Forgive all my sins.
19 Watch my enemies, for they outnumber me;
they hate me and want to harm me.
20 Protect me and deliver me!
Please do not let me be humiliated,
for I have taken shelter in you.
21 May integrity and godliness protect me,
for I rely on you.
22 O God, rescue Israel
from all their distress!

25:8 The mercy of God is as sufficient for the pardon of the greatest sins as for the least, and that because his mercy is infinite. That which is infinite is as much above what is great as it is above what is small. Thus God being infinitely great, he is as much above kings as he is above beggars; he is as much above the highest angel as he is above the meanest worm. One infinite measure does not come any nearer to the extent of what is infinite than another. So the mercy of God being infinite, it must be as sufficient for the pardon of all sin as of one. If one of the least sins be not beyond the mercy of God, so neither are the greatest, or ten thousand of them.

JONATHAN EDWARDS
(1703–1758)
THE COMPLETE WORKS

PSALM 26

By David.

1 Vindicate me, O LORD,
for I have integrity,
and I trust in the LORD without wavering.
2 Examine me, O LORD, and test me.
Evaluate my inner thoughts and motives.
3 For I am ever aware of your faithfulness,
and your loyalty continually motivates me.
4 I do not associate with deceitful men,
or consort with those who are dishonest.
5 I hate the mob of evil men,
and do not associate with the wicked.
6 I maintain a pure lifestyle,
so I can appear before your altar, O LORD,
7 to give you thanks,
and to tell about all your amazing deeds.
8 O LORD, I love the temple where you live,
the place where your splendor is revealed.
9 Do not sweep me away with sinners,
or execute me along with violent people,
10 who are always ready to do wrong
or offer a bribe.
11 But I have integrity.
Rescue me and have mercy on me!
12 I am safe,
and among the worshipers I will praise the LORD.

26:1–12 The petition for judgment does indeed appear to be dangerous, but a separation from evil people is recognized to be an appropriate request from one who is well deserving. Therefore this request does not arise from the detestable pride in merits, it is the just petition of a faithful servant asking to be separated from the most vile in order not to have a portion with wicked people. The psalmist walks in innocence because he puts his hope in the Lord, as he says later; nor does he find confidence in his own powers but in God's generosity. A fitting proof of this matter follows, for he maintains that he has not been weakened in his trust in the Lord. This is the innocence he spoke about earlier, namely his confidence in God's power that no weakness of sin is able to weigh him down.

CASSIODORUS **(C. 485–C. 585)**
EXPLANATION OF THE PSALMS

PSALM 27

By David.

1 The LORD is my light and my salvation.
I fear no one.
The LORD protects my life.
I am afraid of no one.
2 When evil men attack me
to devour my flesh,
when my adversaries and enemies attack me,
they stumble and fall.
3 Even when an army is deployed against me,
I do not fear.
Even when war is imminent,
I remain confident.
4 I have asked the LORD for one thing—
this is what I desire!
I want to live in the LORD's house all the days of my life,
so I can gaze at the splendor of the LORD
and contemplate in his temple.
5 He will surely give me shelter in the day of danger;
he will hide me in his home.
He will place me on an inaccessible rocky summit.
6 Now I will triumph
over my enemies who surround me.
I will offer sacrifices in his dwelling place and shout for joy.
I will sing praises to the LORD.
7 Hear me, O LORD, when I cry out.
Have mercy on me and answer me.
8 My heart tells me to pray to you,
and I do pray to you, O LORD.

27:1–14 Whoever is in covenant with God has solid grounds to expect from God direction, comfort, and deliverance in every trouble. By virtue of the covenant of grace, David said, "The LORD is my light and my salvation." When we have fastened our faith on God, then we may with reason defy our enemies and say with the prophet, "I fear no one." When our enemies appear strong and we know that we are weak, we should place the Lord's strength against our temptations so that we may resist all fear, as David taught, "The LORD protects my life. I am afraid of no one."

DAVID DICKSON **(1583–1663)**
EXPLICATION OF THE FIRST FIFTY PSALMS

9 Do not reject me.
Do not push your servant away in anger.
You are my deliverer.
Do not forsake or abandon me,
O God who vindicates me.
10 Even if my father and mother abandoned me,
the LORD would take me in.
11 Teach me how you want me to live, LORD;
lead me along a level path because of those who wait to ambush me.
12 Do not turn me over to my enemies,
for false witnesses who want to destroy me testify against me.
13 Where would I be if I did not believe I would experience
the LORD's favor in the land of the living?
14 Rely on the LORD!
Be strong and confident!
Rely on the LORD!

PSALM 28

By David.

1 To you, O LORD, I cry out!
My Protector, do not ignore me.
If you do not respond to me,
I will join those who are descending into the grave.
2 Hear my plea for mercy when I cry out to you for help,
when I lift my hands toward your holy temple.
3 Do not drag me away with evil men,
with those who behave wickedly,
who talk so friendly to their neighbors,
while they plan to harm them.
4 Pay them back for their evil deeds.
Pay them back for what they do.
Punish them.
5 For they do not understand the LORD's actions,
or the way he carries out justice.
The LORD will permanently demolish them.
6 The LORD deserves praise,
for he has heard my plea for mercy.
7 The LORD strengthens and protects me;
I trust in him with all my heart.
I am rescued and my heart is full of joy;
I will sing to him in gratitude.
8 The LORD strengthens his people;
he protects and delivers his chosen king.
9 Deliver your people.
Empower the nation that belongs to you.
Care for them like a shepherd and carry them in your arms at all times!

PSALM 29

A psalm of David.

1 Acknowledge the LORD, you heavenly beings,
acknowledge the LORD's majesty and power.
2 Acknowledge the majesty of the LORD's reputation.
Worship the LORD in holy attire.
3 The LORD's shout is heard over the water;
the majestic God thunders,
the LORD appears over the surging water.

28:1–9 David sings this psalm in the person of those who have come to faith in Christ, and with entreaty he calls on Christ for assistance. The psalm was spoken by David when he was pursued by Saul and was the object of schemes on the part of those who seemed to be friends but betrayed him and tried to reveal his whereabouts to Saul. This psalm, and in fact the psalms before it as well, are suited to everyone encountering calamities of this kind: Like blessed David it is possible for the person intent on persevering both to petition God and to secure his providence.

THEODORET OF CYR
(C. 393–C. 458)
COMMENTARY ON THE PSALMS

29:1–11 By his Word he terrifies, punishes, and even plunges into hell alive the proud who resist God. On the other hand, the Word of God makes it so that there is nothing inaccessible to his saints; in fact, those who rely on the power of the Word of God can pass through anything, even opposing the gates of hell. Thus the Word of God or the voice of the Lord is so effective that it functions differently in different circumstances. The arrogant and despisers of the Word perish by it. And the people of God are also challenged by the Word and strengthened to worship God and praise his glory. Indeed this people cannot perish in mighty waters and the shadow of death! Their King and Governor is the eternal Lord: He comforts them against all the powers of both the world and hell so that they can receive the promises of God. In short, this blessing—that is, his eternal grace and peace—he lavishes on them.

JOHANNES BUGENHAGEN
(1485–1558)
INTERPRETATION OF THE PSALMS

4 The LORD's shout is powerful;
the LORD's shout is majestic.
5 The LORD's shout breaks the cedars;
the LORD shatters the cedars of Lebanon.
6 He makes them skip like a calf,
Lebanon and Sirion like a young ox.
7 The LORD's shout strikes with flaming fire.
8 The LORD's shout shakes the wilderness;
the LORD shakes the wilderness of Kadesh.
9 The LORD's shout bends the large trees
and strips the leaves from the forests.
Everyone in his temple says, "Majestic!"
10 The LORD sits enthroned over the engulfing waters;
the LORD sits enthroned as the eternal king.
11 The LORD gives his people strength;
the LORD grants his people security.

PSALM 30

A psalm, a song used at the dedication of the temple; by David.

1 I will praise you, O LORD, for you lifted me up
and did not allow my enemies to gloat over me.
2 O LORD my God,
I cried out to you and you healed me.
3 O LORD, you pulled me up from Sheol;
you rescued me from among those descending into the grave.
4 Sing to the LORD, you faithful followers of his;
give thanks to his holy name.
5 For his anger lasts only a brief moment,
and his good favor restores one's life.
One may experience sorrow during the night,
but joy arrives in the morning.
6 In my self-confidence I said,
"I will never be shaken."
7 O LORD, in your good favor you made me secure.
Then you rejected me and I was terrified.
8 To you, O LORD, I cried out;
I begged the Lord for mercy:
9 "What profit is there in taking my life,
in my descending into the Pit?
Can the dust of the grave praise you?
Can it declare your loyalty?
10 Hear, O LORD, and have mercy on me.
O LORD, deliver me."
11 Then you turned my lament into dancing;
you removed my sackcloth and covered me with joy.
12 So now my heart will sing to you and not be silent;
O LORD my God, I will always give thanks to you.

PSALM 31

For the music director, a psalm of David.

1 In you, O LORD, I have taken shelter.
Never let me be humiliated.
Vindicate me by rescuing me.
2 Listen to me.
Quickly deliver me.
Be my protector and refuge,
a stronghold where I can be safe.
3 For you are my high ridge and my stronghold;

30:4 People do not sing to the Lord by simply uttering the words of the psalm with their mouths, but all who send up the psalmody from a clean heart and who are holy, maintaining righteousness toward God, these are able to sing to God, harmoniously guided by the spiritual rhythms. How many stand there coming from fornication? How many from theft? How many concealing in their hearts deceit? How many lying? They think they are singing, although in truth they are not singing. For the scripture invites the saint to the singing of psalms. "The bad tree bears bad fruit" (Matt 7:17). Therefore make the tree good and its fruits good. Cleanse your hearts in order that you may bear fruit in the Spirit and may be able, after becoming saints, to sing psalms intelligently to the Lord.

BASIL THE GREAT (330–379)
HOMILIES ON THE PSALMS

31:1–8 If you put your trust in money, you are paying futile regard to vain things; if you put your trust in high office or some exalted rank in human government, you are paying futile regard to vain things. When you put your trust in all these, either you expire and leave them all behind, or they will crumble while you are still alive, and what you trusted will have let you down. For my part, I do not put my trust in empty things as they do or pay futile regard to them; I have put my trust in the Lord.

AUGUSTINE (354–430)
EXPOSITIONS ON THE PSALMS

for the sake of your own reputation you lead me and guide me.
4 You will free me from the net they hid for me,
for you are my place of refuge.
5 Into your hand I entrust my life;
you will rescue me, O LORD, the faithful God.
6 I hate those who serve worthless idols,
but I trust in the LORD.
7 I will be happy and rejoice in your faithfulness,
because you notice my pain
and you are aware of how distressed I am.
8 You do not deliver me over to the power of the enemy;
you enable me to stand in a wide open place.
9 Have mercy on me, LORD, for I am in distress!
My eyes grow dim from suffering.
I have lost my strength.
10 For my life nears its end in pain;
my years draw to a close as I groan.
My strength fails me because of my sin,
and my bones become brittle.
11 Because of all my enemies, people disdain me;
my neighbors are appalled by my suffering—
those who know me are horrified by my condition;
those who see me in the street run away from me.
12 I am forgotten, like a dead man no one thinks about;
I am regarded as worthless, like a broken jar.
13 For I hear what so many are saying,
the terrifying news that comes from every direction.
When they plot together against me,
they figure out how they can take my life.
14 But I trust in you, O LORD!
I declare, "You are my God!"
15 You determine my destiny.
Rescue me from the power of my enemies and those who chase me.
16 Smile on your servant.
Deliver me because of your faithfulness.
17 O LORD, do not let me be humiliated,
for I call out to you.
May evil men be humiliated.
May they go wailing to the grave.
18 May lying lips be silenced—
lips that speak defiantly against the innocent
with arrogance and contempt.
19 How great is your favor,
which you store up for your loyal followers.
In plain sight of everyone you bestow it on those who take shelter in you.
20 You hide them with you, where they are safe from the attacks of men;
you conceal them in a shelter, where they are safe from slanderous attacks.
21 The LORD deserves praise
for he demonstrated his amazing faithfulness to me
when I was besieged by enemies.
22 I jumped to conclusions and said,
"I am cut off from your presence!"
But you heard my plea for mercy when I cried out to you for help.

23 Love the LORD, all you faithful followers of his!
The LORD protects those who have integrity,
but he pays back in full the one who acts arrogantly.
24 Be strong and confident,
all you who wait on the LORD.

PSALM 32

By David; a well-written song.

1 How blessed is the one whose rebellious acts are forgiven,
whose sin is pardoned.
2 How blessed is the one whose wrongdoing the LORD does not punish,
in whose spirit there is no deceit.
3 When I refused to confess my sin,
my whole body wasted away,
while I groaned in pain all day long.
4 For day and night you tormented me;
you tried to destroy me in the intense heat of summer. *Selah*
5 Then I confessed my sin;
I no longer covered up my wrongdoing.
I said, "I will confess my rebellious acts to the LORD."
And then you forgave my sins. *Selah*
6 For this reason every one of your faithful followers should pray to you
while there is a window of opportunity.
Certainly when the surging water rises,
it will not reach them.
7 You are my hiding place;
you protect me from distress.
You surround me with shouts of joy from those celebrating deliverance. *Selah*
8 I will instruct and teach you about how you should live.
I will advise you as I look you in the eye.
9 Do not be like an unintelligent horse or mule,
which will not obey you
unless they are controlled by a bridle and bit.
10 An evil person suffers much pain,
but the LORD's faithfulness overwhelms the one who trusts in him.
11 Rejoice in the LORD and be happy, you who are godly!
Shout for joy, all you who are morally upright!

32:1–11 We believe that all our justification rests on the remission of our sins in which also is our only blessedness, as the psalmist says. We therefore reject all other means of justification before God, and without claiming any virtue or merit, we rest simply in the obedience of Jesus Christ, which is imputed to us as much to blot out all our sins as to make us find grace and favor in the sight of God. And in fact we believe that in falling away from this foundation, however slightly, we could not find rest elsewhere but should always be troubled. For we are never at peace with God until we resolve to be loved in Jesus Christ, for of ourselves we are worthy of hatred.

GALLIC CONFESSION (1560)

PSALM 33

1 You godly ones, shout for joy because of the LORD!
It is appropriate for the morally upright to offer him praise.
2 Give thanks to the LORD with the harp.
Sing to him to the accompaniment of a ten-stringed instrument.
3 Sing to him a new song.
Play skillfully as you shout out your praises to him.
4 For the LORD's decrees are just,
and everything he does is fair.
5 He promotes equity and justice;
the LORD's faithfulness extends throughout the earth.
6 By the LORD's decree the heavens were made,
and by the breath of his mouth all the starry hosts.

33:1–22 Perhaps no figure of speech represents God in a more gracious light than when he is spoken of as stooping from his throne to attend to the wants and to behold the woes of humankind. Though leagues of distance lie between the finite creature and the infinite Creator, yet there are links uniting both. Your sigh is able to move the heart of Jehovah, your whisper can incline his ear unto you, your prayer can stay his hand, and your faith can move his arm. Don't think that God sits on high taking no account of you. Remember that however poor and needy you are, yet the Lord thinks of you. "He is the one who forms every human heart, and takes note of all their actions."

CHARLES SPURGEON
(1834–1892)
MORNING AND EVENING

7 He piles up the water of the sea;
he puts the oceans in storehouses.
8 Let the whole earth fear the LORD.
Let all who live in the world stand in awe of him.
9 For he spoke, and it came into existence.
He issued the decree, and it stood firm.
10 The LORD frustrates the decisions of the nations;
he nullifies the plans of the peoples.
11 The LORD's decisions stand forever;
his plans abide throughout the ages.
12 How blessed is the nation whose God is the LORD,
the people whom he has chosen to be his special
possession.
13 The LORD watches from heaven;
he sees all people.
14 From the place where he lives he looks carefully
at all the earth's inhabitants.
15 He is the one who forms every human heart,
and takes note of all their actions.
16 No king is delivered by his vast army;
a warrior is not saved by his great might.
17 A horse disappoints those who trust in it for victory;
despite its great strength, it cannot deliver.
18 Look, the LORD takes notice of his loyal followers,
those who wait for him to demonstrate his faithfulness
19 by saving their lives from death
and sustaining them during times of famine.
20 We wait for the LORD;
he is our deliverer and shield.
21 For our hearts rejoice in him,
for we trust in his holy name.
22 May we experience your faithfulness, O LORD,
for we wait for you.

PSALM 34

By David, when he pretended to be insane before Abimelech, causing the king to send him away.

1 I will praise the LORD at all times;
my mouth will continually praise him.
2 I will boast in the LORD;
let the oppressed hear and rejoice.
3 Magnify the LORD with me.
Let us praise his name together.
4 I sought the LORD's help and he answered me;
he delivered me from all my fears.
5 Look to him and be radiant;
do not let your faces be ashamed.
6 This oppressed man cried out and the LORD heard;
he saved him from all his troubles.
7 The angel of the LORD camps around
the LORD's loyal followers and delivers them.
8 Taste and see that the LORD is good.
How blessed is the one who takes shelter in him.
9 Fear the LORD, you chosen people of his,
for those who fear him lack nothing.
10 Even young lions sometimes lack food and are hungry,
but those who seek the LORD lack no good thing.
11 Come children. Listen to me.
I will teach you what it means to fear the LORD.

34:1–11 This psalm, which has given healing to many a wounded conscience, comes from the depths of a conscience that itself has been wounded and healed. One must be very dull of hearing not to feel how it throbs with emotion and is in fact a gush of rapture from a heart experiencing in its freshness the new joy of forgiveness. Then note the remarkable accumulation of clauses, all expressing substantially the same thing, but expressing it with a difference. The psalmist's heart is too full to be emptied by one utterance. He turns his jewel, as it were, round and round, and at each turn it reflects the light from a different angle.

ALEXANDER MACLAREN
(1826–1910)
EXPOSITIONS OF THE HOLY SCRIPTURES

12 Do you want to really live?
Would you love to live a long, happy life?
13 Then make sure you don't speak evil words
or use deceptive speech.
14 Turn away from evil and do what is right.
Strive for peace and promote it.
15 The LORD pays attention to the godly
and hears their cry for help.
16 But the LORD opposes evildoers
and wipes out all memory of them from the earth.
17 The godly cry out and the LORD hears;
he saves them from all their troubles.
18 The LORD is near the brokenhearted;
he delivers those who are discouraged.
19 The godly face many dangers,
but the LORD saves them from each one of them.
20 He protects all his bones;
not one of them is broken.
21 Evil people self-destruct;
those who hate the godly are punished.
22 The LORD rescues his servants;
all who take shelter in him escape punishment.

PSALM 35

By David.

35:1–28 David prayed to God to manifest himself in his trial. God is our Friend, no matter who is our enemy. By the Spirit of prophecy, David foretold the just judgments of God that would come upon his enemies for their great wickedness. These are predictions, they look forward and show the doom of the enemies of Christ and his kingdom. The psalmist here proposes to serve and glorify God with all his strength. If such language may be applied to outward salvation, how much more will it apply to heavenly things in Christ Jesus!

MATTHEW HENRY **(1662–1714)**
COMMENTARY ON THE WHOLE BIBLE

1 O LORD, fight those who fight with me.
Attack those who attack me.
2 Grab your small shield and large shield,
and rise up to help me.
3 Use your spear and lance against those who chase me.
Assure me with these words: "I am your deliverer."
4 May those who seek my life be embarrassed and
humiliated.
May those who plan to harm me be turned back and
ashamed.
5 May they be like wind-driven chaff,
as the angel of the LORD attacks them.
6 May their path be dark and slippery,
as the angel of the LORD chases them.
7 I did not harm them, but they hid a net to catch me
and dug a pit to trap me.
8 Let destruction take them by surprise.
Let the net they hid catch them.
Let them fall into destruction.
9 Then I will rejoice in the LORD
and be happy because of his deliverance.
10 With all my strength I will say,
"O LORD, who can compare to you?
You rescue the oppressed from those who try to
overpower them,
the oppressed and needy from those who try to rob
them."
11 Violent men perjure themselves,
and falsely accuse me.
12 They repay me evil for the good I have done;
I am overwhelmed with sorrow.
13 When they were sick, I wore sackcloth,
and refrained from eating food.
(If I am lying, may my prayers go unanswered.)

14 I mourned for them as I would for a friend or my
brother.
I bowed down in sorrow as if I were mourning for my
mother.
15 But when I stumbled, they rejoiced and gathered
together;
they gathered together to ambush me.
They tore at me without stopping to rest.
16 When I tripped, they taunted me relentlessly,
and tried to bite me.
17 O Lord, how long are you going to watch this?
Rescue me from their destructive attacks;
guard my life from the young lions.
18 Then I will give you thanks in the great assembly;
I will praise you before a large crowd of people.
19 Do not let those who are my enemies for no reason
gloat over me.
Do not let those who hate me without cause carry out
their wicked schemes.
20 For they do not try to make peace with others,
but plan ways to deceive those who live peacefully in
the land.
21 They are ready to devour me;
they say, "Aha! Aha! We've got you!"
22 But you take notice, LORD; do not be silent!
O Lord, do not remain far away from me.
23 Rouse yourself, wake up and vindicate me.
My God and Lord, defend my just cause.
24 Vindicate me by your justice, O LORD my God.
Do not let them gloat over me.
25 Do not let them say to themselves, "Aha! We have what
we wanted!"
Do not let them say, "We have devoured him."
26 May those who rejoice in my troubles be totally
embarrassed and ashamed.
May those who arrogantly taunt me be covered with
shame and humiliation.
27 May those who desire my vindication shout for joy and
rejoice.
May they continually say, "May the LORD be praised, for
he wants his servant to be secure."
28 Then I will tell others about your justice,
and praise you all day long.

PSALM 36

For the music director, an oracle, written by the LORD's servant David.

1 An evil man is rebellious to the core.
He does not fear God,
2 for he is too proud
to recognize and give up his sin.
3 The words he speaks are sinful and deceitful;
he does not care about doing what is wise and right.
4 While he lies in bed he plans ways to sin.
He is committed to a sinful lifestyle;
he does not reject what is evil.
5 O LORD, your loyal love reaches to the sky,
your faithfulness to the clouds.
6 Your justice is like the highest mountains,

36:1–12 "They are abundantly satisfied with the fullness of Your house" (NKJV). This expression is here directed to the situation of good people. So this heavenly inebriation blocks the remembrance of worldly matters and causes fleshly things to depart from the mind, just as the intoxication of wine separates our actions from our senses. What an incredibly praiseworthy inebriation! This intoxication we must pursue in all our prayers as the source of moderation and for the soundness of mind that is acquired through it. This inebriation does not produce tipsiness, confusion, delirium, or blackouts. But the healthier the soul becomes, the more it is filled with drunkenness. So let us consume this drink eagerly, not with our physical lips, but with the purest disposition of the heart. From this drink one does not receive temporal happiness but rather the joys of eternal life.

CASSIODORUS (C. 485–C. 585)
EXPLANATION OF THE PSALMS

your fairness like the deepest sea;
you, LORD, preserve mankind and the animal kingdom.
7 How precious is your loyal love, O God!
The human race finds shelter under your wings.
8 They are filled with food from your house,
and you allow them to drink from the river of your delicacies.
9 For with you is the fountain of life;
in your light we see light.
10 Extend your loyal love to your faithful followers,
and vindicate the morally upright.
11 Do not let arrogant men overtake me,
or let evil men make me homeless.
12 I can see the evildoers! They have fallen.
They have been knocked down and are unable to get up.

PSALM 37

By David.

1 Do not fret when wicked men seem to succeed.
Do not envy evildoers.
2 For they will quickly dry up like grass,
and wither away like plants.
3 Trust in the LORD and do what is right.
Settle in the land and maintain your integrity.
4 Then you will take delight in the LORD,
and he will answer your prayers.
5 Commit your future to the LORD.
Trust in him, and he will act on your behalf.
6 He will vindicate you in broad daylight,
and publicly defend your just cause.
7 Wait patiently for the LORD!
Wait confidently for him!
Do not fret over the apparent success of a sinner,
a man who carries out wicked schemes.
8 Do not be angry and frustrated.
Do not fret. That only leads to trouble.
9 Wicked men will be wiped out,
but those who rely on the LORD are the ones who will possess the land.
10 Evil men will soon disappear;
you will stare at the spot where they once were, but they will be gone.
11 But the oppressed will possess the land
and enjoy great prosperity.
12 Evil men plot against the godly
and viciously attack them.
13 The Lord laughs in disgust at them,
for he knows that their day is coming.
14 Evil men draw their swords
and prepare their bows,
to bring down the oppressed and needy,
and to slaughter those who are godly.
15 Their swords will pierce their own hearts,
and their bows will be broken.
16 The little bit that a godly man owns is better than
the wealth of many evil men,
17 for evil men will lose their power,
but the LORD sustains the godly.
18 The LORD watches over the innocent day by day,

37:1–40 It seems as if David composed this psalm concerning the difficult trials he experienced within himself as he was stalked by godless Saul, and therefore in his deep misery he must have seen his enemies' good fortune and affluence. For in this he takes hold of a salutary teaching that we should become neither enraged nor resentful because of the prosperity of the godless; instead we should steadfastly endure by faith in God, in innocence and piety—whatever objections we encounter that our flesh introduces.

RUDOLF GWALTHER
(1519–1586)
THE PSALTER

and they possess a permanent inheritance.
19 They will not be ashamed when hard times come;
when famine comes they will have enough to eat.
20 But evil men will die;
the LORD's enemies will be incinerated—
they will go up in smoke.
21 Evil men borrow, but do not repay their debt,
but the godly show compassion and are generous.
22 Surely those favored by the LORD will possess the land,
but those rejected by him will be wiped out.
23 The LORD grants success to the one
whose behavior he finds commendable.
24 Even if he trips, he will not fall headlong,
for the LORD holds his hand.
25 I was once young, now I am old.
I have never seen the godly abandoned,
or their children forced to search for food.
26 All day long they show compassion and lend to others,
and their children are blessed.
27 Turn away from evil. Do what is right.
Then you will enjoy lasting security.
28 For the LORD promotes justice,
and never abandons his faithful followers.
They are permanently secure,
but the children of the wicked are wiped out.
29 The godly will possess the land
and will dwell in it permanently.
30 The godly speak wise words
and promote justice.
31 The law of their God controls their thinking;
their feet do not slip.
32 The wicked set an ambush for the godly
and try to kill them.
33 But the LORD does not surrender the godly,
or allow them to be condemned in a court of law.
34 Rely on the LORD. Obey his commands.
Then he will permit you to possess the land;
you will see the demise of the wicked.
35 I have seen ruthless, wicked people
growing in influence, like a green tree grows in its
native soil.
36 But then one passes by, and suddenly they have
disappeared.
I looked for them, but they could not be found.
37 Take note of the one who has integrity. Observe the
upright.
For the one who promotes peace has a future.
38 Sinful rebels are totally destroyed;
the wicked have no future.
39 But the LORD delivers the godly;
he protects them in times of trouble.
40 The LORD helps them and rescues them;
he rescues them from the wicked and delivers them,
for they seek his protection.

PSALM 38

A psalm of David, written to get God's attention.

1 O LORD, do not continue to rebuke me in your anger.
Do not continue to punish me in your raging fury.

38:1–22 The title "A Psalm of David. To bring to remembrance" (NKJV) in Hebrew means "to remember what has been done," that is, "for confession of our sins." According to the apostle, "Christ redeemed us from the curse of the law by becoming a curse for us" (Gal 3:13) and "He himself bore our sins" (1 Pet 2:24). Therefore this psalm is said in David's person. In it he recalls and confesses our sins for us to God the Father and intercedes for his people's liberation—that is us, through himself and in himself.

MARTIN LUTHER **(1483–1546)**
GLOSSA ON THE PSALMS

2 For your arrows pierce me,
and your hand presses me down.
3 My whole body is sick because of your judgment;
I am deprived of health because of my sin.
4 For my sins overwhelm me;
like a heavy load, they are too much for me to bear.
5 My wounds are infected and starting to smell,
because of my foolish sins.
6 I am dazed and completely humiliated;
all day long I walk around mourning.
7 For I am overcome with shame,
and my whole body is sick.
8 I am numb with pain and severely battered;
I groan loudly because of the anxiety I feel.
9 O Lord, you understand my heart's desire;
my groaning is not hidden from you.
10 My heart beats quickly;
my strength leaves me.
I can hardly see.
11 Because of my condition, even my friends and
acquaintances keep their distance;
my neighbors stand far away.
12 Those who seek my life try to entrap me;
those who want to harm me speak destructive words.
All day long they say deceitful things.
13 But I am like a deaf man—I hear nothing;
I am like a mute who cannot speak.
14 I am like a man who cannot hear
and is incapable of arguing his defense.
15 Yet I wait for you, O LORD!
You will respond, O Lord, my God!
16 I have prayed for deliverance, because otherwise they
will gloat over me;
when my foot slips they will arrogantly taunt me.
17 For I am about to stumble,
and I am in constant pain.
18 Yes, I confess my wrongdoing,
and I am concerned about my sins.
19 But those who are my enemies for no reason are
numerous;
those who hate me without cause outnumber me.
20 They repay me evil for the good I have done;
though I have tried to do good to them, they hurl
accusations at me.
21 Do not abandon me, O LORD.
My God, do not remain far away from me.
22 Hurry and help me, O Lord, my deliverer.

PSALM 39

For the music director, Jeduthun; a psalm of David.

1 I decided, "I will watch what I say
and make sure I do not sin with my tongue.
I will put a muzzle over my mouth
while in the presence of an evil person."
2 I was stone silent;
I held back the urge to speak.
My frustration grew;
3 my anxiety intensified.
As I thought about it, I became impatient.

39:1–13 "I will watch what I say and make sure I do not sin with my tongue." Fellow pilgrim, say not in your heart, *I will go hither and thither, and I shall not sin*, for you are never so out of danger of sinning as to boast of security. There is a robber at every turn of the road to rob you of your jewels; there is a temptation in every mercy; there is a snare in every joy; and if you ever reach heaven, it will be a miracle of divine grace to be ascribed entirely to your Father's power. Be on your guard. There is nothing in this world to foster a Christian's piety but everything to destroy it. How anxious should you be to look up to God that he may keep you!

CHARLES SPURGEON
(1834–1892)
MORNING AND EVENING

Finally I spoke these words:
4 "O LORD, help me understand my mortality
and the brevity of life.
Let me realize how quickly my life will pass.
5 Look, you make my days short lived,
and my life span is nothing from your perspective.
Surely all people, even those who seem secure, are
nothing but vapor. *Selah*
6 Surely people go through life as mere ghosts.
Surely they accumulate worthless wealth
without knowing who will eventually haul it away."
7 But now, O Lord, upon what am I relying?
You are my only hope!
8 Deliver me from all my sins of rebellion.
Do not make me the object of fools' insults.
9 I am silent and cannot open my mouth
because of what you have done.
10 Please stop wounding me.
You have almost beaten me to death.
11 You severely discipline people for their sins;
like a moth you slowly devour their strength.
Surely all people are a mere vapor. *Selah*
12 Hear my prayer, O LORD.
Listen to my cry for help.
Do not ignore my sobbing.
For I am a resident foreigner with you,
a temporary settler, just as all my ancestors were.
13 Turn your angry gaze away from me, so I can be happy
before I pass away.

PSALM 40

For the music director, a psalm of David.

1 I relied completely on the LORD,
and he turned toward me
and heard my cry for help.
2 He lifted me out of the watery pit,
out of the slimy mud.
He placed my feet on a rock
and gave me secure footing.
3 He gave me reason to sing a new song,
praising our God.
May many see what God has done,
so that they might swear allegiance to him and trust in
the LORD.
4 How blessed is the one who trusts in the LORD
and does not seek help from the proud or from liars.
5 O LORD, my God, you have accomplished many things;
you have done amazing things and carried out your
purposes for us.
No one can thwart you.
I want to declare your deeds and talk about them,
but they are too numerous to recount.
6 Receiving sacrifices and offerings are not your primary
concern.
You make that quite clear to me.
You do not ask for burnt sacrifices and sin offerings.
7 Then I say,
"Look, I come!
What is written in the scroll pertains to me.

40:1–17 The psalmist amplifies the greatness of God's goodness by the mass of evils from which God had liberated him. In this way they surrounded him not only once so that, to the judgment of the flesh, it would seem impossible to escape; even if he had ever emerged from one calamity, another calamity, frequently more serious, immediately threatened and overwhelmed him. And when external foes ceased their raging, immediately a great many sins disturbed his conscience. For in this way the Lord had decided to test his eminent friend as an example to all believers so that he would be a suitable type of Christ the Lord, who endured far greater things—even the cross of death itself for the sake of the elect.

KONRAD PELLIKAN
(1478–1556)
COMMENTARY ON THE PSALMS

8 I want to do what pleases you, my God.
Your law dominates my thoughts."
9 I have told the great assembly about your justice.
Look, I spare no words.
O LORD, you know this is true.
10 I have not failed to tell about your justice;
I spoke about your reliability and deliverance.
I have not neglected to tell the great assembly about
your loyal love and faithfulness.
11 O LORD, you do not withhold your compassion from me.
May your loyal love and faithfulness continually protect
me!
12 For innumerable dangers surround me.
My sins overtake me
so I am unable to see;
they outnumber the hairs of my head
so my strength fails me.
13 Please be willing, O LORD, to rescue me!
O LORD, hurry and help me!
14 May those who are trying to snatch away my life
be totally embarrassed and ashamed.
May those who want to harm me
be turned back and ashamed.
15 May those who say to me, "Aha! Aha!"
be humiliated and disgraced.
16 May all those who seek you be happy and rejoice in you.
May those who love to experience your deliverance say
continually,
"May the LORD be praised!"
17 I am oppressed and needy.
May the Lord pay attention to me.
You are my helper and my deliverer.
O my God, do not delay.

PSALM 41

For the music director, a psalm of David.

1 How blessed is the one who treats the poor properly.
When trouble comes, may the LORD deliver him.
2 May the LORD protect him and save his life.
May he be blessed in the land.
Do not turn him over to his enemies.
3 The LORD supports him on his sickbed;
you have healed him from his illness.
4 As for me, I said:
"O LORD, have mercy on me!
Heal me, for I have sinned against you.
5 My enemies ask this cruel question about me,
'When will he finally die and be forgotten?'
6 When someone comes to visit, he pretends to be
friendly;
he thinks of ways to defame me,
and when he leaves he slanders me.
7 All who hate me whisper insults about me to one another;
they plan ways to harm me.
8 They say,
'An awful disease overwhelms him,
and now that he is bedridden he will never recover.'
9 Even my close friend whom I trusted,
he who shared meals with me, has turned against me.

41:1–13 The grace of consolation must be noted because although every affliction and sickness come from the Lord, nothing less than this is ascribed to the Lord, that he guards and sustains his own people during tribulations sent by himself. What else does this guarding and sustaining indicate than that every affliction of the godly is a sign of the affection of God, by which he instructs and chastises his own people? We see here that desire of the ungodly is vain and useless by which they seek the destruction of the godly unless the Lord should give the godly into their hands. Therefore all our salvation is in the hand of the Lord.

WOLFGANG MUSCULUS
(1497–1563)
COMMENTARY ON THE PSALMS

10 As for you, O LORD, have mercy on me and raise me up,
so I can pay them back!"
11 By this I know that you are pleased with me,
for my enemy does not triumph over me.
12 As for me, you uphold me because of my integrity;
you allow me permanent access to your presence.
13 The LORD God of Israel deserves praise
in the future and forevermore.
We agree! We agree!

BOOK 2 (PSALMS 42–72)

PSALM 42

For the music director, a well-written song by the Korahites.

1 As a deer longs for streams of water,
so I long for you, O God!
2 I thirst for God,
for the living God.
I say, "When will I be able to go and appear in God's
presence?"
3 I cannot eat; I weep day and night.
All day long they say to me, "Where is your God?"
4 I will remember and weep.
For I was once walking along with the great throng to
the temple of God,
shouting and giving thanks along with the crowd as we
celebrated the holy festival.
5 Why are you depressed, O my soul?
Why are you upset?
Wait for God!
For I will again give thanks
to my God for his saving intervention.
6 I am depressed,
so I will pray to you while in the region of the upper Jordan,
from Hermon, from Mount Mizar.
7 One deep stream calls out to another at the sound of
your waterfalls;
all your billows and waves overwhelm me.
8 By day the LORD decrees his loyal love,
and by night he gives me a song,
a prayer to the God of my life.
9 I will pray to God, my high ridge:
"Why do you ignore me?
Why must I walk around mourning
because my enemies oppress me?"
10 My enemies' taunts cut me to the bone,
as they say to me all day long, "Where is your God?"
11 Why are you depressed, O my soul?
Why are you upset?
Wait for God!
For I will again give thanks
to my God for his saving intervention.

PSALM 43

1 Vindicate me, O God!
Fight for me against an ungodly nation.
Deliver me from deceitful and evil men.
2 For you are the God who shelters me.
Why do you reject me?

42:1–11 We ought to learn from this that although we are deprived of the helps that God has appointed for the edification of our faith and piety, it is nevertheless our duty to be diligent in stirring up our minds that we may never suffer ourselves to be forgetful of God. But above all this is to be observed, that as we have seen the psalmist contending courageously against his own affections, so now we here see by what means he steadfastly maintained his ground. He did this by having recourse to the help of God and taking refuge in it as in a holy sanctuary. Unless God imparts strength to us, how shall we be able to subdue the many evil thoughts that constantly arise in our minds? "I will pray to God, my high ridge."

JOHN CALVIN (1509–1564)
COMPLETE COMMENTARY ON THE BIBLE

43:1–5 This psalm is connected to the previous psalm with regard to words and subject and explains these words: "By night he gives me a song, a prayer to the God of my life" (Ps 42:8). What and how he prays stand here, namely, that God himself would be his Judge and would sustain the right cause or teaching against the godless, so that the true light and truth would remain and constantly shine in the house of God; that is, that God's Word would always be rightly and purely taught. Through this the miserable are consoled and refreshed. They praise and thank God. They are joyful and of good cheer in God, and they stand firm against all misfortune that comes their way.

NIKOLAUS SELNECKER
(1530–1592)
THE WHOLE PSALTER

44:1–26 Our ancestors, as heirs and next of kin of the patriarchs, were planted in the promised land. They did not gain this by any merits of their own. It was not Moses who led them in, for fear they should attribute it to the law and not to grace. For the law examines our merits, but grace looks to faith. How excellently the apostle followed the faith of his ancestors when he said, "Neither the one who plants counts for anything, nor the one who waters, but God who causes the growth" (1 Cor 3:7). It was not Joshua, son of Nun, even though he led the people in and planted them—but God who gave the increase. "You, by your power, defeated nations and settled our fathers on their land." To him first be the glory.

AMBROSE **(C. 339–C. 397)**
EXPLANATION OF TWELVE PSALMS

Why must I walk around mourning
because my enemies oppress me?
3 Reveal your light and your faithfulness.
They will lead me;
they will escort me back to your holy hill,
and to the place where you live.
4 Then I will go to the altar of God,
to the God who gives me ecstatic joy,
so that I may express my thanks to you, O God, my God,
with a harp.
5 Why are you depressed, O my soul?
Why are you upset?
Wait for God!
For I will again give thanks
to my God for his saving intervention.

PSALM 44

For the music director, by the Korahites; a well-written song.

1 O God, we have clearly heard;
our ancestors have told us
what you did in their days,
in ancient times.
2 You, by your power, defeated nations and settled our
fathers on their land;
you crushed the people living there and enabled our
ancestors to occupy it.
3 For they did not conquer the land by their swords,
and they did not prevail by their strength,
but rather by your power, strength, and good favor,
for you were partial to them.
4 You are my king, O God.
Decree Jacob's deliverance.
5 By your power we will drive back our enemies;
by your strength we will trample down our foes.
6 For I do not trust in my bow,
and I do not prevail by my sword.
7 For you deliver us from our enemies;
you humiliate those who hate us.
8 In God we boast all day long,
and we will continually give thanks to your name. *Selah*
9 But you rejected and embarrassed us.
You did not go into battle with our armies.
10 You made us retreat from the enemy.
Those who hate us take whatever they want from us.
11 You handed us over like sheep to be eaten;
you scattered us among the nations.
12 You sold your people for a pittance;
you did not ask a high price for them.
13 You made us an object of disdain to our neighbors;
those who live on our borders taunt and insult us.
14 You made us an object of ridicule among the nations;
foreigners treat us with contempt.
15 All day long I feel humiliated
and am overwhelmed with shame,
16 before the vindictive enemy
who ridicules and insults me.
17 All this has happened to us, even though we have not
rejected you
or violated your covenant with us.

18 We have not been unfaithful,
nor have we disobeyed your commands.
19 Yet you have battered us, leaving us a heap of ruins
overrun by wild dogs;
you have covered us with darkness.
20 If we had rejected our God,
and spread out our hands in prayer to another god,
21 would not God discover it,
for he knows a person's secret thoughts?
22 Yet because of you we are killed all day long;
we are treated like sheep at the slaughtering block.
23 Rouse yourself! Why do you sleep, O Lord?
Wake up! Do not reject us forever.
24 Why do you look the other way,
and ignore the way we are oppressed and mistreated?
25 For we lie in the dirt,
with our bellies pressed to the ground.
26 Rise up and help us.
Rescue us because of your loyal love.

PSALM 45

For the music director, according to the tune of "Lilies"; by the Korahites, a well-written poem, a love song.

1 My heart is stirred by a beautiful song.
I say, "I have composed this special song for the king;
my tongue is as skilled as the stylus of an experienced
scribe."
2 You are the most handsome of all men.
You speak in an impressive and fitting manner.
For this reason God grants you continual blessings.
3 Strap your sword to your thigh, O warrior.
Appear in your majestic splendor.
4 Appear in your majesty and be victorious.
Ride forth for the sake of what is right,
on behalf of justice.
Then your right hand will accomplish mighty acts.
5 Your arrows are sharp
and penetrate the hearts of the king's enemies.
Nations fall at your feet.
6 Your throne, O God, is permanent.
The scepter of your kingdom is a scepter of justice.
7 You love justice and hate evil.
For this reason God, your God, has anointed you
with the oil of joy, elevating you above your
companions.
8 All your garments are perfumed with myrrh, aloes, and
cassia.
From the luxurious palaces comes the music of stringed
instruments that makes you happy.
9 Princesses are among your honored women.
Your bride stands at your right hand, wearing jewelry
made with gold from Ophir.
10 Listen, O princess.
Observe and pay attention!
Forget your homeland and your family.
11 Then the king will be attracted by your beauty.
After all, he is your master. Submit to him.
12 Rich people from Tyre
will seek your favor by bringing a gift.

45:1 If things do not begin at the heart, whatever we do about spiritual things are of no value, of no use. We may perform duties, we may pray and preach and hear; but if these things do not spring from the heart, that is, from faith and love and delight working in the heart, all is lost. A sacrifice without a heart, a silly dove that has no heart, are things God abhors. The heart of the psalmist was in this matter, and if our heart be in it, it will be a duty, in our measure and proportion, good and acceptable with God, as it was with him.

JOHN OWEN (1616–1683)
THE WORKS

13 The princess looks absolutely magnificent,
decked out in pearls and clothed in a brocade trimmed
with gold.
14 In embroidered robes she is escorted to the king.
Her attendants, the maidens of honor who follow her,
are led before you.
15 They are bubbling with joy as they walk in procession
and enter the royal palace.
16 Your sons will carry on the dynasty of your ancestors;
you will make them princes throughout the land.
17 I will proclaim your greatness through the coming
years,
then the nations will praise you forever.

PSALM 46

For the music director, by the Korahites;
according to the alamoth *style; a song.*

1 God is our strong refuge;
he is truly our helper in times of trouble.
2 For this reason we do not fear when the earth shakes,
and the mountains tumble into the depths of the sea,
3 when its waves crash and foam,
and the mountains shake before the surging sea. *Selah*
4 The river's channels bring joy to the city of God,
the special, holy dwelling place of the Most High.
5 God lives within it, it cannot be moved.
God rescues it at the break of dawn.
6 Nations are in uproar, kingdoms are overthrown.
God gives a shout, the earth dissolves.
7 The LORD of Heaven's Armies is on our side.
The God of Jacob is our stronghold. *Selah*
8 Come, Witness the exploits of the LORD,
who brings devastation to the earth.
9 He brings an end to wars throughout the earth.
He shatters the bow and breaks the spear;
he burns the shields with fire.
10 He says, "Stop your striving and recognize that I am
God.
I will be exalted over the nations! I will be exalted over
the earth!"
11 The LORD of Heaven's Armies is on our side!
The God of Jacob is our stronghold! *Selah*

46:1–11 One thing you must flee: sin. And one refuge from evil must be sought: God. Do not trust in princes, do not be exalted in the uncertainty of wealth, do not be proud of bodily strength, and do not pursue the splendor of human glory. None of these things saves you; all are transient, all are deceptive. There is one refuge, God. God is the true aid for the righteous. Just as a certain general equipped with a noble, heavy-armed force is always ready to give help to an oppressed district, so God is our helper and an ally to everyone who is waging war against the wiliness of the devil, and he sends out ministering spirits for the safety of those who are in need.

BASIL THE GREAT **(330–379)**
HOMILIES ON THE PSALMS

PSALM 47

For the music director, by the Korahites; a psalm.

1 All you nations, clap your hands.
Shout out to God in celebration.
2 For the LORD Most High is awe-inspiring;
he is the great king who rules the whole earth!
3 He subdued nations beneath us
and countries under our feet.
4 He picked out for us a special land
to be a source of pride for Jacob, whom he loves. *Selah*
5 God has ascended his throne amid loud shouts;
the LORD has ascended amid the blaring of ram's horns.
6 Sing to God! Sing!
Sing to our king! Sing!
7 For God is king of the whole earth.
Sing a well-written song.

47:1–9 Our joy and our victory over all our enemies, which Christ has purchased and brings to all believers in every nation, are the matter of Christ's praise and declare that he is God who, having in his humanity suffered and wrestled against sin, Satan, death, hell, and the curse of the law did, by the power of his divinity, prevail before he brought joy to the Gentiles. His triumph presupposes his victory, and his victory presupposes his battle before he overcame, and the commanding of the Gentiles—"All you nations, clap your hands. Shout out to God in celebration"—presupposes their interest in the victory, for they are bidden to shout to God the triumphant who, in this entire psalm, is the Redeemer, Christ. And he is God separately from the Father and the Holy Spirit, yet here he is distinctly to be praised for this his work of victorious redemption of sinners. Therefore it is said with distinct relation to his person, "Shout out to God in celebration."

DAVID DICKSON **(1583–1663)**
EXPLICATION OF THE FIRST FIFTY PSALMS

8 God reigns over the nations.
God sits on his holy throne.
9 The nobles of the nations assemble,
along with the people of the God of Abraham,
for God has authority over the rulers of the earth.
He is highly exalted.

PSALM 48

A song, a psalm by the Korahites.

1 The LORD is great and certainly worthy of praise
in the city of our God, his holy hill.
2 It is lofty and pleasing to look at,
a source of joy to the whole earth.
Mount Zion resembles the peaks of Zaphon;
it is the city of the great king.
3 God is in its fortresses;
he reveals himself as its defender.
4 For look, the kings assemble;
they advance together.
5 As soon as they see, they are shocked;
they are terrified, they quickly retreat.
6 Look at them shake uncontrollably,
like a woman writhing in childbirth.
7 With an east wind
you shatter the large ships.
8 We heard about God's mighty deeds; now we have seen them,
in the city of the LORD of Heaven's Armies,
in the city of our God.
God makes it permanently secure. *Selah*
9 Within your temple
we reflect on your loyal love, O God.
10 The praise you receive as far away as the ends of the earth
is worthy of your reputation, O God.
You execute justice.
11 Mount Zion rejoices;
the towns of Judah are happy,
because of your acts of judgment.
12 Walk around Zion. Encircle it.
Count its towers.
13 Consider its defenses.
Walk through its fortresses,
so you can tell the next generation about it.
14 For God, our God, is our defender forever.
He guides us.

PSALM 49

For the music director, a psalm by the Korahites.

1 Listen to this, all you nations.
Pay attention, all you inhabitants of the world.
2 Pay attention, all you people,
both rich and poor.
3 I will declare a wise saying;
I will share my profound thoughts.
4 I will learn a song that imparts wisdom;
I will then sing my insightful song to the accompaniment of a harp.
5 Why should I be afraid in times of trouble,

48:7 We should no longer put our trust in setting our sails in the favorable tide of worldly prosperity; our foundation must be in Zion. There we must find our stability and not be tossed about by every gust of teaching. Those whose sails are swollen with the uncertain fortunes of this life are liable to be capsized, and all the pride of the Gentiles must be subjected to Christ: "With an east wind you shatter the large ships."

AUGUSTINE **(354–430)**
EXPOSITIONS ON THE PSALMS

49:1–20 If God wants his word to be understood, why does he speak in parables and riddles? The fact that in times past God taught by parables but in these last days has revealed himself fully by the Lord Jesus Christ indicates to us that God wished to give his message to human beings in a gentle and attractive way. As it says in Psalm 49: "I will declare a wise saying; I will share my profound thoughts. I will learn a song that imparts wisdom; I will then sing my insightful song to the accompaniment of a harp." The heavenly and divine wisdom reveals its will to human beings in the form of sweet parables so that those who might otherwise be dull and unwilling are persuaded to listen, and the truth that is discovered is received the more firmly and valued the more highly, and the divine lesson is busy and active all the longer in the understanding, and its roots sink deeper into the heart.

ULRICH ZWINGLI **(1484–1531)**
OF THE CLARITY AND CERTAINTY OF THE WORD OF GOD

MAXIMUS THE CONFESSOR:

A TONGUE AND HAND FOR TRUTH

c. 580–662

Jesus once asked his listeners, *Is your eye or hand causing you to sin?* If so, he said, it would be better to gouge out your eye or cut off your hand and enter heaven than to preserve both only to have your entire body end up in hell (Matt 5:29). This is but one motivator in the persistent willingness of Christians to undergo suffering and martyrdom for the sake of truth. Maximus the Confessor stands among those who risked—and eventually gave—life and limb for the sake of truth.

Born to a noble Christian family in Constantinople in 580, Maximus grew up to be a high-ranking advisor (the personal secretary) to Emperor Heraclius. Shortly after his appointment, Maximus soured on his position in the court, believing he could no longer support the emperor. He left his civil servant position and took up residency at a monastery in Carthage. While there he got wind of a rising controversy within the church: *Monothelitism*, a heresy born from a political compromise. But for Maximus, the peace of the city should never override the commitment to true doctrine.

For two centuries there had been an ongoing conflict within the church and the broader Mediterranean region between the Monophysites and those ascribing to the Council of Chalcedon. Monophysites argued that Christ had one single nature uniting his divinity and humanity into a composite incarnation of the Word. But the Chalcedonian definition insisted that Christ's two natures, divine and human, remain united in the person of Christ without confusion, change, division, or separation.

In an effort to quell the conflict and bring order to the region, Heraclius wanted a compromise: Although Christ had two natures, he had one will. The emperor drafted a statement declaring Monothelite compromise to be the official doctrine of the state, requiring citizens and clergy to believe, support, and teach it. Maximus was outraged at the political meddling not to mention the theological confusion. He went into action.

He traveled to Rome and petitioned the pope and bishops to stand firmly opposed to the innovation. Maximus believed that Monothelitism would destroy the biblical and theological understanding of Christ, for the teaching diminished Jesus' humanity. Perhaps Maximus had in mind the maxim of Gregory of Nazianzus: "What the Son has not assumed he cannot heal." In order for Christ to heal humanity of sin, he must have taken up every aspect of human nature—body, mind, and even a human will. Maximus and others argued that one single will would surely be divine, overwhelming Jesus' human nature. Instead, he argued for and defended *Dyothelitism*: Christ had two natures and two wills. If Christ did not have a human will, he could not have identified with humanity as a full human. And if he was not fully human, he could not fully save, rescue, and heal us.

In 649, Maximus joined hundreds of clergymen and Pope Martin to defy the state order concerning adopting Monothelitism. They were arrested, charged with treason, brought before a state tribunal, and ordered to recant. Maximus refused and paid the price. Both his right hand and tongue were cut off to ensure he could no longer write or speak about the orthodox truth of the person of Christ. He was then sent into exile, where he remained until his death in 662. Though Maximus did not live to see it, his insistence on the dual wills of Christ was vindicated at the Third Council of Constantinople, which permanently established Dyothelitism as a doctrine of the church. Today he is recognized as a father of the church by both the Orthodox and Catholic churches.

IMPORTANT WORKS

THE ASCETIC LIFE
DISPUTATIONS WITH PYRRHUS
COMMENTARY ON THE LORD'S PRAYER
CENTURIES ON LOVE

when the sinful deeds of deceptive men threaten to
overwhelm me?
6 They trust in their wealth
and boast in their great riches.
7 Certainly a man cannot rescue his brother;
he cannot pay God an adequate ransom price
8 (the ransom price for a human life is too high,
and people go to their final destiny),
9 so that he might continue to live forever
and not experience death.
10 Surely one sees that even wise people die;
fools and spiritually insensitive people all
pass away
and leave their wealth to others.
11 Their grave becomes their permanent residence,
their eternal dwelling place.
They name their lands after themselves,
12 but, despite their wealth, people do not last.
They are like animals that perish.
13 This is the destiny of fools,
and of those who approve of their philosophy. *Selah*
14 They will travel to Sheol like sheep,
with death as their shepherd.
The godly will rule over them when the day of
vindication dawns.
Sheol will consume their bodies, and they will no
longer live in impressive houses.
15 But God will rescue my life from the power
of Sheol;
certainly he will pull me to safety. *Selah*
16 Do not be afraid when a man becomes rich
and his wealth multiplies.
17 For he will take nothing with him when he dies;
his wealth will not follow him down into the grave.
18 He pronounces this blessing on himself while he is
alive:
"May men praise you, for you have done well."

19 But he will join his ancestors;
they will never again see the light of day.
20 Wealthy people do not understand;
they are like animals that perish.

PSALM 50

A psalm by Asaph.

1 El, God, the LORD has spoken,
and summoned the earth to come from the east and west.
2 From Zion, the most beautiful of all places,
God has come in splendor.
3 "May our God come
and not be silent."
Consuming fire goes ahead of him,
and all around him a storm rages.
4 He summons the heavens above,
as well as the earth, so that he might judge his people.
5 He says:
"Assemble my covenant people before me,
those who ratified a covenant with me by sacrifice."
6 The heavens declare his fairness,
for God is judge. *Selah*
7 He says:
"Listen, my people. I am speaking!
Listen, Israel. I am accusing you.
I am God, your God!
8 I am not condemning you because of your sacrifices,
or because of your burnt sacrifices that you continually offer me.
9 I do not need to take a bull from your household
or goats from your sheepfolds.
10 For every wild animal in the forest belongs to me,
as well as the cattle that graze on a thousand hills.
11 I keep track of every bird in the hills,
and the insects of the field are mine.
12 Even if I were hungry, I would not tell you,
for the world and all it contains belong to me.
13 Do I eat the flesh of bulls?
Do I drink the blood of goats?
14 Present to God a thank offering.
Repay your vows to the Most High.
15 Pray to me when you are in trouble.
I will deliver you, and you will honor me."
16 God says this to the evildoer:
"How can you declare my commands,
and talk about my covenant?
17 For you hate instruction
and reject my words.
18 When you see a thief, you join him;
you associate with men who are unfaithful to their wives.
19 You do damage with words,
and use your tongue to deceive.
20 You plot against your brother;
you slander your own brother.
21 When you did these things, I was silent,
so you thought I was exactly like you.

50:1–23 To obey is better than sacrifice, and to love God and our neighbor better than all burnt offerings. But we are here warned not to rest in these performances. And let us beware of resting in any form. God demands the heart, and how can human inventions please him when repentance, faith, and holiness are neglected? In the day of distress we must apply to the Lord by fervent prayer. Our troubles, though we see them coming from God's hand, must drive us to him, not from him. We must acknowledge him in all our ways, depend upon his wisdom, power, and goodness, and refer ourselves wholly to him and so give him glory. Thus must we keep up communion with God, meeting him with prayers under trials and with praises in deliverances. Believing supplicants shall not only be graciously answered as to their petition, and so have cause for praising God, but shall also have grace to praise him.

MATTHEW HENRY **(1662–1714)**
COMMENTARY ON THE WHOLE BIBLE

But now I will condemn you
and state my case against you.
22 Carefully consider this, you who reject God.
Otherwise I will rip you to shreds
and no one will be able to rescue you.
23 Whoever presents a thank offering honors me.
To whoever obeys my commands, I will reveal my power
to deliver."

PSALM 51

For the music director, a psalm of David, written when Nathan the prophet confronted him after David's affair with Bathsheba.

1 Have mercy on me, O God, because of your loyal love.
Because of your great compassion, wipe away my
rebellious acts.
2 Wash away my wrongdoing.
Cleanse me of my sin.
3 For I am aware of my rebellious acts;
I am forever conscious of my sin.
4 Against you—you above all—I have sinned;
I have done what is evil in your sight.
So you are just when you confront me;
you are right when you condemn me.
5 Look, I was guilty of sin from birth,
a sinner the moment my mother conceived me.
6 Look, you desire integrity in the inner man;
you want me to possess wisdom.
7 Cleanse me with hyssop and I will be pure;
wash me and I will be whiter than snow.
8 Grant me the ultimate joy of being forgiven.
May the bones you crushed rejoice.
9 Hide your face from my sins.
Wipe away all my guilt.
10 Create for me a pure heart, O God.
Renew a resolute spirit within me.
11 Do not reject me.
Do not take your Holy Spirit away from me.
12 Let me again experience the joy of your deliverance.
Sustain me by giving me the desire to obey.
13 Then I will teach rebels your merciful ways,
and sinners will turn to you.
14 Rescue me from the guilt of murder, O God, the God
who delivers me.
Then my tongue will shout for joy because of your
righteousness.
15 O Lord, give me the words.
Then my mouth will praise you.
16 Certainly you do not want a sacrifice, or else I would
offer it;
you do not desire a burnt sacrifice.
17 The sacrifice God desires is a humble spirit—
O God, a humble and repentant heart you will not
reject.
18 Because you favor Zion, do what is good for her.
Fortify the walls of Jerusalem.
19 Then you will accept the proper sacrifices, burnt
sacrifices and whole offerings;
then bulls will be sacrificed on your altar.

51:1–19 A defilement of mud attaches to us from without, therefore we quickly put it away, but the other sin is generated from within where it is more difficult to wash it off and to cleanse ourselves from it. "For out of the heart" (it is said) "come evil ideas, murder, adultery, sexual immorality, theft, false testimony, slander" (Matt 15:19). Thus the prophet said, "Create for me a pure heart, O God." . . . Other things too must be added to humbleness of mind if it is such as the blessed David knew when he said, "O God, a humble and repentant heart you will not reject." For that which is broken does not rise up, does not strike, but is ready to be ill treated and itself does not rise up. Such is contrition of heart: Though it is insulted, though it is enticed by evil, it is quiet and is not eager for vengeance.

CHRYSOSTOM (C. 347–407)
ON THE EPISTLE TO THE HEBREWS

PSALM 52

For the music director, a well-written song by David. It was written when Doeg the Edomite went and informed Saul: "David has arrived at the home of Ahimelech."

1 Why do you boast about your evil plans, O powerful
man?
God's loyal love protects me all day long.
2 Your tongue carries out your destructive plans;
it is as effective as a sharp razor, O deceiver.
3 You love evil more than good,
lies more than speaking the truth. *Selah*
4 You love to use all the words that destroy,
and the tongue that deceives.
5 Yet God will make you a permanent heap of ruins.
He will scoop you up and remove you from your home;
he will uproot you from the land of the living. *Selah*
6 When the godly see this, they will be filled with awe,
and will mock the evildoer, saying:
7 "Look, here is the man who would not make God his
protector.
He trusted in his great wealth
and was confident about his plans to destroy others."
8 But I am like a flourishing olive tree in the house of God;
I continually trust in God's loyal love.
9 I will continually thank you when you execute judgment;
I will rely on you, for your loyal followers know you are
good.

52:1–9 The tongue, when it is abused, is a world of wickedness setting the world on fire, as it itself is set on fire from hell by Satan. Whatever mischief the devil can suggest or a wicked heart can devise is given vent by the tongue, and so the tongue is charged with devising mischief. The smooth communication of a wicked device does not hide the mischief from God's sight or extenuate the fault of the person, but rather through its cunning and power it helps the mischief. Moreover, when a person tells only part of the tale, the part that serves his own interests, but reserves that part that might declare the innocence of another, even if the first part of the tale is true, this is evil lying, a murdering and devouring speech full of deceit.

DAVID DICKSON **(1583–1663)**
EXPLICATION OF THE FIRST FIFTY PSALMS

PSALM 53

For the music director, according to the machalath *style; a well-written song by David.*

1 Fools say to themselves, "There is no God."
They sin and commit evil deeds;
none of them does what is right.
2 God looks down from heaven at the human race,
to see if there is anyone who is wise and seeks God.
3 Everyone rejects God;
they are all morally corrupt.
None of them does what is right,
not even one!
4 All those who behave wickedly do not understand—
those who devour my people as if they were eating bread
and do not call out to God.
5 They are absolutely terrified,
even by things that do not normally cause fear.
For God annihilates those who attack you.
You are able to humiliate them because God has
rejected them.
6 I wish the deliverance of Israel would come from Zion!
When God restores the well-being of his people,
may Jacob rejoice,
may Israel be happy!

53:1–6 David here describes the misery, weakness, nothingness, sorrow, and distress of all human nature. For the psalm is a penitential sermon and laments our whole being, birth, reason, sense, spirit, heart, and will. This doctrine of our corrupt human nature is badly needed in the congregation of God, that it might be maintained forever, that we would recognize ourselves for what we are, consider and weep for our misery and nothingness, and learn the proper attitude—*I am nothing and am good for nothing*—so we might not become proud or overconfident or trust in any merit or work of our own but live solely on the mere grace and mercy of God that he has shown us in his Son.

NIKOLAUS SELNECKER
(1530–1592)
THE WHOLE PSALTER

PSALM 54

For the music director, to be accompanied by stringed instruments; a well-written song by David. It was written when the Ziphites came and informed Saul: "David is hiding with us."

1 O God, deliver me by your name.
Vindicate me by your power.

2 O God, listen to my prayer.
Pay attention to what I say.
3 For foreigners attack me;
ruthless men, who do not respect God, seek my life.
Selah
4 Look, God is my deliverer.
The Lord is among those who support me.
5 May those who wait to ambush me be repaid for their
evil.
As a demonstration of your faithfulness, destroy them.
6 With a freewill offering I will sacrifice to you.
I will give thanks to your name, O LORD, for it is good.
7 Surely he rescues me from all trouble,
and I triumph over my enemies.

PSALM 55

For the music director, to be accompanied by stringed instruments; a well-written song by David.

1 Listen, O God, to my prayer.
Do not ignore my appeal for mercy.
2 Pay attention to me and answer me.
I am so upset and distressed, I am beside myself,
3 because of what the enemy says,
and because of how the wicked pressure me,
for they hurl trouble down upon me
and angrily attack me.
4 My heart beats violently within me;
the horrors of death overcome me.
5 Fear and panic overpower me;
terror overwhelms me.
6 I say, "I wish I had wings like a dove.
I would fly away and settle in a safe place.
7 Look, I will escape to a distant place;
I will stay in the wilderness. *Selah*
8 I will hurry off to a place that is safe
from the strong wind and the gale."
9 Confuse them, O Lord.
Frustrate their plans.
For I see violence and conflict in the city.
10 Day and night they walk around on its walls,
while wickedness and destruction are within it.
11 Disaster is within it;
violence and deceit do not depart from its public
square.
12 Indeed, it is not an enemy who insults me,
or else I could bear it;
it is not one who hates me who arrogantly taunts me,
or else I could hide from him.
13 But it is you, a man like me,
my close friend in whom I confided.
14 We would share personal thoughts with each other;
in God's temple we would walk together among the
crowd.
15 May death destroy them.
May they go down alive into Sheol.
For evil is in their dwelling place and in their midst.
16 As for me, I will call out to God,
and the LORD will deliver me.
17 During the evening, morning, and noontime

54:1–7 You are my Savior; all around me are my foes and their eager helpers. No shelter is permitted me. But you, O God, will give me refuge and deliver me from all my enemies. By your name, by your great and glorious nature, employ all your attributes for me. "O God, listen to my prayer." This has ever been the defense of saints. As long as God has an open ear, we cannot be shut up in trouble. All other weapons may be useless, but prayer is evermore available.

CHARLES SPURGEON
(1834–1892)
THE TREASURY OF DAVID

55:1–23 Almighty, eternal God, the world is not to be trusted. Your beloved Son himself was betrayed by his disciple Judas; everywhere in all places infidelity and injustice blossom. And nevertheless all people want to be innocent and pure; they offer good works out of a false heart. Therefore I ask that you would govern me with your Holy Spirit so that I would not become impatient but instead cling to your Word and promise, trust and hope in you, and carefully execute my office with devotion and diligence in good conscience; that I would learn to cast all my cares and concerns on you who will not let me and all the righteous remain eternally in discord, even though the world makes much discord for us. I hope in you. And I will, with your help, break through all misery into eternal life and laud and praise you and your Son and the Holy Spirit in eternity. Amen.

JOHANN ARNDT **(1555–1621)**
TRUE CHRISTIANITY

I will lament and moan,
and he will hear me.
18 He will rescue me and protect me from those who attack me,
even though they greatly outnumber me.
19 God, the one who has reigned as king from long ago,
will hear and humiliate them. *Selah*
They refuse to change,
and do not fear God.
20 He attacks his friends;
he breaks his solemn promises to them.
21 His words are as smooth as butter,
but he harbors animosity in his heart.
His words seem softer than oil,
but they are really like sharp swords.
22 Throw your burden upon the LORD,
and he will sustain you.
He will never allow the godly to be shaken.
23 But you, O God, will bring them down to the deep Pit.
Violent and deceitful people will not live even half a normal life-span.
But as for me, I trust in you.

PSALM 56

For the music director, according to the yonath-elem-rekhoqim *style; a prayer of David, written when the Philistines captured him in Gath.*

1 Have mercy on me, O God, for men are attacking me.
All day long hostile enemies are tormenting me.
2 Those who anticipate my defeat attack me all day long.
Indeed, many are fighting against me, O Exalted One.
3 When I am afraid,
I trust in you.
4 In God—I boast in his promise—
in God I trust; I am not afraid.
What can mere men do to me?
5 All day long they cause me trouble;
they make a habit of plotting my demise.
6 They stalk and lurk;
they watch my every step,
as they prepare to take my life.
7 Because they are bent on violence, do not let them escape.
In your anger bring down the nations, O God.
8 You keep track of my misery.
Put my tears in your leather container.
Are they not recorded in your scroll?
9 My enemies will turn back when I cry out to you for help;
I know that God is on my side.
10 In God—I boast in his promise—
in the LORD—I boast in his promise—
11 in God I trust; I am not afraid.
What can mere men do to me?
12 I am obligated to fulfill the vows I made to you, O God;
I will give you the thank offerings you deserve,
13 when you deliver my life from death.
You keep my feet from stumbling,
so that I might serve God as I enjoy life.

56:1–13 David made no pretensions to that lofty heroism that condemns danger, and yet while he allowed that he felt fear, he declared his fixed resolution to persist in a confident expectation of the divine favor. The true proof of faith consists in this, that when we feel the solicitations of natural fear, we can resist them and prevent them from obtaining an undue ascendancy. In a tranquil state of the mind, there is no scope for the exercise of hope. At such times it lies dormant, and its power is displayed to advantage only when we see it elevating the soul under dejection, calming its agitations, or soothing its distractions. This was the manner in which it manifested itself in David who feared and yet trusted, who was sensible of the greatness of his danger and yet quieted his mind with the confident hope of the divine deliverance.

JOHN CALVIN **(1509–1564)**
COMPLETE COMMENTARY ON THE BIBLE

PSALM 57

For the music director, according to the al-taschcheth *style; a prayer of David, written when he fled from Saul into the cave.*

1 Have mercy on me, O God. Have mercy on me.
For in you I have taken shelter.
In the shadow of your wings I take shelter
until trouble passes.
2 I cry out for help to God Most High,
to the God who vindicates me.
3 May he send help from heaven and deliver me
from my enemies who hurl insults. *Selah*
May God send his loyal love and faithfulness.
4 I am surrounded by lions;
I lie down among those who want to devour me,
men whose teeth are spears and arrows,
whose tongues are sharp swords.
5 Rise up above the sky, O God.
May your splendor cover the whole earth.
6 They have prepared a net to trap me;
I am discouraged.
They have dug a pit for me.
They will fall into it. *Selah*
7 I am determined, O God. I am determined.
I will sing and praise you.
8 Awake, my soul!
Awake, O stringed instrument and harp!
I will wake up at dawn.
9 I will give you thanks before the nations, O Lord.
I will sing praises to you before foreigners.
10 For your loyal love extends beyond the sky,
and your faithfulness reaches the clouds.
11 Rise up above the sky, O God.
May your splendor cover the whole earth.

PSALM 58

For the music director, according to the al-taschcheth *style; a prayer of David.*

1 Do you rulers really pronounce just decisions?
Do you judge people fairly?
2 No! You plan how to do what is unjust;
you deal out violence in the earth.
3 The wicked turn aside from birth;
liars go astray as soon as they are born.
4 Their venom is like that of a snake,
like a deaf serpent that does not hear,
5 that does not respond to the magicians,
or to a skilled snake charmer.
6 O God, break the teeth in their mouths!
Smash the jawbones of the lions, O LORD.
7 Let them disappear like water that flows away.
Let them wither like grass.
8 Let them be like a snail that melts away as it moves along.
Let them be like stillborn babies that never see the sun.
9 Before the kindling is even placed under your pots,
he will sweep it away along with both the raw and cooked meat.

57:1–11 The heart prepared for praising God is not idle. For the mouth speaks out of the abundance of the heart. Thus the one affected for the glory of God, which is in the heart, breaks forth into song and vocal praise of God; just as the heart filled with mourning and sadness boils up in wailing and tears, a joyful heart boils up in laughter and the face with cheerfulness. Thus it is fitting when he said, "I am determined, O God. I am determined. I will sing and praise you." He expressed exuberance and passion for praising God, namely in that he did not simply desire to sing but also to sing with the lyre and stringed musical instruments, and that in the morning. Here he promised for himself that in the morning with the greatest joy, he desired to seek the church of God, and in the middle of it and in the sight of all, to praise and extol the Lord with all his strength.

WOLFGANG MUSCULUS
(1497–1563)
COMMENTARY ON THE PSALMS

58:4 Consider what a misfortune it would be for us to fall down of our own accord from the nature of human beings to that of beasts. For to serve the belly, to be possessed by the desire of riches, to be given to anger, to bite, to kick, we become not human beings but beasts. Nay, even the beasts have each, as one may say, one single passion, and that by nature. But people, when they have cast away the dominion of reason, torn themselves from the commonwealth of God's devising, and given themselves up to all the passions, are no longer merely beasts but a kind of many-formed motley monster; nor have they even the excuse from nature, for all their wickedness proceeds from deliberate choice and determination.

CHRYSOSTOM **(C. 347–407)**
HOMILIES ON THE GOSPEL OF JOHN

10 The godly will rejoice when they see vengeance carried out;
they will bathe their feet in the blood of the wicked.
11 Then observers will say,
"Yes indeed, the godly are rewarded.
Yes indeed, there is a God who judges in the earth."

PSALM 59

For the music director, according to the al-tashcheth *style; a prayer of David, written when Saul sent men to surround his house and murder him.*

1 Deliver me from my enemies, my God.
Protect me from those who attack me.
2 Deliver me from evildoers.
Rescue me from violent men.
3 For look, they wait to ambush me;
powerful men stalk me,
but not because I have rebelled or sinned, O LORD.
4 Though I have done nothing wrong, they are anxious to attack.
Spring into action and help me. Take notice of me.
5 You, O LORD God of Heaven's Armies, the God of Israel,
rouse yourself and punish all the nations.
Have no mercy on any treacherous evildoers. *Selah*
6 They return in the evening;
they growl like dogs
and prowl around outside the city.
7 Look, they hurl insults at me
and openly threaten to kill me,
for they say,
"Who hears?"
8 But you, O LORD, laugh in disgust at them;
you taunt all the nations.
9 You are my source of strength. I will wait for you.
For God is my refuge.
10 The God who loves me will help me;
God will enable me to triumph over my enemies.
11 Do not strike them dead suddenly,
because then my people might forget the lesson.
Use your power to make them homeless vagabonds and then bring them down,
O Lord who shields us.
12 They speak sinful words.
So let them be trapped by their own pride
and by the curses and lies they speak.
13 Angrily wipe them out. Wipe them out so they vanish.
Let them know that God rules
over Jacob and to the ends of the earth. *Selah*
14 They return in the evening;
they growl like dogs
and prowl around outside the city.
15 They wander around looking for something to eat;
they refuse to sleep until they are full.
16 As for me, I will sing about your strength;
I will praise your loyal love in the morning.
For you are my refuge
and my place of shelter when I face trouble.
17 You are my source of strength. I will sing praises to you.
For God is my refuge, the God who loves me.

59:1–17 It is the common course of all people who pretend to any piety or knowledge of God to pray to God against their enemies. But it must be the care of all truly and solidly religious people to consider well first what enemies they pray against; whether they are such as David's enemies, who violently persecuted him without any just provocation. Yes, he sought peace and did his utmost to win them by his gentleness and the like. So we hope our prayers might be available and at least not unacceptable. But if we make people our foes by any proud, insolent, or unjust actions, or if on apprehension of just provocation we think to bear ourselves on God's protection of assistance before we ourselves have used all fair and charitable means of reconciliation (which God himself requires from our hands), we may sooner expect to make God our enemy by our prayers than he will grant us our requests on such weak and ungodly grounds.

***THE WESTMINSTER ANNOTATIONS* (1683)**

PSALM 60

For the music director, according to the shushan-eduth *style; a prayer of David written to instruct others. It was written when he fought against Aram Naharaim and Aram Zobah. That was when Joab turned back and struck down 12,000 Edomites in the Valley of Salt.*

1 O God, you have rejected us.
You suddenly turned on us in your anger.
Please restore us!
2 You made the earth quake; you split it open.
Repair its breaches, for it is ready to fall.
3 You have made your people experience hard times;
you have made us drink intoxicating wine.
4 You have given your loyal followers a rallying flag,
so that they might seek safety from the bow. *Selah*
5 Deliver by your power and answer me,
so that the ones you love may be safe.
6 God has spoken in his sanctuary:
"I will triumph. I will parcel out Shechem;
the Valley of Sukkoth I will measure off.
7 Gilead belongs to me,
as does Manasseh.
Ephraim is my helmet,
Judah my royal scepter.
8 Moab is my washbasin.
I will make Edom serve me.
I will shout in triumph over Philistia."
9 Who will lead me into the fortified city?
Who will bring me to Edom?
10 Have you not rejected us, O God?
O God, you do not go into battle with our armies.
11 Give us help against the enemy,
for any help men might offer is futile.
12 By God's power we will conquer;
he will trample down our enemies.

PSALM 61

For the music director, to be played on a stringed instrument; written by David.

1 O God, hear my cry for help.
Pay attention to my prayer.
2 From the remotest place on earth
I call out to you in my despair.
Lead me up to a rocky summit where I can be safe.
3 Indeed, you are my shelter,
a strong tower that protects me from the enemy.
4 I will be a permanent guest in your home;
I will find shelter in the protection of your wings. *Selah*
5 For you, O God, hear my vows;
you grant me the reward that belongs to your loyal followers.
6 Give the king long life.
Make his lifetime span several generations.
7 May he reign forever before God.
Decree that your loyal love and faithfulness should protect him.
8 Then I will sing praises to your name continually,
as I fulfill my vows day after day.

60:1–12 This is the use of the psalm, that we should first sustain ourselves by the promise that confirms that the church will remain, it will be victorious, and in this hope we should endure the toils of teaching. Second, by this example we should seek and expect help from God, so that we would not depend on human plans and protections, but in true dangers our minds would confidently lean on faith.

PHILIP MELANCHTHON
(1497–1560)
COMMENTS ON THE PSALMS

61:1–8 David begins with prayers and tears but ends with praise. Thus the soul, being lifted up to God, returns to the enjoyment of itself. Wherever we are, we have liberty to draw near to God and may find a way open to the throne of grace. And that which separates us from other comforts should drive us nearer to God, the fountain of all comfort. God's power and promise are a rock that is higher than we are. This rock is Christ. On the divine mercy, as on a rock, David desired to rest his soul; but he was like a shipwrecked sailor, exposed to the billows at the bottom of a rock too high for him to climb without help. David found that he could not be fixed on the rock of salvation unless the Lord placed him upon it. As there is safety in him, and none in ourselves, let us pray to be led to and fixed upon Christ our rock.

MATTHEW HENRY **(1662–1714)**
COMMENTARY ON THE WHOLE BIBLE

PSALM 62

For the music director, Jeduthun; a psalm of David.

1 For God alone I patiently wait;
he is the one who delivers me.
2 He alone is my protector and deliverer.
He is my refuge; I will not be upended.
3 How long will you threaten a man like me?
All of you are murderers,
as dangerous as a leaning wall or an unstable fence.
4 They spend all their time planning how to bring their
victim down.
They love to use deceit;
they pronounce blessings with their mouths,
but inwardly they utter curses. *Selah*
5 Patiently wait for God alone, my soul!
For he is the one who gives me hope.
6 He alone is my protector and deliverer.
He is my refuge; I will not be shaken.
7 God delivers me and exalts me;
God is my strong protector and my shelter.
8 Trust in him at all times, you people!
Pour out your hearts before him.
God is our shelter. *Selah*
9 Men are nothing but a mere breath;
human beings are unreliable.
When they are weighed in the scales,
all of them together are lighter than air.
10 Do not trust in what you can gain by oppression.
Do not put false confidence in what you can gain by
robbery.
If wealth increases, do not become attached to it.
11 God has declared one principle;
two principles I have heard:
God is strong,
12 and you, O Lord, demonstrate loyal love.
For you repay men for what they do.

62:1–12 Let me commend to you a life of trust in God in temporal things. Trusting in God, you will not be compelled to mourn because you have used sinful means to grow rich. Serve God with integrity, and if you achieve no success, at least no sin will lie upon your conscience. Trusting God, you will not be guilty of self-contradiction. Those who trust in craft sail this way today and that way the next like a vessel tossed about by the fickle wind; but those who trust in the Lord are like a vessel propelled by steam: She cuts through the waves, defies the wind, and makes one bright, silvery, straightforward track to her destined haven. Be a person with living principles within; never bow to the varying customs of worldly wisdom. Walk in your path of integrity with steadfast steps and show that you are invincibly strong in the strength that confidence in God alone can confer. Thus you will be delivered from worrying care, you will not be troubled with evil tidings, your heart will be fixed, trusting in the Lord.

CHARLES SPURGEON
(1834–1892)
MORNING AND EVENING

PSALM 63

A psalm of David, written when he was in the Judean wilderness.

1 O God, you are my God. I long for you.
My soul thirsts for you,
my flesh yearns for you,
in a dry and parched land where there is no water.
2 Yes, in the sanctuary I have seen you,
and witnessed your power and splendor.
3 Because experiencing your loyal love is better than life
itself,
my lips will praise you.
4 For this reason I will praise you while I live;
in your name I will lift up my hands.
5 As with choice meat you satisfy my soul.
My mouth joyfully praises you,
6 whenever I remember you on my bed,
and think about you during the nighttime hours.
7 For you are my deliverer;
under your wings I rejoice.
8 My soul pursues you;
your right hand upholds me.
9 Enemies seek to destroy my life,

63:1–11 From this one word that God is "my deliverer," I make account that we have both these notions: First, that God has not left me to myself but has come to my succor and has helped me; and then that God does not act apart from me, rather he has been my help, but he has left something for me to do with him and by his help. My security for the future in this consideration of what is past lies not only in this, that God has delivered me, but in this also, that he has delivered me by way of a help, and help always assumes an endeavor and cooperation in one who is helped. God did not elect me as a helper, create me, redeem me, or convert me by way of helping me; for he alone did all, and he had no use at all of me. God infuses his grace first the first way, merely as a giver, entirely all of himself; but his subsequent graces he infuses as a helper, therefore we call them auxiliary graces, helping graces, and we always receive them when we endeavor to make use of his former grace.

JOHN DONNE **(1572–1631)**
THE WORKS

but they will descend into the depths of the earth.
10 Each one will be handed over to the sword;
their corpses will be eaten by jackals.
11 But the king will rejoice in God;
everyone who takes oaths in his name will boast,
for the mouths of those who speak lies will be shut up.

PSALM 64

For the music director, a psalm of David.

1 Listen to me, O God, as I offer my lament!
Protect my life from the enemy's terrifying attacks.
2 Hide me from the plots of evil men,
from the crowd of evildoers.
3 They sharpen their tongues like swords;
they aim their arrows, a slanderous charge,
4 in order to shoot down the innocent in secluded places.
They shoot at him suddenly and are unafraid of retaliation.
5 They encourage one another to carry out their evil deed.
They plan how to hide snares
and boast, "Who will see them?"
6 They devise unjust schemes;
they disguise a well-conceived plot.
Man's inner thoughts cannot be discovered.
7 But God will shoot at them;
suddenly they will be wounded by an arrow.
8 Their slander will bring about their demise.
All who see them will shudder,
9 and all people will fear.
They will proclaim what God has done,
and reflect on his deeds.
10 The godly will rejoice in the LORD
and take shelter in him.
All the morally upright will boast.

PSALM 65

For the music director, a psalm of David, a song.

1 Praise awaits you, O God, in Zion.
Vows made to you are fulfilled.
2 You hear prayers;
all people approach you.
3 Our record of sins overwhelms me,
but you forgive our acts of rebellion.
4 How blessed is the one whom you choose
and allow to live in your palace courts.
May we be satisfied with the good things of your house—
your holy palace.
5 You answer our prayers by performing awesome acts of deliverance,
O God, our savior.
All the ends of the earth trust in you,
as well as those living across the wide seas.
6 You created the mountains by your power
and demonstrated your strength.
7 You calmed the raging seas
and their roaring waves,
as well as the commotion made by the nations.

64:1–10 David begins by saying that he prays earnestly and with vehemence, stating at the same time what renders this necessary. The voice is heard in prayer proportionally to the earnestness and ardor we feel. He condescended upon the circumstances of distress in which he was presently placed and took notice of the dangers to which his life was exposed from enemies. His praying that God would protect his life proves that it must have been in danger at this time. In the second verse he intimates that his enemies were numerous and that, without divine assistance, he would be unable to sustain their attacks. He solicits the compassion of God by complaining of the number that were banded against him. I may add that there is an implied plea for strengthening his cause in prayer in what he says of the malice and wickedness of those who were opposed to him; for the more cruel and unjust the conduct of our enemies may be, we have proportionally the better ground to believe that God will interpose in our behalf.

JOHN CALVIN **(1509–1564)**
COMPLETE COMMENTARY ON THE BIBLE

65:1–13 This psalm or hymn written to the praise of God first teaches that his benefits are never rightly acknowledged and praised anywhere except in his holy congregations. Second, it commands us to admire three very important things and to give thanks to God for them. The first, and by far the greatest, is that God gathers a church to himself in which he wants to be glorified, and where he answers prayers, where he pardon sins—indeed, he never ceases to keep all kinds of blessings on the church and to guard it most powerfully. The second thing is that he sustains human society by establishing and maintaining governments in the midst of such great tumults. The third thing is that from heaven he so abundantly and generously supplies everything necessary for this life.

THEODORE BEZA **(1519–1605)**
THE PSALMS OF DAVID

8 Even those living in the remotest areas are awestruck
by your acts;
you cause those living in the east and west to praise
you.
9 You visit the earth and give it rain;
you make it rich and fertile.
God's streams are full of water;
you provide grain for the people of the earth,
for you have prepared the earth in this way.
10 You saturate its furrows,
and soak its plowed ground.
With rain showers you soften its soil,
and make its crops grow.
11 You crown the year with your good blessings,
and you leave abundance in your wake.
12 The pastures in the wilderness glisten with moisture,
and the hills are clothed with joy.
13 The meadows are clothed with sheep,
and the valleys are covered with grain.
They shout joyfully, yes, they sing.

PSALM 66

For the music director, a song, a psalm.

1 Shout out praise to God, all the earth!
2 Sing praises about the majesty of his reputation.
Give him the honor he deserves!
3 Say to God:
"How awesome are your deeds!
Because of your great power your enemies cower in fear
before you.
4 All the earth worships you
and sings praises to you.
They sing praises to your name." *Selah*
5 Come and witness God's exploits!
His acts on behalf of people are awesome.
6 He turned the sea into dry land;
they passed through the river on foot.
Let us rejoice in him there.
7 He rules by his power forever;
he watches the nations.
Stubborn rebels should not exalt themselves. *Selah*
8 Praise our God, you nations.
Loudly proclaim his praise.
9 He preserves our lives
and does not allow our feet to slip.
10 For you, O God, tested us;
you purified us like refined silver.
11 You led us into a trap;
you caused us to suffer.
12 You allowed men to ride over our heads;
we passed through fire and water,
but you brought us out into a wide open place.
13 I will enter your temple with burnt sacrifices;
I will fulfill the vows I made to you,
14 which my lips uttered
and my mouth spoke when I was in trouble.
15 I will offer up to you fattened animals as burnt
sacrifices,
along with the smell of sacrificial rams.

66:1–20 The psalmist powerfully infuses here an essential doctrine: Prayers to God must be poured out from a pure and unstained conscience. For God does not listen to sinners, and the speech of the impious is sin before God. If anyone therefore feels that his conscience is panged with some wicked deed, he should earnestly repent and seek pardon for his transgressions before he seeks either deliverance from dangers or assistance in toil or defense against enemies. For unless he has been reconciled to God, his prayers will not be heard. If anyone is not conscious of some wicked deed in himself, nevertheless he should acknowledge his weakness and beg for the remission of his sins through the Mediator. Then he should walk in simplicity and uprightness and wait on God's help and deliverance.

TILEMANN HESHUSIUS
(1527–1588)
COMMENTARY ON THE PSALMS

I will offer cattle and goats. *Selah*
16 Come! Listen, all you who are loyal to God.
I will declare what he has done for me.
17 I cried out to him for help
and praised him with my tongue.
18 If I had harbored sin in my heart,
the Lord would not have listened.
19 However, God heard;
he listened to my prayer.
20 God deserves praise,
for he did not reject my prayer
or abandon his love for me.

PSALM 67

For the music director, to be accompanied by stringed instruments; a psalm, a song.

1 May God show us his favor and bless us.
May he smile on us. *Selah*
2 Then those living on earth will know what you are like;
all nations will know how you deliver your people.
3 Let the nations thank you, O God.
Let all the nations thank you.
4 Let foreigners rejoice and celebrate.
For you execute justice among the nations
and govern the people living on earth. *Selah*
5 Let the nations thank you, O God.
Let all the nations thank you.
6 The earth yields its crops.
May God, our God, bless us.
7 May God bless us.
Then all the ends of the earth will give him the honor
he deserves.

PSALM 68

For the music director, by David, a psalm, a song.

1 God springs into action.
His enemies scatter;
his adversaries run from him.
2 As smoke is driven away by the wind, so you drive them
away.
As wax melts before fire,
so the wicked are destroyed before God.
3 But the godly are happy;
they rejoice before God
and are overcome with joy.
4 Sing to God! Sing praises to his name.
Exalt the one who rides on the clouds.
For the LORD is his name.
Rejoice before him.
5 He is a father to the fatherless
and an advocate for widows.
God rules from his holy dwelling place.
6 God settles in their own homes those who have been
deserted;
he frees prisoners and grants them prosperity.
But sinful rebels live in the desert.
7 O God, when you lead your people into battle,
when you march through the wastelands, *Selah*
8 the earth shakes.

67:1–7 Who does not earnestly praise and glorify God—the eternal source of all good—and acknowledge him? This God they know judges, that is, rules and controls all people and indeed does so with the same equity and indulgence so that those who trust in him and hand themselves over to be led by him never lack any good. For this reason indeed there is gladness as well as clapping concerning which the psalmist says, "Let the nations thank you, O God. Let all the nations thank you." He repeats this verse about the burning zeal of glorifying God among all the nations so that he might magnify this happiness that the saints enjoy as the Lord speaks the law and his own Spirit leads them. The more the knowledge of God increases, the more the enjoyment of the same increases, and accordingly the highest delight of the soul to which no greater desire can be imagined than to praise God everywhere.

MARTIN BUCER **(1491–1551)**
HOLY PSALMS

68:1–6 If you ever wish to associate with someone, make sure that you do not give your attention to those who enjoy health and wealth and fame as the world sees it, but take care of those in affliction, those in critical circumstances, those in prison, those who are utterly deserted and enjoy no consolation. Put a high value on associating with these, for from them you shall receive much profit, you will be a better lover of the true wisdom, and you will do all for the glory of God. And if you must visit someone, prefer to pay this honor to orphans, widows, and those in want rather than to those who enjoy reputation and fame. God is "a father to the fatherless and an advocate for widows."

CHRYSOSTOM **(C. 347–407)**
BAPTISMAL INSTRUCTIONS

Yes, the heavens pour down rain
before God, the God of Sinai,
before God, the God of Israel.
9 O God, you cause abundant showers to fall on your
chosen people.
When they are tired, you sustain them,
10 for you live among them.
You sustain the oppressed with your good blessings,
O God.
11 The Lord speaks;
many, many women spread the good news.
12 Kings leading armies run away—they run away!
The lovely lady of the house divides up the loot.
13 When you lie down among the sheepfolds,
the wings of the dove are covered with silver
and with glittering gold.
14 When the Sovereign One scatters kings,
let it snow on Zalmon.
15 The mountain of Bashan is a towering mountain;
the mountain of Bashan is a mountain with many
peaks.
16 Why do you look with envy, O mountains with many
peaks,
at the mountain where God has decided to live?
Indeed the LORD will live there permanently.
17 God has countless chariots;
they number in the thousands.
The Lord comes from Sinai in holy splendor.
18 You ascend on high;
you have taken many captives.
You receive tribute from men,
including even sinful rebels.
Indeed, the LORD God lives there.
19 The Lord deserves praise.
Day after day he carries our burden,
the God who delivers us. *Selah*
20 Our God is a God who delivers;
the LORD, the Sovereign Lord, can rescue from death.
21 Indeed, God strikes the heads of his enemies,
the hairy foreheads of those who persist in rebellion.
22 The Lord says,
"I will retrieve them from Bashan.
I will bring them back from the depths of the sea,
23 so that your feet may stomp in their blood,
and your dogs may eat their portion of the enemies'
corpses."
24 They see your processions, O God—
the processions of my God, my king, who marches along
in holy splendor.
25 Singers walk in front;
musicians follow playing their stringed instruments,
in the midst of young women playing tambourines.
26 In your large assemblies praise God,
the LORD, in the assemblies of Israel.
27 There is little Benjamin, their ruler,
and the princes of Judah in their robes,
along with the princes of Zebulun and the princes of
Naphtali.
28 God has decreed that you will be powerful.

O God, you who have acted on our behalf, demonstrate
your power.
29 Because of your temple in Jerusalem,
kings bring tribute to you.
30 Sound your battle cry against the wild beast of the
reeds,
and the nations that assemble like a herd of calves led
by bulls.
They humble themselves and offer gold and silver as
tribute.
God scatters the nations that like to do battle.
31 They come with red cloth from Egypt.
Ethiopia voluntarily offers tribute to God.
32 O kingdoms of the earth, sing to God.
Sing praises to the Lord, *Selah*
33 to the one who rides through the sky from ancient times.
Look! He thunders loudly.
34 Acknowledge God's power,
his sovereignty over Israel,
and the power he reveals in the skies.
35 You are awe inspiring, O God, as you emerge from your
holy temple.
It is the God of Israel who gives the people power and
strength.
God deserves praise!

PSALM 69

For the music director, according to the tune of "Lilies"; by David.

1 Deliver me, O God,
for the water has reached my neck.
2 I sink into the deep mire
where there is no solid ground;
I am in deep water,
and the current overpowers me.
3 I am exhausted from shouting for help.
My throat is sore;
my eyes grow tired from looking for my God.
4 Those who hate me without cause
are more numerous than the hairs of my head.
Those who want to destroy me,
my enemies for no reason,
outnumber me.
They make me repay what I did not steal.
5 O God, you are aware of my foolish sins;
my guilt is not hidden from you.
6 Let none who rely on you be disgraced because of me,
O Sovereign LORD of Heaven's Armies.
Let none who seek you be ashamed because of me,
O God of Israel.
7 For I suffer humiliation for your sake
and am thoroughly disgraced.
8 My own brothers treat me like a stranger;
they act as if I were a foreigner.
9 Certainly zeal for your house consumes me;
I endure the insults of those who insult you.
10 I weep and refrain from eating food,
which causes others to insult me.
11 I wear sackcloth
and they ridicule me.

69:1–36 Grace does not abound except where sin and wretchedness abound, for it is not possible to make the mercy of God large and good unless a person first makes his miseries large and evil or recognizes them to be such. To make God's mercy great is not, as is commonly supposed, to think that God considers sins as small or that he does not punish them. For how can one who regards evil as something small regard as something great the good by means of which the evil is removed? Hence our total concern must be to magnify and aggravate our sins and thus always to accuse them more and more and earnestly judge and condemn them. The more deeply people condemn themselves and magnify their sins, the more are they fit for the mercy and grace of God.

MARTIN LUTHER **(1483–1546)**
GLOSSA ON THE PSALMS

12 Those who sit at the city gate gossip about me;
drunkards mock me in their songs.
13 O LORD, may you hear my prayer and be favorably
disposed to me.
O God, because of your great loyal love,
answer me with your faithful deliverance.
14 Rescue me from the mud. Don't let me sink.
Deliver me from those who hate me,
from the deep water.
15 Don't let the current overpower me.
Don't let the deep swallow me up.
Don't let the Pit devour me.
16 Answer me, O LORD, for your loyal love is good.
Because of your great compassion, turn toward me.
17 Do not ignore your servant,
for I am in trouble. Answer me right away.
18 Come near me and redeem me.
Because of my enemies, rescue me.
19 You know how I am insulted, humiliated, and
disgraced;
you can see all my enemies.
20 Their insults are painful and make me lose heart;
I look for sympathy, but receive none,
for comforters, but find none.
21 They put bitter poison into my food,
and to quench my thirst they give me vinegar to drink.
22 May their dining table become a trap before them.
May it be a snare for that group of friends.
23 May their eyes be blinded.
Make them shake violently.
24 Pour out your judgment on them.
May your raging anger overtake them.
25 May their camp become desolate,
their tents uninhabited.
26 For they harass the one whom you discipline;
they spread the news about the suffering of those
whom you punish.
27 Hold them accountable for all their sins.
Do not vindicate them.
28 May their names be deleted from the scroll of the
living.
Do not let their names be listed with the godly.
29 I am oppressed and suffering.
O God, deliver and protect me.
30 I will sing praises to God's name.
I will magnify him as I give him thanks.
31 That will please the LORD more than an ox or a bull
with horns and hooves.
32 The oppressed look on—let them rejoice.
You who seek God, may you be encouraged.
33 For the LORD listens to the needy;
he does not despise his captive people.
34 Let the heavens and the earth praise him,
along with the seas and everything that swims in them.
35 For God will deliver Zion
and rebuild the cities of Judah,
and his people will again live in them and possess Zion.
36 The descendants of his servants will inherit it,
and those who are loyal to him will live in it.

PSALM 70

For the music director, by David; written to get God's attention.

1 O God, please be willing to rescue me.
O LORD, hurry and help me.
2 May those who are trying to take my life
be embarrassed and ashamed.
May those who want to harm me
be turned back and ashamed.
3 May those who say, "Aha! Aha!"
be driven back and disgraced.
4 May all those who seek you be happy and rejoice in you.
May those who love to experience your deliverance say
continually,
"May God be praised!"
5 I am oppressed and needy.
O God, hurry to me.
You are my helper and my deliverer.
O LORD, do not delay.

70:1–5 A godly person in extreme distress may call earnestly on God to hurry his deliverance, and there is no hurt in that. Indeed, God is well pleased with our earnestness, and sometimes we reap the fruit of this in present help and deliverance according to our own desire and the intention of our prayers. In our earnestness, however, there must also be a resolution of patience and submission. With that belief and assurance, we must understand that God's time, be it sooner or later, is our best time, even though present sense and weak flesh suggest contrary.

THE WESTMINSTER ANNOTATIONS
(1683)

PSALM 71

1 In you, O LORD, I have taken shelter.
Never let me be humiliated.
2 Vindicate me by rescuing me.
Listen to me. Deliver me.
3 Be my protector and refuge,
a stronghold where I can be safe.
For you are my high ridge and my stronghold.
4 My God, rescue me from the power of the wicked,
from the hand of the cruel oppressor.
5 For you are my hope;
O Sovereign LORD, I have trusted in you since I was
young.
6 I have leaned on you since birth;
you pulled me from my mother's womb.
I praise you continually.
7 Many are appalled when they see me,
but you are my secure shelter.
8 I praise you constantly
and speak of your splendor all day long.
9 Do not reject me in my old age.
When my strength fails, do not abandon me.
10 For my enemies talk about me;
those waiting for a chance to kill me plot my demise.
11 They say, "God has abandoned him.
Run and seize him, for there is no one who will rescue
him."
12 O God, do not remain far away from me.
My God, hurry and help me.
13 May my accusers be humiliated and defeated.
May those who want to harm me be covered with scorn
and disgrace.
14 As for me, I will wait continually,
and will continue to praise you.
15 I will tell about your justice,
and all day long proclaim your salvation,
though I cannot fathom its full extent.
16 I will come and tell about the mighty acts of the
Sovereign LORD.
I will proclaim your justice—yours alone.

71:1–24 Verse 14 has two things. First, the psalmist wants constantly to hope, of course, for the help of the Lord. It is his self-control that said, "My God, hurry and help me." Although he longs for the help of God to come quickly, nevertheless he indicates that he will not despair even if he is not delivered immediately. Second he said he will "continue to praise [God]." This relates to the hope of deliverance. Here again he was moved by what he said, "I will wait continually." Because that relates to the desire to proclaim the praise of God, he indicates that he wants to magnify the praise of God and to have material from which he could add praises to those he had so far proclaimed. Daily the wicked hunt for new ways to add to their past sins; in the same way, by contrast, the pious with fervent longing daily hunt for new ways to add to the surplus of God's praise.

WOLFGANG MUSCULUS
(1497–1563)
COMMENTARY ON THE PSALMS

17 O God, you have taught me since I was young,
and I am still declaring your amazing deeds.
18 Even when I am old and gray,
O God, do not abandon me,
until I tell the next generation about your strength
and those coming after me about your power.
19 Your justice, O God, extends to the skies above;
you have done great things.
O God, who can compare to you?
20 Though you have allowed me to experience much
trouble and distress,
revive me once again.
Bring me up once again from the depths of the earth.
21 Raise me to a position of great honor.
Turn and comfort me.
22 I will express my thanks to you with a stringed
instrument,
praising your faithfulness, O my God.
I will sing praises to you accompanied by a harp,
O Holy One of Israel.
23 My lips will shout for joy. Yes, I will sing your praises.
I will praise you when you rescue me.
24 All day long my tongue will also tell about your justice,
for those who want to harm me will be embarrassed
and ashamed.

PSALM 72

For Solomon.

1 O God, grant the king the ability to make just decisions.
Grant the king's son the ability to make fair decisions.
2 Then he will judge your people fairly
and your oppressed ones equitably.
3 The mountains will bring news of peace to the people,
and the hills will announce justice.
4 He will defend the oppressed among the people;
he will deliver the children of the poor
and crush the oppressor.
5 People will fear you as long as the sun and moon remain
in the sky,
for generation after generation.
6 He will descend like rain on the mown grass,
like showers that drench the earth.
7 During his days the godly will flourish;
peace will prevail as long as the moon remains in the
sky.
8 May he rule from sea to sea,
and from the Euphrates River to the ends of the earth.
9 Before him the coastlands will bow down,
and his enemies will lick the dust.
10 The kings of Tarshish and the coastlands will offer gifts;
the kings of Sheba and Seba will bring tribute.
11 All kings will bow down to him;
all nations will serve him.
12 For he will rescue the needy when they cry out for help,
and the oppressed who have no defender.
13 He will take pity on the poor and needy;
the lives of the needy he will save.
14 From harm and violence he will defend them;
he will value their lives.

72:1–20 This is a glorious prophecy about the Lord Christ and his kingdom, that he is truly God whom the sun and moon will fear and all kings will worship and everyone will honor as long as sun and moon endure. Yet the beloved cross should also be part of this life so that true believers in Christ must often suffer, shed their blood, and die. But their death and blood will be dear and precious before God. The psalm promises that we who are weary and heavy-laden and have all kinds of inward and outward crosses shall be helped and counseled. God will be near, around, under, in, and for us. He will minister to our needs and himself be our Lord and King and protect and preserve to all eternity.

NIKOLAUS SELNECKER
(1530–1592)
THE WHOLE PSALTER

15 May he live! May they offer him gold from Sheba.
May they continually pray for him.
May they pronounce blessings on him all day long.
16 May there be an abundance of grain in the earth;
on the tops of the mountains may it sway.
May its fruit trees flourish like the forests of Lebanon.
May its crops be as abundant as the grass of the earth.
17 May his fame endure.
May his dynasty last as long as the sun remains in the sky.
May they use his name when they formulate their
blessings.
May all nations consider him to be favored by God.
18 The LORD God, the God of Israel, deserves praise.
He alone accomplishes amazing things.
19 His glorious name deserves praise forevermore.
May his majestic splendor fill the whole earth.
We agree! We agree!
20 This collection of the prayers of David son of Jesse ends
here.

BOOK 3 (PSALMS 73–89)

PSALM 73

A psalm by Asaph.

1 Certainly God is good to Israel,
and to those whose motives are pure.
2 But as for me, my feet almost slipped;
my feet almost slid out from under me.
3 For I envied those who are proud,
as I observed the prosperity of the wicked.
4 For they suffer no pain;
their bodies are strong and well fed.
5 They are immune to the trouble common to men;
they do not suffer as other men do.
6 Arrogance is their necklace,
and violence covers them like clothing.
7 Their prosperity causes them to do wrong;
their thoughts are sinful.
8 They mock and say evil things;
they proudly threaten violence.
9 They speak as if they rule in heaven,
and lay claim to the earth.
10 Therefore they have more than enough food to eat
and even suck up the water of the sea.
11 They say, "How does God know what we do?
Is the Most High aware of what goes on?"
12 Take a good look. This is what the wicked are like,
those who always have it so easy and get richer and
richer.
13 I concluded, "Surely in vain I have kept my motives pure
and maintained a pure lifestyle.
14 I suffer all day long
and am punished every morning."
15 If I had publicized these thoughts,
I would have betrayed your people.
16 When I tried to make sense of this,
it was troubling to me.
17 Then I entered the precincts of God's temple
and understood the destiny of the wicked.

73:1–28 "You guide me by your wise advice." The psalmist resolved that God's counsel should guide him. A sense of our own folly is a great step toward being wise when it leads us to rely on the wisdom of the Lord. "You guide" is a blessed expression of confidence. He was sure that the Lord would not decline the condescending task. *Blessed be You, O God, that we may trust you to guide us now and guide us even to the end!* After this guidance through life, the psalmist anticipates a divine reception at last—"And then you will lead me to a position of honor." What a thought for you, believer! God himself will receive you to glory—you! Wandering, erring, straying, yet you will be brought safe at last to glory! This is your portion; live on it this day.

CHARLES SPURGEON
(1834–1892)
MORNING AND EVENING

18 Surely you put them in slippery places;
you bring them down to ruin.
19 How desolate they become in a mere moment.
Terrifying judgments make their demise
complete.
20 They are like a dream after one wakes up.
O Lord, when you awake you will despise them.
21 Yes, my spirit was bitter,
and my insides felt sharp pain.
22 I was ignorant and lacked insight;
I was as senseless as an animal before you.
23 But I am continually with you;
you hold my right hand.
24 You guide me by your wise advice,
and then you will lead me to a position of honor.
25 Whom do I have in heaven but you?
On earth there is no one I desire but you.
26 My flesh and my heart may grow weak,
but God always protects my heart and gives me
stability.
27 Yes, look! Those far from you die;
you destroy everyone who is unfaithful to you.
28 But as for me, God's presence is all I need.
I have made the Sovereign LORD my shelter,
as I declare all the things you have done.

PSALM 74

A well-written song by Asaph.

1 Why, O God, have you permanently rejected us?
Why does your anger burn against the sheep of your
pasture?
2 Remember your people whom you acquired in ancient
times,
whom you rescued so they could be your very own
nation,
as well as Mount Zion, where you dwell.
3 Hurry to the permanent ruins,
and to all the damage the enemy has done to the
temple.
4 Your enemies roar in the middle of your sanctuary;
they set up their battle flags.
5 They invade like lumberjacks
swinging their axes in a thick forest.
6 And now they are tearing down all its engravings
with axes and crowbars.
7 They set your sanctuary on fire;
they desecrate your dwelling place by knocking it to the
ground.
8 They say to themselves,
"We will oppress all of them."
They burn down all the places in the land where people
worship God.
9 We do not see any signs of God's presence;
there are no longer any prophets,
and we have no one to tell us how long this will last.
10 How long, O God, will the adversary hurl insults?
Will the enemy blaspheme your name forever?
11 Why do you remain inactive?
Intervene and destroy him.

74:1–23 "You destroyed the sea by your strength." The Lord the Savior repeats the miracles he had once done among the nation of the Jews. For he strengthened the watery deeps of the Red Sea when the water was divided in two walls so as to make the ship-traversing sea into a path of dry land. "You shattered the heads of the sea monster in the water." The mystery of the earlier miracle explains well enough that that prefigurement of the crossing of the Red Sea was pointing to the waters of holy baptism, where the heads of dragons, that is of unclean spirits, were made nothing because the salvific font makes clean the souls that the demons make unclean with the filth of their sins.

CASSIODORUS (C. 485–C. 585)
EXPLANATION OF THE PSALMS

12 But God has been my king from ancient times,
performing acts of deliverance on the earth.
13 You destroyed the sea by your strength;
you shattered the heads of the sea monster in the water.
14 You crushed the heads of Leviathan;
you fed him to the people who live along the coast.
15 You broke open the spring and the stream;
you dried up perpetually flowing rivers.
16 You established the cycle of day and night;
you put the moon and sun in place.
17 You set up all the boundaries of the earth;
you created the cycle of summer and winter.
18 Remember how the enemy hurls insults, O LORD,
and how a foolish nation blasphemes your name.
19 Do not hand the life of your dove over to a wild animal.
Do not continue to disregard the lives of your oppressed people.
20 Remember your covenant promises,
for the dark regions of the earth are full of places where violence rules.
21 Do not let the afflicted be turned back in shame.
Let the oppressed and poor praise your name.
22 Rise up, O God. Defend your honor.
Remember how fools insult you all day long.
23 Do not disregard what your enemies say
or the unceasing shouts of those who defy you.

PSALM 75

For the music director, according to the al-tashcheth *style; a psalm of Asaph, a song.*

1 We give thanks to you, O God. We give thanks.
You reveal your presence;
people tell about your amazing deeds.
2 God says,
"At the appointed times,
I judge fairly.
3 When the earth and all its inhabitants dissolve in fear,
I make its pillars secure." *Selah*
4 I say to the proud, "Do not be proud,"
and to the wicked, "Do not be so confident of victory.
5 Do not be so certain you have won.
Do not speak with your head held so high.
6 For victory does not come from the east or west,
or from the wilderness.
7 For God is the judge.
He brings one down and exalts another.
8 For the LORD holds in his hand a cup
full of foaming wine mixed with spices,
and pours it out.
Surely all the wicked of the earth
will slurp it up and drink it to its very last drop."
9 As for me, I will continually tell what you have done;
I will sing praises to the God of Jacob.
10 God says,
"I will bring down all the power of the wicked;
the godly will be victorious."

75:1–10 After the psalm had said, "Do not be so certain you have won. Do not speak with your head held so high," it went on immediately: "For victory does not come from the east or west, or from the wilderness. For God is the judge. He brings one down and exalts another." The psalmist sees two kinds of people: one full of pride, the other confessing; one speaking justly, the other speaking unjustly. Who is speaking justly? The one who says "I have sinned." And who is speaking unjustly? The one who says, "It is not I who sinned, it is my luck that sinned, my fate that sinned." So when you see two people, one speaking equity, the other iniquity, one humble, the other proud, do not be surprised that it goes on to say, "God is the judge. He brings one down and exalts another."

AUGUSTINE (354–430)
SERMONS

PSALM 76

For the music director, to be accompanied by stringed instruments; a psalm of Asaph, a song.

1 God has revealed himself in Judah;
in Israel his reputation is great.
2 He lives in Salem;
he dwells in Zion.
3 There he shattered the arrows,
the shield, the sword, and the rest of the weapons of war. *Selah*
4 You shine brightly and reveal your majesty,
as you descend from the hills where you killed your prey.
5 The bravehearted were plundered;
they "fell asleep."
All the warriors were helpless.
6 At the sound of your battle cry, O God of Jacob,
both rider and horse "fell asleep."
7 You are awesome! Yes, you!
Who can withstand your intense anger?
8 From heaven you announced what their punishment would be.
The earth was afraid and silent
9 when God arose to execute judgment,
and to deliver all the oppressed of the earth. *Selah*
10 Certainly your angry judgment upon men will bring you praise;
you reveal your anger in full measure.
11 Make vows to the LORD your God and repay them.
Let all those who surround him bring tribute to the awesome one.
12 He humbles princes;
the kings of the earth regard him as awesome.

76:1–12 Let those to whom the Lord has given stout hearts, strong hands, and great success watch carefully over their own spirits, lest they be led aside into any way against the mind of God. Great endowments are ofttimes great temptations. "Your presumptuous heart has deceived you—you who reside in the safety of the rocky cliffs, whose home is high in the mountains. You think to yourself, 'No one can bring me down to the ground!'" (Obad v. 3). Though people have courage and might and former successes accompany them, yet when they engage themselves against the Lord or any way of his, vanity, weakness, and disappointment will be the issue thereof.

JOHN OWEN **(1616–1683)**
THE WORKS

PSALM 77

For the music director, Jeduthun; a psalm of Asaph.

1 I will cry out to God and call for help.
I will cry out to God and he will pay attention to me.
2 In my time of trouble I sought the Lord.
I kept my hand raised in prayer throughout the night.
I refused to be comforted.
3 I said, "I will remember God while I groan;
I will think about him while my strength leaves me." *Selah*
4 You held my eyelids open;
I was troubled and could not speak.
5 I thought about the days of old,
about ancient times.
6 I said, "During the night I will remember the song I once sang;
I will think very carefully."
I tried to make sense of what was happening.
7 I asked, "Will the Lord reject me forever?
Will he never again show me his favor?
8 Has his loyal love disappeared forever?
Has his promise failed forever?
9 Has God forgotten to be merciful?
Has his anger stifled his compassion?" *Selah*

77:1–5 "I was troubled and could not speak." It often happens that the remembrance of God in the time of adversity aggravates the anguish of the godly as, for example, when they entertain the thought that he is angry with them. The prophet, however, does not mean that his heart was thrown into new distress whenever God was brought to his recollection: He laments only that no consolation proceeded from God to afford him relief, and this is a trial that is very hard to bear. When the remembrance of God does not afford repose or tranquility to our minds, we are ready to think that he is sporting with us. We are nevertheless taught from this passage that however much we may experience fretting, sorrow, and disquietude, we must persevere in calling upon God even in the midst of all these impediments.

JOHN CALVIN **(1509–1564)**
COMPLETE COMMENTARY ON THE BIBLE

10 Then I said, "I am sickened by the thought
that the Most High might become inactive.
11 I will remember the works of the LORD.
Yes, I will remember the amazing things you did long
ago.
12 I will think about all you have done;
I will reflect upon your deeds."
13 O God, your deeds are extraordinary.
What god can compare to our great God?
14 You are the God who does amazing things;
you have revealed your strength among the nations.
15 You delivered your people by your strength—
the children of Jacob and Joseph. *Selah*
16 The waters saw you, O God,
the waters saw you and trembled.
Yes, the depths of the sea shook with fear.
17 The clouds poured down rain;
the skies thundered.
Yes, your arrows flashed about.
18 Your thunderous voice was heard in the wind;
the lightning bolts lit up the world.
The earth trembled and shook.
19 You walked through the sea;
you passed through the surging waters,
but left no footprints.
20 You led your people like a flock of sheep,
by the hand of Moses and Aaron.

PSALM 78

A well-written song by Asaph.

1 Pay attention, my people, to my instruction.
Listen to the words I speak.
2 I will sing a song that imparts wisdom;
I will make insightful observations about the past.
3 What we have heard and learned—
that which our ancestors have told us—
4 we will not hide from their descendants.
We will tell the next generation
about the LORD's praiseworthy acts,
about his strength and the amazing things he has done.
5 He established a rule in Jacob;
he set up a law in Israel.
He commanded our ancestors
to make his deeds known to their descendants,
6 so that the next generation, children yet to be born,
might know about them.
They will grow up and tell their descendants about
them.
7 Then they will place their confidence in God.
They will not forget the works of God,
and they will obey his commands.
8 Then they will not be like their ancestors,
who were a stubborn and rebellious generation,
a generation that was not committed
and faithful to God.
9 The Ephraimites were armed with bows,
but they retreated in the day of battle.
10 They did not keep their covenant with God,
and they refused to obey his law.

78:1–72 Sin dispirits people and takes away the heart. Forgetfulness of God's works is the cause of disobedience to his laws. This narrative relates a struggle between God's goodness and human badness. The Lord hears all our murmurings and distrusts and is much displeased. Those who will not believe the power of God's mercy shall feel the fire of his indignation. Those cannot be said to trust in God's salvation as their happiness at last who cannot trust his providence in the way to it. To all who, by faith and prayer, ask, seek, and knock, these doors of heaven shall at any time be opened; and our distrust of God is a great aggravation of our sins. Let not those who receive mercy from God be thereby made bold to sin, for the mercies they receive will hasten its punishment; yet let not those who are under divine rebukes for sin be discouraged from repentance. The Holy One of Israel will do what is most for his own glory, and what is most for their good.

MATTHEW HENRY (1662–1714)
COMMENTARY ON THE WHOLE BIBLE

11 They forgot what he had done,
the amazing things he had shown them.
12 He did amazing things in the sight of their ancestors,
in the land of Egypt, in the region of Zoan.
13 He divided the sea and led them across it;
he made the water stand in a heap.
14 He led them with a cloud by day
and with the light of a fire all night long.
15 He broke open rocks in the wilderness
and gave them enough water to fill the depths of the sea.
16 He caused streams to flow from the rock
and made the water flow like rivers.
17 Yet they continued to sin against him
and rebelled against the Most High in the desert.
18 They willfully challenged God
by asking for food to satisfy their appetite.
19 They insulted God, saying,
"Is God really able to give us food in the wilderness?
20 Yes, he struck a rock and water flowed out;
streams gushed forth.
But can he also give us food?
Will he provide meat for his people?"
21 When the LORD heard this, he was furious.
A fire broke out against Jacob,
and his anger flared up against Israel,
22 because they did not have faith in God
and did not trust his ability to deliver them.
23 He gave a command to the clouds above
and opened the doors in the sky.
24 He rained down manna for them to eat;
he gave them the grain of heaven.
25 Man ate the food of the mighty ones.
He sent them more than enough to eat.
26 He brought the east wind through the sky
and by his strength led forth the south wind.
27 He rained down meat on them like dust,
birds as numerous as the sand on the seashores.
28 He caused them to fall right in the middle of their camp,
all around their homes.
29 They ate until they were beyond full;
he gave them what they desired.
30 They were not yet filled up;
their food was still in their mouths
31 when the anger of God flared up against them.
He killed some of the strongest of them;
he brought the young men of Israel to their knees.
32 Despite all this, they continued to sin,
and did not trust him to do amazing things.
33 So he caused them to die unsatisfied
and filled with terror.
34 When he struck them down, they sought his favor;
they turned back and longed for God.
35 They remembered that God was their protector
and that God Most High was their deliverer.
36 But they deceived him with their words
and lied to him.
37 They were not really committed to him,
and they were unfaithful to his covenant.

38 Yet he is compassionate.
He forgives sin and does not destroy.
He often holds back his anger
and does not stir up his fury.
39 He remembered that they were made of flesh
and were like a wind that blows past and does not
return.
40 How often they rebelled against him in the wilderness
and insulted him in the wastelands.
41 They again challenged God
and offended the Holy One of Israel.
42 They did not remember what he had done,
how he delivered them from the enemy,
43 when he performed his awesome deeds in Egypt
and his acts of judgment in the region of Zoan.
44 He turned their rivers into blood,
and they could not drink from their streams.
45 He sent swarms of biting insects against them,
as well as frogs that overran their land.
46 He gave their crops to the grasshopper,
the fruit of their labor to the locust.
47 He destroyed their vines with hail
and their sycamore-fig trees with driving rain.
48 He rained hail down on their cattle
and hurled lightning bolts down on their livestock.
49 His raging anger lashed out against them.
He sent fury, rage, and trouble
as messengers who bring disaster.
50 He sent his anger in full force.
He did not spare them from death;
he handed their lives over to destruction.
51 He struck down all the firstborn in Egypt,
the firstfruits of their reproductive power in the tents
of Ham.
52 Yet he brought out his people like sheep;
he led them through the wilderness like a flock.
53 He guided them safely along, and they were not afraid;
but the sea covered their enemies.
54 He brought them to the border of his holy land,
to this mountainous land that his right hand
acquired.
55 He drove the nations out from before them;
he assigned them their tribal allotments
and allowed the tribes of Israel to settle down.
56 Yet they challenged and defied God Most High
and did not obey his commands.
57 They were unfaithful and acted as treacherously as
their ancestors;
they were as unreliable as a malfunctioning bow.
58 They made him angry with their pagan shrines
and made him jealous with their idols.
59 God heard and was angry;
he completely rejected Israel.
60 He abandoned the sanctuary at Shiloh,
the tent where he lived among men.
61 He allowed the symbol of his strong presence to be
captured;
he gave the symbol of his splendor into the hand of the
enemy.

THE BELGIC CONFESSION (1561)

WRITTEN BY GUIDO de Bres, a pastor and former student of John Calvin, this confession was an attempt to persuade King Philip II of Spain to protect the Protestants who were being persecuted for their faith. In light of persecution of Protestants during its time, the articles on the church are particularly compelling. Here are selected portions.

ARTICLE 27: THE HOLY CATHOLIC CHURCH

WE BELIEVE and confess one single catholic or universal church—a holy congregation and gathering of true Christian believers awaiting their entire salvation in Jesus Christ, being washed by his blood and sanctified and sealed by the Holy Spirit. This church has existed from the beginning of the world and will last until the end, as appears from the fact that Christ is an eternal King who cannot be without subjects. And this holy church is preserved by God against the rage of the whole world, even though for a time it may appear very small to human eyes—as though it were snuffed out. For example, during the very dangerous time of Ahab, the Lord preserved for himself 7,000 who did not bend their knees to Baal. And so this holy church is not confined, bound, or limited to a certain place or certain people. But it is spread and dispersed throughout the entire world, though still joined and united in heart and will, in one and the same Spirit, by the power of faith.

ARTICLE 28: THE OBLIGATIONS OF CHURCH MEMBERS

WE BELIEVE that since this holy assembly and congregation is the gathering of those who are saved and there is no salvation apart from it, people ought not to withdraw from it, content to be by themselves, regardless of their status or condition. But all people are obliged to join and unite with it, keeping the unity of the church by submitting to its instruction and discipline, by bending their necks under the yoke of Jesus Christ, and by serving to build up one another, according to the gifts God has given them as members of each other in the same body. And to preserve this unity more effectively, it is the duty of all believers, according to God's Word, to separate themselves from those who do not belong to the church in order to join this assembly wherever God has established it, even if civil authorities and royal decrees forbid and death and physical punishment result. And so, all who withdraw from the church or do not join it act contrary to God's ordinance.

62 He delivered his people over to the sword
and was angry with his chosen nation.
63 Fire consumed their young men,
and their virgins remained unmarried.
64 Their priests fell by the sword,
but their widows did not weep.
65 But then the Lord awoke from his sleep;
he was like a warrior in a drunken rage.
66 He drove his enemies back;
he made them a permanent target for insults.
67 He rejected the tent of Joseph;
he did not choose the tribe of Ephraim.
68 He chose the tribe of Judah
and Mount Zion, which he loves.
69 He made his sanctuary as enduring as the heavens
above,
as secure as the earth, which he established
permanently.
70 He chose David, his servant,
and took him from the sheepfolds.
71 He took him away from following the mother sheep,
and made him the shepherd of Jacob, his people,
and of Israel, his chosen nation.
72 David cared for them with pure motives;
he led them with skill.

PSALM 79

A psalm of Asaph.

1 O God, foreigners have invaded your chosen land;
they have polluted your holy temple
and turned Jerusalem into a heap of ruins.
2 They have given the corpses of your servants
to the birds of the sky,
the flesh of your loyal followers
to the beasts of the earth.
3 They have made their blood flow like water
all around Jerusalem, and there is no one to bury them.
4 We have become an object of disdain to our neighbors;
those who live on our borders taunt and insult us.
5 How long will this go on, O LORD?
Will you stay angry forever?
How long will your rage burn like fire?
6 Pour out your anger on the nations that do not
acknowledge you,

79:1–13 "Why should the nations say, 'Where is their God?'" The family of Christ is furnished with its reply: Our God is everywhere present, wholly everywhere; not confined to any place. He can be present unperceived and be absent without moving. When he exposes us to adversities, it is either to prove our perfections or correct our imperfections; and in return for our patient endurance of the sufferings of time, he reserves for us an everlasting reward. But who are you that we should deign to speak with you even about your own gods, much less about our God, who is "more awesome than all gods. For all the gods of the nations are worthless, but the LORD made the sky" (Ps 96:4–5)?

AUGUSTINE **(354–430)**
CITY OF GOD

on the kingdoms that do not pray to you.
7 For they have devoured Jacob
and destroyed his home.
8 Do not hold us accountable for the sins of earlier generations.
Quickly send your compassion our way,
for we are in serious trouble.
9 Help us, O God, our deliverer!
For the sake of your glorious reputation, rescue us.
Forgive our sins for the sake of your reputation.
10 Why should the nations say, "Where is their God?"
Before our very eyes may the shed blood of your servants
be avenged among the nations.
11 Listen to the painful cries of the prisoners.
Use your great strength to set free those condemned to die.
12 Pay back our neighbors in full.
May they be insulted the same way they insulted you, O Lord.
13 Then we, your people, the sheep of your pasture,
will continually thank you.
We will tell coming generations of your praiseworthy acts.

PSALM 80

For the music director, according to the shushan-eduth *style; a psalm of Asaph.*

1 O Shepherd of Israel, pay attention,
you who lead Joseph like a flock of sheep.
You who sit enthroned above the cherubim, reveal your splendor.
2 In the sight of Ephraim, Benjamin, and Manasseh reveal your power.
Come and deliver us.
3 O God, restore us.
Smile on us. Then we will be delivered.
4 O LORD God of Heaven's Armies,
how long will you remain angry at your people while they pray to you?
5 You have given them tears as food;
you have made them drink tears by the measure.
6 You have made our neighbors dislike us
and our enemies insult us.
7 O God of Heaven's Armies, restore us.
Smile on us. Then we will be delivered.
8 You uprooted a vine from Egypt;
you drove out nations and transplanted it.
9 You cleared the ground for it;
it took root
and filled the land.
10 The mountains were covered by its shadow,
the highest cedars by its branches.
11 Its branches reached the Mediterranean Sea,
and its shoots the Euphrates River.
12 Why did you break down its walls,
so that all who pass by pluck its fruit?
13 The wild boars of the forest ruin it;
the insects of the field feed on it.

80:1–19 In the Old Testament God's justice orders a year's punishment to make up for the sin of one day. In other words, the people were tormented in the desert for forty years because of the defection of forty days. What will happen to us if, after receiving the grace of Christ who redeemed us with his own blood, we still take pleasure in committing not only slight sins but perhaps even criminal offenses? As I have frequently advised, if a person knows he has committed some serious sin, he should have recourse to the remedies of repentance while there is still time. Indeed, conversion in the present life and penance that is fruitfully performed bring a swift cure to wounds of this kind, for repentance not only heals a past wound but also guards the soul against further injury through sin.

CAESARIUS OF ARLES
(C. 468–542)
SERMONS

14 O God of Heaven's Armies, come back.
Look down from heaven and take notice.
Take care of this vine,
15 the root your right hand planted,
the shoot you made to grow.
16 It is burned and cut down.
May those who did this die because you are displeased
with them.
17 May you give support to the one you have
chosen,
to the one whom you raised up for yourself.
18 Then we will not turn away from you.
Revive us and we will pray to you.
19 O LORD God of Heaven's Armies, restore us.
Smile on us. Then we will be delivered.

PSALM 81

For the music director, according to the gittith *style; by Asaph.*

1 Shout for joy to God, our source of strength!
Shout out to the God of Jacob!
2 Sing a song and play the tambourine,
the pleasant-sounding harp, and the ten-stringed
instrument.
3 Sound the ram's horn on the day of the new moon
and on the day of the full moon when our festival
begins.
4 For observing the festival is a requirement for
Israel;
it is an ordinance given by the God of Jacob.
5 He decreed it as a regulation in Joseph,
when he attacked the land of Egypt.
I heard a voice I did not recognize.
6 It said: "I removed the burden from his shoulder;
his hands were released from holding the basket.
7 In your distress you called out and I rescued you.
I answered you from a dark thundercloud.
I tested you at the waters of Meribah. *Selah*
8 I said, 'Listen, my people!
I will warn you.
O Israel, if only you would obey me!
9 There must be no other god among you.
You must not worship a foreign god.
10 I am the LORD, your God,
the one who brought you out of the land of Egypt.
Open your mouth wide and I will fill it.'
11 But my people did not obey me;
Israel did not submit to me.
12 I gave them over to their stubborn desires;
they did what seemed right to them.
13 If only my people would obey me!
If only Israel would keep my commands!
14 Then I would quickly subdue their enemies,
and attack their adversaries."
15 (May those who hate the LORD cower in fear before
him.
May they be permanently humiliated.)
16 "I would feed Israel the best wheat,
and would satisfy your appetite with honey from the
rocky cliffs."

81:1–16 "Sound the ram's horn on the day of the new moon, and on the day of the full moon when our festival begins." We must also consider that we are commanded through the instruments of the musical discipline both to play the lyre for the Lord and to observe the day of solemnity so that every action of ours may be directed to the Lord and offered to his ears in most pleasant music, just as musical instruments are directed toward a sweet-sounding melody and coalesce smoothly into one harmony.

CASSIODORUS (C. 485–C. 585)
EXPLANATION OF THE PSALMS

PSALM 82

A psalm of Asaph.

1 God stands in the assembly of El;
in the midst of the gods he renders judgment.
2 He says, "How long will you make unjust legal decisions
and show favoritism to the wicked? *Selah*
3 Defend the cause of the poor and the fatherless.
Vindicate the oppressed and suffering.
4 Rescue the poor and needy.
Deliver them from the power of the wicked.
5 They neither know nor understand.
They stumble around in the dark,
while all the foundations of the earth crumble.
6 I thought, 'You are gods;
all of you are sons of the Most High.'
7 Yet you will die like mortals;
you will fall like all the other rulers."
8 Rise up, O God, and execute judgment on the earth!
For you own all the nations.

82:8 Often were the righteous given into the hands of the wicked, not that the latter might be honored but that the former might be tested; and though the wicked come, as it is written, to an awful death, nevertheless for the present the godly are a laughingstock while the goodness of God and the great treasuries of what is in store for each of them hereafter are concealed. Then indeed word and deed and thought will be weighed in the just balances of God as he arises to judge the earth, gathering together counsel and works and revealing what he had kept sealed up.

GREGORY OF NAZIANZUS
(C. 329–390)
ORATIONS

PSALM 83

A song, a psalm of Asaph.

1 O God, do not be silent.
Do not ignore us. Do not be inactive, O God.
2 For look, your enemies are making a commotion;
those who hate you are hostile.
3 They carefully plot against your people,
and make plans to harm the ones you cherish.
4 They say, "Come on, let's annihilate them so they are no longer a nation.
Then the name of Israel will be remembered no more."
5 Yes, they devise a unified strategy;
they form an alliance against you.
6 It includes the tents of Edom and the Ishmaelites,
Moab and the Hagrites,
7 Gebal, Ammon, and Amalek,
Philistia, and the inhabitants of Tyre.
8 Even Assyria has allied with them,
lending its strength to the descendants of Lot. *Selah*
9 Do to them as you did to Midian—
as you did to Sisera and Jabin at the Kishon River.
10 They were destroyed at Endor;
their corpses were like manure on the ground.
11 Make their nobles like Oreb and Zeeb,
and all their rulers like Zebah and Zalmunna,
12 who said, "Let's take over the pastures of God."
13 O my God, make them like dead thistles,
like dead weeds blown away by the wind.
14 Like the fire that burns down the forest,
or the flames that consume the mountainsides,
15 chase them with your gale winds
and terrify them with your windstorm.
16 Cover their faces with shame,
so they might seek you, O LORD.
17 May they be humiliated and continually terrified.
May they die in shame.
18 Then they will know that you alone are the LORD,
the Most High over all the earth.

83:13–18 When present felicity accompanies the life of a sinner, since whereby he is shown to be exalted, thereby it is brought about that he should cease to be. Hence again it is written, "O my God, make them like dead thistles." But to us the things that are behind are the goods of the present world, which we leave behind us, but the things that are before are those that are eternal and permanent, to which we are called. The sinner therefore, when he is advanced in the present life, is made to be as a thistle since, while falling in the things that are before, he is lifted up in the things that are behind. For when he enjoys in this life the glory that he must leave behind, he falls from that which comes after this life.

GREGORY THE GREAT
(C. 540–604)
LETTERS

PSALM 84

For the music director, according to the gittith *style; written by the Korahites, a psalm.*

1 How lovely is the place where you live,
O LORD of Heaven's Armies!
2 I desperately want to be
in the courts of the LORD's temple.
My heart and my entire being shout for joy
to the living God.
3 Even the birds find a home there,
and the swallow builds a nest
where she can protect her young
near your altars, O LORD of Heaven's Armies,
my King and my God.
4 How blessed are those who live in your temple
and praise you continually. *Selah*
5 How blessed are those who find their strength in you
and long to travel the roads that lead to your temple.
6 As they pass through the Baca Valley,
he provides a spring for them.
The rain even covers it with pools of water.
7 They are sustained as they travel along;
each one appears before God in Zion.
8 O LORD God of Heaven's Armies,
hear my prayer.
Listen, O God of Jacob. *Selah*
9 O God, take notice of our shield.
Show concern for your chosen king.
10 Certainly spending just one day in your temple courts is better
than spending a thousand elsewhere.
I would rather stand at the entrance to the temple of my God
than live in the tents of the wicked.
11 For the LORD God is our sovereign protector.
The LORD bestows favor and honor;
he withholds no good thing from those who have integrity.
12 O LORD of Heaven's Armies,
how blessed are those who trust in you.

84:1–12 "They are sustained as they travel along." Or "They go from strength to strength" (KJV). Usually if we are walking we go from strength to weakness; we start fresh and in good order for our journey, but by and by the road is rough, and the sun is hot, we sit down by the wayside, and then again painfully pursue our weary way. But the Christian pilgrim, having obtained fresh supplies of grace, is as vigorous after years of toilsome travel and struggle as when he first set out. He may not be quite so elated and buoyant, or perhaps quite so hot and hasty in his zeal as he once was, but he is much stronger in all that constitutes real power and travels, if more slowly, far more surely. Fretful spirits sit down and trouble themselves about the future. "Alas!" say they, "we go from affliction to affliction." Very true, O you of little faith, but then you go from strength to strength also. You will never find a bundle of affliction that has not bound up in the midst of it sufficient grace.

CHARLES SPURGEON
(1834–1892)
MORNING AND EVENING

PSALM 85

For the music director, written by the Korahites, a psalm.

1 O LORD, you showed favor to your land;
you restored the well-being of Jacob.
2 You pardoned the wrongdoing of your people;
you forgave all their sin. *Selah*
3 You withdrew all your fury;
you turned back from your raging anger.
4 Restore us, O God our deliverer.
Do not be displeased with us.
5 Will you stay mad at us forever?
Will you remain angry throughout future generations?
6 Will you not revive us once more?
Then your people will rejoice in you.
7 O LORD, show us your loyal love.
Bestow on us your deliverance.
8 I will listen to what God the LORD says.
For he will make peace with his people, his faithful followers.

85:8–13 We were wolves. "All of us . . . were by nature children of wrath even as the rest" (Eph 2:3). But the sheep died and turned us into sheep. "Look, the Lamb of God who takes away the sin," not of this person or that, but "of the world" (John 1:29). So then let us claim no credit for anything we are, provided it is by faith in him we are whatever we are—let us claim no credit for ourselves, or we may lose what we have received. But for whatever we have received let us give him the glory, him the honor, and may he water the seeds he has sown. What would our land have if he had not sown anything? He too sends the rain. He does not abandon what he has sown. "The LORD will bestow his good blessings, and our land will yield its crops."

AUGUSTINE **(354–430)**
SERMONS

86:1–17 The Word is our educator who heals the unnatural passions of our soul with his counsel. The art of healing, strictly speaking, is the relief of the ills of the body, an art learned through human wisdom. Yet the only true divine healer of human sickness, the holy comforter of the soul when it is ill, is the Word of the Father. Scripture says, "Protect me . . . You are my God; deliver your servant who trusts in you. Have mercy on me, O LORD, for I cry out to you all day long." In the words of Democritus, "The healer, by his art, cures the body of its diseases, but it is wisdom that rids the spirit of its ills." The good educator of little ones, however, Wisdom, the Word of the Father who created human beings, concerns himself with the whole creation, as the physician of the whole person heals both body and soul.

CLEMENT OF ALEXANDRIA
(C. 150–C. 215)
CHRIST THE EDUCATOR

Yet they must not return to their foolish ways.
9 Certainly his loyal followers will soon experience his deliverance;
then his splendor will again appear in our land.
10 Loyal love and faithfulness meet;
deliverance and peace greet each other with a kiss.
11 Faithfulness grows from the ground,
and deliverance looks down from the sky.
12 Yes, the LORD will bestow his good blessings,
and our land will yield its crops.
13 Deliverance goes before him,
and prepares a pathway for him.

PSALM 86

A prayer of David.

1 Listen, O LORD. Answer me.
For I am oppressed and needy.
2 Protect me, for I am loyal.
You are my God; deliver your servant who trusts in you.
3 Have mercy on me, O Lord,
for I cry out to you all day long.
4 Make your servant glad,
for to you, O Lord, I pray.
5 Certainly, O Lord, you are kind and forgiving,
and show great faithfulness to all who cry out to you.
6 O LORD, hear my prayer.
Pay attention to my plea for mercy.
7 In my time of trouble I cry out to you,
for you will answer me.
8 None can compare to you among the gods, O Lord.
Your exploits are incomparable.
9 All the nations, whom you created,
will come and worship you, O Lord.
They will honor your name.
10 For you are great and do amazing things.
You alone are God.
11 O LORD, teach me how you want me to live.
Then I will obey your commands.
Make me wholeheartedly committed to you.
12 O Lord, my God, I will give you thanks with my whole heart.
I will honor your name continually.
13 For you will extend your great loyal love to me
and will deliver my life from the depths of Sheol.
14 O God, arrogant men attack me;
a gang of ruthless men, who do not respect you, seek my life.
15 But you, O Lord, are a compassionate and merciful God.
You are patient and demonstrate great loyal love and faithfulness.
16 Turn toward me and have mercy on me.
Give your servant your strength.
Deliver this son of your female servant.
17 Show me evidence of your favor.
Then those who hate me will see it and be ashamed,
for you, O LORD, will help me and comfort me.

PSALM 87

Written by the Korahites; a psalm, a song.

1 The LORD's city is in the holy hills.
2 The LORD loves the gates of Zion
more than all the dwelling places of Jacob.
3 People say wonderful things about you,
O city of God. *Selah*
4 I mention Rahab and Babylon to my followers.
Here are Philistia and Tyre, along with Ethiopia.
It is said of them, "This one was born there."
5 But it is said of Zion's residents,
"Each one of these was born in her,
and the Most High makes her secure."
6 The LORD writes in the census book of the nations,
"This one was born there." *Selah*
7 As for the singers, as well as the pipers—
all of them sing within your walls.

PSALM 88

A song, a psalm written by the Korahites, for the music director, according to the machalath-leannoth *style; a well-written song by Heman the Ezrahite.*

1 O LORD God who delivers me,
by day I cry out
and at night I pray before you.
2 Listen to my prayer.
Pay attention to my cry for help.
3 For my life is filled with troubles,
and I am ready to enter Sheol.
4 They treat me like those who descend into the grave.
I am like a helpless man,
5 adrift among the dead,
like corpses lying in the grave
whom you remember no more
and who are cut off from your power.
6 You place me in the lowest regions of the Pit,
in the dark places, in the watery depths.
7 Your anger bears down on me,
and you overwhelm me with all your waves. *Selah*
8 You cause those who know me to keep their distance;
you make me an appalling sight to them.
I am trapped and cannot get free.
9 My eyes grow weak because of oppression.
I call out to you, O LORD, all day long;
I spread out my hands in prayer to you.
10 Do you accomplish amazing things for the dead?
Do the departed spirits rise up and give you thanks? *Selah*
11 Is your loyal love proclaimed in the grave,
or your faithfulness in the place of the dead?
12 Are your amazing deeds experienced in the dark region,
or your deliverance in the land of oblivion?
13 As for me, I cry out to you, O LORD;
in the morning my prayer confronts you.
14 O LORD, why do you reject me,
and pay no attention to me?
15 I am oppressed and have been on the verge of death
since my youth.

87:1–7 Pass now to the others who were saved by repentance. Perhaps someone will say, "I have committed fornication and adultery. I have defiled my body with every excess. Can there be salvation for me?" Fix your eyes on Rahab, and look for salvation for yourself too. For observe how she was saved. She said only this: "For the LORD your God is God in heaven above and on earth below!" (Josh 2:11). If you want scriptural testimony of her salvation, you have it recorded in the Psalms: "I mention Rahab and Babylon to my followers." O the great lovingkindness of God, which is mindful of sinners in scripture. He did not say merely, "I will mention Rahab and Babylon," but added "to my followers." The salvation procured by repentance is open to everyone.

CYRIL OF JERUSALEM
(C. 313–386)
CATECHETICAL LECTURES

88:1–18 Greatly may good people be afflicted, and such dismal thoughts may they have about their afflictions, and such dark conclusions may they make about their end, through the power of melancholy and the weakness of faith. The psalmist complained most of God's displeasure. Even the children of God's love may sometimes think themselves children of wrath, and no outward trouble can be so hard upon them as that. Probably the psalmist described his own case, yet he leads to Christ. Thus are we called to look unto Jesus, wounded and bruised for our iniquities. The wrath of God poured the greatest bitterness into his cup. This weighed him down into darkness and the deep. No one could share in the sufferings by which other people were to be redeemed. All forsook him and fled. Oftentimes, blessed Jesus, do we forsake you; but do not forsake us, O take not your Holy Spirit from us.

MATTHEW HENRY **(1662–1714)**
COMMENTARY ON THE WHOLE BIBLE

I have been subjected to your horrors and am numb with pain.
16 Your anger overwhelms me;
your terrors destroy me.
17 They surround me like water all day long;
they join forces and encircle me.
18 You cause my friends and neighbors to keep their distance;
those who know me leave me alone in the darkness.

PSALM 89

A well-written song by Ethan the Ezrahite.

1 I will sing continually about the LORD's faithful deeds;
to future generations I will proclaim your faithfulness.
2 For I say, "Loyal love is permanently established;
in the skies you set up your faithfulness."
3 The LORD said,
"I have made a covenant with my chosen one;
I have made a promise on oath to David, my servant:
4 'I will give you an eternal dynasty
and establish your throne throughout future generations.'" *Selah*
5 O LORD, the heavens praise your amazing deeds,
as well as your faithfulness in the angelic assembly.
6 For who in the skies can compare to the LORD?
Who is like the LORD among the heavenly beings,
7 a God who is honored in the great angelic assembly,
and more awesome than all who surround him?
8 O LORD God of Heaven's Armies!
Who is strong like you, O LORD?
Your faithfulness surrounds you.
9 You rule over the proud sea.
When its waves surge, you calm them.
10 You crushed the Proud One and killed it;
with your strong arm you scattered your enemies.
11 The heavens belong to you, as does the earth.
You made the world and all it contains.
12 You created the north and the south.
Tabor and Hermon rejoice in your name.
13 Your arm is powerful,
your hand strong,
your right hand victorious.
14 Equity and justice are the foundation of your throne.
Loyal love and faithfulness characterize your rule.
15 How blessed are the people who worship you!
O LORD, they experience your favor.
16 They rejoice in your name all day long,
and are vindicated by your justice.
17 For you give them splendor and strength.
By your favor we are victorious.
18 For our shield belongs to the LORD,
our king to the Holy One of Israel.
19 Then you spoke through a vision to your faithful followers and said:
"I have placed a young hero over a warrior;
I have raised up a young man from the people.
20 I have discovered David, my servant.
With my holy oil I have anointed him as king.

89:1–52 We suffer these things because of our fault and of our deserving, as the divine judgment has forewarned us, saying, "If they break my rules and do not keep my commandments, I will punish their rebellion by beating them with a club, their sin by inflicting them with bruises." We therefore who neither please God with our good deeds nor satisfy him for our sins feel the rods and the lashes. Let us ask from the depth of our heart and with our whole mind the mercy of God because he himself adds this, saying, "But I will not remove my loyal love from him." Let us ask and we receive; and if there is delay and tardiness in our receiving because we have offended gravely, let us knock because to him who also knocks it is opened.

CYPRIAN OF CARTHAGE
(C. 210–258)
LETTERS

21 My hand will support him,
and my arm will strengthen him.
22 No enemy will be able to exact tribute from him;
a violent oppressor will not be able to humiliate him.
23 I will crush his enemies before him;
I will strike down those who hate him.
24 He will experience my faithfulness and loyal love,
and by my name he will win victories.
25 I will place his hand over the sea,
his right hand over the rivers.
26 He will call out to me,
'You are my father, my God, and the protector who delivers me.'
27 I will appoint him to be my firstborn son,
the most exalted of the earth's kings.
28 I will always extend my loyal love to him,
and my covenant with him is secure.
29 I will give him an eternal dynasty
and make his throne as enduring as the skies above.
30 If his sons reject my law
and disobey my regulations,
31 if they break my rules
and do not keep my commandments,
32 I will punish their rebellion by beating them with a club,
their sin by inflicting them with bruises.
33 But I will not remove my loyal love from him
nor be unfaithful to my promise.
34 I will not break my covenant
or go back on what I promised.
35 Once and for all I have vowed by my own holiness,
I will never deceive David.
36 His dynasty will last forever.
His throne will endure before me, like the sun;
37 it will remain stable, like the moon.
His throne will endure like the skies." *Selah*
38 But you have spurned and rejected him;
you are angry with your chosen king.
39 You have repudiated your covenant with your servant;
you have thrown his crown to the ground.
40 You have broken down all his walls;
you have made his strongholds a heap of ruins.
41 All who pass by have robbed him;
he has become an object of disdain to his neighbors.
42 You have allowed his adversaries to be victorious
and all his enemies to rejoice.
43 You turn back his sword from the adversary
and have not sustained him in battle.
44 You have brought to an end his splendor
and have knocked his throne to the ground.
45 You have cut short his youth
and have covered him with shame. *Selah*
46 How long, O LORD, will this last?
Will you remain hidden forever?
Will your anger continue to burn like fire?
47 Take note of my brief lifespan.
Why do you make all people so mortal?
48 No man can live on without experiencing death
or deliver his life from the power of Sheol. *Selah*

49 Where are your earlier faithful deeds, O Lord,
the ones performed in accordance with your reliable
oath to David?
50 Take note, O Lord, of the way your servants are taunted
and of how I must bear so many insults from people.
51 Your enemies, O LORD, hurl insults;
they insult your chosen king as they dog his footsteps.
52 The LORD deserves praise forevermore!
We agree! We agree!

BOOK 4 (PSALMS 90–106)

PSALM 90

A prayer of Moses, the man of God.

1 O Lord, you have been our protector through all
generations.
2 Even before the mountains came into existence,
or you brought the world into being,
you were the eternal God.
3 You make mankind return to the dust,
and say, "Return, O people."
4 Yes, in your eyes a thousand years
are like yesterday that quickly passes,
or like one of the divisions of the nighttime.
5 You bring their lives to an end and they "fall asleep."
In the morning they are like the grass that
sprouts up;
6 In the morning it glistens and sprouts up;
at evening time it withers and dries up.
7 Yes, we are consumed by your anger;
we are terrified by your wrath.
8 You are aware of our sins;
you even know about our hidden sins.
9 Yes, throughout all our days we experience your raging
fury;
the years of our lives pass quickly, like a sigh.
10 The days of our lives add up to 70 years,
or 80, if one is especially strong.
But even one's best years are marred by trouble and
oppression.
Yes, they pass quickly and we fly away.
11 Who can really fathom the intensity of your anger?
Your raging fury causes people to fear you.
12 So teach us to consider our mortality,
so that we might live wisely.
13 Turn back toward us, O LORD.
How long must this suffering last?
Have pity on your servants.
14 Satisfy us in the morning with your loyal love.
Then we will shout for joy and be happy all our days.
15 Make us happy in proportion to the days you have
afflicted us,
in proportion to the years we have experienced
trouble.
16 May your servants see your work.
May their sons see your majesty.
17 May our Sovereign God extend his favor to us.
Make our endeavors successful.
Yes, make them successful.

90:10 Sin at first brought death into the world, so sin did afterward shorten the age of human beings before the flood: The patriarchs lived almost to a thousand years. But the sin that brought the flood took away one half of people's age. At the confusion of Babylon it was shortened again in the same manner. After the death of the patriarchs, when the true worship of God was very much declined in their families and the rest of humankind was overrun with superstition and idolatry, the life span was shortened again. And at the frequent murmurings and provokings of God in the wilderness, a third part more or thereabouts were cut off from the age of human beings. And though the sins of humankind have been very great and universal since that time, yet the age of a person's life has not been shortened anymore because a shorter space would hardly have been sufficient for the finding out and improvement of arts and sciences, as well as for other reasons.

JONATHAN EDWARDS
(1703–1758)
THE COMPLETE WORKS

PSALM 91

1 As for you, the one who lives in the shelter of the
Most High,
and resides in the protective shadow of the Sovereign
One—
2 I say this about the LORD, my shelter and my
stronghold,
my God in whom I trust—
3 he will certainly rescue you from the snare of the
hunter
and from the destructive plague.
4 He will shelter you with his wings;
you will find safety under his wings.
His faithfulness is like a shield or a protective wall.
5 You need not fear the terrors of the night,
the arrow that flies by day,
6 the plague that stalks in the darkness,
or the disease that ravages at noon.
7 Though a thousand may fall beside you,
and a multitude on your right side,
it will not reach you.
8 Certainly you will see it with your very own eyes—
you will see the wicked paid back.
9 For you have taken refuge in the LORD,
my shelter, the Most High.
10 No harm will overtake you;
no illness will come near your home.
11 For he will order his angels
to protect you in all you do.
12 They will lift you up in their hands,
so you will not slip and fall on a stone.
13 You will subdue a lion and a snake;
you will trample underfoot a young lion and a serpent.
14 The LORD says,
"Because he is devoted to me, I will deliver him;
I will protect him because he is loyal to me.
15 When he calls out to me, I will answer him.
I will be with him when he is in trouble;
I will rescue him and bring him honor.
16 I will satisfy him with long life
and will let him see my salvation."

91:1–16 Be the terror what it may, the promise is that the believer will not be afraid. Why should he? God our Father is here and will be here all through the lonely hours; He is an almighty watcher, a sleepless guardian, a faithful friend. Nothing can happen without his direction, for even hell itself is under his control. We who rest in Jesus are saved through rich mercy. If we give way to foolish fear, we will lead others to doubt the reality of godliness. We ought to be afraid of being afraid, lest we should vex the Holy Spirit by foolish distrust. God has not forgotten to be gracious or shut up his tender mercies; it may be night in the soul, but there need be no terror, for the God of love changes not. Children of light are now enabled to prove their adoption by trusting in their heavenly Father as hypocrites cannot do.

CHARLES SPURGEON
(1834–1892)
MORNING AND EVENING

PSALM 92

A psalm; a song for the Sabbath day.

1 It is fitting to thank the LORD,
and to sing praises to your name, O Most High.
2 It is fitting to proclaim your loyal love in the morning
and your faithfulness during the night,
3 to the accompaniment of a ten-stringed instrument
and a lyre,
to the accompaniment of the meditative tone of the harp.
4 For you, O LORD, have made me happy by your work.
I will sing for joy because of what you have done.
5 How great are your works, O LORD!
Your plans are very intricate!
6 The spiritually insensitive do not recognize this;
the fool does not understand this.
7 When the wicked sprout up like grass,
and all the evildoers glisten,

92:1–15 "The godly grow like a palm tree." Now these words make known that the soul acquires height and straightness of stature and sweetness from beautiful deeds. But there is another quality that is found in the palm: a single, white heart that is wholly suitable for work (or useful for being worked). And this must be found in righteous persons, for their heart must be single and simple, and it must be accustomed to look toward God only. Now the heart of the palm tree is also white by reason of that fire that it possesses naturally, and all the service of righteous people is in their heart; and the hollowness and the evenness of the tops of the leaves typify the setting up of sharpness of the soul of the righteous person against those who slander others.

DESERT FATHERS **(C. 270)**

it is so that they may be annihilated.
8 But you, O LORD, reign forever.
9 Indeed, look at your enemies, O LORD.
Indeed, look at how your enemies perish.
All the evildoers are scattered.
10 You exalt my horn like that of a wild ox.
I am covered with fresh oil.
11 I gloat in triumph over those who tried to ambush me;
I hear the defeated cries of the evil foes who attacked
me.
12 The godly grow like a palm tree;
they grow high like a cedar in Lebanon.
13 Planted in the LORD's house,
they grow in the courts of our God.
14 They bear fruit even when they are old;
they are filled with vitality and have many leaves.
15 So they proclaim that the LORD, my Protector,
is just and never unfair.

PSALM 93

1 The LORD reigns.
He is robed in majesty.
The LORD is robed;
he wears strength around his waist.
Indeed, the world is established; it cannot be moved.
2 Your throne has been secure from ancient times;
you have always been king.
3 The waves roar, O LORD,
the waves roar,
the waves roar and crash.
4 Above the sound of the surging water,
and the mighty waves of the sea,
the LORD sits enthroned in majesty.
5 The rules you set down are completely reliable.
Holiness aptly adorns your house, O LORD, forever.

PSALM 94

1 O LORD, the God who avenges!
O God who avenges, reveal your splendor.
2 Rise up, O judge of the earth.
Pay back the proud.
3 O LORD, how long will the wicked,
how long will the wicked celebrate?
4 They spew out threats and speak defiantly;
all the evildoers boast.
5 O LORD, they crush your people;
they oppress the nation that belongs to you.
6 They kill the widow and the resident foreigner,
and they murder the fatherless.
7 Then they say, "The LORD does not see this;
the God of Jacob does not take notice of it."
8 Take notice of this, you ignorant people.
You fools, when will you ever understand?
9 Does the one who makes the human ear not hear?
Does the one who forms the human eye not see?
10 Does the one who disciplines the nations not punish?
He is the one who imparts knowledge to human beings!
11 The LORD knows that peoples' thoughts
are morally bankrupt.

93:1–5 To sit at the right hand of the Father is a mystery belonging to the incarnation. For it does not befit that incorporeal nature without the assumption of flesh; neither is the excellency of a heavenly seat sought for the divine nature but for the human. Thus it is said of him, "Your throne has been secure from ancient times; you have always been king." The seat, then, on which the Lord Jesus was to sit was prepared from everlasting; in his name "every knee will bow—in heaven and on earth and under the earth—and every tongue confess that Jesus Christ is Lord to the glory of God the Father" (Phil 2:10–11).

RUFINUS OF AQUILEIA
(C. 344–411)
A COMMENTARY ON THE APOSTLES' CREED

94:1–23 The one who arranged the contest helps the contestant. God, you see, does not watch you in the ring in the same way as people watch a charioteer; they know how to shout, they do not know how to help. God does not watch you battling in the ring in the same way as the president at the games watches an athlete and prepares a crown of leaves for the winner; he does not know how to give strength to the man struggling in the arena, and he cannot do it anyhow—after all he is a man, not God. And perhaps while he is watching, he endures more weariness sitting there than the other does as he wrestles. God, you see, when he watches his champions helps them when they call on him. I mean, it is the voice of his athlete in the psalm, "If I say, 'My foot is slipping,' your loyal love, O LORD, supports me." So, my brothers and sisters, do not let us be slow about it; let us ask, let us seek, let us knock.

AUGUSTINE **(354–430)**
SERMONS

12 How blessed is the one whom you instruct,
O LORD,
the one whom you teach from your law
13 in order to protect him from times of trouble,
until the wicked are destroyed.
14 Certainly the LORD does not forsake his people;
he does not abandon the nation that belongs
to him.
15 For justice will prevail,
and all the morally upright will be vindicated.
16 Who will rise up to defend me against the wicked?
Who will stand up for me against the evildoers?
17 If the LORD had not helped me,
I would soon have dwelt in the silence of death.
18 If I say, "My foot is slipping,"
your loyal love, O LORD, supports me.
19 When worries threaten to overwhelm me,
your soothing touch makes me happy.
20 Cruel rulers are not your allies,
those who make oppressive laws.
21 They conspire against the blameless
and condemn to death the innocent.
22 But the LORD will protect me,
and my God will shelter me.
23 He will pay them back for their sin.
He will destroy them because of their evil;
the LORD our God will destroy them.

PSALM 95

1 Come, let us sing for joy to the LORD.
Let us shout out praises to our Protector who
delivers us.
2 Let us enter his presence with thanksgiving.
Let us shout out to him in celebration.
3 For the LORD is a great God,
a great king who is superior to all gods.
4 The depths of the earth are in his hand,
and the mountain peaks belong to him.
5 The sea is his, for he made it.
His hands formed the dry land.
6 Come, let us bow down and worship.
Let us kneel before the LORD, our Creator.
7 For he is our God;
we are the people of his pasture,
the sheep he owns.
Today, if only you would obey him.
8 He says, "Do not be stubborn like they were at
Meribah,
like they were that day at Massah in the wilderness,
9 where your ancestors challenged my authority
and tried my patience, even though they had seen my
work.
10 For 40 years I was continually disgusted with that
generation,
and I said, 'These people desire to go astray;
they do not obey my commands.'
11 So I made a vow in my anger,
'They will never enter into the resting place I had set
aside for them.'"

95:1–11 No one should continue a longer time in sin out of hope for the mercy of God since no one wishes to be ill for a longer time in the body because of the hope for future health. Those who decline to give up their vices and promise themselves forgiveness from God are thus frequently visited beforehand by the sudden fury of God, so that they find neither time for conversion nor the blessing of forgiveness. Therefore holy scripture mercifully forewarns each one of us when it says, "Do not delay to turn back to the Lord, and do not postpone it from day to day; for suddenly the wrath of the Lord will come upon you, and at the time of punishment you will perish" (Sir 5:7 NRSV). Blessed David also says, "Today, if only you would obey him. He says, 'Do not be stubborn.'"

FULGENTIUS OF RUSPE
(C. 462–C. 527)
ON THE FORGIVENESS OF SINS

PSALM 96

1 Sing to the LORD a new song.
Sing to the LORD, all the earth.
2 Sing to the LORD. Praise his name.
Announce every day how he delivers.
3 Tell the nations about his splendor.
Tell all the nations about his amazing deeds.
4 For the LORD is great and certainly worthy
of praise;
he is more awesome than all gods.
5 For all the gods of the nations are worthless,
but the LORD made the sky.
6 Majestic splendor emanates from him;
his sanctuary is firmly established and beautiful.
7 Ascribe to the LORD, O families of the nations,
ascribe to the LORD splendor and strength.
8 Ascribe to the LORD the splendor he deserves.
Bring an offering and enter his courts.
9 Worship the LORD in holy attire.
Tremble before him, all the earth.
10 Say among the nations, "The LORD reigns!
The world is established; it cannot be moved.
He judges the nations fairly."
11 Let the sky rejoice, and the earth be happy.
Let the sea and everything in it shout.
12 Let the fields and everything in them celebrate.
Then let the trees of the forest shout with joy
13 before the LORD, for he comes.
For he comes to judge the earth.
He judges the world fairly
and the nations in accordance with his justice.

96:1–13 In Psalm 96 the coming of the Lord to humankind is again foretold, and that a new song, by which is meant the new covenant, will be sung by the whole earth at his coming, not by the Jewish race; and that the good news will no longer be for Israel but for all the nations, since it says that the Lord who is to come will be their King. Who could this be but God the Word who, intending to judge the world in righteousness and the human race in truth, considers all people in the world equally worthy of his call and consequently of the salvation of God?

EUSEBIUS OF CAESAREA
(C. 260–339)
THE PROOF OF THE GOSPEL

PSALM 97

1 The LORD reigns.
Let the earth be happy.
Let the many coastlands rejoice.
2 Dark clouds surround him;
equity and justice are the foundation of his
throne.
3 Fire goes before him;
on every side it burns up his enemies.
4 His lightning bolts light up the world;
the earth sees and trembles.
5 The mountains melt like wax before the LORD,
before the Lord of the whole earth.
6 The sky declares his justice,
and all the nations see his splendor.
7 All who worship idols are ashamed,
those who boast about worthless idols.
All the gods bow down before him.
8 Zion hears and rejoices,
the towns of Judah are happy,
because of your judgments, O LORD.
9 For you, O LORD, are the Most High over the whole
earth;
you are elevated high above all gods.
10 You who love the LORD, hate evil!
He protects the lives of his faithful followers;
he delivers them from the power of the wicked.

97:2–5 Now I return to the principle that defines that all things that have come from nothing shall return at last to nothing. For God would not have made any perishable thing out of what was eternal, that is to say, out of matter; neither out of greater things would he have created inferior ones. To his character it would be more agreeable to produce greater things out of inferior ones, in other words, what is eternal out of what is perishable. This is the promise he makes even to our flesh, and it has been his will to deposit within us this pledge of his own virtue and power in order that we may believe that he has actually awakened the universe out of nothing, as if it had been steeped in death, in the sense, of course, of its previous nonexistence for the purpose of its coming into existence.

TERTULLIAN (155–C. 220)
AGAINST HERMOGENES

11 The godly bask in the light;
the morally upright experience joy.
12 You godly ones, rejoice in the LORD.
Give thanks to his holy name.

PSALM 98

A psalm.

1 Sing to the LORD a new song,
for he performs amazing deeds.
His right hand and his mighty arm
accomplish deliverance.
2 The LORD demonstrates his power to deliver;
in the sight of the nations he reveals his justice.
3 He remains loyal and faithful to the family of Israel.
All the ends of the earth see our God deliver us.
4 Shout out praises to the LORD, all the earth.
Break out in a joyful shout and sing!
5 Sing to the LORD accompanied by a harp,
accompanied by a harp and the sound of music.
6 With trumpets and the blaring of the ram's horn,
shout out praises before the king, the LORD.
7 Let the sea and everything in it shout,
along with the world and those who live in it.
8 Let the rivers clap their hands!
Let the mountains sing in unison
9 before the LORD.
For he comes to judge the earth.
He judges the world fairly,
and the nations in a just manner.

PSALM 99

1 The LORD reigns!
The nations tremble.
He sits enthroned above the cherubim;
the earth shakes.
2 The LORD is elevated in Zion;
he is exalted over all the nations.
3 Let them praise your great and awesome name.
He is holy!
4 The king is strong;
he loves justice.
You ensure that legal decisions will be made
fairly;
you promote justice and equity in Jacob.
5 Praise the LORD our God.
Worship before his footstool.
He is holy!
6 Moses and Aaron were among his priests;
Samuel was one of those who prayed to him.
They prayed to the LORD and he answered them.
7 He spoke to them from a pillar of cloud;
they obeyed his regulations and the ordinance he
gave them.
8 O LORD our God, you answered them.
They found you to be a forgiving God,
but also one who punished their sinful deeds.
9 Praise the LORD our God!
Worship on his holy hill,
for the LORD our God is holy.

98:3 The psalmist very properly observes that God in redeeming the world remembered his truth, which he had given to his people. This implies that he was influenced by no other motive than that of faithfully performing what he had himself promised. The more clearly to show that the promise was not grounded at all on the merit or righteousness of humankind, he mentions the goodness of God first, and afterward his faithfulness that stood connected with it. The cause, in short, was not to be found out of God himself, but in his mere good pleasure, which had been testified long before to Abraham and his posterity. When it is added, "All the ends of the earth see our God deliver us," this is not merely commendatory of the greatness of the salvation, meaning that it should be so illustrious that the report of it would reach the ends of the earth, but it signifies that the nations formerly immersed in delusions and superstitions would participate in it.

JOHN CALVIN **(1509–1564)**
COMPLETE COMMENTARY ON THE BIBLE

99:1–9 Let there be in everyone faith and ripeness of character, not one without the other, but let both meet together in one with good works and deeds. For this reason the writer of Hebrews wishes that we should be imitators of those who, as he said, "through faith and perseverance" (Heb 6:12) possess the promises made to Abraham, who by patience was found worthy to receive and to possess the grace of the blessing promised to him. David the prophet warns us that we should be imitators of holy Aaron and has set him amongst the saints of God to be imitated by us, saying, "Moses and Aaron were among his priests; Samuel was one of those who prayed to him."

AMBROSE **(C. 339–C. 397)**
LETTERS

GREGORY THE GREAT:

THE EVANGELIST OF EUROPE

c. 540–604

Gregory is one of only three popes to have received "the Great" designation (the others being Leo the Great and Nicholas the Great)—and for good reason. He was the most important church and political leader in the early Middle Ages, and during his tenure he reshaped and revitalized virtually every aspect of the church's life and practice.

Born in a noble Roman family around 540, Gregory lost his father at a young age. He became a monk in early adulthood, having given much of his considerable inheritance to the poor and using the rest to found monasteries. Gregory attacked his duties with tremendous energy; he restored discipline where the church had slid into corruption, protected Jewish people from persecution, and restored the church's focus on caring for the poor. He also displayed a remarkable knack for handling political and military threats, making peace with several groups of barbarian invaders—and in many cases, winning them over to Christ. Perhaps his most lasting legacy was his evangelization of the Germanic people of Europe.

In his historical accounts of English Christianity, Bede tells us that as a young boy, Gregory witnessed the slave trade show in Rome. "How sad that handsome folk are still in the grasp of the author of darkness," Gregory remarked of the young British boys, "and that faces of such beauty conceal minds ignorant of God's grace!" He believed that "it is right that they should become fellow-heirs with the angels in heaven." This early pity later compelled him to launch missions throughout modern-day France and Germany, which emphasized care and patience in a gradual process of evangelization. In his own words: "It is undoubtedly impossible to cut away everything at once from hard hearts, since one who strives to ascend to the highest place must needs rise by steps or paces, and not by leaps."

Gregory wanted the light of Christ to pierce the desolate land, so he dispatched a young monk named Augustine (not to be confused with Augustine of Hippo) to lead a group of missionaries into Western Europe. The journey was rough, but Gregory encouraged them to press on "with all possible earnestness and zeal . . . being assured that much labor is followed by an eternal reward." After finally arriving, they made a connection with King Ethelbert, ruler of the Kent kingdom. Ethelbert was intrigued by their message and invited them to stay and preach the gospel. Eventually he converted to the faith, which led to other kings' believing and the gospel spreading throughout Britain.

Pope Gregory's designation for himself was not "the Great," but "the Servant of Servants of God." He is also rightly known as the evangelist of Europe, with Venerable Bede saying that the man "transformed our still idolatrous nation into a church of Christ . . . While other popes devoted themselves to building churches and enriching them with costly ornaments, Gregory's sole concern was to save souls."

IMPORTANT WORKS

ON PASTORAL CARE

LIFE OF OUR MOST HOLY FATHER ST. BENEDICT

PSALM 100

A thanksgiving psalm.

1 Shout out praises to the LORD, all the earth!
2 Worship the LORD with joy.
Enter his presence with joyful singing.
3 Acknowledge that the LORD is God.
He made us and we belong to him,
we are his people, the sheep of his pasture.
4 Enter his gates with thanksgiving
and his courts with praise.
Give him thanks.
Praise his name.
5 For the LORD is good.
His loyal love endures,
and he is faithful through all generations.

PSALM 101

A psalm of David.

1 I will sing about loyalty and justice.
To you, O LORD, I will sing praises.
2 I will walk in the way of integrity.
When will you come to me?
I will conduct my business with integrity in the midst of my palace.
3 I will not even consider doing what is dishonest.
I hate doing evil;
I will have no part of it.
4 I will have nothing to do with a perverse person;
I will not permit evil.
5 I will destroy anyone who slanders his neighbor in secret.
I will not tolerate anyone who has a haughty demeanor and an arrogant attitude.
6 I will favor the honest people of the land
and allow them to live with me.
Those who walk in the way of integrity will attend me.
7 Deceitful people will not live in my palace.
Liars will not be welcome in my presence.
8 Each morning I will destroy all the wicked people in the land
and remove all evildoers from the city of the LORD.

PSALM 102

The prayer of an oppressed man, as he grows faint and pours out his lament before the LORD.

1 O LORD, hear my prayer.
Pay attention to my cry for help.
2 Do not ignore me in my time of trouble.
Listen to me.
When I call out to you, quickly answer me.
3 For my days go up in smoke,
and my bones are charred as in a fireplace.
4 My heart is parched and withered like grass,
for I am unable to eat food.
5 Because of the anxiety that makes me groan,
my bones protrude from my skin.
6 I am like an owl in the wilderness;
I am like a screech owl among the ruins.
7 I stay awake;

100:1–5 Delight in divine service is a token of acceptance. Those who serve God with a sad countenance because they do what is unpleasant to them are not serving him at all; they bring the form of homage, but the life is absent. Our God requires no slaves to grace his throne; he is the Lord of the empire of love and would have his servants dressed in the livery of joy. The Lord looks at the heart, and if he sees that we serve him from force and not because we love him, he will reject our offering. Service coupled with cheerfulness is heart-service and therefore true. Reader, do you serve the Lord with gladness? Let us show to the people of the world, who think our religion to be slavery, that it is to us a delight and a joy! Let our gladness proclaim that we serve a good Master.

CHARLES SPURGEON
(1834–1892)
MORNING AND EVENING

101:1–8 The power of the Lord always shows either mercy or judgment. But neither mercy is found without his judgment nor his judgment found without his mercy, for both of them join in mutual alliance. Nor does any deed of his appear that does not seem to be filled with all virtues. For just as he said "loyalty and justice" here, in another place he says "deliverance and peace" (Ps 85:10) instead of these two names, and again, "loyal love and faithfulness" (Ps. 85:10) so that everywhere he might show that God is affectionate and just. You see then that these two are linked together to each other and shine once they have been set in their places. Therefore let sinners, who wickedly despair of their salvation, listen to the merciful Lord. In these two words all the works of the Lord and the edification of the entire church have manifestly been told.

CASSIODORUS **(C. 485–C. 585)**
EXPLANATION OF THE PSALMS

102:1–28 "I am unable to eat food. Because of the anxiety that makes me groan, my bones protrude from my skin." The word of God is our soul's bread: Just as ordinary bread nourishes the body, so the word from heaven nourishes the soul's substance. In passing on the prayer, Christ said as much to the apostles: "Give us each day our daily bread" (Luke 11:3). So whoever forgets to eat it, that is, to be active (action, after all, constituting the eating of the spiritual bread), this one's heart is stricken and dried up like hay. As the heart too when suffering from a dearth of the Word is then stricken and dries up, the flower of virtue no longer has the strength to bloom.

THEODORET OF CYR
(C. 393–C. 458)
COMMENTARY ON THE PSALMS

I am like a solitary bird on a roof.
8 All day long my enemies taunt me;
those who mock me use my name in their curses.
9 For I eat ashes as if they were bread,
and mix my drink with my tears,
10 because of your anger and raging fury.
Indeed, you pick me up and throw me away.
11 My days are coming to an end,
and I am withered like grass.
12 But you, O LORD, rule forever,
and your reputation endures.
13 You will rise up and have compassion on Zion.
For it is time to have mercy on her,
for the appointed time has come.
14 Indeed, your servants take delight in her stones
and feel compassion for the dust of her ruins.
15 The nations will respect the reputation of the LORD,
and all the kings of the earth will respect his splendor
16 when the LORD rebuilds Zion
and reveals his splendor,
17 when he responds to the prayer of the destitute
and does not reject their request.
18 The account of his intervention will be recorded for
future generations;
people yet to be born will praise the LORD.
19 For he will look down from his sanctuary above;
from heaven the LORD will look toward earth,
20 in order to hear the painful cries of the prisoners
and to set free those condemned to die,
21 so they may proclaim the name of the LORD in Zion
and praise him in Jerusalem
22 when the nations gather together,
and the kingdoms pay tribute to the LORD.
23 He has taken away my strength in the middle of life;
he has cut short my days.
24 I say, "O my God, please do not take me away in the
middle of my life.
You endure through all generations.
25 In earlier times you established the earth;
the skies are your handiwork.
26 They will perish,
but you will endure.
They will wear out like a garment;
like clothes you will remove them and they will
disappear.
27 But you remain;
your years do not come to an end.
28 The children of your servants will settle down here,
and their descendants will live securely in your
presence."

PSALM 103

By David.

1 Praise the LORD, O my soul.
With all that is within me, praise his holy name.
2 Praise the LORD, O my soul.
Do not forget all his kind deeds.
3 He is the one who forgives all your sins,
who heals all your diseases,

4 who delivers your life from the Pit,
who crowns you with his loyal love and compassion,
5 who satisfies your life with good things,
so your youth is renewed like an eagle's.
6 The LORD does what is fair,
and executes justice for all the oppressed.
7 The LORD revealed his faithful acts to Moses,
his deeds to the Israelites.
8 The LORD is compassionate and merciful;
he is patient and demonstrates great loyal love.
9 He does not always accuse
and does not stay angry.
10 He does not deal with us as our sins deserve;
he does not repay us as our misdeeds deserve.
11 For as the skies are high above the earth,
so his loyal love towers over his faithful followers.
12 As far as the eastern horizon is from the west,
so he removes the guilt of our rebellious actions from us.
13 As a father has compassion on his children,
so the LORD has compassion on his faithful followers.
14 For he knows what we are made of;
he realizes we are made of clay.
15 A person's life is like grass.
Like a flower in the field it flourishes,
16 but when the hot wind blows, it disappears,
and one can no longer even spot the place where it once grew.
17 But the LORD continually shows loyal love to his faithful followers
and is faithful to their descendants,
18 to those who keep his covenant,
who are careful to obey his commands.
19 The LORD has established his throne in heaven;
his kingdom extends over everything.
20 Praise the LORD, you angels of his,
you powerful warriors who carry out his decrees
and obey his orders.
21 Praise the LORD, all you warriors of his,
you servants of his who carry out his desires.
22 Praise the LORD, all that he has made,
in all the regions of his kingdom.
Praise the LORD, O my soul.

PSALM 104

1 Praise the LORD, O my soul!
O LORD my God, you are magnificent.
You are robed in splendor and majesty.
2 He covers himself with light as if it were a garment.
He stretches out the skies like a tent curtain
3 and lays the beams of the upper rooms of his palace on the rain clouds.
He makes the clouds his chariot
and travels on the wings of the wind.
4 He makes the winds his messengers
and the flaming fire his attendant.
5 He established the earth on its foundations;
it will never be moved.
6 The watery deep covered it like a garment;
the waters reached above the mountains.

103:6–14 Remember, Lord, that you have made me weak. Remember that "we are made of clay." How will I be able to stand unless you direct your care always so as to strengthen this clay, so that my strength may proceed from your countenance? "When you ignore them, they panic" (Ps 104:29). You have nothing to behold in me but the contagion of sins. It is no use either to be abandoned or to be examined, for even while we are being looked on, we are committing offenses. Still, we can hold that God does not reject those whom he looks on because he makes clean those whom he beholds. A fire blazes before him that burns away sin.

AMBROSE **(C. 339–C. 397)**
THE PRAYER OF JOB AND DAVID

104:1–23 Let the pagan philosophers then say distinctly that the great diversity among the products of the earth is not the work of Providence but that a certain fortuitous concurrence of atoms gave birth to qualities so diverse. We Christians, however, who are devoted to the worship of the only God who created these things, feel grateful for them to him who made them because not only for us but also on our account for the animals that are subject to us he has prepared such a home, seeing "he provides grass for the cattle, and crops for people to cultivate, so they can produce food from the ground, as well as wine that makes people glad, and olive oil to make their faces shine, as well as bread that sustains them."

ORIGEN **(C. 185–C. 253)**
CONTRA CELSUM

7 Your shout made the waters retreat;
at the sound of your thunderous voice they hurried off—
8 as the mountains rose up
and the valleys went down—
to the place you appointed for them.
9 You set up a boundary for them that they could not
cross,
so that they would not cover the earth again.
10 He turns springs into streams;
they flow between the mountains.
11 They provide water for all the animals in the field;
the wild donkeys quench their thirst.
12 The birds of the sky live beside them;
they chirp among the bushes.
13 He waters the mountains from the upper rooms of his
palace;
the earth is full of the fruit you cause to grow.
14 He provides grass for the cattle
and crops for people to cultivate,
so they can produce food from the ground
15 as well as wine that makes people glad,
and olive oil to make their faces shine
as well as bread that sustains them.
16 The trees of the LORD receive all the rain they need,
the cedars of Lebanon that he planted,
17 where the birds make nests
near the evergreens in which the herons live.
18 The wild goats live in the high mountains;
the rock badgers find safety in the cliffs.
19 He made the moon to mark the months,
and the sun sets according to a regular schedule.
20 You make it dark and night comes,
during which all the beasts of the forest prowl around.
21 The lions roar for prey,
seeking their food from God.
22 When the sun rises, they withdraw
and sleep in their dens.
23 People then go out to do their work,
and they labor until evening.
24 How many living things you have made, O LORD!
You have exhibited great skill in making all of them;
the earth is full of the living things you have made.
25 Over here is the deep, wide sea,
which teems with innumerable swimming creatures,
living things both small and large.
26 The ships travel there,
and over here swims the whale you made to play in it.
27 All your creatures wait for you
to provide them with food on a regular basis.
28 You give food to them and they receive it;
you open your hand and they are filled with food.
29 When you ignore them, they panic.
When you take away their life's breath,
they die and return to dust.
30 When you send your life-giving breath, they are created,
and you replenish the surface of the ground.
31 May the splendor of the LORD endure.
May the LORD find pleasure in the living things he has
made.

32 He looks down on the earth and it shakes;
he touches the mountains and they start to smolder.
33 I will sing to the LORD as long as I live;
I will sing praise to my God as long as I exist.
34 May my thoughts be pleasing to him.
I will rejoice in the LORD.
35 May sinners disappear from the earth,
and the wicked vanish.
Praise the LORD, O my soul.
Praise the LORD.

PSALM 105

1 Give thanks to the LORD.
Call on his name.
Make known his accomplishments among the nations.
2 Sing to him.
Make music to him.
Tell about all his miraculous deeds.
3 Boast about his holy name.
Let the hearts of those who seek the LORD rejoice.
4 Seek the LORD and the strength he gives.
Seek his presence continually.
5 Recall the miraculous deeds he performed,
his mighty acts and the judgments he decreed,
6 O children of Abraham, God's servant,
you descendants of Jacob, God's chosen ones.
7 He is the LORD our God;
he carries out judgment throughout the earth.
8 He always remembers his covenantal decree,
the promise he made to a thousand generations—
9 the promise he made to Abraham,
the promise he made by oath to Isaac.
10 He gave it to Jacob as a decree,
to Israel as a lasting promise,
11 saying, "To you I will give the land of Canaan
as the portion of your inheritance."
12 When they were few in number,
just a very few, and resident foreigners within it,
13 they wandered from nation to nation,
and from one kingdom to another.
14 He let no one oppress them;
he disciplined kings for their sake,
15 saying, "Don't touch my chosen ones.
Don't harm my prophets."
16 He called down a famine upon the earth;
he cut off all the food supply.
17 He sent a man ahead of them—
Joseph was sold as a servant.
18 The shackles hurt his feet;
his neck was placed in an iron collar,
19 until the time when his prediction came true.
The LORD's word proved him right.
20 The king authorized his release;
the ruler of nations set him free.
21 He put him in charge of his palace,
and made him manager of all his property,
22 giving him authority to imprison his officials
and to teach his advisers.
23 Israel moved to Egypt;

105:1–45 Let us remember the Redeemer's marvelous works, his wonders, and the judgments of his mouth. See the special care God took of his people in the wilderness. All the benefits bestowed on Israel as a nation were shadows of spiritual blessings with which we are blessed in Christ Jesus. Having redeemed us with his blood, restored our souls to holiness, and set us at liberty from Satan's bondage, he guides and guards us all the way. He satisfies our souls with the bread of heaven and the water of life from the Rock of salvation, and he will bring us safely to heaven. He redeems his servants from all iniquity and purifies them unto himself to be a peculiar people, zealous of good works.

MATTHEW HENRY **(1662–1714)**
COMMENTARY ON THE WHOLE BIBLE

Jacob lived for a time in the land of Ham.
24 The LORD made his people very fruitful
and made them more numerous than their enemies.
25 He caused the Egyptians to hate his people
and to mistreat his servants.
26 He sent his servant Moses,
and Aaron, whom he had chosen.
27 They executed his miraculous signs among them
and his amazing deeds in the land of Ham.
28 He made it dark;
Moses and Aaron did not disobey his orders.
29 He turned the Egyptians' water into blood
and killed their fish.
30 Their land was overrun by frogs,
which even got into the rooms of their kings.
31 He ordered flies to come;
gnats invaded their whole territory.
32 He sent hail along with the rain;
there was lightning in their land.
33 He destroyed their vines and fig trees
and broke the trees throughout their territory.
34 He ordered locusts to come,
innumerable grasshoppers.
35 They ate all the vegetation in their land
and devoured the crops of their fields.
36 He struck down all the firstborn in their land,
the firstfruits of their reproductive power.
37 He brought his people out enriched with silver and gold;
none of his tribes stumbled.
38 Egypt was happy when they left,
for they were afraid of them.
39 He spread out a cloud for a cover,
and provided a fire to light up the night.
40 They asked for food, and he sent quail;
he satisfied them with food from the sky.
41 He opened up a rock and water flowed out;
a river ran through dry regions.
42 Yes, he remembered the sacred promise
he made to Abraham his servant.
43 When he led his people out, they rejoiced;
his chosen ones shouted with joy.
44 He handed the territory of nations over to them,
and they took possession of what other peoples had produced,
45 so that they might keep his commands
and obey his laws.
Praise the LORD.

PSALM 106

1 Praise the LORD.
Give thanks to the LORD, for he is good,
and his loyal love endures.
2 Who can adequately recount the LORD's mighty acts
or relate all his praiseworthy deeds?
3 How blessed are those who promote justice
and do what is right all the time.
4 Remember me, O LORD, when you show favor to your people.

106:1–48 The object of our inquiry in the case of God is before all things the indications of his goodness. For as David says, he had not come to save us had not goodness created in him such a purpose, and yet his goodness had not advanced his purpose had not wisdom given efficacy to his love for man. In what way then is wisdom contemplated in combination with goodness? In the actual events that have taken place. One cannot observe a good purpose in the abstract; a purpose cannot possibly be revealed unless it has the light of some events upon it. Well, the things accomplished, progressing as they did in orderly series and sequence, reveal the wisdom and the skill of the divine economy. And since wisdom when combined with justice absolutely becomes a virtue, if it be disjoined from justice it cannot in itself alone be good.

GREGORY OF NYSSA
(C. 335–C. 395)
DOGMATIC TREATISES

Pay attention to me, when you deliver,
5 so I may see the prosperity of your chosen ones,
rejoice along with your nation,
and boast along with the people who belong to you.
6 We have sinned like our ancestors;
we have done wrong, we have done evil.
7 Our ancestors in Egypt failed to appreciate your
miraculous deeds.
They failed to remember your many acts of loyal love,
and they rebelled at the sea, by the Red Sea.
8 Yet he delivered them for the sake of his reputation
that he might reveal his power.
9 He shouted at the Red Sea and it dried up;
he led them through the deep water as if it were a
desert.
10 He delivered them from the power of the one who
hated them
and rescued them from the power of the enemy.
11 The water covered their enemies;
not even one of them survived.
12 They believed his promises;
they sang praises to him.
13 They quickly forgot what he had done;
they did not wait for his instructions.
14 In the wilderness they had an insatiable craving for meat;
they challenged God in the wastelands.
15 He granted their request,
then struck them with a disease.
16 In the camp they resented Moses
and Aaron the LORD's holy priest.
17 The earth opened up and swallowed Dathan;
it engulfed the group led by Abiram.
18 Fire burned their group;
the flames scorched the wicked.
19 They made an image of a calf at Horeb
and worshiped a metal idol.
20 They traded their majestic God
for the image of an ox that eats grass.
21 They rejected the God who delivered them,
the one who performed great deeds in Egypt,
22 amazing feats in the land of Ham,
mighty acts by the Red Sea.
23 He threatened to destroy them,
but Moses, his chosen one, interceded with him
and turned back his destructive anger.
24 They rejected the fruitful land;
they did not believe his promise.
25 They grumbled in their tents;
they did not obey the LORD.
26 So he made a solemn vow
that he would make them die in the wilderness,
27 make their descendants die among the nations,
and scatter them among foreign lands.
28 They worshiped Baal of Peor
and ate sacrifices offered to the dead.
29 They made the LORD angry by their actions,
and a plague broke out among them.
30 Phinehas took a stand and intervened,
and the plague subsided.

31 This was credited to Phinehas as a righteous act
for all generations to come.
32 They made him angry by the waters of Meribah,
and Moses suffered because of them,
33 for they aroused his temper,
and he spoke rashly.
34 They did not destroy the nations,
as the LORD had commanded them to do.
35 They mixed in with the nations
and learned their ways.
36 They worshiped their idols,
which became a snare to them.
37 They sacrificed their sons and daughters to demons.
38 They shed innocent blood—
the blood of their sons and daughters,
whom they sacrificed to the idols of Canaan.
The land was polluted by bloodshed.
39 They were defiled by their deeds
and unfaithful in their actions.
40 So the LORD was angry with his people
and despised the people who belonged to him.
41 He handed them over to the nations,
and those who hated them ruled over them.
42 Their enemies oppressed them;
they were subject to their authority.
43 Many times he delivered them,
but they had a rebellious attitude
and degraded themselves by their sin.
44 Yet he took notice of their distress,
when he heard their cry for help.
45 He remembered his covenant with them
and relented because of his great loyal love.
46 He caused all their conquerors
to have pity on them.
47 Deliver us, O LORD, our God.
Gather us from among the nations.
Then we will give thanks to your holy name,
and boast about your praiseworthy deeds.
48 The LORD God of Israel deserves praise,
in the future and forevermore.
Let all the people say, "We agree! Praise the LORD!"

BOOK 5 (PSALMS 107–150)

PSALM 107

1 Give thanks to the LORD, for he is good,
and his loyal love endures.
2 Let those delivered by the LORD speak out,
those whom he delivered from the power of the enemy
3 and gathered from foreign lands,
from east and west,
from north and south.
4 They wandered through the wilderness, in a
wasteland;
they found no road to a city in which to live.
5 They were hungry and thirsty;
they fainted from exhaustion.
6 They cried out to the LORD in their distress;
he delivered them from their troubles.

107:1–43 "Let those delivered by the LORD speak out." Beloved, the sweetest and the loudest note in our songs of praise should be of redeeming love. God's redeeming acts toward his chosen are forever the favorite themes of their praise. If we know what redemption means, let us not withhold our sonnets of thanksgiving. We have been redeemed from the power of our corruptions, uplifted from the depth of sin in which we were naturally plunged. We have been led to the cross of Christ—our shackles of guilt have been broken off; we are no longer slaves but children of the living God. Even now by faith we wave the palm branch and wrap ourselves about with the fair linen that is to be our everlasting array, and shall we not unceasingly give thanks to the Lord our Redeemer? Child of God, can you be silent?

CHARLES SPURGEON
(1834–1892)
MORNING AND EVENING

7 He led them on a level road
that they might find a city in which to live.
8 Let them give thanks to the LORD for his loyal love
and for the amazing things he has done for people.
9 For he has satisfied those who thirst,
and those who hunger he has filled with food.
10 They sat in utter darkness,
bound in painful iron chains
11 because they had rebelled against God's commands
and rejected the instructions of the Most High.
12 So he used suffering to humble them;
they stumbled and no one helped them up.
13 They cried out to the LORD in their distress;
he delivered them from their troubles.
14 He brought them out of the utter darkness
and tore off their shackles.
15 Let them give thanks to the LORD for his loyal love
and for the amazing things he has done for people.
16 For he shattered the bronze gates
and hacked through the iron bars.
17 They acted like fools in their rebellious ways
and suffered because of their sins.
18 They lost their appetite for all food,
and they drew near the gates of death.
19 They cried out to the LORD in their distress;
he delivered them from their troubles.
20 He sent them an assuring word and healed them;
he rescued them from the pits where they were trapped.
21 Let them give thanks to the LORD for his loyal love
and for the amazing things he has done for people.
22 Let them present thank offerings,
and loudly proclaim what he has done.
23 Some traveled on the sea in ships
and carried cargo over the vast waters.
24 They witnessed the acts of the LORD,
his amazing feats on the deep water.
25 He gave the order for a windstorm,
and it stirred up the waves of the sea.
26 They reached up to the sky,
then dropped into the depths.
The sailors' strength left them because the danger was
so great.
27 They swayed and staggered like drunks,
and all their skill proved ineffective.
28 They cried out to the LORD in their distress;
he delivered them from their troubles.
29 He calmed the storm,
and the waves grew silent.
30 The sailors rejoiced because the waves grew quiet,
and he led them to the harbor they desired.
31 Let them give thanks to the LORD for his loyal love
and for the amazing things he has done for people.
32 Let them exalt him in the assembly of the people.
Let them praise him in the place where the leaders
preside.
33 He turned streams into a desert,
springs of water into arid land,
34 and a fruitful land into a barren place,
because of the sin of its inhabitants.

35 As for his people, he turned a desert into a pool of water
and a dry land into springs of water.
36 He allowed the hungry to settle there,
and they established a city in which to live.
37 They cultivated fields
and planted vineyards,
which yielded a harvest of fruit.
38 He blessed them so that they became very numerous.
He would not allow their cattle to decrease in number.
39 As for their enemies, they decreased in number and
were beaten down,
because of painful distress and suffering.
40 He would pour contempt upon princes,
and he made them wander in a wasteland with no road.
41 Yet he protected the needy from oppression
and cared for his families like a flock of sheep.
42 When the godly see this, they rejoice,
and every sinner shuts his mouth.
43 Whoever is wise, let him take note of these things.
Let them consider the LORD's acts of loyal love.

PSALM 108

A song, a psalm of David.

1 I am determined, O God.
I will sing and praise you with my whole heart.
2 Awake, O stringed instrument and harp.
I will wake up at dawn.
3 I will give you thanks before the nations, O LORD.
I will sing praises to you before foreigners.
4 For your loyal love extends beyond the sky,
and your faithfulness reaches the clouds.
5 Rise up above the sky, O God.
May your splendor cover the whole earth.
6 Deliver by your power and answer me,
so that the ones you love may be safe.
7 God has spoken in his sanctuary:
"I will triumph! I will parcel out Shechem;
the Valley of Sukkoth I will measure off.
8 Gilead belongs to me,
as does Manasseh.
Ephraim is my helmet,
Judah my royal scepter.
9 Moab is my washbasin.
I will make Edom serve me.
I will shout in triumph over Philistia."
10 Who will lead me into the fortified city?
Who will bring me to Edom?
11 Have you not rejected us, O God?
O God, you do not go into battle with our armies.
12 Give us help against the enemy,
for any help men might offer is futile.
13 By God's power we will conquer;
he will trample down our enemies.

108:4 Some have said that God is the soul of the world; others that his power does not extend to earth but only to heaven. Some, laboring under a similar delusion, misinterpret the text "and your faithfulness reaches the clouds" and have dared to limit the providence of God to the skies and heaven and to alienate from God the things on earth, forgetting the psalm that says, "If I were to ascend to heaven, you would be there. If I were to sprawl out in Sheol, there you would be" (Ps 139:8). For if there is nothing higher than heaven and the underworld is deeper than the earth, he who rules the lower regions reaches the earth also.

CYRIL OF JERUSALEM
(C. 313–386)
CATECHETICAL LECTURES

PSALM 109

For the music director, a psalm of David.

1 O God whom I praise, do not ignore me.
2 For they say cruel and deceptive things to me;
they lie to me.

GIUSEPPE ANGELI, ***ELIJAH TAKEN UP IN A CHARIOT OF FIRE*** (1740/1755)

(Public Domain. Courtesy of the National Gallery of Art, Washington, D.C.)

HENRY OSSAWA TANNER, ***THE ANNUNCIATION*** (1898)

(Public Domain)

3 They surround me and say hateful things;
they attack me for no reason.
4 They repay my love with accusations,
but I continue to pray.
5 They repay me evil for good
and hate for love.
6 Appoint an evil man to testify against him.
May an accuser stand at his right side.
7 When he is judged, he will be found guilty.
Then his prayer will be regarded as sinful.
8 May his days be few.
May another take his job.
9 May his children be fatherless,
and his wife a widow.
10 May his children roam around begging,
asking for handouts as they leave their ruined home.
11 May the creditor seize all he owns.
May strangers loot his property.
12 May no one show him kindness.
May no one have compassion on his fatherless children.
13 May his descendants be cut off.
May the memory of them be wiped out by the time the
next generation arrives.
14 May his ancestors' sins be remembered by the LORD.
May his mother's sin not be forgotten.
15 May the LORD be constantly aware of them
and cut off the memory of his children from the earth.
16 For he never bothered to show kindness;
he harassed the oppressed and needy
and killed the disheartened.
17 He loved to curse others, so those curses have come
upon him.
He had no desire to bless anyone, so he has experienced
no blessings.
18 He made cursing a way of life,
so curses poured into his stomach like water
and seeped into his bones like oil.
19 May a curse attach itself to him, like a garment one
puts on,
or a belt one wears continually.
20 May the LORD repay my accusers in this way,
those who say evil things about me.
21 O Sovereign LORD,
intervene on my behalf for the sake of your reputation.
Because your loyal love is good, deliver me.
22 For I am oppressed and needy,
and my heart beats violently within me.
23 I am fading away like a shadow at the end of the day;
I am shaken off like a locust.
24 I am so starved my knees shake;
I have turned into skin and bones.
25 I am disdained by them.
When they see me, they shake their heads.
26 Help me, O LORD my God.
Because you are faithful to me, deliver me.
27 Then they will realize this is your work
and that you, LORD, have accomplished it.
28 They curse, but you will bless.
When they attack, they will be humiliated,

109:1–5 Lying tongues were busy against the reputation of David, but he did not defend himself; he moved the case into a higher court and pleaded before the great King himself. Prayer is the safest method of replying to words of hatred. The psalmist prayed in no cold-hearted manner; he gave himself to the exercise—threw his whole soul and heart into it—straining every sinew and muscle, as Jacob did when wrestling with the angel. Continuance and perseverance are intended in the expression of our text. David did not cry once then relapse into silence; his holy clamor was continued till it brought down the blessing. Prayer must not be our chance work but our daily business, our habit and vocation. As artists give themselves to their models, and poets to their classical pursuits, so must we addict ourselves to prayer.

CHARLES SPURGEON
(1834–1892)
MORNING AND EVENING

but your servant will rejoice.
29 My accusers will be covered with shame
and draped in humiliation as if it were a robe.
30 I will thank the LORD profusely.
In the middle of a crowd I will praise him,
31 because he stands at the right hand of the needy
to deliver him from those who threaten his life.

PSALM 110

A psalm of David.

1 Here is the LORD's proclamation to my lord:
"Sit down at my right hand until I make your enemies
your footstool."
2 The LORD extends your dominion from Zion.
Rule in the midst of your enemies.
3 Your people willingly follow you when you go into
battle.
On the holy hills at sunrise the dew of your youth
belongs to you.
4 The LORD makes this promise on oath and will not
revoke it:
"You are an eternal priest after the pattern of
Melchizedek."
5 O Lord, at your right hand
he strikes down kings in the day he unleashes
his anger.
6 He executes judgment against the nations.
He fills the valleys with corpses;
he shatters their heads over the vast battlefield.
7 From the stream along the road he drinks;
then he lifts up his head.

PSALM 111

1 Praise the LORD!
I will give thanks to the LORD with my whole heart,
in the assembly of the godly and the congregation.
2 The LORD's deeds are great,
eagerly awaited by all who desire them.
3 His work is majestic and glorious,
and his faithfulness endures forever.
4 He does amazing things that will be remembered;
the LORD is merciful and compassionate.
5 He gives food to his faithful followers;
he always remembers his covenant.
6 He announced that he would do mighty deeds for his
people,
giving them a land that belonged to other nations.
7 His acts are characterized by faithfulness and justice;
all his precepts are reliable.
8 They are forever firm
and should be faithfully and properly carried out.
9 He delivered his people;
he ordained that his covenant be observed forever.
His name is holy and awesome.
10 To obey the LORD is the fundamental principle for wise
living;
all who carry out his precepts acquire good moral
insight.
He will receive praise forever.

110:1–7 That this psalm belongs to the Messiah is abundantly evident both from the express testimony of the New Testament and from the consent of the ancient Hebrew authoritative teachers. Of him it is directly and immediately to be understood, the Spirit of God wisely so ordering this matter that it might be a convincing testimony against the unbelieving Jews concerning the true Messiah and concerning the nature and quality of his kingdom: his prophetic office, his priestly office, his kingly office, and his states of humiliation and exaltation.

JOHN WESLEY (1703–1791)
EXPLANATORY NOTES ON THE BIBLE

111:10 It has been a subject of remark how extremely frequent is the intercourse that heretics hold with magicians, with charlatans, with astrologers, and with philosophers. And the reason is that they are people who devote themselves to curious questions. "Seek and you will find" (Matt 7:7) is everywhere in their minds. Thus from the very nature of their conduct may be estimated the quality of their faith. They say that God is not to be feared; therefore all things are, in their view, free and unchecked. Where, however, is God not feared except where he is not? Where God is not, there truth also is not. Where there is no truth, then naturally enough there is also such a discipline as theirs. But where God is, there exists "the beginning of wisdom [which] is to fear the LORD" (Prov 9:10). Where the fear of God is, there is seriousness, an honorable and yet thoughtful diligence, and God in all things.

TERTULLIAN (155–C. 220)
AGAINST MARCION

PSALM 112

1 Praise the LORD!
How blessed is the one who obeys the LORD,
who takes great delight in keeping his commands.
2 His descendants will be powerful on the earth;
the godly will be blessed.
3 His house contains wealth and riches;
his integrity endures.
4 In the darkness a light shines for the godly,
for each one who is merciful, compassionate, and just.
5 It goes well for the one who generously lends money
and conducts his business honestly.
6 For he will never be shaken;
others will always remember one who is just.
7 He does not fear bad news.
He is confident; he trusts in the LORD.
8 His resolve is firm; he will not succumb to fear
before he looks in triumph on his enemies.
9 He generously gives to the needy;
his integrity endures.
He will be vindicated and honored.
10 When the wicked see this, they will worry;
they will grind their teeth in frustration and
melt away.
The desire of the wicked will perish.

PSALM 113

1 Praise the LORD.
Praise, you servants of the LORD,
praise the name of the LORD.
2 May the LORD's name be praised
now and forevermore.
3 From east to west
the LORD's name is deserving of praise.
4 The LORD is exalted over all the nations;
his splendor reaches beyond the sky.
5 Who can compare to the LORD our God,
who sits on a high throne?
6 He bends down to look
at the sky and the earth.
7 He raises the poor from the dirt
and lifts up the needy from the garbage pile
8 that he might seat him with princes,
with the princes of his people.
9 He makes the barren woman of the family
a happy mother of children.
Praise the LORD.

PSALM 114

1 When Israel left Egypt,
when the family of Jacob left a foreign nation behind,
2 Judah became his sanctuary,
Israel his kingdom.
3 The sea looked and fled;
the Jordan River turned back.
4 The mountains skipped like rams,
the hills like lambs.
5 Why do you flee, O sea?
Why do you turn back, O Jordan River?

112:1–10 "He does not fear bad news. He is confident; he trusts in the LORD." Christian, you ought not to dread the arrival of evil tidings; if you are distressed by them, what do you have more than other people? Others have not your God to fly to; they have never proved his faithfulness as you have done, and it is no wonder if they are bowed down with alarm. But you profess to be of another spirit; you have been begotten again unto a lively hope, and your heart lives in heaven and not on earthly things. Trust in the Lord, and wait patiently for him. If you give way to fear when you hear of evil tidings, you will be unable to meet the trouble with that calm composure that nerves for duty and sustains under adversity. Take courage, and relying in sure confidence upon the faithfulness of your covenant God, "do not let your hearts be distressed or lacking in courage" (John 14:27).

CHARLES SPURGEON
(1834–1892)
MORNING AND EVENING

113:1–9 "Who can compare to the LORD our God, who sits on a high throne? He bends down to look at the sky and the earth." God, no doubt, casts his eyes on the lowly, he who laid bare the relics of the holy martyrs of his church, lying hid under the lowly turf, their souls in heaven, their bodies in the earth: "He raises the poor from the dirt, and lifts up the needy from the garbage pile," placing him, as you see, with the princes of his people. Whom are we to think of as the princes of his people if not the holy martyrs?

AMBROSE **(C. 339–C. 397)**
LETTERS

114:1–8 When the divine scripture says, "Let the sky rejoice, and the earth be happy" (Ps 96:11), it is the angels in heaven and the people on earth who are invited to rejoice. For the scripture is wont to speak of inanimate things as though they were animate. For example: "The sea looked and fled; the Jordan River turned back." And again: "Why do you flee, O sea? Why do you turn back, O Jordan River?" Mountains too and hills are asked the reason for their leaping in the same way as we are wont to say, *The city was gathered together* when we do not mean the buildings but the inhabitants of the city. "The heavens declare the glory of God" (Ps 19:1) does not mean that they send forth a voice that can be heard by bodily ears, but that from their own greatness they bring before our minds the power of the Creator; and when we contemplate their beauty, we praise the Maker as the Master Craftsman.

JOHN OF DAMASCUS
(C. 675–749)
AN EXACT EXPOSITION OF THE ORTHODOX FAITH

115:1–18 The psalmist shows the folly of the worshipers of idols. It is folly to trust in dead images, but it is wisdom to trust in the living God, for he is a help and a shield to those who trust in him. He is ever found faithful. And the Lord is to be praised: His goodness is large, for he has given the earth to the children of men for their use. The souls of the faithful, after they are delivered from the burdens of the flesh, are still praising him, but the dead body cannot praise God: Death puts an end to our glorifying him in this world of trial and conflict. Therefore we will seek to do the more for God. We will not only do it ourselves but will engage others to do it, to praise him when we are gone. Lord, you are the only object for faith and love. Help us to praise you while living and when dying that your name may be the first and last upon our lips: And let the sweet savor of your name refresh our souls forever.

MATTHEW HENRY **(1662–1714)**
COMMENTARY ON THE WHOLE BIBLE

6 Why do you skip like rams, O mountains,
like lambs, O hills?
7 Tremble, O earth, before the Lord—
before the God of Jacob,
8 who turned a rock into a pool of water,
a hard rock into springs of water.

PSALM 115

1 Not to us, O LORD, not to us,
but to your name bring honor,
for the sake of your loyal love and faithfulness.
2 Why should the nations say,
"Where is their God?"
3 Our God is in heaven.
He does whatever he pleases.
4 Their idols are made of silver and gold—
they are man-made.
5 They have mouths, but cannot speak;
eyes, but cannot see;
6 ears, but cannot hear;
noses, but cannot smell;
7 hands, but cannot touch;
feet, but cannot walk.
They cannot even clear their throats.
8 Those who make them will end up like them,
as will everyone who trusts in them.
9 O Israel, trust in the LORD.
He is their deliverer and protector.
10 O family of Aaron, trust in the LORD.
He is their deliverer and protector.
11 You loyal followers of the LORD, trust in the LORD.
He is their deliverer and protector.
12 The LORD takes notice of us; he will bless—
he will bless the family of Israel,
he will bless the family of Aaron.
13 He will bless his loyal followers,
both young and old.
14 May he increase your numbers,
yours and your children's.
15 May you be blessed by the LORD,
the Creator of heaven and earth.
16 The heavens belong to the LORD,
but the earth he has given to mankind.
17 The dead do not praise the LORD,
nor do any of those who descend into the silence of death.
18 But we will praise the LORD
now and forevermore.
Praise the LORD!

PSALM 116

1 I love the LORD
because he heard my plea for mercy
2 and listened to me.
As long as I live, I will call to him when I need help.
3 The ropes of death tightened around me,
the snares of Sheol confronted me.
I was confronted with trouble and sorrow.
4 I called on the name of the LORD,

"Please, LORD, rescue my life!"
5 The LORD is merciful and fair;
our God is compassionate.
6 The LORD protects the untrained;
I was in serious trouble and he delivered me.
7 Rest once more, my soul,
for the LORD has vindicated you.
8 Yes, LORD, you rescued my life from death,
kept my eyes from tears
and my feet from stumbling.
9 I will serve the LORD
in the land of the living.
10 I had faith when I said,
"I am severely oppressed."
11 I rashly declared,
"All men are liars."
12 How can I repay the LORD
for all his acts of kindness to me?
13 I will celebrate my deliverance
and call on the name of the LORD.
14 I will fulfill my vows to the LORD
before all his people.
15 The LORD values
the lives of his faithful followers.
16 Yes, LORD! I am indeed your servant;
I am your servant, the son of your female servant.
You saved me from death.
17 I will present a thank offering to you,
and call on the name of the LORD.
18 I will fulfill my vows to the LORD
before all his people,
19 in the courts of the LORD's temple,
in your midst, O Jerusalem.
Praise the LORD!

116:1–19 "I love the LORD," the psalmist says, "because he heard my plea for mercy, and listened to me." Now, God is good and the first and most perfect of good things. Therefore I have loved God who is the highest of objects to be desired, and I have received with joy sufferings for his sake. The psalmist demonstrates the hope stored up for those who receive sufferings because of their devoutness. "Rest once more, my soul, for the LORD has vindicated you." And these words seem to have equal weight with the words of the apostle: "Who will separate us from the love of Christ? Will trouble, or distress, or persecution, or famine, or nakedness, or danger, or sword?" (Rom 8:35). Therefore I have loved all these things knowing that I endure the dangers for the sake of piety under the hands of the Lord of the universe who sees and bestows the reward.

BASIL THE GREAT **(330–379)**
HOMILIES ON THE PSALMS

PSALM 117

1 Praise the LORD, all you nations.
Applaud him, all you foreigners.
2 For his loyal love towers over us,
and the LORD's faithfulness endures.
Praise the LORD.

117:1–2 "His loyal love towers over us" since the furious tongues of hostile nations have yielded to his name, through which we have been freed: "and the LORD's faithfulness endures," whether in those things he promised to the righteous or in those he has threatened to the ungodly.

AUGUSTINE **(354–430)**
EXPOSITIONS ON THE PSALMS

PSALM 118

1 Give thanks to the LORD, for he is good,
and his loyal love endures.
2 Let Israel say,
"Yes, his loyal love endures."
3 Let the family of Aaron say,
"Yes, his loyal love endures."
4 Let the loyal followers of the LORD say,
"Yes, his loyal love endures."
5 In my distress I cried out to the LORD.
The LORD answered me and put me in a wide open place.
6 The LORD is on my side; I am not afraid.
What can people do to me?
7 The LORD is on my side as my helper.
I look in triumph on those who hate me.
8 It is better to take shelter in the LORD
than to trust in people.

118:1–29 "Open for me the gates of the just king's temple. I will enter through them and give thanks to the LORD. This is the LORD's gate—the godly enter through it." Although many gates have been set open, yet this is that gate in Christ by which all they who have entered in and have directed their way in holiness and righteousness are blessed, doing all things without disorder. Let people be faithful; let them be powerful in the utterance of knowledge; let them be wise in judging of words; let them be pure in all their deeds; yet the more they seem to be superior to others in these respects, the humbler ought they to be and to seek the common good of all and not merely their own advantage.

CLEMENT OF ROME **(D. 99)**
FIRST CLEMENT

9 It is better to take shelter in the LORD
than to trust in princes.
10 All the nations surrounded me.
Indeed, in the name of the LORD I pushed them away.
11 They surrounded me, yes, they surrounded me.
Indeed, in the name of the LORD I pushed them away.
12 They surrounded me like bees.
But they disappeared as quickly as a fire among
thorns.
Indeed, in the name of the LORD I pushed them away.
13 "You aggressively attacked me and tried to knock me
down,
but the LORD helped me.
14 The LORD gives me strength and protects me;
he has become my deliverer."
15 They celebrate deliverance in the tents of the godly.
The LORD's right hand conquers.
16 The LORD's right hand gives victory;
the LORD's right hand conquers.
17 I will not die, but live,
and I will proclaim what the LORD has done.
18 The LORD severely punished me,
but he did not hand me over to death.
19 Open for me the gates of the just king's temple.
I will enter through them and give thanks to the LORD.
20 This is the LORD's gate—
the godly enter through it.
21 I will give you thanks, for you answered me,
and have become my deliverer.
22 The stone that the builders discarded
has become the cornerstone.
23 This is the LORD's work.
We consider it amazing!
24 This is the day the LORD has brought about.
We will be happy and rejoice in it.
25 Please, LORD, deliver!
Please, LORD, grant us success!
26 May the one who comes in the name of the LORD be
blessed.
We will pronounce blessings on you in the LORD's
temple.
27 The LORD is God, and he has delivered us.
Tie the offering with ropes
to the horns of the altar.
28 You are my God, and I will give you thanks.
You are my God, and I will praise you.
29 Give thanks to the LORD, for he is good
and his loyal love endures.

PSALM 119

א (*ALEF*)

1 How blessed are those whose actions are blameless,
who obey the law of the LORD.
2 How blessed are those who observe his rules
and seek him with all their heart,
3 who, moreover, do no wrong,
but follow in his footsteps.
4 You demand that your precepts
be carefully kept.

5 If only I were predisposed
to keep your statutes.
6 Then I would not be ashamed,
if I were focused on all your commands.
7 I will give you sincere thanks
when I learn your just regulations.
8 I will keep your statutes.
Do not completely abandon me.

ב (*BET*)

9 How can a young person maintain a pure life?
By guarding it according to your instructions.
10 With all my heart I seek you.
Do not allow me to stray from your commands.
11 In my heart I store up your words,
so I might not sin against you.
12 You deserve praise, O LORD.
Teach me your statutes.
13 With my lips I proclaim
all the regulations you have revealed.
14 I rejoice in the lifestyle prescribed by your rules
as if they were riches of all kinds.
15 I will meditate on your precepts
and focus on your behavior.
16 I find delight in your statutes;
I do not forget your instructions.

ג (*GIMEL*)

17 Be kind to your servant.
Then I will live and keep your instructions.
18 Open my eyes so I can truly see
the marvelous things in your law.
19 I am a resident foreigner in this land.
Do not hide your commands from me.
20 I desperately long to know
your regulations at all times.
21 You reprimand arrogant people.
Those who stray from your commands are doomed.
22 Spare me shame and humiliation,
for I observe your rules.
23 Though rulers plot and slander me,
your servant meditates on your statutes.
24 Yes, I find delight in your rules;
they give me guidance.

ד (*DALET*)

25 I collapse in the dirt.
Revive me with your word.
26 I told you about my ways and you answered me.
Teach me your statutes.
27 Help me to understand what your precepts mean.
Then I can meditate on your marvelous teachings.
28 I collapse from grief.
Sustain me by your word.
29 Remove me from the path of deceit.
Graciously give me your law.
30 I choose the path of faithfulness;
I am committed to your regulations.
31 I hold fast to your rules.

119:17–24 We should ask the Father of the Word during each individual reading, "whenever Moses is read" (2 Cor 3:15), that he might fulfill even in us that which is written in the Psalms: "Open my eyes so I can truly see the marvelous things in your law." For unless he himself opens our eyes, how shall we be able to see these great mysteries that are fashioned in the patriarchs, that are pictured now in terms of wells, now in marriages, now in births, now even in barrenness?

ORIGEN (C. 185–C. 253)
HOMILIES ON GENESIS

O LORD, do not let me be ashamed.
32 I run along the path of your commands,
for you enable me to do so.

119:33–40 "Give me a desire for your rules, rather than for wealth gained unjustly." The psalmist mentions this in particular because it is most opposite to God's testimonies and does most commonly hinder people from receiving his Word and from profiting by it, and because it is most pernicious, as being the root of all evil.

JOHN WESLEY **(1703–1791)**
EXPLANATORY NOTES ON THE BIBLE

ה (*HE*)

33 Teach me, O LORD, the lifestyle prescribed by your statutes
so that I might observe it continually.
34 Give me understanding so that I might observe your law
and keep it with all my heart.
35 Guide me in the path of your commands,
for I delight to walk in it.
36 Give me a desire for your rules,
rather than for wealth gained unjustly.
37 Turn my eyes away from what is worthless.
Revive me with your word.
38 Confirm to your servant your promise,
which you made to the one who honors you.
39 Take away the insults that I dread.
Indeed, your regulations are good.
40 Look, I long for your precepts.
Revive me with your deliverance.

ו (*VAV*)

41 May I experience your loyal love, O LORD,
and your deliverance, as you promised.
42 Then I will have a reply for the one who insults me,
for I trust in your word.
43 Do not completely deprive me of a truthful testimony,
for I await your justice.
44 Then I will keep your law continually
now and for all time.
45 I will be secure,
for I seek your precepts.
46 I will speak about your regulations before kings
and not be ashamed.
47 I will find delight in your commands,
which I love.
48 I will lift my hands to your commands,
which I love,
and I will meditate on your statutes.

ז (*ZAYIN*)

49 Remember your word to your servant,
for you have given me hope.
50 This is what comforts me in my trouble,
for your promise revives me.
51 Arrogant people do nothing but scoff at me.
Yet I do not turn aside from your law.
52 I remember your ancient regulations,
O LORD, and console myself.
53 Rage takes hold of me because of the wicked,
those who reject your law.
54 Your statutes have been my songs
in the house where I live.
55 I remember your name during the night, O LORD,
and I will keep your law.
56 This has been my practice,
for I observe your precepts.

ח (*KHET*)

57 The LORD is my source of security.
I have determined to follow your instructions.
58 I seek your favor with all my heart.
Have mercy on me as you promised.
59 I consider my actions
and follow your rules.
60 I keep your commands eagerly
and without delay.
61 The ropes of the wicked tighten around me,
but I do not forget your law.
62 In the middle of the night I arise to thank you
for your just regulations.
63 I am a friend to all your loyal followers
and to those who keep your precepts.
64 O LORD, your loyal love fills the earth.
Teach me your statutes!

ט (*TET*)

65 You are good to your servant,
O LORD, just as you promised.
66 Teach me proper discernment and understanding.
For I consider your commands to be reliable.
67 Before I was afflicted I used to stray off,
but now I keep your instructions.
68 You are good and you do good.
Teach me your statutes.
69 Arrogant people smear my reputation with lies,
but I observe your precepts with all my heart.
70 Their hearts are calloused,
but I find delight in your law.
71 It was good for me to suffer
so that I might learn your statutes.
72 The law you have revealed is more important
to me
than thousands of pieces of gold and silver.

י (*YOD*)

73 Your hands made me and formed me.
Give me understanding so that I might learn your
commands.
74 Your loyal followers will be glad when they see me,
for I find hope in your word.
75 I know, LORD, that your regulations are just.
You disciplined me because of your faithful devotion
to me.
76 May your loyal love console me,
as you promised your servant.
77 May I experience your compassion so I might
live.
For I find delight in your law.
78 May the arrogant be humiliated, for they have
slandered me.
But I meditate on your precepts.
79 May your loyal followers turn to me,
those who know your rules.
80 May I be fully committed to your statutes,
so that I might not be ashamed.

כ (*KAF*)

81 I desperately long for your deliverance.
I find hope in your word.
82 My eyes grow tired as I wait for your promise to be fulfilled.
I say, "When will you comfort me?"
83 For I am like a wineskin dried up in smoke.
I do not forget your statutes.
84 How long must your servant endure this?
When will you judge those who pursue me?
85 The arrogant dig pits to trap me,
which violates your law.
86 All your commands are reliable.
I am pursued without reason. Help me!
87 They have almost destroyed me here on the earth,
but I do not reject your precepts.
88 Revive me with your loyal love
that I might keep the rules you have revealed.

ל (*LAMED*)

89 O LORD, your instructions endure;
they stand secure in heaven.
90 You demonstrate your faithfulness to all generations.
You established the earth and it stood firm.
91 Today they stand firm by your decrees,
for all things are your servants.
92 If I had not found encouragement in your law,
I would have died in my sorrow.
93 I will never forget your precepts,
for by them you have revived me.
94 I belong to you. Deliver me!
For I seek your precepts.
95 The wicked prepare to kill me,
yet I concentrate on your rules.
96 I realize that everything has its limits,
but your commands are beyond full comprehension.

מ (*MEM*)

97 O how I love your law!
All day long I meditate on it.
98 Your commandments make me wiser than my enemies,
for I am always aware of them.
99 I have more insight than all my teachers,
for I meditate on your rules.
100 I am more discerning than those older than I,
for I observe your precepts.
101 I stay away from every evil path,
so that I might keep your instructions.
102 I do not turn aside from your regulations,
for you teach me.
103 Your words are sweeter
in my mouth than honey!
104 Your precepts give me discernment.
Therefore I hate all deceitful actions.

נ (*NUN*)

105 Your word is a lamp to walk by
and a light to illumine my path.
106 I have vowed and solemnly sworn
to keep your just regulations.

119:97–104 The soul presses forward for a glimpse of hidden mysteries, to the very abode of the Word, to the very dwelling place of that highest Good and his light and brightness. In that bosom and secret dwelling place of the Father, the soul hastens to hear his words and, having heard them, finds them sweeter than all things. Let the prophet who has tasted this sweetness teach you when he says, "Your words are sweeter in my mouth than honey!" What else can a soul desire when it has once tasted the sweetness of the Word, when it has once seen its brightness? How great is the glory of that divine Essence, how great the graces of the Word at which even angels wish to gaze!

AMBROSE (C. 339–C. 397)
LETTERS

107 I am suffering terribly.
O LORD, revive me with your word.
108 O LORD, please accept the freewill offerings of my praise.
Teach me your regulations.
109 My life is in continual danger,
but I do not forget your law.
110 The wicked lay a trap for me,
but I do not wander from your precepts.
111 I claim your rules as my permanent possession,
for they give me joy.
112 I am determined to obey your statutes
at all times, to the very end.

ס (*SAMEK*)

113 I hate people with divided loyalties,
but I love your law.
114 You are my hiding place and my shield.
I find hope in your word.
115 Turn away from me, you evil men,
so that I can observe the commands of my God.
116 Sustain me as you promised, so that I will live.
Do not disappoint me.
117 Support me so that I will be delivered.
Then I will focus on your statutes continually.
118 You despise all who stray from your statutes,
for such people are deceptive and unreliable.
119 You remove all the wicked of the earth like slag.
Therefore I love your rules.
120 My body trembles because I fear you;
I am afraid of your judgments.

ע (*AYIN*)

121 I do what is fair and right.
Do not abandon me to my oppressors.
122 Guarantee the welfare of your servant.
Do not let the arrogant oppress me.
123 My eyes grow tired as I wait for your deliverance,
for your reliable promise to be fulfilled.
124 Show your servant your loyal love.
Teach me your statutes.
125 I am your servant. Give me insight,
so that I can understand your rules.
126 It is time for the LORD to act—
they break your law.
127 For this reason I love your commands
more than gold, even purest gold.
128 For this reason I carefully follow all your precepts.
I hate all deceitful actions.

פ (*PE*)

129 Your rules are marvelous.
Therefore I observe them.
130 Your instructions are a doorway through which light
shines.
They give insight to the untrained.
131 I open my mouth and pant,
because I long for your commands.
132 Turn toward me and extend mercy to me,
as you typically do to your loyal followers.

119:121–128 The blessed psalmist asks the Lord for understanding by which he can recognize God's commands, which he well knew were written in the Book of the Law, when he says, "I am your servant. Give me insight, so that I can understand your rules." Certainly he was in possession of understanding, which had been granted to him by nature, and also had at his fingers' ends a knowledge of God's commands that were preserved in writing in the law. Still he prayed to the Lord that he might learn this more thoroughly because he knew that what came to him by nature would never be sufficient for him unless his understanding was enlightened by the Lord.

JOHN CASSIAN
(C. 360–C. 435)
THE CONFERENCES

119:129–136 This free will will be as free as it is sound, and as sound as it is submissive to divine mercy and grace. Therefore it prays with faith, "Direct my steps by your word. Do not let any sin dominate me." It prays, it does not promise; it confesses, it does not declare itself; it begs for the fullest liberty, it does not boast of its own power. It is not everyone who trusts in his own strength, but everyone who calls on the name of the Lord who will be saved. Therefore those who believe rightly believe that they may call on him in whom they have believed and may be strong to do what they have learned in the precepts of the law, since faith obtains what the law commands.

AUGUSTINE **(354–430)**
LETTERS

133 Direct my steps by your word.
Do not let any sin dominate me.
134 Deliver me from oppressive men,
so that I can keep your precepts.
135 Smile on your servant.
Teach me your statutes!
136 Tears stream down from my eyes,
because people do not keep your law.

צ (*TSADE*)

137 You are just, O LORD,
and your judgments are fair.
138 The rules you impose are just
and absolutely reliable.
139 My zeal consumes me,
for my enemies forget your instructions.
140 Your word is absolutely pure,
and your servant loves it.
141 I am insignificant and despised,
yet I do not forget your precepts.
142 Your justice endures,
and your law is reliable.
143 Distress and hardship confront me,
yet I find delight in your commands.
144 Your rules remain just.
Give me insight so that I can live.

ק (*QOF*)

145 I cried out with all my heart, "Answer me, O LORD!
I will observe your statutes."
146 I cried out to you, "Deliver me,
so that I can keep your rules."
147 I am up before dawn crying for help.
I find hope in your word.
148 My eyes anticipate the nighttime hours
so that I can meditate on your word.
149 Listen to me because of your loyal love.
O LORD, revive me, as you typically do.
150 Those who are eager to do wrong draw near;
they are far from your law.
151 You are near, O LORD,
and all your commands are reliable.
152 I learned long ago that
you ordained your rules to last.

ר (*RESH*)

153 See my pain and rescue me.
For I do not forget your law.
154 Fight for me and defend me.
Revive me with your word.
155 The wicked have no chance for deliverance,
for they do not seek your statutes.
156 Your compassion is great, O LORD.
Revive me, as you typically do.
157 The enemies who chase me are numerous.
Yet I do not turn aside from your rules.
158 I take note of the treacherous and despise them,
because they do not keep your instructions.
159 See how I love your precepts.

O LORD, revive me with your loyal love.
160 Your instructions are totally reliable;
all your just regulations endure.

ש (*SIN/SHIN*)

161 Rulers pursue me for no reason,
yet I am more afraid of disobeying your instructions.
162 I rejoice in your instructions,
like one who finds much plunder.
163 I hate and despise deceit;
I love your law.
164 Seven times a day I praise you
because of your just regulations.
165 Those who love your law are completely secure;
nothing causes them to stumble.
166 I hope for your deliverance, O LORD,
and I obey your commands.
167 I keep your rules;
I love them greatly.
168 I keep your precepts and rules,
for you are aware of everything I do.

ת (*TAV*)

169 Listen to my cry for help, O LORD.
Give me insight by your word.
170 Listen to my appeal for mercy.
Deliver me, as you promised.
171 May praise flow freely from my lips,
for you teach me your statutes.
172 May my tongue sing about your instructions,
for all your commands are just.
173 May your hand help me,
for I choose to obey your precepts.
174 I long for your deliverance, O LORD;
I find delight in your law.
175 May I live and praise you.
May your regulations help me.
176 I have wandered off like a lost sheep.
Come looking for your servant,
for I do not forget your commands.

PSALM 120

A song of ascents.

1 In my distress I cried out
to the LORD and he answered me.
2 I said, "O LORD, rescue me
from those who lie with their lips
and those who deceive with their tongues."
3 How will he severely punish you,
you deceptive talker?
4 Here's how! With the sharp arrows of warriors,
with arrowheads forged over the hot coals.
5 How miserable I am.
For I have lived temporarily in Meshech;
I have resided among the tents of Kedar.
6 For too long I have had to reside
with those who hate peace.
7 I am committed to peace,
but when I speak, they want to make war.

120:1–7 It was none other than God whom David implored for his deliverance: "In my distress I cried out to the LORD and he answered me." To him also giving thanks, he spoke the words of the song in the day in which the Lord delivered him from the hand of all his enemies and from the hand of Saul, saying, "I love you, LORD, my source of strength! The LORD is my high ridge, my stronghold, my deliverer" (Ps 18:1–2). And Paul, after enduring many persecutions, to none other than God gave thanks, saying, "I endured these persecutions and the Lord delivered me from them all" (2 Tim 3:11).

ATHANASIUS (C. 296–373)
FOUR DISCOURSES AGAINST THE ARIANS

PSALM 121

A song of ascents.

1 I look up toward the hills.
From where does my help come?
2 My help comes from the LORD,
the Creator of heaven and earth.
3 May he not allow your foot to slip.
May your Protector not sleep.
4 Look! Israel's Protector
does not sleep or slumber.
5 The LORD is your protector;
the LORD is the shade at your right hand.
6 The sun will not harm you by day,
or the moon by night.
7 The LORD will protect you from all harm;
he will protect your life.
8 The LORD will protect you in all you do,
now and forevermore.

121:1–8 Say, "I look up toward the hills. From where does my help come?" in such a way that you add to it immediately, "My help comes from the LORD, the Creator of heaven and earth." Therefore let us lift our eyes to the hills from which help shall come to us. Yet it is not the hills themselves in which our hope is to be placed, for the hills receive what they may present to us. Therefore we must put our hope in that place from which the hills also receive. When we lift our eyes to the scriptures because the scriptures were delivered through people, we lift our eyes to the hills from which help will come to us; and yet since they who wrote the scriptures were themselves people, they were not providing enlightenment from themselves. Rather Christ was the true light who enlightens everyone coming into the world.

AUGUSTINE **(354–430)**
TRACTATES ON THE GOSPEL OF JOHN

PSALM 122

A song of ascents; by David.

1 I was glad because they said to me,
"We will go to the LORD's temple."
2 Our feet are standing
inside your gates, O Jerusalem.
3 Jerusalem is a city designed
to accommodate an assembly.
4 The tribes go up there,
the tribes of the LORD,
where it is required that Israel
give thanks to the name of the LORD.
5 Indeed, the leaders sit there on thrones and make legal decisions,
on the thrones of the house of David.
6 Pray for the peace of Jerusalem.
May those who love her prosper.
7 May there be peace inside your defenses
and prosperity inside your fortresses.
8 For the sake of my brothers and my neighbors
I will say, "May there be peace in you."
9 For the sake of the temple of the LORD our God
I will pray for you to prosper.

122:1 "I was glad because they said to me, 'We will go to the LORD's temple.'" By this example we are taught that our joy, in like manner, should be doubled when God by his Holy Spirit not only spurs each of us to the obedience of his Word but also produces the same effect upon others, that we may be united together in the same faith. So stubborn and rebellious is human nature that the great majority of humankind invariably murmurs against God whenever he speaks. We have therefore no small ground for rejoicing when all harmoniously rank themselves with us on the side of God. Those who translate deduce this meaning: *I take delight in the company of those who allure me to the service of God and offer themselves to me as companions that we may go to the sanctuary together.*

JOHN CALVIN **(1509–1564)**
COMPLETE COMMENTARY ON THE BIBLE

PSALM 123

A song of ascents.

1 I look up toward you,
the one enthroned in heaven.
2 Look, as the eyes of servants look to the hand of their master,
as the eyes of a female servant look to the hand of her mistress,
so our eyes will look to the LORD, our God, until he shows us favor.
3 Show us favor, O LORD, show us favor!
For we have had our fill of humiliation, and then some.
4 We have had our fill
of the taunts of the self-assured,
of the contempt of the proud.

123:1–2 When we look upon the Lord and our eyes are on him so that we say, "Look, as the eyes of servants look to the hand of their master, as the eyes of a female servant look to the hand of her mistress, so our eyes will look to the LORD, our God, until he shows us favor," then we, as it were, draw the eye of the Lord to watch over us.

BASIL THE GREAT **(330–379)**
HOMILIES ON THE PSALMS

PSALM 124

A song of ascents; by David.

1 "If the LORD had not been on our side"—
let Israel say this.—
2 if the LORD had not been on our side,
when men attacked us,
3 they would have swallowed us alive,
when their anger raged against us.
4 The water would have overpowered us;
the current would have overwhelmed us.
5 The raging water
would have overwhelmed us.
6 The LORD deserves praise,
for he did not hand us over as prey to their teeth.
7 We escaped with our lives, like a bird from a hunter's snare.
The snare broke, and we escaped.
8 Our deliverer is the LORD,
the Creator of heaven and earth.

PSALM 125

A song of ascents.

1 Those who trust in the LORD are like Mount Zion,
which cannot be moved and will endure forever.
2 As the mountains surround Jerusalem,
so the LORD surrounds his people,
now and forevermore.
3 Indeed, the scepter of a wicked king will not settle
upon the allotted land of the godly.
Otherwise the godly
might do what is wrong.
4 Do good, O LORD, to those who are good,
to the morally upright.
5 As for those who are bent on traveling a sinful path,
may the LORD remove them, along with those who behave wickedly.
May Israel experience peace.

PSALM 126

A song of ascents.

1 When the LORD restored the well-being of Zion,
we thought we were dreaming.
2 At that time we laughed loudly
and shouted for joy.
At that time the nations said,
"The LORD has accomplished great things for these people."
3 The LORD did indeed accomplish great things for us.
We were happy.
4 O LORD, restore our well-being,
just as the streams in the arid south are replenished.
5 Those who shed tears as they plant
will shout for joy when they reap the harvest.
6 The one who weeps as he walks along, carrying his bag of seed,
will certainly come in with a shout of joy, carrying his sheaves of grain.

124:5–7 What is our duty but to praise and give thanks to God, the King of all? Let us first exclaim in the words of the Psalms, "The LORD deserves praise, for he did not hand us over as prey to their teeth." Therefore let us, performing our vows to the Lord and confessing our sins, keep the feast to the Lord in conversation, moral conduct, and manner of life, praising our Lord who has chastened us a little but has not utterly failed or forsaken us or altogether kept silent from us. Having brought us out of the deceitful and famous Egypt of the opponents of Christ, he has caused us to pass through many trials and afflictions, as it were in the wilderness, to his holy church. On this account especially I both give thanks to God myself and exhort you to thank him with me.

ATHANASIUS **(C. 296–373)**
FESTAL LETTERS

125:4–5 God is good, but he is also just, and it is the nature of the just to reward in proportion to merit, as it is written: "Do good, O LORD, to those who are good, to the morally upright. As for those who are bent on traveling a sinful path, may the LORD remove them, along with those who behave wickedly." He is merciful, but he is also a judge, for "he promotes equity and justice," says the psalmist (Ps 33:5). You see with what discernment he bestows mercy, neither being merciful without judgment nor judging without mercy. Let us not therefore know God by halves. He who causes the sun to rise also strikes people with blindness. He who sends the rain also causes the rain of fire. By the one he manifests his goodness, by the other his severity. For the one let us love him, for the other let us fear him.

BASIL THE GREAT **(330–379)**
THE LONG RULES

126:1–6 Some Christians are sadly prone to look on the dark side of everything and to dwell more upon what they have gone through than upon what God has done for them. In looking back we would be wrong to deny that we have been in the Slough of Despond and have crept along the Valley of Humiliation, but we would be equally wicked to forget that we have been through them safely and profitably. Our griefs cannot mar the melody of our praise; we reckon them to be the bass part of our life's song: "The LORD did indeed accomplish great things for us. We were happy."

CHARLES SPURGEON
(1834–1892)
MORNING AND EVENING

127:1–5 We must trust in God for success in all enterprises and for children. Children are the chief of these blessings only from God's blessing, even as an inheritance is not the fruit of a man's own labor but the gift of God.

JOHN WESLEY (1703–1791)
EXPLANATORY NOTES ON THE BIBLE

128:1–6 When the psalmist says, "How blessed is every one of the LORD's loyal followers," he shows that they are not blessed who fear with troubled mind the dangers of the world when temporal property is lost. For those dangers make people wretched when they torment them with groundless fear. In contrast, the fear of the Lord descends from love, is born of charity, and is begotten of sweetness. A pious fear comforts the fearful and refreshes the afflicted and does not know how to lack joy. How advantageous fear is if children are taught by it! What sort of learning there is which is given with sweet affection!

CASSIODORUS (C. 485–C. 585)
EXPLANATION OF THE PSALMS

129:4 The Lord bears with the long furrows of the wicked, but he will surely make them cease from their plowing before he has done with them. He has cut asunder the cords of the wicked. He does not unfasten but cuts asunder the harness the ungodly use in their labor of hate. Never has God used a nation to chastise his Israel without destroying that nation when the chastisement has come to a close: He hates those who hurt his people even though he permits that hate to triumph for a while for his own purpose.

CHARLES SPURGEON
(1834–1892)
THE TREASURY OF DAVID

PSALM 127

A song of ascents; by Solomon.

1 If the LORD does not build a house,
then those who build it work in vain.
If the LORD does not guard a city,
then the watchman stands guard in vain.
2 It is vain for you to rise early, come home late,
and work so hard for your food.
Yes, he provides for those whom he loves even when
they sleep.
3 Yes, sons are a gift from the LORD;
the fruit of the womb is a reward.
4 Sons born during one's youth
are like arrows in a warrior's hand.
5 How blessed is the man who fills his quiver
with them.
They will not be put to shame when they confront
enemies at the city gate.

PSALM 128

A song of ascents.

1 How blessed is every one of the LORD's loyal
followers,
each one who keeps his commands.
2 You will eat what you worked so hard to
grow.
You will be blessed and secure.
3 Your wife will be like a fruitful vine
in the inner rooms of your house;
your children will be like olive branches,
as they sit all around your table.
4 Yes indeed, the man who fears the LORD
will be blessed in this way.
5 May the LORD bless you from Zion
that you might see Jerusalem prosper
all the days of your life
6 and that you might see your grandchildren.
May Israel experience peace.

PSALM 129

A song of ascents.

1 "Since my youth they have often attacked me,"
let Israel say.
2 "Since my youth they have often attacked me,
but they have not defeated me.
3 The plowers plowed my back;
they made their furrows long.
4 The LORD is just;
he cut the ropes of the wicked."
5 May all who hate Zion
be humiliated and turned back.
6 May they be like the grass on the rooftops,
which withers before one can even pull it up,
7 which cannot fill the reaper's hand
or the lap of the one who gathers the grain.
8 Those who pass by will not say,
"May you experience the LORD's blessing!
We pronounce a blessing on you in the name of
the LORD."

PSALM 130

A song of ascents.

1 From the deep water I cry out to you, O LORD.
2 O Lord, listen to me.
Pay attention to my plea for mercy.
3 If you, O LORD, were to keep track of sins,
O Lord, who could stand before you?
4 But you are willing to forgive
so that you might be honored.
5 I rely on the LORD.
I rely on him with my whole being;
I wait for his assuring word.
6 I yearn for the Lord,
more than watchmen do for the morning,
yes, more than watchmen do for the morning.
7 O Israel, hope in the LORD,
for the LORD exhibits loyal love
and is more than willing to deliver.
8 He will deliver Israel
from all their sins.

PSALM 131

A song of ascents; by David.

1 O LORD, my heart is not proud,
nor do I have a haughty look.
I do not have great aspirations,
or concern myself with things that are beyond me.
2 Indeed, I have calmed and quieted myself
like a weaned child with its mother;
I am content like a young child.
3 O Israel, hope in the LORD
now and forevermore!

PSALM 132

A song of ascents.

1 O LORD, for David's sake remember
all his strenuous effort
2 and how he made a vow to the LORD,
and swore an oath to the Powerful One of Jacob.
3 He said, "I will not enter my own home,
or get into my bed.
4 I will not allow my eyes to sleep
or my eyelids to slumber,
5 until I find a place for the LORD,
a fine dwelling place for the Powerful One of Jacob."
6 Look, we heard about it in Ephrathah;
we found it in the territory of Jaar.
7 Let us go to his dwelling place.
Let us worship before his footstool.
8 Ascend, O LORD, to your resting place,
you and the ark of your strength.
9 May your priests be clothed with integrity.
May your loyal followers shout for joy.
10 For the sake of David, your servant,
do not reject your chosen king.
11 The LORD made a reliable promise to David;
he will not go back on his word.
He said, "I will place one of your descendants on your
throne.

130:1–8 All people by the law must fall before God forever, for they have broken it but cannot make amends for the transgression. But considering the mercy of God, faith lays hold of that end of the promise that is in the Bible; hope lays hold of that end of the promise that is fastened to the mercy seat. For the promise is like a mighty cable that is fastened by one end to a ship and by the other to the anchor: the soul is the ship where faith is, and to which the end of this cable is fastened, but hope is the anchor that is at the other end of this cable. Thus faith and hope getting hold of both ends of the promise carry it safely all away.

JOHN BUNYAN **(1628–1688)**
ISRAEL'S HOPE ENCOURAGED

131:1–3 David exhorts and directs the people of God constantly and perpetually to place all their hopes and confidence in God. He exhorts them to hope and directs them in the right way of hoping and trusting God. He does this by first providing his own example: He professes his humility and so denies the opposite of this hope that is presumption and self-conceit. Second, he declares his submission and absolute resignation to the will of God. Both together teach us this lesson: that a holy, humble heart that is content to live at God's finding can best trust in God.

THOMAS MANTON
(1620–1677)
THE COMPLETE WORKS

132:1–18 With David the covenant was made, and therefore his name is pleaded on behalf of his descendants and the people who would be blessed by his dynasty. The request is that the Lord would "remember," and this is a word full of meaning. The plea is urged with God that he would bless the family of David for the sake of their progenitor; how much stronger is our master argument in prayer that God would deal well with us for Jesus' sake! David had no personal merit; the plea is based upon the covenant graciously made with him; but Jesus has merits that are his own—these we may urge without hesitation. When the Lord was angry with the reigning prince, the people cried, *Lord, remember David*; and when they needed any special blessing, again they sang it. This was good pleading, but it was not so good as ours, which runs *Lord, remember Jesus and all his afflictions*.

CHARLES SPURGEON
(1834–1892)
THE TREASURY OF DAVID

12 If your sons keep my covenant
and the rules I teach them,
their sons will also sit on your throne forever."
13 Certainly the LORD has chosen Zion;
he decided to make it his home.
14 He said, "This will be my resting place forever;
I will live here, for I have chosen it.
15 I will abundantly supply what she needs;
I will give her poor all the food they need.
16 I will protect her priests,
and her godly people will shout exuberantly.
17 There I will make David strong;
I have determined that my chosen king's dynasty will continue.
18 I will humiliate his enemies,
and his crown will shine."

PSALM 133

A song of ascents; by David.

1 Look! How good and how pleasant it is
when brothers truly live in unity.
2 It is like fine oil poured on the head,
which flows down the beard—
Aaron's beard,
and then flows down his garments.
3 It is like the dew of Hermon,
which flows down upon the hills of Zion.
Indeed, that is where the LORD has decreed
a blessing will be available—eternal life.

PSALM 134

A song of ascents.

1 Attention! Praise the LORD,
all you servants of the LORD
who serve in the LORD's temple during the night.
2 Lift your hands toward the sanctuary
and praise the LORD.
3 May the LORD, the Creator of heaven and earth,
bless you from Zion.

PSALM 135

1 Praise the LORD.
Praise the name of the LORD.
Offer praise, you servants of the LORD,
2 who serve in the LORD's temple,
in the courts of the temple of our God.
3 Praise the LORD, for the LORD is good.
Sing praises to his name, for it is pleasant.
4 Indeed, the LORD has chosen Jacob for himself,
Israel to be his special possession.
5 Yes, I know the LORD is great,
and our Lord is superior to all gods.
6 He does whatever he pleases
in heaven and on earth,
in the seas and all the ocean depths.
7 He causes the clouds to arise from the end of the earth,
makes lightning bolts accompany the rain,
and brings the wind out of his storehouses.
8 He struck down the firstborn of Egypt,

133:1–3 "Look! How good and how pleasant it is when brothers truly live in unity." In a spiritual dwelling, I interpret it, and in a concord that is in God, and in the unity of the faith that distinguishes this pleasant dwelling according to truth. This indeed was illustrated more beautifully in Aaron and the priests clothed with honor, as ointment on the head, nurturing the highest understanding and leading even to the end of wisdom. For in this dwelling the Lord has promised blessing and eternal life. Apprehending, therefore, the importance of this utterance of the prophet, we have spoken this present brotherly word for love's sake and by no means seeking, or meaning to seek, our own things.

ZEPHYRINUS (D. 217)
EPISTLES OF ZEPHYRINUS

134:1–3 He who stands in the courts is not confined but in some fashion is enlarged. Remain in this enlargement, and you can love your enemy because you do not love things in which an enemy could confine you. How can you be understood to stand in the courts? Stand in charity, and you stand in the courts. Breadth lies in charity, confinement in hatred.

AUGUSTINE (354–430)
EXPOSITIONS ON THE PSALMS

including both men and animals.
9 He performed awesome deeds and acts of judgment
in your midst, O Egypt,
against Pharaoh and all his servants.
10 He defeated many nations,
and killed mighty kings—
11 Sihon, king of the Amorites,
and Og, king of Bashan,
and all the kingdoms of Canaan.
12 He gave their land as an inheritance,
as an inheritance to Israel his people.
13 O LORD, your name endures,
your reputation, O LORD, lasts.
14 For the LORD vindicates his people
and has compassion on his servants.
15 The nations' idols are made of silver and gold;
they are man-made.
16 They have mouths, but cannot speak,
eyes, but cannot see,
17 and ears, but cannot hear.
Indeed, they cannot breathe.
18 Those who make them will end up like them,
as will everyone who trusts in them.
19 O family of Israel, praise the LORD.
O family of Aaron, praise the LORD.
20 O family of Levi, praise the LORD.
You loyal followers of the LORD, praise the LORD.
21 The LORD deserves praise in Zion—
he who dwells in Jerusalem.
Praise the LORD.

PSALM 136

1 Give thanks to the LORD, for he is good,
for his loyal love endures.
2 Give thanks to the God of gods,
for his loyal love endures.
3 Give thanks to the Lord of lords,
for his loyal love endures.
4 To the one who performs magnificent, amazing deeds
all by himself,
for his loyal love endures.
5 To the one who used wisdom to make the heavens,
for his loyal love endures.
6 To the one who spread out the earth over the water,
for his loyal love endures.
7 To the one who made the great lights,
for his loyal love endures,
8 the sun to rule by day,
for his loyal love endures,
9 the moon and stars to rule by night,
for his loyal love endures.
10 To the one who struck down the firstborn of Egypt,
for his loyal love endures,
11 and led Israel out from their midst,
for his loyal love endures,
12 with a strong hand and an outstretched arm,
for his loyal love endures.
13 To the one who divided the Red Sea in two,
for his loyal love endures,

135:1–21 Providence, then, is the solicitude that God has for existing things. And again, providence is that will of God by which all existing things receive suitable guidance through to their end. But if providence is God's will, then according to right reason, everything that has come about through providence has quite necessarily come about in the best manner and that most befitting God, so that it could not have happened in a better way. God is both Creator and Provider, and his power of creating, sustaining, and providing is his goodwill. For "he does whatever he pleases in heaven and on earth, in the seas and all the ocean depths," and none resist his will. He willed all things to be made, and they were made; he wills the world to endure, and it does endure; and all things whatsoever he wills are done.

JOHN OF DAMASCUS
(C. 675–749)
AN EXACT EXPOSITION OF THE ORTHODOX FAITH

136:1–26 The psalmist reminds the Lord's people that unless they are constant in his praises, they are chargeable with defrauding him of what is justly due him for his benefits. And in mentioning each benefit, he takes particular notice of the "loyal love" of God to teach us how necessary it is to the proper celebration of his praises that we view everything we receive from him as being bestowed gratuitously. Human beings may not deny the divine goodness to be the source and fountain of all their blessings, but the graciousness of his bounty is far from being fully and sincerely recognized, though the greatest stress is laid upon it in scripture.

JOHN CALVIN **(1509–1564)**
COMPLETE COMMENTARY ON THE BIBLE

14 and led Israel through its midst,
for his loyal love endures,
15 and tossed Pharaoh and his army into the Red Sea,
for his loyal love endures.
16 To the one who led his people through the wilderness,
for his loyal love endures.
17 To the one who struck down great kings,
for his loyal love endures,
18 and killed powerful kings,
for his loyal love endures,
19 Sihon, king of the Amorites,
for his loyal love endures,
20 Og, king of Bashan,
for his loyal love endures,
21 and gave their land as an inheritance,
for his loyal love endures,
22 as an inheritance to Israel his servant,
for his loyal love endures.
23 To the one who remembered us when we were down,
for his loyal love endures,
24 and snatched us away from our enemies,
for his loyal love endures.
25 To the one who gives food to all living things,
for his loyal love endures.
26 Give thanks to the God of heaven,
for his loyal love endures!

PSALM 137

1 By the rivers of Babylon
we sit down and weep
when we remember Zion.
2 On the poplars in her midst
we hang our harps,
3 for there our captors ask us to compose songs;
those who mock us demand that we be happy, saying:
"Sing for us a song about Zion!"
4 How can we sing a song to the LORD
in a foreign land?
5 If I forget you, O Jerusalem,
may my right hand be crippled.
6 May my tongue stick to the roof of my mouth,
if I do not remember you,
and do not give Jerusalem priority
over whatever gives me the most joy.
7 Remember, O LORD, what the Edomites did
on the day Jerusalem fell.
They said, "Tear it down, tear it down,
right to its very foundation!"
8 O daughter Babylon, soon to be devastated,
how blessed will be the one who repays you
for what you dished out to us.
9 How blessed will be the one who grabs your babies
and smashes them on a rock.

PSALM 138

By David.

1 I will give you thanks with all my heart;
before the heavenly assembly I will sing praises to you.
2 I will bow down toward your holy temple

137:1–9 Those who are exiles and banished from their ancestral homes, which the holy law of Moses had assigned them, will be entangled in the errors of the world, thus you hear the psalmist saying: "By the rivers of Babylon we sit down and weep when we remember Zion." He sets forth the wailings of those who have fallen and shows that they who are living in this condition of passing time and changing circumstances ought to repent after the example of those who, as a reward for sin, had been led into miserable captivity.

AMBROSE **(C. 339–C. 397)**
CONCERNING REPENTANCE

138:1–8 "Let them sing about the LORD's deeds." The time when Christians begin to sing of the ways of the Lord is when they first lose their burden at the foot of the cross. Not even the songs of the angels seem so sweet as the first song of rapture that gushes from the inmost soul of the forgiven child of God. But it is not only at the commencement of the Christian life that believers have reason for song; as long as they live they discover cause to sing of the ways of the Lord, and their experience of his constant loving-kindness leads them to say, "I will praise the LORD at all times; my mouth will continually praise him" (Ps 34:1). See to it that you magnify the Lord this day.

CHARLES SPURGEON
(1834–1892)
MORNING AND EVENING

and give thanks to your name,
because of your loyal love and faithfulness,
for you have exalted your promise above the entire sky.
3 When I cried out for help, you answered me.
You made me bold and energized me.
4 Let all the kings of the earth give thanks to you,
O LORD,
when they hear the words you speak.
5 Let them sing about the LORD's deeds,
for the LORD's splendor is magnificent.
6 Though the LORD is exalted, he looks after the lowly,
and from far away humbles the proud.
7 Even when I must walk in the midst of danger, you
revive me.
You oppose my angry enemies,
and your right hand delivers me.
8 The LORD avenges me.
O LORD, your loyal love endures.
Do not abandon those whom you have made.

PSALM 139

For the music director, a psalm of David.

1 O LORD, you examine me and know me.
2 You know when I sit down and when I get up;
even from far away you understand my motives.
3 You carefully observe me when I travel or when I lie
down to rest;
you are aware of everything I do.
4 Certainly my tongue does not frame a word
without you, O LORD, being thoroughly aware of it.
5 You squeeze me in from behind and in front;
you place your hand on me.
6 Your knowledge is beyond my comprehension;
it is so far beyond me, I am unable to fathom it.
7 Where can I go to escape your Spirit?
Where can I flee to escape your presence?
8 If I were to ascend to heaven, you would be there.
If I were to sprawl out in Sheol, there you would be.
9 If I were to fly away on the wings of the dawn
and settle down on the other side of the sea,
10 even there your hand would guide me,
your right hand would grab hold of me.
11 If I were to say, "Certainly the darkness will cover me,
and the light will turn to night all around me,"
12 even the darkness is not too dark for you to see,
and the night is as bright as day;
darkness and light are the same to you.
13 Certainly you made my mind and heart;
you wove me together in my mother's womb.
14 I will give you thanks because your deeds are awesome
and amazing.
You knew me thoroughly;
15 my bones were not hidden from you,
when I was made in secret
and sewed together in the depths of the earth.
16 Your eyes saw me when I was inside the womb.
All the days ordained for me
were recorded in your scroll
before one of them came into existence.

139:1–24 Meditate on the omniscience of God, which the psalmist represents by that perfect knowledge that God had of all his actions, his sitting down and his rising up, and of his thoughts, so that God knew his thoughts afar. Then he represents it by the impossibility of fleeing from the divine presence so that if he should go to heaven, hide himself in hell, or fly to the uttermost parts of the sea, yet he would not be hid from God. Then he represents it by the knowledge God had of him while in his mother's womb. And last of all, the psalmist improves this meditation upon God's all-seeing eye in begging of God that he would search and try him to see if there was any wicked way in him and lead him in the way everlasting.

JONATHAN EDWARDS
(1703–1758)
THE COMPLETE WORKS

17 How difficult it is for me to fathom your thoughts about
me, O God!
How vast is their sum total.
18 If I tried to count them,
they would outnumber the grains of sand.
Even if I finished counting them,
I would still have to contend with you.
19 If only you would kill the wicked, O God!
Get away from me, you violent men!
20 They rebel against you and act deceitfully;
your enemies lie.
21 O LORD, do I not hate those who hate you
and despise those who oppose you?
22 I absolutely hate them;
they have become my enemies.
23 Examine me, O God, and probe my thoughts.
Test me, and know my concerns.
24 See if there is any idolatrous way in me,
and lead me in the everlasting way.

PSALM 140

For the music director, a psalm of David.

1 O LORD, rescue me from wicked men.
Protect me from violent men,
2 who plan ways to harm me.
All day long they stir up conflict.
3 Their tongues wound like a serpent;
a viper's venom is behind their lips. *Selah*
4 O LORD, shelter me from the power of the wicked.
Protect me from violent men,
who plan to knock me over.
5 Proud men hide a snare for me;
evil men spread a net by the path.
They set traps for me. *Selah*
6 I say to the LORD, "You are my God."
O LORD, pay attention to my plea for mercy.
7 O Sovereign LORD, my strong deliverer,
you shield my head in the day of battle.
8 O LORD, do not let the wicked have their way.
Do not allow their plan to succeed when they attack.
Selah
9 As for the heads of those who surround me—
may the harm done by their lips overwhelm them.
10 May he rain down fiery coals upon them.
May he throw them into the fire.
From bottomless pits they will not escape.
11 A slanderer will not endure on the earth;
calamity will hunt down a violent man and strike him
down.
12 I know that the LORD defends the cause of the
oppressed
and vindicates the poor.
13 Certainly the godly will give thanks to your name;
the morally upright will live in your presence.

140:1–13 Where, after all, does evil come to a human being from but from a human being? Count how many evils people suffer from outwardly. Those that are not evidently caused by other people are extremely few. Of evils coming to a human being from a human being there are plenty. Thefts come from a human being, adultery with his wife he suffers from a man, his servant is induced to do something unlawful by a human being, he is hoodwinked by a human being, he is outlawed by a human being, he is overthrown by a human being, he is taken prisoner by a human being. "O LORD, rescue me from wicked men"!

AUGUSTINE **(354–430)**
SERMONS

PSALM 141

A psalm of David.

1 O LORD, I cry out to you. Come quickly to me.
Pay attention to me when I cry out to you.

2 May you accept my prayer like incense,
my uplifted hands like the evening offering.
3 O LORD, place a guard on my mouth.
Protect the opening of my lips.
4 Do not let me have evil desires
or participate in sinful activities
with men who behave wickedly.
I will not eat their delicacies.
5 May the godly strike me in love and correct me.
May my head not refuse choice oil.
Indeed, my prayer is a witness against their evil deeds.
6 They will be thrown over the side of a cliff by their judges.
They will listen to my words, for they are pleasant.
7 As when one plows and breaks up the soil,
so our bones are scattered at the mouth of Sheol.
8 Surely I am looking to you, O Sovereign LORD.
In you I take shelter.
Do not expose me to danger.
9 Protect me from the snare they have laid for me
and the traps the evildoers have set.
10 Let the wicked fall into their own nets,
while I escape.

141:1–10 And he prays constantly who unites prayer with the deeds required and right deeds with prayer. For the only way we can accept the command to "constantly pray" (1 Thess 5:17) as referring to a real possibility is by saying that the entire life of the saint taken as a whole is a single great prayer. What is customarily called "prayer" is then a part of this prayer. Now prayer in the ordinary sense ought to be made no less than three times each day. This is evident from the story of Daniel, who prayed three times a day when such great peril had been devised for him. And the last time of prayer is indicated by "my uplifted hands like the evening offering." Indeed, we do not even complete the nighttime properly without that prayer.

ORIGEN **(C. 185–C. 253)**
ON PRAYER

PSALM 142

A well-written song by David, when he was in the cave; a prayer.

1 To the LORD I cry out;
to the LORD I plead for mercy.
2 I pour out my lament before him;
I tell him about my troubles.
3 Even when my strength leaves me,
you watch my footsteps.
In the path where I walk
they have hidden a trap for me.
4 Look to the right and see.
No one cares about me.
I have nowhere to run;
no one is concerned about my life.
5 I cry out to you, O LORD;
I say, "You are my shelter,
my security in the land of the living."
6 Listen to my cry for help,
for I am in serious trouble.
Rescue me from those who chase me,
for they are stronger than I am.
7 Free me from prison
that I may give thanks to your name.
Because of me the godly will assemble,
for you will vindicate me.

142:1–7 David said that he was not paralyzed with fear, that he did not in a paroxysm of fury take vengeance upon his enemy as he easily might have done, and that he was not actuated by despair to take away his life but composedly addressed himself to the exercise of prayer. To pour out one's thoughts and tell over one's afflictions implies the reverse of those perplexing anxieties that people brood over inwardly to their own distress, and by which they torture themselves and are chafed by their afflictions rather than led to God. In short, we are left to infer that while he did not give way before others to loud and senseless lamentations, neither did he suffer himself to be tormented with inward and suppressed cares but made known his griefs with unsuspecting confidence to the Lord.

JOHN CALVIN **(1509–1564)**
COMPLETE COMMENTARY ON THE BIBLE

PSALM 143

A psalm of David.

1 O LORD, hear my prayer.
Pay attention to my plea for help.
Because of your faithfulness and justice, answer me.
2 Do not sit in judgment on your servant,
for no one alive is innocent before you.
3 Certainly my enemies chase me.
They smash me into the ground.

They force me to live in dark regions,
like those who have been dead for ages.
4 My strength leaves me;
I am absolutely shocked.
5 I recall the old days.
I meditate on all you have done;
I reflect on your accomplishments.
6 I spread my hands out to you in prayer;
my soul thirsts for you in a parched land. *Selah*
7 Answer me quickly, LORD.
My strength is fading.
Do not reject me,
or I will join those descending into the grave.
8 May I hear about your loyal love in the morning,
for I trust in you.
Show me the way I should go,
because I long for you.
9 Rescue me from my enemies, O LORD.
I run to you for protection.
10 Teach me to do what pleases you,
for you are my God.
May your kind presence
lead me into a level land.
11 O LORD, for the sake of your reputation, revive me.
Because of your justice, rescue me from trouble.
12 As a demonstration of your loyal love, destroy my enemies.
Annihilate all who threaten my life,
for I am your servant.

143:1–12 Let us entreat the help of the grace of this Spirit in all our actions, dearly beloved. Let us all, individually and collectively, say to the Lord, "May your kind presence lead me into a level land." And so it will come to pass that the one who came down on the apostles and declared to them the things that were to come may disclose also to our minds the joys of the life to come. May he kindly set us on fire to seek these joys, with the cooperation of the one who is accustomed both to promise and to give him to his faithful, Jesus Christ our Lord, who lives and reigns with the Father in the unity of the Holy Spirit, God forever and ever. Amen.

VENERABLE BEDE
(C. 672–735)
HOMILIES ON THE GOSPELS

PSALM 144

By David.

1 The LORD, my Protector, deserves praise—
the one who trains my hands for battle
and my fingers for war,
2 who loves me and is my stronghold,
my refuge and my deliverer,
my shield and the one in whom I take shelter,
who makes nations submit to me.
3 O LORD, of what importance is the human race that you should notice them?
Of what importance is mankind that you should be concerned about them?
4 People are like a vapor,
their days like a shadow that disappears.
5 O LORD, make the sky sink and come down.
Touch the mountains and make them smolder.
6 Hurl lightning bolts and scatter the enemy.
Shoot your arrows and rout them.
7 Reach down from above.
Grab me and rescue me from the surging water,
from the power of foreigners
8 who speak lies
and make false promises.
9 O God, I will sing a new song to you.
Accompanied by a ten-stringed instrument, I will sing praises to you,
10 the one who delivers kings
and rescued David his servant from a deadly sword.

144:1–15 The prophet reminds us in Psalm 144 that people are said to be blessed in two ways when he says, "How blessed are the people who experience these things" and appends, "How blessed are the people whose God is the LORD." Therefore the blessed of the world are those who are supported by very great security and persevere in constant joy and worldly abundance. But the psalmist excellently applied "people" to those who are not removed from their plan by any adversity but firmly planted with a stable mind, and he confirmed in the contemplation of heavenly matters, they always remain dauntless.

CASSIODORUS **(C. 485–C. 585)**
EXPLANATION OF THE PSALMS

11 Grab me and rescue me from the power of foreigners
who speak lies
and make false promises.
12 Then our sons will be like plants,
that quickly grow to full size.
Our daughters will be like corner pillars,
carved like those in a palace.
13 Our storehouses will be full,
providing all kinds of food.
Our sheep will multiply by the thousands
and fill our pastures.
14 Our cattle will be weighted down with produce.
No one will break through our walls,
no one will be taken captive,
and there will be no terrified cries in our city squares.
15 How blessed are the people who experience these
things.
How blessed are the people whose God is the LORD.

PSALM 145

A psalm of praise; by David.

1 I will extol you, my God, O King.
I will praise your name continually.
2 Every day I will praise you.
I will praise your name continually.
3 The LORD is great and certainly worthy of praise.
No one can fathom his greatness.
4 One generation will praise your deeds to another
and tell about your mighty acts.
5 I will focus on your honor and majestic splendor
and your amazing deeds.
6 They will proclaim the power of your awesome acts.
I will declare your great deeds.
7 They will talk about the fame of your great kindness
and sing about your justice.
8 The LORD is merciful and compassionate;
he is patient and demonstrates great loyal love.
9 The LORD is good to all
and has compassion on all he has made.
10 All your works will give thanks to you, LORD.
Your loyal followers will praise you.
11 They will proclaim the splendor of your kingdom;
they will tell about your power,
12 so that mankind might acknowledge your mighty acts
and the majestic splendor of your kingdom.
13 Your kingdom is an eternal kingdom,
and your dominion endures through all generations.
14 The LORD supports all who fall
and lifts up all who are bent over.
15 Everything looks to you in anticipation,
and you provide them with food on a regular basis.
16 You open your hand
and fill every living thing with the food it desires.
17 The LORD is just in all his actions
and exhibits love in all he does.
18 The LORD is near all who cry out to him,
all who cry out to him sincerely.
19 He satisfies the desire of his loyal followers;
he hears their cry for help and delivers them.

145:3 Now if anyone should ask for some interpretation, description, and explanation of the divine essence, we are not going to deny that in this kind of wisdom we are unlearned. The fact that the divine greatness has no limit is proclaimed by prophecy, which declares expressly that of his splendor, his glory, and his holiness there is no end. If his surroundings have no limit, much more is he himself in his essence, whatever it may be, comprehended by no limitation in any way. If then interpretation by way of words and names implies by its meaning some sort of comprehension of the subject, and if, on the other hand, that which is unlimited cannot be comprehended, no one could reasonably blame us for ignorance if we are not bold in respect of what none should venture upon. For by what name can I describe the incomprehensible?

GREGORY OF NYSSA
(C. 335–C. 395)
AGAINST EUNOMIUS

20 The LORD protects all those who love him,
but he destroys all the wicked.
21 My mouth will praise the LORD.
Let all who live praise his holy name forever.

PSALM 146

1 Praise the LORD.
Praise the LORD, O my soul.
2 I will praise the LORD as long as I live.
I will sing praises to my God as long as I exist.
3 Do not trust in princes,
or in human beings, who cannot deliver.
4 Their life's breath departs, they return to the ground.
On that day their plans die.
5 How blessed is the one whose helper is the God of Jacob,
whose hope is in the LORD his God.
6 The one who made heaven and earth,
the sea, and all that is in them,
who remains forever faithful,
7 vindicates the oppressed,
and gives food to the hungry.
The LORD releases the imprisoned.
8 The LORD gives sight to the blind.
The LORD lifts up all who are bent over.
The LORD loves the godly.
9 The LORD protects the resident foreigner.
He lifts up the fatherless and the widow,
but he opposes the wicked.
10 The LORD rules forever,
your God, O Zion, throughout the generations to come.
Praise the LORD!

146:1–10 Do not grieve too much for orphans and widows. We have a greater Guardian whose law it is that all should take good care of orphans and widows and about whom the psalmist says, "[The Lord] lifts up the fatherless and the widow, but he opposes the wicked." Only let us put the rudders of our lives in his hands, and we shall meet with an unfailing providence. His guardianship will be surer than can be that of any human being. He is nearer to us than father and mother, for he is our Maker and Creator.

THEODORET OF CYR
(C. 393–C. 458)
LETTERS

PSALM 147

1 Praise the LORD,
for it is good to sing praises to our God.
Yes, praise is pleasant and appropriate.
2 The LORD rebuilds Jerusalem
and gathers the exiles of Israel.
3 He heals the brokenhearted
and bandages their wounds.
4 He counts the number of the stars;
he names all of them.
5 Our Lord is great and has awesome power;
there is no limit to his wisdom.
6 The LORD lifts up the oppressed,
but knocks the wicked to the ground.
7 Offer to the LORD a song of thanks.
Sing praises to our God to the accompaniment of a harp.
8 He covers the sky with clouds,
provides the earth with rain,
and causes grass to grow on the hillsides.
9 He gives food to the animals
and to the young ravens when they chirp.
10 He is not enamored with the strength of a horse,
nor is he impressed by the warrior's strong legs.
11 The LORD takes delight in his faithful followers
and in those who wait for his loyal love.
12 Extol the LORD, O Jerusalem.

147:1–20 Whatever pains and difficulties we may have endured in this world, everything that comes to an end is in fact nothing. Good things are coming that will not come to an end; it is through toils and troubles that we come to them. But when we get there, no one can tear us away from them. The gates of Jerusalem are closed, their bars are also put in place so that it may be said to that city, "Extol the LORD, O Jerusalem. Praise your God, O Zion. For he makes the bars of your gates strong. He blesses your children within you. He brings peace to your territory." The gates being shut, the bars bolted home, no friend can go out, no enemy come in. There we are to enjoy true and real security if here we have not let go of true reality.

AUGUSTINE **(354–430)**
SERMONS

Praise your God, O Zion.
13 For he makes the bars of your gates strong.
He blesses your children within you.
14 He brings peace to your territory.
He abundantly provides for you the best grain.
15 He sends his command through the earth;
swiftly his order reaches its destination.
16 He sends the snow that is white like wool;
he spreads the frost that is white like ashes.
17 He throws his hailstones like crumbs.
Who can withstand the cold wind he sends?
18 He then orders it all to melt;
he breathes on it, and the water flows.
19 He proclaims his word to Jacob,
his statutes and regulations to Israel.
20 He has not done so with any other nation;
they are not aware of his regulations.
Praise the LORD!

PSALM 148

1 Praise the LORD.
Praise the LORD from the sky.
Praise him in the heavens.
2 Praise him, all his angels.
Praise him, all his heavenly assembly.
3 Praise him, O sun and moon.
Praise him, all you shiny stars.
4 Praise him, O highest heaven
and you waters above the sky.
5 Let them praise the name of the LORD,
for he gave the command and they came into existence.
6 He established them so they would endure;
he issued a decree that will not be revoked.
7 Praise the LORD from the earth,
you sea creatures and all you ocean depths,
8 O fire and hail, snow and clouds,
O stormy wind that carries out his orders,
9 you mountains and all you hills,
you fruit trees and all you cedars,
10 you animals and all you cattle,
you creeping things and birds,
11 you kings of the earth and all you nations,
you princes and all you leaders on the earth,
12 you young men and young women,
you elderly, along with you children.
13 Let them praise the name of the LORD,
for his name alone is exalted;
his majesty extends over the earth and sky.
14 He has made his people victorious
and given all his loyal followers reason to praise—
the Israelites, the people who are close to him.
Praise the LORD!

PSALM 149

1 Praise the LORD.
Sing to the LORD a new song.
Praise him in the assembly of the godly.
2 Let Israel rejoice in their Creator.
Let the people of Zion delight in their King.

148:1–14 "For he gave the command and they came into existence." For God to have commanded is to have created; the command is creation. He spoke, and they were made, according to that which is written in Genesis: God said, and God created; that is, God the Father gave the command, and God the Son created. Someone may say he is the greater who gives the command, and he is the lesser to whom it is given. It is just as blasphemous to believe this of the Son against the Father as it is to believe it of the Father against the Son. "For he gave the command and they came into existence." One nature both commands and creates; God gives the order, God fulfills it. A painter bids a painter paint, and the painter paints what he has bid be painted.

JEROME **(C. 342–420)**
HOMILIES ON THE PSALMS

149:1–9 "The LORD takes delight in his people." How comprehensive is the love of Jesus! There is no part of his people's interests that he does not consider, and nothing concerns their welfare that is not important to him. Believer, rest assured that the heart of Jesus cares about your humbler affairs. The breadth of his tender love is such that you may resort to him in all matters; for in all your afflictions he is afflicted, and as a father pities his children, so does he pity you. Oh, what a heart is his that does not merely comprehend the persons of his people but comprehends also the diverse and innumerable concerns of all those persons! O my soul, go to your rest rejoicing, for you are no desolate wanderer but a beloved child, watched over, cared for, supplied, and defended by your Lord.

CHARLES SPURGEON
(1834–1892)
MORNING AND EVENING

VENERABLE BEDE:

HISTORIAN OF THE CHURCH IN BRITAIN

c. 672–735

Bede was born around 672 in a recently Christianized region of Britain. His grandparents had been Anglo-Saxon pagans. As a child, he studied in a monastery, where he gained an education under the monastic system and served the church. The young man grew in his mastery of Latin to the point that it supplanted his own native tongue. He also grew in familiarity with Greek in a way that was unusual for Western Europe, which equipped him to write exegetical commentaries and preserve copies of Greek and Latin classic philosophical and literary texts. His most significant contribution, however, was as a historian.

Bede's magnum opus was *Ecclesiastical History of the English People*, a monumental achievement chronicling the historical events of the English church from Augustine to his own time. Three themes dominated the work: He brought together the varying English peoples under one historical roof, helping secure a single English self-identity; he favored the Roman church and supported its Latin practices; and he offered examples of political, monastic, and ecclesial models of behavior in the interest of fostering a Christianized society. Although he himself was a Saxon, he portrayed the Celtic Christians of the region attractively. He also favored Roman forms of the Christian faith in doctrine and practice over those of Constantinople and the East.

Additionally, Bede was instrumental in popularizing the BC and AD dating system. Offered first by the monk Dionysius Exiguus around 525, the method replaced the secular dating system of Rome, which pegged history to the years of Roman political leaders. Dionysius refused to mark time using the persecutors of Christians, so he devised a system that placed Christ's birth at its center. It wasn't until Bede utilized the system, however, that it became widely used.

Beyond Venerable Bede's work of preserving important classical texts for the Middle Ages and offering exegetical commentaries for the Bible, he instilled in the habitants of Britain a sense of their identity, ultimately giving the communion of saints in Britain a greater understanding of their place within the sovereign work of God.

IMPORTANT WORKS

ECCLESIASTICAL HISTORY OF THE ENGLISH PEOPLE

ON THE RECKONING OF TIME

3 Let them praise his name with dancing.
Let them sing praises to him to the accompaniment of
the tambourine and harp.
4 For the LORD takes delight in his people;
he exalts the oppressed by delivering them.
5 Let the godly rejoice because of their vindication.
Let them shout for joy upon their beds.
6 May the praises of God be in their mouths
and a two-edged sword in their hands,
7 in order to take revenge on the nations
and punish foreigners.
8 The godly bind their enemies' kings in chains
and their nobles in iron shackles,
9 and execute the judgment to which their enemies have
been sentenced.
All his loyal followers will be vindicated.
Praise the LORD.

PSALM 150

1 Praise the LORD!
Praise God in his sanctuary;
praise him in the sky, which testifies to his strength!
2 Praise him for his mighty acts;
praise him for his surpassing greatness!
3 Praise him with the blast of the horn;
praise him with the lyre and the harp!
4 Praise him with the tambourine and with dancing;
praise him with stringed instruments and the flute!
5 Praise him with loud cymbals;
praise him with clanging cymbals!
6 Let everything that has breath praise the LORD!
Praise the LORD!

150:1 The psalmist, in order to awaken people who grow languid in God's praises, bids them lift their eyes toward the heavenly sanctuary. That the majesty of God may be duly reverenced, the psalmist represents him as presiding on his throne in the heavens. If we would have our minds kindled to engage in this religious service, let us meditate upon his power and greatness, which will speedily dispel all such insensibility. Though our minds can never take in this immensity, the mere taste of it will deeply affect us. And God will not reject such praises as we offer according to our capacity.

JOHN CALVIN (1509–1564)
COMPLETE COMMENTARY ON THE BIBLE

AUTHOR	AUDIENCE	DATE	PURPOSE	THEMES
King Solomon and other wise men	The people of Israel	Primarily during Solomon's reign (970–930 BC)	The book of Proverbs is a collection of Israel's ancient wisdom, given to guide the reader out of foolishness and to embrace the fear of the Lord.	Wisdom; practical living; and the fear of the Lord

What is a proverb? Didymus the Blind provides a helpful definition as well as historical insight behind the name:

> A proverb is a saying such as, "War is pleasant to the inexperienced," or "A drop constantly falling hollows a stone." The name *proverb* derived from the fact that once roads were marked off with no signs . . . Ancient people set them in certain places and then inscribed them with certain information and questions. So they fulfilled two purposes: On the one hand, they indicated to the traveler the length of the journey; on the other, when one read the inscription and kept busy comprehending it, one was relieved of weariness. Therefore a road is called in Greek *oimos*, from which is derived the word *paroimia*, which means "proverb."

Like those ancient paths, wisdom helps us on our way through the world. It offers signposts, road markers leading to life. John Wesley summarizes the scope and structure of this book of Proverbs in this way: "The nine first chapters are as a preface exhorting us to the study and practice of wisdom and warning us against the things that would hinder it. We have then the first volume of Solomon's Proverbs, chapters 10–24. After that a second volume, chapters 25–29. And then Agur's prophecy, chapter 30. And Lemuel's, chapter 31."

The topics covered in this collection are nearly exhaustive: negative character traits like anger, hatred, pride, self-glory, and stubbornness; positive character traits like faithful love, humility, loyalty, self-control, and teachability; negative conduct like gossip and meddling; positive conduct like moderation and purity; the benefits of discipline and consequences for laziness; the need for justice; advice to families on training children, developing peaceful relationships; the qualities of a godly and noble wife; prosperity and poverty; the rewards of righteousness; and wisdom itself, including how to identify it, get it, keep it, and apply it.

One of the singular contributions of the book of Proverbs has been to impress upon believers the value of wisdom for wisdom's sake. You'll notice from the list of topics that many of the proverbs are not primarily theological in nature. Consequently, these nuggets of wisdom are applicable to everyone, everywhere, in every age. That's not to say there is no religious value in obtaining wisdom. Far from it. In fact, Solomon insists in the preface to the book the very opposite: "The beginning of wisdom is to fear the Lord, and acknowledging the Holy One is understanding" (9:10).

PROVERBS

The fear of the Lord is a major theme in Proverbs, appearing in nearly every chapter. Here fear isn't dread or anxiety but *reverential awe*. It is orienting one's life, affections, and impulses around the Lord and his ways, which unlocks the kind of knowledge, understanding, and wisdom that leads to the good, blessed life. Several early church fathers understood this fear as *piety*. As Didymus the Blind explained, "To know goodness is not sufficient to reach blessedness if one does not put goodness into practice with works. Piety toward God is actually the beginning of knowledge." Chrysostom said, "Piety . . . acts as a fountain and source for discerning the divine according to our inner being so that we may see the true light, hear the secret oracles, be nourished with the bread of life, obtain the fragrance of Christ and learn the doctrine of this life. When we have piety, our senses too are allied with us, when neither our eyes see nor our mouth speaks evil."

While this godly fear moves the wise toward righteous living, it also moves them away from evil and wickedness. According to Ambrose, "He who fears the Lord departs from error and directs his ways to the path of virtue. Except a man fear the Lord, he is unable to renounce sin." Theodoret of Cyr argued, "To the atheist is the name *fool* most accurately applied in truth and nature: If the fear of God is the beginning of wisdom, lack of fear and denial of him would be the opposite of wisdom." It is when we orient our affections toward the Lord that we attain what the book of Proverbs promises: not merely wisdom, but the blessings that come from it.

The book of Proverbs offers "a new way of writing," explained John Wesley,

> wherein divine wisdom is taught us in Proverbs or short sentences . . . And these Proverbs of Solomon are not merely a collection of the wise sayings that had been formerly delivered but were the dictates of the Spirit of God in Solomon, so that it is God by Solomon that here speaks to us . . . The scope of all is to direct us so to order our conversation that we may see the salvation of God.

INTRODUCTION TO THE BOOK

1 The proverbs of Solomon, son of David, king of Israel:
2 To learn wisdom and moral instruction,
to discern wise counsel.
3 To receive moral instruction in skillful living,
with righteousness, justice, and equity.
4 To impart shrewdness to the morally naive,
a discerning plan to the young person.
5 (Let the wise also hear and gain instruction,
and let the discerning acquire guidance!)
6 To discern the meaning of a proverb and a parable,
the sayings of the wise and their riddles.

INTRODUCTION TO THE THEME OF THE BOOK

7 Fearing the LORD is the beginning of discernment,
but fools have despised wisdom and moral instruction.
8 Listen, my child, to the instruction from your father,
and do not forsake the teaching from your mother.
9 For they will be like an elegant garland on your head,
and like pendants around your neck.

ADMONITION TO AVOID EASY BUT UNJUST RICHES

10 My child, if sinners try to entice you,
do not consent!
11 If they say, "Come with us!
We will lie in wait to shed blood;
we will ambush an innocent person capriciously.
12 We will swallow them alive like Sheol,
those full of vigor like those going down to the Pit.
13 We will seize all kinds of precious wealth;
we will fill our houses with plunder.
14 Join with us!
We will all share equally in what we steal."
15 My child, do not go down their way,
withhold yourself from their path;
16 for they are eager to inflict harm,
and they hasten to shed blood.
17 Surely it is futile to spread a net
in plain sight of any bird,
18 but these men lie in wait for their own blood;
they ambush their own lives!
19 Such are the ways of all who gain profit unjustly;
it takes away the life of those who obtain it!

WARNING AGAINST DISREGARDING WISDOM

20 Wisdom calls out in the street,
she shouts loudly in the plazas;
21 at the head of the noisy streets she calls,
in the entrances of the gates in the city she utters her words:
22 "How long will you simpletons love naiveté?
How long have mockers delighted in mockery?
And how long will fools hate knowledge?
23 You should respond to my rebuke.
Then I would pour out my thoughts to you;
I would make my words known to you.
24 However, because I called but you refused to listen,
because I stretched out my hand but no one was paying
attention,

1:20–33 Solomon here declares how dangerous it is not to hearken to the calls of God. Three sorts of persons are here called by him: (1) *Simpletons.* Sinners are fond of their simple notions of good and evil, and they flatter themselves in their wickedness. (2) *Mockers.* Proud, jovial people who make a jest of everything. (3) *Fools.* The worst of fools hate to be taught and have a rooted dislike of serious godliness. We do not make a right use of reproofs if we do not turn from evil to what is good. The promises are very encouraging. People cannot turn by any power of their own, but God answers, "I would pour out my thoughts to you." Special grace is needful to sincere conversion. But that grace shall never be denied to any who seek it.

MATTHEW HENRY (1662–1714)
COMMENTARY ON THE WHOLE BIBLE

25 and you neglected all my advice,
and did not comply with my rebuke,
26 so I myself will laugh when disaster strikes you;
I will mock when what you dread comes,
27 when what you dread comes like a whirlwind,
and disaster strikes you like a devastating storm,
when distressing trouble comes on you.
28 Then they will call to me, but I will not answer;
they will diligently seek me, but they will not find me.
29 Because they hated moral knowledge
and did not choose to fear the LORD,
30 they did not comply with my advice;
they spurned all my rebuke.
31 Therefore they will eat from the fruit of their way,
and they will be stuffed full of their own counsel.
32 For the waywardness of the
simpletons will kill them,
and the careless ease of fools will destroy them.
33 But the one who listens to me will live in security
and will be at ease from the dread of harm."

BENEFITS OF SEEKING WISDOM

2 My child, if you receive my words,
and store up my commands inside yourself,
2 by making your ear attentive to wisdom
and by turning your heart to understanding,
3 indeed, if you call out for discernment—
shout loudly for understanding—
4 if you seek it like silver
and search for it like hidden treasure,
5 then you will understand how to fear the LORD,
and you will discover knowledge about God.
6 For the LORD gives wisdom,
and from his mouth comes knowledge and understanding.
7 He stores up effective counsel for the upright
and is like a shield for those who live with integrity,
8 to guard the paths of the righteous
and to protect the way of his pious ones.
9 Then you will understand righteousness and justice
and equity—every good way.
10 For wisdom will enter your heart,
and moral knowledge will be attractive to you.
11 Discretion will protect you;
understanding will guard you
12 to deliver you from the way of the wicked,
from those speaking perversity,
13 who leave the upright paths
to walk on the dark ways,
14 who delight in doing evil;
they rejoice in perverse evil,
15 whose paths are morally crooked
and who are devious in their ways,
16 to deliver you from the adulterous woman,
from the loose woman who has flattered you with her words,
17 who leaves the husband from her younger days
and has ignored her marriage covenant made before God.
18 For she has set her house by death
and her paths by the place of the departed spirits.

2:1–22 Students of these revered writings should be advised not only to learn the kinds of expressions in the holy scriptures, to notice carefully how they are customarily expressed there, and to remember them, but also to pray that they may understand them, and this is chiefly and especially necessary. Indeed, in these books they are studying earnestly they read that "the LORD gives wisdom, and from his mouth comes knowledge and understanding." It is from him that they have received that zeal for study, if it is endowed with piety.

AUGUSTINE **(354–430)**
CHRISTIAN INSTRUCTION

19 None who go in to her will return,
nor will they reach the paths of life.
20 So you will walk in the way of good people
and will keep on the paths of the righteous.
21 For the upright will reside in the land,
and those with integrity will remain in it,
22 but the wicked will be removed from the land,
and the treacherous will be torn away from it.

EXHORTATIONS TO SEEK WISDOM AND WALK WITH THE LORD

3 My child, do not forget my teaching,
but let your heart keep my commandments,
2 for they will provide a long and full life
and well-being for you.
3 Do not let mercy and truth leave you;
bind them around your neck,
write them on the tablet of your heart.
4 Then you will find favor and good understanding
in the sight of God and people.
5 Trust in the LORD with all your heart,
and do not rely on your own understanding.
6 Acknowledge him in all your ways,
and he will make your paths straight.
7 Do not be wise in your own estimation;
fear the LORD and turn away from evil.
8 This will bring healing to your body
and refreshment to your inner self.
9 Honor the LORD from your wealth
and from the firstfruits of all your crops;
10 then your barns will be filled completely,
and your vats will overflow with new wine.
11 My child, do not despise discipline from the LORD,
and do not loathe his rebuke.
12 For the LORD disciplines those he loves,
just as a father disciplines the son in whom he delights.

BLESSINGS OF OBTAINING WISDOM

13 Blessed is the one who has found wisdom
and the one who obtains understanding.
14 For her benefit is more profitable than silver,
and her gain is better than gold.
15 She is more precious than rubies,
and none of the things you desire can compare with her.
16 Long life is in her right hand;
in her left hand are riches and honor.
17 Her ways are very pleasant,
and all her paths are peaceful.
18 She is like a tree of life to those who grasp onto her,
and everyone who takes hold of her will be blessed.
19 By wisdom the LORD laid the foundation of the earth;
he established the heavens by understanding.
20 By his knowledge the primordial sea was broken open,
so that the clouds drip down dew.
21 My child, do not let them escape from your sight;
safeguard sound wisdom and discretion.
22 So they will become life for your soul
and grace around your neck.
23 Then you will walk on your way with security,

3:13–35 Wisdom is the compass by which human beings are to steer across the trackless waste of life. Those who are in a wilderness infested with robbers must handle matters wisely if they would journey safely. If, trained by the great Teacher, we follow where he leads, we shall find good even while in this dark abode; there are celestial fruits to be gathered this side of Eden's bowery and songs of paradise to be sung amid the groves of earth. Let us listen to the voice of the Lord, for he has declared the secret; he has revealed to the people wherein true wisdom lies.

CHARLES SPURGEON
(1834–1892)
MORNING AND EVENING

and you will not stumble.
24 When you lie down you will not be filled with fear;
when you lie down your sleep will be pleasant.
25 Do not be afraid of sudden disaster
or when destruction overtakes the wicked;
26 for the LORD will be the source of your confidence,
and he will guard your foot from being caught in
a trap.

WISDOM DEMONSTRATED IN RELATIONSHIPS WITH PEOPLE

27 Do not withhold good from those who need it
when you have the ability to help.
28 Do not say to your neighbor, "Go! Return tomorrow
and I will give it," when you have it with you at the time.
29 Do not plot evil against your neighbor
when he dwells by you unsuspectingly.
30 Do not accuse anyone without legitimate cause
if he has not treated you wrongly.
31 Do not envy a violent man,
and do not choose any of his ways;
32 for one who goes astray is an abomination to the LORD,
but he reveals his intimate counsel to the upright.
33 The LORD's curse is on the household of the wicked,
but he blesses the home of the righteous.
34 With arrogant scoffers he is scornful,
yet he shows favor to the humble.
35 The wise inherit honor,
but he holds fools up to public contempt.

ADMONITION TO FOLLOW RIGHTEOUSNESS AND AVOID WICKEDNESS

4 Listen, children, to a father's instruction,
and pay attention so that you may gain discernment.
2 Because I hereby give you good instruction,
do not forsake my teaching.

3 When I was a son to my father,
a tender, only child before my mother,
4 he taught me, and he said to me:
"Let your heart lay hold of my words;
keep my commands so that you will live.
5 Acquire wisdom, acquire understanding;
do not forget and do not turn aside from the words I
speak.
6 Do not forsake wisdom, and she will protect you;
love her, and she will guard you.
7 Wisdom is supreme—so acquire wisdom,
and whatever you acquire, acquire understanding!
8 Esteem her highly and she will exalt you;
she will honor you if you embrace her.
9 She will place a fair garland on your head;
she will bestow a beautiful crown on you."
10 Listen, my child, and accept my words
so that the years of your life will be many.
11 I hereby guide you in the way of wisdom,
and I lead you in upright paths.
12 When you walk, your steps will not be hampered,
and when you run, you will not stumble.

4:8–18 It has been said by inspiration: *Hear, my son, and receive my words, that you may have the many ways of life. For I teach the ways of wisdom so that the fountains fail you not that gush forth from the earth itself.* Not only did he enumerate several ways of salvation for any one righteous person, but he added many other ways of many righteous people, speaking thus: "The path of the righteous is like the bright morning light." The commandments and the modes of preparatory training are to be regarded as the ways and appliances of life.

CLEMENT OF ALEXANDRIA **(C. 150–C. 215)**
STROMATEIS

13 Hold on to instruction, do not let it go;
protect it, because it is your life.
14 Do not enter the path of the wicked
or walk in the way of those who are evil.
15 Avoid it, do not go on it;
turn away from it, and go on.
16 For they cannot sleep unless they cause harm;
they are robbed of sleep until they make someone
stumble.
17 Indeed they have eaten bread gained from wickedness
and drink wine obtained from violence.
18 But the path of the righteous is like the bright morning
light,
growing brighter and brighter until full day.
19 The way of the wicked is like gloomy darkness;
they do not know what they stumble over.

20 My child, pay attention to my words;
listen attentively to my sayings.
21 Do not let them depart from your sight;
guard them within your heart,
22 for they are life to those who find them
and healing to one's entire body.
23 Guard your heart with all vigilance,
for from it are the sources of life.
24 Remove perverse speech from your mouth;
keep devious talk far from your lips.
25 Let your eyes look directly in front of you,
and let your gaze look straight before you.
26 Make the path for your feet level,
so that all your ways may be established.
27 Do not turn to the right or to the left;
turn yourself away from evil.

ADMONITION TO AVOID SEDUCTION TO EVIL

5 My child, be attentive to my wisdom;
pay close attention to my understanding,
2 in order to safeguard discretion
and that your lips may guard knowledge.
3 For the lips of the adulterous woman drip honey,
and her seductive words are smoother than olive oil,
4 but in the end she is bitter as wormwood,
sharp as a two-edged sword.
5 Her feet go down to death;
her steps lead straight to the grave.
6 Lest she should make level the path leading to life,
her paths have wandered, but she is not able to
discern it.
7 So now, children, listen to me;
do not turn aside from the words I speak.
8 Keep yourself far from her,
and do not go near the door of her house,
9 lest you give your vigor to others
and your years to a cruel person,
10 lest strangers devour your strength
and your labor benefit another man's house.
11 And at the end of your life you will groan
when your flesh and your body are wasted away.
12 And you will say, "How I hated discipline!

5:1–14 Even when the sinner looks for gratification, he doesn't find the fruit of his sin pleasant. And "the lips of the adulterous woman drip honey, and her seductive words are smoother than olive oil, but in the end she is bitter as wormwood, sharp as a two-edged sword." So he eats and is quite pleased for a little while. Then, when it is too late, when he has cut off his soul from God, he rejects it. But the fool does not know that those who are cut off from God shall perish.

ATHANASIUS (C. 296–373)
LETTERS

My heart spurned reproof!
13 For I did not obey my teachers,
and I did not heed my instructors.
14 I almost came to complete ruin
in the midst of the whole congregation!"
15 Drink water from your own cistern
and running water from your own well.
16 Should your springs be dispersed outside,
your streams of water in the wide plazas?
17 Let them be for yourself alone
and not for strangers with you.
18 May your fountain be blessed,
and may you rejoice in the wife you married in your
youth—
19 a loving doe, a graceful deer;
may her breasts satisfy you at all times;
may you be captivated by her love always.
20 But why should you be captivated, my son, by an
adulteress,
and embrace the bosom of a different woman?
21 For the ways of a person are in front of the LORD's eyes,
and the LORD weighs all that person's paths.
22 The wicked will be captured by his own iniquities,
and he will be held by the cords of his own sin.
23 He will die because there was no discipline;
because of the greatness of his folly he will reel.

ADMONITIONS AND WARNINGS AGAINST DANGEROUS AND DESTRUCTIVE ACTS

6 My child, if you have made a pledge for your neighbor,
if you have become a guarantor for a stranger,
2 if you have been ensnared by the words you have
uttered
and have been caught by the words you have spoken,
3 then, my child, do this in order to deliver yourself,
because you have fallen into your neighbor's power:
Go, humble yourself,
and appeal firmly to your neighbor.
4 Permit no sleep to your eyes
or slumber to your eyelids.
5 Deliver yourself like a gazelle from a snare
and like a bird from the trap of the fowler.
6 Go to the ant, you sluggard;
observe her ways and be wise!
7 It has no commander,
overseer, or ruler,
8 yet it would prepare its food in the summer;
it gathered at the harvest what it will eat.
9 How long, you sluggard, will you lie there?
When will you rise from your sleep?
10 A little sleep, a little slumber,
a little folding of the hands to relax,
11 and your poverty will come like a robber,
and your need like an armed man.
12 A worthless and wicked person
walks around saying perverse things;
13 he winks with his eyes,
signals with his feet,
and points with his fingers;

6:12–19 The six capital crimes enumerated here are nevertheless like minor faults when compared with the sowing of discord, since the deed that fractures the unity and fraternity achieved by the grace of the Holy Spirit is surely a greater sin. For anyone can raise his eyes boastfully, lie with the tongue, pollute himself with murder, plot to harm his neighbor, subject his members to other offenses, and give false testimony against another. But it must not be thought that what he names with his lying tongue is all the same, for he is able to tell a lie without doing so against a neighbor . . . Each reprobate, I say, can bring evil upon himself or upon others yet without harming the peace of the church. But what heretics do is more serious, they who destroy the harmony of fraternal unity by sowing discord.

VENERABLE BEDE
(C. 672–735)
COMMENTARY ON PROVERBS

14 he plots evil with perverse thoughts in his heart;
he spreads contention at all times.
15 Therefore, his disaster will come suddenly;
in an instant he will be broken, and there will be no
remedy.
16 There are six things that the LORD hates,
even seven things that are an abomination to him:
17 haughty eyes, a lying tongue,
and hands that shed innocent blood,
18 a heart that devises wicked plans,
feet that are swift to run to evil,
19 a false witness who pours out lies,
and a person who spreads discord among family
members.
20 My child, guard the commands of your father
and do not forsake the instruction of your mother.
21 Bind them on your heart continually;
fasten them around your neck.
22 When you walk about, they will guide you;
when you lie down, they will watch over you;
when you wake up, they will talk to you.
23 For the commandments are like a lamp;
instruction is like a light,
and rebukes of discipline are like the road leading to life
24 by keeping you from the evil woman,
from the smooth tongue of the loose woman.
25 Do not lust in your heart for her beauty,
and do not let her captivate you with her alluring eyes;
26 for on account of a prostitute one is brought down to a
loaf of bread,
but the wife of another man preys on your precious life.
27 Can a man hold fire against his chest
without burning his clothes?
28 Can a man walk on hot coals
without scorching his feet?
29 So it is with the one who sleeps with his neighbor's wife;
no one who touches her will escape punishment.
30 People do not despise a thief when he steals
to fulfill his need when he is hungry.
31 Yet if he is caught he must repay seven times over;
he might even have to give all the wealth of his house.
32 A man who commits adultery with a woman lacks
sense;
whoever does it destroys his own life.
33 He will be beaten and despised,
and his reproach will not be wiped away;
34 for jealousy kindles a husband's rage,
and he will not show mercy when he takes revenge.
35 He will not consider any compensation;
he will not be willing, even if you multiply the
compensation.

ADMONITION TO AVOID THE WILES OF THE ADULTERESS

7 My child, devote yourself to my words
and store up my commands inside yourself.
2 Keep my commands so that you may live,
and obey my instruction as your most prized
possession.

3 Bind them on your forearm;
write them on the tablet of your heart.
4 Say to wisdom, "You are my sister,"
and call understanding a close relative
5 so that they may keep you from the adulterous woman,
from the loose woman who has flattered you with her
words.
6 For at the window of my house
through my window lattice I looked out,
7 and I saw among the naive—
I discerned among the youths—
a young man who lacked sense.
8 He was passing by the street near her corner,
making his way along the road to her house
9 in the twilight, the evening,
in the dark of the night.
10 Suddenly a woman came out to meet him!
She was dressed like a prostitute and with secret intent.
11 (She is loud and rebellious;
she does not remain at home—
12 at one time outside, at another in the wide plazas,
and by every corner she lies in wait.)
13 So she grabbed him and kissed him,
and with a bold expression she said to him,
14 "I have meat from my peace offerings at home;
today I have fulfilled my vows!
15 That is why I came out to meet you,
to look for you, and I found you!
16 I have spread my bed with elegant coverings,
with richly colored fabric from Egypt.
17 I have perfumed my bed
with myrrh, aloes, and cinnamon.
18 Come, let's drink deeply of lovemaking until morning;
let's delight ourselves with love's pleasures.
19 For my husband is not at home;
he has gone on a journey of some distance.
20 He has taken a bag of money with him;
he will not return until the end of the month."
21 She turned him aside with her persuasions;
with her smooth talk she was enticing him along.
22 Suddenly he was going after her
like an ox that goes to the slaughter,
like a stag prancing into a trapper's snare
23 till an arrow pierces his liver—
like a bird hurrying into a trap,
and he does not know that it will cost him his life.
24 So now, sons, listen to me,
and pay attention to the words I speak.
25 Do not let your heart turn aside to her ways—
do not wander into her pathways;
26 for she has brought down many fatally wounded,
and all those she has slain are many.
27 Her house is the way to the grave,
going down to the chambers of death.

THE APPEAL OF WISDOM

8 Does not wisdom call out?
Does not understanding raise her voice?
2 At the top of the prominent places along the way,

7:6–23 Here in the words of Solomon we behold the very picture of a wanton woman. What other than worldly pleasure is more characteristic of a prostitute who makes her entrance stealthily into the house, first making tentative explorations with her eyes and then entering quickly, while you concentrate the gaze of your soul outward on the public square, that is, on the streets frequented by passersby and not inward on the mysteries of the law? Pleasure dissipates its fragrance because it has not the fragrance of Christ. Pleasure looks for treasures, it promises kingdoms, it assures lasting loves, it pledges undreamed-of intimacies, instruction without a guardian, and conversation without hindrance. Pleasure promises a life bereft of anxiety, a sleep devoid of disturbance, and wants that cannot be satiated.

AMBROSE **(C. 339–C. 397)**
CAIN AND ABEL

8:1–34 Wisdom here is Christ. Seek him early, seek him earnestly, seek him before anything else. Christ never said, *Seek in vain*. Those who love Christ are such as have seen his loveliness and have had his love shed abroad in their hearts; therefore they are happy. Christ, by his Spirit, guides believers into all truth and so leads them in the way of righteousness, and they walk after the Spirit. Christ is wisdom, and he is life to all believers.

MATTHEW HENRY (1662–1714)
COMMENTARY ON THE WHOLE BIBLE

at the intersection of the paths she has taken her
stand;
3 beside the gates opening into the city,
at the entrance of the doorways she cries out:
4 "To you, O people, I call out,
and my voice calls to all mankind.
5 You who are naive, discern wisdom!
And you fools, understand discernment!
6 Listen, for I will speak excellent things,
and my lips will utter what is right.
7 For my mouth speaks truth,
and my lips hate wickedness.
8 All the words of my mouth are righteous;
there is nothing in them twisted or crooked.
9 All of them are clear to the discerning
and upright to those who find knowledge.
10 Receive my instruction rather than silver,
and knowledge rather than choice gold.
11 For wisdom is better than rubies,
and desirable things cannot be compared to her.
12 "I, wisdom, have dwelt with prudence,
and I find knowledge and discretion.
13 The fear of the LORD is to hate evil;
I hate arrogant pride and the evil way
and perverse utterances.
14 Counsel and sound wisdom belong to me;
I possess understanding and might.
15 By me, kings reign,
and by me, potentates decree righteousness;
16 by me, princes rule,
as well as nobles and all righteous judges.
17 I will love those who love me,
and those who seek me diligently will find me.
18 Riches and honor are with me,
long-lasting wealth and righteousness.
19 My fruit is better than the purest gold,
and my harvest is better than choice silver.
20 I walk in the path of righteousness,
in the pathway of justice,
21 that I may cause those who love me to inherit wealth,
and that I may fill their treasuries.
22 The LORD created me as the beginning of his works,
before his deeds of long ago.
23 From eternity I have been fashioned,
from the beginning, from before the world existed.
24 When there were no deep oceans I was born,
when there were no springs overflowing with water;
25 before the mountains were set in place—
before the hills—I was born,
26 before he made the earth and its fields,
or the top soil of the world.
27 When he established the heavens, I was there;
when he marked out the horizon over the face of the
deep,
28 when he established the clouds above,
when he secured the fountains of the deep,
29 when he gave the sea his decree
that the waters should not pass over his command,
when he marked out the foundations of the earth,

30 then I was beside him as a master craftsman,
and I was his delight day by day,
rejoicing before him at all times,
31 rejoicing in the habitable part of his earth,
and delighting in its people.

32 "So now, children, listen to me;
blessed are those who keep my ways.
33 Listen to my instruction so that you may be wise,
and do not neglect it.
34 Blessed is the one who listens to me,
watching at my doors day by day,
waiting beside my doorway.
35 For the one who finds me has found life
and received favor from the LORD.
36 But the one who misses me brings harm to himself;
all who hate me love death."

THE CONSEQUENCES OF ACCEPTING WISDOM OR FOLLY

9 Wisdom has built her house;
she has carved out its seven pillars.
2 She has prepared her meat, she has mixed her wine;
she also has arranged her table.
3 She has sent out her female servants;
she calls out on the highest places of the city.
4 "Whoever is naive, let him turn in here."
To those who lack understanding, she has said,
5 "Come, eat some of my food,
and drink some of the wine I have mixed.
6 Abandon your foolish ways so that you may live,
and proceed in the way of understanding."
7 Whoever corrects a mocker is asking for insult;
whoever reproves a wicked person receives abuse.
8 Do not reprove a mocker, or he will hate you;
reprove a wise person, and he will love you.
9 Give instruction to a wise person, and he will become
wiser still;
teach a righteous person, and he will add to his
learning.
10 The beginning of wisdom is to fear the LORD,
and acknowledging the Holy One is understanding.
11 For because of me your days will be many,
and years will be added to your life.
12 If you are wise, you are wise to your own advantage,
but if you have mocked, you alone must bear it.
13 The woman called Folly is brash;
she is naive and does not know anything.
14 And she has sat down at the door of her house,
on a seat at the highest point of the city,
15 calling out to those who are passing by her in the
way,
who go straight on their way.
16 "Whoever is naive, let him turn in here,"
To those who lack understanding she has said,
17 "Stolen waters are sweet,
and food obtained in secret is pleasant!"
18 But they do not realize that the dead are there,
that her guests are in the depths of the grave.

9:9–13 Wisely to give and humbly to receive reproof requires much prayer, self-denial, love, and sincerity. Faithful are the wounds of a friend. Wisdom's free and gracious invitation has been set before us. And we might almost ask, who could resist it? Now we have an allure from the opposite direction, for sin is no less keen to destroy than wisdom is to save. The delight of the soul fixed on anything but God and his grace is spiritual adultery.

CHARLES BRIDGES
(1794–1869)
AN EXPOSITION OF THE BOOK OF PROVERBS

BERNARD OF CLAIRVAUX:

THE SWEET-TONGUED DOCTOR
1090–1153

Bernard of Clairvaux is said to have been one of the most influential leaders of the church during the height of the Middle Ages. Indeed, the twelfth century is sometimes called the "Age of Bernard," and his vision of mystical piety and practical Christian discipleship remains influential, both directly and indirectly, in the life of the church today.

Born in 1090 to noble parents in the Burgundy region of France, as a young adult Bernard became involved with the upstart Cistercian monastic order in Citeaux, a reform movement seeking to recapture Benedict's original vision for a dedicated monastic life. Three years later, Bernard founded an offshoot monastery in Clairvaux, which would remain his home until his death. From there he played a variety of roles, but he is most known for his sermons and reflections on the Christian life.

One such work is *On Considerations*, which Bernard wrote to his former disciple, Pope Eugene III. Its themes include knowing God and Christian maturity; the four virtues of justice, temperance, prudence, and fortitude; and the necessity of attending to one's spiritual and intellectual life. It was originally meant to be a single volume but extended to five by the time of his death. Other important works include: *On Humility*, in which Bernard commented on the three degrees of humility and twelve degrees of pride; *On the Love of God*, in which he discusses four degrees of love—love of self for the sake of self, love of God for the sake of self, love of God for the sake of God, and love of self for the sake of God; and *Concerning Grace and Free Will*, in which he explores the complexities of human freedom along a threefold pattern—of nature, of grace, of glory—as well as grace's necessity for salvation in relation to human choice and merit.

Bernard's commentary and sermons on the Song of Solomon have proved especially significant for the church's understanding of personal devotion to Christ. His work hews closely to historical interpretations from early church fathers like Origen and Ambrose, who allegorized the song as a spiritual depiction of the relationship between Christ and the church, or between Christ and the Christian. Desire is an important ingredient in pursuing God, Bernard taught; the tenderness and longing that should characterize a marriage relationship between humans is but an image and reflection of the deeper spiritual relationship between God and his church.

That even the great Reformers Martin Luther and John Calvin appreciated the mystical piety and literary contribution of Bernard of Clairvaux speaks volumes. Well beyond his death in 1153, the sweet-tongued meditations and instructions by the "mellifluous doctor," as he is known in the Catholic Church, have continued to impact the discipleship of Christians through the centuries.

IMPORTANT WORKS

CHRISTIAN THEOLOGY

EXPOSITION OF THE EPISTLE TO THE ROMANS

YES AND NO

THE FIRST COLLECTION OF SOLOMONIC PROVERBS

10 The proverbs of Solomon:

A wise child makes a father rejoice,
but a foolish child is a grief to his mother.
2 Treasures gained by wickedness do not profit,
but righteousness delivers from death.
3 The LORD satisfies the appetite of the righteous,
but he thwarts the craving of the wicked.
4 The one who is lazy becomes poor,
but the one who works diligently becomes wealthy.
5 The one who gathers crops in the summer is a wise son,
but the one who sleeps during harvest is a shameful son.
6 Blessings are on the head of the righteous,
but the speech of the wicked conceals violence.
7 The memory of the righteous is a blessing,
but the reputation of the wicked will rot.
8 The wise person accepts instructions,
but the one who speaks foolishness will come to ruin.
9 The one who conducts himself in integrity will live securely,
but the one who behaves perversely will be found out.
10 The one who winks his eye causes trouble,
and the one who speaks foolishness will come to ruin.
11 The speech of the righteous is a fountain of life,
but the speech of the wicked conceals violence.
12 Hatred stirs up dissension,
but love covers all transgressions.
13 Wisdom is found in the words of the discerning person,
but the one who lacks sense will be disciplined.
14 Those who are wise store up knowledge,
but foolish speech leads to imminent destruction.
15 The wealth of a rich person is like a fortified city,
but the poor are brought to ruin by their poverty.
16 The reward that the righteous receive is life;
the recompense that the wicked receive is judgment.
17 The one who heeds instruction is on the way to life,
but the one who rejects rebuke goes astray.
18 The one who conceals hatred utters lies,
and the one who spreads slander is certainly a fool.
19 When words abound, transgression is inevitable,
but the one who restrains his words is wise.
20 What the righteous say is like the best silver,
but what the wicked think is of little value.
21 The teaching of the righteous feeds many,
but fools die for lack of sense.
22 The blessing from the LORD makes a person rich,
and he adds no sorrow to it.
23 Carrying out a wicked scheme is enjoyable to a fool,
and so is wisdom for the one who has discernment.
24 What the wicked fears will come on him;
what the righteous desire will be granted.
25 When the storm passes through, the wicked are swept away,
but the righteous are an everlasting foundation.
26 Like vinegar to the teeth and like smoke to the eyes,
so is the sluggard to those who send him.

10:25 "When the storm passes through, the wicked are swept away, but the righteous are an everlasting foundation." When temptation attacks, the wicked easily sin. On the other hand, the righteous are saved for eternity when they conquer temptation through patience and a soul of gratitude toward God. Notice how safe righteousness is: The righteous are saved when they avoid evil, are on the defensive, and stand firm constantly. The wicked, on the other hand, are thrown to the ground even when the disturbance or temptation has not attacked completely. Therefore those who ignore the just judgment of God easily sin.

CHRYSOSTOM **(C. 347–407)**
COMMENTARY ON THE PROVERBS OF SOLOMON

27 Fearing the LORD prolongs life,
but the life span of the wicked will be shortened.
28 The hope of the righteous is joy,
but the expectation of the wicked perishes.
29 The way of the LORD is like a stronghold for the upright,
but it is destruction to evildoers.
30 The righteous will never be moved,
but the wicked will not inhabit the land.
31 The speech of the righteous bears the fruit of wisdom,
but the one who speaks perversion will be destroyed.
32 The lips of the righteous know what is pleasing,
but the speech of the wicked is perverse.

11 The LORD abhors dishonest scales,
but an accurate weight is his delight.
2 After pride came, disgrace followed;
but wisdom came with humility.
3 The integrity of the upright guides them,
but the crookedness of the treacherous destroys them.
4 Wealth does not profit in the day of wrath,
but righteousness delivers from death.
5 The righteousness of the blameless will make their way smooth,
but the wicked will fall through their own wickedness.
6 The righteousness of the upright will deliver them,
but the treacherous will be ensnared by their own desires.
7 When a wicked person dies, his expectation perishes,
and hope based on power has perished.
8 A righteous person was delivered out of trouble,
then a wicked person took his place.
9 With his speech the godless person destroys his neighbor,
but by knowledge the righteous will be delivered.
10 When the righteous do well, the city rejoices;
when the wicked perish, there is joy.
11 A city is exalted by the blessing provided from the upright,
but it is destroyed by the counsel of the wicked.
12 The one who denounces his neighbor lacks sense,
but a discerning person keeps silent.
13 The one who goes about slandering others reveals secrets,
but the one who is trustworthy conceals a matter.
14 When there is no guidance a nation falls,
but there is success in the abundance of counselors.
15 The one who has put up security for a stranger will surely have trouble,
but whoever avoids shaking hands is secure.
16 A generous woman gains honor,
and ruthless men seize wealth.
17 A kind person benefits himself,
but a cruel person brings himself trouble.
18 The wicked person earns deceitful wages,
but the one who sows righteousness reaps a genuine reward.
19 True righteousness leads to life,
but the one who pursues evil pursues it to his own death.
20 The LORD abhors those who are perverse in heart,
but those who are blameless in their ways are his delight.

11:1–31 "A generous person will be enriched, and the one who provides water for others will himself be satisfied" (11:25). We are here taught the great lesson that to get, we must give; that to accumulate, we must scatter; that to make ourselves happy, we must make others happy; and that in order to become spiritually vigorous, we must seek the spiritual good of others. In watering others, we are ourselves watered. We have latent talents and dormant faculties that are brought to light by exercise. We do not know what tender sympathies we possess until we try to dry the widow's tears and soothe the orphan's grief. The poor widow of Zarephath gave from her scanty store a supply for the prophet's wants, and from that day she never again knew what want was. Give then, and it shall be given unto you, good measure, pressed down, and running over.

CHARLES SPURGEON
(1834–1892)
MORNING AND EVENING

21 Be assured that the evil person will not be unpunished,
but the descendants of the righteous have escaped harm.
22 Like a gold ring in a pig's snout
is a beautiful woman who rejects discretion.
23 The desire of the righteous is only good,
but the expectation of the wicked is wrath.
24 One person is generous and yet grows more wealthy,
but another withholds more than he should and comes
to poverty.
25 A generous person will be enriched,
and the one who provides water for others will himself
be satisfied.
26 People will curse the one who withholds grain,
but they will praise the one who sells it.
27 The one who diligently seeks good seeks favor,
but the one who searches for evil—it will come to him.
28 The one who trusts in his riches will fall,
but the righteous will flourish like a green leaf.
29 The one who troubles his family will inherit nothing,
and the fool will be a servant to the wise person.
30 The fruit of the righteous is like a tree producing life,
and the one who wins souls is wise.
31 If the righteous are recompensed on earth,
how much more the wicked sinner!

12 The one who loves discipline loves knowledge,
but the one who hates reproof is stupid.
2 A good person obtains favor from the LORD,
but the LORD condemns a person with wicked schemes.
3 No one can be established through wickedness,
but a righteous root cannot be moved.
4 A noble wife is the crown of her husband,
but the wife who acts shamefully is like rottenness in
his bones.
5 The plans of the righteous are just;
the counsels of the wicked are deceitful.
6 The words of the wicked lie in wait to shed innocent blood,
but the words of the upright will deliver them.
7 The wicked are overthrown and perish,
but the righteous household will stand.
8 A person will be praised in accordance with his wisdom,
but the one with a bewildered mind will be despised.
9 Better is a person of humble standing who works for
himself,
than one who pretends to be somebody important yet
has no food.
10 A righteous person cares for the life of his animal,
but even the most compassionate acts of the wicked are
cruel.
11 The one who works his field will have plenty of food,
but whoever chases daydreams lacks sense.
12 The wicked person has desired the stronghold of the
wicked,
but the root of the righteous will yield fruit.
13 The evil person is ensnared by the transgression of his
speech,
but the righteous person escapes out of trouble.
14 A person will be satisfied with good from the fruit of his
words,
and the work of his hands will be rendered to him.

12:10 It must be remembered that people are required to practice justice even in dealing with animals. Solomon condemns injustice to our neighbors the more severely when he says, "A righteous person cares for the life of his animal." In a word, we are to do what is right voluntarily and freely, and each of us is responsible for doing his duty. If animals are entitled to their food, much less should we wait for human beings to plague us before we give them their rights.

JOHN CALVIN **(1509–1564)**
COMPLETE COMMENTARY ON THE BIBLE

15 The way of a fool is right in his own opinion,
but the one who listens to advice is wise.
16 A fool's annoyance is known at once,
but the prudent conceals dishonor.
17 The faithful witness tells what is right,
but a false witness speaks deceit.
18 Speaking recklessly is like the thrusts of a sword,
but the words of the wise bring healing.
19 The one who tells the truth will endure forever,
but the one who lies will last only for a moment.
20 Deceit is in the heart of those who plot evil,
but those who promote peace have joy.
21 No harm will be directed at the righteous,
but the wicked are filled with calamity.
22 The LORD abhors a person who lies,
but those who deal truthfully are his delight.
23 The shrewd person conceals knowledge,
but foolish people proclaim folly.
24 The diligent person will rule,
but the slothful will be put to forced labor.
25 Anxiety in a person's heart weighs him down,
but an encouraging word brings him joy.
26 The righteous person is cautious in his friendship,
but the way of the wicked leads them astray.
27 The lazy person does not roast his prey,
but personal possessions are precious to the diligent.
28 In the path of righteousness there is life,
but another path leads to death.

13 A wise son accepts his father's discipline,
but a scoffer has never listened to rebuke.
2 From the fruit of his speech a person eats good things,
but the treacherous desire the fruit of violence.
3 The one who guards his words guards his life;
whoever is talkative will come to ruin.
4 The appetite of the sluggard craves but gets nothing,
but the desire of the diligent will be abundantly
satisfied.
5 The righteous person will reject anything false,
but the wicked person will act in shameful disgrace.
6 Righteousness guards the one who lives with integrity,
but wickedness overthrows the sinner.
7 There is one who pretends to be rich and yet has
nothing;
another pretends to be poor and yet possesses great
wealth.
8 The ransom of a person's life is his wealth,
thus the poor person has never heard a threat.
9 The light of the righteous shines brightly,
but the lamp of the wicked goes out.
10 With pride comes only contention,
but wisdom is with the well-advised.
11 Wealth gained quickly will dwindle away,
but the one who gathers it little by little will become rich.
12 Hope deferred makes the heart sick,
but a longing fulfilled is like a tree of life.
13 The one who despises instruction will pay the penalty,
but whoever esteems direction will be rewarded.
14 Instruction from the wise is like a life-giving fountain,
to turn a person from deadly snares.

13:8 The riches of a person ought to work to the redemption of his soul, not to its destruction. Wealth is redemption if one uses it well. It is a snare if one does not know how to use it. For what is a person's money if not provision for the journey? A great amount is a burden; a little is useful. We are wayfarers in this life; many are walking along, but a person needs to make a good passage. The Lord Jesus is with him who makes a good passage.

AMBROSE (C. 339–C. 397)
LETTERS

15 Keen insight wins favor,
but the conduct of the treacherous ends in destruction.
16 Every shrewd person acts with knowledge,
but a fool displays his folly.
17 An unreliable messenger falls into trouble,
but a faithful envoy brings healing.
18 The one who neglects discipline ends up in poverty and
shame,
but the one who accepts reproof is honored.
19 A desire fulfilled will be sweet to the soul,
but fools abhor turning away from evil.
20 The one who associates with the wise grows wise,
but a companion of fools suffers harm.
21 Calamity pursues sinners,
but prosperity rewards the righteous.
22 A good person leaves an inheritance for his
grandchildren,
but the wealth of a sinner is stored up for the righteous.
23 Abundant food may come from the field of the poor,
but it is swept away by injustice.
24 The one who spares his rod hates his child,
but the one who loves his child is diligent in
disciplining him.
25 The righteous has enough food to satisfy his appetite,
but the belly of the wicked will be empty.

14 Every wise woman has built her household,
but a foolish woman tears it down with her own hands.
2 The one who walks in his uprightness fears the LORD,
but the one who is perverted in his ways despises him.
3 In the speech of a fool is a rod for his back,
but the words of the wise protect them.
4 Where there are no oxen, the feeding trough is clean,
but an abundant harvest is produced by strong oxen.
5 A truthful witness does not lie,
but a false witness breathes out lies.
6 The scorner sought wisdom—there was none,
but understanding was easy for a discerning person.
7 Walk abreast with a foolish person,
and you do not understand wise counsel.
8 The wisdom of the shrewd person is to discern his way,
but the folly of fools is deception.
9 Fools mock at reparation,
but among the upright there is favor.
10 The heart knows its own bitterness,
and with its joy no one else can share.
11 The household of the wicked will be destroyed,
but the tent of the upright will flourish.
12 There is a way that seems right to a person,
but its end is the way that leads to death.
13 Even in laughter the heart may ache,
and the end of joy may be grief.
14 The backslider will be paid back from his own ways,
but a good person will be rewarded for his.
15 A naive person will believe anything,
but the shrewd person discerns his steps.
16 A wise person is cautious and turns from evil,
but a fool throws off restraint and is overconfident.
17 A person who has a quick temper will do foolish things,
and a person with crafty schemes will be hated.

14:12 "There is a way that seems right to a person, but its end is the way that leads to death." You see, ignorance is also clearly condemned in this text, since people think otherwise and fall into hades, seemingly having the truth. "There are many plans," he says, "in a person's mind"; but still it is not the person's will, which is uncertain and doubtful and changeable, that prevails but "the counsel of the LORD" (Prov 19:21).

JEROME (C. 342–420)
AGAINST THE PELAGIANS

18 The naive have inherited folly,
but the shrewd will be crowned with knowledge.
19 Bad people have bowed before good people,
and wicked people have bowed at the gates of someone righteous.
20 A poor person will be disliked even by his neighbors,
but those who love the rich are many.
21 The one who despises his neighbor sins,
but whoever is kind to the needy is blessed.
22 Do not those who devise evil go astray?
But those who plan good exhibit faithful covenant love.
23 In all hard work there is profit,
but merely talking about it only brings poverty.
24 The crown of the wise is their riches,
but the folly of fools is folly.
25 A truthful witness rescues lives,
but one who testifies falsely betrays them.
26 In the fear of the LORD one has strong confidence,
and it will be a refuge for his children.
27 The fear of the LORD is like a life-giving fountain,
to turn people from deadly snares.
28 A king's glory is the abundance of people,
but the lack of subjects is the ruin of a ruler.
29 Someone with great understanding is slow to anger,
but the one who has a quick temper exalts folly.
30 A tranquil spirit revives the body,
but envy is rottenness to the bones.
31 The one who oppresses the poor has insulted his Creator,
but whoever honors him shows favor to the needy.
32 An evil person will be thrown down through his wickedness,
but a righteous person takes refuge in his integrity.
33 Wisdom rests in the heart of the discerning;
it is not known in the inner parts of fools.
34 Righteousness exalts a nation,
but sin is a disgrace to any people.
35 The king shows favor to a wise servant,
but his wrath falls on one who acts shamefully.

15 A gentle response turns away anger,
but a harsh word stirs up wrath.
2 The tongue of the wise treats knowledge correctly,
but the mouth of the fool spouts out folly.
3 The eyes of the LORD are in every place,
keeping watch on those who are evil and those who are good.
4 Speech that heals is like a life-giving tree,
but a perverse speech breaks the spirit.
5 A fool rejects his father's discipline,
but whoever heeds reproof shows good sense.
6 In the house of the righteous is abundant wealth,
but the income of the wicked will be ruined.
7 The lips of the wise spread knowledge,
but not so the heart of fools.
8 The LORD abhors the sacrifice of the wicked,
but the prayer of the upright pleases him.
9 The LORD abhors the way of the wicked,
but he will love those who pursue righteousness.
10 Severe discipline is for the one who abandons the way;

15:1–2 Our Lord gave most of his assistance with persuasion rather than with admonition. Gentle showers soften the earth and thoroughly penetrate it, but a beating rain hardens and compresses the surface of the earth so that it will not be absorbed. "A harsh word stirs up wrath," and with it comes injury. Whenever a harsh word opens a door, anger enters in, and on the heels of anger, injury.

EPHREM THE SYRIAN
(C. 306–373)
COMMENTARY ON THE PROVERBS OF SOLOMON

the one who hates reproof will die.
11 Death and Destruction are before the LORD—
how much more the hearts of humans!
12 The scorner will not love one who corrects him;
he will not go to the wise.
13 A joyful heart makes the face cheerful,
but by a painful heart the spirit is broken.
14 The discerning mind seeks knowledge,
but the mouth of fools feeds on folly.
15 All the days of the afflicted are bad,
but one with a cheerful heart has a continual feast.
16 Better is little with the fear of the LORD
than great wealth and turmoil with it.
17 Better a meal of vegetables where there is love
than a fattened ox where there is hatred.
18 A quick-tempered person stirs up dissension,
but one who is slow to anger calms a quarrel.
19 The way of the sluggard is like a hedge of thorns,
but the path of the upright is like a highway.
20 A wise child brings joy to his father,
but a foolish person despises his mother.
21 Folly is a joy to one who lacks sense,
but one who has understanding follows an upright
course.
22 Plans fail when there is no counsel,
but with abundant advisers they are established.
23 A person has joy in giving an appropriate answer,
and a word at the right time—how good it is!
24 The path of life is upward for the wise person,
to keep him from going downward to Sheol.
25 The LORD tears down the house of the proud,
but he maintains the boundaries of the widow.
26 The LORD abhors the plans of the wicked,
but pleasant words are pure.
27 The one who is greedy for gain troubles his household,
but whoever hates bribes will live.
28 The heart of the righteous considers how to answer,
but the mouth of the wicked pours out evil things.
29 The LORD is far from the wicked,
but he hears the prayer of the righteous.
30 A bright look brings joy to the heart,
and good news gives health to the body.
31 The person who hears the reproof that leads to life
is at home among the wise.
32 The one who refuses correction despises himself,
but whoever listens to reproof acquires
understanding.
33 The fear of the LORD provides wise instruction,
and before honor comes humility.

16 The intentions of the heart belong to a man,
but the answer of the tongue comes from the LORD.
2 All a person's ways seem right in his own opinion,
but the LORD evaluates the motives.
3 Commit your works to the LORD,
and your plans will be established.
4 The LORD has worked everything for his own ends—
even the wicked for the day of disaster.
5 The LORD abhors every arrogant person;
rest assured that they will not go unpunished.

16:4 The making of the wicked, here mentioned, is a work of Providence. God makes men wicked by so disposing and ordering things in his providence that they, in consequence of his disposals, especially in his permission or withholding restraints, do continue in wickedness or are hardened in it. God's distinguishing dealing toward humankind might be expressed thus—that God makes both the righteous and the wicked in the same sense—whom he will he has mercy on and makes righteous, and whom he will he hardens and leaves to wickedness. It is probable that by making the wicked, here is intended a judicial proceeding and a punishment of sin, though it be a mere sovereign proceeding in God that he distinguishes some by not executing this punishment upon them.

JONATHAN EDWARDS
(1703–1758)
SELECTIONS FROM THE UNPUBLISHED WRITINGS

6 Through loyal love and truth iniquity is appeased;
through fearing the LORD one avoids evil.
7 When a person's ways are pleasing to the LORD,
he even reconciles his enemies to himself.
8 Better to have a little with righteousness
than to have abundant income without justice.
9 A person plans his course,
but the LORD directs his steps.
10 The divine verdict is in the words of the king;
his pronouncements must not act treacherously
against justice.
11 Honest scales and balances are from the LORD;
all the weights in the bag are his handiwork.
12 Doing wickedness is an abomination to kings,
because a throne is established in righteousness.
13 The delight of a king is righteous counsel,
and he will love the one who speaks uprightly.
14 A king's wrath is like a messenger of death,
but a wise person appeases it.
15 In the light of the king's face there is life,
and his favor is like the clouds of the spring rain.
16 How much better it is to acquire wisdom than gold;
to acquire understanding is more desirable than silver.
17 The highway of the upright is to turn away from evil;
the one who guards his way safeguards his life.
18 Pride goes before destruction
and a haughty spirit before a fall.
19 It is better to be lowly in spirit with the afflicted
than to share the spoils with the proud.
20 The one who deals wisely in a matter will find success,
and blessed is the one who trusts in the LORD.
21 The one who is wise in heart is called discerning,
and kind speech increases persuasiveness.
22 Insight is like a life-giving fountain to the one who
possesses it,
but folly leads to the discipline of fools.
23 A wise person's heart makes his speech wise,
and it adds persuasiveness to his words.
24 Pleasant words are like a honeycomb,
sweet to the soul and healing to the bones.
25 There is a way that seems right to a person,
but its end is the way that leads to death.
26 A laborer's appetite has labored for him,
for his hunger has pressed him to work.
27 A wicked scoundrel digs up evil,
and his slander is like a scorching fire.
28 A perverse person spreads dissension,
and a gossip separates the closest friends.
29 A violent person entices his neighbor,
and then leads him down a path that is terrible.
30 The one who winks his eyes devises perverse things,
and one who compresses his lips has accomplished evil.
31 Gray hair is like a crown of glory;
it is attained in the path of righteousness.
32 Better to be slow to anger than to be a mighty warrior,
and one who controls his temper is better than one who
captures a city.
33 The dice are thrown into the lap,
but their every decision is from the LORD.

17 Better is a dry crust of bread where there is quietness
than a house full of feasting with strife.
2 A servant who acts wisely will rule
over an heir who behaves shamefully
and will share the inheritance along with the relatives.
3 The crucible is for refining silver and the furnace is for gold;
likewise the LORD tests hearts.
4 One who acts wickedly pays attention to evil counsel;
a liar listens to a malicious tongue.
5 The one who mocks the poor has insulted his Creator;
whoever rejoices over disaster will not go unpunished.
6 Grandchildren are like a crown to the elderly,
and the glory of children is their parents.
7 Excessive speech is not becoming for a fool;
how much less are lies for a ruler!
8 A bribe works like a charm for the one who offers it;
in whatever he does he succeeds.
9 The one who forgives an offense seeks love,
but whoever repeats a matter separates close friends.
10 A rebuke makes a greater impression on a discerning person
than a hundred blows on a fool.
11 An evil person seeks only rebellion,
and so a cruel messenger will be sent against him.
12 It is better for a person to meet a mother bear being robbed of her cubs
than to encounter a fool in his folly.
13 As for the one who repays evil for good,
evil will not leave his house.
14 Starting a quarrel is like letting out water;
abandon strife before it breaks out!
15 The one who acquits the guilty and the one who condemns the innocent—
both of them are an abomination to the LORD.
16 What's the point of a fool having money in hand
to buy wisdom when his head is empty?
17 A friend loves at all times,
and a relative is born to help in adversity.
18 The one who lacks sense strikes hands in pledge
and puts up financial security for his neighbor.
19 The one who loves a quarrel loves transgression;
whoever builds his gate high seeks destruction.
20 The one who has a perverse heart does not find good,
and the one who is deceitful in speech falls into trouble.
21 Whoever brings a fool into the world does so to his grief,
and the father of a fool has no joy.
22 A cheerful heart brings good healing,
but a crushed spirit dries up the bones.
23 A wicked person receives a bribe secretly
to pervert the ways of justice.
24 Wisdom is directly in front of the discerning person,
but the eyes of a fool run to the ends of the earth.
25 A foolish child is a grief to his father
and bitterness to the mother who bore him.
26 It is terrible to punish a righteous person,
and to flog honorable men is wrong.
27 The truly wise person restrains his words,
and the one who stays calm is discerning.

17:14 **The indolent mind for the most part lapses by degrees into downfall. We neglect to guard against idle words, and so we go on to hurtful ones. At first it pleases us to talk of the affairs of others; afterward the tongue gnaws with detraction at the lives of those of whom we talk. Then at last we break out into open slanders. Thus are pricking thorns sown, quarrels arise, the torches of enmities are kindled, and peace of heart is extinguished. Therefore it is well said by Solomon, "Starting a quarrel is like letting out water." For to let out water is to let loose the tongue to a flurry of speech.**

GREGORY THE GREAT
(C. 540–604)
PASTORAL CARE

28 Even a fool who remains silent is considered wise,
and the one who holds his tongue is deemed discerning.
18 One who has isolated himself seeks his own desires;
he rejects all sound judgment.
2 A fool takes no pleasure in understanding
but only in disclosing what is on his mind.
3 When a wicked person arrives, contempt shows up with him,
and with shame comes a reproach.
4 The words of a person's mouth are like deep waters,
and the fountain of wisdom is like a flowing brook.
5 It is terrible to show partiality to the wicked
by depriving a righteous man of justice.
6 The lips of a fool enter into strife,
and his mouth invites a flogging.
7 The mouth of a fool is his ruin,
and his lips are a snare for his life.
8 The words of a gossip are like choice morsels,
and they have gone down into the person's innermost being.
9 The one who is slack in his work
is a brother to one who destroys.
10 The name of the LORD is like a strong tower;
the righteous person runs to it and is set safely on high.
11 The wealth of a rich person is like a strong city,
and it is like a high wall in his imagination.
12 Before destruction the heart of a person is proud,
but humility comes before honor.
13 The one who gives an answer before he listens—
that is his folly and his shame.
14 A person's spirit sustains him through sickness—
but who can bear a crushed spirit?
15 The discerning person acquires knowledge,
and the wise person seeks knowledge.
16 A person's gift makes room for him
and leads him before important people.
17 The first to state his case seems right,
until his opponent begins to cross-examine him.
18 A toss of a coin ends disputes
and settles the issue between strong opponents.
19 A relative offended is harder to reach than a strong city,
and disputes are like the barred gates of a fortified citadel.
20 From the fruit of a person's mouth his stomach will be satisfied;
with the product of his lips he will be satisfied.
21 Death and life are in the power of the tongue,
and those who love its use will eat its fruit.
22 The one who has found a good wife has found what goodness is
and obtained a delightful gift from the LORD.
23 A poor person makes supplications,
but a rich man answers harshly.
24 There are companions who harm one another,
but there is a friend who sticks closer than a brother.
19 Better is a poor person who walks in his integrity
than one who is perverse in his speech and is a fool.
2 It is dangerous to have zeal without knowledge,
and the one who acts hastily makes poor choices.

18:12 A haughty heart is the prophetic prelude of evil. Pride is as safely the sign of destruction as the change of mercury in the weatherglass is the sign of rain, and far more infallibly so than that. When people have ridden the high horse, destruction has always overtaken them. God hates high looks and never fails to bring them down. Are you glorying in your graces or your talents? If we forget to live at the foot of the cross in deepest lowliness of spirit, God will not forget to make us smart under his rod. A destruction will come to you. Therefore "if people want to boast about this: They should boast that they understand and know me" (Jer 9:24).

CHARLES SPURGEON
(1834–1892)
MORING AND EVENING

3 A person's folly subverts his way,
and his heart rages against the LORD.
4 Wealth adds many friends,
but a poor person is separated from his friend.
5 A false witness will not go unpunished,
and the one who spouts out lies will not escape
punishment.
6 Many people entreat the favor of a generous person,
and everyone is the friend of the person who gives gifts.
7 All the relatives of a poor person hate him;
how much more do his friends avoid him—
one who chases words, which are nothing.
8 The one who acquires understanding loves himself;
the one who preserves understanding will prosper.
9 A false witness will not go unpunished,
and the one who spouts out lies will perish.
10 Luxury is not appropriate for a fool;
how much less for a servant to rule over princes!
11 A person's wisdom has made him slow to anger,
and it is his glory to overlook an offense.
12 A king's wrath is like the roar of a lion,
but his favor is like dew on the grass.
13 A foolish child is the ruin of his father,
and a contentious wife is like a constant dripping.
14 A house and wealth are inherited from parents,
but a prudent wife is from the LORD.
15 Laziness brings on a deep sleep,
and the idle person will go hungry.
16 The one who obeys commandments guards his life;
the one who despises his ways will die.
17 The one who is gracious to the poor lends to the LORD,
and the LORD will repay him for his good deed.
18 Discipline your child, for there is hope,
but do not set your heart on causing his death.
19 A person with great anger bears the penalty,
but if you deliver him from it once, you will have to do
it again.
20 Listen to advice and receive discipline,
that you may become wise by the end of your life.
21 There are many plans in a person's mind,
but it is the counsel of the LORD that will stand.
22 What is desirable for a person is to show loyal love,
and a poor person is better than a liar.
23 Fearing the LORD leads to life,
and one who does so will live satisfied; he will not be
afflicted by calamity.
24 The sluggard has plunged his hand into the dish,
and he will not even bring it back to his mouth!
25 Flog a scorner, and as a result the simpleton will learn
prudence;
correct a discerning person, and as a result he will
understand knowledge.
26 The one who robs his father and chases away his
mother
is a son who brings shame and disgrace.
27 If you stop listening to instruction, my child,
you will stray from the words of knowledge.
28 A crooked witness scorns justice,
and the mouth of the wicked devours iniquity.

19:17 Love for the poor is precious in the sight of God. Do you feel pleasure in being praised when you have any friends or relatives feasting with you? I tell you of something far better: Angels shall praise your bounty, and the rational powers above and holy men as well, and he too shall accept it who transcends all and who loves mercy and is kind. Lend to him fearing nothing, and you will receive with interest whatever you gave, for "the one," it says, "who is gracious to the poor lends to the LORD."

CYRIL OF ALEXANDRIA
(C. 376–444)
COMMENTARY ON LUKE

29 Penalties have been prepared for scorners,
and floggings for the backs of fools.

20 Wine is a mocker and strong drink is a brawler;
whoever goes astray by them is not wise.
2 The king's terrifying anger is like the roar of a lion;
whoever provokes him sins against himself.
3 It is an honor for a person to cease from strife,
but every fool quarrels.
4 The sluggard will not plow during the planting season,
so at harvest time he asks for grain but has nothing.
5 Counsel in a person's heart is like deep water,
but an understanding person draws it out.
6 Many people profess their loyalty,
but a faithful person—who can find?
7 The righteous person behaves in integrity;
blessed are his children after him.
8 A king sitting on the throne to judge
separates out all evil with his eyes.
9 Who can say, "I have kept my heart clean;
I am pure from my sin"?
10 Diverse weights and diverse measures—
the LORD abhors both of them.
11 Even a young man is known by his actions,
whether his activity is pure and whether it is right.
12 The ear that hears and the eye that sees—
the LORD has made them both.
13 Do not love sleep, lest you become impoverished;
open your eyes so that you might be satisfied with food.
14 "It's worthless! It's worthless!" says the buyer,
but when he goes on his way, he boasts.
15 There is gold and an abundance of rubies,
but words of knowledge are like a precious jewel.
16 Take a man's garment when he has given security for a stranger,
and hold him in pledge on behalf of strangers.
17 Bread gained by deceit tastes sweet to a person,
but afterward his mouth will be filled with gravel.
18 Plans are established by counsel,
so make war with guidance.
19 The one who goes about gossiping reveals secrets;
therefore do not associate with someone who is always opening his mouth.
20 The one who curses his father and his mother,
his lamp will be extinguished in the blackest darkness.
21 An inheritance gained easily in the beginning
will not be blessed in the end.
22 Do not say, "I will pay back evil!"
Wait for the LORD, so that he may vindicate you.
23 The LORD abhors differing weights,
and dishonest scales are wicked.
24 The steps of a person are ordained by the LORD—
so how can anyone understand his own way?
25 It is a snare for a person to rashly cry, "Holy!"
and only afterward to consider what he has vowed.
26 A wise king separates out the wicked;
he turns the threshing wheel over them.
27 The human spirit is like the lamp of the LORD,
searching all his innermost parts.
28 Loyal love and truth preserve a king,

20:21 When people burn to be filled at once with all manner of wealth, let them hear what scripture says. For certainly those who are determined to increase their wealth do not seek to avoid sin, and being caught like birds while looking greedily at the bait of earthly things, they are not aware they are being strangled in the noose of sin. Let them hear what scripture says, "An inheritance gained easily in the beginning will not be blessed in the end." For indeed we derive our beginning from this life that we may come to the destiny of blessing. They who make haste to an inheritance in the beginning cut off from themselves the destiny of blessing in the end. When they solicit very much or succeed in obtaining all that they have solicited, let them hear what scripture says: "For what does it benefit a person if he gains the whole world but forfeits his life?" (Matt 16:26).

GREGORY THE GREAT
(C. 540–604)
PASTORAL CARE

and his throne is upheld by loyal love.
29 The glory of young men is their strength,
and the splendor of old men is gray hair.
30 Beatings and wounds cleanse away evil,
and floggings cleanse the innermost being.
21 The king's heart is in the hand of the LORD like channels of water;
he turns it wherever he wants.
2 All a person's ways seem right in his own opinion,
but the LORD evaluates his thoughts.
3 To do righteousness and justice
is more acceptable to the LORD than sacrifice.
4 Haughty eyes and a proud heart—
what the wicked cultivate is sin.
5 The plans of the diligent lead only to plenty,
but everyone who is hasty comes only to poverty.
6 Making a fortune by a lying tongue is like a vapor driven back and forth;
they seek death.
7 The violence done by the wicked will drag them away
because they have refused to do what is right.
8 The way of the guilty person is devious,
but as for the pure, his way is upright.
9 It is better to live on a corner of the housetop
than to share a house with a quarrelsome wife.
10 The appetite of the wicked has desired evil;
his neighbor is shown no favor in his eyes.
11 When a scorner is punished, the naive becomes wise;
when a wise person is instructed, he gains knowledge.
12 The Righteous One considers the house of the wicked;
he overthrows the wicked to their ruin.
13 The one who shuts his ears to the cry of the poor,
he too will cry out and will not be answered.
14 A gift given in secret subdues anger,
and a bribe given secretly subdues strong wrath.
15 Doing justice brings joy to the righteous
and terror to those who do evil.
16 The one who wanders from the way of wisdom
will end up in the company of the departed.
17 The one who loves pleasure will be a poor person;
whoever loves wine and anointing oil will not be rich.
18 The wicked become a ransom for the righteous,
and the treacherous are taken in the place of the upright.
19 It is better to live in the wilderness
than with a quarrelsome and easily provoked woman.
20 There is desirable treasure and olive oil in the dwelling of the wise,
but a foolish person devours all he has.
21 The one who pursues righteousness and love
finds life, bounty, and honor.
22 A wise man went up against the city of the mighty
and brought down the stronghold in which they trust.
23 The one who guards his mouth and his tongue
keeps his life from troubles.
24 A proud and arrogant person, whose name is "Scoffer,"
acts with overbearing pride.
25 What the sluggard desires will kill him,
for his hands have refused to work.

21:1 And the Word also says by Solomon, "By me kings reign, and by me potentates decree righteousness; by me princes rule, as well as nobles and all righteous judges" (Prov 8:15–16). Paul the apostle also says upon this same subject: "Let every person be subject to the governing authorities. For there is no authority except by God's appointment, and the authorities that exist have been instituted by God" (Rom 13:1). Now that he spoke these words, not in regard to angelical powers or of invisible rulers but of actual human authorities, he shows when he says, "For this reason you also pay taxes, for the authorities are God's servants devoted to governing" (Rom 13:6). This also the Lord confirmed when he gave directions that tribute should be paid to the tax-gatherers for himself and Peter; as Paul said, government "is God's servant for your well-being" (Rom 13:4).

IRENAEUS (C. 130–C. 202)
AGAINST HERESIES

26 All day long he has craved greedily,
but the righteous person gives and does not hold back.
27 The wicked person's sacrifice is an abomination;
how much more when he brings it with evil intent!
28 A lying witness will perish,
but the one who reports accurately speaks forever.
29 A wicked person has put on a bold face,
but as for the upright, he establishes his ways.
30 There is no wisdom and there is no understanding,
and there is no counsel against the LORD.
31 A horse is prepared for the day of battle,
but the victory is from the LORD.

22 A good name is to be chosen rather than great wealth,
good favor more than silver or gold.
2 The rich and the poor are met together;
the LORD is the Creator of them both.
3 A shrewd person saw danger and hid himself,
but the naive passed on by and paid for it.
4 The reward for humility and fearing the LORD
is riches and honor and life.
5 Thorns and snares are in the path of the perverse,
but the one who guards himself keeps far from them.
6 Train a child in the way that he should go,
and when he is old he will not turn from it.
7 The rich rule over the poor,
and the borrower is servant to the lender.
8 The one who sows iniquity will reap trouble,
and the rod of his fury will end.
9 A generous person will be blessed,
for he has given some of his food to the poor.
10 Drive out the scorner and contention will leave;
strife and insults will cease.
11 The one who loves a pure heart
and whose speech is gracious—the king will be his friend.
12 The eyes of the LORD watched over a cause
and subverted the words of the treacherous person.
13 The sluggard has said, "There is a lion outside!
I will be killed in the middle of the streets!"
14 The mouth of an adulteress is like a deep pit;
the one against whom the LORD is angry will fall into it.
15 Folly is bound up in the heart of a child,
but the rod of discipline will drive it far from him.
16 The one who oppresses the poor to increase his own gain
and the one who gives to the rich—both end up only in poverty.

THE SAYINGS OF THE WISE

17 Incline your ear and listen to the words of the wise,
and apply your mind to my instruction.
18 For it is pleasing if you keep these sayings within you,
and they are ready on your lips.
19 So that your confidence may be in the LORD,
I hereby make them known to you today—even you.
20 Have I not written thirty sayings for you,
sayings of counsel and knowledge,
21 to show you true and reliable words,
so that you may give accurate answers to those who sent you?

22:20–21 We are instructed by scripture itself in regard to the ideas we ought to form of it. In the Proverbs of Solomon we find the following laid down respecting the consideration of holy scripture: "Have I not written thirty sayings for you, sayings of counsel and knowledge, to show you true and reliable words, so that you may give accurate answers to those who sent you?" Each one then ought to describe in his own mind the understanding of the divine letters in order that all the simpler individuals may be edified, so to speak, by the very body of scripture; for if some have commenced to make considerable progress and are able to see something more, they may be edified by the very soul of scripture.

ORIGEN **(C. 185–C. 253)**
ON FIRST PRINCIPLES

22 Do not exploit a poor person because he is poor
and do not crush the needy in court,
23 for the LORD will plead their case
and will rob the life of those who are robbing them.
24 Do not make friends with an angry person,
and do not associate with a wrathful person,
25 lest you learn his ways
and entangle yourself in a snare.
26 Do not be one who strikes hands in pledge
or who puts up security for debts.
27 If you do not have enough to pay,
your bed will be taken right out from under you!
28 Do not move an ancient boundary stone
that was put in place by your ancestors.
29 You have seen a person skilled in his work—
he will take his position before kings;
he will not take his position before obscure people.

23 When you sit down to eat with a ruler,
consider carefully what is before you,
2 and put a knife to your throat
if you possess a large appetite.
3 Do not crave that ruler's delicacies,
for that food is deceptive.
4 Do not wear yourself out to become rich;
be wise enough to restrain yourself.
5 When you gaze upon riches, they are gone,
for they surely make wings for themselves
and fly off into the sky like an eagle!
6 Do not eat the food of a stingy person,
do not crave his delicacies;
7 for he is like someone who has calculated the cost in his mind.
"Eat and drink," he says to you,
but his heart is not with you;
8 you will vomit up the little bit you have eaten
and will have wasted your pleasant words.
9 Do not speak in the ears of a fool,
for he will despise the wisdom of your words.
10 Do not move an ancient boundary stone
or take over the fields of the fatherless,
11 for their Protector is strong;
he will plead their case against you.
12 Apply your heart to instruction
and your ears to the words of knowledge.
13 Do not withhold discipline from a child;
even if you strike him with the rod, he will not die.
14 If you strike him with the rod,
you will deliver him from death.
15 My child, if your heart is wise,
then my heart also will be glad;
16 my soul will rejoice
when your lips speak what is right.
17 Do not let your heart envy sinners,
but rather be zealous in fearing the LORD all the time.
18 For surely there is a future,
and your hope will not be cut off.
19 Listen, my child, and be wise,
and guide your heart on the right way.

23:12 This counsel is repeatedly given in the book of Proverbs. The best-taught and the most advanced Christians will be the most earnest in seeking more instruction. They will gladly sit at the feet of the Lord's ministers to hear the words of knowledge. Observe the link between the heart and ears. The heart that is otherwise open to sound advice may be shut against Christ and his teaching. It may be closed up in unbelief, prejudice, indifference, and the love of pleasure. A listless heart can, therefore, produce a careless ear. But when the heart is graciously opened and enlightened, the ears instantly become attentive. Awakened spiritual desire brings prayer, and prayer brings blessing.

CHARLES BRIDGES
(1794–1869)
AN EXPOSITION OF THE BOOK OF PROVERBS

20 Do not spend time among drunkards,
among those who eat too much meat,
21 because drunkards and gluttons become impoverished,
and drowsiness clothes them with rags.
22 Listen to your father who gave you life,
and do not despise your mother when she is old.
23 Acquire truth and do not sell it—
wisdom, and discipline, and understanding.
24 The father of a righteous person will rejoice greatly;
whoever fathers a wise child will have joy in him.
25 May your father and your mother have joy;
may she who bore you rejoice.
26 Give me your heart, my son,
and let your eyes observe my ways;
27 for a prostitute is like a deep pit;
a harlot is like a narrow well.
28 Indeed, she lies in wait like a robber
and increases the unfaithful among men.
29 Who has woe? Who has sorrow?
Who has contentions? Who has complaints?
Who has wounds without cause? Who has dullness of
the eyes?
30 Those who linger over wine,
those who go looking for mixed wine.
31 Do not look on the wine when it is red,
when it sparkles in the cup,
when it goes down smoothly.
32 Afterward it bites like a snake
and stings like a viper.
33 Your eyes will see strange things,
and your mind will speak perverse things.
34 And you will be like one who lies down in the midst of
the sea,
and like one who lies down on the top of the rigging.
35 You will say, "They have struck me, but I am not
harmed!
They beat me, but I did not know it!
When will I awake? I will look for another drink."

24 Do not envy evil people
do not desire to be with them;
2 for their hearts contemplate violence,
and their lips speak harm.
3 By wisdom a house is built,
and through understanding it is established;
4 by knowledge its rooms are filled
with all kinds of precious and pleasing treasures.
5 A wise warrior is strong,
and a man of knowledge makes his strength stronger;
6 for with guidance you wage your war,
and with numerous advisers there is victory.
7 Wisdom is unattainable for a fool;
in court he does not open his mouth.
8 The one who plans to do evil
will be called a scheming person.
9 A foolish scheme is sin,
and the scorner is an abomination to people.
10 You have slacked off in the day of trouble—
your strength is small!
11 Deliver those being taken away to death,

and hold back those slipping to the slaughter.
12 If you say, "But we did not know about this,"
won't the one who evaluates hearts discern it?
Won't the one who guards your life realize
and repay each person according to his deeds?
13 Eat honey, my child, for it is good,
and honey from the honeycomb is sweet to your taste.
14 Likewise, know that wisdom is sweet to your soul;
if you have found it, you have a future,
and your hope will not be cut off.
15 Do not lie in wait like the wicked against the place
where the righteous live;
do not assault his home.
16 Indeed a righteous person will fall seven times, and
then get up again,
but the guilty will collapse in calamity.
17 Do not rejoice when your enemy falls,
and when he stumbles do not let your heart rejoice,
18 lest the LORD see it, and be displeased,
and turn his wrath away from him.
19 Do not fret because of evil people
or be envious of wicked people,
20 for the evil person has no future,
and the lamp of the wicked will be extinguished.
21 Fear the LORD, my child, as well as the king,
and do not associate with rebels,
22 for suddenly their destruction will overtake them,
and who knows the ruinous judgment both the LORD
and the king can bring?

FURTHER SAYINGS OF THE WISE

23 These sayings also are from the wise:
To show partiality in judgment is terrible:
24 The one who says to the guilty, "You are innocent,"
peoples will curse him, and nations will
denounce him.
25 But there will be delight for those who convict the
guilty,
and a pleasing blessing will come on them.
26 Like a kiss on the lips
is the one who gives an honest answer.
27 Establish your work outside and get your fields ready;
afterward build your house.
28 Do not be a witness against your neighbor without
cause,
and do not deceive with your words.
29 Do not say, "I will do to him just as he has done to me;
I will pay him back according to what he has done."
30 I passed by the field of a sluggard,
by the vineyard of one who lacks sense.
31 I saw that thorns had grown up all over it;
the ground was covered with weeds,
and its stone wall was broken down.
32 Then I scrutinized it. I was putting my mind to it—
I saw; I took in a lesson:
33 "A little sleep, a little slumber,
a little folding of the hands to relax,
34 and your poverty will come like a bandit,
and your need like an armed robber."

24:33 The worst of sluggards—they ask for only a little slumber, a little folding of the hands to sleep is all they crave, and they have a crowd of reasons to show that this indulgence is a very proper one. Yet by these littles the day ebbs out, the time for labor is all gone, and the field is grown over with thorns. It is by little procrastinations that people ruin their souls. Like sands from an hourglass, time passes, life is wasted by driblets, and seasons of grace are lost by little slumbers. As yet, faith and holy decision are timely. May we obtain them this night.

CHARLES SPURGEON
(1834–1892)
MORNING AND EVENING

PROVERBS OF SOLOMON COLLECTED BY HEZEKIAH

25 These also are proverbs of Solomon, which the men of
King Hezekiah of Judah copied:

2 It is the glory of God to conceal a matter,
and it is the glory of a king to search out a matter.
3 As the heaven is high and the earth is deep
so the hearts of kings are unsearchable.
4 Remove the dross from the silver,
and material for the silversmith will emerge;
5 remove the wicked from before the king,
and his throne will be established in righteousness.
6 Do not honor yourself before the king,
and do not stand in the place of great men;
7 for it is better for him to say to you, "Come up here,"
than to put you lower before a prince,
whom your eyes have seen.
8 Do not go out hastily to litigation,
or what will you do afterward
when your neighbor puts you to shame?
9 When you argue a case with your neighbor,
do not reveal the secret of another person,
10 lest the one who hears it put you to shame
and your infamy will never go away.
11 Like apples of gold in settings of silver,
so is a word skillfully spoken.
12 Like an earring of gold and an ornament of fine gold,
so is a wise reprover to the ear of the one who listens.
13 Like the cold of snow in the time of harvest,
so is a faithful messenger to those who send him,
for he refreshes the heart of his masters.
14 Like cloudy skies and wind that produce no rain,
so is the one who boasts of a gift not given.
15 Through patience a ruler can be persuaded,
and a soft tongue can break a bone.
16 You have found honey—eat only what is sufficient for you,
lest you become stuffed with it and vomit it up.
17 Don't set foot too frequently in your neighbor's house,
lest he become weary of you and hate you.
18 Like a club or a sword or a sharp arrow,
so is the one who testifies against his neighbor as a false
witness.
19 Like a bad tooth or a foot out of joint,
so is confidence in an unfaithful person at the time of
trouble.
20 Like one who takes off a garment on a cold day
or like vinegar poured on soda,
so is one who sings songs to a heavy heart.
21 If your enemy is hungry, give him food to eat,
and if he is thirsty, give him water to drink,
22 for you will heap coals of fire on his head,
and the LORD will reward you.
23 The north wind brings forth rain,
and a gossiping tongue brings forth an angry look.
24 It is better to live on a corner of the housetop
than in a house in company with a quarrelsome wife.
25 Like cold water to a weary person,
so is good news from a distant land.

25:21–22 When you piously do good to your enemy, however wicked and cruel, savage and unfeeling he may be, he at length sometimes blushes and grieves, beginning to repent of what he has done. Then, when he has begun to do penance, his rational sense, that is, his head, begins to be kindled with the fire of charity. One who before was inclined to harbor wrath against you like a cold maniac now begins to love you with his whole heart through being kindled with spiritual warmth arising from your kindness.

CAESARIUS OF ARLES
(C. 468–542)
SERMONS

26 Like a muddied spring and a polluted well,
so is a righteous person who gives way before the wicked.
27 It is not good to eat too much honey,
nor is it honorable for people to seek their own glory.
28 Like a city that is broken down and without a wall,
so is a person who cannot control his temper.

26 Like snow in summer or rain in harvest,
so honor is not fitting for a fool.
2 Like a fluttering bird or like a flying swallow,
so a curse without cause does not come to rest.
3 A whip for the horse and a bridle for the donkey,
and a rod for the backs of fools!
4 Do not answer a fool according to his folly,
lest you yourself also be like him.
5 Answer a fool according to his folly,
lest he be wise in his own opinion.
6 Like cutting off the feet or drinking violence,
so is sending a message by the hand of a fool.
7 Like legs dangle uselessly from the lame,
so a proverb dangles in the mouth of fools.
8 Like tying a stone in a sling,
so is giving honor to a fool.
9 Like a thorn has gone up into the hand of a drunkard,
so a proverb has gone up into the mouth of a fool.
10 Like an archer who wounds at random,
so is the one who hires a fool or hires any passerby.
11 Like a dog that returns to its vomit,
so a fool repeats his folly.
12 You have seen a man wise in his own opinion—
there is more hope for a fool than for him.
13 The sluggard has said, "There is a lion in the road!
A lion in the streets!"
14 Like a door that turns on its hinges,
so a sluggard turns on his bed.
15 The sluggard has plunged his hand in the dish;
he is too lazy to bring it back to his mouth.
16 The sluggard is wiser in his own opinion
than seven people who respond with good sense.
17 Like one who grabs a wild dog by the ears,
so is the person passing by who becomes furious over a quarrel not his own.
18 Like a madman who shoots
firebrands and deadly arrows,
19 so is a person who has deceived his neighbor,
and said, "Was I not only joking?"
20 Where there is no wood, a fire goes out,
and where there is no gossip, contention ceases.
21 Like charcoal is to burning coals, and wood to fire,
so is a contentious person to kindle strife.
22 The words of a gossip are like choice morsels;
and they have gone down into a person's innermost being.
23 Like a coating of glaze over earthenware
are fervent lips with an evil heart.
24 The one who hates others disguises it with his lips,
but he stores up deceit within him.
25 When he speaks graciously, do not believe him,
for there are seven abominations within him.

26:4 Your flight is a good one if you do not answer the fool according to his folly. Your flight is good if you direct your footsteps away from the countenance of fools. Indeed, one swiftly goes astray with bad guide, but if you wish your flight to be a good one, remove your ways far from their words.

AMBROSE (C. 339–C. 397)
FLIGHT FROM THE WORLD

26 Though his hatred may be concealed by deceit,
his evil will be uncovered in the assembly.
27 The one who digs a pit will fall into it;
the one who rolls a stone—it will come back on him.
28 A lying tongue hates those crushed by it,
and a flattering mouth works ruin.

27 Do not boast about tomorrow;
for you do not know what a day may bring forth.
2 Let another praise you, and not your own mouth;
someone else, and not your own lips.
3 A stone is heavy and sand is weighty,
but vexation by a fool is more burdensome than the two
of them.
4 Wrath is cruel and anger is overwhelming,
but who can stand before jealousy?
5 Better is open rebuke
than hidden love.
6 Faithful are the wounds of a friend,
but the kisses of an enemy are excessive.
7 The one whose appetite is satisfied loathes honey,
but to the hungry mouth every bitter thing is sweet.
8 Like a bird that wanders from its nest,
so is a person who wanders from his home.
9 Ointment and incense make the heart rejoice,
likewise the sweetness of one's friend from sincere counsel.
10 Do not forsake your friend and your father's friend,
and do not enter your brother's house in the day of your
disaster;
a neighbor nearby is better than a brother far away.
11 Be wise, my son, and make my heart glad,
so that I may answer anyone who taunts me.
12 A shrewd person saw danger—he hid himself;
the naive passed right on by—they had to pay for it.
13 Take a man's garment when he has given security for a
stranger,
and hold him in pledge on behalf of a stranger.
14 If someone blesses his neighbor with a loud voice early
in the morning,
it will be counted as a curse to him.
15 A continual dripping on a rainy day—
a contentious wife makes herself like that.
16 Whoever contains her has contained the wind
or can grasp oil with his right hand.
17 As iron sharpens iron,
so a person sharpens his friend.
18 The one who tends a fig tree will eat its fruit,
and whoever takes care of his master will be honored.
19 As in water the face is reflected as a face,
so a person's heart reflects the person.
20 As Death and Destruction are never satisfied,
so the eyes of a person are never satisfied.
21 As the crucible is for silver and the furnace is for gold,
so a person must put his praise to the test.
22 If you should pound the fool in the mortar
among the grain with the pestle,
his foolishness would not depart from him.
23 Pay careful attention to the condition of your flocks,
set your mind on your herds,
24 for riches do not last forever,

27:21 By temptations, O Lord, are we daily tried; yes, unceasingly are we tried. Our daily "furnace" is the human tongue. Regarding this matter you know the groans of my heart and the rivers of my eyes. For I am not able to ascertain how far I am clean of this plague, and I stand in great fear of my secret faults that your eyes perceive, though mine do not. For in other kinds of temptations I have some sort of power of examining myself, but in this, hardly any. For, both as regards the pleasures of the flesh and an idle curiosity, I see how far I have been able to hold my mind in check when I do without them, either voluntarily or by reason of their not being at hand; for then I inquire of myself how much more or less troublesome it is to me not to have them.

AUGUSTINE (354–430)
CONFESSIONS

nor does a crown last from generation to generation.
25 When the hay is removed and new grass appears,
and the grass from the hills is gathered in,
26 the lambs will be for your clothing,
and the goats will be for the price of a field.
27 And there will be enough goat's milk for your food,
for the food of your household,
and for the sustenance of your servant girls.

28 The wicked person fled, though no one was pursuing,
but the righteous person can be as confident as a lion.
2 When a country is rebellious it has many princes,
but by someone who is discerning and knowledgeable
order is maintained.
3 A poor person who oppresses the weak
is like a driving rain without food.
4 Those who forsake the law praise the wicked,
but those who keep the law contend with them.
5 Evil people do not understand justice,
but those who seek the LORD understand it all.
6 A poor person who walks in his integrity is better
than one who is perverse in his ways even though he is
rich.
7 The one who keeps the law is a discerning child,
but a companion of gluttons brings shame to his parents.
8 The one who increases his wealth by increasing interest
gathers it for someone who is gracious to the needy.
9 The one who turns away his ear from hearing the law,
even his prayer is an abomination.
10 The one who leads the upright astray in an evil way
will himself fall into his own pit,
but the blameless will inherit what is good.
11 A rich person is wise in his own opinion,
but a discerning poor person can evaluate him properly.
12 When the righteous rejoice, great is the glory,
but when the wicked rise to power, people are sought
out.
13 The one who covers his transgressions will not prosper,
but whoever confesses them and forsakes them will
find mercy.
14 Blessed is the one who is always cautious,
but whoever hardens his heart will fall into evil.
15 Like a roaring lion or a roving bear,
so is a wicked ruler over a poor people.
16 The prince who is a great oppressor lacks wisdom,
but the one who hates unjust gain will prolong his days.
17 The one who is tormented by the murder of another
will flee to the pit;
let no one support him.
18 The one who walks blamelessly will be delivered,
but whoever is perverse in his ways will fall at once.
19 The one who works his land will be satisfied with food,
but whoever chases daydreams will have his fill of
poverty.
20 A faithful person will have an abundance of blessings,
but the one who hastens to gain riches will not go
unpunished.
21 To show partiality is terrible,
for a person will transgress over the smallest piece of
bread.

28:9 Just as scripture says, "The one who turns away his ear from hearing the law, even his prayer is an abomination." Why should we be surprised, then, if God is slow to hear our petitions when we on our part are slow to hear God's command or pay no attention whatever to it?

GREGORY THE GREAT
(C. 540–604)
LETTERS

22 The stingy person hastens after riches
and does not know that poverty will overtake him.
23 The one who reproves another will in the end find more favor
than the one who flatters with the tongue.
24 The one who robs his father and mother and says,
"There is no transgression,"
is a companion to the one who destroys.
25 The greedy person stirs up dissension,
but the one who trusts in the LORD will prosper.
26 The one who trusts in his own heart is a fool,
but the one who walks in wisdom will escape.
27 The one who gives to the poor will not lack,
but whoever shuts his eyes to them will receive many curses.
28 When the wicked gain control, people hide themselves,
but when they perish, the righteous increase.

29 The one who stiffens his neck after numerous rebukes
will suddenly be destroyed without remedy.
2 When the righteous become numerous, the people rejoice;
when the wicked rule, the people groan.
3 The man who loves wisdom brings joy to his father,
but whoever associates with prostitutes wastes his wealth.
4 A king brings stability to a land by justice,
but one who exacts tribute tears it down.
5 The one who flatters his neighbor
spreads a net for his steps.
6 In the transgression of an evil person there is a snare,
but a righteous person can sing and rejoice.
7 The righteous person cares for the legal rights of the poor;
the wicked person does not understand such knowledge.
8 Scornful people inflame a city,
but those who are wise turn away wrath.
9 When a wise person goes to court with a foolish person,
there is no peace whether he is angry or laughs.
10 Bloodthirsty people hate someone with integrity;
as for the upright, they seek his life.
11 A fool lets fly with all his temper,
but a wise person keeps it back.
12 If a ruler listens to lies,
all his ministers will be wicked.
13 The poor person and the oppressor have this in common:
The LORD gives light to the eyes of them both.
14 If a king judges the poor in truth,
his throne will be established forever.
15 A rod and reproof impart wisdom,
but a child who is unrestrained brings shame to his mother.
16 When the wicked increase, transgression increases,
but the righteous will see their downfall.
17 Discipline your child, and he will give you rest;
he will bring you happiness.
18 When there is no prophetic vision the people cast off restraint,
but the one who keeps the law, blessed is he!

29:11 We ought to restrain every movement of anger and moderate it under the direction of discretion that we may not by blind rage be hurried into that which is condemned by Solomon: "A fool lets fly with all his temper, but a wise person keeps it back." That is to say, a fool is inflamed by the passion of his anger to avenge himself, but a wise person, by the maturity of reflection and moderation, diminishes it little by little and gets rid of it.

JOHN CASSIAN
(C. 360–C. 435)
THE CONFERENCES

19 A servant cannot be corrected by words,
for although he understands, there is no answer.
20 You have seen someone who is hasty in his words—
there is more hope for a fool than for him.
21 If someone pampers his servant from youth,
he will be a weakling in the end.
22 An angry person stirs up dissension,
and a wrathful person is abounding in transgression.
23 A person's pride will bring him low,
but one who has a lowly spirit will gain honor.
24 Whoever shares with a thief is his own enemy;
he hears the oath to testify, but does not talk.
25 The fear of people becomes a snare,
but whoever trusts in the LORD will be set on high.
26 Many people seek the face of a ruler,
but it is from the LORD that one receives justice.
27 An unjust person is an abomination to the righteous,
and the one who lives an upright life is an abomination
to the wicked.

THE WORDS OF AGUR

30 The words of Agur, the son of Jakeh; an oracle:
This man says to Ithiel, to Ithiel and to Ukal:
2 Surely I am more brutish than any other human being,
and I do not have human understanding;
3 I have not learned wisdom,
nor can I have knowledge of the Holy One.
4 Who has ascended into heaven, and then descended?
Who has gathered up the winds in his fists?
Who has bound up the waters in his cloak?
Who has established all the ends of the earth?
What is his name, and what is his son's name? Surely
you can know!
5 Every word of God is purified;
he is like a shield for those who take refuge in him.
6 Do not add to his words,
lest he reprove you and prove you to be a liar.
7 Two things I have asked from you;
do not refuse me before I die:
8 Remove falsehood and lies far from me;
do not give me poverty or riches;
feed me with my allotted portion of bread,
9 lest I become satisfied and act deceptively
and say, "Who is the LORD?"
Or lest I become poor and steal
and demean the name of my God.
10 Do not slander a servant to his master,
lest he curse you, and you are found guilty.
11 There is a generation who curse their fathers
and do not bless their mothers.
12 There is a generation who are pure in their own
opinion
and yet are not washed from their filthiness.
13 There is a generation whose eyes are so lofty
and whose eyelids are lifted up disdainfully.
14 There is a generation whose teeth are like swords
and whose molars are like knives
to devour the poor from the earth
and the needy from among the human race.

30:8 What does not war against us? Riches, beauty, pleasure, power, authority, envy, glory, pride? For not only does our own glory war against us, forbidding us to descend to humility, but also the glory of others, leading us to envy and ill nature. From people proceed wickedness, plots, deceits, slanders, and assaults innumerable. Would you that I should tell you from the beginning what took captive the first created? Pleasure, and eating, and the love of dominion. What the son who came next after him? Grudging and envy. What those in the time of Noah? Fleshly pleasures and the evils issuing from them. What his son? Insolence and irreverence. What the Sodomites? Insolence, wantonness, and fullness of bread. But often even poverty has this effect. On this account a certain wise man said, "Do not give me poverty or riches." But it is neither poverty nor riches, but the will that cannot use either of them.

CHRYSOSTOM (C. 347–407)
HOMILIES ON THE FIRST EPISTLE OF PAUL TO THE THESSALONIANS

15 The leech has two daughters:
"Give! Give!"
There are three things that will never be satisfied,
four that have never said, "Enough"—
16 the grave, the barren womb;
earth has not been satisfied with water;
and fire has never said, "Enough!"
17 The eye that mocks at a father
and despises obeying a mother—
the ravens of the valley will peck it out,
and the young vultures will eat it.
18 There are three things that are too wonderful for me,
four that I do not understand:
19 the way of an eagle in the sky,
the way of a snake on a rock,
the way of a ship in the sea,
and the way of a man with a woman.
20 This is the way of an adulterous woman:
She has eaten and wiped her mouth
and has said, "I have not done wrong."
21 Under three things the earth has trembled,
and under four things it cannot bear up:
22 under a servant who becomes king,
under a fool who becomes stuffed with food,
23 under an unloved woman who becomes married,
and under a female servant who dispossesses her
mistress.
24 There are four things on earth that are small,
but they are exceedingly wise:
25 Ants are creatures with little strength,
but they prepare their food in the summer;
26 rock badgers are creatures with little power,
but they make their homes in the crags;
27 locusts have no king,
but they all go forward by ranks;
28 a lizard you can catch with the hand,
but it gets into the palaces of the king.
29 There are three things that are magnificent in their step,
four things that move about magnificently:
30 a lion, mightiest of the beasts,
who does not retreat from anything;
31 a strutting rooster, a male goat,
and a king with his army around him.
32 If you have done foolishly by exalting yourself
or if you have planned evil,
put your hand over your mouth!
33 For as the churning of milk produces butter
and as punching the nose produces blood,
so stirring up anger produces strife.

THE WORDS OF LEMUEL

31 The words of King Lemuel, an oracle that his mother
taught him:
2 O my son, O son of my womb,
O son of my vows,
3 do not give your strength to women,
nor your ways to that which ruins kings.
4 It is not for kings, O Lemuel,
it is not for kings to drink wine

or for rulers to crave strong drink,
5 lest they drink and forget what is decreed
and remove from all the poor their legal rights.
6 Give strong drink to the one who is perishing
and wine to those who are bitterly distressed;
7 let them drink and forget their poverty,
and remember their misery no more.
8 Open your mouth on behalf of those unable to speak,
for the legal rights of all the dying.
9 Open your mouth, judge in righteousness,
and plead the cause of the poor and needy.

THE WIFE OF NOBLE CHARACTER

10 Who can find a wife of noble character?
For her value is far more than rubies.
11 Her husband's heart has trusted her,
and he does not lack the dividends.
12 She has rewarded him with good and not harm
all the days of her life.
13 She sought out wool and flax,
then worked happily with her hands.
14 She was like the merchant ships;
she would bring in her food from afar.
15 Then she rose while it was still night,
and provided food for her household and a portion to
her female servants.
16 She considered a field and bought it;
from her own income she planted a vineyard.
17 She clothed herself in might,
and she strengthened her arms.
18 She perceived that her merchandise was good.
Her lamp would not go out in the night.
19 She extended her hands to the spool,
and her hands grasped the spindle.
20 She opened her hand to the poor,
and extended her hands to the needy.
21 She would not fear for her household in winter,
because all her household were clothed with scarlet,
22 because she had made coverings for herself;
and because her clothing was fine linen and purple.
23 Her husband is well known in the city gate
when he sits with the elders of the land.
24 She made linen garments then sold them
and traded belts to the merchants;
25 her clothing was strong and splendid;
and she laughed at the time to come.
26 She has opened her mouth with wisdom,
with loving instruction on her tongue.
27 Watching over the ways of her household,
she would not eat the bread of idleness.
28 Her children have risen and called her blessed;
her husband also has praised her:
29 "Many daughters have done valiantly,
but you have surpassed them all!"
30 Charm is deceitful and beauty is fleeting.
A woman who fears the LORD—she makes herself
praiseworthy.
31 Give her credit for what she has accomplished,
and let her works praise her in the city gates.

31:10–31 The divinely inspired Solomon in his instructive wisdom praises the woman who keeps her house and loves her husband. And in contrast to the woman who wanders abroad, who is uncontrolled and dishonorable, who hunts precious souls with wanton ways and words, he praises her who is engaged honorably at home, who performs her womanly duties with fearless courage, her hands constantly holding the spindle as she prepares double cloaks for her husband, who buys a field in season and carefully provides food for her servants, receives her friends at a bountiful table, and who exhibits all other qualities for which he extols in song the modest and industrious woman.

GREGORY OF NAZIANZUS
(C. 329–390)
ORATIONS

AUTHOR	AUDIENCE	DATE	PURPOSE	THEMES
Unknown; possibly King Solomon	The people of Israel	Unknown; possibly as early as the tenth century BC	This book was written to explore the full range of human experience in order to arrive at the purpose of life: to fear God and keep his commands.	The meaningful life; the emptiness of life; the human experience; the fear of God; and obedience

The quest for a meaningful life is as old as humanity itself. Every culture has offered its answers, and the Israelites were no different. In Ecclesiastes the full range of human experience is explored in the search for the good life. In the end Solomon discovers that "on earth" (1:9) all is vanity, but in God's presence there is meaning and purpose. Therefore the best we can do with the life we've been given is to fear God and keep his commands.

The book of Ecclesiastes has been a source of inspiration for every generation, but it has also been a source of frustration: The book is a puzzle that requires diligence to uncover its meaning. Gregory of Nyssa explained the book's function and benefits for the believing community: "The teaching of Ecclesiastes pertains only to suitable behavior in the church, that is, how to direct a person in virtue. This book aims to elevate our minds above the senses, to abandon great, brilliant, and noble appearances, to transcend the senses, and to attain what transcends them."

The main voice in this wisdom book is "the Teacher, the son of David, king in Jerusalem" (1:1), which has traditionally been understood to be Solomon. John Wesley offered important insight into the book's composition, which frames the scope of Solomon's discourse:

> That he wrote it in his old age is more than probable from diverse passages in it as that he did it after his buildings, which yet took up 20 years of his life, and after some considerable enjoyment of them and planting of gardens and orchards and reaping the fruit of them, and after long and much consideration and experience of all those methods in which men expect to find happiness.

The opening words represent Solomon's thinking after considering his experience, which sets the course for the rest of the book: "Absolutely futile! Everything is futile!" (1:2). Gregory of Nyssa explained, "[Futility] may be described as something which lacks existence but exists only in the utterance of this word. The reality behind the word is nonexistent; only the letters transmit a useless, empty sound." Another word for *futile* is "meaningless" or "absurd"—the opposite of that which will bring self-fulfillment. Solomon looked across the vast expanse of human experience and concluded that most of the activities we commit ourselves to are utterly devoid of lasting meaning. Augustine called this the "false life" and encouraged the communion of saints to "let them lay hold of true life"—which is what Solomon's work is concerned with.

ECCLESIASTES

The book of Ecclesiastes is wisdom literature, for Solomon's concern was to bring order to his own life as well as his readers'. Solomon searched far and wide for the truth: "I decided to carefully and thoroughly examine all that has been accomplished on earth . . . to discern the benefit of wisdom and knowledge over foolish behavior and ideas" (1:13, 17). Part of his answer was found in recognizing that much of life is meaningless and absurd.

One of the more well-known sections opines, "For everything there is an appointed time . . . for every activity on earth" (3:1). He advises, "In times of prosperity be joyful, but in times of adversity consider this: God has made one as well as the other, so that no one can discover what the future holds" (7:14). In his own life, Solomon had seen both of these principles at work: "Sometimes a righteous person dies prematurely in spite of his righteousness, and sometimes a wicked person lives long in spite of his evil deeds" (7:15). He saw examples of wisdom that impressed him, and he shared them. He also shared proverbs like this one: "Because of laziness the roof caves in, and because of idle hands the house leaks" (10:18).

In the end, the Teacher recognized that his only hope and source for knowledge, wisdom, and meaning in life is the Lord: "Having heard everything, I have reached this conclusion: Fear God and keep his commandments, because this is the whole duty of man. For God will evaluate every deed, including every secret thing, whether good or evil" (12:13–14). From the Shepherd of Hermes to Augustine, Anselm to Aquinas, Luther to Calvin, Kierkegaard to Bonhoeffer and beyond, the communion of saints has cherished these words as the high-water mark for a meaningful life.

Solomon wrote his book, explained John Wesley,

> to describe man's true happiness and the way leading to it. This he does both negatively, proving that it is not to be found either in secular wisdom, in sensual pleasures, in worldly greatness and glory, in abundance of riches, or in a vain profession of religion; and positively, showing that it is to be had only in the fear of God and obedience to his laws, which alone can give a man a cheerful enjoyment of his present comforts and an assurance of his everlasting happiness.

We would all do well to pay close attention to Solomon's words in order to find the way of meaning, the way of happiness, through the fear of God.

1:1–18 Nothing can satisfy the human race but the Lord's love and the Lord's own self. Solomon, the wisest of men, was permitted to make experiments for us all and to do for us what we must not dare to do for ourselves. Here is his testimony in his own words: "Absolutely futile!" Nothing but weariness of spirit. This was his verdict when he had trodden the whole round of pleasure. To embrace our Lord Jesus, to dwell in his love, and to be fully assured of union with him—this is all in all. Dear reader, if you roam the world around, you will see no sights like a sight of the Savior's face; if you could have all the comforts of life, yet you lost your Savior, you would be wretched. But if you win Christ, then you will yet be satisfied with favor and full of the goodness of the Lord.

CHARLES SPURGEON
(1834–1892)
MORNING AND EVENING

TITLE

1 The words of the Teacher, the son of David, king in Jerusalem:

INTRODUCTION: UTTER FUTILITY

2 "Futile! Futile!" laments the Teacher.
"Absolutely futile! Everything is futile!"

FUTILITY ILLUSTRATED FROM NATURE

3 What benefit do people get from all the effort
which they expend on earth?
4 A generation comes and a generation goes,
but the earth remains the same through the ages.
5 The sun rises and the sun sets;
it hurries away to a place from which it rises again.
6 The wind goes to the south and circles around to the north;
round and round the wind goes and on its rounds it returns.
7 All the streams flow into the sea, but the sea is not full,
and to the place where the streams flow, there they will flow again.
8 All this monotony is tiresome; no one can bear to describe it.
The eye is never satisfied with seeing, nor is the ear ever content with hearing.
9 What exists now is what will be,
and what has been done is what will be done;
there is nothing truly new on earth.
10 Is there anything about which someone can say, "Look at this! It is new"?
It was already done long ago, before our time.
11 No one remembers the former events,
nor will anyone remember the events that are yet to happen;
they will not be remembered by the future generations.

FUTILITY OF SECULAR ACCOMPLISHMENT

12 I, the Teacher, have been king over Israel in Jerusalem.
13 I decided to carefully and thoroughly examine
all that has been accomplished on earth.
I concluded: God has given people a burdensome task
that keeps them occupied.
14 I reflected on everything that is accomplished by man on earth,
and I concluded: Everything he has accomplished is futile—like chasing the wind!
15 What is bent cannot be straightened,
and what is missing cannot be supplied.

FUTILITY OF SECULAR WISDOM

16 I thought to myself,
"I have become much wiser than any of my predecessors who ruled over Jerusalem;
I have acquired much wisdom and knowledge."
17 So I decided to discern the benefit of wisdom and knowledge over foolish behavior and ideas;
however, I concluded that even this endeavor is like trying to chase the wind.

18 For with great wisdom comes great frustration;
whoever increases his knowledge merely increases his heartache.

FUTILITY OF SELF-INDULGENT PLEASURE

2 I thought to myself,
"Come now, I will try self-indulgent pleasure to see if it is worthwhile."
But I found that it also is futile.
2 I said of partying, "It is folly,"
and of self-indulgent pleasure, "It accomplishes nothing!"
3 I thought deeply about the effects of indulging myself with wine
(all the while my mind was guiding me with wisdom)
and the effects of behaving foolishly,
so that I might discover what is profitable
for people to do on earth during the few days of their lives.

FUTILITY OF MATERIALISM

4 I increased my possessions:
I built houses for myself;
I planted vineyards for myself.
5 I designed royal gardens and parks for myself,
and I planted all kinds of fruit trees in them.
6 I constructed pools of water for myself,
to irrigate my grove of flourishing trees.
7 I purchased male and female slaves,
and I owned slaves who were born in my house;
I also possessed more livestock—both herds and flocks—
than any of my predecessors in Jerusalem.
8 I also amassed silver and gold for myself,
as well as valuable treasures taken from kingdoms and provinces.
I acquired male singers and female singers for myself,
and what gives a man sensual delight—a harem of beautiful concubines.
9 So I was far wealthier than all my predecessors in Jerusalem,
yet I maintained my objectivity.
10 I did not restrain myself from getting whatever I wanted;
I did not deny myself anything that would bring me pleasure.
So all my accomplishments gave me joy;
this was my reward for all my effort.
11 Yet when I reflected on everything I had accomplished
and on all the effort that I had expended to accomplish it,
I concluded: "All these achievements and possessions are ultimately profitless—
like chasing the wind!
There is nothing gained from them on earth."

WISDOM IS BETTER THAN FOLLY

12 Next, I decided to consider wisdom, as well as foolish behavior and ideas.
For what more can the king's successor do than what the king has already done?

2:12–26 "I decided to consider wisdom, as well as foolish behavior and ideas." To speak now of the troubles of this life, he has taken his soul in vain who is constructing the things of the world and building the things of the body. We arise each day to eat and drink, yet no one is filled so that he does not hunger and thirst after a short time. Daily we seek profit, and to greed there is set no limit. "The eye is never satisfied with seeing, nor the ear ever content with hearing" (Eccl 1:8). He who loves silver will not be satisfied with silver. There is no limit to toil, and there is no profit in abundance.

AMBROSE **(C. 339–C. 397)**
DEATH AS A GOOD

13 I realized that wisdom is preferable to folly,
just as light is preferable to darkness:
14 The wise man can see where he is going, but the fool walks in darkness.
Yet I also realized that the same fate happens to them both.
15 So I thought to myself, "The fate of the fool will happen even to me!
Then what did I gain by becoming so excessively wise?"
So I lamented to myself,
"The benefits of wisdom are ultimately meaningless!"
16 For the wise man, like the fool, will not be remembered for very long,
because in the days to come, both will already have been forgotten.
Alas, the wise man dies—just like the fool!
17 So I loathed life because what
happens on earth seems awful to me;
for all the benefits of wisdom are futile—like chasing the wind.

FUTILITY OF BEING A WORKAHOLIC

18 So I loathed all the fruit of my effort,
for which I worked so hard on earth,
because I must leave it behind in the hands of my successor.
19 Who knows if he will be a wise man or a fool?
Yet he will be master over all the fruit of my labor
for which I worked so wisely on earth.
This also is futile!
20 So I began to despair about all the fruit of my labor
for which I worked so hard on earth.
21 For a man may do his work with wisdom, knowledge, and skill;
however, he must hand over the fruit of his labor as an inheritance
to someone else who did not work for it.
This also is futile, and an awful injustice!

PAINFUL DAYS AND RESTLESS NIGHTS

22 What does a man acquire from all his labor
and from the anxiety that accompanies his toil on earth?
23 For all day long his work produces pain and frustration,
and even at night his mind cannot relax.
This also is futile!

ENJOY WORK AND ITS BENEFITS

24 There is nothing better for people than to eat and drink,
and to find enjoyment in their work.
I also perceived that this ability to find enjoyment comes from God.
25 For no one can eat and drink
or experience joy apart from him.
26 For to the one who pleases him, God gives wisdom, knowledge, and joy,
but to the sinner, he gives the task of amassing wealth—
only to give it to the one who pleases God.
This task of the wicked is futile—like chasing the wind!

A TIME FOR ALL EVENTS IN LIFE

3 For everything there is an appointed time,
and an appropriate time for every activity on earth:
2 A time to be born, and a time to die;
a time to plant, and a time to uproot what was planted;
3 a time to kill, and a time to heal;
a time to break down, and a time to build up;
4 a time to weep, and a time to laugh;
a time to mourn, and a time to dance.
5 A time to throw away stones, and a time to gather stones;
a time to embrace, and a time to refrain from embracing;
6 a time to search, and a time to give something up as lost;
a time to keep, and a time to throw away;
7 a time to rip, and a time to sew;
a time to keep silent, and a time to speak.
8 A time to love, and a time to hate;
a time for war, and a time for peace.

MAN IS IGNORANT OF GOD'S TIMING

9 What benefit can a worker gain from his toil?
10 I have observed the burden
that God has given to people to keep them occupied.
11 God has made everything fit beautifully in its appropriate time,
but he has also placed ignorance in the human heart
so that people cannot discover what God has ordained,
from the beginning to the end of their lives.

ENJOY LIFE IN THE PRESENT

12 I have concluded that there is nothing better for people
than to be happy and to enjoy
themselves as long as they live,
13 and also that everyone should eat and drink, and find enjoyment in all his toil,
for these things are a gift from God.

GOD'S SOVEREIGNTY

14 I also know that whatever God does will endure forever;
nothing can be added to it, and nothing taken away from it.
God has made it this way, so that men will fear him.
15 Whatever exists now has already been, and whatever will be has already been;
for God will seek to do again what has occurred in the past.

THE PROBLEM OF INJUSTICE AND OPPRESSION

16 I saw something else on earth:
In the place of justice, there was wickedness,
and in the place of fairness, there was wickedness.
17 I thought to myself, "God will judge both the righteous and the wicked;
for there is an appropriate time for every activity,
and there is a time of judgment for every deed."
18 I also thought to myself, "It is for the sake of people,
so God can clearly show them that they are like animals.

3:16—4:3 "God will judge both the righteous and the wicked." There will be no person of our times who will be able at that judgment to find an excuse for unbelief when everyone shall call on Christ: the upright for justice, the perjurer for deceit, the king for power and the soldier for battle, the husband to maintain his authority and the wife to show her submission, the father for command and the son for obedience, the master for his right to rule and the servant for his subjection, the humble for piety and the proud for ambition, the rich to distribute and the poor to receive, the drunkard at his wine cups and the beggar at the gate, the good person that he may excel in virtue and the bad one that he may cheat, the Christian worshiper and the pagan sycophant. All have the name of Christ upon their lips, and with whatever intention and formula they invoke him, without doubt they shall render an account of it to him whom they invoke.

AUGUSTINE **(354–430)**
LETTERS

19 For the fate of humans and the fate of animals are the
same:
As one dies, so dies the other; both have the same
breath.
There is no advantage for humans over animals,
for both are fleeting.
20 Both go to the same place;
both come from the dust,
and to dust both return.
21 Who really knows if the human spirit ascends upward,
and the animal's spirit descends into the earth?"
22 So I perceived there is nothing better than for people to
enjoy their work
because that is their reward;
for who can show them what the future holds?

EVIL OPPRESSION ON EARTH

4 So I again considered all the oppression that
continually occurs on earth.
This is what I saw:
The oppressed were in tears, but no one was comforting
them;
no one delivers them from the power of their
oppressors.
2 So I considered those who are dead and gone
more fortunate than those who are still alive.
3 But better than both is the one who has not been born
and has not seen the evil things that are done on earth.

LABOR MOTIVATED BY ENVY

4 Then I considered all the skillful work that is done:
Surely it is nothing more than competition between
one person and another.
This also is profitless—like chasing the wind.
5 The fool folds his hands and does no work,
so he has nothing to eat but his own flesh.
6 Better is one handful with some rest
than two hands full of toil and chasing the wind.

LABOR MOTIVATED BY GREED

7 So I again considered another futile thing on earth:
8 A man who is all alone with no companion—
he has no children nor siblings;
yet there is no end to all his toil,
and he is never satisfied with riches.
He laments, "For whom am I toiling and depriving
myself of pleasure?"
This also is futile and a burdensome task!

LABOR IS BENEFICIAL WHEN ITS REWARDS ARE SHARED

9 Two people are better than one
because they can reap more benefit from their labor.
10 For if they fall, one will help his companion up,
but pity the person who falls down and has no one to
help him up.
11 Furthermore, if two lie down together, they can keep
each other warm,
but how can one person keep warm by himself?

12 Although an assailant may overpower one person,
two can withstand him.
Moreover, a three-stranded cord is not quickly broken.

LABOR MOTIVATED BY PRESTIGE SEEKING

13 A poor but wise youth is better than an old and foolish king
who no longer knows how to receive advice.
14 For he came out of prison to become king,
even though he had been born poor in what would become his kingdom.
15 I considered all the living who walk on earth,
as well as the successor who would arise in his place.
16 There is no end to all the people nor to the past generations,
yet future generations will not rejoice in him.
This also is profitless and like chasing the wind.

RASH VOWS

5 Be careful what you do when you go to the temple of God;
draw near to listen rather than to offer a sacrifice like fools,
for they do not realize that they are doing wrong.
2 Do not be rash with your mouth or hasty in your heart to bring up a matter before God,
for God is in heaven and you are on earth!
Therefore, let your words be few.
3 Just as dreams come when there are many cares,
so the rash vow of a fool occurs when there are many words.
4 When you make a vow to God, do not delay in paying it.
For God takes no pleasure in fools:
Pay what you vow!
5 It is better for you not to vow
than to vow and not pay it.
6 Do not let your mouth cause you to sin,
and do not tell the priest, "It was a mistake!"
Why make God angry at you
so that he would destroy the work of your hands?
7 Just as there is futility in many dreams,
so also in many words.
Therefore, fear God.

GOVERNMENT CORRUPTION

8 If you see the extortion of the poor,
or the perversion of justice and fairness in the government,
do not be astonished by the matter.
For the high official is watched by a higher official,
and there are higher ones over them!
9 The produce of the land is seized by all of them,
even the king is served by the fields.

COVETOUSNESS

10 The one who loves money will never be satisfied with money;
he who loves wealth will never be satisfied with his income.
This also is futile.

5:8–20 If, he says, you see among people those on the one hand who are oppressed and those on the other who do wrong in judgment, and still others who practice justice, do not be amazed that this occurs as if there were no divine foresight. Rather, know that God guards everything through Christ and that he also exercises his provision over everything through his holy angels, who excel in their knowledge of earthly events. God is the ruler of the world that he created, and he allots suffering to those who prefer greed and the vanity of this life to knowledge of Christ. But to those who live their lives in goodness, conduct themselves with courage, and serve justly, he grants the knowledge of God and a peaceful rest. He grants this whether their knowledge was small or great here. But in the end, he will receive these good folk, while those who were filled with wickedness will find no rest from the worm produced by their evil.

EVAGRIUS PONTICUS
(345–399)
SCHOLIA ON ECCLESIASTES

11 When someone's prosperity increases, those who consume it also increase;
so what does its owner gain, except that he gets to see it with his eyes?
12 The sleep of the laborer is pleasant—whether he eats little or much—
but the wealth of the rich will not allow him to sleep.

MATERIALISM THWARTS ENJOYMENT OF LIFE

13 Here is a misfortune on earth that I have seen:
Wealth hoarded by its owner to his own misery.
14 Then that wealth was lost through bad luck;
although he fathered a son, he has nothing left to give him.
15 Just as he came forth from his mother's womb, naked will he return as he came,
and he will take nothing in his hand that he may carry away from his toil.
16 This is another misfortune:
Just as he came, so will he go.
What did he gain from toiling for the wind?
17 Surely, he ate in darkness every day of his life,
and he suffered greatly with sickness and anger.

ENJOY THE FRUIT OF YOUR LABOR

18 I have seen personally what is the only beneficial and appropriate course of action for people:
to eat and drink, and find enjoyment in all their hard work on earth
during the few days of their life that God has given them,
for this is their reward.
19 To every man whom God has given wealth and possessions,
he has also given him the ability
to eat from them, to receive his reward, and to find enjoyment in his toil;
these things are the gift of God.
20 For he does not think much about the fleeting days of his life
because God keeps him preoccupied with the joy he derives from his activity.

NOT EVERYONE ENJOYS LIFE

6 Here is another misfortune that I have seen on earth,
and it weighs heavily on people:
2 God gives a man riches, property, and wealth
so that he lacks nothing that his heart desires,
yet God does not enable him to enjoy the fruit of his labor—
instead, someone else enjoys it!
This is fruitless and a grave misfortune.
3 Even if a man fathers a hundred children and lives many years,
even if he lives a long, long time, but cannot enjoy his prosperity—
even if he were to live forever—
I would say, "A stillborn child is better off than he is."
4 Though the stillborn child came into the world for no reason and departed into darkness,

though its name is shrouded in darkness,
5 though it never saw the light of day nor knew anything,
yet it has more rest than that man—
6 if he should live a thousand years twice, yet does not enjoy his prosperity.
For both of them die!
7 All man's labor is for nothing more than to fill his stomach—
yet his appetite is never satisfied!
8 So what advantage does a wise man have over a fool?
And what advantage does a pauper gain by knowing how to survive?
9 It is better to be content with what the eyes can see
than for one's heart always to crave more.
This continual longing is futile—like chasing the wind.

THE FUTILE WAY LIFE WORKS

10 Whatever has happened was foreordained,
and what happens to a person was also foreknown.
It is useless for him to argue with God about his fate
because God is more powerful than he is.
11 The more one argues with words, the less he accomplishes.
How does that benefit him?
12 For no one knows what is best for a person during his life—
during the few days of his fleeting life—
for they pass away like a shadow.
Nor can anyone tell him what the future will hold for him on earth.

LIFE IS BRIEF AND DEATH IS CERTAIN

7 A good reputation is better than precious perfume;
likewise, the day of one's death is better than the day of one's birth.
2 It is better to go to a funeral
than a feast.
For death is the destiny of every person,
and the living should take this to heart.
3 Sorrow is better than laughter
because sober reflection is good for the heart.
4 The heart of the wise is in the house of mourning,
but the heart of fools is in the house of merrymaking.

FRIVOLOUS LIVING VERSUS WISDOM

5 It is better for a person to receive a rebuke from those who are wise
than to listen to the song of fools.
6 For like the crackling of quick-burning thorns under a cooking pot,
so is the laughter of the fool.
This kind of folly also is useless.

HUMAN WISDOM OVERTURNED BY ADVERSITY

7 Surely oppression can turn a wise person into a fool;
likewise, a bribe corrupts the heart.
8 The end of a matter is better than its beginning;
likewise, patience is better than pride.

6:10 There is a certain sphere in which God has placed man, certain limits by which his attainments in the world and the degree of his worldly happiness are circumscribed, which limits men have come to in time past, and it is a vain imagination for any to expect to exceed those limits. Whatever men attain to, still they are but men. He that made him gave him his name, Adam, which implies that he is dust; and let him be never so greedy, aspiring, busy, restless, and grasping in his pursuits, and vast in his expectations, or he never will be anymore. Man in his first transgression was ambitious of getting above his limits, of being as a god, and this disposition is common among humankind. But he that is mightier than man has set his limits, and it is in vain to contend with him.

JONATHAN EDWARDS
(1703–1758)
SELECTIONS FROM THE UNPUBLISHED WRITINGS

9 Do not let yourself be quickly provoked,
for anger resides in the lap of fools.
10 Do not say, "Why were the old days better than these days?"
for it is not wise to ask that.

WISDOM CAN LENGTHEN ONE'S LIFE

11 Wisdom, like an inheritance, is a good thing;
it benefits those who see the light of day.
12 For wisdom provides protection,
just as money provides protection.
But the advantage of knowledge is this:
Wisdom preserves the life of its owner.

WISDOM ACKNOWLEDGES GOD'S ORCHESTRATION OF LIFE

13 Consider the work of God:
For who can make straight what he has bent?
14 In times of prosperity be joyful,
but in times of adversity consider this:
God has made one as well as the other,
so that no one can discover what the future holds.

EXCEPTIONS TO THE LAW OF RETRIBUTION

15 During the days of my fleeting life I have seen both of these things:
Sometimes a righteous person dies prematurely in spite of his righteousness,
and sometimes a wicked person lives long in spite of his evil deeds.
16 So do not be excessively righteous or excessively wise;
otherwise you might be disappointed.
17 Do not be excessively wicked and do not be a fool;
otherwise you might die before your time.
18 It is best to take hold of one warning without letting go of the other warning;
for the one who fears God will follow both warnings.

WISDOM NEEDED BECAUSE NO ONE IS TRULY RIGHTEOUS

19 Wisdom gives a wise person more protection
than ten rulers in a city.
20 For there is not one truly righteous person on the earth
who continually does good and never sins.
21 Also, do not pay attention to everything that people say;
otherwise, you might even hear your servant cursing you.
22 For you know in your own heart
that you also have cursed others many times.

HUMAN WISDOM IS LIMITED

23 I have examined all this by wisdom;
I said, "I am determined to comprehend this"—but it was beyond my grasp.
24 Whatever has happened is beyond human understanding;
it is far deeper than anyone can fathom.

7:13–15 "Consider the work of God." His wise, just, and powerful government of all events is proposed as the last and best remedy against all murmurings. No one can correct or alter any of God's works, and therefore all fretting at the injuries of people or calamities of times is not only sinful, but also vain and fruitless. This implies that there is a hand of God in all human actions, either affecting them if they be good, or permitting them if they be bad, and ordering and overruling them whether they be good or bad. Consider that it is God's hand and therefore submit to it: Consider also why God sends it, for what sins and with what design. God has wisely ordained that prosperity and adversity should succeed one another. No one might be able to foresee what shall befall afterward, and therefore one might live in a constant dependence upon God and neither despair in trouble nor be secure or presumptuous in prosperity.

JOHN WESLEY (1703–1791)
EXPLANATORY NOTES ON THE BIBLE

TRUE RIGHTEOUSNESS AND WISDOM ARE VIRTUALLY NONEXISTENT

25 I tried to understand, examine, and comprehend
the role of wisdom in the scheme of things,
and to understand the stupidity of wickedness and the
insanity of folly.
26 I discovered this:
More bitter than death is the kind of woman who is like
a hunter's snare;
her heart is like a hunter's net, and her hands are like
prison chains.
The man who pleases God escapes her,
but the sinner is captured by her.
27 The Teacher says:
I discovered this while trying to discover the scheme of
things, item by item.
28 What I have continually sought, I have not found;
I have found only one upright man among a thousand,
but I have not found one upright woman among all of
them.
29 This alone have I discovered: God made humankind
upright,
but they have sought many evil schemes.

HUMAN GOVERNMENT DEMONSTRATES LIMITATIONS OF WISDOM

8 Who is a wise person? Who knows the solution to a
problem?
A person's wisdom brightens his appearance and
softens his harsh countenance.
2 Obey the king's command,
because you took an oath before God to be loyal to him.
3 Do not rush out of the king's presence in haste—do not
delay when the matter is unpleasant,
for he can do whatever he pleases.
4 Surely the king's authority is absolute;
no one can say to him, "What are you doing?"
5 Whoever obeys his command will not experience harm,
and a wise person knows the proper time and
procedure.
6 For there is a proper time and procedure for every
matter,
for the oppression of the king is severe upon his victim.
7 Surely no one knows the future,
and no one can tell another person what will happen.
8 Just as no one has power over the wind to restrain it,
so no one has power over the day of his death.
Just as no one can be discharged during the battle,
so wickedness cannot rescue the wicked.
9 While applying my mind to everything that happens in
this world, I have seen all this:
Sometimes one person dominates other people to their
harm.

CONTRADICTIONS TO THE LAW OF RETRIBUTION

10 Not only that, but I have seen the wicked approaching
and entering the temple,
and as they left the holy temple, they
boasted in the city that they had done so.

8:10–17 Let them rest assured that punishment shall be inflicted on the wicked and rewards shall be bestowed upon the righteous by him who deals with everyone as each deserves. He will proportion his rewards to the good that each has done and to the account of himself that he is able to give. And let all know that the good shall be advanced to a higher state, and that the wicked shall be delivered over to sufferings and torments in punishment of their licentiousness and depravity, their cowardice, timidity, and all their follies.

ORIGEN (C. 185–C. 253)
CONTRA CELSUM

This also is an enigma.
11 When a sentence is not executed at once against a crime,
the human heart is encouraged to do evil.
12 Even though a sinner might commit a hundred crimes and still live a long time,
yet I know that it will go well with God-fearing people—
for they stand in fear before him.
13 But it will not go well with the wicked,
nor will they prolong their days like a shadow,
because they do not stand in fear before God.
14 Here is another enigma that occurs on earth:
Sometimes there are righteous people who get what the wicked deserve,
and sometimes there are wicked people who get what the righteous deserve.
I said, "This also is an enigma."

ENJOY LIFE IN SPITE OF ITS INJUSTICES

15 So I recommend the enjoyment of life,
for there is nothing better on earth for a person to do except to eat, drink, and enjoy life.
So joy will accompany him in his toil
during the days of his life that God gives him on earth.

LIMITATIONS OF HUMAN WISDOM

16 When I tried to gain wisdom
and to observe the activity on earth—
even though it prevents anyone from sleeping day or night—
17 then I discerned all that God has done:
No one really comprehends what happens on earth.
Despite all human efforts to discover it, no one can ever grasp it.
Even if a wise person claimed that he understood,
he would not really comprehend it.

EVERYONE WILL DIE

9 So I reflected on all this, attempting to clear it all up.
I concluded that the righteous and the wise, as well as their works, are in the hand of God;
whether a person will be loved or hated—
no one knows what lies ahead.
2 Everyone shares the same fate—
the righteous and the wicked,
the good and the bad,
the ceremonially clean and unclean,
those who offer sacrifices and those who do not.
What happens to the good person, also happens to the sinner;
what happens to those who make vows, also happens to those who are afraid to make vows.
3 This is the unfortunate fact about everything that happens on earth:
The same fate awaits everyone.
In addition to this, the hearts of all people are full of evil,
and there is folly in their hearts during their lives—then they die.

9:1–12 "Whatever you find to do with your hands" refers to works that are possible. One good deed is worth more than a thousand brilliant theories. Let us not wait for large opportunities or for a different kind of work but do just the things we "find to do" day by day. Serve God now, but be careful as to the way in which you perform what you find to do—"do it with all your might." Whatever you do for Christ, throw your whole soul into it. Do not give Christ a little slurred labor done as a matter of course now and then; when you serve him, do it with heart and soul and strength. Let us seek his help; let us proceed with prayer and faith, and when we have done what we find to do with our hands, let us wait upon the Lord for his blessing. What we do will be well done and will not fail in its effect.

CHARLES SPURGEON
(1834–1892)
MORNING AND EVENING

BETTER TO BE POOR BUT ALIVE THAN RICH BUT DEAD

4 But whoever is among the living has hope;
a live dog is better than a dead lion.
5 For the living know that they will die, but the dead do not know anything;
they have no further reward—and even the memory of them disappears.
6 What they loved, as well as what they hated and envied, perished long ago,
and they no longer have a part in anything that happens on earth.

LIFE IS BRIEF, SO CHERISH ITS JOYS

7 Go, eat your food with joy,
and drink your wine with a happy heart,
because God has already approved your works.
8 Let your clothes always be white,
and do not spare precious ointment on your head.
9 Enjoy life with your beloved wife during all the days of your fleeting life
that God has given you on earth during all your fleeting days;
for that is your reward in life and in your burdensome work on earth.
10 Whatever you find to do with your hands,
do it with all your might,
because there is neither work nor planning nor knowledge nor wisdom in the grave,
the place where you will eventually go.

WISDOM CANNOT PROTECT AGAINST SEEMINGLY CHANCE EVENTS

11 Again, I observed this on the earth:
The race is not always won by the swiftest,
the battle is not always won by the strongest;
prosperity does not always belong to those who are the wisest;
wealth does not always belong to those who are the most discerning,
nor does success always come to those with the most knowledge—
for time and chance may overcome them all.
12 Surely, no one knows his appointed time.
Like fish that are caught in a deadly net and like birds that are caught in a snare—
just like them, all people are ensnared at an unfortunate time that falls upon them suddenly.

MOST PEOPLE ARE NOT RECEPTIVE TO WISE COUNSEL

13 This is what I also observed about wisdom on earth,
and it is a great burden to me:
14 There was once a small city with a few men in it,
and a mighty king attacked it, besieging it and building strong siege works against it.
15 However, a poor but wise man lived in the city,
and he could have delivered the city by his wisdom,
but no one listened to that poor man.

16 So I concluded that wisdom is better than might,
but a poor man's wisdom is despised; no one ever listens to his advice.

WISDOM VERSUS FOOLS, SIN, AND FOLLY

17 The words of the wise are heard in quiet,
more than the shouting of a ruler is heard among fools.
18 Wisdom is better than weapons of war,
but one sinner can destroy much that is good.

10 One dead fly makes the perfumer's ointment give off a rancid stench,
so a little folly can outweigh much wisdom.

WISDOM CAN BE NULLIFIED BY THE CAPRICE OF RULERS

2 A wise person's good sense protects him,
but a fool's lack of sense leaves him vulnerable.
3 Even when a fool walks along the road he lacks sense
and shows everyone what a fool he is.
4 If the anger of the ruler flares up against you, do not resign from your position,
for a calm response can undo great offenses.
5 I have seen another misfortune on the earth:
It is an error a ruler makes.
6 Fools are placed in many positions of authority,
while wealthy men sit in lowly positions.
7 I have seen slaves on horseback
and princes walking on foot like slaves.

WISDOM IS NEEDED TO AVERT DANGERS IN EVERYDAY LIFE

8 One who digs a pit may fall into it,
and one who breaks through a wall may be bitten by a snake.
9 One who quarries stones may be injured by them;
one who splits logs may be endangered by them.
10 If an iron axhead is blunt and a workman does not sharpen its edge,
he must exert a great deal of effort;
so wisdom has the advantage of giving success.
11 If the snake should bite before it is charmed,
the snake charmer is in trouble.

WORDS AND WORKS OF WISE MEN AND FOOLS

12 The words of a wise person win him favor,
but the words of a fool are self-destructive.
13 At the beginning his words are foolish
and at the end his talk is wicked madness,
14 yet a fool keeps on babbling.
No one knows what will happen;
who can tell him what will happen in the future?
15 The toil of a stupid fool wears him out,
because he does not even know the way to the city.

THE PROBLEM WITH FOOLISH RULERS

16 Woe to you, O land, when your king is childish
and your princes feast in the morning.

10:3–6 The true cause of the blessedness of the good is found to be this, that they cleave to him who supremely is. And if we ask the cause of the misery of the bad, it occurs to us, and not unreasonably, that they are miserable because they have forsaken him who supremely is and have turned to themselves who have no such essence. And this vice, what else is it called than pride? For "pride is the beginning of sin" (Sir 10:13 KJV). They were unwilling to preserve their strength for God; and as adherence to God was the condition of their enjoying an ampler being, they diminished it by preferring themselves to him. This was the first defect and the first impoverishment and the first flaw of their nature. Their nature was created not indeed supremely existent, but finding its blessedness in the enjoyment of the Supreme Being, while by abandoning him it should become a nature with a less-ample existence and therefore wretched.

AUGUSTINE (354–430)
CITY OF GOD

17 Blessed are you, O land, when your king is the son of nobility,
and your princes feast at the proper time—with self-control and not in drunkenness.
18 Because of laziness the roof caves in,
and because of idle hands the house leaks.
19 Feasts are made for laughter,
and wine makes life merry,
but money is the answer for everything.
20 Do not curse a king even in your thoughts,
and do not curse the rich while in your bedroom;
for a bird might report what you are thinking,
or some winged creature might repeat your words.

IGNORANCE OF THE FUTURE DEMANDS DILIGENCE IN THE PRESENT

11 Send your grain overseas,
for after many days you will get a return.
2 Divide your merchandise among seven or even eight investments,
for you do not know what calamity may happen on earth.
3 If the clouds are full of rain, they will empty themselves on the earth,
and whether a tree falls to the south or to the north, the tree will lie wherever it falls.
4 He who watches the wind will not sow,
and he who observes the clouds will not reap.
5 Just as you do not know the path of the wind
or how the bones form in the womb of a pregnant woman,
so you do not know the work of God who makes everything.
6 Sow your seed in the morning,
and do not stop working until the evening;
for you do not know which activity will succeed—
whether this one or that one, or whether both will prosper equally.

LIFE SHOULD BE ENJOYED BECAUSE DEATH IS INEVITABLE

7 Light is sweet,
and it is pleasant for a person to see the sun.
8 So, if a man lives many years, let him rejoice in them all,
but let him remember that the days of darkness will be many—all that is about to come is obscure.

ENJOY LIFE TO THE FULLEST UNDER THE FEAR OF GOD

9 Rejoice, young man, while you are young,
and let your heart cheer you in the days of your youth.
Follow the impulses of your heart and the desires of your eyes,
but know that God will judge your motives and actions.
10 Banish emotional stress from your mind
and put away pain from your body;
for youth and the prime of life are fleeting.

11:1–8 It happens with most people that they give indeed, but they do not do so freely and readily, which is a greater and more perfect thing than the mere act of offering itself. It is far better to be generous to the unworthy for the sake of the worthy than to deprive the worthy out of fear of the unworthy. This seems to have a bearing on our duty of casting bread upon the waters, not that it may be swept away or perish in the eyes of the just examiner, but that it may come to that place where all our goods will be stored up. And it will be there to meet us in due time, even though we may think otherwise.

GREGORY OF NAZIANZUS
(C. 329–390)
ORATIONS

12:1–14 Let us indeed "fear God and keep his commandments," for all persons were born for this purpose, that knowing their Creator they might venerate him with fear, honor, and observance of the commandments. When the time of judgment arrives, whatever we have done will stand under judgment and await the double sentence that all persons will receive for their work, whether they have done evil or good. We will be held accountable on the day of judgment for what we were able to do, "including every secret thing, whether good or evil." But because fear belongs to slaves and perfect love drives fear away, fear has a double meaning in divine scripture, for beginners and for the perfect. The fear of him who has been perfected in virtue, I believe, is expressed here: "Those who seek the LORD lack no good thing" (Ps 34:10).

JEROME **(C. 342–420)**
COMMENTARY ON ECCLESIASTES

FEAR GOD NOW BECAUSE OLD AGE AND DEATH COME QUICKLY

12 So remember your Creator in the days of your youth—
before the difficult days come
and the years draw near when you will say, "I have no pleasure in them";
2 before the sun and the light of the moon and the stars grow dark,
and the clouds disappear after the rain;
3 when those who keep watch over the house begin to tremble,
and the virile men begin to stoop over,
and the grinders begin to cease because they grow few,
and those who look through the windows grow dim,
4 and the doors along the street are shut;
when the sound of the grinding mill grows low,
and one is awakened by the sound of a bird,
and all their songs grow faint,
5 and they are afraid of heights and the dangers in the street;
the almond blossoms grow white,
and the grasshopper drags itself along,
and the caper berry shrivels up—
because man goes to his eternal home,
and the mourners go about in the streets—
6 before the silver cord is removed,
or the golden bowl is broken,
or the pitcher is shattered at the well,
or the water wheel is broken at the cistern—
7 and the dust returns to the earth as it was,
and the life's breath returns to God who gave it.

CONCLUDING REFRAIN: THE TEACHER RESTATES HIS THESIS

8 "Absolutely futile!" laments the Teacher,
"All these things are futile!"

CONCLUDING EPILOGUE: THE TEACHER'S ADVICE IS WISE

9 Not only was the Teacher wise,
but he also taught knowledge to the people;
he carefully evaluated and arranged many proverbs.
10 The Teacher sought to find delightful words
and to write accurately truthful sayings.
11 The words of the sages are like prods,
and the collected sayings are like firmly fixed nails;
they are given by one shepherd.

CONCLUDING EXHORTATION: FEAR GOD AND OBEY HIS COMMANDS

12 Be warned, my son, of anything in addition to them.
There is no end to the making of many books,
and much study is exhausting to the body.

13 Having heard everything, I have reached this
conclusion:
Fear God and keep his commandments,
because this is the whole duty of man.
14 For God will evaluate every deed,
including every secret thing, whether good or evil.

AUTHOR	AUDIENCE	DATE	PURPOSE	THEMES
Unknown; possibly King Solomon	The people of Israel	Unknown; possibly as early as the tenth century BC	Song of Solomon is a wisdom poem that extols the virtue of love and the passion shared between a husband and wife; some have understood it as an allegorical portrayal of the love shared between God and his people, Christ and the church.	Love and marriage; and God's love for his people

Song of Solomon is a unique wisdom poem full of romantic love and passion. The song has had a varied history of interpretation through the years. Some have understood it as an allegory about the love of God for his people or Christ for the church. Other believe the song extols the virtues of the love shared between a husband and wife.

Bernard of Clairvaux, known for his magisterial commentary on the song, reflected the earlier tendency among the patristics, including Origen, to interpret the song as allegory:

> [The Song] was a special divine impulse that inspired these songs of his that now celebrate the praises of Christ and his church, the gift of holy love, the sacrament of endless union with God. Here too are expressed the mounting desires of the soul, its marriage song, an exultation of spirit poured forth in figurative language pregnant with delight . . . Because of its excellence, I consider this nuptial song to be well deserving of the title that so remarkably designates it, the Song of Solomon, just as he in whose honor it is sung is uniquely proclaimed King of kings and Lord of lords.

John Wesley agreed: "The design of the book in general is to describe the love and happy marriage of two persons, but it is not to be understood concerning Solomon and Pharaoh's daughter but concerning God, or Christ, and his church and people." He said the bride/bridegroom language is evident of this interpretation, which Matthew Henry also noted: "This book is a divine allegory, which represents the love between Christ and his church of true believers under figures taken from the relation and affection that subsist between a bridegroom and his espoused bride; an emblem often employed in scripture as describing the nearest, firmest, and most sure relation."

SONG OF SOLOMON

Martin Luther agreed with the medievalists before him that the song pointed to deeper spiritual truths beyond itself but in a political sense, as he states in his preface: "I think it is a song in which Solomon honors God with his praises; he gives him thanks for his divinely established and confirmed kingdom and government; he prays for the preservation and extension of this his kingdom. He makes God the bridegroom and his [Solomon's] people the bride."

And yet many modern interpreters disagree, believing the song to be an ancient erotic poem that offers wisdom on love. Whether an erotic Hebrew love poem or an allegory of Christ and the church (or a combination of the two), Song of Solomon "stands at a point where all the [other songs] culminate," wrote Bernard of Clairvaux.

> Only the couch of the Spirit can inspire a song like this, and only personal experience can unfold its meaning. Let those who are versed in the mystery revel in it; let all others burn with desire rather to attain to this experience than merely to learn about it. For it is not a melody that resounds abroad but the very music of the heart, not a trilling on the lips but an inward pulsing of delight, a harmony not of voices but of wills. It is a tune you will not hear in the streets, these notes do not sound where crowds assemble; only the singer hears it and the one to whom he sings—the lover and the beloved. It is preeminently a marriage song telling of chaste souls in loving embrace, of their wills in sweet concord, of the mutual exchange of the heart's affections.

1:1–17 "Solomon's Most Excellent Love Song." And so this might well be called, whether you consider the author of it, who was a great prince and the wisest of all mortal men; or the subject of it, which is not Solomon, but one greater than Solomon, even Christ, and his marriage with the church; or the matter of it, which is most lofty, containing in it the noblest of all the mysteries contained either in the Old or the New Testament; most pious and pathetical, breathing forth the hottest flames of love between Christ and his people, most sweet and comfortable, and useful to all who read it with serious and Christian eyes.

JOHN WESLEY **(1703–1791)**
EXPLANATORY NOTES ON THE BIBLE

TITLE/SUPERSCRIPTION

1 Solomon's Most Excellent Love Song.

THE DESIRE FOR LOVE

The Beloved to Her Lover:

2 Oh, how I wish you would kiss me passionately!
For your lovemaking is more delightful than wine.
3 The fragrance of your colognes is delightful;
your name is like the finest perfume.
No wonder the young women adore you!
4 Draw me after you; let us hurry!
May the king bring me into his bedroom chambers!

The Maidens to the Lover:

We will rejoice and delight in you;
we will praise your love more than wine.

The Beloved to Her Lover:

How rightly the young women adore you!

THE COUNTRY MAIDEN AND THE DAUGHTERS OF JERUSALEM

The Beloved to the Maidens:

5 I am dark but lovely, O maidens of Jerusalem,
dark like the tents of Qedar,
lovely like the tent curtains of Salmah.
6 Do not stare at me because I am dark,
for the sun has burned my skin.
My brothers were angry with me;
they made me the keeper of the vineyards.
Alas, my own vineyard I could not keep!

THE SHEPHERD AND THE SHEPHERDESS

The Beloved to Her Lover:

7 Tell me, O you whom my heart loves,
where do you pasture your sheep?
Where do you rest your sheep during the midday heat?
Tell me lest I wander around
beside the flocks of your companions!

The Lover to His Beloved:

8 If you do not know, O most beautiful of women,
simply follow the tracks of my flock,
and pasture your little lambs
beside the tents of the shepherds.

THE BEAUTIFUL MARE AND THE FRAGRANT MYRRH

The Lover to His Beloved:

9 O my beloved, you are like a mare
among Pharaoh's stallions.
10 Your cheeks are beautiful with ornaments;
your neck is lovely with strings of jewels.
11 We will make for you gold ornaments
studded with silver.

The Beloved about Her Lover:

12 While the king was at his banqueting table,
my nard gave forth its fragrance.

13 My beloved is like a fragrant pouch of myrrh
spending the night between my breasts.
14 My beloved is like a cluster of henna blossoms
in the vineyards of En Gedi.

MUTUAL PRAISE AND ADMIRATION

The Lover to His Beloved:

15 Oh, how beautiful you are, my beloved!
Oh, how beautiful you are!
Your eyes are like doves!

The Beloved to Her Lover:

16 Oh, how handsome you are, my lover!
Oh, how delightful you are!
The lush foliage is our canopied bed;
17 the cedars are the beams of our bedroom chamber;
the pines are the rafters of our bedroom.

THE LILY AMONG THE THORNS AND THE APPLE TREE IN THE FOREST

The Beloved to Her Lover:

2 I am a meadow flower from Sharon,
a lily from the valleys.

The Lover to His Beloved:

2 Like a lily among the thorns,
so is my darling among the maidens.

The Beloved about Her Lover:

3 Like an apple tree among the trees of the forest,
so is my beloved among the young men.
I delight to sit in his shade,
and his fruit is sweet to my taste.

THE BANQUET HALL FOR THE LOVESICK

The Beloved about Her Lover:

4 He brought me into the banquet hall,
and he looked at me lovingly.
5 Sustain me with raisin cakes,
refresh me with apples,
for I am faint with love.

THE DOUBLE REFRAIN: EMBRACING AND ADJURATION

6 His left hand is under my head,
and his right hand embraces me.

The Beloved to the Maidens:

7 I admonish you, O maidens of Jerusalem,
by the gazelles and by the young does of the open fields:
Do not awaken or arouse love until it pleases!

THE ARRIVAL OF THE LOVER

The Beloved about Her Lover:

8 Listen! My lover is approaching!
Look! Here he comes,
leaping over the mountains,
bounding over the hills!

2:6–17 "My lover is mine and I am his." There is no doubt that in this passage a shared love blazes up, but a love in which one of them experiences the highest felicity while the other shows marvelous condescension. This is no betrothal or union of equals here. Who could lay claim to any clear knowledge of the nature of this token of love in which she glories, bestowed upon her and repaid again by her? Who indeed except one worthy himself of a like experience, being pure in soul and holy in body? Its reality is in the affections; it is not to be attained by reason but by affections by conformity. How few there are who can say: "We all, with unveiled faces reflecting the glory of the Lord, are being transformed into the same image from one degree of glory to another, which is from the Lord, who is the Spirit" (2 Cor 3:18).

BERNARD OF CLAIRVAUX
(1090–1153)
ON THE SONG OF SOLOMON

9 My lover is like a gazelle or a young stag.
Look! There he stands behind our wall,
gazing through the window,
peering through the lattice.

THE SEASON OF LOVE AND THE SONG OF THE TURTLEDOVE

The Lover to His Beloved:

10 My lover spoke to me, saying:
"Arise, my darling;
My beautiful one, come away with me!
11 Look! The winter has passed,
the winter rains are over and gone.
12 Blossoms have appeared in the land;
the time for pruning and singing has come;
the voice of the turtledove is heard in our land.
13 The fig tree has ripened its figs;
the vines have blossomed and give off their fragrance.
Arise, come away my darling;
my beautiful one, come away with me!"

THE DOVE IN THE CLEFTS OF EN GEDI

The Lover to His Beloved:

14 O my dove, in the clefts of the rock,
in the hiding places of the mountain crags,
let me see your face;
let me hear your voice;
for your voice is sweet,
and your face is lovely.

THE FOXES IN THE VINEYARD

The Beloved to Her Lover:

15 Catch the foxes for us,
the little foxes,
that ruin the vineyards—
for our vineyard is in bloom.

POETIC REFRAIN: MUTUAL POSSESSION

The Beloved about Her Lover:

16 My lover is mine and I am his;
he grazes among the lilies.

THE GAZELLE AND THE RUGGED MOUNTAINS

The Beloved to Her Lover:

17 Until the dawn arrives and the shadows flee,
turn, my beloved—
be like a gazelle or a young stag
on the mountain gorges.

THE LOST LOVER IS FOUND

The Beloved about Her Lover:

3 All night long on my bed
I longed for my lover.
I longed for him, but he never appeared.
2 "I will arise and look all around throughout the town,
and throughout the streets and squares;
I will search for my beloved."
I searched for him, but I did not find him.

3 The night watchmen found me—the ones who guard
the city walls.
"Have you seen my beloved?"
4 Scarcely had I passed them by
when I found my beloved!
I held onto him tightly and would not let him go
until I brought him to my mother's house,
to the bedroom chamber of the one who conceived me.

THE ADJURATION REFRAIN

The Beloved to the Maidens:

5 I admonish you, O maidens of Jerusalem,
by the gazelles and by the young does of the open fields:
"Do not awaken or arouse love until it pleases!"

THE ROYAL WEDDING PROCESSION

The Speaker:

6 Who is this coming up from the wilderness
like a column of smoke,
like a fragrant billow of myrrh and frankincense,
every kind of fragrant powder of the traveling
merchants?
7 Look! It is Solomon's portable couch!
It is surrounded by sixty warriors,
some of Israel's mightiest warriors.
8 All of them are skilled with a sword,
well trained in the art of warfare.
Each has his sword at his side,
to guard against the terrors of the night.
9 King Solomon made a sedan chair for himself
of wood imported from Lebanon.
10 Its posts were made of silver;
its back was made of gold.
Its seat was upholstered with purple wool;
its interior was inlaid with leather by the maidens of
Jerusalem.
11 Come out, O maidens of Zion,
and gaze upon King Solomon!
He is wearing the crown with which his mother
crowned him
on his wedding day,
on the most joyous day of his life!

THE WEDDING NIGHT: PRAISE OF THE BRIDE

The Lover to His Beloved:

4 Oh, you are beautiful, my darling!
Oh, you are beautiful!
Your eyes behind your veil are like doves.
Your hair is like a flock of female goats
descending from Mount Gilead.
2 Your teeth are like a flock of newly shorn sheep
coming up from the washing place;
each of them has a twin,
and not one of them is missing.
3 Your lips are like a scarlet thread;
your mouth is lovely.
Your forehead behind your veil
is like a slice of pomegranate.
4 Your neck is like the tower of David

3:6–11 A crown is the top of earthly glory, the culminating point of human dignity. When God puts a crown upon the head and a scepter into the hand of a man, he engraves upon that man (in a qualified sense) both his name and the lively characters of his majesty and authority. Yet there is always a reservation and salvo to the divine prerogative to displace at pleasure and set it upon what head he shall please. Though dominion be not founded in grace, yet grace both embellishes and secures the dominion of men. The coronation day of a king is, in a sense, the marriage day betwixt him and his people and is accordingly solemnized with all the signs and demonstrations of joy and gladness. Thus when the crown of Israel was set upon the head of Solomon, the scripture represents their exuberant joy in an elegant and lofty hyperbole.

JOHN FLAVEL **(1627–1691)**
THE WORKS

4:3 "Your lips are like a scarlet thread." There is probably a special respect to the speech of the saints in prayer, which is dyed in the blood of Christ, and by this means becomes pleasant and acceptable and of an attractive influence, like a scarlet cord to draw down blessings. The prayers of saints are lovely and prevalent only through the incense of Christ's merits.

JONATHAN EDWARDS
(1703–1758)
THE COMPLETE WORKS

built with courses of stones;
one thousand shields are hung on it—
all shields of valiant warriors.
5 Your two breasts are like two fawns,
twins of the gazelle
grazing among the lilies.
6 Until the dawn arrives
and the shadows flee,
I will go up to the mountain of myrrh
and to the hill of frankincense.
7 You are altogether beautiful, my darling!
There is no blemish in you!

THE WEDDING NIGHT: BEAUTIFUL AS LEBANON

8 Come with me from Lebanon, my bride;
come with me from Lebanon.
Descend from the crest of Amana,
from the top of Senir, the summit of Hermon,
from the lions' dens
and the mountain haunts of the leopards.
9 You have stolen my heart, my sister, my bride!
You have stolen my heart with one glance of your
eyes,
with one jewel of your necklace.
10 How delightful is your love, my sister, my bride!
How much better is your love than wine;
the fragrance of your perfume is better than any spice!
11 Your lips drip sweetness like the honeycomb,
my bride;
honey and milk are under your tongue.
The fragrance of your garments is like the fragrance of
Lebanon.

THE WEDDING NIGHT: THE DELIGHTFUL GARDEN

The Lover to His Beloved:

12 You are a locked garden, my sister, my bride;
you are an enclosed spring, a sealed-up fountain.
13 Your shoots are a royal garden full of pomegranates
with choice fruits:
henna with nard,
14 nard and saffron,
calamus and cinnamon with every kind of spice,
myrrh and aloes with all the finest spices.
15 You are a garden spring,
a well of fresh water flowing down from Lebanon.

The Beloved to Her Lover:

16 Awake, O north wind; come, O south wind!
Blow on my garden so that its fragrant spices may send
out their sweet smell.
May my beloved come into his garden
and eat its delightful fruit!

The Lover to His Beloved:

5 I have entered my garden, O my sister, my bride;
I have gathered my myrrh with my balsam spice.
I have eaten my honeycomb and my honey;
I have drunk my wine and my milk!

The Poet to the Couple:
Eat, friends, and drink!
Drink freely, O lovers!

THE TRIALS OF LOVE: THE BELOVED'S DREAM OF LOSING HER LOVER

The Beloved about Her Lover:
2 I was asleep, but my mind was dreaming.
Listen! My lover is knocking at the door!

The Lover to His Beloved:
"Open for me, my sister, my darling,
my dove, my flawless one!
My head is drenched with dew,
my hair with the dampness of the night."

The Beloved to Her Lover:
3 "I have already taken off my robe—must I put it on again?
I have already washed my feet—must I soil them again?"
4 My lover thrust his hand through the hole,
and my feelings were stirred for him.
5 I arose to open for my beloved;
my hands dripped with myrrh—
my fingers flowed with myrrh
on the handles of the lock.
6 I opened for my beloved,
but my lover had already turned and gone away.
I fell into despair when he departed.
I looked for him but did not find him;
I called him, but he did not answer me.
7 The watchmen found me as they made their rounds in the city.
They beat me; they bruised me;
they took away my cloak, those watchmen on the walls!

THE TRIUMPH OF LOVE: THE BELOVED PRAISES HER LOVER

The Beloved to the Maidens:
8 I admonish you, O maidens of Jerusalem—
If you find my beloved, what will you tell him?
Tell him that I am lovesick!

The Maidens to the Beloved:
9 Why is your beloved better than others,
O most beautiful of women?
Why is your beloved better than others,
that you would admonish us in this manner?

The Beloved to the Maidens:
10 My beloved is dazzling and ruddy;
he stands out in comparison to all other men.
11 His head is like the purest gold.
His hair is curly—black like a raven.
12 His eyes are like doves by streams of water,
washed in milk, mounted like jewels.
13 His cheeks are like garden beds full of balsam trees
yielding perfume.

5:2–8 Even though you are asleep, if only Christ has come to know the devotion of your soul, he comes and knocks at your door and says, "Open for me, my sister." "Sister" is well put because the marriage of the Word and the soul is spiritual. For souls do not know covenants of wedlock or the ways of bodily union, but they are like the angels in heaven. "Open," therefore, "for me"; do not open to the adversary or give place to the devil. "Open for me," do not be confined but expand, and I will fill you. And because, in my passage through the world, I have found very much trouble and vexation and have not readily had a place to rest, then open that the Son of Man may rest his head on you, for he has no rest save on one who is humble and quiet.

AMBROSE **(C. 339–C. 397)**
CONCERNING VIRGINS

His lips are like lilies dripping with drops of myrrh.
14 His arms are like rods of gold set with chrysolite.
His abdomen is like polished ivory inlaid with
sapphires.
15 His legs are like pillars of marble set on bases of pure
gold.
His appearance is like Lebanon, choice as its cedars.
16 His mouth is very sweet;
he is totally desirable.
This is my beloved!
This is my companion, O maidens of
Jerusalem!

THE LOST LOVER FOUND

The Maidens to the Beloved:

6 Where has your beloved gone,
O most beautiful among women?
Where has your beloved turned?
Tell us, that we may seek him with you.

The Beloved to the Maidens:

2 My beloved has gone down to his garden,
to the flowerbeds of balsam spices,
to graze in the gardens,
and to gather lilies.

POETIC REFRAIN: MUTUAL POSSESSION

The Beloved about Her Lover:

3 I am my lover's, and my lover is mine;
he grazes among the lilies.

THE RENEWAL OF LOVE

The Lover to His Beloved:

4 My darling, you are as beautiful as Tirzah,
as lovely as Jerusalem,
as awe-inspiring as bannered armies.
5 Turn your eyes away from me—
they overwhelm me!
Your hair is like a flock of goats
descending from Mount Gilead.
6 Your teeth are like a flock of sheep
coming up from the washing;
each has its twin;
not one of them is missing.
7 Like a slice of pomegranate
is your forehead behind your veil.
8 There may be sixty queens,
and eighty concubines,
and young women without number.
9 But she is unique,
my dove, my perfect one!
She is the special daughter of her mother;
she is the favorite of the one who bore her.
The maidens saw her and complimented
her;
the queens and concubines praised her:
10 "Who is this who appears like the dawn?
Beautiful as the moon, bright as the sun,
awe-inspiring as the stars in procession?"

6:4–10 All the real excellence and holiness on earth center in the church. Christ goes forth subduing his enemies while his followers gain victories over the world, the flesh, and the devil. He shows the tenderness of a Redeemer, the delight he takes in his redeemed people, and the workings of his own grace in them. True believers alone can possess the beauty of holiness. And when their real character is known, it will be commended. Both the church and believers, at their first conversion, look forth as the morning, their light being small but increasing. As to their sanctification, they are fair as the moon, deriving all their light, grace, and holiness from Christ; and as to justification, clear as the sun, clothed with Christ, the Sun of Righteousness, and fighting the good fight of faith under the banners of Christ against all spiritual enemies.

MATTHEW HENRY (1662–1714)
COMMENTARY ON THE WHOLE BIBLE

THE RETURN TO THE VINEYARDS

The Lover to His Beloved:

11 I went down to the orchard of walnut
trees,
to look for the blossoms of the valley,
to see if the vines had budded
or if the pomegranates were in bloom.
12 I was beside myself with joy!
There please give me your myrrh,
O daughter of my princely people.

THE LOVE SONG AND DANCE

The Lover to His Beloved:

13 Turn, turn, O Perfect One!
Turn, turn, that I may stare at you!

The Beloved to Her Lover:

Why do you gaze upon the Perfect One
like the dance of the Mahanaim?

The Lover to His Beloved:

7 How beautiful are your sandaled feet,
O nobleman's daughter!
The curves of your thighs are like jewels,
the work of the hands of a master craftsman.
2 Your navel is a round mixing bowl—
may it never lack mixed wine!
Your belly is a mound of wheat,
encircled by lilies.
3 Your two breasts are like two fawns,
twins of a gazelle.
4 Your neck is like a tower made of ivory.
Your eyes are the pools in Heshbon
by the gate of Bath Rabbim.
Your nose is like the tower of Lebanon
overlooking Damascus.
5 Your head crowns you like Mount Carmel.
The locks of your hair are like royal
tapestries—
the king is held captive in its tresses!
6 How beautiful you are! How lovely,
O love, with your delights!

THE PALM TREE AND THE PALM TREE CLIMBER

The Lover to His Beloved:

7 Your stature is like a palm tree,
and your breasts are like clusters of grapes.
8 I want to climb the palm tree
and take hold of its fruit stalks.
May your breasts be like the clusters of grapes,
and may the fragrance of your breath be like apples!
9 May your mouth be like the best wine,
flowing smoothly for my beloved,
gliding gently over our lips as we sleep together.

POETIC REFRAIN: MUTUAL POSSESSION

The Beloved about Her Lover:

10 I am my beloved's,
and he desires me!

7:10–13 The spouse desires to give to Jesus all that she produces. Our heart has "every delicacy, both new and old," and they are laid up for our beloved. Let us survey our stores. We have new fruits. We desire to feel new life, new joy, new gratitude. We wish to make new resolves and carry them out by new labors. Our heart blossoms with new prayers, and our soul is pledging herself to new efforts. There is our first love: a choice fruit that Jesus delights in. There is our first faith: that simple faith by which, having nothing, we became possessors of all things. There is our joy when first we knew the Lord: let us revive it. Let our many fruits be laid up only for our beloved; let us display them when he is with us and not hold them up before the gaze of men.

CHARLES SPURGEON
(1834–1892)
MORNING AND EVENING

THE JOURNEY TO THE COUNTRYSIDE

The Beloved to Her Lover:

11 Come, my beloved; let us go to the countryside;
let us spend the night in the villages.
12 Let us rise early to go to the vineyards,
to see if the vines have budded,
to see if their blossoms have opened,
if the pomegranates are in bloom—
there I will give you my love.
13 The mandrakes send out their fragrance;
over our door is every delicacy,
both new and old, which I have stored up for you, my lover.

THE BELOVED'S WISH SONG

The Beloved to Her Lover:

8 Oh, how I wish you were my little brother,
nursing at my mother's breasts;
if I saw you outside, I could kiss you—
surely no one would despise me!
2 I would lead you and bring you to my mother's house,
the one who taught me.
I would give you spiced wine to drink,
the nectar of my pomegranates.

DOUBLE REFRAIN: EMBRACING AND ADJURATION

The Beloved about Her Lover:

3 His left hand is under my head,
and his right hand embraces me.

The Beloved to the Maidens:

4 I admonish you, O maidens of Jerusalem:
"Do not arouse or awaken love until it pleases!"

THE AWAKENING OF LOVE

The Maidens about His Beloved:

5 Who is this coming up from the wilderness,
leaning on her beloved?

The Beloved to Her Lover:

Under the apple tree I aroused you;
there your mother conceived you;
there she who bore you was in labor of childbirth.

THE NATURE OF TRUE LOVE

The Beloved to Her Lover:

6 Set me like a cylinder seal over your heart,
like a signet on your arm.
For love is as strong as death;
passion is as unrelenting as Sheol.
Its flames burst forth;
it is a blazing flame.
7 Surging waters cannot quench love;
floodwaters cannot overflow it.
If someone were to offer all his possessions to buy love,
the offer would be utterly despised.

THE BROTHER'S PLAN AND THE SISTER'S REWARD

The Beloved's Brothers:

8 We have a little sister,
and as yet she has no breasts.
What shall we do for our sister
on the day when she is spoken for?
9 If she is a wall,
we will build on her a battlement of silver;
but if she is a door,
we will barricade her with boards of cedar.

The Beloved:

10 I was a wall,
and my breasts were like fortress towers.
Then I found favor in his eyes.

SOLOMON'S VINEYARD AND THE BELOVED'S VINEYARD

The Beloved to Her Lover:

11 Solomon had a vineyard at Baal Hamon;
he leased out the vineyard to those who maintained it.
Each was to bring 1,000 shekels of silver for its fruit.
12 My vineyard, which belongs to me, is at my disposal alone.
The thousand shekels belong to you, O Solomon,
and 200 shekels belong to those who maintain it for its fruit.

EPILOGUE: THE LOVER'S REQUEST AND HIS BELOVED'S INVITATION

The Lover to His Beloved:

13 O you who stay in the gardens,
my companions are listening attentively for your voice;
let me be the one to hear it!

The Beloved to Her Lover:

14 Make haste, my beloved!
Be like a gazelle or a young stag
on the mountains of spices.

8:14 By saying "Make haste, my beloved!" Christ makes heard the voice that he desires to hear. Through this it is confessed that he alone on the earth, alone among all humankind (true man, but born in an ineffable manner), alone found to be a foreigner and pilgrim, alone fleeing the sordid lifestyle of humanity, alone ascending the prophesied "mountains of spices," he alone in every way is made Lord of heaven and earth. It shows that he alone fled both interior and exterior sin. He alone, who would bind the devil, fugitive of heaven, is himself a fugitive of the earth in the midst of a perverse and depraved nation.

APONIUS (C. 600)
EXPOSITION OF SONG OF SOLOMON

AUTHOR	AUDIENCE	DATE	PURPOSE	THEMES
Isaiah	The people of Judah and Jerusalem	Between 740 and 680 BC	Isaiah was commissioned by the Lord to proclaim a message of impending judgment on his people for sins, while also assuring them of future restoration.	Vindication for God's people; the hope of redemption; the promised Messiah; and insights into the person and work of Christ

All who take delight in the holy scriptures are familiarly acquainted with the writings of the prophet Isaiah," wrote John Calvin. He summarizes the nature and scope of Isaiah's prophetic work:

> In his prophecies he takes a wide range, surveys those nations that power, wealth, learning, or commerce had raised to the highest celebrity in those remote times, and describes their rise and fall, and wonderful revolutions, so eagerly traced lay us in the page of history, as the execution of Jehovah's counsels and the arrangements of unerring wisdom. But chiefly does he pour out rich instruction concerning the Messiah, whose life and sufferings and death and glorious reign he delineates so faithfully and with such thrilling interest that he has obtained the appellation of "the evangelical prophet."

The prophetic ministry of Isaiah began in a dramatic encounter with the Lord one day in the temple. The Lord commissioned him to proclaim to his people a message of coming judgment for their wickedness and comfort for a future restoration. Significant among these assurances of hope are the numerous prophetic words that addressed the coming Messiah, who would come as a Suffering Servant to redeem and restore the world.

"For a child has been born to us, a son has been given to us," Isaiah announced. "He shoulders responsibility and is called Wonderful Adviser, Mighty God, Everlasting Father, Prince of Peace" (9:6). Christians have universally understood these words as an oracle referring to Jesus Christ and have leveraged this language to explain Jesus' dual nature as both God and man. Note this comment from Augustine:

> We read, "For a child has been born to us" because we see him in the nature of a servant, which he had because the Virgin conceived and brought forth a son. However, because it was the Word of God who became flesh in order to dwell among us, and because he remains what he was (that is, really God hidden in the flesh), we use the words of the angel Gabriel and call his name "Immanuel." He is properly called "God with us" to avoid thinking of God as one person and the humanity [in Christ] as another.

This child is described this way: "A shoot will grow out of Jesse's root stock, a bud will sprout from his roots," indicating the Davidic lineage of Christ. What is more, "at that time a root from Jesse will stand like a signal flag for the nations. Nations will look to him for guidance" (11:1, 10), showing that Christ was meant to save both Jew and Gentile

alike. In one of the more memorable sections, the details of the Suffering Servant align perfectly with the life and death of Jesus. "Look, my servant . . ." begins Isaiah 52:13—53:12, which Ephrem the Syrian explained: "These words certainly concern our Lord. Indeed, he was called a servant by his Father because, in the first place, he was sent by his Father in order to fulfill his will in procuring salvation for all humankind, and in the second place because he assumed the aspect of a servant."

The section climaxes with the suffering death of Christ, in which "He was wounded because of our rebellious deeds, crushed because of our sins . . . He was treated harshly and afflicted . . . Like a lamb led to the slaughtering block . . . he did not even open his mouth," all in order to save us, for "because of his wounds we have been healed" (53:5, 7). This passage has offered the church rich language for exploring the theological significance of our salvation and the depths to which Christ went to redeem lost humanity. "Alone did he assume the penalties of our wicked deeds," explained Eusebius of Caesarea, "not when we were half-dead but even when already altogether foul and stinking in tombs and graves." John Wesley echoes this comment, explaining that Christ died "for the guilt of their sins, which he had voluntarily taken upon himself, and for the expiation of their sins, which was hereby purchased. Those punishments by which our peace, our reconciliation to God, was to be purchased were laid upon him by God's justice with his own consent. By his sufferings we are saved from our sins."

Further, chapter 61 was quoted by Jesus himself in Luke 4 to explain the nature of his ministry and announce the passage's fulfillment in and through his life. The early church fathers drew from this passage insights into Jesus' nature. Irenaeus wrote, "For inasmuch as the Word of God was man from the root of Jesse and son of Abraham, in this respect did the Spirit of God rest on him and anoint him to preach the gospel to the lowly." Ephrem the Syrian echoed this understanding: "Therefore, after being incarnated and clothed with a human body, as is said, he has received the Spirit and has been anointed with the Spirit." He also drew Trinitarian doctrine from this passage, saying, "That Spirit that proceeds from the Father and is his essence is in me, I who am the Word and the Son of the Father, and through my incarnation I received the anointment of the economy of salvation."

Of Isaiah the prophet John Wesley concluded, "Undoubtedly he was the prince of all the prophets." More important is what he concluded about the book of Isaiah: "He so evidently and fully describes the person, offices, sufferings, and kingdom of Christ that some of the ancients called him the fifth Evangelist." This prophetic work then is sometimes called the "fifth Gospel," for it showcases the person and work of Jesus. Spend time with these words of the evangelical prophet to deepen your understanding of your Savior, Jesus the Messiah.

HEADING

1 Here is the message about Judah and Jerusalem that was revealed to Isaiah son of Amoz during the time when Uzziah, Jotham, Ahaz, and Hezekiah reigned over Judah.

OBEDIENCE, NOT SACRIFICE

2 Listen, O heavens,
pay attention, O earth!
For the LORD speaks:
"I raised children, I brought them up,
but they have rebelled against me!
3 An ox recognizes its owner,
a donkey recognizes where its owner puts its food;
but Israel does not recognize me,
my people do not understand."
4 Beware sinful nation,
the people weighed down by evil deeds.
They are offspring who do wrong,
children who do wicked things.
They have abandoned the LORD,
and rejected the Holy One of Israel.
They are alienated from him.
5 Why do you insist on being battered?
Why do you continue to rebel?
Your head has a massive wound,
your whole heart is sick.
6 From the soles of your feet to your head,
there is no spot that is unharmed.
There are only bruises, cuts,
and open wounds.
They have not been cleansed or bandaged,
nor have they been treated with olive oil.
7 Your land is devastated,
your cities burned with fire.
Right before your eyes your crops
are being destroyed by foreign invaders.
They leave behind devastation and destruction.
8 Daughter Zion is left isolated,
like a hut in a vineyard
or a shelter in a cucumber field;
she is a besieged city.
9 If the LORD of Heaven's Armies had not left us a few
survivors,
we would have quickly been like Sodom,
we would have become like Gomorrah.
10 Listen to the LORD's message,
you leaders of Sodom!
Pay attention to our God's rebuke,
people of Gomorrah!
11 "Of what importance to me are your many sacrifices?"
says the LORD.
"I have had my fill of burnt sacrifices,
of rams and the fat from steers.
The blood of bulls, lambs, and goats
I do not want.
12 When you enter my presence,
do you actually think I want this—
animals trampling on my courtyards?
13 Do not bring any more meaningless offerings;

I consider your incense detestable!
You observe new moon festivals, Sabbaths, and convocations,
but I cannot tolerate sin-stained celebrations!
14 I hate your new moon festivals and assemblies;
they are a burden
that I am tired of carrying.
15 When you spread out your hands in prayer,
I look the other way;
when you offer your many prayers,
I do not listen
because your hands are covered with blood.
16 Wash! Cleanse yourselves!
Remove your sinful deeds
from my sight.
Stop sinning.
17 Learn to do what is right.
Promote justice.
Give the oppressed reason to celebrate.
Take up the cause of the orphan.
Defend the rights of the widow.

18 "Come, let's consider your options," says the LORD.
"Though your sins have stained you like the color red,
you can become white like snow;
though they are as easy to see as the color scarlet,
you can become white like wool.
19 If you have a willing attitude and obey,
then you will again eat the good crops of the land.
20 But if you refuse and rebel,
you will be devoured by the sword."
Know for certain that the LORD has spoken.

PURIFYING JUDGMENT

21 How tragic that the once-faithful city
has become a prostitute!
She was once a center of justice;
fairness resided in her—
but now only murderers!
22 Your silver has become scum,
your beer is diluted with water.
23 Your officials are rebels,
they associate with thieves.
All of them love bribery,
and look for payoffs.
They do not take up the cause of the orphan
or defend the rights of the widow.
24 Therefore, the Sovereign LORD of Heaven's Armies,
the Powerful One of Israel, says this:
"Ah, I will seek vengeance against my adversaries,
I will take revenge against my enemies.
25 I will attack you;
I will purify your metal with flux.
I will remove all your slag.
26 I will reestablish honest judges as in former times,
wise advisers as in earlier days.
Then you will be called, 'The Just City,
Faithful Town.'"
27 Zion will be freed by justice

1:12–20 We have the gracious invitation, "Come, let's consider your options." Do you think God is going to reason with people whose hands are dripping with blood and before they ask forgiveness and mercy? Will God reason with people living in rebellion against him? No. But if we turn from and confess our sin, then he will reason with us and pardon us. "The wicked need to abandon their lifestyle and sinful people their plans. They should return to the LORD, and he will show mercy to them, and to their God, for he will freely forgive them" (Isa 55:7). The moment people are willing to part with their sins, God meets them in grace and offers them peace and pardon.

D. L. MOODY **(1837–1899)**
SOVEREIGN GRACE

and her returnees by righteousness.
28 All rebellious sinners will be shattered,
those who abandon the LORD will perish.
29 Indeed, they will be ashamed of the sacred trees
you find so desirable;
you will be embarrassed because of the sacred orchards
where you choose to worship.
30 For you will be like a tree whose leaves wither,
like an orchard that is unwatered.
31 The powerful will be like a thread of yarn,
their deeds like a spark;
both will burn together,
and no one will put out the fire.

THE FUTURE GLORY OF JERUSALEM

2 Here is the message about Judah and Jerusalem that was
revealed to Isaiah son of Amoz.
2 In future days
the mountain of the LORD's temple will endure
as the most important of mountains
and will be the most prominent of hills.
All the nations will stream to it;
3 many peoples will come and say,
"Come, let us go up to the LORD's mountain,
to the temple of the God of Jacob,
so he can teach us his requirements,
and we can follow his standards."
For Zion will be the center for moral instruction;
the LORD's message will issue from Jerusalem.
4 He will judge disputes between nations;
he will settle cases for many peoples.
They will beat their swords into plowshares,
and their spears into pruning hooks.
Nations will not take up the sword against other
nations,
and they will no longer train for war.
5 O descendants of Jacob,
come, let us walk in the LORD's guiding light.

THE LORD'S DAY OF JUDGMENT

6 Indeed, O LORD, you have abandoned your people,
the descendants of Jacob.
For diviners from the east are everywhere;
they consult omen readers like the Philistines do.
Plenty of foreigners are around.
7 Their land is full of gold and silver;
there is no end to their wealth.
Their land is full of horses;
there is no end to their chariots.
8 Their land is full of worthless idols;
they worship the product of their own hands,
what their own fingers have fashioned.
9 Men bow down to them in homage,
they lie flat on the ground in worship.
Don't spare them!
10 Go up into the rocky cliffs,
hide in the ground.
Get away from the dreadful judgment of the LORD,
from his royal splendor!

2:5–22 Not only do human beings make gods for themselves from statues, but you will also find them making gods for themselves from their imaginations. For such people can imagine another god and creator of the world in a system different from the divine plan of the world recorded by the Spirit, other than the true world. So too I believe is the case either among the Greeks who generate opinions, so to speak, of this philosophy or that, or among the heretics, the first who generate opinions. These have made idols for themselves and figments of the soul, and by turning to them "they worship the product of their own hands" since they accept as truth their own fabrications.

ORIGEN (C. 185–C. 253)
HOMILIES ON JEREMIAH

11 Proud men will be brought low,
arrogant men will be humiliated;
the LORD alone will be exalted
in that day.
12 Indeed, the LORD of Heaven's Armies has planned a day
of judgment
for all the high and mighty;
for all who are proud—they will be humiliated;
13 for all the cedars of Lebanon
that are so high and mighty,
for all the oaks of Bashan,
14 for all the tall mountains,
for all the high hills,
15 for every high tower,
for every fortified wall,
16 for all the large ships,
for all the impressive ships.
17 Proud men will be humiliated,
arrogant men will be brought low;
the LORD alone will be exalted
in that day.
18 The worthless idols will be completely eliminated.
19 They will go into caves in the rocky cliffs
and into holes in the ground
trying to escape the dreadful judgment of the LORD
and his royal splendor,
when he rises up to terrify the earth.
20 At that time men will throw
their silver and gold idols,
which they made for themselves to worship,
into the caves where rodents and bats live,
21 so they themselves can go into the crevices of the rocky
cliffs
and the openings under the rocky overhangs,
trying to escape the dreadful judgment of the LORD
and his royal splendor,
when he rises up to terrify the earth.
22 Stop trusting in human beings,
whose life's breath is in their nostrils.
For why should they be given special
consideration?

A COMING LEADERSHIP CRISIS

3 Look, the Sovereign LORD of Heaven's Armies
is about to remove from Jerusalem and Judah
every source of security, including
all the food and water,
2 the mighty men and warriors,
judges and prophets,
omen readers and leaders,
3 captains of groups of 50,
the respected citizens,
advisers and those skilled in magical arts,
and those who know incantations.
4 The LORD says, "I will make youths their officials;
malicious young men will rule over them.
5 The people will treat each other harshly;
men will oppose each other;
neighbors will fight.

Youths will proudly defy the elderly
and riffraff will challenge those who were once respected.
6 Indeed, a man will grab his brother
right in his father's house and say,
'You own a coat—
you be our leader!
This heap of ruins will be under your control.'
7 At that time the brother will shout,
'I am no doctor,
I have no food or coat in my house;
don't make me a leader of the people!'"
8 Jerusalem certainly stumbles,
Judah falls,
for their words and their actions offend the LORD;
they rebel against his royal authority.
9 The look on their faces testifies to their guilt;
like the people of Sodom they openly boast of their sin.
Woe to them!
For they bring disaster on themselves.
10 Tell the innocent it will go well with them,
for they will be rewarded for what they have done.
11 Woe to the wicked sinners!
For they will get exactly what they deserve.
12 Oppressors treat my people cruelly;
creditors rule over them.
My people, your leaders mislead you;
they give you confusing directions.
13 The LORD takes his position to judge;
he stands up to pass sentence on his people.
14 The LORD comes to pronounce judgment
on the leaders of his people and their officials.
He says, "It is you who have ruined the vineyard!
You have stashed in your houses what you have stolen
from the poor.
15 Why do you crush my people
and grind the faces of the poor?"
The Sovereign LORD of Heaven's Armies has spoken.

3:9–10 If they are not afraid of being wicked, they should at least be ashamed of being seen for what they are. Often a sin that is concealed is avoided because a mind that is ashamed to be taken for what it does not fear to be in fact is sometimes ashamed to be in fact what it avoids appearing to be. On the other hand, when people are shamelessly and notoriously wicked, then the more freely they commit every kind of evil, the more they think it lawful, and in imagining it lawful they are thereby without doubt immersed in it all the more. Therefore it is written, "Like the people of Sodom they openly boast of their sin." For if Sodom had concealed its sin, it would still have sinned, but in fear. But it had completely lost the curb of fear in that it did not seek even darkness in its sinning. For sin in words is sin in act, but sin that is cried out is sin committed with deliberation.

GREGORY THE GREAT
(C. 540–604)
PASTORAL CARE

WASHING AWAY IMPURITY

16 The LORD says,
"The women of Zion are proud.
They walk with their heads high
and flirt with their eyes.
They skip along
and the jewelry on their ankles jingles.
17 So the Lord will afflict the foreheads of Zion's women
with skin diseases;
the LORD will make the front of their heads bald."

18 At that time the Lord will remove their beautiful ankle
jewelry, neck ornaments, crescent-shaped ornaments, 19 earrings, bracelets, veils, 20 headdresses, ankle ornaments, sashes,
sachets, amulets, 21 rings, nose rings, 22 festive dresses, robes,
shawls, purses, 23 garments, vests, head coverings, and gowns.
24 A putrid stench will replace the smell of spices,
a rope will replace a belt,
baldness will replace braided locks of hair,
a sackcloth garment will replace a fine robe,
and a prisoner's brand will replace beauty.

25 Your men will fall by the sword,
your strong men will die in battle.
26 Her gates will mourn and lament;
deprived of her people, she will sit on the ground.
4 Seven women will grab hold of
one man at that time.
They will say, "We will provide our own food,
we will provide our own clothes;
but let us belong to you—
take away our shame!"

CLEANSING AND PROTECTION FROM THE LORD

2 At that time
the crops given by the LORD will bring admiration and honor;
the produce of the land will be a source of pride and delight
to those who remain in Israel.
3 Those remaining in Zion, those left in Jerusalem,
will be called "holy,"
all in Jerusalem who are destined to live.
4 At that time the Lord will wash the excrement from Zion's women,
he will rinse the bloodstains from Jerusalem's midst,
as he comes to judge
and to bring devastation.
5 Then the LORD will create
over all Mount Zion
and over its convocations
a cloud and smoke by day
and a bright flame of fire by night;
indeed a canopy will accompany the LORD's glorious presence.
6 By day it will be a shelter to provide shade from the heat,
as well as safety and protection from the heavy downpour.

A LOVE SONG GONE SOUR

5 I will sing to my love—
a song to my lover about his vineyard.
My love had a vineyard
on a fertile hill.
2 He built a hedge around it, removed its stones,
and planted a vine.
He built a tower in the middle of it
and constructed a winepress.
He waited for it to produce edible grapes,
but it produced sour ones instead.
3 So now, residents of Jerusalem,
people of Judah,
you decide between me and my vineyard!
4 What more can I do for my vineyard
beyond what I have already done?
When I waited for it to produce edible grapes,
why did it produce sour ones instead?
5 Now I will inform you
what I am about to do to my vineyard:

4:2–4 The Lord gave of his generosity in that he arranged to liberate the human race from the crime of its transgression through his only begotten Son. Concerning this, Isaiah, looking toward the time of human redemption, said, "In that day the Branch of the LORD shall be beautiful and glorious; and the fruit of the earth shall be excellent and appealing" (NKJV). The Branch of the Lord was in magnificence and glory when the undying Son of God, appearing temporally in the flesh as a bright light, poured out upon the world the greatness of his heavenly virtues. The fruit of the earth became "excellent and appealing" when the mortal flesh that God received from our nature, already rendered immortal by virtue of the resurrection, was raised up to heaven.

VENERABLE BEDE
(C. 672–735)
HOMILIES ON THE GOSPELS

I will remove its hedge and turn it into pasture,
I will break its wall and allow animals to graze there.
6 I will make it a wasteland;
no one will prune its vines or hoe its ground,
and thorns and briers will grow there.
I will order the clouds
not to drop any rain on it.
7 Indeed, Israel is the vineyard of the LORD of Heaven's Armies,
the people of Judah are the cultivated place in which he took delight.
He waited for justice, but look what he got—disobedience!
He waited for fairness, but look what he got—cries for help!

DISASTER IS COMING

8 Beware, those who accumulate houses,
who also accumulate field after field
until there is no land left,
and you are the only landowners remaining within the land.
9 The LORD of Heaven's Armies told me this:
"Many houses will certainly become desolate,
large, impressive houses will have no one living in them.
10 Indeed, a large vineyard will produce just a few gallons,
and enough seed to yield several bushels will produce less than a bushel."
11 Beware, those who get up early to drink beer,
those who keep drinking long after dark
until they are intoxicated with wine.
12 They have stringed instruments, tambourines, flutes,
and wine at their parties.
So they do not recognize what the LORD is doing,
they do not perceive what he is bringing about.
13 Therefore my people will be deported
because of their lack of understanding.
Their leaders will have nothing to eat,
their masses will have nothing to drink.
14 So Death will open up its throat,
and open wide its mouth;
Zion's dignitaries and masses will descend into it,
including those who revel and celebrate within her.
15 Men will be humiliated,
they will be brought low;
the proud will be brought low.
16 The LORD of Heaven's Armies will be exalted when he punishes,
the holy God's authority will be recognized when he judges.
17 Lambs will graze as if in their pastures,
amid the ruins the rich sojourners will graze.
18 Beware, those who pull evil along using cords of emptiness are as good as dead,
who pull sin as with cart ropes.
19 They say, "Let him hurry, let him act quickly,
so we can see;
let the plan of the Holy One of Israel take shape and come to pass,
then we will know it!"

5:8–30 Here is a woe to those who set their hearts on the wealth of the world. Not that it is sinful for those who have a house and a field to purchase another, but the fault is that they never know when they have enough. Covetousness is idolatry; and while many envy prosperous, wretched people, the Lord denounces awful woes upon them. How applicable to many among us! Here is woe to those who dote upon the pleasures and the delights of sense. Those are in a woeful condition who set up sin, who exert themselves to gratify their base lusts. They confound and overthrow distinctions between good and evil. They prefer their own reasonings to divine revelations, their own devices to the counsels and commands of God. They deem it prudent and politic to continue profitable sins and to neglect self-denying duties. Their judges perverted justice. Every sin needs some other to conceal it.

MATTHEW HENRY **(1662–1714)**
COMMENTARY ON THE WHOLE BIBLE

20 Beware, those who call evil good and good evil,
who turn darkness into light and light into darkness,
who turn bitter into sweet and sweet into bitter.
21 Beware, those who think they are wise,
those who think they possess understanding.
22 Beware, those who are champions at drinking,
who display great courage when mixing strong drinks.
23 They pronounce the guilty innocent for a payoff,
they ignore the just cause of the innocent.
24 Therefore, as flaming fire devours straw
and dry grass disintegrates in the flames,
so their root will rot,
and their flower will blow away like dust.
For they have rejected the law of the LORD of Heaven's Armies,
they have spurned the commands of the Holy One of Israel.
25 So the LORD is furious with his people;
he lifts his hand and strikes them.
The mountains shake,
and corpses lie like manure in the middle of the streets.
Despite all this, his anger does not subside,
and his hand is ready to strike again.
26 He lifts a signal flag for a distant nation,
he whistles for it to come from the far regions of the earth.
Look, they come quickly and swiftly.
27 None tire or stumble,
they don't stop to nap or sleep.
They don't loosen their belts
or unstrap their sandals to rest.
28 Their arrows are sharpened,
and all their bows are prepared.
The hooves of their horses are hard as flint,
and their chariot wheels are like a windstorm.
29 Their roar is like a lion's;
they roar like young lions.
They growl and seize their prey;
they drag it away and no one can come to the rescue.
30 At that time they will growl over their prey,
it will sound like sea waves crashing against rocks.
One will look out over the land and see the darkness of disaster,
clouds will turn the light into darkness.

ISAIAH'S COMMISSION

6 In the year of King Uzziah's death, I saw the Lord seated on a
high, elevated throne. The hem of his robe filled the temple.
2 Seraphs stood over him; each one had six wings. With two
wings they covered their faces, with two they covered their
feet, and they used the remaining two to fly. 3 They called out to
one another, "Holy, holy, holy is the LORD of Heaven's Armies!
His majestic splendor fills the entire earth!" 4 The sound of
their voices shook the door frames, and the temple was filled
with smoke.
5 I said, "Woe to me! I am destroyed, for my lips are contaminated by sin, and I live among people whose lips are contaminated by sin. My eyes have seen the king, the LORD of Heaven's
Armies." 6 But then one of the seraphs flew toward me. In his

6:9–13 Behold mercy and judgment: mercy upon the elect who have obtained the justice of God, but judgment upon the others who have been blinded. And yet the former have believed because they have willed, while the latter have not believed because they have not willed. Hence mercy and judgment were brought about in their own wills. Clearly this election is through grace, not at all through merits.

AUGUSTINE (354–430)
PREDESTINATION OF THE SAINTS

hand was a hot coal he had taken from the altar with tongs.
7He touched my mouth with it and said, "Look, this coal has
touched your lips. Your evil is removed; your sin is forgiven." 8I
heard the voice of the Lord say, "Whom will I send? Who will
go on our behalf?" I answered, "Here I am, send me!" 9He said,
"Go and tell these people:

"'Listen continually, but don't understand.
Look continually, but don't perceive.'
10 Make the hearts of these people calloused;
make their ears deaf and their eyes blind.
Otherwise they might see with their eyes and hear with their ears,
their hearts might understand and they might repent and be healed."
11 I replied, "How long, Lord?" He said,
"Until cities are in ruins and unpopulated,
and houses are uninhabited,
and the land is ruined and devastated,
12 and the LORD has sent the people off to a distant place,
and the very heart of the land is completely abandoned.
13 Even if only a tenth of the people remain in the land,
it will again be destroyed,
like one of the large sacred trees or an Asherah pole,
when a sacred pillar on a high place is thrown down.
That sacred pillar symbolizes the special chosen family."

AHAZ RECEIVES A SIGN

7 During the reign of Ahaz son of Jotham, son of Uzziah, king
of Judah, King Rezin of Syria and King Pekah son of Remaliah
of Israel marched up to Jerusalem to do battle, but they were
unable to prevail against it.

2It was reported to the family of David, "Syria has allied with
Ephraim." They and their people were emotionally shaken, just
as the trees of the forest shake before the wind. 3So the LORD
told Isaiah, "Go out with your son Shear Jashub and meet Ahaz
at the end of the conduit of the upper pool that is located on
the road to the field where they wash and dry cloth. 4Tell him,
'Make sure you stay calm! Don't be afraid. Don't be intimidated
by these two stubs of smoking logs, or by the raging anger of
Rezin, Syria, and the son of Remaliah. 5Syria has plotted with
Ephraim and the son of Remaliah to bring about your demise.
6They say, "Let's attack Judah, terrorize it, and conquer it. Then
we'll set up the son of Tabeel as its king." 7For this reason the
Sovereign LORD says:

"'It will not take place;
it will not happen.
8 For Syria's leader is Damascus,
and the leader of Damascus is Rezin.
Within 65 years Ephraim will no longer exist as a nation.
9 Ephraim's leader is Samaria,
and Samaria's leader is the son of Remaliah.
If your faith does not remain firm,
then you will not remain secure.'"

10The LORD again spoke to Ahaz: 11"Ask for a confirming sign
from the LORD your God. You can even ask for something miraculous." 12But Ahaz responded, "I don't want to ask; I don't want
to put the LORD to a test." 13So Isaiah replied, "Pay attention,

THOMAS AQUINAS:

SYSTEMATIC THEOLOGIAN *PAR EXCELLENCE*

c. 1224–1274

The legacy of Thomas Aquinas can hardly be overstated given his considerable influence upon Western thought generally and the Catholic Church specifically. He was born to a wealthy family around 1224 in Roccasecca, Italy, and received his primary education at a monastery founded by Benedict of Nursia. He continued his education at the University of Naples. During this period, the Greek philosopher Aristotle was rediscovered in the West, and his distinctive philosophical approach began to augment and challenge the Catholic Church's indebtedness to Plato and Platonism. Aquinas was at the forefront of this shift, spending much of his life reconciling Aristotle's philosophy with the Christian faith.

It is important to keep in mind that Aquinas was a scholastic theologian who sought the fundamental unity of theology and philosophy. His magnum opus, the *Summa Theologica*, was a systematic work that integrated Aristotelian thought with Christian theology. A *summa* was literally a summary of a particular subject, in this case the Christian faith. Aquinas's *Summa Theologica* contains four main parts consisting of individual articles and covers topics as diverse as the nature and character of God; the nature of mankind and the will, virtue, sin, and grace; the nature of faith, knowledge, belief, love, and vices; and the person and work of Christ, sacraments, and forgiveness. Central to the *Summa*'s task is an attempt to leverage Aristotle in service to the Christian faith, particularly in the matter of how reason and revelation are related. While Aquinas believed that no one could receive a full knowledge of the truth, he argued there was some truth everywhere that was accessible to everyone. For Aquinas, that Aristotle could know a great deal of metaphysical truth without the benefit of Christian revelation and faith was significant; it proved that much could be discerned through reason alone, unaided by revelation: "Faith presupposes reason as grace presupposed nature." He wanted to show how natural knowledge and the fundamental truths of reality could be understood through reason unaided by special acts of divine grace. He did, however, believe some things required special revelation, particularly the truths of faith necessary for salvation. Yet even these revealed truths compatible with reasoned truth. The entire *Summa* reflects a synergistic relationship between revealed truths and reasoned truths.

The evangelical Protestant theologian R. C. Sproul said of this systematic theologian *par excellence*, "We need an Aquinas. We need a titanic thinker who will not abandon truth for safety." In a world where faith and reason are all too often pitted against each other, Aquinas can help us remember that there is a better way.

IMPORTANT WORKS

SUMMA CONTRA GENTILES

SUMMA THEOLOGICA

7:10–25 Again hear what was prophesied through Isaiah the prophet, that the Messiah would be born of a virgin. Through the prophetic spirit God announced beforehand that things that are unimaginable and believed to be impossible for human beings would take place in order that when they occurred they would be believed and received by faith because they had been promised. The phrase "Behold, the virgin shall conceive" (NKJV) means that the virgin would conceive without intercourse. If she had in fact had intercourse with someone, she would not have been a virgin. God's power came on the virgin, overshadowed her, and caused her to conceive while she remained a virgin.

JUSTIN MARTYR (C. 100–C. 165)
FIRST APOLOGY

family of David. Do you consider it too insignificant to try the
patience of men? Is that why you are also trying the patience
of my God? 14For this reason the Lord himself will give you a
confirming sign. Look, this young woman is about to conceive
and will give birth to a son. You, young woman, will name him
Immanuel. 15He will eat sour milk and honey, which will help
him know how to reject evil and choose what is right. 16Here is
why this will be so: Before the child knows how to reject evil and
choose what is right, the land whose two kings you fear will be
desolate. 17The LORD will bring on you, your people, and your
father's family a time unlike any since Ephraim departed from
Judah—the king of Assyria!"
18At that time the LORD will whistle for flies from the distant
streams of Egypt and for bees from the land of Assyria. 19All of
them will come and make their home in the ravines between
the cliffs and in the crevices of the cliffs, in all the thornbushes,
and in all the watering holes. 20At that time the Lord will use a
razor hired from the banks of the Euphrates River, the king of
Assyria, to shave the hair off the head and private parts; it will
also shave off the beard. 21At that time a man will keep alive
a young cow from the herd and a couple of goats. 22From the
abundance of milk they produce, he will have sour milk for his
meals. Indeed, everyone left in the heart of the land will eat
sour milk and honey. 23At that time every place where there
had been 1,000 vines worth 1,000 silver shekels will be overrun
with thorns and briers. 24With bow and arrow people will hunt
there, for the whole land will be covered with thorns and briers.
25They will stay away from all the hills that were cultivated for
fear of the thorns and briers. Cattle will graze there, and sheep
will trample on them.

A CHILD IS BORN FOR A SIGN

8 The LORD told me, "Take a large tablet and inscribe these
words on it with an ordinary stylus: 'Maher Shalal Hash Baz.'
2Then I will summon as my reliable witnesses Uriah the priest
and Zechariah son of Jeberekiah." 3I then approached the prophetess for marital relations; she conceived and gave birth to a
son. The LORD told me, "Name him Maher Shalal Hash Baz,
4for before the child knows how to cry out 'My father' or 'My
mother,' the wealth of Damascus and the plunder of Samaria
will be carried off by the king of Assyria."
5The LORD spoke to me again: 6"These people have rejected the gently flowing waters of Shiloah and melt in fear over
Rezin and the son of Remaliah. 7So look, the Lord is bringing
up against them the turbulent and mighty waters of the Euphrates River—the king of Assyria and all his majestic power.
It will reach flood stage and overflow its banks. 8It will spill
into Judah, flooding and engulfing, as it reaches to the necks
of its victims. He will spread his wings out over your entire
land, O Immanuel."

9 You will be broken, O nations;
you will be shattered!
Pay attention, all you distant lands of the earth.
Get ready for battle, and you will be shattered!
Get ready for battle, and you will be shattered!
10 Devise your strategy, but it will be thwarted.
Issue your orders, but they will not be
executed!
For God is with us!

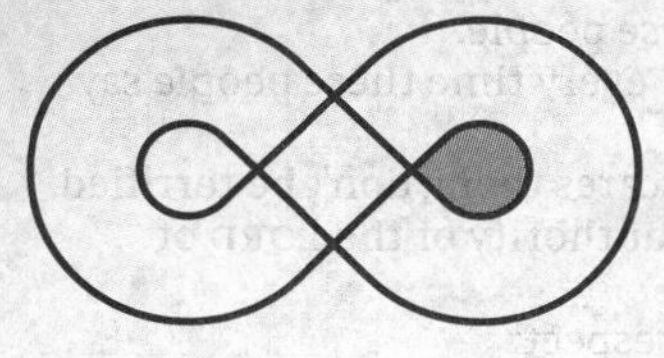

THIRTY-NINE ARTICLES OF RELIGION (1563)

THE ARTICLES OF the church of England were originally written by Archbishop Thomas Cranmer (1552) with later edits made by Archbishop Matthew Parker (1562), Queen Elizabeth (1563), and Bishop John Jewel (1571). One notable focus of the Articles of Religion is that on Scripture.

6. OF THE SUFFICIENCY OF THE HOLY SCRIPTURES FOR SALVATION

HOLY SCRIPTURE containeth all things necessary to salvation, so that whatsoever is not read therein nor may be proved thereby is not to be required of any man, that it should be believed as an article of the Faith, or be thought requisite or necessary to salvation. In the name of the Holy Scripture we do understand those canonical books of the Old and New Testaments, of whose authority was never any doubt in the church . . . And the other books the church doth read for example of life and instruction of manners; but yet doth it not apply them to establish any doctrine.

7. OF THE OLD TESTAMENT

THE OLD Testament is not contrary to the New: for both in the Old and New Testament everlasting life is offered to mankind by Christ, who is the only mediator between God and man, being both God and man. Wherefore they are not to be heard which feign that the old Fathers did look only for transitory promises. Although the Law given from God by Moses, as touching ceremonies and rites, does not bind Christian men, nor the civil precepts thereof ought of necessity to be received in any commonwealth; yet notwithstanding, no Christian man whatsoever is free from the obedience of the Commandments which are called moral.

8:11–22 It is no new thing if a great multitude of persons, and almost all who boast that they belong to the church, stumble against God. Yet let us constantly adhere to him, however small may be our numbers. Isaiah declares that those who refuse to trust in God will not escape without being punished. The threatening runs thus: "Many will stumble over the stone and the rock, and will fall and be seriously injured." This agrees with the former metaphor in which he compared God to a stone. Christ has alluded to that metaphor, including both clauses. "The one who falls on this stone will be broken to pieces, and the one on whom it falls will be crushed" (Matt 21:44). Let not the ungodly therefore imagine that they are stronger or wiser than God; for they will find that he excels them in strength and wisdom, and that to their destruction.

JOHN CALVIN (1509–1564)
COMPLETE COMMENTARY ON THE BIBLE

9:1–7 Listen to what Isaiah predicted: He will be "called Wonderful Adviser, Mighty God, Everlasting Father, Prince of Peace." No one could say this of a mere man. No man from the beginning of time has been called Mighty God or Everlasting Father of the world to come or the Prince of Peace. For Isaiah said, "Of the increase of His . . . peace there will be no end" (NKJV). And this peace has spread over the whole earth and sea, over the world where people dwell and where no one lives, over mountains, woodlands and hills, starting from that day on which he was going to leave his disciples and said to them, "My peace I give to you; I do not give it to you as the world does" (John 14:27). Why did Christ speak in this way? Because the peace that comes from a human being is easily destroyed and subject to many changes. But Christ's peace is strong, unshaken, firm, fixed, steadfast, immune to death, and unending.

CHRYSOSTOM (C. 347–407)
DEMONSTRATIONS AGAINST THE PAGANS

THE LORD ENCOURAGES ISAIAH

11 Indeed this is what the LORD told me quite forcefully. He
warned me not to act like these people:

12 "Do not say, 'Conspiracy,' every time these people say
the word.
Don't be afraid of what scares them; don't be terrified.
13 You must recognize the authority of the LORD of
Heaven's Armies.
He is the one you must respect;
he is the one you must fear.
14 He will become a sanctuary,
but a stone that makes a person trip
and a rock that makes one stumble—
to the two houses of Israel.
He will become a trap and a snare
to the residents of Jerusalem.
15 Many will stumble over the stone and the rock,
and will fall and be seriously injured,
and will be ensnared and captured."
16 Tie up the scroll as legal evidence,
seal the official record of God's instructions, and give it
to my followers.
17 I will wait patiently for the LORD,
who has rejected the family of Jacob;
I will wait for him.

18 Look, I and the sons whom the LORD has given me are
reminders and object lessons in Israel, sent from
the LORD of Heaven's Armies, who lives on Mount
Zion.

DARKNESS TURNS TO LIGHT AS AN IDEAL KING ARRIVES

19 They will say to you, "Seek oracles at the pits used to conjure
up underworld spirits, from the magicians who chirp and mut-
ter incantations. Should people not seek oracles from their
gods, by asking the dead about the destiny of the living?" 20 Then
you must recall the LORD's instructions and the prophetic testimony of what would happen. Certainly they say such things
because their minds are spiritually darkened. 21 They will pass
through the land destitute and starving. Their hunger will make
them angry, and they will curse their king and their God as
they look upward. 22 When one looks out over the land, he sees
distress and darkness, gloom and anxiety, darkness and people
9 forced from the land. 1 The gloom will be dispelled for those
who were anxious.

In earlier times he humiliated
the land of Zebulun,
and the land of Naphtali;
but now he brings honor
to the way of the sea,
the region beyond the Jordan,
and Galilee of the nations.
2 The people walking in darkness
see a bright light;
light shines
on those who live in a land of deep darkness.
3 You have enlarged the nation;
you give them great joy.

They rejoice in your presence
as harvesters rejoice;
as warriors celebrate when they divide up the plunder.
4 For their oppressive yoke
and the club that strikes their shoulders,
the cudgel the oppressor uses on them,
you have shattered, as in the day of Midian's defeat.
5 Indeed every boot that marches and shakes the earth
and every garment dragged through blood
is used as fuel for the fire.
6 For a child has been born to us,
a son has been given to us.
He shoulders responsibility
and is called
Wonderful Adviser,
Mighty God,
Everlasting Father,
Prince of Peace.
7 His dominion will be vast,
and he will bring immeasurable prosperity.
He will rule on David's throne
and over David's kingdom,
establishing it and strengthening it
by promoting justice and fairness,
from this time forward and forevermore.
The zeal of the LORD of Heaven's Armies will
accomplish this.

GOD'S JUDGMENT INTENSIFIES

8 The Lord decreed judgment on Jacob,
and it fell on Israel.
9 All the people were aware of it,
the people of Ephraim and those living in Samaria.
Yet with pride and an arrogant attitude, they said,
10 "The bricks have fallen,
but we will rebuild with chiseled stone;
the sycamore fig trees have been cut down,
but we will replace them with cedars."
11 Then the LORD provoked their adversaries to attack
them,
he stirred up their enemies—
12 Syria from the east,
and the Philistines from the west;
they gobbled up Israelite territory.
Despite all this, his anger does not subside,
and his hand is ready to strike again.
13 The people did not return to the one who struck them,
they did not seek reconciliation with the LORD of
Heaven's Armies.
14 So the LORD cut off Israel's head and tail,
both the shoots and stalk in one day.
15 The leaders and the highly respected people are the head,
the prophets who teach lies are the tail.
16 The leaders of this nation were misleading people,
and the people being led were destroyed.
17 So the Lord was not pleased with their young men,
he took no pity on their orphans and widows;
for the whole nation was godless and did wicked things,
every mouth was speaking disgraceful words.

Despite all this, his anger does not subside,
and his hand is ready to strike again.
18 For evil burned like a fire,
it consumed thorns and briers;
it burned up the thickets of the forest,
and they went up in smoke.
19 Because of the anger of the LORD of Heaven's Armies,
the land was scorched,
and the people became fuel for the fire.
People had no compassion on one another.
20 They devoured on the right, but were still hungry;
they ate on the left, but were not satisfied.
People even ate the flesh of their own arm!
21 Manasseh fought against Ephraim,
and Ephraim against Manasseh;
together they fought against Judah.
Despite all this, his anger does not subside,
and his hand is ready to strike again.
10 Beware, those who enact unjust policies
those who are always instituting unfair regulations,
2 to keep the poor from getting fair treatment
and to deprive the oppressed among my people of justice,
so they can steal what widows own
and loot what belongs to orphans.
3 What will you do on judgment day,
when destruction arrives from a distant place?
To whom will you run for help?
Where will you leave your wealth?
4 You will have no place to go, except to kneel with the prisoners
or to fall among those who have been killed.
Despite all this, his anger does not subside,
and his hand is ready to strike again.

THE LORD TURNS ON ARROGANT ASSYRIA

5 "Beware, Assyria, the club I use to vent my anger,
a cudgel with which I angrily punish.
6 I sent him against a godless nation,
I ordered him to attack the people with whom I was angry,
to take plunder and to carry away loot,
to trample them down like dirt in the streets.
7 But he does not agree with this;
his mind does not reason this way,
for his goal is to destroy
and to eliminate many nations.
8 Indeed, he says:
'Are not my officials all kings?
9 Is not Calneh like Carchemish?
Hamath like Arpad?
Samaria like Damascus?
10 I overpowered kingdoms ruled by idols,
whose carved images were more impressive than Jerusalem's or Samaria's.
11 As I have done to Samaria and its idols,
so I will do to Jerusalem and its idols."

12 But when the Lord finishes judging Mount Zion and Jerusalem, then he will punish the king of Assyria for what he

has proudly planned and for the arrogant attitude he displays.
13 For he says:

"By my strong hand I have accomplished this,
by my strategy that I devised.
I invaded the territory of nations
and looted their storehouses.
Like a mighty conqueror, I brought down rulers.
14 My hand discovered the wealth of the nations, as if it were in a nest;
as one gathers up abandoned eggs,
I gathered up the whole earth.
There was no wing flapping
or open mouth chirping."
15 Does an ax exalt itself over the one who wields it
or a saw magnify itself over the one who cuts with it?
As if a scepter should brandish the one who raises it
or a staff should lift up what is not made of wood!
16 For this reason the Sovereign LORD of Heaven's Armies
will make his healthy ones emaciated.
His majestic glory will go up in smoke.
17 The Light of Israel will become a fire,
their Holy One will become a flame;
it will burn and consume the Assyrian king's briers
and his thorns in one day.
18 The splendor of his forest and his orchard
will be completely destroyed,
as when a sick man's life ebbs away.
19 There will be so few trees left in his forest,
a child will be able to count them.

20 At that time those left in Israel, those who remain of the
family of Jacob, will no longer rely on a foreign leader that abuses them. Instead they will truly rely on the LORD, the Holy One
of Israel. 21 A remnant will come back, a remnant of Jacob, to the
mighty God. 22 For though your people, Israel, are as numerous
as the sand on the seashore, only a remnant will come back.
Destruction has been decreed; just punishment is about to en-
gulf you. 23 The Sovereign LORD of Heaven's Armies is certainly
ready to carry out the decreed destruction throughout the land.
24 So here is what the Sovereign LORD of Heaven's Armies
says: "My people who live in Zion, do not be afraid of Assyria,
even though they beat you with a club and lift their cudgel
against you as Egypt did. 25 For very soon my fury will subside,
and my anger will be directed toward their destruction." 26 The
LORD of Heaven's Armies is about to beat them with a whip,
similar to the way he struck down Midian at the rock of Oreb. He
will use his staff against the sea, lifting it up as he did in Egypt.

27 At that time
the LORD will remove their burden from your shoulders
and their yoke from your neck;
the yoke will be taken off because your neck will be too large.
28 They attacked Aiath,
moved through Migron,
depositing their supplies at Micmash.
29 They went through the pass,
spent the night at Geba.
Ramah trembled,
Gibeah of Saul ran away.

10:20–23 The "remnant" means the Jews who have believed in Christ. Many of them, we remember, did believe in the days of the apostles, and even today there are some converts, although very few. And it is their own scriptures that bear witness that it is not we who are the inventors of the prophecies touching Christ. That is why many of them, who pondered these prophecies before his Passion and more especially after his resurrection, have come to believe in him as was foretold: "For though your people, Israel, are as numerous as the sand on the seashore, only a remnant will come back."

AUGUSTINE **(354–430)**
EXPOSITIONS ON THE PSALMS

30 Shout out, daughter of Gallim!
Pay attention, Laishah!
Answer her, Anathoth!
31 Madmenah flees,
the residents of Gebim have hidden.
32 This very day, standing in Nob,
they shake their fist at Daughter Zion's mountain—
at the hill of Jerusalem.
33 Look, the Sovereign LORD of Heaven's Armies
is ready to cut off the branches with terrifying power.
The tallest trees will be cut down,
the loftiest ones will be brought low.
34 The thickets of the forest will be chopped down with
an ax,
and mighty Lebanon will fall.

AN IDEAL KING ESTABLISHES A KINGDOM OF PEACE

11 A shoot will grow out of Jesse's root stock,
a bud will sprout from his roots.
2 The LORD's Spirit will rest on him—
a Spirit that gives extraordinary wisdom,
a Spirit that provides the ability to execute plans,
a Spirit that produces absolute loyalty to the LORD.
3 He will take delight in obeying the LORD.
He will not judge by mere appearances
or make decisions on the basis of hearsay.
4 He will treat the poor fairly
and make right decisions for the downtrodden of the
earth.
He will strike the earth with the rod of his mouth
and order the wicked to be executed.
5 Justice will be like a belt around his waist,
integrity will be like a belt around his hips.
6 A wolf will reside with a lamb,
and a leopard will lie down with a young goat;
an ox and a young lion will graze together,
as a small child leads them along.
7 A cow and a bear will graze together,
their young will lie down together.
A lion, like an ox, will eat straw.
8 A baby will play
over the hole of a snake;
over the nest of a serpent
an infant will put his hand.
9 They will no longer injure or destroy
on my entire royal mountain.
For there will be universal submission to the LORD's
sovereignty,
just as the waters completely cover the sea.

ISRAEL IS RECLAIMED AND REUNITED

10 At that time a root from Jesse will stand like a signal flag
for the nations. Nations will look to him for guidance, and his
residence will be majestic. 11 At that time the Lord will again
lift his hand to reclaim the remnant of his people from Assyria,
Egypt, Pathros, Cush, Elam, Shinar, Hamath, and the seacoasts.
12 He will lift a signal flag for the nations;
he will gather Israel's dispersed people

11:1–16 The Messiah is called a "Branch" (NKJV). The words signify a small, tender product; "a shoot" such as is easily broken off. He comes forth out of the stem of Jesse; when the royal family was cut down and almost leveled with the ground, it would sprout again. The house of David was brought very low at the time of Christ's birth. The Messiah thus gave early notice that his kingdom was not of this world. But the Holy Spirit, in all his gifts and graces, shall rest and abide upon him; he shall have the fullness of the Godhead dwelling in him. The Messiah would be just and righteous in all his government. His threats shall be executed by the working of his Spirit according to his word. There shall be great peace and quiet under his government. God's people shall be delivered, not only from evil, but from the fear of it.

MATTHEW HENRY **(1662–1714)**
COMMENTARY ON THE WHOLE BIBLE

and assemble Judah's scattered people
from the four corners of the earth.
13 Ephraim's jealousy will end,
and Judah's hostility will be eliminated.
Ephraim will no longer be jealous of Judah,
and Judah will no longer be hostile toward Ephraim.
14 They will swoop down on the Philistine hills to the
west;
together they will loot the people of the east.
They will take over Edom and Moab,
and the Ammonites will be their subjects.
15 The LORD will divide the gulf of the Egyptian Sea;
he will wave his hand over the Euphrates River and
send a strong wind;
he will turn it into seven dried-up streams
and enable them to walk across in their sandals.
16 There will be a highway leading out of Assyria
for the remnant of his people,
just as there was for Israel,
when they went up from the land of Egypt.

12 At that time you will say:
"I praise you, O LORD,
for even though you were angry with me,
your anger subsided, and you consoled me.
2 Look, God is my deliverer!
I will trust in him and not fear.
For the LORD gives me strength and protects me;
he has become my deliverer."
3 Joyfully you will draw water
from the springs of deliverance.
4 At that time you will say:
"Praise the LORD!
Ask him for help!
Publicize his mighty acts among the nations.
Make it known that he is unique.
5 Sing to the LORD, for he has done magnificent things;
let this be known throughout the earth.
6 Cry out and shout for joy, O citizens of Zion,
for the Holy One of Israel acts mightily among you!"

12:1–6 Christ's wounds were redolent with the fragrance of grace, not the stench of repentance. Hence it was not death's decay that flowed from his wounds, as is the case with all other human beings, but it was the fountain of eternal life, as scripture teaches us: "Joyfully you will draw water from the springs of deliverance." His wounds gushed forth that we might drink of salvation. All sinners of the world will drink to overthrow sin, but each person must be considered individually. Christ was afflicted with miseries to make blessed those who were ensconced in misery. The very one who was made sorrowful by the Lord Jesus Christ will bring joy to Christ and will be made joyful by Christ.

AMBROSE **(C. 339–C. 397)**
EXPLANATION OF TWELVE PSALMS

THE LORD WILL JUDGE BABYLON

13 This is an oracle about Babylon that Isaiah son of Amoz
saw:
2 On a bare hill raise a signal flag;
shout to them,
wave your hand
so they might enter the gates of the princes!
3 I have given orders to my chosen soldiers;
I have summoned the warriors through whom I will
vent my anger—
my boasting, arrogant ones.
4 There is a loud noise on the mountains—
it sounds like a large army!
There is great commotion among the kingdoms—
nations are being assembled!
The LORD of Heaven's Armies is mustering
forces for battle.
5 They come from a distant land,
from the horizon.

It is the LORD with his instruments of judgment
coming to destroy the whole earth.
6 Wail, for the LORD's day of judgment is near;
it comes with all the destructive power of the Sovereign
One.
7 For this reason all hands hang limp,
every human heart loses its courage.
8 They panic—
cramps and pain seize hold of them
like those of a woman who is straining to give birth.
They look at one another in astonishment;
their faces are flushed red.
9 Look, the LORD's day of judgment is coming;
it is a day of cruelty and savage, raging anger,
destroying the earth
and annihilating its sinners.
10 Indeed the stars in the sky and their constellations
no longer give out their light;
the sun is darkened as soon as it rises,
and the moon does not shine.
11 I will punish the world for its evil
and wicked people for their sin.
I will put an end to the pride of the insolent,
I will bring down the arrogance of tyrants.
12 I will make human beings more scarce than pure
gold
and people more scarce than gold from Ophir.
13 So I will shake the heavens,
and the earth will shake loose from its foundation,
because of the fury of the LORD of Heaven's Armies,
in the day he vents his raging anger.
14 Like a frightened gazelle
or a sheep with no shepherd,
each will turn toward home,
each will run to his homeland.
15 Everyone who is caught will be stabbed;
everyone who is seized will die by the sword.
16 Their children will be smashed to pieces before their
very eyes;
their houses will be looted
and their wives raped.
17 Look, I am stirring up the Medes to attack them;
they are not concerned about silver,
nor are they interested in gold.
18 Their arrows will cut young men to ribbons;
they have no compassion on a person's offspring;
they will not look with pity on children.
19 Babylon, the most admired of kingdoms,
the Chaldeans' source of honor and pride,
will be destroyed by God
just as Sodom and Gomorrah were.
20 No one will live there again;
no one will ever reside there again.
No bedouin will camp there,
no shepherds will rest their flocks there.
21 Wild animals will rest there,
the ruined houses will be full of hyenas.
Ostriches will live there,
wild goats will skip among the ruins.

13:19–22 Babylon represents the wicked; by her being destroyed, never to be built or inhabited again, is represented the eternal destruction of the congregation of the wicked; by those doleful creatures here mentioned as possessing of Babylon are represented devils that the wicked shall be left to the possession of forever. Babylon, after its destruction, full of these creatures, represents the wicked in its state of punishment. Therefore the apostle John, when speaking of the destruction of mystical Babylon and alluding to this that is said of old Babylon, says expressly, "She has become a lair for demons, a haunt for every unclean spirit" (Rev 18:2).

JONATHAN EDWARDS
(1703–1758)
THE COMPLETE WORKS

22 Wild dogs will yip in her ruined fortresses,
jackals will yelp in the once-splendid palaces.
Her time is almost up,
her days will not be prolonged.

14 The LORD will certainly have compassion on Jacob; he
will again choose Israel as his special people and restore
them to their land. Resident foreigners will join them and
unite with the family of Jacob. 2Nations will take them and
bring them back to their own place. Then the family of Israel
will make foreigners their servants as they settle in the LORD's
land. They will make their captors captives and rule over the
ones who oppressed them. 3When the LORD gives you relief
from your suffering and anxiety and from the hard labor that
you were made to perform, 4you will taunt the king of Babylon
with these words:

"Look how the oppressor has met his end!
Hostility has ceased!
5 The LORD has broken the club of the wicked,
the scepter of rulers.
6 It furiously struck down nations
with unceasing blows.
It angrily ruled over nations,
oppressing them without restraint.
7 The whole earth rests and is quiet;
they break into song.
8 The evergreens also rejoice over your demise,
as do the cedars of Lebanon, singing,
'Since you fell asleep,
no woodsman comes up to chop us down!'
9 Sheol below is stirred up about you,
ready to meet you when you arrive.
It rouses the spirits of the dead for you,
all the former leaders of the earth;
it makes all the former kings of the nations
rise from their thrones.
10 All of them respond to you, saying:
'You too have become weak like us!
You have become just like us!
11 Your splendor has been brought down to Sheol,
as well as the sound of your stringed instruments.
You lie on a bed of maggots,
with a blanket of worms over you.'

12 "Look how you have fallen from the sky,
O shining one, son of the dawn!
You have been cut down to the ground,
O conqueror of the nations!
13 You said to yourself,
'I will climb up to the sky.
Above the stars of El
I will set up my throne.
I will rule on the mountain of assembly
on the remote slopes of Zaphon.
14 I will climb up to the tops of the clouds;
I will make myself like the Most High!'
15 But you were brought down to Sheol,
to the remote slopes of the Pit.

14:12–21 If we were to render a literal translation from the Hebrew, verse 12 would read, "How you have fallen from heaven, howling son of the dawn." And he who was formerly so glorious that he was compared to a bearer of lightning is now told that he must weep and mourn. Just as Lucifer scatters the darkness, it says, glowing and shining with a golden hue, so also your stepping forth to the peoples and the public seemed like a shining star. But you who spoke with arrogance, who wounded the nations, fell to the earth. You said, *I have obtained so great a power that heaven should stand still for me, and the stars above deserve to be thrown under my feet.* Nor was his pride satisfied with desire for the heavens, but it would break forth with such madness that he would claim for himself likeness to God.

JEROME (C. 342–420)
COMMENTARY ON ISAIAH

16 Those who see you stare at you,
they look at you carefully, thinking:
'Is this the man who shook the earth,
the one who made kingdoms tremble?
17 Is this the one who made the world like a wilderness,
who ruined its cities
and refused to free his prisoners so they could return
home?'
18 As for all the kings of the nations,
all of them lie down in splendor,
each in his own tomb.
19 But you have been thrown out of your grave
like a shoot that is thrown away.
You lie among the slain,
among those who have been slashed by the sword,
among those headed for the stones of the Pit,
as if you were a mangled corpse.
20 You will not be buried with them,
because you destroyed your land
and killed your people.

"The offspring of the wicked
will never be mentioned again.
21 Prepare to execute his sons
for the sins their ancestors have committed.
They must not rise up and take possession of the earth
or fill the surface of the world with cities.

22 "I will rise up against them,"
says the LORD of Heaven's Armies.
"I will blot out all remembrance of Babylon and destroy
all her people,
including the offspring she produces,"
says the LORD.
23 "I will turn her into a place that is overrun with wild
animals
and covered with pools of stagnant water.
I will get rid of her, just as one sweeps away dirt with a
broom,"
says the LORD of Heaven's Armies.

24 The LORD of Heaven's Armies makes this solemn vow:
"Be sure of this:
Just as I have intended, so it will be;
just as I have planned, it will happen.
25 I will break Assyria in my land,
I will trample them underfoot on my hills.
Their yoke will be removed from my people,
the burden will be lifted from their shoulders.
26 This is the plan I have devised for the whole earth;
my hand is ready to strike all the nations."
27 Indeed, the LORD of Heaven's Armies has a plan,
and who can possibly frustrate it?
His hand is ready to strike,
and who can possibly stop it?

THE LORD WILL JUDGE THE PHILISTINES

28 This oracle came in the year that King Ahaz died:
29 Don't be so happy, all you Philistines,

just because the club that beat you has been broken!
For a viper will grow out of the serpent's root,
and its fruit will be a darting adder.
30 The poor will graze in my pastures;
the needy will rest securely.
But I will kill your root by famine;
it will put to death all your survivors.
31 Wail, O city gate!
Cry out, O city!
Melt with fear, all you Philistines!
For out of the north comes a cloud of smoke,
and there are no stragglers in its ranks.
32 How will they respond to the messengers of this nation?
Indeed, the LORD has made Zion secure;
the oppressed among his people will find safety in her.

THE LORD WILL JUDGE MOAB

15 This is an oracle about Moab:
Indeed, in a night it is devastated,
Ar of Moab is destroyed!
Indeed, in a night it is devastated,
Kir of Moab is destroyed!
2 They went up to the temple;
the people of Dibon went up to the high places to lament.
Because of what happened to Nebo and Medeba, Moab wails.
Every head is shaved bare,
every beard is trimmed off.
3 In their streets they wear sackcloth;
on their roofs and in their town squares
all of them wail;
they fall down weeping.
4 The people of Heshbon and Elealeh cry out;
their voices are heard as far away as Jahaz.
For this reason Moab's soldiers shout in distress;
their courage wavers.
5 My heart cries out because of Moab's plight
and for the fugitives stretched out as far as Zoar and Eglath Shelishiyah.
For they weep as they make their way up the ascent of Luhith;
they loudly lament their demise on the road to Horonaim.
6 For the waters of Nimrim are gone;
the grass is dried up,
the vegetation has disappeared,
and there are no plants.
7 For this reason what they have made and stored up,
they carry over the Stream of the Poplars.
8 Indeed, the cries of distress echo throughout Moabite territory;
their wailing can be heard in Eglaim and Beer Elim.
9 Indeed, the waters of Dimon are full of blood!
Indeed, I will heap even more trouble on Dimon.
A lion will attack the Moabite fugitives
and the people left in the land.
16 Send rams as tribute to the ruler of the land,
from Sela in the wilderness
to the hill of Daughter Zion.

15:1–9 Here the prophet prophesies against the Moabites and threatens destruction. We ought to remember the design of these predictions. It cannot be believed that they were of any advantage to the Moabites; it was therefore to believers. The first reason was that when they saw so many changes taking place, cities overturned, kingdoms destroyed and succeeding one another, they might not think that this world is governed by the blind violence of fortune but might acknowledge the providence of God. If nothing had been foretold, the minds of human beings, having a strong tendency to foolishness and being strangely blind to the works of God, might have been disposed to attribute all this to chance; but when they had been forewarned by the prophets, they beheld the judgments of God as from a lofty watchtower.

JOHN CALVIN **(1509–1564)**
COMPLETE COMMENTARY ON THE BIBLE

2 At the fords of the Arnon
the Moabite women are like a bird
that flies about when forced from its nest.
3 "Bring a plan, make a decision.
Provide some shade in the middle of the day.
Hide the fugitives! Do not betray the one who tries to escape.
4 Please let the Moabite fugitives live among you.
Hide them from the destroyer!"
Certainly the one who applies pressure will cease;
the destroyer will come to an end;
those who trample will disappear from the earth.
5 Then a trustworthy king will be established;
he will rule in a reliable manner,
this one from David's family.
He will be sure to make just decisions
and will be experienced in executing justice.
6 We have heard about Moab's pride—
their great arrogance—
their boasting, pride, and excess.
But their boastful claims are empty.
7 So Moab wails over its demise—
they all wail!
Completely devastated, they moan
about what has happened to the raisin cakes of Kir Hareseth.
8 For the fields of Heshbon are dried up,
as well as the vines of Sibmah.
The rulers of the nations trample all over its vines,
which reach Jazer and spread to the wilderness;
their shoots spread out and cross the sea.
9 So I weep along with Jazer
over the vines of Sibmah.
I will saturate you with my tears, Heshbon and Elealeh,
for the conquering invaders shout triumphantly
over your fruit and crops.
10 Joy and happiness disappear from the orchards,
and in the vineyards no one rejoices or shouts;
no one treads out juice in the wine vats—
I have brought the joyful shouts to an end.
11 So my heart constantly sighs for Moab, like the strumming of a harp,
my inner being sighs for Kir Hareseth.
12 When the Moabites plead with all their might at their high places
and enter their temples to pray, their prayers will be ineffective.

13 This is the message the LORD previously announced about
Moab. 14 Now the LORD makes this announcement: "Within exactly three years Moab's splendor will disappear, along with all her many people; there will be only a few insignificant survivors left."

THE LORD WILL JUDGE DAMASCUS

17 This is an oracle about Damascus:
"Look, Damascus is no longer a city,
it is a heap of ruins!
2 The cities of Aroer are abandoned.
They will be used for herds,

16:3 I know of two kinds of light. The one is the light of our ruling power directing our steps according to the will of God; the other is a deceitful and meddling one, quite contrary to the true light though pretending to be that light that it may cheat us by its appearance. This really is darkness yet has the appearance of noonday, the high perfection of light. And so I read that passage of those who continually flee in darkness at noonday; for this is really night and yet is thought to be bright light by those who have been ruined by luxury. Let us lay hold of the Godhead; let us lay hold of the first and brightest Light. Let us walk toward him shining before our feet stumble upon the dark. While it is day let us walk honestly as in the day, not in rioting and drunkenness, not in chambering and wantonness, which are the dishonesties of the night.

GREGORY OF NAZIANZUS
(C. 329–390)
ORATIONS

which will lie down there in peace.
3 Fortified cities will disappear from Ephraim,
and Damascus will lose its kingdom.
The survivors in Syria
will end up like the splendor of the Israelites,"
says the LORD of Heaven's Armies.
4 "At that time
Jacob's splendor will be greatly diminished,
and he will become skin and bones.
5 It will be as when one gathers the grain harvest
and his hand gleans the ear of grain.
It will be like one gathering the ears of grain
in the Valley of Rephaim.
6 There will be some left behind,
as when an olive tree is beaten—
two or three ripe olives remain toward the very top,
four or five on its fruitful branches,"
says the LORD God of Israel.
7 At that time men will trust in their Creator;
they will depend on the Holy One of Israel.
8 They will no longer trust in the altars their hands made,
or depend on the Asherah poles and incense altars their fingers made.
9 At that time their fortified cities will be
like the abandoned summits of the Amorites,
which they abandoned because of the Israelites;
there will be desolation.
10 For you ignore the God who rescues you;
you pay no attention to your strong protector.
So this is what happens:
You cultivate beautiful plants
and plant exotic vines.
11 The day you begin cultivating, you do what you can to make it grow;
the morning you begin planting, you do what you can to make it sprout.
Yet the harvest will disappear in the day of disease
and incurable pain.
12 Beware, you many nations massing together,
those who make a commotion as loud as the roaring of the sea's waves.
Beware, you people making such an uproar,
those who make an uproar as loud as the roaring of powerful waves.
13 Though these people make an uproar as loud as the roaring of powerful waves,
when he shouts at them, they will flee to a distant land,
driven before the wind like dead weeds on the hills
or like dead thistles before a strong gale.
14 In the evening there is sudden terror;
by morning they vanish.
This is the fate of those who try to plunder us,
the destiny of those who try to loot us!

THE LORD WILL JUDGE A DISTANT LAND IN THE SOUTH

18 Beware, land of buzzing wings,
the one beyond the rivers of Cush,
2 that sends messengers by sea,

17:10–11 These words concern Judah's alliance with Damascus, which Isaiah was dead against. Isaiah saw that it would only precipitate the Assyrian invasion, as in fact it did. The image of planting a garden of pleasures and "foreign seedlings" (NKJV) refers to sensuous idolatry as well as to the entangling alliance. Then follows a contemptuous description of the rapid growth of this alliance and of the care with which Israel cultivated it. "The day you begin cultivating, you do what you can to make it grow," and next morning it was in blossom, so sedulously had they nursed and fostered it. Then comes the smiting contrast of what it was all for: "Yet the harvest will disappear in a day of disease and incurable pain." All this God-forgetting life of pleasure-seeking and idolatry is bringing on a terrible, inevitable consummation, and every man shall inherit the consequences of his deeds.

ALEXANDER MACLAREN
(1826–1910)
EXPOSITIONS OF THE HOLY SCRIPTURES

18:3–4 The assurance God gives to his prophet to be given to his people—that though he might seem for a time to sit by as an unconcerned spectator, yet he would certainly and seasonably appear for the comfort of his people and the confusion of his and their enemies. When he says, "I will wait and watch from my place," it is not as if he were weary of governing the world. The great God has a perfect, undisturbed enjoyment of himself in the midst of all the agitations and changes of this world. And though he may sometimes seem to his people as if he took no notice, yet even then he knows very well what people are doing and what he himself will do.

MATTHEW HENRY (1662–1714)
COMMENTARY ON THE WHOLE BIBLE

who glide over the water's surface in boats made of papyrus.
Go, you swift messengers,
to a nation of tall, smooth-skinned people,
to a people that are feared far and wide,
to a nation strong and victorious,
whose land rivers divide.
3 All you who live in the world,
who reside on the earth,
you will see a signal flag raised on the mountains;
you will hear a trumpet being blown.
4 For this is what the LORD has told me:
"I will wait and watch from my place,
like scorching heat produced by the sunlight,
like a cloud of mist in the heat of harvest."
5 For before the harvest, when the bud has sprouted
and the ripening fruit appears,
he will cut off the unproductive shoots with pruning knives;
he will prune the tendrils.
6 They will all be left for the birds of the hills
and the wild animals;
the birds will eat them during the summer,
and all the wild animals will eat them during the winter.
7 At that time
tribute will be brought to the LORD of Heaven's Armies
by a people that are tall and smooth-skinned,
a people that are feared far and wide,
a nation strong and victorious,
whose land rivers divide.
The tribute will be brought to the place where the LORD of Heaven's Armies has chosen to reside, on Mount Zion.

THE LORD WILL JUDGE EGYPT

19 This is an oracle about Egypt:
Look, the LORD rides on a swift-moving cloud
and approaches Egypt.
The idols of Egypt tremble before him;
the Egyptians lose their courage.
2 "I will provoke civil strife in Egypt:
brothers will fight with one another,
as will neighbors,
cities, and kingdoms.
3 The Egyptians will panic,
and I will confuse their strategy.
They will seek guidance from the idols and from the spirits of the dead,
from the pits used to conjure up underworld spirits,
and from the magicians.
4 I will hand Egypt over to a harsh master;
a powerful king will rule over them,"
says the Sovereign LORD of Heaven's Armies.
5 The water of the sea will be dried up,
and the river will dry up and be empty.
6 The canals will stink;
the streams of Egypt will trickle and then dry up;
the bulrushes and reeds will decay,
7 along with the plants by the mouth of the river.

All the cultivated land near the river
will turn to dust and be blown away.
8 The fishermen will mourn and lament;
all those who cast a fishhook into the river,
and those who spread out a net on the water's surface
will grieve.
9 Those who make clothes from combed flax will be
embarrassed;
those who weave will turn pale.
10 Those who make cloth will be demoralized;
all the hired workers will be depressed.
11 The officials of Zoan are nothing but fools;
Pharaoh's wise advisers give stupid advice.
How dare you say to Pharaoh,
"I am one of the sages,
one well versed in the writings of the ancient kings"?
12 But where, oh where, are your wise men?
Let them tell you, let them find out
what the LORD of Heaven's Armies has planned for Egypt.
13 The officials of Zoan are fools,
the officials of Memphis are misled;
the rulers of her tribes lead Egypt astray.
14 The LORD has made them undiscerning;
they lead Egypt astray in all she does,
so that she is like a drunk sliding around in his own
vomit.
15 Egypt will not be able to do a thing,
head or tail, shoots or stalk.

16 At that time the Egyptians will be like women. They will
tremble and fear because the LORD of Heaven's Armies bran-
dishes his fist against them. 17 The land of Judah will humiliate
Egypt. Everyone who hears about Judah will be afraid because
of what the LORD of Heaven's Armies is planning to do to them.
18 At that time five cities in the land of Egypt will speak the
language of Canaan and swear allegiance to the LORD of Heav-
en's Armies. One will be called the City of the Sun. 19 At that
time there will be an altar for the LORD in the middle of the
land of Egypt, as well as a sacred pillar dedicated to the LORD
at its border. 20 It will become a visual reminder in the land of
Egypt of the LORD of Heaven's Armies. When they cry out to
the LORD because of oppressors, he will send them a deliverer
and defender who will rescue them. 21 The LORD will reveal
himself to the Egyptians, and they will acknowledge the LORD's
authority at that time. They will present sacrifices and offerings;
they will make vows to the LORD and fulfill them. 22 The LORD
will strike Egypt, striking and then healing them. They will turn
to the LORD, and he will listen to their prayers and heal them.
23 At that time there will be a highway from Egypt to Assyria.
The Assyrians will visit Egypt, and the Egyptians will visit Assyria. The Egyptians and Assyrians will worship together. 24 At
that time Israel will be the third member of the group, along
with Egypt and Assyria, and will be a recipient of blessing in the
earth. 25 The LORD of Heaven's Armies will pronounce a blessing
over the earth, saying, "Blessed be my people, Egypt, and the
work of my hands, Assyria, and my special possession, Israel!"
20 The LORD revealed the following message during the year
in which King Sargon of Assyria sent his commanding
general to Ashdod, and he fought against it and captured it. 2 At

19:18–25 Here is a wonderful display of the grace of God in this promise to Egypt—the nation that was the type of God's enemies—yet the grace of God is to come to Egypt. And if Assyria shall be saved, have confidence in God for those who are often worse than heathens, and you shall have your reward in that day when he of the pierced hand shall distribute crowns to those who faithfully serve him. Take courage—your work of faith and labor of love are not in vain in the Lord and will do wonders yet to the praise of his grace.

CHARLES SPURGEON
(1834–1892)
METROPOLITAN TABERNACLE SERMONS

20:3–4 Someone perhaps will say, *Was it not disgraceful for a man to walk unclothed among the people since he must meet both men and women?* Consider what this act represented and what was the reason for this outward show; it was that Israel's youth would be led away into exile and walk "in the same way that my servant Isaiah has walked around," he says, "in undergarments and barefoot." This might have been expressed in words, but God chose to enforce it by an example that the very sight might strike more terror, and what they shrank from in the body of the prophet they might utterly dread for themselves. Wherein lay the greater abhorrence: in the body of the prophet or in the sins of the unbelievers?

AMBROSE **(C. 339–C. 397)**
LETTERS

that time the LORD announced through Isaiah son of Amoz:
"Go, remove the sackcloth from your waist and take your sandals off your feet." He did as instructed and walked around in
undergarments and barefoot.
3 Later the LORD explained, "In
the same way that my servant Isaiah has walked around in undergarments and barefoot for the past three years, as an object
lesson and omen pertaining to Egypt and Cush,
4 so the king of
Assyria will lead away the captives of Egypt and the exiles of
Cush, both young and old. They will be in undergarments and
barefoot, with the buttocks exposed; the Egyptians will be publicly humiliated.
5 Those who put their hope in Cush and took
pride in Egypt will be afraid and embarrassed.
6 At that time
those who live on this coast will say, 'Look what has happened
to our source of hope to whom we fled for help, expecting to
be rescued from the king of Assyria! How can we escape now?'"

THE LORD WILL JUDGE BABYLON

21 This is an oracle about the wilderness by the Sea:
Like strong winds blowing in the south,
one invades from the wilderness,
from a land that is feared.
2 I have received a distressing message:
"The deceiver deceives,
the destroyer destroys.
Attack, you Elamites!
Lay siege, you Medes!
I will put an end to all the groaning."
3 For this reason my stomach churns;
cramps overwhelm me
like the contractions of a woman in labor.
I am disturbed by what I hear,
horrified by what I see.
4 My heart palpitates,
I shake in fear;
the twilight I desired
has brought me terror.
5 Arrange the table,
lay out the carpet,
eat and drink!
Get up, you officers,
smear oil on the shields!

6 For this is what the Lord has told me:
"Go, post a guard!
He must report what he sees.
7 When he sees chariots,
teams of horses,
riders on donkeys,
riders on camels,
he must be alert,
very alert."
8 Then the guard cries out:
"On the watchtower, O Lord,
I stand all day long;
at my post
I am stationed every night.
9 Look what's coming!
A charioteer,
a team of horses."

When questioned, he replies,
"Babylon has fallen, fallen!
All the idols of her gods lie shattered on the ground!"
10 O my downtrodden people, crushed like stalks on the threshing floor,
what I have heard
from the LORD of Heaven's Armies,
the God of Israel,
I have reported to you.

BAD NEWS FOR SEIR

11 This is an oracle about Dumah:
Someone calls to me from Seir,
"Watchman, what is left of the night?
Watchman, what is left of the night?"
12 The watchman replies,
"Morning is coming, but then night.
If you want to ask, ask;
come back again."

THE LORD WILL JUDGE ARABIA

13 This is an oracle about Arabia:
In the thicket of Arabia you spend the night,
you Dedanite caravans.
14 Bring out some water for the thirsty.
You who live in the land of Tema,
bring some food for the fugitives.
15 For they flee from the swords—
from the drawn sword,
and from the battle-ready bow,
and from the severity of the battle.

16 For this is what the Lord has told me: "Within exactly one
year all the splendor of Kedar will come to an end. 17 Just a
handful of archers, the warriors of Kedar, will be left." Indeed,
the LORD God of Israel has spoken.

THE LORD WILL JUDGE JERUSALEM

22 This is an oracle about the Valley of Vision:
What is the reason
that all of you go up to the rooftops?
2 The noisy city is full of raucous sounds;
the town is filled with revelry.
Your slain were not cut down by the sword;
they did not die in battle.
3 All your leaders ran away together—
they fled to a distant place;
all your refugees were captured together—
they were captured without a single arrow being shot.
4 So I say:
"Don't look at me!
I am weeping bitterly.
Don't try to console me
concerning the destruction of my defenseless people."
5 For the Sovereign LORD of Heaven's Armies
has planned a day of panic, defeat, and confusion.
In the Valley of Vision people shout
and cry out to the hill.

21:11–12 If you enjoy all the prosperity that the world can afford, of what value will it be when night comes? On the other hand, if you experience here one continued night of affliction, it will soon pass away and no more be remembered when once the bright morn of everlasting day shall have risen for you. Learn then to despise the pleasure of sense and to endure with fortitude the troubles of life. Set eternity before you and keep it ever in your view, and then, though your night be long, the day shall soon arise upon you when "your sun will no longer set," but "the LORD will be your permanent source of light" (Isa 60:20).

CHARLES SIMEON
(1759–1836)
HORAE HOMILETICAE

22:1–14 Have you slipped? Rise up. Have you sinned? Cease. Do not, because of certain human considerations, hesitate to come to me. Do not lose heart; be mindful of the days of old. There is salvation; there is amendment. Have courage; do not despair. There is no law that passes sentence of death without pity but grace exceeding the chastisement awaits the amendment. Not yet have the doors been closed; the Bridegroom listens; sin is not the master. Again take up the struggle; do not draw back, but pity yourself and all of us in Jesus Christ our Lord, to whom be glory and might now and forever, for ages of ages. Amen.

BASIL THE GREAT **(330–379)**
LETTERS

6 The Elamites picked up the quiver
and came with chariots and horsemen;
the men of Kir prepared the shield.
7 Your very best valleys were full of chariots;
horsemen confidently took their positions at the gate.
8 They removed the defenses of Judah.
At that time you looked
for the weapons in the House of the Forest.
9 You saw the many breaks
in the walls of the City of David;
you stored up water in the lower pool.
10 You counted the houses in Jerusalem
and demolished houses so you could have material to
reinforce the wall.
11 You made a reservoir between the two walls
for the water of the old pool—
but you did not trust in the one who made it;
you did not depend on the one who formed it long ago.
12 At that time the Sovereign LORD of Heaven's Armies
called for weeping and mourning,
for shaved heads and sackcloth.
13 But look, there is outright celebration!
You say, "Kill the ox and slaughter the sheep,
eat meat and drink wine.
Eat and drink, for tomorrow we die!"

14 The LORD of Heaven's Armies told me this: "Certainly this
sin will not be forgiven as long as you live," says the Sovereign
LORD of Heaven's Armies.
15 This is what the Sovereign LORD of Heaven's Armies says:
"Go visit this administrator, Shebna, who supervises the
palace, and tell him:
16 'What right do you have to be here? What relatives do
you have buried here?
Why do you chisel out a tomb for yourself here?
He chisels out his burial site in an elevated place,
he carves out his tomb on a cliff.
17 Look, the LORD will throw you far away, you mere man!
He will wrap you up tightly.
18 He will wind you up tightly into a ball
and throw you into a wide, open land.
There you will die,
and there with you will be your impressive chariots,
which bring disgrace to the house of your master.
19 I will remove you from your office;
you will be thrown down from your position.

20 "'At that time I will summon my servant Eliakim, son of
Hilkiah. 21 I will put your robe on him, tie your belt around him,
and transfer your authority to him. He will become a protector of the residents of Jerusalem and of the people of Judah.
22 I will place the key to the house of David on his shoulder.
When he opens the door, no one can close it; when he closes
the door, no one can open it. 23 I will fasten him like a peg into
a solid place; he will bring honor and respect to his father's
family. 24 His father's family will gain increasing prominence
because of him, including the offspring and the offshoots. All
the small containers, including the bowls and all the jars, will
hang from this peg.'

[25]"At that time," says the LORD of Heaven's Armies, "the peg fastened into a solid place will come loose. It will be cut off and fall, and the load hanging on it will be cut off." Indeed, the LORD has spoken.

THE LORD WILL JUDGE TYRE

23 This is an oracle about Tyre:
Wail, you large ships,
for the port is too devastated to enter!
From the land of Cyprus this news is announced to them.
2 Lament, you residents of the coast,
you merchants of Sidon who travel over the sea,
whose agents sail over [3]the deep waters.
Grain from the Shihor region,
crops grown near the Nile she receives;
she is the trade center of the nations.
4 Be ashamed, O Sidon,
for the sea says this, O fortress of the sea:
"I have not gone into labor
or given birth;
I have not raised young men
or brought up young women."
5 When the news reaches Egypt,
they will be shaken by what has happened to Tyre.
6 Travel to Tarshish!
Wail, you residents of the coast!
7 Is this really your boisterous city
whose origins are in the distant past
and whose feet led her to a distant land to reside?
8 Who planned this for royal Tyre,
whose merchants are princes,
whose traders are the dignitaries of the earth?
9 The LORD of Heaven's Armies planned it—
to dishonor the pride that comes from all her beauty,
to humiliate all the dignitaries of the earth.
10 Daughter Tarshish, travel back to your land, as one
crosses the Nile;
there is no longer any marketplace in Tyre.
11 The LORD stretched out his hand over the sea,
he shook kingdoms;
he gave the order
to destroy Canaan's fortresses.
12 He said,
"You will no longer celebrate,
oppressed virgin daughter Sidon!
Get up, travel to Cyprus,
but you will find no relief there."
13 Look at the land of the Chaldeans,
these people who have lost their identity!
The Assyrians have made it a home for wild animals.
They erected their siege towers,
demolished its fortresses,
and turned it into a heap of ruins.
14 Wail, you large ships,
for your fortress is destroyed!

[15]At that time Tyre will be forgotten for 70 years, the typical life span of a king. At the end of 70 years Tyre will try to attract attention again, like the prostitute in the popular song:

23:4 Sidon is brought to shame by the voice of the sea when the life of one who is fortified and supposedly steadfast is reprobated in comparison with the lives of those who are worldly and are being tossed about in this world. For often there are those who, returning to the Lord after their sins of the flesh, convince themselves to be the more zealous in doing good works as they realize they were worthy of condemnation for their deeds. And often certain people who persevere in preserving the integrity of the flesh, on perceiving that they have less to deplore, think to themselves that the innocence of their lives is sufficient and do not arouse themselves by zealously striving to be fervent in spirit.

GREGORY THE GREAT
(C. 540–604)
PASTORAL CARE

16 “Take the harp,
go through the city,
forgotten prostitute!
Play it well,
play lots of songs,
so you’ll be noticed.”

17 At the end of 70 years the LORD will revive Tyre. She will
start making money again by selling her services to all the earth’s
kingdoms. 18 Her profits and earnings will be set apart for the
LORD. They will not be stored up or accumulated, for her profits
will be given to those who live in the LORD’s presence and will be
used to purchase large quantities of food and beautiful clothes.

THE LORD WILL JUDGE THE EARTH

24 Look, the LORD is ready to devastate the earth
and leave it in ruins;
he will mar its surface
and scatter its inhabitants.
2 Everyone will suffer—the priest as well as the people,
the master as well as the servant,
the elegant lady as well as the female attendant,
the seller as well as the buyer,
the borrower as well as the lender,
the creditor as well as the debtor.
3 The earth will be completely devastated
and thoroughly ransacked.
For the LORD has decreed this judgment.
4 The earth dries up and withers,
the world shrivels up and withers;
the prominent people of the earth fade away.
5 The earth is defiled by its inhabitants,
for they have violated laws,
disregarded the regulation,
and broken the permanent treaty.
6 So a treaty curse devours the earth;
its inhabitants pay for their guilt.
This is why the inhabitants of the earth disappear,
and are reduced to just a handful of people.
7 The new wine dries up,
the vines shrivel up,
all those who like to celebrate groan.
8 The happy sound of the tambourines stops,
the revelry of those who celebrate comes to a halt,
the happy sound of the harp ceases.
9 They no longer sing and drink wine;
the beer tastes bitter to those who drink it.
10 The ruined town is shattered;
all the houses are shut up tight.
11 They howl in the streets because of what happened to
the wine;
all joy turns to sorrow;
celebrations disappear from the earth.
12 The city is left in ruins;
the gate is reduced to rubble.
13 This is what will happen throughout the earth,
among the nations.
It will be like when they beat an olive tree,
and just a few olives are left at the end of the harvest.

14 They lift their voices and shout joyfully;
they praise the majesty of the LORD in the west.
15 So in the east extol the LORD,
along the seacoasts extol the fame of the LORD God of Israel.
16 From the ends of the earth we hear songs—
the Just One is majestic.
But I say, "I'm wasting away! I'm wasting away! I'm doomed!
Deceivers deceive, deceivers thoroughly deceive!"
17 Terror, pit, and snare
are ready to overtake you, inhabitants of the earth!
18 The one who runs away from the sound of the terror
will fall into the pit;
the one who climbs out of the pit
will be trapped by the snare.
For the floodgates of the heavens are opened up
and the foundations of the earth shake.
19 The earth is broken in pieces,
the earth is ripped to shreds,
the earth shakes violently.
20 The earth will stagger around like a drunk;
it will sway back and forth like a hut in a windstorm.
Its sin will weigh it down,
and it will fall and never get up again.

THE LORD WILL BECOME KING

21 At that time the LORD will punish
the heavenly forces in the heavens
and the earthly kings on the earth.
22 They will be imprisoned in a pit,
locked up in a prison,
and after staying there for a long time, they will be punished.
23 The full moon will be covered up,
the bright sun will be darkened;
for the LORD of Heaven's Armies will rule
on Mount Zion in Jerusalem
in the presence of his assembly, in majestic splendor.

25 O LORD, you are my God!
I will exalt you in praise, I will extol your fame.
For you have done extraordinary things,
and executed plans made long ago exactly as you decreed.
2 Indeed, you have made the city into a heap of rubble,
the fortified town into a heap of ruins;
the fortress of foreigners is no longer a city,
it will never be rebuilt.
3 So a strong nation will extol you;
the towns of powerful nations will fear you.
4 For you are a protector for the poor,
a protector for the needy in their distress,
a shelter from the rainstorm,
a shade from the heat.
Though the breath of tyrants is like a winter rainstorm,
5 like heat in a dry land,
you humble the boasting foreigners.
Just as the shadow of a cloud causes the heat to subside,
so he causes the song of tyrants to cease.

24:23 Isaiah was pricked by the thorn of sin; you are decked with the flowers of virtue. "The full moon will be covered up, the bright sun will be darkened; for the LORD of Heaven's Armies will rule." The moon is ashamed, the sun is confounded, and the sky covered with sackcloth. Shall we fearlessly and joyously, as though we were free from all sin, face the majesty of the Judge? After all, the mountains shall melt away, that is, all who are lifted up by pride and all the host of the heavens, whether they are stars or angelic powers, shall fade away like heavens when the heavens shall be rolled together as a scroll.

JEROME (C. 342–420)
AGAINST THE PELAGIANS

25:1–12 "He will swallow up death permanently. The Sovereign LORD will wipe away the tears from every face." Death overcame our forefather Adam on account of his transgression and like a fierce wild animal it pounced on him and carried him off amid lamentation and loud wailing. People wept and grieved because death ruled over all the earth. But all this came to an end with Christ. Striking down death, he rose up on the third day and became the way by which human nature would rid itself of corruption. He became the firstborn of the dead and the firstfruits of those who have fallen asleep. We who come afterward will certainly follow the firstfruits. He turned suffering into joy, and we cast off our sackcloth. We put on the joy given by God so that we can rejoice and say, "Where, O death, is your victory?" (1 Cor 15:55). Therefore every tear is taken away.

CYRIL OF ALEXANDRIA
(C. 376–444)
THIRD LETTER TO NESTORIUS

26:1–19 "Trust in the LORD from this time forward, even in YAH, the LORD, an enduring protector!" Seeing that we have such a God to trust, let us rest upon him with all our weight; let us resolutely drive out all unbelief and endeavor to get rid of doubts and fears, which so much mar our comfort, since there is no excuse for fear where God is the foundation of our trust. How ungenerous, how unkind is our conduct when we put so little confidence in our heavenly Father who has never failed us and who never will. We should speak well of our God. There is none like him in the heaven above or the earth beneath. We have been in many trials, but we have never yet been cast where we could not find in our God all that we needed. Let us then be encouraged to trust in the Lord forever, assured that his everlasting strength will be, as it has been, our succor and stay.

CHARLES SPURGEON
(1834–1892)
MORNING AND EVENING

6 The LORD of Heaven's Armies will hold a banquet for all the nations on this mountain.
At this banquet there will be plenty of meat and aged wine—
tender meat and choicest wine.
7 On this mountain he will swallow up
the shroud that is over all the peoples,
the woven covering that is over all the nations;
8 he will swallow up death permanently.
The Sovereign LORD will wipe away the tears from every face,
and remove his people's disgrace from all the earth.
Indeed, the LORD has announced it!
9 At that time they will say,
"Look, here is our God!
We waited for him, and he delivered us.
Here is the LORD! We waited for him.
Let's rejoice and celebrate his deliverance!"
10 For the LORD's power will make this mountain secure.
Moab will be trampled down where it stands,
as a heap of straw is trampled down in a manure pile.
11 Moab will spread out its hands in the middle of it,
just as a swimmer spreads his hands to swim;
the LORD will bring down Moab's pride as it spreads its hands.
12 The fortified city (along with the very tops of your walls) he will knock down,
he will bring it down, he will throw it down to the dusty ground.

JUDAH WILL CELEBRATE

26 At that time this song will be sung in the land of Judah:
"We have a strong city!
The LORD's deliverance, like walls and a rampart, makes it secure.
2 Open the gates so a righteous nation can enter—
one that remains trustworthy.
3 You keep completely safe the people who maintain their faith,
for they trust in you.
4 Trust in the LORD from this time forward,
even in YAH, the LORD, an enduring protector!
5 Indeed, the LORD knocks down those who live in a high place,
he brings down an elevated town;
he brings it down to the ground,
he throws it down to the dust.
6 It is trampled underfoot
by the feet of the oppressed,
by the soles of the poor."

GOD'S PEOPLE ANTICIPATE VINDICATION

7 The way of the righteous is level,
the path of the righteous that you prepare is straight.
8 Yes, as your judgments unfold,
O LORD, we wait for you.
We desire your fame and reputation to grow.
9 I look for you during the night;
my spirit within me seeks you at dawn;

for when your judgments come upon the earth,
those who live in the world learn about justice.
10 If the wicked are shown mercy,
they do not learn about justice.
Even in a land where right is rewarded, they act unjustly;
they do not see the LORD's majesty revealed.
11 O LORD, you are ready to act,
but they don't even notice.
They will see and be put to shame by your angry judgment against humankind;
yes, fire will consume your enemies.
12 O LORD, you make us secure,
for even all we have accomplished you have done for us.
13 O LORD, our God,
masters other than you have ruled us,
but we praise your name alone.
14 The dead do not come back to life,
the spirits of the dead do not rise.
That is because you came in judgment and destroyed them,
you wiped out all memory of them.
15 You have made the nation larger, O LORD;
you have made the nation larger and revealed your splendor;
you have extended all the borders of the land.
16 O LORD, in distress they looked for you;
they uttered incantations because of your discipline.
17 As when a pregnant woman gets ready to deliver
and strains and cries out because of her labor pains,
so were we because of you, O LORD.
18 We were pregnant, we strained,
we gave birth, as it were, to wind.
We cannot produce deliverance on the earth;
no people are born to populate the world.
19 Your dead will come back to life;
your corpses will rise up.
Wake up and shout joyfully, you who live in the ground!
For you will grow like plants drenched with the morning dew,
and the earth will bring forth its dead spirits.
20 Go, my people! Enter your inner rooms!
Close your doors behind you!
Hide for a little while,
until his angry judgment is over.
21 For look, the LORD is coming out of the place where he lives
to punish the sin of those who live on the earth.
The earth will display the blood shed on it;
it will no longer cover up its slain.

27 At that time the LORD will punish
with his destructive, great, and powerful sword
Leviathan the fast-moving serpent,
Leviathan the squirming serpent;
he will kill the sea monster.
2 When that time comes,
sing about a delightful vineyard!
3 "I, the LORD, protect it;
I water it regularly.

27:2–13 "I am not angry." This verse contains excellent consolation, for it expresses the incredible warmth of love that the Lord bears toward his people though they are of a wicked and rebellious disposition. God assumes, as we shall see, the character of a father. He shows that he cannot hate his elect so as not to bear fatherly kindness toward them even while he visits them with very severe punishments. Our heavenly Father wishes us to take hold of his power and goodness that we may know how great it is and may partake of it more and more abundantly; for he would wish to deal with us on the same familiar terms as with his children if we did not prevent him by our wickedness. He declares that willingly and most earnestly he hastens to blot out all our offenses.

JOHN CALVIN **(1509–1564)**
COMPLETE COMMENTARY ON THE BIBLE

I guard it night and day,
so no one can harm it.
4 I am not angry.
I wish I could confront some thorns and briers!
Then I would march against them for battle;
I would set them all on fire,
5 unless they became my subjects
and made peace with me;
let them make peace with me."

6 The time is coming when Jacob will take root;
Israel will blossom and grow branches.
The produce will fill the surface of the world.
7 Has the LORD struck down Israel as he did their
oppressors?
Has Israel been killed like their enemies?
8 When you summon her for divorce, you prosecute her;
he drives her away with his strong wind in the day of
the east wind.
9 So in this way Jacob's sin will be forgiven,
and this is how they will show they are finished sinning:
They will make all the stones of the altars
like crushed limestone,
and the Asherah poles and the incense altars will no
longer stand.
10 For the fortified city is left alone;
it is a deserted settlement
and abandoned like the wilderness.
Calves graze there;
they lie down there
and eat its branches bare.
11 When its branches get brittle, they break;
women come and use them for kindling.
For these people lack understanding,
therefore the one who made them has no compassion
on them;
the one who formed them has no mercy on them.

12 At that time the LORD will shake the tree, from the Euphrates River to the Stream of Egypt. Then you will be gathered
up one by one, O Israelites. 13 At that time a large trumpet will
be blown, and the ones lost in the land of Assyria will come, as
well as the refugees in the land of Egypt. They will worship the
LORD on the holy mountain in Jerusalem.

THE LORD WILL JUDGE EPHRAIM

28 The splendid crown of Ephraim's drunkards is doomed,
the withering flower, its beautiful splendor,
situated at the head of a rich valley,
the crown of those overcome with wine.
2 Look, the Lord sends a strong, powerful one.
With the force of a hailstorm or a destructive
windstorm,
with the might of a driving, torrential rainstorm,
he will knock that crown to the ground with his hand.
3 The splendid crown of Ephraim's drunkards
will be trampled underfoot.
4 The withering flower, its beautiful splendor,
situated at the head of a rich valley,

will be like an early fig before harvest—
as soon as someone notices it,
he grabs it and swallows it.
5 At that time the LORD of Heaven's Armies will become
a beautiful crown
and a splendid diadem for the remnant of his people.
6 He will give discernment to the one who makes judicial
decisions
and strength to those who defend the city from attackers.
7 Even these men stagger because of wine;
they stumble around because of beer—
priests and prophets stagger because of beer,
they are confused because of wine,
they stumble around because of beer;
they stagger while seeing prophetic visions,
they totter while making legal decisions.
8 Indeed, all the tables
are covered with vomit,
with filth, leaving no clean place.
9 Who is the LORD trying to teach?
To whom is he explaining a message?
To those just weaned from milk!
To those just taken from their mother's breast!
10 Indeed, they will hear meaningless gibberish,
senseless babbling,
a syllable here, a syllable there.
11 For with mocking lips and a foreign tongue
he will speak to these people.
12 In the past he said to them,
"This is where security can be found.
Provide security for the one who is exhausted.
This is where rest can be found."
But they refused to listen.
13 So the LORD's message to them will sound like
meaningless gibberish,
senseless babbling,
a syllable here, a syllable there.
As a result, they will fall on their backsides when they
try to walk,
and be injured, ensnared, and captured.

THE LORD WILL JUDGE JERUSALEM

14 Therefore, listen to the LORD's message,
you who mock,
you rulers of these people
who reside in Jerusalem.
15 For you say,
"We have made a treaty with death,
with Sheol we have made an agreement.
When the overwhelming judgment sweeps by
it will not reach us.
For we have made a lie our refuge,
we have hidden ourselves in a deceitful word."

16 Therefore, this is what the Sovereign LORD, says:
"Look, I am laying a stone in Zion,
an approved stone,
set in place as a precious cornerstone for the
foundation.

28:16–22 Here is a promise of Christ as the only foundation of hope for escaping the wrath to come. This foundation was laid in Zion, in the eternal counsels of God. This foundation is a stone, firm and able to support his church. It is a tried stone, a chosen stone, approved of God, and it never failed any who made trial of it—a cornerstone, binding together the whole building and bearing the whole weight, precious in the sight of the Lord and of every believer, a sure foundation on which to build. And he who in any age or nation shall believe this testimony and rest all his hopes and his never-dying soul on this foundation shall never be confounded.

MATTHEW HENRY **(1662–1714)**
COMMENTARY ON THE WHOLE BIBLE

The one who maintains his faith will not panic.
17 I will make justice the measuring line,
fairness the plumb line;
hail will sweep away the unreliable refuge,
the floodwaters will overwhelm the hiding place.
18 Your treaty with death will be dissolved;
your agreement with Sheol will not last.
When the overwhelming judgment sweeps by,
you will be overrun by it.
19 Whenever it sweeps by, it will overtake you;
indeed, every morning it will sweep by,
it will come through during the day and the night."
When this announcement is understood,
it will cause nothing but terror.
20 For the bed is too short to stretch out on,
and the blanket is too narrow to wrap around oneself.
21 For the LORD will rise up, as he did at Mount Perazim;
he will rouse himself, as he did in the Valley of Gibeon,
to accomplish his work,
his peculiar work,
to perform his task,
his strange task.
22 So now, do not mock,
or your chains will become heavier!
For I have heard a message about decreed destruction,
from the Sovereign LORD of Heaven's Armies against
the entire land.
23 Pay attention and listen to my message.
Be attentive and listen to what I have to say!
24 Does a farmer just keep on plowing at planting time?
Does he keep breaking up and harrowing his ground?
25 Once he has leveled its surface,
does he not scatter the seed of the caraway plant,
sow the seed of the cumin plant,
and plant the wheat, barley, and grain in their
designated places?
26 His God instructs him;
he teaches him the principles of agriculture.
27 Certainly caraway seed is not threshed with a sledge,
nor is the wheel of a cart rolled over cumin seed.
Certainly caraway seed is beaten with a stick
and cumin seed with a flail.
28 Grain is crushed,
though one certainly does not thresh it forever.
The wheel of one's wagon rolls over it,
but his horses do not crush it.
29 This also comes from the LORD of Heaven's Armies,
who gives supernatural guidance and imparts great
wisdom.

ARIEL IS BESIEGED

29 Ariel is as good as dead—
Ariel, the town David besieged!
Keep observing your annual rituals;
celebrate your festivals on schedule.
2 I will threaten Ariel,
and she will mourn intensely
and become like an altar hearth before me.
3 I will lay siege to you on all sides;

I will besiege you with troops;
I will raise siege works against you.
4 You will fall;
while lying on the ground you will speak;
from the dust where you lie, your words will be heard.
Your voice will sound like a spirit speaking from the underworld;
from the dust you will chirp as if muttering an incantation.
5 But the horde of invaders will be like fine dust,
the horde of tyrants like chaff that is blown away.
It will happen suddenly, in a flash.
6 Judgment will come from the LORD of Heaven's Armies,
accompanied by thunder, earthquake, and a loud noise,
by a strong gale, a windstorm, and a consuming flame of fire.
7 It will be like a dream, a night vision.
There will be a horde from all the nations that fight against Ariel,
those who attack her and her stronghold and besiege her.
8 It will be like a hungry man dreaming that he is eating,
only to awaken and find that his stomach is empty.
It will be like a thirsty man dreaming that he is drinking,
only to awaken and find that he is still weak and his thirst unquenched.
So it will be for the horde from all the nations
that fight against Mount Zion.

GOD'S PEOPLE ARE SPIRITUALLY INSENSITIVE

9 You will be shocked and amazed!
You are totally blind!
They are drunk, but not because of wine;
they stagger, but not because of beer.
10 For the LORD has poured out on you
a strong urge to sleep deeply.
He has shut your eyes (you prophets),
and covered your heads (you seers).

11 To you this entire prophetic revelation is like words in a
sealed scroll. When they hand it to one who can read and say,
"Read this," he responds, "I can't, because it is sealed."
12 Or when
they hand the scroll to one who can't read and say, "Read this,"
he says, "I can't read."

13 The Lord says,
"These people say they are loyal to me;
they say wonderful things about me,
but they are not really loyal to me.
Their worship consists of
nothing but man-made ritual.
14 Therefore I will again do an amazing thing for these people—
an absolutely extraordinary deed.
Wise men will have nothing to say,
the sages will have no explanations."
15 Those who try to hide their plans from the LORD are as good as dead,
who do their work in secret and boast,

29:9–16 According to what the prophet says, "These people say they are loyal to me; they say wonderful things about me, but they are not really loyal to me." To them the Holy Spirit exclaims, "God says this to the evildoer: 'How can you declare my commands, and talk about my covenant?'" (Ps 50:16). It is as if he were saying it does you no good to praise God. It is profitable for those who live well to praise him, but if you praise him and do not abandon your sins, it avails nothing. Again, if when you have begun to live well you attribute it to your own merits, you do not yet praise God. I do not want you to be a robber deriding the cross of our Lord, but neither do I want you as his temple to throw away his merits in you and conceal his wounds.

CAESARIUS OF ARLES
(C. 468–542)
SERMONS

"Who sees us? Who knows what we're doing?"
16 Your thinking is perverse!
Should the potter be regarded as clay?
Should the thing made say about its maker, "He didn't
make me"?
Or should the pottery say about the potter, "He doesn't
understand"?

CHANGES ARE COMING

17 In just a very short time
Lebanon will turn into an orchard,
and the orchard will be considered a forest.
18 At that time the deaf will be able to hear words read
from a scroll,
and the eyes of the blind will be able to see through
deep darkness.
19 The downtrodden will again rejoice in the LORD;
the poor among humankind will take delight in the
Holy One of Israel.
20 For tyrants will disappear,
those who taunt will vanish,
and all those who love to do wrong will be
eliminated—
21 those who bear false testimony against a person,
who entrap the one who arbitrates at the city gate
and deprive the innocent of justice by making false
charges.
22 So this is what the LORD, the one who delivered
Abraham, has said to the family of Jacob:
"Jacob will no longer be ashamed;
their faces will no longer show their embarrassment.
23 For when they see their children,
whom I will produce among them,
they will honor my name.
They will honor the Holy One of Jacob;
they will respect the God of Israel.
24 Those who stray morally will gain understanding;
those who complain will acquire insight.

EGYPT WILL PROVE UNRELIABLE

30 "The rebellious children are as good as dead," says the
LORD,
"those who make plans without consulting me,
who form alliances without consulting my Spirit,
and thereby compound their sin.
2 They travel down to Egypt
without seeking my will,
seeking Pharaoh's protection,
and looking for safety in Egypt's protective shade.
3 But Pharaoh's protection will bring you nothing but
shame
and the safety of Egypt's protective shade nothing but
humiliation.
4 Though his officials are in Zoan
and his messengers arrive at Hanes,
5 all will be put to shame
because of a nation that cannot help them,
who cannot give them aid or help,
but only shame and disgrace."

6 This is an oracle about the animals in the Negev:
Through a land of distress and danger,
inhabited by lionesses and roaring lions,
by snakes and darting adders,
they transport their wealth on the backs of
donkeys,
their riches on the humps of camels,
to a nation that cannot help them.
7 Egypt is totally incapable of helping.
For this reason I call her
"Proud one who is silenced."
8 Now go, write it down on a tablet in their presence
inscribe it on a scroll
so that it might be preserved for a future time
as an enduring witness.
9 For these are rebellious people—
they are lying children,
children unwilling to obey the LORD's law.
10 They say to the visionaries, "See no more visions!"
and to the seers, "Don't relate messages to us about
what is right!
Tell us nice things;
relate deceptive messages.
11 Turn aside from the way;
stray off the path.
Remove from our presence the Holy One of Israel."

12 For this reason this is what the Holy One of Israel says:
"You have rejected this message;
you trust instead in your ability to oppress and trick,
and rely on that kind of behavior.
13 So this sin will become your downfall.
You will be like a high wall
that bulges and cracks and is ready to collapse;
it crumbles suddenly, in a flash.
14 It shatters in pieces like a clay jar,
so shattered to bits that none of it can be salvaged.
Among its fragments one cannot find a shard large
enough
to scoop a hot coal from a fire
or to skim off water from a cistern."

15 For this is what the Sovereign LORD, the Holy One of Israel
says:
"If you repented and patiently waited for me, you would
be delivered;
if you calmly trusted in me, you would find strength,
but you are unwilling.
16 You say, 'No, we will flee on horses,'
so you will indeed flee.
You say, 'We will ride on fast horses,'
so your pursuers will be fast.
17 One thousand will scurry at the battle cry of one enemy
soldier;
at the battle cry of five enemy soldiers you will all run
away,
until the remaining few are as isolated
as a flagpole on a mountaintop
or a signal flag on a hill."

30:18–26 The divine protection is always inseparably present to us, and so great is the love of the Creator for his creature that his providence not only stands by it but even goes constantly before it. When he notices goodwill making an appearance in us, at once he enlightens and encourages it and spurs it on to salvation, giving increase to what he himself planted and saw arise from our own efforts. For, he says, "before they even call out, I will respond; while they are still speaking, I will hear" (Isa 65:24). And again: "When he hears your cry of despair, he will indeed show you mercy; when he hears it, he will respond to you." Not only does he graciously inspire holy desires, he also arranges favorable moments in one's life and the possibility of good results, and he shows the way of salvation to those who are straying.

JOHN CASSIAN
(C. 360–C. 435)
THE CONFERENCES

THE LORD WILL NOT ABANDON HIS PEOPLE

18 For this reason the LORD is ready to show you mercy;
he sits on his throne, ready to have compassion on you.
Indeed, the LORD is a just God;
all who wait for him in faith will be blessed.
19 For people will live in Zion;
in Jerusalem you will weep no more.
When he hears your cry of despair, he will indeed show
you mercy;
when he hears it, he will respond to you.
20 The Lord will give you distress to eat
and suffering to drink;
but your teachers will no longer be hidden;
your eyes will see them.
21 You will hear a word spoken behind you, saying,
"This is the correct way, walk in it,"
whether you are heading to the right or the left.
22 You will desecrate your silver-plated idols
and your gold-plated images.
You will throw them away as if they were a menstrual
rag,
saying to them, "Get out!"
23 He will water the seed you plant in the ground,
and the ground will produce crops in abundance.
At that time your cattle will graze in wide pastures.
24 The oxen and donkeys used in plowing
will eat seasoned feed winnowed with a shovel and
pitchfork.
25 On every high mountain
and every high hill
there will be streams flowing with water,
at the time of great slaughter when the fortified towers
collapse.
26 The light of the full moon will be like the sun's glare,
and the sun's glare will be seven times brighter,
like the light of seven days,
when the LORD binds up his people's fractured bones
and heals their severe wound.
27 Look, the name of the LORD comes from a distant place
in raging anger and awesome splendor.
He speaks angrily,
and his word is like destructive fire.
28 His battle cry overwhelms like a flooding river
that reaches one's neck.
He shakes the nations in a sieve that isolates the chaff;
he puts a bit into the mouth of the nations and leads
them to destruction.
29 You will sing
as you do in the evening when you are celebrating a
festival.
You will be happy like one who plays a flute
as he goes to the mountain of the LORD, the Rock who
shelters Israel.
30 The LORD will give a mighty shout
and intervene in power,
with furious anger and flaming, destructive fire,
with a driving rainstorm and hailstones.
31 Indeed, the LORD's shout will shatter Assyria;
he will beat them with a club.

32 Every blow from his punishing cudgel
with which the LORD will beat them
will be accompanied by music from the tambourine and
harp,
and he will attack them with his weapons.
33 For the burial place is already prepared;
it has been made deep and wide for the king.
The firewood is piled high on it.
The LORD's breath, like a stream flowing with
brimstone,
will ignite it.

EGYPT WILL DISAPPOINT

31 Those who go down to Egypt for help are as good as
dead;
those who rely on war horses
and trust in Egypt's many chariots
and in their many, many horsemen.
But they do not rely on the Holy One of Israel
and do not seek help from the LORD.
2 Yet he too is wise and he will bring disaster;
he does not retract his decree.
He will attack the wicked nation
and the nation that helps those who commit sin.
3 The Egyptians are mere humans, not God;
their horses are made of flesh, not spirit.
The LORD will strike with his hand;
the one who helps will stumble
and the one being helped will fall.
Together they will perish.

THE LORD WILL DEFEND ZION

4 Indeed, this is what the LORD has said to me:
"The LORD will be like a growling lion,
like a young lion growling over its prey.
Though a whole group of shepherds gathers against it,
it is not afraid of their shouts
or intimidated by their yelling.
In this same way the LORD of Heaven's Armies will
descend
to do battle on Mount Zion and on its hill.
5 Just as birds hover over a nest,
so the LORD of Heaven's Armies will protect
Jerusalem.
He will protect and deliver it;
as he passes over he will rescue it."

6 You Israelites! Return to the one you have so blatantly rebelled against! 7 For at that time every one will get rid of the
silver and gold idols your hands sinfully made.
8 "Assyria will fall by a sword, but not one human made;
a sword not made by humankind will destroy them.
They will run away from this sword
and their young men will be forced to do hard labor.
9 They will surrender their stronghold because of fear;
their officers will be afraid of the LORD's battle flag."
This is what the LORD says—
the one whose fire is in Zion,
whose firepot is in Jerusalem.

31:1–3 Let our course take us to regions above because it is better to ascend. As we read today, "Those who go down to Egypt for help are as good as dead." Surely it is not wrong to go to Egypt, but to change to the ways of the Egyptians, to change to the violence of their treachery and to the ugliness of their wantonness—this is wrong. Those who change in this way descend, and those who descend fall. Let us keep away then from the Egyptian, but let us not keep away from God.

AMBROSE **(C. 339–C. 397)**
LETTERS

JUSTICE AND WISDOM WILL PREVAIL

32 Look, a king will promote fairness;
officials will promote justice.
2 Each of them will be like a shelter from the wind
and a refuge from a rainstorm;
like streams of water in a dry region
and like the shade of a large cliff in a parched land.
3 Eyes will no longer be blind
and ears will be attentive.
4 The mind that acts rashly will possess discernment,
and the tongue that stutters will speak with ease and clarity.
5 A fool will no longer be called honorable;
a deceiver will no longer be called principled.
6 For a fool speaks disgraceful things;
his mind plans out sinful deeds.
He commits godless deeds
and says misleading things about the LORD;
he gives the hungry nothing to satisfy their appetite
and gives the thirsty nothing to drink.
7 A deceiver's methods are evil;
he dreams up evil plans
to ruin the poor with lies,
even when the needy are in the right.
8 An honorable man makes honorable plans;
his honorable character gives him security.

THE LORD WILL GIVE TRUE SECURITY

9 You complacent women,
get up and listen to me!
You carefree daughters,
pay attention to what I say!
10 In a year's time
you carefree ones will shake with fear,
for the grape harvest will fail,
and the fruit harvest will not arrive.
11 Tremble, you complacent ones!
Shake with fear, you carefree ones!
Strip off your clothes and expose yourselves—
put sackcloth around your waists.
12 Mourn over the field,
over the delightful fields
and the fruitful vine.
13 Mourn over the land of my people,
which is overgrown with thorns and briers,
and over all the once-happy houses
in the city filled with revelry.
14 For the fortress is neglected;
the once-crowded city is abandoned.
Hill and watchtower
are permanently uninhabited.
Wild donkeys love to go there,
and flocks graze there.
15 This desolation will continue until new life is poured out on us from heaven.
Then the wilderness will become an orchard
and the orchard will be considered a forest.
16 Justice will settle down in the wilderness
and fairness will live in the orchard.

32:9–15 If those very persons who, amid the darkness of the present life, shine bright by virtuous attainments—if they also cannot be void of contagion, with what guilt of wickedness are those bound who still live after the flesh? If those persons cannot be free from sin who are already walking in the way of heavenly desires, what about those who still lie under the loads of sinful habits who, abandoned to the gratifications of their fleshly part, still bear the yoke of rottenness? It is said by Isaiah, "Mourn over the land of my people, which is overgrown with thorns and briers, and over all the once-happy houses in the city filled with revelry." The "city filled with revelry" is the mind of the wicked, which neglects to regard the punishments that are destined to come in the gratification of the flesh, and going away from itself, it revels in empty mirth.

GREGORY THE GREAT
(C. 540–604)
MORALS ON THE BOOK OF JOB

17 Fairness will produce peace
and result in lasting security.
18 My people will live in peaceful settlements,
in secure homes,
and in safe, quiet places.
19 Even if the forest is destroyed
and the city is annihilated,
20 you will be blessed,
you who plant seed by all the banks of the streams,
you who let your ox and donkey graze.

THE LORD WILL RESTORE ZION

33 The destroyer is as good as dead,
you who have not been destroyed!
The deceitful one is as good as dead,
the one whom others have not deceived!
When you are through destroying, you will be
destroyed;
when you finish deceiving, others will deceive you!
2 LORD, be merciful to us! We wait for you.
Give us strength each morning.
Deliver us when distress comes.
3 The nations run away when they hear a loud noise;
the nations scatter when you spring into action!
4 Your plunder disappears as if locusts were eating it;
they swarm over it like locusts.
5 The LORD is exalted,
indeed, he lives in heaven;
he fills Zion with justice and fairness.
6 He is your constant source of stability;
he abundantly provides safety and great wisdom;
he gives all this to those who fear him.
7 Look, ambassadors cry out in the streets;
messengers sent to make peace weep bitterly.
8 Highways are empty;
there are no travelers.
Treaties are broken;
witnesses are despised;
human life is treated with disrespect.
9 The land dries up and withers away;
the forest of Lebanon shrivels up and decays.
Sharon is like the arid rift valley;
Bashan and Carmel are parched.
10 "Now I will rise up," says the LORD.
"Now I will exalt myself;
now I will magnify myself.
11 You conceive straw,
you give birth to chaff;
your breath is a fire that destroys you.
12 The nations will be burned to ashes;
like thornbushes that have been cut down, they will be
set on fire.
13 You who are far away, listen to what I have done!
You who are close by, recognize my strength."
14 Sinners are afraid in Zion;
panic grips the godless.
They say, "Who among us can coexist with destructive
fire?
Who among us can coexist with unquenchable fire?"

33:14–24 This speaks of two different sorts of people who dwell in Zion, the true citizens and the sinners. The one should "see a wide land" and should be led away captive thither, as it was threatened to the children of Israel that they should be driven out of their own land and carried captive to a far country. But the other should "see a king in his splendor." While the sinners are cast out of their own land to the ends of the earth and made slaves, you will dwell quietly in the land of Israel under the peaceable and happy government of your own prince, the King of Zion. The reward promised to the righteous is dwelling under the safe and prosperous government of their own king.

JONATHAN EDWARDS
(1703–1758)
THE COMPLETE WORKS

15 The one who lives uprightly
and speaks honestly,
the one who refuses to profit from oppressive measures
and rejects a bribe,
the one who does not plot violent crimes
and does not seek to harm others—
16 this is the person who will live in a secure place;
he will find safety in the rocky, mountain strongholds;
he will have food
and a constant supply of water.
17 You will see a king in his splendor;
you will see a wide land.
18 Your mind will recall the terror you experienced,
and you will ask yourselves, "Where is the scribe?
Where is the one who weighs the money?
Where is the one who counts the towers?"
19 You will no longer see a defiant people
whose language you do not comprehend,
whose derisive speech you do not understand.
20 Look at Zion, the city where we hold religious festivals!
You will see Jerusalem,
a peaceful settlement,
a tent that stays put;
its stakes will never be pulled up;
none of its ropes will snap in two.
21 Instead the LORD will rule there as our mighty king.
Rivers and wide streams will flow through it;
no war galley will enter;
no large ships will sail through.
22 For the LORD, our ruler,
the LORD, our commander,
the LORD, our king—
he will deliver us.
23 Though at this time your ropes are slack,
the mast is not secured,
and the sail is not unfurled,
at that time you will divide up a great quantity of loot;
even the lame will drag off plunder.
24 No resident of Zion will say, "I am ill";
the people who live there will have their sin forgiven.

THE LORD WILL JUDGE EDOM

34 Come near, you nations, and listen!
Pay attention, you people!
The earth and everything it contains must listen,
the world and everything that lives in it.
2 For the LORD is angry at all the nations
and furious with all their armies.
He will annihilate them and slaughter them.
3 Their slain will be left unburied,
their corpses will stink;
the hills will soak up their blood.
4 All the stars in the sky will fade away,
the sky will roll up like a scroll;
all its stars will wither,
like a leaf withers and falls from a vine
or a fig withers and falls from a tree.
5 He says, "Indeed, my sword has slaughtered heavenly
powers.

34:1–4 So our Lord Jesus Christ comes from heaven, and he comes with glory at the last day to bring this world to its close. For this world will accomplish its course, and the world that once came into being is hereafter to be renewed. For seeing that corruption, theft, adultery, and every form of sin has been poured out on the earth, and in the world fresh blood has been ever mingled with previous blood, this astonishing habitation filled with iniquity is not to last. This world passes away that the fairer world may be revealed. Now would you have this proved by the express words of scripture? Listen to these from Isaiah: "All the stars in the sky will fade away, the sky will roll up like a scroll; all its stars will wither, like a leaf withers and falls from a vine or a fig withers and falls from a tree."

CYRIL OF JERUSALEM
(C. 313–386)
CATECHETICAL LECTURES

Look, it now descends on Edom,
on the people I will annihilate in judgment."
6 The LORD's sword is dripping with blood,
it is covered with fat;
it drips with the blood of young rams and goats
and is covered with the fat of rams' kidneys.
For the LORD is holding a sacrifice in Bozrah,
a bloody slaughter in the land of Edom.
7 Wild oxen will be slaughtered along with them,
as well as strong bulls.
Their land is drenched with blood,
their soil is covered with fat.
8 For the LORD has planned a day of revenge,
a time when he will repay Edom for her hostility toward
Zion.
9 Edom's streams will be turned into pitch
and her soil into brimstone;
her land will become burning pitch.
10 Night and day it will burn;
its smoke will ascend continually.
Generation after generation it will be a wasteland,
and no one will ever pass through it again.
11 Owls and wild animals will live there,
all kinds of wild birds will settle in it.
The LORD will stretch out over her
the measuring line of ruin
and the plumb line of destruction.
12 Her nobles will have nothing left to call a kingdom,
and all her officials will disappear.
13 Her fortresses will be overgrown with thorns;
thickets and weeds will grow in her fortified cities.
Jackals will settle there;
ostriches will live there.
14 Wild animals and wild dogs will congregate there;
wild goats will bleat to one another.
Yes, nocturnal animals will rest there
and make for themselves a nest.
15 Owls will make nests and lay eggs there;
they will hatch them and protect them.
Yes, hawks will gather there,
each with its mate.
16 Carefully read the scroll of the LORD!
Not one of these creatures will be missing,
none will lack a mate.
For the LORD has issued the decree,
and his own Spirit gathers them.
17 He assigns them their allotment;
he measures out their assigned place.
They will live there permanently;
they will settle in it through successive
generations.

THE LAND AND ITS PEOPLE ARE TRANSFORMED

35 Let the wilderness and desert be happy;
let the arid rift valley rejoice and bloom like a lily!
2 Let it richly bloom;
let it rejoice and shout with delight!
It is given the grandeur of Lebanon,
the splendor of Carmel and Sharon.

35:1–10 The prophecy here disguises under the word "desert" the church of the Gentiles, which for long years deserted of God is being evangelized by those of whom we are speaking, and it says that besides other blessings the glory of Lebanon will be given to the desert. Now it is customary to call Jerusalem Lebanon allegorically. This prophecy before us therefore teaches that by God's presence with humanity, the glory of Lebanon will be given to that which is called "desert," that is to say, the church of the Gentiles.

EUSEBIUS OF CAESAREA
(C. 260–339)
THE PROOF OF THE GOSPEL

They will see the grandeur of the LORD,
the splendor of our God.
3 Strengthen the hands that have gone limp,
steady the knees that shake.
4 Tell those who panic,
"Be strong! Do not fear!
Look, your God comes to avenge;
with divine retribution he comes to deliver you."
5 Then blind eyes will open,
deaf ears will hear.
6 Then the lame will leap like a deer,
the mute tongue will shout for joy;
for water will burst forth in the wilderness,
streams in the arid rift valley.
7 The dry soil will become a pool of water,
the parched ground springs of water.
Where jackals once lived and sprawled out,
grass, reeds, and papyrus will grow.
8 A thoroughfare will be there—
it will be called the Way of Holiness.
The unclean will not travel on it;
it is reserved for those authorized to use it—
fools will not stray into it.
9 No lions will be there,
no ferocious wild animals will be on it—
they will not be found there.
Those delivered from bondage will travel on it,
10 those whom the LORD has ransomed will return that way.
They will enter Zion with a happy shout.
Unending joy will crown them,
happiness and joy will overwhelm them;
grief and suffering will disappear.

36:1–22 "What is your source of confidence?" Reader, this is an important question. "I trust," says the Christian, "in a triune God. I trust the Father, believing that he has chosen me from before the foundations of the world; I trust him to bring me home to his own house where the many mansions are. I trust the Son to take away all my sins by his own sacrifice and to adorn me with his perfect righteousness. And I trust the Holy Spirit—he has begun to save me from my inbred sins; I trust him to drive them all out." Happy are you, reader, if this confidence is yours!

CHARLES SPURGEON
(1834–1892)
MORNING AND EVENING

SENNACHERIB INVADES JUDAH

36 In the fourteenth year of King Hezekiah's reign, King Sennacherib of Assyria marched up against all the fortified
cities of Judah and captured them. [2]The king of Assyria sent
his chief adviser from Lachish to King Hezekiah in Jerusalem,
along with a large army. The chief adviser stood at the conduit
of the upper pool that is located on the road to the field where
they wash and dry cloth. [3]Eliakim son of Hilkiah, the palace
supervisor, accompanied by Shebna the scribe and Joah son
of Asaph, the secretary, went out to meet him.

[4]The chief adviser said to them, "Tell Hezekiah: 'This is what
the great king, the king of Assyria, says: "What is your source of
confidence? [5]Your claim to have a strategy and military strength
is just empty talk. In whom are you trusting, that you would
dare to rebel against me? [6]Look, you must be trusting in Egypt,
that splintered reed staff. If someone leans on it for support,
it punctures his hand and wounds him. That is what Pharaoh
king of Egypt does to all who trust in him! [7]Perhaps you will
tell me, 'We are trusting in the LORD our God.' But Hezekiah
is the one who eliminated his high places and altars and then
told the people of Judah and Jerusalem, 'You must worship at
this altar.' [8]Now make a deal with my master the king of Assyria, and I will give you 2,000 horses, provided you can find
enough riders for them. [9]Certainly you will not refuse one of
my master's minor officials and trust in Egypt for chariots and

horsemen. 10Furthermore it was by the command of the LORD
that I marched up against this land to destroy it. The LORD told
me, 'March up against this land and destroy it!'"'"
11Eliakim, Shebna, and Joah said to the chief adviser, "Speak
to your servants in Aramaic, for we understand it. Don't speak
with us in the Judahite dialect in the hearing of the people who
are on the wall." 12But the chief adviser said, "My master did not
send me to speak these words only to your master and to you. His
message is also for the men who sit on the wall, for they will eat
their own excrement and drink their own urine along with you!"
13The chief adviser then stood there and called out loudly in
the Judahite dialect, "Listen to the message of the great king, the
king of Assyria. 14This is what the king says: 'Don't let Hezekiah
mislead you, for he is not able to rescue you! 15Don't let Hezekiah
talk you into trusting in the LORD by saying, "The LORD will certainly rescue us; this city will not be handed over to the king of
Assyria." 16Don't listen to Hezekiah!' For this is what the king of
Assyria says, 'Send me a token of your submission and surrender
to me. Then each of you may eat from his own vine and fig tree
and drink water from his own cistern, 17until I come and take
you to a land just like your own—a land of grain and new wine,
a land of bread and vineyards. 18Hezekiah is misleading you
when he says, "The LORD will rescue us." Have any of the gods
of the nations rescued their lands from the power of the king of
Assyria? 19Where are the gods of Hamath and Arpad? Where are
the gods of Sepharvaim? Indeed, did any gods rescue Samaria
from my power? 20Who among all the gods of these lands have
rescued their lands from my power? So how can the LORD rescue Jerusalem from my power?'" 21They were silent and did
not respond, for the king had ordered, "Don't respond to him."
22Eliakim son of Hilkiah, the palace supervisor, accompanied
by Shebna the scribe and Joah son of Asaph, the secretary, went
to Hezekiah with their clothes torn and reported to him what
the chief adviser had said.

37 When King Hezekiah heard this, he tore his clothes, put
on sackcloth, and went to the LORD's temple. 2Eliakim the
palace supervisor, Shebna the scribe, and the leading priests,
clothed in sackcloth, sent this message to the prophet Isaiah
son of Amoz: 3"This is what Hezekiah says: 'This is a day of distress, insults, and humiliation, as when a baby is ready to leave
the birth canal but the mother lacks the strength to push it
through. 4Perhaps the LORD your God will hear all these things
the chief adviser has spoken on behalf of his master, the king of
Assyria, who sent him to taunt the living God. When the LORD
your God hears, perhaps he will punish him for the things he
has said. So pray for this remnant that remains.'"
5When King Hezekiah's servants came to Isaiah, 6Isaiah said
to them, "Tell your master this: 'This is what the LORD has said:
"Don't be afraid because of the things you have heard—these
insults the king of Assyria's servants have hurled against me.
7Look, I will take control of his mind; he will receive a report
and return to his own land. I will cut him down with a sword
in his own land."'"
8When the chief adviser heard the king of Assyria had departed from Lachish, he left and went to Libnah, where the king was
campaigning. 9The king heard that King Tirhakah of Ethiopia
was marching out to fight him. He again sent messengers to
Hezekiah, ordering them: 10"Tell King Hezekiah of Judah this:
'Don't let your God in whom you trust mislead you when he says,

37:6–20 Against the blasphemies of King Sennacherib, Hezekiah's customary armory failed. So he went back to the temple and opened his letter before the Lord. Previously he was silent, for he did not dare to open his mouth in the temple for fear of the Lord. Now, however, because he had already heard Isaiah saying, "Don't be afraid because of the things you have heard—these insults the king of Assyria's servants have hurled against me," and so on, he beseeched the Lord boldly and claimed that the Lord alone is the living God. It also postulates vengeance, that through this opportunity all kingdoms would recognize that there is only one God, who is able to deliver his own from peril.

JEROME **(C. 342–420)**
COMMENTARY ON ISAIAH

"Jerusalem will not be handed over to the king of Assyria." [11]Cer-
tainly you have heard how the kings of Assyria have annihilated
all lands. Do you really think you will be rescued? [12]Were the nations whom my predecessors destroyed—the nations of Gozan,
Haran, Rezeph, and the people of Eden in Telassar—rescued by
their gods? [13]Where is the king of Hamath or the king of Arpad
or the kings of Lair, Sepharvaim, Hena, and Ivvah?'"

[14]Hezekiah took the letter from the messengers and read it.
Then Hezekiah went up to the LORD's temple and spread it out
before the LORD. [15]Hezekiah prayed before the LORD: [16]"O LORD
of Heaven's Armies, O God of Israel, who is enthroned on the
cherubim! You alone are God over all the kingdoms of the earth.
You made the sky and the earth. [17]Pay attention, LORD, and
hear! Open your eyes, LORD, and observe! Listen to this entire
message Sennacherib sent and how he taunts the living God!
[18]It is true, LORD, that the kings of Assyria have destroyed all
the nations and their lands. [19]They have burned the gods of
the nations, for they are not really gods, but only the product
of human hands manufactured from wood and stone. That is
why the Assyrians could destroy them. [20]Now, O LORD our God,
rescue us from his power, so all the kingdoms of the earth may
know that you alone are the LORD."

[21]Isaiah son of Amoz sent this message to Hezekiah: "This
is what the LORD God of Israel has said: 'As to what you have
prayed to me concerning King Sennacherib of Assyria, [22]this
is what the LORD says about him:

"'The virgin daughter Zion
despises you—she makes fun of you;
daughter Jerusalem
shakes her head after you.

[23] "'Whom have you taunted and hurled insults at?
At whom have you shouted
and looked so arrogantly?
At the Holy One of Israel!
[24] Through your messengers you taunted the Lord,
"With my many chariots I climbed up
the high mountains,
the slopes of Lebanon.
I cut down its tall cedars
and its best evergreens.
I invaded its remotest regions,
its thickest woods.
[25] I dug wells
and drank water.
With the soles of my feet I dried up
all the rivers of Egypt."'

[26] "Certainly you must have heard!
Long ago I worked it out,
in ancient times I planned it,
and now I am bringing it to pass.
The plan is this:
Fortified cities will crash
into heaps of ruins.
[27] Their residents are powerless;
they are terrified and ashamed.
They are as short-lived as plants in the field
or green vegetation.

37:14-20 Against the blasphemies of King Sennacherib, Hezekiah's customary armory failed. So he went back to the temple and opened his letter before the Lord. Previously he was silent, for he did not dare to open his mouth in the temple for fear of the Lord. Now, however, because he had already heard Isaiah saying, "Don't be afraid because of the things you have heard—those insults the king of Assyria's servants have hurled against me," and so on, he beseeched the Lord boldly and claimed that the Lord alone is the living God. He also postulates vengeance, that through this opportunity all kingdoms would recognize that there is only one God who is able to deliver his own from evil.

JEROME (c. 342–420)
COMMENTARY ON ISAIAH

They are as short-lived as grass on the rooftops
when it is scorched by the east wind.
28 I know where you live
and everything you do
and how you rage against me.
29 Because you rage against me
and the uproar you create has reached my ears,
I will put my hook in your nose,
and my bit between your lips,
and I will lead you back
the way you came.

30"This will be your reminder that I have spoken the truth:
This year you will eat what grows wild, and next year what grows
on its own. But the year after that you will plant seed and harvest
crops; you will plant vines and consume their produce. 31Those
who remain in Judah will take root in the ground and bear fruit.
32 "For a remnant will leave Jerusalem;
survivors will come out of Mount Zion.
The zeal of the LORD of Heaven's Armies will
accomplish this.

33 "So this is what the LORD says about the king of Assyria:
"'He will not enter this city,
nor will he shoot an arrow here.
He will not attack it with his shielded warriors,
nor will he build siege works against it.
34 He will go back the way he came—
he will not enter this city,' says the LORD.
35 I will shield this city and rescue it
for the sake of my reputation and because of my
promise to David my servant."

36The angel of the LORD went out and killed 185,000 troops
in the Assyrian camp. When they got up early the next morning,
there were all the corpses! 37So King Sennacherib of Assyria
broke camp and went on his way. He went home and stayed in
Nineveh. 38One day, as he was worshiping in the temple of his
god Nisroch, his sons Adrammelech and Sharezer struck him
down with the sword. They ran away to the land of Ararat; his
son Esarhaddon replaced him as king.

THE LORD HEARS HEZEKIAH'S PRAYER

38 In those days Hezekiah was stricken with a terminal illness. The prophet Isaiah son of Amoz visited him and
told him, "This is what the LORD says, 'Give instructions to
your household, for you are about to die; you will not get well.'"
2Hezekiah turned his face to the wall and prayed to the LORD,
3"Please, LORD. Remember how I have served you faithfully and
with wholehearted devotion, and how I have carried out your
will." Then Hezekiah wept bitterly.
4The LORD's message came to Isaiah, 5"Go and tell Hezekiah:
'This is what the LORD God of your ancestor David says: "I have
heard your prayer; I have seen your tears. Look, I will add 15
years to your life. 6I will also rescue you and this city from the
king of Assyria. I will shield this city."'" 7Isaiah replied, "This is
your sign from the LORD confirming that the LORD will do what
he has said: 8Look, I will make the shadow go back 10 steps on
the stairs of Ahaz." And then the shadow went back 10 steps.

38:1–22 Hezekiah had been at the brink of the grave. A serious view of death is the way to get just thoughts of the mercy of life and to have access to being useful for God in the world. This speaks of a high esteem of God and his service. This will be to a spiritual person in a spiritual frame the most desirable thing in life: to praise or glorify God in the world, to speak of the perfections of his nature and show forth the praises of him who has called us to the advancement of his kingdom here under the sun.

THOMAS BOSTON (1676–1732)
THE COMPLETE WORKS

HEZEKIAH'S SONG OF THANKS

9 This is the prayer of King Hezekiah of Judah when he was sick
and then recovered from his illness:

10 "I thought,
'In the middle of my life I must walk through the gates
of Sheol,
I am deprived of the rest of my years.'

11 "I thought,
'I will no longer see the LORD in the land of the living,
I will no longer look on humankind with the
inhabitants of the world.
12 My dwelling place is removed and taken away from me
as a shepherd's tent.
I rolled up my life like a weaver rolls cloth;
from the loom he cuts me off.
You turn day into night and end my life.
13 I cry out until morning;
like a lion he shatters all my bones;
you turn day into night and end my life.
14 Like a swallow or a thrush I chirp,
I coo like a dove;
my eyes grow tired from looking up to the sky.
O Lord, I am oppressed;
help me!
15 What can I say?
He has decreed and acted.
I will walk slowly all my years because I am overcome
with grief.
16 O Lord, your decrees can give men life;
may years of life be restored to me.
Restore my health and preserve my life.'

17 "Look, the grief I experienced was for my benefit.
You delivered me from the Pit of oblivion.
For you removed all my sins from your sight.
18 Indeed Sheol does not give you thanks;
death does not praise you.
Those who descend into the Pit do not anticipate your
faithfulness.
19 The living person, the living person, he gives you
thanks,
as I do today.
A father tells his sons about your faithfulness.
20 The LORD is about to deliver me,
and we will celebrate with music
for the rest of our lives in the LORD's temple."

21 (Isaiah ordered, "Let them take a fig cake and apply it to the
ulcerated sore and he will get well." 22 Hezekiah said, "What is
the confirming sign that I will go up to the LORD's temple?")

MESSENGERS FROM BABYLON VISIT HEZEKIAH

39 At that time Merodach Baladan son of Baladan, king of
Babylon, sent letters and a gift to Hezekiah, for he heard
that Hezekiah had been ill and had recovered. 2 Hezekiah welcomed them and showed them his storehouse with its silver,
gold, spices, and high-quality olive oil, as well as his whole armory and everything in his treasuries. Hezekiah showed them

39:1–8 In the parable of the rich man, he flattered himself about the increase of his fields. But God said to him, "You fool! This very night your life will be demanded back from you, but who will get what you have prepared for yourself?" (Luke 12:20). It was the same way when King Hezekiah heard from Isaiah the sad doom of his kingdom after he had gloried before the envoys of Babylon in his treasures and the deposits of his precious things.

TERTULLIAN (155–C. 220)
AGAINST MARCION

everything in his palace and in his whole kingdom. [3]Isaiah the prophet visited King Hezekiah and asked him, "What did these men say? Where do they come from?" Hezekiah replied, "They come from the distant land of Babylon." [4]Isaiah asked, "What have they seen in your palace?" Hezekiah replied, "They have seen everything in my palace. I showed them everything in my treasuries." [5]Isaiah said to Hezekiah, "Listen to the message of the LORD of Heaven's Armies: [6]'Look, a time is coming when everything in your palace and the things your ancestors have accumulated to this day will be carried away to Babylon; nothing will be left,' says the LORD. [7]'Some of your very own descendants whom you father will be taken away and will be made eunuchs in the palace of the king of Babylon.'" [8]Hezekiah said to Isaiah, "The LORD's message that you have announced is appropriate." Then he thought, "For there will be peace and stability during my lifetime."

THE LORD RETURNS TO JERUSALEM

40 "Comfort, comfort my people,"
says your God.
2 "Speak kindly to Jerusalem and tell her
that her time of warfare is over,
that her punishment is completed.
For the LORD has made her pay double for all her sins."
3 A voice cries out,
"In the wilderness clear a way for the LORD;
build a level road through the rift valley for our God.
4 Every valley must be elevated
and every mountain and hill leveled.
The rough terrain will become a level plain,
the rugged landscape a wide valley.
5 The splendor of the LORD will be revealed,
and all people will see it at the same time.
For the LORD has decreed it."
6 A voice says, "Cry out!"
Another asks, "What should I cry out?"
The first voice responds: "All people are like grass,
and all their promises are like the flowers in the field.
7 The grass dries up,
the flowers wither,
when the wind sent by the LORD blows on them.
Surely humanity is like grass.
8 The grass dries up,
the flowers wither,
but the decree of our God is forever reliable."
9 Go up on a high mountain, O herald Zion.
Shout out loudly, O herald Jerusalem!
Shout, don't be afraid!
Say to the towns of Judah,
"Here is your God!"
10 Look, the Sovereign LORD comes as a victorious
warrior;
his military power establishes his rule.
Look, his reward is with him;
his prize goes before him.
11 Like a shepherd he tends his flock;
he gathers up the lambs with his arm;
he carries them close to his heart;
he leads the ewes along.

40:1–8 The true consolation, the genuine comfort, and the real deliverance from the iniquities of humankind is the incarnation of our God and Savior. Now the first who acted as herald of this event was the inspired John the Baptist. As for John, whom the Pharisees asked whether he himself was the Christ, he declared on his part: "I am the voice of one shouting in the wilderness, 'Make straight the way for the Lord,' as the prophet Isaiah said" (John 1:23). *I am not God the Word but a voice, for it is as a herald that I am announcing God the Word, who is incarnate.* He has clearly shown by these terms the facility of the evangelical proclamation: Thanks to this facility, in a short time it filled the whole world.

THEODORET OF CYR
(C. 393–C. 458)
COMMENTARY ON ISAIAH

THE LORD IS INCOMPARABLE

12 Who has measured out the waters in the hollow of his hand,
or carefully measured the sky,
or carefully weighed the soil of the earth,
or weighed the mountains in a balance,
or the hills on scales?
13 Who comprehends the mind of the LORD,
or gives him instruction as his counselor?
14 From whom does he receive directions?
Who teaches him the correct way to do things,
or imparts knowledge to him,
or instructs him in skillful design?
15 Look, the nations are like a drop in a bucket;
they are regarded as dust on the scales.
He lifts the coastlands as if they were dust.
16 Not even Lebanon could supply enough firewood for a sacrifice;
its wild animals would not provide enough burnt offerings.
17 All the nations are insignificant before him;
they are regarded as absolutely nothing.
18 To whom can you compare God?
To what image can you liken him?
19 A craftsman casts an idol;
a metalsmith overlays it with gold
and forges silver chains for it.
20 To make a contribution one selects wood that will not rot;
he then seeks a skilled craftsman
to make an idol that will not fall over.
21 Do you not know?
Do you not hear?
Has it not been told to you since the very beginning?
Have you not understood from the time the earth's foundations were made?
22 He is the one who sits on the earth's horizon;
its inhabitants are like grasshoppers before him.
He is the one who stretches out the sky like a thin curtain,
and spreads it out like a pitched tent.
23 He is the one who reduces rulers to nothing;
he makes the earth's leaders insignificant.
24 Indeed, they are barely planted;
yes, they are barely sown;
yes, they barely take root in the earth,
and then he blows on them, causing them to dry up,
and the wind carries them away like straw.
25 "To whom can you compare me? Whom do I resemble?"
says the Holy One.
26 Look up at the sky!
Who created all these heavenly lights?
He is the one who leads out their ranks;
he calls them all by name.
Because of his absolute power and awesome strength,
not one of them is missing.
27 Why do you say, Jacob,
Why do you say, Israel,
"The LORD is not aware of what is happening to me;
my God is not concerned with my vindication"?

28 Do you not know?
Have you not heard?
The LORD is an eternal God,
the Creator of the whole earth.
He does not get tired or weary;
there is no limit to his wisdom.
29 He gives strength to those who are tired;
to the ones who lack power, he gives renewed energy.
30 Even youths get tired and weary;
even strong young men clumsily stumble.
31 But those who wait for the LORD's help find renewed strength;
they rise up as if they had eagles' wings,
they run without growing weary,
they walk without getting tired.

THE LORD CHALLENGES THE NATIONS

41 "Listen to me in silence, you coastlands!
Let the nations find renewed strength!
Let them approach and then speak;
let us come together for debate.
2 Who stirs up this one from the east?
Who officially commissions him for service?
He hands nations over to him
and enables him to subdue kings.
He makes them like dust with his sword,
like windblown straw with his bow.
3 He pursues them and passes by unharmed;
he advances with great speed.
4 Who acts and carries out decrees?
Who summons the successive generations from the beginning?
I, the LORD, am present at the very beginning,
and at the very end—I am the one.
5 The coastlands see and are afraid;
the whole earth trembles;
they approach and come.
6 They help one another;
one says to the other, 'Be strong!'
7 The craftsman encourages the metalsmith,
the one who wields the hammer encourages the one who pounds on the anvil.
He approves the quality of the welding,
and nails it down so it won't fall over.

THE LORD ENCOURAGES HIS PEOPLE

8 "You, my servant Israel,
Jacob, whom I have chosen,
offspring of Abraham my friend,
9 you whom I am bringing back from the earth's extremities
and have summoned from the remote regions—
I told you, 'You are my servant.'
I have chosen you and not rejected you.
10 Don't be afraid, for I am with you!
Don't be frightened, for I am your God!
I strengthen you—
yes, I help you—
yes, I uphold you with my victorious right hand!

41:1–20 God speaks with tenderness, "Don't be afraid, I am helping you"; he is not only within call but present with you. Are you weak? *I will strengthen you.* Are you in want of friends? *I will help you in the time of need.* Are you ready to fall? *I will uphold you with the right hand that is full of righteousness.* There are those who strive with God's people, who seek their ruin. Let not God's people render evil for evil but wait on God's time. Our way to heaven lies through the wilderness of this world. These blessings are kept for the poor in spirit who long for divine enlightening, pardon, and holiness. And God will render their barren souls fruitful in the grace of his Spirit, that all who behold may consider it.

MATTHEW HENRY (1662–1714)
COMMENTARY ON THE WHOLE BIBLE

11 Look, all who were angry at you will be ashamed and
humiliated;
your adversaries will be reduced to nothing and perish.
12 When you will look for your opponents, you will not
find them;
your enemies will be reduced to absolutely nothing.
13 For I am the LORD your God,
the one who takes hold of your right hand,
who says to you, 'Don't be afraid, I am helping you.'
14 Don't be afraid, despised, insignificant Jacob,
men of Israel.
I am helping you," says the LORD,
your Protector, the Holy One of Israel.
15 "Look, I am making you like a sharp threshing sledge,
new and double-edged.
You will thresh the mountains and crush them;
you will make the hills like straw.
16 You will winnow them and the wind will blow them
away;
the wind will scatter them.
You will rejoice in the LORD;
you will boast in the Holy One of Israel.
17 The oppressed and the poor look for water, but there is
none;
their tongues are parched from thirst.
I, the LORD, will respond to their prayers;
I, the God of Israel, will not abandon them.
18 I will make streams flow down the slopes
and produce springs in the middle of the valleys.
I will turn the wilderness into a pool of water
and the arid land into springs.
19 I will make cedars, acacias, myrtles, and olive trees grow
in the wilderness;
I will make evergreens, firs, and cypresses grow together
in the arid rift valley.
20 I will do this so people will observe and recognize,
so they will pay attention and understand
that the LORD's power has accomplished this,
and that the Holy One of Israel has brought it into
being.

THE LORD CHALLENGES THE PAGAN GODS

21 "Present your argument," says the LORD.
"Produce your evidence," says Jacob's King.
22 "Let them produce evidence! Let them tell us what will
happen!
Tell us about your earlier predictive oracles,
so we may examine them and see how they were
fulfilled.
Or decree for us some future events!
23 Predict how future events will turn out,
so we might know you are gods.
Yes, do something good or something bad,
so we might be frightened and in awe.
24 Look, you are nothing, and your accomplishments are
nonexistent;
the one who chooses to worship you is disgusting.
25 I have stirred up one out of the north and he advances,
one from the eastern horizon who prays in my name.

He steps on rulers as if they were clay,
like a potter treading the clay.
26 Who decreed this from the beginning, so we could know?
Who announced it ahead of time, so we could say, 'He's correct'?
Indeed, none of them decreed it.
Indeed, none of them announced it.
Indeed, no one heard you say anything!
27 I first decreed to Zion, 'Look, here's what will happen!'
I sent a herald to Jerusalem.
28 I look, but there is no one,
among them there is no one who serves as an adviser
that I might ask questions and receive answers.
29 Look, all of them are nothing,
their accomplishments are nonexistent;
their metal images lack any real substance.

THE LORD COMMISSIONS HIS SPECIAL SERVANT

42 "Here is my servant whom I support,
my chosen one in whom I take pleasure.
I have placed my Spirit on him;
he will make just decrees for the nations.
2 He will not cry out or shout;
he will not publicize himself in the streets.
3 A crushed reed he will not break,
a dim wick he will not extinguish;
he will faithfully make just decrees.
4 He will not grow dim or be crushed
before establishing justice on the earth;
the coastlands will wait in anticipation for his decrees."
5 This is what the true God, the LORD, says—
the one who created the sky and stretched it out,
the one who fashioned the earth and everything that lives on it,
the one who gives breath to the people on it,
and life to those who live on it:
6 "I, the LORD, officially commission you;
I take hold of your hand.
I protect you and make you a covenant mediator for people
and a light to the nations,
7 to open blind eyes,
to release prisoners from dungeons,
those who live in darkness from prisons.

THE LORD INTERVENES

8 "I am the LORD! That is my name!
I will not share my glory with anyone else
or the praise due me with idols.
9 Look, my earlier predictive oracles have come to pass;
now I announce new events.
Before they begin to occur,
I reveal them to you."

10 Sing to the LORD a brand new song!
Praise him from the horizon of the earth,
you who go down to the sea and everything that lives in it,
you coastlands and those who live there.

42:1–4 The prophet foretells the coming of the Messiah. "Here is my servant," *whom I will enable to do and suffer all those things that belong to his office, chosen by me to do this great work.* "In whom I take pleasure," *both for himself and for all his people, being fully satisfied with that sacrifice that he shall offer up to me.* He shall publish or show the law, will, and counsel of God concerning people's salvation, not only to the Jews, but also to the heathen nations. Christ will establish "justice on the earth"—the law of God or the doctrine of the gospel, which he will bring forth with or according to truth, that is, truly and faithfully.

JOHN WESLEY (1703–1791)
EXPLANATORY NOTES ON THE BIBLE

11 Let the wilderness and its cities shout out,
the towns where the nomads of Kedar live.
Let the residents of Sela shout joyfully;
let them shout loudly from the mountaintops.
12 Let them give the LORD the honor he deserves;
let them praise his deeds in the coastlands.
13 The LORD emerges like a hero,
like a warrior he inspires himself for battle;
he shouts, yes, he yells,
he shows his enemies his power.
14 "I have been inactive for a long time;
I kept quiet and held back.
Like a woman in labor I groan;
I pant and gasp.
15 I will make the trees on the mountains and hills wither up;
I will dry up all their vegetation.
I will turn streams into islands
and dry up pools of water.
16 I will lead the blind along an unfamiliar way;
I will guide them down paths they have never traveled.
I will turn the darkness in front of them into light
and level out the rough ground.
This is what I will do for them.
I will not abandon them.
17 Those who trust in idols
will turn back and be utterly humiliated,
those who say to metal images, 'You are our gods.'

THE LORD REASONS WITH HIS PEOPLE

18 "Listen, you deaf ones!
Take notice, you blind ones!
19 My servant is truly blind,
my messenger is truly deaf.
My covenant partner, the servant of the LORD, is truly blind.
20 You see many things, but don't comprehend;
their ears are open, but do not hear."
21 The LORD wanted to exhibit his justice
by magnifying his law and displaying it.
22 But these people are looted and plundered;
all of them are trapped in pits
and held captive in prisons.
They were carried away as loot with no one to rescue them;
they were carried away as plunder, and no one says,
"Bring that back!"
23 Who among you will pay attention to this?
Who will listen attentively in the future?
24 Who handed Jacob over to the robber?
Who handed Israel over to the looters?
Was it not the LORD, against whom we sinned?
They refused to follow his commands;
they disobeyed his law.
25 So he poured out his fierce anger on them,
along with the devastation of war.
Its flames encircled them, but they did not realize it;
it burned against them, but they did not take it to heart.

THE LORD WILL RESCUE HIS PEOPLE

43 Now, this is what the LORD says,
the one who created you, O Jacob,
and formed you, O Israel:
"Don't be afraid, for I will protect you.
I call you by name, you are mine.
2 When you pass through the waters, I am with you;
when you pass through the streams, they will not
overwhelm you.
When you walk through the fire, you will not be burned;
the flames will not harm you.
3 For I am the LORD your God,
the Holy One of Israel, your deliverer.
I have handed over Egypt as a ransom price,
Ethiopia and Seba in place of you.
4 Since you are precious and special in my sight
and I love you,
I will hand over people in place of you,
nations in place of your life.
5 Don't be afraid, for I am with you.
From the east I will bring your descendants;
from the west I will gather you.
6 I will say to the north, 'Hand them over!'
and to the south, 'Don't hold any back!'
Bring my sons from distant lands,
and my daughters from the remote regions of the earth,
7 everyone who belongs to me,
whom I created for my glory,
whom I formed—yes, whom I made."

THE LORD DECLARES HIS SOVEREIGNTY

8 Bring out the people who are blind, even though they
have eyes,
those who are deaf, even though they have ears!
9 All nations gather together,
the peoples assemble.
Who among them announced this?
Who predicted earlier events for us?
Let them produce their witnesses to testify they were
right;
let them listen and affirm, "It is true."
10 "You are my witnesses," says the LORD,
"my servant whom I have chosen
so that you may consider and believe in me,
and understand that I am he.
No god was formed before me,
and none will outlive me.
11 I, I am the LORD,
and there is no deliverer besides me.
12 I decreed and delivered and proclaimed,
and there was no other god among you.
You are my witnesses," says the LORD, "that I am God.
13 From this day forward I am he;
no one can deliver from my power;
I will act, and who can prevent it?"

THE LORD WILL DO SOMETHING NEW

14 This is what the LORD says,
your Protector, the Holy One of Israel:

43:10–11 God exists, and his essence is incomprehensible. Those who believe in sacred scripture have no doubt that he is one and not several. And through the mouth of the prophet Isaiah: "No god was formed before me, and none will outlive me. I, I am," he says, "the LORD, and there is no deliverer besides me." The divinity is perfect and without deficiency in goodness or wisdom or power. He is without beginning, without end, eternal, uncircumscribed; to put it simply, he is perfect in all things.

JOHN OF DAMASCUS
(C. 675–749)
AN EXACT EXPOSITION OF THE ORTHODOX FAITH

"For your sake I send to Babylon
and make them all fugitives,
turning the Babylonians' joyful shouts into mourning
songs.
15 I am the LORD, your Holy One,
the one who created Israel, your King."
16 This is what the LORD says,
the one who made a road through the sea,
a pathway through the surging waters,
17 the one who led chariots and horses to destruction,
together with a mighty army.
They fell down, never to rise again;
they were extinguished, put out like a burning wick:
18 "Don't remember these earlier events;
don't recall these former events.

19 "Look, I am about to do something new.
Now it begins to happen! Do you not recognize it?
Yes, I will make a road in the wilderness
and paths in the wastelands.
20 The wild animals honor me,
the jackals and ostriches,
because I put water in the wilderness
and streams in the wastelands
to quench the thirst of my chosen people,
21 the people whom I formed for myself,
so they might praise me.

THE LORD REBUKES HIS PEOPLE

22 "But you did not call for me, O Jacob;
you did not long for me, O Israel.
23 You did not bring me lambs for your burnt offerings;
you did not honor me with your sacrifices.
I did not burden you with offerings;
I did not make you weary by demanding incense.
24 You did not buy me aromatic reeds;
you did not present to me the fat of your sacrifices.
Yet you burdened me with your sins;
you made me weary with your evil deeds.
25 I, I am the one who blots out your rebellious deeds for
my sake;
your sins I do not remember.
26 Remind me of what happened. Let's debate!
You, prove to me that you are right!
27 The father of your nation sinned;
your spokesmen rebelled against me.
28 So I defiled your holy princes,
and handed Jacob over to destruction,
and subjected Israel to humiliating abuse.

THE LORD WILL RENEW ISRAEL

44 "Now, listen, Jacob my servant,
Israel whom I have chosen!"
2 This is what the LORD, the one who made you, says—
the one who formed you in the womb and helps you:
"Don't be afraid, my servant Jacob,
Jeshurun, whom I have chosen.
3 For I will pour water on the parched ground
and cause streams to flow on the dry land.

I will pour my Spirit on your offspring
and my blessing on your children.
4 They will sprout up like a tree in the grass,
like poplars beside channels of water.
5 One will say, 'I belong to the LORD,'
and another will use the name 'Jacob.'
One will write on his hand, 'The LORD's,'
and use the name 'Israel.'"

THE ABSURDITY OF IDOLATRY

6 This is what the LORD, Israel's King, says,
their Protector, the LORD of Heaven's Armies:
"I am the first and I am the last,
there is no God but me.
7 Who is like me? Let him make his claim!
Let him announce it and explain it to me—
since I established an ancient people—
let them announce future events.
8 Don't panic! Don't be afraid!
Did I not tell you beforehand and decree it?
You are my witnesses! Is there any God but me?
There is no other sheltering rock; I know of none.
9 All who form idols are nothing;
the things in which they delight are worthless.
Their witnesses cannot see;
they recognize nothing, so they are put to shame.
10 Who forms a god and casts an idol
that will prove worthless?
11 Look, all his associates will be put to shame;
the craftsmen are mere humans.
Let them all assemble and take their stand.
They will panic and be put to shame.
12 A blacksmith works with his tool
and forges metal over the coals.
He forms it with hammers;
he makes it with his strong arm.
He gets hungry and loses his energy;
he drinks no water and gets tired.
13 A carpenter takes measurements;
he marks out an outline of its form;
he scrapes it with chisels
and marks it with a compass.
He patterns it after the human form,
like a well-built human being,
and puts it in a shrine.
14 He cuts down cedars
and acquires a cypress or an oak.
He gets trees from the forest;
he plants a cedar and the rain makes it grow.
15 A man uses it to make a fire;
he takes some of it and warms himself.
Yes, he kindles a fire and bakes bread.
Then he makes a god and worships it;
he makes an idol and bows down to it.
16 Half of it he burns in the fire—
over that half he cooks meat;
he roasts a meal and fills himself.
Yes, he warms himself and says,
'Ah! I am warm as I look at the fire.'

44:9–20 The prophet teaches that the Creator gave the forests and woods on the mountains to supply food and fuel and for the sake of human bodies. They, however, take a holm oak, an oak, or a cedar that God has planted and watered to create gods. If it is a god, Isaiah says, the whole of the wood should be divine. Is not the wood that is put into the fire of the same kind as that you worship? How therefore can you cast aside the one and adore the other? Foolishness has mastered them; they have lost the faculty of reasoning and are slaves to folly. This is why I will put my Spirit on your descendants, so that they will be delivered from error, for in no other way can they receive the truth.

THEODORET OF CYR
(C. 393–C. 458)
COMMENTARY ON ISAIAH

17 With the rest of it he makes a god, his idol;
he bows down to it and worships it.
He prays to it, saying,
'Rescue me, for you are my god!'
18 They do not comprehend or understand,
for their eyes are blind and cannot see;
their minds do not discern.
19 No one thinks to himself,
nor do they comprehend or understand and say to themselves:
'I burned half of it in the fire—
yes, I baked bread over the coals;
I roasted meat and ate it.
With the rest of it should I make a disgusting idol?
Should I bow down to dry wood?'
20 He feeds on ashes;
his deceived mind misleads him.
He cannot rescue himself,
nor does he say, 'Is this not a false god I hold in my right hand?'
21 Remember these things, O Jacob,
O Israel, for you are my servant.
I formed you to be my servant;
O Israel, I will not forget you!
22 I remove the guilt of your rebellious deeds as if they were a cloud,
the guilt of your sins as if they were a cloud.
Come back to me, for I protect you."
23 Shout for joy, O sky, for the LORD intervenes;
shout out, you subterranean regions of the earth.
O mountains, give a joyful shout;
you too, O forest and all your trees!
For the LORD protects Jacob;
he reveals his splendor through Israel.

THE LORD EMPOWERS CYRUS

24 This is what the LORD, your Protector, says,
the one who formed you in the womb:
"I am the LORD, who made everything,
who alone stretched out the sky,
who fashioned the earth all by myself,
25 who frustrates the omens of the empty talkers
and humiliates the omen readers,
who overturns the counsel of the wise men
and makes their advice seem foolish,
26 who fulfills the oracles of his prophetic servants
and brings to pass the announcements of his messengers,
who says about Jerusalem, 'She will be inhabited,'
and about the towns of Judah, 'They will be rebuilt,
her ruins I will raise up,'
27 who says to the deep sea, 'Be dry!
I will dry up your sea currents,'
28 who commissions Cyrus, the one I appointed as shepherd
to carry out all my wishes
and to decree concerning Jerusalem, 'She will be rebuilt,'
and concerning the temple, 'It will be reconstructed.'

45 "This is what the LORD says to his chosen one,
to Cyrus, whose right hand I hold
in order to subdue nations before him
and disarm kings,
to open doors before him
so gates remain unclosed:

2 'I will go before you
and level mountains.
Bronze doors I will shatter
and iron bars I will hack through.
3 I will give you hidden treasures,
riches stashed away in secret places,
so you may recognize that I am the LORD,
the one who calls you by name, the God of Israel.
4 For the sake of my servant Jacob,
Israel, my chosen one,
I call you by name
and give you a title of respect, even though you do not submit to me.
5 I am the LORD, I have no peer,
there is no God but me.
I arm you for battle, even though you do not recognize me.
6 I do this so people will recognize from east to west
that there is no God but me;
I am the LORD, I have no peer.
7 I am the one who forms light
and creates darkness;
the one who brings about peace
and creates calamity.
I am the LORD, who accomplishes all these things.
8 O sky, rain down from above!
Let the clouds send down showers of deliverance!
Let the earth absorb it so salvation may grow
and deliverance may sprout up along with it.
I, the LORD, create it.'"

THE LORD GIVES A WARNING

9 One who argues with his Creator is in grave danger,
one who is like a mere shard among the other shards on the ground!
The clay should not say to the potter,
"What in the world are you doing?
Your work lacks skill!"
10 Danger awaits one who says to his father,
"What in the world are you fathering?"
and to his mother,
"What in the world are you bringing forth?"
11 This is what the LORD says,
the Holy One of Israel, the one who formed him,
concerning things to come:
"How dare you question me about my children!
How dare you tell me what to do with the work of my own hands!
12 I made the earth;
I created the people who live on it.
It was me—my hands stretched out the sky.
I give orders to all the heavenly lights.

45:2 Let us not fear punishment. By this faith we shall escape punishment. This is the correct attitude of the servants of God. For if those who were brought up under the old dispensation, when death was not yet slain, before his "bronze doors" or "iron bars" so nobly encountered their end, how destitute of all defense or excuse shall we be if, after having had the benefit of such great grace, we attain not even to the same measure of virtue as they did.

CHRYSOSTOM (C. 347–407)
HOMILIES ON STATUTES

13 It is me—I stir him up and commission him;
I will make all his ways level.
He will rebuild my city;
he will send my exiled people home,
but not for a price or a bribe,"
says the LORD of Heaven's Armies.

THE LORD IS THE NATIONS' ONLY HOPE

14 This is what the LORD says:
"The profit of Egypt and the revenue of Ethiopia,
along with the Sabeans, those tall men,
will be brought to you and become yours.
They will walk behind you, coming along in chains.
They will bow down to you
and pray to you:
'Truly God is with you; he has no peer;
there is no other God!'"
15 Yes, you are a God who keeps hidden,
O God of Israel, deliverer!
16 They will all be ashamed and embarrassed;
those who fashion idols will all be humiliated.
17 Israel will be delivered once and for all by the LORD;
you will never again be ashamed or humiliated.
18 For this is what the LORD says,
the one who created the sky—
he is the true God,
the one who formed the earth and made it;
he established it,
he did not create it without order,
he formed it to be inhabited:
"I am the LORD, I have no peer.
19 I have not spoken in secret,
in some hidden place.
I did not tell Jacob's descendants,
'Seek me in vain!'
I am the LORD,
the one who speaks honestly,
who makes reliable announcements.
20 Gather together and come!
Approach together, you refugees from the nations.
Those who carry wooden idols know nothing,
those who pray to a god that cannot deliver.
21 Tell me! Present the evidence!
Let them consult with one another.
Who predicted this in the past?
Who announced it beforehand?
Was it not I, the LORD?
I have no peer, there is no God but me,
a God who vindicates and delivers;
there is none but me.
22 Turn to me so you can be delivered,
all you who live in the earth's remote regions!
For I am God, and I have no peer.
23 I solemnly make this oath—
what I say is true and reliable:
'Surely every knee will bow to me,
every tongue will solemnly affirm;
24 they will say about me,
"Yes, the LORD is a powerful deliverer."'"

All who are angry at him will cower before him.
25 All the descendants of Israel will be vindicated by the LORD
and will boast in him.

THE LORD CARRIES HIS PEOPLE

46 Bel kneels down,
Nebo bends low.
Their images weigh down animals and beasts.
Your heavy images are burdensome to tired animals.
2 Together they bend low and kneel down;
they are unable to rescue the images;
they themselves head off into captivity.
3 "Listen to me, O family of Jacob,
all you who are left from the family of Israel,
you who have been carried from birth,
you who have been supported from the time you left the womb.
4 Even when you are old, I will take care of you,
even when you have gray hair, I will carry you.
I made you and I will support you;
I will carry you and rescue you.
5 To whom can you compare and liken me?
Tell me whom you think I resemble, so we can be compared!
6 Those who empty out gold from a purse
and weigh out silver on the scale
hire a metalsmith, who makes it into a god.
They then bow down and worship it.
7 They put it on their shoulder and carry it;
they put it in its place and it just stands there;
it does not move from its place.
Even when someone cries out to it, it does not reply;
it does not deliver him from his distress.
8 Remember this, so you can be brave.
Think about it, you rebels!
9 Remember what I accomplished in antiquity.
Truly I am God, I have no peer;
I am God, and there is none like me,
10 who announces the end from the beginning
and reveals beforehand what has not yet occurred;
who says, 'My plan will be realized,
I will accomplish what I desire;'
11 who summons an eagle from the east,
from a distant land, one who carries out my plan.
Yes, I have decreed,
yes, I will bring it to pass;
I have formulated a plan,
yes, I will carry it out.
12 Listen to me, you stubborn people,
you who distance yourselves from doing what is right.
13 I am bringing my deliverance near, it is not far away;
I am bringing my salvation near, it does not wait.
I will save Zion;
I will adorn Israel with my splendor.

46:1–13 These idols are imitations that cannot save those who carry them and are nothing other than burdens for the priests and weigh them down to the point of exhaustion. And when captivity came, these were carried off first of all due to the value of the metals from which they were made, and they were not able to free the souls of those carrying them. For it is not as dumb imitations they had a life and any feeling of pain, but they are figuratively ascribed soul and body parts though having none. So it could be said that this error of idolatry was the greatest burden among the nations, one that pressed its worshipers down into the ground and could not save and, in fact, made their souls captive to the devil and his demons.

JEROME (C. 342–420)
COMMENTARY ON ISAIAH

JOHN HUS:

BOHEMIAN PRE-REFORMATION REFORMER

c. 1369–1415

John Hus has been called a Reformer before the Reformation and rightly so. Following the lead of another ecclesial reformer, John Wycliffe, Hus fought against abuses in the church, took aim at the church's hierarchy, and preached sermons throughout Czechoslovakia and Germany calling for reform.

Born in Bohemia around 1369, as a young person he traveled to Prague where he earned multiple degrees at the University of Prague, serving as rector and dean of faculty after graduating. While there he garnered a large following of Bohemians known as Hussites, who shared his concerns for the needs of lay Christians and for addressing abuses by the church leadership. His criticisms closely mirror those of another scourge of the Catholic Church of the time, John Wycliffe, whose writings had made their way to Bohemia.

From 1414 to 1418, the Council of Constance met primarily to address a schism in the Catholic Church that had resulted in competing papacies. But this council also addressed the teachings of Wycliffe and Hus. Pope Leo condemned Hus's teachings, saying: "Very great offense is given to God from the prolonged and manifold heresy of the Bohemians, and scandal is cause to the Christian people." The council condemned his teachings as "notoriously heretical," arguing that they had "long ago been rejected and condemned by holy fathers and by general councils."

What had Hus taught that was so troublesome? Much of the controversy stemmed from his doctrine of the church. Hus argued "there is only one holy universal church, which is the total number of those predestined to salvation." In short, his view identified the "church" not with the institutional structure visible on earth but the invisible, spiritual community of God's people—which challenged the existing ecclesial hierarchy. He also challenged the pope, agreeing with Wycliffe that it was Christ alone, not the vicar of Christ, who was the head of the church. "Peter neither was nor is the head of the holy catholic church," he said. Furthermore, Hus claimed that "the papal dignity originated with the emperor, and the primacy and institution of the pope emanated from imperial power," suggesting that the papacy came from the state rather than directly from God.

On July 5, 1415, the council condemned Hus to death and burned him at the stake the next day. Reportedly he said, "You are now roasting a goose, but God will awaken a swan whom you will not burn or roast." And indeed, Hus's efforts for reform did not die with him but found new life a hundred years later in Wittenberg, Germany.

IMPORTANT WORKS

THE CHURCH

THE LETTERS OF JOHN HUS

BABYLON WILL FALL

47 "Fall down! Sit in the dirt,
O virgin daughter Babylon!
Sit on the ground, not on a throne,
O daughter of the Babylonians!
Indeed, you will no longer be called delicate and pampered.
2 Pick up millstones and grind flour.
Remove your veil,
strip off your skirt,
expose your legs,
cross the streams.
3 Let your naked body be exposed.
Your shame will be on display!
I will get revenge;
I will not have pity on anyone,"
4 says our Protector—
the LORD of Heaven's Armies is his name,
the Holy One of Israel.
5 "Sit silently! Go to a hiding place,
O daughter of the Babylonians!
Indeed, you will no longer be called 'Queen of kingdoms.'
6 I was angry at my people;
I defiled my special possession
and handed them over to you.
You showed them no mercy;
you even placed a very heavy burden on old people.
7 You said,
'I will rule forever as permanent queen!'
You did not think about these things;
you did not consider how it would turn out.
8 So now, listen to this,
O one who lives so lavishly,
who lives securely,
who says to herself,
'I am unique! No one can compare to me!
I will never have to live as a widow;
I will never lose my children.'
9 Both of these will come upon you
suddenly, in one day!
You will lose your children and be widowed.
You will be overwhelmed by these tragedies,
despite your many incantations
and your numerous amulets.
10 You were complacent in your evil deeds;
you thought, 'No one sees me.'
Your self-professed wisdom and knowledge lead you astray,
when you say, 'I am unique! No one can compare to me!'
11 Disaster will overtake you;
you will not know how to charm it away.
Destruction will fall on you;
you will not be able to appease it.
Calamity will strike you suddenly,
before you recognize it.
12 Persist in trusting your amulets
and your many incantations,
which you have faithfully recited since your youth!

47:4 Can Babylon be destroyed? Babylon is strong, who shall bring down her power? Yes, there is one who can do it. Here then we have this glorious title of the Lord for the comfort of his people in their distress and the terror of their enemies in their pride: the "LORD of Heaven's Armies." This title is in itself a very fearful one first because all creatures in heaven and in earth are his armies. He is the absolute great Lord over them all. Second, in regard to that special providence of God in the great affairs of wars and battles in the world: The providence of God is great in all wars, but especially in those wars that concern his people. I do not know any one thing wherein the providence of God is more fully set out in scripture than in the workings of it about wars.

JEREMIAH BURROUGHS
(1599–1646)
THE GLORIOUS NAME OF GOD THE LORD OF HOSTS

Maybe you will be successful—
maybe you will scare away disaster.
13 You are tired out from listening to so much advice.
Let them take their stand—
the ones who see omens in the sky,
who gaze at the stars,
who make monthly predictions—
let them rescue you from the disaster that is about to
overtake you!
14 Look, they are like straw
that the fire burns up;
they cannot rescue themselves
from the heat of the flames.
There are no coals to warm them,
no firelight to enjoy.
15 They will disappoint you,
those you have so faithfully dealt with since your youth.
Each strays off in his own direction,
leaving no one to rescue you."

THE LORD APPEALS TO THE EXILES

48 Listen to this, O family of Jacob,
you who are called by the name "Israel,"
and are descended from Judah,
who take oaths in the name of the LORD
and invoke the God of Israel—
but not in an honest and just manner.
2 Indeed, they live in the holy city;
they trust in the God of Israel,
whose name is the LORD of Heaven's Armies.
3 "I announced events beforehand,
I issued the decrees and made the predictions;
suddenly I acted and they came to pass.
4 I did this because I know how stubborn you are.
Your neck muscles are like iron
and your forehead like bronze.
5 I announced them to you beforehand;
before they happened, I predicted them for you,
so you could never say,
'My image did these things,
my idol, my cast image, decreed them.'
6 You have heard; now look at all the evidence!
Will you not admit that what I say is true?
From this point on I am announcing to you new events
that are previously unrevealed and you do not know
about.
7 Now they come into being, not in the past;
before today you did not hear about them,
so you could not say,
'Yes, I know about them.'
8 You did not hear,
you do not know,
you were not told beforehand.
For I know that you are very deceitful;
you were labeled a rebel from birth.
9 For the sake of my reputation I hold back my anger;
for the sake of my prestige I restrain myself from
destroying you.
10 Look, I have refined you, but not as silver;

48:4 Perchance he will say to me, who is not reformed even by blows, I know that you are obstinate and your neck is an iron sinew, and for nothing comes correction from heaven and the scourges. As I once reprimanded you by the mouth of Jeremiah: "The process of refining them has proved useless. The wicked have not been purged" (Jer 6:29). May it not be that I should ever, among other chastisements, be thus approached by him who is good, and yet by my own contrariness continue to walk against his goodness. This causes God to walk against me in fury.

GREGORY OF NAZIANZUS
(C. 329–390)
ON HIS FATHER'S SILENCE

I have purified you in the furnace of misery.
11 For my sake alone I will act,
for how can I allow my name to be defiled?
I will not share my glory with anyone else!
12 Listen to me, O Jacob,
Israel, whom I summoned.
I am the one;
I am present at the very beginning
and at the very end.
13 Yes, my hand founded the earth;
my right hand spread out the sky.
I summon them;
they stand together.
14 All of you, gather together and listen!
Who among them announced these things?
The LORD's ally will carry out his desire against Babylon;
he will exert his power against the Babylonians.
15 I, I have spoken—
yes, I have summoned him;
I lead him and he will succeed.
16 Approach me—listen to this!
From the very first I have not spoken in secret;
when it happens, I am there."
So now, the Sovereign LORD has sent me, accompanied by his Spirit.
17 This is what the LORD, your Protector, says,
the Holy One of Israel:
"I am the LORD your God,
who teaches you how to succeed,
who leads you in the way you should go.
18 If only you had obeyed my commandments,
prosperity would have flowed to you like a river,
deliverance would have come to you like the waves of the sea.
19 Your descendants would have been as numerous as sand
and your children like its granules.
Their name would not have been cut off
and eliminated from my presence.
20 Leave Babylon!
Flee from the Babylonians!
Announce it with a shout of joy!
Make this known—
proclaim it throughout the earth!
Say, 'The LORD protects his servant Jacob.
21 They do not thirst as he leads them through dry regions;
he makes water flow out of a rock for them;
he splits open a rock and water flows out.'
22 There will be no prosperity for the wicked," says the LORD.

DELIVERY OF THE EXILES

49 Listen to me, you coastlands!
Pay attention, you people who live far away!
The LORD summoned me from birth;
he commissioned me when my mother brought me into the world.

2 He made my mouth like a sharp sword,
he hid me in the hollow of his hand;
he made me like a sharpened arrow,
he hid me in his quiver.
3 He said to me, "You are my servant,
Israel, through whom I will reveal my splendor."
4 But I thought, "I have worked in vain;
I have expended my energy for absolutely nothing."
But the LORD will vindicate me;
my God will reward me.
5 So now the LORD says,
the one who formed me from birth to be his servant—
he did this to restore Jacob to himself,
so that Israel might be gathered to him;
and I will be honored in the LORD's sight,
for my God is my source of strength—
6 he says, "Is it too insignificant a task for you to be my servant,
to reestablish the tribes of Jacob,
and restore the remnant of Israel?
I will make you a light to the nations,
so you can bring my deliverance to the remote regions of the earth."
7 This is what the LORD,
the Protector of Israel, their Holy One, says
to the one who is despised and rejected by nations,
a servant of rulers:
"Kings will see and rise in respect,
princes will bow down,
because of the faithful LORD,
the Holy One of Israel who has chosen you."

8 This is what the LORD says:
"At the time I decide to show my favor, I will respond to you;
in the day of deliverance I will help you;
I will protect you and make you a covenant mediator for people,
to rebuild the land
and to reassign the desolate property.
9 You will say to the prisoners, 'Come out,'
and to those who are in dark dungeons, 'Emerge.'
They will graze beside the roads;
on all the slopes they will find pasture.
10 They will not be hungry or thirsty;
the sun's oppressive heat will not beat down on them,
for one who has compassion on them will guide them;
he will lead them to springs of water.
11 I will make all my mountains into a road;
I will construct my roadways."
12 Look, they come from far away!
Look, some come from the north and west,
and others from the land of Sinim.
13 Shout for joy, O sky!
Rejoice, O earth!
Let the mountains give a joyful shout!
For the LORD consoles his people
and shows compassion to the oppressed.

THE LORD REMEMBERS ZION

14 "Zion said, 'The LORD has abandoned me,
the Lord has forgotten me.'
15 Can a woman forget her baby who nurses at her breast?
Can she withhold compassion from the child she has borne?
Even if mothers were to forget,
I could never forget you!
16 Look, I have inscribed your name on my palms;
your walls are constantly before me.
17 Your children hurry back,
while those who destroyed and devastated you depart.
18 Look all around you!
All of them gather to you.
As surely as I live," says the LORD,
"you will certainly wear all of them like jewelry;
you will put them on as if you were a bride.
19 Yes, your land lies in ruins;
it is desolate and devastated.
But now you will be too small to hold your residents,
and those who devoured you will be far away.
20 Yet the children born during your time of bereavement
will say within your hearing,
'This place is too cramped for us,
make room for us so we can live here.'
21 Then you will think to yourself,
'Who bore these children for me?
I was bereaved and barren,
dismissed and divorced.
Who raised these children?
Look, I was left all alone;
where did these children come from?'"

22 This is what the Sovereign LORD says:
"Look I will raise my hand to the nations;
I will raise my signal flag to the peoples.
They will bring your sons in their arms
and carry your daughters on their shoulders.
23 Kings will be your children's guardians;
their princesses will nurse your children.
With their faces to the ground they will bow down to you,
and they will lick the dirt on your feet.
Then you will recognize that I am the LORD;
those who wait patiently for me are not put to shame.
24 Can spoils be taken from a warrior,
or captives be rescued from a conqueror?
25 Indeed," says the LORD,
"captives will be taken from a warrior;
spoils will be rescued from a conqueror.
I will oppose your adversary
and I will rescue your children.
26 I will make your oppressors eat their own flesh;
they will get drunk on their own blood, as if it were wine.
Then all humankind will recognize that
I am the LORD, your Deliverer,
your Protector, the Powerful One of Jacob."

49:14–26 God's love is not only unchangeable but also unfailing. In Isaiah we read: "Can a woman forget her baby who nurses at her breast? Can she withhold compassion from the child she has borne?" The strongest human love that we know of is a mother's love. A mother's love endures through all. But let me tell you that no mother's love is to be compared with the love of God; it does not measure the height or the depth of God's love. Think of the love that God must have had when he gave his Son to die for the world. It seems to me as if it required more love for the Father to give his Son than for the Son to die. Oh, the love that God must have had for the world when he gave his Son to die for it!

D. L. MOODY (1837–1899)
THE WAY TO GOD AND HOW TO FIND IT

50 This is what the LORD says:
"Where is your mother's divorce certificate
by which I divorced her?
Or to which of my creditors did I sell you?
Look, you were sold because of your sins;
because of your rebellious acts I divorced your mother.
2 Why does no one challenge me when I come?
Why does no one respond when I call?
Is my hand too weak to deliver you?
Do I lack the power to rescue you?
Look, with a mere shout I can dry up the sea;
I can turn streams into a desert,
so the fish rot away and die
from lack of water.
3 I can clothe the sky in darkness;
I can cover it with sackcloth."

THE SERVANT PERSEVERES

4 The Sovereign LORD has given me the capacity to be his spokesman,
so that I know how to help the weary.
He wakes me up every morning;
he makes me alert so I can listen attentively as disciples do.
5 The Sovereign LORD has spoken to me clearly;
I have not rebelled,
I have not turned back.
6 I offered my back to those who attacked,
my jaws to those who tore out my beard;
I did not hide my face
from insults and spitting.
7 But the Sovereign LORD helps me,
so I am not humiliated.
For that reason I am steadfastly resolved;
I know I will not be put to shame.
8 The one who vindicates me is close by.
Who dares to argue with me? Let us confront each other!
Who is my accuser? Let him challenge me!
9 Look, the Sovereign LORD helps me.
Who dares to condemn me?
Look, all of them will wear out like clothes;
a moth will eat away at them.
10 Who among you fears the LORD?
Who obeys his servant?
Whoever walks in deep darkness,
without light,
should trust in the name of the LORD
and rely on his God.
11 Look, all of you who start a fire
and who equip yourselves with flaming arrows,
walk in the light of the fire you started
and among the flaming arrows you ignited!
This is what you will receive from me:
You will lie down in a place of pain.

THERE IS HOPE FOR THE FUTURE

51 "Listen to me, you who pursue godliness,
who seek the LORD.
Look at the rock from which you were chiseled,

50:6–9 Our Lord and Savior Jesus Christ comes before us when he would show people how to suffer, who when he was struck bore it patiently, being reviled he reviled not again, when he suffered he threatened not, but he gave his back to the attackers and his cheeks to buffetings, and he turned not his face from spitting. And at last he was willingly led to death that we might behold in him the image of all that is virtuous and immortal, and that we, conducting ourselves after these examples, might truly tread on serpents and scorpions and on all the power of the enemy.

ATHANASIUS (C. 296–373)
LETTERS

at the quarry from which you were dug.
2 Look at Abraham, your father,
and Sarah, who gave you birth.
When I summoned him, he was a lone individual,
but I blessed him and gave him numerous descendants.
3 Certainly the LORD will console Zion;
he will console all her ruins.
He will make her wilderness like Eden,
her arid rift valley like the garden of the LORD.
Happiness and joy will be restored to her,
thanksgiving and the sound of music.
4 Pay attention to me, my people.
Listen to me, my people!
For I will issue a decree,
I will make my justice a light to the nations.
5 I am ready to vindicate,
I am ready to deliver,
I will establish justice among the nations.
The coastlands wait patiently for me;
they wait in anticipation for the revelation of my power.
6 Look up at the sky.
Look at the earth below.
For the sky will dissipate like smoke,
and the earth will wear out like clothes;
its residents will die like gnats.
But the deliverance I give is permanent;
the vindication I provide will not disappear.
7 Listen to me, you who know what is right,
you people who are aware of my law.
Don't be afraid of the insults of men;
don't be discouraged because of their abuse.
8 For a moth will eat away at them like clothes;
a clothes moth will devour them like wool.
But the vindication I provide will be permanent;
the deliverance I give will last."
9 Wake up! Wake up!
Clothe yourself with strength, O arm of the LORD!
Wake up as in former times, as in antiquity.
Did you not smash the Proud One?
Did you not wound the sea monster?
10 Did you not dry up the sea,
the waters of the great deep?
Did you not make a path through the depths of the sea,
so those delivered from bondage could cross over?
11 Those whom the LORD has ransomed will return;
they will enter Zion with a happy shout.
Unending joy will crown them,
happiness and joy will overwhelm them;
grief and suffering will disappear.
12 "I, I am the one who consoles you.
Why are you afraid of mortal men,
of mere human beings who are as short-lived as grass?
13 Why do you forget the LORD, who made you,
who stretched out the sky
and founded the earth?
Why do you constantly tremble all day long
at the anger of the oppressor,
when he makes plans to destroy?
Where is the anger of the oppressor?

14 The one who suffers will soon be released;
he will not die in prison,
he will not go hungry.
15 I am the LORD your God,
who churns up the sea so that its waves surge.
The LORD of Heaven's Armies is his name!

ZION'S TIME TO CELEBRATE

16 "I commission you as my spokesman;
I cover you with the palm of my hand
to establish the sky and to found the earth,
to say to Zion, 'You are my people.'"
17 Wake up! Wake up!
Get up, O Jerusalem!
You drank from the cup the LORD passed to you,
which was full of his anger.
You drained dry
the goblet full of intoxicating wine.
18 There was no one to lead her
among all the children she bore;
there was no one to take her by the hand
among all the children she raised.
19 These double disasters confronted you.
But who feels sorry for you?
Destruction and devastation,
famine and sword.
But who consoles you?
20 Your children faint;
they lie at the head of every street
like an antelope in a snare.
They are left in a stupor by the LORD's anger,
by the battle cry of your God.
21 So listen to this, oppressed one,
who is drunk, but not from wine.
22 This is what your Sovereign LORD, even your God who
judges his people says:
"Look, I have removed from your hand
the cup of intoxicating wine,
the goblet full of my anger.
You will no longer have to drink it.
23 I will put it into the hand of your tormentors
who said to you, 'Lie down, so we can walk over you.'
You made your back like the ground
and like the street for those who walked over you."

51:17–23 Fury is in proportion to transgressions, even though God abates to all some of what is their due and dilutes with compassion the unmixed draught of his wrath. For he inclines from severity to indulgence toward those who accept chastisement with fear and who after a slight affliction conceive and are in pain with conversion and bring forth the perfect spirit of salvation. But he nevertheless reserves the dregs, the last drop of his anger, that he may pour it out entire on those who, instead of being healed by his kindness, grow obdurate like the hard-hearted Pharaoh.

GREGORY OF NAZIANZUS
(C. 329–390)
ON HIS FATHER'S SILENCE

52 Wake up! Wake up!
Clothe yourself with strength, O Zion!
Put on your beautiful clothes,
O Jerusalem, holy city.
For uncircumcised and unclean pagans
will no longer invade you.
2 Shake off the dirt!
Get up, captive Jerusalem.
Take off the iron chains around your neck,
O captive daughter Zion.

3 For this is what the LORD says:
"You were sold for nothing,
and you will not be redeemed for money."

[4]For this is what the Sovereign LORD says:
"In the beginning my people went to live temporarily
in Egypt;
Assyria oppressed them for no good reason.
5 And now, what do we have here?" says the LORD.
"Indeed my people have been carried away for nothing,
those who rule over them taunt," says the LORD,
"and my name is constantly slandered all day long.
6 For this reason my people will know my name;
for this reason they will know at that time that I am the
one who says,
'Here I am.'"
7 How delightful it is to see approaching over the mountains
the feet of a messenger who announces peace,
a messenger who brings good news, who announces
deliverance,
who says to Zion, "Your God reigns!"
8 Listen, your watchmen shout;
in unison they shout for joy,
for they see with their very own eyes
the LORD's return to Zion.
9 In unison give a joyful shout,
O ruins of Jerusalem!
For the LORD consoles his people;
he protects Jerusalem.
10 The LORD reveals his royal power
in the sight of all the nations;
the entire earth sees
our God deliver.
11 Leave! Leave! Get out of there!
Don't touch anything unclean!
Get out of it!
Stay pure, you who carry the LORD's holy items.
12 Yet do not depart quickly
or leave in a panic.
For the LORD goes before you;
the God of Israel is your rear guard.

THE LORD WILL VINDICATE HIS SERVANT

13 Look, my servant will succeed!
He will be elevated, lifted high, and greatly exalted—
14 (just as many were horrified by the sight of you)
he was so disfigured he no longer looked like a man;
his form was so marred he no longer looked human—
15 so now he will startle many nations.
Kings will be shocked by his exaltation,
for they will witness something unannounced to them,
and they will understand something they had not
heard about.

53 Who would have believed what we just heard?
When was the LORD's power revealed through him?
2 He sprouted up like a twig before God,
like a root out of parched soil;
he had no stately form or majesty that might catch our
attention,
no special appearance that we should want to follow him.
3 He was despised and rejected by people,
one who experienced pain and was acquainted with
illness;

52:13—53:12 As a sheep he is led to the slaughter, but he is the Shepherd of Israel and now of the whole world also. As a Lamb he is silent, yet he is the Word and is proclaimed by the voice of one crying in the wilderness. He is bruised and wounded, but he heals every disease and every infirmity. He is lifted up and nailed to the tree, but by the tree of life he restores us, yes, he saves even the robber crucified with him. He dies, but he gives life, and by his death he destroys death. He is buried, but he rises again; he goes down into hell, but he brings up the souls; he ascends to heaven and shall come again to judge the living and the dead.

GREGORY OF NAZIANZUS
(C. 329–390)
ON THE SON

people hid their faces from him;
he was despised, and we considered him insignificant.
4 But he lifted up our illnesses,
he carried our pain;
even though we thought he was being punished,
attacked by God, and afflicted for something he had done.
5 He was wounded because of our rebellious deeds,
crushed because of our sins;
he endured punishment that made us well;
because of his wounds we have been healed.
6 All of us had wandered off like sheep;
each of us had strayed off on his own path,
but the LORD caused the sin of all of us to attack him.
7 He was treated harshly and afflicted,
but he did not even open his mouth.
Like a lamb led to the slaughtering block,
like a sheep silent before her shearers,
he did not even open his mouth.
8 He was led away after an unjust trial—
but who even cared?
Indeed, he was cut off from the land of the living;
because of the rebellion of his own people he was wounded.
9 They intended to bury him with criminals,
but he ended up in a rich man's tomb
because he had committed no violent deeds,
nor had he spoken deceitfully.
10 Though the LORD desired to crush him and make him ill,
once restitution is made,
he will see descendants and enjoy long life,
and the LORD's purpose will be accomplished through him.
11 Having suffered, he will reflect on his work,
he will be satisfied when he understands what he has done.
"My servant will acquit many,
for he carried their sins.
12 So I will assign him a portion with the multitudes,
he will divide the spoils of victory with the powerful,
because he willingly submitted to death
and was numbered with the rebels,
when he lifted up the sin of many
and intervened on behalf of the rebels."

ZION WILL BE SECURE

54 "Shout for joy, O barren one who has not given birth!
Give a joyful shout and cry out, you who have not been in labor!
For the children of the desolate one are more numerous
than the children of the married woman," says the LORD.
2 Make your tent larger,
stretch your tent curtains farther out!
Spare no effort,
lengthen your ropes,
and pound your stakes deep.

54:1–8 Jesus the Redeemer is altogether ours and ours forever. All the offices of Christ are held on our behalf. He is King for us, Priest for us, and Prophet for us. Whenever we read a new title of the Redeemer, let us appropriate him as ours under that name as much as under any other. He blushes not to acknowledge himself our Lord Jesus Christ, though he is the blessed and only Potentate, the King of kings, and Lord of lords. Christ everywhere and every way is our Christ, forever and ever most richly to enjoy. O my soul, by the power of the Holy Spirit call him this day your Redeemer.

CHARLES SPURGEON
(1834–1892)
MORNING AND EVENING

3 For you will spread out to the right and to the left;
your children will conquer nations
and will resettle desolate cities.
4 Don't be afraid, for you will not be put to shame.
Don't be intimidated, for you will not be humiliated.
You will forget about the shame you experienced in
your youth;
you will no longer remember the disgrace of your
abandonment.
5 For your husband is the one who made you—
the LORD of Heaven's Armies is his name.
He is your Protector, the Holy One of Israel.
He is called "God of the entire earth."
6 "Indeed, the LORD will call you back
like a wife who has been abandoned and suffers from
depression,
like a young wife when she has been rejected," says your
God.
7 "For a short time I abandoned you,
but with great compassion I will gather you.
8 In a burst of anger I rejected you momentarily,
but with lasting devotion I will have compassion on
you,"
says your Protector, the LORD.
9 "As far as I am concerned, this is like in Noah's time,
when I vowed that the waters of Noah's flood would
never again cover the earth.
In the same way I have vowed that I will not be angry at
you or shout at you.
10 Even if the mountains are removed
and the hills displaced,
my devotion will not be removed from you,
nor will my covenant of friendship be displaced,"
says the LORD, the one who has compassion on you.
11 "O afflicted one, driven away, and unconsoled!
Look, I am about to set your stones in antimony
and lay your foundation with lapis lazuli.
12 I will make your pinnacles out of gems,
your gates out of beryl,
and your outer wall out of beautiful stones.
13 All your children will be followers of the LORD,
and your children will enjoy great prosperity.
14 You will be reestablished when I vindicate you.
You will not experience oppression;
indeed, you will not be afraid.
You will not be terrified,
for nothing frightening will come near you.
15 If anyone dares to challenge you, it will not be my
doing!
Whoever tries to challenge you will be defeated.
16 Look, I create the craftsman,
who fans the coals into a fire
and forges a weapon.
I create the destroyer so he might devastate.
17 No weapon forged to be used against you will succeed;
you will refute everyone who tries to accuse you.
This is what the LORD will do for his servants—
I will vindicate them,"
says the LORD.

THE LORD GIVES AN INVITATION

55 "Hey, all who are thirsty, come to the water!
You who have no money, come!
Buy and eat!
Come! Buy wine and milk
without money and without cost.
2 Why pay money for something that will not nourish you?
Why spend your hard-earned money on something that will not satisfy?
Listen carefully to me and eat what is nourishing!
Enjoy fine food.
3 Pay attention and come to me.
Listen, so you can live.
Then I will make an unconditional covenantal promise to you,
just like the reliable covenantal promises I made to David.
4 Look, I made him a witness to nations,
a ruler and commander of nations."
5 Look, you will summon nations you did not previously know;
nations that did not previously know you will run to you,
because of the LORD your God,
the Holy One of Israel,
for he bestows honor on you.
6 Seek the LORD while he makes himself available;
call to him while he is nearby!
7 The wicked need to abandon their lifestyle
and sinful people their plans.
They should return to the LORD, and he will show mercy to them,
and to their God, for he will freely forgive them.
8 "Indeed, my plans are not like your plans,
and my deeds are not like your deeds," says the LORD,
9 "for just as the sky is higher than the earth,
so my deeds are superior to your deeds
and my plans superior to your plans.
10 The rain and snow fall from the sky
and do not return,
but instead water the earth
and make it produce and yield crops,
and provide seed for the planter and food for those who must eat.
11 In the same way, the promise that I make
does not return to me, having accomplished nothing.
No, it is realized as I desire
and is fulfilled as I intend."
12 Indeed you will go out with joy;
you will be led along in peace;
the mountains and hills will give a joyful shout before you,
and all the trees in the field will clap their hands.
13 Evergreens will grow in place of thornbushes;
firs will grow in place of nettles;
they will be a monument to the LORD,
a permanent reminder that will remain.

55:1–13 To whom this offer is made? It is to everyone thirsty and penniless. People who know what it is they sorely need are blessed. Those who feel only dimly that they need something and do not know that it is God are condemned to wander in a dry and thirsty land where no water is and where their hearts gape, parched and cracked like the soil upon which they tread. Understand your thirst. Interpret your desires aright. Open your eyes to your need and be sure of this, that mountains of money, the clearest insight into intellectual problems, fame, love, family, a happy home, and an abundance of all things that you can desire will leave a central, aching emptiness that nothing and no person but God can ever fill. Oh, that we all knew what these yearnings of our hearts mean!

ALEXANDER MACLAREN
(1826–1910)
EXPOSITIONS OF THE HOLY SCRIPTURES

THE LORD INVITES OUTSIDERS TO ENTER

56 This is what the LORD says,
"Promote justice! Do what is right!
For I am ready to deliver you;
I am ready to vindicate you openly.
2 The people who do this will be blessed,
the people who commit themselves to obedience,
who observe the Sabbath and do not defile it,
who refrain from doing anything that is wrong.
3 No foreigner who becomes a follower of the LORD
should say,
'The LORD will certainly exclude me from his people.'
The eunuch should not say,
'Look, I am like a dried-up tree.'"

4 For this is what the LORD says:
"For the eunuchs who observe my Sabbaths
and choose what pleases me
and are faithful to my covenant,
5 I will set up within my temple and my walls a
monument
that will be better than sons and daughters.
I will set up a permanent monument for them that will
remain.
6 As for foreigners who become followers of the LORD
and serve him,
who love the name of the LORD and want to be his
servants—
all who observe the Sabbath and do not defile it,
and who are faithful to my covenant—
7 I will bring them to my holy mountain;
I will make them happy in the temple where people
pray to me.
Their burnt offerings and sacrifices will be accepted on
my altar,
for my temple will be known as a temple where all
nations may pray."
8 The Sovereign LORD says this,
the one who gathers the dispersed of Israel:
"I will still gather them up."

THE LORD DENOUNCES ISRAEL'S PAGANISM

9 All you wild animals in the fields, come and devour,
all you wild animals in the forest!
10 All their watchmen are blind,
they are unaware.
All of them are like mute dogs,
unable to bark.
They pant, lie down,
and love to snooze.
11 The dogs have big appetites;
they are never full.
They are shepherds who have no understanding;
they all go their own way,
each one looking for monetary gain.
12 Each one says,
"Come on, I'll get some wine!
Let's guzzle some beer!
Tomorrow will be just like today!

56:1–8 Now, instead of sacrifices we offer to God praises, thanksgivings, good works, and finally ourselves. When he declares that they shall be acceptable, let us not imagine that this arises from their own value or excellence but from God's undeserved kindness. For he might justly reject them if he looked at them in themselves. This ought to excite in us a strong desire to worship God when we see that our works, which are of no value, are accepted by God as if they had been pure sacrifices.

JOHN CALVIN (1509–1564)
COMPLETE COMMENTARY ON THE BIBLE

We'll have everything we want!"

57 The godly perish,
but no one cares.
Honest people disappear,
when no one minds
that the godly disappear because of evil.
2 Those who live uprightly enter a place of peace;
they rest on their beds.

3 "But approach, you sons of omen readers,
you offspring of adulteresses and prostitutes!
4 At whom are you laughing?
At whom are you opening your mouth
and sticking out your tongue?
You are the children of rebels,
the offspring of liars,
5 you who inflame your lusts among the oaks and under every green tree,
who slaughter children near the streams under the rocky overhangs.
6 Among the smooth stones of the stream are the idols you love;
they, they are the object of your devotion.
You pour out liquid offerings to them,
you make an offering.
Because of these things how can I relent from judgment?
7 On every high, elevated hill you prepare your bed;
you go up there to offer sacrifices.
8 Behind the door and doorpost you put your symbols.
Indeed, you depart from me and go up
and invite them into bed with you.
You purchase favors from them;
you love their bed,
and gaze longingly on their naked bodies.
9 You take olive oil as tribute to your king,
along with many perfumes.
You send your messengers to a distant place;
you go all the way to Sheol.
10 Because of the long distance you must travel, you get tired,
but you do not say, 'I give up.'
You get renewed energy,
so you don't collapse.
11 Whom are you worried about?
Whom do you fear, that you would act so deceitfully
and not remember me
or think about me?
Because I have been silent for so long,
you are not afraid of me.
12 I will denounce your so-called righteousness and your deeds,
but they will not help you.
13 When you cry out for help, let your idols help you!
The wind blows them all away,
a breeze carries them away.
But the one who looks to me for help will inherit the land
and will have access to my holy mountain."

14 He says,
"Build it! Build it! Clear a way!
Remove all the obstacles out of the way of my people!"
15 For this is what the high and exalted one says,
the one who rules forever, whose name is holy:
"I dwell in an exalted and holy place,
but also with the discouraged and humiliated,
in order to cheer up the humiliated
and to encourage the discouraged.
16 For I will not be hostile forever
or perpetually angry,
for then man's spirit would grow faint before me,
the life-giving breath I created.
17 I was angry because of their sinful greed;
I attacked them and angrily rejected them,
yet they remained disobedient and stubborn.
18 I have seen their behavior,
but I will heal them. I will lead them,
and I will provide comfort to them and those who
mourn with them.
19 I am the one who gives them reason to celebrate.
Complete prosperity is available both to those who are
far away and those who are nearby,"
says the LORD, "and I will heal them.
20 But the wicked are like a surging sea
that is unable to be quiet;
its waves toss up mud and sand.
21 There will be no prosperity," says my God, "for the
wicked."

57:15 The blessed prophets, when the Lord of the universe promises what is great and godly to them, were filled with much wonder at his glory and mercy and, as if responding from excitement, they ran to give praise. We find the prophet doing precisely that here. The Lord says these things but has to add "exalted," that is, he who is by nature over and above all things that have come to be. "I dwell in an exalted and holy place" means again that he is in the unshakeable upper reaches and that this divine and lofty nature is in the inexpressible transcendence that is above.

CYRIL OF ALEXANDRIA
(C. 376–444)
COMMENTARY ON ISAIAH

THE LORD DESIRES GENUINE DEVOTION

58 "Shout loudly! Don't be quiet!
Yell as loudly as a trumpet!
Confront my people with their rebellious deeds;
confront Jacob's family with their sin.
2 They seek me day after day;
they want to know my requirements,
like a nation that does what is right
and does not reject the law of their God.
They ask me for just decrees;
they want to be near God.
3 They lament, 'Why don't you notice when we fast?
Why don't you pay attention when we humble
ourselves?'
Look, at the same time you fast, you satisfy your selfish
desires,
you oppress your workers.
4 Look, your fasting is accompanied by arguments,
brawls,
and fistfights.
Do not fast as you do today,
trying to make your voice heard in heaven.
5 Is this really the kind of fasting I want?
Do I want a day when people merely humble
themselves,
bowing their heads like a reed
and stretching out on sackcloth and ashes?
Is this really what you call a fast,
a day that is pleasing to the LORD?

58:1–5 We are commanded to cry out and to cry forcefully and not to spare our voice, lest we lose our salvation. "Shout loudly! Don't be quiet!" Isaiah says. That is, do not pass over sinners' wickedness by keeping silent and by being considerate of their shame but inconsiderate of their well-being, for by keeping silent you have made worse the wounds that you ought to have healed by crying out. A trumpet is necessary for sinners; it not only penetrates their ears but should strike their hearts as well; it should not delight with its melody but chastise when it has been heard; it should encourage the bravehearted to righteousness while it should turn the cowardly from their crimes.

MAXIMUS OF TURIN
(C. 380–C. 465)
SERMONS

6 No, this is the kind of fast I want:
I want you to remove the sinful chains,
to tear away the ropes of the burdensome yoke,
to set free the oppressed,
and to break every burdensome yoke.
7 I want you to share your food with the hungry
and to provide shelter for homeless, oppressed people.
When you see someone naked, clothe them!
Don't turn your back on your own flesh and blood.
8 Then your light will shine like the sunrise;
your restoration will quickly arrive;
your godly behavior will go before you,
and the LORD's splendor will be your rear guard.
9 Then you will call out, and the LORD will respond;
you will cry out, and he will reply, 'Here I am.'
You must remove the burdensome yoke from among you
and stop pointing fingers and speaking sinfully.
10 You must actively help the hungry
and feed the oppressed.
Then your light will dispel the darkness,
and your darkness will be transformed into noonday.
11 The LORD will continually lead you;
he will feed you even in parched regions.
He will give you renewed strength,
and you will be like a well-watered garden,
like a spring that continually produces water.
12 Your perpetual ruins will be rebuilt;
you will reestablish the ancient foundations.
You will be called, 'The one who repairs broken walls,
the one who makes the streets inhabitable again.'
13 You must observe the Sabbath
rather than doing anything you please on my holy day.
You must look forward to the Sabbath
and treat the LORD's holy day with respect.
You must treat it with respect by refraining from your normal activities
and by refraining from your selfish pursuits and from making business deals.
14 Then you will find joy in your relationship to the LORD,
and I will give you great prosperity,
and cause crops to grow on the land I gave to your ancestor Jacob."
Know for certain that the LORD has spoken.

INJUSTICE BRINGS ALIENATION FROM GOD

59 Look, the LORD's hand is not too weak to deliver you;
his ear is not too deaf to hear you.
2 But your sinful acts have alienated you from your God;
your sins have caused him to reject you and not listen to your prayers.
3 For your hands are stained with blood
and your fingers with sin;
your lips speak lies,
your tongue utters malicious words.
4 No one is concerned about justice;
no one sets forth his case truthfully.
They depend on false words and tell lies;
they conceive of oppression
and give birth to sin.

5 They hatch the eggs of a poisonous snake
and spin a spider's web.
Whoever eats their eggs will die,
a poisonous snake is hatched.
6 Their webs cannot be used for clothing;
they cannot cover themselves with what they make.
Their deeds are sinful;
they commit violent crimes.
7 They are eager to do evil,
quick to shed innocent blood.
Their thoughts are sinful;
they crush and destroy.
8 They are unfamiliar with peace;
their deeds are unjust.
They use deceitful methods,
and whoever deals with them is unfamiliar with peace.

ISRAEL CONFESSES ITS SIN

9 For this reason deliverance is far from us
and salvation does not reach us.
We wait for light, but see only darkness;
we wait for a bright light, but live in deep darkness.
10 We grope along the wall like the blind,
we grope like those who cannot see;
we stumble at noontime as if it were evening.
Though others are strong, we are like dead men.
11 We all growl like bears,
we coo mournfully like doves;
we wait for deliverance, but there is none,
for salvation, but it is far from us.
12 For you are aware of our many rebellious deeds,
and our sins testify against us;
indeed, we are aware of our rebellious deeds;
we know our sins all too well.
13 We have rebelled and tried to deceive the LORD;
we turned back from following our God.
We stir up oppression and rebellion;
we tell lies we concocted in our minds.
14 Justice is driven back;
godliness stands far off.
Indeed, honesty stumbles in the city square
and morality is not even able to enter.
15 Honesty has disappeared;
the one who tries to avoid evil is robbed.
The LORD watches and is displeased,
for there is no justice.

THE LORD INTERVENES

16 He sees there is no advocate;
he is shocked that no one intervenes.
So he takes matters into his own hands;
his desire for justice drives him on.
17 He wears his desire for justice like body armor,
and his desire to deliver is like a helmet on his head.
He puts on the garments of vengeance
and wears zeal like a robe.
18 He repays them for what they have done,
dispensing angry judgment to his adversaries
and punishing his enemies.

59:9–15 Isaiah puts their accusation categorically: "Honesty stumbles in the city square." It has vanished, he says, because deceit has veiled it. "And morality is not even able to enter." For they have not stopped taking the opposite route. He has shown how truth has departed: They did not want to consider their duty, he says, but they have distorted their intelligence so as not to understand what ought to be done and what is useful. "Honesty has disappeared; the one who tries to avoid evil is robbed." They have distanced themselves so far from the truth that they openly combat those who turn away from perversity and choose the good.

THEODORET OF CYR
(C. 393–C. 458)
COMMENTARY ON ISAIAH

He repays the coastlands.
19 In the west, people respect the LORD's reputation;
in the east they recognize his splendor.
For he comes like a rushing stream
driven on by wind sent from the LORD.
20 "A protector comes to Zion,
to those in Jacob who repent of their rebellious deeds,"
says the LORD.

21 "As for me, this is my promise to them," says the LORD.
"My Spirit, who is upon you, and my words, which I have placed
in your mouth, will not depart from your mouth or from the
mouths of your children and descendants from this time forward," says the LORD.

ZION'S FUTURE SPLENDOR

60 "Arise! Shine! For your light arrives!
The splendor of the LORD shines on you!
2 For, look, darkness covers the earth
and deep darkness covers the nations,
but the LORD shines on you;
his splendor appears over you.
3 Nations come to your light,
kings to your bright light.
4 Look all around you!
They all gather and come to you—
your sons come from far away,
and your daughters are escorted by guardians.
5 Then you will look and smile,
you will be excited and your heart will swell with pride.
For the riches of distant lands will belong to you,
and the wealth of nations will come to you.
6 Camel caravans will cover your roads,
young camels from Midian and Ephah.
All the merchants of Sheba will come,
bringing gold and incense
and singing praises to the LORD.
7 All the sheep of Kedar will be gathered to you;
the rams of Nebaioth will be available to you as
sacrifices.
They will go up on my altar acceptably,
and I will bestow honor on my majestic temple.
8 Who are these who float along like a cloud,
who fly like doves to their shelters?
9 Indeed, the coastlands look eagerly for me;
the large ships are in the lead,
bringing your sons from far away,
along with their silver and gold,
to honor the LORD your God,
the Holy One of Israel, for he has bestowed honor on
you.
10 Foreigners will rebuild your walls;
their kings will serve you.
Even though I struck you down in my anger,
I will restore my favor and have compassion on you.
11 Your gates will remain open at all times;
they will not be shut during the day or at night
so that the wealth of nations may be delivered,
with their kings leading the way.

60:1–18 Shine, shine, O new Jerusalem, for the glory of the Lord shines on you! Rejoice and be glad, O Zion! Christ is risen, and he has crushed death and raised the dead: Rejoice, therefore, O nations of the earth! Shine, shine, O new Jerusalem, for the glory of the Lord has risen over you. Cry out now and rejoice, O Zion; and you, the pure one, the Mother of God, exult in the resurrection of the one to whom you gave birth. On this day the whole creation rejoices and exults, for Christ is risen and hades plundered.

JOHN OF DAMASCUS
(C. 675–749)
THE CANON OF PASCHA

12 Indeed, nations or kingdoms that do not serve you will perish;
such nations will definitely be destroyed.
13 The splendor of Lebanon will come to you,
its evergreens, firs, and cypresses together,
to beautify my palace;
I will bestow honor on my throne room.
14 The children of your oppressors will come bowing to you;
all who treated you with disrespect will bow down at your feet.
They will call you, 'The City of the LORD,
Zion of the Holy One of Israel.'
15 You were once abandoned
and despised, with no one passing through,
but I will make you a permanent source of pride
and joy to coming generations.
16 You will drink the milk of nations;
you will nurse at the breasts of kings.
Then you will recognize that I, the LORD, am your Deliverer,
your Protector, the Powerful One of Jacob.
17 Instead of bronze, I will bring you gold;
instead of iron, I will bring you silver;
instead of wood, I will bring you bronze;
instead of stones, I will bring you iron.
I will make prosperity your overseer,
and vindication your sovereign ruler.
18 Sounds of violence will no longer be heard in your land,
or the sounds of destruction and devastation within your borders.
You will name your walls, 'Deliverance'
and your gates, 'Praise.'
19 The sun will no longer supply light for you by day,
nor will the moon's brightness shine on you;
the LORD will be your permanent source of light—
the splendor of your God will shine upon you.
20 Your sun will no longer set;
your moon will not disappear;
the LORD will be your permanent source of light;
your time of sorrow will be over.
21 All your people will be godly;
they will possess the land permanently.
I will plant them like a shoot;
they will be the product of my labor,
through whom I reveal my splendor.
22 The least of you will multiply into a thousand;
the smallest of you will become a large nation.
When the right time comes, I the LORD will quickly do this!"

THE LORD WILL REJUVENATE HIS PEOPLE

61 The Spirit of the Sovereign LORD is upon me,
because the LORD has chosen me.
He has commissioned me to encourage the poor,
to help the brokenhearted,
to decree the release of captives
and the freeing of prisoners,

61:1–3 The Spirit of God descended on him, the Spirit of him who had promised by the prophets that he would anoint him, so that we, receiving from the abundance of his unction, might be saved. Such then is the witness of Matthew. In the name of Christ is implied he who anoints, he who is anointed, and the unction itself with which he is anointed. And it is the Father who anoints but the Son who is anointed by the Spirit, who is the unction, as the Word declares by Isaiah: "The Spirit of the Sovereign LORD is upon me, because the LORD has chosen me"—pointing out the anointing Father, the anointed Son, and the unction, which is the Spirit.

IRENAEUS **(C. 130–C. 202)**
AGAINST HERESIES

2 to announce the year when the LORD will show his
favor,
the day when our God will seek vengeance,
to console all who mourn,
3 to strengthen those who mourn in Zion
by giving them a turban, instead of ashes,
oil symbolizing joy, instead of mourning,
a garment symbolizing praise, instead of
discouragement.
They will be called oaks of righteousness,
trees planted by the LORD to reveal his splendor.
4 They will rebuild the perpetual ruins
and restore the places that were desolate;
they will reestablish the ruined cities,
the places that have been desolate since ancient times.
5 "Foreigners will take care of your sheep;
foreigners will work in your fields and vineyards.
6 You will be called, 'the LORD's priests,
servants of our God.'
You will enjoy the wealth of nations
and boast about the riches you receive from them.
7 Instead of shame, you will get a double portion;
instead of humiliation, they will rejoice over the land
they receive.
Yes, they will possess a double portion in their land
and experience lasting joy.
8 For I, the LORD, love justice
and hate robbery and sin.
I will repay them because of my faithfulness;
I will make a permanent covenant with them.
9 Their descendants will be known among the nations,
their offspring among the peoples.
All who see them will recognize that
the LORD has blessed them."
10 I will greatly rejoice in the LORD;
I will be overjoyed because of my God.
For he clothes me in garments of deliverance;
he puts on me a robe symbolizing vindication.
I look like a bridegroom when he wears a turban as a
priest would;
I look like a bride when she puts on her jewelry.
11 For just as the ground produces its crops
and a garden yields its produce,
so the Sovereign LORD will cause deliverance to grow
and give his people reason to praise him in the sight of
all the nations.

62:1–12 God's professing people must be a praying people. It is a sign that God is coming to a people in mercy when he pours out a spirit of prayer upon them. Let us delight in attending the courts of the Lord that we may enjoy the consolations of his Spirit. A way shall be made for Christ's salvation; all difficulties shall be removed. He brings a reward of comfort and peace with him but a work of humiliation and reformation before him; and they shall be called "The Holy People, the Ones Protected by the LORD."

MATTHEW HENRY (1662–1714)
COMMENTARY ON THE WHOLE BIBLE

THE LORD TAKES DELIGHT IN ZION

62 For the sake of Zion I will not be silent;
for the sake of Jerusalem I will not be quiet,
until her vindication shines brightly
and her deliverance burns like a torch.
2 Nations will see your vindication,
and all kings your splendor.
You will be called by a new name
that the LORD himself will give you.
3 You will be a majestic crown in the hand of the LORD,
a royal turban in the hand of your God.
4 You will no longer be called, "Abandoned,"

and your land will no longer be called "Desolate."
Indeed, you will be called "My Delight is in Her"
and your land "Married."
For the LORD will take delight in you,
and your land will be married to him.
5 As a young man marries a young woman,
so your sons will marry you.
As a bridegroom rejoices over a bride,
so your God will rejoice over you.
6 I post watchmen on your walls, O Jerusalem;
they should keep praying all day and all night.
You who pray to the LORD, don't be silent!
7 Don't allow him to rest until he reestablishes
Jerusalem,
until he makes Jerusalem the pride of the earth.
8 The LORD swears an oath by his right hand,
by his strong arm:
"I will never again give your grain
to your enemies as food,
and foreigners will not drink your wine,
which you worked hard to produce.

9 "But those who harvest the grain will eat it,
and will praise the LORD.
Those who pick the grapes will drink the wine
in the courts of my holy sanctuary."
10 Come through! Come through the gates!
Prepare the way for the people!
Build it—build the roadway!
Remove the stones.
Lift a signal flag for the nations.
11 Look, the LORD announces to the entire earth:
"Say to Daughter Zion,
'Look, your deliverer comes!
Look, his reward is with him,
and his reward goes before him!'"
12 They will be called, "The Holy People,
the Ones Protected by the LORD."
You will be called, "Sought After,
City Not Abandoned."

THE VICTORIOUS DIVINE WARRIOR

63 Who is this who comes from Edom,
dressed in bright red, coming from Bozrah?
Who is this one wearing royal attire,
who marches confidently because of his great strength?
"It is I, the one who announces vindication,
and who is able to deliver!"
2 Why are your clothes red?
Why do you look like someone who has stomped on
grapes in a vat?
3 "I have stomped grapes in the winepress all by myself;
no one from the nations joined me.
I stomped on them in my anger;
I trampled them down in my rage.
Their juice splashed on my garments
and stained all my clothes.
4 For I looked forward to the day of vengeance,
and then payback time arrived.

63:1–14 "I, the one who announces vindication, and who is able to deliver!" By the words "to deliver" we understand the whole of the great work of salvation, from the first holy desire onward to complete sanctification. Christ is not only "able to deliver" those who repent, but also he is able to make people repent. He will carry those to heaven who believe; but he is, moreover, mighty to give people new hearts and to work faith in them. The life of a believer is a series of miracles wrought by the mighty God. He is mighty to keep his people holy after he has made them so and to preserve them in his fear and love until he consummates their spiritual existence in heaven.

CHARLES SPURGEON
(1834–1892)
MORNING AND EVENING

5 I looked, but there was no one to help;
I was shocked because there was no one offering support.
So my right arm accomplished deliverance;
my raging anger drove me on.
6 I trampled nations in my anger;
I made them drunk in my rage;
I splashed their blood on the ground."

A PRAYER FOR DIVINE INTERVENTION

7 I will tell of the faithful acts of the LORD,
of the LORD's praiseworthy deeds.
I will tell about all the LORD did for us,
the many good things he did for the family of Israel,
because of his compassion and great faithfulness.
8 He said, "Certainly they will be my people,
children who are not disloyal."
He became their deliverer.
9 Through all that they suffered, he suffered too.
The messenger sent from his very presence delivered them.
In his love and mercy he protected them;
he lifted them up and carried them throughout ancient times.
10 But they rebelled and offended his Holy Spirit,
so he turned into an enemy
and fought against them.
11 His people remembered the ancient times.
Where is the one who brought them up out of the sea,
along with the shepherd of his flock?
Where is the one who placed his Holy Spirit among them,
12 the one who made his majestic power available to Moses,
who divided the water before them,
gaining for himself a lasting reputation,
13 who led them through the deep water?
Like a horse running through the wilderness they did not stumble.
14 As an animal that goes down into a valley to graze,
so the Spirit of the LORD granted them rest.
In this way you guided your people,
gaining for yourself an honored reputation.
15 Look down from heaven and take notice,
from your holy, majestic palace!
Where are your zeal and power?
Do not hold back your tender compassion!
16 For you are our father,
though Abraham does not know us
and Israel does not recognize us.
You, LORD, are our father;
you have been called our Protector from ancient times.
17 Why, LORD, do you make us stray from your ways
and make our minds stubborn so that we do not obey you?
Return for the sake of your servants,
the tribes of your inheritance!
18 For a short time your special nation possessed a land,
but then our adversaries knocked down your holy sanctuary.

19 We existed from ancient times,
but you did not rule over them;
they were not your subjects.

64 If only you would tear apart the sky and come down!
The mountains would tremble before you!
2 As when fire ignites dry wood
or fire makes water boil,
let your adversaries know who you are,
and may the nations shake at your presence!
3 When you performed awesome deeds that took us by surprise,
you came down, and the mountains trembled before you.
4 Since ancient times no one has heard or perceived,
no eye has seen any God besides you,
who intervenes for those who wait for him.
5 You assist those who delight in doing what is right,
who observe your commandments.
Look, you were angry because we violated them continually.
How then can we be saved?
6 We are all like one who is unclean,
all our so-called righteous acts are like a menstrual rag in your sight.
We all wither like a leaf;
our sins carry us away like the wind.
7 No one invokes your name,
or makes an effort to take hold of you.
For you have rejected us
and handed us over to our own sins.
8 Yet, LORD, you are our father.
We are the clay, and you are our potter;
we are all the product of your labor.
9 LORD, do not be too angry!
Do not hold our sins against us continually.
Take a good look at your people, at all of us.
10 Your chosen cities have become a wilderness;
Zion has become a wilderness,
Jerusalem, a desolate ruin.
11 Our holy temple, our pride and joy,
the place where our ancestors praised you,
has been burned with fire;
all our prized possessions have been destroyed.
12 In light of all this, how can you still hold back, LORD?
How can you be silent and continue to humiliate us?

64:1–12 The divine is invisible in nature. "No one has ever seen God" (John 1:18). But God can be seen by the eyes of faith from those things that happen without explanation and beyond speech. For the invisible things, since the foundation of the world, are clearly understood by the things that are made, that is, his heavenly power and Godhead. For he is often recognized through those in whom he works the good and makes a sign of the serenity dwelling in him, marvelously saving those deprived of all hope, and he extends a saving hand from the ground to those lying on the earth. In like manner, they who make this prayer say, "Since ancient times no one has heard or perceived, no eye has seen any God besides you, who intervenes for those who wait for him."

CYRIL OF ALEXANDRIA
(C. 376–444)
COMMENTARY ON ISAIAH

THE LORD WILL DISTINGUISH BETWEEN SINNERS AND THE GODLY

65 "I made myself available to those who did not ask for me;
I appeared to those who did not look for me.
I said, 'Here I am! Here I am!'
to a nation that did not invoke my name.
2 I spread out my hands all day long
to my rebellious people,
who lived in a way that is morally unacceptable
and who did what they desired.
3 These people continually and blatantly offend me
as they sacrifice in their sacred orchards
and burn incense on brick altars.

65:2 If, dearly beloved, we comprehend faithfully and wisely the beginning of our creation, we shall find that human beings were made in God's image to the end that they might imitate the Creator and that our race attains its highest natural dignity by the form of the divine goodness being reflected in us, as in a mirror. And assuredly to this form the Savior's grace is daily restoring us, as long as that which in the first Adam fell is raised up again in the second. And the cause of our restoration is nothing else but the mercy of God, whom we would not have loved unless he had first loved us and dispelled the darkness of our ignorance by the light of his truth.

LEO THE GREAT **(C. 400–461)**
SERMONS

4 They sit among the tombs
and keep watch all night long.
They eat pork
and broth from unclean sacrificial meat is in their pans.
5 They say, 'Keep to yourself!
Don't get near me, for I am holier than you!'
These people are like smoke in my nostrils,
like a fire that keeps burning all day long.
6 Look, I have decreed:
I will not keep silent, but will pay them back;
I will pay them back exactly what they deserve,
7 for your sins and your ancestors' sins," says the LORD.
"Because they burned incense on the mountains
and offended me on the hills,
I will punish them in full measure."

8 This is what the LORD says:
"When juice is discovered in a cluster of grapes,
someone says, 'Don't destroy it, for it contains juice.'
So I will do for the sake of my servants—
I will not destroy everyone.
9 I will bring forth descendants from Jacob
and from Judah people to take possession of my mountains.
My chosen ones will take possession of the land;
my servants will live there.
10 Sharon will become a pasture for sheep,
and the Valley of Achor a place where cattle graze;
they will belong to my people, who seek me.
11 But as for you who abandon the LORD
and forget about worshiping at my holy mountain,
who prepare a feast for the god called 'Fortune,'
and fill up wine jugs for the god called 'Destiny'—
12 I predestine you to die by the sword,
all of you will kneel down at the slaughtering block,
because I called to you, and you did not respond;
I spoke and you did not listen.
You did evil before me;
you chose to do what displeases me."

13 So this is what the Sovereign LORD says:
"Look, my servants will eat, but you will be hungry.
Look, my servants will drink, but you will be thirsty.
Look, my servants will rejoice, but you will be humiliated.
14 Look, my servants will shout for joy as happiness fills their hearts.
But you will cry out as sorrow fills your hearts;
you will wail because your spirits will be crushed.
15 Your names will live on in the curse formulas of my chosen ones.
The Sovereign LORD will kill you,
but he will give his servants another name.
16 Whoever pronounces a blessing in the earth
will do so in the name of the faithful God;
whoever makes an oath in the earth
will do so in the name of the faithful God.
For past problems will be forgotten;
I will no longer think about them.

17 For look, I am ready to create
new heavens and a new earth!
The former ones will not be remembered;
no one will think about them anymore.
18 But be happy and rejoice forevermore
over what I am about to create!
For look, I am ready to create Jerusalem to be a source
of joy,
and her people to be a source of happiness.
19 Jerusalem will bring me joy,
and my people will bring me happiness.
The sound of weeping or cries of sorrow
will never be heard in her again.
20 Never again will one of her infants live just a few days
or an old man die before his time.
Indeed, no one will die before the age of one hundred;
anyone who fails to reach the age of one hundred will
be considered cursed.
21 They will build houses and live in them;
they will plant vineyards and eat their fruit.
22 No longer will they build a house only to have another
live in it,
or plant a vineyard only to have another eat its fruit,
for my people will live as long as trees,
and my chosen ones will enjoy to the fullest what they
have produced.
23 They will not work in vain
or give birth to children that will experience
disaster.
For the LORD will bless their children
and their descendants.
24 Before they even call out, I will respond;
while they are still speaking, I will hear.
25 A wolf and a lamb will graze together;
a lion, like an ox, will eat straw,
and a snake's food will be dirt.
They will no longer injure or destroy
on my entire royal mountain," says the LORD.

66 This is what the LORD says:
"The heavens are my throne
and the earth is my footstool.
Where then is the house you will build for me?
Where is the place where I will rest?
2 My hand made them;
that is how they came to be," says the LORD.

"I show special favor to the humble and contrite,
who respect what I have to say.
3 The one who slaughters a bull also strikes down
a man;
the one who sacrifices a lamb also breaks a dog's neck;
the one who presents an offering includes pig's blood
with it;
the one who offers incense also praises an idol.
They have decided to behave this way;
they enjoy these disgusting practices.
4 So I will choose severe punishment for them;
I will bring on them what they dread
because I called, and no one responded.

I spoke and they did not listen.
They did evil before me;
they chose to do what displeases me."
5 Listen to the LORD's message,
you who respect his word!

"Your countrymen, who hate you
and exclude you, supposedly for the sake of my name,
say, 'May the LORD be glorified,
then we will witness your joy.'
But they will be put to shame.
6 The sound of battle comes from the city;
the sound comes from the temple!
It is the sound of the LORD paying back his
enemies.
7 Before she goes into labor, she gives birth!
Before her contractions begin, she delivers a boy!
8 Who has ever heard of such a thing?
Who has ever seen this?
Can a country be brought forth in one day?
Can a nation be born in a single moment?
Yet as soon as Zion goes into labor she gives birth to
sons!
9 Do I bring a baby to the birth opening and then not
deliver it?"
asks the LORD.
"Or do I bring a baby to the point of delivery and then
hold it back?"
asks your God.
10 "Be happy for Jerusalem
and rejoice with her, all you who love her!
Share in her great joy,
all you who have mourned over her!
11 For you will nurse from her satisfying breasts and be
nourished;
you will feed with joy from her milk-filled breasts."

12 For this is what the LORD says:
"Look, I am ready to extend to her prosperity that will
flow like a river,
the riches of nations will flow into her like a stream
that floods its banks.
You will nurse from her breast and be carried at her
side;
you will play on her knees.
13 As a mother consoles a child,
so I will console you,
and you will be consoled over Jerusalem."
14 When you see this, you will be happy,
and you will be revived.
The LORD will reveal his power to his servants
and his anger to his enemies.
15 For look, the LORD comes with fire;
his chariots come like a windstorm
to reveal his raging anger,
his battle cry, and his flaming arrows.
16 For the LORD judges all humanity
with fire and his sword;
the LORD will kill many.

[17]"As for those who consecrate and ritually purify themselves
so they can follow their leader and worship in the sacred orchards, those who eat the flesh of pigs and other disgusting
creatures, like mice—they will all be destroyed together," says
the LORD. [18]"I hate their deeds and thoughts! So I am coming
to gather all the nations and ethnic groups; they will come and
witness my splendor. [19]I will perform a mighty act among them
and then send some of those who remain to the nations—to
Tarshish, Pul, Lud (known for its archers), Tubal, Javan, and to
the distant coastlands that have not heard about me or seen
my splendor. They will tell the nations of my splendor. [20]They
will bring back all your countrymen from all the nations as
an offering to the LORD. They will bring them on horses, in
chariots, in wagons, on mules, and on camels to my holy hill
Jerusalem," says the LORD, "just as the Israelites bring offerings
to the LORD's temple in ritually pure containers. [21]And I will
choose some of them as priests and Levites," says the LORD.
[22]"For just as the new heavens and the new earth I am about to
make will remain standing before me," says the LORD, "so your
descendants and your name will remain. [23]From one month
to the next and from one Sabbath to the next, all people will
come to worship me," says the LORD. [24]"They will go out and
observe the corpses of those who rebelled against me, for the
maggots that eat them will not die, and the fire that consumes
them will not die out. All people will find the sight abhorrent."

66:18–22 Here Isaiah promises that the restoration of the church shall be of such a nature that it shall last forever. When he speaks of "new heavens" and a "new earth," he looks to the reign of Christ, by whom all things have been renewed. The design of this newness is that the condition of the church may always continue to be prosperous and happy. And as God will establish the world that it may never perish, so the succession of the church shall be perpetual that it may be prolonged through all ages. In a word, he explains what he had formerly said about renewing the world, that none may think that this relates to trees, beasts, or the order of the stars; for it must be referred to the inward renewal of humankind.

JOHN CALVIN (1509–1564)
COMPLETE COMMENTARY ON THE BIBLE

AUTHOR	AUDIENCE	DATE	PURPOSE	THEMES
Jeremiah	The people of Judah and Jerusalem during the reigns of their last five kings	Between 626 and 586 BC	Jeremiah wrote to call God's people from their wicked ways in order to avoid the coming divine judgment while also offering the hope of forgiveness, redemption, and restoration.	Judgment; repentance; forgiveness and redemption; rescue and restoration; and the new covenant

Jeremiah is a prophetic book that is both a warning and an offer of hope. In it the prophet calls God's people to turn from their wicked ways in order to avoid judgment and instead to live faithfully. He holds out the possibility of forgiveness, redemption, and restoration. "The general subject of his prophecies," explained Matthew Henry, "is the idolatry and other sins of the Jews; the judgments by which they were threatened, with references to their future restoration and deliverance, and promises of the Messiah. They are remarkable for plain and faithful reproofs, affectionate expostulations, and awful warnings."

The book launches with the call of God on Jeremiah's life. He commissions him to bear a message of judgment, which stems from two sins his people have committed repeatedly: "They have rejected me, the fountain of life-giving water, and they have dug cisterns for themselves, cracked cisterns that cannot even hold water" (2:13). John Wesley explained the living water was "a metaphor taken from springs, called 'living,' because they never cease, or intermit; such had God's care and kindness been over them"—which Israel had forsaken. And the cisterns were "either their idols, which are empty, vain things that never answer expectation, or the Assyrians and Egyptians. Indeed, all other supports that are trusted to besides God are but broken vessels"—which God's people had willingly embraced in place of the Lord.

Yet the Lord was gracious and compassionate, for he invited his people to return to him, declaring, "'I will not continue to look on you with displeasure. For I am merciful,' says the LORD. 'I will not be angry with you forever'" (3:12). They refused. "This has happened because these people have rejected my laws that I gave them," said the Lord, "they have not obeyed me or followed those laws . . . I will scatter them among nations that neither they nor their ancestors have known anything about. I will send people chasing after them with swords until I have destroyed them" (9:13, 16). And he did so at the hand of the Assyrians, Egyptians, and Babylonians, bringing judgment upon his people. Over the years the communion of saints has drawn important lessons from this urgent warning against unrepentance and impending judgment.

Judgment breaks forth against Judah when Babylon attacks the city of Jerusalem. "Listen, you who sit enthroned above the valley on a rocky plateau. I am opposed to you," said the Lord. ". . . I will punish you as your deeds deserve" (21:13–14). John Calvin explained, "God threatens that he would render to the Jews what they merited because they had not ceased to provoke his wrath." Judah and her kings had forsaken the Lord's covenant and as a result, they would be destroyed.

EL GRECO, ***THE ADORATION OF THE SHEPHERDS*** (1605–1610)

REMBRANDT, ***THE STORM ON THE SEA OF GALILEE*** (1633)

JEREMIAH

Yet there was also a promise for the people: "A new time will certainly come when I will raise up for them a righteous branch, a descendant of David. He will rule over them with wisdom and understanding and will do what is just and right in the land," said the Lord (23:5). The church has understood this branch to be Christ and this passage to be a prophetic declaration of God's redemption in the midst of judgment. Leo the Great voices this collective interpretation:

> There was only one remedy in the secret of the divine plan that could help the fallen living in the general ruin of the entire human race. This remedy was that one of the sons of Adam should be born free and innocent of original transgression to prevail for the rest by his example and by his merits . . . . David's Lord was made David's Son, and from the fruit of the promised branch sprang.

The book of Jeremiah records a time when the Lord told the prophet to buy a field. This would seem like an odd request, for the armies of Babylon were on the verge of destroying the city and conquering it. Why buy a field that would soon become occupied by an invading country? The secret was in the Lord's prophetic utterance: "Houses, fields, and vineyards will again be bought in this land" (32:15). On the precipice of destruction, the Lord promised restoration. As Matthew Henry explained, purchasing this land "was to signify, that though Jerusalem was besieged and the whole country likely to be laid waste, yet the time would come when houses, and fields, and vineyards should be again possessed."

The Lord came to Jeremiah with a second word: "I will most surely heal the wounds of this city and restore it and its people to health. I will show them abundant peace and security. I will restore Judah and Israel and will rebuild them as they were in days of old" (33:6–7). Not only would the Lord restore the land and return the captives to it, but he also promised that he would "purify them from all the sin that they committed against me. I will forgive all their sins that they committed in rebelling against me" (33:8). John Calvin explained, "It was needful for the Prophet to . . . [represent] the greatness of their sins that he might on the other hand extol the mercy of God."

The high point of this prophetic book comes when Jeremiah prophesies the "new covenant" (31:33–34). For generations, the book of Jeremiah has reminded believers that alongside God's judgment and destruction are his promised forgiveness and redemption.

THE SUPERSCRIPTION

1 The following is a record of what Jeremiah son of Hilkiah
prophesied. He was one of the priests who lived at Anathoth in the territory of the tribe of Benjamin. 2The LORD's
message came to him in the thirteenth year that Josiah son
of Amon ruled over Judah. 3It also came in the days of Jehoiakim, son of Josiah, king of Judah, and continued until
the eleventh year of Zedekiah, son of Josiah, king of Judah,
until the people of Jerusalem were taken into exile in the
fifth month of that year.

JEREMIAH'S CALL AND COMMISSION

4The LORD's message came to me,

5 "Before I formed you in your mother's womb, I chose
you.
Before you were born, I set you apart.
I appointed you to be a prophet to the nations."

6I answered, "Oh, Sovereign LORD, Really I do not know
how to speak well enough for that, for I am too young."
7The LORD said to me, "Do not say, 'I am too young.' But go
to whomever I send you and say whatever I tell you. 8Do
not be afraid of those to whom I send you, for I will be with
you to protect you," says the LORD. 9Then the LORD reached
out his hand and touched my mouth and said to me, "I will
most assuredly give you the words you are to speak for me.
10Know for certain that I hereby give you the authority to announce to nations and kingdoms that they will be uprooted
and torn down, destroyed and demolished, rebuilt and firmly
planted."

1:4–10 God also mentions the task for which he selected Jeremiah: "I appointed you to be a prophet to the nations." Thus Jeremiah prophesies not only concerning the fortunes of the Jews but also the other nations. "I answered, 'Oh, Sovereign LORD, Really I do not know how to speak well enough for that, for I am too young.'" The prophet recognized the one addressing him. This is why he called him by a title having to do with lordship. Jeremiah imitates Moses' timidity by saying youth is not up to prophesying. The Lord, however, urges him not to put forward the excuse of youthfulness but to do as he is told.

THEODORET OF CYR
(C. 393–C. 458)
COMMENTARY ON JEREMIAH

VISIONS CONFIRMING JEREMIAH'S CALL AND COMMISSION

11Later the LORD's message came to me, "What do you see, Jeremiah?" I answered, "I see a branch of an almond tree." 12Then
the LORD said, "You have observed correctly. This means I am
watching to make sure my threats are carried out."

13The LORD's message came to me a second time, "What do
you see?" I answered, "I see a pot of boiling water; it is tipped
away from the north." 14Then the LORD said, "From the north
destruction will break out on all who live in the land. 15For I
will soon summon all the peoples of the kingdoms of the north,"
says the LORD. "They will come and their kings will set up their
thrones near the entrances of the gates of Jerusalem. They will
attack all the walls surrounding it and all the towns in Judah.
16In this way I will pass sentence on the people of Jerusalem
and Judah because of all their wickedness. For they rejected
me and offered sacrifices to other gods, worshiping what they
made with their own hands.

17"But you, Jeremiah, get yourself ready! Go and tell these
people everything I instruct you to say. Do not be terrified of
them, or I will give you good reason to be terrified of them.
18I, the LORD, hereby promise to make you as strong as a fortified city, an iron pillar, and a bronze wall. You will be able
to stand up against all who live in the land, including the
kings of Judah, its officials, its priests, and all the people of
the land. 19They will attack you but they will not be able to
overcome you, for I will be with you to rescue you," says the
LORD.

THE LORD RECALLS ISRAEL'S EARLIER FAITHFULNESS

2 The LORD's message came to me, 2 "Go and declare in the
hearing of the people of Jerusalem: 'This is what the LORD
says: "I have fond memories of you, how devoted you were to
me in your early years. I remember how you loved me like a
new bride; you followed me through the wilderness, through
a land that had never been planted. 3 Israel was set apart to
the LORD; they were like the firstfruits of a harvest to him. All
who tried to devour them were punished; disaster came upon
them," says the LORD.'"

THE LORD REMINDS THEM OF THE UNFAITHFULNESS OF THEIR ANCESTORS

4 Now listen to the LORD's message, you descendants of Jacob,
all you family groups from the nation of Israel.
5 This is what the LORD says:
"What fault could your ancestors have possibly found in me
that they strayed so far from me?
They paid allegiance to worthless idols, and so became worthless to me.
6 They did not ask,
'Where is the LORD who delivered us out of Egypt,
who brought us through the wilderness,
through a land of valleys and gorges,
through a land of desert and deep darkness,
through a land in which no one travels,
and where no one lives?'
7 I brought you into a fertile land
so you could enjoy its fruits and its rich bounty.
But when you entered my land, you defiled it;
you made the land I call my own loathsome to me.
8 Your priests did not ask, 'Where is the LORD?'
Those responsible for teaching my law did not really know me.
Your rulers rebelled against me.
Your prophets prophesied in the name of the god Baal.
They all worshiped idols that could not help them.

THE LORD CHARGES CONTEMPORARY ISRAEL WITH SPIRITUAL ADULTERY

9 "So, once more I will state my case against you," says the LORD.
"I will also state it against your children and grandchildren.
10 Go west across the sea to the coasts of Cyprus and see.
Send someone east to Kedar and have them look carefully.
See if such a thing as this has ever happened:
11 Has a nation ever changed its gods
(even though they are not really gods at all)?
But my people have exchanged me, their glorious God,
for a god that cannot help them at all!
12 Be amazed at this, O heavens.
Be shocked and utterly dumbfounded,"
says the LORD.

13 "Do so because my people have committed a double
wrong:
They have rejected me,
the fountain of life-giving water,
and they have dug cisterns for themselves,
cracked cisterns that cannot even hold water.

ISRAEL'S RELIANCE ON FOREIGN ALLIANCES (NOT ON GOD)

14 "Israel is not a slave, is he?
He was not born into slavery, was he?
If not, why then is he being carried off?
15 Like lions his enemies roar victoriously over him;
they raise their voices in triumph.
They have laid his land waste;
his cities have been burned down and deserted.
16 Even the soldiers from Memphis and Tahpanhes
have cracked your skulls, people of Israel.
17 You have brought all this on yourself, Israel,
by deserting the LORD your God when he was leading
you along the right path.
18 What good will it do you then to go down to Egypt
to seek help from the Egyptians?
What good will it do you to go over to Assyria
to seek help from the Assyrians?
19 Your own wickedness will bring about your
punishment.
Your unfaithful acts will bring down discipline on you.
Know, then, and realize how utterly harmful
it was for you to reject me, the LORD your God,
to show no respect for me,"
says the Sovereign LORD of Heaven's Armies.

2:14–28 By sundry miracles, by diverse mercies, Jehovah had proved himself worthy of Israel's trust. Yet they forsook their own true and living God and followed after false gods. Constantly did the Lord reprove them for this infatuation: *What have you to do in the way of Egypt, to drink the waters of the muddy river?* Is there not here a word of warning to the Christian? O true believer, you have tasted of better drink than the muddy river of this world's pleasure can give you. You have had fellowship with Christ; you have obtained the joy of seeing Jesus and leaning your head upon his bosom. Have you eaten the bread of angels, and can you live on husks? The waters of Sihor may be sweet to the Egyptians, but they will prove only bitterness to you.

CHARLES SPURGEON
(1834–1892)
MORNING AND EVENING

THE LORD EXPRESSES HIS EXASPERATION AT JUDAH'S PERSISTENT IDOLATRY

20 "Indeed, long ago you threw off my authority
and refused to be subject to me.
You said, 'I will not serve you.'
Instead, you gave yourself to other gods on every high
hill
and under every green tree,
like a prostitute sprawls out before her lovers.
21 I planted you in the land
like a special vine of the very best stock.
Why in the world have you turned into something like
a wild vine
that produces rotten, foul-smelling grapes?
22 You can try to wash away your guilt with a strong
detergent.
You can use as much soap as you want.
But the stain of your guilt is still there for me to see,"
says the Sovereign LORD.
23 "How can you say, 'I have not made myself unclean.
I have not paid allegiance to the gods called Baal.'
Just look at the way you have behaved in the Valley of
Hinnom!
Think about the things you have done there!
You are like a flighty, young female camel
that rushes here and there, crisscrossing its path.

24 You are like a wild female donkey brought up in the wilderness.
In her lust she sniffs the wind to get the scent of a male.
No one can hold her back when she is in heat.
None of the males need wear themselves out chasing after her.
At mating time she is easy to find.
25 Do not chase after other gods until your shoes wear out
and your throats become dry.
But you say, 'It is useless for you to try and stop me
because I love those foreign gods and want to pursue them!'
26 Just as a thief has to suffer dishonor when he is caught,
so the people of Israel will suffer dishonor for what they have done.
So will their kings and officials,
their priests and their prophets.
27 They say to a wooden idol, 'You are my father.'
They say to a stone image, 'You gave birth to me.'
Yes, they have turned away from me instead of turning to me.
Yet when they are in trouble, they say, 'Come and save us!'
28 But where are the gods you made for yourselves?
Let them save you when you are in trouble.
The sad fact is that you have as many gods
as you have towns, Judah.
29 Why do you try to refute me?
All of you have rebelled against me,"
says the LORD.
30 "It did no good for me to punish your people.
They did not respond to such correction.
You slaughtered your prophets
like a voracious lion."
31 You people of this generation,
listen to the LORD's message:
"Have I been like a wilderness to you, Israel?
Have I been like a dark and dangerous land to you?
Why then do you say, 'We are free to wander.
We will not come to you anymore?'
32 Does a young woman forget to put on her jewels?
Does a bride forget to put on her bridal attire?
But my people have forgotten me
for more days than can even be counted.

33 "My, how good you have become
at chasing after your lovers!
Why, you could even teach prostitutes a thing or two!
34 Even your clothes are stained with
the lifeblood of the poor who had not done anything wrong;
you did not catch them breaking into your homes.
Yet, in spite of all these things you have done,
35 you say, 'I have not done anything wrong,
so the LORD cannot really be angry with me any more.'
But, watch out! I will bring down judgment on you
because you say, 'I have not committed any sin.'
36 Why do you constantly go about
changing your political allegiances?

You will get no help from Egypt
just as you got no help from Assyria.
37 Moreover, you will come away from Egypt
with your hands covering your faces in sorrow and shame
because the LORD will not allow your reliance on them to be successful
and you will not gain any help from them.

3

"If a man divorces his wife
and she leaves him and becomes another man's wife,
he may not take her back again.
Doing that would utterly defile the land.
But you, Israel, have given yourself as a prostitute to many gods.
So what makes you think you can return to me?"
says the LORD.
2 "Look up at the hilltops and consider this.
Where have you not been ravished?
You waited for those gods like a thief lying in wait in the wilderness.
You defiled the land by your wicked prostitution to other gods.
3 That is why the rains have been withheld
and the spring rains have not come.
Yet in spite of this you are obstinate as a prostitute.
You refuse to be ashamed of what you have done.
4 Even now you say to me, 'You are my father!
You have been my faithful companion ever since I was young.
5 You will not always be angry with me, will you?
You will not be mad at me forever, will you?'
That is what you say,
but you continually do all the evil that you can."

3:6–18 It is a wonderful forbearance and kindness that God, finding his favor neglected and rejected, should yet persevere and invite people again and again to repent. Who would thus patiently bear the loathing of one's favor and kindness? But we see that God does not immediately reject the tardy and the slothful but adds new stimulants that he might at length move them. That no terror might hinder them to repent, God here declares that he would become their husband. The sum of what he says is, *I have once embraced you with the love of a husband; you have indeed become alienated from me, but return, and I am ready to forgive and to receive you as though you had always been faithful to me.*

JOHN CALVIN (1509–1564)
COMPLETE COMMENTARY ON THE BIBLE

[6]When Josiah was king of Judah, the LORD said to me, "Jeremiah, you have no doubt seen what wayward Israel has done.
You have seen how she went up to every high hill and under
every green tree to give herself like a prostitute to other gods.
[7]Yet even after she had done all that, I thought that she might
come back to me. But she did not. Her sister, unfaithful Judah,
saw what she did. [8]She also saw that, because of wayward Israel's
adulterous worship of other gods, I sent her away and gave her
divorce papers. But still her unfaithful sister Judah was not
afraid, and she too went and gave herself like a prostitute to
other gods. [9]Because she took her prostitution so lightly, she
defiled the land through her adulterous worship of gods made
of wood and stone. [10]In spite of all this, Israel's sister, unfaithful
Judah, has not turned back to me with any sincerity; she has
only pretended to do so," says the LORD. [11]Then the LORD said
to me, "Under the circumstances, wayward Israel could even
be considered less guilty than unfaithful Judah.

THE LORD CALLS ON ISRAEL AND JUDAH TO REPENT

[12]"Go and shout this message to my people in the countries in
the north. Tell them:
'Come back to me, wayward Israel,' says the LORD.
'I will not continue to look on you with displeasure.

For I am merciful,' says the LORD.
'I will not be angry with you forever.
13 However, you must confess that you have done wrong
and that you have rebelled against the LORD your God.
You must confess that you have given yourself to
foreign gods under every green tree
and have not obeyed my commands,' says the LORD.

14"Come back to me, my wayward sons," says the LORD, "for I
am your true master. If you do, I will take one of you from each
town and two of you from each family group, and I will bring
you back to Zion. 15I will give you leaders who will be faithful to
me. They will lead you with knowledge and insight. 16In those
days, your population will greatly increase in the land. At that
time," says the LORD, "people will no longer talk about having
the ark that contains the LORD's covenant with us. They will
not call it to mind, remember it, or miss it. No, that will not
be done anymore! 17At that time the city of Jerusalem will be
called the LORD's throne. All nations will gather there in Jerusalem to honor the LORD's name. They will no longer follow the
stubborn inclinations of their own evil hearts. 18At that time
the nation of Judah and the nation of Israel will be reunited.
Together they will come back from a land in the north to the
land that I gave to your ancestors as a permanent possession.
19 "I thought to myself,
'Oh what a joy it would be for me to treat you like a son!
What a joy it would be for me to give you a pleasant
land,
the most beautiful piece of property there is in all the
world!'
I thought you would call me 'Father'
and would never cease being loyal to me.
20 But, you have been unfaithful to me, nation of Israel,
like an unfaithful wife who has left her husband,"
says the LORD.
21 "A noise is heard on the hilltops.
It is the sound of the people of Israel crying and
pleading to their gods.
Indeed they have followed sinful ways;
they have forgotten to be true to the LORD their God.
22 Come back to me, you wayward people.
I want to cure your waywardness.
Say, 'Here we are. We come to you
because you are the LORD our God.
23 We know our noisy worship of false gods
on the hills and mountains did not help us.
We know that the LORD our God
is the only one who can deliver Israel.
24 From earliest times our worship of that shameful god,
Baal,
has taken away all that our ancestors worked for.
It has taken away our flocks and our herds
and even our sons and daughters.
25 Let us acknowledge our shame.
Let us bear the disgrace that we deserve.
For we have sinned against the LORD our God,
both we and our ancestors.
From earliest times to this very day
we have not obeyed the LORD our God.'

4 "If you, Israel, want to come back," says the LORD,
"if you want to come back to me,
you must get those disgusting idols out of my sight
and must no longer go astray.
2 You must be truthful, honest, and upright
when you take an oath saying, 'As surely as the LORD lives!'
If you do, the nations will pray to be as blessed by him
as you are
and will make him the object of their boasting."
3 Yes, this is what the LORD has said
to the people of Judah and Jerusalem:
"Break up your unplowed ground, do not cast seeds
among thorns.
4 Commit yourselves to the LORD;
dedicate your hearts to me
people of Judah and inhabitants of Jerusalem.
Otherwise, my anger will blaze up like a flaming fire
against you
that no one will be able to extinguish.
That will happen because of the evil you have done."

WARNING OF COMING JUDGMENT

5 The LORD said,
"Announce this in Judah and proclaim it in Jerusalem:
'Sound the trumpet throughout the land!'
Shout out loudly,
'Gather together! Let us flee into the fortified cities!'
6 Raise a signal flag that tells people to go to Zion.
Run for safety! Do not delay!
For I am about to bring disaster out of the north.
It will bring great destruction.
7 Like a lion that has come up from its lair,
the one who destroys nations has set out from his home
base.
He is coming out to lay your land waste.
Your cities will become ruins and lie uninhabited.
8 So put on sackcloth!
Mourn and wail, saying,
'The fierce anger of the LORD
has not turned away from us!'
9 When this happens," says the LORD,
"the king and his officials will lose their courage.
The priests will be struck with horror,
and the prophets will be speechless in astonishment."

10 In response to all this I said, "Ah, Sovereign LORD, you have
surely allowed the people of Judah and Jerusalem to be deceived
by those who say, 'You will be safe!' But in fact a sword is already
at our throats."

11 At that time the people of Judah and Jerusalem will be
told,
"A scorching wind will sweep down
from the hilltops in the wilderness on my dear people.
It will not be a gentle breeze
for winnowing the grain and blowing away the chaff.
12 No, a wind too strong for that will come at my bidding.
Yes, even now I, myself, am calling down judgment on
them.
13 Look! The enemy is approaching like gathering clouds.

The roar of his chariots is like that of a whirlwind.
His horses move more swiftly than eagles."
I cry out, "We are doomed, for we will be destroyed!"
14 O people of Jerusalem, purify your hearts from evil
so that you may yet be delivered.
How long will you continue to harbor up
wicked schemes within you?
15 For messengers are coming, heralding disaster,
from the city of Dan and from the hills of Ephraim.
16 They are saying,
"Announce to the surrounding nations,
'The enemy is coming!'
Proclaim this message to Jerusalem:
'Those who besiege cities are coming from a distant land.
They are ready to raise the battle cry against the towns
in Judah.'
17 They will surround Jerusalem
like men guarding a field
because they have rebelled against me,"
says the LORD.
18 "The way you have lived and the things you have done
will bring this on you.
This is the punishment you deserve, and it will be
painful indeed.
The pain will be so bad it will pierce your heart."

19 I said,
"Oh, the feeling in the pit of my stomach!
I writhe in anguish.
Oh, the pain in my heart!
My heart pounds within me.
I cannot keep silent.
For I hear the sound of the trumpet;
the sound of the battle cry pierces my soul!
20 I see one destruction after another taking place,
so that the whole land lies in ruins.
I see our tents suddenly destroyed,
their curtains torn down in a mere instant.
21 How long must I see the enemy's battle flags
and hear the military signals of their bugles?"

22 The LORD answered,
"This will happen because my people are foolish.
They do not know me.
They are like children who have no sense.
They have no understanding.
They are skilled at doing evil.
They do not know how to do good."
23 I looked at the land and saw that it was an empty
wasteland.
I looked up at the sky, and its light had vanished.
24 I looked at the mountains and saw that they were shaking.
All the hills were swaying back and forth!
25 I looked and saw that there were no more people
and that all the birds in the sky had flown away.
26 I looked and saw that the fruitful land had become a
desert
and that all the cities had been laid in ruins.

4:14–18 To pray with unwashed hands is a thing of no consequence, but to pray with an unclean conscience is the worst of all evils. Listen to what was said to the Jews, who were much concerned about such exterior purification: "Purify your hearts from evil . . . How long will you continue to harbor up wicked schemes within you?" Let us also wash our hearts, not with filth but with pure water, with almsgiving and not with covetousness.

CHRYSOSTOM **(C. 347–407)**
HOMILIES ON THE GOSPEL OF JOHN

The LORD had brought this all about
because of his blazing anger.
27 All this will happen because the LORD said,
"The whole land will be desolate;
however, I will not completely destroy it.
28 Because of this, the land will mourn
and the sky above will grow black.
For I have made my purpose known,
and I will not relent or turn back from carrying it out."
29 At the sound of the approaching horsemen and archers
the people of every town will flee.
Some of them will hide in the thickets.
Others will climb up among the rocks.
All the cities will be deserted.
No one will remain in them.
30 And you, Zion, city doomed to destruction,
you accomplish nothing by wearing a beautiful dress,
decking yourself out in jewels of gold,
and putting on eye shadow!
You are making yourself beautiful for nothing.
Your lovers spurn you.
They want to kill you.
31 In fact, I hear a cry like that of a woman in labor,
a cry of anguish like that of a woman giving birth to her first baby.
It is the cry of Daughter Zion gasping for breath,
reaching out for help, saying, "I am done in!
My life is ebbing away before these murderers!"

JUDAH IS JUSTLY DESERVING OF COMING JUDGMENT

5:1–17 In this chapter we learn that supplications are brought for the correction of our faults. This is why Jeremiah says, "Even when you punish these people, they feel no remorse. Even when you nearly destroy them, they refuse to be corrected." For the Israelites were improved through many torments and chastisements and were found to have no shame for their faults after all of this, but with rock-hard shamelessness on their brow, they would not convert to the better way.

JEROME (C. 342–420)
COMMENTARY ON JEREMIAH

5 The LORD said,
"Go up and down through the streets of Jerusalem.
Look around and see for yourselves.
Search through its public squares.
See if any of you can find a single person
who deals honestly and tries to be truthful.
If you can, then I will not punish this city.
2 These people make promises in the name of the LORD.
But the fact is, what they swear to is really a lie."
3 LORD, I know you look for faithfulness.
But even when you punish these people, they feel no remorse.
Even when you nearly destroy them, they refuse to be corrected.
They have become as hardheaded as a rock.
They refuse to change their ways.
4 I thought, "Surely it is only the ignorant poor who act this way.
They act like fools because they do not know what the LORD demands.
They do not know what their God requires of them.
5 I will go to the leaders
and speak with them.
Surely they know what the LORD demands.
Surely they know what their God requires of them."
Yet all of them, too, have rejected his authority
and refuse to submit to him.

6 So like a lion from the thicket, their enemies will kill
them.
Like a wolf from the rift valley, they will destroy them.
Like a leopard, they will lie in wait outside their cities
and totally destroy anyone who ventures out.
For they have rebelled so much
and done so many unfaithful things.

7 The LORD asked,
"How can I leave you unpunished, Jerusalem?
Your people have rejected me
and have worshiped gods that are not gods at all.
Even though I supplied all their needs, they were like
an unfaithful wife to me.
They went flocking to the houses of prostitutes.
8 They are like lusty, well-fed stallions.
Each of them lusts after his neighbor's wife.
9 I will surely punish them for doing such things!" says
the LORD.
"I will surely bring retribution on such a nation as this!"
10 The LORD commanded the enemy,
"March through the vineyards of Israel and Judah and
ruin them.
But do not destroy them completely.
Strip off their branches
for these people do not belong to the LORD.
11 For the nations of Israel and Judah
have been very unfaithful to me,"
says the LORD.
12 "These people have denied what the LORD says.
They have said, 'That is not so!
No harm will come to us.
We will not experience war and famine.
13 The prophets will prove to be full of wind.
The LORD has not spoken through them.
So, let what they say happen to them.'"

14 Because of that, the LORD God of Heaven's Armies said
to me:
"Because these people have spoken like this,
I will make the words that I put in your mouth like fire.
And I will make this people like wood,
which the fiery judgments you speak will burn up."
15 The LORD says, "Listen, nation of Israel!
I am about to bring a nation from far away to attack
you.
It will be a nation that was founded long ago
and has lasted for a long time.
It will be a nation whose language you will not know.
Its people will speak words that you will not be able to
understand.
16 All its soldiers are strong and mighty.
Their arrows will send you to your grave.
17 They will eat up your crops and your food.
They will kill off your sons and your daughters.
They will eat up your sheep and your cattle.
They will destroy your vines and your fig trees.
Their weapons will batter down
the fortified cities you trust in.

18 "Yet even then I will not completely destroy you," says the
LORD. 19 "So then, Jeremiah, when your people ask, 'Why has the
LORD our God done all this to us?' tell them, 'It is because you
rejected me and served foreign gods in your own land. So you
must serve foreigners in a land that does not belong to you.'

20 "Proclaim this message among the descendants of
Jacob.
Make it known throughout Judah.
21 Tell them: 'Hear this,
you foolish people who have no understanding,
who have eyes but do not discern,
who have ears but do not perceive:
22 "You should fear me!" says the LORD.
"You should tremble in awe before me!
I made the sand to be a boundary for the sea,
a permanent barrier that it can never cross.
Its waves may roll, but they can never prevail.
They may roar, but they can never cross beyond that
boundary."
23 But these people have stubborn and rebellious hearts.
They have turned aside and gone their own way.
24 They do not say to themselves,
"Let us revere the LORD our God.
It is he who gives us the autumn rains and the spring
rains at the proper time.
It is he who assures us of the regular weeks of harvest."
25 Your misdeeds have stopped these things from coming.
Your sins have deprived you of my bounty.'
26 Indeed, there are wicked scoundrels among my people.
They lie in wait like bird catchers hiding in ambush.
They set deadly traps to catch people.
27 Like a cage filled with the birds that have been caught,
their houses are filled with the gains of their fraud and
deceit.
That is how they have gotten so rich and powerful.
28 That is how they have grown fat and sleek.
There is no limit to the evil things they do.
They do not plead the cause of the fatherless in such a
way as to win it.
They do not defend the rights of the poor.
29 I will certainly punish them for doing such things!" says
the LORD.
"I will certainly bring retribution on such a nation as
this!
30 Something horrible and shocking
is going on in the land of Judah:
31 The prophets prophesy lies.
The priests exercise power by their own authority.
And my people love to have it this way.
But they will not be able to help you when the time of
judgment comes!

6:1–30 Oh that human beings would be wise for their souls! "Ask where the old, reliable paths are": The way of godliness and righteousness has always been the way God has owned and blessed. When you have found the good way, go on in it—you will find abundant recompense at your journey's end. But if people will not obey the voice of God and flee to his appointed refuge, it will plainly appear at the day of judgment that they are ruined because they reject God's Word. Saints may rejoice in hope of God's mercies, though they see them only in the promise; sinners must mourn for fear of God's judgments, though they see them only in the threats.

MATTHEW HENRY **(1662–1714)**
COMMENTARY ON THE WHOLE BIBLE

THE DESTRUCTION OF JERUSALEM DEPICTED

6 "Run for safety, people of Benjamin!
Get out of Jerusalem!
Sound the trumpet in Tekoa!
Light the signal fires at Beth Hakkerem!
For disaster lurks out of the north;
it will bring great destruction.

2 I will destroy Daughter Zion,
who is as delicate and defenseless as a young maiden.
3 Kings will attack her with their armies.
They will encamp in siege all around her.
Each of them will devastate the portion assigned to him.
4 They will say, 'Prepare to do battle against it!
Come on! Let's attack it at noon!'
But later they will say, 'Woe to us!
For the day is almost over,
and the shadows of evening are getting long.
5 So come on, let's go ahead and attack it by night
and destroy all its fortified buildings.'
6 All this is because the LORD of Heaven's Armies has
said:
'Cut down the trees around Jerusalem
and build up a siege ramp against its walls.
This is the city that is to be punished.
Nothing but oppression happens in it.
7 As a well continually pours out fresh water,
so it continually pours out wicked deeds.
Sounds of violence and destruction echo throughout it.
All I see are sick and wounded people.'
8 So take warning, Jerusalem,
or I will abandon you in disgust
and make you desolate,
a place where no one can live."

9 This is what the LORD of Heaven's Armies said to me:
"Those who remain in Israel will be
like the grapes thoroughly gleaned from a vine.
So go over them again, as though you were a grape
harvester
passing your hand over the branches one last time."

10 I answered,
"Who would listen
if I spoke to them and warned them?
Their ears are so closed
that they cannot hear!
Indeed, the LORD's message is offensive to them.
They do not like it at all.
11 I am as full of anger as you are, LORD.
I am tired of trying to hold it in."

The LORD answered,
"Vent it, then, on the children who play in the street
and on the young men who are gathered together.
Husbands and wives are to be included,
as well as the old and those who are advanced in years.
12 Their houses will be turned over to others
as will their fields and their wives.
For I will unleash my power
against those who live in this land,"
says the LORD.
13 "That is because, from the least important to the most
important of them,
all of them are greedy for dishonest gain.
Prophets and priests alike,
all of them practice deceit.

14 They offer only superficial help
for the harm my people have suffered.
They say, 'Everything will be all right!'
But everything is not all right!
15 Are they ashamed because they have done such
shameful things?
No, they are not at all ashamed.
They do not even know how to blush!
So they will die, just like others have died.
They will be brought to ruin when I punish them,"
says the LORD.

16 The LORD said to his people:
"You are standing at the crossroads. So consider your
path.
Ask where the old, reliable paths are.
Ask where the path is that leads to blessing and
follow it.
If you do, you will find rest for your souls."
But they said, "We will not follow it!"
17 The LORD said,
"I appointed prophets as watchmen to warn you, saying,
'Pay attention to the warning sound of the trumpet!'"
But they said, "We will not pay attention!"

18 So the LORD said,
"Hear, you nations!
Be witnesses and take note of what will happen to these
people.
19 Hear this, you peoples of the earth:
'Take note! I am about to bring disaster on these people.
It will come as punishment for their scheming.
For they have paid no attention to what I have said,
and they have rejected my law.
20 I take no delight when they offer up to me
frankincense that comes from Sheba
or sweet-smelling cane imported from a faraway land.
I cannot accept the burnt offerings they bring me.
I get no pleasure from the sacrifices they offer to me.'"

21 So, this is what the LORD says:
"I will assuredly make these people stumble to their
doom.
Parents and children will stumble and fall to their
destruction.
Friends and neighbors will die."

22 This is what the LORD says:
"Beware! An army is coming from a land in the north.
A mighty nation is stirring into action in faraway parts
of the earth.
23 Its soldiers are armed with bows and spears.
They are cruel and show no mercy.
They sound like the roaring sea
as they ride forth on their horses.
Lined up in formation like men going into battle
to attack you, Daughter Zion."
24 The people cry out, "We have heard reports about them.

We have become helpless with fear!
Anguish grips us,
agony like that of a woman giving birth to a baby!
25 Do not go out into the countryside.
Do not travel on the roads.
For the enemy is there with sword in hand.
They are spreading terror everywhere."
26 So I said, "Oh, my dear people, put on sackcloth
and roll in ashes.
Mourn with painful sobs
as though you had lost your only child.
For any moment now that destructive army
will come against us."

27 The LORD said to me,
"I have made you like a metal assayer
to test my people like ore.
You are to observe them
and evaluate how they behave."

28 I reported,
"All of them are the most stubborn of rebels!
They are as hard as bronze or iron.
They go about telling lies.
They all deal corruptly.
29 The fiery bellows of judgment burn fiercely.
But there is too much dross to be removed.
The process of refining them has proved useless.
The wicked have not been purged.
30 They are regarded as 'rejected silver'
because the LORD rejects them."

FAULTY RELIGION AND UNETHICAL BEHAVIOR WILL LEAD TO JUDGMENT

7 The LORD said to Jeremiah: 2 "Stand in the gate of the LORD's
temple and proclaim this message: 'Listen to the LORD's message, all you people of Judah who have passed through these
gates to worship the LORD. 3 The LORD of Heaven's Armies, the
God of Israel, says: Change the way you have been living and
do what is right. If you do, I will allow you to continue to live
in this land. 4 Stop putting your confidence in the false belief
that says, "We are safe! The temple of the LORD is here! The
temple of the LORD is here! The temple of the LORD is here!"
5 You must change the way you have been living and do what is
right. You must treat one another fairly. 6 Stop oppressing resident foreigners who live in your land, children who have lost
their fathers, and women who have lost their husbands. Stop
killing innocent people in this land. Stop paying allegiance to
other gods. That will only bring about your ruin. 7 If you stop
doing these things, I will allow you to continue to live in this
land that I gave to your ancestors as a lasting possession.
8 "'But just look at you! You are putting your confidence in
a false belief that will not deliver you. 9 You steal. You murder.
You commit adultery. You lie when you swear on oath. You sacrifice to the god Baal. You pay allegiance to other gods whom
you have not previously known. 10 Then you come and stand in
my presence in this temple I have claimed as my own and say,
"We are safe!" You think you are so safe that you go on doing all
those hateful sins! 11 Do you think this temple I have claimed

7:1–27 "Stop putting your confidence in the false belief that says, 'We are safe! The temple of the LORD is here!'" They are only trying to assure you that you will never be left by God as though God would decide to preserve his blessed temple and would save his priests even though they are wicked. No! Do not find hope in those who flatter you with these words. If you have not corrected what you are doing, then you are no temple of God, and God will not save you on account of the sacredness of his temple that you desecrate. His soul is disgusted by the multitude of your sacrifices that you offer in your wickedness.

EPHREM THE SYRIAN
(C. 306–373)
COMMENTARY ON JEREMIAH

as my own is to be a hideout for robbers? You had better take
note! I have seen for myself what you have done! says the LORD.
[12]So, go to the place in Shiloh where I allowed myself to be
worshiped in the early days. See what I did to it because of
the wicked things my people Israel did. [13]You also have done
all these things, says the LORD, and I have spoken to you over
and over again. But you have not listened! You have refused to
respond when I called you to repent! [14]So I will destroy this
temple that I have claimed as my own, this temple that you
are trusting to protect you. I will destroy this place that I gave
to you and your ancestors, just like I destroyed Shiloh. [15]And I
will drive you out of my sight just like I drove out your relatives,
the people of Israel.'

[16]"But as for you, Jeremiah, do not pray for these people. Do
not raise a cry of prayer for them! Do not plead with me to save
them, because I will not listen to you. [17]Do you see what they
are doing in the towns of Judah and in the streets of Jerusalem?
[18]Children are gathering firewood, fathers are building fires
with it, and women are mixing dough to bake cakes to offer
to the goddess they call the Queen of Heaven. They are also
pouring out drink offerings to other gods. They seem to do
all this just to trouble me. [19]But I am not really the one being
troubled! says the LORD. Rather they are bringing trouble on
themselves to their own shame! [20]So, the Sovereign LORD says,
my raging fury will be poured out on this land. It will be poured
out on human beings and animals, on trees and crops. And it
will burn like a fire that cannot be extinguished.

[21]"The LORD of Heaven's Armies, the God of Israel, says to
the people of Judah: 'You might as well go ahead and add the
meat of your burnt offerings to that of the other sacrifices and
eat it, too! [22]Consider this: When I spoke to your ancestors after
I brought them out of Egypt, I did not merely give them commands about burnt offerings and sacrifices. [23]I also explicitly
commanded them: "Obey me. If you do, I will be your God and
you will be my people. Live exactly the way I tell you and things
will go well with you." [24]But they did not listen to me or pay
any attention to me. They followed the stubborn inclinations
of their own wicked hearts. They acted worse and worse instead
of better. [25]From the time your ancestors departed the land of
Egypt until now, I sent my servants the prophets to you again
and again, day after day. [26]But your ancestors did not listen to
me nor pay attention to me. They became obstinate and were
more wicked than even their own forefathers.'"

[27]Then the LORD said to me, "When you tell them all this,
they will not listen to you. When you call out to them, they will
not respond to you. [28]So tell them: 'This is a nation that has not
obeyed the LORD their God and has not accepted correction.
Faithfulness is nowhere to be found in it. These people do not
even profess it anymore. [29]So mourn, you people of this nation.
Cut off your hair and throw it away. Sing a song of mourning
on the hilltops. For the LORD has decided to reject and forsake
this generation that has provoked his wrath!'"

[30]The LORD says, "I have rejected them because the people
of Judah have done what I consider evil. They have set up their
disgusting idols in the temple that I have claimed for my own
and have defiled it. [31]They have also built places of worship in a
place called Topheth in the Valley of Ben Hinnom so that they
can sacrifice their sons and daughters by fire. That is something
I never commanded them to do! Indeed, it never even entered

my mind to command such a thing! [32]So, watch out!" says the
LORD. "The time will soon come when people will no longer call
those places Topheth or the Valley of Ben Hinnom. But they
will call that valley the Valley of Slaughter, and they will bury so
many people in Topheth that they will run out of room. [33]Then
the dead bodies of these people will be left on the ground for
the birds and wild animals to eat. There will not be any survivors to scare them away. [34]I will put an end to the sounds of
joy and gladness or the glad celebration of brides and grooms
throughout the towns of Judah and the streets of Jerusalem.
For the whole land will become a desolate wasteland."

8 The LORD says, "When that time comes, the bones of the kings
of Judah and its leaders, the bones of the priests and prophets,
and of all the other people who lived in Jerusalem will be dug up
from their graves. [2]They will be spread out and exposed to the
sun, the moon, and the stars. These are things they adored and
served, things to which they paid allegiance, from which they
sought guidance and worshiped. The bones of these people will
never be regathered and reburied. They will be like manure used
to fertilize the ground. [3]However, I will leave some of these wicked people alive and banish them to other places. But wherever
these people who survive may go, they will wish they had died
rather than lived," says the LORD of Heaven's Armies.

WILLFUL DISREGARD OF GOD WILL LEAD TO DESTRUCTION

[4]The LORD said to me,
"Tell them, 'The LORD says,
Do people not get back up when they fall down?
Do they not turn around when they go the wrong way?
5 Why, then, do these people of Jerusalem
continually turn away from me in apostasy?
They hold fast to their deception.
They refuse to turn back to me.
6 I have listened to them very carefully,
but they do not speak honestly.
None of them regrets the evil he has done.
None of them says, "I have done wrong!"
All of them persist in their own wayward course
like a horse charging recklessly into battle.
7 Even the stork knows
when it is time to move on.
The turtledove, swallow, and crane
recognize the normal times for their migration.
But my people pay no attention
to what I, the LORD, require of them.
8 How can you say, "We are wise!
We have the law of the LORD"?
The truth is, those who teach it have used their writings
to make it say what it does not really mean.
9 Your wise men will be put to shame.
They will be dumbfounded and be brought to judgment.
Since they have rejected the LORD's message,
what wisdom do they really have?
10 So I will give their wives to other men
and their fields to new owners.
For from the least important to the most important of them,
all of them are greedy for dishonest gain.

Prophets and priests alike
all practice deceit.
[11] They offer only superficial help
for the hurt my dear people have suffered.
They say, "Everything will be all right!"
But everything is not all right.
[12] Are they ashamed because they have done such
disgusting things?
No, they are not at all ashamed!
They do not even know how to blush.
So they will die just like others have died.
They will be brought to ruin when I punish them,
says the LORD.
[13] I will take away their harvests, says the LORD.
There will be no grapes on their vines.
There will be no figs on their fig trees.
Even the leaves on their trees will wither.
The crops that I gave them will be taken away.'"

JEREMIAH LAMENTS OVER THE COMING DESTRUCTION

[14]The people say,
"Why are we just sitting here?
Let us gather together inside the fortified cities.
Let us at least die there fighting,
since the LORD our God has condemned us to die.
He has condemned us to drink the poison waters of
judgment
because we have sinned against him.
[15] We hoped for good fortune, but nothing good has come
of it.
We hoped for a time of relief, but instead we experience
terror.
[16] The snorting of the enemy's horses
is already being heard in the city of Dan.
The sound of the neighing of their stallions
causes the whole land to tremble with fear.
They are coming to destroy the land and everything in
it.
They are coming to destroy the cities and everyone who
lives in them."

[17]The LORD says,
"Yes indeed, I am sending an enemy against you
that will be like poisonous snakes that cannot be
charmed away.
And they will inflict fatal wounds on you."

[18]Then I said,
"There is no cure for my grief!
I am sick at heart!
[19] I hear my dear people crying out
throughout the length and breadth of the land.
They are crying, 'Is the LORD no longer in Zion?
Is her divine King no longer there?'"
The LORD answers,
"Why then do they provoke me to anger with their
images,
with their worthless foreign idols?"

8:18—9:11 Let us collect ourselves, I exhort you. There are daily wars, submersions of towns, innumerable destructions all around us, and on every side the wrath of God is enclosing us as in a net. Each one of us has much anxiety over how he may add to his wealth; no one has anxiety over how he may save his own soul. I see that our wound is grievous, that our calamity is beyond comfort, that woes have overtaken us that exceed the consolation. We are undone. "I wish that my head were a well full of water and my eyes were a fountain full of tears" that I might lament. Let us weep, beloved, let us groan.

CHRYSOSTOM (C. 347–407)
ON THE EPISTLE TO THE HEBREWS

20 "They cry, 'Harvest time has come and gone and the
summer is over,
and still we have not been delivered.'
21 My heart is crushed because my dear people are being
crushed.
I go about crying and grieving. I am overwhelmed with
dismay.
22 There is still medicinal ointment available in Gilead!
There is still a physician there!
Why then have my dear people
not been restored to health?
9 I wish that my head were a well full of water
and my eyes were a fountain full of tears!
If they were, I could cry day and night
for those of my dear people who have been killed.
2 I wish I had a lodging place in the wilderness
where I could spend some time like a weary traveler.
Then I would desert my people
and walk away from them
because they are all unfaithful to God,
a congregation of people that has been disloyal to him."

THE LORD LAMENTS THAT HE HAS NO CHOICE BUT TO JUDGE THEM

3 The LORD says,
"These people are like soldiers who have readied their
bows.
Their tongues are always ready to shoot out lies.
They have become powerful in the land,
but they have not done so by honest means.
Indeed, they do one evil thing after another
and do not pay attention to me.
4 Everyone must be on his guard around his friends.
He must not even trust any of his relatives.
For every one of them will find some way to cheat him.
And all his friends will tell lies about him.
5 One friend deceives another,
and no one tells the truth.
These people have trained themselves to tell lies.
They do wrong and are unable to repent.
6 They do one act of violence after another,
and one deceitful thing after another.
They refuse to pay attention to me,"
says the LORD.

7 Therefore the LORD of Heaven's Armies says:
"I will now purify them in the fires of affliction and test
them.
The wickedness of my dear people has left me no choice.
What else can I do?
8 Their tongues are like deadly arrows.
They are always telling lies.
Friendly words for their neighbors come from their
mouths,
but their minds are thinking up ways to trap them.
9 I will certainly punish them for doing such things!" says
the LORD.
"I will certainly bring retribution on such a nation as
this!"

THE COMING DESTRUCTION CALLS FOR MOURNING

10 I said,
"I will weep and mourn for the grasslands on the mountains;
I will sing a mournful song for the pastures in the wilderness
because they are so scorched no one travels through them.
The sound of livestock is no longer heard there.
Even the birds in the sky and the wild animals in the fields
have fled and are gone."

11 The LORD said,
"I will make Jerusalem a heap of ruins.
Jackals will make their home there.
I will destroy the towns of Judah
so that no one will be able to live in them."

12 I said,
"Who is wise enough to understand why this has happened?
Who has a word from the LORD that can explain it?
Why does the land lie in ruins?
Why is it as scorched as a desert through which no one travels?"

13 The LORD answered, "This has happened because these
people have rejected my laws that I gave them. They have not
obeyed me or followed those laws. 14 Instead they have followed
the stubborn inclinations of their own hearts. They have paid
allegiance to the gods called Baal, as their fathers taught them
to do. 15 So then, listen to what I, the LORD of Heaven's Armies,
the God of Israel, say, 'I will make these people eat the bitter
food of suffering and drink the poison water of judgment. 16 I
will scatter them among nations that neither they nor their ancestors have known anything about. I will send people chasing
after them with swords until I have destroyed them.'"

17 The LORD of Heaven's Armies told me to say to this people:
"Take note of what I say.
Call for the women who mourn for the dead!
Summon those who are the most skilled at it!"
18 I said, "Indeed, let them come quickly and sing a song of mourning for us.
Let them wail loudly until tears stream from our own eyes
and our eyelids overflow with water.
19 For the sound of wailing is soon to be heard in Zion,
'We are utterly ruined! We are completely disgraced!
For we have left our land,
for our houses have been torn down!'"

20 I said,
"So now, you wailing women, listen to the LORD's message.
Open your ears to the message from his mouth.
Teach your daughters this mournful song,
and let every woman teach her neighbor this lament.

21 'Death has climbed in through our windows.
It has entered into our fortified houses.
It has taken away our children who play in the streets.
It has taken away our young men who gather in the city squares.'
22 Tell your daughters and neighbors, 'The LORD says:
"The dead bodies of people will lie scattered everywhere
like manure scattered on a field.
They will lie scattered on the ground
like grain that has been cut down but has not been gathered."'"

23 The LORD says,
"Wise people should not boast that they are wise.
Powerful people should not boast that they are powerful.
Rich people should not boast that they are rich.
24 If people want to boast, they should boast about this:
They should boast that they understand and know me.
They should boast that they know and understand
that I, the LORD, act out of faithfulness, fairness, and justice in the earth
and that I desire people to do these things,"
says the LORD.

25 The LORD says, "Watch out! The time is soon coming when
I will punish all those who are circumcised only in the flesh.
26 That is, I will punish the Egyptians, the Judeans, the Edomites,
the Ammonites, the Moabites, and all the desert people who
cut their hair short at the temples. I will do so because none of
the people of those nations are really circumcised in the LORD's
sight. Moreover, none of the people of Israel are circumcised
when it comes to their hearts."

THE LORD, NOT IDOLS, IS THE ONLY WORTHY OBJECT OF WORSHIP

10 You people of Israel, listen to what the LORD has to say to you.
2 The LORD says:
"Do not start following pagan religious practices.
Do not be in awe of signs that occur in the sky
even though the nations hold them in awe.
3 For the religion of these people is worthless.
They cut down a tree in the forest,
and a craftsman makes it into an idol with his tools.
4 He decorates it with overlays of silver and gold.
He uses hammer and nails to fasten it together
so that it will not fall over.
5 Such idols are like scarecrows in a cucumber field.
They cannot talk.
They must be carried
because they cannot walk.
Do not be afraid of them
because they cannot hurt you.
And they do not have any power to help you."

6 I said,
"There is no one like you, LORD.
You are great,
and you are renowned for your power.

10:1–16 We ought to believe that God is good, eternal, perfect, almighty, and true, such as we find him in the Law and the Prophets and the rest of the holy scriptures, for otherwise there is no God. For he who is God must be good, seeing that fullness of goodness is of the nature of God. God, who made time, cannot be in time. Again, God cannot be imperfect, for a lesser being is plainly imperfect, seeing that it lacks somewhat whereby it could be made equal to a greater. This, then, is the teaching of our faith—that God is not evil, that with God nothing is impossible, that God does not exist in time, that God is beneath no being.

AMBROSE (C. 339–C. 397)
ON THE CHRISTIAN FAITH

7 Everyone should revere you, O King of all nations,
because you deserve to be revered.
For there is no one like you
among any of the wise people of the nations nor among
any of their kings.
8 The people of those nations are both stupid and foolish.
Instruction from a wooden idol is worthless!
9 Hammered-out silver is brought from Tarshish
and gold is brought from Ufaz to cover those idols.
They are the handiwork of carpenters and goldsmiths.
They are clothed in blue and purple clothes.
They are all made by skillful workers.
10 The LORD is the only true God.
He is the living God and the everlasting King.
When he shows his anger, the earth shakes.
None of the nations can stand up to his fury.
11 You people of Israel should tell those nations this:
'These gods did not make heaven and earth.
They will disappear from the earth and from under the
heavens.'
12 The LORD is the one who by his power made the earth.
He is the one who by his wisdom established the world.
And by his understanding, he spread out the skies.
13 When his voice thunders, the heavenly ocean roars.
He makes the clouds rise from the far-off horizons.
He makes the lightning flash out in the midst of the
rain.
He unleashes the wind from the places where he stores
it.
14 All these idolaters will prove to be stupid and ignorant.
Every goldsmith will be disgraced by the idol he made.
For the image he forges is merely a sham.
There is no breath in any of those idols.
15 They are worthless, mere objects to be mocked.
When the time comes to punish them, they will be
destroyed.
16 The LORD, who is the inheritance of Jacob's
descendants, is not like them.
He is the one who created everything.
And the people of Israel are those he claims as his own.
His name is the LORD of Heaven's Armies."

JEREMIAH LAMENTS FOR AND PRAYS FOR THE PEOPLE SOON TO BE JUDGED

17 "Gather your belongings together and prepare to leave
the land,
you people of Jerusalem who are being besieged.
18 For the LORD says, 'I will now throw out
those who live in this land.
I will bring so much trouble on them
that they will actually feel it.'
19 And I cried out, 'We are doomed!
Our wound is severe!'
We once thought, 'This is only an illness.
And we will be able to bear it.'
20 But our tents have been destroyed.
The ropes that held them in place have been ripped
apart.
Our children are gone and are not coming back.

There is no survivor to put our tents back up,
no one left to hang their tent curtains in place.
21 For our leaders are stupid.
They have not sought the LORD's advice.
So they do not act wisely,
and the people they are responsible for have all been scattered.
22 Listen! News is coming even now.
The rumble of a great army is heard approaching from a land in the north.
It is coming to turn the towns of Judah into rubble,
places where only jackals live.
23 LORD, we know that people do not control their own destiny.
It is not in their power to determine what will happen to them.
24 Correct us, LORD, but only in due measure.
Do not punish us in anger, or you will reduce us to nothing.
25 Vent your anger on the nations that do not acknowledge you.
Vent it on the peoples who do not worship you.
For they have destroyed the people of Jacob.
They have completely destroyed them
and left their homeland in utter ruin."

THE PEOPLE HAVE VIOLATED THEIR COVENANT WITH GOD

11 The LORD said to Jeremiah: [2]"Hear the terms of the covenant I made with Israel and pass them on to the people of
Judah and the citizens of Jerusalem. [3]Tell them that the LORD,
the God of Israel, says, 'Anyone who does not keep the terms of
the covenant will be under a curse. [4]Those are the terms that
I charged your ancestors to keep when I brought them out of
Egypt, that place that was like an iron-smelting furnace. I said
at that time, "Obey me and carry out the terms of the covenant
exactly as I commanded you. If you do, you will be my people
and I will be your God. [5]Then I will keep the promise I swore on
oath to your ancestors to give them a land flowing with milk
and honey." That is the very land that you still live in today.'"
And I responded, "Amen. Let it be so, LORD."
[6]The LORD said to me, "Announce all the following words in
the towns of Judah and in the streets of Jerusalem: 'Listen to
the terms of my covenant with you and carry them out! [7]For
I solemnly warned your ancestors to obey me. I warned them
again and again, ever since I delivered them out of Egypt until
this very day. [8]But they did not listen to me or pay any attention
to me! Each one of them followed the stubborn inclinations of
his own wicked heart. So I brought on them all the punishments
threatened in the covenant because they did not carry out its
terms as I commanded them to do.'"
[9]The LORD said to me, "The people of Judah and the citizens
of Jerusalem have plotted rebellion against me. [10]They have
gone back to the evil ways of their ancestors of old who refused
to obey what I told them. They, too, have paid allegiance to other
gods and worshiped them. Both the nation of Israel and the
nation of Judah have violated the covenant I made with their
ancestors. [11]So I, the LORD, say this: 'I will soon bring disaster
on them that they will not be able to escape! When they cry

11:1–17 "I brought on them all the punishments threatened in the covenant because they did not carry out its terms as I commanded them to do." God gave the Israelites over to noteworthy punishments; sometimes they served the Ammonites, other times the Moabites, and still other times other foreigners. The phrase "have plotted rebellion" means "They have gone back to the evil ways of their ancestors of old who refused to obey what I told them." The Lord indicates as much also through the things that are brought against them. "They, too, have paid allegiance to other gods and worshiped them." *For this reason*, the Lord said, *I will surround them with misfortunes of all kinds. They will not even enjoy any help from the gods who are revered by them.*

THEODORET OF CYR
(C. 393–C. 458)
COMMENTARY ON JEREMIAH

out to me for help, I will not listen to them. [12]Then those living
in the towns of Judah and in Jerusalem will go and cry out for
help to the gods to whom they have been sacrificing. However,
those gods will by no means be able to save them when disaster
strikes them. [13]This is in spite of the fact that the people of
Judah have as many gods as they have towns and the citizens
of Jerusalem have set up as many altars to sacrifice to that disgusting god, Baal, as they have streets in the city!' [14]But as for
you, Jeremiah, do not pray for these people. Do not raise a cry
of prayer for them. For I will not listen to them when they call
out to me for help when disaster strikes them."

[15]The LORD says to the people of Judah,
"What right do you have to be in my temple, my beloved
people?
Many of you have done wicked things.
Can your acts of treachery be so easily canceled by
sacred offerings
that you take joy in doing evil even while you make
them?

16 I, the LORD, once called you a thriving olive tree,
one that produced beautiful fruit.
But I will set you on fire,
fire that will blaze with a mighty roar.
Then all your branches will be good for nothing.

17 For though I, the LORD of Heaven's Armies, planted you
in the land,
I now decree that disaster will come on you
because the nations of Israel and Judah have done evil
and have made me angry by offering sacrifices to the
god Baal."

A PLOT AGAINST JEREMIAH IS REVEALED AND HE COMPLAINS OF INJUSTICE

18 The LORD gave me knowledge, that I might have
understanding.
Then he showed me what the people were doing.

19 Before this I had been like a docile lamb ready to be led
to the slaughter.
I did not know they were making plans to kill me.
I did not know they were saying,
"Let's destroy the tree along with its fruit!
Let's remove Jeremiah from the world of the living
so people will not even be reminded of him anymore."

[20]So I said,
"O LORD of Heaven's Armies, you are a just judge!
You examine people's hearts and minds.
I want to see you pay them back for what they have
done
because I trust you to vindicate my cause."

[21]Then the LORD told me about some men from Anathoth
who were threatening to kill me. They had threatened, "Stop
prophesying in the name of the LORD or we will kill you!" [22]So
the LORD of Heaven's Armies said, "I will surely punish them!
Their young men will be killed in battle. Their sons and daughters will die of starvation. [23]Not one of them will survive. I will
bring disaster on those men from Anathoth who threatened
you. A day of reckoning is coming for them."

JEREMIAH APPEALS TO GOD

12 LORD, you have always been fair
whenever I have complained to you.
However, I would like to speak with you about the
disposition of justice.
Why are wicked people successful?
Why do all dishonest people have such easy lives?
2 You plant them like trees, and they put down their
roots.
They grow prosperous and are very fruitful.
They always talk about you,
but they really care nothing about you.
3 But you, LORD, know all about me.
You watch me and test my devotion to you.
Drag these wicked men away like sheep to be slaughtered!
Appoint a time when they will be killed!
4 How long must the land be parched
and the grass in every field be withered?
How long must the animals and the birds die
because of the wickedness of the people who live in this
land?
For these people boast,
"God will not see what happens to us."

GOD ANSWERS JEREMIAH

5 The LORD answered,
"If you have raced on foot against men and they have
worn you out,
how will you be able to compete with horses?
And if you feel secure only in safe and open country,
how will you manage in the thick undergrowth along
the Jordan River?
6 As a matter of fact, even your own brothers
and the members of your own family have betrayed you
as well.
Even they have plotted to do away with you.
So do not trust them even when they say kind things to
you.
7 "I will abandon my nation.
I will forsake the people I call my own.
I will turn my beloved people
over to the power of their enemies.
8 The people I call my own have turned on me
like a lion in the forest.
They have roared defiantly at me,
so I will treat them as though I hate them.
9 The people I call my own attack me like birds of prey or
like hyenas.
But other birds of prey are all around them.
Let all the nations gather together like wild beasts.
Let them come and destroy these people I call my own.
10 Many foreign rulers will ruin the land where I planted
my people.
They will trample all over my chosen land.
They will turn my beautiful land
into a desolate wilderness.
11 They will lay it waste.
It will lie parched and empty before me.

12:1–17 It seems here that Jeremiah is beginning a dispute with God: Why is God merciful to the wicked when they certainly do not deserve his mercy because their hearts are hard and stubborn? Truly, Jeremiah is not the only one who asks this question. Many righteous people wanted to know as if they debated with God about his multitude of mercies to sinners. But they all had one goal—to call sinners to repentance. For he is good and slow to anger to the sons of Adam, and as a hospitable Father, he showers them with his gifts. Jeremiah had the same goal: by fear and promises to wake up and to call Israel to serve their God.

EPHREM THE SYRIAN
(C. 306–373)
COMMENTARY ON JEREMIAH

The whole land will be laid waste,
but no one living in it will pay any heed.
12 A destructive army will come marching
over the hilltops in the wilderness.
For the LORD will use them as his destructive weapon
against everyone from one end of the land to the other.
No one will be safe.
13 My people will sow wheat, but will harvest weeds.
They will work until they are exhausted, but will get
nothing from it.
They will be disappointed in their harvests
because the LORD will take them away in his fierce anger.

14“I, the LORD, also have something to say concerning the
wicked nations who surround my land and have attacked and
plundered the land that I gave to my people as a permanent
possession. I say: ‘I will uproot the people of those nations from
their land, and I will free the people of Judah who have been
taken there. 15But after I have uprooted the people of those
nations, I will relent and have pity on them. I will restore the
people of each of those nations to their own lands and to their
own country. 16But they must make sure to learn to follow the
religious practices of my people. Once they taught my people
to swear their oaths using the name of the god Baal. But then,
they must swear oaths using my name, saying, “As surely as
the LORD lives, I swear.” If they do these things, then they will
be included among the people I call my own. 17But I will completely uproot and destroy any of those nations that will not
pay heed,’” says the LORD.

AN OBJECT LESSON FROM RUINED LINEN SHORTS

13 The LORD said to me, “Go and buy some linen shorts and
put them on. Do not put them in water.” 2So I bought the
shorts in keeping with the LORD’s instructions and put them on.
3Then the LORD’s message came to me again, 4“Take the shorts
that you bought and are wearing and go at once to Perath. Bury
the shorts there in a crack in the rocks.” 5So I went and buried
them at Perath as the LORD had ordered me to do. 6Many days
later the LORD said to me, “Go at once to Perath and get the
shorts I ordered you to bury there.” 7So I went to Perath and dug
up the shorts from the place where I had buried them. I found
that they were ruined; they were good for nothing.

8Then the LORD’s message came to me, 9“I, the LORD, say:
‘This shows how I will ruin the highly exalted position in which
Judah and Jerusalem take pride. 10These wicked people refuse
to obey what I have said. They follow the stubborn inclinations
of their own hearts and pay allegiance to other gods by worshiping and serving them. So they will become just like these
linen shorts that are good for nothing. 11For,’ I say, ‘just as shorts
cling tightly to a person’s body, so I bound the whole nation of
Israel and the whole nation of Judah tightly to me.’ I intended
for them to be my special people and to bring me fame, honor,
and praise. But they would not obey me.

12“So tell them, ‘The LORD, the God of Israel, says: “Every wine
jar is made to be filled with wine.”’ And they will probably say to
you, ‘Do you not think we know that every wine jar is supposed
to be filled with wine?’ 13Then tell them, ‘The LORD says: “I
will soon fill all the people who live in this land with stupor.

THOMAS À KEMPIS:

A VISION OF CHRIST-IMITATION

1380–1471

Thomas Hammerken was born in 1380 near Dusseldorf, Germany, to working-class parents. Better known as Thomas à Kempis, when he was thirteen he left home and traveled to the Netherlands where he joined the Brethren of the Common Life. This community of ministers and laypeople who renounced worldliness shaped and launched his most important work, *The Imitation of Christ*.

As Christianity's most-read book next to the Bible itself, *The Imitation of Christ* is both a realistic and aspirational work outlining the travails and complexities of human existence while offering a vision for life shaped by Christ. One can see a strong influence from the Brethren of the Common Life upon the work, for its spirituality is Christocentric in orientation with an emphasis on zealous devotion rather than speculative dogma. For example, Thomas declared that the "Trinity is better pleased by adoration than by speculation," pointedly calling readers to move beyond doctrinal precision and into genuine worship. For Thomas, Christ imitation is not only for the purpose of being wholly "in Christ" as Paul teaches, but also for inviting Christ to live wholly in his people.

Imitation is composed of four parts (and was originally circulated as four stand-alone books): Admonition of the Spiritual Life, Admonition of the Inner Life, Of Internal Consolation, and A Devout Exhortation to the Holy Communion. Each part is composed of a series of devotion-length meditations meant to draw the reader deeper into Christ and his life with the aim of inner transformation. Chapter 1 sets forth this dual aim:

> *"The one who follows me will never walk in darkness," says the Lord (John 8:12). By these words of Christ we are advised to imitate his life and habits if we wish to be truly enlightened and free from all blindness of heart. Let our chief effort, therefore, be to study the life of Jesus Christ. The teaching of Christ is more excellent than all the advice of the saints, and he who has his spirit will find in it a hidden manna . . . Yet whoever wishes to understand fully the words of Christ must try to pattern his whole life on that of Christ.*

Leading up to his death in 1471, Thomas à Kempis served at the monastery of Saint Agnes in Zwolle, where he was canon of Saint Augustine. He is rightly remembered and revered for the vision of Christ imitation he offered generations of Christians both in his book and by his example.

IMPORTANT WORKS

THE IMITATION OF CHRIST

PRAYERS AND MEDITATIONS ON THE LIFE OF CHRIST

MEDITATIONS ON THE INCARNATION OF CHRIST

FOUNDERS OF THE NEW DEVOTION

I will also fill the kings from David's dynasty, the priests, the
prophets, and the citizens of Jerusalem with stupor. 14 And I will
smash them like wine bottles against one another, children and
parents alike. I will not show any pity, mercy, or compassion.
Nothing will keep me from destroying them,' says the LORD."

15 Then I said to the people of Judah:
"Listen and pay attention! Do not be arrogant!
For the LORD has spoken.
16 Show the LORD your God the respect that is due him.
Do it before he brings the darkness of disaster.
Do it before you stumble into distress
like a traveler on the mountains at twilight.
Do it before he turns the light of deliverance you hope for
into the darkness and gloom of exile.
17 But if you will not pay attention to this warning,
I will weep alone because of your arrogant pride.
I will weep bitterly, and my eyes will overflow with tears
because you, the LORD's flock, will be carried into exile."

18 The LORD told me:
"Tell the king and the queen mother,
'Surrender your thrones,
for your glorious crowns
will be removed from your heads.
19 The gates of the towns in southern Judah will be shut tight.
No one will be able to go in or out of them.
All Judah will be carried off into exile.
They will be completely carried off into exile.'"

20 Then I said,
"Look up, Jerusalem, and see
the enemy that is coming from the north.
Where now is the flock of people that were entrusted to your care?
Where now are the 'sheep' that you take such pride in?
21 What will you say when the LORD appoints as rulers over you those allies
that you, yourself, had actually prepared as such?
Then anguish and agony will grip you
like that of a woman giving birth to a baby.
22 You will probably ask yourself,
'Why have these things happened to me?
Why have I been treated like a disgraced adulteress
whose skirt has been torn off and her limbs exposed?'
It is because you have sinned so much.
23 But there is little hope for you ever doing good,
you who are so accustomed to doing evil.
Can an Ethiopian change the color of his skin?
Can a leopard remove its spots?

24 "The LORD says,
'That is why I will scatter your people like chaff
that is blown away by a desert wind.
25 This is your fate,
the destiny to which I have appointed you
because you have forgotten me
and have trusted in false gods.

13:23 What says the prophet? If the leopard cannot change his spots, these people, having learned evil, are not able to do good. He doesn't say that the doing of virtue is impossible to them, but that because they will not, they cannot. It was impossible for the prophet to lie; yet it was not on that account impossible that they should believe. For it was possible, even had they believed, that he should remain true, since he would not have prophesied these things if they had been about to believe. "Why then," says someone, "did he not say so?" Because scripture has certain idiomatic phrases of this kind, and it is needful to make allowance for its laws.

CHRYSOSTOM (C. 347–407)
HOMILIES ON THE GOSPEL OF JOHN

26 So I will pull your skirt up over your face
and expose you to shame like a disgraced adulteress!
27 People of Jerusalem, I have seen your adulterous
worship,
your shameless prostitution to, and your lustful pursuit
of, other gods.
I have seen your disgusting acts of worship
on the hills throughout the countryside.
You are doomed to destruction!
How long will you continue to be unclean?'"

A LAMENT OVER THE RAVAGES OF DROUGHT

14 This was the LORD's message to Jeremiah about the
drought.
2 "The people of Judah are in mourning.
The people in her cities are pining away.
They lie on the ground expressing their sorrow.
Cries of distress come up to me from Jerusalem.
3 The leading men of the cities send their servants for
water.
They go to the cisterns, but they do not find any water
there.
They return with their containers empty.
Disappointed and dismayed, they bury their faces in
their hands.
4 They are dismayed because the ground is cracked
because there has been no rain in the land.
The farmers, too, are dismayed
and bury their faces in their hands.
5 Even the doe abandons her newborn fawn in the field
because there is no grass.
6 Wild donkeys stand on the hilltops
and pant for breath like jackals.
Their eyes are strained looking for food,
because there is none to be found."

7 Then I said,
"O LORD, intervene for the honor of your name
even though our sins speak out against us.
Indeed, we have turned away from you many times.
We have sinned against you.
8 You have been the object of Israel's hopes.
You have saved them when they were in trouble.
Why have you become like a resident foreigner in the
land?
Why have you become like a traveler who only stops in
to spend the night?
9 Why should you be like someone who is helpless,
like a champion who cannot save anyone?
You are indeed with us,
and we belong to you.
Do not abandon us!"

10 Then the LORD spoke about these people.
"They truly love to go astray.
They cannot keep from running away from me.
So I am not pleased with them.
I will now call to mind the wrongs they have done
and punish them for their sins."

14:10–18 Though the faithful are disturbed by many inquietudes, cares, anxieties, and fears, still God ever preserves them; and the firmness of their faith within continues, though it may happen that they are apparently not only shaken, but even stagger and fall. But God gives to the unbelieving their just reward who derogate from his power, while they place their safety on human beings or on idols, for they never find where they may safely stand. On this account he says, *Therefore the Lord does not accept them, that is, God will not give them courage: no,* he says, "I will now call to mind the wrongs they have done and punish them for their sins." In short, he teaches us that so grievous was the wickedness of that people that there was no place for the mercy of God.

JOHN CALVIN **(1509–1564)**
COMPLETE COMMENTARY ON THE BIBLE

JUDGMENT FOR BELIEVING THE MISLEADING LIES OF THE FALSE PROPHETS

11 Then the LORD said to me, "Do not pray for good to come to
these people! 12 Even if they fast, I will not hear their cries for
help. Even if they offer burnt offerings and grain offerings, I
will not accept them. Instead, I will kill them through wars,
famines, and plagues."

13 Then I said, "Oh, Sovereign LORD, look! The prophets are
telling them that you said, 'You will not experience war or suffer
famine. I will give you lasting peace and prosperity in this land.'"

14 Then the LORD said to me, "Those prophets are prophesying
lies while claiming my authority! I did not send them. I did not
commission them. I did not speak to them. They are prophesying
to these people false visions, worthless predictions, and the delusions of their own mind. 15 I did not send those prophets, though
they claim to be prophesying in my name. They may be saying,
'No war or famine will happen in this land.' But I, the LORD, say
this about them: 'War and starvation will kill those prophets.'
16 The people to whom they are prophesying will die through war
and famine. Their bodies will be thrown out into the streets of
Jerusalem, and there will be no one to bury them. This will happen
to the men and their wives, their sons, and their daughters. For I
will pour out on them the destruction they deserve."

LAMENT OVER PRESENT DESTRUCTION AND THREAT OF MORE TO COME

17 "Tell these people this, Jeremiah:
'My eyes overflow with tears
day and night without ceasing.
For my people, my dear children, have suffered a crushing blow.
They have suffered a serious wound.
18 If I go out into the countryside,
I see those who have been killed in battle.
If I go into the city,
I see those who are sick because of starvation.
For both prophet and priest—
they go peddling in the land
but they are not humbled.'"

19 Then I said,
"LORD, have you completely rejected the nation of Judah?
Do you despise the city of Zion?
Why have you struck us with such force
that we are beyond recovery?
We hope for peace, but nothing good has come of it.
We hope for a time of relief from our troubles, but experience terror.
20 LORD, we confess that we have been wicked.
We confess that our ancestors have done wrong.
We have indeed sinned against you.
21 For the honor of your name, do not treat Jerusalem with contempt.
Do not treat with disdain the place where your glorious throne sits.
Be mindful of your covenant with us. Do not break it.
22 Do any of the worthless idols of the nations cause rain to fall?

Do the skies themselves send showers?
Is it not you, O LORD our God, who does this?
So we put our hopes in you
because you alone do all this."

15 Then the LORD said to me, "Even if Moses and Samuel
stood before me pleading for these people, I would not
feel pity for them! Get them away from me! Tell them to go
away! 2If they ask you, 'Where should we go?' tell them the
LORD says this:

'Those who are destined to die of disease will go to
death by disease.
Those who are destined to die in war will go to death in
war.
Those who are destined to die of starvation will go to
death by starvation.
Those who are destined to go into exile will go into
exile.'

3"I will punish them in four different ways: I will have war
kill them; I will have dogs drag off their dead bodies; I will have
birds and wild beasts devour and destroy their corpses. 4I will
make all the people in all the kingdoms of the world horrified
at what has happened to them because of what Hezekiah's son
Manasseh, king of Judah, did in Jerusalem."

5The LORD cried out,
"Who in the world will have pity on you, Jerusalem?
Who will grieve over you?
Who will stop long enough
to inquire about how you are doing?
6 I, the LORD, say: 'You people have deserted me;
you keep turning your back on me.'
So I have unleashed my power against you and have
begun to destroy you.
I have grown tired of feeling sorry for you!"

7The LORD continued,
"In every town in the land I will purge them
like straw blown away by the wind.
I will destroy my people.
I will kill off their children.
I will do so because they did not change their
behavior.
8 Their widows will become in my sight more
numerous
than the grains of sand on the seashores.
At noontime I will bring a destroyer
against the mothers of their young men.
I will cause anguish and terror
to fall suddenly upon them.
9 The mother who had seven children will grow faint.
All the breath will go out of her.
Her pride and joy will be taken from her in the prime of
their life.
It will seem as if the sun had set while it was still day.
She will suffer shame and humiliation.
I will cause any of them who are still left alive
to be killed in war by the onslaughts of their enemies,"
says the LORD.

15:9 "'In that day,' says the Sovereign LORD, 'I will make the sun set at noon and make the earth dark in the middle of the day'" (Amos 8:9). This plainly announced that obscuration of the sun that at the time of Jesus' crucifixion took place from the sixth hour onward. Jeremiah speaks concerning Jerusalem: "It will seem as if the sun had set while it was still day. She will suffer shame and humiliation. I will cause any of them who are still left alive to be killed in war by the onslaughts of their enemies." Those who spoke of God's having slumbered and taken sleep, and of Jesus' having risen again because the Lord sustained him, and who enjoined the principalities of heaven to set open the everlasting doors that the King of glory might go in, proclaimed beforehand his resurrection from the dead through the Father's power and his reception into heaven.

IRENAEUS (C. 130–C. 202)
AGAINST HERESIES

JEREMIAH COMPLAINS ABOUT HIS LOT AND THE LORD RESPONDS

10 I said,
"Oh, mother, how I regret that you ever gave birth to me!
I am always starting arguments and quarrels with the people of this land.
I have not lent money to anyone, and I have not borrowed from anyone.
Yet all these people are treating me with contempt."

11 The LORD said,
"Jerusalem, I will surely send you away for your own good.
I will surely bring the enemy upon you in a time of trouble and distress.
12 Can you people who are like iron and bronze
break that iron fist from the north?
13 I will give away your wealth and your treasures as plunder.
I will give it away free of charge for the sins you have committed throughout your land.
14 I will make you serve your enemies in a land that you know nothing about.
For my anger is like a fire that will burn against you."

15 I said,
"LORD, you know how I suffer.
Take thought of me and care for me.
Pay back for me those who have been persecuting me.
Do not be so patient with them that you allow them to kill me.
Be mindful of how I have put up with their insults for your sake.
16 As your words came to me, I drank them in,
and they filled my heart with joy and happiness
because I belong to you, O LORD God of Heaven's Armies.
17 I did not spend my time in the company of other people,
laughing and having a good time.
I stayed to myself because I felt obligated to you
and because I was filled with anger at what they had done.
18 Why must I continually suffer such painful anguish?
Why must I endure the sting of their insults like an incurable wound?
Will you let me down when I need you,
like a brook one goes to for water but that cannot be relied on?"

19 Because of this, the LORD said,
"You must repent of such words and thoughts!
If you do, I will restore you to the privilege of serving me.
If you say what is worthwhile instead of what is worthless,
I will again allow you to be my spokesman.
They must become as you have been.
You must not become like them.

20 I will make you as strong as a wall to these people,
a fortified wall of bronze.
They will attack you,
but they will not be able to overcome you.
For I will be with you to rescue you and deliver you,"
says the LORD.
21 "I will deliver you from the power of the wicked.
I will free you from the clutches of violent people."

JEREMIAH FORBIDDEN TO MARRY, TO MOURN, OR TO FEAST

16 The LORD's message came to me, [2]"Do not get married and
do not have children here in this land. [3]For I, the LORD,
tell you what will happen to the children who are born here
in this land and to the men and women who are their mothers and fathers. [4]They will die of deadly diseases. No one will
mourn for them. They will not be buried. Their dead bodies
will lie like manure spread on the ground. They will be killed
in war or die of starvation. Their corpses will be food for the
birds and wild animals.
[5]"Moreover I, the LORD, tell you: 'Do not go into a house
where they are having a funeral meal. Do not go there to mourn
and express your sorrow for them. For I have stopped showing
them my good favor, my love, and my compassion. I, the LORD,
so affirm it! [6]Rich and poor alike will die in this land. They will
not be buried or mourned. People will not cut their bodies or
shave off their hair to show their grief for them. [7]No one will
take any food to those who mourn for the dead to comfort them.
No one will give them any wine to drink to console them for
the loss of their father or mother.
[8]"'Do not go to a house where people are feasting and sit
down to eat and drink with them either. [9]For I, the LORD of
Heaven's Armies, the God of Israel, tell you what will happen.
I will put an end to the sounds of joy and gladness, to the glad
celebration of brides and grooms in this land. You and the rest
of the people will live to see this happen.'

THE LORD PROMISES EXILE BUT ALSO RESTORATION

[10]"When you tell these people about all this, they will undoubtedly ask you, 'Why has the LORD threatened us with such great
disaster? What wrong have we done? What sin have we done to
offend the LORD our God?' [11]Then tell them that the LORD says,
'It is because your ancestors rejected me and paid allegiance to
other gods. They have served them and worshiped them. But
they have rejected me and not obeyed my law. [12]And you have
acted even more wickedly than your ancestors! Each one of
you has followed the stubborn inclinations of your own wicked heart and not obeyed me. [13]So I will throw you out of this
land into a land that neither you nor your ancestors have ever
known. There you must worship other gods day and night, for
I will show you no mercy.'
[14]"Yet I, the LORD, say: 'A new time will certainly come. People
now affirm their oaths with "I swear as surely as the LORD lives
who delivered the people of Israel out of Egypt." [15]But in that
time they will affirm them with "I swear as surely as the LORD
lives who delivered the people of Israel from the land of the north
and from all the other lands where he had banished them." At
that time I will bring them back to the land I gave their ancestors.

16:14–21 It is truly said that "what they make are not gods at all," for the objects of our foolish love are very doubtful blessings, the solace they yield us now is dangerous, and the help they can give us in the hour of trouble is little indeed. Why then are we so bewitched with vanities? We pity the poor heathen who adore a god of stone. Where is the vast superiority between a god of flesh and one of wood? The heathen bows to a false deity, but the true God he has never known; we commit two evils inasmuch as we forsake the living God and turn to idols. May the Lord purge us all from this grievous iniquity!

CHARLES SPURGEON
(1834–1892)
MORNING AND EVENING

16 "But for now I, the LORD, say: 'I will send many enemies
who will catch these people like fishermen. After that I will
send others who will hunt them out like hunters from all the
mountains, all the hills, and the crevices in the rocks. 17 For I
see everything they do. Their wicked ways are not hidden from
me. Their sin is not hidden away where I cannot see it. 18 Before
I restore them I will punish them in full for their sins and the
wrongs they have done. For they have polluted my land with
the lifeless statues of their disgusting idols. They have filled
the land I have claimed as my own with their detestable idols.'

19 Then I said,

"LORD, you give me strength and protect me.
You are the one I can run to for safety when I am in
trouble.
Nations from all over the earth
will come to you and say,
'Our ancestors had nothing but false gods—
worthless idols that could not help them at all.'
20 Can people make their own gods?
No, what they make are not gods at all."

21 The LORD said,

"So I will now let this wicked people know—
I will let them know my mighty power in judgment.
Then they will know that my name is the LORD.

17 "The sin of Judah is engraved with an iron chisel
on their stone-hard hearts.
It is inscribed with a diamond point
on the horns of their altars.
2 Their children are always thinking about their altars
and their sacred poles dedicated to the goddess
Asherah,
set up beside the green trees on the high hills
3 and on the mountains and in the fields.
I will give your wealth and all your treasures away as
plunder.
I will give it away as the price for the sins you have
committed throughout your land.
4 You will lose your hold on the land
that I gave to you as a permanent possession.
I will make you serve your enemies in a land that you
know nothing about.
For you have made my anger burn like a fire that will
never be put out."

INDIVIDUALS ARE CHALLENGED TO PUT THEIR TRUST IN THE LORD

5 The LORD says,

"I will put a curse on people
who trust in mere human beings,
who depend on mere flesh and blood for their
strength,
and whose hearts have turned away from the LORD.
6 They will be like a shrub in the arid rift valley.
They will not experience good things even when they
happen.
It will be as though they were growing in the stony
wastes in the wilderness,
in a salt land where no one can live.

7 My blessing is on those people who trust in me,
who put their confidence in me.
8 They will be like a tree planted near a stream
whose roots spread out toward the water.
It has nothing to fear when the heat comes.
Its leaves are always green.
It has no need to be concerned in a year of drought.
It does not stop bearing fruit.
9 The human mind is more deceitful than anything else.
It is incurably bad. Who can understand it?
10 I, the LORD, probe into people's minds.
I examine people's hearts.
I deal with each person according to how he has behaved.
I give them what they deserve based on what they have done.
11 The person who gathers wealth by unjust means
is like the partridge that broods over eggs but does not hatch them.
Before his life is half over, he will lose his ill-gotten gains.
At the end of his life, it will be clear he was a fool."

JEREMIAH APPEALS TO THE LORD FOR VINDICATION

12 Then I said,
"LORD, from the very beginning
you have been seated on your glorious throne on high.
You are the place where we can find refuge.
13 You are the one in whom Israel may find hope.
All who leave you will suffer shame.
Those who turn away from you will be consigned to the netherworld.
For they have rejected you, the LORD, the fountain of life.
14 LORD, grant me relief from my suffering
so that I may have some relief;
rescue me from those who persecute me
so that I may be rescued, for you give me reason to praise!
15 Listen to what they are saying to me,
'Where are the things the LORD threatens us with?
May it please happen!'

16 But I have not pestered you to bring disaster.
I have not desired the time of irreparable devastation.
You know that.
You are fully aware of every word that I have spoken.
17 Do not cause me dismay!
You are my source of safety in times of trouble.
18 May those who persecute me be disgraced.
Do not let me be disgraced.
May they be dismayed.
Do not let me be dismayed.
Bring days of disaster on them.
Bring on them the destruction they deserve."

17:16–18 What we find in these verses is a confirmation that when the prophet Jeremiah, and other inspired penmen of the Old Testament, imprecated judgments on their enemies, those parts of their writings are not of private interpretation, nor did they therein express their private inclinations and desires; they spoke prophetically the mind of God, cursed them in the name of the Lord, or foretold that these judgments should come. For here Jeremiah solemnly appeals to God that he had not desired the woeful day—yet he prays that the evil day might be brought on his enemies.

JONATHAN EDWARDS
(1703–1758)
SELECTIONS FROM THE UNPUBLISHED WRITINGS

OBSERVANCE OF THE SABBATH DAY IS A KEY TO THE FUTURE

19 The LORD told me, "Go and stand in the People's Gate through
which the kings of Judah enter and leave the city. Then go and
stand in all the other gates of the city of Jerusalem. 20 And then
announce to them, 'Listen to the LORD's message, you kings of
Judah, and everyone from Judah, and all you citizens of Jerusalem,
those who pass through these gates. 21 The LORD says, Be very
careful if you value your lives! Do not carry any loads in through
the gates of Jerusalem on the Sabbath day. 22 Do not carry any
loads out of your houses or do any work on the Sabbath day.
But observe the Sabbath day as a day set apart to the LORD, as
I commanded your ancestors. 23 Your ancestors, however, did
not listen to me or pay any attention to me. They stubbornly
refused to pay attention or to respond to any discipline.' 24 The
LORD says, 'You must make sure to obey me. You must not bring
any loads through the gates of this city on the Sabbath day. You
must set the Sabbath day apart to me. You must not do any work
on that day. 25 If you do this, then the kings and princes who follow in David's succession and ride in chariots or on horses will
continue to enter through these gates, as well as their officials
and the people of Judah and the citizens of Jerusalem. This city
will always be filled with people. 26 Then people will come here
from the towns in Judah, from the villages surrounding Jerusalem, from the territory of Benjamin, from the foothills, from the
southern hill country, and from the southern part of Judah. They
will come bringing offerings to the temple of the LORD: burnt
offerings, sacrifices, grain offerings, and incense along with their
thank offerings. 27 But you must obey me and set the Sabbath day
apart to me. You must not carry any loads in through the gates of
Jerusalem on the Sabbath day. If you disobey, I will set the gates
of Jerusalem on fire. It will burn down all the fortified dwellings
in Jerusalem and no one will be able to put it out.'"

AN OBJECT LESSON FROM THE MAKING OF POTTERY

18 The LORD said to Jeremiah: 2 "Go down at once to the potter's house. I will speak to you further there." 3 So I went
down to the potter's house and found him working at his wheel.
4 Now and then there would be something wrong with the pot he
was molding from the clay with his hands. So he would rework
the clay into another kind of pot as he saw fit.

5 Then the LORD's message came to me, 6 "I, the LORD, say:
'O nation of Israel, can I not deal with you as this potter deals
with the clay? In my hands, you, O nation of Israel, are just
like the clay in this potter's hand.' 7 There are times, Jeremiah,
when I threaten to uproot, tear down, and destroy a nation or
kingdom. 8 But if that nation I threatened stops doing wrong,
I will cancel the destruction I intended to do to it. 9 And there
are times when I promise to build up and establish a nation or
kingdom. 10 But if that nation does what displeases me and does
not obey me, then I will cancel the good I promised to do to it.
11 So now, tell the people of Judah and the citizens of Jerusalem
this: The LORD says, 'I am preparing to bring disaster on you! I
am making plans to punish you. So, every one of you, stop the
evil things you have been doing. Correct the way you have been
living and do what is right.' 12 But they just keep saying, 'We do
not care what you say! We will do whatever we want to do! We
will continue to behave wickedly and stubbornly!'"

18:1–17 When God wished to hold out good hopes to his people, he brought the prophet to a potter's house and showed him a vessel of clay that was in the hands of the potter, falling to the ground. He brought Jeremiah to say, "Can I not deal with you as this potter deals with the clay? In my hands, you, O nation of Israel, are just like the clay in this potter's hand." *If this potter has taken up and remodeled his vessel that has fallen, shall I not much rather be able to restore you when you have fallen?* It is possible therefore for God not only to restore those who are made of clay through the washing of regeneration, but also to bring them back again to their original state on their careful repentance those who have received the power of the Spirit and have fallen from grace into ruin.

CHRYSOSTOM (C. 347–407)
INSTRUCTIONS TO CATECHUMENS

13 Therefore, the LORD says,
"Ask the people of other nations
whether they have heard of anything like this.
Israel should have been like a virgin,
but she has done something utterly revolting!
14 Does the snow ever completely vanish from the rocky
slopes of Lebanon?
Do the cool waters from those distant mountains ever
cease to flow?
15 Yet my people have forgotten me
and offered sacrifices to worthless idols.
This makes them stumble along in the way they
live
and leave the old reliable path of their fathers.
They have left them to walk in bypaths,
in roads that are not smooth and level.
16 So their land will become an object of horror.
People will forever hiss out their scorn over it.
All who pass that way will be filled with horror
and will shake their heads in derision.
17 I will scatter them before their enemies
like dust blowing in front of a burning east wind.
I will turn my back on them and not look favorably
on them
when disaster strikes them."

JEREMIAH PETITIONS THE LORD TO PUNISH THOSE WHO ATTACK HIM

18 Then some people said, "Come on! Let us consider how to
deal with Jeremiah! There will still be priests to instruct us,
wise men to give us advice, and prophets to declare God's word.
Come on! Let's bring charges against him and get rid of him!
Then we will not need to pay attention to anything he says."
19 Then I said,
"LORD, pay attention to me.
Listen to what my enemies are saying.
20 Should good be paid back with evil?
Yet they are virtually digging a pit to kill me.
Just remember how I stood before you
pleading on their behalf
to keep you from venting your anger on them.
21 So let their children die of starvation.
Let them be cut down by the sword.
Let their wives lose their husbands and children.
Let the older men die of disease
and the younger men die by the sword in battle.
22 Let cries of terror be heard in their houses
when you send bands of raiders unexpectedly to
plunder them.
For they have virtually dug a pit to capture me
and have hidden traps for me to step into.
23 But you, LORD, know
all their plots to kill me.
Do not pardon their crimes!
Do not ignore their sins as though you had erased
them.
Let them be brought down in defeat before
you.
Deal with them while you are still angry!"

19:1–15 Sometimes holy scripture may, by an improper use of terms, call afflictions "evils" because they are imagined to be evils by those on whom they are brought for their good. The Lord says in Jeremiah, "I will smash this nation and this city as though it were a potter's vessel," that is, sorrows and losses with which they shall for the present be chastened for their souls' health, and so they shall at length be driven to return and hurry back to me whom in their prosperity they scorned. And so we cannot in any way assert that these afflictions were originally evil, for they are good for many and ultimately offer occasions for eternal bliss. Therefore all those things that are thought to be evils should not be counted as evils but as things indifferent. For in the end they will not be what he thinks who brought them on us in his rage and fury, but what he makes them who endures them.

JOHN CASSIAN
(C. 360–C. 435)
THE CONFERENCES

AN OBJECT LESSON FROM A BROKEN CLAY JAR

19 The LORD told Jeremiah, "Go and buy a clay jar from a
potter. Take with you some of the leaders of the people
and some of the leaders of the priests. [2]Go out to the part of
the Hinnom Valley that is near the entrance of the Potsherd
Gate. Announce there what I tell you. [3]Say, 'Listen to the LORD's
message, you kings of Judah and citizens of Jerusalem! This is
what the LORD of Heaven's Armies, the God of Israel, has said,
"Look here! I am about to bring a disaster on this place that
will make the ears of everyone who hears about it ring. [4]I will
do so because these people have rejected me and have defiled
this place. They have offered sacrifices in it to other gods that
neither they nor their ancestors nor the kings of Judah knew
anything about. They have filled it with the blood of innocent
children. [5]They have built places here for worship of the god
Baal so that they could sacrifice their children as burnt offerings to him in the fire. Such sacrifices are something I never
commanded them to make. They are something I never told
them to do! Indeed, such a thing never even entered my mind.
[6]So I, the LORD, say: 'The time will soon come that people will
no longer call this place Topheth or the Hinnom Valley. But
they will call this valley the Valley of Slaughter! [7]In this place
I will thwart the plans of the people of Judah and Jerusalem. I
will deliver them over to the power of their enemies who are
seeking to kill them. They will die by the sword at the hands
of their enemies. I will make their dead bodies food for the
birds and wild beasts to eat. [8]I will make this city an object of
horror, a thing to be hissed at. All who pass by it will be filled
with horror and will hiss out their scorn because of all the disasters that have happened to it. [9]I will reduce the people of
this city to desperate straits during the siege imposed on it by
their enemies who are seeking to kill them. I will make them
so desperate that they will eat the flesh of their own sons and
daughters and the flesh of one another."'"'

[10]The LORD continued, "Now break the jar in front of those
who have come here with you. [11]Tell them the LORD of Heaven's
Armies says, 'I will do just as Jeremiah has done. I will smash this
nation and this city as though it were a potter's vessel that is
broken beyond repair. The dead will be buried here in Topheth
until there is no more room to bury them.' [12]I, the LORD, say:
'That is how I will deal with this city and its citizens. I will make
it like Topheth. [13]The houses in Jerusalem and the houses of the
kings of Judah will be defiled by dead bodies just like this place,
Topheth. For they offered sacrifice to the stars and poured out
drink offerings to other gods on the roofs of those houses.'"

[14]Then Jeremiah left Topheth where the LORD had sent him
to give that prophecy. He went to the LORD's temple and stood
in its courtyard and called out to all the people. [15]"The LORD
of Heaven's Armies, the God of Israel, says, 'I will soon bring
on this city and all the towns surrounding it all the disaster I
threatened to do to it. I will do so because they have stubbornly
refused to pay any attention to what I have said!'"

JEREMIAH IS FLOGGED AND PUT IN A CELL

20 Now Pashhur son of Immer heard Jeremiah prophesy
these things. He was the priest who was chief of security
in the LORD's temple. [2]When he heard Jeremiah's prophecy, he
had the prophet flogged. Then he put him in the stocks that

were at the Upper Gate of Benjamin in the LORD's temple. [3]But
the next day Pashhur released Jeremiah from the stocks. When
he did, Jeremiah said to him, "The LORD's name for you is not
'Pashhur' but 'Terror is Everywhere.' [4]For the LORD says, 'I will
make both you and your friends terrified of what will happen to
you. You will see all of them die by the swords of their enemies.
I will hand all the people of Judah over to the king of Babylon.
He will carry some of them away into exile in Babylon, and he
will kill others of them with the sword. [5]I will hand over all the
wealth of this city to their enemies. I will hand over to them
all the fruits of the labor of the people of this city and all their
prized possessions, as well as all the treasures of the kings of
Judah. Their enemies will seize it all as plunder and carry it
off to Babylon. [6]You, Pashhur, and all your household will go
into exile in Babylon. You will die there, and you will be buried
there. The same thing will happen to all your friends to whom
you have prophesied lies.'"

JEREMIAH COMPLAINS ABOUT THE REACTION TO HIS MINISTRY

[7] LORD, you coerced me into being a prophet,
and I allowed you to do it.
You overcame my resistance and prevailed over me.
Now I have become a constant laughingstock.
Everyone ridicules me.
[8] For whenever I prophesy, I must cry out,
"Violence and destruction are coming!"
This message from the LORD has made me
an object of continual insults and derision.
[9] Sometimes I think, "I will make no mention of his
message.
I will not speak as his messenger anymore."
But then his message becomes like a fire
locked up inside of me, burning in my heart and soul.
I grow weary of trying to hold it in;
I cannot contain it.
[10] I hear many whispering words of intrigue against me.
Those who would cause me terror are everywhere!
They are saying, "Come on, let's publicly denounce him!"
All my so-called friends are just watching for
something that would lead to my downfall.
They say, "Perhaps he can be enticed into slipping up,
so we can prevail over him and get our revenge on him."
[11] But the LORD is with me to help me like an awe-
inspiring warrior.
Therefore those who persecute me will fail and will not
prevail over me.
They will be thoroughly disgraced because they did not
succeed.
Their disgrace will never be forgotten.
[12] O LORD of Heaven's Armies, you test and prove the
righteous.
You see into people's hearts and minds.
Pay them back for what they have done
because I trust you to vindicate my cause.
[13] Sing to the LORD! Praise the LORD!
For he rescues the oppressed from the clutches of
evildoers.
[14] Cursed be the day I was born!

20:12 God does not hold out against his children when they beg his pity. And for you he will pray purely, held in high honor as an angel of God and grieved not by you but for you. This is sincere repentance. "God will not be made a fool" (Gal 6:7), nor does he give heed to vain words. For he alone searches the innermost recesses of the heart, hears those who are in the fire, listens to those who supplicate in the whale's belly, and is near to all who believe and far from the ungodly if they do not repent.

CLEMENT OF ALEXANDRIA
(C. 150–C. 215)
WHO IS THE RICH MAN THAT SHALL BE SAVED

May that day not be blessed when my mother gave
birth to me.
15 Cursed be the man
who made my father very glad
when he brought him the news
that a baby boy had been born to him!
16 May that man be like the cities
that the LORD destroyed without showing any mercy.
May he hear a cry of distress in the morning
and a battle cry at noon.
17 For he did not kill me before I came from the womb,
making my pregnant mother's womb my grave forever.
18 Why did I ever come forth from my mother's womb?
All I experience is trouble and grief,
and I spend my days in shame.

THE LORD WILL HAND JERUSALEM OVER TO ENEMIES

21 The LORD spoke to Jeremiah when King Zedekiah sent
to him Pashhur son of Malkijah and the priest Zephaniah son of Maaseiah. Zedekiah sent them to Jeremiah to
ask, 2"Please ask the LORD to come and help us, because King
Nebuchadnezzar of Babylon is attacking us. Maybe the LORD
will perform one of his miracles as in times past and make him
stop attacking us and leave." 3Jeremiah answered them, "Tell
Zedekiah 4that the LORD, the God of Israel, says, 'The forces at
your disposal are now outside the walls fighting against King
Nebuchadnezzar of Babylon and the Babylonians who have you
under siege. I will gather those forces back inside the city. 5In
anger, in fury, and in wrath I myself will fight against you with
my mighty power and great strength. 6I will kill everything
living in Jerusalem, people and animals alike. They will die from
terrible diseases. 7Then I, the LORD, promise that I will hand
over King Zedekiah of Judah, his officials, and any of the people
who survive the war, starvation, and disease. I will hand them
over to King Nebuchadnezzar of Babylon and to their enemies
who want to kill them. He will slaughter them with the sword.
He will not show them any mercy, compassion, or pity.'
8"But tell the people of Jerusalem that the LORD says, 'I will
give you a choice between two courses of action. One will result
in life; the other will result in death. 9Those who stay in this city
will die in battle or of starvation or disease. Those who leave
the city and surrender to the Babylonians who are besieging
it will live. They will escape with their lives. 10For I, the LORD,
say that I am determined not to deliver this city but to bring
disaster on it. It will be handed over to the king of Babylon, and
he will destroy it with fire.'"

WARNINGS TO THE ROYAL COURT

11The LORD told me to say to the royal court of Judah:
"Listen to the LORD's message,
12 O royal family descended from David.
The LORD says:
'See to it that people each day are judged fairly.
Deliver those who have been robbed from those who
oppress them.
Otherwise, my wrath will blaze out against you.
It will burn like a fire that cannot be put out
because of the evil that you have done.

21:8 Do not take into account every sin of your servants, but cleanse us with the cleansing of your truth and direct our steps to walk in holiness and righteousness and purity of heart and to do what is good and pleasing in your sight. Yes, Lord, let your face shine on us in peace for our good that we may be sheltered by your mighty hand and delivered from every sin by your uplifted arm; deliver us as well from those who hate us unjustly. Give harmony and peace to us and to all who dwell on the earth, just as you did to our ancestors when they reverently called on you in faith and truth, that we may be saved while we render obedience to your almighty and most excellent name.

CLEMENT OF ROME **(D. 99)**
FIRST CLEMENT

13 Listen, you who sit enthroned above the valley on a
rocky plateau.
I am opposed to you,' says the LORD.
'You boast, "No one can swoop down on us.
No one can penetrate into our places of refuge."
14 But I will punish you as your deeds deserve,'
says the LORD.
'I will set fire to your palace;
it will burn up everything around it.'"

22 The LORD told me, "Go down to the palace of the king of
Judah. Give him a message from me there. 2 Say: 'Listen,
O king of Judah who follows in David's succession. You, your
officials, and your subjects who pass through the gates of this
palace must listen to the LORD's message. 3 The LORD says, "Do
what is just and right. Deliver those who have been robbed
from those who oppress them. Do not exploit or mistreat resident foreigners who live in your land, children who have no
fathers, or widows. Do not kill innocent people in this land. 4 If
you are careful to obey these commands, then the kings who
follow in David's succession and ride in chariots or on horses
will continue to come through the gates of this palace, as will
their officials and their subjects. 5 But, if you do not obey these
commands, I solemnly swear that this palace will become a pile
of rubble. I, the LORD, affirm it!"'
6 "For the LORD says concerning the palace of the king of
Judah,

"'This place looks like a veritable forest of Gilead to me.
It is like the wooded heights of Lebanon in my eyes.
But I swear that I will make it like a wilderness
whose towns have all been deserted.
7 I will send men against it to destroy it
with their axes and hatchets.
They will hack up its fine cedar panels and columns
and throw them into the fire.

8 "'People from other nations will pass by this city. They will
ask one another, "Why has the LORD done such a thing to this
great city?" 9 The answer will come back, "It is because they
broke their covenant with the LORD their God and worshiped
and served other gods."

JUDGMENT ON JEHOAHAZ

10 "'Do not weep for the king who was killed.
Do not grieve for him.
But weep mournfully for the king who has gone into
exile.
For he will never return to see his native land again.

11 "'For the LORD has spoken about Shallum son of Josiah,
who succeeded his father as king of Judah but was carried off
into exile. He has said, "He will never return to this land. 12 For
he will die in the country where they took him as a captive. He
will never see this land again."

JUDGMENT ON JEHOIAKIM

13 "'Sure to be judged is the king who builds his palace
using injustice
and treats people unfairly while adding its upper rooms.

22:11–23 Here is a sentence of death upon one king, the wicked son of a very pious father. Josiah was prevented from seeing the evil to come in this world; dying saints may be justly envied, while living sinners are justly pitied. Here is the doom of Jehoiakim. He made no conscience of shedding innocent blood. Covetousness, which is the root of all evil, was at the bottom of all. Jehoiakim knew that his father found the way of duty to be the way of comfort, yet he would not tread in his steps. He would die unlamented, hated for oppression and cruelty.

MATTHEW HENRY **(1662–1714)**
COMMENTARY ON THE WHOLE BIBLE

He makes his countrymen work for him for nothing.
He does not pay them for their labor.
14 He says, "I will build myself a large palace
with spacious upper rooms."
He cuts windows in its walls,
panels it with cedar, and paints its rooms red.
15 Does it make you any more of a king
that you outstrip everyone else in building with cedar?
Just think about your father.
He was content that he had food and drink.
He did what was just and right.
So things went well with him.
16 He upheld the cause of the poor and needy.
So things went well for Judah.'
The LORD says,
'That is a good example of what it means to know me.
17 But you are always thinking and looking
for ways to increase your wealth by dishonest means.
Your eyes and your heart are set
on killing some innocent person
and committing fraud and oppression.'"

18 So the LORD has this to say about Josiah's son, King Je-
hoiakim of Judah:
"People will not mourn for him, saying,
'This makes me sad, my brother!
This makes me sad, my sister!'
They will not mourn for him, saying,
'Poor, poor lord! Poor, poor majesty!'
19 He will be left unburied just like a dead donkey.
His body will be dragged off and thrown outside the
gates of Jerusalem.

WARNING TO JERUSALEM

20 "People of Jerusalem, go up to Lebanon and cry out in
mourning.
Go to the land of Bashan and cry out loudly.
Cry out in mourning from the mountains of Moab.
For your allies have all been defeated.
21 While you were feeling secure I gave you warning.
But you said, 'I refuse to listen to you.'
That is the way you have acted from your earliest
history onward.
Indeed, you have never paid attention to me.
22 My judgment will carry off all your leaders like a storm
wind!
Your allies will go into captivity.
Then you will certainly be disgraced and put to shame
because of all the wickedness you have done.
23 You may feel as secure as a bird
nesting in the cedars of Lebanon.
But O how you will groan when the pains of judgment
come on you.
They will be like those of a woman giving birth to a baby."

JECONIAH WILL BE PERMANENTLY EXILED

24 The LORD says, "As surely as I am the living God, you, Jeconiah,
king of Judah, son of Jehoiakim, will not be the earthly representative of my authority. Indeed, I will take that right away

from you. 25 I will hand you over to those who want to take your
life and of whom you are afraid. I will hand you over to King
Nebuchadnezzar of Babylon and his Babylonian soldiers. 26 I
will force you and your mother who gave you birth into exile.
You will be exiled to a country where neither of you were born,
and you will both die there. 27 You will never come back to this
land that you will long to return to!

28 "This man, Jeconiah, will be like a broken pot someone
threw away.
He will be like a clay vessel that no one wants.
Why will he and his children be forced into exile?
Why will they be thrown out into a country they know
nothing about?
29 O Land, land, land of Judah!
Listen to the LORD's message."

30 The LORD says,
"Enroll this man in the register as though he were
childless.
Enroll him as a man who will not enjoy success during
his lifetime.
For none of his sons will succeed in occupying the
throne of David
or ever succeed in ruling over Judah."

NEW LEADERS OVER A REGATHERED REMNANT

23 The LORD says, "The leaders of my people are sure to be
judged. They were supposed to watch over my people
like shepherds watch over their sheep. But they are causing
my people to be destroyed and scattered." 2 So the LORD God of
Israel has this to say about the leaders who are ruling over his
people: "You have caused my people to be dispersed and driven
into exile. You have not taken care of them. So I will punish you
for the evil that you have done. I, the LORD, affirm it! 3 Then I
myself will regather those of my people who are still alive from
all the countries where I have driven them. I will bring them
back to their homeland. They will greatly increase in number.
4 I will install rulers over them who will care for them. Then
they will no longer need to fear or be terrified. None of them
will turn up missing. I, the LORD, promise it!

5 "I, the LORD, promise that a new time will certainly come
when I will raise up for them a righteous branch, a
descendant of David.
He will rule over them with wisdom and understanding
and will do what is just and right in the land.
6 Under his rule Judah will enjoy safety
and Israel will live in security.
This is the name he will go by:
'The LORD has provided us with justice.'

7 "So I, the LORD, say: 'A new time will certainly come. People
now affirm their oaths with, "I swear as surely as the LORD lives
who delivered the people of Israel out of Egypt." 8 But at that
time they will affirm them with, "I swear as surely as the LORD
lives who delivered the descendants of the former nation of
Israel from the land of the north and from all the other lands
where he had banished them." At that time they will live in
their own land.'"

23:1–8 The prophecy proclaims the everlasting nature of grace. Therefore it is clear that these things were fulfilled during the lifetimes of the apostles, for they alone had the gift of the Holy Spirit. The Jews shamelessly endeavor to apply this to Zerubbabel. But they need to understand that he was no king—just a popular leader. Neither is the meaning of the name appropriate to him, the word meaning "the Lord our righteousness." Since, however, he was a type of Christ the Lord and brought back the captives from Babylon to Judah, just as the Lord transferred those enslaved by the devil to truth, anyone applying this to him in the manner of a type would do nothing beyond reason. It is necessary that we understand, however, that it is the Lord Jesus Christ, a descendant of David according to the flesh, who is proclaimed by the prophets as "the righteous branch," "the righteous king" and "the Lord of righteousness."

THEODORET OF CYR
(C. 393–C. 458)
COMMENTARY ON JEREMIAH

ORACLES AGAINST THE FALSE PROPHETS

9 Here is what the LORD says concerning the false prophets:
"My heart and my mind are deeply disturbed.
I tremble all over.
I am like a drunk person,
like a person who has had too much wine,
because of the way the LORD
and his holy word are being mistreated.
10 For the land is full of people unfaithful to him.
They live wicked lives, and they misuse their power.
So the land is dried up because it is under his curse.
The pastures in the wilderness are withered."

11 Moreover, the LORD says,
"Both the prophets and priests are godless.
I have even found them doing evil in my temple.
12 So the paths they follow will be dark and slippery.
They will stumble and fall headlong.
For I will bring disaster on them.
A day of reckoning is coming for them."
The LORD affirms it!
13 The LORD says, "I saw the prophets of Samaria
doing something that was disgusting.
They prophesied in the name of the god Baal
and led my people Israel astray.
14 But I see the prophets of Jerusalem
doing something just as shocking.
They are unfaithful to me
and continually prophesy lies.
So they give encouragement to people who are doing evil,
with the result that they do not stop their evildoing.
I consider all of them as bad as the people of Sodom,
and the citizens of Jerusalem as bad as the people of Gomorrah.
15 So then I, the LORD of Heaven's Armies,
have something to say concerning the prophets of Jerusalem:
'I will make these prophets eat the bitter food of suffering
and drink the poison water of judgment.
For the prophets of Jerusalem are the reason
that ungodliness has spread throughout the land.'"

16 The LORD of Heaven's Armies says to the people of Jerusalem:
"Do not listen to what
those prophets are saying to you.
They are filling you with false hopes.
They are reporting visions of their own imaginations,
not something the LORD has given them to say.
17 They continually say to those who reject what the LORD has said,
'Things will go well for you!'
They say to all those who follow the stubborn inclinations of their own hearts,
'Nothing bad will happen to you!'
18 Yet which of them has ever stood in the LORD's inner circle
so they could see and hear what he has to say?

Which of them have ever paid attention or listened to
what he has said?
19 But just watch! The wrath of the LORD
will come like a storm!
Like a raging storm it will rage down
on the heads of those who are wicked.
20 The anger of the LORD will not turn back
until he has fully carried out his intended purposes.
In future days
you people will come to understand this clearly.
21 I did not send those prophets,
yet they were in a hurry to give their message.
I did not tell them anything,
yet they prophesied anyway.
22 But if they had stood in my inner circle,
they would have proclaimed my message to my people.
They would have caused my people to turn from their
wicked ways
and stop doing the evil things they are doing.
23 Do you people think that I am some local deity
and not the transcendent God?" the LORD asks.
24 "Do you really think anyone can hide himself
where I cannot see him?" the LORD asks.
"Do you not know that I am everywhere?"
the LORD asks.

25 The LORD says, "I have heard what those prophets who
are prophesying lies in my name are saying. They are saying, 'I
have had a dream! I have had a dream!' 26 Those prophets are
just prophesying lies. They are prophesying the delusions of
their own minds. 27 How long will they go on plotting to make
my people forget who I am through the dreams they tell one
another? That is just as bad as what their ancestors did when
they forgot who I am by worshiping the god Baal. 28 Let the
prophet who has had a dream go ahead and tell his dream. Let
the person who has received my message report that message
faithfully. What is like straw cannot compare to what is like
grain! I, the LORD, affirm it! 29 My message is like a fire that
purges dross. It is like a hammer that breaks a rock in pieces. I,
the LORD, so affirm it! 30 So I, the LORD, affirm that I am opposed
to those prophets who steal messages from one another that
they claim are from me. 31 I, the LORD, affirm that I am opposed
to those prophets who are using their own tongues to declare,
'The LORD declares.' 32 I, the LORD, affirm that I am opposed to
those prophets who dream up lies and report them. They are
misleading my people with their reckless lies. I did not send
them. I did not commission them. They are not helping these
people at all. I, the LORD, affirm it!"

33 The LORD said to me, "Jeremiah, when one of these people,
or a prophet, or a priest asks you, 'What burdensome message
do you have from the LORD?' Tell them, 'You are the burden,
and I will cast you away. I, the LORD, affirm it! 34 I will punish
any prophet, priest, or other person who says, "The LORD's
message is burdensome." I will punish both that person and
his whole family.'"

35 So I, Jeremiah, tell you, "Each of you people should say to his
friend or his relative, 'How did the LORD answer? Or what did
the LORD say?' 36 You must no longer say that the LORD's message is burdensome. For what is 'burdensome' really pertains to

what a person himself says. You are misrepresenting the words of our God, the living God, the LORD of Heaven's Armies. [37]Each of you should merely ask the prophet, 'What answer did the LORD give you?' Or 'what did the LORD say?' [38]But just suppose you continue to say, 'The message of the LORD is burdensome.' Here is what the LORD says will happen: 'I sent word to you that you must not say, "The LORD's message is burdensome." But you used the words, "The LORD's message is burdensome," anyway. [39]So I will carry you far off and throw you away. I will send both you and the city I gave to you and to your ancestors out of my sight. [40]I will bring on you lasting shame and lasting disgrace that will never be forgotten!'"

GOOD FIGS AND BAD FIGS

24 The LORD showed me two baskets of figs sitting before his temple. This happened after King Nebuchadnezzar of Babylon deported Jehoiakim's son, King Jeconiah of Judah. He deported him and the leaders of Judah from Jerusalem, along with the craftsmen and metal workers, and took them to Babylon. [2]One basket had very good-looking figs in it. They looked like those that had ripened early. The other basket had very bad-looking figs in it, so bad they could not be eaten. [3]The LORD said to me, "What do you see, Jeremiah?" I answered, "I see figs. The good ones look very good. But the bad ones look very bad, so bad that they cannot be eaten."

[4]The LORD's message came to me, [5]"I, the LORD, the God of Israel, say: 'The exiles of Judah whom I sent away from here to the land of Babylon are like those good figs. I consider them to be good. [6]I will look after their welfare and will restore them to this land. There I will build them up and will not tear them down. I will plant them firmly in the land and will not uproot them. [7]I will give them the desire to acknowledge that I am the LORD. I will be their God, and they will be my people. For they will wholeheartedly return to me.'

[8]"I, the LORD, also solemnly assert: 'King Zedekiah of Judah, his officials, and the people who remain in Jerusalem or who have gone to live in Egypt are like those bad figs. I consider them to be just like those bad figs that are so bad they cannot be eaten. [9]I will bring such disaster on them that all the kingdoms of the earth will be horrified. I will make them an object of reproach, a proverbial example of disaster. I will make them an object of ridicule, an example to be used in curses. That is how they will be remembered wherever I banish them. [10]I will bring war, starvation, and disease on them until they are completely destroyed from the land I gave them and their ancestors.'"

24:1–10 The prophet had hitherto spoken of the alleviation of punishment, as though he had said, *God will stretch forth his hand to restore his people to their own country*. But now the prophet speaks of a much more excellent favor, that God would not only mitigate punishment but would also inwardly change and reform their hearts so that they would not only return to their own country but would also become a true church. Now God promised that he would bring them, not only to enjoy temporal and fading blessings, but also eternal salvation, for they would truly fear and serve him. Jeremiah, after having spoken of the people's restoration, justly exalted this favor above everything else, that the people would repent so that they would not only fully partake of all the blessings they could expect but would also worship God in sincerity and truth.

JOHN CALVIN **(1509–1564)**
COMPLETE COMMENTARY ON THE BIBLE

SEVENTY YEARS OF SERVITUDE FOR FAILURE TO GIVE HEED

25 In the fourth year that Jehoiakim son of Josiah was king of Judah, the LORD spoke to Jeremiah concerning all the people of Judah. (That was the same as the first year that Nebuchadnezzar was king of Babylon.) [2]So the prophet Jeremiah spoke to all the people of Judah and to all the people who were living in Jerusalem. [3]"For the last 23 years, from the thirteenth year that Josiah son of Amon was ruling in Judah until now, the LORD's messages have come to me, and I have told them to you over and over again. But you would not listen. [4]Over and over again the LORD has sent his servants the prophets to you. But you have not listened or paid attention. [5]He said through

them, 'Each of you must turn from your wicked ways and stop doing the evil things you are doing. If you do, I will allow you to continue to live here in the land that I gave to you and your ancestors as a lasting possession. 6Do not pay allegiance to other gods and worship and serve them. Do not make me angry by the things that you do. Then I will not cause you any harm.' 7So, now the LORD says, 'You have not listened to me. But you have made me angry by the things that you have done. Thus you have brought harm on yourselves.'

8"Therefore, the LORD of Heaven's Armies says, 'You have not listened to what I said. 9So I, the LORD, affirm that I will send for all the peoples of the north and my servant, King Nebuchadnezzar of Babylon. I will bring them against this land and its inhabitants and all the nations that surround it. I will utterly destroy the land, its inhabitants, and all the surrounding nations and make them everlasting ruins. I will make them objects of horror and hissing scorn. 10I will put an end to the sounds of joy and gladness and the glad celebration of brides and grooms in these lands. I will put an end to the sound of people grinding meal. I will put an end to lamps shining in their houses. 11This whole area will become a desolate wasteland. These nations will be subject to the king of Babylon for 70 years.'

12"'But when the seventy years are over, I will punish the king of Babylon and his nation for their sins. I will make the land of Babylon an everlasting ruin. I, the LORD, affirm it! 13I will bring on that land everything that I said I would. I will bring on it everything that is written in this book. I will bring on it everything that Jeremiah has prophesied against all the nations. 14For many nations and great kings will make slaves of the king of Babylon and his nation too. I will repay them for all they have done.'"

JUDAH AND THE NATIONS WILL EXPERIENCE GOD'S WRATH

15So the LORD, the God of Israel, spoke to me in a vision: "Take this cup from my hand. It is filled with the wine of my wrath. Take it and make the nations to whom I send you drink it. 16When they have drunk it, they will stagger to and fro and act insane. For I will send wars sweeping through them."

17So I took the cup from the LORD's hand. I made all the nations to whom he sent me drink the wine of his wrath. 18I made Jerusalem and the cities of Judah, its kings and its officials drink it. I did it so Judah would become a ruin. I did it so Judah, its kings, and its officials would become an object of horror and of hissing scorn, an example used in curses. Such is already becoming the case! 19I made all these other people drink it: Pharaoh, king of Egypt; his attendants, his officials, his people, 20the foreigners living in Egypt; all the kings of the land of Uz; all the kings of the land of the Philistines, the people of Ashkelon, Gaza, Ekron, the people who had been left alive from Ashdod; 21all the people of Edom, Moab, Ammon; 22all the kings of Tyre, all the kings of Sidon; all the kings of the coastlands along the sea; 23the people of Dedan, Tema, Buz, all the desert people who cut their hair short at the temples; 24all the kings of Arabia who live in the desert; 25all the kings of Zimri; all the kings of Elam; all the kings of Media; 26all the kings of the north, whether near or far from one another; and all the other kingdoms that are on the face of the earth. After all of them have drunk the wine of the LORD's wrath, the king of Babylon must drink it.

25:1–14 Unless the Jews laid aside their vanities and returned to their God, he would bestow the inheritance of eternal life on foreign nations and collect to himself a more faithful people out of those who were aliens by birth. For the prophet Jeremiah says, "Over and over again the LORD has sent his servants the prophets to you. But you have not listened or paid attention. He said through them, 'Each of you must turn from your wicked ways and stop doing the evil things you are doing. If you do, I will allow you to continue to live here in the land that I gave to you and your ancestors as a lasting possession . . . Do not make me angry by the things that you do. Then I will not cause you any harm.'"

LACTANTIUS **(C. 250–C. 325)**
DIVINE INSTITUTES

27Then the LORD said to me, "Tell them that the LORD of
Heaven's Armies, the God of Israel, says, 'Drink this cup until
you get drunk and vomit. Drink until you fall down and can't
get up. For I will send wars sweeping through you.' 28If they
refuse to take the cup from your hand and drink it, tell them
that the LORD of Heaven's Armies says, 'You most certainly
must drink it! 29For take note, I am already beginning to bring
disaster on the city that I call my own. So how can you possibly
avoid being punished? You will not go unpunished. For I am
proclaiming war against all who live on the earth. I, the LORD
of Heaven's Armies, affirm it!'

30"Then, Jeremiah, make the following prophecy against
them:

'Like a lion about to attack, the LORD will roar from the heights of heaven;
from his holy dwelling on high he will roar loudly.
He will roar mightily against his land.
He will shout in triumph, like those stomping juice from the grapes,
against all those who live on the earth.
31 The sounds of battle will resound to the ends of the earth.
For the LORD will bring charges against the nations.
He will pass judgment on all humankind
and will hand the wicked over to be killed in war.'
The LORD so affirms it!
32 The LORD of Heaven's Armies says,
'Disaster will soon come on one nation after another.
A mighty storm of military destruction is rising up
from the distant parts of the earth.'
33 Those who have been killed by the LORD at that time
will be scattered from one end of the earth to the other.
They will not be mourned over, gathered up, or buried.
Their dead bodies will lie scattered over the ground like manure.
34 Wail and cry out in anguish, you rulers!
Roll in the dust, you who shepherd flocks of people!
The time for you to be slaughtered has come.
You will lie scattered and fallen like broken pieces of fine pottery.
35 The leaders will not be able to run away and hide.
The shepherds of the flocks will not be able to escape.
36 Listen to the cries of anguish of the leaders.
Listen to the wails of the shepherds of the flocks.
They are wailing because the LORD
is about to destroy their lands.
37 Their peaceful dwelling places will be laid waste
by the fierce anger of the LORD.
38 The LORD is like a lion who has left his lair.
So their lands will certainly be laid waste
by the warfare of the oppressive nation
and by the fierce anger of the LORD."

JEREMIAH IS PUT ON TRIAL AS A FALSE PROPHET

26 The LORD spoke to Jeremiah at the beginning of the reign
of Josiah's son, King Jehoiakim of Judah. 2The LORD said,
"Go stand in the courtyard of the LORD's temple. Speak out to all
the people who are coming from the towns of Judah to worship

in the LORD's temple. Tell them everything I command you to
tell them. Do not leave out a single word. 3Maybe they will pay
attention and each of them will stop living the evil way they
do. If they do that, then I will forgo destroying them as I had
intended to do because of the wicked things they have been
doing. 4Tell them that the LORD says, 'You must obey me; you
must live according to the way I have instructed you in my laws.
5You must pay attention to the exhortations of my servants
the prophets. I have sent them to you over and over again. But
you have not paid any attention to them. 6If you do not obey
me, then I will do to this temple what I did to Shiloh. And I will
make this city an example to be used in curses by people from
all the nations on the earth.'"

7The priests, the prophets, and all the people heard Jeremiah
say these things in the LORD's temple. 8Jeremiah had just barely
finished saying all the LORD had commanded him to say to all
the people when all at once some of the priests, the prophets,
and the people grabbed him and shouted, "You deserve to die!
9How dare you claim the LORD's authority to prophesy such
things! How dare you claim his authority to prophesy that this
temple will become like Shiloh and that this city will become
an uninhabited ruin!" Then all the people crowded around Jeremiah in the LORD's temple.

10However, some of the officials of Judah heard about what
was happening, and they rushed up to the LORD's temple from
the royal palace. They set up court at the entrance of the New
Gate of the LORD's temple. 11Then the priests and the prophets made their charges before the officials and all the people.
They said, "This man should be condemned to die because he
prophesied against this city. You have heard him do so with
your own ears."

12Then Jeremiah made his defense before all the officials
and all the people. "The LORD sent me to prophesy everything
you have heard me say against this temple and against this
city. 13But correct the way you have been living and do what is
right. Obey the LORD your God. If you do, the LORD will forgo
destroying you as he threatened he would. 14As to my case, I am
in your power. Do to me what you deem fair and proper. 15But
you should take careful note of this: If you put me to death, you
will bring on yourselves and this city and those who live in it
the guilt of murdering an innocent man. For the LORD has sent
me to speak all this where you can hear it. That is the truth!"

16Then the officials and all the people rendered their verdict
to the priests and the prophets. They said, "This man should
not be condemned to die. For he has spoken to us under the
authority of the LORD our God." 17Then some of the elders of
Judah stepped forward and spoke to all the people gathered
there. They said, 18"Micah from Moresheth prophesied during
the time Hezekiah was king of Judah. He told all the people of
Judah, 'The LORD of Heaven's Armies says,

"'Zion will become a plowed field.
Jerusalem will become a pile of rubble.
The temple mount will become a mere wooded ridge."'

19"King Hezekiah and all the people of Judah did not put
him to death, did they? Did not Hezekiah show reverence for
the LORD and seek the LORD's favor? Did not the LORD forgo
destroying them as he threatened he would? But we are on the
verge of bringing great disaster on ourselves."

26:2 "Do not leave out a single word." God has trusted the prophet to preach clearly and simply and to leave nothing out: *Be genuine, bold, and speak out; do not abbreviate what you say. Then they will understand what I am planning insofar as they want to turn from their malice and toward me and if from now on they do not make excuses.* When an adversary is not present, then one is brave; but when he is present, then one is either very fearful and remains very quiet or one plays the hypocrite and wastes the opportunity, so that one takes all the power from the words. When one neither brings the matter forward nor speaks out loudly, then one allows everyone to have an excuse for his vices. Therefore the prophet must speak out concerning these vices in an unvarnished, clear, and direct way.

ULRICH ZWINGLI **(1484–1531)**
SERMONS

[20]Now there was another man who prophesied as the LORD's representative against this city and this land just as Jeremiah did. His name was Uriah son of Shemaiah from Kiriath Jearim. [21]When King Jehoiakim and all his bodyguards and officials heard what he was prophesying, the king sought to have him executed. But Uriah found out about it and fled to Egypt out of fear. [22]However, King Jehoiakim sent some men to Egypt, including Elnathan son of Achbor, [23]and they brought Uriah back from there. They took him to King Jehoiakim, who had him executed and had his body thrown into the burial place of the common people.

[24]However, Ahikam son of Shaphan used his influence to keep Jeremiah from being handed over and executed by the people.

JEREMIAH COUNSELS SUBMISSION TO BABYLON

27 The LORD spoke to Jeremiah early in the reign of Josiah's son, King Zedekiah of Judah. [2]The LORD told me, "Make a yoke out of leather straps and wooden crossbars and put it on your neck. [3]Use it to send messages to the kings of Edom, Moab, Ammon, Tyre, and Sidon. Send them through the envoys who have come to Jerusalem to King Zedekiah of Judah. [4]Charge them to give their masters a message from me. Tell them, 'The LORD of Heaven's Armies, the God of Israel, says to give your masters this message: [5]"I made the earth and the people and animals on it by my mighty power and great strength, and I give it to whomever I see fit. [6]I have at this time placed all these nations of yours under the power of my servant, King Nebuchadnezzar of Babylon. I have even made all the wild animals subject to him. [7]All nations must serve him and his son and grandson until the time comes for his own nation to fall. Then many nations and great kings will in turn subjugate Babylon. [8]But suppose a nation or a kingdom will not be subject to King Nebuchadnezzar of Babylon. Suppose it will not submit to the yoke of servitude to him. I, the LORD, affirm that I will punish that nation. I will use the king of Babylon to punish it with war, starvation, and disease until I have destroyed it. [9]So do not listen to your prophets or to those who claim to predict the future by divination, by dreams, by consulting the dead, or by practicing magic. They keep telling you, 'You do not need to be subject to the king of Babylon.' [10]Do not listen to them, because their prophecies are lies. Listening to them will only cause you to be taken far away from your native land. I will drive you out of your country and you will die in exile. [11]Things will go better for the nation that submits to the yoke of servitude to the king of Babylon and is subject to him. I will leave that nation in its native land. Its people can continue to farm it and live in it. I, the LORD, affirm it!"'"

[12]I told King Zedekiah of Judah the same thing. I said, "Submit to the yoke of servitude to the king of Babylon. Be subject to him and his people. Then you will continue to live. [13]There is no reason why you and your people should die in war or from starvation or disease. That's what the LORD says will happen to any nation that will not be subject to the king of Babylon. [14]'Do not listen to the prophets who are telling you that you do not need to serve the king of Babylon. For they are prophesying lies to you. [15]For I, the LORD, affirm that I did not send them. They are prophesying lies to you in my name. If you listen to

27:12 Jeremiah was set over kingdoms and nations, for the doctrine taught by the prophets is higher than all earthly rankings. Jeremiah was indeed one of the people and did not exempt himself from the authority of the king. Nor did he pretend that he was released from the laws because he possessed that high dignity by which he was superior to kings. The prophet kept himself in his own rank like others, and yet when he had to exercise his spiritual jurisdiction in God's name, he spared neither the king nor his counselors; for he knew that his doctrine was above all kings.

JOHN CALVIN **(1509–1564)**
COMPLETE COMMENTARY ON THE BIBLE

them, I will drive you and the prophets who are prophesying
lies out of the land and you will all die in exile.'"
16 I also told the priests and all the people, "The LORD says,
'Do not listen to what your prophets are saying. They are prophesying to you that the valuable articles taken from the LORD's
temple will be brought back from Babylon very soon. But they
are prophesying a lie to you. 17 Do not listen to them. Be subject
to the king of Babylon. Then you will continue to live. Why
should this city be made a pile of rubble?'" 18 I also told them,
"If they are really prophets and the LORD is speaking to them,
let them pray earnestly to the LORD of Heaven's Armies. Let
them plead with him not to let the valuable articles that are still
left in the LORD's temple, in the royal palace of Judah, and in
Jerusalem be taken away to Babylon. 19 For the LORD of Heaven's
Armies has already spoken about the two bronze pillars, the
large bronze basin called 'The Sea,' and the movable bronze
stands. He has already spoken about the rest of the valuable
articles that are left in this city. 20 He has already spoken about
these things that King Nebuchadnezzar of Babylon did not take
away when he carried Jehoiakim's son King Jeconiah of Judah
and the nobles of Judah and Jerusalem away as captives from
Jerusalem to Babylon. 21 Indeed, the LORD of Heaven's Armies,
the God of Israel, has already spoken about the valuable articles
that are left in the LORD's temple, in the royal palace of Judah,
and in Jerusalem. 22 He has said, 'They will be carried off to
Babylon. They will remain there until it is time for me to show
consideration for them again. Then I will bring them back and
restore them to this place. I, the LORD, affirm this!'"

JEREMIAH CONFRONTED BY A FALSE PROPHET

28 The following events occurred in that same year, early
in the reign of King Zedekiah of Judah. To be more precise, it was the fifth month of the fourth year of his reign. The
prophet Hananiah son of Azzur, who was from Gibeon, spoke
to Jeremiah in the LORD's temple in the presence of the priests
and all the people: 2 "The LORD of Heaven's Armies, the God of
Israel, says, 'I will break the yoke of servitude to the king of
Babylon. 3 Before two years are over, I will bring back to this
place everything that King Nebuchadnezzar of Babylon took
from it and carried away to Babylon. 4 I will also bring back to
this place Jehoiakim's son King Jeconiah of Judah and all the
exiles who were taken to Babylon.' Indeed, the LORD affirms, 'I
will break the yoke of servitude to the king of Babylon.'"
5 Then the prophet Jeremiah responded to the prophet Hananiah in the presence of the priests and all the people who were
standing in the LORD's temple. 6 The prophet Jeremiah said,
"Amen! May the LORD do all this! May the LORD make your
prophecy come true! May he bring back to this place from
Babylon all the valuable articles taken from the LORD's temple and the people who were carried into exile. 7 But listen to
what I say to you and to all these people. 8 From earliest times,
the prophets who preceded you and me invariably prophesied
war, disaster, and plagues against many countries and great
kingdoms. 9 So if a prophet prophesied peace and prosperity,
it was only known that the LORD truly sent him when what he
prophesied came true."
10 The prophet Hananiah then took the yoke off the prophet
Jeremiah's neck and broke it. 11 Then he spoke up in the presence of all the people. "The LORD says, 'In the same way I will

break the yoke of servitude of all the nations to King Nebuchadnezzar of Babylon before two years are over.'" After he heard this, the prophet Jeremiah departed and went on his way. [12]But shortly after the prophet Hananiah had broken the yoke off the prophet Jeremiah's neck, the LORD's message came to Jeremiah. [13]"Go and tell Hananiah that the LORD says, 'You have indeed broken the wooden yoke. But you have only succeeded in replacing it with an iron one! [14]For the LORD of Heaven's Armies, the God of Israel, says, "I have put an irresistible yoke of servitude on all these nations so they will serve King Nebuchadnezzar of Babylon. And they will indeed serve him. I have even given him control over the wild animals."'" [15]Then the prophet Jeremiah told the prophet Hananiah, "Listen, Hananiah! The LORD did not send you! You are making these people trust in a lie. [16]So the LORD says, 'I will most assuredly remove you from the face of the earth. You will die this very year because you have counseled rebellion against the LORD.'"

[17]In the seventh month of that very same year the prophet Hananiah died.

28:13–14 One king of Judah had already been carried off to Babylon and the throne refilled by his brother, a puppet of the conquerors. This shadow of a king, with the bulk of the nation, was eager for revolt. Jeremiah had almost single-handedly to stem the tide of the popular wish. He steadfastly preached submission, not so much to Nebuchadnezzar as to God, who had sent the invaders as chastisement. The lesson was a difficult one to learn—that to throw off legitimate authority is to bind on a worse tyranny. To some kind of yoke all of us must bend our necks, and if we slip them out we do not thereby become independent but simply bring on ourselves a heavier pressure of a harder bondage.

ALEXANDER MACLAREN
(1826–1910)
EXPOSITIONS OF THE HOLY SCRIPTURES

JEREMIAH'S LETTER TO THE EXILES

29 The prophet Jeremiah sent a letter to the exiles Nebuchadnezzar had carried off from Jerusalem to Babylon. It was addressed to the elders who were left among the exiles, to the priests, to the prophets, and to all the other people who were exiled in Babylon. [2]He sent it after King Jeconiah, the queen mother, the palace officials, the leaders of Judah and Jerusalem, the craftsmen, and the metal workers had been exiled from Jerusalem. [3]He sent it with Elasah son of Shaphan and Gemariah son of Hilkiah. King Zedekiah of Judah had sent these men to Babylon to King Nebuchadnezzar of Babylon. The letter said:

[4]"The LORD of Heaven's Armies, the God of Israel, says to all those he sent into exile to Babylon from Jerusalem, [5]'Build houses and settle down. Plant gardens and eat what they produce. [6]Marry and have sons and daughters. Find wives for your sons and allow your daughters to get married so that they too can have sons and daughters. Grow in number; do not dwindle away. [7]Work to see that the city where I sent you as exiles enjoys peace and prosperity. Pray to the LORD for it. For as it prospers you will prosper.'

[8]"For the LORD of Heaven's Armies, the God of Israel, says, 'Do not let the prophets among you or those who claim to be able to predict the future by divination deceive you. And do not pay any attention to the dreams that you are encouraging them to dream. [9]They are prophesying lies to you and claiming my authority to do so. But I did not send them. I, the LORD, affirm it!'

[10]"For the LORD says, 'Only when the seventy years of Babylonian rule are over will I again take up consideration for you. Then I will fulfill my gracious promise to you and restore you to your homeland. [11]For I know what I have planned for you,' says the LORD. 'I have plans to prosper you, not to harm you. I have plans to give you a future filled with hope. [12]When you call out to me and come to me in prayer, I will hear your prayers. [13]When you seek me in prayer and worship, you will find me available to you. If you seek me with all your heart and soul, [14]I will make myself available to you,' says the LORD. 'Then I will reverse your plight and will regather you from all the nations and all the places where I have exiled you,' says the LORD. 'I will bring you back to the place from which I exiled you.'

29:7 The apostle admonished the church to pray for kings and those in authority, assigning as the reason "that we may live a peaceful and quiet life in all godliness and dignity" (1 Tim 2:2). And the prophet Jeremiah, when predicting the captivity that was to befall the ancient people of God and giving them the divine command to go obediently to Babylonia and thus serve their God, counseled them also to pray for Babylonia, saying, "as it prospers you will prosper."

AUGUSTINE **(354–430)**
CITY OF GOD

15“You say, ‘The LORD has raised up prophets of good news for us here in Babylon.’ 16But just listen to what the LORD has to say about the king who occupies David’s throne and all your fellow countrymen who are still living in this city of Jerusalem and were not carried off into exile with you. 17The LORD of Heaven’s Armies says, ‘I will bring war, starvation, and disease on them. I will treat them like figs that are so rotten they cannot be eaten. 18I will chase after them with war, starvation, and disease. I will make all the kingdoms of the earth horrified at what happens to them. I will make them examples of those who are cursed, objects of horror, hissing scorn, and ridicule among all the nations where I exile them. 19For they have not paid attention to what I said to them through my servants the prophets whom I sent to them over and over again,’ says the LORD. ‘And you exiles have not paid any attention to them either,’ says the LORD. 20‘So pay attention to the LORD’s message, all you exiles whom I have sent to Babylon from Jerusalem.’

21“The LORD of Heaven’s Armies, the God of Israel, also has something to say about Ahab son of Kolaiah and Zedekiah son of Maaseiah, who are prophesying lies to you and claiming my authority to do so. ‘I will hand them over to King Nebuchadnezzar of Babylon, and he will execute them before your very eyes. 22And all the exiles of Judah who are in Babylon will use them as examples when they put a curse on anyone. They will say, “May the LORD treat you like Zedekiah and Ahab whom the king of Babylon roasted to death in the fire!” 23This will happen to them because they have done what is shameful in Israel. They have committed adultery with their neighbors’ wives and have spoken lies while claiming my authority. They have spoken words that I did not command them to speak. I know what they have done. I have been a witness to it,’ says the LORD.”

A RESPONSE TO THE LETTER AND A SUBSEQUENT LETTER

24The LORD told Jeremiah, “Tell Shemaiah the Nehelamite 25that the LORD of Heaven’s Armies, the God of Israel, has a message for him. Tell him, ‘On your own initiative you sent a letter to the priest Zephaniah son of Maaseiah and to all the other priests and to all the people in Jerusalem. In your letter you said to Zephaniah, 26“The LORD has made you priest in place of Jehoiada. He has put you in charge in the LORD’s temple of controlling any lunatic who pretends to be a prophet. And it is your duty to put any such person in the stocks with an iron collar around his neck. 27You should have reprimanded Jeremiah from Anathoth who is pretending to be a prophet among you! 28For he has even sent a message to us here in Babylon. He wrote and told us, ‘You will be there a long time. Build houses and settle down. Plant gardens and eat what they produce.’”’”

29Zephaniah the priest read that letter to the prophet Jeremiah. 30Then the LORD’s message came to Jeremiah: 31“Send a message to all the exiles in Babylon. Tell them, ‘The LORD has spoken about Shemaiah the Nehelamite: “Shemaiah has spoken to you as a prophet even though I did not send him. He is making you trust in a lie. 32Because he has done this,” the LORD says, “I will punish Shemaiah the Nehelamite and his whole family. There will not be any of them left to experience the good things that I will do for my people. I, the LORD, affirm it! For he counseled rebellion against the LORD.”’”

30:1–24 This passage is not simply about biological children of Abraham but about children of promise. Only in this more mysterious sense was the word of Jeremiah fulfilled, "They will be subject to the LORD their God and to the Davidic ruler whom I will raise up as king over them." The Jews did not have peace. After they were conquered by the Chaldeans, they never were free from fear and oppression from other foreign nations. These words of the prophet—"The descendants of Jacob will return to their land and enjoy peace. They will be secure and no one will terrify them"—were not fulfilled for Jews. All prophets who prophesied after the Babylonian captivity say that during their time Jews were not free from fear and wars with neighboring nations. And even though they served the Lord their God and did not worship pagan gods, they were oppressed.

EPHREM THE SYRIAN
(C. 306–373)
COMMENTARY ON JEREMIAH

INTRODUCTION TO THE BOOK OF CONSOLATION

30 The LORD spoke to Jeremiah. [2]"The LORD God of Israel
says, 'Write everything that I am about to tell you in a
scroll. [3]For I, the LORD, affirm that the time will come when I
will reverse the plight of my people, Israel and Judah,' says the
LORD. 'I will bring them back to the land I gave their ancestors,
and they will take possession of it once again.'"

ISRAEL AND JUDAH WILL BE DELIVERED AFTER A TIME OF DEEP DISTRESS

[4]So here is what the LORD has to say about Israel and Judah.
[5]Yes, here is what he says:
"You hear cries of panic and of terror;
there is no peace in sight.
6 Ask yourselves this and consider it carefully:
Have you ever seen a man give birth to a baby?
Why then do I see all these strong men
grabbing their stomachs in pain like a woman giving birth?
And why do their faces
turn so deathly pale?
7 Alas, what a terrible time of trouble it is!
There has never been any like it.
It is a time of trouble for the descendants of Jacob,
but some of them will be rescued out of it.
8 When the time for them to be rescued comes,"
says the LORD of Heaven's Armies,
"I will rescue you from foreign subjugation.
I will deliver you from captivity.
Foreigners will then no longer subjugate them.
9 But they will be subject to the LORD their God
and to the Davidic ruler whom I will raise up as king over them.
10 So I, the LORD, tell you not to be afraid,
you descendants of Jacob, my servants.
Do not be terrified, people of Israel.
For I will rescue you and your descendants
from a faraway land where you are captives.
The descendants of Jacob will return to their land and enjoy peace.
They will be secure, and no one will terrify them.
11 For I, the LORD, affirm that
I will be with you and will rescue you.
I will completely destroy all the nations where I scattered you.
But I will not completely destroy you.
I will indeed discipline you, but only in due measure.
I will not allow you to go entirely unpunished."

THE LORD WILL HEAL THE WOUNDS OF JUDAH

[12]Moreover, the LORD says to the people of Zion:
"Your injuries are incurable;
your wounds are severe.
13 There is no one to plead your cause.
There are no remedies for your wounds.
There is no healing for you.
14 All your allies have abandoned you.
They no longer have any concern for you.

For I have attacked you like an enemy would.
I have chastened you cruelly.
For your wickedness is so great
and your sin is so much.
15 Why do you complain about your injuries,
that your pain is incurable?
I have done all this to you
because your wickedness is so great
and your sin is so much.
16 But all who destroyed you will be destroyed.
All your enemies will go into exile.
Those who plundered you will be plundered.
I will cause those who pillaged you to be pillaged.
17 Yes, I will restore you to health.
I will heal your wounds.
I, the LORD, affirm it!
For you have been called an outcast,
Zion, whom no one cares for."

THE LORD WILL RESTORE ISRAEL AND JUDAH

18 The LORD says:
"I will restore the ruined houses of the descendants of Jacob.
I will show compassion on their ruined homes.
Every city will be rebuilt on its former ruins.
Every fortified dwelling will occupy its traditional site.
19 Out of those places you will hear songs of thanksgiving
and the sounds of laughter and merriment.
I will increase their number, and they will not dwindle away.
I will bring them honor, and they will no longer be despised.
20 The descendants of Jacob will enjoy their former privileges.
Their community will be reestablished in my favor,
and I will punish all who try to oppress them.
21 One of their own people will be their leader.
Their ruler will come from their own number.
I will invite him to approach me, and he will do so.
For no one would dare approach me on his own.
I, the LORD, affirm it!
22 Then you will again be my people,
and I will be your God.
23 Just watch! The wrath of the LORD
will come like a storm.
Like a raging storm it will rage down
on the heads of those who are wicked.
24 The anger of the LORD will not turn back
until he has fully carried out his intended purposes.
In future days you will come to understand this.
31 At that time I will be the God of all the clans of Israel,
and they will be my people.
I, the LORD, affirm it!"

ISRAEL WILL BE RESTORED AND JOIN JUDAH IN WORSHIP

2 The LORD says:
"The people of Israel who survived
death at the hands of the enemy

31:1–3 There is a most glorious connection subsisting between the Lord and his people: He is their God, even "the God of all the clans of Israel"; and they are his people, devoted altogether to his service. He is the God of every individual as much as if no other object of his love existed in the whole creation besides, and they are his exclusively and without reserve. Is it any peculiar fitness in this or that man that occasions God to single him out as an object to be drawn by him, or is the mercy vouchsafed by God to whomsoever he will, according to his own sovereign will and pleasure? We cannot hesitate to declare that the whole salvation, from first to last, is purely of grace.

CHARLES SIMEON
(1759–1836)
HORAE HOMILETICAE

will find favor in the wilderness
as they journey to find rest for themselves.
3 In a faraway land the LORD will manifest himself to them.
He will say to them, 'I have loved you with an everlasting love.
That is why I have continued to be faithful to you.
4 I will rebuild you, my dear children Israel,
so that you will once again be built up.
Once again you will take up the tambourine
and join in the happy throng of dancers.
5 Once again you will plant vineyards
on the hills of Samaria.
Those who plant them
will once again enjoy their fruit.
6 Yes, a time is coming
when watchmen will call out on the mountains of Ephraim,
"Come! Let us go to Zion
to worship the LORD our God!"'"

7 Moreover, the LORD says:
"Sing for joy for the descendants of Jacob.
Utter glad shouts for that foremost of the nations.
Make your praises heard.
Then say, 'LORD, rescue your people.
Deliver those of Israel who remain alive.'
8 Then I will reply, 'I will bring them back from the land of the north.
I will gather them in from the distant parts of the earth.
Blind and lame people will come with them,
so will pregnant women and women about to give birth.
A vast throng of people will come back here.
9 They will come back shedding tears of contrition.
I will bring them back praying prayers of repentance.
I will lead them besides streams of water,
along smooth paths where they will never stumble.
I will do this because I am Israel's father;
Ephraim is my firstborn son.'

10 "Listen to the LORD's message, O nations.
Proclaim it in the faraway lands along the sea.
Say, 'The one who scattered Israel will regather them.
He will watch over his people like a shepherd watches over his flock.'
11 For the LORD will rescue the descendants of Jacob.
He will secure their release from those who had overpowered them.
12 They will come and shout for joy on Mount Zion.
They will be radiant with joy over the good things the LORD provides,
the grain, the fresh wine, the olive oil,
the young sheep, and the calves he has given to them.
They will be like a well-watered garden
and will not grow faint or weary any more.
13 The LORD says, 'At that time young women will dance and be glad.
Young men and old men will rejoice.
I will turn their grief into gladness.

I will give them comfort and joy in place of their sorrow.
14 I will provide the priests with abundant provisions.
My people will be filled to the full with the good things
I provide.'

15 The LORD says:
"A sound is heard in Ramah,
a sound of crying in bitter grief.
It is the sound of Rachel weeping for her children
and refusing to be comforted, because her children are
gone."
16 The LORD says to her,
"Stop crying! Do not shed any more tears.
For your heartfelt repentance will be rewarded.
Your children will return from the land of the enemy.
I, the LORD, affirm it!
17 Indeed, there is hope for your posterity.
Your children will return to their own territory.
I, the LORD, affirm it!
18 I have indeed heard the people of Israel say mournfully,
'We were like a calf untrained to the yoke.
You disciplined us, and we learned from it.
Let us come back to you and we will do so,
for you are the LORD our God.
19 For after we turned away from you we repented.
After we came to our senses we struck our thigh in
sorrow.
We are ashamed and humiliated
because of the disgraceful things we did previously.'
20 Indeed, the people of Israel are my dear children.
They are the children I take delight in.
For even though I must often rebuke them,
I still remember them with fondness.
So I am deeply moved with pity for them
and will surely have compassion on them.
I, the LORD, affirm it!
21 I will say, 'My dear children of Israel, keep in mind
the road you took when you were carried off.
Mark off in your minds the landmarks.
Make a mental note of telltale signs marking the way
back.
Return, my dear children of Israel.
Return to these cities of yours.
22 How long will you vacillate,
you who were once like an unfaithful daughter?
For I, the LORD, promise to bring about something new
on the earth,
something as unique as a woman protecting a man!'"

JUDAH WILL BE RESTORED

23 The LORD of Heaven's Armies, the God of Israel, says,
"I will restore the people of Judah to their land and to
their towns.
When I do, they will again say of Jerusalem,
'May the LORD bless you, you holy mountain,
the place where righteousness dwells.'
24 The land of Judah will be inhabited by people who live
in its towns,
as well as by farmers and shepherds with their flocks.

25 I will fully satisfy the needs of those who are
weary
and fully refresh the souls of those who are faint.
26 Then they will say, 'Under these conditions I can enjoy
sweet sleep
when I wake up and look around.'

ISRAEL AND JUDAH WILL BE REPOPULATED

27"Indeed, a time is coming," says the LORD, "when I will cause
people and animals to sprout up in the lands of Israel and Judah. 28In the past I saw to it that they were uprooted and torn
down, that they were destroyed and demolished and brought
disaster. But now I will see to it that they are built up and firmly
planted. I, the LORD, affirm it!

THE LORD WILL MAKE A NEW COVENANT WITH ISRAEL AND JUDAH

29"When that time comes, people will no longer say, 'The parents
have eaten sour grapes, but the children's teeth have grown
numb.' 30Rather, each person will die for his own sins. The teeth
of the person who eats the sour grapes will themselves grow
numb.

31"Indeed, a time is coming," says the LORD, "when I will make
a new covenant with the people of Israel and Judah. 32It will not
be like the old covenant that I made with their ancestors when
I delivered them from Egypt. For they violated that covenant,
even though I was like a faithful husband to them," says the
LORD. 33"But I will make a new covenant with the whole nation
of Israel after I plant them back in the land," says the LORD. "I
will put my law within them and write it on their hearts and
minds. I will be their God, and they will be my people.

34"People will no longer need to teach their neighbors and
relatives to know me. For all of them, from the least important
to the most important, will know me," says the LORD. "For I
will forgive their sin and will no longer call to mind the wrong
they have done."

THE LORD GUARANTEES ISRAEL'S CONTINUANCE

35 The LORD has made a promise to Israel.
He promises it as the one who fixed the sun to give
light by day
and the moon and stars to give light by night.
He promises it as the one who stirs up the sea so that
its waves roll.
His name is the LORD of Heaven's Armies.
36 The LORD affirms, "The descendants of Israel will not
cease forever to be a nation in my sight.
That could only happen if the fixed ordering of the
heavenly lights
were to cease to operate before me."
37 The LORD says, "I will not reject all the descendants of
Israel
because of all that they have done.
That could only happen if the heavens above could be
measured
or the foundations of the earth below could all be
explored,"
says the LORD.

JERUSALEM WILL BE ENLARGED

38“Indeed a time is coming,” says the LORD, “when the city of Jerusalem will be rebuilt as my special city. It will be built from the Tower of Hananel westward to the Corner Gate. 39The boundary line will extend beyond that, straight west from there to the Hill of Gareb and then turn southward to Goah. 40The whole valley where dead bodies and sacrificial ashes are thrown, and all the terraced fields out to the Kidron Valley on the east as far north as the corner of the Horse Gate, will be included within this city that is sacred to the LORD. The city will never again be torn down or destroyed.”

JEREMIAH BUYS A FIELD

32 In the tenth year that Zedekiah was ruling over Judah the LORD spoke to Jeremiah. That was the same as the eighteenth year of Nebuchadnezzar.

2Now at that time, the armies of the king of Babylon were besieging Jerusalem. The prophet Jeremiah was confined in the courtyard of the guardhouse attached to the royal palace of Judah. 3For King Zedekiah had confined Jeremiah there after he had reproved him for prophesying as he did. He had asked Jeremiah, “Why do you keep prophesying these things? Why do you keep saying that the LORD says, ‘I will hand this city over to the king of Babylon? I will let him capture it. 4King Zedekiah of Judah will not escape from the Babylonians. He will certainly be handed over to the king of Babylon. He must answer personally to the king of Babylon and confront him face to face. 5Zedekiah will be carried off to Babylon and will remain there until I have fully dealt with him. I, the LORD, affirm it! Even if you continue to fight against the Babylonians, you cannot win.’”

6So now, Jeremiah said, “The LORD’s message came to me, 7‘Hanamel, the son of your uncle Shallum, will come to you soon. He will say to you, “Buy my field at Anathoth because you are entitled as my closest relative to buy it.”’ 8And then my cousin Hanamel did come to me in the courtyard of the guardhouse in keeping with the LORD’s message. He said to me, ‘Buy my field that is at Anathoth in the territory of the tribe of Benjamin. Buy it for yourself since you are entitled as my closest relative to take possession of it for yourself.’ When this happened, I recognized that the LORD had indeed spoken to me. 9So I bought the field at Anathoth from my cousin Hanamel. I weighed out seven ounces of silver and gave it to him to pay for it. 10I signed the deed of purchase, sealed it, and had some men serve as witnesses to the purchase. I weighed out the silver for him on a scale. 11There were two copies of the deed of purchase. One was sealed and contained the order of transfer and the conditions of purchase. The other was left unsealed. 12I took both copies of the deed of purchase and gave them to Baruch son of Neriah, the son of Mahseiah. I gave them to him in the presence of my cousin Hanamel, the witnesses who had signed the deed of purchase, and all the Judeans who were housed in the courtyard of the guardhouse. 13In the presence of all these people I instructed Baruch, 14‘The LORD of Heaven’s Armies, the God of Israel, says, “Take these documents, both the sealed copy of the deed of purchase and the unsealed copy. Put them in a clay jar so that they may be preserved for a long time to come.”’ 15For the LORD of Heaven’s Armies, the God of Israel, says, ‘Houses, fields, and vineyards will again be bought in this land.’

JEREMIAH'S PRAYER OF PRAISE AND BEWILDERMENT

16“After I had given the copies of the deed of purchase to Baruch son of Neriah, I prayed to the LORD, 17‘Oh, Sovereign LORD, you did indeed make heaven and earth by your mighty power and great strength. Nothing is too hard for you! 18You show unfailing love to thousands. But you also punish children for the sins of their parents. You are the great and powerful God whose name is the LORD of Heaven's Armies. 19You plan great things and you do mighty deeds. You see everything people do. You reward each of them for the way they live and for the things they do. 20You did miracles and amazing deeds in the land of Egypt that have had lasting effect. By this means you gained both in Israel and among humankind a renown that lasts to this day. 21You used your mighty power and your great strength to perform miracles and amazing deeds and to bring great terror on the Egyptians. By this means you brought your people Israel out of the land of Egypt. 22You kept the promise that you swore on oath to their ancestors. You gave them a land flowing with milk and honey. 23But when they came in and took possession of it, they did not obey you or live as you had instructed them. They did not do anything that you commanded them to do. So you brought all this disaster on them. 24Even now siege ramps have been built up around the city in order to capture it. War, starvation, and disease are sure to make the city fall into the hands of the Babylonians who are attacking it. LORD, you threatened that this would happen. Now you can see that it is already taking place. 25The city is sure to fall into the hands of the Babylonians. Yet, in spite of this, you, Sovereign LORD, have said to me, “Buy that field with silver and have the transaction legally witnessed.”’”

THE LORD ANSWERS JEREMIAH'S PRAYER

26The LORD's message came to Jeremiah: 27“I am the LORD, the God of all humankind. There is, indeed, nothing too difficult for me. 28Therefore I, the LORD, say: ‘I will indeed hand this city over to King Nebuchadnezzar of Babylon and the Babylonian army. They will capture it. 29The Babylonian soldiers that are attacking this city will break into it and set it on fire. They will burn it down along with the houses where people have made me angry by offering sacrifices to the god Baal and by pouring out drink offerings to other gods on their rooftops. 30This will happen because the people of Israel and Judah have repeatedly done what displeases me from their earliest history until now and because they have repeatedly made me angry by the things they have done. I, the LORD, affirm it! 31This will happen because the people of this city have aroused my anger and my wrath since the time they built it until now. They have made me so angry that I am determined to remove it from my sight. 32I am determined to do so because the people of Israel and Judah have made me angry with all their wickedness—they, their kings, their officials, their priests, their prophets, and especially the people of Judah and the citizens of Jerusalem have done this wickedness. 33They have turned away from me instead of turning to me. I tried over and over again to instruct them, but they did not listen and respond to correction. 34They set up their disgusting idols in the temple that I have claimed for my own and defiled it. 35They built places of worship for the god Baal in the Valley of Ben Hinnom so that they could sacrifice their sons and daughters to the god Molech. Such a disgusting practice was not something I commanded them to do. It never even entered my mind to command them to do such a thing! So Judah is certainly liable for punishment.’

36“You and your people are right in saying, ‘War, starvation, and disease are sure to make this city fall into the hands of the king of Babylon.’ But now I, the LORD God of Israel, have something further to say about this city: 37‘I will certainly regather my people from all the countries where I have exiled them in my anger, fury, and great wrath. I will bring them back to this place and allow them to live here in safety. 38They will be my people, and I will be their God. 39I will give them a single-minded purpose to live in a way that always shows respect for me. They will want to do that for their own good and the good of the children who descend from them. 40I will make a lasting covenant with them that I will never stop doing good to them. I will fill their hearts and minds with respect for me so that they will never again turn away from me. 41I will take delight in doing good to them. I will faithfully and wholeheartedly plant them firmly in the land.’

42“For I, the LORD, say: ‘I will surely bring on these people all the good fortune that I am hereby promising them. I will be just as sure to do that as I have been in bringing all this great disaster on them. 43You and your people are saying that this land will become desolate, uninhabited by either people or animals. You are saying that it will be handed over to the Babylonians. But fields will again be bought in this land. 44Fields will again be bought with silver, and deeds of purchase signed, sealed, and witnessed. This will happen in the territory of Benjamin, the villages surrounding Jerusalem, the towns in Judah, the southern hill country, the foothills, and southern Judah. For I will restore them to their land. I, the LORD, affirm it!’”

THE LORD PROMISES A SECOND TIME TO RESTORE ISRAEL AND JUDAH

33 The LORD’s message came to Jeremiah a second time while he was still confined in the courtyard of the guardhouse. 2“I, the LORD, do these things. I, the LORD, form the plan to bring them about. I am known as the LORD. I say to you, 3‘Call on me in prayer, and I will answer you. I will show you great and mysterious things that you still do not know about.’ 4For I, the LORD God of Israel, have something more to say about the houses in this city and the royal buildings of Judah that have been torn down for defenses against the siege ramps and military incursions of the Babylonians: 5‘The defenders of the city will go out and fight with the Babylonians. But they will only fill those houses and buildings with the dead bodies of the people that I will kill in my anger and my wrath. That will happen because I have decided to turn my back on this city on account of the wicked things they have done. 6But I will most surely heal the wounds of this city and restore it and its people to health. I will show them abundant peace and security. 7I will restore Judah and Israel and will rebuild them as they were in days of old. 8I will purify them from all the sin that they committed against me. I will forgive all their sins that they committed in rebelling against me. 9All the nations will hear about all the good things that I will do for them. This city will bring me fame, honor, and praise before them for the joy that I bring it. The nations will tremble in awe at all the peace and prosperity that I will provide for it.’

32:39–41 The prophet Jeremiah, speaking in the person of God, clearly tells us that the fear of God by which we can hold on to him comes from the Lord: *I shall give them one heart and one way so that they may fear me during all their days, so that all will be well for them and for their children after them. And I will make an everlasting covenant with them, and I shall not cease to do good things for them, and, as a gift, I shall put fear of me in their hearts so that they may never go away from me.*

JOHN CASSIAN
(C. 360–C. 435)
THE CONFERENCES

33:1–17 “Call on me in prayer and I will answer you. I will show you great and mysterious things that you still do not know about.” There is an upper realm of rapture, of communion, and of conscious union with Christ that is far from being the common dwelling place of believers. There are heights in experimental knowledge of the things of God that the eagle’s eye of acumen and philosophic thought has never seen: God alone can bear us there, but the chariot in which he takes us up is prevailing prayer. If you would reach to something higher than ordinary groveling experience, look to the Rock that is higher than you, and gaze with the eye of faith through the window of importunate prayer. When you open the window on your side, it will not be bolted on the other.

CHARLES SPURGEON
(1834–1892)
MORNING AND EVENING

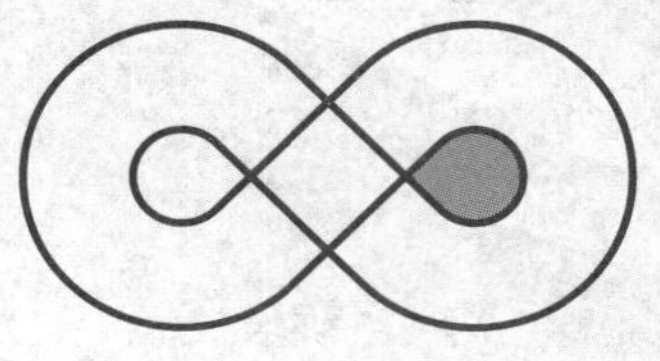

THE HEIDELBERG CONFESSION (1563)

THE PRIMARY ARCHITECT of the Heidelberg Confession was Zacharias Ursinus, a prominent professor of theology at the University of Heidelberg in Germany. The catechism outlines a faithful Christian life utilizing the framework of the Ten Commandments and the Lord's Prayer as well as expounding on the doctrines of patristic Christianity defined in the Apostles' Creed. The pastoral encouragement in the first and last sections set this confession apart.

1. WHAT IS YOUR ONLY COMFORT IN LIFE AND DEATH?

THAT I am not my own but belong with body and soul, both in life and in death, to my faithful Savior Jesus Christ. He has fully paid for all my sins with his precious blood and has set me free from all the power of the devil. He also preserves me in such a way that without the will of my heavenly Father, not a hair can fall from my head; indeed, all things must work together for my salvation. Therefore, by his Holy Spirit he also assures me of eternal life and makes me heartily willing and ready from now on to live for him.

2. WHAT DO YOU NEED TO KNOW IN ORDER TO LIVE AND DIE IN THE JOY OF THIS COMFORT?

FIRST, HOW great my sins and misery are; second, how I am delivered from all my sins and misery; third, how I am to be thankful to God for such deliverance.

26. WHAT DO YOU BELIEVE WHEN YOU SAY, "I BELIEVE IN GOD, THE FATHER ALMIGHTY, CREATOR OF HEAVEN AND EARTH"?

THAT THE eternal Father of our Lord Jesus Christ, who out of nothing created heaven and earth and everything in them, who still upholds and rules them by his eternal counsel and providence, is my God and Father because of Christ the Son.

35. WHAT DOES IT MEAN THAT HE "WAS CONCEIVED BY THE HOLY SPIRIT AND BORN OF THE VIRGIN MARY"?

THAT THE eternal Son of God, who is and remains true and eternal God, took to himself, through the working of the Holy Spirit, from the flesh and blood of the Virgin Mary, a truly human nature so that he might also become David's true descendant, like his brothers and sisters in every way except for sin.

53. WHAT DO YOU BELIEVE CONCERNING "THE HOLY SPIRIT"?

FIRST, THAT the Spirit, with the Father and the Son, is eternal God. Second, that the Spirit is given also to me so that, through true faith, he makes me share in Christ and all his benefits through true faith, comforts me, and will remain with me forever.

10"I, the LORD, say: 'You and your people are saying about
this place, "It lies in ruins. There are no people or animals in
it." That is true. The towns of Judah and the streets of Jerusalem will soon be desolate, uninhabited either by people or by
animals. But happy sounds will again be heard in these places.
11Once again there will be sounds of joy and gladness and the
glad celebrations of brides and grooms. Once again people will
bring their thank offerings to the temple of the LORD and will
say, "Give thanks to the LORD of Heaven's Armies. For the LORD
is good and his unfailing love lasts forever." For I, the LORD,
affirm that I will restore the land to what it was in days of old.'
12"I, the LORD of Heaven's Armies, say: 'This place will indeed
lie in ruins. There will be no people or animals in it. But there
will again be in it and in its towns sheepfolds where shepherds
can rest their sheep. 13I, the LORD, say that shepherds will once
again count their sheep as they pass into the fold. They will do
this in all the towns in the hill country, the foothills, the Negev,
the territory of Benjamin, the villages surrounding Jerusalem,
and the towns of Judah.'

THE LORD REAFFIRMS HIS COVENANT WITH DAVID, ISRAEL, AND LEVI

14"I, the LORD, affirm: 'The time will certainly come when I will
fulfill my gracious promise concerning the nations of Israel and
Judah. 15In those days and at that time I will raise up for them
a righteous descendant of David.

"'He will do what is just and right in the land. 16Under his
rule Judah will enjoy safety and Jerusalem will live in security.
At that time Jerusalem will be called "The LORD has provided
us with justice." 17For I, the LORD, promise: "David will never
lack a successor to occupy the throne over the nation of Israel.

[18]Nor will the Levitical priests ever lack someone to stand before me and continually offer up burnt offerings, sacrifice cereal
offerings, and offer the other sacrifices.'"'"
[19]The LORD's message came to Jeremiah another time: [20]"I,
the LORD, make the following promise: 'I have made a covenant
with the day and with the night that they will always come at
their proper times. Only if you people could break that covenant
[21]could my covenant with my servant David and my covenant
with the Levites ever be broken. So David will by all means
always have a descendant to occupy his throne as king and the
Levites will by all means always have priests who will minister
before me. [22]I will make the children who follow one another
in the line of my servant David very numerous. I will also make
the Levites who minister before me very numerous. I will make
them all as numerous as the stars in the sky and as the sands
that are on the seashore.'"
[23]The LORD's message came to Jeremiah another time: [24]"You
have surely noticed what these people are saying, haven't you?
They are saying, 'The LORD has rejected the two families of
Israel and Judah that he chose.' So they have little regard that
my people will ever again be a nation. [25]But I, the LORD, make
the following promise: 'I have made a covenant governing the
coming of day and night. I have established the fixed laws governing heaven and earth. [26]Just as surely as I have done this,
so surely will I never reject the descendants of Jacob. Nor will I
ever refuse to choose one of my servant David's descendants to
rule over the descendants of Abraham, Isaac, and Jacob. Indeed,
I will restore them and show mercy to them.'"

THE LORD MAKES AN OMINOUS PROMISE TO ZEDEKIAH

34 The LORD's message came to Jeremiah while King Nebuchadnezzar of Babylon was attacking Jerusalem and the
towns around it with a large army. This army consisted of troops
from his own army and from the kingdoms and peoples of the
lands under his dominion. [2]This is what the LORD God of Israel
told Jeremiah, "Go, speak to King Zedekiah of Judah. Tell him,
'This is what the LORD has said: "Take note! I am going to hand
this city over to the king of Babylon, and he will burn it down.
[3]You yourself will not escape his clutches but will certainly be
captured and handed over to him. You must confront the king
of Babylon face to face and answer to him personally. Then you
must go to Babylon."' [4]However, listen to the LORD's message,
King Zedekiah of Judah. This is what the LORD has said: 'You
will not die in battle or be executed. [5]You will die a peaceful
death. They will burn incense at your burial just as they did at
the burial of your ancestors, the former kings who preceded
you. They will mourn for you, saying, "Alas, master!" Indeed, you
have my own word on this. I, the LORD, affirm it!'"
[6]The prophet Jeremiah told all these things to King Zedekiah
of Judah in Jerusalem. [7]He did this while the army of the king
of Babylon was attacking Jerusalem and the cities of Lachish
and Azekah. He was attacking these cities because they were
the only fortified cities of Judah that were still holding out.

THE LORD THREATENS TO DESTROY THOSE WHO WRONGED THEIR SLAVES

[8]The LORD spoke to Jeremiah after King Zedekiah had made a
covenant with all the people in Jerusalem to grant their slaves

34:6–7 The kingdom of Judah was so far weakened that out of so many cities only three walled ones were left subject to the king. All the other ones had been occupied or destroyed by the Babylonians. The greatest malice had led the unfortunate kings of Israel and Judah to the point that nothing of the beautiful and powerful kingdom of Solomon remained except three cities that were themselves soon to be destroyed.

KONRAD PELLIKAN
(1478–1556)
COMMENTARY ON JEREMIAH

their freedom. 9 Everyone was supposed to free their male and female Hebrew slaves. No one was supposed to keep a fellow Judean enslaved. 10 All the people and their leaders had agreed to this. They had agreed to free their male and female slaves and not keep them enslaved any longer. They originally complied with the covenant and freed them. 11 But later they changed their minds. They took back their male and female slaves that they had freed and forced them to be slaves again. 12 The LORD's message came to Jeremiah, 13 "The LORD God of Israel has a message for you: 'I made a covenant with your ancestors when I brought them out of Egypt where they had been slaves. It stipulated, 14 "Every seven years each of you must free any fellow Hebrews who have sold themselves to you. After they have served you for six years, you shall set them free." But your ancestors did not obey me or pay any attention to me. 15 Recently, however, you yourselves showed a change of heart and did what is pleasing to me. You granted your fellow countrymen their freedom, and you made a covenant to that effect in my presence in the house that I have claimed for my own. 16 But then you turned right around and showed that you did not honor me. Each of you took back your male and female slaves, whom you had freed as they desired, and you forced them to be your slaves again. 17 So I, the LORD, say: "You have not really obeyed me and granted freedom to your neighbor and fellow countryman. Therefore, I will grant you freedom, the freedom to die in war, or by starvation, or disease. I, the LORD, affirm it! I will make all the kingdoms of the earth horrified at what happens to you. 18 I will punish those people who have violated their covenant with me. I will make them like the calf they cut in two and passed between its pieces. I will do so because they did not keep the terms of the covenant they made in my presence. 19 I will punish the leaders of Judah and Jerusalem, the court officials, the priests, and all the other people of the land who passed between the pieces of the calf. 20 I will hand them over to their enemies who want to kill them. Their dead bodies will become food for the birds and the wild animals. 21 I will also hand King Zedekiah of Judah and his officials over to their enemies who want to kill them. I will hand them over to the army of the king of Babylon, even though they have temporarily withdrawn from attacking you. 22 For I, the LORD, affirm that I will soon give the order and bring them back to this city. They will fight against it and capture it and burn it down. I will also make the towns of Judah desolate so that there will be no one living in them."'"

JUDAH'S UNFAITHFULNESS CONTRASTED WITH THE RECHABITES' FAITHFULNESS

35 The LORD spoke to Jeremiah when Jehoiakim son of Josiah was ruling over Judah: 2 "Go to the Rechabite community. Invite them to come into one of the side rooms of the LORD's temple and offer them some wine to drink." 3 So I went and got Jaazaniah son of Jeremiah the grandson of Habazziniah, his brothers, all his sons, and all the rest of the Rechabite community. 4 I took them to the LORD's temple. I took them into the room where the disciples of the prophet Hanan son of Igdaliah stayed. That room was next to the one where the temple officers stayed and above the room where Maaseiah son of Shallum, one of the doorkeepers of the temple, stayed. 5 Then I set cups and pitchers full of wine in front of the members of the Rechabite community and said to them, "Have some wine."

35:1–19 Here the prophet, that he might move the Jews more deeply, promised a reward to the sons of Jonadab because they obeyed their father, and he promised them a blessing from God. This is nothing strange; this precept was not inconsistent with God's law, and God approved of their obedience. God has prescribed how he would have us to worship him; whatever therefore people bring in of themselves is wholly impious, for it adulterates the pure worship of God and further, when necessity is laid on consciences, it is a tyrannical bondage. Such was not the object of Jonadab, for what he commanded his posterity was useful and referred only to the things of this life, and it did not bind their consciences, for when it was necessary they moved to Jerusalem and dwelt as others do in houses.

JOHN CALVIN **(1509–1564)**
COMPLETE COMMENTARY ON THE BIBLE

6But they answered, "We do not drink wine because our ancestor Jonadab son of Rechab commanded us not to. He told us, 'You and your children must never drink wine. 7Do not build houses. Do not plant crops. Do not plant a vineyard or own one. Live in tents all your lives. If you do these things you will live a long time in the land that you wander about on.' 8We and our wives and our sons and daughters have obeyed everything our ancestor Jonadab son of Rechab commanded us. We have never drunk wine. 9We have not built any houses to live in. We do not own any vineyards, fields, or crops. 10We have lived in tents. We have obeyed our ancestor Jonadab and done exactly as he commanded us. 11But when King Nebuchadnezzar of Babylon invaded the land we said, 'Let's get up and go to Jerusalem to get away from the Babylonian and Aramean armies.' That is why we are staying here in Jerusalem."

12Then the LORD's message came to Jeremiah. 13The LORD of Heaven's Armies, the God of Israel, told him, "Go and speak to the people of Judah and the citizens of Jerusalem. Tell them, 'I, the LORD, say: "You must learn a lesson from this about obeying what I say. 14Jonadab son of Rechab ordered his descendants not to drink wine. His orders have been carried out. To this day his descendants have drunk no wine because they have obeyed what their ancestor commanded them. But I have spoken to you over and over again, but you have not obeyed me. 15I sent all my servants the prophets to warn you over and over again. They said, 'Every one of you, stop doing the evil things you have been doing and do what is right. Do not pay allegiance to other gods and worship them. Then you can continue to live in this land that I gave to you and your ancestors.' But you did not pay any attention or listen to me. 16Yes, the descendants of Jonadab son of Rechab have carried out the orders that their ancestor gave them. But you people have not obeyed me! 17So I, the LORD God of Heaven's Armies, the God of Israel, say: 'I will soon bring on Judah and all the citizens of Jerusalem all the disaster that I threatened to bring on them. I will do this because I spoke to them but they did not listen. I called out to them but they did not answer.'"'"

18Then Jeremiah spoke to the Rechabite community, "The LORD of Heaven's Armies, the God of Israel says, 'You have obeyed the orders of your ancestor Jonadab. You have followed all his instructions. You have done exactly as he commanded you.' 19So the LORD of Heaven's Armies, the God of Israel, says, 'Jonadab son of Rechab will never lack a male descendant to serve me.'"

JEHOIAKIM BURNS THE SCROLL CONTAINING THE LORD'S MESSAGES

36 The LORD spoke to Jeremiah in the fourth year that Jehoiakim son of Josiah was ruling over Judah: 2"Get a scroll. Write on it everything I have told you to say about Israel, Judah, and all the other nations since I began to speak to you in the reign of Josiah until now. 3Perhaps when the people of Judah hear about all the disaster I intend to bring on them, they will all stop doing the evil things they have been doing. If they do, I will forgive their sins and the wicked things they have done."

4So Jeremiah summoned Baruch son of Neriah. Then, Baruch wrote down in a scroll all the LORD's words that he had told to Jeremiah as they came from his mouth. 5Then Jeremiah told Baruch, "I am no longer allowed to go into the LORD's temple.

36:1–32 The wretched Jehoiakim seems to have had all the vices of Eastern sovereigns. He was covetous, cruel, tyrannous, lawless, heartless, senseless. Jeremiah, who had been prophesying for some 30 years and had already been in peril of his life from the godless tyrant on the throne, was led to collect in one book his scattered prophecies and read them to the people gathered for the fast. That reading had no effect. The roll was then read to the princes and in them roused fear and interested curiosity and kindly desire for the safety of Jeremiah and Baruch, his amanuensis. It was next read to the king, and he cut the roll leaf by leaf and threw it on the brasier, not afraid or penitent but enraged and eager to capture Jeremiah and Baruch. The burnt roll was reproduced by God's command.

ALEXANDER MACLAREN
(1826–1910)
EXPOSITIONS OF THE HOLY SCRIPTURES

[6]So you go there the next time all the people of Judah come in from their towns to fast in the LORD's temple. Read out loud where all of them can hear you what I told you the LORD said, which you wrote in the scroll. [7]Perhaps then they will ask the LORD for mercy and will all stop doing the evil things they have been doing. For the LORD has threatened to bring great anger and wrath against these people."

[8]So Baruch son of Neriah did exactly what the prophet Jeremiah told him to do. He read what the LORD had said from the scroll in the temple of the LORD. [9]All the people living in Jerusalem and all the people who came into Jerusalem from the towns of Judah observed a fast before the LORD. The fast took place in the ninth month of the fifth year that Jehoiakim son of Josiah was ruling over Judah. [10]At that time Baruch went into the temple of the LORD. He stood in the entrance of the room of Gemariah the son of Shaphan who had been the royal secretary. That room was in the upper court near the entrance of the New Gate. There, where all the people could hear him, he read from the scroll what Jeremiah had said.

[11]Micaiah, who was the son of Gemariah and the grandson of Shaphan, heard Baruch read from the scroll everything the LORD had said. [12]He went down to the chamber of the royal secretary in the king's palace and found all the court officials in session there. Elishama the royal secretary, Delaiah son of Shemaiah, Elnathan son of Achbor, Gemariah son of Shaphan, Zedekiah son of Hananiah, and all the other officials were seated there. [13]Micaiah told them everything he had heard Baruch read from the scroll in the hearing of the people. [14]All the officials sent Jehudi, who was the son of Nethaniah, the son of Shelemiah, the son of Cushi, to Baruch. They ordered him to tell Baruch, "Come here and bring with you the scroll you read in the hearing of the people." So Baruch son of Neriah went to them, carrying the scroll in his hand. [15]They said to him, "Please sit down and read it to us." So Baruch sat down and read it to them. [16]When they had heard it all, they expressed their alarm to one another. Then they said to Baruch, "We must certainly give the king a report about everything you have read!" [17]Then they asked Baruch, "How did you come to write all these words? Do they actually come from Jeremiah's mouth?" [18]Baruch answered, "Yes, they came from his own mouth. He dictated all these words to me, and I wrote them down in ink on this scroll." [19]Then the officials said to Baruch, "You and Jeremiah must go and hide. You must not let anyone know where you are."

[20]The officials put the scroll in the room of Elishama, the royal secretary, for safekeeping. Then they went to the court and reported everything to the king. [21]The king sent Jehudi to get the scroll. He went and got it from the room of Elishama, the royal secretary. Then he himself read it to the king and all the officials who were standing around him. [22]Since it was the ninth month of the year, the king was sitting in his winter quarters. A fire was burning in the firepot in front of him. [23]As soon as Jehudi had read three or four columns of the scroll, the king would cut them off with a penknife and throw them on the fire in the firepot. He kept doing so until the whole scroll was burned up in the fire. [24]Neither he nor any of his attendants showed any alarm when they heard all that had been read. Nor did they tear their clothes to show any grief or sorrow. [25]The king did not even listen to Elnathan,

Delaiah, and Gemariah, who had urged him not to burn the scroll. [26]He also ordered Jerahmeel, who was one of the royal princes, Seraiah son of Azriel, and Shelemiah son of Abdeel to arrest the scribe Baruch and the prophet Jeremiah. However, the LORD hid them.

BARUCH AND JEREMIAH WRITE ANOTHER SCROLL

[27]The LORD's message came to Jeremiah after the king had burned the scroll with the words Baruch had written down at Jeremiah's dictation. [28]"Get another scroll and write on it everything that was written on the original scroll that King Jehoiakim of Judah burned. [29]Tell King Jehoiakim of Judah, 'The LORD says, "You burned the scroll. You asked Jeremiah, 'How dare you write in this scroll that the king of Babylon will certainly come and destroy this land and wipe out all the people and animals on it?'" [30]So the LORD says concerning King Jehoiakim of Judah, "None of his line will occupy the throne of David. His dead body will be thrown out to be exposed to scorching heat by day and frost by night. [31]I will punish him and his descendants and the officials who serve him for the wicked things they have done. I will bring on them, the citizens of Jerusalem and the people of Judah, all the disaster that I told them about and that they ignored."'" [32]Then Jeremiah got another scroll and gave it to the scribe Baruch son of Neriah. As Jeremiah dictated, Baruch wrote on this scroll everything that had been on the scroll that King Jehoiakim of Judah burned in the fire. They also added on this scroll several other messages of the same kind.

INTRODUCTION TO INCIDENTS DURING THE REIGN OF ZEDEKIAH

37 Zedekiah son of Josiah succeeded Jeconiah son of Jehoiakim as king. He was elevated to the throne of the land of Judah by King Nebuchadnezzar of Babylon. [2]Neither he nor the officials who served him nor the people of Judah paid any attention to what the LORD said through the prophet Jeremiah.

THE LORD RESPONDS TO ZEDEKIAH'S HOPE FOR HELP

[3]King Zedekiah sent Jehucal son of Shelemiah and the priest Zephaniah son of Maaseiah to the prophet Jeremiah to say, "Please pray to the LORD our God on our behalf." [4](Now Jeremiah had not yet been put in prison. So he was still free to come and go among the people as he pleased. [5]At that time the Babylonian forces had temporarily given up their siege against Jerusalem. They had had it under siege, but withdrew when they heard that the army of Pharaoh had set out from Egypt.) [6]The LORD's message came to the prophet Jeremiah, [7]"This is what the LORD God of Israel has said, 'This is what you must say to the king of Judah who sent you to seek my help. "Beware, Pharaoh's army that was on its way to help you is about to go back home to Egypt. [8]Then the Babylonian forces will return. They will attack the city and will capture it and burn it down. [9]Moreover, I, the LORD, warn you not to deceive yourselves into thinking that the Babylonian forces will go away and leave you alone. For they will not go away. [10]For even if you were to defeat all the Babylonian forces fighting against you so badly that only wounded men were left lying in their tents, they would get up and burn this city down."'"

JEREMIAH IS CHARGED WITH DESERTING, ARRESTED, AND IMPRISONED

[11]The following events also occurred while the Babylonian
forces had temporarily withdrawn from Jerusalem because
the army of Pharaoh was coming. [12]Jeremiah started to leave
Jerusalem to go to the territory of Benjamin. He wanted to make
sure he got his share of the property that was being divided up
among his family there. [13]But he only got as far as the Benjamin
Gate. There an officer in charge of the guards named Irijah,
who was the son of Shelemiah and the grandson of Hananiah,
stopped him. He seized Jeremiah and said, "You are deserting
to the Babylonians!" [14]Jeremiah answered, "That's a lie! I am
not deserting to the Babylonians." But Irijah would not listen
to him. Irijah put Jeremiah under arrest and took him to the
officials. [15]The officials were very angry with Jeremiah. They
had him flogged and put in prison in the house of Jonathan,
the royal secretary, which they had converted into a place for
confining prisoners.

[16]So Jeremiah was put in prison in a cell in the dungeon in
Jonathan's house. He was kept there for a long time. [17]Then King
Zedekiah had him brought to the palace. There he questioned
him privately and asked him, "Is there any message from the
LORD?" Jeremiah answered, "Yes, there is." Then he announced,
"You will be handed over to the king of Babylon." [18]Then Jeremiah asked King Zedekiah, "What crime have I committed against
you, or the officials who serve you, or the people of Judah? What
have I done to make you people throw me into prison? [19]Where
now are the prophets who prophesied to you that the king of
Babylon would not attack you or this land? [20]But now please
listen, your royal Majesty, and grant my plea for mercy. Do not
send me back to the house of Jonathan, the royal secretary. If
you do, I will die there." [21]Then King Zedekiah ordered that
Jeremiah be committed to the courtyard of the guardhouse.
He also ordered that a loaf of bread be given to him every day
from the bakers' street until all the bread in the city was gone.
So Jeremiah was kept in the courtyard of the guardhouse.

37:17–21 The king asked as one who hoped that the prophet could be moved either by the authority of the palace or certainly by his distaste for prison to predict a more generous fate. The constancy and fortitude of the prophet are most worthy of praise. He not only repeated and inculcated the Word of God—even if it could come back by way of his neck (as they say)—but also with a full heart he reprimanded the godless cruelty of the king, and from the outcome itself and the present calamities he argued that those false prophets were vain. But the fact that Jeremiah demanded a less severe prison was not a lack of courage. The prophet sought a modest concession since he was to be imprisoned. Nevertheless, he was prepared to suffer every sort of extreme rather than give up as a public crier of the truth.

JOHANNES PAPPUS
(1549–1610)
ON ALL THE PROPHETS

JEREMIAH IS CHARGED WITH TREASON AND PUT IN A CISTERN TO DIE

38 Now Shephatiah son of Mattan, Gedaliah son of Pashhur,
Jehucal son of Shelemiah, and Pashhur son of Malkijah
had heard the things that Jeremiah had been telling the people. They had heard him say, [2]"The LORD says, 'Those who stay
in this city will die in battle or of starvation or disease. Those
who leave the city and surrender to the Babylonians will live.
They will escape with their lives.'" [3]They had also heard him
say, "The LORD says, 'This city will certainly be handed over
to the army of the king of Babylon. They will capture it.'" [4]So
these officials said to the king, "This man must be put to death.
For he is demoralizing the soldiers who are left in the city as
well as all the other people there by these things he is saying.
This man is not seeking to help these people but is trying to
harm them." [5]King Zedekiah said to them, "Very well, you can
do what you want with him. For I cannot do anything to stop
you." [6]So the officials took Jeremiah and put him in the cistern
of Malkijah, one of the royal princes, that was in the courtyard
of the guardhouse. There was no water in the cistern, only mud.
So when they lowered Jeremiah into the cistern with ropes he
sank in the mud.

38:1–13 Jeremiah was put into a dungeon. Many of God's faithful witnesses have been privately put away in prisons. Ebed Melech was an Ethiopian who spoke to the king faithfully: "Those men have been very wicked in all that they have done to the prophet Jeremiah." See how God can raise up friends for his people in distress. Orders were given for the prophet's release, and Ebed Melech saw him pulled up. Let this encourage us to appear boldly for God. Special notice is taken of his tenderness for Jeremiah. What do we behold in the different characters then, but the same we behold in the different characters now, that the Lord's children are conformed to his example and the children of Satan to their master?

MATTHEW HENRY **(1662–1714)**
COMMENTARY ON THE WHOLE BIBLE

AN ETHIOPIAN OFFICIAL RESCUES JEREMIAH FROM THE CISTERN

[7]An Ethiopian, Ebed Melech, a court official in the royal palace, heard that Jeremiah had been put in the cistern. While the king was holding court at the Benjamin Gate, [8]Ebed Melech departed the palace and went to speak to the king. He said to him, [9]"Your royal Majesty, those men have been very wicked in all that they have done to the prophet Jeremiah. They have thrown him into a cistern, and he is sure to die of starvation there because there is no food left in the city." [10]Then the king gave Ebed Melech the Ethiopian the following order: "Take 30 men with you from here and go pull the prophet Jeremiah out of the cistern before he dies." [11]So Ebed Melech took the men with him and went to a room under the treasure room in the palace. He got some worn-out clothes and old rags from there and let them down by ropes to Jeremiah in the cistern. [12]Ebed Melech called down to Jeremiah, "Put these rags and worn-out clothes under your armpits to pad the ropes." Jeremiah did as Ebed Melech instructed. [13]So they pulled Jeremiah up from the cistern with ropes. Jeremiah, however, still remained confined to the courtyard of the guardhouse.

JEREMIAH RESPONDS TO ZEDEKIAH'S REQUEST FOR SECRET ADVICE

[14]Some time later Zedekiah sent and had Jeremiah brought to him at the third entrance of the LORD's temple. The king said to Jeremiah, "I would like to ask you a question. Do not hide anything from me when you answer." [15]Jeremiah said to Zedekiah, "If I answer you, you will certainly kill me. If I give you advice, you will not listen to me." [16]So King Zedekiah made a secret promise to Jeremiah and sealed it with an oath. He promised, "As surely as the LORD lives who has given us life and breath, I promise you this: I will not kill you or hand you over to those men who want to kill you."

[17]Then Jeremiah said to Zedekiah, "The LORD God of Heaven's Armies, the God of Israel, says, 'You must surrender to the officers of the king of Babylon. If you do, your life will be spared and this city will not be burned down. Indeed, you and your whole family will be spared. [18]But if you do not surrender to the officers of the king of Babylon, this city will be handed over to the Babylonians, and they will burn it down. You yourself will not escape from them.'" [19]Then King Zedekiah said to Jeremiah, "I am afraid of the Judeans who have deserted to the Babylonians. The Babylonians might hand me over to them, and they will torture me." [20]Then Jeremiah answered, "You will not be handed over to them. Please obey the LORD by doing what I have been telling you. Then all will go well with you, and your life will be spared. [21]But if you refuse to surrender, the LORD has shown me a vision of what will happen. Here is what I saw: [22]All the women who are left in the royal palace of Judah will be led out to the officers of the king of Babylon. They will taunt you saying:

"'Your trusted friends misled you;
they have gotten the best of you.
Now that your feet are stuck in the mud,
they have turned their backs on you.'

[23]"All your wives and your children will be turned over to the Babylonians. You yourself will not escape from them but will be captured by the king of Babylon. This city will be burned down."

[24]Then Zedekiah told Jeremiah, "Do not let anyone know about the conversation we have had. If you do, you will die. [25]The officials may hear that I have talked with you. They may come to you and say, 'Tell us what you said to the king and what the king said to you. Do not hide anything from us. If you do, we will kill you.' [26]If they do this, tell them, 'I was pleading with the king not to send me back to die in the dungeon of Jonathan's house.'" [27]All the officials did indeed come and question Jeremiah. He told them exactly what the king had instructed him to say. They stopped questioning him any further because no one had actually heard their conversation. [28]So Jeremiah remained confined in the courtyard of the guardhouse until the day Jerusalem was captured.

THE FALL OF JERUSALEM AND ITS AFTERMATH

The following events occurred when Jerusalem was captured.

39 King Nebuchadnezzar of Babylon came against Jerusalem with his whole army and laid siege to it. The siege began in the tenth month of the ninth year that Zedekiah ruled over Judah. [2]It lasted until the ninth day of the fourth month of Zedekiah's eleventh year. On that day they broke through the city walls. [3]Then Nergal Sharezer of Samgar, Nebo Sarsekim (who was a chief officer), Nergal Sharezer (who was a high official), and all the other officers of the king of Babylon came and set up quarters in the Middle Gate. [4]When King Zedekiah of Judah and all his soldiers saw them, they tried to escape. They departed from the city during the night. They took a path through the king's garden and passed out through the gate between the two walls. Then they headed for the rift valley. [5]But the Babylonian army chased after them. They caught up with Zedekiah in the plains of Jericho and captured him. They took him to King Nebuchadnezzar of Babylon at Riblah in the territory of Hamath, and Nebuchadnezzar passed sentence on him there. [6]There at Riblah the king of Babylon had Zedekiah's sons put to death while Zedekiah was forced to watch. The king of Babylon also had all the nobles of Judah put to death. [7]Then he had Zedekiah's eyes put out and had him bound in chains to be led off to Babylon. [8]The Babylonians burned down the royal palace, the temple of the LORD, and the people's homes, and they tore down the wall of Jerusalem. [9]Then Nebuzaradan, the captain of the royal guard, took captive the rest of the people who were left in the city. He carried them off to Babylon along with the people who had deserted to him. [10]But he left behind in the land of Judah some of the poor people who owned nothing. He gave them fields and vineyards at that time.

[11]Now King Nebuchadnezzar of Babylon had issued orders concerning Jeremiah. He had passed them on through Nebuzaradan, the captain of his royal guard, [12]"Find Jeremiah and look out for him. Do not do anything to harm him, but do with him whatever he tells you." [13]So Nebuzaradan (the captain of the royal guard), Nebushazban (who was a chief officer), Nergal Sharezer (who was a high official), and all the other officers of the king of Babylon [14]sent and had Jeremiah brought from the courtyard of the guardhouse. They turned him over to Gedaliah, the son of Ahikam and the grandson of Shaphan, to take him home with him. But Jeremiah stayed among the people.

39:11–18 The Jews did not want to pay attention to the divine words, and they subjected the prophets to punishments of every kind. The promise of God surely obtained its fulfillment. When God appointed Jeremiah a prophet, he promised to make him irresistible and like an iron pillar and a bronze wall because on the one hand they would wage war against him, but on the other hand they would not prevail. Nebuzaradan and all the company of rulers summoned Jeremiah from the prison and handed him over to Gedaliah, whom he had ordered to rule over the remnant in Judah. And the prophet thought that it was worth noting that the things spoken beforehand by God concerning Ebed Melech were fulfilled. For with him, nothing is uncared for or lacking reward.

THEODORET OF CYR
(C. 393–C. 458)
COMMENTARY ON JEREMIAH

EBED MELECH IS PROMISED DELIVERANCE BECAUSE OF HIS FAITH

15 Now the LORD's message had come to Jeremiah while he was
still confined in the courtyard of the guardhouse, 16 "Go and tell
Ebed Melech the Nubian, 'This is what the LORD of Heaven's
Armies, the God of Israel, has said, "I will carry out against this
city what I promised. It will mean disaster and not good fortune
for it. When that disaster happens, you will be there to see it.
17 But I will rescue you when it happens. I, the LORD, affirm it! You
will not be handed over to those whom you fear. 18 I will certainly
save you. You will not fall victim to violence. You will escape
with your life because you trust in me. I, the LORD, affirm it!"'"

JEREMIAH IS SET FREE A SECOND TIME

40 The LORD spoke to Jeremiah after Nebuzaradan the captain of the royal guard had set him free at Ramah. He
had taken him there in chains along with all the people from
Jerusalem and Judah who were being carried off to exile to
Babylon. 2 The captain of the royal guard took Jeremiah aside
and said to him, "The LORD your God threatened this place with
this disaster. 3 Now he has brought it about. The LORD has done
just as he threatened to do. This disaster has happened because
you people sinned against the LORD and did not obey him. 4 But
now, Jeremiah, today I will set you free from the chains on your
wrists. If you would like to come to Babylon with me, come
along and I will take care of you. But if you prefer not to come
to Babylon with me, you are not required to do so. You are free
to go anywhere in the land you want to go. Go wherever you
choose." 5 Before Jeremiah could turn to leave, the captain of
the guard added, "Go back to Gedaliah, the son of Ahikam and
grandson of Shaphan, whom the king of Babylon appointed to
govern the towns of Judah. Go back and live with him among
the people. Or go wherever else you choose." Then the captain
of the guard gave Jeremiah some food and a present and let him
go. 6 So Jeremiah went to Gedaliah son of Ahikam at Mizpah and
lived there with him. He stayed there to live among the people
who had been left in the land of Judah.

A SMALL JUDEAN PROVINCE IS ESTABLISHED AT MIZPAH

7 Now some of the officers of the Judean army and their troops
had been hiding in the countryside. They heard that the king of
Babylon had appointed Gedaliah son of Ahikam to govern the
country. They also heard that he had been put in charge over
the men, women, and children from the poorer classes of the
land who had not been carried off into exile in Babylon. 8 So all
these officers and their troops came to Gedaliah at Mizpah. The
officers who came were Ishmael son of Nethaniah, Johanan and
Jonathan the sons of Kareah, Seraiah son of Tanhumeth, the
sons of Ephai the Netophathite, and Jezaniah son of the Maacathite. 9 Gedaliah, the son of Ahikam and grandson of Shaphan,
took an oath so as to give them and their troops some assurance
of safety. "Do not be afraid to submit to the Babylonians. Settle down in the land and submit to the king of Babylon. Then
things will go well for you. 10 I for my part will stay at Mizpah to
represent you before the Babylonians whenever they come to
us. You for your part go ahead and harvest the wine, the dates,
the figs, and the olive oil, and store them in jars. Go ahead and
settle down in the towns that you have taken over." 11 Moreover,

40:1–6 This heathen captain acknowledged the hand of the Lord and suggested that his master, the king of Babylon himself, and the rest of the generals were only instruments the Lord made use of, which is very piously as well as wisely said. Nebuzaradan went on to observe the cause of all this: "This disaster has happened because you people sinned against the LORD and did not obey him"—meaning not Jeremiah particularly but his countrymen. Here he vindicated the justice of God and ascribed the ruin of this people, not to the valor of Nebuchadnezzar and his captains; nor to the strength, courage, and skillfulness of his army; nor to any righteousness and merits of the king of Babylon; nor to the justness of his cause; but to the sins of the people.

JOHN GILL (1697–1771)
EXPOSITION OF THE WHOLE BIBLE

all the Judeans who were in Moab, Ammon, Edom, and all the other countries heard what had happened. They heard that the king of Babylon had allowed some people to stay in Judah and that he had appointed Gedaliah, the son of Ahikam and grandson of Shaphan, to govern them. [12]So all these Judeans returned to the land of Judah from the places where they had been scattered. They came to Gedaliah at Mizpah. Thus they harvested a large amount of wine and dates and figs.

ISHMAEL MURDERS GEDALIAH AND CARRIES OFF THE JUDEANS AT MIZPAH AS CAPTIVES

[13]Johanan, son of Kareah, and all the officers of the troops that had been hiding in the open country came to Gedaliah at Mizpah. [14]They said to him, "Are you at all aware that King Baalis of Ammon has sent Ishmael son of Nethaniah to kill you?" But Gedaliah son of Ahikam would not believe them. [15]Then Johanan son of Kareah spoke privately to Gedaliah there at Mizpah, "Let me go and kill Ishmael the son of Nethaniah before anyone knows about it. Otherwise he will kill you and all the Judeans who have rallied around you will be scattered. Then what remains of Judah will disappear." [16]But Gedaliah son of Ahikam said to Johanan son of Kareah, "Do not do that because what you are saying about Ishmael is not true."

41 But in the seventh month Ishmael, the son of Nethaniah and grandson of Elishama, who was a member of the royal family and had been one of Zedekiah's chief officers, came with 10 of his men to Gedaliah son of Ahikam at Mizpah. While they were eating a meal together with him there at Mizpah, [2]Ishmael son of Nethaniah and the 10 men who were with him stood up, pulled out their swords, and killed Gedaliah, the son of Ahikam and grandson of Shaphan. Thus Ishmael killed the man that the king of Babylon had appointed to govern the country. [3]Ishmael also killed all the Judeans who were with Gedaliah at Mizpah and the Babylonian soldiers who happened to be there.

[4]On the day after Gedaliah had been murdered, before anyone even knew about it, [5]80 men arrived from Shechem, Shiloh, and Samaria. They had shaved off their beards, torn their clothes, and cut themselves to show they were mourning. They were carrying grain offerings and incense to present at the temple of the LORD in Jerusalem. [6]Ishmael son of Nethaniah went out from Mizpah to meet them. He was pretending to cry as he walked along. When he met them, he said to them, "Come with me to meet Gedaliah son of Ahikam." [7]But as soon as they were inside the city, Ishmael son of Nethaniah and the men who were with him slaughtered them and threw their bodies in a cistern. [8]But there were 10 men among them who said to Ishmael, "Do not kill us. For we will give you the stores of wheat, barley, olive oil, and honey we have hidden in a field." So he spared their lives and did not kill them along with the rest. [9]Now the cistern where Ishmael threw all the dead bodies of those he had killed was a large one that King Asa had constructed as part of his defenses against King Baasha of Israel. Ishmael son of Nethaniah filled it with dead bodies. [10]Then Ishmael took captive all the people who were still left alive in Mizpah. This included the royal princesses and all the rest of the people in Mizpah that Nebuzaradan, the captain of the royal guard, had put under the authority of Gedaliah son of Ahikam. Ishmael son of Nethaniah took all these people captive and set out to cross over to the Ammonites.

41:4–18 Here Jeremiah relates another circumstance in the nefarious conduct of Ishmael: that by flattery he enticed simple men who feared no evil while pretending kindness to them. The slaughter was in itself very detestable, but added to it was the most abominable deceit, for he pretended to weep with them and offered an act of kindness in order to bring them to Gedaliah, and then he treacherously killed them. Here also is set before us the inscrutable purpose of God: that he suffered unhappy men to have been thus slain by robbers. But God has hidden ways by which he provides for the salvation of his people. It was, in short, better for them to have been removed than to have been under the necessity of suffering many miseries yet again.

JOHN CALVIN **(1509–1564)**
COMPLETE COMMENTARY ON THE BIBLE

JOHANAN RESCUES THE PEOPLE ISHMAEL HAD CARRIED OFF

[11]Johanan son of Kareah and all the army officers who were with
him heard about all the atrocities that Ishmael son of Nethaniah had committed. [12]So they took all their troops and went to
fight against Ishmael son of Nethaniah. They caught up with
him near the large pool at Gibeon. [13]When all the people that
Ishmael had taken captive saw Johanan son of Kareah and all
the army officers with him, they were glad. [14]All those people
that Ishmael had taken captive from Mizpah turned and went
over to Johanan son of Kareah. [15]But Ishmael son of Nethaniah
managed to escape from Johanan along with eight of his men,
and he went on over to Ammon.

[16]Johanan son of Kareah and all the army officers who were
with him led off all the people who had been left alive at Mizpah. They had rescued them from Ishmael son of Nethaniah
after he killed Gedaliah son of Ahikam. They led off the men,
women, children, soldiers, and court officials whom they had
brought away from Gibeon. [17]They set out to go to Egypt to get
away from the Babylonians, but stopped at Geruth Kimham
near Bethlehem. [18]They were afraid of what the Babylonians
might do because Ishmael son of Nethaniah had killed Gedaliah son of Ahikam, whom the king of Babylon had appointed
to govern the country.

THE SURVIVORS ASK THE LORD FOR ADVICE BUT REFUSE TO FOLLOW IT

42 Then all the army officers, including Johanan son of
Kareah and Jezaniah son of Hoshaiah and all the people
of every class, went to the prophet Jeremiah. [2]They said to him,
"Please grant our request and pray to the LORD your God for
all those of us who are still left alive here. For, as you yourself
can see, there are only a few of us left out of the many there
were before. [3]Pray that the LORD your God will tell us where
we should go and what we should do." [4]The prophet Jeremiah
answered them, "Agreed! I will indeed pray to the LORD your
God as you have asked. I will tell you everything the LORD replies in response to you. I will not keep anything back from you."
[5]They answered Jeremiah, "May the LORD be a true and faithful
witness against us if we do not do just as the LORD your God
sends you to tell us to do. [6]We will obey what the LORD our God
to whom we are sending you tells us to do. It does not matter
whether we like what he tells us or not. We will obey what he
tells us to do so that things will go well for us."

[7]Ten days later the LORD's message came to Jeremiah. [8]So
Jeremiah summoned Johanan son of Kareah and all the army
officers who were with him and all the people of every class.
[9]Then Jeremiah said to them, "You sent me to the LORD God of
Israel to make your request known to him. Here is what he says
to you: [10]'If you will only stay in this land, I will build you up. I
will not tear you down. I will firmly plant you. I will not uproot
you. For I am filled with sorrow because of the disaster that I
have brought on you. [11]Do not be afraid of the king of Babylon
whom you now fear. Do not be afraid of him because I will be
with you to save you and to rescue you from his power. I, the
LORD, affirm it! [12]I will have compassion on you so that he in
turn will have mercy on you and allow you to return to your land.'

[13]"You must not disobey the LORD your God by saying, 'We
will not stay in this land.' [14]You must not say, 'No, we will not

42:1—43:2 The prophet, by inspiration of the Spirit of God, commanded the people to "stay in this land." Jeremiah also promised them that God would "firmly plant" them, he would repent of the plagues he had brought upon them, and he would deliver them from the king of Babylon. If, however, they did not obey the voice of the Lord but went against his command to Egypt then the very plagues they feared would come upon them. But when the prophet of God had declared this clear sentence and will of God and asked for their answer, they said, "You are telling a lie!" Thus they refused the counsel of God and followed their own fantasies.

JOHN KNOX (C. 1514–1572)
ADMONITION TO THE PROFESSORS OF GOD'S TRUTH IN ENGLAND

stay. Instead we will go and live in the land of Egypt where we will not face war, or hear the enemy's trumpet calls, or starve for lack of food.' [15]If you people who remain in Judah do that, then listen to the LORD's message. This is what the LORD of Heaven's Armies, the God of Israel, has said, 'If you are so determined to go to Egypt that you go and settle there, [16]the wars you fear will catch up with you there in the land of Egypt. The starvation you are worried about will follow you there to Egypt. You will die there. [17]All the people who are determined to go and settle in Egypt will die from war, starvation, or disease. No one will survive or escape the disaster I will bring on them.' [18]For the LORD of Heaven's Armies, the God of Israel, says, 'If you go to Egypt, I will pour out my wrath on you just as I poured out my anger and wrath on the citizens of Jerusalem. You will become an object of horror and ridicule, an example of those who have been cursed and that people use in pronouncing a curse. You will never see this place again.'

[19]"The LORD has told you people who remain in Judah, 'Do not go to Egypt.' Be very sure of this: I warn you here and now. [20]You are making a fatal mistake. For you sent me to the LORD your God and asked me, 'Pray to the LORD our God for us. Tell us what the LORD our God says, and we will do it.' [21]This day I have told you what he said. But you do not want to obey the LORD your God by doing what he sent me to tell you. [22]So now be very sure of this: You will die from war, starvation, or disease in the place where you want to go and live."

43 Jeremiah finished telling all the people all these things the LORD their God had sent him to tell them. [2]Then Azariah son of Hoshaiah, Johanan son of Kareah, and other arrogant men said to Jeremiah, "You are telling a lie! The LORD our God did not send you to tell us, 'You must not go to Egypt and settle there.' [3]But Baruch son of Neriah is stirring you up against us. He wants to hand us over to the Babylonians so that they will kill us or carry us off into exile in Babylon." [4]So Johanan son of Kareah, all the army officers, and all the rest of the people did not obey the LORD's command to stay in the land of Judah. [5]Instead Johanan son of Kareah and all the army officers led off all the Judean remnant who had come back to live in the land of Judah from all the nations where they had been scattered. [6]They also led off all the men, women, children, and royal princesses that Nebuzaradan, the captain of the royal guard, had left with Gedaliah, the son of Ahikam and grandson of Shaphan; this included the prophet Jeremiah and Baruch son of Neriah. [7]They went on to Egypt because they refused to obey the LORD, and came to Tahpanhes.

JEREMIAH PREDICTS THAT NEBUCHADNEZZAR WILL PLUNDER EGYPT AND ITS GODS

[8]At Tahpanhes the LORD's message came to Jeremiah: [9]"Take some large stones and bury them in the mortar of the clay pavement at the entrance of Pharaoh's residence here in Tahpanhes. Do it while the people of Judah present there are watching. [10]Then tell them, 'The LORD of Heaven's Armies, the God of Israel, says, "I will bring my servant King Nebuchadnezzar of Babylon. I will set his throne over these stones that I have buried. He will pitch his royal tent over them. [11]He will come and attack Egypt. Those who are destined to die of disease will die of disease. Those who are destined to be carried off into exile will be carried off into exile. Those who are destined to die in

war will die in war. [12]He will set fire to the temples of the gods of Egypt. He will burn their gods or carry them off as captives. He will pick Egypt clean like a shepherd picks the lice from his clothing. He will leave there unharmed. [13]He will demolish the sacred pillars in the temple of the sun in Egypt and will burn down the temples of the gods of Egypt.'"

THE LORD WILL PUNISH THE JUDEAN EXILES IN EGYPT FOR THEIR IDOLATRY

44 The LORD spoke to Jeremiah concerning all the Judeans who were living in the land of Egypt, those in Migdol, Tahpanhes, Memphis, and in the region of southern Egypt: [2]"The LORD of Heaven's Armies, the God of Israel, says, 'You have seen all the disaster I brought on Jerusalem and all the towns of Judah. Indeed, they now lie in ruins and are deserted. [3]This happened because of the wickedness the people living there did. They made me angry by worshiping and offering sacrifices to other gods whom neither they nor you nor your ancestors previously knew. [4]I sent my servants the prophets to you people over and over again warning you not to do this disgusting thing I hate. [5]But the people of Jerusalem and Judah would not listen or pay any attention. They would not stop the wickedness they were doing nor quit sacrificing to other gods. [6]So my anger and my wrath were poured out and burned like a fire through the towns of Judah and the streets of Jerusalem. That is why they have become the desolate ruins that they are today.'

[7]"So now the LORD God of Heaven's Armies, the God of Israel, asks, 'Why will you do such great harm to yourselves? Why should every man, woman, child, and baby of yours be destroyed from the midst of Judah? Why should you leave yourselves without a remnant? [8]That is what will result from your making me angry by what you are doing. You are making me angry by sacrificing to other gods here in the land of Egypt where you live. You will be destroyed for doing that! You will become an example used in curses and an object of ridicule among all the nations of the earth. [9]Have you forgotten all the wicked things that have been done in the towns of Judah and in the streets of Jerusalem by your ancestors, by the kings of Judah and their wives, and by you and your wives? [10]To this day your people have shown no contrition! They have not revered me nor followed the laws and statutes I commanded you and your ancestors.'

[11]"Because of this, the LORD of Heaven's Armies, the God of Israel, says, 'I am determined to bring disaster on you, even to the point of destroying all the Judeans here. [12]I will see to it that all the Judean remnant that was determined to go and live in the land of Egypt will be destroyed. Here in the land of Egypt they will fall in battle or perish from starvation. People of every class will die in war or from starvation. They will become an object of horror and ridicule, an example of those who have been cursed and that people use in pronouncing a curse. [13]I will punish those who live in the land of Egypt with war, starvation, and disease, just as I punished Jerusalem. [14]None of the Judean remnant who have come to live in the land of Egypt will escape or survive to return to the land of Judah. Though they long to return and live there, none of them shall return except a few fugitives.'"

[15]Then all the men who were aware that their wives were sacrificing to other gods, as well as all their wives, answered Jeremiah—there was a great crowd of them representing all the people who lived in northern and southern Egypt—[16]"We

44:1–30 What was the reason for this calamity? It was because the Jews were so arrogant and obstinate. They immediately forgot what God had done for them and attributed the miracles to others who were not gods. And they said to Jeremiah, "We will not listen to what you claim the LORD has spoken to us! . . . We will sacrifice and pour out drink offerings to the goddess called the Queen of Heaven . . . For then we had plenty of food, were well off, and had no troubles." The inspired prophets then foretold what would happen to the Jews so that they would ascribe none of the events to idols but would believe that both punishments and blessings always came from God: The punishment came for their sins and the blessings because of God's love and kindness.

CHRYSOSTOM **(C. 347–407)**
DISCOURSES AGAINST JUDAIZING CHRISTIANS

will not listen to what you claim the LORD has spoken to us!
17 Instead we will do everything we vowed we would do. We will
sacrifice and pour out drink offerings to the goddess called the
Queen of Heaven just as we and our ancestors, our kings, and
our leaders previously did in the towns of Judah and in the
streets of Jerusalem. For then we had plenty of food, were well
off, and had no troubles. 18 But ever since we stopped sacrificing
and pouring out drink offerings to the Queen of Heaven, we
have been in great need. Our people have died in wars or of
starvation." 19 The women added, "We did indeed sacrifice and
pour out drink offerings to the Queen of Heaven. But it was
with the full knowledge and approval of our husbands that we
made cakes in her image and poured out drink offerings to her."

20 Then Jeremiah replied to all the people, both men and
women, who responded to him in this way: 21 "The LORD did indeed remember and call to mind what you did! He remembered
the incense you and your ancestors, your kings, your leaders,
and all the rest of the people of the land offered to other gods
in the towns of Judah and in the streets of Jerusalem. 22 Finally
the LORD could no longer endure your wicked deeds and the
disgusting things you did. That is why your land has become
the desolate, uninhabited ruin that it is today. That is why it
has become a proverbial example used in curses. 23 You have
sacrificed to other gods. You have sinned against the LORD!
You have not obeyed the LORD! You have not followed his laws,
his statutes, and his decrees. That is why this disaster that is
evident to this day has happened to you."

24 Then Jeremiah spoke to all the people, particularly to all
the women, "Listen to the LORD's message, all you people of
Judah who are in Egypt. 25 This is what the LORD of Heaven's
Armies, the God of Israel, has said, 'You women have confirmed
by your actions what you vowed with your lips! You said, "We
will certainly carry out our vows to sacrifice and pour out drink
offerings to the Queen of Heaven." Well, then fulfill your vows!
Carry them out!' 26 But listen to the LORD's message, all you people of Judah who are living in the land of Egypt: The LORD says,
'I hereby swear by my own great name that none of the people
of Judah who are living anywhere in Egypt will ever again invoke
my name in their oaths! Never again will any of them use it in
an oath saying, "As surely as the Sovereign LORD lives." 27 I will
indeed see to it that disaster, not prosperity, happens to them.
All the people of Judah who are in the land of Egypt will die in
war or from starvation until not one of them is left. 28 Some
who survive the battle will return to the land of Judah from the
land of Egypt. But they will be very few indeed! Then the Judean
remnant who have come to live in the land of Egypt will know
whose word proves true, mine or theirs.' 29 Moreover the LORD
says, 'I will make something happen to prove that I will punish
you in this place. I will do it so that you will know that my threats
to bring disaster on you will prove true. 30 I, the LORD, promise
that I will hand Pharaoh Hophra king of Egypt over to his enemies who are seeking to kill him. I will do that just as surely as
I handed King Zedekiah of Judah over to King Nebuchadnezzar
of Babylon, his enemy who was seeking to kill him.'"

BARUCH IS REBUKED BUT ALSO COMFORTED

45 The prophet Jeremiah spoke to Baruch son of Neriah while
he was writing down in a scroll the words that Jeremiah
spoke to him. (This happened in the fourth year that Jehoiakim

45:1–5 After King Jehoiakim burned the scroll, God bid Jeremiah and Baruch to write another scroll wherein were written the same things. But now Baruch began to be discouraged by considering what things were likely to befall him by the writing and publishing of this second roll. Though before he acted valiantly and seemed to stand like an oak, yet now his heart shook like a leaf, and his complaint was bitter: "The LORD has added sorrow to my suffering." Should he be troubled for his own peace and safety and desire to live at quiet and ease when all was going to wreck and ruin? God promised to spare his life, nothing else—safety in the midst of so great a calamity.

THOMAS MANTON
(1620–1677)
THE COMPLETE WORKS

son of Josiah was ruling over Judah.) [2]Jeremiah said, "The LORD
God of Israel has a message for you, Baruch. [3]'You have said, "I
feel so hopeless! For the LORD has added sorrow to my suffering.
I am worn out from groaning. I can't find any rest."'"

[4]The LORD told Jeremiah, "Tell Baruch, 'The LORD says, "I
am about to tear down what I have built and to uproot what I
have planted. I will do this throughout the whole earth. [5]Are
you looking for great things for yourself? Do not look for such
things. For I, the LORD, affirm that I am about to bring disaster
on all humanity. But I will allow you to escape with your life
wherever you go."'"

PROPHECIES AGAINST FOREIGN NATIONS

46 This was the LORD's message to the prophet Jeremiah
about the nations.

THE PROPHECY ABOUT EGYPT'S DEFEAT AT CARCHEMISH

[2]He spoke about Egypt and the army of Pharaoh Necho king
of Egypt, which was encamped along the Euphrates River at
Carchemish. Now this was the army that King Nebuchadnezzar
of Babylon defeated in the fourth year that Jehoiakim son of
Josiah was ruling over Judah:

3 "Fall into ranks with your shields ready!
Prepare to march into battle!
4 Harness the horses to the chariots;
mount your horses!
Take your positions with helmets on;
ready your spears!
Put on the armor!

5 "What do I see?
The soldiers are frightened.
They are retreating.
They are being scattered.
They have fled for refuge
without looking back.
Terror is all around them," says the LORD.
6 "But even the swiftest cannot get away.
Even the strongest cannot escape.
There in the north by the Euphrates River
they have stumbled and fallen in defeat.
7 Who is this that rises like the Nile,
like its streams turbulent at flood stage?
8 Egypt rises like the Nile,
like its streams turbulent at flood stage.
Egypt said, 'I will arise and cover the earth.
I will destroy cities and the people who inhabit them.'
9 Go ahead and charge into battle, you horsemen!
Drive furiously, you charioteers!
Let the soldiers march out into battle,
those from Ethiopia and Libya who carry shields,
and those from Lydia who are armed with the bow.
10 But that day belongs to the Sovereign LORD of Heaven's
Armies.
It is a day of reckoning when he will pay back his
adversaries.
His sword will devour them until its appetite is
satisfied.

It will drink its fill from their blood!
Indeed it will be a sacrifice for the Sovereign LORD of Heaven's Armies
in the land of the north by the Euphrates River.
11 Go up to Gilead and get medicinal ointment,
you dear poor people of Egypt.
But it will prove useless no matter how much medicine you use;
there will be no healing for you.
12 The nations have heard of your shameful defeat.
Your cries of distress fill the earth.
One soldier has stumbled over another,
and both of them have fallen down defeated."

THE LORD PREDICTS THAT NEBUCHADNEZZAR WILL ATTACK AND PLUNDER EGYPT

13 The LORD spoke to the prophet Jeremiah about Nebuchad-
nezzar coming to attack the land of Egypt:
14 "Make an announcement throughout Egypt.
Proclaim it in Migdol, Memphis, and Tahpanhes.
'Take your positions and prepare to do battle.
For the enemy army is destroying all the nations around you.'
15 Why will your soldiers be defeated?
They will not stand because I, the LORD, will thrust them down.
16 I will make many stumble.
They will fall over one another in their hurry to flee.
They will say, 'Get up!
Let's go back to our own people.
Let's go back to our homelands
because the enemy is coming to destroy us.'
17 There at home they will say, 'Pharaoh king of Egypt is just a big noise!
He has let the most opportune moment pass by.'
18 I the King, whose name is the LORD of Heaven's Armies, swear this:
'I swear as surely as I live that a conqueror is coming.
He will be as imposing as Mount Tabor is among the mountains,
as Mount Carmel is against the backdrop of the sea.
19 Pack your bags for exile,
you inhabitants of poor dear Egypt.
For Memphis will be laid waste.
It will lie in ruins and be uninhabited.
20 Egypt is like a beautiful young cow.
But northern armies will attack her like swarms of stinging flies.
21 Even her mercenaries
will prove to be like pampered, well-fed calves.
For they too will turn and run away.
They will not stand their ground
when the time for them to be destroyed comes,
the time for them to be punished.
22 Egypt will run away, hissing like a snake,
as the enemy comes marching up in force.
They will come against her with axes
as if they were woodsmen chopping down trees.

23 The population of Egypt is like a vast, impenetrable forest.
But I, the LORD, affirm that the enemy will cut them down.
For those who chop them down will be more numerous than locusts.
They will be too numerous to count.
24 Poor dear Egypt will be put to shame.
She will be handed over to the people from the north.'"

25 The LORD of Heaven's Armies, the God of Israel, says, "I will
punish Amon, the god of Thebes. I will punish Egypt, its gods,
and its kings. I will punish Pharaoh and all who trust in him. 26 I
will hand them over to Nebuchadnezzar and his troops, who
want to kill them. But later on, people will live in Egypt again
as they did in former times. I, the LORD, affirm it!"

A PROMISE OF HOPE FOR ISRAEL

27 "You descendants of Jacob, my servants, do not be afraid;
do not be terrified, people of Israel.
For I will rescue you and your descendants
from the faraway lands where you are captives.
The descendants of Jacob will return to their land and enjoy peace.
They will be secure, and no one will terrify them.
28 I, the LORD, tell you not to be afraid,
you descendants of Jacob, my servant,
for I am with you.
Though I completely destroy all the nations where I scatter you,
I will not completely destroy you.
I will indeed discipline you but only in due measure.
I will not allow you to go entirely unpunished."

46:27–28 "You descendants of Jacob, my servants, do not be afraid." Having spoken of some comfort regarding Egypt, Jeremiah now found it necessary to speak to the Israelites lest they should in their sufferings be overwhelmed with despair. The nations would be stricken and never recover again, and they would have only some outwardly tolerable presence in this world. But to Israel he said, *I will be favorable in respect to the best things and will restore to you the exercise of true religion and finally bestow on you everlasting life.* So being in misery is like a tree in winter that seems to be dead. But having sap in its root, the tree will be restored and will be full of green leaves and will flourish.

JOHN MAYER **(1650–1712)**
COMMENTARY UPON ALL THE PROPHETS

JUDGMENT ON THE PHILISTINE CITIES

47 This was the LORD's message to the prophet Jeremiah about the Philistines before Pharaoh attacked Gaza:
2 "Look! Enemies are gathering in the north like water rising in a river.
They will be like an overflowing stream.
They will overwhelm the whole country and everything in it like a flood.
They will overwhelm the cities and their inhabitants.
People will cry out in alarm.
Everyone living in the country will cry out in pain.
3 Fathers will hear the hoofbeats of the enemies' horses,
the clatter of their chariots and the rumbling of their wheels.
They will not turn back to save their children
because they will be paralyzed with fear.
4 For the time has come
to destroy all the Philistines.
The time has come to destroy all the help
that remains for Tyre and Sidon.
For I, the LORD, will destroy the Philistines,
that remnant that came from the island of Crete.
5 The people of Gaza will shave their heads in mourning.
The people of Ashkelon will be struck dumb.

47:1–7 Jeremiah prophesied here against the Philistines, who were enemies to the Israelites and had contrived against them many cruel and unjust things. There is then no doubt but that God intended to testify, by this prophecy, his love toward the Israelites, for he undertook their cause and avenged the wrongs done to them. We hence perceive why God had predicted the ruin of the Philistines, even that the Israelites might know his paternal love toward them as he set himself against their enemies; and thus he gave them a reason for patience because it behooved them to wait until God fulfilled this prophecy.

JOHN CALVIN **(1509–1564)**
COMPLETE COMMENTARY ON THE BIBLE

How long will you gash yourselves to show your sorrow,
you who remain of Philistia's power?
6 How long will you cry out, 'Oh, sword of the LORD,
how long will it be before you stop killing?
Go back into your sheath;
stay there and rest!'
7 But how can it rest
when I, the LORD, have given it orders?
I have ordered it to attack
the people of Ashkelon and the seacoast."

JUDGMENT AGAINST MOAB

48 The LORD of Heaven's Armies, the God of Israel, spoke about Moab:
"Sure to be judged is Nebo! Indeed, it will be destroyed.
Kiriathaim will suffer disgrace. It will be captured!
Its fortress will suffer disgrace. It will be torn down!
2 People will not praise Moab anymore.
The enemy will capture Heshbon and plot how to destroy Moab,
saying, 'Come, let's put an end to that nation!'
City of Madmen, you will also be destroyed.
A destructive army will march against you.
3 Cries of anguish will arise in Horonaim,
'Oh, the ruin and great destruction!'

4 "Moab will be crushed.
Her children will cry out in distress.
5 Indeed they will climb the slopes of Luhith,
weeping continually as they go.
For on the road down to Horonaim
they will hear the cries of distress over the destruction.
6 They will hear, 'Run! Save yourselves;
even if you must be like a lonely shrub in the wilderness!'

7 "Moab, you trust in the things you do and in your riches.
So you too will be conquered.
Your god Chemosh will go into exile
along with his priests and his officials.
8 The destroyer will come against every town.
Not one town will escape.
The towns in the valley will be destroyed.
The cities on the high plain will be laid waste.
I, the LORD, have spoken.
9 Set up a gravestone for Moab,
for it will certainly be laid in ruins!
Its cities will be laid waste
and become uninhabited.
10 A curse on anyone who is lax in doing the LORD's work!
A curse on anyone who keeps from carrying out his destruction!

11 "From its earliest days Moab has lived undisturbed.
It has never been taken into exile.
Its people are like wine allowed to settle undisturbed on its dregs,
never poured out from one jar to another.
They are like wine that tastes like it always did,
whose aroma has remained unchanged.

48:1–47 The Chaldeans were to destroy the Moabites. The cities would be laid in ruins, and the country would be wasted. There would be great sorrow. If any could give wings to sinners, still they could not fly out of the reach of divine indignation. The destruction of Moab is further prophesied to awaken them by national repentance and reformation to prevent the trouble, or by a personal repentance and reformation to prepare for it. Yet it is not perpetual destruction. The chapter ends with a promise of their return out of captivity in the latter days. Even with Moabites God would not contend forever, nor be always filled with wrath. The Jews compare it to the days of the Messiah; then the captives of the Gentiles, under the yoke of sin and Satan, will be brought back by divine grace, which will make them free indeed.

MATTHEW HENRY **(1662–1714)**
COMMENTARY ON THE WHOLE BIBLE

12 But the time is coming when I will send
men against Moab who will empty it out.
They will empty the towns of their people,
then will lay those towns in ruins.
I, the LORD, affirm it!
13 The people of Moab will be disappointed by their god
Chemosh.
They will be as disappointed as the people of Israel
were
when they put their trust in the calf god at Bethel.
14 How can you men of Moab say, 'We are heroes,
men who are mighty in battle?'
15 Moab will be destroyed. Its towns will be invaded.
Its finest young men will be slaughtered.
I, the King, the LORD of Heaven's Armies, affirm it!
16 Moab's destruction is at hand.
Disaster will come on it quickly.
17 Mourn for that nation, all you nations living around it,
all you nations that know of its fame.
Mourn and say, 'Alas, its powerful influence has been
broken!
Its glory and power have been done away with!'
18 Come down from your place of honor;
sit on the dry ground, you who live in Dibon.
For the one who will destroy Moab will attack you;
he will destroy your fortifications.
19 You who live in Aroer,
stand by the road and watch.
Question the man who is fleeing and the woman who is
escaping.
Ask them, 'What has happened?'
20 They will answer, 'Moab is disgraced, for it has fallen!
Wail and cry out in mourning!
Announce along the Arnon River
that Moab has been destroyed.'

21 "Judgment will come on the cities on the high plain: on
Holon, Jahzah, and Mephaath; 22 on Dibon, Nebo, and Beth Diblathaim; 23 on Kiriathaim, Beth Gamul, and Beth Meon; 24 on
Kerioth and Bozrah. It will come on all the towns of Moab, both
far and near. 25 Moab's might will be crushed. Its power will be
broken. I, the LORD, affirm it!
26 "Moab has vaunted itself against me.
So make him drunk with the wine of my wrath
until he splashes around in his own vomit,
until others treat him as a laughingstock.
27 For did not you people of Moab laugh at the people of
Israel?
Did you think that they were nothing but thieves,
that you shook your head in contempt
every time you talked about them?
28 Leave your towns, you inhabitants of Moab.
Go and live in the cliffs.
Be like a dove that makes its nest
high on the sides of a ravine.
29 I have heard how proud the people of Moab are,
I know how haughty they are.
I have heard how arrogant, proud, and haughty they are,
what a high opinion they have of themselves.

30 I, the LORD, affirm that I know how arrogant they are.
But their pride is ill founded.
Their boastings will prove to be false.
31 So I will weep with sorrow for Moab.
I will cry out in sadness for all Moab.
I will moan for the people of Kir Heres.
32 I will weep for the grapevines of Sibmah
just like the town of Jazer weeps over them.
Their branches once spread as far as the Dead Sea.
They reached as far as the town of Jazer.
The destroyer will ravage
her fig, date, and grape crops.
33 Joy and gladness will disappear
from the fruitful land of Moab.
I will stop the flow of wine from the winepresses.
No one will stomp on the grapes there and shout for joy.
The shouts there will be shouts of soldiers,
not the shouts of those making wine.
34 Cries of anguish raised from Heshbon and Elealeh
will be sounded as far as Jahaz.
They will be sounded from Zoar as far as Horonaim and
Eglath Shelishiyah.
For even the waters of Nimrim will be dried up.
35 I will put an end in Moab
to those who make offerings at her places of worship.
I will put an end to those who sacrifice to other gods.
I, the LORD, affirm it!
36 So my heart moans for Moab
like a flute playing a funeral song.
Yes, like a flute playing a funeral song,
my heart moans for the people of Kir Heres.
For the wealth they have gained will perish.
37 For all of them will shave their heads in mourning.
They will all cut off their beards to show their sorrow.
They will all make gashes in their hands.
They will all put on sackcloth.
38 On all the housetops in Moab
and in all its public squares,
there will be nothing but mourning.
For I will break Moab like an unwanted jar.
I, the LORD, affirm it!
39 Oh, how shattered Moab will be!
Oh, how her people will wail!
Oh, how she will turn away in shame!
Moab will become an object of ridicule,
a terrifying sight to all the nations that surround her."

40 For the LORD says,
"Look! Like an eagle with outspread wings
a nation will swoop down on Moab.
41 Her towns will be captured;
her fortresses will be taken.
At that time the soldiers of Moab will be frightened
like a woman in labor.
42 Moab will be destroyed and no longer be a nation
because she has vaunted herself against the LORD.
43 Terror, pits, and traps are in store
for the people who live in Moab.
I, the LORD, affirm it!

44 Anyone who flees at the sound of terror
will fall into a pit.
Anyone who climbs out of the pit
will be caught in a trap.
For the time is coming
when I will punish the people of Moab.
I, the LORD, affirm it!
45 In the shadows of the walls of Heshbon
those trying to escape will stand helpless.
For a fire will burst forth from Heshbon.
Flames will shoot out from the former territory of
Sihon.
They will burn the foreheads of the people of Moab,
the skulls of those war-loving people.
46 Moab, you are doomed!
You people who worship Chemosh will be destroyed.
Your sons will be taken away captive.
Your daughters will be carried away into exile.
47 Yet in future days
I will reverse Moab's ill fortune,"
says the LORD.

The judgment against Moab ends here.

JUDGMENT AGAINST AMMON

49 The LORD spoke about the Ammonites:
"Do you think there are not any people of the nation of
Israel remaining?
Do you think there are not any of them remaining to
reinherit their land?
Is that why you people who worship the god Milcom
have taken possession of the territory of Gad and live in
his cities?
2 Because you did that,
I, the LORD, affirm that a time is coming
when I will make Rabbah, the capital city of Ammon,
hear the sound of the battle cry.
It will become a mound covered with ruins.
Its villages will be burned to the ground.
Then Israel will take back its land
from those who took their land from them.
I, the LORD, affirm it!
3 Wail, you people in Heshbon, because Ai in Ammon is
destroyed.
Cry out in anguish, you people in the villages
surrounding Rabbah.
Put on sackcloth and cry out in mourning.
Run about covered with gashes.
For your god Milcom will go into exile
along with his priests and officials.
4 Why do you brag about your great power?
Your power is ebbing away, you rebellious people of
Ammon,
who trust in your riches and say,
'Who would dare to attack us?'
5 I will bring terror on you from every side,"
says the Sovereign LORD of Heaven's Armies.
"You will be scattered in every direction.
No one will gather the fugitives back together.

6 Yet in days to come
I will reverse Ammon's ill fortune,"
says the LORD.

JUDGMENT AGAINST EDOM

7The LORD of Heaven's Armies spoke about Edom:
"Is wisdom no longer to be found in Teman?
Can Edom's counselors not give her any good advice?
Has all their wisdom turned bad?
8 Turn and flee! Take up refuge in remote places,
you people who live in Dedan.
For I will bring disaster on the descendants of Esau.
I have decided it is time for me to punish them.
9 If grape pickers came to pick your grapes,
would they not leave a few grapes behind?
If robbers came at night,
would they not pillage only what they needed?
10 But I will strip everything away from Esau's
descendants.
I will uncover their hiding places so they cannot hide.
Their children, relatives, and neighbors will all be
destroyed.
Not one of them will be left!
11 Leave your orphans behind, and I will keep them alive.
Your widows, too, can depend on me."

12For the LORD says, "If even those who did not deserve to
drink from the cup of my wrath must drink from it, do you
think you will go unpunished? You will not go unpunished, but
must certainly drink from the cup of my wrath. 13For I solemnly
swear," says the LORD, "that Bozrah will become a pile of ruins.
It will become an object of horror and ridicule, an example to be
used in curses. All the towns around it will lie in ruins forever."

14 I said, "I have heard a message from the LORD.
A messenger has been sent among the nations to say,
'Gather your armies and march out against her!
Prepare to do battle with her!'"
15 The LORD says to Edom,
"I will certainly make you small among nations.
I will make you despised by all humankind.
16 The terror you inspire in others
and the arrogance of your heart have deceived you.
You may make your home in the clefts of the rocks;
you may occupy the highest places in the hills.
But even if you made your home where the eagles nest,
I would bring you down from there,"
says the LORD.
17 "Edom will become an object of horror.
All who pass by it will be filled with horror;
they will hiss out their scorn
because of all the disasters that have happened to it.
18 Edom will be destroyed like Sodom and Gomorrah
and the towns that were around them.
No one will live there.
No human being will settle in it,"
says the LORD.
19 "A lion coming up from the thick undergrowth along
the Jordan
scatters the sheep in the pastureland around it.

So too I will chase the Edomites off their land.
Then I will appoint over it whomever I choose.
For there is no one like me, and there is no one who can call me to account.
There is no ruler who can stand up against me.
20 So listen to what I, the LORD, have planned against Edom,
what I intend to do to the people who live in Teman.
Their little ones will be dragged off.
I will completely destroy their land because of what they have done.
21 The people of the earth will quake when they hear of their downfall.
Their cries of anguish will be heard all the way to the Gulf of Aqaba.
22 Look! Like an eagle with outspread wings,
a nation will soar up and swoop down on Bozrah.
At that time the soldiers of Edom will be as fearful
as a woman in labor."

JUDGMENT AGAINST DAMASCUS

23 The LORD spoke about Damascus:
"The people of Hamath and Arpad will be dismayed
because they have heard bad news.
Their courage will melt away because of worry.
Their hearts will not be able to rest.
24 The people of Damascus will lose heart and turn to flee.
Panic will grip them.
Pain and anguish will seize them
like a woman in labor.
25 How deserted will that once-famous city be,
that city that was once filled with joy!
26 For her young men will fall in her city squares.
All her soldiers will be destroyed at that time,"
says the LORD of Heaven's Armies.
27 "I will set fire to the walls of Damascus;
it will burn up the palaces of Ben Hadad."

49:23–27 "There is trouble on the sea; it cannot be quiet" (NKJV). Little know we what trouble may be upon the sea at this moment. We are safe in our quiet chamber, but far away on the salt sea the hurricane may be cruelly seeking for the lives of men. Hear how the death fiends howl among the cordage, how every timber starts as the waves beat like battering rams upon the vessel! This is not our rest, and the restless billows tell us so. There is a land where there is no more sea—our faces are steadfastly set toward it; we are going to the place of which the Lord has spoken. Till then, we cast our sorrows on the Lord who trod the sea of old, and who makes a way for his people through the depths thereof.

CHARLES SPURGEON
(1834–1892)
MORNING AND EVENING

JUDGMENT AGAINST KEDAR AND HAZOR

28 The LORD spoke about Kedar and the kingdoms of Hazor that King Nebuchadnezzar of Babylon conquered:
"Army of Babylon, go and attack Kedar.
Lay waste those who live in the eastern desert.
29 Their tents and their flocks will be taken away.
Their tent curtains, equipment, and camels will be carried off.
People will shout to them,
'Terror is all around you!'"
30 The LORD says, "Flee quickly, you who live in Hazor.
Take up refuge in remote places.
For King Nebuchadnezzar of Babylon has laid out plans to attack you.
He has formed his strategy on how to defeat you."
31 The LORD says, "Army of Babylon, go and attack
a nation that lives in peace and security.
They have no gates or walls to protect them.
They live all alone.
32 Their camels will be taken as plunder.

Their vast herds will be taken as spoil.
I will scatter to the four winds
those desert peoples who cut their hair short at the temples.
I will bring disaster against them
from every direction," says the LORD.
33 "Hazor will become a permanent wasteland,
a place where only jackals live.
No one will live there.
No human being will settle in it."

JUDGMENT AGAINST ELAM

34This was the LORD's message to the prophet Jeremiah about
Elam, which came early in the reign of King Zedekiah of Judah.
35The LORD of Heaven's Armies said:
"I will kill all the archers of Elam,
who are the chief source of her military might.
36 I will cause enemies to blow through Elam from every direction
like the winds blowing in from the four quarters of heaven.
I will scatter the people of Elam to the four winds.
There will not be any nation where the refugees of Elam will not go.
37 I will make the people of Elam terrified of their enemies,
who are seeking to kill them.
I will vent my fierce anger
and bring disaster upon them," says the LORD.
"I will send armies chasing after them
until I have completely destroyed them.
38 I will establish my sovereignty over Elam.
I will destroy their king and their leaders," says the LORD.
39 "Yet in future days
I will reverse Elam's ill fortune,"
says the LORD.

JUDGMENT AGAINST BABYLON

50 The LORD spoke concerning Babylon and the land of Bab-
ylonia through the prophet Jeremiah.
2 "Announce the news among the nations! Proclaim it!
Signal for people to pay attention.
Declare the news! Do not hide it! Say:
'Babylon will be captured.
Bel will be put to shame.
Marduk will be dismayed.
Babylon's idols will be put to shame;
her disgusting images will be dismayed.
3 For a nation from the north will attack Babylon;
it will lay her land waste.
People and animals will flee out of it.
No one will inhabit it.'

4 "When that time comes," says the LORD,
"the people of Israel and Judah will return to the land together.
They will come back with tears of repentance
as they seek the LORD their God.

50:1–7 "My people have been lost sheep. Their shepherds have allowed them to go astray." We are all one body and one sheep. The unity arises through love and truth and the choice of good. Thus every Israelite is one according to the true relationship. For we are all one body and one loaf of bread, and we partake of one Spirit. But a sheep that goes astray is one who in word and practice does not join the hunt of what is proper, either by not seeking or by not finding. And the one who knows and does what concerns knowledge does not go astray. But the one who goes astray is driven out by lions. For your adversary the devil prowls around like a roaring lion, seeking someone to devour. And also already young lions roaring to seize and seek from God food for themselves lay snares for the righteous.

ORIGEN (C. 185–C. 253)
FRAGMENTS ON JOB

5 They will ask the way to Zion;
they will turn their faces toward it.
They will come and bind themselves to the LORD
in a lasting covenant that will never be forgotten.

6 "My people have been lost sheep.
Their shepherds have allowed them to go astray.
They have wandered around in the mountains.
They have roamed from one mountain and hill to another.
They have forgotten their resting place.
7 All who encountered them devoured them.
Their enemies who did this said, 'We are not liable for punishment!
For those people have sinned against the LORD, their true pasture.
They have sinned against the LORD in whom their ancestors trusted.'

8 "People of Judah, get out of Babylon quickly!
Leave the land of Babylonia!
Be the first to depart.
Be like the male goats that lead the herd.
9 For I will rouse into action and bring against Babylon
a host of mighty nations from the land of the north.
They will set up their battle lines against her.
They will come from the north and capture her.
Their arrows will be like a skilled soldier
who does not return from the battle empty-handed.
10 Babylonia will be plundered.
Those who plunder it will take all they want,"
says the LORD.
11 "People of Babylonia, you plundered my people.
That made you happy and glad.
You frolic about like calves in a pasture.
Your joyous sounds are like the neighs of a stallion.
12 But Babylonia will be put to great shame.
The land where you were born will be disgraced.
Indeed, Babylonia will become the least important of all nations.
It will become a dry and barren desert.
13 After I vent my wrath on it, Babylon will be uninhabited.
It will be totally desolate.
All who pass by will be filled with horror and will hiss out their scorn
because of all the disasters that have happened to it.

14 "Take up your battle positions all around Babylon,
all you soldiers who are armed with bows.
Shoot all your arrows at her! Do not hold any back!
For she has sinned against the LORD.
15 Shout the battle cry from all around the city.
She will throw up her hands in surrender;
her towers will fall.
Her walls will be torn down.
Because I, the LORD, am wreaking revenge,
take out your vengeance on her!
Do to her as she has done!

DESIDERIUS ERASMUS:

A CHRISTIAN HUMANIST

c. 1469–1536

Born around 1469 in Rotterdam, Holland, Desiderius Erasmus was educated in a parochial school run by reforming lay Christians after his parents died. The Brethren of the Common Life, as they were known, emphasized prayer, meditation, devotion, and personal study, a spirituality that would find its way into Erasmus's own legacy.

As a young man he joined an Augustinian monastery before going on to be ordained into the priesthood in 1492. He was always more of a scholar than a pastor and devoted his time to writing and learning. He was particularly drawn to an emerging way of thinking that was transforming Europe called *humanism*. The cry of the humanists was *ad fontes*—"to the source"—reflecting their interest in rediscovering classical philosophy. Erasmus was enamored with mining the ancient philosophies for practical guidance for the good life, which he combined with his own practical Christian piety. His understanding of Christ was also practical and driven by Jesus' teachings and moral example. He had hoped this philosophical movement would mend the corruption he and many others identified in the Roman Catholic Church.

In *Enchiridion* Erasmus outlined the essential nature of the Christian life. Influenced by the early church fathers Origen and Clement, he tended to interpret scripture allegorically and understood discipleship in spiritualized terms. He envisioned such a life joining together both mind and spirit. His second book, *The Praise of Folly*, took to task the rote religiosity of the Catholic Church with all its relics and rituals, pilgrimages and penitence, monasticism and asceticism. All these things he called "Folly," satirizing the pseudo spirituality as superstitious and the ecclesial hierarchy as corrupt.

As a humanist, Erasmus went back to the sources, which included the original sources of scripture in Hebrew and Greek. His most important work was his construction of a critical edition of the Greek New Testament. It was controversial, given the fact that the only authoritative biblical text at the time was the Latin Vulgate of Jerome; Erasmus's new edition, based on newly discovered Greek manuscripts, revealed potential deficiencies in the Vulgate. Yet Erasmus's work mirrored the very impulse that originally motivated Jerome: He wanted the Bible translated into the vernacular of the people, and he hoped his effort would serve as an important foundation for such translations. This hope was fulfilled beyond all expectations: In subsequent centuries, multiple translations of the Bible relied on Erasmus's Greek New Testament—including Luther's German Bible, the King James Version, and the Spanish Reina-Valera translation, solidifying Erasmus's legacy as a Christian humanist.

IMPORTANT WORKS

ENCHIRIDION

THE PRAISE OF FOLLY

ON THE FREEDOM OF THE WILL

16 Kill all the farmers who sow the seed in the land of
Babylon;
kill all those who wield the sickle at harvest time.
Let all the foreigners return to their own people.
Let them hurry back to their own lands
to escape destruction by that enemy army.

17 "The people of Israel are like scattered sheep
that lions have chased away.
First the king of Assyria devoured them.
Now, last of all, King Nebuchadnezzar of Babylon has
gnawed their bones.
18 So I, the LORD of Heaven's Armies, the God of Israel,
say:
'I will punish the king of Babylon and his land
just as I punished the king of Assyria.
19 But I will restore the flock of Israel to their own
pasture.
They will graze on Mount Carmel and the land of
Bashan.
They will eat until they are full
on the hills of Ephraim and the land of Gilead.
20 When that time comes,
no guilt will be found in Israel.
No sin will be found in Judah.
For I will forgive those of them I have allowed to
survive.
I, the LORD, affirm it!'"
21 The LORD says,
"Attack the land of Merathaim
and the people who live in Pekod.
Pursue, kill, and completely destroy them!
Do just as I have commanded you!
22 The noise of battle can be heard in the land of
Babylonia.
There is the sound of great destruction.
23 Babylon hammered the whole world to pieces.
But see how that 'hammer' has been broken and
shattered!
See what an object of horror
Babylon has become among the nations!
24 I set a trap for you, Babylon;
you were caught before you knew it.
You fought against me;
so you were found and captured.
25 I have opened up the place where my weapons are
stored.
I have brought out the weapons for carrying out my
wrath.
For I, the Sovereign LORD of Heaven's Armies,
have work to carry out in the land of Babylonia.
26 Come from far away and attack Babylonia!
Open up the places where she stores her grain.
Pile her up in ruins. Destroy her completely!
Do not leave anyone alive!
27 Kill all her soldiers.
Let them be slaughtered.
They are doomed, for their day of reckoning has come,
the time for them to be punished.

28 Listen! Fugitives and refugees are coming from the land
of Babylon.
They are coming to Zion to declare there
how the LORD our God is getting revenge,
getting revenge for what they have done to his temple.

29 "Call for archers to come against Babylon!
Summon against her all who draw the bow.
Set up camp all around the city.
Do not allow anyone to escape!
Pay her back for what she has done.
Do to her what she has done to others.
For she has proudly defied me,
the Holy One of Israel.
30 So her young men will fall in her city squares.
All her soldiers will be destroyed at that time,"
says the LORD.
31 "Listen! I am opposed to you, you proud city,"
says the Sovereign LORD of Heaven's Armies.
"Indeed, your day of reckoning has come,
the time when I will punish you.
32 You will stumble and fall, you proud city;
no one will help you get up.
I will set fire to your towns;
it will burn up everything that surrounds you."
33 The LORD of Heaven's Armies says,
"The people of Israel are oppressed.
So too are the people of Judah.
All those who took them captive are holding them
prisoners.
They refuse to set them free.
34 But the one who will rescue them is strong.
His name is the LORD of Heaven's Armies.
He will strongly champion their cause.
As a result he will bring peace and rest to the earth,
but trouble and turmoil to the people who inhabit
Babylonia.

35 "Destructive forces will come against the Babylonians,"
says the LORD.
"They will come against the people who inhabit
Babylonia,
against her leaders and her men of wisdom.
36 Destructive forces will come against her false prophets;
they will be shown to be fools!
Destructive forces will come against her soldiers;
they will be filled with terror!
37 Destructive forces will come against her horses and her
chariots.
Destructive forces will come against all the foreign
troops within her;
they will be as frightened as women!
Destructive forces will come against her treasures;
they will be taken away as plunder!
38 A drought will come upon her land;
her rivers and canals will be dried up.
All this will happen because her land is filled with idols.
Her people act like madmen because of those idols they
fear.

39 Therefore desert creatures and jackals will live there;
ostriches too will dwell in it.
But no people will ever live there again;
no one will dwell there for all time to come.
40 I will destroy Babylonia just as I did
Sodom and Gomorrah and the neighboring towns.
No one will live there;
no human being will settle in it,"
says the LORD.
41 "Look! An army is about to come from the north.
A mighty nation and many kings are stirring into
action
in faraway parts of the earth.
42 Its soldiers are armed with bows and spears.
They are cruel and show no mercy.
They sound like the roaring sea
as they ride forth on their horses.
Lined up in formation like men going into battle,
they are coming against you, fair Babylon.
43 The king of Babylon will become paralyzed with fear
when he hears news of their coming.
Anguish will grip him,
agony like that of a woman giving birth to a baby.

44 "A lion coming up from the thick undergrowth along
the Jordan
scatters the sheep in the pastureland around it.
So too I will chase the Babylonians off their land;
then I will appoint over it whomever I choose.
For there is no one like me.
There is no one who can call me to account.
There is no ruler that can stand up against me.
45 So listen to what I, the LORD, have planned against
Babylon,
what I intend to do to the people who inhabit the land
of Babylonia.
Their little ones will be dragged off like sheep.
I will completely destroy their land because of what
they have done.
46 The people of the earth will quake when they hear
Babylon has been captured.
Her cries of anguish will be heard by the other
nations."

51 The LORD says:
"I will cause a destructive wind to blow
against Babylon and the people who inhabit
Babylonia.
2 I will send people to winnow Babylonia like a wind
blowing away chaff.
They will winnow her and strip her land bare.
This will happen when they come against her from
every direction,
when it is time to destroy her.
3 Do not give her archers time to string their bows
or to put on their coats of armor.
Do not spare any of her young men.
Completely destroy her whole army.
4 Let them fall slain in the land of Babylonia,
mortally wounded in the streets of her cities.

5 "For Israel and Judah will not be forsaken
by their God, the LORD of Heaven's Armies.
For the land of Babylonia is full of guilt
against the Holy One of Israel.
6 Get out of Babylonia quickly, you foreign people.
Flee to save your lives.
Do not let yourselves be killed because of her sins,
for it is time for the LORD to wreak his revenge.
He will pay Babylonia back for what she has done.
7 Babylonia had been a gold cup in the LORD's hand;
she had made the whole world drunk.
The nations had drunk from the wine of her wrath,
so they have all gone mad.
8 But suddenly Babylonia will fall and be destroyed.
Cry out in mourning over it!
Get medicine for her wounds;
perhaps she can be healed!
9 Foreigners living there will say,
'We tried to heal her, but she could not be healed.
Let's leave Babylonia and each go back to his own country.
For judgment on her will be vast in its proportions.
It will be like it is piled up to heaven, stacked up into the clouds.'
10 The exiles from Judah will say,
'The LORD has brought about a great deliverance for us!
Come on, let's go and proclaim in Zion
what the LORD our God has done!'

11 "Sharpen your arrows!
Fill your quivers!
The LORD will arouse a spirit of hostility in the kings of Media,
for he intends to destroy Babylonia.
For that is how the LORD will get his revenge—
how he will get his revenge for the Babylonians' destruction of his temple.
12 Give the signal to attack Babylon's wall!
Bring more guards;
post them all around the city.
Put men in ambush,
for the LORD will do what he has planned.
He will do what he said he would do to the people of Babylon.
13 "You who live along the rivers of Babylon,
the time of your end has come.
You who are rich in plundered treasure,
it is time for your lives to be cut off.
14 The LORD of Heaven's Armies has solemnly sworn,
'I will fill your land with enemy soldiers.
They will swarm over it like locusts.
They will raise up shouts of victory over it.'
15 He is the one who by his power made the earth.
He is the one who by his wisdom fixed the world in place;
by his understanding, he spread out the heavens.
16 When his voice thunders, the waters in the heavens roar.

He makes the clouds rise from the far-off horizons;
he makes the lightning flash out in the midst of the rain.
He unleashes the wind from the places where he stores it;
17 all idolaters will prove to be stupid and ignorant.
Every goldsmith will be disgraced by the idol he made.
For the image he forges is merely a sham;
there is no breath in any of those idols.
18 They are worthless, objects to be ridiculed.
When the time comes to punish them, they will be destroyed.
19 The LORD, who is the portion of the descendants of Jacob, is not like them.
For he is the one who created everything,
including the people of Israel whom he claims as his own.
His name is the LORD of Heaven's Armies.

20 "Babylon, you are my war club,
my weapon for battle.
I used you to smash nations.
I used you to destroy kingdoms.
21 I used you to smash horses and their riders.
I used you to smash chariots and their drivers.
22 I used you to smash men and women.
I used you to smash old men and young men.
I used you to smash young men and young women.
23 I used you to smash shepherds and their flocks.
I used you to smash farmers and their teams of oxen.
I used you to smash governors and leaders.

24 "But I will repay Babylon
and all who live in Babylonia
for all the wicked things they did in Zion
right before the eyes of you Judeans,"
says the LORD.
25 The LORD says, "Beware! I am opposed to you, Babylon!
You are like a destructive mountain that destroys all the earth.
I will unleash my power against you;
I will roll you off the cliffs and make you like a burned-out mountain.
26 No one will use any of your stones as a cornerstone;
no one will use any of them in the foundation of his house.
For you will lie desolate forever,"
says the LORD.
27 "Raise up battle flags throughout the lands.
Sound the trumpets calling the nations to do battle.
Prepare the nations to do battle against Babylonia.
Call for these kingdoms to attack her:
Ararat, Minni, and Ashkenaz.
Appoint a commander to lead the attack.
Send horses against her like a swarm of locusts.
28 Prepare the nations to do battle against her.
Prepare the kings of the Medes.
Prepare their governors and all their leaders.
Prepare all the countries they rule to do battle against her.

29 The earth will tremble and writhe in agony;
for the LORD will carry out his plan.
He plans to make the land of Babylonia
a wasteland where no one lives.
30 The soldiers of Babylonia will stop fighting.
They will remain in their fortified cities.
They will lose their strength to do battle.
They will be as frightened as women.
The houses in her cities will be set on fire.
The gates of her cities will be broken down.
31 One runner after another will come to the king of
Babylon;
one messenger after another will come bringing news.
They will bring news to the king of Babylon
that his whole city has been captured.
32 They will report that the fords have been captured,
the reed marshes have been burned,
the soldiers are terrified.
33 For the LORD of Heaven's Armies, the God of Israel,
says,
'Fair Babylon will be like a threshing floor
that has been trampled flat for harvest.
The time for her to be cut down and harvested
will come very soon.'

34 "King Nebuchadnezzar of Babylon
devoured me and drove my people out.
Like a monster from the deep he swallowed me.
He filled his belly with my riches;
he made me an empty dish.
He completely cleaned me out."
35 The person who lives in Zion says,
"May Babylon pay for the violence done to me and to
my relatives."
Jerusalem says,
"May those living in Babylonia pay for the bloodshed of
my people."
36 Therefore the LORD says,
"I will stand up for your cause.
I will pay the Babylonians back for what they have done
to you.
I will dry up their sea;
I will make their springs run dry.
37 Babylon will become a heap of ruins.
Jackals will make their home there.
It will become an object of horror and of hissing
scorn,
a place where no one lives.
38 The Babylonians are all like lions roaring for prey;
they are like lion cubs growling for something to eat.
39 When their appetites are all stirred up,
I will set out a banquet for them.
I will make them drunk
so that they will pass out,
they will fall asleep forever,
they will never wake up,"
says the LORD.
40 "I will lead them off to be slaughtered
like lambs, rams, and male goats.

41 "See how Babylon has been captured!
See how the pride of the whole earth has been taken!
See what an object of horror
Babylon has become among the nations!
42 The sea has swept over Babylon.
She has been covered by a multitude of its waves.
43 The towns of Babylonia have become heaps of ruins.
She has become a dry and barren desert.
No one lives in those towns any more;
no one even passes through them.
44 I will punish the god Bel in Babylon.
I will make him spit out what he has swallowed.
The nations will not come streaming to him any longer.
Indeed, the walls of Babylon will fall.

45 "Get out of Babylon, my people!
Flee to save your lives
from the fierce anger of the LORD!
46 Do not lose your courage or become afraid
because of the reports that are heard in the land.
For a report will come in one year.
Another report will follow it in the next.
There will be violence in the land
with ruler fighting against ruler.

47 "So the time will certainly come
when I will punish the idols of Babylon.
Her whole land will be put to shame.
All her mortally wounded will collapse in her midst.
48 Then heaven and earth and all that is in them
will sing for joy over Babylon.
For destroyers from the north will attack it,"
says the LORD.
49 "Babylon must fall
because of the Israelites she has killed,
just as the earth's mortally wounded fell
because of Babylon.
50 You who have escaped the sword,
go, do not delay.
Remember the LORD in a faraway land.
Think about Jerusalem.
51 'We are ashamed because we have been insulted.
Our faces show our disgrace.
For foreigners have invaded
the holy rooms in the LORD's temple.'
52 Yes, but the time will certainly come," says the LORD,
"when I will punish her idols.
Throughout her land the mortally wounded will
groan.
53 Even if Babylon climbs high into the sky
and fortifies her elevated stronghold,
I will send destroyers against her,"
says the LORD.

54 Cries of anguish will come from Babylon,
the sound of great destruction from the land of the
Babylonians.
55 For the LORD is ready to destroy Babylon,
and put an end to her loud noise.

51:49–57 The prophet said that the time would come when God would take vengeance on the idols of Babylon. And thus God claimed for himself that power that seemed then to have almost disappeared; for with the temple being overthrown, the Babylonians seemed in a manner to triumph over him. "Yes, but the time will certainly come," that is, *Though you are confounded, yet God will give you a reason for glorying, so that you shall again sing joyfully his praises.* By these words he reminded us that we are to cherish the hope of the promises until God completes his work.

JOHN CALVIN (1509–1564)
COMPLETE COMMENTARY ON THE BIBLE

Their waves will roar like turbulent waters.
They will make a deafening noise.
56 For a destroyer is attacking Babylon.
Her warriors will be captured;
their bows will be broken.
For the LORD is a God who punishes;
he pays back in full.
57 "I will make her officials and wise men drunk,
along with her governors, leaders, and warriors.
They will fall asleep forever and never wake up,"
says the King whose name is the LORD of Heaven's
Armies.

58 This is what the LORD of Heaven's Armies says,
"Babylon's thick wall will be completely demolished.
Her high gates will be set on fire.
The peoples strive for what does not satisfy.
The nations grow weary trying to get what will be
destroyed."

59 This is the order Jeremiah the prophet gave to Seraiah son
of Neriah, son of Mahseiah, when he went to King Zedekiah of
Judah in Babylon during the fourth year of his reign. (Seraiah
was a quartermaster.) 60 Jeremiah recorded on one scroll all the
judgments that would come upon Babylon—all these prophecies written about Babylon. 61 Then Jeremiah said to Seraiah,
"When you arrive in Babylon, make sure you read aloud all these
prophecies. 62 Then say, 'O LORD, you have announced that you
will destroy this place so that no people or animals live in it any
longer. Certainly it will lie desolate forever!' 63 When you finish
reading this scroll aloud, tie a stone to it and throw it into the
middle of the Euphrates River. 64 Then say, 'In the same way
Babylon will sink and never rise again because of the disaster
I am ready to bring upon her; they will grow faint.'"
The prophecies of Jeremiah end here.

THE FALL OF JERUSALEM

52 Zedekiah was twenty-one years old when he became king,
and he ruled in Jerusalem for 11 years. His mother's name
was Hamutal daughter of Jeremiah, from Libnah. 2 He did what
displeased the LORD just as Jehoiakim had done.
3 What follows is a record of what happened to Jerusalem
and Judah because of the LORD's anger when he drove them
out of his sight. Zedekiah rebelled against the king of Babylon.
4 King Nebuchadnezzar of Babylon came against Jerusalem with
his whole army and set up camp outside it. They built siege
ramps all around it. He arrived on the tenth day of the tenth
month in the ninth year that Zedekiah ruled over Judah. 5 The
city remained under siege until Zedekiah's eleventh year. 6 By
the ninth day of the fourth month the famine in the city was
so severe the residents had no food. 7 They broke through the
city walls, and all the soldiers tried to escape. They left the city
during the night. They went through the gate between the two
walls that is near the king's garden. (The Babylonians had the
city surrounded.) Then they headed for the rift valley. 8 But the
Babylonian army chased after the king. They caught up with
Zedekiah in the plains of Jericho, and his entire army deserted
him. 9 They captured him and brought him up to the king of
Babylon at Riblah in the territory of Hamath, and he passed

sentence on him there. 10The king of Babylon had Zedekiah's sons put to death while Zedekiah was forced to watch. He also had all the nobles of Judah put to death there at Riblah. 11He had Zedekiah's eyes put out and had him bound in chains. Then the king of Babylon had him led off to Babylon, and he was imprisoned there until the day he died.

12On the tenth day of the fifth month, in the nineteenth year of King Nebuchadnezzar of Babylon, Nebuzaradan, the captain of the royal guard who served the king of Babylon, arrived in Jerusalem. 13He burned down the LORD's temple, the royal palace, and all the houses in Jerusalem, including every large house. 14The whole Babylonian army that came with the captain of the royal guard tore down the walls that surrounded Jerusalem. 15Nebuzaradan, the captain of the royal guard, took into exile some of the poor, the rest of the people who remained in the city, those who had deserted to the king of Babylon, and the rest of the craftsmen. 16But he left behind some of the poor and gave them fields and vineyards.

17The Babylonians broke the two bronze pillars in the temple of the LORD, as well as the movable stands and the large bronze basin called "The Sea." They took all the bronze to Babylon. 18They also took the pots, shovels, trimming shears, basins, pans, and all the bronze utensils used by the priests. 19The captain of the royal guard took the gold and silver bowls, censers, basins, pots, lampstands, pans, and vessels. 20The bronze of the items that King Solomon made for the LORD's temple (including the two pillars, the large bronze basin called "The Sea," the 12 bronze bulls under "The Sea," and the movable stands) was too heavy to be weighed. 21Each of the pillars was about 27 feet high, about 18 feet in circumference, three inches thick, and hollow. 22The bronze top of one pillar was about 7½ feet high and had bronze latticework and pomegranate-shaped ornaments all around it. The second pillar with its pomegranate-shaped ornaments was like it. 23There were 96 pomegranate-shaped ornaments on the sides; in all there were 100 pomegranate-shaped ornaments over the latticework that went around it.

24The captain of the royal guard took Seraiah the chief priest, Zephaniah the priest who was second in rank, and the three doorkeepers. 25From the city he took an official who was in charge of the soldiers, seven of the king's advisers who were discovered in the city, an official army secretary who drafted citizens for military service, and 60 citizens who were discovered in the middle of the city. 26Nebuzaradan, the captain of the royal guard, took them and brought them to the king of Babylon at Riblah. 27The king of Babylon ordered them to be executed at Riblah in the territory of Hamath.

So Judah was taken into exile away from its land. 28Here is the official record of the number of people Nebuchadnezzar carried into exile: In the seventh year, 3,023 Jews; 29in Nebuchadnezzar's eighteenth year, 832 people from Jerusalem; 30in Nebuchadnezzar's twenty-third year, Nebuzaradan, the captain of the royal guard, carried into exile 745 Judeans. In all, 4,600 people went into exile.

JEHOIACHIN IN EXILE

31In the thirty-seventh year of the exile of King Jehoiachin of Judah, on the twenty-fifth day of the twelfth month, King Evil Merodach of Babylon, in the first year of his reign, pardoned

52:28–34 Here ends the history of the kingdom of Judah. I shall only observe the severe judgment of God upon this people, whose kingdom was made up of the two tribes of Judah and Benjamin and half the tribe of Manasseh. In the numbering of the persons belonging to these two tribes (counting half of the number of the tribe of Manasseh), we find 126,100; we find of them 148,150. Here we find no more of them carried into captivity than 4,600. From this we may judge what a multitude of them were slain by the sword, by the famine, and pestilence! It is a dreadful thing to fall into the hands of the living God, to mock his messengers, despise his words, and misuse his prophets, till there be no remedy.

JOHN WESLEY (1703–1791)
EXPLANATORY NOTES ON THE BIBLE

King Jehoiachin of Judah and released him from prison. [32]He
spoke kindly to him and gave him a more prestigious position
than the other kings who were with him in Babylon. [33]Jehoia-
chin took off his prison clothes and ate daily in the king's presence for the rest of his life. [34]He was given daily provisions by
the king of Babylon for the rest of his life until the day he died.

AUTHOR	AUDIENCE	DATE	PURPOSE	THEMES
Probably Jeremiah	Jews in Babylonian exile who were lamenting the destruction of Jerusalem	Shortly after the fall of Jerusalem in 586 BC	As its name suggests, this book is an honest lament over suffering, though it is mourning with hope because of God's covenant and character.	Lament; suffering; the Lord's goodness and mercy; prayer and worship

"Alas! The city once full of people now sits all alone! The prominent lady among the nations has become a widow! The princess who once ruled the provinces has become a forced laborer!" (1:1). So begins the book of Lamentations, a unique poem within the Hebrew scriptures. It records the deep grief and sadness experienced by the people of Judah when Jerusalem was destroyed. The book offers honest laments over the existence of suffering and the ongoing struggles of the human condition while directing our attention toward God's covenant and character.

Throughout church history this book has served as a point of reflection on pain and loss. John Calvin provided an apt summation of the purpose and scope of the book:

> [Jeremiah's] object was to show that though nothing in the land appeared but desolation, and the temple being destroyed, the covenant of God appeared as made void, and thus all hope of salvation had been cut off, yet hope still remained, provided the people sought God in true repentance and faith; and he thus proceeded in the course of his calling and made it evident that his doctrine would not be without benefit.

These two themes—destruction and suffering; God's covenant and salvation—frame this book and highlight its benefit to the church.

John Wesley noted that the book "has its name from the subject matter of it, which is Lamentation." A *lament* is a passionate expression of grief caused by either outside events or one's own behavior. In the case of Israel both causes were present. "Her foes subjugated her; her enemies are at ease. For the Lord afflicted her because of her many acts of rebellion. Her children went away captive before the enemy" (1:5). The adversary Jeremiah spoke about was Babylon, which conquered and destroyed Jerusalem in 586 BC, taking its inhabitants into captivity. "That the occasion was the miseries of the people, by reason of the famine, sword, and captivity, is evident," explained John Wesley. He continued, "The design of the writing, as to those whom it immediately concerned, is plain and obvious, namely to affect the people with those judgments that came upon them for their sins: as to us (upon whom the ends of the world are come) to mind us to take heed of their sins lest we be sharers in their plagues."

The book climaxes in chapter 3 with the first-person account of Jeremiah complaining about his miserable condition and petitioning God for mercy. He urged, "Let us carefully examine our ways, and let us return to the Lord." Why? Because of this important fact: "We have blatantly rebelled." As a result he can say to God, "You have not forgiven. You shrouded yourself with anger and then pursued us; you killed without mercy"

LAMENTATIONS

(3:40, 42–43). The poet recognized Jerusalem's destruction was self-inflicted, having been the fulfillment of God's promises to curse his people for their willful disobedience and rebellion against him.

Despite his affliction and wandering, despite his downcast soul, the poet says: "I have hope: The Lord's loyal kindness never ceases . . . your faithfulness is abundant!" (3:21–23). Despite this theme of suffering as a result of sin, Jeremiah has a robust theology that understands God's covenant and character. He wrote:

> "My portion is the Lord," I have said to myself, so I will put my hope in him. The Lord is good to those who trust in him, to the one who seeks him. It is good to wait patiently for deliverance from the Lord . . . For the Lord will not reject us forever. Though he causes us grief, he then has compassion on us according to the abundance of his loyal kindness. (3:24–26, 31–32).

Goodness is an important, anchoring character quality of the Lord frequently cited in the Bible. Origen noted, "As therefore God is frequently called *good* in the Old Testament, so also the Father of our Lord Jesus Christ is styled just in the Gospels." Theodore of Cyr encouraged, "Let us not murmur at the storm that has arisen, for the Lord of all knows what is good for us." Jeremiah appealed to the Lord's goodness, beseeching him to intervene and offering a paradigm for our own prayers: "Why do you keep on forgetting us? Why do you forsake us so long? Bring us back to yourself, O Lord, so that we may return to you; renew our life as in days before, unless you have utterly rejected us and are angry with us beyond measure" (5:20–22).

In recounting the message of Lamentations, Athanasius explained that our sufferings

> avail nothing against the multitude of God's tender mercies; for we shall quickly recover from them since they are merely temporal, but God is always gracious, pouring out his tender mercies on those who please him . . . For all present matters are trifling compared with those that are future; the sufferings of this present time not being worthy to be compared with the hope that is to come.

Look to the book of Lamentations when life turns dark to find words for your own honest laments, as well as a reminder of the Lord's goodness. "His compassions never end. They are fresh every morning" (3:22–23).

LAMENTATIONS

THE PROPHET SPEAKS

1:1–15 Bringing someone to his senses is censure, which makes one think. Bewailing one's fate is latent censure and artfully helps to bring salvation, albeit under stealth. The Lord made use of this by Jeremiah: "The prominent lady among the nations has become a widow!" In the end, the system God pursues to inspire fear is the source of salvation. And it is the prerogative of goodness to save. For it is indeed noble not to sin, but it is good also for the sinner to repent, just as it is best to be always in good health but well to recover from disease. Sick, we truly stand in need of the Savior; having wandered, of one to guide us; blind, of one to lead us to the light; dead, we need life; sheep, we need a shepherd; we who are children need a tutor, while universal humanity stands in need of Jesus; so that we may not continue intractable and sinners to the end and thus fall into condemnation but may be separated from the chaff and stored up in the paternal garner.

CLEMENT OF ALEXANDRIA
(C. 150–C. 215)
CHRIST THE EDUCATOR

א (*ALEF*)

1 Alas! The city once full of people
now sits all alone!
The prominent lady among the nations
has become a widow!
The princess who once ruled the
provinces
has become a forced laborer!

ב (*BET*)

2 She weeps bitterly at night;
tears stream down her cheeks.
She has no one to comfort her
among all her lovers.
All her friends have betrayed her;
they have become her enemies.

ג (*GIMEL*)

3 Judah has departed into exile
under affliction and harsh oppression.
She lives among the nations;
she has found no resting place.
All who pursued her overtook her
in narrow straits.

ד (*DALET*)

4 The roads to Zion mourn
because no one travels to the festivals.
All her city gates are deserted;
her priests groan.
Her virgins grieve;
she is in bitter anguish!

ה (*HE*)

5 Her foes subjugated her;
her enemies are at ease.
For the LORD afflicted her
because of her many acts of rebellion.
Her children went away
captive before the enemy.

ו (*VAV*)

6 All of Daughter Zion's splendor
has departed.
Her leaders became like deer;
they found no pasture,
so they were too exhausted to escape
from the hunter.

ז (*ZAYIN*)

7 Jerusalem remembers,
when she became a poor homeless person,
all her treasures
that she owned in days of old.
When her people fell into an enemy's grip,
none of her allies came to her rescue.
Her enemies gloated over her;
they sneered at her downfall.

ח (*KHET*)

8 Jerusalem committed terrible sin;
therefore she became an object of scorn.
All who admired her have despised her
because they have seen her nakedness.
She groans aloud
and turns away in shame.

ט (*TET*)

9 Her menstrual flow has soiled her clothing;
she did not consider the consequences of her sin.
Her demise was astonishing,
and there was no one to comfort her.
She cried, "Look, O LORD, on my affliction
because my enemy boasts!"

י (*YOD*)

10 An enemy grabbed
all her valuables.
Indeed she watched in horror as Gentiles
invaded her holy temple—
those whom you had commanded:
"They must not enter your assembly place."

כ (*KAF*)

11 All her people groaned
as they searched for a morsel of bread.
They exchanged their valuables
for just enough food
to stay alive.

JERUSALEM SPEAKS

"Look, O LORD! Consider
that I have become worthless!"

ל (*LAMED*)

12 Is it nothing to you, all you who pass by on
the road?
Look and see!
Is there any pain like mine?
The Lord has afflicted me,
he has inflicted it on me
when he burned with anger.

מ (*MEM*)

13 He sent down fire
into my bones, and it overcame them.
He spread out a trapper's net for my feet;
he made me turn back.
He has made me desolate;
I am faint all day long.

נ (*NUN*)

14 My sins are bound around my neck like a yoke;
they are fastened together by his hand.
He has placed his yoke on my neck;
he has sapped my strength.
The Lord has handed me over
to those whom I cannot resist.

ס (***SAMEK***)

15 He rounded up all my mighty ones;
the Lord did this in my midst.
He summoned an assembly against me
to shatter my young men.
The Lord has stomped like grapes
the virgin daughter, Judah.

ע (***AYIN***)

16 I weep because of these things;
my eyes flow with tears.
For there is no one in sight who can comfort me
or encourage me.
My children are desolated
because an enemy has prevailed.

THE PROPHET SPEAKS

פ (***PE***)

17 Zion spread out her hands,
but there is no one to comfort her.
The LORD has issued a decree against Jacob;
his neighbors have become his enemies.
Jerusalem has become
like filthy garbage in their midst.

JERUSALEM SPEAKS

צ (***TSADE***)

18 The LORD is right to judge me!
Yes, I rebelled against his commands.
Please listen, all you nations,
and look at my suffering!
My young women and men
have gone into exile.

ק (***QOF***)

19 I called for my lovers,
but they had deceived me.
My priests and my elders
perished in the city.
Truly they had searched for food
to keep themselves alive.

ר (***RESH***)

20 Look, O LORD! I am distressed;
my stomach is in knots!
My heart is pounding inside me.
Yes, I was terribly rebellious!
Out in the street the sword bereaves a mother of her children;
inside the house death is present.

ש (***SIN/SHIN***)

21 They have heard that I groan,
yet there is no one to comfort me.
All my enemies have heard of my trouble;
they are glad that you have brought it about.
Bring about the day of judgment that you promised
so that they may end up like me!

ת (*TAV*)

22 Let all their wickedness come before you;
afflict them
just as you have afflicted me
because of all my acts of rebellion.
For my groans are many,
and my heart is sick with sorrow.

THE PROPHET SPEAKS

א (*ALEF*)

2 Alas! The Lord has covered
Daughter Zion with his anger.
He has thrown down the splendor of Israel
from heaven to earth;
he did not protect his temple
when he displayed his anger.

ב (*BET*)

2 The Lord destroyed mercilessly
all the homes of Jacob's descendants.
In his anger he tore down
the fortified cities of Daughter Judah.
He knocked to the ground and
humiliated
the kingdom and its rulers.

ג (*GIMEL*)

3 In fierce anger he destroyed
the whole army of Israel.
He withdrew his right hand
as the enemy attacked.
He was like a raging fire in the land
of Jacob;
it consumed everything around it.

ד (*DALET*)

4 He prepared his bow like an enemy;
his right hand was ready to shoot.
Like a foe he killed everyone,
even our strong young men;
he has poured out his anger like fire
on the tent of Daughter Zion.

ה (*HE*)

5 The Lord, like an enemy,
destroyed Israel.
He destroyed all her palaces;
he ruined her fortified cities.
He made everyone in Daughter Judah
mourn and lament.

ו (*VAV*)

6 He destroyed his temple as if it were a
vineyard;
he destroyed his appointed meeting place.
The LORD has made those in Zion forget
both the festivals and the Sabbaths.
In his fierce anger he has spurned
both king and priest.

2:1–9 Now, when Jerusalem was reduced to desolation, there was an abolition of God's covenant. We must, however, observe at the same time that the prophet did not mean here to invalidate the fidelity or constancy of God, but thus to rouse the attention of his own people who had become torpid in their sloth. But it was impossible that anyone should really call on God except he was humbled in mind and brought the sacrifice of which we have spoken, even a humble and contrite spirit. It was then the prophet's object to soften the hardness he knew prevailed in almost the whole people.

JOHN CALVIN **(1509–1564)**
COMPLETE COMMENTARY ON THE BIBLE

ז (*ZAYIN*)
7 The Lord rejected his altar
and abhorred his temple.
He handed over to the enemy
Jerusalem's palace walls;
the enemy shouted in the LORD's temple
as if it were a feast day.

ח (*KHET*)
8 The LORD was determined to tear down
Daughter Zion's wall.
He prepared to knock it down;
he did not withdraw his hand from destroying.
He made the ramparts and fortified walls
lament;
together they mourned their ruin.

ט (*TET*)
9 Her city gates have fallen to the ground;
he smashed to bits the bars that lock her gates.
Her king and princes were taken into exile;
there is no more guidance available.
As for her prophets,
they no longer receive a vision from the LORD.

י (*YOD*)
10 The elders of Daughter Zion
sit on the ground in silence.
They have thrown dirt on their heads;
they have dressed in sackcloth.
Jerusalem's young women stare down at the ground.

כ (*KAF*)
11 My eyes are worn out from weeping;
my stomach is in knots.
My heart is poured out on the ground
due to the destruction of my helpless people;
children and infants faint
in the town squares.

ל (*LAMED*)
12 Children say to their mothers,
"Where are food and drink?"
They faint like a wounded warrior
in the city squares.
They die slowly
in their mothers' arms.

מ (*MEM*)
13 With what can I equate you?
To what can I compare you, O Daughter
Jerusalem?
To what can I liken you
so that I might comfort you, O Virgin Daughter
Zion?
Your wound is as deep as the sea.
Who can heal you?

נ (*NUN*)
14 Your prophets saw visions for you
that were worthless whitewash.
They failed to expose your sin
so as to restore your fortunes.
They saw oracles for you
that were worthless lies.

ס (*SAMEK*)
15 All who passed by on the road
clapped their hands to mock you.
They sneered and shook their heads
at Daughter Jerusalem.
"Ha! Is this the city they called
'the perfection of beauty,
the source of joy of the whole earth!'?"

פ (*PE*)
16 All your enemies
gloated over you.
They sneered and gnashed their teeth;
they said, "We have destroyed her!
Ha! We have waited a long time for this day.
We have lived to see it!"

ע (*AYIN*)
17 The LORD has done what he planned;
he has fulfilled his promise
that he threatened long ago:
He has overthrown you without mercy
and has enabled the enemy to gloat over you;
he has exalted your adversaries' power.

צ (*TSADE*)
18 Cry out from your heart to the Lord,
O wall of Daughter Zion!
Make your tears flow like a river
all day and all night long!
Do not rest;
do not let your tears stop!

ק (*QOF*)
19 Get up! Cry out in the night
when the night watches start!
Pour out your heart like water
before the face of the Lord!
Lift up your hands to him
for your children's lives;
they are fainting from hunger
at every street corner.

JERUSALEM SPEAKS

ר (*RESH*)
20 Look, O LORD! Consider!
Whom have you ever afflicted like this?
Should women eat their offspring,
their healthy infants?
Should priest and prophet
be killed in the Lord's sanctuary?

ש (*SIN/SHIN*)

21 The young boys and old men
lie dead on the ground in the streets.
My young women and my young men
have fallen by the sword.
You killed them when you were angry;
you slaughtered them without mercy.

ת (*TAV*)

22 As if it were a feast day, you call
enemies to terrify me on every side.
On the day of the LORD's anger
no one escaped or survived.
My enemy has finished off
those healthy infants whom I bore and raised.

THE PROPHET SPEAKS

א (*ALEF*)

3 I am the man who has experienced affliction
from the rod of the LORD's wrath.
2 He drove me into captivity and made me walk
in darkness and not light.
3 He repeatedly attacks me;
he turns his hand against me all day long.

ב (*BET*)

4 He has made my mortal skin waste away;
he has broken my bones.
5 He has besieged and surrounded me
with bitter hardship.
6 He has made me reside in deepest darkness
like those who died long ago.

ג (*GIMEL*)

7 He has walled me in so that I cannot get out;
he has weighted me down with heavy prison
chains.
8 Also, when I cry out desperately for help,
he has shut out my prayer.
9 He has blocked every road I take with a wall of hewn
stones;
he has made every path impassable.

ד (*DALET*)

10 To me he is like a bear lying in ambush,
like a hidden lion stalking its prey.
11 He has obstructed my paths and torn me to
pieces;
he has made me desolate.
12 He drew his bow and made me
the target for his arrow.

ה (*HE*)

13 He shot his arrows
into my heart.
14 I have become the laughingstock of all people,
their mocking song all day long.
15 He has given me my fill of bitter herbs
and made me drunk with bitterness.

3:1–24 "'My portion is the LORD,' I have said to myself." It is not "The Lord is partly my portion" nor "The Lord is in my portion," but he himself makes up the sum total of my soul's inheritance. Within the circumference of that circle lies all that we possess or desire. The Lord is my portion—not his grace merely, nor his love, nor his covenant, but Jehovah himself. He has chosen us for his portion, and we have chosen him for ours. The Lord is our all-sufficient portion. God fills himself; and if God is all-sufficient in himself, he must be all-sufficient for us. All that we can wish for is to be found in our divine portion so that we ask, "Whom do I have in heaven but you? On earth there is no one I desire but you" (Ps 73:25).

CHARLES SPURGEON
(1834–1892)
MORNING AND EVENING

ו (*VAV*)
16 He ground my teeth in gravel;
he trampled me in the dust.
17 I am deprived of peace;
I have forgotten what happiness is.
18 So I said, "My endurance has expired;
I have lost all hope of deliverance from
the LORD."

ז (*ZAYIN*)
19 Remember my impoverished and homeless
condition,
which is a bitter poison.
20 I continually think about this,
and I am depressed.
21 But this I call to mind;
therefore I have hope:

ח (*KHET*)
22 The LORD's loyal kindness never ceases;
his compassions never end.
23 They are fresh every morning;
your faithfulness is abundant!
24 "My portion is the LORD," I have said to myself,
so I will put my hope in him.

ט (*TET*)
25 The LORD is good to those who trust in him,
to the one who seeks him.
26 It is good to wait patiently
for deliverance from the LORD.
27 It is good for a man
to bear the yoke while he is young.

י (*YOD*)
28 Let a person sit alone in silence,
when the LORD is disciplining him.
29 Let him bury his face in the dust;
perhaps there is hope.
30 Let him offer his cheek to the one who hits him;
let him have his fill of insults.

כ (*KAF*)
31 For the Lord will not
reject us forever.
32 Though he causes us grief, he then has compassion
on us
according to the abundance of his loyal
kindness.
33 For he is not predisposed to afflict
or to grieve people.

ל (*LAMED*)
34 To crush underfoot
all the earth's prisoners,
35 to deprive a person of his rights
in the presence of the Most High,
36 to defraud a person in a lawsuit—
the Lord does not approve of such things!

מ (*MEM*)
37 Whose command was ever fulfilled
unless the Lord decreed it?
38 Is it not from the mouth of the Most High that
everything comes—
both calamity and blessing?
39 Why should any living person complain
when punished for his sins?

נ (*NUN*)
40 Let us carefully examine our ways,
and let us return to the LORD.
41 Let us lift up our hearts and our hands
to God in heaven:
42 "We have blatantly rebelled;
you have not forgiven."

ס (*SAMEK*)
43 You shrouded yourself with anger and then pursued us;
you killed without mercy.
44 You shrouded yourself with a cloud
so that no prayer could get through.
45 You make us like filthy scum
in the estimation of the nations.

פ (*PE*)
46 All our enemies have gloated over us;
47 panic and pitfall have come upon us,
devastation and destruction.
48 Streams of tears flow from my eyes
because my people are destroyed.

ע (*AYIN*)
49 Tears flow from my eyes and will not stop;
there will be no break
50 until the LORD looks down from heaven
and sees what has happened.
51 What my eyes see grieves me—
all the suffering of the daughters in my city.

צ (*TSADE*)
52 For no good reason my enemies
hunted me down like a bird.
53 They shut me up in a pit
and threw stones at me.
54 The waters closed over my head;
I thought I was about to die.

ק (*QOF*)
55 I have called on your name, O LORD,
from the deepest pit.
56 You heard my plea:
"Do not close your ears to my cry for relief!"
57 You came near on the day I called to you;
you said, "Do not fear!"

ר (*RESH*)
58 O Lord, you championed my cause;
you redeemed my life.

59 You have seen the wrong done to me,
O LORD;
pronounce judgment on my behalf!
60 You have seen all their vengeance,
all their plots against me.

ש (*SIN/SHIN*)
61 You have heard their taunts, O LORD,
all their plots against me.
62 My assailants revile and conspire
against me all day long.
63 Watch them from morning to evening;
I am the object of their mocking songs.

ת (*TAV*)
64 Pay them back what they deserve, O LORD,
according to what they have done.
65 Give them a distraught heart;
may your curse be on them!
66 Pursue them in anger and eradicate them
from under the LORD's heaven.

THE PROPHET SPEAKS

א (*ALEF*)
4 Alas! Gold has lost its luster;
pure gold loses value.
Jewels are scattered
on every street corner.

ב (*BET*)
2 The precious sons of Zion
were worth their weight in gold—
Alas!—but now they are treated like broken
clay pots,
made by a potter.

ג (*GIMEL*)
3 Even the jackals nurse their young
at their breast,
but my people are cruel,
like ostriches in the wilderness.

ד (*DALET*)
4 The infant's tongue sticks
to the roof of its mouth due to thirst;
little children beg for bread,
but no one gives them even a morsel.

ה (*HE*)
5 Those who once feasted on delicacies
are now starving to death in the streets.
Those who grew up wearing expensive clothes
are now dying amid garbage.

ו (*VAV*)
6 The punishment of my people
exceeds that of Sodom,
which was overthrown in a moment
with no one to help her.

4:1–22 The horrors of the siege and destruction of Jerusalem are again described. Beholding the sad consequences of sin in the church of old, let us seriously consider to what the same causes may justly bring down the church now. Our anointed King alone is the life of our souls; we may safely live under his shadow and rejoice in him in the midst of our enemies, for he is the true God and eternal life. Here it is foretold that an end should be put to Zion's troubles—not the fullness of punishment deserved, but of what God has determined to inflict. An end shall be put to Edom's triumphs. All the troubles of the church and of the believer will soon be accomplished, and the doom of their enemies approaches. Edom here represents all the enemies of the church. It shows the need of that grace in Christ Jesus that the sin and corruption of all humankind make so necessary.

MATTHEW HENRY (1662–1714)
COMMENTARY ON THE WHOLE BIBLE

ז (*ZAYIN*)
7 Our consecrated ones were brighter than snow,
whiter than milk;
their bodies more ruddy than corals,
their hair like lapis lazuli.

ח (*KHET*)
8 Now their appearance is darker than soot;
they are not recognized in the streets.
Their skin has shriveled on their bones;
it is dried up, like tree bark.

ט (*TET*)
9 Those who die by the sword are better off
than those who die of hunger,
those who waste away,
struck down from lack of food.

י (*YOD*)
10 The hands of tenderhearted women
cooked their own children,
who became their food,
when my people were destroyed.

כ (*KAF*)
11 The LORD fully vented his wrath;
he poured out his fierce anger.
He started a fire in Zion;
it consumed her foundations.

ל (*LAMED*)
12 Neither the kings of the earth
nor the people of the lands ever thought
that enemy or foe could enter
the gates of Jerusalem.

מ (*MEM*)
13 But it happened due to the sins of her prophets
and the iniquities of her priests,
who poured out in her midst
the blood of the righteous.

נ (*NUN*)
14 They wander blindly through the streets,
defiled by the blood they shed,
while no one dares
to touch their garments.

ס (*SAMEK*)
15 People cry to them, “Turn away! You are unclean!
Turn away! Turn away! Don’t touch us!”
So they have fled and wander about;
but the nations say, “They may not stay here any longer.”

פ (*PE*)
16 The LORD himself has scattered them;
he no longer watches over them.
They did not honor the priests;
they did not show favor to the elders.

THE PEOPLE OF JERUSALEM LAMENT

ע (*AYIN*)

17 Our eyes continually failed us
as we looked in vain for help.
From our watchtowers we watched
for a nation that could not rescue us.

צ (*TSADE*)

18 Our enemies hunted us down at every step
so that we could not walk about in our streets.
Our end drew near, our days were numbered,
for our end had come!

ק (*QOF*)

19 Those who pursued us were swifter
than eagles in the sky.
They chased us over the mountains;
they ambushed us in the wilderness.

ר (*RESH*)

20 Our very life breath—the LORD's anointed king—
was caught in their traps,
of whom we thought,
"Under his protection we will survive among the
nations."

THE PROPHET SPEAKS

ש (*SIN/SHIN*)

21 Rejoice and be glad for now, O people of Edom,
who reside in the land of Uz.
But the cup of judgment will pass to you also;
you will get drunk and take off your clothes.

ת (*TAV*)

22 O people of Zion, your punishment will come to an end;
he will not prolong your exile.
But, O people of Edom, he will punish your sin
and reveal your offenses!

THE PEOPLE OF JERUSALEM PRAY

5 O LORD, reflect on what has happened to us;
consider and look at our disgrace.
2 Our inheritance is turned over to strangers;
foreigners now occupy our homes.
3 We have become fatherless orphans;
our mothers have become widows.
4 We must pay money for our own water;
we must buy our own wood at a steep price.
5 We are pursued—they are breathing down our
necks;
we are weary and have no rest.
6 We have submitted to Egypt and Assyria
in order to buy food to eat.
7 Our forefathers sinned and are dead,
but we suffer their punishment.
8 Slaves rule over us;
there is no one to rescue us from their power.
9 At the risk of our lives we get our food
because robbers lurk in the wilderness.

5:1–22 We think that God disregards our miseries, or we imagine that his back is turned to us when he does not immediately assist us. But he is simply to be asked to look, for as soon as he is pleased to look on the evils we suffer, aid is at the same time prepared for us. The remedy is to raise up our eyes to God, for however confounded things may be in the world, yet he remains always the same. His truth may indeed be hidden from us, yet it remains in him. In short, were the world to change and perish a hundred times, nothing could ever affect the immutability of God. There is then no doubt but that the prophet wished to take courage and to raise himself up to a firm hope when he exclaimed, "You, O LORD, reign forever"!

JOHN CALVIN **(1509–1564)**
COMPLETE COMMENTARY ON THE BIBLE

10 Our skin is as hot as an oven
due to a fever from hunger.
11 They raped women in Zion,
virgins in the towns of Judah.
12 Princes were hung by their hands;
elders were mistreated.
13 The young men perform menial labor;
boys stagger from their labor.
14 The elders are gone from the city gate;
the young men have stopped playing their music.
15 Our hearts no longer have any joy;
our dancing is turned to mourning.
16 The crown has fallen from our head;
woe to us, for we have sinned!
17 Because of this, our hearts are sick;
because of these things, we can hardly see through our
tears.
18 For wild animals are prowling over Mount Zion,
which lies desolate.
19 But you, O LORD, reign forever;
your throne endures from generation to generation.
20 Why do you keep on forgetting us?
Why do you forsake us so long?
21 Bring us back to yourself, O LORD, so that we may
return to you;
renew our life as in days before,
22 unless you have utterly rejected us
and are angry with us beyond measure.

AUTHOR	AUDIENCE	DATE	PURPOSE	THEMES
Ezekiel	Jews who were taken captive to Babylon in 597 BC	Between 593 and 571 BC	Ezekiel wrote his prophetic work to comfort the exiles in Babylon; tell of Jerusalem's impending destruction; call God's people to repentance, obedience, and holiness; and assure them of their ultimate deliverance and restoration.	Judgment and destruction; wickedness and disobedience; repentance and obedience; and deliverance and restoration

Throughout church history the book of Ezekiel has often been regarded as a difficult book to understand. As John Wesley explained, "There is much in this book which is very mysterious, especially in the beginning and latter end of it. But tho' the visions are intricate, the sermons are plain, and the design of them is to show God's people their transgressions." Yet he pointed out that "though the reproofs and threatenings are very sharp, yet toward the close we have very comfortable promises to be fulfilled in the kingdom of the Messiah, of whom indeed Ezekiel speaks less than almost any of the prophets." Alongside Ezekiel's pronouncements of judgment are prophetic utterances of deliverance and restoration.

Martin Luther summarized the prophetic mission of Ezekiel this way:

> God raised up in Babylon this prophet Ezekiel to encourage the captives and to prophesy against the false prophets at Jerusalem, as well as to substantiate the word of Jeremiah. Ezekiel does this thoroughly; he prophesies much harder and far more than Jeremiah that Jerusalem shall be destroyed and the people perish along with the king and princes. Yet he promises also that the captives shall return home to the land of Judah. This is the most important thing that Ezekiel did in his time.

Ezekiel wrote his prophetic work to comfort the exiles in Babylon; tell of Jerusalem's impending destruction; call God's people to repentance, obedience, and holiness; and assure them of their ultimate deliverance and restoration. Ezekiel 1–11 outlines the prophet's call to ministry and the ensuing prophetic visions and announcements against Israel, which culminated in the departing of the Lord's glory from the temple; Ezekiel 12–32 contains his prophetic utterances of judgment and destruction against Jerusalem, condemning their hypocrisy, idolatry, and pagan practices and recounting their past failures and disobedience; Ezekiel 33–39 is more hopeful, focused on a future restoration for Judah in which their enemies are vanquished and the Lord shepherds them under a new covenant of peace; and Ezekiel 40–48 offers a final, detailed vision of a restored new temple, presaging the lasting restoration of God's people.

The purpose and nature of God's judgments is a prominent theme in this book, which closely follows an examination of the Lord's attributes in relation to his covenant promises. In Exodus the Lord had formed a relationship with the Israelites based on a covenant; he pledged to be their God and bless them with land, protection, and provision.

EZEKIEL

In turn Israel was called to "love the Lord your God with your whole mind, your whole being, and all your strength" (Deut 6:5) and to faithfully obey all of the words of the covenant. They repeatedly failed, and now their time of judgment had finally come.

The phrase "Then you will know that I am the Lord" foreshadows this coming destruction as well as Israel's future restoration (Ezek 6:7). Repeated 22 times throughout Ezekiel, "knowing" isn't about factual knowledge but an intimacy of relationship that comes from experiential understanding. In this case the destruction is meant to be a revelatory experience leading the people to their senses so they might return to him. "God's wrath is never so hot against his people," English non-Conformist clergyman William Greenhill wrote, "but he will show mercy to some. God would bring a sweeping judgment, lay mountains, hills, rivers, valleys, cities, high places, altars, idols, images, waste and desolate; yet he would have a remnant, preserve some, when they dwelled in the midsts of their enemies, among Babylonians and other nations."

The book of Ezekiel culminates in a vision of a restored future temple that coincides with the restoration of Israel. The prophet offers a detailed description of everything from the gates to the inner and outer courts to the rooms for sacrifice preparation to the measurements of the temple itself. The most important part of the vision, however, is when God's glory returns to the temple: "The glory of the Lord came into the temple by way of the gate that faces east. Then a wind lifted me up and brought me to the inner court; I watched the glory of the Lord filling the temple" (43:4–5). The glory that once came to destroy the city had returned to reform it and dwell within it again. Jerome related this filling to our own lives: "When his face is revealed and we contemplate the glory of God, we are reformed in the image of the Creator."

The book of Ezekiel is the perfect marriage of destruction and deliverance, for as John Calvin remarked,

> All threats are vain without a taste of the mercy of God. The prophets always argue with men with no other intention than that of stirring them up to penitence, which they could never effect unless God could be reconciled to those who had been alienated from him. This then is the reason why our Prophet, as well as Jeremiah, when they reprove the people, temper their asperity by the interposition of promises.

1:1–28 This vision in the first part of Ezekiel is a revelation of the kingdom of Christ in faith here upon earth, in all four corners of the whole world. The four wheels run alike, for all churches in the whole world have one and the same harmonious course in faith, hope, love, the cross, and all spiritual things; they are driven from within by one Spirit. Now the four living creatures go with the wheels forward, backward, upward, and to both sides. And the living creatures and the wheels hold firmly and surely together so that the chariot is one, without any external hitching, fastening, or yoking. Thus everything is in fours: four living creatures, four faces, feet, hands, and wings to each living creature, and four wheels and four spokes to a wheel. This signifies that Christendom, or the kingdom of Christ in faith, is to go to the four corners, that is, into all the world.

MARTIN LUTHER (1483–1546)
A NEW PREFACE TO THE PROPHET EZEKIEL

A VISION OF GOD'S GLORY

1 In the thirtieth year, on the fifth day of the fourth month, while I was among the exiles at the Kebar River, the heavens opened and I saw a divine vision. [2](On the fifth day of the month—it was the fifth year of King Jehoiachin's exile—[3]the LORD's message came to the priest Ezekiel the son of Buzi, at the Kebar River in the land of the Babylonians. The hand of the LORD came on him there.)

[4]As I watched, I noticed a windstorm coming from the north—an enormous cloud, with lightning flashing, such that bright light rimmed it and came from it like glowing amber from the middle of a fire. [5]In the fire were what looked like four living beings. In their appearance they had human form, [6]but each had four faces and four wings. [7]Their legs were straight, but the soles of their feet were like calves' feet. They gleamed like polished bronze. [8]They had human hands under their wings on their four sides. As for the faces and wings of the four of them, [9]their wings touched each other; they did not turn as they moved, but went straight ahead.

[10]Their faces had this appearance: Each of the four had the face of a man, with the face of a lion on the right, the face of an ox on the left, and also the face of an eagle. [11]Their wings were spread out above them; each had two wings touching the wings of one of the other beings on either side and two wings covering their bodies. [12]Each moved straight ahead—wherever the spirit would go, they would go, without turning as they went. [13]In the middle of the living beings was something like burning coals of fire or like torches. It moved back and forth among the living beings. It was bright, and lightning was flashing out of the fire. [14]The living beings moved backward and forward as quickly as flashes of lightning.

[15]Then I looked, and I saw one wheel on the ground beside each of the four beings. [16]The appearance of the wheels and their construction was like gleaming jasper, and all four wheels looked alike. Their structure was like a wheel within a wheel. [17]When they moved they would go in any of the four directions they faced without turning as they moved. [18]Their rims were high and awesome, and the rims of all four wheels were full of eyes all around.

[19]When the living beings moved, the wheels beside them moved; when the living beings rose up from the ground, the wheels rose up too. [20]Wherever the spirit would go, they would go, and the wheels would rise up beside them because the spirit of the living being was in the wheel. [21]When the living beings moved, the wheels moved, and when they stopped moving, the wheels stopped. When they rose up from the ground, the wheels rose up from the ground; the wheels rose up beside them because the spirit of the living being was in the wheel.

[22]Over the heads of the living beings was something like a platform, glittering awesomely like ice, stretched out over their heads. [23]Under the platform their wings were stretched out, each toward the other. Each of the beings also had two wings covering its body. [24]When they moved, I heard the sound of their wings—it was like the sound of rushing waters, or the voice of the Sovereign One, or the tumult of an army. When they stood still, they lowered their wings.

[25]Then there was a voice from above the platform over their heads when they stood still. [26]Above the platform over their heads was something like a sapphire shaped like a throne. High

above on the throne was a form that appeared to be a man. 27I
saw an amber glow like a fire enclosed all around from his waist
up. From his waist down I saw something that looked like fire.
There was a brilliant light around it, 28like the appearance of a
rainbow in the clouds after the rain. This was the appearance
of the surrounding brilliant light; it looked like the glory of the
LORD. When I saw it, I threw myself face down, and I heard a
voice speaking.

EZEKIEL'S COMMISSION

2 He said to me, "Son of man, stand on your feet and I will
speak with you." 2As he spoke to me, a wind came into
me and stood me on my feet, and I heard the one speaking
to me.
3He said to me, "Son of man, I am sending you to the house
of Israel, to rebellious nations who have rebelled against me;
both they and their fathers have revolted against me to this
very day. 4The people to whom I am sending you are obstinate
and hard-hearted, and you must say to them, 'This is what the
Sovereign LORD says.' 5And as for them, whether they listen
or not—for they are a rebellious house—they will know that a
prophet has been among them. 6But you, son of man, do not
fear them, and do not fear their words. Even though briers and
thorns surround you and you live among scorpions—do not fear
their words and do not be terrified of the looks they give you,
for they are a rebellious house! 7You must speak my words to
them whether they listen or not, for they are rebellious. 8As
for you, son of man, listen to what I am saying to you: Do not
rebel like that rebellious house! Open your mouth and eat what
I am giving you."
9Then I looked and realized a hand was stretched out to me,
and in it was a written scroll. 10He unrolled it before me, and it
had writing on the front and back; written on it were laments,
mourning, and woe.

3 He said to me, "Son of man, eat what you see in front of you—
eat this scroll—and then go and speak to the house of Israel."
2So I opened my mouth and he fed me the scroll.
3He said to me, "Son of man, feed your stomach and fill your
belly with this scroll I am giving to you." So I ate it, and it was
sweet like honey in my mouth.
4He said to me, "Son of man, go to the house of Israel and
speak my words to them. 5For you are not being sent to a people of unintelligible speech and difficult language, but to the
house of Israel—6not to many peoples of unintelligible speech
and difficult language, whose words you cannot understand.
Surely if I had sent you to them, they would listen to you! 7But
the house of Israel is unwilling to listen to you, because they
are not willing to listen to me, for the whole house of Israel is
hardheaded and hardhearted.
8"I have made your face adamant to match their faces, and
your forehead hard to match their foreheads. 9I have made
your forehead harder than flint—like diamond! Do not fear
them or be terrified of the looks they give you, for they are a
rebellious house."
10And he said to me, "Son of man, take all my words that I
speak to you to heart and listen carefully. 11Go to the exiles, to
your fellow countrymen, and speak to them. Say to them, 'This
is what the Sovereign LORD says,' whether they pay attention
or not."

2:1–10 The Lord Christ is full of compassion. Ezekiel fell down on his face (see 1:28). The glory of the vision and greatness of him who sat on the throne had conquered and felled our prophet to the earth. There he lay as a man wounded, without strength. Christ left him not in this condition but spoke, and that kindly to him. Our prophet was down at the end of the last chapter, and in the beginning of this he is up again. The humbling from the sight of God, his glory and greatness, is the most effective humbling; and the speediest, most effectual, and sweetest comfort does follow it. The Lord loves to encourage people to their duty. He says not here, "Stand on your feet" only, which might have sufficed, but he makes a promise, "and I will speak with you."

WILLIAM GREENHILL
(1591–1671)
AN EXPOSITION OF EZEKIEL

3:1–27 "The whole house of Israel is hardheaded and hardhearted." Come, my heart, consider how far you have a share in this universal accusation. The first charge is hardness of forehead, a want of holy shame, an unhallowed boldness in evil. Alas! If my forehead were not harder than flint, I should have far more holy fear and a far deeper contrition of spirit. The second charge is hardheartedness, and I must not venture to plead innocent here. I am not affected by the death of Jesus as I ought to be; neither am I moved by the ruin of my fellow human beings or the wickedness of the times as I should be. Blessed be the name of the Lord, the disease is not incurable, the Savior's precious blood is the universal solvent, and me, even me it will effectually soften till my heart melts as wax before the fire.

CHARLES SPURGEON
(1834–1892)
MORNING AND EVENING

EZEKIEL BEFORE THE EXILES

12Then a wind lifted me up and I heard a great rumbling sound
behind me as the glory of the LORD rose from its place, 13and
the sound of the living beings' wings brushing against each
other, and the sound of the wheels alongside them, a great
rumbling sound. 14A wind lifted me up and carried me away. I
went bitterly, my spirit full of fury, and the hand of the LORD
rested powerfully on me. 15I came to the exiles at Tel Abib, who
lived by the Kebar River. I sat dumbfounded among them there,
where they were living, for seven days.

16At the end of seven days the LORD's message came to me:
17"Son of man, I have appointed you a watchman for the house
of Israel. Whenever you hear a word from my mouth, you must
give them a warning from me. 18When I say to the wicked, 'You
will certainly die,' and you do not warn him—you do not speak
out to warn the wicked to turn from his wicked lifestyle so
that he may live—that wicked person will die for his iniquity,
but I will hold you accountable for his death. 19But as for you,
if you warn the wicked and he does not turn from his wicked
deed and from his wicked lifestyle, he will die for his iniquity
but you will have saved your own life.

20"When a righteous person turns from his righteousness and
commits iniquity, and I set an obstacle before him, he will die. If
you have not warned him, he will die for his sin. The righteous
deeds he performed will not be considered, but I will hold you
accountable for his death. 21However, if you warn the righteous
person not to sin, and he does not sin, he will certainly live
because he was warned, and you will have saved your own life."

ISOLATED AND SILENCED

22The hand of the LORD rested on me there, and he said to me,
"Get up, go out to the valley, and I will speak with you there."
23So I got up and went out to the valley, and the glory of the
LORD was standing there, just like the glory I had seen by the
Kebar River, and I threw myself face down.

24Then a wind came into me and stood me on my feet. The
LORD spoke to me and said, "Go shut yourself in your house.
25As for you, son of man, they will put ropes on you and tie you
up with them, so you cannot go out among them. 26I will make
your tongue stick to the roof of your mouth so that you will
be silent and unable to reprove them, for they are a rebellious
house. 27But when I speak with you, I will loosen your tongue
and you must say to them, 'This is what the Sovereign LORD
says.' Those who listen will listen, but the indifferent will refuse,
for they are a rebellious house.

OMINOUS OBJECT LESSONS

4 "And you, son of man, take a brick and set it in front of you.
Inscribe a city on it—Jerusalem. 2Lay siege to it! Build siege
works against it. Erect a siege ramp against it! Post soldiers
outside it and station battering rams around it. 3Then for your
part take an iron frying pan and set it up as an iron wall between
you and the city. Set your face toward it. It is to be under siege;
you are to besiege it. This is a sign for the house of Israel.

4"Also for your part lie on your left side and place the iniquity
of the house of Israel on it. For the number of days you lie on
your side you will bear their iniquity. 5I have determined that
the number of the years of their iniquity are to be the number of
days for you—390 days. So bear the iniquity of the house of Israel.

4:1–17 We know that this is the customary manner of scripture because God reckons sins to the third and fourth generation. When therefore God wished the ten tribes to be dragged into exile, then he punished them for their wickedness 390 years. Afterward he bore with the city of Jerusalem for a certain time that he should not utterly blot out the memory of the people. On the whole then, God wished to show the people that they had abused his forbearance too much and too long. The Israelites indeed began to turn aside from the true worship of God while the temple still remained pure, but at length the tribe of Judah, by degenerating, became guilty of the same impiety. Almighty God, since you have thus far sustained us by your inestimable clemency, grant that we may not abuse your goodness and provoke your vengeance against us.

JOHN CALVIN (1509–1564)
COMPLETE COMMENTARY ON THE BIBLE

6"When you have completed these days, then lie down a second time, but on your right side, and bear the iniquity of the
house of Judah 40 days—I have assigned one day for each year.
7You must turn your face toward the siege of Jerusalem with
your arm bared and prophesy against it. 8Look here: I will tie
you up with ropes, so you cannot turn from one side to the
other until you complete the days of your siege.

9"As for you, take wheat, barley, beans, lentils, millet, and
spelt, put them in a single container, and make food from them
for yourself. For the same number of days that you lie on your
side—390 days—you will eat it. 10The food you eat will be eight
ounces a day by weight; you must eat it at fixed times. 11And you
must drink water by measure, a pint and a half; you must drink
it at fixed times. 12And you must eat the food as you would a
barley cake. You must bake it in front of them over a fire made
with dried human excrement." 13And the LORD said, "This is
how the people of Israel will eat their unclean food among the
nations where I will banish them."

14And I said, "Ah, Sovereign LORD, I have never been ceremonially defiled before. I have never eaten a carcass or an animal
torn by wild beasts; from my youth up, unclean meat has never
entered my mouth."

15So he said to me, "All right then, I will substitute cow's
manure instead of human excrement. You will cook your food
over it."

16Then he said to me, "Son of man, I am about to remove
the bread supply in Jerusalem. They will eat their bread ration
anxiously, and they will drink their water ration in terror 17be-
cause they will lack bread and water. Each one will be terrified,
and they will rot for their iniquity.

5 "As for you, son of man, take a sharp sword and use it as a
barber's razor. Shave off some of the hair from your head and
your beard. Then take scales and divide up the hair you cut off.
2Burn a third of it in the fire inside the city when the days of
your siege are completed. Take a third and slash it with a sword
all around the city. Scatter a third to the wind, and I will unleash
a sword behind them. 3But take a few strands of hair from those
and tie them in the ends of your garment. 4Again, take more of
them and throw them into the fire, and burn them up. From
there a fire will spread to all the house of Israel.

5"This is what the Sovereign LORD says: This is Jerusalem; I
placed her in the center of the nations with countries all around
her. 6Then she defied my regulations and my statutes, becoming
more wicked than the nations and the countries around her.
Indeed, they have rejected my regulations, and they do not
follow my statutes.

7"Therefore this is what the Sovereign LORD says: Because
you are more arrogant than the nations around you, you have
not followed my statutes and have not carried out my regulations. You have not even carried out the regulations of the
nations around you!

8"Therefore this is what the Sovereign LORD says: I—even I—
am against you, and I will execute judgment among you while
the nations watch. 9I will do to you what I have never done
before and will never do again because of all your abominable practices. 10Therefore, fathers will eat their sons within
you, Jerusalem, and sons will eat their fathers. I will execute
judgments on you, and I will scatter any survivors to the
winds.

5:1–17 The prophet must shave off the hair of his head and beard, which signifies God's utter rejecting and abandoning of that people. To whatever refuge sinners flee, the fire and sword of God's wrath will consume them. Who is able to stand in God's sight when he is angry? There is a day coming when the Lord will not spare. Let us endeavor to adorn the doctrine of God our Savior in all things. Sooner or later God's Word will prove itself true.

MATTHEW HENRY **(1662–1714)**
COMMENTARY ON THE WHOLE BIBLE

[11]"Therefore, as surely as I live, says the Sovereign LORD, because you defiled my sanctuary with all your detestable idols and with all your abominable practices, I will withdraw; my eye will not pity you, nor will I spare you. [12]A third of your people will die of plague or be overcome by the famine within you. A third of your people will fall by the sword surrounding you, and a third I will scatter to the winds. I will unleash a sword behind them. [13]Then my anger will be fully vented; I will exhaust my rage on them, and I will be appeased. Then they will know that I, the LORD, have spoken in my jealousy when I have fully vented my rage against them.

[14]"I will make you desolate and an object of scorn among the nations around you, in the sight of everyone who passes by. [15]You will be an object of scorn and taunting, a prime example of destruction among the nations around you when I execute judgments against you in anger and raging fury. I, the LORD, have spoken! [16]I will shoot against them deadly, destructive arrows of famine, which I will shoot to destroy you. I will prolong a famine on you and will remove the bread supply. [17]I will send famine and wild beasts against you, and they will take your children from you. Plague and bloodshed will overwhelm you, and I will bring a sword against you. I, the LORD, have spoken!"

JUDGMENT ON THE MOUNTAINS OF ISRAEL

6 The LORD's message came to me: [2]"Son of man, turn toward the mountains of Israel and prophesy against them. [3]Say, 'Mountains of Israel, hear the word of the Sovereign LORD! This is what the Sovereign LORD says to the mountains and the hills, to the ravines and the valleys: I am bringing a sword against you, and I will destroy your high places. [4]Your altars will be ruined and your incense altars will be broken. I will throw down your slain in front of your idols. [5]I will place the corpses of the people of Israel in front of their idols, and I will scatter your bones around your altars. [6]In all your dwellings, the cities will be laid waste and the high places ruined so that your altars will be laid waste and ruined, your idols will be shattered and demolished, your incense altars will be broken down, and your works wiped out. [7]The slain will fall among you and then you will know that I am the LORD.

[8]"'But I will spare some of you. Some will escape the sword when you are scattered in foreign lands. [9]Then your survivors will remember me among the nations where they are exiled. They will realize how I was crushed by their unfaithful heart that turned from me and by their eyes that lusted after their idols. They will loathe themselves because of the evil they have done and because of all their abominable practices. [10]They will know that I am the LORD; my threats to bring this catastrophe on them were not empty.

[11]"'This is what the Sovereign LORD says: Clap your hands, stamp your feet, and say, "Ah!" because of all the evil, abominable practices of the house of Israel, for they will fall by the sword, famine, and pestilence. [12]The one far away will die by pestilence, the one close by will fall by the sword, and whoever is left and has escaped these will die by famine. I will fully vent my rage against them. [13]Then you will know that I am the LORD when their dead lie among their idols around their altars, on every high hill and on all the mountaintops, under every green tree and every leafy oak—the places where they have offered fragrant incense to all their idols. [14]I will stretch out my hand against

6:1–3 Ezekiel is not ordered to urge the Israelites to repentance or to threaten them with the punishment that still remained, he is ordered to turn his proclamation to the hills and mountains and valleys. Thus God indirectly demonstrates first that the Israelites were deaf and then unworthy of the trouble that Ezekiel would spend in teaching them. God therefore requires the mountains to listen, to show people that an inanimate object can be given understanding, causing them to examine their own stupidity.

JOHN CALVIN (1509–1564)
COMPLETE COMMENTARY ON THE BIBLE

them and make the land a desolate waste from the wilderness
to Riblah, in all the places where they live. Then they will know
that I am the LORD.'"

THE END ARRIVES

7 The LORD's message came to me: 2"You, son of man—this is
what the Sovereign LORD says to the land of Israel: An end!
The end is coming on the four corners of the land! 3The end
is now upon you, and I will release my anger against you. I will
judge you according to your behavior; I will hold you accountable for all your abominable practices. 4My eye will not pity
you; I will not spare you. For I will hold you responsible for
your behavior, and you will suffer the consequences of your
abominable practices. Then you will know that I am the LORD!

5"This is what the Sovereign LORD says: A disaster—a one-of-
a-kind disaster—is coming! 6An end comes—the end comes! It
has awakened against you! Look, it is coming! 7Doom is coming
upon you who live in the land! The time is coming, the day
is near. There are sounds of tumult, not shouts of joy, on the
mountains. 8Soon now I will pour out my rage on you; I will fully
vent my anger against you. I will judge you according to your
behavior. I will hold you accountable for all your abominable
practices. 9My eye will not pity you; I will not spare you. For
your behavior I will hold you accountable, and you will suffer
the consequences of your abominable practices. Then you will
know that it is I, the LORD, who is striking you.

10"Look, the day! Look, it is coming! Doom has gone out! The
staff has budded, pride has blossomed! 11Violence has grown
into a staff that supports wickedness. Not one of them will be
left—not from their crowd, not from their wealth, not from
their prominence. 12The time has come; the day has struck! The
customer should not rejoice, nor the seller mourn; for divine
wrath comes against their whole crowd. 13The customer will no
longer pay the seller while both parties are alive, for the vision
against their whole crowd will not be revoked. Each person, for
his iniquity, will fail to preserve his life.

14"They have blown the trumpet and everyone is ready, but
no one goes to battle, because my anger is against their whole
crowd. 15The sword is outside; pestilence and famine are inside
the house. Whoever is in the open field will die by the sword,
and famine and pestilence will consume everyone in the city.
16Their survivors will escape to the mountains and become
like doves of the valleys; all of them will moan—each one for
his iniquity. 17All their hands will hang limp; their knees will
be wet with urine. 18They will wear sackcloth, terror will cover
them; shame will be on all their faces, and all their heads will
be shaved bald. 19They will discard their silver in the streets,
and their gold will be treated like filth. Their silver and gold
will not be able to deliver them on the day of the LORD's fury.
They will not satisfy their hunger or fill their stomachs because their wealth was the obstacle leading to their iniquity.
20They rendered the beauty of his ornaments into pride, and
with it they made their abominable images—their detestable
idols. Therefore I will render it filthy to them. 21I will give it to
foreigners as loot, to the world's wicked ones as plunder, and
they will desecrate it. 22I will turn my face away from them,
and they will desecrate my treasured place. Vandals will enter
it and desecrate it. 23(Make the chain, because the land is full
of murder and the city is full of violence.) 24I will bring the

7:12 "The customer should not rejoice, nor the seller mourn." Here it may be asked, *What occasion would the seller here have to mourn more than the buyer?* Answer: The prophet here has respect to buyers and sellers of inheritances. Inheritances were not wont to be sold in Israel unless people had become poor and were obliged to sell their inheritance, and it was looked upon as a great calamity to people when they were thus obliged. Therefore God, in mercy and tenderness, required that the land should not be sold forever, but that a redemption should be granted. But at this time, neither had the seller any occasion to mourn nor the buyer to rejoice, for it made no alteration in the circumstances of one or the other because the whole land was about to be broken up and left desolate, and they were all to be carried away out of it into captivity.

JONATHAN EDWARDS
(1703–1758)
SELECTIONS FROM THE UNPUBLISHED WRITINGS

most wicked of the nations, and they will take possession of
their houses. I will put an end to the arrogance of the strong,
and their sanctuaries will be desecrated. 25Terror is coming!
They will seek peace, but find none. 26Disaster after disaster
will come, and one rumor after another. They will seek a vision
from a prophet; priestly instruction will disappear, along with
counsel from the elders. 27The king will mourn and the prince
will be clothed with shuddering; the hands of the people of
the land will tremble. Based on their behavior I will deal with
them, and by their standard of justice I will judge them. Then
they will know that I am the LORD!"

A DESECRATED TEMPLE

8 In the sixth year, in the sixth month, on the fifth of the month,
as I was sitting in my house with the elders of Judah sitting
in front of me, the hand of the Sovereign LORD seized me. 2As
I watched, I noticed a form that appeared to be a man. From
his waist downward was something like fire, and from his waist
upward something like a brightness, like an amber glow. 3He
stretched out the form of a hand and grabbed me by a lock of
hair on my head. Then a wind lifted me up between the earth and
sky and brought me to Jerusalem by divine visions, to the door of
the inner gate that faces north where the statue that provokes to
jealousy was located. 4Then I perceived that the glory of the God
of Israel was there, as in the vision I had seen earlier in the valley.

5He said to me, "Son of man, look up toward the north." So I
looked up toward the north, and I noticed to the north of the
altar gate was this statue of jealousy at the entrance.

6He said to me, "Son of man, do you see what they are doing—
the great abominations that the people of Israel are practicing
here, to drive me far from my sanctuary? But you will see greater
abominations than these!"

7He brought me to the entrance of the court, and as I watched,
I noticed a hole in the wall. 8He said to me, "Son of man, dig
into the wall." So I dug into the wall and discovered a doorway.

9He said to me, "Go in and see the evil abominations they are
practicing here." 10So I went in and looked. I noticed every figure
of creeping thing and beast—detestable images—and every idol
of the house of Israel, engraved on the wall all around. 11Seventy
men from the elders of the house of Israel (with Jaazaniah son
of Shaphan standing among them) were standing in front of
them, each with a censer in his hand, and fragrant vapors from
a cloud of incense were swirling upward.

12He said to me, "Do you see, son of man, what the elders of
the house of Israel are doing in the dark, each in the chamber
of his idolatrous images? For they think, 'The LORD does not see
us! The LORD has abandoned the land!'" 13He said to me, "You
will see them practicing even greater abominations!"

14Then he brought me to the entrance of the north gate of
the LORD's house. I noticed women sitting there weeping for
Tammuz. 15He said to me, "Do you see this, son of man? You
will see even greater abominations than these!"

16Then he brought me to the inner court of the LORD's house.
Right there at the entrance to the LORD's temple, between
the porch and the altar, were about 25 men with their backs
to the LORD's temple, facing east—they were worshiping the
sun toward the east!

17He said to me, "Do you see, son of man? Is it a trivial thing
that the house of Judah commits these abominations they are

8:1–18 Why is it that people are so daring, impudent, and resolute in sinning because they never consider that God sees and takes notice? What wickedness will a person not commit when the sense of God's omniscience is blotted out? "Do you see, son of man, what the elders of the house of Israel are doing in the dark, each in the chamber of his idolatrous images? For they think, 'The LORD does not see us!'" That made them bold in sin. Oh, that you would but much and often think of this all-knowledge of God. Keep the sense of it always on your mind. Wherever you are, remember this, God sees you and observes all your actions.

MATTHEW MEADE
(C. 1630–1699)
EZEKIEL

practicing here? For they have filled the land with violence
and provoked me to anger still further. Look, they are putting
the branch to their nose! 18Therefore I will act with fury! My
eye will not pity them nor will I spare them. When they have
shouted in my ears, I will not listen to them."

THE EXECUTION OF IDOLATERS

9 Then he shouted in my ears, "Approach, you who are to visit
destruction on the city, each with his destructive weapon in
his hand!" 2Next I noticed six men coming from the direction
of the upper gate that faces north, each with his war club in his
hand. Among them was a man dressed in linen with a writing
kit at his side. They came and stood beside the bronze altar.
3Then the glory of the God of Israel went up from the cherub
where it had rested to the threshold of the temple. He called
to the man dressed in linen who had the writing kit at his side.
4The LORD said to him, "Go through the city of Jerusalem and
put a mark on the foreheads of the people who moan and groan
over all the abominations practiced in it."
5While I listened, he said to the others, "Go through the city
after him and strike people down; do not let your eye pity nor
spare anyone! 6Old men, young men, young women, little children, and women—wipe them out! But do not touch anyone
who has the mark. Begin at my sanctuary!" So they began with
the elders who were at the front of the temple.
7He said to them, "Defile the temple and fill the courtyards
with corpses. Go!" So they went out and struck people down
throughout the city. 8While they were striking them down, I
was left alone, and I threw myself face down and cried out, "Ah,
Sovereign LORD! Will you destroy the entire remnant of Israel
when you pour out your fury on Jerusalem?"
9He said to me, "The sin of the house of Israel and Judah is
extremely great; the land is full of murder, and the city is full
of corruption, for they say, 'The LORD has abandoned the land,
and the LORD does not see!' 10But as for me, my eye will not
pity them nor will I spare them; I hereby repay them for what
they have done."
11Next I noticed the man dressed in linen with the writing kit at his side bringing back word: "I have done just as you
commanded me."

GOD'S GLORY LEAVES THE TEMPLE

10 As I watched, I saw on the platform above the top of the
cherubim something like a sapphire, resembling the shape
of a throne, appearing above them. 2The LORD said to the man
dressed in linen, "Go between the wheelwork underneath the
cherubim. Fill your hands with burning coals from among the
cherubim and scatter them over the city." He went as I watched.
3(The cherubim were standing on the south side of the temple when the man went in, and a cloud filled the inner court.)
4Then the glory of the LORD arose from the cherub and moved
to the threshold of the temple. The temple was filled with the
cloud while the court was filled with the brightness of the
LORD's glory. 5The sound of the wings of the cherubim could
be heard from the outer court, like the sound of the Sovereign
God when he speaks.
6When the LORD commanded the man dressed in linen,
"Take fire from within the wheelwork, from among the cherubim," the man went in and stood by one of the wheels. 7Then

9:1–11 There is a forehead of the inner self. That is where those people were marked, to save them from being wiped out. At least they were pained by the sins they saw, and by their very pain they set themselves apart. They are marked with a sign in secret; they escape harm in public. The destroyer is sent next and is told to destroy the people: "But do not touch anyone who has the mark." What a sure guarantee has been given you, my brothers and sisters, you among this people who are groaning and grieving over the wicked deeds committed in your midst and are not committing them!

AUGUSTINE **(354–430)**
SERMONS

10:1–22 We know with what confidence the Jews boasted that they should be safe continually under the protection of God. They did not think it possible that God would ever leave them. So they sinned without restraint, and while they drove him far away from them by their crimes, yet they wished to have him in some way bound to them. Hence it follows that God with his angels, when the temple was left, deserted the Jews so that for the future they would boast themselves in vain to be safe under his protection. The visible appearance of the temple was taken away, but meanwhile, since the temple was founded on the promise of God, it stood among its ruins. Now then we understand in what sense God left his temple and yet did not in any way break his promise.

JOHN CALVIN **(1509–1564)**
COMPLETE COMMENTARY ON THE BIBLE

one of the cherubim stretched out his hand toward the fire that was among the cherubim. He took some and put it into the hands of the man dressed in linen, who took it and left. 8(The cherubim appeared to have the form of human hands under their wings.)

9As I watched, I noticed four wheels by the cherubim, one wheel beside each cherub; the wheels gleamed like jasper. 10As for their appearance, all four of them looked the same, something like a wheel within a wheel. 11When they moved, they would go in any of the four directions they faced without turning as they moved; in the direction the head would turn they would follow without turning as they moved, 12along with their entire bodies, their backs, their hands, and their wings. The wheels of the four of them were full of eyes all around. 13As for their wheels, they were called "the wheelwork" as I listened. 14Each of the cherubim had four faces: The first was the face of a cherub, the second that of a man, the third that of a lion, and the fourth that of an eagle.

15The cherubim rose up; these were the living beings I saw at the Kebar River. 16When the cherubim moved, the wheels moved beside them; when the cherubim spread their wings to rise from the ground, the wheels did not move from their side. 17When the cherubim stood still, the wheels stood still, and when they rose up, the wheels rose up with them, for the spirit of the living beings was in the wheels.

18Then the glory of the LORD moved away from the threshold of the temple and stopped above the cherubim. 19The cherubim spread their wings, and they rose up from the earth while I watched (when they went, the wheels went alongside them). They stopped at the entrance to the east gate of the LORD's temple as the glory of the God of Israel hovered above them.

20These were the living creatures that I saw at the Kebar River underneath the God of Israel; I knew that they were cherubim. 21Each had four faces; each had four wings and the form of human hands under the wings. 22As for the form of their faces, they were the faces whose appearance I had seen at the Kebar River. Each one moved straight ahead.

THE FALL OF JERUSALEM

11 A wind lifted me up and brought me to the east gate of the LORD's temple that faces the east. There, at the entrance of the gate, I noticed 25 men. Among them I saw Jaazaniah son of Azzur and Pelatiah son of Benaiah, officials of the people. 2The LORD said to me, "Son of man, these are the men who plot evil and give wicked advice in this city. 3They say, 'The time is not near to build houses; the city is a cooking pot, and we are the meat in it.' 4Therefore, prophesy against them! Prophesy, son of man!"

5Then the Spirit of the LORD came upon me and said to me, "Say: 'This is what the LORD says: This is what you are thinking, O house of Israel; I know what goes through your minds. 6You have killed many people in this city; you have filled its streets with corpses.' 7Therefore, this is what the Sovereign LORD says: 'The corpses you have dumped in the midst of the city are the meat, and this city is the cooking pot, but I will take you out of it. 8You fear the sword, so the sword I will bring against you,' declares the Sovereign LORD. 9'But I will take you out of the city. And I will hand you over to foreigners. I will execute judgments on you. 10You will die by the sword; I will judge you at

11:1–13 People chief in dignity and place are for the most part corrupt. Here the twenty-five, who bore the sway in the city and had great power, were all joined together in wickedness. Isaiah called their rulers "leaders of Sodom" (Isa 1:10) because of their extreme wickedness. The prophet thought the great ones, who had great obligations on them to honor God, who knew what pertained to worship and justice, would hearken to him. But they cast off all respect, subjugation, and obedience to the law of God. They followed their own wills, lusts, humors; they regarded neither equity nor honesty. They were far worse than the poorer sort whom the prophet had tried also. Are not too many of the great ones among us corrupt, loose, and enemies to Christ and his kingdom?

WILLIAM GREENHILL
(1591–1671)
AN EXPOSITION OF EZEKIEL

FRANCIS OF ASSISI:

THE SAINT OF POVERTY

1182–1226

Perhaps one of the most beloved of the medieval saints, by Catholics and non-Catholics alike, Francis of Assisi is for many the exemplar *par excellence* of Christian piety and Christlikeness. Born in 1182 to a wealthy merchant in the central Italian city of Assisi, Francis exhibited a commitment to self-denial, austerity, and a lifetime of service that began in his youth.

After a lengthy illness brought about his conversion to the Christian faith, Francis renounced his attachment to the world and pledged himself to "Lady Poverty," vowing to follow the lifestyle Christ himself led. Eventually, in responding to Matthew 10:5–16 with literal devotion, Francis permanently renounced money and possessions and devoted himself to freely giving as he had freely received.

Francis attracted a group of men who were similarly committed to his simple, humble living. They were gathered into the *Ordo Fraternum Minorum*, the "Order of the Little Brothers" or "Friars Minor," as they were known. Francis wrote three rules that were instrumental in providing guiding principles for their asceticism and vows, of which poverty was central, both for individuals and a community. His *Regula Prima* built on the first set, maintaining the scripture citations and prayers while adopting increased regulations in response to his community's changing needs. In 1223 he helped compose the *Regula Bullata*, a series of rules that fostered a more structured, intentional life as a fixed community.

Aside from his commitment to poverty and service, Francis was also known for his special attention to and communion with nature. He referred to "Brother sun" and "Sister moon," "Brother wind" and "Sister water" in his *Canticle of the Sun*. There is also an apocryphal story of Francis preaching to the birds.

Francis of Assisi was recognized as a saint shortly after his death in 1226. His example of imitating Christ through self-denial, piety, and service is perhaps best encapsulated in the Peace Prayer of Saint Francis:

Lord, make me an instrument
of your peace: where there
is hatred, let me sow love;
where there is injury, pardon;
where there is doubt, faith;
where there is despair, hope;
where there is darkness, light;
where there is sadness, joy.

O divine Master, grant that I
may not so much seek to be
consoled as to console, to be
understood as to understand,
to be loved as to love. For it is
in giving that we receive, it is
in pardoning that we are pardoned, and it is in dying that
we are born to eternal life.
Amen.

IMPORTANT WORKS

CANTICLE OF THE SUN
REGULA NON BULLATA, THE EARLIER RULE
REGULA BULLATA, THE LATER RULE

the border of Israel. Then you will know that I am the LORD.
11This city will not be a cooking pot for you, and you will not be
meat within it; I will judge you at the border of Israel. 12Then
you will know that I am the LORD, whose statutes you have
not followed and whose regulations you have not carried out.
Instead you have behaved according to the regulations of the
nations around you!'"

13Now, while I was prophesying, Pelatiah son of Benaiah
died. Then I threw myself face down and cried out with a loud
voice, "Alas, Sovereign LORD! You are completely wiping out
the remnant of Israel!"

14Then the LORD's message came to me: 15"Son of man, your
brothers, your relatives, and the whole house of Israel, all of
them are those to whom the inhabitants of Jerusalem have
said, 'They have gone far away from the LORD; to us this land
has been given as a possession.'

16"Therefore say: 'This is what the Sovereign LORD says: Although I have removed them far away among the nations and
have dispersed them among the countries, I have been a little
sanctuary for them among the lands where they have gone.'

17"Therefore say: 'This is what the Sovereign LORD says:
When I regather you from the peoples and assemble you from
the lands where you have been dispersed, I will give you back
the country of Israel.'

18"When they return to it, they will remove from it all its
detestable things and all its abominations. 19I will give them
one heart and I will put a new spirit within them; I will remove
the hearts of stone from their bodies and I will give them tender
hearts, 20so that they may follow my statutes and observe my
regulations and carry them out. Then they will be my people,
and I will be their God. 21But those whose hearts are devoted
to detestable things and abominations, I hereby repay them
for what they have done, says the Sovereign LORD."

22Then the cherubim spread their wings with their wheels
alongside them while the glory of the God of Israel hovered
above them. 23The glory of the LORD rose up from within the
city and stopped over the mountain east of it. 24Then a wind
lifted me up and carried me to the exiles in Babylonia, in the
vision given to me by the Spirit of God.

Then the vision I had seen went up from me. 25So I told the
exiles everything the LORD had shown me.

PREVIEWING THE EXILE

12 The LORD's message came to me: 2"Son of man, you are
living in the midst of a rebellious house. They have eyes
to see, but do not see, and ears to hear, but do not hear, because
they are a rebellious house.

3"Therefore, son of man, pack up your belongings as if for
exile. During the day, while they are watching, pretend to go
into exile. Go from where you live to another place. Perhaps
they will understand, although they are a rebellious house.
4Bring out your belongings packed for exile during the day
while they are watching. And go out at evening, while they are
watching, as if for exile. 5While they are watching, dig a hole in
the wall and carry your belongings out through it. 6While they
are watching, raise your baggage onto your shoulder and carry
it out in the dark. You must cover your face so that you cannot
see the ground because I have made you an object lesson to
the house of Israel."

12:1–28 Ezekiel had been proclaiming the fall of Jerusalem to the exiles whose captivity preceded it by a few years, and he was confronted by the incredulity that fancied that it had a great many facts to support it. The prophets had cried wolf so long that their alarms were disbelieved altogether. Even the people who did not go the length of utter unbelief in the prophetic threat took the comfortable conclusion that these threats had reference to a future date, and they needed not to trouble themselves about them. So the imagined distance of fulfilment turned the edge of the plainest denunciations and was like wool stuffed in the people's ears to deaden the reverberations of the thunder.

ALEXANDER MACLAREN
(1826–1910)
EXPOSITIONS OF THE HOLY SCRIPTURES

7So I did just as I was commanded. I carried out my belongings packed for exile during the day, and at evening I dug myself
a hole through the wall with my hands. I went out in the darkness, carrying my baggage on my shoulder while they watched.
8The LORD's message came to me in the morning: 9"Son of
man, has not the house of Israel, that rebellious house, said
to you, 'What are you doing?' 10Say to them, 'This is what the
Sovereign LORD says: The prince will raise this burden in Jerusalem, and all the house of Israel within it.' 11Say, 'I am an
object lesson for you. Just as I have done, so it will be done to
them; they will go into exile and captivity.'
12"The prince who is among them will raise his belongings
onto his shoulder in darkness and will go out. He will dig a
hole in the wall to leave through. He will cover his face so that
he cannot see the land with his eyes. 13But I will throw my
net over him, and he will be caught in my snare. I will bring
him to Babylon, the land of the Chaldeans (but he will not see
it), and there he will die. 14All his retinue—his attendants and
his troops—I will scatter to every wind; I will unleash a sword
behind them.
15"Then they will know that I am the LORD when I disperse
them among the nations and scatter them among foreign
countries. 16But I will let a small number of them survive the
sword, famine, and pestilence, so that they can confess all their
abominable practices to the nations where they go. Then they
will know that I am the LORD."
17The LORD's message came to me: 18"Son of man, eat your
bread with trembling and drink your water with anxious shaking. 19Then say to the people of the land, 'This is what the Sovereign LORD says about the inhabitants of Jerusalem and of
the land of Israel: They will eat their bread with anxiety and
drink their water in fright, for their land will be stripped bare
of all it contains because of the violence of all who live in it.
20The inhabited towns will be left in ruins, and the land will be
devastated. Then you will know that I am the LORD.'"
21The LORD's message came to me: 22"Son of man, what is
this proverb you have in the land of Israel, 'The days pass slowly, and every vision fails'? 23Therefore tell them, 'This is what
the Sovereign LORD says: I hereby end this proverb; they will
not recite it in Israel any longer.' But say to them, 'The days
are at hand when every vision will be fulfilled. 24For there will
no longer be any false visions or flattering omens amidst the
house of Israel. 25For I, the LORD, will speak. Whatever word I
speak will be accomplished. It will not be delayed any longer.
Indeed in your days, O rebellious house, I will speak the word
and accomplish it, declares the Sovereign LORD.'"
26The LORD's message came to me: 27"Take note, son of man,
the house of Israel is saying, 'The vision that he sees is for distant days; he is prophesying about the far future.' 28Therefore
say to them, 'This is what the Sovereign LORD says: None of my
words will be delayed any longer! The word I speak will come
to pass, declares the Sovereign LORD.'"

FALSE PROPHETS DENOUNCED

13 Then the LORD's message came to me: 2"Son of man,
prophesy against the prophets of Israel who are now
prophesying. Say to the prophets who prophesy from their
imagination: 'Listen to the LORD's message! 3This is what the
Sovereign LORD says: Woe to the foolish prophets who follow

13:1–23 Of all beasts the fox is the most subtle and dangerous for getting into and hurting the vineyard through any breach he finds in the hedge or wall. For this reason, false prophets among the Jews were compared with foxes, and such they are to the church of God in any place. The breach is made by sin. This the true prophet sought to make up by exhorting and stirring to repentance. By earnest prayer to God he stood in the day of battle to keep out enemies from coming to destroy it, as Moses by prayer is said to have stood in the gap. But these false prophets, on the contrary, craftily misled the people, whereby they were brought into danger and gaps were made instead of being hedged up, for which Ezekiel protested against them as pernicious beasts, and such are also called foxes.

JOHN MAYER **(1583–1664)**
COMMENTARY UPON ALL THE PROPHETS

their own spirit but have seen nothing! 4Your prophets have
become like jackals among the ruins, O Israel. 5You have not
gone up in the breaks in the wall, nor repaired a wall for the
house of Israel that it would stand strong in the battle on the
day of the LORD. 6They see delusion and their omens are a lie.
They say, "The LORD declares," though the LORD has not sent
them; yet they expect their word to be confirmed. 7Have you
not seen a false vision and announced a lying omen when you
say, "The LORD declares," although I myself never spoke?

8"'Therefore, this is what the Sovereign LORD says: Because
you have spoken false words and forecast delusion, look, I am
against you, declares the Sovereign LORD. 9My hand will be
against the prophets who see delusion and announce lying
omens. They will not be included in the council of my people,
nor be written in the registry of the house of Israel, nor enter
the land of Israel. Then you will know that I am the Sovereign
LORD.

10"'This is because they have led my people astray saying,
"All is well," when things are not well. When anyone builds a
wall without mortar, they coat it with whitewash. 11Tell the
ones who coat it with whitewash that it will fall. When there
is a deluge of rain, hailstones will fall and a violent wind will
break out. 12When the wall has collapsed, people will ask you,
"Where is the whitewash you coated it with?"

13"'Therefore this is what the Sovereign LORD says: In my
rage I will make a violent wind break out. In my anger there will
be a deluge of rain and hailstones in destructive fury. 14I will
break down the wall you coated with whitewash and knock it to
the ground so that its foundation is exposed. When it falls you
will be destroyed beneath it, and you will know that I am the
LORD. 15I will vent my rage against the wall and against those
who coated it with whitewash. Then I will say to you, "The wall
is no more and those who whitewashed it are no more—16those
prophets of Israel who would prophesy about Jerusalem and
would see visions of peace for it, when there was no peace,"
declares the Sovereign LORD.'

17"As for you, son of man, turn toward the daughters of your
people who are prophesying from their imagination. Prophesy
against them 18and say 'This is what the Sovereign LORD says:
Woe to those who sew bands on all their wrists and make headbands for heads of every size to entrap people's lives! Will you
entrap my people's lives, yet preserve your own lives? 19You
have profaned me among my people for handfuls of barley and
scraps of bread. You have put to death people who should not
die and kept alive those who should not live by your lies to my
people, who listen to lies!

20"'Therefore, this is what the Sovereign LORD says: Take
note that I am against your wristbands with which you entrap
people's lives like birds. I will tear them from your arms and
will release the people's lives, which you hunt like birds. 21I will
tear off your headbands and rescue my people from your power;
they will no longer be prey in your hands. Then you will know
that I am the LORD. 22This is because you have disheartened
the righteous person with lies (although I have not grieved
him), and because you have encouraged the wicked person not
to turn from his evil conduct and preserve his life. 23Therefore
you will no longer see false visions and practice divination. I
will rescue my people from your power, and you will know that
I am the LORD.'"

WELL-DESERVED JUDGMENT

14 Then some men from Israel's elders came to me and sat
down in front of me. [2]The LORD's message came to me:
[3]"Son of man, these men have erected their idols in their hearts
and placed the obstacle leading to their iniquity right before
their faces. Should I really allow them to seek me? [4]Therefore
speak to them and say to them, 'This is what the Sovereign
LORD says: When anyone from the house of Israel erects his
idols in his heart and sets the obstacle leading to his iniquity
before his face, and then consults a prophet, I, the LORD, am determined to answer him personally according to the enormity
of his idolatry. [5]I will do this in order to capture the hearts of
the house of Israel, who have alienated themselves from me
on account of all their idols.'

[6]"Therefore say to the house of Israel, 'This is what the Sovereign LORD says: Return! Turn from your idols, and turn your
faces away from your abominations. [7]For when anyone from
the house of Israel, or the resident foreigner who lives in Israel,
separates himself from me and erects his idols in his heart and
sets the obstacle leading to his iniquity before his face, and then
consults a prophet to seek something from me, I, the LORD,
am determined to answer him personally. [8]I will set my face
against that person and will make him an object lesson and a
byword and will cut him off from among my people. Then you
will know that I am the LORD.

[9]"'As for the prophet, if he is made a fool by being deceived
into speaking a prophetic word—I, the LORD, have made a fool
of that prophet, and I will stretch out my hand against him and
destroy him from among my people Israel. [10]They will bear
their punishment; the punishment of the one who sought an
oracle will be the same as the punishment of the prophet who
gave it [11]so that the house of Israel will no longer go astray
from me, nor continue to defile themselves by all their sins.
They will be my people, and I will be their God, declares the
Sovereign LORD.'"

[12]The LORD's message came to me: [13]"Son of man, suppose a
country sins against me by being unfaithful and I stretch out my
hand against it, cut off its bread supply, cause famine to come
on it, and kill both people and animals. [14]Even if these three
men, Noah, Daniel, and Job, were in it, they would save only their
own lives by their righteousness, declares the Sovereign LORD.

[15]"Suppose I were to send wild animals through the land and
kill its children, leaving it desolate, without travelers due to the
wild animals. [16]Even if these three men were in it, as surely as
I live, declares the Sovereign LORD, they could not save their
own sons or daughters; they would save only their own lives,
and the land would become desolate.

[17]"Or suppose I were to bring a sword against that land and
say, 'Let a sword pass through the land,' and I were to kill both
people and animals. [18]Even if these three men were in it, as
surely as I live, declares the Sovereign LORD, they could not
save their own sons or daughters—they would save only their
own lives.

[19]"Or suppose I were to send a plague into that land and
pour out my rage on it with bloodshed, killing both people and
animals. [20]Even if Noah, Daniel, and Job were in it, as surely as
I live, declares the Sovereign LORD, they could not save their
own son or daughter; they would save only their own lives by
their righteousness.

14:12–23 Who was more righteous than Noah? Who more glorious than Daniel? Who was more diligent in good works than Job? And yet God said that if they should ask, he would not grant. When the prophet Ezekiel interceded for the sins of the people, God said, "Even if these three men . . . were in it, they would save only their own lives by their righteousness." Therefore not all that is sought is in the prejudgment of the seeker but in the decision of the giver, and human opinion takes or assumes nothing to itself unless the divine pleasure also assents.

CYPRIAN OF CARTHAGE
(C. 210–258)
THE LAPSED

21"For this is what the Sovereign LORD says: How much worse will it be when I send my four terrible judgments—sword, famine, wild animals, and plague—to Jerusalem to kill both people and animals! 22Yet some survivors will be left in it, sons and daughters who will be brought out. They will come out to you, and when you see their behavior and their deeds, you will be consoled about the catastrophe I have brought on Jerusalem—for everything I brought on it. 23They will console you when you see their behavior and their deeds, because you will know that it was not without reason that I have done everything that I have done in it, declares the Sovereign LORD."

BURNING A USELESS VINE

15 The LORD's message came to me: 2"Son of man, of all the woody branches among the trees of the forest, what happens to the wood of the vine? 3Can wood be taken from it to make anything useful? Or can anyone make a peg from it to hang things on? 4No! It is thrown in the fire for fuel; when the fire has burned up both ends of it and it is charred in the middle, will it be useful for anything? 5Indeed! If it was not made into anything useful when it was whole, how much less can it be made into anything when the fire has burned it up and it is charred?

6"Therefore, this is what the Sovereign LORD says: Like the wood of the vine is among the trees of the forest that I have provided as fuel for the fire—so I will provide the residents of Jerusalem as fuel. 7I will set my face against them—although they have escaped from the fire, the fire will still consume them! Then you will know that I am the LORD, when I set my face against them. 8I will make the land desolate because they have acted unfaithfully, declares the Sovereign LORD."

15:5 The wood of the vine is contemptible if it abide not in the vine as it is glorious while so abiding. As the Lord says of them in the prophet Ezekiel, when cut off they are of no use for any purpose of the farmer and can be applied to no labor of the mechanic. The branch is suitable only for one of two things, either the vine or the fire: If it is not in the vine, its place will be in the fire; and that it may escape the latter, may it have its place in the vine.

AUGUSTINE (354–430)
SOLILOQUIES

GOD'S UNFAITHFUL BRIDE

16 The LORD's message came to me: 2"Son of man, confront Jerusalem with her abominable practices 3and say, 'This is what the Sovereign LORD says to Jerusalem: Your origin and your birth were in the land of the Canaanites; your father was an Amorite and your mother a Hittite. 4As for your birth, on the day you were born your umbilical cord was not cut, nor were you washed in water; you were certainly not rubbed down with salt, nor wrapped with blankets. 5No eye took pity on you to do even one of these things for you to spare you; you were thrown out into the open field because you were detested on the day you were born.

6"'I passed by you and saw you kicking around helplessly in your blood. I said to you as you lay there in your blood, "Live!" I said to you as you lay there in your blood, "Live!" 7I made you plentiful like sprouts in a field; you grew tall and came of age so that you could wear jewelry. Your breasts had formed and your hair had grown, but you were still naked and bare.

8"'Then I passed by you and watched you, noticing that you had reached the age for love. I spread my cloak over you and covered your nakedness. I swore a solemn oath to you and entered into a marriage covenant with you, declares the Sovereign LORD, and you became mine.

9"'Then I bathed you in water, washed the blood off you, and anointed you with fragrant oil. 10I dressed you in embroidered clothing and put fine leather sandals on your feet. I wrapped you with fine linen and covered you with silk. 11I adorned you with jewelry. I put bracelets on your hands and a necklace

16:1–30 When God says, "Live!" it includes many things. Here is judicial life. The sinner is ready to be condemned, but the mighty one says, "Live," and he rises pardoned and absolved. It is spiritual life. We knew not Jesus—our eyes could not see Christ, our ears could not hear his voice—Jehovah said "Live," and we were quickened who were dead in trespasses and sins. Moreover, it includes glory life, which is the perfection of spiritual life. "I said to you . . . in your blood, 'Live!'" and that word rolls on through all the years of time till death comes, and in the midst of the shadows of death, the Lord's voice is still heard, "Live!" In the morning of the resurrection it is that same voice that is echoed by the archangel, "Live!" and holy spirits rise to heaven to be blest forever in the glory of their God.

CHARLES SPURGEON
(1834–1892)
MORNING AND EVENING

around your neck. [12]I put a ring in your nose, earrings on your
ears, and a beautiful crown on your head. [13]You were adorned
with gold and silver, while your clothing was of fine linen, silk,
and embroidery. You ate the finest flour, honey, and olive oil.
You became extremely beautiful and attained the position of
royalty. [14]Your fame spread among the nations because of your
beauty; your beauty was perfect because of the splendor that I
bestowed on you, declares the Sovereign LORD.

[15]"'But you trusted in your beauty and capitalized on your
fame by becoming a prostitute. You offered your sexual favors to
every man who passed by so that your beauty became his. [16]You
took some of your clothing and made for yourself decorated
high places; you engaged in prostitution on them. You went to
him to become his. [17]You also took your beautiful jewelry, made
of my gold and my silver I had given to you, and made for yourself male images and engaged in prostitution with them. [18]You
took your embroidered clothing and used it to cover them; you
offered my olive oil and my incense to them. [19]As for my food
that I gave you—the fine flour, olive oil, and honey I fed you—
you placed it before them as a soothing aroma. That is exactly
what happened, declares the Sovereign LORD.

[20]"'You took your sons and your daughters whom you bore
to me and you sacrificed them as food for the idols to eat. As
if your prostitution was not enough, [21]you slaughtered my
children and sacrificed them to the idols. [22]And with all your
abominable practices and prostitution you did not remember
the days of your youth when you were naked and bare, kicking
around in your blood.

[23]"'After all your evil—"Woe! Woe to you!" declares the Sovereign LORD—[24]you built yourself a chamber and put up a pavilion
in every public square. [25]At the head of every street you erected
your pavilion, and you disgraced your beauty when you spread
your legs to every passerby and multiplied your promiscuity.
[26]You engaged in prostitution with the Egyptians, your lustful
neighbors, multiplying your promiscuity and provoking me to
anger. [27]So see here, I have stretched out my hand against you
and cut off your rations. I have delivered you into the power of
those who hate you, the daughters of the Philistines, who were
ashamed of your obscene conduct. [28]You engaged in prostitution with the Assyrians because your desires were insatiable;
you prostituted yourself with them and yet you were still not
satisfied. [29]Then you multiplied your promiscuity to the land of
merchants, Babylonia, but you were not satisfied there either.

[30]"'How sick is your heart, declares the Sovereign LORD,
when you perform all these acts, the deeds of a bold prostitute.
[31]When you built your chamber at the head of every street and
put up your pavilion in every public square, you were not like
a prostitute, because you scoffed at payment.

[32]"'Adulterous wife, who prefers strangers instead of her
own husband! [33]All prostitutes receive payment, but instead
you give gifts to every one of your lovers. You bribe them to
come to you from all around for your sexual favors! [34]You were
different from other prostitutes because no one solicited you.
When you gave payment and no payment was given to you, you
became the opposite!

[35]"'Therefore, you prostitute, listen to the LORD's message!
[36]This is what the Sovereign LORD says: Because your lust was
poured out and your nakedness was uncovered in your prostitution with your lovers, and because of all your detestable idols,

and because of the blood of your children you have given to them,
[37]therefore, take note: I am about to gather all your lovers whom
you enjoyed, both all those you loved and all those you hated. I
will gather them against you from all around, and I will expose
your nakedness to them, and they will see all your nakedness.
[38]I will punish you as an adulteress and murderer deserves. I
will avenge your bloody deeds with furious rage. [39]I will give
you into their hands, and they will destroy your chambers and
tear down your pavilions. They will strip you of your clothing
and take your beautiful jewelry and leave you naked and bare.
[40]They will summon a mob who will stone you and hack you in
pieces with their swords. [41]They will burn down your houses
and execute judgments on you in front of many women. Thus I
will put a stop to your prostitution, and you will no longer give
gifts to your clients. [42]I will exhaust my rage on you, and then my
fury will turn from you. I will calm down and no longer be angry.

[43]"'Because you did not remember the days of your youth
and have enraged me with all these deeds, I hereby repay you
for what you have done, declares the Sovereign LORD. Have you
not engaged in prostitution on top of all your other abominable
practices?

[44]"'Observe—everyone who quotes proverbs will quote this
proverb about you: "Like mother, like daughter." [45]You are the
daughter of your mother, who detested her husband and her
sons, and you are the sister of your sisters, who detested their
husbands and their sons. Your mother was a Hittite and your
father an Amorite. [46]Your older sister was Samaria, who lived
north of you with her daughters, and your younger sister, who
lived south of you, was Sodom with her daughters. [47]Have you
not copied their behavior and practiced their abominable
deeds? In a short time you became even more depraved in all
your conduct than they were! [48]As surely as I live, declares the
Sovereign LORD, your sister Sodom and her daughters never
behaved as wickedly as you and your daughters have behaved.

[49]"'See here—this was the iniquity of your sister Sodom: She
and her daughters had majesty, abundance of food, and enjoyed carefree ease, but they did not help the poor and needy.
[50]They were haughty and practiced abominable deeds before
me. Therefore, when I saw it I removed them. [51]Samaria has
not committed half the sins you have; you have done more
abominable deeds than they did. You have made your sisters
appear righteous with all the abominable things you have done.
[52]So now, bear your disgrace, because you have given your sisters reason to justify their behavior. Because the sins you have
committed were more abominable than those of your sisters;
they have become more righteous than you. So now, be ashamed
and bear the disgrace of making your sisters appear righteous.

[53]"'I will restore their fortunes, the fortunes of Sodom and
her daughters, and the fortunes of Samaria and her daughters
(along with your fortunes among them), [54]so that you may bear
your disgrace and be ashamed of all you have done in consoling
them. [55]As for your sisters, Sodom and her daughters will be
restored to their former status, Samaria and her daughters will
be restored to their former status, and you and your daughters
will be restored to your former status. [56]In your days of majesty,
was not Sodom your sister a byword in your mouth, [57]before
your evil was exposed? Now you have become an object of scorn
to the daughters of Aram and all those around her and to the
daughters of the Philistines—those all around you who despise

you. [58]You must bear your punishment for your obscene conduct and your abominable practices, declares the LORD.
[59]"'For this is what the Sovereign LORD says: I will deal with
you according to what you have done when you despised your
oath by breaking your covenant. [60]Yet I will remember the
covenant I made with you in the days of your youth, and I will
establish a lasting covenant with you. [61]Then you will remember
your conduct and be ashamed when you receive your older and
younger sisters. I will give them to you as daughters, but not on
account of my covenant with you. [62]I will establish my covenant
with you, and then you will know that I am the LORD. [63]Then
you will remember, be ashamed, and remain silent because of
your disgrace when I make atonement for all you have done,
declares the Sovereign LORD.'"

A PARABLE OF TWO EAGLES AND A VINE

17 The LORD's message came to me: [2]"Son of man, offer a
riddle and tell a parable to the house of Israel. [3]Say to
them: 'This is what the Sovereign LORD says:

"'A great eagle with broad wings, long feathers,
with full plumage that was multihued,
came to Lebanon and took the top of the cedar.
4 He plucked off its topmost shoot;
he brought it to a land of merchants
and planted it in a city of traders.
5 He took one of the seedlings of the land,
placed it in a cultivated plot;
a shoot by abundant water,
like a willow he planted it.
6 It sprouted and became a vine,
spreading low to the ground;
its branches turning toward him, its roots were under itself.
So it became a vine; it produced shoots and sent out branches.

7 "'There was another great eagle
with broad wings and thick plumage.
Now this vine twisted its roots toward him
and sent its branches toward him
to be watered from the soil where it was planted.
8 In a good field, by abundant waters, it was planted
to grow branches, bear fruit, and become a beautiful vine.'

[9]"Say to them: 'This is what the Sovereign LORD says:
"'Will it prosper?
Will he not rip out its roots
and cause its fruit to rot and wither?
All its foliage will wither.
No strong arm or large army
will be needed to pull it out by its roots.
10 Consider! It is planted, but will it prosper?
Will it not wither completely when the east wind blows on it?
Will it not wither in the soil where it sprouted?'"

[11]Then the LORD's message came to me: [12]"Say to the rebellious house of Israel: 'Don't you know what these things mean?'
Say: 'See here, the king of Babylon came to Jerusalem and took

17:1–24 These verses contain a promise of mercy. And it is no mean promise, but an exceeding great and precious promise, namely of Christ and his kingdom. The Lord having resolved and sworn to the rooting up of the Jewish vine, namely the destruction of Zedekiah, his princes, nobles, city, people, and laying all waste: What will now become of his promise to Abraham, to David, and to others that out of their loins and seed should come a blessing to all nations, that the Messiah should spring out of their root? If all Judah is rooted up and carried out into Babylon, what truth is there in the promise of God? How will this be made good that has proceeded out of his sacred lips? What? Will the God of truth be unfaithful and fail now? No, says the Lord, *I am mindful of what I have promised. And though you see not how it shall be accomplished, I do. I have ways not thought of by you.*

WILLIAM GREENHILL
(1591–1671)
AN EXPOSITION OF EZEKIEL

her king and her officials prisoner and brought them to himself
in Babylon. 13He took one from the royal family, made a treaty
with him, and put him under oath. He then took the leaders of
the land 14so it would be a lowly kingdom that could not rise on
its own but had to keep its treaty with him in order to stand.
15But this one from Israel's royal family rebelled against the
king of Babylon by sending his emissaries to Egypt to obtain
horses and a large army. Will he prosper? Will the one doing
these things escape? Can he break the covenant and escape?
16"'As surely as I live, declares the Sovereign LORD, surely in
the city of the king who crowned him, whose oath he despised
and whose covenant he broke—in the middle of Babylon he
will die! 17Pharaoh with his great army and mighty horde will
not help him in battle, when siege ramps are erected and siege
walls are built to kill many people. 18He despised the oath by
breaking the covenant. Take note—he gave his promise and did
all these things. He will not escape!
19"'Therefore this is what the Sovereign LORD says: As surely
as I live, I will certainly repay him for despising my oath and
breaking my covenant! 20I will throw my net over him and he
will be caught in my snare; I will bring him to Babylon and
judge him there because of the unfaithfulness he committed
against me. 21All the choice men among his troops will die by
the sword, and the survivors will be scattered to every wind.
Then you will know that I, the LORD, have spoken!
22"'This is what the Sovereign LORD says:

"'I will take a sprig from the lofty top of the cedar and
plant it.
I will pluck from the top one of its tender twigs;
I myself will plant it on a high and lofty mountain.
23 I will plant it on a high mountain of Israel,
and it will raise branches and produce fruit and become
a beautiful cedar.
Every bird will live under it;
every winged creature will live in the shade of its
branches.
24 All the trees of the field will know that I am the LORD.
I make the high tree low; I raise up the low tree.
I make the green tree wither, and I make the dry tree
sprout.
I, the LORD, have spoken, and I will do it!'"

INDIVIDUAL RETRIBUTION

18 The LORD's message came to me: 2"What do you mean by
quoting this proverb concerning the land of Israel:

"'The fathers eat sour grapes,
And the children's teeth become numb?'

3"As surely as I live, declares the Sovereign LORD, you will
not quote this proverb in Israel anymore! 4Indeed! All lives are
mine—the life of the father as well as the life of the son is mine.
The one who sins will die.
5"Suppose a man is righteous. He practices what is just and
right; 6does not eat pagan sacrifices on the mountains or pray
to the idols of the house of Israel; does not defile his neighbor's
wife; does not approach a woman for marital relations during
her period; 7does not oppress anyone, but gives the debtor back
whatever was given in pledge; does not commit robbery, but
gives his bread to the hungry and clothes the naked; 8does not

engage in usury or charge interest, but refrains from wrongdoing; promotes true justice between men; 9 and follows my
statutes and observes my regulations by carrying them out.
That man is righteous; he will certainly live, declares the Sovereign LORD.
10 "Suppose such a man has a violent son who sheds blood
and does any of these things mentioned previously 11 (though
the father did not do any of them). He eats pagan sacrifices
on the mountains, defiles his neighbor's wife, 12 oppresses
the poor and the needy, commits robbery, does not give back
what was given in pledge, prays to idols, performs abominable
acts, 13 engages in usury, and charges interest. Will he live? He
will not! Because he has done all these abominable deeds he
will certainly die. He will bear the responsibility for his own
death.
14 "But suppose he in turn has a son who notices all the sins
his father commits, considers them, and does not follow his
father's example. 15 He does not eat pagan sacrifices on the
mountains, does not pray to the idols of the house of Israel,
does not defile his neighbor's wife, 16 does not oppress anyone or keep what has been given in pledge, does not commit
robbery, gives his food to the hungry and clothes the naked,
17 refrains from wrongdoing, does not engage in usury or charge
interest, carries out my regulations, and follows my statutes.
He will not die for his father's iniquity; he will surely live. 18 As
for his father, because he practices extortion, robs his brother,
and does what is not good among his people, he will die for
his iniquity.
19 "Yet you say, 'Why should the son not suffer for his father's
iniquity?' When the son does what is just and right, and observes all my statutes and carries them out, he will surely live.
20 The person who sins is the one who will die. A son will not
suffer for his father's iniquity, and a father will not suffer for
his son's iniquity; the righteous person will be judged according
to his righteousness and the wicked person according to his
wickedness.
21 "But if the wicked person turns from all the sin he has
committed and observes all my statutes and does what is just
and right, he will surely live; he will not die. 22 None of the sins
he has committed will be held against him; because of the righteousness he has done, he will live. 23 Do I actually delight in
the death of the wicked, declares the Sovereign LORD? Do I not
prefer that he turn from his wicked conduct and live?
24 "But if a righteous man turns away from his righteousness
and practices wrongdoing according to all the abominable practices the wicked carry out, will he live? All his righteous acts
will not be remembered; because of the unfaithful acts he has
done and the sin he has committed, he will die.
25 "Yet you say, 'The Lord's conduct is unjust!' Hear, O house
of Israel: Is my conduct unjust? Is it not your conduct that is
unjust? 26 When a righteous person turns back from his righteousness and practices wrongdoing, he will die for it; because
of the wrongdoing he has done, he will die. 27 When a wicked
person turns from the wickedness he has committed and does
what is just and right, he will preserve his life. 28 Because he
considered and turned from all the sins he had done, he will
surely live; he will not die. 29 Yet the house of Israel says, 'The
Lord's conduct is unjust!' Is my conduct unjust, O house of Israel? Is it not your conduct that is unjust?

18:19–32 "Do I actually delight in the death of the wicked, declares the Sovereign LORD? Do I not prefer that he turn from his wicked conduct and live?" The words are proposed by way of interrogation in which form of speech there is more evidence, efficacy, life, and convincing force. That is to say, *You know it is evident that I have no such desire, no such pleasure. It dare not enter into your thoughts that I should take pleasure in the bare destruction of the creature.* God had rather his conversion. In both are implied two great truths; namely, the connection between sin and death, repentance and life, wicked and die, return and live. God does not obscurely nullify or disown his judgments and execution according to that law or give you any hopes that his law should not be executed, but he tells you what he takes pleasure in—rather in the conversion than in the destruction of the creature.

THOMAS MANTON
(1620–1677)
THE COMPLETE WORKS

30"Therefore, I will judge each person according to his conduct, O house of Israel, declares the Sovereign LORD. Repent and
turn from all your wickedness; then it will not be an obstacle
leading to iniquity. 31 Throw away all your sins you have committed and fashion yourselves a new heart and a new spirit! Why
should you die, O house of Israel? 32 For I take no delight in the
death of anyone, declares the Sovereign LORD. Repent and live!

19:1–14 Here the prophet, using the image of a lion, informs us that whatever evils happened to the Israelites could not be imputed to others. Ezekiel confirms what we formerly saw, that the Jews were not afflicted without deserving it. But he uses, as I have said, a simile taken from lions. He calls the nation itself a "lioness," for when he treats of the mother of the people we know that the offspring is considered. He says therefore that the people were full of insolence.

JOHN CALVIN (1509–1564)
COMPLETE COMMENTARY ON THE BIBLE

LAMENT FOR THE PRINCES OF ISRAEL

19 "And you, sing a lament for the princes of Israel, 2 and say:
"'What a lioness was your mother among the lions!
She lay among young lions; she reared her cubs.
3 She reared one of her cubs; he became a young lion.
He learned to tear prey; he devoured people.
4 The nations heard about him; he was trapped in their pit.
They brought him with hooks to the land of Egypt.

5 "'When she realized that she waited in vain, her hope was lost.
She took another of her cubs and made him a young lion.
6 He walked about among the lions; he became a young lion.
He learned to tear prey; he devoured people.
7 He broke down their strongholds and devastated their cities.
The land and everything in it was frightened at the sound of his roaring.
8 The nations—the surrounding regions—attacked him.
They threw their net over him; he was caught in their pit.
9 They put him in a collar with hooks;
they brought him to the king of Babylon;
they brought him to prison
so that his voice would not be heard
any longer on the mountains of Israel.

10 "'Your mother was like a vine in your vineyard, planted by water.
It was fruitful and full of branches because it was well-watered.
11 Its boughs were strong, fit for rulers' scepters; it reached up into the clouds.
It stood out because of its height and its many branches.
12 But it was plucked up in anger; it was thrown down to the ground.
The east wind dried up its fruit;
its strong branches broke off and withered—
a fire consumed them.
13 Now it is planted in the wilderness,
in a dry and thirsty land.
14 A fire has gone out from its branch; it has consumed its shoot and its fruit.
No strong branch was left in it, nor a scepter to rule.'

"This is a lament song, and has become a lament song."

ISRAEL'S REBELLION

20 In the seventh year, in the fifth month, on the tenth of the month, some of the elders of Israel came to seek the LORD, and they sat down in front of me. 2The LORD's message came to me: 3"Son of man, speak to the elders of Israel, and tell them: 'This is what the Sovereign LORD says: Are you coming to seek me? As surely as I live, I will not allow you to seek me, declares the Sovereign LORD.' 4Are you willing to pronounce judgment on them? Are you willing to pronounce judgment, son of man? Then confront them with the abominable practices of their fathers, 5and say to them:

"'This is what the Sovereign LORD says: On the day I chose Israel I swore to the descendants of the house of Jacob and made myself known to them in the land of Egypt. I swore to them, "I am the LORD your God." 6On that day I swore to bring them out of the land of Egypt to a land that I had picked out for them, a land flowing with milk and honey, the most beautiful of all lands. 7I said to them, "Each of you must get rid of the detestable idols you keep before you, and do not defile yourselves with the idols of Egypt; I am the LORD your God." 8But they rebelled against me and refused to listen to me; no one got rid of their detestable idols, nor did they abandon the idols of Egypt. Then I decided to pour out my rage on them and fully vent my anger against them in the midst of the land of Egypt. 9I acted for the sake of my reputation, so that I would not be profaned before the nations among whom they lived, before whom I revealed myself by bringing them out of the land of Egypt.

10"'So I brought them out of the land of Egypt and led them to the wilderness. 11I gave them my statutes and revealed my regulations to them. The one who carries them out will live by them! 12I also gave them my Sabbaths as a reminder of our relationship, so that they would know that I, the LORD, sanctify them. 13But the house of Israel rebelled against me in the wilderness; they did not follow my statutes and they rejected my regulations (the one who obeys them will live by them), and they utterly desecrated my Sabbaths. So I decided to pour out my rage on them in the wilderness and destroy them. 14I acted for the sake of my reputation, so that I would not be profaned before the nations in whose sight I had brought them out. 15I also swore to them in the wilderness that I would not bring them to the land I had given them—a land flowing with milk and honey, the most beautiful of all lands. 16I did this because they rejected my regulations, did not follow my statutes, and desecrated my Sabbaths; for their hearts followed their idols. 17Yet I had pity on them and did not destroy them, so I did not make an end of them in the wilderness.

18"'But I said to their children in the wilderness, "Do not follow the practices of your fathers; do not observe their regulations, nor defile yourselves with their idols. 19I am the LORD your God; follow my statutes, observe my regulations, and carry them out. 20Treat my Sabbaths as holy and they will be a reminder of our relationship, and then you will know that I am the LORD your God." 21But the children rebelled against me, did not follow my statutes, did not observe my regulations by carrying them out (the one who obeys them will live by them), and desecrated my Sabbaths. I decided to pour out my rage on them and fully vent my anger against them in the wilderness. 22But I refrained from doing so and acted instead for the sake of my reputation, so that I would not be profaned before the

20:1–32 Out of his grace the Lord makes this covenant with us: *Do this and live*. Now because no one can perfectly keep the commandments and so attain to life, to the law of doing is added the law of believing. Because of our imperfections, we should repent of our sins with the uttermost of our power, turn from them, and believe in Christ so that perfect justification and salvation may be attained. And so it is not in vain that God bids us to do this and live, which he knows we cannot exactly do. But we who repent of our failings and do what we can, the Son of God puts to his helping hand and both obeys perfectly for us and pays his blood for a ransom of our failings, whereby we come undoubtedly to live indeed.

JOHN MAYER **(1583–1664)**
COMMENTARY UPON ALL THE PROPHETS

nations in whose sight I had brought them out. [23]I also swore to them in the wilderness that I would scatter them among the nations and disperse them throughout the lands. [24]I did this because they did not observe my regulations, they rejected my statutes, they desecrated my Sabbaths, and their eyes were fixed on their fathers' idols. [25]I also gave them decrees that were not good and regulations by which they could not live. [26]I declared them to be defiled because of their sacrifices—they caused all their firstborn to pass through the fire—so that I might devastate them, so that they would know that I am the LORD.'

[27]"Therefore, speak to the house of Israel, son of man, and tell them, 'This is what the Sovereign LORD says: In this way too your fathers blasphemed me when they were unfaithful to me. [28]I brought them to the land that I swore to give them, but whenever they saw any high hill or leafy tree, they offered their sacrifices there and presented the offerings that provoked me to anger. They offered their soothing aroma there and poured out their drink offerings. [29]So I said to them, "What is this high place you go to?"' (So it is called "High Place" to this day.)

[30]"Therefore say to the house of Israel, 'This is what the Sovereign LORD says: Will you defile yourselves like your fathers and engage in prostitution with detestable idols? [31]When you present your sacrifices—when you make your sons pass through the fire—you defile yourselves with all your idols to this very day. Will I allow you to seek me, O house of Israel? As surely as I live, declares the Sovereign LORD, I will not allow you to seek me!

[32]"'What you plan will never happen. You say, "We will be like the nations, like the clans of the lands, who serve gods of wood and stone." [33]As surely as I live, declares the Sovereign LORD, with a powerful hand and an outstretched arm and with an outpouring of rage, I will be king over you. [34]I will bring you out from the nations and will gather you from the lands where you are scattered, with a powerful hand and an outstretched arm and with an outpouring of rage! [35]I will bring you into the wilderness of the nations, and there I will enter into judgment with you face-to-face. [36]Just as I entered into judgment with your fathers in the wilderness of the land of Egypt, so I will enter into judgment with you, declares the Sovereign LORD. [37]I will make you pass under the shepherd's staff, and I will bring you into the bond of the covenant. [38]I will eliminate from among you the rebels and those who revolt against me. I will bring them out from the land where they have been residing, but they will not come to the land of Israel. Then you will know that I am the LORD.

[39]"'As for you, O house of Israel, this is what the Sovereign LORD says: Each of you go and serve your idols, if you will not listen to me. But my holy name will not be profaned again by your sacrifices and your idols. [40]For there on my holy mountain, the high mountain of Israel, declares the Sovereign LORD, all the house of Israel will serve me, all of them in the land. I will accept them there, and there I will seek your contributions and your choice gifts, with all your holy things. [41]When I bring you out from the nations and gather you from the lands where you are scattered, I will accept you along with your soothing aroma. I will display my holiness among you in the sight of the nations. [42]Then you will know that I am the LORD when I bring you to the land of Israel, to the land I swore to give to

your fathers. 43And there you will remember your conduct
and all your deeds by which you defiled yourselves. You will
despise yourselves because of all the evil deeds you have done.
44Then you will know that I am the LORD, when I deal with
you for the sake of my reputation and not according to your
wicked conduct and corrupt deeds, O house of Israel, declares
the Sovereign LORD.'"

PROPHECY AGAINST THE SOUTH

45The LORD's message came to me: 46"Son of man, turn toward
the south, and speak out against the south. Prophesy against the
open scrub land of the Negev, 47and say to the scrub land of the
Negev, 'Listen to the LORD's message! This is what the Sovereign
LORD has said: Look here, I am about to start a fire in you, and
it will devour every green tree and every dry tree in you. The
flaming fire will not be extinguished, and the whole surface of
the ground from the Negev to the north will be scorched by it.
48And everyone will see that I, the LORD, have burned it; it will
not be extinguished.'"

49Then I said, "O Sovereign LORD! They are saying of me, 'Does
he not simply speak in eloquent figures of speech?'"

THE SWORD OF JUDGMENT

21 The LORD's message came to me: 2"Son of man, turn toward Jerusalem and speak out against the sanctuaries.
Prophesy against the land of Israel 3and say to them, 'This is
what the LORD says: Look, I am against you. I will draw my sword
from its sheath and cut off from you both the righteous and
the wicked. 4Because I will cut off from you both the righteous
and the wicked, my sword will go out from its sheath against
everyone from the south to the north. 5Then everyone will know
that I am the LORD, who drew my sword from its sheath—it will
not be sheathed again!'

6"And you, son of man, groan with an aching heart and bitterness; groan before their eyes. 7When they ask you, 'Why are
you groaning?' you will reply, 'Because of the report that has
come. Every heart will melt with fear and every hand will be
limp; everyone will faint, and every knee will be wet with urine.'
Pay attention—it is coming and it will happen, declares the
Sovereign LORD."

8The LORD's message came to me: 9"Son of man, prophesy
and say: 'This is what the Lord says:

"'A sword, a sword is sharpened
and also polished.
10 It is sharpened for slaughter;
it is polished to flash like lightning!

"'Should we rejoice in the scepter of my son? No! The sword
despises every tree!

11 "'He gave it to be polished,
to be grasped in the hand—
the sword is sharpened, it is polished—
giving it into the hand of the executioner.
12 Cry out and moan, son of man,
for it is wielded against my people,
against all the princes of Israel.
They are delivered up to the sword, along with my
people.
Therefore, strike your thigh.

21:1–32 It is declared that the Lord is about to cut off Jerusalem and the whole land, that all might know it was his decree against a wicked and rebellious people. By the Spirit of prophecy Ezekiel foresaw Nebuchadnezzar's march from Babylon, which he would determine by divination. The Lord would overturn the government of Judah. This seems to foretell the overturnings of the Jewish nation to the present day, and the troubles of states and kingdoms that shall make way for establishing the Messiah's kingdom throughout the earth. The Lord secretly leads all to adopt his wise designs. And in the midst of the most tremendous warnings of wrath, we still hear of mercy, and some mention of him through whom mercy is shown to sinful men. Let us be thankful to be employed as instruments of mercy; let us use our understandings in doing good.

MATTHEW HENRY **(1662–1714)**
COMMENTARY ON THE WHOLE BIBLE

13"'For testing will come, and what will happen when the
scepter, which the sword despises, is no more? declares the
Sovereign LORD.'

14 "And you, son of man, prophesy,
and clap your hands together.
Let the sword strike twice, even three times!
It is a sword for slaughter,
a sword for the great slaughter surrounding them.
15 So hearts melt with fear and many stumble.
At all their gates I have stationed the sword for
slaughter.
Ah! It is made to flash, it is drawn for slaughter!
16 Cut sharply on the right!
Swing to the left,
wherever your edge is appointed to strike.
17 I too will clap my hands together,
I will exhaust my rage;
I, the LORD, have spoken."

18The LORD's message came to me: 19"You, son of man, mark
out two routes for the king of Babylon's sword to take; both of
them will originate in a single land. Make a signpost and put it
at the beginning of the road leading to the city. 20Mark out the
routes for the sword to take: 'Rabbah of the Ammonites' and
'Judah with Jerusalem in it.' 21For the king of Babylon stands at
the fork in the road at the head of the two routes. He looks for
omens: He shakes arrows, he consults idols, he examines animal
livers. 22Into his right hand comes the portent for Jerusalem—to
set up battering rams, to give the signal for slaughter, to shout
out the battle cry, to set up battering rams against the gates,
to erect a siege ramp, and to build a siege wall. 23But those in
Jerusalem will view it as a false omen. They have sworn solemn
oaths, but the king of Babylon will accuse them of violations
in order to seize them.

24"Therefore this is what the Sovereign LORD says: 'Because
you have brought up your own guilt by uncovering your transgressions and revealing your sins through all your actions, for
this reason you will be taken by force.

25 "'As for you, profane and wicked prince of Israel,
whose day has come, the time of final punishment,
26 this is what the Sovereign LORD says:
Tear off the turban;
take off the crown!
Things must change.
Exalt the lowly;
bring low the exalted!
27 A total ruin I will make it!
Indeed, this will not be
until he comes to whom is the right, and I will give it
to him.'

28"As for you, son of man, prophesy and say, 'This is what the
Sovereign LORD says concerning the Ammonites and their
coming humiliation:

"'A sword, a sword drawn for slaughter,
polished to consume, to flash like lightning—
29 while seeing false visions about you
and reading lying omens about you—
to place you on the necks of the profane wicked,

whose day has come,
the time of final punishment.
30 Return it to its sheath!
In the place where you were created,
in your native land, I will judge you.
31 I will pour out my anger on you;
the fire of my fury I will blow on you.
I will hand you over to brutal men,
who are skilled in destruction.
32 You will become fuel for the fire—
your blood will stain the middle of the land;
you will no longer be remembered,
for I, the LORD, have spoken.'"

THE SINS OF JERUSALEM

22 The LORD's message came to me: 2"As for you, son of man,
are you willing to pronounce judgment? Are you willing
to pronounce judgment on the bloody city? Then confront
her with all her abominable deeds! 3Then say, 'This is what the
Sovereign LORD says: O city, who spills blood within herself
(which brings on her doom), and who makes herself idols (which
results in impurity), 4you are guilty because of the blood you
shed and defiled by the idols you made. You have hastened the
day of your doom; the end of your years has come. Therefore
I will make you an object of scorn to the nations, an object to
be mocked by all lands. 5Those both near and far from you will
mock you, you with your bad reputation, full of turmoil.

6"'See how each of the princes of Israel living within you has
used his authority to shed blood. 7They have treated father and
mother with contempt within you; they have oppressed the
resident foreigner among you; they have wronged the orphan
and the widow within you. 8You have despised my holy things
and desecrated my Sabbaths! 9Slanderous men shed blood
within you. Those who live within you eat pagan sacrifices on
the mountains; they commit obscene acts among you. 10They
have sexual relations with their father's wife within you; they
violate women during their menstrual period within you. 11One
commits an abominable act with his neighbor's wife; another
obscenely defiles his daughter-in-law; another violates his sister—his father's daughter—within you. 12They take bribes within you to shed blood. You engage in usury and charge interest;
you extort money from your neighbors. You have forgotten me,
declares the Sovereign LORD.

13"'See, I strike my hands together at the dishonest profit you
have made and at the bloodshed they have done among you.
14Can your heart endure or can your hands be strong when I
deal with you? I, the LORD, have spoken, and I will do it! 15I will
scatter you among the nations and disperse you among various
countries; I will remove your impurity from you. 16You will be
profaned within yourself in the sight of the nations; then you
will know that I am the LORD.'"

17The LORD's message came to me: 18"Son of man, the house
of Israel has become slag to me. All of them are like bronze, tin,
iron, and lead in the furnace; they are the worthless slag of silver.
19Therefore this is what the Sovereign LORD says: 'Because all
of you have become slag, look out! I am about to gather you in
the middle of Jerusalem. 20As silver, bronze, iron, lead, and tin
are gathered in a furnace so that the fire can blow on them to
melt them, so I will gather you in my anger and in my rage. I will

22:1–31 "You are guilty because of the blood you shed." You will not be punished on account of another's sins, but you will be punished because of your murders and injustices and your many idolatries. Read "you have sinned" where the text has "O city, who spills blood" or "you are guilty"; that is, you are the guilty party, and you are openly and manifestly found with the pollution of sin. By your evil deeds, you have hastened your years and your visitation, the time of your departure, captivity, and destruction. Your total wickedness calls forth a severe judgment.

JOHANNES OECOLAMPADIUS
(1482–1531)
COMMENTARY ON EZEKIEL

deposit you there and melt you. 21 I will gather you and blow on
you with the fire of my fury, and you will be melted in it. 22 As
silver is melted in a furnace, so you will be melted in it, and you
will know that I, the LORD, have poured out my anger on you.'"
23 The LORD's message came to me: 24 "Son of man, say to her:
'You are a land that receives no rain or showers in the day of my
anger.' 25 Her princes within her are like a roaring lion tearing
its prey; they have devoured lives. They take away riches and
valuable things; they have made many women widows within it.
26 Her priests abuse my law and have desecrated my holy things.
They do not distinguish between the holy and the profane or
recognize any distinction between the unclean and the clean.
They ignore my Sabbaths, and I am profaned in their midst.
27 Her officials are like wolves in her midst rending their prey—
shedding blood and destroying lives—so they can get dishonest
profit. 28 Her prophets coat their messages with whitewash.
They see false visions and announce lying omens for them,
saying, 'This is what the Sovereign LORD says,' when the LORD
has not spoken. 29 The people of the land have practiced extortion and committed robbery. They have wronged the poor and
needy; they have oppressed the resident foreigner and denied
them justice.
30 "I looked for a man from among them who would repair
the wall and stand in the gap before me on behalf of the land,
so that I would not destroy it, but I found no one. 31 So I have
poured my anger on them and destroyed them with the fire of
my fury. I hereby repay them for what they have done, declares
the Sovereign LORD."

TWO SISTERS

23 The LORD's message came to me: 2 "Son of man, there were
two women who were daughters of the same mother.
3 They engaged in prostitution in Egypt; in their youth they
engaged in prostitution. Their breasts were squeezed there;
lovers fondled their virgin nipples there. 4 Oholah was the name
of the older and Oholibah the name of her younger sister. They
became mine and gave birth to sons and daughters. Oholah is
Samaria, and Oholibah is Jerusalem.
5 "Oholah engaged in prostitution while she was mine. She
lusted after her lovers, the Assyrians—warriors 6 clothed in
blue, governors and officials, all of them desirable young men,
horsemen riding on horses. 7 She bestowed her sexual favors
on them; all of them were the choicest young men of Assyria.
She defiled herself with all whom she desired—with all their
idols. 8 She did not abandon the prostitution she had practiced
in Egypt, for in her youth men went to bed with her, fondled
her virgin breasts, and ravished her. 9 Therefore I handed her
over to her lovers, the Assyrians for whom she lusted. 10 They
exposed her nakedness, seized her sons and daughters, and
killed her with the sword. She became notorious among women,
and they executed judgments against her.
11 "Her sister Oholibah watched this, but she became more
corrupt in her lust than her sister had been, and her acts of
prostitution were more numerous than those of her sister.
12 She lusted after the Assyrians—governors and officials, warriors in full armor, horsemen riding on horses, all of them desirable young men. 13 I saw that she was defiled; both of them
followed the same path. 14 But she increased her prostitution.
She saw men carved on the wall, images of the Chaldeans carved

23:1–49 The principal crime of the human race, the highest guilt charged upon the world, the whole procuring cause of judgment is idolatry. The essence of fraud is that any should seize what is another's or refuse to another his due; and of course, fraud done toward man is a name of greatest crime. Well, but idolatry does fraud to God by refusing him and conferring on others his honors so that to fraud it also conjoins. After such crimes so pernicious, so devouring of salvation, all other crimes also, after some manner and separately disposed in order, find their own essence represented in idolatry.

TERTULLIAN (155–C. 220)
ON IDOLATRY

in bright red, [15]wearing belts on their waists and flowing turbans on their heads, all of them looking like officers, the image of Babylonians whose native land is Chaldea. [16]When she saw them, she lusted after them and sent messengers to them in Chaldea. [17]The Babylonians crawled into bed with her. They defiled her with their lust; after she was defiled by them, she became disgusted with them. [18]When she lustfully exposed her nakedness, I was disgusted with her, just as I had been disgusted with her sister. [19]Yet she increased her prostitution, remembering the days of her youth when she engaged in prostitution in the land of Egypt. [20]She lusted after her lovers there, whose genitals were like those of donkeys and whose emission was like that of stallions. [21]This is how you assessed the obscene conduct of your youth, when the Egyptians fondled your nipples and squeezed your young breasts.

[22]"Therefore, Oholibah, this is what the Sovereign LORD says: Look here, I am about to stir up against you the lovers with whom you were disgusted; I will bring them against you from every side: [23]the Babylonians and all the Chaldeans, Pekod, Shoa, and Koa, and all the Assyrians with them, desirable young men, all of them governors and officials, officers and nobles, all of them riding on horses. [24]They will attack you with weapons, chariots, wagons, and with a huge army; they will array themselves against you on every side with large shields, small shields, and helmets. I will assign them the task of judgment; they will punish you according to their laws. [25]I will direct my jealous anger against you, and they will deal with you in rage. They will cut off your nose and your ears, and your survivors will die by the sword. They will seize your sons and daughters, and your survivors will be consumed by fire. [26]They will strip your clothes off you and take away your beautiful jewelry. [27]So I will put an end to your obscene conduct and your prostitution that you have practiced in the land of Egypt. You will not seek their help or remember Egypt anymore.

[28]"For this is what the Sovereign LORD says: Look here, I am about to deliver you over to those whom you hate, to those with whom you were disgusted. [29]They will treat you with hatred, take away all you have labored for, and leave you naked and bare. Your nakedness will be exposed, just as when you engaged in prostitution and obscene conduct. [30]I will do these things to you because you engaged in prostitution with the nations, polluting yourself with their idols. [31]You have followed the ways of your sister, so I will place her cup of judgment in your hand. [32]This is what the Sovereign LORD says: 'You will drink your sister's deep and wide cup; you will be scorned and derided, for it holds a great deal. [33]You will be overcome by drunkenness and sorrow. The cup of your sister Samaria is a cup of horror and desolation. [34]You will drain it dry, gnaw its pieces, and tear out your breasts, for I have spoken, declares the Sovereign LORD.'

[35]"Therefore this is what the Sovereign LORD says: Because you have forgotten me and completely disregarded me, you must bear now the punishment for your obscene conduct and prostitution."

[36]The LORD said to me: "Son of man, are you willing to pronounce judgment on Oholah and Oholibah? Then declare to them their abominable deeds! [37]For they have committed adultery, and blood is on their hands. They have committed adultery with their idols; and their sons, whom they bore to me, they have passed through the fire as food to their idols.

[38]Moreover, they have done this to me: In the very same day they desecrated my sanctuary and profaned my Sabbaths. [39]On the same day they slaughtered their sons for their idols, they came to my sanctuary to desecrate it. This is what they have done in the middle of my house.

[40]"They even sent for men from far away; when the messenger arrived, those men set out. For them you bathed, painted your eyes, and decorated yourself with jewelry. [41]You sat on a magnificent couch, with a table arranged in front of it where you placed my incense and my olive oil. [42]The sound of a carefree crowd accompanied her, including all kinds of men; even Sabeans were brought from the desert. The sisters put bracelets on their wrists and beautiful crowns on their heads. [43]Then I said about the one worn out by adultery, 'Now they will commit immoral acts with her.' [44]They slept with her the way someone sleeps with a prostitute. In this way they slept with Oholah and Oholibah, promiscuous women. [45]But upright men will punish them appropriately for their adultery and bloodshed, because they are adulteresses and blood is on their hands.

[46]"For this is what the Sovereign LORD says: Bring up an army against them and subject them to terror and plunder. [47]That army will pelt them with stones and slash them with their swords; they will kill their sons and daughters and burn their houses. [48]I will put an end to the obscene conduct in the land; all the women will learn a lesson from this and not engage in obscene conduct. [49]They will repay you for your obscene conduct, and you will be punished for idol worship. Then you will know that I am the Sovereign LORD."

THE BOILING POT

24 The LORD's message came to me in the ninth year, in the tenth month, on the tenth day of the month: [2]"Son of man, write down the name of this day, this very day. The king of Babylon has laid siege to Jerusalem this very day. [3]Recite a proverb to this rebellious house and say to them, 'This is what the Sovereign LORD says:

"'Set on the pot, set it on,
pour water in it too;
[4] add the pieces of meat to it,
every good piece,
the thigh and the shoulder;
fill it with choice bones.
[5] Take the choice bone of the flock,
heap up wood under it;
boil rapidly,
and boil its bones in it.

[6]"'Therefore this is what the Sovereign LORD says:
Woe to the city of bloodshed,
the pot whose rot is in it,
whose rot has not been removed from it!
Empty it piece by piece.
No lot has fallen on it.
[7] For her blood was in it;
she poured it on an exposed rock;
she did not pour it on the ground to cover it up with dust.
[8] To arouse anger, to take vengeance,
I have placed her blood on an exposed rock so that it
cannot be covered up.

24:1–24 "I tried to cleanse you, but you are not clean." To be sure, all sins have been remitted and covered, but they have not yet been completely cleansed away. Not only do the dregs of lust, pride, hatred, wrath, and other desires cling to us, but also inner evils and hidden stains, doubts about God, unbelief, impatience, and murmurings. This is where God's game begins, not that we must be destroyed, but that he may examine us and lead us to a knowledge of our foulness, yet not in such a way that we despair, but rather that we cry to him, invoke his mercy, and learn that he shows his mercy wondrously.

MARTIN LUTHER **(1483–1546)**
LECTURES ON GENESIS

9"'Therefore this is what the Sovereign LORD says:
Woe to the city of bloodshed!
I will also make the pile high.
10 Pile up the wood, kindle the fire;
cook the meat well, mix in the spices,
and let the bones be charred.
11 Set the empty pot on the coals,
until it becomes hot and its copper glows,
until its uncleanness melts within it and its rot is
consumed.
12 It has tried my patience;
yet its thick rot is not removed from it.
Subject its rot to the fire!
13 You mix uncleanness with obscene conduct.
I tried to cleanse you, but you are not clean.
You will not be cleansed from your uncleanness
until I have exhausted my anger on you.

14"'I, the LORD, have spoken; judgment is coming and I will
act! I will not relent, or show pity, or be sorry! I will judge you
according to your conduct and your deeds, declares the Sovereign LORD.'"

EZEKIEL'S WIFE DIES

15The LORD's message came to me: 16"Son of man, realize that
I am about to take the delight of your eyes away from you with
a jolt, but you must not mourn or weep or shed tears. 17Groan
to moan for the dead, but do not perform mourning rites. Bind
on your turban and put your sandals on your feet. Do not cover
your lip and do not eat food brought by others."
18So I spoke to the people in the morning, and my wife died
in the evening. In the morning I acted just as I was commanded.
19Then the people said to me, "Will you not tell us what these
things you are doing mean for us?"
20So I said to them: "The LORD's message came to me: 21Say
to the house of Israel, 'This is what the Sovereign LORD says:
Realize I am about to desecrate my sanctuary—the source of
your confident pride, the object in which your eyes delight, and
your life's passion. Your very own sons and daughters whom
you have left behind will die by the sword. 22Then you will do as
I have done: You will not cover your lip or eat food brought by
others. 23Your turbans will be on your heads and your sandals
on your feet; you will not mourn or weep, but you will rot for
your iniquities and groan among yourselves. 24Ezekiel will be
an object lesson for you; you will do all that he has done. When
it happens, then you will know that I am the Sovereign LORD.'
25"And you, son of man, this is what will happen on the day I
take from them their stronghold—their beautiful source of joy,
the object in which their eyes delight, and the main concern of
their lives, as well as their sons and daughters: 26On that day
a fugitive will come to you to report the news. 27On that day
you will be able to speak again; you will talk with the fugitive
and be silent no longer. You will be an object lesson for them,
and they will know that I am the LORD."

A PROPHECY AGAINST AMMON

25 The LORD's message came to me: 2"Son of man, turn toward the Ammonites and prophesy against them. 3Say to
the Ammonites, 'Hear the word of the Sovereign LORD. This is

25:1—26:21 The prophet now prophesies against the Ammonites, Moabites, Edomites, and Philistines because they rejoiced at the destruction of Jerusalem and the temple as bearing always a deadly hatred against the Jews because of their religion. From this note how great a sin it is for the wicked and those seduced by error in religion to hate the professors of the truth. For this the wrath of God shall burn against them until they be destroyed, and likewise it shall be to all wicked people who rejoice at the fall of God's people.

JOHN MAYER **(1583–1664)**
COMMENTARY UPON ALL THE PROPHETS

what the Sovereign LORD says: You said "Aha!" about my sanctuary when it was desecrated, about the land of Israel when it was made desolate, and about the house of Judah when they went into exile. [4]So take note, I am about to make you slaves of the tribes of the east. They will make camps among you and pitch their tents among you. They will eat your fruit and drink your milk. [5]I will make Rabbah a pasture for camels and Ammon a resting place for sheep. Then you will know that I am the LORD. [6]For this is what the Sovereign LORD says: Because you clapped your hands, stamped your feet, and rejoiced with intense scorn over the land of Israel, [7]take note—I have stretched out my hand against you, and I will hand you over as plunder to the nations. I will cut you off from the peoples and make you perish from the lands. I will destroy you; then you will know that I am the LORD.'"

A PROPHECY AGAINST MOAB

[8]"This is what the Sovereign LORD says: 'Moab and Seir say, "Look, the house of Judah is like all the other nations." [9]So look, I am about to open up Moab's flank, eliminating the cities, including its frontier cities, the beauty of the land—Beth Jeshimoth, Baal Meon, and Kiriathaim. [10]I will hand it over, along with the Ammonites, to the tribes of the east, so that the Ammonites will no longer be remembered among the nations. [11]I will execute judgments against Moab. Then they will know that I am the LORD.'"

A PROPHECY AGAINST EDOM

[12]"This is what the Sovereign LORD says: 'Edom has taken vengeance against the house of Judah; they have made themselves fully culpable by taking vengeance on them. [13]So this is what the Sovereign LORD says: I will stretch out my hand against Edom, and I will kill the people and animals within her, and I will make her desolate; from Teman to Dedan they will die by the sword. [14]I will exact my vengeance upon Edom by the hand of my people Israel. They will carry out in Edom my anger and rage; they will experience my vengeance, declares the Sovereign LORD.'"

A PROPHECY AGAINST PHILISTIA

[15]"This is what the Sovereign LORD says: 'The Philistines have exacted merciless revenge, showing intense scorn in their effort to destroy Judah with unrelenting hostility. [16]So this is what the Sovereign LORD says: Take note, I am about to stretch out my hand against the Philistines. I will kill the Kerethites and destroy those who remain on the seacoast. [17]I will exact great vengeance upon them with angry rebukes. Then they will know that I am the LORD, when I exact my vengeance upon them.'"

A PROPHECY AGAINST TYRE

26 In the eleventh year, on the first day of the month, the LORD's message came to me: [2]"Son of man, because Tyre has said about Jerusalem, 'Aha, the gateway of the peoples is broken; it has swung open to me. I will become rich, now that she has been destroyed,' [3]therefore this is what the Sovereign LORD says: Look, I am against you, O Tyre! I will bring up many nations against you, as the sea brings up its waves. [4]They will destroy the walls of Tyre and break down her towers. I will scrape her soil from her and make her a bare rock. [5]She

will be a place where fishing nets are spread, surrounded by
the sea. For I have spoken, declares the Sovereign LORD. She
will become plunder for the nations, 6and her daughters who
are in the field will be slaughtered by the sword. Then they will
know that I am the LORD.
7"For this is what the Sovereign LORD says: Take note that
I am about to bring King Nebuchadrezzar of Babylon, king of
kings, against Tyre from the north, with horses, chariots, and
horsemen, an army and hordes of people. 8He will kill your
daughters in the field with the sword. He will build a siege wall
against you, erect a siege ramp against you, and raise a great
shield against you. 9He will direct the blows of his battering
rams against your walls and tear down your towers with his
weapons. 10He will cover you with the dust kicked up by his
many horses. Your walls will shake from the noise of the horsemen, wheels, and chariots when he enters your gates like those
who invade through a city's broken walls. 11With his horses'
hooves he will trample all your streets. He will kill your people
with the sword, and your strong pillars will tumble down to the
ground. 12They will steal your wealth and loot your merchandise. They will tear down your walls and destroy your luxurious
homes. Your stones, your trees, and your soil he will throw into
the water. 13I will silence the noise of your songs; the sound
of your harps will be heard no more. 14I will make you a bare
rock; you will be a place where fishing nets are spread. You will
never be built again, for I, the LORD, have spoken, declares the
Sovereign LORD.
15"This is what the Sovereign LORD says to Tyre: Oh, how
the coastlands will shake at the sound of your fall, when the
wounded groan at the massive slaughter in your midst! 16All the
princes of the sea will vacate their thrones. They will remove
their robes and strip off their embroidered clothes; they will
clothe themselves with trembling. They will sit on the ground;
they will tremble continually and be shocked at what has happened to you. 17They will sing this lament over you:

"'How you have perished—you have vanished from the
seas,
O renowned city, once mighty in the sea,
she and her inhabitants, who spread their terror!
18 Now the coastlands will tremble on the day of your fall;
the coastlands by the sea will be terrified by your
passing.'

19"For this is what the Sovereign LORD says: When I make
you desolate like the uninhabited cities, when I bring up the
deep over you and the surging waters overwhelm you, 20then
I will bring you down to bygone people, to be with those who
descend to the Pit. I will make you live in the lower parts of
the earth among the primeval ruins, with those who descend
to the Pit, so that you will not be inhabited or stand in the
land of the living. 21I will bring terrors on you, and you will be
no more! Though you are sought after, you will never be found
again, declares the Sovereign LORD."

A LAMENT FOR TYRE

27 The LORD's message came to me: 2"You, son of man, sing a
lament for Tyre. 3Say to Tyre, who sits at the entrance of
the sea, merchant to the peoples on many coasts, 'This is what
the Sovereign LORD says:

27:1–36 No situation, strength, or outward advantage can secure proud cities. Tyre was compassed about with great waters judged by all to be impregnable. God's design was to ruin Tyre for its pride, and he found out a way and means to do it. Let cities be built where they will, in the deeps, on rocky mountains—God can bring destruction on them. Tyre was as strong a place as the world had. Tyre was as rich a place as any under heaven. Yet these kept it not from being brought into great waters. What powers or art of humankind can keep off the wind from a ship when it is at sea? It is not in the power of all the seamen or mariners in the world to do it. Neither can any number of people keep off a judgment of God when it is coming on a sinful place.

WILLIAM GREENHILL
(1591–1671)
AN EXPOSITION OF EZEKIEL

"'O Tyre, you have said, "I am perfectly beautiful."
4 Your borders are in the heart of the seas;
your builders have perfected your beauty.
5 They crafted all your planks out of fir trees from Senir;
they took a cedar from Lebanon to make your mast.
6 They made your oars from oaks of Bashan;
they made your deck with cypress wood from the coasts of Cyprus.
7 Fine linen from Egypt, woven with patterns, was used for your sail
to serve as your banner;
blue and purple from the coastlands of Elishah were used for your deck's awning.
8 The leaders of Sidon and Arvad were your rowers;
your skilled men, O Tyre, were your captains.
9 The elders of Gebal and her skilled men were within you, mending cracks;
all the ships of the sea and their mariners were within you to trade for your merchandise.
10 Men of Persia, Lud, and Put were in your army, men of war.
They hung shield and helmet on you; they gave you your splendor.
11 The Arvadites joined your army on your walls all around,
and the Gammadites were in your towers.
They hung their quivers on your walls all around;
they perfected your beauty.

12"'Tarshish was your trade partner because of your abundant wealth; they exchanged silver, iron, tin, and lead for your
products. 13Javan, Tubal, and Meshech were your clients; they
exchanged slaves and bronze items for your merchandise.
14Beth Togarmah exchanged horses, chargers, and mules for
your products. 15The Dedanites were your clients. Many coastlands were your customers; they paid you with ivory tusks and
ebony. 16Edom was your trade partner because of the abundance
of your goods; they exchanged turquoise, purple, embroidered
work, fine linen, coral, and rubies for your products. 17Judah and
the land of Israel were your clients; they traded wheat from
Minnith, millet, honey, olive oil, and balm for your merchandise.
18Damascus was your trade partner because of the abundance
of your goods and of all your wealth: wine from Helbon, white
wool from Zahar, 19and casks of wine from Izal they exchanged
for your products. Wrought iron, cassia, and sweet cane were
among your merchandise. 20Dedan was your client in saddle-
cloths for riding. 21Arabia and all the princes of Kedar were
your trade partners; for lambs, rams, and goats they traded
with you. 22The merchants of Sheba and Raamah engaged in
trade with you; they traded the best kinds of spices along with
precious stones and gold for your products. 23Haran, Kanneh,
Eden, merchants from Sheba, Asshur, and Kilmad were your
clients. 24They traded with you choice garments, purple clothes
and embroidered work, and multicolored carpets bound and re-
inforced with cords; these were among your merchandise. 25The
ships of Tarshish were the transports for your merchandise.

"'So you were filled and weighed down in the heart of the seas.
26 Your rowers have brought you into surging waters.
The east wind has wrecked you in the heart of the seas.

27 Your wealth, products, and merchandise, your sailors
and captains,
your ship's carpenters, your merchants,
and all your fighting men within you,
along with all your crew who are in you,
will fall into the heart of the seas on the day of your
downfall.
28 At the sound of your captains' cries the waves will surge;
29 They will descend from their ships—all who handle the
oar,
the sailors and all the sea captains—they will stand on
the land.
30 They will lament loudly over you and cry bitterly.
They will throw dust on their heads and roll in the
ashes;
31 they will tear out their hair because of you and put on
sackcloth,
and they will weep bitterly over you with intense
mourning.
32 As they wail they will lament over you, chanting:
"Who was like Tyre, like a tower in the midst of the
sea?"
33 When your products went out from the seas,
you satisfied many peoples;
with the abundance of your wealth and merchandise
you enriched the kings of the earth.
34 Now you are wrecked by the seas, in the depths of the
waters;
your merchandise and all your company have sunk
along with you.
35 All the inhabitants of the coastlands are shocked at you,
and their kings are horribly afraid—their faces are
troubled.
36 The traders among the peoples hiss at you;
you have become a horror, and will be no more.'"

A PROPHECY AGAINST THE KING OF TYRE

28 The LORD's message came to me: 2"Son of man, say to the
prince of Tyre, 'This is what the Sovereign LORD says:
"'Your heart is proud and you said, "I am a god;
I sit in the seat of gods, in the heart of the seas"—
yet you are a man and not a god,
though you think you are godlike.
3 Look, you are wiser than Daniel;
no secret is hidden from you.
4 By your wisdom and understanding you have gained
wealth for yourself;
you have amassed gold and silver in your treasuries.
5 By your great skill in trade you have increased your
wealth,
and your heart is proud because of your wealth.

6 "'Therefore this is what the Sovereign LORD says:
Because you think you are godlike,
7 I am about to bring foreigners against you, the most
terrifying of nations.
They will draw their swords against the grandeur made
by your wisdom,
and they will defile your splendor.

28:1–26 Especially all spiritual pride is of the devil. Those who indulge therein must expect to perish. The Sidonites were borderers upon the land of Israel, and they might have learned to glorify the Lord; instead of that, they seduced Israel to the worship of their idols. War and pestilence are God's messengers; but he will be glorified in restoring his people to their former safety and prosperity. God will cure them of their sins and ease them of their troubles. This promise will at length fully come to pass in the heavenly Canaan, when all the saints shall be gathered together, everything that offends shall be removed, all griefs and fears forever banished. Happy then is the church of God, and every living member of it, though poor, afflicted, and despised; for the Lord will display his truth, power, and mercy in the salvation and happiness of his redeemed people.

MATTHEW HENRY **(1662–1714)**
COMMENTARY ON THE WHOLE BIBLE

8 They will bring you down to the Pit, and you will die
violently in the heart of the seas.
9 Will you still say, "I am a god," before the one who kills
you—
though you are a man and not a god—
when you are in the power of those who wound you?
10 You will die the death of the uncircumcised by the hand
of foreigners;
for I have spoken, declares the Sovereign LORD.'"

11 The LORD's message came to me: 12 "Son of man, sing a
lament for the king of Tyre, and say to him, 'This is what the
Sovereign LORD says:
"'You were the sealer of perfection,
full of wisdom, and perfect in beauty.
13 You were in Eden, the garden of God.
Every precious stone was your covering,
the ruby, topaz, and emerald,
the chrysolite, onyx, and jasper,
the sapphire, turquoise, and beryl;
your settings and mounts were made of gold.
On the day you were created they were prepared.
14 I placed you there with an anointed guardian cherub;
you were on the holy mountain of God;
you walked about amidst fiery stones.
15 You were blameless in your behavior from the day you
were created,
until sin was discovered in you.
16 In the abundance of your trade you were filled with
violence, and you sinned;
so I defiled you and banished you from the mountain
of God—
the guardian cherub expelled you from the midst of the
stones of fire.
17 Your heart was proud because of your beauty;
you corrupted your wisdom on account of your
splendor.
I threw you down to the ground;
I placed you before kings, that they might see you.
18 By the multitude of your iniquities, through the
sinfulness of your trade,
you desecrated your sanctuaries.
So I drew fire out from within you;
it consumed you,
and I turned you to ashes on the earth
before the eyes of all who saw you.
19 All who know you among the peoples are shocked at
you;
you have become terrified and will be no more.'"

A PROPHECY AGAINST SIDON

20 The LORD's message came to me: 21 "Son of man, turn toward
Sidon and prophesy against it. 22 Say, 'This is what the Sovereign
LORD says:
"'Look, I am against you, Sidon,
and I will magnify myself in your midst.
Then they will know that I am the LORD
when I execute judgments on her
and reveal my sovereign power in her.

23 I will send a plague into the city and bloodshed into its
streets;
the slain will fall within it, by the sword that attacks it
from every side.
Then they will know that I am the LORD.

24"'No longer will Israel suffer from the sharp briers or painful thorns of all who surround and scorn them. Then they will
know that I am the Sovereign LORD.
25"'This is what the Sovereign LORD says: When I regather
the house of Israel from the peoples where they are dispersed,
I will reveal my sovereign power over them in the sight of the
nations, and they will live in their land that I gave to my servant Jacob. 26They will live securely in it; they will build houses
and plant vineyards. They will live securely when I execute my
judgments on all those who scorn them and surround them.
Then they will know that I am the LORD their God.'"

A PROPHECY AGAINST EGYPT

29 In the tenth year, in the tenth month, on the twelfth day
of the month, the LORD's message came to me: 2"Son of
man, turn toward Pharaoh king of Egypt and prophesy against
him and against all Egypt. 3Tell them, 'This is what the Sovereign LORD says:
"'Look, I am against you, Pharaoh king of Egypt,
the great monster lying in the midst of its waterways,
who has said, "My Nile is my own, I made it for myself."
4 I will put hooks in your jaws
and stick the fish of your waterways to your scales.
I will haul you up from the midst of your waterways,
and all the fish of your waterways will stick to your
scales.
5 I will leave you in the wilderness,
you and all the fish of your waterways;
you will fall in the open field and will not be gathered
up or collected.
I have given you as food to the beasts of the earth and
the birds of the skies.
6 Then all those living in Egypt will know that I am the
LORD
because they were a reed staff for the house of Israel;
7 when they grasped you with their hand, you broke and
tore their shoulders,
and when they leaned on you, you splintered and
caused their legs to be unsteady.

8"'Therefore, this is what the Sovereign LORD says: Look, I am
about to bring a sword against you, and I will kill every person
and every animal. 9The land of Egypt will become a desolate
ruin. Then they will know that I am the LORD.
"'Because he said, "The Nile is mine and I made it," 10I am
against you and your waterways. I will turn the land of Egypt
into an utter desolate ruin from Migdol to Syene, as far as the
border with Ethiopia. 11No human foot will pass through it, and
no animal's foot will pass through it; it will be uninhabited for
40 years. 12I will turn the land of Egypt into a desolation in the
midst of desolate lands; for 40 years her cities will lie desolate
in the midst of ruined cities. I will scatter Egypt among the
nations and disperse them among foreign countries.

29:1–21 It is a dreadful thing to have the Lord declare himself to be an enemy to a king, to a state, to any. "Look, I am against you, Pharaoh king of Egypt." Therefore the king would be more and more disabled. His princes became fools, his wise counselors brutish, a perverse and seducing spirit was in the midst of them. God being against Pharaoh, all his counselors and enterprises were blasted, all his forces broken, all his cities made desolate, and all his people consumed or carried into captivity. After days of mirth come days of sorrow. Egypt had seen many days of prosperity and rejoicing and now its summer was over, and winter coming on it and black, cloudy, stormy, terrible days were at hand. Mirth and jollity are thrust out the door after a few days by their contrary. Babylon had its days of delight. It was given to pleasure, but suddenly there was a change.

WILLIAM GREENHILL
(1591–1671)
AN EXPOSITION OF EZEKIEL

13"'For this is what the Sovereign LORD says: At the end of
40 years I will gather Egypt from the peoples where they were
scattered. 14I will restore the fortunes of Egypt and will bring
them back to the land of Pathros, to the land of their origin;
there they will be an insignificant kingdom. 15It will be the
most insignificant of the kingdoms; it will never again exalt
itself over the nations. I will make them so small that they
will not rule over the nations. 16It will never again be Israel's
source of confidence, but a reminder of how they sinned by
turning to Egypt for help. Then they will know that I am the
Sovereign LORD.'"

17In the twenty-seventh year, in the first month, on the first
day of the month, the LORD's message came to me: 18"Son of
man, King Nebuchadrezzar of Babylon made his army labor
hard against Tyre. Every head was rubbed bald and every shoulder rubbed bare; yet he and his army received no wages from
Tyre for the work he carried out against it. 19Therefore this is
what the Sovereign LORD says: Look, I am about to give the land
of Egypt to King Nebuchadrezzar of Babylon. He will carry off
her wealth, capture her loot, and seize her plunder; it will be
his army's wages. 20I have given him the land of Egypt as his
compensation for attacking Tyre, because they did it for me,
declares the Sovereign LORD. 21On that day I will make Israel
powerful, and I will give you the right to be heard among them.
Then they will know that I am the LORD."

A LAMENT OVER EGYPT

30 The LORD's message came to me: 2"Son of man, prophesy
and say, 'This is what the Sovereign LORD says:

"'Wail, "Alas, the day is here!"
3 For the day is near,
the day of the LORD is near;
it will be a day of storm clouds,
it will be a time of judgment for the nations.
4 A sword will come against Egypt
and panic will overtake Ethiopia
when the slain fall in Egypt
and they carry away her wealth
and dismantle her foundations.

5Ethiopia, Put, Lud, all the foreigners, Libya, and the people
of the covenant land will die by the sword along with them.

6 "'This is what the LORD says:
Egypt's supporters will fall;
her confident pride will crumble.
From Migdol to Syene they will die by the sword
within her,
declares the Sovereign LORD.
7 They will be desolate among desolate lands,
and their cities will be among ruined cities.
8 They will know that I am the LORD
when I ignite a fire in Egypt
and all her allies are defeated.

9"'On that day messengers will go out from me in
ships to frighten overconfident Ethiopia; panic will overtake them on the day of Egypt's doom; for beware—it is
coming!

30:9 Those rulers whom God had set over humankind, having become rebellious and tyrannical, took in hand to assail their people and to rout them utterly, as the prophet Ezekiel mystically intimates when he says, "On that day messengers will go out from me in ships to frighten overconfident Ethiopia; panic will overtake them on the day of Egypt's doom; for beware—it is coming!" Having stripped them then of their almighty power, Christ is said to have triumphed and to have delivered to people the power that was taken from them, as also he said to his disciples in the Gospel, "Look, I have given you authority to tread on snakes and scorpions and on the full force of the enemy, and nothing will hurt you" (Luke 10:19). The cross of Christ then brought those who had wrongfully abused the authority that they had received into subjection to those who had before been in subjection to them.

JEROME **(C. 342–420)**
A COMMENTARY ON THE APOSTLES' CREED

10 "'This is what the Sovereign LORD says:
I will put an end to the hordes of Egypt,
by the hand of King Nebuchadrezzar of Babylon.
11 He and his people with him,
the most terrifying of the nations,
will be brought there to destroy the land.
They will draw their swords against Egypt
and fill the land with corpses.
12 I will dry up the waterways
and hand the land over to evil men.
I will make the land and everything in it desolate by the hand of foreigners.
I, the LORD, have spoken!
13 "'This is what the Sovereign LORD says:
I will destroy the idols,
and put an end to the gods of Memphis.
There will no longer be a prince from the land of Egypt;
so I will make the land of Egypt fearful.
14 I will desolate Pathros,
I will ignite a fire in Zoan,
and I will execute judgments on Thebes.
15 I will pour out my anger upon Pelusium,
the stronghold of Egypt;
I will cut off the hordes of Thebes.
16 I will ignite a fire in Egypt;
Syene will writhe in agony,
Thebes will be broken down,
and Memphis will face enemies every day.
17 The young men of On and of Pi Beseth will die by the sword;
and the cities will go into captivity.
18 In Tahpanhes the day will be dark
when I break the yoke of Egypt there.
Her confident pride will cease within her;
a cloud will cover her, and her daughters will go into captivity.
19 I will execute judgments on Egypt.
Then they will know that I am the LORD.'"

20 In the eleventh year, in the first month, on the seventh day
of the month, the LORD's message came to me: 21 "Son of man,
I have broken the arm of Pharaoh king of Egypt. Look, it has
not been bandaged for healing or set with a dressing so that it
might become strong enough to grasp a sword. 22 Therefore this
is what the Sovereign LORD says: Look, I am against Pharaoh
king of Egypt, and I will break his arms, the strong arm and
the broken one, and I will make the sword drop from his hand.
23 I will scatter the Egyptians among the nations and disperse
them among foreign countries. 24 I will strengthen the arms
of the king of Babylon, and I will place my sword in his hand,
but I will break the arms of Pharaoh, and he will groan like the
fatally wounded before the king of Babylon. 25 I will strengthen
the arms of the king of Babylon, but the arms of Pharaoh will
fall limp. Then they will know that I am the LORD when I place
my sword in the hand of the king of Babylon and he extends it
against the land of Egypt. 26 I will scatter the Egyptians among
the nations and disperse them among foreign countries. Then
they will know that I am the LORD."

31:1–18 The same argument of threatening Pharaoh and his land with destruction is here further prosecuted at another time the same year. This time, however, by the example of the king of Assyria, his greatness and fall are set forth. For his pride he was as a most high cedar cut down, and so he shows Pharaoh should not be spared. If he would not be moved by anything yet spoken by way of a formal denunciation, he might by the example of his peer, who was yet superior to him in dominion by far, be moved, humble himself, and repent.

JOHN MAYER **(1583–1664)**
COMMENTARY UPON ALL THE PROPHETS

A CEDAR IN LEBANON

31 In the eleventh year, in the third month, on the first day
of the month, the LORD's message came to me: 2"Son of
man, say to Pharaoh king of Egypt and his hordes:

"'Who are you like in your greatness?
3 Consider Assyria, a cedar in Lebanon,
with beautiful branches, like a forest giving shade,
and extremely tall;
its top reached into the clouds.
4 The water made it grow;
underground springs made it grow tall.
Rivers flowed all around the place it was planted,
while smaller channels watered all the trees of the field.
5 Therefore it grew taller than all the trees of the field;
its boughs grew large and its branches grew long,
because of the plentiful water in its shoots.
6 All the birds of the sky nested in its boughs;
under its branches all the beasts of the field gave birth;
in its shade all the great nations lived.
7 It was beautiful in its loftiness, in the length of its branches;
for its roots went down deep to plentiful waters.
8 The cedars in the garden of God could not eclipse it,
nor could the fir trees match its boughs;
the plane trees were as nothing compared to its branches;
no tree in the garden of God could rival its beauty.
9 I made it beautiful with its many branches;
all the trees of Eden, in the garden of God, envied it.

10"'Therefore this is what the Sovereign LORD says: Because it
was tall in stature, and its top reached into the clouds, and it was
proud of its height, 11I gave it over to the leader of the nations.
He has judged it thoroughly, as its sinfulness deserves. I have
thrown it out. 12Foreigners from the most terrifying nations
have cut it down and left it to lie there on the mountains. In all
the valleys its branches have fallen, and its boughs lie broken in
the ravines of the land. All the peoples of the land have departed from its shade and left it. 13On its ruins all the birds of the
sky will live, and all the wild animals will walk on its branches.
14For this reason no watered trees will grow so tall; their tops
will not reach into the clouds, nor will the well-watered ones
grow that high. For all of them have been appointed to die in
the lower parts of the earth; they will be among mere mortals,
with those who descend to the Pit.

15"'This is what the Sovereign LORD says: On the day it went
down to Sheol I caused observers to lament. I covered it with the
deep and held back its rivers; its plentiful water was restrained.
I clothed Lebanon in black for it, and all the trees of the field
wilted because of it. 16I made the nations shake at the sound
of its fall, when I threw it down to Sheol, along with those who
descend to the Pit. Then all the trees of Eden, the choicest and
the best of Lebanon, all that were well-watered, were comforted
in the earth below. 17Those who lived in its shade, its allies among
the nations, also went down with it to Sheol, to those killed by
the sword. 18Which of the trees of Eden was like you in majesty
and loftiness? You will be brought down with the trees of Eden
to the lower parts of the earth; you will lie among the uncircumcised, with those killed by the sword! This is what will happen
to Pharaoh and all his hordes, declares the Sovereign LORD.'"

LAMENTATION OVER PHARAOH AND EGYPT

32 In the twelfth year, in the twelfth month, on the first
of the month, the LORD's message came to me: 2"Son of
man, sing a lament for Pharaoh king of Egypt, and say to him:
"'You were like a lion among the nations,
but you are a monster in the seas;
you thrash about in your streams,
stir up the water with your feet,
and muddy your streams.

3"'This is what the Sovereign LORD says:
"'I will throw my net over you in the assembly of many peoples;
and they will haul you up in my dragnet.
4 I will leave you on the ground,
I will fling you on the open field,
I will allow all the birds of the sky to settle on you,
and I will permit all the wild animals to gorge themselves on you.
5 I will put your flesh on the mountains,
and fill the valleys with your maggot-infested carcass.
6 I will drench the land with the flow
of your blood up to the mountains,
and the ravines will be full of your blood.
7 When I extinguish you, I will cover the sky;
I will darken its stars.
I will cover the sun with a cloud,
and the moon will not shine.
8 I will darken all the lights in the sky over you,
and I will darken your land,
declares the Sovereign LORD.
9 I will disturb many peoples
when I bring about your destruction among the nations,
among countries you do not know.
10 I will shock many peoples with you,
and their kings will shiver with horror because of you.
When I brandish my sword before them,
every moment each one will tremble for his life, on the day of your fall.

11"'For this is what the Sovereign LORD says:
"'The sword of the king of Babylon will attack you.
12 By the swords of the mighty warriors I will cause your hordes to fall—
all of them are the most terrifying among the nations.
They will devastate the pride of Egypt,
and all its hordes will be destroyed.
13 I will destroy all its cattle beside the plentiful waters;
and no human foot will disturb the waters again,
nor will the hooves of cattle disturb them.
14 Then I will make their waters calm
and will make their streams flow like olive oil, declares the Sovereign LORD.
15 When I turn the land of Egypt into desolation
and the land is destitute of everything that fills it,
when I strike all those who live in it,
then they will know that I am the LORD.'

32:1–32 The waters of Egypt shall run like olive oil, which signifies there should be universal sadness and heaviness upon the whole nation. God can soon empty those of this world's goods who have the greatest fullness of them. How weak and helpless, compared to God, are the most powerful of humankind! The destruction of Egypt was a type of the destruction of the enemies of Christ; here is plain allusion to the everlasting ruin of impenitent sinners. How are people deceived by Satan! Surely people disquiet themselves in vain whether they pursue wealth, fame, power, or pleasure. The hour comes when all who are in their graves shall hear the voice of Christ and shall come forth; those who have done good to the resurrection of life, and those who have done evil to the resurrection of damnation.

MATTHEW HENRY **(1662–1714)**
COMMENTARY ON THE WHOLE BIBLE

16 This is a lament; they will chant it.
The daughters of the nations will chant it.
They will chant it over Egypt and over all her hordes,
declares the Sovereign LORD."

17 In the twelfth year, on the fifteenth day of the month, the
LORD's message came to me: 18 "Son of man, wail over the horde
of Egypt. Bring it down; bring her and the daughters of powerful
nations down to the lower parts of the earth, along with those
who descend to the Pit. 19 Say to them, 'Whom do you surpass
in beauty? Go down and be laid to rest with the uncircumcised!'
20 They will fall among those killed by the sword. The sword is
drawn; they carry her and all her hordes away. 21 The bravest of
the warriors will speak to him from the midst of Sheol along
with his allies, saying: 'The uncircumcised have come down;
they lie still, killed by the sword.'

22 "Assyria is there with all her assembly around her grave, all
of them struck down by the sword. 23 Their graves are located in
the remote slopes of the Pit. Her assembly is around her grave,
all of them struck down by the sword, those who spread terror
in the land of the living.

24 "Elam is there with all her hordes around her grave; all of
them struck down by the sword. They went down uncircumcised
to the lower parts of the earth, those who spread terror in the
land of the living. Now they will bear their shame with those who
descend to the Pit. 25 Among the dead they have made a bed for
her, along with all her hordes around her grave. All of them are
uncircumcised, killed by the sword, for their terror had spread
in the land of the living. They bear their shame along with those
who descend to the Pit; they are placed among the dead.

26 "Meshech Tubal is there, along with all her hordes around
her grave. All of them are uncircumcised, killed by the sword,
for they spread their terror in the land of the living. 27 They do
not lie with the fallen warriors of ancient times, who went down
to Sheol with their weapons of war, having their swords placed
under their heads and their shields on their bones, when the
terror of these warriors was in the land of the living.

28 "But as for you, in the midst of the uncircumcised you will
be broken, and you will lie with those killed by the sword.

29 "Edom is there with her kings and all her princes. Despite
their might they are laid with those killed by the sword; they
lie with the uncircumcised and those who descend to the Pit.

30 "All the leaders of the north are there, along with all the
Sidonians; despite their might they have gone down in shameful terror with the dead. They lie uncircumcised with those
killed by the sword and bear their shame with those who descend to the Pit.

31 "Pharaoh will see them and be consoled over all his hordes
who were killed by the sword, Pharaoh and all his army, declares
the Sovereign LORD. 32 Indeed, I terrified him in the land of the
living, yet he will lie in the midst of the uncircumcised with
those killed by the sword, Pharaoh and all his hordes, declares
the Sovereign LORD."

EZEKIEL ISRAEL'S WATCHMAN

33 The LORD's message came to me: 2 "Son of man, speak to
your people, and say to them, 'Suppose I bring a sword
against the land, and the people of the land take one man from
their borders and make him their watchman. 3 He sees the sword

coming against the land, blows the trumpet, and warns the people, [4]but there is one who hears the sound of the trumpet yet
does not heed the warning. Then the sword comes and sweeps
him away. He will be responsible for his own death. [5]He heard
the sound of the trumpet but did not heed the warning, so he
is responsible for himself. If he had heeded the warning, he
would have saved his life. [6]But suppose the watchman sees
the sword coming and does not blow the trumpet to warn the
people. Then the sword comes and takes one of their lives. He
is swept away for his iniquity, but I will hold the watchman
accountable for that person's death.'

[7]"As for you, son of man, I have made you a watchman for
the house of Israel. Whenever you hear a word from my mouth,
you must warn them on my behalf. [8]When I say to the wicked,
'O wicked man, you must certainly die,' and you do not warn
the wicked about his behavior, the wicked man will die for his
iniquity, but I will hold you accountable for his death. [9]But if
you warn the wicked man to change his behavior, and he refuses to change, he will die for his iniquity, but you have saved
your own life.

[10]"And you, son of man, say to the house of Israel, 'This is what
you have said: "Our rebellious acts and our sins have caught up
with us, and we are wasting away because of them. How then
can we live?"' [11]Say to them, 'As surely as I live, declares the
Sovereign LORD, I take no pleasure in the death of the wicked, but prefer that the wicked change his behavior and live.
Turn back, turn back from your evil deeds! Why should you
die, O house of Israel?'

[12]"And you, son of man, say to your people, 'The righteousness
of the righteous will not deliver him if he rebels. As for the wicked, his wickedness will not make him stumble if he turns from
it. The righteous will not be able to live by his righteousness if
he sins.' [13]Suppose I tell the righteous that he will certainly live,
but he becomes confident in his righteousness and commits
iniquity. None of his righteous deeds will be remembered; because of the iniquity he has committed he will die. [14]Suppose
I say to the wicked, 'You must certainly die,' but he turns from
his sin and does what is just and right. [15]He returns what was
taken in pledge, pays back what he has stolen, and follows the
statutes that give life, committing no iniquity. He will certainly
live—he will not die. [16]None of the sins he has committed will
be counted against him. He has done what is just and right; he
will certainly live.

[17]"Yet your people say, 'The behavior of the Lord is not right,'
when it is their behavior that is not right. [18]When a righteous
man turns from his godliness and commits iniquity, he will
die for it. [19]When the wicked turns from his sin and does what
is just and right, he will live because of it. [20]Yet you say, 'The
behavior of the Lord is not right.' House of Israel, I will judge
each of you according to his behavior."

THE FALL OF JERUSALEM

[21]In the twelfth year of our exile, in the tenth month, on the
fifth of the month, a refugee came to me from Jerusalem saying,
"The city has been defeated!" [22]Now the hand of the LORD had
been on me the evening before the refugee reached me, but
the LORD opened my mouth by the time the refugee arrived
in the morning; he opened my mouth and I was able to speak
once more. [23]The LORD's message came to me: [24]"Son of man,

33:12–20 Nature itself teaches us all to lay the blame of evil works on the doers; and therefore when we see any heinous thing done, a principle of justice does provoke us to inquire after him who did it that the evil of the work may return the evil of the shame on the author. It is indeed confessed by all that Satan is the cause, but he does not force people to sin but tempts them to it and leaves it to their own wills. It lies, therefore, between God and the sinner: One of them must be the principal cause of all this misery, for there is no other to cast it on. And God disclaims it. He will not take it on him. And the wicked disclaim it usually, and they will not take it on them. This is the controversy that is here managed in this text.

RICHARD BAXTER **(1615–1691)**
COMMENTARY ON THE PROPHET EZEKIEL

the ones living in these ruins in the land of Israel are saying, 'Abraham was only one man, yet he possessed the land, but we are many; surely the land has been given to us for a possession.' 25 Therefore say to them, 'This is what the Sovereign LORD says: You eat the meat with the blood still in it, pray to your idols, and shed blood. Do you really think you will possess the land? 26 You rely on your swords and commit abominable deeds; each of you defiles his neighbor's wife. Will you possess the land?'

27 "This is what you must say to them, 'This is what the Sovereign LORD says: As surely as I live, those living in the ruins will die by the sword, those in the open field I will give to the wild beasts for food, and those who are in the strongholds and caves will die of disease. 28 I will turn the land into a desolate ruin; her confident pride will come to an end. The mountains of Israel will be so desolate no one will pass through them. 29 Then they will know that I am the LORD when I turn the land into a desolate ruin because of all the abominable deeds they have committed.'

30 "But as for you, son of man, your people (who are talking about you by the walls and at the doors of the houses) say to one another, 'Come hear the word that comes from the LORD.' 31 They come to you in crowds, and they sit in front of you as my people. They hear your words, but do not obey them. For they talk lustfully, and their heart is set on their own advantage. 32 Realize that to them you are like a sensual song, a beautiful voice, and skilled musician. They hear your words, but they do not obey them. 33 When all this comes true—and it certainly will—then they will know that a prophet was among them."

A PROPHECY AGAINST FALSE SHEPHERDS

34 The LORD's message came to me: 2 "Son of man, prophesy against the shepherds of Israel; prophesy, and say to them—to the shepherds: 'This is what the Sovereign LORD says: Woe to the shepherds of Israel who have been feeding themselves! Should not shepherds feed the flock? 3 You eat the fat, you clothe yourselves with the wool, you slaughter the choice animals, but you do not feed the sheep! 4 You have not strengthened the weak, healed the sick, bandaged the injured, brought back the strays, or sought the lost, but with force and harshness you have ruled over them. 5 They were scattered because they had no shepherd, and they became food for every wild beast. 6 My sheep wandered over all the mountains and on every high hill. My sheep were scattered over the entire face of the earth with no one looking or searching for them.

7 "'Therefore, you shepherds, listen to the LORD's message: 8 As surely as I live, declares the Sovereign LORD, my sheep have become prey and have become food for all the wild beasts. There was no shepherd, and my shepherds did not search for my flock, but fed themselves and did not feed my sheep. 9 Therefore, you shepherds, listen to the LORD's message. 10 This is what the Sovereign LORD says: Look, I am against the shepherds, and I will demand my sheep from their hand. I will no longer let them be shepherds; the shepherds will not feed themselves anymore. I will rescue my sheep from their mouths, so that they will no longer be food for them.

11 "'For this is what the Sovereign LORD says: Look, I myself will search for my sheep and seek them out. 12 As a shepherd seeks out his flock when he is among his scattered sheep, so I will seek out my flock. I will rescue them from all the places

34:4 Do you see a shepherd's vigilance? Do you see his heightened interest? What excuse could they have to whom rational flocks are entrusted but who are guilty of great negligence and day after day, in the prophet's words, slaughter some of them and look on without intending to take any care of others made the prey of wild beasts or the spoils of other people—even when the labor involved is slight and attention easy? It is a soul, after all, that is to be instructed, but that involves much labor for body and soul.

CHRYSOSTOM **(C. 347–407)**
HOMILIES ON GENESIS

where they have been scattered on a cloudy, dark day. 13 I will
bring them out from among the peoples and gather them from
foreign countries; I will bring them to their own land. I will feed
them on the mountains of Israel, by the streams and all the inhabited places of the land. 14 In a good pasture I will feed them;
the mountain heights of Israel will be their pasture. There they
will lie down in a lush pasture, and they will feed on rich grass
on the mountains of Israel. 15 I myself will feed my sheep and I
myself will make them lie down, declares the Sovereign LORD.
16 I will seek the lost and bring back the strays; I will bandage
the injured and strengthen the sick, but the fat and the strong
I will destroy. I will feed them—with judgment!
17 "'As for you, my sheep, this is what the Sovereign LORD
says: Look, I am about to judge between one sheep and another,
between rams and goats. 18 Is it not enough for you to feed on the
good pasture that you must trample the rest of your pastures
with your feet? When you drink clean water, must you muddy
the rest of the water by trampling it with your feet? 19 As for
my sheep, they must eat what you trampled with your feet and
drink what you have muddied with your feet!
20 "'Therefore, this is what the Sovereign LORD says to them:
Look, I myself will judge between the fat sheep and the lean
sheep. 21 Because you push with your side and your shoulder,
and thrust your horns at all the weak sheep until you scatter
them abroad, 22 I will save my sheep; they will no longer be prey.
I will judge between one sheep and another.
23 "'I will set one shepherd over them, and he will feed them—
namely, my servant David. He will feed them and will be their
shepherd. 24 I, the LORD, will be their God, and my servant David
will be prince among them; I, the LORD, have spoken!
25 "'I will make a covenant of peace with them and will rid the
land of wild beasts, so that they can live securely in the wilderness and even sleep in the woods. 26 I will turn them and the
regions around my hill into a blessing. I will make showers come
down in their season; they will be showers that bring blessing.
27 The trees of the field will yield their fruit and the earth will
yield its crops. They will live securely on their land; they will
know that I am the LORD, when I break the bars of their yoke
and rescue them from the hand of those who enslaved them.
28 They will no longer be prey for the nations, and the wild beasts
will not devour them. They will live securely, and no one will
make them afraid. 29 I will prepare for them a healthy planting.
They will no longer be victims of famine in the land and will no
longer bear the insults of the nations. 30 Then they will know
that I, the LORD their God, am with them and that they are my
people, the house of Israel, declares the Sovereign LORD. 31 And
you, my sheep, the sheep of my pasture, are my people, and I
am your God, declares the Sovereign LORD.'"

PROPHECY AGAINST MOUNT SEIR

35 The LORD's message came to me: 2 "Son of man, turn toward Mount Seir and prophesy against it. 3 Say to it, 'This
is what the Sovereign LORD says:

"'Look, I am against you, Mount Seir;
I will stretch out my hand against you
and turn you into a desolate ruin.
4 I will lay waste your cities,
and you will become desolate.
Then you will know that I am the LORD!

35:1–15 Edom's princes saw the whole country left desolate and counted upon its easy conquest, but there was one great difficulty in their way—"the LORD was there"—and in his presence lay the special security of the chosen land. Whatever may be the machinations and devices of the enemies of God's people, the saints are God's heritage, and he is in the midst of them and will protect his own. What comfort this assurance yields us in our troubles and spiritual conflicts! We are constantly opposed and yet perpetually preserved! The only reason that anything virtuous or lovely survives in us is this: The Lord is there. Beloved, from the first of a Christian's life to the last, the only reason that he does not perish is because the Lord is there.

CHARLES SPURGEON
(1834–1892)
MORNING AND EVENING

5“‘You have shown unrelenting hostility and poured the
people of Israel onto the blades of a sword at the time of their
calamity, at the time of their final punishment. 6Therefore, as
surely as I live, declares the Sovereign LORD, I will subject you
to bloodshed, and bloodshed will pursue you. Since you did not
hate bloodshed, bloodshed will pursue you. 7I will turn Mount
Seir into a desolate ruin; I will cut off from it the one who passes through or returns. 8I will fill its mountains with its dead;
on your hills and in your valleys and in all your ravines, those
killed by the sword will fall. 9I will turn you into a perpetual
desolation, and your cities will not be inhabited. Then you will
know that I am the LORD.

10“‘You said, “These two nations, these two lands will be mine,
and we will possess them,” (although the LORD was there);
11therefore, as surely as I live, declares the Sovereign LORD, I
will deal with you according to your anger and your envy, by
which you acted spitefully against them. I will reveal myself to
them when I judge you. 12Then you will know that I, the LORD,
have heard all the insults you spoke against the mountains of
Israel, saying, “They are desolate; they have been given to us for
food.” 13You exalted yourselves against me with your speech
and hurled many insults against me—I have heard them all!
14This is what the Sovereign LORD says: While the whole earth
rejoices, I will turn you into a desolation. 15As you rejoiced over
the inheritance of the house of Israel because it was desolate,
so will I deal with you—you will be desolate, Mount Seir, and
all Edom—all of it! Then they will know that I am the LORD.’”

BLESSINGS ON THE MOUNTAINS OF ISRAEL

36 “As for you, son of man, prophesy to the mountains of
Israel, and say: ‘O mountains of Israel, listen to the LORD’s
message! 2This is what the Sovereign LORD says: The enemy
has spoken against you, saying “Aha!” and, “The ancient heights
have become our property!”’ 3So prophesy and say: ‘This is what
the Sovereign LORD says: Surely because they have made you
desolate and crushed you from all directions, so that you have
become the property of the rest of the nations, and have become
the subject of gossip and slander among the people, 4therefore,
O mountains of Israel, hear the word of the Sovereign LORD.
This is what the Sovereign LORD says to the mountains and
hills, the ravines and valleys, and to the desolate ruins and the
abandoned cities that have become prey and an object of derision to the rest of the nations round about; 5therefore, this
is what the Sovereign LORD says: Surely I have spoken in the
fire of my zeal against the rest of the nations and against all
Edom, who with great joy and utter contempt have made my
land their property and prey, because of its pasture.’

6“Therefore prophesy concerning the land of Israel, and say
to the mountains and hills, the ravines and valleys, ‘This is what
the Sovereign LORD says: Look, I have spoken in my zeal and in
my anger because you have endured the insults of the nations.
7So this is what the Sovereign LORD says: I vow that the nations
around you will endure insults as well.

8“‘But you, mountains of Israel, will grow your branches and
bear your fruit for my people Israel, for they will arrive soon.
9For indeed, I am on your side; I will turn to you, and you will
be plowed and planted. 10I will multiply your people—the whole
house of Israel, all of it. The cities will be populated and the
ruins rebuilt. 11I will increase the number of people and animals

on you; they will increase and be fruitful. I will cause you to be inhabited as in ancient times and will do more good for you than at the beginning of your history. Then you will know that I am the LORD. 12I will lead people, my people Israel, across you; they will possess you, and you will become their inheritance. No longer will you bereave them of their children.

13"'This is what the Sovereign LORD says: Because they are saying to you, "You are a devourer of men and bereave your nation of children," 14therefore you will no longer devour people and no longer bereave your nation of children, declares the Sovereign LORD. 15I will no longer subject you to the nations' insults; no longer will you bear the shame of the peoples, and no longer will you bereave your nation, declares the Sovereign LORD.'"

16The LORD's message came to me: 17"Son of man, when the house of Israel was living on their own land, they defiled it by their behavior and their deeds. In my sight their behavior was like the uncleanness of a woman having her monthly period. 18So I poured my anger on them because of the blood they shed on the land and because of the idols with which they defiled it. 19I scattered them among the nations; they were dispersed throughout foreign countries. In accordance with their behavior and their deeds I judged them. 20But when they arrived in the nations where they went, they profaned my holy name. It was said of them, 'These are the people of the LORD, yet they have departed from his land.' 21I was concerned for my holy reputation, which the house of Israel profaned among the nations where they went.

22"Therefore say to the house of Israel, 'This is what the Sovereign LORD says: It is not for your sake that I am about to act, O house of Israel, but for the sake of my holy reputation, which you profaned among the nations where you went. 23I will magnify my great name that has been profaned among the nations, which you have profaned among them. The nations will know that I am the LORD, declares the Sovereign LORD, when I magnify myself among you in their sight.

24"'I will take you from the nations and gather you from all the countries; then I will bring you to your land. 25I will sprinkle you with pure water, and you will be clean from all your impurities. I will purify you from all your idols. 26I will give you a new heart, and I will put a new spirit within you. I will remove the heart of stone from your body and give you a heart of flesh. 27I will put my Spirit within you; I will take the initiative, and you will obey my statutes and carefully observe my regulations. 28Then you will live in the land I gave to your fathers; you will be my people, and I will be your God. 29I will save you from all your uncleanness. I will call for the grain and multiply it; I will not bring a famine on you. 30I will multiply the fruit of the trees and the produce of the fields, so that you will never again suffer the disgrace of famine among the nations. 31Then you will remember your evil behavior and your deeds that were not good; you will loathe yourselves on account of your sins and your abominable deeds. 32Understand that it is not for your sake I am about to act, declares the Sovereign LORD. Be ashamed and embarrassed by your behavior, O house of Israel.

33"'This is what the Sovereign LORD says: In the day I cleanse you from all your sins, I will populate the cities, and the ruins will be rebuilt. 34The desolate land will be plowed, instead of being desolate in the sight of everyone who passes by. 35They

36:16–38 When God has a purpose to show mercy, he never wants a reason in himself, though there can be none found in us why he should. The deliverances he works for his people are on the account of the covenant. What does this point to? Ezekiel tells you: "I will take you from the nations and gather you from all the countries; then I will bring you to your land." Deliverance and repentance came together. They were so far from repenting of sin in their captivity that they continued in their wickedness to the great reproach of God among the heathens. They had no expectation of deliverance, and where there is no faith there can be no fitness for it. Therefore when God does deliver them, he tells them it was not for their sakes; as if he had said, *I do it not because of your worthiness for it, but for the glory of my own name.*

MATTHEW MEADE
(C. 1630–1699)
EZEKIEL

will say, "This desolate land has become like the garden of Eden; the ruined, desolate, and destroyed cities are now fortified and inhabited." 36Then the nations that remain around you will know that I, the LORD, have rebuilt the ruins and replanted what was desolate. I, the LORD, have spoken—and I will do it!'

37"This is what the Sovereign LORD says: I will allow the house of Israel to ask me to do this for them: I will multiply their people like sheep. 38Like the sheep for offerings, like the sheep of Jerusalem during her appointed feasts, so the ruined cities will be filled with flocks of people. Then they will know that I am the LORD."

THE VALLEY OF DRY BONES

37 The hand of the LORD was on me, and he brought me out by the Spirit of the LORD and placed me in the midst of the valley, and it was full of bones. 2He made me walk all around among them. I realized there were a great many bones in the valley, and they were very dry. 3He said to me, "Son of man, can these bones live?" I said to him, "Sovereign LORD, you know." 4Then he said to me, "Prophesy over these bones, and tell them: 'Dry bones, listen to the LORD's message. 5This is what the Sovereign LORD says to these bones: Look, I am about to infuse breath into you and you will live. 6I will put tendons on you and muscles over you and will cover you with skin; I will put breath in you, and you will live. Then you will know that I am the LORD.'"

7So I prophesied as I was commanded. There was a sound when I prophesied—I heard a rattling, and the bones came together, bone to bone. 8As I watched, I saw tendons on them, then muscles appeared, and skin covered over them from above, but there was no breath in them.

9He said to me, "Prophesy to the breath—prophesy, son of man—and say to the breath: 'This is what the Sovereign LORD says: Come from the four winds, O breath, and breathe on these corpses so that they may live.'" 10So I prophesied as I was commanded, and the breath came into them; they lived and stood on their feet, an extremely great army.

11Then he said to me, "Son of man, these bones are all the house of Israel. Look, they are saying, 'Our bones are dry, our hope has perished; we are cut off.' 12Therefore prophesy, and tell them, 'This is what the Sovereign LORD says: Look, I am about to open your graves and will raise you from your graves, my people. I will bring you to the land of Israel. 13Then you will know that I am the LORD, when I open your graves and raise you from your graves, my people. 14I will place my breath in you and you will live; I will give you rest in your own land. Then you will know that I am the LORD—I have spoken and I will act, declares the LORD.'"

15The LORD's message came to me: 16"As for you, son of man, take one branch and write on it, 'For Judah and for the Israelites associated with him.' Then take another branch and write on it, 'For Joseph, the branch of Ephraim, and all the house of Israel associated with him.' 17Join them as one stick; they will be as one in your hand. 18When your people say to you, 'Will you not tell us what these things mean?' 19tell them, 'This is what the Sovereign LORD says: Look, I am about to take the branch of Joseph that is in the hand of Ephraim and the tribes of Israel associated with him, and I will place them on the stick of Judah and make them into one stick—they will be one in my hand.'

37:1–14 In the resurrection people shall have their own bodies and souls again. This vision of the dry bones is held to be a lively representation of the resurrection. And see there, the bones came together, the same bones that were united before were united again in this resurrection; and the sinews, the flesh, the skin that belong to them formerly, the same came and covered them again; so the same souls, the same breath, came and entered them, and they lived. The prophet calls for the soul of everybody here to come from the "four winds," that is, from those parts where they were. Had they been in the bones or dust of the earth or vanished into nothing, the Lord would not have directed the prophet to have called for them from all parts of the world.

WILLIAM GREENHILL
(1591–1671)
AN EXPOSITION OF EZEKIEL

20The sticks you write on will be in your hand in front of them.
21Then tell them, 'This is what the Sovereign LORD says: Look, I
am about to take the Israelites from among the nations where
they have gone. I will gather them from round about and bring
them to their land. 22I will make them one nation in the land,
on the mountains of Israel, and one king will rule over them
all. They will never again be two nations and never again be
divided into two kingdoms. 23They will not defile themselves
with their idols, their detestable things, and all their rebellious
deeds. I will save them from all their unfaithfulness by which
they sinned. I will purify them; they will become my people,
and I will become their God.
24"'My servant David will be king over them; there will be
one shepherd for all of them. They will follow my regulations
and carefully observe my statutes. 25They will live in the land
I gave to my servant Jacob, in which your fathers lived; they
will live in it—they and their children and their grandchildren
forever. David my servant will be prince over them forever. 26I
will make a covenant of peace with them; it will be a perpetual covenant with them. I will establish them, increase their
numbers, and place my sanctuary among them forever. 27My
dwelling place will be with them; I will be their God, and they
will be my people. 28Then, when my sanctuary is among them
forever, the nations will know that I, the LORD, sanctify Israel.'"

A PROPHECY AGAINST GOG

38 The LORD's message came to me: 2"Son of man, turn
toward Gog, of the land of Magog, the chief prince of
Meshech and Tubal. Prophesy against him 3and say: 'This is
what the Sovereign LORD says: Look, I am against you, Gog,
chief prince of Meshech and Tubal. 4I will turn you around,
put hooks into your jaws, and bring you out with all your army,
horses, and horsemen, all of them fully armed, a great company
with shields of different types, all of them armed with swords.
5Persia, Ethiopia, and Put are with them, all of them with shields
and helmets. 6They are joined by Gomer with all its troops and
by Beth Togarmah from the remote parts of the north with all
its troops—many peoples are with you.
7"'Be ready and stay ready, you and all your companies assembled around you, and be a guard for them. 8After many
days you will be summoned; in the latter years you will come
to a land restored from the ravages of war, from many peoples
gathered on the mountains of Israel that had long been in ruins.
Its people were brought out from the peoples, and all of them
will be living securely. 9You will advance; you will come like a
storm. You will be like a cloud covering the earth, you, all your
troops, and the many other peoples with you.
10"'This is what the Sovereign LORD says: On that day
thoughts will come into your mind, and you will devise an evil
plan. 11You will say, "I will invade a land of unwalled towns; I
will advance against those living quietly in security—all of them
living without walls and barred gates—12to loot and plunder,
to attack the inhabited ruins and the people gathered from
the nations, who are acquiring cattle and goods, who live at
the center of the earth." 13Sheba and Dedan and the traders of
Tarshish with all its young warriors will say to you, "Have you
come to loot? Have you assembled your armies to plunder, to
carry away silver and gold, to take away cattle and goods, to
haul away a great amount of spoils?"'

[14]"Therefore, prophesy, son of man, and say to Gog: 'This is
what the Sovereign LORD says: On that day when my people
Israel are living securely, you will take notice [15]and come from
your place, from the remote parts of the north, you and many
peoples with you, all of them riding on horses, a great company
and a vast army. [16]You will advance against my people Israel
like a cloud covering the earth. In future days I will bring you
against my land so that the nations may acknowledge me, when
before their eyes I magnify myself through you, O Gog.
[17]"'This is what the Sovereign LORD says: Are you the one
of whom I spoke in former days by my servants the prophets
of Israel, who prophesied in those days that I would bring you
against them? [18]On that day, when Gog invades the land of Israel, declares the Sovereign LORD, my rage will mount up in my
anger. [19]In my zeal, in the fire of my fury, I declare that on that
day there will be a great earthquake in the land of Israel. [20]The
fish of the sea, the birds of the sky, the wild beasts, all the things
that creep on the ground, and all people who live on the face of
the earth will shake at my presence. The mountains will topple,
the cliffs will fall, and every wall will fall to the ground. [21]I will
call for a sword to attack Gog on all my mountains, declares the
Sovereign LORD; every man's sword will be against his brother.
[22]I will judge him with plague and bloodshed. I will rain down
on him, his troops, and the many peoples who are with him a
torrential downpour, hailstones, fire, and brimstone. [23]I will
exalt and magnify myself; I will reveal myself before many nations. Then they will know that I am the LORD.'

39 "As for you, son of man, prophesy against Gog, and say:
'This is what the Sovereign LORD says: Look, I am against
you, O Gog, chief prince of Meshech and Tubal! [2]I will turn you
around and drag you along; I will lead you up from the remotest parts of the north and bring you against the mountains of
Israel. [3]I will knock your bow out of your left hand and make
your arrows fall from your right hand. [4]You will fall dead on
the mountains of Israel, you and all your troops and the people
who are with you. I give you as food to every kind of bird and
every wild beast. [5]You will fall dead in the open field; for I have
spoken, declares the Sovereign LORD. [6]I will send fire on Magog
and those who live securely in the coastlands; then they will
know that I am the LORD.
[7]"'I will make my holy name known in the midst of my people Israel; I will not let my holy name be profaned anymore.
Then the nations will know that I am the LORD, the Holy One
of Israel. [8]Realize that it is coming and it will be done, declares
the Sovereign LORD. It is the day I have spoken about.
[9]"'Then those who live in the cities of Israel will go out and
use the weapons for kindling—the shields, bows and arrows,
war clubs and spears—they will burn them for seven years.
[10]They will not need to take wood from the field or cut down
trees from the forests because they will make fires with the
weapons. They will take the loot from those who looted them
and seize the plunder of those who plundered them, declares
the Sovereign LORD.
[11]"'On that day I will assign Gog a grave in Israel. It will be the
valley of those who travel east of the sea; it will block the way of
the travelers. There they will bury Gog and all his horde; they
will call it the Valley of Hamon Gog. [12]For seven months Israel
will bury them, in order to cleanse the land. [13]All the people of
the land will bury them, and it will be a memorial for them on

38:18–23 This prophecy is of great troubles to come to the Jews. It then tells of deliverance from this trouble by God's judging their enemies. This was very useful for them that when they should afterward be thus tried, they might not despair or be discomfited as thinking that all promises of happiness after their deliverance out of captivity would now come to naught. As it is here said, although their sufferings should be great, yet they should not be but by divine dispensation, and that they should in a short time be delivered from them again.

JOHN MAYER **(1583–1664)**
COMMENTARY UPON ALL THE PROPHETS

39:10–12 That Gog is the Goth, whose coming forth we have already seen, and over whom victory in days to come is promised, according to the word of the Lord: "They will take the loot from those who looted them and seize the plunder of those who plundered them, declares the Sovereign LORD. On that day I will assign Gog"—that is, the Goths—"a grave in Israel. It will be the valley of those who travel east of the sea; it will block the way of the travelers. There they will bury Gog and all his horde; they will call it the Valley of Hamon Gog. For seven months Israel will bury them, in order to cleanse the land."

AMBROSE **(C. 339–C. 397)**
ON THE CHRISTIAN FAITH

the day I magnify myself, declares the Sovereign LORD. [14]They
will designate men to scout continually through the land, burying those who remain on the surface of the ground, in order to
cleanse it. They will search for seven full months. [15]When the
scouts survey the land and see a human bone, they will place a
sign by it, until those assigned to burial duty have buried it in
the valley of Hamon Gog. [16](A city by the name of Hamonah
will also be there.) They will cleanse the land.'
[17]"As for you, son of man, this is what the Sovereign LORD
says: Tell every kind of bird and every wild beast: 'Assemble and
come! Gather from all around to my slaughter that I am going
to make for you, a great slaughter on the mountains of Israel!
You will eat flesh and drink blood. [18]You will eat the flesh of
warriors and drink the blood of the princes of the earth—the
rams, lambs, goats, and bulls, all of them fattened animals of
Bashan. [19]You will eat fat until you are full and drink blood until
you are drunk at my slaughter that I have made for you. [20]You
will fill up at my table with horses and charioteers, with warriors
and all the soldiers,' declares the Sovereign LORD.
[21]"I will display my majesty among the nations. All the nations will witness the judgment I have executed and the power
I have exhibited among them. [22]Then the house of Israel will
know that I am the LORD their God, from that day forward.
[23]The nations will know that the house of Israel went into exile
due to their iniquity, for they were unfaithful to me. So I hid my
face from them and handed them over to their enemies; all of
them died by the sword. [24]According to their uncleanness and
rebellion I have dealt with them, and I hid my face from them.
[25]"Therefore this is what the Sovereign LORD says: Now I will
restore the fortunes of Jacob, and I will have mercy on the entire
house of Israel. I will be zealous for my holy name. [26]They will
bear their shame for all their unfaithful acts against me, when
they live securely on their land with no one to make them afraid.
[27]When I have brought them back from the peoples and gathered them from the countries of their enemies, I will magnify
myself among them in the sight of many nations. [28]Then they
will know that I am the LORD their God because I sent them
into exile among the nations and then gathered them into
their own land. I will not leave any of them in exile any longer.
[29]I will no longer hide my face from them, when I pour out my
Spirit on the house of Israel, declares the Sovereign LORD."

VISION OF THE NEW TEMPLE

40 In the twenty-fifth year of our exile, at the beginning of
the year, on the tenth day of the month, in the fourteenth
year after the city was struck down, on this very day, the hand
of the LORD was on me, and he brought me there. [2]By divine
visions he brought me to the land of Israel and placed me on a
very high mountain, and on it was a structure like a city, to the
south. [3]When he brought me there, I saw a man whose appearance was like bronze, with a linen cord and a measuring stick in
his hand. He was standing in the gateway. [4]The man said to me,
"Son of man, watch closely, listen carefully, and pay attention to
everything I show you, for you have been brought here so that I
can show it to you. Tell the house of Israel everything you see."
[5]I saw a wall all around the outside of the temple. In the
man's hand was a measuring stick 10½ feet long. He measured
the thickness of the wall as 10½ feet and its height as 10½ feet.
[6]Then he went to the gate facing east. He climbed its steps

40:1–49 Here is a vision beginning at chapter 40 and continuing to the end of the book, which is justly looked upon to be one of the most difficult portions in all the Book of God. When we despair to be satisfied as to any difficulty we meet with, let us bless God that our salvation does not depend upon it, but that things necessary are plain enough; and let us wait till God shall reveal even this unto us. This chapter describes two outward courts of the temple. Whether the personage here mentioned was the Son of God or a created angel is not clear. But Christ is both our altar and our sacrifice, to whom we must look with faith in all approaches to God; and he is salvation in the midst of the earth to be looked unto from all quarters.

MATTHEW HENRY (1662–1714)
COMMENTARY ON THE WHOLE BIBLE

and measured the threshold of the gate as 10½ feet deep. 7The
alcoves were 10½ feet long and 10½ feet wide; between the
alcoves were 8¾ feet. The threshold of the gate by the porch
of the gate facing inward was 10½ feet. 8Then he measured the
porch of the gate facing inward as 10½ feet. 9He measured the
porch of the gate as 14 feet and its jambs as 3½ feet; the porch of
the gate faced inward. 10There were three alcoves on each side
of the east gate; the three had the same measurement, and the
jambs on either side had the same measurement. 11He measured the width of the entrance of the gateway as 17½ feet and
the length of the gateway as 22¾ feet. 12There was a barrier in
front of the alcoves, 1¾ feet on either side; the alcoves were 10½
feet on either side. 13He measured the gateway from the roof
of one alcove to the roof of the other, a width of 43¾ feet from
one entrance to the opposite one. 14He measured the porch at
105 feet high; the gateway went all around to the jamb of the
courtyard. 15From the front of the entrance gate to the porch
of the inner gate was 87½ feet. 16There were closed windows
toward the alcoves and toward their jambs within the gate all
around, and likewise for the porches. There were windows all
around the inside, and on each jamb were decorative palm trees.

17Then he brought me to the outer court. I saw chambers
there and a pavement made for the court all around; 30 chambers faced the pavement. 18The pavement was beside the gates,
corresponding to the length of the gates; this was the lower
pavement. 19Then he measured the width from before the lower
gate to the front of the exterior of the inner court as 175 feet
on the east and on the north.

20He measured the length and width of the gate of the outer
court that faces north. 21Its alcoves, three on each side, and its
jambs and porches had the same measurement as the first gate;
87½ feet long and 43¾ feet wide. 22Its windows, its porches,
and its decorative palm trees had the same measurement as
the gate that faced east. Seven steps led up to it, and its porch
was in front of them. 23Opposite the gate on the north and the
east was a gate of the inner court; he measured the distance
from gate to gate at 175 feet.

24Then he led me toward the south. I saw a gate on the south.
He measured its jambs and its porches; they had the same dimensions as the others. 25There were windows all around it
and its porches, like the windows of the others, 87½ feet long
and 43¾ feet wide. 26There were seven steps going up to it; its
porches were in front of them. It had decorative palm trees
on its jambs, one on either side. 27The inner court had a gate
toward the south; he measured it from gate to gate toward the
south as 175 feet.

28Then he brought me to the inner court by the south gate.
He measured the south gate; it had the same dimensions as
the others. 29Its alcoves, its jambs, and its porches had the same
dimensions as the others, and there were windows all around
it and its porches; its length was 87½ feet and its width 43¾
feet. 30There were porches all around, 43¾ feet long and 8¾
feet wide. 31Its porches faced the outer court, and decorative
palm trees were on its jambs, and its stairway had eight steps.

32Then he brought me to the inner court on the east side. He
measured the gate; it had the same dimensions as the others.
33Its alcoves, its jambs, and its porches had the same dimensions as the others, and there were windows all around it and
its porches; its length was 87½ feet and its width 43¾ feet. 34Its

porches faced the outer court, it had decorative palm trees on its jambs, and its stairway had eight steps.

[35]Then he brought me to the north gate, and he measured it; it had the same dimensions as the others—[36]its alcoves, its jambs, and its porches. It had windows all around it; its length was 87½ feet and its width 43¾ feet. [37]Its jambs faced the outer court, and it had decorative palm trees on its jambs on either side, and its stairway had eight steps.

[38]There was a chamber with its door by the porch of the gate; there they washed the burnt offering. [39]In the porch of the gate were two tables on either side on which to slaughter the burnt offering, the sin offering, and the guilt offering. [40]On the outside of the porch as one goes up at the entrance of the north gate were two tables, and on the other side of the porch of the gate were two tables. [41]Four tables were on each side of the gate, eight tables on which the sacrifices were to be slaughtered. [42]The four tables for the burnt offering were of carved stone, 32 inches long, 32 inches wide, and 21 inches high. They would put the instruments that they used to slaughter the burnt offering and the sacrifice on them. [43]There were hooks 3 inches long fastened in the house all around, and on the tables was the flesh of the offering.

[44]On the outside of the inner gate were chambers for the singers of the inner court, one at the side of the north gate facing south, and the other at the side of the south gate facing north. [45]He said to me, "This chamber that faces south is for the priests who keep charge of the temple, [46]and the chamber that faces north is for the priests who keep charge of the altar. These are the descendants of Zadok, from the descendants of Levi, who may approach the LORD to minister to him." [47]He measured the court as a square 175 feet long and 175 feet wide; the altar was in front of the temple.

[48]Then he brought me to the porch of the temple and measured the jambs of the porch as 8¾ feet on either side; the width of the gate was 24½ feet, and the sides were 5¼ feet on each side. [49]The length of the porch was 35 feet and the width 19¼ feet; steps led up to it, and there were pillars beside the jambs on either side.

THE INNER TEMPLE

41 Then he brought me to the outer sanctuary and measured the jambs; the jambs were 10½ feet wide on each side. [2]The width of the entrance was 17½ feet, and the sides of the entrance were 8¾ feet on each side. He measured the length of the outer sanctuary as 70 feet and its width as 35 feet.

[3]Then he went into the inner sanctuary and measured the jambs of the entrance as 3½ feet, the entrance as 10½ feet, and the width of the entrance as 12¼ feet. [4]Then he measured its length as 35 feet and its width as 35 feet, before the outer sanctuary. He said to me, "This is the Most Holy Place."

[5]Then he measured the wall of the temple as 10½ feet and the width of the side chambers as 7 feet, all around the temple. [6]The side chambers were in three stories, one above the other, 30 in each story. There were offsets in the wall all around to serve as supports for the side chambers, so that the supports were not in the wall of the temple. [7]The side chambers surrounding the temple were wider at each successive story, for the structure surrounding the temple went up story by story all around the temple. For this reason the width of the temple increased as it

41:1—42:14 Now we are come to the gate of the temple. The leaves of this gate or door were folding. For by this means a young disciple may easily be mistaken thinking that the whole passage when yet but a part was open. So that I say a newcomer, if he judged by present sight, especially if he saw but little, might easily be mistaken; therefore such for the most part are most horribly afraid that they shall never get in there. Is this not the case with your soul? So it seems to you that you are too big, so great, so pot-bellied a sinner. But O you sinner, fear not, the doors are folding doors and may be opened wider, and wider again after that. Therefore, when you come to this gate and imagine there is not space enough for you to enter, knock, and it will be wider opened to you, and you will be received.

JOHN BUNYAN **(1628–1688)**
SOLOMON'S TEMPLE SPIRITUALIZED

went up, and one went up from the lowest story to the highest
by the way of the middle story.
[8]I saw that the temple had a raised platform all around; the
foundations of the side chambers were a full measuring stick of
10½ feet high. [9]The width of the outer wall of the side chambers
was 8¾ feet, and the open area between the side chambers of
the temple [10]and the chambers of the court was 35 feet in width
all around the temple on every side. [11]There were entrances
from the side chambers toward the open area, one entrance
toward the north, and another entrance toward the south; the
width of the open area was 8¾ feet all around.
[12]The building that was facing the temple courtyard at the
west side was 122½ feet wide; the wall of the building was 8¾
feet thick all around, and its length 157½ feet.
[13]Then he measured the temple as 175 feet long, the courtyard of the temple and the building and its walls as 175 feet
long, [14]and also the width of the front of the temple and the
courtyard on the east as 175 feet.
[15]Then he measured the length of the building facing the
courtyard at the rear of the temple, with its galleries on either
side as 175 feet.

The interior of the outer sanctuary and the porch of the
court, [16]as well as the thresholds, narrow windows, and galleries
all around on three sides facing the threshold, were paneled
with wood all around, from the ground up to the windows (now
the windows were covered), [17]to the space above the entrance,
to the inner room, and on the outside and on all the walls in the
inner room and outside, by measurement. [18]It was made with
cherubim and decorative palm trees, with a palm tree between
each cherub. Each cherub had two faces: [19]a human face toward
the palm tree on one side and a lion's face toward the palm
tree on the other side. They were carved on the whole temple
all around; [20]from the ground to the area above the entrance,
cherubim and decorative palm trees were carved on the wall
of the outer sanctuary. [21]The doorposts of the outer sanctuary
were square. In front of the sanctuary one doorpost looked just
like the other. [22]The altar was of wood, 5¼ feet high, with its
length 3½ feet; its corners, its length, and its walls were of wood.
He said to me, "This is the table that is before the LORD." [23]The
outer sanctuary and the inner sanctuary each had a double
door. [24]Each of the doors had two leaves, two swinging leaves;
two leaves for one door and two leaves for the other. [25]On the
doors of the outer sanctuary were carved cherubim and palm
trees, like those carved on the walls, and there was a canopy of
wood on the front of the outside porch. [26]There were narrow
windows and decorative palm trees on either side of the side
walls of the porch; this is what the side chambers of the temple
and the canopies were like.

CHAMBERS FOR THE TEMPLE

42 Then he led me out to the outer court, toward the north,
and brought me to the chamber that was opposite the
courtyard and opposite the building on the north. [2]Its length
was 175 feet on the north side, and its width 87½ feet. [3]Opposite
the 35 feet that belonged to the inner court, and opposite the
pavement that belonged to the outer court, gallery faced gallery
in the three stories. [4]In front of the chambers was a walkway on
the inner side, 17½ feet wide at a distance of 1¾ feet, and their
entrances were on the north. [5]Now the upper chambers were

narrower, because the galleries took more space from them than from the lower and middle chambers of the building. 6For they were in three stories and had no pillars like the pillars of the courts; therefore, the upper chambers were set back from the ground more than the lower and middle ones. 7As for the outer wall by the side of the chambers, toward the outer court facing the chambers, it was 87½ feet long. 8For the chambers on the outer court were 87½ feet long, while those facing the temple were 175 feet long. 9Below these chambers was a passage on the east side as one enters from the outer court.

10At the beginning of the wall of the court toward the south, facing the courtyard and the building, were chambers 11like those on the north with a passage in front of them. The chambers that were toward the south were the same length and width as those on the north, and had matching exits and entrances and arrangements. 12There was an opening at the head of the passage, the passage in front of the corresponding wall toward the east when one enters.

13Then he said to me, "The north chambers and the south chambers that face the courtyard are holy chambers where the priests who approach the LORD will eat the most holy offerings. There they will place the most holy offerings—the grain offering, the sin offering, and the guilt offering, because the place is holy. 14When the priests enter, then they will not go out from the sanctuary to the outer court without taking off their garments in which they minister, for these are holy; they will put on other garments, then they will go near the places where the people are."

15Now when he had finished measuring the interior of the temple, he led me out by the gate that faces east and measured all around. 16He measured the east side with the measuring stick as 875 feet by the measuring stick. 17He measured the north side as 875 feet by the measuring stick. 18He measured the south side as 875 feet by the measuring stick. 19He turned to the west side and measured 875 feet by the measuring stick. 20He measured it on all four sides. It had a wall around it, 875 feet long and 875 feet wide, to separate the holy and common places.

THE GLORY RETURNS TO THE TEMPLE

43 Then he brought me to the gate that faced toward the east. 2I saw the glory of the God of Israel coming from the east; the sound was like that of rushing water, and the earth radiated his glory. 3It was like the vision I saw when he came to destroy the city, and the vision I saw by the Kebar River. I threw myself face down. 4The glory of the LORD came into the temple by way of the gate that faces east. 5Then a wind lifted me up and brought me to the inner court; I watched the glory of the LORD filling the temple.

6I heard someone speaking to me from the temple, while the man was standing beside me. 7He said to me: "Son of man, this is the place of my throne and the place for the soles of my feet, where I will live among the people of Israel forever. The house of Israel will no longer profane my holy name, neither they nor their kings, by their spiritual prostitution or by the pillars of their kings set up when they die. 8When they placed their threshold by my threshold and their doorpost by my doorpost, with only the wall between me and them, they profaned my holy name by the abominable deeds they committed. So I consumed them in my anger. 9Now they must put away their

43:1–27 **The sins of Israel caused the glory of the Lord to go out of his house, but now the repentance of Israel is blessed with the return of this glory. The throne of his grace is in his temple. In the dispensations of grace, God manifests himself a king speaking after the manner of men. This is the first comprehensive rule: Holiness becomes God's house, and this relative holiness referred to personal and real holiness. Those who give themselves to God shall be accepted of God, their persons first and then their performances, through the mediator.**

JOHN WESLEY **(1703–1791)**
EXPLANATORY NOTES ON THE BIBLE

spiritual prostitution and the pillars of their kings far from me, and then I will live among them forever.

10"As for you, son of man, describe the temple to the house of Israel, so that they will be ashamed of their sins and measure the pattern. 11When they are ashamed of all that they have done, make known to them the design of the temple—its pattern, its exits and entrances, and its whole design—all its statutes, its entire design, and all its laws; write it all down in their sight, so that they may observe its entire design and all its statutes and do them.

12"This is the law of the temple: The entire area on top of the mountain all around will be most holy. Indeed, this is the law of the temple.

THE ALTAR

13"And these are the measurements of the altar: Its base is 1¾ feet high and 1¾ feet wide, and its border 9 inches on its edge. This is to be the height of the altar. 14From the base of the ground to the lower ledge is 3½ feet, and the width 1¾ feet; and from the smaller ledge to the larger ledge, 7 feet, and the width 1¾ feet; 15and the altar hearth, 7 feet, and from the altar hearth four horns projecting upward. 16Now the altar hearth is a perfect square, 21 feet long and 21 feet wide. 17The ledge is 24½ feet long and 24½ feet wide on four sides; the border around it is 10½ inches, and its surrounding base 1¾ feet. Its steps face east."

18Then he said to me: "Son of man, this is what the Sovereign LORD says: These are the statutes of the altar: On the day it is built to offer up burnt offerings on it and to sprinkle blood on it, 19you will give a young bull for a sin offering to the Levitical priests who are descended from Zadok, who approach me to minister to me, declares the Sovereign LORD. 20You will take some of its blood and place it on the four horns of the altar, on the four corners of the ledge, and on the border all around; you will purify it and make atonement for it. 21You will also take the bull for the sin offering, and it will be burned in the appointed place in the temple, outside the sanctuary.

22"On the second day, you will offer a male goat without blemish for a sin offering. They will purify the altar just as they purified it with the bull. 23When you have finished purifying it, you will offer an unblemished young bull and an unblemished ram from the flock. 24You will present them before the LORD, and the priests will scatter salt on them and offer them up as a burnt offering to the LORD.

25"For seven days you will provide every day a goat for a sin offering; a young bull and a ram from the flock, both without blemish, will be provided. 26For seven days they will make atonement for the altar and cleanse it, so they will consecrate it. 27When the prescribed period is over, on the eighth day and thereafter the priests will offer up on the altar your burnt offerings and your peace offerings; I will accept you, declares the Sovereign LORD."

THE CLOSED GATE

44 Then he brought me back by way of the outer gate of the sanctuary that faces east, but it was shut. 2The LORD said to me: "This gate will be shut; it will not be opened, and no one will enter by it. For the LORD, the God of Israel, has entered by it; therefore it will remain shut. 3Only the prince may sit in it

to eat a sacrificial meal before the LORD; he will enter by way
of the porch of the gate and will go out by the same way."
4Then he brought me by way of the north gate to the front of
the temple. As I watched, I noticed the glory of the LORD filling
the LORD's temple, and I threw myself face down. 5The LORD
said to me: "Son of man, pay attention, watch closely, and listen
carefully to everything I tell you concerning all the statutes of
the LORD's house and all its laws. Pay attention to the entrances
to the temple with all the exits of the sanctuary. 6Say to the
rebellious, to the house of Israel, 'This is what the Sovereign
LORD says: Enough of all your abominable practices, O house
of Israel! 7When you bring foreigners, those uncircumcised in
heart and in flesh, into my sanctuary, you desecrate it—even
my house—when you offer my food, the fat and the blood. You
have broken my covenant by all your abominable practices. 8You
have not kept charge of my holy things, but you have assigned
foreigners to keep charge of my sanctuary for you. 9This is what
the Sovereign LORD says: No foreigner who is uncircumcised
in heart and flesh among all the foreigners who are among the
people of Israel will enter into my sanctuary.
10"'But the Levites who went far from me, straying off from
me after their idols when Israel went astray, will be responsible
for their sin. 11Yet they will be ministers in my sanctuary, having
oversight at the gates of the temple, and serving the temple.
They will slaughter the burnt offerings and the sacrifices for the
people, and they will stand before them to minister to them.
12Because they used to minister to them before their idols and
became a sinful obstacle to the house of Israel, consequently
I have made a vow concerning them, declares the Sovereign
LORD, that they will be responsible for their sin. 13They will not
come near me to serve me as priest, nor will they come near
any of my holy things, the things that are most sacred. They will
bear the shame of the abominable deeds they have committed.
14Yet I will appoint them to keep charge of the temple, all its
service, and all that will be done in it.

THE LEVITICAL PRIESTS

15"'But the Levitical priests, the descendants of Zadok who
kept the charge of my sanctuary when the people of Israel went
astray from me, will approach me to minister to me; they will
stand before me to offer me the fat and the blood, declares the
Sovereign LORD. 16They will enter my sanctuary and approach
my table to minister to me; they will keep my charge.
17"'When they enter the gates of the inner court, they must
wear linen garments; they must not have any wool on them
when they minister in the inner gates of the court and in the
temple. 18Linen turbans will be on their heads and linen undergarments will be around their waists; they must not bind
themselves with anything that causes sweat. 19When they go
out to the outer court to the people, they must remove the
garments they were ministering in and place them in the holy
chambers; they must put on other garments so that they will
not transmit holiness to the people with their garments.
20"'They must not shave their heads nor let their hair grow
long; they must only trim their heads. 21No priest may drink
wine when he enters the inner court. 22They must not marry
a widow or a divorcee, but they may marry a virgin from the
house of Israel or a widow who is a priest's widow. 23Moreover,
they will teach my people the difference between the holy and

44:9–27 The Lord called those who would not believe "foreigners." Only those who lived purely were true priests of God. Therefore, of all the circumcised tribes, those anointed to be high priests, kings, and prophets were reckoned more holy. He commanded them not to touch dead bodies or approach the dead—not that the body was polluted, but sin and disobedience were incarnate, embodied, and dead, and therefore abominable. It was only when a father and mother, a son and daughter died, that the priest was allowed to enter because these were related only by flesh and seed; to them the priest was indebted for the immediate cause of his entrance into life. And they purified themselves seven days, the period in which creation was consummated. For on the seventh day the rest is celebrated; and on the eighth he brings a propitiation, as is written in Ezekiel, according to which propitiation the promise is to be received.

CLEMENT OF ALEXANDRIA
(C. 150–C. 215)
STROMATEIS

the common and show them how to distinguish between the
ceremonially unclean and the clean.
24“‘In a controversy they will act as judges; they will judge
according to my ordinances. They will keep my laws and my
statutes regarding all my appointed festivals and will observe
my Sabbaths.
25“‘They must not come near a dead person or they will be
defiled; however, for father, mother, son, daughter, brother, or
unmarried sister, they may defile themselves. 26After a priest
has become ceremonially clean, they must count off a period of
seven days for him. 27On the day he enters the sanctuary into
the inner court to serve in the sanctuary, he must offer his sin
offering, declares the Sovereign LORD.
28“‘This will be their inheritance: I am their inheritance, and
you must give them no property in Israel; I am their property.
29They may eat the grain offering, the sin offering, and the guilt
offering, and every devoted thing in Israel will be theirs. 30The
first of all the firstfruits and all contributions of any kind will be
for the priests; you will also give to the priest the first portion
of your dough, so that a blessing may rest on your house. 31The
priests will not eat any bird or animal that has died a natural
death or was torn to pieces by a wild animal.

THE LORD'S PORTION OF THE LAND

45 “‘When you allot the land as an inheritance, you will offer
an allotment to the LORD, a holy portion from the land;
the length will be 8¼ miles and the width 3⅓ miles. This entire
area will be holy. 2Of this area a square 875 feet by 875 feet will
be designated for the sanctuary, with 87½ feet set aside for its
open space round about. 3From this measured area you will
measure a length of 8¼ miles and a width of 3⅓ miles; in it will
be the sanctuary, the Most Holy Place. 4It will be a holy portion
of the land; it will be for the priests, the ministers of the sanctuary who approach the LORD to minister to him. It will be a
place for their houses and a holy place for the sanctuary. 5An
area 8¼ miles in length and 3⅓ miles in width will be for the
Levites, who minister at the temple, as the place for the cities
in which they will live.
6“‘Alongside the portion set apart as the holy allotment, you
will allot for the city an area 1⅔ miles wide and 8¼ miles long;
it will be for the whole house of Israel.
7“‘For the prince there will be land on both sides of the holy
allotment and the allotted city, on the west side and on the
east side; it will be comparable in length to one of the portions,
from the west border to the east border 8of the land. This will
be his property in Israel. My princes will no longer oppress
my people, but the land will be allotted to the house of Israel
according to their tribes.
9“‘This is what the Sovereign LORD says: Enough, you princes
of Israel! Put away violence and destruction and do what is just
and right. Put an end to your evictions of my people, declares
the Sovereign LORD. 10You must use just balances, a just dry
measure (an ephah), and a just liquid measure (a bath). 11The
dry and liquid measures will be the same: The bath will contain
a tenth of a homer, and the ephah a tenth of a homer; the homer
will be the standard measure. 12The shekel will be 20 gerahs.
Sixty shekels will be a mina for you.
13“‘This is the offering you must offer: a sixth of an ephah
from a homer of wheat, a sixth of an ephah from a homer of

45:9–12 Godliness without honesty will neither please God nor avail to the benefit of any people. Be it therefore enacted that princes do not oppress their subjects but duly and faithfully administer justice among them. Note, even princes and great men who have long done amiss must at length think it high time to reform and amend. Let them now remove violence and spoil; let them drop wrongful demands, cancel wrongful usages, and turn out those from employments under them who do violence. Let them take away their exactions, ease their subjects of those taxes they find lie heavily upon them, and let them execute judgment and justice according to the law. Note, all princes, but especially the princes of Israel, are concerned to do justice, for of their people God says, *They are my people*, and they in a special manner rule for God.

MATTHEW HENRY **(1662–1714)**
COMMENTARY ON THE WHOLE BIBLE

barley, 14and as the prescribed portion of olive oil, one-tenth of a
bath from each cor (which is ten baths or a homer, for ten baths
make a homer); 15and one sheep from each flock of 200, from
the watered places of Israel, for a grain offering, burnt offering,
and peace offering, to make atonement for them, declares the
Sovereign LORD. 16All the people of the land will contribute to
this offering for the prince of Israel. 17It will be the duty of the
prince to provide the burnt offerings, the grain offering, and
the drink offering at festivals, on the new moons and Sabbaths,
at all the appointed feasts of the house of Israel; he will provide
the sin offering, the grain offering, the burnt offering, and the
peace offerings to make atonement for the house of Israel.

18"'This is what the Sovereign LORD says: In the first month,
on the first day of the month, you must take an unblemished
young bull and purify the sanctuary. 19The priest will take some
of the blood of the sin offering and place it on the doorpost of
the temple, on the four corners of the ledge of the altar, and on
the doorpost of the gate of the inner court. 20This is what you
must do on the seventh day of the month for anyone who sins
inadvertently or through ignorance; so you will make atonement for the temple.

21"'In the first month, on the fourteenth day of the month,
you will celebrate the Passover, and for the seven days of the
festival bread made without yeast will be eaten. 22On that day
the prince will provide for himself and for all the people of
the land a bull for a sin offering. 23And during the seven days
of the feast he will provide as a burnt offering to the LORD
seven bulls and seven rams, all without blemish, on each of the
seven days, and a male goat daily for a sin offering. 24He will
provide as a grain offering an ephah for each bull, an ephah
for each ram, and a gallon of olive oil for each ephah of grain.
25In the seventh month, on the fifteenth day of the month,
at the feast, he will make the same provisions for the sin offering, burnt offering, and grain offering, and for the olive oil,
for the seven days.

THE PRINCE'S OFFERINGS

46 "'This is what the Sovereign LORD says: The gate of the
inner court that faces east will be closed six working
days, but on the Sabbath day it will be opened and on the day
of the new moon it will be opened. 2The prince will enter by
way of the porch of the gate from the outside and will stand
by the doorpost of the gate. The priests will provide his burnt
offering and his peace offerings, and he will bow down at the
threshold of the gate and then go out. But the gate will not be
closed until evening. 3The people of the land will bow down
at the entrance of that gate before the LORD on the Sabbaths
and on the new moons. 4The burnt offering that the prince will
offer to the LORD on the Sabbath day will be six unblemished
lambs and one unblemished ram. 5The grain offering will be
an ephah with the ram, and the grain offering with the lambs
will be as much as he is able to give, and a gallon of olive oil
with an ephah. 6On the day of the new moon he will offer an
unblemished young bull and six lambs and a ram, all without
blemish. 7He will provide a grain offering: an ephah with the
bull and an ephah with the ram, and with the lambs as much
as he wishes, and a gallon of olive oil with each ephah of grain.
8When the prince enters, he will come by way of the porch of
the gate and will go out the same way.

46:1 The reason why these two occasions gain so marked a place now is obvious. Those who are of God are no longer entering into rest; they have gone in. Sabbath-keeping no longer remains for the people of God. Glory dwells in the land, and Israel is there gathered out of the lands. They have been led forth by the right way, they are come to a city of habitation, yea to his city, for this is its true and deep and worthy boast: as we shall hear, Jehovah is there. The Sabbath therefore naturally is now made much of. But so is the new moon. Israel, which had long waned and disappeared, now renews its light, never more to withdraw itself. The new moon therefore fitly marks Israel restored now and forevermore.

WILLIAM KELLY (1821–1906)
NOTES ON EZEKIEL

9"'When the people of the land come before the LORD at
the appointed feasts, whoever enters by way of the north
gate to worship will go out by way of the south gate; whoever enters by way of the south gate will go out by way of the
north gate. No one will return by way of the gate they entered
but will go out straight ahead. 10When they come in, the
prince will come in with them, and when they go out, he will
go out.
11"'At the festivals and at the appointed feasts the grain offering will be an ephah with the bull and an ephah with the
ram, and with the lambs as much as one is able, and a gallon
of olive oil with each ephah of grain. 12When the prince provides a freewill offering, a burnt offering, or peace offerings as
a voluntary offering to the LORD, the gate facing east will be
opened for him, and he will provide his burnt offering and his
peace offerings just as he did on the Sabbath. Then he will go
out, and the gate will be closed after he goes out.
13"'You will provide a lamb a year old without blemish for
a burnt offering daily to the LORD; morning by morning he
will provide it. 14And you will provide a grain offering with it
morning by morning, a sixth of an ephah and a third of a gallon
of olive oil to moisten the choice flour, as a grain offering to the
LORD; this is a perpetual statute. 15Thus they will provide the
lamb, the grain offering, and the olive oil morning by morning
as a perpetual burnt offering.
16"'This is what the Sovereign LORD says: If the prince should
give a gift to one of his sons as his inheritance, it will belong
to his sons; it is their property by inheritance. 17But if he gives
a gift from his inheritance to one of his servants, it will be his
until the year of liberty; then it will revert to the prince. His
inheritance will only remain with his sons. 18The prince will
not take away any of the people's inheritance by oppressively
removing them from their property. He will give his sons an
inheritance from his own possessions so that my people will
not be scattered, each from his own property.'"

19Then he brought me through the entrance, which was at
the side of the gate, into the holy chambers for the priests,
which faced north. There I saw a place at the extreme western
end. 20He said to me, "This is the place where the priests will
boil the guilt offering and the sin offering and where they will
bake the grain offering, so that they do not bring them out to
the outer court to transmit holiness to the people."

21Then he brought me out to the outer court and led me past
the four corners of the court, and I noticed that in every corner
of the court there was another court. 22In the four corners of
the court were small courts, 70 feet in length and 52½ feet in
width; the four were all the same size. 23There was a row of
masonry around each of the four courts, and places for boiling
offerings were made under the rows all around. 24Then he said
to me, "These are the houses for boiling, where the ministers
of the temple boil the sacrifices of the people."

WATER FROM THE TEMPLE

47 Then he brought me back to the entrance of the temple.
I noticed that water was flowing from under the threshold of the temple toward the east (for the temple faced east).
The water was flowing down from under the right side of the
temple, from south of the altar. 2He led me out by way of the
north gate and brought me around the outside of the outer

gate that faces toward the east; I noticed that the water was trickling out from the south side.

3When the man went out toward the east with a measuring line in his hand, he measured 1,750 feet, and then he led me through water, which was ankle deep. 4Again he measured 1,750 feet and led me through the water, which was now knee deep. Once more he measured 1,750 feet and led me through the water, which was waist deep. 5Again he measured 1,750 feet, and it was a river I could not cross, for the water had risen; it was deep enough to swim in, a river that could not be crossed. 6He said to me, "Son of man, have you seen this?"

Then he led me back to the bank of the river. 7When I had returned, I noticed a vast number of trees on the banks of the river, on both sides. 8He said to me, "These waters go out toward the eastern region and flow down into the rift valley; when they enter the Dead Sea, where the sea is stagnant, the waters become fresh. 9Every living creature that swarms where the river flows will live; there will be many fish, for these waters flow there. It will become fresh, and everything will live where the river flows. 10Fishermen will stand beside it; from En Gedi to En Eglaim they will spread nets. They will catch many kinds of fish, like the fish of the Great Sea. 11But its swamps and its marshes will not become fresh; they will remain salty. 12On both sides of the river's banks, every kind of tree will grow for food. Their leaves will not wither nor will their fruit fail, but they will bear fruit every month because their water source flows from the sanctuary. Their fruit will be for food and their leaves for healing."

BOUNDARIES FOR THE LAND

13This is what the Sovereign LORD says: "Here are the borders you will observe as you allot the land to the 12 tribes of Israel. (Joseph will have two portions.) 14You must divide it equally just as I vowed to give it to your forefathers; this land will be assigned as your inheritance.

15"This will be the border of the land: On the north side, from the Great Sea by way of Hethlon to the entrance of Zedad; 16Hamath, Berothah, Sibraim, which is between the border of Damascus and the border of Hamath, as far as Hazer Hattikon, which is on the border of Hauran. 17The border will run from the sea to Hazar Enan, at the border of Damascus, and on the north is the border of Hamath. This is the north side. 18On the east side, between Hauran and Damascus, and between Gilead and the land of Israel, will be the Jordan. You will measure from the border to the eastern sea. This is the east side. 19On the south side it will run from Tamar to the waters of Meribah Kadesh, the river, to the Great Sea. This is the south side. 20On the west side the Great Sea will be the boundary to a point opposite Lebo Hamath. This is the west side.

21"This is how you will divide this land for yourselves among the tribes of Israel. 22You must allot it as an inheritance among yourselves and for the resident foreigners who live among you, who have fathered sons among you. You must treat them as native-born among the people of Israel; they will be allotted an inheritance with you among the tribes of Israel. 23In whatever tribe the resident foreigner lives, there you will give him his inheritance," declares the Sovereign LORD.

47:13–23 According to the letter these words were not fulfilled after the return from Babylon, but mystically under the gospel they were. (1) Then here is held out to us the great extent and largeness of the church under Christ and the gospel. The Christian church is larger than the Jewish that was shut up in one nation; now it reaches to all nations. (2) Those who are subjects or members of this church are not hypocrites but Israelites—true Israelites, such as Nathanael was; of Jews inwardly, such as are circumcised in heart and spirit; of such as are enrolled in heaven; of sealed ones, and these stood with the Lamb on Mount Zion. (3) The privileges of this church equally belong to all the members of it. (4) The state of Christians in the church, and all the spiritual blessings they have therein, are of free grace and mercy.

WILLIAM GREENHILL
(1591–1671)
AN EXPOSITION OF EZEKIEL

THE TRIBAL PORTIONS

48 "These are the names of the tribes: From the northern end beside the road of Hethlon to Lebo Hamath, as far as Hazar Enan (which is on the border of Damascus, toward the north beside Hamath), extending from the east side to the west, Dan will have one portion. 2 Next to the border of Dan, from the east side to the west side, Asher will have one portion. 3 Next to the border of Asher from the east side to the west side, Naphtali will have one portion. 4 Next to the border of Naphtali from the east side to the west side, Manasseh will have one portion. 5 Next to the border of Manasseh from the east side to the west side, Ephraim will have one portion. 6 Next to the border of Ephraim from the east side to the west side, Reuben will have one portion. 7 Next to the border of Reuben from the east side to the west side, Judah will have one portion.

8 "Next to the border of Judah from the east side to the west side will be the allotment you must set apart. It is to be 8¼ miles wide and the same length as one of the tribal portions, from the east side to the west side; the sanctuary will be in the middle of it. 9 The allotment you set apart to the LORD will be 8¼ miles in length and 3⅓ miles in width. 10 These will be the allotments for the holy portion: for the priests, toward the north 8¼ miles in length, toward the west 3⅓ miles in width, toward the east 3⅓ miles in width, and toward the south 8¼ miles in length; the sanctuary of the LORD will be in the middle. 11 This will be for the priests who are set apart from the descendants of Zadok who kept my charge and did not go astray when the people of Israel strayed off, as the Levites did. 12 It will be their portion from the allotment of the land, a Most Holy Place, next to the border of the Levites.

13 "Alongside the border of the priests, the Levites will have an allotment 8¼ miles in length and 3⅓ miles in width. The whole length will be 8¼ miles and the width 3⅓ miles. 14 They must not sell or exchange any of it; they must not transfer this choice portion of land, for it is set apart to the LORD.

15 "The remainder, 1⅔ miles in width and 8¼ miles in length, will be for common use by the city, for houses and for open space. The city will be in the middle of it; 16 these will be its measurements: The north side will be 1½ miles, the south side 1½ miles, the east side 1½ miles, and the west side 1½ miles. 17 The city will have open spaces: On the north there will be 437½ feet, on the south 437½ feet, on the east 437½ feet, and on the west 437½ feet. 18 The remainder of the length alongside the holy allotment will be 3⅓ miles to the east and 3⅓ miles toward the west, and it will be beside the holy allotment. Its produce will be for food for the workers of the city. 19 The workers of the city from all the tribes of Israel will cultivate it. 20 The whole allotment will be 8¼ miles square; you must set apart the holy allotment with the possession of the city.

21 "The rest, on both sides of the holy allotment and the property of the city, will belong to the prince. Extending from the 8¼ miles of the holy allotment to the east border and westward from the 8¼ miles to the west border, alongside the portions, it will belong to the prince. The holy allotment and the sanctuary of the temple will be in the middle of it. 22 The property of the Levites and of the city will be in the middle of that which belongs to the prince. The portion between the border of Judah and the border of Benjamin will be for the prince.

23“As for the rest of the tribes: From the east side to the west side, Benjamin will have one portion. 24Next to the border of Benjamin, from the east side to the west side, Simeon will have one portion. 25Next to the border of Simeon, from the east side to the west side, Issachar will have one portion. 26Next to the border of Issachar, from the east side to the west side, Zebulun will have one portion. 27Next to the border of Zebulun, from the east side to the west side, Gad will have one portion. 28Next to the border of Gad, at the south side, the border will run from Tamar to the waters of Meribah Kadesh, to the Stream of Egypt, and on to the Great Sea. 29This is the land that you will allot to the tribes of Israel, and these are their portions, declares the Sovereign LORD.

30“These are the exits of the city: On the north side, 1½ miles by measure, 31the gates of the city will be named for the tribes of Israel. There will be three gates to the north: one gate for Reuben, one gate for Judah, and one gate for Levi. 32On the east side, 1½ miles in length, there will be three gates: one gate for Joseph, one gate for Benjamin, and one gate for Dan. 33On the south side, 1½ miles by measure, there will be three gates: one gate for Simeon, one gate for Issachar, and one gate for Zebulun. 34On the west side, 1½ miles in length, there will be three gates: one gate for Gad, one gate for Asher, and one gate for Naphtali. 35The circumference of the city will be 6 miles. The name of the city from that day forward will be: ‘The LORD Is There.’”

48:35 It is esteemed by the prophet to be the highest blessing that could come upon a city that its name should be “The LORD Is There.” Even Jerusalem, in its best estate, would have this for its crowning blessing. Do we reckon the presence of the Lord to be the greatest of blessings? When God shall bless his ancient people and restore them to their land, and the temple shall be rebuilt, and all the glory of the latter days shall arrive, this will still be the peculiar glory of it all, that the Lord is there. Where God is present, the preservation of purity will be found. Where God is, there is the constant renewal of vitality. When the Lord is there, there is continuing power. When the Lord is there, is sure to be happiness.

CHARLES SPURGEON
(1834–1892)
METROPOLITAN TABERNACLE SERMONS

AUTHOR	AUDIENCE	DATE	PURPOSE	THEMES
Daniel	The Jewish exiles in Babylon	About 530 BC	Daniel wrote this book to Jews living in exile to remind them of God's sovereign control and exhort them to trust in his providence, live in obedience to his commands, and hold out hope for God's future promises.	The sovereignty of God; holy living within a wicked culture; and trust and hope in the midst of trials

Daniel is one of the better-known books of the Major Prophets, for its central character has been offered in various profiles down through the centuries as a model of holy devotion, faithfulness, and virtue. Yet the book is more than a moralistic character profile; Daniel wrote this volume to Jews living in exile to remind them of God's sovereign control. He exhorted them to trust in the Lord's providence, rely on his promises, and live in obedience to his commands as they looked forward to the fulfillment of his plans.

"Though there are considerable difficulties in explaining the prophetical meaning of some passages in this book," Matthew Henry noted, "we always find encouragement to faith and hope, examples worthy of imitation, and something to direct our thoughts to Christ Jesus upon the cross and on his glorious throne." Further, Jerome stressed in his preface, "none of the prophets has so clearly spoken concerning Christ as has this prophet Daniel. For not only did he assert that he would come, a prediction common to other prophets as well, but he also set forth the very time at which he would come."

One of the important issues of faith and hope mentioned by Matthew Henry is the significant theme of the sovereignty of God woven throughout this book. God is portrayed as sovereign over his creation, the King of kings and Lord of lords: He determines the course of human events, even raising and deposing kings; he holds the lives of individuals and nations in his hands; and he is "great and awesome" (9:4), maintaining his covenant of love with his people. This theme is summarized by none other than the pagan king Darius who declared: "[The God of Daniel] is the living God; he endures forever. His kingdom will not be destroyed; his authority is forever. He rescues and delivers and performs signs and wonders in the heavens and on the earth" (6:26–27).

Although the sovereignty of God is a dominant theme throughout Daniel, also prevalent is the idea that God's people are to separate themselves from the surrounding culture as they seek to live obedient to God's commands, as Daniel himself did: "Daniel made up his mind that he would not defile himself . . . He therefore asked the overseer of the court officials for permission not to defile himself" (1:8). Hippolytus commented on this passage: "Daniel kept the covenant of the fathers and did not transgress the law given by Moses but feared the God proclaimed by him. These, though captives in

a strange land, were not seduced by delicate meats, nor were they slaves to the pleasures of wine, nor were they caught by the bait of princely glory."

The early church wove the narrative of the blazing furnace of chapter 3 into martyrdom tracts. In his exhortation to martyrdom, Origen wrote, "Let us imitate those holy men so that we may experience the heavenly dew that quenches every fire that arises in us and cools our governing mind." In his commentary on Daniel, Hippolytus encouraged the martyr who follows in the footsteps of brave Shadrach, Meshach, and Abednego that the Holy Spirit would be with him, as he was with them: "Behold the Holy Spirit as it is manifest in the martyrs' eloquent speech, comforting them and consoling them and encouraging them to disregard death." The Reformers noted their refusal to commit idolatry and commended these men for their confession of faith.

John Calvin believed the book of Daniel illustrates "how God proves the faith of his people in these days by various trials; and how with wonderful wisdom he has taken care to strengthen their minds by ancient examples that they should never be weakened by the concussion of the severest storms and tempests; or at least, if they should totter at all, that they should never finally fall away." He encouraged believers that as their life's course is impeded by many obstacles, whoever diligently reads this book "will find in it whatever is needed by a voluntary and active runner to guide him from the starting post to the goal, while good and strenuous wrestlers will experimentally acknowledge that they have been sufficiently prepared for the contest." Believers should take heart whenever they are presented with diverse trials and tribulations, learning from the book of Daniel that God will never leave them and is sovereign over their circumstances.

Martin Luther found in this book a worthy example in Daniel: "From this book we see what an excellent and great man Daniel was, before both God and the world." Not only do believers who engage Daniel's story find in him a worthy example, but they also discover a God who is sovereign over the affairs of men and women, providing comfort and resilience.

1:1–21 Daniel and his friends were held captive in the king's palace and daily brought the king's food. Indeed, the food in itself was not foul, but when the prohibition of God was added to it, the matter was settled. Since it was so regarded by God, whose will is always good, whoever accepted such food became defiled because of disobedience. To demonstrate their faith, Daniel and his companions were tested for ten days. They appeared far better in body and more handsome in appearance than the youths who enjoyed the king's table. God does not desert those who firmly cling to the word of God. It is the power of the Lord that made the food of those youths efficacious, and without his power it would have been worthless and ineffective before the world.

HEINRICH BULLINGER
(1504–1575)
DANIEL, THE MOST WISE PROPHET

DANIEL FINDS FAVOR IN BABYLON

1 In the third year of the reign of King Jehoiakim of Judah, King
Nebuchadnezzar of Babylon advanced against Jerusalem and
laid it under siege. 2Now the Lord delivered King Jehoiakim
of Judah into his power, along with some of the vessels of the
temple of God. He brought them to the land of Babylonia to the
temple of his god and put the vessels in the treasury of his god.
3The king commanded Ashpenaz, who was in charge of his
court officials, to choose some of the Israelites who were of
royal and noble descent—4young men in whom there was no
physical defect and who were handsome, well versed in all kinds
of wisdom, well educated and having keen insight, and who
were capable of entering the king's royal service—and to teach
them the literature and language of the Babylonians. 5So the
king assigned them a daily ration from his royal delicacies and
from the wine he himself drank. They were to be trained for
the next three years. At the end of that time they were to enter
the king's service. 6As it turned out, among these young men
were some from Judah: Daniel, Hananiah, Mishael, and Azariah.
7But the overseer of the court officials renamed them. He gave
Daniel the name Belteshazzar, Hananiah he named Shadrach,
Mishael he named Meshach, and Azariah he named Abednego.
8But Daniel made up his mind that he would not defile himself with the royal delicacies or the royal wine. He therefore
asked the overseer of the court officials for permission not to
defile himself. 9Then God made the overseer of the court officials sympathetic to Daniel. 10But he responded to Daniel, "I
fear my master the king. He is the one who has decided your
food and drink. What would happen if he saw that you looked
malnourished in comparison to the other young men your age?
If that happened, you would endanger my life with the king!"
11Daniel then spoke to the warden whom the overseer of the
court officials had appointed over Daniel, Hananiah, Mishael,
and Azariah: 12"Please test your servants for 10 days by providing
us with some vegetables to eat and water to drink. 13Then compare our appearance with that of the young men who are eating
the royal delicacies; deal with us in light of what you see." 14So
the warden agreed to their proposal and tested them for 10 days.
15At the end of the 10 days their appearance was better and
their bodies were healthier than all the young men who had been
eating the royal delicacies. 16So the warden removed the delicacies
and the wine from their diet and gave them a diet of vegetables
instead. 17Now as for these four young men, God endowed them
with knowledge and skill in all sorts of literature and wisdom—and
Daniel had insight into all kinds of visions and dreams.
18When the time appointed by the king arrived, the overseer
of the court officials brought them into Nebuchadnezzar's presence. 19When the king spoke with them, he did not find among
the entire group anyone like Daniel, Hananiah, Mishael, or
Azariah. So they entered the king's service. 20In every matter of
wisdom and insight the king asked them about, he found them
to be 10 times better than any of the magicians and astrologers
that were in his entire empire. 21Now Daniel lived on until the
first year of Cyrus the king.

NEBUCHADNEZZAR HAS A DISTURBING DREAM

2 In the second year of his reign Nebuchadnezzar had many
dreams. His mind was disturbed, and he suffered from in-
somnia. 2The king issued an order to summon the magicians,

astrologers, sorcerers, and wise men in order to explain his
dreams to him. So they came and awaited the king's instructions.
3The king told them, "I have had a dream, and I am anxious
to understand the dream." 4The wise men replied to the king:
[What follows is in Aramaic] "O king, live forever! Tell your servants the dream, and we will disclose its interpretation." 5The
king replied to the wise men, "My decision is firm. If you do not
inform me of both the dream and its interpretation, you will be
dismembered and your homes reduced to rubble! 6But if you
can disclose the dream and its interpretation, you will receive
from me gifts, a reward, and considerable honor. So disclose
to me the dream and its interpretation." 7They again replied,
"Let the king inform us of the dream; then we will disclose its
interpretation." 8The king replied, "I know for sure that you
are attempting to gain time, because you see that my decision
is firm. 9If you don't inform me of the dream, there is only one
thing that is going to happen to you. For you have agreed among
yourselves to report to me something false and deceitful until
such time as things might change. So tell me the dream, and I
will have confidence that you can disclose its interpretation."
10The wise men replied to the king, "There is no man on earth
who is able to disclose the king's secret, for no king, regardless
of his position and power, has ever requested such a thing from
any magician, astrologer, or wise man. 11What the king is asking
is too difficult, and no one exists who can disclose it to the
king, except for the gods—but they don't live among mortals!"
12Because of this the king got furiously angry and gave orders
to destroy all the wise men of Babylon. 13So a decree went out,
and the wise men were about to be executed. They also sought
Daniel and his friends so that they could be executed.
14Then Daniel spoke with prudent counsel to Arioch, who
was in charge of the king's executioners and who had gone out
to execute the wise men of Babylon. 15He inquired of Arioch the
king's deputy, "Why is the decree from the king so urgent?" Then
Arioch informed Daniel about the matter. 16So Daniel went in
and requested the king to grant him time, that he might disclose the interpretation to the king. 17Then Daniel went to his
home and informed his friends Hananiah, Mishael, and Azariah
of the matter. 18He asked them to pray for mercy from the God
of heaven concerning this mystery so that he and his friends
would not be destroyed along with the rest of the wise men of
Babylon. 19Then in a night vision the mystery was revealed to
Daniel. So Daniel praised the God of heaven, 20saying:

"Let the name of God be praised forever and ever,
for wisdom and power belong to him.
21 He changes times and seasons,
deposing some kings
and establishing others.
He gives wisdom to the wise;
he imparts knowledge to those with understanding;
22 he reveals deep and hidden things.
He knows what is in the darkness,
and light resides with him.
23 O God of my fathers, I acknowledge and glorify you,
for you have bestowed wisdom and power on me.
Now you have enabled me to understand what we
requested from you.
For you have enabled us to understand the king's
dilemma."

2:14–23 "Let the name of God be praised forever and ever," Daniel blessed the name of God. This is the voice of all the saints of God, those who prosper and those who do not. Here he gave thanks for the mercy of God, which has been shown to the ancestors, to the chosen people, and those to whom have been given the greatest promises. Among other people, Daniel said, *I acknowledge you to be the God of wisdom and power, bestowing many favors among my ancestors and their posterity, never ceasing to bless us despite our sins.*

JOHANNES OECOLAMPADIUS
(1482–1531)
COMMENTARY ON DANIEL

24 Then Daniel went in to see Arioch (whom the king had appointed to destroy the wise men of Babylon). He came and said to him, "Don't destroy the wise men of Babylon! Escort me to the king, and I will disclose the interpretation to him."

25 So Arioch quickly ushered Daniel into the king's presence, saying to him, "I have found a man from the captives of Judah who can make known the interpretation to the king." 26 The king then asked Daniel (whose name was also Belteshazzar), "Are you able to make known to me the dream that I saw, as well as its interpretation?" 27 Daniel replied to the king, "The mystery that the king is asking about is such that no wise men, astrologers, magicians, or diviners can possibly disclose it to the king. 28 However, there is a God in heaven who reveals mysteries, and he has made known to King Nebuchadnezzar what will happen in the times to come. The dream and the visions you had while lying on your bed are as follows:

29 "As for you, O king, while you were in your bed your thoughts turned to future things. The revealer of mysteries has made known to you what will take place. 30 As for me, this mystery was revealed to me not because I possess more wisdom than any other living person, but so that the king may understand the interpretation and comprehend the thoughts of your mind.

31 "You, O king, were watching as a great statue—one of impressive size and extraordinary brightness—was standing before you. Its appearance caused alarm. 32 As for that statue, its head was of fine gold, its chest and arms were of silver, its belly and thighs were of bronze. 33 Its legs were of iron; its feet were partly of iron and partly of clay. 34 You were watching as a stone was cut out, but not by human hands. It struck the statue on its iron and clay feet, breaking them in pieces. 35 Then the iron, clay, bronze, silver, and gold were broken in pieces without distinction and became like chaff from the summer threshing floors that the wind carries away. Not a trace of them could be found. But the stone that struck the statue became a large mountain that filled the entire earth. 36 This was the dream. Now we will set forth before the king its interpretation.

DANIEL INTERPRETS NEBUCHADNEZZAR'S DREAM

37 "You, O king, are the king of kings. The God of heaven has granted you sovereignty, power, strength, and honor. 38 Wherever human beings, wild animals, and birds of the sky live—he has given them into your power. He has given you authority over them all. You are the head of gold. 39 Now after you another kingdom will arise, one inferior to yours. Then a third kingdom, one of bronze, will rule in all the earth. 40 Then there will be a fourth kingdom, one strong like iron. Just like iron breaks in pieces and shatters everything, and as iron breaks in pieces all these metals, so it will break in pieces and crush the others. 41 In that you were seeing feet and toes partly of wet clay and partly of iron, so this will be a divided kingdom. Some of the strength of iron will be in it, for you saw iron mixed with wet clay. 42 In that the toes of the feet were partly of iron and partly of clay, the latter stages of this kingdom will be partly strong and partly fragile. 43 And in that you saw iron mixed with wet clay, so people will be mixed with one another without adhering to one another, just as iron does not mix with clay. 44 In the days of those kings the God of heaven will raise up an everlasting kingdom that will not be destroyed and a kingdom that will

not be left to another people. It will break in pieces and bring about the demise of all these kingdoms. But it will stand forever. [45]You saw that a stone was cut from a mountain, but not by human hands; it smashed the iron, bronze, clay, silver, and gold into pieces. The great God has made known to the king what will occur in the future. The dream is certain, and its interpretation is reliable."

[46]Then King Nebuchadnezzar bowed down with his face to the ground and paid homage to Daniel. He gave orders to offer sacrifice and incense to him. [47]The king replied to Daniel, "Certainly your God is a God of gods and Lord of kings and revealer of mysteries, for you were able to reveal this mystery!" [48]Then the king elevated Daniel to high position and bestowed on him many marvelous gifts. He granted him authority over the entire province of Babylon and made him the main prefect over all the wise men of Babylon. [49]And at Daniel's request, the king appointed Shadrach, Meshach, and Abednego over the administration of the province of Babylon. Daniel himself served in the king's court.

DANIEL'S FRIENDS ARE TESTED

3 King Nebuchadnezzar had a golden statue made. It was 90 feet tall and 9 feet wide. He erected it on the plain of Dura in the province of Babylon. [2]Then King Nebuchadnezzar sent out a summons to assemble the satraps, prefects, governors, counselors, treasurers, judges, magistrates, and all the other authorities of the province to attend the dedication of the statue that he had erected. [3]So the satraps, prefects, governors, counselors, treasurers, judges, magistrates, and all the other provincial authorities assembled for the dedication of the statue that King Nebuchadnezzar had erected. They were standing in front of the statue that Nebuchadnezzar had erected.

[4]Then the herald made a loud proclamation: "To you, O peoples, nations, and language groups, the following command is given: [5]When you hear the sound of the horn, flute, zither, trigon, harp, pipes, and all kinds of music, you must bow down and pay homage to the golden statue that King Nebuchadnezzar has erected. [6]Whoever does not bow down and pay homage will immediately be thrown into the midst of a furnace of blazing fire!" [7]Therefore when they all heard the sound of the horn, flute, zither, trigon, harp, pipes, and all kinds of music, all the peoples, nations, and language groups began bowing down and paying homage to the golden statue that King Nebuchadnezzar had erected.

[8]Now at that time certain Chaldeans came forward and brought malicious accusations against the Jews. [9]They said to King Nebuchadnezzar, "O king, live forever! [10]You have issued an edict, O king, that everyone must bow down and pay homage to the golden statue when they hear the sound of the horn, flute, zither, trigon, harp, pipes, and all kinds of music. [11]And whoever does not bow down and pay homage must be thrown into the midst of a furnace of blazing fire. [12]But there are Jewish men whom you appointed over the administration of the province of Babylon—Shadrach, Meshach, and Abednego—and these men have not shown proper respect to you, O king. They don't serve your gods, and they don't pay homage to the golden statue that you have erected."

[13]Then Nebuchadnezzar in a fit of rage demanded that they bring Shadrach, Meshach, and Abednego before him. So they brought them before the king. [14]Nebuchadnezzar said to them,

3:1–25 The narrative of the manly courage and marvelous deliverance of the three holy children, or rather champions, is well calculated to excite in the minds of believers firmness and steadfastness in upholding the truth. Lose all rather than lose your integrity. Be not guided by the will-o'-the-wisp of policy, but by the pole-star of divine authority. Follow the right at all hazards. When you see no present advantage, walk by faith and not by sight. To wear a guileless spirit, to have a heart void of offense, to have the favor and smile of God is greater riches than the mines of Ophir could yield, or the traffic of Tyre could win. An ounce of heartsease is worth a ton of gold.

CHARLES SPURGEON
(1834–1892)
MORNING AND EVENING

"Is it true, Shadrach, Meshach, and Abednego, that you don't
serve my gods and that you don't pay homage to the golden
statue that I erected? [15]Now if you are ready, when you hear the
sound of the horn, flute, zither, trigon, harp, pipes, and all kinds
of music, you must bow down and pay homage to the statue that
I had made. If you don't pay homage to it, you will immediately
be thrown into the midst of the furnace of blazing fire. Now, who
is that god who can rescue you from my power?" [16]Shadrach,
Meshach, and Abednego replied to King Nebuchadnezzar, "We
do not need to give you a reply concerning this. [17]If our God
whom we are serving exists, he is able to rescue us from the
furnace of blazing fire, and he will rescue us, O king, from your
power as well. [18]But if he does not, let it be known to you, O king,
that we don't serve your gods, and we will not pay homage to
the golden statue that you have erected."

[19]Then Nebuchadnezzar was filled with rage, and his disposition changed toward Shadrach, Meshach, and Abednego. He
gave orders to heat the furnace seven times hotter than it was
normally heated. [20]He ordered strong soldiers in his army to
tie up Shadrach, Meshach, and Abednego and to throw them
into the furnace of blazing fire. [21]So those men were tied up
while still wearing their cloaks, trousers, turbans, and other
clothes, and were thrown into the furnace of blazing fire. [22]But
since the king's command was so urgent, and the furnace was
so excessively hot, the men who escorted Shadrach, Meshach,
and Abednego were killed by the leaping flames. [23]But those
three men, Shadrach, Meshach, and Abednego, fell into the
furnace of blazing fire while still securely bound.

GOD DELIVERS HIS SERVANTS

[24]Then King Nebuchadnezzar was startled and quickly got up.
He said to his ministers, "Wasn't it three men that we tied up
and threw into the fire?" They replied to the king, "For sure,
O king." [25]He answered, "But I see four men, untied and walking
around in the midst of the fire! No harm has come to them!
And the appearance of the fourth is like that of a god!" [26]Then
Nebuchadnezzar approached the door of the furnace of blazing
fire. He called out, "Shadrach, Meshach, and Abednego, servants
of the most high God, come out! Come here!"

Then Shadrach, Meshach, and Abednego emerged from the
fire. [27]Once the satraps, prefects, governors, and ministers of
the king had gathered around, they saw that those men were
physically unharmed by the fire. The hair of their heads was not
singed, nor were their trousers damaged. Not even the smell
of fire was to be found on them!

[28]Nebuchadnezzar exclaimed, "Praised be the God of
Shadrach, Meshach, and Abednego, who has sent forth his angel
and has rescued his servants who trusted in him, ignoring the
edict of the king and giving up their bodies rather than serve or
pay homage to any god other than their God! [29]I hereby decree
that any people, nation, or language group that blasphemes the
God of Shadrach, Meshach, or Abednego will be dismembered
and his home reduced to rubble! For there exists no other god
who can deliver in this way." [30]Then Nebuchadnezzar promoted
Shadrach, Meshach, and Abednego in the province of Babylon.

4 King Nebuchadnezzar, to all peoples, nations, and language
groups that live in all the land: "Peace and prosperity! [2]I am
delighted to tell you about the signs and wonders that the most
high God has done for me.

3 "How great are his signs!
How mighty are his wonders!
His kingdom will last forever,
and his authority continues from one generation to the next."

NEBUCHADNEZZAR DREAMS OF A TREE CHOPPED DOWN

4 I, Nebuchadnezzar, was relaxing in my home, living luxuriously in my palace. 5 I saw a dream that frightened me badly. The
things I imagined while lying on my bed—these visions of my
mind—were terrifying me. 6 So I issued an order for all the wise
men of Babylon to be brought before me so that they could make
known to me the interpretation of the dream. 7 When the magicians, astrologers, wise men, and diviners entered, I recounted
the dream for them. But they were unable to make known its
interpretation to me. 8 Later Daniel entered (whose name is
Belteshazzar after the name of my god, and in whom there is a
spirit of the holy gods). I recounted the dream for him as well,
9 saying, "Belteshazzar, chief of the magicians, in whom I know
there to be a spirit of the holy gods and whom no mystery baffles,
consider my dream that I saw and set forth its interpretation!
10 Here are the visions of my mind while I was on my bed.

"While I was watching,
there was a tree in the middle of the land.
It was enormously tall.
11 The tree grew large and strong.
Its top reached far into the sky;
it could be seen from the borders of all the land.
12 Its foliage was attractive and its fruit plentiful;
on it there was food enough for all.
Under it the wild animals used to seek shade,
and in its branches the birds of the sky used to nest.
All creatures used to feed themselves from it.

13 "While I was watching in my mind's visions on my bed,
a holy sentinel came down from heaven.
14 He called out loudly as follows:
'Chop down the tree and lop off its branches!
Strip off its foliage
and scatter its fruit!
Let the animals flee from under it
and the birds from its branches.
15 But leave its taproot in the ground,
with a band of iron and bronze around it
surrounded by the grass of the field.
Let it become damp with the dew of the sky,
and let it live with the animals in the grass of the land.
16 Let his mind be altered from that of a human being,
and let an animal's mind be given to him,
and let seven periods of time go by for him.
17 This announcement is by the decree of the sentinels;
this decision is by the pronouncement of the holy ones,
so that those who are alive may understand
that the Most High has authority over human kingdoms,
and he bestows them on whomever he wishes.
He establishes over them even the lowliest of human beings.'

4:1–37 Nebuchadnezzar's conceptions of the true God were but momentary, and hence he suffered the punishment due to such great ingratitude. When people add sin to sin, God loosens their reins and allows them to destroy themselves. Although Nebuchadnezzar seemed to receive with the greatest modesty what God had manifested by his dream, yet he professed with his mouth what he did not really possess. And he shows this sufficiently because when he ought to be afraid and cautious, he does not lay aside his pride but glories in himself as a king of kings, and in Babylon as the queen of the whole world! Since then he spoke so confidently after being admonished by the prophet, we perceive how little he had profited by his dream. But God wished in this way to render him more inexcusable, and although he did not bring forth fruit immediately, yet a long time afterward, when God touched his mind, he very properly recognized this punishment to have been divinely inflicted.

JOHN CALVIN **(1509–1564)**
COMPLETE COMMENTARY ON THE BIBLE

[18]"This is the dream that I, King Nebuchadnezzar, saw. Now you, Belteshazzar, declare its interpretation, for none of the wise men in my kingdom are able to make known to me the interpretation. But you can do so, for a spirit of the holy gods is in you."

DANIEL INTERPRETS NEBUCHADNEZZAR'S DREAM

[19]Then Daniel (whose name is also Belteshazzar) was upset for a brief time; his thoughts were alarming him. The king said, "Belteshazzar, don't let the dream and its interpretation alarm you." But Belteshazzar replied, "Sir, if only the dream were for your enemies and its interpretation applied to your adversaries! [20]The tree that you saw that grew large and strong, whose top reached to the sky, and that could be seen in all the land, [21]whose foliage was attractive and its fruit plentiful, and from which there was food available for all, under whose branches wild animals used to live, and in whose branches birds of the sky used to nest—[22]it is you, O king! For you have become great and strong. Your greatness is such that it reaches to heaven and your authority to the ends of the earth. [23]As for the king seeing a holy sentinel coming down from heaven and saying, 'Chop down the tree and destroy it, but leave its taproot in the ground, with a band of iron and bronze around it, surrounded by the grass of the field. Let it become damp with the dew of the sky, and let it live with the wild animals, until seven periods of time go by for him'—[24]this is the interpretation, O king. It is the decision of the Most High that this has happened to my lord the king. [25]You will be driven from human society, and you will live with the wild animals. You will be fed grass like oxen, and you will become damp with the dew of the sky. Seven periods of time will pass by for you before you understand that the Most High is ruler over human kingdoms and gives them to whomever he wishes. [26]They said to leave the taproot of the tree, for your kingdom will be restored to you when you come to understand that heaven rules. [27]Therefore, O king, may my advice be pleasing to you. Break away from your sins by doing what is right, and from your iniquities by showing mercy to the poor. Perhaps your prosperity will be prolonged."

[28]Now all this happened to King Nebuchadnezzar. [29]After 12 months, he happened to be walking around on the battlements of the royal palace of Babylon. [30]The king uttered these words: "Is this not the great Babylon that I have built for a royal residence by my own mighty strength and for my majestic honor?" [31]While these words were still on the king's lips, a voice came down from heaven: "It is hereby announced to you, King Nebuchadnezzar, that your kingdom has been removed from you! [32]You will be driven from human society, and you will live with the wild animals. You will be fed grass like oxen, and seven periods of time will pass by for you before you understand that the Most High is ruler over human kingdoms and gives them to whomever he wishes."

[33]Now in that very moment this pronouncement about Nebuchadnezzar came true. He was driven from human society, he ate grass like oxen, and his body became damp with the dew of the sky, until his hair became long like an eagle's feathers and his nails like a bird's claws.

[34]But at the end of the appointed time I, Nebuchadnezzar, looked up toward heaven, and my sanity returned to me.

I extolled the Most High,
and I praised and glorified the one who lives forever.
For his authority is an everlasting authority,
and his kingdom extends from one generation to the next.
35 All the inhabitants of the earth are regarded as nothing.
He does as he wishes with the army of heaven
and with those who inhabit the earth.
No one slaps his hand
and says to him, "What have you done?"

36 At that time my sanity returned to me. I was restored to
the honor of my kingdom, and my splendor returned to me.
My ministers and my nobles were seeking me out, and I was
reinstated over my kingdom. I became even greater than before.
37 Now I, Nebuchadnezzar, praise and exalt and glorify the King
of heaven, for all his deeds are right and his ways are just. He is
able to bring down those who live in pride.

BELSHAZZAR SEES MYSTERIOUS HANDWRITING ON A WALL

5 King Belshazzar prepared a great banquet for 1,000 of his
nobles, and he was drinking wine in front of them all. 2 While
under the influence of the wine, Belshazzar issued an order
to bring in the gold and silver vessels—the ones that Nebuchadnezzar his father had confiscated from the temple in
Jerusalem—so that the king and his nobles, together with his
wives and his concubines, could drink from them. 3 So they
brought the gold and silver vessels that had been confiscated
from the temple, the house of God in Jerusalem, and the king
and his nobles, together with his wives and concubines, drank
from them. 4 As they drank wine, they praised the gods of gold
and silver, bronze, iron, wood, and stone.
5 At that very moment the fingers of a human hand appeared
and wrote on the plaster of the royal palace wall, opposite the
lampstand. The king was watching the back of the hand that was
writing. 6 Then all the color drained from the king's face, and he
became alarmed. The joints of his hips gave way, and his knees
began knocking together. 7 The king called out loudly to summon
the astrologers, wise men, and diviners. The king proclaimed to the
wise men of Babylon that anyone who could read this inscription
and disclose its interpretation would be clothed in purple and have
a golden collar placed on his neck and be third ruler in the kingdom.
8 So all the king's wise men came in, but they were unable to
read the writing or to make known its interpretation to the
king. 9 Then King Belshazzar was very terrified, and he was visibly shaken. His nobles were completely dumbfounded.
10 Due to the noise caused by the king and his nobles, the
queen mother then entered the banquet room. She said,
"O king, live forever! Don't be alarmed! Don't be shaken! 11 There
is a man in your kingdom who has within him a spirit of the
holy gods. In the days of your father, he proved to have insight,
discernment, and wisdom like that of the gods. King Nebuchadnezzar your father appointed him chief of the magicians,
astrologers, wise men, and diviners. 12 Thus there was found
in this man Daniel, whom the king renamed Belteshazzar, an
extraordinary spirit, knowledge, and skill to interpret dreams,
explain riddles, and solve difficult problems. Now summon
Daniel, and he will disclose the interpretation."

5:1–30 Previously Daniel showed the king's repentance and propagation of true worship, on whom God bestowed rewards. Now he adds a contrary example of an impious king, restoring idolatry and not repenting, whom God punished and removed from power. Belshazzar ruled and fell into idolatry. As it is testified, he was an enemy of true doctrine, sanctioned idolatry, profaned the Jewish vessels, and with great contempt insulted God. Swift punishment followed these blasphemies; according to the law, "the LORD will not hold guiltless anyone who takes his name in vain" (Exod 20:7). This history admonishes us concerning the horrible power of the devil, who in all ages uses the greatest authorities to sanction idolatry and harass the church. This history also urges rulers to piety and warns the impious of punishment.

PHILIP MELANCHTHON
(1497–1560)
COMMENTARY ON THE PROPHET DANIEL

13 So Daniel was brought in before the king. The king said to Daniel, "Are you that Daniel who is one of the captives of Judah, whom my father the king brought from Judah? 14 I have heard about you, how there is a spirit of the gods in you, and how you have insight, discernment, and extraordinary wisdom. 15 Now the wise men and astrologers were brought before me to read this writing and make known to me its interpretation. But they were unable to disclose the interpretation of the message. 16 However, I have heard that you are able to provide interpretations and to solve difficult problems. Now if you are able to read this writing and make known to me its interpretation, you will wear purple and have a golden collar around your neck and be third ruler in the kingdom."

DANIEL INTERPRETS THE HANDWRITING ON THE WALL

17 But Daniel replied to the king, "Keep your gifts, and give your rewards to someone else. However, I will read the writing for the king and make known its interpretation. 18 As for you, O king, the most high God bestowed on your father Nebuchadnezzar a kingdom, greatness, honor, and majesty. 19 Due to the greatness that he bestowed on him, all peoples, nations, and language groups were trembling with fear before him. He killed whom he wished, he spared whom he wished, he exalted whom he wished, and he brought low whom he wished. 20 And when his mind became arrogant and his spirit filled with pride, he was deposed from his royal throne, and his honor was removed from him. 21 He was driven from human society; his mind was changed to that of an animal. He lived with the wild donkeys, he was fed grass like oxen, and his body became damp with the dew of the sky, until he came to understand that the most high God rules over human kingdoms, and he appoints over them whomever he wishes.

22 "But you, his son Belshazzar, have not humbled yourself, although you knew all this. 23 Instead, you have exalted yourself against the Lord of heaven. You brought before you the vessels from his temple, and you and your nobles, together with your wives and concubines, drank wine from them. You praised the gods of silver, gold, bronze, iron, wood, and stone—gods that cannot see or hear or comprehend. But you have not glorified the God who has in his control your very breath and all your ways! 24 Therefore the palm of a hand was sent from him, and this writing was inscribed.

25 "This is the writing that was inscribed: MENE, MENE, TEQEL, and PHARSIN. 26 This is the interpretation of the words: As for *Mene*—God has numbered your kingdom's days and brought it to an end. 27 As for *Teqel*—you are weighed on the balances and found to be lacking. 28 As for *Peres*—your kingdom is divided and given over to the Medes and Persians."

29 Then, on Belshazzar's orders, Daniel was clothed in purple, a golden collar was placed around his neck, and he was proclaimed third ruler in the kingdom. 30 And that very night Belshazzar, the Babylonian king, was killed. 31 So Darius the Mede took control of the kingdom when he was about sixty-two years old.

DANIEL IS THROWN INTO A LIONS' DEN

6 It seemed like a good idea to Darius to appoint over the kingdom 120 satraps who would be in charge of the entire kingdom. 2 Over them would be three supervisors, one of whom

was Daniel. These satraps were accountable to them, so that
the king's interests might not incur damage. [3]Now this Daniel
was distinguishing himself above the other supervisors and the
satraps, for he had an extraordinary spirit. In fact, the king intended to appoint him over the entire kingdom. [4]Consequently
the supervisors and satraps were trying to find some pretext
against Daniel in connection with administrative matters. But
they were unable to find any such damaging evidence because he
was trustworthy and guilty of no negligence or corruption. [5]So
these men concluded, "We won't find any pretext against this
man Daniel unless it is in connection with the law of his God."
[6]So these supervisors and satraps came by collusion to the
king and said to him, "O King Darius, live forever! [7]To all the
supervisors of the kingdom, the prefects, satraps, counselors,
and governors it seemed like a good idea for a royal edict to
be issued and an interdict to be enforced. For the next 30 days
anyone who prays to any god or human other than you, O king,
should be thrown into a den of lions. [8]Now let the king issue a
written interdict so that it cannot be altered, according to the
law of the Medes and Persians, which cannot be changed." [9]So
King Darius issued the written interdict.
[10]When Daniel realized that a written decree had been issued, he entered his home, where the windows in his upper
room opened toward Jerusalem. Three times daily he was kneeling and offering prayers and thanks to his God just as he had
been accustomed to do previously. [11]Then those officials who
had gone to the king came by collusion and found Daniel praying and asking for help before his God. [12]So they approached
the king and said to him, "Did you not issue an edict to the
effect that for the next 30 days anyone who prays to any god or
human other than to you, O king, would be thrown into a den of
lions?" The king replied, "That is correct, according to the law
of the Medes and Persians, which cannot be changed." [13]Then
they said to the king, "Daniel, who is one of the captives from
Judah, pays no attention to you, O king, or to the edict that you
issued. Three times daily he offers his prayer."
[14]When the king heard this, he was very upset and began
thinking about how he might rescue Daniel. Until late afternoon he was struggling to find a way to rescue him. [15]Then
those men came by collusion to the king and said to him, "Recall, O king, that it is a law of the Medes and Persians that no
edict or decree that the king issues can be changed." [16]So the
king gave the order, and Daniel was brought and thrown into
a den of lions. The king consoled Daniel by saying, "Your God
whom you continually serve will rescue you!" [17]Then a stone
was brought and placed over the opening to the den. The king
sealed it with his signet ring and with those of his nobles so that
nothing could be changed with regard to Daniel. [18]Then the king
departed to his palace. But he spent the night without eating,
and no diversions were brought to him. He was unable to sleep.

GOD RESCUES DANIEL FROM THE LIONS

[19]In the morning, at the earliest sign of daylight, the king got
up and rushed to the lions' den. [20]As he approached the den,
he called out to Daniel in a worried voice, "Daniel, servant of
the living God, was your God whom you continually serve able
to rescue you from the lions?"
[21]Then Daniel spoke to the king, "O king, live forever! [22]My
God sent his angel and closed the lions' mouths so that they

6:1–9 Nothing is more repugnant than envy: It pressured the supervisors and satraps into committing impiety and caused an impious decree to be published forbidding those intent on offering prayers to God; they prevented not only themselves from doing it but also all others subject to royal control. In surrendering to envy, they did not understand that the king could not supply everything to petitioners, such as health, life, fathering children, abundance of rain, and anything else that we receive when we ask it of God. Losing their senses, they ascribed to the king what belongs to God and persuaded the foolish king to reach the same verdict and ratify their request.

THEODORET OF CYR
(C. 393–C. 458)
COMMENTARY ON DANIEL

have not harmed me because I was found to be innocent before
him. Nor have I done any harm to you, O king."
[23]Then the king was delighted and gave an order to haul
Daniel up from the den. So Daniel was hauled up out of the
den. He had no injury of any kind because he had trusted in
his God. [24]The king gave another order, and those men who had
maliciously accused Daniel were brought and thrown into the
lions' den—they, their children, and their wives. They did not
even reach the bottom of the den before the lions overpowered
them and crushed all their bones.
[25]Then King Darius wrote to all the peoples, nations, and
language groups who were living in all the land: "Peace and
prosperity! [26]I have issued an edict that throughout all the
dominion of my kingdom people are to revere and fear the
God of Daniel.

"For he is the living God;
he endures forever.
His kingdom will not be destroyed;
his authority is forever.
[27] He rescues and delivers
and performs signs and wonders
in the heavens and on the earth.
He has rescued Daniel from the power of the lions!"

[28]So this Daniel prospered during the reign of Darius and
the reign of Cyrus the Persian.

DANIEL HAS A VISION OF FOUR ANIMALS COMING UP FROM THE SEA

7 In the first year of King Belshazzar of Babylon, Daniel had
a dream filled with visions while he was lying on his bed.
Then he wrote down the dream in summary fashion. [2]Daniel
explained: "I was watching in my vision during the night as
the four winds of the sky were stirring up the great sea. [3]Then
four large beasts came up from the sea; they were different
from one another.
[4]"The first one was like a lion with eagles' wings. As I watched,
its wings were pulled off, and it was lifted up from the ground.
It was made to stand on two feet like a human being, and a
human mind was given to it.
[5]"Then a second beast appeared, like a bear. It was raised up
on one side, and there were three ribs in its mouth between its
teeth. It was told, 'Get up and devour much flesh!'
[6]"After these things, as I was watching, another beast like a
leopard appeared, with four bird-like wings on its back. This
beast had four heads, and ruling authority was given to it.
[7]"After these things, as I was watching in the night visions a
fourth beast appeared—one dreadful, terrible, and very strong.
It had two large rows of iron teeth. It devoured and crushed, and
anything that was left it trampled with its feet. It was different
from all the beasts that came before it, and it had 10 horns.
[8]"As I was contemplating the horns, another horn—a small
one—came up between them, and three of the former horns
were torn out by the roots to make room for it. This horn had
eyes resembling human eyes and a mouth speaking arrogant
things.

[9]"While I was watching,
thrones were set up,
and the Ancient of Days took his seat.

RAPHAEL, ***THE TRANSFIGURATION*** (1516–1520)

(Public Domain)

DIEGO VELÁZQUEZ, ***CRISTO CRUCIFICADO*** (1632)

(Public Domain)

His attire was white like snow;
the hair of his head was like lamb's wool.
His throne was ablaze with fire,
and its wheels were all aflame.
10 A river of fire was streaming forth
and proceeding from his presence.
Many thousands were ministering to him;
many tens of thousands stood ready to serve him.
The court convened,
and the books were opened.

11"Then I kept on watching because of the arrogant words
of the horn that was speaking. I was watching until the beast
was killed and its body destroyed and thrown into the flaming
fire. 12As for the rest of the beasts, their ruling authority had
already been removed, though they were permitted to go on
living for a time and a season.
13 "I was watching in the night visions,
And with the clouds of the sky,
one like a son of man was approaching.
He went up to the Ancient of Days
and was escorted before him.
14 To him was given ruling authority, honor, and
sovereignty.
All peoples, nations, and language groups were serving
him.
His authority is eternal and will not pass away.
His kingdom will not be destroyed.

AN ANGEL INTERPRETS DANIEL'S VISION

15"As for me, Daniel, my spirit was distressed, and the visions
of my mind were alarming me. 16I approached one of those
standing nearby and asked him about the meaning of all this.
So he spoke with me and revealed to me the interpretation
of the vision: 17'These large beasts, which are four in number,
represent four kings who will arise from the earth. 18The holy
ones of the Most High will receive the kingdom and will take
possession of the kingdom forever and ever.'
19"Then I wanted to know the meaning of the fourth beast,
which was different from all the others. It was very dreadful,
with two rows of iron teeth and bronze claws, and it devoured,
crushed, and trampled anything that was left with its feet. 20I
also wanted to know the meaning of the 10 horns on its head,
and of that other horn that came up and before which three others fell. This was the horn that had eyes and a mouth speaking
arrogant things, whose appearance was more formidable than
the others. 21While I was watching, that horn began to wage
war against the holy ones and was defeating them, 22until the
Ancient of Days arrived and judgment was rendered in favor
of the holy ones of the Most High. Then the time came for the
holy ones to take possession of the kingdom.
23"This is what he told me:
'The fourth beast means that there will be a fourth
kingdom on earth
that will differ from all the other kingdoms.
It will devour all the earth
and will trample and crush it.
24 The 10 horns mean that 10 kings
will arise from that kingdom.

7:15–28 Let us examine the reasons why God reveals these things. The human mind desires knowledge of the future with such perverse curiosity. But in fact God makes known great things from the beginning: the advent of his Son, the future judgment, the resurrection of the dead, the eternal punishment of the wicked, the eternal glory of believers, and the exact succession or order of the kingdoms before the final judgment. God did not reveal these things in vain but that his will would be carefully considered. And indeed, this doctrine taught Daniel and others about eternal life and the future judgment. We know with certainty that this doctrine, which Daniel professed, is divine, and we will not allow it to be taken away from us.

PHILIP MELANCHTHON
(1497–1560)
COMMENTARY ON THE PROPHET DANIEL

Another king will arise after them,
but he will be different from the earlier ones.
He will humiliate three kings.
25 He will speak words against the Most High.
He will harass the holy ones of the Most High
continually.
His intention will be to change times established by
law.
The holy ones will be delivered into his hand
for a time, times, and half a time.
26 But the court will convene, and his ruling authority will
be removed—
destroyed and abolished forever!
27 Then the kingdom, authority,
and greatness of the kingdoms under the whole heaven
will be delivered to the people of the holy ones of the
Most High.
His kingdom is an eternal kingdom;
all authorities will serve him and obey him.'

[28]"This is the conclusion of the matter. As for me, Daniel, my
thoughts troubled me greatly, and the color drained from my
face. But I kept the matter to myself."

DANIEL HAS A VISION OF A GOAT AND A RAM

8 In the third year of King Belshazzar's reign, a vision appeared
to me, Daniel, after the one that had appeared to me previously. [2]In this vision I saw myself in Susa the citadel, which is
located in the province of Elam. In the vision I saw myself at the
Ulai Canal. [3]I looked up and saw a ram with two horns standing
at the canal. Its two horns were both long, but one was longer
than the other. The longer one was coming up after the shorter
one. [4]I saw that the ram was butting westward, northward, and
southward. No animal was able to stand before it, and there
was none who could deliver from its power. It did as it pleased
and acted arrogantly.
[5]While I was contemplating all this, a male goat was coming
from the west over the surface of all the land without touching the ground. This goat had a conspicuous horn between its
eyes. [6]It came to the two-horned ram that I had seen standing
beside the canal and rushed against it with raging strength. [7]I
saw it approaching the ram. It went into a fit of rage against
the ram and struck it and broke off its two horns. The ram had
no ability to resist it. The goat hurled the ram to the ground
and trampled it. No one could deliver the ram from its power.
[8]The male goat acted even more arrogantly. But no sooner had
the large horn become strong than it was broken, and there
arose four conspicuous horns in its place, extending toward
the four winds of the sky.
[9]From one of them came a small horn, but it grew to be very
great toward the south and the east and toward the beautiful
land. [10]It grew so great it reached the army of heaven, and it
brought about the fall of some of the army and some of the
stars to the ground, where it trampled them. [11]It also acted
arrogantly against the Prince of the army, from whom the daily
sacrifice was removed and whose sanctuary was thrown down.
[12]The army was given over, along with the daily sacrifice, in the
course of his sinful rebellion. It hurled truth to the ground and
enjoyed success.

8:1–27 The eternal Son of God stood before the prophet in the appearance of a man and directed the angel Gabriel to explain the vision. Daniel's fainting and astonishment at the prospect of evils he saw coming on his people and the church confirm the opinion that long-continued calamities were foretold. The vision being ended, a charge was given to Daniel to keep it private for the present. He kept it to himself and went on to do the duty of his place. As long as we live in this world, we must have something to do in it, and even those whom God has most honored must not think themselves above their business. Nor must the pleasure of communion with God take us from the duties of our callings, but we must in them abide with God.

MATTHEW HENRY **(1662–1714)**
COMMENTARY ON THE WHOLE BIBLE

[13]Then I heard a holy one speaking. Another holy one said to the one who was speaking, "To what period of time does the vision pertain—this vision concerning the daily sacrifice and the destructive act of rebellion and the giving over of both the sanctuary and army to be trampled?" [14]He said to me, "To 2,300 evenings and mornings; then the sanctuary will be put right again."

AN ANGEL INTERPRETS DANIEL'S VISION

[15]While I, Daniel, was watching the vision, I sought to understand it. Now one who appeared to be a man was standing before me. [16]Then I heard a human voice coming from between the banks of the Ulai. It called out, "Gabriel, enable this person to understand the vision." [17]So he approached the place where I was standing. As he came, I felt terrified and fell flat on the ground. Then he said to me, "Understand, son of man, that the vision pertains to the time of the end." [18]As he spoke with me, I fell into a trance with my face to the ground. But he touched me and stood me upright.

[19]Then he said, "I am going to inform you about what will happen in the latter time of wrath, for the vision pertains to the appointed time of the end. [20]The ram that you saw with the two horns stands for the kings of Media and Persia. [21]The male goat is the king of Greece, and the large horn between its eyes is the first king. [22]The horn that was broken and in whose place there arose four others stands for four kingdoms that will arise from his nation, though they will not have his strength. [23]Toward the end of their rule, when rebellious acts are complete, a rash and deceitful king will arise. [24]His power will be great, but it will not be by his strength alone. He will cause terrible destruction. He will be successful in what he undertakes. He will destroy powerful people and the people of the holy ones. [25]By his treachery he will succeed through deceit. He will have an arrogant attitude, and he will destroy many who are unaware of his schemes. He will rise up against the Prince of princes, yet he will be broken apart—but not by human agency. [26]The vision of the evenings and mornings that was told to you is correct. But you should seal up the vision, for it refers to a time many days from now."

[27]I, Daniel, was exhausted and sick for days. Then I got up and again carried out the king's business. But I was astonished at the vision, and there was no one to explain it.

DANIEL PRAYS FOR HIS PEOPLE

9 In the first year of Darius son of Ahasuerus, who was of Median descent and who had been appointed king over the Babylonian empire—[2]in the first year of his reign I, Daniel, came to understand from the sacred books that the number of years for the fulfilling of the desolation of Jerusalem, which had come as the LORD's message to the prophet Jeremiah, would be 70 years. [3]So I turned my attention to the Lord God to implore him by prayer and requests, with fasting, sackcloth, and ashes. [4]I prayed to the LORD my God, confessing in this way:

"O Lord, great and awesome God who is faithful to his covenant with those who love him and keep his commandments, [5]we have sinned! We have done what is wrong and wicked; we have rebelled by turning away from your commandments and standards. [6]We have not paid attention to your servants the prophets, who spoke by your authority to our kings, our leaders, and our ancestors, and to all the inhabitants of the land as well.

[7]"You are righteous, O Lord, but we are humiliated this day—the people of Judah and the inhabitants of Jerusalem and all

9:1–27 This chapter contains a compendium of the most important articles of faith: God, sin, the forgiveness of sins, penance, faith, prayer, the Messiah, the end of the Jewish people, the antichrist, and the destruction of the world. To this point in the book, Daniel has described the monarchies and memorable events in his history. Now as if to analyze these things that follow the monarchy in which he lived, which is to say of the Medes and Persians, he recites the remarkable revelation concerning the restoration of the Israelite people, the renewal of Jerusalem, and the coming Messiah. Daniel understood that God so loved and preserved the Israelite people that he bestowed on them and adorned them with kindness and miracles for this very reason—so that he might exhibit to them the Messiah, who would conquer the devil, redeem the human race from sin, and save them from eternal condemnation.

JOHANN WIGAND
(C. 1523–1587)
BRIEF EXPOSITION ON THE PROPHET DANIEL

Israel, both near and far away in all the countries in which you
have scattered them because they have behaved unfaithfully
toward you. [8]O LORD, we have been humiliated—our kings, our
leaders, and our ancestors—because we have sinned against you.
[9]Yet the Lord our God is compassionate and forgiving, even
though we have rebelled against him. [10]We have not obeyed
the LORD our God by living according to his laws that he set
before us through his servants the prophets.

[11]"All Israel has broken your law and turned away by not obeying you. Therefore you have poured out on us the judgment solemnly threatened in the law of Moses the servant of God, for we
have sinned against you. [12]He has carried out his threats against
us and our rulers who were over us by bringing great calamity
on us—what has happened to Jerusalem has never been equaled
under all heaven! [13]Just as it is written in the law of Moses, so all
this calamity has come on us. Still we have not tried to pacify
the LORD our God by turning back from our sin and by seeking
wisdom from your reliable moral standards. [14]The LORD was
mindful of the calamity, and he brought it on us. For the LORD
our God is just in all he has done, and we have not obeyed him.

[15]"Now, O Lord our God, who brought your people out of the
land of Egypt with great power and made a name for yourself
that is remembered to this day—we have sinned and behaved
wickedly. [16]O Lord, according to all your justice, please turn your
raging anger away from your city Jerusalem, your holy mountain. For due to our sins and the iniquities of our ancestors,
Jerusalem and your people are mocked by all our neighbors.

[17]"So now, our God, accept the prayer and requests of your
servant, and show favor to your devastated sanctuary for
your own sake. [18]Listen attentively, my God, and hear! Open
your eyes and look on our desolated ruins and the city called
by your name. For it is not because of our own righteous deeds
that we are praying to you, but because your compassion is
abundant. [19]O Lord, hear! O Lord, forgive! O Lord, pay attention,
and act! Don't delay, for your own sake, O my God! For your city
and your people are called by your name."

GABRIEL GIVES TO DANIEL A PROPHECY OF 70 WEEKS

[20]While I was still speaking and praying, confessing my sin and the
sin of my people Israel and presenting my request before the LORD
my God concerning his holy mountain—[21]yes, while I was still
praying, the man Gabriel, whom I had seen previously in a vision,
was approaching me in my state of extreme weariness, around the
time of the evening offering. [22]He spoke with me, instructing me
as follows: "Daniel, I have now come to impart understanding to
you. [23]At the beginning of your requests a message went out, and
I have come to convey it to you, for you are of great value in God's
sight. Therefore consider the message and understand the vision:

24 "Seventy weeks have been determined
concerning your people and your holy city
to put an end to rebellion,
to bring sin to completion,
to atone for iniquity,
to bring in perpetual righteousness,
to seal up the prophetic vision,
and to anoint a Most Holy Place.

25 So know and understand:
From the issuing of the command to restore and rebuild

be afraid, you who are highly valued. Peace be to you! Be strong!
Be really strong!" When he spoke to me, I was strengthened. I said,
"Sir, you may speak now, for you have given me strength." 20He
said, "Do you know why I have come to you? Now I am about to
return to engage in battle with the prince of Persia. When I go, the
prince of Greece is coming. 21However, I will first tell you what is
written in a dependable book. (There is no one who strengthens
me against these princes, except Michael your prince.
11 "And in the first year of Darius the Mede, I stood to
strengthen him and to provide protection for him.) 2Now
I will tell you the truth.

THE ANGEL GIVES A MESSAGE TO DANIEL

"Three more kings will arise for Persia. Then a fourth king will
be unusually rich, more so than all who preceded him. When
he has amassed power through his riches, he will stir up everyone against the kingdom of Greece. 3Then a powerful king
will arise, exercising great authority and doing as he pleases.
4Shortly after his rise to power, his kingdom will be broken up
and distributed toward the four winds of the sky—but not to
his posterity or with the authority he exercised, for his kingdom will be uprooted and distributed to others besides these.

5"Then the king of the south and one of his subordinates will
grow strong. His subordinate will resist him and will rule a kingdom greater than his. 6After some years have passed, they will
form an alliance. Then the daughter of the king of the south will
come to the king of the north to make an agreement, but she
will not retain her power, nor will he continue in his strength.
She, together with the one who brought her, her child, and her
benefactor will all be delivered over at that time.

7"There will arise in his place one from her family line who
will come against their army and will enter the stronghold of the
king of the north and will move against them successfully. 8He
will also take their gods into captivity to Egypt, along with their
cast images and prized utensils of silver and gold. Then he will
withdraw for some years from the king of the north. 9Then the
king of the north will advance against the empire of the king of
the south, but will withdraw to his own land. 10His sons will wage
war, mustering a large army that will advance like an overflowing
river and carrying the battle all the way to the enemy's fortress.

11"Then the king of the south will be enraged and will march
out to fight against the king of the north, who will also muster
a large army, but that army will be delivered into his hand.
12When the army is taken away, the king of the south will become arrogant. He will be responsible for the death of thousands and thousands of people, but he will not continue to
prevail. 13For the king of the north will again muster an army,
one larger than before. At the end of some years he will advance
with a huge army and enormous supplies.

14"In those times many will oppose the king of the south.
Those who are violent among your own people will rise up in
confirmation of the vision, but they will falter. 15Then the king
of the north will advance and will build siege mounds and capture a well-fortified city. The forces of the south will not prevail,
not even his finest contingents. They will have no strength to
prevail. 16The one advancing against him will do as he pleases,
and no one will be able to stand before him. He will prevail in
the beautiful land, and its annihilation will be within his power.
17His intention will be to come with the strength of his entire

Jerusalem until an anointed one, a prince arrives,
there will be a period of seven weeks and sixty-two weeks.
It will again be built, with plaza and moat,
but in distressful times.
26 Now after the sixty-two weeks,
an anointed one will be cut off and have nothing.
As for the city and the sanctuary,
the people of the coming prince will destroy them.
But his end will come speedily like a flood.
Until the end of the war that has been decreed
there will be destruction.
27 He will confirm a covenant with many for one week.
But in the middle of that week
he will bring sacrifices and offerings to a halt.
On the wing of abominations will come one who destroys,
until the decreed end is poured out on the one who
destroys."

AN ANGEL APPEARS TO DANIEL

10 In the third year of King Cyrus of Persia a message was
revealed to Daniel (who was also called Belteshazzar). This
message was true and concerned a great war. He understood
the message and gained insight by the vision.
2 In those days I, Daniel, was mourning for three whole weeks.
3 I ate no choice food, no meat or wine came to my lips, nor did
I anoint myself with oil until the end of those three weeks.
4 On the twenty-fourth day of the first month I was beside
the great river, the Tigris. 5 I looked up and saw a man clothed in
linen; around his waist was a belt made of gold from Ufaz. 6 His
body resembled yellow jasper, and his face had an appearance
like lightning. His eyes were like blazing torches; his arms and
feet had the gleam of polished bronze. His voice thundered
forth like the sound of a large crowd.
7 Only I, Daniel, saw the vision; the men who were with me did
not see it. On the contrary, they were overcome with fright and ran
away to hide. 8 I alone was left to see this great vision. My strength
drained from me, and my vigor disappeared; I was without energy.
9 I listened to his voice, and as I did so I fell into a trance-like sleep
with my face to the ground. 10 Then a hand touched me and set
me on my hands and knees. 11 He said to me, "Daniel, you are of
great value. Understand the words that I am about to speak to
you. So stand up, for I have now been sent to you." When he said
this to me, I stood up shaking. 12 Then he said to me, "Don't be
afraid, Daniel, for from the very first day you applied your mind to
understand and to humble yourself before your God, your words
were heard. I have come in response to your words. 13 However,
the prince of the kingdom of Persia was opposing me for 21 days.
But Michael, one of the leading princes, came to help me, because
I was left there with the kings of Persia. 14 Now I have come to
help you understand what will happen to your people in future
days, for the vision pertains to days to come."
15 While he was saying this to me, I was flat on the ground and
unable to speak. 16 Then one who appeared to be a human being
was touching my lips. I opened my mouth and started to speak,
saying to the one who was standing before me, "Sir, due to the
vision, anxiety has gripped me and I have no strength. 17 How,
sir, am I able to speak with you? My strength is gone, and I am
breathless." 18 Then the one who appeared to be a human being
touched me again and strengthened me. 19 He said to me, "Don't

10:12 Daniel heard from the angel that on the very first day he had begun to pray and to afflict himself before God, his words had been heard and granted. The question arises why, if he had been heard, was the angel not sent to him right away? Well, by reason of the delay an opportunity was afforded him of praying to the Lord at greater length, so that in proportion as his earnest desire was intensified, he might deserve to hear more than he would otherwise. And as for the angel's statement, "I have come in response to your words," his meaning is this: *After you began to invoke God's mercy by good works and tearful supplication and fasting, then I for my part embraced the opportunity of entering in before God and praying for you.*

JEROME **(C. 342–420)**
COMMENTARY ON DANIEL

kingdom, and he will form alliances. He will give the king of the south a daughter in marriage in order to destroy the kingdom, but it will not turn out to his advantage. 18Then he will turn his attention to the coastal regions and will capture many of them. But a commander will bring his shameful conduct to a halt; in addition, he will make him pay for his shameful conduct. 19He will then turn his attention to the fortresses of his own land, but he will stumble and fall, not to be found again. 20There will arise after him one who will send out an exactor of tribute to enhance the splendor of the kingdom, but after a few days he will be destroyed, though not in anger or battle.

21"Then there will arise in his place a despicable person to whom the royal honor has not been rightfully conferred. He will come on the scene in a time of prosperity and will seize the kingdom through deceit. 22Armies will be suddenly swept away in defeat before him; both they and a covenant leader will be destroyed. 23After entering into an alliance with him, he will behave treacherously; he will ascend to power with only a small force. 24In a time of prosperity for the most productive areas of the province, he will come and accomplish what neither his fathers nor their fathers accomplished. He will distribute loot, spoils, and property to his followers, and he will devise plans against fortified cities, but not for long. 25He will rouse his strength and enthusiasm against the king of the south with a large army. The king of the south will wage war with a large and very powerful army, but he will not be able to prevail because of the plans devised against him. 26Those who share the king's fine food will attempt to destroy him, and his army will be swept away; many will be killed in battle. 27These two kings, their minds filled with evil intentions, will trade lies with one another at the same table. But it will not succeed, for there is still an end at the appointed time. 28Then the king of the north will return to his own land with much property. His mind will be set against the holy covenant. He will take action, and then return to his own land. 29At an appointed time he will again invade the south, but this latter visit will not turn out the way the former one did. 30The ships of Kittim will come against him, leaving him disheartened. He will turn back and direct his indignation against the holy covenant. He will return and honor those who forsake the holy covenant. 31His forces will rise up and profane the fortified sanctuary, stopping the daily sacrifice. In its place they will set up the abomination that causes desolation. 32Then with smooth words he will defile those who have rejected the covenant. But the people who are loyal to their God will act valiantly. 33These who are wise among the people will teach the masses. However, they will fall by the sword and by the flame, and they will be imprisoned and plundered for some time. 34When they stumble, they will be granted some help. But many will unite with them deceitfully. 35Even some of the wise will stumble, resulting in their refinement, purification, and cleansing until the time of the end, for it is still for the appointed time.

36"Then the king will do as he pleases. He will exalt and magnify himself above every deity, and he will utter presumptuous things against the God of gods. He will succeed until the time of wrath is completed, for what has been decreed must occur. 37He will not respect the gods of his fathers—not even the god loved by women. He will not respect any god; he will elevate himself above them all. 38What he will honor is a god of fortresses—a god his fathers did not acknowledge he will honor with gold, silver, valuable stones,

11:29–39 "The people who are loyal to their God will act valiantly. These who are wise among the people will teach the masses." Every believer understands that to know God is the highest and best form of knowledge; and this spiritual knowledge is a source of strength to Christians. Knowledge strengthens love as well as faith. Knowledge opens the door, and then through that door we see our Savior. Knowledge also strengthens hope. How can we hope for a thing if we do not know of its existence? Hope may be the telescope, but till we receive instruction our ignorance stands in the front of the glass. Knowledge removes the interposing object, and when we look through the bright optic glass we discern the glory to be revealed and anticipate it with joyous confidence. Knowledge supplies us reasons for patience. Nor is there one single grace of the Christian that, under God, will not be fostered and brought to perfection by holy knowledge. How important then is it that we should grow not only in grace but also in the knowledge of our Lord and Savior Jesus Christ.

CHARLES SPURGEON
(1834–1892)
MORNING AND EVENING

JOHN WYCLIFFE:

ENGLISH PRE-REFORMATION REFORMER

c. 1325–1384

Every era seems to have people who were ahead of their time, advocating revolution well before the actual event. Such a person was John Wycliffe, whom many see as a pre-Reformation Reformer who both anticipated the sixteenth-century movement and laid the foundation for many of the Reformers' arguments.

Born in Yorkshire, England, in 1325, Wycliffe as a young man rose to master of Balliol College at Oxford University, quickly garnering a reputation as an able scholar. He leveraged this position to advocate for ecclesial reform, specifically calling for significant change to church structure and governance. Wycliffe believed the papacy was rife with corruption and that individual churches should be governed by God through local parish overseers rather than the hierarchy of Rome.

Nearly 150 years before Martin Luther would launch the actual Reformation, Wycliffe anticipated Luther's criticism against an important penitential practice of the Catholic Church: indulgences. He excoriated as being both rife with corruption and theologically untenable the practice of the pope's agents selling scripts that granted remittance of the punishment of sins. His harsh criticism has led modern biographers to suggest that Wycliffe's work was vital for motivating and enabling this aspect of the Reformation's critique of the Roman Catholic Church.

Coinciding with his attacks on ecclesial corruption and practices was an ardent advocacy for the supremacy of scripture as authoritative for faith and life. The generations of Christian tradition leading up to Wycliffe's fourteenth-century era had held the great tradition of the Christian faith alongside the Bible with special emphasis on the church's interpretive authority in connection with scripture. In 1378 Wycliffe wrote a corrective: *On the Truth of the Holy Scriptures*, in which he argued, "Holy scripture is the highest authority for every Christian and the standard of all faith and of all human perfection," an affirmation of the Bible's supreme and unique authority in the life of the church that reverberated all the way to the Reformation.

Perhaps stemming from this commitment, he developed five rules for studying the Bible: "Obtain a reliable text, understand the logic of scripture, compare the parts of scripture with one another, maintain an attitude of humble seeking, and receive the instruction of the Spirit." This passion for personal Bible study drove his translation of the Latin version of the Bible, known as the Vulgate, into the vernacular Middle English.

Wycliffe's bold advocacy for ecclesial reform and passion for bringing the Bible into the common language of the day has rightly earned him recognition as an important figure in the growth of the church.

IMPORTANT WORKS

ON THE TRUTH OF THE HOLY SCRIPTURES

THE POWER OF THE PAPACY

ON THE CHURCH

and treasured commodities. 39He will attack mighty fortresses,
aided by a foreign deity. To those who recognize him he will grant
considerable honor. He will place them in authority over many
people, and he will parcel out land for a price.
40"At the time of the end the king of the south will attack
him. Then the king of the north will storm against him with
chariots, horsemen, and a large armada of ships. He will invade lands, passing through them like an overflowing river.
41Then he will enter the beautiful land. Many will fall, but these
will escape: Edom, Moab, and the Ammonite leadership. 42He
will extend his power against other lands; the land of Egypt will
not escape. 43He will have control over the hidden stores of
gold and silver, as well as all the treasures of Egypt. Libyans and
Ethiopians will submit to him. 44But reports will trouble him
from the east and north, and he will set out in a tremendous
rage to destroy and wipe out many. 45He will pitch his royal
tents between the seas toward the beautiful holy mountain.
But he will come to his end, with no one to help him.

12 "At that time Michael,
the great prince who watches over your people,
will arise.
There will be a time of distress
unlike any other from the nation's beginning
up to that time.
But at that time your own people,
all those whose names are found written in the book,
will escape.
2 Many of those who sleep
in the dusty ground will awake—
some to everlasting life,
and others to shame and everlasting abhorrence.
3 But the wise will shine
like the brightness of the heavenly expanse.
And those bringing many to righteousness
will be like the stars forever and ever.

4"But you, Daniel, close up these words and seal the book
until the time of the end. Many will dash about, and knowledge
will increase."
5I, Daniel, watched as two others stood there, one on each
side of the river. 6One said to the man clothed in linen who
was above the waters of the river, "When will the end of these
wondrous events occur?" 7Then I heard the man clothed in
linen who was over the waters of the river as he raised both his
right and left hands to the sky and made an oath by the one
who lives forever: "It is for a time, times, and half a time. Then,
when the power of the one who shatters the holy people has
been exhausted, all these things will be finished."
8I heard, but I did not understand. So I said, "Sir, what will
happen after these things?" 9He said, "Go, Daniel. For these matters are closed and sealed until the time of the end. 10Many will
be purified, made clean, and refined, but the wicked will go on
being wicked. None of the wicked will understand, though the
wise will understand. 11From the time that the daily sacrifice
is removed and the abomination that causes desolation is set
in place, there are 1,290 days. 12Blessed is the one who waits
and attains to the 1,335 days. 13But you should go your way until
the end. You will rest, and then at the end of the days you will
arise to receive what you have been allotted."

12:1–13 We here perceive the angel teaching the same truth as Paul delivered in other words, namely, we are dead, and our life is hidden with Christ; it shall then be made manifest when he shall appear in the heavens. We must hold this first of all, that God is sufficiently powerful to defend us, and we need not hesitate in feeling ourselves safe under his hand and protection. Our salvation is secure, but we still hope for it, as Paul says in another passage. What is hoped for is not seen, says he. This shows us how completely seasonable is the transition from this doctrine respecting God's elect to the last advent of Christ.

JOHN CALVIN (1509–1564)
COMPLETE COMMENTARY ON THE BIBLE

AUTHOR	AUDIENCE	DATE	PURPOSE	THEMES
Hosea	Primarily the northern kingdom of Israel	Probably after the fall of the northern capital, Samaria, in 722 BC	Hosea wrote to expose Israel's unfaithfulness to the Lord, offering both warnings of impending judgment and the hope of restoration.	Sin and rebellion; idolatry; judgment; and mercy and grace

Hosea is part of a collection of prophetic books known in Christian tradition as the Minor Prophets. The designation *minor* doesn't mean *lesser*, only shorter writings. In Jewish tradition this collection is known as the Book of the Twelve, representing a single unit of prophetic literature calling on the children of Israel to repent and return to the Lord, warning against judgment for their rebellion, and offering hope for renewal. Hosea is the first of those twelve prophets.

Hosea wrote to expose Israel's unfaithfulness to the Lord, offering both warnings of impending judgment and the hope of restoration. Theodore of Mopsuestia explained that Hosea "would show how the Israelites were responsible for the coming disasters, having set aside worship and adoration of God while showering all their attention on idols and demons. Hosea was also to make it clear that this was not happening by chance. Rather its occurrence had been told and foreseen well in advance by God." Similarly John Wesley noted, "The scope of his prophecy is to reprove sin and denounce judgments against a people that would not be reformed." And yet Matthew Henry also revealed how Hosea "invites them to repentance with promises of mercy and gospel predictions of the future restoration of the Israelites and of the Jews, and their final conversion to Christianity."

The central organizing theme in this book is the motif of marriage, a metaphor employed by the Lord himself here and elsewhere. Its purpose in Hosea was to show Israel's idolatry for what it was: spiritual adultery. "Go marry a prostitute who will bear illegitimate children," God said to Hosea, "because the nation continually commits spiritual prostitution by turning away from the LORD" (1:2). John Calvin noted how interpreters have struggled with this passage, wondering why the Lord would have a prophet marry a prostitute. He explained: "The beginning, then, of what the Lord spoke by Hosea was this, *This people are an adulterous race, all are born, as it were, of a harlot, the kingdom of Israel is the filthiest brothel; and I now repudiate and reject them, I no longer own them as my children* . . . [Here] he exhibited in his assumed character a living image of the baseness of the people."

While it seems Hosea's marriage to a harlot literally happened, its purpose was to provide an allegory for the people of Israel so that they might understand the gravity of their idolatry, which had the same effect on their relationship to the Lord as a cheating wife's behavior would have on her relationship to her husband. He said,

> Plead earnestly with your mother (for she is not my wife, and I am not her husband), so that she might put an end to her adulterous lifestyle, and turn away from her sexually immoral behavior. Otherwise, I will strip her

> naked, and expose her like she was when she was born. I will turn her land into a wilderness and make her country a parched land, so that I might kill her with thirst. (2:2–3).

As anyone would feel on the receiving end of adultery, the Lord was angry. Not only because "they have broken their covenant with me and have rebelled against my law," God says, but because of their idolatry: "O Samaria, he has rejected your calf idol. My anger burns against them! They will not survive much longer without being punished" (8:1, 5).

Hosea urges God's people, "Come on! Let's return to the LORD. He himself has torn us to pieces, but he will heal us! He has injured us, but he will bandage our wounds!" (6:1). To illustrate the facts in dramatic fashion, the Lord told Hosea to buy back his wife after she had continued her harlotry and receive her in love: "Go, show love to your wife again, even though she loves another man and continually commits adultery. Likewise, the LORD loves the Israelites although they turn to other gods and love to offer raisin cakes to idols" (3:1).

An important corollary to the Lord's judgment for rebellious disobedience is his love and grace. He longs for us to return to him so that he can heal us and bind up our wounds. Though in one breath the Lord pledges to "punish Jacob according to his ways and repay him according to his deeds" (12:2), in the next he promises, "I will heal their waywardness and love them freely, for my anger will turn away from them" (14:4). Mathew Henry commented that when God's people seek the Lord's face, "they shall not seek it in vain. His anger is turned from them. Whom God loves, he loves freely; not because they deserve it, but of his own good pleasure."

The book of Hosea reminds us that the Lord's threat of judgment is always accompanied by the offer of salvation. May we examine our own lives through the lens of this prophetic work, confronting our own adulterous hearts in order to repent and experience God's grace and mercy.

1:1–11 "Go marry a prostitute who will bear illegitimate children conceived *through prostitution,* because the nation continually commits spiritual prostitution by turning away from the LORD." Such a woman consorted with men and idols. God represented through Gomer, the woman of prostitution, the community of the ten tribes who openly practiced the worship of idols. God may order a prophet to do what is unsuitable and inconvenient. In fact, it was typical for the hard and stubborn heart of the people of Israel to despise actively the words before their eyes, which showed the afflictions coming their way. And so, if God punishes the holy prophets because of the people, he will punish even more the people themselves in order that, after being confronted with the outrage of these terrifying actions, they may be frightened and turn away from their crimes.

ISHODAD OF MERV **(850)**
COMMENTARY ON HOSEA

SUPERSCRIPTION

1 This is the LORD's message that came to Hosea son of Beeri
during the time of Uzziah, Jotham, Ahaz, and Hezekiah, kings
of Judah, and during the time of Jeroboam son of Joash, king
of Israel.

SYMBOLS OF SIN AND JUDGMENT: THE PROSTITUTE AND HER CHILDREN

2 When the LORD first spoke through Hosea, he said to him, "Go
marry a prostitute who will bear illegitimate children conceived
through prostitution because the nation continually commits
spiritual prostitution by turning away from the LORD." 3 So Hosea
married Gomer, the daughter of Diblaim. Then she conceived
and gave birth to a son for him. 4 Then the LORD said to Hosea,
"Name him 'Jezreel,' because in a little while I will punish the
dynasty of Jehu on account of the bloodshed in the valley of Jezreel, and I will put an end to the kingdom of Israel. 5 At that time,
I will destroy the military power of Israel in the valley of Jezreel."
6 She conceived again and gave birth to a daughter. Then the
LORD said to him, "Name her 'No Pity' (Lo-Ruhamah) because
I will no longer have pity on the nation of Israel. For I will certainly not forgive their guilt. 7 But I will have pity on the nation
of Judah. I will deliver them by the LORD their God; I will not
deliver them by the warrior's bow, by sword, by military victory,
by chariot horses, or by chariots."
8 When she had weaned "No Pity" (Lo-Ruhamah), she conceived again and gave birth to another son. 9 Then the LORD
said: "Name him 'Not My People' (Lo-Ammi) because you are
not my people and I am not your God."

THE RESTORATION OF ISRAEL

10 "However, in the future the number of the people of Israel
will be like the sand of the sea that can be neither measured nor
numbered. Although it was said to them, 'You are not my people,'
it will be said to them, 'You are children of the living God!' 11 Then
the people of Judah and the people of Israel will be gathered
together. They will appoint for themselves one leader, and will
flourish in the land. Certainly, the day of Jezreel will be great!

2 "Then you will call your brother, 'My People' (Ammi)! You
will call your sister, 'Pity' (Ruhamah)!

IDOLATROUS ISRAEL WILL BE PUNISHED LIKE A PROSTITUTE

2 "Plead earnestly with your mother
(for she is not my wife, and I am not her husband),
so that she might put an end to her adulterous lifestyle
and turn away from her sexually immoral behavior.
3 Otherwise, I will strip her naked
and expose her like she was when she was born.
I will turn her land into a wilderness
and make her country a parched land,
so that I might kill her with thirst.
4 I will have no pity on her children
because they are children conceived in adultery.
5 For their mother has committed adultery;
she who conceived them has acted shamefully.
For she said, 'I will seek out my lovers;
they are the ones who give me my bread and my water,
my wool, my flax, my olive oil, and my wine.'

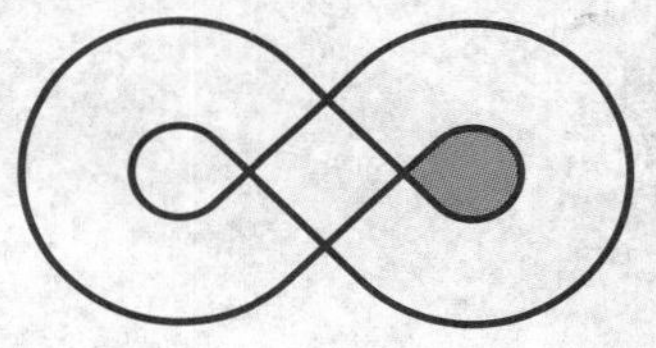

CANONS OF DORT

(1618–1619)

THE CANONS WERE adopted by the Synod of Dort in order to articulate a response to the Five Main Points of Doctrine in Dispute (Remonstrance of 1610) from proponents of Arminian theology. There are four parts to the confession, each one beginning with an exposition of the Reformed doctrine held by the Synod and ending with a response to particular points of disagreement. This selection demonstrates the doctrinal dialogue:

SECTION 1, ARTICLE 7: ELECTION

ELECTION IS God's unchangeable purpose by which he did the following: before the foundation of the world, by sheer grace, according to the free good pleasure of his will, God chose in Christ to salvation a definite number of particular people out of the entire human race, which had fallen by its own fault from its original innocence into sin and ruin. Those chosen were neither better nor more deserving than the others but lay with them in the common misery. God did this in Christ, whom he also appointed from eternity to be the mediator, the head of all those chosen, and the foundation of their salvation. And so God decreed to give to Christ those chosen for salvation and to call and draw them effectively into Christ's fellowship through the Word and Spirit. In other words, God decreed to grant them true faith in Christ, to justify them, to sanctify them, and finally, after powerfully preserving them in the fellowship of the Son, to glorify them.

SECTION 3, ARTICLE 12: REGENERATION A SUPERNATURAL WORK

AND THIS is the regeneration, the new creation, the raising from the dead, and the making alive so clearly proclaimed in the Scriptures, which God works in us without our help. But this certainly does not happen only by outward teaching, by moral persuasion, or by such a way of working that, after God's work is done, it remains in human power whether or not to be reborn or converted. Rather, it is an entirely supernatural work, one that is at the same time most

THE LORD'S DISCIPLINE WILL BRING ISRAEL BACK

6 "Therefore, I will soon fence her in with thorns;
I will wall her in so that she cannot find her way.
7 Then she will pursue her lovers, but she will not catch them;
she will seek them, but she will not find them.
Then she will say,
'I will go back to my husband,
because I was better off then than I am now.'

AGRICULTURAL FERTILITY WITHDRAWN FROM ISRAEL

8 "Yet until now she has refused to acknowledge that I was the one
who gave her the grain, the new wine, and the olive oil;
and that it was I who lavished on her the silver and gold—
that they used in worshiping Baal!
9 Therefore, I will take back my grain during the harvest time
and my new wine when it ripens;
I will take away my wool and my flax
that I had provided in order to clothe her.
10 Soon I will expose her lewd nakedness in front of her lovers,
and no one will be able to rescue her from me!
11 I will put an end to all her celebrations:
her annual religious festivals,
monthly new moon celebrations,
and weekly Sabbath festivities—
all her appointed festivals.
12 I will destroy her vines and fig trees,
about which she said, 'These are my wages for prostitution
that my lovers gave to me!'
I will turn her cultivated vines and fig trees into an uncultivated thicket,
so that wild animals will devour them.
13 I will punish her for the festival days
when she burned incense to the Baal idols;
she adorned herself with earrings and jewelry,
and went after her lovers,
but she forgot me!" says the LORD.

FUTURE REPENTANCE AND RESTORATION OF ISRAEL

14 "However, in the future I will allure her;
I will lead her back into the wilderness
and speak tenderly to her.
15 From there I will give back her vineyards to her
and turn the 'Valley of Trouble' into an 'Opportunity for Hope.'
There she will sing as she did when she was young,
when she came up from the land of Egypt.
16 At that time," declares the LORD,
"you will call me, 'My husband';
you will never again call me, 'My master.'
17 For I will remove the names of the Baal idols from your lips,
so that you will never again utter their names!

2:15—3:5 It was God's purpose to keep in firm hope the minds of the faithful during the exile lest being overwhelmed with despair, they should wholly faint. The prophet had before spoken of God's reconciliation with his people, and he magnificently extolled that favor when he said, "I will give back her vineyards to her, and turn the 'Valley of Trouble' into an 'Opportunity for Hope.'" But in the meantime the daily misery of the people continued. God had indeed determined to remove them into Babylon. They might therefore have despaired under that calamity, as though every hope of deliverance was wholly taken from them. Hence the prophet now shows that God would so restore the people to favor as not immediately to blot out every remembrance of his wrath, but that his purpose was to continue for a time some measure of his severity.

JOHN CALVIN **(1509–1564)**
COMPLETE COMMENTARY ON THE BIBLE

AN ILLUSTRATION OF GOD'S LOVE FOR IDOLATROUS ISRAEL

3 The LORD said to me, "Go, show love to your wife again, even
though she loves another man and continually commits
adultery. Likewise, the LORD loves the Israelites although they
turn to other gods and love to offer raisin cakes to idols." [2]So
I paid 15 shekels of silver and about seven bushels of barley to
purchase her. [3]Then I told her, "You must live with me many
days; you must not commit adultery or become joined to another man, and I also will wait for you." [4]For the Israelites must
live many days without a king or prince, without sacrifice or
sacred fertility pillar, without ephod or idols. [5]Afterward, the
Israelites will turn and seek the LORD their God and their Davidic king. Then they will submit to the LORD in fear and receive
his blessings in future days.

THE LORD'S COVENANT LAWSUIT AGAINST THE NATION ISRAEL

4 Listen to the LORD's message, you Israelites!
For the LORD has a covenant lawsuit against the people
of Israel.
For there is neither faithfulness nor loyalty in the land,
nor do they acknowledge God.
2 There is only cursing, lying, murder, stealing, and
adultery.
They resort to violence and bloodshed.
3 Therefore the land will mourn,
and all its inhabitants will perish.
The wild animals, the birds of the sky,
and even the fish in the sea will perish.

THE LORD'S DISPUTE AGAINST THE SINFUL PRIESTHOOD

4 Do not let anyone accuse or contend against anyone
else,
for my case is against you priests!
5 You stumble day and night,
and the false prophets stumble with you;
you have destroyed your own people.
6 You have destroyed my people
by failing to acknowledge me!
Because you refuse to acknowledge me,
I will reject you as my priests.
Because you reject the law of your God,
I will reject your descendants.
7 The more the priests increased in numbers,
the more they rebelled against me.
They have turned their glorious calling
into a shameful disgrace!
8 They feed on the sin offerings of my people;
their appetites long for their iniquity!
9 I will deal with the people and priests together:
I will punish them both for their ways,
and I will repay them for their deeds.
10 They will eat, but not be satisfied;
they will engage in prostitution, but not increase in
numbers
because they have abandoned the LORD
by pursuing other gods.

powerful and most pleasing, a marvelous, hidden, and inexpressible work, which is not less than or inferior in power to that of creation or of raising the dead, as Scripture (inspired by the author of this work) teaches. As a result, all those in whose hearts God works in this marvelous way are certainly, unfailingly, and effectively reborn and do actually believe. And then the will, now renewed, is not only activated and motivated by God, but in being activated by God is also itself active. For this reason, people themselves, by that grace which they have received, are also rightly said to believe and to repent.

SECTION 4, ARTICLE 3: GOD'S PRESERVATION OF THE CONVERTED

BECAUSE OF these remnants of sin dwelling in them and also because of the temptations of the world and Satan, those who have been converted could not remain standing in this grace if left to their own resources. But God is faithful, mercifully strengthening them in the grace once conferred on them and powerfully preserving them in it to the end.

NEW COVENANT RELATIONSHIP WITH REPENTANT ISRAEL

18 "At that time I will make a covenant for them with the
wild animals,
the birds of the air, and the creatures that crawl on the
ground.
I will abolish the warrior's bow and sword—
that is, every weapon of warfare—from the land,
and I will allow them to live securely.
19 I will commit myself to you forever;
I will commit myself to you in righteousness and justice,
in steadfast love and tender compassion.
20 I will commit myself to you in faithfulness;
then you will acknowledge the LORD.

AGRICULTURAL FERTILITY RESTORED TO THE REPENTANT NATION

21 "At that time, I will willingly respond," declares the LORD.
"I will respond to the sky,
and the sky will respond to the ground;
22 then the ground will respond to the grain, the new
wine, and the olive oil;
and they will respond to 'God Plants' (Jezreel)!
23 Then I will plant her as my own in the land.
I will have pity on 'No Pity' (Lo-Ruhamah).
I will say to 'Not My People' (Lo-Ammi), 'You are my
people!'
And he will say, 'You are my God!'"

SUPERFICIAL REPENTANCE BREEDS FALSE ASSURANCE OF GOD'S FORGIVENESS

6 Come on! Let's return to the LORD.
He himself has torn us to pieces,
but he will heal us!
He has injured us,
but he will bandage our wounds!
2 He will restore us in a very short time;
he will heal us in a little while,
so that we may live in his presence.
3 So let us search for him!
Let us seek to know the LORD!
He will come to our rescue as certainly as the appearance of the dawn,
as certainly as the winter rain comes,
as certainly as the spring rain that waters the land.

TRANSITORY FAITHFULNESS AND IMMINENT JUDGMENT

4 What am I going to do with you, O Ephraim?
What am I going to do with you, O Judah?
For your faithfulness is as fleeting as the morning mist;
it disappears as quickly as dawn's dew.
5 Therefore, I will certainly cut you into pieces at the hands of the prophets;
I will certainly kill you in fulfillment of my oracles of judgment,
for my judgment will come forth like the light of the dawn.
6 For I delight in faithfulness, not simply in sacrifice;
I delight in acknowledging God, not simply in whole burnt offerings.

INDICTMENTS AGAINST THE CITIES OF ISRAEL AND JUDAH

7 At Adam they broke the covenant;
Oh how they were unfaithful to me!
8 Gilead is a city full of evildoers;
its streets are stained with bloody footprints!
9 The company of priests is like a gang of robbers,
lying in ambush to pounce on a victim.
They commit murder on the road to Shechem;
they have done heinous crimes!
10 I have seen a disgusting thing in the house of Israel:
There Ephraim commits prostitution with other gods,
and Israel defiles itself.
11 I have appointed a time to reap judgment for you also, O Judah!

IF ISRAEL WOULD REPENT OF SIN, GOD WOULD RELENT OF JUDGMENT

7 Whenever I want to restore the fortunes of my people,
whenever I want to heal Israel,
the sin of Ephraim is revealed,
and the evil deeds of Samaria are exposed.
For they do what is wrong;
thieves break into houses,
and gangs rob people out in the streets.

6:1–11 The beginning of repentance is a sense of God's mercy; that is, when people are persuaded that God is ready to give pardon, they then begin to gather courage to repent. And for this purpose I have quoted that remarkable verse in Psalm 130, "You are willing to forgive, so that you might be honored" (v. 4). For it cannot be that people will obey God with true and sincere hearts except a taste of his goodness allures them, and they can certainly determine that they shall not return to him in vain but that he will be ready to pardon them. This is the meaning of the words: "Come on! Let's return to the LORD. He himself has torn us to pieces, but he will heal us!" (Hos 6:1). That is, God has not inflicted on us deadly wounds, but he has struck that he might heal.

JOHN CALVIN **(1509–1564)**
COMPLETE COMMENTARY ON THE BIBLE

2 They do not realize
that I remember all their wicked deeds.
Their evil deeds have now surrounded them;
their sinful deeds are always before me.

POLITICAL INTRIGUE AND CONSPIRACY IN THE PALACE

3 The royal advisers delight the king with their evil schemes;
the princes make him glad with their lies.
4 They are all like bakers;
they are like a smoldering oven;
they are like a baker who does not stoke the fire
until the kneaded dough is ready for baking.
5 At the celebration of their king,
his princes become inflamed with wine;
they conspire with evildoers.
6 They approach him, all the while plotting against him.
Their hearts are like an oven;
their anger smolders all night long,
but in the morning it bursts into a flaming fire.
7 All of them are blazing like an oven;
they devour their rulers.
All their kings fall,
and none of them call on me!

ISRAEL LACKS DISCERNMENT AND REFUSES TO REPENT

8 Ephraim has mixed itself like flour among the nations;
Ephraim is like a ruined cake of bread that is scorched on one side.
9 Foreigners are consuming what his strenuous labor produced,
but he does not recognize it.
His head is filled with gray hair,
but he does not realize it.
10 The arrogance of Israel testifies against him,
yet they refuse to return to the LORD their God.
In spite of all this they refuse to seek him.

ISRAEL TURNS TO ASSYRIA AND EGYPT FOR HELP

11 Ephraim has been like a dove,
easily deceived and lacking discernment.
They called to Egypt for help;
they turned to Assyria for protection.
12 I will throw my bird net over them while they are flying;
I will bring them down like birds in the sky;
I will discipline them when I hear them flocking together.

ISRAEL HAS TURNED AWAY FROM THE LORD

13 Woe to them! For they have fled from me!
Destruction to them! For they have rebelled against me!
I want to deliver them,
but they have lied to me.

7:11–16 If birds do not hold to the narrow path with cautious and careful restraint as they go their way, making their airy progress through the void thanks to their marvelous skill, the earth, which is the natural mooring for everyone and the most solid and safe foundation for all, becomes for them a present and manifest danger—not because its nature is changed but because they fall precipitously upon it by the weight of their body. Similarly, the unwearying goodness of God and his unchangeable substance itself certainly hurt no one, but we ourselves bring death upon ourselves by falling from the heights to the depths. For this very fall means death for the one who falls. For it is said: "Woe to them! For they have fled from me! Destruction to them! For they have rebelled against me!"

JOHN CASSIAN
(C. 360–C. 435)
THE CONFERENCES

14 They do not pray to me,
but howl in distress on their beds;
they slash themselves for grain and new wine,
but turn away from me.
15 Although I trained and strengthened them,
they plot evil against me!
16 They turn to Baal;
they are like an unreliable bow.
Their leaders will fall by the sword
because their prayers to Baal have made
me angry.
So people will disdain them in the land of
Egypt.

GOD WILL RAISE UP THE ASSYRIANS TO ATTACK ISRAEL

8 Sound the alarm!
An eagle looms over the temple of the LORD!
For they have broken their covenant with me
and have rebelled against my law.
2 Israel cries out to me,
"My God, we acknowledge you!"
3 But Israel has rejected what is morally good;
so an enemy will pursue him.

THE POLITICAL AND CULTIC SIN OF ISRAEL

4 They enthroned kings without my consent.
They appointed princes without my approval.
They made idols out of their silver and gold,
but they will be destroyed!
5 O Samaria, he has rejected your calf idol.
My anger burns against them!
They will not survive much longer without being
punished,
even though they are Israelites!
6 That idol was made by a workman—it is not God!
The calf idol of Samaria will be broken to bits.

THE FERTILITY CULTISTS WILL BECOME INFERTILE

7 They sow the wind,
and so they will reap the whirlwind!
The stalk does not have any standing grain;
it will not produce any flour.
Even if it were to yield grain,
foreigners would swallow it all up.
8 Israel will be swallowed up among the nations;
they will be like a worthless piece of pottery.

ISRAEL'S HIRED LOVERS

9 They have gone up to Assyria,
like a wild donkey that wanders off.
Ephraim has hired prostitutes as lovers.
10 Even though they have hired lovers among
the nations,
I will soon gather them together for judgment.
Then they will begin to waste away
under the oppression of a mighty king.

8:1–14 You did not fear God, nor did you reverence others or feel shame before your friends. So you have suffered shipwreck of all things at once. You have stripped yourselves of every good thing at the same time. You who were announcing your ardor for the kingdom have fallen from the kingdom. You who were inspiring all with a reverence for the doctrine did not have the fear of God before your eyes. You who were preaching holiness are now found to be polluted. You who through your guidance point out the punishment of God have drawn down chastisement upon yourself. How shall I grieve for you? The morning star, which rose early, has fallen and shattered upon the earth. How did the worthy son of Zion instantly become like a polluted vessel, "like a worthless piece of pottery"?

BASIL THE GREAT **(330–379)**
LETTERS

SACRIFICES INEFFECTIVE WITHOUT MORAL OBEDIENCE

11 Although Ephraim has built many altars for sin offerings,
these have become altars for sinning.
12 I spelled out my law for him in great detail,
but they regard it as something totally unknown to them.
13 They offer up sacrificial gifts to me
and eat the meat,
but the LORD does not accept their sacrifices.
Soon he will remember their wrongdoing;
he will punish their sins,
and they will return to Egypt.
14 Israel has forgotten his Maker and built royal palaces,
and Judah has built many fortified cities.
But I will send fire on their cities;
it will consume their royal citadels.

FERTILITY CULT FESTIVALS HAVE INTOXICATED ISRAEL

9 O Israel, do not rejoice jubilantly like the nations,
for you are unfaithful to your God.
You love to receive a prostitute's wages
on all the floors where you thresh your grain.
2 Threshing floors and wine vats will not feed the people,
and new wine only deceives them.

ASSYRIAN EXILE WILL REVERSE THE EGYPTIAN EXODUS

3 They will not remain in the LORD's land.
Ephraim will return to Egypt;
they will eat ritually unclean food in Assyria.
4 They will not pour out drink offerings of wine to the LORD;
they will not please him with their sacrifices.
Their sacrifices will be like bread eaten while in mourning;
all those who eat them will make themselves ritually unclean.
For their bread will be only to satisfy their appetite;
it will not come into the temple of the LORD.
5 So what will you do on the festival day,
on the festival days of the LORD?

NO ESCAPE FOR THE ISRAELITES THIS TIME

6 Look! Even if they flee from the destruction,
Egypt will take hold of them,
and Memphis will bury them.
The weeds will inherit the silver they treasure—
thornbushes will occupy their homes.
7 The time of judgment is about to arrive!
The time of retribution is imminent!
Israel will be humbled!

ISRAEL REJECTS HOSEA'S PROPHETIC EXHORTATIONS

The prophet is considered a fool—
the inspired man is viewed as a madman—
because of the multitude of your sins
and your intense animosity.

9:1–7 It is not fitting for you to rejoice and exult like the rest of the peoples. For they did not receive any teaching that might lead them to piety, but you, after much instruction and knowledge of God, rebelled against the knowledge that had been given to you because of the depravity of your opinion and turned to the worship of the idols.

THEODORE OF MOPSUESTIA (C. 350–428)
COMMENTARY ON HOSEA

8 The prophet is a watchman over Ephraim on behalf
of God,
yet traps are laid for him along all his paths;
animosity rages against him in the land of his God.

THE BEST OF TIMES, THE WORST OF TIMES

9 They have sunk deep into corruption
as in the days of Gibeah.
He will remember their wrongdoing.
He will repay them for their sins.
10 When I found Israel, it was like finding grapes in the
wilderness.
I viewed your ancestors like an early fig on a fig tree in
its first season.
Then they came to Baal Peor, and they dedicated
themselves to shame—
they became as detestable as what they loved.

THE FERTILITY WORSHIPERS WILL BECOME INFERTILE

11 Ephraim will be like a bird;
what they value will fly away.
They will not bear children—
they will not enjoy pregnancy—
they will not even conceive!
12 Even if they raise their children,
I will take away every last one of them.
Woe to them!
For I will turn away from them.
13 Ephraim, as I have seen, has given their children for
prey;
Ephraim will bear his sons for slaughter.
14 Give them, O LORD—
what will you give them?
Give them wombs that miscarry,
and breasts that cannot nurse!
15 Because of all their evil in Gilgal,
I hate them there.
On account of their evil deeds,
I will drive them out of my land.
I will no longer love them;
all their rulers are rebels.
16 Ephraim will be struck down—
their root will be dried up;
they will not yield any fruit.
Even if they do bear children,
I will kill their precious offspring.
17 My God will reject them,
for they have not obeyed him;
so they will be fugitives among the
nations.

ISRAEL IS GUILTY OF FERTILITY CULT WORSHIP

10 Israel was a fertile vine
that yielded fruit.
As his fruit multiplied,
he multiplied altars to Baal.
As his land prospered,
they adorned the fertility pillars.

10:1–15 A vine is valuable only for its fruit, but Israel now brought no fruit to perfection. The people's hearts were divided. God is the Sovereign of the heart; he will have all or none. Were the stream of the heart wholly after God, it would run strongly and bear down all before it. The people's promises to covenant with God were false. Even the proceeding of justice was as poisonous hemlock. Alas, how empty a vine is the visible church even at this day! Let them cleanse their hearts from all corrupt affections and lusts and be a broken and contrite spirit. Let them abound in works of piety toward God and of justice and charity toward one another: herein let them sow to the Spirit. Come and seek the Lord, and your hope in him shall not deceive you.

MATTHEW HENRY (1662–1714)
COMMENTARY ON THE WHOLE BIBLE

2 Their hearts are slipping;
soon they will be punished for their guilt.
The LORD will break their altars;
he will completely destroy their fertility pillars.

THE LORD WILL PUNISH ISRAEL BY REMOVING ITS KINGS

3 Very soon they will say, "We have no king
since we did not fear the LORD.
But what can a king do for us anyway?"
4 They utter empty words,
taking false oaths and making empty agreements.
Therefore legal disputes sprout up
like poisonous weeds in the furrows of a plowed field.

THE CALF IDOL AND IDOLATERS OF SAMARIA WILL BE EXILED

5 The inhabitants of Samaria will lament over the calf
idol of Beth Aven.
Its people will mourn over it;
its idolatrous priests will wail over it,
because its splendor will be taken from them into exile.
6 Even the calf idol will be carried to Assyria
as tribute for the great king.
Ephraim will be disgraced;
Israel will be put to shame because of its wooden idol.
7 Samaria and its king will be carried off
like a twig on the surface of the waters.
8 The high places of the "House of Wickedness" will be
destroyed;
it is the place where Israel sins.
Thorns and thistles will grow up over its altars.
Then they will say to the mountains, "Cover us!"
and to the hills, "Fall on us!"

FAILURE TO LEARN FROM THE SIN AND JUDGMENT OF GIBEAH

9 "O Israel, you have sinned since the time of Gibeah,
and there you have remained.
Did not war overtake the evildoers in Gibeah?
10 When I please, I will discipline them;
I will gather nations together to attack them,
to bind them in chains for their two sins.

FERTILITY IMAGERY: PLOWING, SOWING, AND REAPING

11 "Ephraim was a well-trained heifer who loved to thresh
grain;
I myself put a fine yoke on her neck.
I will harness Ephraim.
Let Judah plow!
Let Jacob break up the unplowed ground for himself!
12 Sow righteousness for yourselves,
reap unfailing love.
Break up the unplowed ground for yourselves,
for it is time to seek the LORD,
until he comes and showers deliverance on you.
13 But you have plowed wickedness;
you have reaped injustice;

you have eaten the fruit of deception.
Because you have depended on your chariots;
you have relied on your many warriors.

BETHEL WILL BE DESTROYED LIKE BETH ARBEL

14 "The roar of battle will rise against your people;
all your fortresses will be devastated,
just as Shalman devastated Beth Arbel on the day of
battle,
when mothers were dashed to the ground with their
children.
15 So will it happen to you, O Bethel,
because of your great wickedness!
When that day dawns,
the king of Israel will be destroyed.

REVERSAL OF THE EXODUS: RETURN TO EGYPT AND EXILE IN ASSYRIA

11 "When Israel was a young man, I loved him like a son,
and I summoned my son out of Egypt.
2 But the more I summoned them,
the farther they departed from me.
They sacrificed to the Baal idols
and burned incense to images.
3 Yet it was I who led Ephraim;
I took them by the arm,
but they did not acknowledge
that I had healed them.
4 I drew them with leather cords,
with straps of hide;
I lifted the yoke from their neck
and gently fed them.
5 They will return to Egypt!
Assyria will rule over them
because they refuse to repent!
6 A sword will flash in their cities;
it will destroy the bars of their city gates,
and will devour them in their fortresses.
7 My people are obsessed with turning away from me;
they call to Baal, but he will never exalt them!

THE DIVINE DILEMMA: JUDGMENT OR MERCY?

8 "How can I give you up, O Ephraim?
How can I surrender you, O Israel?
How can I treat you like Admah?
How can I make you like Zeboyim?
I have had a change of heart.
All my tender compassions are aroused.
9 I cannot carry out my fierce anger!
I cannot totally destroy Ephraim!
Because I am God, and not man—the Holy One among
you—
I will not come in wrath!

GOD WILL RESTORE THE EXILES TO ISRAEL

10 "He will roar like a lion,
and they will follow the LORD;
when he roars,
his children will come trembling from the west.

11:1–11 I recalled the people from Egypt and freed them from that harsh servitude, but they proved ungrateful to me and opted for the worship of idols. Though I was the one who taught them to walk, showed them paternal affection, and applied all kinds of healing to them, they refused to acknowledge me, even though I protected them from manifold destruction at the hands of the invaders as if clutching them to me in love. It is in love that even now I care for them and invest them in these chastisements. "I have had a change of heart. All my tender compassions are aroused. I cannot carry out my fierce anger! I cannot totally destroy Ephraim." God imitates a father and mother who are naturally worried and cannot turn away from their children for too long.

THEODORET OF CYR
(C. 393–C. 458)
COMMENTARY ON HOSEA

11 They will return in fear and trembling
like birds from Egypt,
like doves from Assyria,
and I will settle them in their homes," declares the LORD.

GOD'S LAWSUIT AGAINST ISRAEL: BREACH OF COVENANT

12 Ephraim has surrounded me with lies;
the house of Israel has surrounded me with deceit.
But Judah still roams about with God;
he remains faithful to the Holy One.

12 Ephraim continually feeds on the wind;
he chases the east wind all day;
he multiplies lies and violence.
They make treaties with Assyria
and send olive oil as tribute to Egypt.
2 The LORD also has a covenant lawsuit against Judah;
he will punish Jacob according to his ways
and repay him according to his deeds.

ISRAEL MUST RETURN TO THE GOD OF JACOB

3 In the womb he attacked his brother;
in his manly vigor he struggled with God.
4 He struggled with an angel and prevailed;
he wept and begged for his favor.
He found God at Bethel,
and there he spoke with him!
5 As for the LORD God Almighty,
the LORD is the name by which he is remembered!
6 But you must return to your God,
by maintaining love and justice
and by waiting for your God to return to you.

12:2–6 "You must return to your God, by maintaining love and justice and by waiting for your God to return to you." Because God loves mercy and justice, he who takes care to do mercy and justice draws near to God. It remains, then, for each to examine himself and for the rich person to take careful inventory of the private resources from which he is to offer gifts to God, to make sure that he has not oppressed a poor person, used force against one weaker than himself, or cheated one dependent upon him, thus exercising license rather than justice. We are bidden to practice fairness and justice also toward those who serve us. Do not employ force because you are in command, and do not take advantage because it is within your power to do so.

BASIL THE GREAT **(330-379)**
ON MERCY AND JUSTICE

THE LORD REFUTES ISRAEL'S FALSE CLAIM OF INNOCENCE

7 The businessmen love to cheat;
they use dishonest scales.
8 Ephraim boasts, "I am very rich!
I have become wealthy!
In all that I have done to gain my wealth,
no one can accuse me of any offense that is actually sinful."

9 "I am the LORD your God who brought you out of Egypt;
I will make you live in tents again as in the days of old.
10 I spoke to the prophets;
I myself revealed many visions;
I spoke in parables through the prophets."
11 Is there idolatry in Gilead?
Certainly its inhabitants will come to nothing!
Do they sacrifice bulls in Gilgal?
Surely their altars will be like stones heaped up on a plowed field!

JACOB IN ARAM, ISRAEL IN EGYPT, AND EPHRAIM IN TROUBLE

12 Jacob fled to the country of Aram,
then Israel worked to acquire a wife;
he tended sheep to pay for her.

13 The LORD brought Israel out of Egypt by a prophet,
and due to a prophet Israel was preserved alive.
14 But Ephraim bitterly provoked him to anger;
so he will hold him accountable for the blood he has shed;
his Lord will repay him for the contempt he has shown.

BAAL WORSHIPERS AND CALF WORSHIPERS TO BE DESTROYED

13 When Ephraim spoke, there was terror;
he was exalted in Israel,
but he became guilty by worshiping Baal and died.
2 Even now they persist in sin!
They make metal images for themselves,
idols that they skillfully fashion from their own silver;
all of them are nothing but the work of craftsmen.
There is a saying about them:
"Those who sacrifice to the calf idol are calf kissers!"
3 Therefore they will disappear like the morning mist,
like early morning dew that evaporates,
like chaff that is blown away from a threshing floor,
like smoke that disappears through an open window.

WELL-FED ISRAEL WILL BE FED TO WILD ANIMALS

4 But I am the LORD your God,
who brought you out of Egypt.
Therefore, you must not acknowledge any God but me.
Except for me there is no Savior.
5 I cared for you in the wilderness,
in the dry desert where no water was.
6 When they were fed, they became satisfied;
when they were satisfied, they became proud;
as a result, they forgot me!
7 So I will pounce on them like a lion;
like a leopard I will lurk by the path.
8 I will attack them like a bear robbed of her cubs—
I will rip open their chests.
I will devour them there like a lion—
like a wild animal would tear them apart.

ISRAEL'S KING UNABLE TO DELIVER THE NATION

9 I will destroy you, O Israel!
Who is there to help you?
10 Where then is your king,
that he may save you in all your cities?
Where are your rulers for whom you asked, saying,
"Give me a king and princes"?
11 I granted you a king in my anger,
and I will take him away in my wrath!

ISRAEL'S PUNISHMENT WILL NOT BE WITHHELD MUCH LONGER

12 The punishment of Ephraim has been decreed;
his punishment is being stored up for the future.
13 The labor pains of a woman will overtake him,
but the baby will lack wisdom;
when the time arrives,
he will not come out of the womb!

13:9 We have here the wail of the parental love of God over the ruin Israel has brought on itself, and that parental love is setting forth the people's true condition in the hope that they may discern it. Thus even the rebuke holds enclosed a promise and a hope. Since God is their help, to depart from him has been ruin and the return to him will be life. Hosea, or rather the Spirit who spoke through Hosea, blended wonderful tenderness with unflinching decision in rebuke and unwavering certainty in foretelling evil with unfaltering hope in the promise of possible blessing. Separation from him has all but destroyed the rebellious, but it has not in the smallest degree affected the fullness of his power or the fervency of his desire to help. God is ready to prove himself the true and only Helper.

ALEXANDER MACLAREN
(1826–1910)
EXPOSITIONS OF THE HOLY SCRIPTURES

THE LORD WILL NOT RELENT FROM THE THREATENED JUDGMENT

14 Will I deliver them from the power of Sheol? No, I will not!
Will I redeem them from death? No, I will not!
O Death, bring on your plagues!
O Sheol, bring on your destruction!
My eyes will not show any compassion!

THE CAPITAL OF THE NORTHERN EMPIRE WILL BE DESTROYED

15 Even though he flourishes like a reed plant,
a scorching east wind will come,
a wind from the LORD rising up from the desert.
As a result, his spring will dry up;
his well will become dry.
That wind will spoil all his delightful foods
in the containers in his storehouse.
16 Samaria will be held guilty
because she rebelled against her God.
They will fall by the sword;
their infants will be dashed to the ground—
their pregnant women will be ripped open.

PROPHETIC CALL TO GENUINE REPENTANCE

14 Return, O Israel, to the LORD your God,
for your sin has been your downfall!
2 Return to the LORD and repent!
Say to him: "Completely forgive our iniquity;
accept our penitential prayer,
that we may offer the praise of our lips as sacrificial bulls.
3 Assyria cannot save us;
we will not ride warhorses.
We will never again say, 'Our gods,'
to what our own hands have made.
For only you will show compassion to Orphan Israel!"

DIVINE PROMISE TO RELENT FROM JUDGMENT AND TO RESTORE BLESSINGS

4 "I will heal their waywardness
and love them freely,
for my anger will turn away from them.
5 I will be like the dew to Israel;
he will blossom like a lily;
he will send down his roots like a cedar of Lebanon.
6 His young shoots will grow;
his splendor will be like an olive tree;
his fragrance like a cedar of Lebanon.
7 People will reside again in his shade;
they will plant and harvest grain in abundance.
They will blossom like a vine,
and his fame will be like the wine from Lebanon.
8 O Ephraim, I do not want to have anything to do with idols anymore!
I will answer him and care for him.
I am like a luxuriant cypress tree;
your fruitfulness comes from me!"

14:1–9 We without any fitness may venture upon the promise of God that was made to us in Christ Jesus when he said, "The one who believes in him is not condemned" (John 3:18). It is blessed to know that the grace of God is free to us at all times, without preparation, without fitness, without money, and without price. These words invite backsliders to return: Indeed, the text was specially written for such—"I will heal their waywardness and love them freely" (Hos 14:4). Backslider! Surely the generosity of the promise will at once break your heart, and you will return and seek your injured Father's face.

CHARLES SPURGEON
(1834–1892)
MORNING AND EVENING

CONCLUDING EXHORTATION

9 Who is wise?
Let him discern these things!
Who is discerning?
Let him understand them!
For the ways of the LORD are right;
the godly walk in them,
but in them the rebellious stumble.

AUTHOR	AUDIENCE	DATE	PURPOSE	THEMES
Joel	The people of Judah	Probably between the late seventh and early fifth centuries BC	Joel wrote his book to interpret a crisis facing the people of Judah as a sign of God's judgment; he warned the situation would get worse, and he called the people to repentance.	Suffering; judgment; confession and repentance; the day of the Lord; and the hope of renewal

Joel is part of a collection of prophetic books known in the Christian tradition as the Minor Prophets, which were shorter prophetic works calling for repentance, warning of impending judgment, and offering hope for renewal. John Wesley succinctly summarized the scope and purpose of this book: "In this prophecy, the desolation made by armies of insects is described; the people are called to repentance; promises are made of mercy to the penitent and of the pouring out of the Spirit in the latter days; the cause of God's people is pleaded against their enemies, and glorious things are spoken of the gospel-Jerusalem."

The book opens with a plague of locusts that had swept across the land, a devastating occurrence for an agriculture-dependent economy. Interpreting the events of the plague and Joel's prophetic words, Theodore of Mopsuestia explained, "In a figurative manner he wants to convey to them the impending troubles; as always, the earlier ones are surpassed by those coming later." He went on to showcase how a series of invasions escalated with successive judgment:

> Tiglath-pileser, king of the Assyrians, came like a cutting locust, he is saying, and laid waste no small proportion of your possessions. After him Shalmaneser [came] like some kind of locust further ravaging your goods. After them Sennacherib [came] like a young locust wreaking general destruction on the Twelve Tribes of Israel. Like some kind of blight in addition to these came the attack of the Babylonians, who took the people of Judah as well and inflicted the evil of captivity on all in common.

Joel's prophecy utilized this existential plight to warn against an even greater threat: the outpouring of God's wrath on the day of the Lord. John Wesley explained this was "a day of greater trouble than yet they felt, troubles which God will heap upon them," which would come about "unless fasting, prayers, and amendment prevent." Through Joel God wanted Zion to "Blow the trumpet . . . sound the alarm signal on my holy mountain! Let all the inhabitants of the land shake with fear, for the day of the Lord is about to come" (2:1). He described it in starkly apocalyptic terms: it was a day of gloom and darkness, a devouring fire leading to destruction and pain. "Who can survive it?" (2:11) Joel asks.

Since the days of the early church fathers, Christian teachers and preachers have applied Joel's warning to the ultimate and final judgment the Lord will execute when Christ returns. This announcement of the day of the Lord is meant to stir God's people to return to the Lord in repentance: "'Yet even now,' the Lord says, 'return to me with all your heart—with fasting, weeping, and mourning. Tear your hearts, not just your garments.' Return to the Lord your God" (2:12–13). And yet Theodore of Cyr noted, "While making threats he has mercy within himself, and he offers it to those who are sorry for their sins." Here we are taken deep into the character of God, for we learn "he is merciful and compassionate, slow to anger and boundless in loyal love—often relenting from calamitous punishment" (2:13). The prophetic pronouncement of judgment for rebellion was meant to provoke the people to repentance, which would lead to restoration and blessing.

This promise of restoration climaxes with a vivid description of the Lord's pity on his people. He promises to send grain and oil to satisfy their hunger; to drive away their enemies far from them; to send rain, both in the autumn and the spring; to "make up for the years that the '*arbeh*-locust consumed your crops—the *yeleq*-locust, the *hasil*-locust, and the *gazam*-locust'—my great army that I sent against you." He promises his people "will have plenty to eat, and your hunger will be fully satisfied . . . My people will never again be put to shame" (2:25–26). "God can as easily restore a rich fruitfulness to the land as he had before rendered it barren by sending devouring insects," John Calvin commented. "[The Lord] says, *When I shall restore you to favor, there will be no army to devour your fruit: the land then will nourish you, for there will be nothing to prevent you to receive its wonted produce*."

Matthew Henry pointed out that "some understand these promises figuratively, as pointing to gospel grace, and as fulfilled in the abundant comforts treasured up for believers in the covenant of grace." Joel paired this prophetic word of immediate reconciliation with another in which the Lord's Spirit would be poured out on his people, signs and wonders would be performed, and an open invitation of reconciliation would be offered to all people so that "everyone who calls on the name of the Lord will be delivered" (2:32). Again, Matthew Henry: "The promise began to be fulfilled on the day of Pentecost, when the Holy Spirit was poured out, and it was continued in the converting grace and miraculous gifts conferred on both Jews and Gentiles."

Joel wrote his book to interpret the agricultural crisis of his people as a sign of God's judgment, warning that the situation would get worse and calling the people to repent. It stands as both a continued warning for God's people as well as a testament to God's gracious desire for reconciliation.

1:1–7 The most aged could not remember such calamities as were about to take place. Armies of insects were coming upon the land to eat the fruits of it. It is expressed so as to apply also to the destruction of the country by a foreign enemy and seems to refer to the devastations of the Chaldeans. God is Lord of hosts, he has every creature at his command, and when he pleases can humble and mortify a proud, rebellious people by the weakest and most contemptible creatures. It is just with God to take away the comforts that are abused to luxury and excess, and the more people place their happiness in the gratifications of sense, the more severe temporal afflictions are upon them. The more earthly delights we make needful to satisfy us, the more we expose ourselves to trouble.

MATTHEW HENRY **(1662–1714)**
COMMENTARY ON THE WHOLE BIBLE

INTRODUCTION

1 This is the LORD's message that came to Joel the son of Pethuel:

A LOCUST PLAGUE FORESHADOWS THE DAY OF THE LORD

2 Listen to this, you elders;
pay attention, all inhabitants of the land.
Has anything like this ever happened in your whole life
or in the lifetime of your ancestors?
3 Tell your children about it;
have your children tell their children,
and their children the following generation.
4 What the *gazam*-locust left the *'arbeh*-locust consumed;
what the *'arbeh*-locust left the *yeleq*-locust consumed;
and what the *yeleq*-locust left the *hasil*-locust consumed.

5 Wake up, you drunkards, and weep!
Wail, all you wine drinkers,
because the sweet wine has been taken away from you.
6 For a nation has invaded my land,
mighty and without number.
Their teeth are lion's teeth;
they have the fangs of a lioness.
7 They have destroyed my vines;
they have turned my fig trees into mere splinters.
They have completely stripped off the bark and thrown it aside;
the twigs are stripped bare.

A CALL TO LAMENT

8 Wail like a young virgin clothed in sackcloth,
lamenting the death of her husband to be.
9 No one brings grain offerings or drink offerings
to the temple of the LORD anymore.
So the priests, those who serve the LORD, are in mourning.
10 The crops of the fields have been destroyed.
The ground is in mourning because the grain has perished.
The fresh wine has dried up;
the olive oil languishes.
11 Be distressed, farmers;
wail, vinedressers, over the wheat and the barley.
For the harvest of the field has perished.
12 The vine has dried up;
the fig tree languishes—
the pomegranate, date, and apple as well.
In fact, all the trees of the field have dried up.
Indeed, the joy of the people has dried up!

13 Get dressed and lament, you priests.
Wail, you who minister at the altar.
Come, spend the night in sackcloth, you servants of my God,
because no one brings grain offerings or drink offerings
to the temple of your God anymore.
14 Announce a holy fast;
proclaim a sacred assembly.

Gather the elders and all the inhabitants of the land
to the temple of the LORD your God,
and cry out to the LORD.
15 How awful that day will be!
For the day of the LORD is near;
it will come as destruction from the Divine Destroyer.
16 Our food has been cut off right before our eyes!
There is no longer any joy or gladness in the temple of
our God.
17 The grains of seed have shriveled beneath their shovels.
Storehouses have been decimated,
and granaries have been torn down
because the grain has dried up.
18 Listen to the cattle groan!
The herds of livestock wander around in confusion
because they have no pasture.
Even the flocks of sheep are suffering.

19 To you, O LORD, I call out for help,
for fire has burned up the pastures of the wilderness,
flames have razed all the trees in the fields.
20 Even the wild animals cry out to you,
for the river beds have dried up;
fire has destroyed the pastures of the wilderness.

THE LOCUSTS' DEVASTATION

2 Blow the trumpet in Zion;
sound the alarm signal on my holy mountain!
Let all the inhabitants of the land shake with fear,
for the day of the LORD is about to come.
Indeed, it is near!
2 It will be a day of dreadful darkness,
a day of foreboding storm clouds,
like blackness spread over the mountains.
It is a huge and powerful army—
there has never been anything like it ever before,
and there will not be anything like it for many
generations to come!

3 Like fire they devour everything in their path;
a flame blazes behind them.
The land looks like the Garden of Eden before them,
but behind them there is only a desolate wilderness—
for nothing escapes them!
4 They look like horses;
they charge ahead like war horses.
5 They sound like chariots rumbling over mountain
tops,
like the crackling of blazing fire consuming stubble,
like the noise of a mighty army being drawn up for
battle.
6 People writhe in fear when they see them.
All their faces turn pale with fright.
7 They charge like warriors;
they scale walls like soldiers.
Each one proceeds on his course;
they do not alter their path.
8 They do not jostle one another;
each of them marches straight ahead.

2:1–11 Joel says, "Let all the inhabitants of the land shake with fear, for the day of the LORD is about to come." For the day of the Lord is great and very terrible, and who shall sustain it? But how incomprehensible and unimaginable that greatness with which he shall come in his second coming! In some degree we estimate correctly if we consider with heedful reflection the momentous circumstances of his first advent. Before he permitted himself to be laid hold of, he questioned his persecutors, saying, "Who are you looking for?" To that they answered, "Jesus the Nazarene." And when he said to them directly, "I am he," he uttered a voice of only the mildest answer and at once prostrated his armed persecutors to the earth (John 18:4–6). What then shall he do when he comes to judge the world, if by one utterance of his voice he struck down his enemies even when he came to be judged?

GREGORY THE GREAT
(C. 540–604)
MORALS ON THE BOOK OF JOB

They burst through the city defenses
and do not break ranks.
9 They rush into the city;
they scale its walls.
They climb up into the houses;
they go in through the windows like a thief.
10 The earth quakes before them;
the sky reverberates.
The sun and the moon grow dark;
the stars refuse to shine.
11 The voice of the LORD thunders as he leads his army.
Indeed, his warriors are innumerable;
Surely his command is carried out!
Yes, the day of the LORD is awesome
and very terrifying—who can survive it?

AN APPEAL FOR REPENTANCE

12 "Yet even now," the LORD says,
"return to me with all your heart—
with fasting, weeping, and mourning.
13 Tear your hearts,
not just your garments."
Return to the LORD your God,
for he is merciful and compassionate,
slow to anger and boundless in loyal love—often
relenting from calamitous punishment.
14 Who knows?
Perhaps he will be compassionate and grant a reprieve,
and leave blessing in his wake—
a meal offering and a drink offering for you to offer to
the LORD your God!

15 Blow the trumpet in Zion.
Announce a holy fast;
proclaim a sacred assembly.
16 Gather the people;
sanctify an assembly!
Gather the elders;
gather the children and the nursing infants.
Let the bridegroom come out from his bedroom
and the bride from her private quarters.
17 Let the priests, those who serve the LORD, weep
from the vestibule all the way back to the altar.
Let them say, "Have pity, O LORD, on your people;
please do not turn over your inheritance to be mocked,
to become a proverb among the nations.
Why should it be said among the peoples,
'Where is their God?'"

THE LORD'S RESPONSE

18 Then the LORD became zealous for his land;
he had compassion on his people.
19 The LORD responded to his people,
"Look! I am about to restore your grain
as well as fresh wine and olive oil.
You will be fully satisfied.
I will never again make you an object of mockery
among the nations.
20 I will remove the one from the north far from you.

I will drive him out to a dry and desolate place.
Those in front will be driven eastward into the Dead
Sea,
and those in back westward into the Mediterranean
Sea.
His stench will rise up as a foul smell."
Indeed, the LORD has accomplished great things!

21 Do not fear, my land.
Rejoice and be glad
because the LORD has accomplished great things!
22 Do not fear, wild animals.
For the pastures of the wilderness are again green with
grass.
Indeed, the trees bear their fruit;
the fig tree and the vine yield to their fullest.
23 Citizens of Zion, rejoice!
Be glad because of what the LORD your God has done!
For he has given to you the early rains as vindication.
He has sent to you the rains—
both the early and the late rains as formerly.
24 The threshing floors are full of grain;
the vats overflow with fresh wine and olive oil.
25 "I will make up for the years
that the *'arbeh*-locust consumed your crops—
the *yeleq*-locust, the *hasil*-locust, and the *gazam*-
locust—
my great army that I sent against you.
26 You will have plenty to eat,
and your hunger will be fully satisfied;
you will praise the name of the LORD your God,
who has acted wondrously in your behalf.
My people will never again be put to shame.
27 You will be convinced that I am in the midst of Israel.
I am the LORD your God; there is no other.
My people will never again be put to shame.

AN OUTPOURING OF THE SPIRIT

28 "After all of this
I will pour out my Spirit on all kinds of people.
Your sons and daughters will prophesy.
Your elderly will have prophetic dreams;
your young men will see visions.
29 Even on male and female servants
I will pour out my Spirit in those days.
30 I will produce portents both in the sky and on the
earth—
blood, fire, and columns of smoke.
31 The sunlight will be turned to darkness
and the moon to the color of blood,
before the day of the LORD comes—
that great and terrible day!
32 It will so happen that
everyone who calls on the name of the LORD will be
delivered.
For on Mount Zion and in Jerusalem there will be those
who survive,
just as the LORD has promised;
the remnant will be those whom the LORD will call.

3:1–6 For those who believe, salvation is in Mount Zion and Jerusalem. In the latter days, the Lord will gather the called remnant from the people of Judah who through the apostles believed. He will return the captives of Judah to Jerusalem. He is the one who came to preach sight to the blind, forgiveness to the captives, and freedom to those who confess the Lord and abide in the church, in which is the vision of peace. But he "will gather all the nations, and bring them down to the Valley of Jehoshaphat. I will enter into judgment against them there." In other words, I will lead you downward and drag you down from the highest heights to the lowest depths.

JEROME **(C. 342–420)**
COMMENTARY ON JOEL

THE LORD PLANS TO JUDGE THE NATIONS

3 "For look! In those days and at that time
I will return the exiles to Judah and Jerusalem.
2 Then I will gather all the nations
and bring them down to the Valley of Jehoshaphat.
I will enter into judgment against them there
concerning my people Israel who are my inheritance,
whom they scattered among the nations.
They partitioned my land,
3 and they cast lots for my people.
They traded a boy for a prostitute;
they sold a little girl for wine so they could drink.
4 Why are you doing these things to me, Tyre and Sidon?
Are you trying to get even with me, land of Philistia?
If you are, I will very quickly repay you for what you
have done!
5 For you took my silver and my gold
and brought my precious valuables to your own palaces.
6 You sold Judeans and Jerusalemites to the Greeks,
removing them far from their own country.
7 Look! I am rousing them from that place to which you
sold them.
I will repay you for what you have done!
8 I will sell your sons and daughters to the people of
Judah.
They will sell them to the Sabeans, a nation far away."
Indeed, the LORD has spoken.

JUDGMENT IN THE VALLEY OF JEHOSHAPHAT

9 Proclaim this among the nations:
"Prepare for a holy war!
Call out the warriors!
Let all these fighting men approach and attack!
10 Beat your plowshares into swords
and your pruning hooks into spears.
Let the weak say, 'I too am a warrior!'
11 Lend your aid and come,
all you surrounding nations,
and gather yourselves to that place."

Bring down, O LORD, your warriors!
12 "Let the nations be roused and let them go up
to the Valley of Jehoshaphat,
for there I will sit in judgment on all the surrounding
nations.
13 Rush forth with the sickle, for the harvest is ripe!
Come, stomp the grapes, for the winepress is full!
The vats overflow.
Indeed, their evil is great!"

14 Crowds, great crowds are in the Valley of Decision,
for the day of the LORD is near in the Valley of Decision!
15 The sun and moon are darkened;
the stars withhold their brightness.
16 The LORD roars from Zion;
from Jerusalem his voice bellows out.
The heavens and the earth shake.
But the LORD is a refuge for his people;
he is a stronghold for the citizens of Israel.

THE LORD'S PRESENCE IN ZION

17 "You will be convinced that I, the LORD, am your God,
dwelling on Zion, my holy mountain.
Jerusalem will be holy—
conquering armies will no longer pass through it.
18 On that day the mountains will drip with sweet wine,
and the hills will flow with milk.
All the dry stream beds of Judah will flow with water.
A spring will flow out from the temple of the LORD,
watering the Valley of Acacia Trees.
19 Egypt will be desolate,
and Edom will be a desolate wilderness
because of the violence they did to the people of Judah,
in whose land they shed innocent blood.
20 But Judah will reside securely forever,
and Jerusalem will be secure from one generation to
the next.
21 I will avenge their blood that I had not previously
acquitted."
It is the LORD who dwells in Zion!

AUTHOR	AUDIENCE	DATE	PURPOSE	THEMES
Amos	Primarily the idolatrous and indulgent people of the northern kingdom	About 760–750 BC	Amos wrote his prophetic work to condemn Israel's lack of concern for social justice and their religious apostasy. He called on the people to care for the poor and vulnerable in society and to destroy their idols, while he also predicted their impending destruction and ultimate restoration.	Social justice; religious apostasy; destruction; and restoration

The book of Amos is a warning of judgment and an offer of restoration. Matthew Henry explained: "[Amos] assures the Twelve Tribes of the destruction of the neighboring nations; and as they at that time gave themselves up to wickedness and idolatry, he reproves the Jewish nation with severity; but he describes the restoration of the church by the Messiah extending to the latter days."

Although Amos promised the destruction of Israel's enemies, most of the book indicts Israel for its own idolatry and injustice. In the first sense Amos is like the other prophets who took Israel to task for breaking their covenant obligations. "Listen, you Israelites, to this message that the Lord is proclaiming against you!" he said. "This message is for the entire clan I brought up from the land of Egypt: 'I have chosen you alone from all the clans of the earth'" (3:1–2). He invoked the memory of the exodus in which the Lord redeemed Israel and ratified a covenant of relationship with the people, choosing and adopting them to be his own possession among all the nations and he their God. Yet, he accused, "you will pick up your images of Sikkuth, your king, and Kiyyun, your star god, which you made for yourselves" (5:26). And for that they would be judged by the Lord and exiled unto destruction.

The book of Amos confronts Israel in another way. Along with the familiar accusation of idolatry, social injustice and oppression are also strongly condemned. Israel sold the innocent and needy for bribes, trampled the poor, and denied justice to the oppressed; the rich "oppress the poor" and "crush the needy" (4:1); they "make the poor pay taxes on their crops and exact a grain tax from them"; the Lord described Israel's "many rebellious acts and your numerous sins. You torment the innocent, you take bribes, and you deny justice to the needy at the city gate" (5:11–12). John Calvin explained Amos's condemnation: "The prophet chiefly reproves them because they oppressed the poor and consumed the needy. Though the rich, no doubt, did other wrongs, yet as they especially exercised cruelty toward the miserable and those who were destitute of every help, this is the reason why the prophet here elates expressly that the poor and the needy were oppressed by the rich." The Lord promised swift judgment in response to their injustice.

Adding to the prophetic literature about the "day of the Lord," Amos explained, "It will bring darkness, not light" (5:18) for all sinners, the nations, and Israel alike. Origen explained this gloom of judgment in stark terms: "If you can envision after the consummation of the world what the gloom is, a gloom that pursues nearly all of the race of humans who are punished for sins. The atmosphere will become dark at that time, and

no longer can anyone ever give glory to God." In the immediacy the Lord promised to send Israel "into exile beyond Damascus" (5:27), which was fulfilled when the Assyrians conquered Israel.

As is consistent with all Hebrew prophetic literature, alongside the Lord's judgment is the promise of restoration:

> I will rebuild the collapsing hut of David. I will seal its gaps, repair its ruins, and restore it to what it was like in days gone by . . . I will bring back my people, Israel; they will rebuild the cities lying in rubble and settle down. They will plant the vineyards and drink the wine they produce; they will grow orchards and eat the fruit they produce. I will plant them on their land, and they will never again be uprooted from the land I have given them. (9:11, 14–15)

The day of restoration Amos speaks about includes the coming day of ultimate renewal in Christ. "Here is another promise literally of abundant plenty to the returned captives," John Wesley explained, "and mystically of abundant grace poured forth in gospel days." He went on to highlight the kind of restoration that God's people will receive:

> The plowman who breaks up the ground and prepares it for sowing shall be ready to tread on the heels of the reaper who shall have a harvest so large that before he can gather it all in, it shall be time to plow the ground again. So great shall their vintage be that e'er the treaders of grapes can have finished their work, the seeds-man shall be sowing his seed against the next season. The vineyards shall be so fruitful and new wine so plentiful as if it ran down from the mountains.

Amos wrote his prophetic work to condemn Israel's injustices against the poor and oppressed and to call them out of their religious apostasy and idolatry. He exhorted them to do what was right by seeking justice and destroying their idols. Along with these exhortations, his prediction of impending destruction for their sins and ultimate restoration stands as a testimony both to God's justice and his mercy. "God marvelously preserves his elect amidst the most fearful confusions and miseries," Matthew Henry commented. "When all seems desperate, he wonderfully revives his church and blesses her with all spiritual blessings in Christ Jesus. And great shall be the glory of that period, in which not one good thing promised shall remain unfulfilled."

INTRODUCTION

1 The following is a record of what Amos prophesied. He was one of the herdsmen from Tekoa. These prophecies about Israel were revealed to him during the time of King Uzziah of Judah and King Jeroboam son of Joash of Israel, two years before the earthquake.

GOD WILL JUDGE THE SURROUNDING NATIONS

2 Amos said:
"The LORD comes roaring out of Zion;
from Jerusalem he comes bellowing!
The shepherds' pastures wilt;
the summit of Carmel withers."

3 This is what the LORD says:
"Because Damascus has committed three crimes—
make that four!—I will not revoke my
decree of judgment.
They ripped through Gilead like threshing sledges with
iron teeth.
4 So I will set Hazael's house on fire;
fire will consume Ben Hadad's fortresses.
5 I will break the bar on the gate of Damascus.
I will remove the ruler from Wicked Valley,
the one who holds the royal scepter from Beth Eden.
The people of Aram will be deported to Kir."
The LORD has spoken!

6 This is what the LORD says:
"Because Gaza has committed three crimes—
make that four!—I will not revoke my decree of
judgment.
They deported a whole community and sold them to
Edom.
7 So I will set Gaza's city wall on fire;
fire will consume her fortresses.
8 I will remove the ruler from Ashdod,
the one who holds the royal scepter from Ashkelon.
I will strike Ekron with my hand;
the rest of the Philistines will also die."
The Sovereign LORD has spoken!

9 This is what the LORD says:
"Because Tyre has committed three crimes—
make that four—I will not revoke my decree of judgment.
They sold a whole community to Edom;
they failed to observe a treaty of brotherhood.
10 So I will set fire to Tyre's city wall;
fire will consume her fortresses."

11 This is what the LORD says:
"Because Edom has committed three crimes—
make that four—I will not revoke my decree of judgment.
He chased his brother with a sword;
he wiped out his allies.
In his anger he tore them apart without stopping to rest;
in his fury he relentlessly attacked them.
12 So I will set Teman on fire;
fire will consume Bozrah's fortresses."

1:3 You must slay the allurements to vice while they are still only thoughts. Be wary and lay claim to the Lord's promise: "Keep me from committing flagrant sins; do not allow such sins to control me. Then I will be blameless, and innocent of blatant rebellion" (Ps 19:13). For elsewhere also the scripture testifies, "I punish the sons, grandsons, and great-grandsons for the sin of the fathers who reject me" (Deut 5:9). That is to say, God will not punish us at once for our thoughts and resolves but will send retribution upon our offspring or upon the evil deeds and habits of sin, which arise out of the offspring. As he says by the mouth of Amos, "Because Damascus has committed three crimes—make that four!—I will not revoke my decree of judgment" (Amos 1:3).

JEROME (C. 342–420)
LETTERS

13This is what the LORD says:
"Because the Ammonites have committed three crimes—
make that four—I will not revoke my decree of judgment.
They ripped open Gilead's pregnant women
so they could expand their territory.
14 So I will set fire to Rabbah's city wall;
fire will consume her fortresses.
War cries will be heard on the day of battle;
a strong gale will blow on the day of the windstorm.
15 Ammon's king will be deported;
he and his officials will be carried off together."
The LORD has spoken!

2 This is what the LORD says:
"Because Moab has committed three crimes—
make that four—I will not revoke my decree of judgment.
They burned the bones of Edom's king into lime.
2 So I will set Moab on fire,
and it will consume Kerioth's fortresses.
Moab will perish in the heat of battle
amid war cries and the blaring of the ram's horn.
3 I will remove Moab's leader;
I will kill all Moab's officials with him."
The LORD has spoken!

4This is what the LORD says:
"Because Judah has committed three covenant
transgressions—
make that four—I will not revoke my decree of judgment.
They rejected the LORD's law;
they did not obey his commands.
Their false gods,
to which their fathers were loyal,
led them astray.
5 So I will set Judah on fire,
and it will consume Jerusalem's fortresses."

GOD WILL JUDGE ISRAEL

6This is what the LORD says:
"Because Israel has committed three covenant
transgressions—
make that four—I will not revoke my decree of judgment.
They sold the innocent for silver,
the needy for a pair of sandals.
7 They trample on the dirt-covered heads of the poor;
they push the destitute away.
A man and his father go to the same girl;
in this way they show disrespect for my moral purity.
8 They stretch out on clothing seized as collateral;
they do so right beside every altar!
They drink wine bought with the fines they have levied;
they do so right in the temple of their God!
9 For Israel's sake I destroyed the Amorites.
They were as tall as cedars
and as strong as oaks,
but I destroyed the fruit on their branches
and their roots in the ground.
10 I brought you up from the land of Egypt;
I led you through the wilderness for 40 years

2:7 In the Pentateuch it is not written that a father and son ought not to have the same concubine, but in the prophet it is thought deserving of the most extreme condemnation. "A man and his father," it is said, "go to the same girl." It makes one reflect upon how many other forms of unclean lust have been found out in the devil's school while divine scripture remains silent about them, not choosing to befoul its dignity with the names of filthy things and condemning their uncleanness in general terms! Recall that the apostle Paul said, "But among you there must not be either sexual immorality, impurity of any kind, or greed, as these are not fitting for the saints" (Eph 5:3). This includes the unspeakable doings of both males and females under the name of uncleanness.

BASIL THE GREAT **(330-379)**
LETTERS

so you could take the Amorites' land as your own.
11 I made some of your sons prophets
and some of your young men Nazirites.
Is this not true, you Israelites?"
The LORD is speaking.
12 "But you made the Nazirites drink wine;
you commanded the prophets, 'Do not prophesy!'
13 Look! I will press you down,
like a cart loaded down with grain presses down.
14 Fast runners will find no place to hide;
strong men will have no strength left;
warriors will not be able to save their lives.
15 Archers will not hold their ground;
fast runners will not save their lives,
nor will those who ride horses.
16 Bravehearted warriors will run away naked in that day."
The LORD is speaking.

EVERY EFFECT HAS ITS CAUSE

3 Listen, you Israelites, to this message that the LORD is proclaiming against you! This message is for the entire clan I
brought up from the land of Egypt:
2 "I have chosen you alone from all the clans of the earth.
Therefore I will punish you for all your sins."
3 Do two walk together without having met?
4 Does a lion roar in the woods if he has not cornered his
prey?
Does a young lion bellow from his den if he has not
caught something?
5 Does a bird swoop down into a trap on the ground if
there is no bait?
Does a trap spring up from the ground unless it has
surely caught something?
6 If an alarm sounds in a city, do people not fear?
If disaster overtakes a city, is the LORD not
responsible?
7 Certainly the Sovereign LORD does nothing without
first revealing his plan to his servants the
prophets.
8 A lion has roared! Who is not afraid?
The Sovereign LORD has spoken. Who can refuse to
prophesy?

3:1–8 Each of us thinks, since he has not been an idolater, since he has not been immoral—would that we were pure in such areas—that after he has been set free from this life, he will be saved. We do not see that "we must all appear before the judgment seat of Christ, so that each one may be paid back according to what he has done while in the body, whether good or evil" (2 Cor 5:10). We do not hear what has been said: "I have chosen you alone from all the clans of the earth. Therefore I will punish you for all"—not just some and not others—"your sins" (Amos 3:2).

ORIGEN (C. 185–C. 253)
HOMILIES ON JEREMIAH

SAMARIA WILL FALL

9 Make this announcement in the fortresses of Ashdod
and in the fortresses in the land of Egypt.
Say this:
"Gather on the hills around Samaria!
Observe the many acts of violence taking place within
the city,
the oppressive deeds occurring in it."
10 "They do not know how to do what is right," the LORD says.
"They store up the spoils of destructive violence in
their fortresses.
11 Therefore," says the Sovereign LORD, "an enemy will
encircle the land.
He will take away your power;
your fortresses will be looted."

12 This is what the LORD says:
"Just as a shepherd salvages from the lion's mouth a
couple of leg bones or a piece of an ear,
so the Israelites who live in Samaria will be salvaged.
They will be left with just a corner of a bed,
and a part of a couch.
13 Listen and warn the family of Jacob!"
The Sovereign LORD, the God who commands armies, is
speaking!

14 "Certainly when I punish Israel for their covenant
transgressions,
I will destroy Bethel's altars.
The horns of the altar will be cut off and fall to the
ground.
15 I will destroy both the winter and summer houses.
The houses filled with ivory will be ruined;
the great houses will be swept away."
The LORD is speaking!

4 Listen to this message, you cows of Bashan who live on
Mount Samaria!
You oppress the poor;
you crush the needy.
You say to your husbands,
"Bring us more to drink!"
2 The Sovereign LORD confirms this oath by his own holy
character:
"Certainly the time is approaching
when you will be carried away in baskets,
every last one of you in fishermen's pots.
3 Each of you will go straight through the gaps in the walls;
you will be thrown out toward Harmon."
The LORD is speaking.

ISRAEL HAS AN APPOINTMENT WITH GOD

4 "Go to Bethel and rebel!
At Gilgal rebel some more!
Bring your sacrifices in the morning,
your tithes on the third day!
5 Burn a thank offering of bread made with yeast!
Make a public display of your voluntary offerings!
For you love to do this, you Israelites."
The Sovereign LORD is speaking.

6 "But surely I gave you no food to eat in all your cities;
you lacked food everywhere you lived.
Still you did not come back to me."
The LORD is speaking.

7 "I withheld rain from you three months before the harvest.
I gave rain to one city, but not to another.
One field would get rain, but the field that received no
rain dried up.
8 People from two or three cities staggered into one city
to get water,
but remained thirsty.
Still you did not come back to me."
The LORD is speaking.

4:6–13 They who refuse to repent do not deserve to be saved by the Lord's visitation or to be healed by temporal afflictions. They are like those who "because they are callous, they have given themselves over to indecency for the practice of every kind of impurity with greediness" (Eph 4:19). In their hardness of heart and with their frequent habit of sinning, they are beyond the purgation of this very brief age and the punishment of the present life. The divine Word reproves them through the prophet: "'I overthrew some of you the way God overthrew Sodom and Gomorrah. You were like a burning stick snatched from the flames. Still you did not come back to me.' The LORD is speaking" (Amos 4:11).

JOHN CASSIAN
(C. 360–C. 435)
THE CONFERENCES

9 “I destroyed your crops with blight and disease.
Locusts kept devouring your orchards, vineyards, fig trees, and olive trees.
Still you did not come back to me.”
The LORD is speaking.

10 “I sent against you a plague like one of the Egyptian plagues.
I killed your young men with the sword,
along with the horses you had captured.
I made the stench from the corpses rise up into your nostrils.
Still you did not come back to me.”
The LORD is speaking.

11 “I overthrew some of you the way God overthrew Sodom and Gomorrah.
You were like a burning stick snatched from the flames.
Still you did not come back to me.”
The LORD is speaking.

12 “Therefore this is what I will do to you, Israel.
Because I will do this to you,
prepare to meet your God, Israel!”

13 For here he is!
He formed the mountains and created the wind.
He reveals his plans to men.
He turns the dawn into darkness
and marches on the heights of the earth.
The LORD God of Heaven’s Armies is his name!

DEATH IS IMMINENT

5 Listen to this funeral song I am ready to sing about you,
family of Israel:
2 “The virgin Israel has fallen down and will not get up again.
She is abandoned on her own land
with no one to help her get up.”

3 The Sovereign LORD says this:
“The city that marches out with a thousand soldiers will have only a hundred left;
the town that marches out with a hundred soldiers will have only ten left for the family of Israel.”

4 The LORD says this to the family of Israel:
“Seek me so you can live!
5 Do not seek Bethel.
Do not visit Gilgal.
Do not journey down to Beer Sheba.
For the people of Gilgal will certainly be carried into exile,
and Bethel will become a place where disaster abounds.”

6 Seek the LORD so you can live!
Otherwise he will break out like fire against Joseph’s family;
the fire will consume,

and no one will be able to quench it and save Bethel.
7 The Israelites turn justice into bitterness;
they throw what is fair and right to the ground.

8 But there is one who made the constellations Pleiades
and Orion;
he can turn the darkness into morning
and daylight into night.
He summons the water of the seas
and pours it out on the earth's surface.
The LORD is his name!
9 He flashes destruction down upon the strong
so that destruction overwhelms the fortified places.

10 The Israelites hate anyone who arbitrates at the city
gate;
they despise anyone who speaks honestly.
11 Therefore, because you make the poor pay taxes on
their crops
and exact a grain tax from them,
you will not live in the houses you built with chiseled
stone,
nor will you drink the wine from the fine vineyards you
planted.
12 Certainly I am aware of your many rebellious acts
and your numerous sins.
You torment the innocent, you take bribes,
and you deny justice to the needy at the city gate.
13 For this reason whoever is smart keeps quiet in such a
time,
for it is an evil time.

14 Seek good and not evil so you can live!
Then the LORD God of Heaven's Armies just might be
with you,
as you claim he is.
15 Hate what is wrong, love what is right.
Promote justice at the city gate.
Maybe the LORD God of Heaven's Armies will have
mercy on those who are left from Joseph.

16 Because of Israel's sins this is what the Lord, the LORD God
of Heaven's Armies, says:
"In all the squares there will be wailing;
in all the streets they will mourn the dead.
They will tell the field workers to lament
and the professional mourners to wail.
17 In all the vineyards there will be wailing,
for I will pass through your midst," says the LORD.

THE LORD DEMANDS JUSTICE

18 Woe to those who wish for the day of the LORD!
Why do you want the LORD's day of judgment to come?
It will bring darkness, not light.
19 Disaster will be inescapable,
as if a man ran from a lion only to meet a bear,
then escaped into a house,
leaned his hand against the wall,
and was bitten by a poisonous snake.

5:16–27 Here the prophet, anticipating an objection, shows that the Israelites deceived themselves, for they believed that God was pacified by their sacrifices: He declares all these to be useless not only because they themselves were impure but also because all their sacrifices were mere profanations. Though the Jews, as to the external form, had not departed from the rule of the law, yet their sacrifices were vicious and repudiated by God. Impurity of heart vitiated all their works, and this was the reason that God rejected everything the Jews thought available for holiness. But different was the design of our prophet: For it was not only for this reason that he blamed the Israelites—because they falsely pretended God's name in their sacrifices—but also because they were apostates; for they had departed from the teaching of the law and built for themselves a spurious temple.

JOHN CALVIN (1509–1564)
COMPLETE COMMENTARY ON THE BIBLE

20 Don't you realize the LORD's day of judgment will bring
darkness, not light—
gloomy blackness, not bright light?

21 "I absolutely despise your festivals!
I get no pleasure from your religious assemblies.
22 Even if you offer me burnt and grain offerings, I will not
be satisfied;
I will not look with favor on your peace offerings of
fattened calves.
23 Take away from me your noisy songs;
I don't want to hear the music of your stringed instruments.
24 Justice must flow like torrents of water,
righteous actions like a stream that never dries up.

25 You did not bring me sacrifices and grain offerings
during the 40 years you spent in the wilderness,
family of Israel.
26 You will pick up your images of Sikkuth, your king,
and Kiyyun, your star god, which you made for
yourselves,
27 and I will drive you into exile beyond Damascus," says
the LORD.
He is called the God of Heaven's Armies.

THE PARTY IS OVER FOR THE RICH

6:1–7 Look, I pray you, at those who stretch themselves upon beds of ivory, whom the divine Amos fitly upbraids, who anoint themselves with the chief ointments, chant to the sound of instruments of music, and attach themselves to transitory things as though they were stable but have not grieved nor had compassion for the affliction of Joseph, though they ought to have been kind to those who had met with disaster before them and by mercy have obtained mercy. As the fir tree should howl because the cedar had fallen, they should be instructed by their neighbors' chastisement and be led by others' ills to regulate their own lives, having the advantage of being saved by their predecessors' fate instead of being themselves a warning to others.

GREGORY OF NAZIANZUS
(C. 329–390)
ON HIS FATHER'S SILENCE

6 Woe to those who live in ease in Zion,
to those who feel secure on Mount Samaria.
They think of themselves as the elite class of the best
nation.
The family of Israel looks to them for leadership.
2 They say to the people:
"Journey over to Calneh and look at it;
then go from there to Hamath-Rabbah;
then go down to Gath of the Philistines.
Are they superior to our two kingdoms?
Is their territory larger than yours?"
3 You refuse to believe a day of disaster will come,
but you establish a reign of violence.
4 They lie around on beds decorated with ivory
and sprawl out on their couches.
They eat lambs from the flock
and calves from the middle of the pen.
5 They sing to the tune of stringed instruments;
like David they invent musical instruments.
6 They drink wine from sacrificial bowls
and pour the very best oils on themselves.
Yet they are not concerned over the ruin of Joseph.
7 Therefore they will now be the first to go into exile,
and the religious banquets where they sprawl on
couches will end.

8 The Sovereign LORD confirms this oath by his very own
life.
The LORD God of Heaven's Armies is speaking:
"I despise Jacob's arrogance;
I hate their fortresses.
I will hand over to their enemies the city of Samaria
and everything in it."

9 If 10 men are left in one house, they too will die. 10 When
their close relatives, the ones who will burn the corpses, pick
up their bodies to remove the bones from the house, they will
say to anyone who is in the inner rooms of the house, "Is anyone else with you?" He will respond, "No one." Then he will say,
"Hush! Don't invoke the LORD's name!"

11 Indeed, look! The LORD is giving the command.
He will smash the large house to bits
and the small house into little pieces.
12 Can horses run on rocky cliffs?
Can one plow the sea with oxen?
Yet you have turned justice into a poisonous plant
and the fruit of righteous actions into a bitter plant.
13 You are happy because you conquered Lo Debar.
You say, "Did we not conquer Karnaim by our own
power?"
14 "Look! I am about to bring a nation against you, family
of Israel,"
the LORD, the God who commands armies, is speaking.
"They will oppress you all the way from Lebo Hamath to
the stream of the rift valley."

SYMBOLIC VISIONS OF JUDGMENT

7 The Sovereign LORD showed me this: I saw him making lo-
custs just as the crops planted late were beginning to sprout.
(The crops planted late sprout after the royal harvest.) 2 When
they had completely consumed the earth's vegetation, I said,
"Sovereign LORD, forgive Israel!
How can Jacob survive?
He is too weak!"

3 The LORD decided not to do this. "It will not happen," the
LORD said.
4 The Sovereign LORD showed me this: I saw the Sovereign
LORD summoning a shower of fire. It consumed the great deep
and devoured the fields. 5 I said,
"Sovereign LORD, stop!
How can Jacob survive?
He is too weak!"

6 The LORD decided not to do this. The Sovereign LORD said,
"This will not happen either."
7 He showed me this: I saw the Lord standing by a tin wall
holding tin in his hand. 8 The LORD said to me, "What do you
see, Amos?" I said, "Tin." The Lord then said,
"Look, I am about to place tin among my people Israel.
I will no longer overlook their sin.
9 Isaac's centers of worship will become desolate;
Israel's holy places will be in ruins.
I will attack Jeroboam's dynasty with the sword."

AMOS CONFRONTS A PRIEST

10 Amaziah the priest of Bethel sent this message to King Jeroboam of Israel: "Amos is conspiring against you in the very
heart of the kingdom of Israel! The land cannot endure all his
prophecies. 11 As a matter of fact, Amos is saying this: 'Jeroboam
will die by the sword, and Israel will certainly be carried into
exile away from its land.'"

7:1–9 God bears long, but he will not bear always with a provoking people. The Lord has many ways of humbling a sinful nation. Whatever trouble we are under, we should be most earnest with God for the forgiveness of sin. Sin will soon make a great people small. See the power of prayer. See how ready, how swift God is to show mercy; how he waits to be gracious. Israel was a wall, a strong wall, but the Lord now seems to stand upon this wall. He measures it; it appears to be a bowing, bulging wall. Thus God would bring the people of Israel to the trial, would discover their wickedness, and the time will come when those who have been spared often shall be spared no longer. But the Lord still calls Israel his people.

MATTHEW HENRY **(1662–1714)**
COMMENTARY ON THE WHOLE BIBLE

MARTIN LUTHER:

TAKING A STAND FOR THE GOSPEL

1483–1546

Martin Luther was born in 1483 to an upper middle-class family in Eisleben, Germany. He studied law as a young man at the University of Erfurt near his hometown at the insistence of his father. One afternoon in 1505, while walking the road home, he was almost killed by a bolt of lightning that struck nearby. In fear he cried out to his patron saint, "Saint Anne, help! I will become a monk!" A few months later he did just that—a move that launched him on the trajectory that led to the Reformation.

Luther described his monastic experience at Saint Augustine's Monastery in Erfurt as *anfechtungen*—an overwhelming experience of spiritual crisis, anxiety, and suffering. For Luther this condition was rooted in his awareness of his own sinfulness, for he was never sure if he had repented enough or if he was truly sorrowful in the first place. He attempted to assuage this inward turmoil through extreme asceticism, including self-flagellation (literally striking oneself with a whip).

It wasn't until he experienced spiritual breakthrough in the tower room of his university that he found what he had been missing. Luther was profoundly troubled by the seeming contradiction of God's grace and righteousness. While studying Romans 1:17 he had an epiphany:

> *At last, by the mercy of God, meditating day and night, I gave heed to the context of the words . . . There I began to understand that the righteousness of God is that by which the righteous lives by a gift of God, namely faith. And this is the meaning: the righteousness of God is revealed by the gospel, namely, the passive righteousness with which merciful God justifies us by faith, as it is written, "The righteous by faith will live."*

Soon Luther was lecturing and writing on this spiritual breakthrough with a newly invigorated emphasis on the gospel. But Luther's theological transformation soon pitted him against one of the church's most corrupt practices. In 1517, an agent of the pope arrived at Wittenberg (where Luther taught theology) peddling indulgences—scripts people could buy for the forgiveness of sins—singing, "As soon as the coin in the coffer rings, a soul from purgatory springs!" This crass, spiritually abusive practice was being used to fund the pope's new cathedral in Rome. Luther rightly saw this manipulative practice as an affront to the gospel of grace and responded with his famous 95 Theses.

The Disputation for Clarifying the Power of Indulgences, as it was known, was a list of 95 points of academic dispute not only condemning indulgences but critically examining a number of other beliefs and practices, including the nature of repentance and penance; purgatory and the afterlife; and the nature of the pope's authority to remit guilt, forgive sins, and grant pardons. Hailed a hero by his German people for his propositions, Luther became the scourge of Rome. The Vatican investigated him and hauled him before ecclesial examining tribunals for examination.

Although there were other actors and the times were ripe for a coming revolution, it is no exaggeration to say that Luther was particularly responsible for launching what became known as the Protestant Reformation. He went on to write tracts, commentaries, and catechisms that contributed to the movement of not only reforming the church but also of reclaiming the gospel, our forgiveness through Christ's death, and the nature of justification by grace through faith.

Luther was excommunicated by the pope in 1520 and was hauled before another tribunal a year later, the Diet of Worms. He was urged to recant his beliefs but responded: "I cannot and will not recant, for going against my conscience is neither safe nor salutary. I can do no other, here I stand, God help me. Amen." Because he neither recanted nor went against his conscience concerning the truth of the gospel, not only was the church reformed but the promises of the gospel were also rediscovered and powerfully communicated again to the people of God.

IMPORTANT WORKS

DISPUTATION ON THE DIVINITY AND HUMANITY OF CHRIST

ON THE BONDAGE OF THE WILL

12 Amaziah then said to Amos, "Leave, you visionary! Run
away to the land of Judah. Earn your living and prophesy there!
13 Don't prophesy at Bethel any longer, for a royal temple and
palace are here."
14 Amos replied to Amaziah, "I was not a prophet by profession. No, I was a herdsman who also took care of sycamore
fig trees. 15 Then the LORD took me from tending flocks and
gave me this commission, 'Go! Prophesy to my people Israel.'
16 So now listen to the LORD's message! You say, 'Don't prophesy
against Israel! Don't preach against the family of Isaac!'
17 "Therefore this is what the LORD says:
'Your wife will become a prostitute in the streets,
and your sons and daughters will die violently.
Your land will be given to others,
and you will die in a foreign land.
Israel will certainly be carried into exile away from its land.'"

MORE VISIONS AND MESSAGES OF JUDGMENT

8 The Sovereign LORD showed me this: I saw a basket of summer fruit. 2 He said, "What do you see, Amos?" I replied, "A
basket of summer fruit." Then the LORD said to me, "The end has
come for my people Israel! I will no longer overlook their sins.
3 The women singing in the temple will wail in that day."
The Sovereign LORD is speaking.
"There will be many corpses littered everywhere! Be quiet!"
4 Listen to this, you who trample the needy
and do away with the destitute in the land.
5 You say,
"When will the new moon festival be over, so we can sell grain?

8:1–14 Wealth is unstable. It is like a wave accustomed to change back and forth due to the violence of the wind. One might suppose that the people of Israel are rich since they have the adoption of sons and divine worship, the promises and the patriarchs. But they have become poor because of their sin against the Lord. They have lacked nourishment in a certain way and have suffered hunger. For when they had put to death the bread of life, a hunger for the bread came upon them. A chastisement for the thirst was imposed on them, but "not a shortage of food or water but an end to divine revelation." Therefore they have wanted and have suffered hunger.

BASIL THE GREAT (330–379)
HOMILIES ON THE PSALMS

When will the Sabbath end, so we can open up the grain bins?
We're eager to sell less for a higher price,
and to cheat the buyer with rigged scales!
6 We're eager to trade silver for the poor,
a pair of sandals for the needy.
We want to mix in some chaff with the grain!"
7 The LORD confirms this oath by the arrogance of Jacob:
"I swear I will never forget all you have done!
8 Because of this the earth will quake,
and all who live in it will mourn.
The whole earth will rise like the Nile River;
it will surge upward and then grow calm, like the Nile in Egypt.
9 In that day," says the Sovereign LORD, "I will make the sun set at noon
and make the earth dark in the middle of the day.
10 I will turn your festivals into funerals
and all your songs into funeral dirges.
I will make everyone wear funeral clothes
and cause every head to be shaved bald.
I will make you mourn as if you had lost your only son;
when it ends it will indeed have been a bitter day.
11 Be certain of this, the time is coming," says the Sovereign LORD,
"when I will send a famine through the land—
not a shortage of food or water
but an end to divine revelation.
12 People will stagger from sea to sea,
and from the north around to the east.
They will wander about looking for a message from the LORD,
but they will not find any.
13 In that day your beautiful young women and your young men will faint from thirst.
14 These are the ones who now take oaths in the name of the sinful idol goddess of Samaria.
They vow, 'As surely as your god lives, O Dan,' or, 'As surely as your beloved one lives, O Beer Sheba!'
But they will fall down and not get up again."

9:1–10 The text says, "I will shake the family of Israel." Precious but much-sifted corn of the Lord's floor, be comforted by the blessed fact that the Lord directs both flail and sieve to his own glory and to your eternal profit. Observe the complete safety of the Lord's wheat; even the least grain has a promise of preservation. God himself sifts them in all places "with all the nations"; he sifts them in the most effectual manner—"It will resemble a sieve being shaken"—and yet for all this, not the smallest, lightest, or most shriveled grain is permitted to fall to the ground. However little we may be, if we are the Lord's, we may rejoice that we are preserved in Christ Jesus.

CHARLES SPURGEON
(1834–1892)
MORNING AND EVENING

9 I saw the Lord standing by the altar and he said,
"Strike the tops of the support pillars, so the thresholds shake!
Knock them down on the heads of all the people,
and I will kill the survivors with the sword.
No one will be able to run away;
no one will be able to escape.
2 Even if they could dig down into the netherworld,
my hand would pull them up from there.
Even if they could climb up to heaven,
I would drag them down from there.
3 Even if they were to hide on the top of Mount Carmel,
I would hunt them down and take them from there.
Even if they tried to hide from me at the bottom of the sea,
from there I would command the Sea Serpent to bite them.

4 Even when their enemies drive them into captivity,
from there I will command the sword to kill them.
I will not let them out of my sight;
they will experience disaster, not prosperity."

5 The Sovereign LORD of Heaven's Armies will do this.
He touches the earth and it dissolves;
all who live on it mourn.
The whole earth rises like the Nile River
and then grows calm like the Nile in Egypt.
6 He builds the upper rooms of his palace in heaven
and sets its foundation supports on the earth.
He summons the water of the sea
and pours it out on the earth's surface.
The LORD is his name.
7 "You Israelites are just like the Ethiopians in my sight,"
says the LORD.
"Certainly I brought Israel up from the land of Egypt,
but I also brought the Philistines from Caphtor and the
Arameans from Kir.
8 Look, the Sovereign LORD is watching the sinful nation,
and I will destroy it from the face of the earth.
But I will not completely destroy the family of Jacob,"
says the LORD.
9 "For look, I am giving a command,
and I will shake the family of Israel together with all the
nations.
It will resemble a sieve being shaken,
when not even a pebble falls to the ground.
10 All the sinners among my people will die by the sword—
the ones who say, 'Disaster will not come near, it will
not confront us.'

THE RESTORATION OF THE DAVIDIC DYNASTY

11 "In that day I will rebuild the collapsing hut
of David.
I will seal its gaps,
repair its ruins,
and restore it to what it was like in days gone by.
12 As a result they will conquer those left in Edom
and all the nations subject to my rule."
The LORD, who is about to do this, is speaking.
13 "Be sure of this, the time is coming," says the LORD,
"when the plowman will catch up to the reaper,
and the one who stomps the grapes will overtake the
planter.
Juice will run down the slopes;
it will flow down all the hillsides.
14 I will bring back my people, Israel;
they will rebuild the cities lying in rubble and settle
down.
They will plant vineyards and drink the wine they
produce;
they will grow orchards and eat the fruit they
produce.
15 I will plant them on their land,
and they will never again be uprooted from the land I
have given them,"
says the LORD your God.

AUTHOR	AUDIENCE	DATE	PURPOSE	THEMES
Obadiah	The people of Judah suffering the treachery of the Edomites, descendants of Esau	Probably the time of the Babylonian attacks on Jerusalem (605–586 BC)	Obadiah wrote not only to warn of God's impending judgment on the nations but also to encourage his people that they would be vindicated and ultimately restored.	God's faithfulness; vindication from enemies; comfort in adversity; justice and restoration; and the day of the Lord

As the shortest book in all the Old Testament, Obadiah is a surprising one because it presents an oracle of judgment in almost vindictive terms against one of Israel's enemies: Edom. The Edomites had been established in the region surrounding Israel since the time of the patriarchs (see Gen 36). A small but strong kingdom, the people were the descendants of Esau, the jilted brother of Jacob who had been denied his father Isaac's blessing due to his brother's cunning. The Israelites had something of a rocky relationship with the small kingdom. For the most part there was a steady if not fragile peace, but at times outright hostility broke out between the two nations. This history of antagonism apparently led Edom to take advantage of God's people when they fell at the hand of the Babylonians, which is the premise of this oracle from Obadiah.

John Calvin explained the purpose of Obadiah's prophetic word in this way:

> The prophet here shows that though the [Edomites] now lived happily, yet in a short time they would be destroyed for they were hated by God, and he shows that this would be the case as we shall see from the contents of this book for the sake of the chosen people. We now then perceive the design of the prophet: as adversity might have weakened the Israelites and even utterly broken them down, the prophet here applies comfort and props up their dejected minds, for the Lord would shortly look on them and take due vengeance on their enemies.

One of the surprising themes of this book is the seeming vindictiveness of God, posing something of a problem to many followers of Jesus and leading some to claim its theology as sub-Christian. "Because you violently slaughtered your relatives, the people of Jacob, shame will cover you, and you will be destroyed forever," wrote the prophet. He continued, making plain that the Edomites not only stood on the sidelines and watched as Jerusalem was sacked but they also "behaved as though [they] were in league with" her enemies (vv. 10–11), joining in the plunder. Ephrem the Syrian noted, "Obadiah shows here that the Edomites must be subjected to captivity because of their pride and the enmity they held against their brothers." And John Calvin commented, "He intimates that the calamity would not be only for a time as in the case of Israel, but that the Lord would execute such a punishment as would prove that the [Edomites] were aliens to him; for God in chastising his church ever observes certain limits, as he never forgets his covenant."

This vindication is given further definition when Obadiah announces the impending "day of the LORD," a day when "as you have done, so it will be done to you. You will get exactly what your deeds deserve" (v. 15). John Wesley noted that this is "the time which

OBADIAH

the Lord has appointed for the punishing of this, and other nations" for their acts, which were "perfidiously, cruelly, and ravenously against Jacob." There is a sense that *lex talionis*, or the law of retribution, is being employed here, meaning people will get what they deserve and the Lord will make things right.

Cyril of Alexandria noted a natural outcome in this oracle for deeds done in the flesh: "For nature is so arranged that everybody receives just treatment, and entirely equal wages are repaid to those who have undertaken similar actions." Jerome recognized an alternative principle here in which the Lord ensures that evil deeds performed against his people are made right since he is personally invested in fair judgment: "Near, O heretic, is the day of the Lord over all the nations. Near is the time of judgment in which all the nations are to be judged. As you have acted against the church, the same pain will come back upon your head, and your iniquities will descend upon the crown of your head."

Further, Obadiah stands with the rest of the prophetic tradition in ensuring that God's people will be delivered, finding ultimate restoration: "The exiles of this fortress of the people of Israel will take possession of what belongs to the people of Canaan as far as Zarephath, and the exiles of Jerusalem who are in Sepharad will take possession of the towns of the Negev. Those who have been delivered will go up on Mount Zion in order to rule over Esau's mountain. Then the LORD will reign as King!" (vv. 20–21). For God's people this oracle represented the Lord's faithfulness and a promise of restoration after exile.

To the early church this book represented something more: an end-times prophecy of God's ultimate gathering. Consider these words from Ephrem the Syrian: "This is the great gathering, which God had promised to bring together again from the four corners of the world. Those who have been saved shall go up to Mount Zion to rule Mount Esau in order to defeat and destroy the nation of the Edomites. And the kingdom shall be the Lord's."

John Calvin concurred: "What then are we to understand by this prophecy? It does unquestionably appear that the prophet speaks here of the kingdom of Christ . . . Hence he shows that [the Jews] should not only be restored to their former condition, but that the kingdom would be increased in splendor and wealth when Christ should come."

Obadiah wrote his oracle not only to warn of God's impending judgment on the nations but also to encourage his people that they would be vindicated and ultimately restored. And it stands as a beacon of God's faithfulness to this day.

GOD'S JUDGMENT ON EDOM

1 The vision that Obadiah saw.
The Sovereign LORD says this concerning Edom:

EDOM'S APPROACHING DESTRUCTION

We have heard a report from the LORD.
An envoy was sent among the nations, saying,
"Arise! Let us make war against Edom!"
2 The LORD says, "Look! I will make you a weak nation;
you will be greatly despised!
3 Your presumptuous heart has deceived you—
you who reside in the safety of the rocky cliffs,
whose home is high in the mountains.
You think to yourself,
'No one can bring me down to the ground!'
4 Even if you were to soar high like an eagle,
even if you were to make your nest among the stars,
I can bring you down even from there!" says the LORD.

5 "If thieves came to rob you during the night,
they would steal only as much as they wanted.
If grape pickers came to harvest your vineyards,
they would leave some behind for the poor.
But you will be totally destroyed!
6 How the people of Esau will be thoroughly plundered!
Their hidden valuables will be ransacked!
7 All your allies will force you from your homeland!
Your treaty partners will deceive you and overpower you.
Your trusted friends will set an ambush for you
that will take you by surprise!

8 "At that time," the LORD says,
"I will destroy the wise sages of Edom,
the advisers from Esau's mountain.
9 Your warriors will be shattered, O Teman,
so that everyone will be destroyed from Esau's mountain!

EDOM'S TREACHERY AGAINST JUDAH

10 "Because you violently slaughtered your relatives, the people of Jacob,
shame will cover you, and you will be destroyed forever.
11 You stood aloof while strangers took his army captive
and foreigners advanced to his gates.
When they cast lots over Jerusalem,
you behaved as though you were in league with them.
12 You should not have gloated when your relatives suffered calamity.
You should not have rejoiced over the people of Judah when they were destroyed.
You should not have boasted when they suffered adversity.
13 You should not have entered the city of my people when they experienced distress.
You should not have joined in gloating over their misfortune when they suffered distress.
You should not have looted their wealth when they endured distress.

14 You should not have stood at the fork in the road to
slaughter those trying to escape.
You should not have captured their refugees when they
suffered adversity.

THE COMING DAY OF THE LORD

15 "For the day of the LORD is approaching for all the
nations!
Just as you have done, so it will be done to you.
You will get exactly what your deeds deserve.
16 For just as you have drunk on my holy mountain,
so all the nations will drink continually.
They will drink, and they will gulp down;
they will be as though they had never been.
17 But on Mount Zion there will be a remnant of those
who escape,
and it will be a holy place once again.
The descendants of Jacob will conquer
those who had conquered them.
18 The descendants of Jacob will be a fire
and the descendants of Joseph a flame.
The descendants of Esau will be like stubble.
They will burn them up and devour them.
There will not be a single survivor of the descendants
of Esau!"
Indeed, the LORD has spoken it.
19 The people of the Negev will take possession of Esau's
mountain,
and the people of the foothills will take
possession of the land of the Philistines.
They will also take possession of the territory of
Ephraim and the territory of Samaria,
and the people of Benjamin will take possession of
Gilead.
20 The exiles of this fortress of the people of Israel
will take possession of what belongs to
the people of Canaan, as far as Zarephath,
and the exiles of Jerusalem who are in Sepharad
will take possession of the towns of the Negev.
21 Those who have been delivered will go up on Mount
Zion
in order to rule over Esau's mountain.
Then the LORD will reign as King!

VV. 17–21 At this place in the text, the migration of Israel back to the land is mentioned, more specifically, from those Jews taken away into Babylon. Perhaps here he is saying that everything that is to the south and to the north and to the east and to the west will be fully occupied by Israel as the people will easily possess the whole region around them. And people will ascend, gathered on top of Zion, which sums up the goal of the prophecy. For the inhabitants of Zion, he says, are saved by God, who will burst through their chains of servitude. At that time he will ascend and take vengeance against Mount Esau. For they will fight against Edom after the time of captivity, and God will rule over all, although God rejected Esau long ago and withdrew from Judah because of apostasy, for they served Baal and the golden calf. But now in mercy and reconciliation he will reign again over them.

CYRIL OF ALEXANDRIA
(C. 376–444)
COMMENTARY ON OBADIAH

AUTHOR	AUDIENCE	DATE	PURPOSE	THEMES
Unknown	The northern kingdom of Israel	Jonah prophesied during the reign of Jeroboam II (793–753 BC); the book was perhaps written between 750 and 725 BC	This book was written to reveal the compassion and grace of God toward all who repent.	Repentance and forgiveness; the people of God; and the character of God

We have here a remarkable instance of God's mercy toward repenting sinners," John Wesley wrote about the book of Jonah. "And in Jonah we have a most remarkable type of our Lord's burial and resurrection." These twin themes have marked how the communion of saints have engaged this important work, the fifth of the Minor Prophets.

For many the story of Jonah is a familiar one: God chose the prophet to preach repentance to Israel's bitter enemy, the Ninevites. Instead of going east toward the city of Nineveh, the prophet went west to a boat in the harbor of Joppa in order to escape. One of the major themes of this book is the compassion and grace God has for all sinners—even those who might seem beyond all hope. Theodoret of Cyr confirmed this aspect of the character of God, drawing a parallel between Jonah's mission and the incarnation of Christ:

> The only begotten Word of God was due to be made manifest to human beings in his human nature and to enlighten all the nations with the light of the knowledge of God; even before his own incarnation he gives the nations a glimpse of his divine care so as to confirm what would happen from what went before, to teach everyone that he is God not only of Jews but also of nations . . . After all, if he had shown no care for the nations before the incarnation, Jews would have formed the impression that he was a different God in doing the opposite to the giver of the law, the former being concerned only with Jews and the latter bestowing attention on all human beings.

Out at sea Jonah was swallowed by a large fish only to be delivered three days later. "His miraculous deliverance from out of the fish," revealed Matthew Henry, "rendered him a type of our blessed Lord, who mentions it so as to show the certain truth of the narrative." The church has universally understood this aspect of Jonah's story to foreshadow Jesus' resurrection. After all, Christ himself referenced Jonah's "burial" in the fish when speaking about his own impending burial: "For just as Jonah was in the belly of the huge fish for three days and three nights, so the Son of Man will be in the heart of the earth for three days and three nights" (Matt 12:40).

Inspired by these words of Christ, Cyril of Jerusalem provided a helpful comparison:

> When we study the story of Jonah the force of the resemblance becomes striking. Jesus was sent to preach repentance. So was Jonah. Though Jonah fled, not knowing what was to come, Jesus came willingly

to grant repentance for salvation. Jonah slumbered in the ship and was fast asleep amid the stormy sea, while Jesus by God's will was sleeping, the sea was stirred up for the purpose of manifesting thereafter the power of him who slept . . . Jonah was cast into the belly of a great fish, but Christ of his own will descended to the abode of the invisible fish of death. He went down of his own will to make death disgorge those it had swallowed up according to the scripture.

Tertullian related Jonah's "resurrection" to both Christ's and our own:

> Jonah was swallowed by the monster of the deep, in whose belly whole ships were devoured, and after three days he was vomited out again safe and sound . . . To what faith do these notable events bear witness, if not to that which ought to inspire in us the belief that they are proofs and documents of our own future and our completed resurrection? To borrow the apostle's phrase, these were figures of ourselves.

The book climaxes with a lesson in the character of God through a curious admission by Jonah: He didn't want to preach repentance to the Gentiles of Nineveh, because he feared they would repent and that God would forgive them, staying his hand of judgment and offering his hand of grace. "This is what I tried to prevent by attempting to escape to Tarshish, because I knew that you are a gracious and compassionate God, slow to anger and abounding in mercy, and one who relents concerning threatened judgment" (4:2). John Calvin commented on this insight into God's character, which countless generations of believers have regarded as well:

> The Lord therefore does here recall us to himself and testifies that he is kind and merciful inasmuch as he is abundant in compassion . . . It is as though he had said that he is not influenced by any regard for our worthiness, and that it is not for merits that he is disposed to mercy when we have sinned and that he receives us into favor; but that he does all this because his goodness is infinite and inexhaustible . . . This slowness to wrath proves that God provides for the salvation of mankind, even when he is provoked by their sins. Though miserable men provoke God daily against themselves, he yet continues to have a regard for their salvation.

Jonah wrote his book to reveal the radical compassion and incredible grace of God toward all who repent. His prophetic words offer us insight into God's character that should comfort us and provoke us to similar compassion and grace.

1:1–15 A certain headstrong prophet ran away from the Lord, crossing the sea from Joppa to Tarshish, as if he could escape from God. But God found him not on land or on sea but in the belly of a beast, where for three days he could not die or even in that way escape from the eyes of God. Is that man not better off who, though he fears the enemy of God, does not flee from but despises him? Who trusts in the protection of God or, if you will, has an even greater fear of God, having stood the longer in his eyes? He says, *He is the Lord, he is mighty, all things are his, and wherever I shall be I am in his hands. Let him do what he will, I shall not run away. If he wishes me to die, let him destroy me, as long as I faithfully serve him.*

TERTULLIAN **(155–C. 220)**
ON FLIGHT AMID PERSECUTION

2:1–10 Hoping for salvation by human resources is no salvation, for mortal means will not drive away death. So those who live in a time of anxiety should be anxious to pray to the Lord of heaven, who dispenses sadness or gladness and who alone by his transcendent sway can ensure that troubles are removed and happy times restored . . . The power of prayers and the healing efficacy of tears in the presence of God our Father is the lesson we must learn from Nineveh saved by its grief . . . So the faith that relies on God should strengthen panicking hearts, and its trust in God should in time of sorrow anticipate untroubled days. For fear of God ensures freedom from fear, whereas the one who does not fear God alone is right to fear everything. Those who have no confidence in Christ as bearer of salvation must put their trust in legions.

PAULINUS OF NOLA
(C. 354–431)
POEMS

JONAH TRIES TO RUN FROM THE LORD

1 The LORD's message came to Jonah son of Amittai, [2]"Go immediately to Nineveh, that large capital city, and announce
judgment against its people because their wickedness has come
to my attention."
[3]Instead, Jonah immediately headed off to Tarshish to escape
from the commission of the LORD. He traveled to Joppa and
found a merchant ship heading to Tarshish. So he paid the
fare and went aboard it to go with them to Tarshish, far away
from the LORD.
[4]But the LORD hurled a powerful wind on the sea. Such a
violent tempest arose on the sea that the ship threatened to
break up! [5]The sailors were so afraid that each cried out to his
own god and they flung the ship's cargo overboard to make
the ship lighter.
Jonah, meanwhile, had gone down into the hold below deck,
had lain down, and was sound asleep. [6]The ship's captain approached him and said, "What are you doing asleep? Get up!
Cry out to your god! Perhaps your god might take notice of us
so that we might not die!"
[7]The sailors said to one another, "Come on, let's cast lots to
find out whose fault it is that this disaster has overtaken us."
So they cast lots, and Jonah was singled out. [8]They said to him,
"Tell us, whose fault is it that this disaster has overtaken us?
What's your occupation? Where do you come from? What's your
country? And who are your people?"
[9]He said to them, "I am a Hebrew, and I worship the LORD, the
God of heaven, who made the sea and the dry land." [10]Hearing
this, the men became even more afraid and said to him, "What
have you done?" (The men said this because they knew that he
was trying to escape from the LORD, because he had previously
told them.) [11]Because the storm was growing worse and worse,
they said to him, "What should we do to you so that the sea will
calm down for us?"
[12]He said to them, "Pick me up and throw me into the sea
so that the sea will calm down for you, because I know it's my
fault you are in this severe storm."
[13]Instead, they tried to row back to land, but they were not
able to do so because the storm kept growing worse and worse.
[14]So they cried out to the LORD, "Oh, please, LORD, don't let us
die on account of this man! Don't hold us guilty of shedding
innocent blood. After all, you, LORD, have done just as you
pleased." [15]So they picked Jonah up and threw him into the sea,
and the sea stopped raging. [16]The men feared the LORD greatly
and earnestly vowed to offer lavish sacrifices to the LORD.

JONAH PRAYS

[17]The LORD sent a huge fish to swallow Jonah, and Jonah was in
the stomach of the fish three days and three nights.

2 Jonah prayed to the LORD his God from the stomach of the
fish [2]and said,

"I called out to the LORD from my distress,
and he answered me;
from the belly of Sheol I cried out for help,
and you heard my prayer.
3 You threw me into the deep waters,
into the middle of the sea;
the ocean current engulfed me;
all the mighty waves you sent swept over me.

4 I thought I had been banished from your sight
and that I would never again see your holy temple.
5 Water engulfed me up to my neck;
the deep ocean surrounded me;
seaweed was wrapped around my head.
6 I went down to the very bottoms of the mountains;
the gates of the netherworld barred me in forever,
but you brought me up from the Pit, O LORD, my God.
7 When my life was ebbing away, I called out to the LORD.
And my prayer came to you, to your holy temple.
8 Those who worship worthless idols forfeit the mercy
that could be theirs.
9 But as for me, I promise to offer a sacrifice to you with a
public declaration of praise;
I will surely do what I have promised.
Salvation belongs to the LORD!"

10 Then the LORD commanded the fish and it vomited Jonah
out onto dry land.

THE PEOPLE OF NINEVEH RESPOND TO JONAH'S WARNING

3 The LORD's message came to Jonah a second time, 2 "Go
immediately to Nineveh, that large city, and proclaim to
it the message that I tell you." 3 So Jonah went immediately to
Nineveh, in keeping with the LORD's message. Now Nineveh
was an enormous city—it required three days to walk through
it! 4 Jonah began to enter the city by going one day's walk, announcing, "At the end of 40 days, Nineveh will be overthrown!"
5 The people of Nineveh believed in God, and they declared
a fast and put on sackcloth, from the greatest to the least of
them. 6 When the news reached the king of Nineveh, he got up
from his throne, took off his royal robe, put on sackcloth, and
sat on ashes. 7 He issued a proclamation and said, "In Nineveh,
by the decree of the king and his nobles: No human or animal,
cattle or sheep, is to taste anything; they must not eat and they
must not drink water. 8 Every person and animal must put on
sackcloth and must cry earnestly to God, and everyone must
turn from their evil way of living and from the violence that
they do. 9 Who knows? Perhaps God might be willing to change
his mind and relent and turn from his fierce anger so that we
might not die." 10 When God saw their actions—that they turned
from their evil way of living—God relented concerning the judgment he had threatened them with and did not destroy them.

JONAH RESPONDS TO GOD'S KINDNESS

4 This displeased Jonah terribly and he became very angry. 2 He
prayed to the LORD and said, "Oh, LORD, this is just what I
thought would happen when I was in my own country. This is
what I tried to prevent by attempting to escape to Tarshish,
because I knew that you are a gracious and compassionate God,
slow to anger and abounding in mercy, and one who relents
concerning threatened judgment. 3 So now, LORD, kill me instead, because I would rather die than live!" 4 The LORD said,
"Are you really so very angry?"
5 Jonah left the city and sat down east of it. He made a shelter
for himself there and sat down under it in the shade to see
what would happen to the city. 6 The LORD God appointed a
little plant and caused it to grow up over Jonah to be a shade

3:1–10 Let us sow in tears so that we may reap in joy. Let us show ourselves people of Nineveh, not of Sodom. Let us amend our wickedness lest we be consumed with it. Let us listen to the preaching of Jonah lest we be overwhelmed by fire and brimstone. And if we have departed from Sodom, let us escape to the mountain. Let us flee to Zoar. Let us enter it as the sun rises. Let us not stay in all the plain. Let us not look around us lest we be frozen into a pillar of salt, a really immoral pillar to accuse the soul that returns to wickedness.

GREGORY OF NAZIANZUS
(C. 329–390)
ORATIONS

4:1–11 "Should I not be more concerned about Nineveh, this enormous city? There are more than 120,000 people in it who do not know right from wrong, as well as many animals." Beside men, women, and children who are in Nineveh, there are many other of my creatures that are not sinful, and my tender mercies are and shall be over all my works. If you would be their butcher, yet I will be their God. Go, Jonah, rest yourself content and be thankful: The goodness that spared Nineveh has spared you in this, your inexcusable forwardness. I will be to repenting Nineveh what I am to you, a God gracious and merciful, slow to anger, and of great kindness, and I will turn from the evil that you and they deserve.

JOHN WESLEY **(1703–1791)**
EXPLANATORY NOTES ON THE BIBLE

over his head to rescue him from his misery. Now Jonah was
very delighted about the little plant.
[7]So God sent a worm at dawn the next day, and it attacked the
little plant so that it dried up. [8]When the sun began to shine,
God sent a hot east wind. So the sun beat down on Jonah's head,
and he grew faint. So he despaired of life and said, "I would
rather die than live!"
[9]God said to Jonah, "Are you really so very angry about the
little plant?" And he said, "I am as angry as I could possibly
be!" [10]The LORD said, "You were upset about this little plant,
something for which you did not work, nor did you do anything
to make it grow. It grew up overnight and died the next day.
[11]Should I not be more concerned about Nineveh, this enormous city? There are more than 120,000 people in it who do
not know right from wrong, as well as many animals."

AUTHOR	AUDIENCE	DATE	PURPOSE	THEMES
Micah	The people of Israel and Judah	Probably between 700 and 650 BC	Micah wrote a message of indictment and judgment to God's people in response to their injustice and idolatry, but through him God also promised one who would bring ultimate peace.	Judgment for wickedness; injustice and oppression; idolatry; redemption and restoration through the coming Messiah; and prophetic insights into Christ

Micah the prophet was explicit in his purpose for writing: "I am full of the courage that the LORD's Spirit gives and have a strong commitment to justice. This enables me to confront Jacob with its rebellion and Israel with its sin" (3:8). Like the other prophets, Micah brought a message of indictment and judgment. His ministry was contemporary with Isaiah's, and he reflected much of the same tenor and tone as Amos. He took to task the people for their long list of social injustices as well as their idolatry—familiar themes in the life of God's people, unfortunately.

"Beware wicked schemers, those who devise calamity as they lie in bed," Micah wrote. "As soon as morning dawns they carry out their plans, because they have the power to do so" (2:1). This evil included coveting, defrauding, and robbing people of their property and inheritance; their judges, prophets, and priests were corrupt. These were among the most common complaints of injustice, which led the Lord to declare, "Because of you, Zion will be plowed up like a field, Jerusalem will become a heap of ruins, and the Temple Mount will become a hill overgrown with brush!" (3:12). He promised the same destruction for their pagan religious practices of witchcraft and idol worship.

As with the other prophets who condemned God's people for their sins and foretold of coming judgment and destruction, Micah also made known God's intent to deliver and restore, particularly with the promised Messiah: "As for you, Bethlehem Ephrathah, seemingly insignificant among the clans of Judah—from you a king will emerge who will rule over Israel on my behalf, one whose origins are in the distant past." Chrysostom voiced what the church has said about this passage from the beginning: "[Micah] revealed Christ's birth in the flesh." Yet until the time of that ruler, Israel would be given up "until the time when the woman in labor gives birth" (5:2–3). The Nestorian bishop Isho'dad of Merv explained that this "means Jerusalem because she is in the pains of labor, which are her afflictions, and waits the birth of her salvation until according to her expectations it sets to her return and her pain's end. But in the same manner they will endure different difficulties until the Virgin gives birth to Christ."

John Calvin recognized that after Micah had reminded Israel "that hard and severe time was nigh," having repeated God's judgments against Israel, "there follows immediately a consolation: we hence see that the prophet, at one time, humbles the children of God and prepares them for enduring the cross; and then he mitigates all sorrow, yea, and makes them to rejoice in the midst of their evils" by promising now "a new Ruler, he promises that there would be again some civil order to be found among the people . . . it was to show that God would again cause a new prince to arise to govern the people. It was therefore a remedy to their devastation." Like others before him, Calvin identified that ruler as Christ and understood this to be a prophetic word announcing God's ultimate rescue and salvation of Israel and all mankind.

Perhaps the more familiar exhortation of Micah comes toward the end when he addresses Israel's pattern of worship and way of living: "He has told you, O man, what is good, and what the Lord really wants from you: He wants you to carry out justice, to love faithfulness, and to live obediently before your God" (6:8).

Micah ended his prophetic work on the same hopeful note most of the prophets did, redirecting the attention of God's people away from judgment and toward mercy according to his covenantal promises: "Who will once again have mercy on us? Who will conquer our evil deeds? Who will hurl all our sins into the depths of the sea? You will be loyal to Jacob and extend your loyal love to Abraham, which you promised on oath to our ancestors in ancient times" (7:19–20). This hope is rooted in the character of God himself, a God whom Micah said was like none other, who pardons our iniquity, passes over our transgressions, lets go of his anger, and delights to offer his people mercy.

Matthew Henry's counsel was right: "Let us remember that the Lord has given the security of his covenant for strong consolation to all who flee for refuge to lay hold on the hope set before them in Christ Jesus."

1:1–16 The prophet here distinctly states that there was a just cause why God denounced so dreadful a judgment on his chosen people: because no portion of the country was free from iniquity. We now understand the prophet's object. As he had before taught how dreadful would be God's vengeance against all the ungodly, so now he mentions their crimes that they might not complain that they were unjustly treated or that God employed too much severity. The prophet then testifies that the punishment, then near at hand, would be just.

JOHN CALVIN (1509–1564)
COMPLETE COMMENTARY ON THE BIBLE

INTRODUCTION

1 This is the LORD's message that came to Micah of Moresheth
during the time of Jotham, Ahaz, and Hezekiah, kings of Judah,
which he saw concerning Samaria and Jerusalem.

THE JUDGE IS COMING

2 Listen, all you nations!
Pay attention, all inhabitants of earth!
The Sovereign LORD will act as a witness against you;
the Lord will accuse you from his majestic palace.
3 Look, the LORD is coming out of his dwelling place!
He will descend and march on the earth's
mountaintops!
4 The mountains will crumble beneath him,
and the valleys will split apart
like wax before a fire,
like water dumped down a steep slope.

5 All this is because of Jacob's rebellion
and the sins of the nation of Israel.
And just what is Jacob's rebellion?
Isn't it Samaria's doings?
And what is Judah's sin?
Isn't it Jerusalem's doings?

6 "I will turn Samaria into a heap of ruins in an open field,
into a place for planting vineyards.
I will dump the rubble of her walls down into the valley
and lay bare her foundations.
7 All her carved idols will be smashed to pieces;
all her metal cult statues will be destroyed by fire.
I will make a waste heap of all her images.
Since she gathered the metal as a prostitute collects
her wages,
the idols will become a prostitute's wages again."
8 For this reason I will mourn and wail;
I will walk around barefoot and without my outer
garments.
I will howl like a wild dog
and screech like an owl.
9 For Samaria's disease is incurable.
It has infected Judah;
it has spread to the leadership of my people
and even to Jerusalem!
10 Don't spread the news in Gath.
Don't shed even a single tear.
In Beth Leaphrah roll about in mourning in the dust!
11 Residents of Shaphir, pass by in nakedness and
humiliation!
The residents of Zaanan have not escaped.
Beth Ezel mourns,
"He takes from you what he desires."
12 Indeed, the residents of Maroth hope for something
good to happen,
though the LORD has sent disaster against the city of
Jerusalem.
13 Residents of Lachish, hitch the horses to the chariots!
You influenced Daughter Zion to sin,
for Israel's rebellious deeds can be traced back to you!

14 Therefore you will have to say farewell to Moresheth
Gath.
The residents of Achzib will be as disappointing
as a dried up well to the kings of Israel.
15 Residents of Mareshah, a conqueror will attack you;
the leaders of Israel shall flee to Adullam.
16 Shave your heads bald as you mourn for the children
you love;
shave your foreheads as bald as an eagle,
for they are taken from you into exile.

LAND ROBBERS WILL LOSE THEIR LAND

2 Beware wicked schemers,
those who devise calamity as they lie in bed.
As soon as morning dawns they carry out their plans,
because they have the power to do so.
2 They confiscate the fields they desire
and seize the houses they want.
They defraud people of their homes
and deprive people of the land they have inherited.

3 Therefore the LORD says this:
"Look, I am devising disaster for this nation!
It will be like a yoke from which you cannot free your
neck.
You will no longer walk proudly,
for it will be a time of catastrophe.
4 In that day people will sing this taunt song to you—
they will mock you with this lament:
'We are completely destroyed;
they sell off the property of my people.
How they remove it from me!
They assign our fields to the conqueror.'"
5 Therefore no one will assign you land in the LORD's
community.

6 "Don't preach with such impassioned rhetoric," they say
excitedly.
"These prophets should not preach of such things;
we will not be overtaken by humiliation."
7 Does the family of Jacob say,
"The LORD's patience can't be exhausted—
he would never do such things"?
To be sure, my commands bring a reward
for those who obey them,
8 but you rise up as an enemy against my people.
You steal a robe from a friend,
from those who pass by peacefully as if returning from
a war.
9 You wrongly evict widows among my people from their
cherished homes.
You defraud their children of their prized
inheritance.
10 But you are the ones who will be forced to leave!
For this land is not secure;
sin will thoroughly destroy it!
11 If a lying windbag should come and say,
'I'll promise you blessings of wine and beer,'
he would be just the right preacher for these people!

2:12–13 Whoever has entered in must not remain in the state wherein he entered but must go forth into the pasture so that entering in should be the beginning; he "will come in and go out, and find pasture" (John 10:9), the perfecting of graces. The one who enters in is contained within the bounds of the world. The one who goes forth goes, as it were, beyond all created things and, counting as nothing all things seen, shall "find pasture" above the heavens and shall feed upon the Word of God and say, "The LORD is my shepherd [and feeds me], I lack nothing" (Ps 23:1). But this going forth can be only through Christ; as it follows, "The LORD himself will lead them" (Mic 2:13).

JEROME (C. 342–420)
COMMENTARY ON MICAH

THE LORD WILL RESTORE HIS PEOPLE

12 "I will certainly gather all of you, O Jacob,
I will certainly assemble those Israelites who remain.
I will bring them together like sheep in a fold,
like a flock in the middle of a pasture;
they will be so numerous that they will make a lot of noise.
13 The one who can break through barriers will lead them out;
they will break out, pass through the gate, and leave.
Their king will advance before them;
the LORD himself will lead them."

GOD WILL JUDGE JUDAH'S SINFUL LEADERS

3 I said,
"Listen, you leaders of Jacob,
you rulers of the nation of Israel!
You ought to know what is just,
2 yet you hate what is good
and love what is evil.
You flay my people's skin
and rip the flesh from their bones.
3 You devour my people's flesh,
strip off their skin,
and crush their bones.
You chop them up like flesh in a pot—
like meat in a kettle.
4 Someday these sinful leaders will cry to the LORD for help,
but he will not answer them.
He will hide his face from them at that time,
because they have done such wicked deeds."

5 This is what the LORD has said about the prophets who
mislead my people,
"If someone gives them enough to eat,
they offer an oracle of peace.
But if someone does not give them food,
they are ready to declare war on him.
6 Therefore night will fall, and you will receive no visions;
it will grow dark, and you will no longer be able to read the omens.
The sun will set on these prophets,
and the daylight will turn to darkness over their heads.
7 The prophets will be ashamed;
the omen readers will be humiliated.
All of them will cover their mouths,
for they will receive no divine oracles."

8 But I am full of the courage that the LORD's Spirit gives
and have a strong commitment to justice.
This enables me to confront Jacob with its rebellion
and Israel with its sin.
9 Listen to this, you leaders of the family of Jacob,
you rulers of the nation of Israel!
You hate justice
and pervert all that is right.
10 You build Zion through bloody crimes,
Jerusalem through unjust violence.

3:8–12 Hence the divine Micah was unable to brook the building of Zion with blood, however you interpret the phrase, and of Jerusalem with iniquity. Meanwhile, these heads of the house of Jacob abhorred justice. The priests were teaching for hire. The prophets were prophesying for money! What does Micah say will be the result of this? "Zion will be plowed up like a field, Jerusalem will become a heap of ruins, and the Temple Mount will become a hill overgrown with brush!" He bewails also the scarcity of the upright, there being scarcely a stalk or a gleaming grape left, since both the prince asks and the judge curries favor, so that his language is almost the same as the mighty David's: "Deliver, LORD! For the godly have disappeared" (Ps 12:1).

GREGORY OF NAZIANZUS
(C. 329–390)
ORATIONS

11 Her leaders take bribes when they decide legal cases,
her priests proclaim rulings for profit,
and her prophets read omens for pay.
Yet they claim to trust the LORD and say,
"The LORD is among us.
Disaster will not overtake us!"
12 Therefore, because of you, Zion will be plowed up like a field,
Jerusalem will become a heap of ruins,
and the Temple Mount will become a hill overgrown with brush!

BETTER DAYS AHEAD FOR JERUSALEM

4 And in future days the LORD's Temple Mount will be the most important mountain of all;
it will be more prominent than other hills.
People will stream to it.
2 Many nations will come, saying,
"Come on! Let's go up to the LORD's mountain,
to the temple of Jacob's God,
so he can teach us his ways
and we can live by his laws."
For instruction will proceed from Zion,
the LORD's message from Jerusalem.
3 He will arbitrate between many peoples
and settle disputes between many distant nations.
They will beat their swords into plowshares
and their spears into pruning hooks.
Nations will not use weapons against other nations,
and they will no longer train for war.
4 Each will sit under his own grapevine
or under his own fig tree without any fear.
The LORD of Heaven's Armies has decreed it.
5 Though all the nations follow their respective gods,
we will follow the LORD our God forever.

RESTORATION WILL FOLLOW CRISIS

6 "In that day," says the LORD, "I will gather the lame
and assemble the outcasts whom I injured.
7 I will transform the lame into the nucleus of a new nation
and those far off into a mighty nation.
The LORD will reign over them on Mount Zion,
from that day forward and forevermore.
8 As for you, watchtower for the flock,
fortress of Daughter Zion—
your former dominion will be restored,
the sovereignty that belongs to Daughter Jerusalem."
9 Jerusalem, why are you now shouting so loudly?
Has your king disappeared?
Has your wise leader been destroyed?
Is this why pain grips you as if you were a woman in labor?
10 Twist and strain, Daughter Zion, as if you were in labor!
For you will leave the city
and live in the open field.
You will go to Babylon,
but there you will be rescued.
There the LORD will deliver you
from the power of your enemies.

4:6—5:1 "Twist and strain, Daughter Zion, as if you were in labor! For you will leave the city and live in the open field. You will go to Babylon, but there you will be rescued." The meaning is that you will go into captivity, people of Zion, to be deported to Babylon, but after years you will come back from there. "Many nations have now assembled against you." That is, in the meantime a mix of many different nations invades you under the command of Gog. The holy places of Zion will be violated and greatly despised. "You will crush many nations. You will devote to the LORD the spoils you take from them and dedicate their wealth to the sovereign Ruler of the whole earth." This will happen when, after taking possession of their land and wealth, you pay the tithe to the Lord of the entire earth.

EPHREM THE SYRIAN
(C. 306–373)
COMMENTARY ON MICAH

11 Many nations have now assembled against you.
They say, "Jerusalem must be desecrated,
so we can gloat over Zion!"
12 But they do not know what the LORD is planning;
they do not understand his strategy.
He has gathered them like stalks of grain to be threshed
at the threshing floor.
13 "Get up and thresh, Daughter Zion!
For I will give you iron horns;
I will give you bronze hooves,
and you will crush many nations."
You will devote to the LORD the spoils you take from
them
and dedicate their wealth to the sovereign Ruler of the
whole earth.

5 But now slash yourself, daughter surrounded by soldiers!
We are besieged!
With a scepter they strike Israel's ruler
on the side of his face.

A KING WILL COME AND A REMNANT WILL PROSPER

2 As for you, Bethlehem Ephrathah,
seemingly insignificant among the clans of Judah—
from you a king will emerge who will rule over Israel on
my behalf,
one whose origins are in the distant past.
3 So the LORD will hand the people of Israel over to their
enemies
until the time when the woman in labor gives birth.
Then the rest of the king's countrymen will return
to be reunited with the people of Israel.
4 He will assume his post and shepherd the people by the
LORD's strength,
by the sovereign authority of the LORD his God.
They will live securely, for at that time he will be honored
even in the distant regions of the earth.
5 He will give us peace.
Should the Assyrians try to invade our land
and attempt to set foot in our fortresses,
we will send against them seven shepherd-rulers,
make that eight commanders.
6 They will rule the land of Assyria with the sword,
the land of Nimrod with a drawn sword.
Our king will rescue us from the Assyrians
should they attempt to invade our land
and try to set foot in our territory.
7 Those survivors from Jacob will live
in the midst of many nations.
They will be like the dew the LORD sends,
like the rain on the grass,
that does not hope for men to come
or wait around for humans to arrive.
8 Those survivors from Jacob will live among the nations,
in the midst of many peoples.
They will be like a lion among the animals of the forest,
like a young lion among the flocks of sheep,
which attacks when it passes through.
It rips its prey and there is no one to stop it.

9 Lift your hand triumphantly against your adversaries;
may all your enemies be destroyed!

THE LORD WILL PURIFY HIS PEOPLE

10 "In that day," says the LORD,
"I will destroy your horses from your midst
and smash your chariots.
11 I will destroy the cities of your land
and tear down all your fortresses.
12 I will remove the sorcery that you practice,
and you will no longer have omen readers living among you.
13 I will remove your idols and sacred pillars from your midst;
you will no longer worship what your own hands made.
14 I will uproot your images of Asherah from your midst
and destroy your idols.
15 With furious anger I will carry out vengeance
on the nations that do not obey me."

THE LORD DEMANDS JUSTICE, NOT RITUAL

6 Listen to what the LORD says:
"Get up! Defend yourself before the mountains.
Present your case before the hills."
2 Hear the LORD's accusation, you mountains,
you enduring foundations of the earth.
For the LORD has a case against his people;
he has a dispute with Israel!
3 "My people, how have I wronged you?
How have I wearied you? Answer me!
4 In fact, I brought you up from the land of Egypt;
I delivered you from that place of slavery.
I sent Moses, Aaron, and Miriam to lead you.
5 My people, recall how King Balak of Moab planned to harm you,
how Balaam son of Beor responded to him.
Recall how you journeyed from Shittim to Gilgal,
so you might acknowledge that the LORD has treated you fairly."

6 With what should I enter the LORD's presence?
With what should I bow before the sovereign God?
Should I enter his presence with burnt offerings,
with year-old calves?
7 Will the LORD accept a thousand rams
or ten thousand streams of olive oil?
Should I give him my firstborn child as payment for my rebellion,
my offspring—my own flesh and blood—for my sin?
8 He has told you, O man, what is good,
and what the LORD really wants from you:
He wants you to carry out justice, to love faithfulness,
and to live obediently before your God.

9 Listen! The LORD is calling to the city!
It is wise to respect your authority, O LORD.
Listen, O nation, and those assembled in the city!
10 "I will not overlook, O sinful house, the dishonest gain you have hoarded away
or the smaller-than-standard measure I hate so much.

6:1–8 Forget about burnt offerings, countless sacrifices, and oblations of firstborn, he is saying. If you are concerned to appease the divinity, practice what God ordered you in the beginning through Moses. What in fact is that? To deliver fair judgment and decision in all cases where you have to choose better from worse, to continue giving evidence of all possible love and fellow feeling to your neighbor, and to put into practice what is pleasing to God in every way.

THEODORE OF MOPSUESTIA **(C. 350–428)**
COMMENTARY ON MICAH

11 I do not condone the use of rigged scales
or a bag of deceptive weights.
12 The city's wealthy people readily resort to violence;
her inhabitants tell lies;
their tongues speak deceptive words.
13 I will strike you brutally
and destroy you because of your sin.
14 You will eat, but not be satisfied.
Even if you have the strength to overtake some prey,
you will not be able to carry it away;
if you do happen to carry away something,
I will deliver it over to the sword.
15 You will plant crops, but will not harvest them;
you will squeeze oil from the olives, but you will have no oil to rub on your bodies;
you will squeeze juice from the grapes, but you will have no wine to drink.
16 You follow Omri's edicts
and all the practices of Ahab's dynasty;
you follow their policies.
Therefore I will make you an appalling sight;
the city's inhabitants will be taunted derisively,
and nations will mock all of you."

MICAH LAMENTS JUDAH'S SIN

7 Woe is me!
For I am like those gathering fruit
and those harvesting grapes,
when there is no grape cluster to eat
and no fresh figs that my stomach craves.
2 Faithful men have disappeared from the land;
there are no godly men left.
They all wait in ambush to shed blood;
they hunt their own brother with a net.
3 They are experts at doing evil;
government officials and judges take bribes,
prominent men announce what they wish,
and then they plan it out.
4 The best of them is like a thorn;
their godly are like a thornbush.
Woe to your watchmen;
your appointed punishment is on the way.
The time of their confusion is now.
5 Do not rely on a friend;
do not trust a companion!
Even with the one who lies in your arms,
do not share secrets!
6 For a son thinks his father is a fool,
a daughter challenges her mother,
and a daughter-in-law her mother-in-law;
a man's enemies are his own family.
7 But I will keep watching for the LORD;
I will wait for the God who delivers me.
My God will listen to me.

JERUSALEM WILL BE VINDICATED

8 My enemies, do not gloat over me!
Though I have fallen, I will get up.
Though I sit in darkness, the LORD will be my light.

7:1–7 Cain and Abel followed in the generation of humankind, and Cain was the first murderer. Afterward a deluge engulfed the earth because of the exceeding wickedness of humanity. Fire came down from heaven upon the people of Sodom because of their corruption. Subsequently God chose Israel, but even Israel became perverse and the chosen race was wounded: While Moses stood on the mountain before God, the people worshiped a calf in place of God. After Moses prophets were sent to heal Israel, but in their exercise of healing they deplored the fact that they could not overcome evil, so that Micah said, "Faithful men have disappeared from the land; there are no godly men left."

CYRIL OF JERUSALEM
(C. 313–386)
CATECHETICAL LECTURES

9 I must endure the LORD's fury,
for I have sinned against him.
But then he will defend my cause
and accomplish justice on my behalf.
He will lead me out into the light;
I will witness his deliverance.
10 When my enemies see this, they will be covered with
shame.
They say to me, "Where is the LORD your God?"
I will gloat over them;
then they will be trampled down
like mud in the streets.
11 It will be a day for rebuilding your walls;
in that day your boundary will be extended.

A CLOSING PRAYER

12 In that day people will come to you
from Assyria as far as Egypt,
from Egypt as far as the Euphrates River,
from the seacoasts and the mountains.
13 The earth will become desolate
because of what its inhabitants have done.
14 Shepherd your people with your rod,
the flock that belongs to you,
the one that lives alone in a thicket,
in the midst of a pastureland.
Allow them to graze in Bashan and Gilead,
as they did in the old days.
15 "As in the days when you departed from the land of
Egypt,
I will show you miraculous deeds."
16 Nations will see this and be disappointed by all their
strength;
they will put their hands over their mouths
and act as if they were deaf.
17 They will lick the dust like a snake,
like serpents crawling on the ground.
They will come trembling from their strongholds
to the LORD our God;
they will be terrified of you.
18 Who is a God like you?
Who forgives sin
and pardons the rebellion
of those who remain among his people?
Who does not stay angry forever,
but delights in showing loyal love?
19 Who will once again have mercy on us?
Who will conquer our evil deeds?
Who will hurl all our sins into the depths of the sea?
20 You will be loyal to Jacob
and extend your loyal love to Abraham,
which you promised on oath to our ancestors in ancient
times.

AUTHOR	AUDIENCE	DATE	PURPOSE	THEMES
Nahum	The people of Judah	Shortly before 612 BC	Nahum wrote this oracle of judgment and retribution against the Assyrian capital of Nineveh.	Wrath and judgment; justice and restoration; and the character of God

The purpose of the book of Nahum can be summarized in a passage from the first chapter: "The Lord is good—indeed, he is a fortress in time of distress, and he protects those who seek refuge in him. But with an overwhelming flood he will make a complete end of Nineveh; he will drive his enemies into darkness" (1:7–8). While the Lord had given the Ninevites a way out from his judgment by sending the prophet Jonah to preach repentance, Nahum now carried a different message: "The Lord is slow to anger but great in power; the Lord will certainly not allow the wicked to go unpunished" (1:3).

The Assyrian Empire dominated the ancient Near East in Nahum's day and had for centuries. And although the Lord had used Assyria to judge and punish his own people for their willful disregard of the covenant and his laws, he made this pledge to his people through his prophet Nahum: "Although I afflicted you, I will afflict you no more" (1:12). As an overview of this book Theodore of Mopsuestia observed:

> While the prophet Jonah reveals [God's mercy toward Nineveh], Nahum mentions the retribution due to be inflicted in many ways on them for displaying their arrogance against both the Israelites and Jerusalem, as well as against the God of all worshiped in the city. Through this it became obvious to everyone that he would not have allowed the Israelites to suffer this fate at their hands if they themselves had not rendered themselves deserving of such sufferings through their impiety.

Issues of justice and mercy abound in this book. In particular one cannot escape the theme of God's wrath in Nahum given that it opens with the sentiment, "The Lord is a zealous and avenging God"; not only does he avenge, the Lord is "very angry," he "takes vengeance against his foes; he sustains his rage against his enemies" (1:2). This wrath of the Lord is described as being "poured out like volcanic fire" (1:6). It is so fearsome that the seas dry up and rivers run dry, the mountains quake before him and melt, and the whole earth trembles. It is clear God's vengeance is total and terrifying. Yet it isn't for naught, for as John Wesley commented, the Lord avenges and administers vengeance "as supreme governor who by office is bound to right the oppressed and to punish the oppressor." Justice is inextricably wrapped up in God's judgment.

NAHUM

This is an important insight, for one can imagine the remnant of Judah suffering under the weight of Assyrian oppression and wondering when the Lord will judge the Assyrians for their arrogance, cruelty, and injustice. Nahum brought the answer. Although the wicked Assyrians had oppressed God's people, Nahum declared: "Never again will the wicked Assyrians invade you; they have been completely destroyed" (1:15). Although "their enemies have plundered them and have destroyed their fields" (2:2), the Lord promised there would be justice. As John Calvin noted, "When the Lord had completed his work on mount Zion and in Jerusalem, he would then turn his vengeance against the Assyrians." Nineveh would pay the price, and the Lord promised to "restore the majesty of Jacob, as well as the majesty of Israel" (2:2).

The prophet stated, "No one can withstand his indignation! No one can resist his fierce anger!" (1:6). When the Lord of hosts declares, *Behold, I am against you*, there is no recourse. He will make things right and bring glory to his name. As Matthew Henry commented, "Nineveh shall not put aside this judgment; there is no counsel or strength against the Lord. God looks upon proud cities, and brings them down . . . Strongholds, even the strongest, are no defense against the judgments of God. They shall be unable to do anything for themselves."

This says something profound about God's character: Not only is he willing to make things right in the world, particularly for his people, but he also has the power to do it. Although he is slow in anger, he is also "great in power" (1:3). No plot or design can either surprise or overtake the Lord, for "he will completely destroy!" (1:9). As John Calvin wrote, "God is able to reduce you to nothing, so that there will be no need to assail you the second time." Nahum revealed that when the Lord is against you, there is no way to escape his judgment. Neither the riches of merchants nor the strength of guards and chariots can thwart his plans, for "the fire will consume you; the sword will cut you down; it will devour you like the young locust would" (3:15).

The Assyrian capital of Nineveh had oppressed God's people for generations. Although the Lord had used them to render judgment against Israel, he would not let their injustice go unpunished forever. Nahum's prophetic word reminds us that when things seem bleak, we must continue to trust him, knowing he is the all-powerful Ruler who has promised to make things right in the end.

1:1–8 "The LORD is slow to anger but great in power; the LORD will certainly not allow the wicked to go unpunished." He does not suddenly and all at once inflict punishment, but only after exercising extreme long-suffering. *You Ninevites are witnesses to this, practicing repentance and finding salvation, and then guilty of extreme wickedness and for a time not paying the penalty for it.* But after putting up with people's wickedness for a long time, he is accustomed to inflict punishment on the unrepentant.

THEODORET OF CYR
(C. 393–C. 458)
COMMENTARY ON NAHUM

INTRODUCTION

1 This is an oracle about Nineveh; the book of the vision of Nahum the Elkoshite:

GOD TAKES VENGEANCE AGAINST HIS ENEMIES

2 The LORD is a zealous and avenging God;
the LORD is avenging and very angry.
The LORD takes vengeance against his foes;
he sustains his rage against his enemies.
3 The LORD is slow to anger but great in power;
the LORD will certainly not allow the wicked to go unpunished.

THE DIVINE WARRIOR DESTROYS HIS ENEMIES BUT PROTECTS HIS PEOPLE

He marches out in the whirlwind and the raging storm;
dark storm clouds billow like dust under his feet.
4 He shouts a battle cry against the sea and makes it dry up;
he makes all the rivers run dry.
Bashan and Carmel wither;
the blossom of Lebanon withers.
5 The mountains tremble before him;
the hills convulse;
the earth is laid waste before him
the world and all its inhabitants are laid waste.
6 No one can withstand his indignation!
No one can resist his fierce anger!
His wrath is poured out like volcanic fire,
boulders are broken up as he approaches.
7 The LORD is good—
indeed, he is a fortress in time of distress,
and he protects those who seek refuge in him.
8 But with an overwhelming flood
he will make a complete end of Nineveh;
he will drive his enemies into darkness.

DENUNCIATION AND DESTRUCTION OF NINEVEH

9 Whatever you plot against the LORD, he will completely destroy!
Distress will not arise a second time.
10 Surely they will be totally consumed
like entangled thornbushes,
like the drink of drunkards,
like very dry stubble.
11 From you, O Nineveh, one has marched forth who plots evil against the LORD,
a wicked military strategist.

ORACLE OF DELIVERANCE TO JUDAH

12 This is what the LORD says:
"Even though they are powerful—
and what is more, even though their army is numerous—
nevertheless, they will be destroyed and trickle away!
Although I afflicted you,
I will afflict you no more.
13 And now, I will break Assyria's yoke bar from your neck;
I will tear apart the shackles that are on you."

ORACLE OF JUDGMENT AGAINST THE KING OF NINEVEH

14 The LORD has issued a decree against you:
"Your dynasty will come to an end.
I will destroy the idols and images in the temples of your gods.
I will desecrate your grave, because you are accursed!"

PROCLAMATION OF THE DELIVERANCE OF JUDAH

15 Look! A herald is running on the mountains!
A messenger is proclaiming deliverance:
"Celebrate your sacred festivals, O Judah!
Fulfill your sacred vows to praise God!
For never again will the wicked Assyrians invade you;
they have been completely destroyed."

PROCLAMATION OF THE DESTRUCTION OF NINEVEH

2 An enemy who will scatter you, Nineveh, has advanced against you!
Guard the rampart!
Watch the road!
Prepare yourselves for battle!
Muster your mighty strength!
2 For the LORD is about to restore the majesty of Jacob,
as well as the majesty of Israel,
though their enemies have plundered them
and have destroyed their fields.

PROPHETIC VISION OF THE FALL OF NINEVEH

3 The shields of his warriors are dyed red;
the mighty soldiers are dressed in scarlet garments.
The chariots are in flashing metal fittings
on the day of battle;
the soldiers brandish their spears.
4 The chariots race madly through the streets,
they rush back and forth in the broad plazas;
they look like lightning bolts,
they dash here and there like flashes of lightning.
5 The commander orders his officers;
they stumble as they advance;
they rush to the city wall,
and they set up the covered siege tower.
6 The sluice gates are opened;
the royal palace is deluged and dissolves.
7 Nineveh is taken into exile and is led away;
her slave girls moan like doves while they beat their breasts.
8 Nineveh was like a pool of water throughout her days,
but now her people are running away;
she cries out: "Stop! Stop!"—
but no one turns back.
9 Her conquerors cry out:
"Plunder the silver! Plunder the gold!"
There is no end to the treasure—
riches of every kind of precious thing.
10 Destruction, devastation, and desolation!
Hearts faint, knees tremble;
every stomach churns, all their faces have turned pale!

2:1–13 The prophet simply teaches us here that God would at length restrain tyrants; for though he hides himself for a time, he never forgets the groans of those whom he sees to be unjustly afflicted. And particularly when tyrants molest the church, it is proved here by the prophet that God will at length be a defender, and hence we ought to consider well these words, "I am against you!" For though God addresses these words only to the Assyrians, yet as he points out the reasons why he rises up with so much displeasure against them, they ought to be extended to all tyrants and to all who exercise cruelty toward distressed and innocent people.

JOHN CALVIN (1509–1564)
COMPLETE COMMENTARY ON THE BIBLE

TAUNT AGAINST THE ONCE-MIGHTY LION

11 Where now is the den of the lions
and the feeding place of the young lions,
where the lion, lioness, and lion cub once prowled
and no one disturbed them?
12 The lion tore apart as much prey as his cubs needed
and strangled prey for his lionesses;
he filled his lairs with prey
and his dens with torn flesh.

BATTLE CRY OF THE DIVINE WARRIOR

13 "I am against you!" declares the LORD of Heaven's
Armies.
"I will burn your chariots with fire;
the sword will devour your young lions.
You will no longer prey upon the land;
the voices of your messengers will no longer
be heard."

REASON FOR JUDGMENT: SINS OF NINEVEH

3 Woe to the city guilty of bloodshed!
She is full of lies;
she is filled with plunder;
she has hoarded her spoil!

3:1–19 The fall of this great city should be a lesson to private persons who increase wealth by fraud and oppression. They are preparing enemies for themselves, and if the Lord sees good to punish them in this world, they will have none to pity them. Strongholds, even the strongest, are no defense against the judgments of God. Those who have done evil to their neighbors will find it come home to them. Nineveh and many other cities, states, and empires have been ruined and should be a warning to us. When the Lord shows himself against a people, everything they trust in must fail or prove a disadvantage, but he continues good to Israel.

MATTHEW HENRY (1662–1714)
COMMENTARY ON THE WHOLE BIBLE

PORTRAYAL OF THE DESTRUCTION OF NINEVEH

2 The chariot drivers will crack their whips;
the chariot wheels will shake the ground.
The chariot horses will gallop;
the war chariots will bolt forward!
3 The charioteers will charge ahead;
their swords will flash
and their spears will glimmer!
There will be many people slain;
there will be piles of the dead
and countless casualties—
so many that people will stumble over the
corpses.

TAUNT AGAINST THE HARLOT CITY

4 Because you have acted like a wanton prostitute—
a seductive mistress who practices sorcery,
who enslaves nations by her harlotry,
and entices peoples by her sorcery—
5 "I am against you," declares the LORD of Heaven's
Armies.
"I will strip off your clothes!
I will show your nakedness to the nations
and your shame to the kingdoms.
6 I will pelt you with filth;
I will treat you with contempt;
I will make you a public spectacle.
7 Everyone who sees you will turn away from you in
disgust;
they will say, 'Nineveh has been devastated!
Who will lament for her?'
There will be no one to comfort you!"

NINEVEH WILL SUFFER THE SAME FATE AS THEBES

8 You are no more secure than Thebes—
she was located on the banks of the Nile;
the waters surrounded her—
her rampart was the sea,
the water was her wall.
9 Cush and Egypt had limitless strength;
Put and the Libyans were among her allies.
10 Yet she went into captivity as an exile;
even her infants were smashed to pieces at the head of every street.
They cast lots for her nobility;
all her dignitaries were bound with chains.
11 You too will act like drunkards;
you will go into hiding;
you too will seek refuge from the enemy.

THE ASSYRIAN DEFENSES WILL FAIL

12 All your fortifications will be like fig trees with first-ripe fruit:
If they are shaken, their figs will fall into the mouth of the eater.
13 Your warriors will be like women in your midst;
the gates of your land will be wide open to your enemies;
fire will consume the bars of your gates.
14 Draw yourselves water for a siege!
Strengthen your fortifications!
Trample the mud and tread the clay!
Make mud bricks to strengthen your walls!
15 There the fire will consume you;
the sword will cut you down;
it will devour you like the young locust would.

THE ASSYRIAN DEFENDERS WILL FLEE

Multiply yourself like the young locust;
multiply yourself like the flying locust!
16 Increase your merchants more than the stars of heaven!
They are like the young locust that sheds its skin and flies away.
17 Your courtiers are like locusts,
your officials are like a swarm of locusts!
They encamp in the walls on a cold day,
yet when the sun rises, they fly away,
and no one knows where they are.

CONCLUDING DIRGE

18 Your shepherds are sleeping, O king of Assyria.
Your officers are slumbering!
Your people are scattered like sheep on the mountains,
and there is no one to regather them.
19 Your destruction is like an incurable wound;
your demise is like a fatal injury.
All who hear what has happened to you will clap their hands for joy,
for no one ever escaped your endless cruelty!

AUTHOR	AUDIENCE	DATE	PURPOSE	THEMES
Habakkuk	The people of Judah	About 605 BC	Habakkuk's prophetic work is a response to the injustice of the day.	Injustice and wickedness; justice and judgment; and righteousness and faith

The book of Habakkuk addresses issues related to ongoing injustice and wickedness: "Why do you force me to witness injustice? Why do you put up with wrongdoing?" and "Why do you put up with such treacherous people? Why do you say nothing when the wicked devour those more righteous than they are?" (1:3, 13). Habakkuk looked around the land at the violence of God's people and their disregard for the covenant and wondered when the Lord would set things right. Theodoret of Cyr understood, commenting on the prophet's indignation in this way:

> There are people who get quite upset at the sight of wrongdoers prospering. Some have doubts as to whether the God of all takes an interest in human beings; others have faith in the talk about providence but are at a loss to explain why God conducts things in this fashion. The remarkable prophet Habakkuk adopted the attitude of the latter, putting the question as though anxious in his own case to learn the reason for what happens and supplying the solution, which the grace of the Spirit provided. He did not, in fact, as some commentators believed, suffer from this complaint; rather he presents the view of the others and supplies instruction on the questions raised.

John Calvin insisted that part of what this passage teaches is "that all who really serve and love God, ought . . . to burn with holy indignation whenever they see wickedness reigning without restraint among men, and especially in the church of God." Habakkuk witnessed the injustice and wrongdoing, the strife and conflict of his people, and appealed to the Lord to do something about it, giving voice to the frustrations of saints down through the ages who have endured similar times. "There is indeed nothing that ought to cause us more grief," Calvin continued, "than to see men raging with profane contempt for God and no regard had for his law and for divine truth, and all order trodden underfoot. When therefore such a confusion appears to us, we must feel roused, if we have in us any spark of religion." He pointed out that there was nothing wrong with Habakkuk's appeal to the Lord, "for wherefore do we pray, but that each of us may unburden his cares, his griefs, and anxieties by pouring them into the bosom of God?"

The Lord replied to Habakkuk in two ways. First he said, "Look at the nations and pay attention! You will be shocked and amazed! For I will do something in your lifetime that you will not believe even though you are forewarned" (1:5). On the one hand this offered assurance of God's impending judgment of evil and putting injustice to rights; he would not tarry forever. On the other it was a lesson to the people of God: God would judge his people for violating their covenant with him; he would not tarry forever. John Calvin agreed: "So then when the people became hardened against all threatening, they thought that God would ever bear with them; hence the prophet expressly declares that the execution of that which they regarded as a fable was near at hand."

The Lord's second response was equally important: "Look, the person whose desires are not upright will faint from exhaustion, but the person of integrity will live because of his faithfulness" (2:4). Many have seen this second answer to be at the core of the book's message, particularly because it is quoted in three important locations in the New Testament: Romans 1:17 (Paul); Galatians 3:11–12 (Paul); and Hebrews 10:37–38 (writer unknown). In light of the world's brokenness and the wickedness of humanity, how should the people of God respond? "The humble and upright one," John Wesley said, "who adores the depth of divine providence, and is persuaded of the truth of divine promises supports himself by a firm expectation of the deliverance of Zion." As history marches forward and we await its ultimate renewal, the righteous continue trusting in the promises of the Lord, not least of which is his promised redemption and the final consummation of his justice.

As is consistent with the other prophets, Habakkuk marries the wrath and judgment of God with his mercy and deliverance. For in the face of injustice and calamity, both at the hand of God and the hands of evildoers, the prophet could claim: "I will rejoice because of the LORD; I will be happy because of the God who delivers me!" Why? Because "The Sovereign LORD is my source of strength. He gives me the agility of a deer; he enables me to negotiate the rugged terrain" (3:18–19).

Perhaps the message of Habakkuk is best summarized by Matthew Henry:

> When we see a day of trouble approach, it concerns us to prepare. A good hope through grace is founded in holy fear. The prophet looked back upon the experiences of the church in former ages and observed what great things God had done for them, and so was he not only recovered but also filled with holy joy. He resolved to delight and triumph in the Lord; for when all is gone, his God is not gone.

May we join Habakkuk in resolving in our hearts to defy injustice with holy joy, and wickedness with the Lord's strength.

1:1–17 *When all things are in disorder, when there is now no regard for equity and justice but people abandon themselves into all kinds of wickedness, how long, Lord, will you take no notice?* God indeed had suspended his judgment, though he had been often solicited to execute it by his prophet. It therefore appears that their wickedness had made such advances that it would be no wonder if they were now severely chastised by the Lord; for they had by their sins not only provoked him against them, but also all the godly and the faithful .

JOHN CALVIN (1509–1564)
COMPLETE COMMENTARY ON THE BIBLE

HABAKKUK COMPLAINS TO THE LORD

1 This is the oracle that the prophet Habakkuk saw:
2 How long, LORD, must I cry for help?
But you do not listen!
I call out to you, "Violence!"
But you do not deliver!
3 Why do you force me to witness injustice?
Why do you put up with wrongdoing?
Destruction and violence confront me;
conflict is present and one must endure strife.
4 For this reason the law lacks power,
and justice is never carried out.
Indeed, the wicked intimidate the innocent.
For this reason justice is perverted.

THE LORD'S SURPRISING ANSWER

5 "Look at the nations and pay attention!
You will be shocked and amazed!
For I will do something in your lifetime
that you will not believe even though you are forewarned.
6 Look, I am about to empower the Babylonians,
that ruthless and greedy nation.
They sweep across the surface of the earth,
seizing dwelling places that do not belong to them.
7 They are frightening and terrifying;
they decide for themselves what is right.
8 Their horses are faster than leopards
and more alert than wolves in the desert.
Their horses gallop,
their horses come a great distance;
like vultures they swoop down quickly to devour their prey.
9 All of them intend to do violence;
every face is determined.
They take prisoners as easily as one scoops up sand.
10 They mock kings
and laugh at rulers.
They laugh at every fortified city;
they build siege ramps and capture them.
11 They sweep by like the wind and pass on.
But the one who considers himself a god will be held guilty."

HABAKKUK VOICES SOME CONCERNS

12 LORD, you have been active from ancient times;
my sovereign God, you are immortal.
LORD, you have made them your instrument of judgment.
Protector, you have appointed them as your instrument of punishment.
13 You are too just to tolerate evil;
you are unable to condone wrongdoing.
So why do you put up with such treacherous people?
Why do you say nothing when the wicked devour those more righteous than they are?
14 You made people like fish in the sea,
like animals in the sea that have no ruler.
15 The Babylonian tyrant pulls them all up with a fishhook;
he hauls them in with his throw net.

When he catches them in his dragnet,
he is very happy.
16 Because of his success he offers sacrifices to his throw net
and burns incense to his dragnet;
for because of them he has plenty of food
and more than enough to eat.
17 Will he then continue to fill and empty his throw net?
Will he always destroy nations and spare none?

2 I will stand at my watch post;
I will remain stationed on the city wall.
I will keep watching so I can see what he says to me
and can know how I should answer
when he counters my argument.

THE LORD ASSURES HABAKKUK

2 The LORD responded:
"Write down this message.
Record it legibly on tablets
so the one who announces it may read it easily.
3 For the message is a witness to what is decreed;
it gives reliable testimony about how matters will turn out.
Even if the message is not fulfilled right away, wait patiently;
for it will certainly come to pass—it will not arrive late.
4 Look, the one whose desires are not upright will faint from exhaustion,
but the person of integrity will live because of his faithfulness.
5 Indeed, wine will betray the proud, restless man!
His appetite is as big as Sheol's;
like death, he is never satisfied.
He gathers all the nations;
he seizes all peoples.

THE PROUD BABYLONIANS ARE AS GOOD AS DEAD

6 "But all these nations will someday taunt him
and ridicule him with proverbial sayings:
'Woe to the one who accumulates what does not belong to him
(how long will this go on?)—
he who gets rich by extortion!'
7 Your creditors will suddenly attack;
those who terrify you will spring into action,
and they will rob you.
8 Because you robbed many countries,
all who are left among the nations will rob you.
You have shed human blood
and committed violent acts against lands, cities, and those who live in them.

9 "The one who builds his house by unjust gain is as good as dead.
He does this so he can build his nest way up high
and escape the clutches of disaster.
10 Your schemes will bring shame to your house.

2:6–14 Woe to him who has a fortune amassed by deceit and builds in blood a city, in other words, his soul. For it is this that is built like a city. Greed does not build it but sets it on fire and burns it. Do you wish to build your city well? "Better is a little with the fear of the LORD than great wealth and turmoil with it" (Prov 15:16). The riches of a person ought to work for the redemption of his soul, not to its destruction. Wealth is redemption if one uses it well; so too it is a snare if one does not know how to use it. For what is a person's money if not provision for the journey?

AMBROSE (C. 339–C. 397)
LETTERS

Because you destroyed many nations, you will
self-destruct.
11 For the stones in the walls will cry out,
and the wooden rafters will answer back.

12 "Woe to the one who builds a city by bloodshed—
he who starts a town by unjust deeds.
13 Be sure of this! The LORD of Heaven's Armies has decreed:
The nations' efforts will go up in smoke;
their exhausting work will be for nothing.
14 For recognition of the LORD's sovereign majesty will fill
the earth
just as the waters fill up the sea.

15 "Woe to you who force your neighbor to drink wine—
you who make others intoxicated
by forcing them to drink from the bowl of your furious
anger
so you can look at their naked bodies.
16 But you will become drunk with shame, not majesty.
Now it is your turn to drink and expose your
uncircumcised foreskin!
The cup of wine in the LORD's right hand is coming to you,
and disgrace will replace your majestic glory!
17 For you will pay in full for your violent acts against
Lebanon;
terrifying judgment will come upon you
because of the way you destroyed the wild animals
living there.
You have shed human blood
and committed violent acts against lands, cities, and
those who live in them.
18 What good is an idol? Why would a craftsman make it?
What good is a metal image that gives misleading
oracles?
Why would its creator place his trust in it
and make such mute, worthless things?
19 Woe to the one who says to wood, 'Wake up!'—
he who says to speechless stone, 'Awake!'
Can it give reliable guidance?
It is overlaid with gold and silver;
it has no life's breath inside it.
20 But the LORD is in his majestic palace.
The whole earth is speechless in his presence!"

HABAKKUK'S VISION OF THE DIVINE WARRIOR

3 This is a prayer of Habakkuk the prophet:
2 LORD, I have heard the report of what you did;
I am awed, LORD, by what you accomplished.
In our time repeat those deeds;
in our time reveal them again.
But when you cause turmoil, remember to show us mercy!
3 God comes from Teman,
the Holy One from Mount Paran. *Selah*
His splendor has covered the skies,
the earth is full of his glory.
4 His brightness will be as lightning;
a two-pronged lightning bolt flashing from his hand.
This is the outward display of his power.

5 Plague will go before him;
pestilence will march right behind him.
6 He took his battle position and shook the earth;
with a mere look he frightened the nations.
The ancient mountains disintegrated;
the primeval hills were flattened.
His are ancient roads.
7 I saw the tents of Cushan overwhelmed by trouble;
the tent curtains of the land of Midian were shaking.
8 Was the LORD mad at the rivers?
Were you angry with the rivers?
Were you enraged at the sea?
Such that you would climb into your horse-drawn
chariots,
your victorious chariots?
9 Your bow is ready for action;
you commission your arrows. *Selah*
You cause flash floods on the earth's surface.
10 When the mountains see you, they shake.
The torrential downpour sweeps through.
The great deep shouts out;
it lifts its hands high.
11 The sun and moon stand still in their courses;
the flash of your arrows drives them away,
the bright light of your lightning-quick spear.
12 You furiously stomp on the earth;
you angrily trample down the nations.
13 You march out to deliver your people,
to deliver your special servant.
You strike the leader of the wicked nation,
laying him open from the lower body to the neck. *Selah*
14 You pierce the heads of his warriors with a spear.
They storm forward to scatter us;
they shout with joy as if they were plundering the poor
with no opposition.
15 But you trample on the sea with your horses,
on the surging, raging waters.

HABAKKUK DECLARES HIS CONFIDENCE

16 I listened and my stomach churned;
the sound made my lips quiver.
My frame went limp, as if my bones were decaying,
and I shook as I tried to walk.
I long for the day of distress
to come upon the people who attack us.
17 When the fig tree does not bud,
and there are no grapes on the vines;
when the olive trees do not produce
and the fields yield no crops;
when the sheep disappear from the pen
and there are no cattle in the stalls—
18 I will rejoice because of the LORD;
I will be happy because of the God who delivers me!
19 The Sovereign LORD is my source of strength.
He gives me the agility of a deer;
he enables me to negotiate the rugged terrain.

(This prayer is for the song leader. It is to be accompanied by stringed instruments.)

3:17–19 Anyone can sing in the day. When the cup is full, they draw inspiration from it. It is easy to sing when we can read the notes by daylight, but they are skillful who sing when there is not a ray of light to read by. People can't make a song in the night by themselves; they may attempt it, but they will find that a song in the night must be divinely inspired. No, it is not in man's power to sing when all is adverse. It was a divine song that Habakkuk sang. Since our Maker gives songs in the night, let us wait upon him for the music. O Chief Musician, let us not remain songless because affliction is upon us, but tune our lips to the melody of thanksgiving.

CHARLES SPURGEON
(1834–1892)
MORNING AND EVENING

AUTHOR	AUDIENCE	DATE	PURPOSE	THEMES
Zephaniah	The people of Judah	Between 640 and 627 BC	Zephaniah wrote his work to complement the previous prophecies of Isaiah and Micah, announcing impending judgment as well as restoration for a faithful remnant of God's people.	The day of the Lord; judgment and destruction; and deliverance and restoration

Following the ministries of Isaiah and Micah, Zephaniah brought an oracle of judgment during the reign of Josiah. Like the prophets before him, he warned the Lord's judgment was nigh, not only for God's people but also for all nations. He also, however, revealed a remnant—upright and repentant Jews who "find safety in the LORD's presence" (3:12) and will be restored. Here is how John Calvin summarized this short but important book of prophecy:

> He first denounces utter destruction on a people who were so perverse that there was no hope of their repentance . . . He afterward repeats again his reproofs and shortly mentions the sins that then prevailed among the elect people of God. At the same time, he turns his discourse to the faithful and exhorts them to patience, setting before them the hope of favor provided they ever looked to the Lord; and provided they relied on the gratuitous covenant that he made with Abraham, and doubted not that he would be a Father to them and also looked, with a tranquil mind, for that redemption that had been promised to them.

Zephaniah's prophecy centers on the "day of the Lord," a day of judgment and destruction, or "a day of vengeance from the Lord," as John Wesley wrote. Matthew Henry explained that "the punishment of presumptuous sinners is a sacrifice to the justice of God . . . in the day of the Lord's judgment, it will clearly appear that those who perish will fall a sacrifice to divine justice for breaking God's law." And consider Gregory the Great's comment on what Zephaniah described:

> The day of the Lord comes full of vengeance and rebuke upon fenced cities and lofty corners, because the wrath of the last judgment both destroys human hearts that have been closed by defenses against the truth and unfolds such as have been folded up in duplicities. For then the fenced cities fall. For souls that God has not penetrated will be damned. Then the lofty corners tumble because hearts that erect themselves in the prudence of insincerity are prostrated by the sentence of righteousness.

Zephaniah reveals this day "is almost here; it is approaching very rapidly!" It is a "day of God's anger" that is meant to "bring distress on the people . . . for they have sinned against the LORD" (1:14–17). Merchants and traders will be wiped out, the wealth of the city will be plundered so that houses will be demolished and vineyards—the symbol of

ZEPHANIAH

prosperity—will lay in ruin. Not only that: "Their blood will be poured out like dirt; their flesh will be scattered like manure" (1:17). This day is meant for all the nations, as well as for the people of Judah. "Beware to the filthy, stained city; the city filled with oppressors!" Zephaniah says of the Lord's Holy City. "She is disobedient; she has refused correction. She does not trust the Lord; she has not sought the advice of her God" (3:1–2). This day of judgment then is in response to sinful rebellion.

And yet there is hope. For Zephaniah revealed the possibility of escaping this day of judgment: "Seek the Lord's favor, all you humble people of the land who have obeyed his commands! Strive to do what is right! Strive to be humble! Maybe you will be protected on the day of the Lord's angry judgment" (2:3). Matthew Henry commented, "The humble, brokenhearted, repenting sinner alone seeks to obtain an interest in this salvation. He will rest his soul on the promise and on Christ, in and through whom it is given. Thus he walks and works as well as lives by faith, perseveres to the end, and is exalted to glory; while those who distrust or despise God's all-sufficiency will not walk uprightly with him."

The Lord holds out this promised deliverance alongside his promised judgment, for Zephaniah revealed the Lord "will leave in your midst a humble and meek group of people, and they will find safety in the Lord's presence" (3:12). He described this people as a righteous, faithful group of believers who will be saved and restored to blessing: "The Lord has removed the judgment against you; he has turned back your enemy" (3:15). Not only that, but the Lord "will then enable the nations to give [him] acceptable praise. All of them will invoke the Lord's name when they pray" (3:9). From Origen to Chrysostom, Calvin to Wesley and beyond, the communion of saints has applied this prophetic word to all who seek the Lord.

In closing his commentary on Zephaniah, Theodoret of Cyr observed:

> The salvation of human beings rests with divine loving-kindness alone: We do not earn it as the wages of righteousness; rather it is a gift of divine goodness . . . We who were once in thrall to the devil but are now freed from that harsh captivity and unmindful of the error of polytheism have become God's own, being famous beyond pagans and barbarians, according to the prophecy, and we who were once far off have become near, according to the divine apostle.

1:1–18 "I will remove . . . those who swear allegiance to the LORD while taking oaths in the name of their 'king.'" Such persons thought themselves safe because they were with both parties: the followers of Jehovah and those who followed a false god. But duplicity is abominable with God. My soul, search yourself this morning and see whether you are guilty of double-dealing. You profess to be a follower of Jesus—do you truly love him? Ask yourself, *Do I rest alone on Jesus crucified and live alone for him? Is it my desire to do so?* If so, blessed be the mighty grace that has led me to salvation; and if not so, O Lord, pardon my sad offense and unite my heart to fear your name.

CHARLES SPURGEON
(1834–1892)
MORNING AND EVENING

INTRODUCTION

1 This is the LORD's message that came to Zephaniah son of Cushi, son of Gedaliah, son of Amariah, son of Hezekiah during the time of Josiah son of Amon, king of Judah:

THE LORD'S DAY OF JUDGMENT IS APPROACHING

2 "I will destroy everything from the face of the earth,"
says the LORD.
3 "I will destroy people and animals;
I will destroy the birds in the sky
and the fish in the sea.
(The idolatrous images of these creatures will be
destroyed along with evil people.)
I will remove humanity from the face of the earth," says
the LORD.
4 "I will attack Judah
and all who live in Jerusalem.
I will remove from this place every trace of Baal
worship,
as well as the very memory of the pagan priests.
5 I will remove those who worship the stars in the sky
from their rooftops,
those who swear allegiance to the LORD while taking
oaths in the name of their 'king,'
6 and those who turn their backs on the LORD
and do not want the LORD's help or guidance."
7 Be silent before the Sovereign LORD,
for the LORD's day of judgment is almost here.
The LORD has prepared a sacrificial meal;
he has ritually purified his guests.
8 "On the day of the LORD's sacrificial meal,
I will punish the princes and the king's sons,
and all who wear foreign styles of clothing.
9 On that day I will punish all who leap over the threshold,
who fill the house of their master with wealth taken by
violence and deceit.
10 On that day," says the LORD,
"a loud cry will go up from the Fish Gate,
wailing from the city's newer district,
and a loud crash from the hills.
11 Wail, you who live in the market district,
for all the merchants will disappear
and those who count money will be removed.
12 At that time I will search through Jerusalem with
lamps.
I will punish the people who are entrenched in their sin,
those who think to themselves,
'The LORD neither rewards nor punishes.'
13 Their wealth will be stolen
and their houses ruined!
They will not live in the houses they have built,
nor will they drink the wine from the vineyards they
have planted.
14 The LORD's great day of judgment is almost here;
it is approaching very rapidly!
There will be a bitter sound on the LORD's day of
judgment;
at that time warriors will cry out in battle.

15 That day will be a day of God's anger,
a day of distress and hardship,
a day of devastation and ruin,
a day of darkness and gloom,
a day of clouds and dark skies,
16 a day of trumpet blasts and battle cries.
Judgment will fall on the fortified cities and the high
corner towers.
17 I will bring distress on the people
and they will stumble like blind men,
for they have sinned against the LORD.
Their blood will be poured out like dirt;
their flesh will be scattered like manure.
18 Neither their silver nor their gold will be able to deliver
them
in the day of the LORD's angry judgment.
The whole earth will be consumed by his fiery wrath.
Indeed, he will bring terrifying destruction on all who
live on the earth."

THE PROPHET WARNS THE PEOPLE

2 Bunch yourselves together like straw, you undesirable
nation,
2 before God's decree becomes reality and the day of
opportunity disappears like windblown chaff,
before the LORD's raging anger overtakes you—
before the day of the LORD's angry judgment overtakes
you!
3 Seek the LORD's favor, all you humble people of the land
who have obeyed his commands!
Strive to do what is right! Strive to be humble!
Maybe you will be protected on the day of the LORD's
angry judgment.

JUDGMENT ON SURROUNDING NATIONS

4 Indeed, Gaza will be deserted
and Ashkelon will become a heap of ruins.
Invaders will drive away the people of Ashdod
by noon,
and Ekron will be overthrown.
5 Beware, you who live by the sea, the people who came
from Crete.
The LORD's message is against you, Canaan, land of the
Philistines:
"I will destroy everyone who lives there!"
6 The seacoast will be used as pasture lands by the
shepherds
and as pens for their flocks.
7 Those who are left from the kingdom of Judah will take
possession of it.
By the sea they will graze,
in the houses of Ashkelon they will lie down in the
evening,
for the LORD their God will intervene for them and
restore their prosperity.
8 "I have heard Moab's taunts
and the Ammonites' insults.
They taunted my people
and verbally harassed those living in Judah.

2:4–15 It was foretold that these nations would come to some place of God, as it has been said, "Nations from all over the earth will come to you" (Jer 16:19). Understand, if you can, that it is to the God of the Christians, who is supreme and the true God, that the people of these nations come not by walking but by believing. For this same announcement has been made in these words by Zephaniah: "The LORD will terrify them, for he will weaken all the gods of the earth. All the distant nations will worship the LORD in their own lands" (Zeph 1:11). One says, *The Gentiles will come to you from everywhere*; the other, *They shall adore him from their own nations.* Therefore they will not be required to withdraw from their own place in coming to him because they will find him in whom they believe in their own hearts.

AUGUSTINE (354–430)
ON FAITH IN THINGS UNSEEN

9 Therefore, as surely as I live," says the LORD of Heaven's
Armies, the God of Israel,
"be certain that Moab will become like Sodom
and the Ammonites like Gomorrah.
They will be overrun by weeds,
filled with salt pits,
and permanently desolate.
Those of my people who are left will plunder their
belongings;
those who are left in Judah will take possession of their
land."
10 This is how they will be repaid for their arrogance,
for they taunted and verbally harassed the people of
the LORD of Heaven's Armies.
11 The LORD will terrify them,
for he will weaken all the gods of the earth.
All the distant nations will worship the LORD in their
own lands.
12 "You Ethiopians will also die by my sword!"
13 The LORD will attack the north
and destroy Assyria.
He will make Nineveh a heap of ruins;
it will be as barren as the desert.
14 Flocks and herds will lie down in the middle of it,
as well as every kind of wild animal.
Owls will sleep in the tops of its support pillars;
they will hoot through the windows.
Rubble will cover the thresholds;
even the cedar work will be exposed to the
elements.
15 This is how the once-proud city will end up—
the city that was so secure.
She thought to herself, "I am unique! No one can
compare to me!"
What a heap of ruins she has become, a place where
wild animals live!
Everyone who passes by her taunts her and shakes his
fist.

JERUSALEM IS CORRUPT

3 Beware to the filthy, stained city;
the city filled with oppressors!
2 She is disobedient;
she has refused correction.
She does not trust the LORD;
she has not sought the advice of her God.
3 Her princes are as fierce as roaring lions;
her rulers are as hungry as wolves in the desert,
who completely devour their prey by
morning.
4 Her prophets are proud;
they are deceitful men.
Her priests have defiled what is holy;
they have broken God's laws.
5 The just LORD resides within her;
he commits no unjust acts.
Every morning he reveals his justice.
At dawn he appears without fail.
Yet the unjust know no shame.

THE LORD'S JUDGMENT WILL PURIFY

6 "I destroyed nations;
their walled cities are in ruins.
I turned their streets into ruins;
no one passes through them.
Their cities are desolate;
no one lives there.
7 I thought, 'Certainly you will respect me!
Now you will accept correction!'
If she had done so, her home would not be destroyed
by all the punishments I have threatened.
But they eagerly sinned
in everything they did.
8 Therefore you must wait patiently for me," says the
LORD,
"for the day when I attack and take plunder.
I have decided to gather nations together
and assemble kingdoms,
so I can pour out my fury on them—
all my raging anger.
For the whole earth will be consumed
by my fiery anger.
9 Know for sure that I will then enable
the nations to give me acceptable praise.
All of them will invoke the LORD's name when they pray
and will worship him in unison.
10 From beyond the rivers of Ethiopia,
those who pray to me, my dispersed people,
will bring me tribute.
11 In that day you will not be ashamed of all your
rebelliousness against me,
for then I will remove from your midst those who
proudly boast,
and you will never again be arrogant on my holy hill.
12 I will leave in your midst a humble and meek group of
people,
and they will find safety in the LORD's presence.
13 The Israelites who remain will not act deceitfully.
They will not lie,
and a deceitful tongue will not be found in their mouths.
Indeed, they will graze peacefully like sheep and lie
down;
no one will terrify them."
14 Shout for joy, Daughter Zion!
Shout out, Israel!
Be happy and boast with all your heart, Daughter
Jerusalem!
15 The LORD has removed the judgment against you;
he has turned back your enemy.
Israel's king, the LORD, is in your midst!
You no longer need to fear disaster.
16 On that day they will say to Jerusalem,
"Don't be afraid, Zion!
Your hands must not be paralyzed from panic!
17 The LORD your God is in your midst;
he is a warrior who can deliver.
He takes great delight in you;
he renews you by his love;
he shouts for joy over you."

3:8–13 Zephaniah takes it now as granted that pride could not be torn away from their hearts except they were wholly cast down and thus made contrite. He then teaches us that as long as they remained whole, they were ever proud, and that hence it was necessary to apply a violent remedy that they might learn meekness and humility. He shows that this was a necessary remedy. How so? Because they would have always conducted themselves arrogantly against God had they not been afflicted. It was therefore needful for them to be in a manner broken because they could not be bent.

JOHN CALVIN **(1509–1564)**
COMPLETE COMMENTARY ON THE BIBLE

18 "As for those who grieve because they cannot attend the
festivals—
I took them away from you;
they became tribute and were a source of shame to you.
19 Look, at that time I will deal with those who mistreated
you.
I will rescue the lame sheep
and gather together the scattered sheep.
I will take away their humiliation
and make the whole earth admire and respect them.
20 At that time I will lead you—
at the time I gather you together.
Be sure of this! I will make all the nations of the earth
respect and admire you
when you see me restore you," says the LORD.

AUTHOR	AUDIENCE	DATE	PURPOSE	THEMES
Haggai	Postexilic Jews living in Judah	520 BC	Haggai wrote to provoke the people of Judah to finish rebuilding the temple, repent of their sins, and make the Lord their priority.	Ruin and rebuilding; confession and repentance; and the Lord's presence

The book of Haggai is addressed to the postexilic people of God who had returned to Judah. Their captivity and return had been the subject of prophetic oracles for many years. And the desolate temple, which lay in ruins before them, was a clear symbol of the Lord's judgment against their wickedness and rebellion, for the temple had been at the center of their religious life and their covenant relationship with him.

The temple in Jerusalem was where the presence of the Lord was made manifest for his people. So when the temple was destroyed, in a very real way it signaled the removal of the Lord himself from among his people. The remnant who had returned from captivity would have already felt far from the Lord, given that their nation had been conquered, their leaders removed and slain, and their precious city, Jerusalem, reduced to rubble. To find the temple in ruin would have confirmed their ruin as by him. They must have wondered if the Lord had turned his back on his people forever.

Under the leadership of Ezra, the people had begun rebuilding the temple, but in fits and starts. Twenty years later, the altar was the only major feature of the temple in operation. God's people had shifted their priorities from the Lord to themselves, and Haggai was sent to call them back to the Lord and remember their covenant with him. Chief among his complaints was their exchanging of zealous faith for material comfort. The people had declared the time wasn't right for rebuilding the Lord's house, yet they had taken great care to rebuild their own houses! "Is it right for you to live in richly paneled houses while my temple is in ruins?" the Lord asked rhetorically (1:4), indicting his people for their mistaken priorities before revealing his discipline.

HAGGAI

Significantly, Haggai prophesied the coming of a greater temple and wrote, "The future splendor of this temple will be greater than that of former times" (2:9). Many believers down through the ages have understood this, at least in part, as a prophecy of the coming of Christ, the greater temple of God's presence amongst the nations. As John Wesley explained, "The first temple had a glory in its magnificent structure, rich ornaments, and costly sacrifices; but this was a worldly glory; that which is here promised is a heavenly glory from the presence of Christ in it. He that was the brightness of his Father's glory, who is the glory of the church, appeared in this second temple."

The final sermon in Haggai reveals Zerubbabel as a type of Christ, a point about which John Calvin wrote: "Zerubbabel was at that time a type of Christ, God declares here that he would be to him as a signet—that is, that his dignity would be esteemed by him . . . God, in short, shows that people gathered under one head would be accepted by him; for Christ was at length to rise, as it is evident, from the seed of Zerubbabel."

Haggai wrote his prophetic work to provoke the people so that they would finish rebuilding the temple, repent of their sins, and make the Lord their priority. May it exhort us to align our own priorities, draw closer to the Lord, and seek his kingdom.

1:1–11 The Lord intends to remind the people of what they have suffered by neglecting the temple. *When you overlooked my house lying in ruins and took an interest in rebuilding your own houses,* he is saying, *then the rain stopped, the land did not yield its crops, and I destroyed all the crops on the ground as though with a sword, striking many times both people and cattle, and in short ruining the fruit of your labors.* He ordered the rebuilding of the temple so that they might observe the law in it and reap the benefit, wanting as he did worship according to the law to be performed until the coming of the Heir, according to the divine apostle.

THEODORE OF MOPSUESTIA **(C. 350–428)**
COMMENTARY ON HAGGAI

INTRODUCTION

1 On the first day of the sixth month of King Darius' second
year, the LORD's message came through the prophet Haggai
to Zerubbabel son of Shealtiel, governor of Judah, and to the
high priest Joshua son of Jehozadak:

THE ACCUSATION OF INDIFFERENCE AGAINST THE PEOPLE

2This is what the LORD of Heaven's Armies has said: "These
people have said, 'The time for rebuilding the LORD's temple
has not yet come.'" 3The LORD's message came through the
prophet Haggai as follows: 4"Is it right for you to live in richly
paneled houses while my temple is in ruins? 5Here then, this
is what the LORD of Heaven's Armies has said: 'Think carefully
about what you are doing. 6You have planted much, but have
harvested little. You eat, but are never filled. You drink, but are
still thirsty. You put on clothes, but are not warm. Those who
earn wages end up with holes in their money bags.'"

CONSEQUENCES OF THE FAILURE TO REBUILD THE TEMPLE

7Moreover, this is what the LORD of Heaven's Armies has said:
"Pay close attention to these things also. 8Go up to the hill country and bring back timber to build the temple. Then I will be
pleased and honored," says the LORD. 9"You expected a large
harvest, but instead there was little. And when you would bring
it home, I would blow it right away. Why?" asks the LORD of
Heaven's Armies. "Because my temple remains in ruins, thanks
to each of you favoring his own house! 10This is why the sky
has held back its dew and the earth its produce. 11Moreover,
I have called for a drought that will affect the fields, the hill
country, the grain, new wine, fresh olive oil, and everything
that grows from the ground; it also will harm people, animals,
and everything they produce."

THE RESPONSE OF THE LEADERS AND THE PEOPLE

12Then Zerubbabel son of Shealtiel and the high priest Joshua
son of Jehozadak, along with the whole remnant of the people,
obeyed the LORD their God. They responded favorably to the
message of the prophet Haggai, who spoke just as the LORD
their God had instructed him, and the people began to respect
the LORD. 13Then Haggai, the LORD's messenger, spoke the
LORD's announcement to the people: "I am with you," decrees
the LORD. 14So the LORD energized and encouraged Zerubbabel
son of Shealtiel, governor of Judah, the high priest Joshua son
of Jehozadak, and the whole remnant of the people. They came
and worked on the temple of their God, the LORD of Heaven's
Armies. 15This took place on the twenty-fourth day of the sixth
month of King Darius' second year.

THE GLORY TO COME

2 On the twenty-first day of the seventh month, the LORD's
message came through the prophet Haggai again: 2"Ask the
following questions to Zerubbabel son of Shealtiel, governor
of Judah, the high priest Joshua son of Jehozadak, and the remnant of the people: 3'Who among you survivors saw the former
splendor of this temple? How does it look to you now? Isn't it
nothing by comparison?' 4Even so, take heart, Zerubbabel,"

decrees the LORD. “Take heart, Joshua son of Jehozadak, the high
priest. And take heart all you citizens of the land,” decrees the
LORD, “and begin to work. For I am with you,” decrees the LORD
of Heaven’s Armies. 5“Do not fear, because I made a promise to
your ancestors when they left Egypt, and my Spirit even now
testifies to you.” 6Moreover, this is what the LORD of Heaven’s
Armies has said: “In just a little while I will once again shake
the sky and the earth, the sea and the dry ground. 7I will also
shake up all the nations, and they will offer their treasures;
then I will fill this temple with glory.” So the LORD of Heaven’s
Armies has said. 8“The silver and gold will be mine,” decrees
the LORD of Heaven’s Armies. 9“The future splendor of this
temple will be greater than that of former times,” the LORD
of Heaven’s Armies has declared. “And in this place I will give
peace,” decrees the LORD of Heaven’s Armies.

THE PROMISED BLESSING

10On the twenty-fourth day of the ninth month of Darius’
second year, the LORD’s message came to the prophet Haggai:
11“This is what the LORD of Heaven’s Armies has said, ‘Ask the
priests about the law. 12If someone carries holy meat in a fold
of his garment and that fold touches bread, a boiled dish, wine,
olive oil, or any other food, will that item become holy?’” The
priests answered, “It will not.” 13Then Haggai asked, “If a person
who is ritually unclean because of touching a dead body comes
in contact with one of these items, will it become unclean?”
The priests answered, “It will be unclean.”

14Then Haggai responded, “‘The people of this nation are
unclean in my sight,’ decrees the LORD. ‘And so is all their effort;
everything they offer is also unclean. 15Now therefore reflect
carefully on the recent past, before one stone was laid on another in the LORD’s temple. 16From that time when one came
expecting a heap of 20 measures, there were only 10; when
one came to the wine vat to draw out 50 measures from it,
there were only 20. 17I struck all the products of your labor with
blight, disease, and hail, and yet you brought nothing to me,’
says the LORD. 18‘Think carefully about the past: from today,
the twenty-fourth day of the ninth month, to the day work on
the temple of the LORD was resumed, think about it. 19The
seed is still in the storehouse, isn’t it? And the vine, fig tree,
pomegranate, and olive tree have not produced. Nevertheless,
from today on I will bless you.’”

ZERUBBABEL THE CHOSEN ONE

20Then the LORD spoke to Haggai a second time on the twenty-
fourth day of the month: 21“Tell Zerubbabel governor of Judah:
‘I am ready to shake the sky and the earth. 22I will overthrow
royal thrones and shatter the might of earthly kingdoms. I will
overthrow chariots and those who ride them, and horses and
their riders will fall as people kill one another. 23On that day,’
says the LORD of Heaven’s Armies, ‘I will take you, Zerubbabel
son of Shealtiel, my servant,’ says the LORD, ‘and I will make
you like a signet ring, for I have chosen you,’ says the LORD of
Heaven’s Armies.”

2:20–23 **“I will take you, Zerubbabel son of Shealtiel, my servant.” He was a type of him who was God’s most beloved Servant. “And I will make you like a signet ring,” which is very highly valued and carefully kept. So shall the antitypical Zerubbabel, the Messiah, be advanced, loved, and inviolably preserved king and supreme over his church. He is indeed the signet on God’s right hand. For all power is given to him and derived from him. In him the great charter of the gospel is signed and sanctified, and it is in him that all the promises of God are yes and amen.**

JOHN WESLEY **(1703–1791)**
EXPLANATORY NOTES ON THE BIBLE

AUTHOR	AUDIENCE	DATE	PURPOSE	THEMES
Zechariah	Postexilic Jews living in Judah	520 to about 480 BC	Zechariah wrote to provoke God's people to finish rebuilding the temple and return to the Lord by addressing their sin and committing themselves anew to the covenant.	God's grace and forgiveness; spiritual renewal; the Messiah; and the end times

Writing as a contemporary of Haggai, Zechariah wrote his prophetic work to Jews who had returned from exile. Zechariah sought to encourage spiritual zeal for rebuilding the temple. He assured God's people that the Lord was with their effort: "I have become compassionate toward Jerusalem and will rebuild my temple in it" (1:16). The first six chapters are dedicated to this return, which is reflected in the opening verses, the core message of the book: "'Turn to me,' says the LORD of Heaven's Armies, 'and I will turn to you,' says the LORD of Heaven's Armies. 'Do not be like your ancestors, to whom the former prophets called out, saying, "This is what the LORD of Heaven's Armies has said, 'Turn now from your evil wickedness'"'" (1:3–4).

"Free will and God's grace are simultaneously commended," Augustine commented on this message. "When God says, 'Turn to me, and I will turn to you,' one of these clauses—that which invites our return to God—evidently belongs to our will; while the other, which promises his return to us, belongs to his grace." Chrysostom agreed, pointing out the curious paradox of this invitation: "Indeed, God is good to everyone, but he shows his patient endurance especially to those who sin. God always seems to be severe to the righteous but good to sinners and quick to clemency."

Perhaps the meaning of the prophet's name is itself an indication of this mercy, for Zechariah means "Yahweh remembers." The Lord remembered the covenant he had made with his people, and he was intent on fulfilling his promises.

Zechariah is said to be the most messianic of all the books in the Old Testament, for it offers important details about the coming Redeemer that were later fulfilled in Christ: "Look—here is the man whose name is Branch" (6:12), the Lord says of Christ's coming. He would be betrayed by "thirty pieces of silver" (11:13) and struck by a "sword" (13:7); the Messiah will be "sitting as king on his throne. Moreover, there will be a priest with him on his throne and they will see eye to eye on everything" (6:13), an indication of his kingship and priesthood. The Messiah would be "humble and riding on a donkey—on a young donkey, the foal of a female donkey" (9:9). For generations the church has recognized the fulfillment of these prophetic oracles in Jesus.

ZECHARIAH

Zechariah offered a glimpse into Israel's future: Israel's enemies will make a final siege against Jerusalem, finding initial victory (14:1–2); the Lord will defend the city of Zion and bring the nations under his judgment (14:3–4, 12–15); the Lord will eventually rule over the earth as King (14:9); all the nations will gather to Zion to worship the Lord, celebrating the Feast of Shelters (14:16); holiness will reign in Zion and among the people of God (14:20–21). Zechariah's words were meant to encourage God's people as they looked forward to God's final act of redemption and vindication, provoking them to anticipate their glorious future with God as King of kings and Lord of lords.

From the earliest days of the church, Christians have understood this prophecy of God's coming kingdom to apply to Christ. As John Calvin explained: "[The] kingdom of Christ, according to the prophetic mode of writing, is here described from its commencement to its end . . . Whenever then the prophets speak of perfection under the reign of Christ, we ought not to confine what they say to one day or to a short time, but we ought to include the whole time from the beginning to the end." The kingdom has already come through Christ's arrival and we await its full consummation, for it has not yet fully arrived.

"This prophecy is suitable to all," wrote Matthew Henry, summarizing the value of this prophetic work "as the scope is to reprove for sin and threaten God's judgments against the impenitent, and to encourage those who feared God with assurances of the mercy God had in store for his church, and especially of the coming of the Messiah, and the setting up of his kingdom in the world."

INTRODUCTION

1 In the eighth month of Darius' second year, the LORD's message came to the prophet Zechariah, son of Berechiah son of Iddo:

2"The LORD was very angry with your ancestors. 3Therefore say to the people: The LORD of Heaven's Armies says, 'Turn to me,' says the LORD of Heaven's Armies, 'and I will turn to you,' says the LORD of Heaven's Armies. 4Do not be like your ancestors, to whom the former prophets called out, saying, 'This is what the LORD of Heaven's Armies has said, "Turn now from your evil wickedness."' But they would by no means obey me," says the LORD. 5"As for your ancestors, where are they? And did the prophets live forever? 6But have my words and statutes, which I commanded my servants the prophets, not outlived your fathers? Then they paid attention and confessed, 'The LORD of Heaven's Armies has indeed done what he said he would do to us, because of our sinful ways.'"

1:1–6 We ought to believe for certain that if our sins cease, the divine mercy will immediately remove the punishments that were due to us. Thus he himself has deigned to promise through the prophet when he said, "'Turn to me,' says the LORD of Heaven's Armies, 'and I will turn to you.'" Therefore let us turn to a better life while the remedies are still in our power. By our good deeds let us summon to mercy the kind and merciful Lord whom we provoked by our sins. According to his usual practice, he will then deign to keep adversities from us and in his clemency to grant us good fortune.

CAESARIUS OF ARLES
(C. 468–542)
SERMONS

THE INTRODUCTION TO THE VISIONS

7On the twenty-fourth day of the eleventh month, the month Shebat, in Darius' second year, the LORD's message came to the prophet Zechariah, son of Berechiah son of Iddo:

THE CONTENT OF THE FIRST VISION

8I was attentive that night and saw a man seated on a red horse that stood among some myrtle trees in the ravine. Behind him were red, sorrel, and white horses.

THE INTERPRETATION OF THE FIRST VISION

9Then I asked one nearby, "What are these, sir?" The angelic messenger who replied to me said, "I will show you what these are." 10Then the man standing among the myrtle trees spoke up and said, "These are the ones whom the LORD has sent to walk about on the earth." 11The riders then agreed with the angel of the LORD, who was standing among the myrtle trees, "We have been walking about on the earth, and now everything is at rest and quiet." 12The angel of the LORD then asked, "O LORD of Heaven's Armies, how long before you have compassion on Jerusalem and the other cities of Judah that you have been so angry with for these 70 years?" 13The LORD then addressed good, comforting words to the angelic messenger who was speaking to me. 14Turning to me, the messenger then said, "Cry out that the LORD of Heaven's Armies says, 'I am very much moved for Jerusalem and for Zion. 15But I am greatly displeased with the nations that take my grace for granted. I was a little displeased with them, but they have only made things worse for themselves.

THE ORACLE OF RESPONSE

16"'Therefore,' this is what the LORD has said, 'I have become compassionate toward Jerusalem and will rebuild my temple in it,' says the LORD of Heaven's Armies. 'Once more a surveyor's measuring line will be stretched out over Jerusalem.' 17Speak up again with the message of the LORD of Heaven's Armies: 'My cities will once more overflow with prosperity, and once more the LORD will comfort Zion and validate his choice of Jerusalem.'"

VISION TWO: THE FOUR HORNS

[18]Once again I looked and this time I saw four horns. [19]So I
asked the angelic messenger who spoke with me, "What are
these?" He replied, "These are the horns that have scattered
Judah, Israel, and Jerusalem." [20]Next the LORD showed me four
blacksmiths. [21]I asked, "What are these going to do?" He answered, "These horns are the ones that have scattered Judah
so that there is no one to be seen. But the blacksmiths have
come to terrify Judah's enemies and cut off the horns of the
nations that have thrust themselves against the land of Judah
in order to scatter its people."

VISION THREE: THE SURVEYOR

2 I looked again, and there was a man with a measuring line
in his hand. [2]I asked, "Where are you going?" He replied,
"To measure Jerusalem in order to determine its width and
its length." [3]At this point the angelic messenger who spoke
to me went out, and another messenger came to meet him
[4]and said to him, "Hurry, speak to this young man as follows:
'Jerusalem will no longer be enclosed by walls because of the
multitude of people and animals there. [5]But I,' the LORD says,
'will be a wall of fire surrounding Jerusalem and the source of
glory in her midst.'"

[6]"You there! Flee from the northland!" says the LORD, "for
like the four winds of heaven I have scattered you," says the
LORD. [7]"Escape, Zion, you who live among the Babylonians!"
[8]For the LORD of Heaven's Armies says: "For his own glory he
has sent me to the nations that plundered you—for anyone
who touches you touches the pupil of his eye. [9]Yes, look here,
I am about to punish them so that they will be looted by their
own slaves." Then you will know that the LORD of Heaven's
Armies has sent me.

[10]"Sing out and be happy, Zion my daughter! For look, I have
come; I will settle in your midst," says the LORD. [11]"Many nations will join themselves to the LORD on the day of salvation,
and they will also be my people. Indeed, I will settle in the midst
of you all. Then you will know that the LORD of Heaven's Armies
has sent me to you. [12]The LORD will take possession of Judah as
his portion in the holy land and he will choose Jerusalem once
again. [13]Be silent in the LORD's presence, all people everywhere,
for he is being moved to action in his holy dwelling place."

2:1–13 The Lord himself has said, "'Many nations will join themselves to the LORD on the day of salvation, and they will also be my people. Indeed, I will settle in the midst of you all." Through another prophet he said, "I am coming to gather all the nations and ethnic groups; they will come and witness my splendor" (Isa 66:18). You come, and what do you bestow upon the nations? "I will perform a mighty act among them" (Isa 66:19). For from my conflict on the cross I will give to each of my soldiers a royal sign to bear upon his forehead. Still another prophet said, "He made the sky ink as he descended; a thick cloud was under his feet" (Ps 18:9). For his coming down from heaven was unknown to humanity.

CYRIL OF JERUSALEM
(C. 313–386)
CATECHETICAL LECTURES

VISION FOUR: THE PRIEST

3 Next I saw Joshua the high priest standing before the angel
of the LORD, with Satan standing at his right hand to accuse
him. [2]The LORD said to Satan, "May the LORD rebuke you, Satan!
May the LORD, who has chosen Jerusalem, rebuke you! Isn't this
man like a burning stick snatched from the fire?" [3]Now Joshua
was dressed in filthy clothes as he stood there before the angel.
[4]The angel spoke up to those standing all around, "Remove
his filthy clothes." Then he said to Joshua, "I have freely forgiv-
en your iniquity and will dress you in fine clothing." [5]Then I
spoke up, "Let a clean turban be put on his head." So they put
a clean turban on his head and clothed him, while the angel of
the LORD stood nearby. [6]Then the angel of the LORD exhorted
Joshua solemnly: [7]"The LORD of Heaven's Armies says, 'If you
follow my ways and keep my requirements, you will be able to
preside over my temple and attend to my courtyards, and I will
allow you to come and go among these others who are standing

3:1–10 The Lord will cause the sins of believers to pass away by his sanctifying grace and will enable them to walk in newness of life. The promises to Joshua look forward to Christ, of whose priesthood Joshua's was a shadow. Whatever trials we pass through, whatever services we perform, our whole dependence must rest on Christ, the Branch of righteousness. He is God's Servant, employed in his work, obedient to his will, devoted to his honor and glory. He is the Branch from which all our fruit must be gathered. We sit down under Christ's shadow with delight and are sheltered by it. And gospel grace, coming with power, makes people forward to draw others to it.

MATTHEW HENRY **(1662–1714)**
COMMENTARY ON THE WHOLE BIBLE

by you. [8]Listen now, Joshua the high priest, both you and your
colleagues who are sitting before you, all of you are a symbol
that I am about to introduce my servant, the Branch. [9]As for
the stone I have set before Joshua—on the one stone there are
seven eyes. I am about to engrave an inscription on it,' says the
LORD of Heaven's Armies, 'to the effect that I will remove the
iniquity of this land in a single day. [10]In that day,' says the LORD
of Heaven's Armies, 'everyone will invite his friend to fellowship
under his vine and under his fig tree.'"

VISION FIVE: THE MENORAH

4 The angelic messenger who had been speaking with me then
returned and woke me, as a person is wakened from sleep.
[2]He asked me, "What do you see?" I replied, "I see a menorah of
pure gold with a receptacle at the top. There are seven lamps at
the top, with seven pipes going to the lamps. [3]There are also two
olive trees beside it, one on the right of the receptacle and the
other on the left." [4]Then I asked the messenger who spoke with
me, "What are these, sir?" [5]He replied, "Don't you know what
these are?" So I responded, "No, sir." [6]Therefore he told me, "This
is the LORD's message to Zerubbabel: 'Not by strength and not
by power, but by my Spirit,' says the LORD of Heaven's Armies.

> 4:1–14 And who shall say to him, *What are you doing?* Indeed, this seems to be one reason—to display his sovereignty—why he chose, before the canon of scripture was settled, to make known his mind in such various methods and to such a variety of his servants and messengers. "The LORD's message came to me as follows: 'The hands of Zerubbabel have laid the foundations of this temple, and his hands will complete it.'" Even their enemies should see the hand and providence of God in the beginning, continuance, and ending of this seemingly improbable and impracticable work. Fear not, though the beginnings are but small. His hands that laid the foundation also shall finish it.
>
> GEORGE WHITEFIELD
> (1714–1770)
> *THE WORKS*

ORACLE OF RESPONSE

[7]"What are you, you great mountain? Because of Zerubbabel
you will become a level plain! And he will bring forth the temple capstone with shoutings of 'Grace! Grace!' because of this."
[8]Moreover, the LORD's message came to me as follows: [9]"The
hands of Zerubbabel have laid the foundations of this temple,
and his hands will complete it. Then you will know that the
LORD of Heaven's Armies has sent me to you. [10]For who dares
make light of small beginnings? These seven eyes will joyfully
look on the tin tablet in Zerubbabel's hand. These are the eyes
of the LORD, which constantly range across the whole earth."
[11]Next I asked the messenger, "What are these two olive trees
on the right and the left of the menorah?" [12]Before he could
reply I asked again, "What are these two extensions of the olive
trees, which are emptying out the golden oil through the two
golden pipes?" [13]He replied, "Don't you know what these are?"
And I said, "No, sir." [14]So he said, "These are the two anointed
ones who stand by the Lord of the whole earth."

VISION SIX: THE FLYING SCROLL

5 Then I turned to look, and there was a flying scroll! [2]Someone
asked me, "What do you see?" I replied, "I see a flying scroll
30 feet long and 15 feet wide." [3]The speaker went on to say,
"This is a curse traveling across the whole earth. For example,
according to the curse whoever steals will be removed from
the community; or on the other hand (according to the curse)
whoever swears falsely will suffer the same fate." [4]"I will send
it out," says the LORD of Heaven's Armies, "and it will enter the
house of the thief and of the person who swears falsely in my
name. It will land in the middle of his house and destroy both
timber and stones."

> 5:1–11 So in the day of judgment, our works will either succor us or plunge us into the depths like people weighted down with a millstone. Iniquity is heavy, supported, as it were, on a talent of lead; avarice is hard to carry; so too all pride and appearance of fraud. Urge the people of the Lord to hope more in the Lord therefore to abound in the riches of simplicity in which they may walk without a snare, without hindrance.
>
> AMBROSE (C. 339–C. 397)
> *LETTERS*

VISION SEVEN: THE EPHAH

[5]After this the angelic messenger who had been speaking to me
went out and said, "Look, see what is leaving." [6]I asked, "What
is it?" And he replied, "It is a basket for measuring grain that

is moving away from here." Moreover, he said, "This is their
'eye' throughout all the earth." 7Then a round lead cover was
raised up, revealing a woman sitting inside the basket. 8He then
said, "This woman represents wickedness," and he pushed her
down into the basket and placed the lead cover on top. 9Then
I looked again and saw two women going forth with the wind
in their wings (they had wings like those of a stork), and they
lifted up the basket between the earth and the sky. 10I asked
the messenger who was speaking to me, "Where are they taking
the basket?" 11He replied, "To build a temple for her in the land
of Babylonia. When it is finished, she will be placed there in
her own residence."

VISION EIGHT: THE CHARIOTS

6 Once more I looked, and this time I saw four chariots emerging from between two mountains of bronze. 2Harnessed to
the first chariot were red horses, to the second black horses,
3to the third white horses, and to the fourth spotted horses,
all of them strong. 4Then I asked the angelic messenger who
was speaking with me, "What are these, sir?" 5The messenger
replied, "These are the four spirits of heaven going out after
presenting themselves before the Lord of all the earth. 6The
chariot with the black horses is going to the north country, and
the white ones are going after them, but the spotted ones are
going to the south country. 7All these strong ones are scatter-
ing; they have sought permission to go and walk about over
the earth." The Lord had said, "Go! Walk about over the earth!"
So they are doing so. 8Then he cried out to me, "Look! The
ones going to the northland have brought me peace about
the northland."

A CONCLUDING ORACLE

9The LORD's message came to me as follows: 10"Choose some
people from among the exiles, namely, Heldai, Tobijah, and
Jedaiah, all who have come from Babylon, and when you have
done so go to the house of Josiah son of Zephaniah. 11Then take
some silver and gold to make a crown and set it on the head
of Joshua the high priest, the son of Jehozadak. 12Then say to
him, 'The LORD of Heaven's Armies says, "Look—here is the
man whose name is Branch, who will sprout up from his place
and build the temple of the LORD. 13Indeed, he will build the
temple of the LORD, and he will be clothed in splendor, sitting
as king on his throne. Moreover, there will be a priest with him
on his throne and they will see eye to eye on everything. 14The
crown will then be turned over to Helem, Tobijah, Jedaiah, and
Hen son of Zephaniah as a memorial in the temple of the LORD.
15Then those who are far away will come and build the temple
of the LORD so that you may know that the LORD of Heaven's
Armies has sent me to you. This will all come to pass if you
completely obey the voice of the LORD your God."'"

THE HYPOCRISY OF FALSE FASTING

7 In King Darius' fourth year, on the fourth day of Kislev, the
ninth month, the LORD's message came to Zechariah. 2Now
the people of Bethel had sent Sharezer and Regem-Melech and
their companions to seek the LORD's favor 3by asking both the
priests of the temple of the LORD of Heaven's Armies and the
prophets, "Should we weep in the fifth month, fasting as we have
done over the years?" 4The message of the LORD of Heaven's

6:9–15 **The simple and true reason why Christ is called the Branch is because he was not like a tall tree, with deep and strong roots, but like a small plant. He is indeed called in another place "a shoot [that] will grow out of Jesse's root stock" (Isa 11:1). This kind of shoot has nothing in it that is illustrious. We hence see that Christ is called the Branch because his beginning was contemptible, so that he was of hardly any repute among heathens; nay even among his own nation. But God intimates at the same time that this little plant would be set by his own hand and thus would gather strength. Though then the beginning of Christ was humble, yet God declares that he would give vigor for continued growth until he should attain to a great height.**

JOHN CALVIN **(1509–1564)**
COMPLETE COMMENTARY ON THE BIBLE

Armies then came to me, 5"Speak to all the people and priests of the land as follows: 'When you fasted and lamented in the fifth and seventh months through all these 70 years, did you truly fast for me—for me, indeed? 6And now when you eat and drink, are you not doing so for yourselves? 7Should you not have obeyed the words that the LORD cried out through the former prophets when Jerusalem was peacefully inhabited and her surrounding cities, the Negev, and the foothills were also populated?'"

8Again the LORD's message came to Zechariah: 9"The LORD of Heaven's Armies said, 'Exercise true judgment and show brotherhood and compassion to each other. 10You must not oppress the widow, the orphan, the resident foreigner, or the poor, nor should anyone secretly plot evil against his fellow citizen.'

7:8–14 What can be more wretched than a person perpetually angry? And just like maniacs who never enjoy tranquility, so also those who are resentful and retain enemies will never have the enjoyment of any peace; they incessantly rage and daily increase the tempest of their thoughts. Do you but mention their enemies, they become furious at once and sustain much inward anguish; and should they by chance get only a bare sight of their enemies, they fear and tremble as if encountering the worst evils.

CHRYSOSTOM **(C. 347–407)**
HOMILIES ON STATUTES

11"But they refused to pay attention, turning away stubbornly and stopping their ears so they could not hear. 12Indeed, they made their hearts as hard as diamond, so that they could not obey the law of Moses and the other words the LORD of Heaven's Armies had sent by his Spirit through the former prophets. Therefore, the LORD of Heaven's Armies poured out great wrath.

13"'Just as I called out, but they would not obey, so they will call out, but I will not listen,' the LORD of Heaven's Armies says. 14'Rather, I will sweep them away in a storm into all the nations they are not familiar with.' Thus the land became desolate because of them, with no one crossing through or returning, for they had made the fruitful land a waste."

THE BLESSING OF TRUE FASTING

8 Then the message of the LORD of Heaven's Armies came to me as follows: 2"The LORD of Heaven's Armies says, 'I am very much concerned for Zion; indeed, I am so concerned for her that my rage will fall on those who hurt her.' 3The LORD says, 'I have returned to Zion and will live within Jerusalem. Now Jerusalem will be called "truthful city," "mountain of the LORD of Heaven's Armies," "holy mountain."' 4Moreover, the LORD of Heaven's Armies says, 'Old men and women will once more live in the plazas of Jerusalem, each one leaning on a cane because of advanced age. 5And the streets of the city will be full of boys and girls playing. 6And,' says the LORD of Heaven's Armies, 'though such a thing may seem to be difficult in the opinion of the small community of those days, will it also appear difficult to me?' asks the LORD of Heaven's Armies.

7"The LORD of Heaven's Armies asserts, 'I am about to save my people from the lands of the east and the west. 8And I will bring them to settle within Jerusalem. They will be my people, and I will be their God, in truth and righteousness.'

9"The LORD of Heaven's Armies also says, 'Gather strength, you who are listening to these words today from the mouths of the prophets who were there at the founding of the house of the LORD of Heaven's Armies, so that the temple might be built. 10Before that time there was no compensation for man or animal, nor was there any relief from adversity for those who came and went, because I had pitted everybody—each one—against everyone else. 11But I will be different now to this remnant of my people from the way I was in those days,' says the LORD of Heaven's Armies, 12'for there will be a peaceful time of sowing, the vine will produce its fruit, and the ground its yield, and the skies will rain down dew. Then I will allow the remnant of my people to possess all these things. 13And it will come about that just as you, both Judah and Israel, were a curse to the nations, so I will save you and you will be a blessing. Do not be afraid! Instead, be strong.'

14"For the LORD of Heaven's Armies says, 'As I had planned to hurt you when your fathers made me angry,' says the LORD of Heaven's Armies, 'and I was not sorry, 15so, to the contrary, I have planned in these days to do good to Jerusalem and Judah—do not fear! 16These are the things you must do: Speak the truth, each of you, to one another. Practice true and righteous judgment in your courts. 17Do not plan evil in your hearts against one another. Do not favor a false oath—these are all things that I hate,' says the LORD."

18The message of the LORD of Heaven's Armies came to me as follows: 19"The LORD of Heaven's Armies says, 'The fast of the fourth, fifth, seventh, and tenth months will become joyful and happy, pleasant feasts for the house of Judah; so love truth and peace.' 20The LORD of Heaven's Armies says, 'It will someday come to pass that people—residents of many cities—will come. 21The inhabitants of one will go to another and say, "Let's go up at once to ask the favor of the LORD, to seek the LORD of Heaven's Armies. Indeed, I'll go with you."' 22Many peoples and powerful nations will come to Jerusalem to seek the LORD of Heaven's Armies and to ask his favor. 23The LORD of Heaven's Armies says, 'In those days 10 people from all languages and nations will grasp hold of—indeed, grab—the robe of one Jew and say, "Let us go with you, for we have heard that God is with you."'"

THE COMING OF THE TRUE KING

9 This is an oracle, the LORD's message concerning the land of Hadrach, with its focus on Damascus:

The eyes of all humanity, especially of the tribes of Israel, are toward the LORD, 2as are those of Hamath also, which adjoins Damascus, Tyre, and Sidon, though they consider themselves to be very wise. 3Tyre built herself a fortification and piled up silver like dust and gold like the mud of the streets. 4Nevertheless the Lord will evict her and shove her fortifications into the sea—she will be consumed by fire. 5Ashkelon will see and be afraid; Gaza will be in great anguish, as will Ekron, for her hope will have been dried up. Gaza will lose her king, and Ashkelon will no longer be inhabited. 6A mongrel people will live in Ashdod, for I will greatly humiliate the Philistines. 7I will take away their abominable religious practices; then those who survive will become a community of believers in our God, like a clan in Judah, and Ekron will be like the Jebusites. 8Then I will surround my temple to protect it like a guard from anyone crossing back and forth; so no one will cross over against them anymore as an oppressor, for now I myself have seen it.

9 Rejoice greatly, daughter of Zion!
Shout, daughter of Jerusalem!
Look! Your king is coming to you:
He is legitimate and victorious,
humble and riding on a donkey—
on a young donkey, the foal of a female donkey.
10 I will remove the chariot from Ephraim
and the warhorse from Jerusalem,
and the battle bow will be removed.

8:19 Let us go quickly to the Lord, who is himself the feast. We must not look at the feast as a time to delight the appetite and overindulge but as a display of virtue. The feasts of the heathen are made up of laziness and greed. Our feasts, on the other hand, are scenes of virtuous activities and the practice of temperance. The prophetic word says it very clearly, "The fast of the fourth, fifth, seventh, and tenth months will become joyful and happy, pleasant feasts for the house of Judah."

ATHANASIUS (C. 296–373)
FESTAL LETTERS

9:9–10 Our Lord Jesus Christ, when he was about to enter Jerusalem, ordered his disciples to get him the donkey with its foal, which was tied at a gate of the village of Bethphage, and he rode upon it as he entered Jerusalem. Since it had been explicitly foretold that the Christ would do precisely this, when he had done it in the sight of all he furnished clear proof that he was the Christ. And yet, even after these things have happened and are proved from the scriptures, you persist in refusing to believe. Zechariah, one of the twelve prophets, predicted this very event when he said, "Rejoice greatly, daughter of Zion! Shout, daughter of Jerusalem! Look! Your king is coming to you: he is legitimate and victorious, humble and riding on a donkey—on a young donkey, the foal of a female donkey."

JUSTIN MARTYR (C. 100–C. 165)
DIALOGUE WITH TRYPHO

Then he will announce peace to the nations.
His dominion will be from sea to sea
and from the Euphrates River to the ends of the earth.

11Moreover, as for you, because of our covenant relationship secured with blood, I will release your prisoners from
the waterless pit. 12Return to the stronghold, you prisoners,
with hope; today I declare that I will return double what was
taken from you. 13I will bend Judah as my bow; I will load the
bow with Ephraim, my arrow. I will stir up your sons, Zion,
against your sons, Greece, and I will make you, Zion, like a
warrior's sword.
14Then the LORD will appear above them, and his arrow will
shoot forth like lightning; the Sovereign LORD will blow the
trumpet and will proceed in the southern storm winds. 15The
LORD of Heaven's Armies will guard them, and they will prevail and overcome with sling stones. Then they will drink and
will become noisy like drunkards, full like the sacrificial basin
or like the corners of the altar. 16On that day the LORD their
God will deliver them as the flock of his people, for they are
the precious stones of a crown sparkling over his land. 17How
precious and fair! Grain will make the young men flourish, and
new wine the young women.

THE RESTORATION OF THE TRUE PEOPLE

10 Ask the LORD for rain in the season of the late spring
rains—the LORD who causes thunderstorms—and he will
give everyone showers of rain and green growth in the field. 2For
the household gods have spoken wickedness, the soothsayers
have seen a lie, and the dreamers have disclosed emptiness and
give comfort in vain. Therefore the people set out like sheep
and become scattered because they have no shepherd. 3"I am
enraged at the shepherds and will punish the lead goats.
"For the LORD of Heaven's Armies has brought blessing to
his flock, the house of Judah, and will transform them into
his majestic warhorse. 4From him will come the cornerstone,
the wall peg, the battle bow, and every ruler. 5And they will be
like warriors trampling the mud of the streets in battle. They
will fight, for the LORD will be with them, and will defeat the
enemy cavalry.
6"I (says the LORD) will strengthen the kingdom of Judah and
deliver the people of Joseph and will bring them back because
of my compassion for them. They will be as though I had never
rejected them, for I am the LORD their God, and therefore I
will hear them. 7The Ephraimites will be like warriors and will
rejoice as if they had drunk wine. Their children will see it and
rejoice; they will celebrate in the things of the LORD. 8I will
signal for them and gather them, for I have already redeemed
them; then they will become as numerous as they were before.
9Though I scatter them among the nations, they will remember
in far-off places—they and their children will survive and return. 10I will bring them back from Egypt and gather them from
Assyria. I will bring them to the lands of Gilead and Lebanon,
and there will not be enough room for them. 11The LORD will
cross the sea of storms and will calm its turbulence. The depths
of the Nile will dry up, the pride of Assyria will be humbled,
and the domination of Egypt will be no more. 12Thus I will
strengthen them by my power, and they will walk about in my
name," says the LORD.

10:1–2 Let us not know God by halves or make his loving-kindness an excuse for our indolence—for this, his thunders, for this, his lightnings—that his goodness may not be held in spite. He who causes the sun to rise also strikes people with blindness. He who sends the rain also causes the rain of fire. By the one he manifests his goodness, by the other, his severity. For the one let us love him, for the other let us fear that it may not be said also to us, "Or do you have contempt for the wealth of his kindness, forbearance, and patience, and yet do not know that God's kindness leads you to repentance?" (Rom 2:4–5).

BASIL THE GREAT (330–379)
THE LONG RULES

THE HISTORY AND FUTURE OF JUDAH'S WICKED KINGS

11 Open your gates, Lebanon,
so that the fire may consume your cedars.
2 Howl, fir tree,
because the cedar has fallen;
the majestic trees have been destroyed.
Howl, oaks of Bashan,
because the impenetrable forest has fallen.
3 Listen to the howling of shepherds,
because their magnificence has been destroyed.
Listen to the roaring of young lions,
because the thickets of the Jordan have been
devastated.

4 The LORD my God says this: "Shepherd the flock set aside
for slaughter. 5 Those who buy them slaughter them and are not
held guilty; those who sell them say, 'Blessed be the LORD, for
I am rich.' Their own shepherds have no compassion for them.
6 Indeed, I will no longer have compassion on the people of the
land," says the LORD, "but instead I will turn every last person
over to his neighbor and his king. They will devastate the land,
and I will not deliver it from them."
7 So I began to shepherd the flock destined for slaughter, the
most afflicted of all the flock. Then I took two staffs, calling one
"Pleasantness" and the other "Union," and I tended the flock.
8 Next I eradicated the three shepherds in one month, for I ran
out of patience with them and, indeed, they detested me as well.
9 I then said, "I will not shepherd you. What is to die, let it die,
and what is to be eradicated, let it be eradicated. As for those
who survive, let them eat each other's flesh!"
10 Then I took my staff "Pleasantness" and cut it in two to annul my covenant that I had made with all the people. 11 So it was
annulled that very day, and then the most afflicted of the flock
who kept faith with me knew that it was the LORD's message.
12 Then I said to them, "If it seems good to you, pay me my
wages, but if not, forget it." So they weighed out my payment—30
pieces of silver. 13 The LORD then said to me, "Throw to the potter
that exorbitant sum at which they valued me!" So I took the 30
pieces of silver and threw them to the potter at the temple of
the LORD. 14 Then I cut the second staff "Union" in two in order
to annul the covenant of brotherhood between Judah and Israel.
15 Again the LORD said to me, "Take up once more the equipment of a foolish shepherd. 16 Indeed, I am about to raise up
a shepherd in the land who will not take heed of the sheep
headed to slaughter, will not seek the scattered, and will not
heal the injured. Moreover, he will not nourish the one that is
healthy, but instead will eat the meat of the fat sheep and tear
off their hooves.
17 "Woe to the worthless shepherd
who abandons the flock!
May a sword fall on his arm and his right eye!
May his arm wither completely away
and his right eye become completely blind!"

THE REPENTANCE OF JUDAH

12 This is an oracle, the LORD's message concerning Israel:
The LORD—he who stretches out the heavens and lays the
foundations of the earth, who forms the human spirit within a

11:4–17 Hear now in regard to thirty pieces of silver: "Then I said to them, 'If it seems good to you, pay me my wages, but if not, forget it.'" One recompense is due me for curing the blind and the lame, and I receive another; instead of thanksgiving, dishonor, and instead of worship, insult. Do you see how scripture foresaw all this? "So they weighed out my payment—thirty pieces of silver." O prophetic accuracy! A great and unerring wisdom of the Holy Spirit! For he did not say ten or twenty but thirty, exactly the right amount. Tell also what happened to this payment, O prophet! The prophet says, "So I took the thirty pieces of silver and threw them to the potter at the temple of the LORD." Compare with the prophecy of the Gospel that says, "So Judas threw the silver coins into the temple and left" (Matt 27:5).

CYRIL OF JERUSALEM
(C. 313–386)
CATECHETICAL LECTURES

person—says, 2“I am about to make Jerusalem a cup that brings
dizziness to all the surrounding nations; indeed, Judah will also
be included when Jerusalem is besieged. 3Moreover, on that day
I will make Jerusalem a heavy burden for all the nations, and all
who try to carry it will be seriously injured; yet all the peoples
of the earth will be assembled against it. 4On that day,” says the
LORD, “I will strike every horse with confusion and its rider with
madness. I will pay close attention to the house of Judah, but
will strike all the horses of the nations with blindness. 5Then
the leaders of Judah will say to themselves, ‘The inhabitants of
Jerusalem are a means of strength to us through their God, the
LORD of Heaven’s Armies.’ 6On that day I will make the leaders
of Judah like an igniter among sticks and a burning torch among
sheaves, and they will burn up all the surrounding nations right
and left. Then the people of Jerusalem will settle once more in
their place, the city of Jerusalem. 7The LORD also will deliver
the homes of Judah first, so that the splendor of the kingship
of David and of the people of Jerusalem may not exceed that
of Judah. 8On that day the LORD himself will defend the inhabitants of Jerusalem, so that the weakest among them will be
like mighty David, and the dynasty of David will be like God,
like the angel of the LORD before them. 9So on that day I will
set out to destroy all the nations that come against Jerusalem.

10“I will pour out on the kingship of David and the population
of Jerusalem a spirit of grace and supplication so that they will
look to me, the one they have pierced. They will lament for
him as one laments for an only son, and there will be a bitter
cry for him like the bitter cry for a firstborn. 11On that day the
lamentation in Jerusalem will be as great as the lamentation at
Hadad Rimmon in the plain of Megiddo. 12The land will mourn,
each clan by itself—the clan of the royal household of David by
itself and their wives by themselves; the clan of the family of
Nathan by itself and their wives by themselves; 13the clan of the
descendants of Levi by itself and their wives by themselves; and
the clan of the Shimeites by itself and their wives by themselves;
14all the clans that remain, each separately with their wives.

12:10–11 The eye that looks to the Pierced One is the eye that weeps for him. O soul, when you come to look where all eyes should look, then your eye begins to weep for that for which all eyes should weep, even the sin that slew your Savior! There is no saving repentance except within sight of the cross. Yet none will look until the Spirit of God inclines them so to do, and he works on none to their salvation unless they yield to his influences and turn their eyes to Jesus.

CHARLES SPURGEON
(1834–1892)
METROPOLITAN TABERNACLE SERMONS

THE REFINEMENT OF JUDAH

13 “In that day there will be a fountain opened up for the
dynasty of David and the people of Jerusalem to cleanse
them from sin and impurity. 2And also on that day,” says the
LORD of Heaven’s Armies, “I will remove the names of the idols
from the land and they will never again be remembered. Moreover, I will remove the prophets and the unclean spirit from
the land. 3Then, if anyone prophesies in spite of this, his father
and mother to whom he was born will say to him, ‘You cannot
live, for you lie in the name of the LORD.’ Then his father and
mother to whom he was born will run him through with a sword
when he prophesies.

4“Therefore, on that day each prophet will be ashamed of his
vision when he prophesies and will no longer wear the hairy
garment of a prophet to deceive the people. 5Instead he will
say, ‘I am no prophet; indeed, I am a farmer, for a man has made
me his indentured servant since my youth.’ 6Then someone
will ask him, ‘What are these wounds on your chest?’ and he
will answer, ‘Some that I received in the house of my friends.’

7 “Awake, sword, against my shepherd,
against the man who is my associate,”
says the LORD of Heaven’s Armies.

"Strike the shepherd that the flock may be scattered;
I will turn my hand against the insignificant ones.
8 It will happen in all the land," says the LORD,
"that two-thirds of the people in it will be cut off and die,
but one-third will be left in it.
9 Then I will bring the remaining third into the fire;
I will refine them like silver is refined
and will test them like gold is tested.
They will call on my name and I will answer;
I will say, 'These are my people,'
and they will say, 'The LORD is our God.'"

THE SOVEREIGNTY OF THE LORD

14 A day of the LORD is about to come when your possessions
will be divided as plunder in your midst. 2For I will gather
all the nations against Jerusalem to wage war; the city will be
taken, its houses plundered, and the women raped. Then half
of the city will go into exile, but the remainder of the people
will not be taken away.
3Then the LORD will go to battle and fight against those nations, just as he fought battles in ancient days. 4On that day his
feet will stand on the Mount of Olives that lies to the east of
Jerusalem, and the Mount of Olives will be split in half from
east to west, leaving a great valley. Half the mountain will move
northward and the other half southward. 5Then you will escape
through my mountain valley, for the valley of the mountains
will extend to Azal. Indeed, you will flee as you fled from the
earthquake in the days of King Uzziah of Judah. Then the LORD
my God will come with all his holy ones with him. 6On that day
there will be no light—the sources of light in the heavens will
congeal. 7It will happen in one day—a day known to the LORD—
not in the day or the night, but in the evening there will be
light. 8Moreover, on that day living waters will flow out from
Jerusalem, half of them to the eastern sea and half of them to
the western sea; it will happen both in summer and in winter.
9The LORD will then be king over all the earth. In that day the
LORD will be seen as one with a single name. 10All the land will
change and become like the rift valley from Geba to Rimmon,
south of Jerusalem. Jerusalem will be raised up and will stay in
its own place from the Benjamin Gate to the site of the First
Gate and on to the Corner Gate, and from the Tower of Hananel
to the royal winepresses. 11And people will settle there, and
there will no longer be the threat of divine extermination—
Jerusalem will dwell in security.
12But this will be the nature of the plague with which the
LORD will strike all the nations that have fought against Jerusalem: Their flesh will decay while they stand on their feet,
their eyes will rot away in their sockets, and their tongues will
dissolve in their mouths. 13On that day there will be great confusion from the LORD among them; they will seize each other
and attack one another violently. 14Moreover, Judah will fight
at Jerusalem, and the wealth of all the surrounding nations will
be gathered up—gold, silver, and clothing in great abundance.
15This is the kind of plague that will devastate horses, mules,
camels, donkeys, and all the other animals in those camps.
16Then all who survive from all the nations that came to
attack Jerusalem will go up annually to worship the King, the
LORD of Heaven's Armies, and to observe the Feast of Shelters.

13:7–9 The same Zechariah foretold that Christ would be struck; after he was crucified, his disciples were dispersed until he rose again from the dead and proved to them that it had been predicted that he would have to suffer. When they were convinced of this, they went out to all the world teaching these things. Thus we are firm in our faith in him and in his doctrine because our faith is grounded upon both the prophets and those who, openly throughout the world, are worshipers of God in the name of the Crucified One. Indeed, Zechariah said, "'Awake, sword, against my shepherd, against the man who is my associate,' says the LORD of Heaven's Armies. 'Strike the shepherd that the flock may be scattered.'"

JUSTIN MARTYR (C. 100–C. 165)
DIALOGUE WITH TRYPHO

14:1–7 The object of the prophet is to comfort the faithful that they might resist whatever evils might be at hand and look for what God promises, even that a church would again emerge, and that God would really prove that Jerusalem was not in vain his sanctuary, where he would bless the remnant that escaped through his wonderful favor. Zechariah here amplifies the favor of God, that he will go forth openly and avowedly carry on war against all the enemies of Jerusalem.

JOHN CALVIN (1509–1564)
COMPLETE COMMENTARY ON THE BIBLE

ULRICH ZWINGLI:

REFORMING THE SACRAMENT OF COMMUNION

1484–1531

If Martin Luther was the spark that started the Protestant Reformation, Ulrich Zwingli was the gasoline that made it spread into a more organized and systematized form. While in agreement with Luther on most doctrinal issues, he expanded the reforming impulse to several important aspects of faith and doctrine—leading to conflicts not only with the Catholic establishment but also with various movements within the Reformation.

Born into an upper middle-class Swiss family on New Year's Day, 1484, Zwingli received a humanist education at the universities of Vienna and Basel, earning theological degrees before becoming a pastor in his hometown. His theological and professional life changed when he met Erasmus in 1516, after which he devoted himself to Erasmus's philosophy, particularly his Christology. Soon he began a significant pastoral post at Grossmünster Church in Zurich on January 1, 1519. This post would serve as the beachhead for his ecclesial reform efforts.

Once the Protestant Reformation began to gain steam, Zwingli was hugely influential in purging Swiss churches of any vestiges of Roman Catholicism, supplanting Catholic masses with Protestant worship practices. He and other Swiss leaders were so successful that by 1530 northern Switzerland was virtually free of any Roman Catholic influence. Much of the abolition movement was external, removing statues and replacing priestly vestments with university-styled ones. But beliefs and practices such as veneration of Mary and purgatory were also banned.

One of Zwingli's most significant reforms brought him into conflict not only with the Catholic church but also with Martin Luther. At issue was the practice of the sacraments generally, and the practice of Communion or the Lord's Supper specifically. A sacrament was considered an outward sign pointing to an inward divine reality. Zwingli did join Luther in rejecting the Roman Catholic view of transubstantiation—the belief that the substance of the Eucharistic elements, the bread and wine, actually become the body and blood of Christ. But Zwingli also rejected Luther's real-presence view—that Christ was really present alongside the Communion elements. Luther, bound by a literal reading of Christ's statement that "this [bread] is my body" (Matt 26:26), argued that Christ's resurrected body was mysteriously omnipresent and was present in a special way "in, with, and under" the elements of the bread and wine.

Instead, Zwingli argued the Lord's Supper was exclusively symbolic, a ceremony of remembrance. He used John 6:63 to make his argument: "Human nature is of no help!" He believed Luther's view smacked of the Catholic view and insisted that believers consume Christ in a spiritual sense only: "To eat the body of Christ spiritually is nothing else than to trust in spirit and heart upon the mercy and goodness of God through Christ, that is, to be sure with unshaken faith that God is going to give us pardon for sins and the joy of everlasting blessedness on account of his Son."

Before he was killed in battle in 1531, Zwingli wrote several important theological works that significantly shaped the course of Protestant Reformed theology. Zwingli's influence is still felt to this day—perhaps most significantly through his teaching that the sacrament of Communion is a symbolic remembrance, which remains standard within many Baptist and evangelical circles today.

IMPORTANT WORKS

ON TRUE AND FALSE RELIGION
ON THE PROVIDENCE OF GOD
A SHORT AND CLEAR EXPOSITION OF THE CHRISTIAN FAITH

17 But if any of the nations anywhere on earth refuse to go up to
Jerusalem to worship the King, the LORD of Heaven's Armies,
they will get no rain. 18 If the Egyptians will not do so, they will
get no rain—instead there will be the kind of plague that the
LORD inflicts on any nations that do not go up to celebrate the
Feast of Shelters. 19 This will be the punishment of Egypt and of
all nations that do not go up to celebrate the Feast of Shelters.
20 On that day the bells of the horses will bear the inscription
"Holy to the LORD." The cooking pots in the LORD's temple will
be as holy as the bowls in front of the altar. 21 Every cooking pot
in Jerusalem and Judah will become holy in the sight of the
LORD of Heaven's Armies, so that all who offer sacrifices may
come and use some of them to boil their sacrifices in them. On
that day there will no longer be a Canaanite in the house of the
LORD of Heaven's Armies.

AUTHOR	AUDIENCE	DATE	PURPOSE	THEMES
Malachi	Postexilic Jews living in Judah	About 430 BC	Malachi wrote to promote religious and social reform, offering an indictment for sin and hope for redemption.	Repentance; social justice; religious reformation; and the coming Messiah

The final book of the Old Testament is the book of Malachi, a prophetic work centering on six arguments that challenged the religious and social life of the people of God who had come out of exile. In the Christian canon the book serves as an important bridge between the Old Testament and the New, between the old covenant under the law and the new covenant under Christ.

In writing to God's people, Malachi "reproves the priests and the people," explained Matthew Henry,

> for the evil practices into which they had fallen and invites them to repentance and reformation, with promises of the blessings to be bestowed at the coming of the Messiah. And now that prophecy was to cease, he speaks clearly of the Messiah as nigh at hand and directs the people of God to keep in remembrance of the law of Moses while they were in expectation of the gospel of Christ.

Remarkably, although a remnant of Israel had been spared and saved thanks to the Lord's providential hand, they "soon returned to their own nature, became unmindful of God's favor, and so gave themselves up to many corruptions," explained John Calvin. "[Their] state was nothing better than that of their fathers before them so that God had, as it were, lost all his labor in chastising them." Not only had the people become corrupted in lifestyles and neglectful of their religious practices, but so had the priesthood.

Malachi begins with the Lord's indictment of the priests who served the postexilic community, for they had defiled his name by offering unclean sacrifices. They had given "blind animals as a sacrifice . . . [also] the lame and sick" (1:8). This was no mere neglect; it was contemptible and deceitful, for they had acceptable sacrifices in their flocks yet sacrificed that which was blemished! Furthermore, although "the lips of a priest should preserve knowledge of sacred things, and people should seek instruction from him because he is the messenger of the Lord of Heaven's Armies," the priests had "turned from the way" and "caused many to violate the law"; they had "corrupted the covenant with Levi" (2:7–8). As John Wesley noted, "It is this [keeping the knowledge of the faith] that their office binds them to; it is the duty of all God's people to know his law, but the priest's duty to know it more than others." On the one hand they had failed to steward this knowledge. On the other the Lord accused, "You are not following after me and are showing partiality in your instruction" (2:9), which earned them the Lord's contempt. In all this the religious life of Israel had been corrupted.

The people of Judah carried this corruption into the larger society as well: "Judah has become disloyal, and unspeakable sins have been committed in Israel and Jerusalem. For Judah has profaned the holy things that the Lord loves and has turned to a foreign god!" (2:11). Marrying foreign women led to idolatry and pagan worship practices, which the Lord had warned against since the time of the exodus. Not only that, but the men had been unfaithful to their wives, which the Lord condemned: "'I hate divorce,' says the Lord God of Israel, 'and the one who is guilty of violence,' says the Lord of Heaven's Armies" (2:16).

Consider Matthew Henry's insight: "Corrupt practices are the fruit of corrupt principles; and he who is false to his God will not be true to his fellow mortals." It is clear from the rest of the Lord's indictments that their principles were indeed corrupt, for he said, "I will come to you in judgment," bearing witness against "those who practice divination; those who commit adultery; those who break promises; and those who exploit workers, widows, and orphans, who refuse to help the resident foreigner" (3:5). As if these evil practices weren't bad enough, the Lord declared them guilty of spiritual corruption as well: "You are indeed robbing me . . . In tithes and contributions!" (3:8).

There is a strong eschatological note in this book, for the Lord promises a coming day when evildoers will be burned to stubble. And yet he also promises to "send my messenger, who will clear the way before me" (3:1). Generations of Christians have understood this messenger to be John the Baptist, who prepared the way for Jesus. A "sun of vindication" is also promised, one who will shine on those who revere his name, bearing "healing wings" (4:2). And a new Elijah is promised "before the great and terrible day of the Lord" (4:5), whom Jesus identified as John the Baptist.

Explained John Calvin, "[Malachi] shows that God would remember his gratuitous covenant, which he had made with their fathers, so that the Redeemer would at length come." For centuries this book has been an important bridge between what God began to do for the Jewish people and what he has accomplished in and through his Son for the sake of Israel and the nations.

1:1–6 The Jews are reminded of God's gratuitous covenant that they might cease to excuse their wickedness in having misused this singular favor. God says that they had been preferred to other people, not on account of their own merit, but because it had pleased God to choose their father Jacob. God had set his love on objects so unworthy. For had they been deserving, they might have boasted that a reward was rendered to them; but as the Lord had gratuitously and of his own good pleasure conferred this benefit on them, their impiety was the less excusable. This baseness then is what our prophet now reprobates.

JOHN CALVIN (1509–1564)
COMPLETE COMMENTARY ON THE BIBLE

INTRODUCTION AND GOD'S ELECTION OF ISRAEL

1 This is an oracle, the LORD's message to Israel through
Malachi:
2"I have shown love to you," says the LORD, but you say, "How
have you shown love to us?"
"Esau was Jacob's brother," the LORD explains, "yet I chose
Jacob 3and rejected Esau. I turned Esau's mountains into a deserted wasteland and gave his territory to the wild jackals."
4Edom says, "Though we are devastated, we will once again
build the ruined places." So the LORD of Heaven's Armies responds, "They indeed may build, but I will overthrow. They will
be known as the land of evil, the people with whom the LORD
is permanently displeased. 5Your eyes will see it, and then you
will say, 'May the LORD be magnified even beyond the border
of Israel!'"

THE SACRILEGE OF PRIESTLY SERVICE

6"A son naturally honors his father and a slave respects his
master. If I am your father, where is my honor? If I am your
master, where is my respect? The LORD of Heaven's Armies
asks you this, you priests who make light of my name! But
you reply, 'How have we made light of your name?' 7You are
offering improper sacrifices on my altar, yet you ask, 'How
have we offended you?' By treating the table of the LORD as if
it is of no importance. 8For when you offer blind animals as a
sacrifice, is that not wrong? And when you offer the lame and
sick, is that not wrong as well? Indeed, try offering them to your
governor! Will he be pleased with you or show you favor?" asks
the LORD of Heaven's Armies. 9"But now plead for God's favor
that he might be gracious to us." "With this kind of offering in
your hands, how can he be pleased with you?" asks the LORD
of Heaven's Armies.
10"I wish that one of you would close the temple doors, so
that you no longer would light useless fires on my altar. I am
not pleased with you," says the LORD of Heaven's Armies, "and
I will no longer accept an offering from you. 11For from the east
to the west my name will be great among the nations. Incense
and pure offerings will be offered in my name everywhere, for
my name will be great among the nations," says the LORD of
Heaven's Armies. 12"But you are profaning it by saying that the
table of the Lord is common and its offerings despicable. 13You
also say, 'How tiresome it is.' You turn up your nose at it," says
the LORD of Heaven's Armies, "and instead bring what is stolen,
lame, or sick. You bring these things for an offering! Should I
accept this from you?" asks the LORD. 14"There will be harsh
condemnation for the hypocrite who has a valuable male animal
in his flock but vows and sacrifices something inferior to the
Lord. For I am a great king," says the LORD of Heaven's Armies,
"and my name is awesome among the nations."

THE SACRILEGE OF THE PRIESTLY MESSAGE

2 "Now, you priests, this commandment is for you. 2If you do
not listen and take seriously the need to honor my name,"
says the LORD of Heaven's Armies, "I will send judgment on
you and turn your blessings into curses—indeed, I have already
done so because you are not taking it to heart. 3I am about to
discipline your children and will spread offal on your faces, the
very offal produced at your festivals, and you will be carried

away along with it. 4Then you will know that I sent this commandment to you so that my covenant may continue to be
with Levi," says the LORD of Heaven's Armies. 5"My covenant
with him was designed to bring life and peace. I gave its statutes to him to fill him with awe, and he indeed revered me
and stood in awe before me. 6He taught what was true; sinful
words were not found on his lips. He walked with me in peace
and integrity, and he turned many people away from sin. 7For
the lips of a priest should preserve knowledge of sacred things,
and people should seek instruction from him because he is
the messenger of the LORD of Heaven's Armies. 8You, however,
have turned from the way. You have caused many to violate
the law; you have corrupted the covenant with Levi," says the
LORD of Heaven's Armies. 9"Therefore, I have caused you to
be ignored and belittled before all people to the extent that
you are not following after me and are showing partiality in
your instruction."

THE REBELLION OF THE PEOPLE

10Do we not all have one father? Did not one God create us?
Why do we betray one another, thus making light of the covenant of our ancestors? 11Judah has become disloyal, and unspeakable sins have been committed in Israel and Jerusalem.
For Judah has profaned the holy things that the LORD loves
and has turned to a foreign god! 12May the LORD cut off from
the community of Jacob every last person who does this, as
well as the person who presents improper offerings to the
LORD of Heaven's Armies!

13You also do this: You cover the altar of the LORD with tears
as you weep and groan, because he no longer pays any attention
to the offering nor accepts it favorably from you. 14Yet you ask,
"Why?" The LORD is testifying against you on behalf of the wife
you married when you were young, to whom you have become
unfaithful even though she is your companion and wife by law.
15No one who has even a small portion of the Spirit in him does
this. What did our ancestor do when seeking a child from God?
Be attentive, then, to your own spirit, for one should not be
disloyal to the wife he took in his youth. 16"I hate divorce," says
the LORD God of Israel, "and the one who is guilty of violence,"
says the LORD of Heaven's Armies. "Pay attention to your conscience, and do not be unfaithful."

RESISTANCE TO THE LORD THROUGH SELF-DECEIT

17You have wearied the LORD with your words. But you say, "How
have we wearied him?" Because you say, "Everyone who does
evil is good in the LORD's opinion, and he delights in them," or,
3 "Where is the God of justice?" 1"I am about to send my messenger, who will clear the way before me. Indeed, the Lord
you are seeking will suddenly come to his temple, and the messenger of the covenant, whom you long for, is certainly coming,"
says the LORD of Heaven's Armies.

2Who can endure the day of his coming? Who can keep
standing when he appears? For he will be like a refiner's fire,
like a launderer's soap. 3He will act like a refiner and purifier
of silver and will cleanse the Levites and refine them like gold
and silver. Then they will offer the LORD a proper offering. 4The
offerings of Judah and Jerusalem will be pleasing to the LORD
as in former times and years past.

2:7–9 In sacred language teachers are sometimes called prophets in that they make manifest the things that are to come. For the language of reproof is the key of discovery because by chiding it discloses the fault of which even he who has committed it is often unaware. Hence through Malachi it is said, "For the lips of a priest should preserve knowledge of sacred things, and people should seek instruction from him." Hence through Isaiah the Lord admonishes, saying, "Shout loudly! Don't be quiet! Yell as loudly as a trumpet!" (Isa 58:1). For it is true that whoever enters on the priesthood undertakes the office of a herald, so to walk, himself crying aloud, before the coming of the judge who follows terribly.

GREGORY THE GREAT
(C. 540–604)
PASTORAL CARE

3:1–7 Malachi prophesied after the return from captivity. Observe how soon a people may forget the mercy of their deliverance. Persons newly come out of a long and tedious captivity should have been more lawful and thankful. But they were tainted by long converse with the heathen and smelled of Babylon when they came back to Zion, having brought home the sins of the country with them where they had been scattered. To such a people is Malachi sent, and his dealing with them is suitable: says he, "'From the days of your ancestors you have ignored my commandments and have not kept them. Return to me, and I will return to you,' says the LORD of Heaven's Armies."

THOMAS MANTON
(1620–1677)
THE COMPLETE WORKS

[5]"I will come to you in judgment. I will be quick to testify against those who practice divination; those who commit adultery; those who break promises; and those who exploit workers, widows, and orphans, who refuse to help the resident foreigner and in this way show they do not fear me," says the LORD of Heaven's Armies.

RESISTANCE TO THE LORD THROUGH SELFISHNESS

[6]"Since, I, the LORD, do not go back on my promises, you, sons of Jacob, have not perished. [7]From the days of your ancestors you have ignored my commandments and have not kept them. Return to me, and I will return to you," says the LORD of Heaven's Armies. "But you say, 'How should we return?' [8]Can a person rob God? You are indeed robbing me, but you say, 'How are we robbing you?' In tithes and contributions! [9]You are bound for judgment because you are robbing me—this whole nation is guilty.

[10]"Bring the entire tithe into the storehouse so that there may be food in my temple. Test me in this matter," says the LORD of Heaven's Armies, "to see if I will not open for you the windows of heaven and pour out blessing for you until there is no room for it all. [11]Then I will stop the plague from ruining your crops, and the vine will not lose its fruit before harvest," says the LORD of Heaven's Armies. [12]"All nations will call you blessed, for you indeed will live in a delightful land," says the LORD of Heaven's Armies.

RESISTANCE TO THE LORD THROUGH SELF-SUFFICIENCY

[13]"You have criticized me sharply," says the LORD, "but you ask, 'How have we criticized you?' [14]You have said, 'It is useless to serve God. How have we been helped by keeping his requirements and going about like mourners before the LORD of Heaven's Armies? [15]So now we consider the arrogant to be blessed; indeed, those who practice evil are successful. In fact, those who challenge God escape!'"

[16]Then those who respected the LORD spoke to one another, and the LORD took notice. A scroll was prepared before him in which were recorded the names of those who respected the LORD and honored his name. [17]"They will belong to me," says the LORD of Heaven's Armies, "in the day when I prepare my own special property. I will spare them as a man spares his son who serves him. [18]Then once more you will see that I make a distinction between the righteous and the wicked, between the one who serves God and the one who does not.

4 "For indeed the day is coming, burning like a furnace, and all the arrogant evildoers will be chaff. The coming day will burn them up," says the LORD of Heaven's Armies. "It will not leave them even a root or branch. [2]But for you who respect my name, the sun of vindication will rise with healing wings, and you will skip about like calves released from the stall. [3]You will trample on the wicked, for they will be like ashes under the soles of your feet on the day that I am preparing," says the LORD of Heaven's Armies.

RESTORATION THROUGH THE LORD

[4]"Remember the law of my servant Moses, to whom at Horeb I gave rules and regulations for all Israel to obey. [5]Look, I will

4:1–6 You know that "the day" of judgment "is coming, burning like a furnace," and the whole earth shall be as lead melting in the fire, and then shall the secret and public deeds of people be made known. Almsgiving, therefore, is good as penance for sin; fasting is better than prayer, but almsgiving is better than both; and "love covers a multitude of sins" (1 Pet 4:8), but prayer from a good conscience delivers from death. Blessed is everyone who is found full of these things; for almsgiving relieves the burden of sin.

PSEUDO-CLEMENT OF ROME (320–380)
2 CLEMENT

send you Elijah the prophet before the great and terrible day of
the LORD arrives. 6He will encourage fathers and their children
to return to me, so that I will not come and strike the earth
with judgment."

THE NEW TESTAMENT

AUTHOR	AUDIENCE	DATE	PURPOSE	THEMES
Matthew, also called Levi	Greek-speaking Jews	Between AD 50 and 70	Matthew wrote his Gospel to reveal Jesus as the long-awaited Messiah in fulfillment of God's promises to the Jewish people.	The Old Testament fulfilled; the kingdom of heaven; Jesus as King; and kingdom living

Matthew wrote his Gospel to reveal Jesus as the long-awaited Messiah in fulfillment of God's promises to his people. The book has a decidedly Jewish emphasis, and it is thoroughly rooted in the messianic expectations of the old covenant. As John Wesley noted, "Matthew particularly points out the fulfilling of the prophecies for the conviction of the Jews." Jesus himself quotes from the Hebrew scriptures many times in order to explain his ministry and the new thing that God had begun through him.

The Jewish story is one that constantly points forward, and Matthew brings about its resolution by explaining how Jesus is King and that his kingdom has now arrived—at least in part. From the beginning, Jesus is revealed as the heir of King David, descended from Abraham's lineage. In doing so Matthew establishes Jesus as the rightful King of Israel. Much of the Gospel outlines the contours of Jesus' reign and what it looks like to live under it.

Over 30 times Matthew makes reference to the "kingdom of heaven," a significant term for Jews loaded with messianic expectations. During the time of Jesus, Jews were living under Roman occupation while awaiting a conquering king who would come and fight for them, cleanse the land of their pagan oppressors, and reestablish the throne of David. But Jesus was a different sort of King, and he brought a different sort of kingdom.

Jesus began his ministry with a call to repentance, telling people the kingdom had come near. This kingdom is described as a mustard seed and yeast, small in stature but powerful in growth. It is like a hidden treasure, he said, and people should do all they can to get it.

If Matthew's Gospel is about a kingdom and King, it's also about the kingdom's citizens and how they are called to live under Christ's lordship. The Sermon on the Mount is a famous expression of what it means to live as a member of Christ's kingdom. Such people are poor in spirit; they are mourners and peacemakers; they are meek, hungry and thirsty for righteousness, and pure in heart. The entrance into Christ's kingdom is small

and narrow, and few find it. Yet it is the way that leads to life. Jesus invites everyone to come, but there is a cost: "If anyone wants to become my follower, he must deny himself, take up his cross, and follow me. For whoever wants to save his life will lose it, but whoever loses his life because of me will find it" (Matt 16:24–25).

One of the unique aspects of Matthew's Gospel account is the sheer number of parables he included. A parable is a rhetorical device Jesus used to teach the truths of God and the kingdom way of living. He would often use a common element from daily life in the first century—dough, nets, farming, a vineyard, a wedding banquet—and tell a short story in order to reveal the secrets of the kingdom.

Theodore of Mopsuestia explained: "It was frequently his habit to make use of parables for at least two reasons: Because he would be speaking about things unseen, so as, by the parable, to make invisible things seen, as far as this was possible. Or it was because of the unworthiness of the hearers, when nothing beneficial would come to them from the things that were said."

In other words, Jesus made the mysteries of heaven known using down-to-earth symbols but also made those mysteries more difficult to comprehend for people who were not truly interested in understanding the ways of God. As John Calvin wrote, "The word of God, in its own nature, is always bright, but its light is choked by the darkness of men." Such is the case with the secrets of the kingdom of heaven.

Matthew's Gospel was regularly cited by early church fathers seeking to understand the mysteries of Christ and his kingdom and his connection with the Old Testament. May our eyes see and our ears hear what King Jesus tells us about his reign and rule over our lives.

THE GENEALOGY OF JESUS CHRIST

1 This is the record of the genealogy of Jesus Christ, the son of David, the son of Abraham.

2Abraham was the father of Isaac, Isaac the father of Jacob, Jacob the father of Judah and his brothers, 3Judah the father of Perez and Zerah (by Tamar), Perez the father of Hezron, Hezron the father of Ram, 4Ram the father of Amminadab, Amminadab the father of Nahshon, Nahshon the father of Salmon, 5Salmon the father of Boaz (by Rahab), Boaz the father of Obed (by Ruth), Obed the father of Jesse, 6and Jesse the father of David the king.

David was the father of Solomon (by the wife of Uriah), 7Solomon the father of Rehoboam, Rehoboam the father of Abijah, Abijah the father of Asa, 8Asa the father of Jehoshaphat, Jehoshaphat the father of Joram, Joram the father of Uzziah, 9Uzziah the father of Jotham, Jotham the father of Ahaz, Ahaz the father of Hezekiah, 10Hezekiah the father of Manasseh, Manasseh the father of Amon, Amon the father of Josiah, 11and Josiah the father of Jeconiah and his brothers, at the time of the deportation to Babylon.

12After the deportation to Babylon, Jeconiah became the father of Shealtiel, Shealtiel the father of Zerubbabel, 13Zerubbabel the father of Abiud, Abiud the father of Eliakim, Eliakim the father of Azor, 14Azor the father of Zadok, Zadok the father of Achim, Achim the father of Eliud, 15Eliud the father of Eleazar, Eleazar the father of Matthan, Matthan the father of Jacob, 16and Jacob the father of Joseph, the husband of Mary, by whom Jesus was born, who is called Christ.

17So all the generations from Abraham to David are fourteen generations, and from David to the deportation to Babylon, fourteen generations, and from the deportation to Babylon to Christ, fourteen generations.

THE BIRTH OF JESUS CHRIST

18Now the birth of Jesus Christ happened this way. While his mother Mary was engaged to Joseph, but before they came together, she was found to be pregnant through the Holy Spirit. 19Because Joseph, her husband to be, was a righteous man, and because he did not want to disgrace her, he intended to divorce her privately. 20When he had contemplated this, an angel of the Lord appeared to him in a dream and said, "Joseph, son of David, do not be afraid to take Mary as your wife because the child conceived in her is from the Holy Spirit. 21She will give birth to a son and you will name him Jesus because he will save his people from their sins." 22This all happened so that what was spoken by the Lord through the prophet would be fulfilled: 23***"Look! The virgin will conceive and give birth to a son, and they will name him Emmanuel,"*** which means ***"God with us."*** 24When Joseph awoke from sleep he did what the angel of the Lord told him. He took his wife, 25but did not have marital relations with her until she gave birth to a son, whom he named Jesus.

1:18–22 **Having established Joseph's faith by all means—by past expectations, by future hopes, by present grace, and by the honor given to himself—the angel then gives expression in support of all these, proclaiming beforehand the good things that are to occur to the world through the Son: Sins are removed once and for all. "He will save his people from their sins." Here again the coming event exceeds all human expectation. From what are the people being saved? Not from warfare or violent men but something far greater: from their own sins, a work that had never been possible to anyone before.**

CHRYSOSTOM (C. 347–407)
HOMILIES ON THE GOSPEL OF MATTHEW

THE VISIT OF THE WISE MEN

2 After Jesus was born in Bethlehem in Judea, in the time of King Herod, wise men from the East came to Jerusalem 2saying, "Where is the one who is born king of the Jews? For we saw his star when it rose and have come to worship him." 3When King Herod heard this he was alarmed, and all Jerusalem with him. 4After assembling all the chief priests and experts

in the law, he asked them where the Christ was to be born.
5"In Bethlehem of Judea," they said, "for it is written this way
by the prophet:
6 ***'And you, Bethlehem,** in the land of **Judah,***
are in no way least among the rulers of Judah,
for out of you will come a ruler who will shepherd my
people Israel.'"

7Then Herod privately summoned the wise men and determined from them when the star had appeared. 8He sent them to
Bethlehem and said, "Go and look carefully for the child. When
you find him, inform me so that I can go and worship him as well."
9After listening to the king they left, and once again the star they
saw when it rose led them until it stopped above the place where
the child was. 10When they saw the star they shouted joyfully.
11As they came into the house and saw the child with Mary his
mother, they bowed down and worshiped him. They opened
their treasure boxes and gave him gifts of gold, frankincense,
and myrrh. 12After being warned in a dream not to return to
Herod, they went back by another route to their own country.

THE ESCAPE TO EGYPT

13After they had gone, an angel of the Lord appeared to Joseph
in a dream and said, "Get up, take the child and his mother and
flee to Egypt, and stay there until I tell you, for Herod is going to
look for the child to kill him." 14Then he got up, took the child
and his mother during the night, and went to Egypt. 15He stayed
there until Herod died. In this way what was spoken by the Lord
through the prophet was fulfilled: ***"I called my Son out of Egypt."***
16When Herod saw that he had been tricked by the wise
men, he became enraged. He sent men to kill all the children
in Bethlehem and throughout the surrounding region from
the age of two and under, according to the time he had learned
from the wise men. 17Then what was spoken by Jeremiah the
prophet was fulfilled:
18 ***"A voice was heard in Ramah,***
weeping and loud wailing,
Rachel weeping for her children,
and she did not want to be comforted, because they were
gone."

THE RETURN TO NAZARETH

19After Herod had died, an angel of the Lord appeared in a
dream to Joseph in Egypt 20saying, "Get up, take the child and
his mother, and go to the land of Israel, for those who were seeking the child's life are dead." 21So he got up and took the child
and his mother and returned to the land of Israel. 22But when
he heard that Archelaus was reigning over Judea in place of his
father Herod, he was afraid to go there. After being warned in a
dream, he went to the regions of Galilee. 23He came to a town
called Nazareth and lived there. Then what had been spoken by
the prophets was fulfilled, that Jesus would be called a Nazarene.

THE MINISTRY OF JOHN THE BAPTIST

3 In those days John the Baptist came into the wilderness of Judea proclaiming, 2"Repent, for the kingdom of heaven is near."
3For he is the one about whom the prophet Isaiah had spoken:
"The voice of one shouting in the wilderness,
'Prepare the way for the Lord, make his paths straight.'"

2:1–12 What joy these wise men felt upon this sight of the star. None know so well as those who, after a long and melancholy night of temptation and desertion, under the power of a spirit of bondage, at length receive the Spirit of adoption, witnessing with their spirits that they are the children of God . . . . The gifts the wise men presented were gold, frankincense, and myrrh. Providence sent these as a seasonable relief to Joseph and Mary in their present poor condition. Thus our heavenly Father, who knows what his children need, uses some as stewards to supply the wants of others and can provide for them even from the ends of the earth.

MATTHEW HENRY **(1662–1714)**
COMMENTARY ON THE WHOLE BIBLE

3:1–12 "Don't think that you can say to yourselves, 'We have Abraham as our Father.'" Rightly did our Lord bear witness to him, saying, "Your father Abraham was overjoyed to see my day, and he saw it and was glad" (John 8:56). For not alone upon Abraham's account did he say these things, but also that he might point out how all who have known God from the beginning and have foretold the advent of Christ have received the revelation from the Son himself. He also in the last times was made visible and passable and spoke with the human race that he might from the stones raise up children unto Abraham and fulfill the promise that God had given him.

IRENAEUS (C. 130–C. 202)
AGAINST HERESIES

4 Now John wore clothing made from camel's hair with a leather belt around his waist, and his diet consisted of locusts and wild honey. 5 Then people from Jerusalem, as well as all Judea and all the region around the Jordan, were going out to him, 6 and he was baptizing them in the Jordan River as they confessed their sins.

7 But when he saw many Pharisees and Sadducees coming to his baptism, he said to them, "You offspring of vipers! Who warned you to flee from the coming wrath? 8 Therefore produce fruit that proves your repentance, 9 and don't think you can say to yourselves, 'We have Abraham as our father.' For I tell you that God can raise up children for Abraham from these stones! 10 Even now the ax is laid at the root of the trees, and every tree that does not produce good fruit will be cut down and thrown into the fire.

11 "I baptize you with water, for repentance, but the one coming after me is more powerful than I am—I am not worthy to carry his sandals! He will baptize you with the Holy Spirit and fire. 12 His winnowing fork is in his hand, and he will clean out his threshing floor and will gather his wheat into the storehouse, but the chaff he will burn up with inextinguishable fire!"

THE BAPTISM OF JESUS

13 Then Jesus came from Galilee to John to be baptized by him in the Jordan River. 14 But John tried to prevent him, saying, "I need to be baptized by you, and yet you come to me?" 15 So Jesus replied to him, "Let it happen now, for it is right for us to fulfill all righteousness." Then John yielded to him. 16 After Jesus was baptized, just as he was coming up out of the water, the heavens opened and he saw the Spirit of God descending like a dove and coming to rest on him. 17 And a voice from heaven said, "This is my one dear Son; in him I take great delight."

THE TEMPTATION OF JESUS

4 Then Jesus was led by the Spirit into the wilderness to be tempted by the devil. 2 After he fasted 40 days and 40 nights he was famished. 3 The tempter came and said to him, "If you are the Son of God, command these stones to become bread." 4 But he answered, "It is written, '***Man does not live by bread alone, but by every word that comes from the mouth of God.***'" 5 Then the devil took him to the holy city, had him stand on the highest point of the temple, 6 and said to him, "If you are the Son of God, throw yourself down. For it is written, '***He will command his angels concerning you***' and '***with their hands they will lift you up, so that you will not strike your foot against a stone.***'" 7 Jesus said to him, "Once again it is written: '***You are not to put the Lord your God to the test.***'" 8 Again, the devil took him to a very high mountain, and showed him all the kingdoms of the world and their grandeur. 9 And he said to him, "I will give you all these things if you throw yourself to the ground and worship me." 10 Then Jesus said to him, "Go away, Satan! For it is written: '***You are to worship the Lord your God and serve*** only ***him.***'" 11 Then the devil left him, and angels came and began ministering to his needs.

PREACHING IN GALILEE

12 Now when Jesus heard that John had been imprisoned, he went into Galilee. 13 While in Galilee, he moved from Nazareth to make his home in Capernaum by the sea, in the region of

Zebulun and Naphtali, [14]so that what was spoken by the prophet Isaiah would be fulfilled:

15 ***"Land of Zebulun and land of Naphtali,***
the way by the sea, beyond the Jordan, Galilee of the
Gentiles—
16 ***the people who sit in darkness have seen a great light,***
and on those who sit in the region and shadow of death a
light has dawned."

[17]From that time Jesus began to preach this message: "Repent, for the kingdom of heaven is near!"

THE CALL OF THE DISCIPLES

[18]As he was walking by the Sea of Galilee he saw two brothers,
Simon (called Peter) and Andrew his brother, casting a net into
the sea (for they were fishermen). [19]He said to them, "Follow me,
and I will turn you into fishers of people!" [20]They left their nets
immediately and followed him. [21]Going on from there he saw
two other brothers, James the son of Zebedee and his brother
John, in a boat with their father Zebedee, mending their nets.
Then he called them. [22]They immediately left the boat and
their father and followed him.

JESUS' HEALING MINISTRY

[23]Jesus went throughout all of Galilee, teaching in their synagogues, preaching the gospel of the kingdom, and healing every
kind of disease and sickness among the people. [24]So a report
about him spread throughout Syria. People brought to him all
who suffered with various illnesses and afflictions, those who
had seizures, paralytics, and those possessed by demons, and
he healed them. [25]And large crowds followed him from Galilee,
the Decapolis, Jerusalem, Judea, and beyond the Jordan River.

THE BEATITUDES

5 When he saw the crowds, he went up the mountain. After
he sat down his disciples came to him. [2]Then he began to
teach them by saying:

3 "Blessed are the poor in spirit, for the kingdom of
heaven belongs to them.
4 Blessed are those who mourn, for they will be
comforted.
5 Blessed are the meek, for they will inherit the earth.
6 Blessed are those who hunger and thirst for
righteousness, for they will be satisfied.
7 Blessed are the merciful, for they will be shown mercy.
8 Blessed are the pure in heart, for they will see God.
9 Blessed are the peacemakers, for they will be called the
children of God.
10 Blessed are those who are persecuted for righteousness,
for the kingdom of heaven belongs to them.
11 Blessed are you when people insult you and persecute
you and say all kinds of evil things about you falsely
on account of me. [12]Rejoice and be glad because
your reward is great in heaven, for they persecuted
the prophets before you in the same way.

SALT AND LIGHT

[13]"You are the salt of the earth. But if salt loses its flavor, how
can it be made salty again? It is no longer good for anything

4:18–21 Our Lord summoned to his side the fishing brothers whom he had chosen from of old. They were busy in a lawful occupation when he called them to be ministers. Our Lord does not call idlers. His word was imperial: "Follow me." His work was appropriate and full of royal promise—"I will turn you into fishers of people!" From this passage we learn that nobody can make a people-fisher but our Lord himself and that those whom he calls can become successful only by following him. No nets can entangle those whom Jesus calls to follow him.

CHARLES SPURGEON
(1834–1892)
METROPOLITAN TABERNACLE SERMONS

except to be thrown out and trampled on by people! [14]You
are the light of the world. A city located on a hill cannot be
hidden. [15]People do not light a lamp and put it under a basket but on a lampstand, and it gives light to all in the house.
[16]In the same way, let your light shine before people, so that
they can see your good deeds and give honor to your Father in
heaven.

FULFILLMENT OF THE LAW AND PROPHETS

[17]"Do not think that I have come to abolish the law or the prophets. I have not come to abolish these things but to fulfill them.
[18]I tell you the truth, until heaven and earth pass away not the
smallest letter or stroke of a letter will pass from the law until
everything takes place. [19]So anyone who breaks one of the least
of these commands and teaches others to do so will be called
least in the kingdom of heaven, but whoever obeys them and
teaches others to do so will be called great in the kingdom of
heaven. [20]For I tell you, unless your righteousness goes beyond
that of the experts in the law and the Pharisees, you will never
enter the kingdom of heaven!

5:17–20 Since we are unable to keep the law and it is impossible for the natural man to do so, Christ came and stepped between the Father and us and prays for us: *Beloved Father, be gracious unto them and forgive them their sins. I will take upon me their transgressions and bear them; I love you with my whole heart, and in addition the entire human race, and this I will prove by shedding my blood for humankind. Moreover, I have fulfilled the law and I did it for their welfare in order that they may partake of my fulfilling the law and thereby come to grace.*

MARTIN LUTHER (1483–1546)
THE CHURCH POSTIL

ANGER AND MURDER

[21]"You have heard that it was said to an older generation, ***'Do not
murder,'*** and 'whoever murders will be subjected to judgment.'
[22]But I say to you that anyone who is angry with a brother will
be subjected to judgment. And whoever insults a brother will
be brought before the council, and whoever says 'Fool' will be
sent to fiery hell. [23]So then, if you bring your gift to the altar and
there you remember that your brother has something against
you, [24]leave your gift there in front of the altar. First go and be
reconciled to your brother and then come and present your
gift. [25]Reach agreement quickly with your accuser while on
the way to court, or he may hand you over to the judge, and
the judge hand you over to the warden, and you will be thrown
into prison. [26]I tell you the truth, you will never get out of there
until you have paid the last penny!

ADULTERY

[27]"You have heard that it was said, ***'Do not commit adultery.'***
[28]But I say to you that whoever looks at a woman to desire her
has already committed adultery with her in his heart. [29]If your
right eye causes you to sin, tear it out and throw it away! It is
better to lose one of your members than to have your whole
body thrown into hell. [30]If your right hand causes you to sin, cut
it off and throw it away! It is better to lose one of your members
than to have your whole body go into hell.

DIVORCE

[31]"It was said, ***'Whoever divorces his wife must give her a legal
document.'*** [32]But I say to you that everyone who divorces his
wife, except for immorality, makes her commit adultery, and
whoever marries a divorced woman commits adultery.

OATHS

[33]"Again, you have heard that it was said to an older generation,
'Do not break an oath, but fulfill your vows to the Lord.' [34]But I
say to you, do not take oaths at all—not by heaven because it
is the throne of God, [35]not by earth because it is his footstool,
and not by Jerusalem because it is the city of the great King.

[36]Do not take an oath by your head because you are not able
to make one hair white or black. [37]Let your word be 'Yes, yes'
or 'No, no.' More than this is from the evil one.

RETALIATION

[38]"You have heard that it was said, '***An eye for an eye and a tooth
for a tooth***.' [39]But I say to you, do not resist the evildoer. But
whoever strikes you on the right cheek, turn the other to him
as well. [40]And if someone wants to sue you and take your tunic,
let him have your coat also. [41]And if anyone forces you to go one
mile, go with him two. [42]Give to the one who asks you, and do
not reject the one who wants to borrow from you.

LOVE FOR ENEMIES

[43]"You have heard that it was said, '***Love your neighbor***' and
'hate your enemy.' [44]But I say to you, love your enemy and pray
for those who persecute you, [45]so that you may be like your
Father in heaven, since he causes the sun to rise on the evil
and the good, and sends rain on the righteous and the unrighteous. [46]For if you love those who love you, what reward do you
have? Even the tax collectors do the same, don't they? [47]And if
you only greet your brothers, what more do you do? Even the
Gentiles do the same, don't they? [48]So then, be perfect, as your
heavenly Father is perfect.

PURE-HEARTED GIVING

6 "Be careful not to display your righteousness merely to be
seen by people. Otherwise you have no reward with your Father in heaven. [2]Thus whenever you do charitable giving, do not
blow a trumpet before you, as the hypocrites do in synagogues
and on streets so that people will praise them. I tell you the
truth, they have their reward! [3]But when you do your giving,
do not let your left hand know what your right hand is doing,
[4]so that your gift may be in secret. And your Father, who sees
in secret, will reward you.

PRIVATE PRAYER

[5]"Whenever you pray, do not be like the hypocrites because
they love to pray while standing in synagogues and on street
corners so that people can see them. Truly I say to you, they
have their reward! [6]But whenever you pray, go into your inner
room, close the door, and pray to your Father in secret. And
your Father, who sees in secret, will reward you. [7]When you
pray, do not babble repetitiously like the Gentiles because they
think that by their many words they will be heard. [8]Do not be
like them, for your Father knows what you need before you ask
him. [9]So pray this way:

"Our Father in heaven, may your name be honored,
10 may your kingdom come,
may your will be done on earth as it is in heaven.
11 Give us today our daily bread,
12 and forgive us our debts, as we ourselves have forgiven
our debtors.
13 And do not lead us into temptation, but deliver us from
the evil one.

[14]"For if you forgive others their sins, your heavenly Father
will also forgive you. [15]But if you do not forgive others, your
Father will not forgive you your sins.

6:5–8 Prayer is mainly to be addressed to God the Father. Pray to your Father who sees you and specially takes note of that which is evidently meant for him only, seeing it is done "in secret," where no eye can see but his own. As the very soul of prayer lies in communion with God, we shall pray best when all our attention is confined to him, and we shall best reach our end of being accepted by him when we have no regard for the opinion of anyone else. Secret prayer is truly heard and openly answered in the Lord's own way and time. Our King reigns "in secret": there he sets up his court, and there will he welcome our approaches. We are not where God sees when we court publicity and pray to obtain credit for our devotion.

CHARLES SPURGEON
(1834–1892)
METROPOLITAN TABERNACLE SERMONS

PROPER FASTING

[16]"When you fast, do not look sullen like the hypocrites, for they make their faces unattractive so that people will see them fasting. I tell you the truth, they have their reward! [17]When you fast, anoint your head and wash your face, [18]so that it will not be obvious to others when you are fasting, but only to your Father who is in secret. And your Father, who sees in secret, will reward you.

LASTING TREASURE

[19]"Do not accumulate for yourselves treasures on earth, where moth and devouring insect destroy and where thieves break in and steal. [20]But accumulate for yourselves treasures in heaven, where moth and devouring insect do not destroy, and thieves do not break in and steal. [21]For where your treasure is, there your heart will be also.

[22]"The eye is the lamp of the body. If then your eye is healthy, your whole body will be full of light. [23]But if your eye is diseased, your whole body will be full of darkness. If then the light in you is darkness, how great is the darkness!

[24]"No one can serve two masters, for either he will hate the one and love the other, or he will be devoted to the one and despise the other. You cannot serve God and money.

DO NOT WORRY

[25]"Therefore I tell you, do not worry about your life, what you will eat or drink, or about your body, what you will wear. Isn't there more to life than food and more to the body than clothing? [26]Look at the birds in the sky: They do not sow, or reap, or gather into barns, yet your heavenly Father feeds them. Aren't you more valuable than they are? [27]And which of you by worrying can add even one hour to his life? [28]Why do you worry about clothing? Think about how the flowers of the field grow; they do not work or spin. [29]Yet I tell you that not even Solomon in all his glory was clothed like one of these! [30]And if this is how God clothes the wild grass, which is here today and tomorrow is tossed into the fire to heat the oven, won't he clothe you even more, you people of little faith? [31]So then, don't worry saying, 'What will we eat?' or 'What will we drink?' or 'What will we wear?' [32]For the unconverted pursue these things, and your heavenly Father knows that you need them. [33]But above all pursue his kingdom and righteousness, and all these things will be given to you as well. [34]So then, do not worry about tomorrow, for tomorrow will worry about itself. Today has enough trouble of its own.

DO NOT JUDGE

7 "Do not judge so that you will not be judged. [2]For by the standard you judge you will be judged, and the measure you use will be the measure you receive. [3]Why do you see the speck in your brother's eye, but fail to see the beam of wood in your own? [4]Or how can you say to your brother, 'Let me remove the speck from your eye,' while there is a beam in your own? [5]You hypocrite! First remove the beam from your own eye, and then you can see clearly to remove the speck from your brother's eye. [6]Do not give what is holy to dogs or throw your pearls before pigs; otherwise they will trample them under their feet and turn around and tear you to pieces.

7:1–6 Our Lord now proceeds to warn us against the chief hindrances of holiness. And how wisely does he begin with judging? Judge not anyone without full, clear, certain knowledge, without absolute necessity, without tender love. With what measure you use, it shall be measured to you! So we may choose for ourselves whether God shall be severe or merciful to us: God and man will favor the candid and benevolent, but they must expect judgment without mercy who have shown no mercy. In particular, why do you open your eyes to any fault of others while you yourself are guilty of a much greater? It is mere hypocrisy to pretend zeal for the amendment of others while we have none for our own.

JOHN WESLEY (1703–1791)
EXPLANATORY NOTES ON THE BIBLE

ASK, SEEK, KNOCK

7“Ask and it will be given to you; seek and you will find; knock
and the door will be opened for you. 8For everyone who asks receives, and the one who seeks finds, and to the one who knocks,
the door will be opened. 9Is there anyone among you who, if his
son asks for bread, will give him a stone? 10Or if he asks for a
fish, will give him a snake? 11If you then, although you are evil,
know how to give good gifts to your children, how much more
will your Father in heaven give good gifts to those who ask him!
12In everything, treat others as you would want them to treat
you, for this fulfills the law and the prophets.

THE NARROW GATE

13“Enter through the narrow gate because the gate is wide and
the way is spacious that leads to destruction, and there are many
who enter through it. 14How narrow is the gate and difficult the
way that leads to life, and there are few who find it!

A TREE AND ITS FRUIT

15“Watch out for false prophets, who come to you in sheep’s
clothing but inwardly are voracious wolves. 16You will recognize
them by their fruit. Grapes are not gathered from thorns or figs
from thistles, are they? 17In the same way, every good tree bears
good fruit, but the bad tree bears bad fruit. 18A good tree is not
able to bear bad fruit, nor a bad tree to bear good fruit. 19Every
tree that does not bear good fruit is cut down and thrown into
the fire. 20So then, you will recognize them by their fruit.

JUDGMENT OF PRETENDERS

21“Not everyone who says to me, ‘Lord, Lord,’ will enter into
the kingdom of heaven—only the one who does the will of my
Father in heaven. 22On that day, many will say to me, ‘Lord, Lord,
didn’t we prophesy in your name, and cast out demons in your
name, and do many powerful deeds in your name?’ 23Then I
will declare to them, ‘I never knew you. Go away from me, you
lawbreakers!’

HEARING AND DOING

24“Everyone who hears these words of mine and does them
is like a wise man who built his house on rock. 25The rain fell,
the flood came, and the winds beat against that house, but it
did not collapse because its foundation had been laid on rock.
26Everyone who hears these words of mine and does not do
them is like a foolish man who built his house on sand. 27The
rain fell, the flood came, and the winds beat against that house,
and it collapsed—it was utterly destroyed!”

28When Jesus finished saying these things, the crowds were
amazed by his teaching, 29because he taught them like one who
had authority, not like their experts in the law.

CLEANSING A LEPER

8 After he came down from the mountain, large crowds followed him. 2And a leper approached and bowed low before
him, saying, “Lord, if you are willing, you can make me clean.”
3He stretched out his hand and touched him saying, “I am willing. Be clean!” Immediately his leprosy was cleansed. 4Then
Jesus said to him, “See that you do not speak to anyone, but go,
show yourself to the priest, and bring the offering that Moses
commanded, as a testimony to them.”

HEALING THE CENTURION'S SERVANT

5When he entered Capernaum, a centurion came to him asking for help: 6"Lord, my servant is lying at home paralyzed, in terrible anguish." 7Jesus said to him, "I will come and heal him." 8But the centurion replied, "Lord, I am not worthy to have you come under my roof! Instead, just say the word and my servant will be healed. 9For I too am a man under authority, with soldiers under me. I say to this one, 'Go!' and he goes, and to another 'Come!' and he comes, and to my slave 'Do this!' and he does it." 10When Jesus heard this he was amazed and said to those who followed him, "I tell you the truth, I have not found such faith in anyone in Israel! 11I tell you, many will come from the east and west to share the banquet with Abraham, Isaac, and Jacob in the kingdom of heaven, 12but the sons of the kingdom will be thrown out into the outer darkness, where there will be weeping and gnashing of teeth." 13Then Jesus said to the centurion, "Go; just as you believed, it will be done for you." And the servant was healed at that hour.

8:5–13 It was a firm persuasion that all power and authority were eminently in Christ and that he could do what he pleased. The great end of Christ in all his miracles was to discover himself to be the Son of God and so by consequence that true Messiah and Savior of the world. Now this centurion, being firmly persuaded of a divine power and authority in Christ, reasoned notably, "Just say the word and my servant will be healed." Here then was the greatness of his faith. The Spirit of God can bless slender motives to a willing heart, and there is a readiness in holy souls to believe sooner and easier than others. Faith is most high when the heart is most low.

THOMAS MANTON
(1620–1677)
THE COMPLETE WORKS

HEALINGS AT PETER'S HOUSE

14Now when Jesus entered Peter's house, he saw his mother-in-law lying down, sick with a fever. 15He touched her hand, and the fever left her. Then she got up and began to serve them. 16When it was evening, many demon-possessed people were brought to him. He drove out the spirits with a word, and healed all who were sick. 17In this way what was spoken by the prophet Isaiah was fulfilled:

"***He took our weaknesses and carried our diseases.***"

CHALLENGING PROFESSED FOLLOWERS

18Now when Jesus saw a large crowd around him, he gave orders to go to the other side of the lake. 19Then an expert in the law came to him and said, "Teacher, I will follow you wherever you go." 20Jesus said to him, "Foxes have dens, and the birds in the sky have nests, but the Son of Man has no place to lay his head." 21Another of the disciples said to him, "Lord, let me first go and bury my father." 22But Jesus said to him, "Follow me, and let the dead bury their own dead."

STILLING OF A STORM

23As he got into the boat, his disciples followed him. 24And a great storm developed on the sea so that the waves began to swamp the boat. But he was asleep. 25So they came and woke him up saying, "Lord, save us! We are about to die!" 26But he said to them, "Why are you cowardly, you people of little faith?" Then he got up and rebuked the winds and the sea, and it was dead calm. 27And the men were amazed and said, "What sort of person is this? Even the winds and the sea obey him!"

HEALING THE GADARENE DEMONIACS

28When he came to the other side, to the region of the Gadarenes, two demon-possessed men coming from the tombs met him. They were extremely violent, so that no one was able to pass by that way. 29They cried out, "Son of God, leave us alone! Have you come here to torment us before the time?" 30A large herd of pigs was feeding some distance from them. 31Then the demons begged him, "If you drive us out, send us into the herd of pigs." 32And he said, "Go!" So they came out and went into the pigs, and the herd rushed down the steep slope into the lake and drowned in the water. 33The herdsmen ran off, went into the town, and told everything that had happened to the demon-possessed men. 34Then the entire town came out to meet Jesus. And when they saw him, they begged him to leave their region.

HEALING AND FORGIVING A PARALYTIC

9 After getting into a boat he crossed to the other side and came to his own town. 2Just then some people brought to him a paralytic lying on a stretcher. When Jesus saw their faith, he said to the paralytic, "Have courage, son! Your sins are forgiven." 3Then some of the experts in the law said to themselves, "This man is blaspheming!" 4When Jesus perceived their thoughts he said, "Why do you respond with evil in your hearts? 5Which is easier, to say, 'Your sins are forgiven' or to say, 'Stand up and walk'? 6But so that you may know that the Son of Man has authority on earth to forgive sins"—then he said to the paralytic—"Stand up, take your stretcher, and go home." 7So he stood up and went home. 8When the crowd saw this, they were afraid and honored God who had given such authority to men.

THE CALL OF MATTHEW; EATING WITH SINNERS

9As Jesus went on from there, he saw a man named Matthew sitting at the tax booth. "Follow me," he said to him. So he got up and followed him. 10As Jesus was having a meal in Matthew's house, many tax collectors and sinners came and ate with Jesus and his disciples. 11When the Pharisees saw this they said to his disciples, "Why does your teacher eat with tax collectors and sinners?" 12When Jesus heard this he said, "Those who are healthy don't need a physician, but those who are sick do. 13Go and learn what this saying means: '***I want mercy and not sacrifice.***' For I did not come to call the righteous, but sinners."

THE SUPERIORITY OF THE NEW

14Then John's disciples came to Jesus and asked, "Why do we and the Pharisees fast often, but your disciples don't fast?" 15Jesus said to them, "The wedding guests cannot mourn while the bridegroom is with them, can they? But the days are coming when the bridegroom will be taken from them, and then they will fast. 16No one sews a patch of unshrunk cloth on an old garment because the patch will pull away from the garment and the tear will be worse. 17And no one pours new wine into old wineskins; otherwise the skins burst and the wine is spilled out and the skins are destroyed. Instead they put new wine into new wineskins and both are preserved."

RESTORATION AND HEALING

18As he was saying these things, a leader came, bowed low before him, and said, "My daughter has just died, but come and lay your hand on her and she will live." 19Jesus and his disciples got up and followed him. 20But a woman who had been suffering from a hemorrhage for 12 years came up behind him and touched the edge of his cloak. 21For she kept saying to herself, "If only I touch his cloak, I will be healed." 22But when Jesus turned and saw her he said, "Have courage, daughter! Your faith has made you well." And the woman was healed from that hour. 23When Jesus entered the leader's house and saw the flute players and the disorderly crowd, 24he said, "Go away, for the girl is not dead but asleep!" And they began making fun of him. 25But when the crowd had been forced outside, he went in and gently took her by the hand, and the girl got up. 26And the news of this spread throughout that region.

9:1–8 Do you see how Jesus is shown to be Creator of both souls and bodies? He heals the paralysis in both soul and body. The healing of the soul is made evident through the healing of the body, even while the body still remains a creature crawling on the ground. The crowds were slow to recognize who he was. He proceeded by his daily actions to arouse them and lift up their thinking. It would have been no small thing for him to be thought greater than all others, as having come from God. If they had established this adequately in their own minds, they would have known in due order that he was indeed the Son of God. But they did not grasp these things clearly. Because of this they did not come close to recognizing who he was.

CHRYSOSTOM **(C. 347–407)**
HOMILIES ON THE GOSPEL OF MATTHEW

HEALING THE BLIND AND MUTE

27 As Jesus went on from there, two blind men began to follow him,
shouting, "Have mercy on us, Son of David!" 28 When he went into
the house, the blind men came to him. Jesus said to them, "Do you
believe that I am able to do this?" They said to him, "Yes, Lord."
29 Then he touched their eyes saying, "Let it be done for you according to your faith." 30 And their eyes were opened. Then Jesus sternly
warned them, "See that no one knows about this!" 31 But they went
out and spread the news about him throughout that entire region.
32 As they were going away, a man who was demon-possessed
and unable to speak was brought to him. 33 After the demon
was cast out, the man who had been mute began to speak. The
crowds were amazed and said, "Never has anything like this
been seen in Israel!" 34 But the Pharisees said, "By the ruler of
demons he casts out demons!"

WORKERS FOR THE HARVEST

35 Then Jesus went throughout all the towns and villages, teaching in their synagogues, preaching the good news of the kingdom, and healing every kind of disease and sickness. 36 When
he saw the crowds, he had compassion on them because they
were bewildered and helpless, like sheep without a shepherd.
37 Then he said to his disciples, "The harvest is plentiful, but
the workers are few. 38 Therefore ask the Lord of the harvest
to send out workers into his harvest-ready fields."

SENDING OUT THE 12 APOSTLES

10 Jesus called his 12 disciples and gave them authority over
unclean spirits so they could cast them out and heal every
kind of disease and sickness. 2 Now these are the names of the
12 apostles: first, Simon (called Peter), and Andrew his brother;
James son of Zebedee and John his brother; 3 Philip and Bartholomew; Thomas and Matthew the tax collector; James the
son of Alphaeus, and Thaddaeus; 4 Simon the Zealot and Judas
Iscariot, who betrayed him.

5 Jesus sent out these 12, instructing them as follows: "Do not
go on a road that leads to Gentile regions and do not enter any
Samaritan town. 6 Go instead to the lost sheep of the house of
Israel. 7 As you go, preach this message: 'The kingdom of heaven
is near!' 8 Heal the sick, raise the dead, cleanse lepers, cast out
demons. Freely you received, freely give. 9 Do not take gold, silver, or copper in your belts; 10 no bag for the journey; or an extra
tunic or sandals or staff; for the worker deserves his provisions.
11 Whenever you enter a town or village, find out who is worthy
there and stay with them until you leave. 12 As you enter the house,
greet those within it. 13 And if the house is worthy, let your peace
come on it, but if it is not worthy, let your peace return to you.
14 And if anyone will not welcome you or listen to your message,
shake the dust off your feet as you leave that house or that town.
15 I tell you the truth, it will be more bearable for the region of
Sodom and Gomorrah on the day of judgment than for that town!

PERSECUTION OF DISCIPLES

16 "I am sending you out like sheep surrounded by wolves, so
be wise as serpents and innocent as doves. 17 Beware of people,
because they will hand you over to councils and flog you in their
synagogues. 18 And you will be brought before governors and
kings because of me, as a witness to them and to the Gentiles.
19 Whenever they hand you over for trial, do not worry about

10:1–15 What kind of people were these disciples? Fishermen and publicans. These "Jesus sent"! Do you perceive the unparalleled magnificence of their ministry? They spoke of new and strange things. Moses and the prophets spoke of temporal promises of an earthly land. The apostles proclaimed the kingdom of heaven and all that this implies. Not only does the loftiness of their message characterize them as greater but also so does the lowly nature of their obedience. They were not reluctant nor irresolute, like those who came before. Instead, warned as they were of perils, wars, and intolerable evils, they received his commands with simple obedience. They immediately became heralds of the coming kingdom.

CHRYSOSTOM (C. 347–407)
HOMILIES ON THE GOSPEL OF MATTHEW

how to speak or what to say, for what you should say will be
given to you at that time. [20]For it is not you speaking, but the
Spirit of your Father speaking through you.
[21]"Brother will hand over brother to death, and a father his
child. Children will rise against parents and have them put to
death. [22]And you will be hated by everyone because of my name.
But the one who endures to the end will be saved! [23]Whenever
they persecute you in one town, flee to another! I tell you the
truth, you will not finish going through all the towns of Israel
before the Son of Man comes.
[24]"A disciple is not greater than his teacher, nor a slave greater than his master. [25]It is enough for the disciple to become like
his teacher, and the slave like his master. If they have called the
head of the house 'Beelzebul,' how much worse will they call
the members of his household!

FEAR GOD, NOT MAN

[26]"Do not be afraid of them, for nothing is hidden that will not
be revealed, and nothing is secret that will not be made known.
[27]What I say to you in the dark, tell in the light, and what is
whispered in your ear, proclaim from the housetops. [28]Do not
be afraid of those who kill the body but cannot kill the soul.
Instead, fear the one who is able to destroy both soul and body
in hell. [29]Aren't two sparrows sold for a penny? Yet not one of
them falls to the ground apart from your Father's will. [30]Even
all the hairs on your head are numbered. [31]So do not be afraid;
you are more valuable than many sparrows.
[32]"Whoever, then, acknowledges me before people, I will acknowledge before my Father in heaven. [33]But whoever denies me
before people, I will deny him also before my Father in heaven.

NOT PEACE, BUT A SWORD

[34]"Do not think that I have come to bring peace to the earth. I
have not come to bring peace but a sword! [35]For I have come to
set *a man against his father, a daughter against her mother, and a*
daughter-in-law against her mother-in-law, [36]*and a man's enemies*
will be the members of his household.
[37]"Whoever loves father or mother more than me is not worthy of me, and whoever loves son or daughter more than me
is not worthy of me. [38]And whoever does not take up his cross
and follow me is not worthy of me. [39]Whoever finds his life
will lose it, and whoever loses his life because of me will find it.

REWARDS

[40]"Whoever receives you receives me, and whoever receives me
receives the one who sent me. [41]Whoever receives a prophet in
the name of a prophet will receive a prophet's reward. Whoever
receives a righteous person in the name of a righteous person
will receive a righteous person's reward. [42]And whoever gives
only a cup of cold water to one of these little ones in the name
of a disciple, I tell you the truth, he will never lose his reward."

11 When Jesus had finished instructing his 12 disciples, he
went on from there to teach and preach in their towns.

JESUS AND JOHN THE BAPTIST

[2]Now when John heard in prison about the deeds Christ had
done, he sent his disciples to ask a question: [3]"Are you the one
who is to come, or should we look for another?" [4]Jesus answered
them, "Go tell John what you hear and see: [5]The blind see, the

JOHN CALVIN:

HERO OF REFORMED THEOLOGY

1509–1564

Other than perhaps Martin Luther, no name is as closely associated with the Protestant Reformation than that of John Calvin. Reformed and Calvinist theology, though not entirely synonymous, are sometimes used interchangeably, revealing the sizable influence the man had during his time and his lasting legacy as a hero of the development and systematization of the Reformation's theology.

Calvin was born into a deeply religious family in 1509 near Noyon, France, where his father was a lawyer for the well-known city cathedral and secretary to the bishop. He received an excellent education from the University of Paris as a teenager, studying philosophy and law before devoting his academic work to theology. During this time he joined a group of French humanists who had been influenced by Erasmus before embracing the Reformation cause in the early 1530s. He described his conversion to Protestantism in this way:

> *What happened first was that by an unexpected conversion, God tamed and made teachable a mind too stubborn for its years. For I was obstinately addicted to the superstitions of the papacy and nothing less could draw me out of so deep a quagmire. And so this mere taste of true godliness that I received set me on fire.*

In short time he fled to Basel under threat of the French Catholic persecution. It was there that he began the work for which he is most known, *Institutes of the Christian Religion*. The work made an immediate impression on the European church embroiled in ecclesial revolution. Initially, he meant it as a six-chapter summary of the essence of the Christian faith, but it eventually ballooned to eighty chapters in its final 1559 form. His magnum opus covered a range of theological topics, including the knowledge of God; the freewill of man; an explanation of the Apostles' Creed; predestination and providence; the sacraments, including baptism and the Lord's Supper and a rejection of the "five false ones"; the church and Christian life; and, of course, justification, grace, faith, and meritorious works.

Calvin explained the benefit of his project:

> *Although the holy scripture contains perfect teaching to which nothing can be added, because our Lord has chosen to unfold the infinite treasures of his wisdom in it; nevertheless, someone who does not have very much practice in using it needs some guidance and direction to know what to look for in it in order not to go astray and wander here and there but to keep a certain path, so as to arrive finally where the Holy Spirit calls him . . . I exhort all who revere the Word of the Lord to read this and impress it in their memory with diligence, if they want first to have a summary of Christian teaching and then an entry point to profit well in reading the Old as well as the New Testament.*

Calvin's *Institutes* became the go-to theological textbook for the

Reformed Christian community, enduring for generations. It has been translated and published multiple times and continues to play a vital role in the theological discussions of the church—making Calvin not merely a hero of Reformed theology but a hero of the faith.

IMPORTANT WORKS

INSTITUTES OF THE CHRISTIAN RELIGION

BIBLE COMMENTARIES

lame walk, lepers are cleansed, the deaf hear, the dead are raised,
and the poor have good news proclaimed to them [6]—and blessed
is anyone who takes no offense at me!"
[7]While they were going away, Jesus began to speak to the
crowd about John: "What did you go out into the wilderness
to see? A reed shaken by the wind? [8]What did you go out to
see? A man dressed in soft clothing? Look, those who wear soft
clothing are in the palaces of kings! [9]What did you go out to
see? A prophet? Yes, I tell you, and more than a prophet! [10]This
is the one about whom it is written:

> "'***Look, I am sending my messenger ahead of you,***
> ***who will prepare your way before you.***'

[11]"I tell you the truth, among those born of women, no one
has arisen greater than John the Baptist. Yet the one who is
least in the kingdom of heaven is greater than he is! [12]From
the days of John the Baptist until now the kingdom of heaven
has suffered violence, and forceful people lay hold of it. [13]For
all the prophets and the law prophesied until John appeared.
[14]And if you are willing to accept it, he is Elijah, who is to come.
[15]The one who has ears had better listen!
[16]"To what should I compare this generation? They are like
children sitting in the marketplaces who call out to one another,

> 17 "'We played the flute for you, yet you did not dance;
> we wailed in mourning, yet you did not weep.'

[18]For John came neither eating nor drinking, and they say, 'He
has a demon!' [19]The Son of Man came eating and drinking, and
they say, 'Look at him, a glutton and a drunk, a friend of tax
collectors and sinners!' But wisdom is vindicated by her deeds."

WOES ON UNREPENTANT CITIES

[20]Then Jesus began to criticize openly the cities in which he had
done many of his miracles because they did not repent. [21]"Woe
to you, Chorazin! Woe to you, Bethsaida! If the miracles done in
you had been done in Tyre and Sidon, they would have repented
long ago in sackcloth and ashes. [22]But I tell you, it will be more
bearable for Tyre and Sidon on the day of judgment than for you!
[23]And you, Capernaum, will you be exalted to heaven? No, you
will be thrown down to Hades! For if the miracles done among
you had been done in Sodom, it would have continued to this
day. [24]But I tell you, it will be more bearable for the region of
Sodom on the day of judgment than for you!"

JESUS' INVITATION

25 At that time Jesus said, "I praise you, Father, Lord of heaven and earth, because you have hidden these things from the wise and intelligent, and have revealed them to little children. 26 Yes, Father, for this was your gracious will. 27 All things have been handed over to me by my Father. No one knows the Son except the Father, and no one knows the Father except the Son and anyone to whom the Son decides to reveal him. 28 Come to me, all you who are weary and burdened, and I will give you rest. 29 Take my yoke on you and learn from me because I am gentle and humble in heart, and you will find rest for your souls. 30 For my yoke is easy to bear, and my load is not hard to carry."

11:25–30 From the very first moment of your spiritual life until you are ushered into glory, Christ's words to you will be: "Come to me." Just as a mother holds out her arms, urging her child to walk by saying, "Come," Jesus does the same. He will always be ahead, bidding you to follow him as a soldier follows his general. He will forever walk before you, paving your way and clearing your path, and you will hear his life-giving voice calling you to follow throughout your days. Even at your solemn hour of death, his sweet words ushering you into his heavenly world will be, "Come, you who are blessed by my Father" (Matt 25:34).

CHARLES SPURGEON
(1834–1892)
MORNING AND EVENING

LORD OF THE SABBATH

12 At that time Jesus went through the grain fields on a Sabbath. His disciples were hungry, and they began to pick heads of wheat and eat them. 2 But when the Pharisees saw this they said to him, "Look, your disciples are doing what is against the law to do on the Sabbath." 3 He said to them, "Haven't you read what David did when he and his companions were hungry—4 how he entered the house of God and ate the sacred bread, which was against the law for him or his companions to eat, but only for the priests? 5 Or have you not read in the law that the priests in the temple desecrate the Sabbath and yet are not guilty? 6 I tell you that something greater than the temple is here. 7 If you had known what this means: '***I want mercy and not sacrifice,***' you would not have condemned the innocent. 8 For the Son of Man is lord of the Sabbath."

9 Then Jesus left that place and entered their synagogue. 10 A man was there who had a withered hand. And they asked Jesus, "Is it lawful to heal on the Sabbath?" so that they could accuse him. 11 He said to them, "Would not any one of you, if he had one sheep that fell into a pit on the Sabbath, take hold of it and lift it out? 12 How much more valuable is a person than a sheep! So it is lawful to do good on the Sabbath." 13 Then he said to the man, "Stretch out your hand." He stretched it out and it was restored, as healthy as the other. 14 But the Pharisees went out and plotted against him, as to how they could assassinate him.

GOD'S SPECIAL SERVANT

15 Now when Jesus learned of this, he went away from there. Great crowds followed him, and he healed them all. 16 But he sternly warned them not to make him known. 17 This fulfilled what was spoken by the prophet Isaiah:

18 ***"Here is my servant whom I have chosen,***
the one I love, in whom I take great delight.
I will put my Spirit on him, and he will proclaim justice to the nations.
19 ***He will not quarrel or cry out,***
nor will anyone hear his voice in the streets.
20 ***He will not break a bruised reed or extinguish a smoldering wick,***
until he brings justice to victory.
21 ***And in his name the Gentiles will hope."***

JESUS AND BEELZEBUL

22 Then they brought to him a demon-possessed man who was blind and mute. Jesus healed him so that he could speak and

see. 23 All the crowds were amazed and said, "Could this one be the Son of David?" 24 But when the Pharisees heard this they said, "He does not cast out demons except by the power of Beelzebul, the ruler of demons!" 25 Now when Jesus realized what they were thinking, he said to them, "Every kingdom divided against itself is destroyed, and no town or house divided against itself will stand. 26 So if Satan casts out Satan, he is divided against himself. How then will his kingdom stand? 27 And if I cast out demons by Beelzebul, by whom do your sons cast them out? For this reason they will be your judges. 28 But if I cast out demons by the Spirit of God, then the kingdom of God has already overtaken you. 29 How else can someone enter a strong man's house and steal his property, unless he first ties up the strong man? Then he can thoroughly plunder the house. 30 Whoever is not with me is against me, and whoever does not gather with me scatters. 31 For this reason I tell you, people will be forgiven for every sin and blasphemy, but the blasphemy against the Spirit will not be forgiven. 32 Whoever speaks a word against the Son of Man will be forgiven. But whoever speaks against the Holy Spirit will not be forgiven, either in this age or in the age to come.

TREES AND THEIR FRUIT

33 "Make a tree good and its fruit will be good, or make a tree bad and its fruit will be bad, for a tree is known by its fruit. 34 Offspring of vipers! How are you able to say anything good, since you are evil? For the mouth speaks from what fills the heart. 35 The good person brings good things out of his good treasury, and the evil person brings evil things out of his evil treasury. 36 I tell you that on the day of judgment, people will give an account for every worthless word they speak. 37 For by your words you will be justified, and by your words you will be condemned."

THE SIGN OF JONAH

38 Then some of the experts in the law along with some Pharisees answered him, "Teacher, we want to see a sign from you." 39 But he answered them, "An evil and adulterous generation asks for a sign, but no sign will be given to it except the sign of the prophet Jonah. 40 For just as Jonah was ***in the belly of the huge fish for three days and three nights,*** so the Son of Man will be in the heart of the earth for three days and three nights. 41 The people of Nineveh will stand up at the judgment with this generation and condemn it because they repented when Jonah preached to them—and now, something greater than Jonah is here! 42 The queen of the South will rise up at the judgment with this generation and condemn it because she came from the ends of the earth to hear the wisdom of Solomon—and now, something greater than Solomon is here!

THE RETURN OF THE UNCLEAN SPIRIT

43 "When an unclean spirit goes out of a person, it passes through waterless places looking for rest but does not find it. 44 Then it says, 'I will return to the home I left.' When it returns, it finds the house empty, swept clean, and put in order. 45 Then it goes and brings with it seven other spirits more evil than itself, and they go in and live there, so the last state of that person is worse than the first. It will be that way for this evil generation as well!"

12:46–50 Jesus' design is to bestow the highest commendation on faith, which is the source and origin of holy obedience and at the same time covers the defects and sins of the flesh that they may not be imputed. Let us perform all that nature can justly claim, and at the same time not be too strongly attached to flesh and blood. As Christ bestows on the disciples of his gospel the inestimable honor of being reckoned as his family, we must be held guilty of the basest ingratitude if we do not disregard all the desires of the flesh and direct every effort toward this object.

JOHN CALVIN (1509–1564)
COMPLETE COMMENTARY ON THE BIBLE

JESUS' TRUE FAMILY

46 While Jesus was still speaking to the crowds, his mother
and brothers came and stood outside, asking to speak to him.
47 Someone told him, "Look, your mother and your brothers are
standing outside wanting to speak to you." 48 To the one who
had said this, Jesus replied, "Who is my mother and who are my
brothers?" 49 And pointing toward his disciples he said, "Here
are my mother and my brothers! 50 For whoever does the will
of my Father in heaven is my brother and sister and mother."

THE PARABLE OF THE SOWER

13 On that day after Jesus went out of the house, he sat by the
lake. 2 And such a large crowd gathered around him that he
got into a boat to sit while the whole crowd stood on the shore.
3 He told them many things in parables, saying: "Listen! A sower
went out to sow. 4 And as he sowed, some seeds fell along the
path, and the birds came and devoured them. 5 Other seeds fell
on rocky ground where they did not have much soil. They sprang
up quickly because the soil was not deep. 6 But when the sun came
up, they were scorched, and because they did not have sufficient
root, they withered. 7 Other seeds fell among the thorns, and they
grew up and choked them. 8 But other seeds fell on good soil and
produced grain, some a hundred times as much, some sixty, and
some thirty. 9 The one who has ears had better listen!"

10 Then the disciples came to him and said, "Why do you speak
to them in parables?" 11 He replied, "You have been given the
opportunity to know the secrets of the kingdom of heaven, but
they have not. 12 For whoever has will be given more, and will
have an abundance. But whoever does not have, even what he
has will be taken from him. 13 For this reason I speak to them in
parables: Although they see they do not see, and although they
hear they do not hear nor do they understand. 14 And concerning
them the prophecy of Isaiah is fulfilled that says:

"'***You will listen carefully yet will never understand,***
you will look closely yet will never comprehend.
15 ***For the heart of this people has become dull;***
they are hard of hearing,
and they have shut their eyes,
so that they would not see with their eyes
and hear with their ears
and understand with their hearts
and turn, and I would heal them.'

16 "But your eyes are blessed because they see, and your ears
because they hear. 17 For I tell you the truth, many prophets and
righteous people longed to see what you see but did not see it,
and to hear what you hear but did not hear it.

18 "So listen to the parable of the sower: 19 When anyone hears
the word about the kingdom and does not understand it, the evil
one comes and snatches what was sown in his heart; this is the
seed sown along the path. 20 The seed sown on rocky ground is the
person who hears the word and immediately receives it with joy.
21 But he has no root in himself and does not endure; when trouble
or persecution comes because of the word, immediately he falls
away. 22 The seed sown among thorns is the person who hears the
word, but worldly cares and the seductiveness of wealth choke the
word, so it produces nothing. 23 But as for the seed sown on good
soil, this is the person who hears the word and understands. He
bears fruit, yielding a hundred, sixty, or thirty times what was sown."

THE PARABLE OF THE WEEDS

24 He presented them with another parable: "The kingdom of
heaven is like a person who sowed good seed in his field. 25 But
while everyone was sleeping, an enemy came and sowed darnel
among the wheat and went away. 26 When the plants sprouted
and produced grain, then the darnel also appeared. 27 So the
slaves of the landowner came and said to him, 'Sir, didn't you
sow good seed in your field? Then where did the darnel come
from?' 28 He said, 'An enemy has done this!' So the slaves replied,
'Do you want us to go and gather it?' 29 But he said, 'No, since in
gathering the darnel you may uproot the wheat along with it.
30 Let both grow together until the harvest. At harvest time I
will tell the reapers, "First collect the darnel and tie it in bundles to be burned, but then gather the wheat into my barn."'"

THE PARABLE OF THE MUSTARD SEED

31 He gave them another parable: "The kingdom of heaven is
like a mustard seed that a man took and sowed in his field.
32 It is the smallest of all the seeds, but when it has grown it is
the greatest garden plant and becomes a tree, so that the wild
birds come and nest in its branches."

THE PARABLE OF THE YEAST

33 He told them another parable: "The kingdom of heaven is
like yeast that a woman took and mixed with three measures
of flour until all the dough had risen."

THE PURPOSE OF PARABLES

34 Jesus spoke all these things in parables to the crowds; he did
not speak to them without a parable. 35 This fulfilled what was
spoken by the prophet:

"I will open my mouth in parables,
I will announce what has been hidden from the
foundation of the world."

EXPLANATION FOR THE DISCIPLES

36 Then he left the crowds and went into the house. And his
disciples came to him saying, "Explain to us the parable of
the darnel in the field." 37 He answered, "The one who sowed
the good seed is the Son of Man. 38 The field is the world and the
good seed are the people of the kingdom. The poisonous weeds
are the people of the evil one, 39 and the enemy who sows them
is the devil. The harvest is the end of the age, and the reapers
are angels. 40 As the poisonous weeds are collected and burned
with fire, so it will be at the end of the age. 41 The Son of Man
will send his angels, and they will gather from his kingdom
everything that causes sin as well as all lawbreakers. 42 They will
throw them into the fiery furnace, where there will be weeping
and gnashing of teeth. 43 Then *the righteous will shine like the*
sun in the kingdom of their Father. The one who has ears had
better listen!

PARABLES ON THE KINGDOM OF HEAVEN

44 "The kingdom of heaven is like a treasure, hidden in a field,
that a person found and hid. Then because of joy he went and
sold all that he had and bought that field.

45 "Again, the kingdom of heaven is like a merchant searching
for fine pearls. 46 When he found a pearl of great value, he went
out and sold everything he had and bought it.

13:24–43 Though gross transgressors and such as openly oppose the gospel ought to be separated from the society of the faithful, yet no human skill can make an exact separation. Those who oppose must not be cut off but instructed, and that with meekness. And though good and bad are together in this world, yet at the great day they shall be parted. Then the righteous and the wicked shall be plainly known; here sometimes it is hard to distinguish between them. Let us, knowing the terrors of the Lord, not do iniquity. At death, believers shall shine forth to themselves; at the great day they shall shine forth before all the world. May we be found of that happy number.

MATTHEW HENRY **(1662–1714)**
COMMENTARY ON THE WHOLE BIBLE

47"Again, the kingdom of heaven is like a net that was cast
into the sea that caught all kinds of fish. 48When it was full, they
pulled it ashore, sat down, and put the good fish into containers
and threw the bad away. 49It will be this way at the end of the age.
Angels will come and separate the evil from the righteous 50and
throw them into the fiery furnace, where there will be weeping
and gnashing of teeth.
51"Have you understood all these things?" They replied, "Yes."
52Then he said to them, "Therefore every expert in the law who
has been trained for the kingdom of heaven is like the owner
of a house who brings out of his treasure what is new and old."

REJECTION AT NAZARETH

53Now when Jesus finished these parables, he moved on from
there. 54Then he came to his hometown and began to teach
the people in their synagogue. They were astonished and said,
"Where did this man get such wisdom and miraculous powers?
55Isn't this the carpenter's son? Isn't his mother named Mary?
And aren't his brothers James, Joseph, Simon, and Judas? 56And
aren't all his sisters here with us? So where did he get all this?"
57And so they took offense at him. But Jesus said to them, "A
prophet is not without honor except in his hometown and in his
own house." 58And he did not do many miracles there because
of their unbelief.

THE DEATH OF JOHN THE BAPTIST

14 At that time Herod the tetrarch heard reports about Jesus,
2and he said to his servants, "This is John the Baptist. He
has been raised from the dead! And because of this, miraculous
powers are at work in him." 3For Herod had arrested John, bound
him, and put him in prison on account of Herodias, his brother
Philip's wife, 4because John had repeatedly told him, "It is not
lawful for you to have her." 5Although Herod wanted to kill John,
he feared the crowd because they accepted John as a prophet.
6But on Herod's birthday, the daughter of Herodias danced
before them and pleased Herod, 7so much that he promised
with an oath to give her whatever she asked. 8Instructed by
her mother, she said, "Give me the head of John the Baptist
here on a platter." 9Although it grieved the king because of his
oath and the dinner guests, he commanded it to be given. 10So
he sent and had John beheaded in the prison. 11His head was
brought on a platter and given to the girl, and she brought it
to her mother. 12Then John's disciples came and took the body
and buried it and went and told Jesus.

THE FEEDING OF THE 5,000

13Now when Jesus heard this he went away from there privately
in a boat to an isolated place. But when the crowd heard about
it, they followed him on foot from the towns. 14As he got out
he saw the large crowd, and he had compassion on them and
healed their sick. 15When evening arrived, his disciples came
to him saying, "This is an isolated place and the hour is already
late. Send the crowds away so that they can go into the villages
and buy food for themselves." 16But he replied, "They don't need
to go. You give them something to eat." 17They said to him, "We
have here only five loaves and two fish." 18"Bring them here to
me," he replied. 19Then he instructed the crowds to sit down on
the grass. He took the five loaves and two fish, and looking up
to heaven he gave thanks and broke the loaves. He gave them

14:13–21 Observe with what discretion the Teacher draws the disciples toward believing. "You give them something to eat." At this point their regard for him was essentially as to a man. In this miracle Jesus was teaching them humility, temperance, charity, to be of like mind toward one another, and to share all things in common. He did so in his choice of location, by providing nothing more than loaves and fishes, by setting the same food before all and having them share it in common. Jesus indeed permitted the crowds to get hungry in order that no one might suppose what took place to be as illusion. For this purpose he also caused just twelve baskets to remain over, that Judas too might bear one. He wanted all the disciples to know his power. He fed their hunger.

CHRYSOSTOM **(C. 347–407)**
HOMILIES ON THE GOSPEL OF MATTHEW

to the disciples, who in turn gave them to the crowds. 20They
all ate and were satisfied, and they picked up the broken pieces
left over, 12 baskets full. 21Not counting women and children,
there were about 5,000 men who ate.

WALKING ON WATER

22Immediately Jesus made the disciples get into the boat and go
ahead of him to the other side, while he dispersed the crowds.
23And after he sent the crowds away, he went up the mountain by
himself to pray. When evening came, he was there alone. 24Mean-
while the boat, already far from land, was taking a beating from
the waves because the wind was against it. 25As the night was ending, Jesus came to them walking on the sea. 26When the disciples
saw him walking on the water they were terrified and said, "It's
a ghost!" and cried out with fear. 27But immediately Jesus spoke
to them: "Have courage! It is I. Do not be afraid." 28Peter said to
him, "Lord, if it is you, order me to come to you on the water." 29So
he said, "Come." Peter got out of the boat, walked on the water,
and came toward Jesus. 30But when he saw the strong wind he
became afraid. And starting to sink, he cried out, "Lord, save me!"
31Immediately Jesus reached out his hand and caught him, saying to him, "You of little faith, why did you doubt?" 32When they
went up into the boat, the wind ceased. 33Then those who were
in the boat worshiped him, saying, "Truly you are the Son of God."
34After they had crossed over, they came to land at Gennesaret. 35When the people there recognized him, they sent
word into all the surrounding area, and they brought all their
sick to him. 36They begged him if they could only touch the
edge of his cloak, and all who touched it were healed.

BREAKING HUMAN TRADITIONS

15 Then Pharisees and experts in the law came from Jerusalem to Jesus and said, 2"Why do your disciples disobey
the tradition of the elders? For they don't wash their hands
when they eat." 3He answered them, "And why do you disobey
the commandment of God because of your tradition? 4For God
said, '***Honor your father and mother***' and '***Whoever insults his
father or mother must be put to death.***' 5But you say, 'If someone tells his father or mother, "Whatever help you would have
received from me is given to God," 6he does not need to honor
his father.' You have nullified the word of God on account of
your tradition. 7Hypocrites! Isaiah prophesied correctly about
you when he said,

8 "'***This people honors me with their lips,***
but their hearts are far from me,
9 ***and they worship me in vain,***
teaching as doctrines the commandments of men.'"

TRUE DEFILEMENT

10Then he called the crowd to him and said, "Listen and understand. 11What defiles a person is not what goes into the
mouth; it is what comes out of the mouth that defiles a person."
12Then the disciples came to him and said, "Do you know that
when the Pharisees heard this saying they were offended?"
13And he replied, "Every plant that my heavenly Father did not
plant will be uprooted. 14Leave them! They are blind guides. If
someone who is blind leads another who is blind, both will fall
into a pit." 15But Peter said to him, "Explain this parable to us."
16Jesus said, "Even after all this, are you still so foolish? 17Don't

you understand that whatever goes into the mouth enters the stomach and then passes out into the sewer? [18]But the things that come out of the mouth come from the heart, and these things defile a person. [19]For out of the heart come evil ideas, murder, adultery, sexual immorality, theft, false testimony, slander. [20]These are the things that defile a person; it is not eating with unwashed hands that defiles a person."

A CANAANITE WOMAN'S FAITH

[21]After going out from there, Jesus went to the region of Tyre and Sidon. [22]A Canaanite woman from that area came and cried out, "Have mercy on me, Lord, Son of David! My daughter is horribly demon-possessed!" [23]But he did not answer her a word. Then his disciples came and begged him, "Send her away because she keeps on crying out after us." [24]So he answered, "I was sent only to the lost sheep of the house of Israel." [25]But she came and bowed down before him and said, "Lord, help me!" [26]"It is not right to take the children's bread and throw it to the dogs," he said. [27]"Yes, Lord," she replied, "but even the dogs eat the crumbs that fall from their masters' table." [28]Then Jesus answered her, "Woman, your faith is great! Let what you want be done for you." And her daughter was healed from that hour.

15:21–28 The woman in this story gained comfort in her misery by thinking great thoughts of Christ. She thought of Jesus as having such an abundance on his table that a crumb would meet her needs. Remember, she was seeking to have a demon cast out of her daughter. This would be a great miracle for her, but because she had such high esteem for Christ she saw it as nothing but a crumb for him to give. The path she took is the royal road to comfort, for focusing your thoughts on your sin alone will drive you to despair, but having great thoughts of Christ will guide you into the haven of peace.

CHARLES SPURGEON
(1834–1892)
MORNING AND EVENING

HEALING MANY OTHERS

[29]When he left there, Jesus went along the Sea of Galilee. Then he went up a mountain, where he sat down. [30]Then large crowds came to him bringing with them the lame, blind, crippled, mute, and many others. They laid them at his feet, and he healed them. [31]As a result, the crowd was amazed when they saw the mute speaking, the crippled healthy, the lame walking, and the blind seeing, and they praised the God of Israel.

THE FEEDING OF THE 4,000

[32]Then Jesus called his disciples and said, "I have compassion on the crowd because they have already been here with me three days and they have nothing to eat. I don't want to send them away hungry since they may faint on the way." [33]The disciples said to him, "Where can we get enough bread in this desolate place to satisfy so great a crowd?" [34]Jesus said to them, "How many loaves do you have?" They replied, "Seven—and a few small fish." [35]After instructing the crowd to sit down on the ground, [36]he took the seven loaves and the fish, and after giving thanks, he broke them and began giving them to the disciples, who then gave them to the crowds. [37]They all ate and were satisfied, and they picked up the broken pieces left over, seven baskets full. [38]Not counting children and women, there were 4,000 men who ate. [39]After sending away the crowd, he got into the boat and went to the region of Magadan.

THE DEMAND FOR A SIGN

16 Now when the Pharisees and Sadducees came to test Jesus, they asked him to show them a sign from heaven. [2]He said, "When evening comes you say, 'It will be fair weather because the sky is red,' [3]and in the morning, 'It will be stormy today because the sky is red and darkening.' You know how to judge correctly the appearance of the sky, but you cannot evaluate the signs of the times. [4]A wicked and adulterous generation asks for a sign, but no sign will be given to it except the sign of Jonah." Then he left them and went away.

THE YEAST OF THE PHARISEES AND SADDUCEES

[5]When the disciples went to the other side, they forgot to take bread. [6]"Watch out," Jesus said to them, "beware of the yeast of the Pharisees and Sadducees." [7]So they began to discuss this among themselves, saying, "It is because we brought no bread." [8]When Jesus learned of this, he said, "You who have such little faith! Why are you arguing among yourselves about having no bread? [9]Do you still not understand? Don't you remember the five loaves for the 5,000, and how many baskets you took up? [10]Or the seven loaves for the 4,000 and how many baskets you took up? [11]How could you not understand that I was not speaking to you about bread? But beware of the yeast of the Pharisees and Sadducees!" [12]Then they understood that he had not told them to be on guard against the yeast in bread, but against the teaching of the Pharisees and Sadducees.

PETER'S CONFESSION

[13]When Jesus came to the area of Caesarea Philippi, he asked his disciples, "Who do people say that the Son of Man is?" [14]They answered, "Some say John the Baptist, others Elijah, and others Jeremiah or one of the prophets." [15]He said to them, "But who do you say that I am?" [16]Simon Peter answered, "You are the Christ, the Son of the living God." [17]And Jesus answered him, "You are blessed, Simon son of Jonah, because flesh and blood did not reveal this to you, but my Father in heaven! [18]And I tell you that you are Peter, and on this rock I will build my church, and the gates of Hades will not overpower it. [19]I will give you the keys of the kingdom of heaven. Whatever you bind on earth will have been bound in heaven, and whatever you release on earth will have been released in heaven." [20]Then he instructed his disciples not to tell anyone that he was the Christ.

FIRST PREDICTION OF JESUS' DEATH AND RESURRECTION

[21]From that time on Jesus began to show his disciples that he must go to Jerusalem and suffer many things at the hands of the elders, chief priests, and experts in the law, and be killed and on the third day be raised. [22]So Peter took him aside and began to rebuke him: "God forbid, Lord! This must not happen to you!" [23]But he turned and said to Peter, "Get behind me, Satan! You are a stumbling block to me because you are not setting your mind on God's interests, but on man's." [24]Then Jesus said to his disciples, "If anyone wants to become my follower, he must deny himself, take up his cross, and follow me. [25]For whoever wants to save his life will lose it, but whoever loses his life because of me will find it. [26]For what does it benefit a person if he gains the whole world but forfeits his life? Or what can a person give in exchange for his life? [27]For the Son of Man will come with his angels in the glory of his Father, and then *he will reward each person according to what he has done.* [28]I tell you the truth, there are some standing here who will not experience death before they see the Son of Man coming in his kingdom."

THE TRANSFIGURATION

17 Six days later Jesus took with him Peter, James, and John the brother of James, and led them privately up a high mountain. [2]And he was transfigured before them. His face shone like the sun, and his clothes became white as light. [3]Then Moses and Elijah also appeared before them, talking with him.

16:13–28 Jesus made it clear that he, the Son of Man, is Christ the Son of the living God. He was acknowledged by Peter as Christ, and then he rebuked Peter who imagined that he was the Christ as the generality of people supposed and was averse to the idea of his suffering: "Whoever wants to save his life will lose it, but whoever loses his life because of me will find it." For these things Christ spoke openly, he being himself the Savior of those who should be delivered over to death for their confession of him and lose their lives.

IRENAEUS (C. 130–C. 202)
AGAINST HERESIES

17:1–13 I have no doubt whatever that Christ came forward of his own accord to offer to the Father the sacrifice of obedience. The disciples were not made aware of this till Christ rose, but the instruction that they now received was intended to be useful at a future period, both to themselves and to us, that no one might take offense at the weakness of Christ as if it were by force and necessity that he had suffered. We are thus taught that he was subjected to death because he wished it to be so; that he was crucified because he offered himself. We are also taught that as long as Christ remained in the world, bearing the form of a servant, nothing had been taken from him for it was of his own accord that he emptied himself.

JOHN CALVIN (1509–1564)
COMPLETE COMMENTARY ON THE BIBLE

[4]So Peter said to Jesus, "Lord, it is good for us to be here. If you want, I will make three shelters—one for you, one for Moses, and one for Elijah." [5]While he was still speaking, a bright cloud overshadowed them, and a voice from the cloud said, "This is my one dear Son, in whom I take great delight. Listen to him!" [6]When the disciples heard this, they were overwhelmed with fear and threw themselves down with their faces to the ground. [7]But Jesus came and touched them. "Get up," he said. "Do not be afraid." [8]When they looked up, all they saw was Jesus alone.

[9]As they were coming down from the mountain, Jesus commanded them, "Do not tell anyone about the vision until the Son of Man is raised from the dead." [10]The disciples asked him, "Why then do the experts in the law say that Elijah must come first?" [11]He answered, "Elijah does indeed come first and will restore all things. [12]And I tell you that Elijah has already come. Yet they did not recognize him, but did to him whatever they wanted. In the same way, the Son of Man will suffer at their hands." [13]Then the disciples understood that he was speaking to them about John the Baptist.

THE DISCIPLES' FAILURE TO HEAL

[14]When they came to the crowd, a man came to him, knelt before him, [15]and said, "Lord, have mercy on my son because he has seizures and suffers terribly, for he often falls into the fire and into the water. [16]I brought him to your disciples, but they were not able to heal him." [17]Jesus answered, "You unbelieving and perverse generation! How much longer must I be with you? How much longer must I endure you? Bring him here to me." [18]Then Jesus rebuked the demon and it came out of him, and the boy was healed from that moment. [19]Then the disciples came to Jesus privately and said, "Why couldn't we cast it out?" [20]He told them, "It was because of your little faith. I tell you the truth, if you have faith the size of a mustard seed, you will say to this mountain, 'Move from here to there,' and it will move; nothing will be impossible for you."§

SECOND PREDICTION OF JESUS' DEATH AND RESURRECTION

[22]When they gathered together in Galilee, Jesus told them, "The Son of Man is going to be betrayed into the hands of men. [23]They will kill him, and on the third day he will be raised." And they became greatly distressed.

THE TEMPLE TAX

[24]After they arrived in Capernaum, the collectors of the temple tax came to Peter and said, "Your teacher pays the double drachma tax, doesn't he?" [25]He said, "Yes." When Peter came into the house, Jesus spoke to him first, "What do you think, Simon? From whom do earthly kings collect tolls or taxes—from their sons or from foreigners?" [26]After he said, "From foreigners," Jesus said to him, "Then the sons are free. [27]But so that we don't offend them, go to the lake and throw out a hook. Take the first fish that comes up, and when you open its mouth, you will find a four-drachma coin. Take that and give it to them for me and you."

QUESTIONS ABOUT THE GREATEST

18 At that time the disciples came to Jesus saying, "Who is the greatest in the kingdom of heaven?" [2]He called a child, had him stand among them, [3]and said, "I tell you the truth,

unless you turn around and become like little children, you will never enter the kingdom of heaven! [4]Whoever then humbles himself like this little child is the greatest in the kingdom of heaven. [5]And whoever welcomes a child like this in my name welcomes me.

[6]"But if anyone causes one of these little ones who believe in me to sin, it would be better for him to have a huge millstone hung around his neck and to be drowned in the open sea. [7]Woe to the world because of stumbling blocks! It is necessary that stumbling blocks come, but woe to the person through whom they come. [8]If your hand or your foot causes you to sin, cut it off and throw it away. It is better for you to enter life crippled or lame than to have two hands or two feet and be thrown into eternal fire. [9]And if your eye causes you to sin, tear it out and throw it away. It is better for you to enter into life with one eye than to have two eyes and be thrown into fiery hell.

THE PARABLE OF THE LOST SHEEP

[10]"See that you do not disdain one of these little ones. For I tell you that their angels in heaven always see the face of my Father in heaven.|| [12]What do you think? If someone owns a hundred sheep and one of them goes astray, will he not leave the ninety-nine on the mountains and go look for the one that went astray? [13]And if he finds it, I tell you the truth, he will rejoice more over it than over the ninety-nine that did not go astray. [14]In the same way, your Father in heaven is not willing that one of these little ones be lost.

RESTORING CHRISTIAN RELATIONSHIPS

[15]"If your brother sins, go and show him his fault when the two of you are alone. If he listens to you, you have regained your brother. [16]But if he does not listen, take one or two others with you, so that ***at the testimony of two or three witnesses every matter may be established.*** [17]If he refuses to listen to them, tell it to the church. If he refuses to listen to the church, treat him like a Gentile or a tax collector.

[18]"I tell you the truth, whatever you bind on earth will have been bound in heaven, and whatever you release on earth will have been released in heaven. [19]Again, I tell you the truth, if two of you on earth agree about whatever you ask, my Father in heaven will do it for you. [20]For where two or three are assembled in my name, I am there among them."

[21]Then Peter came to him and said, "Lord, how many times must I forgive my brother who sins against me? As many as seven times?" [22]Jesus said to him, "Not seven times, I tell you, but seventy-seven times!

THE PARABLE OF THE UNFORGIVING SLAVE

[23]"For this reason, the kingdom of heaven is like a king who wanted to settle accounts with his slaves. [24]As he began settling his accounts, a man who owed 10,000 talents was brought to him. [25]Because he was not able to repay it, the lord ordered him to be sold, along with his wife, children, and whatever he possessed, and repayment to be made. [26]Then the slave threw himself to the ground before him, saying, 'Be patient with me, and I will repay you everything.' [27]The lord had compassion on that slave and released him, and forgave him the debt. [28]After he went out, that same slave found one of his fellow slaves who owed him 100 silver coins. So he grabbed him by the throat

18:1–5 Just as a child does not persist in anger, does not long remember injury suffered, does not think one thing and say another, so you too, unless you have similar innocence and purity of mind, will not be able to enter the kingdom of heaven. Or it might be taken in another way: "Whoever then humbles himself like this little child is the greatest in the kingdom of heaven," Jesus said, which implies, *Anyone who imitates me and humiliates himself following my example, so that he abases himself as much as I abased myself in accepting the form of a Servant, will enter the kingdom of heaven.*

JEROME (C. 342–420)
COMMENTARY ON MATTHEW

and started to choke him, saying, 'Pay back what you owe me!'
29Then his fellow slave threw himself down and begged him, 'Be
patient with me, and I will repay you.' 30But he refused. Instead,
he went out and threw him in prison until he repaid the debt.
31When his fellow slaves saw what had happened, they were
very upset and went and told their lord everything that had
taken place. 32Then his lord called the first slave and said to
him, 'Evil slave! I forgave you all that debt because you begged
me! 33Should you not have shown mercy to your fellow slave,
just as I showed it to you?' 34And in anger his lord turned him
over to the prison guards to torture him until he repaid all he
owed. 35So also my heavenly Father will do to you, if each of you
does not forgive your brother from your heart."

QUESTIONS ABOUT DIVORCE

19 Now when Jesus finished these sayings, he left Galilee and
went to the region of Judea beyond the Jordan River. 2Large
crowds followed him, and he healed them there.
3Then some Pharisees came to him in order to test him.
They asked, "Is it lawful to divorce a wife for any cause?" 4He
answered, "Have you not read that from the beginning the Creator ***made them male and female,*** 5and said, '***For this reason a***
man will leave his father and mother and will be united with his
wife, and the two will become one flesh'? 6So they are no longer
two, but one flesh. Therefore what God has joined together,
let no one separate." 7They said to him, "Why then did Moses
command us *to give* ***a certificate of dismissal*** *and to divorce* her?"
8Jesus said to them, "Moses permitted you to divorce your wives
because of your hard hearts, but from the beginning it was not
this way. 9Now I say to you that whoever divorces his wife, except
for immorality, and marries another commits adultery." 10The
disciples said to him, "If this is the case of a husband with a wife,
it is better not to marry!" 11He said to them, "Not everyone can
accept this statement, except those to whom it has been given.
12For there are some eunuchs who were that way from birth,
and some who were made eunuchs by others, and some who
became eunuchs for the sake of the kingdom of heaven. The
one who is able to accept this should accept it."

JESUS AND LITTLE CHILDREN

13Then little children were brought to him for him to lay his
hands on them and pray. But the disciples scolded those who
brought them. 14But Jesus said, "Let the little children come
to me and do not try to stop them, for the kingdom of heaven
belongs to such as these." 15And he placed his hands on them
and went on his way.

THE RICH YOUNG MAN

16Now someone came up to him and said, "Teacher, what good
thing must I do to gain eternal life?" 17He said to him, "Why do
you ask me about what is good? There is only one who is good.
But if you want to enter into life, keep the commandments."
18"Which ones?" he asked. Jesus replied, "***Do not murder, do not***
commit adultery, do not steal, do not give false testimony, 19***hon-***
or your father and mother, and ***love your neighbor as yourself.***"
20The young man said to him, "I have wholeheartedly obeyed
all these laws. What do I still lack?" 21Jesus said to him, "If you
wish to be perfect, go sell your possessions and give the money
to the poor, and you will have treasure in heaven. Then come,

19:16–30 We should consider how much eternal life is to be loved when this miserable life that must at some time be ended is so loved. Consider how much that life is to be loved when it is a life you never end. You love this life, where you work so much, run, are busy, pant. In this busy life the obligations can scarcely be counted: sowing, plowing, working new land, sailing, grinding, cooking, weaving. And after all this hard work your life comes to an end. Look at what you suffer in this wretched life that you so love. And do you think that you will always live and never die? Learn therefore to seek eternal life, where you will not endure these things but will reign with God forever.

AUGUSTINE **(354–430)**
SERMONS

follow me." [22]But when the young man heard this he went away sorrowful, for he was very rich.

[23]Then Jesus said to his disciples, "I tell you the truth, it will be hard for a rich person to enter the kingdom of heaven! [24]Again I say, it is easier for a camel to go through the eye of a needle than for a rich person to enter into the kingdom of God." [25]The disciples were greatly astonished when they heard this and said, "Then who can be saved?" [26]Jesus looked at them and replied, "This is impossible for mere humans, but for God all things are possible." [27]Then Peter said to him, "Look, we have left everything to follow you! What then will there be for us?" [28]Jesus said to them, "I tell you the truth: In the age when all things are renewed, when the Son of Man sits on his glorious throne, you who have followed me will also sit on 12 thrones, judging the 12 tribes of Israel. [29]And whoever has left houses or brothers or sisters or father or mother or children or fields for my sake will receive a hundred times as much and will inherit eternal life. [30]But many who are first will be last, and the last first.

WORKERS IN THE VINEYARD

20 "For the kingdom of heaven is like a landowner who went out early in the morning to hire workers for his vineyard. [2]And after agreeing with the workers for the standard wage, he sent them into his vineyard. [3]When it was about nine o'clock in the morning, he went out again and saw others standing around in the marketplace without work. [4]He said to them, 'You go into the vineyard too, and I will give you whatever is right.' [5]So they went. When he went out again about noon and three o'clock that afternoon, he did the same thing. [6]And about five o'clock that afternoon he went out and found others standing around, and said to them, 'Why are you standing here all day without work?' [7]They said to him, 'Because no one hired us.' He said to them, 'You go and work in the vineyard too.' [8]When it was evening the owner of the vineyard said to his manager, 'Call the workers and pay them their wages starting with the last hired until the first.' [9]When those hired about five o'clock came, each received a full day's pay. [10]And when those hired first came, they thought they would receive more. But each one also received the standard wage. [11]When they received it, they began to complain against the landowner, [12]saying, 'These last fellows worked one hour, and you have made them equal to us who bore the hardship and burning heat of the day.' [13]And the landowner replied to one of them, 'Friend, I am not treating you unfairly. Didn't you agree with me to work for the standard wage? [14]Take what is yours and go. I want to give to this last man the same as I gave to you. [15]Am I not permitted to do what I want with what belongs to me? Or are you envious because I am generous?' [16]So the last will be first, and the first last."

THIRD PREDICTION OF JESUS' DEATH AND RESURRECTION

[17]As Jesus was going up to Jerusalem, he took the twelve aside privately and said to them on the way, [18]"Look, we are going up to Jerusalem, and the Son of Man will be handed over to the chief priests and the experts in the law. They will condemn him to death, [19]and will turn him over to the Gentiles to be mocked and flogged severely and crucified. Yet on the third day, he will be raised."

20:20–28 The servant who serves for love is highest in the hierarchy of heaven. We may well take the lesson to ourselves. If we are ever to be near the right and the left of the Master in his kingdom, there is only one way, and that is to make self abdicate its authority as the center of our lives and to enthrone there Christ, and for his sake all our brethren. Be ambitious to be first, but remember, noblesse oblige. He who is first must become last. He who is Servant of all is Master of all. That is the only mastery that is worth anything, the devotion of hearts that circle round the source from which they draw light and warmth.

ALEXANDER MACLAREN
(1826–1910)
EXPOSITIONS OF THE HOLY SCRIPTURES

A REQUEST FOR JAMES AND JOHN

20 Then the mother of the sons of Zebedee came to him with
her sons, and kneeling down she asked him for a favor. 21 He
said to her, "What do you want?" She replied, "Permit these
two sons of mine to sit, one at your right hand and one at your
left, in your kingdom." 22 Jesus answered, "You don't know what
you are asking! Are you able to drink the cup I am about to
drink?" They said to him, "We are able." 23 He told them, "You
will drink my cup, but to sit at my right and at my left is not
mine to give. Rather, it is for those for whom it has been prepared by my Father."
24 Now when the other 10 heard this, they were angry with the
two brothers. 25 But Jesus called them and said, "You know that
the rulers of the Gentiles lord it over them, and those in high
positions use their authority over them. 26 It must not be this
way among you! Instead whoever wants to be great among you
must be your servant, 27 and whoever wants to be first among
you must be your slave—28 just as the Son of Man did not come to
be served but to serve, and to give his life as a ransom for many."

TWO BLIND MEN HEALED

29 As they were leaving Jericho, a large crowd followed them.
30 Two blind men were sitting by the road. When they heard that
Jesus was passing by, they shouted, "Have mercy on us, Lord, Son
of David!" 31 The crowd scolded them to get them to be quiet.
But they shouted even more loudly, "Lord, have mercy on us,
Son of David!" 32 Jesus stopped, called them, and said, "What do
you want me to do for you?" 33 They said to him, "Lord, let our
eyes be opened." 34 Moved with compassion, Jesus touched their
eyes. Immediately they received their sight and followed him.

21:1–11 The path of humility seems to lead him who walks in it a diverse way from the path of honor; one seems to tend downward and the other upward. Yet indeed they both meet and become the same, both carry a man to the same place: The donkey was a token both of kingly honor and great humility. The donkey, the symbol of humility, carried a king on his back, and on a donkey does the King of glory ascend into the city and temple of the great King, as by humiliation Christ ascended into heaven. The donkey on which Christ rode was a colt on which never man sat. So Christ's humiliation was now such as there never had been a parallel of, nor anything like it, and it carried him into glory as unparalleled.

JONATHAN EDWARDS
(1703–1758)
SELECTIONS FROM THE UNPUBLISHED WRITINGS

THE TRIUMPHAL ENTRY

21 Now when they approached Jerusalem and came to Bethphage, at the Mount of Olives, Jesus sent two disciples,
2 telling them, "Go to the village ahead of you. Right away you
will find a donkey tied there, and a colt with her. Untie them
and bring them to me. 3 If anyone says anything to you, you are
to say, 'The Lord needs them,' and he will send them at once."
4 This took place to fulfill what was spoken by the prophet:
5 ***"Tell the people of Zion,***
'Look, your king is coming to you,
unassuming and seated on a donkey,
and on a colt, the foal of a donkey.'"
6 So the disciples went and did as Jesus had instructed them.
7 They brought the donkey and the colt and placed their cloaks
on them, and he sat on them. 8 A very large crowd spread their
cloaks on the road. Others cut branches from the trees and
spread them on the road. 9 The crowds that went ahead of him
and those following kept shouting, "*Hosanna* to the Son of David!
Blessed is the one who comes in the name of the Lord! *Hosanna*
in the highest!" 10 As he entered Jerusalem the whole city was
thrown into an uproar, saying, "Who is this?" 11 And the crowds
were saying, "This is the prophet Jesus, from Nazareth in Galilee."

CLEANSING THE TEMPLE

12 Then Jesus entered the temple area and drove out all those
who were selling and buying in the temple courts and turned
over the tables of the money changers and the chairs of those

selling doves. 13 And he said to them, "It is written, '***My house***
will be called a house of prayer, ' but you are turning it into ***a***
den of robbers !"
14 The blind and lame came to him in the temple courts, and
he healed them. 15 But when the chief priests and the experts
in the law saw the wonderful things he did and heard the children crying out in the temple courts, "Hosanna to the Son of
David," they became indignant 16 and said to him, "Do you hear
what they are saying?" Jesus said to them, "Yes. Have you never
read, '***Out of the mouths of children and nursing infants you have***
prepared praise for yourself '?" 17 And leaving them, he went out
of the city to Bethany and spent the night there.

THE WITHERED FIG TREE

18 Now early in the morning, as he returned to the city, he was
hungry. 19 After noticing a fig tree by the road he went to it, but
found nothing on it except leaves. He said to it, "Never again
will there be fruit from you!" And the fig tree withered at once.
20 When the disciples saw it they were amazed, saying, "How did
the fig tree wither so quickly?" 21 Jesus answered them, "I tell
you the truth, if you have faith and do not doubt, not only will
you do what was done to the fig tree, but even if you say to this
mountain, 'Be lifted up and thrown into the sea,' it will happen.
22 And whatever you ask in prayer, if you believe, you will receive."

THE AUTHORITY OF JESUS

23 Now after Jesus entered the temple courts, the chief priests
and elders of the people came up to him as he was teaching and
said, "By what authority are you doing these things, and who gave
you this authority?" 24 Jesus answered them, "I will also ask you
one question. If you answer me then I will also tell you by what
authority I do these things. 25 Where did John's baptism come
from? From heaven or from people?" They discussed this among
themselves, saying, "If we say, 'From heaven,' he will say, 'Then
why did you not believe him?' 26 But if we say, 'From people,' we
fear the crowd, for they all consider John to be a prophet." 27 So
they answered Jesus, "We don't know." Then he said to them,
"Neither will I tell you by what authority I am doing these things.

THE PARABLE OF THE TWO SONS

28 "What do you think? A man had two sons. He went to the
first and said, 'Son, go and work in the vineyard today.' 29 The
boy answered, 'I will not.' But later he had a change of heart
and went. 30 The father went to the other son and said the same
thing. This boy answered, 'I will, sir,' but did not go. 31 Which of
the two did his father's will?" They said, "The first." Jesus said
to them, "I tell you the truth, tax collectors and prostitutes will
go ahead of you into the kingdom of God! 32 For John came to
you in the way of righteousness, and you did not believe him.
But the tax collectors and prostitutes did believe. Although you
saw this, you did not later change your minds and believe him.

THE PARABLE OF THE TENANTS

33 "Listen to another parable: There was a landowner who
planted a vineyard. He put a fence around it, dug a pit for its
winepress, and built a watchtower. Then he leased it to tenant
farmers and went on a journey. 34 When the harvest time was
near, he sent his slaves to the tenants to collect his portion of
the crop. 35 But the tenants seized his slaves, beat one, killed

another, and stoned another. 36Again he sent other slaves, more than the first, and they treated them the same way. 37Finally he sent his son to them, saying, 'They will respect my son.' 38But when the tenants saw the son, they said to themselves, 'This is the heir. Come, let's kill him and get his inheritance!' 39So they seized him, threw him out of the vineyard, and killed him. 40Now when the owner of the vineyard comes, what will he do to those tenants?" 41They said to him, "He will utterly destroy those evil men! Then he will lease the vineyard to other tenants who will give him his portion at the harvest."

42Jesus said to them, "Have you never read in the scriptures:

"'***The stone the builders rejected has become the***
cornerstone.
This is from the Lord, and it is marvelous in our eyes'?

43"For this reason I tell you that the kingdom of God will be taken from you and given to a people who will produce its fruit. 44The one who falls on this stone will be broken to pieces, and the one on whom it falls will be crushed." 45When the chief priests and the Pharisees heard his parables, they realized that he was speaking about them. 46They wanted to arrest him, but they were afraid of the crowds because the crowds regarded him as a prophet.

THE PARABLE OF THE WEDDING BANQUET

22 Jesus spoke to them again in parables, saying: 2"The kingdom of heaven can be compared to a king who gave a wedding banquet for his son. 3He sent his slaves to summon those who had been invited to the banquet, but they would not come. 4Again he sent other slaves, saying, 'Tell those who have been invited, "Look! The feast I have prepared for you is ready. My oxen and fattened cattle have been slaughtered, and everything is ready. Come to the wedding banquet."' 5But they were indifferent and went away, one to his farm, another to his business. 6The rest seized his slaves, insolently mistreated them, and killed them. 7The king was furious! He sent his soldiers, and they put those murderers to death and set their city on fire. 8Then he said to his slaves, 'The wedding is ready, but the ones who had been invited were not worthy. 9So go into the main streets and invite everyone you find to the wedding banquet.' 10And those slaves went out into the streets and gathered all they found, both bad and good, and the wedding hall was filled with guests. 11But when the king came in to see the wedding guests, he saw a man there who was not wearing wedding clothes. 12And he said to him, 'Friend, how did you get in here without wedding clothes?' But he had nothing to say. 13Then the king said to his attendants, 'Tie him up hand and foot and throw him into the outer darkness, where there will be weeping and gnashing of teeth!' 14For many are called, but few are chosen."

PAYING TAXES TO CAESAR

15Then the Pharisees went out and planned together to entrap him with his own words. 16They sent to him their disciples along with the Herodians, saying, "Teacher, we know that you are truthful and teach the way of God in accordance with the truth. You do not court anyone's favor because you show no partiality. 17Tell us then, what do you think? Is it right to pay taxes to Caesar or not?"

22:1–14 Those who were first bid to the great wedding feast were the Jews. They would not come. Now the gospel is preached to all sorts of people in all nations—yet the same sinful rejection of the invitation is constantly being repeated. God, in his infinite mercy, is sending his gospel to the poorest and the vilest of humankind. Many of them do come and thus the Lord provokes you to jealousy by a people who were not a people. The king's servants "gathered all they found, both bad and good." The best gathering into the visible church is sure to be a mixture—there will be some coming into it who should not be there.

CHARLES SPURGEON
(1834–1892)
METROPOLITAN TABERNACLE SERMONS

[18]But Jesus realized their evil intentions and said, "Hypocrites! Why are you testing me? [19]Show me the coin used for the tax." So they brought him a denarius. [20]Jesus said to them, "Whose image is this, and whose inscription?" [21]They replied, "Caesar's." He said to them, "Then give to Caesar the things that are Caesar's, and to God the things that are God's." [22]Now when they heard this they were stunned, and they left him and went away.

MARRIAGE AND THE RESURRECTION

[23]The same day Sadducees (who say there is no resurrection) came to him and asked him, [24]"Teacher, Moses said, '***If a man dies without having children, his brother must marry the widow and father children for his brother.***' [25]Now there were seven brothers among us. The first one married and died, and since he had no children he left his wife to his brother. [26]The second did the same, and the third, down to the seventh. [27]Last of all, the woman died. [28]In the resurrection, therefore, whose wife of the seven will she be? For they all had married her." [29]Jesus answered them, "You are deceived because you don't know the scriptures or the power of God. [30]For in the resurrection they neither marry nor are given in marriage, but are like angels in heaven. [31]Now as for the resurrection of the dead, have you not read what was spoken to you by God, [32]'***I am the God of Abraham, the God of Isaac, and the God of Jacob***'? He is not the God of the dead but of the living!" [33]When the crowds heard this, they were amazed at his teaching.

THE GREATEST COMMANDMENT

[34]Now when the Pharisees heard that he had silenced the Sadducees, they assembled together. [35]And one of them, an expert in religious law, asked him a question to test him: [36]"Teacher, which commandment in the law is the greatest?" [37]Jesus said to him, "'***Love the Lord your God with all your heart, with all your soul, and with all your mind.***' [38]This is the first and greatest commandment. [39]The second is like it: '***Love your neighbor as yourself.***' [40]All the law and the prophets depend on these two commandments."

THE MESSIAH: DAVID'S SON AND LORD

[41]While the Pharisees were assembled, Jesus asked them a question: [42]"What do you think about the Christ? Whose son is he?" They said, "The son of David." [43]He said to them, "How then does David by the Spirit call him 'Lord,' saying,

> [44] "'***The Lord said to my lord,***
> "***Sit at my right hand,***
> ***until I put your enemies under your feet***"'?

[45]If David then calls him 'Lord,' how can he be his son?" [46]No one was able to answer him a word, and from that day on no one dared to question him any longer.

SEVEN WOES

23 Then Jesus said to the crowds and to his disciples, [2]"The experts in the law and the Pharisees sit on Moses' seat. [3]Therefore pay attention to what they tell you and do it. But do not do what they do, for they do not practice what they teach. [4]They tie up heavy loads, hard to carry, and put them on men's shoulders, but they themselves are not willing even to lift a finger to move them. [5]They do all their deeds to be seen by people, for they make their phylacteries wide and their tassels long. [6]They love the place of honor at banquets and the

23:1–36 The scribes and Pharisees were enemies to the gospel of Christ and therefore to the salvation of people's souls. Gain being their godliness, by a thousand devices they made religion give way to their worldly interests. They were very strict and precise in smaller matters of the law but careless and loose in weightier matters. While they would seem to be godly, they were neither sober nor righteous. We sometimes think if we had lived when Christ was upon earth that we should not have despised and rejected him, as people then did; yet Christ in his Spirit, in his Word, in his ministers is still no better treated. And it is just with God to give those up to their hearts' lusts who obstinately persist in gratifying them.

MATTHEW HENRY **(1662–1714)**
COMMENTARY ON THE WHOLE BIBLE

best seats in the synagogues 7and elaborate greetings in the
marketplaces and to have people call them ‘Rabbi.’ 8But you
are not to be called ‘Rabbi,’ for you have one Teacher and you
are all brothers. 9And call no one your ‘father’ on earth, for
you have one Father, who is in heaven. 10Nor are you to be called
‘teacher,’ for you have one Teacher, the Christ. 11The greatest
among you will be your servant. 12And whoever exalts himself
will be humbled, and whoever humbles himself will be exalted.

13“But woe to you, experts in the law and you Pharisees, hypocrites! You keep locking people out of the kingdom of heaven!
For you neither enter nor permit those trying to enter to go in.

15“Woe to you, experts in the law and you Pharisees, hypocrites! You cross land and sea to make one convert, and when
you get one, you make him twice as much a child of hell as
yourselves!

16“Woe to you, blind guides, who say, ‘Whoever swears by
the temple is bound by nothing. But whoever swears by the
gold of the temple is bound by the oath.’ 17Blind fools! Which
is greater, the gold or the temple that makes the gold sacred?
18And, ‘Whoever swears by the altar is bound by nothing. But if
anyone swears by the gift on it he is bound by the oath.’ 19You are
blind! For which is greater, the gift or the altar that makes the
gift sacred? 20So whoever swears by the altar swears by it and by
everything on it. 21And whoever swears by the temple swears
by it and the one who dwells in it. 22And whoever swears by
heaven swears by the throne of God and the one who sits on it.

23“Woe to you, experts in the law and you Pharisees, hypocrites! You give a tenth of mint, dill, and cumin, yet you neglect
what is more important in the law—justice, mercy, and faithfulness! You should have done these things without neglecting the
others. 24Blind guides! You strain out a gnat yet swallow a camel!

25“Woe to you, experts in the law and you Pharisees, hypocrites! You clean the outside of the cup and the dish, but inside
they are full of greed and self-indulgence. 26Blind Pharisee! First
clean the inside of the cup, so that the outside may become
clean too!

27“Woe to you, experts in the law and you Pharisees, hypocrites! You are like whitewashed tombs that look beautiful
on the outside but inside are full of the bones of the dead and
of everything unclean. 28In the same way, on the outside you
look righteous to people, but inside you are full of hypocrisy
and lawlessness.

29“Woe to you, experts in the law and you Pharisees, hypocrites! You build tombs for the prophets and decorate the
graves of the righteous. 30And you say, ‘If we had lived in the
days of our ancestors, we would not have participated with
them in shedding the blood of the prophets.’ 31By saying this
you testify against yourselves that you are descendants of those
who murdered the prophets. 32Fill up then the measure of your
ancestors! 33You snakes, you offspring of vipers! How will you
escape being condemned to hell?

34“For this reason I am sending you prophets and wise men
and experts in the law, some of whom you will kill and crucify,
and some you will flog in your synagogues and pursue from
town to town, 35so that on you will come all the righteous blood
shed on earth, from the blood of righteous Abel to the blood
of Zechariah son of Barachiah, whom you murdered between
the temple and the altar. 36I tell you the truth, this generation
will be held responsible for all these things!

JUDGMENT ON ISRAEL

37“O Jerusalem, Jerusalem, you who kill the prophets and stone
those who are sent to you! How often I have longed to gather
your children together as a hen gathers her chicks under her
wings, but you would have none of it! 38Look, your house is left to
you desolate! 39For I tell you, you will not see me from now until
you say, ‘***Blessed is the one who comes in the name of the Lord!***’”

THE DESTRUCTION OF THE TEMPLE

24 Now as Jesus was going out of the temple courts and
walking away, his disciples came to show him the temple
buildings. 2And he said to them, “Do you see all these things?
I tell you the truth, not one stone will be left on another. All
will be torn down!”

SIGNS OF THE END OF THE AGE

3As he was sitting on the Mount of Olives, his disciples came to
him privately and said, “Tell us, when will these things happen?
And what will be the sign of your coming and of the end of the
age?” 4Jesus answered them, “Watch out that no one misleads
you. 5For many will come in my name, saying, ‘I am the Christ,’
and they will mislead many. 6You will hear of wars and rumors
of wars. Make sure that you are not alarmed, for this must happen, but the end is still to come. 7For nation will rise up in arms
against nation, and kingdom against kingdom. And there will
be famines and earthquakes in various places. 8All these things
are the beginning of birth pains.

PERSECUTION OF DISCIPLES

9“Then they will hand you over to be persecuted and will kill
you. You will be hated by all the nations because of my name.
10Then many will be led into sin, and they will betray one another and hate one another. 11And many false prophets will appear
and deceive many, 12and because lawlessness will increase so
much, the love of many will grow cold. 13But the person who
endures to the end will be saved. 14And this gospel of the kingdom will be preached throughout the whole inhabited earth
as a testimony to all the nations, and then the end will come.

THE ABOMINATION OF DESOLATION

15“So when you see *the abomination of desolation*—spoken
about by Daniel the prophet—standing in the holy place” (let
the reader understand), 16“then those in Judea must flee to the
mountains. 17The one on the roof must not come down to take
anything out of his house, 18and the one in the field must not
turn back to get his cloak. 19Woe to those who are pregnant and
to those who are nursing their babies in those days! 20Pray that
your flight may not be in winter or on a Sabbath. 21For then
there will be great suffering unlike anything that has happened
from the beginning of the world until now, or ever will happen.
22And if those days had not been cut short, no one would be
saved. But for the sake of the elect those days will be cut short.
23Then if anyone says to you, ‘Look, here is the Christ!’ or ‘There
he is!’ do not believe him. 24For false messiahs and false prophets will appear and perform great signs and wonders to deceive,
if possible, even the elect. 25Remember, I have told you ahead
of time. 26So then, if someone says to you, ‘Look, he is in the
wilderness,’ do not go out, or ‘Look, he is in the inner rooms,’ do
not believe him. 27For just like the lightning comes from the

24:1–28 Our Savior’s words might be applied to almost any period of the world’s history. Earth has seldom had a long spell of quiet—there have almost always been both the realities of war and the rumors of war. “Make sure that you are not alarmed” is a timely message—“for this must happen.” Therefore let us not be surprised or alarmed. The destruction of Jerusalem was the beginning of the end—but “the end is still to come.” This prophecy ought both to warn the disciples of Christ what they may expect and wean them from the world where all these and greater sorrows are to be experienced!

CHARLES SPURGEON (1834–1892)
METROPOLITAN TABERNACLE SERMONS

east and flashes to the west, so the coming of the Son of Man
will be. 28Wherever the corpse is, there the vultures will gather.

THE ARRIVAL OF THE SON OF MAN

29"Immediately after the suffering of those days, *the sun will be*
darkened, and the moon will not give its light; the stars will fall from
heaven, and the powers of heaven will be shaken. 30Then the sign
of the Son of Man will appear in heaven, and all the tribes of the
earth will mourn. They will see *the Son of Man arriving on the*
clouds of heaven with power and great glory. 31And he will send
his angels with a loud trumpet blast, and they will gather his
elect from the four winds, from one end of heaven to the other.

THE PARABLE OF THE FIG TREE

32"Learn this parable from the fig tree: Whenever its branch
becomes tender and puts out its leaves, you know that summer
is near. 33So also you, when you see all these things, know that he
is near, right at the door. 34I tell you the truth, this generation
will not pass away until all these things take place. 35Heaven
and earth will pass away, but my words will never pass away.

BE READY!

36"But as for that day and hour no one knows it—not even the
angels in heaven—except the Father alone. 37For just like the
days of Noah were, so the coming of the Son of Man will be.
38For in those days before the flood, people were eating and
drinking, marrying and giving in marriage, until the day Noah
entered the ark. 39And they knew nothing until the flood came
and took them all away. It will be the same at the coming of
the Son of Man. 40Then there will be two men in the field; one
will be taken and one left. 41There will be two women grinding
grain with a mill; one will be taken and one left.
42"Therefore stay alert because you do not know on what day
your Lord will come. 43But understand this: If the owner of the
house had known at what time of night the thief was coming,
he would have been alert and would not have let his house be
broken into. 44Therefore you also must be ready because the
Son of Man will come at an hour when you do not expect him.

THE FAITHFUL AND WISE SLAVE

45"Who then is the faithful and wise slave, whom the master
has put in charge of his household, to give the other slaves
their food at the proper time? 46Blessed is that slave whom the
master finds at work when he comes. 47I tell you the truth, the
master will put him in charge of all his possessions. 48But if that
evil slave should say to himself, 'My master is staying away a
long time,' 49and he begins to beat his fellow slaves and to eat
and drink with drunkards, 50then the master of that slave will
come on a day when he does not expect him and at an hour
he does not foresee, 51and will cut him in two, and assign him
a place with the hypocrites, where there will be weeping and
gnashing of teeth.

THE PARABLE OF THE 10 VIRGINS

25 "At that time the kingdom of heaven will be like 10 virgins
who took their lamps and went out to meet the bridegroom. 2Five of the virgins were foolish, and five were wise. 3When
the foolish ones took their lamps, they did not take extra olive
oil with them. 4But the wise ones took flasks of olive oil with

their lamps. [5]When the bridegroom was delayed a long time,
they all became drowsy and fell asleep. [6]But at midnight there
was a shout, 'Look, the bridegroom is here! Come out to meet
him.' [7]Then all the virgins woke up and trimmed their lamps.
[8]The foolish ones said to the wise, 'Give us some of your oil because our lamps are going out.' [9]'No,' they replied. 'There won't
be enough for you and for us. Go instead to those who sell oil and
buy some for yourselves.' [10]But while they had gone to buy it, the
bridegroom arrived, and those who were ready went inside with
him to the wedding banquet. Then the door was shut. [11]Later,
the other virgins came too, saying, 'Lord, lord! Let us in!' [12]But he
replied, 'I tell you the truth, I do not know you!' [13]Therefore stay
alert because you do not know the day or the hour.

THE PARABLE OF THE TALENTS

[14]"For it is like a man going on a journey, who summoned his
slaves and entrusted his property to them. [15]To one he gave five
talents, to another two, and to another one, each according to his
ability. Then he went on his journey. [16]The one who had received
five talents went off right away and put his money to work and
gained five more. [17]In the same way, the one who had two gained
two more. [18]But the one who had received one talent went out
and dug a hole in the ground and hid his master's money in it.
[19]After a long time, the master of those slaves came and settled
his accounts with them. [20]The one who had received the five
talents came and brought five more, saying, 'Sir, you entrusted
me with five talents. See, I have gained five more.' [21]His master
answered, 'Well done, good and faithful slave! You have been
faithful in a few things. I will put you in charge of many things.
Enter into the joy of your master.' [22]The one with the two talents
also came and said, 'Sir, you entrusted two talents to me. See, I
have gained two more.' [23]His master answered, 'Well done, good
and faithful slave! You have been faithful with a few things. I
will put you in charge of many things. Enter into the joy of your
master.' [24]Then the one who had received the one talent came
and said, 'Sir, I knew that you were a hard man, harvesting where
you did not sow, and gathering where you did not scatter seed,
[25]so I was afraid, and I went and hid your talent in the ground.
See, you have what is yours.' [26]But his master answered, 'Evil and
lazy slave! So you knew that I harvest where I didn't sow and
gather where I didn't scatter? [27]Then you should have deposited
my money with the bankers, and on my return I would have received my money back with interest! [28]Therefore take the talent
from him and give it to the one who has 10. [29]For the one who
has will be given more, and he will have more than enough. But
the one who does not have, even what he has will be taken from
him. [30]And throw that worthless slave into the outer darkness,
where there will be weeping and gnashing of teeth.'

THE JUDGMENT

[31]"When the Son of Man comes in his glory and all the angels
with him, then he will sit on his glorious throne. [32]All the nations will be assembled before him, and he will separate people
one from another like a shepherd separates the sheep from the
goats. [33]He will put the sheep on his right and the goats on his
left. [34]Then the king will say to those on his right, 'Come, you
who are blessed by my Father, inherit the kingdom prepared
for you from the foundation of the world. [35]For I was hungry
and you gave me food, I was thirsty and you gave me something

25:31–45 This sign of the cross will be in the heavens when the Lord comes to judge. Then all the servants of the cross, who during life made themselves one with the Crucified, will draw near with great trust to Christ, the Judge. Why then do you fear to take up the cross when through it you can win a kingdom? In the cross is salvation, in the cross is life, in the cross is protection from enemies, in the cross is infusion of heavenly sweetness, in the cross is strength of mind, in the cross is joy of spirit, in the cross is highest virtue, in the cross is perfect holiness. There is no salvation of soul nor hope of everlasting life but in the cross.

THOMAS À KEMPIS
(C. 1380–1471)
THE IMITATION OF CHRIST

to drink, I was a stranger and you invited me in, [36]I was naked
and you gave me clothing, I was sick and you took care of me,
I was in prison and you visited me.' [37]Then the righteous will
answer him, 'Lord, when did we see you hungry and feed you,
or thirsty and give you something to drink? [38]When did we
see you a stranger and invite you in, or naked and clothe you?
[39]When did we see you sick or in prison and visit you?' [40]And
the king will answer them, 'I tell you the truth, just as you did
it for one of the least of these brothers or sisters of mine, you
did it for me.'

[41]"Then he will say to those on his left, 'Depart from me, you
accursed, into the eternal fire that has been prepared for the
devil and his angels! [42]For I was hungry and you gave me nothing
to eat, I was thirsty and you gave me nothing to drink. [43]I was a
stranger and you did not receive me as a guest, naked and you
did not clothe me, sick and in prison and you did not visit me.'
[44]Then they too will answer, 'Lord, when did we see you hungry
or thirsty or a stranger or naked or sick or in prison, and did not
give you whatever you needed?' [45]Then he will answer them, 'I
tell you the truth, just as you did not do it for one of the least
of these, you did not do it for me.' [46]And these will depart into
eternal punishment, but the righteous into eternal life."

THE PLOT AGAINST JESUS

26 When Jesus had finished saying all these things, he told
his disciples, [2]"You know that after two days the Passover is coming, and the Son of Man will be handed over to be
crucified." [3]Then the chief priests and the elders of the people
met together in the palace of the high priest, who was named
Caiaphas. [4]They planned to arrest Jesus by stealth and kill him.
[5]But they said, "Not during the feast, so that there won't be a
riot among the people."

JESUS' ANOINTING

[6]Now while Jesus was in Bethany at the house of Simon the
leper, [7]a woman came to him with an alabaster jar of expensive
perfumed oil, and she poured it on his head as he was at the
table. [8]When the disciples saw this, they became indignant and
said, "Why this waste? [9]It could have been sold at a high price
and the money given to the poor!" [10]When Jesus learned of this,
he said to them, "Why are you bothering this woman? She has
done a good service for me. [11]For you will always have the poor
with you, but you will not always have me! [12]When she poured
this oil on my body, she did it to prepare me for burial. [13]I tell
you the truth, wherever this gospel is proclaimed in the whole
world, what she has done will also be told in memory of her."

THE PLAN TO BETRAY JESUS

[14]Then one of the twelve, the one named Judas Iscariot, went
to the chief priests [15]and said, "What will you give me to betray
him into your hands?" So they set out 30 silver coins for him.
[16]From that time on, Judas began looking for an opportunity
to betray him.

THE PASSOVER

[17]Now on the first day of the Feast of Unleavened Bread the
disciples came to Jesus and said, "Where do you want us to
prepare for you to eat the Passover?" [18]He said, "Go into the
city to a certain man and tell him, 'The Teacher says, "My time

is near. I will observe the Passover with my disciples at your
house."'" [19]So the disciples did as Jesus had instructed them,
and they prepared the Passover. [20]When it was evening, he took
his place at the table with the twelve. [21]And while they were
eating he said, "I tell you the truth, one of you will betray me."
[22]They became greatly distressed and each one began to say
to him, "Surely not I, Lord?" [23]He answered, "The one who has
dipped his hand into the bowl with me will betray me. [24]The
Son of Man will go as it is written about him, but woe to that
man by whom the Son of Man is betrayed! It would be better
for him if he had never been born." [25]Then Judas, the one who
would betray him, said, "Surely not I, Rabbi?" Jesus replied, "You
have said it yourself."

THE LORD'S SUPPER

[26]While they were eating, Jesus took bread, and after giving
thanks he broke it, gave it to his disciples, and said, "Take, eat,
this is my body." [27]And after taking the cup and giving thanks,
he gave it to them, saying, "Drink from it, all of you, [28]for this
is my blood, the blood of the covenant, that is poured out for
many for the forgiveness of sins. [29]I tell you, from now on I will
not drink of this fruit of the vine until that day when I drink it
new with you in my Father's kingdom." [30]After singing a hymn,
they went out to the Mount of Olives.

THE PREDICTION OF PETER'S DENIAL

[31]Then Jesus said to them, "This night you will all fall away
because of me, for it is written:

> "'***I will strike the shepherd,***
> ***and the sheep of the flock will be scattered.***'

[32]But after I am raised, I will go ahead of you into Galilee." [33]Pe-
ter said to him, "If they all fall away because of you, I will never
fall away!" [34]Jesus said to him, "I tell you the truth, on this night,
before the rooster crows, you will deny me three times." [35]Peter
said to him, "Even if I must die with you, I will never deny you."
And all the disciples said the same thing.

GETHSEMANE

[36]Then Jesus went with them to a place called Gethsemane,
and he said to the disciples, "Sit here while I go over there and
pray." [37]He took with him Peter and the two sons of Zebedee,
and he became anguished and distressed. [38]Then he said to
them, "My soul is deeply grieved, even to the point of death.
Remain here and stay awake with me." [39]Going a little farther,
he threw himself down with his face to the ground and prayed,
"My Father, if possible, let this cup pass from me! Yet not what
I will, but what you will." [40]Then he came to the disciples and
found them sleeping. He said to Peter, "So, couldn't you stay
awake with me for one hour? [41]Stay awake and pray that you
will not fall into temptation. The spirit is willing, but the flesh
is weak." [42]He went away a second time and prayed, "My Father,
if this cup cannot be taken away unless I drink it, your will must
be done." [43]He came again and found them sleeping; they could
not keep their eyes open. [44]So leaving them again, he went away
and prayed for the third time, saying the same thing once more.
[45]Then he came to the disciples and said to them, "Are you still
sleeping and resting? Look, the hour is approaching, and the
Son of Man is betrayed into the hands of sinners. [46]Get up, let
us go. Look! My betrayer is approaching!"

26:36–46 We learn a great deal from the instructive characteristics of our Savior's prayer during this time of severe trial. The first thing to note is that it was lonely prayer, for he withdrew from even his three most favored disciples. Christ's prayer also was humble prayer. If this is the Master's position, what should be yours as his humble servant? His prayer also was filial prayer, prayer befitting a child of the Father. By pleading your adoption as his child, you will find a fortress of protection through your times of trial. So do not be afraid to say, "My Father" (26:39), "Hear my cry for help. Pay attention to my prayer" (Ps 61:1).

CHARLES SPURGEON
(1834–1892)
MORNING AND EVENING

BETRAYAL AND ARREST

47 While he was still speaking, Judas, one of the twelve, arrived.
With him was a large crowd armed with swords and clubs, sent by
the chief priests and elders of the people. 48 (Now the betrayer had
given them a sign, saying, "The one I kiss is the man. Arrest him!")
49 Immediately he went up to Jesus and said, "Greetings, Rabbi,"
and kissed him. 50 Jesus said to him, "Friend, do what you are here
to do." Then they came and took hold of Jesus and arrested him.
51 But one of those with Jesus grabbed his sword, drew it out, and
struck the high priest's slave, cutting off his ear. 52 Then Jesus
said to him, "Put your sword back in its place! For all who take
hold of the sword will die by the sword. 53 Or do you think that I
cannot call on my Father and that he would send me more than
12 legions of angels right now? 54 How then would the scriptures
that say it must happen this way be fulfilled?" 55 At that moment
Jesus said to the crowd, "Have you come out with swords and
clubs to arrest me like you would an outlaw? Day after day I sat
teaching in the temple courts, yet you did not arrest me. 56 But
this has happened so that the scriptures of the prophets would
be fulfilled." Then all the disciples left him and fled.

CONDEMNED BY THE SANHEDRIN

57 Now the ones who had arrested Jesus led him to Caiaphas, the
high priest, in whose house the experts in the law and the elders
had gathered. 58 But Peter was following him from a distance, all
the way to the high priest's courtyard. After going in, he sat with
the guards to see the outcome. 59 The chief priests and the whole
Sanhedrin were trying to find false testimony against Jesus so that
they could put him to death. 60 But they did not find anything,
though many false witnesses came forward. Finally two came
forward 61 and declared, "This man said, 'I am able to destroy the
temple of God and rebuild it in three days.'" 62 So the high priest
stood up and said to him, "Have you no answer? What is this that
they are testifying against you?" 63 But Jesus was silent. The high
priest said to him, "I charge you under oath by the living God, tell
us if you are the Christ, the Son of God." 64 Jesus said to him, "You
have said it yourself. But I tell you, from now on you will see the
Son of Man *sitting at the right hand* of the Power and *coming on
the clouds of heaven*." 65 Then the high priest tore his clothes and
declared, "He has blasphemed! Why do we still need witnesses?
Now you have heard the blasphemy! 66 What is your verdict?" They
answered, "He is guilty and deserves death." 67 Then they spat in
his face and struck him with their fists. And some slapped him,
68 saying, "Prophesy for us, you Christ! Who hit you?"

PETER'S DENIALS

69 Now Peter was sitting outside in the courtyard. A slave girl
came to him and said, "You also were with Jesus the Galilean."
70 But he denied it in front of them all: "I don't know what you're
talking about!" 71 When he went out to the gateway, another
slave girl saw him and said to the people there, "This man was
with Jesus the Nazarene." 72 He denied it again with an oath,
"I do not know the man!" 73 After a little while, those standing
there came up to Peter and said, "You really are one of them
too—even your accent gives you away!" 74 At that he began to
curse, and he swore with an oath, "I do not know the man!" At
that moment a rooster crowed. 75 Then Peter remembered what
Jesus had said: "Before the rooster crows, you will deny me three
times." And he went outside and wept bitterly.

JESUS BROUGHT BEFORE PILATE

27 When it was early in the morning, all the chief priests and the elders of the people plotted against Jesus to execute him. 2 They tied him up, led him away, and handed him over to Pilate the governor.

JUDAS' SUICIDE

3 Now when Judas, who had betrayed him, saw that Jesus had been condemned, he regretted what he had done and returned the 30 silver coins to the chief priests and the elders, 4 saying, "I have sinned by betraying innocent blood!" But they said, "What is that to us? You take care of it yourself!" 5 So Judas threw the silver coins into the temple and left. Then he went out and hanged himself. 6 The chief priests took the silver and said, "It is not lawful to put this into the temple treasury, since it is blood money." 7 After consulting together they bought the Potter's Field with it, as a burial place for foreigners. 8 For this reason that field has been called the "Field of Blood" to this day. 9 Then what was spoken by Jeremiah the prophet was fulfilled: *"They took the 30 silver coins, the price of the one whose price had been set by the people of Israel,* 10 *and they gave them for the potter's field, as the Lord commanded me."*

JESUS AND PILATE

11 Then Jesus stood before the governor, and the governor asked him, "Are you the king of the Jews?" Jesus said, "You say so." 12 But when he was accused by the chief priests and the elders, he did not respond. 13 Then Pilate said to him, "Don't you hear how many charges they are bringing against you?" 14 But he did not answer even one accusation, so that the governor was quite amazed.

15 During the feast the governor was accustomed to release one prisoner to the crowd, whomever they wanted. 16 At that time they had in custody a notorious prisoner named Jesus Barabbas. 17 So after they had assembled, Pilate said to them, "Whom do you want me to release for you, Jesus Barabbas or Jesus who is called the Christ?" 18 (For he knew that they had handed him over because of envy.) 19 As he was sitting on the judgment seat, his wife sent a message to him: "Have nothing to do with that innocent man; I have suffered greatly as a result of a dream about him today." 20 But the chief priests and the elders persuaded the crowds to ask for Barabbas and to have Jesus killed. 21 The governor asked them, "Which of the two do you want me to release for you?" And they said, "Barabbas!" 22 Pilate said to them, "Then what should I do with Jesus who is called the Christ?" They all said, "Crucify him!" 23 He asked, "Why? What wrong has he done?" But they shouted more insistently, "Crucify him!"

JESUS IS CONDEMNED AND MOCKED

24 When Pilate saw that he could do nothing, but that instead a riot was starting, he took some water, washed his hands before the crowd and said, "I am innocent of this man's blood. You take care of it yourselves!" 25 In reply all the people said, "Let his blood be on us and on our children!" 26 Then he released Barabbas for them. But after he had Jesus flogged, he handed him over to be crucified. 27 Then the governor's soldiers took Jesus into the governor's residence and gathered the whole cohort around him. 28 They stripped him and put a scarlet robe around him,

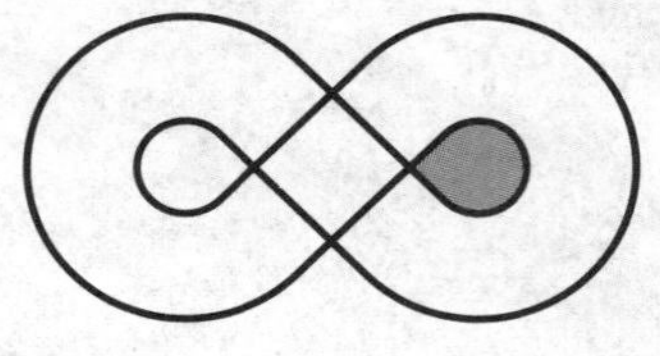

THE WESTMINSTER CATECHISM (1646–1648)

THE LARGER AND Shorter Westminster Catechisms offer questions and answers covering a wide array of important doctrinal topics. The Catechisms particularly focus on declaring what Scripture teaches regarding the doctrines of salvation and the Christian life, along with sections on the Ten Commandments, the sacraments, and the Lord's Prayer. The shorter Catechism is intended for the individual while the Larger Catechism is intended for the church as a community. This selection of teachings is from the Larger Catechism.

QUESTION 1: WHAT IS THE CHIEF AND HIGHEST END OF MAN?

ANSWER: MAN'S chief and highest end is to glorify God, and fully to enjoy him forever.

QUESTION 5: WHAT DO THE SCRIPTURES PRINCIPALLY TEACH?

ANSWER: THE Scriptures principally teach what man is to believe concerning God, and what duty God requires of man.

QUESTION 24: WHAT IS SIN?

ANSWER: SIN is any want of conformity unto, or transgression of, any law of God, given as a rule to the reasonable creature.

QUESTION 91: WHAT IS THE DUTY WHICH GOD REQUIRETH OF MAN?

ANSWER: THE duty which God requireth of man is obedience to his revealed will.

QUESTION 49: HOW DID CHRIST HUMBLE HIMSELF IN HIS DEATH?

ANSWER: CHRIST humbled himself in his death in that having been betrayed by Judas, forsaken by his disciples, scorned and rejected by the world, condemned by Pilate, and tormented by his persecutors; having also conflicted with the terrors of death and the powers of darkness, felt and borne the weight of God's wrath, he laid down his life an offering for sin, enduring the painful, shameful, and cursed death of the cross.

QUESTION 59: WHO ARE MADE PARTAKERS OF REDEMPTION THROUGH CHRIST?

ANSWER: REDEMPTION is certainly applied, and effectually communicated, to all those for whom Christ hath purchased it; who are in time by the Holy Ghost enabled to believe in Christ according to the gospel.

QUESTION 70: WHAT IS JUSTIFICATION?

ANSWER: JUSTIFICATION is an act of God's free grace unto sinners, in which he pardoneth all their sins, accepteth and accounteth their persons righteous in his sight; not for anything wrought in them or done by them, but only for the perfect obedience and full satisfaction of Christ, by God imputed to them and received by faith alone.

QUESTION 73: HOW DOTH FAITH JUSTIFY A SINNER IN THE SIGHT OF GOD?

ANSWER: FAITH justifies a sinner in the sight of God, not because of those other graces which do always accompany it, or of good works that are the fruits of it, nor as if the grace of faith, or any act thereof, were imputed to him for his justification; but only as it is an instrument by which he receiveth and applieth Christ and his righteousness.

[29]and after braiding a crown of thorns, they put it on his head. They put a staff in his right hand, and kneeling down before him, they mocked him: "Hail, king of the Jews!" [30]They spat on him and took the staff and struck him repeatedly on the head. [31]When they had mocked him, they stripped him of the robe and put his own clothes back on him. Then they led him away to crucify him.

THE CRUCIFIXION

[32]As they were going out, they found a man from Cyrene named Simon, whom they forced to carry his cross. [33]They came to a place called Golgotha (which means "Place of the Skull") [34]and offered Jesus wine mixed with gall to drink. But after tasting it, he would not drink it. [35]When they had crucified him, *they divided his clothes by throwing dice.* [36]Then they sat down and kept guard over him there. [37]Above his head they put the charge against him, which read: "This is Jesus, the king of the Jews." [38]Then two outlaws were crucified with him, one on his right and one on his left. [39]Those who passed by defamed him, shaking their heads [40]and saying, "You who can destroy the temple and rebuild it in three days, save yourself! If you are God's Son, come down from the cross!" [41]In the same way even the chief priests—together with the experts in the law and elders—were mocking him: [42]"He saved others, but he cannot save himself! He is the king of Israel! If he comes down now from the cross, we will believe in him! [43]*He trusts in God—let God, if he wants to, deliver him now* because he said, 'I am God's Son'!" [44]The robbers who were crucified with him also spoke abusively to him.

JESUS' DEATH

[45]Now from noon until three, darkness came over all the land. [46]At about three o'clock Jesus shouted with a loud voice, "*Eli, Eli, lema sabachthani?*" that is, "***My God, my God, why have you forsaken me?***" [47]When some of the bystanders heard it, they said, "This man is calling for Elijah." [48]Immediately one of them ran and got a sponge, filled it with sour wine, put it on a stick, and gave it to him to drink. [49]But the rest said, "Leave him alone! Let's see if Elijah will come to save him." [50]Then Jesus cried out again with a loud voice and gave up his spirit. [51]Just then the temple curtain was torn in two, from top to bottom. The earth shook and the rocks were split apart. [52]And tombs were opened, and the bodies of many saints who had died were raised. [53](They came out of the tombs after his resurrection and went into the holy city and appeared to many people.) [54]Now when the centurion and those with him who were guarding Jesus saw the earthquake and what took place, they were extremely terrified and said, "Truly this one was God's Son!" [55]Many women who had followed Jesus from Galilee and given him support were also there, watching from a distance. [56]Among them were Mary Magdalene, Mary the mother of James and Joseph, and the mother of the sons of Zebedee.

27:45–55 No mean miracle was accomplished in the tearing of so strong and thick a veil. The old law of ordinances was put away. That rent also revealed all the hidden things of the old dispensation: The mercy seat could now be seen, and the glory of God gleamed forth above it. By the death of our Lord Jesus we have a clear revelation of God, for he was "not like Moses who used to put a veil over his face" (2 Cor 3:13). Life and immortality are now brought to light, and things that have been hidden since the foundation of the world are manifest in him. Hence access to God is now permitted and is the privilege of every believer in Christ Jesus.

CHARLES SPURGEON
(1834–1892)
METROPOLITAN TABERNACLE SERMONS

JESUS' BURIAL

[57]Now when it was evening, there came a rich man from Arimathea, named Joseph, who was also a disciple of Jesus. [58]He went to Pilate and asked for the body of Jesus. Then Pilate ordered that it be given to him. [59]Joseph took the body, wrapped it in a clean linen cloth, [60]and placed it in his own new tomb that he had cut in the rock. Then he rolled a great stone across the

entrance of the tomb and went away. 61 (Now Mary Magdalene
and the other Mary were sitting there, opposite the tomb.)

THE GUARD AT THE TOMB

62 The next day (which is after the day of preparation) the chief
priests and the Pharisees assembled before Pilate 63 and said,
"Sir, we remember that while that deceiver was still alive he
said, 'After three days I will rise again.' 64 So give orders to secure
the tomb until the third day. Otherwise his disciples may come
and steal his body and say to the people, 'He has been raised
from the dead,' and the last deception will be worse than the
first." 65 Pilate said to them, "Take a guard of soldiers. Go and
make it as secure as you can." 66 So they went with the soldiers
of the guard and made the tomb secure by sealing the stone.

THE RESURRECTION

28 Now after the Sabbath, at dawn on the first day of the
week, Mary Magdalene and the other Mary went to look
at the tomb. 2 Suddenly there was a severe earthquake, for an
angel of the Lord descending from heaven came and rolled away
the stone and sat on it. 3 His appearance was like lightning, and
his clothes were white as snow. 4 The guards were shaken and
became like dead men because they were so afraid of him. 5 But
the angel said to the women, "Do not be afraid; I know that
you are looking for Jesus, who was crucified. 6 He is not here,
for he has been raised, just as he said. Come and see the place
where he was lying. 7 Then go quickly and tell his disciples, 'He
has been raised from the dead. He is going ahead of you into
Galilee. You will see him there.' Listen, I have told you!" 8 So they
left the tomb quickly, with fear and great joy, and ran to tell his
disciples. 9 But Jesus met them, saying, "Greetings!" They came
to him, held on to his feet and worshiped him. 10 Then Jesus
said to them, "Do not be afraid. Go and tell my brothers to go
to Galilee. They will see me there."

THE GUARDS' REPORT

11 While they were going, some of the guards went into the city
and told the chief priests everything that had happened. 12 After
they had assembled with the elders and formed a plan, they
gave a large sum of money to the soldiers, 13 telling them, "You
are to say, 'His disciples came at night and stole his body while
we were asleep.' 14 If this matter is heard before the governor,
we will satisfy him and keep you out of trouble." 15 So they took
the money and did as they were instructed. And this story is
told among the Jews to this day.

THE GREAT COMMISSION

16 So the 11 disciples went to Galilee to the mountain Jesus had
designated. 17 When they saw him, they worshiped him, but
some doubted. 18 Then Jesus came up and said to them, "All
authority in heaven and on earth has been given to me. 19 Therefore go and make disciples of all nations, baptizing them in the
name of the Father and the Son and the Holy Spirit, 20 teaching
them to obey everything I have commanded you. And remember, I am with you always, to the end of the age."

28:1–10 The angels remind the women that Christ had earlier told them about these events, but they did not believe or understand him. Such a message is certain proof that although the angels are totally pure and holy spirits and we are only poor sinners, nevertheless they do not shun or despise us but rather want to be good friends with us. And the angels come with two commands: The first is that the women should not be frightened by their appearance; the other command is that they should quickly go forth and announce the resurrection to the disciples. We should be very glad in both these parts, for the angel says first, "Do not be afraid; I know that you are looking for Jesus, who was crucified. He is not here, for he has been raised."

MARTIN LUTHER **(1483–1546)**
THE FRUIT OF CHRIST'S RESURRECTION

AUTHOR	AUDIENCE	DATE	PURPOSE	THEMES
John Mark	Mostly Gentile Christians, probably in the church at Rome	Between the AD mid-50s and late 60s	Mark wrote his account to present Jesus as the suffering Messiah and call believers to deny themselves and follow him.	The person of Jesus; Jesus' messianic mission; and the kingdom of God

Mark's main purpose for penning his portrait of Jesus is revealed at the climax of his account with the declaration of Peter in 8:29. After Jesus asked him, "Who do you say that I am?" Peter answered, "You are the Christ." Jesus was the long-awaited Christ, the Messiah of Israel who would finally bring justice and peace to his people. Yet he wasn't the Messiah the Jews were expecting, a conquering king who would trounce the Romans. Instead, he was the one who would "suffer many things and be rejected by the elders, chief priests, and experts in the law, and be killed, and after three days rise again" (8:31). It is this pattern of self-denial that Jesus invites people into: "If anyone wants to become my follower, he must deny himself, take up his cross, and follow me. For whoever wants to save his life will lose it, but whoever loses his life because of me and because of the gospel will save it" (8:34–35). From the opening of his book, Mark presents Christ as the Lord who suffers, who calls people into his kingdom as subjects who join him in suffering.

"The beginning of the gospel of Jesus Christ, the Son of God" (1:1)—this is how the book of Mark opens. Those two titles—*Christ* and *Son of God*—summarize Jesus' person: He brought the salvation God promised from the beginning, showing and sharing the love of God as God himself. And while Mark writes about Jesus' teachings and miraculous works, the most significant aspect of Mark's biographical account is Jesus' death on the cross. One person has called the Gospel of Mark a passion narrative preceded by a lengthy introduction! One-third of the book chronicles Jesus' passion, the week of events that culminated with his death. Throughout his Gospel, Mark makes reference to the climactic moment of the cross, showing that it wasn't a tragic accident but part of God's sovereign plan for humanity. It is through his work on the cross that Jesus is most fully revealed. This is the testimony of the Roman centurion who watched as Jesus died and said, "Truly this man was God's Son!" (15:39).

MARK

Mark's account of Jesus' life includes a recurring theme that has come to be known as the Messianic Secret. As you read through this Gospel, you'll notice that Jesus guards against making known his identity as Messiah. For instance, when Peter declares Jesus is the Christ, the Messiah, Jesus "warned [the disciples] not to tell anyone about him" (8:30). And when he healed people, he often wanted them to keep his power a secret too. Even the demons were silenced! Part of the reason why he kept his identity a secret is because broadcasting it would have drawn unnecessary attention from the religious and political elite. It might also have been misunderstood by the crowds. Ultimately, his identity as the Messiah was hidden until it could be fully revealed through the cross and the empty tomb.

From the beginning of Jesus' ministry, he called people to follow him. Jesus invited people from every walk of life to follow him. Such discipleship was marked by self-denial (submitting to Christ's lordship), bearing one's cross (submitting to God's will through radical commitment), and daily following the teachings of Jesus (submitting to his instruction for every area of life). At the heart of these commitments was faith, a full trust in Jesus and his work.

THE MINISTRY OF JOHN THE BAPTIST

1 The beginning of the gospel of Jesus Christ, the Son of God.
2 As it is written in the prophet Isaiah,

"Look, I am sending my messenger ahead of you,
who will prepare your way,
3 *the voice of one shouting in the wilderness,*
'Prepare the way for the Lord,
make his paths straight.'"

4 In the wilderness John the baptizer began preaching a baptism of repentance for the forgiveness of sins. 5 People from the
whole Judean countryside and all of Jerusalem were going out
to him, and he was baptizing them in the Jordan River as they
confessed their sins. 6 John wore a garment made of camel's
hair with a leather belt around his waist, and he ate locusts
and wild honey. 7 He proclaimed, "One more powerful than I am
is coming after me; I am not worthy to bend down and untie
the strap of his sandals. 8 I baptize you with water, but he will
baptize you with the Holy Spirit."

THE BAPTISM AND TEMPTATION OF JESUS

9 Now in those days Jesus came from Nazareth in Galilee and
was baptized by John in the Jordan River. 10 And just as Jesus
was coming up out of the water, he saw the heavens splitting
apart and the Spirit descending on him like a dove. 11 And a
voice came from heaven: "You are my one dear Son; in you I
take great delight." 12 The Spirit immediately drove him into
the wilderness. 13 He was in the wilderness 40 days, enduring
temptations from Satan. He was with wild animals, and angels
were ministering to his needs.

PREACHING IN GALILEE AND THE CALL OF THE DISCIPLES

14 Now after John was imprisoned, Jesus went into Galilee and
proclaimed the gospel of God. 15 He said, "The time is fulfilled
and the kingdom of God is near. Repent and believe the gospel!"
16 As he went along the Sea of Galilee, he saw Simon and Andrew, Simon's brother, casting a net into the sea (for they were
fishermen). 17 Jesus said to them, "Follow me, and I will turn you
into fishers of people!" 18 They left their nets immediately and
followed him. 19 Going on a little farther, he saw James, the son
of Zebedee, and John his brother in their boat mending nets.
20 Immediately he called them, and they left their father Zebedee in the boat with the hired men and followed him.

JESUS' AUTHORITY

21 Then they went to Capernaum. When the Sabbath came, Jesus
went into the synagogue and began to teach. 22 The people there
were amazed by his teaching because he taught them like one
who had authority, not like the experts in the law. 23 Just then
there was a man in their synagogue with an unclean spirit, and he
cried out, 24 "Leave us alone, Jesus the Nazarene! Have you come
to destroy us? I know who you are—the Holy One of God!" 25 But
Jesus rebuked him: "Silence! Come out of him!" 26 After throwing
him into convulsions, the unclean spirit cried out with a loud voice
and came out of him. 27 They were all amazed so that they asked
each other, "What is this? A new teaching with authority! He even
commands the unclean spirits and they obey him." 28 So the news
about him spread quickly throughout all the region around Galilee.

1:14–15 After God had done everything by the ministry of angels and of prophets and of the law and nothing came of it, and it was well nigh come to this, that humankind had been made in vain, brought into the world in vain, no, rather to their ruin—when all were absolutely perishing, more fearfully than in the deluge, he devised this dispensation—that is by grace—that it might not be in vain, might not be to no purpose that humanity was created. At that time when they were on the very point of perishing, then they were rescued.

CHRYSOSTOM (C. 347–407)
HOMILIES ON THE EPISTLE OF PAUL TO THE EPHESIANS

HEALINGS AT SIMON'S HOUSE

29 Now as soon as they left the synagogue, they entered Simon
and Andrew's house, with James and John. 30 Simon's mother-
in-law was lying down, sick with a fever, so they spoke to Jesus
at once about her. 31 He came and raised her up by gently taking
her hand. Then the fever left her and she began to serve them.
32 When it was evening, after sunset, they brought to him all who
were sick and demon-possessed. 33 The whole town gathered
by the door. 34 So he healed many who were sick with various
diseases and drove out many demons. But he would not permit
the demons to speak because they knew him.

PRAYING AND PREACHING

35 Then Jesus got up early in the morning when it was still very
dark, departed, and went out to a deserted place, and there he
spent time in prayer. 36 Simon and his companions searched for
him. 37 When they found him, they said, "Everyone is looking for
you." 38 He replied, "Let us go elsewhere, into the surrounding
villages, so that I can preach there too. For that is what I came
out here to do." 39 So he went into all of Galilee preaching in
their synagogues and casting out demons.

CLEANSING A LEPER

40 Now a leper came to him and fell to his knees, asking for help.
"If you are willing, you can make me clean," he said. 41 Moved
with indignation, Jesus stretched out his hand and touched
him, saying, "I am willing. Be clean!" 42 The leprosy left him at
once, and he was clean. 43 Immediately Jesus sent the man away
with a very strong warning. 44 He told him, "See that you do not
say anything to anyone, but go, show yourself to a priest, and
bring the offering that Moses commanded for your cleansing,
as a testimony to them." 45 But as the man went out he began to
announce it publicly and spread the story widely, so that Jesus
was no longer able to enter any town openly but stayed outside
in remote places. Still they kept coming to him from everywhere.

HEALING AND FORGIVING A PARALYTIC

2 Now after some days, when he returned to Capernaum, the
news spread that he was at home. 2 So many gathered that
there was no longer any room, not even by the door, and he
preached the word to them. 3 Some people came bringing to
him a paralytic, carried by four of them. 4 When they were not
able to bring him in because of the crowd, they removed the
roof above Jesus. Then, after tearing it out, they lowered the
stretcher the paralytic was lying on. 5 When Jesus saw their
faith, he said to the paralytic, "Son, your sins are forgiven." 6 Now
some of the experts in the law were sitting there, turning these
things over in their minds: 7 "Why does this man speak this way?
He is blaspheming! Who can forgive sins but God alone?" 8 Now
immediately, when Jesus realized in his spirit that they were
contemplating such thoughts, he said to them, "Why are you
thinking such things in your hearts? 9 Which is easier, to say to
the paralytic, 'Your sins are forgiven,' or to say, 'Stand up, take
your stretcher, and walk'? 10 But so that you may know that the
Son of Man has authority on earth to forgive sins,"—he said to
the paralytic—11 "I tell you, stand up, take your stretcher, and go
home." 12 And immediately the man stood up, took his stretcher,
and went out in front of them all. They were all amazed and
glorified God, saying, "We have never seen anything like this!"

THE CALL OF LEVI; EATING WITH SINNERS

13 Jesus went out again by the sea. The whole crowd came to
him, and he taught them. 14 As he went along, he saw Levi, the
son of Alphaeus, sitting at the tax booth. "Follow me," he said
to him. And he got up and followed him. 15 As Jesus was having
a meal in Levi's home, many tax collectors and sinners were
eating with Jesus and his disciples, for there were many who
followed him. 16 When the experts in the law and the Pharisees
saw that he was eating with sinners and tax collectors, they
said to his disciples, "Why does he eat with tax collectors and
sinners?" 17 When Jesus heard this he said to them, "Those who
are healthy don't need a physician, but those who are sick do. I
have not come to call the righteous, but sinners."

THE SUPERIORITY OF THE NEW

18 Now John's disciples and the Pharisees were fasting. So they
came to Jesus and said, "Why do the disciples of John and the
disciples of the Pharisees fast, but your disciples don't fast?"
19 Jesus said to them, "The wedding guests cannot fast while
the bridegroom is with them, can they? As long as they have
the bridegroom with them they do not fast. 20 But the days are
coming when the bridegroom will be taken from them, and
at that time they will fast. 21 No one sews a patch of unshrunk
cloth on an old garment; otherwise, the patch pulls away from
it, the new from the old, and the tear becomes worse. 22 And no
one pours new wine into old wineskins; otherwise, the wine
will burst the skins, and both the wine and the skins will be
destroyed. Instead new wine is poured into new wineskins."

2:23—3:6 In the synagogue of the Jews was a man who had a withered hand. The ones who stood by were withered in their minds. Before doing the work, the Savior first softened them up in advance with words so as to tame the wildness of their understanding, asking, "Is it lawful to do good on the Sabbath?" If a person falls into a hole on a Sabbath, Jews are permitted to pull the person out. In this way the law agrees that things relating to preservation may be done, hence Jews prepare meals on the Sabbath. When he asked them about a point on which they could hardly disagree—*Is it permitted to do good?*—they did not even so much as say yes because by then they were not in a good temper.

ATHANASIUS (C. 296–373)
LETTERS

LORD OF THE SABBATH

23 Jesus was going through the grain fields on a Sabbath, and his
disciples began to pick some heads of wheat as they made their
way. 24 So the Pharisees said to him, "Look, why are they doing
what is against the law on the Sabbath?" 25 He said to them,
"Have you never read what David did when he was in need and
he and his companions were hungry—26 how he entered the
house of God when Abiathar was high priest and ate the sacred
bread, which is against the law for any but the priests to eat,
and also gave it to his companions?" 27 Then he said to them,
"The Sabbath was made for people, not people for the Sabbath.
28 For this reason the Son of Man is lord even of the Sabbath."

HEALING A WITHERED HAND

3 Then Jesus entered the synagogue again, and a man was there
who had a withered hand. 2 They watched Jesus closely to see
if he would heal him on the Sabbath, so that they could accuse
him. 3 So he said to the man who had the withered hand, "Stand
up among all these people." 4 Then he said to them, "Is it lawful to
do good on the Sabbath, or evil, to save a life or destroy it?" But
they were silent. 5 After looking around at them in anger, grieved
by the hardness of their hearts, he said to the man, "Stretch out
your hand." He stretched it out, and his hand was restored. 6 So
the Pharisees went out immediately and began plotting with
the Herodians, as to how they could assassinate him.

CROWDS BY THE SEA

7 Then Jesus went away with his disciples to the sea, and a great
multitude from Galilee followed him. And from Judea, 8 Jerusalem, Idumea, beyond the Jordan River, and around Tyre and

MARTIN BUCER:

UNSUNG REFORMATION HERO
1491–1551

The names Martin Luther and John Calvin are probably familiar given they are nearly synonymous with the Protestant Reformation. But what about Martin Bucer, the theologian from Strassburg, Germany? Although he left no Bucerian legacy, as Luther did with Lutheranism or Calvin with Calvinism, he helped shape the Reformation from behind the scenes.

Born in 1491 to a working-class family of barrel makers in the free city of Alsace within the Holy Roman Empire, Bucer became a novice within the Dominican religious order after his primary education in 1507. Three years later he became a friar. But he soon began to follow Martin Luther after being persuaded by Luther's full-throated defense of his views in Heidelberg. He was fiercely committed to Luther and his teachings but was no less committed to working as a peacemaker. For example, he attempted to mediate between Luther and Ulrich Zwingli during their conflict over the nature of the Lord's Supper. Bucer's impulse toward reconciliation extended not only to followers of Luther and Zwingli, but also to the Anabaptists and the Roman Catholic Church, demonstrating his commitment to the unity of the entire body of Christ even in the midst of serious conflict. His open-mindedness, desire for peaceful reconciliation, and ongoing quest for Christian unity was recognized amongst his contemporaries as an important contribution to the Reformation cause.

Bucer was also influential in organizing the Protestant church in Strassburg and establishing it as a potential center for the Protestant church, a new Rome or new Jerusalem. His work *On the Kingdom of Christ*, written to King Edward VI, sought to influence the direction of English Christianity by infusing the established church with the principles of the Reformation and shaping the national and ecclesial life of England. In this work he exhorted Christian government leaders to "firmly restore for their peoples the blessed kingdom of the Son of God, our only Redeemer . . . [to] renew, institute, and establish the administration not only of religion but also of all other parts of the common life according to the purpose of Christ our Savior and supreme King." This was not a systematic theology, but rather an irenic vision for the ideal society, rooted in a God-centered government under the unity of Christian fellowship.

A largely unsung hero of the Reformation, Bucer deserves to be honored along with Luther and Calvin given his influence behind the scenes of the Reformation and his being embraced by Anglicans, Puritans, Lutherans, and Calvinists alike.

IMPORTANT WORKS

ON THE KINGDOM OF CHRIST

ON THE TRUE CURE OF SOULS

DIALOGUES ON THE CHRISTIAN MAGISTRATE

Sidon a great multitude came to him when they heard about
the things he had done. [9]Because of the crowd, he told his disciples to have a small boat ready for him so the crowd would
not press toward him. [10]For he had healed many, so that all
who were afflicted with diseases pressed toward him in order
to touch him. [11]And whenever the unclean spirits saw him,
they fell down before him and cried out, "You are the Son of
God." [12]But he sternly ordered them not to make him known.

APPOINTING THE 12 APOSTLES

[13]Now Jesus went up the mountain and called for those he
wanted, and they came to him. [14]He appointed 12 so that they
would be with him and he could send them to preach [15]and
to have authority to cast out demons. [16]To Simon he gave the
name Peter; [17]to James and his brother John, the sons of Zebedee, he gave the name Boanerges (that is, "sons of thunder");
[18]and Andrew, Philip, Bartholomew, Matthew, Thomas, James
the son of Alphaeus, Thaddaeus, Simon the Zealot, [19]and Judas
Iscariot, who betrayed him.

JESUS AND BEELZEBUL

[20]Now Jesus went home, and a crowd gathered so that they
were not able to eat. [21]When his family heard this they went
out to restrain him, for they said, "He is out of his mind." [22]The
experts in the law who came down from Jerusalem said, "He
is possessed by Beelzebul," and, "By the ruler of demons he
casts out demons!" [23]So he called them and spoke to them in
parables: "How can Satan cast out Satan? [24]If a kingdom is divided against itself, that kingdom will not be able to stand. [25]If
a house is divided against itself, that house will not be able to
stand. [26]And if Satan rises against himself and is divided, he is
not able to stand and his end has come. [27]But no one is able to
enter a strong man's house and steal his property unless he first
ties up the strong man. Then he can thoroughly plunder his
house. [28]I tell you the truth, people will be forgiven for all sins,
even all the blasphemies they utter. [29]But whoever blasphemes
against the Holy Spirit will never be forgiven, but is guilty of an
eternal sin" [30](because they said, "He has an unclean spirit").

JESUS' TRUE FAMILY

[31]Then Jesus' mother and his brothers came. Standing outside,
they sent word to him, to summon him. [32]A crowd was sitting
around him and they said to him, "Look, your mother and your
brothers are outside looking for you." [33]He answered them and
said, "Who are my mother and my brothers?" [34]And looking at
those who were sitting around him in a circle, he said, "Here
are my mother and my brothers! [35]For whoever does the will
of God is my brother and sister and mother."

THE PARABLE OF THE SOWER

4 Again he began to teach by the lake. Such a large crowd gathered around him that he got into a boat on the lake and sat
there while the whole crowd was on the shore by the lake. [2]He
taught them many things in parables, and in his teaching said
to them: [3]"Listen! A sower went out to sow. [4]And as he sowed,
some seed fell along the path, and the birds came and devoured
it. [5]Other seed fell on rocky ground where it did not have much
soil. It sprang up at once because the soil was not deep. [6]When
the sun came up it was scorched, and because it did not have

4:1–20 **Since we could not enter in, for our sins had shut the door to us, he came out to us. He came to till and to take care of the earth: to sow the word of compassion. For here he calls his teaching seed, the souls of people a plowed field, and himself the sower. As the sower fairly and indiscriminately disperses seed broadly over all his field, so does God offer gifts to all, making no distinction between rich and poor, wise and foolish, lazy or diligent, brave or cowardly. He addresses everyone, fulfilling his part, although knowing the results beforehand.**

CHRYSOSTOM **(C. 347–407)**
ON TEMPERANCE

sufficient root, it withered. 7 Other seed fell among the thorns,
and they grew up and choked it, and it did not produce grain.
8 But other seed fell on good soil and produced grain, sprouting
and growing; some yielded thirty times as much, some sixty,
and some a hundred times." 9 And he said, "Whoever has ears
to hear had better listen!"

THE PURPOSE OF PARABLES

10 When he was alone, those around him with the twelve asked
him about the parables. 11 He said to them, "The secret of the
kingdom of God has been given to you. But to those outside,
everything is in parables,

12 "so that ***although they look they may look but not see,***
and although they hear they may hear but not
understand,
so they may not repent and be forgiven."

13 He said to them, "Don't you understand this parable? Then
how will you understand any parable? 14 The sower sows the
word. 15 These are the ones on the path where the word is sown:
Whenever they hear, immediately Satan comes and snatches
the word that was sown in them. 16 These are the ones sown on
rocky ground: As soon as they hear the word, they receive it with
joy. 17 But they have no root in themselves and do not endure.
Then, when trouble or persecution comes because of the word,
immediately they fall away. 18 Others are the ones sown among
thorns: They are those who hear the word, 19 but worldly cares,
the seductiveness of wealth, and the desire for other things
come in and choke the word, and it produces nothing. 20 But
these are the ones sown on good soil: They hear the word and
receive it and bear fruit, one thirty times as much, one sixty,
and one a hundred."

THE PARABLE OF THE LAMP

21 He also said to them, "A lamp isn't brought to be put under a
basket or under a bed, is it? Isn't it to be placed on a lampstand?
22 For nothing is hidden except to be revealed, and nothing
concealed except to be brought to light. 23 If anyone has ears
to hear, he had better listen!" 24 And he said to them, "Take care
about what you hear. The measure you use will be the measure
you receive, and more will be added to you. 25 For whoever has
will be given more, but whoever does not have, even what he
has will be taken from him."

THE PARABLE OF THE GROWING SEED

26 He also said, "The kingdom of God is like someone who spreads
seed on the ground. 27 He goes to sleep and gets up, night and
day, and the seed sprouts and grows, though he does not know
how. 28 By itself the soil produces a crop, first the stalk, then
the head, then the full grain in the head. 29 And when the grain
is ripe, he sends in the sickle because the harvest has come."

THE PARABLE OF THE MUSTARD SEED

30 He also asked, "To what can we compare the kingdom of God,
or what parable can we use to present it? 31 It is like a mustard
seed that when sown in the ground, even though it is the smallest of all the seeds in the ground—32 when it is sown, it grows
up, becomes the greatest of all garden plants, and grows large
branches so that the wild birds can nest in its shade."

THE USE OF PARABLES

33 So with many parables like these, he spoke the word to them,
as they were able to hear. 34 He did not speak to them without
a parable. But privately he explained everything to his own
disciples.

STILLING OF A STORM

35 On that day, when evening came, Jesus said to his disciples,
"Let's go across to the other side of the lake." 36 So after leaving
the crowd, they took him along, just as he was, in the boat, and
other boats were with him. 37 Now a great windstorm developed
and the waves were breaking into the boat, so that the boat
was nearly swamped. 38 But he was in the stern, sleeping on a
cushion. They woke him up and said to him, "Teacher, don't
you care that we are about to die?" 39 So he got up and rebuked
the wind, and said to the sea, "Be quiet! Calm down!" Then the
wind stopped, and it was dead calm. 40 And he said to them,
"Why are you cowardly? Do you still not have faith?" 41 They
were overwhelmed by fear and said to one another, "Who then
is this? Even the wind and sea obey him!"

HEALING OF A DEMONIAC

5 So they came to the other side of the lake, to the region of the
Gerasenes. 2 Just as Jesus was getting out of the boat, a man
with an unclean spirit came from the tombs and met him. 3 He
lived among the tombs, and no one could bind him anymore,
not even with a chain. 4 For his hands and feet had often been
bound with chains and shackles, but he had torn the chains
apart and broken the shackles in pieces. No one was strong
enough to subdue him. 5 Each night and every day among the
tombs and in the mountains, he would cry out and cut himself
with stones. 6 When he saw Jesus from a distance, he ran and
bowed down before him. 7 Then he cried out with a loud voice,
"Leave me alone, Jesus, Son of the Most High God! I implore
you by God—do not torment me!" 8 (For Jesus had said to him,
"Come out of that man, you unclean spirit!") 9 Jesus asked him,
"What is your name?" And he said, "My name is Legion, for we
are many." 10 He begged Jesus repeatedly not to send them out
of the region. 11 There on the hillside, a great herd of pigs was
feeding. 12 And the demonic spirits begged him, "Send us into
the pigs. Let us enter them." 13 Jesus gave them permission.
So the unclean spirits came out and went into the pigs. Then
the herd rushed down the steep slope into the lake, and about
2,000 were drowned in the lake.

14 Now the herdsmen ran off and spread the news in the
town and countryside, and the people went out to see what
had happened. 15 They came to Jesus and saw the demon-
possessed man sitting there, clothed, and in his right mind—
the one who had the "Legion"—and they were afraid. 16 Those
who had seen what had happened to the demon-possessed
man reported it, and they also told about the pigs. 17 Then
they began to beg Jesus to leave their region. 18 As he was
getting into the boat the man who had been demon-possessed
asked if he could go with him. 19 But Jesus did not permit him
to do so. Instead, he said to him, "Go to your home and to
your people and tell them what the Lord has done for you,
that he had mercy on you." 20 So he went away and began to
proclaim in the Decapolis what Jesus had done for him, and
all were amazed.

5:1–20 God's supremacy and loftiness and Christ's nature are recognized but only the more abhorred: "Even the demons believe . . . and tremble with fear" (Jas 2:19). Christ's mere presence makes the flock of obscene creatures nested in the man uneasy, like bats in a cave who flutter against a light. They shrink from him and shudderingly renounce all connection with him, as if their cries would alter facts or make him relax his grip. How striking is Christ's unmoved calm in the face of all this fury! He is always laconic in dealing with demoniacs; and no doubt his tranquil presence helped to calm the man however it excited the demons.

ALEXANDER MACLAREN
(1826–1910)
EXPOSITIONS OF THE HOLY SCRIPTURES

RESTORATION AND HEALING

[21]When Jesus had crossed again in a boat to the other side, a large crowd gathered around him, and he was by the sea. [22]Then one of the synagogue leaders, named Jairus, came up, and when he saw Jesus, he fell at his feet. [23]He asked him urgently, "My little daughter is near death. Come and lay your hands on her so that she may be healed and live." [24]Jesus went with him, and a large crowd followed and pressed around him.

[25]Now a woman was there who had been suffering from a hemorrhage for 12 years. [26]She had endured a great deal under the care of many doctors and had spent all that she had. Yet instead of getting better, she grew worse. [27]When she heard about Jesus, she came up behind him in the crowd and touched his cloak, [28]for she kept saying, "If only I touch his clothes, I will be healed." [29]At once the bleeding stopped, and she felt in her body that she was healed of her disease. [30]Jesus knew at once that power had gone out from him. He turned around in the crowd and said, "Who touched my clothes?" [31]His disciples said to him, "You see the crowd pressing against you and you say, 'Who touched me?'" [32]But he looked around to see who had done it. [33]Then the woman, with fear and trembling, knowing what had happened to her, came and fell down before him and told him the whole truth. [34]He said to her, "Daughter, your faith has made you well. Go in peace, and be healed of your disease."

[35]While he was still speaking, people came from the synagogue leader's house saying, "Your daughter has died. Why trouble the teacher any longer?" [36]But Jesus, paying no attention to what was said, told the synagogue leader, "Do not be afraid; just believe." [37]He did not let anyone follow him except Peter, James, and John, the brother of James. [38]They came to the house of the synagogue leader where he saw noisy confusion and people weeping and wailing loudly. [39]When he entered he said to them, "Why are you distressed and weeping? The child is not dead but asleep!" [40]And they began making fun of him. But he forced them all outside, and he took the child's father and mother and his own companions and went into the room where the child was. [41]Then, gently taking the child by the hand, he said to her, "*Talitha koum*," which means, "Little girl, I say to you, get up." [42]The girl got up at once and began to walk around (she was twelve years old). They were completely astonished at this. [43]He strictly ordered that no one should know about this, and told them to give her something to eat.

REJECTION AT NAZARETH

6 Now Jesus left that place and came to his hometown, and his disciples followed him. [2]When the Sabbath came, he began to teach in the synagogue. Many who heard him were astonished, saying, "Where did he get these ideas? And what is this wisdom that has been given to him? What are these miracles that are done through his hands? [3]Isn't this the carpenter, the son of Mary and brother of James, Joses, Judas, and Simon? And aren't his sisters here with us?" And so they took offense at him. [4]Then Jesus said to them, "A prophet is not without honor except in his hometown, and among his relatives, and in his own house." [5]He was not able to do a miracle there, except to lay his hands on a few sick people and heal them. [6]And he was amazed because of their unbelief. Then he went around among the villages and taught.

6:1–6 Certainly unbelievers, as far as lies in their power, bind up the hands of God by their obstinacy; not that God is overcome as if he were an inferior, but because they do not permit him to display his power. We must observe, however, what Mark adds, that some sick people, notwithstanding, were cured; for hence we infer that the goodness of Christ strove with their malice and triumphed over every obstacle. We have experience of the same thing daily with respect to God, for though he justly and reluctantly restrains his power because the entrance to us is shut against him, yet we see that he opens up a path for himself where none exists and ceases not to bestow favors upon us.

JOHN CALVIN **(1509–1564)**
COMPLETE COMMENTARY ON THE BIBLE

SENDING OUT THE 12 APOSTLES

[7]Jesus called the twelve and began to send them out two by two.
He gave them authority over the unclean spirits. [8]He instructed
them to take nothing for the journey except a staff—no bread,
no bag, no money in their belts—[9]and to put on sandals but not
to wear two tunics. [10]He said to them, "Wherever you enter a
house, stay there until you leave the area. [11]If a place will not
welcome you or listen to you, as you go out from there, shake
the dust off your feet as a testimony against them." [12]So they
went out and preached that all should repent. [13]They cast out
many demons and anointed many sick people with olive oil
and healed them.

THE DEATH OF JOHN THE BAPTIST

[14]Now King Herod heard this, for Jesus' name had become
known. Some were saying, "John the baptizer has been raised
from the dead, and because of this, miraculous powers are at
work in him." [15]Others said, "He is Elijah." Others said, "He is a
prophet, like one of the prophets from the past." [16]But when
Herod heard this, he said, "John, whom I beheaded, has been
raised!" [17]For Herod himself had sent men, arrested John, and
bound him in prison on account of Herodias, his brother Philip's
wife, because Herod had married her. [18]For John had repeatedly
told Herod, "It is not lawful for you to have your brother's wife."
[19]So Herodias nursed a grudge against him and wanted to kill
him. But she could not [20]because Herod stood in awe of John
and protected him, since he knew that John was a righteous and
holy man. When Herod heard him, he was thoroughly baffled,
and yet he liked to listen to John.

[21]But a suitable day came, when Herod gave a banquet on
his birthday for his court officials, military commanders, and
leaders of Galilee. [22]When his daughter Herodias came in and
danced, she pleased Herod and his dinner guests. The king
said to the girl, "Ask me for whatever you want and I will give
it to you." [23]He swore to her, "Whatever you ask I will give
you, up to half my kingdom." [24]So she went out and said to
her mother, "What should I ask for?" Her mother said, "The
head of John the baptizer." [25]Immediately she hurried back to
the king and made her request: "I want the head of John the
Baptist on a platter immediately." [26]Although it grieved the
king deeply, he did not want to reject her request because of
his oath and his guests. [27]So the king sent an executioner at
once to bring John's head, and he went and beheaded John
in prison. [28]He brought his head on a platter and gave it to
the girl, and the girl gave it to her mother. [29]When John's
disciples heard this, they came and took his body and placed
it in a tomb.

THE FEEDING OF THE 5,000

[30]Then the apostles gathered around Jesus and told him everything they had done and taught. [31]He said to them, "Come with
me privately to an isolated place and rest a while" (for many
were coming and going, and there was no time to eat). [32]So
they went away by themselves in a boat to some remote place.
[33]But many saw them leaving and recognized them, and they
hurried on foot from all the towns and arrived there ahead of
them. [34]As Jesus came ashore he saw the large crowd, and he
had compassion on them because they were like sheep without
a shepherd. So he taught them many things.

35 When it was already late, his disciples came to him and
said, "This is an isolated place and it is already very late. 36 Send
them away so that they can go into the surrounding countryside
and villages and buy something for themselves to eat." 37 But
he answered them, "You give them something to eat." And they
said, "Should we go and buy bread for 200 silver coins and give
it to them to eat?" 38 He said to them, "How many loaves do you
have? Go and see." When they found out, they said, "Five—and
two fish." 39 Then he directed them all to sit down in groups on
the green grass. 40 So they reclined in groups of hundreds and
fifties. 41 He took the five loaves and the two fish, and looking
up to heaven, he gave thanks and broke the loaves. He gave
them to his disciples to serve the people, and he divided the
two fish among them all. 42 They all ate and were satisfied, 43 and
they picked up the broken pieces and fish that were left over,
12 baskets full. 44 Now there were 5,000 men who ate the bread.

WALKING ON WATER

45 Immediately Jesus made his disciples get into the boat and go
on ahead to the other side, to Bethsaida, while he dispersed the
crowd. 46 After saying goodbye to them, he went to the mountain
to pray. 47 When evening came, the boat was in the middle of the
sea and he was alone on the land. 48 He saw them straining at the
oars because the wind was against them. As the night was ending,
he came to them walking on the sea, for he wanted to pass by them.
49 When they saw him walking on the water they thought he was
a ghost. They cried out, 50 for they all saw him and were terrified.
But immediately he spoke to them: "Have courage! It is I. Do not
be afraid." 51 Then he went up with them into the boat, and the
wind ceased. They were completely astonished, 52 because they did
not understand about the loaves, but their hearts were hardened.

HEALING THE SICK

53 After they had crossed over, they came to land at Gennesaret
and anchored there. 54 As they got out of the boat, people immediately recognized Jesus. 55 They ran through that whole
region and began to bring the sick on mats to wherever he
was rumored to be. 56 And wherever he would go—into villages,
towns, or countryside—they would place the sick in the marketplaces, and would ask him if they could just touch the edge
of his cloak, and all who touched it were healed.

BREAKING HUMAN TRADITIONS

7 Now the Pharisees and some of the experts in the law who
came from Jerusalem gathered around him. 2 And they saw
that some of Jesus' disciples ate their bread with unclean hands,
that is, unwashed. 3 (For the Pharisees and all the Jews do not
eat unless they perform a ritual washing, holding fast to the
tradition of the elders. 4 And when they come from the marketplace, they do not eat unless they wash. They hold fast to many
other traditions: the washing of cups, pots, kettles, and dining
couches.) 5 The Pharisees and the experts in the law asked him,
"Why do your disciples not live according to the tradition of the
elders, but eat with unwashed hands?" 6 He said to them, "Isaiah prophesied correctly about you hypocrites, as it is written:

> "'***This people honors me with their lips,***
> ***but their hearts are far from me.***
> 7 ***They worship me in vain,***
> ***teaching as doctrine the commandments of men.***'

7:1–23 What obstinacy or what presumption to prefer human tradition to divine ordinance and not to observe that God is indignant and angry as often as human tradition relaxes and passes by the divine precepts, as he cries out and says by Isaiah the prophet, "This people honors me with their lips, but their heart is far from me. They worship me in vain, teaching as doctrine the commandments of men" (Isa 29:13; Mark 7:6–7). Also the Lord in the gospel, similarly rebuking and reproving, says, "Having no regard for the command of God, you hold fast to human tradition."

CYPRIAN OF CARTHAGE
(C. 210–258)
THE EPISTLES

[8]Having no regard for the command of God, you hold fast to human tradition." [9]He also said to them, "You neatly reject the commandment of God in order to set up your tradition. [10]For Moses said, '***Honor your father and your mother,***' and, '***Whoever insults his father or mother must be put to death.***' [11]But you say that if anyone tells his father or mother, 'Whatever help you would have received from me is *corban*' (that is, a gift for God), [12]then you no longer permit him to do anything for his father or mother. [13]Thus you nullify the word of God by your tradition that you have handed down. And you do many things like this."

[14]Then he called the crowd again and said to them, "Listen to me, everyone, and understand. [15]There is nothing outside of a person that can defile him by going into him. Rather, it is what comes out of a person that defiles him."*

[17]Now when Jesus had left the crowd and entered the house, his disciples asked him about the parable. [18]He said to them, "Are you so foolish? Don't you understand that whatever goes into a person from outside cannot defile him? [19]For it does not enter his heart but his stomach, and then goes out into the sewer." (This means all foods are clean.) [20]He said, "What comes out of a person defiles him. [21]For from within, out of the human heart, come evil ideas, sexual immorality, theft, murder, [22]adultery, greed, evil, deceit, debauchery, envy, slander, pride, and folly. [23]All these evils come from within and defile a person."

A SYROPHOENICIAN WOMAN'S FAITH

[24]After Jesus left there, he went to the region of Tyre. When he went into a house, he did not want anyone to know, but he was not able to escape notice. [25]Instead, a woman whose young daughter had an unclean spirit immediately heard about him and came and fell at his feet. [26]The woman was a Greek, of Syrophoenician origin. She asked him to cast the demon out of her daughter. [27]He said to her, "Let the children be satisfied first, for it is not right to take the children's bread and to throw it to the dogs." [28]She answered, "Yes, Lord, but even the dogs under the table eat the children's crumbs." [29]Then he said to her, "Because you said this, you may go. The demon has left your daughter." [30]She went home and found the child lying on the bed, and the demon gone.

HEALING A DEAF MUTE

[31]Then Jesus went out again from the region of Tyre and came through Sidon to the Sea of Galilee in the region of the Decapolis. [32]They brought to him a deaf man who had difficulty speaking, and they asked him to place his hands on him. [33]After Jesus took him aside privately, away from the crowd, he put his fingers in the man's ears, and after spitting, he touched his tongue. [34]Then he looked up to heaven and said with a sigh, "*Ephphatha*" (that is, "Be opened"). [35]And immediately the man's ears were opened, his tongue loosened, and he spoke plainly. [36]Jesus ordered them not to tell anyone. But as much as he ordered them not to do this, they proclaimed it all the more. [37]People were completely astounded and said, "He has done everything well. He even makes the deaf hear and the mute speak."

THE FEEDING OF THE 4,000

8 In those days there was another large crowd with nothing to eat. So Jesus called his disciples and said to them, [2]"I have compassion on the crowd because they have already been here with me three days, and they have nothing to eat. [3]If I send them home

---

8:1–11 The disciples manifest excessive stupidity in not remembering, at least, that earlier proof of the power and grace of Christ that they might have applied to the case in hand. As if they had never seen anything of the same sort, they forget to apply to him for relief. There is not a day on which a similar indifference does not steal upon us; and we ought to be the more careful not to allow our minds to be drawn away from the contemplation of divine benefits, that the experience of the past may lead us to expect for the future the same assistance that God has already bestowed upon us.

JOHN CALVIN (1509–1564)
COMPLETE COMMENTARY ON THE BIBLE

hungry, they will faint on the way, and some of them have come
from a great distance." 4His disciples answered him, "Where can
someone get enough bread in this desolate place to satisfy these
people?" 5He asked them, "How many loaves do you have?" They
replied, "Seven." 6Then he directed the crowd to sit down on the
ground. After he took the seven loaves and gave thanks, he broke
them and began giving them to the disciples to serve. So they
served the crowd. 7They also had a few small fish. After giving
thanks for these, he told them to serve these as well. 8Everyone
ate and was satisfied, and they picked up the broken pieces left
over, seven baskets full. 9There were about 4,000 who ate. Then
he dismissed them. 10Immediately he got into a boat with his
disciples and went to the district of Dalmanutha.

THE DEMAND FOR A SIGN

11Then the Pharisees came and began to argue with Jesus, asking for a sign from heaven to test him. 12Sighing deeply in his
spirit he said, "Why does this generation look for a sign? I tell
you the truth, no sign will be given to this generation." 13Then
he left them, got back into the boat, and went to the other side.

THE YEAST OF THE PHARISEES AND HEROD

14Now they had forgotten to take bread, except for one loaf they
had with them in the boat. 15And Jesus ordered them, "Watch
out! Beware of the yeast of the Pharisees and the yeast of Herod!"
16So they began to discuss with one another about having no
bread. 17When he learned of this, Jesus said to them, "Why are
you arguing about having no bread? Do you still not see or understand? Have your hearts been hardened? 18Though you have
eyes, don't you see? And though you have ears, can't you hear?
Don't you remember? 19When I broke the five loaves for the
5,000, how many baskets full of pieces did you pick up?" They
replied, "Twelve." 20"When I broke the seven loaves for the 4,000,
how many baskets full of pieces did you pick up?" They replied,
"Seven." 21Then he said to them, "Do you still not understand?"

A TWO-STAGE HEALING

22Then they came to Bethsaida. They brought a blind man to
Jesus and asked him to touch him. 23He took the blind man by
the hand and brought him outside of the village. Then he spit
on his eyes, placed his hands on his eyes and asked, "Do you
see anything?" 24Regaining his sight he said, "I see people, but
they look like trees walking." 25Then Jesus placed his hands
on the man's eyes again. And he opened his eyes, his sight was
restored, and he saw everything clearly. 26Jesus sent him home,
saying, "Do not even go into the village."

PETER'S CONFESSION

27Then Jesus and his disciples went to the villages of Caesarea
Philippi. On the way he asked his disciples, "Who do people say
that I am?" 28They said, "John the Baptist, others say Elijah, and
still others, one of the prophets." 29He asked them, "But who do
you say that I am?" Peter answered him, "You are the Christ."
30Then he warned them not to tell anyone about him.

FIRST PREDICTION OF JESUS' DEATH AND RESURRECTION

31Then Jesus began to teach them that the Son of Man must
suffer many things and be rejected by the elders, chief priests,

and experts in the law, and be killed, and after three days rise
again. 32He spoke openly about this. So Peter took him aside
and began to rebuke him. 33But after turning and looking at
his disciples, he rebuked Peter and said, "Get behind me, Satan.
You are not setting your mind on God's interests, but on man's."

FOLLOWING JESUS

34Then Jesus called the crowd, along with his disciples, and
said to them, "If anyone wants to become my follower, he must
deny himself, take up his cross, and follow me. 35For whoever
wants to save his life will lose it, but whoever loses his life because of me and because of the gospel will save it. 36For what
benefit is it for a person to gain the whole world, yet forfeit his
life? 37What can a person give in exchange for his life? 38For if
anyone is ashamed of me and my words in this adulterous and
sinful generation, the Son of Man will also be ashamed of him
when he comes in the glory of his Father with the holy angels."

9 1And he said to them, "I tell you the truth, there are some
standing here who will not experience death before they see
the kingdom of God come with power."

THE TRANSFIGURATION

2Six days later Jesus took with him Peter, James, and John and
led them alone up a high mountain privately. And he was transfigured before them, 3and his clothes became radiantly white,
more so than any launderer in the world could bleach them.
4Then Elijah appeared before them along with Moses, and they
were talking with Jesus. 5So Peter said to Jesus, "Rabbi, it is good
for us to be here. Let us make three shelters—one for you, one
for Moses, and one for Elijah." 6(For they were afraid, and he did
not know what to say.) 7Then a cloud overshadowed them, and
a voice came from the cloud, "This is my one dear Son. Listen
to him!" 8Suddenly when they looked around, they saw no one
with them any more except Jesus.

9As they were coming down from the mountain, he gave them
orders not to tell anyone what they had seen until after the Son
of Man had risen from the dead. 10They kept this statement to
themselves, discussing what this rising from the dead meant.
11Then they asked him, "Why do the experts in the law say
that Elijah must come first?" 12He said to them, "Elijah does
indeed come first, and restores all things. And why is it written
that the Son of Man must suffer many things and be despised?
13But I tell you that Elijah has certainly come, and they did to
him whatever they wanted, just as it is written about him."

THE DISCIPLES' FAILURE TO HEAL

14When they came to the disciples, they saw a large crowd
around them and experts in the law arguing with them. 15When
the whole crowd saw him, they were amazed and ran at once
and greeted him. 16He asked them, "What are you arguing about
with them?" 17A member of the crowd said to him, "Teacher,
I brought you my son, who is possessed by a spirit that makes
him mute. 18Whenever it seizes him, it throws him down, and
he foams at the mouth, grinds his teeth, and becomes rigid. I
asked your disciples to cast it out, but they were not able to do
so." 19He answered them, "You unbelieving generation! How
much longer must I be with you? How much longer must I
endure you? Bring him to me." 20So they brought the boy to
him. When the spirit saw him, it immediately threw the boy

9:4 When the Son of God in his transfiguration is so understood and beheld as if his face were a sun, and his clothes white as the light itself, immediately it will appear to those who behold Jesus in this way that he is conversing with Moses (the law) and Elijah (the prophets), holding conversation not with one prophet only but symbolically with all the prophets.

ORIGEN **(C. 185–C. 253)**
COMMENTARY ON THE GOSPEL OF MATTHEW

into a convulsion. He fell on the ground and rolled around,
foaming at the mouth. 21 Jesus asked his father, "How long has
this been happening to him?" And he said, "From childhood.
22 It has often thrown him into fire or water to destroy him. But
if you are able to do anything, have compassion on us and help
us." 23 Then Jesus said to him, "'If you are able?' All things are
possible for the one who believes." 24 Immediately the father of
the boy cried out and said, "I believe; help my unbelief!"
25 Now when Jesus saw that a crowd was quickly gathering, he
rebuked the unclean spirit, saying to it, "Mute and deaf spirit,
I command you, come out of him and never enter him again."
26 It shrieked, threw him into terrible convulsions, and came
out. The boy looked so much like a corpse that many said, "He
is dead!" 27 But Jesus gently took his hand and raised him to his
feet, and he stood up.
28 Then, after he went into the house, his disciples asked him
privately, "Why couldn't we cast it out?" 29 He told them, "This
kind can come out only by prayer."

SECOND PREDICTION OF JESUS' DEATH AND RESURRECTION

30 They went out from there and passed through Galilee. But
Jesus did not want anyone to know, 31 for he was teaching his
disciples and telling them, "The Son of Man will be betrayed
into the hands of men. They will kill him, and after three days
he will rise." 32 But they did not understand this statement and
were afraid to ask him.

QUESTIONS ABOUT THE GREATEST

33 Then they came to Capernaum. After Jesus was inside the
house he asked them, "What were you discussing on the way?"
34 But they were silent, for on the way they had argued with one
another about who was the greatest. 35 After he sat down, he
called the twelve and said to them, "If anyone wants to be first,
he must be last of all and servant of all." 36 He took a little child
and had him stand among them. Taking him in his arms, he
said to them, 37 "Whoever welcomes one of these little children
in my name welcomes me, and whoever welcomes me does not
welcome me but the one who sent me."

ON JESUS' SIDE

38 John said to him, "Teacher, we saw someone casting out demons in your name, and we tried to stop him because he was
not following us." 39 But Jesus said, "Do not stop him because no
one who does a miracle in my name will be able soon afterward
to say anything bad about me. 40 For whoever is not against us
is for us. 41 For I tell you the truth, whoever gives you a cup of
water because you bear Christ's name will never lose his reward.
42 "If anyone causes one of these little ones who believe in
me to sin, it would be better for him to have a huge millstone
tied around his neck and to be thrown into the sea. 43 If your
hand causes you to sin, cut it off! It is better for you to enter
into life crippled than to have two hands and go into hell, to
the unquenchable fire.† 45 If your foot causes you to sin, cut it
off! It is better to enter life lame than to have two feet and be
thrown into hell.‡ 47 If your eye causes you to sin, tear it out! It
is better to enter into the kingdom of God with one eye than
to have two eyes and be thrown into hell, 48 where their worm
never dies and the fire is never quenched. 49 Everyone will be

salted with fire. 50Salt is good, but if it loses its saltiness, how
can you make it salty again? Have salt in yourselves, and be at
peace with each other."

10:1–12 It is abundantly clear that God ordained monogamy at the beginning as a pattern for posterity. For after he had made Adam, he borrowed from his loins one alone. One woman only did he design for man. What kind of yoke is that of two believers who share one hope, one desire, one discipline, one service? They enjoy kinship in spirit and in flesh. Truly they are two in one flesh. Where the flesh is one, the spirit is one as well. Neither hides anything from the other. Neither neglects the other. Neither is troublesome to the other.

TERTULLIAN (155–C. 220)
EXHORTATION TO CHASTITY AND TO HIS WIFE

DIVORCE

10 Then Jesus left that place and went to the region of Judea
and beyond the Jordan River. Again crowds gathered to
him, and again, as was his custom, he taught them. 2Then some
Pharisees came, and to test him they asked, "Is it lawful for a
man to divorce his wife?" 3He answered them, "What did Moses
command you?" 4They said, "Moses permitted a man *to write*
a certificate of dismissal *and to divorce* her." 5But Jesus said to
them, "He wrote this commandment for you because of your
hard hearts. 6But from the beginning of creation ***he made them***
male and female. 7***For this reason a man will leave his father and***
mother, 8***and the two will become one flesh.*** So they are no longer
two, but one flesh. 9Therefore what God has joined together,
let no one separate."

10In the house once again, the disciples asked him about
this. 11So he told them, "Whoever divorces his wife and marries
another commits adultery against her. 12And if she divorces her
husband and marries another, she commits adultery."

JESUS AND LITTLE CHILDREN

13Now people were bringing little children to him for him to
touch, but the disciples scolded those who brought them. 14But
when Jesus saw this, he was indignant and said to them, "Let
the little children come to me and do not try to stop them, for
the kingdom of God belongs to such as these. 15I tell you the
truth, whoever does not receive the kingdom of God like a child
will never enter it." 16After he took the children in his arms, he
placed his hands on them and blessed them.

THE RICH MAN

17Now as Jesus was starting out on his way, someone ran up
to him, fell on his knees, and said, "Good teacher, what must
I do to inherit eternal life?" 18Jesus said to him, "Why do you
call me good? No one is good except God alone. 19You know
the commandments: '***Do not murder, do not commit adultery,***
do not steal, do not give false testimony, *do not defraud,* ***honor***
your father and mother.'" 20The man said to him, "Teacher, I
have wholeheartedly obeyed all these laws since my youth."
21As Jesus looked at him, he felt love for him and said, "You
lack one thing. Go, sell whatever you have and give the money
to the poor, and you will have treasure in heaven. Then come,
follow me." 22But at this statement, the man looked sad and
went away sorrowful, for he was very rich.

23Then Jesus looked around and said to his disciples, "How
hard it is for the rich to enter the kingdom of God!" 24The disciples were astonished at these words. But again Jesus said to
them, "Children, how hard it is to enter the kingdom of God! 25It
is easier for a camel to go through the eye of a needle than for
a rich person to enter the kingdom of God." 26They were even
more astonished and said to one another, "Then who can be
saved?" 27Jesus looked at them and replied, "This is impossible
for mere humans, but not for God; all things are possible for God."

28Peter began to speak to him, "Look, we have left everything to follow you!" 29Jesus said, "I tell you the truth, there is
no one who has left home or brothers or sisters or mother or

father or children or fields for my sake and for the sake of the
gospel 30who will not receive in this age a hundred times as
much—homes, brothers, sisters, mothers, children, fields, all
with persecutions—and in the age to come, eternal life. 31But
many who are first will be last, and the last first."

THIRD PREDICTION OF JESUS' DEATH AND RESURRECTION

32They were on the way, going up to Jerusalem. Jesus was going
ahead of them, and they were amazed, but those who followed
were afraid. He took the twelve aside again and began to tell
them what was going to happen to him. 33"Look, we are going
up to Jerusalem, and the Son of Man will be handed over to the
chief priests and experts in the law. They will condemn him to
death and will turn him over to the Gentiles. 34They will mock
him, spit on him, flog him severely, and kill him. Yet after three
days, he will rise again."

THE REQUEST OF JAMES AND JOHN

35Then James and John, the sons of Zebedee, came to him and
said, "Teacher, we want you to do for us whatever we ask." 36He said
to them, "What do you want me to do for you?" 37They said to
him, "Permit one of us to sit at your right hand and the other
at your left in your glory." 38But Jesus said to them, "You don't
know what you are asking! Are you able to drink the cup I drink
or be baptized with the baptism I experience?" 39They said to
him, "We are able." Then Jesus said to them, "You will drink
the cup I drink, and you will be baptized with the baptism I
experience, 40but to sit at my right or at my left is not mine to
give. It is for those for whom it has been prepared."

41Now when the other 10 heard this, they became angry with
James and John. 42Jesus called them and said to them, "You know
that those who are recognized as rulers of the Gentiles lord it
over them, and those in high positions use their authority over
them. 43But it is not this way among you. Instead whoever wants
to be great among you must be your servant, 44and whoever
wants to be first among you must be the slave of all. 45For even
the Son of Man did not come to be served but to serve, and to
give his life as a ransom for many."

HEALING BLIND BARTIMAEUS

46They came to Jericho. As Jesus and his disciples and a large
crowd were leaving Jericho, Bartimaeus the son of Timaeus, a
blind beggar, was sitting by the road. 47When he heard that it
was Jesus the Nazarene, he began to shout, "Jesus, Son of David,
have mercy on me!" 48Many scolded him to get him to be quiet,
but he shouted all the more, "Son of David, have mercy on me!"
49Jesus stopped and said, "Call him." So they called the blind
man and said to him, "Have courage! Get up! He is calling you."
50He threw off his cloak, jumped up, and came to Jesus. 51Then
Jesus said to him, "What do you want me to do for you?" The
blind man replied, "Rabbi, let me see again." 52Jesus said to him,
"Go, your faith has healed you." Immediately he regained his
sight and followed him on the road.

THE TRIUMPHAL ENTRY

11 Now as they approached Jerusalem, near Bethphage and
Bethany, at the Mount of Olives, Jesus sent two of his disciples 2and said to them, "Go to the village ahead of you. As soon

11:1–11 Christ's coming into Jerusalem remarkably shows that he was not afraid of the power and malice of his enemies. This would encourage his disciples who were full of fear. But all marked his humiliation, and these matters teach how ill it becomes Christians to take a lofty viewpoint when Christ was so far from claiming it! They welcomed his person: "Blessed is the one who comes," the he who should come so often promised, so long expected; he comes in the name of the Lord. Let him have our best affections; he is a blessed Savior and brings blessings to us, and blessed be he who sent him. Praises be to our God who is in the highest heavens, over all, God blessed forever.

MATTHEW HENRY **(1662–1714)**
COMMENTARY ON THE WHOLE BIBLE

as you enter it, you will find a colt tied there that has never been
ridden. Untie it and bring it here. 3If anyone says to you, 'Why are
you doing this?' say, 'The Lord needs it and will send it back here
soon.'" 4So they went and found a colt tied at a door, outside in the
street, and untied it. 5Some people standing there said to them,
"What are you doing, untying that colt?" 6They replied as Jesus had
told them, and the bystanders let them go. 7Then they brought
the colt to Jesus, threw their cloaks on it, and he sat on it. 8Many
spread their cloaks on the road and others spread branches they
had cut in the fields. 9Both those who went ahead and those who
followed kept shouting, "***Hosanna! Blessed is the one who comes in***
the name of the Lord! 10Blessed is the coming kingdom of our father
David! Hosanna in the highest!" 11Then Jesus entered Jerusalem
and went to the temple. And after looking around at everything,
he went out to Bethany with the twelve since it was already late.

CURSING OF THE FIG TREE

12Now the next day, as they went out from Bethany, he was
hungry. 13After noticing in the distance a fig tree with leaves,
he went to see if he could find any fruit on it. When he came
to it he found nothing but leaves, for it was not the season for
figs. 14He said to it, "May no one ever eat fruit from you again."
And his disciples heard it.

CLEANSING THE TEMPLE

15Then they came to Jerusalem. Jesus entered the temple area
and began to drive out those who were selling and buying in the
temple courts. He turned over the tables of the money changers
and the chairs of those selling doves, 16and he would not permit anyone to carry merchandise through the temple courts.
17Then he began to teach them and said, "Is it not written: '***My***
house will be called a house of prayer for all nations'? But you
have turned it into ***a den of robbers***!" 18The chief priests and
the experts in the law heard it, and they considered how they
could assassinate him, for they feared him because the whole
crowd was amazed by his teaching. 19When evening came, Jesus
and his disciples went out of the city.

THE WITHERED FIG TREE

20In the morning as they passed by, they saw the fig tree withered from the roots. 21Peter remembered and said to him, "Rabbi, look! The fig tree you cursed has withered." 22Jesus said to
them, "Have faith in God. 23I tell you the truth, if someone
says to this mountain, 'Be lifted up and thrown into the sea,'
and does not doubt in his heart but believes that what he says
will happen, it will be done for him. 24For this reason I tell you,
whatever you pray and ask for, believe that you have received
it, and it will be yours. 25Whenever you stand praying, if you
have anything against anyone, forgive him, so that your Father
in heaven will also forgive you your sins."§

THE AUTHORITY OF JESUS

27They came again to Jerusalem. While Jesus was walking in the
temple courts, the chief priests, the experts in the law, and the
elders came up to him 28and said, "By what authority are you
doing these things? Or who gave you this authority to do these
things?" 29Jesus said to them, "I will ask you one question. Answer me and I will tell you by what authority I do these things:
30John's baptism—was it from heaven or from people? Answer

me." 31They discussed with one another, saying, "If we say, 'From
heaven,' he will say, 'Then why did you not believe him?' 32But
if we say, 'From people...'" (they feared the crowd, for they all
considered John to be truly a prophet). 33So they answered
Jesus, "We don't know." Then Jesus said to them, "Neither will
I tell you by what authority I am doing these things."

THE PARABLE OF THE TENANTS

12 Then he began to speak to them in parables: "A man planted a vineyard. He put a fence around it, dug a pit for its
winepress, and built a watchtower. Then he leased it to tenant
farmers and went on a journey. 2At harvest time he sent a slave
to the tenants to collect from them his portion of the crop.
3But those tenants seized his slave, beat him, and sent him
away empty-handed. 4So he sent another slave to them again.
This one they struck on the head and treated outrageously. 5He
sent another, and that one they killed. This happened to many
others, some of whom were beaten, others killed. 6He had one
left, his one dear son. Finally he sent him to them, saying, 'They
will respect my son.' 7But those tenants said to one another,
'This is the heir. Come, let's kill him and the inheritance will be
ours!' 8So they seized him, killed him, and threw his body out
of the vineyard. 9What then will the owner of the vineyard do?
He will come and destroy those tenants and give the vineyard
to others. 10Have you not read this scripture:

"'***The stone the builders rejected has become the***
cornerstone.
11 ***This is from the Lord, and it is marvelous in our eyes***'?"

12Now they wanted to arrest him (but they feared the crowd),
because they realized that he told this parable against them.
So they left him and went away.

PAYING TAXES TO CAESAR

13Then they sent some of the Pharisees and Herodians to trap
him with his own words. 14When they came they said to him,
"Teacher, we know that you are truthful and do not court anyone's favor because you show no partiality but teach the way
of God in accordance with the truth. Is it right to pay taxes to
Caesar or not? Should we pay or shouldn't we?" 15But he saw
through their hypocrisy and said to them, "Why are you testing me? Bring me a denarius and let me look at it." 16So they
brought one, and he said to them, "Whose image is this, and
whose inscription?" They replied, "Caesar's." 17Then Jesus said
to them, "Give to Caesar the things that are Caesar's, and to God
the things that are God's." And they were utterly amazed at him.

MARRIAGE AND THE RESURRECTION

18Sadducees (who say there is no resurrection) also came to
him and asked him, 19"Teacher, Moses wrote for us: '***If a man's***
brother dies and leaves a wife but no children, that man must
marry the widow and father children for his brother.' 20There
were seven brothers. The first one married, and when he died
he had no children. 21The second married her and died without
any children, and likewise the third. 22None of the seven had
children. Finally, the woman died too. 23In the resurrection,
when they rise again, whose wife will she be? For all seven had
married her." 24Jesus said to them, "Aren't you deceived for this
reason because you don't know the scriptures or the power of
God? 25For when they rise from the dead, they neither marry

nor are given in marriage, but are like angels in heaven. [26]Now as for the dead being raised, have you not read in the book of Moses, in the passage about the bush, how God said to him, '*I am the God of Abraham, the God of Isaac, and the God of Jacob*'? [27]He is not the God of the dead but of the living. You are badly mistaken!"

THE GREATEST COMMANDMENT

[28]Now one of the experts in the law came and heard them debating. When he saw that Jesus answered them well, he asked him, "Which commandment is the most important of all?" [29]Jesus answered, "The most important is: '***Listen, Israel, the Lord our God, the Lord is one.*** [30]***Love the Lord your God with all your heart, with all your soul, with all your mind, and with all your strength.***' [31]The second is: '***Love your neighbor as yourself.***' There is no other commandment greater than these." [32]The expert in the law said to him, "That is true, Teacher; you are right to say that ***he is one, and there is no one else besides him.*** [33]And ***to love him with all your heart, with all your mind, and with all your strength*** and ***to love your neighbor as yourself*** is more important than all burnt offerings and sacrifices." [34]When Jesus saw that he had answered thoughtfully, he said to him, "You are not far from the kingdom of God." Then no one dared any longer to question him.

12:29–34 We owe all our love to God alone—that is, the whole strength and capacity of our understanding, will, and affections. To love and serve him with all the united powers of the soul in their utmost vigor and to love our neighbor as ourselves; to maintain the same equitable and charitable temper and behavior toward all people, as we, in like circumstances, would wish from them toward ourselves, is a more necessary and important duty than offering the most noble and costly sacrifices.

JOHN WESLEY (1703–1791)
EXPLANATORY NOTES ON THE BIBLE

THE MESSIAH: DAVID'S SON AND LORD

[35]While Jesus was teaching in the temple courts, he said, "How is it that the experts in the law say that the Christ is David's son? [36]David himself, by the Holy Spirit, said,

> "'***The Lord said to my lord,***
> ***"Sit at my right hand,***
> ***until I put your enemies under your feet."***'

[37]If David himself calls him 'Lord,' how can he be his son?" And the large crowd was listening to him with delight.

WARNINGS ABOUT EXPERTS IN THE LAW

[38]In his teaching Jesus also said, "Watch out for the experts in the law. They like walking around in long robes and elaborate greetings in the marketplaces, [39]and the best seats in the synagogues and the places of honor at banquets. [40]They devour widows' property, and as a show make long prayers. These men will receive a more severe punishment."

THE WIDOW'S OFFERING

[41]Then he sat down opposite the offering box, and watched the crowd putting coins into it. Many rich people were throwing in large amounts. [42]And a poor widow came and put in two small copper coins, worth less than a penny. [43]He called his disciples and said to them, "I tell you the truth, this poor widow has put more into the offering box than all the others. [44]For they all gave out of their wealth. But she, out of her poverty, put in what she had to live on, everything she had."

THE DESTRUCTION OF THE TEMPLE

13 Now as Jesus was going out of the temple courts, one of his disciples said to him, "Teacher, look at these tremendous stones and buildings!" [2]Jesus said to him, "Do you see these great buildings? Not one stone will be left on another. All will be torn down!"

SIGNS OF THE END OF THE AGE

[3]So while he was sitting on the Mount of Olives opposite the
temple, Peter, James, John, and Andrew asked him privately,
[4]"Tell us, when will these things happen? And what will be the
sign that all these things are about to take place?" [5]Jesus began
to say to them, "Watch out that no one misleads you. [6]Many will
come in my name, saying, 'I am he,' and they will mislead many.
[7]When you hear of wars and rumors of wars, do not be alarmed.
These things must happen, but the end is still to come. [8]For
nation will rise up in arms against nation, and kingdom against
kingdom. There will be earthquakes in various places, and there
will be famines. These are but the beginning of birth pains.

PERSECUTION OF DISCIPLES

[9]"You must watch out for yourselves. You will be handed over to
councils and beaten in the synagogues. You will stand before governors and kings because of me, as a witness to them. [10]First the
gospel must be preached to all nations. [11]When they arrest you
and hand you over for trial, do not worry about what to speak. But
say whatever is given you at that time, for it is not you speaking,
but the Holy Spirit. [12]Brother will hand over brother to death,
and a father his child. Children will rise against parents and have
them put to death. [13]You will be hated by everyone because of
my name. But the one who endures to the end will be saved.

THE ABOMINATION OF DESOLATION

[14]"But when you see *the abomination of desolation* standing
where it should not be" (let the reader understand), "then those
in Judea must flee to the mountains. [15]The one on the roof must
not come down or go inside to take anything out of his house.
[16]The one in the field must not turn back to get his cloak. [17]Woe
to those who are pregnant and to those who are nursing their
babies in those days! [18]Pray that it may not be in winter. [19]For
in those days there will be suffering unlike anything that has
happened from the beginning of the creation that God created
until now, or ever will happen. [20]And if the Lord had not cut
short those days, no one would be saved. But because of the
elect, whom he chose, he has cut them short. [21]Then if anyone
says to you, 'Look, here is the Christ!' or 'Look, there he is!' do
not believe him. [22]For false messiahs and false prophets will
appear and perform signs and wonders to deceive, if possible,
the elect. [23]Be careful! I have told you everything ahead of time.

THE ARRIVAL OF THE SON OF MAN

[24]"But in those days, after that suffering, *the sun will be darkened
and the moon will not give its light;* [25]*the stars will be falling from
heaven, and the powers in the heavens will be shaken.* [26]Then everyone will see *the Son of Man arriving in the clouds* with great
power and glory. [27]Then he will send angels and they will gather
his elect from the four winds, from the ends of the earth to the
ends of heaven.

THE PARABLE OF THE FIG TREE

[28]"Learn this parable from the fig tree: Whenever its branch
becomes tender and puts out its leaves, you know that summer
is near. [29]So also you, when you see these things happening, know
that he is near, right at the door. [30]I tell you the truth, this generation will not pass away until all these things take place. [31]Heaven
and earth will pass away, but my words will never pass away.

13:1–13 The Lord exhorts us to wait with patient and reverent faith until the end comes, for "the one who endures to the end will be saved." It is neither a blessed nothingness that awaits us, nor is nonexistence the fruit, nor annihilation the appointed reward of faith. Rather the end is the final attainment of the promised blessedness. They are blessed who endure until the goal of perfect happiness is reached, when the expectation of faith reaches toward complete fulfillment. Their end is to abide with unbroken rest in that condition toward which they are presently pressing.

HILARY OF POITIERS
(C. 310–C. 367)
ON THE TRINITY

BE READY!

32“But as for that day or hour no one knows it—neither the
angels in heaven, nor the Son—except the Father. 33Watch out!
Stay alert! For you do not know when the time will come. 34It
is like a man going on a journey. He left his house and put his
slaves in charge, assigning to each his work, and commanded the
doorkeeper to stay alert. 35Stay alert, then, because you do not
know when the owner of the house will return—whether during
evening, at midnight, when the rooster crows, or at dawn—36or
else he might find you asleep when he returns suddenly. 37What
I say to you I say to everyone: Stay alert!”

THE PLOT AGAINST JESUS

14 Two days before the Passover and the Feast of Unleavened
Bread, the chief priests and the experts in the law were
trying to find a way to arrest Jesus by stealth and kill him. 2For
they said, “Not during the feast, so there won’t be a riot among
the people.”

JESUS’ ANOINTING

3Now while Jesus was in Bethany at the house of Simon the
leper, reclining at the table, a woman came with an alabaster jar of costly aromatic oil from pure nard. After breaking
open the jar, she poured it on his head. 4But some who were
present indignantly said to one another, “Why this waste of
expensive ointment? 5It could have been sold for more than
300 silver coins and the money given to the poor!” So they
spoke angrily to her. 6But Jesus said, “Leave her alone. Why
are you bothering her? She has done a good service for me.
7For you will always have the poor with you, and you can do
good for them whenever you want. But you will not always
have me! 8She did what she could. She anointed my body beforehand for burial. 9I tell you the truth, wherever the gospel
is proclaimed in the whole world, what she has done will also
be told in memory of her.”

14:3–9 What Mary once did as a type, the entire church and every perfect soul should do always. We anoint our Lord’s head when we cherish the glory of his divinity along with that of his humanity with the worthy sweetness of faith, hope, and charity, and when we spread the praise of his name by living uprightly. We anoint our Lord’s feet when we renew his poor by a word of consolation so that they may not lose hope when they are under duress. We wipe the feet of these same ones with our hair when we share some of what is superfluous to us to alleviate the wants of the needy.

VENERABLE BEDE
(C. 672–735)
EXPOSITION ON THE GOSPEL OF MARK

THE PLAN TO BETRAY JESUS

10Then Judas Iscariot, one of the twelve, went to the chief priests
to betray Jesus into their hands. 11When they heard this, they
were delighted and promised to give him money. So Judas began
looking for an opportunity to betray him.

THE PASSOVER

12Now on the first day of the Feast of Unleavened Bread, when
the Passover lamb is sacrificed, Jesus’ disciples said to him,
“Where do you want us to prepare for you to eat the Passover?”
13He sent two of his disciples and told them, “Go into the city,
and a man carrying a jar of water will meet you. Follow him.
14Wherever he enters, tell the owner of the house, ‘The Teacher
says, “Where is my guest room where I may eat the Passover
with my disciples?”’ 15He will show you a large room upstairs,
furnished and ready. Make preparations for us there.” 16So the
disciples left, went into the city, and found things just as he had
told them, and they prepared the Passover.

17Then, when it was evening, he came to the house with
the twelve. 18While they were at the table eating, Jesus said, “I
tell you the truth, one of you eating with me will betray me.”
19They were distressed, and one by one said to him, “Surely
not I?” 20He said to them, “It is one of the twelve, one who dips

his hand with me into the bowl. [21]For the Son of Man will go as it is written about him, but woe to that man by whom the Son of Man is betrayed! It would be better for him if he had never been born."

THE LORD'S SUPPER

[22]While they were eating, he took bread, and after giving thanks he broke it, gave it to them, and said, "Take it. This is my body." [23]And after taking the cup and giving thanks, he gave it to them, and they all drank from it. [24]He said to them, "This is my blood, the blood of the covenant, that is poured out for many. [25]I tell you the truth, I will no longer drink of the fruit of the vine until that day when I drink it new in the kingdom of God." [26]After singing a hymn, they went out to the Mount of Olives.

THE PREDICTION OF PETER'S DENIAL

[27]Then Jesus said to them, "You will all fall away, for it is written,

> "'***I will strike the shepherd,***
> ***and the sheep will be scattered.***'

[28]But after I am raised, I will go ahead of you into Galilee." [29]Peter said to him, "Even if they all fall away, I will not!" [30]Jesus said to him, "I tell you the truth, today—this very night—before a rooster crows twice, you will deny me three times." [31]But Peter insisted emphatically, "Even if I must die with you, I will never deny you." And all of them said the same thing.

GETHSEMANE

[32]Then they went to a place called Gethsemane, and Jesus said to his disciples, "Sit here while I pray." [33]He took Peter, James, and John with him, and became very troubled and distressed. [34]He said to them, "My soul is deeply grieved, even to the point of death. Remain here and stay alert." [35]Going a little farther, he threw himself to the ground and prayed that if it were possible the hour would pass from him. [36]He said, "*Abba,* Father, all things are possible for you. Take this cup away from me. Yet not what I will, but what you will." [37]Then he came and found them sleeping, and said to Peter, "Simon, are you sleeping? Couldn't you stay awake for one hour? [38]Stay awake and pray that you will not fall into temptation. The spirit is willing, but the flesh is weak." [39]He went away again and prayed the same thing. [40]When he came again he found them sleeping; they could not keep their eyes open. And they did not know what to tell him. [41]He came a third time and said to them, "Are you still sleeping and resting? Enough of that! The hour has come. Look, the Son of Man is betrayed into the hands of sinners. [42]Get up, let us go. Look! My betrayer is approaching!"

BETRAYAL AND ARREST

[43]Right away, while Jesus was still speaking, Judas, one of the twelve, arrived. With him came a crowd armed with swords and clubs, sent by the chief priests and experts in the law and elders. [44](Now the betrayer had given them a sign, saying, "The one I kiss is the man. Arrest him and lead him away under guard.") [45]When Judas arrived, he went up to Jesus immediately and said, "Rabbi!" and kissed him. [46]Then they took hold of him and arrested him. [47]One of the bystanders drew his sword and struck the high priest's slave, cutting off his ear. [48]Jesus said to them, "Have you come with swords and clubs to arrest me like you would an outlaw? [49]Day after day I was with you, teaching

in the temple courts, yet you did not arrest me. But this has
happened so that the scriptures would be fulfilled." 50 Then all
the disciples left him and fled. 51 A young man was following
him, wearing only a linen cloth. They tried to arrest him, 52 but
he ran off naked, leaving his linen cloth behind.

CONDEMNED BY THE SANHEDRIN

53 Then they led Jesus to the high priest, and all the chief priests
and elders and experts in the law came together. 54 And Peter
had followed him from a distance, up to the high priest's courtyard. He was sitting with the guards and warming himself by
the fire. 55 The chief priests and the whole Sanhedrin were
looking for evidence against Jesus so that they could put him
to death, but they did not find anything. 56 Many gave false testimony against him, but their testimony did not agree. 57 Some
stood up and gave this false testimony against him: 58 "We heard
him say, 'I will destroy this temple made with hands and in
three days build another not made with hands.'" 59 Yet even on
this point their testimony did not agree. 60 Then the high priest
stood up before them and asked Jesus, "Have you no answer?
What is this that they are testifying against you?" 61 But he was
silent and did not answer. Again the high priest questioned
him, "Are you the Christ, the Son of the Blessed One?" 62 "I
am," said Jesus, "and you will see *the Son of Man sitting at the
right hand* of the Power and *coming with the clouds of heaven.*"
63 Then the high priest tore his clothes and said, "Why do we
still need witnesses? 64 You have heard the blasphemy! What
is your verdict?" They all condemned him as deserving death.
65 Then some began to spit on him, and to blindfold him, and
to strike him with their fists, saying, "Prophesy!" The guards
also took him and beat him.

PETER'S DENIALS

66 Now while Peter was below in the courtyard, one of the high
priest's slave girls came by. 67 When she saw Peter warming
himself, she looked directly at him and said, "You also were
with that Nazarene, Jesus." 68 But he denied it: "I don't even
understand what you're talking about!" Then he went out
to the gateway, and a rooster crowed. 69 When the slave girl
saw him, she began again to say to the bystanders, "This man
is one of them." 70 But he denied it again. A short time later
the bystanders again said to Peter, "You must be one of them
because you are also a Galilean." 71 Then he began to curse,
and he swore with an oath, "I do not know this man you are
talking about!" 72 Immediately a rooster crowed a second time.
Then Peter remembered what Jesus had said to him: "Before
a rooster crows twice, you will deny me three times." And he
broke down and wept.

JESUS BROUGHT BEFORE PILATE

15 Early in the morning, after forming a plan, the chief
priests with the elders and the experts in the law and
the whole Sanhedrin tied Jesus up, led him away, and handed
him over to Pilate. 2 So Pilate asked him, "Are you the king of the
Jews?" He replied, "You say so." 3 Then the chief priests began
to accuse him repeatedly. 4 So Pilate asked him again, "Have
you nothing to say? See how many charges they are bringing
against you!" 5 But Jesus made no further reply, so that Pilate
was amazed.

JESUS AND BARABBAS

6 During the feast it was customary to release one prisoner to the people, whomever they requested. 7 A man named Barabbas was imprisoned with rebels who had committed murder during an insurrection. 8 Then the crowd came up and began to ask Pilate to release a prisoner for them, as was his custom. 9 So Pilate asked them, "Do you want me to release the king of the Jews for you?" 10 (For he knew that the chief priests had handed him over because of envy.) 11 But the chief priests stirred up the crowd to have him release Barabbas instead. 12 So Pilate spoke to them again, "Then what do you want me to do with the one you call king of the Jews?" 13 They shouted back, "Crucify him!" 14 Pilate asked them, "Why? What has he done wrong?" But they shouted more insistently, "Crucify him!" 15 Because he wanted to satisfy the crowd, Pilate released Barabbas for them. Then, after he had Jesus flogged, he handed him over to be crucified.

JESUS IS MOCKED

16 So the soldiers led him into the palace (that is, the governor's residence) and called together the whole cohort. 17 They put a purple cloak on him and after braiding a crown of thorns, they put it on him. 18 They began to salute him: "Hail, king of the Jews!" 19 Again and again they struck him on the head with a staff and spit on him. Then they knelt down and paid homage to him. 20 When they had finished mocking him, they stripped him of the purple cloak and put his own clothes back on him. Then they led him away to crucify him.

THE CRUCIFIXION

21 The soldiers forced a passerby to carry his cross, Simon of Cyrene, who was coming in from the country (he was the father of Alexander and Rufus). 22 They brought Jesus to a place called Golgotha (which is translated, "Place of the Skull"). 23 They offered him wine mixed with myrrh, but he did not take it. 24 Then they crucified him and *divided his clothes, throwing dice* for them, to decide what each would take. 25 It was nine o'clock in the morning when they crucified him. 26 The inscription of the charge against him read, "The king of the Jews." 27 And they crucified two outlaws with him, one on his right and one on his left.|| 29 Those who passed by defamed him, shaking their heads and saying, "Aha! You who can destroy the temple and rebuild it in three days, 30 save yourself and come down from the cross!" 31 In the same way even the chief priests—together with the experts in the law—were mocking him among themselves: "He saved others, but he cannot save himself! 32 Let the Christ, the king of Israel, come down from the cross now, that we may see and believe!" Those who were crucified with him also spoke abusively to him.

JESUS' DEATH

33 Now when it was noon, darkness came over the whole land until three in the afternoon. 34 Around three o'clock Jesus cried out with a loud voice, "*Eloi, Eloi, lema sabachthani?*" which means, ***"My God, my God, why have you forsaken me?"*** 35 When some of the bystanders heard it they said, "Listen, he is calling for Elijah!" 36 Then someone ran, filled a sponge with sour wine, put it on a stick, and gave it to him to drink, saying, "Leave him alone! Let's see if Elijah will come to take him down!" 37 But Jesus cried

15:33–41 As being man he is amazed. Neither his power nor his Godhead is amazed, but his soul; he is amazed by consequence of having taken human infirmity upon him. Seeing, then, that he took upon himself a soul he also took the affections of a soul, for God could not have been distressed or have died in respect of his being God. Finally, he cried, "My God, my God, why have you forsaken me?" As being man therefore he speaks, bearing with him my terrors, for when we are in the midst of dangers we think ourself abandoned by God. As man therefore he is distressed, as man he weeps, as man he is crucified.

AMBROSE **(C. 339–C. 397)**
ON THE CHRISTIAN FAITH

out with a loud voice and breathed his last. 38And the temple curtain was torn in two, from top to bottom. 39Now when
the centurion, who stood in front of him, saw how he died, he
said, "Truly this man was God's Son!" 40There were also women,
watching from a distance. Among them were Mary Magdalene,
and Mary the mother of James the younger and of Joses, and
Salome. 41When he was in Galilee, they had followed him and
given him support. Many other women who had come up with
him to Jerusalem were there too.

JESUS' BURIAL

42Now when evening had already come, since it was the day of
preparation (that is, the day before the Sabbath), 43Joseph of
Arimathea, a highly regarded member of the council, who was
himself looking forward to the kingdom of God, went boldly
to Pilate and asked for the body of Jesus. 44Pilate was surprised
that he was already dead. He called the centurion and asked
him if he had been dead for some time. 45When Pilate was
informed by the centurion, he gave the body to Joseph. 46Af-
ter Joseph bought a linen cloth and took down the body, he
wrapped it in the linen and placed it in a tomb cut out of the
rock. Then he rolled a stone across the entrance of the tomb.
47Mary Magdalene and Mary the mother of Joses saw where
the body was placed.

THE RESURRECTION

16 When the Sabbath was over, Mary Magdalene, Mary the
mother of James, and Salome bought aromatic spices so
that they might go and anoint him. 2And very early on the first
day of the week, at sunrise, they went to the tomb. 3They had
been asking each other, "Who will roll away the stone for us from
the entrance to the tomb?" 4But when they looked up, they saw
that the stone, which was very large, had been rolled back. 5Then
as they went into the tomb, they saw a young man dressed in
a white robe sitting on the right side; and they were alarmed.
6But he said to them, "Do not be alarmed. You are looking for
Jesus the Nazarene, who was crucified. He has been raised! He
is not here. Look, there is the place where they laid him. 7But go,
tell his disciples, even Peter, that he is going ahead of you into
Galilee. You will see him there, just as he told you." 8Then they
went out and ran from the tomb, for terror and bewilderment
had seized them. And they said nothing to anyone, because
they were afraid.◖

> 16:1–8 He came down, he took upon himself, he endured, he vanquished, he restored. He came down from the throne of God to wretched mortal: he took upon himself mortality; he endured affliction and pain and ignominy; he vanquished death, he restored mankind. Stand still, my soul, and with holy astonishment gaze on the series of wonders, this inestimable complication of mercies; consider the greatness of his love.
>
> AUGUSTINE **(354–430)**
> ***SERMONS***

THE LONGER ENDING OF MARK

9[[Early on the first day of the week, after he arose, he appeared
first to Mary Magdalene, from whom he had driven out seven
demons. 10She went out and told those who were with him,
while they were mourning and weeping. 11And when they
heard that he was alive and had been seen by her, they did
not believe.

12After this he appeared in a different form to two of them
while they were on their way to the country. 13They went back
and told the rest, but they did not believe them. 14Then he appeared to the Eleven themselves, while they were eating, and he
rebuked them for their unbelief and hardness of heart because
they did not believe those who had seen him resurrected. 15He
said to them, "Go into all the world and preach the gospel to
every creature. 16The one who believes and is baptized will be

anointed to preach good news to the poor, heal the brokenhearted, set the captives free, liberate the oppressed, and proclaim the acceptable year of the Lord (4:18–19). His ministry inaugurated God's kingdom on earth, and he told his disciples to proclaim its nearness while also promising its ultimate fulfillment. His ultimate act was for the whole world—for everyone who would believe in him. He bore their sins through Roman crucifixion before being vindicated by the Father through the resurrection and exalted to his right hand through the ascension.

The third person of the Trinity, the Holy Spirit, is also prominently featured in Luke's Gospel. Referenced nearly 20 times, he was present from the beginning, coming upon Mary to conceive and birth God the Son (1:35). Then at Jesus' baptism, the Holy Spirit "descended on him in bodily form like a dove" (3:22), validating and energizing his ministry. The Holy Spirit empowered Jesus to accomplish the will of the Father. And Jesus himself promised the Spirit would be poured out upon his people, an event that finds fulfillment in Acts.

Finally, Luke's account of Jesus' life and ministry offers us important commentary on those considered the least in society. Women are an important part of his story, a remarkable fact given the way women were viewed in Jesus' day. In Luke's Gospel, women are exemplary, illustrating how to live pious and devout lives. Examples include women of wealth, such as Joanna, who helped fund the mission of Jesus and his disciples (8:3). Other examples include women of humbler means, like the sinful woman who washed Jesus' feet with her tears and wiped them with her hair (7:36–50). And women were the first to behold his resurrection, exhibiting deep faith by their testimony (24:1–11).

Luke pays special attention to another marginalized group: the poor, revealing God's care for those society neglects. From the blind and the lame to the leper, Luke puts Jesus' concern—and by extension, God's concern—for the downtrodden on display.

Perhaps this entry from the *Book of Common Prayer* (1549) is an appropriate prayer to have in your mind as you read Luke for yourself: "Almighty God, who called Luke the physician—whose praise is in his Gospel—to be a physician of the soul: May it please you by the wholesome medicine of his holy doctrine to heal all the diseases of our soul: through your Son Jesus Christ our Lord. Amen."

EXPLANATORY PREFACE

1 Now many have undertaken to compile an account of the
things that have been fulfilled among us, 2like the accounts
passed on to us by those who were eyewitnesses and servants of
the word from the beginning. 3So it seemed good to me as well,
because I have followed all things carefully from the beginning,
to write an orderly account for you, most excellent Theophilus,
4so that you may know for certain the things you were taught.

BIRTH ANNOUNCEMENT OF JOHN THE BAPTIST

5During the reign of Herod king of Judea, there lived a priest
named Zechariah who belonged to the priestly division of Abijah, and he had a wife named Elizabeth, who was a descendant of
Aaron. 6They were both righteous in the sight of God, following
all the commandments and ordinances of the Lord blamelessly.
7But they did not have a child because Elizabeth was barren,
and they were both very old.

8Now while Zechariah was serving as priest before God when
his division was on duty, 9he was chosen by lot, according to
the custom of the priesthood, to enter the Holy Place of the
Lord and burn incense. 10Now the whole crowd of people were
praying outside at the hour of the incense offering. 11An angel
of the Lord, standing on the right side of the altar of incense,
appeared to him. 12And Zechariah, visibly shaken when he saw
the angel, was seized with fear. 13But the angel said to him, "Do
not be afraid, Zechariah, for your prayer has been heard, and
your wife Elizabeth will bear you a son; you will name him John.
14Joy and gladness will come to you, and many will rejoice at
his birth, 15for he will be great in the sight of the Lord. He must
never drink wine or strong drink, and he will be filled with
the Holy Spirit, even before his birth. 16He will turn many of
the people of Israel to the Lord their God. 17And he will go as
forerunner before the Lord in the spirit and power of Elijah,
to turn the hearts of the fathers back to their children and the
disobedient to the wisdom of the just, to make ready for the
Lord a people prepared for him."

18Zechariah said to the angel, "How can I be sure of this?
For I am an old man, and my wife is old as well." 19The angel
answered him, "I am Gabriel, who stands in the presence of
God, and I was sent to speak to you and to bring you this good
news. 20And now because you did not believe my words, which
will be fulfilled in their time, you will be silent, unable to speak,
until the day these things take place."

21Now the people were waiting for Zechariah, and they began
to wonder why he was delayed in the Holy Place. 22When he
came out, he was not able to speak to them. They realized that
he had seen a vision in the Holy Place because he was making
signs to them and remained unable to speak. 23When his time
of service was over, he went to his home.

24After some time his wife Elizabeth became pregnant, and
for five months she kept herself in seclusion. She said, 25"This
is what the Lord has done for me at the time when he has been
gracious to me, to take away my disgrace among people."

BIRTH ANNOUNCEMENT OF JESUS THE MESSIAH

26In the sixth month of Elizabeth's pregnancy, the angel Gabriel
was sent by God to a town of Galilee called Nazareth, 27to a
virgin engaged to a man whose name was Joseph, a descendant of David, and the virgin's name was Mary. 28The angel

1:26–38 Behold, just consider what an unimaginable miracle I must announce to you. You will not give up your chaste being, and yet you will be pregnant in your womb with a Son. To understand that this is a great thing devised by God long ago, remember what the prophet Isaiah prophesied many hundreds of years ago concerning it: "Look, this young woman is about to conceive and will give birth to a son" (Isa 7:14). You yourself are this virgin who was in God's Word and mind long, long ago. In you will be fulfilled what has been hoped for so ardently for several thousand years. In you the one promised in paradise will begin to be what he is not, even if he is everything!

CATHARINA REGINA VON GREIFFENBERG
(1633–1694)
MEDITATIONS ON THE INCARNATION, PASSION, AND DEATH OF JESUS CHRIST

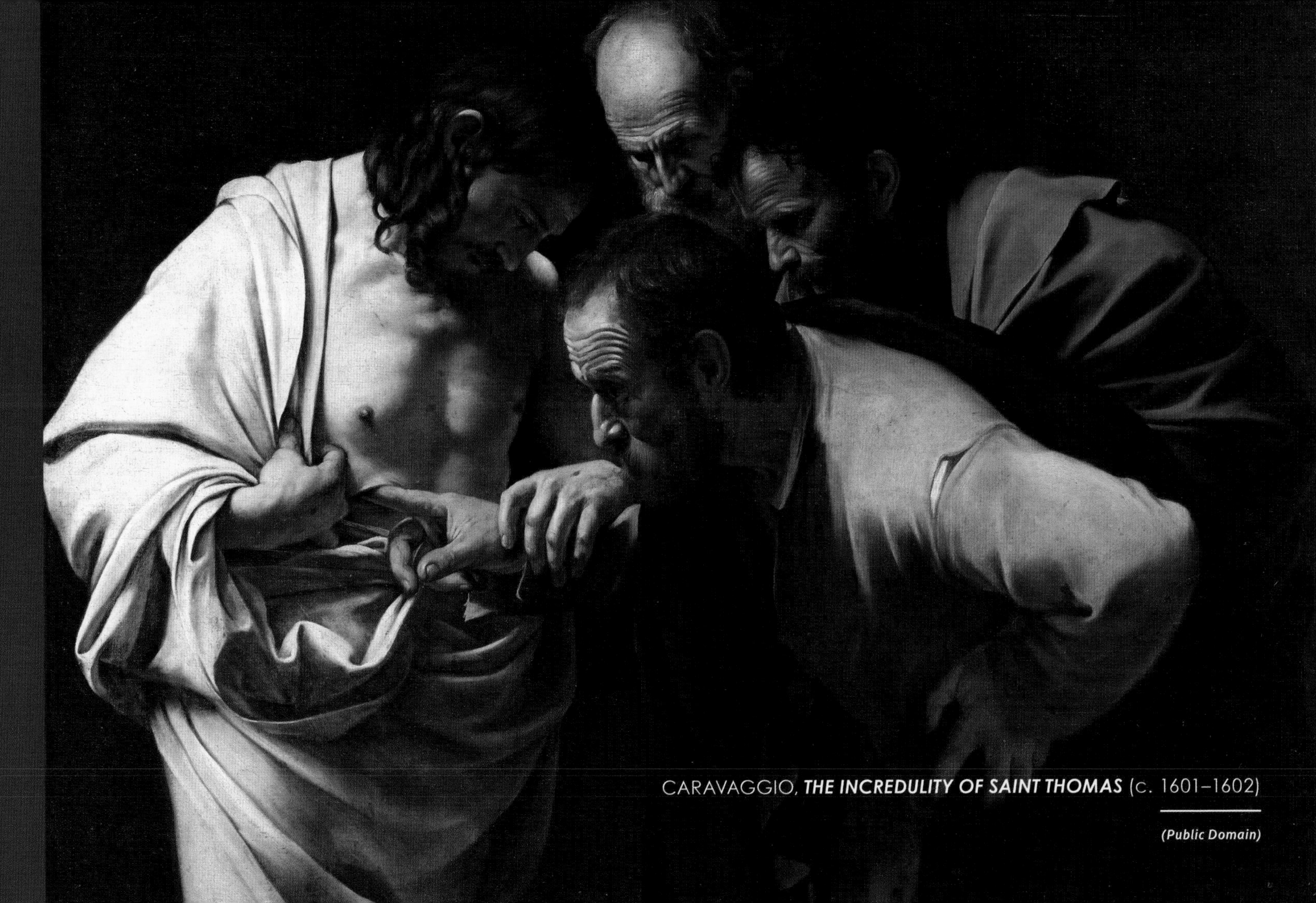

CARAVAGGIO, ***THE INCREDULITY OF SAINT THOMAS*** (c. 1601–1602)

(Public Domain)

THE APOSTLE PAUL, **ST. SOPHIA CATHEDRAL OF KYEV** (1000)

(Public Domain)

came to her and said, "Greetings, favored one, the Lord is with
you!" [29]But she was greatly troubled by his words and began
to wonder about the meaning of this greeting. [30]So the angel
said to her, "Do not be afraid, Mary, for you have found favor
with God! [31]Listen: You will become pregnant and give birth
to a son, and you will name him Jesus. [32]He will be great and
will be called the Son of the Most High, and the Lord God will
give him the throne of his father David. [33]He will reign over
the house of Jacob forever, and his kingdom will never end."
[34]Mary said to the angel, "How will this be, since I have not
been intimate with a man?" [35]The angel replied, "The Holy
Spirit will come upon you, and the power of the Most High
will overshadow you. Therefore the child to be born will be
holy; he will be called the Son of God.

[36]"And look, your relative Elizabeth has also become pregnant with a son in her old age—although she was called barren,
she is now in her sixth month! [37]For nothing will be impossible
with God." [38]So Mary said, "Yes, I am a servant of the Lord; let
this happen to me according to your word." Then the angel
departed from her.

MARY AND ELIZABETH

[39]In those days Mary got up and went hurriedly into the hill
country, to a town of Judah, [40]and entered Zechariah's house
and greeted Elizabeth. [41]When Elizabeth heard Mary's greeting,
the baby leaped in her womb, and Elizabeth was filled with the
Holy Spirit. [42]She exclaimed with a loud voice, "Blessed are you
among women, and blessed is the child in your womb! [43]And
who am I that the mother of my Lord should come and visit
me? [44]For the instant the sound of your greeting reached my
ears, the baby in my womb leaped for joy. [45]And blessed is she
who believed that what was spoken to her by the Lord would
be fulfilled."

MARY'S HYMN OF PRAISE

[46]And Mary said,

"My soul exalts the Lord,
47 and my spirit has begun to rejoice in God my Savior,
48 because he has looked upon the humble state of his servant.
For from now on all generations will call me blessed,
49 because he who is mighty has done great things for me,
and holy is his name;
50 from generation to generation he is merciful to those who fear him.
51 He has demonstrated power with his arm; he has scattered those whose pride wells up from the sheer arrogance of their hearts.
52 He has brought down the mighty from their thrones,
and has lifted up those of lowly position;
53 he has filled the hungry with good things, and has sent the rich away empty.
54 He has helped his servant Israel, remembering his mercy,
55 as he promised to our ancestors, to Abraham and to his descendants forever."

[56]So Mary stayed with Elizabeth about three months and
then returned to her home.

THE BIRTH OF JOHN

57 Now the time came for Elizabeth to have her baby, and she
gave birth to a son. 58 Her neighbors and relatives heard that the
Lord had shown great mercy to her, and they rejoiced with her.
59 On the eighth day they came to circumcise the child, and
they wanted to name him Zechariah after his father. 60 But his
mother replied, "No! He must be named John." 61 They said to
her, "But none of your relatives bears this name." 62 So they made
signs to the baby's father, inquiring what he wanted to name his
son. 63 He asked for a writing tablet and wrote, "His name is John."
And they were all amazed. 64 Immediately Zechariah's mouth was
opened and his tongue released, and he spoke, blessing God. 65 All
their neighbors were filled with fear, and throughout the entire
hill country of Judea all these things were talked about. 66 All who
heard these things kept them in their hearts, saying, "What then
will this child be?" For the Lord's hand was indeed with him.

ZECHARIAH'S PRAISE AND PREDICTION

67 Then his father Zechariah was filled with the Holy Spirit
and prophesied,

68 "Blessed be the Lord God of Israel,
because he has come to help and has redeemed his people.
69 For he has raised up a horn of salvation for us in the
house of his servant David,
70 as he spoke through the mouth of his holy prophets
from long ago,
71 that we should be saved from our enemies
and from the hand of all who hate us.
72 He has done this to show mercy to our ancestors,
and to remember his holy covenant—
73 the oath that he swore to our ancestor Abraham.
This oath grants
74 that we, being rescued from the hand of our enemies,
may serve him without fear,
75 in holiness and righteousness before him for as long as
we live.
76 And you, child, will be called the prophet of the Most High.
For you will go before the Lord to prepare his ways,
77 to give his people knowledge of salvation through the
forgiveness of their sins.
78 Because of our God's tender mercy,
the dawn will break upon us from on high
79 to give light to those who sit in darkness and in the
shadow of death,
to guide our feet into the way of peace."

80 And the child kept growing and becoming strong in spirit,
and he was in the wilderness until the day he was revealed to
Israel.

THE CENSUS AND THE BIRTH OF JESUS

2 Now in those days a decree went out from Caesar Augustus
to register all the empire for taxes. 2 This was the first registration, taken when Quirinius was governor of Syria. 3 Everyone
went to his own town to be registered. 4 So Joseph also went
up from the town of Nazareth in Galilee to Judea, to the city
of David called Bethlehem, because he was of the house and
family line of David. 5 He went to be registered with Mary, who
was promised in marriage to him, and who was expecting a

child. 6While they were there, the time came for her to deliver
her child. 7And she gave birth to her firstborn son and wrapped
him in strips of cloth and laid him in a manger, because there
was no place for them in the inn.

THE SHEPHERDS' VISIT

8Now there were shepherds nearby living out in the field, keeping guard over their flock at night. 9An angel of the Lord appeared to them, and the glory of the Lord shone around them,
and they were absolutely terrified. 10But the angel said to them,
"Do not be afraid! Listen carefully, for I proclaim to you good
news that brings great joy to all the people: 11Today your Savior
is born in the city of David. He is Christ the Lord. 12This will be
a sign for you: You will find a baby wrapped in strips of cloth and
lying in a manger." 13Suddenly a vast, heavenly army appeared
with the angel, praising God and saying,

14 "Glory to God in the highest,
and on earth peace among people with whom he is
pleased!"

15When the angels left them and went back to heaven, the
shepherds said to one another, "Let us go over to Bethlehem
and see this thing that has taken place, that the Lord has made
known to us." 16So they hurried off and located Mary and Joseph,
and found the baby lying in a manger. 17When they saw him,
they related what they had been told about this child, 18and all
who heard it were astonished at what the shepherds said. 19But
Mary treasured up all these words, pondering in her heart what
they might mean. 20So the shepherds returned, glorifying and
praising God for all they had heard and seen; everything was
just as they had been told.

21At the end of eight days, when he was circumcised, he was
named Jesus, the name given by the angel before he was conceived in the womb.

JESUS' PRESENTATION AT THE TEMPLE

22Now when the time came for their purification according to
the law of Moses, Joseph and Mary brought Jesus up to Jerusalem to present him to the Lord 23(just as it is written in the law
of the Lord, "*Every firstborn male will be set apart to the Lord*"),
24and to offer a sacrifice according to what is specified in the
law of the Lord, ***a pair of doves or two young pigeons.***

THE PROPHECY OF SIMEON

25Now there was a man in Jerusalem named Simeon who was
righteous and devout, looking for the restoration of Israel, and
the Holy Spirit was upon him. 26It had been revealed to him by
the Holy Spirit that he would not die before he had seen the
Lord's Christ. 27So Simeon, directed by the Spirit, came into
the temple courts, and when the parents brought in the child
Jesus to do for him what was customary according to the law,
28Simeon took him in his arms and blessed God, saying,

29 "Now, according to your word, Sovereign Lord, permit
your servant to depart in peace.
30 For my eyes have seen your salvation
31 that you have prepared in the presence of all peoples:
32 a light,
for revelation to the Gentiles
and for glory to your people Israel."

2:8–20 The word *gospel* means a good, joyful message that is the proclamation of the new covenant. The angel says, *I bring you good news of great joy.* Where is it? Listen again. "Today your Savior is born in the city of David. He is Christ the Lord." Whoever preaches him rightly preaches the gospel and pure joy. How can a heart hear of greater joy than that Christ is given to him as his own? He not only says that Christ is born but he also makes his birth our own by saying "your Savior." Therefore the gospel not only teaches the history and events of Christ but also makes him our own and gives him to all who believe it, which is the true and proper nature of the gospel.

MARTIN LUTHER **(1483–1546)**
THE CHURCH POSTIL

[33]So the child's father and mother were amazed at what was said about him. [34]Then Simeon blessed them and said to his mother Mary, "Listen carefully: This child is destined to be the cause of the falling and rising of many in Israel and to be a sign that will be rejected. [35]Indeed, as a result of him the thoughts of many hearts will be revealed—and a sword will pierce your own soul as well!"

THE TESTIMONY OF ANNA

[36]There was also a prophetess, Anna the daughter of Phanuel, of the tribe of Asher. She was very old, having been married to her husband for seven years until his death. [37]She had lived as a widow since then for eighty-four years. She never left the temple, worshiping with fasting and prayer night and day. [38]At that moment, she came up to them and began to give thanks to God and to speak about the child to all who were waiting for the redemption of Jerusalem.

[39]So when Joseph and Mary had performed everything according to the law of the Lord, they returned to Galilee, to their own town of Nazareth. [40]And the child grew and became strong, filled with wisdom, and the favor of God was upon him.

JESUS IN THE TEMPLE

[41]Now Jesus' parents went to Jerusalem every year for the Feast of the Passover. [42]When he was twelve years old, they went up according to custom. [43]But when the feast was over, as they were returning home, the boy Jesus stayed behind in Jerusalem. His parents did not know it, [44]but (because they assumed that he was in their group of travelers) they went a day's journey. Then they began to look for him among their relatives and acquaintances. [45]When they did not find him, they returned to Jerusalem to look for him. [46]After three days they found him in the temple courts, sitting among the teachers, listening to them and asking them questions. [47]And all who heard Jesus were astonished at his understanding and his answers. [48]When his parents saw him, they were overwhelmed. His mother said to him, "Child, why have you treated us like this? Look, your father and I have been looking for you anxiously." [49]But he replied, "Why were you looking for me? Didn't you know that I must be in my Father's house?" [50]Yet his parents did not understand the remark he made to them. [51]Then he went down with them and came to Nazareth, and was obedient to them. But his mother kept all these things in her heart.

[52]And Jesus increased in wisdom and in stature and in favor with God and with people.

THE MINISTRY OF JOHN THE BAPTIST

3 In the fifteenth year of the reign of Tiberius Caesar, when Pontius Pilate was governor of Judea, and Herod was tetrarch of Galilee, and his brother Philip was tetrarch of the region of Iturea and Trachonitis, and Lysanias was tetrarch of Abilene, [2]during the high priesthood of Annas and Caiaphas, the word of God came to John the son of Zechariah in the wilderness. [3]He went into all the region around the Jordan River, preaching a baptism of repentance for the forgiveness of sins.

[4]As it is written in the book of the words of the prophet Isaiah,

> ***"The voice of one shouting in the wilderness:***
> ***'Prepare the way for the Lord,***
> ***make his paths straight.***

3:1–6 The precursor of Christ—the voice of one crying in the wilderness—preaches in the desert of the soul that has known no peace. Not only then, but even now, a bright and burning lamp first comes and preaches the baptism of repentance for the forgiveness of sins. What way are we to prepare for the Lord? Surely not a material way. Can the Word of God go on such a journey? Should not the way be prepared for the Lord within? Should not straight and level paths be built in our hearts? This is the way by which the Word of God has entered. That Word dwells in the spaces of the human heart.

ORIGEN (C. 185–C. 253)
HOMILIES ON THE GOSPEL OF LUKE

5 ***Every valley will be filled,***
and every mountain and hill will be brought low,
and the crooked will be made straight,
and the rough ways will be made smooth,
6 ***and all humanity will see the salvation of God.'***"

7 So John said to the crowds that came out to be baptized
by him, "You offspring of vipers! Who warned you to flee from
the coming wrath? 8 Therefore produce fruit that proves your
repentance, and don't begin to say to yourselves, 'We have Abraham as our father.' For I tell you that God can raise up children
for Abraham from these stones! 9 Even now the ax is laid at the
root of the trees, and every tree that does not produce good
fruit will be cut down and thrown into the fire."
10 So the crowds were asking him, "What then should we do?"
11 John answered them, "The person who has two tunics must
share with the person who has none, and the person who has
food must do likewise." 12 Tax collectors also came to be baptized, and they said to him, "Teacher, what should we do?" 13 He
told them, "Collect no more than you are required to." 14 Then
some soldiers also asked him, "And as for us—what should we
do?" He told them, "Take money from no one by violence or by
false accusation, and be content with your pay."
15 While the people were filled with anticipation and they
all wondered whether perhaps John could be the Christ, 16 John
answered them all, "I baptize you with water, but one more
powerful than I am is coming—I am not worthy to untie the
strap of his sandals. He will baptize you with the Holy Spirit
and fire. 17 His winnowing fork is in his hand to clean out his
threshing floor and to gather the wheat into his storehouse,
but the chaff he will burn up with inextinguishable fire."
18 And in this way, with many other exhortations, John proclaimed good news to the people. 19 But when John rebuked
Herod the tetrarch because of Herodias, his brother's wife, and
because of all the evil deeds that he had done, 20 Herod added
this to them all: He locked up John in prison.

THE BAPTISM OF JESUS

21 Now when all the people were baptized, Jesus also was baptized. And while he was praying, the heavens opened, 22 and the
Holy Spirit descended on him in bodily form like a dove. And
a voice came from heaven, "You are my one dear Son; in you I
take great delight."

THE GENEALOGY OF JESUS

23 So Jesus, when he began his ministry, was about thirty years
old. He was the son (as was supposed) of Joseph, the son of
Heli, 24 the son of Matthat, the son of Levi, the son of Melchi,
the son of Jannai, the son of Joseph, 25 the son of Mattathias,
the son of Amos, the son of Nahum, the son of Esli, the son of
Naggai, 26 the son of Maath, the son of Mattathias, the son of
Semein, the son of Josech, the son of Joda, 27 the son of Joanan,
the son of Rhesa, the son of Zerubbabel, the son of Shealtiel,
the son of Neri, 28 the son of Melchi, the son of Addi, the son of
Cosam, the son of Elmadam, the son of Er, 29 the son of Joshua,
the son of Eliezer, the son of Jorim, the son of Matthat, the son
of Levi, 30 the son of Simeon, the son of Judah, the son of Joseph,
the son of Jonam, the son of Eliakim, 31 the son of Melea, the
son of Menna, the son of Mattatha, the son of Nathan, the son

of David, [32]the son of Jesse, the son of Obed, the son of Boaz, the son of Sala, the son of Nahshon, [33]the son of Amminadab, the son of Admin, the son of Arni, the son of Hezron, the son of Perez, the son of Judah, [34]the son of Jacob, the son of Isaac, the son of Abraham, the son of Terah, the son of Nahor, [35]the son of Serug, the son of Reu, the son of Peleg, the son of Eber, the son of Shelah, [36]the son of Cainan, the son of Arphaxad, the son of Shem, the son of Noah, the son of Lamech, [37]the son of Methuselah, the son of Enoch, the son of Jared, the son of Mahalalel, the son of Kenan, [38]the son of Enosh, the son of Seth, the son of Adam, the son of God.

4:1–13 The things that form the substance of innumerable evils are these: to be a slave to the belly, to do anything for vainglory, to be in subjection to the madness of riches—that accursed one set last the most powerful of all. In this way Christ taught us by fleeing to God for refuge, and neither to be depressed in famine as believing in God who is able to feed even with a word, nor amidst whatever good things we may receive to tempt him who gave them, but to be content with the glory which is from above, and on every occasion to despise what is beyond our need. For nothing so makes us fall under the power of the devil as longing for more and loving covetousness.

CHRYSOSTOM (C. 347–407)
HOMILIES ON THE GOSPEL OF MATTHEW

THE TEMPTATION OF JESUS

4 Then Jesus, full of the Holy Spirit, returned from the Jordan River and was led by the Spirit in the wilderness, [2]where for forty days he endured temptations from the devil. He ate nothing during those days, and when they were completed, he was famished. [3]The devil said to him, "If you are the Son of God, command this stone to become bread." [4]Jesus answered him, "It is written, '***Man does not live by bread alone.***'"

[5]Then the devil led him up to a high place and showed him in a flash all the kingdoms of the world. [6]And he said to him, "To you I will grant this whole realm—and the glory that goes along with it, for it has been relinquished to me, and I can give it to anyone I wish. [7]So then, if you will worship me, all this will be yours." [8]Jesus answered him, "It is written, '***You are to worship the Lord your God and serve*** *only* ***him.***'"

[9]Then the devil brought him to Jerusalem, had him stand on the highest point of the temple, and said to him, "If you are the Son of God, throw yourself down from here, [10]for it is written, '***He will command his angels concerning you, to protect you,***' [11]and '***with their hands they will lift you up, so that you will not strike your foot against a stone.***'" [12]Jesus answered him, "It is said, '***You are not to put the Lord your God to the test.***'" [13]So when the devil had completed every temptation, he departed from him until a more opportune time.

THE BEGINNING OF JESUS' MINISTRY IN GALILEE

[14]Then Jesus, in the power of the Spirit, returned to Galilee, and news about him spread throughout the surrounding countryside. [15]He began to teach in their synagogues and was praised by all.

REJECTION AT NAZARETH

[16]Now Jesus came to Nazareth, where he had been brought up, and went into the synagogue on the Sabbath day, as was his custom. He stood up to read, [17]and the scroll of the prophet Isaiah was given to him. He unrolled the scroll and found the place where it was written,

[18]"***The Spirit of the Lord is upon me,***
because he has anointed me to proclaim good news to the poor.
He has sent me to proclaim release to the captives
and the regaining of sight to the blind,
to set free those who are oppressed,
[19]***to proclaim the year of the Lord's favor.***"

[20]Then he rolled up the scroll, gave it back to the attendant, and sat down. The eyes of everyone in the synagogue were fixed

on him. 21 Then he began to tell them, "Today this scripture has
been fulfilled even as you heard it being read." 22 All were speaking
well of him, and were amazed at the gracious words coming out
of his mouth. They said, "Isn't this Joseph's son?" 23 Jesus said to
them, "No doubt you will quote to me the proverb, 'Physician,
heal yourself!' and say, 'What we have heard that you did in Capernaum, do here in your hometown too.'" 24 And he added, "I tell
you the truth, no prophet is acceptable in his hometown. 25 But
in truth I tell you, there were many widows in Israel in Elijah's
days, when the sky was shut up three and a half years and there
was a great famine over all the land. 26 Yet Elijah was sent to none
of them, but only to a woman who was a widow at Zarephath in
Sidon. 27 And there were many lepers in Israel in the time of the
prophet Elisha, yet none of them was cleansed except Naaman
the Syrian." 28 When they heard this, all the people in the synagogue were filled with rage. 29 They got up, forced him out of the
town, and brought him to the brow of the hill on which their town
was built, so that they could throw him down the cliff. 30 But he
passed through the crowd and went on his way.

MINISTRY IN CAPERNAUM

31 So he went down to Capernaum, a town in Galilee, and on the
Sabbath he began to teach the people. 32 They were amazed at
his teaching because he spoke with authority.

33 Now in the synagogue there was a man who had the spirit
of an unclean demon, and he cried out with a loud voice, 34 "Ha!
Leave us alone, Jesus the Nazarene! Have you come to destroy
us? I know who you are—the Holy One of God." 35 But Jesus rebuked him: "Silence! Come out of him!" Then, after the demon
threw the man down in their midst, he came out of him without
hurting him. 36 They were all amazed and began to say to one
another, "What's happening here? For with authority and power
he commands the unclean spirits, and they come out!" 37 So the
news about him spread into all areas of the region.

38 After Jesus left the synagogue, he entered Simon's house.
Now Simon's mother-in-law was suffering from a high fever,
and they asked Jesus to help her. 39 So he stood over her, commanded the fever, and it left her. Immediately she got up and
began to serve them.

40 As the sun was setting, all those who had any relatives sick
with various diseases brought them to Jesus. He placed his
hands on every one of them and healed them. 41 Demons also
came out of many, crying out, "You are the Son of God!" But he
rebuked them and would not allow them to speak because they
knew that he was the Christ.

42 The next morning Jesus departed and went to a deserted
place. Yet the crowds were seeking him, and they came to him
and tried to keep him from leaving them. 43 But Jesus said to
them, "I must proclaim the good news of the kingdom of God
to the other towns too, for that is what I was sent to do." 44 So
he continued to preach in the synagogues of Judea.

THE CALL OF THE DISCIPLES

5 Now Jesus was standing by the Lake of Gennesaret, and the
crowd was pressing around him to hear the word of God. 2 He
saw two boats by the lake, but the fishermen had gotten out of
them and were washing their nets. 3 He got into one of the boats,
which was Simon's, and asked him to put out a little way from
the shore. Then Jesus sat down and taught the crowds from

the boat. 4When he had finished speaking, he said to Simon,
"Put out into the deep water and lower your nets for a catch."
5Simon answered, "Master, we worked hard all night and caught
nothing! But at your word I will lower the nets." 6When they
had done this, they caught so many fish that their nets started
to tear. 7So they motioned to their partners in the other boat
to come and help them. And they came and filled both boats,
so that they were about to sink. 8But when Simon Peter saw it,
he fell down at Jesus' knees, saying, "Go away from me, Lord, for
I am a sinful man!" 9For Peter and all who were with him were
astonished at the catch of fish that they had taken, 10and so were
James and John, Zebedee's sons, who were Simon's business
partners. Then Jesus said to Simon, "Do not be afraid; from now
on you will be catching people!" 11So when they had brought
their boats to shore, they left everything and followed him.

HEALING A LEPER

12While Jesus was in one of the towns, a man came to him who
was covered with leprosy. When he saw Jesus, he bowed down
with his face to the ground and begged him, "Lord, if you are
willing, you can make me clean." 13So he stretched out his hand
and touched him, saying, "I am willing. Be clean!" And immediately the leprosy left him. 14Then he ordered the man to tell no
one, but commanded him, "Go and show yourself to a priest, and
bring the offering for your cleansing, as Moses commanded, as
a testimony to them." 15But the news about him spread even
more, and large crowds were gathering together to hear him
and to be healed of their illnesses. 16Yet Jesus himself frequently
withdrew to the wilderness and prayed.

HEALING AND FORGIVING A PARALYTIC

17Now on one of those days, while he was teaching, there were
Pharisees and teachers of the law sitting nearby (who had come
from every village of Galilee and Judea and from Jerusalem), and
the power of the Lord was with him to heal. 18Just then some
men showed up, carrying a paralyzed man on a stretcher. They
were trying to bring him in and place him before Jesus. 19But
since they found no way to carry him in because of the crowd,
they went up on the roof and let him down on the stretcher
through the roof tiles right in front of Jesus. 20When Jesus saw
their faith, he said, "Friend, your sins are forgiven." 21Then the
experts in the law and the Pharisees began to think to themselves, "Who is this man who is uttering blasphemies? Who
can forgive sins but God alone?" 22When Jesus perceived their
hostile thoughts, he said to them, "Why are you raising objections within yourselves? 23Which is easier, to say, 'Your sins are
forgiven,' or to say, 'Stand up and walk'? 24But so that you may
know that the Son of Man has authority on earth to forgive
sins"—he said to the paralyzed man—"I tell you, stand up, take
your stretcher and go home." 25Immediately he stood up before
them, picked up the stretcher he had been lying on, and went
home, glorifying God. 26Then astonishment seized them all,
and they glorified God. They were filled with awe, saying, "We
have seen incredible things today."

THE CALL OF LEVI; EATING WITH SINNERS

27After this, Jesus went out and saw a tax collector named Levi
sitting at the tax booth. "Follow me," he said to him. 28And he
got up and followed him, leaving everything behind.

5:27–32 Christ went in with sinners, not to join with them in their sins but to heal them of their sins. They who are whole need not a physician but they who are sick. It is as if Christ had said, *You Pharisees think yourselves righteous persons, you need no Savior; but these poor publicans are sick and ready to die, and I come as a physician to cure them; therefore be not angry at a work of mercy*. This sin-sickness has produced many direful effects: division, oppression, bloodshed. Now what remains but that we should go to the Great Physician? God can with a word heal; he can give repentance as well as deliverance.

THOMAS WATSON
(1620–1687)
BODY OF DIVINITY

29 Then Levi gave a great banquet in his house for Jesus, and
there was a large crowd of tax collectors and others sitting at
the table with them. 30 But the Pharisees and their experts in
the law complained to his disciples, saying, "Why do you eat
and drink with tax collectors and sinners?" 31 Jesus answered
them, "Those who are well don't need a physician, but those
who are sick do. 32 I have not come to call the righteous, but
sinners to repentance."

THE SUPERIORITY OF THE NEW

33 Then they said to him, "John's disciples frequently fast and
pray, and so do the disciples of the Pharisees, but yours continue
to eat and drink." 34 So Jesus said to them, "You cannot make
the wedding guests fast while the bridegroom is with them, can
you? 35 But those days are coming, and when the bridegroom
is taken from them, at that time they will fast." 36 He also told
them a parable: "No one tears a patch from a new garment
and sews it on an old garment. If he does, he will have torn the
new, and the piece from the new will not match the old. 37 And
no one pours new wine into old wineskins. If he does, the new
wine will burst the skins and will be spilled, and the skins will
be destroyed. 38 Instead new wine must be poured into new
wineskins. 39 No one after drinking old wine wants the new, for
he says, 'The old is good enough.'"

LORD OF THE SABBATH

6 Jesus was going through the grain fields on a Sabbath, and his
disciples picked some heads of wheat, rubbed them in their
hands, and ate them. 2 But some of the Pharisees said, "Why
are you doing what is against the law on the Sabbath?" 3 Jesus
answered them, "Haven't you read what David did when he and
his companions were hungry—4 how he entered the house of
God, took and ate the sacred bread, which is not lawful for any
to eat but the priests alone, and gave it to his companions?"
5 Then he said to them, "The Son of Man is lord of the Sabbath."

HEALING A WITHERED HAND

6 On another Sabbath, Jesus entered the synagogue and was
teaching. Now a man was there whose right hand was withered.
7 The experts in the law and the Pharisees watched Jesus closely
to see if he would heal on the Sabbath, so that they could find a
reason to accuse him. 8 But he knew their thoughts, and said to
the man who had the withered hand, "Get up and stand here."
So he rose and stood there. 9 Then Jesus said to them, "I ask you,
is it lawful to do good on the Sabbath or to do evil, to save a life
or to destroy it?" 10 After looking around at them all, he said to
the man, "Stretch out your hand." The man did so, and his hand
was restored. 11 But they were filled with mindless rage and
began debating with one another what they would do to Jesus.

CHOOSING THE 12 APOSTLES

12 Now it was during this time that Jesus went out to the mountain to pray, and he spent all night in prayer to God. 13 When
morning came, he called his disciples and chose 12 of them,
whom he also named apostles: 14 Simon (whom he named Peter),
and his brother Andrew; and James, John, Philip, Bartholomew,
15 Matthew, Thomas, James the son of Alphaeus, Simon who was
called the Zealot, 16 Judas the son of James, and Judas Iscariot,
who became a traitor.

6:1–11 We should note that Jesus cured the man with his word alone, not moving his hand or any external thing, as he commonly did at other times. The reason for this was that they would have less of an excuse to make false or petty objections against him. For how could he violate or break the Sabbath with a word? He placed the man with the withered hand in the center so that they might be able to clearly see his misery and so count it a good and charitable deed to heal him, even though it was a Sabbath day. And then, by skillful questioning, he admonished them that there is no time when it is unlawful to do good, much less on the Sabbath. For to do a holy thing according to charity on the holy day follows the commandment of the Lord.

MARTIN BUCER **(1491–1551)**
ECCLESIASTICAL EXPOSITION UPON SAINT MATTHEW

THE SERMON ON THE PLAIN

17Then he came down with them and stood on a level place. And
a large number of his disciples had gathered along with a vast
multitude from all over Judea, from Jerusalem, and from the
seacoast of Tyre and Sidon. They came to hear him and to be
healed of their diseases, 18and those who suffered from unclean
spirits were cured. 19The whole crowd was trying to touch him
because power was coming out from him and healing them all.
20Then he looked up at his disciples and said:

"Blessed are you who are poor, for the kingdom of God
belongs to you.
21 Blessed are you who hunger now, for you will be
satisfied.
Blessed are you who weep now, for you will laugh.
22 Blessed are you when people hate you, and when they
exclude you and insult you and reject you as evil
on account of the Son of Man! 23Rejoice in that
day, and jump for joy because your reward is great
in heaven. For their ancestors did the same things
to the prophets.
24 But woe to you who are rich, for you have received your
comfort already.
25 Woe to you who are well satisfied with food now, for you
will be hungry.
Woe to you who laugh now, for you will mourn and
weep.
26 Woe to you when all people speak well of you, for
their ancestors did the same things to the false
prophets.

27"But I say to you who are listening: Love your enemies, do
good to those who hate you, 28bless those who curse you, pray
for those who mistreat you. 29To the person who strikes you
on the cheek, offer the other as well, and from the person who
takes away your coat, do not withhold your tunic either. 30Give
to everyone who asks you, and do not ask for your possessions
back from the person who takes them away. 31Treat others in
the same way that you would want them to treat you.
32"If you love those who love you, what credit is that to you?
For even sinners love those who love them. 33And if you do good
to those who do good to you, what credit is that to you? Even
sinners do the same. 34And if you lend to those from whom you
hope to be repaid, what credit is that to you? Even sinners lend
to sinners, so that they may be repaid in full. 35But love your
enemies, and do good, and lend, expecting nothing back. Then
your reward will be great, and you will be sons of the Most High,
because he is kind to ungrateful and evil people. 36Be merciful,
just as your Father is merciful.

DO NOT JUDGE OTHERS

37"Do not judge, and you will not be judged; do not condemn,
and you will not be condemned; forgive, and you will be forgiv-
en. 38Give, and it will be given to you: A good measure, pressed
down, shaken together, running over, will be poured into your
lap. For the measure you use will be the measure you receive."
39He also told them a parable: "Someone who is blind cannot
lead another who is blind, can he? Won't they both fall into a
pit? 40A disciple is not greater than his teacher, but everyone
when fully trained will be like his teacher. 41Why do you see the

speck in your brother's eye, but fail to see the beam of wood in
your own? 42How can you say to your brother, 'Brother, let me
remove the speck from your eye,' while you yourself don't see
the beam in your own? You hypocrite! First remove the beam
from your own eye, and then you can see clearly to remove the
speck from your brother's eye.
43"For no good tree bears bad fruit, nor again does a bad tree
bear good fruit, 44for each tree is known by its own fruit. For
figs are not gathered from thorns, nor are grapes picked from
brambles. 45The good person out of the good treasury of his
heart produces good, and the evil person out of his evil treasury
produces evil, for his mouth speaks from what fills his heart.
46"Why do you call me 'Lord, Lord,' and don't do what I tell
you?
47"Everyone who comes to me and listens to my words and
puts them into practice—I will show you what he is like: 48He
is like a man building a house, who dug down deep and laid
the foundation on bedrock. When a flood came, the river burst
against that house but could not shake it because it had been
well built. 49But the person who hears and does not put my
words into practice is like a man who built a house on the
ground without a foundation. When the river burst against
that house, it collapsed immediately and was utterly destroyed!"

HEALING THE CENTURION'S SLAVE

7 After Jesus had finished teaching all this to the people, he
entered Capernaum. 2A centurion there had a slave who was
highly regarded, but who was sick and at the point of death.
3When the centurion heard about Jesus, he sent some Jewish
elders to him, asking him to come and heal his slave. 4When
they came to Jesus, they urged him earnestly, "He is worthy
to have you do this for him 5because he loves our nation and
even built our synagogue." 6So Jesus went with them. When he
was not far from the house, the centurion sent friends to say
to him, "Lord, do not trouble yourself, for I am not worthy to
have you come under my roof! 7That is why I did not presume
to come to you. Instead, say the word, and my servant must be
healed. 8For I too am a man set under authority, with soldiers
under me. I say to this one, 'Go!' and he goes, and to another,
'Come!' and he comes, and to my slave, 'Do this!' and he does
it." 9When Jesus heard this, he was amazed at him. He turned
and said to the crowd that followed him, "I tell you, not even in
Israel have I found such faith!" 10So when those who had been
sent returned to the house, they found the slave well.

RAISING A WIDOW'S SON

11Soon afterward Jesus went to a town called Nain, and his disciples and a large crowd went with him. 12As he approached
the town gate, a man who had died was being carried out, the
only son of his mother (who was a widow), and a large crowd
from the town was with her. 13When the Lord saw her, he had
compassion for her and said to her, "Do not weep." 14Then he
came up and touched the bier, and those who carried it stood
still. He said, "Young man, I say to you, get up!" 15So the dead
man sat up and began to speak, and Jesus gave him back to his
mother. 16Fear seized them all, and they began to glorify God,
saying, "A great prophet has appeared among us!" and "God has
come to help his people!" 17This report about Jesus circulated
throughout Judea and all the surrounding country.

7:18–35 There were certain people who prided themselves upon their performance of what was required by the law, namely the scribes, Pharisees, and others of their party. Jesus proves that those who believe in him are superior to them. He uses as an example one who was the best of their whole class, the blessed Baptizer. Jesus affirmed that John is a prophet or rather above the measure of the prophets. Christ also says that among those born of women no one had arisen greater than him in the righteousness that is by the law. He is not greater in legal righteousness but in the kingdom of God, in faith and the glories that result from faith. Faith crowns those who receive it with glories that surpass the law.

CYRIL OF ALEXANDRIA
(C. 376–444)
COMMENTARY ON LUKE

JESUS AND JOHN THE BAPTIST

18 John's disciples informed him about all these things. So John called two of his disciples 19 and sent them to Jesus to ask, "Are you the one who is to come, or should we look for another?" 20 When the men came to Jesus, they said, "John the Baptist has sent us to you to ask, 'Are you the one who is to come, or should we look for another?'" 21 At that very time Jesus cured many people of diseases, sicknesses, and evil spirits, and granted sight to many who were blind. 22 So he answered them, "Go tell John what you have seen and heard: The blind see, the lame walk, lepers are cleansed, the deaf hear, the dead are raised, the poor have good news proclaimed to them. 23 Blessed is anyone who takes no offense at me."

24 When John's messengers had gone, Jesus began to speak to the crowds about John: "What did you go out into the wilderness to see? A reed shaken by the wind? 25 What did you go out to see? A man dressed in soft clothing? Look, those who wear soft clothing and live in luxury are in the royal palaces! 26 What did you go out to see? A prophet? Yes, I tell you, and more than a prophet. 27 This is the one about whom it is written, '***Look, I am sending my messenger ahead of you, who will prepare your way before you.***' 28 I tell you, among those born of women no one is greater than John. Yet the one who is least in the kingdom of God is greater than he is." 29 (Now all the people who heard this, even the tax collectors, acknowledged God's justice because they had been baptized with John's baptism. 30 However, the Pharisees and the experts in religious law rejected God's purpose for themselves because they had not been baptized by John.)

31 "To what then should I compare the people of this generation, and what are they like? 32 They are like children sitting in the marketplace and calling out to one another,

"'We played the flute for you, yet you did not dance;
we wailed in mourning, yet you did not weep.'

33 For John the Baptist has come eating no bread and drinking no wine, and you say, 'He has a demon!' 34 The Son of Man has come eating and drinking, and you say, 'Look at him, a glutton and a drunk, a friend of tax collectors and sinners!' 35 But wisdom is vindicated by all her children."

JESUS' ANOINTING

36 Now one of the Pharisees asked Jesus to have dinner with him, so he went into the Pharisee's house and took his place at the table. 37 Then when a woman of that town, who was a sinner, learned that Jesus was dining at the Pharisee's house, she brought an alabaster jar of perfumed oil. 38 As she stood behind him at his feet, weeping, she began to wet his feet with her tears. She wiped them with her hair, kissed them, and anointed them with the perfumed oil. 39 Now when the Pharisee who had invited him saw this, he said to himself, "If this man were a prophet, he would know who and what kind of woman this is who is touching him, that she is a sinner." 40 So Jesus answered him, "Simon, I have something to say to you." He replied, "Say it, Teacher." 41 "A certain creditor had two debtors; one owed him 500 silver coins, and the other 50. 42 When they could not pay, he canceled the debts of both. Now which of them will love him more?" 43 Simon answered, "I suppose the one who had the bigger debt canceled." Jesus said to him, "You have judged rightly." 44 Then, turning toward the woman, he said to Simon, "Do you see this woman? I entered your house. You

gave me no water for my feet, but she has wet my feet with
her tears and wiped them with her hair. 45You gave me no kiss
of greeting, but from the time I entered she has not stopped
kissing my feet. 46You did not anoint my head with oil, but she
has anointed my feet with perfumed oil. 47Therefore I tell you,
her sins, which were many, are forgiven, thus she loved much;
but the one who is forgiven little loves little." 48Then Jesus said
to her, "Your sins are forgiven." 49But those who were at the
table with him began to say among themselves, "Who is this,
who even forgives sins?" 50He said to the woman, "Your faith
has saved you; go in peace."

JESUS' MINISTRY AND THE HELP OF WOMEN

8 Sometime afterward he went on through towns and villages,
preaching and proclaiming the good news of the kingdom of
God. The twelve were with him, 2and also some women who had
been healed of evil spirits and disabilities: Mary (called Magdalene), from whom seven demons had gone out, 3and Joanna
the wife of Cuza (Herod's household manager), Susanna, and
many others who provided for them out of their own resources.

THE PARABLE OF THE SOWER

4While a large crowd was gathering and people were coming
to Jesus from one town after another, he spoke to them in a
parable: 5"A sower went out to sow his seed. And as he sowed,
some fell along the path and was trampled on, and the wild birds
devoured it. 6Other seed fell on rock, and when it came up, it
withered because it had no moisture. 7Other seed fell among
the thorns, and they grew up with it and choked it. 8But other
seed fell on good soil and grew, and it produced a hundred times
as much grain." As he said this, he called out, "The one who has
ears to hear had better listen!"

9Then his disciples asked him what this parable meant. 10He
said, "You have been given the opportunity to know the secrets
of the kingdom of God, but for others they are in parables, so
that ***although they see they may not see, and although they hear***
they may not understand.

11"Now the parable means this: The seed is the word of God.
12Those along the path are the ones who have heard; then the
devil comes and takes away the word from their hearts, so
that they may not believe and be saved. 13Those on the rock
are the ones who receive the word with joy when they hear it,
but they have no root. They believe for a while, but in a time
of testing fall away. 14As for the seed that fell among thorns,
these are the ones who hear, but as they go on their way they
are choked by the worries and riches and pleasures of life, and
their fruit does not mature. 15But as for the seed that landed
on good soil, these are the ones who, after hearing the word,
cling to it with an honest and good heart, and bear fruit with
steadfast endurance.

SHOWING THE LIGHT

16"No one lights a lamp and then covers it with a jar or puts
it under a bed, but puts it on a lampstand so that those who
come in can see the light. 17For nothing is hidden that will
not be revealed, and nothing concealed that will not be made
known and brought to light. 18So listen carefully, for whoever
has will be given more, but whoever does not have, even what
he thinks he has will be taken from him."

JESUS' TRUE FAMILY

[19]Now Jesus' mother and his brothers came to him, but they
could not get near him because of the crowd. [20]So he was told,
"Your mother and your brothers are standing outside, wanting to see you." [21]But he replied to them, "My mother and my
brothers are those who hear the word of God and do it."

STILLING OF A STORM

[22]One day Jesus got into a boat with his disciples and said to
them, "Let's go across to the other side of the lake." So they set
out, [23]and as they sailed he fell asleep. Now a violent windstorm
came down on the lake, and the boat started filling up with
water, and they were in danger. [24]They came and woke him,
saying, "Master, Master, we are about to die!" So he got up and
rebuked the wind and the raging waves; they died down, and
it was calm. [25]Then he said to them, "Where is your faith?" But
they were afraid and amazed, saying to one another, "Who then
is this? He commands even the winds and the water, and they
obey him!"

8:22–39 He who was sleeping was awakened and cast the sea into a sleep. He reveals the wakefulness of his divinity that never sleeps by the wakefulness of the sea that was now sleeping. He rebuked the wind, and it became still. What is this power, or what is this goodness of Jesus? See, he subjected by force that which was not his. Our Lord showed that he was the Son of the Creator by means of the wind of the sea.

ERASMUS **(1466–1536)**
AN ECCLESIASTICAL EXPOSITION UPON SAINT LUKE

HEALING OF A DEMONIAC

[26]So they sailed over to the region of the Gerasenes, which is
opposite Galilee. [27]As Jesus stepped ashore, a certain man from
the town met him who was possessed by demons. For a long
time this man had worn no clothes and had not lived in a house,
but among the tombs. [28]When he saw Jesus, he cried out, fell
down before him, and shouted with a loud voice, "Leave me
alone, Jesus, Son of the Most High God! I beg you, do not torment me!" [29]For Jesus had started commanding the evil spirit
to come out of the man. (For it had seized him many times, so
he would be bound with chains and shackles and kept under
guard. But he would break the restraints and be driven by the
demon into deserted places.) [30]Jesus then asked him, "What
is your name?" He said, "Legion," because many demons had
entered him. [31]And they began to beg him not to order them
to depart into the abyss. [32]Now a large herd of pigs was feeding
there on the hillside, and the demonic spirits begged Jesus to let
them go into them. He gave them permission. [33]So the demons
came out of the man and went into the pigs, and the herd of
pigs rushed down the steep slope into the lake and drowned.
[34]When the herdsmen saw what had happened, they ran off and
spread the news in the town and countryside. [35]So the people
went out to see what had happened, and they came to Jesus.
They found the man from whom the demons had gone out,
sitting at Jesus' feet, clothed and in his right mind, and they
were afraid. [36]Those who had seen it told them how the man
who had been demon-possessed had been healed. [37]Then all the
people of the Gerasenes and the surrounding region asked Jesus
to leave them alone, for they were seized with great fear. So he
got into the boat and left. [38]The man from whom the demons
had gone out begged to go with him, but Jesus sent him away,
saying, [39]"Return to your home, and declare what God has done
for you." So he went away, proclaiming throughout the whole
town what Jesus had done for him.

RESTORATION AND HEALING

[40]Now when Jesus returned, the crowd welcomed him because
they were all waiting for him. [41]Then a man named Jairus, who
was a leader of the synagogue, came up. Falling at Jesus' feet,

JOHN KNOX:

FATHER OF SCOTTISH PROTESTANTISM

c. 1510–1572

John Knox was born around 1510 in a town near Edinburgh, Scotland. At fifteen he studied theology at Saint Andrews University and shortly after graduation began to work as a tutor to Scottish nobility. It was around this time that the political and religious climate turned combustible.

The Scottish people were frustrated with the Catholic Church's religious scandals and its role in their political oppression. A wave of Lutheran literature making its way across the English Channel from Europe fomented the English Reformation and influenced the burgeoning Scottish Reformation. The Catholic Church in England and Scotland attempted to suppress these movements and proceeded to arrest, torture, and burn at the stake hundreds of Protestants.

In the 1540s Knox became acquainted with these Reformers, converting to their theological views and taking up their cause for his Scottish people. This was a violent period in which ecclesial revolutionaries sought to purge the country of everything Catholic, resorting at times to murder. Knox was caught up in one of their plots and was eventually imprisoned on a slave galley ship off the coast of France. Upon release he joined the Reformation work of Edward VI's court to reshape the English church. But when Mary Tudor ascended to the throne, he was forced into exile during her Protestant purge.

Knox fled to Geneva where he met Reformed Protestantism's most venerated hero: John Calvin. Not only had Knox soaked up Calvin's theology, but he had also learned from his polity, believing he had found a new form of ecclesial government that would put to rest lingering questions left over from Catholicism. In due course, Knox had become a sort of de facto leader of the exiled English people in Geneva, running the church community under the presbyterian congregational form of governance.

Upon his eventual return to Scotland, Knox brought the Calvinism that had won him over in Geneva. He moved to make the presbyterian form of ecclesiastical government the norm for the church in his home country. In 1560 he and a small group were commissioned by the Scottish Parliament to create a confession of faith for the church of Scotland. Within four days they had sketched what would become the foundational document for the national church, incorporating the political and theological ideals of Calvinism as well as its presbyterian form of government with its representative assembly of elders, over and against the episcopal form that the Church of England had embraced. Knox's leadership made Reformed Protestantism the national religion of Scotland, making him uniquely important in the formation of the Presbyterian Church of Scotland—and, by extension, in the development of the Presbyterian church more broadly, which today includes millions of members worldwide.

IMPORTANT WORKS

HISTORY OF THE REFORMATION OF RELIGION IN SCOTLAND

THE SCOTS CONFESSION

he pleaded with him to come to his house, 42 because he had
an only daughter, about twelve years old, and she was dying.
As Jesus was on his way, the crowds pressed around him.
43 Now a woman was there who had been suffering from a hemorrhage for twelve years but could not be healed by anyone.
44 She came up behind Jesus and touched the edge of his cloak,
and at once the bleeding stopped. 45 Then Jesus asked, "Who
was it who touched me?" When they all denied it, Peter said,
"Master, the crowds are surrounding you and pressing against
you!" 46 But Jesus said, "Someone touched me, for I know that
power has gone out from me." 47 When the woman saw that
she could not escape notice, she came trembling and fell down
before him. In the presence of all the people, she explained
why she had touched him and how she had been immediately
healed. 48 Then he said to her, "Daughter, your faith has made
you well. Go in peace."

49 While he was still speaking, someone from the synagogue
leader's house came and said, "Your daughter is dead; do not
trouble the teacher any longer." 50 But when Jesus heard this, he
told him, "Do not be afraid; just believe, and she will be healed."
51 Now when he came to the house, Jesus did not let anyone go
in with him except Peter, John, and James, and the child's father
and mother. 52 Now they were all wailing and mourning for her,
but he said, "Stop your weeping; she is not dead but asleep!"
53 And they began making fun of him because they knew that
she was dead. 54 But Jesus gently took her by the hand and said,
"Child, get up." 55 Her spirit returned, and she got up immediately. Then he told them to give her something to eat. 56 Her
parents were astonished, but he ordered them to tell no one
what had happened.

THE SENDING OF THE 12 APOSTLES

9 After Jesus called the twelve together, he gave them power
and authority over all demons and to cure diseases, 2 and
he sent them out to proclaim the kingdom of God and to heal
the sick. 3 He said to them, "Take nothing for your journey—no
staff, no bag, no bread, no money, and do not take an extra tunic. 4 Whatever house you enter, stay there until you leave the
area. 5 Wherever they do not receive you, as you leave that town,
shake the dust off your feet as a testimony against them." 6 Then
they departed and went throughout the villages, proclaiming
the good news and healing people everywhere.

HEROD'S CONFUSION ABOUT JESUS

7 Now Herod the tetrarch heard about everything that was happening, and he was thoroughly perplexed because some people
were saying that John had been raised from the dead, 8 while
others were saying that Elijah had appeared, and still others
that one of the prophets of long ago had risen. 9 Herod said, "I
had John beheaded, but who is this about whom I hear such
things?" So Herod wanted to learn about Jesus.

THE FEEDING OF THE 5,000

10 When the apostles returned, they told Jesus everything they
had done. Then he took them with him and they withdrew
privately to a town called Bethsaida. 11 But when the crowds
found out, they followed him. He welcomed them, spoke to
them about the kingdom of God, and cured those who needed
healing. 12 Now the day began to draw to a close, so the twelve

9:10–17 These things are spoken to commend the power of Christ and to set forth the miracle, so that no one might think that not everyone ate of these loaves, or that perhaps everyone ate but not enough to be satisfied. In this example we see the riches of the glory of God by which he feeds those who are his, that they are not only satisfied with what he gives them but also have a great surplus remaining for them. We are also taught here to beware that we do not lose the remnant of those good things with which we are fed.

PHILIP MELANCHTHON
(1497–1560)
AN ECCLESIASTICAL EXPOSITION UPON SAINT MATTHEW

came and said to Jesus, "Send the crowd away, so they can go into the surrounding villages and countryside and find lodging and food because we are in an isolated place." 13But he said to them, "You give them something to eat." They replied, "We have no more than five loaves and two fish—unless we go and buy food for all these people." 14(Now about 5,000 men were there.) Then he said to his disciples, "Have them sit down in groups of about fifty each." 15So they did as Jesus directed, and the people all sat down.

16Then he took the five loaves and the two fish, and looking up to heaven he gave thanks and broke them. He gave them to the disciples to set before the crowd. 17They all ate and were satisfied, and what was left over was picked up—12 baskets of broken pieces.

PETER'S CONFESSION

18Once when Jesus was praying by himself and his disciples were nearby, he asked them, "Who do the crowds say that I am?" 19They answered, "John the Baptist; others say Elijah; and still others that one of the prophets of long ago has risen." 20Then he said to them, "But who do you say that I am?" Peter answered, "The Christ of God." 21But he forcefully commanded them not to tell this to anyone, 22saying, "The Son of Man must suffer many things and be rejected by the elders, chief priests, and experts in the law, and be killed, and on the third day be raised."

A CALL TO DISCIPLESHIP

23Then he said to them all, "If anyone wants to become my follower, he must deny himself, take up his cross daily, and follow me. 24For whoever wants to save his life will lose it, but whoever loses his life because of me will save it. 25For what does it benefit a person if he gains the whole world but loses or forfeits himself? 26For whoever is ashamed of me and my words, the Son of Man will be ashamed of that person when he comes in his glory and in the glory of the Father and of the holy angels. 27But I tell you most certainly, there are some standing here who will not experience death before they see the kingdom of God."

THE TRANSFIGURATION

28Now about eight days after these sayings, Jesus took with him Peter, John, and James, and went up the mountain to pray. 29As he was praying, the appearance of his face was transformed, and his clothes became very bright, a brilliant white. 30Then two men, Moses and Elijah, began talking with him. 31They appeared in glorious splendor and spoke about his departure that he was about to carry out at Jerusalem. 32Now Peter and those with him were quite sleepy, but as they became fully awake, they saw his glory and the two men standing with him. 33Then as the men were starting to leave, Peter said to Jesus, "Master, it is good for us to be here. Let us make three shelters, one for you and one for Moses and one for Elijah"—not knowing what he was saying. 34As he was saying this, a cloud came and overshadowed them, and they were afraid as they entered the cloud. 35Then a voice came from the cloud, saying, "This is my Son, my Chosen One. Listen to him!" 36After the voice had spoken, Jesus was found alone. So they kept silent and told no one at that time anything of what they had seen.

HEALING A BOY WITH AN UNCLEAN SPIRIT

[37]Now on the next day, when they had come down from the mountain, a large crowd met him. [38]Then a man from the crowd cried out, "Teacher, I beg you to look at my son—he is my only child! [39]A spirit seizes him, and he suddenly screams; it throws him into convulsions and causes him to foam at the mouth. It hardly ever leaves him alone, torturing him severely. [40]I begged your disciples to cast it out, but they could not do so." [41]Jesus answered, "You unbelieving and perverse generation! How much longer must I be with you and endure you? Bring your son here." [42]As the boy was approaching, the demon threw him to the ground and shook him with convulsions. But Jesus rebuked the unclean spirit, healed the boy, and gave him back to his father. [43]Then they were all astonished at the mighty power of God.

ANOTHER PREDICTION OF JESUS' SUFFERING

But while the entire crowd was amazed at everything Jesus was doing, he said to his disciples, [44]"Take these words to heart, for the Son of Man is going to be betrayed into the hands of men." [45]But they did not understand this statement; its meaning had been concealed from them, so that they could not grasp it. Yet they were afraid to ask him about this statement.

CONCERNING THE GREATEST

[46]Now an argument started among the disciples as to which of them might be the greatest. [47]But when Jesus discerned their innermost thoughts, he took a child, had him stand by his side, [48]and said to them, "Whoever welcomes this child in my name welcomes me, and whoever welcomes me welcomes the one who sent me, for the one who is least among you all is the one who is great."

ON THE RIGHT SIDE

[49]John answered, "Master, we saw someone casting out demons in your name, and we tried to stop him because he is not a disciple along with us." [50]But Jesus said to him, "Do not stop him, for whoever is not against you is for you."

REJECTION IN SAMARIA

[51]Now when the days drew near for him to be taken up, Jesus set out resolutely to go to Jerusalem. [52]He sent messengers on ahead of him. As they went along, they entered a Samaritan village to make things ready in advance for him, [53]but the villagers refused to welcome him because he was determined to go to Jerusalem. [54]Now when his disciples James and John saw this, they said, "Lord, do you want us *to call fire to come down from heaven and consume them*?" [55]But Jesus turned and rebuked them, [56]and they went on to another village.

CHALLENGING PROFESSED FOLLOWERS

[57]As they were walking along the road, someone said to him, "I will follow you wherever you go." [58]Jesus said to him, "Foxes have dens and the birds in the sky have nests, but the Son of Man has no place to lay his head." [59]Jesus said to another, "Follow me." But he replied, "Lord, first let me go and bury my father." [60]But Jesus said to him, "Let the dead bury their own dead, but as for you, go and proclaim the kingdom of God." [61]Yet another said, "I will follow you, Lord, but first let me say goodbye to my family." [62]Jesus said to him, "No one who puts his hand to the plow and looks back is fit for the kingdom of God."

THE MISSION OF THE SEVENTY-TWO

10 After this the Lord appointed seventy-two others and sent them on ahead of him two by two into every town and place where he himself was about to go. [2]He said to them, "The harvest is plentiful, but the workers are few. Therefore ask the Lord of the harvest to send out workers into his harvest. [3]Go! I am sending you out like lambs surrounded by wolves. [4]Do not carry a money bag, a traveler's bag, or sandals, and greet no one on the road. [5]Whenever you enter a house, first say, 'May peace be on this house!' [6]And if a peace-loving person is there, your peace will remain on him, but if not, it will return to you. [7]Stay in that same house, eating and drinking what they give you, for the worker deserves his pay. Do not move around from house to house. [8]Whenever you enter a town and the people welcome you, eat what is set before you. [9]Heal the sick in that town and say to them, 'The kingdom of God has come upon you!' [10]But whenever you enter a town and the people do not welcome you, go into its streets and say, [11]'Even the dust of your town that clings to our feet we wipe off against you. Nevertheless know this: The kingdom of God has come.' [12]I tell you, it will be more bearable on that day for Sodom than for that town!

[13]"Woe to you, Chorazin! Woe to you, Bethsaida! For if the miracles done in you had been done in Tyre and Sidon, they would have repented long ago, sitting in sackcloth and ashes. [14]But it will be more bearable for Tyre and Sidon in the judgment than for you! [15]And you, Capernaum, will you be exalted to heaven? No, you will be thrown down to Hades!

[16]"The one who listens to you listens to me, and the one who rejects you rejects me, and the one who rejects me rejects the one who sent me."

[17]Then the seventy-two returned with joy, saying, "Lord, even the demons submit to us in your name!" [18]So he said to them, "I saw Satan fall like lightning from heaven. [19]Look, I have given you authority to tread on snakes and scorpions and on the full force of the enemy, and nothing will hurt you. [20]Nevertheless, do not rejoice that the spirits submit to you, but rejoice that your names stand written in heaven."

[21]On that same occasion Jesus rejoiced in the Holy Spirit and said, "I praise you, Father, Lord of heaven and earth, because you have hidden these things from the wise and intelligent and revealed them to little children. Yes, Father, for this was your gracious will. [22]All things have been given to me by my Father. No one knows who the Son is except the Father, or who the Father is except the Son and anyone to whom the Son decides to reveal him."

[23]Then Jesus turned to his disciples and said privately, "Blessed are the eyes that see what you see! [24]For I tell you that many prophets and kings longed to see what you see but did not see it, and to hear what you hear but did not hear it."

THE PARABLE OF THE GOOD SAMARITAN

[25]Now an expert in religious law stood up to test Jesus, saying, "Teacher, what must I do to inherit eternal life?" [26]He said to him, "What is written in the law? How do you understand it?" [27]The expert answered, "***Love the Lord your God with all your heart, with all your soul, with all your strength, and with all your mind,*** and ***love your neighbor as yourself.***" [28]Jesus said to him, "You have answered correctly; do this, and you will live."

10:17–20 For we ought to remember how, when the disciples returned with joy from preaching and said to their heavenly Master, "Lord, even the demons submit to us in your name!" they straightway heard, "Do not rejoice that the spirits submit to you." For they had set their minds on private and temporal gladness when they rejoiced in the miracles. But they are recalled from private to common, from temporal to eternal gladness, when it is said to them, "Rejoice that your names stand written in heaven." For not all the elect work miracles, and yet the names of all of them are kept enrolled in heaven. For to the disciples of the truth there should not be joy save for that good that they have in common with all, and in which they have no end to their gladness.

GREGORY THE GREAT
(C. 540–604)
LETTERS

29 But the expert, wanting to justify himself, said to Jesus, "And
who is my neighbor?" 30 Jesus replied, "A man was going down
from Jerusalem to Jericho, and fell into the hands of robbers, who
stripped him, beat him up, and went off, leaving him half dead.
31 Now by chance a priest was going down that road, but when
he saw the injured man, he passed by on the other side. 32 So too
a Levite, when he came up to the place and saw him, passed by
on the other side. 33 But a Samaritan who was traveling came to
where the injured man was, and when he saw him, he felt compassion for him. 34 He went up to him and bandaged his wounds,
pouring olive oil and wine on them. Then he put him on his own
animal, brought him to an inn, and took care of him. 35 The next
day he took out two silver coins and gave them to the innkeeper,
saying, 'Take care of him, and whatever else you spend, I will repay
you when I come back this way.' 36 Which of these three do you
think became a neighbor to the man who fell into the hands of
the robbers?" 37 The expert in religious law said, "The one who
showed mercy to him." So Jesus said to him, "Go and do the same."

JESUS AND MARTHA

38 Now as they went on their way, Jesus entered a certain village where a woman named Martha welcomed him as a guest.
39 She had a sister named Mary, who sat at the Lord's feet and
listened to what he said. 40 But Martha was distracted with all
the preparations she had to make, so she came up to him and
said, "Lord, don't you care that my sister has left me to do all
the work alone? Tell her to help me." 41 But the Lord answered
her, "Martha, Martha, you are worried and troubled about many
things, 42 but one thing is needed. Mary has chosen the best
part; it will not be taken away from her."

INSTRUCTIONS ON PRAYER

11 Now Jesus was praying in a certain place. When he stopped,
one of his disciples said to him, "Lord, teach us to pray,
just as John taught his disciples." 2 So he said to them, "When
you pray, say:

"'Father, may your name be honored;
may your kingdom come.
3 Give us each day our daily bread,
4 and forgive us our sins,
for we also forgive everyone who sins against us.
And do not lead us into temptation.'"

5 Then he said to them, "Suppose one of you has a friend,
and you go to him at midnight and say to him, 'Friend, lend me
three loaves of bread, 6 because a friend of mine has stopped
here while on a journey, and I have nothing to set before him.'
7 Then he will reply from inside, 'Do not bother me. The door is
already shut, and my children and I are in bed. I cannot get up
and give you anything.' 8 I tell you, even though the man inside
will not get up and give him anything because he is his friend,
yet because of the first man's sheer persistence he will get up
and give him whatever he needs.
9 "So I tell you: Ask, and it will be given to you; seek, and you
will find; knock, and the door will be opened for you. 10 For everyone who asks receives, and the one who seeks finds, and to the
one who knocks, the door will be opened. 11 What father among
you, if your son asks for a fish, will give him a snake instead of
a fish? 12 Or if he asks for an egg, will give him a scorpion? 13 If

11:5–13 Desiring that we arrive at the joys of the heavenly kingdom, our Lord and Savior taught us to ask these joys of him and promised that he would give them to us if we asked for them. Dearly beloved, we earnestly and with our whole heart must ponder these words of our Lord. He bears witness that the kingdom of heaven is not given to, found by, and opened to those who are idle and unoccupied but to those who ask for it, seek after it, and knock at its gates. The gate of the kingdom must be asked for by praying. It must be sought after by living properly. It must be knocked at by persevering.

VENERABLE BEDE
(C. 672–735)
HOMILIES ON THE GOSPELS

you then, although you are evil, know how to give good gifts to
your children, how much more will the heavenly Father give
the Holy Spirit to those who ask him!"

JESUS AND BEELZEBUL

14Now he was casting out a demon that was mute. When the
demon had gone out, the man who had been mute began to
speak, and the crowds were amazed. 15But some of them said,
"By the power of Beelzebul, the ruler of demons, he casts out
demons!" 16Others, to test him, began asking for a sign from
heaven. 17But Jesus, realizing their thoughts, said to them, "Every kingdom divided against itself is destroyed, and a divided
household falls. 18So if Satan too is divided against himself,
how will his kingdom stand? I ask you this because you claim
that I cast out demons by Beelzebul. 19Now if I cast out demons
by Beelzebul, by whom do your sons cast them out? Therefore
they will be your judges. 20But if I cast out demons by the finger
of God, then the kingdom of God has already overtaken you.
21When a strong man, fully armed, guards his own palace, his
possessions are safe. 22But when a stronger man attacks and
conquers him, he takes away the first man's armor on which the
man relied and divides up his plunder. 23Whoever is not with
me is against me, and whoever does not gather with me scatters.

RESPONSE TO JESUS' WORK

24"When an unclean spirit goes out of a person, it passes through
waterless places looking for rest but not finding any. Then it says,
'I will return to the home I left.' 25When it returns, it finds the
house swept clean and put in order. 26Then it goes and brings
seven other spirits more evil than itself, and they go in and live
there, so the last state of that person is worse than the first."
27As he said these things, a woman in the crowd spoke out
to him, "Blessed is the womb that bore you and the breasts at
which you nursed!" 28But he replied, "Blessed rather are those
who hear the word of God and obey it!"

THE SIGN OF JONAH

29As the crowds were increasing, Jesus began to say, "This generation is a wicked generation; it looks for a sign, but no sign
will be given to it except the sign of Jonah. 30For just as Jonah
became a sign to the people of Nineveh, so the Son of Man
will be a sign to this generation. 31The queen of the South will
rise up at the judgment with the people of this generation and
condemn them, because she came from the ends of the earth to
hear the wisdom of Solomon—and now, something greater than
Solomon is here! 32The people of Nineveh will stand up at the
judgment with this generation and condemn it, because they
repented when Jonah preached to them—and now, something
greater than Jonah is here!

INTERNAL LIGHT

33"No one after lighting a lamp puts it in a hidden place or
under a basket, but on a lampstand, so that those who come
in can see the light. 34Your eye is the lamp of your body. When
your eye is healthy, your whole body is full of light, but when it
is diseased, your body is full of darkness. 35Therefore see to it
that the light in you is not darkness. 36If then your whole body
is full of light, with no part in the dark, it will be as full of light
as when the light of a lamp shines on you."

REBUKING THE PHARISEES AND EXPERTS IN THE LAW

37 As he spoke, a Pharisee invited Jesus to have a meal with him, so he went in and took his place at the table. 38 The Pharisee was astonished when he saw that Jesus did not first wash his hands before the meal. 39 But the Lord said to him, "Now you Pharisees clean the outside of the cup and the plate, but inside you are full of greed and wickedness. 40 You fools! Didn't the one who made the outside make the inside as well? 41 But give from your heart to those in need, and then everything will be clean for you.

42 "But woe to you Pharisees! You give a tenth of your mint, rue, and every herb, yet you neglect justice and love for God! But you should have done these things without neglecting the others. 43 Woe to you Pharisees! You love the best seats in the synagogues and elaborate greetings in the marketplaces! 44 Woe to you! You are like unmarked graves, and people walk over them without realizing it!"

45 One of the experts in religious law answered him, "Teacher, when you say these things, you insult us too." 46 But Jesus replied, "Woe to you experts in religious law as well! You load people down with burdens difficult to bear, yet you yourselves refuse to touch the burdens with even one of your fingers! 47 Woe to you! You build the tombs of the prophets whom your ancestors killed. 48 So you testify that you approve of the deeds of your ancestors because they killed the prophets and you build their tombs! 49 For this reason also the wisdom of God said, 'I will send them prophets and apostles, some of whom they will kill and persecute,' 50 so that this generation may be held accountable for the blood of all the prophets that has been shed since the beginning of the world, 51 from the blood of Abel to the blood of Zechariah, who was killed between the altar and the sanctuary. Yes, I tell you, it will be charged against this generation. 52 Woe to you experts in religious law! You have taken away the key to knowledge! You did not go in yourselves, and you hindered those who were going in."

53 When he went out from there, the experts in the law and the Pharisees began to oppose him bitterly and to ask him hostile questions about many things, 54 plotting against him to catch him in something he might say.

FEAR GOD, NOT PEOPLE

12 Meanwhile, when many thousands of the crowd had gathered so that they were trampling on one another, Jesus began to speak first to his disciples, "Be on your guard against the yeast of the Pharisees, which is hypocrisy. 2 Nothing is hidden that will not be revealed, and nothing is secret that will not be made known. 3 So then whatever you have said in the dark will be heard in the light, and what you have whispered in private rooms will be proclaimed from the housetops.

4 "I tell you, my friends, do not be afraid of those who kill the body, and after that have nothing more they can do. 5 But I will warn you whom you should fear: Fear the one who, after the killing, has authority to throw you into hell. Yes, I tell you, fear him! 6 Aren't five sparrows sold for two pennies? Yet not one of them is forgotten before God. 7 In fact, even the hairs on your head are all numbered. Do not be afraid; you are more valuable than many sparrows.

8 "I tell you, whoever acknowledges me before men, the Son of Man will also acknowledge before God's angels. 9 But the one

12:1–11 In the Gospel the Lord speaks and says, "Whoever acknowledges me before men, the Son of Man will also acknowledge before God's angels. But the one who denies me before men will be denied before God's angels." If he does not deny him who denies, neither does he confess him that confesses; the gospel cannot be sound in one part and waver in another. Either both must stand firm, or both must lose the force of truth. If they who deny shall not be guilty of a crime, neither shall they who confess receive the reward of a virtue. Again, if faith that has conquered be crowned, it is of necessity that faithlessness that is conquered should be punished. Thus the martyrs can either do nothing if the gospel may be broken; or if the gospel cannot be broken, they can do nothing against the gospel since they become martyrs on account of the gospel. Let no one decry the dignity of martyrs, let no one degrade their glories and their crowns.

CYPRIAN OF CARTHAGE
(C. 210–258)
LETTERS

who denies me before men will be denied before God's angels.
[10]And everyone who speaks a word against the Son of Man will
be forgiven, but the person who blasphemes against the Holy
Spirit will not be forgiven. [11]But when they bring you before the
synagogues, the rulers, and the authorities, do not worry about
how you should make your defense or what you should say, [12]for
the Holy Spirit will teach you at that moment what you must say."

THE PARABLE OF THE RICH LANDOWNER

[13]Then someone from the crowd said to him, "Teacher, tell my
brother to divide the inheritance with me." [14]But Jesus said to
him, "Man, who made me a judge or arbitrator between you
two?" [15]Then he said to them, "Watch out and guard yourself
from all types of greed because one's life does not consist in the
abundance of his possessions." [16]He then told them a parable:
"The land of a certain rich man produced an abundant crop, [17]so
he thought to himself, 'What should I do, for I have nowhere to
store my crops?' [18]Then he said, 'I will do this: I will tear down
my barns and build bigger ones, and there I will store all my
grain and my goods. [19]And I will say to myself, "You have plenty
of goods stored up for many years; relax, eat, drink, celebrate!"'
[20]But God said to him, 'You fool! This very night your life will
be demanded back from you, but who will get what you have
prepared for yourself?' [21]So it is with the one who stores up
riches for himself, but is not rich toward God."

EXHORTATION NOT TO WORRY

[22]Then Jesus said to his disciples, "Therefore I tell you, do not
worry about your life, what you will eat, or about your body,
what you will wear. [23]For there is more to life than food, and
more to the body than clothing. [24]Consider the ravens: They
do not sow or reap, they have no storeroom or barn, yet God
feeds them. How much more valuable are you than the birds!
[25]And which of you by worrying can add an hour to his life?
[26]So if you cannot do such a very little thing as this, why do
you worry about the rest? [27]Consider how the flowers grow;
they do not work or spin. Yet I tell you, not even Solomon in
all his glory was clothed like one of these! [28]And if this is how
God clothes the wild grass, which is here today and tomorrow
is tossed into the fire to heat the oven, how much more will
he clothe you, you people of little faith! [29]So do not be overly
concerned about what you will eat and what you will drink,
and do not worry about such things. [30]For all the nations of
the world pursue these things, and your Father knows that you
need them. [31]Instead, pursue his kingdom, and these things
will be given to you as well.

[32]"Do not be afraid, little flock, for your Father is well pleased
to give you the kingdom. [33]Sell your possessions and give to the
poor. Provide yourselves purses that do not wear out—a treasure
in heaven that never decreases, where no thief approaches
and no moth destroys. [34]For where your treasure is, there your
heart will be also.

CALL TO FAITHFUL STEWARDSHIP

[35]"Get dressed for service and keep your lamps burning; [36]be
like people waiting for their master to come back from the
wedding celebration, so that when he comes and knocks, they
can immediately open the door for him. [37]Blessed are those
slaves whom their master finds alert when he returns! I tell you

the truth, he will dress himself to serve, have them take their
place at the table, and will come and wait on them! 38 Even if
he comes in the second or third watch of the night and finds
them alert, blessed are those slaves! 39 But understand this: If
the owner of the house had known at what hour the thief was
coming, he would not have let his house be broken into. 40 You
also must be ready because the Son of Man will come at an
hour when you do not expect him."

41 Then Peter said, "Lord, are you telling this parable for us or
for everyone?" 42 The Lord replied, "Who then is the faithful and
wise manager, whom the master puts in charge of his household
servants, to give them their allowance of food at the proper time?
43 Blessed is that slave whom his master finds at work when he
returns. 44 I tell you the truth, the master will put him in charge
of all his possessions. 45 But if that slave should say to himself, 'My
master is delayed in returning,' and he begins to beat the other
slaves, both men and women, and to eat, drink, and get drunk,
46 then the master of that slave will come on a day when he does
not expect him and at an hour he does not foresee, and will cut
him in two, and assign him a place with the unfaithful. 47 That
servant who knew his master's will but did not get ready or do
what his master asked will receive a severe beating. 48 But the
one who did not know his master's will and did things worthy
of punishment will receive a light beating. From everyone who
has been given much, much will be required, and from the one
who has been entrusted with much, even more will be asked.

NOT PEACE, BUT DIVISION

49 "I have come to bring fire on the earth—and how I wish it
were already kindled! 50 I have a baptism to undergo, and how
distressed I am until it is finished! 51 Do you think I have come
to bring peace on earth? No, I tell you, but rather division! 52 For
from now on there will be five in one household divided, three
against two and two against three. 53 They will be divided, father
against son and son against father, mother against daughter and
daughter against mother, mother-in-law against her daughter-
in-law and daughter-in-law against mother-in-law."

READING THE SIGNS

54 Jesus also said to the crowds, "When you see a cloud rising in
the west, you say at once, 'A rainstorm is coming,' and it does.
55 And when you see the south wind blowing, you say, 'There will
be scorching heat,' and there is. 56 You hypocrites! You know how
to interpret the appearance of the earth and the sky, but how
can you not know how to interpret the present time?

CLEAR THE DEBTS

57 "And why don't you judge for yourselves what is right? 58 As
you are going with your accuser before the magistrate, make
an effort to settle with him on the way, so that he will not drag
you before the judge, and the judge hand you over to the officer, and the officer throw you into prison. 59 I tell you, you will
never get out of there until you have paid the very last cent!"

A CALL TO REPENT

13 Now there were some present on that occasion who told
him about the Galileans whose blood Pilate had mixed
with their sacrifices. 2 He answered them, "Do you think these
Galileans were worse sinners than all the other Galileans

because they suffered these things? 3No, I tell you! But unless you repent, you will all perish as well! 4Or those eighteen who were killed when the tower in Siloam fell on them, do you think they were worse offenders than all the others who live in Jerusalem? 5No, I tell you! But unless you repent you will all perish as well!"

WARNING TO ISRAEL TO BEAR FRUIT

6Then Jesus told this parable: "A man had a fig tree planted in his vineyard, and he came looking for fruit on it and found none. 7So he said to the worker who tended the vineyard, 'For three years now, I have come looking for fruit on this fig tree, and each time I inspect it I find none. Cut it down! Why should it continue to deplete the soil?' 8But the worker answered him, 'Sir, leave it alone this year too, until I dig around it and put fertilizer on it. 9Then if it bears fruit next year, very well, but if not, you can cut it down.'"

HEALING ON THE SABBATH

10Now he was teaching in one of the synagogues on the Sabbath, 11and a woman was there who had been disabled by a spirit for eighteen years. She was bent over and could not straighten herself up completely. 12When Jesus saw her, he called her to him and said, "Woman, you are freed from your infirmity." 13Then he placed his hands on her, and immediately she straightened up and praised God. 14But the president of the synagogue, indignant because Jesus had healed on the Sabbath, said to the crowd, "There are six days on which work should be done! So come and be healed on those days, and not on the Sabbath day." 15Then the Lord answered him, "You hypocrites! Does not each of you on the Sabbath untie his ox or his donkey from its stall and lead it to water? 16Then shouldn't this woman, a daughter of Abraham whom Satan bound for eighteen long years, be released from this imprisonment on the Sabbath day?" 17When he said this, all his adversaries were humiliated, but the entire crowd was rejoicing at all the wonderful things he was doing.

13:10–17 Let us hold on to this blessed truth and never let it go. Let us never despair about our own salvation. Our sins may be countless; our lives may have spent years in worldliness and folly; our youth may have been wasted in soul-defiling excesses of which we are greatly ashamed. But if we are willing to commit our souls to Christ, there is hope. He can heal us completely and say, "You are freed from your infirmity."

J. C. RYLE **(1816–1900)**
EXPOSITORY THOUGHTS ON THE GOSPELS

ON THE KINGDOM OF GOD

18Thus Jesus asked, "What is the kingdom of God like? To what should I compare it? 19It is like a mustard seed that a man took and sowed in his garden. It grew and became a tree, and the wild birds nested in its branches."

20Again he said, "To what should I compare the kingdom of God? 21It is like yeast that a woman took and mixed with three measures of flour until all the dough had risen."

THE NARROW DOOR

22Then Jesus traveled throughout towns and villages, teaching and making his way toward Jerusalem. 23Someone asked him, "Lord, will only a few be saved?" So he said to them, 24"Exert every effort to enter through the narrow door because many, I tell you, will try to enter and will not be able to. 25Once the head of the house gets up and shuts the door, then you will stand outside and start to knock on the door and beg him, 'Lord, let us in!' But he will answer you, 'I don't know where you come from.' 26Then you will begin to say, 'We ate and drank in your presence, and you taught in our streets.' 27But he will reply, 'I don't know where you come from! Go away from me, all you evildoers!' 28There will be weeping and gnashing of teeth when you see Abraham,

Isaac, Jacob, and all the prophets in the kingdom of God but
you yourselves thrown out. [29]Then people will come from east
and west, and from north and south, and take their places at
the banquet table in the kingdom of God. [30]But indeed, some
are last who will be first, and some are first who will be last."

GOING TO JERUSALEM

[31]At that time, some Pharisees came up and said to Jesus, "Get
away from here because Herod wants to kill you." [32]But he said
to them, "Go and tell that fox, 'Look, I am casting out demons
and performing healings today and tomorrow, and on the third
day I will complete my work. [33]Nevertheless I must go on my
way today and tomorrow and the next day, because it is impossible that a prophet should be killed outside Jerusalem.' [34]O Jerusalem, Jerusalem, you who kill the prophets and stone those
who are sent to you! How often I have longed to gather your
children together as a hen gathers her chicks under her wings,
but you would have none of it! [35]Look, your house is forsaken!
And I tell you, you will not see me until you say, '***Blessed is the
one who comes in the name of the Lord!***'"

HEALING AGAIN ON THE SABBATH

14 Now one Sabbath when Jesus went to dine at the house of
a leader of the Pharisees, they were watching him closely.
[2]There right in front of him was a man whose body was swollen
with fluid. [3]So Jesus asked the experts in religious law and the
Pharisees, "Is it lawful to heal on the Sabbath or not?" [4]But they
remained silent. So Jesus took hold of the man, healed him, and
sent him away. [5]Then he said to them, "Which of you, if you have
a son or an ox that has fallen into a well on a Sabbath day, will
not immediately pull him out?" [6]But they could not reply to this.

ON SEEKING SEATS OF HONOR

[7]Then when Jesus noticed how the guests chose the places of
honor, he told them a parable. He said to them, [8]"When you are
invited by someone to a wedding feast, do not take the place
of honor because a person more distinguished than you may
have been invited by your host. [9]So the host who invited both
of you will come and say to you, 'Give this man your place.' Then,
ashamed, you will begin to move to the least important place.
[10]But when you are invited, go and take the least important
place, so that when your host approaches he will say to you,
'Friend, move up here to a better place.' Then you will be honored in the presence of all who share the meal with you. [11]For
everyone who exalts himself will be humbled, but the one who
humbles himself will be exalted."

[12]He said also to the man who had invited him, "When you
host a dinner or a banquet, don't invite your friends or your
brothers or your relatives or rich neighbors so you can be invited by them in return and get repaid. [13]But when you host
an elaborate meal, invite the poor, the crippled, the lame, and
the blind. [14]Then you will be blessed because they cannot repay
you, for you will be repaid at the resurrection of the righteous."

THE PARABLE OF THE GREAT BANQUET

[15]When one of those at the meal with Jesus heard this, he said
to him, "Blessed is everyone who will feast in the kingdom of
God!" [16]But Jesus said to him, "A man once gave a great banquet
and invited many guests. [17]At the time for the banquet he sent

14:7–14 Although true believers will never forget the sacredness of their new position and will never lose the sense of holy awe surrounding it, the ongoing walk with Christ causes the earlier feelings of fear and terror to subside. As believers mature, they reverently and submissively approach the Lord's throne and see a God of love, goodness, and mercy and more fully realize the covenant character of God. Thus the believer is invited "to a better place" and is able to exercise the privilege of rejoicing in God and drawing closer to him in holy confidence while saying "Abba, Father" (Rom 8:15).

CHARLES SPURGEON
(1834–1892)
METROPOLITAN TABERNACLE SERMONS

his slave to tell those who had been invited, 'Come, because
everything is now ready.' [18]But one after another they all began
to make excuses. The first said to him, 'I have bought a field,
and I must go out and see it. Please excuse me.' [19]Another said,
'I have bought five yoke of oxen, and I am going out to examine
them. Please excuse me.' [20]Another said, 'I just got married, and
I cannot come.' [21]So the slave came back and reported this to
his master. Then the master of the household was furious and
said to his slave, 'Go out quickly to the streets and alleys of
the city, and bring in the poor, the crippled, the blind, and the
lame.' [22]Then the slave said, 'Sir, what you instructed has been
done, and there is still room.' [23]So the master said to his slave,
'Go out to the highways and country roads and urge people to
come in, so that my house will be filled. [24]For I tell you, not one
of those individuals who were invited will taste my banquet!'"

COUNTING THE COST

[25]Now large crowds were accompanying Jesus, and turning to
them he said, [26]"If anyone comes to me and does not hate his
own father and mother, and wife and children, and brothers and
sisters, and even his own life, he cannot be my disciple. [27]Who-
ever does not carry his own cross and follow me cannot be my
disciple. [28]For which of you, wanting to build a tower, doesn't sit
down first and compute the cost to see if he has enough money
to complete it? [29]Otherwise, when he has laid a foundation and
is not able to finish the tower, all who see it will begin to make
fun of him. [30]They will say, 'This man began to build and was
not able to finish!' [31]Or what king, going out to confront another
king in battle, will not sit down first and determine whether he
is able with 10,000 to oppose the one coming against him with
20,000? [32]If he cannot succeed, he will send a representative
while the other is still a long way off and ask for terms of peace.
[33]In the same way therefore not one of you can be my disciple
if he does not renounce all his own possessions.

[34]"Salt is good, but if salt loses its flavor, how can its flavor
be restored? [35]It is of no value for the soil or for the manure
pile; it is to be thrown out. The one who has ears to hear had
better listen!"

THE PARABLE OF THE LOST SHEEP AND COIN

15 Now all the tax collectors and sinners were coming to hear
him. [2]But the Pharisees and the experts in the law were
complaining, "This man welcomes sinners and eats with them."

[3]So Jesus told them this parable: [4]"Which one of you, if he
has a hundred sheep and loses one of them, would not leave the
ninety-nine in the open pasture and go look for the one that is
lost until he finds it? [5]Then when he has found it, he places it on
his shoulders, rejoicing. [6]Returning home, he calls together his
friends and neighbors, telling them, 'Rejoice with me because I
have found my sheep that was lost.' [7]I tell you, in the same way
there will be more joy in heaven over one sinner who repents than
over ninety-nine righteous people who have no need to repent.

[8]"Or what woman, if she has ten silver coins and loses one
of them, does not light a lamp, sweep the house, and search
thoroughly until she finds it? [9]Then when she has found it, she
calls together her friends and neighbors, saying, 'Rejoice with
me, for I have found the coin that I had lost.' [10]In the same way,
I tell you, there is joy in the presence of God's angels over one
sinner who repents."

THE PARABLE OF THE COMPASSIONATE FATHER

11 Then Jesus said, "A man had two sons. 12 The younger of
them said to his father, 'Father, give me the share of the estate that will belong to me.' So he divided his assets between
them. 13 After a few days, the younger son gathered together
all he had and left on a journey to a distant country, and
there he squandered his wealth with a wild lifestyle. 14 Then
after he had spent everything, a severe famine took place in
that country, and he began to be in need. 15 So he went and
worked for one of the citizens of that country, who sent him
to his fields to feed pigs. 16 He was longing to eat the carob
pods the pigs were eating, but no one gave him anything.
17 But when he came to his senses, he said, 'How many of my
father's hired workers have food enough to spare, but here I
am dying from hunger! 18 I will get up and go to my father and
say to him, "Father, I have sinned against heaven and against
you. 19 I am no longer worthy to be called your son; treat me
like one of your hired workers."' 20 So he got up and went to
his father. But while he was still a long way from home his
father saw him, and his heart went out to him; he ran and
hugged his son and kissed him. 21 Then his son said to him,
'Father, I have sinned against heaven and against you; I am
no longer worthy to be called your son.' 22 But the father said
to his slaves, 'Hurry! Bring the best robe, and put it on him!
Put a ring on his finger and sandals on his feet! 23 Bring the
fattened calf and kill it! Let us eat and celebrate, 24 because
this son of mine was dead, and is alive again—he was lost and
is found!' So they began to celebrate.

25 "Now his older son was in the field. As he came and approached the house, he heard music and dancing. 26 So he called
one of the slaves and asked what was happening. 27 The slave
replied, 'Your brother has returned, and your father has killed
the fattened calf because he got his son back safe and sound.'
28 But the older son became angry and refused to go in. His
father came out and appealed to him, 29 but he answered his
father, 'Look! These many years I have worked like a slave for
you, and I never disobeyed your commands. Yet you never gave
me even a goat so that I could celebrate with my friends! 30 But
when this son of yours came back, who has devoured your assets
with prostitutes, you killed the fattened calf for him!' 31 Then
the father said to him, 'Son, you are always with me, and everything that belongs to me is yours. 32 It was appropriate to
celebrate and be glad, for your brother was dead, and is alive;
he was lost and is found.'"

THE PARABLE OF THE CLEVER STEWARD

16 Jesus also said to the disciples, "There was a rich man
who was informed of accusations that his manager was
wasting his assets. 2 So he called the manager in and said to
him, 'What is this I hear about you? Turn in the account of your
administration, because you can no longer be my manager.'
3 Then the manager said to himself, 'What should I do, since
my master is taking my position away from me? I'm not strong
enough to dig, and I'm too ashamed to beg. 4 I know what to
do so that when I am put out of management, people will
welcome me into their homes.' 5 So he contacted his master's
debtors one by one. He asked the first, 'How much do you
owe my master?' 6 The man replied, '100 measures of olive
oil.' The manager said to him, 'Take your bill, sit down quickly,

15:11–32 The old father sees a long way off, for dim eyes can see a long distance when the son is the object. His heart moves within him, and he has compassion on him. "He ran." It would have been sufficient for him to have stood because he was old and an offended father. But love descends rather than ascends: The son goes to the father, the father runs to the son. He speaks not a single word—his joy was too great to be uttered—but he kisses him, giving him the badge of peace, love, and reconciliation. Through this example is declared the great goodness of God, who most mercifully pardons the sins of the truly penitent.

EDWARD LEIGH **(1602–1671)**
ANNOTATIONS UPON SAINT LUKE

16:1–13 Remember, my beloved, and compare and consider in your mind, who is there of former generations who has been left in this world so as to continue forever? Death has led away the former generations, the great ones and the mighty and the subtle. Who is there that acquired great possessions, and at the time when he departed took them with him? That which was gathered together from the earth returns back into its bosom, and naked does a man depart from his possessions. And our Lord commanded them that acquire possessions to make for themselves friends in heaven and also to lay up treasures there.

GREGORY THE GREAT
(C. 540–604)
DEMONSTRATIONS

and write 50.' [7]Then he said to another, 'And how much do you owe?' The second man replied, '100 measures of wheat.' The manager said to him, 'Take your bill, and write 80.' [8]The master commended the dishonest manager because he acted shrewdly. For the people of this world are more shrewd in dealing with their contemporaries than the people of light. [9]And I tell you, make friends for yourselves by how you use worldly wealth, so that when it runs out, you will be welcomed into the eternal homes.

[10]"The one who is faithful in a very little is also faithful in much, and the one who is dishonest in a very little is also dishonest in much. [11]If then you haven't been trustworthy in handling worldly wealth, who will entrust you with the true riches? [12]And if you haven't been trustworthy with someone else's property, who will give you your own? [13]No servant can serve two masters, for either he will hate the one and love the other, or he will be devoted to the one and despise the other. You cannot serve God and money."

MORE WARNINGS ABOUT THE PHARISEES

[14]The Pharisees (who loved money) heard all this and ridiculed him. [15]But Jesus said to them, "You are the ones who justify yourselves in men's eyes, but God knows your hearts. For what is highly prized among men is utterly detestable in God's sight.

[16]"The law and the prophets were in force until John; since then, the good news of the kingdom of God has been proclaimed, and everyone is urged to enter it. [17]But it is easier for heaven and earth to pass away than for one tiny stroke of a letter in the law to become void.

[18]"Everyone who divorces his wife and marries someone else commits adultery, and the one who marries a woman divorced from her husband commits adultery.

THE RICH MAN AND LAZARUS

[19]"There was a rich man who dressed in purple and fine linen and who feasted sumptuously every day. [20]But at his gate lay a poor man named Lazarus whose body was covered with sores, [21]who longed to eat what fell from the rich man's table. In addition, the dogs came and licked his sores.

[22]"Now the poor man died and was carried by the angels to Abraham's side. The rich man also died and was buried. [23]And in Hades, as he was in torment, he looked up and saw Abraham far off with Lazarus at his side. [24]So he called out, 'Father Abraham, have mercy on me, and send Lazarus to dip the tip of his finger in water and cool my tongue because I am in anguish in this fire.' [25]But Abraham said, 'Child, remember that in your lifetime you received your good things and Lazarus likewise bad things, but now he is comforted here and you are in anguish. [26]Besides all this, a great chasm has been fixed between us, so that those who want to cross over from here to you cannot do so, and no one can cross from there to us.' [27]So the rich man said, 'Then I beg you, father—send Lazarus to my father's house [28](for I have five brothers) to warn them so that they don't come into this place of torment.' [29]But Abraham said, 'They have Moses and the prophets; they must respond to them.' [30]Then the rich man said, 'No, father Abraham, but if someone from the dead goes to them, they will repent.' [31]He replied to him, 'If they do not respond to Moses and the prophets, they will not be convinced even if someone rises from the dead.'"

SIN, FORGIVENESS, FAITH, AND SERVICE

17 Jesus said to his disciples, "Stumbling blocks are sure to
come, but woe to the one through whom they come! [2]It
would be better for him to have a millstone tied around his
neck and be thrown into the sea than for him to cause one of
these little ones to sin. [3]Watch yourselves! If your brother sins,
rebuke him. If he repents, forgive him. [4]Even if he sins against
you seven times in a day, and seven times returns to you saying,
'I repent,' you must forgive him."
[5]The apostles said to the Lord, "Increase our faith!" [6]So the
Lord replied, "If you had faith the size of a mustard seed, you
could say to this black mulberry tree, 'Be pulled out by the roots
and planted in the sea,' and it would obey you.
[7]"Would any one of you say to your slave who comes in from
the field after plowing or shepherding sheep, 'Come at once and
sit down for a meal'? [8]Won't the master instead say to him, 'Get
my dinner ready, and make yourself ready to serve me while I
eat and drink. Then you may eat and drink'? [9]He won't thank
the slave because he did what he was told, will he? [10]So you
too, when you have done everything you were commanded to
do, should say, 'We are slaves undeserving of special praise; we
have only done what was our duty.'"

THE GRATEFUL LEPER

[11]Now on the way to Jerusalem, Jesus was passing along between
Samaria and Galilee. [12]As he was entering a village, ten men
with leprosy met him. They stood at a distance, [13]raised their
voices and said, "Jesus, Master, have mercy on us." [14]When he
saw them he said, "Go and show yourselves to the priests." And
as they went along, they were cleansed. [15]Then one of them,
when he saw he was healed, turned back, praising God with a
loud voice. [16]He fell with his face to the ground at Jesus' feet
and thanked him. (Now he was a Samaritan.) [17]Then Jesus said,
"Were not ten cleansed? Where are the other nine? [18]Was no
one found to turn back and give praise to God except this foreigner?" [19]Then he said to the man, "Get up and go your way.
Your faith has made you well."

THE COMING OF THE KINGDOM

[20]Now at one point the Pharisees asked Jesus when the kingdom
of God was coming, so he answered, "The kingdom of God is not
coming with signs to be observed, [21]nor will they say, 'Look, here
it is!' or 'There!' For indeed, the kingdom of God is in your midst."

THE COMING OF THE SON OF MAN

[22]Then he said to the disciples, "The days are coming when
you will desire to see one of the days of the Son of Man, and
you will not see it. [23]Then people will say to you, 'Look, there
he is!' or 'Look, here he is!' Do not go out or chase after them.
[24]For just like the lightning flashes and lights up the sky from
one side to the other, so will the Son of Man be in his day.
[25]But first he must suffer many things and be rejected by this
generation. [26]Just as it was in the days of Noah, so too it will
be in the days of the Son of Man. [27]People were eating, they
were drinking, they were marrying, they were being given in
marriage—right up to the day Noah entered the ark. Then the
flood came and destroyed them all. [28]Likewise, just as it was in
the days of Lot, people were eating, drinking, buying, selling,
planting, building; [29]but on the day Lot went out from Sodom,

17:20 When our gaze has wandered ever so little from him, let us turn the eyes of the soul back to him and recall our mental gaze as in a perfectly straight direction. For everything depends on the inward frame of mind, and when the devil has been expelled from this and sins no longer reign in it, it follows that the kingdom of God is founded in us, as the evangelist says: "The kingdom of God is not coming with signs to be observed, nor will they say, 'Look, here it is!' or 'There!' For indeed, the kingdom of God is in your midst."

JOHN CASSIAN
(C. 360–C. 435)
THE CONFERENCES

fire and sulfur rained down from heaven and destroyed them
all. 30 It will be the same on the day the Son of Man is revealed.
31 On that day, anyone who is on the roof, with his goods in the
house, must not come down to take them away, and likewise
the person in the field must not turn back. 32 Remember Lot's
wife! 33 Whoever tries to keep his life will lose it, but whoever
loses his life will preserve it. 34 I tell you, in that night there will
be two people in one bed; one will be taken and the other left.
35 There will be two women grinding grain together; one will
be taken and the other left."*

37 Then the disciples said to him, "Where, Lord?" He replied to
them, "Where the dead body is, there the vultures will gather."

PRAYER AND THE PARABLE OF THE PERSISTENT WIDOW

18 Then Jesus told them a parable to show them they should
always pray and not lose heart. 2 He said, "In a certain city
there was a judge who neither feared God nor respected people.
3 There was also a widow in that city who kept coming to him
and saying, 'Give me justice against my adversary.' 4 For a while
he refused, but later on he said to himself, 'Though I neither
fear God nor have regard for people, 5 yet because this widow
keeps on bothering me, I will give her justice, or in the end she
will wear me out by her unending pleas.'" 6 And the Lord said,
"Listen to what the unrighteous judge says! 7 Won't God give
justice to his chosen ones, who cry out to him day and night?
Will he delay long to help them? 8 I tell you, he will give them
justice speedily. Nevertheless, when the Son of Man comes,
will he find faith on earth?"

THE PARABLE OF THE PHARISEE AND TAX COLLECTOR

9 Jesus also told this parable to some who were confident that
they were righteous and looked down on everyone else. 10 "Two
men went up to the temple to pray, one a Pharisee and the
other a tax collector. 11 The Pharisee stood and prayed about
himself like this: 'God, I thank you that I am not like other
people: extortionists, unrighteous people, adulterers—or even
like this tax collector. 12 I fast twice a week; I give a tenth of
everything I get.' 13 The tax collector, however, stood far off and
would not even look up to heaven, but beat his breast and said,
'God, be merciful to me, sinner that I am!' 14 I tell you that this
man went down to his home justified rather than the Pharisee.
For everyone who exalts himself will be humbled, but he who
humbles himself will be exalted."

JESUS AND LITTLE CHILDREN

15 Now people were even bringing their babies to him for him to
touch. But when the disciples saw it, they began to scold those
who brought them. 16 But Jesus called for the children, saying,
"Let the little children come to me and do not try to stop them,
for the kingdom of God belongs to such as these. 17 I tell you
the truth, whoever does not receive the kingdom of God like a
child will never enter it."

THE WEALTHY RULER

18 Now a certain leader asked him, "Good teacher, what must
I do to inherit eternal life?" 19 Jesus said to him, "Why do you
call me good? No one is good except God alone. 20 You know the

18:9–17 How useful and necessary a medicine is repentance! People who remember that they are only human will readily understand this. The Pharisee was not rejoicing so much in his own clean bill of health as in comparing it with the diseases of others. He came to the doctor. It would have been more worthwhile to inform him by confession of the things that were wrong with himself instead of keeping his wounds secret and having the nerve to crow over the scars of others. It is not surprising that the tax collector went away cured, since he had not been ashamed of showing where he felt pain.

AUGUSTINE **(354–430)**
SERMONS

commandments: '***Do not commit adultery, do not murder, do not***
steal, do not give false testimony, honor your father and mother.'"
21 The man replied, "I have wholeheartedly obeyed all these laws
since my youth." 22 When Jesus heard this, he said to him, "One
thing you still lack. Sell all that you have and give the money
to the poor, and you will have treasure in heaven. Then come,
follow me." 23 But when the man heard this, he became very sad,
for he was extremely wealthy. 24 When Jesus noticed this, he said,
"How hard it is for the rich to enter the kingdom of God! 25 In
fact, it is easier for a camel to go through the eye of a needle than
for a rich person to enter the kingdom of God." 26 Those who
heard this said, "Then who can be saved?" 27 He replied, "What
is impossible for mere humans is possible for God." 28 And Peter
said, "Look, we have left everything we own to follow you! 29 Then
Jesus said to them, "I tell you the truth, there is no one who has
left home or wife or brothers or parents or children for the sake
of God's kingdom 30 who will not receive many times more in
this age—and in the age to come, eternal life."

ANOTHER PREDICTION OF JESUS' PASSION

31 Then Jesus took the twelve aside and said to them, "Look,
we are going up to Jerusalem, and everything that is written
about the Son of Man by the prophets will be accomplished.
32 For he will be handed over to the Gentiles; he will be mocked,
mistreated, and spat on. 33 They will flog him severely and kill
him. Yet on the third day he will rise again." 34 But the twelve
understood none of these things. This saying was hidden from
them, and they did not grasp what Jesus meant.

HEALING A BLIND MAN

35 As Jesus approached Jericho, a blind man was sitting by the
road begging. 36 When he heard a crowd going by, he asked what
was going on. 37 They told him, "Jesus the Nazarene is passing
by." 38 So he called out, "Jesus, Son of David, have mercy on me!"
39 And those who were in front scolded him to get him to be
quiet, but he shouted even more, "Son of David, have mercy on
me!" 40 So Jesus stopped and ordered the beggar to be brought
to him. When the man came near, Jesus asked him, 41 "What do
you want me to do for you?" He replied, "Lord, let me see again."
42 Jesus said to him, "Receive your sight; your faith has healed
you." 43 And immediately he regained his sight and followed
Jesus, praising God. When all the people saw it, they too gave
praise to God.

JESUS AND ZACCHAEUS

19 Jesus entered Jericho and was passing through it. 2 Now a
man named Zacchaeus was there; he was a chief tax collector and was rich. 3 He was trying to get a look at Jesus, but
being a short man he could not see over the crowd. 4 So he ran
on ahead and climbed up into a sycamore tree to see him because Jesus was going to pass that way. 5 And when Jesus came
to that place, he looked up and said to him, "Zacchaeus, come
down quickly because I must stay at your house today." 6 So he
came down quickly and welcomed Jesus joyfully. 7 And when
the people saw it, they all complained, "He has gone in to be
the guest of a man who is a sinner." 8 But Zacchaeus stopped
and said to the Lord, "Look, Lord, half of my possessions I now
give to the poor, and if I have cheated anyone of anything, I
am paying back four times as much!" 9 Then Jesus said to him,

"Today salvation has come to this household because he too
is a son of Abraham! 10For the Son of Man came to seek and
to save the lost."

THE PARABLE OF THE TEN MINAS

11While the people were listening to these things, Jesus proceeded to tell a parable because he was near to Jerusalem, and
because they thought that the kingdom of God was going to
appear immediately. 12Therefore he said, "A nobleman went to
a distant country to receive for himself a kingdom and then
return. 13And he summoned ten of his slaves, gave them ten
minas, and said to them, 'Do business with these until I come
back.' 14But his citizens hated him and sent a delegation after him, saying, 'We do not want this man to be king over us!'
15When he returned after receiving the kingdom, he summoned
these slaves to whom he had given the money. He wanted to
know how much they had earned by trading. 16So the first one
came before him and said, 'Sir, your mina has made ten minas
more.' 17And the king said to him, 'Well done, good slave! Because you have been faithful in a very small matter, you will have
authority over ten cities.' 18Then the second one came and said,
'Sir, your mina has made five minas.' 19So the king said to him,
'And you are to be over five cities.' 20Then another slave came
and said, 'Sir, here is your mina that I put away for safekeeping
in a piece of cloth. 21For I was afraid of you because you are a
severe man. You withdraw what you did not deposit and reap
what you did not sow.' 22The king said to him, 'I will judge you
by your own words, you wicked slave! So you knew, did you,
that I was a severe man, withdrawing what I didn't deposit and
reaping what I didn't sow? 23Why then didn't you put my money
in the bank, so that when I returned I could have collected it
with interest?' 24And he said to his attendants, 'Take the mina
from him, and give it to the one who has ten.' 25But they said to
him, 'Sir, he has ten minas already!' 26'I tell you that everyone
who has will be given more, but from the one who does not
have, even what he has will be taken away. 27But as for these
enemies of mine who did not want me to be their king, bring
them here and slaughter them in front of me!'"

THE TRIUMPHAL ENTRY

28After Jesus had said this, he continued on ahead, going up to Jerusalem. 29Now when he approached Bethphage and Bethany, at
the place called the Mount of Olives, he sent two of the disciples,
30telling them, "Go to the village ahead of you. When you enter it,
you will find a colt tied there that has never been ridden. Untie
it and bring it here. 31If anyone asks you, 'Why are you untying
it?' just say, 'The Lord needs it.'" 32So those who were sent ahead
found it exactly as he had told them. 33As they were untying the
colt, its owners asked them, "Why are you untying that colt?"
34They replied, "The Lord needs it." 35Then they brought it to
Jesus, threw their cloaks on the colt, and had Jesus get on it.
36As he rode along, they spread their cloaks on the road. 37As he
approached the road leading down from the Mount of Olives, the
whole crowd of his disciples began to rejoice and praise God with
a loud voice for all the mighty works they had seen: 38"***Blessed is
the king who comes in the name of the Lord!*** Peace in heaven and
glory in the highest!" 39But some of the Pharisees in the crowd
said to him, "Teacher, rebuke your disciples." 40He answered, "I
tell you, if they keep silent, the very stones will cry out!"

19:11–27 The gifts of God are given for this purpose of God: that until Christ comes to judge the living and the dead, everyone may be occupied in increasing the riches of our Lord and to exercise faith and charity in themselves. For when the Lord gave these minas to his servants, he commanded them saying, "Do business with these until I come back."

JOHANNES BRENZ
(1499–1570)
ECCLESIASTICAL EXPOSITION UPON SAINT LUKE

JESUS WEEPS FOR JERUSALEM UNDER JUDGMENT

41 Now when Jesus approached and saw the city, he wept over it, 42 saying, "If you had only known on this day, even you, the things that make for peace! But now they are hidden from your eyes. 43 For the days will come upon you when your enemies will build an embankment against you and surround you and close in on you from every side. 44 They will demolish you—you and your children within your walls—and they will not leave within you one stone on top of another because you did not recognize the time of your visitation from God."

CLEANSING THE TEMPLE

45 Then Jesus entered the temple courts and began to drive out those who were selling things there, 46 saying to them, "It is written, '***My house will be a house of prayer,***' but you have turned it into ***a den of robbers***!"

47 Jesus was teaching daily in the temple courts. The chief priests and the experts in the law and the prominent leaders among the people were seeking to assassinate him, 48 but they could not find a way to do it, for all the people hung on his words.

THE AUTHORITY OF JESUS

20 Now one day, as Jesus was teaching the people in the temple courts and proclaiming the gospel, the chief priests and the experts in the law with the elders came up 2 and said to him, "Tell us: By what authority are you doing these things? Or who is it who gave you this authority?" 3 He answered them, "I will also ask you a question, and you tell me: 4 John's baptism—was it from heaven or from people?" 5 So they discussed it with one another, saying, "If we say, 'From heaven,' he will say, 'Why did you not believe him?' 6 But if we say, 'From people,' all the people will stone us because they are convinced that John was a prophet." 7 So they replied that they did not know where it came from. 8 Then Jesus said to them, "Neither will I tell you by whose authority I do these things."

THE PARABLE OF THE TENANTS

9 Then he began to tell the people this parable: "A man planted a vineyard, leased it to tenant farmers, and went on a journey for a long time. 10 When harvest time came, he sent a slave to the tenants so that they would give him his portion of the crop. However, the tenants beat his slave and sent him away empty-handed. 11 So he sent another slave. They beat this one too, treated him outrageously, and sent him away empty-handed. 12 So he sent still a third. They even wounded this one and threw him out. 13 Then the owner of the vineyard said, 'What should I do? I will send my one dear son; perhaps they will respect him.' 14 But when the tenants saw him, they said to one another, 'This is the heir; let's kill him so the inheritance will be ours!' 15 So they threw him out of the vineyard and killed him. What then will the owner of the vineyard do to them? 16 He will come and destroy those tenants and give the vineyard to others." When the people heard this, they said, "May this never happen!" 17 But Jesus looked straight at them and said, "Then what is the meaning of that which is written: '***The stone the builders rejected has become the cornerstone***'? 18 Everyone who falls on this stone will be broken to pieces, and the one on whom it falls will be crushed." 19 Then the experts in the law and the

20:1–19 Having silenced to an extent the priests, Pharisees, scribes, and the leaders among the people, the Lord added a parable that placed before their eyes their incurable malice. They had been encouraged by God to amend in many ways but were always becoming progressively worse, disdaining the law, killing the prophets, and after this they would kill the Son of God. Now, this certainly is the vineyard of the Lord of the Sabbath, which he brought up out of Egypt and established in the promised land. He provided a temple and added priests, judges, leaders, and doctors: He omitted nothing that pertained to their care. But this well-tended and cared-for vineyard, which was long expected to produce good grapes, in the end produced wild grapes through the fault of the laborers.

ERASMUS **(1466–1536)**
AN ECCLESIASTICAL EXPOSITION UPON SAINT LUKE

chief priests wanted to arrest him that very hour because they
realized he had told this parable against them. But they were
afraid of the people.

PAYING TAXES TO CAESAR

[20]Then they watched him carefully and sent spies who pretended to be sincere. They wanted to take advantage of what he
might say so that they could deliver him up to the authority and
jurisdiction of the governor. [21]Thus they asked him, "Teacher,
we know that you speak and teach correctly, and show no partiality, but teach the way of God in accordance with the truth.
[22]Is it right for us to pay the tribute tax to Caesar or not?" [23]But
Jesus perceived their deceit and said to them, [24]"Show me a
denarius. Whose image and inscription are on it?" They said,
"Caesar's." [25]So he said to them, "Then give to Caesar the things
that are Caesar's, and to God the things that are God's." [26]Thus
they were unable in the presence of the people to trap him
with his own words. And stunned by his answer, they fell silent.

MARRIAGE AND THE RESURRECTION

[27]Now some Sadducees (who contend that there is no resurrection) came to him. [28]They asked him, "Teacher, Moses wrote
for us that ***if a man's brother dies leaving*** a wife but ***no children,***
that man must marry the widow and father children for his broth-
er. [29]Now there were seven brothers. The first one married a
woman and died without children. [30]The second [31]and then the
third married her, and in this same way all seven died, leaving
no children. [32]Finally the woman died too. [33]In the resurrection, therefore, whose wife will the woman be? For all seven
had married her."

[34]So Jesus said to them, "The people of this age marry and are
given in marriage. [35]But those who are regarded as worthy to
share in that age and in the resurrection from the dead neither
marry nor are given in marriage. [36]In fact, they can no longer
die because they are equal to angels and are sons of God, since
they are sons of the resurrection. [37]But even Moses revealed
that the dead are raised in the passage about the bush, where
he calls the Lord ***the God of Abraham and the God of Isaac and***
the God of Jacob. [38]Now he is not God of the dead, but of the
living, for all live before him." [39]Then some of the experts in
the law answered, "Teacher, you have spoken well!" [40]For they
did not dare any longer to ask him anything.

THE MESSIAH: DAVID'S SON AND LORD

[41]But he said to them, "How is it that they say that the Christ
is David's son? [42]For David himself says in the book of Psalms,

'***The Lord said to my lord,***
"***Sit at my right hand,***
[43] ***until I make your enemies a footstool for your feet.***"'

[44]If David then calls him 'Lord,' how can he be his son?"

JESUS WARNS THE DISCIPLES AGAINST PRIDE

[45]As all the people were listening, Jesus said to his disciples,
[46]"Beware of the experts in the law. They like walking around
in long robes, and they love elaborate greetings in the marketplaces and the best seats in the synagogues and the places
of honor at banquets. [47]They devour widows' property, and
as a show make long prayers. They will receive a more severe
punishment."

THE WIDOW'S OFFERING

21 Jesus looked up and saw the rich putting their gifts into the offering box. 2He also saw a poor widow put in two small copper coins. 3He said, "I tell you the truth, this poor widow has put in more than all of them. 4For they all offered their gifts out of their wealth. But she, out of her poverty, put in everything she had to live on."

THE SIGNS OF THE END OF THE AGE

5Now while some were speaking about the temple, how it was adorned with beautiful stones and offerings, Jesus said, 6"As for these things that you are gazing at, the days will come when not one stone will be left on another. All will be torn down!" 7So they asked him, "Teacher, when will these things happen? And what will be the sign that these things are about to take place?" 8He said, "Watch out that you are not misled. For many will come in my name, saying, 'I am he,' and, 'The time is near.' Do not follow them! 9And when you hear of wars and rebellions, do not be afraid. For these things must happen first, but the end will not come at once."

21:5–24 Christ's second advent from heaven will not happen secretly but will be illustrious and terrifying. In the glory of God the Father, he will descend with the holy angels guarding him to judge the world in righteousness. Jesus gives clear and evident signs of the time when the consummation of the world draws near. He says that there will be wars, turmoil, famines, and epidemics everywhere. There will be terrors from heaven and great signs. The unendurable fear of those things that are coming will be sufficient for the destruction of many.

CYRIL OF ALEXANDRIA
(C. 376–444)
COMMENTARY ON LUKE

PERSECUTION OF DISCIPLES

10Then he said to them, "Nation will rise up in arms against nation, and kingdom against kingdom. 11There will be great earthquakes, and famines and plagues in various places, and there will be terrifying sights and great signs from heaven. 12But before all this, they will seize you and persecute you, handing you over to the synagogues and prisons. You will be brought before kings and governors because of my name. 13This will be a time for you to serve as witnesses. 14Therefore be resolved not to rehearse ahead of time how to make your defense. 15For I will give you the words along with the wisdom that none of your adversaries will be able to withstand or contradict. 16You will be betrayed even by parents, brothers, relatives, and friends, and they will have some of you put to death. 17You will be hated by everyone because of my name. 18Yet not a hair of your head will perish. 19By your endurance you will gain your lives.

THE DESOLATION OF JERUSALEM

20"But when you see Jerusalem surrounded by armies, then know that its desolation has come near. 21Then those who are in Judea must flee to the mountains. Those who are inside the city must depart. Those who are out in the country must not enter it, 22because these are days of vengeance, to fulfill all that is written. 23Woe to those who are pregnant and to those who are nursing their babies in those days! For there will be great distress on the earth and wrath against this people. 24They will fall by the edge of the sword and be led away as captives among all nations. Jerusalem will be trampled down by the Gentiles until the times of the Gentiles are fulfilled.

THE ARRIVAL OF THE SON OF MAN

25"And there will be signs in the sun and moon and stars, and on the earth nations will be in distress, anxious over the roaring of the sea and the surging waves. 26People will be fainting from fear and from the expectation of what is coming on the world, for *the powers of the heavens will be shaken.* 27Then they will see *the Son of Man arriving in a cloud* with power and great glory. 28But when these things begin to happen, stand up and raise your heads because your redemption is drawing near."

THE PARABLE OF THE FIG TREE

29 Then he told them a parable: "Look at the fig tree and all the
other trees. 30 When they sprout leaves, you see for yourselves
and know that summer is now near. 31 So also you, when you
see these things happening, know that the kingdom of God is
near. 32 I tell you the truth, this generation will not pass away
until all these things take place. 33 Heaven and earth will pass
away, but my words will never pass away.

BE READY!

34 "But be on your guard so that your hearts are not weighed
down with dissipation and drunkenness and the worries of this
life, and that day close down upon you suddenly like a trap. 35 For
it will overtake all who live on the face of the whole earth. 36 But
stay alert at all times, praying that you may have strength to
escape all these things that must happen, and to stand before
the Son of Man."

37 So every day Jesus was teaching in the temple courts, but
at night he went and stayed on the Mount of Olives. 38 And all
the people came to him early in the morning to listen to him
in the temple courts.

JUDAS' DECISION TO BETRAY JESUS

22 Now the Feast of Unleavened Bread, which is called the
Passover, was approaching. 2 The chief priests and the
experts in the law were trying to find some way to execute
Jesus, for they were afraid of the people.

3 Then Satan entered Judas, the one called Iscariot, who
was one of the twelve. 4 He went away and discussed with the
chief priests and officers of the temple guard how he might
betray Jesus, handing him over to them. 5 They were delighted
and arranged to give him money. 6 So Judas agreed and began
looking for an opportunity to betray Jesus when no crowd
was present.

THE PASSOVER

7 Then the day for the feast of Unleavened Bread came, on which
the Passover lamb had to be sacrificed. 8 Jesus sent Peter and
John, saying, "Go and prepare the Passover for us to eat." 9 They
said to him, "Where do you want us to prepare it?" 10 He said to
them, "Listen, when you have entered the city, a man carrying
a jar of water will meet you. Follow him into the house that he
enters, 11 and tell the owner of the house, 'The Teacher says to
you, "Where is the guest room where I may eat the Passover
with my disciples?"' 12 Then he will show you a large furnished
room upstairs. Make preparations there." 13 So they went and
found things just as he had told them, and they prepared the
Passover.

THE LORD'S SUPPER

14 Now when the hour came, Jesus took his place at the table
and the apostles joined him. 15 And he said to them, "I have
earnestly desired to eat this Passover with you before I suffer.
16 For I tell you, I will not eat it again until it is fulfilled in the
kingdom of God." 17 Then he took a cup, and after giving thanks
he said, "Take this and divide it among yourselves. 18 For I tell
you that from now on I will not drink of the fruit of the vine
until the kingdom of God comes." 19 Then he took bread, and
after giving thanks he broke it and gave it to them, saying, "This

is my body which is given for you. Do this in remembrance of
me.” 20 And in the same way he took the cup after they had
eaten, saying, “This cup that is poured out for you is the new
covenant in my blood.

A FINAL DISCOURSE

21 “But look, the hand of the one who betrays me is with me
on the table. 22 For the Son of Man is to go just as it has been
determined, but woe to that man by whom he is betrayed!”
23 So they began to question one another as to which of them
it could possibly be who would do this.
24 A dispute also started among them over which of them was
to be regarded as the greatest. 25 So Jesus said to them, “The kings
of the Gentiles lord it over them, and those in authority over
them are called ‘benefactors.’ 26 Not so with you; instead the one
who is greatest among you must become like the youngest, and
the leader like the one who serves. 27 For who is greater, the one
who is seated at the table, or the one who serves? Is it not the one
who is seated at the table? But I am among you as one who serves.
28 “You are the ones who have remained with me in my trials.
29 Thus I grant to you a kingdom, just as my Father granted to
me, 30 that you may eat and drink at my table in my kingdom,
and you will sit on thrones judging the 12 tribes of Israel.
31 “Simon, Simon, pay attention! Satan has demanded to have
you all, to sift you like wheat, 32 but I have prayed for you, Simon, that your faith may not fail. When you have turned back,
strengthen your brothers.” 33 But Peter said to him, “Lord, I
am ready to go with you both to prison and to death!” 34 Jesus
replied, “I tell you, Peter, the rooster will not crow today until
you have denied three times that you know me.”
35 Then Jesus said to them, “When I sent you out with no
money bag, or traveler’s bag, or sandals, you didn’t lack anything, did you?” They replied, “Nothing.” 36 He said to them, “But
now, the one who has a money bag must take it, and likewise a
traveler’s bag too. And the one who has no sword must sell his
cloak and buy one. 37 For I tell you that this scripture must be
fulfilled in me, ‘***And he was counted with the transgressors.***’ For
what is written about me is being fulfilled.” 38 So they said, “Look,
Lord, here are two swords.” Then he told them, “It is enough.”

ON THE MOUNT OF OLIVES

39 Then Jesus went out and made his way, as he customarily
did, to the Mount of Olives, and the disciples followed him.
40 When he came to the place, he said to them, “Pray that you
will not fall into temptation.” 41 He went away from them
about a stone’s throw, knelt down, and prayed, 42 “Father, if
you are willing, take this cup away from me. Yet not my will
but yours be done.” [43 Then an angel from heaven appeared
to him and strengthened him. 44 And in his anguish he prayed
more earnestly, and his sweat was like drops of blood falling
to the ground.]† 45 When he got up from prayer, he came to the
disciples and found them sleeping, exhausted from grief. 46 So
he said to them, “Why are you sleeping? Get up and pray that
you will not fall into temptation!”

BETRAYAL AND ARREST

47 While he was still speaking, suddenly a crowd appeared, and
the man named Judas, one of the twelve, was leading them. He
walked up to Jesus to kiss him. 48 But Jesus said to him, “Judas,

22:31–34 What an encouragement to know of our Redeemer’s never-ceasing intercession for us! Actually we know very little of how much we owe to our Savior’s prayers. But once we reach the mountaintops of heaven and look back on the paths the Lord our God has led us, oh, how we will praise him—he who before his Father’s eternal throne thwarted the mischief Satan was doing on earth! Oh, how we will thank him for never keeping his peace, but instead, day and night, pointing to the wounds in his hands and carrying our names on his breastplate! Even before Satan had begun to tempt us, Jesus obstructed our enemy’s way and entered a plea in heaven. Mercy outran malice!

CHARLES SPURGEON
(1834–1892)
MORNING AND EVENING

would you betray the Son of Man with a kiss?" 49When those who were around him saw what was about to happen, they said, "Lord, should we use our swords?" 50Then one of them struck the high priest's slave, cutting off his right ear. 51But Jesus said, "Enough of this!" And he touched the man's ear and healed him. 52Then Jesus said to the chief priests, the officers of the temple guard, and the elders who had come out to get him, "Have you come out with swords and clubs like you would against an outlaw? 53Day after day when I was with you in the temple courts, you did not arrest me. But this is your hour, and that of the power of darkness!"

JESUS' CONDEMNATION AND PETER'S DENIALS

54Then they arrested Jesus, led him away, and brought him into the high priest's house. But Peter was following at a distance. 55When they had made a fire in the middle of the courtyard and sat down together, Peter sat down among them. 56Then a slave girl, seeing him as he sat in the firelight, stared at him and said, "This man was with him too!" 57But Peter denied it: "Woman, I don't know him!" 58Then a little later someone else saw him and said, "You are one of them too." But Peter said, "Man, I am not!" 59And after about an hour still another insisted, "Certainly this man was with him because he too is a Galilean." 60But Peter said, "Man, I don't know what you're talking about!" At that moment, while he was still speaking, a rooster crowed. 61Then the Lord turned and looked straight at Peter, and Peter remembered the word of the Lord, how he had said to him, "Before a rooster crows today, you will deny me three times." 62And he went outside and wept bitterly.

63Now the men who were holding Jesus under guard began to mock him and beat him. 64They blindfolded him and asked him repeatedly, "Prophesy! Who hit you?" 65They also said many other things against him, reviling him.

66When day came, the council of the elders of the people gathered together, both the chief priests and the experts in the law. Then they led Jesus away to their council 67and said, "If you are the Christ, tell us." But he said to them, "If I tell you, you will not believe, 68and if I ask you, you will not answer. 69But from now on *the Son of Man will be seated at the right hand* of the power of God." 70So they all said, "Are you the Son of God, then?" He answered them, "You say that I am." 71Then they said, "Why do we need further testimony? We have heard it ourselves from his own lips!"

JESUS BROUGHT BEFORE PILATE

23 Then the whole group of them rose up and brought Jesus before Pilate. 2They began to accuse him, saying, "We found this man subverting our nation, forbidding us to pay the tribute tax to Caesar and claiming that he himself is Christ, a king." 3So Pilate asked Jesus, "Are you the king of the Jews?" He replied, "You say so." 4Then Pilate said to the chief priests and the crowds, "I find no basis for an accusation against this man." 5But they persisted in saying, "He incites the people by teaching throughout all Judea. It started in Galilee and ended up here!"

JESUS BROUGHT BEFORE HEROD

6Now when Pilate heard this, he asked whether the man was a Galilean. 7When he learned that he was from Herod's jurisdiction, he sent him over to Herod, who also happened to be in Jerusalem at that time. [8]When Herod saw Jesus, he was very glad, for he had long desired to see him because he had heard about him and was hoping to see him perform some miraculous sign. [9]So Herod questioned him at considerable length; Jesus gave him no answer. [10]The chief priests and the experts in the law were there, vehemently accusing him. [11]Even Herod with his soldiers treated him with contempt and mocked him. Then, dressing him in elegant clothes, Herod sent him back to Pilate. [12]That very day Herod and Pilate became friends with each other, for prior to this they had been enemies.

JESUS BROUGHT BEFORE THE CROWD

[13]Then Pilate called together the chief priests, the leaders, and the people, [14]and said to them, "You brought me this man as one who was misleading the people. When I examined him before you, I did not find this man guilty of anything you accused him of doing. [15]Neither did Herod, for he sent him back to us. Look, he has done nothing deserving death. [16]I will therefore have him flogged and release him."‡

[18]But they all shouted out together, "Take this man away! Release Barabbas for us!" [19](This was a man who had been thrown into prison for an insurrection started in the city, and for murder.) [20]Pilate addressed them once again because he wanted to release Jesus. [21]But they kept on shouting, "Crucify, crucify him!" [22]A third time he said to them, "Why? What wrong has he done? I have found him guilty of no crime deserving death. I will therefore flog him and release him." [23]But they were insistent, demanding with loud shouts that he be crucified. And their shouts prevailed. [24]So Pilate decided that their demand should be granted. [25]He released the man they asked for, who had been thrown in prison for insurrection and murder. But he handed Jesus over to their will.

THE CRUCIFIXION

[26]As they led him away, they seized Simon of Cyrene, who was coming in from the country. They placed the cross on his back and made him carry it behind Jesus. [27]A great number of the people followed him, among them women who were mourning and wailing for him. [28]But Jesus turned to them and said, "Daughters of Jerusalem, do not weep for me, but weep for yourselves and for your children. [29]For this is certain: The days are coming when they will say, 'Blessed are the barren, the wombs that never bore children, and the breasts that never nursed!' [30]Then they will begin *to say to the mountains, 'Fall on us!' and to the hills, 'Cover us!'* [31]For if such things are done when the wood is green, what will happen when it is dry?"

[32]Two other criminals were also led away to be executed with him. [33]So when they came to the place that is called "The Skull," they crucified him there, along with the criminals, one on his right and one on his left. [34][But Jesus said, "Father, forgive them, for they don't know what they are doing."]§ Then *they threw dice to divide his clothes.* [35]The people also stood there watching, but the leaders ridiculed him, saying, "He saved others. Let him save himself if he is the Christ of God, his chosen one!" [36]The soldiers also mocked him, coming up and offering him sour wine, [37]and saying, "If you are the king of the Jews, save yourself!" [38]There was also an inscription over him, "This is the king of the Jews."

[39]One of the criminals who was hanging there railed at him, saying, "Aren't you the Christ? Save yourself and us!" [40]But the

other rebuked him, saying, "Don't you fear God, since you are under the same sentence of condemnation? [41]And we rightly so, for we are getting what we deserve for what we did, but this man has done nothing wrong." [42]Then he said, "Jesus, remember me when you come in your kingdom." [43]And Jesus said to him, "I tell you the truth, today you will be with me in paradise."

[44]It was now about noon, and darkness came over the whole land until three in the afternoon, [45]because the sun's light failed. The temple curtain was torn in two. [46]Then Jesus, calling out with a loud voice, said, "Father, ***into your hands I commit my spirit!***" And after he said this he breathed his last.

[47]Now when the centurion saw what had happened, he praised God and said, "Certainly this man was innocent!" [48]And all the crowds that had assembled for this spectacle, when they saw what had taken place, returned home beating their breasts. [49]And all those who knew Jesus stood at a distance, and the women who had followed him from Galilee saw these things.

23:46 During this fearful torture Jesus' faith remained uninjured so that while he complained of being forsaken, he still relied on the aid of God as at hand. No one who considers that Christ undertook the office of mediator on the condition of suffering our condemnation, both in his body and in his soul, will think it strange that he maintained a struggle with the sorrows of death, as if an offended God had thrown him into a whirlpool of afflictions.

JOHN CALVIN **(1509–1564)**
COMPLETE COMMENTARY ON THE BIBLE

JESUS' BURIAL

[50]Now there was a man named Joseph who was a member of the council, a good and righteous man. [51](He had not consented to their plan and action.) He was from the Judean town of Arimathea, and was looking forward to the kingdom of God. [52]He went to Pilate and asked for the body of Jesus. [53]Then he took it down, wrapped it in a linen cloth, and placed it in a tomb cut out of the rock, where no one had yet been buried. [54]It was the day of preparation, and the Sabbath was beginning. [55]The women who had accompanied Jesus from Galilee followed, and they saw the tomb and how his body was laid in it. [56]Then they returned and prepared aromatic spices and perfumes.

On the Sabbath they rested according to the commandment.

THE RESURRECTION

24 Now on the first day of the week, at early dawn, the women went to the tomb, taking the aromatic spices they had prepared. [2]They found that the stone had been rolled away from the tomb, [3]but when they went in, they did not find the body of the Lord Jesus. [4]While they were perplexed about this, suddenly two men stood beside them in dazzling attire. [5]The women were terribly frightened and bowed their faces to the ground, but the men said to them, "Why do you look for the living among the dead? [6]He is not here, but has been raised! Remember how he told you, while he was still in Galilee, [7]that the Son of Man must be delivered into the hands of sinful men, and be crucified, and on the third day rise again." [8]Then the women remembered his words, [9]and when they returned from the tomb, they told all these things to the eleven and to all the rest. [10]Now it was Mary Magdalene, Joanna, Mary the mother of James, and the other women with them who told these things to the apostles. [11]But these words seemed like pure nonsense to them, and they did not believe them. [12]But Peter got up and ran to the tomb. He bent down and saw only the strips of linen cloth; then he went home, wondering what had happened.

24:1–12 We may wonder that these disciples—who believed Jesus to be the Son of God and the true Messiah, who had been so often told that he must die and rise again and then enter into his glory, who had seen him more than once raise the dead—should be so backward to believe his raising himself. But all our mistakes in religion spring from ignorance or forgetfulness of the words Christ has spoken. There are many things puzzling and perplexing to us that would be plain and profitable if we rightly understood the words of Christ.

MATTHEW HENRY **(1662–1714)**
COMMENTARY ON THE WHOLE BIBLE

JESUS WALKS THE ROAD TO EMMAUS

[13]Now that very day two of them were on their way to a village called Emmaus, about seven miles from Jerusalem. [14]They were talking to each other about all the things that had happened. [15]While they were talking and debating these things, Jesus

himself approached and began to accompany them 16(but their
eyes were kept from recognizing him). 17Then he said to them,
“What are these matters you are discussing so intently as you
walk along?” And they stood still, looking sad. 18Then one of
them, named Cleopas, answered him, “Are you the only visitor
to Jerusalem who doesn’t know the things that have happened
there in these days?” 19He said to them, “What things?” “The
things concerning Jesus the Nazarene,” they replied, “a man
who, with his powerful deeds and words, proved to be a prophet
before God and all the people; 20and how our chief priests and
leaders handed him over to be condemned to death, and crucified him. 21But we had hoped that he was the one who was
going to redeem Israel. Not only this, but it is now the third day
since these things happened. 22Furthermore, some women of
our group amazed us. They were at the tomb early this morning,
23and when they did not find his body, they came back and said
they had seen a vision of angels, who said he was alive. 24Then
some of those who were with us went to the tomb and found it
just as the women had said, but they did not see him.” 25So he
said to them, “You foolish people—how slow of heart to believe
all that the prophets have spoken! 26Wasn’t it necessary for the
Christ to suffer these things and enter into his glory?” 27Then
beginning with Moses and all the prophets, he interpreted to
them the things written about himself in all the scriptures.

28So they approached the village where they were going. He
acted as though he wanted to go farther, 29but they urged him,
“Stay with us because it is getting toward evening and the day
is almost done.” So he went in to stay with them.

30When he had taken his place at the table with them, he
took the bread, blessed and broke it, and gave it to them. 31At
this point their eyes were opened and they recognized him.
Then he vanished out of their sight. 32They said to each other,
“Didn’t our hearts burn within us while he was speaking with
us on the road, while he was explaining the scriptures to us?”
33So they got up that very hour and returned to Jerusalem. They
found the eleven and those with them gathered together 34and
saying, “The Lord has really risen and has appeared to Simon!”
35Then they told what had happened on the road, and how they
recognized him when he broke the bread.

JESUS MAKES A FINAL APPEARANCE

36While they were saying these things, Jesus himself stood
among them and said to them, “Peace be with you.” 37But they
were startled and terrified, thinking they saw a ghost. 38Then
he said to them, “Why are you frightened, and why do doubts
arise in your hearts? 39Look at my hands and my feet; it’s me!
Touch me and see; a ghost does not have flesh and bones like
you see I have.” 40When he had said this, he showed them his
hands and his feet. 41And while they still could not believe it
(because of their joy) and were amazed, he said to them, “Do
you have anything here to eat?” 42So they gave him a piece of
broiled fish, 43and he took it and ate it in front of them.

JESUS’ FINAL COMMISSION

44Then he said to them, “These are my words that I spoke to
you while I was still with you, that everything written about
me in the law of Moses and the prophets and the psalms must
be fulfilled.” 45Then he opened their minds so they could understand the scriptures, 46and said to them, “Thus it stands

written that the Christ would suffer and would rise from the
dead on the third day, [47]and repentance for the forgiveness of
sins would be proclaimed in his name to all nations, beginning
from Jerusalem. [48]You are witnesses of these things. [49]And look,
I am sending you what my Father promised. But stay in the city
until you have been clothed with power from on high."

JESUS' DEPARTURE

[50]Then Jesus led them out as far as Bethany, and lifting up his
hands, he blessed them. [51]Now during the blessing he departed
and was taken up into heaven. [52]So they worshiped him and
returned to Jerusalem with great joy, [53]and were continually
in the temple courts blessing God.

AUTHOR	AUDIENCE	DATE	PURPOSE	THEMES
John	Primarily Gentile believers and seeking unbelievers	Between AD 50 and 85	John wrote his biographical account of Jesus' life, death, and resurrection so that people would know he is the Messiah and experience eternal life in his name.	Belief in Jesus; the person of Jesus; the Holy Spirit; and eternal life

John's compelling reason for writing his biography about Jesus is clear from the Gospel itself: "These are recorded so that you may believe that Jesus is the Christ, the Son of God, and that by believing you may have life in his name" (20:31). He wanted Jewish people in particular to believe that Jesus was the long-awaited Messiah, the one God had promised long ago to set the world right. And he wanted them and people everywhere to experience the fullness of life by believing. The word *believe* is a major feature of John's Gospel, appearing nearly 100 times, and the object to which belief is directed is Jesus. It is by believing "in him" (3:16) that we are forgiven of our sins, saved from death, and given eternal life.

Jesus' identity is a significant theme of John's biography. As Matthew Henry explained, "The design of this Gospel appears to be to convey to the Christian world just notions of the real nature, office, and character of that divine Teacher who came to instruct and to redeem mankind." John's answer to the question "Who is Jesus?" is that he is the Son of God, the chosen one, the Messiah, true God from true God. This latter characteristic of Jesus' identity was particularly crucial for the early church, which became embroiled in questions concerning the divinity and nature of Jesus. John revealed from the start: "In the beginning was the Word, and the Word was with God, and the Word was fully God" (1:1). Chrysostom notes, "While all the other Evangelists begin with the incarnation . . . John, passing by everything else—his conception, his birth, his education, and his growth—speaks immediately of his eternal generation" from God the Father.

John's Gospel reveals that Jesus, the Son of God, did what God the Father sent him to do. He received everyone the Father sent him, drawing them close and giving them life. He spoke only what the Father commanded him to say. And he was glorified by the Father in his obedience to death. In many ways then John revealed to us God the Father alongside Jesus the Son. Ultimately, we see Jesus is God himself, eternal but coming to earth in flesh and blood, full of grace and truth.

JOHN

Alongside the person of Christ, we gain great insight into the person and work of the Holy Spirit. More is revealed in John's Gospel than in any other about the third person of the Trinity. We see that the Spirit came down from heaven at Jesus' baptism and empowered him for ministry. Jesus himself promised the Holy Spirit as a gift to believers, an advocate to lead them into the truth. Throughout church history, the communion of saints has used John's Gospel to teach on the vital doctrine of the Holy Spirit.

According to the Nicene Creed, orthodox Christians have always looked forward to the hope and promise of "life of the world to come." This is the eternal life John speaks of throughout his Gospel. "This is the way God loved the world: He gave his one and only Son, so that everyone who believes in him will not perish but have eternal life" (3:16). But this eternal life isn't reserved exclusively for the afterlife. John wrote, "In him was life, and the life was the light of mankind" (1:4), now as much as later. Jesus promised the woman at the well "living water" (4:10), which was meant to satiate our thirst now, in this life. And yet this life is meant to go on forever, for Christ has promised to come back and take us to the place he has prepared for us, to live with him forever (14:1–4).

For generations, John 3:16 has been an anchor verse for the Christian faith, for it succinctly expresses the greatest gift ever given. The Venerable Bede's comment on this verse summarizes the message of John's Gospel: "Our Redeemer and Maker, who was Son of God before the ages, became Son of Man at the end of ages. Thus the one who, through the power of his divinity, had created us to enjoy the happiness of everlasting life might himself restore us, through the weakness of our humanity, to recover the life we had lost."

1:1–5 If the Son was not made, then he is not a creature; but if he is not a creature, then he is of the same substance with the Father. For all substance that is not God is creature, and all that is not creature is God. And if the Son is not of the same substance with the Father, then he is a substance that was made; and if he is a substance that was made, then all things were not made by him; but "all things were created by him," therefore he is of one and the same substance with the Father. And so he is not only God but also very God.

AUGUSTINE **(354–430)**
ON THE TRINITY

THE PROLOGUE TO THE GOSPEL

1 In the beginning was the Word, and the Word was with God,
and the Word was fully God. 2The Word was with God in the
beginning. 3All things were created by him, and apart from
him not one thing was created that has been created. 4*In him
was life,* and the life was the light of mankind. 5And the light
shines on in the darkness, but the darkness has not mastered it.
6A man came, sent from God, whose name was John. 7He
came as a witness to testify about the light, so that everyone
might believe through him. 8He himself was not the light, but
he came to testify about the light. 9The true light, who gives
light to everyone, was coming into the world. 10He was in the
world, and the world was created by him, but the world did
not recognize him. 11He came to what was his own, but his
own people did not receive him. 12But to all who have received
him—those who believe in his name—he has given the right to
become God's children—13children not born by human parents
or by human desire or a husband's decision, but by God.
14Now the Word became flesh and took up residence among
us. We saw his glory—the glory of the one and only, full of grace
and truth, who came from the Father. 15John testified about
him and shouted out, "This one was the one about whom I
said, 'He who comes after me is greater than I am, because he
existed before me.'" 16For we have all received from his fullness
one gracious gift after another. 17For the law was given through
Moses, but grace and truth came about through Jesus Christ.
18No one has ever seen God. The only one, himself God, who
is in closest fellowship with the Father, has made God known.

THE TESTIMONY OF JOHN THE BAPTIST

19Now this was John's testimony when the Jewish leaders sent
priests and Levites from Jerusalem to ask him, "Who are you?"
20He confessed—he did not deny but confessed—"I am not the
Christ!" 21So they asked him, "Then who are you? Are you Elijah?" He said, "I am not!" "Are you the Prophet?" He answered,
"No!" 22Then they said to him, "Who are you? Tell us so that
we can give an answer to those who sent us. What do you say
about yourself?"
23John said, "I am ***the voice of one shouting in the wilderness,***
'Make straight the way for the Lord,' as the prophet Isaiah said."
24(Now they had been sent from the Pharisees.) 25So they asked
John, "Why then are you baptizing if you are not the Christ, nor
Elijah, nor the Prophet?"
26John answered them, "I baptize with water. Among you
stands one whom you do not recognize, 27who is coming after
me. I am not worthy to untie the strap of his sandal!" 28These
things happened in Bethany across the Jordan River where
John was baptizing.
29On the next day John saw Jesus coming toward him and
said, "Look, the Lamb of God who takes away the sin of the
world! 30This is the one about whom I said, 'After me comes a
man who is greater than I am, because he existed before me.'
31I did not recognize him, but I came baptizing with water so
that he could be revealed to Israel."
32Then John testified, "I saw the Spirit descending like a dove
from heaven, and it remained on him. 33And I did not recognize him, but the one who sent me to baptize with water said
to me, 'The one on whom you see the Spirit descending and
remaining—this is the one who baptizes with the Holy Spirit.'

[34]I have both seen and testified that this man is the Chosen
One of God."
[35]Again the next day John was standing there with two of
his disciples. [36]Gazing at Jesus as he walked by, he said, "Look,
the Lamb of God!" [37]When John's two disciples heard him say
this, they followed Jesus. [38]Jesus turned around and saw them
following and said to them, "What do you want?" So they said
to him, "Rabbi" (which is translated Teacher), "where are you
staying?" [39]Jesus answered, "Come and you will see." So they
came and saw where he was staying, and they stayed with him
that day. Now it was about four o'clock in the afternoon.

ANDREW'S DECLARATION

[40]Andrew, the brother of Simon Peter, was one of the two disciples who heard what John said and followed Jesus. [41]He first
found his own brother Simon and told him, "We have found the
Messiah!" (which is translated Christ). [42]Andrew brought Simon
to Jesus. Jesus looked at him and said, "You are Simon, the son
of John. You will be called Cephas" (which is translated Peter).

THE CALLING OF MORE DISCIPLES

[43]On the next day Jesus wanted to set out for Galilee. He found
Philip and said to him, "Follow me." [44](Now Philip was from
Bethsaida, the town of Andrew and Peter.) [45]Philip found Nathanael and told him, "We have found the one Moses wrote
about in the law, and the prophets also wrote about—Jesus of
Nazareth, the son of Joseph." [46]Nathanael replied, "Can anything
good come out of Nazareth?" Philip replied, "Come and see."
[47]Jesus saw Nathanael coming toward him and exclaimed,
"Look, a true Israelite *in whom there is no deceit!*" [48]Nathanael
asked him, "How do you know me?" Jesus replied, "Before Philip called you, when you were under the fig tree, I saw you."
[49]Nathanael answered him, "Rabbi, you are the Son of God;
you are the king of Israel!" [50]Jesus said to him, "Because I told
you that I saw you under the fig tree, do you believe? You will
see greater things than these." [51]He continued, "I tell all of you
the solemn truth—you will see heaven opened and the angels
of God ascending and descending on the Son of Man."

TURNING WATER INTO WINE

2 Now on the third day there was a wedding at Cana in Galilee.
Jesus' mother was there, [2]and Jesus and his disciples were also
invited to the wedding. [3]When the wine ran out, Jesus' mother
said to him, "They have no wine left." [4]Jesus replied, "Woman,
why are you saying this to me? My time has not yet come." [5]His
mother told the servants, "Whatever he tells you, do it."
[6]Now there were six stone water jars there for Jewish ceremonial washing, each holding 20 or 30 gallons. [7]Jesus told the
servants, "Fill the water jars with water." So they filled them
up to the very top. [8]Then he told them, "Now draw some out
and take it to the head steward," and they did. [9]When the head
steward tasted the water that had been turned to wine, not
knowing where it came from (though the servants who had
drawn the water knew), he called the bridegroom [10]and said to
him, "Everyone serves the good wine first, and then the cheaper
wine when the guests are drunk. You have kept the good wine
until now!" [11]Jesus did this as the first of his miraculous signs,
in Cana of Galilee. In this way he revealed his glory, and his
disciples believed in him.

CLEANSING THE TEMPLE

[12]After this he went down to Capernaum with his mother and
brothers and his disciples, and they stayed there a few days.
[13]Now the Jewish Feast of Passover was near, so Jesus went up
to Jerusalem.
[14]He found in the temple courts those who were selling
oxen and sheep and doves, and the money changers sitting at
tables. [15]So he made a whip of cords and drove them all out of
the temple courts, with the sheep and the oxen. He scattered
the coins of the money changers and overturned their tables.
[16]To those who sold the doves he said, "Take these things away
from here! Do not make my Father's house a marketplace!"
[17]His disciples remembered that it was written, ***"Zeal for your
house will devour me."***
[18]So then the Jewish leaders responded, "What sign can you
show us, since you are doing these things?" [19]Jesus replied, "Destroy this temple and in three days I will raise it up again."
[20]Then the Jewish leaders said to him, "This temple has been
under construction for 46 years, and are you going to raise it
up in three days?" [21]But Jesus was speaking about the temple
of his body. [22]So after he was raised from the dead, his disciples remembered that he had said this, and they believed the
scripture and the saying that Jesus had spoken.

2:13–25 The Messiah was the king and priest of God's people. He had come to save humankind and to reform the true religion of his Father, which at that time was distorted by many foolish traditions and crazy things. But the temple was the workshop of religion. And so it was fitting that he hastens straight to the temple and drives out the sellers and buyers. For it is the duty of a king to liberate his oppressed people. And it is the duty of a priest to cleanse religion when it has been defiled and to build it up when it has collapsed. Here our most excellent Lord shows himself to be the Messiah of God's people who had come to declare God's glory, to reform his church, and to save his people.

HEINRICH BULLINGER
(1504–1575)
COMMENTARY ON JOHN

JESUS AT THE PASSOVER FEAST

[23]Now while Jesus was in Jerusalem at the Feast of the Passover, many people believed in his name because they saw the
miraculous signs he was doing. [24]But Jesus would not entrust
himself to them because he knew all people. [25]He did not
need anyone to testify about man, for he knew what was in
man.

CONVERSATION WITH NICODEMUS

3 Now a certain man, a Pharisee named Nicodemus, who was a
member of the Jewish ruling council, [2]came to Jesus at night
and said to him, "Rabbi, we know that you are a teacher who
has come from God. For no one could perform the miraculous
signs that you do unless God is with him." [3]Jesus replied, "I tell
you the solemn truth, unless a person is born from above, he
cannot see the kingdom of God." [4]Nicodemus said to him, "How
can a man be born when he is old? He cannot enter his mother's
womb and be born a second time, can he?"
[5]Jesus answered, "I tell you the solemn truth, unless a person
is born of water and spirit, he cannot enter the kingdom of
God. [6]What is born of the flesh is flesh, and what is born of the
Spirit is spirit. [7]Do not be amazed that I said to you, 'You must
all be born from above.' [8]The wind blows wherever it will, and
you hear the sound it makes, but do not know where it comes
from and where it is going. So it is with everyone who is born
of the Spirit."
[9]Nicodemus replied, "How can these things be?" [10]Jesus answered, "Are you the teacher of Israel and yet you don't understand these things? [11]I tell you the solemn truth, we speak about
what we know and testify about what we have seen, but you
people do not accept our testimony. [12]If I have told you people
about earthly things and you don't believe, how will you believe
if I tell you about heavenly things? [13]No one has ascended into
heaven except the one who descended from heaven—the Son
of Man. [14]Just as Moses *lifted up the serpent in the wilderness,*

3:1–21 Nicodemus knew only one birth from Adam and Eve. He did not yet know the birth from God and the church. He knew only the parents who beget death. He did not yet know the parents who beget life. He knew only the parents who beget those who will succeed them. He did not yet know the parents who, living forever, beget those who will remain. Therefore, although there are two births, he knew only one. One is from earth, the other from heaven. One is from the flesh, the other from the Spirit. One is from mortality, the other from eternity. One is from male and female, the other from God and the church. But these two are each individual instances. Neither the one nor the other can be repeated.

AUGUSTINE **(354–430)**
TRACTATES ON THE GOSPEL OF JOHN

so must the Son of Man be lifted up, 15so that everyone who
believes in him may have eternal life."
16For this is the way God loved the world: He gave his one and
only Son, so that everyone who believes in him will not perish
but have eternal life. 17For God did not send his Son into the
world to condemn the world, but that the world should be saved
through him. 18The one who believes in him is not condemned.
The one who does not believe has been condemned already,
because he has not believed in the name of the one and only
Son of God. 19Now this is the basis for judging: that the light
has come into the world and people loved the darkness rather
than the light because their deeds were evil. 20For everyone
who does evil deeds hates the light and does not come to the
light, so that their deeds will not be exposed. 21But the one who
practices the truth comes to the light, so that it may be plainly
evident that his deeds have been done in God.

FURTHER TESTIMONY ABOUT JESUS BY JOHN THE BAPTIST

22After this, Jesus and his disciples came into Judean territory,
and there he spent time with them and was baptizing. 23John
was also baptizing at Aenon near Salim because water was plentiful there, and people were coming to him and being baptized.
24(For John had not yet been thrown into prison.)
25Now a dispute came about between some of John's disciples
and a certain Jew concerning ceremonial washing. 26So they
came to John and said to him, "Rabbi, the one who was with
you on the other side of the Jordan River, about whom you
testified—see, he is baptizing, and everyone is flocking to him!"
27John replied, "No one can receive anything unless it has
been given to him from heaven. 28You yourselves can testify
that I said, 'I am not the Christ,' but rather, 'I have been sent
before him.' 29The one who has the bride is the bridegroom.
The friend of the bridegroom, who stands by and listens for
him, rejoices greatly when he hears the bridegroom's voice.
This then is my joy, and it is complete. 30He must become more
important while I become less important."
31The one who comes from above is superior to all. The one
who is from the earth belongs to the earth and speaks about
earthly things. The one who comes from heaven is superior
to all. 32He testifies about what he has seen and heard, but
no one accepts his testimony. 33The one who has accepted his
testimony has confirmed clearly that God is truthful. 34For the
one whom God has sent speaks the words of God, for he does
not give the Spirit sparingly. 35The Father loves the Son and has
placed all things under his authority. 36The one who believes in
the Son has eternal life. The one who rejects the Son will not
see life, but God's wrath remains on him.

DEPARTURE FROM JUDEA

4 Now when Jesus knew that the Pharisees had heard that he
was winning and baptizing more disciples than John 2(although Jesus himself was not baptizing, but his disciples were),
3he left Judea and set out once more for Galilee.

CONVERSATION WITH A SAMARITAN WOMAN

4But he had to pass through Samaria. 5Now he came to a Samaritan town called Sychar, near the plot of land that Jacob
had given to his son Joseph. 6Jacob's well was there, so Jesus,

since he was tired from the journey, sat right down beside the well. It was about noon.

7 A Samaritan woman came to draw water. Jesus said to her, "Give me some water to drink." 8 (For his disciples had gone off into the town to buy supplies.) 9 So the Samaritan woman said to him, "How can you—a Jew—ask me, a Samaritan woman, for water to drink?" (For Jews use nothing in common with Samaritans.)

10 Jesus answered her, "If you had known the gift of God and who it is who said to you, 'Give me some water to drink,' you would have asked him, and he would have given you living water." 11 "Sir," the woman said to him, "you have no bucket and the well is deep; where then do you get this living water? 12 Surely you're not greater than our ancestor Jacob, are you? For he gave us this well and drank from it himself, along with his sons and his livestock."

13 Jesus replied, "Everyone who drinks some of this water will be thirsty again. 14 But whoever drinks some of the water that I will give him will never be thirsty again, but the water that I will give him will become in him a fountain of water springing up to eternal life." 15 The woman said to him, "Sir, give me this water, so that I will not be thirsty or have to come here to draw water." 16 He said to her, "Go call your husband and come back here." 17 The woman replied, "I have no husband." Jesus said to her, "Right you are when you said, 'I have no husband,' 18 for you have had five husbands, and the man you are living with now is not your husband. This you said truthfully!"

19 The woman said to him, "Sir, I see that you are a prophet. 20 Our fathers worshiped on this mountain, and you people say that the place where people must worship is in Jerusalem." 21 Jesus said to her, "Believe me, woman, a time is coming when you will worship the Father neither on this mountain nor in Jerusalem. 22 You people worship what you do not know. We worship what we know because salvation is from the Jews. 23 But a time is coming—and now is here—when the true worshipers will worship the Father in spirit and truth, for the Father seeks such people to be his worshipers. 24 God is spirit, and the people who worship him must worship in spirit and truth." 25 The woman said to him, "I know that Messiah is coming" (the one called Christ); "whenever he comes, he will tell us everything." 26 Jesus said to her, "I, the one speaking to you, am he."

THE DISCIPLES RETURN

27 Now at that very moment his disciples came back. They were shocked because he was speaking with a woman. However, no one said, "What do you want?" or "Why are you speaking with her?" 28 Then the woman left her water jar, went off into the town and said to the people, 29 "Come, see a man who told me everything I ever did. Surely he can't be the Messiah, can he?" 30 So they left the town and began coming to him.

WORKERS FOR THE HARVEST

31 Meanwhile the disciples were urging him, "Rabbi, eat something." 32 But he said to them, "I have food to eat that you know nothing about." 33 So the disciples began to say to one another, "No one brought him anything to eat, did they?" 34 Jesus said to them, "My food is to do the will of the one who sent me and to complete his work. 35 Don't you say, 'There are four more months

4:27–38 Jesus was always seizing opportunities for bringing people away from worry about material things to eagerness for spiritual things. Just as he had led the woman from the mention of water to a knowledge of the gospel faith, he likewise drew the still untrained disciples from the circumstance of food to eagerness for spreading the gospel. In the earlier instance perhaps he was not thirsty for well water; and if he was thirsty, he thirsted more for the salvation of humankind; nonetheless, he took the opportunity for a holy conversation from the feelings of a woman who had come to draw water. Similarly now, though he was hungry in the manner of all flesh, he had a greater hunger to save the human race for whose sake he had come from heaven.

ERASMUS **(1466–1536)**
PARAPHRASE OF THE GOSPEL OF JOHN

and then comes the harvest?' I tell you, look up and see that
the fields are already white for harvest! 36The one who reaps
receives pay and gathers fruit for eternal life, so that the one
who sows and the one who reaps can rejoice together. 37For in
this instance the saying is true, 'One sows and another reaps.'
38I sent you to reap what you did not work for; others have
labored and you have entered into their labor."

THE SAMARITANS RESPOND

39Now many Samaritans from that town believed in him because of the report of the woman who testified, "He told me
everything I ever did." 40So when the Samaritans came to him,
they began asking him to stay with them. He stayed there two
days, 41and because of his word many more believed. 42They
said to the woman, "No longer do we believe because of your
words, for we have heard for ourselves, and we know that this
one really is the Savior of the world."

ONWARD TO GALILEE

43After the two days he departed from there to Galilee. 44(For
Jesus himself had testified that a prophet has no honor in his
own country.) 45So when he came to Galilee, the Galileans welcomed him because they had seen all the things he had done
in Jerusalem at the feast (for they themselves had gone to the
feast).

HEALING THE ROYAL OFFICIAL'S SON

46Now he came again to Cana in Galilee where he had made
the water wine. In Capernaum there was a certain royal official
whose son was sick. 47When he heard that Jesus had come back
from Judea to Galilee, he went to him and begged him to come
down and heal his son, who was about to die. 48So Jesus said to
him, "Unless you people see signs and wonders you will never
believe!" 49"Sir," the official said to him, "come down before
my child dies." 50Jesus told him, "Go home; your son will live."
The man believed the word that Jesus spoke to him, and set
off for home.
51While he was on his way down, his slaves met him and
told him that his son was going to live. 52So he asked them the
time when his condition began to improve, and they told him,
"Yesterday at one o'clock in the afternoon the fever left him."
53Then the father realized that it was the very time Jesus had
said to him, "Your son will live," and he himself believed along
with his entire household. 54Jesus did this as his second miraculous sign when he returned from Judea to Galilee.

HEALING A PARALYTIC AT THE POOL OF BETHESDA

5 After this there was a Jewish feast, and Jesus went up to Jerusalem. 2Now there is in Jerusalem by the Sheep Gate a pool
called *Bethzatha* in Aramaic, which has five covered walkways.
3A great number of sick, blind, lame, and paralyzed people were
lying in these walkways.|| 5Now a man was there who had been
disabled for 38 years. 6When Jesus saw him lying there and when
he realized that the man had been disabled a long time already,
he said to him, "Do you want to become well?" 7The sick man
answered him, "Sir, I have no one to put me into the pool when
the water is stirred up. While I am trying to get into the water,
someone else goes down there before me." 8Jesus said to him,

5:1–15 Years are short to the happy and healthy, but thirty-eight years of disease must have dragged a very weary length along the life of the poor man. When Jesus therefore healed him by a word while he lay at the pool of Bethesda, he was delightfully sensible of a change. Yet the poor man was ignorant of the author of his cure; he knew not the sacredness of his person, the offices he sustained, or the errand that brought him among humanity. The cure of his ignorance, however, soon followed the cure of his infirmity, for he was visited by the Lord in the temple; and after that gracious manifestation, he was found testifying that "Jesus was the one who had made him well."

CHARLES SPURGEON
(1834–1892)
MORNING AND EVENING

"Stand up! Pick up your mat and walk." [9]Immediately the man
was healed, and he picked up his mat and started walking. (Now
that day was a Sabbath.)
[10]So the Jewish leaders said to the man who had been healed,
"It is the Sabbath, and you are not permitted to carry your mat."
[11]But he answered them, "The man who made me well said to
me, 'Pick up your mat and walk.'" [12]They asked him, "Who is the
man who said to you, 'Pick up your mat and walk'?" [13]But the
man who had been healed did not know who it was, for Jesus
had slipped out, since there was a crowd in that place.
[14]After this Jesus found him at the temple and said to him,
"Look, you have become well. Don't sin any more, lest anything
worse happen to you." [15]The man went away and informed the
Jewish leaders that Jesus was the one who had made him well.

RESPONDING TO JEWISH LEADERS

[16]Now because Jesus was doing these things on the Sabbath,
the Jewish leaders began persecuting him. [17]So he told them,
"My Father is working until now, and I too am working." [18]For
this reason the Jewish leaders were trying even harder to kill
him because not only was he breaking the Sabbath, but he was
also calling God his own Father, thus making himself equal
with God.
[19]So Jesus answered them, "I tell you the solemn truth, the
Son can do nothing on his own initiative, but only what he
sees the Father doing. For whatever the Father does, the Son
does likewise. [20]For the Father loves the Son and shows him
everything he does, and will show him greater deeds than
these, so that you will be amazed. [21]For just as the Father
raises the dead and gives them life, so also the Son gives life
to whomever he wishes. [22]Furthermore, the Father does not
judge anyone, but has assigned all judgment to the Son, [23]so
that all people will honor the Son just as they honor the Father. The one who does not honor the Son does not honor the
Father who sent him.
[24]"I tell you the solemn truth, the one who hears my message
and believes the one who sent me has eternal life and will not
be condemned, but has crossed over from death to life. [25]I tell
you the solemn truth, a time is coming—and is now here—when
the dead will hear the voice of the Son of God, and those who
hear will live. [26]For just as the Father has life in himself, thus
he has granted the Son to have life in himself, [27]and he has
granted the Son authority to execute judgment because he is
the Son of Man.
[28]"Do not be amazed at this because a time is coming when
all who are in the tombs will hear his voice [29]and will come
out—the ones who have done what is good to the resurrection
resulting in life, and the ones who have done what is evil to the
resurrection resulting in condemnation. [30]I can do nothing on
my own initiative. Just as I hear, I judge, and my judgment is
just because I do not seek my own will, but the will of the one
who sent me.

MORE TESTIMONY ABOUT JESUS

[31]"If I testify about myself, my testimony is not true. [32]There is
another who testifies about me, and I know the testimony he
testifies about me is true. [33]You have sent to John, and he has
testified to the truth. [34](I do not accept human testimony, but
I say this so that you may be saved.) [35]He was a lamp that was

burning and shining, and you wanted to rejoice greatly for a
short time in his light.
[36]"But I have a testimony greater than that from John. For
the deeds that the Father has assigned me to complete—the
deeds I am now doing—testify about me that the Father has
sent me. [37]And the Father who sent me has himself testified
about me. You people have never heard his voice nor seen
his form at any time, [38]nor do you have his word residing in
you because you do not believe the one whom he sent. [39]You
study the scriptures thoroughly because you think in them
you possess eternal life, and it is these same scriptures that
testify about me, [40]but you are not willing to come to me so
that you may have life.
[41]"I do not accept praise from people, [42]but I know you, that
you do not have the love of God within you. [43]I have come in
my Father's name, and you do not accept me. If someone else
comes in his own name, you will accept him. [44]How can you
believe, if you accept praise from one another and don't seek
the praise that comes from the only God?
[45]"Do not suppose that I will accuse you before the Father.
The one who accuses you is Moses, in whom you have placed
your hope. [46]If you believed Moses, you would believe me because he wrote about me. [47]But if you do not believe what Moses
wrote, how will you believe my words?"

THE FEEDING OF THE 5,000

6 After this Jesus went away to the other side of the Sea of
Galilee (also called the Sea of Tiberias). [2]A large crowd was
following him because they were observing the miraculous
signs he was performing on the sick. [3]So Jesus went on up the
mountainside and sat down there with his disciples. [4](Now
the Jewish Feast of the Passover was near.) [5]Then Jesus, when
he looked up and saw that a large crowd was coming to him,
said to Philip, "Where can we buy bread so that these people
may eat?" [6](Now Jesus said this to test him, for he knew what
he was going to do.) [7]Philip replied, "200 silver coins worth
of bread would not be enough for them, for each one to get a
little." [8]One of Jesus' disciples, Andrew, Simon Peter's brother,
said to him, [9]"Here is a boy who has five barley loaves and two
fish, but what good are these for so many people?"
[10]Jesus said, "Have the people sit down." (Now there was a
lot of grass in that place.) So the men sat down, about 5,000 in
number. [11]Then Jesus took the loaves, and when he had given
thanks, he distributed the bread to those who were seated.
He then did the same with the fish, as much as they wanted. [12]When they were all satisfied, Jesus said to his disciples,
"Gather up the broken pieces that are left over, so that nothing
is wasted." [13]So they gathered them up and filled 12 baskets
with broken pieces from the five barley loaves left over by the
people who had eaten.
[14]Now when the people saw the miraculous sign that Jesus
performed, they began to say to one another, "This is certainly
the Prophet who is to come into the world." [15]Then Jesus, because
he knew they were going to come and seize him by force to
make him king, withdrew again up the mountainside alone.

WALKING ON WATER

[16]Now when evening came, his disciples went down to the lake,
[17]got into a boat, and started to cross the lake to Capernaum. (It

6:1–14 Philip reveals his unbelief. And with his statement he provides an example of the wisdom of the flesh. For our reason, endowed as it is with fleshly eyes, can look no further than to the present state of affairs into matters of the flesh, to food and money. When these things have run out, it despairs, not knowing where to turn. But faith, because it has spiritual eyes, does not cling to visible things but looks to invisible things, to another world, where it finds God promising all the best things, abounding in every good thing, and kindly directing us to all the things we need to live. What then? You will have enough if you have enough belief. Miserly and wicked people do not believe, and so they possess nothing and have nothing.

JOHANNES BRENZ
(1499–1570)
COMMENTARY ON JOHN

had already become dark, and Jesus had not yet come to them.)
[18]By now a strong wind was blowing and the sea was getting
rough. [19]Then, when they had rowed about three or four miles,
they caught sight of Jesus walking on the lake, approaching
the boat, and they were frightened. [20]But he said to them, "It
is I. Do not be afraid." [21]Then they wanted to take him into the
boat, and immediately the boat came to the land where they
had been heading.

[22]The next day the crowd that remained on the other side
of the lake realized that only one small boat had been there,
and that Jesus had not boarded it with his disciples, but that
his disciples had gone away alone. [23]Other boats from Tiberias came to shore near the place where they had eaten the
bread after the Lord had given thanks. [24]So when the crowd
realized that neither Jesus nor his disciples were there,
they got into the boats and came to Capernaum looking for
Jesus.

JESUS' DISCOURSE ABOUT THE BREAD OF LIFE

[25]When they found him on the other side of the lake, they said
to him, "Rabbi, when did you get here?" [26]Jesus replied, "I tell
you the solemn truth, you are looking for me not because you
saw miraculous signs, but because you ate all the loaves of bread
you wanted. [27]Do not work for the food that disappears, but for
the food that remains to eternal life—the food which the Son
of Man will give to you. For God the Father has put his seal of
approval on him."

[28]So then they said to him, "What must we do to accomplish
the deeds God requires?" [29]Jesus replied, "This is the deed God
requires—to believe in the one whom he sent." [30]So they said to
him, "Then what miraculous sign will you perform, so that we
may see it and believe you? What will you do? [31]Our ancestors
ate the manna in the wilderness, just as it is written, '***He gave
them bread from heaven to eat.***'"

[32]Then Jesus told them, "I tell you the solemn truth, it is
not Moses who has given you the bread from heaven, but my
Father is giving you the true bread from heaven. [33]For the
bread of God is the one who comes down from heaven and
gives life to the world." [34]So they said to him, "Sir, give us this
bread all the time!"

[35]Jesus said to them, "I am the bread of life. The one who
comes to me will never go hungry, and the one who believes
in me will never be thirsty. [36]But I told you that you have seen
me and still do not believe. [37]Everyone whom the Father gives
me will come to me, and the one who comes to me I will never
send away. [38]For I have come down from heaven not to do my
own will but the will of the one who sent me. [39]Now this is the
will of the one who sent me—that I should not lose one person
of every one he has given me, but raise them all up at the last
day. [40]For this is the will of my Father—for everyone who looks
on the Son and believes in him to have eternal life, and I will
raise him up at the last day."

[41]Then the Jews who were hostile to Jesus began complaining
about him because he said, "I am the bread that came down
from heaven," [42]and they said, "Isn't this Jesus the son of Joseph,
whose father and mother we know? How can he now say, 'I have
come down from heaven'?" [43]Jesus replied, "Do not complain
about me to one another. [44]No one can come to me unless the
Father who sent me draws him, and I will raise him up at the last

day. [45]It is written in the prophets, ‘***And they will all be taught by***
God.’ Everyone who hears and learns from the Father comes to
me. [46](Not that anyone has seen the Father except the one who
is from God—he has seen the Father.) [47]I tell you the solemn
truth, the one who believes has eternal life. [48]I am the bread
of life. [49]Your ancestors ate the manna in the wilderness, and
they died. [50]This is the bread that has come down from heaven,
so that a person may eat from it and not die. [51]I am the living
bread that came down from heaven. If anyone eats from this
bread he will live forever. The bread that I will give for the life
of the world is my flesh.”

[52]Then the Jews who were hostile to Jesus began to argue
with one another, “How can this man give us his flesh to eat?”
[53]Jesus said to them, “I tell you the solemn truth, unless you
eat the flesh of the Son of Man and drink his blood, you have
no life in yourselves. [54]The one who eats my flesh and drinks
my blood has eternal life, and I will raise him up on the last day.
[55]For my flesh is true food, and my blood is true drink. [56]The
one who eats my flesh and drinks my blood resides in me, and
I in him. [57]Just as the living Father sent me, and I live because
of the Father, so the one who consumes me will live because of
me. [58]This is the bread that came down from heaven; it is not
like the bread your ancestors ate, but then later died. The one
who eats this bread will live forever.”

MANY FOLLOWERS DEPART

[59]Jesus said these things while he was teaching in the synagogue in Capernaum. [60]Then many of his disciples, when
they heard these things, said, “This is a difficult saying! Who
can understand it?” [61]When Jesus was aware that his disciples were complaining about this, he said to them, “Does this
cause you to be offended? [62]Then what if you see the Son of
Man ascending where he was before? [63]The Spirit is the one
who gives life; human nature is of no help! The words that I
have spoken to you are spirit and are life. [64]But there are some
of you who do not believe.” (For Jesus had already known from
the beginning who those were who did not believe, and who
it was who would betray him.) [65]So Jesus added, “Because of
this I told you that no one can come to me unless the Father
has allowed him to come.”

PETER'S CONFESSION

[66]After this many of his disciples quit following him and did
not accompany him any longer. [67]So Jesus said to the twelve,
“You don't want to go away too, do you?” [68]Simon Peter answered him, “Lord, to whom would we go? You have the words
of eternal life. [69]We have come to believe and to know that you
are the Holy One of God!” [70]Jesus replied, “Didn't I choose you,
the twelve, and yet one of you is the devil?” [71](Now he said this
about Judas son of Simon Iscariot, for Judas, one of the twelve,
was going to betray him.)

THE FEAST OF SHELTERS

7 After this Jesus traveled throughout Galilee. He stayed out
of Judea because the Jewish leaders wanted to kill him. [2]Now
the Jewish Feast of Shelters was near. [3]So Jesus' brothers advised
him, “Leave here and go to Judea so your disciples may see your
miracles that you are performing. [4]For no one who seeks to
make a reputation for himself does anything in secret. If you

are doing these things, show yourself to the world." 5(For not even his own brothers believed in him.)

6So Jesus replied, "My time has not yet arrived, but you are ready at any opportunity! 7The world cannot hate you, but it hates me because I am testifying about it that its deeds are evil. 8You go up to the feast yourselves. I am not going up to this feast because my time has not yet fully arrived." 9When he had said this, he remained in Galilee.

10But when his brothers had gone up to the feast, then Jesus himself also went up, not openly but in secret. 11So the Jewish leaders were looking for him at the feast, asking, "Where is he?" 12There was a lot of grumbling about him among the crowds. Some were saying, "He is a good man," but others, "He deceives the common people." 13However, no one spoke openly about him for fear of the Jewish leaders.

TEACHING IN THE TEMPLE

14When the feast was half over, Jesus went up to the temple courts and began to teach. 15Then the Jewish leaders were astonished and said, "How does this man know so much when he has never had formal instruction?" 16So Jesus replied, "My teaching is not from me, but from the one who sent me. 17If anyone wants to do God's will, he will know about my teaching, whether it is from God or whether I speak from my own authority. 18The person who speaks on his own authority desires to receive honor for himself; the one who desires the honor of the one who sent him is a man of integrity, and there is no unrighteousness in him. 19Hasn't Moses given you the law? Yet not one of you keeps the law! Why do you want to kill me?"

20The crowd answered, "You're possessed by a demon! Who is trying to kill you?" 21Jesus replied, "I performed one miracle and you are all amazed. 22However, because Moses gave you the practice of circumcision (not that it came from Moses, but from the forefathers), you circumcise a male child on the Sabbath. 23But if a male child is circumcised on the Sabbath so that the law of Moses is not broken, why are you angry with me because I made a man completely well on the Sabbath? 24Do not judge according to external appearance, but judge with proper judgment."

QUESTIONS ABOUT JESUS' IDENTITY

25Then some of the residents of Jerusalem began to say, "Isn't this the man they are trying to kill? 26Yet here he is, speaking publicly, and they are saying nothing to him. Do the ruling authorities really know that this man is the Christ? 27But we know where this man comes from. Whenever the Christ comes, no one will know where he comes from."

28Then Jesus, while teaching in the temple courts, cried out, "You both know me and know where I come from! And I have not come on my own initiative, but the one who sent me is true. You do not know him, 29but I know him because I have come from him and he sent me."

30So then they tried to seize Jesus, but no one laid a hand on him because his time had not yet come. 31Yet many of the crowd believed in him and said, "Whenever the Christ comes, he won't perform more miraculous signs than this man did, will he?"

32The Pharisees heard the crowd murmuring these things about Jesus, so the chief priests and the Pharisees sent officers

7:10–24 **If anyone of any nation seeks to do the will of God, he shall know whether the doctrine is of God. Only those who hate the truth shall be given up to errors that will be fatal. Surely it was as agreeable to the design of the Sabbath to restore health to the afflicted as to administer an outward rite. Jesus told the crowd to decide on his conduct according to the spiritual import of the divine law. We must not judge concerning any by their outward appearance but by their worth, and by the gifts and graces of God's Spirit in them.**

MATTHEW HENRY **(1662–1714)**
COMMENTARY ON THE WHOLE BIBLE

to arrest him. [33]Then Jesus said, "I will be with you for only a little while longer, and then I am going to the one who sent me. [34]You will look for me but will not find me, and where I am you cannot come."

[35]Then the Jewish leaders said to one another, "Where is he going to go that we cannot find him? He is not going to go to the Jewish people dispersed among the Greeks and teach the Greeks, is he? [36]What did he mean by saying, 'You will look for me but will not find me, and where I am you cannot come'?"

TEACHING ABOUT THE SPIRIT

[37]On the last day of the feast, the greatest day, Jesus stood up and shouted out, "If anyone is thirsty, let him come to me, and [38]let the one who believes in me drink. Just as the scripture says, '***From within him will flow rivers of living water.***'" [39](Now he said this about the Spirit, whom those who believed in him were going to receive, for the Spirit had not yet been given because Jesus was not yet glorified.)

DIFFERING OPINIONS ABOUT JESUS

[40]When they heard these words, some of the crowd began to say, "This really is the Prophet!" [41]Others said, "This is the Christ!" But still others said, "No, for the Christ doesn't come from Galilee, does he? [42]Don't the scriptures say that the Christ is *a descendant of David* and *comes from Bethlehem,* the village where David lived?" [43]So there was a division in the crowd because of Jesus. [44]Some of them were wanting to seize him, but no one laid a hand on him.

LACK OF BELIEF

[45]Then the officers returned to the chief priests and Pharisees, who said to them, "Why didn't you bring him back with you?" [46]The officers replied, "No one ever spoke like this man!" [47]Then the Pharisees answered, "You haven't been deceived too, have you? [48]None of the members of the ruling council or the Pharisees have believed in him, have they? [49]But this rabble who do not know the law are accursed!"

[50]Nicodemus, who had gone to Jesus before and who was one of the rulers, said, [51]"Our law doesn't condemn a man unless it first hears from him and learns what he is doing, does it?" [52]They replied, "You aren't from Galilee too, are you? Investigate carefully and you will see that no prophet comes from Galilee!"

A WOMAN CAUGHT IN ADULTERY

8 [53][[And each one departed to his own house. [1]But Jesus went to the Mount of Olives. [2]Early in the morning he came to the temple courts again. All the people came to him, and he sat down and began to teach them. [3]The experts in the law and the Pharisees brought a woman who had been caught committing adultery. They made her stand in front of them [4]and said to Jesus, "Teacher, this woman was caught in the very act of adultery. [5]In the law *Moses commanded us to stone to death* such women. What then do you say?" [6](Now they were asking this in an attempt to trap him, so that they could bring charges against him.) Jesus bent down and wrote on the ground with his finger. [7]When they persisted in asking him, he stood up straight and replied, "Whoever among you is guiltless may be the first to throw a stone at her." [8]Then he bent over again and wrote on the ground.

8:1–12 He who had come to forgive sins said, "Whoever among you is guiltless may be the first to throw a stone at her." What a splendid answer or rather suggestion! If they had been prepared to throw a single stone at the sinner, they would have received the prompt rejoinder, *The judgment you judge with shall be pronounced on you. You have condemned; condemned you shall be.* They, however, knew their own consciences. Turning one after the other, they, from the eldest to the youngest—that is what the evangelist said—all went out. The Holy Spirit, you see, had said, "All have turned away, together they have become worthless; there is no one who shows kindness, not even one" (Rom 3:12).

AUGUSTINE **(354–430)**
SERMONS

9 Now when they heard this, they began to drift away one
at a time, starting with the older ones, until Jesus was left
alone with the woman standing before him. 10 Jesus stood up
straight and said to her, "Woman, where are they? Did no one
condemn you?" 11 She replied, "No one, Lord." And Jesus said,
"I do not condemn you either. Go, and from now on do not sin
any more."]]

JESUS AS THE LIGHT OF THE WORLD

12 Then Jesus spoke out again, "I am the light of the world! The
one who follows me will never walk in darkness but will have
the light of life." 13 So the Pharisees objected, "You testify about
yourself; your testimony is not true!" 14 Jesus answered, "Even if I
testify about myself, my testimony is true because I know where
I came from and where I am going. But you people do not know
where I came from or where I am going. 15 You people judge by
outward appearances; I do not judge anyone. 16 But if I judge,
my evaluation is accurate because I am not alone when I judge,
but I and the Father who sent me do so together. 17 It is written
in your law that *the testimony of two men is true.* 18 I testify about
myself and the Father who sent me testifies about me."

19 Then they began asking him, "Who is your father?" Jesus
answered, "You do not know either me or my Father. If you
knew me you would know my Father too." 20 (Jesus spoke these
words near the offering box while he was teaching in the temple courts. No one seized him because his time had not yet
come.)

WHERE JESUS CAME FROM AND WHERE HE IS GOING

21 Then Jesus said to them again, "I am going away, and you will
look for me but will die in your sin. Where I am going you cannot
come." 22 So the Jewish leaders began to say, "Perhaps he is going
to kill himself because he says, 'Where I am going you cannot
come.'" 23 Jesus replied, "You people are from below; I am from
above. You people are from this world; I am not from this world.
24 Thus I told you that you will die in your sins. For unless you
believe that I am he, you will die in your sins."

25 So they said to him, "Who are you?" Jesus replied, "What I
have told you from the beginning. 26 I have many things to say
and to judge about you, but the Father who sent me is truthful,
and the things I have heard from him I speak to the world."
27 (They did not understand that he was telling them about
his Father.)

28 Then Jesus said, "When you lift up the Son of Man, then you
will know that I am he, and I do nothing on my own initiative,
but I speak just what the Father taught me. 29 And the one who
sent me is with me. He has not left me alone because I always
do those things that please him." 30 While he was saying these
things, many people believed in him.

ABRAHAM'S CHILDREN AND THE DEVIL'S CHILDREN

31 Then Jesus said to those Judeans who had believed him, "If you
continue to follow my teaching, you are really my disciples 32 and
you will know the truth, and the truth will set you free." 33 "We
are descendants of Abraham," they replied, "and have never
been anyone's slaves! How can you say, 'You will become free'?"
34 Jesus answered them, "I tell you the solemn truth, everyone

MENNO SIMONS:

TAKING CHRISTIANITY BACK TO ITS ROOTS

c. 1496–1561

Like most movements, the Protestant Reformation was diverse in its direction and leadership. It is often divided into two broad categories: the magisterial Reformers, such as Luther, Calvin, and Zwingli; and the radical Reformers, known mostly as the Anabaptists.

The radical Reformation leaders wanted to take Protestant Christianity "back to the roots" of the New Testament by peeling back the layers of medieval Christianity as well as the Augustinianism and Constantinianism they insisted had tarnished the pure Christian faith. Some have called them the "Protestants of Protestants," for they insisted Luther and company didn't go far enough in purifying the church from Roman Catholicism. They desired to complete the Protestant Reformation project by taking Christianity back to the beginning: apostolic Christianity. And Menno Simons led the charge.

Simons was born in 1496 within the coastal region of the Netherlands and Belgium. He was ordained in 1524 as a Roman Catholic priest, and during the course of his parish ministry he became acquainted with the writings of Luther, Zwingli, and other Reformers. Yet it wasn't until his brother was killed for being a radical Reformer in 1535 that he had a conversion experience. As he framed it:

> *My heart trembled within me. I prayed to God with sighs and tears that he would give to me, a sorrowing sinner, the gift of his grace, create within me a clean heart, and graciously through the merits of the crimson blood of Christ forgive my unclean walk and frivolous easy life and bestow upon me wisdom, Spirit, courage, and a manly spirit.*

This confession—with repentance of sins, receipt of the Holy Spirit, and a cleansing toward perfection—would become a paradigm for Anabaptist spirituality and salvation theology.

The radical Reformers' work of further reforming Christian theology extended to their theology of salvation and the sacraments. Simons didn't agree with Luther that Christ's righteousness is merely imputed and insisted that through Christ a born-again believer actually becomes righteous, since genuine faith results in righteous living. And he rejected predestination and the strong monergism of the Reformers.

Menno Simons's legacy is evident not only in his enduring paradigm of salvation but also in the denomination that bears his name: the Mennonites. His early efforts at organizing underground radical Reformer groups into Anabaptist congregations continues to bear fruit, and he remains an inspiration to all those in the communion of saints who seek to remind Christianity of its roots.

IMPORTANT WORKS

THE FOUNDATION OF CHRISTIAN DOCTRINE

THE INCARNATION OF OUR LORD

WORKS OF JAMES ARMINIUS, 3 VOLS.

who practices sin is a slave of sin. [35]The slave does not remain
in the family forever, but the son remains forever. [36]So if the
son sets you free, you will be really free. [37]I know that you are
Abraham's descendants. But you want to kill me because my
teaching makes no progress among you. [38]I am telling you the
things I have seen while with the Father; as for you, practice
the things you have heard from the Father!"

[39]They answered him, "Abraham is our father!" Jesus replied,
"If you are Abraham's children, you would be doing the deeds
of Abraham. [40]But now you are trying to kill me, a man who has
told you the truth I heard from God. Abraham did not do this!
[41]You people are doing the deeds of your father."

Then they said to Jesus, "We were not born as a result of
immorality! We have only one Father, God himself." [42]Jesus
replied, "If God were your Father, you would love me, for I have
come from God and am now here. I have not come on my own
initiative, but he sent me. [43]Why don't you understand what I
am saying? It is because you cannot accept my teaching. [44]You
people are from your father the devil, and you want to do what
your father desires. He was a murderer from the beginning,
and does not uphold the truth because there is no truth in
him. Whenever he lies, he speaks according to his own nature
because he is a liar and the father of lies. [45]But because I am
telling you the truth, you do not believe me. [46]Who among you
can prove me guilty of any sin? If I am telling you the truth, why
don't you believe me? [47]The one who belongs to God listens and
responds to God's words. You don't listen and respond because
you don't belong to God."

[48]The Judeans replied, "Aren't we correct in saying that
you are a Samaritan and are possessed by a demon?" [49]Jesus
answered, "I am not possessed by a demon, but I honor my
Father—and yet you dishonor me. [50]I am not trying to get praise
for myself. There is one who demands it, and he also judges. [51]I
tell you the solemn truth, if anyone obeys my teaching, he will
never see death."

[52]Then the Judeans responded, "Now we know you're possessed by a demon! Both Abraham and the prophets died, and
yet you say, 'If anyone obeys my teaching, he will never experience death.' [53]You aren't greater than our father Abraham
who died, are you? And the prophets died too! Who do you
claim to be?" [54]Jesus replied, "If I glorify myself, my glory is
worthless. The one who glorifies me is my Father, about whom
you people say, 'He is our God.' [55]Yet you do not know him, but
I know him. If I were to say that I do not know him, I would
be a liar like you. But I do know him, and I obey his teaching.
[56]Your father Abraham was overjoyed to see my day, and he
saw it and was glad."

[57]Then the Judeans replied, "You are not yet fifty years old!
Have you seen Abraham?" [58]Jesus said to them, "I tell you the
solemn truth, before Abraham came into existence, I am!"
[59]Then they picked up stones to throw at him, but Jesus was
hidden from them and went out from the temple area.

HEALING A MAN BORN BLIND

9 Now as Jesus was passing by, he saw a man who had been blind
from birth. [2]His disciples asked him, "Rabbi, who committed the sin that caused him to be born blind, this man or his
parents?" [3]Jesus answered, "Neither this man nor his parents
sinned, but he was born blind so that the acts of God may be

revealed through what happens to him. 4We must perform the
deeds of the one who sent me as long as it is daytime. Night is
coming when no one can work. 5As long as I am in the world,
I am the light of the world." 6Having said this, he spat on the
ground and made some mud with the saliva. He smeared
the mud on the blind man's eyes 7and said to him, "Go wash in
the pool of Siloam" (which is translated "sent"). So the blind
man went away and washed, and came back seeing.
8Then the neighbors and the people who had seen him previously as a beggar began saying, "Is this not the man who used
to sit and beg?" 9Some people said, "This is the man!" while
others said, "No, but he looks like him." The man himself kept
insisting, "I am the one!" 10So they asked him, "How then were
you made to see?" 11He replied, "The man called Jesus made
mud, smeared it on my eyes and told me, 'Go to Siloam and
wash.' So I went and washed, and was able to see." 12They said
to him, "Where is that man?" He replied, "I don't know."

THE PHARISEES' REACTION TO THE HEALING

13They brought the man who used to be blind to the Pharisees.
14(Now the day on which Jesus made the mud and caused him
to see was a Sabbath.) 15So the Pharisees asked him again how
he had gained his sight. He replied, "He put mud on my eyes
and I washed, and now I am able to see."
16Then some of the Pharisees began to say, "This man is not
from God because he does not observe the Sabbath." But others
said, "How can a man who is a sinner perform such miraculous
signs?" Thus there was a division among them. 17So again they
asked the man who used to be blind, "What do you say about
him, since he caused you to see?" "He is a prophet," the man
replied.
18Now the Jewish religious leaders refused to believe that
he had really been blind and had gained his sight until at
last they summoned the parents of the man who had become
able to see. 19They asked the parents, "Is this your son, whom
you say was born blind? Then how does he now see?" 20So his
parents replied, "We know that this is our son and that he
was born blind. 21But we do not know how he is now able to
see, nor do we know who caused him to see. Ask him, he is a
mature adult. He will speak for himself." 22(His parents said
these things because they were afraid of the Jewish religious
leaders. For the Jewish leaders had already agreed that anyone
who confessed Jesus to be the Christ would be put out of the
synagogue. 23For this reason his parents said, "He is a mature
adult, ask him.")
24Then they summoned the man who used to be blind a
second time and said to him, "Promise before God to tell the
truth. We know that this man is a sinner." 25He replied, "I do
not know whether he is a sinner. I do know one thing—that
although I was blind, now I can see." 26Then they said to him,
"What did he do to you? How did he cause you to see?" 27He
answered, "I told you already and you didn't listen. Why do you
want to hear it again? You people don't want to become his
disciples too, do you?"
28They heaped insults on him, saying, "You are his disciple!
We are disciples of Moses! 29We know that God has spoken to
Moses! We do not know where this man comes from!" 30The
man replied, "This is a remarkable thing that you don't know
where he comes from, yet he caused me to see! 31We know that

9:30–33 The healed man brings in the miracle everywhere as evidence because they could not invalidate it. And he draws his own inferences from it too. When he has an opportunity, he turns their own words against them and defends Jesus: "We know that God doesn't listen to sinners."

CHRYSOSTOM **(C. 347–407)**
HOMILIES ON THE GOSPEL OF JOHN

God doesn't listen to sinners, but if anyone is devout and does his will, God listens to him. 32Never before has anyone heard of someone causing a man born blind to see. 33If this man were not from God, he could do nothing." 34They replied, "You were born completely in sinfulness, and yet you presume to teach us?" So they threw him out.

THE MAN'S RESPONSE TO JESUS

35Jesus heard that they had thrown him out, so he found the man and said to him, "Do you believe in the Son of Man?" 36The man replied, "And who is he, sir, that I may believe in him?" 37Jesus told him, "You have seen him; he is the one speaking with you." [38He said, "Lord, I believe," and he worshiped him. 39Jesus said,]* "For judgment I have come into this world, so that those who do not see may gain their sight, and the ones who see may become blind."

40Some of the Pharisees who were with him heard this and asked him, "We are not blind too, are we?" 41Jesus replied, "If you were blind, you would not be guilty of sin, but now because you claim that you can see, your guilt remains.

JESUS AS THE GOOD SHEPHERD

10 "I tell you the solemn truth, the one who does not enter the sheepfold by the door, but climbs in some other way, is a thief and a robber. 2The one who enters by the door is the shepherd of the sheep. 3The doorkeeper opens the door for him, and the sheep hear his voice. He calls his own sheep by name and leads them out. 4When he has brought all his own sheep out, he goes ahead of them, and the sheep follow him because they recognize his voice. 5They will never follow a stranger, but will run away from him because they do not recognize the stranger's voice." 6Jesus told them this parable, but they did not understand what he was saying to them.

7So Jesus said again, "I tell you the solemn truth, I am the door for the sheep. 8All who came before me were thieves and robbers, but the sheep did not listen to them. 9I am the door. If anyone enters through me, he will be saved, and will come in and go out, and find pasture. 10The thief comes only to steal and kill and destroy; I have come so that they may have life, and may have it abundantly.

11"I am the good shepherd. The good shepherd lays down his life for the sheep. 12The hired hand, who is not a shepherd and does not own sheep, sees the wolf coming and abandons the sheep and runs away. So the wolf attacks the sheep and scatters them. 13Because he is a hired hand and is not concerned about the sheep, he runs away.

14"I am the good shepherd. I know my own and my own know me—15just as the Father knows me and I know the Father—and I lay down my life for the sheep. 16I have other sheep that do not come from this sheepfold. I must bring them too, and they will listen to my voice, so that there will be one flock and one shepherd. 17This is why the Father loves me—because I lay down my life, so that I may take it back again. 18No one takes it away from me, but I lay it down of my own free will. I have the authority to lay it down, and I have the authority to take it back again. This commandment I received from my Father."

19Another sharp division took place among the Jewish people because of these words. 20Many of them were saying, "He is

possessed by a demon and has lost his mind! Why do you listen
to him?" 21 Others said, "These are not the words of someone
possessed by a demon. A demon cannot cause the blind to see,
can it?"

JESUS AT THE FEAST OF DEDICATION

22 Then came the feast of the Dedication in Jerusalem. 23 It was
winter, and Jesus was walking in the temple area in Solomon's
Portico. 24 The Jewish leaders surrounded him and asked, "How
long will you keep us in suspense? If you are the Christ, tell us
plainly." 25 Jesus replied, "I told you and you do not believe. The
deeds I do in my Father's name testify about me. 26 But you
refuse to believe because you are not my sheep. 27 My sheep
listen to my voice, and I know them, and they follow me. 28 I
give them eternal life, and they will never perish; no one will
snatch them from my hand. 29 My Father, who has given them
to me, is greater than all, and no one can snatch them from my
Father's hand. 30 The Father and I are one."

31 The Jewish leaders picked up rocks again to stone him to
death. 32 Jesus said to them, "I have shown you many good deeds
from the Father. For which one of them are you going to stone
me?" 33 The Jewish leaders replied, "We are not going to stone
you for a good deed but for blasphemy because you, a man, are
claiming to be God."

34 Jesus answered, "Is it not written in your law, '***I said, you are***
gods'? 35 If those people to whom the word of God came were
called 'gods' (and the scripture cannot be broken), 36 do you say
about the one whom the Father set apart and sent into the
world, 'You are blaspheming,' because I said, 'I am the Son of
God'? 37 If I do not perform the deeds of my Father, do not believe
me. 38 But if I do them, even if you do not believe me, believe the
deeds, so that you may come to know and understand that I am
in the Father and the Father is in me." 39 Then they attempted
again to seize him, but he escaped their clutches.

40 Jesus went back across the Jordan River again to the place
where John had been baptizing at an earlier time, and he stayed
there. 41 Many came to him and began to say, "John performed
no miraculous sign, but everything John said about this man
was true!" 42 And many believed in Jesus there.

THE DEATH OF LAZARUS

11 Now a certain man named Lazarus was sick. He was from
Bethany, the village where Mary and her sister Martha
lived. 2 (Now it was Mary who anointed the Lord with perfumed
oil and wiped his feet dry with her hair, whose brother Lazarus
was sick.) 3 So the sisters sent a message to Jesus, "Lord, look,
the one you love is sick." 4 When Jesus heard this, he said, "This
sickness will not lead to death, but to God's glory, so that the Son
of God may be glorified through it." 5 (Now Jesus loved Martha
and her sister and Lazarus.)

6 So when he heard that Lazarus was sick, he remained in the
place where he was for two more days. 7 Then after this, he said
to his disciples, "Let us go to Judea again." 8 The disciples replied,
"Rabbi, the Jewish leaders were just now trying to stone you
to death! Are you going there again?" 9 Jesus replied, "Are there
not 12 hours in a day? If anyone walks around in the daytime,
he does not stumble because he sees the light of this world.
10 But if anyone walks around at night, he stumbles because
the light is not in him."

10:31–39 Christ's works of power and mercy proclaim him to be over all, God-blessed forevermore, that all may know and believe he is in the Father and the Father is in him. Whom the Father sends he sanctifies. The holy God will reward and therefore will employ none but such as he makes holy. The Father was in the Son so that by divine power he wrought his miracles; the Son was so in the Father that he knew the whole of his mind. This we cannot by searching find out to perfection, but we may know and believe these declarations of Christ.

MATTHEW HENRY (1662–1714)
COMMENTARY ON THE WHOLE BIBLE

11:1–16 A man was raised up by him who made humankind. The Lord Jesus Christ is the only one of the Father by whom all things were made. And if all things were made by him, why is anyone amazed that one was raised by him when so many are daily brought into the world by his power? It is a greater deed to create men and women than to raise them again from the dead. Yet he decided both to create and to raise again; to create all, to resuscitate some.

AUGUSTINE (354–430)
TRACTATES ON THE GOSPEL OF JOHN

11After he said this, he added, "Our friend Lazarus has fallen
asleep. But I am going there to awaken him." 12Then the disciples replied, "Lord, if he has fallen asleep, he will recover." 13(Now
Jesus had been talking about his death, but they thought he
had been talking about real sleep.)

14Then Jesus told them plainly, "Lazarus has died, 15and I am
glad for your sake that I was not there, so that you may believe.
But let us go to him." 16So Thomas (called Didymus) said to his
fellow disciples, "Let us go too, so that we may die with him."

SPEAKING WITH MARTHA AND MARY

17When Jesus arrived, he found that Lazarus had been in the
tomb four days already. 18(Now Bethany was less than two miles
from Jerusalem, 19so many of the Jewish people of the region
had come to Martha and Mary to console them over the loss of
their brother.) 20So when Martha heard that Jesus was coming,
she went out to meet him, but Mary was sitting in the house.
21Martha said to Jesus, "Lord, if you had been here, my brother
would not have died. 22But even now I know that whatever you
ask from God, God will grant you."

23Jesus replied, "Your brother will come back to life again."
24Martha said, "I know that he will come back to life again in
the resurrection at the last day." 25Jesus said to her, "I am the
resurrection and the life. The one who believes in me will live
even if he dies, 26and the one who lives and believes in me
will never die. Do you believe this?" 27She replied, "Yes, Lord,
I believe that you are the Christ, the Son of God who comes
into the world."

28And when she had said this, Martha went and called her
sister Mary, saying privately, "The Teacher is here and is asking
for you." 29So when Mary heard this, she got up quickly and went
to him. 30(Now Jesus had not yet entered the village, but was still
in the place where Martha had come out to meet him.) 31Then
the people who were with Mary in the house consoling her saw
her get up quickly and go out. They followed her because they
thought she was going to the tomb to weep there.

32Now when Mary came to the place where Jesus was and
saw him, she fell at his feet and said to him, "Lord, if you had
been here, my brother would not have died." 33When Jesus saw
her weeping, and the people who had come with her weeping, he was intensely moved in spirit and greatly distressed.
34He asked, "Where have you laid him?" They replied, "Lord,
come and see." 35Jesus wept. 36Thus the people who had come
to mourn said, "Look how much he loved him!" 37But some
of them said, "This is the man who caused the blind man to
see! Couldn't he have done something to keep Lazarus from
dying?"

LAZARUS RAISED FROM THE DEAD

38Jesus, intensely moved again, came to the tomb. (Now it was
a cave, and a stone was placed across it.) 39Jesus said, "Take
away the stone." Martha, the sister of the deceased, replied,
"Lord, by this time the body will have a bad smell because
he has been buried four days." 40Jesus responded, "Didn't I
tell you that if you believe, you would see the glory of God?"
41So they took away the stone. Jesus looked upward and said,
"Father, I thank you that you have listened to me. 42I knew
that you always listen to me, but I said this for the sake of
the crowd standing around here, that they may believe that

you sent me." [43]When he had said this, he shouted in a loud
voice, "Lazarus, come out!" [44]The one who had died came out,
his feet and hands tied up with strips of cloth, and a cloth
wrapped around his face. Jesus said to them, "Unwrap him
and let him go."

THE RESPONSE OF THE JEWISH LEADERS

[45]Then many of the people, who had come with Mary and had
seen the things Jesus did, believed in him. [46]But some of them
went to the Pharisees and reported to them what Jesus had
done. [47]So the chief priests and the Pharisees called the council
together and said, "What are we doing? For this man is performing many miraculous signs. [48]If we allow him to go on in this
way, everyone will believe in him, and the Romans will come
and take away our sanctuary and our nation."

[49]Then one of them, Caiaphas, who was high priest that year,
said, "You know nothing at all! [50]You do not realize that it is
more to your advantage to have one man die for the people
than for the whole nation to perish." [51](Now he did not say
this on his own, but because he was high priest that year, he
prophesied that Jesus was going to die for the Jewish nation,
[52]and not for the Jewish nation only, but to gather together into
one the children of God who are scattered.) [53]So from that day
they planned together to kill him.

[54]Thus Jesus no longer went around publicly among the
Judeans, but went away from there to the region near the wilderness, to a town called Ephraim, and stayed there with his
disciples. [55]Now the Jewish Feast of Passover was near, and
many people went up to Jerusalem from the rural areas before
the Passover to cleanse themselves ritually. [56]Thus they were
looking for Jesus, and saying to one another as they stood in
the temple courts, "What do you think? That he won't come to
the feast?" [57](Now the chief priests and the Pharisees had given
orders that anyone who knew where Jesus was should report
it, so that they could arrest him.)

JESUS' ANOINTING

12 Then, six days before the Passover, Jesus came to Bethany,
where Lazarus lived, whom he had raised from the dead.
[2]So they prepared a dinner for Jesus there. Martha was serving,
and Lazarus was among those present at the table with him.
[3]Then Mary took three quarters of a pound of expensive aromatic oil from pure nard and anointed the feet of Jesus. She
then wiped his feet dry with her hair. (Now the house was filled
with the fragrance of the perfumed oil.) [4]But Judas Iscariot,
one of his disciples (the one who was going to betray him) said,
[5]"Why wasn't this oil sold for 300 silver coins and the money
given to the poor?" [6](Now Judas said this not because he was
concerned about the poor, but because he was a thief. As keeper
of the money box, he used to steal what was put into it.) [7]So
Jesus said, "Leave her alone. She has kept it for the day of my
burial. [8]For you will always have the poor with you, but you will
not always have me!"

[9]Now a large crowd of Judeans learned that Jesus was there,
and so they came not only because of him but also to see
Lazarus whom he had raised from the dead. [10]So the chief
priests planned to kill Lazarus too, [11]for on account of him
many of the Jewish people from Jerusalem were going away
and believing in Jesus.

12:1–8 So powerful is the praise of a good work of this kind that it exhorts all of us to fill the Lord's head with fragrant and rich works so that it may be said also of us that we have done a good work on his head. Because as long as we are in this life, we will always have the poor with us, and those who have advanced in word and have become rich in the wisdom of God need to care for them, but this cannot be equal to having always with them, by night and day, the Son of God, the Word and wisdom of God, and whatever also the Lord our Savior is.

ORIGEN (C. 185–C. 253)
COMMENTARY ON THE GOSPEL OF MATTHEW

THE TRIUMPHAL ENTRY

12 The next day the large crowd that had come to the feast heard
that Jesus was coming to Jerusalem. 13 So they took branches
of palm trees and went out to meet him. They began to shout,
"***Hosanna! Blessed is the one who comes in the name of the Lord!***
Blessed is the king of Israel!" 14 Jesus found a young donkey
and sat on it, just as it is written, 15 "***Do not be afraid, people of
Zion; look, your king is coming, seated on a donkey's colt!***" 16 (His
disciples did not understand these things when they first happened, but when Jesus was glorified, then they remembered
that these things were written about him and that these things
had happened to him.)
17 So the crowd who had been with him when he called
Lazarus out of the tomb and raised him from the dead were
continuing to testify about it. 18 Because they had heard that
Jesus had performed this miraculous sign, the crowd went out
to meet him. 19 Thus the Pharisees said to one another, "You see
that you can do nothing. Look, the world has run off after him!"

SEEKERS

20 Now some Greeks were among those who had gone up to
worship at the feast. 21 So these approached Philip, who was
from Bethsaida in Galilee, and requested, "Sir, we would like to
see Jesus." 22 Philip went and told Andrew, and they both went
and told Jesus. 23 Jesus replied, "The time has come for the Son
of Man to be glorified. 24 I tell you the solemn truth, unless a
kernel of wheat falls into the ground and dies, it remains by
itself alone. But if it dies, it produces much grain. 25 The one
who loves his life destroys it, and the one who hates his life in
this world guards it for eternal life. 26 If anyone wants to serve
me, he must follow me, and where I am, my servant will be too.
If anyone serves me, the Father will honor him.
27 "Now my soul is greatly distressed. And what should I
say? 'Father, deliver me from this hour'? No, but for this very
reason I have come to this hour. 28 Father, glorify your name."
Then a voice came from heaven, "I have glorified it, and I will
glorify it again." 29 The crowd that stood there and heard the
voice said that it had thundered. Others said that an angel
had spoken to him. 30 Jesus said, "This voice has not come for
my benefit but for yours. 31 Now is the judgment of this world;
now the ruler of this world will be driven out. 32 And I, when
I am lifted up from the earth, will draw all people to myself."
33 (Now he said this to indicate clearly what kind of death he
was going to die.)
34 Then the crowd responded, "We have heard from the law
that *the Christ will remain forever.* How can you say, 'The Son
of Man must be lifted up'? Who is this Son of Man?" 35 Jesus
replied, "The light is with you for a little while longer. Walk
while you have the light, so that the darkness may not overtake
you. The one who walks in the darkness does not know where
he is going. 36 While you have the light, believe in the light, so
that you may become sons of light." When Jesus had said these
things, he went away and hid himself from them.

THE OUTCOME OF JESUS' PUBLIC MINISTRY FORETOLD

37 Although Jesus had performed so many miraculous signs
before them, they still refused to believe in him, 38 so that the
word of the prophet Isaiah would be fulfilled. He said, "***Lord,***

who has believed our message, and to whom has the arm of the
***Lord been revealed?*"** 39For this reason they could not believe
because again Isaiah said,
40 ***"He has blinded their eyes***
and hardened their heart,
so that they would not see with their eyes
and understand with their heart,
and turn to me, and I would heal them."
41Isaiah said these things because he saw Christ's glory and
spoke about him.
42Nevertheless, even among the rulers many believed in him,
but because of the Pharisees they would not confess Jesus to be
the Christ, so that they would not be put out of the synagogue.
43For they loved praise from men more than praise from God.

JESUS' FINAL PUBLIC WORDS

44But Jesus shouted out, "The one who believes in me does
not believe in me, but in the one who sent me, 45and the one
who sees me sees the one who sent me. 46I have come as a light
into the world, so that everyone who believes in me should not
remain in darkness. 47If anyone hears my words and does not
obey them, I do not judge him. For I have not come to judge the
world, but to save the world. 48The one who rejects me and does
not accept my words has a judge; the word I have spoken will
judge him at the last day. 49For I have not spoken from my own
authority, but the Father himself who sent me has commanded
me what I should say and what I should speak. 50And I know
that his commandment is eternal life. Thus the things I say, I
say just as the Father has told me."

WASHING THE DISCIPLES' FEET

13 Just before the Passover Feast, Jesus knew that his time
had come to depart from this world to the Father. Having
loved his own who were in the world, he now loved them to the
very end. 2The evening meal was in progress, and the devil had
already put into the heart of Judas Iscariot, Simon's son, that he
should betray Jesus. 3Because Jesus knew that the Father had
handed all things over to him, and that he had come from God
and was going back to God, 4he got up from the meal, removed
his outer clothes, took a towel and tied it around himself. 5He
poured water into the washbasin and began to wash the disciples' feet and to dry them with the towel he had wrapped
around himself.
6Then he came to Simon Peter. Peter said to him, "Lord, are
you going to wash my feet?" 7Jesus replied, "You do not understand what I am doing now, but you will understand after these
things." 8Peter said to him, "You will never wash my feet!" Jesus
replied, "If I do not wash you, you have no share with me." 9Si-
mon Peter said to him, "Lord, wash not only my feet but also my
hands and my head!" 10Jesus replied, "The one who has bathed
needs only to wash his feet, but is completely clean. And you
disciples are clean, but not every one of you." 11(For Jesus knew
the one who was going to betray him. For this reason he said,
"Not every one of you is clean.")
12So when Jesus had washed their feet and put his outer
clothing back on, he took his place at the table again and said
to them, "Do you understand what I have done for you? 13You
call me 'Teacher' and 'Lord,' and do so correctly, for that is what
I am. 14If I then, your Lord and Teacher, have washed your feet,

13:1–17 Observe how not only by the washing but also in another way Christ exhibits humility. For it was not before reclining, but after they had all sat down, then he arose. In the next place, he does not merely wash them, but he does so after taking off his garments. And he did not even stop here, but he girded himself with a towel. Nor was he satisfied with this, but himself filled the basin and did not ask another to fill it. He did all these things himself, showing by all of them that we must do such things when we are engaged in well doing, not merely for the sake of appearance but with every effort.

CHRYSOSTOM (C. 347–407)
HOMILIES ON THE GOSPEL OF JOHN

you too ought to wash one another's feet. 15For I have given you
an example—you should do just as I have done for you. 16I tell
you the solemn truth, the slave is not greater than his master,
nor is the one who is sent as a messenger greater than the one
who sent him. 17If you understand these things, you will be
blessed if you do them.

THE ANNOUNCEMENT OF JESUS' BETRAYAL

18"What I am saying does not refer to all of you. I know the
ones I have chosen. But this is to fulfill the scripture, '***The one
who eats my bread has turned against me.***' 19I am telling you
this now, before it happens, so that when it happens you may
believe that I am he. 20I tell you the solemn truth, whoever
accepts the one I send accepts me, and whoever accepts me
accepts the one who sent me."

21When he had said these things, Jesus was greatly distressed in spirit, and testified, "I tell you the solemn truth,
one of you will betray me." 22The disciples began to look at one
another, worried and perplexed to know which of them he was
talking about. 23One of his disciples, the one Jesus loved, was at
the table to the right of Jesus in a place of honor. 24So Simon
Peter gestured to this disciple to ask Jesus who it was he was
referring to. 25Then the disciple whom Jesus loved leaned back
against Jesus' chest and asked him, "Lord, who is it?" 26Jesus
replied, "It is the one to whom I will give this piece of bread
after I have dipped it in the dish." Then he dipped the piece
of bread in the dish and gave it to Judas Iscariot, Simon's son.
27And after Judas took the piece of bread, Satan entered into
him. Jesus said to him, "What you are about to do, do quickly."
28(Now none of those present at the table understood why
Jesus said this to Judas. 29Some thought that because Judas
had the money box, Jesus was telling him to buy whatever
they needed for the feast, or to give something to the poor.)
30Judas took the piece of bread and went out immediately.
(Now it was night.)

THE PREDICTION OF PETER'S DENIAL

31When Judas had gone out, Jesus said, "Now the Son of Man
is glorified, and God is glorified in him. 32If God is glorified in
him, God will also glorify him in himself, and he will glorify him
right away. 33Children, I am still with you for a little while. You
will look for me, and just as I said to the Jewish religious leaders,
'Where I am going you cannot come,' now I tell you the same.
34"I give you a new commandment—to love one another. Just
as I have loved you, you also are to love one another. 35Everyone
will know by this that you are my disciples—if you have love
for one another."

36Simon Peter said to him, "Lord, where are you going?" Jesus
replied, "Where I am going, you cannot follow me now, but you
will follow later." 37Peter said to him, "Lord, why can't I follow
you now? I will lay down my life for you!" 38Jesus answered, "Will
you lay down your life for me? I tell you the solemn truth, the
rooster will not crow until you have denied me three times!

JESUS' PARTING WORDS TO HIS DISCIPLES

14 "Do not let your hearts be distressed. You believe in God;
believe also in me. 2There are many dwelling places in
my Father's house. Otherwise, I would have told you, because
I am going away to make ready a place for you. 3And if I go and

14:1–6 He who is the way does not lead us into byways or trackless wastes. He who is the truth does not mock us with lies. He who is the life does not betray us into delusions, which are death. He himself has chosen these winning names to indicate the methods that he has appointed for our salvation. As the way, he will guide us to the truth. As the truth, he will establish us in the life. And therefore it is all important for us to know what the mysterious mode is that he reveals for attaining this life. "No one comes to the Father except through me." The way to the Father is through the Son.

HILARY OF POITIERS
(C. 310–C. 367)
ON THE TRINITY

make ready a place for you, I will come again and take you to
be with me, so that where I am you may be too. 4And you know
the way where I am going."
5Thomas said, "Lord, we don't know where you are going. How
can we know the way?" 6Jesus replied, "I am the way, and the
truth, and the life. No one comes to the Father except through
me. 7If you have known me, you will know my Father too. And
from now on you do know him and have seen him."
8Philip said, "Lord, show us the Father, and we will be content." 9Jesus replied, "Have I been with you for so long and yet
you have not known me, Philip? The person who has seen me
has seen the Father! How can you say, 'Show us the Father'? 10Do
you not believe that I am in the Father, and the Father is in me?
The words that I say to you, I do not speak on my own initiative,
but the Father residing in me performs his miraculous deeds.
11Believe me that I am in the Father, and the Father is in me,
but if you do not believe me, believe because of the miraculous
deeds themselves. 12I tell you the solemn truth, the person
who believes in me will perform the miraculous deeds that I
am doing, and will perform greater deeds than these because
I am going to the Father. 13And I will do whatever you ask in
my name, so that the Father may be glorified in the Son. 14If
you ask me anything in my name, I will do it.

TEACHING ON THE HOLY SPIRIT

15"If you love me, you will obey my commandments. 16Then I
will ask the Father, and he will give you another Advocate to be
with you forever—17the Spirit of truth, whom the world cannot
accept because it does not see him or know him. But you know
him because he resides with you and will be in you.
18"I will not abandon you as orphans, I will come to you. 19In
a little while the world will not see me any longer, but you will
see me; because I live, you will live too. 20You will know at that
time that I am in my Father and you are in me and I am in you.
21The person who has my commandments and obeys them is
the one who loves me. The one who loves me will be loved by
my Father, and I will love him and will reveal myself to him."
22"Lord," Judas (not Judas Iscariot) said, "what has happened
that you are going to reveal yourself to us and not to the world?"
23Jesus replied, "If anyone loves me, he will obey my word, and
my Father will love him, and we will come to him and take up
residence with him. 24The person who does not love me does
not obey my words. And the word you hear is not mine, but the
Father's who sent me.
25"I have spoken these things while staying with you. 26But
the Advocate, the Holy Spirit, whom the Father will send in my
name, will teach you everything and will cause you to remember
everything I said to you.
27"Peace I leave with you; my peace I give to you; I do not give
it to you as the world does. Do not let your hearts be distressed
or lacking in courage. 28You heard me say to you, 'I am going
away and I am coming back to you.' If you loved me, you would
be glad that I am going to the Father because the Father is
greater than I am. 29I have told you now before it happens, so
that when it happens you may believe. 30I will not speak with
you much longer, for the ruler of this world is coming. He has
no power over me, 31but I am doing just what the Father commanded me, so that the world may know that I love the Father.
Get up, let us go from here.

THE VINE AND THE BRANCHES

15 “I am the true vine and my Father is the gardener. [2]He takes away every branch that does not bear fruit in me. He prunes every branch that bears fruit so that it will bear more fruit. [3]You are clean already because of the word that I have spoken to you. [4]Remain in me, and I will remain in you. Just as the branch cannot bear fruit by itself, unless it remains in the vine, so neither can you unless you remain in me.

[5]“I am the vine; you are the branches. The one who remains in me—and I in him—bears much fruit because apart from me you can accomplish nothing. [6]If anyone does not remain in me, he is thrown out like a branch and dries up; and such branches are gathered up and thrown into the fire and are burned up. [7]If you remain in me and my words remain in you, ask whatever you want, and it will be done for you. [8]My Father is honored by this, that you bear much fruit and show that you are my disciples.

[9]“Just as the Father has loved me, I have also loved you; remain in my love. [10]If you obey my commandments, you will remain in my love, just as I have obeyed my Father’s commandments and remain in his love. [11]I have told you these things so that my joy may be in you, and your joy may be complete. [12]My commandment is this—to love one another just as I have loved you. [13]No one has greater love than this—that one lays down his life for his friends. [14]You are my friends if you do what I command you. [15]I no longer call you slaves because the slave does not understand what his master is doing. But I have called you friends because I have revealed to you everything I heard from my Father. [16]You did not choose me, but I chose you and appointed you to go and bear fruit, fruit that remains, so that whatever you ask the Father in my name he will give you. [17]This I command you—to love one another.

THE WORLD’S HATRED

[18]“If the world hates you, be aware that it hated me first. [19]If you belonged to the world, the world would love you as its own. However, because you do not belong to the world, but I chose you out of the world, for this reason the world hates you. [20]Remember what I told you, ‘A slave is not greater than his master.’ If they persecuted me, they will also persecute you. If they obeyed my word, they will obey yours too. [21]But they will do all these things to you on account of my name because they do not know the one who sent me. [22]If I had not come and spoken to them, they would not be guilty of sin. But they no longer have any excuse for their sin. [23]The one who hates me hates my Father too. [24]If I had not performed among them the miraculous deeds that no one else did, they would not be guilty of sin. But now they have seen the deeds and have hated both me and my Father. [25]Now this happened to fulfill the word that is written in their law, ‘***They hated me without reason.***’ [26]When the Advocate comes, whom I will send you from the Father—the Spirit of truth who goes out from the Father—he will testify about me, [27]and you also will testify because you have been with me from the beginning.

16 “I have told you all these things so that you will not fall away. [2]They will put you out of the synagogue, yet a time is coming when the one who kills you will think he is offering service to God. [3]They will do these things because they have not known the Father or me. [4]But I have told you these things

---

15:9–17 “I have called you friends, because I have revealed to you everything I heard from my Father.” And once more, “You are my friends if you do what I command you.” You see then that there are different stages of perfection and that we are called by the Lord from high things to still higher in such a way that he who has become blessed and perfect in the fear of God—going, as it is written, “from strength to strength” (Ps 84:7 NKJV) and from one perfection to another, that is, mounting with an eager soul from fear to hope—is summoned in the end to that still more blessed stage, which is love.

JOHN CASSIAN
(C. 360–C. 435)
THE CONFERENCES

so that when their time comes, you will remember that I told you about them.

"I did not tell you these things from the beginning because I was with you. 5But now I am going to the one who sent me, and not one of you is asking me, 'Where are you going?' 6Instead your hearts are filled with sadness because I have said these things to you. 7But I tell you the truth, it is to your advantage that I am going away. For if I do not go away, the Advocate will not come to you, but if I go, I will send him to you. 8And when he comes, he will prove the world wrong concerning sin and righteousness and judgment—9concerning sin because they do not believe in me; 10concerning righteousness because I am going to the Father and you will see me no longer; 11and concerning judgment because the ruler of this world has been condemned.

12"I have many more things to say to you, but you cannot bear them now. 13But when he, the Spirit of truth, comes, he will guide you into all truth. For he will not speak on his own authority, but will speak whatever he hears and will tell you what is to come. 14He will glorify me because he will receive from me what is mine and will tell it to you. 15Everything that the Father has is mine; that is why I said the Spirit will receive from me what is mine and will tell it to you. 16In a little while you will see me no longer; again after a little while, you will see me."

17Then some of his disciples said to one another, "What is the meaning of what he is saying, 'In a little while you will not see me; again after a little while, you will see me,' and 'because I am going to the Father'?" 18So they kept on repeating, "What is the meaning of what he says, 'In a little while'? We do not understand what he is talking about."

19Jesus could see that they wanted to ask him about these things, so he said to them, "Are you asking each other about this—that I said, 'In a little while you will not see me; again after a little while, you will see me'? 20I tell you the solemn truth, you will weep and wail, but the world will rejoice; you will be sad, but your sadness will turn into joy. 21When a woman gives birth, she has distress because her time has come, but when her child is born, she no longer remembers the suffering because of her joy that a human being has been born into the world. 22So also you have sorrow now, but *I will see you again, and your hearts will rejoice, and no one will take your joy away from you.* 23At that time you will ask me nothing. I tell you the solemn truth, whatever you ask the Father in my name he will give you. 24Until now you have not asked for anything in my name. Ask and you will receive it, so that your joy may be complete.

25"I have told you these things in obscure figures of speech; a time is coming when I will no longer speak to you in obscure figures, but will tell you plainly about the Father. 26At that time you will ask in my name, and I do not say that I will ask the Father on your behalf. 27For the Father himself loves you because you have loved me and have believed that I came from God. 28I came from the Father and entered into the world, but in turn, I am leaving the world and going back to the Father."

29His disciples said, "Look, now you are speaking plainly and not in obscure figures of speech! 30Now we know that you know everything and do not need anyone to ask you anything. Because of this we believe that you have come from God."

31Jesus replied, "Do you now believe? 32Look, a time is coming—and has come—when you will be scattered, each one

16:25–33 In coming to the world, Christ came forth in such a sense from the Father that he did not leave the Father behind. And when he leaves the world, he goes to the Father in such a sense that he does not forsake the world. For he came forth from the Father because he is of the Father. And he came into the world in showing to the world his bodily form that he had received from the Virgin. He left the world by a bodily withdrawal, he proceeded to the Father by his ascension as man, but he did not forsake the world in the ruling activity of his presence.

AUGUSTINE **(354–430)**
TRACTATES ON THE GOSPEL OF JOHN

to his own home, and I will be left alone. Yet I am not alone
because my Father is with me. 33 I have told you these things so
that in me you may have peace. In the world you have trouble
and suffering, but take courage—I have conquered the world."

JESUS PRAYS FOR THE FATHER TO GLORIFY HIM

17 When Jesus had finished saying these things, he looked
upward to heaven and said, "Father, the time has come.
Glorify your Son, so that your Son may glorify you—2 just as
you have given him authority over all humanity, so that he
may give eternal life to everyone you have given him. 3 Now
this is eternal life—that they know you, the only true God,
and Jesus Christ, whom you sent. 4 I glorified you on earth by
completing the work you gave me to do. 5 And now, Father,
glorify me at your side with the glory I had with you before
the world was created.

JESUS PRAYS FOR THE DISCIPLES

6 "I have revealed your name to the men you gave me out of
the world. They belonged to you, and you gave them to me,
and they have obeyed your word. 7 Now they understand that
everything you have given me comes from you, 8 because I
have given them the words you have given me. They accepted
them and really understand that I came from you, and they
believed that you sent me. 9 I am praying on behalf of them. I
am not praying on behalf of the world, but on behalf of those
you have given me because they belong to you. 10 Everything I
have belongs to you, and everything you have belongs to me,
and I have been glorified by them. 11 I am no longer in the
world, but they are in the world, and I am coming to you. Holy
Father, keep them safe in your name that you have given me,
so that they may be one just as we are one. 12 When I was with
them I kept them safe and watched over them in your name
that you have given me. Not one of them was lost except the
one destined for destruction, so that the scripture could be
fulfilled. 13 But now I am coming to you, and I am saying these
things in the world, so they may experience my joy completed
in themselves. 14 I have given them your word, and the world
has hated them because they do not belong to the world, just
as I do not belong to the world. 15 I am not asking you to take
them out of the world, but that you keep them safe from the
evil one. 16 They do not belong to the world just as I do not
belong to the world. 17 Set them apart in the truth; your word
is truth. 18 Just as you sent me into the world, so I sent them
into the world. 19 And I set myself apart on their behalf, so that
they too may be truly set apart.

JESUS PRAYS FOR BELIEVERS EVERYWHERE

20 "I am not praying only on their behalf, but also on behalf of
those who believe in me through their testimony, 21 that they
will all be one, just as you, Father, are in me and I am in you. I
pray that they will be in us, so that the world will believe that
you sent me. 22 The glory you gave to me I have given to them,
that they may be one just as we are one—23 I in them and you
in me—that they may be completely one, so that the world will
know that you sent me, and you have loved them just as you
have loved me.

24 "Father, I want those you have given me to be with me
where I am, so that they can see my glory that you gave me

17:20–26 If we believe in Christ through the doctrine of the gospel, we ought to entertain no doubt that we are already gathered with the apostles into his faithful protection, so that not one of us shall perish. This prayer of Christ is a safe harbor, and whoever retreats into it is safe from all danger of shipwreck; for it is as if Christ had solemnly sworn that he will devote his care and diligence to our salvation. There is nothing therefore that ought more powerfully to excite us to embrace the gospel, for as it is an inestimable blessing that we are presented to God by the hand of Christ to be preserved from destruction, so we ought justly to love it and to care for it above all things else.

JOHN CALVIN **(1509–1564)**
COMPLETE COMMENTARY ON THE BIBLE

because you loved me before the creation of the world. 25Righ-
teous Father, even if the world does not know you, I know you,
and these men know that you sent me. 26I made known your
name to them, and I will continue to make it known, so that
the love you have loved me with may be in them, and I may
be in them."

BETRAYAL AND ARREST

18 When he had said these things, Jesus went out with his
disciples across the Kidron Valley. There was an orchard
there, and he and his disciples went into it. 2(Now Judas, the
one who betrayed him, knew the place too, because Jesus had
met there many times with his disciples.) 3So Judas obtained
a squad of soldiers and some officers of the chief priests and
Pharisees. They came to the orchard with lanterns and torches
and weapons.

4Then Jesus, because he knew everything that was going to
happen to him, came and asked them, "Who are you looking
for?" 5They replied, "Jesus the Nazarene." He told them, "I am
he." (Now Judas, the one who betrayed him, was standing there
with them.) 6So when Jesus said to them, "I am he," they retreated and fell to the ground. 7Then Jesus asked them again, "Who
are you looking for?" And they said, "Jesus the Nazarene." 8Jesus
replied, "I told you that I am he. If you are looking for me, let
these men go." 9He said this to fulfill the word he had spoken,
"I have not lost a single one of those whom you gave me."
10Then Simon Peter, who had a sword, pulled it out and struck
the high priest's slave, cutting off his right ear. (Now the slave's
name was Malchus.) 11But Jesus said to Peter, "Put your sword
back into its sheath! Am I not to drink the cup that the Father
has given me?"

JESUS BEFORE ANNAS

12Then the squad of soldiers with their commanding officer and
the officers of the Jewish leaders arrested Jesus and tied him
up. 13They brought him first to Annas, for he was the father-
in-law of Caiaphas, who was high priest that year. 14(Now it was
Caiaphas who had advised the Jewish leaders that it was to their
advantage that one man die for the people.)

PETER'S FIRST DENIAL

15Simon Peter and another disciple followed them as they
brought Jesus to Annas. (Now the other disciple was acquainted with the high priest, and he went with Jesus into the high
priest's courtyard.) 16But Peter was left standing outside by the
door. So the other disciple who was acquainted with the high
priest came out and spoke to the slave girl who watched the
door, and brought Peter inside. 17The girl who was the doorkeeper said to Peter, "You're not one of this man's disciples too, are
you?" He replied, "I am not." 18(Now the slaves and the guards
were standing around a charcoal fire they had made, warming
themselves because it was cold. Peter also was standing with
them, warming himself.)

JESUS QUESTIONED BY ANNAS

19While this was happening, the high priest questioned Jesus
about his disciples and about his teaching. 20Jesus replied, "I
have spoken publicly to the world. I always taught in the synagogues and in the temple courts, where all the Jewish people

18:1–12 When the people would have forced our Lord Jesus to a crown, he withdrew, but when they came to force him to a cross, he offered himself. He showed plainly what he could have done; when he struck them down he could have struck them dead, but he would not do so. Christ set us an example of meekness in sufferings. We were bound with the cords of our iniquities, with the yoke of our transgressions. Christ, being made a sin offering for us, to free us from those bonds, himself submitted to be bound for us. To his bonds we owe our liberty; thus the Son makes us free.

MATTHEW HENRY **(1662–1714)**
COMMENTARY ON THE WHOLE BIBLE

assemble together. I have said nothing in secret. 21 Why do you
ask me? Ask those who heard what I said. They know what I
said." 22 When Jesus had said this, one of the high priest's officers who stood nearby struck him on the face and said, "Is that
the way you answer the high priest?" 23 Jesus replied, "If I have
said something wrong, confirm what is wrong. But if I spoke
correctly, why strike me?" 24 Then Annas sent him, still tied up,
to Caiaphas the high priest.

PETER'S SECOND AND THIRD DENIALS

25 Meanwhile Simon Peter was standing in the courtyard warming himself. They said to him, "You aren't one of his disciples
too, are you?" Peter denied it: "I am not!" 26 One of the high
priest's slaves, a relative of the man whose ear Peter had cut off,
said, "Did I not see you in the orchard with him?" 27 Then Peter
denied it again, and immediately a rooster crowed.

JESUS BROUGHT BEFORE PILATE

28 Then they brought Jesus from Caiaphas to the Roman governor's residence. (Now it was very early morning.) They did not go
into the governor's residence so they would not be ceremonially
defiled, but could eat the Passover meal. 29 So Pilate came outside to them and said, "What accusation do you bring against
this man?" 30 They replied, "If this man were not a criminal, we
would not have handed him over to you."

31 Pilate told them, "Take him yourselves and pass judgment
on him according to your own law!" The Jewish leaders replied,
"We cannot legally put anyone to death." 32 (This happened to
fulfill the word Jesus had spoken when he indicated what kind
of death he was going to die.)

PILATE QUESTIONS JESUS

33 So Pilate went back into the governor's residence, summoned
Jesus, and asked him, "Are you the king of the Jews?" 34 Jesus
replied, "Are you saying this on your own initiative, or have
others told you about me?" 35 Pilate answered, "I am not a Jew,
am I? Your own people and your chief priests handed you over
to me. What have you done?"

36 Jesus replied, "My kingdom is not from this world. If my
kingdom were from this world, my servants would be fighting
to keep me from being handed over to the Jewish authorities.
But as it is, my kingdom is not from here." 37 Then Pilate said, "So
you are a king!" Jesus replied, "You say that I am a king. For this
reason I was born, and for this reason I came into the world—to
testify to the truth. Everyone who belongs to the truth listens
to my voice." 38 Pilate asked, "What is truth?"

When he had said this he went back outside to the Jewish
leaders and announced, "I find no basis for an accusation against
him. 39 But it is your custom that I release one prisoner for you
at the Passover. So do you want me to release for you the king
of the Jews?" 40 Then they shouted back, "Not this man, but
Barabbas!" (Now Barabbas was a revolutionary.)

PILATE TRIES TO RELEASE JESUS

19 Then Pilate took Jesus and had him flogged severely. 2 The
soldiers braided a crown of thorns and put it on his head,
and they clothed him in a purple robe. 3 They came up to him
again and again and said, "Hail, king of the Jews!" And they
struck him repeatedly in the face.

4 Again Pilate went out and said to the Jewish leaders, "Look, I am bringing him out to you, so that you may know that I find no reason for an accusation against him." 5 So Jesus came outside, wearing the crown of thorns and the purple robe. Pilate said to them, "Look, here is the man!" 6 When the chief priests and their officers saw him, they shouted out, "Crucify him! Crucify him!" Pilate said, "You take him and crucify him! Certainly I find no reason for an accusation against him!" 7 The Jewish leaders replied, "We have a law, and according to our law he ought to die because he claimed to be the Son of God!"

8 When Pilate heard what they said, he was more afraid than ever, 9 and he went back into the governor's residence and said to Jesus, "Where do you come from?" But Jesus gave him no answer. 10 So Pilate said, "Do you refuse to speak to me? Don't you know I have the authority to release you and to crucify you?" 11 Jesus replied, "You would have no authority over me at all, unless it was given to you from above. Therefore the one who handed me over to you is guilty of greater sin."

12 From this point on, Pilate tried to release him. But the Jewish leaders shouted out, "If you release this man, you are no friend of Caesar! Everyone who claims to be a king opposes Caesar!" 13 When Pilate heard these words he brought Jesus outside and sat down on the judgment seat in the place called "The Stone Pavement" (*Gabbatha* in Aramaic). 14 (Now it was the day of preparation for the Passover, about noon.) Pilate said to the Jewish leaders, "Look, here is your king!"

15 Then they shouted out, "Away with him! Away with him! Crucify him!" Pilate asked, "Shall I crucify your king?" The high priests replied, "We have no king except Caesar!" 16 Then Pilate handed him over to them to be crucified.

THE CRUCIFIXION

So they took Jesus, 17 and carrying his own cross he went out to the place called "The Place of the Skull" (called in Aramaic *Golgotha*). 18 There they crucified him along with two others, one on each side, with Jesus in the middle. 19 Pilate also had a notice written and fastened to the cross, which read: "Jesus the Nazarene, the king of the Jews." 20 Thus many of the Jewish residents of Jerusalem read this notice because the place where Jesus was crucified was near the city, and the notice was written in Aramaic, Latin, and Greek. 21 Then the chief priests of the Jews said to Pilate, "Do not write, 'The king of the Jews,' but rather, 'This man said, I am king of the Jews.'" 22 Pilate answered, "What I have written, I have written."

23 Now when the soldiers crucified Jesus, they took his clothes and made four shares, one for each soldier, and the tunic remained. (Now the tunic was seamless, woven from top to bottom as a single piece.) 24 So the soldiers said to one another, "Let's not tear it, but throw dice to see who will get it." This took place to fulfill the scripture that says, "***They divided my garments among them, and for my clothing they threw dice.***" So the soldiers did these things.

25 Now standing beside Jesus' cross were his mother, his mother's sister, Mary the wife of Clopas, and Mary Magdalene. 26 So when Jesus saw his mother and the disciple whom he loved standing there, he said to his mother, "Woman, look, here is your son!" 27 He then said to his disciple, "Look, here is your mother!" From that very time the disciple took her into his own home.

19:17–24 We ought to consider, on the one hand, the dreadful weight of God's wrath against sin, and on the other hand, his infinite goodness toward us. In no other way could our guilt be removed than by the Son of God becoming a curse for us. If God declares that our salvation was so dear to him that he did not spare his only begotten Son, what abundant goodness and what astonishing grace do we here behold! Whoever then takes a just view of the causes of the death of Christ, together with the advantage that it yields to us, will regard it as an invaluable token and pledge of the power, wisdom, righteousness, and goodness of God.

JOHN CALVIN **(1509–1564)**
COMPLETE COMMENTARY ON THE BIBLE

JESUS' DEATH

[28]After this Jesus, realizing that by this time everything was completed, said (in order to fulfill the scripture), "I am thirsty!" [29]A jar full of sour wine was there, so they put a sponge soaked in sour wine on a branch of hyssop and lifted it to his mouth. [30]When he had received the sour wine, Jesus said, "It is completed!" Then he bowed his head and gave up his spirit.

[31]Then because it was the day of preparation, so that the bodies should not stay on the crosses on the Sabbath (for that Sabbath was an especially important one), the Jewish leaders asked Pilate to have the victims' legs broken and the bodies taken down. [32]So the soldiers came and broke the legs of the two men who had been crucified with Jesus, first the one and then the other. [33]But when they came to Jesus and saw that he was already dead, they did not break his legs. [34]But one of the soldiers pierced his side with a spear, and blood and water flowed out immediately. [35]And the person who saw it has testified (and his testimony is true, and he knows that he is telling the truth), so that you also may believe. [36]For these things happened so that the scripture would be fulfilled, ***"Not a bone of his will be broken."*** [37]And again another scripture says, ***"They will look on the one whom they have pierced."***

JESUS' BURIAL

[38]After this, Joseph of Arimathea, a disciple of Jesus (but secretly because he feared the Jewish leaders), asked Pilate if he could remove the body of Jesus. Pilate gave him permission, so he went and took the body away. [39]Nicodemus, the man who had previously come to Jesus at night, accompanied Joseph, carrying a mixture of myrrh and aloes weighing about 75 pounds. [40]Then they took Jesus' body and wrapped it, with the aromatic spices, in strips of linen cloth according to Jewish burial customs. [41]Now at the place where Jesus was crucified there was a garden, and in the garden was a new tomb where no one had yet been buried. [42]And so, because it was the Jewish day of preparation and the tomb was nearby, they placed Jesus' body there.

THE RESURRECTION

20 Now very early on the first day of the week, while it was still dark, Mary Magdalene came to the tomb and saw that the stone had been moved away from the entrance. [2]So she went running to Simon Peter and the other disciple whom Jesus loved and told them, "They have taken the Lord from the tomb, and we don't know where they have put him!" [3]Then Peter and the other disciple set out to go to the tomb. [4]The two were running together, but the other disciple ran faster than Peter and reached the tomb first. [5]He bent down and saw the strips of linen cloth lying there, but he did not go in. [6]Then Simon Peter, who had been following him, arrived and went right into the tomb. He saw the strips of linen cloth lying there, [7]and the face cloth, which had been around Jesus' head, not lying with the strips of linen cloth but rolled up in a place by itself. [8]Then the other disciple, who had reached the tomb first, came in, and he saw and believed. [9](For they did not yet understand the scripture that Jesus must rise from the dead.)

JESUS' APPEARANCE TO MARY MAGDALENE

[10]So the disciples went back to their homes. [11]But Mary stood outside the tomb weeping. As she wept, she bent down and looked into the tomb. [12]And she saw two angels in white sitting where Jesus' body had been lying, one at the head and one at the feet. [13]They said to her, "Woman, why are you weeping?" Mary replied, "They have taken my Lord away, and I do not know where they have put him!" [14]When she had said this, she turned around and saw Jesus standing there, but she did not know that it was Jesus.

[15]Jesus said to her, "Woman, why are you weeping? Who are you looking for?" Because she thought he was the gardener, she said to him, "Sir, if you have carried him away, tell me where you have put him, and I will take him." [16]Jesus said to her, "Mary." She turned and said to him in Aramaic, "*Rabboni*" (which means "Teacher"). [17]Jesus replied, "Do not touch me, for I have not yet ascended to my Father. Go to my brothers and tell them, 'I am ascending to my Father and your Father, to my God and your God.'" [18]Mary Magdalene came and informed the disciples, "I have seen the Lord!" And she told them what Jesus had said to her.

JESUS' APPEARANCE TO THE DISCIPLES

[19]On the evening of that day, the first day of the week, the disciples had gathered together and locked the doors of the place because they were afraid of the Jewish leaders. Jesus came and stood among them and said to them, "Peace be with you." [20]When he had said this, he showed them his hands and his side. Then the disciples rejoiced when they saw the Lord. [21]So Jesus said to them again, "Peace be with you. Just as the Father has sent me, I also send you." [22]And after he said this, he breathed on them and said, "Receive the Holy Spirit. [23]If you forgive anyone's sins, they are forgiven; if you retain anyone's sins, they are retained."

THE RESPONSE OF THOMAS

[24]Now Thomas (called Didymus), one of the twelve, was not with them when Jesus came. [25]The other disciples told him, "We have seen the Lord!" But he replied, "Unless I see the wounds from the nails in his hands, and put my finger into the wounds from the nails, and put my hand into his side, I will never believe it!"

[26]Eight days later the disciples were again together in the house, and Thomas was with them. Although the doors were locked, Jesus came and stood among them and said, "Peace be with you!" [27]Then he said to Thomas, "Put your finger here, and examine my hands. Extend your hand and put it into my side. Do not continue in your unbelief, but believe." [28]Thomas replied to him, "My Lord and my God!" [29]Jesus said to him, "Have you believed because you have seen me? Blessed are the people who have not seen and yet have believed."

[30]Now Jesus performed many other miraculous signs in the presence of the disciples, which are not recorded in this book. [31]But these are recorded so that you may believe that Jesus is the Christ, the Son of God, and that by believing you may have life in his name.

JESUS' APPEARANCE TO THE DISCIPLES IN GALILEE

21 After this Jesus revealed himself again to the disciples by the Sea of Tiberias. Now this is how he did so. [2]Simon Peter, Thomas (called Didymus), Nathanael (who was from Cana

20:19–23 Jesus did not remain in death's power. The wounds that his body had received from the iron of the nails and spear offered no impediment to his rising again. After his resurrection he showed himself whenever he wanted to his disciples. When he wished to be present with them, he was in their midst without being seen, needing no entrance through open doors. All these occurrences, and whatever other similar facts we know about his life, require no further argument to show that they are signs of deity and of a sublime and supreme power.

GREGORY OF NYSSA
(C. 335–C. 395)
THE GREAT CATECHISM

in Galilee), the sons of Zebedee, and two other disciples of his were together. [3]Simon Peter told them, "I am going fishing." "We will go with you," they replied. They went out and got into the boat, but that night they caught nothing.

[4]When it was already very early morning, Jesus stood on the beach, but the disciples did not know that it was Jesus. [5]So Jesus said to them, "Children, you don't have any fish, do you?" They replied, "No." [6]He told them, "Throw your net on the right side of the boat, and you will find some." So they threw the net and were not able to pull it in because of the large number of fish.

[7]Then the disciple whom Jesus loved said to Peter, "It is the Lord!" So Simon Peter, when he heard that it was the Lord, tucked in his outer garment (for he had nothing on underneath it), and plunged into the sea. [8]Meanwhile the other disciples came with the boat, dragging the net full of fish, for they were not far from land, only about a hundred yards.

[9]When they got out on the beach, they saw a charcoal fire ready with a fish placed on it, and bread. [10]Jesus said, "Bring some of the fish you have just now caught." [11]So Simon Peter went aboard and pulled the net to shore. It was full of large fish, 153, but although there were so many, the net was not torn. [12]"Come, have breakfast," Jesus said. But none of the disciples dared to ask him, "Who are you?" because they knew it was the Lord. [13]Jesus came and took the bread and gave it to them, and did the same with the fish. [14]This was now the third time Jesus was revealed to the disciples after he was raised from the dead.

PETER'S RESTORATION

[15]Then when they had finished breakfast, Jesus said to Simon Peter, "Simon, son of John, do you love me more than these do?" He replied, "Yes, Lord, you know I love you." Jesus told him, "Feed my lambs." [16]Jesus said a second time, "Simon, son of John, do you love me?" He replied, "Yes, Lord, you know I love you." Jesus told him, "Shepherd my sheep." [17]Jesus said a third time, "Simon, son of John, do you love me?" Peter was distressed that Jesus asked him a third time, "Do you love me?" and said, "Lord, you know everything. You know that I love you." Jesus replied, "Feed my sheep. [18]I tell you the solemn truth, when you were young, you tied your clothes around you and went wherever you wanted, but when you are old, you will stretch out your hands, and others will tie you up and bring you where you do not want to go." [19](Now Jesus said this to indicate clearly by what kind of death Peter was going to glorify God.) After he said this, Jesus told Peter, "Follow me."

PETER AND THE DISCIPLE JESUS LOVED

[20]Peter turned around and saw the disciple whom Jesus loved following them. (This was the disciple who had leaned back against Jesus' chest at the meal and asked, "Lord, who is the one who is going to betray you?") [21]So when Peter saw him, he asked Jesus, "Lord, what about him?" [22]Jesus replied, "If I want him to live until I come back, what concern is that of yours? You follow me!" [23]So the saying circulated among the brothers and sisters that this disciple was not going to die. But Jesus did not say to him that he was not going to die, but rather, "If I want him to live until I come back, what concern is that of yours?"

A FINAL NOTE

24This is the disciple who testifies about these things and has
written these things, and we know that his testimony is true.
25There are many other things that Jesus did. If every one of
them were written down, I suppose the whole world would not
have room for the books that would be written.

21:24–25 We are lost in the deepest amazement that such a nature, preeminent above all others, should have divested itself of its condition of majesty and become man and tabernacled among men, as the grace that was poured upon his lips testifies, and as his heavenly Father bore him witness, and as is confessed by the various signs and wonders and miracles that were performed by him. He also sent the prophets as his forerunners and the messengers of his advent, and after his ascension into heaven made his holy apostles, men ignorant and unlearned but who were filled with the power of his divinity, to itinerate throughout the world that they might gather together out of every race and every nation a multitude of devout believers in himself.

ORIGEN (C. 185–C. 253)
ON FIRST PRINCIPLES

AUTHOR	AUDIENCE	DATE	PURPOSE	THEMES
Luke, a Gentile physician and missionary companion of Paul	Addressed to Theophilus but intended for all believers	About AD 63 or later	Luke wrote to explain how the gospel of Jesus Christ spread rapidly from Jerusalem through the whole Roman Empire—from its Jewish roots to the Gentile world, fulfilling God's promises.	The lordship of Jesus; the work and power of the Holy Spirit; the salvation of the world; the mission of the church; and discipleship

In this second of two volumes examining Jesus and his movement, the focus shifts from what Jesus did and taught to what he continued to do and teach through his apostles, empowered by the Holy Spirit. Luke gives us a vivid portrayal of the earliest followers of Jesus. There are also biographical accounts of the church's major leaders, who spread the good news about Jesus throughout Jerusalem and into the wider Roman Empire.

The evangelist Luke wrote Acts as a follow-up to the Gospel that bears his name in order to inform Theophilus and all lovers of God concerning the mighty works accomplished in and through Jesus' followers. Combined, Luke and Acts cover six decades of God's action in the world through his Son and his followers. In his history of the early church, Luke confirmed that the people of God are those who follow Jesus and that the life and work of the Messiah are continued through his church.

In his lauded commentary series, Matthew Henry described this book as uniting the Gospels to the Epistles and outlined its purpose in this way: "1) to relate in what manner the gifts of the Holy Spirit were communicated on the day of Pentecost, and the miracles performed by the apostles, to confirm the truth of Christianity, as showing that Christ's declarations were really fulfilled; 2) to prove the claim of the Gentiles to be admitted into the church of Christ."

Luke begins his second volume where his first ended: Christ's ascension into the heavens and his exaltation at the Father's right hand. From there Jesus' disciples bear witness to Jesus "in Jerusalem, and in all Judea and Samaria, and to the farthest parts of the earth" (1:8). In essence their witness was to the good news of his life, death, and resurrection and what that news means for all who accept their message: forgiveness, salvation, and eternal life in Jesus' name. In fact, Jesus' name is referenced over 50 times in Acts, signifying that he alone possesses the power to rescue humanity. Acts makes it clear that "everyone who calls on the name of the Lord will be saved" (2:21). Through dreams, providential encounters, and councils, God reiterates that his promised salvation by grace through faith isn't reserved for Jews alone, but for the entire world.

ACTS

While Jesus was clearly at the center of Luke's Gospel, he is no less so in Acts, though now the story unfolds with Jesus at work in the lives of his people through the Holy Spirit. The Holy Spirit is referenced almost twice as often in Acts than in Luke. The Holy Spirit is given to all God's people who believe in his Son, not merely a holy, select few. The church carries out the mission of God by the power of the Holy Spirit, bearing witness to his gospel and performing mighty wonders for his name's sake.

The task of witnessing isn't easy—far from it. Jesus himself promised that the world "will seize you and persecute you" (Luke 21:12). Throughout Acts early Christians were persecuted and their plans opposed. Yet, through the Holy Spirit, they overcame, the church grew, and the kingdom of God expanded. The apostles healed people and cast out demons. They also cared for one another and the world around them. As in Luke's Gospel, the poor feature prominently in Acts; Luke emphasizes that it is the church's responsibility to care for those in need. We show our commitment to Christ's entire mission and message when we live lives devoted to loving God and neighbor, pray without ceasing, and persevere with faith through every trial.

One Reformation leader, Johann Spangenberg, suggested the title of this book should be changed from "the Acts of the Apostles" to "the Acts of Christ," for the stories of the apostles described in it are "not what they have done from their own power but what they have done in the power of our Lord Jesus Christ."

1:1–8 Great is the praise of the apostles when they have been entrusted with such a charge, that is to say, the salvation of the world. Words full of the Spirit! This he hints at in the expression "by the Holy Spirit." "The words that I have spoken to you are spirit," he had said earlier (John 6:63), inducing in the hearer a desire for learning the commandments and establishing the authority of the apostles, since it is the words of the Spirit they are to speak, and the commandments of Christ.

CHRYSOSTOM **(C. 347–407)**
HOMILIES ON THE ACTS OF THE APOSTLES

JESUS ASCENDS TO HEAVEN

1 I wrote the former account, Theophilus, about all that Jesus began to do and teach [2]until the day he was taken up to heaven, after he had given orders by the Holy Spirit to the apostles he had chosen. [3]To the same apostles also, after his suffering, he presented himself alive with many convincing proofs. He was seen by them over a forty-day period and spoke about matters concerning the kingdom of God. [4]While he was with them, he declared, "Do not leave Jerusalem, but wait there for what my Father promised, which you heard about from me. [5]For John baptized with water, but you will be baptized with the Holy Spirit not many days from now."

[6]So when they had gathered together, they began to ask him, "Lord, is this the time when you are restoring the kingdom to Israel?" [7]He told them, "You are not permitted to know the times or periods that the Father has set by his own authority. [8]But you will receive power when the Holy Spirit has come upon you, and you will be my witnesses in Jerusalem, and in all Judea and Samaria, and to the farthest parts of the earth." [9]After he had said this, while they were watching, he was lifted up and a cloud hid him from their sight. [10]As they were still staring into the sky while he was going, suddenly two men in white clothing stood near them [11]and said, "Men of Galilee, why do you stand here looking up into the sky? This same Jesus who has been taken up from you into heaven will come back in the same way you saw him go into heaven."

A REPLACEMENT FOR JUDAS IS CHOSEN

[12]Then they returned to Jerusalem from the mountain called the Mount of Olives (which is near Jerusalem, a Sabbath day's journey away). [13]When they had entered Jerusalem, they went to the upstairs room where they were staying. Peter and John, and James, and Andrew, Philip and Thomas, Bartholomew and Matthew, James son of Alphaeus and Simon the Zealot, and Judas son of James were there. [14]All these continued together in prayer with one mind, together with the women, along with Mary the mother of Jesus, and his brothers. [15]In those days Peter stood up among the believers (a gathering of about 120 people) and said, [16]"Brothers, the scripture had to be fulfilled that the Holy Spirit foretold through David concerning Judas—who became the guide for those who arrested Jesus—[17]for he was counted as one of us and received a share in this ministry." [18](Now this man Judas acquired a field with the reward of his unjust deed, and falling headfirst he burst open in the middle and all his intestines gushed out. [19]This became known to all who lived in Jerusalem, so that in their own language they called that field *Hakeldama,* that is, "Field of Blood.") [20]"For it is written in the book of Psalms, '***Let his house become deserted, and let there be no one to live in it,***' and '***Let another take his position of responsibility.***' [21]Thus one of the men who have accompanied us during all the time the Lord Jesus associated with us, [22]beginning from his baptism by John until the day he was taken up from us—one of these must become a witness of his resurrection together with us." [23]So they proposed two candidates: Joseph called Barsabbas (also called Justus) and Matthias. [24]Then they prayed, "Lord, you know the hearts of all. Show us which one of these two you have chosen [25]to assume the task of this service and apostleship from which Judas turned aside to go to his own place." [26]Then they cast lots for them, and the one chosen was Matthias; so he was counted with the eleven apostles.

THE HOLY SPIRIT AND THE DAY OF PENTECOST

2 Now when the day of Pentecost had come, they were all together in one place. 2Suddenly a sound like a violent wind
blowing came from heaven and filled the entire house where
they were sitting. 3And tongues spreading out like a fire appeared to them and came to rest on each one of them. 4All of
them were filled with the Holy Spirit, and they began to speak
in other languages as the Spirit enabled them.
5Now there were devout Jews from every nation under heav-
en residing in Jerusalem. 6When this sound occurred, a crowd
gathered and was in confusion because each one heard them
speaking in his own language. 7Completely baffled, they said,
"Aren't all these who are speaking Galileans? 8And how is it that
each one of us hears them in our own native language? 9Par-
thians, Medes, Elamites, and residents of Mesopotamia, Judea
and Cappadocia, Pontus and the province of Asia, 10Phrygia
and Pamphylia, Egypt and the parts of Libya near Cyrene, and
visitors from Rome, 11both Jews and proselytes, Cretans and
Arabs—we hear them speaking in our own languages about the
great deeds God has done!" 12All were astounded and greatly
confused, saying to one another, "What does this mean?" 13But
others jeered at the speakers, saying, "They are drunk on new
wine!"

2:1–13 What teacher can be found so great as to teach men all at once things that they have not learned? The Holy Spirit taught them many languages at once. What a contrast of their long ignorance in time past to their sudden, complete, varied, and unaccustomed exercise of these languages! The multitude of the hearers was confounded as at Babylon. For in Babylon's confusion of tongues there was division of purpose because their thought was at enmity with God; but here at Pentecost minds were restored and united because the object of interest was godly.

CYRIL OF JERUSALEM
(C. 313–386)
CATECHETICAL LECTURES

PETER'S ADDRESS ON THE DAY OF PENTECOST

14But Peter stood up with the eleven, raised his voice, and addressed them: "You men of Judea and all you who live in Jerusalem, know this and listen carefully to what I say. 15In spite
of what you think, these men are not drunk, for it is only nine
o'clock in the morning. 16But this is what was spoken about
through the prophet Joel:

17 ***'And** in the last days **it will be,'** God says,*
'that I will pour out my Spirit on all people,
and your sons and your daughters will prophesy,
and your young men will see visions,
and your old men will dream dreams.
18 ***Even on my servants, both men and women,***
I will pour out my Spirit in those days, and they will prophesy.
19 ***And I will perform wonders in the sky above***
and miraculous signs on the earth below,
blood and fire and clouds of smoke.
20 ***The sun will be changed to darkness***
and the moon to blood
before the great and glorious day of the Lord comes.
21 ***And then everyone who calls on the name of the Lord will be saved.'***

22"Men of Israel, listen to these words: Jesus the Nazarene, a
man clearly attested to you by God with powerful deeds, wonders, and miraculous signs that God performed among you
through him, just as you yourselves know—23this man, who was
handed over by the predetermined plan and foreknowledge
of God, you executed by nailing him to a cross at the hands of
Gentiles. 24But God raised him up, having released him from
the pains of death because it was not possible for him to be
held in its power. 25For David says about him,

'I saw the Lord always in front of me,
for he is at my right hand so that I will not be shaken.

[26] ***Therefore my heart was glad and my tongue rejoiced;***
my body also will live in hope,
[27] ***because you will not leave my soul in Hades,***
nor permit your Holy One to experience decay.
[28] ***You have made known to me the paths of life;***
you will make me full of joy with your presence.'

[29]"Brothers, I can speak confidently to you about our forefather David, that he both died and was buried, and his tomb
is with us to this day. [30]So then, because he was a prophet and
knew that God *had sworn to him with an oath to seat one of his*
descendants on his throne, [31]David by foreseeing this spoke about
the resurrection of the Christ, that *he was neither abandoned to*
Hades, nor did his body *experience decay.* [32]This Jesus God raised
up, and we are all witnesses of it. [33]So then, exalted to the right
hand of God, and having received the promise of the Holy Spirit
from the Father, he has poured out what you both see and hear.
[34]For David did not ascend into heaven, but he himself says,
'The Lord said to my lord,
"Sit at my right hand
[35] ***until I make your enemies a footstool for your feet."'***
[36]Therefore let all the house of Israel know beyond a doubt
that God has made this Jesus whom you crucified both Lord
and Christ."

THE RESPONSE TO PETER'S ADDRESS

[37]Now when they heard this, they were acutely distressed and said
to Peter and the rest of the apostles, "What should we do, brothers?" [38]Peter said to them, "Repent, and each one of you be baptized
in the name of Jesus Christ for the forgiveness of your sins, and
you will receive the gift of the Holy Spirit. [39]For the promise is
for you and your children, and for all who are far away, as many as
the Lord our God will call to himself." [40]With many other words
he testified and exhorted them saying, "Save yourselves from this
perverse generation!" [41]So those who accepted his message were
baptized, and that day about 3,000 people were added.

THE FELLOWSHIP OF THE EARLY BELIEVERS

[42]They were devoting themselves to the apostles' teaching and
to fellowship, to the breaking of bread and to prayer. [43]Reveren-
tial awe came over everyone, and many wonders and miraculous
signs came about by the apostles. [44]All who believed were together and held everything in common, [45]and they began selling
their property and possessions and distributing the proceeds
to everyone, as anyone had need. [46]Every day they continued
to gather together by common consent in the temple courts,
breaking bread from house to house, sharing their food with
glad and humble hearts, [47]praising God and having the good
will of all the people. And the Lord was adding to their number
every day those who were being saved.

PETER AND JOHN HEAL A LAME MAN AT THE TEMPLE

3 Now Peter and John were going up to the temple at the time
for prayer, at three o'clock in the afternoon. [2]And a man lame
from birth was being carried up, who was placed at the temple
gate called "the Beautiful Gate" every day so he could beg for
money from those going into the temple courts. [3]When he saw
Peter and John about to go into the temple courts, he asked

them for money. [4]Peter looked directly at him (as did John) and
said, "Look at us!" [5]So the lame man paid attention to them,
expecting to receive something from them. [6]But Peter said, "I
have no silver or gold, but what I do have I give you. In the name
of Jesus Christ the Nazarene, stand up and walk!" [7]Then Peter
took hold of him by the right hand and raised him up, and at
once the man's feet and ankles were made strong. [8]He jumped
up, stood and began walking around, and he entered the temple
courts with them, walking and leaping and praising God. [9]All
the people saw him walking and praising God, [10]and they recognized him as the man who used to sit and ask for donations
at the Beautiful Gate of the temple, and they were filled with
astonishment and amazement at what had happened to him.

PETER ADDRESSES THE CROWD

[11]While the man was hanging on to Peter and John, all the people, completely astounded, ran together to them in the covered
walkway called Solomon's Portico. [12]When Peter saw this, he
declared to the people, "Men of Israel, why are you amazed at
this? Why do you stare at us as if we had made this man walk
by our own power or piety? [13]The God of Abraham, Isaac, and
Jacob, the God of our forefathers, has glorified his servant Jesus,
whom you handed over and rejected in the presence of Pilate
after he had decided to release him. [14]But you rejected the Holy
and Righteous One and asked that a man who was a murderer
be released to you. [15]You killed the Originator of life, whom God
raised from the dead. To this fact we are witnesses! [16]And on
the basis of faith in Jesus' name, his very name has made this
man—whom you see and know—strong. The faith that is through
Jesus has given him this complete health in the presence of you
all. [17]And now, brothers, I know you acted in ignorance, as your
rulers did too. [18]But the things God foretold long ago through
all the prophets—that his Christ would suffer—he has fulfilled
in this way. [19]Therefore repent and turn back so that your sins
may be wiped out, [20]so that times of refreshing may come from
the presence of the Lord, and so that he may send the Messiah
appointed for you—that is, Jesus. [21]This one heaven must receive until the time all things are restored, which God declared
from times long ago through his holy prophets. [22]Moses said,
'***The Lord your God will raise up for you a prophet like me from***
among your brothers. You must obey him in everything he tells you.
[23]***Every person who does not obey that prophet will be destroyed***
and thus removed from the people.' [24]And all the prophets, from
Samuel and those who followed him, have spoken about and
announced these days. [25]You are the sons of the prophets and
of the covenant that God made with your ancestors, saying to
Abraham, '***And in your descendants all the nations of the earth will***
be blessed.' [26]God raised up his servant and sent him first to you,
to bless you by turning each one of you from your iniquities."

THE ARREST AND TRIAL OF PETER AND JOHN

4 While Peter and John were speaking to the people, the priests
and the commander of the temple guard and the Sadducees
came up to them, [2]angry because they were teaching the people and announcing in Jesus the resurrection of the dead. [3]So
they seized them and put them in jail until the next day (for
it was already evening). [4]But many of those who had listened
to the message believed, and the number of the men came to
about 5,000.

3:11–26 Moses instituted the Jewish church: Christ instituted the Christian. With the prophesying of Moses was soon joined the effect, the deliverance of Israel from Egypt: with the prophesying of Christ that grand effect, the deliverance of his people from sin and death. Those who could not bear the voice of God yet desired to hear that of Moses. Much more do those who are wearied with the law desire to hear the voice of Christ. Moses spoke to the people all, and only those things that God had commanded him: so did Christ. But though he was like Moses, yet he was infinitely superior to him in person as well as in office.

JOHN WESLEY (1703–1791)
EXPLANATORY NOTES ON THE BIBLE

[5]On the next day, their rulers, elders, and experts in the law came together in Jerusalem. [6]Annas the high priest was there, and Caiaphas, John, Alexander, and others who were members of the high priest's family. [7]After making Peter and John stand in their midst, they began to inquire, "By what power or by what name did you do this?" [8]Then Peter, filled with the Holy Spirit, replied, "Rulers of the people and elders, [9]if we are being examined today for a good deed done to a sick man—by what means this man was healed—[10]let it be known to all of you and to all the people of Israel that by the name of Jesus Christ the Nazarene whom you crucified, whom God raised from the dead, this man stands before you healthy. [11]This Jesus is ***the stone that was rejected by*** you, ***the builders, that has become the cornerstone.*** [12]And there is salvation in no one else, for there is no other name under heaven given among people by which we must be saved."

[13]When they saw the boldness of Peter and John, and discovered that they were uneducated and ordinary men, they were amazed and recognized these men had been with Jesus. [14]And because they saw the man who had been healed standing with them, they had nothing to say against this. [15]But when they had ordered them to go outside the council, they began to confer with one another, [16]saying, "What should we do with these men? For it is plain to all who live in Jerusalem that a notable miraculous sign has come about through them, and we cannot deny it. [17]But to keep this matter from spreading any further among the people, let us warn them to speak no more to anyone in this name." [18]And they called them in and ordered them not to speak or teach at all in the name of Jesus. [19]But Peter and John replied, "Whether it is right before God to obey you rather than God, you decide, [20]for it is impossible for us not to speak about what we have seen and heard." [21]After threatening them further, they released them, for they could not find how to punish them on account of the people, because they were all praising God for what had happened. [22]For the man, on whom this miraculous sign of healing had been performed, was over forty years old.

4:13–22 **A Christian should be a striking likeness of Jesus Christ. You have read lives of Christ, beautifully and eloquently written, but the best life of Christ is his living biography written out in the words and actions of his people. Be like Jesus, very valiant for your God. Imitate him in your loving spirit; think kindly, speak kindly, and do kindly that others may say of you, "He has been with Jesus."**

CHARLES SPURGEON
(1834–1892)
MORNING AND EVENING

THE FOLLOWERS OF JESUS PRAY FOR BOLDNESS

[23]When they were released, Peter and John went to their fellow believers and reported everything the high priests and the elders had said to them. [24]When they heard this, they raised their voices to God with one mind and said, "Master of all, you who made the heaven, the earth, the sea, and everything that is in them, [25]who said by the Holy Spirit through your servant David our forefather,

'Why do the nations rage,
and the peoples plot foolish things?
[26] ***The kings of the earth stood together,***
and the rulers assembled together,
against the Lord and against his Christ.'

[27]"For indeed both Herod and Pontius Pilate, with the Gentiles and the people of Israel, assembled together in this city against your holy servant Jesus, whom you anointed, [28]to do as much as your power and your plan had decided beforehand would happen. [29]And now, Lord, pay attention to their threats, and grant to your servants to speak your message with great courage, [30]while you extend your hand to heal, and to bring

about miraculous signs and wonders through the name of your
holy servant Jesus." 31 When they had prayed, the place where
they were assembled together was shaken, and they were all
filled with the Holy Spirit and began to speak the word of God
courageously.

CONDITIONS AMONG THE EARLY BELIEVERS

32 The group of those who believed were of one heart and mind,
and no one said that any of his possessions was his own, but
everything was held in common. 33 With great power the apostles were giving testimony to the resurrection of the Lord Jesus,
and great grace was on them all. 34 For there was no one needy
among them because those who were owners of land or houses
were selling them and bringing the proceeds from the sales
35 and placing them at the apostles' feet. The proceeds were
distributed to each, as anyone had need. 36 So Joseph, a Levite
who was a native of Cyprus, called by the apostles Barnabas
(which is translated "son of encouragement"), 37 sold a field
that belonged to him and brought the money and placed it at
the apostles' feet.

THE JUDGMENT ON ANANIAS AND SAPPHIRA

5 Now a man named Ananias, together with Sapphira his wife,
sold a piece of property. 2 He kept back for himself part of the
proceeds with his wife's knowledge; he brought only part of it
and placed it at the apostles' feet. 3 But Peter said, "Ananias,
why has Satan filled your heart to lie to the Holy Spirit and
keep back for yourself part of the proceeds from the sale of the
land? 4 Before it was sold, did it not belong to you? And when
it was sold, was the money not at your disposal? How have you
thought up this deed in your heart? You have not lied to people
but to God!"

5 When Ananias heard these words he collapsed and died, and
great fear gripped all who heard about it. 6 So the young men
came, wrapped him up, carried him out, and buried him. 7 After
an interval of about three hours, his wife came in, but she did
not know what had happened. 8 Peter said to her, "Tell me, were
the two of you paid this amount for the land?" Sapphira said,
"Yes, that much." 9 Peter then told her, "Why have you agreed
together to test the Spirit of the Lord? Look! The feet of those
who have buried your husband are at the door, and they will
carry you out!" 10 At once she collapsed at his feet and died. So
when the young men came in, they found her dead, and they
carried her out and buried her beside her husband. 11 Great fear
gripped the whole church and all who heard about these things.

THE APOSTLES PERFORM MIRACULOUS SIGNS AND WONDERS

12 Now many miraculous signs and wonders came about among
the people through the hands of the apostles. By common
consent they were all meeting together in Solomon's Portico.
13 None of the rest dared to join them, but the people held them
in high honor. 14 More and more believers in the Lord were
added to their number, crowds of both men and women. 15 Thus
they even carried the sick out into the streets and put them on
cots and pallets, so that when Peter came by at least his shadow
would fall on some of them. 16 A crowd of people from the towns
around Jerusalem also came together, bringing the sick and
those troubled by unclean spirits. They were all being healed.

FURTHER TROUBLE FOR THE APOSTLES

[17]Now the high priest rose up, and all those with him (that is, the religious party of the Sadducees), and they were filled with jealousy. [18]They laid hands on the apostles and put them in a public jail. [19]But during the night an angel of the Lord opened the doors of the prison, led them out, and said, [20]"Go and stand in the temple courts and proclaim to the people all the words of this life." [21]When they heard this, they entered the temple courts at daybreak and began teaching.

Now when the high priest and those who were with him arrived, they summoned the Sanhedrin—that is, the whole high council of the Israelites—and sent to the jail to have the apostles brought before them. [22]But the officers who came for them did not find them in the prison, so they returned and reported, [23]"We found the jail locked securely and the guards standing at the doors, but when we opened them, we found no one inside." [24]Now when the commander of the temple guard and the chief priests heard this report, they were greatly puzzled concerning it, wondering what this could be. [25]But someone came and reported to them, "Look! The men you put in prison are standing in the temple courts and teaching the people!" [26]Then the commander of the temple guard went with the officers and brought the apostles without the use of force (for they were afraid of being stoned by the people).

[27]When they had brought them, they stood them before the council, and the high priest questioned them, [28]saying, "We gave you strict orders not to teach in this name. Look, you have filled Jerusalem with your teaching, and you intend to bring this man's blood on us!" [29]But Peter and the apostles replied, "We must obey God rather than people. [30]The God of our forefathers raised up Jesus, whom you seized and killed by hanging him on a tree. [31]God exalted him to his right hand as Leader and Savior, to give repentance to Israel and forgiveness of sins. [32]And we are witnesses of these events, and so is the Holy Spirit whom God has given to those who obey him."

[33]Now when they heard this, they became furious and wanted to execute them. [34]But a Pharisee whose name was Gamaliel, a teacher of the law who was respected by all the people, stood up in the council and ordered the men to be put outside for a short time. [35]Then he said to the council, "Men of Israel, pay close attention to what you are about to do to these men. [36]For sometime ago Theudas rose up, claiming to be somebody, and about 400 men joined him. He was killed, and all who followed him were dispersed and nothing came of it. [37]After him Judas the Galilean arose in the days of the census and incited people to follow him in revolt. He too was killed, and all who followed him were scattered. [38]So in this case I say to you, stay away from these men and leave them alone because if this plan or this undertaking originates with people, it will come to nothing, [39]but if it is from God, you will not be able to stop them, or you may even be found fighting against God." He convinced them, [40]and they summoned the apostles and had them beaten. Then they ordered them not to speak in the name of Jesus and released them. [41]So they left the council rejoicing because they had been considered worthy to suffer dishonor for the sake of the name. [42]And every day both in the temple courts and from house to house, they did not stop teaching and proclaiming the good news that Jesus was the Christ.

5:22–42 The Lord brought the apostles out of prison, not because he wished to deliver them from the hand of their enemies forever, for later on he allowed them to be brought back again. But by this miracle he meant to demonstrate that they were in his hand and care for the defense of faith in his gospel, partly in order that the church might find fresh encouragement from the event and partly to leave the ungodly without any excuse. For that reason we must not always hope, not even are we to desire, that God may deliver us from death; the proper thing for us is to be content that our life is protected by his hand as needs be.

JOHN CALVIN **(1509–1564)**
COMPLETE COMMENTARY ON THE BIBLE

THE APPOINTMENT OF THE FIRST SEVEN DEACONS

6 Now in those days, when the disciples were growing in number, a complaint arose on the part of the Greek-speaking Jews against the native Hebraic Jews because their widows were being overlooked in the daily distribution of food. 2 So the twelve called the whole group of the disciples together and said, "It is not right for us to neglect the word of God to wait on tables. 3 But carefully select from among you, brothers, seven men who are well-attested, full of the Spirit and of wisdom, whom we may put in charge of this necessary task. 4 But we will devote ourselves to prayer and to the ministry of the word." 5 The proposal pleased the entire group, so they chose Stephen, a man full of faith and of the Holy Spirit, with Philip, Prochorus, Nicanor, Timon, Parmenas, and Nicolas, a Gentile convert to Judaism from Antioch. 6 They stood these men before the apostles, who prayed and placed their hands on them. 7 The word of God continued to spread, the number of disciples in Jerusalem increased greatly, and a large group of priests became obedient to the faith.

STEPHEN IS ARRESTED

8 Now Stephen, full of grace and power, was performing great wonders and miraculous signs among the people. 9 But some men from the Synagogue of the Freedmen (as it was called), both Cyrenians and Alexandrians, as well as some from Cilicia and the province of Asia, stood up and argued with Stephen. 10 Yet they were not able to resist the wisdom and the Spirit with which he spoke. 11 Then they secretly instigated some men to say, "We have heard this man speaking blasphemous words against Moses and God." 12 They incited the people, the elders, and the experts in the law; then they approached Stephen, seized him, and brought him before the council. 13 They brought forward false witnesses who said, "This man does not stop saying things against this holy place and the law. 14 For we have heard him saying that Jesus the Nazarene will destroy this place and change the customs that Moses handed down to us." 15 All who were sitting in the council looked intently at Stephen and saw his face was like the face of an angel.

STEPHEN'S DEFENSE BEFORE THE COUNCIL

7 Then the high priest said, "Are these things true?" 2 So he replied, "Brothers and fathers, listen to me. The God of glory appeared to our forefather Abraham when he was in Mesopotamia, before he settled in Haran, 3 and said to him, '***Go out from your country and from your relatives, and come to the land I will show you.***' 4 Then he went out from the country of the Chaldeans and settled in Haran. After his father died, God made him move to this country where you now live. 5 He did not give any of it to him for an inheritance, not even a foot of ground, yet God promised *to give it to him as his possession, and to his descendants after him,* even though Abraham as yet had no child. 6 But God spoke as follows: 'Your ***descendants will be foreigners in a foreign country, whose citizens will enslave them and mistreat them for 400 years.*** 7 ***But I will punish the nation they serve as slaves,*** ' said God, '***and after these things they will come out of there*** and *worship me in this place.*' 8 Then God gave Abraham the covenant of circumcision, and so he became the father of Isaac and circumcised him when he was eight days

6:1–7 The apostles seemed to think that it was a very important business to look after a handful of poor widows and see that they had their fair share in the dispensing of the modest charity of the Jerusalem church, when they said that for such a purely secular thing as that a man would need to be "full of the Spirit and wisdom." "Wisdom" here, I suppose, means practical sagacity, common sense, the power of picking out an impostor. Very commonplace virtues—but the apostles evidently thought that such everyday operations were not too secular and commonplace to owe their origin to the communication to men of the fullness of the Holy Spirit. The only power for Christian service is the power that comes from being clothed with God's Spirit.

ALEXANDER MACLAREN
(1826–1910)
EXPOSITIONS OF THE HOLY SCRIPTURES

old, and Isaac became the father of Jacob, and Jacob of the 12 patriarchs. [9]The patriarchs, because they were jealous of Joseph, sold him into Egypt. But God was with him, [10]and rescued him from all his troubles, and granted him favor and wisdom in the presence of Pharaoh, king of Egypt, who made him ruler over Egypt and over all his household. [11]Then a famine occurred throughout Egypt and Canaan, causing great suffering, and our ancestors could not find food. [12]So when Jacob heard that there was grain in Egypt, he sent our ancestors there the first time. [13]On their second visit Joseph made himself known to his brothers again, and Joseph's family became known to Pharaoh. [14]So Joseph sent a message and invited his father Jacob and all his relatives to come, seventy-five people in all. [15]So Jacob went down to Egypt and died there, along with our ancestors, [16]and their bones were later moved to Shechem and placed in the tomb that Abraham had bought for a certain sum of money from the sons of Hamor in Shechem.

[17]"But as the time drew near for God to fulfill the promise he had declared to Abraham, the people increased greatly in number in Egypt, [18]until ***another king who did not know about Joseph ruled over Egypt.*** [19]This was the one who exploited our people and was cruel to our ancestors, forcing them to abandon their infants so they would die. [20]At that time Moses was born, and he was beautiful to God. For three months he was brought up in his father's house, [21]and when he had been abandoned, Pharaoh's daughter adopted him and brought him up as her own son. [22]So Moses was trained in all the wisdom of the Egyptians and was powerful in his words and deeds. [23]But when he was about forty years old, it entered his mind to visit his fellow countrymen the Israelites. [24]When he saw one of them being hurt unfairly, Moses came to his defense and avenged the person who was mistreated by striking down the Egyptian. [25]He thought his own people would understand that God was delivering them through him, but they did not understand. [26]The next day Moses saw two men fighting and tried to make peace between them, saying, 'Men, you are brothers; why are you hurting one another?' [27]But the man who was unfairly hurting his neighbor pushed Moses aside, saying, '***Who made you a ruler and judge over us?*** [28]***You don't want to kill me the way you killed the Egyptian yesterday, do you?***' [29]When the man said this, Moses fled and became a foreigner in the land of Midian, where he became the father of two sons.

[30]"After forty years had passed, *an angel appeared to him in the desert of Mount Sinai, in the flame of a burning bush.* [31]When Moses saw it, he was amazed at the sight, and when he approached to investigate, there came the voice of the Lord, [32]'***I am the God of your forefathers, the God of Abraham, Isaac, and Jacob.***' Moses began to tremble and did not dare to look more closely. [33]***But the Lord said to him, 'Take the sandals off your feet, for the place where you are standing is holy ground.*** [34]***I have certainly seen the suffering of my people who are in Egypt and have heard their groaning, and I have come down to rescue them. Now come, I will send you to Egypt.***' [35]This same Moses they had rejected, saying, '***Who made you a ruler and judge?***' God sent as both ruler and deliverer through the hand of the angel who appeared to him in the bush. [36]This man led them out, performing wonders and miraculous signs in the land of Egypt, at the Red Sea, and in the wilderness for forty years. [37]This is the Moses who said to the Israelites, '***God will raise up for you***

7:17–43 Notice how clearly Jesus of Nazareth has been represented in Moses. The people of Israel refused Moses, who was still unknown, saying, "Who made you a ruler and a judge over us?" In the same way, Jesus heard from our people, "By what authority are you doing these things?" (Mark 11:28). They did not yet know that God at that time, through pity for our race, sent the leader and prince of liberty and the author of eternal life. And indeed God exalted Moses, though despised by his own, and made him leader, ruler, and liberator of his people. What Moses was to one people, this truly Jesus of Nazareth is to all who are willing to follow his lead.

ERASMUS (1466–1536)
PARAPHRASE OF THE ACTS OF THE APOSTLES

a prophet like me from among your brothers.' 38This is the man
who was in the congregation in the wilderness with the angel
who spoke to him at Mount Sinai, and with our ancestors, and
he received living oracles to give to you. 39Our ancestors were
unwilling to obey him, but pushed him aside and turned back
to Egypt in their hearts, 40saying to Aaron, '***Make us gods who
will go in front of us, for this Moses, who led us out of the land of
Egypt—we do not know what has happened to him!'*** 41At that time
they made an idol in the form of a calf, brought a sacrifice to
the idol, and began rejoicing in the works of their hands. 42But
God turned away from them and gave them over to worship the
host of heaven, as it is written in the book of the prophets: '***It
was not to me that you offered slain animals and sacrifices forty
years in the wilderness, was it, house of Israel? 43But you took
along the tabernacle of Moloch and the star of the god Rephan,
the images you made to worship, but I will deport you beyond
Babylon.'*** 44Our ancestors had the tabernacle of testimony in
the wilderness, just as God who spoke to Moses ordered him to
make it according to the design he had seen. 45Our ancestors
received possession of it and brought it in with Joshua when
they dispossessed the nations that God drove out before our
ancestors, until the time of David. 46He found favor with God
and asked that he could find a dwelling place for the house
of Jacob. 47But Solomon built a house for him. 48Yet the Most
High does not live in houses made by human hands, as the
prophet says,

49 '***Heaven is my throne,***
and earth is the footstool for my feet.
What kind of house will you build for me, says the Lord,
or what is my resting place?
50 ***Did my hand not make all these things?'***

51"You stubborn people, with uncircumcised hearts and ears!
You are always resisting the Holy Spirit, like your ancestors did!
52Which of the prophets did your ancestors not persecute? They
killed those who foretold long ago the coming of the Righteous
One, whose betrayers and murderers you have now become!
53You received the law by decrees given by angels, but you did
not obey it."

STEPHEN IS KILLED

54When they heard these things, they became furious and
ground their teeth at him. 55But Stephen, full of the Holy Spirit,
looked intently toward heaven and saw the glory of God, and
Jesus standing at the right hand of God. 56"Look!" he said. "I see
the heavens opened, and the Son of Man standing at the right
hand of God!" 57But they covered their ears, shouting out with
a loud voice, and rushed at him with one intent. 58When they
had driven him out of the city, they began to stone him, and the
witnesses laid their cloaks at the feet of a young man named
Saul. 59They continued to stone Stephen while he prayed, "Lord
Jesus, receive my spirit!" 60Then he fell to his knees and cried
out with a loud voice, "Lord, do not hold this sin against them!"
8 When he had said this, he died. 1And Saul agreed completely
with killing him.

SAUL BEGINS TO PERSECUTE THE CHURCH

Now on that day a great persecution began against the church
in Jerusalem, and all except the apostles were forced to scatter

8:1–8 Jewish malice could do nothing against the apostles, nor for that matter could it do anything against the others except by the permission of the Lord Jesus. The Lord Jesus had permitted this so that under pressure of persecution they would flee from city to city. This was not so much a matter of terror on the part of the disciples as of divine dispensation, that as the seed was broadly spread, an abundant harvest of evangelical confession would quickly appear.

ERASMUS **(1466–1536)**
PARAPHRASE OF THE ACTS OF THE APOSTLES

throughout the regions of Judea and Samaria. 2Some devout
men buried Stephen and made loud lamentation over him.
3But Saul was trying to destroy the church; entering one house
after another, he dragged off both men and women and put
them in prison.

PHILIP PREACHES IN SAMARIA

4Now those who had been forced to scatter went around proclaiming the good news of the word. 5Philip went down to the
main city of Samaria and began proclaiming the Christ to them.
6The crowds were paying attention with one mind to what
Philip said, as they heard and saw the miraculous signs he was
performing. 7For unclean spirits, crying with loud shrieks, were
coming out of many who were possessed, and many paralyzed
and lame people were healed. 8So there was great joy in that city.
9Now in that city was a man named Simon, who had been
practicing magic and amazing the people of Samaria, claiming
to be someone great. 10All the people, from the least to the
greatest, paid close attention to him, saying, "This man is the
power of God that is called 'Great.'" 11And they paid close attention to him because he had amazed them for a long time with
his magic. 12But when they believed Philip as he was proclaiming the good news about the kingdom of God and the name of
Jesus Christ, they began to be baptized, both men and women.
13Even Simon himself believed, and after he was baptized, he
stayed close to Philip constantly, and when he saw the signs and
great miracles that were occurring, he was amazed.

14Now when the apostles in Jerusalem heard that Samaria
had accepted the word of God, they sent Peter and John to them.
15These two went down and prayed for them so that they would
receive the Holy Spirit. 16(For the Spirit had not yet come upon
any of them, but they had only been baptized in the name of
the Lord Jesus.) 17Then Peter and John placed their hands on
the Samaritans, and they received the Holy Spirit.

18Now Simon, when he saw that the Spirit was given through
the laying on of the apostles' hands, offered them money, 19say-
ing, "Give me this power too, so that everyone I place my hands
on may receive the Holy Spirit." 20But Peter said to him, "May
your silver perish with you because you thought you could acquire God's gift with money! 21You have no share or part in this
matter because your heart is not right before God! 22Therefore
repent of this wickedness of yours, and pray to the Lord that
he may perhaps forgive you for the intent of your heart. 23For
I see that you are bitterly envious and in bondage to sin." 24But
Simon replied, "You pray to the Lord for me so that nothing of
what you have said may happen to me."

25So after Peter and John had solemnly testified and spoken
the word of the Lord, they started back to Jerusalem, proclaiming the good news to many Samaritan villages as they went.

PHILIP AND THE ETHIOPIAN EUNUCH

26Then an angel of the Lord said to Philip, "Get up and go south
on the road that goes down from Jerusalem to Gaza." (This is
a desert road.) 27So he got up and went. There he met an Ethiopian eunuch, a court official of Candace, queen of the Ethiopians, who was in charge of all her treasury. He had come to
Jerusalem to worship, 28and was returning home, sitting in his
chariot, reading the prophet Isaiah. 29Then the Spirit said to
Philip, "Go over and join this chariot." 30So Philip ran up to it

and heard the man reading the prophet Isaiah. He asked him, "Do you understand what you're reading?" 31The man replied, "How in the world can I, unless someone guides me?" So he invited Philip to come up and sit with him. 32Now the passage of scripture the man was reading was this:

"He was led like a sheep to slaughter,
and like a lamb before its shearer is silent,
so he did not open his mouth.
33 *In humiliation justice was taken from him.*
Who can describe his posterity?
For his life was taken away from the earth."

34Then the eunuch said to Philip, "Please tell me, who is the prophet saying this about—himself or someone else?" 35So Philip started speaking, and beginning with this scripture proclaimed the good news about Jesus to him. 36Now as they were going along the road, they came to some water, and the eunuch said, "Look, there is water! What is to stop me from being baptized?"† 38So he ordered the chariot to stop, and both Philip and the eunuch went down into the water, and Philip baptized him. 39Now when they came up out of the water, the Spirit of the Lord snatched Philip away, and the eunuch did not see him any more, but went on his way rejoicing. 40Philip, however, found himself at Azotus, and as he passed through the area, he proclaimed the good news to all the towns until he came to Caesarea.

THE CONVERSION OF SAUL

9 Meanwhile Saul, still breathing out threats to murder the Lord's disciples, went to the high priest 2and requested letters from him to the synagogues in Damascus, so that if he found any who belonged to the Way, either men or women, he could bring them as prisoners to Jerusalem. 3As he was going along, approaching Damascus, suddenly a light from heaven flashed around him. 4He fell to the ground and heard a voice saying to him, "Saul, Saul, why are you persecuting me?" 5So he said, "Who are you, Lord?" He replied, "I am Jesus whom you are persecuting! 6But stand up and enter the city, and you will be told what you must do." 7(Now the men who were traveling with him stood there speechless because they heard the voice but saw no one.) 8So Saul got up from the ground, but although his eyes were open, he could see nothing. Leading him by the hand, his companions brought him into Damascus. 9For three days he could not see, and he neither ate nor drank anything.

10Now there was a disciple in Damascus named Ananias. The Lord said to him in a vision, "Ananias," and he replied, "Here I am, Lord." 11Then the Lord told him, "Get up and go to the street called 'Straight,' and at Judas' house look for a man from Tarsus named Saul. For he is praying, 12and he has seen in a vision a man named Ananias come in and place his hands on him so that he may see again." 13But Ananias replied, "Lord, I have heard from many people about this man, how much harm he has done to your saints in Jerusalem, 14and here he has authority from the chief priests to imprison all who call on your name!" 15But the Lord said to him, "Go, because this man is my chosen instrument to carry my name before Gentiles and kings and the people of Israel. 16For I will show him how much he must suffer for the sake of my name." 17So Ananias departed and entered the house, placed his hands on Saul and said, "Brother Saul, the

9:1–22 While Saul is breathing out slaughter, he is thrown to the ground by the voice of Christ from heaven the persecutor, he is raised up the preacher. Christ then by one word laid Saul low and raised up Paul; that is, he laid low the proud and raised up the humble. He the least made great, not by himself, but by him whom he once persecuted, was sent to the Gentiles, from a robber become a shepherd, from a wolf a sheep. He, the least apostle, was sent to the Gentiles and labored much among the Gentiles, and through him the Gentiles believed.

AUGUSTINE (354–430)
SERMONS

Lord Jesus, who appeared to you on the road as you came here, has sent me so that you may see again and be filled with the Holy Spirit." [18]Immediately something like scales fell from his eyes, and he could see again. He got up and was baptized, [19]and after taking some food, his strength returned.

For several days he was with the disciples in Damascus, [20]and immediately he began to proclaim Jesus in the synagogues, saying, "This man is the Son of God." [21]All who heard him were amazed and were saying, "Is this not the man who in Jerusalem was ravaging those who call on this name, and who had come here to bring them as prisoners to the chief priests?" [22]But Saul became more and more capable, and was causing consternation among the Jews who lived in Damascus by proving that Jesus is the Christ.

SAUL'S ESCAPE FROM DAMASCUS

[23]Now after some days had passed, the Jews plotted together to kill him, [24]but Saul learned of their plot against him. They were also watching the city gates day and night so that they could kill him. [25]But his disciples took him at night and let him down through an opening in the wall by lowering him in a basket.

SAUL RETURNS TO JERUSALEM

[26]When he arrived in Jerusalem, he attempted to associate with the disciples, and they were all afraid of him because they did not believe that he was a disciple. [27]But Barnabas took Saul, brought him to the apostles, and related to them how he had seen the Lord on the road, that the Lord had spoken to him, and how in Damascus he had spoken out boldly in the name of Jesus. [28]So he was staying with them, associating openly with them in Jerusalem, speaking out boldly in the name of the Lord. [29]He was speaking and debating with the Greek-speaking Jews, but they were trying to kill him. [30]When the brothers found out about this, they brought him down to Caesarea and sent him away to Tarsus.

[31]Then the church throughout Judea, Galilee, and Samaria experienced peace and thus was strengthened. Living in the fear of the Lord and in the encouragement of the Holy Spirit, the church increased in numbers.

PETER HEALS AENEAS

[32]Now as Peter was traveling around from place to place, he also came down to the saints who lived in Lydda. [33]He found there a man named Aeneas who had been confined to a mattress for eight years because he was paralyzed. [34]Peter said to him, "Aeneas, Jesus the Christ heals you. Get up and make your own bed!" And immediately he got up. [35]All those who lived in Lydda and Sharon saw him, and they turned to the Lord.

PETER RAISES DORCAS

[36]Now in Joppa there was a disciple named Tabitha (which in translation means Dorcas). She was continually doing good deeds and acts of charity. [37]At that time she became sick and died. When they had washed her body, they placed it in an upstairs room. [38]Because Lydda was near Joppa, when the disciples heard that Peter was there, they sent two men to him and urged him, "Come to us without delay." [39]So Peter got up and went with them, and when he arrived they brought him to the upper room. All the widows stood beside him, crying

and showing him the tunics and other clothing Dorcas used to make while she was with them. 40 But Peter sent them all outside, knelt down, and prayed. Turning to the body, he said, "Tabitha, get up." Then she opened her eyes, and when she saw Peter, she sat up. 41 He gave her his hand and helped her get up. Then he called the saints and widows and presented her alive. 42 This became known throughout all Joppa, and many believed in the Lord. 43 So Peter stayed many days in Joppa with a man named Simon, a tanner.

PETER VISITS CORNELIUS

10 Now there was a man in Caesarea named Cornelius, a centurion of what was known as the Italian Cohort. 2 He was a devout, God-fearing man, as was all his household; he did many acts of charity for the people and prayed to God regularly. 3 About three o'clock one afternoon he saw clearly in a vision an angel of God who came in and said to him, "Cornelius." 4 Staring at him and becoming greatly afraid, Cornelius replied, "What is it, Lord?" The angel said to him, "Your prayers and your acts of charity have gone up as a memorial before God. 5 Now send men to Joppa and summon a man named Simon, who is called Peter. 6 This man is staying as a guest with a man named Simon, a tanner, whose house is by the sea." 7 When the angel who had spoken to him departed, Cornelius called two of his personal servants and a devout soldier from among those who served him, 8 and when he had explained everything to them, he sent them to Joppa.

9 About noon the next day, while they were on their way and approaching the city, Peter went up on the roof to pray. 10 He became hungry and wanted to eat, but while they were preparing the meal, a trance came over him. 11 He saw heaven opened and an object something like a large sheet descending, being let down to earth by its four corners. 12 In it were all kinds of four-footed animals and reptiles of the earth and wild birds. 13 Then a voice said to him, "Get up, Peter; slaughter and eat!" 14 But Peter said, "Certainly not, Lord, for I have never eaten anything defiled and ritually unclean!" 15 The voice spoke to him again, a second time, "What God has made clean, you must not consider ritually unclean!" 16 This happened three times, and immediately the object was taken up into heaven.

17 Now while Peter was puzzling over what the vision he had seen could signify, the men sent by Cornelius had learned where Simon's house was and approached the gate. 18 They called out to ask if Simon, known as Peter, was staying there as a guest. 19 While Peter was still thinking seriously about the vision, the Spirit said to him, "Look! Three men are looking for you. 20 But get up, go down, and accompany them without hesitation because I have sent them." 21 So Peter went down to the men and said, "Here I am, the person you're looking for. Why have you come?" 22 They said, "Cornelius the centurion, a righteous and God-fearing man, well spoken of by the whole Jewish nation, was directed by a holy angel to summon you to his house and to hear a message from you." 23 So Peter invited them in and entertained them as guests.

On the next day he got up and set out with them, and some of the brothers from Joppa accompanied him. 24 The following day he entered Caesarea. Now Cornelius was waiting anxiously for them and had called together his relatives and close friends. 25 So when Peter came in, Cornelius met him, fell at his feet, and

10:1–23 Peter is taught that people are no longer divided as they used to be and that a Jew is no different from a Greek. From this Peter is warned not to shrink afterward from the Gentiles as unclean. Peter would never have dared to open the gate of heaven to the Gentiles unless God himself had removed the wall and thrown open a plain way and entrance for all. This vision is of no small value for us. For when it teaches that the separation between Jews and Gentiles was only temporary, it is just as if God proclaimed from heaven that he is gathering all the peoples of the world into his grace so that he may be God of all.

JOHN CALVIN (1509–1564)
COMPLETE COMMENTARY ON THE BIBLE

WILLIAM TYNDALE:

CHAMPION OF THE ENGLISH BIBLE

c. 1494–1536

In the twenty-first century we take for granted the number of English-language Bibles available to read for personal devotions and study. Yet there was a time when the average English-speaking person could not read the Bible in his or her own language. William Tyndale was an early champion in the effort to change that.

Born around 1494 in Gloucestershire, England, Tyndale studied at Oxford and Cambridge and served as chaplain to an English nobleman and tutor to his grandchildren. During this time Tyndale was inspired to translate the Bible anew into the language of his people. Inspired by Desiderius Erasmus's improved Greek New Testament, John Wycliffe's translation of the Vulgate into Middle English, and Martin Luther's new German translation, Tyndale wanted to put the Word of God into the vernacular of the English people. He proposed the ambitious project to the bishop of London, Cuthbert Tunstall, but he refused. Sometime in 1525 he traveled to Wittenberg, Germany, where he began the translation process using Luther's Bible as a model.

In March 1526, copies of Tyndale's New Testament and Pentateuch translation began reaching the English shores, alarming Bishop Tunstall. He was so alarmed that he thought it best to buy up all the copies so as to stem the flow, which had the inadvertent effect of providing the necessary funds for Tyndale's second edition. The controversy stemmed in part from how Tyndale translated some of the words and phrases. But most of the concern was over the threat to Roman Catholic ecclesial control and the ability of Christians to read the Bible in their own language. Tyndale's translation was banned from the church and from England, and he was forced to flee to Belgium for refuge from Henry VIII and Tunstall.

Tyndale wrote in the Prologue to his finished edition,

> *I have here translated (brethren and sisters most dear and tenderly beloved in Christ), the New Testament for your spiritual edifying, consolation and solace: exhorting instantly and beseeching those that are better seen in the tongues than I, and that have higher gifts of grace to interpret the sense of the scripture, and meaning of the Spirit, than I, to consider and ponder my labor, and that with the spirit of meekness.*

Here is how he rendered arguably the most famous verse in all the Bible, John 3:16: "*For God so loveth the worlde yt he hath geven his only sonne that none that beleve in him shuld perisshe: but shuld have everlastinge lyfe.*"

Through his translation, Tyndale has been credited with popularizing the English word *atonement* to describe the effectual death of Christ for our sins. And several phrases from his work have become commonplace: "let there be light," from the creation account; "my brother's keeper," from the Cain and Abel drama; and "it came to pass" from the nativity story of Jesus' birth. Not only was Tyndale's translation popular among the people of the English-speaking world, but it also went on to impact future translations, including the Great Bible of

1539, the Geneva Bible of 1560, and the King James Version of 1611.

On October 6, 1536, Tyndale was sentenced to death by strangulation after having been found guilty of heresy for his translating efforts. His dying words were a prayer: "Lord! Open the king of England's eyes." This prayer was powerfully answered when the so-called Great Bible, based almost entirely upon Tyndale's work, was authorized by King Henry VIII—just two years after he ordered Tyndale's martyrdom.

IMPORTANT WORKS

THE TYNDALE BIBLE

THE OBEDIENCE OF A CHRISTIAN MAN

THE PRACTYSE OF PRELATES

worshiped him. 26But Peter helped him up, saying, "Stand up.
I too am a mere mortal." 27Peter continued talking with him
as he went in, and he found many people gathered together.
28He said to them, "You know that it is unlawful for a Jew to
associate with or visit a Gentile, yet God has shown me that I
should call no person defiled or ritually unclean. 29Therefore
when you sent for me, I came without any objection. Now may I
ask why you sent for me?" 30Cornelius replied, "Four days ago at
this very hour, at three o'clock in the afternoon, I was praying in
my house, and suddenly a man in shining clothing stood before
me 31and said, 'Cornelius, your prayer has been heard and your
acts of charity have been remembered before God. 32Therefore
send to Joppa and summon Simon, who is called Peter. This
man is staying as a guest in the house of Simon the tanner, by
the sea.' 33Therefore I sent for you at once, and you were kind
enough to come. So now we are all here in the presence of God to
listen to everything the Lord has commanded you to say to us."
34Then Peter started speaking: "I now truly understand that
God does not show favoritism in dealing with people, 35but in
every nation the person who fears him and does what is right
is welcomed before him. 36You know the message he sent to the
people of Israel, proclaiming the good news of peace through
Jesus Christ (he is Lord of all)—37you know what happened
throughout Judea, beginning from Galilee after the baptism
that John announced: 38with respect to Jesus from Nazareth,
that God anointed him with the Holy Spirit and with power. He
went around doing good and healing all who were oppressed by
the devil because God was with him. 39We are witnesses of all
the things he did both in Judea and in Jerusalem. They killed
him by hanging him on a tree, 40but God raised him up on the
third day and caused him to be seen, 41not by all the people,
but by us, the witnesses God had already chosen, who ate and
drank with him after he rose from the dead. 42He commanded
us to preach to the people and to warn them that he is the one
appointed by God as judge of the living and the dead. 43About
him all the prophets testify, that everyone who believes in him
receives forgiveness of sins through his name."

THE GENTILES RECEIVE THE HOLY SPIRIT

[44]While Peter was still speaking these words, the Holy Spirit
fell on all those who heard the message. [45]The circumcised
believers who had accompanied Peter were greatly astonished
that the gift of the Holy Spirit had been poured out even on
the Gentiles, [46]for they heard them speaking in tongues and
praising God. Then Peter said, [47]"No one can withhold the water
for these people to be baptized, who have received the Holy
Spirit just as we did, can he?" [48]So he gave orders to have them
baptized in the name of Jesus Christ. Then they asked him to
stay for several days.

PETER DEFENDS HIS ACTIONS TO THE JERUSALEM CHURCH

11 Now the apostles and the brothers who were throughout
Judea heard that the Gentiles too had accepted the word
of God. [2]So when Peter went up to Jerusalem, the circumcised
believers took issue with him, [3]saying, "You went to uncircumcised men and shared a meal with them." [4]But Peter began and
explained it to them point by point, saying, [5]"I was in the city of
Joppa praying, and in a trance I saw a vision, an object something
like a large sheet descending, being let down from heaven by
its four corners, and it came to me. [6]As I stared I looked into it
and saw four-footed animals of the earth, wild animals, reptiles,
and wild birds. [7]I also heard a voice saying to me, 'Get up, Peter;
slaughter and eat!' [8]But I said, 'Certainly not, Lord, for nothing
defiled or ritually unclean has ever entered my mouth!' [9]But
the voice replied a second time from heaven, 'What God has
made clean, you must not consider ritually unclean!' [10]This
happened three times, and then everything was pulled up to
heaven again. [11]At that very moment, three men sent to me
from Caesarea approached the house where we were staying.
[12]The Spirit told me to accompany them without hesitation.
These six brothers also went with me, and we entered the man's
house. [13]He informed us how he had seen an angel standing in
his house and saying, 'Send to Joppa and summon Simon, who
is called Peter, [14]who will speak a message to you by which you
and your entire household will be saved.' [15]Then as I began to
speak, the Holy Spirit fell on them just as he did on us at the
beginning. [16]And I remembered the word of the Lord, as he
used to say, 'John baptized with water, but you will be baptized
with the Holy Spirit.' [17]Therefore if God gave them the same
gift as he also gave us after believing in the Lord Jesus Christ,
who was I to hinder God?" [18]When they heard this, they ceased
their objections and praised God, saying, "So then, God has
granted the repentance that leads to life even to the Gentiles."

> 11:1–18 "If God gave them the same gift as he also gave us after believing in the Lord Jesus Christ," he says, "who was I to hinder God?" To silence them more effectively, Peter added "the same gift." Do you see how he does not allow them to have less? "When they heard this, they ceased their objections and praised God, saying, 'So then, God has granted the repentance that leads to life even to the Gentiles.'" Do you see how it all came about through the oratory of Peter, who did well to report the events? They glorified God because he had given them repentance. They were humbled by these words. From this point on the door of faith was open to the Gentiles.
>
> CHRYSOSTOM (C. 347–407)
> *HOMILIES ON THE ACTS OF THE APOSTLES*

ACTIVITY IN THE CHURCH AT ANTIOCH

[19]Now those who had been scattered because of the persecution
that took place over Stephen went as far as Phoenicia, Cyprus,
and Antioch, speaking the message to no one but Jews. [20]But
there were some men from Cyprus and Cyrene among them
who came to Antioch and began to speak to the Greeks too,
proclaiming the good news of the Lord Jesus. [21]The hand of the
Lord was with them, and a great number who believed turned
to the Lord. [22]A report about them came to the attention of
the church in Jerusalem, and they sent Barnabas to Antioch.
[23]When he came and saw the grace of God, he rejoiced and
encouraged them all to remain true to the Lord with devoted

hearts, 24because he was a good man, full of the Holy Spirit
and of faith, and a significant number of people were brought
to the Lord. 25Then Barnabas departed for Tarsus to look for
Saul, 26and when he found him, he brought him to Antioch. So
for a whole year Barnabas and Saul met with the church and
taught a significant number of people. Now it was in Antioch
that the disciples were first called Christians.

FAMINE RELIEF FOR JUDEA

27At that time some prophets came down from Jerusalem to
Antioch. 28One of them, named Agabus, got up and predicted
by the Spirit that a severe famine was about to come over the
whole inhabited world. (This took place during the reign of
Claudius.) 29So the disciples, each in accordance with his financial ability, decided to send relief to the brothers living in
Judea. 30They did so, sending their financial aid to the elders
by Barnabas and Saul.

JAMES IS KILLED AND PETER IMPRISONED

12 About that time King Herod laid hands on some from the
church to harm them. 2He had James, the brother of John,
executed with a sword. 3When he saw that this pleased the Jews,
he proceeded to arrest Peter too. (This took place during the feast
of Unleavened Bread.) 4When he had seized him, he put him in
prison, handing him over to four squads of soldiers to guard
him. Herod planned to bring him out for public trial after the
Passover. 5So Peter was kept in prison, but those in the church
were earnestly praying to God for him. 6On that very night before
Herod was going to bring him out for trial, Peter was sleeping
between two soldiers, bound with two chains, while guards in
front of the door were keeping watch over the prison. 7Suddenly
an angel of the Lord appeared, and a light shone in the prison
cell. He struck Peter on the side and woke him up, saying, "Get
up quickly!" And the chains fell off Peter's wrists. 8The angel
said to him, "Fasten your belt and put on your sandals." Peter
did so. Then the angel said to him, "Put on your cloak and follow
me." 9Peter went out and followed him; he did not realize that
what was happening through the angel was real, but thought he
was seeing a vision. 10After they had passed the first and second
guards, they came to the iron gate leading into the city. It opened
for them by itself, and they went outside and walked down one
narrow street, when at once the angel left him. 11When Peter
came to himself, he said, "Now I know for certain that the Lord
has sent his angel and rescued me from the hand of Herod and
from everything the Jewish people were expecting to happen."
12When Peter realized this, he went to the house of Mary,
the mother of John Mark, where many people had gathered
together and were praying. 13When he knocked at the door of
the outer gate, a slave girl named Rhoda answered. 14When she
recognized Peter's voice, she was so overjoyed she did not open
the gate, but ran back in and told them that Peter was standing
at the gate. 15But they said to her, "You've lost your mind!" But
she kept insisting that it was Peter, and they kept saying, "It
is his angel!" 16Now Peter continued knocking, and when they
opened the door and saw him, they were greatly astonished.
17He motioned to them with his hand to be quiet and then
related how the Lord had brought him out of the prison. He
said, "Tell James and the brothers these things," and then he
left and went to another place.

12:5–21 A prisoner escaping might be glad to make a bolt for it, dressed or undressed. It would have been quite as easy for the angel to have whisked him out of the cell and put him down at Mary's door, but that was not to be the way. Peter was led past all the obstacles—"The first and second guards, [and] they came to the iron gate leading into the city," which was no doubt bolted and barred. There was a leisurely procession through the prison. Why? Because Omnipotence is never in a hurry, and God, not only in his judgments but in his mercies, very often works slowly, as becomes his majesty. We are impatient and hurry our work over; God works slowly for he works certainly.

ALEXANDER MACLAREN
(1826–1910)
EXPOSITIONS OF THE HOLY SCRIPTURES

18At daybreak there was great consternation among the soldiers over what had become of Peter. 19When Herod had searched for him and did not find him, he questioned the guards and commanded that they be led away to execution. Then Herod went down from Judea to Caesarea and stayed there.

20Now Herod was having an angry quarrel with the people of Tyre and Sidon. So they joined together and presented themselves before him. And after convincing Blastus, the king's personal assistant, to help them, they asked for peace because their country's food supply was provided by the king's country. 21On a day determined in advance, Herod put on his royal robes, sat down on the judgment seat, and made a speech to them. 22But the crowd began to shout, "The voice of a god, and not of a man!" 23Immediately an angel of the Lord struck Herod down because he did not give the glory to God, and he was eaten by worms and died. 24But the word of God kept on increasing and multiplying.

25So Barnabas and Saul returned to Jerusalem when they had completed their mission, bringing along with them John Mark.

THE CHURCH AT ANTIOCH COMMISSIONS BARNABAS AND SAUL

13 Now there were these prophets and teachers in the church at Antioch: Barnabas, Simeon called Niger, Lucius the Cyrenian, Manaen (a close friend of Herod the tetrarch from childhood) and Saul. 2While they were serving the Lord and fasting, the Holy Spirit said, "Set apart for me Barnabas and Saul for the work to which I have called them." 3Then, after they had fasted and prayed and placed their hands on them, they sent them off.

PAUL AND BARNABAS PREACH IN CYPRUS

4So Barnabas and Saul, sent out by the Holy Spirit, went down to Seleucia, and from there they sailed to Cyprus. 5When they arrived in Salamis, they began to proclaim the word of God in the Jewish synagogues. (Now they also had John as their assistant.) 6When they had crossed over the whole island as far as Paphos, they found a magician, a Jewish false prophet named Bar-Jesus, 7who was with the proconsul Sergius Paulus, an intelligent man. The proconsul summoned Barnabas and Saul and wanted to hear the word of God. 8But the magician Elymas (for that is the way his name is translated) opposed them, trying to turn the proconsul away from the faith. 9But Saul (also known as Paul), filled with the Holy Spirit, stared straight at him 10and said, "You who are full of all deceit and all wrongdoing, you son of the devil, you enemy of all righteousness—will you not stop making crooked the straight paths of the Lord? 11Now look, the hand of the Lord is against you, and you will be blind, unable to see the sun for a time!" Immediately mistiness and darkness came over him, and he went around seeking people to lead him by the hand. 12Then when the proconsul saw what had happened, he believed because he was greatly astounded at the teaching about the Lord.

PAUL AND BARNABAS AT PISIDIAN ANTIOCH

13Then Paul and his companions put out to sea from Paphos and came to Perga in Pamphylia, but John left them and returned to Jerusalem. 14Moving on from Perga, they arrived at Pisidian Antioch, and on the Sabbath day they went into the synagogue

13:13–33 The glory of this good news about Christ is infinitely greater and higher than all kingdoms, riches, and glory of the world, even heaven and earth. For what can all this do for me if I do not have this word of salvation and eternal life? For when it comes to sin or death or danger, I must indeed say, *Away with everything that is good and joyous to this world, so that I may have and hear just this good news of salvation sent from Christ!* This you must know and cling to, that only this word grants eternal peace and joy, and it must be believed even if it seems totally contrary to everything. Do not follow yourself or your feelings but cling tightly to the divine, eternal, ineffable truth that he has spoken and promulgated.

MARTIN LUTHER **(1483–1546)**
POSTIL ON EASTER TUESDAY

and sat down. 15After the reading from the law and the prophets, the leaders of the synagogue sent them a message, saying, "Brothers, if you have any message of exhortation for the people, speak it." 16So Paul stood up, gestured with his hand and said, "Men of Israel, and you Gentiles who fear God, listen: 17The God of this people Israel chose our ancestors and made the people great during their stay as foreigners in the country of Egypt, and with uplifted arm he led them out of it. 18For a period of about forty years he put up with them in the wilderness. 19After he had destroyed seven nations in the land of Canaan, he gave his people their land as an inheritance. 20All this took about 450 years. After this he gave them judges until the time of Samuel the prophet. 21Then they asked for a king, and God gave them Saul son of Kish, a man from the tribe of Benjamin, who ruled forty years. 22After removing him, God raised up David their king. He testified about him: '***I have found David*** the son of Jesse ***to be a man after my heart,*** who will accomplish everything I want him to do.' 23From the descendants of this man God brought to Israel a Savior, Jesus, just as he promised. 24Before Jesus arrived, John had proclaimed a baptism for repentance to all the people of Israel. 25But while John was completing his mission, he said repeatedly, 'What do you think I am? I am not he. But look, one is coming after me. I am not worthy to untie the sandals on his feet!' 26Brothers, descendants of Abraham's family, and those Gentiles among you who fear God, the message of this salvation has been sent to us. 27For the people who live in Jerusalem and their rulers did not recognize him, and they fulfilled the sayings of the prophets that are read every Sabbath by condemning him. 28Though they found no basis for a death sentence, they asked Pilate to have him executed. 29When they had accomplished everything that was written about him, they took him down from the cross and placed him in a tomb. 30But God raised him from the dead, 31and for many days he appeared to those who had accompanied him from Galilee to Jerusalem. These are now his witnesses to the people. 32And we proclaim to you the good news about the promise to our ancestors, 33that this promise God has fulfilled to us, their children, by raising Jesus, as also it is written in the second psalm, '***You are my Son; today I have fathered you.***' 34But regarding the fact that he has raised Jesus from the dead, never again to be in a state of decay, God has spoken in this way: '***I will give you the holy and trustworthy promises made to David.***' 35Therefore he also says in another psalm, '***You will not permit your Holy One to experience decay.***' 36For David, after he had served God's purpose in his own generation, died, was buried with his ancestors, and experienced decay, 37but the one whom God raised up did not experience decay. 38Therefore let it be known to you, brothers, that through this one forgiveness of sins is proclaimed to you, 39and by this one everyone who believes is justified from everything from which the law of Moses could not justify you. 40Watch out, then, that what is spoken about by the prophets does not happen to you:

41 ***'Look, you scoffers; be amazed and perish!***
For I am doing a work in your days,
a work you would never believe, even if someone tells you.'"

42As Paul and Barnabas were going out, the people were urging them to speak about these things on the next Sabbath. 43When the meeting of the synagogue had broken up, many of the Jews and God-fearing proselytes followed Paul and Barnabas, who were speaking with them and were persuading them to continue in the grace of God.

[44]On the next Sabbath almost the whole city assembled together to hear the word of the Lord. [45]But when the Jews saw the crowds, they were filled with jealousy, and they began to contradict what Paul was saying by reviling him. [46]Both Paul and Barnabas replied courageously, "It was necessary to speak the word of God to you first. Since you reject it and do not consider yourselves worthy of eternal life, we are turning to the Gentiles. [47]For this is what the Lord has commanded us: '*I have appointed you to be a light for the Gentiles, to bring salvation to the ends of the earth.*'" [48]When the Gentiles heard this, they began to rejoice and praise the word of the Lord, and all who had been appointed for eternal life believed. [49]So the word of the Lord was spreading through the entire region. [50]But the Jews incited the God-fearing women of high social standing and the prominent men of the city, stirred up persecution against Paul and Barnabas, and threw them out of their region. [51]So after they shook the dust off their feet in protest against them, they went to Iconium. [52]And the disciples were filled with joy and with the Holy Spirit.

PAUL AND BARNABAS AT ICONIUM

14 The same thing happened in Iconium when Paul and Barnabas went into the Jewish synagogue and spoke in such a way that a large group of both Jews and Greeks believed. [2]But the Jews who refused to believe stirred up the Gentiles and poisoned their minds against the brothers. [3]So they stayed there for a considerable time, speaking out courageously for the Lord, who testified to the message of his grace, granting miraculous signs and wonders to be performed through their hands. [4]But the population of the city was divided; some sided with the Jews, and some with the apostles. [5]When both the Gentiles and the Jews (together with their rulers) made an attempt to mistreat them and stone them, [6]Paul and Barnabas learned about it and fled to the Lycaonian cities of Lystra and Derbe and the surrounding region. [7]There they continued to proclaim the good news.

PAUL AND BARNABAS AT LYSTRA

[8]In Lystra sat a man who could not use his feet, lame from birth, who had never walked. [9]This man was listening to Paul as he was speaking. When Paul stared intently at him and saw he had faith to be healed, [10]he said with a loud voice, "Stand upright on your feet." And the man leaped up and began walking. [11]So when the crowds saw what Paul had done, they shouted in the Lycaonian language, "The gods have come down to us in human form!" [12]They began to call Barnabas Zeus and Paul Hermes, because he was the chief speaker. [13]The priest of the temple of Zeus, located just outside the city, brought bulls and garlands to the city gates; he and the crowds wanted to offer sacrifices to them. [14]But when the apostles Barnabas and Paul heard about it, they tore their clothes and rushed out into the crowd, shouting, [15]"Men, why are you doing these things? We too are men, with human natures just like you! We are proclaiming the good news to you, so that you should turn from these worthless things to the living God, who made the heaven, the earth, the sea, and everything that is in them. [16]In past generations he

14:8–18 God, being good and loving and caring for the souls made by him—since he is by nature invisible and incomprehensible, for which reason the race of humans was likely to miss the way to the knowledge of him—for this cause God by his own Word gave the universe the order it has in order that since he is by nature invisible, people might be enabled to know him at any rate by his works. For often the artist even when not seen is known by his works, so by the order of the universe one ought to perceive God its Maker and artificer, even though he be not seen with the bodily eyes.

ATHANASIUS **(C. 296–373)**
AGAINST THE HEATHEN

allowed all the nations to go their own ways, [17]yet he did not leave himself without a witness by doing good, by giving you rain from heaven and fruitful seasons, satisfying you with food and your hearts with joy." [18]Even by saying these things, they scarcely persuaded the crowds not to offer sacrifice to them.

[19]But Jews came from Antioch and Iconium, and after winning the crowds over, they stoned Paul and dragged him out of the city, presuming him to be dead. [20]But after the disciples had surrounded him, he got up and went back into the city. On the next day he left with Barnabas for Derbe.

PAUL AND BARNABAS RETURN TO ANTIOCH IN SYRIA

[21]After they had proclaimed the good news in that city and made many disciples, they returned to Lystra, to Iconium, and to Antioch. [22]They strengthened the souls of the disciples and encouraged them to continue in the faith, saying, "We must enter the kingdom of God through many persecutions." [23]When they had appointed elders for them in the various churches, with prayer and fasting they entrusted them to the protection of the Lord in whom they had believed. [24]Then they passed through Pisidia and came into Pamphylia, [25]and when they had spoken the word in Perga, they went down to Attalia. [26]From there they sailed back to Antioch, where they had been commended to the grace of God for the work they had now completed. [27]When they arrived and gathered the church together, they reported all the things God had done with them, and that he had opened a door of faith for the Gentiles. [28]So they spent considerable time with the disciples.

THE JERUSALEM COUNCIL

15 Now some men came down from Judea and began to teach the brothers, "Unless you are circumcised according to the custom of Moses, you cannot be saved." [2]When Paul and Barnabas had a major argument and debate with them, the church appointed Paul and Barnabas and some others from among them to go up to meet with the apostles and elders in Jerusalem about this point of disagreement. [3]So they were sent on their way by the church, and as they passed through both Phoenicia and Samaria, they were relating at length the conversion of the Gentiles and bringing great joy to all the brothers. [4]When they arrived in Jerusalem, they were received by the church and the apostles and the elders, and they reported all the things God had done with them. [5]But some from the religious party of the Pharisees who had believed stood up and said, "It is necessary to circumcise the Gentiles and to order them to observe the law of Moses."

[6]Both the apostles and the elders met together to deliberate about this matter. [7]After there had been much debate, Peter stood up and said to them, "Brothers, you know that some time ago God chose me to preach to the Gentiles so they would hear the message of the gospel and believe. [8]And God, who knows the heart, has testified to them by giving them the Holy Spirit just as he did to us, [9]and he made no distinction between them and us, cleansing their hearts by faith. [10]So now why are you putting God to the test by placing on the neck of the disciples a yoke that neither our ancestors nor we have been able to bear? [11]On the contrary, we believe that we are saved through the grace of the Lord Jesus, in the same way as they are."

15:6–21 The apostle Peter declared that the church was built by the Holy Spirit. For you read that he said: "God, who knows the heart, as testified to them by giving them the Holy Spirit just as he did to us, and he made no distinction between them and us, cleansing their hearts by faith." As Christ is the cornerstone who joined together both peoples into one, so too the Holy Spirit made no distinction between the hearts of each people but united them.

AMBROSE **(C. 339–C. 397)**
ON THE HOLY SPIRIT

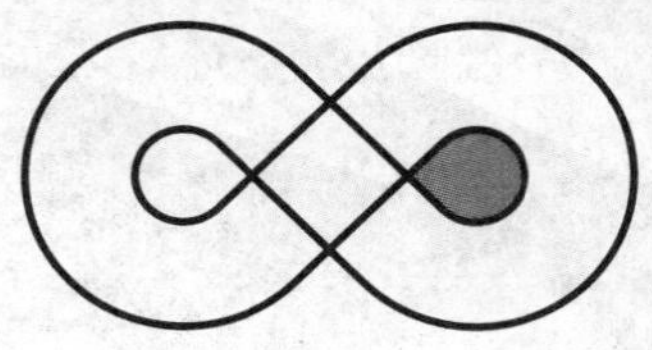

LONDON BAPTIST CONFESSION

(1677–1689)

THE LONDON CONFESSION is the classic summary of faith in the Baptist tradition. For many Baptists it has long been the standard of teaching and basis for association. Of particular interest is the section on Christian liberty and conscience, a belief that permeates Baptist polity and its involvement in the public square. In the defense of liberty, Baptists have experienced intense persecution in their attempts to advance religious freedom.

CHAPTER 21: OF CHRISTIAN LIBERTY AND LIBERTY OF CONSCIENCE

THE LIBERTY which Christ hath purchased for believers under the gospel consists in their freedom from the guilt of sin, the condemning wrath of God, the rigor and curse of the law, and in their being delivered from this present evil world, bondage to Satan, and dominion of sin, from the evil of afflictions, the fear and sting of death, the victory of the grave, and ever- lasting damnation: as also in their free access to God, and their yielding obedience unto him, not out of slavish fear, but a childlike love and willing mind. All which were common also to believers under the law for the substance of them; but under the New Testament the liberty of Christians is further enlarged, in their freedom from the yoke of a ceremonial law, to which the Jewish church was subjected, and in greater boldness of access to the throne of grace, and in fuller communications of the free Spirit of God, than believers under the law did ordinarily partake of.

GOD ALONE is Lord of the conscience and hath left it free from the doctrines and commandments of men which are in anything contrary to his Word, or not contained in it. So that to believe such doctrines, or obey such commands out of conscience, is to betray true liberty of conscience; and the requiring of an implicit faith, an absolute and blind obedience, is to destroy liberty of conscience and reason also.

THEY WHO upon pretense of Christian liberty do practice any sin or cherish any sinful lust, as they do thereby pervert the main design of the grace of the gospel to their own destruction, so they wholly destroy the end of Christian liberty, which is, that being delivered out of the hands of all our enemies, we might serve the Lord without fear, in holiness and righteousness before him, all the days of our lives.

12 The whole group kept quiet and listened to Barnabas and
Paul while they explained all the miraculous signs and wonders God had done among the Gentiles through them. 13 After
they stopped speaking, James replied, "Brothers, listen to me.
14 Simeon has explained how God first concerned himself to
select from among the Gentiles a people for his name. 15 The
words of the prophets agree with this, as it is written,

16 *'After this I will return,*
and I will rebuild the fallen tent of David;
I will rebuild its ruins and restore it,
17 *so that the rest of humanity may seek the Lord,*
namely, all the Gentiles I have called to be my own,' says
the Lord, who makes these things 18 known from long
ago.

19 "Therefore I conclude that we should not cause extra
difficulty for those among the Gentiles who are turning to
God, 20 but that we should write them a letter telling them
to abstain from things defiled by idols and from sexual immorality and from what has been strangled and from blood.
21 For Moses has had those who proclaim him in every town
from ancient times, because he is read aloud in the synagogues
every Sabbath."
22 Then the apostles and elders, with the whole church, decided to send men chosen from among them, Judas called Barsabbas and Silas, leaders among the brothers, to Antioch with
Paul and Barnabas. 23 They sent this letter with them:

From the apostles and elders, your brothers, to the
Gentile brothers and sisters in Antioch, Syria, and Cilicia,
greetings! 24 Since we have heard that some have gone
out from among us with no orders from us and have confused you, upsetting your minds by what they said, 25 we
have unanimously decided to choose men to send to you
along with our dear friends Barnabas and Paul, 26 who
have risked their lives for the name of our Lord Jesus
Christ. 27 Therefore we are sending Judas and Silas who
will tell you these things themselves in person. 28 For
it seemed best to the Holy Spirit and to us not to place
any greater burden on you than these necessary rules:
29 that you abstain from meat that has been sacrificed to
idols and from blood and from what has been strangled
and from sexual immorality. If you keep yourselves from
doing these things, you will do well. Farewell.

30 So when they were dismissed, they went down to Antioch, and after gathering the entire group together, they delivered the letter. 31 When they read it aloud, the people rejoiced at its encouragement. 32 Both Judas and Silas, who were prophets themselves, encouraged and strengthened the brothers with a long speech. 33 After they had spent some time there, they were sent off in peace by the brothers to those who had sent them.‡ 35 But Paul and Barnabas remained in Antioch, teaching and proclaiming (along with many others) the word of the Lord.

PAUL AND BARNABAS PART COMPANY

36 After some days Paul said to Barnabas, "Let's return and visit the brothers in every town where we proclaimed the word of the Lord to see how they are doing." 37 Barnabas wanted to bring John called Mark along with them too, 38 but Paul insisted that they should not take along this one who had left them in Pamphylia and had not accompanied them in the work. 39 They had a sharp disagreement, so that they parted company. Barnabas took along Mark and sailed away to Cyprus, 40 but Paul chose Silas and set out, commended to the grace of the Lord by the brothers and sisters. 41 He passed through Syria and Cilicia, strengthening the churches.

TIMOTHY JOINS PAUL AND SILAS

16 He also came to Derbe and to Lystra. A disciple named Timothy was there, the son of a Jewish woman who was a believer, but whose father was a Greek. 2 The brothers in Lystra and Iconium spoke well of him. 3 Paul wanted Timothy to accompany him, and he took him and circumcised him because of the Jews who were in those places, for they all knew that his father was Greek. 4 As they went through the towns, they passed on the decrees that had been decided on by the apostles and elders in Jerusalem for the Gentile believers to obey. 5 So the churches were being strengthened in the faith and were increasing in number every day.

PAUL'S VISION OF THE MACEDONIAN MAN

6 They went through the region of Phrygia and Galatia, having been prevented by the Holy Spirit from speaking the message in the province of Asia. 7 When they came to Mysia, they attempted to go into Bithynia, but the Spirit of Jesus did not allow them to do this, 8 so they passed through Mysia and went down to Troas. 9 A vision appeared to Paul during the night: A Macedonian man was standing there urging him, "Come over to Macedonia and help us!" 10 After Paul saw the vision, we attempted immediately to go over to Macedonia, concluding that God had called us to proclaim the good news to them.

ARRIVAL AT PHILIPPI

11 We put out to sea from Troas and sailed a straight course to Samothrace, the next day to Neapolis, 12 and from there to Philippi, which is a leading city of that district of Macedonia, a Roman colony. We stayed in this city for some days. 13 On the Sabbath day we went outside the city gate to the side of the river, where we thought there would be a place of prayer, and we sat down and began to speak to the women who had assembled there. 14 A woman named Lydia, a dealer in purple cloth from the city of Thyatira, a God-fearing woman, listened to us. The Lord opened her heart to respond to what Paul was saying.

15After she and her household were baptized, she urged us, "If
you consider me to be a believer in the Lord, come and stay in
my house." And she persuaded us.

PAUL AND SILAS ARE THROWN INTO PRISON

16Now as we were going to the place of prayer, a slave girl met
us who had a spirit that enabled her to foretell the future by
supernatural means. She brought her owners a great profit by
fortune-telling. 17She followed behind Paul and us and kept
crying out, "These men are servants of the Most High God, who
are proclaiming to you the way of salvation." 18She continued
to do this for many days. But Paul became greatly annoyed, and
turned and said to the spirit, "I command you in the name of
Jesus Christ to come out of her!" And it came out of her at once.
19But when her owners saw their hope of profit was gone, they
seized Paul and Silas and dragged them into the marketplace
before the authorities. 20When they had brought them before
the magistrates, they said, "These men are throwing our city
into confusion. They are Jews 21and are advocating customs that
are not lawful for us to accept or practice, since we are Romans."
22The crowd joined the attack against them, and the magistrates tore the clothes off Paul and Silas and ordered them
to be beaten with rods. 23After they had beaten them severely,
they threw them into prison and commanded the jailer to guard
them securely. 24Receiving such orders, he threw them in the
inner cell and fastened their feet in the stocks.

25About midnight Paul and Silas were praying and singing
hymns to God, and the rest of the prisoners were listening to
them. 26Suddenly a great earthquake occurred, so that the foundations of the prison were shaken. Immediately all the doors
flew open, and the bonds of all the prisoners came loose. 27When
the jailer woke up and saw the doors of the prison standing
open, he drew his sword and was about to kill himself because
he assumed the prisoners had escaped. 28But Paul called out
loudly, "Do not harm yourself, for we are all here!" 29Calling for
lights, the jailer rushed in and fell down trembling at the feet
of Paul and Silas. 30Then he brought them outside and asked,
"Sirs, what must I do to be saved?" 31They replied, "Believe in
the Lord Jesus and you will be saved, you and your household."
32Then they spoke the word of the Lord to him, along with all
those who were in his house. 33At that hour of the night he took
them and washed their wounds; then he and all his family were
baptized right away. 34The jailer brought them into his house
and set food before them, and he rejoiced greatly that he had
come to believe in God, together with his entire household.
35At daybreak the magistrates sent their police officers, saying,
"Release those men." 36The jailer reported these words to Paul,
saying, "The magistrates have sent orders to release you. So
come out now and go in peace." 37But Paul said to the police
officers, "They had us beaten in public without a proper trial—
even though we are Roman citizens—and they threw us in prison.
And now they want to send us away secretly? Absolutely not!
They themselves must come and escort us out!" 38The police
officers reported these words to the magistrates. They were
frightened when they heard Paul and Silas were Roman citizens
39and came and apologized to them. After they brought them
out, they asked them repeatedly to leave the city. 40When they
came out of the prison, they entered Lydia's house, and when
they saw the brothers, they encouraged them and then departed.

16:16–34 Observe that the jailer did not respond because he had been saved, but because he was astonished by their virtue. Here they only showed him the doors opened and it opened the doors of his heart, loosened the double chains, and kindled the light. For the light in his heart was bright. He washed their wounds; he himself was washed of his sins. He fed and was fed. "And he rejoiced greatly," it says. And yet it was nothing but words alone and good hope.

CHRYSOSTOM **(C. 347–407)**
HOMILIES ON THE ACTS OF THE APOSTLES

PAUL AND SILAS AT THESSALONICA

17 After they traveled through Amphipolis and Apollonia, they came to Thessalonica, where there was a Jewish synagogue. 2 Paul went to the Jews in the synagogue, as he customarily did, and on three Sabbath days he addressed them from the scriptures, 3 explaining and demonstrating that the Christ had to suffer and to rise from the dead, saying, "This Jesus I am proclaiming to you is the Christ." 4 Some of them were persuaded and joined Paul and Silas, along with a large group of God-fearing Greeks and quite a few prominent women. 5 But the Jews became jealous, and gathering together some worthless men from the rabble in the marketplace, they formed a mob and set the city in an uproar. They attacked Jason's house, trying to find Paul and Silas to bring them out to the assembly. 6 When they did not find them, they dragged Jason and some of the brothers before the city officials, screaming, "These people who have stirred up trouble throughout the world have come here too, 7 and Jason has welcomed them as guests! They are all acting against Caesar's decrees, saying there is another king named Jesus!" 8 They caused confusion among the crowd and the city officials who heard these things. 9 After the city officials had received bail from Jason and the others, they released them.

PAUL AND SILAS AT BEREA

10 The brothers sent Paul and Silas off to Berea at once, during the night. When they arrived, they went to the Jewish synagogue. 11 These Jews were more open-minded than those in Thessalonica, for they eagerly received the message, examining the scriptures carefully every day to see if these things were so. 12 Therefore many of them believed, along with quite a few prominent Greek women and men. 13 But when the Jews from Thessalonica heard that Paul had also proclaimed the word of God in Berea, they came there too, inciting and disturbing the crowds. 14 Then the brothers sent Paul away to the coast at once, but Silas and Timothy remained in Berea. 15 Those who accompanied Paul escorted him as far as Athens, and after receiving an order for Silas and Timothy to come to him as soon as possible, they left.

PAUL AT ATHENS

17:16–32 Paul fixes the wandering attention of blind philosophers [Epicureans and Stoics], proclaiming to them an unknown and yet not a new God. The way is open; God is ready to be found: "He now commands all people everywhere to repent." This universal demand of repentance declared universal guilt in the strongest manner and admirably confronted the pride of the haughtiest Stoic of them all. God raising Jesus demonstrated hereby that he was to be the glorious judge of all.

JOHN WESLEY (1703–1791)
EXPLANATORY NOTES ON THE BIBLE

16 While Paul was waiting for them in Athens, his spirit was greatly upset because he saw the city was full of idols. 17 So he was addressing the Jews and the God-fearing Gentiles in the synagogue, and in the marketplace every day those who happened to be there. 18 Also some of the Epicurean and Stoic philosophers were conversing with him, and some were asking, "What does this foolish babbler want to say?" Others said, "He seems to be a proclaimer of foreign gods." (They said this because he was proclaiming the good news about Jesus and the resurrection.) 19 So they took Paul and brought him to the Areopagus, saying, "May we know what this new teaching is that you are proclaiming? 20 For you are bringing some surprising things to our ears, so we want to know what they mean." 21 (All the Athenians and the foreigners who lived there used to spend their time in nothing else than telling or listening to something new.)

22 So Paul stood before the Areopagus and said, "Men of Athens, I see that you are very religious in all respects. 23 For as I went around and observed closely your objects of worship, I

even found an altar with this inscription: 'To an unknown god.'
Therefore what you worship without knowing it, this I proclaim
to you. [24]The God who made the world and everything in it,
who is Lord of heaven and earth, does not live in temples made
by human hands, [25]nor is he served by human hands, as if he
needed anything, because he himself gives life and breath and
everything to everyone. [26]From one man he made every nation
of the human race to inhabit the entire earth, determining
their set times and the fixed limits of the places where they
would live, [27]so that they would search for God and perhaps
grope around for him and find him, though he is not far from
each one of us. [28]For in him we live and move about and exist, as even some of your own poets have said, 'For we too are
his offspring.' [29]So since we are God's offspring, we should not
think the deity is like gold or silver or stone, an image made
by human skill and imagination. [30]Therefore, although God
has overlooked such times of ignorance, he now commands
all people everywhere to repent, [31]because he has set a day
on which he is going to judge the world in righteousness, by a
man whom he designated, having provided proof to everyone
by raising him from the dead."
[32]Now when they heard about the resurrection from the
dead, some began to scoff, but others said, "We will hear you
again about this." [33]So Paul left the Areopagus. [34]But some people joined him and believed. Among them were Dionysius, who
was a member of the Areopagus, a woman named Damaris, and
others with them.

PAUL AT CORINTH

18 After this Paul departed from Athens and went to Corinth.
[2]There he found a Jew named Aquila, a native of Pontus,
who had recently come from Italy with his wife Priscilla, because Claudius had ordered all the Jews to depart from Rome.
Paul approached them, [3]and because he worked at the same
trade, he stayed with them and worked with them (for they
were tentmakers by trade). [4]He addressed both Jews and Greeks
in the synagogue every Sabbath, attempting to persuade them.
[5]Now when Silas and Timothy arrived from Macedonia, Paul
became wholly absorbed with proclaiming the word, testifying
to the Jews that Jesus was the Christ. [6]When they opposed him
and reviled him, he protested by shaking out his clothes and
said to them, "Your blood be on your own heads! I am guiltless!
From now on I will go to the Gentiles!" [7]Then Paul left the synagogue and went to the house of a person named Titius Justus, a
Gentile who worshiped God, whose house was next door to the
synagogue. [8]Crispus, the president of the synagogue, believed
in the Lord together with his entire household, and many of
the Corinthians who heard about it believed and were baptized.
[9]The Lord said to Paul by a vision in the night, "Do not be afraid,
but speak and do not be silent [10]because I am with you, and no
one will assault you to harm you because I have many people in
this city." [11]So he stayed there a year and six months, teaching
the word of God among them.

PAUL BEFORE THE PROCONSUL GALLIO

[12]Now while Gallio was proconsul of Achaia, the Jews attacked
Paul together and brought him before the judgment seat, [13]say-
ing, "This man is persuading people to worship God in a way
contrary to the law!" [14]But just as Paul was about to speak, Gallio

18:1–17 Tens of thousands of redeemed ones are not regenerated yet, but regenerated they must be; and this is our comfort when we go forth to them with the quickening Word of God. Poor, ignorant souls, they know nothing about prayer for themselves, but Jesus prays for them. Their names are on his breastplate, and ere long they must bow their stubborn knee, breathing the penitential sigh before the throne of grace. The predestinated moment has not struck, but when it comes they shall obey, for God will have his own; they must, for the Spirit is not to be withstood when he comes forth with fullness of power—they must become the willing servants of the living God.

CHARLES SPURGEON
(1834–1892)
MORNING AND EVENING

said to the Jews, "If it were a matter of some crime or serious
piece of villainy, I would have been justified in accepting the
complaint of you Jews, [15]but since it concerns points of disagreement about words and names and your own law, settle it
yourselves. I will not be a judge of these things!" [16]Then he had
them forced away from the judgment seat. [17]So they all seized
Sosthenes, the president of the synagogue, and began to beat
him in front of the judgment seat. Yet none of these things
were of any concern to Gallio.

PAUL RETURNS TO ANTIOCH IN SYRIA

[18]Paul, after staying many more days in Corinth, said farewell to
the brothers and sailed away to Syria accompanied by Priscilla
and Aquila. He had his hair cut off at Cenchrea because he had
made a vow. [19]When they reached Ephesus, Paul left Priscilla
and Aquila behind there, but he himself went into the synagogue and addressed the Jews. [20]When they asked him to stay
longer, he would not consent, [21]but said farewell to them and
added, "I will come back to you again if God wills." Then he set
sail from Ephesus, [22]and when he arrived at Caesarea, he went
up and greeted the church at Jerusalem and then went down to
Antioch. [23]After he spent some time there, Paul left and went
through the region of Galatia and Phrygia, strengthening all
the disciples.

APOLLOS BEGINS HIS MINISTRY

[24]Now a Jew named Apollos, a native of Alexandria, arrived
in Ephesus. He was an eloquent speaker, well-versed in the
scriptures. [25]He had been instructed in the way of the Lord,
and with great enthusiasm he spoke and taught accurately the
facts about Jesus, although he knew only the baptism of John.
[26]He began to speak out fearlessly in the synagogue, but when
Priscilla and Aquila heard him, they took him aside and explained the way of God to him more accurately. [27]When Apollos
wanted to cross over to Achaia, the brothers encouraged him
and wrote to the disciples to welcome him. When he arrived,
he assisted greatly those who had believed by grace, [28]for he
refuted the Jews vigorously in public debate, demonstrating
from the scriptures that the Christ was Jesus.

DISCIPLES OF JOHN THE BAPTIST AT EPHESUS

19 While Apollos was in Corinth, Paul went through the in-
land regions and came to Ephesus. He found some disciples there [2]and said to them, "Did you receive the Holy Spirit
when you believed?" They replied, "No, we have not even heard
that there is a Holy Spirit." [3]So Paul said, "Into what then were
you baptized?" "Into John's baptism," they replied. [4]Paul said,
"John baptized with a baptism of repentance, telling the people to believe in the one who was to come after him, that is, in
Jesus." [5]When they heard this, they were baptized in the name
of the Lord Jesus, [6]and when Paul placed his hands on them,
the Holy Spirit came upon them, and they began to speak in
tongues and to prophesy. [7](Now there were about 12 men in all.)

PAUL CONTINUES TO MINISTER AT EPHESUS

[8]So Paul entered the synagogue and spoke out fearlessly for
three months, addressing and convincing them about the kingdom of God. [9]But when some were stubborn and refused to
believe, reviling the Way before the congregation, he left them

and took the disciples with him, addressing them every day in
the lecture hall of Tyrannus. 10 This went on for two years, so
that all who lived in the province of Asia, both Jews and Greeks,
heard the word of the Lord.

THE SEVEN SONS OF SCEVA

11 God was performing extraordinary miracles by Paul's hands,
12 so that when even handkerchiefs or aprons that had touched
his body were brought to the sick, their diseases left them
and the evil spirits went out of them. 13 But some itinerant
Jewish exorcists tried to invoke the name of the Lord Jesus
over those who were possessed by evil spirits, saying, "I sternly
warn you by Jesus whom Paul preaches." 14 (Now seven sons
of a man named Sceva, a Jewish high priest, were doing this.)
15 But the evil spirit replied to them, "I know about Jesus and
I am acquainted with Paul, but who are you?" 16 Then the man
who was possessed by the evil spirit jumped on them and
beat them all into submission. He prevailed against them so
that they fled from that house naked and wounded. 17 This
became known to all who lived in Ephesus, both Jews and
Greeks; fear came over them all, and the name of the Lord Jesus
was praised. 18 Many of those who had believed came forward,
confessing and making their deeds known. 19 Large numbers
of those who had practiced magic collected their books and
burned them up in the presence of everyone. When the value
of the books was added up, it was found to total 50,000 silver
coins. 20 In this way the word of the Lord continued to grow
in power and to prevail.

A RIOT IN EPHESUS

21 Now after all these things had taken place, Paul resolved to
go to Jerusalem, passing through Macedonia and Achaia. He
said, "After I have been there, I must also see Rome." 22 So after
sending two of his assistants, Timothy and Erastus, to Macedonia, he himself stayed on for a while in the province of Asia.
23 At that time a great disturbance took place concerning the
Way. 24 For a man named Demetrius, a silversmith who made
silver shrines of Artemis, brought a great deal of business to
the craftsmen. 25 He gathered these together, along with the
workmen in similar trades, and said, "Men, you know that our
prosperity comes from this business. 26 And you see and hear
that this Paul has persuaded and turned away a large crowd,
not only in Ephesus but in practically all of the province of
Asia, by saying that gods made by hands are not gods at all.
27 There is danger not only that this business of ours will come
into disrepute, but also that the temple of the great goddess
Artemis will be regarded as nothing, and she whom all the
province of Asia and the world worship will suffer the loss of
her greatness."

28 When they heard this they became enraged and began
to shout, "Great is Artemis of the Ephesians!" 29 The city was
filled with the uproar, and the crowd rushed to the theater
together, dragging with them Gaius and Aristarchus, the
Macedonians who were Paul's traveling companions. 30 But
when Paul wanted to enter the public assembly, the disciples
would not let him. 31 Even some of the provincial authorities
who were his friends sent a message to him, urging him not to
venture into the theater. 32 So then some were shouting one
thing, some another, for the assembly was in confusion, and

19:21–40 This crowd that was so unruly just moments before dispersed peacefully. Here we see the provident care of God by which he delivers his children. As this same God is accustomed to raise the waves of the sea with sudden blasts of wind and suddenly quiets them again, in the same way he tests his children with dreadful storms of danger, and when he sees fit he still restores them without any harm. Therefore, trusting his goodness and power, let us persevere with stout courage, assuring ourselves that through Christ Jesus our Lord and most faithful and invincible defender that we have the upper hand against the efforts of the wicked.

RUDOLF GWALTHER
(1519–1586)
HOMILIES

most of them did not know why they had met together. 33 Some
of the crowd concluded it was about Alexander because the
Jews had pushed him to the front. Alexander, gesturing with
his hand, was wanting to make a defense before the public
assembly. 34 But when they recognized that he was a Jew, they
all shouted in unison, "Great is Artemis of the Ephesians!" for
about two hours. 35 After the city secretary quieted the crowd,
he said, "Men of Ephesus, what person is there who does not
know that the city of the Ephesians is the keeper of the temple
of the great Artemis and of her image that fell from heaven?
36 So because these facts are indisputable, you must keep quiet
and not do anything reckless. 37 For you have brought these men
here who are neither temple robbers nor blasphemers of our
goddess. 38 If then Demetrius and the craftsmen who are with
him have a complaint against someone, the courts are open
and there are proconsuls; let them bring charges against one
another there. 39 But if you want anything in addition, it will
have to be settled in a legal assembly. 40 For we are in danger
of being charged with rioting today, since there is no cause we
can give to explain this disorderly gathering." 41 After he had
said this, he dismissed the assembly.

PAUL TRAVELS THROUGH MACEDONIA AND GREECE

20 After the disturbance had ended, Paul sent for the disciples, and after encouraging them and saying farewell,
he left to go to Macedonia. 2 After he had gone through those
regions and spoken many words of encouragement to the believers there, he came to Greece, 3 where he stayed for three
months. Because the Jews had made a plot against him as he was
intending to sail for Syria, he decided to return through Macedonia. 4 Paul was accompanied by Sopater son of Pyrrhus from
Berea, Aristarchus and Secundus from Thessalonica, Gaius from
Derbe, and Timothy, as well as Tychicus and Trophimus
from the province of Asia. 5 These had gone on ahead and were
waiting for us in Troas. 6 We sailed away from Philippi after the
days of Unleavened Bread, and within five days we came to the
others in Troas, where we stayed for seven days. 7 On the first
day of the week, when we met to break bread, Paul began to
speak to the people, and because he intended to leave the next
day, he extended his message until midnight. 8 (Now there were
many lamps in the upstairs room where we were meeting.) 9 A
young man named Eutychus, who was sitting in the window,
was sinking into a deep sleep while Paul continued to speak for
a long time. Fast asleep, he fell down from the third story and
was picked up dead. 10 But Paul went down, threw himself on
the young man, put his arms around him, and said, "Do not be
distressed, for he is still alive!" 11 Then Paul went back upstairs,
and after he had broken bread and eaten, he talked with them a
long time, until dawn. Then he left. 12 They took the boy home
alive and were greatly comforted.

THE VOYAGE TO MILETUS

13 We went on ahead to the ship and put out to sea for Assos,
intending to take Paul aboard there, for he had arranged it this
way. He himself was intending to go there by land. 14 When he
met us in Assos, we took him aboard and went to Mitylene.
15 We set sail from there, and on the following day we arrived
off Chios. The next day we approached Samos, and the day after

that we arrived at Miletus. 16For Paul had decided to sail past
Ephesus so as not to spend time in the province of Asia, for he
was hurrying to arrive in Jerusalem, if possible, by the day of
Pentecost. 17From Miletus he sent a message to Ephesus, telling
the elders of the church to come to him.
18When they arrived, he said to them, "You yourselves know
how I lived the whole time I was with you, from the first day I set
foot in the province of Asia, 19serving the Lord with all humility
and with tears, and with the trials that happened to me because
of the plots of the Jews. 20You know that I did not hold back from
proclaiming to you anything that would be helpful, and from
teaching you publicly and from house to house, 21testifying to
both Jews and Greeks about repentance toward God and faith in
our Lord Jesus. 22And now, compelled by the Spirit, I am going
to Jerusalem without knowing what will happen to me there,
23except that the Holy Spirit warns me in town after town that
imprisonment and persecutions are waiting for me. 24But I do
not consider my life worth anything to myself, so that I may
finish my task and the ministry that I received from the Lord
Jesus, to testify to the good news of God's grace.
25"And now I know that none of you among whom I went
around proclaiming the kingdom will see me again. 26There-
fore I declare to you today that I am innocent of the blood of
you all. 27For I did not hold back from announcing to you the
whole purpose of God. 28Watch out for yourselves and for all
the flock of which the Holy Spirit has made you overseers, to
shepherd the church of God that he obtained with the blood
of his own Son. 29I know that after I am gone fierce wolves will
come in among you, not sparing the flock. 30Even from among
your own group men will arise, teaching perversions of the
truth to draw the disciples away after them. 31Therefore be
alert, remembering that night and day for three years I did not
stop warning each one of you with tears. 32And now I entrust
you to God and to the message of his grace. This message is
able to build you up and give you an inheritance among all
those who are sanctified. 33I have desired no one's silver or gold
or clothing. 34You yourselves know that these hands of mine
provided for my needs and the needs of those who were with
me. 35By all these things, I have shown you that by working in
this way we must help the weak, and remember the words of
the Lord Jesus that he himself said, 'It is more blessed to give
than to receive.'"
36When he had said these things, he knelt down with them
all and prayed. 37They all began to weep loudly, and hugged Paul
and kissed him, 38especially saddened by what he had said, that
they were not going to see him again. Then they accompanied
him to the ship.

PAUL'S JOURNEY TO JERUSALEM

21 After we tore ourselves away from them, we put out to
sea, and sailing a straight course, we came to Cos, on the
next day to Rhodes, and from there to Patara. 2We found a ship
crossing over to Phoenicia, went aboard, and put out to sea.
3After we sighted Cyprus and left it behind on our port side,
we sailed on to Syria and put in at Tyre because the ship was to
unload its cargo there. 4After we located the disciples, we stayed
there seven days. They repeatedly told Paul through the Spirit
not to set foot in Jerusalem. 5When our time was over, we left
and went on our way. All of them, with their wives and children,

20:25–38 See that the work of saving grace be thoroughly wrought in your own soul. Take heed to yourself, lest you be void of that saving grace of God that you offer to others and lest, while you proclaim to the world the necessity of a Savior, your own heart should neglect him and his saving benefits. Take heed therefore to yourself first that you be what you persuade others to be and heartily entertain that Savior whom you offer to them. Oh, what aggravated misery is this, to perish in the midst of plenty—to famish with the bread of life in our hands while we offer it to others.

RICHARD BAXTER **(1615–1691)**
THE REFORMED PASTOR

21:1–25 The motion of the clouds is not spontaneous, but they move as they are moved by the winds; neither can gospel ministers choose their own stations and govern their own motions but must go when and where the Spirit and providence of God directs and guides them. This journey was full of danger; Paul foresaw his business was not only to plant the gospel at Jerusalem with his doctrine but to water it also with his blood; but so effectually was his will determined by the will of God that he cheerfully complied with his duty therein, whatsoever difficulties and dangers did attend it.

JOHN FLAVEL **(1627–1691)**
THE WORKS

accompanied us outside of the city. After kneeling down on the beach and praying, [6]we said farewell to one another. Then we went aboard the ship, and they returned to their own homes. [7]We continued the voyage from Tyre and arrived at Ptolemais, and when we had greeted the brothers, we stayed with them for one day. [8]On the next day we left and came to Caesarea, and entered the house of Philip the evangelist, who was one of the seven, and stayed with him. [9](He had four unmarried daughters who prophesied.)

[10]While we remained there for a number of days, a prophet named Agabus came down from Judea. [11]He came to us, took Paul's belt, tied his own hands and feet with it, and said, "The Holy Spirit says this: 'This is the way the Jews in Jerusalem will tie up the man whose belt this is and will hand him over to the Gentiles.'" [12]When we heard this, both we and the local people begged him not to go up to Jerusalem. [13]Then Paul replied, "What are you doing, weeping and breaking my heart? For I am ready not only to be tied up, but even to die in Jerusalem for the name of the Lord Jesus." [14]Because he could not be persuaded, we said no more except, "The Lord's will be done."

[15]After these days we got ready and started up to Jerusalem. [16]Some of the disciples from Caesarea came along with us too, and brought us to the house of Mnason of Cyprus, a disciple from the earliest times, with whom we were to stay. [17]When we arrived in Jerusalem, the brothers welcomed us gladly. [18]The next day Paul went in with us to see James, and all the elders were there. [19]When Paul had greeted them, he began to explain in detail what God had done among the Gentiles through his ministry. [20]When they heard this, they praised God. Then they said to him, "You see, brother, how many thousands of Jews there are who have believed, and they are all ardent observers of the law. [21]They have been informed about you—that you teach all the Jews now living among the Gentiles to abandon Moses, telling them not to circumcise their children or live according to our customs. [22]What then should we do? They will no doubt hear that you have come. [23]So do what we tell you: We have four men who have taken a vow; [24]take them and purify yourself along with them and pay their expenses, so that they may have their heads shaved. Then everyone will know there is nothing in what they have been told about you, but that you yourself live in conformity with the law. [25]But regarding the Gentiles who have believed, we have written a letter, having decided that they should avoid meat that has been sacrificed to idols and blood and what has been strangled and sexual immorality." [26]Then Paul took the men the next day, and after he had purified himself along with them, he went to the temple and gave notice of the completion of the days of purification, when the sacrifice would be offered for each of them. [27]When the seven days were almost over, the Jews from the province of Asia who had seen him in the temple area stirred up the whole crowd and seized him, [28]shouting, "Men of Israel, help! This is the man who teaches everyone everywhere against our people, our law, and this sanctuary! Furthermore he has brought Greeks into the inner courts of the temple and made this holy place ritually unclean!" [29](For they had seen Trophimus the Ephesian in the city with him previously, and they assumed Paul had brought him into the inner temple courts.) [30]The whole city was stirred up, and the people rushed together. They seized Paul and dragged him out

of the temple courts, and immediately the doors were shut.
31While they were trying to kill him, a report was sent up to
the commanding officer of the cohort that all Jerusalem was
in confusion. 32He immediately took soldiers and centurions
and ran down to the crowd. When they saw the commanding
officer and the soldiers, they stopped beating Paul. 33Then the
commanding officer came up and arrested him and ordered
him to be tied up with two chains; he then asked who he was
and what he had done. 34But some in the crowd shouted one
thing, and others something else, and when the commanding
officer was unable to find out the truth because of the disturbance, he ordered Paul to be brought into the barracks. 35When
he came to the steps, Paul had to be carried by the soldiers
because of the violence of the mob, 36for a crowd of people followed them, screaming, "Away with him!" 37As Paul was about
to be brought into the barracks, he said to the commanding
officer, "May I say something to you?" The officer replied, "Do
you know Greek? 38Then you're not that Egyptian who started
a rebellion and led the 4,000 men of the 'Assassins' into the
wilderness sometime ago?" 39Paul answered, "I am a Jew from
Tarsus in Cilicia, a citizen of an important city. Please allow me
to speak to the people." 40When the commanding officer had
given him permission, Paul stood on the steps and gestured
to the people with his hand. When they had become silent, he
addressed them in Aramaic,

PAUL'S DEFENSE

22 "Brothers and fathers, listen to my defense that I now
make to you." 2(When they heard that he was addressing
them in Aramaic, they became even quieter.) Then Paul said,
3"I am a Jew, born in Tarsus in Cilicia, but brought up in this
city, educated with strictness under Gamaliel according to
the law of our ancestors, and was zealous for God just as all
of you are today. 4I persecuted this Way even to the point of
death, tying up both men and women and putting them in
prison, 5as both the high priest and the whole council of elders
can testify about me. From them I also received letters to the
brothers in Damascus, and I was on my way to make arrests
there and bring the prisoners to Jerusalem to be punished. 6As
I was en route and near Damascus, about noon a very bright
light from heaven suddenly flashed around me. 7Then I fell
to the ground and heard a voice saying to me, 'Saul, Saul, why
are you persecuting me?' 8I answered, 'Who are you, Lord?'
He said to me, 'I am Jesus the Nazarene, whom you are persecuting.' 9Those who were with me saw the light, but did not
understand the voice of the one who was speaking to me. 10So
I asked, 'What should I do, Lord?' The Lord said to me, 'Get up
and go to Damascus; there you will be told about everything
that you have been designated to do.' 11Since I could not see
because of the brilliance of that light, I came to Damascus
led by the hand of those who were with me. 12A man named
Ananias, a devout man according to the law, well spoken of by
all the Jews who live there, 13came to me and stood beside me
and said to me, 'Brother Saul, regain your sight!' And at that
very moment I looked up and saw him. 14Then he said, 'The
God of our ancestors has already chosen you to know his will,
to see the Righteous One, and to hear a command from his
mouth, 15because you will be his witness to all people of what
you have seen and heard. 16And now what are you waiting for?

22:1–21 We have heard that there is a resurrection and ten thousand good things; therefore we ought to bear witness to this before all. If we say that there is a resurrection and ten thousand good things but then look down upon others and prefer the things here, who will believe us? For all people pay attention not to what we say but to what we do. This is what witnesses are for: They persuade not those who know but those who do not. Let us become trustworthy witnesses. How will we become trustworthy? By the life we lead.

CHRYSOSTOM **(C. 347–407)**
HOMILIES ON THE ACTS OF THE APOSTLES

Get up, be baptized, and have your sins washed away, calling
on his name.' [17]When I returned to Jerusalem and was praying
in the temple, I fell into a trance [18]and saw the Lord saying
to me, 'Hurry and get out of Jerusalem quickly because they
will not accept your testimony about me.' [19]I replied, 'Lord,
they themselves know that I imprisoned and beat those in
the various synagogues who believed in you. [20]And when the
blood of your witness Stephen was shed, I myself was standing
nearby, approving, and guarding the cloaks of those who were
killing him.' [21]Then he said to me, 'Go, because I will send you
far away to the Gentiles.'"

THE ROMAN COMMANDER QUESTIONS PAUL

[22]The crowd was listening to him until he said this. Then they
raised their voices and shouted, "Away with this man from the
earth! For he should not be allowed to live!" [23]While they were
screaming and throwing off their cloaks and tossing dust in
the air, [24]the commanding officer ordered Paul to be brought
back into the barracks. He told them to interrogate Paul by
beating him with a lash so that he could find out the reason
the crowd was shouting at Paul in this way. [25]When they had
stretched him out for the lash, Paul said to the centurion
standing nearby, "Is it legal for you to lash a man who is a
Roman citizen without a proper trial?" [26]When the centurion
heard this, he went to the commanding officer and reported
it, saying, "What are you about to do? For this man is a Roman
citizen." [27]So the commanding officer came and asked Paul,
"Tell me, are you a Roman citizen?" He replied, "Yes." [28]The
commanding officer answered, "I acquired this citizenship
with a large sum of money." "But I was even born a citizen,"
Paul replied. [29]Then those who were about to interrogate
him stayed away from him, and the commanding officer was
frightened when he realized that Paul was a Roman citizen
and that he had had him tied up.

PAUL BEFORE THE SANHEDRIN

[30]The next day, because the commanding officer wanted to
know the true reason Paul was being accused by the Jews, he
released him and ordered the chief priests and the whole council to assemble. He then brought Paul down and had him stand
before them.

23 Paul looked directly at the council and said, "Brothers,
I have lived my life with a clear conscience before God
to this day." [2]At that the high priest Ananias ordered those
standing near Paul to strike him on the mouth. [3]Then Paul said
to him, "God is going to strike you, you whitewashed wall! Do
you sit there judging me according to the law, and in violation
of the law you order me to be struck?" [4]Those standing near
him said, "Do you dare insult God's high priest?" [5]Paul replied,
"I did not realize, brothers, that he was the high priest, for it is
written, '***You must not speak evil about a ruler of your people.***'"
[6]Then when Paul noticed that part of them were Sadducees
and the others Pharisees, he shouted out in the council, "Brothers, I am a Pharisee, a son of Pharisees. I am on trial concerning
the hope of the resurrection of the dead!" [7]When he said this, an
argument began between the Pharisees and the Sadducees, and
the assembly was divided. [8](For the Sadducees say there is no
resurrection, or angel, or spirit, but the Pharisees acknowledge
them all.) [9]There was a great commotion, and some experts in

23:1–35 When the apostle Paul was smitten on the face before the high priest he said, "God is going to strike you, you whitewashed wall!" With deep insight beholding that the priesthood of the Jews was already become foul with muddy lusts, this priesthood he saw in spirit to be ready to pass away through vengeance of the Lord when he spoke those words. Yet he had his heart ready not only to receive other blows on the cheek but also to suffer for the truth any torments whatever with love of them from whom he should suffer the same.

AUGUSTINE (354–430)
ON LYING

the law from the party of the Pharisees stood up and protested
strongly, "We find nothing wrong with this man. What if a spirit
or an angel has spoken to him?" [10]When the argument became
so great the commanding officer feared that they would tear
Paul to pieces, he ordered the detachment to go down, take
him away from them by force, and bring him into the barracks.
[11]The following night the Lord stood near Paul and said,
"Have courage, for just as you have testified about me in Jerusalem, so you must also testify in Rome."

THE PLOT TO KILL PAUL

[12]When morning came, the Jews formed a conspiracy and bound
themselves with an oath not to eat or drink anything until they
had killed Paul. [13]There were more than forty of them who
formed this conspiracy. [14]They went to the chief priests and
the elders and said, "We have bound ourselves with a solemn
oath not to partake of anything until we have killed Paul. [15]So
now you and the council request the commanding officer to
bring him down to you, as if you were going to determine his
case by conducting a more thorough inquiry. We are ready to
kill him before he comes near this place."
[16]But when the son of Paul's sister heard about the ambush, he came and entered the barracks and told Paul. [17]Paul
called one of the centurions and said, "Take this young man
to the commanding officer, for he has something to report
to him." [18]So the centurion took him and brought him to the
commanding officer and said, "The prisoner Paul called me
and asked me to bring this young man to you because he has
something to tell you." [19]The commanding officer took him by
the hand, withdrew privately, and asked, "What is it that you
want to report to me?" [20]He replied, "The Jews have agreed
to ask you to bring Paul down to the council tomorrow, as if
they were going to inquire more thoroughly about him. [21]So
do not let them persuade you to do this because more than
forty of them are lying in ambush for him. They have bound
themselves with an oath not to eat or drink anything until
they have killed him, and now they are ready, waiting for you
to agree to their request." [22]Then the commanding officer sent
the young man away, directing him, "Tell no one that you have
reported these things to me." [23]Then he summoned two of
the centurions and said, "Make ready 200 soldiers to go to
Caesarea along with 70 horsemen and 200 spearmen by nine
o'clock tonight, [24]and provide mounts for Paul to ride so that
he may be brought safely to Felix the governor." [25]He wrote a
letter that went like this:

> [26]Claudius Lysias to His Excellency Governor Felix,
> greetings. [27]This man was seized by the Jews and
> they were about to kill him, when I came up with the
> detachment and rescued him because I had learned
> that he was a Roman citizen. [28]Since I wanted to know
> what charge they were accusing him of, I brought him
> down to their council. [29]I found he was accused with
> reference to controversial questions about their law,
> but no charge against him deserved death or impris-
> onment. [30]When I was informed there would be a
> plot against this man, I sent him to you at once, also
> ordering his accusers to state their charges against
> him before you.

31 So the soldiers, in accordance with their orders, took Paul and brought him to Antipatris during the night. 32 The next day they let the horsemen go on with him, and they returned to the barracks. 33 When the horsemen came to Caesarea and delivered the letter to the governor, they also presented Paul to him. 34 When the governor had read the letter, he asked what province he was from. When he learned that he was from Cilicia, 35 he said, "I will give you a hearing when your accusers arrive too." Then he ordered that Paul be kept under guard in Herod's palace.

THE ACCUSATIONS AGAINST PAUL

24 After five days the high priest Ananias came down with some elders and an attorney named Tertullus, and they brought formal charges against Paul to the governor. 2 When Paul had been summoned, Tertullus began to accuse him, saying, "We have experienced a lengthy time of peace through your rule, and reforms are being made in this nation through your foresight. 3 Most excellent Felix, we acknowledge this everywhere and in every way with all gratitude. 4 But so that I may not delay you any further, I beg you to hear us briefly with your customary graciousness. 5 For we have found this man to be a troublemaker, one who stirs up riots among all the Jews throughout the world, and a ringleader of the sect of the Nazarenes. 6 He even tried to desecrate the temple, so we arrested him.§ 8 When you examine him yourself, you will be able to learn from him about all these things we are accusing him of doing." 9 The Jews also joined in the verbal attack, claiming that these things were true.

PAUL'S DEFENSE BEFORE FELIX

10 When the governor gestured for him to speak, Paul replied, "Because I know that you have been a judge over this nation for many years, I confidently make my defense. 11 As you can verify for yourself, not more than 12 days ago I went up to Jerusalem to worship. 12 They did not find me arguing with anyone or stirring up a crowd in the temple courts or in the synagogues or throughout the city, 13 nor can they prove to you the things they are accusing me of doing. 14 But I confess this to you, that I worship the God of our ancestors according to the Way (which they call a sect), believing everything that is according to the law and that is written in the prophets. 15 I have a hope in God (a hope that these men themselves accept too) that there is going to be a resurrection of both the righteous and the unrighteous. 16 This is the reason I do my best to always have a clear conscience toward God and toward people. 17 After several years I came to bring to my people gifts for the poor and to present offerings, 18 which I was doing when they found me in the temple, ritually purified, without a crowd or a disturbance. 19 But there are some Jews from the province of Asia who should be here before you and bring charges, if they have anything against me. 20 Or these men here should tell what crime they found me guilty of when I stood before the council, 21 other than this one thing I shouted out while I stood before them: 'I am on trial before you today concerning the resurrection of the dead.'"

22 Then Felix, who understood the facts concerning the Way more accurately, adjourned their hearing, saying, "When Lysias the commanding officer comes down, I will decide your

case." 23He ordered the centurion to guard Paul, but to let him have some freedom, and not to prevent any of his friends from meeting his needs.

PAUL SPEAKS REPEATEDLY TO FELIX

24Some days later, when Felix arrived with his wife Drusilla, who was Jewish, he sent for Paul and heard him speak about faith in Christ Jesus. 25While Paul was discussing righteousness, self-control, and the coming judgment, Felix became frightened and said, "Go away for now, and when I have an opportunity, I will send for you." 26At the same time he was also hoping that Paul would give him money, and for this reason he sent for Paul as often as possible and talked with him. 27After two years had passed, Porcius Festus succeeded Felix, and because he wanted to do the Jews a favor, Felix left Paul in prison.

PAUL APPEALS TO CAESAR

25 Now three days after Festus arrived in the province, he went up to Jerusalem from Caesarea. 2So the chief priests and the most prominent men of the Jews brought formal charges against Paul to him. 3Requesting him to do them a favor against Paul, they urged Festus to summon him to Jerusalem, planning an ambush to kill him along the way. 4Then Festus replied that Paul was being kept at Caesarea, and he himself intended to go there shortly. 5"So," he said, "let your leaders go down there with me, and if this man has done anything wrong, they may bring charges against him."

6After Festus had stayed not more than eight or ten days among them, he went down to Caesarea, and the next day he sat on the judgment seat and ordered Paul to be brought. 7When he arrived, the Jews who had come down from Jerusalem stood around him, bringing many serious charges that they were not able to prove. 8Paul said in his defense, "I have committed no offense against the Jewish law or against the temple or against Caesar." 9But Festus, wanting to do the Jews a favor, asked Paul, "Are you willing to go up to Jerusalem and be tried before me there on these charges?" 10Paul replied, "I am standing before Caesar's judgment seat, where I should be tried. I have done nothing wrong to the Jews, as you also know very well. 11If then I am in the wrong and have done anything that deserves death, I am not trying to escape dying, but if not one of their charges against me is true, no one can hand me over to them. I appeal to Caesar!" 12Then, after conferring with his council, Festus replied, "You have appealed to Caesar; to Caesar you will go!"

FESTUS ASKS KING AGRIPPA FOR ADVICE

13After several days had passed, King Agrippa and Bernice arrived at Caesarea to pay their respects to Festus. 14While they were staying there many days, Festus explained Paul's case to the king to get his opinion, saying, "There is a man left here as a prisoner by Felix. 15When I was in Jerusalem, the chief priests and the elders of the Jews informed me about him, asking for a sentence of condemnation against him. 16I answered them that it was not the custom of the Romans to hand over anyone before the accused had met his accusers face-to-face and had been given an opportunity to make a defense against the accusation. 17So after they came back here with me, I did not postpone the case, but the next day I sat on the judgment seat

24:22–27 Paul disclosed to Felix what he had before concealed—the way of salvation. This way does not consist in the observances of the law, as the Jews thought, but in trust in Jesus Christ, whom the Jews had crucified. Through baptism all the sins of our former life are once for all abolished so that those who have been reborn into him may henceforth live pure and holy lives according to the rule of the gospel, doing so until the same Jesus who gave himself for the salvation of the human race returns in exultation with the glory of the Father, judge of the living and the dead.

ERASMUS **(1466–1536)**
PARAPHRASE OF THE ACTS OF THE APOSTLES

25:13–27 This is a singular example of God's goodness by which he offers the salvation that is purchased by Christ to such wicked stock. For their great-grandfather was Herod the Great who laid in wait for Christ, being newborn, and commanded the cruelest murder of the infants of Bethlehem. Their father, Agrippa, killed James and cast the apostle Peter into prison, meaning to have him put to death as well. Agrippa and Bernice, born of such progenitors as these, hear Paul preach the gospel of salvation. Let these things serve to instruct us so that we condemn no one rashly because of his ancestors, seeing that in the genealogy of Christ are numbered many defamed people, so that no one should doubt that Christ belongs chiefly to sinners.

RUDOLF GWALTHER
(1519–1586)
HOMILIES

and ordered the man to be brought. [18]When his accusers stood
up, they did not charge him with any of the evil deeds I had
suspected. [19]Rather they had several points of disagreement
with him about their own religion and about a man named
Jesus who was dead, whom Paul claimed to be alive. [20]Because
I was at a loss how I could investigate these matters, I asked if
he were willing to go to Jerusalem and be tried there on these
charges. [21]But when Paul appealed to be kept in custody for the
decision of His Majesty the Emperor, I ordered him to be kept
under guard until I could send him to Caesar." [22]Agrippa said to
Festus, "I would also like to hear the man myself." "Tomorrow,"
he replied, "you will hear him."

PAUL BEFORE KING AGRIPPA AND BERNICE

[23]So the next day Agrippa and Bernice came with great pomp
and entered the audience hall, along with the senior military
officers and the prominent men of the city. When Festus gave
the order, Paul was brought in. [24]Then Festus said, "King Agrippa, and all you who are present here with us, you see this man
about whom the entire Jewish populace petitioned me both
in Jerusalem and here, shouting loudly that he ought not to
live any longer. [25]But I found that he had done nothing that
deserved death, and when he appealed to His Majesty the
Emperor, I decided to send him. [26]But I have nothing definite
to write to my lord about him. Therefore I have brought him
before you all, and especially before you, King Agrippa, so that
after this preliminary hearing I may have something to write.
[27]For it seems unreasonable to me to send a prisoner without
clearly indicating the charges against him."

PAUL OFFERS HIS DEFENSE

26 So Agrippa said to Paul, "You have permission to speak
for yourself." Then Paul held out his hand and began his
defense:

[2]"Regarding all the things I have been accused of by the Jews,
King Agrippa, I consider myself fortunate that I am about to
make my defense before you today, [3]because you are especially
familiar with all the customs and controversial issues of the
Jews. Therefore I ask you to listen to me patiently. [4]Now all
the Jews know the way I lived from my youth, spending my life
from the beginning among my own people and in Jerusalem.
[5]They know because they have known me from time past, if
they are willing to testify, that according to the strictest party
of our religion, I lived as a Pharisee. [6]And now I stand here
on trial because of my hope in the promise made by God to
our ancestors, [7]a promise that our 12 tribes hope to attain
as they earnestly serve God night and day. Concerning this
hope the Jews are accusing me, Your Majesty! [8]Why do you
people think it is unbelievable that God raises the dead? [9]Of
course, I myself was convinced that it was necessary to do
many things hostile to the name of Jesus the Nazarene. [10]And
that is what I did in Jerusalem: Not only did I lock up many
of the saints in prisons by the authority I received from the
chief priests, but I also cast my vote against them when they
were sentenced to death. [11]I punished them often in all the
synagogues and tried to force them to blaspheme. Because I
was so furiously enraged at them, I went to persecute them
even in foreign cities.

26:1–23 Paul is a witness worthy of belief because after doing countless things—fighting and killing the faithful—he was so suddenly changed. Paul shows he had been rightly persuaded and not deceived by the light, by the prophets, by the facts, by the events that were unfolding at that very moment. In order that he may not appear to be an innovator, even though he could speak of such great things, he takes refuge once more in the prophets, and he puts them forth for public scrutiny. This is more trustworthy, as it happens in the present; but since he alone had seen, again he is confirmed by the prophets.

CHRYSOSTOM **(C. 347-407)**
CATENA ON THE ACTS OF THE APOSTLES

12“While doing this very thing, as I was going to Damascus
with authority and complete power from the chief priests,
13about noon along the road, Your Majesty, I saw a light from
heaven, brighter than the sun, shining everywhere around
me and those traveling with me. 14When we had all fallen to
the ground, I heard a voice saying to me in Aramaic, ‘Saul,
Saul, why are you persecuting me? You are hurting yourself
by kicking against the goads.’ 15So I said, ‘Who are you, Lord?’
And the Lord replied, ‘I am Jesus whom you are persecuting.
16But get up and stand on your feet, for I have appeared to
you for this reason, to designate you in advance as a servant
and witness to the things you have seen and to the things
in which I will appear to you. 17I will rescue you from your
own people and from the Gentiles, to whom I am sending
you 18to open their eyes so that they turn from darkness to
light and from the power of Satan to God, so that they may
receive forgiveness of sins and a share among those who are
sanctified by faith in me.’

19“Therefore, King Agrippa, I was not disobedient to the
heavenly vision, 20but I declared to those in Damascus first,
and then to those in Jerusalem and in all Judea, and to the
Gentiles, that they should repent and turn to God, performing
deeds consistent with repentance. 21For this reason the Jews,
after they seized me while I was in the temple courts, were
trying to kill me. 22I have experienced help from God to this
day, and so I stand testifying to both small and great, saying
nothing except what the prophets and Moses said was going
to happen: 23that the Christ was to suffer and be the first to
rise from the dead, to proclaim light both to our people and
to the Gentiles.”

24As Paul was saying these things in his defense, Festus
exclaimed loudly, “You have lost your mind, Paul! Your great
learning is driving you insane!” 25But Paul replied, “I have not
lost my mind, most excellent Festus, but am speaking true and
rational words. 26For the king knows about these things, and
I am speaking freely to him because I cannot believe that any
of these things has escaped his notice, for this was not done in
a corner. 27Do you believe the prophets, King Agrippa? I know
that you believe.” 28Agrippa said to Paul, “In such a short time
are you persuading me to become a Christian?” 29Paul replied, “I
pray to God that whether in a short or a long time not only you
but also all those who are listening to me today could become
such as I am, except for these chains.”

30So the king got up, and with him the governor and Bernice
and those sitting with them, 31and as they were leaving they
said to one another, “This man is not doing anything deserving
death or imprisonment.” 32Agrippa said to Festus, “This man
could have been released if he had not appealed to Caesar.”

PAUL AND COMPANY SAIL FOR ROME

27 When it was decided we would sail to Italy, they handed
over Paul and some other prisoners to a centurion of the
Augustan Cohort named Julius. 2We went on board a ship from
Adramyttium that was about to sail to various ports along the
coast of the province of Asia and put out to sea, accompanied
by Aristarchus, a Macedonian from Thessalonica. 3The next
day we put in at Sidon, and Julius, treating Paul kindly, allowed
him to go to his friends so they could provide him with what
he needed. 4From there we put out to sea and sailed under the

lee of Cyprus because the winds were against us. [5]After we had sailed across the open sea off Cilicia and Pamphylia, we put in at Myra in Lycia. [6]There the centurion found a ship from Alexandria sailing for Italy, and he put us aboard it. [7]We sailed slowly for many days and arrived with difficulty off Cnidus. Because the wind prevented us from going any farther, we sailed under the lee of Crete off Salmone. [8]With difficulty we sailed along the coast of Crete and came to a place called Fair Havens that was near the town of Lasea.

CAUGHT IN A VIOLENT STORM

[9]Since considerable time had passed and the voyage was now dangerous because the fast was already over, Paul advised them, [10]"Men, I can see the voyage is going to end in disaster and great loss not only of the cargo and the ship, but also of our lives." [11]But the centurion was more convinced by the captain and the ship's owner than by what Paul said. [12]Because the harbor was not suitable to spend the winter in, the majority decided to put out to sea from there. They hoped that somehow they could reach Phoenix, a harbor of Crete facing southwest and northwest, and spend the winter there. [13]When a gentle south wind sprang up, they thought they could carry out their purpose, so they weighed anchor and sailed close along the coast of Crete. [14]Not long after this, a hurricane-force wind called the northeaster blew down from the island. [15]When the ship was caught in it and could not head into the wind, we gave way to it and were driven along. [16]As we ran under the lee of a small island called Cauda, we were able with difficulty to get the ship's boat under control. [17]After the crew had hoisted it aboard, they used supports to undergird the ship. Fearing they would run aground on the Syrtis, they lowered the sea anchor, thus letting themselves be driven along. [18]The next day, because we were violently battered by the storm, they began throwing the cargo overboard, [19]and on the third day they threw the ship's gear overboard with their own hands. [20]When neither sun nor stars appeared for many days and a violent storm continued to batter us, we finally abandoned all hope of being saved.

[21]Since many of them had no desire to eat, Paul stood up among them and said, "Men, you should have listened to me and not put out to sea from Crete, thus avoiding this damage and loss. [22]And now I advise you to keep up your courage, for there will be no loss of life among you, but only the ship will be lost. [23]For last night an angel of the God to whom I belong and whom I serve came to me [24]and said, 'Do not be afraid, Paul! You must stand before Caesar, and God has graciously granted you the safety of all who are sailing with you.' [25]Therefore keep up your courage, men, for I have faith in God that it will be just as I have been told. [26]But we must run aground on some island."

[27]When the fourteenth night had come, while we were being driven across the Adriatic Sea, about midnight the sailors suspected they were approaching some land. [28]They took soundings and found the water was twenty fathoms deep; when they had sailed a little farther they took soundings again and found it was fifteen fathoms deep. [29]Because they were afraid that we would run aground on the rocky coast, they threw out four anchors from the stern and wished for day to appear. [30]Then when the sailors tried to escape from the ship and were lowering the

27:13–38 Duty is ours, events are God's; we do not trust God but tempt him when we say we put ourselves under his protection if we do not use proper means for our safety. Happy those who have such a one as Paul in their company, who not only had intercourse with heaven but was also of an enlivening spirit to those about him. The sorrow of the world works death, while joy in God is life and peace in the greatest distresses and dangers. And the salvation he reveals must be waited for in use of the means he appoints.

MATTHEW HENRY (1662–1714)
COMMENTARY ON THE WHOLE BIBLE

ship's boat into the sea, pretending that they were going to put
out anchors from the bow, [31] Paul said to the centurion and the
soldiers, "Unless these men stay with the ship, you cannot be
saved." [32]Then the soldiers cut the ropes of the ship's boat and
let it drift away.

[33]As day was about to dawn, Paul urged them all to take some
food, saying, "Today is the fourteenth day you have been in
suspense and have gone without food; you have eaten nothing.
[34]Therefore I urge you to take some food, for this is important
for your survival. For not one of you will lose a hair from his
head." [35]After he said this, Paul took bread and gave thanks to
God in front of them all, broke it, and began to eat. [36]So all of
them were encouraged and took food themselves. [37](We were
in all 276 persons on the ship.) [38]When they had eaten enough
to be satisfied, they lightened the ship by throwing the wheat
into the sea.

PAUL IS SHIPWRECKED

[39]When day came, they did not recognize the land, but they
noticed a bay with a beach, where they decided to run the
ship aground if they could. [40]So they slipped the anchors and
left them in the sea, at the same time loosening the linkage
that bound the steering oars together. Then they hoisted the
foresail to the wind and steered toward the beach. [41] But they
encountered a patch of crosscurrents and ran the ship aground;
the bow stuck fast and could not be moved, but the stern was
being broken up by the force of the waves. [42]Now the soldiers'
plan was to kill the prisoners so that none of them would escape by swimming away. [43]But the centurion, wanting to save
Paul's life, prevented them from carrying out their plan. He
ordered those who could swim to jump overboard first and
get to land, [44]and the rest were to follow, some on planks and
some on pieces of the ship. And in this way all were brought
safely to land.

PAUL ON MALTA

28 After we had safely reached shore, we learned that the
island was called Malta. [2]The local inhabitants showed
us extraordinary kindness, for they built a fire and welcomed
us all because it had started to rain and was cold. [3]When Paul
had gathered a bundle of brushwood and was putting it on the
fire, a viper came out because of the heat and fastened itself
on his hand. [4]When the local people saw the creature hanging
from Paul's hand, they said to one another, "No doubt this man
is a murderer! Although he has escaped from the sea, Justice
herself has not allowed him to live!" [5]However, Paul shook the
creature off into the fire and suffered no harm. [6]But they were
expecting that he was going to swell up or suddenly drop dead.
So after they had waited a long time and had seen nothing
unusual happen to him, they changed their minds and said
he was a god.

[7]Now in the region around that place were fields belonging to the chief official of the island, named Publius, who
welcomed us and entertained us hospitably as guests for
three days. [8]The father of Publius lay sick in bed, suffering
from fever and dysentery. Paul went in to see him and after
praying, placed his hands on him and healed him. [9]After this
had happened, many of the people on the island who were
sick also came and were healed. [10]They also bestowed many

honors, and when we were preparing to sail, they gave us all
the supplies we needed.

PAUL FINALLY REACHES ROME

[11]After three months we put out to sea in an Alexandrian ship
that had wintered at the island and had the "Heavenly Twins" as
its figurehead. [12]We put in at Syracuse and stayed there three
days. [13]From there we cast off and arrived at Rhegium, and
after one day a south wind sprang up and on the second day
we came to Puteoli. [14]There we found some brothers and were
invited to stay with them seven days. And in this way we came
to Rome. [15]The brothers from there, when they heard about us,
came as far as the Forum of Appius and Three Taverns to meet
us. When he saw them, Paul thanked God and took courage.
[16]When we entered Rome, Paul was allowed to live by himself,
with the soldier who was guarding him.

28:11–16 Paul's living situation was a great favor, no doubt, but do not forget that he had to have his right hand chained to the left hand of the soldier day and night and that was not very pleasant either for him or for the soldier. Yet he thus had an opportunity of personal intercourse with the soldiers of the Pretorian guard, and as they were continually being changed, Paul no doubt had opportunities of conversation with hundreds of them, and thus the gospel was spread in a very unlikely quarter. That is a wonderful way of preaching: When they were chained hand to hand, there was no getting away from what Paul had to say.

CHARLES SPURGEON
(1834–1892)
METROPOLITAN TABERNACLE SERMONS

PAUL ADDRESSES THE JEWISH COMMUNITY IN ROME

[17]After three days Paul called the local Jewish leaders together. When they had assembled, he said to them, "Brothers, although I had done nothing against our people or the
customs of our ancestors, from Jerusalem I was handed over
as a prisoner to the Romans. [18]When they had heard my case,
they wanted to release me because there was no basis for a
death sentence against me. [19]But when the Jews objected, I
was forced to appeal to Caesar—not that I had some charge
to bring against my own people. [20]So for this reason I have
asked to see you and speak with you, for I am bound with this
chain because of the hope of Israel." [21]They replied, "We have
received no letters from Judea about you, nor have any of the
brothers come from there and reported or said anything bad
about you. [22]But we would like to hear from you what you
think, for regarding this sect we know that people everywhere
speak against it."

[23]They set a day to meet with him, and they came to him
where he was staying in even greater numbers. From morning
until evening he explained things to them, testifying about
the kingdom of God and trying to convince them about Jesus
from both the law of Moses and the prophets. [24]Some were
convinced by what he said, but others refused to believe. [25]So
they began to leave, unable to agree among themselves, after
Paul made one last statement: "The Holy Spirit spoke rightly to your ancestors through the prophet Isaiah [26]when he
said,

'Go to this people and say,
"You will keep on hearing, but will never understand,
and you will keep on looking, but will never
perceive.
[27] ***For the heart of this people has become dull,***
and their ears are hard of hearing,
and they have closed their eyes,
so that they would not see with their eyes
and hear with their ears
and understand with their heart
and turn, and I would heal them."'

[28]"Therefore be advised that this salvation from God has
been sent to the Gentiles; they will listen!"||

[30]Paul lived there two whole years in his own rented quarters
and welcomed all who came to him, [31]proclaiming the kingdom
of God and teaching about the Lord Jesus Christ with complete
boldness and without restriction.

AUTHOR	AUDIENCE	DATE	PURPOSE	THEMES
Paul	The church in Rome, predominantly Gentile but including a minority of Jews	About AD 57	Paul wrote his epistle to Christians living in Rome to explore and explain the fullness of the gospel, God's plan to make a way of salvation for all people, Jews and Gentiles alike.	The gospel; God's wrath and love; justification by faith; the Christian life; and Jews and Gentiles

On no other portion of the New Testament have people commented more than the epistle to the Romans—and rightly so. It contains a detailed summary of our Christian faith, the essence of the gospel. As John Calvin wrote in his introduction to his commentary on Romans: "When anyone gains a knowledge of this Epistle, he has an entrance opened to him to all the most hidden treasures of scripture." Those treasures are the gospel.

Paul was eager to visit the Christians in Rome for this very reason: "I am eager also to preach the gospel to you" (1:15). He wrote his letter to explain and explore the fullness of God's plan to make a way of salvation for all people, Jew and Gentile alike. He clearly articulated this message of Christ's good news in a way that has resonated from the early church to the Reformation and down to the present day—stabilizing and shaping the communion of saints for generations.

Paul was passionately unashamed about the gospel, "for it is God's power for salvation to everyone who believes, to the Jew first and also to the Greek. For the righteousness of God is revealed in the gospel from faith to faith, just as it is written, 'The righteous by faith will live'" (1:16–17). And this is why the gospel is central to Paul's teaching ministry and to this letter. The gospel is good news because it has the power to rescue all people from evil, sin, and death, reconciling them to God and transforming their hearts with God's own righteousness.

Almost from the start Paul roots the good news in God's wrath, for you cannot fully understand the depths of God's love until you understand God's wrath. Without discrimination "the wrath of God is revealed from heaven against all ungodliness and unrighteousness of people" (1:18). Apart from Christ, everyone—Jew and Gentile alike—is in rebellion and deserving of God's wrath. Paul wrote, "All have sinned and fall short of the glory of God" (3:23). And while he also wrote "The payoff of sin is death," he went on to say, "but the gift of God is eternal life in Christ Jesus our Lord" (6:23). In chapter 5, we find the perfect comingling of God's wrath and love: "God demonstrates his own love for us, in that while we were still sinners, Christ died for us" (5:8). Despite God's wrath toward sin, we can be made right with God, justified, and saved.

At the heart of the Reformation was the desire to recapture the truth at the heart of Paul's letter: "We consider that a person is declared righteous by faith apart from the works of the law" (3:28). From Augustine to Martin Luther to Billy Graham, Christians have understood that we are all guilty before God for our sins. But how do we become

ROMANS

right with God and rightly oriented toward others? Paul is clear: "Because we have now been declared righteous by his blood, we will be saved through him from God's wrath" (5:9). The law was originally given for our benefit, to reveal our sins and bring life. But because we were mired in sin, it brought death. So here is what God did: "For God achieved what the law could not do because it was weakened through the flesh. By sending his own Son in the likeness of sinful flesh and concerning sin, he condemned sin in the flesh, so that the righteous requirement of the law may be fulfilled in us, who do not walk according to the flesh but according to the Spirit" (8:3–4). Because Christ fulfilled the law on our behalf, not only are we *declared* righteous, we are also *made* righteous.

Our salvation from sin isn't Paul's only concern. He wrote to the Roman Christians to explain their freedom from sin in order to experience life by the Spirit. He makes this contrast explicit: "(For if you live according to the flesh, you will die), but if by the Spirit you put to death the deeds of the body you will live" (8:13). This life is possible because "the Spirit of the one who raised Jesus from the dead . . . will also make your mortal bodies alive through his Spirit who lives in you" (8:11). This same Spirit brought about our adoption as children of God so that we share in Christ's glory and are helped in our weakness. When we live by the Spirit we will "present [our] bodies as a sacrifice—alive, holy, and pleasing to God—which is [our] reasonable service," and no longer be conformed to the world but "be transformed by the renewing of [our] mind[s]" (12:1–2); hate what is evil, cling to the good; show brotherly love and honor; "live decently as in the daytime, not in carousing and drunkenness, not in sexual immorality or sensuality, not in discord and jealousy" (13:13); and exhibit a number of other behaviors that reflect the righteousness of God.

Finally, Paul is interested to show that the promises of God contained in the gospel are "to the Jew first and also to the Greek" (1:16); justification by grace through faith is for everyone. Since all people are under God's wrath apart from Christ, all are in need of salvation in Christ. Paul shows how, though the Jewish people were first gifted God's promise of salvation, Gentiles have been "grafted in" (11:23). As Abraham was justified by faith, all people can be justified by the same faith.

It's no wonder this epistle of Paul's has been commented on more than any other book in the New Testament, for it contains the essence of our faith: God's gospel call to every person on the planet.

SALUTATION

1 From Paul, a slave of Christ Jesus, called to be an apostle, set
apart for the gospel of God. [2]This gospel he promised beforehand through his prophets in the holy scriptures, [3]concerning
his Son who was a descendant of David with reference to the
flesh, [4]who was appointed the Son-of-God-in-power according to the Holy Spirit by the resurrection from the dead, Jesus
Christ our Lord. [5]Through him we have received grace and our
apostleship to bring about the obedience of faith among all
the Gentiles on behalf of his name. [6]You also are among them,
called to belong to Jesus Christ. [7]To all those loved by God in
Rome, called to be saints: Grace and peace to you from God our
Father and the Lord Jesus Christ!

PAUL'S DESIRE TO VISIT ROME

[8]First of all, I thank my God through Jesus Christ for all of you,
because your faith is proclaimed throughout the whole world.
[9]For God, whom I serve in my spirit in the gospel of his Son, is
my witness that I continually remember you, [10]and I always ask
in my prayers if, perhaps now at last, I may succeed in visiting
you according to the will of God. [11]For I long to see you, so
that I may impart to you some spiritual gift to strengthen you,
[12]that is, that we may be mutually comforted by one another's
faith, both yours and mine. [13]I do not want you to be unaware,
brothers and sisters, that I often intended to come to you (and
was prevented until now), so that I may have some fruit even
among you, just as I already have among the rest of the Gentiles.
[14]I am a debtor both to the Greeks and to the barbarians, both
to the wise and to the foolish. [15]Thus I am eager also to preach
the gospel to you who are in Rome.

THE POWER OF THE GOSPEL

[16]For I am not ashamed of the gospel, for it is God's power for
salvation to everyone who believes, to the Jew first and also to
the Greek. [17]For the righteousness of God is revealed in the
gospel from faith to faith, just as it is written, ***"The righteous
by faith will live."***

THE CONDEMNATION OF THE UNRIGHTEOUS

[18]For the wrath of God is revealed from heaven against all ungodliness and unrighteousness of people who suppress the
truth by their unrighteousness, [19]because what can be known
about God is plain to them, because God has made it plain
to them. [20]For since the creation of the world his invisible
attributes—his eternal power and divine nature—have been
clearly seen because they are understood through what has
been made. So people are without excuse. [21]For although they
knew God, they did not glorify him as God or give him thanks,
but they became futile in their thoughts, and their senseless
hearts were darkened. [22]Although they claimed to be wise, they
became fools [23]and exchanged the glory of the immortal God
for an image resembling mortal human beings or birds or four-
footed animals or reptiles.
[24]Therefore God gave them over in the desires of their hearts
to impurity, to dishonor their bodies among themselves. [25]They
exchanged the truth of God for a lie and worshiped and served the
creation rather than the Creator, who is blessed forever! Amen.
[26]For this reason God gave them over to dishonorable passions. For their women exchanged the natural sexual relations

1:18–32 **The apostle begins to show that all human beings need the salvation of the gospel because none could obtain the favor of God or escape his wrath by their own works. For no man can plead that he has fulfilled all his obligations to God and to his neighbor; nor can any truly say that he has fully acted up to the light afforded him. There never yet was a person who had not reason to lament his strong corruptions. Therefore this chapter is a call to self-examination, the end of which should be a deep conviction of sin and of the necessity of deliverance from a state of condemnation.**

MATTHEW HENRY **(1662–1714)**
COMMENTARY ON THE WHOLE BIBLE

for unnatural ones, 27and likewise the men also abandoned
natural relations with women and were inflamed in their passions for one another. Men committed shameless acts with
men and received in themselves the due penalty for their error.
28And just as they did not see fit to acknowledge God, God
gave them over to a depraved mind, to do what should not be
done. 29They are filled with every kind of unrighteousness, wickedness, covetousness, malice. They are rife with envy, murder,
strife, deceit, hostility. They are gossips, 30slanderers, haters
of God, insolent, arrogant, boastful, contrivers of all sorts of
evil, disobedient to parents, 31senseless, covenant-breakers,
heartless, ruthless. 32Although they fully know God's righteous
decree that those who practice such things deserve to die, they
not only do them but also approve of those who practice them.

THE CONDEMNATION OF THE MORALIST

2 Therefore you are without excuse, whoever you are, when
you judge someone else. For on whatever grounds you judge
another, you condemn yourself, because you who judge practice the same things. 2Now we know that God's judgment is in
accordance with truth against those who practice such things.
3And do you think, whoever you are, when you judge those
who practice such things and yet do them yourself, that you
will escape God's judgment? 4Or do you have contempt for the
wealth of his kindness, forbearance, and patience, and yet do
not know that God's kindness leads you to repentance? 5But
because of your stubbornness and your unrepentant heart, you
are storing up wrath for yourselves in the day of wrath, when
God's righteous judgment is revealed! 6He ***will reward each one
according to his works***: 7eternal life to those who by perseverance in good works seek glory and honor and immortality, 8but
wrath and anger to those who live in selfish ambition and do
not obey the truth but follow unrighteousness. 9There will be
affliction and distress on everyone who does evil, on the Jew
first and also the Greek, 10but glory and honor and peace for
everyone who does good, for the Jew first and also the Greek.
11For there is no partiality with God. 12For all who have sinned
apart from the law will also perish apart from the law, and all
who have sinned under the law will be judged by the law. 13For
it is not those who hear the law who are righteous before God,
but those who do the law will be declared righteous. 14For whenever the Gentiles, who do not have the law, do by nature the
things required by the law, these who do not have the law are
a law to themselves. 15They show that the work of the law is
written in their hearts, as their conscience bears witness and
their conflicting thoughts accuse or else defend them, 16on the
day when God will judge the secrets of human hearts, according
to my gospel through Christ Jesus.

2:14–16 **If God will judge the secrets of men, surely the God who will judge is he to whom belong both the law and that nature that is the rule for those who do not know the law. But how will he conduct this judgment? "According to my gospel," says the apostle, "through Christ Jesus." The law and nature are vindicated by the gospel and Christ.**

TERTULLIAN **(155–C. 220)**
AGAINST MARCION

THE CONDEMNATION OF THE JEW

17But if you call yourself a Jew and rely on the law and boast
of your relationship to God 18and know his will and approve
the superior things because you receive instruction from the
law, 19and if you are convinced that you yourself are a guide
to the blind, a light to those who are in darkness, 20an educator of the senseless, a teacher of little children, because you
have in the law the essential features of knowledge and of the
truth—21therefore you who teach someone else, do you not
teach yourself? You who preach against stealing, do you steal?

22 You who tell others not to commit adultery, do you commit
adultery? You who abhor idols, do you rob temples? 23 You who
boast in the law dishonor God by transgressing the law! 24 For
just as it is written, "***the name of God is being blasphemed among***
the Gentiles because of you."
25 For circumcision has its value if you practice the law, but
if you break the law, your circumcision has become uncircumcision. 26 Therefore if the uncircumcised man obeys the righteous requirements of the law, will not his uncircumcision be
regarded as circumcision? 27 And the physically uncircumcised
man, by keeping the law, will judge you to be the transgressor
of the law, even though you have the letter and circumcision!
28 For a person is not a Jew who is one outwardly, nor is circumcision something that is outward in the flesh, 29 but someone
is a Jew who is one inwardly, and circumcision is of the heart
by the Spirit and not by the letter. This person's praise is not
from people but from God.

3 Therefore what advantage does the Jew have, or what is the
value of circumcision? 2 Actually, there are many advantages.
First of all, the Jews were entrusted with the oracles of God.
3 What then? If some were unfaithful, their unfaithfulness will
not nullify God's faithfulness, will it? 4 Absolutely not! Let God
be proven true, and every human being shown up as a liar, just
as it is written: "***so that you will be justified in your words and***
will prevail when you are judged."
5 But if our unrighteousness demonstrates the righteousness
of God, what shall we say? The God who inflicts wrath is not
unrighteous, is he? (I am speaking in human terms.) 6 Absolutely
not! For otherwise how could God judge the world? 7 For if by my
lie the truth of God enhances his glory, why am I still actually
being judged as a sinner? 8 And why not say, "Let us do evil so
that good may come of it"?—as some who slander us allege that
we say. (Their condemnation is deserved!)

THE CONDEMNATION OF THE WORLD

9 What then? Are we better off? Certainly not, for we have already
charged that Jews and Greeks alike are all under sin, 10 just as
it is written:

"There is no one righteous, not even one,
11 ***there is no one who understands,***
there is no one who seeks God.
12 ***All have turned away,***
together they have become worthless;
there is no one who shows kindness, not even one."
13 ***"Their throats are open graves,***
they deceive with their tongues,
the poison of asps is under their lips."
14 ***"Their mouths are full of cursing and bitterness."***
15 ***"Their feet are swift to shed blood,***
16 ***ruin and misery are in their paths,***
17 ***and the way of peace they have not known."***
18 ***"There is no fear of God before their eyes."***

19 Now we know that whatever the law says, it says to those
who are under the law, so that every mouth may be silenced
and the whole world may be held accountable to God. 20 For *no*
one is declared righteous before him by the works of the law, for
through the law comes the knowledge of sin. 21 But now apart
from the law the righteousness of God (although it is attested

by the law and the prophets) has been disclosed—[22]namely, the
righteousness of God through the faithfulness of Jesus Christ
for all who believe. For there is no distinction, [23]for all have
sinned and fall short of the glory of God. [24]But they are justified
freely by his grace through the redemption that is in Christ
Jesus. [25]God publicly displayed him at his death as the mercy
seat accessible through faith. This was to demonstrate his righteousness because God in his forbearance had passed over the
sins previously committed. [26]This was also to demonstrate his
righteousness in the present time, so that he would be just and
the justifier of the one who lives because of Jesus' faithfulness.

[27]Where, then, is boasting? It is excluded! By what principle?
Of works? No, but by the principle of faith! [28]For we consider
that a person is declared righteous by faith apart from the works
of the law. [29]Or is God the God of the Jews only? Is he not the
God of the Gentiles too? Yes, of the Gentiles too! [30]Since God
is one, he will justify the circumcised by faith and the uncircumcised through faith. [31]Do we then nullify the law through
faith? Absolutely not! Instead we uphold the law.

THE ILLUSTRATION OF JUSTIFICATION

4 What then shall we say that Abraham, our ancestor according
to the flesh, has discovered regarding this matter? [2]For if
Abraham was declared righteous by works, he has something to
boast about—but not before God. [3]For what does the scripture
say? "***Abraham believed God, and it was credited to him as righteousness.***" [4]Now to the one who works, his pay is not credited
due to grace but due to obligation. [5]But to the one who does
not work, but believes in the one who declares the ungodly
righteous, his faith is credited as righteousness.

[6]So even David himself speaks regarding the blessedness of
the man to whom God credits righteousness apart from works:

[7]"***Blessed are those whose lawless deeds are forgiven, and***
whose sins are covered;
[8] ***blessed is the one against whom the Lord will never count***
sin."

[9]Is this blessedness then for the circumcision or also for
the uncircumcision? For we say, "***faith was credited to** Abraham*
as righteousness." [10]How then was it credited to him? Was he
circumcised at the time, or not? No, he was not circumcised but
uncircumcised! [11]And he received the sign of circumcision as
a seal of the righteousness that he had by faith while he was
still uncircumcised, so that he would become the father of all
those who believe but have never been circumcised, that they
too could have righteousness credited to them. [12]And he is also
the father of the circumcised, who are not only circumcised,
but who also walk in the footsteps of the faith that our father
Abraham possessed when he was still uncircumcised.

[13]For the promise to Abraham or to his descendants that he
would inherit the world was not fulfilled through the law, but
through the righteousness that comes by faith. [14]For if they
become heirs by the law, faith is empty and the promise is nullified. [15]For the law brings wrath, because where there is no law
there is no transgression either. [16]For this reason it is by faith
so that it may be by grace, with the result that the promise may
be certain to all the descendants—not only to those who are
under the law, but also to those who have the faith of Abraham,
who is the father of us all [17](as it is written, "***I have made you***

3:21–26 As long then as the former time endured, God permitted us to be borne along by unruly impulses. This was not that he at all delighted in our sins, but that he simply endured them. Yet the one love of God did not regard us with hatred, thrust us away, or remember our iniquity against us but showed great long-suffering and bore with us. He took on him the burden of our iniquities, he gave his own Son as a ransom for us. For what was capable of covering our sins other than his righteousness? By whom was it possible that we, the wicked and ungodly, could be justified other than by the only Son of God?

EPISTLE OF MATHETES TO DIOGNETUS **(130)**

4:1–25 Faith is precious because it believes in the future, even against what it now sees or knows. For it consoles itself in this hope, that it is God who promises. Paul claims that Abraham is worthy of praise because he strengthened his weakness by faith so that he believed that with God's help he could do what he knew was impossible by the laws of the universe. He was of great merit before God because he believed God over against his own knowledge. Paul therefore urges the Gentiles to believe as firmly as Abraham did so that they might receive the promise of God and his grace without any hesitation.

AMBROSIASTER **(C. 330)**
COMMENTARY ON PAUL'S EPISTLES

the father of many nations"). He is our father in the presence
of God whom he believed—the God who makes the dead alive
and summons the things that do not yet exist as though they
already do. 18Against hope Abraham believed in hope with the
result that he became ***the father of many nations*** according to the
pronouncement, "***so will your descendants be.***" 19Without being
weak in faith, he considered his own body as dead (because he
was about one hundred years old) and the deadness of Sarah's
womb. 20He did not waver in unbelief about the promise of God
but was strengthened in faith, giving glory to God. 21He was fully
convinced that what God promised he was also able to do. 22So
indeed it was credited to Abraham as righteousness.
23But the statement ***it was credited to him*** was not written
only for Abraham's sake, 24but also for our sake, to whom it
will be credited, those who believe in the one who raised Jesus
our Lord from the dead. 25He was given over because of our
transgressions and was raised for the sake of our justification.

THE EXPECTATION OF JUSTIFICATION

5 Therefore, since we have been declared righteous by faith, we
have peace with God through our Lord Jesus Christ, 2through
whom we have also obtained access into this grace in which
we stand, and we rejoice in the hope of God's glory. 3Not only
this, but we also rejoice in sufferings, knowing that suffering
produces endurance, 4and endurance, character, and character,
hope. 5And hope does not disappoint, because the love of God
has been poured out in our hearts through the Holy Spirit who
was given to us.
6For while we were still helpless, at the right time Christ died
for the ungodly. 7(For rarely will anyone die for a righteous person, though for a good person perhaps someone might possibly
dare to die.) 8But God demonstrates his own love for us, in that
while we were still sinners, Christ died for us. 9Much more then,
because we have now been declared righteous by his blood, we
will be saved through him from God's wrath. 10For if while we
were enemies we were reconciled to God through the death of
his Son, how much more, since we have been reconciled, will
we be saved by his life? 11Not only this, but we also rejoice in
God through our Lord Jesus Christ, through whom we have now
received this reconciliation.

5:1–5 This is the true fortitude that Christ's warrior has who receives not the crown unless he strives lawfully. Or does that call to fortitude seem to you but a poor one: "Suffering produces endurance, and endurance, character, and character, hope"? See how many a contest there is, yet but one crown! That call was given by Paul who was strengthened in Christ Jesus and whose flesh had no rest. Affliction on all sides, fighting without, and fears within. And though in dangers, in countless labors, in prisons, in deaths, he was not broken in spirit but fought so as to become more powerful through his infirmities.

AMBROSE (C. 339–C. 397)
ON THE DUTIES OF THE CLERGY

THE AMPLIFICATION OF JUSTIFICATION

12So then, just as sin entered the world through one man and
death through sin, and so death spread to all people because
all sinned—13for before the law was given, sin was in the world,
but there is no accounting for sin when there is no law. 14Yet
death reigned from Adam until Moses even over those who
did not sin in the same way that Adam (who is a type of the
coming one) transgressed. 15But the gracious gift is not like the
transgression. For if the many died through the transgression of
the one man, how much more did the grace of God and the gift
by the grace of the one man Jesus Christ multiply to the many!
16And the gift is not like the one who sinned. For judgment,
resulting from the one transgression, led to condemnation,
but the gracious gift from the many failures led to justification.
17For if, by the transgression of the one man, death reigned
through the one, how much more will those who receive the
abundance of grace and of the gift of righteousness reign in life
through the one, Jesus Christ!

IGNATIUS OF LOYOLA:

FOUNDER OF THE SOCIETY OF JESUS

c. 1491–1556

Early sixteenth-century Europe was a tumultuous place religiously and politically, thanks to Martin Luther and his compatriots. The Catholic Church responded in a number of ways. While the Inquisition was the defensive response to the Reformation, a new religious order organized by Ignatius of Loyola was the offensive weapon the Counter-Reformation used to push back against Protestantism and call dedicated soldiers of Christ to personal piety and devotion.

Ignatius was born to an upper-class family in northern Spain around 1491. At eighteen he entered military service where, when he was thirty, his right leg was shattered by a cannonball. The experience proved providential, for while recovering in the city of Loyola after several surgeries he had a profound conversion experience. He ventured to the Benedictine monastery Santa Maria de Montserrat and placed his sword on the altar—signaling his new life of service to Christ as his soldier on the battlefield of faith. For the next year he would seclude himself near Barcelona, living an ascetic lifestyle and seeking how best to serve Christ. It was then that he began his magisterial *Spiritual Exercises*.

According to Ignatius, *Spiritual Exercises* is meant to be a

> *way of examining one's conscience, of meditating, of contemplating, of praying vocally and mentally, and of performing other spiritual actions . . . For as strolling, walking, and running are bodily exercises, so every way of preparing and disposing the soul to rid itself of all the disordered tendencies, and, after it is rid, to seek and find the divine will as to the management of one's life for the salvation of the soul, is called a spiritual exercise.*

Eventually, a new religious order rose up based on the lifestyle described in Ignatius's *Spiritual Exercises*: the Society of Jesus, commonly known as the Jesuits.

After Ignatius had spent nearly a decade pursuing education at the University of Alcalá de Henares and University of Paris, he gathered several like-minded students who had similarly devoted themselves to being soldiers of Christ. Their religious order was officially recognized by Pope Paul III on September 27, 1540, with the expressed mission "To serve only God and the Roman pontiff, his vicar on earth, after a solemn vow of perpetual chastity."

Ignatius's work lives on through the Society of Jesus, which has established institutes of higher learning across continental Europe and engaged in missionary activity throughout the world. Like Ignatius himself, the Jesuits are known for their vows of poverty and chastity, rigorous philosophical and theological study, and the defense and propagation of the Christian faith.

IMPORTANT WORKS

SPIRITUAL EXERCISES

THE CONSTITUTION OF THE JESUITS

[18]Consequently, just as condemnation for all people came through one transgression, so too through the one righteous act came righteousness leading to life for all people. [19]For just as through the disobedience of the one man many were constituted sinners, so also through the obedience of one man many will be constituted righteous. [20]Now the law came in so that the transgression may increase, but where sin increased, grace multiplied all the more, [21]so that just as sin reigned in death, so also grace will reign through righteousness to eternal life through Jesus Christ our Lord.

THE BELIEVER'S FREEDOM FROM SIN'S DOMINATION

6 What shall we say then? Are we to remain in sin so that grace may increase? [2]Absolutely not! How can we who died to sin still live in it? [3]Or do you not know that as many as were baptized into Christ Jesus were baptized into his death? [4]Therefore we have been buried with him through baptism into death, in order that just as Christ was raised from the dead through the glory of the Father, so we too may live a new life.

[5]For if we have become united with him in the likeness of his death, we will certainly also be united in the likeness of his resurrection. [6]We know that our old man was crucified with him so that the body of sin would no longer dominate us, so that we would no longer be enslaved to sin. [7](For someone who has died has been freed from sin.)

[8]Now if we died with Christ, we believe that we will also live with him. [9]We know that since Christ has been raised from the dead, he is never going to die again; death no longer has mastery over him. [10]For the death he died, he died to sin once for all, but the life he lives, he lives to God. [11]So you too consider yourselves dead to sin, but alive to God in Christ Jesus.

[12]Therefore do not let sin reign in your mortal body so that you obey its desires, [13]and do not present your members to sin as instruments to be used for unrighteousness, but present yourselves to God as those who are alive from the dead and your members to God as instruments to be used for righteousness. [14]For sin will have no mastery over you, because you are not under law but under grace.

THE BELIEVER'S ENSLAVEMENT TO GOD'S RIGHTEOUSNESS

[15]What then? Shall we sin because we are not under law but under grace? Absolutely not! [16]Do you not know that if you present yourselves as obedient slaves, you are slaves of the one you obey, either of sin resulting in death, or obedience resulting in righteousness? [17]But thanks be to God that though you were slaves to sin, you obeyed from the heart that pattern of teaching you were entrusted to, [18]and having been freed from sin, you became enslaved to righteousness. [19](I am speaking in human terms because of the weakness of your flesh.) For just as you once presented your members as slaves to impurity and lawlessness leading to more lawlessness, so now present your members as slaves to righteousness leading to sanctification. [20]For when you were slaves of sin, you were free with regard to righteousness.

[21]So what benefit did you then reap from those things that you are now ashamed of? For the end of those things is death. [22]But now, freed from sin and enslaved to God, you have your benefit leading to sanctification, and the end is eternal life.

6:15–23 After shaming his readers by mentioning their slavery, Paul recalls the benefits they have received. He shows that they were set free from very great evils indeed. In the past you did not split your service between righteousness and sin but were wholly given over to sin. So now that you have come over to the side of righteousness, you should do the same thing and give yourself over entirely to righteousness. Instead of the shame and death you deserved before, you now have the hope of attaining holiness and eternal life. Note how Paul says that some things have already been given while others are still hoped for, but that the former point to the latter. Thus if we can come to holiness now, we can be assured of obtaining eternal life in the future.

CHRYSOSTOM **(C. 347–407)**
HOMILIES ON THE EPISTLE OF PAUL TO THE ROMANS

23For the payoff of sin is death, but the gift of God is eternal
life in Christ Jesus our Lord.

THE BELIEVER'S RELATIONSHIP TO THE LAW

7 Or do you not know, brothers and sisters (for I am speaking
to those who know the law), that the law is lord over a person
as long as he lives? 2For a married woman is bound by law to
her husband as long as he lives, but if her husband dies, she is
released from the law of the marriage. 3So then, if she is joined
to another man while her husband is alive, she will be called an
adulteress. But if her husband dies, she is free from that law,
and if she is joined to another man, she is not an adulteress.
4So, my brothers and sisters, you also died to the law through
the body of Christ, so that you could be joined to another, to
the one who was raised from the dead, to bear fruit to God. 5For
when we were in the flesh, the sinful desires, aroused by the
law, were active in the members of our body to bear fruit for
death. 6But now we have been released from the law, because
we have died to what controlled us, so that we may serve in
the new life of the Spirit and not under the old written code.
7What shall we say then? Is the law sin? Absolutely not!
Certainly, I would not have known sin except through the law.
For indeed I would not have known what it means to desire
something belonging to someone else if the law had not said,
"***Do not covet.***" 8But sin, seizing the opportunity through the
commandment, produced in me all kinds of wrong desires.
For apart from the law, sin is dead. 9And I was once alive apart
from the law, but with the coming of the commandment, sin
became alive 10and I died. So I found that the very commandment that was intended to bring life brought death! 11For sin,
seizing the opportunity through the commandment, deceived
me and through it I died. 12So then, the law is holy, and the
commandment is holy, righteous, and good.
13Did that which is good, then, become death to me? Absolutely
not! But sin, so that it would be shown to be sin, produced death
in me through what is good, so that through the commandment
sin would become utterly sinful. 14For we know that the law is
spiritual—but I am unspiritual, sold into slavery to sin. 15For I don't
understand what I am doing. For I do not do what I want—instead,
I do what I hate. 16But if I do what I don't want, I agree that the law
is good. 17But now it is no longer me doing it, but sin that lives in
me. 18For I know that nothing good lives in me, that is, in my flesh.
For I want to do the good, but I cannot do it. 19For I do not do the
good I want, but I do the very evil I do not want! 20Now if I do what
I do not want, it is no longer me doing it but sin that lives in me.
21So, I find the law that when I want to do good, evil is present
with me. 22For I delight in the law of God in my inner being.
23But I see a different law in my members waging war against
the law of my mind and making me captive to the law of sin that
is in my members. 24Wretched man that I am! Who will rescue
me from this body of death? 25Thanks be to God through Jesus
Christ our Lord! So then, I myself serve the law of God with my
mind, but with my flesh I serve the law of sin.

7:13–25 It was sin that was made death to me by the good law. The consequence was that inbred sin, thus driving furiously in spite of the commandment, became exceeding sinful, the guilt thereof being greatly aggravated. The struggle is now come to the height: And the man finding there is no help in himself begins almost unaware to pray, *Who shall deliver me?* He then seeks and looks for deliverance till God in Christ appears to answer his question. That is, *God will deliver me through Christ.* The apostle beautifully interweaves his assertion with thanksgiving, the hymn of praise answering in a manner to the voice of sorrow.

JOHN WESLEY **(1703–1791)**
EXPLANATORY NOTES ON THE BIBLE

THE BELIEVER'S RELATIONSHIP TO THE HOLY SPIRIT

8 There is therefore now no condemnation for those who are
in Christ Jesus. 2For the law of the life-giving Spirit in Christ
Jesus has set you free from the law of sin and death. 3For God

achieved what the law could not do because it was weakened
through the flesh. By sending his own Son in the likeness of sinful
flesh and concerning sin, he condemned sin in the flesh, 4so that
the righteous requirement of the law may be fulfilled in us, who
do not walk according to the flesh but according to the Spirit.

5For those who live according to the flesh have their outlook
shaped by the things of the flesh, but those who live according
to the Spirit have their outlook shaped by the things of the
Spirit. 6For the outlook of the flesh is death, but the outlook of
the Spirit is life and peace, 7because the outlook of the flesh is
hostile to God, for it does not submit to the law of God, nor is
it able to do so. 8Those who are in the flesh cannot please God.
9You, however, are not in the flesh but in the Spirit, if indeed
the Spirit of God lives in you. Now if anyone does not have the
Spirit of Christ, this person does not belong to him. 10But if
Christ is in you, your body is dead because of sin, but the Spirit
is your life because of righteousness. 11Moreover if the Spirit
of the one who raised Jesus from the dead lives in you, the one
who raised Christ from the dead will also make your mortal
bodies alive through his Spirit who lives in you.

12So then, brothers and sisters, we are under obligation, not
to the flesh, to live according to the flesh 13(for if you live according to the flesh, you will die), but if by the Spirit you put to
death the deeds of the body, you will live. 14For all who are led by
the Spirit of God are the sons of God. 15For you did not receive
the spirit of slavery leading again to fear, but you received the
Spirit of adoption, by whom we cry, "*Abba,* Father." 16The Spirit
himself bears witness to our spirit that we are God's children.
17And if children, then heirs (namely, heirs of God and also
fellow heirs with Christ)—if indeed we suffer with him so we
may also be glorified with him.

18For I consider that our present sufferings cannot even be
compared to the coming glory that will be revealed to us. 19For
the creation eagerly waits for the revelation of the sons of God.
20For the creation was subjected to futility—not willingly but
because of God who subjected it—in hope 21that the creation
itself will also be set free from the bondage of decay into the
glorious freedom of God's children. 22For we know that the whole
creation groans and suffers together until now. 23Not only this,
but we ourselves also, who have the firstfruits of the Spirit, groan
inwardly as we eagerly await our adoption, the redemption of
our bodies. 24For in hope we were saved. Now hope that is seen is
not hope, because who hopes for what he sees? 25But if we hope
for what we do not see, we eagerly wait for it with endurance.

26In the same way, the Spirit helps us in our weakness, for
we do not know how we should pray, but the Spirit himself
intercedes for us with inexpressible groanings. 27And he who
searches our hearts knows the mind of the Spirit, because the
Spirit intercedes on behalf of the saints according to God's
will. 28And we know that all things work together for good for
those who love God, who are called according to his purpose,
29because those whom he foreknew he also predestined to be
conformed to the image of his Son, that his Son would be the
firstborn among many brothers and sisters. 30And those he
predestined, he also called; and those he called, he also justified;
and those he justified, he also glorified.

31What then shall we say about these things? If God is for
us, who can be against us? 32Indeed, he who did not spare his
own Son, but gave him up for us all—how will he not also, along

with him, freely give us all things? 33Who will bring any charge against God's elect? It is God who justifies. 34Who is the one who will condemn? Christ is the one who died (and more than that, he was raised), who is at the right hand of God, and who also is interceding for us. 35Who will separate us from the love of Christ? Will trouble, or distress, or persecution, or famine, or nakedness, or danger, or sword? 36As it is written, ***"For your sake we encounter death all day long; we were considered as sheep to be slaughtered."*** 37No, in all these things we have complete victory through him who loved us! 38For I am convinced that neither death, nor life, nor angels, nor heavenly rulers, nor things that are present, nor things to come, nor powers, 39nor height, nor depth, nor anything else in creation will be able to separate us from the love of God in Christ Jesus our Lord.

ISRAEL'S REJECTION CONSIDERED

9 I am telling the truth in Christ (I am not lying!), for my conscience assures me in the Holy Spirit—2I have great sorrow and unceasing anguish in my heart. 3For I could wish that I myself were accursed—cut off from Christ—for the sake of my people, my fellow countrymen, 4who are Israelites. To them belong the adoption as sons, the glory, the covenants, the giving of the law, the temple worship, and the promises. 5To them belong the patriarchs, and from them, by human descent, came the Christ, who is God over all, blessed forever! Amen.

6It is not as though the word of God had failed. For not all those who are descended from Israel are truly Israel, 7nor are all the children Abraham's true descendants; rather ***"through Isaac will your descendants be counted."*** 8This means it is not the children of the flesh who are the children of God; rather, the children of promise are counted as descendants. 9For this is what the promise declared: ***"About a year from now I will return and Sarah will have a son."*** 10Not only that, but when Rebekah had conceived children by one man, our ancestor Isaac—11even before they were born or had done anything good or bad (so that God's purpose in election would stand, not by works but by his calling)—12it was said to her, ***"The older will serve the younger,"*** 13just as it is written: ***"Jacob I loved, but Esau I hated."***

14What shall we say then? Is there injustice with God? Absolutely not! 15For he says to Moses: ***"I will have mercy on whom I have mercy, and I will have compassion on whom I have compassion."*** 16So then, it does not depend on human desire or exertion, but on God who shows mercy. 17For the scripture says to Pharaoh: ***"For this very purpose I have raised you up, that I may demonstrate my power in you, and that my name may be proclaimed in all the earth."*** 18So then, God has mercy on whom he chooses to have mercy, and he hardens whom he chooses to harden.

19You will say to me then, "Why does he still find fault? For who has ever resisted his will?" 20But who indeed are you—a mere human being—to talk back to God? ***Does what is molded say to the molder, "Why have you made me like this?"*** 21Has the potter no right to make from the same lump of clay one vessel for special use and another for ordinary use? 22But what if God, willing to demonstrate his wrath and to make known his power, has endured with much patience the objects of wrath prepared for destruction? 23And what if he is willing to make known the wealth of his glory on the objects of mercy that he has prepared beforehand for glory—24even us, whom he has

8:31–39 Paul does not say it is God who forgave our sins, but what is much greater, "It is God who justifies." For when the Judge's sentence declares us just, what signifies the accuser? Who then is to condemn us since God crowns us and Christ was put to death for us, and not only was put to death but also after this intercedes for us? For he was not contented with being put to death alone. And this is a sign for the most part of very great love, to be doing not only what falls to his lot but also to address another on this behalf. For this is all he meant to signify by the interceding: Intercession is a sign of love.

CHRYSOSTOM **(C. 347–407)**
HOMILIES ON THE EPISTLE OF PAUL TO THE ROMANS

9:1–33 Paul teaches the godly that we understand the lofty and hidden mystery of election most correctly only when we consider the immense majesty of God and in turn confess the worthlessness of our nature, and we entrust ourselves entirely to the divine will and power and allow ourselves to be shaped as clay is handled and shaped by the potter. A human being does not have any grounds for complaining. In vain the wicked strive to excuse themselves and release themselves from blame. On the last day God will exercise his judgment with perfect justice.

TILEMANN HESHUSIUS
(1527–1588)
COMMENTARY ON ROMANS

called, not only from the Jews but also from the Gentiles? 25 As
he also says in Hosea:

"I will call those who were not my people, 'My people,' and
I will call her who was unloved, 'My beloved.'"
26 *"And in the very place where it was said to them, 'You are*
not my people,'
there they will be called 'sons of the living God.'"

27 And Isaiah cries out on behalf of Israel, *"Though the number*
of the children of Israel are as the sand of the sea, only the remnant
will be saved, 28 *for the Lord will execute his sentence on the earth*
completely and quickly." 29 Just as Isaiah predicted,

"If the Lord of Heaven's Armies had not left us
descendants,
we would have become like Sodom,
and we would have resembled Gomorrah."

ISRAEL'S REJECTION CULPABLE

30 What shall we say then?—that the Gentiles who did not pursue
righteousness obtained it, that is, a righteousness that is by
faith, 31 but Israel even though pursuing a law of righteousness
did not attain it. 32 Why not? Because they pursued it not by
faith but (as if it were possible) by works. They stumbled over
the stumbling stone, 33 just as it is written,

"Look, I am laying in Zion a stone that will cause people
to stumble
and a rock that will make them fall,
yet the one who believes in him will not be put to shame."

10 Brothers and sisters, my heart's desire and prayer to God
on behalf of my fellow Israelites is for their salvation. 2 For
I can testify that they are zealous for God, but their zeal is not
in line with the truth. 3 For ignoring the righteousness that
comes from God and seeking instead to establish their own
righteousness, they did not submit to God's righteousness.
4 For Christ is the end of the law, with the result that there is
righteousness for everyone who believes.

5 For Moses writes about the righteousness that is by the
law: *"The one who does these things will live by them."* 6 But the
righteousness that is by faith says: *"Do not say in your heart,*
'Who will ascend into heaven?'" (that is, to bring Christ down)
7 or *"Who will descend into the abyss?"* (that is, to bring Christ
up from the dead). 8 But what does it say? *"The word is near you,*
in your mouth and in your heart" (that is, the word of faith that
we preach), 9 because if you confess with your mouth that Jesus
is Lord and believe in your heart that God raised him from
the dead, you will be saved. 10 For with the heart one believes
and thus has righteousness and with the mouth one confesses
and thus has salvation. 11 For the scripture says, *"Everyone who*
believes in him will not be put to shame." 12 For there is no distinction between the Jew and the Greek, for the same Lord is
Lord of all, who richly blesses all who call on him. 13 For *everyone*
who calls on the name of the Lord will be saved.

14 How are they to call on one they have not believed in? And
how are they to believe in one they have not heard of? And how
are they to hear without someone preaching to them? 15 And
how are they to preach unless they are sent? As it is written,
"How timely is the arrival of those who proclaim the good news."
16 But not all have obeyed the good news, for Isaiah says, *"Lord,*

10:1–13 God requires both of these things: your heart and your mouth—your heart so that you may believe and your mouth that you may confess what you believe. And by this faith and by this confession God gives you two things: justification (because you believe with your heart) and salvation (because by confessing with the mouth what you believe, you thereby fortify your own faith and increase it).

JUAN DE VALDÉS
(C. 1490–1541)
COMMENTARY ON ROMANS

who has believed our report?" [17]Consequently faith comes from
what is heard, and what is heard comes through the preached
word of Christ.
[18]But I ask, have they not heard? Yes, they have: ***Their voice
has gone out to all the earth, and their words to the ends of the
world.*** [19]But again I ask, didn't Israel understand? First Moses
says, ***"I will make you jealous by those who are not a nation; with
a senseless nation I will provoke you to anger."*** [20]And Isaiah is
even bold enough to say, ***"I was found by those who did not seek
me; I became well known to those who did not ask for me."*** [21]But
about Israel he says, ***"All day long I held out my hands to this
disobedient and stubborn people!"***

ISRAEL'S REJECTION NOT COMPLETE NOR FINAL

11 So I ask, God has not rejected his people, has he? Absolutely not! For I too am an Israelite, a descendant of Abraham,
from the tribe of Benjamin. [2]God has not rejected his people
whom he foreknew! Do you not know what the scripture says
about Elijah, how he pleads with God against Israel? [3]"Lord,
***they have killed your prophets; they have demolished your altars;
I alone am left, and they are seeking my life!"*** [4]But what was the
divine response to him? ***"I have kept*** for myself ***7,000 people
who have not bent the knee to Baal."***
[5]So in the same way at the present time there is a remnant
chosen by grace. [6]And if it is by grace, it is no longer by works,
otherwise grace would no longer be grace. [7]What then? Israel
failed to obtain what it was diligently seeking, but the elect
obtained it. The rest were hardened, [8]as it is written,

"God gave them a spirit of stupor,
eyes that would not see and ears that would not hear,
to this very day."

[9]And David says,

"Let their table become a snare and trap,
a stumbling block and a retribution for them;
10 ***let their eyes be darkened so that they may not see,***
and make their backs bend continually."

[11]I ask then, they did not stumble into an irrevocable fall,
did they? Absolutely not! But by their transgression salvation
has come to the Gentiles, to make Israel jealous. [12]Now if their
transgression means riches for the world and their defeat
means riches for the Gentiles, how much more will their full
restoration bring?
[13]Now I am speaking to you Gentiles. Seeing that I am an
apostle to the Gentiles, I magnify my ministry, [14]if somehow I
could provoke my people to jealousy and save some of them.
[15]For if their rejection is the reconciliation of the world, what
will their acceptance be but life from the dead? [16]If the first
portion of the dough offered is holy, then the whole batch is
holy, and if the root is holy, so too are the branches.
[17]Now if some of the branches were broken off, and you, a wild
olive shoot, were grafted in among them and participated in the
richness of the olive root, [18]do not boast over the branches. But
if you boast, remember that you do not support the root, but
the root supports you. [19]Then you will say, "The branches were
broken off so that I could be grafted in." [20]Granted! They were
broken off because of their unbelief, but you stand by faith. Do

11:1–36 Multitudes of Gentiles were made heirs of Abraham's faith, holiness, and blessedness. Still, the restoration of the Jews is far less improbable than the call of the Gentiles to be the children of Abraham. Jews are still to be favored for the sake of their pious fathers. True grace seeks not to confine God's favor. Those who find mercy themselves should endeavor that through their mercy others also may obtain mercy. And the continued care of the Lord toward that people, and the final mercy and blessed restoration intended for them, show the patience and love of God.

MATTHEW HENRY **(1662–1714)**
COMMENTARY ON THE WHOLE BIBLE

not be arrogant, but fear! [21]For if God did not spare the natural
branches, perhaps he will not spare you. [22]Notice therefore
the kindness and harshness of God—harshness toward those
who have fallen, but God's kindness toward you, provided you
continue in his kindness; otherwise you also will be cut off.
[23]And even they—if they do not continue in their unbelief—
will be grafted in, for God is able to graft them in again. [24]For
if you were cut off from what is by nature a wild olive tree, and
grafted, contrary to nature, into a cultivated olive tree, how
much more will these natural branches be grafted back into
their own olive tree?

[25]For I do not want you to be ignorant of this mystery, brothers and sisters, so that you may not be conceited: A partial
hardening has happened to Israel until the full number of the
Gentiles has come in. [26]And so all Israel will be saved, as it is
written:

"The Deliverer will come out of Zion;
he will remove ungodliness from Jacob.
27 ***And this is my covenant with them,***
when I take away their sins."

[28]In regard to the gospel they are enemies for your sake,
but in regard to election they are dearly loved for the sake of
the fathers. [29]For the gifts and the call of God are irrevocable.
[30]Just as you were formerly disobedient to God, but have now
received mercy due to their disobedience, [31]so they too have
now been disobedient in order that, by the mercy shown to you,
they too may now receive mercy. [32]For God has consigned all
people to disobedience so that he may show mercy to them all.

[33]Oh, the depth of the riches and wisdom and knowledge
of God! How unsearchable are his judgments and how unfathomable his ways!

34 ***For who has known the mind of the Lord,***
or who has been his counselor?
35 ***Or who has first given to God***
that God needs to repay him?

[36]For from him and through him and to him are all things.
To him be glory forever! Amen.

CONSECRATION OF THE BELIEVER'S LIFE

12 Therefore I exhort you, brothers and sisters, by the mercies
of God, to present your bodies as a sacrifice—alive, holy,
and pleasing to God—which is your reasonable service. [2]Do not
be conformed to this present world, but be transformed by
the renewing of your mind, so that you may test and approve
what is the will of God—what is good and well-pleasing and
perfect.

CONDUCT IN HUMILITY

[3]For by the grace given to me I say to every one of you not to
think more highly of yourself than you ought to think, but to
think with sober discernment, as God has distributed to each
of you a measure of faith. [4]For just as in one body we have many
members, and not all the members serve the same function,
[5]so we who are many are one body in Christ, and individually
we are members who belong to one another. [6]And we have
different gifts according to the grace given to us. If the gift
is prophecy, that individual must use it in proportion to his

12:1–2 If the body, which is less than the soul and which the soul uses as a servant or a tool, is a sacrifice when it is used well and rightly for the service of God, how much more so is the soul when it offers itself to God? In this way, aflame in the fire of divine love and with the dross of worldly desire melted away, it is remolded into the unchangeable form of God and becomes beautiful in his sight by reason of the bounty of beauty he has bestowed upon it.

AUGUSTINE (354–430)
CITY OF GOD

faith. 7If it is service, he must serve; if it is teaching, he must teach; 8if it is exhortation, he must exhort; if it is contributing, he must do so with sincerity; if it is leadership, he must do so with diligence; if it is showing mercy, he must do so with cheerfulness.

CONDUCT IN LOVE

9Love must be without hypocrisy. Abhor what is evil, cling to what is good. 10Be devoted to one another with mutual love, showing eagerness in honoring one another. 11Do not lag in zeal, be enthusiastic in spirit, serve the Lord. 12Rejoice in hope, endure in suffering, persist in prayer. 13Contribute to the needs of the saints, pursue hospitality. 14Bless those who persecute you, bless and do not curse. 15Rejoice with those who rejoice, weep with those who weep. 16Live in harmony with one another; do not be haughty but associate with the lowly. Do not be conceited. 17Do not repay anyone evil for evil; consider what is good before all people. 18If possible, so far as it depends on you, live peaceably with all people. 19Do not avenge yourselves, dear friends, but give place to God's wrath, for it is written, ***"Vengeance is mine, I will repay,"*** says the Lord. 20Rather, ***if your enemy is hungry, feed him; if he is thirsty, give him a drink; for in doing this you will be heaping burning coals on his head.*** 21Do not be overcome by evil, but overcome evil with good.

SUBMISSION TO CIVIL GOVERNMENT

13 Let every person be subject to the governing authorities. For there is no authority except by God's appointment, and the authorities that exist have been instituted by God. 2So the person who resists such authority resists the ordinance of God, and those who resist will incur judgment 3(for rulers cause no fear for good conduct but for bad). Do you desire not to fear authority? Do good and you will receive its commendation 4because it is God's servant for your well-being. But be afraid if you do wrong because government does not bear the sword for nothing. It is God's servant to administer punishment on the person who does wrong. 5Therefore it is necessary to be in subjection, not only because of the wrath of the authorities but also because of your conscience. 6For this reason you also pay taxes, for the authorities are God's servants devoted to governing. 7Pay everyone what is owed: taxes to whom taxes are due, revenue to whom revenue is due, respect to whom respect is due, honor to whom honor is due.

EXHORTATION TO LOVE NEIGHBORS

8Owe no one anything, except to love one another, for the one who loves his neighbor has fulfilled the law. 9For the commandments, ***"Do not commit adultery, do not murder, do not steal, do not covet,"*** (and if there is any other commandment) are summed up in this, ***"Love your neighbor as yourself."*** 10Love does no wrong to a neighbor. Therefore love is the fulfillment of the law.

MOTIVATION TO GODLY CONDUCT

11And do this because we know the time, that it is already the hour for us to awake from sleep, for our salvation is now nearer than when we became believers. 12The night has advanced toward dawn; the day is near. So then we must lay aside the

13:8–14 The rule of love is that one should wish his friend to have all the good things he wants to have himself and should not wish the evils to befall his friend that he wishes to avoid himself. He shows this benevolence to all men. No evil must be done to any. Love of one's neighbor works no evil. Let us then love even our enemies as we are commanded if we wish to be truly unconquered.

AUGUSTINE **(354–430)**
OF TRUE RELIGION

works of darkness, and put on the weapons of light. [13]Let us live
decently as in the daytime, not in carousing and drunkenness,
not in sexual immorality and sensuality, not in discord and
jealousy. [14]Instead, put on the Lord Jesus Christ, and make no
provision for the flesh to arouse its desires.

EXHORTATION TO MUTUAL FORBEARANCE

14 Now receive the one who is weak in the faith, and do
not have disputes over differing opinions. [2]One person
believes in eating everything, but the weak person eats only
vegetables. [3]The one who eats everything must not despise the
one who does not, and the one who abstains must not judge
the one who eats everything, for God has accepted him. [4]Who
are you to pass judgment on another's servant? Before his own
master he stands or falls. And he will stand, for the Lord is able
to make him stand.

[5]One person regards one day holier than other days, and
another regards them all alike. Each must be fully convinced
in his own mind. [6]The one who observes the day does it for
the Lord. The one who eats, eats for the Lord because he gives
thanks to God, and the one who abstains from eating abstains
for the Lord, and he gives thanks to God. [7]For none of us lives
for himself and none dies for himself. [8]If we live, we live for
the Lord; if we die, we die for the Lord. Therefore, whether we
live or die, we are the Lord's. [9]For this reason Christ died and
returned to life, so that he may be the Lord of both the dead
and the living.

[10]But you who eat vegetables only—why do you judge your
brother or sister? And you who eat everything—why do you
despise your brother or sister? For we will all stand before the
judgment seat of God. [11]For it is written, ***"As I live, says the Lord,***
every knee will bow to me, and every tongue will give praise to
God." [12]Therefore, each of us will give an account of himself
to God.

EXHORTATION FOR THE STRONG NOT TO DESTROY THE WEAK

[13]Therefore we must not pass judgment on one another, but
rather determine never to place an obstacle or a trap before a
brother or sister. [14]I know and am convinced in the Lord Jesus
that there is nothing unclean in itself; still, it is unclean to the
one who considers it unclean. [15]For if your brother or sister is
distressed because of what you eat, you are no longer walking
in love. Do not destroy by your food someone for whom Christ
died. [16]Therefore do not let what you consider good be spoken
of as evil. [17]For the kingdom of God does not consist of food
and drink, but righteousness, peace, and joy in the Holy Spirit.
[18]For the one who serves Christ in this way is pleasing to God
and approved by people.

[19]So then, let us pursue what makes for peace and for building up one another. [20]Do not destroy the work of God for the
sake of food. For although all things are clean, it is wrong to
cause anyone to stumble by what you eat. [21]It is good not to eat
meat or drink wine or to do anything that causes your brother to stumble. [22]The faith you have, keep to yourself before
God. Blessed is the one who does not judge himself by what
he approves. [23]But the man who doubts is condemned if he
eats, because he does not do so from faith, and whatever is not
from faith is sin.

14:14–23 "If your brother or sister is distressed because of what you eat, you are no longer walking in love. Do not destroy by your food someone for whom Christ died." That is as much as to say, *Will you not in your food put yourself as much out of the way as to restrain your appetite?* Otherwise you expose your brother to be destroyed, him for whom Christ put himself so much out of the way as to die to save him from being destroyed.

JONATHAN EDWARDS
(1703–1758)
SELECTIONS FROM THE UNPUBLISHED WRITINGS

EXHORTATION FOR THE STRONG TO HELP THE WEAK

15 But we who are strong ought to bear with the failings of the weak, and not just please ourselves. 2Let each of us please his neighbor for his good to build him up. 3For even Christ did not please himself, but just as it is written, "***The insults of those who insult you have fallen on me.***" 4For everything that was written in former times was written for our instruction, so that through endurance and through encouragement of the scriptures we may have hope. 5Now may the God of endurance and comfort give you unity with one another in accordance with Christ Jesus, 6so that together you may with one voice glorify the God and Father of our Lord Jesus Christ.

EXHORTATION TO MUTUAL ACCEPTANCE

7Receive one another, then, just as Christ also received you, to God's glory. 8For I tell you that Christ has become a servant of the circumcised on behalf of God's truth to confirm the promises made to the fathers, 9and thus the Gentiles glorify God for his mercy. As it is written, "***Because of this I will confess you among the Gentiles, and I will sing praises to your name.***" 10And again it says: "***Rejoice, O Gentiles, with his people.***" 11And again, "***Praise the Lord all you Gentiles, and let all the peoples praise him.***" 12And again Isaiah says, "***The root of Jesse will come, and the one who rises to rule over the Gentiles, in him will the Gentiles hope.***" 13Now may the God of hope fill you with all joy and peace as you believe in him, so that you may abound in hope by the power of the Holy Spirit.

PAUL'S MOTIVATION FOR WRITING THE LETTER

14But I myself am fully convinced about you, my brothers and sisters, that you yourselves are full of goodness, filled with all knowledge, and able to instruct one another. 15But I have written more boldly to you on some points so as to remind you, because of the grace given to me by God 16to be a minister of Christ Jesus to the Gentiles. I serve the gospel of God like a priest, so that the Gentiles may become an acceptable offering, sanctified by the Holy Spirit.

17So I boast in Christ Jesus about the things that pertain to God. 18For I will not dare to speak of anything except what Christ has accomplished through me in order to bring about the obedience of the Gentiles, by word and deed, 19in the power of signs and wonders, in the power of the Spirit of God. So from Jerusalem even as far as Illyricum I have fully preached the gospel of Christ. 20And in this way I desire to preach where Christ has not been named, so as not to build on another person's foundation, 21but as it is written: "***Those who were not told about him will see, and those who have not heard will understand.***"

PAUL'S INTENTION OF VISITING THE ROMANS

22This is the reason I was often hindered from coming to you. 23But now there is nothing more to keep me in these regions, and I have for many years desired to come to you 24when I go to Spain. For I hope to visit you when I pass through and that you will help me on my journey there, after I have enjoyed your company for a while.

25But now I go to Jerusalem to minister to the saints. 26For Macedonia and Achaia are pleased to make some contribution

15:1–13 Should not we be humble, self-denying, and ready to consider one another who are members one of another? This like-mindedness must be according to the precept of Christ, according to his pattern and example. Our divine Master invites his disciples and encourages them by showing himself as meek and lowly in spirit. The same disposition ought to mark the conduct of his servants. The great end in all our actions must be that God may be glorified; nothing more advances this than the mutual love and kindness of those who profess religion.

MATTHEW HENRY **(1662–1714)**
COMMENTARY ON THE WHOLE BIBLE

for the poor among the saints in Jerusalem. [27]For they were
pleased to do this, and indeed they are indebted to the Jerusalem saints. For if the Gentiles have shared in their spiritual
things, they are obligated also to minister to them in material
things. [28]Therefore after I have completed this and have safely
delivered this bounty to them, I will set out for Spain by way of
you, [29]and I know that when I come to you, I will come in the
fullness of Christ's blessing.
[30]Now I urge you, brothers and sisters, through our Lord Jesus
Christ and through the love of the Spirit, to join fervently with
me in prayer to God on my behalf. [31]Pray that I may be rescued
from those who are disobedient in Judea and that my ministry in Jerusalem may be acceptable to the saints, [32]so that by
God's will I may come to you with joy and be refreshed in your
company. [33]Now may the God of peace be with all of you. Amen.

PERSONAL GREETINGS

16 Now I commend to you our sister Phoebe, who is a servant
of the church in Cenchrea, [2]so that you may welcome her
in the Lord in a way worthy of the saints and provide her with
whatever help she may need from you, for she has been a great
help to many, including me.
[3]Greet Prisca and Aquila, my fellow workers in Christ Jesus,
[4]who risked their own necks for my life. Not only I, but all the
churches of the Gentiles are grateful to them. [5]Also greet the
church in their house. Greet my dear friend Epenetus, who
was the first convert to Christ in the province of Asia. [6]Greet
Mary, who has worked very hard for you. [7]Greet Andronicus
and Junia, my compatriots and my fellow prisoners. They are
well known to the apostles, and they were in Christ before me.
[8]Greet Ampliatus, my dear friend in the Lord. [9]Greet Urbanus,
our fellow worker in Christ, and my good friend Stachys. [10]Greet
Apelles, who is approved in Christ. Greet those who belong to
the household of Aristobulus. [11]Greet Herodion, my compatriot.
Greet those in the household of Narcissus who are in the Lord.
[12]Greet Tryphena and Tryphosa, laborers in the Lord. Greet my
dear friend Persis, who has worked hard in the Lord. [13]Greet Ru-
fus, chosen in the Lord, and his mother who was also a mother
to me. [14]Greet Asyncritus, Phlegon, Hermes, Patrobas, Hermas,
and the brothers and sisters with them. [15]Greet Philologus and
Julia, Nereus and his sister, and Olympas, and all the believers
who are with them. [16]Greet one another with a holy kiss. All
the churches of Christ greet you.
[17]Now I urge you, brothers and sisters, to watch out for those
who create dissensions and obstacles contrary to the teaching
that you learned. Avoid them! [18]For these are the kind who do
not serve our Lord Christ, but their own appetites. By their
smooth talk and flattery they deceive the minds of the naive.
[19]Your obedience is known to all and thus I rejoice over you.
But I want you to be wise in what is good and innocent in what
is evil. [20]The God of peace will quickly crush Satan under your
feet. The grace of our Lord Jesus be with you.
[21]Timothy, my fellow worker, greets you; so do Lucius, Jason,
and Sosipater, my compatriots. [22]I, Tertius, who am writing this
letter, greet you in the Lord. [23]Gaius, who is host to me and to
the whole church, greets you. Erastus the city treasurer and
our brother Quartus greet you.◖
[25]Now to him who is able to strengthen you according to
my gospel and the proclamation of Jesus Christ, according to

the revelation of the mystery that had been kept secret for long ages, [26]but now is disclosed, and through the prophetic scriptures has been made known to all the nations, according to the command of the eternal God, to bring about the obedience of faith—[27]to the only wise God, through Jesus Christ, be glory forever! Amen.

16:25–27 Paul gives glory to God the Father. God decreed that every creature was to be saved by coming to a knowledge of the truth. For the truth of this mystery had been indicated by the prophets in symbols, and it was known only to God. This wisdom is Jesus Christ, who is from God and was with God forever. Without Christ nothing is complete because all things are through him. It is acknowledged that praise is given to God the Father through him because it is understood that "through Jesus Christ" means through his wisdom, in whom he has saved believers. Therefore glory to the Father through the Son is glory to both in the Holy Spirit because both are in the one glory.

AMBROSIASTER **(C. 330)**
COMMENTARY ON PAUL'S EPISTLES

AUTHOR	AUDIENCE	DATE	PURPOSE	THEMES
Paul	Believers at Corinth whose church was being torn apart by factions and spiritual immaturity	AD 55	Paul wrote this epistle to Christians in Corinth to confront and correct problems within the church and to answer questions they had regarding the Christian faith.	The nature of the gospel; the nature of the church; the Christian life; and hope in Christ

Corinth was a powerful cultural and financial center within the Roman Empire, full of prosperity and decadence. It makes sense that a church in such a city would face unique challenges—many of which find parallels in our modern world. Paul wrote his epistle to confront and correct a number of problems the church in Corinth was facing in such a culture of corruption. The believers there needed guidance for living within a system that seemed to oppose its values at every turn. Paul exhorted them to practice unity, and he confronted their divisions and quarrels head-on. Addressing sexual sin was important, for rampant immorality existed within the Corinthian church. Paul also offered direction for living together as God's family, urging those believers to love each other completely and maintain their services in an orderly manner, especially the commemoration of the Lord's Supper.

But 1 Corinthians isn't all confrontation. Paul also instructed his brothers and sisters in vital truths of the faith: reconciling devotion to Christ with food sacrificed to idols, explaining freedom in Christ, exploring the nature of spiritual gifts, and understanding the truth about the resurrection at the end of the age. Paul wrote his epistle as the founding father of the community, having planted the church at Corinth during his third missionary journey. Its message of correction and teaching on issues of the faith have made it a vital book in every generation, no less so in ours, for the cosmopolitan, individualistic, polytheistic nation of Corinth often mirrors the culture of our own day.

Paul sums up the basics of the Christian faith with a statement of orthodoxy found near the end of his epistle: "For I passed on to you as of first importance what I also received—that Christ died for our sins according to the scriptures, and that he was buried, and that he was raised on the third day according to the scriptures, and that he appeared to Cephas, then to the twelve" (15:3–5). He explains he received these teachings from others and passed them along as primary tenets of the faith. The early church understood this as the rule of faith, and these core beliefs of Christianity have been maintained through the centuries in every faithful branch of the church. They reflect what Paul taught: Christ's death for our sins; that he died and was buried; and that he rose again to new life, paving the way for our own new life and salvation.

1 CORINTHIANS

Ecclesiology is concerned with the nature of the church, and this letter is a primary course in that study. Paul addresses a number of issues, including jealousy and quarreling, which leads to disunity and division; the nature of church leadership and ministry; open sexual immorality; the abuse of Holy Communion; the nature of spiritual gifts and their purpose; and orderliness in worship. Paul reminds the Corinthians—and us—that the church is Christ's body, united and in need of all its parts.

Paul stated, "You were bought at a price. Therefore glorify God with your body" (6:20). As believers we do not have the freedom to live as we wish; rather what matters for our ethical life as followers of Christ is "keeping God's commandments" (7:19).

"I believe in . . . the resurrection of the body and the life everlasting." So ends the anchoring creed of our faith, the Apostles' Creed. This important outro is rooted in 1 Corinthians 15. In closing his epistle, Paul confronted a distortion of the basic belief that Christ has been raised from the dead. He is the "firstfruits of those who have fallen asleep" (15:20). Our future hope is not in heaven but in the resurrection, which is why Christ's own resurrection is so important. Paul writes, "If Christ has not been raised, then our preaching is futile and your faith is empty . . . And if Christ has not been raised, your faith is useless; you are still in your sins" (15:14, 17). The fact of the empty tomb has been the central pillar of the Christian faith from the beginning; it is the *why* of Christianity. We believe what we believe because Christ lives. And because he lives we have the hope of new, resurrected life.

Martin Luther summarizes 1 Corinthians perfectly: "In this epistle Saint Paul exhorts the Corinthians to be one in faith and love, and to see to it that they learn well the chief thing, namely, that Christ is our salvation, the thing over which all reason and wisdom stumbles."

SALUTATION

1 From Paul, called to be an apostle of Christ Jesus by the will of God, and Sosthenes, our brother, [2]to the church of God that is in Corinth, to those who are sanctified in Christ Jesus, and called to be saints, with all those in every place who call on the name of our Lord Jesus Christ, their Lord and ours. [3]Grace and peace to you from God our Father and the Lord Jesus Christ!

THANKSGIVING

[4]I always thank my God for you because of the grace of God that was given to you in Christ Jesus. [5]For you were made rich in every way in him, in all your speech and in every kind of knowledge—[6]just as the testimony about Christ has been confirmed among you—[7]so that you do not lack any spiritual gift as you wait for the revelation of our Lord Jesus Christ. [8]He will also strengthen you to the end, so that you will be blameless on the day of our Lord Jesus Christ. [9]God is faithful, by whom you were called into fellowship with his son, Jesus Christ our Lord.

DIVISIONS IN THE CHURCH

[10]I urge you, brothers and sisters, by the name of our Lord Jesus Christ, to agree together, to end your divisions, and to be united by the same mind and purpose. [11]For members of Chloe's household have made it clear to me, my brothers and sisters, that there are quarrels among you. [12]Now I mean this, that each of you is saying, "I am with Paul," or "I am with Apollos," or "I am with Cephas," or "I am with Christ." [13]Is Christ divided? Paul wasn't crucified for you, was he? Or were you in fact baptized in the name of Paul? [14]I thank God that I did not baptize any of you except Crispus and Gaius, [15]so that no one can say that you were baptized in my name! [16](I also baptized the household of Stephanus. Otherwise, I do not remember whether I baptized anyone else.) [17]For Christ did not send me to baptize, but to preach the gospel—and not with clever speech, so that the cross of Christ would not become useless.

THE MESSAGE OF THE CROSS

[18]For the message about the cross is foolishness to those who are perishing, but to us who are being saved it is the power of God. [19]For it is written, ***"I will destroy the wisdom of the wise, and I will thwart the cleverness of the intelligent."*** [20]Where is the wise man? Where is the expert in the Mosaic law? Where is the debater of this age? Has God not made the wisdom of the world foolish? [21]For since in the wisdom of God the world by its wisdom did not know God, God was pleased to save those who believe by the foolishness of preaching. [22]For Jews demand miraculous signs and Greeks ask for wisdom, [23]but we preach about a crucified Christ, a stumbling block to Jews and foolishness to Gentiles. [24]But to those who are called, both Jews and Greeks, Christ is the power of God and the wisdom of God. [25]For the foolishness of God is wiser than human wisdom, and the weakness of God is stronger than human strength.

[26]Think about the circumstances of your call, brothers and sisters. Not many were wise by human standards, not many were powerful, not many were born to a privileged position. [27]But God chose what the world thinks foolish to shame the wise, and God chose what the world thinks weak to shame the strong. [28]God chose what is low and despised in the world, what is regarded as nothing, to set aside what is regarded as something,

1:18–25 **The cross of Christ is indeed a stumbling block to those who do not believe, but to the believing it is salvation and life eternal. "Where is the wise man? . . . Where is the debater of this age?" Where is the boasting of those who are called mighty? The Son of God, who was begotten before time began and established all things according to the will of the Father, was conceived in the womb of Mary, according to the appointment of God, of the seed of David, and by the Holy Spirit. For says the scripture, "Behold, the virgin shall conceive and bear a Son, and shall call His name Immanuel" (Isa 7:14 NKJV).**

IGNATIUS OF ANTIOCH
(C. 110)
EPISTLES

29so that no one can boast in his presence. 30He is the reason
you have a relationship with Christ Jesus, who became for us
wisdom from God, and righteousness and sanctification and
redemption, 31so that, as it is written, ***"Let the one who boasts,
boast in the Lord."***

2 When I came to you, brothers and sisters, I did not come
with superior eloquence or wisdom as I proclaimed the testimony of God. 2For I decided to be concerned about nothing
among you except Jesus Christ, and him crucified. 3And I was
with you in weakness and in fear and with much trembling.
4My conversation and my preaching were not with persuasive
words of wisdom, but with a demonstration of the Spirit and
of power, 5so that your faith would not be based on human
wisdom but on the power of God.

WISDOM FROM GOD

6Now we do speak wisdom among the mature, but not a wisdom of this age or of the rulers of this age, who are perishing.
7Instead we speak the wisdom of God, hidden in a mystery, that
God determined before the ages for our glory. 8None of the rulers of this age understood it. If they had known it, they would
not have crucified the Lord of glory. 9But just as it is written,
***"Things that no eye has seen, or ear heard, or mind imagined,
are the things God has prepared for those who love him."*** 10God
has revealed these to us by the Spirit. For the Spirit searches
all things, even the deep things of God. 11For who among men
knows the things of a man except the man's spirit within him?
So too, no one knows the things of God except the Spirit of God.
12Now we have not received the spirit of the world, but the
Spirit who is from God, so that we may know the things that are
freely given to us by God. 13And we speak about these things, not
with words taught us by human wisdom, but with those taught
by the Spirit, explaining spiritual things to spiritual people.
14The unbeliever does not receive the things of the Spirit of
God, for they are foolishness to him. And he cannot understand
them, because they are spiritually discerned. 15The one who is
spiritual discerns all things, yet he himself is understood by no
one. 16***For who has known the mind of the Lord, so as to advise
him?*** But we have the mind of Christ.

IMMATURITY AND SELF-DECEPTION

3 So, brothers and sisters, I could not speak to you as spiritual
people, but instead as people of the flesh, as infants in Christ.
2I fed you milk, not solid food, for you were not yet ready. In fact,
you are still not ready, 3for you are still influenced by the flesh.
For since there is still jealousy and dissension among you, are
you not influenced by the flesh and behaving like unregenerate
people? 4For whenever someone says, "I am with Paul," or "I am
with Apollos," are you not merely human?
5What is Apollos, really? Or what is Paul? Servants through
whom you came to believe, and each of us in the ministry the
Lord gave us. 6I planted, Apollos watered, but God caused it to
grow. 7So neither the one who plants counts for anything, nor
the one who waters, but God who causes the growth. 8The one
who plants and the one who waters work as one, but each will
receive his reward according to his work. 9We are coworkers belonging to God. You are God's field, God's building. 10According
to the grace of God given to me, like a skilled master-builder
I laid a foundation, but someone else builds on it. And each

2:6–16 He who has the Spirit of God to teach him truth, he is not in those things subject to the judgment or correction of any of the wise men of this world. Says the apostle, "Who has known the mind of the Lord, so as to advise him? But we have the mind of Christ." A man who has the mind of Christ is taught by his Spirit; if he should be subject to the judgment and correction of men, that would argue that the mind of the Lord itself was subject to human correction.

JONATHAN EDWARDS
(1703–1758)
THE COMPLETE WORKS

3:5–23 Even when people have taught badly, the name of Christ endures because it is the foundation, although the bad teaching collapses. Nobody can lay another foundation because even if some people are heretics they do not teach except in the name of Christ. Through the dignity of his name, they try to make contradictory and absurd ideas acceptable. Knowing that their thoughts are vain, God rebukes their wisdom in order to prove that they are foolish, showing that what they thought was false is true and vice versa. Human reasoning is unwise and weak, so one should not glory in man but in God whose word cannot be altered. Whatever human beings think apart from God is foolishness.

AMBROSIASTER (C. 330)
COMMENTARY ON PAUL'S EPISTLES

4:6–13 The concern of ministers of Christ and other believers should be this: first that they seek the kingdom of God before all things from their hearts, and second that they are prepared to endure every circumstance for the sake of the name of Christ. Now if it happens that they are held in high esteem and experience peace, that's okay. For even Paul knew not only hunger but also abundance and plenty. But if the Christian faces the cross, persecution, and contempt on account of Christ, this also should be borne and endured in the faith and love of Christ.

WOLFGANG MUSCULUS
(1497–1563)
COMMENTARY ON PAUL'S FIRST LETTER TO THE CORINTHIANS

one must be careful how he builds. 11For no one can lay any
foundation other than what is being laid, which is Jesus Christ.
12If anyone builds on the foundation with gold, silver, precious
stones, wood, hay, or straw, 13each builder's work will be plainly
seen, for the Day will make it clear, because it will be revealed
by fire. And the fire will test what kind of work each has done.
14If what someone has built survives, he will receive a reward.
15If someone's work is burned up, he will suffer loss. He himself
will be saved, but only as through fire.
16Do you not know that you are God's temple and that God's
Spirit lives in you? 17If someone destroys God's temple, God will
destroy him. For God's temple is holy, which is what you are.
18Guard against self-deception, each of you. If someone
among you thinks he is wise in this age, let him become foolish so that he can become wise. 19For the wisdom of this age
is foolishness with God. As it is written, "***He catches the wise in
their craftiness.***" 20And again, "***The Lord knows that the thoughts
of the wise are futile.***" 21So then, no more boasting about mere
mortals! For everything belongs to you, 22whether Paul or Apollos or Cephas or the world or life or death or the present or the
future. Everything belongs to you, 23and you belong to Christ,
and Christ belongs to God.

THE APOSTLES' MINISTRY

4 One should think about us this way—as servants of Christ
and stewards of the mysteries of God. 2Now what is sought in
stewards is that one be found faithful. 3So for me, it is a minor
matter that I am judged by you or by any human court. In fact,
I do not even judge myself. 4For I am not aware of anything
against myself, but I am not acquitted because of this. The one
who judges me is the Lord. 5So then, do not judge anything
before the time. Wait until the Lord comes. He will bring to
light the hidden things of darkness and reveal the motives of
hearts. Then each will receive recognition from God.
6I have applied these things to myself and Apollos because
of you, brothers and sisters, so that through us you may learn
"not to go beyond what is written," so that none of you will be
puffed up in favor of the one against the other. 7For who con-
cedes you any superiority? What do you have that you did not
receive? And if you received it, why do you boast as though you
did not? 8Already you are satisfied! Already you are rich! You
have become kings without us! I wish you had become kings so
that we could reign with you! 9For, I think, God has exhibited
us apostles last of all, as men condemned to die, because we
have become a spectacle to the world, both to angels and to
people. 10We are fools for Christ, but you are wise in Christ!
We are weak, but you are strong! You are distinguished, we are
dishonored! 11To the present hour we are hungry and thirsty,
poorly clothed, brutally treated, and without a roof over our
heads. 12We do hard work, toiling with our own hands. When
we are verbally abused, we respond with a blessing, when persecuted, we endure, 13when people lie about us, we answer in
a friendly manner. We are the world's dirt and scum, even now.

A FATHER'S WARNING

14I am not writing these things to shame you, but to correct
you as my dear children. 15For though you may have 10,000
guardians in Christ, you do not have many fathers, because
I became your father in Christ Jesus through the gospel. 16I

encourage you, then, be imitators of me. [17]For this reason, I have sent Timothy to you, who is my dear and faithful son in the Lord. He will remind you of my ways in Christ, as I teach them everywhere in every church. [18]Some have become arrogant, as if I were not coming to you. [19]But I will come to you soon, if the Lord is willing, and I will find out not only the talk of these arrogant people, but also their power. [20]For the kingdom of God is demonstrated not in idle talk but with power. [21]What do you want? Shall I come to you with a rod of discipline or with love and a spirit of gentleness?

CHURCH DISCIPLINE

5 It is actually reported that sexual immorality exists among you, the kind of immorality that is not permitted even among the Gentiles, so that someone is cohabiting with his father's wife. [2]And you are proud! Shouldn't you have been deeply sorrowful instead and removed the one who did this from among you? [3]For even though I am absent physically, I am present in spirit. And I have already judged the one who did this, just as though I were present. [4]When you gather together in the name of our Lord Jesus, and I am with you in spirit, along with the power of our Lord Jesus, [5]hand this man over to Satan for the destruction of the flesh, so that his spirit may be saved in the day of the Lord.

[6]Your boasting is not good. Don't you know that a little yeast affects the whole batch of dough? [7]Clean out the old yeast so that you may be a new batch of dough—you are, in fact, without yeast. For Christ, our Passover lamb, has been sacrificed. [8]So then, let us celebrate the festival, not with the old yeast, the yeast of vice and evil, but with the bread without yeast, the bread of sincerity and truth.

[9]I wrote you in my letter not to associate with sexually immoral people. [10]In no way did I mean the immoral people of this world, or the greedy and swindlers and idolaters, since you would then have to go out of the world. [11]But now I am writing to you not to associate with anyone who calls himself a Christian who is sexually immoral, or greedy, or an idolater, or verbally abusive, or a drunkard, or a swindler. Do not even eat with such a person. [12]For what do I have to do with judging those outside? Are you not to judge those inside? [13]But God will judge those outside. *Remove the evil person from among you.*

5:1–12 Mark Paul's energy. He suffers them not even to wait for his presence, nor to receive him first and then pass the sentence; but as if on the point of expelling some contagion before it has spread itself into the rest of the body, he hastens to restrain it. And therefore he subjoins the clause, "I have already judged the one who did this, just as though I were present." These things moreover he said to frighten them, as one who knew what was to be done and determined there. Paul permits them not to have any other device. For when the first transgressor escapes punishment, speedily will others also commit the same faults.

CHRYSOSTOM **(C. 347–407)**
HOMILIES ON THE EPISTLES OF PAUL TO THE CORINTHIANS

LAWSUITS

6 When any of you has a legal dispute with another, does he dare go to court before the unrighteous rather than before the saints? [2]Or do you not know that the saints will judge the world? And if the world is to be judged by you, are you not competent to settle trivial suits? [3]Do you not know that we will judge angels? Why not ordinary matters! [4]So if you have ordinary lawsuits, do you appoint as judges those who have no standing in the church? [5]I say this to your shame! Is there no one among you wise enough to settle disputes between fellow Christians? [6]Instead, does a Christian sue a Christian, and do this before unbelievers? [7]The fact that you have lawsuits among yourselves demonstrates that you have already been defeated. Why not rather be wronged? Why not rather be cheated? [8]But you yourselves wrong and cheat, and you do this to your brothers and sisters!

[9]Do you not know that the unrighteous will not inherit the kingdom of God? Do not be deceived! The sexually immoral,

6:1–8 Here Paul begins to reprove another fault among the Corinthians—an excessive fondness for litigation, which took its rise from avarice. Now this reproof consists of two parts. The first is that by bringing their disputes before the tribunals of the wicked, they by this means made the gospel contemptible and exposed it to derision. The second is that while Christians ought to endure injuries with patience, they inflicted injury on others rather than allow themselves to be subjected to any inconvenience.

JOHN CALVIN **(1509–1564)**
COMPLETE COMMENTARY ON THE BIBLE

JOHN WESLEY:

FATHER OF METHODISM

1703–1791

John Wesley was an unassuming figure who left a tremendous legacy. He traveled up to 5,000 miles a year on horseback for decades to preach more than 40,000 sermons. He published over 5,000 pamphlets and books. And he was personally devoted to the methodical pursuit of holiness and the study of scripture. His lifetime of tireless discipleship, evangelism, and service sparked a movement that eventually evolved into a major Christian denomination: Methodism.

Born in 1703 to an Anglican priest near Epworth, England, Wesley studied at Oxford University. He excelled in languages and classical studies and found spiritual resonance with the writings of the early church fathers as he studied for ministry in the Church of England. During this time, along with George Whitefield and his brother, Charles, he founded a small society of dedicated Christians. Derisively labeled the Holy Club by fellow students, this group sought to follow a life of self-denial and service to the world, particularly the poor and incarcerated. Because of their methodical approach to holy living, with self-imposed guidelines for everything from prayer and fasting to scripture study and daily acts of charity, Wesley and his compatriots were sometimes called Methodists. The name stuck. Although Wesley never sought to establish a new denomination, the Methodist societies that proliferated in England and North America became increasingly distinctive in their teachings and practices and ultimately split from the Anglican church after Wesley's death.

Methodism is a "religion of the heart," for spiritual experience is essential for the denomination. Perhaps this emphasis stems from John's own religious experience, in which the knowledge of biblical truth was closely accompanied by an inward response. When he heard Martin Luther's preface to the Epistle to the Romans, he felt his "heart strangely warmed." As he put it: "I felt I did trust in Christ, Christ alone for my salvation and an assurance was given me that he had taken away my sins, even mine, and saved me from the law of sin and death." This experiential focus would be taken on the road through numerous revivals, ranging from fields to fish markets, prisons to town squares. In a journal entry from 1739, Wesley described such an experience amongst 60 believers: "The power of God came mightily upon us, insomuch that many cried out for exceeding joy, and many fell to the ground."

Outward marks of transforming experience, beyond mere intellectual assent to orthodoxy, were central to the Methodist understanding of a genuine Christian life. In his *Nature, Design, and General Rules of the United Societies*, Wesley said Methodists would be marked by three things: "Avoiding all known sin, doing good after [God's] power, and attending all the ordinances of God." Prayer, obedience to scripture, reliance on the Holy Spirit, and a conscious effort toward Christian perfection were all characteristic of the Methodist movement. This latter characteristic in particular was a distinctive emphasis for Wesley, who believed it was possible for believers to be entirely sanctified. He took seriously Jesus' injunction, "Be perfect, as your heavenly Father is perfect" (Matt 5:48). In *A Plain Account of Christian Perfection* he said, "If the love of God fill all the heart, there can be no sin therein," for he was convinced of the "impossibility of being half a Christian." He determined "to be all-devoted to God, to give him all my soul, my body, and my substance," and he expected every other Christian to do the same, insisting "that Christians are saved in this world from all sin, from all unrighteousness, that they are now in such a sense perfect as not to commit sin, and to be freed from evil thoughts and evil tempers."

When Wesley died in 1791, Methodism had grown into an alternative to the Anglican Church in England, and it became the dominant denomination in America by the time of the Civil War. Many Christians today know the joy of a transformative, personal Christian faith thanks to Wesley's pursuit of holiness.

IMPORTANT WORKS

A PLAIN ACCOUNT OF CHRISTIAN PERFECTION

HYMNS AND SACRED POEMS

idolaters, adulterers, passive homosexual partners, practicing
homosexuals, 10thieves, the greedy, drunkards, the verbally
abusive, and swindlers will not inherit the kingdom of God.
11Some of you once lived this way. But you were washed, you
were sanctified, you were justified in the name of the Lord Jesus
Christ and by the Spirit of our God.

FLEE SEXUAL IMMORALITY

12"All things are lawful for me"—but not everything is beneficial.
"All things are lawful for me"—but I will not be controlled by
anything. 13"Food is for the stomach and the stomach is for
food, but God will do away with both." The body is not for sexual
immorality, but for the Lord, and the Lord for the body. 14Now
God indeed raised the Lord and he will raise us by his power.
15Do you not know that your bodies are members of Christ?
Should I take the members of Christ and make them members
of a prostitute? Never! 16Or do you not know that anyone who
is united with a prostitute is one body with her? For it is said,
"The two will become one flesh." 17But the one united with the
Lord is one spirit with him. 18Flee sexual immorality! "Every
sin a person commits is outside of the body"—but the immoral
person sins against his own body. 19Or do you not know that
your body is the temple of the Holy Spirit who is in you, whom
you have from God, and you are not your own? 20For you were
bought at a price. Therefore glorify God with your body.

CELIBACY AND MARRIAGE

7 Now with regard to the issues you wrote about: "It is good
for a man not to have sexual relations with a woman." 2But
because of immoralities, each man should have relations with
his own wife and each woman with her own husband. 3A husband should fulfill his marital responsibility to his wife, and
likewise a wife to her husband. 4It is not the wife who has the

7:1–16 Paul would that all believers who are now unmarried would remain single for the kingdom of heaven's sake. Paul having tasted the sweetness of this liberty wished others to enjoy it as well as himself, but everyone has his proper gift from God. All people cannot receive this saying save they, the happy few, to whom it is given, though our Lord has not left any commandment concerning it. The various stations of life, and various relations to everyone, let him take care to discharge his duty therein. The gospel annuls none of these.

JOHN WESLEY (1703–1791)
EXPLANATORY NOTES ON THE BIBLE

rights to her own body, but the husband. In the same way, it is not the husband who has the rights to his own body, but the wife. [5]Do not deprive each other, except by mutual agreement for a specified time, so that you may devote yourselves to prayer. Then resume your relationship, so that Satan may not tempt you because of your lack of self-control. [6]I say this as a concession, not as a command. [7]I wish that everyone was as I am. But each has his own gift from God, one this way, another that.

[8]To the unmarried and widows I say that it is best for them to remain as I am. [9]But if they do not have self-control, let them get married. For it is better to marry than to burn with sexual desire.

[10]To the married I give this command—not I, but the Lord—a wife should not divorce a husband [11](but if she does, let her remain unmarried, or be reconciled to her husband), and a husband should not divorce his wife.

[12]To the rest I say—I, not the Lord—if a brother has a wife who is not a believer and she is happy to live with him, he should not divorce her. [13]And if a woman has a husband who is not a believer and he is happy to live with her, she should not divorce him. [14]For the unbelieving husband is sanctified because of the wife, and the unbelieving wife because of her husband. Otherwise your children are unclean, but now they are holy. [15]But if the unbeliever wants a divorce, let it take place. In these circumstances the brother or sister is not bound. God has called you in peace. [16]For how do you know, wife, whether you will bring your husband to salvation? Or how do you know, husband, whether you will bring your wife to salvation?

THE CIRCUMSTANCES OF YOUR CALLING

[17]Nevertheless, as the Lord has assigned to each one, as God has called each person, so must he live. I give this sort of direction in all the churches. [18]Was anyone called after he had been circumcised? He should not try to undo his circumcision. Was anyone called who is uncircumcised? He should not get circumcised. [19]Circumcision is nothing and uncircumcision is nothing. Instead, keeping God's commandments is what counts. [20]Let each one remain in that situation in life in which he was called. [21]Were you called as a slave? Do not worry about it. But if indeed you are able to be free, make the most of the opportunity. [22]For the one who was called in the Lord as a slave is the Lord's freedman. In the same way, the one who was called as a free person is Christ's slave. [23]You were bought with a price. Do not become slaves of men. [24]In whatever situation someone was called, brothers and sisters, let him remain in it with God.

REMAINING UNMARRIED

[25]With regard to the question about people who have never married, I have no command from the Lord, but I give my opinion as one shown mercy by the Lord to be trustworthy. [26]Because of the impending crisis I think it best for you to remain as you are. [27]The one bound to a wife should not seek divorce. The one released from a wife should not seek marriage. [28]But if you marry, you have not sinned. And if a virgin marries, she has not sinned. But those who marry will face difficult circumstances, and I am trying to spare you such problems. [29]And I say this, brothers and sisters: The time is short. So then those who have wives should be as those who have none, [30]those with tears like those not weeping, those who rejoice like those not rejoicing,

those who buy like those without possessions, [31]those who use the world as though they were not using it to the full. For the present shape of this world is passing away.

[32]And I want you to be free from concern. An unmarried man is concerned about the things of the Lord, how to please the Lord. [33]But a married man is concerned about the things of the world, how to please his wife, [34]and he is divided. An unmarried woman or a virgin is concerned about the things of the Lord, to be holy both in body and spirit. But a married woman is concerned about the things of the world, how to please her husband. [35]I am saying this for your benefit, not to place a limitation on you, but so that without distraction you may give notable and constant service to the Lord.

[36]If anyone thinks he is acting inappropriately toward his virgin, if she is past the bloom of youth and it seems necessary, he should do what he wishes; he does not sin. Let them marry. [37]But the man who is firm in his commitment, and is under no necessity but has control over his will, and has decided in his own mind to keep his own virgin, does well. [38]So then, the one who marries his own virgin does well, but the one who does not, does better.

[39]A wife is bound as long as her husband is living. But if her husband dies, she is free to marry anyone she wishes (only someone in the Lord). [40]But in my opinion, she will be happier if she remains as she is—and I think that I too have the Spirit of God!

FOOD SACRIFICED TO IDOLS

8 With regard to food sacrificed to idols, we know that "we all have knowledge." Knowledge puffs up, but love builds up. [2]If someone thinks he knows something, he does not yet know to the degree that he needs to know. [3]But if someone loves God, he is known by God.

[4]With regard then to eating food sacrificed to idols, we know that "an idol in this world is nothing," and that "there is no God but one." [5]If after all there are so-called gods, whether in heaven or on earth (as there are many gods and many lords), [6]yet for us there is one God, the Father, from whom are all things and for whom we live, and one Lord, Jesus Christ, through whom are all things and through whom we live.

[7]But this knowledge is not shared by all. And some, by being accustomed to idols in former times, eat this food as an idol sacrifice, and their conscience, because it is weak, is defiled. [8]Now food will not bring us close to God. We are no worse if we do not eat and no better if we do. [9]But be careful that this liberty of yours does not become a hindrance to the weak. [10]For if someone weak sees you who possess knowledge dining in an idol's temple, will not his conscience be "strengthened" to eat food offered to idols? [11]So by your knowledge the weak brother or sister, for whom Christ died, is destroyed. [12]If you sin against your brothers or sisters in this way and wound their weak conscience, you sin against Christ. [13]For this reason, if food causes my brother or sister to sin, I will never eat meat again, so that I may not cause one of them to sin.

THE RIGHTS OF AN APOSTLE

9 Am I not free? Am I not an apostle? Have I not seen Jesus our Lord? Are you not my work in the Lord? [2]If I am not an apostle to others, at least I am to you, for you are the confirming sign of my apostleship in the Lord. [3]This is my defense to those who examine me. [4]Do we not have the right to financial

8:1–13 Paul rebukes those who think they are wiser than the rest by saying that everybody possesses knowledge. If anyone has knowledge but lacks love, not only will he gain nothing more, but he will also be cast down from what he already has. Knowledge is not productive of love, but rather it prevents the unwary from acquiring it by puffing him up and elating him. Arrogance causes divisions, but love draws people together and leads to true knowledge.

CHRYSOSTOM **(C. 347-407)**
HOMILIES ON THE EPISTLES OF PAUL TO THE CORINTHIANS

support? 5 Do we not have the right to the company of a believing wife, like the other apostles and the Lord's brothers and Cephas? 6 Or do only Barnabas and I lack the right not to work? 7 Who ever serves in the army at his own expense? Who plants a vineyard and does not eat its fruit? Who tends a flock and does not consume its milk? 8 Am I saying these things only on the basis of common sense, or does the law not say this as well? 9 For it is written in the law of Moses, "***Do not muzzle an ox while it is treading out the grain.***" God is not concerned here about oxen, is he? 10 Or is he not surely speaking for our benefit? It was written for us, because the one plowing and threshing ought to work in hope of enjoying the harvest. 11 If we sowed spiritual blessings among you, is it too much to reap material things from you? 12 If others receive this right from you, are we not more deserving?

But we have not made use of this right. Instead we endure everything so that we may not be a hindrance to the gospel of Christ. 13 Don't you know that those who serve in the temple eat food from the temple, and those who serve at the altar receive a part of the offerings? 14 In the same way the Lord commanded those who proclaim the gospel to receive their living by the gospel. 15 But I have not used any of these rights. And I am not writing these things so that something will be done for me. In fact, it would be better for me to die than—no one will deprive me of my reason for boasting! 16 For if I preach the gospel, I have no reason for boasting, because I am compelled to do this. Woe to me if I do not preach the gospel! 17 For if I do this voluntarily, I have a reward. But if I do it unwillingly, I am entrusted with a responsibility. 18 What then is my reward? That when I preach the gospel I may offer the gospel free of charge, and so not make full use of my rights in the gospel.

19 For since I am free from all I can make myself a slave to all, in order to gain even more people. 20 To the Jews I became like a Jew to gain the Jews. To those under the law I became like one under the law (though I myself am not under the law) to gain those under the law. 21 To those free from the law I became like one free from the law (though I am not free from God's law but under the law of Christ) to gain those free from the law. 22 To the weak I became weak in order to gain the weak. I have become all things to all people, so that by all means I may save some. 23 I do all these things because of the gospel, so that I can be a participant in it.

24 Do you not know that all the runners in a stadium compete, but only one receives the prize? So run to win. 25 Each competitor must exercise self-control in everything. They do it to receive a perishable crown, but we an imperishable one. 26 So I do not run uncertainly or box like one who hits only air. 27 Instead I subdue my body and make it my slave, so that after preaching to others I myself will not be disqualified.

9:19–23 Paul is free from all human claims because he preached the gospel without getting any praise for it and never wanted anything from anyone, except his or her salvation. Did Paul merely pretend to be all things to all men, in the way that flatterers do? No. He was a man of God and a doctor of the spirit who could diagnose every pain, and with great diligence he tended them and sympathized with them all. We all have something or other in common with everyone. This empathy is what Paul embodied in dealing with each particular person.

AMBROSIASTER (C. 330)
COMMENTARY ON PAUL'S EPISTLES

LEARNING FROM ISRAEL'S FAILURES

10 For I do not want you to be unaware, brothers and sisters, that our fathers were all under the cloud and all passed through the sea, 2 and all were baptized into Moses in the cloud and in the sea, 3 and all ate the same spiritual food, 4 and all drank the same spiritual drink. For they were all drinking from the spiritual rock that followed them, and the rock was Christ. 5 But God was not pleased with most of them, for they were cut down in the wilderness. 6 These things happened as examples for us, so that we will not crave evil things as they did. 7So do not be idolaters, as some of them were. As it is written, "***The people sat down to eat and drink and rose up to play.***" 8And let us not be immoral, as some of them were, and 23,000 died in a single day. 9And let us not put Christ to the test, as some of them did, and were destroyed by snakes. 10And do not complain, as some of them did, and were killed by the destroying angel. 11These things happened to them as examples and were written for our instruction, on whom the ends of the ages have come. 12So let the one who thinks he is standing be careful that he does not fall. 13No trial has overtaken you that is not faced by others. And God is faithful: He will not let you be tried beyond what you are able to bear, but with the trial will also provide a way out so that you may be able to endure it.

AVOID IDOL FEASTS

14So then, my dear friends, flee from idolatry. 15I am speaking to thoughtful people. Consider what I say. 16Is not the cup of blessing that we bless a sharing in the blood of Christ? Is not the bread that we break a sharing in the body of Christ? 17Because there is one bread, we who are many are one body, for we all share the one bread. 18Look at the people of Israel. Are not those who eat the sacrifices partners in the altar? 19Am I saying that idols or food sacrificed to them amount to anything? 20No, I mean that what the pagans sacrifice is to demons and not to God. I do not want you to be partners with demons. 21You cannot drink the cup of the Lord and the cup of demons. You cannot take part in the table of the Lord and the table of demons. 22Or are we trying to provoke the Lord to jealousy? Are we really stronger than he is?

LIVE TO GLORIFY GOD

23"Everything is lawful," but not everything is beneficial. "Everything is lawful," but not everything builds others up. 24Do not seek your own good, but the good of the other person. 25Eat anything that is sold in the marketplace without questions of conscience, 26for *the earth and its abundance are the Lord's.* 27If an unbeliever invites you to dinner and you want to go, eat whatever is served without asking questions of conscience. 28But if someone says to you, "This is from a sacrifice," do not eat, because of the one who told you and because of conscience—29I do not mean yours but the other person's. For why is my freedom being judged by another's conscience? 30If I partake with thankfulness, why am I blamed for the food that I give thanks for? 31So whether you eat or drink, or whatever you do, do everything for the glory of God. 32Do not give offense to Jews or Greeks or to the church of God, 33just as I also try to please everyone in all things. I do not seek my own benefit, but the benefit of many, so that they may be saved.

11 1Be imitators of me, just as I also am of Christ.

WOMEN'S HEAD COVERINGS

2I praise you because you remember me in everything and maintain the traditions just as I passed them on to you. 3But I want you to know that Christ is the head of every man, and the man is the head of a woman, and God is the head of Christ. 4Any man who prays or prophesies with his head covered disgraces his head. 5But any woman who prays or prophesies with her head uncovered disgraces her head, for it is one and the same

10:1–13 He who boasts of grace has little grace to boast of. Some who do this imagine that their graces can keep them, knowing not that the stream must flow constantly from the fountainhead or else the brook will soon be dry. If a continuous stream of oil comes not to the lamp, though it burns brightly today, it will smoke tomorrow, and noxious will be its scent. Take heed that you do not glory in your graces, but let all your glorying and confidence be in Christ and his strength, for this is the only way you can be kept from falling.

CHARLES SPURGEON
(1834–1892)
MORNING AND EVENING

thing as having a shaved head. 6For if a woman will not cover
her head, she should cut off her hair. But if it is disgraceful for
a woman to have her hair cut off or her head shaved, she should
cover her head. 7For a man should not have his head covered,
since he is the image and glory of God. But the woman is the
glory of the man. 8For man did not come from woman, but
woman from man. 9Neither was man created for the sake of
woman, but woman for man. 10For this reason a woman should
have a symbol of authority on her head, because of the angels.
11In any case, in the Lord woman is not independent of man,
nor is man independent of woman. 12For just as woman came
from man, so man comes through woman. But all things come
from God. 13Judge for yourselves: Is it proper for a woman to
pray to God with her head uncovered? 14Does not nature itself
teach you that if a man has long hair, it is a disgrace for him,
15but if a woman has long hair, it is her glory? For her hair is
given to her for a covering. 16If anyone intends to quarrel about
this, we have no other practice, nor do the churches of God.

THE LORD'S SUPPER

17Now in giving the following instruction I do not praise you,
because you come together not for the better but for the worse.
18For in the first place, when you come together as a church
I hear there are divisions among you, and in part I believe it.
19For there must in fact be divisions among you, so that those
of you who are approved may be evident. 20Now when you come
together at the same place, you are not really eating the Lord's
Supper. 21For when it is time to eat, everyone proceeds with his
own supper. One is hungry and another becomes drunk. 22Do
you not have houses so that you can eat and drink? Or are you
trying to show contempt for the church of God by shaming
those who have nothing? What should I say to you? Should I
praise you? I will not praise you for this!

23For I received from the Lord what I also passed on to you,
that the Lord Jesus on the night in which he was betrayed took
bread, 24and after he had given thanks he broke it and said, "This
is my body, which is for you. Do this in remembrance of me." 25In
the same way, he also took the cup after supper, saying, "This cup
is the new covenant in my blood. Do this, every time you drink
it, in remembrance of me." 26For every time you eat this bread
and drink the cup, you proclaim the Lord's death until he comes.

27For this reason, whoever eats the bread or drinks the cup of
the Lord in an unworthy manner will be guilty of the body and
blood of the Lord. 28A person should examine himself first, and
in this way let him eat the bread and drink of the cup. 29For the
one who eats and drinks without careful regard for the body eats
and drinks judgment against himself. 30That is why many of you
are weak and sick, and quite a few are dead. 31But if we examined
ourselves, we would not be judged. 32But when we are judged by
the Lord, we are disciplined so that we may not be condemned
with the world. 33So then, my brothers and sisters, when you come
together to eat, wait for one another. 34If anyone is hungry, let
him eat at home, so that when you assemble it does not lead to
judgment. I will give directions about other matters when I come.

11:23–34 Christ is near each of us that we may make him the very food of our spirits. The true life of the believer is just the feeding of our souls upon him, our minds accepting, meditating upon, digesting the truths that are incarnated in Jesus, our hearts feeding upon the love that is so tender and close, the whole nature finding its nourishment in Jesus Christ. You are Christians in the measure in which the very strength of your spirits and sustenance of all your faculties are found in loving communion with the living Lord.

ALEXANDER MACLAREN
(1826–1910)
EXPOSITIONS OF THE HOLY SCRIPTURES

SPIRITUAL GIFTS

12 With regard to spiritual gifts, brothers and sisters, I do
not want you to be uninformed. 2You know that when
you were pagans you were often led astray by speechless idols,

however you were led. [3]So I want you to understand that no one speaking by the Spirit of God says, "Jesus is cursed," and no one can say, "Jesus is Lord," except by the Holy Spirit.

[4]Now there are different gifts, but the same Spirit. [5]And there are different ministries, but the same Lord. [6]And there are different results, but the same God who produces all of them in everyone. [7]To each person the manifestation of the Spirit is given for the benefit of all. [8]For one person is given through the Spirit the message of wisdom, and another the message of knowledge according to the same Spirit, [9]to another faith by the same Spirit, and to another gifts of healing by the one Spirit, [10]to another performance of miracles, to another prophecy, and to another discernment of spirits, to another different kinds of tongues, and to another the interpretation of tongues. [11]It is one and the same Spirit, distributing as he decides to each person, who produces all these things.

DIFFERENT MEMBERS IN ONE BODY

[12]For just as the body is one and yet has many members, and all the members of the body—though many—are one body, so too is Christ. [13]For in one Spirit we were all baptized into one body. Whether Jews or Greeks or slaves or free, we were all made to drink of the one Spirit. [14]For in fact the body is not a single member, but many. [15]If the foot says, "Since I am not a hand, I am not part of the body," it does not lose its membership in the body because of that. [16]And if the ear says, "Since I am not an eye, I am not part of the body," it does not lose its membership in the body because of that. [17]If the whole body were an eye, what part would do the hearing? If the whole were an ear, what part would exercise the sense of smell? [18]But as a matter of fact, God has placed each of the members in the body just as he decided. [19]If they were all the same member, where would the body be? [20]So now there are many members, but one body. [21]The eye cannot say to the hand, "I do not need you," nor in turn can the head say to the foot, "I do not need you." [22]On the contrary, those members that seem to be weaker are essential, [23]and those members we consider less honorable we clothe with greater honor, and our unpresentable members are clothed with dignity, [24]but our presentable members do not need this. Instead, God has blended together the body, giving greater honor to the lesser member, [25]so that there may be no division in the body, but the members may have mutual concern for one another. [26]If one member suffers, everyone suffers with it. If a member is honored, all rejoice with it.

[27]Now you are Christ's body, and each of you is a member of it. [28]And God has placed in the church first apostles, second prophets, third teachers, then miracles, gifts of healing, helps, gifts of leadership, different kinds of tongues. [29]Not all are apostles, are they? Not all are prophets, are they? Not all are teachers, are they? Not all perform miracles, do they? [30]Not all have gifts of healing, do they? Not all speak in tongues, do they? Not all interpret, do they? [31]But you should be eager for the greater gifts.

And now I will show you a way that is beyond comparison.

THE WAY OF LOVE

13 If I speak in the tongues of men and of angels, but I do not have love, I am a noisy gong or a clanging cymbal. [2]And if I have prophecy, and know all mysteries and all knowledge, and

12:1–11 The Holy Spirit, being one and of one nature and indivisible, imparts to each one his grace "as he decides." Though the Spirit is one in nature, yet by the will of God and in the name of the Son, he brings about many virtuous effects. For he employs the tongue of one for wisdom, illumines the soul of another by prophecy, to another he grants the power of driving out devils, to another the gift of interpreting the sacred scriptures. He acts differently in different persons, though he himself is not diverse.

CYRIL OF JERUSALEM
(C. 313–386)
CATECHETICAL LECTURES

13:1–13 Faith has its seat purely in the understanding of divine things and an apprehension of their reality. Hope has its seat both in the understanding and natural will or inclination and apprehends not only the reality of divine things but also our interest in them. Love has its seat in the spiritual will and apprehends divine things as amiable. These three, when joined together and united in one, constitute saving faith, or the soul's savingly embracing Christ and Christianity. But of these three constituents of justifying faith, love is the greatest; the other two are the body, that is, the soul.

JONATHAN EDWARDS
(1703–1758)
THE COMPLETE WORKS

if I have all faith so that I can remove mountains, but do not have love, I am nothing. 3If I give away everything I own, and if I give over my body in order to boast, but do not have love, I receive no benefit.

4Love is patient, love is kind, it is not envious. Love does not brag, it is not puffed up. 5It is not rude, it is not self-serving, it is not easily angered or resentful. 6It is not glad about injustice, but rejoices in the truth. 7It bears all things, believes all things, hopes all things, endures all things.

8Love never ends. But if there are prophecies, they will be set aside; if there are tongues, they will cease; if there is knowledge, it will be set aside. 9For we know in part, and we prophesy in part, 10but when what is perfect comes, the partial will be set aside. 11When I was a child, I talked like a child, I thought like a child, I reasoned like a child. But when I became an adult, I set aside childish ways. 12For now we see in a mirror indirectly, but then we will see face to face. Now I know in part, but then I will know fully, just as I have been fully known. 13And now these three remain: faith, hope, and love. But the greatest of these is love.

PROPHECY AND TONGUES

14 Pursue love and be eager for the spiritual gifts, especially that you may prophesy. 2For the one speaking in a tongue does not speak to people but to God, for no one understands; he is speaking mysteries by the Spirit. 3But the one who prophesies speaks to people for their strengthening, encouragement, and consolation. 4The one who speaks in a tongue builds himself up, but the one who prophesies builds up the church. 5I wish you all spoke in tongues, but even more that you would prophesy. The one who prophesies is greater than the one who speaks in tongues, unless he interprets so that the church may be strengthened.

6Now, brothers and sisters, if I come to you speaking in tongues, how will I help you unless I speak to you with a revelation or with knowledge or prophecy or teaching? 7It is similar for lifeless things that make a sound, like a flute or harp. Unless they make a distinction in the notes, how can what is played on the flute or harp be understood? 8If, for example, the trumpet makes an unclear sound, who will get ready for battle? 9It is the same for you. If you do not speak clearly with your tongue, how will anyone know what is being said? For you will be speaking into the air. 10There are probably many kinds of languages in the world, and none is without meaning. 11If then I do not know the meaning of a language, I will be a foreigner to the speaker and the speaker a foreigner to me. 12It is the same with you. Since you are eager for manifestations of the Spirit, seek to abound in order to strengthen the church.

13So then, one who speaks in a tongue should pray that he may interpret. 14If I pray in a tongue, my spirit prays, but my mind is unproductive. 15What should I do? I will pray with my spirit, but I will also pray with my mind. I will sing praises with my spirit, but I will also sing praises with my mind. 16Otherwise, if you are praising God with your spirit, how can someone without the gift say "Amen" to your thanksgiving, since he does not know what you are saying? 17For you are certainly giving thanks well, but the other person is not strengthened. 18I thank God that I speak in tongues more than all of you, 19but in the church I want to speak five words with my mind to instruct others, rather than ten thousand words in a tongue.

20Brothers and sisters, do not be children in your thinking.
Instead, be infants in evil, but in your thinking be mature. 21It
is written in the law: ***"By people with strange tongues and by the***
lips of strangers I will speak to this people, yet not even in this way
will they listen to me," says the Lord. 22So then, tongues are a
sign not for believers but for unbelievers. Prophecy, however, is
not for unbelievers but for believers. 23So if the whole church
comes together and all speak in tongues, and unbelievers or
uninformed people enter, will they not say that you have lost
your minds? 24But if all prophesy, and an unbeliever or uninformed person enters, he will be convicted by all, he will be
called to account by all. 25The secrets of his heart are disclosed,
and in this way he will fall down with his face to the ground and
worship God, declaring, "God is really among you."

CHURCH ORDER

26What should you do then, brothers and sisters? When you
come together, each one has a song, has a lesson, has a revelation, has a tongue, has an interpretation. Let all these things be
done for the strengthening of the church. 27If someone speaks
in a tongue, it should be two, or at the most three, one after
the other, and someone must interpret. 28But if there is no
interpreter, he should be silent in the church. Let him speak
to himself and to God. 29Two or three prophets should speak
and the others should evaluate what is said. 30And if someone
sitting down receives a revelation, the person who is speaking
should conclude. 31For you can all prophesy one after another,
so all can learn and be encouraged. 32Indeed, the spirits of the
prophets are subject to the prophets, 33for God is not characterized by disorder but by peace.

As in all the churches of the saints, 34the women should be
silent in the churches, for they are not permitted to speak.
Rather, let them be in submission, as in fact the law says. 35If
they want to find out about something, they should ask their
husbands at home, because it is disgraceful for a woman to
speak in church. 36Did the word of God begin with you, or did
it come to you alone?

37If anyone considers himself a prophet or spiritual person,
he should acknowledge that what I write to you is the Lord's
command. 38If someone does not recognize this, he is not recognized. 39So then, brothers and sisters, be eager to prophesy,
and do not forbid anyone from speaking in tongues. 40And do
everything in a decent and orderly manner.

CHRIST'S RESURRECTION

15 Now I want to make clear for you, brothers and sisters, the
gospel that I preached to you, that you received and on
which you stand, 2and by which you are being saved, if you hold
firmly to the message I preached to you—unless you believed
in vain. 3For I passed on to you as of first importance what I
also received—that Christ died for our sins according to the
scriptures, 4and that he was buried, and that he was raised on
the third day according to the scriptures, 5and that he appeared
to Cephas, then to the twelve. 6Then he appeared to more than
500 of the brothers and sisters at one time, most of whom are
still alive, though some have fallen asleep. 7Then he appeared
to James, then to all the apostles. 8Last of all, as though to one
born at the wrong time, he appeared to me also. 9For I am the
least of the apostles, unworthy to be called an apostle, because

14:26–40 I have exercised myself in the holy scriptures and godly matters for more than 48 years now and never abandoned the grace of God. I never got bogged down hearing, learning, and following until the day of the death of my dear and good husband. I could now teach others and with the elderly Anna prophesy about Christ to those who are waiting for redemption and praise the Lord. But considering that I must appropriately be submissive under the man's office, according to the teaching of Saint Paul, I myself seek to hear others and to be exhorted as far as they speak the truth! But where that is not so, then I would tell you and not keep silent but speak, point out, and answer your wrong preaching and insulting words about the innocent.

KATHARINA SCHÜTZ ZELL
(C. 1497–1562)
LETTER TO CASPAR SCHWENCKFELD

15:1–19 Paul ascribes to divine grace all that was valuable in him. True believers, though not ignorant of what the Lord has done for, in, and by them, yet when they look at their whole conduct and their obligations they are led to feel that none are so worthless as they are. All true Christians believe that Jesus Christ, him crucified, and then risen from the dead is the sun and substance of Christianity. All the apostles agreed in this testimony; by this faith they lived, and in this faith they died.

MATTHEW HENRY **(1662–1714)**
COMMENTARY ON THE WHOLE BIBLE

I persecuted the church of God. 10 But by the grace of God I am
what I am, and his grace to me has not been in vain. In fact,
I worked harder than all of them—yet not I, but the grace of
God with me. 11 Whether then it was I or they, this is the way
we preach and this is the way you believed.

NO RESURRECTION?

12 Now if Christ is being preached as raised from the dead,
how can some of you say there is no resurrection of the dead?
13 But if there is no resurrection of the dead, then not even
Christ has been raised. 14 And if Christ has not been raised, then
our preaching is futile and your faith is empty. 15 Also, we are
found to be false witnesses about God, because we have testified against God that he raised Christ from the dead, when in
reality he did not raise him, if indeed the dead are not raised.
16 For if the dead are not raised, then not even Christ has been
raised. 17 And if Christ has not been raised, your faith is useless;
you are still in your sins. 18 Furthermore, those who have fallen
asleep in Christ have also perished. 19 For if only in this life we
have hope in Christ, we should be pitied more than anyone.

20 But now Christ has been raised from the dead, the firstfruits of those who have fallen asleep. 21 For since death came
through a man, the resurrection of the dead also came through
a man. 22 For just as in Adam all die, so also in Christ all will be
made alive. 23 But each in his own order: Christ, the firstfruits;
then when Christ comes, those who belong to him. 24 Then
comes the end, when he hands over the kingdom to God the
Father, when he has brought to an end all rule and all authority
and power. 25 For he must reign until he has put all his enemies
under his feet. 26 The last enemy to be eliminated is death. 27 For
he has put everything in subjection under his feet. But when it
says "everything" has been put in subjection, it is clear that this
does not include the one who put everything in subjection to
him. 28 And when all things are subjected to him, then the Son
himself will be subjected to the one who subjected everything
to him, so that God may be all in all.

29 Otherwise, what will those do who are baptized for the
dead? If the dead are not raised at all, then why are they baptized for them? 30 Why too are we in danger every hour? 31 Every
day I am in danger of death! This is as sure as my boasting in
you, which I have in Christ Jesus our Lord. 32 If from a human
point of view I fought with wild beasts at Ephesus, what did it
benefit me? If the dead are not raised, *let us eat and drink, for
tomorrow we die.* 33 Do not be deceived: "Bad company corrupts
good morals." 34 Sober up as you should, and stop sinning! For
some have no knowledge of God—I say this to your shame!

THE RESURRECTION BODY

35 But someone will say, "How are the dead raised? With what
kind of body will they come?" 36 Fool! What you sow will not
come to life unless it dies. 37 And what you sow is not the body
that is to be, but a bare seed—perhaps of wheat or something
else. 38 But God gives it a body just as he planned, and to each of
the seeds a body of its own. 39 All flesh is not the same: People
have one flesh, animals have another, birds and fish another.
40 And there are heavenly bodies and earthly bodies. The glory of the heavenly body is one sort and the earthly another.
41 There is one glory of the sun, and another glory of the moon
and another glory of the stars, for star differs from star in glory.

42It is the same with the resurrection of the dead. What is
sown is perishable, what is raised is imperishable. 43It is sown in
dishonor, it is raised in glory; it is sown in weakness, it is raised
in power; 44it is sown a natural body, it is raised a spiritual body.
If there is a natural body, there is also a spiritual body. 45So also
it is written, "***The first man, Adam, became a living person***"; the
last Adam became a life-giving spirit. 46However, the spiritual
did not come first, but the natural, and then the spiritual. 47The
first man is from the earth, made of dust; the second man is
from heaven. 48Like the one made of dust, so too are those
made of dust, and like the one from heaven, so too those who
are heavenly. 49And just as we have borne the image of the man
of dust, let us also bear the image of the man of heaven.

50Now this is what I am saying, brothers and sisters: Flesh and
blood cannot inherit the kingdom of God, nor does the perishable
inherit the imperishable. 51Listen, I will tell you a mystery: We
will not all sleep, but we will all be changed—52in a moment, in
the blinking of an eye, at the last trumpet. For the trumpet will
sound, and the dead will be raised imperishable, and we will
be changed. 53For this perishable body must put on the imperishable, and this mortal body must put on immortality. 54Now
when this perishable puts on the imperishable, and this mortal
puts on immortality, then the saying that is written will happen,

"***Death has been swallowed up in victory.***"
55 "***Where, O death, is your victory?***
Where, O death, is your sting?"

56The sting of death is sin, and the power of sin is the law. 57But
thanks be to God, who gives us the victory through our Lord
Jesus Christ! 58So then, dear brothers and sisters, be firm. Do
not be moved! Always be outstanding in the work of the Lord,
knowing that your labor is not in vain in the Lord.

A COLLECTION TO AID JEWISH CHRISTIANS

16 With regard to the collection for the saints, please follow
the directions that I gave to the churches of Galatia: 2On
the first day of the week, each of you should set aside some
income and save it to the extent that God has blessed you, so
that a collection will not have to be made when I come. 3Then,
when I arrive, I will send those whom you approve with letters
of explanation to carry your gift to Jerusalem. 4And if it seems
advisable that I should go also, they will go with me.

PAUL'S PLANS TO VISIT

5But I will come to you after I have gone through Macedonia—for I will be going through Macedonia—6and perhaps I
will stay with you, or even spend the winter, so that you can
send me on my journey, wherever I go. 7For I do not want to see
you now in passing, since I hope to spend some time with you,
if the Lord allows. 8But I will stay in Ephesus until Pentecost,
9because a door of great opportunity stands wide open for me,
but there are many opponents.

10Now if Timothy comes, see that he has nothing to fear
among you, for he is doing the Lord's work, as I am too. 11So
then, let no one treat him with contempt. But send him on his
way in peace so that he may come to me. For I am expecting
him with the brothers.

12With regard to our brother Apollos: I strongly encouraged
him to visit you with the other brothers, but it was simply not his
intention to come now. He will come when he has the opportunity.

16:13–17 Paul's readers were to be watchful in case they were secretly attacked in their faith. They were to stand firm, being bold in confessing what they had been taught. They were to be strong in both word and deed because it is the right combination of these that enables people to mature.

AMBROSIASTER (C. 330)
COMMENTARY ON PAUL'S EPISTLES

FINAL CHALLENGE AND BLESSING

13Stay alert, stand firm in the faith, show courage, be strong.
14Everything you do should be done in love.
15Now, brothers and sisters, you know about the household
of Stephanus, that as the first converts of Achaia, they devoted
themselves to ministry for the saints. I urge you 16also to submit
to people like this, and to everyone who cooperates in the work
and labors hard. 17I was glad about the arrival of Stephanus,
Fortunatus, and Achaicus because they have supplied the fellowship with you that I lacked. 18For they refreshed my spirit
and yours. So then, recognize people like this.
19The churches in the province of Asia send greetings to
you. Aquila and Prisca greet you warmly in the Lord, with the
church that meets in their house. 20All the brothers and sisters
send greetings. Greet one another with a holy kiss.
21I, Paul, send this greeting with my own hand.
22Let anyone who has no love for the Lord be accursed. Our
Lord, come!
23The grace of the Lord Jesus be with you.
24My love be with all of you in Christ Jesus.

AUTHOR	AUDIENCE	DATE	PURPOSE	THEMES
Paul	The church in Corinth	AD 55	Paul wrote another letter to the Corinthian believers to clarify aspects of the faith and confront the false apostles who had created division within the community.	The person and work of Christ; nature of the gospel; and Christian life and generosity

Evidence within the letter itself suggests that this epistle from Paul to Christians in Corinth was probably not the second letter he wrote. It was probably the third or fourth such letter. He wrote what we call the Second Epistle to the Corinthians in order to defend his ministry from the arrival of "super-apostles" (11:5) who leveled accusations against Paul and preached a different Jesus, a different Spirit, and a different gospel.

After opening with an apology for not yet coming to visit, Paul expresses his joy at the Corinthians' repentance and the fruit they've experienced as a result of their obedience to the truth found in his previous letter. Then he "focuses on the stubbornness of those who remain incorrigible," as Ambrosiaster explained. Throughout the letter we learn more about the nature of the gospel and about Paul's own suffering on its behalf, both of which inform our own faith.

We discover in Paul's letter important truths about Christ—truths that were especially vital to the early church. For one, Christ became incarnate: "Although he was rich, he became poor for your sakes, so that you by his poverty could become rich" (8:9). That the Son of God came to earth and lived as a human is central to Christ's identity and purpose. He is the "image of God" (4:4) in whose face shines the glory of God (4:6). Becoming poor for our sakes didn't end with his becoming human but with his death on the cross. Christ came so that God could "[reconcile] us to himself through Christ" (5:18). How did he accomplish this? "God made the one who did not know sin to be sin for us, so that in him we would become the righteousness of God" (5:21).

Paul emphasized an important aspect of the gospel in 2 Corinthians: "If anyone is in Christ, he is a new creation; what is old has passed away—look, what is new has come!" (5:17). "In Christ," an important theological concept for Paul, we are given a new nature so that who and what we were before Christ have been transformed into something entirely new. This is good news indeed, made possible because we have been "reconciled"—a relational term that describes friendship where there was once enmity. And all of this was accomplished by God who "in Christ . . . was reconciling the world to himself, not counting people's trespasses against them" (5:19). This reflects the Reformers' cry *Sola Christus*, Christ alone. For it is only in and through Christ's work on the cross that we experience reconciliation with God.

2 CORINTHIANS

We have been made ambassadors (5:18) of this reconciliation. This is a political term meant to remind us of our new allegiance to Christ and his kingdom. Mysteriously, we have been given a "ministry of reconciliation" (5:18). Our message is the same as Paul's: "Be reconciled to God!" (5:20). In the rest of the letter, Paul explained how it looks to take on such a ministry: Comfort for others is rooted in God's own comfort for us; generosity toward others is rooted in Christ's own selflessness; such a ministry is parental so that we give of ourselves as "parents for their children" (12:14).

As he did in his other letters, Paul cast a strong vision of the Christian life for the Corinthians. We are to come out from the world and be separate, guarding ourselves against becoming "partners with those who do not believe" (6:14); we are to live life deliberately, "[cleansing] ourselves from everything that could defile the body and the spirit, and thus accomplish holiness out of reverence for God" (7:1); in this life, "even if our physical body is wearing away, our inner person is being renewed day by day" (4:16); and the more we suffer and experience weakness, the more we understand the truth of Christ's words: "My grace is enough for you, for my power is made perfect in weakness" (12:9).

One final aspect of the Christian life Paul addressed is generosity, which was one of the reasons he wrote the epistle in the first place. He wanted to impress upon this church how generously the poor Macedonians gave to his collection for impoverished believers in Jerusalem (see Rom 15:26). Paul compares such generosity to Christ's own generosity—he became poor "that you by his poverty could become rich" (8:9). It's dependent upon "eagerness" (8:12), rather than what one does or does not have, and should come out of a heart that gives "as he has decided in his heart, not reluctantly or under compulsion" (9:7).

The second epistle of Paul the apostle to the Corinthians explores the reality that in Christ we have been reconciled to God and have experienced the new-creation life he promised. At the end of his letter, Paul provides an apt exhortation: "Put yourselves to the test to see if you are in the faith; examine yourselves! Or do you not recognize regarding yourselves that Jesus Christ is in you"? (13:5).

SALUTATION

1 From Paul, an apostle of Christ Jesus by the will of God, and
Timothy our brother, to the church of God that is in Corinth,
with all the saints who are in all Achaia. [2]Grace and peace to
you from God our Father and the Lord Jesus Christ!

THANKSGIVING FOR GOD'S COMFORT

[3]Blessed is the God and Father of our Lord Jesus Christ, the
Father of mercies and God of all comfort, [4]who comforts us in all
our troubles so that we may be able to comfort those experiencing any trouble with the comfort with which we ourselves are
comforted by God. [5]For just as the sufferings of Christ overflow
toward us, so also our comfort through Christ overflows to you.
[6]But if we are afflicted, it is for your comfort and salvation; if
we are comforted, it is for your comfort that you experience
in your patient endurance of the same sufferings that we also
suffer. [7]And our hope for you is steadfast because we know
that as you share in our sufferings, so also you will share in
our comfort. [8]For we do not want you to be unaware, brothers
and sisters, regarding the affliction that happened to us in the
province of Asia, that we were burdened excessively, beyond
our strength, so that we despaired even of living. [9]Indeed we
felt as if the sentence of death had been passed against us, so
that we would not trust in ourselves but in God who raises the
dead. [10]He delivered us from so great a risk of death, and he will
deliver us. We have set our hope on him that he will deliver us
yet again, [11]as you also join in helping us by prayer, so that many
people may give thanks to God on our behalf for the gracious
gift given to us through the help of many.

1:8–9 Let us remember the labors of those who went before us, and what we endure will not be hard, for we must through many tribulations enter into the kingdom of God. "We were burdened excessively, beyond our strength, so that we despaired even of living. Indeed we felt as if the sentence of death had been passed against us, so that we would not trust in ourselves but in God." And yet the sufferings of this present time are not worthy to be compared with the supervening glory that shall be revealed in us. How then can we who are weak sheep pass without labor through the heat of this world where we know that even rams have suffered under heavy toil?

GREGORY THE GREAT
(C. 540–604)
LETTERS

PAUL DEFENDS HIS CHANGED PLANS

[12]For our reason for confidence is this: The testimony of our conscience, that with pure motives and sincerity which are from
God—not by human wisdom but by the grace of God—we conducted ourselves in the world, and all the more toward you. [13]For we
do not write you anything other than what you can read and also
understand. But I hope that you will understand completely [14]just
as also you have partly understood us, that we are your source of
pride just as you also are ours in the day of the Lord Jesus. [15]And
with this confidence I intended to come to you first so that you
would get a second opportunity to see us, [16]and through your help
to go on into Macedonia and then from Macedonia to come back
to you and be helped on our way into Judea by you. [17]Therefore
when I was planning to do this, I did not do so without thinking
about what I was doing, did I? Or do I make my plans according
to mere human standards so that I would be saying both "Yes,
yes" and "No, no" at the same time? [18]But as God is faithful, our
message to you is not "Yes" and "No." [19]For the Son of God, Jesus
Christ, the one who was proclaimed among you by us—by me and
Silvanus and Timothy—was not "Yes" and "No," but it has always
been "Yes" in him. [20]For every one of God's promises are "Yes" in
him; therefore also through him the "Amen" is spoken, to the
glory we give to God. [21]But it is God who establishes us together
with you in Christ and who anointed us, [22]who also sealed us and
gave us the Spirit in our hearts as a down payment.

WHY PAUL POSTPONED HIS VISIT

[23]Now I appeal to God as my witness, that to spare you I did
not come again to Corinth. [24]I do not mean that we rule over

your faith, but we are workers with you for your joy, because
2 by faith you stand firm. 1So I made up my own mind not to
pay you another painful visit. 2For if I make you sad, who
would be left to make me glad but the one I caused to be sad?
3And I wrote this very thing to you, so that when I came I would
not have sadness from those who ought to make me rejoice,
since I am confident in you all that my joy would be yours. 4For
out of great distress and anguish of heart I wrote to you with
many tears, not to make you sad, but to let you know the love
that I have especially for you. 5But if anyone has caused sadness,
he has not saddened me alone, but to some extent (not to exaggerate) he has saddened all of you as well. 6This punishment
on such an individual by the majority is enough for him, 7so
that now instead you should rather forgive and comfort him.
This will keep him from being overwhelmed by excessive grief
to the point of despair. 8Therefore I urge you to reaffirm your
love for him. 9For this reason also I wrote you: to test you to see
if you are obedient in everything. 10If you forgive anyone for
anything, I also forgive him—for indeed what I have forgiven
(if I have forgiven anything) I did so for you in the presence of
Christ, 11so that we may not be exploited by Satan (for we are
not ignorant of his schemes). 12Now when I arrived in Troas
to proclaim the gospel of Christ, even though the Lord had
opened a door of opportunity for me, 13I had no relief in my
spirit, because I did not find my brother Titus there. So I said
goodbye to them and set out for Macedonia.

APOSTOLIC MINISTRY

14But thanks be to God who always leads us in triumphal procession in Christ and who makes known through us the fragrance
that consists of the knowledge of him in every place. 15For we
are a sweet aroma of Christ to God among those who are being
saved and among those who are perishing—16to the latter an
odor from death to death, but to the former a fragrance from
life to life. And who is adequate for these things? 17For we are
not like so many others, hucksters who peddle the word of God
for profit, but we are speaking in Christ before God as persons
of sincerity, as persons sent from God.

A LIVING LETTER

3 Are we beginning to commend ourselves again? We don't
need letters of recommendation to you or from you as some
other people do, do we? 2You yourselves are our letter, written
on our hearts, known and read by everyone, 3revealing that
you are a letter of Christ, delivered by us, written not with ink
but by the Spirit of the living God, not *on stone tablets* but on
tablets of human hearts.

4Now we have such confidence in God through Christ. 5Not
that we are adequate in ourselves to consider anything as if it
were coming from ourselves, but our adequacy is from God,
6who made us adequate to be servants of a new covenant not
based on the letter but on the Spirit, for the letter kills, but
the Spirit gives life.

THE GREATER GLORY OF THE SPIRIT'S MINISTRY

7But if the ministry that produced death—carved in letters *on
stone tablets*—came with glory, so that the Israelites could not
keep their eyes fixed on the face of Moses because of the glory
of his face (a glory which was made ineffective), 8how much

2:14–17 Whether a person is saved or lost, the gospel continues to have its own power. The light, even when it blinds someone, is still light. Honey, though it is bitter to those who are sick, is still sweet. So also the gospel has a sweet savor to all, even if those who do not believe it are lost. If anyone is lost he has only himself to blame. Soothing ointment is said to suffocate pigs. Light is blinding to the weak. It is in the nature of good things not only to correct what is close to them but also to destroy the opposite, and in this way their power is displayed.

CHRYSOSTOM **(C. 347–407)**
HOMILIES ON THE EPISTLES OF PAUL TO THE CORINTHIANS

3:7–18 The law is our tutor; a tutor brings us to the master; Christ is our only Master. A tutor is feared, the master points out the way to salvation. Fear brings us to liberty, liberty to faith, faith to love, love obtains adoption, adoption an inheritance. Therefore where there is faith there is freedom, for a slave acts in fear, a free man through faith. The one is under the letter, the other under grace; the one in slavery, the other in the spirit; for "where the Spirit of the Lord is present, there is freedom."

AMBROSE **(C. 339–C. 397)**
LETTERS

more glorious will the ministry of the Spirit be? 9For if there
was glory in the ministry that produced condemnation, how
much more does the ministry that produces righteousness
excel in glory! 10For indeed, what had been glorious now has
no glory because of the tremendously greater glory of what
replaced it. 11For if what was made ineffective came with glory,
how much more has what remains come in glory! 12Therefore,
since we have such a hope, we behave with great boldness, 13and
not like Moses who used to put a veil over his face to keep the
Israelites from staring at the result of the glory that was made
ineffective. 14But their minds were closed. For to this very day,
the same veil remains when they hear the old covenant read. It
has not been removed because only in Christ is it taken away.
15But until this very day whenever Moses is read, a veil lies over
their minds, 16but when one turns to the Lord, *the veil is removed.*
17Now the Lord is the Spirit, and where the Spirit of the Lord
is present, there is freedom. 18And we all, with unveiled faces
reflecting the glory of the Lord, are being transformed into the
same image from one degree of glory to another, which is from
the Lord, who is the Spirit.

PAUL'S PERSEVERANCE IN MINISTRY

4 Therefore, since we have this ministry, just as God has shown
us mercy, we do not become discouraged. 2But we have rejected shameful hidden deeds, not behaving with deceptiveness
or distorting the word of God, but by open proclamation of the
truth we commend ourselves to everyone's conscience before
God. 3But even if our gospel is veiled, it is veiled only to those
who are perishing, 4among whom the god of this age has blinded
the minds of those who do not believe so they would not see
the light of the glorious gospel of Christ, who is the image of
God. 5For we do not proclaim ourselves, but Jesus Christ as Lord,
and ourselves as your slaves for Jesus' sake. 6For God, who said
"*Let light shine out of darkness,*" is the one who shined in our
hearts to give us the light of the glorious knowledge of God in
the face of Christ.

AN ETERNAL WEIGHT OF GLORY

7But we have this treasure in clay jars, so that the extraordinary power belongs to God and does not come from us. 8We
are experiencing trouble on every side, but are not crushed; we
are perplexed, but not driven to despair; 9we are persecuted,
but not abandoned; we are knocked down, but not destroyed,
10always carrying around in our body the death of Jesus, so that
the life of Jesus may also be made visible in our body. 11For we
who are alive are constantly being handed over to death for
Jesus' sake, so that the life of Jesus may also be made visible in
our mortal body. 12As a result, death is at work in us, but life
is at work in you. 13But since we have the same spirit of faith
as that shown in what has been written, "***I believed; therefore***
I spoke," we also believe, therefore we also speak. 14We do so
because we know that the one who raised up Jesus will also raise
us up with Jesus and will bring us with you into his presence.
15For all these things are for your sake, so that the grace that
is including more and more people may cause thanksgiving to
increase to the glory of God. 16Therefore we do not despair, but
even if our physical body is wearing away, our inner person is
being renewed day by day. 17For our momentary, light suffering
is producing for us an eternal weight of glory far beyond all

4:1–6 Knowing Christ we learn that it is necessary for our lives to be illuminated by the rays of the true light. Virtues are the rays of "the sun of vindication" (Mal 4:2) streaming forth for our illumination through which we "lay aside the works of darkness" so that we "live decently as in the daytime" (Rom 13:12–13), and "we have rejected shameful hidden deeds" (2 Cor 4:2). By doing all things in the light, we become the light itself so that it shines before others, which is the peculiar quality of light. And if we recognize Christ as sanctification, in whom every action is steadfast and pure, let us prove by our lives that we ourselves stand apart, being ourselves true sharers of his name, coinciding in deed and not just in word with the power of his sanctification.

GREGORY OF NYSSA
(C. 335–C. 395)
ON PERFECTION

comparison 18because we are not looking at what can be seen
but at what cannot be seen. For what can be seen is temporary,
but what cannot be seen is eternal.

LIVING BY FAITH, NOT BY SIGHT

5 For we know that if our earthly house, the tent we live in, is
dismantled, we have a building from God, a house not built by
human hands, that is eternal in the heavens. 2For in this earthly house we groan, because we desire to put on our heavenly
dwelling, 3if indeed, after we have put on our heavenly house,
we will not be found naked. 4For we groan while we are in this
tent, since we are weighed down, because we do not want to be
unclothed, but clothed, so that what is mortal may be swallowed
up by life. 5Now the one who prepared us for this very purpose
is God, who gave us the Spirit as a down payment. 6Therefore
we are always full of courage, and we know that as long as we
are alive here on earth we are absent from the Lord—7for we live
by faith, not by sight. 8Thus we are full of courage and would
prefer to be away from the body and at home with the Lord. 9So
then whether we are alive or away, we make it our ambition to
please him. 10For we must all appear before the judgment seat
of Christ, so that each one may be paid back according to what
he has done while in the body, whether good or evil.

THE MESSAGE OF RECONCILIATION

11Therefore, because we know the fear of the Lord, we try to
persuade people, but we are well known to God, and I hope we
are well known to your consciences too. 12We are not trying to
commend ourselves to you again, but are giving you an opportunity to be proud of us, so that you may be able to answer those
who take pride in outward appearance and not in what is in the
heart. 13For if we are out of our minds, it is for God; if we are of
sound mind, it is for you. 14For the love of Christ controls us,
since we have concluded this, that Christ died for all; therefore
all have died. 15And he died for all so that those who live should
no longer live for themselves but for him who died for them and
was raised. 16So then from now on we acknowledge no one from
an outward human point of view. Even though we have known
Christ from such a human point of view, now we do not know
him in that way any longer. 17So then, if anyone is in Christ, he
is a new creation; what is old has passed away—look, what is new
has come! 18And all these things are from God who reconciled us
to himself through Christ and who has given us the ministry of
reconciliation. 19In other words, in Christ God was reconciling the
world to himself, not counting people's trespasses against them,
and he has given us the message of reconciliation. 20Therefore we
are ambassadors for Christ, as though God were making his plea
through us. We plead with you on Christ's behalf, "Be reconciled
to God!" 21God made the one who did not know sin to be sin for
us, so that in him we would become the righteousness of God.

GOD'S SUFFERING SERVANTS

6 Now because we are fellow workers, we also urge you not to
receive the grace of God in vain. 2For he says, "***I heard you at
the acceptable time, and in the day of salvation I helped you.***" Look,
now is ***the acceptable time;*** look, now is ***the day of salvation***! 3We
do not give anyone an occasion for taking an offense in anything,
so that no fault may be found with our ministry. 4But as God's
servants, we have commended ourselves in every way, with

5:1–8 There is not one body that we now use in lowliness and corruption and a different one that we are to use hereafter in incorruption and power: This same body, having cast off the weaknesses of its present existence, will be transformed into a thing of glory and made spiritual. The result is that what was a vessel of dishonor shall itself be purified and become a vessel of honor and a habitation of blessedness. We are made certain of this fact by the statement of the apostle Paul in which he says, "We have a building from God, a house not built by human hands, that is eternal in the heavens."

ORIGEN (C. 185–C. 253)
ON FIRST PRINCIPLES

6:1–10 When can the upright man be alone, since he is always with God? For he is "as unknown, and yet well-known; as dying and yet—see!—we continue to live; as those who are scourged and yet not executed; as sorrowful, but always rejoicing, as poor but making many rich, as having nothing, and yet possessing everything." For the upright man regards nothing but what is consistent and virtuous. And so although he seems poor to another he is rich to himself, for his worth is taken not at the value of the things that are temporal but of the things that are eternal.

AMBROSE (C. 339–C. 397)
ON THE DUTIES OF THE CLERGY

GEORGE WHITEFIELD:

THE SPARK OF THE GREAT AWAKENING
1714–1770

Religious revival has been the hallmark of the church from the very beginning when Peter addressed the crowds in Jerusalem on the day of Pentecost. At various times and in various ways, the Spirit of God has continued to move among his creatures, awakening them to their sin, provoking them to repentance, and calling them to relationship through his love. One such season occurred around 1740 sparked by British Methodist preacher George Whitefield.

Born and raised in a home of modest means near Gloucester, England, Whitefield self-confessed to being "addicted to lying, filthy talk, and foolish jesting" when he was a youth. But while studying at Oxford, he met John and Charles Wesley, joining their Holy Club. It was there he had a radical, life-altering experience: "I thirst! I thirst!" Whitefield said he cried from his bed one night. "Soon after this, I found and felt in myself that I was delivered from the burden that had so heavily oppressed me! The spirit of mourning was taken away from me, and I knew what it was truly to rejoice in God my Savior." A year later in 1736 he was ordained as an Anglican priest and began an itinerant preaching ministry, packing the pews and increasing in reputation as a preacher capable of captivating a crowd.

After traveling as a missionary to Georgia in 1737 to start an orphanage and aid in evangelizing the colonies, he returned to England a year later where he began preaching in the fields after many Anglican bishops closed their pulpits to him. Coal miners would be his first field parishioners. In 1739 he preached the gospel to miners coming out from their mines, reporting: "They were glad to hear of Jesus who was a friend to publicans and came not to call the righteous but sinners to repentance. The first discovery of their being affected was the sight of the white gutters made by their tears, which plentifully fell down their black cheeks as they came out of their coal pits." The crowds swelled as he continued his preaching ministry, and John Wesley joined him on his circuits.

But Whitefield's legacy would be cemented in America, to which he returned on several occasions, and where he would spark the Great Awakening with a 45-day tour through New England, preaching 145 sermons. Consider how one person responded: "Hearing him preach gave me a heart wound [so that] by God's blessing, my old foundation was broken up and I saw that my righteousness would not save me." Even Benjamin Franklin was impressed, believing Whitefield could project his voice to speak to 30,000 people, and saying, "It was wonderful to see the change soon made by his preaching in the manners of the inhabitants." This evangelistic fervor wasn't limited to northeastern America; Whitefield also ministered throughout Scotland and Wales in 1741 and 1742. He preached from February to August during the Cambuslang Awakening in Scotland, where he witnessed thousands praying, confessing, and receiving the Lord through a movement of God's Spirit.

John Wesley offered these words at Whitefield's funeral in 1770: "Have we read or heard of anyone who has been the blessed instrument of bringing so many sinners from darkness to light, and from the power of Satan unto God?" Although Whitefield preached thousands of sermons reaching perhaps millions of people throughout England and America over the course of his lifetime, Whitefield the man had this to say about his own legacy: "Let the name of George Whitefield perish so long as Christ is exalted."

IMPORTANT WORKS

COMMENTARIES
SERMONS

great endurance, in persecutions, in difficulties, in distresses,
[5]in beatings, in imprisonments, in riots, in troubles, in sleepless nights, in hunger, [6]by purity, by knowledge, by patience, by
benevolence, by the Holy Spirit, by genuine love, [7]by truthful
teaching, by the power of God, with weapons of righteousness
both for the right hand and for the left, [8]through glory and
dishonor, through slander and praise; regarded as impostors,
and yet true; [9]as unknown, and yet well-known; as dying and
yet—see!—we continue to live; as those who are scourged and
yet not executed; [10]as sorrowful, but always rejoicing; as poor,
but making many rich; as having nothing, and yet possessing
everything.
[11]We have spoken freely to you, Corinthians; our heart has
been opened wide to you. [12]Our affection for you is not restricted, but you are restricted in your affections for us. [13]Now as
a fair exchange—I speak as to my children—open wide your
hearts to us also.

UNEQUAL PARTNERS

[14]Do not become partners with those who do not believe, for
what partnership is there between righteousness and lawlessness, or what fellowship does light have with darkness? [15]And
what agreement does Christ have with Beliar? Or what does
a believer share in common with an unbeliever? [16]And what
mutual agreement does the temple of God have with idols? For
we are the temple of the living God, just as God said, ***"I will live
in them and will walk among them, and I will be their God, and
they will be my people."*** [17]Therefore "***come out from their midst,
and be separate,***" says the Lord, "***and touch no unclean thing,*** *and
I will welcome you,* [18]*and I will be a father to you, and you will be
my sons and daughters,*" says the All-Powerful Lord.

SELF-PURIFICATION

7 Therefore, since we have these promises, dear friends, let us
cleanse ourselves from everything that could defile the body
and the spirit, and thus accomplish holiness out of reverence
for God. [2]Make room for us in your hearts; we have wronged no
one; we have ruined no one; we have exploited no one. [3]I do not
say this to condemn you, for I told you before that you are in
our hearts so that we die together and live together with you.

7:1–12 Sorrow according to the will of God, tending to the glory of God and wrought by the Spirit of God, renders the heart humble, contrite, submissive, disposed to mortify every sin and to walk in newness of life. And this repentance is connected with saving faith in Christ and an interest in his atonement. Where the heart is changed, the life and actions will be changed. Repentance wrought indignation at sin, at self, at the tempter and his instruments. Deep humility before God and hatred of all sin, with faith in Christ and a new heart and a new life, make repentance unto salvation. May the Lord bestow it on every one of us.

MATTHEW HENRY (1662–1714)
COMMENTARY ON THE WHOLE BIBLE

A LETTER THAT CAUSED SADNESS

4I have great confidence in you; I take great pride on your behalf.
I am filled with encouragement; I am overflowing with joy in
the midst of all our suffering. 5For even when we came into
Macedonia, our body had no rest at all, but we were troubled in
every way—struggles from the outside, fears from within. 6But
God, who encourages the downhearted, encouraged us by the
arrival of Titus. 7We were encouraged not only by his arrival,
but also by the encouragement you gave him, as he reported to
us your longing, your mourning, your deep concern for me, so
that I rejoiced more than ever. 8For even if I made you sad by
my letter, I do not regret having written it (even though I did
regret it, for I see that my letter made you sad, though only for
a short time). 9Now I rejoice, not because you were made sad,
but because you were made sad to the point of repentance.
For you were made sad as God intended, so that you were not
harmed in any way by us. 10For sadness as intended by God
produces a repentance that leads to salvation, leaving no regret,
but worldly sadness brings about death. 11For see what this very
thing, this sadness as God intended, has produced in you: what
eagerness, what defense of yourselves, what indignation, what
alarm, what longing, what deep concern, what punishment!
In everything you have proved yourselves to be innocent in
this matter. 12So then, even though I wrote to you, it was not
on account of the one who did wrong or on account of the one
who was wronged, but to reveal to you your eagerness on our
behalf before God. 13Therefore we have been encouraged. And
in addition to our own encouragement, we rejoiced even more
at the joy of Titus because all of you have refreshed his spirit.
14For if I have boasted to him about anything concerning you,
I have not been embarrassed by you, but just as everything
we said to you was true, so our boasting to Titus about you
has proved true as well. 15And his affection for you is much
greater when he remembers the obedience of you all, how you
welcomed him with fear and trembling. 16I rejoice because in
everything I am fully confident in you.

COMPLETING THE COLLECTION FOR THE SAINTS

8 Now we make known to you, brothers and sisters, the grace
of God given to the churches of Macedonia, 2that during
a severe ordeal of suffering, their abundant joy and their extreme poverty have overflowed in the wealth of their generosity. 3For I testify, they gave according to their means and
beyond their means. They did so voluntarily, 4begging us with
great earnestness for the blessing and fellowship of helping
the saints. 5And they did this not just as we had hoped, but
they gave themselves first to the Lord and to us by the will
of God. 6Thus we urged Titus that, just as he had previously begun this work, so also he should complete this act of
kindness for you. 7But as you excel in everything—in faith,
in speech, in knowledge, and in all eagerness and in the love
from us that is in you—make sure that you excel in this act of
kindness too. 8I am not saying this as a command, but I am
testing the genuineness of your love by comparison with the
eagerness of others. 9For you know the grace of our Lord Jesus
Christ, that although he was rich, he became poor for your
sakes, so that you by his poverty could become rich. 10So here
is my opinion on this matter: It is to your advantage, since

8:1–7 The affliction of the Macedonians did not lead only to sorrow but also to great rejoicing and generosity. Paul said this in order to prepare the Corinthians to be noble and firm in their sufferings. For they were not merely to be afflicted, they were to use their afflictions as a means of growing in joy. The greatness of the Macedonians can be seen from the fact that they gave voluntarily in spite of their poverty. The secret of the Macedonians' zeal was that first they gave themselves to the Lord. Everything else flowed from that. As a result, when they showed mercy they were not filled with pride but rather displayed great humility and heavenly wisdom.

CHRYSOSTOM **(C. 347–407)**
HOMILIES ON THE EPISTLES OF PAUL TO THE CORINTHIANS

you made a good start last year both in your giving and your
desire to give, [11]to finish what you started, so that just as you
wanted to do it eagerly, you can also complete it according to
your means. [12]For if the eagerness is present, the gift itself is
acceptable according to whatever one has, not according to
what he does not have. [13]For I do not say this so there would
be relief for others and suffering for you, but as a matter of
equality. [14]At the present time, your abundance will meet
their need, so that one day their abundance may also meet
your need, and thus there may be equality, [15]as it is written:
***"The one who gathered much did not have too much, and the
one who gathered little did not have too little."***

THE MISSION OF TITUS

[16]But thanks be to God who put in the heart of Titus the same
devotion I have for you, [17]because he not only accepted our
request, but since he was very eager, he is coming to you of his
own accord. [18]And we are sending along with him the brother
who is praised by all the churches for his work in spreading
the gospel. [19]In addition, this brother has also been chosen
by the churches as our traveling companion as we administer
this generous gift to the glory of the Lord himself and to show
our readiness to help. [20]We did this as a precaution so that no
one should blame us in regard to this generous gift we are ad-
ministering. [21]For we are *concerned about what is right not only
before the Lord but also before men.* [22]And we are sending with
them our brother whom we have tested many times and found
eager in many matters, but who now is much more eager than
ever because of the great confidence he has in you. [23]If there is
any question about Titus, he is my partner and fellow worker
among you; if there is any question about our brothers, they
are messengers of the churches, a glory to Christ. [24]Therefore
show them openly before the churches the proof of your love
and of our pride in you.

PREPARING THE GIFT

9 For it is not necessary for me to write you about this service to the saints [2]because I know your eagerness to help.
I keep boasting to the Macedonians about this eagerness of
yours, that Achaia has been ready to give since last year, and
your zeal to participate has stirred up most of them. [3]But I
am sending these brothers so that our boasting about you
may not be empty in this case, so that you may be ready just
as I kept telling them. [4]For if any of the Macedonians should
come with me and find that you are not ready to give, we
would be humiliated (not to mention you) by this confidence
we had in you. [5]Therefore I thought it necessary to urge these
brothers to go to you in advance and to arrange ahead of time
the generous contribution you had promised, so this may be
ready as a generous gift and not as something you feel forced
to do. [6]My point is this: The person who sows sparingly will
also reap sparingly, and the person who sows generously will
also reap generously. [7]Each one of you should give just as he
has decided in his heart, not reluctantly or under compulsion,
because God loves a cheerful giver. [8]And God is able to make
all grace overflow to you so that because you have enough of
everything in every way at all times, you will overflow in every
good work. [9]Just as it is written, ***"He has scattered widely, he
has given to the poor; his righteousness remains forever."*** [10]Now

9:1–15 Now we can go on to speak of kindness, which breaks up into two parts, goodwill and liberality. To exist in perfection kindness must consist of these two qualities. It is not enough just to wish well; we must also do well. Nor again is it enough to do well unless this springs from a good source, even from a goodwill. "God loves a cheerful giver."

AMBROSE **(C. 339–C. 397)**
ON THE DUTIES OF THE CLERGY

God who provides seed for the sower and bread for food will
provide and multiply your supply of seed and will cause the
harvest of your righteousness to grow. 11You will be enriched
in every way so that you may be generous on every occasion,
which is producing through us thanksgiving to God, 12because
the service of this ministry is not only providing for the needs
of the saints but is also overflowing with many thanks to God.
13Through the evidence of this service they will glorify God
because of your obedience to your confession in the gospel of
Christ and the generosity of your sharing with them and with
everyone. 14And in their prayers on your behalf, they long for
you because of the extraordinary grace God has shown to you.
15Thanks be to God for his indescribable gift!

PAUL'S AUTHORITY FROM THE LORD

10 Now I, Paul, appeal to you personally by the meekness and
gentleness of Christ (I who am meek when present among
you, but am full of courage toward you when away!)—2now I
ask that when I am present I may not have to be bold with the
confidence that (I expect) I will dare to use against some who
consider us to be behaving according to human standards. 3For
though we live as human beings, we do not wage war according
to human standards, 4for the weapons of our warfare are not
human weapons, but are made powerful by God for tearing
down strongholds. We tear down arguments 5and every arrogant obstacle that is raised up against the knowledge of God,
and we take every thought captive to make it obey Christ. 6We
are also ready to punish every act of disobedience, whenever
your obedience is complete. 7You are looking at outward appearances. If anyone is confident that he belongs to Christ,
he should reflect on this again: Just as he himself belongs to
Christ, so too do we. 8For if I boast somewhat more about our
authority that the Lord gave us for building you up and not
for tearing you down, I will not be ashamed of doing so. 9I do
not want to seem as though I am trying to terrify you with
my letters, 10because some say, "His letters are weighty and
forceful, but his physical presence is weak and his speech is
of no account." 11Let such a person consider this: What we say
by letters when we are absent, we also are in actions when we
are present.

10:1–6 Though faith and prayer belong also to the Christian armor, yet the Word of God seems to be here chiefly intended as a wall or rampart. If we bring every thought, or rather faculty of the mind, into captivity to the obedience of Christ, those evil reasonings are destroyed. The mind itself being overcome and taken captive lays down all authority of its own and entirely gives itself up to perform, for the time to come, for Christ its conqueror, the obedience of faith.

JOHN WESLEY (1703–1791)
EXPLANATORY NOTES ON THE BIBLE

PAUL'S MISSION

12For we would not dare to classify or compare ourselves with
some of those who recommend themselves. But when they
measure themselves by themselves and compare themselves
with themselves, they are without understanding. 13But we will
not boast beyond certain limits, but will confine our boasting
according to the limits of the work to which God has appointed
us, that reaches even as far as you. 14For we were not overextend-
ing ourselves, as though we did not reach as far as you, because
we were the first to reach as far as you with the gospel about
Christ. 15Nor do we boast beyond certain limits in the work
done by others, but we hope that as your faith continues to
grow, our work may be greatly expanded among you according
to our limits, 16so that we may preach the gospel in the regions
that lie beyond you, and not boast of work already done in another person's area. 17But ***the one who boasts must boast in the
Lord.*** 18For it is not the person who commends himself who is
approved, but the person the Lord commends.

PAUL AND HIS OPPONENTS

11 I wish that you would be patient with me in a little foolishness, but indeed you are being patient with me! [2]For I
am jealous for you with godly jealousy, because I promised you
in marriage to one husband, to present you as a pure virgin to
Christ. [3]But I am afraid that just as the serpent deceived Eve
by his treachery, your minds may be led astray from a sincere
and pure devotion to Christ. [4]For if someone comes and proclaims another Jesus different from the one we proclaimed, or
if you receive a different spirit than the one you received, or a
different gospel than the one you accepted, you put up with it
well enough! [5]For I consider myself not at all inferior to those
"super-apostles." [6]And even if I am unskilled in speaking, yet I
am certainly not so in knowledge. Indeed, we have made this
plain to you in everything in every way. [7]Or did I commit a sin
by humbling myself so that you could be exalted, because I
proclaimed the gospel of God to you free of charge? [8]I robbed
other churches by receiving support from them so that I could
serve you! [9]When I was with you and was in need, I was not a
burden to anyone, for the brothers who came from Macedonia
fully supplied my needs. I kept myself from being a burden to
you in any way, and will continue to do so. [10]As the truth of
Christ is in me, this boasting of mine will not be stopped in
the regions of Achaia. [11]Why? Because I do not love you? God
knows I do! [12]And what I am doing I will continue to do, so that
I may eliminate any opportunity for those who want a chance to
be regarded as our equals in the things they boast about. [13]For
such people are false apostles, deceitful workers, disguising
themselves as apostles of Christ. [14]And no wonder, for even
Satan disguises himself as an angel of light. [15]Therefore it is
not surprising his servants also disguise themselves as servants
of righteousness, whose end will correspond to their actions.

PAUL'S SUFFERINGS FOR CHRIST

[16]I say again, let no one think that I am a fool. But if you do,
then at least accept me as a fool, so that I too may boast a little.
[17]What I am saying with this boastful confidence I do not say
the way the Lord would. Instead it is, as it were, foolishness.
[18]Since many are boasting according to human standards, I
too will boast. [19]For since you are so wise, you put up with fools
gladly. [20]For you put up with it if someone makes slaves of you,
if someone exploits you, if someone takes advantage of you, if
someone behaves arrogantly toward you, if someone strikes you
in the face. [21](To my disgrace I must say that we were too weak
for that!) But whatever anyone else dares to boast about (I am
speaking foolishly), I also dare to boast about the same thing.
[22]Are they Hebrews? So am I. Are they Israelites? So am I. Are
they descendants of Abraham? So am I. [23]Are they servants of
Christ? (I am talking like I am out of my mind!) I am even more
so: with much greater labors, with far more imprisonments,
with more severe beatings, facing death many times. [24]Five
times I received from the Jews forty lashes less one. [25]Three times
I was beaten with a rod. Once I received a stoning. Three times I
suffered shipwreck. A night and a day I spent adrift in the
open sea. [26]I have been on journeys many times, in dangers
from rivers, in dangers from robbers, in dangers from my own
countrymen, in dangers from Gentiles, in dangers in the city,
in dangers in the wilderness, in dangers at sea, in dangers from
false brothers, [27]in hard work and toil, through many sleepless

11:5–15 There are many wolves going about in sheep's clothing; they possess nonetheless both talons and teeth. They wrap themselves in the gentle creature's hide and with this disguise deceive the innocent only to inject with their teeth the deadly poison of their irreligion. We therefore need the grace of God, a sober mind, and watchful eyes so as not to eat tares for wheat and come to harm for not knowing better; so as not to mistake the wolf for a sheep and be ravaged; and so as not to take the death-dealing devil for a good angel and be devoured.

CYRIL OF JERUSALEM
(C. 313–386)
CATECHETICAL LECTURES

nights, in hunger and thirst, many times without food, in cold and without enough clothing. [28]Apart from other things, there is the daily pressure on me of my anxious concern for all the churches. [29]Who is weak, and I am not weak? Who is led into sin, and I do not burn with indignation? [30]If I must boast, I will boast about the things that show my weakness. [31]The God and Father of the Lord Jesus, who is blessed forever, knows I am not lying. [32]In Damascus, the governor under King Aretas was guarding the city of Damascus in order to arrest me, [33]but I was let down in a rope-basket through a window in the city wall, and escaped his hands.

PAUL'S THORN IN THE FLESH

12 It is necessary to go on boasting. Though it is not profitable, I will go on to visions and revelations from the Lord. [2]I know a man in Christ who fourteen years ago (whether in the body or out of the body I do not know, God knows) was caught up to the third heaven. [3]And I know that this man (whether in the body or apart from the body I do not know, God knows) [4]was caught up into paradise and heard things too sacred to be put into words, things that a person is not permitted to speak. [5]On behalf of such an individual I will boast, but on my own behalf I will not boast, except about my weaknesses. [6]For even if I wish to boast, I will not be a fool, for I would be telling the truth, but I refrain from this so that no one may regard me beyond what he sees in me or what he hears from me, [7]even because of the extraordinary character of the revelations. Therefore, so that I would not become arrogant, a thorn in the flesh was given to me, a messenger of Satan to trouble me—so that I would not become arrogant. [8]I asked the Lord three times about this, that it would depart from me. [9]But he said to me, "My grace is enough for you, for my power is made perfect in weakness." So then, I will boast most gladly about my weaknesses, so that the power of Christ may reside in me. [10]Therefore I am content with weaknesses, with insults, with troubles, with persecutions and difficulties for the sake of Christ, for whenever I am weak, then I am strong.

12:1–6 For truly the great grounds of boasting were those that he had recounted, those of his trials; he has, however, other things to tell of such as concern the revelations, the unspeakable mysteries. And therefore, says he, "it is not profitable," by which he means *lest it lift me up to pride.* But our knowing of them ourselves does not lift us up as much as our publishing them to others. Good deeds will not puff anybody up unless they are witnessed to and remarked upon by others.

CHRYSOSTOM **(C. 347–407)**
HOMILIES ON THE EPISTLES OF PAUL TO THE CORINTHIANS

THE SIGNS OF AN APOSTLE

[11]I have become a fool. You yourselves forced me to do it, for I should have been commended by you. For I lack nothing in comparison to those "super-apostles," even though I am nothing. [12]Indeed, the signs of an apostle were performed among you with great perseverance by signs and wonders and powerful deeds. [13]For how were you treated worse than the other churches, except that I myself was not a burden to you? Forgive me this injustice! [14]Look, for the third time I am ready to come to you, and I will not be a burden to you, because I do not want your possessions, but you. For children should not have to save up for their parents, but parents for their children. [15]Now I will most gladly spend and be spent for your lives! If I love you more, am I to be loved less? [16]But be that as it may, I have not burdened you. Yet because I was a crafty person, I took you in by deceit! [17]I have not taken advantage of you through anyone I have sent to you, have I? [18]I urged Titus to visit you, and I sent our brother along with him. Titus did not take advantage of you, did he? Did we not conduct ourselves in the same spirit? Did we not behave in the same way? [19]Have you been thinking all this time that we have been defending ourselves to you? We are speaking in

Christ before God, and everything we do, dear friends, is to build
you up. 20For I am afraid that somehow when I come I will not
find you what I wish, and you will find me not what you wish.
I am afraid that somehow there may be quarreling, jealousy,
intense anger, selfish ambition, slander, gossip, arrogance, and
disorder. 21I am afraid that when I come again, my God may
humiliate me before you, and I will grieve for many of those
who previously sinned and have not repented of the impurity,
sexual immorality, and licentiousness that they have practiced.

PAUL'S THIRD VISIT TO CORINTH

13 This is the third time I am coming to visit you. ***By the
testimony of two or three witnesses every matter will be established.*** 2I said before when I was present the second time
and now, though absent, I say again to those who sinned previously and to all the rest, that if I come again, I will not spare
anyone, 3since you are demanding proof that Christ is speaking
through me. He is not weak toward you but is powerful among
you. 4For indeed he was crucified by reason of weakness, but he
lives because of God's power. For we also are weak in him, but
we will live together with him, because of God's power toward
you. 5Put yourselves to the test to see if you are in the faith;
examine yourselves! Or do you not recognize regarding yourselves that Jesus Christ is in you—unless, indeed, you fail the
test! 6And I hope that you will realize that we have not failed
the test! 7Now we pray to God that you may not do anything
wrong, not so that we may appear to have passed the test, but
so that you may do what is right even if we may appear to have
failed the test. 8For we cannot do anything against the truth,
but only for the sake of the truth. 9For we rejoice whenever we
are weak, but you are strong. And we pray for this: that you may
become fully qualified. 10Because of this I am writing these
things while absent, so that when I arrive I may not have to
deal harshly with you by using my authority—the Lord gave it
to me for building up, not for tearing down!

FINAL EXHORTATIONS AND GREETINGS

11Finally, brothers and sisters, rejoice, set things right, be encouraged, agree with one another, live in peace, and the God
of love and peace will be with you. 12Greet one another with a
holy kiss. All the saints greet you. 13The grace of the Lord Jesus
Christ and the love of God and the fellowship of the Holy Spirit
be with you all.

13:1–10 The most desirable thing we can ask of God is to be kept from sin that we may not do evil. We have far more need to pray that we may not do evil than that we may not suffer evil. The apostle not only desired that they might be kept from sin but also that they might grow in grace and increase in holiness. We should be glad for others to be strong in the grace of Christ, though it may be the means of showing our own weakness.

MATTHEW HENRY **(1662–1714)**
COMMENTARY ON THE WHOLE BIBLE

AUTHOR	AUDIENCE	DATE	PURPOSE	THEMES
Paul	Churches in southern Galatia, and perhaps northern Galatia, founded by Paul during his missionary journey	AD 48, or in the 50s	Paul wrote to confront false teachers who were attempting to add works of the law to the gospel of grace.	The gospel of grace; justification by faith; works of the law; and freedom in Christ

The Christian humanist Erasmus provided an explanation of the epistle of Paul the apostle to the Galatians that generally represents how the communion of saints have received and understood this foundational letter: "In this epistle Paul is concerned about the same matter that he discusses everywhere else. He wants to call people from the bondage of Moses' law to the grace of the gospel." Paul wrote to the community of believers in Galatia because he was alarmed at how they had deserted the gospel for a distortion of the truth.

People known as Judaizers had slipped in among the believers of Galatia and were twisting the gospel by insisting that the Gentile believers adopt Jewish customs and works of the law, such as circumcision, in order to experience God's salvation. They were adding to the gospel, nullifying justification by grace through faith by requiring works of the law. Paul confronted this perversion by reminding the Galatians of the apostles' message, showing how grace has always been at the heart of God's promises. Paul was passionate about the issue: "May I never boast except in the cross of our Lord Jesus Christ" (6:14).

The message of Galatians—the centrality of the cross—was vital to the Reformers' efforts during the sixteenth century to bring the church back to the essence of the Christian faith. In opposing the Judaizers, Paul asserted that people were justified by grace through faith, not works of the law (see 2:16). The Reformers were reminded by Paul that grace is something entirely of God and leveraged this message to confront those they saw as the "Judaizers" of their own day: those who sought to burden followers of Christ by insisting on a system of works-based justification. It is the essence of God's good news in Christ, the gospel, that he loved us by his own free choice, not because we earned or merited his favor with works.

GALATIANS

To speak about justification is to speak about how people become right with God and are declared not guilty. Martin Luther said the doctrine of justification by grace through faith was vital to the health and stability of Christianity "because if this article stands, the church stands; if this article collapses, the church collapses." Just as Luther did for his generation, every believer needs to defend the preeminence of grace in the gospel message. We do this by returning, again and again, to the essence of the good news: "[Jesus Christ] gave himself for our sins to rescue us from this present evil age according to the will of our God and Father" (1:4).

Paul argued that grace has been at the heart of God's story since the beginning: "Just as Abraham believed God, and it was credited to him as righteousness, so then, understand that those who believe are the sons of Abraham" (3:6–7). Those who try to earn God's favor are cursed because no one can fulfill the works of the law. The law was always meant to be temporary, to serve as a signpost until Christ could fulfill its requirements (see 3:24).

Luther was right: The church rises or falls on the foundation of justification by grace through faith. The temptation to add works of merit to the gospel of grace is a strong one. May we join Paul in boasting in nothing else but the cross of Christ, which releases us from the bondage of merit and enjoins us to glory in the gospel of grace.

1:1–10 The gospel is the happy and blessed news that the human race has been saved, and by it repentance and the forgiveness of sins are preached in the name of Jesus Christ alone. There are two things we have to learn if we are going to fight against the impostors of our own time. The first is the nature of the gospel itself. The second is that it is that gospel that the apostles actually preached. When we understand this we shall see why nothing should be added to their teaching, nor should it be altered in anyway.

RUDOLF GWALTHER
(1519–1586)
SERMONS ON GALATIANS

SALUTATION

1 From Paul, an apostle (not from men, nor by human agency,
but by Jesus Christ and God the Father who raised him from
the dead) [2]and all the brothers with me, to the churches of
Galatia. [3]Grace and peace to you from God the Father and our
Lord Jesus Christ, [4]who gave himself for our sins to rescue us
from this present evil age according to the will of our God and
Father, [5]to whom be glory forever and ever! Amen.

OCCASION OF THE LETTER

[6]I am astonished that you are so quickly deserting the one who
called you by the grace of Christ and are following a different
gospel—[7]not that there really is another gospel, but there are
some who are disturbing you and wanting to distort the gospel of Christ. [8]But even if we (or an angel from heaven) should
preach a gospel contrary to the one we preached to you, let
him be condemned to hell! [9]As we have said before, and now
I say again, if any one is preaching to you a gospel contrary to
what you received, let him be condemned to hell! [10]Am I now
trying to gain the approval of people, or of God? Or am I trying
to please people? If I were still trying to please people, I would
not be a slave of Christ!

PAUL'S VINDICATION OF HIS APOSTLESHIP

[11]Now I want you to know, brothers and sisters, that the gospel
I preached is not of human origin. [12]For I did not receive it
or learn it from any human source; instead I received it by a
revelation of Jesus Christ.

[13]For you have heard of my former way of life in Judaism,
how I was savagely persecuting the church of God and trying
to destroy it. [14]I was advancing in Judaism beyond many of my
contemporaries in my nation, and was extremely zealous for
the traditions of my ancestors. [15]But when the one who set
me apart from birth and called me by his grace was pleased
[16]to reveal his Son in me so that I could preach him among
the Gentiles, I did not go to ask advice from any human being,
[17]nor did I go up to Jerusalem to see those who were apostles
before me, but right away I departed to Arabia, and then returned to Damascus.

[18]Then after three years I went up to Jerusalem to visit
Cephas and get information from him, and I stayed with him
fifteen days. [19]But I saw none of the other apostles except James
the Lord's brother. [20]I assure you that, before God, I am not
lying about what I am writing to you! [21]Afterward I went to the
regions of Syria and Cilicia. [22]But I was personally unknown
to the churches of Judea that are in Christ. [23]They were only
hearing, "The one who once persecuted us is now proclaiming
the good news of the faith he once tried to destroy." [24]So they
glorified God because of me.

CONFIRMATION FROM THE JERUSALEM APOSTLES

2 Then after fourteen years I went up to Jerusalem again with
Barnabas, taking Titus along too. [2]I went there because of
a revelation and presented to them the gospel that I preach
among the Gentiles. But I did so only in a private meeting with
the influential people, to make sure that I was not running—or
had not run—in vain. [3]Yet not even Titus, who was with me,
was compelled to be circumcised, although he was a Greek.

2:1–10 When Paul speaks of the truth of the gospel, he implies by contrast a false gospel. The true gospel has that we are justified by faith alone. The false gospel has that we are justified by faith but not without the deeds of the law. Faith is able to justify because it apprehends Christ the Redeemer. Human reason can think only in terms of the law. It mumbles, *This I have done, this I have not done.* But faith looks to Jesus Christ, the Son of God, given to death for the sins of the whole world. To turn one's eyes away from Jesus means to turn them to the law. True faith lays hold of Christ and leans on him alone.

MARTIN LUTHER **(1483–1546)**
COMMENTARY ON GALATIANS

[4]Now this matter arose because of the false brothers with false pretenses who slipped in unnoticed to spy on our freedom that we have in Christ Jesus, to make us slaves. [5]But we did not surrender to them even for a moment, in order that the truth of the gospel would remain with you.

[6]But from those who were influential (whatever they were makes no difference to me; God shows no favoritism between people)—those influential leaders added nothing to my message. [7]On the contrary, when they saw that I was entrusted with the gospel to the uncircumcised just as Peter was entrusted with the gospel to the circumcised [8](for he who empowered Peter for his apostleship to the circumcised also empowered me for my apostleship to the Gentiles) [9]and when James, Cephas, and John, who had a reputation as pillars, recognized the grace that had been given to me, they gave to Barnabas and me the right hand of fellowship, agreeing that we would go to the Gentiles and they to the circumcised. [10]They requested only that we remember the poor, the very thing I also was eager to do.

PAUL REBUKES PETER

[11]But when Cephas came to Antioch, I opposed him to his face, because he had clearly done wrong. [12]Until certain people came from James, he had been eating with the Gentiles. But when they arrived, he stopped doing this and separated himself because he was afraid of those who were pro-circumcision. [13]And the rest of the Jews also joined with him in this hypocrisy, so that even Barnabas was led astray with them by their hypocrisy. [14]But when I saw that they were not behaving consistently with the truth of the gospel, I said to Cephas in front of them all, "If you, although you are a Jew, live like a Gentile and not like a Jew, how can you try to force the Gentiles to live like Jews?"

THE JUSTIFICATION OF JEWS AND GENTILES

[15]We are Jews by birth and not Gentile sinners, [16]yet we know that no one is justified by the works of the law but by the faithfulness of Jesus Christ. And we have come to believe in Christ Jesus, so that we may be justified by the faithfulness of Christ and not by the works of the law, because by the works of the law no one will be justified. [17]But if while seeking to be justified in Christ we ourselves have also been found to be sinners, is Christ then one who encourages sin? Absolutely not! [18]But if I build up again those things I once destroyed, I demonstrate that I am one who breaks God's law. [19]For through the law I died to the law so that I may live to God. [20]I have been crucified with Christ, and it is no longer I who live, but Christ lives in me. So the life I now live in the body, I live because of the faithfulness of the Son of God, who loved me and gave himself for me. [21]I do not set aside God's grace, because if righteousness could come through the law, then Christ died for nothing!

JUSTIFICATION BY LAW OR BY FAITH?

3 You foolish Galatians! Who has cast a spell on you? Before your eyes Jesus Christ was vividly portrayed as crucified! [2]The only thing I want to learn from you is this: Did you receive the Spirit by doing the works of the law or by believing what you heard? [3]Are you so foolish? Although you began with the

3:1–14 What does he mean by this phrase "before your eyes"? Paul is illustrating the power of faith, which is able to see even things far off. And he said not "crucified" but "portrayed as crucified," showing that with the eyes of faith the Galatians saw more accurately than those who were there and witnessed the events. And he says this both to reprimand and to commend them. He commends the Galatians for having received the facts with such enthusiasm. He blames them because having seen Christ stripped, crucified, nailed, spat on, mocked, drinking vinegar, insulted by thieves, and pierced with a spear, they have forsaken this man and run back to the law, showing no awareness of Christ's sufferings.

CHRYSOSTOM (C. 347–407)
HOMILIES ON GALATIANS

Spirit, are you now trying to finish by human effort? 4Have
you suffered so many things for nothing?—if indeed it was for
nothing. 5Does God then give you the Spirit and work miracles
among you by your doing the works of the law or by your believing what you heard?
6Just as Abraham ***believed God, and it was credited to him as***
righteousness, 7so then, understand that those who believe are
the sons of Abraham. 8And the scripture, foreseeing that God
would justify the Gentiles by faith, proclaimed the gospel to
Abraham ahead of time, saying, "***All the nations will be blessed***
in you." 9So then those who believe are blessed along with
Abraham the believer. 10For all who rely on doing the works
of the law are under a curse because it is written, "***Cursed is***
everyone who does not keep on doing everything written in the
book of the law." 11Now it is clear no one is justified before
God by the law because ***the righteous one will live by faith.***
12But the law is not based on faith, but ***the one who does*** the
works of the law ***will live by them.*** 13Christ redeemed us from
the curse of the law by becoming a curse for us (because it is
written, "***Cursed is everyone who hangs on a tree***") 14in order
that in Christ Jesus the blessing of Abraham would come
to the Gentiles, so that we could receive the promise of the
Spirit by faith.

INHERITANCE COMES FROM PROMISES AND NOT LAW

15Brothers and sisters, I offer an example from everyday life:
When a covenant has been ratified, even though it is only a
human contract, no one can set it aside or add anything to
it. 16Now the promises were spoken to Abraham and to his
descendant. Scripture does not say, "and to the descendants,"
referring to many, but "***and to your descendant,***" referring to one,
who is Christ. 17What I am saying is this: The law that came 430
years later does not cancel a covenant previously ratified by
God, so as to invalidate the promise. 18For if the inheritance is
based on the law, it is no longer based on the promise, but God
graciously gave it to Abraham through the promise.
19Why then was the law given? It was added because of
transgressions, until the arrival of the descendant to whom
the promise had been made. It was administered through
angels by an intermediary. 20Now an intermediary is not for
one party alone, but God is one. 21Is the law therefore opposed to the promises of God? Absolutely not! For if a law
had been given that was able to give life, then righteousness
would certainly have come by the law. 22But the scripture
imprisoned everything under sin so that the promise could
be given—because of the faithfulness of Jesus Christ—to those
who believe.

SONS OF GOD ARE HEIRS OF PROMISE

23Now before faith came we were held in custody under the
law, being kept as prisoners until the coming faith would be
revealed. 24Thus the law had become our guardian until Christ,
so that we could be declared righteous by faith. 25But now that
faith has come, we are no longer under a guardian. 26For in
Christ Jesus you are all sons of God through faith. 27For all of
you who were baptized into Christ have clothed yourselves
with Christ. 28There is neither Jew nor Greek, there is neither
slave nor free, there is neither male nor female—for all of you

are one in Christ Jesus. 29And if you belong to Christ, then you
are Abraham's descendants, heirs according to the promise.
4 Now I mean that the heir, as long as he is a minor, is no different from a slave, though he is the owner of everything. 2But
he is under guardians and managers until the date set by his
father. 3So also we, when we were minors, were enslaved under
the basic forces of the world. 4But when the appropriate time
had come, God sent out his Son, born of a woman, born under
the law, 5to redeem those who were under the law, so that we
may be adopted as sons with full rights. 6And because you are
sons, God sent the Spirit of his Son into our hearts, who calls
"*Abba!* Father!" 7So you are no longer a slave but a son, and if
you are a son, then you are also an heir through God.

HEIRS OF PROMISE ARE NOT TO RETURN TO LAW

8Formerly when you did not know God, you were enslaved to
beings that by nature are not gods at all. 9But now that you have
come to know God (or rather to be known by God), how can you
turn back again to the weak and worthless basic forces? Do you
want to be enslaved to them all over again? 10You are observing
religious days and months and seasons and years. 11I fear for
you that my work for you may have been in vain. 12I beg you,
brothers and sisters, become like me, because I have become
like you. You have done me no wrong!

PERSONAL APPEAL OF PAUL

13But you know it was because of a physical illness that I first
proclaimed the gospel to you, 14and though my physical condition put you to the test, you did not despise or reject me.
Instead, you welcomed me as though I were an angel of God,
as though I were Christ Jesus himself! 15Where then is your
sense of happiness now? For I testify about you that if it were
possible, you would have pulled out your eyes and given them
to me! 16So then, have I become your enemy by telling you
the truth?

17They court you eagerly, but for no good purpose; they want
to exclude you, so that you would seek them eagerly. 18However,
it is good to be sought eagerly for a good purpose at all times,
and not only when I am present with you. 19My children—I
am again undergoing birth pains until Christ is formed in you!
20I wish I could be with you now and change my tone of voice,
because I am perplexed about you.

AN APPEAL FROM ALLEGORY

21Tell me, you who want to be under the law, do you not understand the law? 22For it is written that Abraham had two sons,
one by the slave woman and the other by the free woman.
23But one, the son by the slave woman, was born by natural
descent, while the other, the son by the free woman, was born
through the promise. 24These things may be treated as an allegory, for these women represent two covenants. One is from
Mount Sinai bearing children for slavery; this is Hagar. 25Now
Hagar represents Mount Sinai in Arabia and corresponds to
the present Jerusalem, for she is in slavery with her children.
26But the Jerusalem above is free, and she is our mother. 27For
it is written:

> ***"Rejoice, O barren woman who does not bear children;***
> ***break forth and shout, you who have no birth pains,***

4:8–20 Righteousness has its basic elements, its own alphabet. This elementary ABC level of righteousness has its place in the law of Moses. But perfect righteousness is that which is found in Christ by faith. When Christ is known by faith, relapsing into a search for righteousness by observing the feasts of the law is nothing other than if someone who was a most learned professor and master of arts should lapse back into learning the alphabet. Who would not be astonished at such stupidity?

JOHANNES BRENZ
(1499–1570)
EXPLANATION OF GALATIANS

JONATHAN EDWARDS:

AMERICA'S PURITAN THEOLOGIAN

1703–1758

Jonathan Edwards, combining a philosopher's mind and a revivalist's heart, produced some of the most influential theological treatises of the American Colonial period, and helped shape the connection between Puritan, Reformed theology and the spiritual renewal of the First Great Awakening.

Edwards was born in Connecticut in 1703. As the grandson of New England's most influential Puritan preacher, Solomon Stoddard, he became his grandfather's associate minister after graduating from Yale College in 1724. He was unique in that he combined a strong Puritan Calvinism with strong pietistic leanings. This pietism was marked by a revivalist flare that placed him at the center of the Great Awakening that dominated the East Coast in the 1740s. Agreeing with German Pietists that true Christianity is heart-centered more than merely an intellectual endeavor, he aimed to pluck the heartstrings of his hearers to bring them to Christian awakening.

One of the dominant themes of his theology was a strong belief in religious experience. Edwards conducted a careful study of the psychology of religion and suggested that the faculty of the will includes something called the "affections": deep, long-lasting beliefs that are powerfully supported by the emotions and always result in action. As he expressed it in *A Treatise Concerning Religious Affection*: "The affections are no other than the more vigorous and sensible exercises of the inclination of the will of the soul . . . by which the soul does not merely perceive and view things but is some way inclined [moved] with respect to the things it views or considers." He recognized that only religious affections that glorified God were true and righteous ones, particularly love for him and neighbor. Religious revival, though ultimately the work of God himself, taps into the great well of the human's affections.

Alongside his strong Pietism was a deep commitment to Puritan Calvinism. He was a fierce defender of Calvinist doctrine in the face of what he perceived to be a tidal wave of Arminianism and theological rationalism affecting the American colonies. Consequently, he spent much time defending God's glory and sovereignty as well as humankind's depravity and bondage to sin. Much of his theology revolved around the hallmarks of Calvinism: Consistent with Calvinist teaching, Edwards argued that humans are totally dependent on God, totally depraved, and in total bondage to sin; he emphasized God's complete sovereignty in all things. But Edwards added a philosophical determinism to his theological writings, arguing that God is the One Cause determining all reality entirely for his glory and honor. His views remain controversial as does his movement toward an utterly deterministic framework for all human activity—an apparent step away from those Reformed and medieval scholars who recognized various kinds of causes (including human freedom) within God's sovereign rule of the world.

Although he is perhaps most remembered by his fire-and-brimstone sermon "Sinners in the Hands of an Angry God," the over 600 sermons he gave over the course of his life were actually marked by a genuine concern to see the people's affections turned toward the beauty and truth of God. He consistently showed a pastoral interest in the souls of men, seeking to draw them toward devotion to God and piety. Edwards continues to inspire and challenge believers today, and his work exemplifies how serious theological work can be a vital source of spiritual awakening and revival.

IMPORTANT WORKS

ON THE NATURE OF TRUE VIRTUE
ON FREEDOM OF THE WILL
A TREATISE CONCERNING RELIGIOUS AFFECTION

because the children of the desolate woman are more numerous
than those of the woman who has a husband."

28 But you, brothers and sisters, are children of the promise
like Isaac. 29 But just as at that time the one born by natural
descent persecuted the one born according to the Spirit, so it
is now. 30 But what does the scripture say? "***Throw out the slave***
woman and her son, for the son of the slave woman will not share
the inheritance with the son" of the free woman. 31 Therefore,
brothers and sisters, we are not children of the slave woman
but of the free woman.

FREEDOM OF THE BELIEVER

5 For freedom Christ has set us free. Stand firm, then, and do
not be subject again to the yoke of slavery. 2 Listen! I, Paul,
tell you that if you let yourselves be circumcised, Christ will
be of no benefit to you at all! 3 And I testify again to every man
who lets himself be circumcised that he is obligated to obey the
whole law. 4 You who are trying to be declared righteous by the
law have been alienated from Christ; you have fallen away from
grace! 5 For through the Spirit, by faith, we wait expectantly for
the hope of righteousness. 6 For in Christ Jesus neither circumcision nor uncircumcision carries any weight—the only thing
that matters is faith working through love.

7 You were running well; who prevented you from obeying
the truth? 8 This persuasion does not come from the one who
calls you! 9 A little yeast makes the whole batch of dough rise!
10 I am confident in the Lord that you will accept no other view.
But the one who is confusing you will pay the penalty, whoever
he may be. 11 Now, brothers and sisters, if I am still preaching
circumcision, why am I still being persecuted? In that case the
offense of the cross has been removed. 12 I wish those agitators
would go so far as to castrate themselves!

PRACTICE LOVE

13 For you were called to freedom, brothers and sisters; only do
not use your freedom as an opportunity to indulge your flesh,
but through love serve one another. 14 For the whole law can be

5:7–15 The whole work of the law is fulfilled by this one command: love. For one who loves another neither murders nor commits adultery nor steals. Now Paul himself adds a text: "You must love your neighbor as yourself." But we ought to understand by "neighbor" every human being and then constantly view Christ as our neighbor. Here Paul now seems to urge the Galatians to avoid discord. And this could happen if they love one another in the Spirit, not in the flesh nor for the works of the flesh nor in natural observances. For he who loves another feels no envy, nor steals from another, nor despises or abuses him.

MARIUS VICTORINUS
(C. 350)
COMMENTARY ON THE LETTER TO THE GALATIANS

summed up in a single commandment, namely, "***You must love your neighbor as yourself.***" [15]However, if you continually bite and devour one another, beware that you are not consumed by one another. [16]But I say, live by the Spirit and you will not carry out the desires of the flesh. [17]For the flesh has desires that are opposed to the Spirit, and the Spirit has desires that are opposed to the flesh, for these are in opposition to each other, so that you cannot do what you want. [18]But if you are led by the Spirit, you are not under the law. [19]Now the works of the flesh are obvious: sexual immorality, impurity, depravity, [20]idolatry, sorcery, hostilities, strife, jealousy, outbursts of anger, selfish rivalries, dissensions, factions, [21]envying, murder, drunkenness, carousing, and similar things. I am warning you, as I had warned you before: Those who practice such things will not inherit the kingdom of God!

[22]But the fruit of the Spirit is love, joy, peace, patience, kindness, goodness, faithfulness, [23]gentleness, and self-control. Against such things there is no law. [24]Now those who belong to Christ have crucified the flesh with its passions and desires. [25]If we live by the Spirit, let us also behave in accordance with the Spirit. [26]Let us not become conceited, provoking one another, being jealous of one another.

SUPPORT ONE ANOTHER

6 Brothers and sisters, if a person is discovered in some sin, you who are spiritual restore such a person in a spirit of gentleness. Pay close attention to yourselves, so that you are not tempted too. [2]Carry one another's burdens, and in this way you will fulfill the law of Christ. [3]For if anyone thinks he is something when he is nothing, he deceives himself. [4]Let each one examine his own work. Then he can take pride in himself and not compare himself with someone else. [5]For each one will carry his own load.

[6]Now the one who receives instruction in the word must share all good things with the one who teaches it. [7]Do not be deceived. God will not be made a fool. For a person will reap what he sows, [8]because the person who sows to his own flesh will reap corruption from the flesh, but the one who sows to the Spirit will reap eternal life from the Spirit. [9]So we must not grow weary in doing good, for in due time we will reap, if we do not give up. [10]So then, whenever we have an opportunity, let us do good to all people, and especially to those who belong to the family of faith.

FINAL INSTRUCTIONS AND BENEDICTION

[11]See what big letters I make as I write to you with my own hand! [12]Those who want to make a good showing in external matters are trying to force you to be circumcised. They do so only to avoid being persecuted for the cross of Christ. [13]For those who are circumcised do not obey the law themselves, but they want you to be circumcised so that they can boast about your flesh. [14]But may I never boast except in the cross of our Lord Jesus Christ, through which the world has been crucified to me, and I to the world. [15]For neither circumcision nor uncircumcision counts for anything; the only thing that matters is a new creation! [16]And all who will behave in accordance with this rule, peace and mercy be on them, and on the Israel of God.

6:11–15 The resurrection of the Savior from the Passion of the cross contains the mystery of the resurrection of the whole body of Christ. But as that material body of Jesus was sacrificed, buried, and afterward raised, so the whole body of Christ's saints is crucified along with him and now lives no longer. For each of them, like Paul, glories in nothing but the cross of our Lord Jesus Christ, through which he is crucified to the world and the world to him.

ORIGEN (C. 185–C. 253)
COMMENTARY ON THE GOSPEL OF JOHN

[17]From now on let no one cause me trouble, for I bear the
marks of Jesus on my body.
[18]The grace of our Lord Jesus Christ be with your spirit,
brothers and sisters. Amen.

AUTHOR	AUDIENCE	DATE	PURPOSE	THEMES
Paul	Believers in the church at Ephesus and probably other Christians in western Asia Minor	Around AD 60	Paul wrote to inform and encourage believers in their faith and lives.	Salvation and grace; unity of Jewish and Gentile believers; Christian living; and Christian identity

This epistle contains the sum total of Paul's preaching," wrote Reformed pastor and professor Johannes Bugenhagen, "and indeed of the gospel, in words that are few but amazingly powerful, so that you do not need to add anything to them." He then summarized the epistle of Paul the apostle to the Ephesians, showing why the communion of saints has valued the letter for generations: "In the first three chapters he preaches the gospel and the freedom and effectiveness of the gospel in the clearest possible way. In the remainder of the epistle, he expounds, after faith by which alone we are justified, the Christian life that ought to be the fruit of inward faith, that is, of justification. He tells each and every one of us what we must do."

Unlike many of Paul's other letters, this one was not written to address specific issues in a church community. It was a general letter written to Gentile believers to encourage and instruct them in their faith. While it was written to "the saints [in Ephesus]" (1:1), the earliest extant manuscripts don't contain that phrase, and it is likely that the letter was meant to be circulated more widely in the surrounding region.

Paul began his letter with a rising chorus of divine acknowledgment, rooting our faith in the spiritual blessings of God made possible through Christ's blood and God's forgiveness, which result in our adoption. The rest of the letter is an exploration of key themes: salvation by grace through faith, a foundational doctrine of the Reformation; God's power and sovereignty; and Christian unity and identity.

Sola fide (faith alone) and *sola gratia* (grace alone) were two of five rallying cries at the heart of the Reformation. Both can be traced to themes Paul addressed in chapter 2, which is principally concerned with salvation by grace through faith. The chapter begins with an honest, sober assessment of our human condition: we were "dead in [our] offenses and sins . . . and were by nature children of wrath" (2:1, 3). This total depravity, as it became known, was expounded in the writings of several of the early church fathers, principally Augustine. Yet "God, being rich in mercy, because of his great love with which he loved us . . . made us alive together with Christ" (2:4–5). This love is spiritually transforming, and saving comes "by grace . . . through faith" (2:8). Its truth anchored the Reformers' efforts to properly orient justification around God's grace and

EPHESIANS

faith and remove it from the realm of human merit, a false doctrine that plagued the early church.

One major theme in Paul's letters is how the promises of God extend to Gentiles (non-Jews). In Ephesians Paul explains how those who had been previously excluded from citizenship in God's family have now been united into one body, one building with Christ as the cornerstone, through Christ's blood. We are now "in Christ," an idea expressed multiple times in various ways throughout the letter. We are no longer who we were—"foreigners and noncitizens, but you are fellow citizens with the saints and members of God's household" (2:19). Our new identity and our blessings as Christians are possible only because of who Christ is.

If the first half of Paul's epistle lays the foundation of Christian orthodoxy (right beliefs), the second half lays the foundation for Christian orthopraxy (right behavior). Beginning with chapter 4, Paul beseeched the saints "live worthily of the calling with which you have been called" (4:1), to live in a way that aligns with their identity in Christ.

We are called to discern not only what teachings we follow but also what patterns of living we practice. We are to "lay aside the old man who is being corrupted in accordance with deceitful desires, to be renewed in the spirit of your mind" (4:22–23). We are to do this by telling the truth, avoiding anger, talking wholesomely, eschewing any hint of sexual immorality, and walking in love and unity. Such ethics have practical implications for every aspect of life, from marriage to parenting to work to leadership.

"Blessed be the God and Father of our Lord Jesus Christ, who has blessed us with every spiritual blessing in the heavenly realms in Christ" (1:3). This letter is written large with those spiritual blessings. As Ambrosiaster explained, "He means not with an earthly but a heavenly blessing, not corruptible but eternal . . . For every gift of God's grace is in Christ." May we live in light of them, putting on the new man "who has been created in God's image—in righteousness and holiness" (4:24).

1:1–13 The wonder is not only that God gave his Son but also that he did so in this way, by sacrificing the one he loved. It is astonishing that he gave the beloved for those who hated him. See how highly he honors us. If even when we hated him and were enemies he gave the beloved, what will he not do for us now?

CHRYSOSTOM **(C. 347–407)**
HOMILIES ON THE EPISTLE OF PAUL TO THE EPHESIANS

SALUTATION

1 From Paul, an apostle of Christ Jesus by the will of God, to the
saints [in Ephesus],* the faithful in Christ Jesus. 2Grace and
peace to you from God our Father and the Lord Jesus Christ!

SPIRITUAL BLESSINGS IN CHRIST

3Blessed is the God and Father of our Lord Jesus Christ, who has
blessed us with every spiritual blessing in the heavenly realms
in Christ. 4For he chose us in Christ before the foundation of the
world that we should be holy and blameless before him in love.
5He did this by predestining us to adoption as his legal heirs
through Jesus Christ, according to the pleasure of his will—6to
the praise of the glory of his grace that he has freely bestowed
on us in his dearly loved Son. 7In him we have redemption
through his blood, the forgiveness of our offenses, according
to the riches of his grace 8that he lavished on us in all wisdom
and insight. 9He did this when he revealed to us the mystery
of his will, according to his good pleasure that he set forth in
Christ, 10toward the administration of the fullness of the times,
to head up all things in Christ—the things in heaven and the
things on earth. 11In Christ we too have been claimed as God's
own possession, since we were predestined according to the
purpose of him who accomplishes all things according to the
counsel of his will 12so that we, who were the first to set our
hope on Christ, would be to the praise of his glory. 13And when
you heard the word of truth (the gospel of your salvation)—
when you believed in Christ—you were marked with the seal
of the promised Holy Spirit, 14who is the down payment of our
inheritance, until the redemption of God's own possession, to
the praise of his glory.

PRAYER FOR WISDOM AND REVELATION

15For this reason, because I have heard of your faith in the
Lord Jesus and your love for all the saints, 16I do not cease to
give thanks for you when I remember you in my prayers. 17I
pray that the God of our Lord Jesus Christ, the glorious Father,
will give you spiritual wisdom and revelation in your growing
knowledge of him, 18—since the eyes of your heart have been
enlightened—so that you can know what is the hope of his
calling, what is the wealth of his glorious inheritance in the
saints, 19and what is the incomparable greatness of his power
toward us who believe, as displayed in the exercise of his immense strength. 20This power he exercised in Christ when he
raised him from the dead and seated him at his right hand in
the heavenly realms 21far above every rule and authority and
power and dominion and every name that is named, not only
in this age but also in the one to come. 22And God *put all things*
under Christ's *feet,* and gave him to the church as head over all
things. 23Now the church is his body, the fullness of him who
fills all in all.

NEW LIFE INDIVIDUALLY

2 And although you were dead in your offenses and sins, 2in
which you formerly lived according to this world's present
path, according to the ruler of the domain of the air, the ruler
of the spirit that is now energizing the sons of disobedience,
3among whom all of us also formerly lived out our lives in the
cravings of our flesh, indulging the desires of the flesh and the
mind, and were by nature children of wrath even as the rest...

2:1–10 The apostle himself, after saying, "By grace you are saved through faith, and this is not from yourselves, it is the gift of God," saw, of course, the possibility that people would think from this statement that good works are not necessary to those who believe, but that faith alone suffices for them; and again, the possibility of people's boasting of their good works as if they were of themselves capable of performing them. To meet these opinions on both sides, he immediately added, "For we are his creative work, having been created in Christ Jesus for good works that God prepared beforehand so we can do them."

AUGUSTINE **(354–430)**
CONFESSIONS

JOHN MARTIN, ***THE LAST JUDGEMENT*** (1853)

(Zuri Swimmer / Alamy Stock Photo)

WILLIAM HOLMAN HUNT, ***THE LIGHT OF THE WORLD*** (1851–1853)

(Public Domain)

4But God, being rich in mercy because of his great love with
which he loved us, 5even though we were dead in offenses, made
us alive together with Christ—by grace you are saved!—6and he
raised us up together with him and seated us together with
him in the heavenly realms in Christ Jesus, 7to demonstrate in
the coming ages the surpassing wealth of his grace in kindness
toward us in Christ Jesus. 8For by grace you are saved through
faith, and this is not from yourselves, it is the gift of God; 9it is
not from works, so that no one can boast. 10For we are his creative work, having been created in Christ Jesus for good works
that God prepared beforehand so we can do them.

NEW LIFE CORPORATELY

11Therefore remember that formerly you, the Gentiles in the
flesh—who are called "uncircumcision" by the so-called "circumcision" that is performed on the body by human hands—12that
you were at that time without the Messiah, alienated from the
citizenship of Israel and strangers to the covenants of promise,
having no hope and without God in the world. 13But now in
Christ Jesus you who used to be far away have been brought
near by the blood of Christ. 14For he is our peace, the one who
made both groups into one and who destroyed the middle wall
of partition, the hostility, 15when he nullified in his flesh the law
of commandments in decrees. He did this to create in himself
one new man out of two, thus making peace, 16and to reconcile
them both in one body to God through the cross, by which the
hostility has been killed. 17And he came and preached peace to
you who were far off and peace to those who were near, 18so that
through him we both have access in one Spirit to the Father.
19So then you are no longer foreigners and noncitizens, but
you are fellow citizens with the saints and members of God's
household, 20because you have been built on the foundation
of the apostles and prophets, with Christ Jesus himself as the
cornerstone. 21In him the whole building, being joined together,
grows into a holy temple in the Lord, 22in whom you also are
being built together into a dwelling place of God in the Spirit.

PAUL'S RELATIONSHIP TO THE DIVINE MYSTERY

3 For this reason I, Paul, the prisoner of Christ Jesus for the sake
of you Gentiles 2if indeed you have heard of the stewardship
of God's grace that was given to me for you, 3that by revelation
the mystery was made known to me, as I wrote before briefly.
4When reading this, you will be able to understand my insight
into the mystery of Christ 5(which was not disclosed to people
in former generations as it has now been revealed to his holy
apostles and prophets by the Spirit), 6namely, that through the
gospel the Gentiles are fellow heirs, fellow members of the body,
and fellow partakers of the promise in Christ Jesus. 7I became
a servant of this gospel according to the gift of God's grace that
was given to me by the exercise of his power. 8To me—less than
the least of all the saints—this grace was given, to proclaim to
the Gentiles the unfathomable riches of Christ 9and to enlight-
en everyone about God's secret plan—the mystery that has been
hidden for ages in God who has created all things. 10The purpose
of this enlightenment is that through the church the multifac-
eted wisdom of God should now be disclosed to the rulers and
the authorities in the heavenly realms. 11This was according
to the eternal purpose that he accomplished in Christ Jesus
our Lord, 12in whom we have boldness and confident access

3:1–21 The knowledge of Christ and of his love is deservedly in this place set down among the most desirable enjoyments of believers in this world. This love of Christ had entered the apostle's heart; he was swallowed up in the meditation and admiration of it and would have all hearts inflamed and affected with it as his was. He earnestly desired that the Ephesians know the love of Christ, that they may experimentally know his love that passes knowledge. Labor to get the clearest and fullest knowledge of Christ and his love that is attainable in this world, though you cannot arrive at a perfect comprehensive knowledge of either.

JOHN FLAVEL **(1627–1691)**
THE WORKS

to God by way of Christ's faithfulness. 13For this reason I ask you not to lose heart because of what I am suffering for you, which is your glory.

PRAYER FOR STRENGTHENED LOVE

14For this reason I kneel before the Father, 15from whom every family in heaven and on earth is named. 16I pray that according to the wealth of his glory he will grant you to be strengthened with power through his Spirit in the inner person, 17that Christ will dwell in your hearts through faith, so that, because you have been rooted and grounded in love, 18you will be able to comprehend with all the saints what is the breadth and length and height and depth, 19and thus to know the love of Christ that surpasses knowledge, so that you will be filled up to all the fullness of God.

20Now to him who by the power that is working within us is able to do far beyond all that we ask or think, 21to him be the glory in the church and in Christ Jesus to all generations, forever and ever. Amen.

LIVE IN UNITY

4 I, therefore, the prisoner for the Lord, urge you to live worthily of the calling with which you have been called, 2with all humility and gentleness, with patience, putting up with one another in love, 3making every effort to keep the unity of the Spirit in the bond of peace. 4There is one body and one Spirit, just as you too were called to the one hope of your calling, 5one Lord, one faith, one baptism, 6one God and Father of all, who is over all and through all and in all.

7But to each one of us grace was given according to the measure of Christ's gift. 8Therefore it says, ***"When he ascended on high he captured captives; he gave gifts to men."*** 9Now what is the meaning of "***he ascended,***" except that he also descended to the lower regions, namely, the earth? 10He, the very one who descended, is also the one who ascended above all the heavens, in order to fill all things. 11And he himself gave some as apostles, some as prophets, some as evangelists, and some as pastors and teachers, 12to equip the saints for the work of ministry, that is, to build up the body of Christ, 13until we all attain to the unity of the faith and of the knowledge of the Son of God—a mature person, attaining to the measure of Christ's full stature. 14So we are no longer to be children, tossed back and forth by waves and carried about by every wind of teaching by the trickery of people who craftily carry out their deceitful schemes. 15But practicing the truth in love, we will in all things grow up into Christ, who is the head. 16From him the whole body grows, fitted and held together through every supporting ligament. As each one does its part, the body builds itself up in love.

4:7–16 The design of these words is to show that the gift of the ministry is an eminent fruit of the exaltation of Christ, and a great expression and pledge of his care and love toward his church. It is the great promise that, under the gospel, Christ would give ministers to his church. It is not from any authority of their own, but it consists in an absolute compliance with the command of Christ; it is but doing what Christ commanded, and that gives virtue, efficacy, and power to it. It is in the name and authority of Jesus Christ alone by which we act; in obedience to that the minister is so constituted and appointed.

JOHN OWEN (1616–1683)
THE WORKS

LIVE IN HOLINESS

17So I say this, and insist in the Lord, that you no longer live as the Gentiles do, in the futility of their thinking. 18They are darkened in their understanding, being alienated from the life of God because of the ignorance that is in them due to the hardness of their hearts. 19Because they are callous, they have given themselves over to indecency for the practice of every kind of impurity with greediness. 20But you did not learn about Christ like this, 21if indeed you heard about him and were taught in him, just as the truth is in Jesus. 22You were taught with

reference to your former way of life to lay aside the old man
who is being corrupted in accordance with deceitful desires, [23]to
be renewed in the spirit of your mind, [24]and to put on the new
man who has been created in God's image—in righteousness
and holiness that comes from truth.

[25]Therefore, having laid aside falsehood, ***each one of you
speak the truth with his neighbor*** because we are members of
one another. [26]***Be angry and do not sin;*** do not let the sun go
down on the cause of your anger. [27]Do not give the devil an
opportunity. [28]The one who steals must steal no longer; instead
he must labor, doing good with his own hands, so that he will
have something to share with the one who has need. [29]You
must let no unwholesome word come out of your mouth, but
only what is beneficial for the building up of the one in need,
that it would give grace to those who hear. [30]And do not grieve
the Holy Spirit of God, by whom you were sealed for the day of
redemption. [31]You must put away all bitterness, anger, wrath,
quarreling, and slanderous talk—indeed all malice. [32]Instead,
be kind to one another, compassionate, forgiving one another,
just as God in Christ also forgave you.

LIVE IN LOVE

5 Therefore, be imitators of God as dearly loved children [2]and
live in love, just as Christ also loved us and gave himself for
us, a sacrificial and fragrant offering to God. [3]But among you
there must not be either sexual immorality, impurity of any
kind, or greed, as these are not fitting for the saints. [4]Neither
should there be vulgar speech, foolish talk, or coarse jesting—
all of which are out of character—but rather thanksgiving. [5]For
you can be confident of this one thing: that no person who is
immoral, impure, or greedy (such a person is an idolater) has
any inheritance in the kingdom of Christ and God.

LIVE IN THE LIGHT

[6]Let nobody deceive you with empty words, for because of these
things God's wrath comes on the sons of disobedience. [7]There-
fore do not be sharers with them, [8]for you were at one time
darkness, but now you are light in the Lord. Live like children
of light—[9]for the fruit of the light consists in all goodness, righteousness, and truth—[10]trying to learn what is pleasing to the
Lord. [11]Do not participate in the unfruitful deeds of darkness,
but rather expose them. [12]For the things they do in secret are
shameful even to mention. [13]But all things being exposed by
the light are made visible. [14]For everything made visible is light,
and for this reason it says:

"Awake, O sleeper!
Rise from the dead,
and Christ will shine on you!"

LIVE WISELY

[15]Therefore consider carefully how you live—not as unwise but
as wise, [16]taking advantage of every opportunity because the
days are evil. [17]For this reason do not be foolish, but be wise by
understanding what the Lord's will is. [18]And do not get drunk with
wine, which is debauchery, but be filled by the Spirit, [19]speaking
to one another in psalms, hymns, and spiritual songs, singing and
making music in your hearts to the Lord, [20]always giving thanks to
God the Father for all things in the name of our Lord Jesus Christ,
[21]and submitting to one another out of reverence for Christ.

5:1–21 Christ, the Sun of Righteousness, has risen. Rise up from the sleep of the age. Walk cautiously and prudently. Cast off folly. Take hold of wisdom. In this way you will be able to avoid changing yourself constantly as you walk through the vicissitudes of the times. Rather you will find a unity within yourself even amid the diversity of the times.

JEROME (C. 342–420)
EPISTLE TO THE EPHESIANS

JOHN BUNYAN:

PURITAN PILGRIM, CHIEF OF SINNERS

1628–1688

The name John Bunyan is synonymous with *spiritual journey*, for his book *Pilgrim's Progress* quickly became a classic work guiding countless people burdened by sin to the cross of Christ and beyond to the Celestial City.

Born to a working-class peasant family in 1628 near Bedford, England, Bunyan was given a brief grammar school education before he began assisting his father as a tinker and was groomed to learn the trade. But at sixteen he was conscripted to serve a four-year military stint, after which he joined the Puritan movement that was sweeping the land, serving as a field preacher. It was then that his life took a dramatic turn.

After Charles II was reinstated as king, so-called Nonconformists such as Bunyan were deemed suspect and arrested. He spent 12 years in prison after refusing to give up field preaching, but this misfortune turned into a source of tremendous blessing for the church: It was in the solitude and suffering of his prison cell that John Bunyan launched his writing career.

His first work was *Grace Abounding*, an autobiographical account of his personal spiritual journey and struggles to find new-creation life in Christ after years of profane, blasphemous living. It also chronicled his quest to discover God's abounding grace and mercy in light of his sinful condition. This journey was in many ways shaped by the Calvinism of his day, which emphasized both man's total depravity and God's predestination of individuals, which led to Bunyan's personal spiritual despair.

Wracked by guilt, he wrote:

> *I had no sooner thus conceived in my mind, but suddenly this conclusion was fastened on my spirit, for the former hint did set my sins again before my face that I had been a great and grievous sinner, and that it was now too late for me to look after heaven; for Christ would not forgive me, nor pardon my transgressions.*

Yet Bunyan slowly began to discover what he had been searching for: grace abounding. His account of his personal journey would serve as a foundation for another book: *Pilgrim's Progress*.

The tenor and tone of this allegory of the Christian's journey is set from the opening paragraph:

> *As I walked through the wilderness of this world, I lighted on a certain place where was a den, and laid me down in that place to sleep; and as I slept, I dreamed a dream. I dreamed, and behold, I saw a man clothed with rags, standing in a certain place, with his face from his own house, a book in his hand, and a great burden upon his back. I looked and saw him open the book, and read therein; and as he read, he wept and trembled; and not being able longer to contain, he brake out with a lamentable cry, saying, "What shall I do?"*

The rest of the book traces the journey of this pilgrim named Christian to discover an answer to that burning question—the same question voiced by the crowd in Acts 2 after Peter's gospel sermon calling for repentance: "What should we do?" (v. 37). Bunyan's own discovery of a righteousness not his own is reflected in Christian's allegorical journey, which climaxes when he comes to the cross and his burden of original sin falls off and is buried in the sepulchre of Christ, never to be seen again. The book ends with Christian's discovery of his heart's desire: the gates of the Celestial City open, even to him.

Hailed as a book that crosses social and cultural barriers, *Pilgrim's Progress* has stood the generational test, impacting countless spiritual journeys. Bunyan saw the book published in 12 editions before his death in 1688, perhaps providing encouragement to his own pilgrim soul's journey to the Celestial City.

IMPORTANT WORKS

GRACE ABOUNDING TO THE CHIEF OF SINNERS

PILGRIM'S PROGRESS

EXHORTATIONS TO HOUSEHOLDS

22Wives, submit to your husbands as to the Lord, 23because
the husband is the head of the wife as also Christ is the head
of the church (he himself being the savior of the body). 24But
as the church submits to Christ, so also wives should submit
to their husbands in everything. 25Husbands, love your wives
just as Christ loved the church and gave himself for her 26to
sanctify her by cleansing her with the washing of the water by
the word, 27so that he may present the church to himself as
glorious—not having a stain or wrinkle, or any such blemish,
but holy and blameless. 28In the same way husbands ought
to love their wives as their own bodies. He who loves his wife
loves himself. 29For no one has ever hated his own body, but
he feeds it and takes care of it, just as Christ also does the
church, 30because we are members of his body. 31***For this rea-***
son a man will leave his father and mother and will be joined to
his wife, and the two will become one flesh. 32This mystery is
great—but I am actually speaking with reference to Christ and
the church. 33Nevertheless, each one of you must also love his
own wife as he loves himself, and the wife must respect her
husband.

6 Children, obey your parents in the Lord, for this is right.
2"***Honor your father and mother,***" which is the first commandment accompanied by a promise, namely, 3"***that it will go well***
with you and that you will live a long time on the earth."

4Fathers, do not provoke your children to anger, but raise
them up in the discipline and instruction of the Lord.

5Slaves, obey your human masters with fear and trembling,
in the sincerity of your heart, as to Christ, 6not like those who
do their work only when someone is watching—as people-
pleasers—but as slaves of Christ doing the will of God from
the heart. 7Obey with enthusiasm, as though serving the Lord
and not people, 8because you know that each person, whether
slave or free, if he does something good, this will be rewarded
by the Lord.

[9]Masters, treat your slaves the same way, giving up the use
of threats, because you know that both you and they have the
same master in heaven, and there is no favoritism with him.

EXHORTATIONS FOR SPIRITUAL WARFARE

[10]Finally, be strengthened in the Lord and in the strength of
his power. [11]Clothe yourselves with the full armor of God, so
that you will be able to stand against the schemes of the devil.
[12]For our struggle is not against flesh and blood, but against
the rulers, against the powers, against the world rulers of this
darkness, against the spiritual forces of evil in the heavens.
[13]For this reason, take up the full armor of God so that you may
be able to stand your ground on the evil day, and having done
everything, to stand. [14]Stand firm therefore, by fastening the
belt of truth around your waist, by putting on the breastplate
of righteousness, [15]by fitting your feet with the preparation
that comes from the good news of peace, [16]and in all of this,
by taking up the shield of faith with which you can extinguish
all the flaming arrows of the evil one. [17]And take *the helmet
of salvation* and the sword of the Spirit (which is the word of
God). [18]With every prayer and petition, pray at all times in the
Spirit, and to this end be alert, with all perseverance and petitions for all the saints. [19]Pray for me also, that I may be given
the right words when I begin to speak—that I may confidently
make known the mystery of the gospel, [20]for which I am an
ambassador in chains. Pray that I may be able to speak boldly
as I ought to speak.

6:10–20 The apostle Paul teaches us that we ought not to give place to the devil but "clothe yourselves" he says, "with the full armor of God, so that you will be able to stand against the schemes of the devil." Paul points out that the saints have to wrestle "not against flesh and blood, but against the rulers, against the powers, against the world rulers of this darkness, against the spiritual forces of evil in the heavens." By all this, holy scripture teaches us that there are certain invisible enemies that fight against us and against whom it commands us to arm ourselves.

ORIGEN (C. 185–C. 253)
ON FIRST PRINCIPLES

FAREWELL COMMENTS

[21]Tychicus, my dear brother and faithful servant in the Lord,
will make everything known to you, so that you too may know
about my circumstances, how I am doing. [22]I have sent him to
you for this very purpose, that you may know our circumstances
and that he may encourage your hearts.

[23]Peace to the brothers and sisters, and love with faith, from
God the Father and the Lord Jesus Christ. [24]Grace be with all
those who love our Lord Jesus Christ with an undying love.

AUTHOR	AUDIENCE	DATE	PURPOSE	THEMES
Paul	The believers at Philippi, a prosperous Roman colony	Around AD 61	Paul wrote to thank the Philippian believers for their partnership in gospel ministry and to encourage them in their faith.	The gospel; the person of Christ; Christian living; and Christian community

Paul wrote his epistle of encouragement to believers in Philippi so that their "love may abound even more and more in knowledge and every kind of insight" (1:9). These brothers and sisters had been faithful partners in Paul's missionary efforts—a ministry that had landed the apostle in chains. He encouraged them not to be afraid of joining him in suffering and adversity. He also cautioned them about the dangers of disunity and false teaching. He pointed to the person and work of Christ, as well as his own living example, to spur them on in their walk with the Lord.

The church has long leaned on the heart of this letter in theological debates concerning the nature of Christ. Chapter 2 contains a hymn of Christ that reveals the majesty of his preexistent glory; the humility of Christ in his earthly sojourn and sacrificial death; and his exaltation as Lord in full, resurrected glory. Eusebius captured well the implications of these truths: "[Paul] acknowledged Christ and no other to be the Son of God. The flesh that Christ assumed was called 'the form of a slave' and 'son of man.' But as to that birth that, unknown to all, was from the Father and before all ages, he was Son of God."

In light of Christ's lordship, Philippians exhorts readers to live under his reign in our everyday lives, "working out your salvation with awe and reverence" knowing "the one bringing forth in you both the desire and the effort—for the sake of his good pleasure—is God" (2:12–13). We work out our salvation by shifting our mindset and attention from earthly cares to the priorities of heaven, since that is where our ultimate citizenship resides. Rejoicing should be a hallmark of our lives on earth, as is putting into practice that which is true and noble.

Christ's lordship over our lives should also impact how we live with one another, for the gospel creates a people who are "of the same mind, by having the same love, being united in spirit, and having one purpose" (2:2). Selfish ambition and acrimonious disputes have no place in the body of Christ. Further, we are to care for one another, sharing our distresses and needs. Reflecting on this mandate, John Calvin wrote, "Now he reckons that the chief indication of a prosperous condition of the church is when mutual agreement prevails in it, and brotherly harmony . . . Hence the beginning of love is harmony of views, but that is not sufficient, unless men's hearts are at the same time joined together in mutual affection." The Reformers viewed the church as a community of love bound together by common beliefs as well as by a common devotion to Christ.

Centuries earlier, Christian thinker Marius Victorinus offered this reflection: "What does he mean by 'the same love'? That you should have the same love for another that the other has for you, not a divided love but a love embedded in life in Christ."

As we approach this book, the words of Lutheran theologian Georg Major on its importance are worth remembering:

> Therefore, let us observe that in this letter to the Philippians a truly fine example of a brave, honest Christian congregation is placed before us. We and other Christian congregations should follow their example so that we too would grow in faith, would remain firm in the confession of pure teaching, would lead a godly and irreproachable life, would hold our pastors in high esteem—just as we see in both Saint Paul and the congregation in Philippi, how sincerely they loved one another and cared for one another. For this reason this letter should become even dearer to us.

1:3–11 Never was anything equal to the yearnings of the apostle, never anything like the sympathy and the affection of the blessed Paul, who made his every prayer on behalf of whole cities and peoples and writes the same to all, "I thank my God every time I remember you. I always pray with joy in my every prayer for all of you." Think how many he had in his mind, whom it was a labor so much as to remember; how many he made mention of in his prayers, giving thanks to God for them all as though he himself had received the greatest blessing.

CHRYSOSTOM **(C. 347–407)**
HOMILIES ON THE EPISTLE OF PAUL TO THE EPHESIANS

SALUTATION

1 From Paul and Timothy, slaves of Christ Jesus, to all the saints in Christ Jesus who are in Philippi, with the overseers and deacons. [2]Grace and peace to you from God our Father and the Lord Jesus Christ!

PRAYER FOR THE CHURCH

[3]I thank my God every time I remember you. [4]I always pray with joy in my every prayer for all of you [5]because of your participation in the gospel from the first day until now. [6]For I am sure of this very thing, that the one who began a good work in you will perfect it until the day of Christ Jesus. [7]For it is right for me to think this about all of you, because I have you in my heart, since both in my imprisonment and in the defense and confirmation of the gospel all of you became partners in God's grace together with me. [8]For God is my witness that I long for all of you with the affection of Christ Jesus. [9]And I pray this, that your love may abound even more and more in knowledge and every kind of insight [10]so that you can decide what is best, and thus be sincere and blameless for the day of Christ, [11]filled with the fruit of righteousness that comes through Jesus Christ to the glory and praise of God.

MINISTRY AS A PRISONER

[12]I want you to know, brothers and sisters, that my situation has actually turned out to advance the gospel: [13]The whole imperial guard and everyone else knows that I am in prison for the sake of Christ, [14]and most of the brothers and sisters, having confidence in the Lord because of my imprisonment, now more than ever dare to speak the word fearlessly.

[15]Some, to be sure, are preaching Christ from envy and rivalry, but others from goodwill. [16]The latter do so from love because they know that I am placed here for the defense of the gospel. [17]The former proclaim Christ from selfish ambition, not sincerely, because they think they can cause trouble for me in my imprisonment. [18]What is the result? Only that in every way, whether in pretense or in truth, Christ is being proclaimed, and in this I rejoice.

Yes, and I will continue to rejoice, [19]for I know that this will turn out for my deliverance through your prayers and the help of the Spirit of Jesus Christ. [20]My confident hope is that I will in no way be ashamed but that with complete boldness, even now as always, Christ will be exalted in my body, whether I live or die. [21]For to me, living is Christ and dying is gain. [22]Now if I am to go on living in the body, this will mean productive work for me, yet I don't know which I prefer: [23]I feel torn between the two because I have a desire to depart and be with Christ, which is better by far, [24]but it is more vital for your sake that I remain in the body. [25]And since I am sure of this, I know that I will remain and continue with all of you for the sake of your progress and joy in the faith, [26]so that what you can be proud of may increase because of me in Christ Jesus, when I come back to you.

[27]Only conduct yourselves in a manner worthy of the gospel of Christ so that—whether I come and see you or whether I remain absent—I should hear that you are standing firm in one spirit, with one mind, by contending side by side for the faith of the gospel, [28]and by not being intimidated in any way by your opponents. This is a sign of their destruction, but of your

salvation—a sign which is from God. 29For it has been granted
to you not only to believe in Christ but also to suffer for him,
30since you are encountering the same conflict that you saw
me face and now hear that I am facing.

CHRISTIAN UNITY AND CHRIST'S HUMILITY

2 Therefore, if there is any encouragement in Christ, any
comfort provided by love, any fellowship in the Spirit, any
affection or mercy, 2complete my joy and be of the same mind,
by having the same love, being united in spirit, and having one
purpose. 3Instead of being motivated by selfish ambition or
vanity, each of you should, in humility, be moved to treat one
another as more important than yourself. 4Each of you should
be concerned not only about your own interests, but about the
interests of others as well. 5You should have the same attitude
toward one another that Christ Jesus had,

6 who, though he existed in the form of God,
did not regard equality with God
as something to be grasped,
7 but emptied himself
by taking on the form of a slave,
by looking like other men,
and by sharing in human nature.
8 He humbled himself
by becoming obedient to the point of death
—even death on a cross!
9 As a result God highly exalted him
and gave him the name
that is above every name,
10 so that at the name of Jesus
every knee will bow
—in heaven and on earth and under the earth—
11 and every tongue confess
that Jesus Christ is Lord
to the glory of God the Father.

LIGHTS IN THE WORLD

12So then, my dear friends, just as you have always obeyed, not
only in my presence but even more in my absence, continue
working out your salvation with awe and reverence, 13for the
one bringing forth in you both the desire and the effort—for
the sake of his good pleasure—is God. 14Do everything without
grumbling or arguing, 15so that you may be blameless and pure,
children of God without blemish though you live in a crooked
and perverse society, in which you shine as lights in the world
16by holding on to the word of life so that on the day of Christ I
will have a reason to boast: that I did not run in vain nor labor
in vain. 17But even if I am being poured out like a drink offering
on the sacrifice and service of your faith, I am glad and rejoice
together with all of you. 18And in the same way you also should
be glad and rejoice together with me.

MODELS FOR MINISTRY

19Now I hope in the Lord Jesus to send Timothy to you soon,
so that I, too, may be encouraged by hearing news about you.
20For there is no one here like him who will readily demonstrate
his deep concern for you. 21Others are busy with their own
concerns, not those of Jesus Christ. 22But you know his qualifications that like a son working with his father, he served with

2:1–11 While on earth, wasn't Christ continually stripping away one robe of honor after another until, finally naked, he was nailed to the cross? Even on the cross, didn't he continue to empty out his inmost self, pouring out his lifeblood and giving his all for us until they laid him in a borrowed tomb? How could our dear Redeemer have been brought any lower? How then can we be proud? As Jesus humbled himself for you, bow yourself in complete humility at his feet, for an awareness of Christ's amazing love for us should have a greater tendency to cause us to humble ourselves than even the consciousness of our own guilt.

CHARLES SPURGEON
(1834–1892)
METROPOLITAN TABERNACLE SERMONS

me in advancing the gospel. [23]So I hope to send him as soon as I know more about my situation, [24]though I am confident in the Lord that I, too, will be coming to see you soon.

[25]But for now I have considered it necessary to send Epaphroditus to you. For he is my brother, coworker and fellow soldier, and your messenger and minister to me in my need. [26]Indeed, he greatly missed all of you and was distressed because you heard that he had been ill. [27]In fact he became so ill that he nearly died. But God showed mercy to him—and not to him only, but also to me—so that I would not have grief on top of grief. [28]Therefore I am all the more eager to send him, so that when you see him again you can rejoice and I can be free from anxiety. [29]So welcome him in the Lord with great joy, and honor people like him, [30]since it was because of the work of Christ that he almost died. He risked his life so that he could make up for your inability to serve me.

TRUE AND FALSE RIGHTEOUSNESS

3 Finally, my brothers and sisters, rejoice in the Lord! To write this again is no trouble to me, and it is a safeguard for you. [2]Beware of the dogs, beware of the evil workers, beware of those who mutilate the flesh! [3]For we are the circumcision, the ones who worship by the Spirit of God, exult in Christ Jesus, and do not rely on human credentials [4]—though mine, too, are significant. If someone thinks he has good reasons to put confidence in human credentials, I have more: [5]I was circumcised on the eighth day, from the people of Israel and the tribe of Benjamin, a Hebrew of Hebrews. I lived according to the law as a Pharisee. [6]In my zeal for God I persecuted the church. According to the righteousness stipulated in the law I was blameless. [7]But these assets I have come to regard as liabilities because of Christ. [8]More than that, I now regard all things as liabilities compared to the far greater value of knowing Christ Jesus my Lord, for whom I have suffered the loss of all things—indeed, I regard them as dung!—that I may gain Christ [9]and be found in him, not because I have my own righteousness derived from the law, but because I have the righteousness that comes by way of Christ's faithfulness—a righteousness from God that is in fact based on Christ's faithfulness. [10]My aim is to know him, to experience the power of his resurrection, to share in his sufferings, and to be like him in his death, [11]and so, somehow, to attain to the resurrection from the dead.

KEEP GOING FORWARD

[12]Not that I have already attained this—that is, I have not already been perfected—but I strive to lay hold of that for which Christ Jesus also laid hold of me. [13]Brothers and sisters, I do not consider myself to have attained this. Instead I am single-minded: Forgetting the things that are behind and reaching out for the things that are ahead, [14]with this goal in mind, I strive toward the prize of the upward call of God in Christ Jesus. [15]Therefore let those of us who are "perfect" embrace this point of view. If you think otherwise, God will reveal to you the error of your ways. [16]Nevertheless, let us live up to the standard that we have already attained.

[17]Be imitators of me, brothers and sisters, and watch carefully those who are living this way, just as you have us as an example. [18]For many live, about whom I have often told you, and now, with tears, I tell you that they are the enemies of the cross of Christ.

3:1–16 Paul deemed all these things to be but loss compared with the knowledge of Christ by faith in his person and salvation. He speaks of all worldly enjoyments and outward privileges that sought a place with Christ in his heart. The believer prefers Christ, knowing that it is better for him to be without all worldly riches than without Christ and his word. There is no getting to heaven as our home but by Christ as our way. True believers, in seeking this assurance as well as to glorify him, will seek more nearly to resemble his sufferings and death by dying to sin and by crucifying the flesh with its affections and lusts.

MATTHEW HENRY (1662–1714)
COMMENTARY ON THE WHOLE BIBLE

[19]Their end is destruction, their god is the belly, they exult in their shame, and they think about earthly things. [20]But our citizenship is in heaven—and we also eagerly await a savior from there, the Lord Jesus Christ, [21]who will transform these humble bodies of ours into the likeness of his glorious body by means of that power by which he is able to subject all things to himself.

CHRISTIAN PRACTICES

4 So then, my brothers and sisters, dear friends whom I long to see, my joy and crown, stand in the Lord in this way, my dear friends!

[2]I appeal to Euodia and to Syntyche to agree in the Lord. [3]Yes, I say also to you, true companion, help them. They have struggled together in the gospel ministry along with me and Clement and my other coworkers, whose names are in the book of life. [4]Rejoice in the Lord always. Again I say, rejoice! [5]Let everyone see your gentleness. The Lord is near! [6]Do not be anxious about anything. Instead, in every situation, through prayer and petition with thanksgiving, tell your requests to God. [7]And the peace of God that surpasses all understanding will guard your hearts and minds in Christ Jesus.

[8]Finally, brothers and sisters, whatever is true, whatever is worthy of respect, whatever is just, whatever is pure, whatever is lovely, whatever is commendable, if something is excellent or praiseworthy, think about these things. [9]And what you learned and received and heard and saw in me, do these things. And the God of peace will be with you.

APPRECIATION FOR SUPPORT

[10]I have great joy in the Lord because now at last you have again expressed your concern for me. (Now I know you were concerned before but had no opportunity to do anything.) [11]I am not saying this because I am in need, for I have learned to be content in any circumstance. [12]I have experienced times of need and times of abundance. In any and every circumstance I have learned the secret of contentment, whether I go satisfied or hungry, have plenty or nothing. [13]I am able to do all things through the one who strengthens me. [14]Nevertheless, you did well to share with me in my trouble.

[15]And as you Philippians know, at the beginning of my gospel ministry, when I left Macedonia, no church shared with me in this matter of giving and receiving except you alone. [16]For even in Thessalonica on more than one occasion you sent something for my need. [17]I do not say this because I am seeking a gift. Rather, I seek the credit that abounds to your account. [18]For I have received everything, and I have plenty. I have all I need because I received from Epaphroditus what you sent—a fragrant offering, an acceptable sacrifice, very pleasing to God. [19]And my God will supply your every need according to his glorious riches in Christ Jesus. [20]May glory be given to God our Father forever and ever. Amen.

FINAL GREETINGS

[21]Give greetings to all the saints in Christ Jesus. The brothers with me here send greetings. [22]All the saints greet you, especially those who belong to Caesar's household. [23]The grace of the Lord Jesus Christ be with your spirit.

4:1–8 Paul writes, "The peace of God . . . will guard your hearts" and "the God of peace will be with you." A carnal heart could be satisfied if it might but have outward peace. But mark how a godly heart goes beyond a carnal one. *I must have the peace of God.* But suppose you have the peace of God, will not that quiet you? *No, I must have the God of peace.* That is, *I must enjoy the God who gives me the peace. I must see from where my peace comes and enjoy the fountain of my peace as well as the stream of my peace.*

JEREMIAH BURROUGHS
(1599–1646)
THE GRACIOUS HEART AND THE CARNAL HEART

AUTHOR	AUDIENCE	DATE	PURPOSE	THEMES
Paul	The believers at Colossae, a church perhaps planted by Paul's coworker, Epaphras	Around AD 60	Paul wrote to demonstrate the supremacy of Christ over every human philosophy and accomplishment.	The supremacy of Christ; the church; the gospel; faith; and the Christian life

Hope is hard to come by these days. Yet it is something for which every human heart has yearned since our first parents were exiled from the garden. In Colossians saints in Christ are offered the hope of God, "laid up for you in heaven . . . the hope of the gospel" (1:5, 23).

For generations the book of Colossians has provided hope for Christians looking to understand what they are to believe and how they are to live, making it a book just as vital for us as it has been in the lives of the saints down through the centuries. Although this book contains only four chapters, it has helped believers from all walks of life express the hope of their faith.

Written by the apostle Paul shortly after he penned his larger letter to the Romans, Colossians traces a number of hope-filled themes that can be summarized by what Paul and Timothy themselves had heard about this community: "your faith in Christ Jesus and the love that you have for all the saints" (1:4). A voice from the sixteenth-century church, Girolamo Zanchi, framed Paul's message to the Colossian believers in this way, showing how it pivots around these two themes of faith and love, believing and living:

> First, he lays out for them a brief sum of the whole of Christian doctrine, just as they had learned also from Epaphras, particularly showing them wherein lies our salvation and what are the true grounds of it. Second, after confirming true doctrine, he refutes its antithesis by arguing against pseudo-apostles. He shows unequivocally that the Mosaic ceremonies have been abolished and that all self-made religion should be avoided as completely futile and displeasing to God. He tells them that they should press on in their zeal for true piety, stripping off the old person and putting on the new.

Throughout history people have struggled to understand how to approach the divine. In some ways, early Christians were no different. As the fourth-century church father Chrysostom explained, "The Colossians used to approach God through angels; they followed many Jewish and Grecian observances. Paul is correcting these practices."

COLOSSIANS

John Calvin echoed this background context: "The Colossians had been instructed in the gospel. But immediately afterward, Satan had crept in with his tares, according to his usual and invariable manner, so that he might there distort right faith."

Paul worked to correct these distorted beliefs by reminding the Colossians (and us) that Christ is the very "image of the invisible God, the firstborn over all creation" (1:15); that the work of Christ "[makes] peace through the blood of his cross" (1:20); and that there are indeed false Christs who will attempt "to captivate you through an empty, deceitful philosophy that is according to human traditions" (2:8).

And yet it's also more than that. Not only had the Colossians struggled with right belief, but they also struggled with right living, which is why Paul encouraged this community of faith to "keep thinking about things above, not things on the earth" (3:2).

Such a shift in mindset should unfold in a way that puts to death fornication and evil desire, covetousness and idolatry; that puts off anger and malice, lying and filthy talk. But it doesn't stop there, for Paul exhorts us to "put on" as much as "put off" (3:8–9). Put on tender mercies and kindness, he says. Put on humility and forgiveness, he encourages. The sixteenth-century pastor and Reformer Martin Luther put it this way: "You must die and be dead to [sin], and then strive for what is righteous, godly, and Christian." This is because a life of hope is found in a life well lived according to the gospel of hope.

The hope of the gospel is "Christ in you, the hope of glory" (1:27), which works within us to draw us nearer to God and make us more like his Son. "Christ in you" is a deposit of hope for a future in which he reconciles all things to himself, "in whom we have redemption, the forgiveness of sins" (1:14)—our ultimate hope.

We need Paul's message to the Colossians in our day as much as they needed it in theirs. These sacred words of hope from the heart of God and the pen of Paul are infused with sacred insights into faith and life that will guide you every day "as the elect of God, holy and dearly loved" (3:12).

1:1–8 In this preface the apostle praises the Colossians. Faith, hope, and love are the nerves and sinews—they are the principal heads of the Christian religion. While Paul congratulates the Colossians on their success, he also prays that God will increase their inheritance steadily and uphold them from that day forward. By rightly dividing these concepts, Paul connects them to their powers and duties: Faith stretches toward Christ Jesus and leans on his merits, love busies itself with everything holy and excellent, and hope perseveres on account of the eternal treasure set aside for us in heaven.

HEINRICH BULLINGER
(1504–1575)
COMMENTARY ON COLOSSIANS

SALUTATION

1 From Paul, an apostle of Christ Jesus by the will of God, and
Timothy our brother, 2to the saints, the faithful brothers
and sisters in Christ, at Colossae. Grace and peace to you from
God our Father!

PAUL'S THANKSGIVING AND PRAYER FOR THE CHURCH

3We always give thanks to God, the Father of our Lord Jesus
Christ, when we pray for you, 4since we heard about your faith
in Christ Jesus and the love that you have for all the saints.
5Your faith and love have arisen from the hope laid up for you
in heaven, which you have heard about in the message of truth,
the gospel 6that has come to you. Just as in the entire world this
gospel is bearing fruit and growing, so it has also been bearing
fruit and growing among you from the first day you heard it and
understood the grace of God in truth. 7You learned the gospel
from Epaphras, our dear fellow slave—a faithful minister of
Christ on our behalf—8who also told us of your love in the Spirit.

PAUL'S PRAYER FOR THE GROWTH OF THE CHURCH

9For this reason we also, from the day we heard about you, have
not ceased praying for you and asking God to fill you with the
knowledge of his will in all spiritual wisdom and understanding, 10so that you may live worthily of the Lord and please him
in all respects—bearing fruit in every good deed, growing in
the knowledge of God, 11being strengthened with all power
according to his glorious might for the display of all patience
and steadfastness, joyfully 12giving thanks to the Father who
has qualified you to share in the saints' inheritance in the light.
13He delivered us from the power of darkness and transferred
us to the kingdom of the Son he loves, 14in whom we have redemption, the forgiveness of sins.

THE SUPREMACY OF CHRIST

15 He is the image of the invisible God, the firstborn over
all creation,
16 for all things in heaven and on earth were created
in him—all things, whether visible or invisible,
whether thrones or dominions, whether
principalities or powers—all things were created
through him and for him.
17 He himself is before all things, and all things are held
together in him.
18 He is the head of the body, the church, as well as the
beginning, the firstborn from the dead, so that he
himself may become first in all things.
19 For God was pleased to have all his fullness dwell in the
Son
20 and through him to reconcile all things to himself by
making peace through the blood of his cross—
through him, whether things on earth or things in
heaven.

PAUL'S GOAL IN MINISTRY

21And you were at one time strangers and enemies in your
minds as expressed through your evil deeds, 22but now he has
reconciled you by his physical body through death to present

you holy, without blemish, and blameless before him—[23]if indeed you remain in the faith, established and firm, without shifting from the hope of the gospel that you heard. This gospel has also been preached in all creation under heaven, and I, Paul, have become its servant.

[24]Now I rejoice in my sufferings for you, and I fill up in my physical body—for the sake of his body, the church—what is lacking in the sufferings of Christ. [25]I became a servant of the church according to the stewardship from God—given to me for you—in order to complete the word of God, [26]that is, the mystery that has been kept hidden from ages and generations, but has now been revealed to his saints. [27]God wanted to make known to them the glorious riches of this mystery among the Gentiles, which is Christ in you, the hope of glory. [28]We proclaim him by instructing and teaching all people with all wisdom so that we may present every person mature in Christ. [29]Toward this goal I also labor, struggling according to his power that powerfully works in me.

2 For I want you to know how great a struggle I have for you, and for those in Laodicea, and for those who have not met me face to face. [2]My goal is that their hearts, having been knit together in love, may be encouraged, and that they may have all the riches that assurance brings in their understanding of the knowledge of the mystery of God, namely, Christ, [3]in whom are hidden all the treasures of wisdom and knowledge. [4]I say this so that no one will deceive you through arguments that sound reasonable. [5]For though I am absent from you in body, I am present with you in spirit, rejoicing to see your morale and the firmness of your faith in Christ.

WARNINGS AGAINST THE ADOPTION OF FALSE PHILOSOPHIES

[6]Therefore, just as you received Christ Jesus as Lord, continue to live your lives in him, [7]rooted and built up in him and firm in your faith just as you were taught, and overflowing with thankfulness. [8]Be careful not to allow anyone to captivate you through an empty, deceitful philosophy that is according to human traditions and the elemental spirits of the world, and not according to Christ. [9]For in him all the fullness of deity lives in bodily form, [10]and you have been filled in him, who is the head over every ruler and authority. [11]In him you also were circumcised—not, however, with a circumcision performed by human hands, but by the removal of the fleshly body, that is, through the circumcision done by Christ. [12]Having been buried with him in baptism, you also have been raised with him through your faith in the power of God who raised him from the dead. [13]And even though you were dead in your transgressions and in the uncircumcision of your flesh, he nevertheless made you alive with him, having forgiven all your transgressions. [14]He has destroyed what was against us, a certificate of indebtedness expressed in decrees opposed to us. He has taken it away by nailing it to the cross. [15]Disarming the rulers and authorities, he has made a public disgrace of them, triumphing over them by the cross.

[16]Therefore do not let anyone judge you with respect to food or drink, or in the matter of a feast, new moon, or Sabbath days—[17]these are only the shadow of the things to come, but the reality is Christ! [18]Let no one who delights in false humility and the worship of angels pass judgment on you. That person

2:1–10 **Believers are filled with all the fullness of God. But in Christ dwells "all the fullness of deity," not only divine powers but also the divine nature, personally, really, substantially. The very substance of God, if one might so speak, dwells in Christ in the fullest sense. And you who believe are "filled in him." Christ is filled with God, and you are filled with Christ. The fullness of Christ overflows his church. He is originally full. We are filled by him with wisdom and holiness.**

JOHN WESLEY **(1703–1791)**
EXPLANATORY NOTES ON THE BIBLE

goes on at great lengths about what he has supposedly seen,
but he is puffed up with empty notions by his fleshly mind.
19He has not held fast to the head from whom the whole body,
supported and knit together through its ligaments and sinews,
grows with a growth that is from God.
20If you have died with Christ to the elemental spirits of the
world, why do you submit to them as though you lived in the
world? 21"Do not handle! Do not taste! Do not touch!" 22These
are all destined to perish with use, founded as they are on human commands and teachings. 23Even though they have the
appearance of wisdom with their self-imposed worship and
humility achieved by an unsparing treatment of the body—a
wisdom with no true value—they in reality result in fleshly
indulgence.

3:1–11 Christ is the nourishment for our life, for what can a Christian truly feed upon but Jesus' flesh and blood? Oh, travel-weary pilgrims in this wilderness of sin, you will never find even a morsel to satisfy the hunger of your spirit unless you find it in Christ! He is the source of peace for our life and all true joy comes from him, and in times of trouble his presence is our comfort. If we live in close fellowship with the Lord Jesus, we will grow to be like him. We will set him before us as our divine example and will seek to walk in his footsteps until he becomes the crown of our life in glory.

CHARLES SPURGEON
(1834–1892)
METROPOLITAN TABERNACLE SERMONS

EXHORTATIONS TO SEEK THE THINGS ABOVE

3 Therefore, if you have been raised with Christ, keep seeking
the things above, where Christ is, seated at the right hand
of God. 2Keep thinking about things above, not things on the
earth, 3for you have died and your life is hidden with Christ in
God. 4When Christ (who is your life) appears, then you too will
be revealed in glory with him. 5So put to death whatever in
your nature belongs to the earth: sexual immorality, impurity,
shameful passion, evil desire, and greed which is idolatry. 6Be-
cause of these things the wrath of God is coming on the sons of
disobedience. 7You also lived your lives in this way at one time,
when you used to live among them. 8But now, put off all such
things as anger, rage, malice, slander, abusive language from
your mouth. 9Do not lie to one another since you have put off
the old man with its practices 10and have been clothed with the
new man that is being renewed in knowledge according to the
image of the one who created it. 11Here there is neither Greek
nor Jew, circumcised or uncircumcised, barbarian, Scythian,
slave or free, but Christ is all and in all.

EXHORTATION TO UNITY AND LOVE

12Therefore, as the elect of God, holy and dearly loved, clothe
yourselves with a heart of mercy, kindness, humility, gentleness,
and patience, 13bearing with one another and forgiving one another, if someone happens to have a complaint against anyone
else. Just as the Lord has forgiven you, so you also forgive others.
14And to all these virtues add love, which is the perfect bond.
15Let the peace of Christ be in control in your heart (for you
were in fact called as one body to this peace), and be thankful.
16Let the word of Christ dwell in you richly, teaching and exhorting one another with all wisdom, singing psalms, hymns,
and spiritual songs, all with grace in your hearts to God. 17And
whatever you do in word or deed, do it all in the name of the
Lord Jesus, giving thanks to God the Father through him.

EXHORTATION TO HOUSEHOLDS

18Wives, submit to your husbands, as is fitting in the Lord.
19Husbands, love your wives and do not be embittered against
them. 20Children, obey your parents in everything, for this is
pleasing in the Lord. 21Fathers, do not provoke your children, so
they will not become disheartened. 22Slaves, obey your earthly
masters in every respect, not only when they are watching—
like those who are strictly people-pleasers—but with a sincere
heart, fearing the Lord. 23Whatever you are doing, work at it

with enthusiasm, as to the Lord and not for people, 24because
you know that you will receive your inheritance from the Lord
as the reward. Serve the Lord Christ. 25For the one who does
wrong will be repaid for his wrong, and there are no exceptions.

4 1Masters, treat your slaves with justice and fairness, because
you know that you also have a master in heaven.

EXHORTATION TO PRAY FOR THE SUCCESS OF PAUL'S MISSION

2Be devoted to prayer, keeping alert in it with thanksgiving.
3At the same time pray for us too, that God may open a door
for the message so that we may proclaim the mystery of Christ,
for which I am in chains. 4Pray that I may make it known as I
should. 5Conduct yourselves with wisdom toward outsiders,
making the most of the opportunities. 6Let your speech always
be gracious, seasoned with salt, so that you may know how you
should answer everyone.

PERSONAL GREETINGS AND INSTRUCTIONS

7Tychicus, a dear brother, faithful minister, and fellow slave in
the Lord, will tell you all the news about me. 8I sent him to you
for this very purpose that you may know how we are doing and
that he may encourage your hearts. 9I sent him with Onesimus,
the faithful and dear brother, who is one of you. They will tell
you about everything here.

10Aristarchus, my fellow prisoner, sends you greetings, as
does Mark, the cousin of Barnabas (about whom you received
instructions; if he comes to you, welcome him). 11And Jesus
who is called Justus also sends greetings. In terms of Jewish
converts, these are the only fellow workers for the kingdom of
God, and they have been a comfort to me. 12Epaphras, who is
one of you and a slave of Christ, greets you. He is always struggling in prayer on your behalf, so that you may stand mature
and fully assured in all the will of God. 13For I can testify that
he has worked hard for you and for those in Laodicea and Hier-
apolis. 14Our dear friend Luke the physician and Demas greet
you. 15Give my greetings to the brothers and sisters who are
in Laodicea and to Nympha and the church that meets in her
house. 16And after you have read this letter, have it read to
the church of Laodicea. In turn, read the letter from Laodicea
as well. 17And tell Archippus, "See to it that you complete the
ministry you received in the Lord."

18I, Paul, write this greeting by my own hand. Remember my
chains. Grace be with you.

4:1–6 We are admonished that the beginning of people's faith is God's gift. How is the door of his Word opened except when the sense of the hearer is opened so that he may believe and, having made a beginning of faith, may admit those things that are declared and reasoned for the purpose of building up wholesome doctrine, lest by a heart closed through unbelief he reject and repel those things that are spoken?

AUGUSTINE **(354–430)**
PREDESTINATION OF THE SAINTS

AUTHOR	AUDIENCE	DATE	PURPOSE	THEMES
Paul	The largely Gentile church in Thessalonica, founded by Paul	Around AD 51	Paul wrote to reinforce what he had taught the Thessalonians concerning the Christian faith and to encourage them as they awaited the future hope Christ promised.	Faith, hope, and love; Christian living; and the second coming of Christ

The first epistle of Paul the apostle to the Thessalonians is believed to be the earliest of Paul's letters, written only 20 years after the death and resurrection of Jesus Christ. Within a short time of planting this church, Paul had concerns: "On hearing . . . that persecutions were raging there," John Calvin wrote,

> [Paul] had sent Timothy with the view of animating them for the conflict, that they might not give way through fear, as human infirmity is apt to do. Having been afterward informed by Timothy respecting their entire condition, he employs various arguments to confirm them in steadfastness of faith as well as in patience should they be called to endure anything for the testimony of the gospel.

Paul wrote to commend the Thessalonian believers for their faith, hope, and love. He exhorts them as a father to live worthy of God's calling. He encourages them to remain pure, to persevere in their faith, and to prepare for Christ's second coming. He urges the Thessalonian believers to "stay alert and sober" (5:6) in steadfast faith as they anticipate the Lord's coming.

Although not an exhaustive exposition of the gospel, 1 Thessalonians does help us to understand the power of the good news more deeply, especially its personal impact on our lives: "For God did not destine us for wrath but for gaining salvation through our Lord Jesus Christ. He died for us." The gospel leads us into a higher way of living: "Whether we are alert or asleep we will come to life together with him" (5:9–10).

Faith and action are consistently paired in scripture, for what we believe impacts how we behave. Paul reminds us that God calls us into a new kingdom and into his glorious way of life in Christ. Therefore we should live in a way that's worthy of the one who has called us, avoiding sexual immorality, doing good to others, and "[living] a decent life before outsiders" (4:12).

1 THESSALONIANS

Finally, Paul wanted to encourage the Thessalonian believers about their future, knowing that death isn't the end: "For if we believe that Jesus died and rose again, so also we believe that God will bring with him those who have fallen asleep as Christians" (4:14). One day Christ will return, and we will be with him forever. We are to avoid speculating about that coming but instead live in eager expectation. As Theodoret of Cyr argued, "The woman who is pregnant knows that she has a fetus in the womb but does not know when birth will occur. So it is with us as we know that the Lord will come, but we do not teach the time itself with certainty."

Matthew Henry offered encouraging words about the pursuit of steadfast faith on display in 1 Thessalonians:

> The apostle prays that they might be sanctified more perfectly, for the best are sanctified but in part while in this world; therefore we should pray for and press toward complete holiness. And as we must fall, if God did not carry on his good work in the soul, we should pray to God to perfect his work till we are presented faultless before the throne of his glory . . . We need no more to make us happy than to know the grace of our Lord Jesus Christ. He is an ever-flowing and an over-flowing fountain of grace to supply all our wants.

SALUTATION

1 From Paul and Silvanus and Timothy, to the church of the
Thessalonians in God the Father and the Lord Jesus Christ.
Grace and peace to you!

THANKSGIVING FOR RESPONSE TO THE GOSPEL

2We thank God always for all of you as we mention you constantly in our prayers, 3because we recall in the presence of our God
and Father your work of faith and labor of love and endurance
of hope in our Lord Jesus Christ. 4We know, brothers and sisters
loved by God, that he has chosen you, 5in that our gospel did
not come to you merely in words, but in power and in the Holy
Spirit and with deep conviction (surely you recall the character
we displayed when we came among you to help you).
6And you became imitators of us and of the Lord when you received the message with joy that comes from the Holy Spirit, despite great affliction. 7As a result you became an example to all the
believers in Macedonia and in Achaia. 8For from you the message of
the Lord has echoed forth not just in Macedonia and Achaia, but in
every place reports of your faith in God have spread, so that we do
not need to say anything. 9For people everywhere report how you
welcomed us and how you turned to God from idols to serve the
living and true God 10and to wait for his Son from heaven, whom he
raised from the dead, Jesus our deliverer from the coming wrath.

1:1–10 After recognizing that this salvation is established through the Father and the Son and the Holy Spirit, shall we fling away "that pattern of teaching" we received (Rom 6:17)? Would it not rather be ground for great groaning if we are found now further off from our salvation "than when we first believed" (Rom 13:11) and deny now what we then received? And whoever does not always keep to and hold fast as a sure protection the confession we recorded at our first admission. when, being delivered "from idols" we came "to serve the living and true God" (1 Thess 1:9)? Them I charge to preserve the faith secure until the day of Christ, preserving, both in the confession of faith and in the doxology, the doctrine taught them at their baptism.

BASIL THE GREAT (330–379)
DE SPIRITU SANCTO

PAUL'S MINISTRY IN THESSALONICA

2 For you yourselves know, brothers and sisters, about our coming to you—it has not proven to be purposeless. 2But although
we suffered earlier and were mistreated in Philippi, as you know,
we had the courage in our God to declare to you the gospel of
God in spite of much opposition. 3For the appeal we make does
not come from error or impurity or with deceit, 4but just as we
have been approved by God to be entrusted with the gospel, so
we declare it, not to please people but God, who examines our
hearts. 5For we never appeared with flattering speech, as you
know, nor with a pretext for greed—God is our witness—6nor to
seek glory from people, either from you or from others, 7although
we could have imposed our weight as apostles of Christ; instead we
became little children among you. Like a nursing mother caring
for her own children, 8with such affection for you we were happy
to share with you not only the gospel of God but also our own lives,
because you had become dear to us. 9For you recall, brothers and
sisters, our toil and drudgery: By working night and day so as not
to impose a burden on any of you, we preached to you the gospel
of God. 10You are witnesses, and so is God, as to how holy and
righteous and blameless our conduct was toward you who believe.
11As you know, we treated each one of you as a father treats his
own children, 12exhorting and encouraging you and insisting that
you live in a way worthy of God who calls you to his own kingdom
and his glory. 13And so we too constantly thank God that when
you received God's message that you heard from us, you accepted
it not as a human message, but as it truly is, God's message, which
is at work among you who believe. 14For you became imitators,
brothers and sisters, of God's churches in Christ Jesus that are in
Judea, because you too suffered the same things from your own
countrymen as they in fact did from the Jews, 15who killed both
the Lord Jesus and the prophets and persecuted us severely. They
are displeasing to God and are opposed to all people 16because
they hinder us from speaking to the Gentiles so that they may

2:1–12 Paul presents in a few words the sum and substance of his exhortations that in magnifying the mercy of God, he admonished his readers not to fail as to their calling. His commendation of the grace of God is contained in the expression "who calls you to his own kingdom." For as our salvation is founded upon God's gracious adoption, every blessing that Christ has brought us is comprehended in this one term. It now remains that we answer God's call, that is, that we show ourselves to be such children to him as he is a Father to us. For he who lives otherwise than as becomes a child of God deserves to be cut off from God's household.

JOHN CALVIN (1509–1564)
COMPLETE COMMENTARY ON THE BIBLE

CHARLES SPURGEON:

PRINCE OF PREACHERS

1834–1892

The communion of saints has been impacted by theologians and evangelists, monks and mystics. Add to that list preachers, those specially called to declare the Word of God to the world. Charles Haddon Spurgeon was one of the most influential preachers and Christian leaders of the nineteenth century, delivering thousands of sermons that have since been translated into many languages and reached millions of people for Christ.

Born into a nominally Anglican family in Essex, England, in 1834, Spurgeon had a dramatic conversion experience to Christ when he was a teenager. Caught in a snowstorm at age fifteen while walking to meet a friend, he was forced to take refuge in a Methodist church. There he was confronted with the text of Isaiah 45:22: "Turn to me so you can be delivered, all you who live in the earth's remote regions! For I am God, and I have no peer." The pastor of the chapel exhorted him: "Young man, look to Jesus Christ. Look!" He did, and he would spend the rest of his life telling every man, woman, and child he encountered of the wondrous love of Jesus. Within a year of his conversion, Spurgeon had preached his first sermon, and within a few months of that sermon he was installed as the pastor of a small Baptist church in Cambridgeshire. Then in 1854 at the age of nineteen, he assumed the pastorate at the famed London Baptist Church New Park Street Chapel. From that platform his preaching fame began to spread.

By twenty-two he had become the most popular preacher of his day, preaching to thousands and reaching more through the regular publication of his sermons. Four years later his church moved into the renovated Metropolitan Tabernacle, which held 6,000 people. In 1857 he spoke to 24,000 at the Crystal Palace. His style of preaching was populist, speaking directly to the common person using the language of the heart and soul to convey the truths of scripture. Although he never gave altar calls, every Sunday he would invite all who were interested in giving their lives to Christ to meet him the next day. Each Monday morning a parishioner or two would seek out Spurgeon, desiring to give their lives to Christ.

"He who searches all hearts," Spurgeon said of his ministry mission, "knows that our aim and object is not to gather a band around self, but to unite a company around the Savior." Spurgeon authored 49 volumes of commentaries, devotionals, and anecdotes and gave nearly 4,000 sermons by the time of his death in 1892, securing his reputation as the prince of preachers.

IMPORTANT WORKS

MORNING AND EVENING DEVOTIONS

THE METROPOLITAN TABERNACLE PULPIT SERMONS, 45 VOLS.

be saved. Thus they constantly fill up their measure of sins, but
wrath has come upon them completely.

FORCED ABSENCE FROM THESSALONICA

[17]But when we were separated from you, brothers and sisters,
for a short time (in presence, not in affection) we became all
the more fervent in our great desire to see you in person. [18]For
we wanted to come to you (I, Paul, in fact tried again and again),
but Satan thwarted us. [19]For who is our hope or joy or crown to
boast of before our Lord Jesus at his coming? Is it not of course
you? [20]For you are our glory and joy!

3:1–5 Do you see how God permits trials and by them stirs up and awakens the disciples and makes them more energetic? Nothing so makes friends and rivets them as firmly as affliction; nothing so fastens and joins the souls of believers; nothing is so timely for us teachers in order that the things said by us may be heard. For when the hearer is living an easy life, listless and indolent, those who try to teach him only annoy him. But when he is in affliction and distress, he longs to hear his teachers. For when he is distressed in his soul, he seeks comfort from all directions in his affliction. And the preaching brings no small comfort.

CHRYSOSTOM **(C. 347–407)**
HOMILIES ON THE ACTS OF THE APOSTLES

3 So when we could bear it no longer, we decided to stay on
in Athens alone. [2]We sent Timothy, our brother and fellow
worker for God in the gospel of Christ, to strengthen you and
encourage you about your faith, [3]so that no one would be shak-
en by these afflictions. For you yourselves know that we are
destined for this. [4]For in fact when we were with you, we were
telling you in advance that we would suffer affliction, and so
it has happened, as you well know. [5]So when I could bear it
no longer, I sent to find out about your faith, for fear that the
tempter somehow tempted you and our toil had proven useless.
[6]But now Timothy has come to us from you and given us the
good news of your faith and love and that you always think of
us with affection and long to see us just as we also long to see
you! [7]So in all our distress and affliction, we were reassured
about you, brothers and sisters, through your faith. [8]For now
we are alive again if you stand firm in the Lord. [9]For how can
we thank God enough for you, for all the joy we feel because of
you before our God? [10]We pray earnestly night and day to see
you in person and make up what may be lacking in your faith.
[11]Now may God our Father himself and our Lord Jesus direct our
way to you. [12]And may the Lord cause you to increase and abound
in love for one another and for all, just as we do for you, [13]so that
your hearts are strengthened in holiness to be blameless before our
God and Father at the coming of our Lord Jesus with all his saints.

A LIFE PLEASING TO GOD

4 Finally then, brothers and sisters, we ask you and urge you in
the Lord Jesus, that as you received instruction from us about
how you must live and please God (as you are in fact living) that
you do so more and more. [2]For you know what commands we
gave you through the Lord Jesus. [3]For this is God's will: that
you become holy, that you keep away from sexual immorality,
[4]that each of you know how to possess his own body in holiness
and honor, [5]not in lustful passion like the Gentiles who do not
know God. [6]In this matter no one should violate the rights of
his brother or take advantage of him, because the Lord is the
avenger in all these cases, as we also told you earlier and warned
you solemnly. [7]For God did not call us to impurity but in holiness. [8]Consequently the one who rejects this is not rejecting
human authority but God, who gives his Holy Spirit to you.
[9]Now on the topic of brotherly love you have no need for
anyone to write you, for you yourselves are taught by God to
love one another. [10]And indeed you are practicing it toward all
the brothers and sisters in all of Macedonia. But we urge you,
brothers and sisters, to do so more and more, [11]to aspire to lead
a quiet life, to attend to your own business, and to work with
your own hands, as we commanded you. [12]In this way you will
live a decent life before outsiders and not be in need.

4:9–12 Paul first began with the soothing application of praise and made their ears submissive and ready for the remedy of the healing words. At last with difficulty he breaks out into that at which he was driving before. He gave the first aim: "Aspire to lead a quiet life." Then Paul added a second: "Attend to your own business." And a third as well: "Work with your own hands, as we commanded you." The outcome is that one who does not dutifully and peacefully work for his daily food with his own hands is sure to view enviously another's gifts and blessings. You see what conditions, serious and shameful, may spring solely from the malady of leisure.

JOHN CASSIAN
(C. 360–C. 435)
INSTITUTES

THE LORD RETURNS FOR BELIEVERS

13Now we do not want you to be uninformed, brothers and
sisters, about those who are asleep, so that you will not grieve
like the rest who have no hope. 14For if we believe that Jesus
died and rose again, so also we believe that God will bring with
him those who have fallen asleep as Christians. 15For we tell
you this by the word of the Lord, that we who are alive, who are
left until the coming of the Lord, will surely not go ahead of
those who have fallen asleep. 16For the Lord himself will come
down from heaven with a shout of command, with the voice
of the archangel, and with the trumpet of God, and the dead
in Christ will rise first. 17Then we who are alive, who are left,
will be suddenly caught up together with them in the clouds
to meet the Lord in the air. And so we will always be with the
Lord. 18Therefore encourage one another with these words.

THE DAY OF THE LORD

5 Now on the topic of times and seasons, brothers and sisters,
you have no need for anything to be written to you. 2For you
know quite well that the day of the Lord will come in the same
way as a thief in the night. 3Now when they are saying, "There
is peace and security," then sudden destruction comes on them,
like labor pains on a pregnant woman, and they will surely not
escape. 4But you, brothers and sisters, are not in the darkness for
the day to overtake you like a thief would. 5For you all are sons of
the light and sons of the day. We are not of the night nor of the
darkness. 6So then we must not sleep as the rest, but must stay
alert and sober. 7For those who sleep, sleep at night, and those
who get drunk are drunk at night. 8But since we are of the day,
we must stay sober *by putting on the breastplate* of faith and love
and as *a helmet* our hope *for salvation.* 9For God did not destine
us for wrath but for gaining salvation through our Lord Jesus
Christ. 10He died for us so that whether we are alert or asleep, we
will come to life together with him. 11Therefore encourage one
another and build up each other, just as you are in fact doing.

5:1–11 Christians who isolate themselves from others and walk through life alone are likely to be drowsy. But if you fellowship with other Christians you will stay wide awake, will be refreshed and encouraged, and will make faster progress on the road to heaven. Dear friends, if you live close to the cross, you will not sleep. Constantly strive to deepen your understanding of the true value of the place where you are going. If you remember your destination is heaven, you will not sleep along the road. Do you desire to sleep while the pearly gates of heaven are open before you, while the songs of angels await your voice, and while a crown of gold awaits your head?

CHARLES SPURGEON
(1834–1892)
MORNING AND EVENING

FINAL INSTRUCTIONS

12Now we ask you, brothers and sisters, to acknowledge those
who labor among you and preside over you in the Lord and admonish you, 13and to esteem them most highly in love because
of their work. Be at peace among yourselves. 14And we urge you,
brothers and sisters, admonish the undisciplined, comfort the
discouraged, help the weak, be patient toward all. 15See that no
one pays back evil for evil to anyone, but always pursue what is
good for one another and for all. 16Always rejoice, 17constantly
pray, 18in everything give thanks. For this is God's will for you
in Christ Jesus. 19Do not extinguish the Spirit. 20Do not treat
prophecies with contempt. 21But examine all things; hold fast
to what is good. 22Stay away from every form of evil.

CONCLUSION

23Now may the God of peace himself make you completely
holy and may your spirit and soul and body be kept entirely
blameless at the coming of our Lord Jesus Christ. 24He who
calls you is trustworthy, and he will in fact do this. 25Brothers
and sisters, pray for us too. 26Greet all the brothers and sisters
with a holy kiss. 27I call on you solemnly in the Lord to have
this letter read to all the brothers and sisters. 28The grace of
our Lord Jesus Christ be with you.

AUTHOR	AUDIENCE	DATE	PURPOSE	THEMES
Paul	The church at Thessalonica	Around AD 51 or 52	Paul wrote to clarify the nature of the last days and exhort the Thessalonians to stand firm.	Suffering and persecution; the second coming of Christ; and idleness and disruption

Every generation must grapple with the teaching of God's Word concerning the last days and be on guard against false teachers who would twist this important doctrine. Apparently, the first generation of believers in Thessalonica were confused about Jesus' second coming. Paul wrote this second epistle to remind them of the truth and encourage them to stand firm in it. He also exhorted them to persevere in the midst of the persecution they were experiencing. Finally, Paul warned the Thessalonians to keep away from busybodies who didn't live according to the gospel, for such people burdened and disrupted the community.

We don't know the precise nature of the persecution in Thessalonica, but it seemed to have increased since Paul wrote the letter we know today as 1 Thessalonians. The apostle wanted to clarify that trials and tribulations had purpose. Not only would God vindicate believers who suffered for their faith, paying back their oppressors in due time, but he also would count the sufferers worthy of the kingdom of God.

Paul revealed the fate of all who persecute God's people: everlasting punishment. This serves as a warning for all who would oppose God, his kingdom, and his people. Not only will such people "undergo the penalty of eternal destruction" but they will also be shut "away from the presence of the Lord and from the glory of his strength" (1:9). This is to be an encouragement for all who suffer under the weight of persecution for they can be sure justice will be served.

False claims about Christ's second coming and the end of the world as we know it must be countered with truth, which Paul supplied to the Thessalonians believers, citing what must take place before Christ returns. Paul also urged his friends to "stand firm and hold on to the traditions that we taught you" (2:15) as they await this coming. Though the "man of lawlessness" (2:3) will come and wreak havoc, the Lord himself will strengthen his followers so they can persevere.

2 THESSALONIANS

Finally, Paul warned against people in the church who were idle and disruptive. He advised the faithful to keep away from such people and have nothing to do with them, for they become a burden to the community. We ourselves must also guard against taking advantage of our local congregations, as such people do, instead earning our living and doing what is good.

In explaining the central point of this letter, Athanasius offers an important word as we prepare for Christ's second coming, standing firm in the truth and living according to the tradition we have received:

> Not to know when the end is, or when the day of the end will occur, is actually a good thing. If people knew the time of the end, they might begin to ignore the present time as they waited for the end days. They might well begin to argue that they should focus only on themselves . . . The Word, then, has concealed both the end of all things and the time of our own death from us, for in the end of all is the end of each, and in the end of each the end of all is comprehended. This is so that, when things remain uncertain and always in prospect, we advance day by day as if summoned, reaching forward to the things before us and forgetting the things behind.

SALUTATION

1 From Paul and Silvanus and Timothy, to the church of the Thessalonians in God our Father and the Lord Jesus Christ. 2 Grace and peace to you from God the Father and the Lord Jesus Christ!

THANKSGIVING

3 We ought to thank God always for you, brothers and sisters, and rightly so, because your faith flourishes more and more and the love of each one of you all for one another is ever greater. 4 As a result we ourselves boast about you in the churches of God for your perseverance and faith in all the persecutions and afflictions you are enduring.

1:3–12 The apostle had given thanks for them. In his thanksgiving he said, "We ought to thank God always for you, brothers and sisters" and in his prayer, "We pray for you always." If you have any success, we always give thanks for you, if any fear or danger of receding from the faith, we always pray for you. The apostle dare not trust the event or force of his own ministry, nor the experiment of their sincerity, but ascribes all to God, commends all to God; the beginning, progress, and end of our salvation comes from him alone. They had begun well, therefore he blessed God; that they might end well, he prays to God, "that our God will make you worthy of his calling."

THOMAS MANTON
(1620–1677)
THE COMPLETE WORKS

ENCOURAGEMENT IN PERSECUTION

5 This is evidence of God's righteous judgment, to make you worthy of the kingdom of God, for which in fact you are suffering. 6 For it is right for God to repay with affliction those who afflict you, 7 and to you who are being afflicted to give rest together with us when the Lord Jesus is revealed from heaven with his mighty angels. 8 *With flaming fire he will mete out punishment on those who do not know God* and do not obey the gospel of our Lord Jesus. 9 They will undergo the penalty of eternal destruction, *away from the presence of the Lord and from the glory of his strength,* 10 when he comes to be glorified among his saints and admired on that day among all who have believed—and you did in fact believe our testimony. 11 And in this regard we pray for you always, that our God will make you worthy of his calling and fulfill by his power your every desire for goodness and every work of faith, 12 that the name of our Lord Jesus may be glorified in you, and you in him, according to the grace of our God and the Lord Jesus Christ.

THE DAY OF THE LORD

2 Now regarding the arrival of our Lord Jesus Christ and our being gathered to be with him, we ask you, brothers and sisters, 2 not to be easily shaken from your composure or disturbed by any kind of spirit or message or letter allegedly from us, to the effect that the day of the Lord is already here. 3 Let no one deceive you in any way. For that day will not arrive until the rebellion comes and the man of lawlessness is revealed, the son of destruction. 4 He opposes *and exalts himself above every* so-called *god* or object of worship, and as a result *he takes his seat* in God's temple, displaying himself as God. 5 Surely you recall that I used to tell you these things while I was still with you. 6 And so you know what holds him back, so that he will be revealed in his own time. 7 For the hidden power of lawlessness is already at work. However, the one who holds him back will do so until he is taken out of the way, 8 and then the lawless one will be revealed, whom the Lord will destroy by the breath of his mouth and wipe out by the manifestation of his arrival. 9 The arrival of the lawless one will be by Satan's working with all kinds of miracles and signs and false wonders, 10 and with every kind of evil deception directed against those who are perishing, because they found no place in their hearts for the truth so as to be saved. 11 Consequently God sends on them a deluding influence so that they will believe what is false. 12 And so all of them who have not believed the truth but have delighted in evil will be condemned.

2:1–16 Faith and holiness must be joined together as well as holiness and happiness. The outward call of God is by the gospel, and this is rendered effectual by the inward working of the Spirit. The belief of the truth brings the sinner to rely on Christ and so to love and obey him; it is sealed by the Holy Spirit upon his heart. We have no certain proof of anything having been delivered by the apostles more than what we find contained in the holy scriptures. Let us then stand fast in the doctrines taught by the apostles and reject all additions and vain traditions.

MATTHEW HENRY **(1662–1714)**
COMMENTARY ON THE WHOLE BIBLE

CALL TO STAND FIRM

13But we ought to thank God always for you, brothers and sisters
loved by the Lord, because God chose you from the beginning
for salvation through sanctification by the Spirit and faith in
the truth. 14He called you to this salvation through our gospel, so that you may possess the glory of our Lord Jesus Christ.
15Therefore, brothers and sisters, stand firm and hold on to the
traditions that we taught you, whether by speech or by letter.
16Now may our Lord Jesus Christ himself and God our Father,
who loved us and by grace gave us eternal comfort and good
hope, 17encourage your hearts and strengthen you in every
good thing you do or say.

REQUEST FOR PRAYER

3 Finally, pray for us, brothers and sisters, that the Lord's
message may spread quickly and be honored as in fact it
was among you, 2and that we may be delivered from perverse
and evil people. For not all have faith. 3But the Lord is faithful,
and he will strengthen you and protect you from the evil one.
4And we are confident about you in the Lord that you are both
doing—and will do—what we are commanding. 5Now may the
Lord direct your hearts toward the love of God and the endurance of Christ.

RESPONSE TO THE UNDISCIPLINED

6But we command you, brothers and sisters, in the name of our
Lord Jesus Christ, to keep away from any brother who lives an
undisciplined life and not according to the tradition they received from us. 7For you know yourselves how you must imitate
us, because we did not behave without discipline among you,
8and we did not eat anyone's food without paying. Instead, in toil
and drudgery we worked night and day in order not to burden
any of you. 9It was not because we do not have that right, but
to give ourselves as an example for you to imitate. 10For even
when we were with you, we used to give you this command: "If
anyone is not willing to work, neither should he eat." 11For we
hear that some among you are living an undisciplined life, not
doing their own work but meddling in the work of others. 12Now
such people we command and urge in the Lord Jesus Christ to
work quietly and so provide their own food to eat. 13But you,
brothers and sisters, do not grow weary in doing what is right.
14But if anyone does not obey our message through this letter,
take note of him and do not associate closely with him, so that
he may be ashamed. 15Yet do not regard him as an enemy, but
admonish him as a brother.

3:6–15 The very people whom in his first epistle Paul had treated with the gentle application of his words he endeavors in his second epistle to heal with severer and sterner remedies. Paul renders this commandment severe by the imprecation of the name of our Lord Jesus Christ. He is concerned that they might again scorn his teaching as merely a human word. And so quite directly, like a well-skilled physician operating on infected limbs to which he could not apply the remedy of a mild treatment, Paul attempts to cure by an incision with a spiritual knife. This is so that the malady of idleness, like some deadly contagion, might not infect even the healthy portion of their limbs by the gradual advance of infection.

JOHN CASSIAN
(C. 360–C. 435)
INSTITUTES

CONCLUSION

16Now may the Lord of peace himself give you peace at all times
and in every way. The Lord be with you all. 17I, Paul, write this
greeting with my own hand, which is how I write in every letter.
18The grace of our Lord Jesus Christ be with you all.

AUTHOR	AUDIENCE	DATE	PURPOSE	THEMES
Paul	Timothy, one of Paul's closest associates, but no doubt intended also for the whole church in Ephesus	About AD 64	Paul wrote to warn Timothy about false teachers and instruct him in the administration of the church.	False teachers; church leadership and administration; and living as God's household

The first epistle of Paul the apostle to Timothy is the first of three letters commonly known as the Pastoral Epistles. They were written by the seasoned missionary Paul as guidance for the care and management of local churches. This letter addresses a number of basic issues confronting young pastor Timothy, including church leadership and administration as well as life and conduct in the household of God. It also addresses the growing threat to the church: "Certain men," said Irenaeus, were "introducing among us false stories and vain genealogies, which serve rather to elicit controversies . . . than to God's work of building up in the faith." The apostle Paul wrote this epistle to his young protégé to exhort him to hold tight to the once-for-all faith entrusted to God's holy people.

Paul brought Timothy along on his missionary journey after the young man was converted to the Christian faith through the apostle's ministry. After spending years planting the church in Ephesus, Paul traveled to Macedonia and left Timothy in charge. The words contained in 1 Timothy are those of a mentor imparting wisdom to his mentee in the faith. Apparently, some in the believing community had abandoned the truth, shipwrecking their lives; others were entertaining and promoting false teaching, which threatened to shipwreck the church. Timothy was called to preserve the true faith—save the ship, so to speak—with sound instruction and leadership, and to help the congregation in Ephesus live that faith as the household of God.

False gospels and false teachers have been around since the earliest days of the church. Young pastor Timothy dealt with them firsthand. Paul instructed Timothy to train leaders in sound doctrine so that the faith handed down from the apostles would continue to be taught without distortion. He also wanted Timothy to confront unorthodox teaching in order to preserve the faith itself, as well as the faith of the Ephesian believers. Two individuals—Hymenaeus and Alexander—were offered as examples of what

1 TIMOTHY

can happen when people accept false doctrine: their faith "suffered shipwreck" and they "blaspheme[d]" (1:19–20). Paul exhorted Timothy to proclaim orthodoxy and live a godly life in faith as he provided sound leadership for God's people in Ephesus.

The instruction in this letter covers a number of practical areas: how to conduct prayer meetings and Christian gatherings; what kind of leaders should oversee God's people; and what makes such people qualified to lead. This last topic is especially important, for much rises and falls on leadership. On this, Paul provided several marks of godly leaders: they live morally upright lives, they live at peace with others, they are generous, their conduct is right and true, and they possess great integrity.

First Timothy offers sound advice for managing God's household. As Athanasius wisely summarized:

> To help prevent people from renouncing godliness when they are persecuted, he urges them to cling to the faith. Just as brothers become strongly knit together when one helps another, so faith and godliness, coming from the same family, cohere together. A person who gives his attention to one of the two is strengthened by the other. Consequently, wishing Timothy to live godly to the end and to fight the battle in faith, Saint Paul says, "Compete well for the faith and lay hold of that eternal life" (6:12).

SALUTATION

1 From Paul, an apostle of Christ Jesus by the command of God
our Savior and of Christ Jesus our hope, 2to Timothy, my genuine child in the faith. Grace, mercy, and peace from God the
Father and Christ Jesus our Lord!

TIMOTHY'S TASK IN EPHESUS

3As I urged you when I was leaving for Macedonia, stay on in
Ephesus to instruct certain people not to spread false teachings, 4nor to occupy themselves with myths and interminable
genealogies. Such things promote useless speculations rather
than God's redemptive plan that operates by faith. 5But the
aim of our instruction is love that comes from a pure heart, a
good conscience, and a sincere faith. 6Some have strayed from
these and turned away to empty discussion. 7They want to be
teachers of the law, but they do not understand what they are
saying or the things they insist on so confidently.
8But we know that the law is good if someone uses it le-
gitimately, 9realizing that law is not intended for a righteous
person, but for lawless and rebellious people, for the ungodly
and sinners, for the unholy and profane, for those who kill their
fathers or mothers, for murderers, 10sexually immoral people,
practicing homosexuals, kidnappers, liars, perjurers—in fact, for
any who live contrary to sound teaching. 11This accords with
the glorious gospel of the blessed God that was entrusted to me.
12I am grateful to the one who has strengthened me, Christ
Jesus our Lord, because he considered me faithful in putting me
into ministry, 13even though I was formerly a blasphemer and a
persecutor, and an arrogant man. But I was treated with mercy
because I acted ignorantly in unbelief, 14and our Lord's grace
was abundant, bringing faith and love in Christ Jesus. 15This
saying is trustworthy and deserves full acceptance: "Christ Jesus
came into the world to save sinners"—and I am the worst of
them! 16But here is why I was treated with mercy: so that in
me as the worst, Christ Jesus could demonstrate his utmost
patience, as an example for those who are going to believe in
him for eternal life. 17Now to the eternal King, immortal, invisible, the only God, be honor and glory forever and ever! Amen.
18I put this charge before you, Timothy my child, in keeping
with the prophecies once spoken about you, in order that with
such encouragement you may fight the good fight. 19To do this
you must hold firmly to faith and a good conscience, which
some have rejected and so have suffered shipwreck in regard
to the faith. 20Among these are Hymenaeus and Alexander,
whom I handed over to Satan to be taught not to blaspheme.

PRAYER FOR ALL PEOPLE

2 First of all, then, I urge that requests, prayers, intercessions, and
thanks be offered on behalf of all people, 2even for kings and all
who are in authority, that we may lead a peaceful and quiet life
in all godliness and dignity. 3Such prayer for all is good and welcomed before God our Savior, 4since he wants all people to be saved
and to come to a knowledge of the truth. 5For there is one God
and one intermediary between God and humanity, Christ Jesus,
himself human, 6who gave himself as a ransom for all, revealing
God's purpose at his appointed time. 7For this I was appointed a
preacher and apostle—I am telling the truth; I am not lying—and
a teacher of the Gentiles in faith and truth. 8So I want the men in
every place to pray, lifting up holy hands without anger or dispute.

1:18—2:7 This passage ought to be carefully observed. We know that the treasure of sound doctrine is invaluable, and therefore there is nothing that we ought to dread more than to have it taken from us. But Paul here informs us that there is only one way of keeping it safe, and that is to secure it by the locks and bars of a good conscience. This is what we experience every day, for how come there are so many who, laying aside the gospel, rush into wicked sects or become involved in monstrous errors? It is because by this kind of blindness God punishes hypocrisy as, on the other hand, a genuine fear of God gives strength for perseverance.

JOHN CALVIN (1509–1564)
COMPLETE COMMENTARY ON THE BIBLE

CONDUCT OF WOMEN

9Likewise the women are to dress in suitable apparel, with
modesty and self-control. Their adornment must not be
with braided hair and gold or pearls or expensive clothing, 10but
with good deeds, as is proper for women who profess reverence
for God. 11A woman must learn quietly with all submissiveness.
12But I do not allow a woman to teach or exercise authority over
a man. She must remain quiet. 13For Adam was formed first
and then Eve. 14And Adam was not deceived, but the woman,
because she was fully deceived, fell into transgression. 15But
she will be delivered through childbearing, if she continues in
faith and love and holiness with self-control.

QUALIFICATIONS FOR OVERSEERS AND DEACONS

3 This saying is trustworthy: "If someone aspires to the office of overseer, he desires a good work." 2The overseer then
must be above reproach, the husband of one wife, temperate,
self-controlled, respectable, hospitable, an able teacher, 3not
a drunkard, not violent, but gentle, not contentious, free from
the love of money. 4He must manage his own household well
and keep his children in control without losing his dignity. 5But
if someone does not know how to manage his own household,
how will he care for the church of God? 6He must not be a
recent convert, or he may become arrogant and fall into the
punishment that the devil will exact. 7And he must be well
thought of by those outside the faith, so that he may not fall
into disgrace and be caught by the devil's trap.
8Deacons likewise must be dignified, not two-faced, not
given to excessive drinking, not greedy for gain, 9holding to
the mystery of the faith with a clear conscience. 10And these
also must be tested first and then let them serve as deacons if
they are found blameless. 11Likewise also their wives must be
dignified, not slanderous, temperate, faithful in every respect.
12Deacons must be husbands of one wife and good managers of
their children and their own households. 13For those who have
served well as deacons gain a good standing for themselves and
great boldness in the faith that is in Christ Jesus.

CONDUCT IN GOD'S CHURCH

14I hope to come to you soon, but I am writing these instructions to you 15in case I am delayed to let you know how people
ought to conduct themselves in the household of God, because
it is the church of the living God, the support and bulwark of
the truth. 16And we all agree, our religion contains amazing
revelation:

He was revealed in the flesh,
vindicated by the Spirit,
seen by angels,
proclaimed among Gentiles,
believed on in the world,
taken up in glory.

TIMOTHY'S MINISTRY IN THE LATER TIMES

4 Now the Spirit explicitly says that in the later times some
will desert the faith and occupy themselves with deceiving
spirits and demonic teachings, 2influenced by the hypocrisy
of liars whose consciences are seared. 3They will prohibit marriage and require abstinence from foods that God created to be

3:1–13 The inspired apostle bids us to take thought, laying injunction upon all who hear, when he says that a leader must be without reproach. Is this all that the apostle cares for, that he who is advanced to the priesthood should be irreproachable? And what is so great an advantage as that all possible qualifications should be included in one? But he knows full well that the subject is molded by the character of his superior and that the upright walk of the guide becomes that of his followers too. For what the Master is, such does he make the disciple to be.

GREGORY OF NYSSA
(C. 335–C. 395)
LETTERS

4:1–11 Great is the gain whereby we attain to godliness, which is rich with God, not indeed in fleeting wealth but in eternal gifts, and in which rests no uncertain trial but grace constant and unending. There is therefore a usefulness connected with the body and also one that has to do with godliness, according to the apostle's division, "Physical exercise has some value, but godliness is valuable in every way."

AMBROSE (C. 339–C. 397)
ON THE DUTIES OF THE CLERGY

received with thanksgiving by those who believe and know the
truth. 4For every creation of God is good, and no food is to be
rejected if it is received with thanksgiving. 5For it is sanctified
by God's word and by prayer.

6By pointing out such things to the brothers and sisters, you
will be a good servant of Christ Jesus, having nourished yourself
on the words of the faith and of the good teaching that you
have followed. 7But reject those myths fit only for the godless
and gullible, and train yourself for godliness. 8For "physical
exercise has some value, but godliness is valuable in every way.
It holds promise for the present life and for the life to come."
9This saying is trustworthy and deserves full acceptance. 10In
fact this is why we work hard and struggle, because we have
set our hope on the living God, who is the Savior of all people,
especially of believers.

11Command and teach these things. 12Let no one look down
on you because you are young, but set an example for the believers in your speech, conduct, love, faithfulness, and purity.
13Until I come, give attention to the public reading of scripture,
to exhortation, to teaching. 14Do not neglect the spiritual gift
you have, given to you and confirmed by prophetic words when
the elders laid hands on you. 15Take pains with these things; be
absorbed in them, so that everyone will see your progress. 16Be
conscientious about how you live and what you teach. Persevere
in this, because by doing so you will save both yourself and
those who listen to you.

INSTRUCTIONS ABOUT SPECIFIC GROUPS

5 Do not address an older man harshly but appeal to him as a
father. Speak to younger men as brothers, 2older women as
mothers, and younger women as sisters—with complete purity.

3Honor widows who are truly in need. 4But if a widow has
children or grandchildren, they should first learn to fulfill their
duty toward their own household and so repay their parents
what is owed them. For this is what pleases God. 5But the widow
who is truly in need, and completely on her own, has set her
hope on God and continues in her pleas and prayers night and
day. 6But the one who lives for pleasure is dead even while she
lives. 7Reinforce these commands, so that they will be beyond
reproach. 8But if someone does not provide for his own, especially his own family, he has denied the faith and is worse than
an unbeliever.

9No widow should be put on the list unless she is at least
sixty years old, was the wife of one husband, 10and has a reputation for good works: as one who has raised children, practiced hospitality, washed the feet of the saints, helped those
in distress—as one who has exhibited all kinds of good works.
11But do not accept younger widows on the list, because their
passions may lead them away from Christ and they will desire
to marry, 12and so incur judgment for breaking their former
pledge. 13And besides that, going around from house to house
they learn to be lazy, and they are not only lazy, but also gossips
and busybodies, talking about things they should not. 14So I
want younger women to marry, raise children, and manage
a household, in order to give the adversary no opportunity
to vilify us. 15For some have already wandered away to follow
Satan. 16If a believing woman has widows in her family, let her
help them. The church should not be burdened so that it may
help the widows who are truly in need.

5:3–16 And what will be said if instructing others, someone neglects his own family, though he has greater capacities and a higher obligation to benefit those near? Will it not be said: *Aha! These Christians are affectionate indeed who neglect their own relatives! They are worse than infidels.* So what? One who does not benefit those far away benefits even less those nearer. What is meant is this: The law of God and of nature is violated by him who does not provide for his own family.

CHRYSOSTOM (C. 347–407)
HOMILIES ON THE FIRST EPISTLE OF PAUL TO TIMOTHY

D. L. MOODY:

EVANGELIZER OF THE WORLD

1837–1899

Born in 1837 to a working-class family in rural Massachusetts, Dwight L. Moody was raised by his mother after the untimely death of his father. At seventeen he moved to Boston to work with his uncle at a shoe shop, where he converted to Christianity and joined a Congregational church. Two years later he moved to Chicago to work as a shoe salesman, though he gave it up for full-time work at the YMCA. This was a period of urban revivalism, and he wanted to play his part. Moody set about creating a Sunday school for poor, immigrant children, which led to the founding in 1864 of Illinois Street Church, which he pastored. After the infamous Chicago fire destroyed his church and home, he spent two years touring England and discovered his calling as an evangelist.

Accompanied by gospel singer Ira Sankey, Moody's work resonated in the British Isles, and he spent a total of six years visiting and evangelizing the region. In 1873 he launched something of a revival in Scotland, leading around 3,000 to Christ in Glasgow. He drew 12,000 people at one London event, cementing his reputation as an evangelist ahead of his return to the United States in 1875. Christian leaders in many major cities requested his services in hopes of replicating his success, and he obliged.

Moody's philosophy of evangelism can be summed up in the words of one of his stock sermons on Christ's return: "I look upon the world as a wrecked vessel. God has given me a lifeboat and said to me, 'Moody, save all you can.'" And so he did.

Moody's evangelistic strategies were effective, but some of his methods drew criticism. His sermons were simple and positive, emphasizing the love of God and omitting preaching about hell and God's wrath. Although he believed in the doctrine of eternal punishment, he explained: "Terror never brought a man in yet." Instead, his sermons focused on three Rs: ruin by sin, redemption by Christ, regeneration by the Holy Spirit. Additionally, he came under criticism from Calvinists for emphasizing a person's individual decision to accept Christ and gain victory over sin as well as God's desire for all to be saved. Though Moody himself believed in the doctrine of election, he remarked, "I don't try to reconcile God's sovereignty with man's free agency" and insisted such doctrinal discussions were not meant for evangelistic revivals. He steadily avoided such debates and controversies, focusing entirely on the work of evangelizing America and Europe.

Church historian David Bebbington writes, "Moody was not just an American evangelist: he exercised a profound and lasting influence over the course of evangelicalism throughout the world." As one of the champions of fundamentalism and an expert evangelist, Moody has inspired generations to know and share the gospel.

IMPORTANT WORKS

HEAVEN

PREVAILING PRAYER

SECRET POWER

17 Elders who provide effective leadership must be counted worthy of double honor, especially those who work hard in speaking and teaching. 18 For the scripture says, "***Do not muzzle an ox while it is treading out the grain,***" and, "The worker deserves his pay." 19 Do not accept an accusation against an elder unless it can be confirmed *by two or three witnesses.* 20 Those guilty of sin must be rebuked before all, as a warning to the rest. 21 Before God and Christ Jesus and the elect angels, I solemnly charge you to carry out these commands without prejudice or favoritism of any kind. 22 Do not lay hands on anyone hastily and so identify with the sins of others. Keep yourself pure. 23 (Stop drinking just water, but use a little wine for your digestion and your frequent illnesses.) 24 The sins of some people are obvious, going before them into judgment, but for others, they show up later. 25 Similarly good works are also obvious, and the ones that are not cannot remain hidden.

6 Those who are under the yoke as slaves must regard their own masters as deserving of full respect. This will prevent the name of God and Christian teaching from being discredited. 2 But those who have believing masters must not show them less respect because they are brothers. Instead they are to serve all the more, because those who benefit from their service are believers and dearly loved.

SUMMARY OF TIMOTHY'S DUTIES

Teach them and exhort them about these things. 3 If someone spreads false teachings and does not agree with sound words (that is, those of our Lord Jesus Christ) and with the teaching that accords with godliness, 4 he is conceited and understands nothing, but has an unhealthy interest in controversies and verbal disputes. This gives rise to envy, dissension, slanders, evil suspicions, 5 and constant bickering by people corrupted in their minds and deprived of the truth, who suppose that godliness is a way of making a profit. 6 Now godliness combined with contentment brings great profit. 7 For we have brought nothing into this world and so we cannot take a single thing out either. 8 But if we have food and shelter, we will be satisfied with that. 9 Those who long to be rich, however, stumble into temptation and a trap and many senseless and harmful desires that plunge people into ruin and destruction. 10 For the love of money is the root of all evils. Some people in reaching for it have strayed from the faith and stabbed themselves with many pains.

11 But you, as a person dedicated to God, keep away from all that. Instead pursue righteousness, godliness, faithfulness, love, endurance, and gentleness. 12 Compete well for the faith and lay hold of that eternal life you were called for and made your good confession for in the presence of many witnesses. 13 I charge you before God who gives life to all things and Christ Jesus who made his good confession before Pontius Pilate, 14 to obey this command without fault or failure until the appearing of our Lord Jesus Christ 15—whose appearing the blessed and only Sovereign, the King of kings and Lord of lords, will reveal at the right time. 16 He alone possesses immortality and lives in unapproachable light, whom no human has ever seen or is able to see. To him be honor and eternal power! Amen.

17 Command those who are rich in this world's goods not to be haughty or to set their hope on riches, which are uncertain, but on God who richly provides us with all things for our

6:3–16 "Now godliness combined with contentment brings great profit." Just look for a sufficiency, look for what is enough, not for more than that. Anything more is a weighing down, not a lifting up of the spirit; a burden, not a reward. "But you, as a person dedicated to God, keep away from all that." You see, Paul said, "Keep away" as from an enemy. You were trying to flee with gold; flee from gold instead. Let your heart flee from it and your use of it need have no worries. Do without greed; don't do without concern for others. There's something you can do with gold if you're its master, not its slave. If you're the master of gold, you can do good with it; if you're its slave, it can do evil with you.

AUGUSTINE **(354–430)**
SERMONS

AUTHOR	AUDIENCE	DATE	PURPOSE	THEMES
Paul	Paul's disciple Timothy, who ministered in Ephesus	About AD 66–67	Paul wrote this epistle toward the end of his life, urging Timothy to faithfully execute his ministry and steward the gospel.	False teaching; suffering and hardship; and the second coming of Christ

This second epistle to Timothy, one of the Pastoral Epistles, was probably one of the last letters Paul wrote. You can almost hear the urgency in his voice as he wrote this last will and testament of sorts, urging Timothy to faithfully execute his ministry and steward the gospel. He included concerns about false teachers and their teaching, as he did in his first letter to Timothy. There are also instructions on living and ministering well. But Paul also wrote to strengthen Timothy so that he would be able to stand under suffering and persecution. The apostle wrote as one on the brink of death, from one minister to another, passing along wisdom, encouragement, and exhortation.

The apostle charged Timothy to remind believers in Ephesus of the gospel's central truth: Christ was crucified for our sins and raised for our new life. Seeds of false doctrine were still being sown by false teachers—those who had "strayed from the truth" (2:18). Timothy was called to handle truth correctly, preach the Word, rebuke false teachers, and endure hardship by standing firm in Christ. For a day would come, Paul wrote, when people would not tolerate the truth; instead they would search for teaching that conforms to "their own desires . . . because they have an insatiable curiosity . . . [and] they will turn away from hearing the truth, but on the other hand they will turn aside to myths" (4:3–4). This was an apt warning for the early church, and it's needed in our day too.

Along with warnings about false teachers, there are exhortations to "accept your share of suffering for the gospel" and "as a good soldier of Christ Jesus" (1:8; 2:3). Paul wrote

enjoyment. [18]Tell them to do good, to be rich in good deeds,
to be generous givers, sharing with others. [19]In this way they
will save up a treasure for themselves as a firm foundation for
the future and so lay hold of what is truly life.

CONCLUSION

[20]O Timothy, protect what has been entrusted to you. Avoid
the profane chatter and absurdities of so-called "knowledge."
[21]By professing it, some have strayed from the faith. Grace be
with you all.

2 TIMOTHY

these words in chains, imprisoned for his steadfast commitment to Christ and his good news. Others through the ages took his words seriously, including Polycarp of Smyrna, Perpetua, John Hus, Martin Luther, Dietrich Bonhoeffer, and others. Paul invites us to join their ranks, but we need not fear, "for God did not give us a Spirit of fear but of power and love and self-control" (1:7).

Finally, Paul offered instruction concerning "the last days" (3:1). He revealed that during this time many people will become lovers of themselves and of money, boasters and blasphemers, unholy and unloving, slanderers and without self-control, and lovers of their own desires rather than lovers of God. He urged believers to flee such people and behavior but warned that all who seek lives of godliness will be persecuted.

Paul's closing words have been a balm of encouragement for the communion of saints stretching from the early church through the Middle Ages through the Reformation and into our day. May they encourage your own faith as well: "I have competed well; I have finished the race; I have kept the faith! Finally the crown of righteousness is reserved for me. The Lord, the righteous Judge, will award it to me in that day—and not to me only, but also to all who have set their affection on his appearing" (4:7–8).

1:1–7 For it requires much zeal to stir up the gift of God. As fire requires fuel, so grace requires our eagerness that it may be ever fervent. It is in our power to kindle or extinguish this grace. By sloth and carelessness it is quenched, and by watchfulness and diligence it is kept alive. For it is in you indeed, but you must render it more vehement, that is, fill it with confidence, with joy and delight. Stand confidently.

CHRYSOSTOM (C. 347–407)
HOMILIES ON THE SECOND EPISTLE OF PAUL TO TIMOTHY

SALUTATION

1 From Paul, an apostle of Christ Jesus by the will of God, to further the promise of life in Christ Jesus, [2]to Timothy, my dear child. Grace, mercy, and peace from God the Father and Christ Jesus our Lord!

THANKSGIVING AND CHARGE TO TIMOTHY

[3]I am thankful to God, whom I have served with a clear conscience as my ancestors did, when I remember you in my prayers as I do constantly night and day. [4]As I remember your tears, I long to see you, so that I may be filled with joy. [5]I recall your sincere faith that was alive first in your grandmother Lois and in your mother Eunice, and I am sure is in you.

[6]Because of this I remind you to rekindle God's gift that you possess through the laying on of my hands. [7]For God did not give us a Spirit of fear but of power and love and self-control. [8]So do not be ashamed of the testimony about our Lord or of me, a prisoner for his sake, but by God's power accept your share of suffering for the gospel. [9]He is the one who saved us and called us with a holy calling, not based on our works but on his own purpose and grace, granted to us in Christ Jesus before time began, [10]but now made visible through the appearing of our Savior Christ Jesus. He has broken the power of death and brought life and immortality to light through the gospel! [11]For this gospel I was appointed a preacher and apostle and teacher. [12]Because of this, in fact, I suffer as I do. But I am not ashamed because I know the one in whom my faith is set and I am convinced that he is able to protect what has been entrusted to me until that day. [13]Hold to the standard of sound words that you heard from me and do so with the faith and love that are in Christ Jesus. [14]Protect that good thing entrusted to you, through the Holy Spirit who lives within us.

[15]You know that everyone in the province of Asia deserted me, including Phygelus and Hermogenes. [16]May the Lord grant mercy to the family of Onesiphorus because he often refreshed me and was not ashamed of my imprisonment. [17]But when he arrived in Rome, he eagerly searched for me and found me. [18]May the Lord grant him to find mercy from the Lord on that day! And you know very well all the ways he served me in Ephesus.

2:1–13 "You, my child, be strong in the grace that is in Christ Jesus. And what you heard me say in the presence of many witnesses entrust to faithful people who will be competent to teach others as well." The blessed apostle delivered these things with a pious caution, aware that they could be easily known and distorted by anyone who does not have faith. How much greater will be our danger if, rashly and without thought, we commit the revelations of God to profane and unworthy people.

HIPPOLYTUS OF ROME
(C. 170–C. 235)
TREATISE ON CHRIST AND ANTICHRIST

SERVING FAITHFULLY DESPITE HARDSHIP

2 So you, my child, be strong in the grace that is in Christ Jesus. [2]And what you heard me say in the presence of many witnesses entrust to faithful people who will be competent to teach others as well. [3]Take your share of suffering as a good soldier of Christ Jesus. [4]No one in military service gets entangled in matters of everyday life; otherwise he will not please the one who recruited him. [5]Also, if anyone competes as an athlete, he will not be crowned as the winner unless he competes according to the rules. [6]The farmer who works hard ought to have the first share of the crops. [7]Think about what I am saying and the Lord will give you understanding of all this.

[8]Remember Jesus Christ, raised from the dead, a descendant of David; such is my gospel, [9]for which I suffer hardship to the point of imprisonment as a criminal, but God's message is not

imprisoned! [10]So I endure all things for the sake of those chosen
by God, that they, too, may obtain salvation in Christ Jesus and
its eternal glory. [11]This saying is trustworthy:
If we died with him, we will also live with him.
12 If we endure, we will also reign with him.
If we deny him, he will also deny us.
13 If we are unfaithful, he remains faithful, since he cannot
deny himself.

DEALING WITH FALSE TEACHERS

[14]Remind people of these things and solemnly charge them
before the Lord not to wrangle over words. This is of no benefit; it just brings ruin on those who listen. [15]Make every
effort to present yourself before God as a proven worker who
does not need to be ashamed, teaching the message of truth
accurately. [16]But avoid profane chatter because those occupied with it will stray further and further into ungodliness,
[17]and their message will spread its infection like gangrene.
Hymenaeus and Philetus are in this group. [18]They have
strayed from the truth by saying that the resurrection has
already occurred, and they are undermining some people's
faith. [19]However, God's solid foundation remains standing,
bearing this seal: "***The Lord knows those who are his,***" and
"Everyone who confesses the name of the Lord must turn
away from evil."
[20]Now in a wealthy home there are not only gold and silver
vessels, but also ones made of wood and of clay, and some are
for honorable use, but others for ignoble use. [21]So if someone
cleanses himself of such behavior, he will be a vessel for honorable use, set apart, useful for the Master, prepared for every
good work. [22]But keep away from youthful passions, and pursue
righteousness, faithfulness, love, and peace, in company with
others who call on the Lord from a pure heart. [23]But reject
foolish and ignorant controversies because you know they
breed infighting. [24]And the Lord's slave must not engage in
heated disputes but be kind toward all, an apt teacher, patient,
[25]correcting opponents with gentleness. Perhaps God will grant
them repentance and then knowledge of the truth, [26]and they
will come to their senses and escape the devil's trap where they
are held captive to do his will.

MINISTRY IN THE LAST DAYS

3 But understand this, that in the last days difficult times
will come. [2]For people will be lovers of themselves, lovers
of money, boastful, arrogant, blasphemers, disobedient to parents, ungrateful, unholy, [3]unloving, irreconcilable, slanderers,
without self-control, savage, opposed to what is good, [4]treach-
erous, reckless, conceited, loving pleasure rather than loving
God. [5]They will maintain the outward appearance of religion
but will have repudiated its power. So avoid people like these.
[6]For some of these insinuate themselves into households and
captivate weak women who are overwhelmed with sins and
led along by various passions. [7]Such women are always seeking instruction, yet never able to arrive at a knowledge of the
truth. [8]And just as Jannes and Jambres opposed Moses, so these
people—who have warped minds and are disqualified in the
faith—also oppose the truth. [9]But they will not go much further,
for their foolishness will be obvious to everyone, just like it was
with Jannes and Jambres.

3:10–17 The scripture is of the Holy Spirit, and its intention is the profit of humankind. For "every scripture," he says, "is inspired by God and useful." The profit is varied and multiform, as the apostle says, "for teaching, for reproof, for correction, and for training in righteousness." Such a gift as this, however, is not within any person's reach to lay hold of. Rather the divine intention lies hidden under the body of the scripture, as it were under a veil, some legislative enactment or some historical narrative being cast over the truths that are contemplated by the mind.

GREGORY OF NYSSA
(C. 335–C. 395)
AGAINST EUNOMIUS

CONTINUE IN WHAT YOU HAVE LEARNED

10You, however, have followed my teaching, my way of life, my
purpose, my faith, my patience, my love, my endurance, 11as
well as the persecutions and sufferings that happened to me
in Antioch, in Iconium, and in Lystra. I endured these persecutions, and the Lord delivered me from them all. 12Now in
fact all who want to live godly lives in Christ Jesus will be persecuted. 13But evil people and charlatans will go from bad to
worse, deceiving others and being deceived themselves. 14You,
however, must continue in the things you have learned and are
confident about. You know who taught you 15and how from
infancy you have known the holy writings, which are able to
give you wisdom for salvation through faith in Christ Jesus.
16Every scripture is inspired by God and useful for teaching, for
reproof, for correction, and for training in righteousness, 17that
the person dedicated to God may be capable and equipped for
every good work.

CHARGE TO TIMOTHY REPEATED

4 I solemnly charge you before God and Christ Jesus, who is
going to judge the living and the dead, and by his appearing
and his kingdom: 2Preach the message, be ready whether it
is convenient or not, reprove, rebuke, exhort with complete
patience and instruction. 3For there will be a time when people will not tolerate sound teaching. Instead, following their
own desires, they will accumulate teachers for themselves
because they have an insatiable curiosity to hear new things.
4And they will turn away from hearing the truth, but on the
other hand they will turn aside to myths. 5You, however, be
self-controlled in all things, endure hardship, do an evangelist's
work, fulfill your ministry. 6For I am already being poured out
as an offering, and the time for me to depart is at hand. 7I have
competed well; I have finished the race; I have kept the faith!
8Finally the crown of righteousness is reserved for me. The
Lord, the righteous Judge, will award it to me in that day—and
not to me only, but also to all who have set their affection on
his appearing.

4:6–8 As a Christian and a minister, Paul had kept the faith, kept the doctrines of the gospel. What comfort will it afford to be able to speak in this manner toward the end of our days! The crown of believers is a crown of righteousness, purchased by the righteousness of Christ. The believer, amid poverty, pain, sickness, and the agonies of death, may rejoice; but if the duties of people's place and station are neglected, their evidence of interest in Christ will be darkened and uncertainty and distress may be expected to cloud and harass their last hours.

MATTHEW HENRY (1662–1714)
COMMENTARY ON THE WHOLE BIBLE

TRAVEL PLANS AND CONCLUDING GREETINGS

9Make every effort to come to me soon. 10For Demas deserted
me, since he loved the present age, and he went to Thessalonica.
Crescens went to Galatia and Titus to Dalmatia. 11Only Luke
is with me. Get Mark and bring him with you because he is a
great help to me in ministry. 12Now I have sent Tychicus to
Ephesus. 13When you come, bring with you the cloak I left in
Troas with Carpas and the scrolls, especially the parchments.
14Alexander the coppersmith did me a great deal of harm. *The
Lord will repay him in keeping with his deeds.* 15You be on guard
against him too, because he vehemently opposed our words.
16At my first defense no one appeared in my support; instead
they all deserted me—may they not be held accountable for
it. 17But the Lord stood by me and strengthened me, so that
through me the message would be fully proclaimed for all the
Gentiles to hear. And so I was delivered from the lion's mouth!
18The Lord will deliver me from every evil deed and will bring
me safely into his heavenly kingdom. To him be glory for ever
and ever! Amen.

[19]Greetings to Prisca and Aquila and the family of Onesiphorus. [20]Erastus stayed in Corinth. Trophimus I left ill in Miletus.
[21]Make every effort to come before winter. Greetings to you
from Eubulus, Pudens, Linus, Claudia, and all the brothers and
sisters. [22]The Lord be with your spirit. Grace be with you.

AUTHOR	AUDIENCE	DATE	PURPOSE	THEMES
Paul	Titus, a trusted Gentile companion of Paul	About AD 63–65	Paul wrote Titus to outline the qualities of a sound church and to remind him of the glories of God's grace.	The gospel and salvation; Christian leadership; and doing good

Matthew Henry explained that the epistle of Paul to Titus "chiefly contains directions to Titus concerning the elders of the church and the manner in which he should give instruction; and the latter part tells him to urge obedience to magistrates, to enforce good works, avoid foolish questions, and shun heresies." In other words, this letter offers the communion of saints plain and simple instructions for conducting church life in any era, at any age.

Paul wrote as a mentor to young Titus, whom he had left in Crete to govern the church. Just as he had in his letter to Timothy, he urged Titus to choose godly men as overseers of the church, men with certain qualifications for leadership. He also offered guidance for refuting false teachers, telling Titus to silence such people and "rebuke them sharply that they may be healthy in the faith" (1:13). He urged the eager pastor to refute false doctrine by teaching what is good and appropriate—both sound doctrine and sound conduct. Right belief (orthodoxy) and right living (orthopraxy) are intimately connected: "For the grace of God has appeared, bringing salvation to all people. It trains us to reject godless ways and worldly desires and to live self-controlled, upright, and godly lives in the present age" (2:11–12).

Paul's identity was caught up in being "a slave of God and apostle of Jesus Christ, to further the faith of God's chosen ones and the knowledge of the truth that is in keeping with godliness" (1:1). He appointed Titus to further his mission, so he outlined what the gospel is all about: eternal life, promised before the beginning of time. Salvation in Christ is offered to all people and is made possible because Christ gave himself up for humanity, redeeming and purifying "from every kind of lawlessness" all who believe (2:14). As such the Christian faith needs to be guarded and preserved by qualified leaders. Otherwise false teachers will inevitably disrupt God's household.

Those who are chosen to lead impact the faith of God's people and their knowledge of the truth of salvation. That's why Paul gave a number of qualifications for appointing overseers: they must be blameless, faithful to their spouses, godly parents, neither overbearing nor quick-tempered, and not drunk, violent, or greedy. Hospitality, goodness, self-control, holiness, and discipline must mark them as well.

Contained in this letter are sound, simple instructions for any pastor or ministry leader charged with stewarding the life of the believing community. As John Calvin noted, "Paul has no other object in view than to support the cause of Titus and to stretch out the hand to assist him in performing the work of the Lord." Following his guidance will help to ensure that the work of the Lord continues in our own churches too.

SALUTATION

1 From Paul, a slave of God and apostle of Jesus Christ, to further the faith of God's chosen ones and the knowledge of the truth that is in keeping with godliness, 2in hope of eternal life, which God, who does not lie, promised before time began. 3But now in his own time he has made his message evident through the preaching I was entrusted with according to the command of God our Savior. 4To Titus, my genuine son in a common faith. Grace and peace from God the Father and Christ Jesus our Savior!

TITUS' TASK ON CRETE

1:5–16 Paul says to Titus, "An elder must be blameless." All the virtues are comprehended in this one word; thus he seems to require an impossible perfection. For if every sin, every idle word is deserving of blame, who is sinless and blameless? Still, he who is chosen to be shepherd of the church must be such compared with other men who are rightly regarded as but a flock of sheep.

JEROME (C. 342–420)
LETTERS

5The reason I left you in Crete was to set in order the remaining matters and to appoint elders in every town, as I directed you. 6An elder must be blameless, the husband of one wife, with faithful children who cannot be charged with dissipation or rebellion. 7For the overseer must be blameless as one entrusted with God's work, not arrogant, not prone to anger, not a drunkard, not violent, not greedy for gain. 8Instead he must be hospitable, devoted to what is good, sensible, upright, devout, and self-controlled. 9He must hold firmly to the faithful message as it has been taught, so that he will be able to give exhortation in such healthy teaching and correct those who speak against it.

10For there are many rebellious people, idle talkers, and deceivers, especially those with Jewish connections, 11who must be silenced because they mislead whole families by teaching for dishonest gain what ought not to be taught. 12A certain one of them, in fact, one of their own prophets, said, "Cretans are always liars, evil beasts, lazy gluttons." 13Such testimony is true. For this reason rebuke them sharply that they may be healthy in the faith 14and not pay attention to Jewish myths and commands of people who reject the truth. 15All is pure to those who are pure. But to those who are corrupt and unbelieving, nothing is pure, but both their minds and consciences are corrupted. 16They profess to know God but with their deeds they deny him, since they are detestable, disobedient, and unfit for any good deed.

CONDUCT CONSISTENT WITH SOUND TEACHING

2:1–10 Foreseeing the snares of the wicked one, I arm you beforehand by my admonitions as my beloved and faithful children in Christ. Therefore, clothing yourself with meekness, become the imitators of his sufferings and of his love. He loved us when he gave himself a ransom for us that he might cleanse us by his blood from our old ungodliness and bestow life on us when we were almost on the point of perishing through the depravity that was in us. Let no one cherish any grudge against his neighbor. For says our Lord, *Forgive, and you shall be forgiven* (see Matt 6:14).

IGNATIUS OF ANTIOCH (C. 110)
EPISTLES

2 But as for you, communicate the behavior that goes with sound teaching. 2Older men are to be temperate, dignified, self-controlled, sound in faith, in love, and in endurance. 3Older women likewise are to exhibit behavior fitting for those who are holy, not slandering, not slaves to excessive drinking, but teaching what is good. 4In this way they will train the younger women to love their husbands, to love their children, 5to be self-controlled, pure, fulfilling their duties at home, kind, being subject to their own husbands, so that the message of God may not be discredited. 6Encourage younger men likewise to be self-controlled, 7showing yourself to be an example of good works in every way. In your teaching show integrity, dignity, 8and a sound message that cannot be criticized, so that any opponent will be at a loss because he has nothing evil to say about us. 9Slaves are to be subject to their own masters in everything, to do what is wanted and not talk back, 10not pilfering, but showing all good faith, in order to bring credit to the teaching of God our Savior in everything.

11For the grace of God has appeared, bringing salvation to
all people. 12It trains us to reject godless ways and worldly desires and to live self-controlled, upright, and godly lives in the
present age, 13as we wait for the happy fulfillment of our hope
in the glorious appearing of our great God and Savior, Jesus
Christ. 14He gave himself for us to set us free from every kind
of lawlessness and to purify for himself a people who are truly
his, who are eager to do good. 15So communicate these things
with the sort of exhortation or rebuke that carries full authority.
Don't let anyone look down on you.

CONDUCT TOWARD THOSE OUTSIDE THE CHURCH

3 Remind them to be subject to rulers and authorities, to be
obedient, to be ready for every good work. 2They must not
slander anyone, but be peaceable, gentle, showing complete
courtesy to all people. 3For we, too, were once foolish, disobedient, misled, enslaved to various passions and desires, spending
our lives in evil and envy, hateful and hating one another. 4But
"when the kindness of God our Savior and his love for mankind
appeared, 5he saved us not by works of righteousness that we
have done but on the basis of his mercy, through the washing
of the new birth and the renewing of the Holy Spirit, 6whom
he poured out on us in full measure through Jesus Christ our
Savior. 7And so, since we have been justified by his grace, we
become heirs with the confident expectation of eternal life."

SUMMARY OF THE LETTER

8This saying is trustworthy, and I want you to insist on such
truths, so that those who have placed their faith in God may
be intent on engaging in good works. These things are good
and beneficial for all people. 9But avoid foolish controversies,
genealogies, quarrels, and fights about the law because they
are useless and empty. 10Reject a divisive person after one or
two warnings. 11You know that such a person is twisted by sin
and is conscious of it himself.

FINAL INSTRUCTIONS AND GREETING

12When I send Artemas or Tychicus to you, do your best to
come to me at Nicopolis, for I have decided to spend the winter
there. 13Make every effort to help Zenas the lawyer and Apollos
on their way; make sure they have what they need. 14Here is
another way that our people can learn to engage in good works
to meet pressing needs and so not be unfruitful. 15Everyone
with me greets you. Greet those who love us in the faith. Grace
be with you all.

3:1–11 We conclude from Paul's words that we bring nothing to God, but that he goes before us by his pure grace. For when he says, "Not by works of righteousness that we have done," he means that we can do nothing but sin till we have been renewed by God. This negative statement depends on the former affirmation by which he said that they were foolish and disobedient till they were created anew in Christ; and indeed, what good work could proceed from so corrupt a mass? Although as long as we are held by the entanglements of sin we carry about a body of death, yet we are certain of our salvation provided that we are ingrafted into Christ by faith.

JOHN CALVIN **(1509–1564)**
COMPLETE COMMENTARY ON THE BIBLE

AUTHOR	AUDIENCE	DATE	PURPOSE	THEMES
Paul	Philemon and the members of the church at Colossae	About AD 60	Paul wrote to urge Philemon to receive his runaway slave, Onesimus, as a brother in the faith.	Christian fellowship; Christian devotion; and brotherly love

Paul wrote Philemon to urge him to forgive and receive a runaway slave named Onesimus. By God's providence Paul had led Onesimus to Christ while in prison. In the spirit of Christian love, the apostle appealed to Philemon to forgive, restore, and reconcile with his slave as a brother in Christ.

Throughout Paul's epistles, one theme emerges repeatedly: Because of Christ's love, believers have been set free from slavery to sin and death; they are forgiven and restored. Paul demonstrates this love by advocating for Onesimus, just as on the cross Christ advocated for sinners before God's throne. Further, Paul humbled himself as Christ did. As an apostle he had the authority to command Philemon to do the right thing. He could have compelled him to relinquish his legal power over his runaway slave. But Paul chose instead to exhort his brother to choose love and peace. Here is how Martin Luther explained it:

> He acts exactly as if he were himself Onesimus who had done wrong. Yet he does this not with force or compulsion, as lay within his rights, but he empties himself of his rights in order to compel Philemon also to waive his rights. What Christ has done for us with God the Father, that Saint Paul does also for Onesimus with Philemon. For Christ emptied himself of his rights (see Phil 2:7) and overcame the Father with love and humility, so that the Father had to put away his wrath and rights and receive us into favor for the sake of Christ.

PHILEMON

Much has been made about the differences between Roman slavery in the first century and its counterpart in eighteenth- and nineteenth-century Britain and the United States. While these differences are important, we should not be too quick to dismiss the evils of slavery in any generation. As believers we must grapple with the Bible's clear teaching about human dignity. Paul himself wrote, "There is neither . . . slave nor free . . . for all of you are one in Christ Jesus" (Gal 3:28). Yet he sent the runaway slave Onesimus back to Philemon, a man who, according to Roman law, could have put Onesimus to death for his desertion.

Paul appealed not to his own authority in his letter to Philemon but to the authority of Christ, who calls us to treat all people with the dignity owed to being created in God's image. He knew that the Spirit of Christ at work in Philemon would bring his actions in line with the gospel of freedom. And by sending Onesimus back, Paul was asking his friend to walk in faith. Slaves run away, but those who find freedom in Christ know that nothing can separate them from the love of God (see Rom 8:31–39). In him we are truly free, even if the world regards us as slaves. In him we have nothing to fear.

VV. 1–25 Shall I show you freedom arising from slavery? There was a certain Onesimus, a slave, a runaway. He escaped and went to Paul. He obtained baptism, washed away his sins, and remained at Paul's feet. Do you see his nobility? Do you see a character that brings freedom? Slave and free are simply names. What is a slave? It is a mere name. How many masters lie drunken upon their beds while slaves stand by sober? Whom shall I call a slave—the one who is sober or the one who is drunk? The one who is the slave of a man or the one who is the captive of passion? The former has his slavery on the outside; the latter wears his captivity on the inside.

CHRYSOSTOM **(C. 347–407)**
HOMILIES ON THE EPISTLE OF PAUL TO PHILEMON

SALUTATION

[1]From Paul, a prisoner of Christ Jesus, and Timothy our brother, to Philemon, our dear friend and colaborer, [2]to Apphia our sister, to Archippus our fellow soldier, and to the church that meets in your house. [3]Grace and peace to you from God our Father and the Lord Jesus Christ!

THANKS FOR PHILEMON'S LOVE AND FAITH

[4]I always thank my God as I remember you in my prayers, [5]because I hear of your faith in the Lord Jesus and your love for all the saints. [6]I pray that the faith you share with us may deepen your understanding of every blessing that belongs to you in Christ. [7]I have had great joy and encouragement because of your love, for the hearts of the saints have been refreshed through you, brother.

PAUL'S REQUEST FOR ONESIMUS

[8]So, although I have quite a lot of confidence in Christ and could command you to do what is proper, [9]I would rather appeal to you on the basis of love—I, Paul, an old man and even now a prisoner for the sake of Christ Jesus—[10]I am appealing to you concerning my child, whose spiritual father I have become during my imprisonment, that is, Onesimus, [11]who was formerly useless to you, but is now useful to you and me. [12]I have sent him (who is my very heart) back to you. [13]I wanted to keep him with me so that he could serve me in your place during my imprisonment for the sake of the gospel. [14]However, without your consent I did not want to do anything so that your good deed would not be out of compulsion, but from your own willingness. [15]For perhaps it was for this reason that he was separated from you for a little while so that you would have him back eternally, [16]no longer as a slave, but more than a slave, as a dear brother. He is especially so to me, and even more so to you now, both humanly speaking and in the Lord. [17]Therefore if you regard me as a partner, accept him as you would me. [18]Now if he has defrauded you of anything or owes you anything, charge what he owes to me. [19]I, Paul, have written this letter with my own hand: I will repay it. I could also mention that you owe me your very self. [20]Yes, brother, let me have some benefit from you in the Lord. Refresh my heart in Christ. [21]Since I was confident that you would obey, I wrote to you because I knew that you would do even more than what I am asking you to do. [22]At the same time also, prepare a place for me to stay, for I hope that through your prayers I will be given back to you.

CONCLUDING GREETINGS

[23]Epaphras, my fellow prisoner in Christ Jesus, greets you. [24]Mark, Aristarchus, Demas, and Luke, my colaborers, greet you too. [25]May the grace of the Lord Jesus Christ be with your spirit.

AUTHOR	AUDIENCE	DATE	PURPOSE	THEMES
Unknown; possibly Apollos or Barnabas	Primarily Jewish Christians	About AD 67–70	The author wrote to Jewish Christians to show them how Christ fulfills every old covenant promise and to warn them against turning back to their old way of life.	The person of Christ; the old covenant; Jewish religious practices; perseverance in faith; and godly living

Perhaps there is no clearer presentation of Jesus Christ as the author of the new covenant than the one found in the book of Hebrews. The writer to the Hebrews wrote to show that the Old Testament finds its full meaning in Jesus Christ. As Matthew Henry explained:

> This epistle shows Christ as the end, foundation, body, and truth of the figures of the law, which of themselves were no virtue for the soul . . . The ceremonial law is full of Christ, and all the gospel is full of Christ; the blessed lines of both Testaments meet in him; and how they both agree and sweetly unite in Jesus Christ is the chief object of the epistle to the Hebrews to discover.

Although tradition has it that Paul wrote this epistle, the author of Hebrews is unknown. But the author's reason for writing is not: "We must pay closer attention to what we have heard, so that we do not drift away" (2:1). Whoever wrote this epistle did so to encourage Jewish believers in their faith and to show them how Jesus fits every Old Testament expectation of the Messiah. The letter is rich in Jewish imagery, recounting Moses and the wilderness, the priestly sacrificial system, the tabernacle, and the temple. The writer deftly bridged the Jewish story and the Jesus story in order to show how Christ fulfills each old covenant promise.

The early church was especially concerned with Christology, the nature of Christ. In Hebrews Jesus is revealed as both divine and human in full measure. The Son is the radiance of God's glory, the exact representation of his being, sustaining all things by his power; he has been exalted in glory at God's right hand in heaven, the Lord over all creation; he was made a little lower than the angels by taking on the flesh and blood of humanity; he was subjected to weakness and temptation so that he might identify with us as our great high priest.

This epistle is a letter to Hebrew people. Thus it is steeped in the Old Testament promises of God and the traditions of Israel. Christ fulfills these promises and is far superior to every religious regulation. The letter climaxes with the rituals of sacrifice, showing how

HEBREWS

Jesus offered himself as the once-for-all sacrifice. Because he made this offering and sat down at God's right hand, there is no longer a need for the blood of animals to cover sin. We are encouraged to draw near to God through this "fresh and living way that he inaugurated for us" (10:20). John Calvin explained:

> Here is the conclusion of the whole argument, that the practice of daily sacrificing is inconsistent with and wholly foreign to the priesthood of Christ; and that hence after his coming the Levitical priests, whose custom and settled practice was daily to offer, were deposed from their office; for the character of things that are contrary is that when one thing is set up, the other falls to the ground. The conclusion then is that the ancient priesthood, which is inconsistent with this, has ceased; for all the saints find a full consecration in the one offering of Christ.

There is a subtle theme that weaves its way from the beginning of the epistle to the end: a warning against falling away. The example of Israel in the wilderness is offered as an illustration of what *not* to do. The author warned against apostasy. Destruction comes when believers taste salvation and then fall away, turning back to the old covenant or by living a life that produces "thorns and thistles" (6:8). Alongside this warning the author called believers to persevere, exhorting them to "hold unwaveringly to the hope that we confess" (10:23). He offered the "great cloud of witnesses" (12:1) to the faith as encouragement for the Christian life. Ultimately, we are to fix our eyes on Jesus in order to run the race set before us and persevere till the end.

Of the epistle to the Hebrews John Calvin wrote, "No doubt the epistle next in importance to that to the Romans is this to the Hebrews. The truths explained in it might, indeed, have been deduced from other portions of scripture; but it is a vast advantage and a great satisfaction to find them expressly set forth and distinctly stated by an inspired apostle." Engage this book yourself to better understand the grandeur and glory of Christ, his once-for-all sacrifice, and his place as the "pioneer and perfecter of our faith" (12:2).

INTRODUCTION: GOD HAS SPOKEN FULLY AND FINALLY IN HIS SON

1 After God spoke long ago in various portions and in various
ways to our ancestors through the prophets, 2in these last
days he has spoken to us in a son, whom he appointed heir of
all things, and through whom he created the world. 3The Son is
the radiance of his glory and the representation of his essence,
and he sustains all things by his powerful word, and so when
he had accomplished cleansing for sins, *he sat down at the right*
hand of the Majesty on high. 4Thus he became so far better than
the angels as he has inherited a name superior to theirs.

1:1–4 Christ always has been the brightness of the Father's glory. It is the same glory, but Christ is its shining forth. And God beholds his image in Christ—*in Christ* is the means by which the glory of the Father shines forth to us. As we see the sun by its light, we see the Father by Christ. He enlightens everyone who is enlightened and is therefore called the Word of God. As Christ dwells in human nature, we can behold better what is near than what is far off. And the brightness is suited to our eyes. The incarnation softens the light. The work of redemption is the greatest revelation of the glory of God in this world.

JONATHAN EDWARDS
(1703–1758)
THE COMPLETE WORKS

THE SON IS SUPERIOR TO ANGELS

5For to which of the angels did God ever say, ***"You are my son!***
Today I have fathered you"? And in another place he says, ***"I will***
be his father and he will be my son." 6But when he again brings
his firstborn into the world, he says, ***"Let all the angels of God***
worship him!" 7And he says of the angels, ***"He makes his angels***
winds and his ministers a flame of fire," 8but of the Son he says,

"Your throne, O God, is forever and ever,
and a righteous scepter is the scepter of your kingdom.
9 ***You have loved righteousness and hated lawlessness.***
So God, your God, has anointed you over your
companions with the oil of rejoicing."

10And,

"You founded the earth in the beginning, Lord,
and the heavens are the works of your hands.
11 ***They will perish, but you continue.***
And they will all grow old like a garment,
12 ***and like a robe you will fold them up***
and like a garment ***they will be changed,***
but you are the same and your years will never run out."

13But to which of the angels has he ever said, ***"Sit at my right***
hand until I make your enemies a footstool for your feet"? 14Are
they not all ministering spirits, sent out to serve those who
will inherit salvation?

WARNING AGAINST DRIFTING AWAY

2 Therefore we must pay closer attention to what we have heard,
so that we do not drift away. 2For if the message spoken through
angels proved to be so firm that every violation or disobedience
received its just penalty, 3how will we escape if we neglect such
a great salvation? It was first communicated through the Lord
and was confirmed to us by those who heard him, 4while God
confirmed their witness with signs and wonders and various miracles and gifts of the Holy Spirit distributed according to his will.

2:1–4 Why then ought we to "pay closer attention"? Lest at any time we should fall away. And here the writer shows the grievousness of this falling away, in that it is a difficult thing for that which has fallen away to return again, inasmuch as it has happened through willful negligence. For scripture says, "Let the one who thinks he is standing be careful that he does not fall" (1 Cor 10:12), showing both the easiness of the fall and the grievousness of the ruin. Our disobedience is not without danger.

CHRYSOSTOM (C. 347–407)
ON THE EPISTLE TO THE HEBREWS

EXPOSITION OF PSALM 8: JESUS AND THE DESTINY OF HUMANITY

5For he did not put the world to come, about which we are
speaking, under the control of angels. 6Instead someone testified somewhere:

"What is man that you think of him or the son of man that
you care for him?
7 ***You made him lower than the angels for a little while.***
You crowned him with glory and honor.
8 ***You put all things under his control."***

For when he ***put all things under his control,*** he left nothing
outside of his control. At present we do not yet see ***all things
under his control,*** [9]but we see Jesus, who was made ***lower than
the angels for a little while,*** now crowned with glory and honor
because he suffered death, so that by God's grace he would experience death on behalf of everyone. [10]For it was fitting for
him, for whom and through whom all things exist, in bringing many sons to glory, to make the pioneer of their salvation
perfect through sufferings. [11]For indeed he who makes holy
and those being made holy all have the same origin, and so
he is not ashamed to call them brothers and sisters, [12]saying,
***"I will proclaim your name to my brothers; in the midst of the
assembly I will praise you."*** [13]Again he says, "I will be confident
in him," and again, ***"Here I am, with the children God has given
me."*** [14]Therefore, since the children share in flesh and blood,
he likewise shared in their humanity, so that through death
he could destroy the one who holds the power of death (that
is, the devil), [15]and set free those who were held in slavery all
their lives by their fear of death. [16]For surely his concern is
not for angels, but he is concerned for Abraham's descendants.
[17]Therefore he had to be made like his brothers and sisters in
every respect, so that he could become a merciful and faithful
high priest in things relating to God, to make atonement for
the sins of the people. [18]For since he himself suffered when he
was tempted, he is able to help those who are tempted.

JESUS AND MOSES

3 Therefore, holy brothers and sisters, partners in a heavenly
calling, take note of Jesus, the apostle and high priest whom
we confess, [2]who is faithful to the one who appointed him, as
Moses was also in God's house. [3]For he has come to deserve
greater glory than Moses, just as the builder of a house deserves greater honor than the house itself! [4]For every house
is built by someone, but the builder of all things is God. [5]Now
Moses was ***faithful in all God's house*** as a servant, to testify to
the things that would be spoken. [6]But Christ is faithful as a son
over God's house. We are of his house, if in fact we hold firmly
to our confidence and the hope we take pride in.

EXPOSITION OF PSALM 95: HEARING GOD'S WORD IN FAITH

[7]Therefore, as the Holy Spirit says,

"Oh, that today you would listen as he speaks!
8 ***Do not harden your hearts as in the rebellion, in the day
of testing in the wilderness.***
9 ***There your fathers tested me and tried me, and they saw
my works for forty years.***
10 ***Therefore, I became provoked at that generation and
said, 'Their hearts are always wandering, and they
have not known my ways.'***
11 ***As I swore in my anger, 'They will never enter my rest!'"***

[12]See to it, brothers and sisters, that none of you has an evil,
unbelieving heart that forsakes the living God. [13]But exhort one
another each day, as long as it is called "Today," that none of you
may become hardened by sin's deception. [14]For we have become
partners with Christ, if in fact we hold our initial confidence firm
until the end. [15]As it says, ***"Oh, that today you would listen as he
speaks! Do not harden your hearts as in the rebellion."*** [16]For which

3:7–19 From hardness comes unbelief. As in bodies the parts that have become callous and hard do not yield to the hands of the physicians, so also souls that are hardened yield not to the Word of God. "See to it . . . that none of you has an evil, unbelieving heart." The writer reminds them of the history in which they had lacked faith. *For if your fathers,* he says, *because they did not hope as they ought to have hoped, suffered these things, much more will you.* Therefore, "exhort one another each day, as long as it is called 'Today'"—that is, edify one another, raise yourselves up, lest the same things should befall you—"that none of you may become hardened by sin's deception."

CHRYSOSTOM (C. 347–407)
ON THE EPISTLE TO THE HEBREWS

ones heard and rebelled? Was it not all who came out of Egypt
under Moses' leadership? [17]And against whom was God provoked
for forty years? Was it not those who sinned, *whose dead bodies fell
in the wilderness*? [18]And to whom did he swear they would never
enter into his rest, except those who were disobedient? [19]So we
see that they could not enter because of unbelief.

GOD'S PROMISED REST

4 Therefore we must be wary that, while the promise of entering his rest remains open, none of you may seem to have
come short of it. [2]For we had good news proclaimed to us just
as they did. But the message they heard did them no good, since
they did not join in with those who heard it in faith. [3]For we
who have believed enter that rest, as he has said, ***"As I swore in
my anger, 'They will never enter my rest!'"*** And yet God's works
were accomplished from the foundation of the world. [4]For he
has spoken somewhere about the seventh day in this way: ***"And
God rested on the seventh day from all his works,"*** [5]but to repeat
the text cited earlier: ***"They will never enter my rest!"*** [6]There-
fore it remains for some to enter it, yet those to whom it was
previously proclaimed did not enter because of disobedience.
[7]So God again ordains a certain day, "Today," speaking through
David after so long a time, as in the words quoted before, ***"Oh,
that today you would listen as he speaks! Do not harden your
hearts."*** [8]For if Joshua had given them rest, God would not have
spoken afterward about another day. [9]Consequently a Sabbath
rest remains for the people of God. [10]For the one who enters
God's rest has also rested from his works, just as God did from
his own works. [11]Thus we must make every effort to enter that
rest, so that no one may fall by following the same pattern of
disobedience. [12]For the word of God is living and active and
sharper than any double-edged sword, piercing even to the
point of dividing soul from spirit, and joints from marrow; it
is able to judge the desires and thoughts of the heart. [13]And
no creature is hidden from God, but everything is naked and
exposed to the eyes of him to whom we must render an account.

JESUS OUR COMPASSIONATE HIGH PRIEST

[14]Therefore since we have a great high priest who has passed
through the heavens, Jesus the Son of God, let us hold fast to
our confession. [15]For we do not have a high priest incapable
of sympathizing with our weaknesses, but one who has been
tempted in every way just as we are, yet without sin. [16]There-
fore let us confidently approach the throne of grace to receive
mercy and find grace whenever we need help.

5 For every high priest is taken from among the people and
appointed to represent them before God, to offer both gifts
and sacrifices for sins. [2]He is able to deal compassionately with
those who are ignorant and erring, since he also is subject to
weakness, [3]and for this reason he is obligated to make sin offerings for himself as well as for the people. [4]And no one assumes
this honor on his own initiative, but only when called to it by
God, as in fact Aaron was. [5]So also Christ did not glorify himself
in becoming high priest, but the one who glorified him was
God, who said to him, ***"You are my Son! Today I have fathered
you,"*** [6]as also in another place God says, ***"You are a priest forever in the order of Melchizedek."*** [7]During his earthly life Christ
offered both requests and supplications, with loud cries and
tears, to the one who was able to save him from death, and he

4:14—5:11 To show that it is eminently the character of the true God that he is a God who hears prayer, he gives free access to himself by prayer. God in his Word manifests himself ready at all times to allow us to come to him. He sits on a throne of grace, and there is no veil to hide this throne and keep us from it. The veil is rent from the top to the bottom; the way is open at all times, and we may go to God as often as we will. Although God is infinitely above us, yet we may come with boldness. "Let us confidently approach the throne of grace to receive mercy and find grace whenever we need help." How wonderful is it that such worms as we should be allowed to come boldly at all times to so great a God!

JONATHAN EDWARDS
(1703–1758)
THE COMPLETE WORKS

was heard because of his devotion. 8Although he was a son, he learned obedience through the things he suffered. 9And by being perfected in this way, he became the source of eternal salvation to all who obey him, 10and he was designated by God as high priest ***in the order of Melchizedek.***

THE NEED TO MOVE ON TO MATURITY

11On this topic we have much to say, and it is difficult to explain, since you have become sluggish in hearing. 12For though you should in fact be teachers by this time, you need someone to teach you the beginning elements of God's utterances. You have gone back to needing milk, not solid food. 13For everyone who lives on milk is inexperienced in the message of righteousness because he is an infant. 14But solid food is for the mature, whose perceptions are trained by practice to discern both good and evil.

6 Therefore we must progress beyond the elementary instructions about Christ and move on to maturity, not laying this foundation again: repentance from dead works and faith in God, 2teaching about ritual washings, laying on of hands, resurrection of the dead, and eternal judgment. 3And this is what we intend to do, if God permits. 4For it is impossible in the case of those who have once been enlightened, tasted the heavenly gift, become partakers of the Holy Spirit, 5tasted the good word of God and the miracles of the coming age, 6and then have committed apostasy, to renew them again to repentance, since they are crucifying the Son of God for themselves all over again and holding him up to contempt. 7For the ground that has soaked up the rain that frequently falls on it and yields useful vegetation for those who tend it receives a blessing from God. 8But if it produces thorns and thistles, it is useless and about to be cursed; its fate is to be burned. 9But in your case, dear friends, even though we speak like this, we are convinced of better things relating to salvation. 10For God is not unjust so as to forget your work and the love you have demonstrated for his name, in having served and continuing to serve the saints. 11But we passionately want each of you to demonstrate the same eagerness for the fulfillment of your hope until the end, 12so that you may not be sluggish, but imitators of those who through faith and perseverance inherit the promises.

13Now when God made his promise to Abraham, since he could swear by no one greater, he swore by himself, 14saying, ***"Surely I will bless you greatly and multiply your descendants abundantly."*** 15And so by persevering, Abraham inherited the promise. 16For people swear by something greater than themselves, and the oath serves as a confirmation to end all dispute. 17In the same way God wanted to demonstrate more clearly to the heirs of the promise that his purpose was unchangeable, and so he intervened with an oath, 18so that we who have found refuge in him may find strong encouragement to hold fast to the hope set before us through two unchangeable things, since it is impossible for God to lie. 19We have this hope as an anchor for the soul, sure and steadfast, which reaches inside behind the curtain, 20where Jesus our forerunner entered on our behalf, since he became ***a priest forever in the order of Melchizedek.***

6:13–20 **Having then this hope, let our souls be bound to him who is faithful in his promises and just in his judgments. It is impossible for God to lie. Let his faith therefore be stirred up again within us, and let us consider that all things are nigh unto him. By the word of his might he established all things, and by his word he can overthrow them. When and as he pleases he will do all things, and none of the things determined by him shall pass away.**

CLEMENT OF ROME **(D. 99)**
FIRST CLEMENT

THE NATURE OF MELCHIZEDEK'S PRIESTHOOD

7 Now this ***Melchizedek, king of Salem, priest of the most high God, met Abraham as he was returning from defeating the kings*** and ***blessed him.*** 2To him also ***Abraham apportioned a***

J. GRESHAM MACHEN:

CHAMPION OF THE FUNDAMENTALS

1881–1937

The editor of *Christian Century*, Charles Clayton Morrison aptly framed the controversy facing the Christian faith a quarter of the way into the twentieth century: "Two worlds have crashed, the world of tradition and the world of modernism." Stepping into the middle of this clash was J. Gresham Machen.

Machen became a primary symbol of the modernist-fundamentalist controversy that arose during this time of religious upheaval, joining the likes of B. B. Warfield, C. I. Scofield, and John Darby. Modernism had emanated from the Enlightenment of the seventeenth century and blossomed in the nineteenth century. As an intellectual mindset, it called into question the previous ways of knowing and experiencing the world, exalting the newly discovered and established scientific principles and methods above tradition. Despite its significant advances in multiple areas, the modernistic mindset at its worst encouraged the wholesale neglect or rejection of the wisdom of the past.

Having studied at Johns Hopkins, Marburg, and Göttingen before taking up a post as a New Testament scholar at Princeton Theological Seminary, Machen entered the fray alongside other fundamentalists. Although he embraced neither their premillennialism nor prohibitionism, he did lead the intellectual charge of preserving the fundamentals of the Christian faith. He believed the crisis of the day lay "chiefly in the intellectual sphere," for the hostility to the gospel by modern culture was "due to the intellectual atmosphere in which men are living."

Machen took issue with two competing responses to this hostility that had arisen within the Christian faith: liberals who subordinated Christianity to culture; and conservatives who wanted to destroy or ignore culture. Instead, he wanted to cultivate and consecrate culture "in service of our God." He wanted the faith to "pervade not merely all nations, but also all human thought," and he urged believers to "go forth joyfully, enthusiastically to make the world subject to God."

Coinciding with this desire was a commitment to the traditional Christian faith, which was both supernatural and biblically based. This put Machen squarely at odds with the culturally accommodating liberalism beholden to modernism. His book *Christianity and Liberalism* was his answer to the clash of cultures, which he saw as being within the church between historic Christian orthodoxy and the modern accommodation of theological liberalism.

"The great redemptive religion," wrote Machen, "which has always been known as Christianity is battling a totally diverse type of religious belief, which is only the more destructive of the Christian faith because it makes use of Christian terminology." Further, "despite the liberal use of traditional phraseology, modern liberalism is not only a different religion from Christianity, but it belongs to a totally different class of religions." He described liberalism as both *un-Christian* and *unscientific*: un-Christian because it jettisoned the central beliefs of Christianity regarding Christ having died to save sinners and rising three days later; unscientific because it neglected the facts of Christianity in favor of "appeals to man's will" and "religious aspiration."

In the end, Machen became alienated from his institution and deemed a troublemaker by the president. He resigned in 1929 and founded a rival seminary, Westminster Theological Seminary. And when he was suspended from ministry with the Presbyterian Church USA in 1936, he helped found an alternative denomination, the Orthodox Presbyterian Church. The next year he passed from this life to the next, leaving a lasting legacy as a champion of the fundamentals of the faith.

IMPORTANT WORKS

CHRISTIANITY AND LIBERALISM

THE CHRISTIAN FAITH IN THE MODERN WORLD

THE CHRISTIAN VIEW OF MAN

tithe of everything. His name first means king of righteousness,
then ***king of Salem,*** that is, king of peace. 3Without father,
without mother, without genealogy, he has neither beginning of days nor end of life but is like the son of God, and he
remains a priest for all time. 4But see how great he must be, if
Abraham the patriarch gave him a tithe of his plunder. 5And
those of the sons of Levi who receive the priestly office have
authorization according to the law to collect a tithe from the
people, that is, from their fellow countrymen, although they,
too, are descendants of Abraham. 6But Melchizedek who does
not share their ancestry collected a tithe from Abraham and
blessed the one who possessed the promise. 7Now without
dispute the inferior is blessed by the superior, 8and in one
case tithes are received by mortal men, while in the other
by him who is affirmed to be alive. 9And it could be said that
Levi himself, who receives tithes, paid a tithe through Abraham. 10For he was still in his ancestor Abraham's loins when
Melchizedek met him.

JESUS AND THE PRIESTHOOD OF MELCHIZEDEK

11So if perfection had in fact been possible through the Levitical priesthood—for on that basis the people received the
law—what further need would there have been for another
priest to arise, said to be in the order of Melchizedek and not
in Aaron's order? 12For when the priesthood changes, a change
in the law must come as well. 13Yet the one these things are
spoken about belongs to a different tribe, and no one from that
tribe has ever officiated at the altar. 14For it is clear that our
Lord is descended from Judah, yet Moses said nothing about
priests in connection with that tribe. 15And this is even clearer
if another priest arises in the likeness of Melchizedek, 16who
has become a priest not by a legal regulation about physical
descent but by the power of an indestructible life. 17For here
is the testimony about him: "***You are a priest forever in the
order of Melchizedek.***" 18On the one hand a former command
is set aside because it is weak and useless, 19for the law made

7:1–21 Just as our Redeemer, when he appeared in the flesh, deigned to become like a king to us by bestowing a heavenly kingdom, so did he become a high priest by offering himself for us as a sacrifice to God with an odor of sweetness. Hence it is written, "For here is the testimony about him: 'You are a priest forever in the order of Melchizedek . . . The Lord has sworn and will not change his mind, 'You are a priest forever.'" Melchizedek, as we read, was a priest of the Most High God long before the time of the priesthood of the law, and he offered bread and wine to the Lord. Our Redeemer is said to be a priest "in the order of Melchizedek" because he put aside the sacrificial victims stipulated by the law and instituted the same type of sacrifice to be offered in the new covenant in the mystery of his own body and blood.

VENERABLE BEDE
(C. 672–735)
HOMILIES ON THE GOSPELS

nothing perfect. On the other hand a better hope is introduced,
through which we draw near to God. 20And since this was not
done without a sworn affirmation—for the others have become priests without a sworn affirmation, 21but Jesus did so
with a sworn affirmation by the one who said to him, ***"The
Lord has sworn and will not change his mind, 'You are a priest
forever'"***—22accordingly Jesus has become the guarantee of a
better covenant. 23And the others who became priests were
numerous because death prevented them from continuing
in office, 24but he holds his priesthood permanently since he
lives forever. 25So he is able to save completely those who come
to God through him because he always lives to intercede for
them. 26For it is indeed fitting for us to have such a high priest:
holy, innocent, undefiled, separate from sinners, and exalted
above the heavens. 27He has no need to do every day what those
priests do, to offer sacrifices first for their own sins and then
for the sins of the people, since he did this in offering himself
once for all. 28For the law appoints as high priests men subject
to weakness, but the word of solemn affirmation that came
after the law appoints a son made perfect forever.

THE HIGH PRIEST OF A BETTER COVENANT

8 Now the main point of what we are saying is this: We have
such a high priest, one who *sat down at the right hand of the
throne of the Majesty in heaven,* 2a minister in the sanctuary
and the true tabernacle that the Lord, not man, set up. 3For
every high priest is appointed to offer both gifts and sacrifices. So this one, too, had to have something to offer. 4Now
if he were on earth, he would not be a priest, since there are
already priests who offer the gifts prescribed by the law. 5The
place where they serve is a sketch and shadow of the heavenly
sanctuary, just as Moses was warned by God as he was about
to complete the tabernacle. For he says, "***See that you make
everything according to the design shown to you on the mountain.***" 6But now Jesus has obtained a superior ministry, since
the covenant that he mediates is also better and is enacted
on better promises.

7For if that first covenant had been faultless, no one would
have looked for a second one. 8But showing its fault, God says
to them,

***"Look, the days are coming, says the Lord, when I will
complete a new covenant with the house of Israel
and with the house of Judah.***

9 ***It will not be like the covenant that I made with their
fathers, on the day when I took them by the hand
to lead them out of Egypt, because they did not
continue in my covenant, and I had no regard for
them, says the Lord.***

10 ***For this is the covenant that I will establish with the house
of Israel after those days, says the Lord. I will put my
laws in their minds, and I will inscribe them on their
hearts. And I will be their God, and they will be my
people.***

11 ***And there will be no need at all for each one to teach his
countryman or each one to teach his brother saying,
'Know the Lord,' since they will all know me, from
the least to the greatest.***

12 ***For I will be merciful toward their evil deeds, and their
sins I will remember no longer."***

8:1–13 Mighty Paul knew that the only begotten God, who has the preeminence in all things, is the author and cause of everything that is good. Paul witnesses to the fact that the creation of all that exists was formed by the only begotten God. On top of this he also testifies that when the original creation of man had decayed and vanished away (to use his own language), and another new creation was formed in Christ, in this too no other than he, the only begotten God, took the lead. But he is himself the firstborn of all that new creation of human beings who are effected by the gospel.

GREGORY OF NYSSA
(C. 335–C. 395)
AGAINST EUNOMIUS

13When he speaks of a new covenant, he makes the first
obsolete. Now what is growing obsolete and aging is about to
disappear.

THE ARRANGEMENT AND RITUAL OF THE EARTHLY SANCTUARY

9 Now the first covenant, in fact, had regulations for worship and its earthly sanctuary. 2For a tent was prepared, the
outer one, which contained the lampstand, the table, and the
presentation of the loaves; this is called the Holy Place. 3And
after the second curtain there was a tent called the holy of
holies. 4It contained the golden altar of incense and the ark of
the covenant covered entirely with gold. In this ark were the
golden urn containing the manna, Aaron's rod that budded,
and the stone tablets of the covenant. 5And above the ark were
the cherubim of glory overshadowing the mercy seat. Now is
not the time to speak of these things in detail. 6So with these
things prepared like this, the priests enter continually into
the outer tent as they perform their duties. 7But only the high
priest enters once a year into the inner tent, and not without
blood that he offers for himself and for the sins of the people
committed in ignorance. 8The Holy Spirit is making clear that
the way into the Holy Place had not yet appeared as long as
the old tabernacle was standing. 9This was a symbol for the
time then present, when gifts and sacrifices were offered that
could not perfect the conscience of the worshiper. 10They
served only for matters of food and drink and various ritual
washings; they are external regulations imposed until the
new order came.

CHRIST'S SERVICE IN THE HEAVENLY SANCTUARY

11But now Christ has come as the high priest of the good things
to come. He passed through the greater and more perfect tent
not made with hands, that is, not of this creation, 12and he entered once for all into the Most Holy Place not by the blood of
goats and calves but by his own blood, and so he himself secured
eternal redemption. 13For if the blood of goats and bulls and
the ashes of a young cow sprinkled on those who are defiled
consecrated them and provided ritual purity, 14how much more
will the blood of Christ, who through the eternal Spirit offered
himself without blemish to God, purify our consciences from
dead works to worship the living God.
15And so he is the mediator of a new covenant, so that those
who are called may receive the eternal inheritance he has promised, since he died to set them free from the violations committed under the first covenant. 16For where there is a will, the
death of the one who made it must be proven. 17For a will takes
effect only at death, since it carries no force while the one who
made it is alive. 18So even the first covenant was inaugurated
with blood. 19For when Moses had spoken every command to
all the people according to the law, he took the blood of calves
and goats with water and scarlet wool and hyssop and sprinkled
both the book itself and all the people, 20and said, ***"This is the
blood of the covenant that God has commanded you to keep."***
21And both the tabernacle and all the utensils of worship he
likewise sprinkled with blood. 22Indeed according to the law
almost everything was purified with blood, and without the
shedding of blood there is no forgiveness. 23So it was necessary

9:6–22 Moving to the contemplation of the blood of the Son of God, our awe is increased. We should shudder to think of the guilt of sin and its terrible penalty that Jesus, the sin-bearer, endured. Blood is all the more priceless when it flows from Immanuel's side. The blood of Jesus sealed God's covenant of grace, guaranteeing it forever. Oh, the delight of being saved upon the sure foundation of God's divine agreements that cannot be dishonored. Salvation by works of the law is a frail and leaky boat whose shipwreck is certain, but the ship of the covenant fears no storms for Jesus' blood ensures it from stem to stern.

CHARLES SPURGEON
(1834–1892)
METROPOLITAN TABERNACLE SERMONS

for the sketches of the things in heaven to be purified with these sacrifices, but the heavenly things themselves required better sacrifices than these. [24]For Christ did not enter a sanctuary made with hands—the representation of the true sanctuary—but into heaven itself, and he appears now in God's presence for us. [25]And he did not enter to offer himself again and again, the way the high priest enters the sanctuary year after year with blood that is not his own, [26]for then he would have had to suffer again and again since the foundation of the world. But now he has appeared once for all at the consummation of the ages to put away sin by his sacrifice. [27]And just as people are appointed to die once, and then to face judgment, [28]so also, after Christ was offered once to *bear the sins of many,* to those who eagerly await him he will appear a second time, not to bear sin but to bring salvation.

CONCLUDING EXPOSITION: OLD AND NEW SACRIFICES CONTRASTED

10 For the law possesses a shadow of the good things to come but not the reality itself, and is therefore completely unable, by the same sacrifices offered continually, year after year, to perfect those who come to worship. [2]For otherwise would they not have ceased to be offered, since the worshipers would have been purified once for all and so have no further consciousness of sin? [3]But in those sacrifices there is a reminder of sins year after year. [4]For it is impossible for the blood of bulls and goats to take away sins. [5]So when he came into the world, he said,

"Sacrifice and offering you did not desire, but a body you
prepared for me.
6 ***Whole burnt offerings and sin-offerings you took no***
delight in.
7 ***Then I said, 'Here I am: I have come—it is written of me in***
the scroll of the book—to do your will, O God.'"

[8]When he says above, "***Sacrifices and offerings*** and ***whole burnt offerings and sin-offerings you did not desire nor did you take delight*** in them" (which are offered according to the law), [9]then he says, "***Here I am: I have come to do your will.***" He does away with the first to establish the second. [10]By his will we have been made holy through the offering of the body of Jesus Christ once for all. [11]And every priest stands day after day serving and offering the same sacrifices again and again—sacrifices that can never take away sins. [12]But when this priest had offered one sacrifice for sins for all time, *he sat down at the right hand* of God, [13]where he is now waiting *until his enemies are made a footstool for his feet.* [14]For by one offering he has perfected for all time those who are made holy. [15]And the Holy Spirit also witnesses to us, for after saying, [16]"***This is the covenant that I will establish with them after those days, says the Lord. I will put my laws on their hearts and I will inscribe them on their minds,***" [17]then he says, "***Their sins and their lawless deeds I will remember no longer.***" [18]Now where there is forgiveness of these, there is no longer any offering for sin.

DRAWING NEAR TO GOD IN ENDURING FAITH

[19]Therefore, brothers and sisters, since we have confidence to enter the sanctuary by the blood of Jesus, [20]by the fresh and living way that he inaugurated for us through the curtain, that

10:5–10 **Not without the Father does he work; not without his Father's will did he offer himself for that most holy Passion, the victim slain for the salvation of the whole world; not without his Father's will concurring did he raise the dead to life. For example, when he was at the point to raise Lazarus to life, he lifted up his eyes and said, "Father, I thank you that you have listened to me" (John 11:41). He said this in order that in the flesh he might still express his oneness with the Father in will and operation, in that the Father hears all and sees all that the Son wills. Therefore also the Father sees the Son's doings, hears the utterances of his will, for the Son made no request and yet said that he had been heard.**

AMBROSE (C. 339–C. 397)
ON THE CHRISTIAN FAITH

is, through his flesh, [21] and since we have a great priest over the house of God, [22]let us draw near with a sincere heart in the assurance that faith brings, because we have had our hearts sprinkled clean from an evil conscience and our bodies washed in pure water. [23]And let us hold unwaveringly to the hope that we confess, for the one who made the promise is trustworthy. [24]And let us take thought of how to spur one another on to love and good works, [25]not abandoning our own meetings, as some are in the habit of doing, but encouraging each other, and even more so because you see the day drawing near.

[26]For if we deliberately keep on sinning after receiving the knowledge of the truth, no further sacrifice for sins is left for us, [27]but only a certain fearful expectation of judgment and *a fury of fire that will consume God's enemies.* [28]Someone who rejected the law of Moses was put to death without mercy *on the testimony of two or three witnesses.* [29]How much greater punishment do you think that person deserves who has contempt for the Son of God, and profanes the blood of the covenant that made him holy, and insults the Spirit of grace? [30]For we know the one who said, "***Vengeance is mine, I will repay,***" and again, "***The Lord will judge his people.***" [31]It is a terrifying thing to fall into the hands of the living God.

[32]But remember the former days when you endured a harsh conflict of suffering after you were enlightened. [33]At times you were publicly exposed to abuse and afflictions, and at other times you came to share with others who were treated in that way. [34]For in fact you shared the sufferings of those in prison, and you accepted the confiscation of your belongings with joy, because you knew that you certainly had a better and lasting possession. [35]So do not throw away your confidence, because it has great reward. [36]For you need endurance in order to do God's will and so receive what is promised. [37]For ***just a little longer*** and ***he who is coming will arrive and not delay.*** [38]***But my righteous one will live by faith, and if he shrinks back, I take no pleasure in him.*** [39]But we are not among those who shrink back and thus perish, but are among those who have faith and preserve their souls.

PEOPLE COMMENDED FOR THEIR FAITH

11 Now faith is being sure of what we hope for, being convinced of what we do not see. [2]For by it the people of old received God's commendation. [3]By faith we understand that the worlds were set in order at God's command, so that the visible has its origin in the invisible. [4]By faith Abel offered God a greater sacrifice than Cain, and through his faith he was commended as righteous because God commended him for his offerings. And through his faith he still speaks, though he is dead. [5]By faith Enoch was taken up so that he did not see death, and he was not to be found because God took him up. For before his removal he had been commended as having pleased God. [6]Now without faith it is impossible to please him, for the one who approaches God must believe that he exists and that he rewards those who seek him. [7]By faith Noah, when he was warned about things not yet seen, with reverent regard constructed an ark for the deliverance of his family. Through faith he condemned the world and became an heir of the righteousness that comes by faith.

[8]By faith Abraham obeyed when he was called to go out to a place he would later receive as an inheritance, and he went out without understanding where he was going. [9]By faith he

11:4–29 **What a beautiful epitaph for all those blessed saints who fell asleep before the coming of our Lord, who all "died in faith without receiving the things promised." They had lived "in faith" for it was their comfort, their guide, their motivation, and their support; and it was in the same spiritual blessing they died, ending their life's song with the same sweet strain in which they had walked for so long. To these saints the pains of death were but the birth pangs of a better life. Therefore take courage as you read this epitaph. Your path through grace is also one of faith. Look anew to Jesus, "the pioneer and perfecter of our faith" (Heb 12:2), thanking him for giving you the gift of precious faith—faith just like that of those souls who are now in glory.**

CHARLES SPURGEON
(1834–1892)
MORNING AND EVENING

lived as a foreigner in the promised land as though it were a foreign country, living in tents with Isaac and Jacob, who were fellow heirs of the same promise. [10]For he was looking forward to the city with firm foundations, whose architect and builder is God. [11]By faith, even though Sarah herself was barren and he was too old, he received the ability to procreate because he regarded the one who had given the promise to be trustworthy. [12]So in fact children were fathered by one man—and this one as good as dead—*like the number of stars in the sky and like the innumerable grains of sand on the seashore.* [13]These all died in faith without receiving the things promised, but they saw them in the distance and welcomed them and acknowledged that they were strangers and foreigners on the earth. [14]For those who speak in such a way make it clear that they are seeking a homeland. [15]In fact, if they had been thinking of the land that they had left, they would have had opportunity to return. [16]But as it is, they aspire to a better land, that is, a heavenly one. Therefore, God is not ashamed to be called their God, for he has prepared a city for them. [17]By faith Abraham, when he was tested, offered up Isaac. He had received the promises, yet he was ready to offer up his only son. [18]God had told him, ***"Through Isaac descendants will carry on your name,"*** [19]and he reasoned that God could even raise him from the dead, and in a sense he received him back from there. [20]By faith also Isaac blessed Jacob and Esau concerning the future. [21]By faith Jacob, as he was dying, blessed each of the sons of Joseph and ***worshiped as he leaned on his staff.*** [22]By faith Joseph, at the end of his life, mentioned the exodus of the sons of Israel and gave instructions about his burial.

[23]By faith, when Moses was born, his parents hid him for three months because they saw the child was beautiful and they were not afraid of the king's edict. [24]By faith, when he grew up, Moses refused to be called the son of Pharaoh's daughter, [25]choosing rather to be ill-treated with the people of God than to enjoy sin's fleeting pleasure. [26]He regarded abuse suffered for Christ to be greater wealth than the treasures of Egypt, for his eyes were fixed on the reward. [27]By faith he left Egypt without fearing the king's anger, for he persevered as though he could see the one who is invisible. [28]By faith he kept the Passover and the sprinkling of the blood, so that the one who destroyed the firstborn would not touch them. [29]By faith they crossed the Red Sea as if on dry ground, but when the Egyptians tried it, they were swallowed up. [30]By faith the walls of Jericho fell after the people marched around them for seven days. [31]By faith Rahab the prostitute escaped the destruction of the disobedient because she welcomed the spies in peace.

[32]And what more shall I say? For time will fail me if I tell of Gideon, Barak, Samson, Jephthah, of David and Samuel and the prophets. [33]Through faith they conquered kingdoms, administered justice, gained what was promised, shut the mouths of lions, [34]quenched raging fire, escaped the edge of the sword, gained strength in weakness, became mighty in battle, put foreign armies to flight, [35]and women received back their dead raised to life. But others were tortured, not accepting release, to obtain resurrection to a better life. [36]And others experienced mocking and flogging, and even chains and imprisonment. [37]They were stoned, sawed apart, murdered with the sword; they went about in sheepskins and goatskins; they were

destitute, afflicted, ill-treated 38(the world was not worthy of
them); they wandered in deserts and mountains and caves and
openings in the earth. 39And these all were commended for
their faith, yet they did not receive what was promised. 40For
God had provided something better for us, so that they would
be made perfect together with us.

THE LORD'S DISCIPLINE

12 Therefore, since we are surrounded by such a great cloud of
witnesses, we must get rid of every weight and the sin that
clings so closely, and run with endurance the race set out for
us, 2keeping our eyes fixed on Jesus, the pioneer and perfecter
of our faith. For the joy set out for him he endured the cross,
disregarding its shame, and *has taken his seat at the right hand of*
the throne of God. 3Think of him who endured such opposition
against himself by sinners, so that you may not grow weary in
your souls and give up. 4You have not yet resisted to the point of
bloodshed in your struggle against sin. 5And have you forgotten
the exhortation addressed to you as sons?

"My son, do not scorn the Lord's discipline
or give up when he corrects you.
6 ***For the Lord disciplines the one he loves and chastises***
every son he accepts."

7Endure your suffering as discipline; God is treating you as
sons. For what son is there that a father does not discipline?
8But if you do not experience discipline, something all sons have
shared in, then you are illegitimate and are not sons. 9Besides,
we have experienced discipline from our earthly fathers and
we respected them; shall we not submit ourselves all the more
to the Father of spirits and receive life? 10For they disciplined
us for a little while as seemed good to them, but he does so for
our benefit, that we may share his holiness. 11Now all discipline
seems painful at the time, not joyful. But later it produces the
fruit of peace and righteousness for those trained by it. 12There-
fore, ***strengthen your listless hands and your weak knees,*** 13and
make straight paths for your feet, so that what is lame may not
be put out of joint but be healed.

DO NOT REJECT GOD'S WARNING

14Pursue peace with everyone, and holiness, for without it no
one will see the Lord. 15See to it that no one comes short of the
grace of God, that no one be like *a bitter root springing up* and
causing trouble, and through it many become defiled. 16And
see to it that no one becomes an immoral or godless person
like Esau, who *sold his own birthright for a single meal.* 17For you
know that later when he wanted to inherit the blessing, he was
rejected, for he found no opportunity for repentance, although
he sought the blessing with tears. 18For you have not come to
something that can be touched, to a burning fire and darkness
and gloom and a whirlwind 19and the blast of a trumpet and a
voice uttering words such that those who heard begged to hear
no more. 20For they could not bear what was commanded: ***"If***
even an animal touches the mountain, it must be stoned." 21In
fact, the scene was so terrifying that Moses said, ***"I shudder***
with fear." 22But you have come to Mount Zion, the city of the
living God, the heavenly Jerusalem, and to myriads of angels,
to the assembly 23and congregation of the firstborn, who are
enrolled in heaven, and to God, the judge of all, and to the spirits

12:1–17 With God nothing that is suffered for his sake, no matter how small, can pass without reward. Be prepared for the fight, then, if you wish to gain the victory. Without struggle you cannot obtain the crown of patience, and if you refuse to suffer you are refusing the crown. But if you desire to be crowned, fight bravely and bear up patiently. Without labor there is no rest and without fighting, no victory.

THOMAS À KEMPIS
(C. 1380–1471)
THE IMITATION OF CHRIST

of the righteous, who have been made perfect, 24and to Jesus,
the mediator of a new covenant, and to the sprinkled blood
that speaks of something better than Abel's does.
25Take care not to refuse the one who is speaking! For if
they did not escape when they refused the one who warned
them on earth, how much less shall we, if we reject the one
who warns from heaven? 26Then his voice shook the earth,
but now he has promised, ***"I will once more shake not only the***
earth but heaven too." 27Now this phrase "***once more***" indicates
the removal of what is shaken, that is, of created things, so that
what is unshaken may remain. 28So since we are receiving an
unshakable kingdom, let us give thanks, and through this let
us offer worship pleasing to God in devotion and awe. 29For our
God is indeed a devouring fire.

FINAL EXHORTATIONS

13 Brotherly love must continue. 2Do not neglect hospitality
because through it some have entertained angels without
knowing it. 3Remember those in prison as though you were
in prison with them, and those ill-treated as though you, too,
felt their torment. 4Marriage must be honored among all and
the marriage bed kept undefiled, for God will judge sexually
immoral people and adulterers. 5Your conduct must be free
from the love of money, and you must be content with what
you have, for he has said, ***"I will never leave you and I will never***
abandon you." 6So we can say with confidence, ***"The Lord is my***
helper, and I will not be afraid. What can people do to me?" 7Re-
member your leaders, who spoke God's message to you; reflect
on the outcome of their lives and imitate their faith. 8Jesus
Christ is the same yesterday and today and forever! 9Do not
be carried away by all sorts of strange teachings. For it is good
for the heart to be strengthened by grace, not ritual meals,
which have never benefited those who participated in them.
10We have an altar that those who serve in the tabernacle have
no right to eat from. 11For the bodies of those animals whose
blood the high priest brings into the sanctuary as an offering
for sin are burned outside the camp. 12Therefore, to sanctify the
people by his own blood, Jesus also suffered outside the camp.
13We must go out to him, then, outside the camp, bearing the
abuse he experienced. 14For here we have no lasting city, but
we seek the city that is to come. 15Through him then let us
continually offer up a sacrifice of praise to God, that is, the fruit
of our lips, acknowledging his name. 16And do not neglect to do
good and to share what you have, for God is pleased with such
sacrifices.
17Obey your leaders and submit to them, for they keep watch
over your souls and will give an account for their work. Let
them do this with joy and not with complaints, for this would
be no advantage for you. 18Pray for us, for we are sure that we
have a clear conscience and desire to conduct ourselves rightly
in every respect. 19I especially ask you to pray that I may be
restored to you very soon.

BENEDICTION AND CONCLUSION

20Now may the God of peace who by the blood of the eternal
covenant brought back from the dead the great shepherd of
the sheep, our Lord Jesus, 21equip you with every good thing to
do his will, working in us what is pleasing before him through
Jesus Christ, to whom be glory forever. Amen.

13:7–21 Living by faith in Christ, set apart to God through his blood, let us willingly separate from this evil world. Let us go forth now by faith and seek in Christ the rest and peace that this world cannot afford us. Let us bring our sacrifices to this our high priest and offer them up by him. The sacrifice of praise to God we should offer always. In this are worship and prayer as well as thanksgiving.

MATTHEW HENRY **(1662–1714)**
COMMENTARY ON THE WHOLE BIBLE

[22]Now I urge you, brothers and sisters, bear with my message
of exhortation, for in fact I have written to you briefly. [23]You
should know that our brother Timothy has been released. If
he comes soon, he will be with me when I see you. [24]Greetings
to all your leaders and all the saints. Those from Italy send you
greetings. [25]Grace be with you all.

AUTHOR	AUDIENCE	DATE	PURPOSE	THEMES
James, the half brother of Jesus and a leader in the Jerusalem church	Jewish Christians, perhaps Jerusalem believers scattered after Stephen's death	Perhaps before AD 50	James wrote to commend a vital Christianity characterized by good deeds and a faith that worked.	The wisdom of God; the law of Moses; faith and good deeds; practical issues of Christian living; and friendship with the world

Though Martin Luther referred to the epistle of James as an "epistle of straw" in his preface to his German translation of the New Testament, this book has made an important contribution to the life of the communion of saints.

James's epistle follows in the great tradition of Jewish wisdom from the Hebrew scriptures, addressing several relevant issues in a way Jewish Christians would have understood. It is clear from the opening that James wrote "to the twelve tribes dispersed abroad" (1:1), encouraging Jewish converts to Christianity throughout the Roman Empire.

As a sort of wisdom sermon, James teaches believers on various topics relevant to Christian living, inspired by the long tradition of Jewish wisdom literature. The Greek word for wisdom, *sophia*, occurs four times in James's letter. The epistle comforts and offers hope to believers in the midst of trials, exhorts believers to live lives of faithful obedience, urges the confirmation of faith with works, provides spiritual instruction for daily living, and promotes conduct that unifies the church.

First, James recognizes the necessity of seeking God's wisdom for life's trials, where insight into the Lord's ways is necessary. The Lord is the source, and he promises we will experience spiritual maturity and lack nothing when we ask for wisdom. Whatever the temptation or trial—whether spiritual or financial, job- or health-related—we will find the guidance we need in this letter when our faith is being challenged. What is more, the epistle of James makes clear that there is always a divine goal in such experiences: "that you will be perfect and complete, not deficient in anything" (1:4).

In referring to "the royal law" (2:8), James makes reference to the law of the Old Testament, quoting Leviticus 19:18: "You shall love your neighbor as yourself." He compares violating this royal law of love to violating the Ten Commandments themselves, revealing the seriousness of living out this aspect of God's Word. In fact James makes a general appeal, saying, "Humbly welcome the message implanted within you" (1:21), exhorting every Christian to "be sure you live out the message and do not merely listen

JAMES

to it and so deceive yourselves. For if someone merely listens to the message and does not live it out," he deceives himself (1:22–23).

This leads to the third item of faith and life James addresses: the connection between faith and good works. One of the ongoing debates surrounding this epistle, and one of the reasons Luther suggested it was empty straw, is the suggestion that James contradicts Paul's teaching on salvation by grace through faith alone. For instance, "You see that a person is justified by works and not by faith alone" (2:24) seems, at first glance, to do just that. But it only seems that way. Rather than undermining or opposing Paul's theology of faith and works, namely that "by grace you are saved through faith, and this is not from yourselves, it is the gift of God" (Eph 2:8), James uses his letter to outline the kind of faith that saves: working faith. He argues, "For just as the body without the spirit is dead, so also faith without works is dead" (2:26).

Finally, the apostle James offered several words addressing practical Christian living: He gave a strong warning against partiality, addressing the enormous gap between the rich and poor at gathered assemblies, which had manifested itself in personal favoritism of those wearing fine clothes. He assured poor believers that God has blessed them with every heavenly privilege and warned the rich against corruption and greed. He chided gossipers and slanderers, exhorting God's children to tame their tongues; railed against every form of wickedness and friendship with the world, from fighting to coveting, lusting to pride; exhorted believers to patiently await the coming of the Lord, persevering as farmers do while waiting for the fullness of their crops; and gave instructions for confession, prayer, and healing.

Unlike Luther, the other great Reformer, John Calvin, commended James's epistle as beneficial to every part of the Christian life: "For there are here remarkable passages on patience, prayer to God, the excellency and fruit of heavenly truth, humility, holy duties, the restraining of the tongue, the cultivation of peace, the repressing of lusts, [and] the contempt of the world."

1:1–18 In temptations and trials the progress of a man is measured; in them opportunity for merit and virtue is made more manifest. When a man is not troubled it is not hard for him to be fervent and devout, but if he bears up patiently in time of adversity, there is hope for great progress. Some, guarded against great temptations, are frequently overcome by small ones in order that, humbled by their weakness in small trials, they may not presume on their own strength in great ones.

THOMAS À KEMPIS
(C. 1380–1471)
THE IMITATION OF CHRIST

SALUTATION

1 From James, a slave of God and the Lord Jesus Christ, to the
12 tribes dispersed abroad. Greetings!

JOY IN TRIALS

2 My brothers and sisters, consider it nothing but joy when you
fall into all sorts of trials, 3 because you know that the testing
of your faith produces endurance. 4 And let endurance have
its perfect effect, so that you will be perfect and complete, not
deficient in anything. 5 But if anyone is deficient in wisdom,
he should ask God, who gives to all generously and without
reprimand, and it will be given to him. 6 But he must ask in faith
without doubting, for the one who doubts is like a wave of the
sea, blown and tossed around by the wind. 7 For that person
must not suppose that he will receive anything from the Lord,
8 since he is a double-minded individual, unstable in all his ways.
9 Now the believer of humble means should take pride
in his high position. 10 But the rich person's pride should be
in his humiliation because he will pass away like a wildflower in
the meadow. 11 For the sun rises with its heat and dries up the
meadow; the petal of the flower falls off and its beauty is lost
forever. So also the rich person in the midst of his pursuits will
wither away. 12 Happy is the one who endures testing because
when he has proven to be genuine, he will receive the crown of
life that God promised to those who love him. 13 Let no one say
when he is tempted, "I am tempted by God," for God cannot be
tempted by evil, and he himself tempts no one. 14 But each one
is tempted when he is lured and enticed by his own desires.
15 Then when desire conceives, it gives birth to sin, and when
sin is full grown, it gives birth to death. 16 Do not be led astray,
my dear brothers and sisters. 17 All generous giving and every
perfect gift is from above, coming down from the Father of lights,
with whom there is no variation or the slightest hint of change.
18 By his sovereign plan he gave us birth through the message
of truth, that we would be a kind of firstfruits of all he created.

LIVING OUT THE MESSAGE

19 Understand this, my dear brothers and sisters! Let every person
be quick to listen, slow to speak, slow to anger. 20 For human anger
does not accomplish God's righteousness. 21 So put away all filth
and evil excess and humbly welcome the message implanted
within you, which is able to save your souls. 22 But be sure you
live out the message and do not merely listen to it and so deceive
yourselves. 23 For if someone merely listens to the message and
does not live it out, he is like someone who gazes at his own
face in a mirror. 24 For he gazes at himself and then goes out and
immediately forgets what sort of person he was. 25 But the one
who peers into the perfect law of liberty and fixes his attention
there, and does not become a forgetful listener but one who lives
it out—he will be blessed in what he does. 26 If someone thinks
he is religious yet does not bridle his tongue, and so deceives his
heart, his religion is futile. 27 Pure and undefiled religion before
God the Father is this: to care for orphans and widows in their
adversity and to keep oneself unstained by the world.

PREJUDICE AND THE LAW OF LOVE

2 My brothers and sisters, do not show prejudice if you possess
faith in our glorious Lord Jesus Christ. 2 For if someone comes
into your assembly wearing a gold ring and fine clothing, and a

poor person enters in filthy clothes, [3]do you pay attention to the one who is finely dressed and say, "You sit here in a good place," and to the poor person, "You stand over there," or "Sit on the floor"? [4]If so, have you not made distinctions among yourselves and become judges with evil motives? [5]Listen, my dear brothers and sisters! Did not God choose the poor in the world to be rich in faith and heirs of the kingdom that he promised to those who love him? [6]But you have dishonored the poor! Are not the rich oppressing you and dragging you into the courts? [7]Do they not blaspheme the good name of the one you belong to? [8]But if you fulfill the royal law as expressed in this scripture, ***"You shall love your neighbor as yourself,"*** you are doing well. [9]But if you show prejudice, you are committing sin and are convicted by the law as violators. [10]For the one who obeys the whole law but fails in one point has become guilty of all of it. [11]For he who said, ***"Do not commit adultery,"*** also said, ***"Do not murder."*** Now if you do not commit adultery but do commit murder, you have become a violator of the law. [12]Speak and act as those who will be judged by a law that gives freedom. [13]For judgment is merciless for the one who has shown no mercy. But mercy triumphs over judgment.

FAITH AND WORKS TOGETHER

[14]What good is it, my brothers and sisters, if someone claims to have faith but does not have works? Can this kind of faith save him? [15]If a brother or sister is poorly clothed and lacks daily food, [16]and one of you says to them, "Go in peace, keep warm and eat well," but you do not give them what the body needs, what good is it? [17]So also faith, if it does not have works, is dead being by itself. [18]But someone will say, "You have faith and I have works." Show me your faith without works and I will show you faith by my works. [19]You believe that God is one; well and good. Even the demons believe that—and tremble with fear.

[20]But would you like evidence, you empty fellow, that faith without works is useless? [21]Was not Abraham our father justified by works when he offered Isaac his son on the altar? [22]You see that his faith was working together with his works and his faith was perfected by works. [23]And the scripture was fulfilled that says, ***"Now Abraham believed God and it was counted to him for righteousness,"*** and *he was called God's friend.* [24]You see that a person is justified by works and not by faith alone. [25]And similarly, was not Rahab the prostitute also justified by works when she welcomed the messengers and sent them out by another way? [26]For just as the body without the spirit is dead, so also faith without works is dead.

THE POWER OF THE TONGUE

3 Not many of you should become teachers, my brothers and sisters, because you know that we will be judged more strictly. [2]For we all stumble in many ways. If someone does not stumble in what he says, he is a perfect individual, able to control the entire body as well. [3]And if we put bits into the mouths of horses to get them to obey us, then we guide their entire bodies. [4]Look at ships too: Though they are so large and driven by harsh winds, they are steered by a tiny rudder wherever the pilot's inclination directs. [5]So, too, the tongue is a small part of the body, yet it has great pretensions. Think how small a flame sets a huge forest ablaze. [6]And the tongue is a fire! The tongue represents the world of wrongdoing among the parts of our

2:1–13 If a man has conducted himself not only as an equal, but even as an inferior, he will plainly obtain a much higher rank of dignity in the judgment of God. What nobility can be so firm, what resources, what power, since God is able to make kings themselves even lower than the lowest? And therefore God has consulted our interest in placing this in particular among the divine precepts: "God opposes the proud, but he gives grace to the humble" (Jas 4:6). And the wholesomeness of this precept teaches that he who shall simply place himself on a level with other men and carry himself with humility is esteemed excellent and illustrious in the sight of God.

LACTANTIUS **(C. 250–C. 325)**
DIVINE INSTITUTES

3:1–12 It is a clear instance of the tongue's deadly poison that it can thus through a monstrous levity transform itself; for when it pretends to bless God, it immediately curses him in his own image even by cursing human beings. It is a hypocrisy not to be borne when people employ the same tongue in blessing God and in cursing others. There can be then no calling on God, and his praises must necessarily cease when evil speaking prevails, for it is impious profanation of God's name when the tongue is virulent toward our brethren and pretends to praise him. He then who truly worships and honors God will be afraid to speak slanderously of man.

JOHN CALVIN **(1509–1564)**
COMPLETE COMMENTARY ON THE BIBLE

H. RICHARD NIEBUHR:

CONNECTING CHRIST AND CULTURE

1894–1962

The perennial problem of the Christian faith has been how to relate to the surrounding culture. H. Richard Niebuhr called this "the enduring problem," and he sought to chart out a useful path.

Niebuhr was born in 1894 to German immigrants in a small town in Missouri. He was the younger brother of the famed theologian Richard Niebuhr, and his father was a minister whose footsteps he would follow into ministry. After being ordained in 1916 and serving in St. Louis after graduating from seminary, he went on to earn his PhD from Yale, where he taught ethics for over 30 years until his death. One of his primary areas of reflection and research was the sovereignty of God and the historical movement of civilization, particularly the role humans play within it. Coinciding with this interest was a second, related concern: the Christian role within the movement of this history. Of particular focus was the relationship between Christ and culture.

Published in 1951, *Christ and Culture* was concerned with what Niebuhr called the "enduring problem" of "the relations of Christianity and civilization being carried on in our time." He acknowledged the problem wasn't a new one, arising from the beginning with Jesus' own life and his situation as a Jew challenging both Jewish and Roman civilizations.. Early Christians living in Rome faced the same challenge, leading all the way to the modern era with issues of pluralism and historical relativism. "Given the two complex realities—Christ and culture," Niebuhr suggested "an infinite dialogue must develop in the Christian conscience and the Christian community," which he summarized in five possible answers.

First, *Christ against culture*, in which Christianity is opposed to civilization and offers it an "either-or" decision; second, *Christ of culture*, in which there is agreement between the two, and Jesus is seen as a hero of history; third, *Christ above culture* is best represented by Thomas Aquinas, in which there is a synthesis of the two; fourth, *Christ and culture in paradox*, a both/and struggle of dueling authority and opposition between the two; and fifth, *Christ transforming culture*, a conversionist solution exemplified by Augustine and John Calvin who saw Christ converting humankind, culture, and all society. Niebuhr understood these five types as mere constructs. Yet he saw in them an "advantage of calling to attention the continuity and significance of the great *motifs* that appear and reappear in the long wrestling of Christians with their enduring problem."

Since Niebuhr's death in 1962, his book's legacy has been mixed. Regardless, it is undeniable that the questions at the intersection of Christianity and civilization he addressed have not changed and will continue to be asked for generations to come. His paradigms continue to "help us gain orientation as we in our own time seek to answer the question of Christ and culture."

IMPORTANT WORKS

CHRIST AND CULTURE

THE KINGDOM OF GOD IN AMERICA

RADICAL MONOTHEISM AND WESTERN CULTURE

bodies. It pollutes the entire body and sets fire to the course
of human existence—and is set on fire by hell.
[7]For every kind of animal, bird, reptile, and sea creature is
subdued and has been subdued by humankind. [8]But no human
being can subdue the tongue; it is a restless evil, full of deadly
poison. [9]With it we bless the Lord and Father, and with it we
curse people made in God's image. [10]From the same mouth
come blessing and cursing. These things should not be so, my
brothers and sisters. [11]A spring does not pour out fresh water
and bitter water from the same opening, does it? [12]Can a fig tree
produce olives, my brothers and sisters, or a vine produce figs?
Neither can a salt water spring produce fresh water.

TRUE WISDOM

[13]Who is wise and understanding among you? By his good conduct he should show his works done in the gentleness that
wisdom brings. [14]But if you have bitter jealousy and selfishness
in your hearts, do not boast and tell lies against the truth. [15]Such
wisdom does not come from above but is earthly, natural, demonic. [16]For where there is jealousy and selfishness, there is
disorder and every evil practice. [17]But the wisdom from above
is first pure, then peaceable, gentle, accommodating, full of
mercy and good fruit, impartial, and not hypocritical. [18]And the
fruit that consists of righteousness is planted in peace among
those who make peace.

PASSIONS AND PRIDE

4 Where do the conflicts and where do the quarrels among
you come from? Is it not from this, from your passions that
battle inside you? [2]You desire and you do not have; you murder
and envy and you cannot obtain; you quarrel and fight. You do
not have because you do not ask; [3]you ask and do not receive
because you ask wrongly, so you can spend it on your passions.
[4]Adulterers, do you not know that friendship with the world
means hostility toward God? So whoever decides to be the
world's friend makes himself God's enemy. [5]Or do you think
the scripture means nothing when it says, "The spirit that God
caused to live within us has an envious yearning"? [6]But he gives
greater grace. Therefore it says, "***God opposes the proud, but he***
gives grace to the humble." [7]So submit to God. But resist the
devil and he will flee from you. [8]Draw near to God and he will
draw near to you. Cleanse your hands, you sinners, and make
your hearts pure, you double-minded. [9]Grieve, mourn, and weep.
Turn your laughter into mourning and your joy into despair.
[10]Humble yourselves before the Lord and he will exalt you.
[11]Do not speak against one another, brothers and sisters. He
who speaks against a fellow believer or judges a fellow believer
speaks against the law and judges the law. But if you judge the
law, you are not a doer of the law but its judge. [12]But there is only
one who is lawgiver and judge—the one who is able to save and
destroy. On the other hand, who are you to judge your neighbor?
[13]Come now, you who say, "Today or tomorrow we will go into
this or that town and spend a year there and do business and make
a profit." [14]You do not know about tomorrow. What is your life
like? For you are a puff of smoke that appears for a short time and
then vanishes. [15]You ought to say instead, "If the Lord is willing,
then we will live and do this or that." [16]But as it is, you boast about
your arrogant plans. All such boasting is evil. [17]So whoever knows
what is good to do and does not do it is guilty of sin.

4:1–12 **Let us clothe ourselves with concord and humility, ever exercising self-control, standing far off from all whispering and evil speaking, being justified by our works and not our words. Let our praise be in God and not of ourselves; for God hates those who commend themselves. Let testimony to our good deeds be borne by others, as it was in the case of our righteous forefathers. Boldness, arrogance, and audacity belong to those who are accursed of God; but moderation, humility, and meekness to such as are blessed by him.**

CLEMENT OF ROME **(D. 99)**
FIRST CLEMENT

WARNING TO THE RICH

5 Come now, you rich! Weep and cry aloud over the miseries
that are coming on you. [2]Your riches have rotted and your
clothing has become moth-eaten. [3]Your gold and silver have
rusted and their rust will be a witness against you. It will consume your flesh like fire. It is in the last days that you have
hoarded treasure! [4]Look, the pay you have held back from the
workers who mowed your fields cries out against you, and the
cries of the reapers have reached the ears of the Lord of Heav-
en's Armies. [5]You have lived indulgently and luxuriously on
the earth. You have fattened your hearts in a day of slaughter.
[6]You have condemned and murdered the righteous person,
although he does not resist you.

PATIENCE IN SUFFERING

[7]So be patient, brothers and sisters, until the Lord's return.
Think of how the farmer waits for the precious fruit of the
ground and is patient for it until it receives the early and late
rains. [8]You also be patient and strengthen your hearts, for the
Lord's return is near. [9]Do not grumble against one another,
brothers and sisters, so that you may not be judged. See, the
judge stands before the gates! [10]As an example of suffering and
patience, brothers and sisters, take the prophets who spoke in
the Lord's name. [11]Think of how we regard as blessed those who
have endured. You have heard of Job's endurance and you have
seen the Lord's purpose, that *the Lord is full of compassion and
mercy.* [12]And above all, my brothers and sisters, do not swear,
either by heaven or by earth or by any other oath. But let your
"Yes" be yes and your "No" be no, so that you may not fall into
judgment.

PRAYER FOR THE SICK

[13]Is anyone among you suffering? He should pray. Is anyone in
good spirits? He should sing praises. [14]Is anyone among you ill?
He should summon the elders of the church, and they should
pray for him and anoint him with olive oil in the name of the
Lord. [15]And the prayer of faith will save the one who is sick
and the Lord will raise him up—and if he has committed sins,
he will be forgiven. [16]So confess your sins to one another and
pray for one another so that you may be healed. The prayer
of a righteous person has great effectiveness. [17]Elijah was a
human being like us, and he prayed earnestly that it would
not rain and there was no rain on the land for three years and
six months! [18]Then he prayed again, and the sky gave rain and
the land sprouted with a harvest.
[19]My brothers and sisters, if anyone among you wanders from
the truth and someone turns him back, [20]he should know that
the one who turns a sinner back from his wandering path will
save that person's soul from death and will cover a multitude
of sins.

5:13–19 **Take everything to God. If you are suffering go in prayer; if you are in joy go in praise. But in any and every case, go. It is strong and reiterated advice, you see. Go continually, go always to God. Go, go because prayer is not of no profit but on the contrary, the "prayer of a righteous person has great effectiveness." The heart of the matter lies in every case in the communion with God that the soul enjoys in prayer. If it be humanity's chief end to glorify God and enjoy him forever, then human beings have attained their end, the sole purpose for which they were made and the entire object for which they exist when they enter into communion with God.**

B. B. WARFIELD **(1851–1921)**
FAITH AND LIFE

AUTHOR	AUDIENCE	DATE	PURPOSE	THEMES
Peter	Gentile and Jewish believers in Pontus, Galatia, Cappadocia, western Asia Minor, and Bithynia	About AD 60–64	Peter wrote to encourage believers in Asia Minor in their suffering and instruct them in holy living as born-again people of God.	The nature of God; the nature of salvation; Christian living; and Christian suffering

There is a wonderful weightiness, and yet liveliness and sweetness, in the epistles of Saint Peter," wrote John Wesley. "His design . . . is to stir up the minds of those to whom he writes, by way of remembrance, and to guard them not only against error but also against doubting. This he does by reminding them of that glorious grace that God had vouchsafed them through the gospel, by which believers are inflamed to bring forth the fruits of faith, hope, love, and patience."

Peter wrote to a number of churches in Asia minor (modern-day Turkey). The Gentile believers there had experienced intense persecution at the hands of their unbelieving neighbors for living the way of Christ, "[suffering] for a short time in various trials" (1:6). He wrote to encourage them in their suffering, which he assured them was not without purpose but would prove their faith genuine—being "much more valuable than gold" (1:7). John Calvin commented on the significance of this testing:

> Gold is, indeed, tried twice by fire: first when it is separated from its dross and then when a judgment is to be formed of its purity. Both modes of trial may very suitably be applied to faith: For when there is much of the dregs of unbelief remaining in us, and when by various afflictions we are refined as it were in God's furnace, the dross of our faith is removed so that it becomes pure and clean before God; and at the same time, a trial of it is made as to whether it be true or fictitious.

Peter had both "modes of trial" in mind as he exhorted believers to live in holiness and purity, ridding themselves of everything contrary to the goodness of the Lord, in order to show their faith true and genuine.

In this epistle, we find on full display the grandeur and glory of the holy Trinity. God the Father elects, dispenses mercy, shields, offers salvation, and judges. Jesus Christ the Son is the Redeemer who provided salvation through his precious blood, "an unblemished and spotless lamb" (1:19); he has been raised from the dead and glorified by God the Father. Of course, all of this was prophesied in ages past when the Spirit of Christ

1 PETER

"testified beforehand about the sufferings appointed for Christ and his subsequent glory" (1:11). This same Spirit is vital to our ongoing Christian life, for he reveals the gospel to us, purifies and sanctifies us, and empowers us to live obedient lives.

We also learn more about the nature of our salvation through Peter's letter. We have been elected according to the foreknowledge of God, having been redeemed not through religious tradition, but by the blood of Christ. Our souls have been purified because of the Lord's graciousness and Christ's suffering for our sins. Our salvation is the result of Christ's sacrifice, for he was an unblemished lamb whose blood paid the price for our sin. And we discover that this sacrifice resulted in us being given a "new birth into a living hope through the resurrection of Jesus Christ from the dead" (1:3). The result is that we are being built into a new spiritual home. Of this new birth the Venerable Bede wrote, "It is well said of this regeneration that it does not come from corruptible seed but operates by the word of the living and eternal God."

Peter exhorts the recipients of his letter to "become holy yourselves in all of your conduct" (1:15), no longer conforming to the evil desires of their previous lives. Didymus the Blind explained, "Since God, who called us to salvation by the gospel, is holy, those who obey his calling must also become holy in all their thoughts and behavior, especially since he who calls us to this also provides the necessary sanctification himself." Through Peter's letter God calls us to rid our lives of sin and live as his chosen people, a royal priesthood, and his special possession.

As foreigners and exiles on this earth, we will suffer grief for we are in conflict with our world as a holy nation set apart for God. Peter's epistle reminds us to take heart. Such persecution proves our faith, and it is a privilege for us to experience such suffering for in doing so we bear the name of Christ.

"I have written to you briefly," Peter explained, "in order to encourage you and testify that this is the true grace of God. Stand fast in it" (5:12). May we heed his exhortations, being sober and vigilant and standing firm in God's grace.

SALUTATION

1 From Peter, an apostle of Jesus Christ, to those temporarily
residing abroad (in Pontus, Galatia, Cappadocia, the province
of Asia, and Bithynia) who are chosen 2according to the foreknowledge of God the Father by being set apart by the Spirit
for obedience and for sprinkling with Jesus Christ's blood. May
grace and peace be yours in full measure!

NEW BIRTH TO JOY AND HOLINESS

3Blessed be the God and Father of our Lord Jesus Christ! By his
great mercy he gave us new birth into a living hope through the
resurrection of Jesus Christ from the dead, 4that is, into an inheritance imperishable, undefiled, and unfading. It is reserved
in heaven for you, 5who by God's power are protected through
faith for a salvation ready to be revealed in the last time. 6This
brings you great joy, although you may have to suffer for a short
time in various trials. 7Such trials show the proven character of
your faith, which is much more valuable than gold—gold that
is tested by fire, even though it is passing away—and will bring
praise and glory and honor when Jesus Christ is revealed. 8You
have not seen him, but you love him. You do not see him now
but you believe in him, and so you rejoice with an indescribable
and glorious joy, 9because you are attaining the goal of your
faith—the salvation of your souls.

10Concerning this salvation, the prophets who predicted the
grace that would come to you searched and investigated carefully. 11They probed into what person or time the Spirit of Christ
within them was indicating when he testified beforehand about
the sufferings appointed for Christ and his subsequent glory.
12They were shown that they were serving not themselves but
you, in regard to the things now announced to you through
those who proclaimed the gospel to you by the Holy Spirit sent
from heaven—things angels long to catch a glimpse of.

13Therefore, get your minds ready for action by being fully
sober, and set your hope completely on the grace that will be
brought to you when Jesus Christ is revealed. 14Like obedient
children, do not comply with the evil urges you used to follow in
your ignorance, 15but, like the Holy One who called you, become
holy yourselves in all of your conduct, 16for it is written, ***"You
shall be holy, because I am holy."*** 17And if you address as Father
the one who impartially judges according to each one's work,
live out the time of your temporary residence here in reverence. 18You know that from your empty way of life inherited
from your ancestors you were ransomed—not by perishable
things like silver or gold, 19but by precious blood like that of an
unblemished and spotless lamb, namely Christ. 20He was foreknown before the foundation of the world but was manifested
in these last times for your sake. 21Through him you now trust
in God, who raised him from the dead and gave him glory, so
that your faith and hope are in God.

22You have purified your souls by obeying the truth in order
to show sincere mutual love. So love one another earnestly from
a pure heart. 23You have been born anew, not from perishable
but from imperishable seed, through the living and enduring
word of God. 24For

all flesh is like grass
and all its glory like the flower of the grass;
the grass withers and the flower falls off,
25 ***but the word of the Lord endures forever.***

1:13–21 **Serve the Lord in fear and truth, as those who have forsaken the vain, empty talk and error of the multitude and believed in him who raised up our Lord Jesus Christ from the dead. "Like obedient children, do not comply with the evil urges you used to follow in your ignorance." Jesus comes as the judge of the living and the dead. He who raised him up from the dead will raise up us also if we do his will, keeping ourselves from all unrighteousness, covetousness, love of money, evil speaking, false witness; not rendering evil for evil, but being mindful of what the Lord said in his teaching: Judge not, that you be not judged; forgive, and it shall be forgiven unto you; be merciful, that you may obtain mercy.**

POLYCARP **(69–155)**
EPISTLE TO THE PHILIPPIANS

And this is the word that was proclaimed to you.

2 So get rid of all evil and all deceit and hypocrisy and envy and all slander. [2]And yearn like newborn infants for pure, spiritual milk, so that by it you may grow up to salvation, [3]if ***you have experienced the Lord's kindness.***

A LIVING STONE, A CHOSEN PEOPLE

[4]So as you come to him, a living stone rejected by men but chosen and precious in God's sight, [5]you yourselves, as living stones, are built up as a spiritual house to be a holy priesthood and to offer spiritual sacrifices that are acceptable to God through Jesus Christ. [6]For it says in scripture, "***Look, I lay in Zion a stone, a chosen and precious cornerstone, and whoever believes in him will never be put to shame.***" [7]So you who believe see his value, but for those who do not believe, ***the stone that the builders rejected has become the cornerstone,*** [8]and ***a stumbling-stone and a rock to trip over.*** They stumble because they disobey the word, as they were destined to do. [9]But you are *a chosen race, a royal priesthood, a holy nation, a people of his own,* so that you may *proclaim the virtues* of the one who called you out of darkness into his marvelous light. [10]You once were ***not a people,*** but now you are God's people. You were ***shown no mercy,*** but now you have received mercy.

[11]Dear friends, I urge you as foreigners and exiles to keep away from fleshly desires that do battle against the soul, [12]and maintain good conduct among the non-Christians, so that though they now malign you as wrongdoers, they may see your good deeds and glorify God when he appears.

SUBMISSION TO AUTHORITIES

[13]Be subject to every human institution for the Lord's sake, whether to a king as supreme [14]or to governors as those he commissions to punish wrongdoers and praise those who do good. [15]For God wants you to silence the ignorance of foolish people by doing good. [16]Live as free people, not using your freedom as a pretext for evil, but as God's slaves. [17]Honor all people, love the family of believers, fear God, honor the king.

[18]Slaves, be subject to your masters with all reverence, not only to those who are good and gentle, but also to those who are perverse. [19]For this finds God's favor, if because of conscience toward God someone endures hardships in suffering unjustly. [20]For what credit is it if you sin and are mistreated and endure it? But if you do good and suffer and so endure, this finds favor with God. [21]For to this you were called, since Christ also suffered for you, leaving an example for you to follow in his steps. [22]He ***committed no*** sin ***nor was deceit found in his mouth.*** [23]When he was maligned, he did not answer back; when he suffered, he threatened no retaliation, but committed himself to God who judges justly. [24]He ***himself bore our sins*** in his body on the tree, that we may cease from sinning and live for righteousness. ***By*** his ***wounds you were healed.*** [25]For you were ***going astray like sheep*** but now you have turned back to the shepherd and guardian of your souls.

WIVES AND HUSBANDS

3 In the same way, wives, be subject to your own husbands. Then, even if some are disobedient to the word, they will be won over without a word by the way you live, [2]when they see your pure and reverent conduct. [3]Let your beauty not be

2:4–12 You, chosen generation, go after him and confound the things that are mighty; go after him, you beautiful feet, and shine in the firmament that the heavens may declare his glory. Shine over all the earth and let the day, lightened by the sun, utter unto day the word of wisdom; and let night, shining by the moon, announce unto night the word of knowledge. The moon and the stars shine for the night, but the night does not obscure them since they illumine it in its degree. Run to and fro everywhere, you holy fires, you beautiful fires for you are the light of the world, nor are you put under a bushel. He to whom you cleave is exalted and has exalted you. Run to and fro and be known unto all nations.

AUGUSTINE (354–430)
CONFESSIONS

DIETRICH BONHOEFFER:

COSTLY DISCIPLESHIP TOGETHER

1906–1945

Dietrich Bonhoeffer was born into a distinguished German family near Berlin. His father was a psychology professor at the university and his mother was a daughter of a countess. Though his immediate family was neither religious nor Christian, at fourteen he told his parents he wanted to study theology and be a pastor when he grew up. Nineteen years later he received his doctorate in theology from the University of Berlin, setting him on a course that would eventually lead to his fateful conflict with the German Nazi state.

Although Adolf von Harnack and his theological liberalism were dominant during Bonhoeffer's academic studies, Bonhoeffer felt a much greater kinship with Karl Barth's critique of both the accommodation to modernism and the rise of fascism. Frustrated and horrified by the German church's willful disregard of the Nazi rise to power—and even complicity in that rise—Bonhoeffer became involved in the Confessing Church, rising to head of their seminary in Finkenwalde. The Confessing Church movement was a revolt against efforts to unify the German churches under the pro-Nazi nationalist church. During this time he wrote two of his most important works: *Life Together* and *The Cost of Discipleship*. His monastic and communal life serving and teaching at the seminary impacted the underlying premise of both books, centering on the nature of Christian commitment to both Christ and his church community.

In *Life Together*, Bonhoeffer opened with Psalm 133:1, extolling the virtues of community and brotherhood: "Look! How good and how pleasant it is when brothers truly live in unity." His book reveals a number of principles of not mere togetherness but "our life together under the Word." Like Barth, Bonhoeffer believed the centrality of Christ was key, for "Christianity means community through Jesus Christ and in Jesus Christ." He went on to suggest that "no Christian community is more or less than this. Whether it be a brief, single encounter or the daily fellowship of years, Christian community is only this. We belong to one another only through and in Jesus Christ."

Considered a Christian classic, *The Cost of Discipleship* is a discourse on the Sermon on the Mount. Originally titled *Nachfolge*—literally, "following"—this book is Bonhoeffer's working out what it means to follow Christ wholeheartedly. In it he makes a sharp distinction between "cheap" and "costly" grace:

> *Cheap grace is the deadly enemy of our church. We are fighting today for costly grace. Cheap grace is the preaching of forgiveness without requiring repentance . . . without discipleship, grace without the cross, grace without Jesus Christ, living and incarnate. Costly grace is the treasure hidden in the field; for the sake of it a man will gladly go and sell all that he has.*

After the Second World War broke out, Bonhoeffer became a lecturer at Union Theological Seminary in America to avoid being drafted into the war, though he realized he had made a mistake and went back to Germany to join the Resistance. He chose the costly route of devotion to Christ and his way, which led to imprisonment in 1943. Two years later he was executed by hanging. His final words reflect his ultimate hope in Christ: "This is the end—for me the beginning of life." Bonhoeffer bore the cost of discipleship, following the way of Christ in a wayward world, until the very end.

IMPORTANT WORKS

THE COST OF DISCIPLESHIP

LIFE TOGETHER

LETTERS AND PAPERS FROM PRISON

external—the braiding of hair and wearing of gold jewelry or fine
clothes—[4]but the inner person of the heart, the lasting beauty of
a gentle and tranquil spirit, which is precious in God's sight. [5]For
in the same way the holy women who hoped in God long ago
adorned themselves by being subject to their husbands, [6]like
Sarah who obeyed Abraham, calling him lord. You become her
children when you do what is good and have no fear in doing so.
[7]Husbands, in the same way, treat your wives with consideration
as the weaker partners and show them honor as fellow heirs of
the grace of life. In this way nothing will hinder your prayers.

SUFFERING FOR DOING GOOD

[8]Finally, all of you be harmonious, sympathetic, affectionate,
compassionate, and humble. [9]Do not return evil for evil or insult for insult, but instead bless others because you were called
to inherit a blessing. [10]For

the one who wants to love life and see good days must
keep his tongue from evil and his lips from uttering
deceit.
[11] ***And he must turn away from evil and do good;***
he must seek peace and pursue it.
[12] ***For the eyes of the Lord are upon the righteous and his***
ears are open to their prayer.
But the Lord's face is against those who do evil.

[13]For who is going to harm you if you are devoted to what
is good? [14]But in fact, if you happen to suffer for doing what
is right, you are blessed. ***But do not be terrified of them or be***
shaken. [15]But set Christ apart as Lord in your hearts and always
be ready to give an answer to anyone who asks about the hope
you possess. [16]Yet do it with courtesy and respect, keeping a
good conscience, so that those who slander your good conduct
in Christ may be put to shame when they accuse you. [17]For it is
better to suffer for doing good, if God wills it, than for doing evil.

[18] Because Christ also suffered once for sins,
the just for the unjust,
to bring you to God,
by being put to death in the flesh
but by being made alive in the spirit.
[19] In it he went and preached to the spirits in prison,

3:13–22 Let us give up vain and fruitless cares and approach to the glorious and venerable rule of our holy calling. Let us attend to what is good, pleasing, and acceptable in the sight of him who formed us. Let us look steadfastly to the blood of Christ and see how precious that blood is to God, which, having been shed for our salvation, has set the grace of repentance before the whole world. Let us turn to every age that has passed and learn that from generation to generation the Lord has granted a place of repentance to all as would be converted to him.

CLEMENT OF ROME (D. 99)
FIRST CLEMENT

[20]after they were disobedient long ago when God patiently waited in the days of Noah as an ark was being constructed. In the ark a few, that is eight souls, were delivered through water. [21]And this prefigured baptism, which now saves you—not the washing off of physical dirt but the pledge of a good conscience to God—through the resurrection of Jesus Christ, [22]who went into heaven and is at the right hand of God with angels and authorities and powers subject to him.

4 So, since Christ suffered in the flesh, you also arm yourselves with the same attitude because the one who has suffered in the flesh has finished with sin, [2]in that he spends the rest of his time on earth concerned about the will of God and not human desires. [3]For the time that has passed was sufficient for you to do what the non-Christians desire. You lived then in debauchery, evil desires, drunkenness, carousing, drinking bouts, and wanton idolatries. [4]So they are astonished when you do not rush with them into the same flood of wickedness, and they vilify you. [5]They will face a reckoning before Jesus Christ who stands ready to judge the living and the dead. [6]Now it was for this very purpose that the gospel was preached to those who are now dead, so that though they were judged in the flesh by human standards they may live spiritually by God's standards.

4:1–6 They are called true Christians who incorporate the life and name of Christ into their own life. For Christ's Passion must be dealt with not in words and a show, but in our lives and in truth. But this kind of meditation is now out of use and very rare, although the epistles of Saint Paul and Saint Peter are full of it. We have changed the essence into a mere show and painted the meditation of Christ's sufferings only in letters and on walls.

MARTIN LUTHER (1483–1546)
CHRIST'S HOLY SUFFERINGS

SERVICE, SUFFERING, AND JUDGMENT

[7]For the culmination of all things is near. So be self-controlled and sober-minded for the sake of prayer. [8]Above all keep your love for one another fervent because ***love covers a multitude of sins.*** [9]Show hospitality to one another without complaining. [10]Just as each one has received a gift, use it to serve one another as good stewards of the varied grace of God. [11]Whoever speaks, let it be with God's words. Whoever serves, do so with the strength that God supplies, so that in everything God will be glorified through Jesus Christ. To him belong the glory and the power forever and ever. Amen.

[12]Dear friends, do not be astonished that a trial by fire is occurring among you, as though something strange were happening to you. [13]But rejoice in the degree that you have shared in the sufferings of Christ, so that when his glory is revealed you may also rejoice and be glad. [14]If you are insulted for the name of Christ, you are blessed, because the Spirit of glory, who is ***the Spirit of God, rests*** on you. [15]But let none of you suffer as a murderer or thief or criminal or as a troublemaker. [16]But if you suffer as a Christian, do not be ashamed, but glorify God that you bear such a name. [17]For it is time for judgment to begin, starting with the house of God. And if it starts with us, what will be the fate of those who are disobedient to the gospel of God? [18]And ***if the righteous are barely saved, what will become of the ungodly and sinners?*** [19]So then let those who suffer according to the will of God entrust their souls to a faithful Creator as they do good.

LEADING AND LIVING IN GOD'S FLOCK

5 So as your fellow elder and a witness of Christ's sufferings and as one who shares in the glory that will be revealed, I urge the elders among you: [2]Give a shepherd's care to God's flock among you, exercising oversight not merely as a duty but willingly under God's direction, not for shameful profit but eagerly. [3]And do not lord it over those entrusted to you, but be examples to the flock. [4]Then when the Chief Shepherd appears, you will receive the crown of glory that never fades away.

[5]In the same way, you who are younger, be subject to the
elders. And all of you, clothe yourselves with humility toward
one another because God ***opposes the proud but gives grace to
the humble.*** [6]And God will exalt you in due time, if you humble
yourselves under his mighty hand [7]by casting all your cares on
him because he cares for you. [8]Be sober and alert. Your enemy
the devil, *like a roaring lion,* is on the prowl looking for someone to devour. [9]Resist him, strong in your faith, because you
know that your brothers and sisters throughout the world are
enduring the same kinds of suffering. [10]And, after you have suffered for a little while, the God of all grace who called you to his
eternal glory in Christ will himself restore, confirm, strengthen,
and establish you. [11]To him belongs the power forever. Amen.

FINAL GREETINGS

[12]Through Silvanus, whom I know to be a faithful brother, I
have written to you briefly, in order to encourage you and testify
that this is the true grace of God. Stand fast in it. [13]The church
in Babylon, chosen together with you, greets you, and so does
Mark, my son. [14]Greet one another with a loving kiss. Peace to
all of you who are in Christ.

5:5–11 We will come again to this Valley of Humiliation. It is the best and most fruitful piece of ground in all those parts. Behold how green this valley is, also how beautified with lilies. I have known many laboring men who have good estates in this Valley of Humiliation, for God resists the proud but gives grace to the humble. Indeed it is a very fruitful soil and does bring forth by handfuls. Some also have wished that the next way to their Father's house were here, that they might be troubled no more with either hills or mountains to go over; but the way is the way, and there is an end.

JOHN BUNYAN
(1628–1688)
THE PILGRIM'S PROGRESS

AUTHOR	AUDIENCE	DATE	PURPOSE	THEMES
Peter	Christians in western Asia Minor	Between AD 65 and 68	Peter wrote to encourage Christians in Asia Minor to live godly lives and warn them against false teaching as they prepare for the coming of the Lord.	The promises of God; confirmation of calling; Christian living; false teaching; and the day of the Lord

The second epistle of Peter opens with a great and glorious truth that anchors the rest of his letter: "[God's] divine power has bestowed on us everything necessary for life and godliness through the rich knowledge of the one who called us by his own glory and excellence. Through these things he has bestowed on us his precious and most magnificent promises, so that by means of what was promised you may become partakers of the divine nature" (1:3–4).

"God has blessed us abundantly," church father Andreas wrote. "We have received thousands of good things as a result of Christ's coming, and through them we can become partakers of the divine nature and be turned toward life and godliness. Therefore we must behave in such a way as to add virtue to faith, and in virtue walk along the way that leads to godliness until we come to the perfection of all good things, which is love."

Peter wrote this second epistle to believers in Asia Minor as one who had witnessed the glory, majesty, and significance of Christ firsthand. He felt compelled to encourage them to live holy, godly lives until the day of Christ's return. He also warned them against false teachers, for destructive heresies threatened their faith. Apparently, such people had encouraged the believers to use their freedom to commit depraved acts and were mocking the truth of Christ's second coming.

Peter's letter exhorts us to confirm our calling and election by living a life that adds to our faith goodness, self-control, godliness, and love. For Peter knowledge is key: knowing we are delivered and growing in the knowledge of Christ leads to an acknowledgment of Christ's lordship and a life of virtue; our faith then will have forward momentum. As Hilary of Arles commented, "Peter is telling us that we should not be content with our baptism but should go on and grow in our faith."

Peter's call to fruitful, holy living is oriented toward one end—*the* end—his ethic is eschatological. We should live with the end in mind, knowing that Christ could come back at any moment: "Since all these things are to melt away in this manner, what sort of people must you be, conducting your lives in holiness and godliness, while waiting for and hastening the coming of the day of God?" (3:11–12). Yes, we are looking forward

2 PETER

to the day when Christ restores the world, but we should live as if that day might be today, "[striving] to be found at peace, without spot or blemish" (3:14). Again, Hilary of Arles explained it well: "You are waiting for the end as the virgins waited for the bridegroom. When he returns, Christ wants to find you spotless in your faith and uncorrupted in the chastity of your body."

Peter follows in a long line of other New Testament writers in warning against false teachers. He was worried such teachers would slip in among the churches and secretly introduce heresies to destroy the believing communities. "Peter says this," Andreas explained, "so that people will not just listen to everyone who claims to be a prophet, without discerning whether he really is or not. He tells them to be careful not to listen to false prophets instead of the true ones."

Such people denied God's sovereignty, mocked Christ's second coming, blasphemed the angels, gave license to sin, and exploited believers with their greed. Although such people "in their destruction they will be destroyed" (2:12), Peter urged the recipients of his letter to guard themselves against the influence of these false teachers, "that you do not get led astray by the error of these unprincipled men and fall from your firm grasp on the truth" (3:17). The Didache, a guide for Christian living from the early church, offered this sound advice toward that end: "Not everyone who speaks in the spirit is a prophet, but only if he follows behaviorally in the path of the Lord. Accordingly, from their conduct the false prophet and the true prophet will be known."

The Venerable Bede offered a closing exhortation to Peter's second epistle, echoing his own closing:

> May glory always be given to God our Lord and Savior, both now when we are still in the flesh and far from him, wandering through the daily pressures of our adversaries, and especially at that future time when he who has been long desired shall come to all the nations and deign to illuminate us by his presence. Meanwhile, as we await that glorious day, let us go on singing: "One day in your temple courts is better than spending a thousand elsewhere" (Ps 84:10).

SALUTATION

1 From Simeon Peter, a slave and apostle of Jesus Christ, to those who through the righteousness of our God and Savior, Jesus Christ, have been granted a faith just as precious as ours. [2]May grace and peace be lavished on you as you grow in the rich knowledge of God and of Jesus our Lord!

BELIEVERS' SALVATION AND THE WORK OF GOD

[3]I can pray this because his divine power has bestowed on us everything necessary for life and godliness through the rich knowledge of the one who called us by his own glory and excellence. [4]Through these things he has bestowed on us his precious and most magnificent promises, so that by means of what was promised you may become partakers of the divine nature, after escaping the worldly corruption that is produced by evil desire. [5]For this very reason, make every effort to add to your faith excellence, to excellence, knowledge; [6]to knowledge, self-control; to self-control, perseverance; to perseverance, godliness; [7]to godliness, brotherly affection; to brotherly affection, unselfish love. [8]For if these things are really yours and are continually increasing, they will keep you from becoming ineffective and unproductive in your pursuit of knowing our Lord Jesus Christ more intimately. [9]But concerning the one who lacks such things—he is blind. That is to say, he is nearsighted, since he has forgotten about the cleansing of his past sins. [10]Therefore, brothers and sisters, make every effort to be sure of your calling and election. For by doing this you will never stumble into sin. [11]For thus an entrance into the eternal kingdom of our Lord and Savior, Jesus Christ, will be richly provided for you.

1:5–11 The apostle had exhorted to give diligence to add to our faith, excellence, and so on and tells us that if we do these things, we shall not be barren and unfruitful in the knowledge. Now he offers another argument, he tells us that to neglect those things is the way to doubtfulness about our condition; he who lacks those things has forgotten that he was purged from his old sins. Therefore the meaning of this verse is to give diligence in those things that you may make your calling and election sure, as is evident by the following clause, "for by doing this you will never stumble into sin."

JONATHAN EDWARDS
(1703–1758)
SELECTIONS FROM THE UNPUBLISHED WRITINGS

SALVATION BASED ON THE WORD OF GOD

[12]Therefore, I intend to remind you constantly of these things even though you know them and are well established in the truth that you now have. [13]Indeed, as long as I am in this tabernacle, I consider it right to stir you up by way of a reminder, [14]since I know that my tabernacle will soon be removed because our Lord Jesus Christ revealed this to me. [15]Indeed, I will also make every effort that, after my departure, you have a testimony of these things.

[16]For we did not follow cleverly concocted fables when we made known to you the power and return of our Lord Jesus Christ; no, we were eyewitnesses of his grandeur. [17]For he received honor and glory from God the Father, when that voice was conveyed to him by the Majestic Glory: "This is my dear Son, in whom I am delighted." [18]When this voice was conveyed from heaven, we ourselves heard it, for we were with him on the holy mountain. [19]Moreover, we possess the prophetic word as an altogether reliable thing. You do well if you pay attention to this as you would to a light shining in a murky place, until the day dawns and the morning star rises in your hearts. [20]Above all, you do well if you recognize this: No prophecy of scripture ever comes about by the prophet's own imagination, [21]for no prophecy was ever borne of human impulse; rather, men carried along by the Holy Spirit spoke from God.

THE FALSE TEACHERS' UNGODLY LIFESTYLE

2 But false prophets arose among the people, just as there will be false teachers among you. These false teachers will infiltrate your midst with destructive heresies, even to the

point of denying the Master who bought them. As a result,
they will bring swift destruction on themselves. [2]And many
will follow their debauched lifestyles. Because of these false
teachers, the way of truth will be slandered. [3]And in their greed
they will exploit you with deceptive words. Their condemnation
pronounced long ago is not sitting idly by; their destruction
is not asleep.
[4]For if God did not spare the angels who sinned, but
threw them into hell and locked them up in chains in utter
darkness, to be kept until the judgment, [5]and if he did not
spare the ancient world, but did protect Noah, a herald of
righteousness, along with seven others, when God brought
a flood on an ungodly world, [6]and if he turned to ashes the
cities of Sodom and Gomorrah when he condemned them to
destruction, having appointed them to serve as an example
to future generations of the ungodly, [7]and if he rescued Lot,
a righteous man in anguish over the debauched lifestyle of
lawless men, [8](for while he lived among them day after day,
that righteous man was tormented in his righteous soul by the
lawless deeds he saw and heard) [9]—if so, then the Lord knows
how to rescue the godly from their trials, and to reserve the
unrighteous for punishment at the day of judgment, [10]especially those who indulge their fleshly desires and who despise
authority.

Brazen and insolent, they are not afraid to insult the glorious ones, [11]yet even angels, who are much more powerful,
do not bring a slanderous judgment against them in the presence of the Lord. [12]But these men, like irrational animals—
creatures of instinct, born to be caught and destroyed—do
not understand whom they are insulting, and consequently in their destruction they will be destroyed, [13]suffering
harm as the wages for their harmful ways. By considering it
a pleasure to carouse in broad daylight, they are stains and
blemishes, indulging in their deceitful pleasures when they
feast together with you. [14]Their eyes, full of adultery, never
stop sinning; they entice unstable people. They have trained
their hearts for greed, these cursed children! [15]By forsaking
the right path they have gone astray, because they followed
the way of Balaam son of Bosor, who loved the wages of unrighteousness, [16]yet was rebuked for his own transgression
(a dumb donkey, speaking with a human voice, restrained the
prophet's madness).
[17]These men are waterless springs and mists driven by a
storm, for whom the utter depths of darkness have been reserved. [18]For by speaking high-sounding but empty words they
are able to entice, with fleshly desires and with debauchery,
people who have just escaped from those who reside in error.
[19]Although these false teachers promise such people freedom,
they themselves are enslaved to immorality. For whatever a
person succumbs to, to that he is enslaved. [20]For if after they
have escaped the filthy things of the world through the rich
knowledge of our Lord and Savior Jesus Christ, they again get
entangled in them and succumb to them, their last state has
become worse for them than their first. [21]For it would have been
better for them never to have known the way of righteousness
than, having known it, to turn back from the holy commandment that had been delivered to them. [22]They are illustrations
of this true proverb: ***"A dog returns to its own vomit,"*** and "A sow,
after washing herself, wallows in the mire."

2:1–22 The apostles have each indicated the appearing of these abominable and ruin-working men, and they have openly announced their lawless deeds. First of all Peter, the rock of the faith, whom Christ our God called blessed, the teacher of the church, the first disciple, he who has the keys of the kingdom, has instructed us to this effect: "These false teachers will infiltrate your midst with destructive heresies, even to the point of denying the Master who bought them." After him, John the theologian and the beloved of Christ, in harmony with him, cries, "By this the children of God and the children of the devil are revealed: Everyone who does not practice righteousness . . . is not of God" (1 John 3:10).

HIPPOLYTUS OF ROME
(C. 170–C. 235)
THE WORKS

3:1–9 While we have opportunity let us turn to God who called us. For if we conquer the soul by not fulfilling its wicked desires, we shall be partakers of the mercy of Jesus. Know that the day of judgment draws nigh like a burning oven and certain of the heavens and all the earth will melt like lead melting in fire, and then will appear the hidden and manifest deeds of humankind. Good, then, is alms as repentance from sin; better is fasting than prayer and alms than both: "Love covers a multitude of sins" (1 Pet 4:8). Blessed is everyone who shall be found complete in these, for alms lightens the burden of sin.

CLEMENT OF ROME **(D. 99)**
FIRST CLEMENT

THE FALSE TEACHERS' DENIAL OF THE LORD'S RETURN

3 Dear friends, this is already the second letter I have written
you, in which I am trying to stir up your pure mind by way
of reminder: 2I want you to recall both the predictions foretold
by the holy prophets and the commandment of the Lord and
Savior through your apostles. 3Above all, understand this: In
the last days blatant scoffers will come, being propelled by their
own evil urges 4and saying, "Where is his promised return? For
ever since our ancestors died, all things have continued as they
were from the beginning of creation." 5For they deliberately
suppress this fact, that by the word of God heavens existed
long ago and an earth was formed out of water and by means
of water. 6Through these things the world existing at that time
was destroyed when it was deluged with water. 7But by the
same word the present heavens and earth have been reserved
for fire, by being kept for the day of judgment and destruction
of the ungodly.
8Now, dear friends, do not let this one thing escape your
notice, that a single day is like a thousand years with the Lord
and a thousand years are like a single day. 9The Lord is not slow
concerning his promise, as some regard slowness, but is being
patient toward you because he does not wish for any to perish
but for all to come to repentance. 10But the day of the Lord will
come like a thief; when it comes, the heavens will disappear
with a horrific noise, and the celestial bodies will melt away in a
blaze, and the earth and every deed done on it will be laid bare.
11Since all these things are to melt away in this manner, what
sort of people must you be, conducting your lives in holiness
and godliness, 12while waiting for and hastening the coming of
the day of God? Because of this day, the heavens will be burned
up and dissolve, and the celestial bodies will melt away in a
blaze! 13But, according to his promise, we are waiting for new
heavens and a new earth, in which righteousness truly resides.

EXHORTATION TO THE FAITHFUL

14Therefore, dear friends, since you are waiting for these things,
strive to be found at peace, without spot or blemish, when you
come into his presence. 15And regard the patience of our Lord
as salvation, just as also our dear brother Paul wrote to you,
according to the wisdom given to him, 16speaking of these
things in all his letters. Some things in these letters are hard
to understand, things the ignorant and unstable twist to their
own destruction, as they also do to the rest of the scriptures.
17Therefore, dear friends, since you have been forewarned, be
on your guard that you do not get led astray by the error of
these unprincipled men and fall from your firm grasp on the
truth. 18But grow in the grace and knowledge of our Lord and
Savior Jesus Christ. To him be the honor both now and on that
eternal day.

AUTHOR	AUDIENCE	DATE	PURPOSE	THEMES
John	Christians in western Asia Minor	Between AD 85 and 95	John wrote to clarify aspects of the faith and encourage believers to hold fast to the teachings of Jesus Christ.	Perseverance in truth; discerning false teachings; the centrality of Jesus Christ; and living out the teachings of Christ

"This book is very sweet to every healthy Christian heart that savors the bread of God," wrote Augustine of the first epistle of John, "and it should constantly be in the mind of God's holy church." He went on to write: "I choose it more particularly because what it specially commends to us is love. The person who possesses the thing that he hears about in this epistle must rejoice when he hears it. His reading will be like oil to a flame . . . For others, the epistle should be like flame set to firewood; if it was not already burning, the touch of the Word may kindle it."

The apostle John wrote to testify to the truth of Jesus Christ, proclaiming the eternal life he offers so that the recipients might experience fellowship and the depth of God's love. He wrote his letter in opposition to false teachers who were bringing division to the community. John urged the believers in Asia Minor to continue walking in the light of truth. Some believe he wrote this letter as a companion to his gospel, for there are shades of similarity between the two documents.

In John's Gospel, the stated goal in writing was "that you may believe that Jesus is the Christ, the Son of God, and that by believing you may have life in his name" (John 20:31). The same goal permeates this letter. The truth about Jesus and the eternal life he offers are squarely in view; false teachers had come to distort both. He urged his readers, "Do not believe every spirit, but test the spirits to determine if they are from God, because many false prophets have gone out into the world" (4:1).

Part of the reason John wrote was because of what he called "antichrists" (2:18)—people who denied the person and work of Christ, people who had gone out into local churches but who weren't actually Christians, who brought only division and confusion. John opposed them by pointing to teachings of the apostles, urging discernment through the Spirit, and exhorting believers to cling to their personal experience of

1 JOHN

God's love. This was how believers in the early church confronted false teachers in their day. The Reformers did the same in theirs. It is up to us to follow their lead in ours.

In John's epistle we gain tremendous insight into the character of God: He is light, which means there is no dark way about him. He faithfully forgives our sins, cleansing us from our unrighteousness. He is Father, Son, and Spirit; he is the very definition of love; he is ultimate truth. John unveils in this epistle a deeper, more profound picture of Christ: He is the eternal "word of life" (1:1) who was with the Father from the beginning; through his blood we are cleansed, for he is our propitiation; he is the promised Messiah, God in the flesh; he who has no sin takes away our sins. Jesus is the Son of God, in whom we believe and trust for eternal life.

The letter reaches its climax with the declaration, "God is love" (4:8). The same John who announced, "This is the way God loved the world" (John 3:16) is the one who wrote of God's burning love for us in this letter: "See what sort of love the Father has given to us: that we should be called God's children—and indeed we are!" (3:1; see 4:7). The Venerable Bede commented on the love of God in this way: "The grace of our Creator is so great that he has allowed us both to know him and to love him, and moreover, to love him as children love a wonderful father." In response, not only are we called to love God our Father, but we are also called to love others with the same furious love.

"Love is so much the gift of God that it is called God," wrote Augustine. This letter unveils the fullness of this love-gift: "By this the love of God is revealed in us: that God has sent his one and only Son into the world so that we may live through him" (4:9). And John proclaimed this eternal life to us in this letter that we might have fellowship with Christ, with God, and with the whole communion of saints.

THE PROLOGUE TO THE LETTER

1 This is what we proclaim to you: what was from the beginning,
what we have heard, what we have seen with our eyes, what
we have looked at and our hands have touched (concerning the
word of life—[2]and the life was revealed, and we have seen and
testify and announce to you the eternal life that was with the
Father and was revealed to us). [3]What we have seen and heard
we announce to you too, so that you may have fellowship with
us (and indeed our fellowship is with the Father and with his
Son Jesus Christ). [4]Thus we are writing these things so that our
joy may be complete.

GOD IS LIGHT, SO WE MUST WALK IN THE LIGHT

[5]Now this is the gospel message we have heard from him and
announce to you: God is light, and in him there is no darkness
at all. [6]If we say we have fellowship with him and yet keep on
walking in the darkness, we are lying and not practicing the
truth. [7]But if we walk in the light as he himself is in the light,
we have fellowship with one another and the blood of Jesus his
Son cleanses us from all sin. [8]If we say we do not bear the guilt
of sin, we are deceiving ourselves and the truth is not in us. [9]But
if we confess our sins, he is faithful and righteous, forgiving us
our sins and cleansing us from all unrighteousness. [10]If we say
we have not sinned, we make him a liar and his word is not in us.

2 [1](My little children, I am writing these things to you so that
you may not sin.) But if anyone does sin, we have an advocate
with the Father, Jesus Christ the Righteous One, [2]and he himself
is the atoning sacrifice for our sins, and not only for our sins
but also for the whole world.

1:5—2:2 In the context the apostle speaks of communion with God. Now communion with God we cannot have till we are reconciled to him by Christ, and none can be looked upon as reconciled to him by Christ but those who endeavor toward conformity to God in purity and holiness. "If we walk in the light as he himself is in the light, we have fellowship with one another and the blood of Jesus his Son cleanses us from all sin." Labor to make your claim more sure. Walk in the light. The ground of comfort is the blood of Christ; the matter of comfort is the covenant; but we must look to our claim and title, or else this grace is not brought home to us, nor are we sanctified and enabled to live to God.

THOMAS MANTON
(1620–1677)
THE COMPLETE WORKS

KEEPING GOD'S COMMANDMENTS

[3]Now by this we know that we have come to know God: if we
keep his commandments. [4]The one who says "I have come to
know God" and yet does not keep his commandments is a liar,
and the truth is not in such a person. [5]But whoever obeys his
word, truly in this person the love of God has been perfected. By
this we know that we are in him. [6]The one who says he resides
in God ought himself to walk just as Jesus walked.

[7]Dear friends, I am not writing a new commandment to you,
but an old commandment which you have had from the beginning. The old commandment is the word that you have already
heard. [8]On the other hand, I am writing a new commandment
to you, which is true in him and in you, because the darkness
is passing away and the true light is already shining. [9]The one
who says he is in the light but still hates his fellow Christian is
still in the darkness. [10]The one who loves his fellow Christian
resides in the light, and there is no cause for stumbling in him.
[11]But the one who hates his fellow Christian is in the darkness,
walks in the darkness, and does not know where he is going
because the darkness has blinded his eyes.

WORDS OF REASSURANCE

[12]I am writing to you, little children, that your sins have been
forgiven because of his name. [13]I am writing to you, fathers,
that you have known him who has been from the beginning. I
am writing to you, young people, that you have conquered the
evil one. [14]I have written to you, children, that you have known
the Father. I have written to you, fathers, that you have known
him who has been from the beginning. I have written to you,

young people, that you are strong, and the word of God resides
in you, and you have conquered the evil one.
15 Do not love the world or the things in the world. If anyone
loves the world, the love of the Father is not in him, 16 because
all that is in the world (the desire of the flesh and the desire of
the eyes and the arrogance produced by material possessions)
is not from the Father, but is from the world. 17 And the world
is passing away with all its desires, but the person who does
the will of God remains forever.

WARNING ABOUT FALSE TEACHERS

18 Children, it is the last hour, and just as you heard that the
antichrist is coming, so now many antichrists have appeared.
We know from this that it is the last hour. 19 They went out
from us, but they did not really belong to us because if they
had belonged to us, they would have remained with us. But
they went out from us to demonstrate that all of them do not
belong to us.
20 Nevertheless you have an anointing from the Holy One,
and you all know. 21 I have not written to you that you do not
know the truth, but that you do know it, and that no lie is of the
truth. 22 Who is the liar but the person who denies that Jesus is
the Christ? This one is the antichrist: the person who denies
the Father and the Son. 23 Everyone who denies the Son does
not have the Father either. The person who confesses the Son
has the Father also.
24 As for you, what you have heard from the beginning must
remain in you. If what you heard from the beginning remains
in you, you also will remain in the Son and in the Father. 25 Now
this is the promise that he himself made to us: eternal life.
26 These things I have written to you about those who are trying
to deceive you.
27 Now as for you, the anointing that you received from him
resides in you, and you have no need for anyone to teach you.
But as his anointing teaches you about all things, it is true and
is not a lie. Just as it has taught you, you reside in him.

CHILDREN OF GOD

28 And now, little children, remain in him, so that when he appears we may have confidence and not shrink away from him in
shame when he comes back. 29 If you know that he is righteous,
you also know that everyone who practices righteousness has
been fathered by him.
3 (See what sort of love the Father has given to us: that we
should be called God's children—and indeed we are! For this
reason the world does not know us: Because it did not know
him. 2 Dear friends, we are God's children now, and what we
will be has not yet been revealed. We know that whenever it is
revealed we will be like him because we will see him just as he
is. 3 And everyone who has this hope focused on him purifies
himself, just as Jesus is pure).
4 Everyone who practices sin also practices lawlessness; indeed, sin is lawlessness. 5 And you know that Jesus was revealed
to take away sins, and in him there is no sin. 6 Everyone who
resides in him does not sin; everyone who sins has neither
seen him nor known him. 7 Little children, let no one deceive
you: The one who practices righteousness is righteous, just as
Jesus is righteous. 8 The one who practices sin is of the devil
because the devil has been sinning from the beginning. For this

purpose the Son of God was revealed: to destroy the works of the devil. [9]Everyone who has been fathered by God does not practice sin because God's seed resides in him, and thus he is not able to sin because he has been fathered by God. [10]By this the children of God and the children of the devil are revealed: Everyone who does not practice righteousness—the one who does not love his fellow Christian—is not of God.

3:10–23 John now shows what true love is, for it would not have been enough to commend it unless its power is understood. As an instance of perfect love, he sets before us the example of Christ; for he, by not sparing his own life, testified how much he loved us. This then is the mark to which he bids the reader to advance. The sum of what is said is that our love is approved when we transfer the love of ourselves to our brothers and sisters so that everyone, in a manner forgetting self, should seek the good of others.

JOHN CALVIN **(1509–1564)**
COMPLETE COMMENTARY ON THE BIBLE

GOD IS LOVE, SO WE MUST LOVE ONE ANOTHER

[11]For this is the gospel message that you have heard from the beginning: that we should love one another, [12]not like Cain who was of the evil one and brutally murdered his brother. And why did he murder him? Because his deeds were evil, but his brother's were righteous.

[13]Therefore do not be surprised, brothers and sisters, if the world hates you. [14]We know that we have crossed over from death to life because we love our fellow Christians. The one who does not love remains in death. [15]Everyone who hates his fellow Christian is a murderer, and you know that no murderer has eternal life residing in him. [16]We have come to know love by this: that Jesus laid down his life for us; thus we ought to lay down our lives for our fellow Christians. [17]But whoever has the world's possessions and sees his fellow Christian in need and shuts off his compassion against him, how can the love of God reside in such a person?

[18]Little children, let us not love with word or with tongue but in deed and truth. [19]And by this we will know that we are of the truth and will convince our conscience in his presence, [20]that if our conscience condemns us, that God is greater than our conscience and knows all things. [21]Dear friends, if our conscience does not condemn us, we have confidence in the presence of God, [22]and whatever we ask we receive from him, because we keep his commandments and do the things that are pleasing to him. [23]Now this is his commandment: that we believe in the name of his Son Jesus Christ and love one another, just as he gave us the commandment. [24]And the person who keeps his commandments resides in God, and God in him. Now by this we know that God resides in us: by the Spirit he has given us.

TESTING THE SPIRITS

4 Dear friends, do not believe every spirit, but test the spirits to determine if they are from God, because many false prophets have gone out into the world. [2]By this you know the Spirit of God: Every spirit that confesses Jesus as the Christ who has come in the flesh is from God, [3]but every spirit that refuses to confess Jesus, that spirit is not from God, and this is the spirit of the antichrist, which you have heard is coming, and now is already in the world.

[4]You are from God, little children, and have conquered them because the one who is in you is greater than the one who is in the world. [5]They are from the world; therefore they speak from the world's perspective and the world listens to them. [6]We are from God; the person who knows God listens to us, but whoever is not from God does not listen to us. By this we know the Spirit of truth and the spirit of deceit.

GOD IS LOVE

[7]Dear friends, let us love one another, because love is from God, and everyone who loves has been fathered by God and knows God. [8]The person who does not love does not know God

because God is love. [9]By this the love of God is revealed in us:
that God has sent his one and only Son into the world so that we
may live through him. [10]In this is love: not that we have loved
God, but that he loved us and sent his Son to be the atoning
sacrifice for our sins.
[11]Dear friends, if God so loved us, then we also ought to love
one another. [12]No one has seen God at any time. If we love one
another, God resides in us, and his love is perfected in us. [13]By
this we know that we reside in God and he in us: in that he has
given us of his Spirit. [14]And we have seen and testify that the
Father has sent the Son to be the Savior of the world.
[15]If anyone confesses that Jesus is the Son of God, God resides in him and he in God. [16]And we have come to know and
to believe the love that God has in us. God is love, and the one
who resides in love resides in God, and God resides in him. [17]By
this love is perfected with us, so that we may have confidence
in the day of judgment, because just as Jesus is, so also are we
in this world. [18]There is no fear in love, but perfect love drives
out fear because fear has to do with punishment. The one who
fears punishment has not been perfected in love. [19]We love
because he loved us first.
[20]If anyone says "I love God" and yet hates his fellow Christian, he is a liar because the one who does not love his fellow
Christian whom he has seen cannot love God whom he has not
seen. [21]And the commandment we have from him is this: that
the one who loves God should love his fellow Christian too.
5 [1]Everyone who believes that Jesus is the Christ has been
fathered by God, and everyone who loves the father loves
the child fathered by him. [2]By this we know that we love the
children of God: whenever we love God and obey his commandments. [3]For this is the love of God: that we keep his commandments. And his commandments do not weigh us down, [4]because
everyone who has been fathered by God conquers the world.

TESTIMONY ABOUT THE SON

This is the conquering power that has conquered the world:
our faith. [5]Now who is the person who has conquered the world
except the one who believes that Jesus is the Son of God? [6]Jesus
Christ is the one who came by water and blood—not by the
water only, but by the water and the blood. And the Spirit is
the one who testifies, because the Spirit is the truth. [7]For there
are three that testify, [8]the Spirit and the water and the blood,
and these three are in agreement.
[9]If we accept the testimony of men, the testimony of God is
greater because this is the testimony of God that he has testified
concerning his Son. [10](The one who believes in the Son of God
has the testimony in himself; the one who does not believe
God has made him a liar because he has not believed in the
testimony that God has testified concerning his Son.) [11]And
this is the testimony: God has given us eternal life, and this
life is in his Son. [12]The one who has the Son has this eternal
life; the one who does not have the Son of God does not have
this eternal life.

ASSURANCE OF ETERNAL LIFE

[13]I have written these things to you who believe in the name of
the Son of God so that you may know that you have eternal life.
[14]And this is the confidence that we have before him: that
whenever we ask anything according to his will, he hears us.

4:7–16 "God is love, and the one who resides in love resides in God"—whether as the fountain of love in its ineffable essence or as the fountain from which he freely gives it to us by his Spirit. If then it can be shown that love can at any time become visible to our bodily eyes, then we grant that possibly God shall be so too; but if love never can become visible, much less can he who is himself its fountain or whatever other figurative name more excellent or more appropriate can be employed in speaking of one so great.

AUGUSTINE (354–430)
LETTERS

[15]And if we know that he hears us in regard to whatever we ask,
then we know that we have the requests that we have asked
from him. [16]If anyone sees his fellow Christian committing a
sin not resulting in death, he should ask, and God will grant
life to the person who commits a sin not resulting in death.
There is a sin resulting in death. I do not say that he should
ask about that. [17]All unrighteousness is sin, but there is sin
not resulting in death.

[18]We know that everyone fathered by God does not sin, but
God protects the one he has fathered, and the evil one cannot
touch him. [19]We know that we are from God, and the whole
world lies in the power of the evil one. [20]And we know that the
Son of God has come and has given us insight to know him who
is true, and we are in him who is true, in his Son Jesus Christ.
This one is the true God and eternal life. [21]Little children, guard
yourselves from idols.

5:18–21 The Son leads believers to the Father, and they are in the love and favor of both, in union with both by the indwelling and working of the Holy Spirit. Happy are those to whom it is given to know that the Son of God is come and to have a heart to trust in and rely on him that is true! May this be our privilege; we shall thus be kept from all idols and false doctrines, from the idolatrous love of worldly objects, and be kept by the power of God through faith unto eternal salvation. To this living and true God be glory and dominion forever and ever. Amen.

MATTHEW HENRY **(1662–1714)**
COMMENTARY ON THE WHOLE BIBLE

AUTHOR	AUDIENCE	DATE	PURPOSE	THEMES
John	The "elect lady and her children," probably a local church in western Asia Minor	Between AD 85 and 95	John wrote to urge believers to continue walking in the truth and practicing the love of Christ and to warn them against false teachers.	Persevering in the truth; brotherly love; and spiritual discernment

False teachings about Christ are as old as the Christian faith itself. That's why this second letter from the apostle John is as relevant in our day as it was in his.

Although the precise recipient of John's letter isn't known, it appears it was directed to a local church in Asia Minor that had been inundated with false teachings about Christ from "deceivers" (v. 7). Even so, this letter is considered one of the so-called Catholic, or General, Epistles—letters written to the universal church rather than an individual community. The early church fathers regarded these Epistles as vitally important because they could be used to defend the faith. Though a short letter, 2 John is an important document for this very reason.

John wrote to men and women already walking in the truth and love of Christ. Having done so he highlighted something important about truth: we can "know" it (v. 1); it "resides in us" and "will be with us forever" (v. 2).

John revealed something else about truth: It is intimately connected with love. According to his epistle, love is not merely an emotion or an affection. We love most when we are walking in the truth. In other words, we love when "we walk according to [God's] commandments" (v. 6). Of course, Jesus Christ himself summarized God's commandments in this way: "'Love the Lord your God with all your heart, with all your soul, and with all your mind' . . . 'Love your neighbor as yourself'" (Matt 22:37, 39). Love, then, has an upward *and* outward trajectory.

It is in this context of truth and love that John issued his warning against deceivers who teach false doctrine. The Venerable Bede explained that John's warnings

> may refer primarily to those who believed that Christ was incarnate but who understood this in the wrong way by denying some aspect of it. Perhaps they rejected the idea that his flesh was real or that his soul was as ours. Or perhaps they refused to accept that he was truly divine, or that his Father was really God or that the Holy Spirit was really Almighty God. John may even be referring to those Jews who, rejecting any link between Jesus and God, deny that Christ has come in the flesh but are waiting for the antichrist, to their own damnation.

These false teachers who had infected this local church were preaching a different gospel about Jesus Christ, claiming that he hadn't been truly human, a heresy akin to Docetism (the false notion that Jesus only appeared to have a physical body, that its form was only an illusion, as were his sufferings). John exhorted believers to guard against such teachings so that they might not lose their reward. He urged them not even to welcome such teachers into their community, for receiving them was tantamount to receiving their ideas and sharing in their evil deeds.

The communion of saints in the twenty-first century would do well to heed these words of John the apostle, lest we become deceived and perpetuate the false teachings of our own day, turning away from love and truth in the process.

VV. 1–13 Deceivers are to outward appearance sheep, for they appear to be like us by what they say in public, repeating the same words as we do, but inwardly they are wolves. Their doctrine is homicidal, conjuring up, as it does, a number of gods and simulating many fathers, but lowering and dividing the Son of God in many ways. These are they against whom the Lord has cautioned us beforehand, and his disciple John commands us to avoid them when he says: "Many deceivers have gone out into the world, people who do not confess Jesus as Christ coming in the flesh. This person is the deceiver and the antichrist! Watch out, so that you do not lose the things we have worked for." And John also said, "By this you know the Spirit of God: Every spirit that confesses Jesus as the Christ who has come in the flesh is from God" (1 John 4:2). We know Jesus Christ to be one and the same who, because of his taking upon him flesh, shall also come in the same flesh in which he suffered, revealing the glory of the Father.

IRENAEUS (C. 130–C. 202)
AGAINST HERESIES

INTRODUCTION AND THANKSGIVING

1 From the elder, to an elect lady and her children, whom I love
in truth (and not I alone, but also all those who know the truth),
2 because of the truth that resides in us and will be with us forever. 3 Grace, mercy, and peace will be with us from God the Father
and from Jesus Christ the Son of the Father, in truth and love.
4 I rejoiced greatly because I have found some of your children
living according to the truth, just as the Father commanded us.

WARNING AGAINST FALSE TEACHERS

5 But now I ask you, lady (not as if I were writing a new commandment to you, but the one we have had from the beginning), that
we love one another. 6 (Now this is love: that we walk according
to his commandments.) This is the commandment, just as you
have heard from the beginning; thus you should walk in it. 7 For
many deceivers have gone out into the world, people who do
not confess Jesus as Christ coming in the flesh. This person is
the deceiver and the antichrist! 8 Watch out, so that you do not
lose the things we have worked for, but receive a full reward.
9 Everyone who goes on ahead and does not remain in the
teaching of Christ does not have God. The one who remains
in this teaching has both the Father and the Son. 10 If anyone
comes to you and does not bring this teaching, do not receive
him into your house and do not give him any greeting 11 because
the person who gives him a greeting shares in his evil deeds.

CONCLUSION

12 Though I have many other things to write to you, I do not
want to do so with paper and ink, but I hope to come visit you
and speak face to face so that our joy may be complete.
13 The children of your elect sister greet you.

AUTHOR	AUDIENCE	DATE	PURPOSE	THEMES
John	Gaius, perhaps a leader in one of the churches in western Asia Minor	Between AD 85 and 95	John wrote to praise Gaius for his hospitality in supporting itinerant teachers, as well as to speak out against the pride and inhospitality of Diotrephes.	Living in the truth of Christ; hospitality; disunity within the church; and imitating what is good

Although the third letter of John is the shortest book in the New Testament, it carries a big message: "Do not imitate what is bad but what is good" (v. 11). The apostle drives home this central point by commending an example of goodness: the letter's recipient, Gaius.

John praised this local church leader for walking in the truth, made evident by his love for both fellow believers and those outside the faith—"strangers" (v. 5). The early church writer Oecumenius said it best: "The person who loves God with heartfelt charity loves in the truth, a point that John often makes in his other letters." The Venerable Bede commented that "Gaius's loyalty is the result of his faith." When we love truth and walk in it, we share that truth by living it out in love.

The apostle made it clear there is also a corollary, a reverse truth, as well: "The one who does good is of God; the one who does what is bad has not seen God" (v. 11). This harsh reality was evidenced in the life of another local Christian leader in Asia Minor, Diotrephes. Apparently, this man was prideful, eager to have the first place in everything. He also stirred up discourse and disunity through malicious gossip and by being inhospitable to Christian teachers. John calls this attitude, and the resulting actions, evil.

3 JOHN

Reflecting on these words and connecting them to John's other teachings about living out the truth of Christ in love, Didymus the Blind wrote, "Light has nothing in common with darkness, and there is no agreement between Christ and Belial [the devil]. The person who does good has Christ, the true light, and not darkness or Belial. But the person who does evil is from Belial and darkness and has not seen God or had any knowledge of him."

Knowing God and doing good are intimately connected. As children of God we are called to do good to all, especially to fellow believers. God defines what is good in his Word and through his commandments. And we ought to imitate those people who, like Demetrius (v. 12), have learned to walk in truth and love.

The great commentary writer Matthew Henry summarized John's letter in this way: "By associating with and copying the example of such Christians, we shall have peace within and live at peace with the brethren; our communications with the Lord's people on earth will be pleasing, and we shall be numbered with them in glory everlasting."

VV. 1–15 Truth must enter into the soul, penetrate and saturate it, or it is of no value. Doctrines held as a matter of creed are like bread in the hand that ministers no nourishment to the frame, but doctrine accepted by the heart is as food digested that, by assimilation, sustains and builds up the body. In us truth must be a living force, an active energy, an indwelling reality, a part of the woof and warp of our being. If it is in us, we cannot henceforth part with it. A man may lose his garments or his limbs, but his inward parts are vital and cannot be torn away without absolute loss of life. A Christian can die but he cannot deny the truth.

CHARLES SPURGEON
(1834–1892)
MORNING AND EVENING

INTRODUCTION AND THANKSGIVING

1 From the elder, to Gaius my dear brother, whom I love in truth.
2 Dear friend, I pray that all may go well with you and that you
may be in good health, just as it is well with your soul. 3 For I
rejoiced greatly when the brothers came and testified to your
truth, just as you are living according to the truth.

4 I have no greater joy than this: to hear that my children are
living according to the truth.

THE CHARGE TO GAIUS

5 Dear friend, you demonstrate faithfulness by whatever you do
for the brothers (even though they are strangers). 6 They have
testified to your love before the church. You will do well to
send them on their way in a manner worthy of God. 7 For they
have gone forth on behalf of "The Name," accepting nothing
from the pagans. 8 Therefore we ought to support such people
so that we become coworkers in cooperation with the truth.

DIOTREPHES THE TROUBLEMAKER

9 I wrote something to the church, but Diotrephes, who loves to
be first among them, does not acknowledge us. 10 Therefore, if I
come, I will call attention to the deeds he is doing—the bringing
of unjustified charges against us with evil words! And not being
content with that, he not only refuses to welcome the brothers
himself, but hinders the people who want to do so and throws
them out of the church! 11 Dear friend, do not imitate what is
bad, but what is good. The one who does good is of God; the one
who does what is bad has not seen God.

WORTHY DEMETRIUS

12 Demetrius has been testified to by all, even by the truth itself.
We also testify to him, and you know that our testimony is true.

CONCLUSION

13 I have many things to write to you, but I do not wish to write
to you with pen and ink. 14 But I hope to see you right away, and
we will speak face to face. 15 Peace be with you. The friends here
greet you. Greet the friends there by name.

AUTHOR	AUDIENCE	DATE	PURPOSE	THEMES
Jude, the half brother of Jesus	Christians who were being threatened by false teachers	Between AD 65 and 80	Jude wrote to warn Christians about false teachers, who had convinced some that their salvation gave them license to sin.	Contending for the faith; living the faith; the character of God; and coming salvation and judgment

While it may not be apparent, the Christian faith has always needed defending from those who try to undermine its tenets. From the beginning, false teachers have attempted to pervert the truth about Jesus or subvert it as a license to sin. Therefore the epistle of Jude is as relevant today as it was when Jude wrote it.

The reason Jude wrote was to exhort believers "to contend earnestly for the faith that was once for all entrusted to the saints" (v. 3). You see, some wolves in sheep's clothing, as Jesus called them, had snuck into the church to spread heresies, creating chaos and confusing believers about the truth of the Christian faith. Although we aren't certain to whom this letter was originally addressed, we know that its recipients had believed the gospel and were now being deceived by false teachers, who twisted the teachings they received from the apostles with ideas foreign to the faith. Jude instructed these churches to preserve, contend, and struggle for the faith.

In Jude "faith" is not simply belief in God but is rather *the* faith—the Christian faith, composed of the teachings passed down by the apostles, inspired by God's Spirit, and based on historical events. Jude used the word "contend" (v. 3), a word often associated with ancient athletic competitions, to describe the task he was setting before the recipients of his letter. In other words, we who know Christ need to exert ourselves as we would in a race or other sporting event, expending great energy in fighting for, preserving, and advancing the one true gospel. We must also defend core beliefs, handing them down carefully from one generation of Christians to the next in order to stem the threat of false teaching.

Yet Jude's concerns go beyond doctrine. How believers live out their faith is as important as what they believe; orthodoxy (right beliefs) and orthopraxy (right living) cannot be separated. The false teachers in Jude's day were threatening this necessary dynamic, having crept into the churches unnoticed. They were "ungodly men who have turned the grace of our God into a license for evil and who deny our only Master and

JUDE

Lord, Jesus Christ" (v. 4). Jude was concerned the false teachers who had twisted the message of the faith would destroy not only believers' faith but also their godliness.

Jude coupled his instructions to preserve sound teaching with instructions to preserve sound living, offering several exhortations. Pressing his point, he issued seven commands toward the close of his letter: build yourself up on the foundation of your holy faith; pray in the Holy Spirit; keep yourself in God's love; look for Christ's eternal mercy; have compassion, especially upon those who doubt; do all you can to help save the lost; and hate all forms of wickedness that defile. The way we contend for the faith is to live it.

Quoting from an ancient Jewish book, 1 Enoch, Jude reveals that God will "execute judgment on all" (v. 15), convicting the ungodly of their ungodliness. This makes the issue of contending for the sound teachings of the Christian faith all the more urgent given the reality of coming judgment.

This epistle also offers the church a rich portrait of God's character. God the Father is described as one who has "called, wrapped in the love of God . . . and kept" his people (v. 1). Through his providential care and loving sovereignty, the God of the universe has chosen us in Christ, enveloping us in his renewing love and guarding our lives for his purposes. He is also a revealing God, for he has delivered to us the truth of his Word. We find the Trinity at work in this letter too, for we are called to pray "in the Holy Spirit," remain "in the love of God [the Father]," and look for "the mercy of our Lord Jesus Christ that brings eternal life" (vv. 20–21). Then there is the majestic hymn of God's glorious character, which keeps us from stumbling, presents us without fault, and is all-wise, glorious, majestic, and powerful (see v. 25).

The Venerable Bede wrote, "All God's chosen people share one common salvation, one faith and one love of Christ," which is why the people of God must continue to contend earnestly for this deposit of truth, entrusted to the saints from generation to generation.

SALUTATION

1 From Jude, a slave of Jesus Christ and brother of James, to those who are called, wrapped in the love of God the Father and kept for Jesus Christ. 2 May mercy, peace, and love be lavished on you!

> VV. 3–18 The taproot of all human miseries lies in the solemn fact of human transgression. Be sure of this: your deepest needs will not be met until the fact of your individual sinfulness and the consequences of that fact are somehow or other dealt with, staunched, and swept away. There is one remedy for the sickness. There is one safety against the danger. There is only one because it is the remedy for all humanity. Jesus Christ deals, as no one else has ever pretended to deal, with this outstanding fact of my transgression and yours. By his death he has saved the world from the danger because he has set right the world's relations to God. Further, Jesus Christ imparts a life that cures the sickness of sin. Jesus Christ heals society by healing the individual.
>
> ALEXANDER MACLAREN
> (1826–1910)
> ***EXPOSITIONS OF THE HOLY SCRIPTURES***

CONDEMNATION OF THE FALSE TEACHERS

3 Dear friends, although I have been eager to write to you about our common salvation, I now feel compelled instead to write to encourage you to contend earnestly for the faith that was once for all entrusted to the saints. 4 For certain men have secretly slipped in among you—men who long ago were marked out for the condemnation I am about to describe—ungodly men who have turned the grace of our God into a license for evil and who deny our only Master and Lord, Jesus Christ.

5 Now I desire to remind you (even though you have been fully informed of these facts once for all) that Jesus, having saved the people out of the land of Egypt, later destroyed those who did not believe. 6 You also know that the angels who did not keep within their proper domain but abandoned their own place of residence, he has kept in eternal chains in utter darkness, locked up for the judgment of the great Day. 7 So also Sodom and Gomorrah and the neighboring towns, since they indulged in sexual immorality and pursued unnatural desire in a way similar to these angels, are now displayed as an example by suffering the punishment of eternal fire.

8 Yet these men, as a result of their dreams, defile the flesh, reject authority, and insult the glorious ones. 9 But even when Michael the archangel was arguing with the devil and debating with him concerning Moses' body, he did not dare to bring a slanderous judgment, but said, "May the Lord rebuke you!" 10 But these men do not understand the things they slander, and they are being destroyed by the very things that, like irrational animals, they instinctively comprehend. 11 Woe to them! For they have traveled down Cain's path, and because of greed have abandoned themselves to Balaam's error; hence, they will certainly perish in Korah's rebellion. 12 These men are dangerous reefs at your love feasts, feasting without reverence, feeding only themselves. They are waterless clouds, carried along by the winds; autumn trees without fruit—twice dead, uprooted; 13 wild sea waves, spewing out the foam of their shame; wayward stars for whom the utter depths of eternal darkness have been reserved.

14 Now Enoch, the seventh in descent beginning with Adam, even prophesied of them, saying, "Look! The Lord is coming with thousands and thousands of his holy ones, 15 to execute judgment on all, and to convict every person of all their thoroughly ungodly deeds that they have committed, and of all the harsh words that ungodly sinners have spoken against him." 16 These people are grumblers and fault-finders who go wherever their desires lead them, and they give bombastic speeches, enchanting folks for their own gain.

EXHORTATION TO THE FAITHFUL

17 But you, dear friends—recall the predictions foretold by the apostles of our Lord Jesus Christ. 18 For they said to you, "At the end of time there will come scoffers, propelled by their own ungodly desires." 19 These people are divisive, worldly, devoid of the Spirit. 20 But you, dear friends, by building yourselves up in your most holy faith, by praying in the Holy Spirit, 21 maintain

yourselves in the love of God while anticipating the mercy of
our Lord Jesus Christ that brings eternal life. 22And have mercy
on those who waver; 23save others by snatching them out of the
fire; have mercy on others, coupled with a fear of God, hating
even the clothes stained by the flesh.

FINAL BLESSING

24Now to the one who is able to keep you from falling, and
to cause you to stand, rejoicing, without blemish before his
glorious presence, 25to the only God our Savior through Jesus
Christ our Lord, be glory, majesty, power, and authority, before
all time, and now, and for all eternity. Amen.

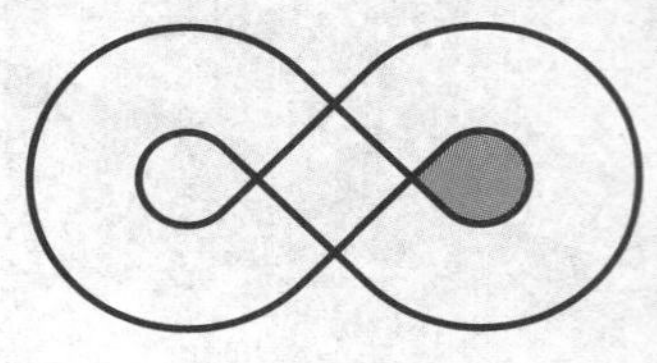

THE LAUSANNE COVENANT (1974)

WHILE THE LAUSANNE Covenant is not a typical creed or confession, it is regarded as one of the most significant statements in modern church history, written to unify the evangelical church around the world. Emerging from the First Lausanne Congress in 1974, with John Stott as its chief architect, it challenged Christians to work together to advance the gospel of Jesus Christ throughout the world. Here are several selections that demonstrate its intent:

4. THE NATURE OF EVANGELISM

TO EVANGELIZE is to spread the good news that Jesus Christ died for our sins and was raised from the dead according to the Scriptures, and that, as the reigning Lord, he now offers the forgiveness of sins and the liberating gifts of the Spirit to all who repent and believe. Our Christian presence in the world is indispensable to evangelism, and so is that kind of dialogue whose purpose is to listen sensitively in order to understand. But evangelism itself is the proclamation of the historical, biblical Christ as Savior and Lord, with a view to persuading people to come to him personally and so be reconciled to God. In issuing the gospel invitation we have no liberty to conceal the cost of discipleship. Jesus still calls all who would follow him to deny themselves, take up their cross, and identify themselves with his new community. The results of evangelism include obedience to Christ, incorporation into his church, and responsible service in the world.

9. THE URGENCY OF THE EVANGELISTIC TASK

MORE THAN two-thirds of all humanity have yet to be evangelized. We are ashamed that so many have been neglected; it is a standing rebuke to us and to the whole church. There is now, however, in many parts of the world, an unprecedented receptivity to the Lord Jesus Christ. We are convinced that this is the time for churches and para-church agencies to pray earnestly for the salvation of the unreached and to launch new efforts to achieve world evangelization. A reduction of foreign missionaries and money in an evangelized country may sometimes be necessary to facilitate the national church's growth in self-reliance and to release resources for unevangelized areas. Missionaries should flow ever more freely from and to all six continents in a spirit of humble service. The goal should be, by all available means and at the earliest possible time, that every person will have the opportunity to hear, to understand, and to receive the good news. We cannot hope to attain this goal without sacrifice. All of us are shocked by the poverty of millions and disturbed by the injustices which cause it. Those of us who live in affluent circumstances accept our duty to develop a simple lifestyle in order to contribute more generously to both relief and evangelism.

AUTHOR	AUDIENCE	DATE	PURPOSE	THEMES
John	Seven churches in western Asia Minor	About AD 95	John wrote in response to a direct revelation of Jesus Christ to encourage believers to persevere under persecution and to offer hope for our future by unveiling certain truths about the end of the age and the second coming of Christ.	The end of days; the person of Jesus Christ; judgment and punishment; and rescue and renewal

Revelation is a unique book within the canon of scripture, and it has a unique history, for as long as saints have been reading the book they have offered countless interpretations. Some have viewed it as a historical window into the late-first-century church, with little connection to succeeding centuries. Others have understood it to contain hidden messages about events that will take place at the end of history. How one interprets this book, perhaps more than any other Bible book, has direct bearing on how one comes to understand its purpose. Today there are generally four streams of interpretation.

- First, the *preterist* view sees most of the book's events as already having been completed. The symbols are about the past, not the future, and the book is meant to extol the faithfulness of God in light of religious persecution, offering the hope of God's ultimate victory over evil.
- Second, the *futurist* view, reflecting modern dispensationalists among others, sees most of the events in Revelation as future occurrences. The symbols point to people, places, and happenings that will be pivotal in the lead up to Christ's second coming. This view offers all believers, in every era, hope for God's final victory and evil's eventual judgment.
- Third, the *historical* view, favored by many of the Reformers, associates the events of church and world history with the events described in the book of Revelation. Those who subscribe to this view read meaning into the text through what has transpired in the past and present while also leaving room for future historical fulfillments. For example, many have attempted to uncover the identity of the beast by associating the diabolical figure with dictators ranging from Hitler to Hussein.
- Fourth, the *idealist* view, often reflected in early church interpretations, seeks the deeper meaning behind the symbols for the church's existence between the first and second comings of Christ. They understand Revelation to be filled with timeless spiritual truths for every church age, including good versus evil, the church's role in the world, and the victory of believers in Christ over Satan.

Some have taken a more eclectic approach to understanding the message behind this apocalyptic book, believing it reviews, previews, identifies, and idealizes history and Christ's command over it in order to encourage believers in all ages to persevere under persecution.

Still others have suggested this book is another gospel of sorts, for it reveals the good news about Jesus in his ascended glory. He is presented as "the faithful witness, the firstborn from among the dead, the ruler over the kings of the earth" (1:5). He is the glorified

REVELATION

Lamb, worthy of praise and power, strength and wisdom, honor and glory. The Lamb is identified as God himself, who is worshiped night and day. Jesus is explicitly identified as the "King of kings and Lord of lords" (19:16). He is judge over all humankind as well as every creature in heaven and on earth. And he is the one who will make all things new.

Reading John's Revelation, one cannot escape the book's emphasis on judgment. Remarkably, Jesus begins with his own church, instructing John to write seven letters to seven churches, most of which needed some form of correction. After Christ judges his own people, he invites John to witness "what must happen after these things" (4:1). From here Christ opens seven seals that in turn unleash judgments upon the earth and its inhabitants. The destruction continues with the seven trumpets and then seven bowls, culminating in the judgment and punishment of Satan and "the dead, the great and the small" (20:12). They are "judged by what was written in the books, according to their deeds" (20:12), and "anyone's name . . . not found written in the book of life, that person was thrown into the lake of fire" (20:15). This judgment is depicted as final and exhaustive, so that evil and wickedness are no more.

The book of Revelation doesn't end in judgment, however. Instead, the final pages of the Bible are spent describing the rescue and renewal of God in the form of a new creation. Yes, the new creation has come now to believers, as Paul wrote, but we await the ultimate re-creation. That will occur when justice is served and Christ himself makes everything new again. In this new creation, God "will wipe away every tear from their eyes, and death will not exist any more—or mourning, or crying, or pain, for the former things have ceased to exist" (21:4). All of this will be for the ones who overcome, for the faithful. Victorious living is faithful living, a major theme of this book.

At the start, Christ reveals to John that "the one who conquers" (2:17) will have the right to eat from the tree of life and will not experience the second death. The overcomers will receive new names, be given authority over the nations, never be blotted from the Book of Life, be pillars in God's temple, and sit with Christ on his throne. Such victory comes by doing Christ's will and by persevering in the midst of persecution and suffering.

The Venerable Bede offered a fitting summary of Revelation: "When the church had been established by the apostles, it was proper that it be revealed by what course the church was to be extended and was to be perfected at the end, so that the preachers of the faith might be strengthened against the adversaries of the world." The church in every era has needed this letter for encouragement while awaiting the end, the day when Christ returns to make all things new.

1:1–8 Those who have more diligently commented on the Revelation understand that what is contained in this revelation had begun immediately after the Passion of our Lord and Savior and therefore was to be fulfilled in the day of judgment. As a result, only a small period of time remained for the times of the antichrist. Therefore, whatever you shall hear in the recitation of the reading, whether it is of the Son of Man or of stars or of angels or of lampstands, or of the four living creatures or of the eagle flying in midheaven, understand that these and everything else are reality in Christ and in the church.

CAESARIUS OF ARLES
(C. 468–542)
EXPOSITION ON THE APOCALYPSE

THE PROLOGUE

1 The revelation of Jesus Christ, which God gave him to show his servants what must happen very soon. He made it clear by sending his angel to his servant John, [2]who then testified to everything that he saw concerning the word of God and the testimony about Jesus Christ. [3]Blessed is the one who reads the words of this prophecy aloud, and blessed are those who hear and obey the things written in it, because the time is near!

[4]From John, to the seven churches that are in the province of Asia: Grace and peace to you from "he who is," and who was, and who is still to come, and from the seven spirits who are before his throne, [5]and from Jesus Christ—the faithful witness, the firstborn from among the dead, the ruler over the kings of the earth. To the one who loves us and has set us free from our sins at the cost of his own blood [6]and has appointed us as a kingdom, as priests serving his God and Father—to him be the glory and the power for ever and ever! Amen.

[7] (Look! *He is returning with the clouds,*
and *every eye will see him,*
even those who pierced him,
and all the tribes on the earth will mourn because of him.
This will certainly come to pass! Amen.)

[8]"I am the Alpha and the Omega," says the Lord God—the one who is, and who was, and who is still to come—the All-Powerful! [9]I, John, your brother and the one who shares with you in the persecution, kingdom, and endurance that are in Jesus, was on the island called Patmos because of the word of God and the testimony about Jesus. [10]I was in the Spirit on the Lord's Day when I heard behind me a loud voice like a trumpet, [11]saying: "Write in a book what you see and send it to the seven churches—to Ephesus, Smyrna, Pergamum, Thyatira, Sardis, Philadelphia, and Laodicea."

[12]I turned to see whose voice was speaking to me, and when I did so, I saw seven golden lampstands, [13]and in the midst of the lampstands was one *like a son of man.* He was dressed in a robe extending down to his feet, and he wore a wide golden belt around his chest. [14]His head and hair were as white as wool, even as white as snow, and his eyes were like a fiery flame. [15]His feet were like polished bronze refined in a furnace, and his voice was like the roar of many waters. [16]He held seven stars in his right hand, and a sharp double-edged sword extended out of his mouth. His face shone like the sun shining at full strength. [17]When I saw him I fell down at his feet as though I were dead, but he placed his right hand on me and said: "Do not be afraid! I am the first and the last, [18]and the one who lives! I was dead, but look, now I am alive—forever and ever—and I hold the keys of death and of Hades! [19]Therefore write what you saw, what is, and what will be after these things. [20]The mystery of the seven stars that you saw in my right hand and the seven golden lampstands is this: The seven stars are the angels of the seven churches, and the seven lampstands are the seven churches.

TO THE CHURCH IN EPHESUS

2 "To the angel of the church in Ephesus, write the following: "This is the solemn pronouncement of the one who has a firm grasp on the seven stars in his right hand—the one who walks among the seven golden lampstands: [2]'I know your works

as well as your labor and steadfast endurance, and that you cannot tolerate evil. You have even put to the test those who refer
to themselves as apostles (but are not), and have discovered that
they are false. [3]I am also aware that you have persisted steadfastly, endured much for the sake of my name, and have not grown
weary. [4]But I have this against you: You have departed from
your first love! [5]Therefore, remember from what high state
you have fallen and repent! Do the deeds you did at the first;
if not, I will come to you and remove your lampstand from its
place—that is, if you do not repent. [6]But you do have this going
for you: You hate what the Nicolaitans practice—practices I also
hate. [7]The one who has an ear had better hear what the Spirit
says to the churches. To the one who conquers, I will permit
him to eat from the tree of life that is in the paradise of God.'

TO THE CHURCH IN SMYRNA

[8]"To the angel of the church in Smyrna write the following:
"This is the solemn pronouncement of the one who is the
first and the last, the one who was dead, but came to life: [9]'I
know the distress you are suffering and your poverty (but you
are rich). I also know the slander against you by those who
call themselves Jews and really are not, but are a synagogue of
Satan. [10]Do not be afraid of the things you are about to suffer.
The devil is about to have some of you thrown into prison so
you may be tested, and you will experience suffering for ten
days. Remain faithful even to the point of death, and I will give
you the crown that is life itself. [11]The one who has an ear had
better hear what the Spirit says to the churches. The one who
conquers will in no way be harmed by the second death.'

TO THE CHURCH IN PERGAMUM

[12]"To the angel of the church in Pergamum write the following:
"This is the solemn pronouncement of the one who has the
sharp double-edged sword: [13]'I know where you live—where
Satan's throne is. Yet you continue to cling to my name, and you
have not denied your faith in me, even in the days of Antipas, my
faithful witness, who was killed in your city where Satan lives.
[14]But I have a few things against you: You have some people there
who follow the teaching of Balaam, who instructed Balak to put
a stumbling block before the people of Israel so they would eat
food sacrificed to idols and commit sexual immorality. [15]In the
same way, there are also some among you who follow the teaching of the Nicolaitans. [16]Therefore, repent! If not, I will come
against you quickly and make war against those people with the
sword of my mouth. [17]The one who has an ear had better hear
what the Spirit says to the churches. To the one who conquers,
I will give him some of the hidden manna, and I will give him a
white stone, and on that stone will be written a new name that
no one can understand except the one who receives it.'

TO THE CHURCH IN THYATIRA

[18]"To the angel of the church in Thyatira write the following:
"This is the solemn pronouncement of the Son of God, the
one who has eyes like a fiery flame and whose feet are like polished bronze: [19]'I know your deeds: your love, faith, service, and
steadfast endurance. In fact, your more recent deeds are greater
than your earlier ones. [20]But I have this against you: You tolerate
that woman Jezebel, who calls herself a prophetess, and by her
teaching deceives my servants to commit sexual immorality and

2:18–29 Although on account of your faithfulness and your service for those in need I acknowledge your piety and your endurance, nonetheless I rightly blame you because you allow the heresy of the Nicolaitans to exist openly. This heresy is figuratively called "Jezebel" because of its impiety and licentiousness. Because of this heresy my servants, through their simplicity of mind, are presented with a stone of stumbling and are drawn toward idolatrous practices from which they had previously fled. You must curb this heresy because it deceitfully calls itself a prophetess, being moved by an evil spirit.

ANDREW OF CAESAREA
(563–614)
COMMENTARY ON THE APOCALYPSE

C. S. LEWIS:

AN ATHEIST TURNED MERE CHRISTIAN

1898–1963

The Oxford scholar Clive Staples Lewis described his conversion to the Christian faith as that of "a prodigal who is brought in kicking, struggling, resentful, and darting his eyes in every direction for a chance to escape." His was a 15-year journey from atheism to Christianity, making him a significant modern apologist for the Christian faith.

Born in 1898 in Belfast, Ireland, Lewis was the son of a lawyer. His mother died early in his childhood. Although he grew up in the Church of Ireland, he was never religious, and in fact he expressed no belief in God at all as a teenager: "I believe in no religion," he told a friend. "There is absolutely no proof of any of them, and from a philosophical standpoint Christianity is not even the best." When he was a soldier in the First World War, he boasted he "never sank so low as to pray" after experiencing the horrors of trench warfare. Yet 15 years later he would write to a childhood friend something very different: "Christianity is God expressing himself through what we call 'real things' . . . namely the actual incarnation, crucifixion, and resurrection."

His journey to the Christian faith is one of the more well-known modern conversion stories. As a teenager he was interested in and fascinated by the occult and paranormal. Later in life he would describe that fascination as "spiritual lust," but it did reflect an atheism that had been established at an early age. Over time his Oxford colleague J. R. R. Tolkien and the works of G. K. Chesterton moved him to confess belief in God. "In the Trinity Term of 1929," he relates in *Surprised by Joy*, "I gave in, and admitted that God was God, and knelt and prayed: perhaps, that night, the most dejected and reluctant convert in all England."

His conversion compelled him to write several books designed as apologies for the Christian faith. One was the classic children's series The Chronicles of Narnia, allegorically depicting such classic Christian themes as creation and the fall, redemption, and ultimate cosmic restoration. His most well-known and beloved book may be *Mere Christianity*, in which he confessed: "All I am doing is to ask people to face the facts—to understand the questions which Christianity claims to answer." The book deals with the "mere-ness" of Christianity, the fundamental beliefs that make the case for the Christian faith.

One of the more enduring arguments of the book concerns Jesus Christ, in which Lewis tried "to prevent anyone saying the really foolish thing that people often say about Him: 'I'm ready to accept Jesus as a great moral teacher, but I don't accept His claim to be God.' That is the one thing we must not say." The argument became the classic liar, lunatic, Lord argument:

> *Either this man [Jesus Christ] was, and is, the Son of God: or else a madman or something worse. You can shut Him up for a fool, you can spit at Him and kill Him as a demon; or you can fall at His feet and call Him Lord and God. But let us not come with any patronizing nonsense about His being a great human teacher. He has not left that open to us. He did not intend to.*

It's no surprise that *Christianity Today* judged the book to be one of the top three most influential Christian books of all time.

Lewis's legacy has been sizable, influencing the conversions of such Christian notables as Charles Colson and Francis Collins. Although self-described as "a most reluctant convert," Lewis was one of the most important writers and Christian thinkers of his generation.

IMPORTANT WORKS

MERE CHRISTIANITY
SURPRISED BY JOY
MIRACLES
THE CHRONICLES OF NARNIA

to eat food sacrificed to idols. 21 I have given her time to repent, but
she is not willing to repent of her sexual immorality. 22 Look! I am
throwing her onto a bed of violent illness, and those who commit
adultery with her into terrible suffering, unless they repent of
her deeds. 23 Furthermore, I will strike her followers with a deadly
disease, and then all the churches will know that I am the one
who searches minds and hearts. I will repay each one of you what
your deeds deserve. 24 But to the rest of you in Thyatira, all who
do not hold to this teaching (who have not learned the so-called
"deep secrets of Satan"), to you I say: I do not put any additional
burden on you. 25 However, hold on to what you have until I come.
26 And to the one who conquers and who continues in my deeds
until the end, I will give him authority over the nations—

27 ***he will rule them with an iron rod,***
and like clay jars he will break them to pieces,

28 just as I have received the right to rule from my Father—and
I will give him the morning star. 29 The one who has an ear had
better hear what the Spirit says to the churches.'

TO THE CHURCH IN SARDIS

3 "To the angel of the church in Sardis write the following:
"This is the solemn pronouncement of the one who holds
the seven spirits of God and the seven stars: 'I know your deeds,
that you have a reputation that you are alive, but in reality you
are dead. 2 Wake up then, and strengthen what remains that was
about to die, because I have not found your deeds complete in
the sight of my God. 3 Therefore, remember what you received
and heard, and obey it, and repent. If you do not wake up, I will
come like a thief, and you will never know at what hour I will
come against you. 4 But you have a few individuals in Sardis
who have not stained their clothes, and they will walk with
me dressed in white because they are worthy. 5 The one who
conquers will be dressed like them in white clothing, and I will
never erase his name from the book of life, but will declare his
name before my Father and before his angels. 6 The one who
has an ear had better hear what the Spirit says to the churches.'

3:1–6 This group of saints refers to those persons who are negligent and behave in a manner other than what they ought in the world, who are vacuous in works and who are Christian only in name. And therefore John exhorts them so that in some way they might reverse themselves from this dangerous negligence and be saved. "Strengthen," he says, "what remains that was about to die, because I have not found your deeds complete in the sight of my God." For it is not sufficient that a tree lives but doesn't give fruit. Neither is it sufficient that one be called a Christian, confess himself to be a Christian, and yet does not do the works of a Christian.

VICTORINUS OF PETOVIUM (D. 304)
COMMENTARY ON THE APOCALYPSE

TO THE CHURCH IN PHILADELPHIA

[7]"To the angel of the church in Philadelphia write the following:
"This is the solemn pronouncement of the Holy One, the
True One, who holds the key of David, who opens doors no one
can shut, and shuts doors no one can open: [8]'I know your deeds.
(Look! I have put in front of you an open door that no one can
shut.) I know that you have little strength, but you have obeyed
my word and have not denied my name. [9]Listen! I am going
to make those people from the synagogue of Satan—who say
they are Jews yet are not, but are lying—look, I will make them
come and bow down at your feet and acknowledge that I have
loved you. [10]Because you have kept my admonition to endure
steadfastly, I will also keep you from the hour of testing that is
about to come on the whole world to test those who live on the
earth. [11]I am coming soon. Hold on to what you have so that no
one can take away your crown. [12]The one who conquers I will
make a pillar in the temple of my God, and he will never depart
from it. I will write on him the name of my God and the name of
the city of my God (the new Jerusalem that comes down out of
heaven from my God), and my new name as well. [13]The one who
has an ear had better hear what the Spirit says to the churches.'

TO THE CHURCH IN LAODICEA

[14]"To the angel of the church in Laodicea write the following:
"This is the solemn pronouncement of the Amen, the faithful
and true witness, the originator of God's creation: [15]'I know your
deeds, that you are neither cold nor hot. I wish you were either
cold or hot! [16]So because you are lukewarm, and neither hot nor
cold, I am going to vomit you out of my mouth! [17]Because you
say, "I am rich and have acquired great wealth, and need nothing,"
but do not realize that you are wretched, pitiful, poor, blind, and
naked, [18]take my advice and buy gold from me refined by fire so
you can become rich! Buy from me white clothing so you can be
clothed and your shameful nakedness will not be exposed, and
buy eye salve to put on your eyes so you can see! [19]All those I love,
I rebuke and discipline. So be earnest and repent! [20]Listen! I am
standing at the door and knocking! If anyone hears my voice
and opens the door I will come into his home and share a meal
with him, and he with me. [21]I will grant the one who conquers
permission to sit with me on my throne, just as I, too, conquered
and sat down with my Father on his throne. [22]The one who has
an ear had better hear what the Spirit says to the churches.'"

THE AMAZING SCENE IN HEAVEN

4 After these things I looked, and there was a door standing
open in heaven! And the first voice I had heard speaking to
me like a trumpet said: "Come up here so that I can show you
what must happen after these things." [2]Immediately I was in
the Spirit, and a throne was standing in heaven with someone
seated on it! [3]And the one seated on it was like jasper and carnelian in appearance, and a rainbow looking like it was made
of emerald encircled the throne. [4]In a circle around the throne
were twenty-four other thrones, and seated on those thrones
were twenty-four elders. They were dressed in white clothing
and had golden crowns on their heads. [5]From the throne came
out flashes of lightning and roaring and crashes of thunder.
Seven flaming torches, which are the seven spirits of God, were
burning in front of the throne, [6]and in front of the throne was
something like a sea of glass, like crystal.

4:1–11 He commands him who prays to seek that he may be glorified also by our life. This very thing he had said before likewise, "Let your light shine before people, so that they can see your good deeds and give honor to your Father in heaven" (Matt 5:16). Yes, and the seraphim giving glory said on this, "Holy holy holy" (Rev 4:8). That is, *Provide,* said he, *that we may live so purely that through us all we may glorify you.* This pertains to perfect self-control, to present to all a life so pure that every one of the beholders may offer to the Lord the praise due to him for this.

CHRYSOSTOM (C. 347–407)
HOMILIES ON THE GOSPEL OF MATTHEW

In the middle of the throne and around the throne were four
living creatures full of eyes in front and in back. 7The first living
creature was like a lion, the second creature like an ox, the third
creature had a face like a man's, and the fourth creature looked
like an eagle flying. 8Each one of the four living creatures had
six wings and was full of eyes all around and inside. They never
rest day or night, saying:

"***Holy, Holy, Holy is the Lord God, the All-Powerful,***
Who was, and who is, and who is still to come!"

9And whenever the living creatures give glory, honor, and
thanks to the one who sits on the throne, who lives forever and
ever, 10the twenty-four elders throw themselves to the ground
before the one who sits on the throne and worship the one
who lives forever and ever, and they offer their crowns before
his throne, saying:

11 "You are worthy, our Lord and God,
to receive glory and honor and power,
since you created all things,
and because of your will they existed and were created!"

THE OPENING OF THE SCROLL

5 Then I saw in the right hand of the one who was seated on
the throne a scroll written on the front and back and sealed
with seven seals. 2And I saw a powerful angel proclaiming in a
loud voice: "Who is worthy to open the scroll and to break its
seals?" 3But no one in heaven or on earth or under the earth
was able to open the scroll or look into it. 4So I began weeping
bitterly because no one was found who was worthy to open the
scroll or to look into it. 5Then one of the elders said to me, "Stop
weeping! Look, the Lion of the tribe of Judah, the root of David,
has conquered; thus he can open the scroll and its seven seals."

6Then I saw standing in the middle of the throne and of the
four living creatures, and in the middle of the elders, a Lamb
that appeared to have been killed. He had seven horns and seven
eyes, which are the seven spirits of God sent out into all the
earth. 7Then he came and took the scroll from the right hand
of the one who was seated on the throne, 8and when he had
taken the scroll, the four living creatures and the twenty-four
elders threw themselves to the ground before the Lamb. Each
of them had a harp and golden bowls full of incense (which
are the prayers of the saints). 9They were singing a new song:

"You are worthy to take the scroll
and to open its seals
because you were killed,
and at the cost of your own blood you have purchased
for God
persons from every tribe, language, people, and nation.
10 You have appointed them as a kingdom and priests to
serve our God, and they will reign on the earth."

11Then I looked and heard the voice of many angels in a circle
around the throne, as well as the living creatures and the elders.
Their number was ten thousand times ten thousand—thousands
times thousands—12all of whom were singing in a loud voice:

"Worthy is the lamb who was killed
to receive power and wealth
and wisdom and might
and honor and glory and praise!"

5:1–14 Jesus is called a lion. He is called a lamb. There is an admirable conjunction of diverse excellencies in Jesus Christ. Though very diverse kinds of creatures, each has peculiar excellencies. The lion excels in strength and in the majesty of his voice. The lamb excels in meekness and patience, besides the excellent nature of the creature as good for food, yielding that which is fit for our clothing, and being suitable to be offered in sacrifice to God. But we see that Christ is in the text compared to both because the diverse excellencies of both wonderfully meet in him.

JONATHAN EDWARDS
(1703–1758)
THE COMPLETE WORKS

13Then I heard every creature—in heaven, on earth, under
the earth, in the sea, and all that is in them—singing:
"To the one seated on the throne and to
the Lamb
be praise, honor, glory, and ruling power forever and
ever!"

14And the four living creatures were saying "Amen," and the
elders threw themselves to the ground and worshiped.

6:1–17 For at that time all shall stand upon the face of the earth, waiting for the coming of the righteous and terrible judge, in fear and trembling unutterable. For the river of fire shall come forth in fury like an angry sea and shall burn up mountains and hills, shall make the sea vanish, and shall dissolve the atmosphere with its heat like wax. The stars of heaven shall fall, the sun shall be turned into darkness, and the moon into blood. The heaven shall be rolled together like a scroll: The whole earth shall be burnt up by reason of the deeds done in it, which people did corruptly. For there shall be the new heaven and the new earth.

HIPPOLYTUS OF ROME
(C. 170–C. 235)
THE WORKS

THE SEVEN SEALS

6 I looked on when the Lamb opened one of the seven seals,
and I heard one of the four living creatures saying with a
thunderous voice, "Come!" 2So I looked, and here came a white
horse! The one who rode it had a bow, and he was given a crown,
and as a conqueror he rode out to conquer.
3Then when the Lamb opened the second seal, I heard the
second living creature saying, "Come!" 4And another horse, fiery
red, came out, and the one who rode it was granted permission
to take peace from the earth so that people would butcher one
another, and he was given a huge sword.
5Then when the Lamb opened the third seal I heard the
third living creature saying, "Come!" So I looked, and here came
a black horse! The one who rode it had a balance scale in his
hand. 6Then I heard something like a voice from among the
four living creatures saying, "A quart of wheat will cost a day's
pay, and three quarts of barley will cost a day's pay. But do not
damage the olive oil and the wine!"
7Then when the Lamb opened the fourth seal I heard the
voice of the fourth living creature saying, "Come!" 8So I looked
and here came a pale green horse! The name of the one who
rode it was Death, and Hades followed right behind. They were
given authority over a fourth of the earth, to kill its population
with the sword, famine, and disease, and by the wild animals
of the earth.
9Now when the Lamb opened the fifth seal, I saw under the
altar the souls of those who had been violently killed because
of the word of God and because of the testimony they had
given. 10They cried out with a loud voice, "How long, Sovereign
Master, holy and true, before you judge those who live on the
earth and avenge our blood?" 11Each of them was given a long
white robe, and they were told to rest for a little longer, until
the full number was reached of both their fellow servants
and their brothers who were going to be killed just as they
had been.
12Then I looked when the Lamb opened the sixth seal, and
a huge earthquake took place; the sun became as black as
sackcloth made of hair, and the full moon became blood red;
13and the stars in the sky fell to the earth like a fig tree drop-
ping its unripe figs when shaken by a fierce wind. 14The sky
was split apart like a scroll being rolled up, and every mountain and island was moved from its place. 15Then the kings of
the earth, the very important people, the generals, the rich,
the powerful, and everyone, slave and free, hid themselves in the
caves and among the rocks of the mountains. 16They said to
the mountains and to the rocks, "Fall on us and hide us from
the face of the one who is seated on the throne and from the
wrath of the Lamb, 17because the great day of their wrath has
come, and who is able to withstand it?"

THE SEALING OF THE 144,000

7 After this I saw four angels standing at the four corners of the
earth, holding back the four winds of the earth so no wind
could blow on the earth, on the sea, or on any tree. 2Then I saw
another angel ascending from the east, who had the seal of the
living God. He shouted out with a loud voice to the four angels
who had been given permission to damage the earth and the
sea: 3"Do not damage the earth or the sea or the trees until we
have put a seal on the foreheads of the servants of our God."
4Now I heard the number of those who were marked with the
seal, 144,000, sealed from all the tribes of the people of Israel:

5 From the tribe of Judah, 12,000 were sealed,
from the tribe of Reuben, 12,000,
from the tribe of Gad, 12,000,
6 from the tribe of Asher, 12,000,
from the tribe of Naphtali, 12,000,
from the tribe of Manasseh, 12,000,
7 from the tribe of Simeon, 12,000,
from the tribe of Levi, 12,000,
from the tribe of Issachar, 12,000,
8 from the tribe of Zebulun, 12,000,
from the tribe of Joseph, 12,000,
from the tribe of Benjamin, 12,000 were sealed.

9After these things I looked, and here was an enormous
crowd that no one could count, made up of persons from every nation, tribe, people, and language, standing before the
throne and before the Lamb dressed in long white robes, and
with palm branches in their hands. 10They were shouting out
in a loud voice,

"Salvation belongs to our God, who is seated on the
throne, and to the Lamb!"

11And all the angels stood there in a circle around the throne
and around the elders and the four living creatures, and they
threw themselves down with their faces to the ground before
the throne and worshiped God, 12saying,

"Amen! Praise and glory,
and wisdom and thanksgiving,
and honor and power and strength
be to our God for ever and ever. Amen!"

13Then one of the elders asked me, "These dressed in long
white robes—who are they and where have they come from?"
14So I said to him, "My lord, you know the answer." Then he
said to me, "These are the ones who have come out of the great
tribulation. They have washed their robes and made them white
in the blood of the Lamb! 15For this reason they are before the
throne of God, and they serve him day and night in his temple,
and the one seated on the throne will shelter them. 16*They will*
never go hungry or be thirsty again, and the sun will not beat down
on them, nor any burning heat, 17because the Lamb in the middle
of the throne will shepherd them and lead them to springs of
living water, *and God will wipe away every tear from their eyes."*

7:9–17 Such a glorious appearance will the faithful servants of God make at last when they have fought the good fight of faith and finished their course. With a loud voice they gave to God and the Lamb the praise of the great salvation. Those who enjoy eternal happiness must and will bless both the Father and the Son; they will do it publicly and with fervor. We see what is the work of heaven, and we ought to begin it now, to have our hearts much in it and to long for that world where our praises, as well as our happiness, will be made perfect.

MATTHEW HENRY **(1662–1714)**
COMMENTARY ON THE WHOLE BIBLE

THE SEVENTH SEAL

8 Now when the Lamb opened the seventh seal there was silence in heaven for about half an hour. 2Then I saw the seven
angels who stand before God, and seven trumpets were given

8:1–13 And what is the loosing of the seventh seal? It is the second coming of Christ and the giving of blessings as rewards. For although some are handed over to the punishment of sinners, nonetheless it is the aim of Christ and the intention of the incarnation that everyone become an heir of his kingdom. Therefore, when the seventh seal was loosed, "there was," it says, "silence in heaven for about half an hour," since the King of creation was coming and every angelic and supernatural power, astounded at the exceeding greatness of the glory of him who was coming, for that reason became silent.

OECUMENIUS
(C. 7TH CENTURY)
COMMENTARY ON THE APOCALYPSE

9:1–12 Death is not only not an evil, but it is even a good thing. As it is written: "People will seek death, but will not be able to find it." They will seek it who shall "begin to say to the mountains, 'Fall on us!' and to the hills, 'Cover us!'" (Luke 23:30). That soul too shall seek it that has sinned. That rich man lying in hell shall seek it who wishes that his tongue should be cooled with the finger of Lazarus.

AMBROSE **(C. 339–C. 397)**
ON THE DEATH OF HIS BROTHER SATYRUS

to them. [3]Another angel holding a golden censer came and was stationed at the altar. A large amount of incense was given to him to offer up, with the prayers of all the saints, on the golden altar that is before the throne. [4]The smoke coming from the incense, along with the prayers of the saints, ascended before God from the angel's hand. [5]Then the angel took the censer, filled it with fire from the altar, and threw it on the earth, and there were crashes of thunder, roaring, flashes of lightning, and an earthquake.

[6]Now the seven angels holding the seven trumpets prepared to blow them.

[7]The first angel blew his trumpet, and there was hail and fire mixed with blood, and it was thrown at the earth so that a third of the earth was burned up, a third of the trees were burned up, and all the green grass was burned up.

[8]Then the second angel blew his trumpet, and something like a great mountain of burning fire was thrown into the sea. A third of the sea became blood, [9]and a third of the creatures living in the sea died, and a third of the ships were completely destroyed.

[10]Then the third angel blew his trumpet, and a huge star burning like a torch fell from the sky; it landed on a third of the rivers and on the springs of water. [11](Now the name of the star is Wormwood.) So a third of the waters became wormwood, and many people died from these waters because they were poisoned.

[12]Then the fourth angel blew his trumpet, and a third of the sun was struck, and a third of the moon, and a third of the stars, so that a third of them were darkened. And there was no light for a third of the day and for a third of the night likewise. [13]Then I looked, and I heard an eagle flying directly overhead, proclaiming with a loud voice, "Woe! Woe! Woe to those who live on the earth because of the remaining sounds of the trumpets of the three angels who are about to blow them!"

9 Then the fifth angel blew his trumpet, and I saw a star that had fallen from the sky to the earth, and he was given the key to the shaft of the abyss. [2]He opened the shaft of the abyss and smoke rose out of it like smoke from a giant furnace. The sun and the air were darkened with smoke from the shaft. [3]Then out of the smoke came locusts onto the earth, and they were given power like that of the scorpions of the earth. [4]They were told not to damage the grass of the earth, or any green plant or tree, but only those people who did not have the seal of God on their forehead. [5]The locusts were not given permission to kill them, but only to torture them for five months, and their torture was like that of a scorpion when it stings a person. [6]In those days people will seek death, but will not be able to find it; they will long to die, but death will flee from them.

[7]Now the locusts looked like horses equipped for battle. On their heads were something like crowns similar to gold, and their faces looked like men's faces. [8]They had hair like women's hair, and their teeth were like lions' teeth. [9]They had breastplates like iron breastplates, and the sound of their wings was like the noise of many horse-drawn chariots charging into battle. [10]They have tails and stingers like scorpions, and their ability to injure people for five months is in their tails. [11]They have as king over them the angel of the abyss, whose name in Hebrew is *Abaddon,* and in Greek, *Apollyon.*

[12]The first woe has passed, but two woes are still coming after these things!

[13]Then the sixth angel blew his trumpet, and I heard a single voice coming from the horns on the golden altar that is before God, [14]saying to the sixth angel, the one holding the trumpet, "Set free the four angels who are bound at the great river Euphrates!" [15]Then the four angels who had been prepared for this hour, day, month, and year were set free to kill a third of humanity. [16]The number of soldiers on horseback was 200,000,000; I heard their number. [17]Now this is what the horses and their riders looked like in my vision: The riders had breastplates that were fiery red, dark blue, and sulfurous yellow in color. The heads of the horses looked like lions' heads, and fire, smoke, and sulfur came out of their mouths. [18]A third of humanity was killed by these three plagues, that is, by the fire, the smoke, and the sulfur that came out of their mouths. [19]For the power of the horses resides in their mouths and in their tails because their tails are like snakes, having heads that inflict injuries. [20]The rest of humanity, who had not been killed by these plagues, did not repent of the works of their hands so that they did not stop worshiping demons and idols made of gold, silver, bronze, stone, and wood—idols that cannot see or hear or walk about. [21]Furthermore, they did not repent of their murders, of their magic spells, of their sexual immorality, or of their stealing.

THE ANGEL WITH THE LITTLE SCROLL

10 Then I saw another powerful angel descending from heaven, wrapped in a cloud, with a rainbow above his head; his face was like the sun, and his legs were like pillars of fire. [2]He held in his hand a little scroll that was open, and he put his right foot on the sea and his left on the land. [3]Then he shouted in a loud voice like a lion roaring, and when he shouted, the seven thunders sounded their voices. [4]When the seven thunders spoke, I was preparing to write, but just then I heard a voice from heaven say, "Seal up what the seven thunders spoke and do not write it down." [5]Then the angel I saw standing on the sea and on the land raised his right hand to heaven [6]and swore by the one who lives forever and ever, who created heaven and what is in it, and the earth and what is in it, and the sea and what is in it, "There will be no more delay! [7]But in the days when the seventh angel is about to blow his trumpet, the mystery of God is completed, just as he has proclaimed to his servants the prophets." [8]Then the voice I had heard from heaven began to speak to me again, "Go and take the open scroll in the hand of the angel who is standing on the sea and on the land." [9]So I went to the angel and asked him to give me the little scroll. He said to me, "Take the scroll and eat it. It will make your stomach bitter, but it will be as sweet as honey in your mouth." [10]So I took the little scroll from the angel's hand and ate it, and it did taste as sweet as honey in my mouth, but when I had eaten it, my stomach became bitter. [11]Then they told me: "You must prophesy again about many peoples, nations, languages, and kings."

THE FATE OF THE TWO WITNESSES

11 Then a measuring rod like a staff was given to me, and I was told, "Get up and measure the temple of God, and the altar, and the ones who worship there. [2]But do not measure the outer courtyard of the temple; leave it out because

10:1–11 Ezekiel received a scroll, but at the command of the Logos he swallowed the book. John also is recorded to have seen and done a similar thing. Paul even "heard things too sacred to be put into words, things that a person is not permitted to speak" (2 Cor 12:4). And it is related of Jesus, who was greater than all these, that he conversed with his disciples in private, but the words he uttered have not been preserved because it appeared to the evangelists that they could not be adequately conveyed to the multitude. And once more John, in teaching us the difference between what ought to be committed to writing and what not, declares that he heard seven thunders instructing him on certain matters and forbidding him to commit their words to writing.

ORIGEN (C. 185–C. 253)
CONTRA CELSUM

11:1–14 God's faithful witnesses prophesy in sackcloth. It shows their afflicted, persecuted state and deep sorrow for the abominations against which they protested. They are supported during their great and hard work till it is done. There is abundant cause to prophesy in sackcloth on account of the state of religion. But the Spirit of life from God quickens dead souls and shall quicken the dead bodies of his people and his dying interest in the world. The revival of God's work and witnesses will strike terror into the souls of his enemies. Where there is guilt, there is fear and a persecuting spirit, though cruel, is a cowardly spirit. It will be no small part of the punishment of persecutors that they see the faithful servants of God honored and advanced.

MATTHEW HENRY **(1662–1714)**
COMMENTARY ON THE WHOLE BIBLE

it has been given to the Gentiles, and they will trample on
the holy city for forty-two months. 3And I will grant my two
witnesses authority to prophesy for 1,260 days, dressed in
sackcloth." 4(These are the two olive trees and the two lampstands that stand before the Lord of the earth.) 5If anyone
wants to harm them, fire comes out of their mouths and
completely consumes their enemies. If anyone wants to harm
them, they must be killed this way. 6These two have the power
to close up the sky so that it does not rain during the time
they are prophesying. They have power to turn the waters
to blood and to strike the earth with every kind of plague
whenever they want. 7When they have completed their testimony, the beast that comes up from the abyss will make war
on them and conquer them and kill them. 8Their corpses will
lie in the street of the great city that is symbolically called
Sodom and Egypt, where their Lord was also crucified. 9For
three and a half days those from every people, tribe, nation,
and language will look at their corpses because they will
not permit them to be placed in a tomb. 10And those who
live on the earth will rejoice over them and celebrate, even
sending gifts to each other because these two prophets had
tormented those who live on the earth. 11But after three and
a half days a breath of life from God entered them, and they
stood on their feet, and tremendous fear seized those who
were watching them. 12Then they heard a loud voice from
heaven saying to them: "Come up here!" So the two prophets
went up to heaven in a cloud while their enemies stared at
them. 13Just then a major earthquake took place and a tenth
of the city collapsed; seven thousand people were killed in
the earthquake, and the rest were terrified and gave glory
to the God of heaven.

14The second woe has come and gone; the third is coming
quickly.

THE SEVENTH TRUMPET

15Then the seventh angel blew his trumpet, and there were
loud voices in heaven saying:

"The kingdom of the world
has become the kingdom of our Lord
and of his Christ,
and he will reign for ever and ever."

16Then the twenty-four elders who are seated on their
thrones before God threw themselves down with their faces
to the ground and worshiped God 17with these words:

"We give you thanks, Lord God, the All-Powerful,
the one who is and who was,
because you have taken your great power
and begun to reign.
18 The nations were enraged,
but your wrath has come,
and the time has come for the dead to be judged,
and the time has come to give to your servants,
the prophets, their reward,
as well as to the saints
and to those who revere your name, both small and great,
and the time has come to destroy those who destroy the earth."

19 Then the temple of God in heaven was opened, and the ark
of his covenant was visible within his temple. And there were
flashes of lightning, roaring, crashes of thunder, an earthquake,
and a great hailstorm.

THE WOMAN, THE CHILD, AND THE DRAGON

12 Then a great sign appeared in heaven: a woman clothed
with the sun, and with the moon under her feet, and on
her head was a crown of twelve stars. 2 She was pregnant and
was screaming in labor pains, struggling to give birth. 3 Then
another sign appeared in heaven: a huge red dragon that had
seven heads and ten horns, and on its heads were seven diadem crowns. 4 Now the dragon's tail swept away a third of the
stars in heaven and hurled them to the earth. Then the dragon
stood before the woman who was about to give birth, so that he
might devour her child as soon as it was born. 5 So the woman
gave birth to a son, a male child, who is going *to rule over all the
nations with an iron rod.* Her child was suddenly caught up to
God and to his throne, 6 and she fled into the wilderness where
a place had been prepared for her by God, so she could be taken
care of for 1,260 days.

WAR IN HEAVEN

7 Then war broke out in heaven: Michael and his angels fought
against the dragon, and the dragon and his angels fought back.
8 But the dragon was not strong enough to prevail, so there was
no longer any place left in heaven for him and his angels. 9 So
that huge dragon—the ancient serpent, the one called the devil
and Satan, who deceives the whole world—was thrown down
to the earth, and his angels along with him. 10 Then I heard a
loud voice in heaven saying,

"The salvation and the power
and the kingdom of our God,
and the ruling authority of his Christ, have now come,
because the accuser of our brothers and sisters,
the one who accuses them day and night before our
God,
has been thrown down.
11 But they overcame him
by the blood of the Lamb
and by the word of their testimony,
and they did not love their lives so much that they were
afraid to die.
12 Therefore you heavens rejoice, and all who reside in
them!
But woe to the earth and the sea
because the devil has come down to you!
He is filled with terrible anger,
for he knows that he only has a little time!"

13 Now when the dragon realized that he had been thrown
down to the earth, he pursued the woman who had given birth
to the male child. 14 But the woman was given the two wings of
a giant eagle so that she could fly out into the wilderness, to the
place God prepared for her, where she is taken care of—away
from the presence of the serpent—for a time, times, and half a
time. 15 Then the serpent spouted water like a river out of his
mouth after the woman in an attempt to sweep her away by a
flood, 16 but the earth came to her rescue; the ground opened

12:1–17 All Jesus' servants will and must fight. The duty of every soldier in the army of the Lord is to fight against the dragon with all his heart, soul, and strength each day. It is foolish for us to expect to serve God without opposition, and the more zealous we are for him the more certain we are to be attacked by the minions of hell. The church may grow lazy, but not so her great enemy. His restless spirit never will allow a pause in the war and would gladly devour the church if he could. But glory be to God that we know the end of the war! "That huge dragon" will be cast down and forever destroyed, while Jesus—and those who are with him—"will receive the crown of life" (Jas 1:12).

CHARLES SPURGEON
(1834–1892)
MORNING AND EVENING

up and swallowed the river that the dragon had spewed from
his mouth. 17 So the dragon became enraged at the woman and
went away to make war on the rest of her children, those who
keep God's commandments and hold to the testimony about
Jesus. 18 And the dragon stood on the sand of the seashore.

> 13:1–18 By "the beast" he means the kingdom of the Antichrist. He will make himself like the Son of God and set himself forward as king. He will order incense-pans to be set up by all everywhere that no person among the saints may be able to buy or sell without first sacrificing, for this is what is meant by the mark received upon the right hand. But having the mystery of God in our heart, we ought in fear to keep faithfully what has been told us by the blessed prophets, in order that when those things come to pass we may be prepared for them and not deceived. For when the times advance, he of whom these things are said will be manifested.
>
> HIPPOLYTUS OF ROME
> (C. 170–C. 235)
> *TREATISE ON CHRIST AND ANTICHRIST*

THE TWO BEASTS

13 Then I saw a beast coming up out of the sea. It had ten
horns and seven heads, and on its horns were ten diadem
crowns, and on its heads a blasphemous name. 2 Now the beast
that I saw was like a leopard, but its feet were like a bear's, and
its mouth was like a lion's mouth. The dragon gave the beast
his power, his throne, and great authority to rule. 3 One of the
beast's heads appeared to have been killed, but the lethal wound
had been healed. And the whole world followed the beast in
amazement; 4 they worshiped the dragon because he had given
ruling authority to the beast, and they worshiped the beast too,
saying: "Who is like the beast?" and "Who is able to make war
against him?" 5 The beast was given a mouth speaking proud
words and blasphemies, and he was permitted to exercise ruling
authority for forty-two months. 6 So the beast opened his mouth
to blaspheme against God—to blaspheme both his name and his
dwelling place, that is, those who dwell in heaven. 7 The beast was
permitted to go to war against the saints and conquer them. He
was given ruling authority over every tribe, people, language,
and nation, 8 and all those who live on the earth will worship
the beast, everyone whose name has not been written since
the foundation of the world in the book of life belonging to the
Lamb who was killed. 9 If anyone has an ear, he had better listen!

10 If anyone is meant for captivity,
into captivity he will go.
If anyone is to be killed by the sword,
then by the sword he must be killed.

This requires steadfast endurance and faith from the saints.
11 Then I saw another beast coming up from the earth. He had
two horns like a lamb, but was speaking like a dragon. 12 He exercised all the ruling authority of the first beast on his behalf, and
made the earth and those who inhabit it worship the first beast,
the one whose lethal wound had been healed. 13 He performed
momentous signs, even making fire come down from heaven to
earth in front of people 14 and, by the signs he was permitted to
perform on behalf of the beast, he deceived those who live on
the earth. He told those who live on the earth to make an image
to the beast who had been wounded by the sword, but still lived.
15 The second beast was empowered to give life to the image of
the first beast so that it could speak, and could cause all those
who did not worship the image of the beast to be killed. 16 He
also caused everyone (small and great, rich and poor, free and
slave) to obtain a mark on their right hand or on their forehead.
17 Thus no one was allowed to buy or sell things unless he bore
the mark of the beast—that is, his name or his number. 18 This
calls for wisdom: Let the one who has insight calculate the beast's
number, for it is man's number, and his number is 666.

AN INTERLUDE: THE SONG OF THE 144,000

14 Then I looked, and here was the Lamb standing on Mount
Zion, and with him were 144,000, who had his name and
his Father's name written on their foreheads. 2 I also heard a

sound coming out of heaven like the sound of many waters
and like the sound of loud thunder. Now the sound I heard was
like that made by harpists playing their harps, [3]and they were
singing a new song before the throne and before the four living
creatures and the elders. No one was able to learn the song
except the 144,000 who had been redeemed from the earth.
[4]These are the ones who have not defiled themselves with
women, for they are virgins. These are the ones who follow the
Lamb wherever he goes. These were redeemed from humanity
as firstfruits to God and to the Lamb, [5]and no lie was found on
their lips; they are blameless.

THREE ANGELS AND THREE MESSAGES

[6]Then I saw another angel flying directly overhead, and he had
an eternal gospel to proclaim to those who live on the earth—to
every nation, tribe, language, and people. [7]He declared in a loud
voice: "Fear God and give him glory because the hour of his
judgment has arrived, and worship the one who made heaven
and earth, the sea and the springs of water!"
[8]A second angel followed the first, declaring: "Fallen, fallen
is Babylon the great city! She made all the nations drink of the
wine of her immoral passion."
[9]A third angel followed the first two, declaring in a loud
voice: "If anyone worships the beast and his image, and takes
the mark on his forehead or his hand, [10]that person will also
drink of the wine of God's anger that has been mixed undi-
luted in the cup of his wrath, and he will be tortured with
fire and sulfur in front of the holy angels and in front of the
Lamb. [11]And the smoke from their torture will go up forever
and ever, and those who worship the beast and his image will
have no rest day or night, along with anyone who receives the
mark of his name." [12]This requires the steadfast endurance of
the saints—those who obey God's commandments and hold to
their faith in Jesus.
[13]Then I heard a voice from heaven say, "Write this:
'Blessed are the dead,
those who die in the Lord from this moment on!'"

"Yes," says the Spirit, "so they can rest from their hard work,
because their deeds will follow them."
[14]Then I looked, and a white cloud appeared, and seated *on
the cloud was one like a son of man!* He had a golden crown on his
head and a sharp sickle in his hand. [15]Then another angel came
out of the temple, shouting in a loud voice to the one seated
on the cloud, "Use your sickle and start to reap, because the
time to reap has come, since the earth's harvest is ripe!" [16]So
the one seated on the cloud swung his sickle over the earth,
and the earth was reaped.
[17]Then another angel came out of the temple in heaven, and
he, too, had a sharp sickle. [18]Another angel, who was in charge
of the fire, came from the altar and called in a loud voice to
the angel who had the sharp sickle, "Use your sharp sickle and
gather the clusters of grapes off the vine of the earth, because
its grapes are now ripe." [19]So the angel swung his sickle over the
earth and gathered the grapes from the vineyard of the earth
and tossed them into the great winepress of the wrath of God.
[20]Then the winepress was stomped outside the city, and blood
poured out of the winepress up to the height of horses' bridles
for a distance of almost 200 miles.

14:1–5 The loud voice of the saints is the great devotion of love that John says he heard from heaven. When he said that those who uttered the voice stood on Mount Zion, it was to indicate that by Mount Zion he referred to nothing other than the church. This is truly to sing to the Lamb who is standing on Mount Zion. Although all the saints are harpists of God who crucify their flesh with its vices and lusts and praise him with psalter and harp, how much more are they who, by the privilege of an angelic purity, render themselves totally a sacrifice to the Lord and in a particular way deny themselves and, taking up their cross, "follow the Lamb wherever he goes"?

VENERABLE BEDE
(C. 672–735)
EXPLANATION OF THE APOCALYPSE

THE FINAL PLAGUES

15 Then I saw another great and astounding sign in heaven:
seven angels who have seven final plagues (they are final
because in them God's anger is completed).
2Then I saw something like a sea of glass mixed with fire,
and those who had conquered the beast and his image and the
number of his name. They were standing by the sea of glass,
holding harps given to them by God. 3They sang the song of
Moses the servant of God and the song of the Lamb:

"Great and astounding are your deeds,
Lord God, the All-Powerful!
Just and true are your ways,
King over the nations!
4 Who will not fear you, O Lord,
and glorify your name, because you alone are holy?
All nations will come and worship before you
for your righteous acts have been revealed."

5After these things I looked, and the temple (the tent of the
testimony) was opened in heaven, 6and the seven angels who
had the seven plagues came out of the temple, dressed in clean
bright linen, wearing wide golden belts around their chests.
7Then one of the four living creatures gave the seven angels
seven golden bowls filled with the wrath of God who lives forever and ever, 8and the temple was filled with smoke from God's
glory and from his power. Thus no one could enter the temple
until the seven plagues from the seven angels were completed.

15:1–8 The "sea of glass mixed with fire" is but a photograph of what John must have seen on many a still morning when the sunrise came blushing over the calm surface. So here, in the solemn pause before the judgment goes forth, there are represented the spirits that have been made wise by conquest, as gathered on the bank of that steadfast ocean lifting up as of old a hymn of triumphant thankfulness. Ever his judgments are right; ever the purpose of his most terrible things is that people may know him and may love him; and ever they who see deepest into the mysteries and understand most truly the realities of the universe will have praise springing to their lips for all that God has done.

ALEXANDER MACLAREN
(1826–1910)
EXPOSITIONS OF THE HOLY SCRIPTURES

THE BOWLS OF GOD'S WRATH

16 Then I heard a loud voice from the temple declaring to
the seven angels: "Go and pour out on the earth the seven
bowls containing God's wrath." 2So the first angel went and
poured out his bowl on the earth. Then ugly and painful sores
appeared on the people who had the mark of the beast and
who worshiped his image.
3Next, the second angel poured out his bowl on the sea, and it
turned into blood, like that of a corpse, and every living creature
that was in the sea died.
4Then the third angel poured out his bowl on the rivers and
the springs of water, and they turned into blood. 5Now I heard
the angel of the waters saying:

"You are just—the one who is and who was,
the Holy One—because you have passed these
judgments,
6 because they poured out the blood of your saints and
prophets,
so you have given them blood to drink. They got what
they deserved!"

7Then I heard the altar reply, "Yes, Lord God, the All-Powerful,
your judgments are true and just!"
8Then the fourth angel poured out his bowl on the sun, and
it was permitted to scorch people with fire. 9Thus people were
scorched by the terrible heat, yet they blasphemed the name
of God, who has ruling authority over these plagues, and they
would not repent and give him glory.
10Then the fifth angel poured out his bowl on the throne
of the beast so that darkness covered his kingdom, and people began to bite their tongues because of their pain. 11They

16:1–21 The whole exodus of the people out of Egypt, which took place under divine guidance, was a type and image of the exodus of the church that should take place from among the Gentiles. And for this reason Jesus leads the church out at last from this world into his own inheritance, which Moses the servant of God did not give but which Jesus the Son of God shall give for an inheritance. And if anyone should pay close attention to those things that are stated by the prophets concerning the time of the end and to those whom John the disciple of the Lord saw in the Apocalypse, he will find that the nations are to receive the same plagues universally, as Egypt once did particularly.

IRENAEUS (C. 130–C. 202)
AGAINST HERESIES

blasphemed the God of heaven because of their sufferings and
because of their sores, but nevertheless they still refused to
repent of their deeds.
12Then the sixth angel poured out his bowl on the great river
Euphrates and dried up its water to prepare the way for the
kings from the east. 13Then I saw three unclean spirits that
looked like frogs coming out of the mouth of the dragon, out
of the mouth of the beast, and out of the mouth of the false
prophet. 14For they are the spirits of the demons performing
signs who go out to the kings of the earth to bring them together
for the battle that will take place on the great day of God, the
All-Powerful.

15 (Look! I will come like a thief!
Blessed is the one who stays alert and does not lose his
clothes so that he will not have to walk around
naked and his shameful condition be seen.)

16Now the spirits gathered the kings and their armies to the
place that is called Armageddon in Hebrew.
17Finally the seventh angel poured out his bowl into the air
and a loud voice came out of the temple from the throne, saying:
"It is done!" 18Then there were flashes of lightning, roaring, and
crashes of thunder, and there was a tremendous earthquake—an
earthquake unequaled since humanity has been on the earth, so
tremendous was that earthquake. 19The great city was split into
three parts, and the cities of the nations collapsed. So Babylon
the great was remembered before God and was given the cup
filled with the wine made of God's furious wrath. 20Every island
fled away, and no mountains could be found. 21And gigantic
hailstones, weighing about a 100 pounds each, fell from heaven
on people, but they blasphemed God because of the plague of
hail, since it was so horrendous.

THE GREAT PROSTITUTE AND THE BEAST

17 Then one of the seven angels who had the seven bowls
came and spoke to me. "Come," he said, "I will show you the
condemnation and punishment of the great prostitute who sits
on many waters, 2with whom the kings of the earth committed
sexual immorality and the earth's inhabitants got drunk with the
wine of her immorality." 3So he carried me away in the Spirit to
a wilderness, and there I saw a woman sitting on a scarlet beast
that was full of blasphemous names and had seven heads and
ten horns. 4Now the woman was dressed in purple and scarlet
clothing, and adorned with gold, precious stones, and pearls. She
held in her hand a golden cup filled with detestable things and
unclean things from her sexual immorality. 5On her forehead
was written a name, a mystery: "Babylon the Great, the Mother of
prostitutes and of the detestable things of the earth." 6I saw that
the woman was drunk with the blood of the saints and the blood
of those who testified to Jesus. I was greatly astounded when I
saw her. 7But the angel said to me, "Why are you astounded? I
will interpret for you the mystery of the woman and of the beast
with the seven heads and ten horns that carries her. 8The beast
you saw was, and is not, but is about to come up from the abyss
and then go to destruction. The inhabitants of the earth—all
those whose names have not been written in the book of life
since the foundation of the world—will be astounded when they
see that the beast was, and is not, but is to come. 9(This requires
a mind that has wisdom.) The seven heads are seven mountains

17:1–6 This woman is clothed in scarlet and purple, for these are symbols of her dominion and rule over all. Therefore she is decorated with precious stones and pearls. The cup indicates the sweetness of evil deeds before they are tasted, and it is gold because such deeds seem precious. Moreover, the cup demonstrates that she is not sated by her evil but pursues further evil with a thirst for her own destruction. Therefore she multiplies abominations for herself, that is, she demands practices that are abominable to God and that she makes the multitude who love the martyrs to drink. In this way she draws, as though it were a sweet drink, the abominable stupor of sin and the pollution of fornication from God.

ANDREW OF CAESAREA
(563–614)
COMMENTARY ON THE APOCALYPSE

the woman sits on. They are also seven kings: [10]five have fallen;
one is, and the other has not yet come, but whenever he does
come, he must remain for only a brief time. [11]The beast that was,
and is not, is himself an eighth king and yet is one of the seven,
and is going to destruction. [12]The ten horns that you saw are
ten kings who have not yet received a kingdom, but will receive
ruling authority as kings with the beast for one hour. [13]These
kings have a single intent, and they will give their power and
authority to the beast. [14]They will make war with the Lamb,
but the Lamb will conquer them, because he is Lord of lords
and King of kings, and those accompanying the Lamb are the
called, chosen, and faithful."

[15]Then the angel said to me, "The waters you saw (where
the prostitute is seated) are peoples, multitudes, nations, and
languages. [16]The ten horns that you saw, and the beast—these
will hate the prostitute and make her desolate and naked. They
will consume her flesh and burn her up with fire. [17]For God
has put into their minds to carry out his purpose by making a
decision to give their royal power to the beast until the words
of God are fulfilled. [18]As for the woman you saw, she is the great
city that has sovereignty over the kings of the earth."

BABYLON IS DESTROYED

18 After these things I saw another angel, who possessed
great authority, coming down out of heaven, and the earth
was lit up by his radiance. [2]He shouted with a powerful voice:

"Fallen, fallen, is Babylon the great!
She has become a lair for demons,
a haunt for every unclean spirit,
a haunt for every unclean bird,
a haunt for every unclean and detested beast.
3 For all the nations have fallen from
the wine of her immoral passion,
and the kings of the earth have committed sexual
immorality with her,
and the merchants of the earth have gotten rich from
the power of her sensual behavior."

[4]Then I heard another voice from heaven saying, "Come out
of her, my people, so you will not take part in her sins and so
you will not receive her plagues, [5]because her sins have piled
up all the way to heaven and God has remembered her crimes.
[6]Repay her the same way she repaid others; pay her back double
corresponding to her deeds. In the cup she mixed, mix double
the amount for her. [7]As much as she exalted herself and lived
in sensual luxury, to this extent give her torment and grief
because she said to herself, 'I rule as queen and am no widow; I
will never experience grief!' [8]For this reason, she will experience
her plagues in a single day: disease, mourning, and famine, and
she will be burned down with fire, because the Lord God who
judges her is powerful!"

[9]Then the kings of the earth who committed immoral acts
with her and lived in sensual luxury with her will weep and wail
for her when they see the smoke from the fire that burns her
up. [10]They will stand a long way off because they are afraid of
her torment, and will say,

"Woe, woe, O great city,
Babylon the powerful city!
For in a single hour your doom has come!"

[11]Then the merchants of the earth will weep and mourn
for her because no one buys their cargo any longer—[12]cargo
such as gold, silver, precious stones, pearls, fine linen, purple
cloth, silk, scarlet cloth, all sorts of things made of citron wood,
all sorts of objects made of ivory, all sorts of things made of
expensive wood, bronze, iron and marble, [13]cinnamon, spice,
incense, perfumed ointment, frankincense, wine, olive oil and
costly flour, wheat, cattle and sheep, horses and four-wheeled
carriages, slaves and human lives.

14 (The ripe fruit you greatly desired
has gone from you,
and all your luxury and splendor
have gone from you—
they will never ever be found again!)

[15]The merchants who sold these things, who got rich from
her, will stand a long way off because they are afraid of her
torment. They will weep and mourn, [16]saying,

"Woe, woe, O great city—
dressed in fine linen, purple and scarlet clothing,
and adorned with gold, precious stones, and pearls—
17 because in a single hour such great wealth has been
destroyed!"

And every ship's captain, and all who sail along the coast—
seamen, and all who make their living from the sea, stood a
long way off [18]and began to shout when they saw the smoke
from the fire that burned her up, "Who is like the great city?"
[19]And they threw dust on their heads and were shouting with
weeping and mourning,

"Woe, Woe, O great city—
in which all those who had ships on the sea got rich
from her wealth—
because in a single hour she has been destroyed!"
20 (Rejoice over her, O heaven,
and you saints and apostles and prophets,
for God has pronounced judgment against her on your
behalf!)

[21]Then one powerful angel picked up a stone like a huge
millstone, threw it into the sea, and said,

"With this kind of sudden violent force
Babylon the great city will be thrown down,
and it will never be found again!
22 And the sound of the harpists, musicians,
flute players, and trumpeters
will never be heard in you again.
No craftsman who practices any trade
will ever be found in you again;
the noise of a mill will never be heard in you again.
23 Even the light from a lamp
will never shine in you again!
The voices of the bridegroom and his bride
will never be heard in you again.
For your merchants were the tycoons of the world,
because all the nations were deceived by your magic spells!
24 The blood of the saints and prophets was found in her,
along with the blood of all those who had been killed on
the earth."

18:9–20 Here it is proclaimed that Babylon the great is fallen and become the habitation of devils, the hold of every foul spirit, and a cage of every unclean and hateful bird; that her sins had reached to heaven and that God had remembered her iniquity; that God gave the commandment to reward her as she had rewarded others, to double unto her double according to her works. And it is declared that these plagues are come upon her in one day—death, mourning, and famine—and that she should be utterly burnt with fire because strong is the Lord who judges her. When the saints in glory shall see the wrath of God executed on ungodly people, it will be no occasion of grief to them, but of rejoicing.

JONATHAN EDWARDS
(1703–1758)
THE COMPLETE WORKS

19:1–10 How great is the Lord Jesus, and how great is his patience, that he who is adored in heaven is not yet avenged on earth! Let us consider his patience in our persecutions and sufferings; let us give an obedience full of expectation to his advent; and let us not hasten, servants as we are, to be defended before our Lord with irreligious and immodest eagerness. Let us rather press onward and labor, watching with our whole heart and steadfast to all endurance, let us keep the Lord's precepts; so that when that day of anger and vengeance shall come, we may not be punished with the impious and sinners but may be honored with the righteous and those who fear God.

CYPRIAN OF CARTHAGE
(C. 210–258)
LETTERS

19 After these things I heard what sounded like the loud voice of a vast throng in heaven, saying,
"Hallelujah! Salvation and glory and power belong to
our God,
2 because his judgments are true and just.
For he has judged the great prostitute
who corrupted the earth with her sexual immorality,
and has avenged the blood of his servants poured out
by her own hands!"

3Then a second time the crowd shouted, "Hallelujah!" The
smoke rises from her forever and ever. 4The twenty-four elders
and the four living creatures threw themselves to the ground
and worshiped God, who was seated on the throne, saying:
"Amen! Hallelujah!"
5Then a voice came from the throne, saying:
"Praise our God
all you his servants,
and all you who fear him,
both the small and the great!"

THE WEDDING CELEBRATION OF THE LAMB

6Then I heard what sounded like the voice of a vast throng,
like the roar of many waters and like loud crashes of thunder.
They were shouting:
"Hallelujah!
For the Lord our God, the All-Powerful, reigns!
7 Let us rejoice and exult
and give him glory,
because the wedding celebration of the Lamb
has come,
and his bride has made herself ready.
8 She was permitted to be dressed in bright, clean, fine
linen" (for the fine linen is the righteous deeds of
the saints).

9Then the angel said to me, "Write the following: Blessed
are those who are invited to the banquet at the wedding celebration of the Lamb!" He also said to me, "These are the true
words of God." 10So I threw myself down at his feet to worship
him, but he said, "Do not do this! I am only a fellow servant with
you and your brothers and sisters who hold to the testimony
about Jesus. Worship God, for the testimony about Jesus is the
spirit of prophecy."

THE SON OF GOD GOES TO WAR

11Then I saw heaven opened and here came a white horse! The
one riding it was called "Faithful" and "True," and with justice
he judges and goes to war. 12His eyes are like a fiery flame and
there are many diadem crowns on his head. He has a name
written that no one knows except himself. 13He is dressed in
clothing dipped in blood, and he is called the Word of God.
14The armies that are in heaven, dressed in white, clean, fine
linen, were following him on white horses. 15From his mouth
extends a sharp sword so that with it he can strike the nations.
He will rule them with an iron rod, and he stomps the winepress
of the furious wrath of God, the All-Powerful. 16He has a name
written on his clothing and on his thigh: "King of kings and
Lord of lords."

17 Then I saw one angel standing in the sun, and he shouted
in a loud voice to all the birds flying high in the sky:
"Come, gather around for the great banquet of God,
18 to eat your fill of the flesh of kings,
the flesh of generals,
the flesh of powerful people,
the flesh of horses and those who ride them,
and the flesh of all people, both free and slave,
and small and great!"

19 Then I saw the beast and the kings of the earth and their
armies assembled to do battle with the one who rode the horse
and with his army. 20 Now the beast was seized, and along with
him the false prophet who had performed the signs on his behalf—signs by which he deceived those who had received the
mark of the beast and those who worshiped his image. Both of
them were thrown alive into the lake of fire burning with sulfur.
21 The others were killed by the sword that extended from the
mouth of the one who rode the horse, and all the birds gorged
themselves with their flesh.

THE THOUSAND-YEAR REIGN

20 Then I saw an angel descending from heaven, holding
in his hand the key to the abyss and a huge chain. 2 He
seized the dragon—the ancient serpent, who is the devil and
Satan—and tied him up for a thousand years. 3 The angel then
threw him into the abyss and locked and sealed it so that he
could not deceive the nations until the one thousand years
were finished. (After these things he must be released for a
brief period of time.)
4 Then I saw thrones and seated on them were those who
had been given authority to judge. I also saw the souls of those
who had been beheaded because of the testimony about Jesus
and because of the word of God. These had not worshiped the
beast or his image and had refused to receive his mark on their
forehead or hand. They came to life and reigned with Christ
for a thousand years. 5 (The rest of the dead did not come to
life until the thousand years were finished.) This is the first
resurrection. 6 Blessed and holy is the one who takes part in the
first resurrection. The second death has no power over them,
but they will be priests of God and of Christ, and they will reign
with him for a thousand years.

SATAN'S FINAL DEFEAT

7 Now when the thousand years are finished, Satan will be released from his prison 8 and will go out to deceive the nations
at the four corners of the earth, Gog and Magog, to bring them
together for the battle. They are as numerous as the grains of
sand in the sea. 9 They went up on the broad plain of the earth
and encircled the camp of the saints and the beloved city, but
fire came down from heaven and devoured them completely.
10 And the devil who deceived them was thrown into the lake
of fire and sulfur, where the beast and the false prophet are too,
and they will be tormented there day and night forever and ever.

THE GREAT WHITE THRONE

11 Then I saw a large white throne and the one who was seated
on it; the earth and the heaven fled from his presence, and no
place was found for them. 12 And I saw the dead, the great and

20:1–15 **After mentioning the devil's chaining for a thousand years and his brief interval of freedom to follow, John sums up the activity of and in the church during the "thousand years." Now there is no question of the last judgment in verse 12. The thrones and the enthroned people are the prelates who govern the church here and now. And the judgment is best interpreted as the one contained in the words, "whatever you bind on earth will have been bound in heaven, and whatever you release on earth will have been released in heaven" (Matt 18:18).**

AUGUSTINE **(354–430)**
CITY OF GOD

the small, standing before the throne. Then books were opened, and another book was opened—the book of life. So the dead were judged by what was written in the books, according to their deeds. [13]The sea gave up the dead that were in it, and Death and Hades gave up the dead that were in them, and each one was judged according to his deeds. [14]Then Death and Hades were thrown into the lake of fire. This is the second death—the lake of fire. [15]If anyone's name was not found written in the book of life, that person was thrown into the lake of fire.

A NEW HEAVEN AND A NEW EARTH

21 Then I saw a new heaven and a new earth, for the first heaven and earth had ceased to exist, and the sea existed no more. [2]And I saw the holy city—the new Jerusalem—descending out of heaven from God, made ready like a bride adorned for her husband. [3]And I heard a loud voice from the throne saying: "Look! The residence of God is among human beings. He will live among them, and they will be his people, and God himself will be with them. [4]He will wipe away every tear from their eyes, and death will not exist any more—or mourning, or crying, or pain, for the former things have ceased to exist."

[5]And the one seated on the throne said: "Look! I am making all things new!" Then he said to me, "Write it down, because these words are reliable and true." [6]He also said to me, "It is done! I am the Alpha and the Omega, the beginning and the end. To the one who is thirsty I will give water free of charge from the spring of the water of life. [7]The one who conquers will inherit these things, and I will be his God and he will be my son. [8]But as for the cowards, unbelievers, detestable persons, murderers, the sexually immoral, and those who practice magic spells, idol worshipers, and all those who lie, their place will be in the lake that burns with fire and sulfur. That is the second death."

THE NEW JERUSALEM DESCENDS

[9]Then one of the seven angels who had the seven bowls full of the seven final plagues came and spoke to me, saying, "Come, I will show you the bride, the wife of the Lamb!" [10]So he took me away in the Spirit to a huge, majestic mountain and showed me the holy city, Jerusalem, descending out of heaven from God. [11]The city possesses the glory of God; its brilliance is like a precious jewel, like a stone of crystal-clear jasper. [12]It has a massive, high wall with twelve gates, with twelve angels at the gates, and the names of the twelve tribes of the nation of Israel are written on the gates. [13]There are three gates on the east side, three gates on the north side, three gates on the south side, and three gates on the west side. [14]The wall of the city has twelve foundations, and on them are the twelve names of the twelve apostles of the Lamb.

[15]The angel who spoke to me had a golden measuring rod with which to measure the city and its foundation stones and wall. [16]Now the city is laid out as a square, its length and width the same. He measured the city with the measuring rod at 1,400 miles (its length and width and height are equal). [17]He also measured its wall, 144 cubits according to human measurement, which is also the angel's. [18]The city's wall is made of jasper and the city is pure gold, like transparent glass. [19]The foundations of the city's wall are decorated with every kind of precious stone. The first foundation is jasper, the second sapphire, the third agate, the fourth emerald, [20]the fifth onyx, the sixth carnelian, the seventh chrysolite, the eighth beryl, the ninth topaz, the

21:9–21 **"And the city is pure gold, like transparent glass." This does most dramatically represent the perfect purity of that city and its inhabitants. The very streets of this heavenly city are so pure that their being like pure gold does not sufficiently represent the purity of them, but they appear also like clear glass or crystal. Christ represents through the saints that he has washed, though they are clean, yet while in this world have defiled feet, they need to be often washing their feet, but in that world their feet shall be perfectly pure so as not at all to defile the streets. This is evidence that what is treated in the two last chapters of Revelation is the heavenly state of the church.**

JONATHAN EDWARDS
(1703–1758)
SELECTIONS FROM THE UNPUBLISHED WRITINGS

tenth chrysoprase, the eleventh jacinth, and the twelfth amethyst. 21 And the twelve gates are twelve pearls—each one of
the gates is made from just one pearl! The main street of the
city is pure gold, like transparent glass.
22 Now I saw no temple in the city, because the Lord God—the
All-Powerful—and the Lamb are its temple. 23 The city does not
need the sun or the moon to shine on it, because the glory of
God lights it up, and its lamp is the Lamb. 24 The nations will
walk by its light, and the kings of the earth will bring their
grandeur into it. 25 Its gates will never be closed during the
day (and there will be no night there). 26 They will bring the
grandeur and the wealth of the nations into it, 27 but nothing
ritually unclean will ever enter into it, nor anyone who does
what is detestable or practices falsehood, but only those whose
names are written in the Lamb's book of life.

22 Then the angel showed me the river of the water of life—
water as clear as crystal—pouring out from the throne of
God and of the Lamb, 2 flowing down the middle of the city's
main street. On each side of the river is the tree of life producing 12 kinds of fruit, yielding its fruit every month of the year.
Its leaves are for the healing of the nations. 3 And there will no
longer be any curse, and the throne of God and the Lamb will
be in the city. His servants will worship him, 4 and they will see
his face, and his name will be on their foreheads. 5 Night will be
no more, and they will not need the light of a lamp or the light
of the sun, because the Lord God will shine on them, and they
will reign forever and ever.

A FINAL REMINDER

6 Then the angel said to me, "These words are reliable and true.
The Lord, the God of the spirits of the prophets, has sent his
angel to show his servants what must happen soon."

7 (Look! I am coming soon!
Blessed is the one who keeps the words of the prophecy
expressed in this book.)

8 I, John, am the one who heard and saw these things, and
when I heard and saw them, I threw myself down to worship
at the feet of the angel who was showing them to me. 9 But he
said to me, "Do not do this! I am a fellow servant with you and
with your brothers the prophets, and with those who obey the
words of this book. Worship God!" 10 Then he said to me, "Do
not seal up the words of the prophecy contained in this book,
because the time is near. 11 The evildoer must continue to do
evil, and the one who is morally filthy must continue to be filthy.
The one who is righteous must continue to act righteously, and
the one who is holy must continue to be holy."

12 (Look! I am coming soon,
and my reward is with me to pay each one according to
what he has done!
13 I am the Alpha and the Omega,
the first and the last,
the beginning and the end!)

14 Blessed are those who wash their robes so they can have
access to the tree of life and can enter into the city by the gates.
15 Outside are the dogs and the sorcerers and the sexually immoral, and the murderers, and the idolaters and everyone who
loves and practices falsehood!

22:12–17 The Holy Spirit and the church call all to come to salvation. And whoever keeps the words of this prophecy and hears him whom the Lord himself has commanded to speak, he is worthy to be taught. Salvation is given without any price and without any barter. Rather he who desires to be saved will enter and will either receive free of charge the regeneration of baptism or he will receive the remedy of repentance without cost or charge. The prophet spoke in a similar manner: "And let the one who is thirsty come; let the one who wants it take the water of life free of charge."

APRINGIUS OF BEJA
(C. 6TH CENTURY)
TRACTATE ON THE APOCALYPSE

[16]"I, Jesus, have sent my angel to testify to you about these things for the churches. I am the root and the descendant of David, the bright morning star!" [17]And the Spirit and the bride say, "Come!" And let the one who hears say: "Come!" And let the one who is thirsty come; let the one who wants it take the water of life free of charge.

[18]I testify to everyone who hears the words of the prophecy contained in this book: If anyone adds to them, God will add to him the plagues described in this book. [19]And if anyone takes away from the words of this book of prophecy, God will take away his share in the tree of life and in the holy city that are described in this book.

[20]The one who testifies to these things says, "Yes, I am coming soon!" Amen! Come, Lord Jesus! [21]The grace of the Lord Jesus be with all.

BIBLIOGRAPHY AND INDEX

à Kempis, Thomas. *The Imitation of Christ.* Matt 25:31–45; Heb 12:1–17; Jas 1:1–18

Airay, Henry. *Lectures on Philippians.* 1 Kgs 18:1–16; 1 Chr 28:1–21

Ambrose. *Cain and Abel.* Exod 8:1–15; Num 15:20; 28:1–31; Prov 7:6–23

——. *Concerning Repentance.* Exod 3:1–5; Ps 137:*1–9*

——. *Concerning Virgins.* 1 Kgs 13:1–10; Song 5:2–8

——. *Concerning Widows.* Judg 4:1–23; Ruth 2:1–16

——. *Death as a Good.* Eccl 2:12–26

——. *Dogmatic Treatises.* Gen 20:1–18

——. *Explanation of Twelve Psalms.* Ps 44:1–26; Isa 12:1–6

——. *Flight from the World.* Prov 26:4

——. *Letters.* Num 16:1–40; Pss 99:1–9; 113:1–9; 119:97–104; Prov 13:8; Isa 20:3–4; 31:1–3; Hab 2:6–14; Zech 5:1–11; 2 Cor 3:7–18

——. *On Abraham.* Gen 17:15–27

——. *On the Christian Faith.* Jer 10:1–16; Ezek 39:10–12; Mark 15:33–41; Heb 10:5–10

——. *On the Death of His Brother Satyrus.* Rev 9:1–12

——. *On the Duties of the Clergy.* Gen 44:16; Num 1:47–53; 31:1–54; Deut 23:19; Josh 9:1–27; 14:6–15; 1 Sam 25:23–31; 2 Sam 3:20–28; Rom 5:1–5; 2 Cor 6:1–10; 9:1–15; 1 Tim 4:1–11

——. *On the Holy Spirit.* Job 33:4; Acts 15:6–21

——. *The Prayer of Job and David.* Ps 103:6–14

Ambrosiaster. *Commentary on Paul's Epistles.* Rom 4:1–25; 16:25–27; 1 Cor 3:5–23; 9:19–23; 16:13–17

Andrew of Caesarea. *Commentary on the Apocalypse.* Rev 2:18–29; 17:1–6

Aphrahat. *Demonstrations.* Deut 4:1–14

Aponius. *Exposition of Song of Songs.* Song 8:14

Apringius of Beja. *Tractate on the Apocalypse.* Rev 22:12–17

Archelaus, *The Acts of the Disputation with the Heresiarch Manes.* Exod 2:1–10

Arndt, Johann. *True Christianity.* 2 Sam 6:12–23; Ps 55:1–23

Athanasius. *Against the Heathen.* Acts 14:8–18

——. *Defense Before Constantius.* Ezra 3:1–13

——. *Encyclical Letter.* Judg 19:22—20:11

——. *Festal Letters.* Esth 9:18–25; Pss 17:15; 124:5–7; Zech 8:19

——. *Four Discourses Against the Arians.* 1 Sam 16:14–15; Ps 120:1–7

——. *Letters.* Prov 5:1–14; Isa 50:6–9; Mark 2:23—3:6

——. *On the Incarnation.* Deut 21:22–23; Job 18:1–21

Augustine. *Anti-Pelagian Writings.* Exod 19:1–25; Deut 30:1–11; 1 Chr 12:1–40; 9:14–17; 16:8–17; Job 6:2–3

——. *Christian Instruction.* Prov 2:1–22

——. *City of God.* Ps 79:1–13; Eccl 10:3–6; Jer 29:7; Rom 12:1–2; Rev 20:1–15

——. *Confessions.* Prov 27:21; Eph 2:1–10; 1 Pet 2:4–12

——. *Expositions on the Psalms.* Pss 9:1–2; 31:1–8; 48:7; 117:1–2; 134:1–3; Isa 10:20–23

——. *Harmony of the Gospels.* 1 Sam 21:1–9

——. *Letters.* Ps 119:129–136; Eccl 3:16—4:3; 1 John 4:7–16

——. *Of True Religion.* Rom 13:8–14

——. *On Christian Doctrine.* Gen 10:1–11:1; 2 Sam 19:1–8

——. *On Faith in Things Unseen.* Zeph 2:4–15

——. *On Grace and Free Will.* 2 Chr 21:1–20; 25:1–28

——. *On Lying.* Acts 23:1–35

——. *On the Trinity.* Exod 24:1–18; John 1:1–5

——. *Predestination of the Saints.* Isa 6:9–13; Col 4:1–6

——. *Questions on Joshua.* Josh 8:1–29

——. *Questions on Exodus.* Exod 6:26–7:13

——. *Questions on Leviticus.* Lev 5:1–13

——. *Sermons.* Lev 12:1–8; Pss 75:1–10; 85:8–13; 94:1–23; 140:1–13; 147:1–20; Ezek 9:1–11; Matt 19:16–30; Mark 16:1–8; Luke 18:9–17; John 8:1–12; Acts 9:1–22; 1 Tim 6:3–16

——. *Soliloquies.* Ezek 15:5

——. *Tractates on the Gospel of John.* Gen 7:7–15; Exod 1:1–22; Num 11:1–15; 21:1–9; Ps 121:1–8; John 3:1–21; 11:1–16; 16:25–33

Basil the Great. *Ascetical Works.* Num 20:1–10; Judg 21:1–25

——. *De Spiritu Sancto.* 1 Thess 1:1–10

——. *Homilies on the Psalms.* Pss 30:4; 46:1–11; 116:1–19; 123:1–2; Amos 8:1–14

——. *Letters.* Isa 22:1–14; Hos 8:1–14; Amos 2:7

——. *On Humility.* Judg 9:22–57

——. *On Mercy and Justice.* Hos 12:2–6
——. *Prolegomena.* Gen 23:1–19
——. *The Long Rules.* Ps 125:4–5; Zech 10:1–2
Baxter, Richard. *Commentary on the Prophet Ezekiel.* Ezek 33:12–20
——. *The Reformed Pastor.* Acts 20:25–38
Bellett, J. G. *The Captives Returned to Jerusalem.* Neh 11:1–36
Bernard of Clairvaux. *On the Song of Solomon.* Song 2:6–17
Beza, Theodore. *The Psalms of David.* Pss 7:1–17; 65:1–13
Blaikie, William Garden. *The First Book of Samuel.* 1 Sam 11:6–8
Bonar, Andrew. *A Commentary on Leviticus.* Lev 2:3–10; 7:11–13
Bonar, Horatius. *Diverse Kinds of Conscience.* Neh 5:15
Boston, Thomas. *The Complete Works.* Isa 38:1–22
Brenz, Johannes. *Commentary on John.* John 6:1–14
——. *Ecclesiastical Exposition upon Saint Luke.* Luke 19:11–27
——. *Explanation of Galatians.* Gal 4:8–20
——. *History of Jehoshaphat.* 2 Chr 17:1–19
Bridges, Charles. *An Exposition of the Book of Proverbs.* Prov 9:9–13; 23:12
Bucer, Martin. *Ecclesiastical Exposition upon Saint Matthew.* Luke 6:1–11
——. *Holy Psalms.* Ps 67:1–7
——. *Instructions on Christian Love.* 1 Kgs 3:1–15
Bugenhagen, Johannes. *Commentary on First Kings.* 1 Kgs 1:1–53; 4:20–34; 17:1–24
——. *Commentary on First Samuel.* 1 Sam 4:1–11; 12:5–12; 17:1–37; 31:1–13
——. *Commentary on Second Kings.* 2 Kgs 14:1–22; 21:1–18
——. *Commentary on Second Samuel.* 2 Sam 8:1–14
——. *Interpretation of the Psalms.* Ps 29:1–11
Bullinger, Heinrich. *Commentary on Colossians.* Col 1:1–8
——. *Commentary on John.* John 2:13–25
——. *Daniel, the Most Wise Prophet.* Dan 1:1–21
——. *Decades.* 2 Sam 12:1–15; 15:13–37; 1 Chr 22:1–19
Bunyan, John. *Grace Abounding to the Chief of Sinners.* Job 21:1–21
——. *Israel's Hope Encouraged.* Ps 130:1–8
——. *Solomon's Temple Spiritualized.* Ezek 41:1—42:14
——. *The Pilgrim's Progress.* 1 Pet 5:5–11
Burroughs, Jeremiah. *The Glorious Name of God the Lord of Hosts.* Isa 47:4
——. *The Gracious Heart and the Carnal Heart.* Phil 4:1–8
——. *The Rare Jewel of Christian Contentment.* Deut 28:15–68
Caesarius of Arles. *Exposition on the Apocalypse.* Rev 1:1–8
——. *Sermons.* Num 17:1–13; Deut 16:18—17:13; Judg 14:1–20; 2 Kgs 5:1–19; Ps 80:1–19; Prov 25:21–22; Isa 29:9–16; Zech 1:1–6
Cajetan, Thomas. *Commentary on the Psalms.* Ps 20:1–9
Calvin, John. *Complete Commentary on the Bible.* Gen 13:1–18; 24:26–28; 33:1–20; 36:1–43; 47:9; Exod 5:1–21; 31:1–11; 39:1–43; Lev 9:1–24; Num 6:22–27; 14:1–10; Deut 9:1–6; 20:5–7; 22:13–30; 34:1–10; Josh 1:6; 17:11–18; 22:10–20; 1 Sam 13:1–16; 2 Sam 1:1–16; 10:1–19; 11:1–27; 13:1–22; 2 Kgs 18:17–37; 1 Chr 19:1—20:8; 2 Chr 6:3–11; Pss 10:1–18; 42:1–11; 56:1–13; 64:1–10; 77:1–5; 98:3; 122:1; 136:1–26; 142:1–7; 150:1; Prov 12:10; Isa 8:11–22; 15:1–9; 27:2–13; 56:1–8; 66:18–22; Jer 3:6–18; 14:10–18; 24:1–10; 27:12; 35:1–19; 41:4–18; 47:1–7; 51:49–57; Lam 2:1–9; 5:1–22; Ezek 4:1–17; 6:1–3; 10:1–22; 19:1–14; Dan 4:1–37; 12:1–13; Hos 2:15—3:5; 6:1–11; Amos 5:16–27; Mic 1:1–16; Nah 2:1–13; Hab 1:1–17; Zeph 3:8–13; Zech 6:9–15; 14:1–7; Mal 1:1–6; Matt 12:46–50; 17:1–13; Mark 6:1–6; 8:1–11; Luke 23:46; John 17:20–26; 19:17–24; Acts 5:22–42; 10:1–23; 1 Cor 6:1–8; 1 Thess 2:1–12; 1 Tim 1:18—2:7; Titus 3:1–11; Jas 3:1–12; 1 John 3:10–23
Carroll, B. H. *Interpretation of the English Bible.* Josh 11:16—12:24
Cassiodorus. *Explanation of the Psalms.* 1 Chr 25:1–31; Pss 13:1–6; 26:1–12; 36:1–12; 74:1–23; 81:1–16; 101:1–8; 128:1–6; 144:1–15
Cassian, John. *Institutes.* 2 Chr 32:24–26; 1 Thess 4:9–12; 2 Thess 3:6–15
——. *The Conferences.* Gen 37:1–5; 40:1–23; Judg 3:1–6; Ps 119:121–128; Prov 29:11; Isa 30:18–26; Jer 19:1–15; 32:39–41; Hos 4:11–19; 7:11–16; Amos 4:6–13; Luke 17:20; John 15:9–17
Chrysostom, John. *Baptismal Instructions.* Ps 68:1–6
——. *Catena on the Acts of the Apostles.* Acts 26:1–23
——. *Commentary on Job.* Job 5:1–16; 32:1–6; 37:1–13
——. *Commentary on the Proverbs of Solomon.* Prov 10:25
——. *Commentary on the Psalms.* Ps 11:1–7
——. *Demonstrations Against the Pagans.* Isa 9:1–7
——. *Discourses Against Judaizing Christians.* Jer 44:1–30

——. *Homilies on Galatians.* Gal 3:1–14
——. *Homilies on Genesis.* Gen 27:1–17; 31:1–21; 39:1–23; 41:1–57; 46:1–26; Lev 17:1–16; Ezek 34:4
——. *Homilies on Statutes.* 2 Chr 3:1–17; Job 2:1–13; Isa 45:2; Zech 7:8–14
——. *Homilies on the Acts of the Apostles.* Acts 1:1–8; 11:1–18; 16:16–34; 22:1–21; 1 Thess 3:1–5
——. *Homilies on the Epistle of Paul to Philemon.* Phlm vv. 1–25
——. *Homilies on the Epistles of Paul to the Corinthians.* 1 Cor 5:1–12; 8:1–13; 2 Cor 2:14–17; 8:1–7; 12:1–6
——. *Homilies on the Epistle of Paul to the Ephesians.* Mark 1:14–15; Eph 1:1–13; Phil 1:3–11
——. *Homilies on the Epistle of Paul to the Romans.* Rom 6:15–23; 8:31–39
——. *Homilies on the First Epistle of Paul to the Thessalonians.* Prov 30:8
——. *Homilies on the First Epistle of Paul to Timothy.* 1 Tim 5:3–16
——. *Homilies on the Gospel of John.* Deut 7:1–11; Ps 58:4; Jer 4:14–18; 13:23; John 9:30–33; 13:1–17
——. *Homilies on the Gospel of Matthew.* Lev 25:35–36; Ruth 4:1–12; Matt 1:18–22; 9:1–8; 10:1–15; 14:13–21; Luke 4:1–13; Rev 4:1–11
——. *Homilies on the Second Epistle of Paul to Timothy.* 2 Tim 1:1–7
——. *Instructions to Catechumens.* Jer 18:1–17
——. *On Temperance.* Mark 4:1–20
——. *On the Epistle to the Hebrews.* Ps 51:1–19; Jer 8:18–9:11; Heb 2:1–4; 3:7–19
——. *On the Priesthood.* Lev 4:1–12
Chytraeus, David. *Commentary on Judges.* Judg 10:6–18
Clement of Alexandria. *Christ the Educator.* Deut 14:3–21; Ps 86:1–17; Lam 1:1–15
——. *Fragments.* 1 Kgs 8:22–53
——. *Stromateis.* Lev 19:9–10; 26:23–24; Prov 4:8–18; Ezek 44:9–27
——. *The Paedagogus.* Deut 31:20
——. *Who Is the Rich Man That Shall Be Saved.* Jer 20:12
Clement of Rome. *First Clement.* Exod 14:15–31; 32:1–35; Josh 2:1–24; 2 Chr 31:14–21; Esth 4:1–17; Job 38:1–41; Ps 118:1–29; Jer 21:8; Heb 6:13–20; Jas 4:1–12; 1 Pet 3:13–22; 2 Pet 3:1–9
——. *Recognitions.* Deut 18:15
Coke, Thomas. *Commentary on the Holy Bible.* Gen 30:1
Constitutions of the Holy Apostles. Lev 18:1–30; Num 12:1–3; 2 Sam 20:1–22
Cumming, John. *Sabbath Morning Readings on the Old Testament.* Exod 37:1–29
Cyprian of Carthage. *Exhortation to Martyrdom.* Exod 4:10–17
——. *Letters.* Gen 14:18–24; Ps 89:1–52; Luke 12:1–11; Rev 19:1–10
——. *The Epistles.* Deut 24:16; Mark 7:1–23
——. *The Lapsed.* Ezek 14:12–23
——. *The Lord's Prayer.* 2 Kgs 24:1–10
——. *The Unity of the Catholic Church.* Lev 10:1–7
Cyril of Alexandria. *Commentary on Isaiah.* Isa 57:15; 64:1–12
——. *Commentary on Luke.* Prov 19:17; Luke 7:18–35; Luke 21:5–24
——. *Commentary on Obadiah.* Obad vv. 17–21
——. *Glaphyra on Genesis.* Gen 35:1–15
——. *Third Letter to Nestorius.* Isa 25:1–12
Cyril of Jerusalem. *Catechetical Lectures.* Exod 33:12–23; Lev 8:1–9; Job 39:1–30, Pss 87:1–7; 108:4; Isa 34:1–4; Mic 7:1–7; Zech 2:1–13; 11:4–17; Acts 2:1–13; 1 Cor 12:1–11; 2 Cor 11:5–15
Daneau, Lambert. *Dialogue of Witches.* 2 Kgs 1:1–15
——. *True and Christian Friendship.* 1 Sam 18:1–16; 23:14–29
Davenant, John. *Exposition on Colossians.* 1 Sam 24:1–22; 2 Kgs 9:14–29
Desert Fathers. Ps 92:1–15
de Valdés, Juán. *Commentary on Romans.* Rom 10:1–13
Dickson, David. *Explication of the First Fifty Psalms.* Pss 27:1–14; 47:1–9; 52:1–9
Didymus the Blind. *Commentary on Job.* Job 9:1–13
Donne, John. *The Works.* Ps 63:1–11
Drelincourt, Charles. *Christian Defense Against the Fear of Death.* 2 Sam 16:15–17:14; 2 Chr 16:7–14
Dyke, Daniel. *The Mystery of Self-Deceiving.* 1 Kgs 15:1–8
Edwards, Jonathan. *Selections from the Unpublished Writings.* Gen 19:1–38; 50:1–25; Num 13:22, 28–33; Deut 33:1–25; Josh 5:1–12; Job 41:11; Prov 16:4; Eccl 6:10; Jer 17:16–18; Matt 21:1–11; Rom 14:14–23; 2 Pet 1:5–11; Rev 21:9–21
——. *The Complete Works.* Exod 25:10–22; Num 23:13–26; Deut 15:11; Job 8:11–22; 27:1–13; Pss 25:8; 90:10; 139:1–24; Song 4:3; Isa 13:19–22; 33:14–24; Ezek 7:12; 1 Cor 2:6–16; 13:1–13; Heb 1:1–4; 4:14–5:11; Rev 5:1–14; 18:9–20
Ephrem the Syrian. *Commentary on Genesis.* Gen 18:1–15

——. *The Way to God and How to Find It.* Isa 49:14–26
Morgan, G. Campbell. *Living Messages of the Books of the Bible.* Esth 1:1–22
Musculus, Wolfgang. *Commentary on Paul's First Letter to the Corinthians.* 1 Cor 4:6–13
——. *Commentary on the Psalms.* Pss 21:1–13; 41:1–13; 57:1–11; 71:1–24
Oecolampadius, Johannes. *Commentary on Daniel.* Dan 2:14–23
——. *Commentary on Ezekiel.* Ezek 22:1–31
Oecumenius. *Commentary on the Apocalypse.* Rev 8:1–13
Olympiodorus. *Commentary on Job.* Job 26:1–14
Origen. *Commentary on the Gospel of John.* Josh 3:1–17; Gal 6:11–15
——. *Commentary on the Gospel of Matthew.* Mark 9:4; John 12:1–8
——. *Contra Celsum.* Ps 104:1–23; Eccl 8:10–17; Rev 10:1–11
——. *Exhortation to Martyrdom.* Num 25:1–17
——. *Fragments on Job.* Job 35:1–16; Jer 50:1–7
——. *Homilies on Genesis.* Num 18:8–20; Neh 1:1–11; Ps 119:17–24
——. *Homilies on Jeremiah.* Isa 2:5–22; Amos 3:1–8
——. *Homilies on Joshua.* Josh 10:28–42; 15:1–12
——. *Homilies on Leviticus.* Exod 30:1–10
——. *Homilies on Numbers.* Num 29:1–11; 33:1–49
——. *Homilies on the Gospel of Luke.* Luke 3:1–6
——. *On First Principles.* Deut 1:1–8; Job 25:4–5; Prov 22:20–21; John 21:24–25; 2 Cor 5:1–8; Eph 6:10–20
——. *On Prayer.* Ps 141:1–10
Osiander, Lucas. *Annotations on First Chronicles.* 1 Chr 10:1–14; 16:7–43; 26:1–19
——. *Annotations on First Samuel.* 1 Sam 5:1–12
Owen, John. *The Works.* Judg 11:1–28; Pss 45:1; 76:1–12; Eph 4:7–16
Pappus, Johann. *On All the Prophets.* Jer 37:17–21
Paterius. *Exposition of the Old and New Testaments.* Num 7:89; 10:1–10
Paulinus of Nola. *Poems.* Jon 2:1–10
Pellikan, Konrad. *Commentary on First Kings.* 1 Kgs 9:1–9
——. *Commentary on Jeremiah.* Jer 34:6–7
——. *Commentary on the Psalms.* Ps 40:1–17
Piscator, Johannes. *Commentary on First Chronicles.* 1 Chr 6:1–53; 14:8–17; 18:1–17; 23:1–32
——. *Commentary on First Kings.* 1 Kgs 10:1–13; 14:1–18
——. *Commentary on Second Kings.* 2 Kgs 6:24–7:3; 12:1–16; 22:1–20
Polycarp. *Epistle to the Philippians.* Ps 4:1–8; 1 Pet 1:13–21
Poole, Matthew. *English Annotations on the Holy Bible.* 1 Sam 14:6
Procopius of Gaza. *Catena on the Octateuch.* Num 26:1–65; 30:1–16
——. *Commentary on Joshua.* Josh 16:1–10
——. *Commentary on Judges.* Judg 5:1–12
Pseudo-Clement of Rome. *2 Clement.* Mal 4:1–6
Reynolds, Edward. *Seven Sermons on Fourteenth Chapter of Hosea.* 1 Sam 1:8–19; 2 Sam 14:1–33; 1 Kgs 12:1–15; 2 Chr 30:1–12
——. *The Sinfulness of Sin.* 2 Sam 23:1–7; 2 Kgs 10:1–32
Rufinus of Aquileia. *A Commentary on the Apostles' Creed.* Ps 93:1–5
Ryle, J. C. *Expository Thoughts on the Gospels.* Luke 13:10–17
Sanderson, Robert. *To the People.* 1 Kgs 21:17–29
Selnecker, Nikolaus. *The Whole Psalter.* Pss 43:1–5; 53:1–6; 72:1–20
Sibbes, Richard. *Between Christ and His Church.* Exod 16:22–31
——. *The Glorious Feast of the Gospel.* Exod 34:19–20
Simeon, Charles. *Horae Homileticae.* Exod 11:7; Judg 17:1–13; 2 Chr 23:1–21; Isa 21:11–12; Jer 31:1–3
Simons, Menno. *True Christian Faith.* 1 Sam 15:1–9; 2 Kgs 23:1–27
Spurgeon, C. H. *Morning and Evening.* Gen 9:8–17; 21:1–7; 29:1–30; 42:1–24; 49:22–28; Exod 22:1–15; Lev 1:1–17; 6:8–13; 13:1–17; Num 32:1–15; Deut 5:23–33; Josh 20:1–9; Judg 7:1–25; 15:1–20; 1 Sam 7:1–17; 27:1–28:2; 2 Sam 5:17–25; 1 Kgs 19:1–18; 1 Chr 5:1–26; Ezra 7:1–28; Neh 3:1–32; 9:1–38; Esth 10:1–3; Job 1:1–12; 10:1–22; 19:1–29; 23:1–17; 29:1–25; 40:1–5; Pss 12:1–8; 22:1–31; 33:1–22; 39:1–13; 62:1–12; 73:1–28; 84:1–12; 91:1–16; 100:1–5; 107:1–43; 109:1–5; 112:1–10; 126:1–6; 138:1–8; 149:1–9; Prov 3:13–35; 11:1–31; 18:12; 24:33; Eccl 1:1–18; 9:1–12; Song 7:10–13; Isa 26:1–19; 36:1–22; 54:1–8; 63:1–14; Jer 2:14–28; 16:14–21; 33:1–17; 49:23–27; Lam 3:1–24; Ezek 3:1–27; 16:1–30; 35:1–15; Dan 3:1–25; 11:29–39; Hos 14:1–9; Amos 9:1–10; Hab 3:17–19; Zeph 1:1–18; Matt 11:25–30; 15:21–28; 26:36–46; Luke 22:31–34; John 5:1–15; Acts 4:13–22; 18:1–17; 1 Cor 10:1–13; 1 Thess 5:1–11; Heb 11:4–29; 3 John vv. 1–15; Rev 12:1–17
——. *Metropolitan Tabernacle Sermons.* Exod 10:12–20; Deut 2:1–7; 2 Chr 27:1–9; Job 15:4; Isa 19:18–25; Ezek 48:35; Hos 5:1–15; Zech 12:10–11; Matt 4:18–21; 6:5–8; 22:1–14; 24:1–28; 27:45–55; Luke 14:7–14; Acts 28:11–16; Phil 2:1–11; Col 3:1–11; Heb 9:6–22

——. *The Treasury of David*. Pss 1:1–2; 54:1–7; 129:4; 132:1–18

Strigel, Viktorin. *Book of Chronicles*. 1 Chr 2:1–17; 8:1–9:2; 11:1–9; 2 Chr 2:1–16; 18:1–27; 29:1–36; 35:1–19

——. *Book of Kings*. 2 Kgs 4:8–37; 11:1–20; 19:1–19; 25:1–21

——. *Book of Samuel*. 1 Sam 3:1–21

Sutcliffe, Joseph. *Commentary on the Old and New Testament*. Deut 26:1–15

Tertullian. *Against Hermogenes*. Ps 97:2–5

——. *Against Marcion*. Exod 21:12–27; Lev 16:1–14; 2 Sam 7:1–17; Ps 111:10; Isa 39:1–8; Rom 2:14–16

——. *Exhortation to Chastity and to His Wife*. Lev 20:1–27; Mark 10:1–12

——. *On Flight Amid Persecution*. Jon 1:1–15

——. *On Idolatry*. Ezek 23:1–49

——. *On Patience*. Gen 15:1–6

——. *On Prayer*. Gen 45:1–15

Theodore of Mopsuestia. *Commentary on Haggai*. Hag 1:1–11

——. *Commentary on Hosea*. Hos 9:1–7

——. *Commentary on Micah*. Mic 6:1–8

Theodoret of Cyr. *Commentary on Daniel*. Dan 6:1–9

——. *Commentary on Hosea*. Hos 11:1–11

——. *Commentary on Isaiah*. Isa 40:1–8; 44:9–20; 59:9–15

——. *Commentary on Jeremiah*. Jer 1:4–10; 11:1–17; 23:1–8; 39:11–18

——. *Commentary on Nahum*. Nah 1:1–8

——. *Commentary on the Psalms*. Pss 28:1–9; 102:1–28

——. *Letters*. Ps 146:1–10

——. *Questions on Exodus*. Exod 40:1–38

——. *Questions on Kings and Chronicles*. 1 Kgs 20:23–43; 2 Chr 15:1–19; 28:1–27

Thomas, W. H. Griffith. *Genesis: A Devotional Commentary*. Gen 34:1–31

Torrey, R. A., *Treasury of Scripture Knowledge*. Num 35:26–28

Tyndale, William. *Doctrinal Treatises and Introductions to Other Portions of Holy Scriptures*. 1 Sam 22:1–5

Venerable Bede. *Commentary on Proverbs*. Prov 6:12–19

——. *Commentary on the Acts of the Apostles*. 2 Chr 9:1–7

——. *Explanation of the Apocalypse*. Rev 14:1–5

——. *Exposition on the Gospel of Mark*. Mark 14:3–9

——. *Homilies on the Gospels*. Exod 27:1–8; Judg 13:1–7; 1 Chr 24:1–31; Ps 143:1–12; Isa 4:2–4; Luke 11:5–13; Heb 7:1–21

——. *On Ezra and Nehemiah*. Ezra 5:1–17; 6:1–22; 10:1–44; Neh 4:1–23; 10:28–39; 13:1–30

——. *On the Tabernacle*. Lev 24:5–9; Num 19:1–22; Josh 18:1–10

Vermigli, Peter. *Commentary on Second Samuel*. 2 Sam 2:1–7

Victorinus, Marius. *Commentary on the Letter to the Galatians*. Gal 5:7–15

Victorinus of Petovium. *Commentary on the Apocalypse*. Rev 3:1–6

Vincent of Lérins. *Commonitorium*. Deut 13:1–18

von Greiffenberg, Catharina Regina. *Meditations on the Incarnation, Passion and Death of Jesus Christ*. Luke 1:26–38

von Molsdorf, Hieronymus Weller. *Annotations on 2 Samuel*. 2 Sam 21:1–14

Warfield, B. B. *Faith and Life*. Jas 5:13–19

Watson, Thomas. *Body of Divinity*. Deut 6:4; Luke 5:27–32

Wesley, John. *Explanatory Notes on the Bible*. Gen 16:1–5; 28:1–9; Exod 17:1–7; 20:18–21; 26:1–37; 35:20–29; 38:1–8; Lev 21:1–24; 27:28–34; Num 4:21–29; 9:15–23; 34:1–15; Deut 10:1–11; 19:15–21; 27:1–10; Josh 7:1–9; 13:1–7; 21:43–45; 2 Sam 4:4–12; 1 Kgs 16:1–7; 2 Kgs 16:15; 1 Chr 7:23; 2 Chr 7:1; Ezra 2:1–70; 8:21–35; Job 17:8; 28:1–28; 36:5–33; 42:7–16; Pss 16:1–11; 19:1–14; 24:1–10; 110:1–7; 119:33–40; 127:1–5; Eccl 7:13–15; Song 1:1–17; Isa 42:1–4; Jer 52:28–34; Ezek 43:1–27; Jon 4:1–11; Hag 2:20–23; Matt 7:1–6; Mark 12:29–34; Acts 3:11–26; 17:16–32; Rom 7:13–25; 1 Cor 7:1–16; 2 Cor 10:1–6; Col 2:1–10

The Westminster Annotations. 1 Chr 13:1–14; 2 Chr 4:1–5:1; 12:1–12; 19:1–11; 26:1–23; 36:15–21; Pss 59:1–17; 70:1–5

Whitefield, George. *The Works*. Gen 22:11–19; Josh 24:1–28; Zech 4:1–14

Wigand, Johann. *Brief Exposition on the Prophet Daniel*. Dan 9:1–27

Willet, Andrew. *A Harmony upon the First Book of Samuel*. 1 Sam 8:1–22

——. *A Harmony upon the Second Book of Samuel*. 2 Sam 18:1–18

Zell, Katharina Schütz. *Letter to Caspar Schwenckfeld*. 1 Cor 14:26–40

Zephyrinus. *Epistles of Zephyrinus*. Ps 133:1–3

Zwingli, Ulrich. *Annotations on Genesis*. Gen 1:26–30

——. *Of the Clarity and Certainty of the Word of God*. Ps 49:1–20

——. *On the Providence of God*. 1 Sam 9:6–26; 1 Kgs 11:15–40; 2 Kgs 20:1–11

——. *Sermons*. Jer 26:2

——. *Warning Against Control of Foreign Lands*. 2 Sam 24:1–17

LIST OF SACRED ARTWORK

1. Andrei Rublev, *The Trinity* (1425). *The Trinity* is an icon painted by the fifteenth-century artist Andrei Rublev. It is one of the most renowned pieces of Russian art and was commissioned to honor Sergius of Radonezh of the Trinity Lavra of Saint Sergius monastery near Moscow. The icon depicts the three angels who visited Abraham in Genesis 18:1–8, but the painting is often interpreted as a symbolic icon of the eternal Holy Trinity. The foundation of the composition of the piece places all haloed figures on the same level, demonstrating that each person of the Trinity is fully God. (*Public Domain*)

2. Thomas Cole, *Expulsion from the Garden of Eden* (1828). The British-born American Thomas Cole is well known for his breathtaking portrayals of the American outdoors. *Expulsion from the Garden of Eden* reflects the philosophy of the Hudson River School, which Cole founded. In the painting, the two realms of Eden and the fallen world meet amidst the lush forest and rugged mountains. Cole's dramatic use of light at the center of the canvas draws the viewer's eyes toward Adam and Eve, who stand on the ominous precipice of the abyss following the fall of humankind in Genesis 3. (*Public Domain*)

3. Francis Danby, *The Deluge* (1840). Danby's use of extravagant movement on a large-scale canvas is epitomized in his painting *The Deluge* ("a severe flood") portraying the narrative of Genesis 6–8. The foreground is chaotic and tragic as God destroys the wicked world and all that is in it with water. The condemned people are fighting for their lives as the stormy sea rages, engulfing the jagged rocks and cracking trees in half. In the corner, an angel mourns a child's death. In the background, Noah's ark is subtly illumined by the few beams of light breaking through the dark clouds. (*Public Domain*)

4. Pieter Bruegel the Elder, *The Tower of Babel* (c. 1563). Pieter Bruegel the Elder, a significant Dutch and Flemish Renaissance artist, painted the tower as an enormous structure with spiraling ramps surrounded by the chaotic movement of antlike workers in a frenzy of activity. Bruegel placed the tower in a coastal landscape to show how the building supplies were transported to the construction site by means of water. The artist is precise in showing a knowledge of building techniques, rendering every detail with precision. Ladders, lifts, a crane, scaffolding, engineers, masons, and laborers all work futilely in this pointless human ambition described in Genesis 11. (*Public Domain*)

5. Caravaggio, *Sacrifice of Isaac* (1603). Very few painters have exercised such great influence as the Italian artist Caravaggio, known as the Master of Darkness and Light. This painting depicts the dramatic scene of Genesis 22 when Abraham is about to sacrifice his bound and defenseless son Isaac. Interrupting the scene, an angel holds back Abraham's knife, redirecting his attention toward a ram to sacrifice in the place of his son. This painting was commissioned by an influential cardinal, Maffeo Barberini, the future Catholic Pope Urban VIII. (*Public Domain*)

6. Rembrandt, *Moses Breaking the Tablets of the Law* (1659). Dutch artist Rembrandt's painting is one of the most recognized pieces depicting Exodus 32. The artist subtly captures the sorrow on Moses' face as he descends the holy mountain to find his people in idolatrous worship, so easily forsaking their saving God. Reproductions of this work fail to capture its halting power over the viewer; in the original piece, Moses is life-size on a canvas that is more than five feet tall and four feet wide. (*Public Domain*)

7. Giuseppe Angeli, *Elijah Taken Up in a Chariot of Fire* (1740/1755). Giuseppe Angeli was an Italian painter of the late Baroque period who was known to paint both religious and secular images. In this painting, Angeli depicts the narrative of 2 Kings 2, when God takes Elijah into the heavens. The vision of the saint's rapture from earth into a fiery chariot among the clouds is full of movement and captures the transformation with both tenacity and warmth. (*Public Domain. Courtesy of the National Gallery of Art, Washington, D.C.*)

8. Henry Ossawa Tanner, *The Annunciation* (1898). Henry Ossawa Tanner, son of a minister, was the first African American painter to earn fame and respect on an international level. In Tanner's *Annunciation*, the brilliant intensity of Gabriel's presence illumines Mary's tapestry-decorated bedroom. The composition of an ordinary adolescent girl in a typical domestic setting in the presence of a heavenly being is a beautiful and stunning depiction of the encounter of Luke 1. (*Public Domain*)

9. El Greco, *The Adoration of the Shepherds* (1605–1610). El Greco was a Greek sculptor, painter, and key participant in the Spanish Renaissance. Like all of El Greco's later works, *The Adoration of the Shepherds* uses distorted poses and perspectives to communicate energy. Contrasts of light, shadow, and color bolster the drama of the narrative. The infant Jesus is glowing, casting light on all around him. The circular arrangement of the figures in dancelike postures gives a sense of celebratory awe and wonder at the arrival of the promised Messiah related in Luke 2. (*Public Domain. Courtesy of The Metropolitan Museum of Art*)

10. Rembrandt, *The Storm on the Sea of Galilee* (1633). Rembrandt was a Dutch Golden Age artist known not only for his artistic skill but also for his ability to seize a viewer's attention with the narrative of his pieces. In this dramatic painting, *The Storm on the Sea of Galilee* from Matthew 8, Mark 4, and Luke 8, the chaotic waters swell and surge outside the boat, yet our attention is drawn to the disarray inside the vessel. Some of the disciples cling to the mast, the others cling to their Master, pleading with him to save their lives. (*Public Domain*)

11. Raphael, *The Transfiguration* (1516–1520). *The Transfiguration* was the last painting Italian Renaissance master Raphael completed before his death. In the painting, the transfigured Christ floats in light and clouds while conversing with Moses and Elijah, a scene taken from Matthew 17 and Mark 9. Peter, James, and John lay fear-filled on the ground beneath Christ. The two-level composition captures both the serenity and terror of this experience, and the darkness of earthly chaos below provides a powerful contrast to the illumined heavens above. (*Public Domain*)

12. Diego Velazquez, *Cristo Crucificado* (1632). Diego Velázquez was a Baroque painter who served as the lead artist in the court of King Philip IV of Spain. Velázquez's depiction of the crucified Christ is at once beautiful and haunting. Christ's pale, dead body seems both serene and dignified. There is no narrative accompaniment—background or other characters—thus Christ hangs dead and alone. Yet the illumined halo reminds the viewer of the sacredness of this solemn moment from Mark 15:37. (*Public Domain*)

13. Caravaggio, *The Incredulity of Saint Thomas* (c. 1601–1602). The striking detail of Caravaggio's painting not only demonstrates his mastery of light and dark pigments but also allows the viewer to step in and experience the incident recorded in John 20. The resurrected Christ exhibits patience in providing Thomas with the physical evidence that he needs to believe. The emphasis of the painting is on the illuminated area where Christ compassionately guides the right hand of Thomas to feel the wound in his open side. (*Public Domain*)

14. The Apostle Paul, St. Sophia Cathedral of Kyev (1000). Beginning in the late fourth century with the construction of Christian basilicas, wall and ceiling mosaics became a significant form of Christian art. As with other religious art forms, the rich imagery of mosaics helped communicate biblical narratives and theological truth to Christian congregations. This Byzantine-styled mosaic of the apostle Paul is from a cathedral in Kyev. In a sense, a mosaic is an appropriate medium to portray Paul, whose life testimony was put together by a broken background and sufferings. (*Public Domain*)

15. John Martin, *The Last Judgement* (1853). *The Last Judgement* is a painting of the main event that takes place in the book of Revelation. Martin has collaged various passages together to provide us with a broader visual of what this day might look like. In the center of the painting, near the top, God sits on a throne in the heavens as Judge over all. He is surrounded by the twenty-four elders clothed in white. The Seventh Seal of Revelation 8 has been opened and the four angels have sounded their trumpets. Near the bottom of the painting, a deep chasm divides humanity into two parts. The evil gathered on the right, to the left on Mount Zion are the redeemed, each called individually to account. (*Public Domain*)

16. William Holman Hunt, *The Light of the World* (1851–1853). *The Light of the World* is an allegorical painting by the English Pre-Raphaelite artist William Holman Hunt (1827–1910). The piece depicts Jesus Christ from Revelation 3:20, knocking on a door overgrown with weeds. There are only two sources providing glowing light in the image, the search lantern and the halo that illumines Jesus' crown of thorns. Many considered the painting the most relevant and vital portrait of Christ of that time. (*Public Domain*)